TENTH EDITION

Business Law and the Regulatory Environment

Concepts and Cases

JANE P. MALLOR

A. JAMES BARNES

THOMAS BOWERS

MICHAEL J. PHILLIPS

ARLEN W. LANGVARDT

all of University of Indiana

Irwin McGraw-Hill

Boston, Massachusetts   Burr Ridge, Illinois   Dubuque, Iowa
Madison, Wisconsin   New York, New York   San Francisco, California   St. Louis, Missouri

Barnes/Dworkin/Richards
Law for Business
Sixth Edition,
1997

Bennett-Alexander/Pincus
Employment Law for Business
Second Edition,
1998

Blackburn/Klayman/Malin
The Legal Environment of
Business
Fifth Edition,
1994

Corley/Reed/Shedd/Morehead
The Legal and Regulatory
Environment of Business
Tenth Edition,
1996

Dunfee, et.al.
Modern Business Law and the
Regulatory Environment
Third Edition,
1996

Dworkin
Contract Law Tutorial Software
1993

Hotchkiss
International Law for Business
1994

Mallor/Barnes/Bower/Phillips/
Langvardt
Business Law and the Regulatory
Environment
Tenth Edition,
1998

McAdams
Law, Business, and Society
Fifth Edition,
1998

McAdams/Pincus
Legal Environment of Business
1997

McCarty/Bagby
The Legal Environment
of Business
Third Edition,
1996

Richards
Law for Global Business
1994

Jane P. Mallor has taught business law at Indiana University since 1976. During that time, she has received several teaching awards, including the Student Alumni Council Senior Faculty Award, the Faculty Colloquium for Excellence in Teaching, and the Amoco Foundation Award for Distinguished Teaching. Mallor received her B.A. from Indiana University and her J.D. from Indiana University School of Law.

A. James Barnes currently is Dean and Professor of Public and Environmental Affairs at Indiana University, as well as Director of the Long Island Lighting Company. He previously won a distinguished teaching award from Indiana University's School of Business. Barnes's government positions include Deputy Administrator of EPA, General Counsel of EPA, General Counsel of the Department of Agriculture, and trial attorney in the Department of Justice. Barnes received his B.A. with honors from Michigan State University and J.D. Cum Laude from Harvard Law School.

Thomas Bowers is Co-Director of The Sports and Entertainment Academy in the MBA Program at Indiana University. He joined the faculty of Indiana University's School of Business after working for the Brooklyn District Attorney and the Enforcement Division of the United States Securities and Exchange Commission in New York City. He has received 12 outstanding teaching awards at Indiana, and is the only two-time recipient of the Indiana University Student Choice Award for outstanding teaching. Bowers graduated Summa Cum Laude from the Ohio State University and earned his J.D. at New York University.

Michael J. Phillips has been teaching business law at Indiana University's School of Business since 1977. During that period, he has won eight best article or comment awards from the *American Business Law Journal.* After filling various editorial board positions, Phillips also served as editor-in-chief of the *Journal* from 1988 to 1990. In addition, he has twice chaired the business law department at Indiana University's School of Business. Phillips received his B.A. from Johns Hopkins University, earned a J.D. from Columbia University, and received L.L.M. and S.J.D. degrees from George Washington University.

Arlen W. Langvardt, Professor of Business Law, joined the Indiana University School of Business faculty after private practice as a trial attorney involved in a variety of legal areas. Langvardt has received several teaching awards at both the undergraduate and M.B.A. levels, as well as Holmes/Cardozo Award from the Academy of Legal Studies in Business. He has published numerous articles in law and business journals. In 1992 he delivered the Boal Memorial Lecture at Georgetown University Law Center. Langvardt received his B.A. with highest honors from Hastings College and J.D. with distinction from the University of Nebraska.

Irwin/McGraw-Hill

A Division of The **McGraw·Hill** Companies

BUSINESS LAW AND THE REGULATORY ENVIRONMENT: CONCEPTS AND CASES

1 2 3 4 5 6 7 8 9 0 VH/VH 9 0 9 8 7

ISBN 0-256-19716-4

Vice president and Editorial director: *Michael W. Junior*
Executive director: *Jerry Saykes*
Marketing manager: *Kenyetta Giles*
Project manager: *Robert A. Preskill*
Production supervisor: *Melonie Salvati*
Designer: *Michael Warrell/Ellen Pettengell*
Compositor: *Carlisle Communications, Ltd.*
Typeface: *10/12 Times Roman*
Printer: *Von Hoffmann Press, Inc.*

Library of Congress Cataloging-in-Publication Data

Business law and the regulatory environment : concepts and cases. —
    10th ed. / Jane P. Mallor . . . [et al.]
        p.   cm. — (Irwin/McGraw-Hill legal studies in business
    series)
      Includes index.
      ISBN 0-256-19716-4 (acid-free paper)
      1. Commercial law—United States—Cases. 2. Commercial law-
    -United States.   I. Mallor, Jane P.   II. Series.
    KF888.B8   1998
    346.7307—dc21   97-25762

http://www.mhhe.com

This is the tenth UCC edition (and the seventeenth overall edition) of a business law text that first appeared in 1935. Throughout its more than 60 years of existence, this book has been a leader and an innovator in the fields of business law and the legal environment of business. One reason for the book's success, we feel, is its clear and comprehensive treatment of the standard topics that form the traditional business law curriculum. Another is its responsiveness to changes in these traditional subjects and to new views about that curriculum. Prominent among the latter are the injection of regulatory materials that has largely defined "legal environment" approach to business law and the more recent emphasis on ethics and international issues.

Continuing Strengths

This edition continues the basic features that have made its predecessors successful. They include:

- *Comprehensive Coverage.* We believe that the text continues to excel both in the number of topics it addresses and the depth of coverage within each topic. This is true both of the basic business law subjects that form the core of the book and also of the regulatory and other subjects that are said to constitute the "legal environment" curriculum.
- *Style and Presentation.* We like to think that this text is written in a style that is direct, lucid, and organized, yet also relatively relaxed and conversational. For this reason, we often have been able to cover certain topics by assigning them as reading without lecturing on them. As always, we continue to employ italics and bold-face to emphasize key points and terms; to make liberal use of examples; to state the elements of a claim or a list of defenses in numbered paragraphs; and to include many charts, figures, and concept summaries.
- *Case Selection.* We try very hard to find cases that clearly illustrate important points made in

the text, that should interest students, and that are fun to teach. Except where older decisions are landmarks or best illustrate particular concepts, we also try to select recent cases. Our collective in-class teaching experience with recent editions has helped us determine which of those cases best meet these criteria.

- *AACSB Curricular Standards.* The AACSB's recent curriculum standards say that both undergraduate and MBA curricula should include ethical and global issues; should address the influence of political, social, legal and regulatory, environmental, and technological issues on business; and should also address the impact of demographic diversity on organizations. In addition to its obvious stress on legal and regulatory issues, the book contains chapters on business ethics, the legal environment for international business, and environmental law, as well as "Ethical and Public Policy Concerns" at the end of all chapters except the ethics chapter. By putting legal changes in their social, political, and economic context, several text chapters enhance students' understanding of how political and social changes influence business and the law. Finally, Chapter 50's discussion of employment discrimination law certainly speaks to the subject of workplace diversity.

Important Changes in this Edition

This edition's lineup of chapters is unchanged from the ninth edition. The most important changes within that lineup follow. Of course, they are in addition to the routine updating, inclusion of new cases, and replacement of problem cases that accompany any new edition.

- Chapter 6 has undergone a fairly significant rewrite. More importantly, the chapter's discussion of property-related intentional torts has been expanded and cases for these torts included.

- Chapter 7's discussion of negligence and strict liability also has received a fairly significant rewrite.

- Chapter 8 incorporates some recent changes in the law regarding the duration of patents, as well as the 1996 Federal Trademark Dilution Act. It also expands the previous edition's discussions of patent infringement, copyright duration, copyright infringement, and the duration of trademarks.

- Chapter 29 includes the 1994 amendments to the Bankruptcy Code.

- Chapters 40–43 contain some new material on nonprofit corporations.

- Chapter 42 contains discussions of two new takeover defenses: golden parachutes and maintaining a corps of friendly shareholders.

- Chapter 44 includes some new material regarding securities offerings on the Internet.

- Chapter 45 now contains the Private Securities Litigation Reform Act of 1995, which limits the liability of most auditors to the amount of the investor's loss for which the auditor actually is responsible. An even more important inclusion is Securities Exchange Act section 10A, which imposes a public watchdog function on independent auditors, requiring them to report their clients' violations of law to the Securities and Exchange Commission.

- Chapter 47 contains some new material on the FTC's Telemarketing Sales Rule.

- Chapter 49 expands the discussion of federal enforcement authorities' recent attitudes toward mergers.

The Package

- *Instructor's Manual.* We have prepared the lengthy instructor's manual for this text. Each chapter in the manual contains outlined suggestions for structuring the presentation of the corresponding text chapter material, provides additional material and examples not mentioned in the text, discusses each text case while providing points for discussion with students, and answers the problem cases. Each text manual chapter also contains suggested answers to the chapter's ethical and public policy concerns.

Finally, the manual includes an answer key for questions presented in the student workbook.

- *Student Workbook.* The student workbook, prepared by Arlen Langvardt and Michael Phillips, contains true-false, multiple-choice, and short essay questions for each chapter.

- *Test Bank.* The text bank, prepared by Thomas Bowers, Arlen Langvardt, and Michael Phillips, contains true-false, multiple-choice, and short-essay questions. For each question, the manual includes an answer, a page reference to that answer, and a rating of the question's difficulty. In addition, a computerized version of the test bank is available. It enables instructors to generate random tests and to add their own questions.

- *Case Videos.* As was true for its predecessor, adopters of the tenth edition can obtain Irwin's 20 case videos for classroom use. These contemporary dramatizations of business law issues sometimes focus on issues within a particular chapter, or may span different chapters. Portions of the case videos are integrated as problem cases in many chapters. They are designated by a video cassette icon ▣ and the term *Video Case.* In addition, Supplementary Video Case Notes, prepared by Richard Finkley of Governors State University, outline the facts, question, issues, and decision for each video segment, and direct instructors to the appropriate chapter. This material is included in the Instructor's Manual.

ACKNOWLEDGMENTS

Through conversations, focus groups, and reviews, you have contributed ideas and time to the development of *Business Law and The Regulatory Environment.* Our sincere appreciation to the following:

Mary Jane Dundas, Arizona State University

James E. Macdonald, Weber State College

Robert D. McNutt, California State University, Northridge

Roscoe Shain, Austin Peay State University

Susan Jarvis, Pan American University

Kay Creasman, Virginia Commonwealth University

Ralph Quinones, Loyola Marymount University

Daniel Reynolds, Middle Tennessee State University

James Van de Bogart, University of Wisconsin-Whitewater

Walter Jensen, Virginia Polytechnic Institute

Michael Howard, University of Iowa

James F. Morgan, California State University-Chico

Wayne Anderson, Southwest Missouri State University

Frank Chong, Southwest Missouri State University

William Elliott, Saginaw Valley State University

Michael Engber, Ball State University

Gene Marsh, The University of Alabama

Gregory Naples, Marquette University

Rick Orsinger, College of DuPage

Dennis Pappas, Columbus State Community College

Robert Peace, North Carolina State University

Carol Rasnic, Virginia Commonwealth University

Linda Samuels, George Mason University

Daphne Sipes, University of Texas at San Antonio

Rodolfo Camacho, Oregon State University

Theodore Dinges, Longview Community College

Carey Mills, Florida Atlantic University

We would also like to express our thanks to Michael B. Metzger, who no longer is participating on the book effective this edition. Mike's continuing administrative responsibilities and his pursuit of important teaching initiatives have precluded his continuing as an author. We are grateful for his many contributions to the book's success.

In addition, we were fortunate to work with the following team of professionals at Irwin/McGraw-Hill in making this book and package a reality: Craig Beytien, Karen Mellon, Robert Preskill, and Jerry Saykes.

Finally, we wish to extend our appreciation to the faculty and students who have made many unsolicited suggestions for improving previous editions.

Jane P. Mallor
A. James Barnes
Thomas Bowers
Michael J. Phillips
Arlen W. Langvardt

BRIEF CONTENTS

CONTENTS

Appendixes

Foundations of American Law

The Nature of Law

T oday, businesspeople confront the law at every turn. For example, business firms continually use the law of property, contract, and agency. Indeed, business could hardly function without these and other basic bodies of law. In addition to assisting business activity, the legal system restricts it as well. Today, government regulates most aspects of a firm's operations—for example, advertising, product safety, employee relations, the issuance of securities, and behavior toward competitors.

Thus, businesspeople constantly use, rely on, react to, plan around—and sometimes violate—innumerable legal rules (or laws). For this reason, managers should have a general knowledge of the legal system and the most important legal rules affecting their firms. This text discusses many such rules, often in detail. But your ability to use and apply the legal rules affecting business is incomplete unless you also understand law's general nature, its functions, and how judges interpret it. This understanding could go some way toward reducing business complaints about the law and lawyers.

To help provide such an understanding, this chapter examines law's nature from four different angles. First, it describes, classifies, and ranks the various kinds of rules that are regarded as law in the United States—the *types of law*. This discussion, however, only partly conveys law's general nature. Thus, the chapter's second section discusses a subject known as *jurisprudence* or legal philosophy. Jurisprudence tries to establish a general definition of law, and each of the competing definitions we examine highlights an important facet of law's many-sided nature. Shifting from the theoretical to the pragmatic, this chapter's third section examines some of the *functions* law serves—what it *does*. The chapter concludes by discussing *legal reasoning,* the set of techniques judges use when interpreting legal rules. This discussion should help dispel the common misconception that the law consists of clear and precise commands that judges merely look up and then mechanically apply. ∽

TYPES AND CLASSIFICATIONS OF LAW

The Types of Law

Constitutions   Constitutions, which exist at the state and federal levels, have two general functions.[1] First, they set up the structure of government for the political unit they control (a state or the federal government). This involves creating the branches and subdivisions of the government and stating the powers given and denied to each. Through its **separation of powers,** for example, the U.S. Constitution establishes a Congress and gives it power to legislate or *make* law in certain areas, provides for a chief executive (the president) whose function is to execute or *enforce* the laws, and helps create a federal judiciary to *interpret* the laws. The U.S. Constitution also structures the relationship between the federal government and the states. In the process, it respects the principle of **federalism** by recognizing the states' power to make law in certain areas.

The second function of constitutions is to prevent other units of government from taking certain actions or passing certain laws. Constitutions do so mainly by prohibiting government action that restricts certain individual rights. The Bill of Rights to the U.S. Constitution is an example.

Statutes   Statutes are laws created by Congress or a state legislature. They are stated in an authoritative form in statute books or codes. As you will see, however, their interpretation and application are often difficult.

Throughout this text, you will encounter state statutes that were originally drafted as **uniform acts.** Uniform acts are model statutes drafted by private bodies of lawyers and/or scholars. They do not become law until they are enacted by a legislature. Their aim is to produce state-by-state uniformity on the subjects they address. Examples include

the Uniform Commercial Code (which deals with a wide range of commercial law subjects), the Uniform Partnership Act, the Revised Uniform Limited Partnership Act, and the Revised Model Business Corporation Act.

Common Law   The common law (also called judge-made law or case law) is that law made and applied by judges as they decide cases not governed by statutes or other types of law. In theory, the common law exists at the state level only. The common law originated in medieval England. It developed from the decisions of judges in settling disputes. Over time, judges began to follow the decisions of other judges in similar cases. This practice became formalized in the doctrine of *stare decisis* (let the decision stand). As you will see later in the chapter, *stare decisis* has enabled the common law to evolve to meet changing social conditions. Thus, the common law rules in force today often differ considerably from the common law rules of earlier times.

The common law came to America with the first English settlers and was applied by courts during the colonial period. It continued to be applied after the Revolution and the adoption of the Constitution, and it still governs many cases today. For example, the rules of tort, contract, and agency discussed in this text are mainly common law rules. However, the states have codified (enacted into statute) some parts of the common law. They also have passed statutes superseding judge-made law in certain situations. As discussed in Chapter 9, for example, the states have established special rules for contract cases involving the sale of goods by enacting Article 2 of the Uniform Commercial Code.

This text's torts, contracts, and agency chapters often refer to the *Restatement* (or *Restatement (Second)*) rule on a particular subject. The *Restatements* are collections of common law (and occasionally statutory) rules covering various areas of the law. Because they are promulgated by the American Law Institute rather than by courts, the *Restatements* are not law and do not bind courts. However, state courts often find *Restatement* rules persuasive and adopt them as common law rules within their states. Usually, the *Restatement* rules are the rules actually followed by a majority of the states. Occasionally, however, the *Restatements* stimulate changes in the common law by stating new rules that the courts later decide to follow.

---

[1]Chapter 3 discusses constitutional law as it applies to government regulation of business.

Equity   The body of law called **equity** has traditionally tried to do discretionary rough justice in situations where common law rules would produce unfair results. In medieval England, common law rules were technical and rigid and the remedies available in common law courts were too few. This meant that some deserving parties could not obtain adequate relief in the common law courts. As a result, the chancellor, the king's most powerful executive officer, began to hear cases that the common law courts could not resolve fairly.

Eventually, separate equity courts emerged to handle the cases heard by the chancellor. These courts took control of a case only when there was no adequate remedy in a regular common law court. In equity courts, procedures were flexible, and rigid rules of law were de-emphasized in favor of general moral maxims. Equity courts also provided several remedies not available in the common law courts (which generally awarded only money damages or the recovery of property). Perhaps the most important of these *equitable remedies* is the **injunction,** a court order forbidding a party to do some act or commanding him to perform some act. Others include the contract remedies of **specific performance** (whereby a party is ordered to perform according to the terms of her contract), **reformation** (in which the court rewrites the contract's terms to reflect the parties' real intentions), and **rescission** (a cancellation of a contract in which the parties are returned to their precontractual position).

Like the common law, equity principles and practices were brought to the American colonies by the English settlers. They continued to be used after the Revolution and the adoption of the Constitution. Over time, however, the once-sharp line between law and equity has become blurred. Most states have abolished separate equity courts, now allowing one court to handle both legal and equitable claims. Also, equitable principles have been blended together with common law rules, and some traditional equity doctrines have been restated as common law or statutory rules. An example is the doctrine of unconscionability discussed in Chapter 15. Finally, courts sometimes combine an award of money damages with an equitable remedy.

Administrative   Regulations   and   Decisions
Throughout this century, the *administrative agencies* established by Congress and the state legislatures and discussed in Chapter 46 have acquired considerable power, importance, and influence over business. A major reason for the rise of administrative agencies was the collection of social and economic problems created by the industrialization of the United States that began late in the 19th century. Because legislatures generally lacked the time and expertise to deal with these problems on a continuing basis, the creation of specialized, expert agencies was almost inevitable.

Administrative agencies get the ability to make law through a *delegation* (or handing over) of power from the legislature. Agencies normally are created by a statute that specifies the areas in which the agency can make law and the scope of its power in each area. Often, these statutory delegations are worded so broadly that the legislature has, in effect, merely pointed to a problem and given the agency wide-ranging powers to deal with it.

The two kinds of law made by administrative agencies are **administrative regulations** and **agency decisions.** Like statutes, administrative regulations appear in a precise form in one authoritative source. However, they differ from statutes because the body enacting them is an agency, not the legislature. In addition, some agencies have an internal court structure that enables them to hear cases arising under the statutes and regulations they enforce. The resulting agency decisions are another kind of law.

Treaties   According to the U.S. Constitution, **treaties** made by the president with foreign governments and approved by two-thirds of the U.S. Senate are "the supreme Law of the Land." As we note shortly, treaties invalidate inconsistent state (and sometimes federal) laws.

Ordinances   State governments have subordinate units that exercise certain functions. Some of these units, such as school districts, have limited powers. Others, such as counties, municipalities, and townships, exercise various governmental functions. The enactments of municipalities are called **ordinances;** zoning ordinances are an example. The enactments of other political subdivisions may also be called ordinances.

Executive Orders   In theory, the president or a state's governor is a chief executive who enforces the laws but has no law-making powers. However, these officials sometimes have the power to issue laws called **executive orders.** This power normally results from a legislative delegation.

Priority Rules

Because the different types of law conflict, rules for determining which type takes priority are necessary. Here, we briefly describe the most important such rules.

1. According to the principle of **federal supremacy,** the U.S. Constitution, federal laws enacted pursuant to it, and treaties are the supreme law of the land. This means that federal law defeats conflicting state law.
2. Constitutions defeat other types of law within their domain. Thus, a state constitution defeats all other state laws inconsistent with it, and the U.S. Constitution defeats inconsistent federal laws.
3. When a treaty conflicts with a federal statute over a purely domestic matter, the measure that is latest in time usually prevails.
4. Within either the state or the federal domain, statutes defeat conflicting laws that depend on a legislative delegation for their validity. For example, a state statute defeats an inconsistent state administrative regulation.
5. State statutes and any laws derived from them by delegation defeat inconsistent common law

---

CONCEPT   REVIEW

The Types of Law Compared

	WHO ENACTS?	STATE AND/OR FEDERAL?	STATED IN ONE AUTHORITATIVE FORM?	REMARKS
Constitutions	U.S. Constitution originally ratified by states; complex amendment process. States may vary.	Both	Yes, but see Chapter 3 on constitutional decision making.	Defeat other forms of positive law within sphere (federal or state)
Statutes	Legislatures	Both	Yes, but see this chapter's discussion of statutory interpretation.	Normally defeat other forms of positive law within sphere (federal or state) except constitutions
Common Law	Courts	In theory, state only	No. See this chapter's discussion of legal reasoning.	Law of tort, contract, and agency mainly common law
Equity	Formerly, equity courts; now usually courts in general	In theory, state only. But equitable principles pervade federal law as well.	No	Traditional separation of law and equity now virtually gone
Administrative Regulations	Administrative agencies	Both	Yes	See Chapter 46
Administrative Decisions	Administrative agencies	Both	No	See Chapter 46
Treaties	President plus two-thirds of Senate	Federal	Yes	Defeat inconsistent state law
Ordinances	Usually, local government bodies	State (mainly local)	Yes	
Executive Orders	Chief executives	Both	Yes	Usually based on delegation from legislature

rules. For example, either a statute or a state administrative regulation defeats a conflicting common law rule.

Classifications of Law

Cutting across the different types of law are three common *classifications* of law. These classifications involve distinctions between: (1) criminal law and civil law, (2) substantive law and procedural law, and (3) public law and private law. One type of law might be classified in each of these ways. For example, a state homicide statute would be criminal, substantive, and public; a rule of contract law would be civil, substantive, and private.

Criminal and Civil Law **Criminal law** is the law under which the government prosecutes someone for committing a crime. It is said to create duties that are owed to the public as a whole. **Civil law** mainly concerns obligations that private parties owe to other private parties. It is the law applied when one private party sues another private party because the second party did not meet a legal duty owed to the first party. (For this purpose, the government may be treated as a private party and thus as a party to a civil suit; for example, a city may sue, or be sued by, a construction contractor.) Criminal penalties (e.g., imprisonment or fines) differ from civil remedies (e.g., money damages or equitable relief). Although most of the legal rules in this text are civil law rules, Chapter 5 deals specifically with the criminal law, and criminal provisions may appear in other chapters.

Even though the civil law and the criminal law are distinct bodies of law, the same behavior can violate both. For instance, if due to A's careless driving his car hits and injures B, A may face both a criminal prosecution by the state and B's civil suit for damages.

Substantive Law and Procedural Law **Substantive law** sets the rights and duties of people as they act in society. **Procedural law** controls the behavior of government bodies (mainly courts) as they establish and enforce rules of substantive law. A statute making murder a crime, for example, is a rule of substantive law. But the rules describing the proper conduct of a criminal trial are procedural. This text mainly discusses substantive law. Chapters 2 and 5, however, examine some of the procedural rules governing civil and criminal cases, respectively.

Public and Private Law **Public law** concerns the powers of government and the relations between government and private parties. Examples include constitutional law, administrative law, and criminal law. **Private law** establishes a framework of legal rules that enables private parties to set the rights and duties they owe each other. Examples include the rules of contract, property, and agency.

JURISPRUDENCE

The types of law sometimes are collectively referred to as *positive law*. Positive law comprises the rules that have been laid down (or posited) by a recognized political authority. Knowing the types of positive law is essential for understanding the American legal system and the business law topics discussed in this text. But defining *law* by listing these different kinds of positive law is much like defining the word *automobile* by describing all the vehicles going by that name. To define law properly, some people say, we need a general description that captures its essence.

The field known as **jurisprudence** or legal philosophy tries to provide such a description. Over time, different schools of jurisprudence have emerged, each with its own distinctive view of law. The differences among these schools are not just academic matters. As Figure 1 suggests, their conceptions of law often affect their approach toward real-life issues.

Legal Positivism

One feature common to all types of positive law is their enactment by a recognized political authority such as a legislature or an administrative agency. This common feature underlies the definition of law adopted by the school of jurisprudence called **legal positivism.** Legal positivists define law as the *command of a recognized political authority.* To the British political philosopher Thomas Hobbes, for instance, "Law properly, is the word of him, that by right hath command over others."

The commands made by recognized political authorities can be good, bad, or indifferent in moral terms. But as Figure 2 demonstrates, to legal positivists such commands are valid law regardless of their goodness or badness. For positivists, in other words, legal validity and moral validity are different

FIGURE 1

A Brief Sketch of the Jurisprudential Schools

	DEFINITION OF LAW	RELATION BETWEEN LAW AND MORALITY	PRACTICAL TENDENCY
Legal Positivism	Command of a recognized political authority	Separate questions: "law is law, just or not"	Valid positive law should be enforced and obeyed, just or not
Natural Law	All commands of recognized political authorities that are not unjust	"Unjust law is not law"	Unjust positive laws should not be enforced and obeyed
American Legal Realism	What public decisionmakers actually do	Unclear	"Law in action" often more important than "law in the books"
Sociological Jurisprudence	Process of social ordering in accordance with dominant social values and interests	Although moral values influence positive law, no way to say whether this is right or wrong	Law inevitably does (and should?) follow dominant social values and interests

FIGURE 2

The Positivist and Natural Law Definitions of Law

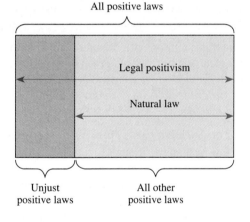

questions. Sometimes this view is expressed by the slogan: "Law is law, just or not." For this reason, some (but not all) positivists say that every properly enacted positive law should be enforced and obeyed, whether just or not. Similarly, positivist judges usually try to enforce the law as written, excluding their own moral views from the process.

Natural Law

At first glance, legal positivism's "law is law, just or not" approach may seem like perfect common sense. But it presents a problem, for it could mean that *any* positive law (no matter how unjust) is valid law and should be enforced and obeyed so long as some recognized political authority (no matter how wicked) enacted it. Here, the school of jurisprudence known as **natural law** takes issue with legal positivism by rejecting the positivist separation of law and morality.

The basic idea behind most systems of natural law is that some higher law or set of universal moral rules binds all human beings in all times and places. The Roman statesman Marcus Cicero described natural law as "the highest reason, implanted in nature, which commands what ought to be done and forbids the opposite." Because this higher law determines what is ultimately good and ultimately bad, it is a criterion for evaluating positive law. To Saint Thomas Aquinas, for example, "every human law has just so much of the nature of law, as it is derived from the law of nature." To be genuine law, in other words, positive law must resemble the law of nature by being good—or at least by not being bad. This suggests the practical natural law definition of law depicted in Figures 1 and 2—that it equals those commands of recognized political authorities that do not offend the higher law by being unjust.

Unjust positive laws, on the other hand, simply are not law. As Cicero put it: "What of the many deadly, the many pestilential statutes which are imposed on peoples? These no more deserve to be called laws than the rules a band of robbers might pass in their assembly." This view sometimes is expressed by the slogan: "An unjust law is not law." Because unjust positive laws are not truly law, many natural law thinkers conclude that they should not be enforced or obeyed.

As compared with positivist judges, therefore, judges influenced by natural law ideas are more likely to read constitutional provisions broadly to strike down positive laws they regard as unjust. They also are more likely to let morality influence their interpretation of the law. Of course, neither judges nor natural law thinkers always agree about what is moral and immoral. This is a major difficulty for the natural law position. This difficulty allows legal positivists to claim that only by keeping legal and moral questions separate can we get any stability and predictability in the law.

American Legal Realism

To some people, the debate between natural law and legal positivism seems unreal. Not only is natural law pie-in-the-sky, such people might say, but sometimes positive law does not mean much either. For example, juries often pay little attention to the legal rules that are supposed to guide their decisions, and prosecutors frequently have discretion whether or not to enforce criminal statutes. In some legal proceedings, moreover, the background, biases, and values of the judge—and not the positive law—determine the result. As the joke goes, justice sometimes is what the judge ate for breakfast.

Remarks like these typify the school of jurisprudence known as **American legal realism.** Legal realists regard the positivist law-in-the-books as less important than the *law in action*—the conduct of those who enforce and interpret the positive law. Thus, American legal realism defines law as the *behavior of public officials (mainly judges) as they deal with matters before the legal system.* Because the actions of such decisionmakers—and not the rules in the books—really affect people's lives, the realists say, this behavior is what counts and what deserves to be called law.

It is doubtful whether the legal realists have ever developed a common position on the relation between law and morality or the duty to obey positive law. But they have been quick to tell judges how to behave. Many realists feel that the modern judge should be a kind of social engineer who weighs all relevant values and considers social science findings when deciding a case. Such a judge would make the positive law only one factor in her decision. Be-

cause judges inevitably base their decisions on personal considerations, the realists seem to say, they should at least do this honestly and intelligently. To promote this kind of decisionmaking, the realists have sometimes favored fuzzy, discretionary rules that allow judges to decide each case according to its unique facts.

Sociological Jurisprudence

The term **sociological jurisprudence** is a general label uniting several different jurisprudential approaches whose common aim is to examine law within its social context. Their outlook is captured by the following quotation from Justice Oliver Wendell Holmes:

The life of the law has not been logic: it has been experience. The felt necessities of the time, the prevalent moral and political theories, intuitions of public policy, avowed or unconscious, even the prejudices which judges share with their fellow-men, have had a good deal more to do than the syllogism in determining the rules by which men should be governed. The law embodies the story of a nation's development through many centuries, and it cannot be dealt with as if it contained only the axioms and corollaries of a book of mathematics.[2]

Despite this common outlook, there is no distinctive sociological definition of law. If one were attempted, it might go as follows: *Law is a process of social ordering reflecting society's dominant interests and values.*

Different Sociological Approaches By examining a few examples of sociological legal thinking, we can put some flesh on the definition just offered. The "dominant interests" portion of the definition is exemplified by the writings of Roscoe Pound, an influential 20th-century American legal philosopher. Pound developed a detailed catalog of the social interests that press on government and the legal system and thus shape positive law. During his life, Pound's catalog changed along with changes in American society. An example of the definition's "dominant values" component is the *historical school* of jurisprudence identified with the 19th-century German legal philosopher Friedrich Karl von Savigny. Savigny saw law as an unplanned, almost unconscious, reflection of the collective spirit (*Volksgeist*) of a particular society. In his view, legal change could only be explained historically, as a slow response to social change.

---

[2]Holmes, *The Common Law* (1881).

By emphasizing the influence of dominant social interests and values, Pound and Savigny undermine the legal positivist view that law is nothing more than the command of some political authority. The early 20th-century Austrian legal philosopher Eugen Ehrlich went even further in rejecting positivism. He did so by distinguishing two different "processes of social ordering" contained within our definition of sociological jurisprudence. The first of these is "state law," or positive law. The second is the "living law," informal social controls such as customs, family ties, and business practices. By regarding both as law, Ehrlich blurred the line between positive law and other kinds of social ordering. In the process, he stimulated people to recognize that positive law is only one element within a spectrum of social controls.

The Implications of Sociological Jurisprudence
Because its definition of law includes social values, sociological jurisprudence seems to resemble natural law. But most sociological thinkers are only concerned with the *fact* that moral values influence

the law, and not with the goodness or badness of those values. In Chapter 20, for instance, we note that laissez-faire economic values were widely shared in 19th-century America and strongly influenced the product liability law of that period. But we do not say whether this was good or bad. Thus, it might seem that sociological jurisprudence gives no practical advice to those who must enforce and obey positive law.

However, sociological jurisprudence has at least one practical implication—a tendency to urge that the law must change to meet changing social conditions and values. This is basically the familiar notion that the law should keep up with the times. Some might stick to this view even when society's values are changing for the worse. To Holmes, for example, "[t]he first requirement of a sound body of law is, that it should correspond with the actual feelings and demands of the community, *whether right or wrong*."[3]

---

[3]The italics have been added for emphasis.

ROCHIN v. CALIFORNIA[4]   342 U.S. 165 (U.S. Sup. Ct. 1952)[4]

I *n 1949, three Los Angeles County deputy sheriffs heard that Antonio Rochin was selling narcotics. In search of evidence, they entered Rochin's home one morning and forced open the door to his bedroom. They spotted two capsules on a nightstand beside the bed on which the half-clad Rochin was sitting. After the deputies asked, "Whose stuff is this?" Rochin quickly put the capsules in his mouth. The deputies then jumped Rochin and tried to force the capsules from his mouth. When this proved unsuccessful, they handcuffed Rochin and took him to a hospital. Over Rochin's opposition, they had a doctor insert a tube into his stomach and force an emetic (vomit-inducing) solution through the tube. This stomach pumping caused Rochin to vomit. Within the material he disgorged were two capsules containing morphine.*

Rochin then was tried and convicted for possessing a morphine preparation in violation of California law. The two morphine capsules were the main evidence against him, and the trial court admitted this evidence over Rochin's objection. An intermediate appellate court and the California Supreme Court affirmed the conviction. Rochin then appealed to the U.S. Supreme Court. The main issue before the Court was whether the methods by which the deputies obtained the capsules violated the Due Process Clause of the U.S. Constitution's Fourteenth Amendment, which states that "No state shall . . . deprive any person of life, liberty, or property, without due process of law."

Note: At the time this case was decided, evidence obtained through a forced stomach pumping probably was admissible in a majority of the states that had considered the question. Also, the Supreme Court did not then require that state courts exclude evidence obtained through an illegal search or seizure. ∽

Frankfurter, Justice   The requirements of due process impose upon this Court an exercise of judgment upon the proceedings resulting in a con-

viction to ascertain whether they offend those canons of decency and fairness which express the notions of justice of English-speaking peoples even toward those charged with the most heinous offenses. These standards of justice are not authoritatively formulated anywhere as though they were

---

[4]At this point, you may want to read this chapter's appendix on the reading and briefing of cases.

specifics. Due process of law is a summarized guarantee of respect for those personal immunities so rooted in the traditions and conscience of our people as to be fundamental, or implicit in the concept of ordered liberty.

The vague contours of the due process clause do not leave judges at large. We may not draw upon our merely personal and private notions and disregard the limits that bind judges. These limits are derived from considerations that are fused in the whole nature of our judicial process. These are considerations deeply rooted in reason and in the compelling traditions of the legal profession. The due process clause places upon this Court the duty of exercising a judgment upon interests of society pushing in opposite directions. Due process thus conceived is not to be derided as a resort to the revival of "natural law."

Applying these general considerations to the present case, we conclude that the proceedings by which this conviction was obtained do more than offend some fastidious squeamishness or private sentimentalism about combatting crime too energetically. This is conduct that shocks the conscience. Illegally breaking into the privacy of Rochin, the struggle to open his mouth and remove what was there, the forcible extraction of his stomach's contents—this course of proceeding is bound to offend even hardened sensibilities. They are methods too close to the rack and the screw to permit of constitutional differentiation.

Judgment reversed in favor of Rochin.

Comparing the Schools

The *Rochin* case helps illustrate the differences among the schools of jurisprudence. To highlight those differences, consider the following questions. Do you believe Justice Frankfurter when he says that the Court's decision is not based on natural law? Is that decision closer to positivism's law-is-law-just-or-not approach, or to natural law's an-unjust-law-is-not-law approach? Do you think that a positivist would like this case? On the other hand, how would a legal realist look at *Rochin?* Specifically, what would such a person probably say about both the Court's decision and the police behavior here? With the benefit of hindsight, finally, it looks as if *Rochin* was a precursor of the many liberal criminal procedure decisions of the 1960s—decisions that probably had their roots in changed social values. If so, what might an exponent of sociological jurisprudence say about *Rochin?*

THE FUNCTIONS OF LAW

In traditional societies, people often viewed law as a set of unchanging rules that deserved obedience because they were part of the natural order of things. By now, however, most lawmakers treat law as a flexible *tool* or *instrument* for the accomplishment of chosen purposes. For example, the law of negotiable instruments discussed later in this text is designed to stimulate commercial activity by promoting the free movement of money substitutes such as promissory notes, checks, and drafts. Throughout the text, moreover, you see courts manipulating existing legal rules to get the results they desire. One strength of this *instrumentalist* attitude is its willingness to adapt the law to further the social good. One weakness is the legal instability and uncertainty those adaptations often produce.

Just as individual legal rules advance specific purposes, *law as a whole* serves many general social functions. Among the most important of those functions are:

1. *Peacekeeping.* The criminal law rules discussed in Chapter 5 best further this basic function of any legal system. Also, as Chapter 2 suggests, one major function of the civil law is the resolution of private disputes.

2. *Checking government power and thereby promoting personal freedom.* Obvious examples are the constitutional restrictions on government regulation in Chapter 3.

3. *Facilitating planning and the realization of reasonable expectations.* The rules of contract law discussed in Chapters 9–18 help fulfill this function of law.

4. *Promoting economic growth through free competition.* The antitrust laws discussed in Chapters 47–49 are among the many legal rules that help perform this function.

5. *Promoting social justice.* Throughout this century, government has intervened in private social and economic affairs to correct perceived

injustices and give all citizens equal access to life's basic goods. One example is the collection of employer–employee regulations treated in Chapter 50.

6. *Protecting the environment.* The most important federal environmental statutes are discussed in Chapter 51.

Obviously, the law's various functions can conflict. The familiar clash between economic growth and environmental protection is an example. The *Rochin* case illustrates the equally familiar conflict between effective law enforcement and the preservation of personal rights. Only rarely does the law achieve one end without sacrificing others to some degree. In law, as in life, there generally is no such thing as a free lunch. Where the law's ends conflict, lawmakers can only try to strike the best possible balance among those ends. This suggests limits on the law's usefulness as a device for promoting particular social goals.

LEGAL REASONING

This text's main aim is to describe the most important legal rules affecting business. Like most other business law texts, it states those rules in what lawyers call "black letter" form, using sentences saying that certain legal consequences will occur if certain events happen. Although it enables a clear statement of the law's commands, this black letter approach can be misleading. It suggests definiteness, certainty, permanence, and predictability—attributes the law frequently lacks. To illustrate this, and to give you some idea how lawyers think, we now discuss the two most important kinds of legal reasoning: **case law reasoning** and **statutory interpretation.**[5] However, we first must examine legal reasoning in general.

Legal reasoning is basically deductive, or syllogistic. The legal rule is the major premise, the facts are the minor premise, and the result is the product of combining the two. Suppose a state statute says that a driver operating an automobile between 55 and 70 miles per hour must pay a $50 fine (the rule or major premise) and that Jim Smith drives his car

at 65 miles per hour (the facts or minor premise). If Jim is arrested, and if the necessary facts can be proved, he will be required to pay the $50 fine. As you will now see, however, legal reasoning often is more difficult than this example would suggest.

Case Law Reasoning

In cases governed by the common law, courts find the appropriate legal rules in prior cases or *precedents.* The standard for choosing and applying prior cases to decide present cases is the doctrine of *stare decisis,* which states that like cases should be decided alike.[6] That is, the present case should be decided in the same way as past cases presenting the same facts and the same legal issues. If a court decides that an alleged precedent is not like the present case and should not control the decision in that case, it *distinguishes* the prior case.[7]

Because every present case differs from the precedents in *some* respect, it is always theoretically possible to distinguish those precedents. For example, one *could* distinguish a prior case because both parties in that case had black hair, while one party in the present case has brown hair. Of course, such distinctions are usually ridiculous, because the differences they identify are insignificant in moral or social policy terms. In other words, a good distinction of a prior case involves a widely accepted ethical or policy reason for treating the present case differently from its predecessor. Because people disagree about moral ideas, public policies, and the degree to which they are accepted, and because all these factors change over time, judges may differ on the wisdom of distinguishing a prior case. This is a significant source of uncertainty in the common law. But it also gives the common law the flexibility to adapt to changing social conditions.

The following *MacPherson* case illustrates the common law's ability to change over time. In the series of New York cases *MacPherson* discusses, the **plaintiff** (the party suing) claimed that the **defendant** (the party being sued) had been negligent in manufacturing or inspecting some product, thus injuring the plaintiff, who later purchased or

---

[5]The reasoning courts employ in constitutional cases resembles that used in common law cases, but often is somewhat looser. For the way courts decide constitutional cases, see Chapter 3.

[6]*Stare decisis* should be distinguished from the doctrine of *res judicata,* which says that a final judicial decision on the merits conclusively settles the rights of *the parties to the case.*

[7]Also, while they exercise the power infrequently, courts sometimes completely *overrule* their prior decisions.

used the product.[8] In the mid-19th century, such suits often failed due to the general rule that a seller or manufacturer was not liable for negligence unless there was *privity of contract* between the defendant and the plaintiff. Privity of contract is the existence of a direct contractual relationship between two parties. Thus, the no-liability-outside-privity rule prevented injured plaintiffs from recovering against a seller or manufacturer who had sold the product to a dealer who resold it to the plaintiff. Over time, however, courts began to allow injured plaintiffs to

recover from sellers or manufacturers with whom they had not directly dealt. These courts were creating *exceptions* to the general rule; that is, they were distinguishing prior cases announcing the rule and creating new rules to govern the situations they distinguished. *MacPherson* describes the gradual enlargement of such an exception in New York. Eventually, the exception "consumed the rule" by covering so many situations that the original rule became insignificant.[9]

_____
[8]Negligence law is discussed in Chapter 7.

_____
[9]The present status of the old no-liability-outside-privity rule in sale-of-goods cases is discussed in Chapter 20.

MACPHERSON v. BUICK MOTOR CO.   111 N.E. 1050 (N.Y. Ct. App. 1916)

One wheel of an automobile manufactured by the Buick Motor Company was made of defective wood. Buick could have discovered the defect had it made a reasonable inspection after it purchased the wheel from another manufacturer. Buick sold the car to a retail dealer, who then sold it to MacPherson. While MacPherson was driving his new Buick, the defective wheel collapsed and he was thrown from the vehicle. He sued Buick for his injuries in a New York trial court, alleging that it had negligently failed to inspect the wheel. Buick's main defense was that it had not dealt directly with MacPherson and thus owed no duty to him. Following trial and appellate court judgments in MacPherson's favor, Buick appealed to the New York Court of Appeals, the state's highest court. ∞

Cardozo, Justice   The foundations of this branch of the law were laid in *Thomas v. Winchester* (1852). A poison was falsely labeled. The sale was made to a druggist, who sold to a customer. The customer recovered damages from the seller who affixed the label. The defendant's negligence, it was said, put human life in imminent danger. A poison, falsely labeled, is likely to injure anyone who gets it. Because the danger is to be foreseen, there is a duty to avoid the injury. *Thomas v. Winchester* became quickly a landmark of the law. In the application of its principle there may, at times, have been uncertainty or even error. There has never been doubt or disavowal of the principle itself.

The chief cases are well known. *Loop v. Litchfield* (1870) was the case of a defect in a small balance wheel used on a circular saw. The manufacturer pointed out the defect to the buyer. The risk can hardly have been an imminent one, for the wheel lasted five years before it broke. In the meanwhile the buyer had made a lease of the machinery. It was held that the manufacturer was not answerable to the lessee. *Loop v. Litchfield* was

followed by *Losee v. Clute* (1873), the case of the explosion of a steam boiler. That decision must be confined to its special facts. It was put upon the ground that the risk of injury was too remote. The buyer had not only accepted the boiler, but had tested it. The manufacturer knew that his own test was not the final one. The finality of the test has a bearing on the measure of diligence owing to persons other than the purchaser.

These early cases suggest a narrow construction of the rule. Later cases evince a more liberal spirit. In *Devlin v. Smith* (1882), the defendant contractor built a scaffold for a painter. The painter's workmen were injured. The contractor was held liable. He knew that the scaffold, if improperly constructed, was a most dangerous trap. He knew that it was to be used by the workmen. Building it for their use, he owed them a duty to build it with care. From *Devlin v. Smith* we turn to *Statler v. Ray Manufacturing Co.* (1909). The defendant manufactured a large coffee urn. It was installed in a restaurant. The urn exploded and injured the plaintiff. We held that the manufacturer was liable. We said that the urn was of such a character that it was liable to become a source of great danger if not carefully and properly constructed.

It may be that *Devlin v. Smith* and *Statler v. Ray Manufacturing Co.* have extended the rule of *Thomas v. Winchester.* If so, this court is committed to the extension. The defendant argues that things imminently dangerous to human life are poisons, explosives, deadly weapons—things whose normal function is to injure or destroy. But whatever the rule in *Thomas v. Winchester* may once have been, it no longer has that restricted meaning. A scaffold is not inherently a destructive instrument. No one thinks of [a coffee urn] as an implement whose normal function is destruction.

We hold, then, that the principle of *Thomas v. Winchester* is not limited to things which are implements of destruction. If the nature of a thing is such that it is reasonably certain to place life and limb in peril when negligently made, it is a thing of danger. If to the element of danger there is added knowledge that the thing will be used by persons other than the purchaser, then, irrespective of

contract, the manufacturer is under a duty to make it carefully.

The nature of an automobile gives warning of probable danger if its construction is defective. This automobile was designed to go 50 miles an hour. Unless its wheels were sound and strong, injury was almost certain. The defendant knew the danger. It knew that the car would be used by persons other than the buyer, a dealer in cars. The dealer was indeed the one person of whom it might be said with some certainty that by him the car would not be used. Yet the defendant would have us say that he was the one person it was under a legal duty to protect. The law does not lead us to so inconsequent a conclusion. Precedents drawn from the age of travel by stagecoach do not fit the conditions of travel today. The principle that the danger must be imminent does not change, but the things subject to the principle do change. They are whatever the needs of life in a developing civilization require them to be.

Judgment for MacPherson affirmed.

Statutory Interpretation

Because statutes are written in one authoritative form, their interpretation might seem easier than case law reasoning. However, this is not so. One reason courts face difficulties when interpreting statutes is the natural ambiguity of language. This is especially true when statutory words are applied to situations the legislature did not foresee. Also, legislators may deliberately use ambiguous language when they are unwilling or unable to deal specifically with each situation the statute was enacted to regulate. When this happens, the legislature expects courts and/or administrative agencies to fill in the details on a case-by-case basis. Other reasons for deliberate ambiguity include the need for legislative compromise and legislators' desire to avoid taking controversial positions.

Due to problems like these, courts need and use various techniques of statutory interpretation. As you will see shortly, different techniques can dictate different results in a particular case. Moreover, judges sometimes employ the techniques in an instrumentalist or result-oriented fashion, emphasiz-

ing the technique that will produce the result they want and downplaying the others. Thus, it is unclear which technique should control when different techniques yield different results. Although there are some "rules" on this subject, judges often ignore them or use them selectively.

Plain Meaning   Courts begin their interpretation of a statute with its actual language. Where the statute's words have a clear, common, accepted meaning, some courts employ the *plain meaning rule*. This rule states that in such cases, the court should simply apply the statute according to the plain, accepted meaning of its words, and should not concern itself with anything else.

Legislative History   Some courts, like the Supreme Court in the following *Weber* case, refuse to follow a statute's plain meaning when its legislative history suggests a different result. And almost all courts resort to legislative history when the statute's language is ambiguous. A statute's legislative history includes the following sources: the reports of investigative committees or law revision commissions that led to the legislation, the hearings of the legislative committee(s) originally considering the legislation, any reports issued by such a committee, legislative debates, the report of a conference committee reconciling two houses' conflicting versions of the law, amendments or defeated amendments to the legislation, other bills not passed by the legislature but proposing similar legislation, and discrepancies between a bill passed by one house and the final version of the statute.

Sometimes a statute's legislative history provides no information or conflicting information about its meaning, its scope, or its purposes. Also, some sources are more authoritative than others. The worth of debates, for instance, may depend on which legislator (e.g., the sponsor of the bill or an uninformed blowhard) is quoted. Some sources are useful only in particular situations; prior unpassed bills and amendments or defeated amendments are examples. To illustrate those sources, consider whether mopeds are covered by an air pollution statute applying to "automobiles, trucks, buses, and other motorized passenger or cargo vehicles." If the statute's original version included mopeds but this reference was removed by amendment, it is unlikely that the legislature wanted mopeds to be covered. The same might be true if six similar unpassed bills had included mopeds but the bill that was eventually passed did not, or if one house had passed a bill including mopeds but mopeds did not appear in the final version of the legislation.

Courts use legislative history in two overlapping but distinguishable ways. They may use it to determine what the legislature thought about the specific meaning of statutory language. They may also use it to determine the overall aim, end, or goal of the legislation. In this second case, they then ask whether a particular interpretation of the statute is consistent with this purpose. To illustrate the difference between these two uses of legislative history, suppose that a court is considering whether our pollution statute's "other motorized passenger or cargo vehicles" language includes battery-powered vehicles. The court might scan the legislative history for specific references to battery-powered vehicles or other indications of what the legislature thought about their inclusion. However, the court might also use the same history to determine the overall aims of the statute, and then ask whether

including battery-powered vehicles is consistent with those aims. Because the history probably would reveal that the statute's purpose was to reduce air pollution from internal combustion engines, the court might well conclude that battery-powered vehicles should not be covered.

General Public Purpose Occasionally, courts construe statutory language in the light of various *general public purposes.* These purposes are not the purposes underlying the statute in question; rather, they are widely accepted general notions of public policy. In one case, for example, the U.S. Supreme Court used the general public policy against racial discrimination in education as one argument for denying tax-exempt status to a private university that discriminated on the basis of race.[10]

Prior Interpretations Courts sometimes follow prior cases (and administrative decisions) interpreting a statute regardless of the statute's plain meaning or its legislative history. The main argument for following these prior interpretations is to promote stability and certainty by preventing each successive court that considers a statute from adopting its own interpretation. The courts' willingness to follow a prior interpretation depends on such factors as the number of past courts adopting the interpretation, the authoritativeness of those courts, and the number of years that the interpretation has been followed. Note that in *Weber,* the Supreme Court arguably did not follow one of its own prior interpretations.

Maxims Maxims are general rules of thumb employed in statutory interpretation. There are many maxims, and courts tend to use them or ignore them at their discretion. One example of a maxim is the *ejusdem generis* rule, which says that when general words follow words of a specific, limited meaning, the general language should be limited to things of the same class as those specifically stated. Suppose that the pollution statute quoted earlier listed 32 types of gas-powered vehicles and ended with the words "and other motorized passenger or cargo vehicles." Here, *ejusdem generis* probably would dictate that battery-powered vehicles not be included.

---

[10]*Bob Jones University v. United States,* 461 U.S. 574 (1983).

UNITED STEELWORKERS v. WEBER   443 U.S. 193 (U.S. Sup. Ct. 1979)

A s part of its collective bargaining agreement with the United Steelworkers of America, the Kaiser Aluminum and Chemical Company established a new on-the-job craft training program at its Gramercy, Louisiana plant. The selection of trainees for the program was based on seniority, but at least 50 percent of the new trainees had to be black until the percentage of black skilled craft workers in the plant approximated the percentage of blacks in the local labor force.

Brian Weber was a rejected white applicant who would have qualified for the program had the racial preference not existed. He sued Kaiser and the union in federal district court, arguing that the racial preference violated Title VII of the 1964 Civil Rights Act. Section 703(a) of the act stated: "It shall be an unlawful employment practice for an employer . . . to discriminate against any individual with respect to his compensation, terms, conditions, or privileges of employment, because of such individual's race, color, religion, sex, or national origin." Section 703(d) had a similar provision specifically forbidding racial discrimination in admission to apprenticeship or other training programs. Weber's suit was successful, and the federal court of appeals affirmed. Kaiser and the union appealed to the U.S. Supreme Court. ∽

Brennan, Justice   The only question before us is whether Title VII forbids private employers and unions from voluntarily agreeing upon bona fide affirmative action plans that accord racial preferences in the manner and for the purpose provided in the Kaiser-USWA plan. That question was expressly left open in *McDonald v. Santa Fe Trail Transp. Co.* (1976), which held, in a case not involving affirmative action, that Title VII protects whites as well as blacks from racial discrimination.

Weber argues that Congress intended in Title VII to prohibit all race-conscious affirmative action plans. His argument rests upon a literal interpretation of sections 703(a) and (d) of the act. Those sections make it unlawful to discriminate because of race in the selection of apprentices for training programs. Since, the argument runs, *McDonald* settled that Title VII forbids discrimination against whites as well as blacks, and since the Kaiser-USWA plan discriminated against white employees solely because they are white, it follows that the plan violates Title VII.

Weber's argument is not without force. But it overlooks the fact that the Kaiser-USWA plan is an affirmative action plan voluntarily adopted by private parties to eliminate traditional patterns of racial segregation. It is a familiar rule, that a thing may be within the letter of the statute and yet not within the statute, because not within its spirit. Sections 703(a) and (d) must therefore be read against the background of the legislative history of Title VII and the historical context from which the act arose. Exami-

nation of these sources makes clear that an interpretation that forbade all race-conscious affirmative action would bring about an end completely at variance with the purpose of the statute and must be rejected.

Congress's primary concern in enacting the prohibition against racial discrimination in Title VII was the plight of the Negro in our economy. Before 1964, blacks were largely relegated to unskilled and semi-skilled jobs. Because of automation the number of such jobs was rapidly decreasing. As a consequence the relative position of the Negro worker was steadily worsening. Congress feared that the goal of the Civil Rights Act—the integration of blacks into the mainstream of American society—could not be achieved unless this trend were reversed. Accordingly, it was clear to Congress that the crux of the problem was to open employment opportunities for Negroes in occupations which have traditionally been closed to them, and it was to this problem that Title VII's prohibition against racial discrimination in employment was primarily addressed.

Given this legislative history, we cannot agree with Weber that Congress intended to prohibit the private sector from taking effective steps to accomplish the goal that Congress designed Title VII to achieve. It would be ironic indeed if a law triggered by a nation's concern over centuries of racial injustice and intended to improve the lot of those who had been excluded from the American dream for so long, constituted the first legislative prohibition of all voluntary, private, race-conscious efforts to abolish traditional patterns of racial segregation and hierarchy.

We need not define the line between permissible and impermissible affirmative action plans. It suffices to hold that the challenged plan falls on the permissible side of the line. The purposes of the plan mirror those of the statute. Both were designed to break down old patterns of racial segregation and hierarchy, and to open employment opportunities for Negroes in occupations which have been traditionally closed to them. At the same time the plan does not unnecessarily trammel the interests of the white employees. Nor does the plan create an absolute bar to the advancement of white employees; half of those trained in the program will be white. Moreover, the plan is a temporary measure. Preferential selection of craft trainees will end as soon as the percentage of black skilled craft workers approximates the percentage of blacks in the local labor force. We conclude therefore that the plan falls within the area of discretion left by Title VII to the private sector voluntarily to adopt affirmative action plans designed to eliminate conspicuous racial imbalance in traditionally segregated job categories.

Judgment reversed in favor of Kaiser and the union.

Limits on the Power of Courts

By now, you may think that anything goes when courts decide common law cases or interpret statutes. However, many factors discourage courts from adopting a totally freewheeling approach. Due to their legal training and mental makeup, judges tend to respect established precedents and the will of the legislature. Many courts issue written opinions, which expose judges to academic and professional criticism. Lower court judges may be discouraged from innovation by the fear of being overruled by a higher court. Finally, political factors inhibit judges. For example, some judges are elected, and even judges with lifetime tenure can sometimes be removed.

An even more fundamental limit on the power of courts is that they cannot make law until some parties present them with a case to decide. In addition, any such case must be a *real dispute;* that is, courts generally limit themselves to genuine, existing "cases or controversies" between real parties with tangible opposing interests in the lawsuit. Thus, courts generally do not issue *advisory opinions* on abstract legal questions unrelated to a genuine dispute, and do not decide *feigned controversies* that parties concoct to get answers to such questions. Also, courts may refuse to decide suits that are insufficiently *ripe* to have matured into a genuine controversy, or that are *moot* because there no longer is a real dispute between the parties. Expressing similar ideas is the doctrine of **standing to sue,** which generally requires that the plaintiff have some direct, tangible, and substantial stake in the outcome of the suit.

Nonetheless, state and federal **declaratory judgment** statutes allow parties to determine their rights and duties even though their controversy has not advanced to the point where harm has occurred and legal relief may be necessary. This enables them to determine their legal position without taking action that could expose them to liability. For example, if Joan thinks that she is not obligated to perform her contract to Jim, she may seek a declaratory judgment on the question rather than risk Jim's lawsuit by breaking the contract. Usually, though, a declaratory judgment is awarded only when the parties' dispute is sufficiently advanced to constitute a real case or controversy.

> ### ETHICAL AND PUBLIC POLICY CONCERNS

1. What might be troubling about the result in this chapter's *Rochin* case? (*Hint:* Today, what aspect of the case is commonly regarded as one of the country's most serious problems?) As discussed in Chapter 4, moral philosophers sometimes distinguish *deontological* ethical theories from *consequentialist* (or teleological) ethical theories. Strict or extreme deontological theories say that certain actions are right or wrong and should be pursued or avoided, no matter what the consequences of doing so. Consequentialist theories, on the other hand, assess the moral worth of actions by looking to their consequences. Which of these approaches best describes the Supreme Court's decision in *Rochin?*

2. Earlier in this chapter, we quoted Justice Holmes's statement that "[t]he first requirement of a sound body of law is, that it should correspond with the actual feelings and demands of the community, whether right or wrong." This statement may mean that the law should reflect prevailing moral views, whatever they happen to be. What is good about such an approach to the law and to lawmaking? What is bad about it?

3. Legal positivists often say that even morally bad laws are still law and that such laws (or some of them, at least) should still be enforced and obeyed. What *moral* arguments can you make for this position?

APPENDIX
READING AND BRIEFING CASES

Throughout this text, you encounter cases—the judicial opinions accompanying court decisions. These cases are highly edited versions of their much longer originals. What follows are a few explanations and pointers to assist you in studying cases.

1. Each case has a *case name* that includes at least some of the parties to the case. Because the order of the parties may change when a case is appealed, do not assume that the first party listed is the plaintiff (the party suing) and the second the defendant (the party being sued). Also, because some cases have many plaintiffs and/or many defendants, the parties discussed in the court's opinion sometimes differ from those found in the case name.

2. Each case also has a *citation*, which includes the volume and page number of the legal reporter in which the full case appears, plus the year the case was decided. *United Steelworkers v. Weber,* for instance, begins on page 193 of volume 443 of the United States Reports (the official reporter for U.S. Supreme Court decisions), and was decided in 1979. (Each of the many different legal reporters has its own abbreviation, and they are too numerous to include here.) In the parenthesis accompanying the date, we also give you some information about the court that decided the case. For example: "U.S. Sup. Ct." is the United States Supreme Court, "3d

Cir." is the U.S. Court of Appeals for the Third Circuit, "S.D.N.Y." is the U.S. District Court for the Southern District of New York, "Minn. Sup. Ct." is the Minnesota Supreme Court, and "Mich. Ct. App." is the Michigan Court of Appeals (a Michigan intermediate appellate court). Chapter 2 describes the various kinds of courts.

3. At the beginning of each case, there is a *statement of facts* containing the most important facts that gave rise to the case.

4. Immediately after the statement of facts, we give you the case's *procedural history.* (Chapter 2 discusses civil procedure and Chapter 5 discusses criminal procedure.) Basically, this history tells you what courts previously handled the case you are reading, and how they dealt with it.

5. Next comes your major concern: the *body of the court's opinion.* Here, the court typically determines the applicable law and applies it to the facts to reach a conclusion. The court's discussion of the relevant law may be elaborate; it can include prior cases, legislative history, applicable public policies, and more. The court's application of the law to the facts usually occurs after it has arrived at the applicable legal rule(s), but also may be intertwined with its legal discussion.

6. At the very end of the case, we complete the procedural history by stating the court's *decision.* For example, "Judgment reversed in favor of Smith" says that a lower court judgment *against* Smith was reversed on appeal, which means that Smith's appeal was successful and Smith wins.

7. The cases' main function is to provide concrete examples of rules stated in the text. (Frequently, the text tells you what point the case illustrates.) In studying law, it is easy to conclude that your task is finished once you have memorized a black letter rule. In real life, however, legal problems rarely present themselves as abstract questions of law; instead, they are hidden in particular situations you encounter or particular actions you take. Without some sense of a legal rule's real-life application, therefore, your knowledge of that rule is incomplete. The cases help provide this sense.

8. You may find it helpful to *brief* the cases. There is no one correct way to brief a case, but most good briefs contain the following elements: (1) a short statement of the relevant facts, (2) the case's prior history, (3) the question(s) or issue(s) the court had to decide, (4) the answer(s) to those question(s), (5) the reasoning the court used to justify its decision, and (6) the final result. Using "P" and "D" for the plaintiff and defendant, a brief of the *Weber* case might look like this:

United Steelworkers v. Weber (p. 15)

Facts   The Ds were a private employer and a union that had voluntarily established a craft training program through a collective bargaining agreement. The procedures for selecting the program's trainees favored black workers over white workers by establishing an effective 50 percent quota for the former. P, a white worker who was denied access to the program, would have qualified had the racial preference not existed.

History   P sued the Ds under Title VII of the 1964 Civil Rights Act, which forbids employment discrimination on the basis of race. He won in federal district court and the court of appeals affirmed. The Ds appealed to the U.S. Supreme Court.

Issue   Does this voluntary racial preference favoring blacks violate Title VII's ban on racial discrimination in employment?

Answer   No.

Reasoning   Even though Title VII's plain meaning favors P and a prior interpretation holds that Title VII forbids racial discrimination against both whites and blacks, neither point is decisive. The reason is that holding for P would frustrate Title VII's purpose. Title VII's legislative history and its historical context make clear that its aim was to integrate blacks into the American mainstream. This was especially true in the area of employment, an area in which blacks were falling behind. The Ds' preference helped further this purpose because it helped blacks get better jobs, and declaring the preference illegal would have frustrated the purpose.

Result   Court of appeals decision reversed; Ds win.

PROBLEM CASES

1. In which way do administrative regulations resemble statutes? In which way do they differ from statutes?

2. Suppose that Congress passes a federal statute that conflicts with a state constitutional provision. The state argues that the constitutional provision should prevail over the statute because constitutions are a higher, more authoritative kind of law than statutes. Is this argument correct? Why or why not?

3. Suppose that someone objects to the president's promulgation of an executive order by claiming that the U.S. Constitution only gives the president the power to *execute* the laws, not the power to make them. What concept explains the president's power to make law through executive orders? Explain its meaning.

4. State A passes a statute declaring that those who sell heroin are to receive a mandatory 30-year prison sentence. Describe this statute in terms of the three classifications of law stated in the text—criminal/civil, substantive/procedural, and public/private.

5. Nation X is a dictatorship in which one ruler has the ultimate lawmaking power. The ruler issues a statute declaring that certain religious minorities are to be exterminated. An international convocation of jurisprudential scholars meets to discuss the question, "Is Nation X's extermination statute truly law?" What would be the typical natural law answer to this question? What would be the typical legal positivist response? Assume that all of those present at the convocation think that Nation X's statute is morally wrong.

6. Nation Y has enacted positive laws forbidding all abnormal sexual relations between consenting adults. However, the police of Nation Y rarely enforce these laws, and even when they do, prosecutors never bring charges against violators. What observation would American legal realists make about this situation? In order to determine what a believer in natural law would think about these laws, what else would you have to know?

7. Many states and localities used to have so-called Sunday Closing laws—statutes or ordinances forbidding the conduct of certain business on Sunday. A few may still do so. Often, these laws have not been obeyed or enforced. What would an extreme legal positivist tend to think about the duty to enforce and obey such laws? What would a natural law exponent who strongly believes in economic freedom tend to think about this question? What about a natural law adherent who is a Christian religious traditionalist? What *observation* would almost any American legal realist make about Sunday Closing laws? Looking at these laws from a sociological perspective, finally, what social factors help explain their original passage, their relative lack of enforcement today, and their continuance on the books despite their lack of enforcement?

8. The Supreme Court of State X is about to decide on the constitutionality of a statute restricting some controversial activity. Three of the court's justices—Justices A, B, and C—are taking the coming decision very seriously. In an effort to determine the true rule of law that governs the case, Justice A is reading and rereading all the relevant precedents and legislative history. In order to determine what result is morally right, Justice B is reading books on moral philosophy. To determine what the public thinks, finally, Justice C is reading every available public opinion poll on the behavior at issue in the case. Which jurisprudential schools do Justices A, B, and C most nearly exemplify?

9. Although you would not know this from reading the *MacPherson* case in this chapter, two of the cases mentioned there distinguished *Thomas v. Winchester* (the case involving the falsely labeled poison) in a certain way. The courts in *Loop v. Litchfield* (the circular saw case) and *Losee v. Clute* (the steam boiler case) both distinguished *Thomas v. Winchester* because in *Thomas,* the thing that caused the injury—a poison—was *by its nature intended to cause harm.* In other words, these courts held that a poison should be treated differently from a circular saw that flies apart, or an exploding steam boiler. If the relevant public policy here is to allow recovery for injuries caused by highly dangerous products, does this distinction make any sense?

10. In 1910, the White Slave Traffic Act (usually known as the Mann Act) went into effect. Congress passed the act in response to an alleged white slave traffic in which gangs of certain nationalities were said to be forcing or luring American women into prostitution. One portion of the act stated that "any person who shall knowingly transport or cause to be transported ... any woman or girl for the purpose of prostitution or debauchery, or for any other immoral purpose, ... shall be deemed guilty of a felony." In 1913, F. Drew Caminetti was indicted for transporting a woman from Sacramento, California, to Reno, Nevada, to be his mistress. Which technique of statutory interpretation would you use in arguing that Caminetti is guilty under the Mann Act? Which technique would you use to argue that Caminetti should not be guilty under the act?

The Resolution of Private Disputes

Most business law courses deal mainly with substantive legal rules—laws that tell people how to behave in organized social life. Examples include the rules of property, contract, tort, and agency law, as well as federal regulation of business. Most of these rules are civil law rules—rules the courts apply in suits between private parties. But what about the courts themselves? And what about the *procedures* courts follow in civil cases? This chapter discusses these and related matters. One of these related subjects, *alternative dispute resolution,* concerns a collection of processes for resolving private disputes outside the regular court system. ∽

STATE COURTS AND THEIR JURISDICTION

The United States has 52 court systems—a federal system, plus a system for each state and the District of Columbia. This section describes the various kinds of state courts. It also considers the kinds of cases they have power to resolve, or their *jurisdiction.*

Courts of Limited Jurisdiction

Minor criminal matters and civil disputes involving small amounts of money frequently are decided in *courts of limited jurisdiction* (also called courts of inferior or special jurisdiction). Examples include justice of the peace courts, traffic courts, probate courts, and small claims courts. Such courts often handle a large number of cases. Their procedures may be informal, the presiding judicial officer may not be a lawyer, and the parties may argue their own cases. Also, courts of limited jurisdiction usually are not courts of record; that is, they ordinarily do not keep a transcript of the testimony and proceedings. Thus, appeals from their decisions require a new trial (a trial *de novo*) in a trial court.

Trial Courts

Courts of limited jurisdiction find the relevant facts, identify the appropriate rule(s) of law, and combine the facts and the law to reach a decision. State trial courts do the same, but differ from inferior courts in at least three ways. First, they are not governed by the limits on civil damages or criminal penalties that govern courts of limited jurisdiction. Thus, cases involving significant dollar amounts or major criminal penalties usually begin at the trial court level. Second, trial courts are courts of record that keep detailed records of their proceedings. Third, the trial court judge almost always is a lawyer. The trial court's fact-finding function may be handled by the judge or by a jury. Determination of the applicable law is the judge's responsibility.

States usually have one trial court for each county. It may be called a circuit, superior, district, county, or common pleas court. Most state trial courts can hear a wide range of civil and criminal cases. They may have civil and criminal divisions. If no court of limited jurisdiction deals with these matters, state trial courts may also contain other divisions such as domestic relations courts, probate courts, and the like.

State Appeals Courts

In general, state appeals (or appellate) courts only decide *legal* questions. They have no jury and their judges do not find the facts. Thus, while appellate courts can correct legal errors made by the trial judge, they usually accept the trial court's findings of fact. Appellate courts also may hear appeals from state administrative agency decisions. Some states have only one appeals court (usually called the supreme court), while others also have an intermediate appellate court. The U.S. Supreme Court sometimes hears appeals from decisions of the state's highest court.

State Court Jurisdiction and Venue

The party who sues in a civil case (the plaintiff) cannot sue the defendant (the party being sued) in any court he chooses. Instead, the chosen court must have **jurisdiction** over the case. Jurisdiction is a court's power to hear a case and to issue a decision binding on the parties. As Figure 1 suggests, in order to render a binding decision in a civil case, a state court must have *both:* (1) subject-matter jurisdiction, and (2) *either* in personam jurisdiction *or* in rem jurisdiction. Even if a court has jurisdiction, it also must meet the state's **venue** requirements in order for the suit to proceed there.

Subject-Matter Jurisdiction   **Subject-matter jurisdiction** is a court's power to decide the *type* of dispute involved in the case. Criminal courts, for example, cannot hear civil matters, and a $500,000 suit for breach of contract cannot proceed in a small claims court.

In Personam Jurisdiction   Even a court with subject-matter jurisdiction cannot decide a civil case unless it also has either **in personam jurisdiction** or **in rem jurisdiction.** In personam jurisdiction is based on the residence, location, or activities of the defendant. A state court has in personam jurisdiction over defendants who are citizens or residents of the state (even if situated out-of-state), who are within the state's borders when process is served against them (even if nonresidents),[1] or who consent to the suit (for instance, by entering the state to defend against it).[2]

In addition, many states have enacted "long-arm" statutes that give their courts in personam jurisdiction over certain out-of-state defendants. Under these statutes, nonresident individuals and businesses become subject to the state's jurisdiction by, for example, doing business within the state, contracting to supply goods or services within the state, or committing a tort (a civil wrong) within the state. As the following *Knowles* case indicates, a state's assertion of in personam jurisdiction over an out-of-state defendant is subject to federal due process standards.

---

[1]Service of process is discussed later in the chapter.

[2]In some states, however, out-of-state defendants may make a *special appearance* to challenge the court's jurisdiction without consenting to that jurisdiction.

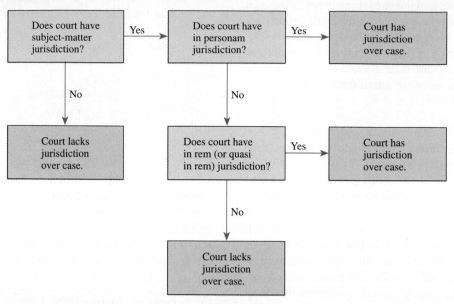

FIGURE I

State Court Jurisdiction

KNOWLES v. MODGLIN   553 So. 2d 563 (Ala. Sup. Ct. 1989)

Albert Knowles, an Alabama truck driver, died of natural causes in California while hauling produce from Alabama to California. After Knowles's body was discovered inside his truck, it was taken to Hems Brothers Mortuaries, where an autopsy was performed by Damon Reference Laboratories at the request of the local coroner. Both Hems and Damon did business in California. After a request from an Alabama funeral home, Hems prepared Knowles's body for shipment and arranged for it to be flown to his home town. Hems billed the Alabama funeral home for these services and for the price of a casket; it also mailed a statement to Knowles's wife.

Mrs. Knowles did not view her husband's body after its return to Alabama and before its burial, and no one positively identified the body as that of Mr. Knowles during this period. After the burial, Mrs. Knowles received an autopsy report from Damon describing a body that was different from her husband's body. As a result, she had the buried body exhumed and personally viewed it to verify that it was her husband's body—which it was. However, Mrs. Knowles also found that the body had been buried nude, had been packed in cotton in a "disaster pouch," was terribly discolored, and was lying in an awkward position. She described it as looking like "a monster."

Mrs. Knowles then sued Hems and Damon in an Alabama trial court for the wrongful mishandling of her husband's body. Both Damon and Hems had no contacts with Alabama other than those just described, and each moved to dismiss the claim because the court lacked in personam jurisdiction. After the court granted Damon's motion but denied Hems's motion, both Mrs. Knowles and Hems appealed to the Alabama Supreme Court. ∞

Houston, Justice   The issue is whether, consistent with the Due Process Clause of the Fourteenth Amendment to the United States Constitution, the defendants have sufficient contacts with this state to make it fair and reasonable to require them to come here to defend against the present action. Due process requires that to subject a defendant to a judgment in personam, he have certain minimum contacts with it such that the maintenance of the suit does not offend traditional notions of fair play and substantive justice. Alabama's long-arm statute has been interpreted to extend the jurisdiction of

Alabama courts to the permissible limits of due process.

A relevant factor in a due process analysis is whether the defendant should have reasonably anticipated that he would be sued in the forum state. In determining [this question], it is essential that there be some act by which the defendant purposefully avails itself of the privilege of conducting activities within the forum state, thus invoking the benefits and protections of its laws. Other relevant factors include the burden placed on the defendant, the interest of the forum state in adjudicating the dispute, the plaintiff's interest in obtaining convenient and effective relief, and the interstate judicial system's interest in obtaining the most efficient resolution of the controversy.

The trial court did not err in dismissing Damon for lack of in personam jurisdiction. It does not appear that Damon ever had any contacts with Alabama, with the exception of mailing the autopsy report to Mrs. Knowles. Damon could not have reasonably anticipated that Mr. Knowles's body would make its way to Alabama, that it would not be positively identified by anyone before burial, and that, thereafter, Damon would be haled into an Alabama court to defend against a suit based on a misdescription contained in the autopsy report.

However, Hems established significant contacts with this state by agreeing to prepare and ship Mr. Knowles's body here. In addition, Hems sold Mrs. Knowles a casket, and later solicited payment by mail in Alabama. Hems purposefully availed itself of the privilege of conducting business in Alabama [and] should have reasonably anticipated being summoned to an Alabama court to answer any charges of misconduct in the handling and shipment of Mr. Knowles's body. Furthermore, given the progress in communications and transportation in recent years, we cannot say that it would be unduly burdensome for Hems to defend against the suit in an Alabama court. Considering the nature of Hems's activity, the resultant foreseeability of its being required to defend an action in Alabama, the obvious interest of the plaintiff in obtaining convenient and effective relief, and the relative lack of inconvenience that would be incurred by Hems in appearing and defending, it is fair and reasonable to require Hems to defend against this action in Alabama.

Trial court decision dismissing Mrs. Knowles's suit against Damon for lack of jurisdiction and finding jurisdiction over Hems affirmed.

In Rem Jurisdiction   **In rem jurisdiction** is based on the presence of *property* within the state. It empowers state courts to determine rights in that property even if the persons whose rights are affected are outside the state's in personam jurisdiction. For example, a state court's decision regarding title to land within the state is said to bind the world.[3]

Venue   Even where a court has jurisdiction, it may be unable to decide the case because **venue** requirements have not been met. Venue presupposes jurisdiction, and venue questions only arise once juris-

diction is established or assumed. In general, a court has venue if it is a territorially fair and convenient forum in which to hear the case. Venue requirements typically are set by state statutes, which normally determine the county in which suit must be brought. For instance, the statute might say that a suit concerning land must be brought in the county where the land is located, and that other suits must be brought in the county where the defendant resides or is doing business. In certain cases where justice so requires, the defendant may obtain a *change of venue.* This can occur when, for example, a fair trial is impossible within a particular county.

FEDERAL COURTS AND THEIR JURISDICTION

Federal District Courts

In the federal system, lawsuits usually begin in the federal district courts, which basically are federal

---

[3]Another form of jurisdiction, *quasi in rem jurisdiction* or *attachment jurisdiction,* also is based on the presence of property within the state. Unlike cases based on in rem jurisdiction, cases based on quasi in rem jurisdiction do not necessarily determine rights in the property itself. Instead, the property is regarded as an extension of the out-of-state defendant, which enables the court to decide claims unrelated to the property. For example, a plaintiff might attach the defendant's bank account in the state where the bank is located, sue the defendant on a tort or contract claim unrelated to the bank account, and recover the amount of the judgment from the account if the suit is successful.

trial courts. Like state trial courts, the federal district courts determine both the facts and the law. The fact-finding function may be entrusted to either the judge or a jury, but determining the law is the judge's responsibility. Each state has at least one district court, and each district court has at least one judge.

District Court Jurisdiction There are many bases of federal district court civil jurisdiction. The two most important are **diversity jurisdiction** and **federal question jurisdiction.** One traditional justification for diversity jurisdiction is to protect out-of-state defendants from potentially biased state courts. Diversity jurisdiction exists when: (1) the suit is between citizens of different states, and (2) the amount in controversy exceeds $75,000. Diversity jurisdiction also exists in certain suits between citizens of a state and citizens or governments of foreign nations where the amount in controversy exceeds $75,000. Under diversity jurisdiction, a corporation normally is a citizen of both the state where it has been incorporated and the state where it has its principal place of business.

Federal question jurisdiction exists when the case arises under the Constitution, laws, or treaties of the United States. The "arises under" requirement normally is met when a right created by federal law is a basic part of the plaintiff's case. There is no amount-in-controversy requirement for federal question jurisdiction.

A district court's diversity or federal question jurisdiction usually includes only those defendants who would be subject to the in personam jurisdiction of the state where the district court sits. Further limiting the plaintiff's choice of federal district courts are the federal system's complex venue requirements, which are beyond the scope of this text.

Concurrent Jurisdiction and Removal The federal district courts have *exclusive jurisdiction* over some matters—for example, patent and copyright cases. This means that such cases must be heard in federal district court. Often, however, the district courts have *concurrent jurisdiction* with state courts; here, both state and federal courts have jurisdiction over the case. For example, a plaintiff might assert state court in personam jurisdiction over an out-of-state defendant or might sue in a

federal district court under that court's diversity jurisdiction. Also, a state court may decide a case involving a federal question if it has jurisdiction over that case. Where concurrent jurisdiction exists and the plaintiff opts for a state court, the defendant sometimes can *remove* the case to an appropriate federal district court.

Specialized Federal Courts

The federal court system also includes certain specialized federal courts, including the Court of Federal Claims (which hears claims against the United States), the Court of International Trade (which is concerned with tariff, customs, import and other trade matters), the Bankruptcy Courts (which operate as adjuncts of the district courts), and the Tax Court (which reviews certain IRS determinations). Usually, the decisions of these courts can be appealed to one or more of the federal courts of appeals.

Federal Courts of Appeals

Like state intermediate appellate courts, the U.S. courts of appeals do not find the facts, and they review only the legal conclusions reached by lower federal courts. As Figure 2 illustrates, there are 13 federal courts of appeals: 11 organized territorially into circuits covering several states each, one for the District of Columbia, and the Court of Appeals for the Federal Circuit.

Except for the Court of Appeals for the Federal Circuit, the most important function of the U.S. courts of appeals is to hear appeals from decisions of the federal district courts. Appeals from a district court ordinarily proceed to the court of appeals for that district court's region. Appeals from the District Court for the Southern District of New York, for example, go to the Second Circuit Court of Appeals. The courts of appeals also hear appeals from the Tax Court, from many administrative agency decisions, and (via appellate panels they appoint) from some Bankruptcy Court decisions. The Court of Appeals for the Federal Circuit hears a wide variety of specialized appeals, including some patent and trademark matters, Court of Federal Claims decisions, and decisions by the Court of International Trade.

FIGURE   2

The Thirteen Federal Judicial Circuits

First Circuit (*Boston, Mass.*) Maine, Massachusetts, New Hampshire, Puerto Rico, Rhode Island

Second Circuit (*New York, N.Y.*) Connecticut, New York, Vermont

Third Circuit (*Philadelphia, Pa.*) Delaware, New Jersey, Pennsylvania, Virgin Islands

Fourth Circuit (*Richmond, Va.*) Maryland, North Carolina, South Carolina, Virginia, West Virginia

Fifth Circuit (*New Orleans, La.*) Louisiana, Mississippi, Texas

Sixth Circuit (*Cincinnati, Ohio*) Kentucky, Michigan, Ohio, Tennessee

Seventh Circuit (*Chicago, Ill.*) Illinois, Indiana, Wisconsin

Eighth Circuit (*St. Louis, Mo.*) Arkansas, Iowa, Minnesota, Missouri, Nebraska, North Dakota, South Dakota

Ninth Circuit (*San Francisco, Calif.*) Alaska, Arizona, California, Guam, Hawaii, Idaho, Montana, Nevada, Northern Mariana Islands, Oregon, Washington

Tenth Circuit (*Denver, Colo.*) Colorado, Kansas, New Mexico, Oklahoma, Utah, Wyoming

Eleventh Circuit (*Atlanta, Ga.*) Alabama, Florida, Georgia

District of Columbia Circuit (*Washington, D.C.*)

Federal Circuit (*Washington, D.C.*)

The U.S. Supreme Court

The United States Supreme Court mainly is an appellate court. Thus, it only considers questions of law when it decides appeals. Most of the appeals handled by the Supreme Court come from the federal courts of appeals and the highest state courts.[4] Today, most appealable decisions from these courts fall within the Supreme Court's *certiorari* jurisdiction, under which the Court has discretion whether or not to hear the appeal. The Court hears only a small percentage of the many appeals it receives through its certiorari jurisdiction.

Virtually all appeals from the federal courts of appeals are within the Court's discretionary certiorari jurisdiction. Appeals from the highest state courts are within the certiorari jurisdiction when: (1) the validity of any treaty or federal statute has

been questioned; (2) the validity of any state statute is questioned because it is repugnant to federal law; or (3) any title, right, privilege, or immunity is claimed under federal law. The Supreme Court usually defers to the highest state courts on questions of state law and does not hear appeals from those courts if the case only involves such questions.

In certain rare situations, finally, the U.S. Supreme Court has **original jurisdiction,** which means that it acts as a trial court. The Supreme Court has *original and exclusive* jurisdiction over all controversies between two or more states. It has *original,* but not exclusive, jurisdiction over cases involving foreign ambassadors, ministers, and like parties; controversies between the United States and a state; and cases where a state proceeds against citizens of another state or against aliens.

Figure 3 combines the federal and state court systems.

---

[4]There are, however, situations in which the Supreme Court will hear appeals directly from the federal district courts.

A Simplified Model of the State and Federal Court Systems

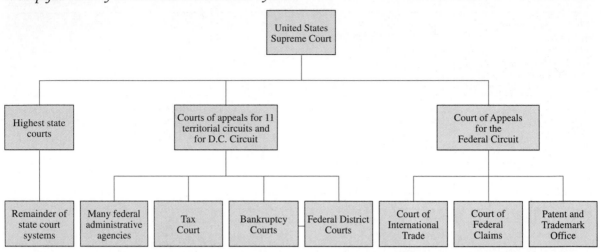

CIVIL PROCEDURE

Civil procedure is the set of legal rules governing the conduct of a trial court case between private parties.[5] Because this law sometimes varies with the jurisdiction in question,[6] the following presentation merely summarizes the most widely accepted rules governing civil cases in state trial courts and the federal district courts. Knowing about these basic procedural matters is useful if you become involved in a civil lawsuit. Such knowledge also helps you understand the cases in this text. Figure 4 presents the major steps through which a civil case normally proceeds and the most significant motions the parties (or *litigants*) can make at each step.

In any civil case, the *adversary system* is at work. Through their attorneys, the litigants present contrary positions of fact or law before a theoretically impartial judge and possibly a jury. To win a civil case, the plaintiff must prove each element of his claim by a *preponderance of the evidence*.[7] That is, the plaintiff must show that the greater weight of the evidence—by *credibility,* not quantity—supports the

existence of each element. In other words, the plaintiff must convince the fact finder that the existence of each factual element is more probable than its nonexistence. Thus, the lawyers for each party present their clients' version of the facts, try to convince the judge or jury that this version is true, and attempt to rebut conflicting factual allegations by the other party. Each attorney also seeks to persuade the judge that her reading of the law is correct.

Service of the Summons

The function of the **summons** is to notify the defendant that he is being sued. The summons typically names the plaintiff and states the time within which the defendant must enter an *appearance* in court (usually through her attorney). In most jurisdictions, it is accompanied by a copy of the plaintiff's complaint (which is described below).

The summons is usually delivered, or served, to the defendant by an appropriate public official after the plaintiff has filed his complaint with the court. To ensure that the defendant is properly notified of the suit, statutes, court rules, and constitutional due process guarantees set standards for proper service of the summons in particular cases. For example, personal delivery of the summons to the defendant almost always meets these standards, and many jurisdictions also permit the summons to be left at the defendant's home or place of business. Service

---

[5]Criminal procedure is discussed in Chapter 5 and the procedures used before administrative agencies in Chapter 46.

[6]In the following discussion, the term *jurisdiction* refers to one of the 50 states, the District of Columbia, or the federal government.

[7]However, as discussed in Chapter 5, in a criminal case the government must prove the elements of the alleged crime *beyond a reasonable doubt.* Other burdens of proof—for example, the clear-and-convincing-evidence standard—exist as well.

The Most Important Stages and Motions in Civil Litigation (Appeals Assumed)

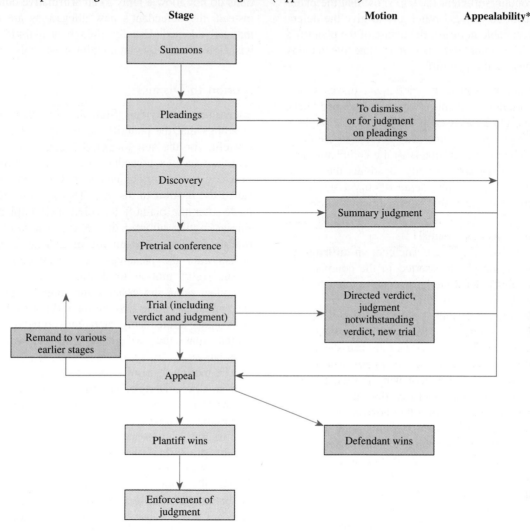

*As discussed later in the chapter, many other trial court rulings also are appealable.

to corporations often may be accomplished by delivery of the summons to the firm's general or managing agent. Many state long-arm statutes permit out-of-state defendants to be served by registered mail. Although inadequate service of process may sometimes defeat the plaintiff's claim, in most jurisdictions the defendant must make his objection early or it will be waived.

The Pleadings

The **pleadings** are the documents the parties file with the court when they first state their respective cases. They include the **complaint,** the **answer,** and (in some jurisdictions) the **reply.** Traditionally, the pleadings' main function was to define and limit the issues to be decided by the court. Thus, only those issues raised in the pleadings were considered part of the case, amendments to the pleadings were rarely granted, and litigants were bound to allegations admitted during the pleadings. Although many jurisdictions retain some of these rules, many also have relaxed them. The main reason is a new view about the purpose behind pleading rules—that their aim is less to define the issues for trial than to give the parties notice of each others' claims.

The Complaint The complaint states the plaintiff's claim in separate, numbered paragraphs. It must contain sufficient facts to show that the plaintiff is entitled to legal relief and to give the defendant reasonable notice of the nature of the plaintiff's claim. The complaint also must state the remedy requested by the plaintiff.

The Answer Unless the defendant makes a successful motion to dismiss (which is described later), she must file an answer to the plaintiff's complaint within a designated time after service of the complaint. The answer responds to the complaint paragraph by paragraph. Usually, it admits the allegations of each paragraph, denies them, or states that the defendant lacks the information to assess the truth or falsity of the allegations (which has much the same effect as a denial).

An answer may also include an **affirmative defense** to the claim asserted in the complaint. A successful affirmative defense enables the defendant to win the case even if all the allegations in the complaint are true and, by themselves, entitle the plaintiff to recover. For example, suppose that the plaintiff bases her suit on a contract that she alleges the defendant has breached (broken). The defendant's answer may admit or deny the existence of the contract or the assertion that the defendant breached it. In addition, the answer may make assertions that, if proven, would show that the defendant has an affirmative defense because the plaintiff's fraud induced the defendant to enter the contract.

Furthermore, the answer may contain a **counterclaim.**[8] A counterclaim is a *new* claim by the defendant arising from the matters stated in the complaint. Unlike an affirmative defense, it is not merely an attack on the plaintiff's claim, but is the *defendant's* attempt to obtain legal relief. In addition to using fraud as an affirmative defense to a plaintiff's contract claim, for example, a defendant might counterclaim for damages caused by that fraud.

The Reply In some jurisdictions, the plaintiff is allowed or required to respond to an affirmative defense or a counterclaim by making a reply. The reply is the plaintiff's point-by-point response (a kind of answer) to the allegations in the affirmative defense or counterclaim. However, many jurisdictions do not allow a reply to an affirmative defense; instead, the defendant's new allegations are automatically denied. Usually, though, a plaintiff who wishes to contest a counterclaim must reply to it.

Motion to Dismiss

Sometimes it is evident from the complaint or the pleadings that the plaintiff has no case. Here, it is wasteful for the suit to proceed further and it is useful to have a procedural device for ending it. This device has various names, but it is commonly called the **motion to dismiss.** This motion often is made after the plaintiff has filed his complaint. A similar motion allowed by some jurisdictions, the **motion for judgment on the pleadings,** normally occurs after the pleadings have been completed. A successful motion to dismiss means that the defendant wins the case; if the motion fails, the case proceeds further. Where the motion to dismiss was made immediately after the complaint, this means that the defendant must answer the complaint.

The motion to dismiss may be made on various grounds—for example, inadequate service of process or lack of jurisdiction. The most important type of motion to dismiss, however, is the motion to dismiss for failure to state a claim upon which relief can be granted, sometimes called the **demurrer.** This motion basically says "So what?" to the factual allegations in the complaint. It asserts that the plaintiff cannot recover even if all these allegations are true because no rule of law entitles him to win on those facts. Suppose that Potter sues Davis on the theory that Davis's bad breath is a form of "olfactory pollution" entitling Potter to recover damages. Potter's complaint describes Davis's breath and the distress it causes Potter in great detail. Even if all of Potter's factual allegations are true, Davis's motion to dismiss almost certainly will succeed. Thus, Davis will win the case, for there is no rule of law allowing a civil recovery for bad breath.

Discovery

Litigants sometimes lack the facts to prove their cases when the suit begins. To help them get those facts and to narrow and clarify the issues for trial,

---

[8]The defendant also may file a *cross-claim* against another party who is a defendant in the plaintiff's suit, and also may file a *third-party complaint* against (or *implead*) some party who is not a defendant in the plaintiff's suit.

all jurisdictions permit the parties to undertake extensive **discovery** of relevant information. The most common kinds of discovery are **depositions** (oral examinations of a party or a party's witness by the other party's attorney), **interrogatories** (written questions directed to a party, answered in writing, and signed under oath), **requests for admissions** (one party's written demand that the other party agree to certain statements of fact or law), **requests for documents and other evidence,** and **physical and mental examinations.** The permissible limits of discovery are set by the trial judge, whose rulings are controlled by the procedural law of the jurisdiction. In an effort to make civil litigation less of a battle of wits or a sporting event and more of a disinterested search for the truth, many jurisdictions have liberalized their discovery rules to give parties freer access to all relevant facts.

The jurisdiction's law of evidence determines whether or when discovery findings are admissible trial evidence. However, almost all jurisdictions allow some discovery findings to be employed at trial for certain purposes. Depositions, for instance, may sometimes be used as "paper testimony" from dead or distant witnesses, or to attack the credibility of a witness whose trial testimony differs from statements she made at the deposition.

Summary Judgment

The **summary judgment** is a device for disposing of relatively clear cases without a trial. It differs from a demurrer because it involves factual determinations. To prevail, the party moving for a summary judgment must show that: (1) there is no genuine issue of material (legally significant) fact, and (2) he is entitled to judgment as a matter of law. A moving party satisfies the first element of the test by using the pleadings, discovery information, and affidavits (signed and sworn statements regarding matters of fact) to show that there is no real question about any significant fact. She satisfies the second element by showing that, given the established facts, the applicable law directs that she win.

Either or both parties may move for a summary judgment. If the court rules in favor of either party, that party wins the case. If no party's motion for summary judgment is granted, the case proceeds to trial. The judge may also grant a partial summary judgment, which settles some issues in the case but leaves the others to be decided at trial.

The Pretrial Conference

Depending on the jurisdiction, a **pretrial conference** is either mandatory or at the discretion of the trial judge. At this conference, the judge meets informally with the attorneys for both litigants. The judge may try to get the attorneys to *stipulate,* or agree to, the resolution of certain issues to simplify the trial. He may also encourage them to get their clients to *settle* the case by coming to an agreement that eliminates the need for a trial. If the case is not settled, the judge enters a pretrial order including the attorneys' stipulations and any other agreements. Ordinarily, this order binds the parties throughout the remainder of the case.

The Trial

Once the case has been through discovery and has survived any pretrial motions, it is set for trial. The trial may be before a judge alone, in which case the judge makes separate findings of fact and law before issuing the court's judgment. But if the right to a jury trial exists and either party demands one, the jury finds the facts while the judge continues to determine legal questions.[9] At a pretrial jury screening process known as *voir dire,* most jurisdictions: (1) allow biased potential jurors to be removed *for cause,* and (2) give the attorney for each party a certain number of *peremptory challenges,* which allow him to remove potential jurors without *any* cause.

The Basic Scenario   At either a judge or a jury trial, the attorneys for each side typically begin by making opening statements explaining what they intend to prove. After this, the plaintiff's witnesses and other evidence are introduced and these witnesses are cross-examined by the defendant's attorney. This may be followed by the plaintiff's re-direct examination of his witnesses, and perhaps by the defendant's recross examination of those same witnesses. Then, using the same procedures, the defendant's evidence is presented. Throughout each side's presentation, the opposing attorney may

---

[9]The rules governing availability of a jury trial are largely beyond the scope of this text. The U.S. Constitution guarantees a jury trial in federal court suits "at common law" whose amount exceeds $20. Most of the states have similar constitutional provisions, often with a higher dollar amount. Also, Congress and the state legislatures may allow jury trials in various other cases.

object to the admission of certain evidence. Using the law of evidence, the judge then decides whether the challenged proof is admissible. After the plaintiff and defendant have completed their initial presentations of evidence, each is allowed to offer evidence rebutting the other's evidence. Once all the evidence has been presented, each attorney makes a closing argument summarizing her position. In nonjury trials, the judge then makes findings of fact and law, renders judgment, and states the relief to which the plaintiff is entitled if the plaintiff is victorious.

Jury Trials Rather than proceeding to decide the case herself, the judge issues a **charge** or **instruction** to the jury at the end of a jury trial. The charge sets out the law applicable to the case. The judge may also summarize the evidence for the jury. Then the jury is supposed to make the necessary fact determinations, apply the law to these, and arrive at a **verdict** upon which the court's **judgment** is based.

The most common verdict is the **general verdict,** which only requires that the jury declare which party wins and the relief (if any) awarded. Because the jury need not state its factual findings or its application of the law to those findings, the general verdict gives the jury freedom to ignore the judge's charge and follow its own inclinations. Arguably, this freedom allows the jury to soften the law's rigors by bringing common sense and community values to bear on the case, but it also weakens the rule of law and allows juries to commit injustices. The **special verdict** is one response to this problem. Here, the jury only makes specific findings of fact, and the judge then applies the law to these findings. The decision whether to utilize a special verdict usually is within the trial judge's discretion.

Directed Verdict Although the general verdict gives the jury considerable power, the American legal system also has devices for limiting that power. The special verdict is one of these devices. Another, the **directed verdict,** essentially takes the case away from the jury and gives a judgment to one party before the jury gets a chance to decide. The motion for a directed verdict can be made by either party; it usually occurs after the other (nonmoving) party has presented her evidence. The moving party basically asserts that, even when read most favorably to the other party, the evidence leads to only one result and need not be considered by the

jury. Courts differ on the test governing a motion for a directed verdict: some deny the motion if there is *any* evidence favoring the nonmoving party, while others deny the motion only if there is *substantial* evidence favoring the nonmoving party.

Judgment Notwithstanding the Verdict On occasion, the case is taken away from the jury and one party wins a judgment even *after* the jury has reached a verdict *against* that party. The device for doing so is the **judgment notwithstanding the verdict** (also known as the judgment *non obstante veredicto* or judgment n.o.v.). Some jurisdictions require that, in order to make a motion for judgment n.o.v, the moving party must previously have moved for a directed verdict. In any event, the standard used to decide the motion for judgment n.o.v. usually is the same standard the jurisdiction uses to decide the motion for a directed verdict.

Motion for New Trial In a wide range of situations that vary among jurisdictions, the losing party can successfully move for a new trial. Acceptable reasons for granting a new trial include errors by the judge during the trial, jury or attorney misconduct, misapplication of the law, new evidence, or an award of excessive damages to the plaintiff.

Appeal

A final judgment generally prevents the parties from relitigating the same claim. But one or more parties still may *appeal* the trial court's decision. Normally, appellate courts only consider alleged errors of law made by the trial court. As Figure 4 indicated earlier in the chapter, among the matters ordinarily considered "legal" and thus appealable are the trial judge's decisions on a motion to dismiss or a motion for judgment on the pleadings, the scope of discovery, a motion for summary judgment, a motion for a directed verdict or for judgment notwithstanding the verdict, and a motion for a new trial. Other matters typically considered appealable include any trial court rulings on service of process, its rulings on the admission of evidence at trial, its legal findings in a nonjury trial, its instruction to the jury in a jury trial, and the damages or other relief awarded.

Among other things, appellate courts may *affirm* the trial court's decision, *reverse* it, or affirm one part of the decision and reverse another part. As Figure 4 also suggests, one of three things ordinarily

The Major Civil Motions Compared

MOTION	WHEN TYPICALLY MADE	BY WHOM TYPICALLY MADE	TYPICAL TEST	TYPICAL EFFECT IF SUCCESSFUL
To Dismiss or for Judgment on the Pleadings	After complaint or pleadings	Defendant	Assuming the facts in the complaint are true, can plaintiff win as a matter of law?	Defendant wins case
For Summary Judgment	Varies; often after discovery	Either party	No genuine issue of material fact, and moving party entitled to judgment as a matter of law	Moving party wins case; partial summary judgment also possible
For Directed Verdict	After other party has presented evidence at trial	Either party	Two versions. Moving party loses if: (1) *any* evidence favoring nonmoving party; or (2) *substantial* evidence favoring nonmoving party	Moving party wins case
For Judgment Notwithstanding Verdict	After adverse jury verdict	Losing party	Same test jurisdiction uses for directed verdict	Moving party wins case
For New Trial	After adverse judgment or jury verdict	Losing party	Wide range of possible grounds	New trial ordered

results from the appellate courts' disposition of the appeal: (1) the plaintiff wins the case; (2) the defendant wins the case; or (3) if the case is reversed in whole or in part, it is *remanded* (returned) to the trial court for further proceedings. For example, if the plaintiff appeals a trial court decision granting the defendant's motion to dismiss and the appellate court(s) affirm that decision, the plaintiff loses. On the other hand, where an appellate court reverses a trial court verdict and judgment in the defendant's favor, the plaintiff might win outright, or the case might be returned to the trial court for further proceedings not inconsistent with the appellate decision.

Enforcing a Judgment

In this text, you occasionally see cases where someone was not sued even though he appeared to be liable to the plaintiff, and where another party was sued instead. One explanation is that the first party was "judgment-proof"—so lacking in assets as to make a civil suit for damages impractical. The other party's financial condition also affects a winning plaintiff's ability to actually recover whatever damages she has been awarded.

When the defendant fails to pay as required after losing a civil suit, the winning plaintiff must enforce the judgment. Ordinarily, the plaintiff will obtain a *writ of execution* enabling the sheriff to seize designated property of the defendant and sell it at a judicial sale to satisfy the judgment. A judgment winner may also use a procedure known as *garnishment* to seize property, money, or wages of the defendant that are in the hands of a third party. If the property needed to satisfy the judgment is located in another state, the plaintiff must use that state's execution or garnishment procedures. Under the U.S. Constitution, the second state must give "full faith and credit" to the judgment of the state where the plaintiff originally sued. Finally, when the court has awarded an equitable remedy such as an injunction, the defendant may be found in contempt of court and subjected to a fine or imprisonment if he fails to obey the court's order.

Class Actions

So far, our civil procedure discussion has proceeded as if the plaintiff and the defendant each were a single party. Actually, several plaintiffs and/or defendants can be parties to one lawsuit. Also, each jurisdiction has procedural rules stating when other parties can be *joined* to a suit that begins without them.

One special type of multiparty suit, the **class action,** allows one or more persons to sue on behalf of themselves and all others who have suffered similar harm from substantially the same wrong. Class action suits by consumers, environmentalists, women, minorities, and other groups now are common events. The usual justifications for the class action are that: (1) it allows legal wrongs causing losses to a large number of widely dispersed parties to be fully compensated, and (2) it promotes economy of judicial effort by combining many similar claims into one suit.

The requirements for a class action vary among jurisdictions. The issues addressed by class action statutes include the following: whether there are questions of law and fact common to all members of the alleged class, whether the class is small enough to allow all of its members to join the case as parties rather than use a class action, and whether the plaintiff(s) and their attorney(s) can competently represent the class without conflicts of interest or other forms of unfairness. To protect the individual class member's right to be heard, some jurisdictions have required that unnamed or absent class members be given notice of the suit if this is reasonably possible. The damages awarded in a successful class action usually are apportioned among the entire class. Establishing the total recovery and distributing it to the class, however, pose problems when the class is large, the class members' injuries are indefinite, or some members cannot be identified.

ALTERNATIVE DISPUTE RESOLUTION

Courts are not the only devices for resolving civil disputes. Nor are they always the best means of doing so. Settling private disputes through the courts can be a cumbersome, lengthy, and expensive process for litigants. With the advent of a litigious society and the increasing caseloads it has produced, handling disputes in this fashion also imposes ever-greater social costs. For these reasons and others, the various forms of **alternative dispute resolution (ADR)** have assumed increasing importance in recent years. Proponents of ADR cite many considerations in its favor—for example: (1) quicker resolution of disputes; (2) lower costs in time, money, and aggravation for the parties; (3) reduced strain on an overloaded court system; (4) the ability to use decision makers with specialized expertise; and (5) flexible compromise decisions that promote and reflect consensus between the parties. Those who are skeptical of ADR worry about its potential for sloppy, biased, and/or lawless decisions. They also worry that it may sometimes mean second-class justice for ordinary people who deal with powerful economic interests. Sometimes, for example, agreements to submit disputes to alternative dispute resolution are buried in complex standard-form contracts drafted by a party with superior size, knowledge, and business sophistication and are unknowingly agreed to by less knowledgeable parties. Such clauses may compel ADR proceedings before decision makers who are biased in favor of the stronger party.

Common Forms of ADR

Settlement   The settlement of a civil suit is not everyone's idea of an alternative dispute resolution mechanism. But it is an important means of avoiding protracted litigation, one that often is a sensible compromise for the parties. Many cases settle at some stage in the civil proceedings described previously. The typical settlement agreement is a contract whereby the defendant agrees to pay the plaintiff a sum of money, in exchange for the plaintiff's promise to release the defendant from liability on the claims in his suit. Although courts want to enforce settlement agreements, such agreements still must satisfy the requirements of contract law discussed later in this text. In some cases, moreover, the court must approve the settlement in order for it to be enforceable. Examples include class actions and litigation involving minors.

Arbitration   Arbitration is the submission of a dispute to a neutral, nonjudicial third party (the *arbitrator*) who issues a binding decision resolving the dispute. Arbitration usually results from the parties' agreement. That agreement normally is made before the dispute arises (most often through an *arbitration clause* in a contract), but it can occur after the dispute begins. Arbitration may also be compelled by statute. One example is the *compulsory arbitration* many states require as part of the collective bargaining process for certain public employees.

Arbitration usually is less formal than regular court proceedings. The arbitrator need not be an attorney; often, she is a professional who may be expert in the subject-matter of the dispute. Although arbitration hearings often resemble civil trials, the applicable procedures, the rules for admission of evidence, and the record-keeping requirements typically are not as rigorous as those governing courts. Also, arbitrators have some freedom to ignore rules of substantive law that would bind a court.

The arbitrator's decision, called an *award,* is filed with a court, which will enforce it if necessary. The losing party may object to the arbitrator's award, but the courts' review of arbitration proceedings is limited. Possible grounds for overturning an arbitration award include: (1) its procurement by fraud, (2) the arbitrator's partiality or corruption, and (3) other misconduct by the arbitrator (e.g., refusing to hear relevant evidence).

Court-Annexed Arbitration In this form of ADR, certain kinds of civil lawsuits are diverted into arbitration. One example might be cases where less than a specified dollar amount is at issue. Most often, court-annexed arbitration is mandatory and is ordered by the judge, but some jurisdictions merely offer litigants the option of arbitration. The losing party in a court-annexed arbitration still has the right to a regular trial.

Mediation In mediation, a neutral third party called a *mediator* helps the parties reach an agreeable, cooperative resolution of their dispute by facilitating communication between them, clarifying their areas of agreement and disagreement, helping them to see each other's viewpoints, suggesting settlement options, and so forth. Unlike arbitrators, mediators cannot make decisions that bind the parties. Instead, a successful mediation process typically results in a *mediation agreement.* Such agreements normally are enforced under regular contract law principles.

Mediation is used in a wide range of situations, including labor, commercial, family, and environmental disputes. It may occur by agreement of the parties after a dispute has arisen. It also may result from a previous contractual agreement by the parties. Increasingly, moreover, court-annexed mediation is either compelled or made available by courts in certain cases.

Summary Jury Trial Sometimes settlement of civil litigation is impeded because the litigants have different perceptions about the merits of their cases. In such cases, the summary jury trial may give either or both parties a needed dose of reality. As its name suggests, the summary jury trial is an abbreviated, nonpublic mock jury trial that does not bind the parties. Often, this "trial" occurs before a real judge, with jurors chosen from the regular pool of jurors. If the parties do not settle after completion of the summary jury trial, they still are entitled to a regular court trial. Also, there is some disagreement over whether courts can compel the parties to undergo a summary jury trial in the first place.

Minitrial A minitrial is an informal, abbreviated private "trial" whose aim is to promote settlement of disputes. Normally, it arises out of a private agreement that also describes the procedures to be followed. In the typical minitrial, counsel for each party present their cases to a panel composed of senior management from each side. Sometimes a neutral advisor such as an attorney or a retired judge presides. This party may also offer an opinion about the case's likely outcome in court. After the presentations, the managers try to negotiate a settlement.

Other ADR Devices Other ADR devices include: (1) *med/arb* (a hybrid of mediation and arbitration in which the third party first acts as a mediator, and then as an arbitrator); (2) the appointment of *magistrates* and *special masters* to perform various tasks during complex litigation in the federal courts; (3) *early neutral evaluation* (ENE) (a court-annexed procedure involving early, objective evaluation of the case by a neutral private attorney with experience in its subject matter); (4) *private judging* (in which litigants hire a private referee to issue a decision that may be binding but that usually does not preclude some recourse to the courts); and (5) *private panels* instituted by an industry or an organization to handle claims of certain kinds (e.g., the Better Business Bureau). Also, some formally legal processes are sometimes called ADR devices; examples include small claims courts and the administrative procedures used to handle claims for veterans' benefits or Social Security benefits.

ETHICAL AND PUBLIC POLICY CONCERNS

1. As you might expect, the arguments against ADR often come from the legal profession. Are these self-serving arguments? Who stands to lose money and influence if ADR becomes more popular? Assuming that these arguments are self-serving, is this fact alone enough to rebut them?

2. The *Knowles* case earlier in this chapter used a style of legal reasoning different from the simple deductive model presented in Chapter 1. This style, which might be called *factor-based balancing,* appears from time to time in this text. Courts using this style of reasoning typically consider several factors (values or policy goals) when deciding. They assess a particular result in light of each factor, trying to determine whether that result advances or frustrates the values embodied in each factor. Then, they try to assess the overall desirability of that result by weighing its positive and negative effects against each other and determining whether the result has a positive or negative effect on balance. Such determinations naturally vary depending on the facts of the case. In *Knowles,* the decision was easy, for almost all the factors the court considered pulled in the same direction.

What is good about this kind of legal decision making? What is bad about it?

3. As noted in Chapter 4, debates in the ethics and business ethics literature have sometimes involved clashes between *utilitarian* ethical theories and *deontological rights-based* ethical theories. Utilitarians normally say that we should maximize total satisfaction, and they tend to approve measures that disadvantage particular individuals so long as those measures actually produce the most overall satisfaction. Such theories occasionally use social wealth maximization as a rough measure of total satisfaction. Deontological rights-based theories generally urge that some rights are so important that they can only be overridden by certain other rights, and *not* by maximum total utility.

Speaking generally, into which category would many foes of ADR fit? Assume that these people oppose ADR because they feel that due to the sloppiness of its procedures, it causes injustices to individuals—injustices that could be avoided were normal court procedures used. Although the use of such procedures costs more money than ADR, they assert, this is of no consequence because basic issues of *justice* are involved.

Speaking generally, into which category would many proponents of ADR fit? Assume that these people stress the social and economic costs created by the court system and argue that the widespread use of ADR would free money and resources for other purposes, thus making people wealthier and happier. This increased wealth and happiness, they would add, easily outweigh the personal suffering caused by whatever injustices ADR permits.

PROBLEMS

1. Peters sues Davis. At trial, Peters's lawyer attempts to introduce certain evidence to help make his case. Davis's attorney objects, and the trial judge refuses to allow the evidence to be admitted. Peters eventually loses the case at the trial court level. He appeals, his attorney arguing that the trial judge's decision not to admit the evidence was erroneous. Davis's attorney argues that the appellate court cannot consider this question, because appellate courts only review errors of *law* (not fact) at the trial court level. Is Davis's attorney correct? Why or why not?

2. Phillips sues Dilks for $500,000 in a state small claims court set up to handle cases where the amount in controversy does not exceed $5,000. The court clearly does not have jurisdiction over the case. What *kind* of jurisdiction is absent here?

3. Dial, a resident of Indiana, vandalizes a parked car in Columbus, Ohio. This action results in harm to the car, and also prevents the owner from using it for a period of time. In the meantime, Dial has fled to Indiana and remains there. The owner, an Ohio resident, plans to sue Dial for trespass to personal property, a tort described in Chapter 6. He claims $5,000 in damages, and wants to sue either in an Ohio trial court or in a federal district court. Do each of these courts have jurisdiction over the case? Why or why not? Assume for purposes of this problem that: (a) subject-matter jurisdiction is present, (b) Dial has had no other contacts with the state of Ohio, and (c) Ohio has a long-arm statute with all the features described in the chapter.

4. State *two* differences between the motion to dismiss for failure to state a claim upon which relief can be granted (or demurrer) and the motion for summary judgment.

5. In a suit by Pierce against Dodge, the jury has rendered a verdict in favor of Dodge. Pierce and her attorney think that the evidence was overwhelmingly in Pierce's favor. They also have reason to believe that the jury was bribed by someone connected with Dodge. What *two* motions can Pierce's attorney make in an attempt to overturn the jury's verdict?

6. While driving to work one day, Dember runs over Pearson, causing him severe injuries. Pearson sues Dember in a state trial court. His complaint alleges that Dember's negligent driving caused his injuries. The law of the state declares that if the plaintiff's own negligence contributed to his injury, the defendant has a complete defense and the plaintiff cannot recover. Dember wants to argue that whether he was negligent or not, Pearson's own negligence helped cause his injuries and that Pearson therefore has no case. In order to be *sure* of his ability to raise this argument at trial, what should Dember's attorney do in response to Pearson's complaint?

7. What is the main difference between a motion for a directed verdict and a motion for judgment notwithstanding the verdict?

8. The state of Mississippi is planning to sue the state of Massachusetts. Mississippi's attorney general wants to sue in an appropriate federal district court. Do the federal district courts have jurisdiction over this case? If not, which federal court does have jurisdiction? You can assume that Mississippi's suit involves issues of federal law, and that the amount in controversy exceeds $75,000.

9. Jackson was born in Texas but has had absolutely no contact with that state for 20 years. Jackson's father dies, and a Texas court interprets his will so that Jackson receives none of his father's property, which is located in Texas. Assume that the court had jurisdiction to make this decision. What *kinds* of jurisdiction did it have?

10. Pike sues Dillon, alleging that his parked car was destroyed due to Dillon's negligent driving. After the pleadings and discovery have been completed, Pike's attorney concludes that the case is an obvious winner on both the facts and the law. What motion should the attorney make in an attempt to win the case without having to go to trial?

11. Does ADR really resolve disputes without any help from the courts? Give two examples of ADR processes that depend on courts for their operation or their effectiveness and state how they depend on the courts.

Business and the Constitution

Constitutions serve two general functions. They set up the structure of government, allocating power among its various branches and subdivisions. Constitutions also prevent government from taking certain actions—especially actions that restrict individual rights. As the following overview of its provisions suggests, the U.S. Constitution performs both these functions.[1] This chapter examines how the Constitution's performance of these functions affects government regulation of business.

AN OVERVIEW OF THE U.S. CONSTITUTION

The U.S. Constitution exhibits the principle of **separation of powers** by giving distinct powers to Congress, the president, and the federal courts. Thus, Article I of the Constitution establishes a Congress composed of a Senate and a House of Representatives, gives it sole power to legislate at the federal level, and sets out rules for the passage of legislation. Also, Article I, section 8 defines when Congress can make law by stating its *legislative powers.* Three of those powers—Congress's commerce, tax, and spending powers—are discussed later in this chapter.

Article II of the Constitution gives the president the *executive power*—the power to execute or enforce the laws passed by Congress. Section 2 of that

---

[1]Appendix A to this book contains the text of the U.S. Constitution.

article lists some other presidential powers, including the powers to command the nation's armed forces and to make treaties. Article III gives the *judicial power* of the United States to the Supreme Court and the other federal courts later established by Congress. Article III also determines the kinds of cases the federal courts can decide.

In addition to creating a separation of powers, Articles I, II, and III of the Constitution also set up a system of **checks and balances** among Congress, the president, and the courts. For example, Article I, section 7 gives the president the power to veto legislation passed by Congress, and also allows Congress to override such a veto by a two-thirds vote of each House. Article I, section 3 and Article II, section 4 provide that the president, the vice president, and other federal officials may be impeached by a two-thirds vote of the Senate. Article II, section 2 says that treaties made by the president must be approved by a two-thirds vote of the Senate. Article III, section 2 gives Congress some control over the Supreme Court's appellate jurisdiction.

Sometimes, the U.S. Constitution also recognizes the principle of **federalism** in the way it structures power relations between the federal government and the states. Article I, section 9 lists certain powers that Congress cannot exercise. The Tenth Amendment provides that those powers the Constitution neither gives to the federal government nor denies to the states are reserved to the states or the people.

Article VI, however, makes the Constitution, laws, and treaties of the United States supreme over state law. As discussed later in this chapter, this means that where the Constitution gives Congress the power to legislate, this principle of **federal supremacy** allows federal statutes to *preempt* inconsistent state laws. The U.S. Constitution also puts specific limits on the states' lawmaking powers. One example from this chapter is Article I, section 10's command that no state shall pass any law impairing the obligation of contracts.

Article V sets the procedures for amending the Constitution. By now, the Constitution has been amended 26 times. The first 10 of these amendments comprise the Bill of Rights. Although the rights stated in the first 10 amendments once applied to the federal government alone, most of them now apply to the states as well. As you will learn, this is due to their *incorporation* within the Due Process

Clause of the Fourteenth Amendment, which applies to the states. This application of federal constitutional principles to the states is another reason why the Constitution gives only partial support to the principle of federalism.

THE EVOLUTION OF THE CONSTITUTION AND THE ROLE OF THE SUPREME COURT

According to Chapter 1's legal realists, written "book law" is less important than what public decision makers *actually do.* Using this approach, we discover a Constitution that differs from the written Constitution just described. For example, the actual powers of today's presidency exceed anything you would expect from reading Article II. As you will see throughout the chapter, moreover, some constitutional provisions now have a different practical meaning than they did when first enacted. American constitutional law is much more evolving than static.

Many of these changes result from the way one public decisionmaker—the U.S. Supreme Court—has interpreted the Constitution over time. In theory, constitutional change can be accomplished through the formal amendment process. Because this process is difficult to use, however, amendments to the Constitution have been relatively infrequent. For better or worse, therefore, the Supreme Court has been the Constitution's main amender. Many factors help explain the Supreme Court's ability and willingness to play this role. Due to their vagueness, some key constitutional provisions invite diverse interpretations; "due process of law" and "equal protection of the laws" are examples. Also, the history surrounding the enactment of constitutional provisions sometimes is sketchy, confused, or contradictory. Probably more important, however, is the perceived need to adapt the Constitution to changing social conditions. As the old saying goes, Supreme Court decisions tend to follow the election returns.

Under the power of **judicial review,** courts can declare the actions of other government bodies unconstitutional. How courts exercise this power depends on how they choose to read the Constitution. This means that courts—especially the Supreme Court—have political power. Indeed, the

Supreme Court's nine justices basically are public policymakers. Thus, their beliefs are important in determining how America is governed. This is why the justices' nomination and confirmation often involve so much political controversy.

But even though the Constitution frequently is what the Supreme Court says it is, the Court's power to shape the Constitution has limits. Some of these limits spring from the Constitution's language, which sometimes is quite clear. Others spring from the judges' adherence to the doctrine of *stare decisis* discussed in Chapter 1. Perhaps the most significant limits on judges' power, however, result from the tension between modern judicial review and democracy. Legislators are chosen by the people, while judges usually are unelected. Today, however, judges exercise political power by declaring the actions of legislatures unconstitutional under standards that are largely of the judiciary's own devising. This naturally leads to charges that courts are undemocratic, elitist institutions, and those charges put political constraints on courts. Those constraints exist because the Supreme Court and other courts depend on the other branches of government—and ultimately on public belief in judges' fidelity to the rule of law—to make their decisions effective. Thus, federal judges may be inhibited from declaring federal statutes unconstitutional because they are wary of power struggles with a more representative body like Congress.

THE COVERAGE AND STRUCTURE OF THIS CHAPTER

This chapter examines certain constitutional provisions that are important to business; it does not discuss constitutional law in its entirety. These provisions help define federal and state power to

regulate the economy. The U.S. Constitution limits government regulatory power in two general ways. First, it restricts *federal* legislative authority by listing the powers Congress can exercise and restricting it to these **enumerated powers.** To be constitutional, that is, federal legislation must be based on a power specifically stated in the Constitution. Second, the U.S. Constitution limits both *state and federal* power by placing certain **independent checks** in the path of each. In effect, the independent checks declare that even if Congress has an enumerated power to act in a particular area or a state constitution authorizes a state to act in a certain way, there still are certain protected spheres into which neither can reach.

As Figure 1 suggests, therefore, a federal law must meet two general tests in order to be constitutional: (1) it must be based on an enumerated power of Congress, and (2) it must not collide with any of the independent checks. For example, Congress has the power to regulate commerce among the states. By itself, this power might allow Congress to pass legislation forbidding women from crossing state lines to buy or sell goods. But such a law, although arguably based on an enumerated power, surely would be unconstitutional. The reason is that it conflicts with an independent check—the equal protection guarantee discussed later in the chapter. Today, the independent checks are the main limitations on congressional power. The most important reason for the 20th-century decline of the enumerated powers limitation is the perceived need for active federal regulation of economic and social life. Recently, however, the enumerated powers limitation has begun to assume a bit more importance.

This chapter begins by discussing the most important state and federal powers to regulate economic matters. Next, the chapter examines certain

Enumerated Powers and Independent Checks

	LAW DOES NOT CONFLICT WITH ANY INDEPENDENT CHECK	LAW CONFLICTS WITH AN INDEPENDENT CHECK
Law Is within Congress's Enumerated Powers	Law is constitutional	Law is unconstitutional
Law Is Not within Congress's Enumerated Powers	Law is unconstitutional	Law is unconstitutional

independent checks that apply to both the federal government and the states. After this, it discusses some independent checks affecting the states alone. The chapter concludes by treating a provision—the Takings Clause of the Fifth Amendment—that both recognizes a governmental power and limits its exercise.

STATE AND FEDERAL POWER TO REGULATE

State Regulatory Power

Although state constitutions may do so, the U.S. Constitution does not list the powers state legislatures can exercise. However, the U.S. Constitution does place certain independent checks in the path of state lawmaking. It also declares that certain powers (e.g., creating currency and taxing imports) can only be exercised by Congress. In many other areas, though, Congress and the state legislatures have *concurrent powers.* Within those areas, both can make law unless Congress preempts state regulation under the supremacy clause. A very important state legislative power that operates concurrently with many congressional powers is the **police power.** The police power is a broad state power to regulate for the public health, safety, morals, and welfare.

Federal Regulatory Power

Article I, section 8 of the U.S. Constitution states a number of ways in which Congress can legislate concerning business and commercial matters. For example, it empowers Congress to coin and borrow money, regulate commerce with foreign nations, establish uniform laws regarding bankruptcies, create post offices, and regulate copyrights and patents. However, the most important congressional powers contained in Article I, section 8 are the powers to regulate commerce among the states, to lay and collect taxes, and to spend for the general welfare. Because they now are read so broadly, these three powers are the main constitutional bases for the extensive federal social and economic regulation that exists today.

The Commerce Power Article I, section 8 states that "The Congress shall have Power. . . To regulate Commerce. . . among the several States." The origi-

nal reason for giving Congress this power to regulate *interstate commerce* was to block the protectionist state restrictions on interstate trade that were common after the Revolution and thus to nationalize economic life. This *Commerce Clause* has two major thrusts. First, as discussed later in the chapter, it is an independent check on state regulation that unduly restricts interstate commerce. Our present concern is the second aspect of the Commerce Clause—its role as a source of congressional regulatory power.

By its literal language, the Commerce Clause simply gives Congress power to regulate commerce that occurs among the states. Today, however, the clause basically is an all-purpose federal police power enabling Congress to regulate most activities within a state's borders (*intrastate* matters). How has this transformation occurred?

The most important step in the transformation was the Supreme Court's conclusion that the power to regulate *interstate* commerce includes the power to regulate *intrastate* activities that affect interstate commerce. For example, in the *Shreveport Rate Cases* (1914), the Supreme Court upheld the Interstate Commerce Commission's regulation of railroad rates within Texas (an intrastate matter outside the language of the Commerce Clause) because those rates affected rail traffic between Texas and Louisiana (an interstate matter within the clause's language). Eventually, this "affecting commerce" doctrine was used to justify federal police power measures with a great intrastate reach. Over 30 years ago, for example, the Supreme Court upheld the application of the 1964 Civil Rights Act's "public accommodations" section to a family-owned restaurant in Birmingham, Alabama. It did so because the restaurant's racial discrimination affected interstate commerce by: (1) reducing the restaurant's business and limiting its purchases of out-of-state meat, and (2) restricting the ability of blacks to travel among the states.

As this example suggests, Congress now can regulate intrastate activities even though they have relatively little impact on commerce among the states. In our highly interdependent society, almost all intrastate activities have *some* effect on interstate commerce. This has led some people to believe that the intrastate reach of the Commerce Clause is virtually unlimited. In the following *Lopez* case, however, the Supreme Court made it clear that the commerce power still has some inherent limits.

UNITED STATES v. LOPEZ   514 U.S. 549 (U.S. Sup. Ct. 1995)

A lfonso Lopez carried a concealed .38 caliber handgun and five bullets into his high school in San Antonio, Texas. For this, he was arrested and charged with violating section 922(q) of the federal Gun-Free School Zones Act of 1990, which forbids the knowing possession of a firearm within a school zone. After being found guilty of violating this statute, Lopez appealed his conviction. His argument was that section 922(q) was unconstitutional because it exceeded Congress's legislative power under the Commerce Clause. Agreeing with this argument, the Fifth Circuit Court of Appeals reversed Lopez's conviction. The government then appealed to the U.S. Supreme Court. ∽

Rehnquist, Chief Justice   The Constitution creates a federal government of enumerated powers. As James Madison wrote, "[t]he powers delegated by the proposed Constitution to the federal government are few and defined. Those which are to remain in the State governments are numerous and indefinite." This division of authority was adopted by the Framers to ensure protection of our fundamental liberties. Just as the separation and independence of the coordinate branches of the federal government serve to prevent the accumulation of excessive power in any one branch, a healthy balance of power between the states and the federal government will reduce the risk of tyranny and abuse from either front.

The Constitution delegates to Congress the power "[t]o regulate commerce with foreign Nations, and among the several States, and with the Indian Tribes." Congress's commerce authority includes the power to regulate those activities having a substantial relation to interstate commerce. The government's essential contention is that section 922(q) is valid because possession of a firearm in a local school zone substantially affect[s] interstate commerce. First, the costs of violent crime are substantial, and through the mechanism of insurance, those costs are spread throughout the population. Second, violent crime reduces the willingness of individuals to travel to areas of the country that are perceived to be unsafe. The government also argues that the presence of guns in schools poses a substantial threat to the educational process by threatening the learning environment. A handicapped educational process, in turn, will result in a less productive citizenry. That, in turn, would have an adverse effect on the nation's economic well-being.

We pause to consider the implications of the government's arguments. The government admits, under its "costs of crime" reasoning, that Congress could regulate not only all violent crime, but all activities that might lead to violent crime, regardless of how tenuously they relate to interstate commerce. Similarly, under the government's "national productivity" reasoning, Congress could regulate any activity that it found was related to the economic productivity of individual citizens: family law (including marriage, divorce, and child custody), for example. Under the theories that the government presents in support of section 922(q), it is difficult to perceive any limitation on federal power, even in areas such as criminal law enforcement or education where States historically have been sovereign. Thus, if we were to accept the government's arguments, we are hard-pressed to posit any activity by an individual that Congress is without power to regulate.

To uphold the government's contentions here, we would have to pile inference upon inference in a manner that would bid fair to convert congressional authority under the Commerce Clause to a general police power of the sort retained by the states. Admittedly, some of our prior cases have taken long steps down that road, giving great deference to congressional action. The broad language in these opinions has suggested the possibility of additional expansion, but we decline here to proceed any further. To do so would require us to conclude that the Constitution's enumeration of powers does not presuppose something not enumerated, and that there will never be a distinction between what is truly national and what is truly local. This we are unwilling to do.

Court of Appeals decision affirmed;
Lopez wins.

The Taxing Power   Article I, section 8 of the Constitution also states that "The Congress shall have Power To lay and collect Taxes, Duties, Imposts and Excises." The main purpose behind this *taxing power* is to raise revenue for the federal government.[2] But the taxing power can also serve as a regulatory device. Because the power to tax is the power to destroy, Congress can regulate by imposing a heavy tax on a disfavored activity. Although some past regulatory taxes have been struck down, today the reach of the taxing power, while poorly defined, still is very broad. Sometimes it is said that a regulatory tax is constitutional if its purpose could be furthered by one of Congress's *other* powers. Due to the broad scope of the commerce power, this may mean that the taxing power has few limits.

The Spending Power   If taxing power regulation uses a federal club, congressional *spending power* regulation employs a federal carrot. After stating the taxing power, Article I, section 8 gives Congress a broad ability to spend for the general welfare. By basing the receipt of federal money on the performance of certain conditions, Congress can use the spending power to advance specific regulatory ends. For instance, conditional federal grants to the states are common today.

Over the past 50 years, congressional spending power regulation invariably has been upheld. Still, there are limits on its use. First, an exercise of the spending power must serve *general* public purposes, and not particular interests. Second, when Congress conditions the receipt of federal money on certain conditions, it must do so clearly. Third, the condition must be reasonably related to the purpose behind the federal expenditure. For example, Congress probably cannot condition a state's receipt of federal highway money on the state's adoption of a one-house legislature.

INDEPENDENT CHECKS ON THE FEDERAL GOVERNMENT AND THE STATES

Even if a regulation is within Congress's enumerated powers or a state's police power, it still is unconstitutional if it collides with one of the Constitution's *independent checks*. This section discusses three checks that limit both federal and state regulation of the economy. These are freedom of speech, due process, and equal protection. Before discussing these guarantees, however, we must consider three preliminary matters.

Incorporation

The Fifth Amendment prevents the federal government from depriving "any person of life, liberty, or property, without due process of law," and the Fourteenth Amendment does the same to the states. The First Amendment, however, applies only to the federal government. And the Fourteenth Amendment merely says that no state shall "deny to any person. . . the equal protection of the laws." Thus, while due process clearly applies to both the federal government and the states, the First Amendment seems to apply only to the federal government and the Equal Protection Clause only to the states. But the First Amendment's free speech guarantee has been included within the "liberty" protected by Fourteenth Amendment due process and thus made applicable to the states. This is part of the process of *incorporation* by which almost all Bill of Rights provisions now apply to the states. The Fourteenth Amendment's equal protection guarantee, on the other hand, has been made applicable to the federal government by incorporating it within the Fifth Amendment's Due Process Clause. Figure 2 summarizes all these points.

Government Action

People often talk as if the Constitution protects them against anyone who might threaten their rights. However, most of the Constitution's individual rights provisions only block the actions of *government* bodies, state and federal.[3] Private behavior that denies individual rights, while perhaps forbidden by statute, is not supposed to be a constitutional matter. This **government action** or **state action**

---

[2]The Constitution imposes some restrictions on the types of taxes that may be used to raise revenue, but these restrictions are beyond the scope of this text.

[3]However, the Thirteenth Amendment, which bans slavery and involuntary servitude throughout the United States, does not have a state action requirement. Also, some state constitutions have individual rights provisions that lack a state action requirement.

FIGURE 2

Why Certain Individual Rights Guarantees Apply to Both the Federal Government and the States

GUARANTEE	WHY APPLICABLE TO STATES	WHY APPLICABLE TO FEDERAL GOVERNMENT
Due Process	Text of Fourteenth Amendment	Text of Fifth Amendment
First Amendment	Incorporation within Fourteenth Amendment	Text of First Amendment
Equal Protection	Text of Fourteenth Amendment	Incorporation within Fifth Amendment

requirement forces courts to distinguish between governmental behavior and private behavior. Their approach to this problem has varied over time.

Before World War II, only formal organs of government such as legislatures, administrative agencies, municipalities, courts, prosecutors, and state universities were deemed state actors. But after the war, the scope of government action increased considerably, with all sorts of traditionally private behavior being subjected to individual rights limitations. In *Marsh v. Alabama* (1946), the Supreme Court treated a privately owned company town's restriction of free expression as government action under the *public function* theory because the town was like a regular municipality in most respects. Also, in *Shelley v. Kraemer* (1948), the Court held that state court enforcement of certain white homeowners' private agreement not to sell their homes to blacks was unconstitutional state action under the Equal Protection Clause. Later, in *Burton v. Wilmington Parking Authority* (1961), the Court concluded that racial discrimination by a privately owned restaurant located in a state-owned and state-operated parking garage was unconstitutional state action, in part because the garage and the restaurant were intertwined in a mutually beneficial "symbiotic" relationship. Among the other factors leading courts to find state action during the 1960s and 1970s were extensive government regulation of private activity and government financial aid to a private actor.

However, the Court severely restricted the reach of state action during the 1970s and 1980s. Now, private behavior is state action only when a regular unit of government is directly *responsible* for the challenged private behavior because it has coerced or encouraged such behavior. Also, the public function doctrine has been limited to situations where a private entity exercises powers that have *traditionally* been *exclusively* reserved to the state; private police protection is a possible example. In addition, government regulation and government funding

now are less important factors in state action determinations. Despite all these changes, however, state action doctrine probably has not returned to its narrow pre–World War II definition, and some uncertainty remains in this area.

To illustrate the Supreme Court's state action cutback, consider its 1982 decision in *Rendell-Baker v. Cohn,* where it rejected various constitutional challenges to the firing of teachers and counselors at a private school for maladjusted high school students because no state action was present. Although the school was extensively regulated by the state, this did not matter because no state regulation compelled or even influenced the challenged firings. Even though the school depended heavily on state funding, this was not sufficient for state action either. The Court also rejected a "symbiosis" argument without much discussion. Finally, it found the public function doctrine inapplicable because the education of maladjusted high school students, while public in nature, is not *exclusively* a state function.

Means-Ends Tests

Throughout this chapter, you will see tests of constitutionality that seem strange at first glance. One example is the test for determining whether laws that discriminate on the basis of sex violate equal protection. This test says that to be constitutional, such laws must be substantially related to the achievement of an important government purpose. The Equal Protection Clause does not contain such language. It simply says that "No State shall. . . deny to any person. . . the equal protection of the laws." What is going on here?

The sex discrimination test just stated is a **means-ends test.** Courts create such tests because no constitutional right is absolute, and because judges therefore must weigh individual rights against the social purposes served by laws that restrict those rights. In other words, means-ends tests determine how courts strike the balance between individual rights and the social needs that may justify their suppression. The "ends" component of a means-ends test specifies how *significant* a social purpose must be in order to justify the restriction of a right. The "means" component states how *effectively* the challenged law must promote that purpose in order to be constitutional. In our sex discrimination test, for example, the challenged law must serve an "important" government purpose (the significance of the end) and must be "substantially" related to the achievement of that purpose (the effectiveness of the means).

Because some constitutional rights are deemed more important than others, courts use tougher tests of constitutionality in such cases and more lenient tests in other situations. Sometimes these tests are long, wordy, and complicated. Throughout the chapter, therefore, we simplify by employing three general kinds of means-ends tests:

1. *The rational basis test.* This is a very relaxed test of constitutionality that challenged laws usually pass with ease. A typical formulation of the rational basis test might say that government action need only have a *reasonable* relation to the achievement of a *legitimate* government purpose to be constitutional.
2. *Intermediate scrutiny.* This comes in many forms; the sex discrimination test we have been discussing is an example.
3. *Full Strict Scrutiny.* Here, the court might say that the challenged law must be *necessary* to the fulfillment of a *compelling* government purpose. Government action that is subjected to this rigorous test of constitutionality almost always is struck down.

Business and the First Amendment

The First Amendment says that "Congress shall make no law. . . abridging the freedom of speech." Despite its absolute language ("*no* law"), the First Amendment does not prohibit every law that restricts speech. As Justice Oliver Wendell Holmes once remarked, the First Amendment does not protect someone who falsely shouts "Fire!" in a crowded theater. But while the First Amendment's free speech guarantee is not absolute, government action restricting speech usually receives very strict judicial scrutiny. One justification for this high level of protection is the "marketplace" rationale. On this view, the free competition of ideas is the surest means of attaining truth and the marketplace of ideas best serves this end when restrictions on speech are kept to a minimum and all viewpoints can be considered.

This chapter does not consider most of the situations in which the First Amendment's free speech guarantee has been applied during the 20th century. Nor does it examine *corporate political speech,* which generally receives full First Amendment protection. Instead, we discuss one First Amendment issue of considerable concern to business—the government's power to regulate *commercial speech.*

Commercial Speech The definition of commercial speech is not completely clear, but most cases on the subject involve commercial advertising. In 1942, the Supreme Court ruled that commercial speech was outside the First Amendment's protection, but the Court reversed its position during the 1970s. Now, restrictions on commercial speech receive an *intermediate* level of means-ends scrutiny that is less rigorous than the full strict scrutiny given laws restricting corporate *political* speech. The test is that laws regulating commercial speech must *directly* advance a *substantial* government interest and must be *no more extensive than necessary* to advance that interest. However, laws regulating false or deceptive commercial speech, or requiring the disclosure of information useful to consumers, get only light scrutiny.

The usual justification for protecting commercial speech is to promote informed consumer choice by removing barriers to the flow of commercial information. The following case is an example. Note the two ways in which the challenged law failed the constitutional test stated earlier.

 licensed Rhode Island liquor store named 44 Liquormart ran a newspaper advertisement containing an implied reference to the bargain prices at which people could buy its liquor. For this reason, the Rhode Island Liquor Control Administrator fined the store $400. The Administrator levied the fine under Rhode Island statutes forbidding public price advertising for alcoholic beverages.

44 Liquormart challenged its fine in federal district court, arguing that the statutes violated the First Amendment. After the district court granted 44 Liquormart's claim, the court of appeals reversed, finding the statutes constitutional. 44 Liquormart then appealed to the U.S. Supreme Court. ∞

Stevens, Justice In *Central Hudson Gas & Electric Corporation v. Public Service Commission* (1980), we considered a regulation completely banning all promotional advertising by electric utilities. Five members of the Court recognized that the state interest in the conservation of energy was substantial, and that there was an immediate connection between advertising and demand for electricity. Nevertheless, they concluded that the regulation was invalid because the Commission had failed to make a showing that a more limited speech regulation would not have adequately served the state's interest. The majority explained that although the special nature of commercial speech may require less than strict review of its regulation, special concerns arise from regulations that entirely suppress commercial speech in order to pursue a nonspeech-related policy. As a result, the Court concluded that special care should attend the review of such blanket bans.

Rhode Island errs in concluding that *all* commercial speech regulations are subject to a similar form of constitutional review. When a state regulates commercial messages to protect consumers from misleading, deceptive, or aggressive sales practices, or requires the disclosure of beneficial consumer information, the purpose of its regulation is consistent with the reasons for according constitutional protection to commercial speech and therefore justifies less than strict review. However, when a state entirely prohibits the dissemination of truthful, nonmisleading commercial messages for reasons unrelated to the preservation of a fair bargaining process, there is far less reason to depart from the rigorous review that the First Amendment generally demands.

Rhode Island's price advertising ban constitutes a blanket prohibition against truthful, nonmisleading speech about a lawful product. The ban serves an end unrelated to consumer protection. Accordingly, we must review the price advertising ban with special care, mindful that speech prohibitions of this type rarely survive constitutional review.

The state argues that the price advertising prohibition should be upheld because it directly advances the state's substantial interest in promoting temperance, and because it is no more extensive than necessary. We cannot agree. Although the record suggests that the price advertising ban may have some impact on the purchasing patterns of temperate drinkers of modest means, the state has presented no evidence to suggest that its speech prohibition will *significantly* reduce marketwide consumption. Moreover, the evidence suggests that the abusive drinker will probably not be deterred by a marginal price increase, and that the true alcoholic may simply reduce his purchases of other necessities. Any conclusion that elimination of the ban would significantly increase alcohol consumption would require the sort of speculation or conjecture that is an unacceptable means of demonstrating that a restriction on commercial speech directly advances the state's asserted interest. Such speculation certainly does not suffice when the state takes aim at accurate commercial information for paternalistic ends.

The state also cannot satisfy the requirement that its restriction on speech be no more excessive than necessary. Higher prices can be maintained either by direct regulation or by increased taxation. Per capita purchases could be limited as is the case with prescription drugs. Even educational campaigns focused on the problems of excessive, or even moderate, drinking might prove to be more effective.

Court of appeals judgment in Rhode Island's favor reversed; 44 Liquormart wins.

Due Process

The Fifth and Fourteenth Amendments require that the federal government and the states observe **due process** when they deprive a person of life, liberty, or property. Due process has both *procedural* and *substantive* meanings.

Procedural Due Process The traditional conception of due process, called **procedural due process,** establishes the *procedures* that government must follow when it takes life, liberty, or property. Although the requirements of procedural due process vary from situation to situation, their core idea is that people are entitled to adequate *notice* of the government action to be taken against them and to some sort of *fair trial or hearing* before that action can occur.

In order to trigger due process protections, the government must deprive a person of life, liberty, or property. Procedural due process *liberty* includes a very broad and poorly defined range of freedoms. It even includes certain interests in personal reputation. For example, the firing of a government employee might require some kind of due process hearing if it is publicized, the fired employee's reputation is sufficiently damaged, and her future employment opportunities are restricted. The Supreme Court has said that procedural due process *property* is not created by the Constitution but by existing rules and understandings that stem from an independent source such as state law. These rules and understandings must give a person a *legitimate claim of entitlement* to a benefit, not merely some need, desire, or expectation for it. This definition includes almost all of the usual forms of property. It also includes the job rights of tenured public employees who can be discharged only for cause, but not the rights of untenured or probationary employees.

Substantive Due Process   Procedural due process does not challenge rules of *substantive law*—the rules that set standards of behavior for organized social life. For example, imagine that State X makes adultery a crime and allows people to be convicted of adultery without a trial. Arguments that adultery should not be a crime go to the substance of the statute, while objections to the lack of a trial are procedural in nature.

Sometimes, the Due Process Clauses have been used to attack the substance of government action.

For our purposes, the most important example of this **substantive due process** occurred early in the 20th century, when courts struck down various kinds of social legislation as denying due process. They did so mainly by reading freedom of contract and other economic rights into the liberty and property protected by the Fifth and Fourteenth Amendments, and then interpreting "due process of law" to require that laws denying such rights be subjected to means-ends scrutiny. The best-known example is the Supreme Court's 1905 decision in *Lochner v. New York,* where it struck down a state law setting maximum hours of work for bakery employees because the statute limited freedom of contract and did not directly advance the legitimate state goal of promoting worker health.

Since 1937, this "economic"form of substantive due process has not been a significant check on government regulation of social and economic matters. Over that period, substantive due process attacks on such regulations have triggered only a lenient kind of rational basis review and thus have little chance of success. In the 1970s and 1980s, however, substantive due process became increasingly important as a device for protecting *noneconomic* rights—most importantly, the constitutional right of privacy.

Is the following *Gore* case consistent with the Court's post-1937 pattern? The case does not use the words "substantive due process," and it claims to apply the procedural due process requirement of fair notice. Yet it seems to use tests of substantive fairness to strike down substantive state action. Indeed, it might be the first case since the 1930s to use due process to knock out substantive government action involving an economic matter.

BMW OF NORTH AMERICA v. GORE   116 S. Ct. 1589 (1996)

Ira Gore bought a new BMW sports sedan for approximately $41,000 from an Alabama BMW dealer. Before the car's sale, its finish had been damaged. As a result, BMW repainted it. BMW's policy was to sell such a repaired car as new without notifying the dealer or the customer if the repair cost was less than 3 percent of the suggested retail price. If the cost exceeded 3 percent, BMW would put the car in company service and then sell it as a used car. Since the cost of repainting Gore's car was about 1.5 percent of its retail price, BMW did not disclose the repainting to the dealer or to Gore.

After Gore eventually discovered the repainting, he sued BMW for fraud in an Alabama trial court, seeking actual damages of $4,000 and punitive damages of $4 million. Gore based the $4 million figure on evidence that throughout the United States, BMW had secretly sold nearly 1,000 refinished cars as new, at a loss to the buyer of $4,000 per car. The jury returned a verdict finding BMW liable for compensatory damages of $4,000 *and punitive damages of $4 million. Alleging that its nondisclosure policy was legal in at least 25 states, BMW appealed. The Alabama Supreme Court upheld the imposition of punitive damages, but reduced the award to $2 million. BMW then appealed to the U.S. Supreme Court.* ∞

Stevens, Justice Punitive damages may properly be imposed to further a state's legitimate interests in punishing unlawful conduct and deterring its repetition. In our federal system, states have considerable flexibility in determining the level of punitive damages that they will allow in different classes of cases and in any particular case. Most states afford the jury similar latitude, requiring only that the damages awarded be reasonably necessary to vindicate the state's legitimate interests in punishment and deterrence. Only when an award can fairly be categorized as grossly excessive in relation to these interests does it enter the zone of arbitrariness that violates due process.

Elementary notions of fairness enshrined in our constitutional jurisprudence dictate that a person receive fair notice not only of the conduct that will subject him to punishment but also of the severity of the penalty that a state may impose. Three guideposts, each of which indicates that BMW did not receive adequate notice of the magnitude of the sanction that Alabama might impose for adhering to the nondisclosure policy, lead us to the conclusion that the $2 million award is grossly excessive.

Degree of Reprehensibility

Perhaps the most important indicium of the reasonableness of a punitive damages award is the degree of reprehensibility of the defendant's conduct. In this case, none of the aggravating factors associated with particularly reprehensible conduct is present. The harm BMW inflicted on Dr. Gore was purely economic. The presale refinishing of the car had no effect on its performance or safety features, or even its appearance. BMW's conduct evinced no indifference to or reckless disregard for the health and safety of others.

Ratio

The second indicium of an unreasonable or excessive punitive damages award is its ratio to the actual harm inflicted on the plaintiff. The $2 million in punitive damages is 500 times the amount of his actual harm. Moreover, there is no suggestion that Gore or any other BMW purchaser was threatened with any additional potential harm by BMW's nondisclosure policy. When the ratio is a breathtaking 500 to 1, the award must surely raise a suspicious judicial eyebrow.

Sanctions for Comparable Misconduct

Comparing the punitive damages award and the civil or criminal penalties that could be imposed for comparable misconduct provides a third indicium of excessiveness. A reviewing court should accord substantial deference to legislative judgments concerning appropriate sanctions for the conduct at issue. The maximum civil penalty authorized by the Alabama legislature for a violation of its Deceptive Trade Practices Act is $2,000. Moreover, at the time BMW's policy was first challenged, there does not appear to have been any judicial decision in Alabama or elsewhere indicating that application of that policy might have to give rise to such severe punishment.

We are not prepared to draw a bright line marking the limits of a constitutionally acceptable punitive damages award. However, we are fully convinced that the grossly excessive award imposed in this case transcends the constitutional limit.

Alabama Supreme Court decision upholding a $2 million punitive damages award against BMW reversed. Case returned to the Alabama courts for proceedings consistent with the U.S. Supreme Court's decision.

Equal Protection

The Fourteenth Amendment's Equal Protection Clause says that "[n]o State shall. . . deny to any person. . . the equal protection of the laws." Because it has been incorporated within Fifth Amend-ment due process, the clause also applies to the federal government. As currently interpreted, the equal protection guarantee applies to all situations in which government *classifies* or *distinguishes* people. The law inevitably makes distinctions among people, benefiting or burdening some groups but not others. The equal protection guarantee sets the standards such distinctions must meet to be constitutional.

The Rational Basis Test The basic equal protection standard is the *rational basis* test described earlier. This is the standard usually applied to social and economic regulations that are challenged as

denying equal protection. Although formulations of the rational basis test vary, here it means that the government's classification must be *reasonably* related to the accomplishment of a *legitimate* public purpose. As the following *Stanglin* case indicates, this lenient test usually does not impede state and federal regulation of social and economic matters.

CITY OF DALLAS v. STANGLIN   490 U.S. 19 (U.S. Sup. Ct. 1989)

The city of Dallas, Texas adopted an ordinance restricting admission to so-called "Class E" dance halls to persons between the ages of 14 and 18. However, it did not impose similar age limitations on most other establishments where teenagers might congregate—for example, skating rinks. Charles Stanglin, who in one building operated both a Class E dance hall and a roller-skating rink, sued for an injunction against enforcement of the ordinance in a Texas trial court. One of his arguments was that the ordinance denied equal protection because its distinction between Class E dance halls and other establishments for teenagers was irrational. The Texas trial court upheld the ordinance, but a higher Texas court struck down its age restriction. The city appealed to the U.S. Supreme Court.

Rehnquist, Chief Justice The Dallas ordinance implicates no suspect class. The question remaining is whether the classification survives rational basis scrutiny under the Equal Protection Clause. The city has chosen to impose a rule that separates 14- to 18-year-olds from what may be the corrupting influences of older teenagers and young adults. An urban planner for the city testified: "Older kids can access drugs and alcohol, and they have more mature sexual attitudes, more liberal sexual attitudes in general. . . . And we're concerned about mixing up these individuals with youngsters [who] have not fully matured."

Stanglin claims that this restriction has no real connection with the city's stated objectives. Except for saloons and teenage dance halls, he argues, teenagers and adults in Dallas may associate with each other, including at the skating area of his rink. We think Stanglin's arguments misapprehend the nature of rational basis scrutiny, which is the most relaxed and tolerant form of judicial scrutiny under the Equal Protection Clause. If the classification has some reasonable basis, it does not offend the Constitution simply because the classification is not

made with mathematical nicety or because in practice it results in some inequality. The rational basis standard is true to the principle that the Fourteenth Amendment gives the federal courts no power to impose upon the states their views of what constitutes wise economic or social policy.

In the local economic sphere, it is only the invidious discrimination, the wholly arbitrary act, which cannot stand consistently with the Fourteenth Amendment. The city could reasonably conclude that teenagers might be susceptible to corrupting influences if permitted to frequent a dance hall with older persons [and that] limiting dance hall contacts between juveniles and adults would make less likely illicit or undesirable juvenile involvement with alcohol, illegal drugs, and promiscuous sex. It is true that the city allows teenagers and adults to roller-skate together, but skating involves less physical contact than dancing. The differences between the two activities may not be striking, but differentiations need not be striking in order to survive rational basis scrutiny.

Texas court decision striking down the age limitation reversed.

Stricter Scrutiny The rational basis test is the basic equal protection standard. Some classifications, however, get tougher means-ends scrutiny. Specifi-

cally, laws that discriminate regarding **fundamental rights** or involve **suspect classifications** now receive more rigorous review. This is a development that mainly began after World War II and that greatly accelerated during the 1960s and 1970s.

The list of rights regarded as "fundamental" for equal protection purposes is not completely clear, but it includes voting, interstate travel, and certain criminal procedure protections. Laws creating unequal enjoyment of these rights receive something resembling full strict scrutiny. In 1969, for instance, the Supreme Court struck down the District of Columbia's one-year residency requirement for receiving welfare benefits because that requirement unequally and impermissibly restricted the right of interstate travel.

Certain "suspect" bases of classification also trigger more rigorous equal protection review. As of late 1996, these **suspect classifications** and the level of scrutiny they attract are as follows:

1. *Race and national origin.* Classifications disadvantaging racial or national minorities receive the strictest kind of strict scrutiny and are almost never constitutional. Still, the Supreme Court has upheld so-called reverse racial discrimination—government action that benefits racial minorities and disadvantages whites. In 1989, however, a majority of the Court concluded that discrimination of this kind should receive the same full strict scrutiny as discrimination *against* racial or national minorities. Reversing a 1990 case, a 1995 Supreme Court decision held that this is true of federal government action as well as state action. It remains to be seen what impact these developments will have on the many federal and state programs preferring racial minorities.

2. *Alienage.* Classifications based on one's status as an alien also receive strict scrutiny of some kind,

but it is doubtful whether this standard is as tough as the full strict scrutiny normally used in race discrimination cases. Under the "political function" exception, moreover, laws restricting aliens from employment in positions that are intimately related to democratic self-government only receive *rational basis* review. This exception has been read broadly to uphold laws excluding aliens from being state troopers, public school teachers, and probation officers.

3. *Sex.* Although sex has never formally been declared a suspect classification, for nearly 20 years laws discriminating on the basis of gender have been subjected to a fairly tough form of *intermediate scrutiny.* As the Court said in 1996, such laws require an "exceedingly persuasive" justification. The usual test is that government action discriminating on the basis of sex must be *substantially* related to the furtherance of an *important* government purpose. Under this test, measures discriminating against women have almost always been struck down. The Supreme Court has said that laws disadvantaging men get the same scrutiny as those disadvantaging women, but this has not prevented the Court from upholding men-only draft registration and a law making statutory rape a crime for men alone.

4. *Illegitimacy* Classifications based on one's illegitimate birth receive a form of *intermediate scrutiny* that probably is less strict than the scrutiny given gender-based classifications. Under this vague standard, the Court has struck down state laws discriminating against illegitimates in areas such as recovery for wrongful death, workers' compensation benefits, social security payments, inheritance, and child support.

C O N C E P T R E V I E W

The Levels of Equal Protection Review: A Rough Summary

Rational Basis Review	1. Most general social and economic regulations 2. Laws discriminating against aliens under the political function exception
Intermediate Scrutiny	1. Sex discrimination against both men and women 2. Discrimination against illegitimates
Full or Nearly Full Strict Scrutiny	1. Discrimination regarding fundamental rights 2. Federal and state racial discrimination against both blacks and whites 3. Most discrimination against aliens 4. National origin discrimination

INDEPENDENT CHECKS APPLYING ONLY TO THE STATES

The Contract Clause

Article I, section 10 of the Constitution says: "No State shall... pass any... Law impairing the Obligation of Contracts." This *Contract Clause* applies to state laws that change the parties' performance obligations under an *existing* contract *after* that contract has been made.[4] The original purpose behind the Contract Clause was to strike down the many debtor relief statutes passed by the states after the Revolution. These statutes impaired the obligations of existing private contracts by relieving debtors of the obligations they owed to contract credi-

---

[4]Also, under the Fifth Amendment's Due Process Clause, standards similar to those described in this section apply to the federal government.

tors. In two early 19th-century cases, however, the Contract Clause also was held to protect the obligations of *governmental* contracts, charters, and grants.

The Contract Clause probably was the most important constitutional check on state regulation of the economy in the 19th century. Beginning in the latter part of that century, though, the clause gradually became subordinate to legislation based on the states' police powers. By the mid-20th century, most observers treated the clause as a constitutional dead letter. In 1977, however, the Supreme Court gave the Contract Clause new life by announcing a fairly strict constitutional test governing situations where a state impairs *its own* contracts, charters, and grants. Such impairments, it said, must be "reasonable and necessary to serve an important public purpose." With one exception in 1978, however, the Court has continued its deference toward state regulations that impair the obligations of *private* contracts. The following *Exxon* case is an example.

EXXON CORPORATION v. EAGERTON 462 U.S. 176 (U.S. Sup. Ct. 1983)

F or years, the Exxon Corporation paid a severance tax on the oil and gas it drilled in Alabama. Under the sales contracts that Exxon made with purchasers of its oil and gas, it was able to pass on any tax increase to the purchasers. In 1979, Alabama raised the severance tax from 4 to 6 percent and forbade producers of oil and gas from passing on the increase to purchasers.

Exxon sued the Alabama commissioner of revenue in an Alabama trial court, seeking a ruling that the pass-on restriction was unconstitutional under the Contract Clause. The trial court found for Exxon, but the Alabama Supreme Court reversed. Exxon appealed to the U.S. Supreme Court. ⌒

Marshall, Justice By barring Exxon from passing the tax increase through to its purchasers, the pass-through prohibition nullified the purchasers' contractual obligations to reimburse Exxon for any severance taxes. While the prohibition thus affects contractual obligations, it does not follow that the prohibition constituted a "Law impairing the Obligation of Contracts" within the meaning of the Contract Clause. Although the language of the Clause is facially absolute, its prohibition must be accommodated to the inherent police power of the state to safeguard the vital interests of its people. If the law were otherwise, one would be able to obtain immunity from state regulation by making private contractual arrangements.

The Contract Clause does not deprive the states of their broad power to adopt general regulatory measures without being concerned that private con-

tracts will be impaired, or even destroyed, as a result. Thus, a state prohibition law may be applied to contracts for the sale of beer that were valid when entered into, a law barring lotteries may be applied to lottery tickets that were valid when issued, and a workmen's compensation law may be applied to employers and employees operating under preexisting contracts of employment that made no provision for work-related injuries.

Like the laws upheld in these cases, the pass-through prohibition did not prescribe a rule limited in effect to contractual obligations or remedies, but instead imposed a generally applicable rule of conduct designed to advance a broad societal interest, protecting consumers from excessive prices. The prohibition applied to all oil and gas producers, regardless of whether they happened to be parties to sale contracts permitting them to pass tax increases through to their purchasers. The effect of the pass-through prohibition on existing contracts that did contain such a provision was incidental to its main effect of shielding consumers from the burden of the tax increase.

Judgment for the commissioner affirmed on the Contract Clause issue. Case returned to the Alabama Supreme Court for consideration of other questions.

Burden on Interstate Commerce

In addition to empowering Congress to regulate interstate commerce, the Commerce Clause also limits the states' ability to *burden* such commerce. This limitation is not expressly stated in the Constitution. Instead, it arises by implication from the Commerce Clause and reflects that clause's original purpose of blocking state protectionism and ensuring free interstate trade. This burden-on-commerce limitation operates independently of congressional legislation under the commerce power or other federal powers. If appropriate federal regulation is present, the preemption questions discussed in the next section may also arise.

Many different state laws can raise burden-on-commerce problems. For example, state regulation of transportation (e.g., limits on train or truck lengths) has been a prolific source of litigation. The same is true of state restrictions on the importation of goods or resources—for example, laws forbidding the sale of out-of-state food products unless they meet certain standards. Such restrictions sometimes benefit local economic interests and reflect their political influence. Burden-on-commerce issues also arise when states try to aid their own residents by blocking the export of scarce or valuable products, thus denying out-of-state buyers access to those products.

Due in part to the many different regulations it has had to consider, the Supreme Court has not adhered to one consistent test for determining when such regulations impermissibly burden interstate commerce. In a 1994 case, the Court said that laws that *discriminate* against interstate commerce must satisfy the strictest scrutiny to be constitutional. Discrimination is *express* when state laws treat local and interstate commerce unequally on their face. In 1992, for example, the Supreme Court considered a 1986 Oklahoma statute that required Oklahoma coal-fired electric generating plants producing power for sale in Oklahoma to burn at least 10 percent Oklahoma-mined coal. The Court said that

because this measure treated Oklahoma coal differently from out-of-state coal, it expressly discriminated against interstate commerce and deserved very strict scrutiny. Because the Court suspected that the Oklahoma statute had protectionist motivations and because the alleged justifications for it were weak, the Court found the law unconstitutional.

State laws might also discriminate even though they are neutral on their face so far as interstate commerce is concerned. This occurs when their *effect* is to burden or hinder such commerce. In one case, for example, the Supreme Court considered a North Carolina statute requiring all closed containers of apples sold within the state to bear only the applicable U.S. grade or standard. Washington State, the nation's largest apple producer, had its own inspection and grading system for Washington apples, a system that generally was regarded as superior to the federal system. The Court struck down the North Carolina statute because it benefited local apple producers by forcing Washington sellers to regrade apples sold in North Carolina (thus raising their costs of doing business) and by undermining the competitive advantage provided by Washington's superior grading system.

On the other hand, state laws that *regulate evenhandedly and have only incidental effects on interstate commerce* are constitutional if they serve legitimate state interests and their local benefits exceed the burden they place on interstate commerce. There is no sharp line between such regulations and those that are almost always unconstitutional under the tests discussed above. In a 1981 Supreme Court case, a state truck-length limitation that differed from the limitations imposed by neighboring states failed to satisfy these tests. First, the Court concluded that the measure did not further the state's legitimate interest in highway safety because the trucks the state banned generally were as safe as those it allowed. Second, whatever marginal safety advantage the law provided was outweighed by the numerous problems it posed for interstate trucking companies.

Finally, laws may unconstitutionally burden interstate commerce when they *directly regulate* that commerce. This can occur, for example, when state price regulations require firms to post the prices at which they will sell within the state and to promise that they will not sell below those prices in other states. Because they affect prices in other states, such regulations directly regulate interstate commerce and usually are unconstitutional.

Federal Preemption

The constitutional principle of **federal supremacy** dictates that where state law conflicts with valid federal law, the federal law is supreme. Where a state law conflicts with a federal statute, the state law is said to be *preempted* by the federal regulation. The central question in most federal preemption cases is Congress's intent. Thus, such cases often present questions of statutory interpretation that can be complex and that are decided on a case-by-case basis.

As the following *Mortier* case suggests, federal preemption of state law generally occurs for one or more of four reasons.

1. *There is a literal conflict between the state and federal measures, so that it is impossible to follow both simultaneously.*

2. *The federal law specifically states that it will preempt state regulation in certain areas.* Similar statements may also appear in the federal statute's legislative history, and courts may find such statements persuasive.

3. *The federal regulation is pervasive.* The fact that Congress has "occupied the field" by regulating a subject in great breadth and/or in considerable detail suggests its intent to displace state regulation of that subject. This may be especially true where Congress has given an administrative agency broad regulatory power in a particular area.

4. *The state regulation is an obstacle to fulfilling the purposes of the federal law.* Here, the party challenging the state law's constitutionality typically claims that the state law interferes with the purposes she attributes to the federal measure (purposes usually found in its legislative history).

WISCONSIN PUBLIC INTERVENOR v. MORTIER   501 U.S. 597 (U.S. Sup. Ct. 1991)

T he small town of Casey in rural Wisconsin adopted an ordinance that regulated the use of pesticides. The ordinance required a permit for applications of pesticides to public lands, private lands subject to public use, and private lands by air. Ralph Mortier applied for a permit to spray a portion of his land from the air. The town granted him a permit, but refused to let him spray by air, and also restricted the areas in which Mortier could spray.

Mortier sued for a declaratory judgment against the ordinance in a state trial court, arguing that it was preempted by the Federal Insecticide, Fungicide, and Rodenticide Act (FIFRA). The Wisconsin Public Intervenor, an assistant attorney general charged with the protection of environmental rights, was admitted as a defendant in Mortier's suit. The trial court decided in Mortier's favor, and the Wisconsin Supreme Court affirmed. The state intervenor appealed to the U.S. Supreme Court. ∽

White, Justice Under the Supremacy Clause, state laws that interfere with, or are contrary to, the laws of Congress are invalid. The ways in which federal law may preempt state law are well established. Congress's intent to supplant state authority in a particular field may be express in the terms of the statute. Absent explicit preemptive language, Congress's intent to supersede state law may nonetheless be implicit if a scheme of federal regulation is so pervasive as to make reasonable the

inference that Congress left no room for the states to supplement it. Even when Congress has not chosen to occupy a particular field, preemption may occur to the extent that state and federal law actually conflict. Such a conflict arises when compliance with both federal and state regulations is a physical impossibility, or when a state law stands as an obstacle to the accomplishment and execution of the full purposes and objectives of Congress.

Applying these principles, we conclude that FIFRA does not preempt the town's ordinance either explicitly, implicitly, or by virtue of an actual conflict. FIFRA nowhere expressly supersedes local regulation of pesticide use.... Likewise, FIFRA fails to provide any clear and manifest indication that Congress sought to supplant local authority over pesticide regulation impliedly. While [its] 1972 amendments turned FIFRA into a comprehensive regulatory statute, the resulting scheme was not so pervasive as to make reasonable the inference that Congress left no room for the states to supplement it. FIFRA addresses numerous aspects of pesticide control in considerable detail, in particular: registration and classification, applicator certification, inspection of pesticide production facilities, and the possible ban and seizure of pesticides that are misbranded or that otherwise fail to meet federal requirements. FIFRA nonetheless leaves substantial portions of the field vacant, including the area at issue in this case. FIFRA nowhere seeks to establish an affirmative permit scheme for the actual use of pesticides. It certainly does not equate registration and labeling requirements with a general approval to apply pesticides throughout the nation without regard to regional and local factors like climate, population, geography, and water supply.

Finally, we discern no actual conflict either between FIFRA and the ordinance before us or between FIFRA and local regulation generally. Mortier does not rely, nor could he, on the theory that compliance with the ordinance and FIFRA is a physical impossibility. Instead, he urges that the town's ordinance stands as an obstacle to the statute's goals of promoting pesticide regulation that is coordinated solely on the federal and state levels, that rests upon some degree of technical expertise, and that does not unduly burden interstate commerce. Each one of these assertions rests on little more than snippets of legislative history and policy speculations. None of them is convincing.

Judgment reversed in favor of the Wisconsin intervenor.

THE TAKINGS CLAUSE

The Fifth Amendment says that "private property [shall not] be taken for public use, without just compensation." This **Takings Clause** has been incorporated within Fourteenth Amendment due process and thus applies to the states. Traditionally, it has often come into play when the government formally condemns land through its power of **eminent domain,**[5] but it has many other applications as well.

The Takings Clause recognizes government's power to take private property and also limits the exercise of that power. It does so by requiring that when *property* is subjected to a governmental *taking,* the taking must be for a *public purpose* and the property owner must receive *just compensation.* We now consider these four aspects of the Takings Clause in turn. Figure 3 describes how they interact.

1. *Property.* The Takings Clause protects other property interests besides land and interests in land. Although its full scope is unclear, the clause has been held to cover takings of personal property, liens, trade secrets, and contract rights.

2. *Taking.* Due to the range of property interests it may cover, the Takings Clause potentially has a broad scope. Another reason for the clause's wide possible application is the range of government activities that may be considered takings. Of course, the government's use of formal *condemnation procedures* to acquire private property almost always is a taking. There also is a taking when the government *physically invades* private property or allows someone else to do so. The following *Lucas* case describes this type of taking.

In addition, it has long been recognized that government *regulation* may so diminish the value of property or the owner's enjoyment of it as to constitute a taking. Land use regulation such as zoning is an example. Among the factors courts consider in such "regulatory taking" cases are the degree to which government deprives the owner of free possession, use, and disposition of his property; the overall economic impact of the regulation on the owner; and how much the regulation interferes with the owner's reasonable investment-backed expectations regarding the future use of the property. As *Lucas* declares, there is an automatic taking where the government denies the owner *all* economically beneficial uses of the land. Where this is not the

---

[5]Eminent domain and the Takings Clause's application to land use problems are discussed in Chapter 24.

FIGURE   **3**

Analyzing a Takings Clause Case

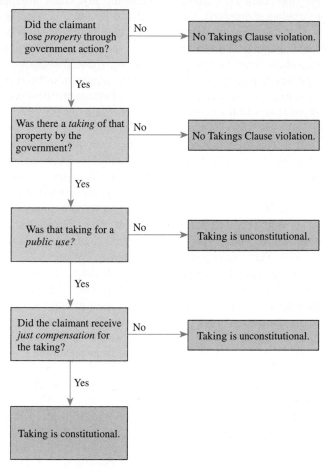

case, courts occasionally apply some form of means-ends scrutiny in determining whether a regulatory taking has occurred.

3. *Public use.* Once a taking of property has occurred, it is unconstitutional unless it is for a public use. Because courts now apply a relaxed version of the rational basis test to resolve "public use" questions, that test is very easy to meet.

4. *Just compensation.* Even if a taking of property is for a public use, it still is unconstitutional if the property owner does not receive just compensation. Although the standards for determining just compensation vary with the circumstances, the basic test is the fair market value of the property at the time of the taking.

LUCAS v. SOUTH CAROLINA COASTAL COUNCIL   505 U.S. 1003 (U.S. Sup. Ct. 1992)

I   n 1986, David Lucas paid $975,000 for two residential lots on the Isle of Palms in Charleston County, South Carolina. His aim was to build single-family homes on the lots. In 1988, however, the South Carolina legislature enacted the Beachfront Management Act, which prevented Lucas from erecting any permanent habitable structures on the two lots. Lucas then sued in a South Carolina trial court, arguing that the state had taken his property without just compensation. The trial court held in his favor, but the South Carolina Supreme Court reversed that decision. Lucas appealed to the U.S. Supreme Court. ∞

Scalia, Justice Prior to Justice Holmes's exposition in *Pennsylvania Coal Co. v. Mahon* (1922), it was generally thought that the Takings Clause reached only a direct appropriation of property, or the functional equivalent of a practical ouster of the owner's possession. That case [gave birth to] the oft-cited maxim that while property may be regulated to a certain extent, if regulation goes too far it will be recognized as a taking. *Mahon* offered little insight into when a given regulation would be seen as going "too far." In the 70-odd years of succeeding "regulatory takings" jurisprudence, we have generally eschewed any set formula for determining how far is too far, preferring to engage in essentially ad hoc factual inquiries.

We have, however, described at least two categories of regulatory action as compensable without case-specific inquiry into the public interest advanced in support of the restraint. The first encompasses regulations that compel the property owner to suffer a physical invasion of his property. In general, no matter how minute the intrusion, and no matter how weighty the public purpose behind it, we have required compensation. For example in *Loretto v. Teleprompter Manhattan CATV Corp.* (1982), we determined that New York's law requiring landlords to allow television cable companies to emplace cable facilities in their apartment buildings constituted a taking, even though the facilities occupied at most only 1½ cubic feet of the landlords' property. The second situation in which we have found categorical treatment appropriate is where the regulation denies all economically beneficial or productive use of land. . . . [W]hen the owner of real property has been called upon to sacrifice *all* economically beneficial uses in the name of the common good, he has suffered a taking. The trial court found Lucas's two beachfront lots to have been rendered valueless by [the state's] enforcement of the coastal-zone construction ban. Under Lucas's theory of the case, which rested upon our "no economically viable use" statements, that finding entitled him to compensation.

Where the state seeks to sustain regulation that deprives land of all economically beneficial use, it may resist compensation only if the logically antecedent inquiry into the nature of the owner's estate shows that the proscribed use interests were not part of his title to begin with. Any limitation so severe [as a regulation that prohibits all economically viable uses of land] cannot be newly legislated (without compensation), but must inhere in the title itself, in the restrictions that background principles of the state's law of property and nuisance already place upon land ownership. A law or decree with such an effect must, in other words, do no more than duplicate the result that could have been achieved in the courts. When, however, a regulation that declares off-limits all economically productive or beneficial uses of land goes beyond what the relevant background principles would dictate, compensation must be paid to sustain it.

It seems unlikely that common-law principles would have prevented the erection of any habitable or productive improvements on Lucas's land. The question, however, is one of state law to be dealt with on remand. [To win,] South Carolina must identify background principles of nuisance and property law that prohibit the uses Lucas now intends in the circumstances in which the property is presently found. Only on this showing can the state fairly claim that, in proscribing all such beneficial uses, the Beachfront Management Act is taking nothing.

South Carolina Supreme Court's judgment against Lucas reversed; case returned to the South Carolina courts for proceedings not inconsistent with the Supreme Court's opinion.

ETHICAL AND PUBLIC POLICY CONCERNS

1. Courts sometimes state which rights are fundamental and protect those rights by imposing tough means-ends scrutiny on laws that restrict them. What fundamental ethical objection almost always applies to such actions by the courts? *Hint:* Look at the section on the evolution of the Constitution and the role of the Supreme Court.

2. Although this chapter is mainly concerned with economic rights, one of the great generalizations about modern American constitutional law is that since 1937 the Supreme Court has shifted from protecting economic rights to protecting personal rights. One example of the Court's former solicitude for economic rights is the doctrine of economic substantive due process mentioned earlier in the chapter. The most important aspect of modern substantive due process, on the other hand, is the constitutional right of privacy. Today, social and economic regulations that are challenged on substantive due process grounds usually get very light means-ends review, while fairly strict scrutiny still applies to some laws that violate privacy rights.

With all of the above in mind, consider the following groups of questions. Throughout, we assume for the sake of argument that it is desirable for courts to give great protection to personal rights.

a. Why are personal rights intrinsically more important than economic rights? Why, for example, is the right to an abortion more important than freedom of contract? Or consider the distinction between a right protected by the old-time substantive due process—the right to pursue a trade, occupation, or profession—and freedom of speech. To ordinary people, which right really matters the most in their daily lives? Finally, aren't freedom of contract and the right to pursue a chosen occupation "personal" rights, too?

b. What are the possible consequences of giving greater protection to economic rights? Would this imperil social and economic regulations intended to protect the poor and the powerless? In considering this question, examine the text's discussion of the Supreme Court's 1905 *Lochner* decision. Even if such regulations would be jeopardized, is this a decisive objection to giving greater protection to economic rights?

On the other hand, would greater constitutional protection for economic rights increase productivity and thereby benefit both rich and poor? Many free-market economists believe that this would happen. But the U.S. economy has grown spectacularly over the last 50 years even though economic rights have received little constitutional protection during that time.

c. If courts ever give economic rights greater protection, could they make intelligent decisions on the questions this would force them to consider? This would require that courts apply tougher means-ends scrutiny to social and economic regulations. This, in turn, probably means that they would have to decide with some precision how well particular statutes advance their pur-

poses. Are courts likely to do a good job if they try this? How much do most lawyers know about these matters?

On the other hand, don't courts sometimes have to consider complex questions of social policy when they apply tough scrutiny to laws that restrict *personal* rights? If so, does this mean that courts also can handle issues related to economic rights?

PROBLEM CASES

1. In *Wickard v. Filburn* (1942), the Supreme Court upheld the Agricultural Adjustment Act's application to a small Ohio wheat farmer named Filburn. In order to raise prices by restricting output, the act empowered the Secretary of Agriculture to proclaim acreage allotments for wheat farmers. Filburn's permitted allotment for 1941 was 11.1 acres. However, he sowed and harvested 23 acres. Some of this wheat was sold locally, but most of it was used on Filburn's farm. For this overproduction, Filburn was assessed a penalty of $117.11. The Court upheld the penalty, reasoning that Congress's commerce power could reach Filburn's actions because of their impact on interstate commerce.

Why did Filburn's behavior have at least *some* effect on interstate commerce? Taken by itself, would that effect be *substantial,* as now required by the *Lopez* case? Assuming for the sake of argument that the answer to this second question is "no," what could the government argue to create a "substantial" effect here?

2. In 1984, Congress passed a statute directing the Secretary of Transportation to withhold a percentage of the federal highway funds due to a state if the state allowed the purchase or possession of alcoholic beverages by those under 21 years of age. South Dakota, which permitted those 19 or older to buy 3.2 beer, sued to have the statute declared unconstitutional. On what enumerated power is this federal law based? Is it a constitutional exercise of that power? If the statute is constitutional, does this mean that South Dakota cannot permit the purchase or consumption of alcoholic beverages by those under 21?

3. The United States Olympic Committee (USOC) is a federally chartered private corporation. Under the Amateur Sports Act, it has broad powers to handle U.S. participation in international athletic competition and to promote amateur athletics within this country. In addition to granting the USOC its charter, Congress imposed certain regulatory requirements upon it and also gave it some funding. Congress also gave the USOC near-exclusive rights in the commercial and promotional use of the term *Olympic*. When the USOC sued to protect those rights, the defendant argued that its discriminatory enforcement of them violated the Equal Protection Clause.

Suppose that you are an attorney for the defendant in this case. Based on the discussion in the text, what arguments would you make for the proposition that the USOC's enforcement of its rights was state action? Do you think that those arguments will succeed today? Why or why not?

4. The Youngs Drug Products Company planned a marketing campaign for its condoms. The campaign involved the unsolicited mass mailing of advertising fliers and other materials to the general public. The mailings were to include: (1) fliers promoting a range of products available in drug stores (including condoms), (2) fliers specifically promoting condoms, and (3) informational pamphlets discussing the usefulness of condoms in preventing venereal disease and aiding family planning. Are Youngs's *fliers* commercial speech? What about the *informational pamphlets?*

5. In 1968, David Roth became an assistant professor of political science at Wisconsin State University–Oshkosh. He did not have academic tenure; indeed, his contract ran for only one year. At the end of that year, Roth was fired without receiving a statement of reasons and a hearing at which to challenge those reasons. Roth later sued the state's Board of Regents, arguing that his firing was unconstitutional because it deprived him of liberty and property without due process of law. Was Roth deprived of liberty or property here? Assume that the firing was not publicized and that Roth's reputation in the community was not damaged to any significant extent.

6. John DiGiovanni was about to sue Brian Doehr for assault and battery in a Connecticut trial court. In order to ensure that funds would be available to satisfy a judgment, DiGiovanni applied for a $75,000 prejudgment attachment on Doehr's home. He did so under a state statute permitting prejudg-

ment attachments on real estate without notice or a hearing if there is probable cause to sustain the plaintiff's claim. Basing its judgment on five one-sentence paragraphs in the affidavit accompanying DiGiovanni's application, the court found probable cause and ordered the requested attachment on Doehr's home.

Shortly thereafter, and before he was served with DiGiovanni's complaint for assault and battery, Doehr received his first notice of the attachment. As required by the statute, he was also informed of his right to a postattachment hearing to challenge the attachment. Rather than pursuing this option, however, Doehr challenged the attachment statute's constitutionality in federal district court, arguing that it violated due process. What *kind* of due process claim is Doehr making? Why? Has he been deprived of liberty or property?

7. One provision of the federal Deficit Reduction Act of 1984 established a 15-month freeze on the fees certain physicians could charge Medicare patients. A group of physicians challenged the constitutionality of this provision, alleging that it restricted freedom of contract in violation of the Fifth Amendment's Due Process Clause. What *kind* of due process attack is this? Will it succeed?

8. The Minnesota legislature passed a statute banning the sale of milk in plastic nonrefillable, nonreusable containers. However, it allowed sales of milk in other nonrefillable, nonreusable containers such as paperboard cartons. One of the justifications for this ban on plastic jugs was that it would ease the state's solid waste disposal problems because plastic jugs occupy more space in landfills than other nonreturnable milk containers. A group of dairy businesses challenged the statute, arguing that its distinction between plastic containers and other containers was unconstitutional under the Equal Protection Clause. What means-ends test or level of scrutiny applies in this case? Under that test, is easing the state's solid waste disposal problems a sufficiently important *end?* Under that test, is there a sufficiently close "fit" between the classification and that end to make the statutory *means* constitutional? In answering the last question, assume for the sake of argument that there were better ways of alleviating the solid waste disposal problem than banning plastic jugs while allowing paperboard cartons.

9. Oklahoma statutes set the age for drinking 3.2 beer at 21 for men and 18 for women. The asserted purpose behind the statutes (and the sex-based classification that they established) was traffic safety. The statutes were challenged as a denial of equal protection by male residents of Oklahoma. What level of scrutiny would this measure receive if *women* had been denied the right to drink 3.2 beer until they were 21 but men had been allowed to consume it at age 18? Should this standard change because the measure discriminates against *men?* Is the male challenge to the statute likely to be successful?

10. Suppose that State X enacts a minimum wage law for women only. Why were such laws subject to a substantive due process attack in the early part of this century? Would such an attack succeed today? How *might* one successfully attack such a law today?

11. After nine years and eight months of service, Perry McClendon was fired from his sales job with the Ingersoll-Rand Company. Believing that Ingersoll-Rand fired him to avoid pension obligations that would have arisen after 10 years of service, McClendon sued the firm for wrongful discharge. During the litigation, Ingersoll-Rand argued that McClendon's common law claim was preempted by the Employee Retirement Income Security Act (ERISA). ERISA has a provision stating that: "[T]he provisions of this subchapter and subchapter III of this chapter shall supersede any and all State laws insofar as they may now or hereafter relate to any employee benefit plan [covered by relevant ERISA provisions]." Does this language preempt McClendon's claim?

12. The Federal Insecticide, Fungicide, and Rodenticide Act (FIFRA) requires that all covered pesticides be registered with the Environmental Protection Agency (EPA) before their sale. In 1972, the act was amended to give applicants for registration broad powers to block the EPA's use and disclosure of trade secrets submitted as part of the registration process. But in 1978 Congress again amended FIFRA to let the EPA disclose such trade secrets to the public on certain occasions and to use secrets submitted by one applicant when reviewing subsequent applications. Its aims were to streamline the registration process, thus making new products available to consumers more quickly. The Monsanto Company, which makes pesticides, sued to have FIFRA's provisions letting the EPA use and disclose applicants' trade secrets declared unconstitutional under the Takings Clause. Are trade secrets "property" for Takings Clause purposes? Is the "public use" test met here? Assuming that federal law gives Monsanto an adequate remedy for any taking that occurs, would such a taking be unconstitutional?

Business Ethics, Corporate Social Responsibility, and the Control and Governance of Corporations

O ver the past 10 to 20 years, ethics has increased its presence in the business curriculum. Ethics courses are a response to socially irresponsible business behavior—behavior in which businesspeople fail to meet basic ethical standards during the course of their work. Ordinarily such failures mean harm to society or to specific third parties. Business ethics courses usually proceed on the theory that such harm can be reduced, and socially responsible business behavior increased, if tomorrow's managers are instructed in their ethical obligations. ∽

THE DEBATE OVER THE LARGE CORPORATION

Business ethics instruction is a relatively recent phenomenon, but it is only the latest stage in a century-long struggle to control corporate misbehavior.[1] In America, large corporations first ap-

---

[1] Of course, many of this chapter's observations apply to other business forms besides corporations.

peared when the country began its rapid industrialization late in the 19th century. Ever since, such firms have been villains to some and heroes to others. Hostility to big business was one theme in the populist movement of the late 19th century, and the control of large corporations preoccupied the progressive movement of the early 20th century. The perceived need to check abuses of business power was a major force behind both the New Deal statutes of the 1930s and the many new federal regulations enacted during the 1960s and 1970s. Much the same motives underlie modern calls for more business ethics instruction.

Over the past 30 years, critics of corporations probably have been more vocal than their defenders. By now, the critics' litany of complaints is very familiar. In the single-minded pursuit of profits, the critics say, corporations despoil the environment, mistreat employees, fire loyal workers at will, abandon local communities without warning, sell shoddy and dangerous products, and corrupt the political process. Underlying these criticisms are some general perceptions about modern business. Large corporations, it is observed, perform such essential national economic functions as raw materials extraction, energy production, the provision of transportation and communications, and military production—functions that many countries entrust to government bodies. How corporations perform these functions is critical to the nation's well-being. Despite their importance, however, corporations are not nearly so accountable to the public as the formal organs of government. For example, the public has little to say about the appointment of their officers and directors. This lack of accountability is made all the more serious, critics maintain, by the tremendous power big corporations wield in many spheres of American life.

These criticisms and perceptions naturally have generated calls for changes in the ways corporations decide and behave. Throughout the 20th century, the law has been the main device for checking corporate misdeeds. However, some observers have come to feel that legal regulation, while an important element in any corporate control scheme, is insufficient by itself. To supplement regulation, they urge that business be led to adhere to standards of ethical or socially responsible behavior higher than those imposed by existing law. One example is the *stakeholder theory* of corporate social responsibility, which says that rather than striving only to maxi-

mize profits for shareholders, a business firm should balance shareholder interests against the interests of other stakeholders such as its employees, managers, suppliers, customers, and local community residents (see Figure 1). To promote such behavior, some corporate critics have proposed significant changes in the internal governance of corporations. Others have urged that the business community's own resources be brought to bear. It is within the latter context that the move toward ethics instruction has arisen.

Despite all the concern about abuses of its power, big business has contributed mightily to the unprecedented material abundance that America has experienced over the last century. In part for this reason, the debate about the modern corporation has not been totally dominated by its critics. In opposition to the critics, defenders of business argue that profit maximization should be its main goal and that the only ethical norms firms must follow are those embodied in the law. In short, they say that the only social responsibility of corporations is to maximize profits within the bounds set by the law.

Unlike stakeholder theory, therefore, this traditional view of corporate social responsibility stresses the interests of the firm's shareholders. Its main justification is economic. When corporations maximize profits under genuinely competitive conditions, their defenders insist, they use scarce economic resources efficiently and thereby maximize productivity. Because "ethical" firms recognize moral duties other than profit maximization and try to serve other constituencies besides shareholders,

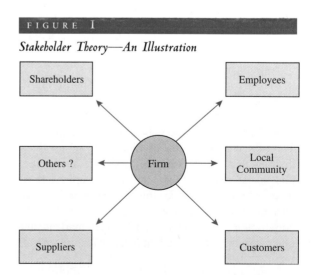

FIGURE 1

Stakeholder Theory—An Illustration

they are not likely to maximize profits. Thus, they should be less efficient and less productive than firms that worry only about the bottom line.

The corporation's defenders also disagree with its critics on a number of specific points raised above. In their view, corporate size is not the issue; what is critical is that firms efficiently *compete.* Because truly competitive markets and other private-sector forces such as unfavorable publicity go some way toward controlling business misbehavior, they add, corporate accountability is not a big problem. Where markets and other private forces fail to curb socially irresponsible conduct, moreover, the law can do the job. Indeed, sometimes the law does that job too well. In the corporate defenders' view of things, business often is hamstrung by a maze of regulations that deter socially valuable profit-seeking without producing comparable benefits.

The Plan of this Chapter

In the preceding discussion, we developed two general views of corporate social responsibility. To defenders of the corporation, the only moral obligations of business are to *maximize profits and to obey the law.* Critics of the corporation naturally want business firms to obey the law. All other things being equal, moreover, most of them have no particular quarrel with profit maximization. But they say that *business should recognize other moral obligations as well.* For example, stakeholder theory tells businesses to balance the interests of their various constituencies. This means that corporations have other moral obligations in addition to the moral obligation to maximize profits for their shareholders. This probably means that under stakeholder theory, profits will be lower than under the first view of corporate social responsibility.

Which view of corporate social responsibility is right? In large measure, the disagreement is *ethical.* In other words, the corporation's critics and its defenders disagree about how things *ought to be.* Thus, the chapter begins by discussing some ethical theories that are relevant to the debate over corporate social responsibility. Then it examines those theories' implications for that debate. After this, the chapter criticizes an assumption often made by the corporation's defenders—that the law, markets, and other private forces adequately check corporate

misbehavior. Then the chapter turns its fire on some assumptions commonly made by the corporation's critics—that ethics instruction and other ethics initiatives from within the business community will significantly reduce corporate misconduct; and that where they fail, changes in corporate governance will do the job. The chapter's last section tries to state some tentative conclusions about the corporate social responsibility debate.

SOME ETHICAL BACKGROUND

What is ethical or socially responsible corporate behavior? This question requires another: What is moral or ethical behavior generally? Of course, a full consideration of moral philosophy is far beyond the scope of this text. Nonetheless, two well-known ethical views have implications for the corporate social responsibility debate. The first of these views is **rights theory**; the other is **utilitarianism.** Before discussing these two views, however, we must consider the difference between **deontological** ethical theories and **consequentialist** (or teleological) theories.

Deontological and Consequentialist Ethical Theories

Suppose that by breaking a contract with another party you could make yourself richer without harming that party in any way. Is it morally right for you to break the contract under these circumstances? Moral philosophers called *consequentialists* generally would answer this question in the affirmative. The rightness or wrongness of an action, consequentialists say, depends on its *consequences.* Here, the consequences of breaking the contract clearly seem favorable: You are better off and the other party is no worse off. Because a consequentialist has to consider *all* of an action's likely consequences, however, he might conclude that you should perform the contract. For example, suppose that by breaking your contract you would encourage other people to break theirs when it would be harmful for them to do so.

Note that by breaking the contract you are breaking the *promise* contained in that contract. To some moral philosophers, promises are sacred (or nearly so). This attitude is an example of *deontological* moral thinking. Strict deontologists say that certain actions are right or wrong *in themselves*—irrespective of their consequences. Thus, a strict deontologist who believes in the sanctity of promises would say that you should never break your contracts, no matter what. Of course, a person can be a deontologist without thinking that promises always should be kept. For example, someone might believe that it is always wrong to take human life, or that people should always tell the truth, but not that promises are sacred.

Few moral philosophers have been strict deontologists. One possible exception, however, was the German philosopher Immanuel Kant (1724–1804). Kant apparently believed that certain moral rules apply universally, irrespective of their consequences. The key to determining these rules was his famous **categorical imperative.** One major formulation of the categorical imperative says: "Act only according to that maxim by which you can at the same time will that it should become a universal law."[2] Suppose you want to borrow some money even though you know that you never will be able to repay the loan. To justify this action, you affirm the following maxim, rule, or principle: "When I believe myself to be in need of money, I will borrow money and promise to repay it, although I know I shall never be able to do so." According to Kant, however, you would not want this maxim to become a universal law. If it did become a universal law, no one would believe in promises to repay debts, and you would be unable to borrow the money you want. Thus, your maxim fails to satisfy the categorical imperative. Unless there is an alternative maxim that justifies such behavior and that can be universalized, it is wrong to falsely promise that you will repay a loan.

Kant also had a second major formulation of the categorical imperative: "Act so that you treat humanity, whether in your own person or in that of another, always as an end and never as a means only." One application of this statement is that we should not use or manipulate other people to serve our own purposes, but instead should appeal to their reason when trying to influence them. In Kant's eyes, if you falsely promise a lender that you will repay the money she lends you, you are *using* that person, because she would not rationally agree to the loan if she knew all the facts.

Strict deontological views like Kant's face an obvious problem—the absolute nature of the duties they assert. Such theories essentially say that we should *always* tell the truth, *never* lie, or *never* kill; and such positions are difficult for most morally reflective people to maintain. Responding to this difficulty, some philosophers have advocated what we will call *mixed deontological theories.* Some theories of this kind say that the rightness or wrongness of actions is not completely determined by their consequences but by their nature and the motives underlying them as well. Another kind of mixed deontological theory emphasizes the notion of **prima facie duties.**[3] Prima facie duties are moral rules that bind us unless they conflict with another, more compelling prima facie duty. In such cases, our *actual duty* is to obey the moral rule that is stronger under the circumstances. For example, your duty to preserve human life should override your duty to tell the truth where lying is necessary to prevent someone from being killed.

Rights Theories

Modern rights theories normally are mixed deontological theories that emphasize rights rather than duties. Such theories usually identify certain fundamental rights, try to justify them and establish their relative importance, and assert that such rights should be honored unless doing so would compromise a more important right. These rights may be either *negative* or *positive.* Negative rights such as freedom of contract, freedom of expression, and the right of privacy are claims that the community should not interfere with certain personal choices. Positive or "welfare" rights such as rights to old-age assistance or unemployment compensation are claims that the community should provide people with certain goods or services. Negative and positive rights differ in *what they require of other people.* Negative rights basically obligate us to leave the rightholder alone when she undertakes certain activities, while positive rights obligate us to do something for the rightholder.

---

[2]This quotation and those that follow can be found in Kant, *Foundations of the Metaphysics of Morals,* 2nd ed. (MacMillan/Library of Liberal Arts paperback 1990), pp. 38–39, 46–47.

---

[3]The notion of prima facie duties comes from W. D. Ross, *The Right and the Good* (1930), pp. 18–34.

Rights theorists naturally disagree about which rights are most important and the weight we should attach to particular rights. But they often agree on two general points:

1. *Where rights-based claims conflict, the right that is stronger under the circumstances wins out.* Thus, Justice Oliver Wendell Holmes's famous statement that no one has the right to shout "Fire!" in a crowded theater basically says that in some cases the rights to life and physical safety overcome free speech rights. Of course, there often is disagreement over the relative strength or importance of competing rights. Another problem, one suggested by the words "under the circumstances," is that our decision to favor one right over another often depends on the *degree* to which each is involved in the case before us. Even though someone might be hurt as a result, for example, most people would agree that someone has the moral right to scream "Fire!" at an outdoor fraternity party.

2. *Rights-based claims overcome utilitarian claims where the two conflict.* Rights, it is frequently said, are "trumps" that defeat arguments based on utility. This is because rights theories are deontological, which means that rights claims defeat the moral claims generated by consequences such as utility. However, some rights theorists say that utility can be considered where no rights are at stake. But what is a utilitarian claim and what is utility?

Utilitarianism

Utilitarianism says that the moral worth of actions depends on *their tendency to maximize utility.*[4] Thus, utilitarianism is a consequentialist ethical theory. In general, maximizing utility means achieving the greatest overall balance of satisfactions over dissatisfactions. The British utilitarian Jeremy Bentham (1748–1832) limited these satisfactions and dissatisfactions to pleasure and pain. Believing Bentham's approach too narrowly hedonistic, later utilitarians such as John Stuart Mill (1806–1873) broadened the notion of utility to include satisfactions such as health, knowledge, friendship, and aesthetic delights. Some modern utilitarians have urged that actions should be judged by their ability to promote the greatest net satisfaction of actual human preferences, whatever their nature. But no matter what the definition used, the aim generally is to maximize *total* or *aggregate* utility, not the individual actor's *own* utility.[5]

Utilitarianism has encountered many criticisms over time. One common objection is that there is no reliable method for measuring utility, however defined. Another is that utilitarianism is indifferent to the manner in which utility is realized. To a committed utilitarian, for example, satisfying sick or perverted desires is better than satisfying healthy ones if the former would generate more utility. So long as total utility is maximized, moreover, utilitarianism seems indifferent to inequalities in its distribution among society's members. Finally, utilitarianism tends to sacrifice personal rights and interests to the maximization of collective utility. If enough Romans congregate to watch the lion devour the Christian, their collective pleasure will outweigh the pain of the Christian, however intense.[6] Similarly, utilitarian calculations might justify evils such as slavery, religious intolerance, infanticide, and the extermination of despised minorities—so long as total net satisfaction is maximized thereby.

ETHICAL THEORY AND THE CORPORATE SOCIAL RESPONSIBILITY DEBATE

Defenders of the corporation generally say that business's only moral obligations are to maximize profits and to obey the law. The corporation's critics, on the other hand, assert that business has other moral obligations as well—obligations that may conflict with profit maximization. Assuming that there is a moral duty to obey the law, what does our brief review of ethical theory suggest about the remaining claims?

---

[4]This is *act-utilitarianism.* Another form of utilitarianism, called *rule-utilitarianism,* says that we should follow the *rule* that would maximize utility if it were consistently followed in like cases. For example, a rule-utilitarian might say that we should never break our promises because if we follow an absolute rule to this effect, we will generate more utility than if we try to make case-by-case judgments. As this example suggests, rule-utilitarianism sometimes resembles deontological theories in its practical results—but not in the reasoning producing those results.

[5]Some utilitarians, however, say that the standard should be *average* utility per capita, not total utility.

[6]M. Sandel, ed., *Liberalism and Its Critics* (1984), p. 2.

Ethical Supports for Profit Maximization

Utilitarianism   The utilitarian argument for profit maximization assumes that material things usually give their possessors utility and that more material things usually mean more utility. The argument also assumes that the efficient allocation and use of society's scarce resources contribute powerfully to material abundance. Finally, the argument assumes that profit maximization under genuinely competitive conditions results in such an allocation and use of society's resources. Figure 2 summarizes the steps in the argument.

Why is there a relationship between profit maximization and efficiency? Firms that efficiently use resources generally can undersell their competitors. As a result, they gain greater sales and reap higher profits. For this reason, they often can outbid less efficient resource users. Hence, scarce resources are allocated efficiently; they flow to the users and uses most highly valued by consumers and best able to give them a maximum return on their expenditures. If corporate managers pursue goals other than profit maximization, resources will not be put to their most efficient uses and society's total wealth will be reduced by the resulting allocational inefficiencies. In other words, corporate social responsibility generally does not come free.

To illustrate the last point, assume for simplicity's sake that there is no foreign competition in the American steel industry and that all domestic steel makers spontaneously decide to observe pollution standards stricter than those imposed by law. Also, assume that the firms know that their buyers may not be willing to pay extra for "responsibly" produced steel. Because such socially responsible behavior costs money, the firms face a dilemma. They can try to pass on the increased costs to buyers in the form of higher prices, thus reducing the buyers' return per dollar spent and, most likely, their ability to make other purchases and their overall utility. Higher prices also might cause some buyers to seek substitutes for steel, with obvious effects on the steel firms' profits and their shareholders' utility. Or the firms might decide to retain existing customers by refusing to increase prices despite the higher costs they face. In this case, the firms almost certainly would have to accept lower profits. If profits fall, dividends and salaries might be reduced, with corresponding utility losses for shareholders and employees. In addition, the firms' ability to bid for scarce resources such as iron ore also might suffer. The likely result is a flow of employees, investment funds, and resources away from those firms. This, in turn, may mean lower steel production, which may also mean lower societal utility. If all these various possible losses in utility exceed the utility gains from reduced pollution, the steel firms' "socially responsible" behavior is wrong from a utilitarian point of view.

As Figure 2 suggests, however, the utilitarian argument for profit maximization depends on at least two further assumptions:

1.   As already mentioned, *profit maximization must occur under conditions of genuine competition.* As Adam Smith observed in his *The Wealth of Nations* over 200 years ago, people in the same business seldom converse, even on social occasions, without the conversation ending in a conspiracy against the public, or in some scheme to raise prices. In other words, competitors often try to thwart the market and maximize their profits by engaging in the various anticompetitive practices described in Chapters 48 and 49, or by using government to restrict competition. To the extent that they succeed, they weaken the link between profit-seeking and efficiency, thereby reducing utility.

For example, industries that get government to give them tariff protection or members of professions who establish government-backed occupational licensing schemes often gain significant protection from competition. This may allow them to restrict output, raise prices, and/or offer lower-quality products or services. To illustrate the point, consider the extreme case in which one firm has a

FIGURE **2**

A Utilitarian Argument for Profit Maximization

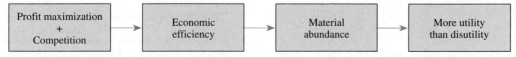

monopoly in a certain product. Economists say that such a firm can maximize its sales revenues and reap monopoly profits by restricting output and raising prices. This results in inefficiencies, because the total amount of goods or services is reduced and purchasers of those goods or services do not receive a maximum return for the higher prices they pay. Outright monopolization is illegal under section 2 of the Sherman Act. But economists often argue that tacit price-fixing agreements among firms in *oligopolistic* industries have similar, if less serious, effects, and that the antitrust laws have done relatively little to curb oligopolistic price-fixing.[7] This is one example of a theme we stress later in the chapter—the law's limits as a corporate control device.

2. *The disutility resulting from profit maximization must not exceed the utility it produces.* This assumption is illustrated by our earlier steel industry example. In that example, it would be difficult to defend profit maximization on utilitarian grounds if the utility gained from reduced pollution exceeded the utility lost due to reduced efficiency. The point is that competitive profit-maximization often has social costs, and sometimes those costs outweigh the material benefits it provides.

Negative Economic Rights   If they exist and are strong enough to outweigh other moral concerns, negative *economic* rights such as freedom of contract and property rights also support profit maximization. They do so mainly by protecting the activities through which profits are made.

For example, suppose that in order to maximize profits, the XYZ Corporation does not provide health insurance for its employees. If XYZ is criticized for failing to respect its employees' alleged positive right to decent health care, it can claim that its employees freely contracted to work on this basis, and that freedom of contract outweighs any right to decent health care. However, this argument faces difficulties if XYZ has greater bargaining power than its employees. To take another example, suppose that the ABC Corporation closes an inefficient plant to improve its profit picture. If members of the affected local community object, ABC might defend its action by saying that it has an absolute or near-absolute right to dispose of its property as it

sees fit. Because the plant is its property, ABC could continue, it is morally entitled to shut down that plant down whenever it desires.

Ethical Supports for the Critics' Position

Positive Rights   The preceding arguments depended on the assumption that negative economic rights are very important, and on the absence of competing moral concerns strong enough to override them. But what if negative economic rights are less important than positive rights of all kinds? First, this would undermine an important defense of profit maximization. Second, it would powerfully justify the view that business has other ethical responsibilities besides maximizing profits. To be sure, some of these positive rights might diminish economic efficiency and productivity. But to a rights theorist, rights trump utilitarian claims.

How can positive rights justify the critics' position in the corporate social responsibility debate? Stakeholder theory provides an example. Suppose that each of the firm's various stakeholders has positive rights of one kind or another. This means that society in general—and the firm in particular—has certain duties to these stakeholders. Figure 3 provides one set of examples. You should be able to think of others.

Kantianism   Kant's categorical imperative also might justify certain moral obligations to the firm's stakeholders.[8] Suppose that, consistent with the second major formulation of Kant's categorical imperative, stakeholders have a right to be treated as ends in themselves and not merely as means. This could mean that they should not be treated as objects to be used for corporate profit and discarded when they cease to be useful. If so, it might be wrong for a corporation to fire workers once their services are no longer required, or to suddenly leave a community with which it has had a long relationship. As discussed earlier, another implication of the categorical imperative is that we should appeal to people's rational nature when trying to influence them or when taking action that affects their interests. This could mean that affected stakeholders

---

[7]See Chapter 48. An oligopolistic industry is one dominated by a few large sellers.

[8]For an argument resembling the one made in this paragraph, see W. Evan and R. Freeman, "A Stakeholder Theory of the Modern Corporation: Kantian Capitalism," in *Ethical Theory and Business,* 3rd. ed., ed. T. Beauchamp and N. Bowie (1988), pp. 97–112.

F I G U R E   3

Positive Rights and Stakeholder Theory (One Example)

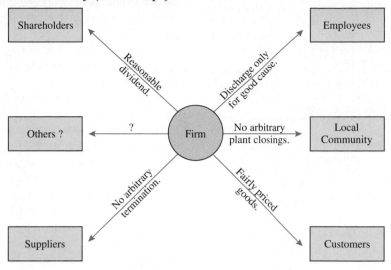

should be allowed to participate in corporate governance, or at least be consulted and have their views taken into account before any adverse action against them can occur. Later in the chapter, we will examine proposals for stakeholder participation in corporate governance.

Utilitarianism   Earlier we observed that for utilitarianism to justify full-fledged profit maximization, the utility profit maximization produces must exceed the disutility it creates. If the balance is always or nearly always unfavorable to profit maximization, maybe corporations should emphasize other goals more and profit maximization less. To make much the same point in a different way, maybe utilitarianism could justify stakeholder theory. Maybe, that is, a world in which businesses recognize all kinds of moral duties to their stakeholders would generate more net utility than a world devoted to profit maximization. To be sure, such a world probably would be poorer than a profit-maximizing world, but it might also be a safer and less anxious one. But then again, maybe material things yield enough extra utility to justify the disutilities created by profit maximization.

PRACTICAL PROBLEMS WITH THE DEFENDERS' POSITION

The previous section suggests that ethical theory does not clearly dictate any particular position on

the corporate social responsibility debate. If so, how else might we evaluate the two views of corporate social responsibility sketched earlier? One possibility is to examine the *factual assumptions* each view makes. This section examines some assumptions made by many people who say that a corporation's main social responsibility is to maximize profits.

Although there often are real ethical differences between the corporation's critics and its defenders, no one thinks that business should maximize profits to the exclusion of everything else. According to the corporation's defenders, business's other (nonprofit-related) responsibilities can be met by obeying the law. This position is plausible only if the law is very effective in controlling corporate misbehavior. Also, the position becomes more plausible if private-sector forces such as markets and public opinion are significant checks on business misconduct. In fact, the corporation's defenders tend to assert—or assume—the truth of both these contentions. Thus, they could say, it is safe to let managers concentrate on profit maximization because the law, the market, and various other private forces do so good a job keeping them in line. Figure 4 summarizes the defenders' major positions. Of course, not every defender of business embraces every one of Figure 4's propositions.

As we will see, however, the defenders' contentions are questionable. Market forces and other private checks, while sometimes effective, offer very incomplete protection against business misconduct.

FIGURE 4

Major Points Argued by Defenders of the Corporation

Overall Position	Business's only moral responsibility is to maximize profits within the bounds set by the law
Preferred Moral Theories	Utilitarianism and rights theories stressing negative economic rights
Other Arguments	1. Markets and other private forces such as protests, publicity, and public opinion are significant checks on business misconduct 2. The law is a very effective (perhaps *too* effective) constraint on business

The law's ability to control such misconduct also has its limits. Thus, it may not be enough for firms simply to seek profits and obey the law. Even if you were convinced by the moral arguments for profit maximization, therefore, you still may want business to have other ethical responsibilities besides simply following the law.

Markets and Other Private Forces

Defenders of profit maximization tend to argue or assume that market forces and other private-sector activities force business to behave in a socially responsible fashion. For such reasons, the corporation's defenders sometimes conclude, there is little need for managers to abandon their profit orientation and the utility it generates. Unfortunately, however, market checks and other forms of private behavior have definite limits as corporate control devices. As a rule, the former only check certain kinds of corporate misbehavior. In addition, many practical obstacles stand in the way of the latter's success.

Market Checks   Market forces clearly can influence corporate behavior for the better. Sooner or later, for example, firms that market defective and/or dangerous products will almost certainly lose business. This possibility naturally stimulates corporate managers to avoid this form of corporate irresponsibility. But are market checks well equipped to stop other forms of real or alleged corporate misbehavior such as overseas bribery, environmental degradation, and poor working conditions? In these cases, consumers of the offending firm's products may not be directly harmed by the firm's wrongdoing and thus may lack strong incentives to act against it. Indeed, they may not even know about the misconduct.

These considerations suggest that while market forces impel firms to offer safe and trouble-free products and services, they are much less effective against corporate irresponsibility that does not involve those products and services. In fact, market forces are not always effective even in the former case. One reason is that people who are injured or otherwise disadvantaged by defective products may not be aware of the harm at the time it occurs. In the past, for instance, many cigarette smokers did not know that cigarette smoking helps cause lung cancer. In some cases, even the *manufacturer itself* is unaware of these "unknown harms." In all these situations, some people will be harmed before the problem is discovered and corrective action taken. A second reason why market forces do not always curb product-related harms, one discussed later in this section, is that business organizations sometimes do not respond rationally to external pressures. This can prevent them from quickly acting on negative information about defective products.

Protest, Publicity, and Public Opinion   Thus, market forces seem to check certain forms of corporate misbehavior but not others. However, other kinds of private activity appear not to have this limitation. Citizens angered by corporate misconduct can organize boycotts (which might also be regarded as a market check), initiate letter-writing campaigns, engage in picketing, and stage demonstrations against the offending firm. Such activities may attract media attention. Or the media itself may uncover and publicize irresponsible corporate behavior. All these forms of private action can provoke government regulation, hurt the firm's image, and expose managers to criticism in their nonbusiness lives. The prospect of such happenings can force managers to change their ways for the better.

Thus, protests, publicity, and public opinion obviously *can* influence business conduct in responsible directions. But how often? Clearly, they cannot work where the offender is unaware of the misbehavior, or where knowledge of the misbehavior stays within the offender's confines. Even if the information becomes public, moreover, how many people will find out? Of those people, how many will view the information negatively? Within that group, how great is the level of concern? For those who are significantly concerned, what are the costs of taking action and the obstacles to organizing for collective action? Finally, how effectively can the offending firm counter any bad publicity that emerges? These questions suggest that a series of conditions normally must be met before protests, publicity, and public opinion can threaten a firm's well-being and thus change its behavior for the better.

The Law

Even the most ardent defender of business probably would admit that markets and free private activity have limitations as corporate control devices. However, he would be less inclined to concede that the law has any such weaknesses. In fact, he might well think that it puts *excessive* restrictions on business, thereby deterring valuable profit-seeking activity.

Throughout this century, the law has been the main means of controlling corporate misdeeds. Lawmakers usually assume that corporations are rational actors that can be deterred from misbehavior by the threats the law presents. Those threats are the sanctions (e.g., fines, civil damages) the law imposes on those who violate its rules. For deterrence to work effectively, corporate decisionmakers must understand when the law's penalties will be imposed, must fear the costs those penalties create, and must act rationally to avoid them.

Unfortunately, the law's ability to control irresponsible corporate behavior, while significant, has limits. Some of the reasons are discussed below. To the extent that these arguments are valid, the profit-maximizers' insistence that legal checks are sufficient to control corporate misbehavior is weakened. If so, then it may make sense to say that business has moral duties that go beyond those stated in the law and to seek additional ways to make firms live up to those duties.

Corporate Influence on the Law's Content One reason the law is an imperfect corporate control device, some argue, is that business has a significant voice in determining its content. Thus, the law sometimes reflects corporate interests. This may allow corporations to engage in unethical behavior that nonetheless is perfectly legal.

The political influence exerted by large corporations is a familiar subject. Because of their size, resources, and sophistication, they have (or can purchase) the ability to influence legislation through methods such as lobbying and contributions to business-oriented political action committees. Even if Congress or a state legislature passes hostile regulation, moreover, business sometimes can blunt its impact. It may use its political influence to reduce the funding received by the agency enforcing the legislation. Over time, business may co-opt the agency by inducing it to take a probusiness view of its functions. One way this occurs is through the continuous exchange of personnel between the agency and the industry it is supposed to regulate in the public interest. Also, an agency, the industry it regulates, and the congressional subcommittee controlling the agency may form a mutually beneficial relationship that is relatively impervious to outside influence (the so-called Iron Triangle).

By now, however, critics of the corporation have also become politically adept and sometimes can counteract corporate political power. Consumer groups and environmental groups are but two examples. More importantly, what is the implication of the previous arguments? That business should have *no* say in determining the rules by which it is governed?

Unknown Harms As noted earlier, for market forces to control corporate behavior, consumers must know that they are being harmed at the time the harm occurs. Reliance on the law involves a similar assumption—that legislators and regulators possess such knowledge. Legal action to control harmful corporate behavior usually will not happen until there is a clear need for it. Yet lawmakers learn about previously unknown harms even later than the business producing those harms or the people suffering them. This means that in some cases, legal action to correct those harms will occur only after they have already taken place. This is an obvious and almost inevitable limitation on the law's effectiveness as a control device.

Are Corporations Always Rational Actors? Another argument against the law's ability to control corporations is that much of their irresponsible behavior results from an *inability to respond sensibly* to legal threats. The law's ability to affect business behavior depends on managers' clear perception of the penalties for illegal actions and their rational response to the resulting risk. To the extent that corporations fail these tests of clear perception and rational response, the law's ability to control them suffers.

But why should we think that business firms sometimes behave irrationally? Normal human failings aside, the main reasons concern some familiar facts about life in organizations. For instance, social psychologists and students of organizational behavior have long been aware of a phenomenon called *risky shift*. This means that a group of people who must reach consensus on an acceptable level of risk often choose a level *higher* than the level they would accept as individuals. Thus, decisions made by a team of managers may create greater legal problems than decisions made by an isolated manager. Also relevant here is the familiar phenomenon of *groupthink*—the tendency for members of a group to internalize the group's values and perceptions and to suppress critical thought. Thus, if our team of managers is planning a highly profitable venture to which the success of each team member is tied, each may minimize the venture's legal problems because these conflict with the group's goals.

Somewhat similar to groupthink is another familiar feature of organizational life: the tendency for *bad news not to get to the top*. When subordinates know that top managers are strongly committed to a particular course of action, they may not report problems for fear of provoking their superiors' disapproval. Ideally, of course, managers should want to be fully apprised of potential legal risks, but occasionally their response is to penalize the bearer of bad news instead. Also, subordinates may distort the information they present to their superiors in order to make their own performance look better than it actually is.

Finally, the complex and unwieldy organizational structures of some modern corporations sometimes diminish their capacity for rational and effective response to legal problems. For example, they may worsen the tendency for bad news not to reach top managers. They also may make it difficult for top managers to ensure that their decisions are fully implemented at lower levels.

Conscious Lawbreaking   Throughout this chapter, we assume that business firms have a moral obligation to obey the law. Yet businesses some-times ignore the law's commands. Unlike the corporate irrationality just discussed, here we have disobedience that is knowing, thought-out, and deliberate. Corporations may conclude that breaking the law poses acceptable risks if the potential benefits are great, the penalties for violation are relatively light, and/or the chances of being sued or prosecuted are low. Sometimes, for example, it may make sense for a firm to continue to market a defect-ridden product rather than redesign it if competitors' products are no better and the costs of paying product liability claims or of procuring product liability insurance are sufficiently low that they can be passed on to consumers.

Other factors increase the likelihood that corporations will engage in conscious lawbreaking. The let's-take-the-risk mentality may be reinforced when the law is (or is perceived to be) uncertain. Corporate or industry norms may regard a measure of illegal (or borderline) behavior as morally acceptable. This is especially likely where corporate managers regard the relevant legal rules as misguided.

The tendency toward conscious lawbreaking could be reduced, many argue, by stiffer penalties and increased enforcement efforts. But corporate political influence may prevent either from occurring. As noted above, business sometimes tries to blunt politically popular legislation by devoting its efforts to such less visible matters as agency funding.

Problems with the Criminal Sanction   The existence of conscious corporate lawbreaking leads naturally to a related subject—the effectiveness of criminal sanctions in the corporate context. As discussed in Chapter 5, both the corporate entity and individual corporation members can be liable for crimes committed in the course of the corporation's business. However, there are reasons to ask how well criminal liability checks corporate misconduct.

Criminal penalties directed at *the corporation itself* are a problematical control device. Such penalties work by deterring future misbehavior. But deterrence requires rationality, and as we have seen, corporate behavior is not always rational. In addition, some corporate crime results from internal bureaucratic malfunctions that the threat of criminal liability is unlikely to eliminate and that are difficult to eliminate in any event. Moreover, the main criminal penalty for corporations is the fine, and many observers believe that the fines now imposed on corporations are too small for effective deterrence. Although bigger fines might work better, corporate political influence could prevent them from ever being enacted or imposed. In addition, such fines involve possible injustices. In all likelihood, the costs they impose ultimately will be passed on to the firm's customers in the form of higher prices—or will fall on its shareholders (as lower dividends) or employees (as lower wages). Usually, these parties are unable to prevent the wrongdoing that gave rise to criminal liability and did not benefit from it. The managers responsible for the crime, on the other hand, may escape any significant financial penalty.

Such problems have led some observers to advocate greater *individual* criminal liability to control corporate misbehavior. Because managers with the power to order or prevent criminal activity would know that *they* will suffer if the activity is detected and a prosecution results, individual sanctions promise significant deterrence of corporate misconduct. In addition, this deterrence could be achieved without unjustly penalizing customers, shareholders, and innocent employees. Despite its apparent attractiveness, however, individual criminal liability suffers from serious problems. Due to the diffused, collective nature of corporate decisionmaking, it often is difficult to pinpoint the people with the necessary mental state for criminal liability. Where a guilty party can be identified, moreover, it may not be a high-level executive. Because bad news tends not to reach the top and because those at the top consciously avoid knowing too much, individual criminal liability often falls on middle-level managers instead. Juries may be unwilling to convict such people if they appear to be scapegoats for someone higher up. Even where either a middle or high-level manager is convicted, moreover, he may not go to jail. Instead, he may merely be fined, and then may be indemnified by the corporation. Even where the convicted party does jail time, he is likely to receive a short sentence in a "country club" institution where early parole is a possibility.

PRACTICAL PROBLEMS WITH THE CRITICS' POSITION

The preceding section concluded that markets and other private-sector forces are useful, but imperfect, checks on corporate misbehavior, and that despite its importance as a corporate control device, the law is not as effective as many people believe. This

---

> **FIGURE 5**
>
> *Major Points Argued by Critics of the Corporation*
>
> | Overall Position | Business has moral obligations that go beyond—and may conflict with—the duty to maximize profits |
> | --- | --- |
> | **Preferred Moral Theories** | Rights theories emphasizing positive rights; Kantianism |
> | **Other Arguments** | 1. Ethics instruction and other ethical initiatives from within the business community can significantly reduce corporate irresponsibility
2. Where these methods fail, changes in the internal governance of corporations will cause them to behave responsibly |

---

suggests that if business misconduct is to be adequately controlled, corporations have to assume other moral duties in addition to maximizing profits and obeying the law. But how can they be led to do so? Critics of the corporation often say that ethics instruction and other ethical initiatives from within the business community can play a significant role in producing such behavior.[9] Where these methods fail, critics often add, certain changes in the internal governance of corporations can cause them to behave more responsibly (see Figure 5). However, all these corporate control tactics face significant objections. First, it is questionable how well many of them will work. Second, some of them may negatively affect both the corporation's internal functioning and its profitability.

Responses from within the Business Community

Ethics Instruction   In a sense, greater ethical awareness and more ethical behavior by business managers are *the* solutions to corporate irresponsibility. If all corporate decisionmakers possess such traits, business misbehavior should fall sharply and the need for other control devices should diminish

---

[9]These methods, of course, often have attracted significant support within the business community as well. Because they generally are consistent with the critics' agenda, however, we include them here.

appreciably. In recent years, business schools have increasingly attempted to advance this goal by injecting ethical considerations into their curricula. Such efforts are attempts to generate socially responsible corporate behavior by changing the outlook of existing and future managers.

Despite its promise, however, ethics instruction faces significant theoretical and practical problems. One concerns the substance of the instruction: Which moral theories and which values should receive emphasis? As this chapter's brief ethics discussion suggests, there is considerable disagreement on these questions. Worse yet, the various ethical theories may not have clear implications for the corporate social responsibility debate.

Even if there is consensus on ethical theory and its implications, moreover, can ethics instruction really instill the chosen values and make them stick after the educational process is completed? Ethics instruction is directed at people whose character— or lack thereof—has largely been formed by the time the instruction occurs. Although ethics instruction should increase the moral awareness of those who are predisposed to listen, its effect on the basically self-interested, indifferent, or unethical is questionable. Furthermore, even those who are positively influenced by ethics instruction may still behave irresponsibly if their careers or their livelihoods require them to act in their employer's financial interest. For the firm itself, ethical behavior may hurt earnings unless all the firm's competitors follow suit. And the thoughtways acquired in a business ethics course may not survive the tendency for organizations to socialize their members to accept the group's goals as paramount.

Corporate or Industry Codes of Ethical Conduct
Over time, many large corporations and several industries have adopted codes of conduct to guide managerial and/or employee decisionmaking. There are two popular views about such codes. One sees them as genuine efforts to foster ethical behavior within a firm or an industry. The other regards them as thinly disguised attempts to make the firm function better, mislead the public into believing that business behaves ethically, forestall legislation that would impose stricter constraints on business, or limit competition under the veil of ethical standards. Even where the first view is correct, moreover, ethical codes do not address all possible forms of corporate misbehavior. Instead, they tend to empha-

size either the behavior required for the firm's effective internal functioning (e.g., not accepting gifts from customers) or the relations between competitors within a particular industry (e.g., prohibitions on certain kinds of advertising).

The Corporate Stewardship Argument   Earlier in the chapter, we suggested that some large, entrenched corporations in oligopolistic industries try to avoid competition by fixing prices and otherwise collaborating among themselves. Such behavior is bad for efficiency and probably for total utility. For certain observers of years past, however, it had great promise for promoting more responsible corporate behavior. Their argument was that once corporations become economically secure, they will be free to behave in a more ethical manner. One proponent of this position, which we call the corporate stewardship argument, contended that modern corporate managers have come to resemble a professional civil service more than a group of property-owning entrepreneurs.[10]

Corporate stewardship is a *possible* consequence of oligopolistic corporations' anticompetitive behavior, but is it a *necessary* result of such behavior? Rather than behaving ethically, such firms might simply try to maximize their return to shareholders, or instead might funnel money toward executive salaries and perquisites, a pleasant work environment, and so forth. Also, large, oligopolistic firms arguably are less accountable to outside forces than smaller businesses in competitive markets. Thus, the incentives for irresponsible behavior may *increase* because large, secure firms can indulge in such behavior with relative impunity.

Stakeholder Theory Revisited   One way for an enlightened "corporate steward" to behave is to follow the stakeholder theory described earlier in this chapter. In other words, such a person might define ethical corporate behavior as the effort to balance the interests of the corporation's various constituencies. If our criticisms of the corporate stewardship argument are valid, it is questionable whether entrenched corporations in oligopolistic industries will behave in this way. But this definition of corporate social responsibility suffers from other problems as well. First, the interests of the relevant constituencies conflict. For instance, consumers'

---

[10]A. Berle, *Power without Property* (1959), p. 113.

interest in lower prices may conflict with employees' interest in higher wages, and perhaps with the surrounding community's interest in environmental protection. From an ethical point of view, moreover, why should a corporation's immediate constituencies be favored over the larger society? For example, firms or industries that corrupt the national political processes to get unjustified tax breaks may well be *helping* their various stakeholders.

The Corporate Governance Agenda

Despite the problems they face, ethics instruction and other efforts from within the business community eventually may generate more responsible corporate conduct. But corporate critics of the 1960s and 1970s chose to encourage it in a more direct fashion. They did so by making various proposals for altering the *internal governance* of corporations. The general aim of such proposals was to give representation to the firm's stakeholders (as well as other groups deemed deserving) and to make corporations more sensitive to their interests.

This text's corporations chapters discuss some of these internal governance proposals, and this chapter supplements that discussion. Although a few such proposals have occasionally been adopted in modified form, public interest in them has diminished since the 1970s. However, they may again become popular if the political and attitudinal winds shift. Here, we discuss three such recommendations—and the problems they present—in general terms. First, however, we must say a few words about intracorporate power relations.

Corporation law gives a corporation's shareholders the power to elect directors who are empowered to manage the corporation. The directors, in turn, typically delegate this power to the corporation's officers while retaining general supervisory powers over them. This formal legal model suggests that the directors have more authority over corporate policy than management, and that corporate policy ultimately is set by the shareholders as they elect the directors. Yet for much of the 20th century it has been widely agreed that management really runs the show within most large corporations, that directors tend to ratify managerial decisions, and that shareholders have little effective control over such decisions. The many reasons for this much-noted *separation of ownership from control* are beyond the

scope of this chapter. Chief among these reasons, however, are the complexity of corporate decision-making and the limited time and expertise directors and shareholders can bring to bear on such matters.

Greater Shareholder Power   Some proposals for changing internal corporate governance say that shareholders should have a greater voice in shaping corporate policy. Specific recommendations include giving shareholders greater power to nominate directors and the ability to adopt resolutions binding the directors.

Of the various corporate governance proposals, granting greater power to shareholders has the least to recommend it. For one thing, such proposals seem unrealistic when we consider the facts of intracorporate life noted above. Of particular importance here is a matter discussed in Chapters 42 and 43—management's tendency to get its way on corporate policy decisions by dominating the proxy machinery through which shareholders usually vote. If shareholders somehow were to exercise greater power, moreover, effective corporate decisionmaking could be impaired as this relatively uninformed group issues edicts to management.

From a corporate control perspective, however, the real problem with giving greater power to shareholders concerns the values they are likely to advance. Although it is conceivable that some corporate managers do not make profit maximization their first priority, the orientation of shareholders almost always is completely pecuniary. For this reason, shareholders are unlikely to initiate or approve corporate actions hostile to profit maximization. The same generally is true of institutional investors such as pension funds and mutual funds, which own significant blocks of stock in many corporations. Such investors tend to follow the "Wall Street Rule," under which they either support management or sell their shares.

Changing the Composition of the Board   Despite the tendency for corporate management to dominate the board of directors, the board's formal legal powers still are considerable. Recognizing this, critics of the corporation have made innumerable recommendations for changing the board's composition to make corporations more representative and more responsible. Some of the recommendations have been fairly modest—for example, creating nominating committees composed of outside directors, requiring that there be more such directors and fewer insiders, and limiting the number of corporate boards on which one individual can serve.[11] More extreme proposals include recommendations that stakeholders or constituencies of all sorts (e.g., labor, government, creditors, local communities, minorities, environmentalists) be represented, that certain directors be assigned special areas of concern (e.g., consumer protection, environmental affairs), and that special committees of the board be given similar functions.

From a corporate social responsibility perspective, the basic problem with all such proposals is that they fail to confront the main reason for management's domination of the board—the limited time, information, and expertise that directors can bring to bear when considering corporate affairs. One solution to this problem is to give outside or constituency directors a full-time staff with the power to dig for information within the corporation. Doing so, however, effectively creates another—perhaps competing—layer of management within the corporate organizational structure. Although this could curtail certain corporate misdeeds, it could also lessen firms' ability to innovate and respond to changing developments, with negative implications for their profitability and the utility they can generate.

Another, more down-to-earth, set of problems with some of these proposals concerns the details of their implementation. Which constituencies deserve representation? How many directors should each constituency have? Within each constituency, what criteria should govern the choice of directors? For example, is it desirable or undesirable that they have business experience?

Finally, in addition to complicating the management structure, these proposals might make the board less cohesive and render it incapable of coherent action. Conflicts among stakeholder representatives or between insiders and outsiders are possible. In fact, the addition of constituency directors might simply mean the intrusion of broader social conflicts into corporate boardrooms. The board, that is, could be divided by disputes among consumers who want lower prices, workers who want higher wages and job security, environmental-

ists who want pollution to cease, and communities that want to preserve jobs and their tax bases. This could render the board incapable of pushing management in responsible directions.

Changes in Management Structure As noted above, one of the great commonplaces about large 20th-century corporations is the separation of ownership from control—the shift of power away from shareholders and directors to the corporation's managers. Because this is where true power resides, some corporate reformers argue, the best way to produce more responsible corporate behavior is to change the corporation's *management structure*.

The main proponent of this view, Christopher Stone, has made several recommendations for such changes.[12] They include the establishment of: (1) specified offices within certain corporations (e.g., offices for environmental affairs, worker safety, and product safety); (2) requirements for holding certain corporate positions (e.g., educational requirements for safety engineers); (3) offices for ensuring that relevant external information (e.g., data from auto repair shops for car manufacturers or data from doctors for drug companies) is received by the corporation; and (4) internal information-flow procedures for ensuring that relevant external information gets to the proper corporate departments (to guarantee, for instance, that bad news gets to the top). Stone and others have also recommended that corporations be required to make internal findings before undertaking certain activities. For example, drug companies might be required to produce a document resembling an environmental impact statement before marketing a new product.

These proposed requirements are procedural in the sense that they do not dictate what decisions a firm should make. Their aim is to ensure that corporations can anticipate problems before they arise so that timely responses are possible. Such requirements probably would not deter a strongly profit-oriented corporation from taking irresponsible actions. It also is possible that the corporate personnel responsible for implementing these requirements could be influenced by a strong internal profit orientation or frozen out of the final decisionmaking process.

---

[11]Inside directors usually are defined as either present or former managers of the firm on whose board they serve; normally, all other directors are regarded as outside directors.

[12]C. Stone, *Where the Law Ends: The Social Control of Corporate Behavior* (1975), Chapters 17–19.

In cases where irresponsible corporate behavior results less from profit-seeking than from faulty perceptions, however, Stone's proposals could have an impact. For example, they may be especially effective in addressing the unknown-harms problem discussed earlier. But such benefits would probably be obtained only at the cost of further organizational complexity, with a consequent reduction in the corporation's ability to make quick responses to changing business conditions.

SUMMARY AND CONCLUSIONS

Critics of the corporation say that business should be held to a standard of socially responsible behavior higher than that imposed by law. Ethics instruction and other ethical initiatives from within businesses can do something to make responsible corporate behavior a reality. And where these fail, changes in internal corporate governance can finish the job. The corporation's defenders, on the other hand, say that the firm's only moral responsibility is to maximize profits within the bounds set by the law. Because the law, markets, and other private forces adequately restrain corporations, they add, this stance will not threaten society.

As this chapter has revealed, neither the corporation's critics nor its defenders have convincingly made their case. To be sure, each position finds some support in ethical theory. But philosophers disagree about the relative merits of these theories (and others). In addition, the more or less factual arguments made by each side have problems. At best, ethics instruction and ethics initiatives from within business can only supplement the other means of controlling corporate misconduct. Worse yet, the critics' proposed changes in corporate governance are likely either to adversely affect organizational effectiveness or to be ineffective—or both. As for the defenders' factual arguments, markets and such other private checks, while important constraints on corporate misconduct, have limited scope. Although the law has long been the main force by which society tries to check business misbehavior, it is far from a perfect control device.

What, then, can safely be said about the social responsibilities of business and the control of corporate misconduct? The three following generalizations strike us as valid.

1. *Competitive profit maximization is an extremely important—perhaps the most important—social responsibility of business.* Although the corporation's critics downplay competitive profit maximization and sometimes subordinate it to other values, they do not really deny this point. The reason is the economic efficiency and material abundance profit-maximizing economic competition produces. For this reason, it finds ready support in utilitarianism. And it also contributes to the realization of certain positive economic rights. Without economic abundance, how likely are positive rights such as the rights to a decent living wage, unemployment compensation, old-age assistance, and adequate health care to be realized?

2. *Competitive profit maximization does not exhaust business's social responsibilities.* In other words, business has other moral obligations in addition to profit maximization. If the law, the market, and other private forces were as effective as the corporation's defenders sometimes seem to think, perhaps we could safely limit business's social responsibilities to profit maximization. In fact, however, they are imperfect control devices. To be sure, this does not directly establish that business has other moral responsibilities besides competitive profit maximization; for that, a moral argument is needed. But the necessary arguments are readily available. As we have seen, positive rights clearly support such duties. In cases where profit-maximizing behavior's disutility exceeds its utility, utilitarianism supports those duties as well.

3. *For all its flaws, the law is—and probably will remain—the most important means by which society controls business misconduct.* This chapter's catalog of the law's imperfections reminds one of the old debate concerning whether a glass filled to its halfway mark is half empty or half full. Overall, the law is probably the best—or the least bad—of the control devices discussed in this chapter. Of these devices, only the law and the various private controls impose real penalties for corporate misbehavior. Although legal norms have no special claim to moral correctness, at least they are arrived at through a fairly open political process in which competing arguments may be weighed and evaluated. This cannot be said about the intuitions of some "responsible" businessperson, the edicts of some "public interest" group, or the theories of some academic economist or philosopher. As a

CONCEPT REVIEW

The Corporate Control Devices Compared: A Tentative Box Score

DEVICE	LIKELY EFFECTIVENESS IN CURBING CORPORATE IRRESPONSIBILITY	POSSIBLE COSTS IN EFFICIENCY AND IN INEFFECTIVE CORPORATE DECISIONMAKING	REMARKS
Ethical Instruction	Will it take? Will it stick? Which values?	Disunity within corporation? Adverse effects on efficiency?	Effects probably long term
Codes of Conduct	Questionable, due to limited scope	Could be anticompetitive	A sham?
Corporate Stewardship	Questionable at best	By hypothesis, firms in question are inefficient oligopolists	Has this really happened? Would such firms necessarily behave ethically?
Advancing Stakeholder Interests	Interests of stakeholders may conflict	Occasional adverse effects on efficiency?	Are interests of stakeholders necessarily congruent with larger social good?
Market Forces and Private Action	Should vary with type of corporate misbehavior	Fairly low. Market forces tend to *promote* efficiency	Fine where they work
Greater Shareholder Power	Poor, due to pecuniary orientation of shareholders	Less coherent decisionmaking?	Maybe the weakest of the bunch
Packing the Board	Likely to be minimal unless the causes of board's subservience are overcome	Could adversely affect corporate decisionmaking and efficiency	Which constituencies and interests deserve representation?
Changing the Internal Management Structure	Probably most effective for unknown harms	Could complicate corporate decisionmaking	Focus on *management* structure an advantage
The Law	Despite limits on effectiveness, has a respectable track record	Can have adverse impact on efficiency	The best of a flawed group?

general rule, finally, the law's commands should have less adverse effect on corporations' internal functioning than many of the corporate reform proposals.

More importantly, the law has a track record as a corporate control device, and that record contains a number of real accomplishments. For example, although the antitrust laws discussed in Chapters 47–49 remain controversial, they have at least eliminated some of the worst anticompetitive abuses that were common before their enactment. If nothing else, similarly, the federal securities regulations

examined in Chapters 44–45 have prevented the shady practices that, some contend, led to the stock market crash of the late 1920s. Although environmentalists often demand more regulation, virtually everyone agrees that the environmental laws treated in Chapter 51 have appreciably improved the quality of our air and water and reduced our exposure to toxic substances. Finally, the various employment regulations discussed in Chapter 50—especially those forbidding employment discrimination—have worked enormous changes in the American workplace over the course of this century.

1. Defenders of the corporation often argue that the principal moral obligation of business is to maximize profits within the law. But are the law's commands necessarily moral? And is there an ethical obligation to obey morally bad laws? What do the *natural law* and *legal positivist* schools of jurisprudence discussed in Chapter 1 say about these questions?

2. Along with five other people, you are exploring a cave beneath the ground. A rainstorm causes the water level in the cave to rise, forcing you to head back to the surface. You are first in line, an extremely fat man is second, and four other people trail the fat man. After you have safely passed through a very narrow opening in the tunnel, the fat man gets stuck in that same opening. Nothing can dislodge him. The rising waters threaten to drown the four people whose path is blocked by the fat man. You just happen to have several sticks of dynamite and some matches with you. Ought you to blow up the fat man? How would a utilitarian answer this question? Do you agree? *Note:* This question asks what you *should* do, not what you could or would do.

3. Is the right to obtain an abortion a negative or a positive right? How about the asserted right to have one's abortion funded by the federal government or the states?

4. Suppose that by keeping your promise to A, you would give her 1,000 units of utility. However, by breaking your promise to A and performing the promised act for B, you would give B 1,001 units of utility. You have not promised B anything, however. Assume that it is impossible to perform for both A and B. Assume also that neither A nor B will suffer disutility from being denied the promise.

What course of action would utilitarianism dictate here? (The question refers to act-utilitarianism; see footnote 4 in this chapter.) What would a person who is a strict deontologist about promises recommend? What about a mixed deontologist who thinks that keeping promises is important but who also recognizes a duty to maximize utility? Which, if any, of your answers would change if, instead of giving B 1,001 units of utility, breaking the promise to A would give B 1 million units of utility? Here, assume again that keeping the promise to A would give A only 1,000 units of utility.

5. A terrorist has planted a nuclear device that soon will totally destroy New York City. Shortly before the device is to go off, the authorities capture the terrorist and begin to interrogate her. The terrorist, however, refuses to tell where the device is hidden. As the deadline approaches, the authorities' thoughts naturally turn to torture. At this point, Newton Kindly, the U.S. Ambassador to the United Nations, says: "We can't do that! This person is a *human being* after all! Human beings have *rights,* among them the right not to be *used* as a means to others' ends without their consent. So what we've got to do is *rationally persuade* this lady to tell us where the bomb is hidden. Our basic principles demand no less."

What basic ethical orientation—consequentialist or deontological—does Newton's speech express? From which specific moral philosopher has Newton apparently gotten inspiration? What would a utilitarian think about Newton's speech? What do you think?

6. The ABC Corporation declares itself a "socially responsible" firm, and defines socially responsible behavior as behavior that maximizes the well-being of its various stakeholders. Then, ABC identifies the following stakeholders to which it feels responsible: its workers, consumers of its products, its shareholders, and the communities where its plants are situated. There are many possibilities, but identify three situations where the interests of two or more of these communities might clash. Feel free to assume whatever facts are necessary to create such conflicting interests.

7. One particular problem discussed in this chapter negatively affects both the ability of markets to control corporate misconduct and the law's ability to control such misconduct. What is that problem? Which of the corporate control devices discussed in this chapter probably is best equipped to address this problem?

8. Unknown to most Americans, the XYZ Corporation, which markets soft drinks, routinely bribes the officials of foreign nations in order to make sales there. Suppose that you are a critic of business who thinks that American firms' overseas bribery is clearly immoral. Which of the following corporate control techniques has the *best* (or least bad) chance of stopping XYZ's overseas bribery? The choices are: (1) market pressure from XYZ's American consumers, (2) XYZ's adoption of the stakeholder theory of corporate social responsibility, (3) giving greater power to XYZ's shareholders, and (4) legal penalties against American firms that engage in overseas bribery. Why are the three options you did *not* pick likely to be inadequate?

9. Many corporations pay quarterly dividends to their shareholders. Over time, the amount of these dividends and their rate of increase depend on the firm's earnings, or profits. All other things being equal, under which theory of corporate social responsibility—the obey-the-law-and-maximize-profits view, or stakeholder theory—are shareholders likely to get higher dividends? Try to formulate a corporate dividend policy that is consistent with stakeholder theory.

10. You have recently been appointed CEO of Pureco Pharmaceutical Corporation. While being briefed on company operations by your vice president for sales, you ask him about the seemingly high volume of business the company is doing in the sale of amphetamines. The vice president reluctantly admits that about 70 percent of Pureco's amphetamine sales are made to small pharmacies in Mexico. When asked why Mexican pharmacies should purchase such high quantities of amphetamines, the vice president says: "Well, I guess they buy them to resell in quantity." "You mean to drug dealers, don't you?" you respond. "Yeah, I guess so," he admits. "This means that a lot of this stuff is probably being smuggled back across the border and sold illegally in the United States, doesn't it?" you ask. "Yeah, probably," he replies, "but let me set you straight on a few things before you get too critical. First, this is a *very* profitable line of business for us, and the last thing you probably want to do as a new CEO is to take action that will negatively affect earnings. Second, we are violating no U.S. or Mexican law when we make these sales. Third, every other major U.S. pharmaceutical firm does the same thing. Fourth, if we stopped tomorrow, that would simply encourage the entry of illicit suppliers who might put *anything* in their drugs. Finally, due to the high R&D costs in this industry, losing the profits from these sales could impair our ability to develop new drugs that could do a lot of good." Should Pureco continue the Mexican sales?

11. Virginia Parker, a new MBA, has recently been hired by the First Planetary Bank. She has received an overseas assignment as assistant director of lending in the bank's office in Chauvinaria. Virginia's boss, Thomas Paine, seems friendly and professional and appears to go out of his way to make her feel welcome in her new position. During their first joint interview with an important local client, however, Tom treats Virginia in an obviously patronizing and demeaning manner, making her get coffee for the men and excluding her from their conversation. After the interview is over, Virginia angrily demands an explanation. Tom appears genuinely surprised and says: "Gee, I'm sorry, but I thought you knew the score here. Chauvinarians just have these archaic attitudes toward women. In fact, we're taking a risk even bringing female managers out here. None of our competitors do, and we'd be committing suicide in a very lucrative market if the Chauvinarians perceived us as treating women like complete equals. Personally, I think their attitudes are nonsense, but business is business. 'When in Rome' and all that, you know."

Is Tom's position ethically justified? Assume that Tom is being honest about his reasons for treating Virginia as he did.

Crimes and Torts

Crimes

When one lists legal topics relevant to business, criminal law may come to mind less readily than contracts, torts, agency, corporations, and various other subjects dealt with in this text. Today, however, business owners (whether sole proprietors or corporate) and their employees are more likely than ever before to come in contact with the criminal justice system. A working understanding of major criminal law concepts therefore has become essential to a manager's education. ∞

THE CRIMINAL LAW

This century has witnessed society's increasing tendency to use the criminal law as a major device for controlling corporate behavior. Many regulatory statutes establish criminal and civil penalties for statutory violations. The criminal penalties often apply to individual employees as well as to their employers.

Advocates of using the criminal law in this way typically argue that doing so achieves a deterrence level superior to that produced by damage awards and other civil remedies. Corporations may be inclined to treat damage awards as simply a business cost and to violate regulatory provisions when doing so makes economic "sense." Criminal prosecutions, however, threaten corporations with the stigma of a criminal conviction. In some cases, the criminal law allows society to penalize corporate employees who would not be directly affected by a civil judgment against their employer. Moreover, by alerting private parties to a violation that could also give rise to a civil damage suit, criminal prosecutions may increase the likelihood that a corporation will bear the full costs of its actions.

Whatever the merit of these arguments, the threat of criminal prosecution plays an undeniable role in today's legal environment of business. Accordingly, this chapter begins by examining the nature and essential components of the criminal law. It then considers various problems encountered in applying the criminal law to the corporate setting.

Nature of Crime

Crimes are *public wrongs*—acts prohibited by the state or federal government. Criminal prosecutions are initiated by a prosecutor (an elected or appointed government employee) in the name of the state or the United States, whichever is appropriate. Persons convicted of crimes bear the *stigma* of a criminal conviction—the social condemnation resulting from being found guilty of a crime. Convicted offenders also face the uniquely coercive force of the *criminal sanction*, society's punishment of those who violate its most important rules. This punishment may be a fine, imprisonment, or, in extreme cases, execution.

Our legal system also contemplates noncriminal consequences for violations of legal duties. For example, the next two chapters deal with *torts*, private wrongs for which the wrongdoer must pay money damages to compensate the harmed victim. In some tort cases, the court may also assess punitive damages in order to punish the wrongdoer. Only the criminal sanction, however, combines the threat to life or liberty with the stigma of conviction. This potent combination makes the criminal sanction "the law's ultimate threat."[1]

Crimes are typically classified as felonies or misdemeanors. A **felony** is a serious crime such as murder, rape, arson, illicit drug-dealing, or a theft offense of sufficient magnitude. Most felonies involve significant moral culpability on the offender's part. Felonies are punishable by lengthy confinement of the convicted offender to a penitentiary, as well as by a fine. A person convicted of a felony may experience other adverse consequences, such as *disenfranchisement* (loss of voting rights) and disqualification from the practice of certain professions (e.g., law or medicine). A **misdemeanor,** on the other hand, is a lesser offense such as disorderly conduct or battery resulting in minor physical harm

to the victim. Misdemeanor offenses usually involve less—sometimes much less—moral culpability than felony offenses. As such, misdemeanors are punishable by lesser fines and/or limited confinement in jail. Depending on their seriousness and potential for harm to the public, traffic violations are classified either as misdemeanors or as less serious **infractions.** Really only quasi-criminal, infractions usually are punishable by fines but not by confinement in jail.

It is a social question whether to classify a given act as criminal. As our social values have changed over time, so have our definitions of criminal conduct.

Purpose of the Criminal Sanction

Much of the disagreement about when the criminal sanction should be employed stems from a dispute over the criminal sanction's purpose. Persons accepting the *utilitarian* view of the criminal sanction believe that *prevention* of socially undesirable behavior is the only proper purpose of criminal penalties. This prevention goal includes three major components: deterrence, rehabilitation, and incapacitation.

Deterrence theorists hold that the threat or imposition of punishment deters the commission of crimes in two different ways. The first, *special deterrence,* occurs when punishment of a convicted offender deters him from committing further crimes. The second, *general deterrence,* results when punishment of a convicted wrongdoer deters other persons from committing a similar offense. Factors influencing the probable effectiveness of deterrence include the respective likelihoods that the crime will be detected, that detection will be followed by prosecution, and that prosecution will result in a conviction. The severity of the probable punishment (should there be a conviction) serves as another key factor. In economic terms, effective deterrence requires that the penalty imposed for an offense, discounted by the likelihood of apprehension and conviction, must equal or exceed the gains to the offender from committing the offense.

A fundamental problem attends deterrence theories: We cannot be certain whether deterrence works because we can never know what the crime rate would be in the absence of punishment. For example, high levels of crime and *recidivism* (repeat

---

[1]H. Packer, *The Limits of the Criminal Sanction* (Stanford, CA: Stanford University Press, 1968), p. 250.

offenses by previously punished offenders) may indicate only that sufficiently severe and certain criminal sanctions have not been employed, not that criminal sanctions in general cannot effectively deter. Deterrence theory's other major problem is its assumption that potential offenders are rational beings who consciously weigh the threat of punishment against the benefits derived from an offense. The threat of punishment, however, may not deter the commission of criminal offenses produced by irrational or unconscious drives.

Rehabilitation of convicted offenders—changing their attitudes or values so that they are not inclined to commit future offenses—serves as another way to prevent undesirable behavior. Critics of rehabilitation commonly point to high rates of recidivism as evidence of the general failure of rehabilitation efforts to date. Even if rehabilitation efforts fail, however, *incapacitation* of convicted offenders re-

sults from their incarceration and thus contributes to the goal of prevention. While imprisoned, offenders have much less ability to commit other crimes.

Prevention is not the only goal advanced for the criminal sanction. Some persons see *retribution*—the infliction of deserved suffering on violators of society's most fundamental rules—as the central focus of criminal punishment. Under this theory, punishment satisfies community and individual desires for revenge, and reinforces important social values. A retributionist therefore is unlikely to see prevention as a sufficient reason to criminalize socially undesirable but morally neutral behavior. When serious moral culpability is present, however, a retributionist is likely to favor punishment even if it would not prevent future offenses.

Figure 1 contains a general discussion of how state and federal law approach the proper determination of a convicted offender's punishment.

FIGURE **1**

A Note on State and Federal Approaches to Sentencing of Convicted Offenders

---

TYPICAL STATE APPROACHES

As a general rule, state laws on criminal punishments seek to further the deterrence, rehabilitation, and incapacitation purposes discussed in the text. State statutes usually set forth ranges of sentences (e.g., minimum and maximum amounts of fines and imprisonment) for each crime established by law. The court sets the convicted offender's sentence within the appropriate range unless the court places the defendant on probation.

Probation is effectively a conditional sentence that suspends the usual imprisonment and/or fine if the offender "toes the line" and meets other judicially imposed conditions for the period specified by the court. It is sometimes granted to first-time offenders and other convicted defendants deemed suitable candidates by the court. In deciding whether to order probation or an appropriate sentence within the statutory range, the court normally places considerable reliance on a presentence investigation conducted by the state probation office. Relevant information revealed in this investigation, coupled with evidence of the offender's prior criminal history, will influence the court in deciding at what point within the statutory range a particular offender's punishment should fall.

THE FEDERAL APPROACH

The federal approach to sentencing was essentially the same until very recent years, when the Federal Sentencing Guidelines set by the U.S. Sentencing Commission took effect. In the Sentencing Reform Act of 1984, Congress created the Sentencing Commission and authorized it to develop sentencing guidelines. Congress thereby sought to reduce judicial discretion in sentencing and to minimize disparities among sentences imposed by judges on similar offenders. The Sentencing Guidelines, which are binding on federal courts and have been criticized by some judges, contain a table with more than 40 levels of seriousness of offense. Where a particular offender's crime and corresponding sentence are listed on the table depends on various factors associated with the offense and on the offender's prior criminal history. The court normally must sentence the defendant to what the table shows, although departures are allowed in the event of exceptional circumstances specified by the court. A special subset of rules known as the Corporate Sentencing Guidelines (discussed later in this chapter) governs the sentencing of organizations convicted of federal crimes.

For various crimes, the Federal Sentencing Guidelines appear to have led to the imposition of more severe—sometimes much more severe—sentences than had previously been the case. Although the prospect of probation for certain offenses still exists, an increased use of incarceration of individuals convicted of serious offenses also appears to have resulted from the Sentencing Guidelines. As for what purposes incarceration should serve, the Sentencing Reform Act specifically rejected rehabilitation as one of them. Instead, the statute stated that the goals of punishment should be education, deterrence, and incapacitation.

Essentials of Crime

To convict a defendant of a crime, the state ordinarily must: (1) demonstrate that his alleged acts violated a criminal statute; (2) prove beyond a reasonable doubt that he committed those acts; and (3) prove that he had the capacity to form a criminal intent.

Prior Statutory Prohibition   Crimes are *statutory* offenses. A given behavior is not a crime unless Congress or a state legislature has criminalized it.[2] The U.S. Constitution prohibits *ex post facto* criminal laws. This means that a defendant's act must have been prohibited by statute at the time she committed it and that the penalty imposed must be the one provided for at the time of her offense.

The Constitution places other limits on legislative power to criminalize behavior. If behavior is constitutionally protected, it cannot be deemed criminal. For example, the right of privacy held implicit in the Constitution caused the Supreme Court, in *Griswold v. Connecticut,* to strike down state statutes that prohibited the use of contraceptive devices and the counseling or assisting of others in the use of such devices.[3] This decision provided the constitutional basis for the Court's historic *Roe v. Wade* decision, which limited the states' power to criminalize abortions.[4]

By prohibiting laws that unreasonably restrict freedom of expression, the First Amendment to the Constitution also plays a major role in limiting legislative power to criminalize behavior. Legislative attempts to hold persons criminally liable for the content of their written or spoken statements are usually suspect under the First Amendment. Various times during the past several years, the Supreme Court has considered the extent to which so-called expressive conduct—an action that expresses a point of view or message regardless of whether written or spoken words accompany the action—merits First Amendment protection against government attempts to criminalize it. Figure 2 contains a discussion of the Court's expressive conduct decisions.

In addition to limiting the sorts of behavior that may be made criminal, the Constitution limits the manner in which behavior may be criminalized. The Due Process Clauses of the Fifth and Fourteenth Amendments require that criminal statutes define the prohibited behavior precisely enough that an ordinary person can understand which behavior violates the law.[5] Statutes that fail to provide such fair notice may be challenged as unconstitutionally vague. The Fourteenth Amendment's Equal Protection Clause[6] prohibits criminal statutes that discriminatorily treat certain persons of the same class or arbitrarily discriminate among different classes of persons.[7] Legislatures usually are extended considerable latitude in making statutory classifications if the classifications have a rational basis. "Suspect" classifications, such as those based on race, are subjected to much closer judicial scrutiny, however.

Finally, the Constitution limits the type of punishment imposed on convicted offenders. The Eighth Amendment forbids "cruel and unusual punishments." This prohibition furnishes, for example, the constitutional basis for judicial decisions establishing limits on the imposition of the death penalty.[8] Although various Supreme Court cases indicate that the Eighth Amendment may bar a sentence whose harshness is disproportionate to the seriousness of the defendant's offense, the Court has signaled that any Eighth Amendment concerns along these lines are unlikely to be triggered unless the sentence–crime disproportionality is exceedingly gross.[9]

Proof Beyond a Reasonable Doubt   The serious matters at stake in a criminal case—the life and liberty of the accused—justify our legal system's placement of significant limits on the government's

---

[2]Infractions of a minor criminal or quasi-criminal nature (such as traffic offenses) are often established by city or county ordinances but will not be considered here. For discussion of ordinances as a type of law, see Chapter 1.

[3]381 U.S. 479 (U.S. Sup. Ct. 1965).

[4]410 U.S. 113 (U.S. Sup. Ct. 1973).

---

[5]Chapter 3 discusses due process in greater detail.

[6]Chapter 3 discusses equal protection in greater detail.

[7]For an example, see *McLaughlin v. Florida,* 379 U.S. 1984 (U.S. Sup. Ct. 1964), where the Court struck down a Florida statute forbidding cohabitation between black males and white females on the ground that no valid statutory purpose justified prohibiting only interracial cohabitation.

[8]See, for example, *Thompson v. Oklahoma,* 487 U.S. 815 (U.S. Sup. Ct. 1988), where the Court held that the Eighth Amendment bars the execution of a defendant who was under 16 years of age at the time of his offense.

[9]See *Harmelin v. Michigan,* 501 U.S. 957 (U.S. Sup. Ct. 1991), where the Court upheld, against an Eighth Amendment–based attack, a statutorily mandated sentence of life imprisonment without parole for persons convicted of possessing 650 or more grams of cocaine.

FIGURE **2**

Supreme Court Decisions Exploring First Amendment Limits on Legislative Power to Criminalize Expressive Conduct

TEXAS V. JOHNSON

In the controversial case of *Texas v. Johnson,* 491 U.S. 397 (U.S. Sup. Ct. 1989), the Court held that Gregory Johnson's burning an American flag during a protest demonstration was protected expressive conduct. The Court reasoned that regardless of the presence or absence of spoken or written words, certain conduct such as flag-burning may be "sufficiently imbued with elements of communication" to come under the First Amendment umbrella. In view of the considerable First Amendment protection extended to political speech—to which Johnson's expressive conduct surely was equivalent—Johnson could not constitutionally be convicted of violating a Texas statute that prohibited the "desecration of a venerated object." A year later, in *U.S. v. Eichman,* 496 U.S. 310 (U.S. Sup. Ct. 1990), the Court used the *Johnson* rationale to strike down a federal statute that criminalized flag-burning.

BARNES V. GLEN THEATRE, INC.

As if the flag-burning decisions somehow were not "hot" enough, the Court's expressive conduct focus then turned to nonobscene nude dancing. In *Barnes v. Glen Theatre, Inc.,* 501 U.S. 560 (U.S. Sup. Ct. 1991), the Court noted that such dancing is expressive conduct "marginally" within the First Amendment's protective scope. Nevertheless, in a plurality decision that did not produce a controlling rationale, the Court concluded that the First Amendment was not violated by Indiana's application of a public indecency statute to nude dancing.

R.A.V. V. CITY OF ST. PAUL

R.A.V. v. City of St. Paul, 505 U.S. 377 (U.S. Sup. Ct. 1992) was a different story, however. There, the Court considered the city's hate-crimes ordinance, which prohibited placing on public or private property "a burning cross" or other symbol "which one knows or has reasonable grounds to know arouses anger, alarm or resentment in others on the basis of race, color, creed, religion or gender." The Court held that the ordinance was an impermissible content-based and viewpoint-based restriction on expressive conduct. The First Amendment thus protected the cross-burning defendants from being convicted of violating the ordinance, even though their behavior was, as the Court acknowledged, "reprehensible."

WISCONSIN V. MITCHELL

Although some observers assumed that *R.A.V.* would dictate a similar outcome in *Wisconsin v. Mitchell,* 508 U.S. 476 (U.S. Sup. Ct. 1993), it did not. Mitchell was convicted of aggravated battery for severely beating a child. On the basis of a Wisconsin statute that authorized the imposition of an enhanced maximum penalty when the offender selected his victim on the basis of the victim's race, Mitchell received a stiffer sentence than otherwise would have been allowed under the law. Rejecting Mitchell's argument that *R.A.V.* controlled and that the enhanced penalty he received was an unconstitutional criminalization of thought and expression, the Court upheld the imposition of the greater sentence. It distinguished *R.A.V.* by observing that the ordinance at issue there was obviously directed at expression, whereas the Wisconsin penalty-enhancement statute under which Mitchell was sentenced was nothing more than a permissible regulation of nonexpressive conduct.

power to convict a person of a crime. One of the most fundamental safeguards is the presumption of innocence; defendants in criminal cases are presumed innocent until proven guilty. The Due Process Clauses require the government to overcome this presumption by proving beyond a reasonable doubt every element of the offense charged against the defendant.[10] Requiring the government to meet this stern burden of proof minimizes the risk of erroneous criminal convictions.[11] It also reflects a strong belief shared by all common law jurisdictions about the proper way to enforce laws and administer justice.

Defendant's Criminal Intent and Capacity
Most serious crimes require *mens rea,* or criminal intent, as an element. The level of fault required for

---

[10]The beyond a reasonable doubt standard required of the government in criminal cases contemplates a stronger and more convincing showing than that required of plaintiffs in civil cases. As explained in Chapter 2, plaintiffs in civil cases need only prove the elements of their claims by a preponderance of the evidence.

[11]The beyond a reasonable doubt standard applies to the conviction phase of a criminal prosecution but not to the sentencing phase. Once the defendant has been convicted of a certain charge, the court determining the appropriate sentence may take into account other charges of which the defendant was acquitted if the conduct underlying those charges has been proven by a preponderance of the evidence. *United States v. Watts,* 1997 U.S. LEXIS 1 (U.S. Sup. Ct. 1997).

a given criminal violation depends on the wording of the statute in question. Many criminal statutes require proof of intentional wrongdoing. Others impose liability for reckless conduct or sometimes mere negligence. In the criminal context, recklessness generally means that the accused consciously disregarded a substantial risk that the harm prohibited by the statute would result from her actions. Negligence, in criminal cases, means that the accused failed to perceive a substantial risk of harm that a reasonable person would have perceived.

Criminal intent may be inferred from an accused's behavior, because a person is normally held to have intended the natural and probable consequences of her acts. The criminal intent requirement furthers the criminal law's general goal of punishing conscious wrongdoers. Accordingly, proof that the defendant had the capacity to form the required intent is a traditional prerequisite of criminal responsibility. The criminal law recognizes three general types of incapacity: *intoxication, infancy,* and *insanity.*

Voluntary intoxication, although not a complete defense to criminal liability, may sometimes diminish the degree of a defendant's liability. This is so because a highly intoxicated person may be incapable of forming the specific criminal intent required for certain crimes. For example, many first-degree murder statutes require proof of *premeditation,* a conscious decision to kill. One who kills while highly intoxicated may be incapable of premeditation—meaning that he would not be guilty of first-degree murder. He may be convicted, however, of another homicide offense that does not require proof of premeditation.[12] Involuntary intoxication may be a complete defense to criminal liability.

The common law usually presumed that children younger than 14 years of age could not form a criminal intent. Today, most states treat juvenile offenders below a certain statutory age (usually 16 or 17) differently from adult offenders, with special juvenile court systems and separate detention facilities. Current juvenile law emphasizes rehabilitation rather than capacity issues. Repeat offenders or offenders charged with very serious offenses, however, may sometimes be treated as adults.

A criminal defendant's insanity may affect a criminal prosecution in various ways. Insanity rendering a defendant incapable of assisting in her defense will delay her trial until she regains sanity. Insanity manifesting itself after conviction, but before sentencing, can delay sentencing until sanity returns. If a condemned prisoner becomes insane while awaiting execution, the Eighth Amendment's prohibition of cruel and unusual punishment serves to bar the execution.[13]

In addition, an accused's insanity at the time the charged act was committed may constitute a complete defense to liability. This possible effect of insanity has generated expressions of public dissatisfaction with the insanity defense, as well as disagreements over the proper basis on which to determine insanity. Courts have adopted various insanity tests in an effort to achieve consistency with the goal of punishing conscious wrongdoers. These tests are *legal* tests, not medical tests. A defendant who was medically insane at the time of the criminal act may still be legally responsible.

The primary common law test for insanity is the *M'Naghten* rule: A criminal defendant is not responsible if, at the time of the offense, he did not know the nature and quality of his act, or, if he did know this, he did not know his act was wrong.[14] Some states have replaced or supplemented this test with the *irresistible impulse* rule, which absolves a defendant of responsibility if mental disease rendered her incapable of controlling her behavior and resisting the impulse to commit a crime. Many jurisdictions apply the American Law Institute's insanity test. Under this test, a defendant is not responsible if, at the time the act was committed, mental disease or defect caused him to lack the substantial capacity to appreciate the wrongfulness of his act or to conform his conduct to the law's requirements.

Public reaction to highly publicized cases in which insanity defenses were raised, however, has spurred two significant trends in recent years. One is a tendency to return to the narrower *M'Naghten* standard or something closely resembling it. Congress has taken such an approach in prescribing the insanity standard applicable in federal criminal

---

[12]A state is free, however, to enact a statute that prohibits consideration of the defendant's voluntary intoxication in the determination of whether the defendant possessed the requisite intent. The Supreme Court recently held that such a statute does not violate the Fourteenth Amendment's Due Process Clause. *Montana v. Egelhoff,* 116 S Ct 2013 (U.S. Sup. Ct. 1996).

[13]*Ford v. Wainwright,* 477 U.S. 399 (U.S. Sup. Ct. 1986).

[14]This rule is derived from *Daniel M'Naghten's Case,* 8 Eng. Reprint 718 (House of Lords 1843).

F I G U R E 3

Essentials of Crime Checklist

- Did the accused violate an existing statute?

- Is the statute constitutionally valid?
  Does it prohibit constitutionally protected
  behavior?
  Does it clearly define the prohibited behavior?

- Did the accused have the required criminal intent?
  Did he have the capacity to form the required
  intent?
  Can the necessary level of intent be inferred from
  his actions?

- Did the state prove each element of the crime
  beyond a reasonable doubt?

cases. The other recent trend is the creation of procedural rules that make it more difficult for defendants to succeed with an insanity defense. Criminal defendants are presumed to be sane. Traditionally, once an accused introduced evidence tending to prove insanity, the government was expected to prove her sanity beyond a reasonable doubt. Today, however, many states and the federal government treat insanity as an affirmative defense under which the defendant bears the burden of proving insanity. In addition, some states have instituted a "guilty, but mentally ill" verdict as an alternative to the traditional "not guilty by reason of insanity" verdict. This alternative allows jurors to convict (rather than acquit) mentally ill defendants, with the assurance that they will receive postconviction treatment.

Figure 3 summarizes the essential components of criminal liability under our legal system.

CRIMINAL PROCEDURE

Criminal Prosecutions

Persons arrested for allegedly committing a crime are taken to the police station and booked. **Booking** is an administrative procedure for recording the suspect's arrest and the alleged offenses involved. In some states, temporary release on bail may be available at this stage. After booking, the police file an arrest report with the prosecutor, who decides whether to charge the suspect with an offense. If she decides to prosecute, the prosecutor prepares a complaint identifying the accused and detailing the charges. Most states require that arrested suspects be taken promptly before a magistrate or other judicial officer (such as a justice of the peace or judge whose court is of limited jurisdiction) for an **initial appearance.** During this appearance, the magistrate informs the accused of the charges against him and outlines the accused's constitutional rights. In misdemeanor cases in which the accused pleads guilty, the sentence may be (but need not be) imposed without a later hearing. If the accused pleads not guilty to the misdemeanor charge, the case is set for trial. In felony cases, as well as misdemeanor cases in which the accused pleads not guilty, the magistrate sets the amount of bail.

In many states, defendants in felony cases are protected against unjustified prosecutions by an additional procedural step, the **preliminary hearing.** The prosecutor must introduce enough evidence at this hearing to persuade a magistrate that there is **probable cause** to believe the accused committed a felony.[15] If persuaded that probable cause exists, the magistrate binds over the defendant for trial in the appropriate court.

After a bindover, the formal charge against the defendant is filed with the trial court. The formal charge consists of either an **information** filed by the prosecutor or an **indictment** returned by a grand jury. Roughly half of the states require that a grand jury approve the decision to prosecute a person for a felony. Grand juries are bodies of citizens selected in the same manner as the members of a trial (petit) jury; often, they are chosen through random drawings from a list of registered voters. Grand juries traditionally included 23 members, with a majority vote being necessary for an indictment. Today, many states have reduced the size of the grand jury. There is also significant variation in the number of votes required for an indictment. Indictment of an accused prior to a preliminary hearing normally eliminates the need for a preliminary hearing because the indictment serves essentially the same function as a magistrate's probable cause determination.

---

[15]The state need not satisfy the beyond a reasonable doubt standard of proof at the preliminary hearing stage. The prosecutor sufficiently establishes probable cause by causing the magistrate to believe it is more likely than not that the defendant committed the felony alleged.

The remainder of the states allow felony defendants to be charged by either indictment or information, at the prosecutor's discretion. An **information** is a formal charge signed by the prosecutor outlining the facts supporting the charges against the defendant. In states allowing felony prosecution by information, prosecutors elect the information method in the vast majority of felony cases. Misdemeanor cases are prosecuted by information in virtually all states.[16]

Once an information or indictment has been filed with a trial court, an *arraignment* occurs. The defendant is brought before the court, informed of the charges, and asked to enter a plea. The defendant may plead guilty, not guilty, or nolo contendere. Although technically not an admission of guilt, nolo contendere pleas indicate that the defendant does not contest the charges. This decision by the defendant will lead to a finding of guilt. Unlike evidence of a guilty plea, however, evidence of a defendant's nolo plea is inadmissible in later civil suits against that defendant based on the same conduct amounting to the criminal violation. Individuals and corporate defendants therefore may find nolo pleas attractive when their chances of mounting a successful defense to the criminal prosecution are poor and the prospect of later civil suits is likely.

At or shortly after the arraignment, the defendant who pleads not guilty chooses the type of trial that will take place. Persons accused of serious crimes for which incarceration for more than six months is possible have a constitutional right to be tried by a jury of their peers. The accused, however, generally may waive this right and opt for a bench trial (i.e., before a judge only).

Constitutional Safeguards

The preceding pages referred to several procedural devices designed to protect persons accused of crime. The Bill of Rights, which consists of the first 10 amendments to the U.S. Constitution, sets forth other rights of criminal defendants. These rights guard against unjustified or erroneous criminal convictions and serve as reminders of government's proper role in the administration of justice in a democratic society. Justice Oliver Wendell Holmes aptly addressed this latter point when he said, "I think it less evil that some criminals should escape than that the government should play an ignoble part." Although the specific language of the Bill of Rights refers only to federal government actions, the U.S. Supreme Court has applied the most important Bill of Rights guarantees to state government actions by "selectively incorporating" those guarantees into the Fourteenth Amendment's Due Process Clause. Once a particular safeguard has been found to be "implicit in the concept of ordered liberty" or "fundamental to the American scheme of justice," it has been applied equally in state and federal criminal trials. This has occurred with the constitutional protections examined earlier in this chapter as well as with the Fourth, Fifth, and Sixth Amendment guarantees discussed in the following pages.

The Fourth Amendment   The Fourth Amendment protects persons against arbitrary and unreasonable governmental violations of their privacy rights. It states:

The right of the people to be secure in their persons, houses, papers, and effects, against unreasonable searches and seizures, shall not be violated, and no Warrants shall issue, but upon probable cause, supported by Oath or affirmation, and particularly describing the place to be searched, and the persons or things to be seized.

Both the language of the amendment and the judicial interpretations it has generated reflect the difficulties inherent in properly balancing citizens' legitimate expectations of privacy and government's legitimate interest in securing evidence of wrongdoing. Citizens are not protected against all searches and seizures—only against unreasonable ones. Because the Fourth Amendment safeguards reasonable privacy expectations, the Supreme Court has extended the amendment's protection to such places or items as private dwellings and immediately surrounding areas (often called the *curtilage*), telephone booths, sealed containers, and first-class mail. The Court has denied protection to places, items, or matters as to which it found no reasonable expectations of privacy, such as open fields, personal bank

---

[16]For federal crimes, a prosecutor in the relevant U.S. Attorney's office files an information to institute the case if the offense involved carries a penalty of not more than one year of imprisonment. Federal prosecutions for more serious crimes with potentially more severe penalties are commenced by means of a grand jury indictment.

records, and voluntary conversations between criminal defendants and government informants. In *United States v. Hall,* which follows, a federal court of appeals considered whether a corporation and one of its executives possessed a reasonable expectation of privacy in the contents of garbage bags placed in a dumpster that was located on the corporation's property.

Even when plainly protected areas or items are involved, not every governmental action is deemed sufficiently intrusive to constitute a search or seizure for Fourth Amendment purposes. Thus, for example, the Supreme Court held that exposing an airline traveler's luggage to a narcotics detection dog in a public place was not a search, considering the minimally intrusive nature of the intrusion and the narrow scope of information it revealed.[17] No seizure occurred, according to the Court in *Florida v. Bostick,* when police boarded a bus at a regular stop and asked a passenger for permission to search his luggage.[18]

In its treatment of the Fourth Amendment's Warrant Clause, the Supreme Court has engaged in similar balancing of individual and governmental interests. The warrant requirement further protects privacy interests by mandating that a judge or magistrate authorize and define the scope of intrusive governmental action. As a general rule, the Court has held that searches carried out without a proper warrant are unreasonable. Nonetheless, the Court has devised a lengthy list of exceptions to this general rule. The Court has upheld warrantless searches of the area within the immediate control of an arrestee, of premises police enter in hot pursuit of an armed suspect, and of automobiles and containers located therein under certain circumstances (due to automobiles' mobile nature). Warrantless seizures of contraband items in the plain view of officers acting lawfully have likewise been upheld. The Court has also authorized customs searches, stop-and-frisk searches for weapons, inventory searches of property in an arrestee's possession, and consensual searches, despite the absence of a warrant in each of these instances. Finally, the Court has upheld warrantless administrative inspections of closely regulated businesses.[19]

---

[17]*United States v. Place,* 426 U.S. 696 (U.S. Sup. Ct. 1983). In this case, however, the Court also held that the warrantless detention of the defendant's luggage for 90 minutes was unlawful, given the fact that the agents in question had several hours' advance notice of the defendant's arrival.

[18]501 U.S. 429 (U.S. Sup. Ct. 1991).

---

[19]See, e.g., *New York v. Burger,* 482 U.S. 691 (U.S. Sup. Ct. 1987).

UNITED STATES v. HALL   47 F. 3d 1091 (11th Cir. 1995)

William T. Parks, a special agent of the U.S. Customs Service, was investigating allegations that Bet-Air, Inc. (a Miami-based seller of spare aviation parts and supplies) had supplied restricted military parts to Iran. Parks entered Bet-Air's property and removed, from a garbage dumpster, a bag of shredded documents. The dumpster was located near the Bet-Air offices in a parking area reserved for the firm's employees. To reach the dumpster, Parks had to travel 40 yards on a private paved road. No signs indicated that the road was private. In later judicial proceedings, Parks testified that at the time he traveled on the road, he did not know he was on Bet-Air's property.

When reconstructed, some of the previously shredded documents contained information seemingly relevant to the investigation. Parks used the shredded documents and the information they revealed as the basis for obtaining a warrant to search the Bet-Air premises. In executing the search warrant, Parks and other law enforcement officers seized numerous documents and Bet-Air records.

A federal grand jury later indicted Bet-Air's chairman, Terrence Hall, and other defendants on various counts related to the alleged supplying of restricted military parts to Iran. Contending that the Fourth Amendment had been violated, Hall filed a motion asking the court to suppress (i.e., exclude) all evidence derived from the warrantless search of the dumpster and all evidence seized during the search of the Bet-Air premises (the search pursuant to the warrant). The federal district court denied Hall's motion. Following a jury trial, Hall was convicted on all counts and sentenced to prison. Hall appealed to the 11th Circuit Court of Appeals. ∽

Hatchett, Circuit Judge   In *California v. Greenwood* (1988), the Supreme Court held that a warrantless search and seizure of garbage left in a plastic bag on the curb in front of, but outside the curtilage of, a private house did not violate the Fourth Amendment. The Court held that such a search would only violate the Fourth Amendment if the persons discarding the garbage manifested a subjective expectation of privacy in their garbage that society accepts as objectively reasonable. The Court concluded that Greenwood had exposed his garbage to the public sufficiently to render his subjective expectation of privacy objectively unreasonable.

Hall points to the fact that Parks obtained documents that were shredded, then placed inside a green garbage bag, which was in turn placed inside a garbage dumpster. We believe that the manner in which Bet-Air disposed of its garbage serves only to demonstrate that Bet-Air manifested a subjective expectation of privacy in its discarded garbage. Whether Parks's actions were proscribed by the Fourth Amendment, however, turns on whether society is prepared to accept Bet-Air's subjective expectation of privacy as objectively reasonable.

It is well established that the Fourth Amendment protections apply [not only to residential property but also] to commercial premises. The Supreme Court's treatment of the expectation of privacy that the owner of commercial property enjoys in such property has differed significantly from the protection accorded an individual's home, [however]. Such distinctions are inevitable given the fundamental difference in the nature and uses of a residence as opposed to commercial property. These distinctions are drawn into sharp focus when, as in this case, the government intrudes into the area immediately surrounding the structure. In order for persons to preserve Fourth Amendment protection in the area immediately surrounding the residence, they must not conduct an activity or leave an object in the plain view of those outside the area. The occupant of a commercial building, in contrast, must take the additional precaution of affirmatively barring the public from the area. The Supreme Court has consistently held that the government is required to obtain a search warrant only when it wishes to search those areas of commercial property from which the public has been excluded.

Relying on the fact that the dumpster was within the "commercial curtilage" of Bet-Air's property and that it could only be accessed by traveling 40 yards on a private road, Hall asserts that the company's subjective expectation of privacy was objectively reasonable. Hall's heavy emphasis on Parks's trespass onto Bet-Air's private property is misplaced. The law of trespass forbids intrusions onto land that the Fourth Amendment would not proscribe. We note that although the road leading to Bet-Air's dumpster was private, the magistrate judge found that no "objective signs of restricted access such as signs, barricades, and the like" were present. Moreover, the magistrate judge also found that at the time Parks traveled the road, he believed it was a public road. [Bet-Air's] failure to exclude the public takes on increased significance when the asserted expectation of privacy is in discarded garbage. A commercial proprietor incurs a diminished expectation of privacy when garbage is placed in a dumpster which is located in a parking lot that the business shares with other businesses, and no steps are taken to limit the public's access to the dumpster. It is common knowledge that commercial dumpsters have long been a source of fruitful exploration for scavengers.

The Supreme Court used the concept of curtilage in *Hester v. United States* (1924) to distinguish between the area outside a person's house which the Fourth Amendment protects, and the open fields, which are afforded no First Amendment protection. The Supreme Court has not squarely addressed the applicability of the common law concept of curtilage to commercial property. Given the Court's view of the relationship between the Fourth Amendment and commercial premises, however, we have little doubt that were the Court to embrace the so-called "business curtilage" concept, it would, at a minimum, require that the commercial proprietor take affirmative steps to exclude the public. In light of Bet-Air's failure to exclude the public from the area immediately surrounding its offices, we refuse to apply the so-called "business curtilage" concept in this case.

[W]e do not believe that Parks infringed upon any societal values the Fourth Amendment protects when he searched Bet-Air's garbage. Bet-Air did not take sufficient steps to restrict the public's access to its discarded garbage; therefore, its subjective expectation of privacy is not one that society is prepared to accept as objectively reasonable.

District court's denial of Hall's suppression motion affirmed.

The exclusionary rule serves as the basic remedial device in cases of Fourth Amendment violations. Under this judicially crafted rule, evidence seized in illegal searches cannot be used in a subsequent trial against an accused whose constitutional rights were violated.[20] Because the exclusionary rule may result in suppression of convincing evidence of crime, it has generated considerable controversy. The rule's supporters regard it as necessary to deter police from violating citizens' constitutional rights. The rule's opponents assert that it has no deterrent effect on police who believed they were acting lawfully. A loudly voiced complaint in some quarters has been that "because of a policeman's error, a criminal goes free."

In recent years, the Court has responded to such criticism by rendering decisions restricting the operation of the exclusionary rule. For example, in *Nix v. Williams,* the Court held that illegally obtained evidence may be introduced at trial if the prosecution convinces the trial judge that the evidence would inevitably have been obtained anyway by lawful means.[21] In *United States v. Leon,* the Court created a "good faith" exception to the exclusionary rule. This exception allows the use of evidence seized by police officers who acted pursuant to a search warrant later held invalid if the officers reasonably believed that the warrant was valid.[22] Although the Court has not extended the good faith exception to the warrantless search setting, it did expand the exception's scope to include searches made in reliance on a statute that is later declared invalid.[23] *Arizona v. Evans,* which follows, provides a further example of the Court's recent inclination to restrict the operation of the exclusionary rule.

---

[20]The Supreme Court initially authorized application of the exclusionary rule in federal criminal cases only. In *Mapp v. Ohio,* 367 U.S. 643 (U.S. Sup. Ct. 1961), the Court made the exclusionary rule applicable to state criminal cases as well.

[21]467 U.S. 431 (U.S. Sup. Ct. 1984).
[22]468 U.S. 897 (U.S. Sup. Ct. 1984).
[23]*Illinois v. Krull,* 480 U.S. 340 (U.S. Sup. Ct. 1987).

ARIZONA v. EVANS 115 S. Ct. 1185 (U.S. Sup. Ct. 1995)

A Phoenix police officer stopped Isaac Evans after seeing him drive the wrong way on a one-way street. During this traffic stop, the officer entered Evans's name into a computer data terminal located in his patrol car. The computer search revealed that there was an outstanding misdemeanor warrant for the arrest of Evans. Based on this warrant, the officer placed Evans under arrest. While Evans was being handcuffed, he dropped a hand-rolled cigarette that, in the officer's judgment, smelled of marijuana. The officer then searched Evans's car and discovered a bag of marijuana under the front seat.

The state charged Evans with possession of marijuana. When the police informed the court that Evans had been arrested pursuant to the warrant listed in the computer records, court personnel discovered that the warrant had been quashed (canceled by the court) 17 days prior to the arrest. Evans filed a motion asking the court to suppress the seized marijuana (i.e., exclude it from evidence) on the theory that it was the fruit of an unlawful arrest. Testimony at the suppression hearing revealed that court employees had failed, in violation of their standard practice, to inform the police that the warrant had been quashed. The trial court granted the suppression motion and ordered that the seized evidence be excluded. The Arizona Court of Appeals reversed, concluding that the exclusionary rule should not be applied when an unlawful arrest resulted from errors of court employees rather than from any errors of police officers. Rejecting the distinction drawn by the Court of Appeals and holding that the exclusionary rule should apply, the Arizona Supreme Court reversed. The U.S. Supreme Court granted the state's petition for certiorari. ⌒

Rehnquist, Chief Justice This case presents the question whether evidence seized in violation of the Fourth Amendment by an officer who acted in reliance on a police record indicating the existence of an outstanding arrest warrant—a record that is later determined to be erroneous—must be suppressed by virtue of the exclusionary rule regardless of the source of the error.

We have recognized . . . that the Fourth Amendment contains no provision expressly precluding the use of evidence obtained in violation of its demands. The exclusionary rule operates as a judicially created remedy designed to safeguard against future violations of Fourth Amendment rights through the rule's general deterrent effect. As with any remedial device, the rule's application has been restricted to those instances where its remedial objectives are thought most efficaciously served.

In *United States v. Leon* (1984), we applied these principles to the context of a police search in which the officers had acted in objectively reasonable reliance on a search warrant, issued by a neutral and detached magistrate, that later was determined to be invalid. [W]e determined that there was no sound reason to apply the exclusionary rule as a means of deterring misconduct on the part of judicial officers who are responsible for issuing warrants. The *Leon* Court then examined whether application of the exclusionary rule could be expected to alter the behavior of the law enforcement officers. We concluded [that] "where the officer's conduct is objectively reasonable, excluding the evidence will not further the ends of the exclusionary rule in any appreciable way. . . . Excluding the evidence can in no way affect his future conduct unless it is to make him less willing to do his duty." Thus, we held that the "marginal or nonexistent benefits produced by suppressing evidence obtained in objectively reasonable reliance on a subsequently invalidated search warrant cannot justify the substantial costs of exclusion."

[Evans] argues that *Whiteley v. Warden, Wyoming State Penitentiary* (1971), compels exclusion of the evidence. Although *Whiteley* clearly retains relevance in determining whether police officers have violated the Fourth Amendment, its precedential value regarding application of the exclusionary rule is dubious. In *Whiteley,* the Court treated identification of a Fourth Amendment violation as synonymous with application of the exclusionary rule to evidence secured incident to that violation. Subsequent case law has rejected this reflexive application of the exclusionary rule. [The] later cases have emphasized that the issue of exclusion is separate from whether the Fourth Amendment has been violated, and exclusion is appropriate only if the remedial objectives of the rule are thought most efficaciously served.

Applying the reasoning of *Leon* to the facts of this case, we conclude that the decision of the Arizona Supreme Court must be reversed. First, as we noted in *Leon,* the exclusionary rule was historically designed as a means of deterring police misconduct, not mistakes by court employees. Second, respondent offers no evidence that court employees are inclined to ignore or subvert the Fourth Amendment or that lawlessness among these actors requires application of the extreme sanction of exclusion. Finally, and most important, there is no basis for believing that application of the exclusionary rule in these circumstances will have a significant effect on court employees responsible for informing the police that a warrant has been quashed. Because court clerks are not adjuncts to the law enforcement team engaged in the often competitive enterprise of ferreting out crime, they have no stake in the outcome of particular criminal cases. The threat of exclusion of evidence could not be expected to deter such individuals from failing to inform police officials that a warrant had been quashed.

If it were indeed a court clerk who was responsible for the erroneous entry on the police computer, application of the exclusionary rule also could not be expected to alter the behavior of the arresting officer. As the trial court in this case stated: "I think the police officer [was] bound to arrest. I think he would [have been] derelict in his duty if he failed to arrest." There is no indication that the arresting officer was not acting objectively reasonably when he relied upon the police computer record. Application of the *Leon* framework supports a categorical exception to the exclusionary rule for clerical errors of court employees.

Decision of Arizona Supreme Court reversed, and case remanded for further proceedings.

The Fifth Amendment   The Fifth Amendment's Due Process Clause guarantees basic procedural and substantive fairness to criminal defendants. In another significant provision, the Fifth Amendment protects against *compelled testimonial self-incrimination* by establishing that "[n]o person . . . shall be compelled in any criminal case to be a witness against himself." This provision prevents the government from coercing a defendant into making incriminating statements and thereby assisting in his own prosecution.

In *Miranda v. Arizona,* the Supreme Court established procedural requirements—the now-familiar *Miranda* warnings—to safeguard this Fifth Amendment right and other constitutional guarantees. The Court did so by requiring police to inform criminal suspects, before commencing custodial interrogation of them, that they have the right to remain silent, that any statements they make may be used as evidence against them, and that they have the right to the presence and assistance of a retained or court-appointed attorney (with court appointment occurring when suspects lack the financial ability to retain counsel).[24] Incriminating statements that the accused makes without first having been given the *Miranda* warnings are inadmissible at trial. If the suspect invokes her right to silence, custodial interrogation must cease. If, on the other hand, the suspect knowingly and voluntarily waives her right to silence after being given the *Miranda* warnings, her statements will be admissible.

The right to silence is limited, however, in various ways. For example, the traditional view that the Fifth Amendment applies only to *testimonial* admissions serves as the basis for allowing the police to compel an accused to furnish nontestimonial evidence such as fingerprints, samples of body fluids, and hair. Recent Supreme Court decisions have recognized further significant limitations on the right to silence. For instance, a longstanding view holds that the right includes a corresponding implicit prohibition of prosecutorial comments at trial about the accused's failure to speak in his own defense. Although Supreme Court decisions still support this prohibition as a general rule, the Court has sometimes allowed prosecutors to use the defendant's pretrial silence to impeach his trial testimony. For example, the Court has held that the Fifth Amendment is not violated by prosecutorial use of a defendant's silence (either prearrest or postarrest, but in advance of any *Miranda* warnings) to discredit his trial testimony that he killed the victim in self-defense.[25]

A similar inclination to narrow *Miranda*'s applicability and effect has also been displayed by the Supreme Court during roughly the past decade. In *Moran v. Burbine,* for instance, the Court upheld a suspect's waiver of his *Miranda* rights and approved the use of his confession at trial, despite the police's failure to notify the suspect that an attorney retained for him by a family member was seeking to contact him.[26] As another example, *Illinois v. Perkins* established that an undercover police officer posing as a fellow inmate need not give a jailed suspect the *Miranda* warnings before asking questions that could lead to incriminating admissions.[27]

The preceding discussion of the privilege against self-incrimination applies to criminal defendants in general. The Fifth Amendment's scope, however, has long been of particular concern to businesspersons charged with crimes. Documentary evidence often is quite important to the government's case in many white-collar crime prosecutions. To what extent does the Fifth Amendment protect business records? More than a century ago, the Supreme Court held, in *Boyd v. United States,* that the Fifth Amendment protects individuals against compelled production of their private papers.[28]

In more recent years, however, the Court has drastically limited the scope of the protection contemplated by *Boyd.* The Court has held various times that the private papers privilege is personal and thus cannot be asserted by a corporation, partnership, or other "collective entity." Because such entities have no Fifth Amendment rights, the Court has held, moreover, that when an organization's individual officer or agent has custody of organization records, the officer or agent cannot assert any personal privilege to prevent their disclosure. This rule holds even if the contents of the records incriminate her personally. Finally, various decisions allow the government to require business proprietors to keep certain records relevant to transactions that are appropriate subjects for government regulation. These "required records" are not entitled to private papers protection. They may be subpoenaed and used against the record-keeper in prosecutions for regulatory violations.

---

[24]384 U.S. 436 (U.S. Sup. Ct. 1966). The portions of the *Miranda* warnings dealing with the right to an attorney further Sixth Amendment interests. The Sixth Amendment is discussed later in this chapter.

[25]*Fletcher v. Weir,* 455 U.S. 603 (U.S. Sup. Ct. 1982); *Jenkins v. Anderson,* 447 U.S. 231 (U.S. Sup. Ct. 1980).

---

[26]475 U.S. 412 (U.S. Sup. Ct. 1986).

[27]496 U.S. 292 (U.S. Sup. Ct. 1990).

[28]116 U.S. 616 (U.S. Sup. Ct. 1886).

The Court's most recent business records decisions cast further doubt on the future of the private papers doctrine. Instead of focusing on whether subpoenaed records are private in nature, the Court now considers whether the *act of producing* the records would be sufficiently testimonial to trigger the privilege against self-incrimination. In *Fisher v. United States,* the Court held that an individual subpoenaed to produce personal documents may assert his Fifth Amendment privilege only if the act of producing the documents would involve incriminating testimonial admissions.[29] This is likely when the individual producing the records is in effect certifying the records' authenticity or admitting the existence of records previously unknown to the government (demonstrating that she had access to the records and, therefore, possible knowledge of any incriminating contents).

In *United States v. Doe,* the Court extended the act-of-production privilege to a sole proprietor whose proprietorship records were subpoenaed.[30] The Court, however, held that normal business records were not themselves protected by the Fifth Amendment because they were voluntarily prepared and thus not the product of compulsion. In view of *Doe*'s emphasis on the testimonial and potentially incriminating nature of the act of producing business records, some observers thought that officers of collective entities under government investigation might be able to assert their personal privileges against self-incrimination as a way to avoid producing incriminating business records. *Braswell v. United States,* however, dashed such hopes, as the Court refused to extend its *Doe* holding to cover a corporation's sole shareholder who acted in his capacity as custodian of corporate records.[31] The Court held that Braswell (the sole shareholder), having chosen to operate his business under the corporate form, was bound by the rule that corporations and similar entities have no Fifth Amendment privilege. Because Braswell acted in a representative capacity in producing the requested records, the government could not make evidentiary use of his act of production. The government, however, was free to use the contents of the records against Braswell and the corporation.

In the following *In re Grand Jury Subpoenas* decision, the Second Circuit Court of Appeals relied heavily on *Braswell* in rejecting a corporate president's Fifth Amendment–based attempt to avoid production of records pertaining to telephone lines listed in the president's name but paid for by the corporation.

---

[29]425 U.S. 391 (U.S. Sup. Ct. 1976).
[30]463 U.S. 605 (U.S. Sup. Ct. 1984).

[31]487 U.S. 99 (U.S. Sup. Ct. 1988).

IN RE GRAND JURY SUBPOENAS DATED OCTOBER 22, 1991, AND NOVEMBER 1, 1991 (U.S.v. DOE)
959 F.2d 1158 (2d Cir. 1992)

A federal grand jury was investigating "John Doe," president and sole shareholder of the corporation "XYZ," concerning possible violations of federal securities and money-laundering statutes. During the investigation, the government learned that XYZ had paid the bills for various telephone lines, including those used by Doe in his homes and car. Grand jury subpoenas duces tecum (i.e., subpoenas calling for production of documents) were then served on the custodian of XYZ's corporate records, on Doe, and on the law firm Paul, Weiss, Rifkind, Wharton & Garrison (Paul-Weiss), which represented Doe. These subpoenas sought production of telephone bills, records, and statements of account regarding certain telephone numbers (including the numbers of the telephone lines in Doe's homes and car).

Paul-Weiss possessed copies of these documents because it had received them from its client, Doe. Paul-Weiss refused, however, to comply with the subpoena. To justify this refusal, Paul-Weiss asserted that any copies of records in its possession were exempted from production due to (1) Doe's Fifth Amendment privilege against self-incrimination, and (2) the attorney–client and attorney-work-product privileges. Contending that the subpoenaed documents amounted to corporate records of XYZ rather than records belonging to or created by Doe, the government maintained that the asserted privileges were inapplicable. The government therefore filed a motion asking the district court to order Paul-Weiss to provide the subpoenaed documents. Doe, who was permitted to intervene in the proceeding, raised the same arguments made by Paul-Weiss in its refusal to comply with the subpoena.

After an evidentiary hearing on the government's motion, the district court determined that the records and documents at issue were those of XYZ rather than Doe. Concluding that requiring Paul-Weiss or Doe to produce the subpoenaed material would not violate Doe's Fifth Amendment rights, the attorney–client privilege, or the attorney-work-product privilege, the district court granted the government's motion and entered an order compelling Paul-Weiss to produce the subpoenaed material. Doe appealed. ∞

Kearse, Circuit Judge Doe contends that enforcement of the subpoena served on Paul-Weiss would violate his Fifth Amendment privilege principally because the act of producing the documents would tend to incriminate him. Preliminarily, we note that when documents have been transferred by a client to his attorney for the purpose of obtaining legal advice and the client claims attorney–client privilege, the attorney may refuse to produce the documents if the client, had he retained possession of them, would have had a Fifth Amendment privilege to refuse production. Accordingly, though Paul-Weiss was in possession of the subpoenaed records, we examine Doe's Fifth Amendment arguments as if Doe himself were the custodian.

The district court found that the subpoenaed records were not Doe's personal records but rather XYZ records. Artificial entities are not protected by the Fifth Amendment's prohibition against compelled self-incrimination. A corporation thus may not claim the privilege for the contents of its subpoenaed corporate records. Moreover, the custodian of corporate records is not entitled to refuse to produce those records on the ground that their contents may incriminate him personally, because they are not his personal records, and hence any incrimination would not be self-incrimination. This is so whether the subpoena for the corporate records is addressed to the corporation or to the custodian. Accordingly, Doe as custodian of XYZ's records is not entitled to prevent compliance with a subpoena calling for those records by asserting that the contents of those records would tend to incriminate him.

Further, the custodian of corporate records has no Fifth Amendment privilege to refuse to produce those records on the ground that the act of production itself would tend to incriminate him. This is the rule because, as pointed out by the Supreme Court in *Braswell v. United States,* "the custodian's act of production is not deemed a personal act, but rather an act of the corporation. Any claim of Fifth Amendment privilege asserted by the agent would be tantamount to a claim of privilege by the corporation—which of course possesses no such privilege." The policy reason for this limitation on the custodian's claim of privilege is that if not for this limitation, governmental efforts to investigate and prosecute white-collar crime by corporations and their agents would be seriously impaired. The fact that the custodian of corporate records is not entitled to assert an individual Fifth Amendment privilege to avoid producing the documents does not mean, however, that the custodian's act of production may be used against him. *Braswell* establishes that the government cannot make evidentiary use of the custodian's act of production.

Doe argues, however, that the above principles do not apply to him because, he contends, the subpoenaed documents are not in fact XYZ corporate records. Doe instead maintains that the records are his, either because they pertain to his personal telephone lines or because he obtained copies of the records from XYZ's files or from the telephone company for his own personal use. We disagree with Doe's characterization of the records. It is superficial for Doe to assert that the original records belonged to him because they pertained to his personal telephone lines. Although the lines may have been listed in his name, there was evidence that XYZ paid all of the bills, that Doe did not reimburse XYZ for these payments, that XYZ deducted the payments on its income tax returns, and that the telephone bills and statements had been stored in corporate files on corporate premises. The district court found that the documents were in fact XYZ corporate records. That finding was amply supported by the evidence.

We also reject Doe's assertion that he owns the subpoenaed records because all that remain in existence are copies. Copies of corporate records do not become the personal property of an individual merely because he caused the copies to be made. Allowing a corporate officer to obtain copies of corporate records and secure for them greater protection than could be enjoyed for the originals would create a rule ripe for abuse.

Further, even if we construed the copies of the telephone company records as papers belonging to Doe, compelled production of those papers would not violate Doe's privilege against self-incrimination. The Fifth Amendment does not proscribe the compelled production of every sort of incriminating evidence. It applies only when the accused is compelled to make a *testimonial* communication that is incriminating. When, as is the case here, the documents sought by the government were not prepared by the person subpoenaed and contain no testimonial declarations by him, a subpoena duces tecum does not compel self-incrimination.

Neither would the act of producing copies of the telephone company statements and bills cause Doe to incriminate himself. The subpoenaed documents were prepared and sent by the telephone company in the ordinary course of its business. There is no dispute that the bills were received or that the bills were paid by XYZ. The mere fact that Doe has or produces the copies of the records will not constitute testimonial self-incrimination.

We conclude that the district court correctly ruled that Doe's Fifth Amendment privilege does not entitle him to prevent Paul-Weiss from complying with the subpoena.

Order compelling Paul-Weiss to produce subpoenaed documents affirmed.

Note: In a later portion of the opinion not set forth here, the Second Circuit concluded that the district court correctly rejected Doe's and Paul-Weiss's attorney–client privilege and attorney-work-product privilege arguments.

Another Fifth Amendment provision worthy of note is the **Double Jeopardy Clause.** This provision protects defendants from multiple criminal prosecutions for the same offense. It prevents an accused from being charged with more than one count of the same statutory violation for one offense, such as being charged with two robbery violations for a one-time robbery of one individual. This clause also prevents a second prosecution for the same offense after the defendant has been acquitted or convicted of that offense. Moreover, it bars the imposition of multiple punishments for the same offense.

The Double Jeopardy Clause does not, however, preclude the possibility that a single criminal act may lead to more than one criminal prosecution. One criminal act may produce several statutory violations, all of which may give rise to prosecution. For example, a defendant who commits rape may also be prosecuted for battery, assault with a deadly weapon, and kidnapping if the facts of the case indicate that the relevant statutes were violated. In addition, the Supreme Court has long used a "same elements" test to determine what constitutes the same offense.[32] This means that a single criminal act with multiple victims (e.g., a restaurant robbery in which several patrons are robbed) could result in several prosecutions because the identity of each victim would be an additional fact or element of proof in each case.

In addition, the Double Jeopardy Clause does not protect against multiple prosecutions by different sovereigns. A conviction or acquittal in a state prosecution does not prevent a subsequent federal prosecution for a federal offense arising out of the same event, or vice versa. This principle was illustrated in recent years by the prosecutions stemming from the highly publicized beating of motorist Rodney King at the hands of Los Angeles police officers. After the officers were found not guilty in state prosecutions stemming from the beating, two of them were found guilty in federal prosecutions for violations of King's civil rights.

Finally, the Double Jeopardy Clause does not bar a private plaintiff from pursuing a *civil* case (normally for one or more of the intentional torts discussed in Chapter 6) against a defendant who was criminally prosecuted by the government for the same alleged conduct. The headline-dominating criminal and civil cases against O.J. Simpson furnish the best-known recent example of this principle.

The Sixth Amendment   The Sixth Amendment contains several provisions applicable to criminal cases. It entitles criminal defendants to a speedy trial by an impartial jury and guarantees them the right to confront and cross-examine the witnesses against them. The Sixth Amendment also gives the accused in a criminal case the right "to have the assistance of counsel" in her defense. This provision has been interpreted to mean not only that the accused may employ her own attorney but also that an indigent criminal defendant is entitled to

---

[32]*United States v. Dixon,* 509 U.S. 688 (U.S. Sup. Ct. 1993); *Blockburger v. United States,* 284 U.S. 299 (U.S. Sup. Ct. 1932).

FIGURE 4

Major Procedural Safeguards

Fourth Amendment

• Prohibits unreasonable searches and seizures

Fifth Amendment

• Due Process Clause
  Presumption of innocence
  Prohibits vague criminal statutes
  Requires basic procedural and substantive fairness
• Right to silence
  Double Jeopardy Clause

Sixth Amendment

• Speedy trial
• Impartial jury
• Confront and cross-examine prosecution's witnesses
• Right to counsel

Eighth Amendment

• Forbids cruel and unusual punishments

---

court-appointed counsel.[33] Included in the previously discussed *Miranda* warnings is a requirement that the police inform the accused of his right to counsel before custodial interrogation begins. *Edwards v. Arizona* established that once the accused has requested the assistance of counsel, he may not as a general rule be interrogated further until counsel is made available to him.[34] The Supreme Court later held that the *Edwards* rule against further questioning is triggered only by an *unambiguous* request for counsel.[35] In *McNeil v. Wisconsin,* the Court provided further latitude for law enforcement officers by holding that if a defendant has made an in-court request for an attorney's assistance regarding a crime with which he has been formally charged, that request does not preclude police interrogation of him—in the absence of counsel—regarding another unrelated crime.[36]

Finally, an accused is entitled to *effective* assistance of counsel. This means that the accused is entitled to representation at a point in the proceedings when an attorney may effectively assist him,[37] and to reasonably competent representation by that attorney. Inadequate assistance of counsel can be a proper basis for setting aside a conviction and ordering a new trial.[38]

Figure 4 summarizes the major procedural safeguards enjoyed by defendants under our criminal justice system.

WHITE–COLLAR CRIMES AND THE DILEMMAS OF CORPORATE CONTROL

Introduction

White-collar crime is the term broadly used to describe a wide variety of nonviolent criminal offenses committed by businesspersons and business organizations. Although this term often includes offenses committed by employees against their employers (such as theft, embezzlement, or accepting a bribe), our discussion will focus on criminal offenses committed by corporate employers and employees against society. Each year, corporate crime costs consumers billions of dollars. It takes various forms, from consumer fraud, securities fraud, and tax evasion to price-fixing, environmental pollution, and other regulatory violations. Corporate crime presents our legal system with a variety of problems—problems we have failed to resolve satisfactorily.

Corporations form the backbone of the most successful economic system in history. They dominate the international economic scene and provide us with substantial benefits in the forms of efficiently produced goods and services. Yet these same corporations may pollute the environment, swindle their customers, produce dangerously defective products, and conspire with others to injure or destroy competition. How are we to achieve effective control over these large organizations so important to our existence? Increasingly, we have come to rely on the criminal law as a major corporate control

---

[33]*Gideon v. Wainwright,* 372 U.S. 335 (U.S. Sup. Ct. 1963).

[34]451 U.S. 477 (U.S. Sup. Ct. 1981).

[35]*Davis v. United States,* 512 U.S. 452 (U.S. Sup. Ct. 1994) (concluding that "Maybe I should talk to a lawyer" was too ambiguous to trigger the *Edwards* rule).

[36]501 U.S. 171 (U.S. Sup. Ct. 1991).

[37]*Powell v. Alabama,* 287 U.S. 45 (U.S. Sup. Ct. 1932).

[38]In *Strickland v. Washington,* 446 U.S. 668 (U.S. Sup. Ct. 1984), the Court held that a defendant's conviction would not be set aside unless his attorney's performance fell below an objective standard of reasonableness and so prejudiced him as to result in the denial of a fair trial. As applied, this standard makes ineffective assistance of counsel claims rather difficult ones for convicted defendants to invoke successfully.

instrument. The criminal law, however, was developed with individual wrongdoers in mind. Who is at fault when a large organization causes social harm? Corporate crime is *organizational* in nature. Any given corporate action may be the product of the combined actions of many individuals acting within the corporate hierarchy. It may be that no individual had sufficient knowledge to possess the *mens rea* necessary for criminal responsibility under traditional criminal law principles. Moreover, criminally penalizing corporations raises special problems in view of the obvious inability to apply standard sanctions such as imprisonment to legal entities.

Evolution of Corporate Criminal Liability

The common law initially rejected the notion that corporations could be criminally responsible for their employees' actions. Early corporations, small in size and number, had little impact on public life. Their small size made it relatively easy to pinpoint individual wrongdoers within the corporation.

As corporations grew in size and power, however, the social need to control their activities grew accordingly. Not coincidentally, the rules governing corporate criminal liability also began to change. Legislatures enacted statutes creating *public welfare offenses* of which corporations were convicted.[39] These regulatory offenses did not require proof of *mens rea*. By the turn of this century, American courts had begun to impose criminal liability on corporations for general criminal offenses that required proof of *mens rea*. This expansion of corporate criminal liability involved imputing the criminal intent of corporate employees to the corporation in a fashion similar to the imposition of tort or contract liability on corporations under the *respondeat superior* doctrine.[40]

Corporations now may face criminal liability for almost any criminal offense if the statute in question indicates a legislative intent to hold corporations responsible. This legislative intent requirement is

sometimes problematic. Many state criminal statutes are based on common law crimes and may contain language suggesting an intent to hold only humans liable. For example, state manslaughter statutes often define the offense as "the killing of one human being by the act of another." When statutes are framed, however, in more general terms—such as by referring to "persons"—courts are generally willing to apply them to corporate defendants.

Corporate Criminal Liability Today

Under the modern rule on corporate criminal liability, a corporation may be held liable for criminal offenses committed by employees who *acted within the scope of their employment and for the benefit of the corporation.* A major corporate criminal liability issue centers around the classes of corporate employees whose intent can be imputed to the corporation. Some commentators argue that a corporation should be criminally responsible only for offenses committed by high corporate officials or those linked to them by authorization or acquiescence. (Virtually all courts impose criminal liability on a corporation under such circumstances.) Such arguments reflect fairness notions, for if any group of corporate employees can fairly be said to constitute a corporation's mind, that group is its top officers and directors.

The problem with imposing corporate liability only on the basis of top corporate officers' actions or knowledge is that such a policy often insulates the corporation from liability. Many corporate offenses may be directly traceable only to middle managers or more subordinate corporate employees. It may be impossible to demonstrate that any higher-level corporate official had sufficient knowledge to constitute *mens rea*. Recognizing this problem, the federal courts have adopted a general rule that a corporation can be criminally liable for the actions of any of its agents, regardless of whether any link between the agents and higher-level corporate officials can be demonstrated.

Problems with Corporate Criminal Liability
Despite the legal theories that justify corporate criminal liability, the punishment of corporations remains problematic. Does a criminal conviction stigmatize a corporation in the same way it stigmatizes an individual? The idea of viewing a corporation as a criminal may be difficult for many people

[39]These statutes followed the lead of early corporate criminal liability cases in which criminal liability was imposed on public corporations such as municipalities—initially the most common type of corporation—for failures to perform such public duties as road and bridge repair.

[40]Chapter 35 discusses *respondeat superior* in detail. For an early landmark case on this subject, see *New York Central & Hudson River R.R. v. United States,* 212 U.S. 481 (U.S. Sup. Ct. 1909).

to embrace. Perhaps the only stigma resulting from a corporate criminal conviction is felt by corporate employees, many of whom are entirely innocent of any wrongdoing. Is it just to punish the innocent in an attempt to punish the guilty?

And what of the cash fine, the primary punishment imposed on convicted corporations? Most critics of contemporary corporate control strategies maintain that fines imposed on convicted corporations tend to be too small to provide effective deterrence. These critics urge the use of fines keyed in some fashion to the corporate defendant's wealth, such as a percentage of the defendant's income or total capital. Larger fines may lead to undesirable results, however, if the corporate defendant ultimately passes along the fines to its customers (through higher prices), shareholders (through lower dividends or no dividends), or employees (through lower wages). Moreover, fines large enough to threaten corporate solvency may harm corporate employees and those economically dependent on the corporation's financial well-being. Most of these persons, however, neither had the power to prevent the violation nor derived any benefit from it. The managers responsible for a violation may avoid the imposition of direct burdens on them when the fine is assessed against the corporation. Given the randomness inherent in criminal fines, legislatures may be unwilling to authorize—and courts reluctant to impose—fines large enough to produce deterrence.

Still other deficiencies make fines less-than-adequate corporate control devices. Fine strategies assume that all corporations are rationally acting profit-maximizers. Fines of sufficient size, it is argued, will erode the profit drive underlying most corporate violations. Numerous studies of actual corporate behavior, however, suggest that many corporations are neither profit-maximizers nor rational actors. Mature firms with well-established market shares may embrace goals other than profit maximization, such as technological prominence, increased market share, or higher employee salaries. In addition, the interests of managers who make corporate decisions and establish corporate policies may not coincide with the long-range economic interests of their corporate employers. The prospect that their employer could have to pay a substantial fine at some future point may not trouble top managers, who tend to have relatively short terms in office and are often compensated in part by large bonuses keyed to year-end profitability.

Individual Liability for Corporate Crime

Individuals committing criminal offenses while acting in corporate capacities have always been personally subjected to criminal liability. Most European nations reject corporate criminal liability and rely exclusively on individual criminal responsibility. In view of the problems associated with imposing criminal liability on corporations, individual liability may seem a more attractive control device. Besides being more consistent with traditional criminal law notions about the personal nature of guilt, individual liability may provide better deterrence than corporate liability if it enables society to use the criminal punishment threat against the persons who make important corporate decisions. The prospect of personal liability may cause individuals to resist corporate pressures to violate the law. If guilty individuals are identified and punished, the criminal law's purposes may be achieved without harm to innocent employees, shareholders, and consumers.

Problems with Individual Liability   Attractive as it may sound, individual liability also poses significant problems when applied to corporate acts. Identifying responsible individuals within the corporate hierarchy becomes difficult—and frequently impossible—if we follow traditional notions and require proof of criminal intent. Business decisions leading to corporate wrongs often result from the collective actions of numerous corporate employees, none of whom had complete knowledge or specific criminal intent. Other corporate crimes are structural in the sense that they result from internal bureaucratic failures rather than the conscious actions of any individual or group.

Proving culpability on the part of high-level executives may be particularly difficult. Bad news sometimes does not reach them; other times, they consciously avoid knowledge that would lead to criminal responsibility. It therefore may be possible to demonstrate culpability only on the part of middle-level managers. Juries may be unwilling to convict such individuals, however, if they seem to be scapegoats for their unindicted superiors. Even when a culpable individual is identified, significant problems can prevent meaningful application of the criminal sanction. The individual in question may have died, retired, or been transferred to another post outside the jurisdiction where the offense occurred. If convicted, white-collar defendants usually are either not imprisoned or imprisoned for a short period of time. This phenomenon is generally attributed to public doubts about the moral culpability involved in certain white-collar offenses and to the positive image that such offenders—often well-educated, well-spoken community leaders—may possess. Most convicted white-collar offenders receive fines that may be small in comparison to their wealth.

These difficulties in imposing criminal penalties on individual corporate employees have led to the creation of regulatory offenses imposing strict or vicarious liability on corporate officers. Strict liability offenses dispense with the requirement of proof of criminal intent on the defendant's part but ordinarily require proof that the defendant committed some wrongful act. Vicarious liability offenses impose criminal liability on a defendant for the acts of third parties (normally, employees under the defendant's personal supervision), but may require proof of some form of *mens rea,* such as the defendant's negligent or reckless failure to supervise. Statutes often combine these two approaches by making corporate executives liable for the acts or omissions of corporate employees without requiring proof of criminal intent on the part of the employees. *United States v. Park,* discussed in Figure 5, is a famous example of such a prosecution.

Critics of strict liability offenses often argue that *mens rea* is a basic principle in our legal system and that it is unjust to stigmatize with a criminal conviction persons who are not morally culpable. In addition, critics commonly doubt that strict liability statutes produce the deterrence sought by their proponents. Such statutes may reduce the moral impact of the criminal sanction if they apply it to

---

FIGURE 5

A Note on United States v. Park, *421 U.S. 658 (U.S. Sup. Ct. 1975)*

FACTS AND PROCEDURAL HISTORY

John R. Park was CEO of Acme Markets, Inc., a national retail food chain with approximately 36,000 employees, 874 retail outlets, and 16 warehouses. Acme and Park were charged with five counts of violating the federal Food, Drug, and Cosmetic Act (the Act) by storing food shipped in interstate commerce in warehouses where it was exposed to rodent contamination. The violations were detected during Food and Drug Administration (FDA) inspections of Acme's Baltimore warehouse. Inspectors saw evidence of rodent infestation and unsanitary conditions, such as mouse droppings on the floor of the hanging meat room and alongside bales of lime Jell-O, and a hole chewed by a rodent in a bale of Jell-O. The FDA notified Park by letter of these findings.

Upon checking with Acme's vice president for legal affairs, Park learned that the Baltimore division vice president "was investigating the situation immediately and would be taking corrective action." An FDA inspection three months after the first one disclosed continued rodent contamination at the Baltimore warehouse despite improved sanitation there. The criminal charges were then filed against Acme and Park. Acme pleaded guilty; Park refused to do so. Park was convicted on each count, but the court of appeals overturned the conviction.

THE SUPREME COURT'S DECISION

The Supreme Court, however, reversed. In sustaining Park's conviction, the Court noted that in view of the substantial public interest in purity of food, the Act did not require awareness of wrongdoing as an element of criminal conduct. This did not mean, however, that a person "remotely entangled in the proscribed shipment" was at risk of being criminally convicted. Instead, the defendant must be shown to have had "a responsible share" in the violation, such as by failing to exercise authority and supervisory responsibility. The Court emphasized that the Act imposes on supervisory personnel the "highest standard of foresight and vigilance." This includes a duty to seek out and remedy violations when they occur, and a duty to implement measures to prevent violations from occurring.

Although one who was "powerless" to prevent or correct the violation cannot be held criminally responsible under the Act, the Court emphasized that Park was hardly powerless. He had the authority and responsibility to prevent or correct the prohibited condition. The evidence showed that prior to the Baltimore warehouse inspections giving rise to the criminal charges, Park was advised by the FDA of unsanitary conditions in another Acme warehouse. According to the Court, Park thus acquired notice—prior to the time that the Baltimore warehouse violations were discovered—that he could not rely on his previously employed system of delegation to subordinates to prevent or correct unsanitary conditions at company warehouses. Despite evidence indicating Park's prior awareness of this system's deficiencies well before the Baltimore violations were discovered, Park had not instituted any new procedures designed to prevent violations of the Act. The Court therefore concluded that his conviction should stand.

relatively trivial offenses. Moreover, they may not result in enough convictions or sufficiently severe penalties to produce deterrence because juries and judges are unwilling to convict or punish defendants who may not be morally culpable. Although statutes creating strict liability offenses are generally held constitutional, they are disfavored by courts. Most courts require a clear indication of a legislative intent to dispense with the *mens rea* element.[41]

Strict liability offenses are also criticized on the ground that even if responsible individuals within the corporation are convicted and punished appropriately, individual liability unaccompanied by corporate liability is unlikely to achieve effective corporate control. If immune from criminal liability, corporations could benefit financially from employees' violations of the law. Individual liability, unlike a corporate fine, does not force a corporation to give up the profits flowing from a violation. Thus, the corporation would have no incentive to avoid future violations. Incarcerated offenders would merely be replaced by others who might eventually yield to the pressures that produced the violations in the first place. Corporate liability, however, may sometimes encourage corporate efforts to prevent future violations. When an offense has occurred but no identifiable individual is sufficiently culpable to justify an individual prosecution of him or her, corporate liability is uniquely appropriate.

New Directions

The preceding discussion suggests that future efforts at corporate control are likely to include both corporate and individual criminal liability. It also suggests, however, that new approaches are necessary if society is to gain more effective control over corporate activities.

Various novel criminal penalties have been suggested in the individual liability setting. For example, white-collar offenders could be deprived of leisure time or sentenced to render public service rather than being incarcerated or fined. Some have even suggested the licensing of managers, with license suspensions as a penalty for offenders. The common thread in these and other similar approaches is an attempt to create penalties that are meaningful yet not so severe that judges and juries are unwilling to impose them.

A promising recent suggestion regarding corporate liability involves imaginative judicial use of corporate probation for convicted corporate offenders. For example, courts could require convicted corporations to do self-studies identifying the source of a violation and proposing appropriate steps to prevent future violations. If bureaucratic failures caused the violation, the court could order a limited restructuring of the corporation's internal decisionmaking processes as a condition of obtaining probation or avoiding a penalty. Possible orders might include requiring the collection and monitoring of the data necessary to discover or prevent future violations and mandating the creation of new executive positions to monitor such data. Restructuring would minimize the previously discussed harm to innocent persons that often accompanies corporate financial penalties. In addition, restructuring could be a more effective way to achieve corporate rehabilitation than relying exclusively on a corporation's desire to avoid future fines as an incentive to police itself. Because restructuring would represent a new form of governmental intrusion into the private sector, however, it should be applied sparingly and with discretion.

The Federal Sentencing Guidelines, discussed earlier in this chapter in Figure 1, contain good reasons for corporations to institute measures to prevent regulatory violations. Under the subset of rules known as the Corporate Sentencing Guidelines, organizations convicted of violating federal law may face greatly increased penalties for certain offenses, with some crimes carrying fines as high as $290 million. The penalty imposed on an organization depends on its "culpability score," which increases (thus calling for a more severe penalty) if, for example, high-level corporate officers were involved in the offense or the organization had a history of such offenses. Even apart from the potentially severe penalties, however, the Corporate Sentencing Guidelines provide an incentive for corporations to adopt compliance programs designed "to prevent and detect violations of the law." The presence of an effective compliance program can reduce the corporation's culpability score for sentencing purposes. Prior to the time the Corporate Sentencing Guidelines took effect, courts generally

---

[41]See, for example, *United States v. U.S. Gypsum Co.,* 425 U.S. 422 (U.S. Sup. Ct. 1978).

concluded that the existence of a compliance program should not operate as a mitigating factor in the sentencing of a convicted organization.

IMPORTANT WHITE–COLLAR CRIMES

Regulatory Offenses

Numerous state and federal regulatory statutes on a wide range of subjects prescribe criminal as well as civil liability for violations. The Food, Drug, and Cosmetic Act, at issue in the case discussed in Figure 5, is an example of such a statute. Several other major federal regulatory offenses are discussed in detail in later chapters. These include violations of the Sherman Antitrust Act, the Securities Act of 1933, the Securities Exchange Act of 1934, the Clean Waters Act of 1972, the Resource Conservation and Recovery Act, and the Electronic Funds Transfer Act.

Fraudulent Acts

Many business crimes involve some fraudulent conduct. In most states, it is a crime to obtain money or property by fraudulent pretenses, issue fraudulent checks, make false credit statements, or give short weights or measures. Certain forms of fraud in bankruptcy proceedings, such as false claims by creditors or fraudulent concealment or transfer of a debtor's assets, are federal criminal offenses.[42] In addition, federal mail fraud and wire fraud statutes make criminal the use of the mail, telephone, or telegrams to accomplish a fraudulent scheme. Another federal law makes it a crime to travel or otherwise use facilities in interstate commerce in order to commit criminal acts.

Bribery

State and federal law have long made it a crime to offer public officials gifts, favors, or anything of value to influence official decisions for private benefit. In 1977, Congress passed the Foreign Corrupt Practices Act, which criminalized giving anything of value to officials of foreign governments in an attempt to influence their official actions.[43] Most states also have enacted commercial bribery statutes that outlaw offering kickbacks and payoffs to private individuals to secure some commercial advantage.

RICO

When Congress passed the Racketeer Influenced and Corrupt Organizations Act (RICO) as part of the Organized Crime Control Act of 1970, lawmakers were primarily concerned about organized crime's increasing entry into legitimate business enterprises. RICO's broad language, however, allows the statute to be applied in a wide variety of cases having nothing to do with organized crime. As a result, RICO has become one of the most controversial pieces of legislation affecting business in our legal history. Supporters of RICO argue that it is an effective and much-needed tool for attacking a broad range of unethical business practices. Its critics, however, see RICO as an overbroad statute that needlessly taints business reputations. Critics also argue that RICO has operated unduly to favor plaintiffs in civil litigation rather than serving as an aid to law enforcement.

Criminal RICO Under RICO, it is a federal crime to: (1) use income derived from a "pattern of racketeering activity" to acquire an interest in an enterprise, (2) acquire or maintain an interest in an enterprise through a pattern of racketeering activity, (3) conduct or participate in the affairs of an enterprise through a pattern of racketeering activity, or (4) conspire to do any of the preceding acts. RICO is a compound statute because it requires proof of "predicate" criminal offenses that constitute the necessary pattern of racketeering activity.

Racketeering activity includes the commission of any of more than 30 state or federal criminal offenses. Although most offenses that qualify (e.g., arson, gambling, extortion) have no relation to normal business transactions, such offenses as mail and wire fraud, securities fraud, and bribery are also included. Thus, almost any business fraud may be alleged to be a racketeering activity. To show a *pattern* of such activity, the prosecution must first

---

[42]Chapter 29 discusses bankruptcy in detail.

[43]Chapter 44 discusses the Foreign Corrupt Practices Act in detail.

prove the defendant's commission of at least two acts of racketeering activity within a 10-year period. The pattern requirement also calls for proof that these acts are related and amount to (or pose the threat of) continuing racketeering activity. Most courts have interpreted the statutory term *enterprise* broadly to include partnerships and unincorporated associations as well as corporations.

Individuals found guilty of RICO violations are subject to substantial fines and imprisonment for up to 20 years. In addition, RICO violators risk the forfeiture of any interest gained in any enterprise as a result of a violation, as well as forfeiture of property derived from the prohibited racketeering activity. To prevent defendants from hiding assets that may be forfeitable upon conviction, federal prosecutors may seek pretrial orders freezing a defendant's assets. Some RICO critics argue that the harm such a freeze may work on a defendant's ability to conduct business, coupled with the threat of forfeiture of most or all of the business upon conviction, has led some defendants to make plea bargains rather than risk all by fighting prosecutions they believe to be unjustified.

Civil RICO Under RICO, the government may also seek various civil penalties for violations. These include divestiture of a defendant's interest in an enterprise, the dissolution or reorganization of the enterprise, and injunctions against future racketeering activities by the defendant.

RICO's most controversial sections, however, are those allowing private individuals to recover treble damages (three times their actual loss) and attorney's fees for injuries caused by a statutory violation. To qualify for recovery under RICO, a plaintiff must prove that the defendant violated RICO's provisions (as explained above) and that the plaintiff was "injured in his business or property" as a result. Aided by the Supreme Court's refusal, in *Sedima, S.P.R.L. v. Imrex Co.,*[44] to give a narrowing construction to the broadly phrased RICO, private plaintiffs have brought a large number of civil RICO cases in recent years. In *Sedima,* the Court rejected, as an erroneous statutory interpretation, some lower federal courts' approach of requiring civil RICO plaintiffs to prove that the defendant had actually been criminally convicted of a predicate offense. In addition, the Court rejected the argument that civil RICO plaintiffs should be expected to prove a "distinct racketeering injury" as a precondition of recovery. The Court acknowledged lower courts' concern about RICO's breadth and noted the fact that most civil RICO suits are filed against legitimate businesses rather than against "the archetypal, intimidating mobster." Nevertheless, the Court observed that "[t]his defect—if defect it is—is inherent in the statute as written, and its correction must lie with Congress."

The *Northwestern Bell* case, which follows, focuses on the necessary "pattern of racketeering activity" element of a RICO claim.

---

[44]473 U.S. 479 (U.S. Sup. Ct. 1985).

H.J. INC. v. NORTHWESTERN BELL TELEPHONE CO. 492 U.S. 229 (U.S. Sup. Ct. 1989)

C*ustomers of Northwestern Bell Telephone Company filed a class action suit alleging violations of RICO based on allegations that between 1980 and 1986, Northwestern Bell sought to influence members of the Minnesota Public Utilities Commission (MPUC) to approve rates for Northwestern in excess of a fair and reasonable amount. They alleged that Northwestern made cash payments to commissioners, negotiated with them regarding future employment, and paid for parties and meals, tickets to sporting events, and airline tickets. These acts, they alleged, were in violation of the state bribery statute and state common law prohibiting bribery. The district court dismissed their civil RICO claims because the complaint failed to allege the "multiple illegal schemes" that the Eighth Circuit Court of Appeals had previously held were necessary to establish a "pattern of racketeering activity" under RICO.* ∽

Brennan, Justice In *Sedima, S.P.R.L. v. Imrex Co.,* we acknowledged concern in some quarters over civil RICO's use against "legitimate" businesses, as well as "mobsters and organized criminals." But we suggested that RICO's expansive uses "appear to be primarily the result of the breadth of the predicate offenses, and the failure of Congress and the courts to develop a meaningful concept of 'pattern.' " Congress has done nothing in the interim to illuminate RICO's key requirement of a pattern of racketeering activity, and developing a meaningful concept of "pattern" within the existing statutory framework has proved to be no easy task.

It is, nevertheless, a task we must undertake in order to decide this case. Our guides must be the text of the statute and its legislative history. We find no support in those sources for the proposition that predicate acts of racketeering may form a pattern only when they are a part of separate illegal schemes. Nor can we agree with those courts that have suggested that a pattern is established by proving two predicate acts, or with *amici* in this case who argue that the word "pattern" refers only to predicates that are indicative of a perpetrator involved in organized crime.

As we remarked in *Sedima,* the section of the statute headed "definitions," section 1961, does not so much define a pattern of racketeering activity as state a minimum necessary condition for the existence of such a pattern. Unlike other provisions in section 1961 that tell us what various concepts used in the Act "mean," section 1961(5) says of the phrase "pattern of racketeering activity" only that it "requires at least two acts of racketeering activity, one of which occurred after October 15, 1970 and the last of which occurred within 10 years after the commission of a prior act of racketeering activity."

Section 1961(5) does indicate that Congress envisioned circumstances in which no more than two predicates would be necessary to establish a pattern. But the statement that a pattern "requires at least" two predicates implies that while two acts are necessary, they may not be sufficient. Section 1961(5) concerns only the minimum *number* of predicates necessary to establish a pattern; and it assumes that there is something to a RICO pattern *beyond* simply the number of predicate acts involved. The legislative history bears out this interpretation, for the principal sponsor of the Senate bill expressly indicated that "proof of two acts of racketeering activity, without more, does not establish a pattern." Section 1961(5) does not identify, though, these additional prerequisites for establishing the existence of a RICO pattern.

In normal usage, the word "pattern" here would be taken to require more than just a multiplicity of racketeering predicates. A "pattern" is an "arrangement or order of things or activity," 11 Oxford English Dictionary 357 (2d ed. 1989). It is not the

number of predicates but the relationship that they bear to each other or to some external organizing principle that renders them "ordered" or "arranged."

RICO's legislative history reveals Congress' intent that to prove a pattern of racketeering activity a plaintiff or prosecutor must show that the racketeering predicates are related, *and* that they amount to or pose a threat of continued criminal activity. In the Organized Crime Control Act of 1970, Congress defined a pattern requirement solely in terms of the *relationship* of the defendant's criminal acts one to another: "criminal conduct forms a pattern if it embraces criminal acts that have the same or similar purposes, results, participants, victims, or methods of commission, or otherwise are interrelated by distinguishing characteristics and are not isolated events." We have no reason to suppose that Congress had in mind for RICO's pattern component any more constrained a notion of the relationships between predicates that would suffice.

RICO's legislative history also tells us, however, that the relatedness of racketeering activities is not alone enough to satisfy the pattern element. It must also be shown that the predicates themselves amount to, or that they otherwise constitute a threat of, *continuing* racketeering activity. It is this aspect of RICO's pattern element that has spawned the "multiple scheme" test adopted by the Court of Appeals in this case. But although proof that a defendant has been involved in multiple criminal schemes would certainly be highly relevant to the inquiry into the continuity of the defendant's racketeering activity, it is implausible to suppose that Congress thought continuity might be shown *only* by proof of multiple schemes. We adopt a less inflexible approach that seems to us to derive from a common-sense, everyday understanding of RICO's language and Congress' gloss on it. What a plaintiff or prosecutor must prove is continuity of racketeering activity, or its threat.

A party alleging a RICO violation may demonstrate continuity over a closed period by proving a series of related predicates extending over a substantial period of time. Predicate acts extending over a few weeks or months and threatening no future criminal conduct do not satisfy this requirement: Congress was concerned in RICO with long-term criminal conduct. Often a RICO action will be brought before continuity can be established in this way. In such cases, liability depends on whether the *threat* of continuity is demonstrated.

The threat of continuity is sufficiently established where the predicates can be attributed to a defendant operating as part of a long-term association that exists for criminal purposes. Such associations include, but extend well beyond, those traditionally grouped under the phrase "organized crime." The continuity requirement is likewise satisfied where it is shown that the predicates are a regular way of conducting defendant's ongoing legitimate business, or of conducting or participating in an ongoing legitimate RICO "enterprise."

Plaintiffs' complaint alleges that at different times over the course of at least a 6-year period the defendants gave five members of the MPUC numerous bribes, in several different forms, with the objective—in which they were allegedly successful—of causing these Commissioners to approve unfair and unreasonable rates. RICO defines bribery as a racketeering activity, so plaintiffs have alleged multiple predicate acts. They may be able to prove that the multiple predicates alleged constitute a "pattern of racketeering activity," in that they satisfy the requirements of relationship and continuity. The acts of bribery alleged are said to be related to a common purpose, to influence Commissioners to win approval of unfairly high rates for Northwestern Bell. Furthermore, the racketeering predicates allegedly occurred over at least a 6-year period, which may be sufficient to satisfy the continuity requirement. Alternatively, a threat of continuity might be established at trial by showing that the alleged bribes were a regular way of conducting or participating in the conduct of the alleged and ongoing RICO enterprise, the MPUC. The Court of Appeals thus erred in affirming the District Court's dismissal of plaintiff's complaint for failure to plead "a pattern of racketeering activity."

Judgment reversed in favor of plaintiffs; case remanded for trial.

Over roughly the past decade, various RICO reform proposals have been unsuccessfully introduced in Congress. A 1995 reform measure that did become law, however, established that a civil RICO case cannot be based on conduct that would have been actionable as securities fraud unless the conduct amounting to securities fraud had resulted in a criminal conviction. Although the Supreme Court has generally continued to regard RICO reform as the task of Congress, the Court has in recent years issued two decisions that critics of frequent uses of civil RICO have found encouraging. Those decisions are discussed in Figure 6.

COMPUTER CRIME

As computers have come to play an increasingly important role in our society, new opportunities for crime have resulted. In some instances, computers may be used to accomplish "traditional" crimes such as theft, embezzlement, espionage, and fraud. In others, computers or the information stored there may be targets of crimes such as unauthorized access, vandalism, tampering, or theft of services. The law's response to computer crimes has evolved with this new technology. For example, computer hacking—once viewed by some as a mischievous but clever activity—can now lead to significant prison sentences and fines.

The technical nature of computer crime tends to complicate its detection and prosecution. Traditional criminal statutes have often proven inadequate because they tend not to address explicitly the types of crime associated with the use of computers. Assume, for example, that a general statute on theft defines the offense in terms of stealing "property," and that the defendant is charged with violating the statute by taking and using computer data without authorization. The court could decide to dismiss this case if categorizing data stored in a computer as "property" strikes the court as a strained interpretation of the statute. Although some courts have interpreted existing criminal laws narrowly so as to exclude instances of computer abuse, other courts have construed them more broadly. In light of the uncertainties attending statutory interpretation, legislatures on the state and federal levels have become increasingly aware of the need to revise their criminal codes to be certain that they explicitly cover computer crime.

Almost all states have now enacted criminal statutes specifically outlawing certain abuses of computers. Common provisions prohibit such acts

FIGURE 6

A Note on Other Civil RICO Decisions of the Supreme Court

HOLMES V. SECURITIES INVESTOR PROTECTION CORP.

In *Holmes v. Securities Investor Protection Corp.,* 503 U.S. 258 (U.S. Sup. Ct. 1992), the Court held that plaintiffs in treble damages cases under RICO must demonstrate that the harm they experienced was directly and proximately caused by the defendants' wrongful conduct. Plaintiffs whose injury was only an indirect result of the defendants' actions do not have legal standing to sue.

The defendant in *Holmes* allegedly engaged in fraudulent stock-manipulation schemes that caused certain broker-dealers to become insolvent and unable to meet their obligations to customers. When the broker-dealers collapsed financially, Securities Investor Protection Corp. (SIPC), a private corporation authorized by federal law, fulfilled its legal obligation to provide funds to satisfy the claims of customers of the insolvent broker-dealers. SIPC then brought a treble damages action under RICO against defendant Holmes on the theory that SIPC, having supplied the funds to pay the customers of the failed broker-dealers, stood in the shoes of the customers in terms of collecting losses caused by Holmes's alleged stock-manipulation schemes. The Court noted that even if SIPC stood in the customers' shoes, any loss being alleged by SIPC was too indirect to support a RICO claim against Holmes. The harm necessary to support a RICO claim would instead have been that experienced by the broker-dealers, whose financial demise presumably stemmed directly from Holmes's actions.

REVES V. ERNST & YOUNG

In recent years, the highly attractive treble damages and attorney's fee provisions in RICO have led to the frequent use of RICO by plaintiffs in commercial fraud cases. Stockbrokers, banks, insurance companies, and accounting firms have been typical targets of such civil suits. In *Reves v. Ernst & Young,* 507 U.S. 170 (U.S. Sup. Ct. 1993), however, the Court limited plaintiffs' ability to use civil RICO against "outside" professionals such as accounting firms when financial institutions involved in fraudulent activities fail. The Court held that accounting firms and "other" outside professionals who performed work for such a financial institution are potentially liable under RICO only if they "participate[d] in the management or operation of the enterprise." Merely providing auditing services to the financial institution, without more, would not be sufficient to constitute participation in the management or operation of the enterprise.

as obtaining access to a computer system without authorization, tampering with files or causing damage to a system (e.g., by spreading a virus or deleting files), invading the privacy of others, using a computer to commit fraud or theft, and trafficking in passwords or access codes.

On the federal level, computer crime has been prosecuted with some success under existing federal statutes, primarily those forbidding mail fraud, wire fraud, transportation of stolen property, and thefts of property. As has been true at the state level, successful prosecution of these cases often depends on broad interpretation of the statutory prerequisites. Another federal law deals more directly with improper uses of computers. Among the crimes covered by this federal statute are intentionally gaining unauthorized access to a computer used by or for the U.S. government, trafficking in passwords and other access devices, and using a computer to obtain government information that is protected from disclosure. It is also a crime to gain unauthorized access to the computer system of a private financial institution that has a connection with the federal government (such as federal insurance for the deposits in the financial institution). In addition, the statute criminalizes the transmission of codes, commands, or information if the transmission was intended to damage such an institution's computers, computer system, data, or programs.

ETHICAL AND PUBLIC POLICY CONCERNS

1. Few issues have managed to provoke more prolonged, heated controversy than the death penalty. Many of the arguments both for and against the death penalty are, at base, ethical arguments. Identify and briefly discuss some fundamental arguments on both sides of the issue.

2. Are strict and vicarious liability ethically defensible? Who would be more likely to support such liability, utilitarians or rights theorists? Which form of liability would rights theorists find more palatable?

3. Business opponents of RICO argue that federal prosecutors sometimes use the threat of asset forfeitures under the RICO statute to coerce business defendants to enter plea agreements that they would not otherwise enter. Assuming that these allegations are true, are such prosecutorial practices defensible?

PROBLEMS AND PROBLEM CASES

1. Two police officers on patrol observed Dickerson leaving an apartment building that the police department considered to be a "crack house," in view of the various drug-related complaints made to the police about the building. Dickerson began walking in the opposite direction after seeing the police car and the officers. Based on Dickerson's behavior and the fact that he had just left a building suspected of being a site of drug traffic, the officers decided to stop Dickerson and investigate further. The officers ordered Dickerson to stop and submit to a patdown search. Although the patdown search revealed no weapons, the officer who conducted the search noted a small lump in a pocket of Dickerson's jacket. The officer knew immediately that the lump was not a weapon but did not know what the lump was on the basis of initially touching it. After probing the lump further, the officer concluded that it could be contraband. The officer removed the "lump," which proved to be a plastic bag containing crack cocaine. Dickerson was arrested and later charged with possession of cocaine. Dickerson moved to suppress (i.e., exclude evidence of) the cocaine, on the ground that his Fourth Amendment rights were violated by the warrantless search and seizure. The trial court denied the motion to suppress, and Dickerson was found guilty. Did the trial court err in concluding that Dickerson's Fourth Amendment rights were not violated and in denying the motion to suppress?

2. Dixon was arrested and indicted for possession of cocaine with intent to distribute. He was then convicted of criminal contempt of court for violating a condition of his release on an unrelated offense. This condition of release had forbidden him from committing any criminal offense. After the conviction of criminal contempt, the trial court dismissed the cocaine indictment on double jeopardy grounds. Was the trial court correct in doing so?

3. Plainclothes police officers were patrolling, in an unmarked car, an area known for illegal drug activity. They passed a truck that had temporary license plates and was stopped at a stop sign. The driver, who appeared to be looking down into the lap of the passenger at his right, kept the truck stopped at the sign for an unusually long time. Suspecting possible unlawful activity, the officers executed a U-turn in order to head back toward the truck. The truck then made a sudden turn without signaling, and sped away at an unreasonable speed. The policemen followed the truck and overtook it when it stopped behind other traffic. When one of the officers approached the driver's side of the truck, he observed two large plastic bags of what appeared to be crack cocaine in the hands of a passenger, Whren. The officers arrested the driver (Brown) and Whren, and then retrieved several types of illegal drugs from the truck. Brown and Whren were indicted for various drug law violations. At a pretrial suppression hearing, they challenged the legality of the officers' stop of the truck and the resulting seizure of drugs. Brown and Whren contended that the officers' asserted traffic violations–related purpose of stopping the truck was pretextual, and that the officers' real purpose in making the stop was their suspicion—not justified by probable cause—that Brown and Whren were engaged in illegal drug activity. The trial court refused, however, to suppress the evidence. Brown and Whren were convicted. The court of appeals affirmed. Before the U.S. Supreme Court, Brown and Whren asserted that the Fourth Amendment test for the validity of a traffic stop should not simply be whether the officer had probable cause to believe that a traffic violation was committed. Instead, they argued, the test should be whether a reasonable officer would have made the traffic stop in the absence of some additional law enforcement objective (such as checking for other unlawful activity). Is the test proposed by Brown and Whren the appropriate one under the Fourth Amendment?

4. Dow Chemical Company operated a 2,000-acre chemical manufacturing facility at Midland, Michigan. The facility consisted of numerous covered buildings, with manufacturing equipment and piping conduits between various buildings plainly visible from the air. Dow maintained elaborate security around the perimeter of the complex to bar ground-level public views of these areas. It also investigated any low-level flights by aircraft over the facility. Dow did not, however, attempt to conceal all manufacturing equipment within the complex from aerial views because the cost would have been prohibitive. With Dow's consent, enforcement officials of the Environmental Protection Agency (EPA) made an on-site inspection of two power plants in this complex. When Dow denied EPA's request for another inspection, EPA did not seek an administrative search warrant. Instead, EPA employed a commercial aerial photographer, who used a standard floor-mounted, precision aerial mapping camera to take photographs of the facility from altitudes of 12,000, 3,000, and 1,200 feet. At all times, the aircraft was lawfully within navigable airspace. EPA did not inform Dow of this aerial photography. Was EPA's taking of aerial photographs of the Dow complex a search prohibited by the Fourth Amendment?

5. Doe, the target of a federal grand jury investigation, was subpoenaed to produce records of his accounts in banks in the Cayman Islands and Bermuda. He produced some records, testified that he had no other records in his possession or control, and invoked the Fifth Amendment when asked to reveal the existence or location of other records. The U.S. branches of Doe's banks cited their nations' bank secrecy laws and refused to comply with subpoenas ordering them to produce records of his accounts. At the government's request, the district court then ordered Doe to sign a consent directive authorizing the banks to turn over records of any and all accounts over which he had a right of withdrawal. The ordered consent directive, however, was to be structured so that it would not be an identification or acknowledgment by Doe of the existence of any such accounts. When Doe refused to obey the court's order, the court found him in contempt. Would being forced to sign the consent directive violate Doe's Fifth Amendment rights?

6. A police officer on drug interdiction patrol stopped Robinette for speeding in a construction zone. After checking Robinette's driver's license, the officer decided not to issue him a ticket. The officer nevertheless asked Robinette to get out of his car. As he issued Robinette a warning and returned his license to him, the officer said, "One more question before you get gone: Are you carrying any illegal contraband in your car? Any weapons of any kind, drugs, anything like that?" Robinette said he was not. The officer then asked Robinette for con-

sent to a search of his car. Robinette consented. The search revealed the presence of illegal drugs. Robinette was arrested and charged with knowing possession of a controlled substance. The trial court denied his motion to suppress the seized drugs. Robinette was convicted. On appeal, Robinette argued that the search and seizure violated the Fourth Amendment because the officer asked him questions about whether contraband was in his car and asked for consent to a search of the car, without first advising him that the traffic stop was over and that he was free to go. Was Robinette correct in arguing that the officer needed to tell him he was free to go before the officer asked further questions and sought consent to a search?

7. The Internal Revenue Service filed a claim in the Chapter 11 bankruptcy proceeding of American Biomaterials Corp. (ABC) in an effort to collect unpaid taxes and penalties from ABC. The bankruptcy court and district court disallowed the penalty portion, which exceeded $120,000. Both courts concluded that ABC's failure to comply with the tax code was the result of embezzlement by two ABC officers. This caused the bankruptcy and district courts to rule that ABC's noncompliance with the tax code was due to reasonable cause rather than willful neglect. On appeal to the Third Circuit Court of Appeals, however, the IRS argued that ABC should be held accountable on a vicarious basis for the actions of its wrongdoing officers, and that the penalties therefore should be assessed against ABC. Was the IRS correct in this argument?

8. Muniz was arrested on a charge of driving under the influence of alcohol. He was taken to a booking center, where he was asked several questions by a police officer without first being given the *Miranda* warnings. Videotape (which included an audio portion) was used to record the questions and Muniz's answers. The officer asked Muniz his name, address, height, weight, eye color, date of birth, and current age. Muniz stumbled over answers to two of these questions. The officer then asked Muniz the date of his sixth birthday, but Muniz did not give the correct date. At a later point, Muniz was read the *Miranda* warnings for the first time. He was later convicted of the charged offense, with the trial court denying his motion to exclude the videotape (both video and audio portions) from evidence. Assume that the video portion of the tape violated neither the Fifth Amendment nor *Miranda*. Should all or any part of the audio portion of the tape (which contained Muniz's stumbling responses to two questions plus his incorrect answer to the sixth birthday date question) have been excluded as a violation of either the Fifth Amendment or *Miranda?*

9. Versaggi was employed by Kodak as a computer technician. Because he was responsible for maintaining and repairing certain telephone systems for the company, he had been given an "accelerator," a security device that allowed him to access the telephone systems operated by two SL-100 computers. On two occasions during the same month, thousands of telephone lines at Kodak's offices and a Kodak industrial complex were shut down and rendered inoperable for up to an hour and a half as a result of a cause that initially was not known. It was later determined that Versaggi had accessed the SL-100 systems and, without authorization, had issued commands that caused the phone lines to shut down. Versaggi was charged with violating New York's computer tampering statute, which read as follows: "A person is guilty of computer tampering . . . when he uses or causes to be used a computer or computer service and having no right to do so . . . intentionally alters in any manner or destroys computer data or a computer program of another person." Versaggi contended that he was not guilty of violating the statute because he did not "alter" any computer programs. Instead, Versaggi maintained, he merely activated existing instructions that commanded the computers to shut down. The trial court concluded that Versaggi violated the computer tampering statute. Was the trial court correct?

10. Following a jury trial, Arlt and Wren were convicted of federal drug and money laundering violations. The trial court sentenced them to prison and imposed a fine on Arlt. Before the criminal trial had started, the federal government had filed a civil forfeiture complaint against Arlt and Wren. In the forfeiture proceeding, the government alleged that property to which Arlt and Wren held title was subject to forfeiture to the government under federal law because the property was connected to drug and money laundering offenses (the same offenses dealt with in the criminal case). The parties agreed to defer litigation of the forfeiture action while the criminal case was pending. More than a year after the criminal trial had concluded, the federal district court ruled in favor of the government in the forfeiture case. The court ordered that the property be forfeited to the government. Arguing that the forfeiture violated the Double Jeopardy Clause, Arlt and Wren appealed. Did the forfeiture violate the Double Jeopardy Clause?

11. In December 1983, a grand jury indicted Automated Medical Laboratories, Inc. (AML), Richmond Plasma Corporation (RPC) (a wholly owned AML subsidiary), and three former RPC managers for engaging in a conspiracy that included falsification of logbooks and records required to be maintained by businesses producing blood plasma. The falsification was designed to conceal from the Food and Drug Administration (FDA) various violations of federal regulations governing the plasmapheresis process and facilities. The evidence introduced at trial indicated that the managers and several other members of the team charged with ensuring compliance with FDA regulations had actively participated in record falsification. AML was convicted and appealed on the ground that there was no evidence that any officer or director of AML knowingly or willfully participated in or authorized the unlawful practices at RPC. Was AML's conviction in the absence of such proof proper?

Intentional Torts

 tort is a *civil wrong* that is not a breach (breaking) of a contract. Tort cases and books on tort law identify different kinds of wrongfulness, culpability, or fault and define them differently. In this chapter and in Chapter 7, we use the following four kinds of wrongfulness.

1. *Intent.* We define intent as the desire to cause certain consequences or substantial certainty that those consequences will result from one's behavior. For example, if D pulls the trigger of a loaded handgun while aiming it at P with the desire to kill P or with a substantial certainty of killing him, and does kill him, D intended to kill P. This chapter discusses several *intentional torts,* most of which require an intent to do something or other.

2. *Recklessness.* The form of intent involving substantial certainty blends by degrees into a different kind of fault—recklessness. We define recklessness as a conscious indifference to a known high risk of harm created by one's behavior. Now suppose that, just because he likes the muzzle flash and the sound, D fires his handgun at random in a crowded subway station. One of D's shots injures P. D acted recklessly if he had no desire to hit P or anyone else and was not substantially certain that anyone would be hit but nonetheless knew that this could easily result from his behavior. Recklessness appears from time to time in this chapter and in Chapter 7.

3. *Negligence.* We define negligence as conduct that falls below the level necessary to protect others against unreasonable risks of harm. In everyday language, negligence is careless behavior. Imagine that, without checking, D pulls the trigger on what he incorrectly and unreasonably thinks is an unloaded handgun. If the gun goes off, killing P, D has negligently caused P's death. Chapter 7 discusses

FIGURE 1

Crimes and Intentional Torts

	CRIMES	INTENTIONAL TORTS
Nature	Criminal	Civil
Type of Law	Mainly statutory	Mainly common law
Actors	Prosecutor versus defendant	Plaintiff versus defendant
Burden	Beyond a reasonable doubt	Preponderance of the evidence
Punishment	Fines, imprisonment, execution	Compensatory and punitive damages

negligence law in detail. Of course, negligence is not always easy to distinguish from recklessness; one difference is that recklessness usually involves a higher probability of harm.

4. *Strict liability.* Strict liability is liability without fault, or liability irrespective of fault. In a strict liability case, the plaintiff need not prove intent, recklessness, negligence, or any other kind of wrongfulness on the defendant's part. However, strict liability is not automatic liability. A plaintiff must prove certain things in any strict liability case, but fault is not one of them. Chapter 7 discusses several kinds of strict liability, some of which are examined more fully in other chapters.

In addition to involving wrongfulness, tort law involves *civil* liability. This distinguishes it from the criminal law, which also involves wrongful behavior. As you saw in Chapter 1, a civil suit is a suit between private parties. In criminal cases, on the other hand, a prosecutor confronts the defendant. Also, the plaintiff's burden of proof in a tort case is the *preponderance of the evidence* rather than the more stringent beyond-a-reasonable-doubt standard normally applied in criminal cases. This means that the greater weight of the evidence introduced at the trial must support the plaintiff's position on every element of the case. Finally, the punishment imposed in civil cases (most often, damages) differs from the punishment imposed in criminal cases (e.g., execution, imprisonment, or a fine). Of course, the same behavior can create both civil and criminal liability. For example, a rapist may be criminally liable for rape and also liable for the torts of assault, battery, false imprisonment, and intentional infliction of emotional distress. Figure 1 summarizes the important differences between criminal and tort liability. ∞

A plaintiff who wins a tort suit usually recovers the **actual damages** or **compensatory damages** that she suffered because of the tort. Depending on the facts of the case, these damages may be for direct and immediate harms, such as physical injuries, medical expenses, and lost pay and benefits, or for harms as intangible as loss of privacy, injury to reputation, and emotional distress. In cases where the defendant's behavior is particularly bad, injured victims may also be able to recover **punitive damages.** Punitive damages are not intended to compensate tort victims for their losses. Instead, they are designed to punish flagrant wrongdoers and to deter them and others from engaging in similar conduct in the future. Theoretically, therefore, punitive damages are reserved for the worst kinds of wrongdoing. Punitive damages have always been controversial, but they have grown more so in recent years due to the size of some punitive damage awards and the perception that juries are awarding them in situations where they are not justified.

INTERFERENCE WITH PERSONAL RIGHTS

Intentional torts break down into three categories: (1) those involving interference with personal rights, (2) those involving interference with property rights, and (3) business or competitive torts. This chapter discusses the first two categories, while Chapter 8 discusses the third.

Battery

Battery is the intentional, harmful or offensive, touching of another without his consent. A contact is *harmful* if it produces bodily injury. However, battery also includes nonharmful contacts that are *offensive*—calculated to offend a reasonable sense of personal dignity. The *intent* required for a battery is either: (1) the intent to cause a harmful or offensive contact, or (2) the intent to cause apprehension that such a contact is imminent. If, in order to scare Pine, Delano threatens to shoot Pine with a gun he mistakenly believes is unloaded, and ends up shooting Pine, Delano would be liable for battery. For battery to occur, moreover, the person who suffers the harmful or offensive contact does not have to be the person whom the wrongdoer intended to injure. Under a general intentional tort concept called *transferred intent,* a defendant who intends to injure one person but actually injures another is liable to the person injured, despite the absence of any specific desire to injure him. So, if Delano throws a rock at Thomas and hits Pike instead, Delano would be liable to Pike for battery.

As the previous examples suggest, the *touching* necessary for battery does not require direct contact between the defendant's body and the plaintiff's body. Thus, Delano would also be liable if he successfully laid a trap for Pike or poisoned him. Furthermore, there is a touching if the defendant causes contact with anything that is attached to the plaintiff's body. If the other elements of a battery are present, therefore, Delano would be liable to Pike if he shoots off Pike's hat. Finally, the plaintiff need not be conscious of the battery at the time it occurs. Thus, Delano would be liable if Delano sneaks up behind Pike and knocks him unconscious, without Pike's ever knowing what hit him.

However, there is no liability for battery if the plaintiff *consented* to the touching. As a general rule, consent must be freely and intelligently given to be a defense to battery. Consent also may be inferred from a person's voluntary participation in an activity, but it is ordinarily limited to contacts that are a normal consequence of the activity. Thus, Joe Frazier would not win a battery suit against Muhammad Ali for injuries he suffered during one of their title fights, but

a quarterback who is knifed by a blitzing linebacker has a valid battery claim. Finally, the law infers consent to many touchings that are customary in normal social life or are reasonably necessary to it. Thus, Pike could not recover in battery if Delano tapped him on the shoulder to ask directions or brushed against him on a crowded street. Of course, many such contacts are not harmful or offensive, either.

Assault

Assault might be defined as an intentional attempt or offer to cause a harmful or offensive contact with another, where the attempt or offer causes a reasonable apprehension of imminent battery in the other person's mind. The necessary *intent* is the same as the intent required for battery. In an assault case, however, it is irrelevant whether the threatened contact actually occurs. Instead, the key thing is the plaintiff's *apprehension* of a harmful or offensive contact. Apprehension is not the same thing as fear; it might be described as a mental state like: "Uh, oh, here comes a battery!" Thus, even the bravest people can be apprehensive and can recover for assault.

This apprehension must concern an *imminent or immediate* battery. Thus, threats of a future battery do not create liability for assault. In addition, the plaintiff must experience apprehension *at the time the threatened battery occurs.* Therefore, if Dillon fires a rifle at Pine from a great distance and misses him, and only later does Pine learn of the attempt on his life, Dillon is not liable to Pine for assault. Finally, the plaintiff's apprehension must be *reasonable.* As a result, threatening words normally are not an assault unless they are accompanied by acts or circumstances indicating the defendant's intent to carry out the threat.

In the following *Brown* case, the court grudgingly upheld a $1 nominal damages award in the plaintiff's favor. Should this award have been for battery, for assault, or for both? Or should the court have held for the defendant instead?

BROWN v. STAUFFER CHEMICAL CO.   539 P. 2d 374 (Mont. Sup. Ct. 1975)

 erry Brown, age 18, was a newly hired hourly worker for the Stauffer Chemical Company. His supervisor was LeRoy Mehring. One day, Mehring entered the office where Brown was working and said, "Let's go, sweetheart." After Brown told Mehring that his name was not sweetheart, Mehring replied, "OK, sweetheart." At this, Brown called Mehring a "scab." After further exchanges between the two men, Mehring told Brown that he was fired. Brown claimed that while he was getting his things together in order to leave, "Mehring continually called me 'sweetheart' as well as obscene names and gave me pats on the rear at different times."

Among Brown's subsequent lawsuits was an assault and battery claim against Mehring. On this claim, the trial court awarded Brown $1 in nominal damages. Mehring appealed. ∞

Castles, Justice   The entire basis for the claimed damages is [that] Mehring called Brown "sweetheart" as well as obscene names and gave Brown pats on the rear at different times. These are all the facts of the so-called assault and battery. Obviously the mere words are not an assault; and certainly in a plant working environment a "pat on the rear" is hardly actionable assault and battery. The entire exchange is insignificant and the law disregards trifles. Even assuming that a battery occurred, the award of nominal damages is all that is required.

The trial court was justified in its ruling that the record disclosed no genuine issue of material fact on punitive damages.

Nominal damages of $1 against Mehring are justified on this record, and this court does not wish to indulge in an extended discussion of law on such a trifling matter.

Trial court nominal damages award in Brown's favor affirmed.

False Imprisonment

False imprisonment is the intentional *confinement* of another person for an *appreciable time* (a few minutes is enough) *without his consent*. The confinement element essentially involves the defendant's keeping the plaintiff within a circle that the defendant has created. It may result from physical barriers to the plaintiff's freedom of movement, such as locking a person in a room with no other doors or windows, or from physical force or the threat of physical force against the plaintiff. Confinement also may result from the assertion of legal authority to detain the plaintiff, or from the detention of the plaintiff's property (e.g., a purse containing a large sum of money). Likewise, a threat to harm another, such as the plaintiff's spouse or child, can also be confinement if it prevents the plaintiff from moving.

The confinement must be *complete*. Partial confinement of another by blocking her path or by depriving her of one means of escape where several exist, such as locking one door of a building having several unlocked doors, is not false imprisonment. The fact that a means of escape exists, however, does not relieve the defendant of liability where the plaintiff cannot reasonably be expected to know of its existence. The same is true if the escape route involves some unreasonable risk of harm to the plaintiff, such as walking a tightrope or climbing out of a second-story window. The confinement also may be complete where using the escape route would involve some affront to the plaintiff's sense of personal dignity; for example, imagine that D steals P's clothes while P is swimming in the nude.

Although there is some disagreement on the subject, courts usually hold that the plaintiff must have *knowledge* of his confinement before liability for false imprisonment arises. In addition, there is no liability where the plaintiff has *consented* to his confinement. Such consent, however, must be freely given; consent in the face of an implied or actual threat of force or an assertion of legal authority by the confiner is not freely given.

Today, many false imprisonment cases involve a store's detention of people suspected of shoplifting. In an attempt to accommodate the legitimate interests of store owners, most states have passed statutes giving them a *conditional privilege* to stop suspected shoplifters. To obtain this defense, the owner usually must act with reasonable cause, act in a reasonable manner, and only detain the suspect for a reasonable length of time. These privilege statutes typically extend to other intentional torts besides false imprisonment. Would such a statute have protected the defendant in the following case?

A cting upon information that someone had just stolen several cartons of cigarettes from the store, the manager of Harvey's Supermarket stepped outside and approached Speight, who had walked out of the store only moments earlier. Upon being asked by the manager if he had anything that did not belong to him, Speight answered, "No, do you want to see?" He then briefly held the sides of his jacket open and let them close, at which point the manager parted the jacket with his hands to see if anything was concealed there. Simultaneously, Speight pointed to another person in the immediate vicinity and said, "I think that is the man you are looking for." The manager then left Speight to pursue this other person. Speight subsequently sued Harvey's for false imprisonment, assault, and battery. After a jury awarded him $2,500 in compensatory damages and $30,000 in punitive damages, Harvey's appealed. ∽

Banke, Chief Judge   Speight testified that the store manager had not been rude to him but stated that he did not consider the manager's conduct in looking inside his jacket as courteous. He admitted that he had invited this search and that the manager had [neither] cursed him nor spoken loudly to him; however, he testified that he felt the manager was angry because of the look in his eyes and the fact that several people had followed the manager out of the store. At trial, Speight testified that the entire encounter had lasted about 45 seconds, whereas during an earlier deposition he had testified that the encounter lasted between 15 and 30 seconds.

According to *Prosser, Law of Torts* (4th ed.), in false imprisonment:

[T]he imprisonment need not be for more than an appreciable length of time, and. . . it is not necessary that any damage result from it other than the confinement itself, since the tort is complete with even a brief restraint of the plaintiff's freedom. . . . It is essential, however, that the restraint be against the plaintiff's will, and if he agrees of his own free choice to surrender his freedom of motion, as by remaining in a room or accompanying the defendant voluntarily, to clear himself of suspicion or to accommodate the desires of another, rather than yielding to the constraint of a threat, then there is no imprisonment.

Speight's testimony fails to establish any involuntary restraint by Harvey's store manager or employees. Although a person need not make an effort to escape or await application of open force before he can recover, there must be restraint whether by force or fear. With regard to the second count of the complaint, Speight admitted that any touching of his person had been invited by him; and such invitation is inconsistent with the torts of assault and battery. The evidence was consequently insufficient to support any recovery.

Judgment reversed in favor of Harvey's.

Infliction of Emotional Distress

For many years, courts refused to allow recovery for purely emotional injuries unless the defendant had committed some recognized tort. Thus, victims of such torts as assault, battery, and false imprisonment could recover for the emotional injuries resulting from these torts, but courts would not recognize an independent tort of infliction of emotional distress. The reasons for this judicial reluctance included a fear of spurious or trivial claims, concerns about proving purely emotional harms, and uncertainty about the proper boundaries of an independent tort.

However, increased confidence in our knowledge about emotional injuries and a greater willingness to compensate such injuries have helped to overcome these judicial impediments. Today, most courts allow recovery for severe emotional distress regardless of whether the elements of any other tort are proven.

The courts are not, however, in complete agreement on the elements of this new tort. All courts require that a wrongdoer's conduct must be *outrageous* before liability for emotional distress arises. The *Restatement (Second) of Torts* speaks of conduct "so outrageous in character, and so extreme in degree, as to go beyond all possible bounds of decency, and to be regarded as atrocious, and utterly intolerable in a civilized community."[1] The courts also agree in requiring *severe* emotional distress. Some courts, however, still fear fictitious claims and also require proof of some bodily harm resulting from the victim's emotional distress. Finally, the *Restatement (Second)* says that the defendant must *intentionally* or *recklessly* inflict the distress in order to be liable.

In addition, some courts say that the plaintiff's distress must be distress that a reasonable person of ordinary sensibilities would suffer. In some cases, therefore, emotionally susceptible people may not recover even though they suffer severe distress.

Even if his distress is unreasonable, however, a hypersensitive person still may win where the defendant acts outrageously by playing upon the sensitivity with knowledge of its existence. The same sometimes is true where the defendant behaves outrageously by abusing a position or relation that gives him authority over another. Examples include employers, police officers, landlords, and school authorities.

The courts also differ in the extent to which they allow recovery for emotional distress suffered as a result of witnessing outrageous conduct directed at persons other than the plaintiff. The *Restatement (Second)* suggests that people be allowed to recover for severe emotional distress resulting from witnessing outrageous behavior toward a member of their immediate family. Where the third person is not a member of the plaintiff's immediate family, the *Restatement (Second)* restricts liability to severe emotional distress that results in some bodily harm.

---

[1] *Restatement (Second) of Torts* § 46, comment d (1965). The other propositions attributed to the *Restatement (Second)* in this section also come from § 46.

WHITE v. MONSANTO CO.   585 So. 2d 1205 (La. Sup. Ct. 1991)

Irma White, a church-going woman in her late 40s, was employed at a Monsanto refinery. While working in the canning department, she and three other employees were told to transfer a corrosive and hazardous chemical from a large container into smaller containers. After they asked for rubber gloves and goggles, a supervisor sent for the equipment. In the meantime, White began cleaning up the work area and one of the other employees went to another area to do some work. The other two employees sat around waiting for the safety equipment, contrary to a work rule requiring employees to busy themselves in such situations.

After learning that the group was idle, Gary McDermott, the canning department foreman, went to the work station. Once there, he launched into a profane one-minute tirade directed at White and the other two workers present, calling them "motherf-----s," accusing them of sitting on their "f-----g asses," and threatening to "show them to the gate." At this, White became upset and began to experience pain in her chest, pounding in her head, and difficulty in breathing. Her family physician met her at the hospital where he admitted her, fearing that she was having a heart attack. She was later diagnosed as having had an acute anxiety reaction.

White later sued McDermott and Monsanto for intentional infliction of emotional distress. After a jury awarded her $60,000, Monsanto and McDermott appealed.

Hall, Justice [Louisiana law] makes worker's compensation an employee's exclusive remedy for a work-related injury caused by a co-employee, except for an intentional tort. The intentional tort alleged in this case is intentional infliction of emotional distress. Most states now recognize intentional infliction of emotional distress as an independent tort, not "parasitic" to a physical injury or a traditional tort such as assault, battery, false imprisonment or the like.

We affirm the viability in Louisiana of a cause of action for intentional infliction of emotional distress. In order to recover, a plaintiff must establish: (1) that the conduct of the defendant was extreme and outrageous, (2) that the emotional distress suffered by the plaintiff was severe, and (3) that the defendant desired to inflict severe emotional distress or knew that severe emotional distress would be certain or substantially certain to result from his conduct.

The conduct must be so outrageous in character, and so extreme in degree, as to go beyond all possible bounds of decency, and to be regarded as atrocious and utterly intolerable in a civilized community. The extreme and outrageous character of the conduct may arise from an abuse by the actor of a position, or a relation with the other, which gives him actual or apparent authority over the other, or power to affect his interests. Thus, many of the cases have involved circumstances arising in the workplace. A plaintiff's status as an employee may entitle him to a greater degree of protection from insult and outrage by a supervisor with authority over him than if he were a stranger. On the other hand, liability does not attach where the actor has done no more than insist upon his legal rights in a permissible way, even though he is aware that such insistence is certain to cause emotional distress. Thus, disciplinary action and conflict in a pressure-packed workplace environment, although calculated to cause some degree of mental anguish, is not ordinarily actionable.

Applying these precepts, we find that White has failed to establish her right to recover from the defendants. The one-minute outburst of profanity does not amount to such extreme and outrageous conduct as to give rise to recovery for intentional infliction of emotional distress. Such conduct, although crude, rough and uncalled for, was not tortious. The brief, isolated instance of improper behavior by the supervisor was the kind of unpleasant experience persons must expect to endure from time to time. The conduct was not more than a person of ordinary sensibilities can be expected to endure. The tirade was directed to all three employees and not just to White. Although White was a decent person and a diligent employee who would not condone the use of vulgar language and who would be upset at being unjustifiably called down at her place of work, there was no evidence that she was particularly susceptible to emotional distress, or that McDermott had knowledge of any such susceptibility. The supervisor did not intend to inflict emotional distress of a severe nature, nor did he believe such a result was substantially certain to follow from his conduct.

Judgment reversed in favor of McDermott and Monsanto

Defamation

The tort of **defamation** protects the individual's interest in his *reputation*. Defamation is ordinarily defined as the (1) unprivileged (2) publication of (3) false and defamatory (4) statements concerning another. Before examining each of these elements, we must consider the distinction between two forms of defamation: **libel** and **slander.**

The Libel–Slander Distinction   Libel refers to written or printed defamations or to other defamations that have a more or less permanent physical form, such as a defamatory picture, sign, or statue. Slander refers to all other defamatory statements— mainly oral defamation. Today, the great majority of courts treat defamatory statements in radio and television broadcasts as libel.

Why does the libel–slander distinction matter? Due to its more permanent nature and the seriousness we usually attach to the written word, recovery for libel is possible without proof of **special damages** (the loss of anything of monetary value) to the plaintiff. Slander, on the other hand, is generally not actionable without proof of special damages, unless the nature of the slanderous statement is so serious that it can be classified as *slander per se*. In slander per se, injury to the plaintiff's reputation is presumed. Slander per se ordinarily includes false and defamatory statements that the plaintiff has: (1) committed a crime involving moral turpitude or potential imprisonment, (2) has a loathsome disease (traditionally, a venereal disease or leprosy), (3) is professionally incompetent or guilty of professional misconduct, or (4) is guilty of serious sexual misconduct (traditionally, unchaste behavior by a woman). The *Starr* case, which follows shortly, presents a variation on this scheme.

False and Defamatory Statement   As noted later, truth is a complete defense in a defamation case. A *defamatory* statement is one that harms the reputation of another by injuring his community's estimation of him or by deterring others from associating or dealing with him. Whether a given statement is defamatory ordinarily is decided by the fact-finder.

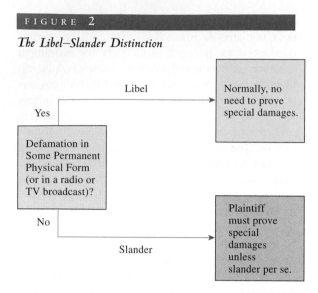

FIGURE **2**

The Libel–Slander Distinction

"Of and Concerning" the Plaintiff

Because defamation aims to protect reputation, an essential element of the tort is that the alleged defamatory statement must be "of and concerning" the plaintiff. That is, the statement must harm the particular plaintiff's reputation. This requirement presents several problems—problems whose many complexities are beyond the scope of this text. Thus, all the rules sketched below have exceptions.

What about allegedly *fictional accounts* whose characters resemble real people? Most courts say that fictional accounts are defamatory if a reasonable reader would identify the plaintiff as the subject of the story. Similarly, *humorous or satirical accounts* ordinarily are not defamation unless a reasonable reader would believe that they purport to describe real events. Likewise, statements of *personal opinion* usually are not defamation because they are not statements of fact concerning the plaintiff.

Do defamatory statements concerning particular *groups* of people also defame the individuals who form those groups? Speaking very generally, an individual member of a defamed group cannot recover for damage to her own reputation unless the group is so small that the statement can reasonably be understood as referring to individual group members.

Finally, the courts have placed some limits on the persons or entities that can suffer injury to reputation. For example, no liability attaches to defamatory statements concerning the dead. Corporations and other business forms have a limited right to reputation and can recover for defamatory statements that harm them in their business or deter others from dealing with them. Statements about a corporation's officers, employees, or shareholders normally are not defamation of the corporation unless such statements also reflect on the manner in which the corporation conducts its business.[2]

Publication

Liability for defamation requires *publication* of the defamatory statement. As a general rule, no widespread communication of a defamatory statement is necessary for publication. Communication of the defamatory statement to *one person* other than the person defamed ordinarily suffices.

So long as no one else receives or overhears it, however, an insulting message communicated directly from the defendant to the plaintiff is not actionable. In this and other cases, moreover, the traditional rule is that the defendant is not liable when *the plaintiff herself* publishes the offensive statement to another. In recent years, some courts have made an exception to this rule in cases where a discharged employee is forced to tell a potential future employer about false and defamatory statements made to her by her prior employer. According to the *Starr* case, however, this "compelled self-disclosure" rule has not found favor with most courts. *Starr* also raises another question on which courts disagree—whether *intracorporate* statements are published. Finally, the general rule is that one who *repeats* or *republishes* a defamatory statement is liable for defamation. This is true even if he identifies the source of the statement or expresses his disagreement with it.

Defenses and Privileges

Even though it is called an intentional tort, defendants are strictly liable for defamation. Because so many defamatory statements have defenses, however, it is questionable whether this technicality matters much. Of course, the *truth* of the defamatory statement is a complete defense to liability. Defamatory statements may be *privileged* as well. Privileges to defamation liability recognize that, in some circumstances, other social

---

[2]As Chapter 8 reveals, statements concerning the quality of a corporation's products or the quality of its title to land or other property may be the basis of an *injurious falsehood* suit.

interests are more important than an individual's right to reputation. Privileges can be *absolute* or *conditional.* Over the past 30 years, moreover, the Supreme Court has created a sort of "constitutional privilege" in certain cases involving public officials and public figures.

An **absolute privilege** shields the author of a defamatory statement regardless of her knowledge, motive, or intent. Where such a privilege applies, it operates as a complete defense to defamation liability. Absolutely privileged statements include those made by participants in judicial proceedings, legislators or witnesses in the course of legislative proceedings, certain executive officials in the course of their official duties, and between spouses in private. In each case, the theory behind the privilege is that complete freedom of expression is essential to the proper functioning of the relevant activity, and that potential liability for defamation would inhibit free expression.

Conditional (or qualified) privileges give the defendant a defense unless the privilege is *abused.* What constitutes abuse varies with the privilege in question. In general, conditional privileges are abused when the statement is made with knowledge of its falsity or reckless disregard of its truth or falsity, when the statement does not advance the purposes behind the privilege, or when it is unnecessarily made to inappropriate people.

There are several conditional privileges. One involves *statements made to advance the publisher's legitimate interests.* For example, a statement reasonably necessary to counteract the plaintiff's defamatory statement about the defendant would be conditionally privileged. One way the defendant might abuse this privilege is by making irrelevant statements that do not advance the goals of the privilege. For instance, Doris might counter Paul's charge of financial corruption by saying that Paul has fathered an illegitimate child. A second conditional privilege involves *statements made to protect the interests of another.* For example, suppose that Peter tells Molly that her fiancé Dave has a criminal record. But Peter would abuse the privilege if he made the statement with knowledge of its falsity or was reckless about its truth or falsity. A third kind of conditional privilege concerns *statements made to promote a common interest.* Intracorporate communications—which may or may not be publications in the first place—are one example. But such communications normally would abuse the privilege if they are made to the public at large. Finally, the privilege called *fair comment* protects fair and accurate media reports of defamatory matter in reports or proceedings of official action or originating from public meetings.

Defamation and the Constitution   Over the past 30 years, a conditional privilege of sorts has emerged from the interaction between defamation law and the First Amendment. The theory behind this "privilege" is that overzealous protection of individual reputation could restrict our constitutionally protected freedoms of speech and of the press and thereby inhibit the flow of information necessary to a free society. In 1964, the Court held that *public officials* seeking to recover for defamatory statements concerning performance of their official duties must prove *actual malice* (knowledge of falsity or reckless disregard for the truth) on the part of a media defendant to recover any damages. The Court subsequently extended the actual malice test to *public figures*—people in the public eye due to: (1) their celebrity status, or (2) their voluntarily involving themselves in matters of public controversy. Later, however, the Court refused to extend the actual-malice test to media defamation of *private citizens* who involuntarily become involved in matters of public concern. Instead, the Court held that to recover compensatory damages such people must prove some degree of fault at least amounting to negligence on the part of the defendant, and that to recover punitive damages they must prove actual malice. Finally, in a 1985 case involving a private figure plaintiff (a construction contractor) and defamatory speech about a matter of purely private concern (a false credit report), the Court upheld a recovery based on the common law strict liability standard.

Thus, the amount of protection the Constitution affords to otherwise defamatory statements appears to depend on two factors: (1) whether the plaintiff is a public figure/official or a private person; and (2) whether the subject matter of the speech at issue is a matter of public concern or private concern. The Court has yet to speak definitively on the standard it will apply to cases involving defamatory statements about private matters concerning public figures and officials.

STARR v. PEARLE VISION, INC. 54 F.3d 1548 (10 th Cir. 1995)

J acqui Starr was general manager of a Pearle Vision retail optical store in Tulsa, Oklahoma. Three Pearle employees met with Starr to discuss a $4,000 deficit in her store's petty cash account. Starr refused to cooperate with the investigation and was officially fired for that reason. The three investigating employees made some allegedly defamatory statements about Starr's situation to two other Pearle employees (named Ballard and Ross) whom they were investigating. Later in April, Starr's successor as store manager told Katherine Winn, a friend of Starr's who was not a Pearle employee, that Starr "is no longer here" and "is in big trouble."

Starr sued Pearle for slander. Her three claims were that: (1) the investigating employees' statements to Ballard and Ross defamed her, (2) she would be required to engage in defamatory self-publication when asked about her previous employment in subsequent job applications, and (3) the new manager's statements to Winn defamed her. After the court granted Pearle's motion for summary judgment on all three claims, Starr appealed. ∞

Ebel, Circuit Judge Under Oklahoma law, slander is a false and unprivileged publication, other than libel, which: (1) charges any person with crime, or with having been indicted, convicted, or punished for crime; (2) imputes in him the present existence of an infectious, contagious, or loathsome disease; (3) tends directly to injure him in respect to his office, profession, trade, or business; (4) imputes to him impotence or want of chastity; or (5) which, by natural consequences, causes actual damage. The first four provisions constitute slander per se, whereas the fifth provision requires a showing of actual damages and thus states a slander per quod rule.

In 1944, the Oklahoma Supreme Court held that intracompany communications do not constitute actionable "publications." Publication is the communication of defamatory matter to a third person, and neither agents nor employees of a company are third persons in relation to the corporation because they are part and parcel of the corporation itself. [The corporation] is but communicating with itself.

Starr next contends that she has been, and will continue to be, forced to reveal the accusations surrounding her termination when applying for other positions. This is the so-called compelled self-publication doctrine, which holds that an individual who only utters the slanderous statement to the victim (and not a third party) may be liable if the victim is compelled to repeat the slander to a third person. The small number of jurisdictions that have embraced the self-publication doctrine articulate two formulations. The first imposes liability if the defendant knew or could have foreseen that the

plaintiff would be *compelled* to repeat the defamatory statement. The second imposes liability if the defendant knew or could have foreseen that the plaintiff was *likely* to repeat the defamatory statement. In the absence of any Oklahoma authority, federal district courts have concluded that Oklahoma would not follow the self-publication theory because the vast majority of states considering the issue reject it. We agree. In any event, here the record does not convince us that Starr was compelled to repeat a slanderous statement to a prospective employer. First, Starr presents no evidence [of such a statement]. Moreover, Pearle's stated reason for terminating Starr was that she failed to cooperate with a company investigation. Thus, Starr would not publish a defamatory statement by informing third parties [of this], because [it] is a true statement.

We must evaluate the statement "she's in big trouble" in the context of the new manager informing Winn that Starr no longer worked at the [store]. Whether this comment imputes the commission of a crime or tends to injure the victim's professional reputation—and therefore constitutes slander per se—is a question for the factfinder. A claim of slander per se renders irrelevant the absence of evidence that a comment actually sullied the victim's reputation.

Summary judgment in Pearle's favor affirmed, except on Starr's claim that the new manager's statement to Winn defamed her. Case returned to the district court for proceedings consistent with the court of appeals' decision.

Invasion of Privacy

In tort law, the term *invasion of privacy* refers to four distinct torts. Each involves a different sense of the term *privacy.*

Intrusion on Personal Solitude or Seclusion

Any intentional intrusion on the solitude or seclusion of another constitutes an invasion of privacy if that intrusion would be *highly offensive to a reasonable individual.* The intrusion in question may be physical, such as an illegal search of a person's home or body or the opening of his mail. It may also be a nonphysical intrusion such as tapping another's telephone, examining her bank account, or subjecting her to harassing telephone calls. However, the tort applies only where there is a *reasonable expectation of privacy.* As a general rule, therefore, there is no liability for examining public records concerning a person, or observing or photographing him in a public place.

Public Disclosure of Private Facts about a Person

Publicizing facts concerning someone's private life can be an invasion of privacy if the publicity would be highly offensive to a reasonable person. The idea is that the public has no legitimate right to know certain aspects of a person's private life. Thus, publicity concerning someone's failure to pay his debts, humiliating illnesses he has suffered, or details about his sex life constitutes an invasion of privacy. Truth is *not* a defense to this type of invasion of privacy because the essence of the tort is giving unjustified publicity to purely private matters. Here, in further contrast to defamation, publicity means a *widespread* dissemination of private details.

Like defamation, this form of invasion of privacy potentially conflicts with the First Amendment. The courts have attempted to resolve this conflict in several ways. First, no liability ordinarily attaches to publicity concerning matters of public record or legitimate public interest. Second, public figures and public officials have no right of privacy concerning information that is reasonably related to their public lives.

False Light

Publicity that places a person in a false light in the public eye can be an invasion of privacy if that false light would be highly offensive to a reasonable person. All that is required is unreasonable and highly objectionable publicity attributing to a person characteristics that he does not possess or beliefs that he does not hold. Examples include signing a person's name to a public letter that violates her deepest beliefs or attributing authorship of an inferior scholarly or artistic work to her. As in defamation cases, truth is an absolute defense to liability. However, it is not necessary that a person be defamed by the false light in which he is placed. Signing a pro-life person's name to a petition urging increased abortion rights would create liability for false light but not for defamation, while signing the same person's name to a petition urging infanticide probably would create liability for both torts.

Due to the overlap between false light and defamation, and the obvious First Amendment issues at stake, defendants in false light cases enjoy constitutional protections similar to those enjoyed by defamation defendants.

Appropriation of Name or Likeness

Liability for invasion of privacy can exist when, without that person's consent, the defendant uses someone's name or likeness to imply his endorsement of a product or service or a nonexistent connection with the defendant's business. As the following *White* case emphasizes, liability extends beyond the use of the plaintiff's name or likeness to include other things associated with the plaintiff.

This form of invasion of privacy recognizes the personal property right connected with a person's identity and his exclusive right to control it. This raises the question whether, or to what extent, public figures have a *right of publicity.* To what extent, that is, do public persons have the right to control the use of their names, likenesses, or other matters associated with their identities? For example, should a well-known movie star have the right to prevent the writing of a book about her life or the televising of a docudrama about her? At this point, the scope of a public person's right of publicity varies greatly from state to state; considerable disagreement exists concerning such issues as its duration and inheritability.

S*amsung Electronics America ran a series of advertisements prepared by David Deutsch Associates in a number of national publications. The ads were set in the 21st century and depicted a current item from the popular culture and a Samsung electronic product. The basic message was that the Samsung products would still be used in the future. By hypothesizing outrageous future outcomes for the cultural items, the ads created humorous effects.*

One of the ads depicted a robot dressed in a wig, gown, and jewelry that Deutsch consciously selected to resemble Vanna White, the hostess of the "Wheel of Fortune" game show. The robot was posed next to a game board that was instantly recognizable as the Wheel of Fortune set, in a stance for which White is famous. The caption of the ad read: "Longest-running game show. 2012 A.D." Deutsch and Samsung referred to the ad as the "Vanna White" ad.

White, who had not consented to the ad, sued Deutsch and Samsung alleging, among other things, violation of her common law right of publicity. After the federal district court granted the defendants' summary judgment motion, White appealed. ∞

Goodwin, Circuit Judge *Eastwood v. Superior Court* (1983) stated that the right of publicity cause of action may be pleaded by alleging: (1) the defendant's use of the plaintiff's identity; (2) the appropriation of plaintiff's name or likeness to defendant's advantage, commercially or otherwise; (3) lack of consent; and (4) resulting injury. The district court dismissed White's claim for failure to satisfy *Eastwood*'s second prong, reasoning that the defendants had not appropriated White's "name or likeness." We agree that the robot ad did not use White's name or likeness. However, the common law right of publicity is not so confined.

The "name or likeness" formulation in *Eastwood* originated not as an element of the right of publicity cause of action, but as a description of the types of cases in which the cause of action had been recognized. The source of this formulation is Prosser, *Privacy,* 48 Cal. L. Rev. 383 (1960), one of the earliest and most enduring articulations of the right of publicity cause of action. Even though Prosser focused on appropriations of name or likeness in discussing the right of publicity, he noted that "[i]t is not impossible that there might be appropriation of the plaintiff's identity, as by impersonation, without the use of either his name or his likeness."

Since Prosser's early formulation, the case law has borne out his insight that the right of publicity is not limited to the appropriation of name or likeness. In *Motschenbacher v. R.J.Reynolds Tobacco Co.* (1974), the defendant used a photo of the plaintiff's race car in a television commercial. Even though the defendant had not appropriated the plaintiff's name or likeness, this court held that Motschenbacher's right of publicity claim should reach the jury. In *Carson v. Here's Johnny Portable Toilets, Inc.* (1983), the defendant marketed portable toilets under the brand name "Here's Johnny"—Johnny Carson's signature "Tonight Show" introduction—without Carson's permission. The Sixth Circuit held that the right was implicated because the defendant had appropriated Carson's identity by using the phrase "Here's Johnny."

Although the defendants in these cases avoided the most obvious means of appropriating the plaintiffs' identities, each of their actions directly implicated the commercial interests which the right of publicity is designed to protect. As the *Carson* court explained:

The right of publicity has developed to protect the commercial interest of celebrities in their identities. The theory of the right is that a celebrity's identity can be valuable in the promotion of products, and the celebrity has an interest that may be protected from the unauthorized commercial exploitation of that identity. If the celebrity's identity is commercially exploited, there has been an invasion of his right whether or not his "name or likeness" is used.

Motschenbacher and *Carson* teach the impossibility of treating the right of publicity as guarding only against a laundry list of specific means of appropriating identity. A rule which says that the right of publicity can be infringed only through the use of nine different methods of appropriating identity merely challenges the clever advertising strategist to come up with the tenth. If we treated the means of appropriation as dispositive in our analysis of the right of publicity, we would not only weaken the right but effectively eviscerate it. The right would fail to protect those plaintiffs most in need of its protection.

Viewed separately, the individual aspects of the ad in the present case say little. Viewed together, they leave little doubt about the celebrity the ad is meant to depict. Indeed, the defendants themselves referred to their ad as the "Vanna White" ad. Because White has alleged facts showing that Samsung and Deutsch appropriated her identity, the district court erred by rejecting her right of publicity claim.

Summary judgment for the defendant reversed. Case remanded for trial.

Misuse of Legal Proceedings

Three intentional torts protect people against the harm that can result from wrongfully instituted legal proceedings. **Malicious prosecution** affords a remedy for the wrongful institution of *criminal proceedings*. Recovery for malicious prosecution requires that: (1) the defendant initiated the proceedings without probable cause to believe that an offense had been committed, (2) the defendant did so for an improper purpose, and (3) the criminal proceedings eventually were terminated in the plaintiff's favor. **Wrongful use of civil proceedings** is designed to protect people from wrongfully instituted *civil* suits. Its elements are very similar to those for malicious prosecution.

Abuse of process imposes liability on those who initiate legal proceedings, whether criminal or civil, for a primary purpose other than the one for which the proceedings were designed. Abuse of process cases often involve situations in which the legal proceedings compel the other person to take some action unrelated to the subject of the suit. For example, Rogers wishes to buy Herbert's property, but Herbert refuses to sell. To pressure him into selling, Rogers files a private nuisance suit against Herbert, contending that Herbert's activities on his land interfere with Rogers' use and enjoyment of his adjoining property. Rogers may be liable to Herbert for abuse of process even though he had probable cause to file the suit and won the suit.

Deceit (Fraud)

Deceit (or fraud) is the formal name for the tort claim that is available to victims of knowing misrepresentations.[3] Liability for deceit usually requires a false statement of material fact, knowingly or recklessly made by the defendant, with the intent to induce reliance by the plaintiff, actual and justifiable reliance by the plaintiff, and harm to the plaintiff due to his reliance. Because most deceit actions arise in a contractual setting, and because a tort action for deceit is only one of the remedies available to a victim of fraud, a fuller discussion of this topic is deferred until Chapter 13.

Can a defendant be liable in deceit for the *nondisclosure* of facts material to the transaction? The following *Maybee* case presents the *Restatement (Second)* rule on this subject.

---

[3]In addition, many states allow tort recovery for *negligent* misrepresentations under one theory or another.

MAYBEE v. JACOBS MOTOR CO.   519 N.W.2d 341 (S.D. Sup. Ct. 1994)

Johnie Maybee purchased a 1984 Chevrolet van from Jacobs Motor Company for $8,700. No one at Jacobs told her that the van's original engine had been replaced with a rebuilt engine using a 1966 engine block. According to Maybee, the salesman with whom she dealt "just said that it was an '84 van that was in good condition and that they had used it around the business." In addition, no Jacobs employee mentioned that the van had dieseling and oil leakage problems. Although Maybee had the opportunity to ask questions and to have the van inspected by a mechanic, she declined.

About one month after the purchase, Maybee's husband took the van to a garage because it had been leaking oil. The mechanic discovered the 1966 block and also determined that the engine was in poor shape.

In addition, an expert witness for Maybee later testified that, due to its high compression ratio, the engine required high-octane aviation fuel for its proper operation. Eventually, Maybee claimed, she parked the van in her yard because it "didn't work."

Maybee sued Jacobs for fraud and deceit. The jury found Jacobs liable, awarding Maybee $14,700 in compensatory damages and $75,000 in punitive damages. Because the $14,700 in compensatory damages was more than 10 times the $1,450 cost of replacing the engine, the trial court ordered a new trial on the damages question. Maybee appealed this order, and Jacobs appealed the jury's determination that it was liable for fraud and deceit. ∞

Henderson, Justice Deceit requires proof that the misrepresentation was material to the formation of the contract and that the other party relied on the misrepresentation to her detriment. Such misrepresentations include true statements which the maker knows or believes to be materially misleading because of the failure to state additional or qualifying matter. [According to] *Restatement (Second) of Torts* section 551(2)(e):

One party to a business transaction is under a duty to exercise reasonable care to disclose to the other before the transaction is consummated. . .

(e) *facts basic to the transaction,* if he knows that the other is about to enter into it under a mistake as to them, and that the other, because of the relationship between them, the customs of the trade or other objective circumstances, would reasonably expect a disclosure of those facts.

When a person purchases a 1984 vehicle, is the presence, within that vehicle, of an engine built for a 1966 model which requires a fuel typically not used by vehicles on the road today, a fact basic to

the transaction? The jury so found and this court finds that the evidence can support such a finding.

Nevertheless, a new trial on all issues is warranted due to our decision on the second issue. During closing argument, *Maybee's counsel stated that $1,500 would compensate his client.* Somehow, the jury calculated compensatory damages at $14,750 and additionally awarded $75,000 in punitive damages. The jury verdict indicates passion and prejudice as well as inconsistencies with the instructions and law. A trial solely on Maybee's damages would require essentially the same evidence as a trial on both the substantive merits of the fraud claim and damages. Because these issues are so interwoven, we find that they are not separable. A new trial on both damages and liability is warranted even though the evidence does support liability, which remains a jury question.

Trial court decision reversed; case returned to the trial court for a new trial on both liability and damages.

INTERFERENCE WITH PROPERTY RIGHTS

Trespass to Land

Trespass to land might be defined as any unauthorized or unprivileged intentional intrusion upon another's real property (land). Such intrusions include: (1) physically entering the plaintiff's land, (2) causing another to do so (e.g., by chasing her onto the land), (3) remaining on the land after one's right to remain has ceased (e.g., staying past the term of a lease), (4) failing to remove from the land anything one has a duty to remove, (5) causing something to enter the land (although some overlap with nuisance exists here), and (6) invading the airspace above the land or the subsurface beneath it

(if property law and federal, state, and local regulations give the plaintiff rights to the airspace or subsurface and do not allow the defendant to intrude).

The intent required for trespass liability is simply the intent to be on the land or to cause it to be invaded. Thus, a person can be liable for trespass even though the trespass resulted from his mistaken belief that his entry was legally justified. Where the trespass is intentional, no actual harm to the land is required for liability, but actual harm is required for reckless or negligent trespasses.

Private Nuisance

In general, a **private nuisance** involves some interference with the plaintiff's use and enjoyment of her land. Unlike trespass to land, nuisance usually does not involve any physical invasion of the plaintiff's property. One source suggests that trespass requires an *invasion of tangible matter,* while nuisance involves other interferences.[4] Examples of such other interferences include odors, noise, smoke, light, and vibration. For nuisance liability to exist, however, the

interference must be *substantial* and *unreasonable.* Finally, the defendant must intend the interference.

Despite the distinction just suggested, some courts have imposed nuisance liability in cases involving apparent invasions of tangible matter such as flooding, dust, and the pollution of a stream. In the following *Burke* case, the court washed its hands of the trespass-nuisance distinction, instead holding that negligence principles should govern the facts before it.

---

[4]*Prosser and Keeton on the Law of Torts,* 5th ed. (1984), p. 71.

BURKE v. BRIGGS   571 A.2d 296 (N.J. App. Ct. 1990)

R obert Briggs and Daniel and Marcia Burke were adjoining suburban homeowners. One day, a large oak tree growing on Briggs's property suddenly fell onto the Burkes' property, causing $7,900 in damages to their garage. The cause of the tree's collapse was unclear, and Briggs denied knowledge of any condition that might have caused it to collapse. After the Burkes sued Briggs in nuisance and moved for summary judgment, the trial court held in their favor. The court ruled that strict liability applied and that Briggs therefore was liable. Briggs appealed. ∽

Scalera, Judge   There is perhaps no more impenetrable jungle in the entire law than that which surrounds the word "nuisance." A private nuisance is based on one's interference with another's use and enjoyment of land. The trespass to land concept has also been applied to cover situations where the actor interferes with one's enjoyment of his land. The distinction between nuisance and trespass has become wavering and uncertain and has often led to results that are difficult to explain.

Neither nuisance nor trespass would result in the application of [strict] liability here, under *Restatement* principles. Such liability without fault should not be imposed, whether [the] activity be classed as a nuisance or a trespass, absent intentional or hazardous activity requiring a higher standard of care, or [for] some compelling policy reason.

In the context of this case, the process of adjudication requires recognition of the reciprocal rights of each owner to reasonable use, and a balancing of

the conflicting interests. Regardless of the label attached, be it nuisance, trespass, or negligence, the issue here should depend on whether the offending landowner has made a negligent or unreasonable use of his land when compared with the rights of the party injured on the adjoining land. Such a determination merits consideration of the various attendant circumstances and factors—such as the nature of the incident; the danger presented by the tree; whether Briggs, by making inspections, could or should have known of its condition; what steps he could have taken to prevent it from falling on plaintiff's property, etc.

Since reasonable care was the proper standard, such an issue was for the jury to determine and was inappropriately disposed of by summary judgment.

Summary judgment in the Burkes' favor reversed; case returned to the trial court.

Conversion

Conversion is the defendant's intentional exercise of dominion or control over the plaintiff's personal property without the plaintiff's consent. Usually, the personal property in question is the plaintiff's

goods.[5] This can happen through the defendant's: (1) *acquisition* of the plaintiff's property (e.g., theft,

---

[5]Chapters 23 and 24 discuss the distinction between personal property and real property.

fraud, and even the purchase of stolen property), (2) *removal* of the plaintiff's property (e.g., taking that property to the dump or moving the plaintiff's car), (3) *transfer* of the plaintiff's property (e.g., selling stolen goods or misdelivering property), (4) *withholding possession* of the plaintiff's property (e.g., refusing to return a car one was to repair), (5) *destruction or alteration* of the plaintiff's property, and (6) *using* the plaintiff's property (e.g., driving a car left with one for storage).

In each case, the necessary intent is merely the intent to exercise dominion or control over the property. Thus, it is possible for the defendant to be liable if she buys or sells stolen property in good faith. However, conversion is limited to *serious* interferences with the plaintiff's property rights. The following *McCray* case lists many of the factors courts use to determine the seriousness of the interference.

If there is a serious interference and conversion, the defendant is liable for the *full value* of the property. What happens when the interference is nonserious? Although it has largely been superseded by conversion and its elements are hazy, a tort called **trespass to personal property** may come into play here. Suppose that Dalton goes to Friendly Motors and asks to test-drive a new Ford Thunderbird. If Dalton either wrecks the car, causing major damage, or drives it across the United States, he is probably liable for conversion and obligated to pay Friendly Motors the reasonable value of the car. On the other hand, if Dalton is merely involved in a fender-bender, or keeps the car for eight hours, he is probably only liable for trespass. Therefore, he is only obligated to pay damages to compensate Friendly for the loss in value of the car or for its loss of use of the car.

McCRAY v. CARSTENSEN 492 N.W.2d 444 (Iowa Ct. App. 1992)

R&J Associates leased commercial real estate from T&C Associates for a one-year period beginning May 1, 1989. The lease required that T&C give R&J ten days' notice before cancellation. R&J operated the leased premises as a bar featuring seminude dancers. However, R&J discontinued the business in March 1990 after losing its dance permit. In late March and early April, T&C noticed that the bar was not open and became aware that R&J had lost its permit. Also, R&J was late on its rent payment and the utility companies were seeking to shut off service to the bar. When T&C informed R&J that its rental payments would be higher if it renewed the lease, R&J denied any interest in renewing it.

For all these reasons, T&C took possession of the premises on April 7, 1990—without giving the required 10 days' notice. On April 18, it leased those premises to a new tenant. About this time, R&J demanded the return of personal property it had left on the premises, and T&C told it to contact the new tenant, adding that there should be no problem with returning the property. After R&J did so, the new tenant told R&J to submit a list of its possessions, because others were also claiming rights to the property left on the premises.

R&J never submitted this list, and it never again contacted T&C about its possessions. Instead, it sued T&C for conversion of those possessions. After the trial court held for T&C, R&J appealed. ∞

Hayden, Judge The fact that T&C locked R&J out of the premises does not necessarily involve sufficient interference with R&J's personal property to constitute conversion. The following factors should be considered in determining the seriousness of the interference: (a) the extent and duration of the actor's dominion or control, (b) the actor's intent to assert a right inconsistent with the other's right of control, (c) the actor's good faith, (d) the extent and duration of the resulting interference with the other's right of control, (e) the harm done to the chattel, and (f) the inconvenience and expense caused to the other.

The fact that T&C failed to provide notice of default does not alone determine whether it converted the property. The issue is whether T&C's actions so seriously interfered with R&J's rights as to require T&C to pay the full value of the property. The following facts support the conclusion that T&C is not liable.

R&J contacted T&C only one time to discuss the return of its personal property. T&C asked R&J to contact the new tenant. The new tenant merely asked R&J to provide a list of its property. R&J failed to provide such a list and never contacted T&C with any complaints about the return of its property. At all times, T&C was willing to release the property and had no intent of denying access to R&J.

T&C acted in good faith when it took possession of the premises. T&C did not assert any rights inconsistent with R&J's rights. T&C also acted in good faith through its efforts to relet the premises.

Finally, the personal property of R&J was not harmed. The items still remain in the building.

We conclude that T&C never interfered so seriously as to constitute a denial of R&J's right to its personal property.

Trial court decision in T&C's favor affirmed.

Other Examples of Intentional Tort Liability

Chapter 8 discusses three additional intentional torts that protect various economic interests and often involve unfair competition. These are: *injurious falsehood* (a kind of business defamation), *intentional interference with contractual relations,* and *interference with prospective advantage.* Chapter 50 examines an intentional tortlike recovery for wrongful discharge called the *public policy* exception to employment at will. In Chapter 53, finally, this text discusses the recoveries some states allow for *bad faith breach of contract.*

ETHICAL AND PUBLIC POLICY CONCERNS

1. Tort law attempts to protect various individual interests by giving persons whose rights are violated by others the ability to sue for money damages. Can monetary awards, however, ever truly compensate persons who have suffered harms such as an invasion of privacy or emotional distress? If not, how do we justify such awards?

2. Safeco Plastics Corporation owns a plant upstream from Morrison's farm. Safeco periodically discharges large amounts of water into the stream, a practice which occasionally results in the flooding of Morrison's property. Assuming that it is cheaper for Safeco to pay damages to Morrison for trespass or nuisance than it is to take corrective steps to prevent the flooding, is it ethically proper for Safeco to continue to flood Morrison's land?

3. Maxwell is defamed by an article in a local newspaper as a result of careless reporting. When confronted with its error, the paper promptly apologizes and runs an article retracting the defamatory statement. Maxwell has noticed no negative effects from the article, but his lawyer advises him that he would have no trouble proving defamation by the

paper and that, as a result, the paper's liability insurance company would probably be eager to settle in the event that Maxwell files suit. Should Maxwell sue?

PROBLEM CASES

1. Betty England worked at a Dairy Queen restaurant owned by S&M Foods in Tallulah, Louisiana. One day while she was at work, her manager, Larry Garley, became upset when several incorrectly prepared hamburgers were returned by a customer. Garley expressed his dissatisfaction by throwing a hamburger that hit England on the leg. Assume that while Garley was not trying to hit England with the hamburger, he was aware that she was substantially certain to be hit as a result of his action. Also, assume that England was not harmed by the hamburger. England sued Garley for battery. Did Garley have the necessary intent for battery liability? Does England's not suffering harm defeat her battery claim?

2. While shopping in a Publix Supermarket, Anthony Gatto was accosted by Publix employees who believed that he had shoplifted some paperback books. Gatto alleged that in the process of trying to get the books from him, Harold Stepp, the store manager, touched "either part of my palm or my wrist or my arms." Gatto later filed suit against Publix for assault, battery, and false imprisonment. At trial, Gatto admitted that he was never prevented from leaving and at all times considered himself free to leave the premises. Was the trial court's directed verdict in favor of Publix on all three tort theories correct?

3. In 1985, Ford Motor Company and its ad agency, Young & Rubicam, Inc., ran a series of 19 television commercials aimed at making an emotional connection with Yuppies, bringing back memories of their college days. Seventies pop songs were sung in each commercial, and the agency tried to get the original artists to sing the songs. One of the songs selected was "Do You Want to Dance," a song from a 1973 Bette Midler album. The agency acquired a license from the copyright holder to use the song, but Midler refused to do the commercial. The agency then hired a former backup singer for Midler to record it, instructing her to "sound as much as possible like the Bette Midler record." After the commercial was aired, a number of people told Midler that it "sounded exactly" like her recording. Midler filed suit against Ford and Young & Rubicam. The trial judge granted summary judgment for the defendants because he believed no legal principle prevented the imitation of Midler's voice. Was the trial judge's decision correct?

4. After Donna Drejza was violently raped by a former boyfriend whom she had voluntarily admitted to her home, the police took her to the Department's Sex Offense Branch, where she was interviewed by Detective Michael Vaccaro. Drejza testified that Vaccaro acted obnoxiously throughout the interview, snickered at her account of the rape, and treated her with scorn, apparently because she had formerly had voluntary sexual relations with her assailant and later had voluntarily admitted him to her home. Due to Vaccaro's behavior, Drejza claimed, she suffered severe emotional distress. Under the definition in the text, would Vaccaro's behavior qualify as "outrageous?" If not, what additional factor might make it outrageous?

5. In February 1986, Lois Grimsley, a 46-year-old security inspector, unexpectedly gave birth in her home less than two days after doctors had told her that her stomach pains were nothing more than a urinary tract infection and a case of hemorrhoids. A reporter from a local newspaper interviewed Grimsley about the birth, and Grimsley provided details about it and posed for a picture with the child. The story appeared in the local paper the following day, was subsequently picked up by the Associated Press, and also appeared in several other newspapers. In July 1986, a synopsis of the article (including a photo of Grimsley and her son) appeared in the "Hard Times" section of *Penthouse* magazine (a section that the magazine describes as "a compendium of bizarre, idiotic, lurid, and ofttimes witless driblets of information culled from the nation's press") under the heading "Birth of a Hemorrhoid." Grimsley filed suit against *Penthouse* for defama-

tion, invasion of privacy, and intentional infliction of mental distress. Should her suit succeed?

6. In September 1987, *The National Enquirer* ran an article reporting Henry Dempsey's harrowing escape from injury or death when he fell out of a small airplane while in flight but clung to the open boarding ladder of the plane, surviving his copilot's landing with only a few scratches. Dempsey had refused to be interviewed for the article, despite repeated attempts by an *Enquirer* reporter to gain an interview. The reporter allegedly came to his home twice, repeatedly drove past his home for three-quarters of an hour after the first refusal, and followed him to a restaurant where she attempted to photograph him and again requested an interview. After the article appeared, Dempsey filed suit against the *Enquirer* for invasion of privacy and intentional infliction of emotional distress. Should Dempsey's suit succeed?

7. Dorothy Yu, an employee of Northwest Pipeline Corporation, was found to have in her possession a confidential personnel document that she was not authorized to possess. She admitted possession and identified Enser, who worked in the records department, as the source of the document. Both Yu and Enser were terminated for violating Northwest's confidentiality policy. Northwest then informed the Utah Job Services that Yu had been fired for this reason and therefore was ineligible for unemployment compensation. Selected nonsupervisory Northwest employees also were informed of the reasons for Yu's termination. Yu filed a defamation suit against Northwest. Should Northwest's motion for summary judgment be granted?

8. Cynthia Cheatham creates unique clothing designs and displays them at bikers' events. At a Chillicothe, Ohio bikers' festival, Cheatham wore one of her designs. The design displayed her bottom through fishnet fabric that replaced cut-out portions of her blue jeans. Later, a drawing reproducing the picture appeared on the front of a T-shirt depicted in an advertisement for shirts made by T-Shurte's. T-Shurte's may have sold at least several hundred T-shirts bearing the drawing. Cheatham sued T-Shurte's for all four forms of invasion of privacy. In each case, give *one* argument *against* her recovering.

9. The Blanks purchased a lot in the Indian Fork subdivision next to a lot owned by Gary Rawson. When Rawson built his home, he located a basketball goal and dog pen immediately next to the

---

property separating the two lots. The Blanks complained to the subdivision developer that Rawson was violating the minimum setback restrictions applicable to the subdivision and were told that Rawson had received permission from the developer to do so. They then filed a nuisance suit against Rawson. At the trial, they alleged that the sound of the basketball hitting the backboard when Rawson's son played was offensive and that when he missed, the ball could come into their yard. They also stated that the dog was a large one and that the pen was not cleaned regularly, with the result that offensive odors continued to reach their property despite the 10-foot privacy fence Rawson had erected between their properties shortly after their complaint against him was filed. Was the trial judge's order forcing Rawson to remove or relocate the goal and the dog pen proper?

10. Moore was receiving treatment for hairy-cell leukemia at a university hospital. After his spleen was removed as part of that treatment, the treating physician and another university employee determined that his cells were unique. Without Moore's knowledge or consent, they applied genetic engineering techniques to his cells, producing a cell-line that they patented and marketed very successfully through agreements with a pharmaceutical company and a biotechnology firm. To further their research, they continued to monitor him and take tissue samples from him for almost seven years after his spleen was removed. When Moore discovered the truth, he filed a conversion suit against the university, which moved to dismiss his claim, arguing that he had no property right in his spleen and that, in any event, his cells were worthless without their subsequent modifications to them. Should Moore's suit survive their motion to dismiss?

11. The Bradleys owned land on Vashon Island in King County, Washington, about four miles north of American Smelting and Refining Company's copper smelter in Ruston, Washington. They sued American on trespass and nuisance theories, arguing that invisible arsenic and cadmium particles emitted by American's smelter had been carried by the wind and deposited on their property. American sought summary judgment on the trespass claim on the grounds that the Bradleys had incurred no actual damages. Even assuming that particles of arsenic and cadmium emitted from American's smelter had settled onto the Bradleys' land, American argued that these materials are innocuous in the tiny concentrations in which they actually had been found in the Bradleys' soil. Assuming American's statements are factually correct, should its motion for summary judgment be granted?

12. The Sanders Lead Company began an operation for recovering lead from used automobile batteries. Adjoining Sanders's operation was farmland owned by J.H. and Sara Borland. Alleging that Sanders's operation had caused a dangerous accumulation of airborne lead particulates and sulfoxide deposits to settle onto their land, the Borlands sued Sanders for trespass to land. Can Sanders be liable for trespass here? Assume that neither Sanders's employees nor its operations ever physically intruded on the Borlands' land.

Negligence and Strict Liability

he Industrial Revolution that changed the face of 19th-century America created serious problems for the law of torts. Railroads, factories, machinery, and new technologies meant increased injuries to people and their property. These injuries did not fit within the intentional torts framework because most of them were unintended. In response, courts created the modern law of **negligence.**

Originally, negligence law was not very kind to injured plaintiffs. One reason, some say, was the fear that if infant industries were held responsible for all the harms they caused, the country's industrial development would be seriously retarded. With the achievement of a viable industrial economy in the 20th century, this feeling has tended to fade. Also fading over the same period was the 19th-century belief that there should be no tort liability without genuine fault on the defendant's part. More and more, the injuries compensated by tort law are now seen as the unavoidable consequences of life in a highly industrialized, high-speed, technologically advanced society. Thus, rather than worrying about fault, modern courts and legislatures sometimes impose tort liability on the party best able to bear the financial costs of these unavoidable consequences—usually, the defendant. As a result, negligence law has become more proplaintiff throughout much of this century. In some cases, moreover, courts and legislatures have imposed **strict liability**—liability without fault—on defendants. Due in part to the financial pressures this increased liability has put on defendants, however, a **tort reform** movement has emerged in recent years. Its main aim is to limit plaintiffs' ability to recover and/or the damages they can receive. ⚭

NEGLIGENCE

Chapter 6 defined negligence as conduct that falls below the level necessary to protect others against unreasonable risks of harm. The *elements* of a negligence case—the things the plaintiff must prove to recover—are: (1) a **breach of duty** by the defendant, (2) **actual injury** suffered by the plaintiff, and (3) actual and proximate **causation** between the breach and the injury. To win, a plaintiff must also overcome any **defenses** to negligence liability raised by the defendant. The two traditional negligence defenses are **contributory negligence** and **assumption of risk.** However, these traditional defenses are being superseded by newer defenses that go by the names **comparative negligence** and **comparative fault.**

Breach of Duty

The Reasonable Person Standard   The basic idea behind negligence law is that each member of society has a duty to behave so as to avoid unreasonable risks of harm to others. This means that each of us must act like a *reasonable person of ordinary prudence in similar circumstances.* If a person's conduct falls below this standard, he has *breached a duty.* This "reasonable person" standard is *objective* in two senses of the term. First, the reasonable person is a hypothetical person with some ideal attributes—not a real human being. Second, the reasonable person standard focuses on behavior rather than on the defendant's subjective mental state. Finally, the standard is *flexible* because it lets courts tailor their decisions to the facts of the case.

How do courts determine this objective yet flexible reasonable person standard in specific cases? They consider and balance certain factors as those factors apply to the situation before them. The most important such factor is the *reasonable foreseeability* of harm. The idea is that the reasonable person

acts so as to avoid reasonably foreseeable risks of harm. Suppose that Donald gets into an automobile accident with Peter after Donald falls asleep at the wheel. Because falling asleep at the wheel involves a foreseeable risk of harm to others, a reasonable person would not behave that way. And because Donald's conduct fell short of this behavioral standard, he has breached a duty to Peter. However, this probably would not be true if Donald's falling asleep at the wheel was due to a sudden, severe, and unforeseeable blackout. On the other hand, there probably *would* be a breach of duty if Donald drove the car after being warned by a doctor that he was subject to sudden blackouts.

Negligence law does not require that we protect others against all foreseeable risks of harm. Instead, the risk created by the defendant's conduct must only be an *unreasonable* one. In determining the reasonableness of the risk, courts consider other factors besides the foreseeability of harm. One such factor is the *seriousness* or *magnitude* of the foreseeable harm. As the seriousness of the harm increases, so does the duty to avoid it. Another factor is the *social utility* of the defendant's conduct. The more valuable that conduct, the less likely that it will be a breach of duty. A further consideration is the *ease or difficulty of avoiding the risk.* Negligence law normally does not require that defendants make superhuman efforts to avoid harm to others. The following *Duncan* case considers some of these factors.

To a limited extent, negligence law also considers the *personal characteristics* of the defendant. For example, children are generally required to act as would a reasonable person of similar age, intelligence, and experience under similar circumstances. People with physical disabilities must act as would a reasonable person with the same disability. Mental deficiencies, however, ordinarily do *not* relieve a person from the duty to conform to the normal reasonable person standard. The same is true of voluntary and negligent intoxication.

Finally, negligence law is sensitive to the *context* in which the defendant acted. For example, someone confronted with an emergency requiring rapid decisions and action need not employ the same level of caution and deliberation as someone in circumstances allowing for calm reflection and deliberate action.

DUNCAN v. UNION PACIFIC RAILROAD CO.   790 P.2d 595 (Utah Ct. App. 1990), *affirmed*, 842 P.2d 832 (Utah Sup. Ct. 1992)

A t about 8:50 P.M. one evening, a Union Pacific train struck an automobile at a crossing with Droubay Road in a rural Utah county, killing all four of the car's occupants. There was no evidence that the train was negligently operated. Three roadside signs warned oncoming motorists about the crossing. Although there were no flashing lights or other mechanical devices at the crossing, nothing obstructed a motorist's view of the tracks for several thousand feet.

The heirs of the accident victims sued Union Pacific for negligent maintenance of the crossing. The possibility that the driver of the car was at fault apparently was not an issue in the case. After Union Pacific successfully moved for summary judgment, the plaintiffs appealed. ∞

Bullock, Senior District Judge Every railroad crossing is hazardous, but, since it is not practicable to eliminate all railroad crossings, the simple existence of a crossing is not in itself a breach of duty. Much of everyday life presents hazards; driving or walking along a street are hazardous, and so are stairs, electricity, and many other things, but we tolerate those hazards because of the impracticability of eliminating them. The question is not whether a hazard existed, but rather whether, under prevailing community standards, the defendant should bear the responsibility to discover and ameliorate a hazard, in light of the practicability of doing so and the costs and benefits to society of requiring the defendant so to act. In the case of railroad crossings, the cost of eliminating the hazard, such as by installing overpasses at all railroad crossings, including rural ones, does not warrant a duty of care so rigorous that simply having a railroad cross a street is tortious. Rather, for a railroad to be liable for a crossing mishap, there must be something about the railroad's right of way that creates a hazard to motorists greater than the hazard presented by the simple fact that the railroad and the street intersect.

It would thus be error to hold that a railroad right of way cannot cross a street. However, for such a crossing, the railroad is required to take every reasonable action to assure the safety of motorists who can reasonably be expected to cross the right of way. In determining what is reasonable under the circumstances of a specific case, the trier of fact must weigh the burden on the railroad, and indirectly on the public, of requiring added precautions, against the benefits that would be derived by the public from such precautions. For example, in [one] case, wild vegetation on the right of way obscured oncoming trains from motorists at the crossing. The cost of removing or maintaining the vegetation was minimal compared to the enormous benefit to the public of being able to see an approaching train at a frequent crossing. The imposition of a tort duty on the railroad to remove or maintain the vegetation was therefore clearly correct.

In this case, there is nothing to indicate what could have made Union Pacific's right of way safer to motorists crossing on Droubay Road. The path of the train is clearly visible to oncoming motorists. Plaintiffs suggest that Union Pacific should have placed warning signs and devices on Droubay Road, including automatic gates blocking traffic on the road from crossing the tracks when a train was approaching. It is not, however, the responsibility of the railroad to place signs and devices on the public road. The design and maintenance of state roads and the control of traffic on state roads are the Utah Department of Transportation's (UDOT's) responsibilities and prerogatives.

The net effect of this holding is that if the railroad's right of way does not negligently obscure an oncoming train, the train is properly operated, and some visible warning sign is present, then the plaintiff is not entitled to relief for an injury at the crossing. We do not consider this outcome to be harsh or unjust, although any tragedy in which life is lost or impaired is regrettable, whatever the cause.

Summary judgment in Union Pacific's favor affirmed.

Special Duties   In some situations, courts have fashioned particular negligence duties rather than applying the general reasonable person standard. When performing their professional duties, for example, professionals such as doctors, lawyers, and accountants generally must exercise the knowledge, skill, and care ordinarily possessed and employed by members of the profession.[1] Also, common carriers and (sometimes) innkeepers are held to an extremely high duty of care approaching strict liability when they are sued for damaging or losing their customers' property. Many courts say that they also must exercise great caution to protect their passengers and lodgers against personal injury—especially against the foreseeable wrongful acts of third persons. This is true even though the law has long refused to recognize any general duty to aid and protect others from third-party wrongdoing unless the defendant's actions foreseeably increased the risk of such wrongdoing. Some recent decisions have imposed a duty on landlords to protect their tenants against the foreseeable criminal acts of others.

Another important set of special duties concerns the duties possessors of land owe toward parties who enter the land. Traditionally, the level of duty that a person in possession of land owes to such parties has depended on whether such persons are invitees, licensees, or trespassers. *Invitees* include: (1) people who enter the land for a purpose connected with the business interests of the possessor, such as customers, delivery persons, or paying boarders; and (2) members of the public who are lawfully on public land such as a park, swimming pool, or government office. *Licensees* are those whose privilege to enter the land depends entirely on the possessor's consent. Licensees include people who are on the land solely for their own purposes, such as someone soliciting money for charity, members of the possessor's household, and social guests. *Trespassers* are persons who enter or remain on another's land without any legal right or privilege to do so.

At common law, a possessor of land owed *invitees* a duty to exercise reasonable care to keep the premises in reasonably safe condition for their use. He also had a duty to protect invitees against dangerous conditions on the premises that he knew about, or reasonably should have discovered, and that they were unlikely to discover. In most cases, he only owed *licensees* a duty to warn them of known dangerous conditions that they were unlikely to discover. The possessor of land owed no duty to *trespassers* to maintain his premises in a safe condition, and only a duty not to willfully and wantonly injure them once their presence was known.

Recent years have seen some tendency to erode these common law distinctions. Many courts no longer distinguish between licensees and invitees, holding that a possessor of land owes the same duties to licensees that he owes to invitees. Also, the courts have made numerous exceptions to the minimal duties that possessors of land owe to trespassers. For example, a higher level of duty is ordinarily owed to trespassers who the possessor of land knows are constantly entering the land (e.g., using a well-worn path across the land), and greater duties are ordinarily owed to children if the possessor of land knows that they are likely to trespass.

In the following case, the court applied the traditional rule on a landowner's liability to an invitee.

---

[1]Chapter 45 discusses professional liability in greater detail.

CULLI v. MARATHON PETROLEUM CO.   862 F.2d 119 (7th. Cir. 1988)

E lizabeth Culli stopped at a 24-hour self-service gas station operated by Marathon Petroleum. She filled her gas tank and then picked up five eight-pack cartons of soda. After paying for the gas, she headed back toward her car. Before Culli reached her car, however, she slipped and fell on a "clearish" slippery substance in a pool approximately 8 to 10 inches in width and length. Culli suffered a compound fracture of her ankle and had to use a wheelchair and walker for several months thereafter.

At the trial of Culli's negligence suit against Marathon, the evidence indicated that the station typically was staffed by one person, who would primarily stay inside and run the cash register, and who also was *responsible for replenishing supplies of the various items sold at the station. The station lot was normally swept once a day during the night shift. There was also testimony that spills generally occurred once or twice each day, and that one employee had asked the station manager to hire more help because the station was understaffed, a request that he relayed to his superiors but that went unheeded. After a jury awarded Culli $87,500, Marathon appealed.* ◠

Will, Senior District Judge The defendant owed the plaintiff invitee the duty of maintaining its property in a reasonably safe condition. This includes a duty to inspect and repair dangerous conditions on the property or give adequate warnings to prevent injury. To be liable, Marathon must have had actual or constructive notice of the dangerous condition. Both parties agree that Marathon did not have actual notice.

Constructive notice can be established under Illinois law under two alternative theories: (1) the dangerous condition existed for a sufficient amount of time so that it would have been discovered by the exercise of ordinary care, or (2) the dangerous condition was part of a pattern of conduct or a recurring incident.

In *Hresil v. Sears, Roebuck & Co.* (1980), plaintiff sought damages for injuries she suffered when she slipped on a "gob" of phlegm in the defendant's self-service store. At the time of her accident, there were few customers in the store and, due to the inactivity in the store at the place where she fell, the foreign substance could have been on the floor for at least 10 minutes. The court found that, as a matter of law, 10 minutes was not long enough to give Sears constructive notice of the gob, and "to charge the store with constructive notice would place upon the store the unfair requirement of the constant patrolling of its aisles."

Because of the lack of testimony establishing how long the substance in this case was present, we do not know if it was present for a period of time which would have placed Marathon on constructive notice of it. It could have been present for a few minutes or several hours. Under the first constructive notice theory, evidence establishing how long the particular substance was present is necessary.

Under the second constructive notice theory, what is needed is a pattern of dangerous conditions which were not attended to within a reasonable time. There was substantial evidence presented at trial establishing that there were spills on a daily basis in the pump area and that the volume of sales on the day in question made it unreasonable for Marathon to sweep the lot only at night and operate for most of the day with only one attendant who was primarily confined to the cash register. The evidence is sufficient to support the jury's verdict that Marathon's maintenance of its property was unreasonable and proximately caused Culli's injury.

Judgment for Culli affirmed.

Negligence Per Se Sometimes courts use statutes, ordinances, and administrative regulations to determine how a reasonable person would behave. Under the doctrine of **negligence per se,** the defendant's violation of such laws may create a breach of duty. In addition to the violation, the plaintiff normally must: (1) be within the class of persons intended to be protected by the statute or other law, and (2) suffer harm of a sort that the statute or other law was intended to protect against. As the following *Baldwin* case illustrates, these requirements can be difficult to apply.

BALDWIN v. GTE SOUTH, INC.   428 S.E.2d 857 (N.C. Ct. App. 1993)

fter a collision between a dump truck and a car at the intersection of two North Carolina roads, the dump truck traveled about 130 feet before hitting a GTE South telephone booth in a grocery store parking lot adjoining one of the roads. The booth was located within the right-of-way for the road it adjoined. Inside the booth was Laura Baldwin, who suffered injuries when the dump truck struck the booth. After settling with the two drivers, Baldwin sued GTE South in negligence. The trial court found in her favor, and GTE South appealed. ⌒

Wells, Judge The [North Carolina] DOT [Department of Transportation] has adopted the following regulation pursuant to its statutory authority: "Telephone pay-station booths or other commercial telephone installations are not permitted on highway rights-of-way, except in rest areas or truck weigh stations." Plaintiff contends that this regulation is aimed at protecting pedestrians using telephone booths from injury caused by vehicular traffic. We disagree.

Violation of a public safety statute is negligence per se. Defendant's violation of a statute, however, will not constitute negligence per se unless plaintiff belongs to the class of persons the statute was intended to protect. We therefore must examine the purpose of the adoption of the DOT telephone regulation.

The general purpose of the laws creating the DOT is that the DOT shall take over, establish, construct, and maintain a statewide system of highways. All the other powers it possesses are incidental to the purpose for which it was created. These powers include the authority to acquire and maintain rights-of-way for roads and highways, including the authority to regulate the use of such rights-of-way. [Specifically, the DOT is empowered by statute] "to make proper and reasonable rules, regulations, and ordinances for the placing or erection of telephone, telegraph, or other poles, signboards, fences, gas, water, sewage, oil, or other pipelines, and other similar obstructions that may, in the

opinion of the Department of Transportation, contribute to the hazard upon any of the [state's] highways or in any wise interfere with the same, and to make reasonable rules and regulations for the proper control thereof."

It is clear that in this legislative scheme, the authority and powers set forth are intended to allow the DOT to protect the integrity of its rights-of-way, which are there to accommodate the construction and maintenance of roads and highways. These circumstances lead us to the conclusion that the DOT prohibition against telephone booths in or upon highway rights-of-way does not include pedestrians within the class of protected persons. While the DOT's regulation may have safety implications, it does not provide a basis for negligence claims by this plaintiff.

Judgment in Baldwin's favor reversed.

Orr, Judge, dissenting The statute was designed to protect the motoring public from the hazards [created by] a car's leaving the travelled portion of a highway and striking a fixed object such as a phone booth. However, to limit protection to the motorist and not include the relatively unprotected person utilizing the phone booth is too restrictive. Under the majority's interpretation, a motorist striking a booth that violates the statute would be covered by the statute, but if that driver parked his car and was injured using the phone booth, no problem would exist.

Injury

A plaintiff in a negligence case must prove not only that the defendant breached a duty owed to the plaintiff, but also that the plaintiff suffered actual injury, and that this injury was to an interest the law seeks to protect. Ordinarily, personal injury to the plaintiff and damage to her property meet this test. Purely monetary damage such as lost profits may sometimes qualify as well. Serious problems arise, however, when the plaintiff's injury is *emotional* in nature.[2]

Negligent Infliction of Emotional Distress As you learned in Chapter 6, the law has long been reluctant to afford recovery for purely emotional harms. This is due, among other things, to the danger of spurious claims and the difficulty of placing a monetary value on emotional injuries. Until fairly recently, most courts would not allow a plaintiff to recover for emotional injuries resulting from a defendant's negligence without some impact or contact with the plaintiff's person. Today, many courts have abandoned this "impact rule" and allow recovery for foreseeable emotional injuries standing alone. Many such courts, however, still require proof that some serious physical injury or symptoms

[2]Another problem of this kind, emotional distress suffered by plaintiffs who witness a negligently caused harm to *another person,* is beyond the scope of this text.

resulted from the plaintiff's emotional distress. Nonetheless, some other courts have dispensed with the injury requirement where the plaintiff has suffered serious emotional distress as a foreseeable consequence of the defendant's negligent conduct.

Causation

Even if the defendant has breached a duty and the plaintiff has suffered actual injury, there is no liability for negligence without the required *causal relationship* between breach and injury. The causation question involves three issues: (1) was there *actual causation* between breach and injury? (2) was the breach a *proximate cause* of the injury? and (3) what was the effect of any *intervening force* arising after the breach and helping to cause the injury?

Actual Causation Suppose that, just as Dave breaches a duty by driving his car at 90 miles per hour on a crowded street, Pete is injured by a falling tree limb five blocks away. If Pete sues Dave for negligence, he may have little trouble proving Dave's breach and his own injury. Yet Pete surely will not recover, because Dave's behavior was not the *actual* cause of Pete's injury. To determine the existence of actual cause, many courts employ a "but for" test. Under this test, a defendant's conduct is the actual cause of a plaintiff's injury if that injury would not have occurred except for (or but for) the defendant's breach of duty. Here, Pete's injury *would* have occurred even if Dave had not breached a duty.

In some cases, however, a person's negligent conduct may combine with another person's negligent conduct to cause a plaintiff's injury. For example, suppose that fires negligently set by Dustin and Dibble combine to burn down Potter's house. If each fire would have destroyed Potter's house on its own, the but-for test would absolve both Dustin and Dibble. In such cases, courts often ask whether each defendant's conduct was a *substantial factor* in bringing about the plaintiff's injury. Under this test, both Dustin and Dibble probably would be liable for Potter's loss.

Proximate Cause Questions of proximate cause assume the existence of actual causation. The proximate cause question arises because it seems unfair to hold a defendant liable for all the injuries actually caused by her breach—no matter how remote, bizarre, or unforeseeable they are. Thus, courts typically say that a negligent defendant is liable only for the *proximate* results of her breach. Proximate cause, then, concerns the required degree of proximity or closeness between the defendant's breach and the injury it actually caused.

The courts have not reached any substantial agreement on the test for determining the proximate cause question. In reality, that question is one of social policy. In deciding which test to adopt, a court must recognize both that negligent defendants can be exposed to catastrophic liability by a lenient test for proximate cause, and also that a restrictive test prevents some innocent victims from recovering any compensation for their losses. Courts have responded in a variety of ways to this difficult choice.

Some courts have said that a negligent defendant is liable only for the "natural and probable consequences" of his actions. Others have limited a negligent person's liability for unforeseeable injuries by saying that he is liable only to plaintiffs who are within the "scope of the foreseeable risk."[3] Such courts hold that if the defendant could not have reasonably foreseen *some* injury to the plaintiff as a result of his actions, he is not liable to the plaintiff for any injury that in fact results from his negligence. On the other hand, a defendant may be liable even for unforeseeable injuries to persons whom he has exposed to some foreseeable risk of harm. In still another approach to the proximate cause question, the *Restatement (Second) of Torts* suggests that a defendant's negligence is not the legal cause of a plaintiff's injury if, looking back after the harm, it appears "highly extraordinary" to the court that the defendant's breach should have brought about the plaintiff's injury.[4] Adopting yet a further approach, the following case basically asks whether the plaintiff's injury was a foreseeable consequence of the defendant's breach. Under this approach, courts first find or assume a breach of duty, and then ask whether, given that breach, the injury was foreseeable.

---

[3]Although this rule is often characterized as a rule of causation, actually it is a rule limiting the defendant's *duty*, because courts adopting the rule hold that a defendant owes *no duty* to those to whom he cannot foresee any injury.

[4]*Restatement (Second) of Torts* § 435(2) (1965).

REPUBLIC OF FRANCE v. UNITED STATES 290 F.2d 395 (5th Cir. 1961)

O*n April 16, 1947, the SS* Grandchamp, *a cargo ship owned by the Republic of France and operated by the French Line, was loading a cargo of Fertilizer Grade Ammonium Nitrate (FGAN) at Texas City, Texas. A fire began on board the ship, apparently as a result of a cigarette or match carelessly discarded by a longshoreman in one of the ship's holds. Despite attempts to put it out, the fire spread quickly. A little over an hour after the fire was first discovered, the* Grandchamp *exploded with tremendous force. Fire and burning debris spread throughout the waterfront, touching off further fires and explosions in other ships, refineries, gasoline storage tanks, and chemical plants. When the conflagration was over, 500 people had been killed, and more than 3,000 had been injured. The evidence indicated that even though ammonium nitrate was known throughout the transportation industry as an oxidizing agent and as a fire hazard, no one aboard the* Grandchamp *made any attempt to prevent smoking in the ship's holds.*

Numerous lawsuits were filed after the incident. In the following opinion, treat the United States (which paid out considerable sums to victims of the disaster) as the plaintiff, and the Republic of France and the French Line as defendants. At trial, the defendants had argued that they should not be liable for claims arising out of the explosion because FGAN was not known to be capable of exploding *under the circumstances of this case. When the federal district court rejected their petition for limitation of liability, they appealed.* ∞

Rives, Circuit Judge In Texas, as elsewhere, not only proximate causal connection but also the very existence of a duty depends upon reasonable foreseeability of consequences. The test of whether a negligent act or omission is a proximate cause of an injury is whether the wrongdoer might by the exercise of ordinary care have foreseen that some similar injury might result from the negligence.

The United States argues with much force that the district court found that fault or negligence of the owners caused the fire and permitted it to increase in intensity, and that the fire caused the disastrous explosion. It insists that that causal connection is sufficient. The fallacy in that chain of argument is that it is only the operation of natural forces theretofore recognized as normal which one is charged with foreseeing.

The district court found it "undoubtedly true that the force and devastating effects of this explosion shocked and surprised the scientific field as well as the transportation industry." The court further found as to ammonium nitrate, which constituted approximately 95 percent of the FGAN, and which, with the benefit of hindsight, we now know to be the explosive part of the mixture:

Despite its use as a principal ingredient of high explosives, at the time of the disaster ammonium nitrate was not, and is not now, classified as an "explosive" for transportation purposes by the Interstate Commerce Commission or the Coast Guard. This is true because it was considered that to cause the detonation of ammonium nitrate, an initial shock or "booster" of considerable magnitude was required. The chances of such an initial or booster detonation being encountered in normal conditions of transportation has always been considered so remote as to be negligible.

Substantially all of the evidence is to the effect that the explosion, as distinguished from the fire, could not reasonably have been foreseen.

It would be ironic indeed if the United States were permitted to impose liability for these claims on the Republic of France and the French Line by claiming now that the officials and employees of the French Government and the master of the *Grandchamp* should have known that FGAN was a dangerous explosive and that an explosion from fire should reasonably have been anticipated.

Judgment reversed in favor of the defendants.

Intervening Forces In some cases, an *intervening force* (or intervening cause) occurring *after* a defendant's negligence may play a significant role in bringing about the plaintiff's injury. For example, suppose that after Davis sets a fire, a high wind springs up and spreads the fire to Parker's home, or that after Davis negligently runs Parker down with his car, a thief steals Parker's wallet while he lies unconscious. If the intervening force is a *foreseeable* one, it usually will *not* relieve the defendant from liability. So, if high winds are a reasonably common occurrence in the locality, Davis probably is liable for the damage to Parker's home even though his fire would not have spread that far under the wind conditions that existed when he started it. Likewise, in our second example, Davis probably is liable for the theft of Parker's wallet if the theft is foreseeable, given the time and location of the accident.

On the other hand, if the intervening force that contributes to the plaintiff's injury is *unforeseeable,* most courts hold that it is a superseding cause that absolves the defendant of any liability for negligence. For example, Dalton negligently starts a fire that causes injury to several persons. The driver of an ambulance summoned to the scene has been drinking on duty and, as a result, loses control of his ambulance and runs up onto a sidewalk, injuring several pedestrians. Most courts would not hold Dalton responsible for the pedestrians' injuries.

One important exception to this second rule concerns unforeseeable intervening causes that produce a harm that is foreseeable because it is identical to the harm risked by the defendant's negligence. Why should the defendant escape liability because an all-too-foreseeable consequence of its conduct came about through unforeseeable means? For example, if the owners of a concert hall negligently fail to install the number of emergency exits required by law, the owners will not escape liability to those burned and trampled during a fire just because that fire was caused by an insane concertgoer who set himself ablaze. The following case applies this rule.

TU LOI v. NEW PLAN REALTY TRUST   1993 U.S. DIST. LEXIS 1189 (E.D. Pa. 1993)

A vehicle driven by Solomon Bomze collided with a vehicle driven by Tu Loi at an intersection in the parking lot of a shopping mall leased and operated by New Plan Realty Trust. The accident occurred because Bomze failed to stop at the intersection. A stop sign previously placed at the crossing had been vandalized the day before the accident, and New Plan had not yet replaced it. However, the word stop was painted in yellow on the asphalt of the lane followed by Bomze.

After the initial collision, Tu Loi left his car to check it for damage. In the meantime, Bomze's car continued in a circular fashion, struck a parked car, and then headed toward Tu Loi, eventually pinning him against his own car and causing him serious injury.

Tu Loi sued New Plan for its negligent failure to maintain proper traffic signs in the mall's parking lot. New Plan moved for summary judgment. ∞

Yohn, Jr., District Judge New Plan's motion presents one issue—whether, as a matter of law, New Plan's negligence, if any, was so remote that it was not the legal cause of the harm suffered by Tu Loi. New Plan believes that what it characterizes as Bomze's extraordinary and unforeseeable conduct following the initial impact between his and Tu Loi's vehicles constitutes a superseding cause that exonerates it from liability. However, in Pennsylvania a tortfeasor is not relieved from liability simply because his victim suffers a foreseeable harm in an unforeseeable manner.

Certainly, if New Plan negligently maintained the traffic signs in the mall's parking lot, a foreseeable result of such negligence would be that somebody driving in the mall could be injured in an automobile accident. Tu Loi was in fact injured in an automobile accident. If the actor's conduct has created or increased the risk that a particular harm will occur, and has been a substantial factor in causing that harm, it is immaterial that the harm is brought about in a manner which no one in his position could possibly be expected to foresee.

New Plan's motion for summary judgment denied.

Generally Accepted Causation Rules Whatever test for proximate cause a court adopts, most courts generally agree on certain basic causation rules. In case of a conflict, these rules supersede the proximate cause and intervening force rules stated earlier. One such rule is that persons guilty of negligence "take their victims as they find them." This means that a negligent defendant is liable for the full extent of his victim's injuries if those injuries are aggravated by some preexisting physical susceptibility of the victim—even though this susceptibility could not have been foreseen. Similarly, negligent defendants normally are liable for diseases contracted by their victims while in a weakened state caused by their injuries. They are *jointly* liable—along with the attending physician—for negligent medical care that their victims receive for their injuries.

Also, negligent defendants ordinarily are responsible for injuries sustained by persons seeking to avoid being injured by the defendant's negligence. For example, if Peters swerves to avoid being hit by Denning's negligently driven car and in the process loses control of her own car and is injured, Denning is liable for Peters's injuries. Finally, it is commonly said that "danger invites rescue." This means that negligent persons are liable to those injured in a nonreckless attempt to rescue the victims of their negligence. This is true even if the rescue attempt was unforeseeable. As a general rule, such nonreckless rescuers also beat the various "contributory fault" defenses discussed later in the chapter.

Res Ipsa Loquitur

In some cases, negligence may be difficult to prove because the defendant has superior knowledge of the circumstances surrounding the plaintiff's injury. It may not be in the defendant's best interests to disclose those circumstances if they point to liability on his part. The classic example is *Byrne v. Boadle,* where a pedestrian was hit on the head by a barrel of flour that fell from a warehouse owned by the defendant.[5] The victim had no way of knowing what caused the barrel to fall; he merely knew he had been injured. The only people likely to know the relevant facts were the owners of the warehouse and

---

[5]2 H. & C. 722 (Eng. 1863).

their employees, but they most likely were the ones responsible for the accident. After observing that "[a] barrel could not roll out of a warehouse without some negligence," the English court required the defendant owner to show that he was not at fault.

Byrne v. Boadle eventually led to the doctrine of *res ipsa loquitur* ("the thing speaks for itself"). *Res ipsa* applies when: (1) the defendant has exclusive control of the instrumentality of harm (and therefore probable knowledge of, and responsibility for, the cause of the harm), (2) the harm that occurred would not ordinarily occur in the absence of negligence, and (3) the plaintiff was in no way responsible for his own injury. What happens when these three elements are satisfied? The answers vary from state to state, but usually this creates an inference or presumption of negligence and causation. In general, the defendant runs a significant risk of losing the case if he does not produce evidence to rebut this inference or presumption.

Negligence Defenses

The common law traditionally recognized two defenses to negligence: **contributory negligence** and **assumption of risk.** In many states, however, one or both of these traditional defenses has been superseded by new defenses called **comparative negligence** and **comparative fault.**

Contributory Negligence Contributory negligence is the plaintiff's failure to exercise reasonable care for her own safety. Where it still applies, contributory negligence is a complete defense for the defendant if it is a *substantial factor* in producing the plaintiff's injury. So, if Parker steps into the path of Dworkin's speeding car without first checking to see whether any cars are coming, Parker would be denied any recovery against Dworkin due to the clear causal relationship between his injury and his failure to exercise reasonable care for his own safety. But if Parker is injured one night when his speeding car crashes into a large, unmarked hole in a city street, and if the accident would have occurred even had Parker been driving at a legal speed, he is not barred from recovering against the city for its negligence.

Traditionally, a contributorily negligent plaintiff could overcome an otherwise-valid contributory negligence defense by showing that the defendant had the **last clear chance** to avoid the injury. The doctrine of last clear chance focuses on who was last at fault *in time*. Therefore, if, despite the plaintiff's contributory negligence, the harm could have been avoided had the defendant exercised reasonable care, the defendant's superior opportunity to avoid the accident makes him more at fault and justifies imposing liability upon him. For example, Preston pulls into the path of Durban's speeding car without looking, causing an accident. When Preston sues, Durban argues that Preston's behavior is contributory negligence. But if Preston can convince the court that Durban had the last clear chance of avoiding the accident, Preston will beat Durban's contributory negligence defense. This might involve demonstrating that Durban was reasonably aware of Preston's plight, had time to act, and had a reasonable option available to him.

Comparative Negligence Traditionally, even a minor failure to exercise reasonable care for one's own safety—only a slight departure from the standard of reasonable self-protectiveness—gave the defendant a *complete* contributory negligence defense. This rule, which some say resulted from the 19th-century desire to protect railroads and infant manufacturing interests from negligence liability, has come under increasing attack in the 20th century. The main reasons are the all-or-nothing situation the traditional rule creates and its harsh impact on many plaintiffs. For example, the rule may prevent slightly negligent plaintiffs from recovering any compensation for their losses, while only marginally more careful plaintiffs get a full recovery.

In response to such complaints, most of the states have adopted **comparative negligence** systems either by statute or by judicial decision. The details of these systems vary, but the principle underlying them is essentially the same: Courts seek to determine the *relative negligence* of the parties and award damages in proportion to the degree of negligence determined. The formula is:

Plaintiff's recovery = Defendant's percentage share of the negligence causing the injury × Plaintiff's provable damages

For example, assume that Dunne negligently injures Porter and Porter suffers $10,000 in damages. A jury determines that Dunne was 80 percent at fault and Porter 20 percent at fault. Under comparative negligence, Porter could recover only $8,000 from Dunne. But what if Dunne's share of the negligence is determined to be 40 percent and Porter's 60 percent? Here, the results vary depending on whether the state in question has adopted a *pure* or a *mixed* comparative negligence system. Under a pure system, courts apply the preceding formula no matter what the plaintiff's and the defendant's percentage shares of the negligence; thus, Porter would recover $4,000 in a pure comparative negligence state. Under a mixed system, the formula operates only when the defendant's share of the negligence is greater than (or, in some states, greater than or equal to) 50 percent. Otherwise, the traditional rule operates. In such states, therefore, Porter would recover nothing. Figure 1 summarizes the rules discussed in this section.

Assumption of Risk Assumption of risk is the plaintiff's *voluntary* consent to a *known* danger. Voluntariness basically means that the plaintiff accepted the risk of her own free will; knowledge means that the nature and extent of the risk was subjectively present to the plaintiff's consciousness. Often, the plaintiff's knowledge and voluntariness are implied from the facts of the case. For example,

---

FIGURE **1**

Plaintiff's Recovery under Contributory and Comparative Negligence Systems

PLAINTIFF'S RELATIVE FAULT	CONTRIBUTORY NEGLIGENCE	COMPARATIVE NEGLIGENCE (PURE)	COMPARATIVE NEGLIGENCE (MIXED)
0%	100%	100%	100%
10	0	90	90
60	0	40	0
90	0	10	0

Pilson voluntarily goes for a ride in Dudley's car, even though Dudley has told Pilson that her car's brakes are not working properly. Pilson probably has assumed the risk of injury from the car's defective brakes.

A plaintiff can also *expressly* assume the risk of injury by entering a contract purporting to relieve the defendant of a duty of care that he would otherwise owe to the plaintiff. Such contract provisions are called *exculpatory clauses.* Chapter 15 discusses exculpatory clauses and the numerous limitations that courts have imposed on their enforceability. The most important such limitations are that the plaintiff have knowledge of the exculpatory clause (which often boils down to a question of its conspicuousness), and that the plaintiff must accept it voluntarily (which does not happen when the defendant has greatly superior bargaining power).

What happens to assumption of risk in comparative negligence states? Some of these states have

eliminated assumption of risk as a separate defense. Some comparative negligence states have also eliminated the traditional doctrine of last clear chance. But how can such rules, which have important policy justifications, be completely discarded? Thus, assumption of risk and last clear chance often are incorporated within the state's comparative negligence scheme. In such states, comparative negligence basically becomes **comparative fault.** Although the terms comparative negligence and comparative fault often are used interchangeably, technically the former only involves negligence and the latter involves all kinds of fault. In a comparative fault state, therefore, the fact finder determines the plaintiff's and the defendant's relative shares of the fault—including assumption of risk and last clear chance—causing the plaintiff's injury. Some states have explicitly adopted comparative fault by statute; the following *Roggow* case provides an example.

ROGGOW v. MINERAL PROCESSING CORP.   698 F. Supp. 1441 (S.D. Ind. 1988)

Charles Roggow, a truck driver, made a delivery of scrap aluminum to a processing plant owned by the Mineral Processing Corporation. After making the delivery, Roggow was to pick up an unloaded trailer. Because Mineral Processing's employees had failed to secure the header bar of the trailer (the part that secures the sides of the trailer to prevent damaging vibration), Roggow had to fasten the bar before leaving the plant. The pin securing the bar had to be set in place at the very top of the trailer, but Mineral Processing had no ladder available. Consequently, Tracy Phillips, a Mineral Processing employee, offered to assist Roggow by placing him in the bucket of a highloader and raising him high enough to set the bar in place. Roggow accepted the offer and succeeded in fastening the header bar, but as Phillips was lowering him to the ground, Phillips's sleeve caught the highloader's dump lever, causing the bucket to overturn and Roggow to fall approximately nine feet onto a concrete floor.

Roggow sued Mineral Processing in negligence for his resulting injuries. After a trial, the jury found Roggow's damages to be $80,000, but reduced his award to $48,000 because they found him to be 40 percent at fault. Roggow moved for a new trial, arguing, among other things, that the trial court erred in refusing to instruct the jury on last clear chance. ∞

Endsley, U.S. Magistrate   This matter was tried under Indiana's Comparative Fault Act (the Act). Prior to the enactment of comparative fault, Indiana followed the common law rule of contributory negligence. This antiquated "all-or-nothing" rule totally bars a plaintiff from recovering damages for injuries if he is guilty of negligence, albeit slight. During the 20th century, common law doctrines were developed to alleviate the harsh results of contributory negligence. Last clear chance [was

one] of those exceptions. Roggow now invites the Court to determine the applicability of this exception to contributory negligence under the Act.

Because no Indiana court has addressed this issue, this federal court must determine how the highest court in Indiana would decide if it were presented with the question. Under the Act, assumed risk [is not] available as [an] absolute defense for the defendant. Specifically, "unreasonable assumption of risk not constituting an enforceable express consent" [is a] factor to be considered by the fact finder when weighing the fault attributable to the individual actors. Similarly, by its definition in the Act, "fault" necessarily includes the factors which make up last clear chance. The Indiana legislature defined fault as "any act or omission that is negligent, willful, wanton, or reckless toward the person or property of the actor or others, but does not include an intentional act. The term also includes unreasonable assumption of risk not constituting an enforceable express consent, . . . and unreasonable failure to avoid an injury or to mitigate damages."

Consequently, just as assumed risk is no longer available to completely excuse the negligence of the defendant, so too [is] last clear chance no longer available to completely excuse the negligence of the plaintiff.

This conclusion is in accord with the holdings and statutes of a majority of states which have addressed the issue. Consequently, failure to give Roggow's tendered instruction was not error in this case.

Roggow's motion for a new trial denied.

STRICT LIABILITY

Strict liability is liability without fault or irrespective of fault. This means that in strict liability cases, the defendant is liable even though he did not intend to cause the harm and did not bring it about through his recklessness or negligence. Also, defendants in strict liability cases traditionally have had fewer defenses to liability than defendants in negligence cases.

The imposition of strict liability is a social policy decision that the risk associated with an activity should be borne by those who pursue it, rather than by innocent people who are exposed to that risk. Such liability has been justified either by the defendant's voluntary decision to engage in a particularly risky activity or, more recently, by the defendant's superior ability to bear losses. Thus, corporations are often thought superior to individuals as risk bearers because they can pass the costs of liability on to consumers in the form of higher prices for goods or services. Through strict liability, therefore, the economic costs created by certain harms are transferred from the victims to defendants to society at large, or "socialized." This strategy often is called *risk spreading* or *socialization of risk.*

When does strict liability apply? The owners of trespassing livestock and the keepers of naturally dangerous wild animals were among the first classes of defendants on whom the courts imposed strict liability. Today, the two most important activities subject to judicially imposed strict liability are abnormally dangerous (or ultrahazardous) activities and the manufacture or sale of defective and unreasonably dangerous products. We discuss the latter in Chapter 20 and the former immediately below. After that, this chapter briefly examines some forms of statutory strict liability.

Abnormally Dangerous Activities

Abnormally dangerous (or ultrahazardous) activities are activities that necessarily involve a risk of harm to others that cannot be eliminated by the exercise of reasonable care. Among the activities treated as abnormally dangerous are blasting, crop dusting, stunt flying, and, in one case, the transportation of large quantities of gasoline by truck. The following *Klein* case discusses the numerous factors that courts sometimes consider before deciding whether a particular activity should be classified as abnormally dangerous. Traditionally, contributory negligence has not been a defense in ultrahazardous activity cases, but assumption of risk has been a defense.

KLEIN v. PYRODYNE CORPORATION   810 P.2d 917 (Wash. Sup. Ct. 1991)

 yrodyne Corporation was hired to display the fireworks at the Western Washington State Fairgrounds in Puyallup, Washington, on July 4, 1987. During the display, one of the 5-inch mortars was knocked into a horizontal position, from which position a rocket inside ignited and flew 500 feet parallel to the earth, exploding near the crowd of onlookers. Danny and Marion Klein were injured by the explosion. They filed a strict liability suit against Pyrodyne. They also argued that Pyrodyne failed to carry out a number of the statutory and regulatory requirements for preparing and setting off fireworks. Pyrodyne argued that the accident was caused by a rocket detonating in its mortar tube without ever leaving the ground, causing another rocket to be knocked over, ignited, and set off horizontally. Pyrodyne moved for summary judgment on the ground that negligence principles should be applied to the case. When the trial court denied its motion and found it strictly liable, Pyrodyne appealed. ∞

Guy, Justice   The modern doctrine of strict liability for abnormally dangerous activities derives from *Rylands v. Fletcher* (Eng. 1866), in which the defendant's reservoir flooded mine shafts on the plaintiff's adjoining land. *Rylands v. Fletcher* has come to stand for the rule that the defendant will be liable when he damages another by a thing or activity unduly dangerous and inappropriate to the place where it is maintained, in the light of the character of that place and its surroundings.

The basic principle of *Rylands v. Fletcher* has been accepted by the *Restatement (Second) of Torts.* Section 519 of the *Restatement* provides that any party carrying on an "abnormally dangerous activity" is strictly liable for the ensuing damages. Section 520 of the *Restatement* lists six factors that are to be considered in determining whether an activity is "abnormally dangerous": (a) a high degree of risk of some harm to the person, land, or chattels of others; (b) the likelihood that the harm that results from it will be great; (c) an inability to eliminate the risk by the exercise of reasonable care; (d) the extent to which the activity is not a matter of common usage; (e) the inappropriateness of the activity to the place where it is carried on; and (f) the extent to which its value to the community is outweighed by its dangerous attributes. The comments to section 520 explain how these factors should be evaluated: "Any one of them is not necessarily sufficient of itself in a particular case, and ordinarily several of them will be required for strict liability. On the other hand, it is not necessary that each of them be present, especially if others weigh heavily."

We find that the factors stated in clauses (a), (b), and (c) are all present in the case of fireworks displays. Any time a person ignites rockets with the intention of sending them aloft to explode in the presence of large crowds of people, a high risk of serious personal injury or property damage is created. That risk arises because of the possibility that a rocket will malfunction or be misdirected. Furthermore, no matter how much care pyrotechnicians exercise, they cannot entirely eliminate the high risk inherent in setting off powerful explosives near crowds.

Pyrodyne argues that the factor stated in clause (d) is not met because fireworks are a common way to celebrate the 4th of July. Although fireworks are frequently and regularly enjoyed by the public, few persons set off special fireworks displays. Indeed, anyone wishing to do so must first obtain a license.

The Puyallup Fairgrounds is an appropriate place for the fireworks show because the audience can be seated at a reasonable distance from the display. Therefore, the clause (e) factor is not present in this case. The factor in clause (f) requires analysis of the extent to which the value of the fireworks to the community outweighs its dangerous attributes. This country has a longstanding tradition of fireworks on the 4th of July. That tradition suggests that we have decided that the value of fireworks on the day celebrating our national independence and unity outweighs the risks of injuries and damage.

In sum, we find that setting off public fireworks displays satisfies four of the six conditions under the *Restatement* test. We therefore hold that conducting public fireworks displays is an abnormally dangerous activity justifying the imposition of strict liability.

Judgment for the Kleins affirmed.

Statutory Strict Liability

Strict liability principles are also embodied in modern legislation. The most important examples are the *Workers' Compensation Acts* passed by most states early in this century, which Chapter 50 discusses in detail. Such statutes allow employees to recover statutorily limited amounts from their employers without any fault on the employer's part or any contributory fault on the employee's part. Employers participate in a compulsory liability insurance system and are expected to pass the costs of the system on to consumers, who then become the ultimate bearers of the human costs of industrial production. Other examples of statutory strict liability include the *Dram Shop statutes* of some states, which impose liability on sellers of alcoholic beverages without proof of negligence when third parties are harmed due to a buyer's intoxication. Also included is the statutory strict liability that some states impose on the operators of aircraft for ground damage resulting from aviation accidents.

TORT REFORM

The risk-spreading strategy just described has not been trouble-free. Over the past 20 years or so, there has been considerable talk about a "crisis" in the liability insurance system. From time to time over that period, the insurance system has been marked by outright refusals of coverage, reductions in coverage, and escalating premiums when coverage remains available. To some, this liability insurance crisis is largely the fault of the insurance industry. Among other things, such people argue that insurers have manufactured the crisis to get unjustified premium increases and to divert attention from insurer mismanagement of invested premium income.

To other observers, however, the reason for the crisis is the explosion in tort liability that has occurred in recent years. Examples include the tendency toward greater imposition of strict liability, increases in the frequency and size of punitive damage awards, and similar increases in awards for noneconomic harms such as pain and suffering. The greater costs this explosion imposes on defendants, these observers say, naturally increase the price and diminish the availability of liability insurance. In some cases, therefore, businesses may be required to self-insure or to "go naked" without insurance coverage. In others, they may be able to obtain insurance—but only at a price that cannot be completely passed on to consumers. Where the costs *can* be fully passed on, the argument continues, they depress the economy by diminishing consumers' purchasing power, adding to inflation, or both. In addition, our argument concludes, the liability explosion impedes the development of new products and technologies that might result in huge awards for injured plaintiffs.

These beliefs have fueled a movement for tort reform. By the mid-1990s, most states had enacted some form of tort reform legislation. Such legislation typically follows one or both of two strategies: (1) limiting defendants' tort *liability* (plaintiffs' ability to get a judgment), and (2) limiting the *damages* plaintiffs can recover once they get a judgment. One example of the former is legislation restricting the liability of social hosts or businesses for the damage caused by intoxicated people to whom they serve alcohol. Perhaps the most common examples of the latter are statutory caps or other limits on recoveries for punitive damages and noneconomic harm.

In addition, local governments in many states now enjoy statutory limits on their liability for negligence, affording them partial relief from negligence claims for improper maintenance of streets and traffic signals—claims that sometimes accompany automobile accident cases. Likewise, physicians in a number of states have received some relief from spiraling liability costs by devices such as caps on the amount recoverable in liability suits and mandatory pretrial mediation of all claims over a prescribed threshold.

The battle for tort reform is far from over, however. Tort reform opponents who lost the fight against tort reform in the legislature have continued it in the courts. They have done so primarily by challenging tort reform measures on state constitutional grounds. Such challenges have succeeded in some states and have been rebuffed in others.

ETHICAL AND PUBLIC POLICY CONCERNS

1. In the famous case of *Palsgraf v. Long Island Railroad,* the plaintiff was injured when a late-boarding train passenger dropped a package of fireworks he was carrying as he attempted to board a train that was pulling out of the station. Two railroad employees were trying to help him board, one pulling and one pushing. The package was jostled loose and exploded on impact. The concussion from the explosion caused some scales to fall on the victim, who was standing several feet away from the action. The defendant railroad escaped liability to the victim because the court found it had no duty to her because its employees could not reasonably have foreseen that they were endangering her by their actions. Yet plainly the harm would not have occurred had the railroad's employees refused to allow the passenger to try to board a moving train. Even if the railroad had no legal duty to Palsgraf, did it have any ethical duty to her?

2. Implicit in the idea of proximate cause is the fact that a negligent defendant can be the actual cause of some plaintiffs' injuries but avoid any liability for those injuries because his negligence was not the proximate cause of such injuries. Is the doctrine of proximate cause ethically justifiable?

3. While proximate cause allows defendants to avoid responsibility for some consequences of their negligence, strict liability imposes liability on persons who participate in abnormally dangerous activities even though they exercised all possible care to avoid injuring anyone. Can such liability be ethically justified?

PROBLEM CASES

1. The Citizens for Bob Olexo Campaign Committee rented three tanks of helium from James Dawes Company. The helium was to be used to fill balloons that were to be handed out to the public during the Belmont County Fair. Although the agreement with Dawes called for the Committee to return the used cylinders, they were left at the fairgrounds leaning up against a commercial building. Philip C. Jeffers III, age 14, attended a football game at the fairgrounds, where he and some friends discovered the tanks. Despite the warning on the tanks which said "CAUTION! HIGH PRESSURE GAS. CAN CAUSE RAPID SUFFOCATION," Jeffers inhaled some helium from one of the tanks, collapsed and died. Jeffers's father sued the Dawes Company, which moved for a summary judgment on a number of grounds, among which was the argument that it owed no duty to Jeffers. Should Dawes's motion be granted?

2. A young man abducted R.M.V., age 10, from the sidewalk in front of her home and dragged her across the street to a vacant apartment at the Chalmette Apartments. He raped her, put her in the closet, told her not to leave, and disappeared. The apartment in question was described by the police officer called to the scene as "empty, filthy, dirty, and full of debris." Glass was broken from its windows and the front door was off its hinges. In the two years prior to the attack on R.M.V., Dallas

police had investigated many serious crimes committed at the Chalmette Apartments complex. A Dallas City Ordinance established minimum standards for property owners, requiring them, among other things, to "keep the doors and windows of a vacant structure or vacant portion of a structure securely closed to prevent unauthorized entry." Gaile Nixon, R.M.V.'s mother, filed a negligence suit against Chalmette's owner and Mr. Property Management Company, Inc., the manager of the complex. Were the defendants correct in arguing that they owed no duty to R.M.V.?

3. On September 3, 1984, Valerie Jones, a lab technician at a Kelco's chemical plant, stole a cupful of sulfuric acid from the plant. After work, she drove to the home of her sister-in-law, Gwendolyn Henry. After a brief verbal altercation with Henry over the fact that Henry, who had been baby-sitting Jones's 2-year-old son, had trimmed the child's hair, she threw the acid in Henry's face. Henry suffered severe and permanent injuries, and Jones was ultimately sentenced to seven years in prison for the attack. Henry filed a negligence suit against Kelco, and a jury awarded her $450,000. Kelco appealed, arguing that it owed no duty to Henry and that, in any event, Jones's act was an intervening cause that relieved it of liability. The evidence at trial indicated that Jones had been a model employee who had to have access to the chemical storage area to perform her duties. Should the jury's verdict be reversed?

4. Emily Hopkins accompanied her son and daughter to an open house to which they had been invited by a realtor. When Hopkins walked down the house's hallway from its laundry room toward its foyer, she fell on a step that led down from the hallway to the foyer, fracturing her ankle. Hopkins failed to see the step because the floors on both levels and on the step were covered with vinyl of the same pattern. Under the traditional categories, is Hopkins better classed as an invitee or a licensee? Which categorization would be more advantageous for her if she sues the realtor for failing to warn her of the hazard?

5. Higgins and some friends went to a night baseball game at Comiskey Park in Chicago. Near the end of the game, Higgins went to the men's room. On his way back to his seat, he walked down a corridor that ran past a concession stand. As he passed the stand, the door to the front of the stand (a 4′ by 6′ sheet of plywood attached to the top of the stand and hooked to an eyelet in the ceiling when opened) fell from its open position and struck him on the head, causing permanent head and neck injuries. None of the eyewitnesses to the incident saw anyone touch either the door or the hook securing it, or do anything that might have caused the door to fall. There was, however, testimony that, just before the door fell, the crowd in the stadium was screaming and stamping, and that one "could feel the place tremble." Higgins sued the Chicago White Sox, owners of the stadium, arguing that *res ipsa loquitur* should be applied to the case. Was he right?

6. Frank Bills was injured when he fell on the exterior landing of his apartment building during a snow and ice storm. The landing was covered with a thin coat of ice. Bills sued his landlord, Willow Run 1 Apartments, in negligence. He argued that his fall would not have occurred if the landing had complied with a local building code. The preface to the building code stated that it was "dedicated to the development of better building construction and greater safety to the public." However, the exact nature of Willow Run's alleged building code violation was unclear. Assuming that Willow Run had violated some building code provision, did it breach a duty to Bills here? If it did breach a duty, what other issue would remain for resolution?

7. A madman ran through the front door of the crowded Concord Cafeteria, threw a five-gallon container of gasoline on the floor, lit a match to the gasoline, and ran away. In the fire that ensued, many patrons were burned and/or suffered smoke inhalation, and others were injured in the chaotic rush to flee the burning building. Assume for the sake of argument that the exits to the cafeteria were inadequate, were inadequately marked, and thus amounted to a breach of duty on Concord's part. Even so, is Concord liable to the injured parties in negligence?

8. Allen Beckett, a fourth-year player on his high school baseball team, was injured when he collided with another player during outfielder practice. The accident occurred after the coach conducting the practice hit a fly ball to Beckett. Beckett called for the ball, but the wind was blowing so hard that neither the coach nor the other players heard him. The coach called for another player to catch the ball, and that player and Beckett collided head-on. Beckett's jaw was broken, and he filed suit against the school, arguing that it had failed to warn him of the danger of such collisions, failed to adequately supervise the practice, and had conducted the practice in an unreasonably dangerous manner. At one point in his testimony Beckett denied that he had ever heard of baseball players colliding and said that he had no knowledge of any accidents happening on baseball fields. Under cross-examination, however, he admitted that his coaches had repeatedly stressed communication among players to avoid accidents, that it was possible on such a windy day for his voice to have gotten lost in the wind, and that the same type of thing could have happened in a game. Was the trial court summary judgment in favor of the school proper?

9. Lee Ann Laird, age 12, was injured when her bicycle was hit by a car driven by Larry Kostman. Lee Ann was in the process of pulling into the street from a driveway, and she emerged from behind a van parked at the curb. At the trial, Kostman testified that he hit his brakes as soon as saw the bicycle. His passenger testified that Laird "came out of nowhere," and that he didn't see her until the moment of impact. Laird testified that she saw Kostman's car turn onto the street from an intersection more than 200 feet from the point of impact, that no more than 2 feet of her bicycle extended into the street from behind the parked van, and that when she tried to move the bike back to avoid the collision, the brakes locked. After the trial judge refused to instruct the jury on the doctrine of last clear chance, the jury ruled in favor of Kostman. Was the trial judge's refusal proper? Assume that traditional negligence rules apply.

10. On January 9, 1979, a railroad car leased by American Cyanamid (American) and containing 20,000 gallons of acrylonitrile manufactured by American, began leaking. At the time, the car was sitting just south of Chicago in the Blue Island yard of the Indiana Harbor Belt Railroad (Indiana) awaiting switching to Conrail for delivery to its final destination. Indiana's employees stopped the leak but were uncertain about how much of the car's contents had escaped. Because acrylonitrile is flammable, highly toxic, and possibly carcinogenic, Illinois authorities ordered homes near the yard temporarily evacuated. Later, it was discovered that only about a quarter of the car's contents had leaked, but the Illinois Department of Environmental Protection, fearing that the soil and water had been contaminated, ordered Indiana to take decontamination measures costing $981,000. Indiana sued American on negligence and strict liability theories seeking to recover its expenses. Evidence introduced at the trial included a list of 125 hazardous materials that are shipped in highest volume on the nation's railroads. Acrylonitrile was the 53rd most hazardous on the list. Was the trial court's entry of summary judgment for Indiana on the strict liability claim proper?

11. Mark Brown sustained serious burns when his rental home was destroyed by a fire. The fire began when Brown attempted to light his oil stove and unknowingly ignited underground natural gas leaking into his home from a damaged gas line several blocks away. The gas leak was caused years earlier, when a firm laying underground telephone cable damaged a gas transmission line owned by Washington Water Power (WWP). Brown sued WWP in strict liability. Under the *Restatement* factors discussed in the *Klein* case, should WWP be liable on the theory that natural gas transmission is an abnormally dangerous activity?

Unfair Competition

This chapter discusses certain legal rules that limit free competition by allowing civil recoveries for abuses of that freedom. These abuses are: (1) patent, copyright, and trademark infringement; (2) the misappropriation of trade secrets; (3) the intentional torts of injurious falsehood, interference with contractual relations, and interference with prospective advantage; and (4) the various forms of unfair competition attacked by section 43(a) of the Lanham Act. Indeed, the term *unfair competition* describes the whole chapter. In general, competition is deemed unfair because: (1) it discourages creative endeavor by robbing creative people of the fruits of their innovations, or (2) it renders commercial life too uncivilized for the law to tolerate. ∞

PROTECTION OF INTELLECTUAL PROPERTY

Patents

A patent can be regarded as an agreement between an inventor and the federal government. Under that agreement, the inventor obtains the exclusive right (for a limited time) to make, use, and sell his invention, in return for making the invention public by giving the government certain information about it. The patent holder's (or **patentee's**) monopoly encourages the creation and disclosure of inventions by stopping third parties from appropriating them once they become public. However, third parties may develop the invention in ways that do not interfere with the patentee's rights.

What Is Patentable? An inventor may patent: (1) a *process* (as described in the following *Diehr* case), (2) a *machine,* (3) a *manufacture* or product, (4) a *composition of matter* (a combination of elements with qualities not present in the elements taken individually, such as a new chemical compound), (5) an *improvement* of any of the above, (6) an *ornamental design* for a product, and (7) a *plant* produced by asexual reproduction. Naturally occurring things (e.g., a new wild plant) and new business methods (e.g., an innovative accounting technique) are not patentable. In addition, as *Diehr* states, abstract ideas, scientific laws, and other mental concepts are not patentable, although their practical applications often are. As *Diehr* also reveals, a computer program may be patentable if it is part of a patentable process. However, it is unclear whether a program is patentable if it stands alone and is not part of a patentable process.[1]

Even though an invention fits within one of the above categories, it is not patentable if it lacks novelty, is obvious, or has no utility, or if the patent applicant is an inappropriate applicant.[2] One aspect of the *novelty* requirement is the rule that no patent should be issued where *before the invention's creation* it has been: (1) known or used in the United States, (2) patented in the United States or a foreign country, or (3) described in a printed publication in the United States or a foreign country. Another aspect is the requirement that no patent should be issued if more than one year before the *patent*

application the invention was: (1) patented in the United States or a foreign country, (2) described in a printed publication in the United States or a foreign country, or (3) in public use or on sale in the United States. In addition, there can be no patent if the invention would have been *obvious* to a person having ordinary skill in the area. A patentable invention must also have *utility,* or usefulness. Finally, there can be no patent if the applicant did not create the invention in question, or if she abandoned the invention. *Creation* problems frequently arise where several people allegedly contributed to the invention. *Abandonment* may be by express statement, such as publicly devoting an invention to humanity, or by implication from conduct, such as delaying for an unreasonable length of time before making a patent application.

Obtaining a Patent The Patent and Trademark Office of the Department of Commerce handles patent applications. The application must include a *specification* describing the invention with sufficient detail and clarity to enable any person skilled in the relevant field to make and use it. The application must also contain a *drawing* when this is necessary for understanding the subject matter to be patented. The Patent Office then determines whether the invention meets the various tests for patentability. If the application is rejected, the applicant may resubmit it. Once any of the applicant's claims have been rejected twice, the applicant may appeal to the Office's Board of Patent Appeals and Interferences. Subsequent appeals to the federal courts are also possible.

---

[1]As discussed later in this chapter, however, computer programs may obtain copyright and trade secret protection.

[2]Plant and design patents are subject to requirements that are slightly different from those stated here.

DIAMOND v. DIEHR 450 U.S. 175 (U.S. Sup. Ct. 1981)

D*iehr and Lutton attempted to obtain a patent covering a process for molding raw, uncured synthetic rubber into cured precision products. The process used a mold for shaping the uncured rubber under heat and pressure and then curing it in the mold. Previous efforts at curing and molding synthetic rubber had suffered from an inability to measure the temperature inside the molding press and thus to determine a precise curing time. Diehr and Lutton's invention involved a process for constantly measuring the temperature inside the mold, feeding this information to a computer that constantly recalculated the curing time, and enabling the computer to signal the molding press to open at the correct instant.*

The patent examiner rejected Diehr and Lutton's patent application. The Patent and Trademark Office Board of Appeals (now the Board of Patent Appeals and Interferences) agreed with the examiner, but the now-defunct Court of Customs and Patent Appeals reversed. The patent office appealed to the U.S. Supreme Court. ∞

Rehnquist, Justice   In defining the nature of a patentable process, this Court has stated:

A process is a mode of treatment of certain materials to produce a given result. It is an act, or a series of acts, performed upon the subject matter to be transformed and reduced to a different state or thing. If new and useful, it is just as patentable as is a piece of machinery. The machinery pointed out as suitable to perform the process may or may not be new or patentable; whilst the process itself may be altogether new and produce an entirely new result.

Recently, we repeated the above definition, adding:

Transformation and reduction of an article to a different state or thing is the clue to the patentability of a process claim that does not include particular machines.

That Diehr and Lutton's claims involve the transformation of an article, raw uncured synthetic rubber, into a different state or thing cannot be disputed. Industrial processes such as this have historically been eligible to receive the protection of our patent laws.

Excluded from patent protection are laws of nature, physical phenomena, and abstract ideas. Only last Term, we explained:

A new mineral discovered in the earth or a new plant found in the wild is not patentable subject matter. Likewise, Einstein could not patent his celebrated law that $E = mc^2$; nor could Newton have patented the law of gravity. Such discoveries are manifestations of nature, free to all men and reserved exclusively to none.

Diehr and Lutton do not seek to patent a mathematical formula. Instead, they seek patent protection for a process of curing synthetic rubber. Their process employs a well-known mathematical equation, but they do not seek to preempt the use of that equation. They seek only to foreclose from others the use of that equation in conjunction with all the other steps in their process. It is now a commonplace that an *application* of a law of nature or mathematical formula to a known structure or process may be deserving of patent protection.

It may later be determined that the process is not deserving of patent protection because it fails to satisfy the statutory conditions of novelty or nonobviousness. A rejection on either of these grounds does not affect the determination that Diehr and Lutton's claims recited subject matter which was eligible for patent protection.

Judgment for Diehr and Lutton affirmed.

Ownership and Transfer of Patent Rights   Until a recent change in federal law, a patent normally gave the patentee exclusive rights to make, use, and sell the patented invention for 17 years from the date the patent was granted. In order to bring the United States into compliance with the General Agreement on Tariffs and Trade (an international agreement commonly known as GATT), Congress amended the patent law to provide that the patentee's exclusive rights to make, use, and sell the patented invention generally exist until the expiration of 20 years from the date the patent application was filed. This duration rule applies to patents that result from applications filed on or after June 8, 1995. (A design patent, however, exists for 14 years from the date it was granted.)

The patentee may transfer ownership of the patent by making a written *assignment* of it to another party. Alternatively, the patentee may retain ownership and *license* others to exercise some or all of the patent rights.

Usually, the party who created the invention is the patent holder. But what happens when the creator of the invention is an employee and her employer seeks rights in her invention? If the invention was developed by an employee *hired to do inventive or creative work,* she must use the invention solely for the employer's benefit and must assign any patents she obtains to the employer. If the employee was hired for purposes *other than invention or creation,* however, she owns any patent she acquires. Finally, regardless of the purpose for which the employee was hired, the *shop right* doctrine gives the employer a nonexclusive, royalty-free *license* to use the employee's invention if it was created on company time and through the use of company facilities. Any patent the employee might retain is still effective against parties other than the employer.

Patent Infringement   Patent infringement occurs when a defendant, without authorization from the patentee, takes action that usurps any of the patentee's rights to make, use, and sell the patented invention. Infringement may be established under principles of *literal* infringement or under a judicially developed approach known as the *doctrine of equivalents.* Infringement is considered to be literal in nature when the subject matter made, used, or sold by the defendant clearly falls within the stated terms of the claim of invention set forth in the successful patent applicant's specification. Under the doctrine of equivalents, a defendant may be held liable for infringement even though the subject matter he made, used, or sold contained elements that were not identical to those described in the patentee's claim of invention, if the elements of the defendant's subject matter nonetheless may be seen as equivalent to those of the patented invention. A traditional formulation of the test posed by the doctrine of equivalents is whether the alleged infringer's subject matter performs substantially the same function as the protected invention in substantially the same way, in order to obtain the same result.

Recently, an alleged infringer sought to convince the U.S. Supreme Court to abolish the doctrine of equivalents on the ground that it effectively allows patentees to extend the scope of patent protection beyond the stated terms approved by the Patent Office when it issued the patent. In *Warner-Jenkinson Co. v. Hilton Davis Chemical Co.,*[3] however, the Court rejected this attack on the doctrine. The Court observed that in view of courts' longstanding use of the doctrine (use in which Congress seemingly acquiesced by not legislatively prohibiting its use), arguments for abolishing the doctrine would be better addressed to Congress. The *Warner-Jenkinson* Court did acknowledge, however, that overly broad application of the doctrine of equivalents could lead to an unwarranted expansion of patent owners' rights. Therefore, the Court held that the doctrine of equivalents must be applied to the *individual elements* of the patentee's claim of invention rather than to the patentee's invention *as a whole.*

One who *actively induces* another's infringement of a patent is liable as an infringer if he knows and intends that the infringement occur. For example, if Ingram directly infringes Paxton's patent on a ma-

chine and Doyle knowingly sold Ingram an instruction manual for the machine, Doyle may be liable as an infringer. Finally, if one knowingly sells a direct patent infringer a component of a patented invention or something useful in employing a patented process, the seller may be liable for *contributory infringement.* Here, the thing sold must be a material part of the invention and must not be a staple article of commerce with some other significant use. Suppose that Irving directly infringes Potter's patent for a radio by selling virtually identical radios. If Davis sells Irving sophisticated circuitry for the radios with knowledge of Irving's infringement, Davis may be liable for contributory infringement, assuming that the circuitry is an important component of the radios and has no other significant uses.

The basic recovery for patent infringement is damages adequate to compensate for the infringement, plus court costs and interest. The damages cannot be less than a reasonable royalty for the use made of the invention by the infringer. The court may in its discretion award damages of up to three times those actually suffered. Finally, injunctive relief is available, and attorney's fees may be awarded in exceptional cases.

Defenses to Patent Infringement One defense to a patent infringement suit is that the subject matter of the alleged infringement is neither within the literal scope of the patent nor substantially equivalent to the patented invention. The alleged infringer may also defend by attacking the validity of the patent. Despite having been approved by the Patent and Trademark Office, patents are sometimes declared invalid when challenged in court.

In appropriate cases, the defendant can assert that the patentee has committed *patent misuse.* This is behavior that unjustifiably exploits the patent monopoly. For example, the patentee may require the purchaser of a license on his patent to buy his unpatented goods, or may tie the obtaining of a license on one of his patented inventions to the purchase of a license on another.[4] One who refuses the patentee's terms and later infringes the patent may escape liability by arguing that the patentee misused his monopoly position.

---

[3]65 U.S.L.W. 4162 (U.S. Sup. Ct. 1997).

[4]Some forms of patent misuse may be antitrust violations. Chapter 49 discusses the interaction between patent law and antitrust law.

Copyrights

Copyright law gives certain exclusive rights to creators of *original works of authorship*. It prevents others from using their work, gives them an incentive to innovate, and thereby benefits society. Yet copyright law also tries to balance these purposes against the equally compelling public interest in the free movement of ideas, information, and commerce. It does so mainly by limiting the intellectual products it protects and by allowing the fair use defense described later.

Coverage Federal copyright law protects a wide range of works of authorship, including books, periodical articles, dramatic and musical compositions, works of art, motion pictures, sound recordings, lectures, computer programs, and architectural plans. To merit copyright protection, such works must be *fixed*—set out in a tangible medium of expression from which they can be perceived, reproduced, or communicated. They also must be *original* (the author's own work) and *creative* (reflecting exercise of the creator's judgment). Unlike the inventions protected by patent law, however, copyrightable works need not be novel.

Copyright protection does not extend to ideas, facts, procedures, processes, systems, methods of operation, concepts, principles, or discoveries *as such*. However, it may protect the *forms and ways in which they are expressed*. The story line of a play, for instance, is protected, but the ideas, themes, or messages underlying it are not. Although there is no copyright protection over facts, the expression in nonfiction works and compilations of fact is protected.

Computer programs involve their own special problems. It is fairly well settled that copyright law protects a program's *object code* (program instructions that are machine-readable but not intelligible to humans) and *source code* (instructions intelligible to humans). But there is less agreement about the copyrightability of a program's nonliteral elements such as its organization, its structure, and its presentation of information on the screen. Most of the courts that have considered the issue hold that nonliteral elements may sometimes be protected by copyright law, but courts differ about the extent of this protection.

Creation, Duration, and Notice A copyright comes into existence upon the creation and fixing of a protected work. Although a copyright owner may register the copyright with the Copyright Office of the Library of Congress, registration is not necessary for the copyright to exist. However, registration normally *is* necessary before the owner can begin a suit for copyright infringement.

For works created in 1978 and thereafter, the copyright usually lasts for *the life of the author plus 50 years*. This basic duration rule does not apply, however, if the copyrighted work is a *work-for-hire*. In that event, the copyright lasts for 100 years from creation of the work or 75 years from first publication of it, whichever comes first. A work-for-hire exists when: (1) an employee, in the course of her regular employment duties, prepares a copyrightable work; or (2) an individual or corporation and an independent contractor (i.e., nonemployee) enter into a written agreement under which the independent contractor is to prepare, for the retaining individual or corporation, one of several types of copyrightable works designated in the Copyright Act. In the first situation, the employer is legally classified as the work's author and copyright owner. In the second situation, the party who (or which) retained the independent contractor is considered the resulting work's author and copyright owner.

Even though it is not required, copyright owners often provide *notice* of the copyright. Federal law authorizes a basic form of notice for use with most copyrighted works. A book, for example, might include the term *Copyright* (or the abbreviation *Copr.* or the symbol ©), the year of its first publication, and the name of the copyright owner in a location likely to give reasonable notice to readers.

Ownership Rights A copyright owner has exclusive rights to reproduce the copyrighted work, prepare derivative works based on it (e.g., a movie version of a novel), and distribute copies of the work by sale or otherwise. With certain copyrighted works, the copyright owner also obtains the exclusive right to perform the work or display it publicly. Copyright ownership initially resides in the creator of the copyrighted work, but the copyright may be transferred to another party. Also, the owner may individually transfer each of the listed rights, or a portion of each, without losing ownership of the remaining rights. Most transfers of copyright ownership require a writing signed by the owner or his agent. The owner may also retain ownership while licensing the copyrighted work or a portion of it.

Infringement Those who violate any of the copyright owner's exclusive rights may be liable for copyright infringement. Infringement is fairly easily proven when direct evidence of significant copying exists; verbatim copying of protected material is an example. Usually, however, proof of infringement involves establishing that: (1) the defendant had *access* to the copyrighted work; (2) the defendant engaged in enough *copying*—either deliberately or subconsciously—that the resemblance between the allegedly infringing work and the copyrighted work does not seem coincidental; and (3) there is *substantial similarity* between the two works.

Access may be proven circumstantially, such as by showing that the copyrighted work was widely circulated. The copying and substantial similarity elements, which closely relate to each other, necessarily involve discretionary case-by-case determinations. Of course, the copying and substantial similarity must exist with regard to the copyrighted work's protected expression. Copying of general ideas, facts, themes, and the like (i.e., copying of unprotected matter) is not infringement. The defendant's having paraphrased protected expression does not constitute a defense to what otherwise appears to be infringement. Neither does the defendant's having credited the copyrighted work as the source from which the defendant borrowed.

The basic recovery for copyright infringement is the owner's actual damages plus the attributable profits received by the infringer. However, the plaintiff may usually elect to receive statutory damages—which fall within certain defined ranges—in lieu of the basic remedy. Injunctive relief and awards of costs and attorney's fees are possible in appropriate cases. Although it seldom does so, the federal government may pursue a criminal copyright infringement prosecution if the infringement was willful and for purposes of commercial advantage or private financial gain.

The Fair Use Defense The fair use defense to a copyright infringement suit requires the weighing of several factors whose application varies from case to case. These factors are: (1) the purpose and character of the use, (2) the nature of the copyrighted work, (3) the amount and substantiality of the portion used in relation to the copyrighted work as a whole, and (4) the effect of the use on the potential market for the copyrighted work or on its value. *Campbell v. Acuff-Rose Music, Inc.*, which follows, discusses the reasons for the fair use defense and applies the fair use factors in the context of an allegedly infringing parody of a copyrighted song.

CAMPBELL v. ACUFF-ROSE MUSIC, INC. 510 U.S. 569 (U.S. Sup. Ct. 1994)

I n 1964, Roy Orbison and William Dees wrote a song titled "Oh, Pretty Woman." They assigned their rights in the song to Acuff-Rose Music, Inc., the copyright owner at all times relevant to this case. In 1989, Luther Campbell, a member of the rap music group known as 2 Live Crew, wrote a parodic version of "Oh, Pretty Woman." The group sought Acuff-Rose's permission to use the parody on an album. Despite Acuff-Rose's denial of permission, 2 Live Crew used the parody on the "As Clean As They Wanna Be" album. Roughly a year after this recording was released (and approximately 250,000 copies had been sold), Acuff-Rose sued 2 Live Crew and its record company for copyright infringement. The federal district court granted summary judgment to the defendants on the ground of fair use. The Sixth Circuit Court of Appeals reversed, holding that the defendants were not entitled to the fair use defense. The U.S. Supreme Court granted certiorari. ∞

Souter, Justice It is uncontested that 2 Live Crew's song would be an infringement . . . , but for a finding of fair use. The fair use doctrine . . . "permits [and requires] courts to avoid rigid application of the copyright statute when, on occasion, it would stifle the very creativity which that law is designed to foster" (quoting *Stewart v. Abend* (1990)).

The first factor in a fair use enquiry is "the purpose and character of the use, including whether such use is of a commercial nature or is for non-profit educational purposes" (quoting Copyright Act, § 107). The enquiry here may be guided by the examples given in . . . § 107, looking to whether the use is for criticism, or comment, or news reporting, and the like. The central purpose of this investigation is to see . . . whether the new work [reflects] a further purpose or different character, altering the [original work] with new expression, meaning, or message; it asks, in other words, whether . . . the new work is "transformative." Although such transformative use is not absolutely necessary for a finding of fair use, . . . transformative works . . . lie at the heart of the fair use doctrine's guarantee of breathing space within the confines of copyright. [T]he more transformative the new work, the less will be the significance of other factors, like commercialism, that may weigh against a finding of fair use.

[P]arody has an obvious claim to transformative value. [I]t can provide social benefit, by shedding light on an earlier work and, in the process, creating a new one. We thus line up with the courts that have held that parody, like other comment or criticism, may claim fair use under § 107. If, [however], the commentary has no critical bearing on the substance or style of the original composition, which the alleged infringer merely uses to get attention or to avoid the drudgery in working up something fresh, the claim to fairness in borrowing from another's work diminishes accordingly (if it does not vanish), and other facts, like the extent of its commerciality, loom larger.

Parody needs to mimic an original to make its point, and so has some claim to use the creation of its victim's . . . imagination. The fact that parody can claim legitimacy for some appropriation does not, [however], tell either parodist or judge much about where to draw the line. [P]arody may or may not be fair use, and . . . , like any other use, [must] be judged case by case.

We have less difficulty in finding [criticism of the original] in 2 Live Crew's song than the Court of Appeals did, although having found it we will not . . . evaluat[e] its quality. Whether . . . parody is in good taste or bad does not . . . matter to fair use. While we might not assign a high rank to the parodic elements here, we think it fair to say that 2 Live Crew's song reasonably could be perceived as commenting on the original. 2 Live Crew juxtaposes the romantic musings of a man whose fantasy comes true, with degrading taunts, a bawdy demand for sex, and a sigh of relief from paternal responsibility. The later words can be taken as a comment on the naivete of the original [and] as a rejection of its sentiment that ignores the ugliness of street life and the debasement that it signifies.

The Court of Appeals, however, immediately cut short the enquiry into 2 Live Crew's fair use claim by confining its treatment of the first factor [to] the commercial nature of the use. In giving virtually

dispositive weight to the commercial nature of the parody, the Court of Appeals erred. The language of the statute makes clear that the commercial or nonprofit educational purpose of a work is only one element of the first factor enquiry. Congress resisted [efforts to create] categories of presumptively fair use. Accordingly, the mere fact that a use is educational and not for profit does not insulate it from a finding of infringement, any more than the commercial character of a use bars a finding of fairness.

If, indeed, commerciality carried presumptive force against a finding of fairness, the presumption would swallow nearly all of the illustrative uses listed in . . . § 107, including news reporting, comment, criticism, teaching, scholarship, and research, since those activities are generally conducted for profit in this country. Congress could not have intended such a rule. [Commercial use merely] "tends to weigh against a finding of fair use" (quoting *Harper & Row Publishers, Inc. v. Nation Enterprises* (1985)). But that is all, and the fact that even the force of that tendency will vary with the context is a further reason against elevating commerciality to hard presumptive significance. The use, for example, of a copyrighted work to advertise a product, even in a parody, will be entitled to less indulgence . . . than the sale of a parody for its own sake.

The second statutory factor, "the nature of the copyrighted work," [recognizes] that some works are closer to the core of intended copyright protection than others, with the consequence that fair use is more difficult to establish when the former works are copied. [T]he Orbison original's creative expression for public dissemination falls within [this] core. [Such a conclusion furnishes little help, however] in separating the fair use sheep from the infringing goats in a parody case, since parodies almost invariably copy from publicly known, expressive works.

The third factor asks whether "the amount and substantiality of the portion used in relation to the copyrighted work as a whole" are reasonable in relation to the purpose of the copying (quoting § 107). The Court of Appeals is . . . correct that this factor calls for thought not only about the quantity of the materials used, but about their quality and importance, too. In *Harper & Row,* for example, the Nation [a magazine] had taken only some 300 words out of President Ford's memoirs, but we signalled the significance of the question in finding them to amount to "the heart of the book." We also agree with the Court of Appeals that whether a "substantial portion of the infringing work was copied verbatim" . . . is a relevant question.

Where we part company with the court below is in applying these guides to parody. Parody's humor, or in any event its comment, necessarily springs from recognizable allusion to its object through distorted imitation. Its art lies in the tension between a known original and its parodic twin. When parody takes aim at a particular original work, the parody must be able to "conjure up" at least enough of that original to make the object of its critical wit recognizable. What makes for this recognition is quotation of the original's most distinctive or memorable features, which the parodist can be sure the audience will know.

[T]he Court of Appeals was insufficiently appreciative of parody's need for the recognizable sight or sound when it ruled 2 Live Crew's use unreasonable as a matter of law. [I]f quotation of the opening riff and the first line [of "Oh, Pretty Woman"] may be said to go to the "heart" of the original, the heart is also what most readily conjures up the song for parody. Copying does not become excessive in relation to parodic purpose merely because the portion taken was the original's heart. If 2 Live Crew had copied a significantly less memorable part . . . , it is difficult to see how its parodic character would have come through.

This is not, of course, to say that anyone who calls himself a parodist can skim the cream and get away scot free. [T]he question of fairness asks what else the parodist did besides [borrow from] the original. It is significant that 2 Live Crew not only copied the first line . . . , but thereafter departed markedly from the Orbison lyrics for its own ends. 2 Live Crew not only copied the bass riff and repeated it, but also produced otherwise distinctive sounds, [added] solos in different keys, and alter[ed] the drum beat. [A]s to the lyrics, we think the Court of Appeals correctly suggested that "no more was taken than necessary." As to the music, we express no opinion whether repetition of the bass riff is excessive copying, and we remand to permit evaluation of the amount taken, in light of the song's parodic purpose and character, its transformative elements, and consideration of the potential for market substitution.

The fourth fair use factor is "the effect of the use upon the potential market for or value of the copyrighted work" (quoting § 107). The enquiry "must take account not only of harm to the original but also of harm to the market for derivative works" (quoting *Harper & Row*). The [Court of Appeals] reasoned that because "the use of the copyrighted work is wholly commercial, we presume a likelihood of future harm to Acuff-Rose exists." [T]he court resolved the fourth factor against 2 Live Crew, just as it had the first, by applying a presumption about the effect of commercial use, a presumption which as applied here we hold to be error. No "presumption" or inference of market harm . . . is applicable to a case involving something beyond mere duplication for commercial purposes. [W]hen a commercial use amounts to mere duplication of the entirety of an original, it clearly . . . serves as a market replacement . . . , making it likely that cognizable market harm to the original will occur. But when . . . the second use is transformative, market substitution is at least less certain, and market harm may not be so readily inferred. Indeed, as to parody, it is more likely that the new work will not affect the market for the original . . . by acting as a substitute for it. This is so because the parody and the original usually serve different market functions.

We do not, of course, suggest that a parody may not harm the market at all, but when a lethal parody, like a scathing theater review, kills demand for the original, it does not produce a harm cognizable under the Copyright Act. [T]he role of the courts is to distinguish between biting criticism that suppresses demand [an effect permitted by law] and copyright infringement, which usurps [demand].

2 Live Crew's song comprises not only parody but also rap music, and the derivative market for rap music is a proper focus of enquiry. Evidence of substantial harm to it would weigh against a finding of fair use, because the licensing of derivatives is an important economic incentive to the creation of originals. Although 2 Live Crew submitted uncontroverted affidavits on the question of market harm to the original, neither they, nor Acuff-Rose, introduced evidence or affidavits addressing the likely effect of 2 Live Crew's parodic rap song on the market for a non-parody, rap version of "Oh, Pretty Woman." The evidentiary hole will doubtless be plugged on remand.

Decision of Court of Appeals reversed and remanded for further proceedings.

Trademarks

Trademarks help purchasers identify favored products and services. For this reason, they also give sellers and manufacturers an incentive to innovate and strive for quality. However, both these ends would be defeated if competitors were free to appropriate each other's trademarks. Thus, the federal Lanham Act protects trademark owners against certain uses of their marks by third parties.[5]

Protected Marks The Lanham Act recognizes four kinds of marks. It defines a **trademark** as any word, name, symbol, device, or combination thereof used by a manufacturer or seller to identify its products and to distinguish them from the products of competitors. Although trademarks consisting of single words or names are most commonly encountered, federal trademark protection has sometimes been extended to colors, pictures, label and package designs, slogans, sounds, arrangements of numbers and/or letters (e.g., "7-Eleven"), and shapes of goods or their containers (e.g., Coca-Cola bottles). *Qualitex Co. v. Jacobson Products Co.,* which follows shortly, contains examples of the wide variety of potentially protectible trademarks.

Service marks resemble trademarks but identify and distinguish services. **Certification marks** certify the origin, materials, quality, method of manufacture, and other aspects of goods and services. Here, the user of the mark and its owner are distinct parties. A retailer, for example, may sell products bearing the Good Housekeeping Seal of Approval. **Collective marks** are trademarks or service marks used by organizations to identify themselves as the source of goods or services. Trade union and trade association marks fall into this category. Although all four kinds of marks receive federal protection, this chapter focuses on trademarks and service marks, using the terms *mark* or *trademark* to refer to both.

Distinctiveness Because their purpose is to help consumers identify products and services, trademarks must be *distinctive* to merit maximum Lanham Act protection. Marks fall into five general categories of distinctiveness (or nondistinctiveness):

1. *Arbitrary or fanciful marks.* These marks are the most distinctive—and the most likely to be protected—because they do not describe the qualities of the product or service they identify. The "Exxon" trademark is an example.

2. *Suggestive marks.* These marks convey the nature of a product or service only through imagination, thought, and perception. They do not actually describe the underlying product or service. A "Dietene" trademark for a dietary food supplement is an example. Although not as clearly distinctive as arbitrary or fanciful marks, suggestive marks are nonetheless classified as distinctive. Hence, they are good candidates for protection.

3. *Descriptive marks.* These marks directly describe the product or service they identify (e.g., "Realemon," for bottled lemon juice). Descriptive marks are not protected unless they acquire *secondary meaning.* This occurs when their identification with a particular source of goods or services has become firmly established in the minds of a substantial number of buyers. "Realemon," of course, now has secondary meaning. Among the factors considered in secondary-meaning determinations are the length of time the mark has been used, the volume of sales associated with that use, and the nature of the advertising employing the mark. When applied to a package delivery service, for instance, the term *overnight* is usually just descriptive and thus not protectible. It may come to deserve trademark protection, however, through long use by a single firm that advertised it extensively and made many sales while doing so. As will be seen, the same approach is taken concerning deceptively misdescriptive and geographically descriptive marks.

4. *Marks that are not inherently distinctive.* Although these marks are not distinctive in the usual senses of arbitrary nature, fanciful quality, or suggestiveness, proof of secondary meaning effectively makes these marks distinctive. They are therefore protectible if secondary meaning exists. The *Qualitex* case deals with a potentially protectible trademark of this type, product color.

5. *Generic terms.* Generic terms (e.g., "diamond" or "truck") simply refer to the general class of which the particular product or service is one example. Because any seller has the right to call a product or service by its common name, generic terms are ineligible for trademark protection.

---

[5]In addition, the owner of a trademark may enjoy legal protection under common law trademark doctrines and state trademark statutes.

Federal Registration   Once the seller of a product or service uses a mark in commerce or forms a bona fide intention to do so very soon, she may apply to register the mark with the U.S. Patent and Trademark Office. The office reviews applications for distinctiveness. Its decision to deny or grant the application may be contested by the applicant or by a party who feels that he would be injured by registration of the mark. Such challenges may eventually reach the federal courts.

Trademarks of sufficient distinctiveness are placed on the Principal Register of the Patent and Trademark Office. A mark's inclusion in the Principal Register: (1) is prima facie evidence of the mark's ownership, validity, and registration (which is useful in trademark infringement suits); (2) gives nationwide constructive notice of the owner's claim of ownership (thus eliminating the need to show that the defendant in an infringement suit had notice of the mark); (3) entitles the mark owner to assistance from the Bureau of Customs in stopping the importation of certain goods that, without the consent of the mark owner, bear a likeness of the mark; and (4) means that the mark will be incontestable after five years of registered status (as described later).

Even though they are not distinctive, certain other marks may merit placement on the Principal Register if they have acquired secondary meaning. These include: (1) marks that are *not inherently distinctive* (as discussed earlier); (2) *descriptive* marks (as discussed earlier); (3) *deceptively misdescriptive* marks (such as "Dura-Skin," for plastic gloves); (4) *geographically descriptive* marks (such as "Indiana-Made"); and (5) marks that are *primarily a surname* (because as matter of general policy, persons who have a certain last name should be fairly free to use that name in connection with their businesses). Once a mark in one of these classifications achieves registered status, the mark's owner obtains the legal benefits described in the previous paragraph.

Regardless of their distinctiveness, however, some kinds of marks are denied placement on the Principal Register. These include marks that: (1) consist of the flags or other insignia of governments; (2) consist of the name, portrait, or signature of a living person who has not given consent to the trademark use; (3) are immoral, deceptive, or scandalous; or (4) are likely to cause confusion because they resemble a mark previously registered or used in the United States.

The *Qualitex* case, which follows, contains the U.S. Supreme Court's answer to a question on which lower courts had split: whether color is eligible for trademark registration and protection. *Qualitex* also addresses a number of related issues that the Trademark Office and courts face in deciding whether a trademark claimed by a party is entitled to registration.

QUALITEX CO. v. JACOBSON PRODUCTS CO.   514 U.S. 159 (U.S. Sup. Ct. 1995)

Qualitex Co. produces pads that dry-cleaning firms use on their presses. Since the 1950s, Qualitex has colored its press pads a shade of green-gold. In 1989, Jacobson Products Co. began producing press pads for sale to dry-cleaning firms. Jacobson colored its pads a green-gold resembling the shade used by Qualitex. In 1991, the U.S. Patent & Trademark Office (PTO) granted Qualitex a trademark registration for the green-gold color (as used on press pads). Qualitex then added a trademark infringement count to an unfair competition lawsuit it had previously filed against Jacobson. Qualitex won the case, but the Ninth Circuit Court of Appeals set aside the judgment in Qualitex's favor on the trademark infringement claim. In the Ninth Circuit's view, the Lanham Act does not allow any party to have "color alone" registered as a trademark. The U.S. Supreme Court granted certiorari. ∽

Breyer, Justice   The question in this case is whether the Lanham Act permits the registration of a trademark that consists, purely and simply, of a color. The courts of appeals have differed as to whether the law recognizes the use of color alone as a trademark.

[T]he Lanham Act . . . would seem to include color within the universe of things that can qualify as a trademark. [It] says that trademarks "includ[e] any word, name, symbol, or device, or combination thereof" (quoting § 1127). Since human beings might use as a "symbol" . . . almost anything . . .

capable of carrying meaning, this language . . . is not restrictive. The courts and the PTO have authorized for use as a mark a particular shape (of a Coca-Cola bottle), a particular sound (of NBC's three chimes), and even a particular scent (of plumeria blossoms on sewing thread). If a shape, a sound, and a fragrance can act as symbols, why . . . can a color not do the same?

A color is also capable of satisfying the more important part of the statutory definition . . . , which requires that a person "us[e]" or "inten[d] to use" the mark "to identify and distinguish his or her goods . . . from those manufactured or sold by others and to indicate the source of the goods" (quoting § 1127). True, a product's color is unlike "fanciful," "arbitrary", or "suggestive" words or designs, which almost *automatically* tell a customer that they refer to a brand. The imaginary word "Suntost" . . . on a jar of orange jam immediately would signal a brand or a product "source"; the jam's orange color does not do so. But, over time, customers may come to treat a particular color on a product or its packaging (say, a color that in context seems unusual, such as pink on a firm's insulating material or red on the head of a large industrial bolt) as signifying a brand. [I]f so, the color would have come to identify and distinguish the goods—i.e., to "indicate" their "source"—much in the way that descriptive words on a product (say, "Trim" on nail clippers . . .) can come to indicate a product's origin. In this circumstance, trademark law says that the word (e.g., "Trim"), although not inherently distinctive, has developed "secondary meaning." "[S]econdary meaning" is acquired when "in the minds of the public, the primary significance of a product feature . . . is to identify the source of the product rather than the product itself" (quoting *Inwood Laboratories, Inc. v. Ives Laboratories, Inc.* (1982)). [I]f trademark law permits a descriptive word with secondary meaning to act as a mark, why would it not permit a color, under similar circumstances, to do the same?

We cannot find . . . any obvious theoretical objection to the use of color alone as a trademark, where that color has attained "secondary meaning" and therefore identifies and distinguishes a particular brand (and thus indicates its "source"). [T]rademark law, by preventing others from copying a source-identifying mark, . . . assures a potential customer that *this* item—the item with this mark—is made by the same producer as other similarly marked items that he or she liked (or disliked) in the past. At the same time, the law helps assure a producer that it (and not an imitating competitor) will reap the financial, reputation-related rewards associated with a desirable product. It is the source-distinguishing ability of a mark—not its ontological status as color, shape, fragrance, word, or sign—that permits it to serve these basic purposes.

Neither can we find a principled objection to the use of color as a mark in the important "functionality" doctrine. [This] doctrine prevents trademark law, which seeks to promote competition by protecting a firm's reputation, from instead inhibiting legitimate competition by allowing a producer to control a useful product feature. It is the province of patent law, not trademark law, to encourage invention by granting inventors a monopoly over new product designs or functions for a limited time, after which competitors are free to use the innovation. If a product's functional features could be used as trademarks, however, a monopoly over such features could be obtained without regard to whether they qualify as patents and could be extended forever (because trademarks may be renewed in perpetuity). "[A] product feature is functional," and cannot serve as a trademark, "if it is essential to the use or purpose of the article or if it affects the cost or quality of the article," that is, if exclusive use of the feature would put competitors at a significant non-reputation-related advantage (quoting *Inwood Laboratories*). Although sometimes color plays an important role (unrelated to source identification) in making a product more desirable, sometimes it does not. [T]his latter fact—that sometimes color is not essential to a product's use or purpose and does not affect cost or quality—indicates that the doctrine of "functionality" does not create an absolute bar to the use of color alone as a mark.

Qualitex's green-gold press pad color . . . acts as a symbol. Having developed secondary meaning (for customers identified the green-gold color as Qualitex's), it identifies the press pads' source. [T]he green-gold color serves no other function. [The district court saw] "no competitive need in the press pad industry for the green-gold color, since other colors are equally usable." Accordingly, unless there is some special reason that convincingly militates against the use of color alone as a trademark, trademark law would protect Qualitex's use of the green-gold color on its press pads.

Jacobson [argues] that there are four [such] reasons. *First,* Jacobson says that if the law permits the use of color as a trademark, it will produce uncertainty and unresolvable court disputes about what shades of a color a competitor may lawfully use. We do not believe, however, that color, in this respect, is special. Courts traditionally decide quite difficult questions about whether two words or phrases or symbols are sufficiently similar, in context, to confuse buyers. Legal standards exist to guide courts in making such comparisons. We do not see why courts could not apply those standards to a color, replicating, if necessary, lighting conditions under which a colored product is normally sold. [C]ourts already have done so in cases where a trademark consists of a color plus a design, [e.g.], a colored symbol such as a gold stripe (around a sewer pipe), a yellow strand of wire rope, or a "brilliant yellow" band (on ampules).

Second, Jacobson argues . . . that colors are in limited supply. Jacobson claims that if one of many competitors can appropriate a particular color for [trademark] use . . . , and each competitor then tries to do the same, the supply of colors will soon be depleted. This [unpersuasive] argument . . . relies on an occasional problem to justify a blanket prohibition. When a color serves as a mark, normally alternative colors will likely be available for similar use by others. Moreover, if that is not so—if a "color depletion" . . . problem does arise—the trademark doctrine of "functionality" normally would . . . prevent the anticompetitive consequences that Jacobson's argument posits.

The functionality doctrine . . . protects competitors against a disadvantage (unrelated to recognition or reputation) that trademark protection might otherwise impose. For example, this Court has written that competitors might be free to copy the color of a medical pill whose color serves to identify the kind of medication (e.g., a type of blood medicine) in addition to its source. [L]ower courts have permitted competitors to copy the green color of farm machinery (because customers wanted their farm equipment to match) and have barred the use of black as a trademark on outboard boat motors (because black

has the special functional attributes of decreasing the apparent size of the motor and ensuring compatibility with many different boat colors). [W]here a color serves a significant nontrademark function . . . , courts will examine whether its use as a mark would permit one competitor . . . to interfere with legitimate (nontrademark-related) competition through actual or potential exclusive use of an important product ingredient. [That examination] ordinarily . . . should prevent the anticompetitive consequences of Jacobson's hypothetical "color depletion" argument . . .

Third, Jacobson points to many older cases . . . in support of its position. [Those] cases, however, interpreted trademark law as it existed [in common law form] *before* 1946, when Congress enacted the Lanham Act [and] significantly changed and liberalized the common law. [I]n 1985, the Federal Circuit [Court of Appeals] considered . . . the Lanham Act's changes . . . and held that trademark protection for color was consistent with the "jurisprudence under the Lanham Act developed in accordance with the statutory principle that if a mark is capable of being or becoming distinctive of [the] applicant's goods in commerce, then it is capable of serving as a trademark" (quoting *In re Owens-Corning Fiberglass Corp.* (1985)). [W]e believe the Federal Circuit was right . . . At a minimum, the Lanham Act's changes left the courts free to reevaluate the preexisting legal precedent which had absolutely forbidden the use of color alone as a trademark.

Fourth, Jacobson argues that there is no need to permit color alone . . . as a trademark because a firm already may use color as part of a trademark, say, as a colored circle or colored letter or colored word . . . [T]his argument begs the question. One can understand why a firm might find it difficult to place a usable symbol or word on a product (say, a large industrial bolt that customers normally see from a distance). [I]n such instances, a firm might want to use color, pure and simple, instead of color as part of a design. [W]e conclude that the Ninth Circuit erred in barring Qualitex's use of color as a trademark.

**Decision of Ninth Circuit Court
of Appeals reversed.**

Transfer of Rights   Due to the purposes underlying trademark law, transferring trademark rights is more difficult than transferring copyright or patent interests. A trademark owner may license the use of the mark, but only if the owner reserves control over the nature and quality of the goods or services as to which the licensee will use the mark. An uncontrolled "naked license" would allow the sale of goods or services bearing the mark but lacking the qualities formerly associated with it, and could confuse purchasers. Trademark rights may also be assigned or sold, but only along with the sale of the goodwill of the business originally using the mark.

Losing Federal Trademark Protection   Federal registration of a trademark lasts for 10 years, with renewals for additional 10-year periods possible. However, trademark protection may be lost before the period expires. The government must cancel a registration six years after its date unless the registrant files with the Patent and Trademark Office, within the fifth and sixth years following the registration date, an affidavit detailing that the mark is in use or explaining its nonuse.

Any person who believes that he is or will be damaged by a mark's registration may petition the Patent and Trademark Office to cancel that registration. Normally, the petition must be filed within five years of the mark's registration, because the mark becomes *incontestable* as regards goods or services with which it has continuously been used for five consecutive years after the registration.[6] A mark's

incontestability means that the permissible grounds for canceling its registration are limited. Even an incontestable mark, however, may be canceled *at any time* if, among other things, it was obtained by fraud, has been abandoned, or has become the generic name for the goods or services it identifies. *Abandonment* may occur through an express statement or agreement to abandon, through the mark's losing its significance as an indication of origin, or through the owner's failure to use it. A mark acquires a *generic meaning* when it comes to refer to a class of products or services rather than a particular product or service. For example, this has happened to such once-protected marks as aspirin, escalator, and thermos.

Trademark Infringement   A trademark is infringed when, without the owner's consent, another party uses a substantially similar mark in connection with the sale of goods or services and this is likely to cause confusion concerning their source or concerning whether there is an endorsement relationship or other affiliation between the mark's owner and the other party. The *Nike* case, which follows shortly, discusses many of the factors courts sift and weigh when determining whether the use is likely to cause confusion. A trademark owner who wins an infringement suit may obtain an injunction against uses of the mark that are likely to cause confusion. In addition, the owner may obtain money damages for provable injury resulting from the infringement and for attributable profits realized by the infringing defendant.

---

[6]The Lanham Act's incontestability provision also imposes on the owner an affidavit requirement resembling the cancellation affidavit requirement just mentioned.

NIKE, INC. v. "JUST DID IT" ENTERPRISES   6 F.3d 1225 (7th Cir. 1993)

S ince the 1970s, Nike, Inc., has used the word NIKE and a swoosh design as trademarks in connection with the footwear, clothing items, and related accessories it produces and sells. Both NIKE and the swoosh design are well-known, federally registered trademarks. Since 1989, Nike has used the now-familiar slogan JUST DO IT in connection with the promotion of its products.

   Michael Stanard began designing and selling t-shirts and sweatshirts that bore the name MIKE and a swoosh design as a takeoff on, and parody of, the Nike trademarks. Stanard, who gave the name "Just Did It" Enterprises to this business venture, chose persons named "Mike" (and their relatives) as his target market. He sought to reach these persons by mailing brochures to them. Nike sued Stanard for trademark infringement. When the federal district court granted summary judgment in favor of Nike, Stanard appealed. ∞

Manion, Judge   Trademarks consist of words or symbols that identify and distinguish goods for the

benefit of consumers. Manufacturers and merchants invest a great deal in trademarks [in the] hope [that] the public at large identifies [them]. When businesses seek the national spotlight, part of the territory includes accepting a certain amount of ridicule. The First Amendment . . . allows such ridicule in the form of parody. But parodies have a legal hurdle to overcome. Federal law prohibits copies or imitations that [are likely to] confuse consumers.

Stanard admitted that his "whole point" was to give someone viewing from a distance the impression that the shirt actually read NIKE [rather than MIKE]. Stanard believes that the word play . . . is humorous and deserves First Amendment protection. He sees this whole matter as a "joke on Nike's image which has become a social phenomenon," a "trick upon the perception of the viewer," and his own "personal pun."

To prevail against an alleged [infringer], the plaintiff must show . . . a likelihood of confusion on the part of the public [as a result of the defendant's use of a substantially similar version of the plaintiff's trademark]. Parodies do not enjoy a dispensation from this standard. If the defendant employs a successful parody, [however,] the customer would not be confused, but amused. The keystone of parody is imitation. A parody must convey two simultaneous—and contradictory—messages: that it is the original, but also that it is not the original. To the extent that it does only the former but not the latter, it is not only a poor parody but also vulnerable under trademark law, since the customer will be confused.

[C]onsumer confusion need not be restricted to a mistake regarding the source of the goods; the court should also consider whether the consumer would believe that the trademark owner sponsored, endorsed, or was otherwise affiliated with the product. What matters [in this case] is whether the "Mike" shirts [were likely to have] confused the consuming public into thinking that they were a Nike product [or a Nike-endorsed product]. We must analyze several factors [that aid in the determination of whether there was] likelihood of confusion.

A. Similarity of Trademarks

Our initial inquiry concerns the degree of similarity between the trademark and [the defendant's version] in appearance and suggestion. The marks [in this case] are no doubt similar; save one letter they are identical. Obviously if a humorist wished to parody NIKE, using a variation of the name or swoosh design would necessitate some identification of the original. The parties do not dispute . . . that a person

could not tell the difference [between MIKE and NIKE] from across the room.

Stanard argues that a customer interested in purchasing a t-shirt or sweatshirt [bearing] the word NIKE and its swoosh design is not interested only in the quality of the merchandise but also in associating with a major sportswear company. NIKE is not merely a brand name . . . but a statement about the person wearing [the shirt]. Thus, whether it connotes a parody depends in large part on whether the public would actually read the t-shirt or sweatshirt in question. That a person cannot tell the difference between the two from across the room matters little. We are dealing here with customer confusion when choosing [whether] to purchase . . . the items, not public confusion at viewing them from afar.

The district court did not compare the slogan JUST DO IT with the name of Stanard's enterprise, JUST DID IT. [H]owever, the comparison is important. Stanard does not sell his shirts off the rack at stores. His was a mail-order business. To purchase a shirt, the customer has to make a check payable to JUST DID IT Enterprises. Not so with Nike. There is no evidence in the record that Nike sells shirts through the mail, or whether consumers can purchase products directly from Nike or must rather go through a dealer. Nike asserts JUST DO IT [as] its slogan, not the name of the business to which customers make checks payable in order to receive Nike products. Certainly Nike would not have us compare the similarity of MIKE and NIKE on actual shirts because the customer never sees the actual MIKE shirt until after purchasing it. Thus, in order for a customer to be confused in this case, he must see MIKE as similar to NIKE, and continue to be confused while making a check out to JUST DID IT Enterprises. A jury could find that MIKE and NIKE, in text, meaning, and pronunciation, are not so similar as to confuse consumers, especially when making the decision to purchase or not to purchase. A jury could also find that ordering a shirt from JUST DID IT Enterprises would not confuse a consumer, considering that Nike uses JUST DO IT only as its slogan.

B. Similarity of Products and Concurrent Uses

Our next inquiry concerns the similarity of the products upon which MIKE and NIKE [appear]. Where the goods are in close competition, trademarks need not be as similar in order to find an infringement. Stanard has [placed his] parody on the same types of items that Nike sells. The district court was thus correct in concluding that . . . Nike's trademark and Stanard's parody dealt with similar products, used for similar purposes.

C. Marketing Channels

Nike obviously markets its products to the general public. Stanard marketed the MIKE shirts strictly by mail-order to people with a first name of Mike. [W]e . . . infer that Stanard specifically targeted his parody to an audience that would appreciate (more so than the general public) the distinction between MIKE and NIKE. [A] jury could find on this record that Stanard uses a completely different marketing channel than Nike. A jury could also conclude that Stanard's targeted market would not have been likely to purchase a shirt emblazoned with NIKE instead of MIKE.

D. Consumer Care

Nike argued, and the district court agreed, that [Stanard's] prices support a conclusion that consumers would not exercise a high degree of care in purchasing [Stanard's] shirts. [W]e cannot agree that . . . customers routinely purchase a $39.95 item [the most expensive of Stanard's shirts] without looking at the product information. [A] jury could conclude that customers take care when purchasing this type of clothing. A jury could also consider evidence of just who would and would not typically purchase a NIKE-labeled shirt. One group of purchasers might seek out the Nike name to ensure top quality and to display to others their good taste for such quality. [O]ther purchasers might resent paying a premium to be a walking billboard and would relish the opportunity to mock trendy folks who wear labels on their sleeves.

E. Trademark Strength

The stronger the trademark the greater [the] protection received from the courts. This factor can also include the likelihood of expansion of the product lines. We agree with the district court's conclusions that Nike's trademarks are widely recognized and deserve protection.

F. Actual Confusion

Proof that a trademark parody actually confuses consumers provides substantial evidence [of] likelihood of confusion. And vice-versa, it is certainly proper for the trial judge to infer from the absence of actual confusion that there was no likelihood of confusion. Nike [presented] no evidence of actual confusion. While actual confusion is not essential to show likelihood of confusion, Nike still must demonstrate why a customer would conclude Stanard's shirt was a Nike product. Nike has not done this, leaving an open question [concerning which] a jury could conclude that Stanard's trademark parody would not likely confuse a purchaser.

G. Intent of the [Alleged Infringer]

An intent on the part of Stanard to palm off his products as those of another would raise an inference that the consumer would likely be confused. An intent to parody, however, raises the opposite inference. Given the parody defense, the question is whether the intent was to confuse or amuse. No one likes to be the butt of a joke. But . . . trademark law [requires that] a likely confusion of source, sponsorship, or affiliation must be proven, which is not the same thing as a "right" not to be made fun of.

The district court concluded that Stanard intended to pass off his merchandise as that of Nike. [In doing so, the court focused] on Stanard's statement that to be initially tricked at first glance from across the room was "the whole point." But a jury could surely conclude that any initial confusion ends with a closer look, when the observer "gets it." Parodies do not exist by mere happenstance. Actual knowledge of the trademark by the presenter as well as the observer or the consumer is virtually required. Throughout this case Stanard has asserted that he intended only to poke fun at Nike's corporate identity. He intended to use his own name to play a witty prank upon the perception of the viewer. Whether a customer would also believe that MIKE was somehow affiliated with NIKE is a disputed issue of fact. [A] jury could infer that Stanard intended to amuse, not confuse, and that MIKE was intended as a parody, not an imitation designed to be passed off to consumers as a Nike product.

[We cannot] conclude as a matter of law that Stanard's parody does or does not confuse the purchasing public. Too many disputed facts require a trial for resolution. The [district] court erred in granting summary judgment to the plaintiff.

Decision of district court reversed and remanded for further proceedings.

The Three Forms of Intellectual Property Compared

	PATENT	COPYRIGHT	TRADEMARK
What Is Protected?	Process, machine, product, composition of matter, improvement, ornamental design, plant produced by asexual reproduction, if *novel, nonobvious,* and *useful*	Wide range of works of authorship that are *fixed, original,* and *creative*	Trademarks, service marks, certification marks, and collective marks of sufficient distinctiveness
Registration Needed?	Yes	Although copyright exists in the absence of registration, registration often necessary for infringement suit	Necessary for infringement suit under Lanham Act section 32(1). Unregistered marks protected under Lanham Act section 43(a), common law, and state statutes.
Duration	20 years from application	Life of author plus 50 years, unless work-for-hire	If registered, 10 years, with 10-year renewals possible
Transferability	By assignment or license	By assignment or license	By assignment or license, though limited
How Infringed	Making, using, or selling patented invention or its substantial equivalent	Violation of owner's exclusive rights to reproduce, prepare derivative works, distribute copies, perform, or display. But *fair use* defense available.	Use of substantially similar version of mark in way that is likely to cause confusion concerning source, endorsement, or affiliation. Dilution cause of action available for famous marks.

Trademark Dilution   Congress recently granted owners of certain marks an alternative to the standard claim of trademark infringement. The Federal Trademark Dilution Act (FTDA), which took effect in 1996 and was placed in the Lanham Act as section 43(c), allows the owner of a "famous" mark to seek legal relief when another party's commercial use of a substantially similar version of the famous mark causes "dilution of [the mark's] distinctive quality." Under the FTDA, a mark need not be a registered mark in order to be "famous." Proof of likelihood of confusion—essential to a claim for trademark infringement—is not required for purposes of this claim of trademark *dilution.* The FTDA provides that if dilution is established, the owner of the famous mark will normally be entitled only to the standard remedy of an injunction against the defendant's continued use of the diluting version of the mark. Damages and the infringer's profits are recoverable by the owner of the famous mark only if the evidence reveals that the defendant willfully sought either to trade on the mark owner's reputation or to cause dilution of the mark.

In view of the recent enactment of the FTDA, few court decisions have been rendered under it. As more FTDA-based cases are decided, courts will have opportunities to interpret a number of the new statute's seemingly ambiguous and broad-ranging provisions.

TRADE SECRETS

The law provides at least two means of protecting creative inventions. Owners of such inventions may go public and obtain monopoly patent rights. As an alternative, they may keep the invention secret and rely on trade secrets law to protect it. Figure 1

FIGURE 1

Patent and Trade Secrets Protection Compared

FACTOR	PATENT LAW	TRADE SECRETS LAW
Range of Protected Matter?	Probably narrower than trade secrets law	Probably broader than patent law
Need to Register?	Yes	No
Burden of Maintaining Secrecy?	No	Yes
Duration	20 years from application	However long secrecy is maintained
Transferability	Fairly easy	Fairly easy
Ability to Keep Knowledge Secret?	No	Yes, if secrecy really maintained
Effective Monopoly over Protected Matter?	Yes	No, because discovery/use by proper means is permissible

sketches some of the advantages and disadvantages of each alternative.

The policies underlying patent protection and trade secrets protection differ. The general aim of patent law is to encourage the creation and disclosure of inventions by granting the patentee a temporary monopoly in the patented invention in exchange for his making it public. Trade secrets, however, are nonpublic by definition. Although protecting trade secrets may stimulate creative activity, it also keeps the information from becoming public knowledge. Thus, the main justification for trade secrets protection is simply to preserve certain standards of commercial morality.

Definition of a Trade Secret

A trade secret can be defined as any secret formula, pattern, process, program, device, method, technique, or compilation of information that is used in the owner's business and that gives its owner an advantage over competitors who do not know it or use it.[7] Examples include chemical formulas, computer software, manufacturing processes, designs for machines, and customer lists. To be protectible, a trade secret must usually have sufficient value or

originality to provide an actual or potential competitive advantage. It need not possess the novelty required for patent protection, however.

The *Mason* case, which follows shortly, considers some factors courts may examine when determining whether a trade secret exists. As several of those factors suggest, a trade secret must actually be *secret*. A substantial measure of secrecy is necessary, but it need not be absolute. Thus, information that becomes public knowledge or becomes generally known in the industry cannot be a trade secret. Similarly, information that is reasonably discoverable by proper means may not be protected. "Proper means" include independent invention of the secret, observation of a publicly displayed product, the owner's advertising, published literature, product analysis, and reverse engineering (starting with a legitimately acquired product and working backward to discover how it was developed).

In addition, a firm claiming a trade secret must usually show that it took *reasonable measures to ensure secrecy*. Examples include advising employees about the secret's secrecy, limiting access to the secret on a need-to-know basis, requiring those given access to sign a nondisclosure agreement, disclosing the secret only on a confidential basis, and controlling access to an office or plant. Computer software licensing agreements commonly forbid the licensee to copy the program except for backup and archival purposes, require the licensee and its employees to sign confidentiality agreements, require those employees to use the program

---

[7]This definition comes mainly from *Restatement (Third) of Unfair Competition* § 39 (1995) with some additions from *Uniform Trade Secrets Act* § 1(4) (1985). Many states have adopted the Uniform Trade Secrets Act (UTSA) in some form. The discussion in this chapter is a composite of the *Restatement's* and the UTSA's rules.

only in the course of their jobs, and require the licensee to use the program only in a central processing unit. Because the owner must only make *reasonable* efforts to ensure secrecy, however, she need not adopt extreme measures to block every ingenious form of industrial espionage.

Ownership and Transfer of Trade Secrets

The owner of a trade secret is usually the person who developed it or the business under whose auspices it was generated. But establishing the ownership of a trade secret can pose problems where an employee develops a secret in the course of her employment. In such cases, courts often find the *employer* to be the owner if: (1) the employee was hired to do creative work related to the secret, (2) the employee agreed not to divulge or use trade secrets, or (3) other employees contributed to the development of the secret. Even where the employee owns the secret, the employer still may obtain a royalty-free license to use it through the shop right doctrine discussed in the section on patents.

The owner of a trade secret may transfer rights in the secret to third parties. This may occur by assignment (in which case the owner loses title) or by license (in which case the owner retains title but allows the transferee certain uses of the secret).

Misappropriation of Trade Secrets

Misappropriation of a trade secret can occur in various ways, most of which involve *disclosure or use* of the secret. For example, misappropriation liability occurs when the secret is disclosed or used by one who did one of the following:

1. Acquired it by *improper means.* Improper means include theft, trespass, wiretapping, spying, bugging, bribery, fraud, impersonation, and eavesdropping.

2. Acquired it from a party who *is known or should be known* to have obtained it by improper means. For example, a free-lance industrial spy might obtain one firm's trade secrets by improper means and sell them to the firm's competitors. If those competitors know or have reason to know that the spy obtained the secrets by improper means, they are liable for misappropriation along with the spy.

3. *Breached a duty of confidentiality regarding the secret.* Where an employer owns a trade secret, for example, an employee is generally bound not to use or disclose it during his employment or thereafter.[8] The employee may, however, utilize general knowledge and skills acquired during her employment.

Remedies for misappropriation of a trade secret include damages, which may involve both the actual loss caused by the misappropriation and the defendant's unjust enrichment. In some states, punitive damages are awarded for willful and malicious misappropriations. Also, an injunction may be issued against actual or threatened misappropriations.

---

[8]This is an application of the agent's duty of loyalty, which is discussed in Chapter 34.

MASON v. JACK DANIEL DISTILLERY   518 So. 2d 130 (Ala. Civ. App. 1987)

Tony Mason created a mixed drink that he named "Lynchburg Lemonade." The drink consisted of Jack Daniel's whiskey, Triple Sec, sweet and sour mix, and 7-Up. Mason served the drink at his restaurant and lounge, where it became very popular. Later, Winston Randle, a sales representative for Jack Daniel Distillery, drank Lynchburg Lemonade while in Mason's restaurant and lounge. Although the source of his information is unclear, he also learned the recipe for the drink at this time. Randle informed his superiors about Lynchburg Lemonade and its recipe, and about one year later Jack Daniel was developing a national promotion campaign for the drink.

Mason, who never received any compensation for this use of Lynchburg Lemonade, sued Jack Daniel and Randle for misappropriation of a trade secret. Mason won a jury verdict. The defendants appealed the trial judge's refusal to grant their motion for a directed verdict. ∽

Holmes, Judge The defendants contend that Mason's recipe for Lynchburg Lemonade was not a trade secret. The *Restatement* [*of Torts*] provides in pertinent part:

A trade secret may consist of any formula, pattern, device, or compilation of information which is used in one's business, and which gives him an opportunity to obtain an advantage over competitors who do not know or use it. . .

An exact definition of a trade secret is not possible. Some factors to be considered in determining whether given information is one's trade secret are: (1) the extent to which the information is known outside of his business; (2) the extent to which it is known by employees and others involved in his business; (3) the extent of measures taken by him to guard the secrecy of his information; (4) the value of the information to him and to his competitors; (5) the amount of effort or money expended by him in developing the information; (6) the ease or difficulty with which the information could be properly acquired or duplicated by others.

Applying these factors to this case, we find that some support and some negate the conclusion that Lynchburg Lemonade was Mason's trade secret.

Mason apparently spent little time, effort, or money in concocting the recipe for Lynchburg Lemonade. He seems to have created the beverage one evening to ease a sore throat. However, he put much effort into making the beverage an exclusive specialty of his restaurant and lounge. Mason testified that Lynchburg Lemonade comprised about a third of his total sales of alcoholic drinks. Obviously, the exclusive sale of Lynchburg Lemonade was of great value to Mason. The beverage could also have been valuable to his competitors in the area.

Mason [also] testified that he told only a few of his employees the recipe. He stated that each one was specifically instructed not to tell anyone the recipe. To prevent customers from learning the recipe, the beverage was mixed in the back of the restaurant and lounge. Mason's efforts to keep the recipe a secret were apparently successful until Randle learned the recipe. It appears that one could not order a Lynchburg Lemonade in any establishment other than that of the plaintiff. Absolute secrecy is not required for the recipe to constitute a trade secret—a substantial element of secrecy is all that is necessary.

The defendants contend that Mason's recipe was not a trade secret because it could be easily duplicated by others. The defendants' [expert] testimony characterized Lynchburg Lemonade as a member of the Collins family of drinks, of which there are dozens, if not hundreds, with essentially the same elements. At least one witness testified that he could duplicate the recipe after tasting a Lynchburg Lemonade. Certainly, this testimony is a strong factor against the conclusion that Mason's recipe was a trade secret. We do not think, however, that this evidence in and of itself could prevent such a conclusion. Rather, this evidence should be weighed and considered along with the evidence tending to show the existence of a trade secret. Courts have protected information as a trade secret despite evidence that it could easily be duplicated by others competent in the given field.

A motion for directed verdict should not be granted if there is a scintilla of evidence supporting an element essential to the plaintiff's claim. Our review of the record indicates that Mason did present a scintilla of evidence that his recipe, or formula, for Lynchburg Lemonade was a trade secret.

Trial court's refusal to grant the defendant's motion for a directed verdict affirmed.

COMMERCIAL TORTS

In addition to the intentional torts discussed in Chapter 6, certain other intentional torts involve business or commercial competition. These torts may help promote innovation by protecting creative businesses against certain competitive abuses. Their main aim, however, is simply to uphold certain minimum standards of commercial morality.

Injurious Falsehood

Injurious falsehood also goes by names such as product disparagement, slander of title, and trade libel. This tort involves the publication of false statements that disparage another's business, property, or title to property, and thus harm her economic interests. One common kind of injurious falsehood involves false statements that disparage either a person's *property rights* in land, things, or intangibles, or their *quality*. The property rights in question include virtually all legally protected property interests that can be sold; examples include leases, mineral rights, trademarks, copyrights, and corporate stock. As the following *Atlas* case indicates, injurious falsehood also includes false statements that harm another's economic interests even though they do not disparage property or property rights as such.

Elements and Damages   In injurious falsehood cases, the plaintiff must prove that the defendant made a false statement of the sort just described, and that the statement was communicated to a third party. The degree of fault required for liability is unclear. Sources often say that the standard is malice, but formulations of this differ. The *Restatement* requires either knowledge that the statement is false, or reckless disregard as to its truth or falsity. There is usually no liability for false statements that are made negligently and in good faith.

The plaintiff must also prove that the false statement played a substantial part in causing him to suffer *special damages*. These may include: losses resulting from the diminished value of disparaged property, the expense of measures for counteracting the false statement (e.g., advertising or litigation expenses), losses resulting from the breach of an existing contract by a third party, and the loss of prospective business. In cases involving the loss of prospective business, the plaintiff is usually required to show that some specific person or persons refused to buy because of the disparagement. As *Atlas* states, however, this rule is often relaxed where these losses are difficult to prove.

The special damages that the plaintiff is required to prove are his usual—and virtually his only—

remedy in injurious falsehood cases. Damages for personal injury or emotional distress, for instance, are generally not recoverable. However, punitive damages and injunctive relief are sometimes obtainable.

Injurious Falsehood and Defamation   Injurious falsehood may or may not overlap with the tort of defamation discussed in Chapter 6. Statements impugning a businessperson's character or conduct are probably defamatory. If the false statement is limited to the plaintiff's business, property, or property rights, on the other hand, his normal claim is for injurious falsehood. Both claims are possible where the injurious falsehood implies something about the plaintiff's character and affects his overall reputation. An example is a defendant's false allegation that the plaintiff knowingly sells dangerous products to children.

Defamation law's absolute and conditional privileges generally apply in injurious falsehood cases.[9] Certain other privileges protect defendants who are sued for injurious falsehood. For example, a rival claimant may in good faith disparage another's property rights by asserting his own competing rights. Similarly, one may make a good faith allegation that a competitor is infringing one's patent, copyright, or trademark. Finally, a person may sometimes make unfavorable comparisons between her own property and that of a competitor. This privilege is generally limited to sales talk asserting the superiority of one's property and does not cover unfavorable statements about a competitor's property.

_____
[9]Chapter 6 discusses those privileges.

Time-Life Books published a book entitled Exercising for Fitness. *The book contained a reproduction of the famous Charles Atlas advertisement in which a 97-pound weakling uses Atlas's Dynamic Tension body-building program to become a real man after a bully kicks sand in his face and the face of his girlfriend. The caption accompanying the reproduction told the book's readers that Atlas's program is a system of isometric exercises. On the same page, the book warned readers about the extreme dangers of isometric exercises.*

Charles Atlas, Ltd. sued Time-Life in federal district court for product disparagement (injurious falsehood). It basically alleged that the book's caption was false because Atlas's method was not isometric, and that this falsehood, coupled with the warning about the dangers of isometric exercises, caused it to suffer economic loss. Time-Life moved to dismiss Atlas's complaint. The question before the court was whether the facts in the complaint were sufficient to state a claim upon which relief could be granted. ∞

Goettel, District Judge   This court cannot say as a matter of law that the alleged misstatements are not reasonably susceptible to a defamatory meaning and that no reasonable reader could conclude that the statements [concern] the plaintiff's product. When the caption is read in conjunction with the text, a reasonable reader could conclude that Atlas markets an isometric exercise program, that isometric exercises are dangerous, and that therefore Atlas's exercise program is dangerous. Whether the trier of fact will conclude that a defamatory connotation was indeed conveyed will have to await trial.

Malice is pleaded adequately. It is extremely questionable whether the plaintiff must show common-law malice to state a claim for product disparagement. Rather, it appears that the plaintiff must show knowledge of the alleged false statement or reckless disregard as to the truth of the statement [citing the *Restatement*]. Atlas alleges that the allegedly false statements were known by Time-Life to be false when they were made, or were made with recklessness, malice, and intent to injure Atlas.

Finally, Atlas has pleaded special damages adequately. According to Atlas, the alleged disparagement has caused it to lose $30,323 in sales and revenues and to expend $14,000 in special advertising expenses and $16,687 in legal expenses to counteract the alleged disparagement. Special damage is the pecuniary loss resulting directly from the effect of a defendant's allegedly wrongful conduct. Among the losses deemed to constitute special damages are the expenses necessary to counteract the alleged wrongful conduct. Thus, Atlas can recover at least the special advertising expenses in-curred to counteract the alleged product disparagement, and the pleading of these expenses is sufficient to support the claim at this stage of the litigation.

Loss of sales is also a proper item of special damages. However, Time-Life argues that Atlas has failed to plead this adequately because it has failed to identify lost customers. Adopting such a rule would be grossly unfair in this case. Atlas sells only through mail orders. It is, therefore, virtually impossible to identify those who did not order Atlas's product because of *Exercising for Fitness*. As Dean Prosser has noted: "[A] more liberal rule has been applied, requiring the plaintiff to be particular only where it is reasonable to expect him to do so. It is probably still the law everywhere that he must either offer the names of those who have failed to purchase or explain why it is impossible for him to do so; but where he cannot, the matter is dealt with by analogy to the proof of lost profits resulting from breach of contract."

Whether legal fees expended to prosecute a claim for product disparagement can be recovered as an item of special damages is an interesting issue. It can be argued that the expenses incurred in bringing the lawsuit are similar to other expenses necessary to counteract the alleged wrongful conduct. Be that as it may, the court need not resolve the question at this time because it has already determined that Atlas has stated a claim for product disparagement.

Time-Life's motion to dismiss denied; Atlas's case continues.

Interference with Contractual Relations

In a suit for intentional interference with contractual relations, one party to a contract claims that the defendant's interference with the other party's performance of the contract wrongly caused the plaintiff to lose the benefit of that performance. One can interfere with the performance of a contract by causing a party to repudiate it, or by wholly or partly preventing that party's performance. The means of interference can range from mere persuasion to threatened or actual violence. The agreement whose performance is checked, however, must be an *existing* contract. This includes contracts that are voidable, unenforceable, or subject to contract defenses, but *not* void bargains, contracts that are illegal on public policy grounds, or contracts to marry. Finally, the defendant must have *intended* to cause the breach; there is usually no liability for negligent contract interferences.

Even if the plaintiff proves these threshold requirements, the defendant is liable only if his behavior was *improper.* The *RAN* case, which follows shortly, lists the factors the *Restatement* uses to decide this question. Despite the flexible, case-by-case nature of such determinations, a few generalizations about improper interference are possible.

1. Where the contract's performance was blocked by such clearly improper means as threats of physical violence, misrepresentations, defamatory statements, bribery, harassment, or bad faith civil or criminal actions, the defendant usually is liable. Liability is also likely where the interference was motivated *solely* by malice, spite, or a simple desire to meddle.

2. If his means and motives are legitimate, a defendant generally escapes liability when his contract interference is in the *public interest*—for example, when he informs an airport that an air traffic controller habitually uses hallucinogenic drugs. The same is true where the defendant acts to *protect a person for whose welfare she is responsible*—for example, where a mother induces a private school to discharge a diseased student who could infect her children.

3. A contract interference resulting from the defendant's good faith effort to protect her own *existing* legal or economic interests usually does not create liability so long as appropriate means are used. For example, a landowner can probably induce his tenant to breach a sublease to a party whose business detracts from the land's value. However, business parties generally cannot interfere with existing contract rights merely to further some *prospective* competitive advantage. For example, a seller cannot entice its competitors' customers to break existing contracts with those competitors. Is the *RAN* case completely consistent with these rules?

4. Finally, competitors are unlikely to incur liability where, as is still often true of employment contracts, the agreement interfered with is *terminable at will.*[10] The reason is that in such cases, the plaintiff has only an expectancy that the contract

[10]Chapter 50 discusses terminable-at-will employment contracts.

will continue, and not a right to have it continued. Thus, a firm that hires away its competitors' at-will employees usually escapes liability.

The basic measure of damages for intentional interference with contractual relations is the value of the lost contract performance. Some courts also award compensatory damages reasonably linked to the interference (including emotional distress and damage to reputation). Sometimes the plaintiff may obtain an injunction prohibiting further interferences.

Interference with Prospective Advantage

The rules and remedies for intentional interference with prospective advantage parallel those for interference with contractual relations. The main difference is that the former tort involves interferences with *prospective* relations rather than existing contracts. The protected future relations are mainly potential contractual relations of a business or commercial sort. Liability for interference with such relations requires intent; negligence does not suffice.

The "improper interference" factors weighed in interference-with-contract cases generally apply to interference with prospective advantage as well. One difference, however, is that interference with prospective advantage can be justified if: (1) the plaintiff and the defendant are in competition for the prospective relation with which the defendant interferes; (2) the defendant's purpose is at least partly competitive; (3) the defendant does not use such improper means as physical threats, misrepresentations, and bad faith lawsuits; and (4) the defendant's behavior does not create an unlawful restraint of trade under the antitrust laws or other regulations. Thus, a competitor ordinarily can win customers by offering lower prices and attract suppliers by offering higher prices. Unless this is otherwise illegal, he can also refuse to deal with suppliers or buyers who also deal with his competitors.

RAN CORPORATION v. HUDESMAN   823 P.2d 646 (Alaska Sup. Ct. 1991)

David Hudesman *leased commercial property housing the Red Dog Saloon to Don Harris, the saloon's owner and operator. The lease said that Harris could assign it to any subtenant or assignee who was financially responsible and would properly care for the premises. It also required that Hudesman consent to such an assignment, but added that this consent could not be withheld* unreasonably. *After Harris decided to relocate his business, he was contacted by Richard Stone, president of* *the RAN Corporation. Stone wanted to use the property for an artifacts gallery. Harris and Stone agreed that Harris would assign the lease for $15,000, conditional on Hudesman's approval.*

About this time, a politically influential man named Jerry Reinwand contacted Hudesman about the property. In exchange for Reinwand's promise to help Hudesman secure government leases for a large building Hudesman owned, Hudesman promised Reinwand that if Harris relocated his business, Reinwand would be assigned the property. Then Hudesman told Harris that he would not consent to Harris's assignment of the lease to RAN, and that Harris would be "looking at litigation" if he tried to assign the lease to Stone. Therefore, Harris told Stone that the deal was off, returned his $15,000 deposit, and assigned the lease to Reinwand for $15,000.

RAN then sued for an injunction to invalidate Reinwand's lease and to enforce its assignment contract with Harris, and also for damages. After RAN settled with several defendants, its main remaining claims were interference with contractual relations and interference with prospective advantage claims against Hudesman. When both parties moved for summary judgment, the trial court held for Hudesman. RAN appealed. ∽

Matthews, Justice The elements of intentional interference with contractual relations are: (1) a contract existed, (2) the defendant knew of the contract and intended to induce a breach, (3) the contract was breached, (4) the defendant's wrongful conduct engendered the breach, (5) the breach caused the plaintiff's damages, and (6) the defendant's conduct was not privileged or justified. The fourth, fifth, and sixth elements also apply to the related tort of intentional interference with prospective economic advantage. As our analysis applies equally to either tort, we will refer to them collectively.

The sixth element is troublingly vague. The *Restatement (Second) of Torts* section 767 speaks not in terms of "privilege," but requires that the actor's conduct not be "improper." Other authorities used the catch word "malice." Regardless of the phrase used, the critical question is what conduct is not "privileged" or "improper" or "malicious." The *Restatement* lists seven factors for consideration: (1) the nature of the actor's conduct, (2) the actor's motive, (3) the interests of the other with which the actor's conduct interferes, (4) the interests sought to be advanced by the actor, (5) the social interests in protecting the freedom of action of the actor and the contractual interests of the other, (6) the proximity or remoteness of the actor's conduct to the interference, and (7) the relations between the parties. While these factors are relevant in some or all incarnations of the interference tort, they are hard to apply in any sort of predictive way.

Instead of relying on the *Restatement* factors, we [have] adopted a test of privilege which hold[s] that where an actor has a direct financial interest, he is privileged to interfere with a contract for economic reasons, but not where he is motivated by spite, malice, or some other improper motive. In our view, this rule applies to this case. A number of other cases have recognized that a landlord has a sufficient interest to interfere with a prospective or actual lease assignment. The right to intervene has also been recognized in the analogous setting of transfers of distributorships.

It seems beyond reasonable argument that an owner of property has a financial interest in the assignment of a lease of the property he owns. An effective lease assignment makes the assignee the tenant of the owner. The tenant has an obligation to pay rent directly to the owner, and the use, or abuse, of the property by the assignee may affect its value to the owner. Further, the owner may know of another potential assignee who will pay more rent than the prospective assignee. Moreover, the owner may wish to terminate the lease based on knowledge of a more profitable use for the property.

Since Hudesman had a direct financial interest in the proposed assignment of the lease, the essential question in determining if interference is justified is whether Hudesman's conduct is motivated by a desire to protect his economic interest, or whether it is motivated by spite, malice, or some other improper objective. As there is no evidence of spite, malice, or other improper objective—Hudesman did not even know RAN Corporation's principals—and since it is clear that Hudesman refused to approve the assignment because he believed that he would receive a greater economic benefit from a tenancy by Reinwand, the interference was justified.

Hudesman's threat of litigation does not seem relevant to RAN's claim for interference. RAN's assignment agreement with Harris was explicitly conditional on Hudesman's approval. When Hudesman disapproved of the assignment, the interference was complete. Hudesman's disapproval may have been a breach of the Hudesman/Harris lease, but it was privileged from a tort standpoint because of Hudesman's preexisting interest as a property owner-lessor. The threat of litigation may, at worst, have been another breach of the Hudesman/Harris

lease. However, it too was not tortious and it was, in any case, superfluous to the interference, because RAN's prospective economic relationship was terminated by Hudesman's disapproval, not by his threat to sue.

Lower court judgment in favor of Hudesman affirmed.

LANHAM ACT SECTION 43(a)

Section 43(a) of the Lanham Act basically creates a federal law of unfair competition. Section 43(a) is not a consumer remedy; it is normally available only to commercial parties, who usually are the defendant's competitors. The section creates civil liability for a wide range of false, misleading, confusing, or deceptive descriptions of fact made in connection with goods or services. Section 43(a)'s many applications include:

1. *Tort claims for "palming off" or "passing off."* This tort involves false representations that are likely to induce third parties to believe that the defendant's goods or services are those of the plaintiff. Such representations include imitations of the plaintiff's trademarks, trade names, packages, labels, containers, employee uniforms, and place of business.

2. *Trade dress infringement claims.* These claims resemble passing-off claims. A product's trade dress is its overall appearance and sales image. Section

43(a) prohibits a party from passing off its goods or services as those of a competitor by employing a substantially similar trade dress that is likely to confuse consumers as to the source of its products or services. For example, a competitor that sells antifreeze in jugs that are similar in size, shape, and color to a well-known competitor's jugs may face section 43(a) liability.

3. *Claims for infringement of both registered and unregistered trademarks.*

4. *Commercial appropriation of name or likeness claims and right of publicity claims* (discussed in Chapter 6).

5. *False advertising claims.* This important application of section 43(a) includes ads that misrepresent the nature, qualities, or characteristics of either the *advertiser's* products and services or a *competitor's* products and services. As the following *Rhone-Poulenc Rorer* case shows, section 43(a) applies to ads that are likely to mislead buyers even if they are not clearly false on their face, and to ads with certain deceptive *omissions*.

ADVENT SYSTEMS LTD. v. UNISYS CORPORATION   925 F.2d 670 (3d Cir. 1991)

I n 1989, Marion Merrell Dow, Inc. (MMD), developed "Cardizem CD," an improved version of a prescription diltiazem drug that MMD had introduced several years earlier. The Food and Drug Administration (FDA) approved Cardizem CD for the treatment of angina and hypertension. Cardizem CD and its predecessor versions generated huge sales figures.

Approximately three years after Cardizem CD came on the market, Rhone-Poulenc Rorer Pharmaceuticals, Inc. (RPR), introduced a prescription diltiazem drug known as "Dilacor XR." It was less expensive than Cardizem CD. Dilacor XR received approval from the FDA for treatment of hypertension but not angina. Physicians may prescribe an FDA-approved drug for nonapproved uses, but federal law prohibits the drug's manufacturer from promoting nonapproved uses. Through an advertising campaign, RPR sought to convince physicians to prescribe Dilacor XR instead of Cardizem CD. MMD responded with advertisements and promotional materials meant to dissuade physicians from prescribing Dilacor XR in place of Cardizem CD.

RPR brought a false advertising lawsuit against MMD under § 43(a) of the Lanham Act. MMD responded with a § 43(a)–based counterclaim alleging false advertising by RPR. The federal district court concluded that early promotional literature distributed by MMD contained false representations about Dilacor XR's bioavailability (the degree to which a drug becomes available to the body's target tissues after administration of the drug). Although the court enjoined these false representations, it declined to award RPR money damages because RPR failed to prove resulting economic harm. The court also concluded that false advertising was not present in MMD's later promotional material, which discussed a specially commissioned study known as the "6730 Study." According to the 6730 Study, Dilacor XR's bioavailability was 74 to 81 percent.

In ruling on MMD's counterclaim, the court held that RPR's advertisements "contain[ed] a hidden message encouraging indiscriminate substitution" by prescribing physicians. This message, the court concluded, was false or misleading because it failed to disclose that Dilacor XR had not been approved by the FDA for treatment of angina. The court therefore ordered RPR to engage in corrective advertising revealing the fact that the FDA had not approved Dilacor XR for the treatment of angina. RPR appealed the adverse portions of the court's rulings on its claim and on MMD's counterclaim. ∽

Loken, Circuit Judge RPR sought to convince prescribing physicians that Dilacor XR is the "same as, only cheaper" than Cardizem CD. MMD's message was, in essence, "not same as," and maybe not cheaper.

MMD's Advertising

The trial evidence showed that MMD's [claims in early promotional literature discussing Dilacor XR's bioavailability were] false because [they] had no substantiation [or were] based upon an obvious misinterpretation of data from prior studies. But MMD's [later] claim of 74% to 81% bioavailability was based upon the specially commissioned 6730 Study.

The Lanham Act prohibits "commercial advertising or promotion [that] misrepresents the nature, characteristics, qualities, or geographic origin of [the advertiser's] or another person's goods, services, or commercial activities." False advertising decisions in other circuits have consistently distinguished between two types of comparative advertising claims: "my product is better than yours," versus "*tests prove* that my product is better than yours." To successfully challenge the first type of claim, a Lanham Act plaintiff must prove that [the] defendant's claim of superiority is false. But to successfully challenge the second type of claim, where [the] defendant has hyped the claim of superiority by attributing it to the results of scientific testing, [the] plaintiff must prove only "that the tests [relied upon] were not sufficiently reliable to permit one to conclude with reasonable certainty that they established the proposition for which they

were cited" (quoting *Castrol, Inc. v. Quaker State Corp.* (2d Cir. 1992)).

RPR concedes that the 6730 Study results support the claims MMD made in its advertising brochure. Thus, the issue before us is whether the advertising was false because the 6730 Study is not a sufficiently reliable basis for comparing the bioavailability of Dilacor XR and Cardizem CD. After carefully reviewing [the parties' conflicting expert testimony on the 6730 Study's design and methodology and the arguments made by RPR concerning studies that reached conclusions different from those of the 6730 Study], we conclude the district court's finding that MMD did not falsely advertise the 6730 Study must be upheld. We note that Lanham Act liability for "tests prove" advertising requires proof that the tests are not "sufficiently reliable" to support the advertised conclusion with "reasonable certainty." To ensure vigorous competition and to protect legitimate commercial speech, courts applying this standard should give advertisers a fair amount of leeway, at least in the absence of a clear intent to deceive or substantial consumer confusion.

RPR also argues that it was entitled to money damages for MMD's earlier false advertising [i.e., the representations that were not based on the 6730 Study]. The plaintiff must prove both actual damages and a causal link between the defendant's violation and those damages. In this case, RPR did not attempt to prove that it incurred increased costs in countering MMD's false advertisements, one well-established method of proving Lanham Act damages. Rather, RPR attempted to prove that MMD's false advertising resulted in $40 to $56 million of lost Dilacor XR sales. However, the district court found that Dilacor XR sales "exceeded [RPR's] initial predictions" and that "Dilacor XR is as well-positioned as should be reasonably expected at this stage in its product history with or without [MMD's] anti-Dilacor campaigns." These findings are not clearly erroneous and are directly responsive to RPR's damage theory. Thus, the district court did not abuse its remedial discretion in declining to award RPR damages.

RPR's Advertising

The district court found that RPR's advertisements conveyed a false hidden message encouraging indiscriminate substitution of Dilacor XR for Cardizem CD. RPR concedes that its advertisements encouraged physicians to consider the two drugs freely substitutable, . . . [b]ut RPR [argues] that the district court erred in ordering corrective advertising disclosing that Dilacor XR is not approved to treat angina.

Regarding the limited FDA approval issue, RPR notes that it has truthfully advertised Dilacor XR as approved for the treatment of hypertension. The district court erred, RPR argues, because a Lanham Act plaintiff alleging that advertising is false because it conveys a false *implicit* message must prove actual consumer confusion, and MMD presented no such proof. We note that [cases other than those relied upon by the plaintiff] have said that implicit falsity should be tested by public reaction, not that a [party] such as MMD *must* prove confusion by

consumer research. But we need not resolve that issue because consumer confusion need not be proved if advertising is literally false.

In assessing whether advertising is literally false, "a court must analyze the message conveyed in full context" (quoting *Castrol, Inc. v. Pennzoil Co.* (3d Cir. 1993)). Here, the record fully supports the district court's finding that RPR's advertisements were literally false. The court focused on RPR advertisements featuring images such as two similar gasoline pumps or airline tickets with dramatically different prices, accompanied by the slogan, "Which one would you choose[?]" The court found that these ads falsely represented that the two drugs may be indiscriminately substituted, in effect, a representation that Dilacor XR has certain qualities that it in fact does not have. Because the implicit message was literally false, the issue became one of remedy—what corrective advertising would be appropriate. The district court determined that the false message would be remedied if RPR adequately explained the differences in the two products, including the fact that Dilacor XR is not approved to treat angina. There was no abuse of discretion in adopting that remedy.

Decision of district court affirmed.

Note: In a portion of the opinion not presented here, the Eighth Circuit Court of Appeals vacated a portion of an order the district court had entered against RPR. Matters relevant to the vacated portion of the order were not included in the above summary of facts and edited version of the Eighth Circuit's opinion.

ETHICAL AND PUBLIC POLICY CONCERNS

1. An ethical theory known as *utilitarianism* says that the test for the moral worth of actions is their ability to produce the greatest degree of aggregate net satisfaction throughout society. Some utilitarians say that satisfaction is maximized when people are best able to realize their individual preferences. Some say that one measure of satisfaction is the creation of economic wealth. Look at the purposes said to underlie trademark law. Are these generally utilitarian? Why or why not?

2. Legal reasoning is sometimes deductive or syllogistic. In such cases, the court states a general rule

as a major premise, treats the facts as a minor premise, and applies the rule to the facts to generate a result. But another style of legal reasoning called *factor-based balancing* proceeds differently. In cases of this kind, the court states various factors that are relevant to its decision and decides by weighing these factors against one another under the facts before it. Which cases in this chapter use this method in whole or in part? Based on those cases, what is good about this style of legal reasoning? Are sensible decisions possible in any other way? On the other hand, what is bad about this decisionmaking process? In answering this last question, consider whether or how well this process enables business parties to predict the legal consequences of their behavior.

1. Huey J. Rivet patented an "amphibious marsh craft" for hauling loads and laying pipeline in swamps. Rivet's model could "walk" over stumps for extended periods while carrying heavy loads. Later, Robert Wilson, who had once worked for Rivet as a welder, began marketing a similar craft. The craft sold by Wilson differed from the craft described in the specification accompanying Rivet's patent application in several respects. Overall, though, the Wilson boat performed much the same functions about as effectively as the Rivet craft, and used much the same engineering techniques and concepts to do so. Has Wilson infringed Rivet's patent?

2. Lorna Nelson, half-sister of the rock star Prince, sued Prince for copyright infringement. She alleged that Prince's hit "U Got the look" infringed her copyrighted song "What's Cooking in this Book." Lorna's song, to which Prince had access, had six verses totaling 35 lines and 176 words. "U Got the look" had eight verses totaling 47 lines and 242 words. The alleged infringements concerned the following verses and words from the two songs:

a. Lorna's verse 2: "I glanced up and saw you, a smile so pretty." *Prince's verses 2 and 7:* "I woke up, I've never seen such a pretty girl."

b. Lorna's verse 3: "Makeup was rolling down my face." *Prince's verse 5:* "A whole hour just to make up your face."

c. Lorna's verse 6: "What's cooking in this book, what's cooking in . . . " *Prince's verses 4 and 6:* "U sho 'nuf do be cooking in my book."

d. Lorna's verses 1 and 6: "Take a look, Take another look." *Prince's verses 1 and 7:* "U got the look."

The main issue in the case was whether there was substantial similarity between the lyrics just quoted. Although you cannot answer this question from the chapter, do you think that these lyrics are sufficiently similar to justify imposing liability on Prince?

3. Irena Narell wrote a book that was a social history of the Bay area Jewish community. Narell's book, titled *Our City: The Jews of San Francisco,* was published in 1981. It sold fewer than 5,000 copies. In 1986, Narell repurchased the copyright

and the remaining inventory from the publisher. Cynthia Freeman's novel, *Illusions of Love,* was published in hardcover in 1984 and in paperback in 1986. Approximately 1 million copies of the novel were sold. *Illusions* told a fictional story about the heir of a large, wealthy Jewish family. In the story, the heir had to choose between his family and a lover from a vastly different background. Freeman consulted and used *Our City* in writing *Illusions.* Portions of *Illusions* were based on historical events described in *Our City. Illusions* also contained several instances of verbatim copying from *Our City.* These instances totaled approximately 300 words. In various other places, *Illusions* contained paraphrases of passages from *Our City.* Narell sued Freeman and her publishers for copyright infringement. The defendants argued that they should be protected against liability by the fair use defense. Should the defendants succeed with the fair use defense?

4. Jack Elo founded Ikon Photographic Corp. (IPC) to market inexpensive 35 mm and 110 mm pocket cameras. IPC applied to register the "Ikon" trademark and its logo but failed to obtain registration on the Principal Register. Later, IPC managed to obtain registration of a separate "Ikon" mark with a stylized "I" logo. Eventually, Nikon, Inc., sued IPC for infringement of the "Nikon" trademark. Nikon primarily manufactures cameras that are more expensive and complicated than those sold by IPC. However, Nikon had also been making point-and-shoot cameras similar to IPC's offerings. Should IPC be held liable for trademark infringement?

5. Levi Strauss & Co. makes Levi jeans. Each pair of Levi jeans has a striking and original back pocket stitching pattern consisting of two intersecting arcs that roughly bisect both pockets. In terms of distinctiveness, what kind of trademark is this? Should such a mark receive strong protection or relatively little protection if Levi Strauss sues another jeans manufacturer for trademark infringement?

6. E. I. du Pont de Nemours & Co. was building a plant to develop a highly secret unpatented process for producing methanol. During the construction, some of its trade secrets were exposed to view from the air because the plant in which they were contained did not yet have a roof. These secrets were photographed from an airplane by two photographers who were hired by persons unknown to take pictures of the new construction. Did this action amount to a misappropriation of Du Pont's trade secrets?

7. Frank and Frances Gardner sued Sailboat Key, Inc., to prevent it from constructing certain improvements pursuant to building permits issued by the city of Miami. Sailboat Key later sued the Gardners for injurious falsehood. It alleged that false statements contained in the Gardners' pleadings in the earlier case caused it to lose its interest in the land where the construction was to occur because it could not obtain financing. The Gardners claimed that defamation law's absolute privilege for statements made in the course of judicial proceedings also applied to this injurious falsehood action, and thus protected them from liability. Are the Gardners correct?

8. A geologist employed by Amoco Production Co. provided an oil wildcatter (a nonemployee of Amoco) with a faxed transmission of a page from a road atlas. On this page, the Amoco geologist had drawn circles indicating the location of potential oil reserve sites. In attempting to identify the sites, Amoco personnel had relied on publicly available information (including U.S. Geologic Survey reports) dealing with fault lines. Amoco identified the sites through use of a microwave radar survey of a geologic formation. The microwave radar detection technology was not something developed by, or exclusive to, Amoco. In litigation against the wildcatter, Amoco contended that the potential oil reserve site information highlighted on the map was an Amoco trade secret. Is Amoco entitled to trade secret protection concerning this information?

9. The New Mexico and Arizona Land Company owned a sizable tract of land in Arizona. It leased a portion of this land, which contained water for grazing, to the Bar J Bar Cattle Company. New Mexico had the right to cancel the lease upon 30 days' notice once it sold the land. Malcolm Pace, who owned a ranch adjoining the Bar J Bar ranch and wanted its water rights, bought the land leased by Bar J Bar from New Mexico. Shortly thereafter, New Mexico gave Bar J Bar 30 days' notice of termination. Bar J Bar sued Pace for intentional interference with contractual relations. One feature of the Bar J Bar lease weakens its chances of recovery against Pace. What is that feature of the lease? *Hint:* The answer requires that you make an

analogy to a subject discussed in this chapter's discussion of intentional interference with contractual relations.

10. After retiring from professional football, ex–Notre Dame and Green Bay Packer star Paul Hornung began a career as a television sports announcer. From the mid-1960s until 1980, he worked as a play-by-play announcer and color commentator at both college and professional games. In 1981 or 1982, the Atlanta television station WTBS contracted with the NCAA to telecast 19 college football games during the 1982 and 1983 seasons. The contract gave the NCAA the right to approve or disapprove any announcer or color commentator used on the broadcasts. When WTBS proposed Hornung as a color analyst for the games, the NCAA rejected him. The stated reasons for Hornung's rejection were his close association with professional football, his suspension for gambling while an NFL player, and his participation in Miller Lite beer commercials. The NCAA, however, itself accepted advertising revenue from the Miller Brewing Company.

Hornung sued the NCAA for intentional interference with prospective advantage. Did he win? Why or why not?

11. A Quaker State Corp. television commercial asserted that "tests prove" the following claim: "At start up Quaker State 10W-30 protects better than any other leading 10W-30 motor oil." The commercial also depicted an engine, superimposed over which were bottles of Quaker State motor oil and four competing oils, including Castrol GTX 10W-30. Nearby was a bar graph displaying the superior speed with which Quaker State oil flows to engine components once the engine is started. Castrol, Inc., sued Quaker State for false advertising under Lanham Act section 43(a). Castrol sought a preliminary injunction against Quaker State's airing the commercial. The evidence presented to the court indicated that Quaker State's oil did indeed reach engine parts faster at start-up than did its competitors' oil, but that this had no discernible effect on engine wear. The apparent reason was that the "residual oil" remaining from prior engine starts protects the engine until new oil arrives. Should an injunction be granted against the airing of the Quaker State commercial?

Contracts

Introduction to Contracts

The law of contracts deals with the enforcement of promises. It is important to realize from the outset of your study of contracts that *not every promise is legally enforceable.* (If every promise were enforceable, this chapter could be one sentence long!) We have all made and broken promises without fear of being sued. If you promise to take a friend out to dinner and then fail to do so, you would be shocked to be sued for breach of contract. What separates such promises from legally enforceable contracts? The law of contracts sorts out what promises are enforceable, to what extent, and how they will be enforced. ∞

THE NATURE OF CONTRACTS

The essence of a contract is that it is a *legally enforceable* promise or set of promises. In other words, when a set of promises has the status of *contract,* a person injured by a breach of that contract is entitled to call on the government (courts) to force the breaching party to honor the contract.

Over the years, the common law courts have developed several basic tests that a promise must meet before it is treated as a contract. These tests comprise the basic elements of contract. Contracts are *agreements* (an *offer,* made and *accepted*) that are *voluntarily* created by persons with the *capacity* to contract. The objectives of the agreement must be *legal* and, in most cases, the agreement must be

FIGURE   **1**

Getting to Contract

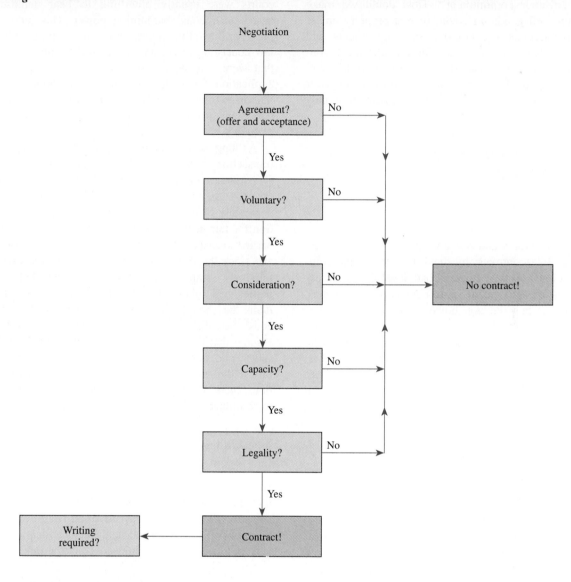

supported by some *consideration* (a bargained-for exchange of legal value). (See Figure 1.) The following chapters discuss each of these elements and other points that are necessary to enable you to distinguish contracts from unenforceable, social promises.

THE FUNCTIONS OF CONTRACTS

Contracts give us the ability to enter into agreements with others with confidence that we may call on the *law*—not merely the good faith of the other party—to make sure that those agreements will be honored. Within limitations that you will study later, *contracting lets us create a type of private law*—the terms of the agreements we make—that governs our relations with others.

Contracts facilitate the planning that is necessary in a modern, industrialized society. Who would invest in a business if she could not rely on the fact that the builders and suppliers of the facilities and equipment, the suppliers of the raw materials necessary to manufacture products, and the customers who agree to purchase those products would all honor their commitments? How could we make loans, sell goods on credit, or rent property unless loan agreements, conditional sales agreements, and leases were backed by the force of the law? Contract, then, is necessary to the world as we know it. Like that world, its particulars tend to change over time, while its general characteristics remain largely stable.

THE EVOLUTION OF CONTRACT LAW

Classical Contract Law

The contract idea is ancient. Thousands of years ago, Egyptians and Mesopotamians recognized devices like contracts; by the 15th century, the common law courts of England had developed a variety of theories to justify enforcing certain promises. Contract law did not, however, assume major importance in our legal system until the 19th century, when many social factors combined to shape the common law of contract. Laissez-faire (free market) economic ideas had a profound influence on public policy thinking during this period, and the Industrial Revolution created the necessity for private planning and certainty in commercial transactions. The typical contract situation in the early decades of the 19th century involved face-to-face transactions between parties with relatively equal bargaining power who dealt with relatively simple goods.

The contract law that emerged from this period was strongly influenced by these factors. Its central principle was *freedom of contract.* Freedom of contract is the idea that contracts should be enforced because they are the products of the free wills of their creators, who should, within broad limits, be free to determine the extent of their obligations. The proper role of the courts in such a system of contract was to enforce these freely made bargains but otherwise to adopt a hands-off stance. Contractual liability should not be imposed unless the parties clearly agreed to assume it, but once an agreement had been made, liability was near absolute. The fact that the items exchanged were of unequal value was usually legally irrelevant. The freedom to make good deals carried with it the risk of making bad deals. As long as a person voluntarily entered a contract, it would generally be enforced against

him, even if the result was grossly unfair. And since equal bargaining power tended to be assumed, the courts were usually unwilling to hear defenses based on unequal bargaining power. This judicial posture allowed the courts to create a pure contract law consisting of precise, clear, and technical rules that were capable of general, almost mechanical, application. Such a law of contract met the needs of the marketplace by affording the predictable and consistent results necessary to facilitate private planning.

As long as most contracts resembled the typical transaction envisioned by 19th-century contract law, such rules made perfect sense. If the parties dealt face-to-face, they were likely to know each other personally or at least to know each other's reputation for fair dealing. Face-to-face deals enabled the parties to inspect the goods in advance of the sale, and since the subject matter of most contracts was relatively simple, the odds were great that the parties had relatively equal knowledge about the items they bought and sold. If the parties also had equal bargaining power, it was probably fair to assume that they were capable of protecting themselves and negotiating an agreement that seemed fair at the time. Given the truth of these assumptions, there was arguably no good reason for judges to scrutinize private contracts for fairness.

The Underlying Assumptions of Contract Law Begin to Shift

America's Industrial Revolution, however, undermined many of the assumptions about the characteristics of the typical contract that had been made in the previous era. Regional, and later national, markets produced longer chains of distribution. This fact, combined with more efficient means of communication, meant that people often contracted with persons whom they did not know for goods that they had never seen. And rapidly developing technology meant that those goods were becoming increasingly complex. Thus, sellers often knew far more about their products than did the buyers with whom they dealt. Finally, the emergence of large business organizations after the Civil War produced obvious disparities of bargaining power in many contract situations. These large organizations found it more efficient to standardize their numerous transactions by employing standard form contracts, which also could be used to exploit disproportionate

Factors that Shaped Modern Contract Law

bargaining power by dictating the terms of their agreements. Figure 2 summarizes the factors that shaped modern contract law.

The upshot of all this is that many contracts today no longer resemble the stereotypical agreements envisioned by the common law of contract. It has been estimated that over 90 percent of all contracts today are form contracts.[1] How should courts respond to contracts where the terms have been dictated by one party to another party who may not have read or understood them, and who, in any event, may have lacked the power to bargain for better terms? Contract law is changing to reflect these changes in social reality. The 20th century has witnessed a dramatic increase in government regulation of private contractual relationships. Think of all the statutes governing the terms of what were once purely private contractual relationships. Legislatures commonly dictate many of the basic terms of insurance contracts. Employment contracts are governed by a host of laws concerning maximum hours worked, minimum wages paid, employer liability for on-the-job injuries, unemployment compensation, and retirement benefits. In some circum-

stances, product liability statutes impose liability on the manufacturers and sellers of products regardless of the terms of their sales contracts. The purpose of much of this regulation has been to protect persons who lack sufficient bargaining power to protect themselves.

Nor have the legislatures been the only source of public supervision of private agreements. Twentieth-century courts have been increasingly concerned with creating contract rules that produce fair results. The result of this concern has been an increasingly hands-on posture by courts that often feel compelled to intervene in private contractual relationships to protect weaker parties. In the name of avoiding injustice, some modern contract doctrines impose contractual liability, or something quite like it, in situations where traditional contract rules would have denied liability. Similarly, other modern contract doctrines allow parties to avoid contract liability in cases where traditional common law rules would have recognized a binding agreement and imposed liability.

How Modern Contract Law Differs from Classical Contract Law

In the process of evolving to accommodate changing social circumstances, the basic nature of contract rules is changing. The precise, technical rules that characterized traditional common law contract are giving way to broader, imprecise standards such as good faith, injustice, reasonableness, and unconscionability. The reason for such standards is clear. If courts are increasingly called on to evaluate private contracts on the basis of fairness, it is necessary to fashion rules that afford the degree of judicial discretion required to reach just decisions in the increasingly complex and varied situations where intervention is needed.

This greater emphasis on fairness, like every other choice made by law, carries with it some cost. Imprecise, discretionary modern contract rules do not produce the same measure of certainty and predictability that their precise and abstract predecessors afforded. And because modern contract rules often impose liability in the absence of the clear consent required by traditional common law contract rules, one price of increased fairness in contract cases has been a diminished ability of private parties to control the nature and extent of their contractual obligations.

[1]Slawson, "Standard Form Contracts and Democratic Control of Lawmaking Power," 84 *Harv. L. Rev.* 529 (1971).

This change in the nature of contract law is far from complete, however. The idea that a contract is an agreement freely entered into by the parties still lies at the heart of contract law today, and contract cases may be found that differ very little in their spirit or ultimate resolution from their 19th-century predecessors. It is probably fair to say, however, that these are most likely to be cases where 19th-century assumptions about the nature of contracts are still largely valid. Thus, these cases involve contracts between parties with relatively equal bargaining power and relatively equal knowledge about the subject of the contract. Despite the existence of such cases, it is evident that contract law is in the process of significant change. Before discussing particular examples of this new thrust in contract law, however, we should familiarize ourselves with the basic contract terminology that is used throughout the text.

BASIC CONTRACT CONCEPTS AND TYPES

Bilateral and Unilateral Contracts

Contracts have traditionally been classified as **bilateral** or **unilateral,** depending on whether one or both of the parties have made a promise. In unilateral contracts, only one party makes a promise. For example, if a homeowner says to a painter, "I will pay you $1,000 if you paint my house," the homeowner has made an offer for a unilateral contract, a contract that will be created only if and when the painter paints the house. If the homeowner instead says to the painter, "If you *promise* to paint my house, I will promise to pay you $1,000," he has asked the painter to commit to painting the house rather than just to perform the act of painting. This offer contemplates the formation of a bilateral contract. If the painter makes the requested promise to paint the house, a bilateral contract is created at that point.

Valid, Unenforceable, Voidable, and Void Contracts

A **valid contract** is one that meets all of the legal requirements for a binding contract. Valid contracts are, therefore, enforceable in court.

An **unenforceable contract** is one that meets the basic legal requirements for a contract but may not be enforceable due to some other legal rule. You'll learn about an example of this in Chapter 16, which discusses the statute of frauds, a rule that requires certain kinds of contracts to be evidenced by a writing. If a contract is one of those for which the statute of frauds requires a writing, but no writing is made, the contract is said to be unenforceable. Another example of an unenforceable contract is an otherwise valid contract whose enforcement is barred by the applicable contract statute of limitations.

Voidable contracts are those in which one or more of the parties have the legal right to cancel their obligations under the contract. For example, a contract that is induced by fraud or duress is voidable (cancellable) at the election of the injured party. Other situations in which contracts are voidable are discussed in Chapters 13 and 14. The important feature of a voidable contract is that the injured party has the *right* to cancel the contract *if he chooses.* That right belongs only to the injured party, and if he does not cancel the contract, it can be enforced by either party.

Void contracts are agreements that create no legal obligations and for which no remedy will be given. Contracts to commit crimes, such as "hit" contracts, are classic examples of void contracts. Illegal contracts such as these are discussed in Chapter 15.

Express and Implied Contracts

In an **express contract,** the parties have directly stated the terms of their contract orally or in writing at the time the contract was formed. However, the mutual agreement necessary to create a contract may also be demonstrated by the conduct of the parties. When the surrounding facts and circumstances indicate that an agreement has in fact been reached, an **implied contract** (also called a contract implied in fact) has been created. When you go to a doctor for treatment, for example, you do not ordinarily state the terms of your agreement in advance, although it is clear that you do, in fact, have an agreement. A court would infer a promise by your doctor to use reasonable care and skill in treating you and a return promise on your part to pay a reasonable fee for her services.

Executed and Executory Contracts

A contract is **executed** when all of the parties have fully performed their contractual duties, and it is

executory until such duties have been fully performed.

Any contract may be described using one or more of the above terms. For example, Eurocars, Inc., orders five new Mercedes-Benz 500 SLs from Mercedes. Mercedes sends Eurocars its standard acknowledgment form accepting the order. The parties have a *valid, express, bilateral* contract that will be *executory* until Mercedes delivers the cars and Eurocars pays for them.

BODIES OF LAW GOVERNING CONTRACTS

Two bodies of law—Article 2 of the Uniform Commercial Code and the common law of contracts—govern contracts today. The Uniform Commercial Code, or UCC, is statutory law in every state. The common law of contracts is court-made law that, like all court-made law, is in a constant state of evolution. Determining what body of law applies to a contract problem is a very important first step in analyzing that problem.

The Uniform Commercial Code: Origin and Purposes

The UCC was created by the American Law Institute and the National Conference of Commissioners on Uniform State Laws. All of the states have adopted it except Louisiana, which has adopted only part of the Code. The drafters of the Code had several purposes in mind, the most obvious of which was to establish a uniform set of rules to govern commercial transactions, which are often conducted across state lines.[2]

In addition to promoting uniformity, the drafters of the Code sought to create a body of rules that would realistically and fairly solve the common problems occurring in everyday commercial transactions. Finally, the drafters tried to formulate rules that would promote fair dealing and higher standards in the marketplace.

The UCC contains nine articles, most of which are discussed in detail in Parts IV, VI, and VII of this book. The most important Code article for our present purposes is Article 2, which deals with the sale of goods. At the time of this writing, revisions to Article 2 are being proposed, including the addition of a new article that would regulate software licenses.

Application of Article 2

Article 2 expressly applies only to *contracts for the sale of goods* [2–102] (the numbers in brackets refer to specific Code sections). The essence of the definition of goods in the UCC [1–105] is that *goods* are *tangible, movable, personal property.* So, contracts for the sale of such items as motor vehicles, books, appliances, and clothing are covered by Article 2.

Application of the Common Law of Contracts

Article 2 of the UCC applies to contracts for the sale of goods, but it does *not* apply to contracts for the sale of real estate or intangibles such as stocks and bonds, because those kinds of property do not constitute goods. Article 2 also does not apply to *service* contracts. Contracts for the sale of real estate, services, and intangibles are governed by the common law of contracts.

Law Governing "Hybrid" Contracts

Many contracts involve a hybrid of both goods and services. As the following *Advent* case illustrates, the test that the courts most frequently use to determine whether Article 2 applies to such a contract is to ask which element, goods or services, *predominates* in the contract. Is the major purpose or thrust of the agreement the rendering of a service, or is it the sale of goods, with any services involved being merely incidental to that sale? This means that contracts calling for services that involve significant elements of personal skill or judgment in addition to goods probably are not governed by Article 2. Construction contracts, remodeling contracts, and auto repair contracts are all examples of mixed goods and services contracts that may be considered outside the scope of the Code.

---

[2]Despite the Code's almost national adoption, however, complete uniformity has not been achieved. Many states have varied or amended the Code's language in specific instances, and some Code provisions were drafted in alternative ways, giving the states more than one version of particular Code provisions to choose from. Also, the various state courts have reached different conclusions about the meaning of particular Code sections. Work is currently under way to revise many basic sections of the Code, so uniformity will continue to be a problem as states adopt the revised sections at different rates and to different degrees.

Advent Systems Limited (Advent), a British company engaged primarily in the production of computer software, developed an electronic document management system (EDMS), a process for transforming engineering drawings and similar documents into a computer database. Unisys Corporation (Unisys), an American computer manufacturer, decided to market Advent's EDMS in the United States. In 1987, Advent and Unisys signed two documents, one labeled "Heads of Agreement" and the other "Distribution Agreement," in which Advent agreed to provide the software and hardware making up the EDMS, as well as sales and marketing material and the technical personnel to work with Unisys employees in building and installing the document systems. The agreement was to continue for two years, subject to automatic renewal or termination on notice.

During the summer of 1987, Unisys attempted to sell the document system to a large oil company but was unsuccessful. Nevertheless, progress on the sales and training programs in the United States was satisfactory. But Unisys, then in the throes of restructuring, decided it would be better off developing its own document system, and in December 1987 it told Advent the agreement was ended. Advent filed suit, alleging breach of contract among other things. Unisys argued that the agreement with Advent was covered by the UCC and that it failed to contain an express quantity provision that the UCC statute of frauds requires. The trial court ruled, however, that the agreements were not covered by the Code because their services aspect predominated. When the jury awarded Advent $4,550,000 for breach of contract, Unisys appealed. ∽

Weis, Circuit Judge As the district court appraised the transaction, provisions for services outweighed those for products and, consequently, the arrangement was not predominantly one for the sale of goods. The agreements provided that Advent was to modify its software and hardware interfaces to run initially on equipment not manufactured by Unisys but eventually on Unisys hardware. "In so far as Advent has successfully completed [some of the processing] of software and hardware interfaces," Unisys promised to reimburse Advent to the extent of $150,000 derived from a "surcharge" on products purchased.

Advent agreed to provide 12 man-weeks of marketing manpower, but with Unisys bearing certain expenses. Advent also undertook to furnish an experienced systems builder to work with Unisys personnel at Advent's prevailing rates, and to provide sales and support training for Unisys staff as well as its customers.

The Distribution Agreement begins with the statement "Unisys desires to purchase, and Advent desires to sell, on a non-exclusive basis, certain of Advent hardware products and software licenses for resale worldwide." Following a heading "Subject Matter of Sales," appears this sentence, "Advent agrees to sell hardware and license software to Unisys, and Unisys agrees to buy from Advent the products listed in Schedule A." Schedule A lists 20 products, such as computer cards, plotters, imagers, scanners and designer systems.

Because software was a major portion of the "products" described in the agreement, this matter requires some discussion. Computer systems consist of "hardware" and "software." Hardware is the computer machinery, its electronic circuitry and peripheral items such as keyboards, readers, scanners and printers. Software is a more elusive concept. Generally speaking, "software" refers to the medium that stores input and output data as well as computer programs. The medium includes hard disks, floppy disks, and magnetic tapes.

In simplistic terms, programs are codes prepared by a programmer that instruct the computer to perform certain functions. When the program is transposed onto a medium compatible with the computer's needs, it becomes software. The increasing frequency of computer products as subjects of commercial litigation has led to controversy over whether software is a "good" or intellectual property. The Code does not specifically mention software.

In the absence of express legislative guidance, courts interpret the Code in the light of commercial and technological developments. The Code is designed "to permit the continued expansion of commercial practices" [1–102(2)(b)]. The Code applies to "transactions in goods" [2–102], which are defined as "all things (including specially manufactured goods) which are moveable at the time of the identification for sale" [2–105(1)].

Our Court has addressed computer package sales in other cases, but has not been required to consider whether the UCC applied to software per se. Computer programs are the product of an intellectual process, but once implanted in a medium are widely distributed to computer owners. An analogy can be drawn to a compact disc recording of an orchestral rendition. The music is produced by the artistry of musicians and in itself is not a "good," but when transferred to a laser-readable disc becomes a readily merchantable commodity. Similarly, when a professor delivers a lecture, it is not a good, but, when transcribed as a book, it becomes a good.

That a computer program may be copyrightable as intellectual property does not alter the fact that once in the form of a floppy disc or other medium, the program is tangible, moveable and available in the marketplace. The fact that some programs may be tailored for specific purposes need not alter their status as "goods" because the Code definition includes "specially manufactured goods." The topic has stimulated academic commentary with the majority espousing the view that software fits with the definition of a "good" in the UCC.

The relationship at issue here is a typical mixed goods and services arrangement. The services are not substantially different from those generally accompanying package sales of computer systems consisting of hardware and software. Although determining the applicability of the UCC to a contract by examining the predominance of goods or services has been criticized, we see no reason to depart from that practice here. We consider the purpose or essence of the contract. Comparing the relative costs of the materials supplied with the costs of the labor may be helpful in this analysis, but not dispositive. In this case the contract's main objective was to transfer "products." The specific provisions for training of Unisys personnel by Advent were but a small part of the parties' contemplated relationship.

The compensation structure of the agreement also focuses on "goods." The projected sales figures introduced during the trial demonstrate that in the contemplation of the parties the sale of goods clearly predominated. The payment provision of $150,000 for developmental work which Advent had previously completed was to be made through individual purchases of software and hardware rather than through the fees for services and is further evidence that the intellectual work was to be subsumed into tangible items for sale.

Applying the UCC to computer software transactions offers substantial benefits to litigants and the courts. The Code offers a uniform body of law on a wide range of questions likely to arise in computer software disputes: implied warranties, consequential damages, disclaimers of liability, the statute of limitations, to name a few. The importance of software to the commercial world and the advantages to be gained by the uniformity inherent in the UCC are strong policy arguments favoring inclusion. The contrary arguments are not persuasive, and we hold that software is a "good" within the definition of the Code.

Judgment reversed and remanded for further proceedings consistent with the court's opinion.

Relationship of the UCC and the Common Law of Contracts

Two important qualifications must be made concerning the application of Code contract principles. First, the Code does not change *all* of the traditional contract rules. Where no specific Code rule exists, traditional contract law rules apply to contracts for the sale of goods. Second, and ultimately far more important, the courts have demonstrated a significant tendency to apply Code contract concepts by analogy to some contracts that are not technically covered by Article 2. For example, the Code concepts of good faith dealing and unconscionability have enjoyed wide application in cases that are technically outside the scope of Article 2. Thus, the Code is an important influence in shaping the evolution of contract law in general, and if this trend toward broader application of Code principles continues, the time may come when the dichotomy between Code principles and traditional contract rules is a thing of the past. (See Figure 3.)

Basic Differences in the Nature of Article 2 and the Common Law of Contracts

Many of the provisions of Article 2 exhibit the basic tendencies of modern contract law discussed earlier in this chapter. Accordingly, they differ from traditional contract law rules in a variety of important ways. The Code is more concerned with rewarding

FIGURE 3

When the Uniform Commercial Code Applies

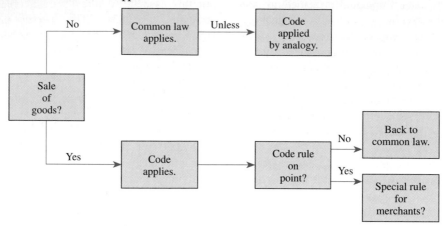

people's legitimate expectations than with technical rules, so it is generally more flexible than contract law. A court that applies the Code is more likely to find that the parties had a contract than is a court that applies contract law [2–204]. In some cases, the Code gives less weight than does contract law to technical requirements such as consideration [2–205 and 2–209].

The drafters of the Code sought to create practical rules to deal with what people actually do in today's marketplace. We live in the day of the form contract, so some of the Code's rules try to deal fairly with that fact [2–205, 2–207, 2–209(2), and 2–302]. The words *reasonable, commercially reasonable,* and *seasonably* (within a reasonable time) are found throughout the Code. This reasonableness standard is different from the hypothetical reasonable person standard in tort law. A court that tries to decide what is reasonable under the Code is more likely to be concerned with what people really do in the marketplace than with what a nonexistent reasonable person would do.

The drafters of the Code wanted to promote fair dealing and higher standards in the marketplace, so they imposed a **duty of good faith** [1–203] in the performance and enforcement of every contract under the Code. Good faith means "honesty in fact," which is required of all parties to sales contracts [1–201(19)]. In addition, merchants are required to observe "reasonable commercial standards of fair dealing" [2–103(1)(b)]. The parties cannot alter this duty of good faith by agreement [1–102(3)]. Finally, the Code expressly recognizes the concept of an **unconscionable contract,** one

that is grossly unfair or one-sided, and it gives the courts broad discretionary powers to deal fairly with such contracts [2–302].[3]

The Code also recognizes that buyers tend to place more reliance on professional sellers and that professionals are generally more knowledgeable and better able to protect themselves than nonprofessionals. So, the Code distinguishes between **merchants** and nonmerchants by holding merchants to a higher standard in some cases [2–201(2), 2–205, and 2–207(2)]. The Code defines the term *merchant* [2–104(1)] on a case-by-case basis. If a person regularly deals in the kind of goods being sold, or pretends to have some special knowledge about the goods, or employed an agent in the sale who fits either of these two descriptions, that person is a merchant for the purposes of the contract in question. So, if you buy a used car from a used-car dealer, the dealer is a merchant for the purposes of your contract. But, if you buy a refrigerator from a used-car dealer, the dealer is probably not a merchant.

RESTATEMENT (SECOND) OF CONTRACTS

Nature and Origins

In 1932, the American Law Institute published the first *Restatement of Contracts,*[4] an attempt to codify

---

[3]Chapter 15 discusses unconscionability in detail.

[4]See Chapter 1 for a general discussion of the *Restatement* phenomenon.

and systematize the soundest principles of contract law gleaned from thousands of often conflicting judicial decisions. As the product of a private organization, the *Restatement* did not have the force of law, but as the considered judgment of some of the leading scholars of the legal profession, it was highly influential in shaping the evolution of contract law. The *Restatement (Second) of Contracts,* issued in 1979, is an attempt to reflect the significant changes that have occurred in contract law in the years following the birth of the first *Restatement.* The *Restatement (Second)* reflects the "shift from rules to standards" in modern contract law—the shift from precise, technical rules to broader, discretionary principles that produce just results.[5] In fact, many *Restatement (Second)* provisions are virtually identical to their Code analogues. For example, the *Restatement (Second)* has explicitly embraced the Code concepts of *good faith*[6] and *unconscionability.*[7]

The *Restatement (Second)* does *not* have the force of law. Nonetheless, it can be and has been influential in shaping the evolution of contract law because courts have the option of adopting a *Restatement (Second)* approach to the contract issues presented in the cases that come before them. Particular approaches suggested by the *Restatement (Second)* will be mentioned in some of the following chapters.

"NONCONTRACT" OBLIGATIONS

Before we proceed to a discussion of the individual elements of contract law, there is one more group of introductory concepts to be considered. Although contract obligations normally require mutual agreement and an exchange of value, there are some circumstances in which the law enforces an obligation to pay for certain losses or benefits even in the absence of mutual agreement and exchange of value. We will refer to these circumstances as "noncontract" obligations because they impose the duty on a person to pay for a loss or benefit yet they do not meet the criteria for formation of a contract. These noncontract doctrines give a person who cannot establish the existence of a contract a chance to obtain compensation.

Quasi-Contract

Requiring all the elements of a binding contract before contractual obligation is imposed can cause injustice in some cases. One person may have provided goods or services to another person who benefited from them but has no contractual obligation to pay for them because no facts exist that would justify a court in implying a promise to pay for them. Such a situation can also arise in cases where the parties contemplated entering into a binding contract but some legal defense exists that prevents the enforcement of the agreement. Consider the following examples:

1. Jones paints Smith's house by mistake, thinking it belongs to Reed. Smith knows that Jones is painting his house but does not inform him of his error. There are no facts from which a court can infer that Jones and Smith have a contract because the parties have had no prior discussions or dealings.

2. Thomas Products fraudulently induces Perkins to buy a household products franchise by grossly misstating the average revenues of its franchisees. Perkins discovers the misrepresentation after he has resold some products that he has received but before he has paid Thomas for them. Perkins elects to rescind (cancel) the franchise contract on the basis of the fraud.

In the preceding examples, both Smith and Perkins have good defenses to contract liability; however, enabling Smith to get a free paint job and Perkins to avoid paying for the goods he resold would *unjustly enrich* them at the expense of Jones and Thomas. To deal with such cases and to prevent such unjust enrichment, the courts imply *as a matter of law* a promise by the benefited party to pay the *reasonable value* of the benefits he received. This idea is called **quasi-contract** (or contract implied in law) because it represents an obligation imposed by law to avoid injustice, not a contractual obligation created by voluntary consent. Quasi-contract liability has been imposed in situations too numerous and varied to detail. In general, however, quasi-contract liability is imposed when one party *confers a benefit* on another who *knowingly accepts it* and *retains it* under circumstances that make it *unjust* to do so without paying for it. So, if Jones painted Smith's house while Smith was away on vacation, Smith would probably not be liable for the reasonable

---

[5]Speidel, "Restatement Second: Omitted Terms and Contract Method," 67 *Cornell L. Rev.* 785, 786 (1982).

[6]*Restatement (Second) of Contracts* § 205 (1981).

[7]*Restatement (Second) of Contracts* § 208 (1981).

value of the paint job because he did *not* knowingly accept it and because he has no way to return it to Jones. The following case, *Anthony Corrado, Inc. v. Menard & Co.*, highlights the central importance of the unjust enrichment idea to quasi-contract liability.

ANTHONY CORRADO, INC. v. MENARD & CO. 589 A.2d 1201 (R.I. Sup. Ct. 1991)

Hart Engineering Company (Hart) was the general contractor for the construction of the Fields Point Waste Water Treatment Facility. Hart posted the necessary bond for the project, and Seaboard Surety Company (Seaboard) wrote the bond. Hart subcontracted with Menard & Co. Building Contractors (Menard) to do the masonry work. Menard purchased certain building materials for the project from Corrado. Corrado supplied the materials but was never paid by either Menard or Hart. Corrado later sued Hart, Seaboard, and Menard. He won a summary judgment against Menard, but the trial court granted summary judgments in favor of Seaboard and Hart because Menard, not Hart or Seaboard, had ordered the materials. Corrado appealed. ⌒

Per Curiam   Corrado argues that under quasi-contract, he had a cause of action against Hart and Seaboard for unjust enrichment. In order to recover under quasi-contract, a plaintiff is required to prove three elements: (1) a benefit must be conferred upon the defendant by the plaintiff, (2) there must be appreciation by the defendant of such a benefit, and (3) there must be an acceptance of such benefit in such circumstances that it would be inequitable for a defendant to retain the benefit without paying the value thereof.

In reviewing a motion for summary judgment, a trial justice must determine, after an examination of the pleadings, affidavits, admissions, and answers to interrogatories, viewed in the light most favorable to the opposing party, whether there is a genuine issue regarding any material fact that must be resolved.

In his affidavit Frank Rampone, president of Hart, avers that from time to time Menard would submit an application for payment and that periodic payments were made to Menard. He further averred that Hart had no contractual relationship with Corrado and that it was Menard's obligation to pay Corrado directly from the periodic payments made to it. Hart never agreed to pay Corrado directly.

It is obvious from the record that there is no genuine issue regarding any material fact that must be resolved. No conflicting evidence was introduced to establish that Menard was not paid in full by Hart. Moreover, there was no evidence that would establish that Hart received any unjust enrichment from Corrado's building materials since Hart made periodic payments to Menard.

Judgment for Hart and Seaboard affirmed.

Promissory Estoppel

Another very important idea that 20th-century courts have developed to deal with the unfairness that would sometimes result from the strict application of traditional contract principles is the doctrine of **promissory estoppel.** In numerous situations one person may *rely* on a promise made by another even though the promise and surrounding circumstances are not sufficient to justify the conclusion that a contract has been created because one or more of the required elements is missing. To allow the person who made such a promise (the promisor) to argue that no contract was created would sometimes work an injustice on the person who relied on the promise (the promisee). For example, in *Ricketts v. Scothorn,* a grandfather's promise to pay his granddaughter interest on a demand note he gave her so that she would not have to work was enforced against him after she had quit her job in reliance on his promise.[8] The Nebraska Supreme Court acknowledged that such promises were traditionally unenforceable because they were gratuitous and not supported by any consideration, but held that the granddaughter's reliance prevented her grandfather

---

[8]57 Neb. 51, 77 N.W. 365 (1898).

from raising his lack of consideration defense. In the early decades of this century, many courts began to extend similar protection to relying promisees. They said that persons who made promises that produced such reliance were *estopped,* or equitably prevented, from raising any defense they had to the enforcement of their promise. Out of such cases grew the doctrine of promissory estoppel. Section 90 of the *Restatement (Second) of Contracts* states:

A promise which the promisor should reasonably expect to induce action or forbearance on the part of the promisee or a third person and which does induce such action or forbearance is binding if injustice can be avoided only by enforcement of the promise. The remedy granted for breach may be limited as justice requires.

Thus, the elements of promissory estoppel are a *promise* that the *promisor should foresee is likely to induce reliance, reliance* on the promise by the promisee, and *injustice* as a result of that reliance. (See Figure 4.)

When you consider these elements, it is obvious that promissory estoppel is fundamentally different from traditional contract principles. Contract is traditionally thought of as protecting *agreements* or

Contract and Noncontract Theories of Recovery

THEORY	KEY CONCEPT	REMEDY
Contract	Voluntary agreement	Enforce promise
Quasi-Contract	Unjust enrichment	Reasonable value of services
Promissory Estoppel	Foreseeable reliance	Enforce promise or recover reliance losses

bargains. Promissory estoppel, on the other hand, protects *reliance.* Early promissory estoppel cases applied the doctrine only to gift promises like the one made by the grandfather in the previous example. As subsequent chapters demonstrate, however, promissory estoppel is now being used by the courts to prevent offerors from revoking their offers, to enforce indefinite promises, and to enforce oral promises that would ordinarily have to be in writing. As the following *Ypsilanti* case demonstrates, however, a promise lies at the heart of promissory estoppel.

YPSILANTI v. GENERAL MOTORS, INC.   506 N.W.2d 556 (Mich. Ct. App. 1993)

General Motors operated two plants in the township of Ypsilanti, Michigan, for a number of years. The Hydra-Matic plant employed approximately 9,000 workers and the Willow Run plant employed more than 4,000. Over the years, the township granted GM 11 tax abatements, 8 at Hydra-Matic and 3 at Willow Run, pursuant to a Michigan statute that authorizes municipalities to grant tax exemptions for businesses that meet the requirements of the act. In 1984, the township approved GM's application for a 12-year, 50 percent abatement of personal property taxes on the corporation's $175 million investment for the introduction of a new car. In April 1988, GM announced that it would produce a new rear-wheel drive vehicle, the Chevrolet Caprice, at Willow Run. Six months later, in 1988, GM applied for a tax abatement for that project, which involved another 12-year, $75 million project. The township approved that application as well.

In December 1991, GM announced that it had decided to consolidate the work being done at Willow Run and Arlington, Texas, at Arlington. GM claims the consolidation was necessary because of the company's record losses and because its Caprice sales had been far less than projected. The township sued GM, pressing a variety of contract claims against GM. The trial court found that there had been no contract between the township and GM, but it did find that GM was bound by promissory estoppel to keep the production of the Caprice line in Willow Run as long as the company produced that model. It enjoined GM "from transferring the production of its Caprice sedan, and Buick and Cadillac [sic, Chevrolet] station wagons, from the Willow Run plant to any other facility." GM appealed.

Per Curiam   The trial court, relying on the background of GM's negotiations for abatements and principally on a statement by Willow Run plant manager Harvey Williams, found that a promise had been made. Williams stated that "[u]pon completion of this project and favorable market demand, it will allow Willow Run to continue production and maintain continuous employment for our employees." The trial court ruled:

In the context of this background, when the plant manager, in the prepared statement on behalf of General Motors stated that, subject to "favorable market demand," General Motors would "continue production and maintain continuous employment" at the Willow Run plant, *it was a promise.* The promise was clearly that if the Township granted the abatement, GM would make the Caprice at Willow Run and not just transfer that work somewhere else.

The elements of promissory estoppel are:

A promise which the promisor should reasonably expect to induce action or forbearance on the part of the promisee or a third person which does induce such action or forbearance is binding if injustice can be avoided only by enforcement of the promise. The remedy granted for breach may be limited as justice requires. [1 *Restatement Contracts 2d,* section 90, p. 242]

Promissory estoppel requires an actual, clear, and definite promise. Further, "reliance is reasonable only if it is induced by an actual promise."

The trial court's finding that GM promised to keep Caprice and station wagon production at Willow Run is clearly erroneous. First, the mere fact that a corporation solicits a tax abatement and persuades a municipality with assurances of jobs cannot be evidence of a promise. The very purpose of tax abatement legislation is to induce companies to locate and to continue business enterprises in the municipality. Second, representations of job creation and retention are a statutory prerequisite. An applicant for an industrial facilities exemption certificate must certify that "completion of the facility is calculated to have the reasonable likelihood to create employment, retain employment, prevent a

loss of employment, or produce energy in the community in which the facility is situated."

Third, the fact that a manufacturer uses hyperbole and puffery in seeking an advantage or concession does not necessarily create such a promise. Turning to the case at bar, almost all the statements the trial court cited as foundations for a promise were, instead, expressions of GM's hopes or expectations of continued employment at Willow Run. The court summarized the corporation's concerted efforts to obtain abatements as follows:

Over the years, GM followed the example set in its first application and a course of conduct developed between GM and the township for the granting of tax abatements. Each time GM wanted an abatement to make a physical change in the plants, it would invite township officials to the plant for a briefing, a tour of the plant, and lunch. The formal application would be submitted and GM officials would appear at a public hearing before the entire Board, which would then approve the application. Each time, the Board was advised, in some specifics, of the impact of the improvements, and presumably the abatement, on production and employment levels in the plant.

The acts cited by the trial court were acts one would naturally expect a company to do in order to introduce and promote an abatement proposal to a municipality. The acts showed only efforts to take advantage of a statutory opportunity. They did not constitute assurances of continued employment.

Even if the finding of a promise could be sustained, reliance on the promise would not have been reasonable. It has never been held that an abatement carries a promise of continued employment. Indeed the history of this case shows that persons involved in the 1988 Willow Run abatement understood that GM was not promising continued employment. In short, GM made no promises.

Reversed in favor of GM.

ETHICAL AND PUBLIC POLICY CONCERNS

1. Compare and contrast the ethical values at the heart of classical contract law with those at the heart of modern contract law. If all contracts today fit the typical model assumed by classical contract law, would we necessarily feel ethically compelled to

treat them differently than they were treated under classical contract law?

2. Do a brief social cost–benefit analysis of the shift from rules to standards that has occurred in modern contract law. Do a contrasting cost–benefit analysis of the rule-oriented approach of classical contract law.

3. The idea that contracts should be enforced because they are voluntary agreements can obviously be justified on ethical grounds. What ethical justifications, if any, can you give for departing from the notion of voluntary agreement in quasi-contract and promissory estoppel cases?

PROBLEM CASES

1. Intending to marry as soon as Donald's divorce became final, Rose Elsten and Donald Cook moved to Tucson in 1969 and lived there together until 1981. Although they did not marry, Rose used Donald's last name and they represented themselves to the community as husband and wife. Both parties worked throughout most of the relationship, pooling their income in two joint accounts and acquiring a house, two cars, and a number of shares of stock, all owned as joint tenants with right of survivorship. Rose left Donald in 1981. Of their joint assets, she received only one car and a few hundred dollars; Donald retained the balance. Rose filed suit against Donald, arguing that he had breached their agreement to share their assets equally. In her deposition she said: "[E]verything we did and purchased, whether it be a vacuum cleaner or a car, was together as husband and wife. It was just something *that we agreed on,* that is how we were going to do it." Did a contract exist?

2. On April 4, 1991, Rutland Lumber Co. hired Milliken & Michael (M & M), a collection agency, to collect a delinquent account of $11,568.38 from Bacon Lumber Co. On April 22, 1991, Fred Netterville Lumber Co. also hired M & M to collect a delinquent account from Bacon in the amount of $23,105.23. Milliken met with some success in collecting this money from Bacon. On April 26, Bacon remitted a $5,000 payment designated as partial payment for the Netterville account. M & M subtracted its $750 collection fee and sent the balance to Netterville. On May 20, Bacon remitted another $5,000 as partial payment for the *Rutland* account. Milliken subtracted its collection fee but mistakenly sent the $4,250 check to Netterville rather than Rutland. Netterville credited Bacon for two payments on its delinquent account in the amount of $10,000, even though the check clearly indicated that it was intended as payment for Rutland. Realizing its mistake, M & M notified Netterville of the error and asked that the payment be returned. Netterville responded by closing its account with M & M and refusing to return the payment. Fred Netterville testified at a later hearing that he would not have employed M & M had he known that it was representing other businesses in collecting from Bacon, and he felt there was a conflict of interest in M & M's representing the two lumber companies. Does Netterville have the obligation to return the money to M & M?

3. Cooper, an attorney, furnished senior White House officials memoranda that saved Salomon Brothers from criminal indictment. Salomon had not requested Cooper's services, nor was Cooper Salomon's attorney. Cooper filed suit against Salomon seeking damages of $530 million plus 50 percent of Salomon's equity. Does quasi-contract obligate Salomon to pay this money to Cooper?

4. Slodov adopted a four-month-old puppy from the Animal Protective League (APL) for a fee of $45, which covered the costs of neutering or spaying, shots, collar, starter kit, and two weeks of veterinary care. She signed an adoption agreement that stipulated that the APL would treat the dog at no cost to Slodov for two weeks after the adoption. According to the agreement, the APL would not be held responsible for any treatment of the dog outside the APL clinic. The dog became ill several times and Slodov took the dog to a private veterinarian rather than to the APL clinic. She then requested that the APL pay the veterinary bills, including advertising costs of placing the dog for adoption, because her landlord would not allow dogs in the apartment, and the APL refused. Slodov brought suit against APL on a variety of theories, including breach of warranties under the UCC. She claimed that the APL was a merchant under the UCC. Was it?

5. Chow arranged through a travel agent to fly from Indianapolis to Singapore on June 27, 1986. Singapore Airlines gave him a round-trip ticket that included a TWA flight to Los Angeles. Shortly before the trip, Chow's flight was rerouted so that he had to fly to St. Louis first and then to San Francisco. During the St. Louis stopover, the flight developed engine trouble, causing a substantial delay. TWA personnel assured Chow that if he missed his connecting flight, TWA would arrange for him to take the next Singapore flight out of San Francisco. After the engine problem was fixed, TWA delayed the flight's departure an additional two hours to board additional passengers. Chow was again assured that if he missed his scheduled flight, TWA would make arrangements for him. Chow missed his Singapore flight by minutes, and was housed overnight at TWA's expense in San Francisco after once more being assured that TWA would make arrangements to get him on the next Singapore flight. When he called Singapore Airlines the next morning to see whether TWA had made him a reservation, Chow was told that no arrangements had been made. When he contacted TWA, he was told TWA would make the arrangements immediately. After waiting several hours, Chow learned TWA had still not made the arrangements and was told that TWA could no longer help him. Because Singapore Airlines no longer had economy class seats available, Chow had to buy a business class seat at an additional cost of $928. When he filed suit against TWA for that amount, TWA argued that the Conditions of Contract printed on Chow's ticket disclaimed any liability for failure to make connections. Did Chow have a valid claim against TWA?

6. Commercial Cornice, a subcontractor, entered a contract with Camel Construction, a general contractor, to furnish labor and materials for a construction project owned by Malarkey's, Inc. Commercial completed its obligations under the contract but only received $78,000 of the $177,773. When Commercial filed suit against Camel and Malarkey's for the remaining $99,773, Malarkey's moved to dismiss Commercial's claims against it on the ground that Commercial's only contract was with Camel. The trial court granted Malarkey's motion, despite the fact that the evidence indicated that Malarkey's had never paid Camel for the work. Was the dismissal of Commercial's claim against Malarkey's proper?

7. Early in 1986, Gray Communications contacted various television tower builders concerning the manufacture and erection of a television tower. After several discussions with Kline Iron & Steel, Gray received a signed written proposal from Kline to build and install the tower for $1,485,368. The proposal said that it could be revoked or modified by Kline prior to acceptance by Gray, and it required Kline's approval after acceptance by Gray.

Gray refused to sign the proposal after Kline would not lower its bid to meet a competitor's lower bid, and Kline filed suit for breach of contract. At trial, Gray argued that no contract existed, and that even if a contract existed it was unenforceable because Gray had never signed the writing the UCC requires for all contracts for $500 or more. Kline argued that the contract was not covered by the UCC because it was a services contract. The evidence at trial indicated that the service component of the agreement amounted at most to 26 percent of the total cost. Should the court apply the UCC?

8. Dr. Monteleone, a neurologist, entered into a lease-purchase agreement for a turnkey computer system from Neilson Business Equipment Center, Inc. The system included both hardware and software recommended by Neilson after two Neilson representatives studied Dr. Monteleone's manual billing system. When the computer was delivered in July 1982, serious problems immediately developed. Neilson's attempts to modify the software, which it had acquired elsewhere and renamed the "Neilson Medical Office Management System," were unsuccessful. Dr. Monteleone notified Neilson that he was terminating the lease for cause and later filed suit against Neilson. The trial court awarded him $34,983.42 in damages for breaches of the implied warranties of merchantability and fitness for a particular purpose. Did the trial court err in holding that the case was governed by the UCC?

9. Stephen Gall and his family became ill after drinking contaminated water supplied to their home by the McKeesport Municipal Water Authority. They filed suit against the utility, arguing, among other things, that the utility had breached the UCC implied warranty of merchantability when it sold them contaminated water. The utility moved to dismiss their complaint, arguing that since water was not "goods," the UCC did not apply. Should the Gall's complaint be dismissed?

10. In February 1981, Salamon, a builder, entered into written agreements to buy two lots owned by Terra for $9,000 each. The agreement provided that Salamon would take possession of the lots by April 15, 1981, but would not have to pay the bulk of the purchase price ($8,500 per lot) until delivery of the deeds in August 1981. Salamon intended to build a house on each lot and then sell the houses to third parties, paying off Terra with the proceeds of the house sales. Salamon partially completed the two houses but was unable either to obtain financing to complete them or to find purchasers for them. Terra extended the date of performance under the purchase agreements by several months, but because Salamon was never able to pay for the lots, he retained ownership of them. Salamon filed a quasi-contract suit against Terra to recover the value of the partially completed houses. The trial judge ruled that Terra had been unjustly enriched in the amount of $15,000. Had Terra been unjustly enriched?

11. ▥ *Video Case.* Stevens went to look at a car owned by Marx that he had seen advertised in the private classified ad section of the newspaper. He wanted to buy the car and tentatively agreed on a price with Marx, but he asked if he could wait until his wife could see the car that evening. Marx agreed, promising in writing not to sell the car to anyone else in the interim. When Stevens and his wife returned to Marx's house that evening, however, they found that Marx had sold the car to another buyer for $100 more than the price Marx and Stevens had discussed. Stevens filed a breach of contract suit against Marx, pointing to a section of the UCC that provides that merchants can't revoke signed written offers. Should Stevens win?

The Agreement: Offer

The concept of mutual agreement lies at the heart of traditional contract law. Courts faced with deciding whether two or more persons entered into a contract look first for an *agreement* between the parties. Because the formation of an agreement is normally a two-step process by which one party makes a proposal and the other responds to the proposal, it is customary to analyze the agreement in two parts: *offer* and *acceptance.* This chapter, which concerns itself with the offer, and the next chapter, which covers acceptance, focus on the tools used by courts to determine whether the parties have reached the kind of agreement that becomes the foundation of a contract. ∾

REQUIREMENTS FOR AN OFFER

An **offer** is the critically important first step in the contract formation process. An offer says, in effect, "This is it—if you agree to these terms, we have a contract." The person who makes an offer (**the offeror**) gives the person to whom she makes the offer (**the offeree**) the power to bind her to a contract simply by accepting the offer.

Not every proposal qualifies as an offer. Some proposals are vague, for example, or made in jest, or thrown out merely as a way of opening negotiations. To distinguish an offer, courts look for three requirements. First, they look for some objective indication of a *present intent to contract* on the part of the offeror. Second, they look for specificity, or *definiteness,* in the terms of the alleged offer. Third, they look to see whether the alleged offer has been *communicated to the offeree.*

The preceding chapter discussed the fact that contracts for the sale of goods are governed by

Article 2 of the UCC whereas contracts for services, real estate, and intangibles are generally governed by the common law of contracts. Common law and UCC standards for contract formation have a great deal in common, but they also differ somewhat. This chapter will point out those areas in which an offer for the sale of goods would be treated somewhat differently than an offer for services, real estate, and intangibles.

Intent to Contract

For a proposal to be considered an offer, the offeror must indicate *present intent to contract.* Present intent means the intent to enter the contract upon acceptance. It signifies that the offeror is not joking, haggling, or equivocating. It makes sense that intent on the part of the offeror would be required for an offer—otherwise, an unwilling person might wrongly be bound to a contract. But what is meant by intent? Should courts look at what the offeror actually in his own mind (*subjectively*) intended? Or should intent be judged by the impression that he has given to the rest of the world through words, acts, and circumstances that *objectively* indicate that intent?

The Objective Theory of Contracts Early American courts took a subjective approach to contract formation, asking whether there was truly a "meeting of the minds" between the parties. This subjective standard, however, created uncertainty in the enforcement of contracts because it left every contract vulnerable to disputes about actual intent. The desire to meet the needs of the marketplace by affording predictable and consistent results in contracts cases dictated a shift toward an *objective theory of contracts.* By the middle of the 19th century, the objective approach to contract formation, which judges agreement by looking at the parties' outward manifestations of intent, was firmly established in American law. Judge Learned Hand once described the effect of the objective contract theory as follows:

A contract has, strictly speaking, nothing to do with the personal, or individual, intent of the parties. A contract is an obligation attached by the mere force of law to certain acts of the parties, usually words, which ordinarily accompany and represent a known intent. If however, it were proved by 20 bishops that either party when he used the words intended something else than the usual meaning which the law imposes on them, he would still be held, unless there were mutual mistake or something else of that sort.[1]

Following the objective theory of contracts, then, an offeror's intent will be judged by an objective standard—that is, what his words, acts, and the circumstances signify about his intent. If a reasonable person familiar with all the circumstances would be justified in believing that the offeror intended to contract, a court would find that the intent requirement of an offer was satisfied even if the offeror himself says that he did not intend to contract.

Definiteness of Terms

If Smith says to Ford, "I'd like to buy your house," and Ford responds, "You've got a deal," has a contract been formed? An obvious problem here is lack of specificity. A proposal that fails to state specifically what the offeror is willing to do and what he asks in return for his performance is unlikely to be considered an offer. One reason for the requirement of definiteness is that definiteness and specificity in an offer tend to indicate an intent to contract, whereas indefiniteness and lack of specificity tend to indicate that the parties are still negotiating and have not yet reached agreement. In the conversation between Smith and Ford, Smith's statement that he'd like to buy Ford's house is merely an invitation to offer or an invitation to negotiate. It indicates a willingness to contract in the future if the parties can reach agreement on mutually acceptable terms, but not a present intent to contract. If, however, Smith sends Ford a detailed and specific written document stating all of the material terms and conditions on which he is willing to buy the house and Ford writes back agreeing to Smith's terms, the parties' intent to contract would be objectively indicated and a contract probably would be created.

A second reason definiteness is important is that courts need to know the terms on which the parties agreed in order to determine if a breach of contract has occurred and calculate a remedy if it has. Keep

---

[1]*Hotchkiss v. National City Bank,* 200 F. 287, 293 (S.D.N.Y. 1911).

in mind that the offer often contains all the terms of the parties' contract. This is so because all that an offeree is allowed to do in most cases is to accept or reject the terms of the offer. If an agreement is too indefinite, a court would not have a basis for giving a remedy if one of the parties alleged that the "contract" was breached.

Definiteness Standards under the Common Law

Classical contract law took the position that courts are contract enforcers, not contract makers. The prospect of enforcing an agreement in which the parties had omitted terms or left terms open for later agreement was unthinkable to courts that took a traditional, hands-off approach to contracts. Traditionally, contract law required a relatively high standard of definiteness for offers, requiring that all the essential terms of a proposed contract be stated in the offer. The traditional insistence on definiteness can serve useful ends. It can prevent a person from being held to an agreement when none was reached or from being bound by a contract term to which he never assented. Often, however, it can operate to frustrate the expectations of parties who intend to contract but, for whatever reason, fail to procure an agreement that specifies all the terms of the contract. The definiteness standard, like much of contract law, is constantly evolving. The trend of modern contract law is to tolerate a lower degree of specificity in agreements than classical contract law would have tolerated. Although it is still unlikely that an agreement that leaves open important aspects of a transaction will be enforced, the following case, *Mears v. Nationwide Mutual Insurance Co.,* provides an example of a contemporary court's approach to definiteness.

MEARS v. NATIONWIDE INSURANCE COMPANY   91 F.3d 1118 (8th Cir. 1996)

N *ationwide traditionally holds a regional convention for its employees every three years. The conventions are intended to boost employee morale by recognizing workplace achievements. Nationwide planned to have a regional convention for the South Central Regional Offices (SOCRO) in July 1994. Nationwide created planning committees, among them a committee responsible for selecting a convention theme. It decided to have a theme contest and drafted the following announcement:*

Special Announcement

The 1994 SOCRO Claims Convention plans are being developed and we need your creativity. We don't know where. We don't know when. And we don't have a theme. That's where you come in. A contest is hereby announced to create a theme. Here's what you could win:

His and Hers Mercedes

An all expense paid trip for two around the world

Additional prize to be announced

(All prizes subject to availability)

Only two rules apply:

1. The slogan is limited to no more than eight words.
2. All entries must be submitted to Linda McCauley, Regional Office by August 1, 1993.

Put your thinking caps on, get those creative juices flowing, tap the far reaches of your mind. Prior themes are not eligible. As you will remember, our 1991 theme was "Our Moving Force is You." Don't delay. Like Ed McMahon says, you can't win if you don't enter.

David Mears, who worked out of his home as a claims adjuster for Nationwide, was one of about 185 SOCRO employees who received the announcement. Mears decided to enter the contest and submitted several themes, including, "At the Top and Still Climbing." Several months after submitting his theme, Mears left Nationwide.

In October 1993, Peterson, a member of the convention theme committee, notified Mears that his theme had been chosen for the 1994 convention. Mears claims that Peterson also told him that he had won two Mercedes-Benz automobiles, a fact that Peterson disputes. In January 1994, Mears spoke with Peterson again to ask about the status of the cars. Peterson warned him that he might not receive the cars for three reasons:

first, Nationwide might change the convention theme; second, Mears was no longer employed by Nationwide, and third, the contest was a joke.

In the end, Nationwide used the theme submitted by Mears for the July convention. The theme appeared on name tags and convention booklets, and provided an overarching message for the convention events. After the convention, Mears spoke with a member of the convention theme committee, who informed Mears that Nationwide never intended to award the two automobiles and offered Mears a restaurant gift certificate instead.

Mears sued Nationwide for breach of contract. At trial, Nationwide admitted that the contest was legitimate, but argued that Mears was not entitled to the two Mercedes-Benz automobiles as a prize. The jury found in favor of Mears and awarded him $60,000, but the court granted judgment for Nationwide as a matter of law on the ground that no contract was formed because the terms were not definite enough to be enforced. Mears appealed. ∞

Magill, Circuit Judge   In order to be binding, a contract must be reasonably certain as to its terms and requirements. A contract is sufficiently certain if it provides a basis for determining the existence of a breach and for giving an appropriate remedy. The law does not favor the destruction of contracts because of uncertainty.

Nationwide's contest notice offered several prizes and gave no indication of which prize the winning theme submitter would receive. However, a contract that is ambiguous can be made certain by the subsequent actions or declarations of the parties.

At trial, both Peterson and Mears testified that she told him that he had won two Mercedes while at a dinner attended by many Nationwide employees. Peterson claimed that she spoke with a facetious tone and, in reality, had no intention of awarding the automobiles. Mears, on the other hand, took Peterson at her word and believed that of the prizes listed on the contest announcement, he had won the Mercedes. It appears that others around Mears also believed that he had won the automobiles. Faced with this factual dispute, the jury had to decide which version of events was more credible. They believed Mears and we perceive no reasoning for undoing this jury determination.

Because the contest contract could be reasonably construed to entitle Mears to two Mercedes-Benz automobiles, the only remaining uncertainty lies in the type of Mercedes to be awarded. There is a wide range of values for Mercedes, depending largely on the model and year. This uncertainty, however, is not fatal. First, contract terms are interpreted with strong determination for what is reasonable. Under reasonable interpretation of the contest contract, the jury could expect the automobiles to be new. Second, when a minor ambiguity exists in a contract, Arkansas law allows the complaining party to insist on the reasonable interpretation that is least favorable to him. Indeed, in *Dolly Parker Motors, Inc. v. Stinson,* the Arkansas Supreme Court held that a contract that specified only the make of the automobile had enough certainty to be enforceable. These two factors, taken together, are sufficient to support the jury's conclusion that Nationwide owed Mears two of Mercedes-Benz's least expensive new automobiles as his contest prize. At trial, Nationwide did not offer any evidence of the price of such Mercedes-Benz. Mears, on the other hand, testified that the least expensive new Mercedes-Benz cost $31,450. He based this figure on information from Mercedes-Benz dealerships in Little Rock and in Fayetteville. In the absence of contrary testimony from Nationwide, the jury reasonably concluded that Mears suffered $60,000 in damages.

For the reasons stated, we reverse the district court's order of judgment as a matter of law and reinstate the jury's verdict for $60,000.

Reversed in favor of Mears.

Definiteness Standards under the UCC   The UCC, with its increased emphasis on furthering people's justifiable expectations and its encouragement of a hands-on approach by the courts, often creates contractual liability in situations where no contract would have resulted at common law. Perhaps no part of the Code better illustrates this basic difference between the UCC and classical common law than does the basic Code section on contract formation [2–204]. This section says that sales contracts under Article 2 can be created "in any manner sufficient to show agreement, including conduct which recognizes the existence of a contract" [2–204(1)]. So, if the parties are acting as though they have a contract by delivering or accepting goods or payment, for example, this may be enough to create a binding contract, even if it is impossible to point to a particular moment in time when the contract was created [2–204(2)].

An important difference between Code and classical common law standards for definiteness is that under the Code, the fact that the parties left open one or more terms of their agreement does not necessarily mean that their agreement is too indefinite to enforce. A sales contract is created if the court finds that the parties intended to make a contract and that their agreement is complete enough to allow the court to reach a fair settlement of their dispute ("a reasonably certain basis for giving an appropriate remedy" [2–204(3)]). If a term is left open in a contract that meets these two standards, that open term or "gap" can be "filled" by inserting a presumption found in the Code's "gap-filling" rules. The gap-filling rules allow courts to fill contract terms left open on matters of price [2–305], quantity [2–306], delivery [2–307, 2–308, and 2–309(1)], and time for payment [2–310] when such terms have been left open by the parties.[2] Of course, if a term was left out because the parties were *unable* to reach agreement about it, this would indicate that the intent to contract was absent and no contract would result, even under the Code's more liberal rules. *Intention is still at the heart of these modern contract rules;* the difference is that courts applying Code principles seek to further the parties' *underlying* intent to contract even though the parties have failed to express their intention about specific aspects of their agreement.

Communication to Offeree

When an offeror communicates the terms of an offer to an offeree, he objectively indicates an intent to be bound by those terms. The fact that an offer has *not* been communicated, on the other hand, may be evidence that the offeror has not yet decided to enter into a binding agreement. For example, assume that

Stevens and Meyer have been negotiating over the sale of Meyer's restaurant. Stevens confides in his friend, Reilly, that he plans to offer Meyer $150,000 for the restaurant. Reilly goes to Meyer and tells Meyer that Stevens has decided to offer him $150,000 for the restaurant and has drawn up a written offer to that effect. After learning the details of the offer from Reilly, Meyer telephones Stevens and says, "I accept your offer." Is Stevens now contractually obligated to buy the restaurant? No. Since *Stevens* did not communicate the proposal to Meyer, there was no offer for Meyer to accept.

SPECIAL OFFER PROBLEM AREAS

Advertisements

Generally speaking, advertisements for the sale of goods at specified prices are *not* considered to be offers. Rather, they are treated as being invitations to offer or negotiate. The same rule is generally applied to signs, handbills, catalogs, price lists, and price quotations. This rule is based on the presumed intent of the sellers involved. It is not reasonable to conclude that a seller who has a limited number of items to sell intends to give every person who sees her ad, sign, or catalog the power to bind her to contract. Thus, if Customer sees Retailer's advertisement of Whizbang XL laptop computers for $2,000 and goes to Retailer's store indicating his intent to buy the computer, Customer is making an offer, which Retailer is free to accept or reject. This is so because *Customer* is manifesting a present intent to contract on the definite terms of the ad.

In some cases, however, particular ads have been held to amount to offers. Such ads are usually highly specific about the nature and number of items offered for sale and what is requested in return. This specificity precludes the possibility that the offeror could become contractually bound to an infinite number of offerees. In addition, many of the ads treated as offers have required some special performance by would-be buyers or have in some other way clearly indicated that immediate action by the buyer creates a binding agreement. The potential for unfairness to those who attempt to accept such ads and their fundamental difference from ordinary ads justify treating them as offers. *Jackson v. Investment Corporation of Palm Beach* presents an example of an advertisement that was held to constitute an offer.

---

[2]Chapter 19 discusses these Code provisions in detail.

J *ohn Jackson read an ad in the* Miami Herald *that stated that the Pic-6 Jackpot for the last evening of the dog track racing season would be $825,000. Jackson went to the track on that date, picked the winner in the six designated races, and won the jackpot. However, Investment Corporation of Palm Beach, the owner of the dog track, contended that it should not have to pay more than $25,000 because it had intended the amount of the jackpot to be $25,000, not $825,000. The mix-up occurred when Investment submitted to the newspaper a prior ad with the following words written on the face of it: "Guaranteed Jackpot $25,000 must go tonight," and the newspaper employee who prepared the final draft of the ad mistook the dollar sign with only one slash-mark to be the number 8. Investment paid Jackson $25,000 on the night of the races but Jackson later brought suit to claim the balance. At trial, the judge instructed the jury that it should find for Investment unless the evidence supported the claim that Investment intended by its newspaper advertisement to make an offer to pay a guaranteed jackpot of $825,000. The jury returned a verdict in favor of Investment and the trial judge entered judgment on the verdict. Jackson appealed, claiming that this instruction to the jury was erroneous.* ∽

Downey, J   There was no evidence adduced that Investment intended the jackpot to be $825,000. Jackson concedes that Investment never intended the jackpot to be the larger amount. The point is that Investment's subjective intent was not material in determining what the contract was between the parties. As the Florida Supreme Court said in *Gendzier v. Bielecki,* quoting from Justice Oliver Wendell Holmes:

The making of a contract depends not on the agreement of two minds in one intention, but on the agreement of two sets of external signs—not on the parties having meant the same thing but on their having said the same thing.

Professor Williston, in his work on Contracts, describes the test as:

[T]he test of the true interpretation of an offer or acceptance is not what the party making it thought it meant or intended it to mean, but what a reasonable person in the position of the parties would have thought it meant. 1 *Williston on Contracts* sec. 94, 339-40.

It appears to us that the law, applicable to offers of a reward, is also applicable to the type of advertisement involved in this case. The offer is a mere proposal or conditional promise which, if accepted before it is revoked, creates a binding contract. We have given due consideration to Investment's argument regarding the advertisement as an "invitation to bargain," but find it inapposite here. The "invitation to bargain" rule appears to be applied in advertising wherein:

Neither the advertiser nor the reader of his notice understands that the latter is empowered to close the deal without further expression by the former. Such advertisements are understood to be mere requests to consider and examine and negotiate; and no one can reasonably regard them otherwise unless the circumstances are exceptional and the words used are very plain and clear. 1 *Corbin on Contracts* sec. 25 (1963).

Here there are no further negotiations indicated. If a member of the public buys a winning ticket on six races, he has accepted the offer and the parties have a contract. We thus hold that the trial court erred in instructing the jury as it did and we reverse the judgment appealed from and remand the cause for a new trial.

Judgment reversed in favor of Jackson.

Rewards

Advertisements offering rewards for lost property, for information, or for the capture of criminals are generally treated as offers for unilateral contracts. To accept the offer and be entitled to the stated reward, offerees must perform the requested act—return the lost property, supply the requested infor- mation, or capture the wanted criminal. Some courts have held that only offerees who started perfor- mance with knowledge of the offer are entitled to the reward. Other courts, however, have indicated the only requirement is that the offeree know of the reward before completing performance. In reality, the result in most such cases probably reflects the court's perception of what is fairer given the facts involved in the particular case at hand.

Auctions

Sellers at auctions are generally treated as making an invitation to offer. Those who bid on offered goods are, therefore, treated as making offers that the owner of the goods may accept or reject. Acceptance occurs only when the auctioneer strikes the goods off to the highest bidder; the auctioneer may withdraw the goods at any time before acceptance. However, when an auction is advertised as being "without reserve," the seller is treated as having made an offer to sell the goods to the highest bidder and the goods cannot be withdrawn after a call for bids has been made unless no bids are made within a reasonable time.[3]

Bids

The bidding process is a fertile source of contract disputes. Advertisements for bids are generally treated as invitations to offer. Those who submit bids are treated as offerors. According to general contract principles, bidders can withdraw their bids at any time prior to acceptance by the offeree inviting the bids and the offeree is free to accept or reject any bid. The previously announced terms of the bidding may alter these rules, however. For example, if the advertisement for bids unconditionally states that the contract will be awarded to the lowest responsible bidder, this will be treated as an offer that is accepted by the lowest bidder. Only proof by the offeror that the lowest bidder is not responsible can prevent the formation of a contract. Also, under some circumstances discussed later in this chapter, promissory estoppel may operate to prevent bidders from withdrawing their bids.

Bids for governmental contracts are generally covered by specific statutes rather than by general

contract principles. Such statutes ordinarily establish the rules governing the bidding process, often require that the contract be awarded to the lowest bidder, and frequently establish special rules or penalties governing the withdrawal of bids.

WHICH TERMS ARE INCLUDED IN THE OFFER?

After making a determination that an offer existed, a court must decide which terms were included in the offer so that it can determine the terms of the parties' contract. Put another way, which terms of the offer are binding on the offeree who accepts it? Should offerees, for example, be bound by fine-print clauses or by clauses on the back of the contract? Originally, the courts tended to hold that offerees were bound by all the terms of the offer on the theory that every person had a duty to protect himself by reading agreements carefully before signing them.

In today's world of lengthy, complex form contracts, however, people often sign agreements that they have not fully read or do not fully understand. Modern courts tend to recognize this fact by saying that offerees are bound only by terms of which they had actual or reasonable notice. If the offeree actually read the term in question, or if a reasonable person should have been aware of it, it will probably become part of the parties' contract. A fine-print provision on the back of a theater ticket would probably not be binding on a theater patron, however, because a reasonable person would not normally expect such a ticket to contain contractual terms. By contrast, the terms printed on a multipage airline ticket might well be considered binding on the purchaser if such documents would be expected to contain terms of the contract. The following case, *ProCD, Inc. v. Zeidenberg,* concerns the enforceability of contract terms contained inside a product package and not read until after the purchase. This is a controversial area, but the *ProCD* case provides rationales for considering such terms to be included in the seller's offer.

---

[3]These rules and others concerned with the sale of goods by auction are contained in section 2–328 of the UCC.

ProCD INC. v. ZEIDENBERG   86 F.3d 1447 (7th Cir. 1996)

 roCD compiled information from more than 3,000 telephone directories into a computer database and sold a version of this database called SelectPhone on CD-ROM discs. The database in SelectPhone cost more than $10 million to compile and is expensive to keep current. For commercial users such as retailers and manufacturers, SelectPhone is a much cheaper alternative *to the expensive mailing lists that such users otherwise would purchase from various information intermediaries. For noncommercial users, SelectPhone has less value, functioning as a substitute for calling long-distance information or other directory. ProCD decided to sell its database to the general public for personal use at a low price (approximately $150 for the set of five discs), while selling to commercial users at a higher price. If ProCD had to recover all of its cost and make a profit by charging a single price—that is, if it could not charge more to commercial users than to the general public—it would have to raise the price substantially above $150. To help ensure that no commercial users purchased the database at the lower, noncommerical price, ProCD marketed the consumer product with a kind of contract that is popularly known as a "shrinkwrap license." A shrinkwrap license limits the ways that the person who acquires computer software can use the software. It gets its name from the fact that retail software packages are covered in plastic or cellophane "shrinkwrap." Every box containing ProCD's consumer product declares that the software comes with restrictions stated in an enclosed license. This license, which is encoded on the CD-ROM disks as well as printed in the manual, and which appears on a user's screen every time the software runs, limits use of the application program and listings to noncommercial purposes.*

Matthew Zeidenberg bought a consumer package of SelectPhone in 1994 from a retail outlet in Madison, Wisconsin, but decided to ignore the license. He formed Silken Mountain Web Services, Inc., to resell the information in the SelectPhone database. The corporation made the database available on the Internet to anyone willing to pay its price—which is less than ProCD charges its commercial customers. Zeidenberg purchased two additional SelectPhone packages, each with an updated version of the database, and made the latest information available over the World Wide Web, for a price, through his corporation. ProCD filed suit against Zeidenberg seeking an injunction against dissemination of the database that exceeds the rights specified in the licenses. The district court held the licenses ineffectual because their terms do not appear on the outside of the package. ProCD appealed. ∞

Easterbrook, Circuit Judge   We treat the licenses as ordinary contracts accompanying the sale of products. Zeidenberg [argues] that placing the package of software on the shelf is an "offer," which the customer "accepts" by paying the asking price and leaving the store with the goods. In Wisconsin, as elsewhere, a contract includes only the terms on which the parties have agreed. One cannot agree to hidden terms. So far, so good—but one of the terms to which Zeidenberg agreed by purchasing the software is that the transaction was subject to a license.

Zeidenberg's position therefore must be that the printed terms on the outside of a box are the parties' contract—except for printed terms that refer to or incorporate other terms. But why would Wisconsin fetter the parties' choice in this way? Vendors can put the entire terms of a contract on the outside of a box only by using microscopic type, removing other information that buyers might find more useful (such as what the software does, and on which computers it works), or both. The "Read Me" included with most software, describing system requirements and potential incompatibilities, may be equivalent to 10 pages of type; warranties and license restrictions take up more space. Notice on the outside, terms on the inside, and a right to return the software for a refund if the terms are unacceptable (a right that the license expressly extends), may

be a means of doing business valuable to buyers and sellers alike.

Transactions in which the exchange of money precedes the communication of terms are common. Consider the purchase of an airline ticket. The traveler calls the carrier or an agent, is quoted a price, reserves a seat, pays, and gets a ticket, in that order. The ticket contains elaborate terms, which the traveler can reject by canceling the reservation. To use the ticket is to accept the terms, even terms that in retrospect are disadvantageous. Consumer goods work the same way. Someone who wants to buy a radio set visits a store, pays, and walks out with a box. Inside the box is a leaflet containing some terms, the most important of which usually is the warranty, read for the first time in the comfort of home. By Zeidenberg's lights, the warranty in the box is irrelevant.

Next consider the software industry itself. Only a minority of sales take place over the counter, where there are boxes to peruse. A customer may place an order by phone in response to a line item in a catalog or a review in a magazine. Much software is ordered over the Internet by purchasers who have never seen the box. Increasingly, software arrives by wire. There is no box; there is only a collection of information that includes data, an application program, instructions, many limitations, and the terms of sale. The user purchases a serial number which activates the software's features. On Zeidenberg's arguments, these unboxed sales are unfettered by terms.

A vendor, as master of the offer, may invite acceptance by conduct and may propose limitations on the kind of conduct that constitutes acceptance. A buyer may accept by performing the acts the vendor proposes to treat as acceptance. And that is what happened. ProCD proposed a contract that a buyer would accept by *using* the software after having an opportunity to read the license at leisure. This Zeidenberg did. He had no choice, because the software splashed the license on the screen and would not let him proceed without indicating acceptance. Ours is not a case in which a consumer opens a package to find an insert saying "you owe us an extra $10,000" and the seller files suit to collect. Any buyer finding such a demand can prevent formation of the contract by returning the package, as can any consumer who concludes that the terms of the license make the software worth less than the purchase price. Zeidenberg inspected the package, tried out the software, learned of the license, and did not reject the goods.

Zeidenberg has not located any case holding that the ordinary terms found in shrinkwrap licenses require any special prominence. In the end, the terms of the license are conceptually identical to the contents of the package. Just as no court would dream of saying that SelectPhone must contain 3,100 phone books rather than 3,000, or must sell for $100 rather than $150—although any of these changes would be welcomed by the customer—so, we believe, Wisconsin would not let the buyer pick and choose among terms. Terms of use are no less a part of "the product" than are the size of the database and the speed with which the software compiles listings. Competition among vendors, not judicial revision of a package's contents, is how consumers are protected in a market economy.

Reversed and remanded in favor of ProCD.

TERMINATION OF OFFERS

After a court has determined the existence and content of an offer, it must determine the duration of the offer. Was the offer still in existence when the offeree attempted to accept it? If not, no contract was created and the offeree is treated as having made an offer that the original offeror is free to accept or reject. This is so because, by attempting to accept an offer that has terminated, the offeree has indicated a present intent to contract on the terms of the original offer though he lacks the power to bind the offeror to a contract due to the original offer's termination.

Terms of the Offer

The offeror is often said to be "the master of the offer." This means that offerors have the power to determine the terms and conditions under which they are bound to a contract. As the following *Newman* case indicates, an offeror may include terms in the offer that limit its effective life. These may be specific terms, such as "you must accept by December 5, 1998," or "this offer is good for five days," or more general terms such as "for immediate acceptance," "prompt wire acceptance," or "by return mail." General time limitation language in an offer can raise difficult problems of interpretation for courts trying to decide whether an offeree accepted before the offer terminated. Even more specific language, such as "this offer is good for five days," can cause problems if the offer does not specify whether the five-day period begins when the offer is sent or when the offeree receives it. Not all courts agree on such questions, so wise offerors should be as specific as possible in stating when their offers terminate.

NEWMAN v. SCHIFF   778 F.2d. 460 (3d Cir. 1985)

 rwin Schiff, a self-styled tax rebel who had made a career out of his tax protest activities, appeared live on the February 7, 1983, CBS News "Nightwatch" program. During the course of the program, which had a viewer participation format, Schiff repeated his longstanding position that "there is nothing in the Internal Revenue Code which says anyone is legally required to pay the tax." Later *in the program, Schiff stated: "If anybody calls this show and cites any section of this Code that says an individual is required to file a tax return, I will pay them $100,000."*

Attorney John Newman failed to see Schiff live on "Nightwatch," but saw a two-minute taped segment of the original "Nightwatch" interview several hours later on the "CBS Morning News." Certain that Schiff's statements were incorrect, Newman telephoned and wrote "CBS Morning News," attempting to accept Schiff's offer by citing Internal Revenue Code provisions requiring individuals to pay federal income tax. CBS forwarded Newman's letter to Schiff, who refused to pay on the ground that Newman had not properly accepted his offer. Newman sued Schiff for breach of contract. The trial court ruled in Schiff's favor, and Newman appealed. ∽

Bright, Senior Circuit Judge   It is a basic legal principle that mutual assent is necessary for the formation of a contract. Courts determine whether the parties expressed their assent to a contract by analyzing their agreement process in terms of offer and acceptance. An offer is the "manifestation of willingness to enter into a bargain, so made as to justify another person in understanding that his assent to that bargain is invited and will conclude it." *Restatement (Second) of Contracts* § 24 (1981). Schiff's statement on "Nightwatch" that he would pay $100,000 to anyone who called the show and cited any section of the Internal Revenue Code "that says an individual is required to file a tax return" constituted a valid offer for a reward. If anyone had called the show and cited the code sections that Newman produced, a contract would have been formed and Schiff would have been obligated to pay the $100,000 reward.

Newman, however, never saw the live CBS "Nightwatch" program on which Schiff appeared and this lawsuit is not predicated on Schiff's "Nightwatch" offer. Newman saw the "CBS Morning News" rebroadcast of Schiff's "Nightwatch" appearance. This rebroadcast served not to re-new or extend Schiff's offer, but rather only to inform viewers that Schiff had made an offer on "Nightwatch." An offeror is the master of his offer and it is clear that Schiff by his words, "If anybody calls this show," limited his offer in time to remain open only until the conclusion of the live "Nightwatch" broadcast. A reasonable person listening to the news rebroadcast could not conclude that the above language constituted a new offer rather than what it actually was, a news report of the offer previously made, which had already expired.

Although Newman has not "won" his lawsuit in the traditional sense of recovering a reward that he sought, he has accomplished an important goal in the public interest of unmasking the "blatant nonsense" dispensed by Schiff. For that he deserves great commendation from the public. Perhaps now CBS and other communication media who have given Schiff's mistaken views widespread publicity will give John Newman equal time in the public interest.

Judgment for Schiff affirmed.

Lapse of Time

Offers that fail to provide a specific time for acceptance are valid for a reasonable time. What constitutes a reasonable time depends on the circumstances surrounding the offer. How long would a reasonable person in the offeree's position believe she had to accept the offer? Offers involving things subject to rapid fluctuations in value, such as stocks, bonds, or commodities futures, have a very brief duration. The same is true for offers involving goods that may spoil, such as produce.

The context of the parties' negotiations is another factor relevant to determining the duration of an offer. For example, most courts hold that when parties bargain face-to-face or over the telephone, the normal time for acceptance does not extend past the conclusion of their conversation unless the offeror indicates a contrary intention. Where negotiations are carried out by mail or telegram, the time for acceptance would ordinarily include at least the normal time for communicating the offer and a prompt response by the offeree. Finally, in cases where the parties have dealt with each other on a regular basis in the past, the timing of their prior transactions would be highly relevant in measuring the reasonable time for acceptance.

Revocation

General Rule: Offers are Revocable   As the masters of their offers, offerors can give offerees the power to bind them to contracts by making offers. They can also terminate that power by revoking their offers. The general common law rule on revocations is that offerors may revoke their offers at any time prior to acceptance, *even if they have promised to hold the offer open for a stated period of time*. In the following situations (summarized in Figure 1), however, offerors are *not* free to revoke their offers:

1. *Options.* An **option** is a separate contract in which an offeror agrees not to revoke her offer for a stated time in exchange for some valuable consideration. You can think of it as a contract in which an offeror sells her right to revoke her offer. For example, Jones, in exchange for $5,000, agrees to give Dewey Development Co. a six-month option to purchase her farm for $550,000. In this situation, Jones would not be free to revoke the offer during the six-month period of the option. The offeree, Dewey Development, has no obligation to accept Jones's offer. In effect, it has merely purchased the right to consider the offer for the stated time without fear that Jones will revoke it. The traditional common law rule on options requires the actual payment of the agreed-on consideration before an option contract becomes enforceable. Therefore, in the above example, if Dewey Development never, in fact, paid the $5,000, no option was created and

Jones could revoke her offer at any time prior to its acceptance by Dewey Development.

2. *Offers for unilateral contracts.* Suppose Franklin makes the following offer for a unilateral contract to Waters: "If you mow my lawn, I'll pay you $25." Given that an offeree in a unilateral contract must fully perform the requested act to accept the offer, can Franklin wait until Waters is almost finished mowing the lawn and then say "I revoke!"? Obviously, the application of the general rule that offerors can revoke at any time before acceptance creates the potential for injustice when applied to offers for unilateral contracts, because it would allow an offeror to revoke after the offeree has begun performance but before he has had a chance to complete it. To prevent injustice to offerees who rely on such offers by beginning performance, two basic approaches are available to modern courts.

Some courts have held that once the offeree has begun to perform, the offeror's power to revoke is suspended for the amount of time reasonably necessary for the offeree to complete performance. Another approach to the unilateral contract dilemma is to hold that a bilateral contract is created once the offeree begins performance.

3. *Promissory estoppel.* In some cases in which the offeree *relies* on the offer being kept open, the doctrine of promissory estoppel can operate to prevent offerors from revoking their offers prior to acceptance. Section 87(2) of the *Restatement (Second)* says:

> An offer which the offeror should reasonably expect to induce action or forbearance of a substantial character on the part of the offeree before acceptance and which does induce such action or forbearance is binding as an option contract to the extent necessary to avoid injustice.

Many of the cases in which promissory estoppel has been used successfully to prevent revocation of offers involve the bidding process. For example, Gigantic General Contractor seeks to get the general contract to build a new high school gymnasium for Shadyside School District. It receives bids from subcontractors. Liny Electric submits the lowest bid to perform the electrical work on the job and Gigantic uses Liny's bid in preparing its bid for the general contract. Here, Liny has made an offer to Gigantic, but Gigantic cannot accept that offer until it knows whether it has gotten the general contract. The school district awards the general contract to Gigantic. Before Gigantic can accept Liny's offer,

---

FIGURE **1**

When Offerors Cannot Revoke

Options	Offeror has promised to hold offer open and has received consideration for that promise
Firm Offers	Merchant offeror makes written offer to buy or sell goods, giving assurances that the offer will be held open
Unilateral Contract Offers	Offeree has started to perform requested act before offeror revokes
Promissory Estoppel	Offeree foreseeably and reasonably relies on offer being held open, and will suffer injustice if it is revoked

however, Liny attempts to revoke it. In this situation, a court could use the doctrine of promissory estoppel to hold that the offer could not be revoked.

4. *Firm offers for the sale of goods [Note: This applies to offers for the sale of goods ONLY!].* The Code makes a major change in the common law rules governing the revocability of offers by recognizing the concept of a **firm offer** [2–205]. Like an option, a firm offer is irrevocable for a period of time. In contrast to an option, however, a firm offer does not require consideration to be given in exchange for the offeror's promise to keep the offer open. Not all offers to buy or sell goods qualify as firm offers, however. To be a firm offer, an offer must:

• Be made by an offeror who is a *merchant.*
• Be contained in a signed writing.[4]
• Give assurances that the offer will be kept open.

An offer to buy or sell goods that fails to satisfy these three requirements is governed by the general common law rule and is revocable at any time prior to acceptance. If an offer *does* meet the requirements of a firm offer, however, it will be irrevocable for the time stated in the offer. If no specific time is stated in the offer, it will be irrevocable for a *reasonable* time. Regardless of the terms of the firm offer, the outer limit on a firm offer's irrevocability is *three months.* For example, if Worldwide Widget makes an offer in a signed writing in which it proposes to sell a quantity of its XL Turbo Widget to Howell Hardware and gives assurances that the offer will be kept open for a year, the offer is a firm offer, but it can be revoked after three months if Howell Hardware has not yet accepted it.

In some cases, however, offerees are the true originators of an assurance term in an offer. When offerees have effective control of the terms of the offer by providing their customers with preprinted purchase order forms or order blanks, they may be tempted to take advantage of their merchant customers by placing an assurance term in their order forms. This would allow offerees to await market developments before deciding whether to fill the order, while their merchant customers, who may have signed the order without reading all of its

terms, would be powerless to revoke. To prevent such unfairness, the Code requires that assurance terms on forms provided by offerees be separately signed by the offeror to effect a firm offer. For example, if Fashionable Mfg. Co. supplies its customer, Retailer, with preprinted order forms that contain a fine-print provision giving assurances that the customer's offer to purchase goods will be held open for one month, the purported promise to keep the offer open would not be enforceable unless Retailer separately signed that provision.

Effectiveness of Revocations   The question of *when* a revocation is effective to terminate an offer is often a critical issue in the contract formation process. For example, Davis offers to landscape Winter's property for $1,500. Two days after making the offer, Davis changes his mind and mails Winter a letter revoking the offer. The next day, Winter, who has not received Davis's letter, telephones Davis and attempts to accept. Contract? Yes. The general rule on this point is that revocations are effective only when they are actually *received* by the offeree.

The only major exception to the general rule on effectiveness of revocations concerns offers to the general public. Because it would be impossible in most cases to reach every offeree with a revocation, it is generally held that a revocation made in the same manner as the offer is effective when published, without proof of communication to the offeree.

Rejection

An offeree may expressly reject an offer by indicating that he is unwilling to accept it. He may also impliedly reject it by making a counteroffer, an offer to contract on terms materially different from the terms of the offer. As a general rule, either form of rejection by the offeree terminates his power to accept the offer. This is so because an offeror who receives a rejection may rely on the offeree's expressed desire not to accept the offer by making another offer to a different offeree.

One exception to the general rule that rejections terminate offers concerns offers that are the subject of an option contract. Some courts hold that a rejection does not terminate an option contract and that the offeree who rejects still has the power to accept the offer later, so long as the acceptance is effective within the option period.

---

[4]Under the UCC [1–201(39)], the word *signed* includes any symbol that a person makes or adopts with the intent to authenticate a writing.

What Terminates Offers?

- Their own terms
- Lapse of time
- Revocation
- Rejection
- Death or insanity of offeror or offeree
- Destruction of subject matter
- Intervening illegality

Effectiveness of Rejections   As a general rule, rejections, like revocations, are effective only when actually received by the offeror. Therefore, an offeree who has mailed a rejection could still change her mind and accept if she communicates the acceptance before the offeror receives the rejection.[5]

Death or Insanity of Either Party

The death or insanity of either party to an offer automatically terminates the offer without notice. A meeting of the minds is obviously impossible when one of the parties has died or become insane.[6]

Destruction of Subject Matter

If, prior to an acceptance of an offer, the subject matter of a proposed contract is destroyed without the knowledge or fault of either party, the offer is terminated.[7] So, if Marks offers to sell Wiggins his lakeside cottage and the cottage is destroyed by fire before Wiggins accepts, the offer was terminated on the destruction of the cottage. Subsequent acceptance by Wiggins would not create a contract.

Intervening Illegality

An offer is terminated if the performance of the contract it proposes becomes illegal before the offer is accepted. So, if a computer manufacturer offered to sell sophisticated computer equipment to another country, but two days later, before the offer was accepted, Congress placed an embargo on all sales to this country, the offer was terminated by the embargo.[8]

1.   Classical contract theory has traditionally found strong ethical justification in the notion of voluntary consent. To parties who want out of their contracts and ask why they should be held to them, the law has often responded: "Because you agreed to them." How does this ethical justification square with the objective theory of contract, which can in some cases result in holding people to agreements that are inconsistent with their subjective intent? Is there some other ethical justification for holding people to the objective manifestations of consent, regardless of their actual or subjective intent?

2.   Compare and contrast the underlying ethical justifications of the classical and modern contract positions on what terms are included in offers. Is it ethical for businesses who deal with consumers or other unsophisticated parties to "hide" contract terms under misleading headings, in small print, or on the reverse side of contracts? What about putting form contracts in complex, technical language that consumers are unlikely to understand?

3.   As you learned earlier in this chapter, there are now a number of exceptions to the traditional rule that offerors can revoke at any time prior to acceptance, even if they have promised not to. Is there an ethical basis for each of these exceptions? If so, what is it?

PROBLEM CASES

1.   In 1989, the New Jersey Highway Authority increased its tolls from 25 cents to 35 cents. In connection with this increase, it authorized the sale

---

[5]Chapter 11 discusses this subject in detail.

[6]Death or insanity of a party that occurs after a contract has been formed can excuse performance in contracts that call for personal services to be performed by the person who has died or become insane. This is discussed in Chapter 18.

[7]In some circumstances, destruction of subject matter can also serve as a legal excuse for a party's failure to perform his obligations under an existing contract. Chapter 18 discusses this subject.

[8]In some circumstances, intervening illegality can also serve as a legal excuse for a party's failure to perform his obligations under an existing contract. Chapter 18 discusses this subject.

of tokens for a discounted price—$10 for a roll of 40 tokens, a savings of $4 per roll for customers—for a limited time. The authority advertised this sale through several media, including signs on the parkway itself. Shortly after the discount sale began, complaints were made that the tokens were not available. The authority explained that the shortage probably resulted from an unanticipated demand for the tokens resulting from purchasers hoarding them. The authority then began limiting the sales to certain days of the week, but even with that limitation, the demand could not be satisfied. Schlictman, a motorist who used the toll roads, sued the authority for breach of contract after trying unsuccessfully, on five different occasions within the authorized sale dates and times, to buy the discounted tokens. What should the result be?

2. In 1985, First Colonial Savings Bank ran a newspaper advertisement that stated in part:

**You Win 2 ways
with First Colonial's
Savings Certificates**

1 Great Gifts   2 & High Interest

Saving at First Colonial is a very rewarding experience. In appreciation for your business we have Great Gifts for you to enjoy *now*—and when your investment matures you get your entire principal back *plus great interest.*

Plan B: 3½ Year Investment

Deposit $14,000 and receive two gifts: a Remington Shotgun and GE CB Radio, OR an RCA 20″ Color-Trac TV, and $20,136.12 upon maturity in 3½ years.

Relying on this ad, the Changs deposited $14,000 with First Colonial on January 3, 1986. They received a color television that day from First Colonial and expected to receive the sum of $20,136.12 upon maturity of the deposit in three and one-half years. First Colonial also gave the Changs a certificate of deposit when they made their deposit. When the Changs returned to liquidate the certificate of deposit upon its maturity, they were informed that the advertisement contained a typographical error and that they should have deposited $15,000 in order to receive the sum of $20,136.12 upon maturity of the certificate of deposit. First Colonial did not inform the Changs, nor were the Changs aware, that the advertisement contained an error until after the certificate of deposit had matured. First Colonial did display in its lobby pamphlets that contained the correct figures when the Changs made their deposit. The Changs sued First Colonial to recover the $1,312.19 difference between the $20,136.12 amount in the advertisement and the $18,823.93 that First Colonial actually paid to the Changs. Will they prevail?

3. On August 4, 1980, Normile made a written offer to buy property owned by Miller. Miller signed and returned the offer after making several substantial changes in its terms and initialing those changes. The executed form was delivered to Normile by Byer, the real estate agent who had shown him the property. In the early afternoon of August 5, 1980, Miller accepted an offer by Segal to buy her property on terms similar to those in the modified offer she had returned to Normile. At 2:00 P.M. that day, Byer told Normile: "You snooze, you lose; the property has been sold." Shortly thereafter, Normile attempted to accept Miller's proposal. Was the trial court correct in ruling that Normile and Miller had no contract?

4. Indian Construction Services (ICS) is a general contractor. AROK Construction Co. is a drywall and stucco contractor. AROK and the principal owners of ICS had entered into contracts on three occasions prior to this case, using in all three situations identical standard form contracts. In 1985, Window Rock Unified School District solicited bids for the services of a general contractor on its construction project. ICS submitted a bid to act as the general contractor, listing AROK in its bid as subcontractor for the drywall and stucco portions of the project. AROK had first submitted its bid over the telephone to ICS for $1.549 million. Before bid closing, however, ICS asked AROK to reduce its bid to $1.42 million. AROK's president told ICS's project manager that AROK would reduce its bid even further to $1.4 million if, as a result, ICS would agree to contract with AROK if the school district awarded the job to ICS. ICS's project manager stated that in exchange for AROK's further reduction to $1.4 million, "If [ICS] gets the job, [AROK] gets a job." AROK sent a letter to ICS confirming the $1.4 million quote and enclosed a detailed bid confirmation. The school district awarded the contract to ICS. After receiving notice to proceed with the project from the school district, ICS requested that AROK perform "value engineering" services with regard to its bid. (Value engineering involves changing the bid structure to lower the overall bid price without changing the profit structure for either the general contractor or the subcontractor.) AROK complied and worked approximately 8 to 10 hours further reducing the subcontract price. Several months later, a dispute arose between ICS and AROK over the amount of the contract price and ICS entered into subcontracts with two other companies to perform the drywall and stucco work. AROK brought suit for breach of contract. ICS contended, however, that the parties failed to specify other terms essential to indicate their intent to be bound: the manner and time of payments, penalty provisions, time for completion, and bonding. ICS argued that as a result of the missing terms, no enforceable contract exists as a matter of law. Is ICS correct?

5. Less than an hour before his estranged wife underwent emergency surgery for an ectopic pregnancy caused by another man, McAdoo was asked to sign a standard form contract prepared by St. John's Episcopal Hospital. McAdoo testified that at the time he signed the form his wife's physical appearance and declared mental state convinced him that she was near death. Further, he stated that, under such circumstances, it did not occur to him to read carefully or question the implications of the papers he was being asked to sign. The form contained a provision that read as follows:

ASSIGNMENT OF INSURANCE BENEFITS: I hereby authorize payment directly to the above named hospital of the hospital expense benefits otherwise payable to me but not to exceed the hospital's regular charges for this period of hospitalization. I understand that I am financially responsible to the hospital for the charges not covered by my group insurance plan.

McAdoo's wife survived and was discharged from St. John's eight days later. McAdoo did not visit her after the day of the operation and had not had any further contact with her when the hospital filed suit against him to collect her hospital bill. Should St. John's be able to enforce the agreement against McAdoo?

6. Phyllis Chaplin filed a class action suit against Consolidated Edison (Con Ed) for allegedly discriminating against epileptics in violation of the Rehabilitation Act of 1973. In August 1981, Con Ed's lawyer sent Chaplin's lawyer a settlement offer. Chaplin's lawyer replied by saying that Chaplin had "objections" to the proposed settlement. On September 16, 1981, Con Ed's lawyer replied, saying: "Any further negotiation is an impossibility; if this agreement is not satisfactory to your client in its present form, I must withdraw all offers of settlement." In a letter dated September 17, 1981, Chaplin's lawyer answered that "after careful consideration" Chaplin still had "objections" to Con Ed's offer. Later, on September 17, a federal appellate court ruled that private suits such as Chaplin's were not allowed under the Rehabilitation Act. On September 30, 1981, Chaplin's lawyer told Con Ed's lawyer Chaplin had had "a change of heart" and was accepting the settlement offer. Con Ed's lawyer replied that the settlement was no longer acceptable. Was Con Ed bound by the settlement offer?

7. Edward Sherman engaged V. R. Brokers as listing agent for the sale of Adgraphics, his business. On December 5, 1985, William Lyon made a written offer to purchase the business for $75,000 and attached certain conditions to the offer. Later the same day, Sherman signed a written counteroffer offering to sell for $80,000 and rejecting two of the conditions contained in Lyon's offer. On December 7, at 11:35 A.M., Lyon signed the counteroffer before a notary public and then brought it to the office of V. R. Brokers around noon on that day. Before Lyon could hand the signed counteroffer to Robert Renault, the principal of V. R. Brokers, Renault told him that Sherman wanted to cancel his counteroffer. Did Sherman have the right to revoke his counteroffer?

8. Mariah Carey is a famous entertainer. Vian, who was Carey's stepfather before she achieved stardom, was in the business of designing, producing, and marketing gift and novelty items. Vian claimed that Carey agreed orally to give him a license to produce "Mariah dolls," which would be statuettes of the singer that would play her most popular songs. Vian asserted that this right was given in exchange for his financial and emotional support of Carey, including picking her up from late-night recording sessions, providing her with the use of a car, paying for dental care, allowing her to use his boat for business meetings and rehearsals, and giving her various items to help furnish her apartment. Vian based his claim of an oral contract on three conversations, twice in the family car and once on Vian's boat. Vian said to Carey, "Don't forget about the Mariah dolls," and "I get the Mariah dolls." According to Vian, on one occasion Carey responded, "Okay" and on other occasions, she merely smiled and nodded. Although Carey admits that Vian mentioned the dolls two or three times, she testified that she thought it was a joke. Claiming that Carey breached the contract to license dolls in her likeness, Vian brought this action for breach of contract. Was a contract formed?

9. In June 1973, Berryman signed an agreement giving Kmoch, a real estate broker, a 120-day option to purchase 960 acres of Berryman's land in exchange for "$10.00 and other valuable consideration," which was never paid. Kmoch hired two agricultural consultants to produce a report that he intended to use in order to interest other investors in joining him to exercise the option. In late July 1973, Berryman telephoned Kmoch and asked to be released from the option agreement. Nothing definite was agreed to, and Berryman later sold the land to another person. In August, Kmoch decided to exercise the option and contacted the local Federal Land Bank representative to make arrangements to buy the land. After being told by the representative that Berryman had sold the property, Kmoch sent Berryman a letter attempting to exercise the option. Kmoch argued that the option was still in effect and that, in any event, Berryman was estopped from revoking it. Was Kmoch right?

10. In August 1994, Auburn Engineers sued Downtown Properties #1, Howard Porter, Jr., and Porter and Associates, Inc., for breach of contract, fraud, and conversion. In August 1995, the defendants' lawyer telephoned Auburn's lawyer and offered to settle all claims for $70,000. Auburn's lawyer rejected this offer. Defendants' lawyer then served Auburn with a written offer of judgment for $70,000. In September 1995, Auburn's lawyer telephoned defendants' lawyer with a counteroffer. While discussing the case, defendants' lawyer discovered an error in the written offer of judgment. The error was that the offer of judgment referred only to Downtown and not to the other two defendants. The defendants' lawyer immediately informed Auburn's lawyer that the offer contained a mistake and that it was revoked, explaining that the

written offer had been intended to reflect the earlier oral offer wherein all three defendants had offered to settle all claims for $70,000. The defendants' lawyer then immediately sent a letter and an amended order of judgment to Auburn's lawyer by fax, informing him that the August 30 offer was revoked. He also notified the clerk of court by fax that the offer of judgment contained an error and that it had been revoked and replaced with an amended offer of judgment. On September 8, 1995, Auburn's lawyer filed a notice of acceptance of both the original offer of judgment of August 30 and the amended offer of September 5. Was a contract formed as to the August 30 offer?

11. *Video Case.* Justin and Judy received a flyer in the mail from a supermarket advertising New York strip steak for $.99 per pound. When they went to the supermarket to buy the steak, however, an employee of the store told them that the ad was an error; the price was intended to be $7.99 per pound, not $.99. The employee pointed to a memo posted in the store that announced that the ad was an error. Was the ad an offer? If it had been an offer, would the memo posted in the store be a valid revocation?

12. *Video Case.* Judy and Justin received a flyer that stated, "Dear Preferred Customer: Special close-out of Ubachi VCRs. Only 3 available at this unbelievable price, first come, first served, no rain checks." Was this an offer?

13. *Video Case.* Judy and Justin saw a newspaper ad for a brand new Mark Twelve Luxury Automobile for $9,999. Although Justin thought the ad might be a typographical mistake, there was no fine print in the ad and the two decided to go to the dealership and see if it would "make good on the offer." Once there, they learned that the price of the car was $29,999, not $9,999. The salesman stated that the advertised price was an obvious typo. Is the dealership obligated to sell the car to Judy and Justin for $9,999?

14. *Video Case.* Jeff visited a car dealership and test-drove a used car. After discussing the price with the salesman, Jake, and learning that he could purchase the car for $500 less than the sticker price, Jeff asked Jake to hold the car for him until 8:00 that evening so that he could bring his wife back to see the car. Jake agreed, writing out a note promising not to sell the car before 8:00 P.M. The note was written on dealership stationery, but Jake did not sign his name. The dealership broke its promise and sold the car to Jones before 8:00 P.M. Was it free to revoke its offer to Jeff? Jones, the new purchaser of the car (and a nonmerchant), later offered in a signed writing to sell the car to Jill and to hold the car for her until she returned with her husband. Could Jones revoke this offer?

15. [img] *Video Case.* Mike, a roofing contractor, had submitted a bid to resurface a roof on the Bobco factory in Industrial Park. He had gotten encouraging signals about getting the job and was just about to get a signed contract to do the work when the Bobco factory was burned to the ground. What is the status of Mike's offer to resurface the roof?

16. [img] *Video Case.* Salesperson takes an order having Customer, who is a merchant, sign the order form. The order form states that the offer will remain open for a length of time. Can Customer revoke the offer?

The Agreement: Acceptance

The preceding chapter discussed the circumstances under which a proposal will constitute the first stage of an agreement: the offer. This chapter focuses on the final stage of forming an agreement: the acceptance. The acceptance is vitally important because it is with the acceptance that the contract is formed. This chapter discusses the requirements for making a valid acceptance as well as the rules concerning the time at which a contract comes into being. ∞

WHAT IS AN ACCEPTANCE?

An **acceptance** is "a manifestation of assent to the terms [of the offer] made by the offeree in the manner invited or required by the offer."[1] In determining if an offeree accepted an offer and created a contract, a court will look for evidence of three factors: (1) the offeree intended to enter the contract, (2) the offeree accepted on the terms proposed by the offeror, and (3) the offeree communicated his acceptance to the offeror.

Intention to Accept

In determining whether an offeree accepted an offer, the court is looking for the same *present intent to contract* on the part of the offeree that it found on the part of the offeror. And, as is true of intent to make an offer, intent to accept is judged by an objective standard. The difference is that the offeree

---

[1]*Restatement (Second) of Contracts* § 50(1) (1981).

must objectively indicate a present intent to contract on the terms of the offer for a contract to result. As the master of the offer, the offeror may specify in detail what behavior is required of the offeree to bind him to a contract. If the offeror does so, the offeree must ordinarily comply with all the terms of the offer before a contract results.

Intent and Acceptance on the Offeror's Terms

Common Law: Traditional "Mirror Image" Rule The traditional contract law rule is that an acceptance must be the *mirror image* of the offer. Attempts by offerees to change the terms of the offer or to add new terms to it are treated as counteroffers because they impliedly indicate an intent by the offeree to reject the offer instead of being bound by its terms. However, recent years have witnessed a judicial tendency to apply the mirror image rule in a more liberal fashion by holding that only *material* (important) variances between an offer and a purported acceptance result in an implied rejection of the offer. You will see an example of that approach in the following *State of Rhode Island Department of Transportation v. Providence and Worcester Railroad Co.* case.

Even under the mirror image rule, no rejection is implied if an offeree merely asks about the terms of the offer without indicating its rejection (an *inquiry regarding terms*), or accepts the offer's terms while complaining about them (a *grumbling acceptance*). Distinguishing among a counteroffer, an inquiry regarding terms, and a grumbling acceptance is often a difficult task. The fundamental issue, however, remains the same: Did the offeree objectively indicate a present intent to be bound by the terms of the offer?

STATE OF RHODE ISLAND DEPARTMENT OF TRANSPORTATION v. PROVIDENCE AND WORCESTER RAILROAD CO.
674 A.2d 1239 (R.I. Sup. Ct. 1996)

Providence and Worcester (P & W) owned a waterfront property in East Providence, Rhode Island. Railroad tracks were situated on the property, but the property was not being used for railroad purposes at the time this case arose. A Rhode Island statute regulated rail properties, providing that all rail properties within the state offered for sale by any railway corporation be offered for sale to the state at the lowest price at which the railway corporation is willing to sell. The statute required railway corporations to notify the state in writing if they desire to sell any rail properties and give the state a period of not more than 30 days from receipt of the notification to accept the offer.

On December 12, 1986, P & W entered into an agreement to sell the property to Promet for $100,000. This agreement was subject to the State of Rhode Island's 30-day option to purchase the property. On that same day, P & W gave written notice to the state that it proposed to sell the property for $100,000 with a closing to be held on January 17, 1986. P & W's letter stated that, "[i]f the State's rights are not exercised within such period, we shall deem ourselves free to sell the property to Promet Corp. in accordance with the terms of the enclosed Real Estate Sales Agreement."

On January 7, 1986, Herbert DeSimone, director of transportation for the state, accepted the offer in writing. In his letter to P & W, DeSimone wrote, "Of course, you understand that certain wording in the Real Estate Sales Agreement relating to 'buyer' and obligations concerning the removal of track would be inappropriate to the purpose of the State's purchase." On April 11, 1986, the state filed suit against P & W, claiming that P & W was refusing to convey the property to the state and was about to convey the property to Promet Corp. in violation of the state's statutory rights. Several days later, P & W conveyed the property to Promet. The state then amended its complaint, asking that the deed to Promet be declared null and void. The trial court found in favor of the state on this issue and P & W appealed. ∞

Lederberg, Justice On appeal, P & W asserted that no contract for the sale of the parcel existed because the state's January 7, 1986, letter did not constitute a valid acceptance of P & W's December 12, 1985, offer. In support of its assertion, P & W argued that the January 7 letter in fact proposed additional terms to the agreement. The letter from DeSimone to P & W provided:

I am writing to you on behalf of the State of Rhode Island to exercise its right to accept the offer to purchase 6.9 acres of land. . . . Of course, you understand that certain wording in the Real Estate Sales Agreement [referring to the agreement between P & W and Promet] relating to 'buyer' and obligations concerning the removal of track would be inappropriate to the purpose of the State's purchase. Please contact Mr. Joseph F. Arruda of this department to arrange for a meeting to revise the existing offer to conform the State's acceptance.

P & W argued that as a matter of law, the letter was nothing more than an invitation to meet and attempt to reach agreement on the terms of the sale. We disagree.

This court has held that a valid acceptance must be definite and unequivocal, and that an acceptance which is equivocal or upon condition or with a limitation is a counteroffer and requires acceptance by the original offeror before a contractual relationship can exist. It is not equivocation, however, if the offeree merely puts into words that which was already reasonably implied in the terms of the offer. It is further the case that an acceptance must receive a reasonable construction and that the mere addition of a collateral or immaterial matter will not prevent the formation of a contract. To transmogrify a purported acceptance into a counteroffer, it must be shown that the acceptance differs in some material respect from the offer.

The state's letter of acceptance points out that the name of the buyer in the original agreement would have to be changed. In our opinion, this statement simply reflected the obvious necessity to replace "the state" for "Promet" as the named buyer in the deed. Moreover, the letter's reference to P & W's obligation to Promet to remove tracks from the property as "inappropriate to the purpose of the State's purchase" did not *add* any terms or conditions to the contract but, instead, constituted a clear benefit to P & W. The state, in fact, relieved P & W from the obligation and expense it otherwise would have incurred in selling the property to Promet. When an offeree, in its acceptance of an offer, absolves the offeror of a material obligation, the rules of contract construction and the rules of common sense preclude construing that absolution as an additional term that invalidates the acceptance. Moreover, DeSimone explicitly and unequivocally stated, "I am writing to you on behalf of the State of Rhode Island to exercise its right to *accept* the offer to purchase" and requested the meeting in order "to revise the existing offer to conform the *State's acceptance.*"

Therefore, we concur with the trial justice who found that the state validly accepted the option extended to it by P & W.

Judgment affirmed in favor of the state.

UCC Standard for Acceptance on the Offeror's Terms: The "Battle of the Forms"   Strictly applying the mirror image rule to modern commercial transactions, most of which are carried out by using preprinted form contracts, would often result in frustrating the parties' true intent. Offerors use standard order forms prepared by their lawyers, and offerees use standard acceptance or acknowledgment forms drafted by their counsel. The odds that these forms will agree in every detail are slight, as are the odds that the parties will read each other's forms in their entirety. Instead, the parties to such transactions are likely to read only crucial provisions concerning the goods ordered, the price, and the delivery date called for, and if these terms are agreeable, believe that they have a contract.

If a dispute arose before the parties started to perform, a court strictly applying the mirror image rule would hold that no contract resulted because the offer and acceptance forms did not match exactly. If a dispute arose after performance had commenced, the court would probably hold that the offeror had impliedly accepted the offeree's counteroffer and was bound by its terms.

Because neither of these results is very satisfactory, the Code, in a very controversial provision often called the "Battle of the Forms" section [2–207] (see Figure 1), has changed the mirror image rule for contracts involving the sale of goods. As you will see in the following *Union Carbide* case, UCC section 2–207 allows the formation of a contract even when there is some variance between the terms of the offer and the terms of the acceptance. It also makes it possible, under *some* circumstances, for a term contained in the acceptance form to become part of the contract. The Code provides that a *definite and timely expression of acceptance* creates a contract, even if it includes terms that are *different from those stated in the offer* or even if it states *additional terms* that the offer did not address [2–207(1)]. An attempted acceptance that *was expressly conditioned* on the offeror's agreement to

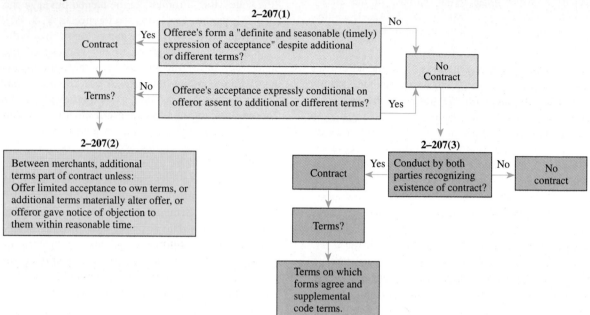

FIGURE I

The "Battle of the Forms"—A Section 2–207 Flowchart

the offeree's terms would *not* be a valid acceptance, however [2–207(1)].

What are the terms of a contract created by the exchange of standardized forms? The *additional* terms contained in the offeree's form are treated as "proposals for addition to the contract." If the parties are both *merchants,* the additional terms become part of the contract *unless:*

1. The offer *expressly limited acceptance* to its own terms.
2. The new terms would *materially alter* the offer, or
3. The offeror gives notice of objection to the new terms within a reasonable time after receiving the acceptance [2–207(2)].

The *Union Carbide* case shows how courts analyze whether a term contained in the acceptance has become part of the contract.

When the offeree has made his acceptance expressly conditional on the offeror's agreement to the new terms or when the offeree's response to the offer is clearly not "an expression of acceptance" (e.g., an express rejection), no contract is created under section 2–207(1). A contract will only result in such cases if the parties engage in conduct that "recognizes the existence of a contract," such as an exchange of performance. Unlike her counterpart under traditional contract principles, however, the offeror who accepts performance in the face of an express rejection or expressly conditional acceptance is not thereby bound to all of the terms contained in the offeree's response. Instead, the Code provides that the terms of a contract created by such performance are those on which the parties' writings *agree,* supplemented by appropriate gap-filling provisions from the Code [2–207(3)].

UNION CARBIDE CORP. v. OSCAR MAYER FOODS CORP. 947 F.2d 1333 (7th Cir. 1991)

Union Carbide sold Oscar Mayer plastic casings that Oscar Mayer uses in manufacturing sausages. The prices in Union Carbide's invoices to Oscar Mayer included two 1 percent sales taxes that are applicable to sales that originate in Chicago. In 1980, another one of Oscar Mayer's suppliers of plastic sausage casings began charging a price that was 1 percent lower than Union Carbide's. This supplier had begun accepting orders at an office outside of Chicago and had decided that therefore it did *not have to pay one of the sales taxes. When Oscar Mayer informed Union Carbide of this, Union Carbide instructed its customers to send their orders to an address outside Chicago, too, and it stopped paying both sales taxes and therefore deleted them from the invoices it sent Oscar Mayer. Thus, Union Carbide had met and indeed beat the other supplier's discount by lowering its price 2 percent compared to the other supplier's reduction of 1 percent.*

In 1988, the Illinois tax authorities decided that the two sales taxes were due notwithstanding the change of address and assessed Union Carbide $88,000 in back taxes on sales to Oscar Mayer and $55,000 in interest on those sales. Union Carbide paid this and then turned around and brought this suit to recover what it had paid from Oscar Mayer, claiming that Oscar Mayer had agreed to indemnify it for all sales tax liability. It relied on the following provision printed on the back of its invoices to Oscar Mayer and also in a "price book" that it sent its customers:

In addition to the purchase price, Buyer shall pay Seller the amount of all governmental taxes . . . that Seller may be required to pay with respect to the production, sale or transportation of any materials delivered hereunder.

The trial court granted a summary judgment in favor of Oscar Mayer, and Union Carbide appealed. ∞

Posner, Circuit Judge The common law rule was that if the purported acceptance of an offer was not identical to the offer, the acceptance was a fresh offer and had to be expressly accepted by the original offeror for the parties to have a contract. This "mirror image" rule was widely believed to take insufficient account of the incorrigible fallibility of human beings engaged in commercial as in other dealings, and is changed by the Uniform Commercial Code, which allows an acceptance to make a contract even if it adds terms to the offer. Moreover, if it is a contract between "merchants" (in the sense of "pros," UCC section 2–104(1)—as Union Carbide and Oscar Mayer are)—the additional terms become part of the contract. But not any additional terms; only those to which the offeror would be unlikely to object, because they fill out the contract in an expectable fashion, and hence do not alter it materially. If a term added by the offeree in his acceptance works a material alteration of the offer, the acceptance is still effective, but the term is not: that is, the contract is enforceable minus the term the offeree tried to add. An alteration is material if consent to it cannot be presumed. What is expectable, hence unsurprising, is okay; what is unexpected, hence surprising, is not.

This is not the end of the analysis, however. Even if the alteration is material, the other party can, of course, decide to accept it. Put differently, consent can be inferred from other things beside the unsurprising character of the new term: even from silence, in the face of a course of dealings that makes it reasonable for the other party to infer consent from a failure to object. An offeror can protect

himself against additional terms, material or not, by expressly limiting acceptance to the terms of the offer.

The record does not reveal the origins of Union Carbide's dealings with Oscar Mayer. All we know is that in 1980 the parties' method of dealing was as follows. Oscar Mayer would from time to time send large purchase orders to Union Carbide which would not be filled immediately but instead would be filed for future reference. When Oscar Mayer actually needed casings it would phone Union Carbide and tell it how many it needed and Union Carbide would ship the casings the next day. After the casings arrived Oscar Mayer would send Union Carbide a purchase order for the shipment on the same form used for the standing orders. These "release orders," as the specific purchase orders were called, were like checks written against a bank account—only this was a sausage-casings account. At about the same time that Oscar Mayer sent Union Carbide a release order, Union Carbide would send Oscar Mayer an invoice for the shipment—and the so-called indemnity clause was on the back of the invoice and also in a price book that Union Carbide sent its customers from time to time. So every actual purchase of sausage casings involved an exchange of four documents: the standing order, the price book, the release order, the invoice. Such a pattern of sequential exchange of documents governing a single sale is a prototypical situation for the application of UCC section 2–207. Union Carbide does not question that for purposes of our decision the purchase orders by Oscar Mayer are the offers and Union Carbide's invoices are the acceptances, and that the price book, if it be assumed to be an offer, was never accepted. So the indemnity clause was binding on Oscar Mayer only if the clause did not work a material alteration of the terms in the purchase orders.

Those orders don't exactly *discuss* taxes, but they contain a space for sales tax to be added into the purchase price, and Union Carbide points out that, consistent with this indication of willingness to pay sales tax, Oscar Mayer paid uncomplainingly all sales taxes that appeared on Union Carbide's invoices. If the sales tax rates had risen, Oscar Mayer would have had to pay the higher rates. What difference does it make, asks Union Carbide, if the increase took the form of an assessment of back taxes? It makes a big difference, amounting to a material alteration to which Oscar Mayer did not consent either explicitly or implicitly. If a tax increase showed up on an invoice, Oscar Mayer

would have to pay but might then decide to cease buying casings from Union Carbide, as it had every right to do; it did not have a requirements contract with Union Carbide but could switch at will to other suppliers some of whom might not be subject to the tax. To assume responsibility for taxes shown on an individual invoice is quite different from assuming an open-ended, indeed incalculable, liability for back taxes. The tax clause altered the contract materially; and since the clause was at best ambiguous, this is not a case where consent can realistically be inferred from Oscar Mayer's silence in the face of a succession of acceptances (Union Carbide's invoices) containing the new term. There was no breach of contract.

Judgment affirmed in favor of Oscar Mayer.

Communication of Acceptance

To accept an offer for a bilateral contract, the offeree must make the promise requested by the offer. In Chapter 10, you learned that an offeror must communicate the terms of his proposal to the offeree before an offer results. This is so because communication is a necessary component of the present intent to contract required for the creation of an offer. For similar reasons, it is generally held that an offeree must communicate his intent to be bound by the offer before a contract can be created. To accept an offer for a unilateral contract, however, the offeree must perform the requested act. The traditional contract law rule on this point assumes that the offeror will learn of the offeree's performance and holds that no further notice from the offeree is necessary to create a contract unless the offeror specifically requests notice.

Manner of Communication   The offeror, as the master of the offer, has the power to specify the precise time, place, and manner in which acceptance must be communicated. This is called a *stipulation.* If the offeror stipulates a particular manner of acceptance, the offeree must respond in this way to form a valid acceptance. Suppose Prompt Printing makes an offer to Jackson and the offer states that Jackson must respond by certified mail. If Jackson deviates from the offer's instructions in any signifi-

cant way, no contract results unless Prompt Printing indicates a willingness to be bound by the deviating acceptance. If, however, the offer merely *suggests* a method or place of communication or is *silent* on such matters, the offeree may accept within a *reasonable time* by *any reasonable means* of communication. So, if Prompt Printing's offer did not *require* any particular manner of accepting the offer, Jackson could accept the offer by any reasonable manner of communication within a reasonable time.

When Is Acceptance Communicated?

Acceptances by Instantaneous Forms of Communication   When the parties are dealing face-to-face, by telephone, or by other means of communication that are virtually instantaneous, there are few problems determining when the acceptance was communicated. As soon as the offeree says, "I accept," or words to that effect, a contract is created, assuming that the offer is still in existence.

Acceptances by Noninstantaneous Forms of Communication   Suppose the circumstances under which the offer was made reasonably led the offeree to believe that acceptance by some noninstantaneous form of communication is acceptable, and the offeree responds by using mail, telegraph, or some other means of communication that creates a time lag between the dispatching of the acceptance and its actual receipt by the offeror. The practical problems involving the timing of acceptance multiply in such transactions. The offeror may be attempting to revoke the offer while the offeree is attempting to accept it. An acceptance may get lost and never be received by the offeror. The time limit for accepting the offer may be rapidly approaching. Was the offer accepted before a revocation was received or before the offer expired? Does a lost acceptance create a contract when it is dispatched, or is it totally ineffective?

Under the so-called *"mailbox rule,"* properly addressed and dispatched acceptances can become effective when they are *dispatched,* even if they are lost and never received by the offeror. The mailbox rule, which is discussed further in the following *Casto v. State Farm Mutual Insurance Co.* case, protects the offeree's reasonable belief that a binding contract was created when the acceptance was dispatched. By the same token, it exposes the offeror to the risk of being bound by an acceptance that she has never received. The offeror, however, has the ability to minimize this risk by stipulating in her offer that she must actually receive the acceptance for it to be effective. Offerors who do this maximize the time that they have to revoke their offers and ensure that they will never be bound by an acceptance that they have not received.

Operation of the Mailbox Rule: Common Law of Contracts   As traditionally applied by the common law of contracts, the mailbox rule would make acceptances effective upon dispatch when the offeree used a manner of communication that was expressly or impliedly **authorized** (invited) by the offeror. Any manner of communication *suggested* by the offeror (e.g., "You may respond by mail") would be expressly authorized, resulting in an acceptance sent by the suggested means being effective on dispatch. Unless circumstances indicated to the contrary, a manner of communication *used by the offeror in making the offer* would be impliedly authorized (e.g., an offer sent by mail would impliedly authorize an acceptance by mail), as would a manner of communication common in the parties' trade or business (e.g., a trade usage in the parties' business that offers are made by mail and accepted by telegram would authorize an acceptance by telegram). Conversely, an improperly dispatched acceptance or one that was sent by some means of

communication that was *nonauthorized* would be effective when *received,* assuming that the offer was still open at that time. This placed on the offeree the risk of the offer being revoked or the acceptance being lost.

The mailbox rule is often applied more liberally by courts today. A modern version of the mailbox rule that is sanctioned by the *Restatement (Second)* holds that an offer that does not indicate otherwise is considered to invite acceptance by *any reasonable means* of communication, and a properly dispatched acceptance sent by a reasonable means of communication within a reasonable time is effective on dispatch.

Operation of the Mailbox Rule: UCC   The UCC, like the *Restatement (Second),* provides that an offer that does not specify a particular means of acceptance is considered to invite acceptance by *any reasonable means* of communication. It also provides that a properly dispatched acceptance sent by a reasonable means of communication within a reasonable time is effective on dispatch. What is reasonable depends on the circumstances in which the offer was made. These include the speed and reliability of the means used by the offeree, the nature of the transaction (e.g., does the agreement involve goods subject to rapid price fluctuations?), the existence of any trade usage governing the transaction, and the existence of prior dealings between the parties (e.g., has the offeree previously used the mail to accept telegraphed offers from the offeror?). So, under proper circumstances, a mailed response to a telegraphed offer or a telegraphed response to a mailed offer might be considered reasonable and therefore effective on dispatch.

What if an offeree attempts to accept the offer by some means that is *unreasonable* under the circumstances or if the acceptance is not properly addressed or dispatched (e.g., misaddressed or accompanied by insufficient postage)? The UCC rejects the traditional rule that such acceptances cannot be effective until received. It provides that an acceptance sent by an unreasonable means would be effective on dispatch *if* it is received within the time that an acceptance by a reasonable means would normally have arrived. The *Casto* case shows what happens when an improperly dispatched acceptance is not received within the time that a properly dispatched acceptance would have been.

CASTO v. STATE FARM MUTUAL INSURANCE CO.   594 N.E.2d 1004 (Ct. App. Ohio 1991)

I
n 1985, State Farm issued Deborah Casto an automobile insurance policy on her Jaguar. Casto also insured a second car, a Porsche, with State Farm. Sometime in September or early October 1987, Casto received two renewal notices for her policy on the Jaguar, indicating that the next premium was due on October 10, 1987. State Farm sent a notice of cancellation on October 16, indicating that the policy would be canceled on October 29. Casto denied having received this notice. On October 20, Casto placed two checks, one for the Jaguar and one for the Porsche, in two preaddressed envelopes that had been supplied by State Farm. She gave these envelopes to Donald Dick, who mailed them on the same day. The envelope containing the Porsche payment was timely delivered to State Farm, but State Farm never received the Jaguar payment, and that policy was canceled.

Casto was involved in an accident on November 20 while driving the Jaguar. When she made a claim with State Farm, she learned that the policy had been canceled. After the accident, the envelope containing the Jaguar payment was returned to her stamped "Returned for postage." Casto brought this declaratory judgment action seeking a declaration that her insurance policy was in effect as of the date of the accident. The trial court rendered a judgment for State Farm and Casto appealed. ∽

Reilly, Presiding Judge   The facts indicate that while the payment was mailed before October 29, it was not received by the insurance company. The issue then is whether the insurance premium is effectively paid on the day it was mailed or the day it is received by the company.

An insurance policy is a contract and the relationship between the insurer and its insured is contractual in nature. The renewal of an insurance policy is generally considered a new contract of insurance to which the requirements of offer and acceptance apply. The well-established general rule of contract formation is that an acceptance transmitted in a form invited by the offer is operative as soon as it is put out of the offeree's possession, regardless of whether it ever reaches the offeror. This is the so-called "mailbox rule" which states that in the absence of any limitation to the contrary in the offer, an acceptance is effective when mailed. One of the parties must bear the risk of loss. As the offeror has the power to condition acceptance of the offer on actual receipt, the courts have uniformly held that, in the absence of language to the contrary, an acceptance is effective when mailed.

To be effective upon mailing, however, the acceptance must be properly dispatched. The offeree must properly address the acceptance and take whatever other precautions as are ordinarily observed in the transmission of similar messages. It is undisputed that State Farm provided Casto with preaddressed envelopes and thus authorized her to mail her premium payments. Furthermore, the renewal notices contain no language requiring actual receipt before payment is deemed effective. Finally, Casto and Donald Dick testified in their depositions that the Jaguar and Porsche payments were mailed on October 20, 1987, nine days before the cancellation date. Their testimony is further supported by the fact that the Porsche payment was actually received by State Farm before the cancellation date. Thus, the only remaining question is whether the payment was properly dispatched.

Casto testified that the check and renewal notice were placed in a preaddressed and stamped envelope. Donald Dick also testified that both envelopes were stamped when he mailed them. Nevertheless, the envelope did not bear any postage when it was returned to Casto. Casto bore the burden of proving that the envelope was stamped when it was mailed. When the findings of fact leave some material fact undetermined, a reviewing court will presume that the issue of fact was not proved by the party having the burden of proof. We thus presume that the trial court concluded that the envelope was not stamped when mailed, and there is sufficient evidence in the record to support such a finding. As the envelope was not properly dispatched, the payment was not effective upon mailing under the facts of this case.

Judgment affirmed in favor of State Farm.

FIGURE 2

Time of Acceptance

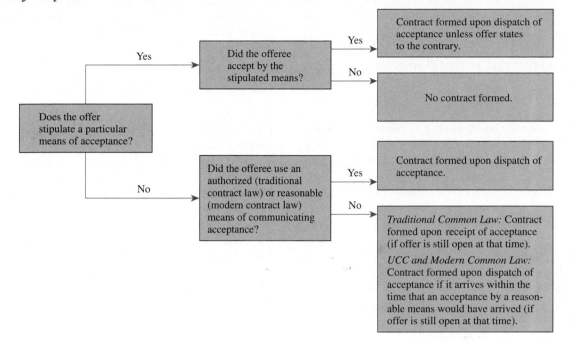

Stipulated Means of Communication   As we discussed earlier, an offer may stipulate the means of communication that the offeree must use to accept by saying, in effect: "You must accept by mail." An acceptance by the stipulated means of communication is effective on dispatch, just like an acceptance by any other reasonable or authorized means of communication (see Figure 2). The difference is that an acceptance by other than the stipulated means does not create a contract because it is an acceptance at variance with the terms of the offer.

SPECIAL ACCEPTANCE PROBLEM AREAS

Acceptance in Unilateral Contracts

A unilateral contract involves the exchange of a promise for an act. To accept an offer to enter such a contract, the offeree must perform the requested act. As you learned in the last chapter, however, courts applying modern contract rules may prevent an offeror from revoking such an offer once the offeree has begun performance. This is achieved by holding either that a bilateral contract is created by

the beginning of performance or that the offeror's power to revoke is suspended for the period of time reasonably necessary for the offeree to complete performance.

Acceptance in Bilateral Contracts

A bilateral contract involves the exchange of a promise for a promise. As a general rule, to accept an offer to enter such a contract, an offeree must *make the promise requested by the offer*. This may be done in a variety of ways. For example, Wallace sends Stevens a detailed offer for the purchase of Stevens's business. Within the time period prescribed by the offer, Stevens sends Wallace a letter that says, "I accept your offer." Stevens has *expressly* accepted Wallace's offer, creating a contract on the terms of the offer. Acceptance, however, can be *implied* as well as express. Offerees who take action that objectively indicates agreement risk the formation of a contract. For example, offerees who act in a manner that is inconsistent with an offeror's ownership of offered property are commonly held to have accepted the offeror's terms. So, if Arnold, a farmer, leaves 10 bushels of corn with Porter, the owner of a grocery store, saying, "Look this corn over. If you want it, it's $5 a bushel," and Porter sells the corn, he has impliedly accepted Arnold's offer. But what if Porter just let the corn sit and, when Arnold returned a week later, Porter told Arnold that he did not want it? Could Porter's failure to act ever amount to an acceptance?

Silence as Acceptance

Since contract law generally requires some objective indication that an offeree intends to contract, the general rule is that an offeree's silence, without more, is *not* an acceptance. In addition, it is generally held that an offeror cannot impose on the offeree a duty to respond to the offer. So, even if Arnold made an offer to sell corn to Porter and said, "If I don't hear from you in three days, I'll assume you're buying the corn," Porter's silence would still not amount to acceptance.

On the other hand, the circumstances of a case sometimes impose a duty on the offeree to reject the offer affirmatively or be bound by its terms. These are cases in which the offeree's silence objectively indicates an intent to accept. Customary trade practice or prior dealings between the parties may indicate that silence signals acceptance. So, if Arnold and Porter had dealt with each other on numerous occasions and Porter had always promptly returned items that he did not want, Porter's silent retention of the goods for a week would probably constitute an acceptance. Likewise, an offeree's silence can also operate as an acceptance if the offeree has indicated that it will. For example, Porter (the *offeree*) tells Arnold, "If you don't hear from me in three days, I accept."

Finally, it is generally held that offerees who accept an offeror's performance knowing what the offeror expects in return for his performance have impliedly accepted the offeror's terms. So, if Apex Paving Corporation offers to do the paving work on a new subdivision being developed by Majestic Homes Corporation, and Majestic fails to respond to Apex's offer but allows Apex to do the work, most courts would hold that Majestic is bound by the terms of Apex's offer.

Acceptance When a Writing Is Anticipated

Frequently, the parties to a contract intend to prepare a written draft of their agreement for both parties to sign. This is a good idea not only because the law requires written evidence of some contracts,[2] but also because it provides written evidence of the terms of the agreement if a dispute arises at a later date. If a dispute arises before such a writing has been prepared or signed, however, a question may arise concerning whether the signing of the agreement was a necessary condition to the creation of a contract. A party to the agreement who now wants out of the deal may argue that the parties did not intend to be bound until both parties signed the writing. As the following *Texaco* case indicates, a clear expression of such an intent by the parties during the negotiation process prevents the formation of a contract until both parties have signed. However, in the absence of such a clear expression of intent, the courts ask whether a reasonable person familiar with all the circumstances of the parties' negotiations would conclude that the parties intended to be bound only when a formal agreement was signed. If it appears that the parties had concluded their negotiations and reached agreement on all the essential aspects of the transaction, most courts would probably find a contract at the time agreement was reached, even though no formal agreement had been signed.

---

[2] Chapter 16 discusses this subject in detail.

TEXACO, INC. v. PENNZOIL CO.   729 S.W.2d 768 (Tex. Ct. App. 1987)

On December 28, 1983, in the wake of well-publicized dissension between the board of directors of Getty Oil Company and Gordon Getty, Pennzoil announced an unsolicited, public tender offer for 16 million shares of Getty Oil at $100 each. Gordon Getty was a director of Getty Oil and the owner, as trustee of the Sarah C. Getty Trust, of 40.2 percent of the 79.1 million outstanding shares of Getty Oil. Shortly thereafter, Pennzoil contacted both Gordon Getty and a representative of the J. Paul Getty Museum, which held 11.8 percent of the shares of Getty Oil, to discuss the tender offer and the possible purchase of Getty Oil.

The parties drafted and signed a Memorandum of Agreement providing that Pennzoil and the Trust (with Gordon Getty as trustee) were to become partners on a ³/₇ths to ⁴/₇ths basis, respectively, in owning and operating Getty Oil. The museum was to receive $110 per share for its 11.8 percent ownership, and all other outstanding public shares were to be cashed in by the company at $110 per share. The memorandum provided that it was subject to the approval of Getty Oil's board. On January 2, 1984, the board voted to reject the memorandum price as too low and made a counterproposal to Pennzoil of $110 per share plus a $10 debenture. On January 3, the board received a revised Pennzoil proposal of $110 per share plus a $3 "stub" that was to be paid after the sale of a Getty Oil subsidiary. After discussion, the board voted 15 to 1 to accept Pennzoil's proposal if the stub price was raised to $5. This counteroffer was accepted by Pennzoil later the same day. On January 4, Getty Oil and Pennzoil issued identical press releases announcing an agreement in principle on the terms of the Memorandum of Agreement. Pennzoil's lawyers began working on a formal transaction agreement describing the deal in more detail than the outline of terms contained in the Memorandum of Agreement and press release.

On January 5, the board of Texaco, which had been in contact with Getty Oil's investment banker, authorized its officers to make an offer for 100 percent of Getty Oil's stock. Texaco first contacted the Getty Museum, which, after discussion, agreed to sell its shares to Texaco. Later that evening, Gordon Getty accepted Texaco's offer of $125 per share. On January 6, the Getty Board voted to withdraw its previous counteroffer to Pennzoil and to accept Texaco's offer. Pennzoil later filed suit against Texaco for tortious interference with its contract with the Getty entities. At trial, Texaco argued, among other things, that no contract had existed between Pennzoil and the Getty entities. The jury disagreed, awarding Pennzoil $7.53 billion in actual damages and $3 billion in punitive damages. Texaco appealed. ∞

Warren, Justice Texaco contends that there was insufficient evidence to support the jury's finding that at the end of the Getty Oil board meeting on January 3, the Getty entities intended to bind themselves to an agreement with Pennzoil. Pennzoil contends that the evidence showed that the parties intended to be bound to the terms in the Memorandum of Agreement plus a price term of $110 plus a $5 stub, even though the parties may have contemplated a later, more formal document to memorialize the agreement already reached. If parties do not intend to be bound to an agreement until it is reduced to writing and signed by both parties, then there is no contract until that event occurs. If there is no understanding that a signed writing is necessary before the parties will be bound, and the parties have agreed upon all substantial terms, then an informal agreement can be binding, even though the parties contemplated evidencing their agreement in a formal document later. It is the parties' expressed intent that controls which rule of contract formation applies. Only the outward expressions of intent are considered—secret or subjective intent is immaterial to the question of whether the parties were bound.

Several factors have been articulated to help determine whether the parties intended to be bound only by a formal, signed writing: (1) whether a party expressly reserved the right to be bound only when a written agreement is signed; (2) whether there was any partial performance by one party that the party disclaiming the contract accepted; (3) whether all essential terms of the alleged contract had been agreed upon; and (4) whether the complexity or magnitude of the transaction was such that a formal, executed writing would normally be expected.

Any intent of the parties not to be bound before signing a formal document is not so clearly expressed in the press release to establish, as a matter of law, that there was no contract at that time. The press release does refer to an agreement "in principle" and states that the "transaction" is subject to execution of a definitive merger agreement. But the release as a whole is worded in indicative terms, not in subjunctive or hypothetical ones. The press release describes what shareholders will receive, what Pennzoil will contribute, that Pennzoil will be granted an option, etc.

We find little relevant partial performance in this case that might show that the parties believed that they were bound by a contract. However, the absence of relevant part performance in this short period of time does not compel the conclusion that no contract existed.

There was sufficient evidence for the jury to conclude that the parties had reached agreement on all essential terms of the transaction with only the mechanics and details left to be supplied by the parties' attorneys. Although there may have been many specific items relating to the transaction agreement draft that had yet to be put in final form, there is sufficient evidence to support a conclusion by the jury that the parties did not consider any of Texaco's asserted "open items" significant obstacles precluding an intent to be bound.

Although the magnitude of the transaction here was such that normally a signed writing would be expected, there was sufficient evidence to support an inference by the jury that that expectation was satisfied here initially by the Memorandum of Agreement, signed by a majority of shareholders of Getty Oil and approved by the board with a higher price, and by the transaction agreement in progress that had been intended to memorialize the agreement previously reached.

Judgment for Pennzoil affirmed.

[*Note:* The court's decision was contingent on a reduction in the punitive damages awarded by the jury from $3 billion to $1 billion. Texaco ultimately sought reorganization under the protection of the Bankruptcy Court and the parties finally settled the case for $3 billion.]

Acceptance of Ambiguous Offers

Although offerors have the power to specify the manner in which their offers can be accepted by requiring that the offeree make a return promise (a bilateral contract) or perform a specific act (a unilateral contract), often an offer is unclear about which form of acceptance is necessary to create a contract. In such a case, the offer may be accepted in any manner that is *reasonable* in light of the circumstances surrounding the offer. Thus, either a promise to perform or performance, if reasonable, creates a contract.

Acceptance by Shipment The Code specifically elaborates on the rule stated in the preceding section by stating that an order requesting prompt or current shipment of goods may be accepted either by a *prompt promise to ship* or by a *prompt or current shipment* of the goods [2–206(1)(b)]. So, if Ampex Corporation orders 500 IBM personal computers from Marks Office Supply, to be shipped immediately, Marks could accept either by promptly promising to ship the goods or by promptly shipping them. If Marks accepts by shipping, any subsequent attempt by Ampex to revoke the order will be ineffective.

What if Marks did not have 500 IBMs in stock and Marks knew that Ampex desperately needed the goods? Marks might be tempted to ship another brand of computers (that is, *nonconforming goods*— goods different from what the buyer ordered), hoping that Ampex would be forced by its circumstances to accept them because by the time they arrived it would be too late to get the correct goods elsewhere. Marks would argue that by shipping the wrong goods it had made a counteroffer because it had not performed the act requested by Ampex's order. If Ampex accepts the goods, Marks could argue that Ampex has impliedly accepted the counteroffer. If Ampex rejects the goods, Marks would arguably have no liability since it did not accept the order.

The Code prevents such a result by providing that prompt shipment of either conforming goods (what the order asked for) or nonconforming goods (something else) operates as an acceptance of the order [2–206(1)(b)]. This protects buyers such as Ampex because sellers who ship the wrong goods have simultaneously accepted their offers and breached the contract by sending the wrong merchandise.[3]

But what if Marks is an honest seller merely trying to help out a customer that has placed a rush order? Must Marks expose itself to liability for breach of contract in the process? The Code prevents such a result by providing that no contract is created if the seller notifies the buyer within a reasonable time that the shipment of nonconforming goods is intended as an accommodation (an attempt to help the buyer) [2–206(1)(b)]. In this case, the shipment is merely a counteroffer that the buyer is free to accept or reject and the seller's notification gives the buyer the opportunity to seek the goods he needs elsewhere.

Who Can Accept an Offer?

As the masters of their offers, offerees have the right to determine who can bind them to a contract.

---

[3]Chapter 19 discusses the rights and responsibilities of the buyer and seller following the shipment of nonconforming goods.

So, the only person with the legal power to accept an offer and create a contract is the *original offeree.* An attempt to accept by anyone other than the offeree is treated as an offer, because the party attempting to accept is indicating a present intent to contract on the original offer's terms. For example, Price offers to sell his car to Waterhouse for $5,000. Anderson learns of the offer, calls Price, and attempts to accept. Anderson has made an offer that Price is free to accept or reject.

ETHICAL AND PUBLIC POLICY CONCERNS

1. It should be apparent to you from the discussion of section 2–207 of the Code, the "Battle of the Forms" section, that the application of that section can sometimes result in a party being held to a contract term that she has not actually consented to. How can this be justified?

2. Compare the ethical standards underlying the traditional contract law approach to the seller who ships nonconforming goods with the ethical standards reflected by section 2–206(1)(b) of the Code.

3. Compare the public policy stances implicit in the different ways in which traditional and modern contract law treat offeree attempts to accept by an nonauthorized or unreasonable means of communication.

PROBLEM CASES

1. On September 24, 1979, Benya's agent presented Stevens and Thompson Paper Company (S&T) with a sales agreement to purchase 5,243 acres of timber land owned by S&T for $605,366.50. S&T's lawyer made several modifications to the agreement, raising the cash to be paid at closing from $5,000 to $10,000, raising the interest rate on the mortgage S&T would hold on the property until it was fully paid for from 9 to 10 percent, providing for quarterly rather than annual payments on the mortgage, and changing the deed S&T was to provide from a warranty to a special warranty deed. S&T's vice president then initialed each change and signed the document, which was mailed back to Benya's agent. In early November, S&T received a new sales agreement from Benya,

which differed from the two previous versions in a number of ways. S&T neither signed this agreement nor responded to it in any way. Later, however, S&T sold the property to someone else. Benya filed suit, claiming that it had a contract with S&T to buy the land. Did it?

2. First Texas Savings Association promoted a "$5,000 Scoreboard Challenge" contest. Contestants who completed an entry form and deposited it with First Texas were eligible for a random drawing. The winner was to receive an $80 savings account with First Texas, plus four tickets to a Dallas Mavericks home basketball game chosen by First Texas. If the Mavericks held their opponent in the chosen game to 89 or fewer points, the winner was to receive an additional $5,000 money market certificate. In October 1982, Jergins deposited a completed entry form with First Texas. On November 1, 1982, First tried to amend the contest rules by posting notice at its branches that the Mavericks would have to hold their opponent to 85 or fewer points before the contest winner would receive the $5,000. In late December, Jergins was notified that she had won the $80 savings account and tickets to the January 22, 1983, game against the Utah Jazz. The notice contained the revised contest terms. The Mavericks held the Jazz to 88 points. Was Jergins entitled to the $5,000?

3. In April 1973, in response to a request from Mobil Chemical for a bid on a two-sided precoater, Egan Machinery submitted a "quotation" describing the components of the precoater and the details of its operation. The quotation stated a price for the precoater but did not contain conditions of sale. In May 1973, Mobil sent Egan a purchase order for the precoater. The purchase order contained the following language:

Important—this order expressly limits acceptance to terms stated herein, and any additional or different terms proposed by the seller are rejected unless expressly agreed to in writing.

Egan responded with an order acknowledgment in May 1973, which provided that:

This order is accepted on the condition that our Standard Conditions of Sale, which are attached hereto and made a part hereof, are accepted by you, notwithstanding any modifying or additive conditions contained on your purchase order. Receipt of this acknowledgment by you without prompt written objection thereto shall constitute an acceptance of these terms and conditions.

One of the terms included in Egan's Standard Conditions required Mobil to indemnify Egan against any liability Egan might incur to persons injured by the precoater if the injury resulted from Mobil's failure to require its employees to follow safety procedures and/or use safety devices while operating it. When a Mobil employee who was injured while operating the precoater later won a $75,000 judgment against Egan, Egan filed suit against Mobil seeking indemnity. Did the indemnity clause become part of the contract?

4. Lambert owned the Rainbow Fruit Co. in Boston, which sold Christmas trees and wreaths at retail during the holiday season. From 1987 through 1989, Lambert bought Christmas trees at wholesale from Joan and Sam Kysar pursuant to a written form contract signed by both parties. The front of the order form contained spaces in which the size, grade, quantity, and price of each Christmas tree order could be filled in; a small space at the bottom of the page, labeled as "other," was used by the parties to note additional terms and conditions. The back of the order form stated the fixed terms of the contract. One of these fixed terms provided that the contract was to be interpreted under the law of the *State of Washington* and any action that might be brought to enforce the contract would be brought in *Clark County, Washington.* In July, the Kysars visited Boston to discuss Lambert's needs for the upcoming Christmas season. On their return to Washington, they sent Lambert an order form, filled out and signed by Joan Kysar. The numbers handwritten on the form by Joan Kysar provided for an order of 2,600 Christmas trees at $11.60 apiece. At the bottom of the form, in the space marked "other," Kysar wrote that the order was "based on 4 loads of 650 trees each. All trucks will be loaded to capacity. 25% deposit . . . balance due on or before 12/10/89." Lambert received the order form in late July, but apparently thought that it overstated the quantity of trees needed for the next season. Writing on the same order form submitted by the Kysars, he changed the notation "4 loads of 650 trees each," to read "3 loads of 550 trees," and changed the total number ordered from "2600" to "1650." Lambert also recomputed the total amount due and the amount of the required 25 percent deposit. He inserted the new figures over Joan Kysar's handwritten figures at the bottom of the form and returned the form to the Kysars. He made no change

to the $11.60 unit price or to any other contract provisions. On November 25, 29, and December 1, in accordance with the instructions on the altered order form, the Kysars sent Lambert the requested 1,650 trees, in three loads, by overland truck. After delivery of the trees, Lambert's inspection allegedly revealed that the trees "were dry, not fresh, and appeared old." The Kysars then sued Lambert in Clark County, Washington, seeking payment for the trees. A dispute arose between the parties about whether the term on the order form stating that lawsuits would be brought in Clark County, Washington, was part of the parties' contract. Was it?

5. On February 21, 1990, Barto went to Estate Motors, Ltd., to buy a new Mercedes-Benz 500SL. Barto was told that because of limited production in Germany and great demand for that model, it would be at least 18 months before a new 500SL could be delivered to him. The salesperson told Barto that Estate Motors would order the car for him if Barto would pay a $500 deposit with the order. Barto agreed and paid Estate Motors $500 with his personal check. Barto and the salesperson then executed a "Retail Buyer's Order" form. The form stated the model, body type, color, and upholstery specifications for the car. No price was specified on the form and neither the dealer nor the salesperson signed in the space provided to indicate the dealer's approval of the order. It stated at the bottom "THIS ORDER IS NOT A BINDING CONTRACT." The reverse side of the form contained 10 additional terms and conditions, including payment in cash or cashier's check upon delivery. On February 22, the day after this form was executed, Estate Motors placed an order with the manufacturer for a new 500SL with the specifications requested by Barto. On February 23, Estate Motors cashed Barto's $500 check. Nine months later, Congress amended the Internal Revenue Code to include a "luxury tax" on purchases of certain passenger vehicles, boats, and aircraft. The statute contained a "pre-existing binding contract" exception that stated that the new tax would not be imposed on sales made after December 31, 1990, if there was a binding contract for the purchase of a covered luxury item in existence as of September 30, 1990. In mid-August of 1991, nearly 18 months after Barto's payment of the $500 deposit and the execution of the order, Estate Motors notified Barto that his Mercedes would be ready for him to pick up on August 30. It also told him for the first time that he would have to pay the luxury tax on his new car ($6,995.00) when he came to pick it up. Barto believed that his car fell within the "pre-existing binding contract" exception to the luxury tax statute because his order for the car had been placed before September 30, 1990. Barto paid for the car and paid the tax, but claimed a refund from the U.S. government on the ground that he had a "binding contract" for the Mercedes-Benz in February of 1990, when the order was placed. The government, however, argued that no contract existed until August 30, 1991, when Barto paid his full purchase price and received his new car. Is Barto right?

6. On January 16, 1987, Koop, an employee of Professional Search, Inc., called Renner, the director of systems software for Northwest Airlines, to inquire about possible job openings in Renner's department. Koop explained to Renner that if Northwest Airlines hired a candidate recommended by Professional Search, Professional Search would be entitled to charge Northwest Airlines 30 percent of the candidate's starting salary. Renner told Koop that a systems analyst position was open and described the job. Renner also stated that Northwest Airlines was not currently interviewing for that position and that Koop should direct further inquiries to Northwest Airlines's human resources department. Later, Koop and Wawrzyniak discussed Wawrzyniak's desire to be placed as a systems analyst and Wawrzyniak signed a placement contract. On January 20, 1987, Koop sent Wawrzyniak's résumé to Renner. He later called Renner, who told him the résumé "looked good." On February 19, Wawrzyniak filled out an application for a systems position with Northwest Airlines, claiming he heard of the opening through a friend. On April 13, Northwest Airlines hired Wawrzyniak. Professional Search claimed that a placement contract had been formed between it and Northwest Airlines, and sought to recover its $12,000 commission. Will Professional Search prevail?

7. In 1986, Mercy Memorial Hospital decided to open an outpatient family practice clinic in Petersburg. It retained a recruiter to identify a private family practitioner. The recruiter brought the hospital and Dr. Kamalnath together. In June 1986, Iacoangeli, the hospital's director of planning and development, wrote Dr. Kamalnath a letter in which he made an offer to her that proposed terms regarding salary, office rental, line of credit for professional and operational expenses, home relocation, and other matters. Dr. Kamalnath did not accept this written offer. Instead, she suggested various changes and additions, principally an increase in the term of employment to three years and a provision that the hospital handle marketing. On June 30, Iacoangeli sent Dr. Kamalnath a second letter incorporating the longer period of employment, subject to annual performance reviews, and proposing other terms. Iacoangeli also prepared several drafts of a proposed contract, but none of these proved satisfactory to Dr. Kamalnath. Dr. Kamalnath nevertheless moved to Petersburg and began work, although she had no signed contract, the parties still differed as to some contractual duties such as the responsibility for certain major expenses, and the clinic was not yet complete. The Petersburg clinic was not as successful as the parties had hoped. Relations between them deteriorated, and the hospital notified Dr. Kamalnath to vacate the clinic in November 1987. Was there a contract between the hospital and Dr. Kamalnath?

8. On March 30, Cushing, a member of an anti-nuclear protest group, applied to the New Hampshire adjutant general's office for permission to hold a dance in the Portsmouth armory. On March 31, the adjutant general mailed a signed contract offer agreeing to rent the armory to the group. The agreement required Cushing to accept by signing a copy of the agreement and returning it to the adjutant general within five days after its receipt. On April 3, Cushing received the offer and signed it. At 6:30 P.M. on April 4, Cushing received a call from the adjutant general attempting to revoke the offer. Cushing told the adjutant general that he had signed the contract and placed it in the office outbox on April 3, customary office practice being to collect all mail from outboxes at the end of the day and deposit it in the U.S. Mail. On April 6, the adjutant general's office received the signed contract in the mail, dated April 3 and postmarked April 5. Assuming Cushing was telling the truth, did the parties have a contract?

9. Reddick bought a life insurance policy on her son from Globe Life Insurance effective December 1, 1987, to December 1, 1988. The policy provided a 31-day grace period after the due date for the payment of a premium, during which time the policy remained in effect. If the payment was not made by the end of the grace period, the policy lapsed. When Reddick did not pay the premium due December 1, 1988, the coverage lapsed. On January 5, 1989, Globe sent Reddick a letter offering to continue the policy if they received her premium by January 20, 1989. Reddick's son died on January 17; on January 20, Reddick called Globe and notified it of his death. They told her the policy had lapsed. She then sent them the premium, which they did not receive until after the 20th. Was Reddick's mailing of the premium on the 20th an effective acceptance?

10. Soldau was fired by Organon, Inc. He received a letter from Organon offering to pay him double the normal severance pay if he would sign a release giving up all claims against the company. The letter incorporated the proposed release, which Soldau signed, dated, and deposited in a mailbox outside a post office. When he returned home, Soldau found that he had received a check from Organon in the amount of the increased severance pay. He returned to the post office and persuaded a postal employee to open the mailbox and retrieve the release. Soldau cashed Organon's check and subsequently filed an age discrimination suit against Organon. Was Soldau bound by the release?

Consideration

One of the things that separates a contract from an unenforceable social promise is that a contract requires voluntary agreement by two or more parties. Not all agreements, however, are enforceable contracts. At a fairly early point in the development of classical contract law, the common law courts decided not to enforce gratuitous (free) promises. Instead, only promises supported by consideration were enforceable in a court of law. This was consistent with the notion that the purpose of contract law was to enforce freely made bargains. As one 19th-century work on contracts put it: "The common law . . . gives effect only to contracts that are founded on the mutual exigencies of men, and does not compel the performance of any merely gratuitous agreements."[1] The concept of consideration distinguishes agreements that the law will enforce from gratuitous promises, which are normally unenforceable. This chapter focuses on the concept of consideration. ∞

THE IDEA OF CONSIDERATION

A common definition of **consideration** is *legal value, bargained for and given in exchange for an act or a promise.* Thus, a promise generally cannot be enforced against the person who made it (the *promisor*) unless the person to whom the promise was made (the *promisee*) has given up something of legal value in exchange for the promise. In effect, the requirement of consideration means that a promisee must pay the price that the promisor asked to gain the right to enforce the promisor's promise. So,

---

[1]T. Metcalf, *Principles of the Law of Contracts* (1874), p. 161.

FIGURE I

The Elements of Consideration

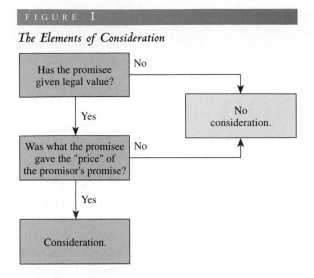

if the promisor did not ask for anything in exchange for making her promise or if what the promisor asked for did not have legal value (e.g., because it was something to which she was already entitled), her promise is not enforceable against her because it is not supported by consideration. Figure 1 illustrates the elements of consideration.

Consider the early case of *Thorne v. Deas,* in which the part owner of a sailing ship named the *Sea Nymph* promised his co-owners that he would insure the ship for an upcoming voyage.[2] He failed to do so, and when the ship was lost at sea, the court found that he was not liable to his co-owners for breaching his promise to insure the ship. Why? Because his promise was purely gratuitous; he had neither asked for nor received anything in exchange for making it. Therefore, it was unenforceable because it was not supported by consideration.

This early example illustrates two important aspects of the consideration requirement. First, the requirement *tended to limit the scope of a promisor's liability for his promises* by insulating him from liability for gratuitous promises and by protecting him against liability for reliance on such promises. Second, the mechanical application of the requirement *often produced unfair results.* This potential for unfairness has produced considerable dissatisfaction with the consideration concept. As the rest of this chapter indicates, the relative importance of consideration in modern contract law has been somewhat eroded by numerous exceptions to

the consideration requirement and by judicial applications of consideration principles designed to produce fair results.

LEGAL VALUE

Consideration can be an act in the case of a unilateral contract or a promise in the case of a bilateral contract. An act or a promise can have legal value in one of two ways. If, in exchange for the promisor's promise, the promisee does, or agrees to do, something he had no prior legal duty to do, that provides legal value. If, in exchange for the promisor's promise, the promisee refrains from doing, or agrees not to do, something she has a legal right to do, that also provides legal value. Note that this definition does not require that an act or a promise have monetary (economic) value to amount to consideration. Thus, in a famous 19th-century case, *Hamer v. Sidway,*[3] an uncle's promise to pay his nephew $5,000 if he refrained from using tobacco, drinking, swearing, and playing cards or billiards for money until his 21st birthday was held to be supported by consideration. Indeed, the nephew had refrained from doing any of these acts, even though he may have benefited from so refraining. He had a legal right to indulge in such activities, yet he had refrained from doing so at his uncle's request and in exchange for his uncle's promise. This was all that was required for consideration.

Adequacy of Consideration

The point that the legal value requirement is not concerned with actual value is further borne out by the fact that the courts generally will not concern themselves with questions regarding the adequacy of the consideration that the promisee gave. This means that as long as the promisee's act or promise satisfies the legal value test, the courts do not ask whether that act or promise was worth what the promisor gave, or promised to give, in return for it. You will see an example of the application of this rule in the following *Brads* case. This rule on adequacy of consideration reflects the laissez-faire assumptions underlying classical contract law. Freedom of contract includes the freedom to make bad bargains as well as good ones, so promisors' prom-

---

[2]4 Johns. 84 (N.Y. 1809).

[3]27 N.E. 256 (N.Y. Ct. App. 1891).

ises are enforceable if they got what they asked for in exchange for making their promises, even if what they asked for was not nearly so valuable in worldly terms as what they promised in return. Also, a court taking a hands-off stance concerning private contracts would be reluctant to step in and second-guess the parties by setting aside a transaction that both parties at one time considered satisfactory. Finally, the rule against considering the adequacy of consideration can promote certainty and predictability in commercial transactions by denying legal effect to what would otherwise be a possible basis for challenging the enforceability of a contract—the inequality of the exchange.

Several qualifications must be made concerning the general rule on adequacy of consideration. First, if the inadequacy of consideration is apparent on the face of the agreement, most courts conclude that the agreement was a disguised gift rather than an enforceable bargain. Thus, an agreement calling for an unequal exchange of money (e.g., $500 for $1,000) or identical goods (20 business law textbooks for 40 identical business law textbooks) and containing no other terms would probably be unenforceable. Gross inadequacy of consideration may also give rise to an

inference of fraud, duress,[4] lack of capacity,[5] unconscionability,[6] or some other independent basis for setting aside a contract. However, inadequacy of consideration, standing alone, is never sufficient to prove lack of true consent or contractual capacity. Although gross inadequacy of consideration is not, by itself, ordinarily a sufficient reason to set aside a contract, the courts may refuse to grant specific performance or other equitable remedies to persons seeking to enforce unfair bargains.

Finally, some agreements recite "$1," or "$1 and other valuable consideration," or some other small amount as consideration for a promise. If no other consideration is actually exchanged, this is called *nominal consideration*. Often, such agreements are attempts to make gratuitous promises look like true bargains by reciting a nonexistent consideration. Most courts refuse to enforce such agreements unless they find that the stated consideration was truly bargained for.

---

[4]Fraud and duress are discussed in Chapter 13.
[5]Lack of capacity is discussed in Chapter 14.
[6]Chapter 15 discusses unconscionability in detail.

BRADS v. FIRST BAPTIST CHURCH OF GERMANTOWN   624N.E.2d 737 (Ohio Ct. App. 1993)

Marvin Brads became pastor of the First Baptist Church of Germantown, Ohio, in January 1958. In June 1971, Brads had a heart attack. While he was recuperating, an officer of the church told Brads that the church had voted to pay his full salary for the remainder of his lifetime. That promise was unperformed because Brads later recovered and returned to work. In April 1980, Brads again had heart problems. On the advice of his doctor, Brads approached the deacons of the church about retirement. Brads proposed that his salary be reduced after retirement through a series of gradual step-downs to an amount approximately one-third of the salary he was then receiving. Brads's proposal was accepted by the deacons. Under the terms of the agreement, the church placed Brads on disability retirement status, conferred an honorary title on him, gave him office space in the church, and allotted him retirement benefits according to the agreed step-down schedule. Brads was required to aid, assist, and advise whomever the church called as a new pastor, to the extent Brads's health would allow. Brads and the church deacons jointly recommended to the congregation that it adopt the agreement, which the congregation did, unanimously. Brads then left his position as pastor and his benefits commenced.

In 1985, the congregation was advised by a church officer that the benefits paid to Brads under the 1980 agreement should continue for Brads's lifetime. The congregation once again unanimously approved and reaffirmed the agreement. Brads received his benefits from 1980 through early July 1990, when he was notified by church officials that he had been dismissed from the membership of the church and that no more payments would be made to him. Other benefits, such as free office space, were also discontinued.

Brads sued the church, claiming that it had breached its contract to pay Brads's retirement benefits for life. At trial, the jury returned a verdict in favor of Brads. The church appealed, contending that there was no consideration to support the promise to pay retirement benefits for life. ∞

Grady, Presiding Judge Consideration is, of course, an element necessary for a binding contract and a complete lack of any consideration is a valid defense to a breach of contract action. Consideration may consist of either a detriment to the promisee or a benefit to the promisor. A benefit may consist of some right, interest, or profit accruing to the promisor, while a detriment may consist of some forbearance, loss, or responsibility given, suffered, or undertaken by the promisee. Absent a showing of fraud, consideration is not deemed legally insufficient merely because it is inadequate.

The evidence demonstrates that in 1980 Brads proposed a gradual reduction in the salary he was being paid to a final amount representing approximately one-third of that salary. According to the evidence presented by Brads, all parties knew and understood this final step-down amount would be paid to Brads for life. Brads was obligated to aid whomever the Church called as a new pastor. The parties jointly prepared an agreement in writing, which was adopted by the congregation in 1980 and readopted in 1985. Over the course of the next 10 years, Brads preached occasionally at First Baptist Church, taught Sunday school classes there, served on the budget committee and helped with administrative matters.

The foregoing evidence demonstrates that the Church received a benefit in the form of Brads's promise to assist a new pastor and that Brads received the benefits of payments, office space and title. Each party performed on these promises to confer an actual benefit on the other. Those benefits were the product of the agreement and subsequent to it. We conclude that there is some competent evidence to demonstrate the existence of consideration by Brads.

Affirmed in favor of Brads.

Illusory Promises: Not Legal Value

For a promise to serve as consideration in a bilateral contract, the promisee must have promised to do, or to refrain from doing, something at the promisor's request. It seems obvious, therefore, that if the promisee's promise is illusory because it really does not bind the promisee to do or refrain from doing anything, such a promise could not serve as consideration. Such agreements are often said to lack the mutuality of obligation required for an agreement to be enforceable. So, a promisee's promise to buy "all the sugar that I want" or to "paint your house if I feel like it" would not be sufficient consideration for a promisor's return promise to sell sugar or hire a painter. In neither case has the promisee given the promisor anything of legal value in exchange for the promisor's promise. Remember, though: So long as the promisee has given legal value, the agreement will be enforceable even though what the promisee gave is worth substantially less than what the promisor promised in return.

Effect of Cancellation or Termination Clauses
The fact that an agreement allows one or both of the parties to cancel or terminate their contractual obligations does not necessarily mean that the party (or parties) with the power to cancel has given an illusory promise. Such provisions are a common and necessary part of many business relationships. The central issue in such cases concerns whether a promise subject to cancellation or termination actually represents a binding obligation. A right to cancel or terminate at any time, for any reason, and without any notice would clearly render illusory any other promise by the party possessing such a right. However, limits on the circumstances under which cancellation may occur (such as a dealer's failure to live up to dealership obligations), or the time in which cancellation may occur (such as no cancellations for the first 90 days), or a requirement of advance notice of cancellation (such as a 30-day notice requirement) would all effectively remove a promise from the illusory category. This is so because in each case the party making such a promise has bound himself to do *something* in exchange for the other party's promise. A party's duty of good faith and fair dealing can also limit the right to terminate and prevent its promise from being considered illusory.

Effect of Output and Requirements Contracts
Contracts in which one party to the agreement agrees to buy all of the other party's production of a particular commodity (*output* contracts) or to supply all of another party's needs for a particular commodity (*requirements* contracts) are common busi-

ness transactions that serve legitimate business purposes. They can reduce a seller's selling costs and provide buyers with a secure source of supply. Prior to the enactment of the UCC, however, many common law courts used to refuse to enforce such agreements on the ground that their failure to specify the quantity of goods to be produced or purchased rendered them illusory. The courts also feared that a party to such an agreement might be tempted to exploit the other party. For example, subsequent market conditions could make it profitable for the seller in an output contract or the buyer in a requirements contract to demand that the other party buy or provide more of the particular commodity than the other party had actually intended to buy or sell. The Code legitimizes requirements and output contracts. It addresses the concern about the potential for exploitation by limiting a party's demands to those quantity needs that occur in *good faith* and are not unreasonably disproportionate to any quantity estimate contained in the contract, or to any normal prior output or requirements if no estimate is stated [2–306(1)]. Chapter 19, Formation and Terms of Sales Contracts, discusses this subject in greater detail.

Effect of Exclusive Dealing Contracts   When a manufacturer of goods enters an agreement giving a distributor the exclusive right to sell the manufacturer's products in a particular territory, does such an agreement impose sufficient obligations on both parties to meet the legal value test? Put another way, does the distributor have any duty to sell the manufacturer's products and does the manufacturer have any duty to supply any particular number of products? Such agreements are commonly encountered in today's business world, and they can serve the legitimate interests of both parties. The Code recognizes this fact by providing that, unless the parties agree to the contrary, an exclusive dealing contract imposes a duty on the distributor to use her best efforts to sell the goods and imposes a reciprocal duty on the manufacturer to use his best efforts to supply the goods [2–306(2)].

Preexisting Duties

The legal value component of our consideration definition requires that promisees do, or promise to do, something in exchange for a promisor's promise that they had no prior legal duty to do. Thus, as a general rule, performing or agreeing to perform a preexisting duty is not consideration. This seems fair because the promisor in such a case has effectively made a gratuitous promise, since she was already entitled to the promisee's performance.

Preexisting Public Duties   Every member of society has a duty to obey the law and refrain from committing crimes or torts. Therefore, a promisee's promise not to commit such an act can never be consideration. So, Thomas's promise to pay Brown $100 a year in exchange for Brown's promise not to burn Thomas's barn would not be enforceable against Thomas. Since Brown has a preexisting duty not to burn Thomas's barn, his promise lacks legal value.

Similarly, public officials, by virtue of their offices, have a preexisting legal duty to perform their public responsibilities. For example, Smith, the owner of a liquor store, promises to pay Fawcett, a police officer whose beat includes Smith's store, $50 a week to keep an eye on the store while walking her beat. Smith's promise is unenforceable because Fawcett has agreed to do something that she already has a duty to do.

Modifications of Contracts and Preexisting Contractual Duties   The most important preexisting duty cases are those involving preexisting *contractual* duties. These cases generally occur when the parties to an existing contract agree to *modify* that contract. As the *Rinck* case (which follows shortly) indicates, the general common law rule on contract modifications holds that an agreement to modify an existing contract requires *some new consideration* to be binding.

For example, Turner enters into a contract with Acme Construction Company for the construction of a new office building for $350,000. When the construction is partially completed, Acme tells Turner that due to rising labor and materials costs it will stop construction unless Turner agrees to pay an extra $50,000. Turner, having already entered into contracts to lease office space in the new building, promises to pay the extra amount. When the construction is finished, Turner refuses to pay more than $350,000. Is Turner's promise to pay the extra $50,000 enforceable against him? No. All Acme has done in exchange for Turner's promise to pay more is build the building, something that Acme had a preexisting contractual duty to do. Therefore, Acme's performance is not consideration for Turner's promise to pay more.

Although the result in the preceding example seems fair (why should Turner have to pay $400,000 for something he had a right to receive for $350,000?) and is consistent with consideration theory, the application of the preexisting duty rule to contract modifications has generated a great deal of criticism. Plainly, the rule can protect a party to a contract such as Turner from being pressured into paying more because the other party to the contract is trying to take advantage of his situation by demanding an additional amount for performance. However, mechanical application of the rule could also produce unfair results when the parties have freely agreed to a fair modification of their contract. Some critics argue that the purpose of contract modification law should be to enforce freely made modifications of existing contracts and to deny enforcement to coerced modifications. Such critics commonly suggest that general principles such as good faith and unconscionability, rather than technical consideration rules, should be used to police contract modifications.

Other observers argue that most courts in fact apply the preexisting duty rule in a manner calculated to reach fair results, because several exceptions to the rule can be used to enforce a fair modification agreement. For example, any new consideration furnished by the promisee provides sufficient consideration to support a promise to modify an existing contract. So, if Acme had promised to finish construction a week before the completion date called for in the original contract, or had promised to make some change in the original

contract specifications such as to install a better grade of carpet, Acme would have done something that it had no legal duty to do in exchange for Turner's new promise. Turner's promise to pay more would then be enforceable because it would be supported by new consideration.

Many courts also enforce an agreement to modify an existing contract if the modification resulted from *unforeseen circumstances* that a party could not reasonably be expected to have foreseen, and which made that party's performance far more difficult than the parties originally anticipated. For example, if Acme had requested the extra payment because abnormal subsurface rock formations made excavation on the construction site far more costly and time-consuming than could have been reasonably expected, many courts would enforce Turner's promise to pay more.

Courts can also enforce fair modification agreements by holding that the parties mutually agreed to terminate their original contract and then entered a new one. Because contracts are created by the will of the parties, they can be terminated in the same fashion. Each party agrees to release the other party from his contractual obligations in exchange for the other party's promise to do the same. Because such a mutual agreement terminates all duties owed under the original agreement, any subsequent agreement by the parties would not be subject to the preexisting duty rule. A court is likely to take this approach, however, only when it is convinced that the modification agreement was fair and free from coercion.

RINCK v. ASSOCIATION OF RESERVE CITY BANKERS   676 A.2d 12 (D.C. Ct. App. 1996)

The Association of Bank Holding Companies (ABHC) hired Sandra Rinck to be its administrative vice president in 1988. In January 1993, ABHC agreed to merge with Association of Reserve City Bankers (ACRB). The parties to the merger agreed that ACRB would be the surviving partner of the merger. The merger agreement also established that Anthony Cluff would become the executive director of the merged corporations. Thomas Ashley, then president of ABHC, would no longer serve the surviving corporation. At least two newspaper articles discussed the merger, and both included comments attributed to Cluff indicating that, aside from the departure of Ashley, no staff cuts were expected.

Cluff and Rinck met to discuss administrative and staffing issues in February 1993. During the meeting, Rinck referred to the newspaper articles and asked whether they were accurate in stating that there would be no terminations other than Ashley's in connection with the merger. Cluff responded that the articles were accurate and that neither she nor any other staff member would be terminated as a result of the merger. While Cluff did not specifically describe Rinck's new position or responsibilities with the surviving corporation, he *led her to believe that her salary and benefits would not be reduced. As a result of this conversation, Rinck did not seek alternative employment and assisted in the accomplishment of the merger.*

In May 1993, the acting president of ABHC, Rippey, informed Rinck that her employment was being terminated effective immediately. The reason he gave for her termination was that there would be no room for her in the merged organization. No other employees were terminated, nor were their salaries or benefits reduced, as a result of the merger. There is evidence that Cluff was responsible for the decision to terminate Rinck. Rinck filed a complaint against ACRB, alleging breach of contract. The trial court granted a summary judgment to ACRB, and Rinck appealed. ∞

Belson, Senior Judge   Rinck contends that her termination amounted to a breach of her employment contract. This court has held:

[t]here is a presumption that a hiring not accompanied by an expression of a specific term of duration creates an employment relationship terminable at will by either party at any time. This presumption can be rebutted by evidence that the parties intended the employment to be for a fixed period, or subject to specific preconditions before termination.

Rinck admitted that Cluff did not mention a specific job title, duties, responsibilities, term, benefits, or wages. However, she avers that Cluff did promise her that she would not be terminated, and that her salary and benefits would not be reduced. We conclude that a statement that an employee will not be terminated for a specific stated reason is analogous to the establishment of preconditions for termination. Cluff's alleged statement that Rinck would not be terminated as a result of the merger was sufficiently clear and unambiguous.

Generally, consideration is necessary to make a promise enforceable. According to the *Restatement of Contracts*:

(1)   To constitute consideration, a performance or a return promise must be bargained for.

(2)   A performance or return promise is bargained for if it is sought by the promisor in exchange for his promise and is given by the promisee in exchange for that promise.

Restatement (Second) of Contracts section 71 (1981).

More than one promise can usually be supported by a single consideration.

Therefore, if a promise of job security is made at the time the parties first enter into the employment contract, the consideration of the employee's services is undoubtedly sufficient to support the various obligations the employer undertakes, including the job security provision.

It is a different situation, however, when an additional promise is made after contractual duties have been undertaken. In general:

[t]he parties to a contract are free to modify that contract by mutual consent. In order to be valid, however, the modification must possess the same elements of consideration as necessary for normal contract formation. *Herson v. Hellman Co.*

The case before us presents the issue of whether additional consideration beyond the continuation of services is required when a promise of job security is made *after* the commencement of employment.

We hold that additional consideration beyond continued employment per se is required to make such a promise enforceable. We are not disposed to encroach on this jurisdiction's long-established presumption of at-will employment. That conclusion, however, does not resolve this case. We must deal with its particular circumstances. The context in which Cluff made the alleged promise of job security to Rinck is significant—a merger was being worked out. Typically mergers involve the consolidation of operations and they often require staff reductions. Rinck was justifiably concerned about her future with the surviving association, especially because she had worked directly for the head of the association that would not survive, and that person would not remain with the merged association. Therefore, Rinck might understandably have inquired about her job security.

Under the circumstance, a finder of fact could reasonably conclude that Rinck gave the associations the benefit of her continued services and her assistance in bringing about the merger because of Cluff's promise, and that she would not have conferred that benefit if he had not made the promise. A finder of fact could also infer that Cluff, in making the promise, sought to have Rinck remain on at that time. Therefore, even though Rinck's merely staying in her job would not normally, in the absence of such a circumstance, amount to consideration that would make binding an employer's statement concerning termination policy, if the jury should find that Cluff in fact made a promise of the nature alleged and that it was because of that promise that Rinck decided to forgo seeking out other employ- ment but instead to remain with the merging associations, her performance would constitute sufficient consideration to create a binding unilateral contract.

Reversed and remanded for further proceedings in favor of Rinck.

Preexisting Duty and Contract Modification under the UCC   The drafters of the Code sought to avoid many of the problems caused by the consideration requirement by dispensing with it in two important situations: As discussed in Chapter 10, The Agreement: Offer, the Code does not require consideration for firm offers [2–205]. The Code also provides that an agreement to modify a contract for the sale of goods needs *no consideration* to be binding [2–209(1)]. For example, Electronics World orders 200 XYZ televisions at $150 per unit from XYZ Corp. Electronics World later seeks to cancel its order, but XYZ refuses to agree to cancellation. Instead, XYZ seeks to mollify a valued customer by offering to reduce the price to $100 per unit. Electronics World agrees, but when the televisions arrive, XYZ bills Electronics World for $150 per unit. Under classical contract principles, XYZ's promise to reduce the price of the goods would not be enforceable because Electronics World has furnished no new consideration in exchange for XYZ's promise. Under the Code, no new consideration is necessary and the agreement to modify the contract is enforceable.

Several things should be made clear about the operation of this Code rule. First, XYZ had no duty to agree to a modification and could have insisted on payment of $150 per unit. Second, as the following *Roth Steel Products* case illustrates, modification agreements under the Code are still subject to scrutiny under the general Code principles of good faith and unconscionability, so unfair agreements or agreements that are the product of coercion are unlikely to be enforced. Finally, the Code contains two provisions to protect people from fictitious claims that an agreement has been modified. If the original agreement requires any modification to be in writing, an oral modification is unenforceable [2–209(2)]. Regardless of what the original agreement says, if the price of the goods in the modified contract is $500 or more, the modification is unenforceable unless the requirements of the Code's statute of frauds section [2–201] are satisfied [2–209(3)].[7]

---

[7]Chapter 16 discusses § 2–201 of the Code in detail.

ROTH STEEL PRODUCTS v. SHARON STEEL CORPORATION   705 F.2d 134 (6th Cir. 1983)

I n November 1972, when conditions in the steel industry were highly competitive and the industry was operating at about 70 percent of its capacity, Sharon Steel Corporation agreed to sell Roth Steel Products several types of steel at prices well below Sharon's published book prices for such steel. These prices were to be effective from January 1 until December 31, 1973.

   In early 1973, however, several factors changed the market for steel. Federal price controls simultaneously discouraged foreign steel imports and encouraged domestic steel producers to export a substantial portion of their production to avoid domestic price controls, sharply reducing the domestic steel supply. In addition, the steel industry experienced substantial increases in labor, raw material, and energy costs, compelling steel producers to increase prices. The increased domestic demand for steel and the attractive export market caused the entire industry to operate at full capacity; as a consequence, nearly every domestic steel producer experienced substantial delays in delivery.

   On March 23, 1973, Sharon notified Roth that it was discontinuing all price discounts. Roth protested, and Sharon agreed to continue to sell at the discount price until June 30, 1973, but refused to sell thereafter unless

Roth agreed to pay a modified price that was higher than that agreed to the previous November but still lower than the book prices Sharon was charging other customers. Because Roth was unable to purchase enough steel elsewhere to meet its production requirements, it agreed to pay the increased prices. When a subsequent dispute arose between the parties over late deliveries and unfilled orders by Sharon in 1974, Roth filed a breach of contract suit against Sharon, arguing, among other things, that the 1973 modification agreement was unenforceable. When the trial court ruled in favor of Roth, Sharon appealed. ⚭

Celebrezze, Senior Circuit Judge   The ability of a party to modify a contract which is subject to Article 2 of the UCC is broader than common law, primarily because the modification needs no consideration to be binding. [UCC Sec. 2–209(1)]. A party's ability to modify an agreement is limited only by Article 2's general obligation of good faith. In determining whether a particular modification was obtained in good faith, a court must make two distinct inquiries: whether the party's conduct is consistent with "reasonable commercial standards of fair dealing in the trade," and whether the parties were in fact motivated to seek modification by an honest desire to compensate for commercial exigencies.

The first inquiry is relatively straightforward; the party asserting the modification must demonstrate that his decision to seek modification was the result of a factor, such as increased costs, which would cause an ordinary merchant to seek a modification of the contract. The second inquiry, regarding the subjective honesty of the parties, is less clearly defined. Essentially, this requires the party asserting the modification to demonstrate that he was, in fact, motivated by a legitimate commercial reason and that such a reason is not offered merely as a pretext. Moreover, the trier of fact must determine whether the means used to obtain the modification are an impermissible attempt to obtain a modification by extortion or overreaching.

The single most important consideration in determining whether the decision to seek a modification is justified is whether, because of changes in the market or other unforeseeable conditions, performance of the contract has come to involve a loss. In this case, the district court found that Sharon suffered substantial losses by performing the contract as modified. We are convinced that unforeseen economic exigencies existed which would prompt an ordinary merchant to seek a modification to avoid a loss on the contract.

The second part of the analysis, honesty in fact, is pivotal. The district court found that Sharon "threatened not to sell Roth any steel if Roth refused to pay increased prices after July 1, 1973" and, consequently, that Sharon acted wrongfully. We believe that the district court's conclusion that Sharon acted in bad faith by using coercive conduct to extract the price modification is not clearly erroneous. Therefore, we hold that Sharon's attempt to modify the November 1972 contract, in order to compensate for increased costs which made performance come to involve a loss, is ineffective because Sharon did not act in a manner consistent with Article 2's requirement of honesty in fact when it refused to perform its remaining obligations under the contract at 1972 prices.

Judgment affirmed in favor of Roth.

Preexisting Duty and Agreements to Settle Debts

One special variant of the preexisting duty rule that causes considerable confusion occurs when a debtor offers to pay a creditor a sum less than the creditor is demanding in exchange for the creditor's promise to accept the part payment as full payment of the debt. If the creditor later sues for the balance of the debt, is the creditor's promise to take less enforceable? The answer depends on the nature of the debt and on the circumstances of the debtor's payment.

Liquidated Debts   A **liquidated debt** is a debt that is both due and certain; that is, the parties have no good faith dispute about either the existence or the amount of the original debt. If a debtor does nothing more than pay less than an amount he clearly owes, how could this be consideration for a creditor's promise to take less? Such a debtor has actually done less than he had a preexisting legal duty to do—namely, to pay the full amount of the debt. For this reason, the creditor's promise to discharge a liquidated debt for part payment of the debt at or after its due date is *unenforceable* for lack of consideration.

For example, Connor borrows $10,000 from Friendly Finance Company, payable in one year. On the day payment is due, Connor sends Friendly a check for $9,000 marked: "Payment in full for all claims Friendly Finance has against me." Friendly cashes Connor's check, thus impliedly promising to accept it as full payment by cashing it, and later sues Connor for $1,000. Friendly is entitled to the $1,000 because Connor has given no consideration to support Friendly's implied promise to accept $9,000 as full payment.

However, had Connor done something he had no preexisting duty to do in exchange for Friendly's promise to settle for part payment, he could enforce Friendly's promise and avoid paying the $1,000. For example, if Connor had paid early, before the loan contract called for payment, or in a different medium of exchange than that called for in the loan contract (such as $4,000 in cash and a car worth $5,000), he would have given consideration for Friendly's promise to accept early or different payment as full payment.

Unliquidated Debts A good faith dispute about either the existence or the amount of a debt makes the debt an **unliquidated debt.** The settlement of an unliquidated debt is called an **accord and satisfaction.**[8] When an accord and satisfaction has occurred, the creditor cannot maintain an action to recover the remainder of the debt that he alleges is due. For example, Computer Corner, a retailer, orders 50 personal computers and associated software packages from Computech for $75,000. After receiving the goods, Computer Corner refuses to pay Computech the full $75,000, arguing that some of the computers were defective and that some of the software it received did not conform to its order. Computer Corner sends Computech a check for $60,000 marked: "Payment in full for all goods received from Computech." A creditor in Computech's position obviously faces a real dilemma. If Computech cashes Computer Corner's check, it will be held to have impliedly promised to accept $60,000 as full payment. Computech's promise to accept part payment as full payment would be enforceable because Computer Corner has given

consideration to support it: Computer Corner has given up its right to have a court determine the amount it owes Computech. This is something that Computer Corner had no duty to do; by giving up this right and the $60,000 in exchange for Computech's implied promise, the consideration requirement is satisfied. The result in this case is supported not only by consideration theory but also by a strong public policy in favor of encouraging parties to settle their disputes out of court. Who would bother to settle disputed claims out of court if settlement agreements were unenforceable?

Computech could refuse to accept Computer Corner's settlement offer and sue for the full $75,000, but doing so involves several risks. A court may decide that Computer Corner's arguments are valid and award Computech less than $60,000. Even if Computech is successful, it may take years to resolve the case in the courts through the expensive and time-consuming litigation process. In addition, there is always the chance that Computer Corner may file for bankruptcy before any judgment can be collected. Faced with such risks, Computech may feel that it has no practical alternative other than to cash Computer Corner's check.[9]

Composition Agreements Composition agreements are agreements between a debtor and two or more creditors who agree to accept as full payment a stated percentage of their liquidated claims against the debtor at or after the date on which those claims are payable. Composition agreements are generally enforced by the courts despite the fact that enforcement appears to be contrary to the general rule on part payment of liquidated debts. Many courts have justified enforcing composition agreements on the ground that the creditors' mutual agreement to accept less than the amount due them provides the necessary consideration. The main reason why creditors agree to compositions is that they fear that their failure to do so may force the debtor into bankruptcy proceedings, in which case they might ultimately recover a smaller percentage of their claims than that agreed to in the composition.

---

[8]Accord and satisfaction is also discussed in Chapter 18.

[9]A new provision of Article 3 of the Uniform Commercial Code, section 3–311, covers accord and satisfaction by use of an instrument such as a "full payment" check. With a few exceptions, the basic provisions of section 3–311 parallel the common law rules regarding accord and satisfaction that are described in this chapter and Chapter 18.

Forbearance to Sue

An agreement by a promisee to refrain, or forbear, from pursuing a legal claim against a promisor can be valid consideration to support a return promise—usually to pay a sum of money—by a promisor. The promisee has agreed not to file suit, something that she has a legal right to do, in exchange for the promisor's promise. The courts do not wish to sanction extortion by allowing people to threaten to file spurious claims against others in the hope that those threatened will agree to some payment to avoid the expense or embarrassment associated with defending a lawsuit. On the other hand, we have a strong public policy favoring private settlement of disputes. Therefore, it is generally said that the promisee must have a good faith belief in the validity of his or her claim before forbearance amounts to consideration.

BARGAINED–FOR EXCHANGE

Up to this point, we have focused on the legal value component of our consideration definition. But the fact that a promisee's act or promise provides legal value is not, in itself, a sufficient basis for finding that it amounted to consideration. In addition, the promisee's act or promise must have been bargained for and given in exchange for the promisor's promise. In effect, it must be the price that the promisor asked for in exchange for making his promise. Over a hundred years ago, Oliver Wendell Holmes, one of our most renowned jurists, expressed this idea when he said, "It is the essence of a consideration that, by the terms of the agreement, it is given and accepted as the motive or inducement of the promise."[10]

Past Consideration

Past consideration—despite its name—is not consideration at all. Past consideration is an act or other benefit given in the past that was *not* given in exchange for the promise in question. Because the past act was not given in exchange for the present promise, it cannot be consideration. Consider again the facts of the famous case of *Hamer v. Sidway,* discussed earlier in this chapter. There, an uncle's promise to pay his nephew $5,000 for refraining

from smoking, drinking, swearing, and other delightful pastimes until his 21st birthday was supported by consideration because the nephew had given legal value by refraining from participating in the prohibited activities. However, what if the uncle had said to his nephew on the eve of his 21st birthday: "Your mother tells me you've been a good lad and abstained from tobacco, hard drink, foul language, and gambling. Such goodness should be rewarded. Tomorrow, I'll give you a check for $5,000." Should the uncle's promise be enforceable against him? Clearly not, because although his nephew's behavior still passes the legal value test, in this case it was not bargained for and given in exchange for the uncle's promise.

Moral Obligation

As a general rule, promises made to satisfy a preexisting moral obligation are unenforceable for lack of consideration. The fact that a promisor or some member of the promisor's family, for example, has received some benefit from the promisee in the past (e.g., food and lodging, or emergency care) would not constitute consideration for a promisor's promise to pay for that benefit, due to the absence of the bargain element. Some courts find this result distressing and enforce such promises despite the absence of consideration. In addition, a few states have passed statutes making promises to pay for past benefits enforceable if such a promise is contained in a writing that clearly expresses the promisor's intent to be bound.

EXCEPTIONS TO THE CONSIDERATION REQUIREMENT

The consideration requirement is a classic example of a traditional contract law rule. It is precise, abstract, and capable of almost mechanical application. It can also, in some instances, result in significant injustice. Modern courts and legislatures have responded to this potential for injustice by carving out numerous exceptions to the requirement of consideration. Some of these exceptions (for example, the Code firm offer and contract modification rules) have already been discussed in this and preceding chapters. In the remaining portion of this chapter, we focus on several other important exceptions to the consideration requirement.

---

[10]O. W. Holmes, *The Common Law* (1881), p. 239.

Consideration

CONSIDERATION*	NOT CONSIDERATION
Doing something you had no preexisting duty to do	Doing something you had a preexisting duty to do
Promising to do something you had no preexisting duty to do	Promising to do something you had a preexisting duty to do
Paying part of a liquidated debt prior to the date the debt is due	Nominal consideration (unless actually bargained for)
Paying a liquidated debt in a different medium of exchange than originally agreed to	Paying part of a liquidated debt at or after the date the debt is due
Agreeing to settle an unliquidated debt	Making an illusory promise
Agreeing not to file suit when you have a good faith belief in your claim's validity	Past consideration
	Preexisting moral obligation

*Assuming bargained for.

Promissory Estoppel

As discussed in Chapter 9, Introduction to Contracts, the doctrine of promissory estoppel first emerged from attempts by courts around the turn of this century to reach just results in donative (gift) promise cases. Classical contract consideration principles did not recognize a promisee's reliance on a donative promise as a sufficient basis for enforcing the promise against the promisor. Instead, donative promises were unenforceable because they were not supported by consideration. In fact, the essence of a donative promise is that it does not seek or require any bargained-for exchange. Yet people continued to act in reliance on donative promises, often to their considerable disadvantage.

Refer to the facts of *Thorne v. Deas,* discussed earlier in this chapter. The co-owners of the *Sea Nymph* clearly relied to their injury on their fellow co-owner's promise to get insurance for the ship. Some courts in the early years of this century began to protect such relying promisees by *estopping* promisors from raising the defense that their promises were not supported by consideration. In a wide variety of cases involving gratuitous agency promises (as in *Thorne v. Deas*), promises of bonuses or pensions made to employees, and promises of gifts of land, courts began to use a promisee's detrimental (harmful) reliance on a donative promise as, in effect, a *substitute for* consideration.

In 1932, the first *Restatement of Contracts* legitimized these cases by expressly recognizing promissory estoppel in section 90. The elements of promissory estoppel were then essentially the same as they are today: a *promise* that the promisor should reasonably expect to induce reliance, *reliance* on the promise by the promisee, and *injustice* to the promisee as a result of that reliance. As the following *Niehaus* case illustrates, promissory estoppel is now widely used as a consideration substitute, not only in donative promise cases but also in cases involving commercial promises contemplating a bargained-for exchange. The construction contract bid cases discussed in Chapter 10 are another example of this expansion of promissory estoppel's reach. In fact, although promissory estoppel has expanded far beyond its initial role as a consideration substitute into other areas of contract law, it is probably fair to say that it is still most widely accepted in the consideration context.

P*atricia Niehaus was an employee of Delaware Valley Medical Center. The medical center distributed an employee handbook that stated that if an employee were granted an approved leave of absence, that employee, at the end of the leave, would be guaranteed the same position or one similar to the position occupied prior to the leave of absence. The handbook also stated, however, that the provisions in the handbook were not to be interpreted as a contract of employment and that either party could terminate the employment relationship at any time. Niehaus made a written request for a nine months' leave, and her request was approved. At the end of her leave, however, Delaware Valley refused to rehire Niehaus for any position. Niehaus sued the medical center for breach of contract and promissory estoppel, and the trial court dismissed her complaint. Niehaus appealed.* ∞

Wieand, Judge The presumption under Pennsylvania law is that all employment is at will and, therefore, an employee may be discharged for any reason or no reason. The medical center contends in this case that because Niehaus was an employee at will, she could be terminated for any reason or no reason, and that it would be absurd to require a rehiring of Niehaus when she could thereafter be discharged immediately. In any event, suggests the employer, there was no consideration for an agreement to rehire Niehaus following an approved leave of absence. It is argued, therefore, that the provision in the handbook is unenforceable.

In the instant case, whether or not there was consideration, the employer's promise is enforceable under principles of promissory estoppel. "A promise which the promisor should expect to induce action or forbearance on the part of the promisee or a third person and which does induce such action or forbearance is binding if injustice can be avoided only by enforcement of the promise." *Restatement (Second) of Contracts* section 90(1). Where an employer expects, if not demands, that its employees abide by a policy expressed with particularity in an employee handbook, an employee may justifiably rely thereon and expect justifiably that the employer will do the same.

Here, the medical center, by its handbook, had guaranteed its employees that if a leave of absence were requested and approved by the employer, then the employee could return at the end of the leave of absence and would be restored to the same or similar position as that occupied by the employee prior to the leave of absence. Under this policy, the employer had a right to expect a stable work force, where employees would take leave of absence only with the employer's consent and approval. An employee who was granted an approved leave of absence, however, could also rely upon the employer's promise that the employee would be rehired. The employer's promise was not illusory. When the employee was induced in fact to seek and obtain an approved leave of absence without pay on the assurance that she could return to the same or similar employment at the expiration of her leave, enforcement of the promise was essential to avoid injustice.

The medical center argues, however, that a cause of action for breach of contract of employment cannot be based on the provisions of the handbook where other language disclaims an intent to form a contract. In this case, Niehaus was initially employed at will. When the employee requested a leave of absence without pay, the employer could have refused to approve it or, indeed, could have revoked its promise of renewed employment at the end of the leave of absence. This it did not do. Instead, it approved the leave of absence in accordance with its handbook promise. It is this approval which thereupon gave rise to an implied contract and not the mere language in the handbook.

We conclude that the trial court erred when it summarily dismissed Niehaus's amended complaint. The complaint is sufficient to allege a cause of action for breach of a contract to rehire.

Reversed in favor of Niehaus and remanded for further proceedings.

Debts Barred by Statutes of Limitations

Statutes of limitations set an express statutory time limit on a person's ability to pursue any legal claim. A creditor who fails to file suit to collect a debt within the time prescribed by the appropriate statute of limitations loses the right to collect it. Many states, however, enforce a new promise by a debtor to pay such a debt, even though technically such promises are not supported by consideration because the creditor has given nothing in exchange for the new promise. Most states afford debtors some protection in such cases, however, by requiring that the new promise be in writing to be enforceable.

Debts Barred by Bankruptcy Discharge

Once a bankrupt debtor is granted a discharge,[11] creditors no longer have the legal right to collect discharged debts. Most states enforce a new promise by the debtor to pay (reaffirm) the debt regardless of whether the creditor has given any consideration to support it. To reduce creditor attempts to pressure debtors to reaffirm, the Bankruptcy Reform Act of 1978 made it much more difficult for debtors to reaffirm debts discharged in bankruptcy proceedings. The act requires that a reaffirmation promise be made prior to the date of the discharge and gives the debtor the right to revoke his promise within 30 days after it becomes enforceable. This act also requires the Bankruptcy Court to counsel individual (as opposed to corporate) debtors about the legal effects of reaffirmation and requires Bankruptcy Court approval of reaffirmations by individual debtors. In addition, a few states require reaffirmation promises to be in writing to be enforceable.

Charitable Subscriptions

Promises to make gifts for charitable or educational purposes are often enforced, despite the absence of consideration, when the institution or organization to which the promise was made has acted in reliance on the promised gift. This result is usually justified on the basis of either promissory estoppel or public policy.

---

[11]Chapter 29 discusses bankruptcy in detail.

1. In this chapter, you learned the general rule that the law does not enforce promises that are not supported by consideration. Are there ethical arguments that one could make to support the proposition that people should generally honor their promises to others regardless of whether they are legally required to do so? What might those arguments be? Do any of them help to explain the doctrine of promissory estoppel as an exception to the consideration requirement?

2. Discuss the public policy behind the rule that courts will not inquire into the adequacy of consideration. What social benefits are purchased by such a rule and at what price?

3. Discuss the ethical dimensions of offers by debtors to satisfy a liquidated debt by part payment before the due date. Are such offers ever ethical? What factors would be relevant in determining whether such an offer was ethical?

PROBLEMS AND PROBLEM CASES

1. Grouse, a recently graduated pharmacist who was working as a retail pharmacist for Richter Drug, applied for a job with Group Health Plan, Inc. Grouse was interviewed at Group Health by Elliott, chief pharmacist, and Shoberg, general manager. On December 4, 1975, Elliott telephoned Grouse at work and offered him a job as a pharmacist at Group Health's St. Louis Park Clinic. Grouse accepted, informing Elliott that he would give Richter two weeks' notice. That afternoon, Grouse received an offer from a Veterans Administration Hospital in Virginia, which he declined because of Group Health's offer. Elliott called back to confirm that Grouse had resigned. Sometime in the next few days, Elliott mentioned to Shoberg that he had hired, or was thinking of hiring, Grouse. Shoberg told him that company hiring requirements included a favorable written reference, a background check, and approval of the general manager. Elliott contacted two faculty members at the University of Minnesota School of Pharmacy, who declined to give references. He also contacted an internship employer and several pharmacies where Grouse had done relief work. Their responses were that they had not had enough exposure to Grouse's work to form a judgment about his capabilities. Because Elliott was unable to supply a favorable reference for Grouse, Shoberg hired another person to fill the position. On December 15, 1975, Grouse called Group Health and reported that he was free to begin work. Elliott informed Grouse that someone else had been hired. Grouse had difficulty regaining full-time employment and suffered wage loss as a result. Does he have any recourse against Group Health?

2. Reames, president and sole shareholder of Reames Foods, recruited and hired Lyon to be a salesperson for the company. Before joining Reames Foods, Lyon had been employed by and was a part owner in the Certified Meat Company. Lyon claims that when Reames approached him about joining the company, he had been concerned about the possibility that Reames might decide to sell the company in the future. Lyon did not want to help build the company's sales over time and then be subject to termination by a new owner after the company was sold. Lyon claimed that he received from Reames and Reames Foods an oral agreement guaranteeing him employment for five years after a change in ownership of the company, but the existence of such an agreement was denied by Reames Foods. Lyon asserted that, in reliance on this oral contract, he sold his ownership interest in the Certified Meat Company, quit his old job, and joined Reames Foods in April 1976. Lyon attempted to get the terms of the alleged oral contract with Reames Foods reduced to writing, but Reames continually put off his requests. Finally, at a meeting in November 1977, after several discussions between Reames and Lyon, Reames handed to Lyon a copy of a document entitled "Work Agreement." This document, which Lyon claims sets forth the terms of the earlier oral agreement, was typed on Reames Foods's letterhead, and was signed by Reames as president and agent of Reames Foods. The document provided in part that:

it is agreed that in event of the sale of the company . . . we of REAMES FOODS, INC. do guarantee and assure Donald F. Lyon of five (5) years continued employment at a minimum of his current salary effective at such time. . . . Donald Lyon agrees that he will, during such period of time, maintain all of his efforts in working for the company and will be employed by no other party during said period of time and said employment may be discontinued at any

time if said Donald F. Lyon fails to perform his work in a manner satisfactory to the Board of Directors.

The document was signed by Reames, but was not signed by Lyon. Reames and Reames Foods claim that this document was merely one of many proposals and counterproposals considered by Lyon and Reames and that it does not amount to an enforceable contract in itself. Reames sold Reames Foods to the T. Marzetti Company in October 1989. In December 1989, Lyon was terminated. Lyon sued Reames and Reames Foods for breach of contract. One of the defendants' defenses was lack of consideration. Was there consideration in this case?

3. In 1977, Dairy Specialties, Inc. (Dairy), hired Gross to develop nondairy products for customers allergic to milk and to serve as general manager. The employment contract was for a term of 15 years and provided for annual wages of $14,400 plus cost-of-living increases. It also provided that when 10 percent of Dairy's gross profits exceeded Gross's annual salary, he would receive the difference between the two figures, and it gave Gross a royalty of 1 percent of the selling price of all products Dairy produced using one or more of Gross's inventions or formulae. This royalty increased to 2 percent after the expiration of the agreement, at which time ownership of the inventions and formulae (which was jointly held during the term of the agreement) would revert to Gross. In 1982, Dairy was bought from its original owner by the Diehl family. The Diehls insisted on renegotiation of Gross's contract with Dairy as a condition of the purchase. Although he was not a party to the sale and received nothing tangible from it, Gross agreed to a new contract that had the same expiration date as the first one but that eliminated his cost-of-living increases, gave Dairy exclusive ownership of his inventions and formulae during and after the term of the agreement, and eliminated his right to royalties after the agreement expired. After the sale, Gross was given additional duties but no additional compensation. In 1984, after a business downturn, Gross was fired. He filed suit, arguing that his termination benefits should be calculated under his original contract. Was the modification of his contract valid?

4. Cash was a staff sergeant in a Missouri National Guard Military Police detachment. At a drill during August or September, Benward, the unit clerk, distributed to all unit members a brochure published by a private organization that offered $50,000 of spousal life insurance coverage. Cash claims that when he first received the application he did not realize that the organization offering the insurance was not associated with the National Guard. After reviewing the application, Cash was uncertain how to obtain coverage under the policy, so he sought help from Benward. Benward allegedly told him to fill out the application and send it to her with a check in the premium amount and she would forward it to the company. Cash completed the application and mailed it to Benward along with a check for the premium amount of $8. Benward does not recall either the discussion or receiving the application and check. Forwarding the spousal life insurance applications was not part of Benward's duties, although Cash assumed it was at the time he sent the application to Benward. In November, after determining that his check had not cleared, Cash approached both Benward and Sisk, Benward's supervisor, and inquired about the status of his check. Benward told him that she did not know anything about either. Sisk told Cash that he had seen a personal check in Benward's desk and that Benward had gotten a new job, and that "between you, me and the fencepost, she trashed your application." Cash claims that Sisk then told him not to worry, that the next month when Cash came back for drill, Sisk would give him a new application and Sisk would help him get it sent in. In December, Sisk gave Cash a new insurance application form and informed Cash that applying for the insurance was something Cash needed to handle himself. Cash did not complete a new form at that time. The night Cash returned home from the December drill, his wife became ill, spent two weeks in the hospital, and died. Cash sued Benward and Sisk for breach of contract. The trial court stated that there had been no consideration to support Benward and Sisk's promises. Was the court correct?

5. White went to the Homewood Fire Department to take a physical agility test to become a firefighter/paramedic. Prior to taking the test, White signed an agreement purporting to release the Village of Homewood from liability for any injuries she might suffer as a result of the agility test. White admitted signing the agreement but stated that she did so just to get the job. Illinois law required the Village to administer the physical agility test, and White had a right to participate. While she was traversing horizontal bars as part of the test, she fell and was injured. White brought suit for her injuries, alleging negligence in administering the test. The defendants moved to dismiss the negligence action asserting that the exculpatory agreement released them from liability. White asserted that the exculpatory agreement was unenforceable because it was not supported by any consideration. Was there consideration to support White's promise to release the Village from liability?

6. Artisoft hired Gould in January 1991 to assemble and coordinate its nationwide sales force. The contract provided that Gould would assume his new position on or before July 29, 1991, but until then, he was to remain in his previous position. The contract also provided that Gould was to relocate to Arizona and that he would sign a noncompetition agreement. In addition to other terms, the contract provided that in addition to his annual salary, Gould was to receive 50 shares of Artisoft stock. The contract also called for a three-month probationary period, during which either Gould or Artisoft could terminate the agreement. When the contract was signed, Artisoft was a privately held Arizona corporation. Plans were in the works, however, to make an initial public offering of Artisoft stock, and in anticipation of that offering, Artisoft was reincorporated in Delaware. On July 26, 1991, the 50 shares of stock referred to in Gould's contract were canceled and converted to 10,000 shares of the reincorporated Delaware corporation. Artisoft terminated Gould's employment less than two weeks after he assumed his new position with the company. After his termination, Gould sued Artisoft for enforcement of Artisoft's promise to provide 50 shares of stock. Gould asserted that he became entitled to the stock upon acceptance of Artisoft's offer and that the right to the stock was unaffected by his termination. Artisoft claimed that the contract lacked consideration. Was there consideration to support Artisoft's promises?

7. Gorham was a store manager for LensCrafters earning $38,000 when he received a phone call from Benson Optical offering him a job. After an interview, he was offered the job of area manager for half of North Carolina plus stores in Kentucky and Florida for $50,000. Terms were discussed over the phone and he was told a confirming letter and packet would follow. When he received nothing, he phoned and was told they were in the mail, and that he should quit his job with LensCrafters, which he did. He declined further negotiations with Lens-

Crafters, flew to Chicago at his own expense, and reported for a nationwide sales meeting, which was his first day of employment. At this meeting, Gorham was "reinterviewed" and then terminated. When he sued for breach of contract, Benson defended by arguing there was no consideration because the promise of employment was unenforceable. Gorham had been promised employment at will, which gave the employer the right to fire him at any time for any reason, including on his first day of work. Can Gorham enforce the promise under the doctrine of promissory estoppel?

8. Passander was executive vice president of Spickelmier Industries. Because Spickelmier was facing financial difficulties, a committee of creditors had been formed to oversee its operations. In November 1971, the committee projected a small profit for the year and recommended that bonuses be given to certain key employees if the profit materialized. This recommendation was adopted by Spickelmier's board of directors in late December, and Passander was promised a $1,500 bonus. In January 1972, however, the board's executive committee discovered that the earlier profit estimates had been overly optimistic and that insufficient funds were available to pay the bonuses. Instead of taking the board's recommendation that the bonuses not be paid, the chairman of the board negotiated a compromise whereby one-half of the originally specified bonus would be paid as planned, with the balance to be paid when funds were available. Passander accepted the half bonus, and later in the month his contract with Spickelmier was renegotiated to provide for a 25 percent salary increase and guaranteed quarterly bonuses of $500. In June 1972, Passander quit his job, later filing suit against Spickelmier for the remaining half of his 1971 bonus. Can he recover it?

9. Kaufmann was employed by Fiduciary Management, Inc. (FMI). In September 1988, Lanier, president and sole shareholder of FMI, signed and gave a letter to Kaufmann, which stated in part:

If your employment is terminated without cause before July 1, 1990, Fiduciary Management, Inc., agrees that within one month of the date on which your full salary ceases to be paid you will receive an additional payment of $150,000.

The context of this letter was that several projects serviced by FMI were experiencing financial difficulties and Lanier's sons advised him that Kaufmann was distracted, that he may have been consid-

ering leaving FMI, and that he needed to focus on his work. The letter was intended to help him focus on his work, presumably by giving him a sense of job security. After receiving the letter, Kaufmann undertook a secret and systematic search for another job. In January 1990, Kaufmann's employment with FMI ceased. He was not paid the $150,000 that had been promised in the letter, and he sued Lanier and FMI to recover the money. Was Lanier's promise to pay $150,000 enforceable?

10. ▣ *Video Case.* See "California Dreaming." Jensen offered Judy, a resident of Chicago, a position in a company in Los Angeles. Jensen gave Judy an employee handbook, extolled the low turnover of his firm's work force, and told her that there was a "no-cut policy." Jensen told Judy that if she decided to relocate within a year, the job was hers. After deciding to accept the job, Judy called Jensen and informed him. She also told him that she did not know how long it would take to sell her house in Chicago, but Jensen told her to give him a call as soon as she arrived in Los Angeles and said, "We're really looking forward to having you on board." Six months later, Judy and her husband quit their jobs, sold their house in Chicago, and moved to Los Angeles. When Judy called Jensen, however, he said that the position they had discussed was not available and the company had no openings. Was the company's promise to hire Judy enforceable?

11. ▣ *Video Case.* See "A Christmas Story." Tinker Construction had a contract with Scroge to build a factory addition for Scroge by a particular date. The contract contained a penalty clause exacting daily penalties for late performance, and Tinker was working hard to complete the building on time. Because prompt completion of the addition was so important to Scroge, however, Scroge offered Tinker a bonus if it completed the factory addition on time. Scroge also learned that the supplier of parts for machinery that he had contracted for had called and said that it could not deliver the parts on Scroge's schedule for the price it had agreed to. Because there was no other supplier, Scroge promised to pay the requested higher price. The factory addition was completed on time and the parts arrived on time. Scroge then refused to pay both the bonus to Tinker and the higher price for the parts. Were these promises enforceable?

See also "The Stock Option" and "A Bedtime Story."

Reality of Consent

I n a complex economy that depends on planning for the future, it is crucial that the law can be counted on to enforce contracts. In some situations, however, there are compelling reasons for permitting people to escape or *avoid* their contracts. An agreement obtained by force, trickery, unfair persuasion, or error is not the product of mutual and voluntary consent. A person who has made an agreement under these circumstances will be able to avoid it because his consent was not *real*.

This chapter discusses five doctrines that permit people to avoid their contracts because of the absence of real consent: misrepresentation, fraud, mistake, duress, and undue influence. Doctrines that involve similar considerations will be discussed in Chapter 14, Capacity to Contract, and in Chapter 15, Illegality. ∞

EFFECT OF DOCTRINES DISCUSSED IN THIS CHAPTER

Contracts induced by misrepresentation, fraud, mistake, duress, or undue influence are generally considered to be **voidable.** This means that the person whose consent was not real has the power to **rescind** (cancel) the contract. A person who rescinds a contract is entitled to the return of anything he gave the other party. By the same token, he must offer to return anything he has received from the other party.

Necessity for Prompt and Unequivocal Rescission

Suppose Johnson, who recently bought a car from Sims Motors, learns that Sims Motors made fraudulent statements to her to induce her to buy the car. She believes the contract was induced by fraud and wants to rescind it. How does she act to protect her rights? To rescind a contract based on fraud or any of the other doctrines discussed in this chapter, she must act promptly and unequivocally. She must object promptly upon learning the facts that give her the right to rescind and must clearly express her intent to cancel the contract. She must also avoid any behavior that would suggest that she affirms or **ratifies** the contract. (Ratification of a voidable contract means that a person who had the right to rescind has elected not to do so. Ratification ends the right to rescind.) This means that she should avoid unreasonable delay in notifying the other party of her rescission, because unreasonable delay communicates that she has ratified the contract. She should also avoid any conduct that would send a "mixed message," such as continuing to accept benefits from the other party or behaving in any other way that is inconsistent with her expressed intent to rescind.

MISREPRESENTATION AND FRAUD

Nature of Misrepresentation

A misrepresentation is an assertion that is not in accord with the truth. When a person enters a contract because of his justifiable reliance on a misrepresentation about some important fact, the contract is voidable.

It is not necessary that the misrepresentation be intentionally deceptive. Misrepresentations can be either "innocent" (not intentionally deceptive) or "fraudulent" (made with knowledge of falsity and intent to deceive). A contract may be voidable even if the person making the misrepresentation believes in good faith that what he says is true. Either innocent misrepresentation or fraud gives the complaining party the right to rescind a contract.

Nature of Fraud

Fraud is the type of misrepresentation that is committed knowingly, with the intent to deceive. The legal term for this knowledge of falsity, which distinguishes fraud from innocent misrepresentation, is **scienter.** A person making a misrepresentation would be considered to do so "knowingly" if

she knew that her statement was false, if she knew that she did not have a basis for making the statement, or even if she just made the statement without being confident that it was true. The intent to deceive can be inferred from the fact that the defendant knowingly made a misstatement of fact to a person who was likely to rely on it.

As is true for innocent misrepresentation, the contract remedy for fraudulent misrepresentation is rescission. The tort liability of a person who commits fraud is different from that of a person who commits innocent misrepresentation, however. A person who commits fraud may be liable for damages, possibly including punitive damages, for the tort of **deceit.**[1] As you will learn in following sections, innocent misrepresentation and fraud share a common core of elements.

Election of Remedies   In some states, a person injured by fraud cannot rescind the contract *and* sue for damages for deceit; he must elect (choose) between these remedies. In other states, however, an injured party may pursue both rescission and damage remedies and does not have to elect between them.[2]

REQUIREMENTS FOR RESCISSION ON THE GROUND OF MISREPRESENTATION

The fact that one of the parties has made an untrue assertion does not in itself make the contract voidable. Courts do not want to permit people who have exercised poor business judgment or poor common sense to avoid their contractual obligations, nor do they want to grant rescission of a contract when there have been only minor and unintentional misstatements of relatively unimportant details. A drastic remedy such as rescission should be used only when a person has been seriously misled about a fact important to the contract by someone he had the right to rely on. A person seeking to rescind a contract on the ground of innocent or fraudulent

---

[1] The tort of deceit is discussed in Chapter 6, Intentional Torts.

[2] Under every state's law, however, a person injured by fraud in a contract for the *sale of goods* can both rescind the contract and sue for damages. This is made clear by section 2–721 of the Uniform Commercial Code, which specifically states that no election of remedies is required in contracts for the sale of goods.

misrepresentation must be able to establish each of the following elements:

1. An untrue assertion of fact was made.
2. The fact asserted was material *or* the assertion was fraudulent.
3. The complaining party entered the contract because of his reliance on the assertion.
4. The reliance of the complaining party was reasonable.

In tort actions in which the plaintiff is seeking to recover damages for deceit, the plaintiff would have to establish a *fifth* element: injury. He would have to prove that he had suffered actual economic injury because of his reliance on the fraudulent assertion. In cases in which the injured person seeks only rescission of the contract, however, proof of economic injury usually is not required.

Untrue Assertion of Fact

To have misrepresentation, one of the parties must have made an untrue assertion of fact or engaged in some conduct that is the equivalent of an untrue assertion of fact. The fact asserted must be a *past or existing fact,* as distinguished from an opinion or a promise or prediction about some future happening.

The **concealment** of a fact through some active conduct intended to prevent the other party from discovering the fact is considered to be the equivalent of an assertion. Like a false statement of fact,

concealment can be the basis for a claim of misrepresentation or fraud. For example, if Summers is offering his house for sale and paints the ceilings to conceal the fact that the roof leaks, his active concealment constitutes an assertion of fact.

Nondisclosure can also be the equivalent of an assertion of fact. Nondisclosure differs from concealment in that concealment involves the active hiding of a fact, while nondisclosure is the failure to volunteer information. Disclosure of a fact—even a fact that will harm the speaker's bargaining position—is required in a number of situations, such as when the person has already offered *some* information but further information is needed to give the other party an accurate picture, or when there is a relationship of trust and confidence between the parties. In recent years, courts and legislatures have tended to impose a duty to disclose when a party has access to information that is not readily available to the other party. This is consistent with modern contract law's emphasis on influencing ethical standards of conduct and achieving fair results. Transactions involving the sale of real estate are among the most common situations in which this duty to disclose arises. Most states now hold that a seller who knows about a latent (hidden) defect that materially affects the value of the property he is selling has the obligation to speak up about this defect. *Stambovsky v. Ackley,* which follows, involves an interesting application of the duty to disclose in the context of a sale of real estate.

STAMBOVSKY v. ACKLEY   572 N.Y.S.2d 672 (N.Y. Sup. Ct. App. Div. 1991)

J effrey Stambovsky, a resident of New York City, contracted to purchase a house in the Village of Nyack, New York, from Helen Ackley. The house was widely reputed to be possessed by poltergeists, which Ackley and members of her family had reportedly seen. Ackley did not tell Stambovsky about the poltergeists before he bought the house. When Stambovsky learned of the house's reputation, however, he promptly commenced this action for rescission. The trial court dismissed his complaint, and Stambovsky appealed. ○

Rubin, Justice The unusual facts of this case clearly warrant a grant of equitable relief to the buyer who, as a resident of New York City, cannot be expected to have any familiarity with the folklore of the Village of Nyack. Not being a "local," Stambovsky could not readily learn that the home he had contracted to purchase is haunted. Whether

the source of the spectral apparitions seen by Ackley are parapsychic or psychogenic, having reported their presence in both a national publication (*Readers' Digest*) and the local press (in 1977 and 1982, respectively), Ackley is estopped to deny their existence and, as a matter of law, the house is haunted. More to the point, however, no divination is required to conclude that it is Ackley's promotional efforts in publicizing her close encounters with these spirits which fostered the home's reputation in the community. In 1989, the house was included in a five-home walking tour of Nyack and described in a November 27th newspaper article as a "riverfront Victorian (with ghost)." The impact of the reputation thus created goes to the very essence of the bargain between the parties, greatly impairing both the value of the property and its potential for resale.

[The court discussed the fact that New York law does not recognize a remedy for damages incurred as a result of the seller's mere silence, applying instead the doctrine of caveat emptor. The court then proceeded to discuss the availability of rescission.]

From the perspective of a person in the position of the plaintiff, a very practical problem arises with respect to the discovery of a paranormal phenomenon: "Who you gonna call?" as the title song to the movie *Ghostbusters* asks. Applying the strict rule of *caveat emptor* to a contract involving a house possessed by poltergeists conjures up visions of a psychic or medium routinely accompanying the structural engineer and Terminix man on an inspection of every home subject to a contract of sale. The doctrine of *caveat emptor* requires that a buyer act prudently to assess the fitness and value of his purchase. It should be apparent, however, that the most meticulous inspection and the search would not reveal the presence of poltergeists at the premises or unearth the property's ghoulish reputation in the community. Therefore, there is no sound policy reason to deny Stambovsky relief for failing to discover a state of affairs which the most prudent purchaser would not be expected to even contemplate.

Where a condition which has been created by the seller materially impairs the value of the contract and is peculiarly within the knowledge of the seller or unlikely to be discovered by a prudent purchaser exercising due care, nondisclosure constitutes a basis for rescission as a matter of equity. Any other outcome places upon the buyer not merely the obligation to exercise care in his purchase but rather to be omniscient with respect to any fact which may affect the bargain. No practical purpose is served by imposing such a burden upon a purchaser. To the contrary, it encourages predatory business practice and offends the principle that equity will suffer no wrong to be without a remedy.

In the case at bar, Ackley deliberately fostered the public belief that her home was possessed. Having undertaken to inform the public at large, to whom she has no legal relationship, about the supernatural occurrences on her property, she may be said to owe no less a duty to her contract vendee. Application of the remedy of rescission is entirely appropriate to relieve the unwitting purchaser from the consequences of a most unnatural bargain.

Judgment modified in favor of Stambovsky, reinstating his action seeking rescission of the contract.

Materiality

If the misrepresentation was innocent, the person seeking to rescind the contract must establish that the fact asserted was **material.** A fact will be considered to be material if it is likely to play a significant role in inducing a reasonable person to enter the contract or if the person asserting the fact knows that the other person is likely to rely on the fact. For example, Rogers, who is trying to sell his car to Ferguson and knows that Ferguson idolizes professional bowlers, tells Ferguson that a professional bowler once rode in the car. Relying on that representation, Ferguson buys the car. Although the fact Rogers asserted might not be important to most people, it would be material here because Rogers knew that his representation would be likely to induce Ferguson to enter the contract.

Even if the fact asserted was not material, the contract may be rescinded if the misrepresentation was *fraudulent*. The rationale for this rule is that a person who fraudulently misrepresents a fact, even one that is not material under the standards previously discussed, should not be able to profit from his intentionally deceptive conduct.

Actual Reliance

Reliance means that a person pursues some course of action because of his faith in an assertion made to

CONCEPT   REVIEW

Misrepresentation and Fraud

	INNOCENT MISREPRESENTATION	FRAUD
Remedy	Rescission	Rescission *and/or* tort action for damages
Elements	1. Untrue assertion of fact (or equivalent) 2. Assertion relates to material fact 3. Actual reliance 4. Justifiable reliance	1. Untrue assertion of fact (or equivalent) 2. Assertion made with knowledge of falsity (scienter) and intent to deceive 3. Actual reliance 4. Justifiable reliance 5. Economic loss (in a tort action for damages)

him. For misrepresentation to exist, there must have been a causal connection between the assertion and the complaining party's decision to enter the contract. If the complaining party knew that the assertion was false or was not aware that an assertion had been made, there has been no reliance.

Justifiable Reliance

Courts also scrutinize the reasonableness of the behavior of the complaining party by requiring that his reliance be *justifiable*. A person does not act justifiably if he relies on an assertion that is obviously false or not to be taken seriously.

One problem involving the justifiable reliance element is determining the extent to which the relying party is responsible for investigating the accuracy of the statement on which he relies. Classical contract law held that a person who did not attempt to discover readily discoverable facts generally was not justified in relying on the other party's statements about them. For example, under traditional law, a person would not be entitled to rely on the other party's assertions about facts that are a matter of public record or that could be discovered through a reasonable inspection of available documents or records. The extent of the responsibility placed on a relying party to conduct an independent investigation has declined in modern contract law, however. Today, a court might be more likely to follow the approach of section 172 of the *Restatement,* which provides that a relying party's failure to discover facts before entering the contract does not make his reliance unjustifiable unless the degree of his fault was so extreme as to amount to a failure to act in good faith and in accordance with reasonable standards of fair dealing. Thus, today's

courts tend to place a greater degree of accountability on the person who makes the assertion rather than the person who relies on the assertion.

MISTAKE

Nature of Mistake

Anyone who enters a contract does so on the basis of his understanding of the facts that are relevant to the contract. His decision about what he is willing to exchange with the other party is based on this understanding. If the parties are wrong about an important fact, the exchange that they make is likely to be quite different than what they contemplated when they entered the contract, and this difference is due to simple error rather than to any external events such as an increase in market price. For example, Fox contracts to sell to Ward a half-carat stone, which both believe to be a tourmaline, at a price of $65. If they are wrong and the stone is actually a diamond worth at least $2,500, Fox will have suffered an unexpected loss and Ward will have reaped an unexpected gain. The contract would not have been made at a price of $65 if the parties' belief about the nature of the stone had been in accord with the facts. In such cases, the person adversely affected by the mistake can avoid the contract under the doctrine of mistake. The purpose of the doctrine of mistake is to prevent unexpected and unbargained for losses that result when the parties are mistaken about a fact central to their contract.

What Is a Mistake?   In ordinary conversation, we may use the term *mistake* to mean an error in judgment or an unfortunate act. In contract law, however, a mistake is a *belief* about a fact that is *not* *in accord with the truth.*[3] The mistake must relate to facts as they exist at the time the contract is created. An erroneous belief or prediction about facts that might occur in the future would not qualify as a mistake.

---

[3]*Restatement (Second) of Contracts* section 151.

As in misrepresentation cases, the complaining party in a mistake case enters a contract because of a belief that is at variance with the actual facts. Mistake is unlike misrepresentation, however, in that the erroneous belief is not the result of the other party's untrue statements.

The *Wilkin v. 1st Source Bank* case, which follows, illustrates the concept and effect of mistake in contract law.

WILKEN v. 1ST SOURCE BANK   548 N.E.2d 170 (Ind. Ct. App. 1990)

Olga Mestrovic, the widow of internationally known sculptor and artist Ivan Mestrovic, owned a large number of works of art created by her late husband. Mrs. Mestrovic died, leaving a will in which she directed that all the works of art created by her husband were to be sold and the proceeds distributed to surviving members of the Mestrovic family. Mrs. Mestrovic also owned real estate at the time of her death. 1st Source Bank, as the personal representative of Mrs. Mestrovic's estate, entered into a contract to sell this real estate to Terrence and Antoinette Wilkin. The purchase agreement provided that certain personal property on the premises would be sold to the Wilkins, too: specifically, the stove, refrigerator, dishwasher, drapes, curtains, sconces, and French doors in the attic.

After taking possession of the property, the Wilkins complained to the bank that the property was left in a cluttered condition and would require substantial cleaning effort. The trust officer of the bank offered the Wilkins two options: Either the bank would obtain a rubbish removal service to clean the property or the Wilkins could clean the property and keep any items of personal property they wanted. The Wilkins opted to clean the property themselves. At the time these arrangements were made, neither the bank nor the Wilkins suspected that any works of art remained on the premises.

During the cleanup efforts, the Wilkins found eight drawings apparently created by Ivan Mestrovic. They also found a plaster sculpture of the figure of Christ with three small children. The Wilkins claimed ownership of these works of art by virtue of their agreement with the bank. The probate court ruled that there was no agreement for the purchase of the artwork, and the Wilkins appealed. ∞

Hoffman, Judge   Mutual assent is a prerequisite to the creation of a contract. Where both parties share a common assumption about a vital fact upon which they based their bargain, and that assumption is false, the transaction may be avoided if because of the mistake a quite different exchange of values occurs from the exchange of values contemplated by the parties. *J. Calamari & J. Perillo, The Law of Contracts* section 9-26 (1987).

The necessity of mutual assent is illustrated in the classic case of *Sherwood v. Walker* (1887). The owners of a blooded cow indicated to the purchaser that the cow was barren. The purchaser appeared to believe that the cow was barren. Consequently, a bargain was made to sell at a price per pound at which the cow would have brought approximately $80.00. Before delivery, it was discovered that the cow was with calf and that she was, therefore, worth

from $750.00 to $1,000.00 The court ruled that the transaction was voidable: "[T]he mistake . . . went to the very nature of the thing. A barren cow is substantially a different creature than a breeding one."

Like the parties in *Sherwood,* the parties in the instant case shared a common presupposition as to the existence of certain facts which proved false. The bank and the Wilkins considered the real estate which the Wilkins had purchased to be cluttered with items of personal property variously characterized as "junk," "stuff," or "trash." Neither party suspected that works of art created by Ivan Mestrovic remained on the premises.

As in *Sherwood,* one party experienced an unexpected, unbargained-for gain while the other experienced an unexpected, unbargained for loss. Because the bank and the Wilkins did not know that the eight drawings and the plaster sculpture were included in the items of personalty that cluttered the real property, the discovery of those works of art by the Wilkins was unexpected. The resultant gain to the Wilkins and loss to the Bank were not contemplated by the parties when the bank agreed that the Wilkins could clean the premises and keep such personal property as they wished.

The following commentary on *Sherwood* is equally applicable to the case at bar:

Here the buyer sought to retain a gain that was produced, not by a subsequent change in circumstances, nor by the favorable resolution of known uncertainties when the contract was made, but by the presence of facts quite different from those on which the parties based their bargain. *Palmer, Mistake and Unjust Enrichment* 16-17 (1962).

The probate court properly concluded that there was no agreement for the purchase, sale, or other disposition of the eight drawings and plaster sculpture.

Judgment for 1st Source Bank affirmed.

Mistakes of Law

A number of the older mistake cases state that mistake about a principle of law will not justify rescission. The rationale for this view was that everyone was presumed to know the law. More modern cases, however, have granted relief even when the mistake is an erroneous belief about some aspect of law.

Negligence and the Right to Avoid for Mistake

Although courts sometimes state that relief will not be granted when a person's mistake was caused by his own negligence, they often have granted rescission even when the mistaken party was somewhat negligent. Section 157 of the *Restatement (Second) of Contracts* focuses on the *degree* of a party's negligence in making the mistake. It states that a person's fault in failing to know or discover facts before entering the contract will not bar relief unless his fault amounted to a failure to act in good faith.

Effect of Mistake

The mere fact that the contracting parties have made a mistake is not, standing alone, a sufficient ground for avoidance of the contract. The right to avoid a contract because of mistake depends on several factors that are discussed in following sections. One important factor that affects the right to avoid is whether the mistake was made by just one of the parties (**unilateral mistake**) or by both parties (**mutual mistake**).

Mutual Mistake

A mutual mistake exists when both parties to the contract have erroneous assumptions about the same fact. When *both* parties are mistaken, the resulting contract can be avoided if the three following elements are present:

1. The mistake relates to a basic assumption on which the contract was made.
2. The mistake has a material effect on the agreed-upon exchange.
3. The party adversely affected by the mistake does not bear the risk of the mistake.[4]

Mistake about a Basic Assumption Even if the mistake is mutual, the adversely affected party will not have the right to avoid the contract unless the mistake concerns a basic assumption on which the contract was based. Assumptions about the identity, existence, quality, or quantity of the subject matter of the contract are among the basic assumptions on which contracts typically are founded. It is not necessary that the parties be consciously aware of the assumption; an assumption may be so basic that they take it for granted. For example, if Peterson contracts to buy a house from Tharp, it is likely that both of them assume at the time of contracting that the house is in existence and that it is legally permissible for the house to be used as a residence.

An assumption would not be considered a basic assumption if it concerns a matter that bears an indirect or collateral relationship to the subject

---

[4]*Restatement (Second) of Contracts* § 152.

matter of the contract. For example, mistakes about matters such as a party's financial ability or market conditions usually would not give rise to avoidance of the contract.

Material Effect on Agreed-Upon Exchange   It is not enough for a person claiming mistake to show that the exchange is something different from what he expected. He must show that the imbalance caused by the mistake is so severe that it would be unfair for the law to require him to perform the contract. He will have a better chance of establishing this element if he can show not only that the contract is *less* desirable for him because of the mistake but also that the other party has received an unbargained-for advantage.

Adversely Affected Party Does Not Bear the Risk of Mistake   Even if the first two elements are present, the person who is adversely affected by the mistake cannot avoid the contract if he is considered to bear the risk of mistake.[5] Courts have the power to allocate the risk of a mistake to the adversely affected person whenever it is reasonable under the circumstances to do so.

One situation in which an adversely affected person would bear the risk of mistake is when he has expressly contracted to do so. For example, if Buyer contracted to accept property "as is," he may be considered to have accepted the risk that his assumption about the quality of the property may be erroneous.

The adversely affected party also bears the risk of mistake when he contracts with *conscious awareness* that he is ignorant or has limited information about a fact—in other words, he *knows that he does not know* the true state of affairs about a particular fact but he binds himself to perform anyway. Suppose someone gives you an old, locked safe. Without trying to open it, you sell it and "all of its contents" to one of your friends for $25. When your friend succeeds in opening the safe, he finds $10,000 in cash. In this case, you would not be able to rescind the contract because, in essence, you gambled on your limited knowledge . . . and lost.

Mutual Mistakes in Drafting Writings

Sometimes, mutual mistake takes the form of erroneous *expression* of an agreement, frequently

caused by a clerical error in drafting or typing a contract, deed, or other document. In such cases, the remedy is *reformation* of the writing rather than avoidance of the contract. Reformation means modification of the written instrument to express the agreement that the parties made but failed to express correctly. Suppose Arnold agrees to sell Barber a vacant lot next to Arnold's home. The vacant lot is "Lot 3, block 1"; Arnold's home is on "Lot 2, block 1." The person typing the contract strikes the wrong key, and the contract reads, "Lot 2, block 1." Neither Arnold nor Barber notices this error when they read and sign the contract, yet clearly they did not intend to have Arnold sell the lot on which his house stands. In such a case, a court will reform the contract to conform to Arnold and Baker's true agreement.

Unilateral Mistake

A unilateral mistake exists when only one of the parties makes a mistake about a basic assumption on which he made the contract. For example, Plummer contracts to buy from Taylor 25 shares of Worthwright Enterprises, Inc., mistakenly believing that he is buying 25 shares of the much more valuable Worthwrite Industries. Taylor knows that the contract is for the sale of shares of Worthwright. Taylor (the "nonmistaken party") is correct in his belief about the identity of the stock he is selling; only Plummer (the "mistaken party") is mistaken in his assumption about the identity of the stock. Does Plummer's unilateral mistake give him the right to avoid the contract? Courts are more likely to allow avoidance of a contract when both parties are mistaken than when only one is mistaken. The rationale for this tendency is that in cases of unilateral mistake, at least one party's assumption about the facts was correct, and allowing avoidance disappoints the reasonable expectations of that nonmistaken party.

It is possible to avoid contracts for unilateral mistake, but to do so, proving the elements necessary for mutual mistake is just a starting point. *In addition to* proving the elements of mistake discussed earlier, a person trying to avoid on the ground of unilateral mistake must show *either* one of the following:

1. *The nonmistaken party caused or had reason to know of the mistake.* Courts permit avoidance in

[5]*Restatement (Second) of Contracts* § 154.

C O N C E P T   R E V I E W

Avoidance on the Ground of Mistake

	MUTUAL MISTAKE	UNILATERAL MISTAKE
Description	Both parties mistaken about same fact	Only one party mistaken about a fact
Needed for Avoidance of Contract	Elements of mistake: 1. Mistake about basic assumption on which contract was made 2. Material effect on agreed exchange 3. Person adversely affected by mistake does not bear the risk of the mistake	Same elements as mutual mistake *Plus* *a.* Nonmistaken party caused mistake or had reason to know of mistake *Or* *b.* Effect of mistake is to make it unconscionable to enforce contract

cases of unilateral mistake if the nonmistaken party caused the mistake, knew of the mistake, or even if the mistake was so obvious that the nonmistaken party had reason to realize that a mistake had been made.[6] For example, Ace Electrical Company makes an error when preparing a bid that it submits to Gorge General Contracting. If the mistake in Ace's bid was so obvious that Gorge knew about it when it accepted Ace's offer, Ace could avoid the contract even though Ace is the only party who was mistaken. The reasoning behind this rule is that the nonmistaken person could have prevented the loss by acting in good faith and informing the person in error that he had made a mistake. It also reflects the judgment that people should not take advantage of the mistakes of others. *Or*

2. *It would be unconscionable to enforce the contract.* A court could also permit avoidance because of unilateral mistake when the effect of the mistake was such that it would be unconscionable to enforce the contract. To show that it would be unconscionable to enforce the contract, the mistaken party would have to show that the consequences of the mistake were severe enough that it would be unreasonably harsh or oppressive to enforce the contract.[7] In the example above, Ace Electrical Company made an error when preparing a bid that it submits to Gorge General Contracting. Suppose that Gorge had no reason to realize that a mistake had been made, and accepted the bid. Ace might show that it

would be unconscionable to enforce the contract by showing that not only will its profit margin not be what Ace contemplated when it made its offer, but also that it would suffer a grave loss by having to perform at the mistaken price.

DURESS

Nature of Duress

Duress is wrongful coercion that induces a person to enter or modify a contract. One kind of duress is physical compulsion to enter a contract. For example, Thorp overpowers Grimes, grasps his hand, and forces him to sign a contract. This kind of duress is rare, but when it occurs, a court would find that the contract was **void.** A far more common type of duress occurs when a person is induced to enter a contract by a *threat* of physical, emotional, or economic harm. In these cases, the contract is considered *voidable* at the option of the victimized person. This is the form of duress addressed in this chapter.

The elements of duress have undergone dramatic changes. Classical contract law took a very narrow view of the type of coercion that constituted duress, limiting duress to threats of imprisonment or serious physical harm. Today, however, courts take a much broader view of the types of coercion that will constitute duress. For example, modern courts recognize that threats to a person's economic interests can be duress.

Elements of Duress

To rescind a contract because of duress, one must be able to establish both of the following elements:

---

[6]*Restatement (Second) of Contracts* § 153.

[7]The concept of unconscionability is developed more fully in Chapter 15.

1. The contract was induced by an improper threat.
2. The victim had no reasonable alternative but to enter the contract.

Improper Threat   It would not be desirable for courts to hold that every kind of threat constituted duress. If they did, the enforceability of all contracts would be in question, because every contract negotiation involves at least the implied threat that a person will not enter into the transaction unless her demands are met. What degree of wrongfulness, then, is required for a threat to constitute duress? Traditionally, a person would have to threaten to do something she was not legally entitled to do—such as threaten to commit a crime or a tort—for that threat to be duress. Some courts still follow that rule. Other courts today follow the *Restatement* position that, to be duress, the threat need not be wrongful or illegal but must be *improper*—that is, improper to use as leverage to induce a contract.

Under some circumstances, threats to institute legal actions can be considered improper threats that will constitute duress. A threat to file either a civil or a criminal suit without a legal basis for doing so would clearly be improper. What of a threat to file a well-founded lawsuit or prosecution? Generally, if there is a good faith dispute over a matter, a person's threat to file a lawsuit to resolve that dispute is *not* considered to be improper. Otherwise, every person who settled a suit out of court could later claim duress. However, if the threat to sue is made in bad faith and for a purpose unrelated to the issues in the lawsuit, the threat can be considered improper. In one case, for example, duress was found when a husband who was in the process of divorcing his wife threatened to sue for custody of their children—something he had the right to do—unless the wife transferred to him stock that she owned in his company.[8]

Victim Had No Reasonable Alternative   The person complaining of duress must be able to prove that the coercive nature of the improper threat was such that he had no reasonable alternative but to enter or modify the contract. Classical contract law applied an objective standard of coercion, which

required that the degree of coercion exercised had to be sufficient to overcome the will of a person of ordinary courage. The more modern standard for coercion focuses on the alternatives open to the complaining party. For example, Barry, a traveling salesman, takes his car to Cheatum Motors for repair. Barry pays Cheatum the full amount previously agreed upon for the repair, but Cheatum refuses to return Barry's car to him unless Barry agrees to pay substantially more than the contract price for the repairs. Because of his urgent need for the return of his car, Barry agrees to do this. In this case, Barry technically had the alternative of filing a legal action to recover his car. However, this would not be a *reasonable alternative* for someone who needs the car urgently because of the time, expense, and uncertainty involved in pursuing a lawsuit. Thus, Barry could avoid his agreement to pay more money under a theory of duress.

Economic Duress   Today, the doctrine of duress is often applied in a business context. *Economic duress,* or *business compulsion,* are terms commonly used to describe situations in which one person induces the formation or modification of a contract by threatening another person's economic interests. A common coercive strategy is to threaten to breach the contract unless the other party agrees to modify its terms. For example, Moore, who has contracted to sell goods to Stephens, knows that Stephens needs timely delivery of the goods. Moore threatens to withhold delivery unless Stephens agrees to pay a higher price. Another common situation involving economic duress occurs when one of the parties offers a disproportionately small amount of money in settlement of a debt and refuses to pay more. Such a strategy exerts great economic pressure on a creditor who is in a desperate financial situation to accept the settlement because he cannot afford the time and expense of bringing a lawsuit.

Classical contract law did not recognize economic duress because this type of hard bargaining was considered neither improper nor coercive. After all, the victim of the sorts of economic pressure described above had at least the theoretical right to file a lawsuit to enforce his rights under the contract. Modern courts recognize that improper economic pressure can prevent a resulting contract or contract modification from being truly voluntary, and the concept of economic duress is well accepted today.

---

[8]*Link v. Link,* 179 S.E.2d 697 (1971).

UNDUE INFLUENCE

Nature of Undue Influence

Undue influence is unfair persuasion. Like duress, undue influence involves wrongful pressure exerted on a person during the bargaining process. In undue influence, however, the pressure is exerted through *persuasion* rather than through coercion. The doctrine of undue influence was developed to give relief to persons who are unfairly persuaded to enter a contract while in a position of weakness that makes them particularly vulnerable to being preyed upon by those they trust or fear. A large proportion of undue influence cases arise after the death of the person who has been the subject of undue influence, when his relatives seek to set aside that person's contracts or wills.

Determining Undue Influence   All contracts are based on persuasion. There is no precise dividing line between permissible persuasion and impermissible persuasion. Nevertheless, several hallmarks of undue influence cases can be identified. Undue influence cases normally involve both of the following elements:

1. The relationship between the parties is either one of trust and confidence or one in which the person exercising the persuasion dominates the person being persuaded.
2. The persuasion is unfair.[9]

Relation between the Parties   Undue influence cases involve people who, though they have capacity to enter a contract, are in a position of particular vulnerability in relationship to the other party to the contract. This relationship can be one of trust and confidence, in which the person being influenced

---

[9]*Restatement (Second) of Contracts* § 177.

---

justifiably believes that the other party is looking out for his interests, or at least that he would not do anything contrary to his welfare. Examples of such relationships would include parent and child, husband and wife, or lawyer and client.

The relationship also can be one in which one of the parties holds dominant psychological power that is not derived from a confidential relationship. For example, Royce, an elderly man, is dependent on his housekeeper, Smith, to care for him. Smith persuades Royce to withdraw most of his life savings from the bank and make an interest-free loan to her. If the persuasion Smith used was unfair, the transaction could be avoided because of undue influence.

Unfair Persuasion   The mere existence of a close or dependent relationship between the parties that results in economic advantage to one of them is not sufficient for undue influence. It must also appear that the weaker person entered the contract because he was subjected to unfair methods of persuasion. In determining this, a court will look at all of the surrounding facts and circumstances. Was the person isolated and rushed into the contract, or did he have access to outsiders for advice and time to consider his alternatives? Was the contract discussed and consummated in the usual time and place that would be expected for such a transaction, or was it discussed or consummated at an unusual time or in an unusual place? Was the contract a reasonably fair one that a person might have entered voluntarily, or was it so lopsided and unfair that one could infer that he probably would not have entered it unless he had been unduly influenced by the other party? The answers to these and similar questions help determine whether the line between permissible and impermissible persuasion has been crossed. The following case, *Goldman v. Bequai,* provides an example of the factors that courts consider in determining undue influence.

GOLDMAN v. BEQUAI   19 F.3d 666 (D.C. Cir. 1994)

lorence Goldman was a woman in her 80s whose husband died after a long bout with Alzheimer's and Parkinson's diseases. For several years prior to her husband's death, Goldman had cared for him at home. During much of her husband's illness and for some time afterward, she was under the care of a psychiatrist, who treated her for depression stemming from the strain and grief she *experienced because of her husband's declining health. August Bequai was an attorney and a long-time friend whom Goldman regarded as almost a member of her family. After the death of Goldman's husband, she looked to Bequai as her adviser and attorney in financial affairs.*

Goldman, her son, and Bequai discussed starting a business that would employ both Goldman and her son. According to Goldman and her son, Bequai had told them that he needed to be listed as an owner of property that Goldman owned on Massachusetts Avenue in Washington, D.C., in order adequately to represent the Goldmans' interests during negotiations over the property. Bequai allegedly told Goldman's son that the transfer would be temporary and solely for the limited purpose of inflating his financial worth on paper while he looked for a business to invest in. In January 1986, three months after her husband's death, Goldman conveyed to Bequai joint tenancy with a right of survivorship (a form of joint ownership) in her condominium in Bethesda, Maryland, and a partnership interest in the Massachusetts Avenue property, for $10 consideration for the transfer of each property.

Goldman had no legal counsel or independent advice of any sort, and she alleges that Bequai did not fully explain the nature of the transactions to her. There were no witnesses to the transactions other than the notary. The Massachusetts Avenue property was sold in 1990 and the proceeds attributed to the Goldman/Bequai partnership were distributed to them. Both Bequai and Goldman were represented at the closing by an attorney hired by Bequai. After the sale of the property, Bequai accompanied Goldman to the bank, where both placed their proceeds in investment accounts that were opened that day. Bequai placed his money in an account he owned jointly with his wife, whereas Goldman placed her share in a joint account with Bequai.

Eventually, Goldman came to feel that Bequai had "deceived" her. In 1991, she brought several claims against Bequai, including fraud and breach of fiduciary duty. The trial court granted a summary judgment for Bequai on the ground that the three-year statute of limitations had run on Goldman's claim. Goldman appealed this ruling, arguing in part that the statute of limitations should be equitably tolled (that is, that time for filing suit should be extended) because Bequai had exercised undue influence on her. ∽

Edwards, Circuit Judge Goldman argued directly and unequivocally that Bequai obtained a joint tenancy in her real estate holdings through the exercise of undue influence over her. Undue influence is a contract doctrine which serves to equitably toll the statute of limitations.

Situations amounting to undue influence may be found when "a party in whom another reposes confidence misuses that confidence to gain his own advantage while the other has been made to feel that the party in question will not act against his welfare." SAMUEL WILLISTON, 13 WILLISTON ON CONTRACTS section 1625 at 776-77.

Whether a plaintiff is subject to undue influence is a question of fact. Both Williston and the *Restatement (Second) of Contracts* agree that the alleged victim's advanced age, mental condition and poor health, as well as the consideration a defendant gave for the benefit conferred by a plaintiff, are factors to be considered in establishing undue influence. Although the District Court made much of the fact that Goldman's psychiatrist stated that she was not mentally *incompetent,* this fact is hardly dispositive of the undue influence issue. Indeed, Williston specifi-

cally states that "[u]ndue influence in its essential elements has no real relation to mental incapacity." 13 WILLISTON section 1625 at 782.

It is a matter of basic contract law that if a plaintiff proves undue influence, the statute of limitations is equitably tolled so long as the influence continues. Goldman has alleged facts which a reasonable jury could find to constitute undue influence. She has suggested that her age, her lack of business experience, her long friendship with and reliance on Bequai, and her mental condition all made her susceptible to Bequai's manipulation. In addition, Goldman argues that Bequai was acting as her attorney, and that he accordingly had both additional influence over her and additional obligations to see to her welfare. Goldman also points to the paltry consideration she received for the enormous benefit she conferred on Bequai. These factors, if proven at trial, have the makings of a classic case of undue influence.

Reversed and remanded for further proceedings in favor of Goldman.

Wrongful Pressure in the Bargaining Process

	DURESS	UNDUE INFLUENCE
Nature of Pressure	Coercion	Unfair persuasion of susceptible individual
Elements	1. Contract induced by improper threat	1. Relationship of trust and confidence or dominance
	2. Threat leaves party no reasonable alternative but to enter or modify contract	2. Unfair persuasion

ETHICAL AND PUBLIC POLICY CONCERNS

1. You read that modern contract law has expanded the circumstances under which a contracting party has the duty to disclose facts material to the contract. Keep in mind that the facts that he is required to disclose would almost always harm his bargaining position—otherwise, he would have been only too happy to have volunteered the information. What are some ethical and public policy justifications for requiring an individual to volunteer information that is contrary to his interests?

2. Do you think the legal rules applied today regarding misrepresentation and duress encourage a higher standard of ethical dealing than did the legal rules applicable under classical contract law?

3. In this chapter, you learned a circumstance under which a contracting party owes a higher duty of conduct to someone with whom he is in a relationship of trust and confidence than he would owe to individuals with whom he stood in an arm's-length relationship. What is the justification for requiring a higher standard of ethical dealing in such relationships? Would you favor the law's imposing the same high standards of conduct in relation to the rest of the world? Why or why not?

PROBLEM CASES

1. After seeing a TV advertisement for Ed Garner's Autorama RV Center, the Hylers went to Autorama, talked with a salesperson, and looked at several recreational vehicles. They explained to the sales-person that they wanted a motor home that Mr. Hyler could drive and maintain. Mr. Hyler was disabled due to a back injury, and the Hylers were very concerned that they get adequate warranty protection on their RV so that Mr. Hyler would not be burdened with maintenance. After several conversations with the salesperson, they purchased a 1992 Lexington Mallard motor home for $62,115 less a trade-in allowance of $16,000 for their old car and trailer. The motor home came with three warranties. The coach was warranted by its manufacturer, Mallard. This warranty stated that if the buyer did not receive satisfactory warranty service from the dealer, the buyer was invited to contact the manufacturer. After several problems arose with the coach that were not corrected to the Hylers' satisfaction, the Hylers attempted to contact Mallard. When they did so, they learned that Mallard had ceased operation and filed a petition for bankruptcy two months prior to the date on which the Hylers purchased their vehicle. The Hylers' attorney wrote Autorama and rescinded the purchase contract, tendering the return of the motor home. Autorama denied the request for rescission. Did the Hylers have the right to rescind?

2. Blubaugh was summoned to his employers' office and told he could resign or he would be terminated from his district manager position. If he resigned and signed a letter releasing the employer from any and all claims he might have against the employer, he would get outplacement counseling and $4,560.78 in addition to the separation pay of $31,382.22 to which he was entitled. Blubaugh signed the agreement and turned in his letter of resignation. Later, at his request, he also received additional compensation for moving expenses.

When Blubaugh subsequently sued for damages relating to his termination, the employer argued his suit was barred by the release agreement. Blubaugh argued the agreement should be set aside on the ground of economic duress since he was in a state of shock and distraught about losing his job when he signed it, he had no opportunity to negotiate terms, and he was not told he could consult with a lawyer or file a grievance. Should the agreement be set aside on the ground of economic duress?

3. The Verbas sold the Rancourts a lakeshore lot in North Hero, Vermont, for $115,000. The Verbas knew that the Rancourts intended to build a residence on the lot in close proximity to the lakeshore. The Rancourts prepared the lakeshore building site by adding fill, but because this site preparation was done without permits, it violated state and federal wetland regulations. They were later ordered to remove all fill placed on the building site. On learning that they could not build near the lake, the Rancourts demanded that the Verbas rescind the transaction, refund the purchase price, and pay damages. The Verbas refused and the Rancourts brought a rescission action based on mutual mistake. Will they win?

4. Odorizzi, an elementary school teacher, was arrested on criminal charges involving illegal sexual activity. After he was arrested, questioned by police, booked, and released on bail, and had gone 40 hours, without sleep, he was visited in his home by the superintendent of the school district and the principal of his school. They told him that they were trying to help him and that they had his best interests at heart. They advised him to resign immediately, stating that there was no time to consult an attorney. They said that if he did not resign immediately, the district would dismiss him and publicize the proceedings, but that if he resigned at once, the incident would not be publicized and would not jeopardize his chances of securing employment as a teacher elsewhere. Odorizzi gave them a written letter of resignation, which they accepted. The criminal charges against Odorizzi were later dismissed, and he sought to resume his employment. When the school district refused to reinstate him, Odorizzi attempted to rescind his letter of resignation on several grounds, including undue influence. (He also alleged duress, but the facts of his case did not constitute duress under applicable state law). Can Odorizzi avoid the contract on the ground of undue influence?

5. The Walkers owned property in Eagle River, Alaska. In 1976, they listed the property for sale with a real estate broker. They signed a multiple listing agreement, which described the property as having 580 feet of highway frontage and stated, "ENGINEER REPORT SAYS OVER 1 MILLION IN GRAVEL ON PROP." A later listing contract signed with the same broker described the property as having 580 feet of highway frontage, but listed the gravel content as "minimum 80,000 cubic yds of gravel." An appraisal prepared to determine the property's value stated that it did not take any gravel into account, but described the ground as "all good gravel base." Cousineau, a contractor who was also in the gravel extraction business, became aware of the property when he saw the multiple listing. After visiting the property with his real estate broker and discussing gravel extraction with Mr. Walker, Cousineau offered to purchase the property. He then attempted to determine the lot's road frontage but was unsuccessful because the property was covered with snow. He was also unsuccessful in obtaining the engineer's report allegedly showing "over 1 million in gravel." Walker admitted at trial that he had never seen a copy of the report, either. Nevertheless, the parties signed and consummated a contract of sale for the purchase price of $385,000. There was no reference to the amount of highway frontage in the purchase agreement. After the sale was completed, Cousineau began developing the property and removing gravel. Cousineau learned that the description of highway frontage contained in the real estate listing was incorrect when a neighbor threatened to sue him for removing gravel from the neighbor's adjacent lot. A subsequent survey revealed that the highway frontage was 410 feet—not 580 feet, as advertised. At about the same time, the gravel ran out after Cousineau had removed only 6,000 cubic yards. Cousineau stopped making payments and informed the Walkers of his intention to rescind the contract. Cousineau brought an action against the Walkers, seeking the return of his money. Does Cousineau have the right to rescind?

6. Boskett, a part-time coin dealer, paid $450 for a dime purportedly minted in 1916 at Denver and two additional coins of relatively small value. After carefully examining the dime, Beachcomber Coins, a retail coin dealer, bought the coin from Boskett for $500. Beachcomber then received an offer from a third party to purchase the dime for $700, subject to certification of its genuineness from the American Numismatic Society. That organization labeled the coin a counterfeit. Can Beachcomber rescind the contract with Boskett on the ground of mistake?

7. [▣▣▣] *Video Case.* Retailer opened a baseball card store in vacant premises next to an existing store. The card shop was very busy on opening day, so Retailer got a clerk from the adjacent store to help out. The clerk knew nothing about baseball cards. A boy who had a large baseball card collection asked to see an Ernie Banks rookie card, which was in a plastic case with an adhesive dot attached that read "1200." The boy asked the salesclerk, "Is it really worth $12?" The salesclerk responded, "I guess so," or "I'm sure it is." The boy bought the card for $12. In fact, the true price intended by Retailer was $1,200. Can Retailer get the card back from the boy?

8. Robert & Wendy Pfister asked Foster & Marshall, a stock brokerage firm, to evaluate some stocks that they owned. One of these stocks was 100 shares of Tracor Computing Corporation. The stock was no longer traded on the New York Stock Exchange. The Pfisters did not know the value of the stock, but they believed it to be of little value. They were surprised when Foster & Marshall told them that the stock was trading at $49.50 under its new name, Continuum Co., Inc., so that the value of the Pfisters' stock was $4,950. They asked Foster & Marshall to recheck the figures and brought their stock certificates in for verification. Based on Foster & Marshall's reassurances that they owned 100 shares of Continuum and that these were worth $4,950, the Pfisters sold the stock to Foster & Marshall. As a result of receiving this money for the stock, the Pfisters made a commitment to build a new home, which before the sale had been a "borderline decision." A year after the transaction, Foster & Marshall discovered that the Tracor Computing stock had been exchanged for Continuum stock at a 10-to-1 ratio and that the Pfisters had owned only 10 shares of Continuum. Foster & Marshall claimed relief under the doctrine of mistake and sued the Pfisters to recover the $4,466.25 it had overpaid them. Will Foster & Marshall win?

9. Snap-On manufactures and sells hand tools to a nationwide network of dealers, each of whom is assigned a marketing territory. The dealers, in turn, resell the tools to professional mechanics. Eulrich, an auto body mechanic who had never before operated a business, entered into a dealership agreement and became a Snap-On dealer in 1986. Eulrich initially invested $22,000 from his savings and promised to pay a balance of $22,500 from the sale of inventory. The dealership agreement included a provision allowing termination of the dealership by either party. It further provided that upon termination, if Snap-On consented, Eulrich could resell to Snap-On any new tools remaining in his possession. From the very beginning, Eulrich's dealership was not profitable. In early 1987, he tried to get a more profitable territory because his territory was not supporting him, but he was told to work the territory harder. Eulrich's supervisors, Kash and Park, insisted that anyone could succeed as a dealer by following Snap-On's sales program. (However, there was evidence that Snap-On's marketing system was designed to provide a maximum number of potential dealers and profit for Snap-On while providing inadequate revenue to support dealers. As a result, dealers quickly failed and were replaced by new recruits.) By the spring of 1987, Eulrich was financially ruined, and informed Kash and Park that he wanted to exercise his rights under the dealership agreement and terminate his dealership. Beginning in April, he attempted to get Kash and Park to "check in" his truck, which he understood would allow him to receive a refund for the tools and the equity in his van. He needed this money to pay his household bills because his dealership had depleted his personal finances. Kash and Park repeatedly put off this check-in until June 1. By that time, as they knew, Eulrich was in serious financial difficulty and could not pay his living expenses, a situation that was aggravated by the fact that Eulrich's wife was ill and required hospitalization but had no medical insurance. On the day of the check-in, after having worked five or six hours to unload the van under trying circumstances, Kash and Park had Eulrich come into Park's office to "do paperwork." Eulrich was physically tired and emotionally drained. In the office, Kash and Park berated Eulrich for his poor business practices. They also presented Eulrich with a number of documents, none of which had been sent to him in advance to review, and told him to sign them. Kash told Eulrich that he would have to sign the papers before he could get any money. When he asked when he would get a check, Park told him that there would be no checks until the inventory was done and all of the papers were signed. Eulrich signed the papers.

Included in the papers that he signed was a "Termination Agreement," which included an agreement by Snap-On to repurchase Eulrich's tool inventory at current dealer cost. Also included in the document was a release of claims which provided that "each party to this Agreement waives any and all claims it may have against the other arising out of the Dealership terminated by this Agreement. . . ." Eulrich was not aware that a release was included in the Termination Agreement, nor was he aware that he had any legal claims against Snap-On. Eulrich later filed a lawsuit against Snap-On, Kash, Park, and another Snap-On supervisor to recover damages for fraud, breach of good faith and fair dealing, and breach of contract arising out of the original dealership contract. The defendants asserted that the release barred these claims. Eulrich sought to rescind the release on a number of grounds, including economic duress. Was this a case of economic duress?

10. Ashton Development hired Rich & Whillock, Inc., to do grading and excavating work on a construction project. The contract specified that removal of any rock encountered would be considered an "extra." After a month's work, Rich & Whillock encountered rock on the project site. Ashton agreed that the rock would have to be blasted and that this would involve extra costs. It directed Rich & Whillock to go ahead with the blasting and bill for the extra cost. Rich & Whillock did so, submitting separate invoices for the regular contract work and the extra blasting work and receiving payment every two weeks. After complet-ing the work, Rich & Whillock submitted a final billing for an additional $72,286.45. This time, Ashton refused to pay. Rich & Whillock communicated that it would "go broke" without this final payment because it was a new business with rented equipment and had numerous subcontractors waiting to be paid. Ashton replied that it would pay $50,000 or nothing. Stating, "I have a check for you, and just take it or leave it, this is all you get. If you don't want this, you have got to sue me," Ashton's agent presented Rich & Whillock with an agreement for a final compromise payment of $50,000. Rich & Whillock signed the settlement agreement and received a $25,000 check after communicating that the agreement was "blackmail" and that it was signing the agreement only because it was necessary in order to survive. Rich & Whillock later signed a release form and received a second check for $25,000. Several months afterward, however, Rich & Whillock sued Ashton for breach of contract, maintaining that the settlement agreement and release should not be enforced. Are the settlement agreement and release voidable?

11. Reed purchased a house from King. Neither King nor his real estate agents told Reed before the sale that a woman and her four children had been murdered there 10 years earlier. Reed learned of the gruesome episode from a neighbor after the sale. She sued King and his real estate agents, seeking rescission and damages on the ground that King should have disclosed the history of the house to her. Can Reed rescind the contract?

Capacity to Contract

One of the major justifications for enforcing a contract is that the parties voluntarily consented to be bound by it. It follows, then, that a person must have the *ability* to give consent before he can be legally bound to an agreement. For truly voluntary agreements to exist, this ability to give consent must involve more than the mere physical ability to say yes or shake hands or sign one's name. Rather, the person's maturity and mental ability must be such that it is fair to presume that he is capable of representing his own interests effectively. This concept is embodied in the legal term *capacity.* ⌇

LACK OF CAPACITY

Capacity means the ability to incur legal obligations and acquire legal rights. Today, the primary classes of people who are considered to lack capacity are minors (who, in legal terms, are known as *infants*), persons suffering from mental illnesses or defects, and intoxicated persons.[1] Contract law gives them the right to *avoid* (escape) contracts that they enter during incapacity. This rule provides a means of protecting people who, because of mental impairment, intoxication, or youth and inexperience, are disadvantaged in the normal give and take of the bargaining process.

Usually, lack of capacity to contract comes up in court in one of two ways. In some cases, it is asserted by a plaintiff as the basis of a lawsuit for the money or other benefits that he gave the other

---

[1] In times past, married women, convicts, and aliens were also among the classes of persons who lacked capacity to contract. These limitations on capacity have been removed by statute and court rule, however.

party under their contract. In others, it arises as a defense to the enforcement of a contract when the defendant is the party who lacked capacity. The responsibility for alleging and proving incapacity is placed on the person who bases his claim or defense on his lack of capacity.

Effect of Lack of Capacity

Normally, a contract in which one or both parties lack capacity because of infancy, mental impairment, or intoxication is considered to be voidable. People whose capacity is impaired in any of these ways are able to enter a contract and enforce it if they wish, but they also have the right to avoid the contract. There are, however, some individuals whose capacity is so impaired that they do not have the ability to form even a voidable contract. A bargain is considered to be void if, at the time of formation of the bargain, a court had already **adjudicated** (adjudged or decreed) one or more of the parties to be mentally incompetent or one or more of the parties was so impaired that he could not even manifest assent (for example, he was comatose or unconscious).

MINORS' CONTRACTS

Minors' Right to Disaffirm

Courts have long recognized that minors are in a vulnerable position in their dealings with adults. Courts granted minors the right to avoid contracts as a means of protecting against their own improvidence and against overreaching by adults. The exercise of this right to avoid a contract is called **disaffirmance.** The right to disaffirm is personal to the minor. That is, only the minor or a legal representative such as a guardian may disaffirm the contract. No formal act or written statement is required to make a valid disaffirmance. Any words or acts that effectively communicate the minor's desire to cancel the contract can constitute disaffirmance.

If, on the other hand, the minor wishes to enforce the contract instead of disaffirming it, the adult party must perform. You can see that the minor's right to disaffirm puts any adult contracting with a minor in an undesirable position: He is bound on the contract unless it is to the minor's advantage to disaffirm it. The right to disaffirm has the effect of discouraging adults from dealing with minors.

Exceptions to the Minor's Right to Disaffirm Not every contract involving a minor is voidable, however. State law often creates statutory exceptions to the minor's right to disaffirm. These statutes prevent minors from disaffirming such transactions as marriage, agreements to support their children, educational loans, life and medical insurance contracts, contracts for transportation by common carriers, and certain types of contracts approved by a court (such as contracts to employ a child actor).

Period of Minority

At common law, the age of majority was 21. However, the ratification in 1971 of the 26th Amendment to the Constitution giving 18-year-olds the right to vote stimulated a trend toward reducing the age of majority. The age of majority has been lowered by 49 states. In almost all of these states, the age of majority for contracting purposes is now 18.

Emancipation

Emancipation is the termination of a parent's right to control a child and receive services and wages from him. There are no formal requirements for emancipation. It can occur by the parent's express or implied consent or by the occurrence of some events such as the marriage of the child. In most states, the mere fact that a minor is emancipated does *not* give him capacity to contract. A person younger than the legal age of majority is generally held to lack capacity to enter a contract, even if he is married and employed full time.

Time of Disaffirmance

Contracts entered during minority that affect title to *real estate* cannot be disaffirmed until majority. This rule is apparently based on the special importance of real estate and on the need to protect a minor from improvidently disaffirming a transaction (such as a mortgage or conveyance) involving real estate. All other contracts entered during minority may be disaffirmed as soon as the contract is formed. The minor's power to avoid his contracts does not end on the day he reaches the age of majority. It continues for a period of time after he reaches majority.

How long after reaching majority does a person retain the right to disaffirm the contracts he made

FIGURE I

Time Line Showing Effect of Ratification

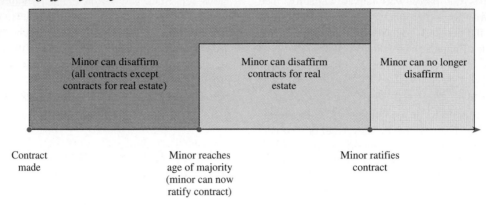

while a minor? A few states have statutes that prescribe a definite time limit on the power of avoidance. In Oklahoma, for example, a person who wishes to disaffirm a contract must do so within one year after reaching majority.[2] In most states, however, there is no set limit on the time during which a person may disaffirm after reaching majority. In determining whether a person has the right to disaffirm, a major factor that courts consider is whether the adult has rendered performance under the contract or relied on the contract. If the adult has relied on the contract or has given something of value to the minor, the minor must disaffirm within a reasonable time after reaching majority. If he delays longer than a period of time that is considered to be reasonable under the circumstances, he will run the risk of *ratifying* (affirming) the contract. (The concept and consequences of ratification are discussed in the next section.) If the adult has neither performed nor relied on the contract, however, the former minor is likely to be accorded a longer period of time in which to disaffirm, sometimes even years after he has reached majority.

Ratification

Though a person has the right to disaffirm contracts made during minority, this right can be given up after the person reaches the age of majority. When a person who has reached majority indicates that he intends to be bound by a contract that he made while still a minor, he surrenders his right to disaffirm. This act of affirming the contract and surrendering the right to avoid the contract is known as **ratification.** Ratification makes a contract valid from its inception. Because ratification represents the former minor's election to be bound by the contract, he cannot later disaffirm. Ratification can be done effectively only after the minor reaches majority. Otherwise, it would be as voidable as the initial contract. The effect of ratification is illustrated in Figure 1.

There are no formal requirements for ratification. Any of the former minor's words or acts after reaching majority that indicate with reasonable clarity his intent to be bound by the contract are sufficient. Ratification can be *expressed* in an oral or written statement, or, as is more often the case, it can be *implied* by conduct on the part of the former minor. Naturally, ratification is clearest when the former minor has made some express statement of his intent to be bound. Predicting whether a court will determine that a contract has been ratified is a bit more difficult when the only evidence of the alleged ratification is the conduct of the minor. A former minor's acceptance or retention of benefits given by the other party for an unreasonable time after he has reached majority can constitute ratification. Also, a former minor's continued performance of his part of the contract after reaching majority has been held to imply his intent to ratify the contract.

Duty to Return Consideration upon Disaffirmance

If neither party has performed his part of the contract, the parties' relationship will simply be

---

[2]Okla. Stat. Ann. tit. 15 sec. 18 (1983).

canceled by the disaffirmance. Since neither party has given anything to the other party, no further adjustments are necessary. But what about the situation where, as is often the case, the minor has paid money to the adult and the adult has given property to the minor? Upon disaffirmance, each party has the duty to return to the other any consideration that the other has given. This means that the minor must return any consideration given to him by the adult that remains in his possession. However, if the minor is unable to return the consideration, most states will still permit him to disaffirm the contract.

The duty to return consideration also means that the minor has the right to recover any consideration he has given to the adult party. He even has the right to recover some property that has been transferred to third parties. One exception to the minor's right to recover property from third parties is found in section 2–403 of the Uniform Commercial Code, however. Under this section, a minor cannot recover *goods* that have been transferred to a good faith purchaser. For example, Simpson, a minor, sells a 1980 Ford to Mort's Car Lot. Mort's then sells the car to Vane, a good faith purchaser. If Simpson disaffirmed the contract with Mort's, he would *not* have the right to recover the Ford from Vane.

Must the Disaffirming Minor Make Restitution? A Split of Authority

If the consideration given by the adult party has been lost, damaged, destroyed, or simply has depreciated in value, is the minor required to make restitution to the adult for the loss? The traditional rule is that the minor who cannot fully return the consideration that was given to her is *not* obligated to pay the adult for the benefits she has received or to compensate the adult for loss or depreciation of the consideration. Some states still follow this traditional rule. (As you will read in the next section, however, a minor's misrepresentation of age can, even in some of these states, make her responsible for reimbursing the other party upon disaffirmance.) The rule that restitution is not required is designed to protect minors by discouraging adults from dealing with them. After all, if an adult knew that he might be able to demand the return of anything that he transferred to a minor, he would have little incentive to refrain from entering into contracts with minors.

The traditional rule, however, can work harsh results for innocent adults who have dealt fairly with minors. It strikes many people as unprincipled that a doctrine intended to protect against unfair exploitation of one class of people can be used to unfairly exploit another class of people. As courts sometimes say, the minor's right to disaffirm was designed to be used as a "shield rather than as a sword." For these reasons, a growing number of states have rejected the traditional rule. The courts and legislatures of these states have adopted rules that require minors who disaffirm their contracts and seek refunds of purchase price to reimburse adults for the use or depreciation of their property. The following case, *Dodson v. Shrader*, follows this approach.

DODSON v. SHRADER   824 W.2d 545 (Tenn. Sup. Ct. 1992)

J oseph Dodson, age 16, bought a 1984 Chevrolet truck from Burns and Mary Shrader, owners of Shrader's Auto Sales, for $4,900 cash. At the time, Burns Shrader, believing Dodson to be 18 or 19, did not ask Dodson's age and Dodson did not volunteer it. Dodson drove the truck for about eight months, when he learned from an auto mechanic that there was a burned valve in the engine. Dodson did not have the money for the repairs, so he continued to drive the truck without repair for another month until the engine "blew up" and stopped operating. He parked the car in the front yard of his parents' house. He then contacted the Shraders, rescinding the purchase of the truck and requesting a full refund. The Shraders refused to accept the truck or to give Dodson a refund. Dodson then filed an action seeking to rescind the contract and recover the amount paid for the truck. Before the court could hear the case, a hit-and-run driver struck Dodson's parked truck, damaging its left front fender. At the time of the circuit court trial, the truck was worth only $500. The Shraders argued that Dodson should be responsible for paying the difference between the present value of the truck and the $4,900 purchase price. The trial court found in Dodson's favor, ordering the Shraders to refund the $4,900 purchase price upon delivery of the truck. The Tennessee Court of Appeals affirmed this judgment, and the Shraders appealed. ∽

O'Brien, Justice The law on the subject of the protection of infants' rights has been slow to evolve. The underlying purpose of the "infancy doctrine" is to protect minors from their lack of judgment and from squandering their wealth through improvident contracts with crafty adults who would take advantage of them in the marketplace.

There is, however, a modern trend among the states, either by judicial action or by statute, in the approach to the problem of balancing the rights of minors against those of innocent merchants. As a result, two minority rules have developed which allow the other party to a contract with a minor to refund less than the full consideration paid in the event of rescission. The first of these minority rules is called the "Benefit Rule." This rule holds that, upon rescission, recovery of the full purchase price is subject to a deduction for the minor's use of the merchandise. This rule recognizes that the traditional rule in regard to necessaries has been extended so far as to hold an infant bound by his contracts, where he failed to restore what he has received under them to the extent of the benefit actually derived by him from what he has received from the other party to the transaction. The other minority rule holds that the minor's recovery of the full purchase price is subject to a deduction for the minor's "use" of the consideration he or she received under the contract, or for the "depreciation" or "deterioration" of the consideration in his or her possession.

We are impressed by the statement made by the Court of Appeals of Ohio:

At a time when we see young persons between 18 and 21 years of age demanding and assuming more responsibilities in their daily lives; when we see such persons charged with the responsibility for committing crimes; when we see such persons being sued in tort claims for acts of negligence; when we see such persons subject to military service; when we see such persons engaged in business and acting in almost all other respects as an adult, it seems timely to re-examine the case law pertaining to contractual rights and responsibilities of infants to see if the law as pronounced and applied by the courts should be redefined.

We state the rule to be followed hereafter, in reference to a contract of a minor, to be where the minor has not been overreached in any way, and there has been no undue influence, and the contract is a fair and reasonable one, and the minor has actually paid money on the purchase price, and taken and used the article purchased, that he ought not to be permitted to recover the amount actually paid, without allowing the vendor of the goods reasonable compensation for the use of, depreciation, and willful or negligent damage to the article purchased, while in his hands. If there has been any fraud or imposition on the part of the seller or if the contract is unfair, or any unfair advantage has been taken of the minor inducing him to make the purchase, then the rule does not apply. This rule will fully and fairly protect the minor against injustice or imposition, and at the same time it will be fair to a business person who has dealt with such minor in good faith.

This rule is best adapted to modern conditions under which minors are permitted to, and do in fact, transact a great deal of business for themselves, long before they have reached the age of legal majority. Many young people work and earn money and collect it and spend it oftentimes without any oversight or restriction. The law does not question their right to buy if they have the money to pay for their purchases. It seems intolerably burdensome of everyone concerned if merchants cannot deal with them safely, in a fair and reasonable way. Further, it does not appear consistent with practice of proper moral influence upon young people, tend to encourage honesty and integrity, or lead them to a good and useful business future if they are taught that they can make purchases with their own money, for their own benefit, and after paying for them, and using them until they are worn out and destroyed, go back and compel the vendor to return to them what they have paid upon the purchase price. Such a doctrine can only lead to the corruption of principles and encourage young people in habits of trickery and dishonesty.

Reversed and remanded in favor of the Shraders.

Effect of Misrepresentation of Age

It is not unheard of for a minor to occasionally pretend to be older than he is. The normal rules dealing with the minor's right to disaffirm and his duties upon disaffirmance can be affected by a minor's misrepresentation of his age.[3] Suppose, for example, that Jones, age 17, wants to lease a car from Acme Auto Rentals, but knows that Acme rents only to people who are at least 18. Jones induces Acme to lease a car to him by showing a false identification that represents his age to be 18. Acme relies on the misrepresentation. Jones wrecks the car, attempts to disaffirm the contract, and asks for the return of his money. What is the effect of Jones's misrepresentation? State law is not uniform on this point.

The traditional rule was that a minor's misrepresentation about his age did not affect his right to disaffirm and did not create any obligation to reimburse the adult for damages or pay for benefits received. The theory behind this rule is that one who lacks capacity cannot acquire it merely by claiming to be of legal age. As you can imagine, this traditional approach does not "sit well" with modern courts, at least in those cases in which the adult has dealt with the minor fairly and in good faith, because it creates severe hardship for innocent adults who have relied on minors' misrepresentations of age.

State law today is fairly evenly divided among those states that take the position that the minor who misrepresents his age will be *estopped* (prevented) from asserting his infancy as a defense and those that will allow a minor to disaffirm regardless of his misrepresentation of age. Among the states that allow disaffirmance despite the minor's misrepresentation, most hold the disaffirming minor responsible for the losses suffered by the adult, either by allowing the adult to counterclaim against the minor for the tort of deceit or by requiring the minor to reimburse the adult for use or depreciation of his property.

Minors' Obligation to Pay Reasonable Value of Necessaries

Though the law regarding minors' contracts is designed to discourage adults from dealing with (and possibly taking advantage of) minors, it would be undesirable for the law to discourage adults from selling minors the items that they need for basic survival. For this reason, disaffirming minors are required to pay the reasonable value of items that have been furnished to them that are classified as **necessaries.** A necessary is something that is essential for the minor's continued existence and general welfare that has not been provided by the minor's parents or guardian. Examples of necessaries include food, clothing, shelter, medical care, tools of the minor's trade, and basic educational or vocational training.

A minor's liability for necessaries supplied to him is **quasi contractual.** That is, the minor is liable for the *reasonable value* of the necessaries that she actually receives. She is not liable for the entire price agreed on if that price exceeds the actual value of the necessaries, and she is not liable for necessaries that she contracted for but did not receive. For example, Joy Jones, a minor, signs a one-year lease for an apartment in Mountain Park at a rent of $300 per month. After living in the apartment for three months, Joy breaks her lease and moves out. Because she is a minor, Joy has the right to disaffirm the lease. If shelter is a necessary in this case, however, she must pay the reasonable value of what she has actually received—three months' rent. If she can establish that the actual value of what she has received is less than $300 per month, she will be bound to pay only that lesser amount. Furthermore, she will not be obligated to pay for the remaining nine months' rent, because she has not received any benefits from the remainder of the lease.

Whether a given item is considered a necessary depends on the facts of a particular case. The minor's age, station in life, and personal circumstances are all relevant to this issue. As is emphasized in the *Webster Street Partnership* case, which follows, an item sold to a minor is not considered a necessary if the minor's parent or guardian has already supplied him with similar items. For this reason, the range of items that will be considered necessaries is broader for married minors and other emancipated minors than it is for unemancipated minors.

[3]You might want to refer back to Chapter 13 to review the elements of misrepresentation.

*W*ebster Street owns real estate in Omaha, Nebraska. On September 18, 1982, Webster Street entered into a written contract to lease an apartment to Matthew Sheridan and Pat Wilwerding for one year at a rental of $250 per month. Although Webster Street did not know this, both Sheridan and Wilwerding were younger than the age of majority (which was 19) when the lease was signed.

Sheridan and Wilwerding paid $150 as a security deposit and rent for the remainder of September and the month of October, for a total of $500. They failed to pay their November rent on time, however, and Webster Street notified them that they would be required to move out unless they paid immediately. Unable to pay rent, Sheridan and Wilwerding moved out of the apartment on November 12. Webster Street later demanded that they pay the expenses it incurred in attempting to rerent the property, rent for the months of November and December (apparently the two months it took to find a new tenant), and assorted damages and fees, amounting to $630.94. Sheridan and Wilwerding refused to pay any of the amount demanded on the ground of minority, and demanded the return of their security deposit. Webster Street then filed this lawsuit. The district court found that the apartment was a necessary and that Sheridan and Wilwerding were liable for the 12 days in November in which they had actually possessed the apartment without paying rent, but that they were entitled to the return of their security deposit. Webster Street appealed from this ruling. ∞

Krivosha, Chief Justice   The privilege of infancy will not enable an infant to escape liability under all circumstances. For example, it is well established that an infant is liable for the value of necessaries furnished him. Just what are necessaries, however, has no exact definition. The term is flexible and varies according to the facts of each individual case. A number of factors must be considered before a court can conclude whether a particular product or service is a necessary. The articles must be useful and suitable. To be necessaries the articles must supply the infant's personal needs, either those of his body or those of his mind. However, the term "necessaries" is not confined to merely such things as are required for bare subsistence. What may be considered necessary for one infant may not be necessaries for another infant whose state is different as to rank, social position, fortune, health, or other circumstances. To enable an infant to contract for articles as necessaries, he must have been in actual need of them, and obliged to procure them for himself. They are not necessaries as to him, however necessary they may be in their nature, if he was already supplied with sufficient articles of the kind, or if he had a parent or guardian who was able and willing to supply them. The burden of proof is on the plaintiff to show that the infant was destitute of the articles and had no way of procuring them except by his own contract.

The undisputed testimony is that both tenants were living away from home, apparently with the understanding that they could return home at any time. It would appear that neither Sheridan nor Wilwerding was in need of shelter but, rather, had chosen to voluntarily leave home, with the understanding that they could return whenever they desired. One may at first blush believe that such a rule is unfair. Yet, on further consideration, the wisdom of such a rule is apparent. If landlords may not contract with minors, except at their peril, they may refuse to do so. In that event, minors who voluntarily leave home but who are free to return will be compelled to return to their parents' home—a result which is desirable. We therefore hold that the district court erred in finding that the apartment was a necessary.

Because the rental of the apartment was not a necessary, the minors had the right to avoid the contract, either during their minority or within a reasonable time after reaching their majority. Disaffirmance by an infant completely puts an end to the contract's existence both as to him and as to the adult with whom he contracted. Because the parties then stand as if no contract had ever existed, the infant can recover payments made to the adult, and the adult is entitled to the return of whatever was received by the infant.

The record shows that Wilwerding clearly disaffirmed the contract during his minority. Moreover, when Webster Street ordered the minors out for failure to pay rent and they vacated the premises, Sheridan likewise disaffirmed the contract. The record indicates that Sheridan reached majority on November 5. To suggest that a lapse of 7 days was not disaffirmance within a reasonable time would be foolish. Once disaffirmed, no contract existed between the parties and the minors were entitled to recover all of the moneys which they paid and to be relieved of any further obligation under the contract. The judgment of the district court is therefore reversed and the cause remanded with directions to vacate the judgment in favor of Webster Street and to enter a judgment in favor of Matthew Sheridan and Pat Wilwerding in the amount of $500, representing September rent in the amount of $100, October rent in the amount of $250, and the security deposit in the amount of $150.

Judgment reversed in favor of Sheridan and Wilwerding.

CAPACITY OF MENTALLY IMPAIRED PERSONS

Theory of Incapacity

Like minors, people who suffer from a mental illness or defect are at a disadvantage in their ability to protect their own interests in the bargaining process. Contract law makes their contracts either void or voidable to protect them from the results of their own impaired perceptions and judgment and from others who might take advantage of them.

Test for Mental Incapacity

Incapacity on grounds of mental illness or defect, which is often referred to in cases and texts as "insanity," encompasses a broad range of causes of impaired mental functioning, such as mental illness, brain damage, mental retardation, or senility. The mere fact that a person suffers from some mental illness or defect does not necessarily mean that he lacks capacity to contract, however. He could still have full capacity unless the defect or illness affects the particular transaction in question.

The usual test for mental incapacity is a *cognitive* one; that is, courts ask whether the person had sufficient mental capacity to understand the nature and effect of the contract. Some courts have criticized the traditional test as unscientific because it does not take into account the fact that a person suffering from a mental illness or defect might be unable to *control* his conduct. Section 15 of the *Restatement (Second) of Contracts* provides that a person's contracts are voidable if he is unable to *act* in a reasonable manner in relation to the transaction and the other party has reason to know of his condition. Where the other party has reason to know of the condition of the mentally impaired person, the *Restatement (Second)* standard would provide protection to people who understood the transaction but, because of some mental defect or illness, were unable to exercise appropriate judgment or to control their conduct effectively. This standard is employed by the court in the following case, *Farnum v. Silvano.*

FARNUM v. SILVANO   540 N.E.2d 202 (App. Ct. of Mass. 1989)

Viola Farnum was 90 years old when she sold her real estate in South Yarmouth to Joseph Silvano, age 24. Farnum knew and trusted Silvano because he had done mowing and landscape work on her property. Although the fair market value of Farnum's property was $115,000 at the time of the sale, she agreed to sell it as well as the furniture and other furnishings in the house for $64,900. Silvano had reason to know of the inadequacy of the purchase price. Farnum's nephew had warned Silvano not to proceed with the sale. In addition, Silvano was able to get a mortgage for $65,000 from the bank to finance the purchase.

Farnum's mental competence had begun to fail seriously three years before the sale to Silvano. She began to engage in aberrant conduct such as lamenting not hearing from her sisters, who were dead, and she would wonder where the people upstairs in her house had gone, when there was no upstairs to her house. She offered to sell her house to a neighbor for $35,000. She became abnormally forgetful, locking herself out of her house *and breaking into it rather than calling on a neighbor with whom she had left a key. She hid her cat to protect it from "the cops." She would express the desire to return to Cape Cod although she was on Cape Cod. She easily became lost. Her sister and nephew had to pay her bills and balance her checkbook. She was hospitalized several times during the three-year period preceding the sale to Silvano. Medical tests revealed organic brain disease.*

During the transaction in question, Farnum was represented by a lawyer selected and paid by Silvano. That lawyer and a lawyer for the bank that was making a loan to Silvano attended the closing at Farnum's house. At the closing, Farnum was cheerful, engaged in pleasantries, and made instant coffee for those present. After the transaction, however, Farnum insisted to others, including her sister and nephew, that she still owned the property. Six months after the conveyance, Farnum was admitted to the hospital for treatment of dementia and seizure disorder. She was discharged to a nursing home.

Farnum's nephew, who was ultimately appointed her guardian, brought this suit on Farnum's behalf to rescind the sale on the ground of Farnum's mental impairment. The trial judge concluded that Farnum had been "aware of what was going on," and denied the rescission. Farnum appealed. ∞

Kass, Judge   On the basis of a finding that Farnum enjoyed a lucid interval when she conveyed her house to Silvano, for approximately half its market value, a Probate Court judge decided that Farnum had capacity to execute the deed. A different test measures competence to enter into a contract and we, therefore, reverse the judgment.

Competence to enter into a contract presupposes something more than a transient surge of lucidity. It involves not merely comprehension of what is "going on," but an ability to comprehend the nature and quality of the transaction, together with an understanding of its significance and consequences. In the act of entering into a contract there are reciprocal obligations, and it is appropriate, when mental incapacity, as here, is manifest, to require a baseline of reasonableness.

In *Krasner v. Berk,* the court cited with approval the synthesis of those principles now appearing in the *Restatement (Second) of Contracts* section 15(1), which regards as voidable a transaction entered into with a person who, "by reason of mental illness or defect (a) . . . is unable to understand in a reasonable manner the nature and consequences of the transaction, or (b) . . . is unable to act in a reasonable manner in relation to the transaction and the other party has reason to know of [the] condition."

Applied to the case at hand, Farnum could be aware that she was selling her house to Silvano for much less than it was worth, while failing to understand the unreasonableness of doing so at a time when she faced serious cash demands for rent, home care, or nursing care charges. That difference between awareness of the surface of a transaction, *i.e.,* that it was happening, and failure to comprehend the unreasonableness and consequences of the transaction by a mentally impaired person was recognized and discussed in *Ortolere v. Teachers' Retirement Bd.* In the Ortolere case, a teacher who was enrolled in a retirement plan suffered a psychotic break. Her age was 60 and she also suffered from cerebral arteriosclerosis. While thus afflicted, Grace Ortolere changed her selection of benefit to choose the maximum retirement allowance during her lifetime with nothing payable after her death— this in the face of severely diminished life expectancy and her husband having given up his employment to care for her full time. The court observed that her selection was so unwise and foolhardy that a fact finder might conclude that it was explainable only as a product of psychosis.

We think Farnum did not possess the requisite contextual understanding. She suffered mental disease which had manifested itself in erratic and irrational conduct and was confirmed by diagnostic test. Her physician did not think she was competent to live alone. Relatively soon after the transaction, Farnum's mental deficits grew so grave that it became necessary to hospitalize her. The man to whom she sold her property for less than its value was not a member of her family or someone who had cared for her for long duration. Farnum was not represented by a lawyer who knew her and considered her overall interests as a primary concern. The mission of the lawyer secured by Silvano, and paid by him, was to effect the transaction. As we have observed, Farnum was faced with growing cash demands for her maintenance, and, in her circumstances, it was not rational to part with a major asset for a cut-rate price.

The decisive factor which we think makes Farnum's delivery of her deed to Silvano voidable was his awareness of Farnum's inability to act in a reasonable manner. Silvano knew or had reason to know of Farnum's impaired condition from her conduct, which at the times material caused concern to her relatives, her neighbors, and her physician. Silvano was aware that he was buying the house for about half its value. He had been specifically warned by Farnum's nephew about the unfairness of the transaction and Farnum's mental disability.

Farnum is entitled to rescission of the conveyance.

Judgment reversed in favor of Farnum.

The Effect of Incapacity Caused by Mental Impairment

The contracts of people who are suffering from a mental defect at the time of contracting are usually considered to be *voidable*. In some situations, however, severe mental or physical impairment may prevent a person from even being able to manifest consent. In such a case, no contract could be formed.

As mentioned at the beginning of this chapter, contract law makes a distinction between a contract involving a person who has been *adjudicated* (judged by a court) incompetent at the time the contract was made and a contract involving a person who was suffering from some mental impairment at the time the contract was entered but whose incompetency was not established until *after* the contract was formed. If a person is under guardianship at the time the contract is formed—that is, if a court has found a person mentally incompetent after holding a hearing on his mental competency and has appointed a guardian for him—the contract is considered *void*. On the other hand, if *after* a contract has been formed, a court finds that the person who manifested consent lacked capacity on grounds of mental illness or defect, the contract is usually considered *voidable* at the election of the party who lacked capacity (or his guardian or personal representative).

The Right to Disaffirm

If a contract is found to be voidable on the ground of mental impairment, the person who lacked capacity at the time the contract was made has the right to disaffirm the contract. A person formerly incapacitated by mental impairment can ratify a contract if he regains his capacity. Thus, if he regains capacity, he must disaffirm the contract unequivocally within a reasonable time, or he will be deemed to have ratified it.

As is true of a disaffirming minor, a person disaffirming on the ground of mental impairment must return any consideration given by the other party that remains in his possession. A person under this type of mental incapacity is liable for the reasonable value of necessaries in the same manner as are minors. Must the incapacitated party reimburse the other party for loss, damage, or depreciation of non-necessaries given to him? This is generally said to depend on whether the contract was basically fair and on whether the other party had reason to be aware of his impairment. If the contract is fair, bargained for in good faith, and the other party had no reasonable cause to know of the incapacity, the contract cannot be disaffirmed unless the other party is placed in *status quo* (the position she was in before the creation of the contract). However, if the other party had reason to know of the incapacity, the incapacitated party is allowed to disaffirm without placing the other party in status quo. This distinction discourages people from attempting to take advantage of mentally impaired people, but it spares those who are dealing in good faith and have no such intent.

CONTRACTS OF INTOXICATED PERSONS

Intoxication and Capacity

Intoxication (either from alcohol or the use of drugs) can deprive a person of capacity to contract. The mere fact that a party to a contract had been drinking when the contract was formed would *not* normally affect his capacity to contract, however. Intoxication is a ground for lack of capacity only when it is so extreme that the person is unable to understand the nature of the business at hand. Section 16 of the *Restatement (Second) of Contracts* further provides that intoxication is a ground for lack of capacity only if *the other party has reason to know* that the affected person is so intoxicated that he cannot understand or act reasonably in relation to the transaction.

The rules governing the capacity of intoxicated persons are very similar to those applied to the capacity of people who are mentally impaired. The basic right to disaffirm contracts made during incapacity, the duties upon disaffirmance, and the possibility of ratification upon regaining capacity are the same for an intoxicated person as for a person under a mental impairment. In practice, however, courts traditionally have been less sympathetic with a person who was intoxicated at the time of contracting than with minors or those suffering from a mental impairment. It is rare for a person to actually escape his contractual obligations on the ground of intoxication. A person incapacitated by intoxication at the time of contracting might nevertheless be bound to his contract if he fails to disaffirm in a timely manner.

ETHICAL AND PUBLIC POLICY CONCERNS

1. You read that the age of majority for contracting purposes is 18 in almost all states today. We all know that maturity at a given age varies greatly from individual to individual. Does it make sense for the law to *presume* that a person is sufficiently mature to be responsible for his agreements merely because he has reached the age of 18? Would public policy be better served if the maturity of contracting parties were determined on a case-by-case basis in the same way that we now determine the capacity of those who are mentally impaired or intoxicated? Why or why not?

2. In *Dodson v. Shrader*, the court rejected the traditional view that minors who no longer have the consideration in their possession can disaffirm their contracts without reimbursing the adult party for use or depreciation of the adult's property. Which rule, the traditional rule or the rule applied in *Dodson*, makes the most sense? Was Judge O'Brien correct in his remark that the traditional rule is inconsistent with "proper moral influence upon young people?" Discuss.

3. In recent years, there has been growing public concern over alcohol and drug abuse. Through legal developments such as vigorous enforcement of drunken driving laws and the imposition of tort liability on the part of alcohol suppliers, the law encourages moderation in the use of alcohol. Yet, the law also makes it possible for a person who is so intoxicated that he does not appreciate the business at hand to escape his contractual obligations. Is this rule about the capacity of intoxicated persons out of step with sound public policy?

PROBLEMS AND PROBLEM CASES

1. Del Bosco, a competitive skier, fell while participating in a Trophy Series Ski Race. She suffered extensive injuries in the fall that resulted in multiple surgeries to repair her leg and ankle. Del Bosco sued the promoter of the race for negligent inspection of the race course. The promoter asserted that Del Bosco's claim was barred because Del Bosco had signed a release form agreeing not to hold the promoter liable for any injuries that she might suffer while skiing. Del Bosco was 14 at the time she signed the contract and 15 at the time she was injured. Del Bosco claimed the release was voidable. Is she correct?

2. Robertson, while a minor, contracted to borrow money from his father for a college education. His father mortgaged his home and took out loans against his life insurance policies to get some of the money he lent to Robertson, who ultimately graduated from dental school. Two years after Robertson's graduation, his father asked him to begin paying back the amount of $30,000 at $400 per month. Robertson agreed to pay $24,000 at $100 per month. He did this for three years before stopping the payments. His father sued for the balance of the debt. Could Robertson disaffirm the contract?

3. Green, age 16, contracted to buy a Camaro from Star Chevrolet. Green lived about six miles from school and one mile from his job, and used the Camaro to go back and forth to school and work. When he did not have the car, he used a car pool to get to school and work. Several months later, the car became inoperable due to a blown head gasket, and Green gave notice of disaffirmance to Star Chevrolet. Star Chevrolet refused to refund the purchase price, claiming, in part, that the car was a necessary. Was it?

4. In 1990, Hannegan, a minor, contracted with Swalberg to buy Swalberg's 1974 Ford truck for $2,500. The fact that Hannegan was a minor apparently was not discussed when they entered the contract. Hannegan paid Swalberg $640 on the date of the sale and promised to pay the balance of $1,860 three months later. Rather than paying the balance, however, Hannegan disaffirmed the contract on the basis of his minority. The truck was worth $700 when Hannegan returned it. Swalberg filed a complaint asking that the contract be enforced or, in the alternative, that the truck be returned and that Hannegan be held responsible for the reasonable value of his use of the truck or for the amount it depreciated while in Hannegan's possession. In a state that applies traditional rules, will Swalberg win?

5. At a time when the age of majority in Ohio was 21, Lee, age 20, contracted to buy a 1964 Plymouth Fury for $1,552 from Haydocy Pontiac. Lee represented herself to be 21 when entering the contract. She paid for the car by trading in another car worth $150 and financing the balance. Immediately following delivery of the car to her, Lee permitted one John Roberts to take possession of it. Roberts delivered the car to someone else, and it was never recovered. Lee failed to make payments on the car, and Haydocy Pontiac sued her to recover the car or the amount due on the contract. Lee repudiated the contract on the ground that she was a minor at the time of purchase. Can Lee disaffirm the contract without reimbursing Haydocy Pontiac for the value of the car?

6. In 1955, the Probate Court of Franklin County adjudged Beard to be mentally incompetent and appointed a guardian for him. Thereafter, in 1978, a successor guardian was appointed for Beard. On February 22, 1989, while still under guardianship, Beard executed a promissory note for $10,254.60 to Huntington National Bank in order to finance the purchase of a 1987 Nissan pickup truck. The flexible interest rate for the note was to be paid over a five-year period, with monthly installments of $170.91. Beard made only a few payments on the note before dying on July 31, 1989. In the four- or five-year period prior to his death, Beard had had several dealings with the bank, including the financing of two other truck purchases. He had maintained a sparkling credit rating, fully repaying his previous loans. Toland was appointed administrator of Beard's estate. When she learned of the outstanding debt to the bank, she returned the car to the bank. The bank sold it and sought to have the estate pay the outstanding debt left after crediting the proceeds of the car and Beard's payments. Toland rejected the bank's claim, contending that the promissory note was invalid because of Beard's lack of capacity. Is she right?

7. In 1987, Hauer suffered a brain injury in a motorcycle accident. She was later adjudicated to be incompetent, resulting in a guardian being appointed by the court. In 1988, Hauer's guardianship was terminated based on a letter from her treating physician, who opined that Hauer had recovered to the point where she had ongoing memory, showed good judgment, was reasonable in her goals and plans, and could manage her own affairs. After the accident, Hauer had a monthly income of $900 from social security disability and the interest from a mutual fund worth approximately $80,000. Eilbes, who was attempting to start a small business, was looking for investors. He learned of Hauer's mutual fund through her daughter and discussed his business several times with Hauer. Hauer was interested in investing in Eilbes's business. Since Hauer could sell her stocks only at certain times, Eilbes suggested that she take out a short-term loan using the stocks as collateral. Eilbes told Hauer that if she loaned him money, he would give her a job, pay her interest on the loan, and pay the loan when it came due. Hauer agreed. Eilbes then contacted the assistant vice president of Union State Bank of Wautoma, Schroeder, to arrange the loan. Schroeder called Hauer's stockbroker to verify the existence of Hauer's fund. During that conversation, the stockbroker told Schroeder that Hauer needed the interest income to live on and that he wished the Bank would not use it as collateral for a loan. (At trial, Schroeder also conceded that it was possible that the stockbroker had told him that Hauer was suffering from brain damage, but he did not specifically recall that part of the conversation). The Bank loaned $30,000 to Hauer with her stock as collateral, and Hauer loaned the entire $30,000 to Eilbes. On the date the loan from the Bank matured, Hauer filed suit to rescind the loan and get her stock back. She could not return the $30,000 because it had been spent. At trial, the jury found that Hauer lacked mental capacity at the time that she entered the loan contract and also that the Bank had failed to act in good faith toward Hauer in the transaction. Will she be able to recover her collateral without liability for the loan proceeds?

8. In December 1989, 16-year-old Travis brought a 1970 Pontiac GTO into M & M Precision Body and Paint to get an estimate on repairs to the vehicle from Mizerski. After examining the vehicle, Mizerski provided Travis with an estimate for $1,550.35 in repairs and informed him that a $1,000 deposit to cover the cost of parts and materials would be required before the work was begun. Travis delivered the vehicle to Mizerski's body shop in April 1990 to have the vehicle repaired. He gave the deposit in the form of a $1,000 cashier's check. In April or May of 1990, Travis and his father went to the body shop to check on the car and to discuss and authorize additional repairs. In July, they returned to the body shop and, after an argument about the balance due, compromised on a balance of $850. This amount was paid to Mizerski in the form of a cashier's check drawn on Travis's parents' account when Travis picked up the vehicle at the end of July. Travis and his father were dissatisfied with Mizerski's workmanship, and after demanding and not receiving resolution of the problems, Travis filed suit to disaffirm the contracts that he had made for the repair work and to get his money back. In a state that follows the traditional approach to the infancy doctrine, will he succeed?

9. 📼 *Video Case.* See "In the Cards." A boy bought an Ernie Banks rookie card for $12 from an inexperienced clerk in a baseball card store owned by Johnson. The card had been marked "1200," and Johnson, who had been away from the store at the time of the sale, had intended the card to be sold for $1,200, not $12. Can Johnson get the card back by asserting the boy's lack of capacity?

Illegality

Although the public interest normally favors the enforcement of contracts, there are times when the interests that usually favor the enforcement of an agreement are subordinated to conflicting social concerns. As you read in Chapter 13, Reality of Consent, and Chapter 14, Capacity to Contract, for example, people who did not truly consent to a contract or who lacked the capacity to contract have the power to cancel their contracts. In these situations, concerns about protecting disadvantaged persons and preserving the integrity of the bargaining process outweigh the usual public interest in enforcing private agreements. Similarly, when an agreement involves an act or promise that violates some legislative or court-made rule, the public interests threatened by the agreement outweigh the interests that favor its enforcement. Such an agreement will be denied enforcement on the ground of *illegality,* even if there is voluntary consent between two parties who have capacity to contract. ∞

MEANING OF ILLEGALITY

When a court says that an agreement is illegal, it does not necessarily mean that the agreement violates a criminal law, although an agreement to commit a crime is one type of illegal agreement. Rather, an agreement is illegal either because the legislature has declared that particular type of contract to be unenforceable or void or because the agreement violates a **public policy** that has been developed by courts or that has been manifested in constitutions, statutes, administrative regulations, or other sources of law.

The term *public policy* is impossible to define precisely. Generally, it is taken to mean a widely shared view about what ideas, interests, institutions, or freedoms promote public welfare. For example, in our society, there are strong public policies favoring the protection of human life and health, free competition, and private property. Judges' and legislators' perceptions of desirable public policy influence the decisions they make about the resolution of cases or the enactment of statutes. Public policy may be based on a prevailing moral code, on an economic philosophy, or on the need to protect a valued social institution such as the family or the judicial system. If the enforcement of an agreement would create a threat to a public policy, a court may determine that it is illegal.

Determining Whether an Agreement Is Illegal

If a statute states that a particular type of agreement is unenforceable or void, courts will apply the statute and refuse to enforce the agreement. Relatively few such statutes exist, however. More frequently, a legislature will forbid certain conduct but will not address the enforceability of contracts that involve the forbidden conduct. In such cases, courts must determine whether the importance of the public policy that underlies the statute in question and the degree of interference with that policy are sufficiently great to outweigh any interests that favor enforcement of the agreement.

In some cases, it is relatively easy to predict that an agreement will be held to be illegal. For example, an agreement to commit a serious crime is certain to be illegal. However, the many laws enacted by legislatures are of differing degrees of importance to the public welfare. The determination of **illegality** would not be so clear if the agreement violated a statute that was of relatively small importance to the public welfare. For example, in one Illinois case,[1] a seller of fertilizer failed to comply with an Illinois statute requiring that a descriptive statement accompany the delivery of the fertilizer. The sellers prepared the statements and offered them to the buyers but did not give them to the buyers at the time of delivery. The court enforced the contract despite the sellers' technical violation of the law because the contract was not seriously injurious to public welfare.

Similarly, the public policies developed by courts are rarely absolute; they, too, depend on a balancing of several factors. In determining whether to hold an agreement illegal, a court will consider the importance of the public policy involved and the extent to which enforcement of the agreement would interfere with that policy. They will also consider the seriousness of any wrongdoing involved in the agreement and how directly that wrongdoing was connected with the agreement.

For purposes of our discussion, illegal agreements will be classified into three main categories: (1) agreements that violate statutes, (2) agreements that violate public policy developed by courts, and (3) unconscionable agreements and contracts of adhesion.

The following case, *Straub v. B.M.T.,* provides an example of a contract that was held to violate public policy.

---

[1]*Amoco Oil Co. v. Toppert,* 56 Ill. App. 3d 1294 (Ill. Ct. App. 1978).

STRAUB v. B.M.T. 626 N.E.2d 848 (Ind. Ct. App. 1993)

Edward Straub and Francine Todd began dating in 1985 when both were teachers at the same elementary school. In late 1986, Todd discussed her desire to have a child with Straub after her doctor informed her that artificial insemination would not work. Straub told Todd that he did not want the responsibility of another family due to his age and the fact that he already had children from a previous marriage. However, when Todd threatened to end their relationship, he agreed to try to impregnate her providing she would sign a "hold harmless" agreement. Straub presented Todd with the following handwritten agreement, which Todd signed:

To Whom it may concern
I Francine Todd in sound mind & fore thought have decided not to marry, but would like to have a baby of my own. To support financially & emotionally, I have approached several men who will not be held responsible financially or emotionally who's [sic] names will be kept secret for life.
Signed Francine Todd
Dec. 15, 1986

After Todd signed the agreement, the couple began to have unprotected sex, and in March 1987, Todd became pregnant. During this period, Todd was not sexually active with any other man. Todd and Straub continued their relationship during Todd's pregnancy and for three years after the birth of their child (B.M.T.), and even after Straub's marriage to someone else, but Straub did not establish a relationship with the child. He stopped seeing Todd after she filed this action on B.M.T.'s behalf to establish paternity. The trial court found that Straub was the biological father of B.M.T. and that he had the obligation to support her. Straub appealed. ∞

Miller, Judge   Indiana has long recognized the obligation of both parents to support their children. A parent's obligations to support his minor child is a basic tenet recognized in this state by statutes that provide civil and criminal sanctions against parents who neglect such duty. In addition, there is a well-established common-law duty and obligation of a *father* to assist in the support of his children.

It is apparent that our legislature has created a strong current public policy (and not merely maintained an ancient one) with the object of protecting the rights of children from the whims of their parents and the power of the state.

Straub first claims that "fundamental contract principles" allow him to contract around his statutory and common law duty to provide support to his daughter. He ignores other rights, such as inheritance. However, this argument fails because it amounts to the contracting away of his daughter's right to support. It is well settled that a parent cannot, by his own contract relieve himself of the legal obligation to support his minor children. In *Ort v. Schage,* we held that an agreement to forgo court ordered child support even in exchange for a benefit (social security payments) to the child is unenforceable because a parent has no right to contract away a child's support benefits.

Although the primary goal of a paternity action is to secure support and education for illegitimate children, a legitimate subsidiary goal of the same action, however, is to protect the public interest by preventing the illegitimate child from becoming a ward of the state. Public policy considerations mandate that the state take an active interest in providing for the welfare of illegitimate children in order to avoid placing an undue burden on taxpayers.

Finally, Straub argues that the agreement signed by Todd should be enforced because he was acting merely as a "sperm donor." He argues that we should follow cases from other jurisdictions which look to the pre-conception intent of the parties involved in deciding whether to enforce their agreement. We first note, of course, arguing that Straub's and Todd's relationship was that of a sperm donor and donee ignores the facts. It is undisputed that Straub and Todd had an ongoing affair, one which began before Todd decided to become pregnant and only ended three years after B.M.T.'s birth.

Straub argues that he should be indemnified against any support claims because Todd is capable of supporting the child on her own and the "economic injury" to Straub due to her "breach of contract" would exceed $100,000. Because this argument merely seeks to circumvent public policy, it, too, must fail. First, because the agreement between the parties is void, there is no enforceable contract to breach. Second, Todd's *present* ability to care for the child on her own and the cost of the support to Straub do not change the law—Straub must provide his share of his daughter's support.

Affirmed in favor of B.M.T.

AGREEMENTS IN VIOLATION OF STATUTE

Agreements Declared Illegal by Statute

State legislatures occasionally enact statutes that declare certain types of agreements unenforceable, void, or voidable. In a case in which a legislature has specifically stated that a particular type of contract is void, a court need only interpret and apply the statute. These statutes differ from state to state. Some are relatively uncommon. For example, an Indiana statute declares surrogate birth contracts to be void.[2] Others, such as *usury statutes* and *wagering statutes,* are common.

Usury Statutes   Federal law and the law of most states set limits on the amount of interest that can be charged for a loan or forbearance (refraining from making a demand for money that is already due). *Usury* means obtaining interest beyond the amount

------

[2]Ind. Code 31-8-2-2 (1988).

that is authorized by law for these transactions. The statutes that define usury and set the maximum permissible limit for interest are not uniform in their prohibitions or their penalties. When a transaction is covered by usury laws and the rate of interest charged for the use of money exceeds the statutory limit, the contract to pay that interest rate is unenforceable.

Wagering Statutes   All states either prohibit or regulate wagering, or gambling. There is a thin line separating wagering, which is illegal, from well-accepted, lawful transactions in which a person will profit from the happening of an uncertain event. The hallmark of a wager is that neither party has any financial stake or interest in the uncertain event except for the stake that he has created by making the bet. The person making a wager *creates* the risk that he may lose the money or property wagered upon the happening of an uncertain event. Suppose Ames bets Baker $20 that the Cubs will win the pennant this year. Ames has no financial interest in a Cubs victory other than that which he has created through his bet. Rather, he has created the risk of losing $20 for the sole purpose of bearing that risk. If, however, people make an agreement about who shall bear an existing risk in which one of them has an actual stake or interest, that is a legal, risk-shifting agreement. Property insurance contracts are classic examples of risk-shifting agreements. The owner of the property pays the insurance company a fee (premium) in return for the company's agreement to bear the risk of the uncertain event that the property will be damaged or destroyed. If, however, the person who takes out the policy had no legitimate economic interest in the insured property (called an **insurable interest** in insurance law), the agreement is an illegal wager.

Agreements that Violate the Public Policy of a Statute

As stated earlier, an agreement can be illegal even if no statute specifically states that that particular sort of agreement is illegal. Legislatures enact statutes in an effort to resolve some particular problem. If courts enforced agreements that involve the violation of a statute, they would frustrate the purpose for which the legislature passed the statute. They would also promote disobedience of the law and disrespect for the courts.

Agreements to Commit a Crime   For the reasons stated above, contracts that require the violation of a criminal statute are illegal. If Grimes promises to pay Judge John Doe a bribe of $5,000 to dismiss a criminal case against Grimes, for example, the agreement is illegal. Sometimes the very formation of a certain type of contract is a crime, even if the acts agreed on are never carried out. An example of this is an agreement to murder another person. Naturally, such agreements are considered illegal under contract law as well as under criminal law.

Agreements that Promote Violations of Statutes   Sometimes a contract of a type that is usually perfectly legal—say, a contract to sell goods—is deemed to be illegal under the circumstances of the case because it promotes or facilitates the violation of a statute. Suppose Davis sells Sims goods on credit. Sims uses the goods in some illegal manner and then refuses to pay Davis for the goods. Can Davis recover the price of the goods from Sims? The answer depends on whether Davis knew of the illegal purpose and whether he intended the sale to further that illegal purpose. Generally speaking, such agreements will be legal unless there is a direct connection between the illegal conduct and the agreement in the form of active, intentional participation in or facilitation of the illegal act. Knowledge of the other party's illegal purpose, standing alone, is generally not sufficient to render an agreement illegal. When a person is aware of the other's illegal purpose *and* actively helps to accomplish that purpose, an otherwise legal agreement—such as a sale of goods—might be labeled illegal.

Licensing Laws: Agreement to Perform an Act for Which a Party Is Not Properly Licensed   Congress and the state legislatures have enacted a variety of statutes that regulate professions and businesses. A common type of regulatory statute is one that requires a person to obtain a license, permit, or registration before engaging in a certain business or profession. For example, state statutes require lawyers, physicians, dentists, teachers, and other professionals to be licensed to practice their professions. In order to obtain the required license, they must meet specified requirements such as attaining a certain educational degree and passing an examination. Real estate brokers, stockbrokers, insurance agents, sellers of liquor and tobacco, pawnbrokers, electricians, barbers, and others too numerous to mention are also often required by state statute to meet licensing requirements to perform services or sell regulated commodities to members of the public.

What is the status of an agreement in which one of the parties agrees to perform an act regulated by state law for which she is not properly licensed? This will often be determined by looking at the purpose of the legislation that the unlicensed party has violated. If the statute is **regulatory**—that is, the purpose of the legislation is to protect the public against dishonest or incompetent practitioners—an agreement by an unlicensed person is generally held to be unenforceable. For example, if Spencer, a first-year law student, agrees to draft a will for Rowen for a fee of $150, Spencer could not enforce the agreement and collect a fee from Rowen for drafting the will because she is not licensed to practice law. This result makes sense, even though it imposes a hardship on Spencer. The public interest in ensuring that people on whose legal advice others rely have an appropriate educational background and proficiency in the subject matter outweighs any interest in seeing that Spencer receives what she bargained for.

On the other hand, where the licensing statute was intended primarily as a **revenue-raising** measure—that is, as a means of collecting money rather than as a means of protecting the public—an agreement to pay a person for performing an act for which she is not licensed will generally be enforced. For example, suppose that in the example used above, Spencer is a lawyer who is licensed to practice law in her state and who met all of her state's educational, testing, and character requirements but neglected to pay her annual registration fee. In this situation, there is no compelling public interest that would justify the harsh measure of refusing enforcement and possibly inflicting forfeiture on the unlicensed person.

Whether a statute is a regulatory statute or a revenue-raising statute depends on the intent of the legislature, which may not always be expressed clearly. Generally, statutes that require proof of character and skill and impose penalties for violation are considered to be regulatory in nature. Their requirements indicate that they were intended for the protection of the public. Those that impose a significant license fee and allow anyone who pays the fee to obtain a license are usually classified as revenue raising. The fact that no requirement other than the payment of the fee is imposed indicates that the purpose of the law is to raise money rather than to protect the public. Because such a statute is not designed for the protection of the public, a violation of the statute is not as threatening to the public interest as is a violation of a regulatory statute.

It would be misleading to imply that cases involving unlicensed parties always follow such a mechanical test. In some cases, courts may grant recovery to an unlicensed party even where a regulatory statute is violated. If the public policy promoted by the statute is relatively trivial in relation to the amount that would be forfeited by the unlicensed person and the unlicensed person is neither dishonest nor incompetent, a court may conclude that the statutory penalty for violation of the regulatory statute is sufficient to protect the public interest and that enforcement of the agreement is appropriate.

CONCEPT REVIEW

Contracts that Violate a Licensing Statute

TYPE OF LICENSING STATUTE	REGULATORY STATUTE	REVENUE RAISING STATUTE
Purpose of Statute	Protect the public welfare	Provide source of revenue
Typical Characteristics of Statute	Require proof of character, skill, and training, and impose penalties for violation	Impose fee with no or few other requirements
Status of Contracts that Violate Statute	Contracts violating statute usually illegal	Contracts violating statute still legal (validity of contract not affected by statute)

AGREEMENTS IN VIOLATION OF PUBLIC POLICY ARTICULATED BY COURTS

Courts have broad discretion to articulate public policy and to decline to lend their powers of enforcement to an agreement that would contravene what they deem to be in the best interests of society. There is no simple rule for determining when a particular agreement is contrary to public policy. Public policy may change with the times; changing social and economic conditions may make behavior that was acceptable in an earlier time unacceptable today, or vice versa. The following are examples of agreements that are frequently considered vulnerable to attack on public policy grounds.

Agreements in Restraint of Competition

The policy against restrictions on competition is one of the oldest public policies declared by the common law. This same policy is also the basis of federal and state antitrust statutes. The policy against restraints on competition is based on the economic judgment that the public interest is best served by free competition. Nevertheless, courts have long recognized that some contractual restrictions on competition serve legitimate business interests and should be enforced. Therefore, agreements that limit competition are scrutinized very closely by the courts to determine whether the restraint imposed is in violation of public policy.

If the *sole* purpose of an agreement is to restrain competition, it violates public policy and is illegal. For example, if Martin and Bloom, who own competing businesses, enter an agreement whereby each agrees not to solicit or sell to the other's customers, such an agreement would be unenforceable. Where the restriction on competition was part of (*ancillary to*) an otherwise legal contract, the result may be different because the parties may have a legitimate interest to be protected by the restriction on competition.

For example, if Martin had *purchased* Bloom's business, the goodwill of the business was part of what she paid for. She has a legitimate interest in making sure that Bloom does not open a competing business soon after the sale and attract away the very customers whose goodwill she paid for. Or suppose that Martin hired Walker to work as a salesperson in her business. She wants to assure herself that she does not disclose trade secrets, confidential information, or lists of regular customers to Walker only to have Walker quit and enter a competing business.

To protect herself, the buyer or the employer in the above examples might bargain for a contractual clause that would provide that the seller or employee agrees not to engage in a particular competing activity in a specified *geographic area* for a specified *time* after the sale of the business or the termination of employment. This type of clause is called an **ancillary covenant not to compete,** or, as it is more commonly known, a **non-competition clause.** They most frequently appear in *employment contracts, contracts for the sale of a business, partnership agreements,* and *small-business buy-sell agreements.* In an employment contract, the non-competition clause might be the only part of the contract that the parties put in writing.

Enforceability of Non-Competition Clauses   Although non-competition clauses restrict competition and thereby affect the public policy favoring free competition, courts enforce them if they meet the following three criteria.

1. *Clause must serve a legitimate business purpose.* This means that the person protected by the clause must have some justifiable interest—such as an interest in protecting goodwill or trade secrets—that is to be protected by the non-competition clause. It also means that the clause must be *ancillary* to, or part of, an otherwise valid contract. For example, a non-competition clause that is one term of an existing employment contract would be ancillary to that contract. By contrast, a promise not to compete would not be enforced if the employee made the promise *after* he had already resigned his job, because the promise not to compete was not ancillary to any existing contract.

2. *The restriction on competition must be reasonable in time, geographic area, and scope.* Another way of stating this is that the restrictions must not be any greater than necessary to protect a legitimate interest. It would be unreasonable for an employer or buyer of a business to restrain the other party from engaging in some activity that is not a competing activity or from doing business in a territory in which the employer or buyer does not do business, because this would not threaten his legitimate interests.

3. *The non-competition clause should not impose an undue hardship.* A court will not enforce a non-competition clause if its restraints are unduly burdensome either on the public or on the party whose ability to compete would be restrained. In one case, for example, the court refused to enforce a non-competition clause against a gastroenterologist because of evidence that the restriction would have imposed a hardship on patients and other physicians requiring his services.[3] Non-competition clauses in employment contracts that have the practical effect of preventing the restrained person from earning a livelihood are unlikely to be enforced as well. This is discussed further in the next section.

Non-Competition Clauses in Employment Contracts   Restrictions on competition work a greater hardship on an employee than on a person who has sold a business. For this reason, courts tend to judge non-competition clauses contained in employment contracts by a stricter standard than they judge similar clauses contained in contracts for the sale of a business. In some states, statutes limit or even prohibit non-competition clauses in employment contracts. In others, there is a trend toward refusing enforcement of these clauses in employment contracts unless the employer can bring forth very good evidence that he has a protectible interest that compels enforcement of the clause. The employer can do this by showing that he has entrusted the employee with trade secrets or confidential information, or that his goodwill with "near-permanent" customers is threatened. In the absence of this kind of proof, a court might conclude that the employer is just trying to avoid competition with a more efficient competitor and refuse enforcement because there is no legitimate business interest that requires protection.

Furthermore, many courts refuse to enforce non-competition clauses if they restrict employees from engaging in a "common calling." A common calling is an occupation that does not require extensive or highly sophisticated training but instead involves relatively simple, repetitive tasks. Under this common calling restriction, various courts have refused to enforce non-competition clauses against salespersons, a barber, and an auto trim repairperson.

The following *John R. Ray* case provides an example of a court's treatment of a non-competition clause in an employment contract.

---

[3]*Iredell Digestive Disease Clinic, P.A. v. Petrozza*, 373 S.E.2d 449 (N.C. Ct. App. 1988).

JOHN R. RAY & SONS, INC. v. STROMAN   923 S.W.2d 80 (Tex. Ct. App. 1996)

Ray & Sons is a family-owned insurance agency. The company hired Stroman as an insurance agent in 1983 pursuant to an employment contract that extended through December 31, 1987. On December 31, 1987, Stroman and Ray & Sons executed a new agreement, entitled "Non-Competition Agreement." This agreement provided that Stroman would not engage in or have an interest in any business that sold insurance policies or engaged in the insurance agency business within Harris County and all adjacent counties for a period of five years from the date of the agreement. It also provided that Stroman would never solicit or accept, or assist or be employed by any other party in soliciting or accepting insurance business from any of Ray & Sons' accounts. In consideration for entering into the agreement, Stroman was to receive a 10 percent ownership interest in the company, which was equivalent to 104 shares of common stock. The company's stock transfer ledger indicates that the stock was issued on December 31, 1987. A stock certificate was prepared in Stroman's name but it was retained by Ray & Sons and not actually placed in Stroman's possession.

In June 1992, four and one-half years after execution of the agreement, Stroman left Ray & Sons and took a job with another insurance agency in Harris County. Stroman offered his shares to Ray & Sons pursuant to a shareholder's agreement, but the company chose not to buy the shares. Ray & Sons took the position that Stroman had breached the agreement and was not entitled to the stock. Stroman filed suit seeking a declaratory judgment that the stock issued in his name should be delivered to him and that the covenant not to compete was unenforceable. The trial court granted summary judgment in favor of Stroman, and Ray & Sons appealed.

O'Neill, Justice Ray & Sons challenges the trial court's finding that the covenant not to compete was an unreasonable restraint of trade and therefore unenforceable. The validity and enforceability of covenants not to compete are governed by sections 15.50-15.52 of the Texas Business and Commerce Code. Section 15.50 provides:

a covenant not to compete is enforceable if it is ancillary to or part of an otherwise enforceable agreement at the time the agreement is made to the extent that it contains limitations as to time, geographical area, and scope of activity to be restrained that are reasonable and do not impose a greater restraint than is necessary to protect the goodwill or other business interest of the promisee.

A covenant not to compete is a restraint of trade and unenforceable as a matter of public policy unless it meets a reasonableness standard. Restraints are unreasonable if they are broader than necessary to protect the legitimate interests of the employer. The Texas Supreme Court has held that an industry-wide exclusion is unreasonable. The court has also held that a covenant not to compete unlimited as to time is unreasonable. In the case of covenants applied to a personal services occupation, such as that of a salesman, a restraint on client solicitation is overbroad and unreasonable when it extends to clients with whom the employee had no dealings during his employment.

In the present case, the agreement created an unenforceable industry-wide exclusion on Stroman's ability to work in the insurance business in and around Harris County. [Another part of the agreement] is similarly unenforceable because it is unlimited as to time and extends to customers with whom Stroman had no association while he was working for Ray & Sons. Furthermore, Ray & Sons has not shown that the limitations were necessary to protect the goodwill or business interests of the company. Therefore, we agree with the trial court that the covenant not to compete is an unreasonable restraint of trade.

The language of the agreement clearly indicates the parties intended the stock to issue in exchange for Stroman's covenant not to compete. Because the covenant not to compete is unenforceable, the stock transfer must also fail.

Affirmed in part in favor of Stroman and modified in part in favor of Ray & Sons.

The Effect of Overly Broad Non-Competition Clauses

The courts of different states treat unreasonably broad non-competition clauses in different ways. Some courts will strike the entire restriction if they find it to be unreasonable and will refuse to grant the buyer or employer any protection. Others will refuse to enforce the restraint as written, but will adjust the clause and impose such restraints as would be reasonable. In case of breach of an enforceable non-competition clause, the person benefited by the clause may seek damages or an injunction (a court order preventing the promisor from violating the covenant).

Exculpatory Clauses

An **exculpatory clause** is a provision in a contract that purports to relieve one of the parties from tort liability. Exculpatory clauses are suspect on public policy grounds for two reasons. First, courts are concerned that a party who can contract away his liability for negligence will not have the incentive to use care to avoid hurting others. Second, courts are concerned that an agreement that accords one party such a powerful advantage might have been the result of the abuse of superior bargaining power rather than truly voluntary choice. Although exculpatory agreements are often said to be "disfavored" in the law, courts do not want to prevent parties who are dealing on a fair and voluntary basis from determining how the risks of their transaction shall be borne if their agreement does not threaten public health or safety.

Courts enforce exculpatory clauses in some cases and refuse to enforce them in others, depending on the circumstances of the case, the identity and relationship of the parties, and the language of the agreement. A few ground rules can be stated. First, an exculpatory clause cannot protect a party from liability for any wrongdoing greater than negligence. One that purports to relieve a person from liability for fraud or some other willful tort will be considered to be against public policy. In some cases, in fact, exculpatory clauses have been invalidated on this ground because of broad language stating that one of the parties was relieved of "all liability." Second, exculpatory clauses will not be effective to exclude tort liability on the part of a party who owes a duty to the public (such as an airline) because this would present an obvious threat to the public health and safety.

A third possible limitation on the enforceability of exculpatory clauses arises from the increasing array of statutes and common law rules that impose certain obligations on one party to a contract for the benefit of the other party to the contract. Workers' compensation statutes and laws requiring landlords to maintain leased property in a habitable condition are examples of such laws. Sometimes the person on whom such an obligation is placed will attempt to escape it by inserting an exculpatory or waiver provision in a contract. Such clauses are often— though not always—found to be against public policy because, if enforced, they would frustrate the very purpose of imposing the duty in question. For example, an employee's agreement to relieve her employer from workers' compensation liability is likely to be held illegal as a violation of public policy.

Even if a clause is not against public policy on any of the above three grounds, a court may still refuse to enforce it if a court finds that the clause was **unconscionable,** a **contract of adhesion,** or some other product of abuse of superior bargaining power. (Unconscionability and contracts of adhesion are discussed later in this chapter.) This determination depends on all of the facts of the case. Facts that tend to show that the exculpatory clause was the product of *knowing* consent will increase the likelihood that it will be enforced. For example, a clause that is written in clear language and conspicuous print is more likely to be enforced than one written in "legalese" and presented in fine print. Facts that tend to show that the exculpatory clause was the product of *voluntary* consent increase the likelihood of enforcement of the clause. For example, a clause contained in a contract for a frivolous or unnecessary activity, such as the Ironman Decathlon in *Milligan v. Big Valley Corporation,* is more likely to be enforced than is an exculpatory clause contained in a contract for a necessary activity such as medical care.

MILLIGAN v. BIG VALLEY CORPORATION   754 P.2d 1063 (Sup. Ct. Wyo. 1988)

Dean Griffin, an expert skier and certified ski instructor, entered the Ironman Decathlon held at the Grand Targhee ski resort, which was owned and operated by Big Valley Corporation. The decathlon was held for fun rather than profit. It consisted of several events, including swimming five pool laps, bowling one line, drinking a quart of beer, throwing darts, and skiing in both downhill and cross-country races. The downhill ski race was the first event in the decathlon. It was held early in the morning before the resort was opened to the public. Prior to the race, Griffin and all of the other downhill contestants were required to sign a document entitled "General Release of Claim." This provided in part:

In consideration of my being allowed to participate in IRONMAN DECATHLON at Targhee Resort, Alta, Wyoming, I irrevocably and forever hereby release and discharge any and all of the employees, agents, or servants and owners of Targhee Resort and the other sponsors of IRONMAN DECATHLON officially connected with this event of and from any and all legal claims or legal liability of any kind involving bodily injury or death sustained by me during my stay at Targhee Resort. I hereby personally assume all risks in connection with said event and I further release the aforementioned resort, its agents, and operators, for any harm which might befall me as a participant in this event, whether foreseen or unforeseen and further save and hold harmless said resort and persons from any claim by me or my family, estate, heirs or assigns. /s/ Dean Griffin 4/13/84

About 10 minutes after the race began, Griffin was found unconscious approximately three-quarters of the way down the mountain. He died a few hours later. No one witnessed the incident that caused his death, but it was speculated that he lost control of his skis and hit a tree.

Elizabeth Milligan, as personal representative for Griffin's estate, filed this wrongful death action against Big Valley on behalf of Griffin's son. The trial court granted a summary judgment in favor of Big Valley on the ground that the exculpatory agreement signed by Griffin released Big Valley from all liability. Milligan appealed.

Cardine, Justice Exculpatory agreements releasing parties from negligence liability for damages or injury are valid and enforceable in Wyoming if they do not violate public policy. Generally, agreements absolving participants and proprietors from negligence liability during hazardous recreational activities are enforceable, subject to willful misconduct limitations.

To determine whether this type of release is valid and enforceable, we consider:

1. Whether there exists a duty to the public;
2. The nature of the service performed;
3. Whether the contract was fairly entered into;
4. Whether the intention of the parties is expressed in clear and unambiguous language.

A duty to the public exists if the nature of the business or service affects the public interest and the service performed is considered an essential service. Types of services thought to be subject to public regulation and therefore demanding a public duty or considered essential have included common carriers, hospitals and doctors, public utilities, innkeepers, public warehousemen, employers, and services involving extra-hazardous activities. Generally, a private recreational business does not qualify as a service demanding a special duty to the public, nor are its services of a special, highly necessary or essential nature. The Ironman Decathlon can best be labeled a recreational type of activity of no great public import.

The agreement in question does not involve severe disparity of bargaining power. A disparity of bargaining power will be found when a contracting party with little or no bargaining strength has no reasonable alternative to entering the contract at the mercy of the other's negligence. For example, a member of the public contracting with a public utility, common carrier, hospital, or employer often has no real choice or alternative and is, therefore, at the mercy of the other. Such is not the case here. Grand Targhee did not force Griffin to ski in the race. Skiing in the race was not a matter of practical necessity for the public, and putting on the race was not an essential service. Thus, no decisive bargaining advantage existed. No evidence suggests that Griffin was unfairly pressured into signing the agreement or that he was deprived of an opportunity to understand its implications.

Milligan argues that the release was entered into unfairly because it contained boilerplate language prepared solely by the resort and was an adhesive contract. The argument is without merit. The mere fact that a contract is on a printed form prepared by one party and offered on a "take it or leave it" basis does not automatically establish it as an adhesive contract. There must be a showing that the parties were greatly disparate in bargaining power and that there was no opportunity for negotiation for services which could not be obtained elsewhere. Here no such showing was made. Indeed, the evidence is to the contrary. The release was fairly executed and satisfies the first three criteria.

The final factor requires us to determine whether the release agreement evidences the parties' intent to release Big Valley from liability for negligent acts in clear and unambiguous language. The language could not be clearer. Examining the release in light of the purpose of the contract, it is clear that the parties intended to release the ski resort and all those involved in the Ironman Decathlon from liability. It is clear that the intent was to release Big Valley from negligence liability. The absence of the word "negligence" is not fatal to an exculpatory clause if the terms of the contract clearly show intent to extinguish liability.

We conclude that the release is not void as a matter of public policy and that Big Valley was entitled to judgment as a matter of law.

Judgment for Big Valley affirmed.

Family Relationships and Public Policy In view of the central position of the family as a valued social institution, it is not surprising that an agreement that unreasonably tends to interfere with family relationships will be considered illegal. Examples of this type of contract include agreements whereby one of the parties agrees to divorce a spouse or agrees not to marry.

In recent years, courts have been presented with an increasing number of agreements between unmarried cohabitants that purport to agree upon the manner in which the parties' property will be shared or divided upon separation. It used to be widely held that contracts between unmarried cohabitants were against public policy because they were based on an immoral relationship. As unmarried cohabitation has become more widespread, however, the law concerning the enforceability of agreements between unmarried couples has changed. For example, in the 1976 case of *Marvin v. Marvin,* the California Supreme Court held that an agreement between an unmarried couple to pool income and share property could be enforceable.[4] Today, most courts hold that agreements between unmarried couples are not against public policy unless they are explicitly based on illegal sexual relations as the consideration for the contract or unless one or more of the parties is married to someone else.

UNFAIRNESS IN AGREEMENTS: CONTRACTS OF ADHESION AND UNCONSCIONABLE CONTRACTS

Under classical contract law, courts were reluctant to inquire into the fairness of an agreement. Because the prevailing social attitudes and economic philosophy strongly favored freedom of contract, American courts took the position that so long as there had been no fraud, duress, misrepresentation, mistake, or undue influence in the bargaining process, unfairness in an agreement entered into by competent adults did not render it unenforceable.

As the changing nature of our society produced many contract situations in which the bargaining positions of the parties were grossly unequal, the classical contract assumption that each party was capable of protecting himself was no longer persuasive. The increasing use of standardized contracts (preprinted contracts) enabled parties with superior bargaining power and business sophistication to virtually dictate contract terms to weaker and less sophisticated parties.

Legislatures responded to this problem by enacting a variety of statutory measures to protect individuals against the abuse of superior bargaining power in specific situations. Examples of such legislation include minimum wage laws and rent control ordinances. Courts became more sensitive to the fact that superior bargaining power often led to **contracts of adhesion** (contracts in which a stronger party is able to determine the terms of a contract, leaving the weaker party no practical choice but to "adhere" to the terms). Some courts responded by borrowing a doctrine that had been

developed and used for a long time in courts of equity,[5] the doctrine of **unconscionability.** Under this doctrine, courts would refuse to grant the equitable remedy of specific performance for breach of a contract if they found the contract to be oppressively unfair. Courts today can use the concepts of unconscionability or adhesion to analyze contracts that are alleged to be so unfair that they should not be enforced.

UNCONSCIONABILITY

One of the most far-reaching efforts to correct abuses of superior bargaining power was the enactment of section 2–302 of the Uniform Commercial Code, which gives courts the power to refuse to enforce all or part of a contract for the sale of goods or to modify such a contract if it is found to be unconscionable. By virtue of its inclusion in Article 2 of the Uniform Commercial Code, the prohibition against unconscionable terms applies to every contract for the sale of goods. The concept of unconscionability is not confined to contracts for the sale of goods, however. Section 208 of the *Restatement (Second) of Contracts,* which closely resembles the unconscionability section of the UCC, provides that courts may decline to enforce unconscionable terms or contracts. The prohibition of unconscionability has been adopted as part of the public policy of many states by courts in cases that did not involve the sale of goods, such as banking transactions and contracts for the sale or rental of real estate. It is therefore fair to state that the concept of unconscionability has become part of the general body of contract law.

Consequences of Unconscionability

The UCC and the *Restatement (Second)* sections on unconscionability give courts the power to manipulate a contract containing an unconscionable provision so as to reach a just result. If a court finds that a contract or a term in a contract is unconscionable, it can do one of three things: it can refuse to enforce the entire agreement; it can refuse to enforce the unconscionable provision but enforce the rest of the contract; or it can "limit the application of the unconscionable clause so as to avoid any unconscionable

---

[4]134 Cal. Rptr. 815 (1976).

[5]Chapter 1 discusses courts of equity.

result." This last alternative has been taken by courts to mean that they can make adjustments in the terms of the contract.

Meaning of Unconscionability

Neither the UCC nor the *Restatement (Second) of Contracts* attempts to define the term *unconscionability*. Though the concept is impossible to define with precision, unconscionability is generally taken to mean the *absence of meaningful choice* together with *terms unreasonably advantageous* to one of the parties.

The facts of each individual case are crucial to determining whether a contract term is unconscionable. Courts will scrutinize the process by which the contract was reached to see if the agreement was reached by fair methods and whether it can fairly be said to be the product of knowing and voluntary consent.

Procedural Unconscionability   Courts and writers often refer to unfairness in the bargaining process as *procedural unconscionability*. Some facts that may point to procedural unconscionability include the use of fine print or inconspicuously placed terms, complex, legalistic language, and high-pressure sales tactics. One of the most significant facts pointing to procedural unconscionability is the lack of voluntariness as shown by a marked imbalance in the parties' bargaining positions, particularly where the weaker party is unable to negotiate more favorable terms because of economic need, lack of time, or market factors. In fact, in most contracts that have been found to be unconscionable, there has been a serious inequality of bargaining power between the parties. It is important to note, however, that the mere existence of unequal bargaining power does not make a contract unconscionable. If it did, every consumer's contract with the telephone company or the electric company would be unenforceable. Rather, in an unconscionable contract, the party with the stronger bargaining power *exploits* that power by driving a bargain containing a term or terms that are so unfair that they "shock the conscience of the court."

Substantive Unconscionability

In addition to looking at facts that might indicate procedural unconscionability, courts will scrutinize the contract terms themselves to determine whether they are oppressive, unreasonably one-sided, or unjustifiably harsh. This aspect of unconscionability is often referred to as *substantive unconscionability*. Examples include situations in which a party to the contract bears a disproportionate amount of the risk or other negative aspects of the transaction and situations in which a party is deprived of a remedy for the other party's breach. In some cases, unconscionability has been found in situations in which the contract provides for a price that is greatly in excess of the usual market price.

There is no mechanical test for determining whether a clause is unconscionable. Generally, in cases in which courts have found a contract term to be unconscionable, there are elements of *both* procedural and substantive unconscionability. Though courts have broad discretion to determine what contracts will be deemed to be unconscionable, it must be remembered that the doctrine of unconscionability is designed to prevent oppression and unfair surprise—not to relieve people of the effects of bad bargains.

The cases concerning unconscionability are quite diverse. Some courts, such as the court in the following case, *Murphy v. McNamara,* have found unconscionability in contracts involving grossly unfair sales prices. Although the doctrine of unconscionability has been raised primarily by victimized consumers, there have been cases in which business-people in an inherently weak bargaining position have been successful in asserting unconscionability.

MURPHY v. McNAMARA   416 A.2d 170 (Conn. Super. Ct. 1979)

C arolyn Murphy, a welfare recipient with four minor children, saw an advertisement in the local newspaper that had been placed by Brian McNamara, a television and stereo dealer. It stated the following:

Why buy when you can rent? Color TV and stereos. *Rent to own!* Use our Rent-to-own plan and let TV Rentals deliver either of these models to your home. *We feature*—Never a repair bill—No deposit—No credit needed—No long term obligation—Weekly or monthly rates available—Order by phone—Call today—Watch color TV tonight.

As a result of this advertisement, Murphy leased a 25-inch Philco color console television set from McNamara under the "Rent to Own" plan. The lease agreement provided that Murphy would pay a $20 delivery charge and 78 weekly payments of $16. At the end of this period, Murphy would own the set. The agreement also provided that the customer could return the set at any time and terminate the lease as long as all rental payments had been made up to the return date. Murphy entered the lease because she believed that she could acquire ownership of a television set without first establishing credit, as was stressed in McNamara's ads. At no time did McNamara inform Murphy that the terms of the lease required her to pay a total of $1,268 for the set. The retail sales price for the same set was $499.

After making $436 in payments over a period of about six months, Murphy read a newspaper article criticizing the lease plan and realized the amount that the agreement required her to pay. She stopped making payments, and McNamara sought to repossess the set, threatening to file a criminal complaint against her if she failed to return it. Murphy, claiming that the agreement was unconscionable, filed suit for an injunction barring McNamara from repossessing the TV set or filing charges against her. ∽

Berdon, Judge An excessive price charged a consumer with unequal bargaining power can constitute a violation of 2–302 of the Uniform Commercial Code. In the case of *Jones v. Star Credit Corp.*, the plaintiffs, welfare recipients, purchased a home freezer unit for $900.00. The freezer had a retail value of approximately $300.00. The court held the contract was unconscionable under 2–302 of the Uniform Commercial Code and reformed the contract by excusing further payments over the $600.00 already paid by the plaintiffs. There have been similar holdings by other courts. The failure on the part of McNamara to advise Murphy of the total price she would be required to pay under the terms of the contract further compounded the unfairness of his trade practices.

In sum, an agreement for the sale of consumer goods entered into with a consumer having unequal bargaining power and which calls for an unconscionable purchase price, constitutes an unfair trade practice. By unequal bargaining power, the court means that at the time the contract was made there was such an inequality of bargaining power (for

example, because of the consumer's need for credit) that the merchant could insist on the inclusion of unconscionable terms in the contract which were not justifiable on the grounds of commercial necessity. The intent of this rule is not to erase the doctrine of freedom of contract, but to make realistic the assumption of the law that the agreement has resulted from real bargaining between parties who had freedom of choice and understanding and ability to negotiate in a meaningful fashion. Viewed in that sense, freedom to contract survives but the marketers of consumer goods are brought to an awareness that the restraint of unconscionability is always hovering over their operations and that courts will employ it to balance the interests of the consumer public and those of the seller.

Injunction granted, prohibiting McNamara from repossessing the TV set, using harassing collection techniques, or filing criminal charges against Murphy, but permitting McNamara to file suit for the difference between the amount Murphy paid and the value of the set.

CONTRACTS OF ADHESION

A contract of adhesion is a contract, usually on a standardized form, offered by a party who is in a superior bargaining position on a "take it or leave it" basis. The person presented with such a contract has no opportunity to negotiate the terms of the contract; they are imposed on him if he wants to receive the goods or services offered by the stronger party. In addition to not having a "say" about the terms of the contract, the person who signs a standardized contract of adhesion may not even

know or understand the terms of the contract that he is signing. When these factors are present, the objective theory of contracts and the normal duty to read contracts before signing them may be modified.

All of us have probably entered contracts of adhesion at one time or another. The mere fact that a contract is a contract of adhesion does not, in and of itself, mean that the contract is unenforceable. Courts will not refuse enforcement to such a contract unless the term complained of is either unconscionable or is a term that the adhering party could not reasonably expect to be included in the form that he was signing.

Unenforceable contracts of adhesion can take different forms. The first is seen when the contract of adhesion contains a term that is harsh or oppressive. In this kind of case, the party offering the contract of adhesion has used his superior bargaining power to dictate unfair terms. Here, the concepts of unconscionability and adhesion overlap. A court may use the word *adhesion* when describing procedural unconscionability.

The second situation in which contracts of adhesion are refused enforcement occurs when a contract of adhesion contains a term that, while it may not be harsh or oppressive, is a term that the adhering party could *not* be expected to have been aware that he

was agreeing to. This type of case relates to the fundamental concept of agreement in an era in which lengthy, complex, standardized contracts are common. If a consumer presented with a contract of adhesion has no opportunity to negotiate terms and signs the contract without knowing or fully understanding what he is signing, is it fair to conclude that he has consented to the terms? It is reasonable to conclude that he has consented at least to the terms that he could have expected to be in the contract, but *not* to any terms that he could not have expected to be contained in the contract. The following case, *Broemmer v. Abortion Services, Inc.,* presents an example of a contract of adhesion that was held to be unenforceable.

BROEMMER v. ABORTION SERVICES OF PHOENIX, LTD.   840 P.2d 1013 (Sup. Ct. Ariz. 1992)

In December 1986, Melinda Broemmer was 21 years old, unmarried, and 16 or 17 weeks pregnant. She was a high school graduate earning less than $100 a week and had no medical benefits. The father-to-be insisted that she have an abortion, but her parents advised against it. Broemmer later described the time as one of considerable confusion and turmoil for her. Broemmer's mother contacted Abortion Services of Phoenix and made an appointment for Broemmer for December 29, 1986. When they arrived at the clinic, Broemmer was escorted into an adjoining room and asked to complete three forms: a consent to treatment form, a questionnaire asking for a detailed medical history, and an agreement to arbitrate. The agreement to arbitrate stated that "any dispute arising between the Parties as a result of the fees and/or services" would be settled by binding arbitration and that "any arbitrators appointed by the AAA [American Arbitration Association] shall be licensed medical doctors who specialize in obstetrics/gynecology." No one made any effort to explain this to Broemmer and she was not provided with a copy of the agreement. She completed all three forms in less than five minutes. After Broemmer returned the forms to the front desk, she was taken into an examination room where preoperation procedures were performed. She was then instructed to return at 7:00 A.M. the next morning. She returned the following day and a physician performed the abortion. As a result of this procedure, Broemmer suffered a punctured uterus, which required medical treatment. Broemmer later filed a malpractice lawsuit against Abortion Services. Abortion Services moved to dismiss the suit on the ground that arbitration was required under the agreement. The trial court granted a summary judgment to Abortion Services. Although the court of appeals found that the agreement to arbitrate was a contract of adhesion, it still affirmed the trial court's judgment because the arbitration agreement was neither unconscionable nor beyond Broemmer's reasonable expectations. Broemmer appealed. ∞

Moeller, Justice The enforceability of the agreement to arbitrate is determined by principles of general contract law. Under those principles, the contract in this case was one of adhesion. An adhesion contract is typically a standardized form offered to consumers of goods and services on essentially a "take it or leave it" basis without affording the consumer a realistic opportunity to

bargain and under such conditions that the consumer cannot obtain the desired product or services except by acquiescing in the form contract.

The printed form agreement signed by Broemmer in this case possesses all the characteristics of a contract of adhesion. The form is a standardized contract offered to Broemmer on a "take it or leave it" basis. In addition to removing from the courts any potential dispute concerning fees or services, the drafter inserted additional terms potentially advantageous to itself requiring that any arbitrator appointed by the American Arbitration Association be a licensed medical doctor specializing in obstetrics/gynecology. The contract was not negotiated but was, instead, prepared by Abortion Services and presented to Broemmer as a condition of treatment. Staff at the clinic neither explained its terms to Broemmer nor indicated that she was free to refuse to sign the form; they merely represented that she had to complete three forms. Applying general contract law to the undisputed facts, the court of appeals correctly held that the contract was one of adhesion.

Our conclusion that the contract was one of adhesion is not, of itself, determinative of its enforceability. To determine whether this contract of adhesion is enforceable, we look to two factors: the reasonable expectations of the adhering party and whether the contract is unconscionable. As the court stated in *Graham v. Scissor-Tail, Inc.*:

Generally speaking, there are two judicially imposed limitations on the enforcement of adhesion contracts. The first is that such a contract or provision which does not fall within the reasonable expectations of the weaker or "adhering" party will not be enforced against him. The second is that a contract or provision, even if consistent with the reasonable expectations of the parties, will be denied enforcement if, considered in its context, it is unduly oppressive or "unconscionable."

Clearly, the issues of knowing consent and reasonable expectations are closely related and intertwined. Although customers typically adhere to standardized agreements and are bound by them without even appearing to know the standard terms in detail, they are not bound to unknown terms which are beyond the range of reasonable expectation. The *Restatement* focuses our attention on whether it was beyond plaintiff's reasonable expectations to expect to arbitrate her medical malpractice claims, which includes waiving her right to a jury trial, as part of the filling out of the three forms. Clearly, there was no conspicuous or explicit waiver of the fundamental right to a jury trial or any evidence that such rights were knowingly, voluntarily, and intelligently waived. The only evidence presented compels a finding that waiver of such fundamental rights was beyond the reasonable expectations of Broemmer. In this case failure to explain to Broemmer that the agreement required all potential disputes, including malpractice disputes, to be heard only by an arbitrator who was a licensed obstetrician/gynecologist requires us to view the "bargaining process" with suspicion. It would be unreasonable to enforce such a critical term against Broemmer when it is not a negotiated term and Abortion Services failed to explain it to her or call her attention to it.

Broemmer was under a great deal of emotional stress, had only a high school education, was not experienced in commercial matters, and is still not sure "what arbitration is." The contract fell outside Broemmer's reasonable expectations and is, therefore, unenforceable. Because of this holding, it is unnecessary for us to determine whether the contract is also unconscionable.

Judgment reversed in favor of Broemmer.

EFFECT OF ILLEGALITY

General Rule

As a general rule, courts will refuse to give any remedy for the breach of an illegal agreement. A court will refuse to enforce an illegal agreement and will also refuse to permit a party who has fully or partially performed her part of the agreement to recover what she has parted with. The reason for this rule is to serve the public interest, not to punish the parties.

In some cases, the public interest is best served by allowing some recovery to one or both of the parties. Such cases constitute exceptions to the "hands off" rule. The following discussion concerns the most common situations in which courts will grant some remedy even though they find the agreement to be illegal.

Excusable Ignorance of Facts or Legislation

Though it is often said that ignorance of the law is no excuse, courts will, under certain circumstances, permit a party to an illegal agreement who was excusably ignorant of facts or legislation that rendered the agreement illegal to recover damages for breach of the agreement. This exception is used where only *one* of the parties acted in ignorance of the illegality of the agreement and the other party was aware that the agreement was illegal. For this exception to apply, the facts or legislation of which the person claiming damages was ignorant must be of a relatively minor character—that is, it must not involve an immoral act or a serious threat to the public welfare. Finally, the person who is claiming damages cannot recover damages for anything that he does after learning of the illegality. For example, Warren enters a contract to perform in a play at Craig's theater. Warren does not know that Craig does not have the license to operate a theater as required by statute. Warren can recover the wages agreed on in the parties' contract for work that he performed before learning of the illegality.

When *both* of the parties are ignorant of facts or legislation of a relatively minor character, courts will not permit them to enforce the agreement and receive what they had bargained for, but they will permit the parties to recover what they have parted with.

Rights of Parties Not Equally in the Wrong

The courts will often permit a party who is not equally in the wrong (in technical legal terms, not *in pari delicto*) to recover what she has parted with under an illegal agreement. One of the most common situations in which this exception is used involves the rights of "protected parties"—people who were intended to be protected by a regulatory statute—who contract with parties who are not properly licensed under that statute. Most regulatory statutes are intended to protect the public. As a general rule, if a person guilty of violating a regulatory statute enters into an agreement with another person for whose protection the statute was adopted, the agreement will be enforceable by the party whom the legislature intended to protect.

Another common situation in which courts will grant a remedy to a party who is not equally in the wrong is one in which the less guilty party has been induced to enter the agreement by misrepresentation, fraud, duress, or undue influence.

Rescission before Performance of Illegal Act

Obviously, public policy is best served by any rule that encourages people not to commit illegal acts.

People who have fully or partially performed their part of an illegal contract have little incentive to raise the question of illegality if they know that they will be unable to recover what they have given because of the courts' hands-off approach to illegal agreements. To encourage people to cancel illegal contracts, courts will allow a person who rescinds such a contract before any illegal act has been performed to recover any consideration that he has given. For example, Dixon, the owner of a restaurant, pays O'Leary, an employee of a competitor's restaurant, $1,000 to obtain some of the competitor's recipes. If Dixon has second thoughts and tells O'Leary the deal is off before receiving any recipes, he can recover the $1,000 he paid O'Leary.

Divisible Contracts

If part of an agreement is legal and part is illegal, the courts will enforce the legal part so long as it is possible to separate the two parts. A contract is said to be *divisible*—that is, the legal part can be separated from the illegal part—if the contract consists of several promises or acts by one party, each of which corresponds with an act or a promise by the other party. In other words, there must be a separate consideration for each promise or act for a contract to be considered divisible.

Where no separate consideration is exchanged for the legal and illegal parts of an agreement, the agreement is said to be *indivisible*. As a general rule, an indivisible contract that contains an illegal part will be entirely unenforceable unless it comes within one of the exceptions discussed above. However, if the major portion of a contract is legal but the contract contains an illegal provision that does not affect the primary, legal portion, courts will often enforce the legal part of the agreement and simply decline to enforce the illegal part. For example, suppose Alberts sells his barbershop to Bates. The contract of sale provides that Alberts will not engage in barbering anywhere in the world for the rest of his life. The major portion of the contract—the sale of the business—is perfectly legal. A provision of the contract—the ancillary covenant not to compete—is overly restrictive, and thus illegal. A court would enforce the sale of the business but modify or refuse to enforce the restraint provision. See Figure 1.

FIGURE I

Effect of Illegality

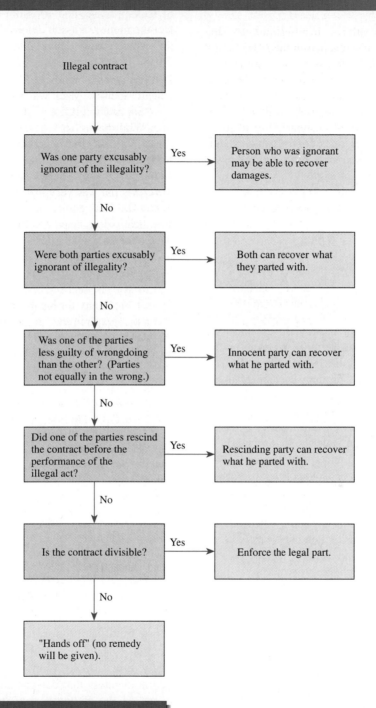

ETHICAL AND PUBLIC POLICY CONCERNS

1. In the *John Ray & Sons* case, the court refused to enforce a non-competition clause in an employment contract. How can this decision be justified?

2. You read that the law makes a distinction between contracts that violate regulatory statutes and contracts that violate revenue-raising statutes. What is the rationale for this distinction? Would it be better for the law simply to hold that *any* contract that violates *any* statute would be illegal? Why or why not?

3. What are some ethical justifications for the decisions that the courts reached in the *Murphy* and *Broemmer* cases? In both cases, the contracts in question were held to be unconscionable even though the individuals who signed the contracts *could have* read them and figured out their obligations. Who should have the responsibility to make sure that the person signing a contract understands his obligations, the person who drafts and offers the contract or the person who signs it?

PROBLEMS AND PROBLEM CASES

1. Isokappacase, a product manufactured by PTX Corp., is used as a starter medium and bacteriophage preventative medium in the production of cheese. Because of its high protein content, Isokappacase can also be used as a yield enhancer by adding it directly into cheese milk. When the product is used in this way, however, federal law requires that the resulting product be labeled as an imitation cheese and that the label list the ingredients in the end product to reflect the characteristics of imitation cheese. Podell, a salesman for Blossom Farm Products, was the sole U.S. distributor of Isokappacase. Over the course of three years, Blossom sold a large volume of Isokappacase to Kasson Cheese. Kasson used Isokappacase as a yield enhancer, introducing it directly into cheese milk to enhance cheese yields from the milk, but it did not label its final product as imitation cheese as required by federal standards. Had Kasson labeled its end product as an imitation cheese, it would have been able to sell the end product for only $.70 per pound rather than the $1.40 per pound it received for selling it as real cheese. Blossom was aware of the fact that Kasson's extremely large volume purchases of the product could only be accounted for by Kasson's use of Isokappacase as a yield enhancer. Podell acknowledged that once he recognized that Kasson was ordering about 100 times more Isokappacase than would be needed if it were using the products as a starter medium, he realized that such large volume orders could only mean that Kasson was using the product as a yield enhancer. Blossom also tacitly knew that Kasson was mislabeling its product. Both Kasson and Blossom benefited economically from this volume purchase and use. Kasson failed to pay Blossom $138,306 for its last order of Isokappacase, and Blossom brought suit to collect the money. Kasson defended on the ground that the contract was illegal. Was it? Must Kasson pay for the Isokappacase?

2. Alack was a member of Vic Tanny International, a health facility. Alack was encouraged to engage in the "Super Circuit," a cardiovascular workout routine. While using an upright row machine during a Super Circuit, the machine's handle disengaged from the weight cable, due to a missing clevis pin, and smashed into Alack's mouth and jaw. Although the clevis pin was very important to user safety, Vic Tanny did not require periodic inspections by any specifically designated employee to make certain that the clevis pin was in place. Alack suffered injuries to his mouth and lips, including several loose and broken teeth, causing Alack to undergo two surgeries and to see his dentist 20 times. Alack brought suit against Vic Tanny for his injuries. Vic Tanny claimed that a paragraph in the "Retail Installment Contract" that Alack signed releases Vic Tanny from "any and all claims" against it. The contract provides:

By the use of the facilities of Seller and/or by the attendance at any of the gymnasiums owned by Seller, the Member expressly agrees that Seller shall not be liable for any damages arising from personal injuries sustained by the Member or his guest in, on or about the premises of the said gymnasiums or as a result of their using the facilities and the equipment therein. By the execution of this agreement Member assumes full responsibility . . . and . . . does hereby fully and forever release and discharge Seller and all associated gymnasiums, their owners, employees and agents from any and all claims, demands, damages, rights of action, or causes of action, present or future, whether the same be known or unknown, anticipated or unanticipated, resulting from or arising out of the Member's or his guests use or intended use of the said gymnasium or the facilities and equipment thereof.

Will this contract be effective in protecting Vic Tanny from liability for its negligence?

3. The Ransburgs, residents of Peoria, Illinois, orally hired David William Haase Associates, a Peoria business that designs and decorates houses, to act as the architect, construction manager, designer, and decorator of a house that the Ransburgs wanted to have built in Vail, Colorado. The parties discussed this project both in Peoria and in Colorado. The parties agreed that Haase would provide budgetary control and monitor every aspect of the design, construction, and furnishing of the house. They also agreed to a construction budget of

$838,000 and a furnishing budget of $107,500, for a total project cost of $949,500. The scheduled completion date was December 18, 1988. Haase was to receive $80,000, including travel and other expenses, as compensation for his services. The Ransburgs ultimately sued Haase, alleging that he failed to compete the project on time, failed to ensure compliance with applicable building codes and easements, and failed to control the budget, so that the total cost of the project exceeded $1 million. Count II of this suit stated an alternative cause of action in which the Ransburgs alleged that Haase had held himself out as an architect but is not a registered architect in Illinois or any other state. Claiming that the contract for architectural services was against public policy, they sought recovery of the fees paid to Haase. Will they prevail?

4. Strickland attempted to bribe Judge Sylvania Woods to show leniency toward one of Strickland's friends who had a case pending before the judge. Judge Woods immediately reported this to the state's attorney and was asked to play along with Strickland until the actual payment of money occurred. Strickland gave $2,500 to the judge, who promptly turned it over to the state's attorney's office. Strickland was indicted for bribery, pled guilty, and was sentenced to a four-year prison term. Three months after the criminal trial, Strickland filed a motion for the return of his $2,500. Will the court order the return of his money?

5. Steamatic of Kansas City, Inc., specialized in cleaning and restoring property damaged by fire, smoke, water, or other elements. It employed Rhea as a marketing representative. His duties included soliciting customers, preparing cost estimates, supervising restoration work, and conducting seminars. At the time of his employment, Rhea signed a non-competition agreement prohibiting him from entering into a business in competition with Steamatic within six counties of the Kansas City area for a period of two years after the termination of his employment with Steamatic. Late in 1987, Rhea decided to leave Steamatic. In contemplation of the move, he secretly extracted the agreement restricting his postemployment activity from the company's files and destroyed it. Steamatic learned of this and discharged Rhea. Steamatic filed suit against Rhea to enforce the non-competition agreement when it learned that he was entering a competing business. Will the non-competition agreement be enforced?

6. Ben Lee Wilson had been licensed to practice architecture in the state of Hawaii, but his license lapsed in 1971 because he failed to pay a required $15 renewal fee. A Hawaii statute provides that any person who practices architecture without having been registered and "without having a valid unexpired certificate of registration . . . shall be fined not more than $500 or imprisoned not more than one year, or both." In 1972, Wilson performed architectural and engineering services for Kealakekua Ranch, for which he billed the Ranch $33,994.36. When the Ranch failed to pay Wilson's fee, he brought an action for breach of contract. What will the result be?

7. Blubaugh, a farmer, leased a Model 6620 combine from John Deere Leasing (JDL). The lease, which was printed on very lightweight paper, provided that Blubaugh would pay four annual rentals of $15,991.37 beginning July 1983 and at the end of the lease term would have the option to purchase the equipment for $27,191.25. On the reverse side of the lease, printed in light-colored fine print, were several terms that spelled out what JDL's remedies would be if Blubaugh failed to make a rental payment. These provisions gave JDL the right to repossess the combine, sell it, and keep the proceeds of such a sale. Even though Blubaugh was only agreeing to rent the combine rather than to buy it, these default provisions also made Blubaugh responsible for an additional amount of money that represented the difference between the "termination value" of the combine (as defined in a complicated formula on the reverse side of the lease) and any money received by JDL if it repossessed and sold the combine. Blubaugh read and signed the front of the contract but did not read the back. His understanding was that he had entered a basic lease with an option to purchase arrangement. His potential liability under the lease was not explained to him by anyone from JDL. Blubaugh paid $30,939.16 toward the first two rental payments, then made no further payments. JDL repossessed the combine and sold it for $42,000. JDL then sued Blubaugh for an additional $12,054.63, which was the amount due under the default clauses on the reverse side of the lease. Blubaugh defended on the ground that the default clauses were unconscionable. Were they?

8. In March 1990, Sanders first contacted Gore, an attorney, on a collection matter. Although both were married to others, Sanders and Gore began having an affair. Sanders alleged that during the affair, Gore persuaded Sanders that he wanted to divorce his wife and marry her. He persuaded her to divorce her husband, representing her in the divorce action. In June 1992, they took a trip to Hawaii where they registered for a promotional tour of time-share condos as "Brent and Brenda Gore." In November 1992, Gore presented Sanders with an engagement ring and asked her to marry him, and Sanders accepted his proposal. The affair continued until December 1993, when Gore told Sanders that he was "too weak" to leave his wife and ended the relationship with Sanders. Sanders brought suit against Gore seeking damages for breach of his promise to marry her. Will she prevail?

9. Hohe, a 15-year-old student at Mission Bay High School, was injured during an annual campus hypnotism show sponsored by the PTSA (Parent, Teacher, and Student Association) as a fundraiser. Hohe was one of 18 or 20 subjects selected at random from a group of many volunteers. Her participation in the "Magic of the Mind Show" was conditioned on signing two release forms. Hohe's father signed a form entitled "Mission Bay High School PTSA Presents Dr. Karl Santo," which stated that he waived "all liability" against the PTSA, high school, and school district. Hohe and her father both signed a second form entitled "KARL SANTO HYPNOTIST," in which they agreed to "indemnify and hold you and any third parties harmless from any and all liability, loss or damage . . . caused by or arising in any manner from my participation in the Magic of the Mind Show." During the course of the show, Hohe was injured when she slid from her chair and also fell to the floor about six times. Hohe sued the school district and the PTSA for her injuries. She argues that the releases she and her father signed are contrary to public policy. Are they?

10. Gianni Sport was a New York manufacturer and distributor of women's clothing. Gantos was a clothing retailer headquartered in Grand Rapids, Michigan. In 1980, Gantos's sales total was 20 times greater than Gianni Sport's, and in this industry, buyers were "in the driver's seat." In June 1980, Gantos submitted to Gianni Sport a purchase order for women's holiday clothing to be delivered on October 10, 1980. The purchase order contained the following clause:

Buyer reserves the right to terminate by notice to Seller all or any part of this Purchase Order with respect to Goods that have not actually been shipped by Seller or as to Goods which are not timely delivered for any reason whatsoever.

Gianni Sport made the goods in question especially for Gantos. This holiday order comprised 20 to 22 percent of Gianni Sport's business. In late September 1980, before the goods were shipped, Gantos canceled the order. Was the cancellation clause unconscionable?

11. On September 29, 1987, Guido, a practicing lawyer, visited Koopman's Academy of Equestrian Arts to inquire about taking horseback riding lessons. At that time, she signed an agreement stating that she agreed to release the owners and managers of the Academy for liability for any injury, loss, or damage that she might suffer as a result of negligence by any of them. Prior to signing, Koopman told Guido that the form "didn't mean anything. It is something that I need to have you sign, because my insurance company won't let me give lessons unless I have people sign this." Guido went ahead and signed the form without reading it because she did not think it was enforceable. Guido took lessons from Koopman as often as twice a week until June 1988, when she was thrown from one of Koopman's horses and injured. Guido sued Koopman for negligence and Koopman asserted the release as a defense. Guido claimed that the release is illegal and unenforceable. Was it?

12. Audley, a professional model, was bitten on the head by an adult male lion with which she had been posing during a photography shoot at Melton's studio. Audley sued Melton, claiming that he failed to take any precautionary action despite noticing that Audley's hair was agitating the lion. Melton moved to dismiss, arguing that the suit was barred by either of two releases that Audley had signed. The first release, which primarily addressed proprietary rights to the photos and negatives, included a sentence that read: "I further release the photographer, his/her agents or assigns from any and all liability whatsoever." The second release stated:

I, *Shannon Audley* realize that working with the wild and potentially dangerous animals (i.e., lion, white tiger, hawk) can create a hazardous situation, resulting in loss of life or limb. I take all responsibility on myself for any event as described above that may take place. I hold Bill Melton and T.I.G.E.R.S. or any of their agents free of any or all liability. I am signing this of my on [*sic*] free will.

Is Melton correct?

Writing

Your study of contract law so far has focused on the requirements for the formation of a valid contract. You should be aware, however, that even when all the elements of a valid contract exist, the enforceability of the contract and the nature of the parties' obligations can be greatly affected by the *form* in which the contract is set out and by the *language* that is used to express the agreement. An otherwise valid contract can become unenforceable if it does not comply with the formalities required by state law. A person may be unable to offer evidence about promises and agreements made in preliminary negotiations be-cause the parties later adopted a written contract that did not contain those terms. And, of course, the legal effect of any contract is determined in large part by the way in which a court interprets the language it contains. This chapter discusses the ways in which the enforceability of a contract and the scope of contractual obligations can be affected by the manner in which people express their agreements. ∞

THE STATUTE OF FRAUDS

Despite what many people believe, there is no general requirement that contracts be in writing. In most situations, oral contracts are legally enforce-able, assuming that they can be proven. Still, oral contracts are less desirable than written contracts in many ways. They are more easily misunderstood or forgotten than written contracts. They are also more subject to the danger that a person might fabricate terms or fraudulently claim to have made an oral contract where none exists.

In 17th-century England, the dangers inherent in oral contracts were exacerbated by a legal rule that prohibited parties to a lawsuit from testifying in their own cases. Since the parties to an oral contract could not give testimony, the only way they could prove the existence of the contract was through the testimony of third parties. As you might expect, third parties were sometimes persuaded to offer false testimony about the existence of contracts. In an attempt to stop the widespread fraud and perjury that resulted, Parliament enacted the Statute of Frauds in 1677. It required written evidence before certain classes of contracts would be enforced. Although the possibility of fraud exists in every contract, the statute focused on contracts in which the potential for fraud was great or the consequences of fraud were especially serious. The legislatures of American states adopted very similar statutes, also known as statutes of frauds. These statutes, which require certain kinds of contracts to be evidenced by a signed writing, are exceptions to the general rule that oral contracts are enforceable.

Statutes of frauds have produced a great deal of litigation, due in part to the public's ignorance of their provisions. It is difficult to imagine an aspect of contract law that is more practical for businesspeople to know about than the circumstances under which an oral contract will not suffice.

EFFECT OF FAILURE TO COMPLY WITH THE STATUTE OF FRAUDS

The statute of frauds applies only to executory contracts. If an oral contract has been completely performed by both parties, the fact that it did not comply with the statute of frauds would not be a ground for rescission of the contract.

What happens if an executory contract is within the statute of frauds but has not been evidenced by the type of writing required by the statute? It is not treated as an illegal contract because the statute of frauds is more of a formal rule than a rule of substantive law. Rather, the contract that fails to comply with the statute of frauds is *unenforceable*. Although the contract will not be enforced, a person who has conferred some benefit on the other party pursuant to the contract can recover the reasonable value of his performance in an action based on *quasi-contract*.

CONTRACTS WITHIN THE STATUTE OF FRAUDS

A contract is said to be "within" the statute of frauds if the statute requires that sort of contract to be evidenced by a writing. In almost all states, the following types of contracts are within the statute of frauds:

1. Collateral contracts in which a person promises to perform the obligation of another person.
2. Contracts for the sale of an interest in real estate.
3. Bilateral contracts that cannot be performed within a year from the date of their formation.
4. Contracts for the sale of goods for a price of $500 or more.
5. Contracts in which an executor or administrator promises to be personally liable for the debt of an estate.
6. Contracts in which marriage is the consideration.

Of this list, the first four sorts of contracts have the most significance today, and our discussion will focus primarily on them.

The statutes of frauds of the various states are not uniform. Some states require written evidence of other contracts in addition to those listed above. For example, a number of states require written evidence of contracts to pay a commission for the sale of real estate. Others require written evidence of ratifications of infants' promises or promises to pay debts that have been barred by the statute of limitations or discharged by bankruptcy.

The following discussion examines in greater detail the sorts of contracts that are within most states' statute of frauds.

Collateral Contracts

A **collateral contract** is one in which one person (the *guarantor*) agrees to pay the debt or obligation that a second person (the *principal debtor*) owes to a third person (the *obligee*) if the principal debtor fails to perform. For example, Cohn, who wants to help Davis establish a business, promises First Bank that he will repay the loan that First Bank makes to Davis if Davis fails to pay it. Here, Cohn is the guarantor, Davis is the principal debtor, and First

FIGURE 1

Collateral Contract

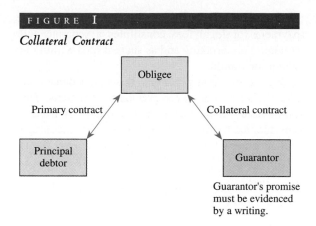

Bank is the obligee. Cohn's promise to First Bank must be in writing to be enforceable.

Figure 1 shows that a collateral contract involves at least three parties and at least two promises to perform (a promise by the principal debtor to pay the obligee and a promise by the guarantor to pay the obligee). In a collateral contract, the guarantor promises to pay *only if the principal debtor fails to do so.* As you will read in the following case, *Crozier and Gudsnuk, P.C. v. Valentine,* the essence of the collateral contract is that the debt or obligation is owed primarily by the principal debtor and the guarantor's debt is *secondary.* Thus, not all three-party transactions are collateral contracts.

When a person undertakes an obligation that is *not* conditioned on the default of another person, and the debt is his own rather than that of another person, his obligation is said to be *original,* not collateral. For example, when Timmons calls Johnson Florist Company and says, "Send flowers to Elrod," Timmons is undertaking an obligation to pay *her own*—not someone else's—debt.

CROZIER AND GUDSNUK P.C. v. VALENTINE 1992 Conn. Super. LEXIS 1179 (Super. Ct. Conn. 1992) No. CV-91-0036504

Michael Valentine, Jr., an adult over the age of 18, was charged with criminal assault. His parents, Lorraine and Michael Valentine, Sr., contacted the law firm of Crozier and Gudsnuk about representing their son in the criminal action. In October 1990, attorney Barbara DeGennaro, an associate in the law firm, agreed to represent Valentine. The law firm claims that Valentine's parents orally agreed to guarantee payment for the legal fees incurred by their son. Approximately 10 days after DeGennaro had agreed to represent Valentine, Mrs. Valentine paid the firm's retainer by signing a check for $250. The law firm represented Valentine in the criminal assault charge until February 25, 1991, when its representation ended at the request of the Valentines. The law firm claims that the reasonable value of the legal services it performed was $4,200. It brought suit against Valentine's parents to recover the legal fees owed to the firm. It asked the court for a prejudgment attachment of the Valentines' home. A hearing was held on this issue.

Jones, Judge The present case involves an alleged oral contract made between a law firm and the parents of an adult child charged in a criminal action. The Statute of Frauds provides that:

No civil action may be maintained in the following cases unless the agreement, or a memorandum of the agreement, is made in writing and signed by the party, or the agent of the party, to be charged ... (2) against any person upon any special promise to answer for the debt, default or miscarriage of another.

The Valentines have raised the Statute of Frauds as a defense, claiming that the oral agreement of guarantee made between the parents and the law firm was a separate, collateral undertaking independent of the law firm's representation of Michael Valentine, Jr. In *Adamowicz v. Stevens,* the court held:

The statute is not a defense if the promise was an original undertaking. Fundamentally the distinction between a contract which falls within the condemnation of the statute of frauds and one which does not is that the former is a collateral undertaking to answer in case of a default on the part of the obligor in the contract, upon whom still rests the primary liability to perform; whereas, in the latter, the obligation assumed is a primary one that the contract shall be performed.

Further, an undertaking by a party not before liable, for the purpose of securing the performance of a duty for which the party for whom the undertaking is made continues liable, is a special promise to answer for the debt, default or miscarriage of another and is within the statute of frauds.

In the present case, only the adult son of the Valentines was legally represented by the law firm. The parents were not charged in any criminal action and received no material benefit from the law firm's representation of Michael Valentine, Jr. If the oral agreement between the parents and the law firm was in fact a separate, collateral undertaking, then the agreement will be within the statute of frauds. From the facts before this court, the parents cannot be seen as principal parties in the legal services agreement between the law firm and their adult son. The record indicates that the oral agreement to guarantee payment for legal fees constitutes a separate and collateral undertaking and as such, it falls within the statute of frauds.

For the foregoing reasons, this Court denies the plaintiff's application for prejudgment remedy. The Court notes in passing that [the statute of frauds] was adopted by the legislature in order to encourage certain contracting parties to put their agreements into writing so as to avoid certain pitfalls.

Plaintiff's application denied in favor of the Valentines.

Exception: Main Purpose or Leading Object Rule   There are some situations in which a contract that is technically collateral is treated like an original contract because the person promising to pay the debt of another does so for the primary purpose of securing some personal benefit. Under the **main purpose** or **leading object** rule, no writing is required where the guarantor makes a collateral promise for the main purpose of obtaining some personal economic advantage. When the consideration given in exchange for the collateral promise is something the guarantor seeks primarily for his own benefit rather than for the benefit of the primary debtor, the contract is outside the statute of frauds and does not have to be in writing. Suppose, for example, that Penn is a major creditor of Widgetmart, a retailer. To help keep Widgetmart afloat and increase the chances that Widgetmart will repay the debt it owes him, Penn orally promises Rex Industries, one of the Widgetmart's suppliers, that he will guarantee Widgetmart's payment for goods that Rex sells to Widgetmart. In this situation, Penn's oral agreement could be enforced under the main purpose rule if the court finds that Penn was acting for his own personal financial benefit.

Interest in Land

Any contract that creates or transfers an interest in land is within the statute of frauds. The inclusion of real estate contracts in the statute of frauds reflects the values of an earlier, agrarian society in which land was the primary basis of wealth. Our legal system historically has treated land as being more important than other forms of property. Courts have interpreted the land provision of the statute of frauds broadly to require written evidence of any transaction that will affect the ownership of an interest in land. Thus, a contract to sell or mortgage real estate must be evidenced by a writing, as must an option to purchase real estate or a contract to grant an easement or permit the mining and removal of minerals on land. A lease is also a transfer of an interest in land, but most states' statutes of frauds do not require leases to be in writing unless they are long-term leases, usually those for one year or more. On the other hand, a contract to erect a building or to insure a building would not be within the real estate provision of the statute of frauds because such contracts do not involve the transfer of interests in land.[1]

Exception: Full Performance by the Vendor   An oral contract for the sale of land that has been completely performed by the vendor (seller) is "taken out of the statute of frauds"—that is, is enforceable without a writing. For example, Peterson and Lincoln enter into an oral contract for the sale of Peterson's farm at an agreed-on price and Peterson, the vendor, delivers a deed to the farm to Lincoln. In this situation, the vendor has completely performed and most states would treat the oral contract as being enforceable.

Exception: Part Performance (Action in Reliance) by the Vendee   When the vendee (purchaser of land) does an act in clear reliance on an oral contract for the sale of land, an equitable doctrine

---

[1]Note, however, that a writing might be required under state insurance statutes.

commonly known as the "part performance doctrine" permits the vendee to enforce the contract notwithstanding the fact that it was oral. The part performance doctrine is based on both evidentiary and reliance considerations. The doctrine recognizes that a person's conduct can "speak louder than words" and can indicate the existence of a contract almost as well as a writing can. The part performance doctrine is also based on the desire to avoid the injustice that would otherwise result if the contract were repudiated after the vendee's reliance.

Under section 129 of the *Restatement (Second) of Contracts,* a contract for the transfer of an interest in land can be enforced even without a writing if the person seeking enforcement:

1. Has *reasonably relied* on the contract and on the other party's assent.
2. Has changed his position to such an extent that *enforcement of the contract is the only way to prevent injustice.*

In other words, the vendee must have done some act in reliance on the contract and the nature of the act must be such that restitution (returning his money) would not be an adequate remedy. The part performance doctrine will not permit the vendee to collect damages for breach of contract, but it will permit him to obtain the equitable remedy of **specific performance,** a remedy whereby the court orders the breaching party to perform his contract.[2]

A vendee's reliance on an oral contract could be shown in many ways. Traditionally, many states have required that the vendee pay part or all of the purchase price and either make substantial improvements on the property or take possession of it. For example, Contreras and Miller orally enter into a contract for the sale of Contreras's land. If Miller pays Contreras a substantial part of the purchase price and either takes possession of the land or begins to make improvements on it, the contract would be enforceable without a writing under the part performance doctrine. These are not the only sorts of acts in reliance that would make an oral contract enforceable, however. Under the *Restatement (Second)* approach, if the promise to transfer land is clearly proven or is admitted by the breaching party, it is not necessary that the act of reliance

include making payment, taking possession, or making improvements.[3] It still is necessary, however, that the reliance be such that restitution would not be an adequate remedy. For this reason, a vendee's payment of the purchase price, standing alone, is usually *not* sufficient for the part performance doctrine.

Contracts that Cannot Be Performed within One Year

A bilateral, executory contract that cannot be performed within one year from the day on which it comes into existence is within the statute of frauds and must be evidenced by a writing. The apparent purpose of this provision is to guard against the risk of faulty or willfully inaccurate recollection of long-term contracts. Courts have tended to construe it very narrowly.

One aspect of this narrow construction is that most states hold that a contract that has been fully performed by *one* of the parties is "taken out of the statute of frauds" and is enforceable without a writing. For example, Nash enters into an oral contract to perform services for Thomas for 13 months. If Nash has already fully performed his part of the contract, Thomas will be required to pay him the contract price.

In addition, this provision of the statute has been held to apply only when the terms of the contract make it impossible for the contract to be completed within one year. If the contract is for an indefinite period of time, it is not within the statute of frauds. This is true even if, in retrospect, the contract was not completed within a year. Thus, Weinberg's agreement to work for Wolf for an indefinite period of time would not have to be evidenced by a writing, even if Weinberg eventually works for Wolf for many years. As demonstrated by *Hodge v. Evans Financial Corporation,* which follows, the mere fact that performance is unlikely to be completed in one year does not bring the contract within the statute of frauds. In most states, a contract "for life" is not within the statute of frauds because it is possible—since death is an uncertain event—for the contract to be performed within a year. In a few states such as New York, contracts for life are within the statute of frauds.

---

[2]Specific performance is discussed in more detail in Chapter 18.

---

[3]*Restatement (Second) of Contracts* § 129, comment *d.*

HODGE v. EVANS FINANCIAL CORPORATION   823 F.2d 559 (D.C. Cir. 1987)

O n two occasions in 1980, Albert Hodge met with John Tilley, president and chief operating officer of Evans Financial Corporation, to discuss Hodge's possible employment by Evans. Hodge was 54 years old at that time and was assistant counsel and assistant secretary of Mellon National Corporation and Mellon Bank of Pittsburgh. During these discussions, Tilley asked Hodge what his conditions were for accepting employment with Evans, and Hodge replied, "No. 1, the job must be permanent. Because of my age, I have a great fear about going back into the marketplace again. I want to be here until I retire." Tilley allegedly responded, "I accept that condition." Regarding his retirement plans, Hodge later testified, "I really questioned whether I was going to go much beyond 65." Hodge subsequently accepted Evans's offer of employment as vice president and general counsel. He moved from Pittsburgh to Washington, D.C., in September 1980 and worked for Evans from that time until he was fired by Tilley on May 7, 1981.

Hodge brought a breach of contract suit against Evans. The case was tried before a jury, which rendered a verdict in favor of Hodge for $175,000. Evans appeals. ⌇

Wald, Chief Justice   Evans argues that the oral employment agreement between Evans and Hodge is unenforceable under the statute of frauds. Because the agreement here contemplated long-term employment for a number of years, Evans argues that the statute requires it to have been in writing in order to be enforceable.

Despite its sweeping terms, the one-year provision of the statute has long been construed narrowly and literally. Under prevailing interpretation, the enforceability of a contract under the statute does not depend on the actual course of subsequent events or on the expectations of the parties. Instead, the statute applies only to those contracts whose performance could not possibly or conceivably be completed within one year. The statute of frauds is thus inapplicable if, at the time the contract is formed, any contingent event could complete the terms of the contract within one year.

Hodge argues that, under this interpretation of the statute of frauds, a permanent or lifetime employment contract does not fall within the statute because it is capable of full performance within one year if the employee were to die within the period. Hodge's view of the statute's application to lifetime or permanent employment contracts has, in fact, been accepted by an overwhelming majority of courts and commentators.

The employment contract in this case cannot reasonably be interpreted as a contract for a specified period of time. Hodge unequivocally alleged a contract for permanent employment, not a contract until he reached age 65 or for any other stated period of time. The fact that Hodge expected to retire at some point does not mean that his contract could not possibly be performed within one year. All employment contracts of permanent, lifetime, or indefinite duration undoubtedly contemplate retirement; such contracts certainly do not mean that employees are bound to work until the moment they drop dead. Hodge's permanent employment contract with Evans could therefore be fully performed, according to its terms, upon Hodge's retirement or upon his death. Under the conventional view the latter possibility is sufficient to take the contract out of the statute. That Hodge expected to retire before he died is completely irrelevant to this case so long as the contract was legally susceptible of performance within one year. The applicability of the statute of frauds does not depend on the expectations of the parties.

We recognize that the conventional view of the statute is somewhat "legalistic." Yet the statute of frauds itself is widely understood as a formal device that shields promise breakers from the consequences of otherwise enforceable agreements. The conventional, narrowing interpretation overwhelmingly adopted by courts and commentators is designed to mollify the often harsh and unintended consequences of the statute. Here the jury concluded, despite Evans's vigorous defense, that Hodge was promised permanent employment and that he was nonetheless fired without cause. Under the traditional, narrow view of the statute, the statute of frauds does not bar the enforcement of such jury verdicts.

Judgment for Hodge affirmed.

Computing Time   In determining whether a contract is within the one-year provision, courts begin counting time on the day when the contract comes into existence. If, under the terms of the contract, it is possible to perform it within one year from this date, the contract does not fall within the statute of frauds and does not have to be in writing. If, however, the terms of the contract make it impossible to complete performance of the contract (without breaching it) within one year from the date on which the contract came into existence, the contract falls within the statute and must meet its requirements to be enforceable. Thus, if Hammer Co. and McCrea agree on August 1, 1997, that McCrea will work for Hammer Co. for one year, beginning October 1, 1997, the terms of the contract dictate that it is not possible to complete performance until October 1, 1998. Because that date is more than one year from the date on which the contract came into existence, the contract falls within the statute of frauds and must be evidenced by a writing to be enforceable.

Sale of Goods for $500 or More

The original English Statute of Frauds required a writing for contracts for the sale of goods for a price of 10 pounds sterling or more. In the United States today, the writing requirement for the sale of goods is governed by section 2–201 of the Uniform Commercial Code. This section provides that contracts for the sale of goods for the price of $500 or more are not enforceable without a writing or other specified evidence that a contract was made. There are a number of alternative ways of satisfying the requirements of section 2–201. These will be explained later in this chapter.

Modifications of Existing Sales Contracts   Just as some contracts to extend the time for performance fall within the one-year provision of the statute of frauds, agreements to modify existing sales contracts can fall within the statute of frauds if the contract as modified is for a price of $500 or more.[4] UCC section 2–209(3) provides that the requirements of the statute of frauds must be satisfied if the contract as modified is within its provisions. For example, if Carroll and Kestler enter into

a contract for the sale of goods at a price of $490, the original contract does *not* fall within the statute of frauds. However, if they later modify the contract by increasing the contract price to $510, the modification falls within the statute of frauds and must meet its requirements to be enforceable.

Promise of Executor or Administrator to Pay a Decedent's Debt Personally

When a person dies, a personal representative is appointed to administer his estate. One of the important tasks of this personal representative, who is called an executor if the person dies leaving a will or an administrator if the person dies without a will, is to pay the debts owed by the decedent. No writing is required when an executor or administrator—acting in his representative capacity—promises to pay the decedent's debts from the funds of the decedent's estate. The statute of frauds requires a writing, however, if the executor, acting in her capacity as a private individual rather than in her representative capacity, promises to pay one of the decedent's debts out of her own (the executor's) funds. For example, Thomas, who has been appointed executor of his Uncle Max's estate, is presented with a bill for $10,500 for medical services rendered to Uncle Max during his last illness by the family doctor, Dr. Barnes. Feeling bad that there are not adequate funds in the estate to compensate Dr. Barnes for his services, Thomas promises to pay Dr. Barnes from his own funds. Thomas's promise would have to be evidenced by a writing to be enforceable.

Contract in which Marriage Is the Consideration

The statute of frauds also requires a writing when marriage is the consideration to support a contract. The marriage provision has been interpreted to be inapplicable to agreements that involve only mutual promises to marry. It can apply to any other contract in which one party's promise is given in exchange for marriage or the promise to marry on the part of the other party. This is true whether the promisor is one of the parties to the marriage or a third party. For example, if Hicks promises to deed his ranch to Everett in exchange for Everett's agreement to marry Hicks's son, Everett could not enforce

---

[4]Modifications of sales contracts are discussed in greater detail in Chapter 12.

CONCEPT REVIEW

Contracts within the Statute of Frauds

PROVISION	DESCRIPTION	EXCEPTIONS (SITUATIONS IN WHICH CONTRACT DOES NOT REQUIRE A WRITING)
Marriage	Contracts, other than mutual promises to marry, where marriage is the consideration	—
Year	Bilateral contracts that, *by their terms,* cannot be performed within one year from the date on which the contract was formed	Full (complete) performance by one of the parties
Land	Contracts that create or transfer an ownership interest in real property	1. Full performance by vendor (vendor deeds property to vendees) or 2. "Part performance" doctrine: Vendee relies on oral contract—for example, by: a. Paying substantial part of purchase price, and b. Taking possession or making improvements
Executor's Promise	Executor promises to pay estate's debt out of his own funds	—
Sale of Goods at Price of $500 or More (UCC § 2–201)	Contracts for the sale of goods for a contract price of $500 or more; also applies to modifications of contracts for goods where price as modified is $500 or more	See alternative ways of satisfying statute of frauds under UCC.
Collateral Contracts, Guaranty	Contracts where promisor promises to pay the debt of another if the primary debtor fails to pay	"Main purpose" or "leading object" exception: Guarantor makes promise primarily for her own economic benefit

Hicks's promise without written evidence of the promise.

Prenuptial (or antenuptial) agreements present a common contemporary application of the marriage provision of the statute of frauds. These are agreements between couples who contemplate marriage. They usually involve such matters as transfers of property, division of property upon divorce or death, and various lifestyle issues. Assuming that marriage or the promise to marry is the consideration supporting these agreements, they are within the statute of frauds and must be evidenced by a writing.[5]

_____

[5]Note, however, that "nonmarital" agreements between unmarried cohabitants who do not plan marriage are not within the marriage provision of the statute of frauds, even though the agreement may concern the same sorts of matters that are typically covered in a prenuptial agreement. The legality of agreements between unmarried cohabitants is discussed in Chapter 15.

MEETING THE REQUIREMENTS OF THE STATUTE OF FRAUDS

Nature of the Writing Required

The statutes of frauds of the various states are not uniform in their formal requirements. However, most states require only a *memorandum* of the parties' agreement; they do not require that the entire contract be in writing. As you will read in the following *Smith v. International Paper Co.* case, essential terms of the contract must be stated in the writing. The memorandum must provide written evidence that a contract was made, but it need not have been created with the intent that the memorandum itself would be binding. In fact, in some cases, written offers that were accepted orally have been held sufficient to satisfy the writing requirement. Typical examples include letters, telegrams, receipts, or any other writing indicating that the parties had a contract. The memorandum need not be made at the same time the contract comes into being; in fact, the memorandum may be made at any time before suit is filed. If a memorandum of the parties' agreement is lost, its loss and its contents may be proven by oral testimony.

SMITH v. INTERNATIONAL PAPER CO.   87 F.3d 245 (8th Cir. 1996)

I n 1989, International Paper (IP) decided to sell its lumberyard in Hannibal, Missouri. Smith, the lumberyard's manager, expressed an interest in buying it. Smith and IP eventually signed an Asset Purchase Agreement dated March 20, 1990 (the "March 20 Agreement"). However, Smith quickly concluded that the purchase price in the March 20 Agreement was too high. Therefore, he did not seek Small Business Administration financing, as the March 20 Agreement required, and notified IP that he did not intend to go forward under that Agreement.

Beginning in July 1990, Smith submitted a series of new purchase offers, which IP rejected. On November 16, he submitted another written offer, "subject to the approval of a local lending institution and the Small Business Administration." Three days later, an IP e-mail message requested confirmation that Smith's latest proposal included an undertaking to retain the lumberyard's employees; Smith agreed. On November 30, there was a telephone conversation between Smith and IP's comptroller. According to Smith, the comptroller orally accepted Smith's November 16 offer, requesting that Smith provide a $10,000 down payment and the requisite financing commitment.

On December 4, Smith mailed IP a $10,000 check and a letter from Hannibal National Bank that was supportive but not a firm loan commitment. IP initially endorsed and deposited Smith's check. However, on December 21, IP wrote Smith rejecting his "conditional" offer. IP then returned Smith's $10,000 and sold the lumberyard for a lower price to a buyer with secure financing. Smith sued, claiming breach of a contract to sell the lumberyard. The trial court granted a summary judgment in favor of IP. Smith appealed. ∞

Per Curiam   To satisfy the Missouri statute of frauds, a writing must contain all the essential terms of the contract and must be signed by the party to be charged. Several documents in combination may supply the essential terms of the contract, as long as one document refers to the other, or their contents clearly show they are related.

We agree with the district court that Smith has not satisfied the statute of frauds. Smith first contends that the March 20 Agreement satisfies the statute because the parties later simply modified its terms. The summary judgment record does not support this modification theory—the March 20 Agreement provides that it may only be modified in writing, none of the later documents refer to that Agreement, and Smith himself testified that the March 20 Agreement "just died" and "went away."

None of the remaining documents, individually or in combination, contain either an offer by IP to sell the lumberyard, or IP's acceptance of an offer by Smith to buy it. IP's e-mail message concerning the retention of employees merely sought to clarify an implied term of Smith's cryptic November 16 offer. IP's deposit of Smith's $10,000 check is insufficient because part payment of the purchase price for real estate [does not remove] an oral contract from the statute of frauds. Smith may not flesh out the terms of the documents with parol evidence to satisfy the statute of frauds.

When the party to be charged is the seller of real estate, there must be a writing signed by that party reflecting a promise to sell. Because Smith failed to come forward with such a writing, the district court properly granted summary judgment dismissing his claim as barred by the statute of frauds.

Affirmed in favor of IP.

Contents of the Memorandum   Although there is a general trend away from requiring complete writings to satisfy the statute of frauds, an adequate memorandum must still contain several things. As you saw in the Smith case, the essential terms of the contract generally must be indicated in the memorandum. States differ in their requirements concerning how specifically the terms must be stated, however. The identity of the parties must be indicated in some way, and the subject matter of the contract must be identified with reasonable certainty. This last requirement causes particular problems in contracts for the sale of land, since many statutes require a detailed description of the property to be sold.

Contents of Memorandum under the UCC The standard for determining the sufficiency of the contents of a memorandum is more flexible in cases concerning contracts for the sale of goods. This looser standard is created by the language of UCC section 2–201, which states that the writing must be sufficient to indicate that a contract for sale has been made between the parties, but a writing can be sufficient even if it omits or incorrectly states a term agreed on. However, the memorandum is not enforceable for more than the quantity of goods stated in the memorandum. Thus, a writing that does not indicate the *quantity* of goods to be sold would not satisfy the Code's writing requirement.

Signature Requirement The memorandum must be signed by the *party to be charged* or his authorized agent. (The party to be charged is the person using the statute of frauds as a defense—generally the defendant unless the statute of frauds is asserted as a defense to a counterclaim.) This means that it is not necessary for purposes of meeting the statute of frauds for both parties' signatures to appear on the document. It is, however, in the best interests of both parties for both signatures to appear on the writing; otherwise, the contract evidenced by the writing is enforceable only against the signing party. Unless the statute expressly provides that the memorandum or contract must be signed at the end, the signature may appear any place on the memorandum. Any writing, mark, initials, stamp, engraving, or other symbol placed or printed on a memorandum will suffice as a signature, as long as the party to be charged intended it to authenticate (indicate the genuineness of) the writing.

Memorandum Consisting of Several Writings In many situations, the elements required for a memorandum are divided among several documents. For example, Wayman and Allen enter into a contract for the sale of real estate, intending to memorialize their agreement in a formal written

document later. While final drafts of a written contract are being prepared, Wayman repudiates the contract. Allen has a copy of an unsigned preliminary draft of the contract that identifies the parties and contains all of the material terms of the parties' agreement, an unsigned note written by Wayman that contains the legal description of the property, and a letter signed by Wayman that refers to the contract and to the other two documents. None of these documents, standing alone, would be sufficient to satisfy the statute of frauds. However, Allen can combine them to meet the requirements of the statute, provided that they all relate to the same agreement. This can be shown by physical attachment, as where the documents are stapled or bound together, or by references in the documents themselves that indicate that they all apply to the same transaction. In some cases, it has also been shown by the fact that the various documents were executed at the same time.

UCC: ALTERNATIVE MEANS OF SATISFYING THE STATUTE OF FRAUDS IN SALE OF GOODS CONTRACTS

As you have learned, the basic requirement of the UCC statute of frauds [2–201] is that a contract for the sale of goods for the purchase price of $500 or more must be evidenced by a written memorandum that indicates the existence of the contract, states the quantity of goods to be sold, and is signed by the party to be charged. Recognizing that the underlying purpose of the statute of frauds is to provide more evidence of the existence of a contract than the mere oral testimony of one of the parties, however, the Code also permits the statute of frauds to be satisfied by any of four other types of evidence. These different methods of satisfying the UCC statute of frauds are depicted in Figure 2. Under the UCC, then, a contract for the sale of goods for a purchase price of $500 or more for which there is no written memorandum signed by the party to be charged can meet the requirements of the statute of frauds in any of the following ways:

1. *Confirmatory memorandum between merchants.* Suppose Gardner and Roth enter into a contract over the telephone for the sale of goods at a price of $5,000. Gardner then sends a memorandum to Roth

FIGURE   2

Satisfying the Statute of Frauds through a Contract for the Sale of Goods with a Price of $500 or More

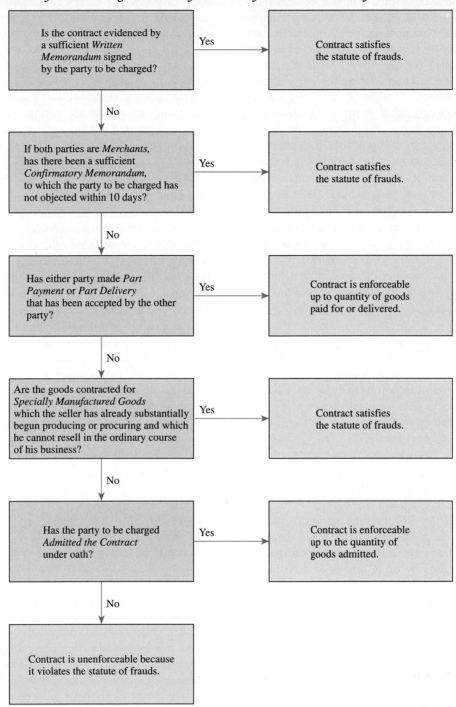

confirming the deal they made orally. If Roth receives the memo and does not object to it, it would be fair to say that the parties' conduct provides some evidence that a contract exists. Under some circumstances, the UCC permits such confirmatory memoranda to satisfy the statute of frauds even though the writing is signed by the party who is seeking to enforce the contract rather than the party against whom enforcement is sought [2–201(2)]. This exception applies only when *both* of the parties to a contract are *merchants*. Furthermore, the memo must be sent within a reasonable time after the contract is made and must be sufficient to bind the person who sent it if enforcement were sought against him (that is, it must indicate that a contract was made, state a quantity, and be signed by the sender). If the party against whom enforcement is sought receives the memo, has reason to know its contents, and yet fails to give written notice of objection to the contents of the memo within 10 days after receiving it, the memo can be introduced to meet the requirements of the statute of frauds.

2. *Part payment or part delivery.* Suppose Rice and Cooper enter a contract for the sale of 1,000 units of goods at $1 each. After Rice has paid $600, Cooper refuses to deliver the goods and asserts the statute of frauds as a defense to enforcement of the contract. The Code permits part payment or part delivery to satisfy the statute of frauds, but only for the quantity of goods that have been delivered or paid for [2–201(3)(c)]. Thus, Cooper would be required to deliver only 600 units rather than the 1,000 units Rice alleges that he agreed to sell.

3. *Admission in pleadings or court.* Another situation in which the UCC statute of frauds can be satisfied without a writing occurs when the party being sued admits the existence of the oral contract in his trial testimony or in any document that he files with the court. For example, Nelson refuses to perform an oral contract he made with Smith for the sale of $2,000 worth of goods, and Smith sues him. If Nelson admits the existence of the oral contract in pleadings or in court proceedings, his admission is sufficient to meet the statute of frauds. This exception is justified by the strong evidence that such an admission provides. After all, what better evidence of a contract can there be than is provided when the party being sued admits under penalty of perjury that a contract exists? When such an admission is made, the statute of frauds is satisfied as to the quantity of goods admitted [2–201(3)(b)]. For example, if Nelson only admits contracting for $1,000 worth of goods, the contract is enforceable only to that extent.

4. *Specially manufactured goods.* Finally, an oral contract within the UCC statute of frauds can be enforced without a writing in some situations involving the sale of specially manufactured goods. This exception to the writing requirement will apply only if the nature of the specially manufactured goods is such that they are not suitable for sale in the ordinary course of the seller's business. Completely executory oral contracts are not enforceable under this exception. The seller must have made a substantial beginning in manufacturing the goods for the buyer, or must have made commitments for their procurement, before receiving notice that the buyer was repudiating the sale [2–201(3)(a)]. For example, Bennett Co. has an oral contract with Stevenson for the sale of $2,500 worth of calendars imprinted with Bennett Co.'s name and address. If Bennett Co. repudiates the contract before Stevenson has made a substantial beginning in manufacturing the calendars, the contract will be unenforceable under the statute of frauds. If, however, Bennett Co. repudiated the contract after Stevenson had made a substantial beginning, the oral contract would be enforceable. The specially manufactured goods provision is based both on the evidentiary value of the seller's conduct and on the need to avoid the injustice that would otherwise result from the seller's reliance.

PROMISSORY ESTOPPEL AND THE STATUTE OF FRAUDS

The statute of frauds, which was created to prevent fraud and perjury, has often been criticized because it can create unjust results. One of the troubling features of the statute is that it can as easily be used to defeat a contract that was actually made as it can to defeat a fictitious agreement. As you have seen, courts and legislatures have created several exceptions to the statute of frauds that reduce the statute's potential for creating unfair results. In recent years, courts in some states have allowed the use of the doctrine of **promissory estoppel**[6] to enable some

---

[6]The doctrine of promissory estoppel is discussed in Chapters 9 and 12.

parties to recover under oral contracts that the statute of frauds would ordinarily render unenforceable.

Courts in these states hold that, when one of the parties would suffer serious losses because of her reliance on an oral contract, the other party is estopped from raising the statute of frauds as a defense. This position has been approved in the *Restatement (Second) of Contracts.* Section 139 of the *Restatement (Second)* provides that a promise that induces action or forbearance can be enforceable notwithstanding the statute of frauds if the reliance was foreseeable to the person making the promise and if injustice can be avoided only by enforcing the promise. The idea behind this section and the cases employing promissory estoppel is that the statute of frauds, which is designed to prevent injustice, should not be allowed to work an injustice. Section 139 and these cases also impliedly recognize the fact that the reliance required by promissory estoppel to some extent provides evidence of the existence of a contract between the parties, since it is unlikely that a person would materially rely on a nonexistent promise.

The use of promissory estoppel as a means of circumventing the statute of frauds is still controversial, however. Many courts fear that enforcing oral contracts on the basis of a party's reliance will essentially negate the statute. In cases involving the UCC statute of frauds, an additional source of concern involves the interpretation of section 2–201. Some courts have construed the provisions listing specific alternative methods of satisfying section 2–201's formal requirements to be *exclusive,* precluding the creation of any further exceptions by courts.

THE PAROL EVIDENCE RULE

Explanation of the Rule

In many situations, contracting parties prefer to express their agreements in writing even when they are not required to do so by the statute of frauds. Written contracts rarely come into being without some prior discussions or negotiations between the parties, however. Various promises, proposals, or representations are usually made by one or both of the parties before the execution of a written contract. What happens when one of those prior promises, proposals, or representations is not included in the terms of the written contract? For example, suppose that Jackson wants to buy Stone's house. During the course of negotiations, Stone states that he will pay for any major repairs that the house needs for the first year that Jackson owns it. The written contract that the parties ultimately sign, however, does not say anything about Stone paying for repairs, and, in fact, states that Jackson will take the house "as is." The furnace breaks down three months after the sale, and Stone refuses to pay for its repair. What is the status of Stone's promise to pay for repairs? The basic problem is one of defining the boundaries of the parties' agreement. Are all the promises made in the process of negotiation part of the contract, or do the terms of the written document that the parties signed supersede any preliminary agreements?

The **parol evidence rule** provides the answer to this question. The term *parol evidence* means written or spoken statements that are *not contained in the written contract.* The parol evidence rule provides that, when parties enter a *written contract* that they intend as a complete **integration** (a complete and final statement of their agreement), a court will not permit the use of evidence of *prior* or *contemporaneous* statements to add to, alter, or contradict the terms of the written contract. This rule is based on the presumption that when people enter into a written contract, the best evidence of their agreement is the written contract itself. It also reflects the idea that later expressions of intent are presumed to prevail over earlier expressions of intent. In the hypothetical case involving Stone and Jackson, assuming that they intended the written contract to be the final integration of their agreement, Jackson would not be able to introduce evidence of Stone's promise to pay for repairs. The effect of excluding preliminary promises or statements from consideration is, of course, to confine the parties' contract to the terms of the written agreement. The lesson to be learned from this example is that people who put their agreements in writing should make sure that all the terms of their agreement are included in the writing. The following case, *Slivinsky v. Watkins-Johnson Company,* illustrates the application of the parol evidence rule.

SLIVINSKY v. WATKINS-JOHNSON COMPANY   270 Cal. Rptr. 585 (Ct. App. 1990)

I n July 1984, Sandra Slivinsky applied for a job as a materials scientist with Watkins-Johnson Company, a large aerospace manufacturer. Directly above the signature line on the application she signed was the statement: "I understand that employment by WATKINS-JOHNSON COMPANY is conditional upon . . . execution of an Employment Agreement. . . . I further understand that if I become employed by Watkins-Johnson Company, there will be no agreement, expressed or implied, between the company and me for any specific period of employment, nor for continuing or long-term employment." Over the next several months, Watkins-Johnson contacted Slivinsky's references, requested her transcripts, and set up a series of interviews. Slivinsky claims that at these interviews she was promised "long-term," "indefinite," and "permanent" employment, not dependent on business cycles, and subject to termination only for cause. Finally, Watkins-Johnson made a verbal offer of employment to Slivinsky and she accepted. On January 7, 1985, which was Slivinsky's first day at work, Slivinsky signed the employee agreement that had been referred to in her employment application. Set apart in bold type, the last paragraph of this agreement provided that there was no express or implied agreement between the parties regarding the duration of her employment and that the employment could be terminated at any time with or without cause.

As a result of the space shuttle Challenger disaster in January 1986, Watkins-Johnson experienced significant business losses and government contract cancellations. The management decided that employee cutbacks were essential to cope with the loss of business. Ultimately, 24 employees, including Slivinsky, were selected for the reduction in force program. Watkins-Johnson terminated her employment in June 1986.

Slivinsky brought suit against Watkins-Johnson for breach of the employment contract, asserting that she had been terminated without cause in violation of the parties' express and implied agreement. She also claimed that the reasons given for her termination were pretextual and that she was really fired for other reasons, such as her supervisor disliking her. The trial court granted Watkins-Johnson's motion for summary judgment, and Slivinsky appealed. ⌒

Cottle, Associate Justice   Slivinsky claims that the parties' employment agreement includes factors such as oral assurances of job security and Watkins-Johnson's personnel policies and practices not to terminate employees except for good cause. Watkins-Johnson [argues] that it is limited to the parties' express written contract defining the employment as at-will.

The dispositive issue, therefore, is whether we can look beyond the four corners of the parties' written agreements to ascertain the complete agreement of the parties. The answer to that question involves application of the parol evidence rule, a rule of substantive law precluding the introduction of evidence which varies or contradicts the terms of an integrated written instrument. If the parties intended that the Application and Employment Agreement constituted an integration, i.e., the final expression of their agreement with respect to grounds for termination, then those agreements may not be contradicted by evidence of any prior agreement or of a contemporaneous oral agreement. No particular form is required for an integrated agreement. When

only part of the agreement is integrated, the parol evidence rule applies to that part.

Applying these standards, we conclude that the contract was integrated with respect to the grounds for termination. Slivinsky's employment application specifically conditioned employment upon execution of an employment agreement. It further provided that if Slivinsky were to become employed by Watkins-Johnson, there "will be no agreement, expressed or implied, . . . for any specific period of employment, nor for continuing or long-term employment." When Slivinsky executed the Employee Agreement, she acknowledged "that there is no agreement, express or implied, between employee and the Company for any specific period of employment, nor for continuing or long-term employment. Employee and the Company each have a right to terminate employment, with or without cause." Reading these documents together, the only reasonable conclusion that can be drawn is that the parties intended that there would be no other agreement regarding termination other than that set forth in the Employee Agreement. Consequently, evidence of an implied agreement which contradicts the terms of the written agreement is not admissible. There cannot be a valid express contract and an implied contract, each embracing the same subject, but requiring different results.

Because we hold that the contract is a contract for employment terminable at will, we do not reach the issues regarding whether good cause existed for Slivinsky's termination based on Watkins-Johnson's decision to reduce its work force. Even if the reduction in force were a pretextual ground for terminating Slivinsky's employment, it would not be actionable with an at-will employment contract unless the employer's motivation for a discharge contravenes some significant public policy principle. No such public policy violation is alleged here.

Judgment for Watkins-Johnson affirmed.

Scope of the Parol Evidence Rule

The parol evidence rule is relevant only in cases in which the parties have expressed their agreement in a written contract. Thus, it would not apply to a case involving an oral contract or to a case in which writings existed that were not intended to embody the final statement of at least part of the parties' contract. The parol evidence rule has been made a part of the law of sales in the Uniform Commercial Code [2–202], so it is applicable to contracts for the sale of goods as well as to contracts governed by the common law of contracts. Furthermore, the rule excludes only evidence of statements made *prior to* or *during* the signing of the written contract. It does not apply to statements made after the signing of the contract. Thus, evidence of subsequent statements is freely admissible.

Admissible Parol Evidence

In some situations, evidence of statements made outside the written contract is admissible notwithstanding the parol evidence rule. Parol evidence is permitted in the situations discussed below either because the writing is not the best evidence of the contract or because the evidence is offered, not to contradict the terms of the writing, but to explain the writing or to challenge the underlying contractual obligation that the writing represents.

1. *Additional terms in partially integrated contracts.* In many instances, parties will desire to introduce evidence of statements or agreements that would supplement rather than contradict the written contract. Whether they can do this depends on whether the written contract is characterized as *completely integrated* or *partially integrated*. A completely integrated contract is one that the parties intend as a *complete and exclusive statement* of their entire agreement. A partially integrated contract is one that expresses the parties' final agreement as to some but not all of the terms of their contract. When a contract is only partially integrated, the parties are permitted to use parol evidence to prove the *additional* terms of their agreement. Such evidence cannot, however, be used to contradict the written terms of the contract. To determine whether a contract is completely or partially integrated, a court must determine the parties' intent. A court judges intent by looking at the language of the contract, the apparent completeness of the writing, and all the surrounding circumstances. It will also consider whether the contract contains a **merger clause** (also known as an **integration clause**). These clauses, which are very common in form contracts and commercial contracts, provide that the written contract is the complete integration of the parties' agreement. They are designed to prevent a party from giving testimony about prior statements or agreements and are generally effective in indicating that the writing was a complete integration. Even though a contract contains a merger clause, parol evidence could be admissible under one of the following exceptions.

2. *Explaining ambiguities.* Parol evidence can be offered to explain an ambiguity in the written contract. Suppose a written contract between Lowen and Matthews provides that Lowen will buy "Matthews's truck," but Matthews has two trucks. The parties could offer evidence of negotiations, statements, and other circumstances preceding the creation of the written contract to identify the truck to which the writing refers. Used in this way, parol evidence helps the court interpret the contract. It does not contradict the written contract.

Parol Evidence Rule

Parol Evidence Rule	Applies when:	Provides that:
	Parties create a writing intended as a final and complete integration of at least part of the parties' contract.	Evidence of statements or promises made before or during the creation of the writing cannot be used to supplement, change, or contradict the terms of the written contract.
But Parol Evidence Can Be Used to	1. Prove consistent, additional terms when the contract is *partially integrated*. 2. Explain an ambiguity in the written contract. 3. Prove that the contract is void, voidable, or unenforceable. 4. Prove that the contract was subject to a condition. 5. Prove that the parties subsequently modified the contract or made a new agreement.	

3. *Circumstances invalidating contract.* Any circumstances that would be relevant to show that a contract is not valid can be proven by parol evidence. For example, evidence that Holden pointed a gun at Dickson and said, "Sign this contract, or I'll kill you," would be admissible to show that the contract was voidable because of duress. Likewise, parol evidence would be admissible to show that a contract was illegal or was induced by fraud, misrepresentation, undue influence, or mistake.

4. *Existence of condition.* It is also permissible to use parol evidence to show that a writing was executed with the understanding that it was *not to take effect until the occurrence of a condition* (a future, uncertain event that creates a duty to perform). Suppose Farnsworth signs a contract to purchase a car with the agreement that the contract is not to be effective unless and until Farnsworth gets a new job. If the written contract is silent about any conditions that must occur before it becomes effective, Farnsworth could introduce parol evidence to prove the existence of the condition. Such proof merely elaborates on, but does not contradict, the terms of the writing.

5. *Subsequent agreements.* As you read earlier, the parol evidence rule does not forbid parties to introduce proof of *subsequent agreements.* This is true even if the terms of the later agreement cancel, subtract from, or add to the obligations stated in the written contract. The idea here is that when a writing is followed by a later statement or agreement, the writing is no longer the best evidence of the agreement. You should be aware, however, that

subsequent modifications of contracts may sometimes be unenforceable due to lack of consideration or failure to comply with the statute of frauds. In addition, contracts sometimes expressly provide that modifications must be written. In this situation, an oral modification would be unenforceable.

INTERPRETATION OF CONTRACTS

Once a court has decided what promises are included in a contract, it is faced with *interpreting* the contract to determine the *meaning* and *legal effect* of the terms used by the parties. Courts have adopted broad, basic standards of interpretation that guide them in the interpretation process.

The court will first attempt to determine the parties' *principal objective.* Every clause will then be determined in the light of this principal objective. Ordinary words will be given their usual meaning and technical words (such as those that have a special meaning in the parties' trade or business) will be given their technical meaning, unless a different meaning was clearly intended.

Guidelines grounded in common sense are also used to determine the relationship of the various terms of the contract. Specific terms that follow general terms are presumed to qualify those general terms. Suppose that a provision that states that the subject of the contract is "guaranteed for one year" is followed by a provision describing the "one-year guarantee against defects in workmanship." Here, it is fair to conclude that the more specific term qualifies the more general term and that the guarantee described in the contract is a guarantee of workmanship only, and not of parts and materials.

Sometimes, there is internal conflict in the terms of an agreement and courts must determine which term should prevail. When the parties use a form contract or some other type of contract that is partially printed and partially handwritten, the handwritten provisions will prevail. If the contract was drafted by one of the parties, any ambiguities will be resolved against the party who drafted the contract.

If both parties to the contract are members of a trade, profession, or community in which certain words are commonly given a particular meaning (this is called a *usage*), the courts will presume that the parties intended the meaning that the usage gives to the terms they use. For example, if the word *dozen* in the bakery business means 13 rather than 12, a contract between two bakers for the purchase of 10 dozen loaves of bread will be presumed to mean 130 loaves of bread rather than 120. Usages can also add provisions to the parties' agreement. If the court finds that a certain practice is a matter of common usage in the parties' trade, it will assume that the parties intended to include that practice in their agreement. If contracting parties are members of the same trade, business, or community but do not intend to be bound by usage, they should specifically say so in their agreement.

ETHICAL AND PUBLIC POLICY CONCERNS

1. The statute of frauds requires written evidence of some, but not all, contracts. Is this defensible from a public policy standpoint? Would it be preferable for the law to simply require that all contracts be evidenced by a writing?

2. What ethical problem was the statute of frauds designed to prevent, and what ethical problem does the statute of frauds create? Is the "cure worse than the disease"?

3. Under the law of some states, the doctrine of promissory estoppel permits the enforcement of promises that induce reliance, even when those promises do not comply with the statute of frauds. Should all states adopt this position? What effect would this have on the statute of frauds?

4. For those parties who draft and proffer standardized form contracts, the parol evidence rule can be a powerful ally because it has the effect of limiting the scope of an integrated, written contract to the terms of the writing. Although statements and promises made to a person before he signs a contract might be highly influential in persuading him to enter the contract, the parol evidence rule effectively prevents these precontract communications from being legally enforceable. Consider also that standardized form contracts are usually drafted for the benefit of and proffered by the more sophisticated and powerful party in a contract (e.g., the insurance company rather than the insured, the automobile dealer rather than the customer, the landlord rather than the tenant). Considering all of this, do you believe that the parol evidence rule promotes ethical behavior?

PROBLEMS AND PROBLEM CASES

1. Golomb allegedly orally agreed to sell to Lee for $275,000 the Ferrari once owned by King Leopold of Belgium. Golomb ultimately refused to sell the car and Lee sued him. At trial, Golomb denied ever promising to sell the car to Lee. Can Lee enforce this alleged promise?

2. Putt owned commercial real estate known as the King Tractor Building, which was located in Corinth, Mississippi. Putt had most recently used it to operate a used car business. In the fall of 1984, the Corinth Gas and Water Department, which is an arm of the City of Corinth, was seeking a building suitable for housing its maintenance department and storing equipment and spare parts. Putt learned about this and approached Gas and Water Department employees telling them his building was for sale for $100,000. One of the employees appeared at the regular monthly meeting of the Utilities Commission and reported his conversation with Putt. After inspection and some negotiation, the parties reached an agreement for the purchase of the building for $95,000. On March 11, 1985, the commission formally approved the purchase, as evidenced in written minutes that specified the parties, description of the property, sales price, and payment of price. The minutes were then signed by the chairman of the commission and attested by the secretary of the commission. Putt readied the property for sale, but a dispute arose between Putt and the city over matters involved with the closing of the sale. The city purchased other property instead and Putt sued the city for breach of contract. The city asserted the statute of frauds as a defense. Does the statute of frauds bar the enforcement of this contract?

3. In September 1983, Campbell Soup Co. and Center State Farms orally agreed to a business relationship under which Center State Farms would take possession of flocks of newborn turkeys, grow the turkeys for several months, and return them to Campbell Soup for use in its food products. Center State Farm agreed to make an initial investment of approximately $150,000 to convert its chicken houses to grow turkeys based on Campbell Soup's agreement to continue the relationship indefinitely. Center State Farm contends that Campbell Soup orally promised "to provide poults, feed and medicine and pay for grown turkeys as long as Center State performed satisfactorily." Center State Farms estimated that it would take approximately 20 years for it to recoup its initial investment. In early 1991, Campbell Soup ended the relationship, and Center State Farms sued it for breach of contract. Campbell Soup contends that the oral agreement claimed by Center State Farms was unenforceable because it was "not to be performed" within one year. Is this a good argument?

4. Green owns a lot (Lot S) in the Manomet section of Plymouth, Massachusetts. In July 1980, she advertised it for sale. On July 11 and 12, the Hickeys discussed with Green purchasing Lot S and orally agreed to a sale for $15,000. On July 12, Green accepted the Hickeys' check for $500. Hickey had left the payee line of the deposit check blank because of uncertainty whether Green or her brother was to receive the check. Hickey asked Green to fill in the appropriate name. Green, however, held the check, did not fill in the payee's name, and neither cashed nor indorsed it. Hickey told Green that his intention was to sell his home and build on the lot he was buying from Green. Relying on the arrangements with Green, the Hickeys advertised their house in newspapers for three days in July. They found a purchaser quickly. Within a short time, they contracted with a purchaser for the sale of their house and accepted the purchaser's deposit check. On the back of this check, above the Hickeys' signatures indorsing the check, was noted: "Deposit on purchase of property at Sachem Rd.

and First St., Manomet, Ma. Sale price, $44,000." On July 24, Green told Hickey that she no longer intended to sell her property to him and instead had decided to sell it to someone else for $16,000. Hickey offered to pay Green $16,000 for the lot, but she refused this offer. The Hickeys then filed a complaint against Green seeking specific performance. Green asserted that relief was barred by the statute of frauds. Is this correct?

5. In June 1976, Moore went to First National Bank and requested the president of the bank to allow his sons, Rocky and Mike, to open an account in the name of Texas Continental Express, Inc. Moore promised to bring his own business to the bank and orally agreed to make good any losses that the bank might incur from receiving dishonored checks from Texas Continental. The bank then furnished regular checking account and bank draft services to Texas Continental. Several years later, Texas Continental wrote checks totaling $448,942.05 that were returned for insufficient funds. Texas Continental did not cover the checks, and the bank turned to Moore for payment. When Moore refused to pay, the bank sued him. Does Moore have a good statute of frauds defense?

6. Bristol Compressors, Inc., was a subsidiary of York International Corp. Bristol's chief operating officer, Young, asked Terwilliger, the company's manager of engineering services, to help develop a new high-efficiency compressor. Young told Terwilliger that if he was successful, he would be taken care of and properly rewarded. Although not part of his general duties at Bristol, Terwilliger accomplished this task. York invested heavily in the invention's marketing and development, and in the years that followed, the compressor was an enormous financial success for the company. On September 13, 1988, Terwilliger executed an assignment agreement whereby he sold and assigned to Bristol his rights in all of his inventions, discoveries, and improvements in the compressor in exchange "for good and valuable consideration received." Two years later, York released Terwilliger as part of a general reduction in the work force. Terwilliger sued York claiming that York breached its promises to compensate him for his invention and the assignment of his patent rights. At trial, the district court held that the parol evidence rule prevented Terwilliger from offering evidence to prove that he had not received consideration for the patent assignment. Could Terwilliger introduce evidence that no consideration was given to him despite the contract's statement that "good and valuable consideration" had been received?

7. Dyer purchased a used Ford from Walt Bennett Ford for $5,895. She signed a written contract, which showed that no taxes were included in the sales price. Dyer contended, however, that the salesperson who negotiated the purchase with her told her both before and after her signing of the contract that the sales tax on the automobile had been paid. The contract Dyer signed contained the following language:

The above comprises the entire agreement pertaining to this purchase and no other agreement of any kind, verbal understanding, representation, or promise whatsoever will be recognized.

It also stated:

This contract constitutes the entire agreement between the parties and no modification hereof shall be valid in any event and Buyer expressly waives the right to rely thereon, unless made in writing, signed by Seller.

Later, when Dyer attempted to license the automobile, she discovered that the Arkansas sales tax had not been paid on it. She paid the sales tax and sued Bennett for breach of contract. What result?

8. Goldstein was a sales representative and regional sales manager with G & O Manufacturing. Kellwood acquired G & O. Goldstein received word from Grossman, the Kellwood president of the G & O facility, that Kellwood wanted him to move to New York. Goldstein expressed his disappointment to McWhite, the head of his division. According to Goldstein, he was playing golf with McWhite when McWhite told him:

Allen, I told you not to worry about Mr. Grossman. You work for Kellwood. You work for me. He cannot fire you and he cannot force you to move to New York. . . . Mr. Grossman will be retiring soon. I don't know exactly when, but he'll be retiring soon. And I guarantee you that I will not make changes with you for at least two years, because that's how long it's going to take to get this mess cleaned up. And don't worry about it. I want you to go back with all the initiative to do your job knowing that you are not going to be fired or your status is not going to change.

McWhite and Goldstein had a similar conversation the next day. Based on these conversations, Goldstein believed that he had a contract for a period of two years after Grossman retired. Grossman retired in March 1993. After these conversations, Goldstein received an offer of employment from Tres Chic Lingerie, but he refused the offer. In April 1993, Gendel, the president of Kellwood, informed Goldstein that he would be transferred to New York. Kellwood attempted to work out an agreement for Grossman to stay in Atlanta on a commissioned sales arrangement, but the parties were unable to reach a final agreement. Kellwood then terminated Goldstein's employment in February 1994. Can Goldstein enforce this alleged oral contract?

9. Grove and Stanfield entered into an arrangement in July 1986 whereby Grove was to receive a 1936 Pontiac from Stanfield in exchange for the performance of reupholstery work on Stanfield's 1953 Cadillac. Grove then took possession of the '36 Pontiac, although he did not receive the title to the car. However, Grove never did the reupholstery. In 1991, some five years after Grove had taken delivery of the Pontiac, Grove paid Stanfield $1,000 and Stanfield assigned the title to Grove. The title certificate, duly notarized and signed by Stanfield, recited that the Pontiac was thereby sold to Grove for $1,000. No other terms of sale are mentioned in the title document, nor are any incorporated by reference. In 1994, Stanfield filed suit against Grove for breach of contract and conversion and asking for the return of the car. He claimed that the parties had entered a contract for the sale of the Pontiac for $9,000 and that the $1,000 that Grove had paid in 1991 was merely for the title and not for the car itself. Is the contract to pay additional money enforceable?

10. The Peoples Bank owned approximately 66 acres, which it offered for sale. Hoping to get a real estate commission, Whatley, an attorney and real estate broker, advertised the property for sale. Whatley showed the property once to Barnes, who on that same day wrote a deposit check for $5,500, 10 percent of the listed purchase price. Although Barnes signed the check, it was Whatley who filled out all the information, including denoting the payee as Whatley Realty Trust Account and making a notation on Barnes's check: "Earnest money on 66.21 acres." Whatley also created a receipt for the check as "Binder on 66.21 acres pending title clearance and 30 days to close." Whatley held Barnes's check and did not deposit it. The next day, Whatley drafted a real estate sales agreement and mailed it to the bank. The bank's vice president signed the agreement and mailed it back to Whatley. The sales contract expressly obligated the bank to pay Whatley a real estate commission "when the sale is consummated." According to the sales contract, "This instrument shall be regarded as an offer by the Purchaser or Seller, who first signs, as to the other and is open for acceptance by the other until 4:00 P.M. on the 7th day of July, 1993." Barnes never signed the real estate sales contract and never accepted the bank's offer by July 7. Rather, on July 1, Barnes stopped payment on his earnest money check and informed Whatley that he was withdrawing his offer to purchase the land. About six weeks later, the bank sold the land to another purchaser, and Whatley did not receive a commission. Whatley sued Barnes to recover $5,000, the amount of the real estate commission to which he would have been entitled had the sale been effectuated. For Whatley to be entitled to a commission, he must have procured a ready, willing, and able purchaser. Was an enforceable contract formed between Barnes and the bank for the sale of the land?

11. *Video Case.* See "Car Deals." Acme Used Cars Sales and Service sold a used car to Jones. Prior to the signing of a written purchase contract, Acme's salesperson told Jones that he "wouldn't find a car like this at any price" and "this car is a crown jewel." However, the purchase order that Jones signed stated that the car was being sold "as is" and that "no warranties or representations concerning the car have been made or given except as contained" in the contract. Jones later discovered that the brakes were defective and needed to be rebuilt. If Jones sued Acme, would the parol evidence rule prevent the admission of testimony about the salesperson's statements?

12. *Video Case.* See "Sour Grapes." Fred, a jelly manufacturer in Chicago, ordered grapes by telephone for a price of $800 from Gus, a grape grower in California. Gus sent a written purchase order confirmation. He also shipped the grapes, but they were spoiled when they arrived. Would the statute of frauds prevent this contract from being enforced?

See also "Software Horror Story" and "A Christmas Story."

Rights of Third Parties

I n preceding chapters, we have emphasized the way in which an agreement
between two or more people creates
legal rights and duties *on the part of
the contracting parties.* Since a contract is founded on the consent of the contracting
parties, it might seem to follow that they are the
only ones who have rights and duties under the
contract. Although this is generally true, there are
two situations in which people who were not parties
to a contract have legally enforceable rights under
it: when a contract has been *assigned* (transferred)
to a third party and when a contract is *intended to
benefit a third person* (a *third-party beneficiary*).
This chapter discusses the circumstances in which
third parties have rights under a contract. ∞

ASSIGNMENT OF CONTRACTS

Contracts give people both rights and duties. If
Murphy buys Wagner's motorcycle and promises to
pay him $1,000 for it, Wagner has the *right* to
receive Murphy's promised performance (the payment of the $1,000) and Murphy has the *duty* to
perform the promise by paying $1,000. In most
situations, contract rights can be transferred to a
third person and contract duties can be delegated to
a third person. The transfer of a *right* under a
contract is called an **assignment.** The appointment
of another person to perform a *duty* under a contract
is called a **delegation.**

Nature of Assignment of Rights

A person who owes a duty to perform under a
contract is called an **obligor.** The person to whom
he owes the duty is called the **obligee.** For example,

FIGURE 1

FIGURE 1

Assignment: Key Terms

OBLIGOR	OBLIGEE	ASSIGNMENT	ASSIGNOR	ASSIGNEE
Person who owes the duty to perform	Person who has the right to receive obligor's performance	Transfer of the right to receive obligor's performance	Obligee who transfers the right to receive obligor's performance	Person to whom the right to receive obligor's performance is transferred

FIGURE 2

Assignment

Before assignment	Assignment	Result of assignment
Owes duty to perform	Transfers right to receive obligor's performance	Owes duty to perform
Obligor → Obligee	Obligee (Assignor) → Assignee	Obligor → Assignee

Samson borrows $500 from Jordan, promising to repay Jordan in six months. Samson, who owes the duty to pay the money, is the obligor, and Jordan, who has the right to receive the money, is the obligee. An assignment occurs when the obligee transfers his right to receive the obligor's performance to a third person. When there has been an assignment, the person making the assignment—the original obligee—is then called the **assignor.** The person to whom the right has been transferred is called the **assignee.** Figure 1 summarizes these key terms.

Suppose that Jordan, the obligee in the example above, assigns his right to receive Samson's payment to Kane. Here, Jordan is the assignor and Kane is the assignee. The relationship between the three parties is represented in Figure 2. Notice that the assignment is a separate transaction: It occurs after the formation of the original contract.

The effect of the assignment is to extinguish the assignor's right to receive performance and to transfer that right to the assignee. In the above example, Kane now owns the right to collect payment from Samson. If Samson fails to pay, Kane, as an assignee, now has the right to file suit against Samson to collect the debt.

People assign rights for a variety of reasons. A person might assign a right to a third party to satisfy a debt that he owes. For example, Jordan, the assignor in the above example, owes money to Kane, so he assigns to Kane the right to receive the $500 that Samson owes him. A person might also sell or pledge the rights owed to him to obtain financing. In the case of a business, the money owed to the business by customers and clients is called *accounts receivable.* A business's accounts receivable are an asset to the business that can be used to raise money in several ways. For example, the business may pledge its accounts receivable as collateral for a loan. Suppose Ace Tree Trimming Co. wants to borrow money from First Bank and gives First Bank a security interest (an interest in the debtor's property that secures the debtor's performance of an obligation) in its accounts receivable.[1] If Ace defaults in its payments to First Bank, First Bank will acquire Ace's rights to collect the accounts receivable. A person might also make an assignment of a contract right as a gift. For example, Lansing owes $2,000 to Father. Father assigns the right to receive Lansing's performance to Son as a graduation gift.

Evolution of the Law Regarding Assignments
Contract rights have not always been transferable. Early common law refused to permit assignment or delegation because debts were considered to be too personal to transfer. A debtor who failed to pay an

---

[1]Security interests in accounts and other property are discussed in Chapter 28.

honest debt was subject to severe penalties, including imprisonment, because such a failure to pay was viewed as the equivalent of theft. The identity of the creditor was of great importance to the debtor, since one creditor might be more lenient than another. Courts also feared that the assignment of debts would stir up unwanted litigation. In an economy that was primarily land-based, the extension of credit was of relatively small importance. As trade increased and became more complex, however, the practice of extending credit became more common. The needs of an increasingly commercial society demanded that people be able to trade freely in intangible assets such as debts. Consequently, the rules of law regarding the assignment of contracts gradually became more liberal. Today, public policy favors free assignability of contracts.

Sources of Assignment Law Today   Legal principles regarding assignment are found not only in the common law of contracts but also in Articles 2 and 9 of the Uniform Commercial Code. Section 2–210 of Article 2 contains principles applicable to assignments of rights under a contract for the sale of *goods*. Article 9 governs security interests in accounts and other contract rights as well as the outright sale of accounts. Article 9's treatment of assignments will be discussed in more detail in Chapter 28, Security Interests in Personal Property, but some provisions of Article 9 relating to assignments will be discussed in this chapter.

Creating an Assignment

An assignment can be made in any way that is sufficient to show the assignor's intent to assign. No formal language is required, and a writing is not necessary unless required by a provision of the statute of frauds or some other statute. Many states do have statutes requiring certain types of assignments to be evidenced by a writing, however. Additionally, an assignment for the purposes of security must meet Article 9's formal requirements for security interests.[2]

It is not necessary that the assignee give any consideration to the assignor in exchange for the assignment. Gratuitous assignments (those for which the assignee gives no value) are generally revocable until such time as the obligor satisfies the

---

[2]These requirements are discussed in Chapter 28.

obligation, however. They can be revoked by the assignor's death or incapacity or by notification of revocation given by the assignor to the assignee.

Assignability of Rights

Most, but not all, contract rights are assignable. Although the free assignability of contract rights performs a valuable function in our modern credit-based economy, assignment is undesirable if it would adversely affect some important public policy or if it would materially vary the bargained-for expectations of the parties. There are several basic limitations on the assignability of contract rights.

First, an assignment will not be effective if it is *contrary to public policy.* For example, most states have enacted statutes that prohibit or regulate a wage earner's assignment of future wages. These statutes are designed to protect people against unwisely impoverishing themselves by signing away their future incomes.

Second, an assignment will not be effective if it *adversely affects the obligor* in some significant way. An assignment is ineffective if it materially changes the obligor's duty or increases the burden or risk on the obligor. Naturally, any assignment will change an obligor's duty to some extent. The obligor will have to pay money or deliver goods or render some other performance to one party instead of to another. These changes are not considered to be sufficiently material to render an assignment ineffective. Thus, a right to receive money or goods or land is generally assignable. In addition, covenants not to compete are generally considered to be assignable to buyers of businesses. For example, Jefferson sells RX Drugstore to Waldman, including in the contract of sale a covenant whereby Jefferson promises not to operate a competing drugstore within a 30-mile radius of RX for 10 years after the sale. Waldman later sells RX to Tharp. Here, Tharp could enforce the covenant not to compete against Jefferson. The reason for permitting assignment of covenants not to compete is that the purpose of such covenants is to protect an asset of the business—goodwill—for which the buyer has paid.

An assignment could be ineffective because of its variation of the obligor's duty, however, if the contract right involved a *personal relationship* or an element of *personal skill, judgment,* or *character.* For this reason, contracts of employment in which an employee works under the direct and personal supervision of an employer cannot be assigned to a new employer. An employer could assign a contract of employment, however, if the assignee-employer could perform the contract without adversely affecting the interests of the employee, such as would be the case when an employment relationship does not involve personal supervision by an individual employer. This point is illustrated by the following case, *Special Products Manufacturing, Inc. v. Douglass.*

A purported assignment is ineffective if it significantly increases the burden of the obligor's performance. For example, if Walker contracts to sell Dwyer all of its requirements of wheat, a purported assignment of Dwyer's rights to a corporation that has much greater requirements of wheat would probably be ineffective because it would significantly increase the burden on Walker.

SPECIAL PRODUCTS MANUFACTURING, INC. v. DOUGLASS   553 N.Y.S. 2d 506 (N.Y.S. Ct., App. Div. 1990)

Thaddeus Douglass was a highly trained servicer of hardness-testing machinery who was employed by Page-Wilson Corporation. In August and April 1983, Douglass signed two employment agreements governing the terms and conditions of his employment with Page-Wilson. The first agreement prohibited Douglass, while he was working for Page-Wilson and for one year after the termination of his employment, from using, to Page-Wilson's detriment, any of its customer lists or other intellectual property acquired from his job there. The second agreement, which applied to the same time period, prohibited Douglass from accepting employment from or serving as a consultant to any business that was in competition with Page-Wilson. In April 1987, Canrad Corporation purchased all assets and contractual rights of Page-Wilson, including Douglass's two employment contracts. Special Products Manufacturing (Special Products), a wholly owned subsidiary of Canrad, assumed plant operations. Douglass worked for Special Products until his resignation in February 1988.

Shortly after that, Special Products filed this lawsuit against Douglass, alleging that Douglass had affixed his name and home telephone number to the machines he serviced, so that the ensuing maintenance calls would reach him personally. It also alleged that, following his resignation, Douglass established a competing business and actively solicited Special Products's clientele. Douglass did not answer the complaint in a timely manner, and, after a long delay, the trial judge entered a default judgment in favor of Special Products. Douglass appealed this order, arguing in part that Special Products did not have the right to enforce the agreements not to compete.

Yesawich, Justice We perceive no merit in the contention that because Douglass entered into the agreements with Page-Wilson, they are unenforceable by Special Products. In an uncontroverted affidavit based upon personal knowledge, Special Products's vice-president of sales avows that Special Products acquired all of Page-Wilson's contract rights, including Douglass's. Douglass's consent was not required to effectuate this transfer. When the original parties to an agreement so intend, a covenant not to compete is freely assignable. Here, such intent is unmistakably evident in the first employment agreement which expressly "inure[s] to the benefit of the successors and assigns of Page-Wilson." And, while the second document contains no similar provision, neither does it specifically forbid assignment. Because executory contracts, which do not involve exceptional personal skills on the part of the assignor and which the assignee can perform without adversely affecting the rights and interests of the adverse party, are freely assignable absent a contractual, statutory or public policy prohibition, a clear and unambiguous prohibition is essential to effectively prevent assignment. Accordingly, the assignment to Special Products perpetuated the restrictive covenant provision, the very terms of which Douglass violated without justification.

Order in favor of Special Products affirmed.

Contract Clauses Prohibiting Assignment A contract right may also be nonassignable because the original contract expressly forbids assignment. For example, leases often contain provisions forbidding assignment or requiring the tenant to obtain the landlord's permission for assignment.[3]

Antiassignment clauses in contracts are generally enforceable. Because of the strong public policy favoring assignability, however, such clauses are often interpreted narrowly. For example, a court might view an assignment made in violation of an antiassignment clause as a breach of contract for which damages may be recovered but not as an invalidation of the assignment. Another tactic is to interpret a contractual ban on assignment as prohibiting only the delegation of duties.

The UCC takes this latter position. Under section 2–210(2), general language prohibiting assignment of "the contract" or "all my rights under the contract" is interpreted as forbidding only the delegation of duties, unless the circumstances indicate to the contrary. Section 2–210 also states that a right to damages for breach of a whole sales contract or a right arising out of the assignor's performance of his entire obligation may be assigned even if a provision of the original sales contract prohibited assignment. In addition, UCC section 9–318(4) invalidates contract terms that prohibit (or require the debtor's consent to) an assignment of an account or creation of a security interest in a right to receive money that is now due or that will become due.

Nature of Assignee's Rights

When an assignment occurs, the assignee is said to "step into the shoes of his assignor." This means that the assignee acquires all of the rights that his assignor had under the contract. The assignee has the right to receive the obligor's performance, and if performance is not forthcoming, the assignee has the right to sue in his own name for breach of the obligation. By the same token, the assignee acquires no greater rights than those possessed by the assignor.

Because the assignee has no greater rights than did the assignor, the obligor may assert any defense or claim against the assignee that he could have asserted against the assignor, subject to certain time limitations discussed below. A contract that is void, voidable, or unenforceable as between the original parties does not become enforceable just because it has been assigned to a third party. For example, if Richards induces Dillman's consent to a contract by duress and subsequently assigns his rights under the contract to Keith, Dillman can assert the doctrine of duress against Keith as a ground for avoiding the contract.

Importance of Notifying the Obligor An assignee should promptly notify the obligor of the assignment. Although notification of the obligor is not necessary for the assignment to be valid, such notice is of great practical importance. One reason notice is important is that an obligor who does not have reason to know of the assignment could render performance to the assignor and claim that his obligation had been discharged by performance. An obligor who renders performance to the assignor without notice of the assignment has no further liability under the contract. For example, McKay borrows $500 from Goodheart, promising to repay the debt by June 1. Goodheart assigns the debt to Rogers, but no one informs McKay of the assignment, and McKay pays the $500 to Goodheart, the assignor. In this case, McKay is not liable for any further payment. But if Rogers had immediately notified McKay of the assignment and, after receiving notice, McKay had mistakenly paid the debt to Goodheart, McKay would still have the legal obligation to pay $500 to Rogers. Having been given adequate notice of the assignment, he may remain liable to the assignee even if he later renders performance to the assignor.

An assignor who accepts performance from the obligor after the assignment holds any benefits that he receives as a trustee for the assignee. If the assignor fails to pay those benefits to the assignee, however, an obligor who has been notified of the assignment and renders performance to the wrong person may have to pay the same debt twice.

An obligor who receives notice of an assignment from the assignee will want to assure himself that the assignment has in fact occurred. He may ask for written evidence of the assignment or contact the assignee and ask for verification of the assignment. Under UCC section 9–318(3), a notification of assignment is ineffective unless it reasonably identifies the rights assigned. If requested by the account debtor (an obligor who owes money for goods sold

---

[3]The assignment of leases is discussed further in Chapter 25.

or leased or services rendered), the assignee must furnish reasonable proof that the assignment has been made, and, unless he does so, the account debtor may disregard the notice and pay the assignor.

Defenses against the Assignee   An assignee's rights in an assignment are subject to the defenses that the obligor could have asserted against the assignor. Keep in mind that the assignee's rights are limited by the terms of the underlying contract between the assignor and the obligor. When defenses arise from the terms or performance of that contract, they can be asserted against the assignee even if they arise after the obligor receives notice of the assignment. For example, on June 1, Worldwide Widgets assigns to First Bank its rights under a contract with Widgetech, Inc. This contract obligates Worldwide Widgets to deliver a quantity of widgets to Widgetech by September 1, in return for which Widgetech is obligated to pay a stated purchase price. First Bank gives prompt notice of the assignment to Widgetech. Worldwide Widget fails to deliver the widgets and Widgetech refuses to pay. If First Bank brought an action against Widgetech to recover the purchase price of the widgets, Widgetech could assert Worldwide Widget's breach as a defense, even though the breach occurred after Widgetech received notice of the assignment.[4]

In determining what other defenses can be asserted against the assignee, the time of notification plays an important role. After notification, as we discussed earlier, payment by the obligor to the assignor will not discharge the obligor.

Subsequent Assignments

An assignee may "reassign" a right to a third party, who would be called a **subassignee.** The subassignee then acquires the rights held by the prior assignee. He should give the obligor prompt notice of the subsequent assignment, because he takes his interest subject to the same principles discussed above regarding the claims and defenses that can be asserted against him.

---

[4]Similarly, if the assignor's rights were subject to discharge because of other factors such as the nonoccurrence of a condition, impossibility, impracticability, or public policy, this can be asserted as a defense against the assignee even if the event occurs after the obligor receives notice of assignment. See *Restatement (Second) of Contracts* § 336(3). The doctrines relating to discharge from performance are explained in Chapter 18.

Successive Assignments

Notice to the obligor may be important in one other situation. If an assignor assigns the same right to two assignees in succession, both of whom pay for the assignment, a question of priority results. An assignor who assigns the same right to different people will be held liable to the assignee who acquires no rights against the obligor, but which assignee is entitled to the obligor's performance? Which assignee will have recourse only against the assignor? There are several views on this point.

In states that follow the "American rule," the first assignee has the better right. This view is based on the rule of property law that a person cannot transfer greater rights in property than he owns. In states that follow the "English rule," however, the assignee who first gives notice of the assignment to the obligor, without knowledge of the other assignee's claim, has the better right. The *Restatement (Second) of Contracts* takes a third position. Section 342 of the *Restatement (Second)* provides that the first assignee has priority unless the subsequent assignee gives value (pays for the assignment) and, without having reason to know of the other assignee's claim, does one of the following: obtains payment of the obligation, gets a judgment against the obligor, obtains a new contract with the obligor by novation, or possesses a writing of a type customarily accepted as a symbol or evidence of the right assigned (such as a passbook for a savings account).

Assignor's Warranty Liability to Assignee

Suppose that Ross, a 16-year-old boy, contracts to buy a used car for $2,000 from Donaldson. Ross pays Donaldson $500 as a down payment and agrees to pay the balance in equal monthly installments. Donaldson assigns his right to receive the balance of the purchase price to Beckman, who pays $1,000 in cash for the assignment. When Beckman later attempts to enforce the contract, however, Ross disaffirms the contract on grounds of lack of capacity. Thus, Beckman has paid $1,000 for a worthless claim. Does Beckman have any recourse against Donaldson? When an assignor is paid for making an assignment, the assignor is held to have made certain implied warranties about the claim assigned.

The assignor implicitly warrants that the claim assigned is valid. This means that the obligor has capacity to contract, the contract is not illegal, the contract is not voidable for any other reason known to the assignor (such as fraud or duress), and the contract has not been discharged prior to assignment. The assignor also warrants that he has good title to the rights assigned and that any written instrument representing the assigned claim is genuine. In addition, the assignor impliedly agrees that he will not do anything to impair the value of the assignment. These guarantees are imposed by law unless the assignment agreement clearly indicates to the contrary. One important aspect of the assigned right that the assignor does not impliedly warrant, however, is that the obligor is solvent.

DELEGATION OF DUTIES

Nature of Delegation

A **delegation** of duties occurs when an obligor indicates his intent to appoint another person to perform his duties under a contract. For example, White owns a furniture store. He has numerous existing contracts to deliver furniture to customers, including a contract to deliver a sofa to Coombs. White is the *obligor* of the duty to deliver the sofa and Coombs is the *obligee*. White decides to sell his business to Rosen. As a part of the sale of the business, White assigns the rights in the existing contracts to Rosen and delegates to him the performance of those contracts, including the duty to deliver the sofa to Coombs. Here, White is the *delegator* and Rosen is the *delegatee*. White is appointing Rosen to carry out his duties to the obligee, Coombs. Figure 3 summarizes the key terms regarding delegation.

In contrast to an assignment of a right, which extinguishes the assignor's right and transfers it to the assignee, the delegation of a *duty* does *not* extinguish the duty owed by the delegator. This point is made in *Rosenberg v. Son, Inc.,* which follows this discussion. The delegator remains liable to the obligee unless the obligee agrees to substitute

the delegatee's promise for that of the delegator (this is called a *novation* and will be discussed in greater detail later in this chapter). This makes sense because, if it were possible for a person to escape his duties under a contract by merely delegating them to another, any party to a contract could avoid liability by delegating duties to an insolvent acquaintance. The significance of an effective delegation is that performance by the delegatee will discharge the delegator. In addition, if the duty is a delegable one, the obligee cannot insist on performance by the delegator; he must accept the performance of the delegatee. The relationship between the parties in a delegation is shown in Figure 4.

Delegable Duties

A duty that can be performed fully by a number of different persons is delegable. Not all duties are delegable, however. The grounds for finding a duty to be nondelegable resemble closely the grounds for finding a right to be nonassignable. A duty is nondelegable if delegation would violate public policy or if the original contract between the parties forbids delegation. In addition, both section 2–210(1) of the UCC and section 318(2) of the *Restatement (Second) of Contracts* take the position that a party to a contract may delegate his duty to perform to another person unless the parties have agreed to the contrary or unless the other party has a *substantial interest* in having the original obligor perform the acts required by the contract. The key factor used in determining whether the obligee has such a substantial interest is the degree to which performance is dependent on the individual traits, skill, or judgment of the person who owes the duty to perform. For example, if Jansen hires Skelton, an artist, to paint her portrait, Skelton could not effectively delegate the duty to paint the portrait to another artist. Similarly, an employee could not normally delegate her duties under an employment contract to some third person, because employment

Delegation: Key Terms

OBLIGOR	OBLIGEE	DELEGATION	DELEGATOR	DELEGATEE
Person who owes the duty to perform	Person who has the right to receive obligor's performance	Appointment of another person to perform the obligor's duty to the obligee	Obligor who appoints another to perform his duty to obligee	Person who is appointed to perform the obligor's duty to the obligee

FIGURE 4

Delegation

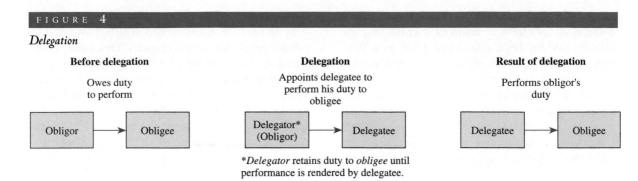

Before delegation — Owes duty to perform: Obligor → Obligee

Delegation — Appoints delegatee to perform his duty to obligee: Delegator* (Obligor) → Delegatee

Result of delegation — Performs obligor's duty: Delegatee → Obligee

*Delegator retains duty to obligee until performance is rendered by delegatee.

contracts are made with the understanding that the person the employer hires will perform the work. The situation in which a person hires a general contractor to perform specific work is distinguishable, however. In that situation, the person hiring the general contractor would normally understand that at least part of the work would be delegated to subcontractors.

Language Creating a Delegation

No special, formal language is necessary to create an effective delegation of duties. In fact, since parties frequently confuse the terms *assignment* and *delegation,* one of the problems frequently presented to courts is determining whether the parties intended an assignment only or both an assignment and a delegation. Unless the agreement indicates a contrary intent, courts tend to interpret assignments as including a delegation of the assignor's duties. Both the UCC 2–210(4) and section 328 of the *Restatement (Second) of Contracts* provide that, unless the language or the circumstances indicate to the contrary, general language of assignment such as language indicating an assignment of "the contract" or of "all my rights under the contract" is to be interpreted as creating *both* an assignment and a delegation.

Assumption of Duties by Delegatee

A delegation gives the delegatee the right to perform the duties of the delegator. The mere fact that duties have been delegated does not always place legal responsibility on the delegatee to perform. The delegatee who fails to perform will not be liable to either the delegator or the obligee unless the delegatee has assumed the duty by expressly or impliedly undertaking the obligation to perform. However,

both section 2–210(4) of the UCC and section 328 of the *Restatement (Second)* provide that an assignee's acceptance of an assignment is to be construed as a promise by him to perform the duties under the contract, unless the language of the assignment or the circumstances indicate to the contrary. Frequently, a term of the contract between the delegator and the delegatee provides that the delegatee assumes responsibility for performance. A common example of this is the assumption of an existing mortgage debt by a purchaser of real estate. Suppose Morgan buys a house from Friedman, agreeing to assume the outstanding mortgage on the property held by First Bank. By this assumption, Morgan undertakes personal liability to both Friedman and First Bank. If Morgan fails to make the mortgage payments, First Bank has a cause of action against Morgan personally. An assumption does *not* release the delegator from liability, however. Rather, it creates a situation in which both the delegator and the assuming delegatee owe duties to the obligee. If the assuming delegatee fails to pay, the delegator can be held liable. Thus, in the example described above, if Morgan fails to make mortgage payments and First Bank is unable to collect the debt from Morgan, Friedman would have secondary liability. Friedman, of course, would have an action against Morgan for breach of their contract.

Discharge of Delegator by Novation

As you have seen, the mere delegation of duties— even when the delegatee assumes those duties— does not release the delegator from his legal obligation to the obligee. A delegator can, however, be discharged from performance by **novation.**

A novation is a particular type of substituted contract in which the obligee agrees to discharge the original obligor and to substitute a new obligor in his place. The effects of a novation are that the original obligor has no further obligation under the contract and the obligee has the right to look to the new obligor for fulfillment of the contract. A novation requires more than the obligee's consent to having the delegatee perform the duties. In the example used above, the mere fact that First Bank accepted mortgage payments from Morgan would not create a novation. Rather, there must be some evidence that the obligee agrees to discharge the old obligor and substitute a new obligor. As you will see in the following *Rosenberg* case, this can be inferred from language of a contract or such other factors as the obligee's conduct or the surrounding circumstances.

ROSENBERG v. SON, INC.   491 N.W.2d 71 (Sup. Ct. N.D. 1992)

I n February 1980, Mary Pratt entered into a contract to buy a Dairy Queen restaurant located in Grand Forks's City Center Mall from Harold and Gladys Rosenberg. The terms of the contract for the franchise, inventory, and equipment were a purchase price totaling $62,000, a $10,000 down payment, and $52,000 due in quarterly payments at 10 percent interest over a 15-year period. The sales contract also contained a provision denying the buyer a right of prepayment for the first five years of the contract. In October 1982, Pratt assigned her rights and delegated her duties under this contract to Son, Inc. The assignment between Pratt and Son contained a "Consent to Assignment" clause, which was signed by the Rosenbergs. It also contained a "save harmless" clause, in which Son promised to indemnify Pratt for any claims, demands, or actions that might result from Son's failure to perform the agreement. After this transaction, Pratt moved to Arizona and had no further knowledge of or involvement with the Dairy Queen business. Also following the assignment, the Dairy Queen was moved from the mall to a different location in Grand Forks.

Son assigned the contract to Merit Corporation in June 1984. This assignment did not include a consent clause, but the Rosenbergs knew of the assignment and apparently acquiesced in it. They accepted a large prepayment from Merit, reducing the principal balance to $25,000. After the assignment, Merit pledged the inventory and equipment of the Dairy Queen as collateral for a loan from Valley Bank and Trust. Payments from Merit to the Rosenbergs continued until June 1988, at which time the payments ceased, leaving an unpaid principal balance of $17,326.24 plus interest. The Rosenbergs attempted collection of the balance from Merit, but Merit filed bankruptcy. The business assets pledged as collateral for the loan from Valley Bank and Trust were repossessed. The Rosenbergs brought this action for collection of the outstanding debt against Son and Pratt. The trial court granted summary judgment in favor of Son and Pratt and against the Rosenbergs, and the Rosenbergs appealed. ∞

Erickstad, Chief Justice   It is a well-established principle in the law of contracts that a contracting party cannot escape its liability on the contract by merely assigning its duties and rights under the contract to a third party. This rule of law applies to all categories of contracts, including contracts for the sale of goods, which is present in the facts of this case.

Thus, when Pratt entered into the "assignment agreement" with Son, a simple assignment alone was insufficient to release her from any further liability on the contract. It is not, however, a legal impossibility for a contracting party to rid itself of an obligation under a contract. It may seek the approval of the other original party for release, and substitute a new party in its place. In such an instance, the transaction is no longer called an assignment; instead, it is called a novation. If a novation occurs in this manner, it must be clear from the terms of the agreement that a novation is intended by all parties involved. Both original parties to the contract must intend and mutually assent to the discharge of the obligor from any further liability on the original contract.

It is evident from the express language of the assignment agreement between Pratt and Son that only an assignment was intended, not a novation. The agreement made no mention of discharging Pratt from any further liability on the contract. To the contrary, the latter part of the agreement contained an indemnity clause holding Pratt harmless in the event of a breach by Son. Thus, it is apparent that Pratt contemplated being held ultimately responsible for performance of the obligation.

Furthermore, the agreement was between Pratt and Son; they were the parties signing the agreement, not the Rosenbergs. An agreement between Pratt and Son cannot unilaterally affect the Rosenbergs' rights under the contract. The Rosenbergs did sign a consent to the assignment at the bottom of the agreement. However, by merely consenting to the assignment the Rosenbergs did not consent to a discharge of the principal obligor—Pratt. Nothing in the language of the consent clause supports such an allegation. A creditor is free to consent to an assignment without releasing the original obligor. Thus, the express language of the agreement and intent of the parties at the time the assignment was made did not contemplate a novation by releasing Pratt and substituting Son in her stead.

The inquiry as to Pratt's liability does not end at this juncture. The trial court released Pratt from any liability on the contract due to the changes or alterations which took place following her assignment to Son. While it is true that Pratt cannot be forced to answer on the contract irrespective of events occurring subsequent to her assignment, it is also true that she cannot be exonerated for every type of alteration or change that may develop.

The buyer can assign his right to the goods or land and can delegate performance of his duty to pay that price. But observe that he remains bound "as before"; the assignee and the seller cannot, by agreement or by waiver, make it the assignor's duty to pay a different price or on different conditions. If the seller is willing to make such a change, he must trust to the assignee alone. 4 *Corbin on Contracts* section 866 at 458–59.

The trial court decided that any alteration in the underlying obligation resulted in a release of Pratt on the contract. It appears that not every type of alteration is sufficient to warrant discharge of the assignor. As suggested by Professor Corbin in the language highlighted above, the alteration must "prejudice the position of the assignor." 4 *Corbin on Contracts* section 866 at 459.

If the changes in the obligation prejudicially affect the assignor, a new agreement has been formed between the assignee and the other original contracting party. More concisely, a novation has occurred and the assignor's original obligation has been discharged. Although we have previously determined that the terms of the assignment agreement between Pratt and Son did not contemplate a novation, there are additional methods of making a novation besides doing so in the express terms of an agreement. The question of whether or not there has been a novation is a question of fact. The trial court should not have granted summary judgment. There are questions of fact remaining as to the result of the changes in the contract. Thus, we reverse the summary judgment and remand for further proceedings.

Reversed and remanded in favor of the Rosenbergs.

THIRD–PARTY BENEFICIARIES

There are many situations in which the performance of a contract would constitute some benefit to a person who was not a party to the contract. Despite the fact that a nonparty may expect to derive advantage from the performance of a contract, the general rule is that no one but the parties to a contract or their assignees can enforce it. In some situations, however, parties contract for the purpose of benefiting some third person. In such cases, the benefit to the third person is an essential part of the contract, not just an incidental result of a contract that was really designed to benefit the parties. Where the parties to a contract *intended* to benefit a third party, courts will give effect to their intent and permit the third party to enforce the contract. Such third parties are called **third-party beneficiaries.**

Figure 5 illustrates the relationship of third-party beneficiaries to the contracting parties.

Intended Beneficiaries versus Incidental Beneficiaries

For a third person (other than an assignee) to have the right to enforce a contract, she must be able to establish that the contract was made with the intent to benefit her. A few courts have required that both parties must have intended to benefit the third party. Most courts, however, have found it to be sufficient if the person to whom the promise to perform was made (the *promisee*) intended to benefit the third party. You will see an example of this in the following *Cherry v. Crow* case. In ascertaining intent to benefit the third party, a court will look at the language used by the parties and all the sur-

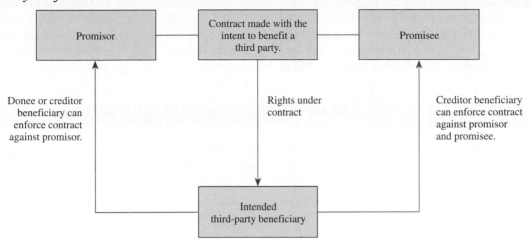

FIGURE   5

Third-Party Beneficiaries

rounding circumstances. One factor that is frequently important in determining intent to benefit is whether the party making the promise to perform (the *promisor*) was to render performance directly to the third party. For example, if Allison contracts with Jones Florist to deliver flowers to Kirsch, the fact that performance was to be rendered to Kirsch would be good evidence that the parties intended to benefit Kirsch. This factor is not conclusive, however. There are some cases in which intent to benefit a third party has been found even though performance was to be rendered to the promisee rather than to the third party. Intended beneficiaries are often classified as either *creditor* or *donee beneficiaries*. These classifications are discussed in greater detail below.

A third party who is unable to establish that the contract was made with the intent to benefit her is called an *incidental beneficiary*. A third party is classified as an incidental beneficiary when the benefit derived by that third party was merely an unintended by-product of a contract that was created for the benefit of those who were parties to it. Incidental beneficiaries acquire no rights under a contract. For example, Hutton contracts with Long Construction Company to build a valuable structure on his land. The performance of the contract would constitute a benefit to Keller, Hutton's next-door neighbor, by increasing the value of Keller's land. The contract between Hutton and Long was made for the purpose of benefiting themselves, however. Any advantage derived by Keller is purely inciden-

tal to their primary purpose. Thus, Keller could not sue and recover damages if either Hutton or Long breaches the contract.

As a general rule, members of the public are held to be incidental beneficiaries of contracts entered into by their municipalities or other governmental units in the regular course of carrying on governmental functions. A member of the public cannot recover a judgment in a suit against a promisor of such a contract, even though all taxpayers will suffer some injury from nonperformance. A different result may be reached, however, if a party contracting with a governmental unit agrees to reimburse members of the public for damages or if the party undertakes to perform some duty for individual members of the public.

Creditor Beneficiaries   If the promisor's performance is intended to satisfy a legal duty that the promisee owes to a third party, the third party is a **creditor beneficiary.** The creditor beneficiary has rights against both the promisee (because of the original obligation) and the promisor. For example, Smith buys a car on credit from Jones Auto Sales. Smith later sells the car to Carmichael, who agrees to pay the balance due on the car to Jones Auto Sales. (Note that Smith is delegating his duty to pay to Carmichael, and Carmichael is assuming the personal obligation to do so.) In this case, Jones Auto Sales is a creditor beneficiary of the contract between Smith and Carmichael. It has rights against both Carmichael and Smith if Carmichael does not perform.

Donee Beneficiaries   If the promisee's primary purpose in contracting is to make a gift of the agreed-on performance to a third party, that third party is classified as a *donee beneficiary.* If the contract is breached, the donee beneficiary will have a cause of action against the promisor, but not against the promisee (donor). For example, Miller contracts with Perpetual Life Insurance Company, agreeing to pay premiums in return for which Perpetual agrees to pay $100,000 to Miller's husband when Miller dies. Miller's husband is a donee beneficiary and can bring suit and recover judgment against Perpetual if Miller dies and Perpetual does not pay.

CHERRY v. CROW   845 F. Supp. 1520 (M. D. Fla. 1994)

The Sheriff of Polk County employed Prison Health Services (PHS) to provide total health care services for inmates and detainees housed within the Polk County Jail and the Polk County Jail Annex. On December 22, 1922, Polk County Sheriff's Department (PCSD) employees booked Eddie Ronald Cherry into the jail to begin serving a 30-day sentence for driving under the influence of alcohol. At the time of his incarceration, Cherry informed the PHS medical staff that he consumed approximately one case of beer daily. Over the next two days, Cherry repeatedly requested medical attention for symptoms related to alcohol withdrawal.

Cherry's wife notified a PCSD employee by phone on December 25 that her husband had a history of delirium tremens ("DTs") during alcohol withdrawal and that he was in immediate need of a doctor's attention. About two hours later, the inmates sharing Cherry's cell asked PCSD employees to check on Cherry's condition. The employees found Cherry in his cell, hallucinating and shaking violently. The PCSD employees notified PHS Nurse Gill, who examined Cherry and reported his symptoms of DTs to PHS Nurse Smith. Nurse Smith requested that Cherry be sent to the infirmary for observation.

At the infirmary, a PCSD employee shackled Cherry, who was still hallucinating, to his bed, with the knowledge and acquiescence of Nurse Smith. The next morning, while still suffering from hallucinations associated with DTs, Cherry either walked or jumped off the end of his bed. Because the leg shackle did not allow his feet to advance beyond the top of the bed, Cherry landed head first on the concrete floor. Cherry died five days later as a result of his injuries. Cherry's wife filed suit on behalf of Cherry's estate against PHS, Nurse Smith, and the PCSD for breach of contract and other claims. The defendants moved to dismiss the suit and strike the complaint. The court's opinion follows. ∞

Kovachevich, District Judge   Defendants assert that no cause of action exists against PHS for breach of contract, in that Cherry was not an intended third party beneficiary of the employment contract between PHS and PCSD.

The Health Services Agreement between PCSD and PHS states:
WHEREAS, the SHERIFF has the statutory and constitutional duty and responsibility to provide necessary and proper medical, psychiatric, dental and other health care services for persons remanded to his care, custody and control within the county correctional system. . . .
WHEREAS, the SHERIFF is desirous of contracting with PHS and PHS is desirous of contracting with the SHERIFF to provide total health care services *for the inmates/ detainees* . . . housed within the county correctional system facilities described above. . .

The right of a third party beneficiary to bring suit under contract as outlined in *American Surety Co. of New York v. Smith* remains clear guidance today. The Supreme Court recognized:

Where, therefore it is manifest from the nature or terms of a contract that the formal parties thereto intended its provisions to be for the benefit of a third party, as well as for the benefit of the formal parties themselves, the benefit to such third parties being the direct and primary object of the contract, or amongst such objects, such third party may maintain an action on the contract even though he is a stranger to the consideration.

The Court finds that PCSD and PHS intended, as a result of their agreement, to benefit persons situated such as Cherry. Accordingly, defendants' motion to dismiss is denied.

Motion denied in favor of Cherry.

Vesting of Beneficiary's Rights

Another possible threat to the interests of the third-party beneficiary is that the promisor and the promisee might modify or discharge their contract so as to extinguish or alter the beneficiary's rights. For example, Gates, who owes $500 to Sorenson, enters into a contract with Connor whereby Connor agrees to pay the $500 to Sorenson. What happens if, before Sorenson is paid, Connor pays the money to Gates and Gates accepts it or Connor and Gates otherwise modify the contract? Courts have held that there is a point at which the rights of the beneficiary vest—that is, the beneficiary's rights cannot be lost by modification or discharge. A modification or discharge that occurs after the beneficiary's rights have vested cannot be asserted as a defense to a suit brought by the beneficiary. The exact time at which the beneficiary's rights vest differs from jurisdiction to jurisdiction. Some courts have held that vesting occurs when the contract is formed, while others hold that vesting does not occur until the beneficiary learns of the contract and consents to it or does some act in reliance on the promise.

The contracting parties' ability to vary the rights of the third-party beneficiary can also be affected by the terms of their agreement. A provision of the contract between the promisor and the promisee stating that the duty to the beneficiary cannot be modified would be effective to prevent modification. Likewise, a contract provision in which the parties specifically reserved the right to change beneficiaries or modify the duty to the beneficiary would be enforced. For example, provisions reserving the right to change beneficiaries are very common in insurance contracts.

ETHICAL AND PUBLIC POLICY CONCERNS

1. You learned that an assignor's rights are extinguished as soon as he assigns them. Should a delegator's duties be extinguished by his delegation of them?

2. Why does public policy favor allowing third parties to enforce contracts made for their benefit? Should incidental beneficiaries have a right to enforce contracts? Why or why not?

PROBLEMS AND PROBLEM CASES

1. In 1974, Spiklevitz loaned money to Vincent and Geraldine Heron. The Herons signed a promissory note agreeing to repay the debt by January 15, 1975. In April 1980, the Herons sold their business to Markmil Corp. At that time, $3,510 of their debt to Spiklevitz remained unpaid. Markmil executed an "Assumption of Obligation," which stated that as part of the purchase price of the Herons' business, Markmil agreed to pay the list of debts written on an attached sheet of paper labeled "Exhibit A." Spiklevitz was listed as a creditor in Exhibit A for the balance owed to him. In June 1981, Spiklevitz sued Markmil to recover the amount remaining due on the note. Is Markmil obligated to pay?

2. Peterson was employed by Post–Newsweek as a newscaster-anchorman on station WTOP–TV (Channel 9) under a three-year employment contract that was to end June 30, 1980, and could be extended for two additional one-year terms at the option of Post–Newsweek. In June 1978, Post–Newsweek sold its operating license to the Evening News Association (Evening News), and Channel 9 was then designated as WDVM–TV. The contract of sale between Post–Newsweek and Evening News provided for the assignment of all contracts, including Peterson's employment contract. Peterson continued working for the station for more than a year after the change of ownership and received all of the compensation and benefits provided by his contract with Post–Newsweek. In early August 1979, he negotiated a new contract with a competing television station and tendered his resignation to Evening News. Evening News sued Peterson. Peterson defended on the ground that his employment contract was not assignable. Is he correct?

3. In May 1978, John and Judith Brooks contracted with Hayes to construct a Windsor Home (a packaged, predesigned, and precut home) on a lot that they owned. Hayes was primarily a real estate broker but also sold Windsor Homes. The construction contract required Hayes to "provide all necessary labor and materials and perform all work of every nature whatsoever to be done in the erection of a residence for" the Brookses. The Brookses and Hayes contemplated that Hayes would hire subcontractors to perform much of the home construction work and Hayes, who had no personal experience in construction, would not control the method of construction. During the construction, the Brookses requested that a "heatilator" be installed as an extra to increase the efficiency of the fireplace. Marr, the mason hired by Hayes to do the fireplace and other masonry work, installed the heatilator. The Brookses moved into the house in the winter of 1978. When they used the fireplace, they smelled smoke in areas of the house remote from the fireplace. Both the Brookses and Hayes hired several masons to inspect the fireplace system, but none of the masons was able to discover the cause of the problem. The Brookses used the fireplace with some frequency until November 1980, when a fire in the home caused structural damage around the fireplace and smoke damage to the house and the couple's personal property. It was discovered that Marr's negligence in installing the heatilator had caused the fire. The Brookses sued both Marr and Hayes. The case against Marr was dismissed because Marr went bankrupt. Is Hayes liable to the Brookses?

4. Andreson went to Monahan Beaches Jewelry Center to shop for a diamond engagement ring for his fiancée, Warren. Andreson told Monahan that the ring was to be given to Warren. Andreson and a salesperson discussed several aspects of the size, type, and style of the ring, and the salesperson made suggestions about what would be likely to be pleasing to Warren. Shortly before Christmas, Monahan sold Andreson a ring, which Monahan represented as being a diamond ring, for $3,974.25. Andreson gave the ring to Warren for Christmas as a symbol of their engagement. Warren soon noticed a small chip in the stone under the setting. She returned the ring to Monahan shortly after the Christmas holidays and Monahan agreed to replace the stone with one of equal or greater value at no charge to Warren. After making this agreement, Warren took the ring to another jeweler to have it appraised. There she learned for the first time that the alleged diamond that Monahan sold to Andreson was in fact nothing more than cut glass or cubic zirconia. Warren filed suit against Monahan on several counts, including breach of contract. Could Warren win a breach of contract suit against Monahan, even though it was her fiancé who purchased the ring?

5. Jones paid Sullivan, the chief of the Addison Police Department, $6,400 in exchange for Sullivan's cooperation in allowing Jones and others to bring marijuana by airplane into the Addison airport without police intervention. Instead of performing the requested service, Sullivan arrested Jones. The $6,400 was turned over to the district attorney's office and was introduced into evidence in the subsequent trial in which Jones was tried for and convicted of bribery. After his conviction, Jones assigned his alleged claim to the $6,400 to Melvyn Bruder. Based on the assignment, Bruder brought suit against the state of Texas to obtain possession of the money. Will he be successful?

6. Post, Lumber, and Samson were construction-related businesses owned and operated by DiPietro. In May 1984, Boynton contracted with DiPietro personally and with Post for the lease of Boynton's property, which contained a sawmill. Lumber and Samson used the millsite along with Post in related businesses. At the same time, Boynton entered into a separate contract with Post, giving it a one-year option to purchase the millsite for $60,000. This option provided that on payment of $6,000 at the time of exercising the option, Boynton would transfer title to the property, and the balance would be financed in a specified way. In October 1984, Post assigned its rights in the option agreement to Lumber. In January 1985, Lumber attempted to exercise the option by sending a $6,000 check to Boynton with a letter expressing its readiness to execute the agreement and advising Boynton that the payment of rent would stop. Boynton cashed Lumber's check but did not respond to the letter. Lumber sent Boynton two more letters seeking to exercise the option before it lapsed, but Boynton did not respond. In later litigation, Boynton contended that the assignment of the option agreement was invalid because he was not notified of it. Is this a good argument?

7. Richard Caldwell, a 13-year-old boy, was swinging on the swing set at his apartment complex when the swing came loose from the frame. Richard broke his ankle in the fall. The swing set had been sold to the apartment complex, which was owned by Marine Creek Partners, by Shade Tree Toys. The contract of sale between Shade Tree and Marine Creek stated as follows:

MAINTENANCE: Maintenance is the responsibility of the purchaser. **All moving parts should be periodically inspected by purchaser and replaced as signs of wear became apparent.** It is recommended that . . . nuts and bolts [be] tightened on a regular basis. A visual inspection should be made by purchaser every three months.

SUPERVISION: ALL PLAYGROUND AREAS AND EQUIPMENT REQUIRE ADULT SUPERVISION.

Richard's parents brought a breach of contract action on a claim of third-party beneficiary status under the swing set sales agreement. Will they win?

8. Harred Fuel owns property in Allentown. Harred leased the property to the Attiyehs, who own and operate the Acorn Hotel. The lease provided that the Attiyehs would maintain liability insurance on the property. Upon the signing of the lease, the Attiyehs assumed operation of the Acorn Hotel and its public bar. Ten years later, Bryan entered the Acorn Hotel, where he was shot and injured. He and his wife sued the Attiyehs, the Acorn Hotel, and Harred Fuel. One of their claims was that Bryan was a third-party beneficiary to the liability insurance clause in the lease. Is this a good argument?

9. Lewis, a dairyman, was a member of the Mountain Empire Dairymen's Association (MEDA). MEDA was the exclusive agent for marketing Lewis's dairy products. Lewis borrowed $194,850 from Mid-States Sales and secured the loan with certain of his cattle and their products. Lewis assigned his right to receive some of the proceeds from the sale of his milk each month to Mid-States, and notified MEDA of the assignment. After paying Mid-States for over a year under this agreement, MEDA received notice from Lewis that he was canceling his membership in MEDA. MEDA notified Mid-States and other assignees of Lewis that Lewis was canceling his membership, and asked them to sign a release of assignment. The other assignees signed the releases, but Mid-States did not. MEDA made the last payout on the milk it sold for Lewis directly to Lewis rather than to Mid-States. After Lewis filed for bankruptcy, Mid-States sued MEDA for the payment. Will it prevail?

10. ▦ *Video Case.* See "Roof Repairs." Roofer contracted with Driscoll Industries to do a roofing job. The job was too big for Roofer to handle, so he delegated his duties under the contract to another company that claimed to do that kind of roofing work all the time. However, the other company did such a poor job that it damaged the heating and cooling systems of the building. Is Roofer liable to Driscoll for the damage done by its delegatee?

See also "TV Repair" and "The Student Loan."

Performance and Remedies

ontracts are generally formed before either of the parties renders any actual performance to the other. A person may be content to bargain for and receive the other person's promise at the formation stage of a contract because this permits him to plan for the future. Ultimately, however, all parties bargain for the *performance* of the promises that have been made to them.

In most contracts, each party carries out his promise and is *discharged* (released from all of his obligations under the contract) when his performance is complete. Sometimes, however, a party fails to perform or performs in an unsatisfactory manner. In such cases, courts are often called on to determine the respective rights and duties of the parties. This frequently involves deciding such questions as whether performance was due, whether the contract was breached, to what extent it was breached, and whether performance was excused. This task is made more difficult by the fact that contracts often fail to specify the consequences of nonperformance or defective performance. In deciding questions involving the performance of contracts and remedies for breach of contract, courts draw on a variety of legal principles that attempt to do justice, prevent forfeiture and unjust enrichment, and effectuate the parties' presumed intent.

This chapter presents an overview of the legal concepts that are used to resolve disputes arising in the performance stage of contracting. It describes how courts determine whether performance is due and what kind of performance is due, the consequences of contract breach, and the excuses for a party's failure to perform. It also includes a discussion of the remedies that are used when a court determines that a contract has been breached. ∞

CONDITIONS

Nature of Conditions

One issue that frequently arises in the performance stage of a contract is whether a party has the duty to perform. Some duties are *unconditional* or *absolute*—that is, the duty to perform does not depend on the occurrence of any further event other than the passage of time. For example, if Root promises to pay Downing $100, Root's duty is unconditional. When a party's duty is unconditional, he has the duty to perform unless his performance is excused. (The various excuses for nonperformance will be discussed later in this chapter.) When a duty is unconditional, the promisor's failure to perform constitutes a *breach of contract.*

In many situations, however, a promisor's duty to perform depends on the occurrence of some event that is called a **condition.** A condition is an uncertain, future event that affects a party's duty to perform. For example, if Melman contracts to buy Lance's house on condition that First Bank approve Melman's application for a mortgage loan by January 10, Melman's duty to buy Lance's house is *conditioned* on the bank's approving his loan application by January 10. When a promisor's duty is conditional, his duty to perform is affected by the occurrence of the condition. In this case, if the condition does not occur, Melman has no duty to buy the house. His failure to buy it because of the nonoccurrence of the condition will *not* constitute a breach of contract. Rather, he is discharged from further obligation under the contract.

Almost any event can be a condition. Some conditions are beyond the control of either party, such as when Morehead promises to buy Pratt's business if the prime rate drops by a specified amount. Others are within the control of a party, such as when one party's performance of a duty under the contract is a condition of the other party's duty to perform.

Types of Conditions

There are two ways of classifying conditions. One way of classifying conditions focuses on the effect of the condition on the duty to perform. The other way focuses on the way in which the condition is created.

Classifications of Conditions Based on Their Effect on the Duty to Perform   As Figure 1 illustrates, conditions vary in their effects on the duty to perform.

1. *Condition precedent.* A condition precedent is a future, uncertain event that creates the duty to perform. If the condition does not occur, performance does not become due. If the condition does occur, the duty to perform arises. The condition at issue in *Beverly Way Associates v. Barham,* which follows this discussion, is an example of a condition precedent.

2. *Concurrent condition.* When the contract calls for the parties to perform at the same time, each person's performance is conditioned on the performance or tender of performance (offer of performance) by the other. Such conditions are called **concurrent conditions.** For example, if Martin promises to buy Johnson's car for $5,000, the parties' respective duties to perform are subject to a concurrent condition. Martin does not have the duty to perform unless Johnson tenders his performance, and vice versa.

3. *Condition subsequent.* A **condition subsequent** is a future, uncertain event that **discharges** the duty to perform. When a duty is subject to a condition subsequent, the duty to perform arises but is discharged if the future, uncertain event occurs. For example, Wilkinson and Jones agree that Wilkinson will begin paying Jones $2,000 per month, but that if XYZ Corporation dissolves, Wilkinson's obligation to pay will cease. In this case, Wilkinson's duty to pay is subject to being discharged by a condition subsequent. The major significance of the distinction between conditions precedent and conditions subsequent is that the plaintiff bears the burden of proving the occurrence of a condition precedent, while the defendant bears the burden of proving the occurrence of a condition subsequent.

Classifications of Conditions Based on the Way in which They Were Created   Another way of classifying conditions is to focus on the means by which the condition was created.

1. *Express condition.* An **express condition** is a condition that is specified in the language of the

FIGURE   I

Effect of Conditions

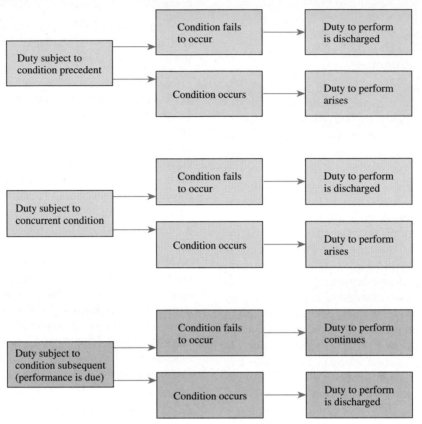

parties' contract. For example, if Grant promises to sell his regular season football tickets to Carson on condition that Indiana University wins the Rose Bowl, Indiana's winning the Rose Bowl is an express condition of Grant's duty to sell the tickets.

When the contract expressly provides that a party's duty is subject to a condition, courts take it very seriously. When a duty is subject to an express condition, that condition must be strictly complied with in order to give rise to the duty to perform.

2. *Implied-in-fact condition.* An **implied-in-fact condition** is one that is not specifically stated by the parties but is *implied* by the nature of the parties' promises. For example, if Summers promises to unload cargo from Knight's ship, the ship's arrival in port would be an implied-in-fact condition of Summer's duty to unload the cargo.

3. *Constructive condition.* **Constructive conditions** (also known as *implied-in-law conditions*) are conditions that are imposed by law rather than by

the agreement of the parties. The law imposes constructive conditions to do justice between the parties. In contracts in which one of the parties is expected to perform before the other, the law normally infers that that performance is a constructive condition of the other party's duty to perform. For example, if Thomas promises to build a house for King, and the parties' understanding is that King will pay Thomas an agreed-on price when the house is built, King's duty to pay is subject to the constructive condition that Thomas complete the house. Without such a constructive condition, a person who did not receive the performance promised him would still have to render his own performance.

Creation of Express Conditions

Although no particular language is required to create an express condition, the conditional nature of promises is usually indicated by such words as *provided that, subject to, on condition that, if, when, while, after,* and *as soon as.* The process of determining the meaning of conditions is not a mechanical one. Courts look at the parties' overall intent as indicated in language of the entire contract.

The following discussion explores two common types of express conditions.

Example of Express Condition: Satisfaction of Third Parties   It is common for building and construction contracts to provide that the property owner's duty to pay is conditioned on the builder's production of certificates to be issued by a specific architect or engineer. These certificates indicate the satisfaction of the architect or engineer with the builder's work. They are often issued at each stage of completion, after the architect or engineer has inspected the work done.

The standard usually used to determine whether the condition has occurred is a *good faith* standard. As a general rule, if the architect or engineer is acting honestly and has some good faith reason for withholding a certificate, the builder cannot recover payments due. In legal terms, the condition that will create the owner's duty to pay has not occurred.

If the builder can prove that the withholding of the certificate was fraudulent or done in bad faith (as a result of collusion with the owner, for example), the court may order that payment be made despite the absence of the certificate. In addition, production of the certificate may be excused by the death, insanity, or incapacitating illness of the named architect or engineer.

Example of Express Condition: Personal Satisfaction   Contracts sometimes provide that a promisee's duty to perform is conditioned on his personal satisfaction with the promisee's performance. For example, Moore commissions Allen to paint a portrait of Moore's wife, but the contract provides that Moore's duty to pay is conditioned on his personal satisfaction with the portrait.

How does a court determine whether the condition of personal satisfaction has occurred? If the court applies a standard of actual, subjective satisfaction and Moore asserts that he is not satisfied, it would be very difficult for Allen to prove that the condition has occurred. If, on the other hand, the court applies an objective, "reasonable person" standard of satisfaction, Allen stands a better chance of proving that the condition has occurred.

In determining which standard of satisfaction to apply, courts distinguish between cases in which the performance bargained for involves personal taste and comfort and cases that involve mechanical fitness or suitability for a particular purpose. If personal taste and comfort are involved, as they would be in the hypothetical case described above, a promisor who is honestly dissatisfied with the promisee's performance has the right to reject the performance without being liable to the promisee. If, however, the performance involves mechanical fitness or suitability, the court will apply a reasonable person test. If the court finds that a reasonable person would be satisfied with the performance, the condition of personal satisfaction has been met and the promisor must accept the performance and pay the contract price. For example, Kitt Manufacturing Company hires Pace to design a conveyor belt system for use in its factory, conditioning its duty to pay on its personal satisfaction with the system. A court would be likely to find that this is a contract involving mechanical fitness and suitability for which an objective test of satisfaction could be used. These standards are illustrated in Figure 2 on page 329. Because the "honest satisfaction" standard involves a danger of forfeiture by the performing party, courts prefer the objective test of satisfaction when objective evaluation is feasible. The following *Beverly Way Associates v. Barham* case discusses a further implication of personal satisfaction conditions.

BEVERLY WAY ASSOCIATES v. BARHAM   276 Cal. Rptr. 240 (Ct. App. Cal. 1990)

n July 7, 1988, Phyllis Barham entered into a contract to sell her residential building in Long Beach, California, to Beverly Way Associates (Beverly Way) for $3.9 million. The contract provided for the opening of escrow (the procedure by which the sale would be consummated) and a closing within 60 days of that time. It also provided that Beverly Way's obligation to purchase the property *"shall be conditioned upon" its approval of a number of specified inspections and documents and delivery of clear title. One of these items was a certified survey of the property that would show all improvements to the property and the location of all exceptions to the title. The contract gave Beverly Way 28 business days in which to inspect and approve documents after having been furnished them by Barham. On November 15, 1988, Barham furnished the material that Beverly Way required, and on December 2, Beverly Way wrote to Barham stating, "We reluctantly disapprove of the matters disclosed on the Survey and relating to the Property." This letter described in detail the reasons for its rejection. The letter expressed the hope that the parties could "keep the deal alive" and proposed two alternatives that would have changed the parties' arrangement substantially. There was no further communication between the parties until February 1989, when Beverly Way sent a second letter stating that it was prepared to waive its objections to the survey and to proceed to close the deal. Barham refused to sell the property and Beverly Way sued for specific performance. The trial court sustained a demurrer in favor of Barham, and Beverly Way appealed.* ∽

Epstein, Judge Both sides to this appeal treat the buyer's right of approval under the contract as a condition precedent in favor of the buyer. They are quite correct in that characterization. "A condition is an event, not certain to occur, which must occur, unless its non-occurrence is excused, before performance under a contract becomes due." (*Rest. 2d, Contracts,* section 224).

We turn to an examination of the nature of the buyer's power to approve the condition precedent and to the effect of its disapproval. Most of the textual and case material on "satisfaction" conditions precedent turns on whether an objective or subjective standard is to be used in reviewing the reasonableness of its exercise. Neither party questions the reasonableness of the buyer's exercise of its approval authority in the December 2, 1988, letter.

The effect of a buyer's power to approve documentation required in a contract for the purchase of real estate "is to give the buyer an option not to consummate the purchase if it fails to meet the condition," at least so long as the buyer acts reasonably and in the exercise of good faith. Stated another way, the contract gives the buyer the power and privilege of termination in the event that it reasonably concludes that the condition has not been fulfilled. Except for the judicial gloss that the power of rejection must be exercised reasonably, the party having the power to approve or reject is in the same position as a contract offeree. It is hornbook law that an unequivocal rejection by an offeree, communicated to the offeror, terminates the offer; even if the offeror does no further act, the offeree cannot later purport to accept the offer and thereby create enforceable contractual rights against the offeror. There can be no question but that Beverly Way exercised its power of disapproval in this case. The December 2, 1988, letter said so expressly. This rejection, communicated to Barham, terminated the contract. It left Beverly Way with no power to create obligations against Barham by a late "waiver" of its objections and acceptance of the proffered documentation.

The fact that Beverly Way considered the existing contract to be at an end is reflected also by its effort to keep the "deal alive" by proposing two entirely new formulations that were novel to the agreement of the parties. It may be inferred that Beverly Way was hoping to find a way to acquire the property, but it cannot be doubted that it was unwilling to do so on the basis of what had been presented by Barham.

Affirmed in favor of Barham.

Excuse of Conditions

In most situations involving conditional duties, the promisor does not have the duty to perform unless and until the condition occurs. There are, however, a variety of situations in which the occurrence of a condition will be excused. In such a case, the person whose duty is conditional will have to perform even though the condition has not occurred.

One ground for excusing a condition is that the occurrence of the condition has been *prevented* or *hindered* by the party who is benefited by the condition. For example, Connor hires Ingle to construct a garage on Connor's land, but when Ingle

FIGURE 2

Duty to Perform Conditioned on "Personal Satisfaction" (a form of express condition precedent)

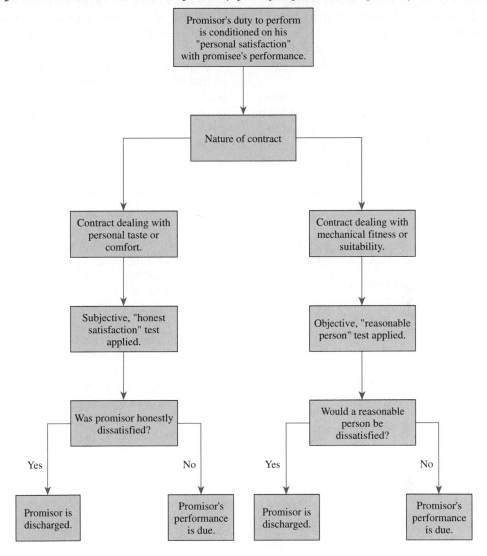

attempts to begin construction, Connor refuses to allow Ingle access to the land. In this case, Connor's duty to pay would normally be subject to a constructive condition that Ingle build the garage. However, since Connor prevented the occurrence of the condition, the condition will be excused, and Ingle can sue Connor for damages for breach of contract even though the condition has not occurred.

Other grounds for excuse of a condition include **waiver** and **estoppel.** When a person whose duty is conditional voluntarily gives up his right to the occurrence of the condition (waiver), the condition

will be excused. Suppose that Buchman contracts to sell his car to Fox on condition that Fox pay him $2,000 by June 14. Fox fails to pay on June 14, but, when he tenders payment on June 20, Buchman accepts and cashes the check without reservation. Buchman has thereby *waived* the condition of payment by June 14.

When a person whose duty is conditional leads the other party to rely on his noninsistence on the condition, the condition will be excused because of estoppel. For example, McDonald agrees to sell his business to Brown on condition that Brown provide a credit report and personal financial statement by July 17. On July 5, McDonald tells Brown that he can have until the end of the month to provide the necessary documents. Relying on McDonald's assurances, Brown does not provide the credit report and financial statement until July 29. In this case, McDonald would be *estopped* (precluded) from claiming that the condition did not occur.

A condition may also be excused when performance of the act that constitutes the condition becomes *impossible*. For example, if a building contract provides that the owner's duty to pay is conditioned on the production of a certificate from a named architect, the condition would be excused if the named architect died or became incapacitated before issuing the certificate.

PERFORMANCE OF CONTRACTS

When a promisor has performed his duties under a contract, he is discharged. Because his performance constitutes the occurrence of a constructive condition, the other party's duty to perform is also triggered, and the person who has performed has the right to receive the other party's performance. In determining whether a promisor is discharged by performance and whether the constructive condition of his performance has been fulfilled, courts must consider the standard of performance expected of him.

Level of Performance Expected of the Promisor

In some situations, no deviation from the promisor's promised performance is tolerated; in others, less-than-perfect performance will be sufficient to discharge the promisor and give him the right to recover under the contract.

1. *Strict performance standard.* A **strict performance** standard is a standard of performance that requires virtually perfect compliance with the contract terms. Remember that when a party's duty is subject to an express condition, that condition must be strictly and completely complied with in order to give rise to a duty of performance. Thus, when a promisor's performance is an express condition of the promisee's duty to perform, that performance must strictly and completely comply with the contract in order to give rise to the other promisee's

duty to perform. For example, if McMillan agrees to pay Jester $500 for painting his house "on condition that" Jester finish the job no later than June 1, 1994, a standard of strict or complete performance would be applied to Jester's performance. If Jester does not finish the job by June 1, his breach will have several consequences. First, since the condition precedent to McMillan's duty to pay has not occurred, McMillan does not have a duty to pay the contract price. Second, since it is now too late for the condition to occur, McMillan is discharged. Third, McMillan can sue Jester for breach of contract. The law's commitment to freedom of contract justifies such results in cases in which the parties have expressly bargained for strict compliance with the terms of the contract.

The strict performance standard is also applied to contractual obligations that can be performed either exactly or to a high degree of perfection. Examples of this type of obligation include promises to pay money, deliver deeds, and, generally, promises to deliver goods. A promisor who performs such promises completely and in strict compliance with the contract is entitled to receive the entire contract price. The promisor whose performance deviates from perfection is not entitled to receive the other party's performance if he does not render perfect performance within an appropriate time. He may, however, be able to recover the value of any benefits that he has conferred on the other party under a theory of quasi-contract.

2. *Substantial performance.* A **substantial performance** standard is a somewhat lower standard of performance that is applied to duties that are difficult to perform without some deviation from perfection *if* performance of those duties is *not* an express condition. A common example of this type of obligation is a promise to erect a building. Other examples include promises to construct roads, to cultivate crops, and to render some types of personal or professional services. Substantial performance is performance that falls short of complete performance in minor respects. As you will see in *M.J. Oldenstedt Plumbing Co., Inc. v. K-Mart Corp.,* which appears later in this chapter, it does not apply when a contracting party has been deprived of a material part of the consideration he bargained for. When a substantial performance standard is applied, the promisor who has substantially performed is discharged. His substantial performance triggers the other party's duty to pay the

Substantial Performance

DEFINITION	APPLICATION	EFFECTS	LIMITATION
Performance that falls short of complete performance in some minor respect but that does not deprive the other party of a material part of the consideration for which he bargained	Applies to performance that (1) is *not* an express condition of the other party's duty to perform and (2) is difficult to do perfectly	Triggers other party's duty to perform; requires other party to pay the contract price minus any damages caused by defects in performance	Breach cannot have been willful

contract price less any damages resulting from the defects in his performance. The obvious purpose behind the doctrine of substantial performance is to prevent forfeiture by a promisor who has given the injured party most of what he bargained for. Substantial performance is generally held to be inapplicable to a situation in which the breach of contract has been *willful,* however.

Good Faith Performance

One of the most significant trends in modern contract law is that courts and legislatures have created a duty to perform in good faith in an expanding range of contracts.[1] The Uniform Commercial Code specifically imposes a duty of good faith in every contract within the scope of any of the articles of the Code [1–203]. A growing number of courts have applied the duty to use good faith in transactions between lenders and their customers as well as insurance contracts, employment contracts, and contracts for the sale of real property.

This obligation to carry out a contract in good faith is usually called the **implied covenant of good faith and fair dealing.** It is a broad and flexible duty that is imposed by law rather than by the agreement of the parties. It is generally taken to mean that neither party to a contract will do anything to prevent the other from obtaining the benefits that he has the right to expect from the parties' agreement or their contractual relationship. The law's purpose in imposing such a term in contracts is to prevent abuses of power and encourage ethical behavior. *Dalton v. Educational Testing Service,* which follows, presents an example of the application of the implied covenant of good faith and fair dealing.

Breach of the implied covenant of good faith gives rise to a contract remedy. In some states, it can also constitute a tort, depending on the severity of the breach. A tort action for breach of the implied covenant of good faith is more likely to be recognized in situations in which a contract involves a special relationship of dependency and trust between the parties or where the public interest is adversely affected by a contracting party's practices. Numerous cases exist, for example, in which insurance companies' bad faith refusal to settle claims or perform duties to their insured and lenders' failure to exercise good faith in their dealings with their customers have led to large damage verdicts. Likewise, in states in which the implied duty of good faith has been held applicable to contracts of employment, employers who discharge employees in bad faith have been held liable for damages.[2]

---

[1]This trend is discussed in Chapter 9.

[2]This is discussed in Chapter 50.

 n May 1991, Brian Dalton took the SAT, which was administered by ETS, at Holy Cross High School in Queens where Dalton was a junior. Six months later, in November, he took the examination a second time, this time at John Bowne High School in Queens, and his combined score increased 410 points. Because Dalton's score increased by more than 350 points, his test results fell within the

ETS category of "Large Score Differences" or "discrepant scores." In accordance with ETS policy, members of the ETS Test Security Office therefore reviewed his May and November answer sheets. Upon a finding of different handwriting, the answer sheets were submitted to a document examiner, who opined that they were completed by separate individuals. Dalton's case was then forwarded to the Board of Review, which preliminarily decided that substantial evidence supported canceling Dalton's November score.

Upon registering for the November SAT, Dalton had signed a statement agreeing to the conditions in the New York state edition of the Registration Bulletin, which reserved to ETS "the right to cancel any test score . . . if ETS believes that there is reason to question the score's validity."

As specified in the Registration Bulletin, ETS apprised Dalton of its preliminary decision to cancel his November SAT score in a letter from Eppinger, a Test Security Specialist. Noting the handwriting disparity and substantial difference between his May and November test results, Eppinger informed Dalton that "the evidence suggests that someone else may have completed your answer sheet and that the questioned scores may be invalid." She advised him that he could supply "any additional information that will help explain" this, or, alternatively, elect one of the other options that were specified in the ETS Registration Bulletin.

Dalton opted to present additional information to the Board of Review, including the following: verification that he was suffering from mononucleosis during the May examination, diagnostic test results from a preparatory course he took prior to the November examination (he had taken no similar course prior to the May SAT) that were consistent with his performance on that test; a statement from an ETS proctor who remembered Dalton's presence during the November examination, and statements from two students—one previously unacquainted with Dalton—that he had been in the classroom during that test. Dalton further provided ETS with a report from a document examiner obtained by his family who concluded that Dalton was the author of both sets of answer sheets.

ETS, after several Board of Review meetings, submitted the various handwriting exemplars to a second document examiner who, like its first, opined that the May and November tests were not completed by the same individual. As a result, ETS continued to question the validity of Dalton's November score. Dalton's father then filed an action against ETS. The trial court found that ETS failed "to make even rudimentary efforts to evaluate or investigate the information" furnished by Dalton, and that it had breached its duty of good faith, thereby breaching its contract. As a remedy for the breach, the trial court ordered ETS to release the November SAT score. The Appellate Division affirmed this ruling, and ETS appealed. ∽

Kaye, Chief Judge By accepting ETS's standardized form agreement when he registered for the November SAT, Dalton entered into a contract with ETS. Implicit in all contracts is a covenant of good faith and fair dealing in the course of contract performance. Encompassed within the implied obligation of each promisor to exercise good faith are "any promises which a reasonable person in the position of the promisee would be justified in understanding were included." This embraces a pledge that neither party shall do anything which will have the effect of destroying or injuring the right of the other party to receive the fruits of the contract. Where the contract contemplates the exercise of discretion, this pledge includes a promise not to act arbitrarily or irrationally in exercising that discretion. The duty of good faith and fair dealing, however, is not without limits, and no obligation can be implied that would be inconsistent with other terms of the contractual relationship.

ETS was under no duty to initiate an external investigation into a questioned score. The contract, however, did require that ETS consider any relevant material that Dalton supplied to the Board of Review. The Registration Bulletin explicitly afforded Dalton the option to provide ETS with relevant information upon notification that ETS questioned the legitimacy of his test score. Having elected to offer this option, it was certainly reasonable to expect that ETS would, at the very least, consider any relevant material submitted in reaching its final decision. Dalton triggered this implied-in-law obligation on the part of ETS by exercising his contractual option to provide ETS with information.

Where ETS refuses to exercise its discretion by declining even to consider relevant material submitted by the test-taker, the legal question is whether this refusal breached an express or implied term of the contract. Here, the courts below agreed that ETS did not consider the relevant information furnished by Dalton. By doing so, ETS failed to comply in good faith with its own test security procedures, thereby breaching its contract with Dalton.

The court modified the remedy ordered at trial by requiring ETS to give good-faith consideration of Dalton's materials rather than requiring ETS to release the scores. Otherwise the court affirmed in favor of Dalton.

BREACH OF CONTRACT

When a person's performance is due, any failure to perform that is not excused is a breach of contract. Not all breaches of contract are of equal seriousness, however. Some are relatively minor deviations, whereas others are so extreme that they deprive the promisee of the essence of what he bargained for. The legal consequences of a given breach depend on the extent of the breach.

At a minimum, a party's breach of contract gives the nonbreaching party the right to sue and recover for any damages caused by that breach. When the breach is serious enough to be called a **material breach,** further legal consequences ensue.

Effect of Material Breach

A material breach occurs when the promisor's performance fails to reach the level of performance that the promisee is justified in expecting under the circumstances. In a situation in which the promisor's performance is judged by a substantial performance standard, saying that he failed to give substantial performance is the same thing as saying that he materially breached the contract. You will see an example of that principle in the following *M.J. Oldenstedt* case.

The party who is injured by a material breach has the right to withhold his own performance. He is discharged from further obligations under the contract and may cancel it. He also has the right to sue for damages for total breach of contract.

Effect of Nonmaterial Breach   By contrast, when the breach is not serious enough to be material, the

nonbreaching party may sue for only those damages caused by the particular breach. In addition, he does not have the right to cancel the contract, although a nonmaterial breach can give him the right to suspend his performance until the breach is remedied. Once the breach is remedied, however, the nonbreaching party must go ahead and render his performance, minus any damages caused by the breach.

Determining the Materiality of the Breach   The standard for determining materiality is a flexible one that takes into account the facts of each individual case. The key question is whether the breach deprives the injured party of the benefits that he reasonably expected. For example, Norman, who is running for mayor, orders campaign literature from Prompt Press, to be delivered in September. Prompt Press's failure to deliver the literature until after the election in November deprives Norman of the essence of what he bargained for and would be considered a material breach.

In determining materiality, courts take into account the extent to which the breaching party will suffer forfeiture if the breach is held to be material. They also consider the magnitude (amount) of the breach and the willfulness or good faith exercised by the breaching party. The timing of the breach can also be important. A breach that occurs early on in the parties' relationship is more likely to be viewed as material than is one that occurs after an extended period of performance. Courts also consider the extent to which the injured party can be adequately compensated by the payment of damages.

M.J. OLDENSTEDT PLUMBING CO., INC. v. K-MART CORP.   629 N.E.2d 214 (Ill. Ct. App. 1994)

uring the summer of 1991, K-Mart Corp. built a new K-Mart store in Bollingbrook, Illinois. Leopardo Construction acted as the general contractor during construction, and Oldenstedt was a subcontractor. In March 1991, Oldenstedt received drawings describing the site utilities and interior plumbing. Oldenstedt agreed to install the site utilities and interior plumbing for $709,500.

The written contract received by Oldenstedt set out the details of the job and Oldenstedt's responsibilities. It stated that Oldenstedt agreed to "supply adequate man power, material and equipment at all times to meet the project schedule" and "cooperate with the Contractor in scheduling and performing the work to avoid conflict, delay in or interference with the work of the Contractor, other subcontractors, or the owner's own forces."

The subcontract agreement called for Oldenstedt to begin the project on May 27, and it began the interior plumbing portion of the project on or about this date. According to Leopardo's work schedule, Oldenstedt's work was to be completed on July 18. Not long after Oldenstedt began work on the project, the project superintendent, Cusimano, became concerned that the plaintiff was working too slowly. He did not begin the site utilities work until June 13. Cusimano had numerous conversations with Oldenstedt at the job site concerning the pace of his work. On June 19, 27, and July 2, Cusimano sent letters to Oldenstedt telling him that he was in breach of the subcontract agreement by failing to work expeditiously and without delay, and that he would have to increase progress.

On July 17, it was clear that Oldenstedt would not finish his work by July 18 as required by the schedule. A meeting was held to establish a new schedule for the site utility work. The new schedule gave Oldenstedt until August 10 to complete his work. Cusimano testified that when he visited the site 10 days later on July 27, Oldenstedt was already 12 to 14 crew days behind schedule. (A crew day is the amount of work that can be accomplished by one crew in one day.) By the last week of July, Oldenstedt had at least two crews working the site each day. When Oldenstedt fell behind the new schedule, Cusimano contacted other plumbing contractors to supplement Oldenstedt's crew and then terminated Oldenstedt, delivering a letter to him that said that he had breached the contract and that the contract was therefore canceled. According to Leopardo, the new contractors had to do substantial remedial work to correct deficient work performed by Oldenstedt as well as complete the job. Oldenstedt filed a suit against Leopardo and others to foreclose a mechanic's lien, alleging breach of contract. Leopardo countersued, alleging breach of contract. The trial court entered judgment in favor of the defendants, and Oldenstedt appealed. ☜

Slater, Presiding Justice   The trial court determined that Oldenstedt breached the contract by failing to perform in a timely and workmanlike manner. The contract required Oldenstedt to comply with Leopardo's project time schedule, to supply adequate man power, material and equipment to meet the schedule, and to cooperate with Leopardo in scheduling and performing the work to avoid delay. Leopardo presented evidence that Oldenstedt failed to meet these requirements. When he was first asked to bring out additional crews, he refused. He then failed to complete his work by July 18 as required by the schedule. Oldenstedt testified that he knew nothing about the time schedule until the middle of June. However, Cusimano testified that Oldenstedt knew about the time schedule from the beginning of the project. Oldenstedt also claimed that the schedule was unreasonable. However, his replacement testified that he could have completed the job in six weeks, the amount of time given Oldenstedt under the original schedule. Finally, Oldenstedt testified that his work was slow in the beginning because he had to wait until K-Mart made a decision about pipe size. However, Cusimano testified that there were other parts of the project

Oldenstedt could have worked on while he waited for that information. When the testimony of witnesses is conflicting, it is within the exclusive province of the trial court, as the trier of fact, to determine the witnesses' credibility and the weight to be given their testimony. The evidence also showed that the parties drafted a revised schedule which extended Oldenstedt's time to perform. Oldenstedt quickly fell behind this schedule as well. Oldenstedt's failure to keep up forced Cusimano to reschedule the work of other trades and jeopardized the completion of the project.

Oldenstedt argues that even if he did breach the contract, it was not a material breach because he was only four days behind schedule when he was terminated on July 29. He reaches this conclusion by arguing that although he was 12 crew days behind schedule, he had three crews working at the site at the time he was terminated. Therefore he could have made up the 12 crew days in only four days. Oldenstedt's claim that he had three crews at the site was disputed by defense witnesses. Moreover, even if he was only four days behind the July 17 schedule, he fell that far behind after only 10 days, and this was the second schedule Oldenstedt failed to maintain. In light of all of the evidence regarding the slow pace of Oldenstedt's work, we find that the trial court's determination that he materially breached the contract was not against the manifest weight of the evidence.

Oldenstedt next contends that the trial court erred in calculating damages. He first argues that he is entitled to the contract price because his work constituted substantial performance of the contract. While it is true that a contract which is substantially performed in a workmanlike manner generally entitled the builder to the contract price, the trial court in this case found that Oldenstedt failed to substantially perform under the terms of the contract. In light of our finding that Oldenstedt materially breached the contract, we agree with the trial court

that Oldenstedt failed to render substantial performance. A builder who fails to substantially perform a contract is not entitled to the contract price. Rather, the builder's right is under a theory of *quantum meruit,* a right to recover only reasonable compensation for value received by the purchaser over and above the injury suffered by the builder's breach. The trial court judge found that the reasonable value of the work and services performed by Oldenstedt was $471,571. The trial court was concerned with determining what Oldenstedt's work was worth, not what it cost. We find that the trial court's determination was well within the range of the evidence.

Affirmed in favor of the defendants.

Time for Performance   A party's failure to perform on time is a breach of contract that may be serious enough to constitute a material breach, or it may be relatively trivial under the circumstances.

At the outset, it is necessary to determine when performance is due. Some contracts specifically state the time for performance, which makes it easy to determine the time for performance. In some contracts that do not specifically state the time for performance, such a time can be inferred from the circumstances surrounding the contract. In the Norman and Prompt Press campaign literature example, the circumstances surrounding the contract probably would have implied that the time for performance was some time before the election, even if the parties had not specified the time for performance. In still other contracts, no time for performance is either stated or implied. When no time for performance is stated or implied, performance must be completed within a "reasonable time," as judged by the circumstances of each case.

Consequences of Late Performance   After a court determines when performance was due, it must determine the consequences of late performance. In some contracts, the parties expressly state that "time is of the essence" or that timely performance is "vital." This means that each party's timely performance by a specific date is an express condition of the other party's duty to perform. Thus, in a contract that contains a time is of the essence

provision, any delay by either party normally constitutes a material breach. Sometimes, courts will imply such a term even when the language of the contract does not state that time is of the essence. A court would be likely to do this if late performance is of little or no value to the promisee. For example, Schrader contracts with the local newspaper to run an advertisement for Christmas trees from December 15, 1994, to December 24, 1994, but the newspaper does not run the ad until December 26, 1994. In this case, the time for performance is an essential part of the contract and the newspaper has committed a material breach.

When a contract does not contain language indicating that time is of the essence and a court determines that the time for performance is not a particularly important part of the contract, the promisee must accept late performance rendered within a reasonable time after performance was due. The promisee is then entitled to deduct or set off from the contract price any losses caused by the delay. Late performance is not a material breach in such cases unless it is unreasonably late.

Anticipatory Repudiation   One type of breach of contract occurs when the promisor indicates before the time for his performance that he is unwilling or unable to carry out the contract. This is called **anticipatory repudiation** or **anticipatory breach.** Anticipatory breach generally constitutes a material breach of contract that discharges the promisee from all further obligation under the contract.

CONCEPT REVIEW

Time for Performance

CONTRACT LANGUAGE	TIME FOR PERFORMANCE	CONSEQUENCES OF LATE PERFORMANCE
"Time is of the essence" or similar language	The time stated in the contract	Material breach
Specific time is stated in or implied by the contract and late performance would have little or no value	The time stated in or implied by the contract	Material breach
Specific time is stated in or implied by the contract, but the time for performance is a relatively unimportant part of the contract	The time stated in or implied by the contract	Not a material breach unless performance is unreasonably late
No time for performance is stated in or implied by the contract	Within a reasonable time	Not material breach unless performance is unreasonably late

In determining what constitutes anticipatory repudiation, courts look for some unequivocal statement or voluntary act that clearly indicates that the promisor cannot or will not perform his duties under the contract. This may take the form of an express statement by the promisor. The promisor's intent not to perform could also be implied from actions of the promisor such as selling to a third party the property that the promisor was obligated to sell to the promisee. For example, if Ross, who is obligated to convey real estate to Davis, conveys the property to some third person instead, Ross has repudiated the contract.

When anticipatory repudiation occurs, the promisee is faced with several choices. For example, Marsh and Davis enter a contract in which Davis agrees to deliver a quantity of bricks to Marsh on September 1, 1994, and Marsh agrees to pay Davis a sum of money in two installments. The agreement specifies that Marsh will pay 50 percent of the purchase price on July 15, 1994, and 50 percent of the purchase price within 30 days after delivery. On July 1, 1994, Davis writes Marsh and unequivocally states that he will not deliver the bricks. Must Marsh go ahead and send the payment that is due on July 15? Must he wait until September 1 to bring suit for total breach of contract? The answer to both questions is no.

When anticipatory repudiation occurs, the non-breaching party is justified in withholding his own performance and suing for damages right away,

without waiting for the time for performance to arrive.[3] If he can show that he was ready, willing, and able to perform his part of the contract, he can recover damages for total breach of the contract. The nonbreaching party is not obligated to do this, however. If he chooses, he may wait until the time for performance in case the other party changes his mind and decides to perform.

Recovery by a Party Who Has Committed Material Breach

A party who has materially breached the contract (that is, has not substantially performed) does not have the right to recover the contract price. If a promisor who has given some performance to the promisee cannot recover under the contract, however, the promisor will face forfeiture and the promisee will have obtained an unearned gain. There are two possible avenues for a party who has committed material breach to obtain some compensation for the performance he has conferred on the nonbreaching party.

1. *Quasi-contract.* A party who has materially breached a contract might recover the reasonable

---

[3]Uniform Commercial Code rules regarding anticipatory repudiation in contracts for the sale of goods are discussed in Chapter 21.

value of any benefits he has conferred on the promisee by bringing an action under quasi-contract.[4] This would enable him to obtain compensation for the value of any performance he has given that has benefited the nonbreaching party. Some courts take the position that a person in material breach should not be able to recover for benefits he has conferred, however.

2. *Partial performance of a divisible contract.* Some contracts are divisible; that is, each party's performance can be divided in two or more parts and each part is exchanged for some corresponding consideration from the other party. For example, if Johnson agrees to mow Peterson's lawn for $20 and clean Peterson's gutters for $50, the contract is divisible. When a promisor performs one part of the contract but materially breaches another part, he can recover at the contract price for the part that he did perform. For example, if Johnson breached his duty to clean the gutters but fully performed his obligation to mow the lawn, he could recover at the contract price for the lawn-mowing part of the contract.

EXCUSES FOR NONPERFORMANCE

Although nonperformance of a duty that has become due will ordinarily constitute a breach of contract, there are some situations in which nonperformance is excused because of factors that arise after the formation of the contract. When this occurs, the person whose performance is made impossible or impracticable by these factors is discharged from further obligation under the contract. The following discussion concerns the most common grounds for excuse of nonperformance.

Impossibility

When performance of a contractual duty becomes impossible after the formation of the contract, the duty will be discharged on grounds of **impossibility**. This does not mean that a person can be discharged

merely because he has contracted to do something that he is simply unable to do or that causes him hardship or difficulty. Impossibility in the legal sense of the word means "it cannot be done by anyone" rather than "I cannot do it." Thus, promisors who find that they have agreed to perform duties that are beyond their capabilities or that turn out to be unprofitable or burdensome are generally not excused from performance of their duties. Impossibility will provide an excuse for nonperformance, however, when some unexpected event arises after the formation of the contract and renders performance objectively impossible. The event that causes the impossibility need not have been entirely unforeseeable. Normally, however, the event will be one that the parties would not have reasonably thought of as a real possibility that would affect performance.

There are a variety of situations in which a person's duty to perform may be discharged on grounds of impossibility. The three most common situations involve illness or death of the promisor, supervening illegality, and destruction of the subject matter of the contract.

Illness or Death of Promisor   Incapacitating illness or death of the promisor excuses nonperformance when the promisor has contracted to perform personal services. For example, if Pauling, a college professor who has a contract with State University to teach for an academic year, dies before the completion of the contract, her estate will not be liable for breach of contract. The promisor's death or illness does not, however, excuse the nonperformance of duties that can be delegated to another, such as the duty to deliver goods, pay money, or convey real estate. For example, if Odell had contracted to convey real estate to Ruskin and died before the closing date, Ruskin could enforce the contract against Odell's estate.

Supervening Illegality   If a statute or governmental regulation enacted after the creation of a contract makes performance of a party's duties illegal, the promisor is excused from performing. Statutes or regulations that merely make performance more difficult or less profitable do not, however, excuse nonperformance. You will see an example of this form of impossibility in the following case, *Centex Corporation v. Dalton.*

---

[4]Quasi-contract is discussed in Chapter 9. It involves the use of the remedy of restitution, which is discussed later in this chapter.

CENTEX CORPORATION v. DALTON 840 S. W. 2d 952 (Sup. Ct. Tex. 1992)

entex is a company engaged in residential and commercial construction and related financial services. John Dalton was an executive of a Texas thrift institution. In 1988, because the flagging Texas economy adversely affected the state's thrift institutions, the Federal Home Loan Bank Board (Bank Board) and other regulatory agencies decided to close, merge, liquidate, or sell several large thrift institutions. This plan was called the "Southwest Plan." In November 1988, Centex contacted Dalton to request that he help Centex acquire certain thrifts made available through the Southwest Plan. A few weeks later, Dalton traveled to Washington, D.C., where he made an unsuccessful bid to acquire a group of thrifts for Centex. While there, Dalton learned about the availability of four central Texas thrifts known as the "Lamb Package." Dalton informed Centex about this, and in December 1988, Centex entered into a letter agreement with Dalton in which it promised to pay Dalton $750,000 over a three-year period if Centex were successful in acquiring the Lamb Package. Before the parties signed this agreement, Centex met with the Bank Board and told it of its intention to pay fees to Dalton on completion of the purchase of the Lamb Package. The Bank Board told Centex that this would be acceptable as long as Centex—rather than any of the thrift institutions in the Lamb Package or any entity formed to acquire the Lamb Package—made the payment to Dalton. Arrangements were made to acquire the Lamb Package, but on December 28, 1988, the night before Centex's acquisition of the Lamb Package was to be finalized, Centex's representative learned that the Bank Board probably would not permit payment of the fees to Dalton. Centex nevertheless went ahead and finalized the purchase of the Lamb Package, forming a wholly owned subsidiary, Texas Trust Savings Bank, as the acquiring entity. At a meeting on December 28, 1988, the Bank Board approved the acquisition of the Lamb Package, conditioned on a prohibition against Texas Trust's direct or indirect payment of finder's fees. The transcript of the meeting shows that members of the Bank Board discussed Texas Trust's planned payment of fees to Dalton, made specific objection to the payment, and requested its general counsel to prepare an amendment to clarify that its prohibition against the payment of fees extended to affiliates of Texas Trust. On January 31, 1989, the Bank Board adopted the amendment proposed by its counsel.

Dalton performed the services required of him under the letter agreement, but Centex did not pay him because of the prohibition imposed by the Bank Board. Dalton brought suit against Centex for breach of contract. The trial court granted a summary judgment in favor of Dalton, awarding him $750,000 in damages plus interest, costs, and attorney's fees. Centex appealed, and the court of appeals affirmed the summary judgment. Centex appealed to the Texas Supreme Court. (In August 1989, while the case was on appeal, a federal statute called the Financial Institutions Reform Recovery and Enforcement Act became effective. This statute abolished the Bank Board, created the Office of Thrift Supervision (OTS), and gave OTS the powers formerly vested in the Bank Board. On December 11, 1990, OTS issued a cease-and-desist order to prevent Centex or Texas Trust from paying any fees to Dalton under the letter agreement.) ∞

Gammage, Justice Centex argues that, because its performance under the letter agreement has been made impracticable by having to comply with the Bank Board's order, its duty to render that performance is discharged. Congress gave the Bank Board power to regulate the acquisition and control of federally insured thrifts by savings and loan holding companies. As a result, the Bank Board's prohibition makes it illegal for Centex to perform under the letter agreement. "Where a party's performance is made impracticable by the occurrence of an event the non-occurrence of which was a basic assumption on which the contract was made, his duty to render that performance is discharged." *Restatement (Second) of Contracts* section 261 (1981). A governmental regulation or order that makes impracticable the performance of a duty "is an event the non-occurrence of which was made a basic assumption on which the contract was made." Consequently, to avoid inconsistency with the Bank Board's prohibition and conflict with federal regulatory law, we must hold that Centex is excused from performance by the doctrine of impossibility.

When courts are asked to excuse a party's performance due to supervening circumstances which made performance impracticable or impossible, they sometimes attempt to allocate the burden of risk and decide who must pay for the unanticipated occurrence. Foreseeability is one factor used to decide which party assumed the risk of supervening impossibility. The foreseeability factor has, however, gradually decreased in importance. Here, one party, Centex, cannot be required to pay, regardless of the foreseeability of the Bank Board's prohibition.

The court of appeals reasoned that the Bank Board's prohibition applied only to Texas Trust and not to Centex. We note, however, that the prohibition forbids not only the direct payment of finder's fees by Centex, which is an affiliate of Texas Trust, but also the indirect payments of such fees. We also note the court of appeals reasoned that, because the obligation of Centex to pay Dalton arose when the letter agreement was signed on December 23, 1988, before the Bank Board's adoption of its prohibition on December 29, 1988, the prohibition did not apply

to the letter agreement. The court of appeals' reasoning was incorrect because the letter agreement is premised on a condition precedent. By the terms of the letter agreement, Dalton's right to enforce it could not accrue until the Bank Board approved the acquisition. Because the Bank Board, in approving the acquisition, prohibited the payment of the finder's fees, thereby invalidating the letter agreement, Dalton's right to enforce the letter agreement never accrued.

The Bank Board's order prohibits Centex's performance under the letter agreement, which otherwise would be enforceable under state contract law. Centex cannot pay Dalton and obey the governmental regulation, which has prohibited the proposed payment. Centex's duty to perform under the letter agreement is excused.

Reversed in favor of Centex.

Destruction of the Subject Matter of the Contract   If something that is essential to the promisor's performance is destroyed after the formation of the contract through no fault of the promisor, the promisor is excused from performing. For example, Woolridge contracts to sell his car to Rivkin. If an explosion destroys the car after the contract has been formed but before Woolridge has made delivery, Woolridge's nonperformance will be excused. The destruction of nonessential items that the promisor intended to use in performing does not excuse nonperformance if substitutes are available, even though securing them makes performance more difficult or less profitable. Suppose that Ace Construction Company had planned to use a particular piece of machinery in fulfilling a contract to build a building for Worldwide Widgets Company. If the piece of machinery is destroyed but substitutes are available, destruction of the machinery before the contract is performed would *not* give Ace an excuse for failing to perform.

Frustration of Venture

Closely associated with impossibility is the doctrine of **frustration of venture** (also known as **commercial frustration** or **frustration of purpose**). This doctrine provides an excuse for nonperformance

when events that occur after the formation of the contract would deprive the promisor of the benefit of return performance. Although courts often include frustration cases within the general terminology of impossibility, frustration can be distinguished from impossibility and impracticability by the fact that the promisor in a frustration case is not necessarily prevented from performing. Rather, in frustration cases, the promisor is excused because the return performance by the other party has become worthless to him. For example, Boyd signs a contract for a one-year membership in an Eden Exercise Salon, for which he agrees to pay $50 per month. One week after signing the contract, Boyd is involved in a serious automobile accident and suffers injuries that cause him to be bedridden for a year. In such a case, the automobile accident and Boyd's resulting injuries did not prevent him from performing his duties under the contract (paying money each month), but this unexpected event does deprive Boyd of the benefit of receiving Eden's return performance. In such a case, a court might excuse Boyd's performance on the ground of frustration of venture.

Commercial Impracticability

Section 2–615 of the Uniform Commercial Code has extended the scope of the common law doctrine of impossibility to cases in which unforeseen developments make performance by the promisor highly impracticable, unreasonably expensive, or of little value to the promisee. Rather than using a standard of impossibility, then, the Code uses the more relaxed standard of **impracticability.** Despite the less stringent standard applied, cases actually excusing nonperformance on grounds of impracticability are relatively rare. To be successful in claiming excuse based on impracticability, a promisor must be able to establish that the event that makes performance impracticable occurred without his fault and that the contract was made with the basic assumption that this event would not occur. This basically means that the event was beyond the scope of the risks that the parties contemplated at the time of contracting and that the promisor did not expressly or impliedly assume the risk that the event would occur.

Case law and official comments to UCC section 2–615 indicate that neither increased cost nor collapse of a market for particular goods is sufficient to excuse nonperformance, because those are the types of business risks that every promisor assumes. However, drastic price increases or severe shortages of goods resulting from unforeseen circumstances such as wars and crop failures can give rise to impracticability.

If the event causing impracticability affects only a part of the seller's capacity to perform, the seller must allocate production and deliveries among customers in a "fair and reasonable" manner and must notify them of any delay or any limited allocation of the goods. You can read more about commercial impracticability in Chapter 21, Performance of Sales Contracts.

OTHER GROUNDS FOR DISCHARGE

Earlier in this chapter, you learned about several situations in which a party's duty to perform could be discharged even though that party had not himself performed. These include the nonoccurrence of a condition precedent or concurrent condition, the occurrence of a condition subsequent, material breach by the other party, and excuse from performance by impossibility, impracticability, or frustration. The following discussion deals with additional ways in which a discharge can occur.

Discharge by Mutual Agreement

Just as contracts are created by mutual agreement, they can also be discharged by *mutual agreement.* An agreement to discharge a contract must be supported by consideration to be enforceable.

Discharge by Accord and Satisfaction

An **accord** is an agreement whereby a promisee who has an existing claim agrees with the promisor that he will accept some performance different from that which was originally agreed on. When the promisor performs the accord, that is called a **satisfaction.**[5] When an accord and satisfaction occurs, the parties are discharged. For example, Root contracts with May to build a garage on May's property for $30,000. After Root has performed his part of the bargain, the parties then agree that instead of paying money, May will transfer a one-year-old Porsche to Root instead. When this is done, both parties are discharged.

Discharge by Waiver

A party to a contract may voluntarily relinquish any right he has under a contract, including the right to receive return performance. Such a relinquishment of rights is known as a **waiver.** If one party tenders an incomplete or defective performance and the other party accepts that performance without objection, knowing that the defects will not be remedied, the party to whom performance was due will have discharged the other party from his duty of performance. For example, a real estate lease requires Long, the tenant, to pay a $5 late charge for late payments of rent. Long pays his rent late each month for five months, but the landlord accepts it without objection and without assessing the late charge. In this situation, the landlord has probably waived his right to collect the late charge.

To avoid waiving rights, a person who has received defective performance should give the other party prompt notice that she expects complete performance and will seek damages if the defects are not corrected.

---

[5]Accord and satisfaction is also discussed in Chapter 12.

Discharge by Alteration

If the contract is represented by a *written* instrument, and one of the parties intentionally makes a material alteration in the instrument without the other's consent, the alteration acts as a discharge of the other party. If the other party consents to the alteration or does not object to it when he learns of it, he is not discharged. Alteration by a third party without the knowledge or consent of the contracting parties does not affect the parties' rights.

Discharge by Statute of Limitations

Courts have long refused to grant a remedy to a person who delays bringing a lawsuit for an unreasonable time. All of the states have enacted statutes known as **statutes of limitation,** which specify the period of time in which a person can bring a lawsuit.

The time period for bringing a contract action varies from state to state, and many states prescribe time periods for cases concerning oral contracts that are different from those for cases concerning written contracts. Section 2–725 of the Uniform Commercial Code provides for a four-year statute of limitations for contracts involving the sale of goods.

The statutory period ordinarily begins to run from the date of the breach. It may be delayed if the party who has the right to sue is under some incapacity at that time (such as minority or insanity) or is beyond the jurisdiction of the state. A person who has breached a contractual duty is discharged from liability for breach if no lawsuit is brought before the statutory period elapses.

Discharge by Decree of Bankruptcy

The contractual obligations of a debtor are generally discharged by a decree of bankruptcy. Bankruptcy is discussed in Chapter 29.

REMEDIES FOR BREACH OF CONTRACT

Our discussion of the performance stage of contracts so far has focused on the circumstances under which a party has the duty to perform or is excused from performing. In situations in which a person is injured by a breach of contract and is unable to obtain compensation by a settlement out of court, a further important issue remains: What remedy will a court fashion to compensate for breach of contract?

Contract law seeks to encourage people to rely on the promises made to them by others. Contract remedies focus on the economic loss caused by breach of contract, not on the moral obligation to perform a promise. The objective of granting a remedy in a case of breach of contract is simply to compensate the injured party.

Types of Contract Remedies

There are a variety of ways in which this can be done. The basic categories of contract remedies include:

1. Legal remedies (money damages).
2. Equitable remedies.
3. Restitution.

The usual remedy is an award of money damages that will compensate the injured party for his losses. This is called a **legal remedy** or **remedy at law,** because the imposition of money damages in our legal system originated in courts of law. Less frequently used but still important are **equitable remedies** such as specific performance. Equitable remedies are those remedies that had their origins in courts of equity rather than in courts of law.[6] Today, they are available at the discretion of the judge. A final possible remedy is **restitution,** which requires the defendant to pay the value of the benefits that the plaintiff has conferred on him.

Interests Protected by Contract Remedies

Remedies for breach of contract protect one or more of the following interests that a promisee may have:[7]

1. *Expectation interest.* A promisee's **expectation interest** is his interest in obtaining the objective or opportunity for gain that he bargained for and "expected." Courts attempt to protect this interest

---

[6]The nature of equitable remedies is also discussed in Chapter 1.

[7]*Restatement (Second) of Contracts* § 344.

by formulating a remedy that will place the promisee in the position he would have been in if the contract had been performed as promised.

2. *Reliance interest.* A promisee's **reliance interest** is his interest in being compensated for losses that he has suffered by changing his position in reliance on the other party's promise. In some cases, such as when a promisee is unable to prove his expectation interest with reasonable certainty, the promisee may seek a remedy to compensate for the loss suffered as a result of relying on the promisor's promise rather than for the expectation of profit.

3. *Restitution interest.* A **restitution interest** is a party's interest in recovering the amount by which he has enriched or benefited the other. Both the reliance and restitution interests involve promisees who have changed their position. The difference between the two is that the reliance interest involves a loss to the promisee that does not benefit the promisor, whereas the restitution interest involves a loss to the promisee that does constitute an unjust enrichment to the promisor. A remedy based on restitution enables a party who has performed or partially performed her contract and has benefited the other party to obtain compensation for the value of the benefits that she has conferred.

LEGAL REMEDIES (DAMAGES)

Limitations on Recovery of Damages in Contract Cases

An injured party's ability to recover damages in a contract action is limited by three principles:

1. *A party can recover damages only for those losses that he can prove with reasonable certainty.* Losses that are purely speculative are not recoverable. Thus, if Jones Publishing Company breaches a contract to publish Powell's memoirs, Powell may not be able to recover damages for lost royalties (her expectation interest), since she may be unable to establish, beyond speculation, how much money she would have earned in royalties if the book had been published. (Note, however, that Powell's reliance interest might be protected here; she could be allowed to recover provable losses incurred in reliance on the contract.)

2. *A breaching party is responsible for paying only those losses that were foreseeable to him at the time*

of contracting. A loss is foreseeable if it would ordinarily be expected to result from a breach or if the breaching party had reason to know of particular circumstances that would make the loss likely. For example, if Prince Manufacturing Company renders late performance in a contract to deliver parts to Cheatum Motors without knowing that Cheatum is shut down waiting for the parts, Prince will not have to pay the business losses that result from Cheatum's having to close its operation.

3. *Plaintiffs injured by a breach of contract have the duty to mitigate (avoid or minimize) damages.* A party cannot recover for losses that he could have avoided without undue risk, burden, or humiliation. For example, an employee who has been wrongfully fired would be entitled to damages equal to his wages for the remainder of the employment period. The employee, however, has the duty to minimize the damages by making reasonable efforts to seek a similar job elsewhere.

Compensatory Damages

Subject to the limitations discussed above, a person who has been injured by a breach of contract is entitled to recover **compensatory damages.** In calculating the compensatory remedy, a court will attempt to protect the expectation interest of the injured party by giving him the "benefit of his bargain" (placing him in the position he would have been in *had the contract been performed as promised*). To do this, the court must compensate the injured person for the provable losses he has suffered as well as for the provable gains that he has been prevented from realizing by the breach of contract. Normally, compensatory damages include one or more of three possible items: loss in value, any allowable consequential damages, and any allowable incidental damages.

1. *Loss in value.* The starting point in calculating compensatory damages is to determine the **loss in value** of the performance that the plaintiff had the right to expect. This is a way of measuring the expectation interest. The calculation of the loss in value experienced by an injured party differs according to the sort of contract involved and the circumstances of the breach. In contracts involving nonperformance of the sale of real estate, for example, courts normally measure loss in value by the difference between the contract price and the market price of the property. Thus, if Willis repudiates a contract with Renfrew whereby Renfrew was to purchase land worth $20,000 from Willis for $10,000, Renfrew's loss in value was $10,000. Where a seller has failed to perform a contract for the sale of goods, courts may measure loss in value by the difference between the contract price and the price that the buyer had to pay to procure substitute goods.[8] In cases in which a party breaches by rendering defective performance—say, by breaching a warranty in the sale of goods—the loss in value would be measured by the difference between the value of the goods if they had been in the condition warranted by the seller and the value of the goods in their defective condition.[9]

2. *Consequential damages.* **Consequential damages** (also called **special damages**) compensate for losses that occur as a consequence of the breach of contract. Consequential losses occur because of some special or unusual circumstances of the particular contractual relationship of the parties. For example, Apex Trucking Company buys a computer system from ABC Computers. The system fails to operate properly, and Apex is forced to pay its employees to perform the tasks manually, spending $10,000 in overtime pay. In this situation, Apex might seek to recover the $10,000 in overtime pay in addition to the loss of value that it has experienced.

Lost profits flowing from a breach of contract can be recovered as consequential damages if they are foreseeable and can be proven with reasonable certainty. It is important to remember, however, that the recovery of consequential damages is subject to the limitations on damage recovery discussed earlier.

3. *Incidental damages.* **Incidental damages** compensate for reasonable costs that the injured party incurs after the breach in an effort to avoid further loss. For example, if Smith Construction Company breaches an employment contract with Brice, Brice could recover as incidental damages those reasonable expenses he must incur in attempting to pro-cure substitute employment, such as long-distance telephone tolls or the cost of printing new résumés.

Alternative Measures of Damages   The foregoing discussion has focused on the most common formulation of damage remedies in contracts cases. The normal measure of compensatory damages is not appropriate in every case, however. When it is not appropriate, a court may use an alternative measure of damages. For example, where a party has suffered losses by performing or preparing to perform, he might seek damages based on his *reliance interest* instead of his expectation interest. In such a case, he would be compensated for the provable losses he suffered by relying on the other party's promise. This measure of damages is often used in cases in which a promise is enforceable under promissory estoppel.[10]

Nominal Damages

Nominal damages are very small damage awards that are given when a technical breach of contract has occurred without causing any actual or provable economic loss. The sums awarded as nominal damages typically vary from 2 cents to a dollar.

Liquidated Damages

The parties to a contract may expressly provide in their contract that a specific sum shall be recoverable if the contract is breached. Such provisions are called **liquidated damages** provisions. For example, Murchison rents space in a shopping mall in which she plans to operate a retail clothing store. She must make improvements in the space before opening the store, and it is very important to her to have the store opened for the Christmas shopping season. She hires Ace Construction Company to construct the improvements. The parties agree to include in the contract a liquidated damages provision stating that, if Ace is late in completing the construction, Murchison will be able to recover a specified sum for each day of delay. Such a provision is highly desirable from Murchison's point of view because, without a liquidated damages provision, she would have a difficult time in establishing

---

[8]Remedies under Article 2 of the Uniform Commercial Code are discussed in detail in Chapter 22.

[9]See Chapter 20 for further discussion of the damages for breach of warranty in the sale of goods.

[10]Promissory estoppel is discussed in Chapters 9 and 12.

the precise losses that would result from delay. Courts scrutinize these agreed-on damages carefully, however.

If the amount specified in a liquidated damages provision is reasonable and if the nature of the contract is such that actual damages would be difficult to determine, a court will enforce the provision. When liquidated damages provisions are enforced, the amount of damages agreed on will be the injured party's exclusive damage remedy. If the amount specified is unreasonably great in relation to the probable loss or injury, however, or if the amount of damages could be readily determined in the event of breach, the courts will declare the provision to be a penalty and will refuse to enforce it. The issue of reasonableness of liquidated damages is presented in the *Luminous Neon, Inc. v. Parscale* case, which follows.

LUMINOUS NEON, INC. v. PARSCALE   836 P.2d 1201 (Ct. App. Kan. 1992)

Rita Parscale, the owner of a restaurant, entered into negotiations to acquire outdoor advertising signs for her business from Luminous Neon. At the outset of the negotiations, Luminous Neon had offered to sell the signs to Parscale for $5,600 plus tax, but Parscale ultimately leased them. Under the terms of the lease, Parscale paid a rental of $191.75 plus tax per month for a term of five years. The lease also contained a liquidated damages clause that required Parscale, in the event of breach, to pay damages equal to 80 percent of the remaining payments due. That 80 percent represented Luminous Neon's expenses incurred in manufacturing, financing, and installing the signs, as well as profit. The 20 percent of the remaining payments that was not included as liquidated damages was for maintenance and service expenses that would not be incurred due to Parscale's breach.

Sometime after Parscale leased the signs, the City of Topeka began construction on a street that limited access to Parscale's business. That construction had an adverse effect on Parscale's business, and it ultimately closed. Parscale stopped making payments on the signs after making a total of 19 payments. Forty-one monthly payments of $191.75 remained due and payable, resulting in liquidated damages, including tax, of $6,651.04. Luminous Neon removed the signs from Parscale's business at her request. The removal added another $300 to the damages. Luminous Neon ultimately sued Parscale to collect this money. The trial court granted Luminous Neon's motion for summary judgment and awarded it $6,951.04. Parscale appealed. ∞

Bullock, Judge   Parscale contends the court erred in granting summary judgment because a material fact existed relating to the liquidated damages claim of Luminous Neon. She argues that Luminous Neon's offer to sell the signs for $5,600 plus tax reveals that the liquidated damages were unreasonable. The contention that only the original sale price of the signs constitutes reasonable damages is not persuasive. There are advantages to be weighed when one considers leasing rather than purchasing an item. However, when one chooses to lease an item and then breaches that lease, it is unreasonable to believe damages should be based upon values attendant to a purchase of that item. By leasing rather than purchasing, Parscale avoided financing charges, insurance, repair, and maintenance expenses. Luminous Neon agreed to maintain the signs during the term of the lease.

The general rule is that courts will "refuse to enforce a liquidated damage provision which fixes damages in an amount grossly disproportionate to the harm actually sustained or likely to be sustained, and under certain circumstances indicative of gross proportion," such a provision will be deemed a penalty. 22 *Am. Jur. 2d, Damages* section 701, p. 758.

Luminous Neon custom designed the signs specifically for Parscale, and, notwithstanding her argument to the contrary, we are not persuaded that the signs are of particular value to Luminous Neon. Moreover, the trial court awarded the signs to Parscale. The damage clause of the lease was not a penalty, and the award did not unjustly enrich Luminous Neon.

Judgment affirmed in favor of Luminous Neon.

Punitive Damages

Punitive damages are damages awarded in addition to the compensatory remedy that are designed to punish a defendant for particularly reprehensible behavior and to deter the defendant and others from committing similar behavior in the future. The traditional rule is that punitive damages are not recoverable in contracts cases unless a specific statutory provision (such as some consumer protection statutes) allows them or the defendant has committed *fraud* or some other independent tort. A few states will permit the use of punitive damages in contracts cases in which the defendant's conduct, though not technically a tort, was malicious, oppressive, or tortious in nature.

Punitive damages have also been awarded in many of the cases involving breach of the implied covenant of good faith. In such cases, courts usually circumvent the traditional rule against awarding punitive damages in contracts cases by holding that breach of the duty of good faith is an independent tort. The availability of punitive damages in such cases operates to deter a contracting party from deliberately disregarding the other party's rights. Insurance companies have been the most frequent target for punitive damages awards in bad faith cases, but employers and banks have also been subjected to punitive damages verdicts.

EQUITABLE REMEDIES

In exceptional cases in which money damages alone are not adequate to fully compensate for a party's injuries, a court may grant an **equitable remedy** either alone or in combination with a legal remedy. Equitable relief is subject to several limitations, however, and will be granted only when justice is served by doing so. The primary equitable remedies for breach of contract are specific performance and injunction.[11]

Specific Performance

Specific performance is an equitable remedy whereby the court orders the breaching party to perform his contractual duties as promised. For example, if Barnes breached a contract to sell a tract of land to Metzger and a court granted specific performance of the contract, the court would require Barnes to deed the land to Metzger. (Metzger, of course, must pay the purchase price.) This remedy can be advantageous to the injured party because he is not faced with the complexities of proving damages, he does not have to worry about whether he can actually collect the damages, and he gets exactly what he bargained for. However, the availability of this remedy is subject to the limitations discussed below.

The Availability of Specific Performance   Specific performance, like other equitable remedies, is available only when the injured party has no adequate remedy at law—in other words, when money damages do not adequately compensate the injured party. This generally requires a showing that the subject of the contract is unique or at least that no substitutes are available. Even if this requirement is met, a court will withhold specific performance if the injured party has acted in bad faith, if he unreasonably delayed in asserting his rights, or if specific performance would require an excessive amount of supervision by the court.

Contracts for the sale of real estate are the most common subjects of specific performance decrees because every tract of real estate is considered to be unique. Specific performance is rarely granted for breach of a contract for the sale of goods because the injured party can usually procure substitute goods. However, there are situations involving sales of goods contracts in which specific performance is given. These cases involve goods that are unique or goods for which no substitute can be found. Examples include antiques, heirlooms, works of art, and objects of purely sentimental value.[12] Specific performance is not available for the breach of a promise to perform a personal service (such as a contract for employment, artistic performance, or consulting services). A decree requiring a person to specifically perform a personal-services contract would probably be ineffective in giving the injured party what he bargained for. It would also require a great deal of supervision by the court. In addition,

---

[11]Another equitable remedy, *reformation,* allows a court to reform or "rewrite" a written contract when the parties have made an error in expressing their agreement. Reformation is discussed, along with the doctrine of mistake, in Chapter 13.

[12]Specific performance under § 2–716(1) of the UCC is discussed in Chapter 22.

an application of specific performance in such cases would amount to a form of involuntary servitude.

Injunction

Injunction is an equitable remedy that is employed in many different contexts and is sometimes used as a remedy for breach of contract. An **injunction** is a court order requiring a person to do something (**mandatory injunction**) or ordering a person to refrain from doing something (**negative injunction**). Unlike legal remedies that apply only when the breach has already occurred, the equitable remedy of injunction can be invoked when a breach has merely been *threatened.* Injunctions are available only when the breach or threatened breach is likely to cause *irreparable injury.*

In the contract context, specific performance is a form of mandatory injunction. Negative injunctions are appropriately used in several situations, such as contract cases in which a party whose duty under the contract is forbearance threatens to breach the contract. For example, Norris sells his restaurant in Gas City, Indiana, to Ford. A term of the contract of sale provides that Norris agrees not to own, operate, or be employed in any restaurant within 30 miles of Gas City for a period of two years after the sale.[13] If Norris threatens to open a new restaurant in Gas City several months after the sale is consummated, a court could *enjoin* Norris from opening the new restaurant.

RESTITUTION

Restitution is a remedy that can be obtained either at law or in equity. Restitution applies when one party's performance or reliance has conferred a benefit on the other. A party's restitution interest is protected by compensating him for the value of benefits he has conferred on the other person.[14] This can be done through **specific restitution,** in which the defendant is required to return the exact property conferred on him by the plaintiff, or **substitutionary restitution,** in which a court awards the plaintiff a sum of money that reflects the amount by which he benefited the defendant. In an action for damages based on quasi-contract, substitutionary restitution would be the remedy.

Restitution can be used in a number of circumstances. Sometimes, parties injured by breach of contract seek restitution as an alternative remedy instead of damages that focus on their expectation interest. In other situations, a *breaching party* who has partially performed seeks restitution for the value of benefits he conferred in excess of the losses he caused. In addition, restitution often applies in cases in which a person rescinds a contract on the grounds of lack of capacity, misrepresentation, fraud, duress, undue influence, or mistake. Upon rescission, each party who has been benefited by the other's performance must compensate the other for the value of the benefit conferred. Another application of restitution occurs when a party to a contract that violates the statute of frauds confers a benefit on the other party. For example, Boyer gives Blake a $10,000 down payment on an oral contract for the sale of a farm. Although the contract is unenforceable (that is, Boyer could not get compensation for his expectation interest), the court would give Boyer restitution of his down payment.

ETHICAL AND PUBLIC POLICY CONCERNS

1. Is it good public policy for a party who has materially breached a contract to be able to obtain restitution for the benefits he has conferred on the nonbreaching party?

2. How does the duty of good faith and fair dealing encourage ethical dealings? Do you see any problems with such a duty?

3. You have seen that contract remedies focus solely on the economic effect of contract breaches rather than on the moral implications of such breaches or the emotional harms that might result from a breach of contract. As a result, contract remedies are much more limited than are remedies in tort cases. Is this sound public policy? Explain.

PROBLEMS AND PROBLEM CASES

1 Linder hired Reale to build a 12 foot by 12 foot extension on his house with a raised wooden deck, sliding glass doors, and a gas-fired barbecue. Their

---

[13]Ancillary covenants not to compete, or non-competition agreements, are discussed in detail in Chapter 15.

[14]Quasi-contract is discussed in detail in Chapter 9.

written contract made no provision regarding obtaining a building permit or compliance with building codes, although it did contain a notation stating "plairs [sic] and permit $500 Dep." The agreed price for the improvements was $22,560. It became evident that several features of the finished addition deviated from the state building code and the building plans that had been approved by the town. Reale had built the crawl space beneath the addition some 4 to 7 inches less than the 18 inches mandated by the state building code, which prevented inspection underneath the addition for structural defects. In addition, Reale sealed the framing of the addition, where substantial problems existed, without a prior inspection by the city building department or his own architect. Serious defects existed in the roof, and the plumbing work was not done by a licensed plumber, although it was later corrected. The steps leading down from the main dwelling to the addition are each 4 inches high rather than the 6 and 8 inches each that appear in the plan. In addition, Reale did no grade survey of the property before building, although expert witnesses testified that a grade survey was necessary to build the addition properly. The city building department initially denied a certificate of occupancy because the architect's affidavit stating that he had inspected the location and that the work had been done in conformity with the approved plans and the state fire and building code, but this was apparently based on false information that Reale gave to the architect. Linder made partial payment under the contract, but withheld $5,855. Reale sued Linder to collect the unpaid balance, claiming that he substantially performed the contract. Did he?

2. Asphalt International chartered a tanker, the *Oswego Tarmac,* from Enterprise Shipping. The contract provided that Enterprise was obligated to maintain the vessel in good order but that it was absolved of responsibility for any loss or damage resulting from a collision and that, if the vessel should be lost, the contract would cease. While loading cargo alongside a pier, the *Oswego Tarmac* was rammed amidships by the bow of the motor vessel *Elektra* with such heavy impact that four of its tanks ruptured and heated asphalt spewed across the harbor. Expert appraisers estimated the cost of repair at not less than $1.5 million. The fair market value of the *Oswego Tarmac* prior to the collision was $750,000. Enterprise advised Asphalt International that the *Oswego Tarmac* was a complete loss.

It refused Asphalt International's request to repair the vehicle. Asphalt International brought suit against Enterprise for breach of contract. Will it be successful?

3. Light contracted to build a house for the Mullers. After the job was completed, the Mullers refused to pay Light the balance they owed him under the contract, claiming that he had done some of the work in an unworkmanlike manner. When Light sued for the money, the Mullers counterclaimed for $5,700 damages for delay under a liquidated damages clause in the contract. The clause provided that Light must pay $100 per day for every day of delay in completion of the construction. The evidence indicated that the rental value of the home was between $400 and $415 per month. Should the liquidated damages provision be enforced?

4. The Warrens hired Denison, a building contractor, to build a house on their property. They executed a written contract in which the Warrens agreed to pay $73,400 for the construction. Denison's construction deviated somewhat from the specifications for the project. These deviations were presumably unintentional, and the cost of repairing them was $1,961.50. The finished house had a market value somewhat higher than the market value would have been without the deviations. The Warrens failed to pay the $48,400 balance due under the contract, alleging that Denison had used poor workmanship in constructing the house and that they were under no obligation to perform further duties under the contract. Are they correct?

5. The Bassos contracted with Dierberg to purchase her property for $1,310,000. One term of the contract stated, "[t]he sale under this contract shall be closed . . . at the office of Community Title Company . . . on May 16, 1988 at 10:00 A.M. . . . Time is of the essence of this contract." After forming the contract, the Bassos assigned their right to purchase Dierberg's property to Miceli and Slonim Development Corp. At 10:00 A.M. on May 16, 1988, Dierberg appeared at Community Title for closing. No representative of Miceli and Slonim was there, nor did anyone from Miceli and Slonim inform Dierberg that there would be any delay in the closing. At 10:20 A.M., Dierberg declared the contract null and void because the closing did not take place as agreed, and she left the title company office shortly thereafter. Dierberg had intended to use the purchase money to close another contract to purchase real estate later in the day. At about 10:30 A.M., a representative of Miceli and Slonim appeared at Community Title to begin the closing, but the representative did not have the funds for payment until 1:30 P.M. Dierberg refused to return to the title company, stating that Miceli and Slonim had breached the contract by failing to tender payment on time. She had already made alternative arrangements to finance her purchase of other real estate to meet her obligation under that contract. Miceli and Slonim sued Dierberg, claiming that the contract did not require closing exactly at 10:00 A.M., but rather some time on the day of May 16. Will they prevail?

6. In 1991, the VanVoorhees poured a foundation on their shorefront lot in Machiasport, Maine. Soon thereafter, they were contacted by Dodge, who described himself as a construction consultant and designer whose job was to "oversee the building of a house." The VanVoorhees ultimately met with Dodge and hired him to design their home and to provide consulting services. Dodge agreed that once construction began, he would provide the Van-Voorhees with materials "at cost." Over the next year, Dodge developed plans for a 2,300-square-foot home. As plans for the home began to crystallize, Dodge sent a letter to the VanVoorhees estimating that the cost of constructing the home would be between $65 and $85 per square foot, which amounted to an estimated cost of construction of between $150,000 and $200,000. The VanVoorhees told Dodge they did not want the cost of the home to exceed $150,000 and Dodge assured them, both verbally and in writing, that he could construct the home at that cost. Construction began on the home in August 1992, with Dodge promising a completion date for at least the home's carriage house apartment of late October or early November of the same year. Dodge was the party responsible for the day-to-day management of the construction site, including the selection and supervision of the subcontractors and the ordering of materials. Although Dodge testified to the contrary, four experienced subcontractors each testified that work on the Van-Voorhees' home suffered because of Dodge's incompetence both as a designer and manager. Subcontractors were repeatedly called to the site when the home was not ready for them to begin their portion of the project, windows were mismeasured, rooms were poorly designed requiring redesigning during the construction process, and certain portions

of the construction occurred out of sequence, resulting in damage to the home and additional cost. As winter approached, the VanVoorhees came to the realization that no part of their new home would be completed when Dodge had promised, and that Dodge had broken his "at cost" promise to them by charging them more than $37,000 for windows that cost approximately $30,000 and were never delivered. In addition, Dodge informed the VanVoorhees that the final cost of construction for the home would exceed his $150,000 estimate by between $80,000 and $90,000. The VanVoorhees discharged Dodge and continued the construction as the weather and their finances allowed. As a result of Dodge's failure to complete the home by November 1992, the VanVoorhees incurred additional rental and living expenses from November 1992 until September 1993. Additionally, by the time of the trial the amount expended to build the house had increased to almost $300,000. The VanVoorhees filed a breach of contract suit against Dodge. Will they prevail?

7. In early 1991, Williams entered into an installment land contract for the purchase of property on Macomb Street, Northwest, in Washington, D.C. Williams agreed to purchase the property for $289,000, with a down payment of $28,900, and a promissory note of $260,100, payable in full within five years. The contract provided that Williams was taking the property "as is," but it obligated the seller to make certain repairs and improvements, including the replacement of all water supply galvanized pipes with copper pipes and the installation of a new roof. The seller was required to provide notice to Williams when the repairs and improvements were finished. Williams then had seven days in which to notify the seller of any complaint or defect in the work. The contract provided that failure to give this notice was deemed a waiver, which relieved the seller of any further liability. The contract also provided that if Williams were to give notice of a defect in repairs, the seller's duty was to enforce its agreement with the contractor doing the repairs. The seller hired contractors to make the required repairs and gave Williams due notice when they were completed. Williams did a walk-through of the property, but did not send the seller a list of any complaints or defects within the required seven-day period. Williams signed a document stating that the seller's "preliminary obligations under the contract had been satisfied." About six months later, in September 1991, Williams discovered that a galvanized pipe located under the bathroom flooring had burst. Several months later, Williams notified the seller that leaking pipes existed in the house. However, he did not ask the seller to take any action against any of the contractors whom seller had hired to do the repair work. In February 1992, Williams discovered that there were large areas of rotten porous wood under the shingles of the roof, and a new roof was recommended. Williams did not make monthly interest payments from October 1991 through August 1992, and failed to carry the requisite insurance on the property as well. In February 1992, the seller filed a complaint against Williams to get possession of the real estate as well as rent, fees, and costs. Williams counterclaimed for breach of contract on the ground of his discovery of "latent defects." Will Williams prevail on his counterclaim?

8. Shirley MacLaine Parker entered into a contract with Twentieth Century-Fox to play the female lead in Fox's contemplated production of a movie entitled *Bloomer Girl.* The contract provided that Fox would pay Parker a minimum "guaranteed compensation" of $53,571.42 per week for 14 weeks, beginning May 23, 1966, for a total of $750,000. Fox decided not to produce the movie, and in a letter dated April 4, 1966, it notified Parker that it would not "comply with our obligations to you under" the written contract. In the same letter, with the professed purpose "to avoid any damage to you," Fox instead offered to employ Parker as the leading actress in another movie, tentatively entitled *Big Country, Big Man.* The compensation offered was identical. Unlike *Bloomer Girl,* however, which was to have been a musical production, *Big Country* was to be a dramatic "western type" movie. *Bloomer Girl* was to have been filmed in California; *Big Country* was to be produced in Australia. Certain other terms of the substitute contract varied from those of the original. Parker was given one week within which to accept. She did not, and the offer lapsed. Parker then filed suit against Fox for recovery of the agreed-on guaranteed compensation. Will she prevail?

9. Ross was recruited to play basketball at Creighton University. He came from an academically disadvantaged background, and at the time he enrolled, Ross was at an academic level far below that of the average Creighton student. Creighton realized Ross's academic limitations when it admitted him, and to induce him to attend and play basketball, assured him that he would receive sufficient tutoring so that he "would receive a meaningful education while at Creighton." Ross attended Creighton from 1978 to 1982. He maintained a D average and earned 96 of the 128 credits needed to graduate. On the advice of the athletics department, he took many of these credits in courses such as marksmanship and theory of basketball, which did not count toward a university degree. He also alleged that the university hired a secretary to read his assignments and prepare and type his papers. When he left Creighton, Ross had the overall language skills of a fourth grader and the reading skills of a seventh grader. He took remedial classes for a year at a preparatory school at Creighton's expense, attending classes with grade-school children, and then enrolled at Roosevelt University. He was forced to withdraw there for lack of funds. Ross sued Creighton for breach of contract, among other theories. Can Ross win this suit?

10. ▣ *Video Case.* See "Roof Repair." Roofer had a contract to repair the roof on the Seaside Hotel. After the formation of the contract, however, extensive flood damage caused the hotel to be condemned. Are the parties' duties under the contract discharged?

See also "Sour Grapes" and "California Dreaming."

Sales

Formation and Terms of Sales Contracts

I n Part 3, Contracts, we introduced the common law rules that govern the creation and performance of contracts generally. Throughout much of history, special rules, known as the law merchant, were developed to control mercantile transactions in goods. Because transactions in goods commonly involve buyers and sellers located in different states—and even different countries—a common body of law to control these transactions can facilitate the smooth flow of commerce. To address this need, a Uniform Sales Act was drafted in the early 1900s and adopted by about two-thirds of the states. Subsequently, the Uniform Commercial Code (UCC or Code) was prepared to simplify and modernize the rules of law governing commercial transactions.

This chapter reviews some Code rules that govern the formation of sales contracts previously discussed. It also covers some key terms in sales contracts, such as delivery terms, title, and risk of loss. Finally, it discusses the rules governing sales on trial, such as sales on approval and consignments. ∞

SALE OF GOODS

The **sale of goods** is the transfer of ownership to tangible personal property in exchange for money, other goods, or the performance of services. The law of sales of goods is codified in Article 2 of the Uniform Commercial Code. While the law of sales is based on the fundamental principles of contract and personal property, it has been modified to

FIGURE 1

Choice of Law

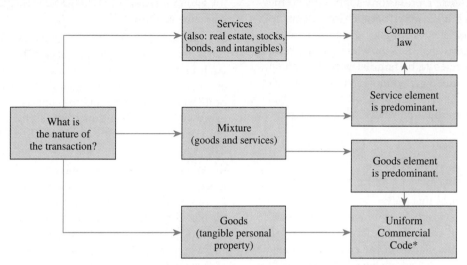

*If there is no specific Uniform Commercial Code provision governing the transaction, use the common law.

accommodate current practices of merchants. In large measure, the Code discarded many technical requirements of earlier law that did not serve any useful purpose in the marketplace and replaced them with rules that are consistent with commercial expectations.

Article 2 of the Code applies only to *transactions in goods*. Thus, it does not cover contracts to provide services or to sell real property. However, some courts have applied the principles set out in the Code to such transactions. When a contract appears to call for the furnishing of both goods and services, a question may arise as to whether the Code applies. For example, the operator of a hair salon may use a commercial permanent solution intended to be used safely on humans that causes injury to a person's head. The injured person then might bring a lawsuit claiming that there was a breach of the Code's warranty of the suitability of the permanent solution. In such cases, the courts commonly see whether the sale of goods is the *predominant* part of the transaction or merely an *incidental* part; where the sale of goods predominates, courts normally apply Article 2. The *Advent Systems Ltd. v. Unisys Corp.* case, which appears in Chapter 9 at page 180, illustrates the type of analysis courts use to determine whether a particular contract should be governed by the Code.

Thus, the first question you should ask when faced with a contracts problem is: Is this a contract for the sale of goods? If it is not, then the principles of common law that were discussed in Part 3, Contracts, apply. If the contract is one for the sale of goods, then the Code applies. This analysis is illustrated in Figure 1.

LEASES

A lease of goods is a transfer of the right to possess and use goods belonging to another. Although the rights of one who leases goods (a lessee) do not constitute ownership of the goods, leasing is mentioned here because it is becoming an increasingly important way of acquiring the use of many kinds of goods, from automobiles to farm equipment. In most states, Article 2 and Article 9 of the UCC are applied to such leases by analogy. However, rules contained in these articles sometimes are inadequate to resolve special problems presented by leasing. For this reason, a new article of the UCC dealing exclusively with leases of goods, Article 2A, was written in 1987. Article 2A has been presented to state legislatures for possible adoption. Forty states have adopted Article 2A as of the time of this writing. Because of space limitations, this textbook does not cover Article 2A in detail.

MERCHANTS

Many of the Code's provisions apply only to **merchants** or to transactions between merchants.[1] In addition, the Code sets a higher standard of conduct for merchants because persons who regularly deal in goods are expected to be familiar with the practices of that trade and with commercial law. Ordinary consumers and nonmerchants, on the other hand, frequently have little knowledge of or experience in these matters.

CODE REQUIREMENTS

The Code requires that parties to sales contracts act in good faith and in a commercially reasonable manner. Further, when a contract contains an unfair or unconscionable clause, or the contract as a whole is unconscionable, the courts have the right to refuse to enforce the unconscionable clause or contract [2–302].[2] The Code's treatment of unconscionability is discussed in detail in Chapter 15, Illegality.

A number of the Code provisions concerning the sale of goods were discussed in the chapters on contracts. The following is a list of some of the important provisions discussed earlier, together with the section of the Code and the chapters in the text where the discussion can be found.

1. *Firm offers.* Under the Code, an offer in writing by a merchant that gives assurance that the offer will be held open is not revocable for lack of consideration during the time stated, or for a reasonable time if no time is stated, up to a period of three months [2–205]. (See Chapter 10, The Agreement: Offer.)

2. *Formation.* Under the Code, a contract for the sale of goods may be made in any manner that shows that the parties reached agreement, even though no particular moment can be pointed to as the time when the contract was made. Where the parties intended to make a contract but left one or more terms open, the contract is valid despite the lack of definiteness so long as the court has a basis for giving a remedy [2–204]. (See Chapter 10, The Agreement: Offer.)

3. *Additional terms in acceptances.* The Code states that an expression of acceptance or written confirmation sent within a reasonable time operates as an acceptance even if it states terms additional to or different from those offered, unless acceptance is expressly made conditional on assent to the additional or different terms [2–207]. (See Chapter 11, The Agreement: Acceptance.)

4. *Statute of frauds.* The **statute of frauds** in the Code applies to the sale of goods at a price of $500 or more. The Code makes special exceptions for written confirmations between merchants, part payment or part delivery, admissions in legal proceedings, and specially manufactured goods [2–201]. (See Chapter 16, Writing.)

TERMS OF THE CONTRACT

General Terms

Within broad limits, the parties to a contract to sell goods may include any terms on which they agree. Many practices have become common in the everyday transactions of business, and under the Code, if a particular matter is not specifically covered in a contract or is unclear, common trade practices are used to fill out the terms of the contract.

The Code sets out in some detail the rights of the parties when they use certain terms, and those meanings apply unless the parties agree otherwise. For example, if a contract includes an open-price clause where the price is to be determined later, or if a contract is silent about price, the price is what would be considered *reasonable* at the time of delivery. If the price is to be fixed by either the buyer or the seller, that person must act in *good faith* in setting the price. However, if it is clear from their negotiations that the parties do not intend to be bound unless they agree on a price, and the price is not agreed on or fixed, no contract results [2–305].

Quantity Terms

In some cases, the parties may state the quantity of goods covered by their sales contract in an indefinite way. Contracts that obligate a buyer to purchase a seller's *output* of a certain item or all of the buyer's

---

[1]Under the Code, a "merchant" is defined as a "person who deals in goods of the kind or otherwise by his occupation holds himself out as having knowledge or skill peculiar to the practices or goods involved in the transaction or to whom such knowledge or skill may be attributed by his employment of an agent or broker or other intermediary who by his occupation holds himself out as having such knowledge or skill" [2–104(1)].

[2]The numbers in brackets refer to sections of the Uniform Commercial Code.

requirements of a certain item are commonly encountered. These contracts caused frequent problems under the common law because of the indefiniteness of the parties' obligations. If the seller decided to double its output, did the buyer have to accept the entire amount? If the market price of the item soared much higher than the contract price, could the buyer double or triple its demands?

Output and Needs Contracts

In an "output" contract, one party is bound to sell its entire output of particular goods and the other party is bound to buy that output. In a "needs" or "requirements" contract, the quantity of goods is based on the needs of the buyer. In determining the quantity of goods to be produced or taken pursuant to an output or needs contract, the rule of *good faith* applies. Thus, no quantity can be demanded or taken that is unreasonably disproportionate to any stated estimate in the contract or to "normal" prior output or requirements if no estimate is stated [2–306(2)].

For example, Farmer contracts to supply Sam's Grocery with all of the apples it requires for sale to customers. If Sam's has sold between 500 and 700 bushels of apples a year over the past 10 years, Farmer could not be required to deliver 5,000 bushels of apples to Sam's one year because Sam had an unusual demand for them. Similarly, it would not be reasonable for Sam to say he would take only 10 bushels one year.

Exclusive Dealing Contracts

The Code takes a similar approach to *exclusive dealing contracts.* Under the common law, these contracts were sources of difficulty due to the indefinite nature of the parties' duties. Did the dealer have to make any effort to sell the manufacturer's products, and did the manufacturer have any duty to supply the dealer? The Code says that unless the parties agree to the contrary, sellers have an obligation to use their best efforts to supply the goods to the buyer and the buyers are obligated to use their best efforts to promote their sale [2–306(2)].

Time for Performance

If no time for performance is stated in the sales contract, a *reasonable time* for performance is im-

plied. If a contract requires successive performances over an indefinite period of time, the contract is valid for a reasonable time; however, either party can terminate it at any time upon the giving of reasonable notice unless the parties have agreed otherwise as to termination [2–309]. For example, Farmer Jack agrees to sell his entire output of apples each fall to a cannery at the then current market price. If the contract does not contain a provision spelling out how and when the contract can be terminated, Farmer Jack can terminate it if he gives the cannery a reasonable time to make arrangements to acquire apples from someone else.

Delivery Terms

Standardized shipping terms that through commercial practice have come to have a specific meaning are customarily used in sales contracts. The terms **FOB (free on board)** and **FAS (free alongside ship)** are basic delivery terms. If the delivery term of the contract is FOB or FAS the place at which the goods originate, the seller is obligated to deliver to the carrier goods that *conform to the contract* and *are properly prepared for shipment* to the buyer, and the seller must make a *reasonable contract for transportation of the goods* on behalf of the buyer. Under such delivery terms, the goods are at the risk of the buyer during transit and he must pay the shipping charges. If the term is *FOB destination,* the seller must deliver the goods to the designated destination and they are at the seller's risk and expense during transit. These terms will be discussed in more detail later in this chapter.

TITLE

Passage of Title

Title to goods cannot pass from the seller to the buyer until the goods are identified to the contract [2–401(1)]. For example, if Seller agrees to sell Buyer 50 chairs and Seller has 500 chairs in his warehouse, title to 50 chairs will not pass from Seller to Buyer until the 50 chairs that Buyer has purchased are selected and identified as the chairs sold to Buyer.

The parties may agree between themselves when title to the goods will pass from the seller to the buyer. If there is no agreement, then the general rule is that the *title to the goods passes to the buyer when the seller completes his obligations as to delivery of the goods:*

1. If the contract requires the seller to "ship" the goods to the buyer, then title passes to the buyer when the seller delivers conforming goods to the carrier.

2. If the contract requires the seller to "deliver" the goods to the buyer, title does not pass to the buyer until the goods are delivered to the buyer and tendered to him.

3. If delivery is to be made without moving the goods, then title passes at the time and place of contracting. An exception is made if title to the goods is represented by a document of title such as a warehouse receipt; then, title passes when the document of title is delivered to the buyer.

4. If the buyer rejects goods tendered to him, title reverts to the seller [2–401(4)].

Importance of Title

At common law, most of the problems relating to risks, insurable interests in goods, remedies, and similar rights and liabilities were determined on the basis of who was the technical title owner at the particular moment the right or liability arose. Under the Code, however, the rights of the seller and buyer and of third persons are determined irrespective of the technicality of who has the title, unless the provision of the Code expressly refers to title.

Determination of who has title to the goods is important in instances in which the rights of the seller's or the buyer's creditors in the goods are an issue. The *O'Donnell v. American Employers Insurance Co.* case, which follows, illustrates another instance in which determination of the title holder may be important—whether the seller's insurance policy covers a particular loss.

O'DONNELL v. AMERICAN EMPLOYERS INSURANCE CO. 622 N.E.2d 570 (Ind. Ct. App. 1993)

O n June 3, 1991, Donald and Sonna Hummel executed a written purchase order invoice for the purchase of a 1989 Chevrolet Corsica from Raisor Pontiac in Lafayette, Indiana. The purchase order indicated that the total retail price of the Corsica would be $7,681.98, that the Hummels would make a cash down payment of $624.50, and that the Purdue Employees Federal Credit Union would be the lienholder for the $7,057.48 balance. The Hummels signed a Retail Installment Contract and Security Agreement with Raisor Pontiac, presented a check for $350.00 and took delivery of the Corsica. The next day, the Hummels gave Raisor Pontiac a second check for $274.50.

On June 5, 1991, Donald Hummel was driving the Corsica when it collided with a vehicle driven by Matthew Lyons. At the time of the accident, Raisor Pontiac held the certificate of title to the Corsica and the vehicle bore an interim license plate. Lyons was injured in the accident and Sean O'Donnell, a passenger in the Lyons' vehicle, died in the collision.

The day after the accident, the Hummel's $274.50 check to Raisor Pontiac was debited to their account, and on June 7, the $350.00 check was debited. Also on June 7, Raisor Pontiac assigned the installment contract with the Hummels to the Credit Union, which remitted a check to Raisor Pontiac for $7,057.48, the amount financed. Raisor Pontiac transferred the certificate of title to the Hummels on June 11.

At the time of the accident, Raisor Pontiac was insured by American Employers Insurance Co. under a policy that covered its ownership, maintenance, or use of covered automobiles. Sean O'Donnell's parents sued Hummel for the wrongful death of their son, alleging that he was negligent in his operation of the automobile at the time of the collision. They also sought a declaratory judgment that the American Employers' policy covered this situation on the grounds that Raisor Pontiac was the owner of the vehicle at the time of the accident. ∞

Najam, Judge Our decision in this case turns on whether the Hummels or Raisor Pontiac owned the vehicle when the accident with Lyons occurred.

In insurance coverage cases, where an automobile dealer sells a vehicle but has not yet transferred the certificate of title to the buyer, ownership of a newly purchased vehicle is established when the evidence shows that the parties have completed the sales transaction. Our courts have recognized several indicia of ownership of an automobile which are considered evidence of a completed sale, including: (1) whether the parties have executed the sales contract; (2) whether the buyer has remitted a down payment; (3) whether the sale was conditioned upon financing and whether financing was obtained; (4) whether the vehicle bears an interim license plate; and (5) whether title has passed from the seller to the buyer. The purchaser's use of an interim license plate is proof of the sale and proof of ownership by the purchaser because the Indiana statute authorizing the use of such plates by the purchaser assumes both the sale of a vehicle and ownership by the purchaser. Further, the purchaser in possession of a vehicle sold under a conditional sales contract, as a conditional vendee, is the owner of that vehicle and is not a permissive user under an insurance policy omnibus clause.

Here, the evidence showed that the Hummels and Raisor Pontiac had executed all documents necessary to complete the sale of the vehicle. The Hummels signed the Purchase Order and financed the vehicle by means of the Installment Contract. The Hummels also remitted two checks constituting a down payment on the vehicle. The first check was dated June 3, 1991, and the second was dated June 4, 1991. The Hummels took delivery of the vehicle on June 3, 1991, and Raisor supplied the Hummels with an interim license plate.

In sum, there was nothing left to be done to transfer ownership of the car to the Hummels except placing title in their name. Numerous indicia of ownership by the Hummels are present in this case and are probative and compelling evidence that Raisor Pontiac and the Hummels had completed the sale before the accident. Likewise, the Hummels and Raisor Pontiac executed an installment contract which made the Hummels conditional vendees and owners of the vehicle for purposes of Indiana's financial responsibility statute. The undisputed material facts support the conclusion that the Hummels owned the vehicle when the accident with the O'Donnells' son and Lyons occurred.

The O'Donnells and Lyons contend nevertheless that Raisor Pontiac, and not the Hummels, owned the vehicle because title had not passed to the Hummels at the time of the accident. The O'Donnells and Lyons rely on the following provision in the Purchase Order which they claim prevented title from passing to the Hummels: "Purchaser shall not have any rights in the Vehicle to be purchased until Dealer receives final payment." American responds that this provision merely permitted Raisor to retain a security interest in the vehicle.

We observe first that under Indiana's version of the Uniform Commercial Code, the question of whether title has passed is no longer decisive in determining the ownership of goods. Whether title has passed is merely one indicium of ownership of property or goods in a sales transaction.

In any event, title to the vehicle had passed to the Hummels at the time of the accident. Indiana Code Section 2–401 applies here and controls:

(1) . . . Any retention or reservation by the seller of the title (property) in goods shipped or delivered to the buyer is limited in effect to a reservation of a security interest . . .

(2) Unless otherwise explicitly agreed, title passes to the buyer at the time and place at which the seller completes his performance with reference to the physical delivery of the goods, despite any reservation of a security interest.

By retaining the vehicle's certificate of title following delivery to the Hummels, Raisor Pontiac retained only a security interest.

We agree that Section 2–401(2) generally permits the parties to form their own agreement concerning the passage of title to goods. However, Section 2–401(1) also provides that "any retention . . . of the title . . . is limited in effect to the reservation of a security interest," a provision which restricts the parties' contractual freedom to delay passage of title by agreement under Section 2–401(2). That language in Section 2–401(1), providing that any retention of title is limited to the reservation of a security interest negates any attempt by the parties to forestall passage of title beyond the moment of final delivery; contract language purporting to do so merely results in a security interest being retained. Therefore, we conclude that parties to a transaction for the sale of goods cannot delay passage of title to those goods past the moment of final delivery.

Judgment affirmed in favor of American Employers Insurance Company.

TITLE AND THIRD PARTIES

Obtaining Good Title

A fundamental rule of property law is that a buyer cannot receive better title to goods than the seller had. If Thief steals a television set from Adler and sells it to Brown, Brown does not get good title to the set, because Thief had no title to it. Adler would have the right to recover the set from Brown. Similarly, if Brown sold the set to Carroll, Carroll could get no better title to it than Brown had. Adler would have the right to recover the set from Carroll.

Under the Code, however, there are several exceptions to the general rule that a buyer cannot get better title to goods than his seller had. The most important exceptions include the following: (1) a person who has a voidable title to goods can pass good title to a bona fide purchaser for value; (2) a person who buys goods in the regular course of a retailer's business takes free of any interests in the goods that the retailer has given to others; and (3) a person who buys goods in the ordinary course of a dealer's business takes free of any claim of a person who entrusted those goods to the dealer.

Transfers of Voidable Title

A seller who has a **voidable title** has the power to pass good title to a *good faith purchaser for value* [2–403(1)]. A seller has a voidable title to goods if he has obtained his title through fraudulent representations. For example, a person would have a voidable title if he obtained goods by impersonating another person or by paying for them with a bad check or if he obtained goods without paying the agreed purchase price when it was agreed that the transaction was to be a cash sale. Under the Code, **good faith** means "honesty in fact in the conduct or transaction concerned" [1–201(19)] and a buyer has given **value** if he has given any consideration sufficient to support a simple contract [1–201(44)].

For example, Jones goes to the ABC Appliance Store, convinces the clerk that he is really Clark, who is a good customer of ABC, and leaves with a stereo charged to Clark's account. If Jones sells the stereo to Davis, who gives Jones value for it and has no knowledge of the fraud that Jones perpetrated on ABC, Davis gets good title to the stereo. ABC cannot recover the stereo from Davis; instead, it must look for Jones, the person who deceived it. In this situation, both ABC and Davis were innocent of wrongdoing, but the law considers Davis to be the more worthy of its protection because ABC was in a better position to have prevented the wrongdoing by Jones and because Davis bought the goods in good faith and for value. The same result would be reached if Jones had given ABC a check that later bounced and then sold the stereo to Davis, who was a good faith purchaser for value. Davis would have good title to the stereo, and ABC would have to pursue its right against Jones on the bounced check.

The *Alsafi Oriental Rugs v. American Loan Co.* case, which follows, illustrates the importance of determining the identity and creditworthiness of a person to whom one sells goods. It also shows the importance of a subsequent buyer qualifying as a good faith purchaser for value so that it is able to get good title from a seller with a voidable title.

ALSAFI ORIENTAL RUGS v. AMERICAN LOAN CO.   864. S.W.2d 41 (Tenn. Ct. App. 1993)

In December 1990, Arlene Bradley entered Alsafi Oriental Rugs and advised the owner that she was an interior decorator and that she was interested in selling some of his rugs to one of her customers. Alsafi did not know Bradley and had never done business with her. However, he allowed her to take three rugs out on consignment with the understanding that she would return them if her customer was not interested. In fact, however, Bradley was not obtaining the rugs for a "customer" but was instead working for another individual, Walid Salaam, a rug dealer.

A friend of Bradley's had introduced her to Salaam earlier. Salaam had advised Bradley and her friend that he was the owner of an oriental rug store that had recently closed but he was attempting to reopen it. He offered to teach them how to become decorators and told them that when his store reopened they could operate out of the store. However, Salaam advised them that until he got his store restocked, he wanted them to "check out" rugs on approval from other rug dealers in town. As they had no experience with oriental rugs, Salaam instructed them what rugs to look for. He then instructed them to go to rug dealers in Memphis and advise them that they were interior decorators with customers that wanted to purchase oriental rugs.

After Bradley obtained possession of three rugs from Alsafi, she turned them over to Salaam, who in turn took them to a pawnshop operated by the American Loan Company. There Salaam pawned the rugs, obtaining approximately $5,000 after filling out the required paperwork. Salaam failed to redeem the rugs. Following the default, the pawnshop gave the appropriate notice that it intended to dispose of them.

In April 1991, Alsafi learned that his rugs were at the pawnshop. After visiting the pawnshop and identifying the three rugs as his, he brought suit to recover possession of them. The trial court held that the rugs had been stolen from Alsafi and awarded him possession of them. The pawnshop appealed. ∽

Tomlin, Presiding Judge   Section 2–403(1) reads as follows:

(1) A purchaser of goods acquires all title which his transferor had or had power to transfer except that a purchaser of limited interest acquires rights only to the extent of the interest purchased. A person with voidable title has power to transfer a good title to a good faith purchaser for value. When goods have been delivered under a transaction of purchase the purchaser has such power even though:

(a) the transferor was deceived as to the identity of the purchaser, or

(b) the delivery was in exchange for a check which is later dishonored, or

(c) it was agreed that the transaction was to be a "cash sale," or

(d) the delivery was procured through fraud punishable as larcenous under the criminal law.

Section 2–403(1) empowers a purchaser with a voidable title to confer good title upon a good faith purchaser for value where the goods were procured through fraud punishable as larcenous under the criminal law. The distinction between theft and fraud in this context is found in the statutory definitions of "delivery" and "purchase." Delivery concerns a voluntary transfer of possession (1–201[14]), and purchase refers to a voluntary transaction creating an interest in property (1–201[32]). As one commentator has pointed out, "a thief who wrongfully takes goods is not a purchaser . . . but a swindler who fraudulently induces the victim to voluntarily deliver them is a purchaser."

In his sworn complaint as well as in his deposition, Alsafi characterized the transfer of possession to Bradley as a consignment—i.e., a voluntary relinquishment of possession to her. She was a purchaser as defined in sections 1–201(33) and 1–201(32). As such, she was empowered by that transaction to pass title to Salaam, who in turn passed title to American Loan Company, a good faith purchaser for value, as found by the trial court, which noted that American Loan Company had no actual knowledge or reason to believe that Salaam was not the true owner of the rugs.

Judgment reversed in favor of American Loan Company.

Buyers in the Ordinary Course of Business

A person who buys goods in the ordinary course of business from a person dealing in goods of that type takes free of any security interest in the goods given by his seller to another person [9–307(1)]. **A buyer in ordinary course** is a person who in good faith and without knowledge that the sale to him is in violation of the ownership rights of a third party buys goods in the ordinary course of business of a person selling goods of that kind, other than a pawnbroker [1–201(9)].

For example, Brown Buick may borrow money from Bank in order to finance its inventory of new Buicks; in turn, Bank may take a security interest in the inventory to secure repayment of the loan. If Carter buys a new Buick from Brown Buick, he gets good title to the Buick free and clear of the Bank's security interest if he is a buyer in the ordinary course of business. The basic purpose of this exception is to protect those who innocently buy from merchants and thereby to promote confidence in such commercial transactions. The exception also reflects the fact that the bank is more interested in the proceeds from the sale than in the inventory. Security interests and the rights of buyers in the ordinary course of business are discussed in more detail in Chapter 28, Security Interests in Personal Property.

Entrusting of Goods

A third exception to the general rule is that if goods are entrusted to a merchant who deals in goods of that kind, the merchant has the power to transfer all

Title and Third Parties

General Rule	A seller cannot pass better title to goods than he has.
Exceptions to General Rule	1. A person who has voidable title to goods can pass good title to a bona fide purchaser for value. 2. A buyer in the ordinary course of a retailer's business takes free of any interests in the goods that the retailer has given to others. 3. A person who buys goods in the ordinary course of a dealer's business takes free of any claims of a person who entrusted those goods to the dealer.

rights of the entruster to a buyer in the ordinary course of business [2–403(2)]. For example, Gail takes her watch to Jeweler, a retail jeweler, to have it repaired, and Jeweler sells the watch to Mary. Mary would acquire good title to the watch, and Gail would have to proceed against Jeweler for conversion of her watch. The purpose behind this rule is to protect commerce by giving confidence to buyers that they will get good title to the goods they buy from merchants in the ordinary course of business. However, a merchant-seller cannot pass good title to stolen goods even if the buyer is a buyer in the ordinary course of business. This is because the original owner did nothing to facilitate the transfer.

RISK OF LOSS

The transportation of goods from sellers to buyers can be a risky business. The carrier of the goods may lose, damage, or destroy them; floods, tornadoes, and other natural catastrophes may take their toll; thieves may steal all or part of the goods. If neither party is at fault for the loss, who should bear the risk? If the buyer has the risk when the goods are damaged or lost, the buyer is liable for the contract price. If the seller has the risk, he is liable for damages unless substitute performance can be tendered.

The common law placed the risk on the party who had technical title at the time of the loss. The Code rejects this approach and provides specific rules governing risk of loss that are designed to provide certainty and to place the risk on the party best able to protect against loss and most likely to be insured against it. Risk of loss under the Code depends on the terms of the parties' agreement, on the moment the loss occurs, and on whether one of the parties was in breach of contract when the loss occurred.

Terms of the Agreement

The contracting parties, subject to the rule of good faith, may specify who has the risk of loss in their agreement [2–509(4)]. This they may do directly or by using certain commonly accepted shipping terms in their contract. In addition, the Code has certain general rules on risk of loss that amplify specific shipping terms and control risk of loss in cases where specific terms are not used [2–509].

Shipment Contracts

If the contract requires the seller to ship the goods by carrier but does not require their delivery to a specific destination, the risk passes to the buyer when the seller delivers the goods to the carrier [2–509(1)(a)]. Shipment contracts are considered to be the normal contract where the seller is required to send goods to the buyer but is not required to guarantee delivery at a particular location.

The following are commonly used shipping terms that create shipment contracts:

1. *FOB (free on board) point of origin.* This term calls for the seller to deliver the goods free of expense and at the seller's risk at the place designated. For example, a contract between a seller located in Chicago and a buyer in New York calls for delivery FOB Chicago. The seller must deliver the goods at his expense and at his risk to a carrier in the place designated in the contract, namely Chicago, and arrange for their carriage. Because the shipment term in this example is FOB Chicago, the seller bears the risk and expense of delivering the goods to the carrier, but the seller is not responsible for delivering the goods to a specific destination. If the term is "FOB vessel, car, or other vehicle," the seller must load the goods on board at his own risk and expense [2–319(1)].

2. *FAS (free alongside ship).* This term is commonly used in maritime contracts and is normally accompanied by the name of a specific vessel and port—for example, "FAS Calgary [the ship], Chicago Port Authority." The seller must deliver the goods alongside the vessel *Calgary* at the Chicago Port Authority at his own risk and expense [2–319(2)].

3. *CIF (cost, insurance, and freight).* This term means that the price of the goods includes the cost of shipping and insuring them. The seller bears this expense and the risk of loading the goods [2–320].

4. *C & F.* This term is the same as CIF, except that the seller is not obligated to insure the goods [2–320].

The *Morauer v. Deak & Co., Inc.* case, which follows, provides an example of the risk borne by a buyer in a shipment contract.

MORAUER v. DEAK & CO., INC.   26 UCC Rep. 1142 (D.C. Super. Ct. 1979)

O*n March 12, 1975, Raymond Morauer contracted with Deak & Co., a dealer in foreign currency, to purchase for investment purposes several bags of silver coins and a quantity of gold coins. He paid for his purchase with personal checks totaling $35,000. After his checks had cleared, he came to Deak's place of business to take delivery. Morauer had a discussion with Deak's assistant manager about the District of Columbia tax on the sale of gold. Both parties agreed that in order to avoid the tax, an admittedly legal endeavor, Deak would ship all of Morauer's gold coins to his residence in suburban Maryland. There was no District of Columbia tax on silver coins, so Morauer took possession of them.*

Deak placed the gold coins in two packages and, as authorized by Morauer, sent the packages to his house by registered mail, return receipt requested. Deak did not insure the packages with the U.S. Postal Service but instead, in accordance with its custom, relied on its own insurance contract with its insurer to cover any risk of loss. Only one package was received by Morauer; however, he did not open it and thus did not realize at the time that he had received only a portion of his gold coins. More than two years later, while making an inventory of his collection, Morauer discovered the problem and notified Deak. By that time, the post office had destroyed its records of the shipment and Deak's insurance coverage for that shipment had expired. Morauer then brought a lawsuit asking the value at their time of purchase of the gold coins that he had not received. ∞

Smith, Judge   The court must determine whether the risk of loss of the gold coins in question passed from the defendant Deak to Morauer upon Deak's delivery of the coins to the Post Office for shipment to Morauer. If so, then Deak is not liable to Morauer for the value of the lost shipment. If the risk of loss did not pass, however, then Deak is liable for the full value of the coins at time of purchase.

The case is governed by section 2–509(1) of the UCC, and the court must determine whether paragraph (a) or paragraph (b) of subsection (1) controls. If the contract was a so-called "shipment" contract, then the risk of loss passed to Morauer, the buyer, on Deak's delivery to the carrier, section 2–509(1) (a), provided, however, that Deak also satisfied the UCC's requirements for a valid "shipment" contract, section 2–504. If, on the other hand, the contract called for delivery at a particular destination, then the risk of loss never passed to Morauer, because the goods were never delivered, and Morauer must prevail, section 2–509(1) (b).

The fact that the parties had agreed that Deak would ship the coins to Morauer's residence in Maryland is not dispositive of this controversy. A "ship to" term in a sales contract has no significance in determining whether the agreement is a "shipment" or "destination" contract. Moreover, there is a preference in the UCC for "shipment" contracts. The drafters of the UCC state the preference and give the reasons for it in the following manner:

For the purposes of subsections (2) and (3) there is omitted from this Article the rule under prior uniform legislation that a term requiring the seller to pay the freight or cost of transportation to the buyer is equivalent to an agreement by the seller to deliver to the buyer or at an agreed destination. This omission is with the specific intention of negating the rule, for under this Article the "shipment" contract is regarded as the normal one and the "destination" contract as the variant type. The seller is not obligated to deliver at a named destination and bear the concurrent risk of loss until arrival, unless he has specifically agreed so to deliver or the commercial understanding of the terms used by the parties contemplates such delivery. Uniform Commercial Code Comment No. 5; Section 2–503.

Here we have an order and payment by Morauer in person to Deak with receipts signed by Kirsch, Deak's agent, indicating Morauer's home address and, in one instance, including the further instruction, "c/o Mrs. Geraldine Morauer." Morauer and Kirsch discussed delivery of the coins, and Morauer decided that to avoid payment of the District of Columbia sales tax, he would have them shipped to his residence. Deak mailed the gold coins in two packages, both of which were properly addressed, stamped and deposited at the United States Post Office. Deak also included the cost of postage as part of Morauer's total bill. Therefore, we hold that Deak was authorized by the contract to ship the gold coins to Morauer by carrier, and that the risk of loss passed from Deak to Morauer on delivery of the packages of coins to the Post Office.

Although the court's finding that the parties were operating under a "shipment" contract puts the risk of loss on Morauer from the time of Deak's delivery to the authorized carrier, there remains the question whether defendant Deak met all the statutory requirements of "shipment" contracts under the applicable UCC section 2–504. That section states:

Where the seller is required or authorized to send the goods to the buyer and the contract does not require him to deliver them at a particular destination, then unless otherwise agreed he must:

(a) put the goods in the possession of such a carrier and make such a contract for their transportation as may be reasonable having regard to the nature of the goods and other circumstances of the case; and

(b) obtain and promptly deliver or tender in due form any document necessary to enable the buyer to obtain possession of the goods or otherwise required by the agreement or by usage of trade; and

(c) promptly notify the buyer of the shipment.

Failure to notify the buyer under paragraph (c) or to make a proper contract under paragraph (a) is a ground for rejection only if material delay or loss ensues.

In the case now before this court Deak followed its regular practice of insuring the shipments with its own insurance company, properly addressed each package and sent both by first-class, registered mail, with a return receipt requested. Deak therefore made all arrangements with the carrier, the United States Postal Service, as were "reasonable having regard to the nature of the goods and other circumstances of the case." Section 2–504(a). Deak had no obligation under paragraph (b) of section 2–504, insofar as there were no documents necessary to enable Morauer to obtain possession of the goods, and none "otherwise required by the agreement or by usage of trade." And finally, Deak was in compliance with section 2–504(c) in that Kirsch notified Morauer of the mailing of the gold coins when Morauer went to Deak's office to take delivery personally of the silver coins he had also purchased.

Judgment in favor of Deak.

Destination Contracts

If the contract requires the seller to deliver the goods to a specific destination, the seller bears the risk and expense of delivery to that destination [2–509(1)(b)]. The following are commonly used shipping terms that create destination contracts:

1. *FOB destination.* An FOB term coupled with the place of destination of the goods puts the expense and risk of delivering the goods to that destination on the seller [2–319(1)(b)]. For example, a contract between a seller in Chicago and a buyer in Phoenix might call for shipment FOB Phoenix. The seller must ship the goods to Phoenix at her own expense,

and she also retains the risk of delivery of the goods to Phoenix.

2. *Ex-ship.* This term does not specify a particular ship, but it places the expense and risk on the seller until the goods are unloaded from whatever ship is used [2–322].

3. *No arrival, no sale.* This term places the expense and risk during shipment on the seller. If the goods fail to arrive through no fault of the seller, the seller has no further liability to the buyer [2–324].

For example, a Chicago-based seller contracts to sell a quantity of shirts to a buyer FOB Phoenix, the buyer's place of business. The shirts are destroyed en route when the truck carrying the shirts is involved in an accident. The risk of the loss of the shirts is on the seller, and the buyer is not obligated to pay for them. The seller may have the right to recover from the trucking company, but between the seller and the buyer, the seller has the risk of loss. If the contract had called for delivery FOB the seller's manufacturing plant, then the risk of loss would have been on the buyer. The buyer would have had to pay for the shirts and then pursue any claims that he had against the trucking company.

Goods in the Possession of Third Parties

If the goods are in the possession of a bailee and are to be delivered without being moved, the risk of loss passes to the buyer upon delivery to him of a negotiable document of title for the goods; if no negotiable document of title has been used, the risk of loss passes when the bailee indicates to the buyer that the buyer has the right to the possession of the goods [2–509(2)]. For example, if Farmer sells Miller a quantity of grain currently stored at Grain Elevator, the risk of loss of the grain will shift from Farmer to Miller (1) when a negotiable warehouse receipt for the grain is delivered to Miller or (2) when Grain Elevator notifies Miller that it is holding the grain for Miller.

Risk Generally

If the transaction does not fall within the situations discussed above, the risk of loss passes to the buyer upon *receipt* of the goods if the seller is a merchant; if the seller is not a merchant, then the risk of loss passes to the buyer upon the *tender of delivery* of the goods to the buyer [2–509(3)]. If Jones bought a television set from ABC Appliance on Monday, intending to pick it up on Thursday, and the set was stolen on Wednesday, the risk of loss remained with ABC. However, if Jones had purchased the set from his next-door neighbor and could have taken delivery of the set on Monday (i.e., delivery was tendered then), the risk of loss was Jones's.

Effect of Breach on Risk of Loss

When a seller tenders goods that do not conform to the contract and the buyer has the right to reject the goods, the risk of loss remains with the seller until

---

Risk of Loss

The point at which the risk of loss or damage to goods identified to a contract passes to the buyer is as follows:

1. If there is an agreement between the parties, the risk of loss passes to the buyer at the time they have agreed to.
2. If the contract requires the seller to ship the goods by carrier but does not require that the seller guarantee their delivery to a specific destination (shipment contract), the risk of loss passes to the buyer when the seller has delivered the goods to the carrier and made an appropriate contract for their carriage.
3. If the contract requires the seller to guarantee delivery of the goods to a specific destination (destination contract), the risk of loss passes to the buyer when the seller delivers the goods to the designated destination.
4. If the goods are in the hands of a third person and the contract calls for delivery without moving the goods, the risk of loss passes to the buyer when the buyer has the power to take possession of the goods—for example, when he receives a document of title.
5. In any situation other than those noted above where the seller is a merchant, the risk of loss passes to the buyer on his receipt of the goods.
6. In any situation other than those noted above where the seller is not a merchant, the risk of loss passes to the buyer on the tender of delivery to the buyer by the seller.
7. When a seller tenders goods that the buyer lawfully could reject because they do not conform to the contract description, the risk of loss stays on the seller until the defect is cured or the buyer accepts them.
8. When a buyer rightfully revokes acceptance of goods, the risk of loss is on the seller from the beginning to the extent it is not covered by the buyer's insurance.
9. If a buyer repudiates a contract for identified, conforming goods before risk of loss has passed to the buyer, the buyer is liable for a commercially reasonable time for any loss or damage to the goods that is not covered by the seller's insurance.

any defect is cured or until the buyer accepts the goods [2–510(1)]. Where the buyer rightfully revokes his acceptance of goods, the risk of loss is with the seller to the extent that any loss is not covered by the buyer's insurance [2–510(2)]. This rule gives the seller the benefit of any insurance carried by the buyer.

For example, if Adler bought a new Buick from Brown Buick that he later returned to Brown because of serious defects in it and if through no fault of Adler the automobile was damaged while in his possession, then the risk of loss would be with Brown. However, if Adler had insurance on the automobile covering the damage to it and recovered from the insurance company, Adler would have to turn the insurance proceeds over to Brown or use them to fix the car before returning it to Brown.

When a buyer repudiates a contract for goods and those goods have already been set aside by the seller, the risk of loss stays with the buyer for a commercially reasonable time after the repudiation if the seller's insurance is not sufficient to cover any loss [2–510(3)]. Suppose Cannery contracts to buy Farmer's entire crop of peaches. Farmer picks the peaches, crates them, tenders delivery to Cannery, and stores them in his barn. Cannery then tells Farmer that it does not intend to honor the contract. Shortly thereafter, but before Farmer has a chance to find another buyer, the peaches are spoiled by a fire. If Farmer's insurance covers only part of the loss, Cannery must bear the rest of the loss.

Insurable Interest

The general practice of insuring risks is recognized and provided for under the Code. A buyer may protect his interest in goods that are the subject matter of a sales contract before he actually obtains title. The buyer obtains an insurable interest in existing goods when they are identified as the goods covered by the contract even though they are in fact nonconforming. The seller retains an insurable interest in goods so long as he has either title or a security interest in them [2–501(2)].

SALES ON TRIAL

A common commercial practice is for a seller of goods to entrust possession of goods to a buyer to either give the buyer an opportunity to decide whether or not to buy them or to try to resell them to a third person. The entrusting may be known as a **sale on approval,** a **sale or return,** or a **consignment,** depending on the terms of the entrusting. Occasionally, the goods may be damaged, destroyed, or stolen, or the creditors of the buyer may try to claim them; on such occasions, the form of the entrusting will determine whether the buyer or the seller had the risk of loss and whether the buyer's creditors can successfully claim the goods.

Sale on Approval

In a sale on approval, the goods are delivered to the buyer with an understanding that he may use or test them for the purpose of determining whether he wishes to buy them [2–326(1)(a)]. In a sale on approval, neither the risk of loss nor title to the goods passes to the buyer until he accepts the goods. The buyer has the right to use the goods in any manner consistent with the purpose of the trial, but any unwarranted exercise of ownership over the goods is considered to be an acceptance of the goods. Similarly, if the buyer fails to notify the seller of his election to return the goods, he is considered to have accepted them [2–327]. For example, if Dealer agrees to let Hughes take a new automobile home to drive for a day to see whether she wants to buy it and Hughes takes the car on a two-week vacation trip, Hughes will be considered to have accepted the automobile because she used it in a manner beyond that contemplated by the trial and as if she were its owner. If Hughes had driven the automobile for a day, decided not to buy it, and parked it in her driveway for two weeks without telling Dealer of her intention to return it, Hughes would also be deemed to have accepted the automobile.

Once the buyer has notified the seller of his election to return the goods, the return of the goods is at the seller's expense and risk. Because the title and risk of loss of goods delivered on a sale on approval remain with the seller, goods held on approval are not subject to the claims of the buyer's creditors until the buyer accepts them [2–326].

Sale or Return

In a sale or return, goods are delivered to a buyer for resale with the understanding that the buyer has the right to return them [2–326(1)(b)]. Under a sale or return, the title and risk of loss are with the buyer. While the goods are in the buyer's possession, they are subject to the claims of his creditors [2–326 and 2–327]. For example, if Publisher delivers some paperbacks to Bookstore on the understanding that Bookstore may return any of the paperbacks that remain unsold at the end of six months, the transaction is a sale or return. If Bookstore is destroyed by a fire, the risk of loss of the paperbacks was Bookstore's and it is responsible to Publisher for the purchase price. Similarly, if Bookstore becomes insolvent and is declared a bankrupt, the paperbacks will be considered part of the bankruptcy estate. If the buyer elects to return goods held on a sale or return basis, the return is at the buyer's risk and expense.

Sale on Consignment

Sometimes, goods are delivered to a merchant on consignment. If the merchant to whom goods are consigned maintains a place of business dealing in goods of that kind under a name other than that of the person consigning the goods, then the consignor must take certain steps to protect his interest in the goods or they will be subject to the claims of the merchant's creditors. The consignor must (1) make sure that a sign indicating the consignor's interest is prominently posted at the place of business, or (2) make sure that the merchant's creditors know that he is generally in the business of selling goods owned by others, or (3) comply with the filing provisions of Article 9 of the Code—Secured Transactions.

For example, Jones operates a retail music store under the name of City Music Store. Baldwin Piano Company delivers some pianos to Jones on consignment. If no notices are posted indicating Baldwin's interest in the pianos, if Jones is not generally known to be selling from a consigned inventory, and if Baldwin does not file its interest with the recording office pursuant to Article 9 of the Code, then the goods are subject to the claims of Jones's creditors. This is crucial to Baldwin because it may have intended to retain title. However, the Code treats a consignment to a person doing business under a name other than that of the consignor as a "sale or return" [2–326(3)]. If Jones did business as the Baldwin Piano Company, Baldwin's interest would be protected from the claims of Jones's creditors without the need for Baldwin to post a sign or to file under Article 9.

The case that follows, *In Re Auclair,* illustrates the risks borne by a person who makes goods available on a sale or return or consignment basis.

IN RE AUCLAIR; MC GREGOR v. JACKSON   131 BR 185 (Bankr. M.D. Ala. 1991)

 dd and Diane Auclair maintained a place of business in Covington County, Alabama, where they operated a gun shop and convenience store named Heath Grocery and Final Chapter Firearms. In November 1989, Luke Jackson delivered about 70 firearms to the Auclairs to sell on consignment. The consignment agreement provided as follows:

I Edd Auclair have received a number of guns, of which a list will be attached and I will sign. As I sell a gun I will pay James E. "Luke" Jackson or Betty King with them giving me a receipt for that particular gun. If something should happen to Luke Jackson the guns are to be returned to Betty King or at that time Betty King and Edd Auclair can enter into an agreement. If something should happen to Edd Auclair, Diane agrees to return all guns that have not been paid for to Luke Jackson or Betty King and pay for any that has [sic] been sold.

The agreement was signed by Jackson, King and the Auclairs.

On June 28, 1990, the Auclairs filed a petition in bankruptcy under Chapter 11 of the Bankruptcy Act. Shortly thereafter, Jackson removed the firearms he had consigned from the Auclairs's store. The bankruptcy trustee representing the Auclairs' creditors claimed that the firearms were the property of the bankruptcy estate. ⌒

Gordon, Bankruptcy Judge   Both parties agree that Section 2–326(3) regarding consignments applies to the facts of this case. Under that subsection, goods delivered on consignment are "deemed to be on sale or return." Thus, by deeming the consignee a purchaser of the goods, the consignor is precluded from asserting an ownership claim to the goods vis-a-vis the consignee's creditors.

Applying that section to the instant case, Jackson is precluded from asserting his ownership of the firearms vis-a-vis the trustee. However, the subsection is not applicable to a consignor who—

(a) Complies with an applicable law providing for a consignor's interest or the like to be evidenced by a sign, or

(b) Establishes that the person conducting the business is generally known by his creditors to be substantially engaged in selling the goods of others, or

(c) Complies with the filing provisions of the article on secured transactions (Article 9)." Section 2–326(3).

Jackson is not protected under (a) because Alabama does not have a sign law applicable to consignments. Jackson is not protected under (c) because he did not comply with the filing provisions of Article 9.

Jackson contends, but has failed to prove, that he is protected under (b). The evidence does not reflect that the debtors were "generally known by [their] creditors to be substantially engaged in selling the goods of others."

Jackson admitted that he did not notify any of the Auclairs' creditors that the firearms were placed with the Auclairs on consignment. The evidence reveals, *at best,* that only one of the Auclairs' 18 creditors had knowledge of the consignment. The court concludes that the debtors were not "generally known by [their] creditors to be substantially engaged in selling" consigned firearms.

The court holds that the firearms in question are property of this bankruptcy estate which the trustee may sell. A separate order will be entered requiring Jackson to deliver the firearms to the trustee and to account for such property or its value. Jackson will have an unsecured claim for the value of the property returned to the trustee, for which he may file a proof of claim in this case.

Judgment in favor of bankruptcy estate and against Jackson.

BULK TRANSFERS

Bulk Transfer Legislation

There is one other situation where the creditors of a party to a sales contract may claim an interest (other than an Article 9 security interest) in the goods. This is in the case of a bulk transfer as covered by Article 6 of the Code. A bulk transfer occurs when a person whose main business is selling goods from stock (a retailer, a wholesaler, and in some cases a manufacturer) sells a major part of the materials, supplies, merchandise, or other inventory of the business in bulk and not in the ordinary course of business [6–102].

The danger in such cases is that financially troubled sellers may secretly dispose of their assets, pocket the proceeds, and disappear. In order to protect such a seller's creditors from being defrauded in this manner, Article 6 is designed to give them notice of the sale and enable them to file any claims they may have against the goods. The seller must give the buyer a sworn list of the seller's creditors and a schedule of the property to be transferred [6–104]. The buyer must keep this list available for inspection and copying by the seller's creditors for six months after the sale [6–104].

Notice to Creditors

The buyer must notify all known creditors of the sale at least 10 days before taking possession of the goods [6–105]. Failure to comply with the requirements means that the buyer holds the goods in trust for the seller's creditors. In some states (Pennsylvania, for example), an optional provision of the Code has been enacted requiring that the proceeds of the bulk transfer be paid to the seller's creditors [6–106].

Statute of Limitations

Creditors have only six months from the time the transfer took place to enforce their rights under Article 6, unless the transfer was concealed from them. In such a case, they have six months after the transfer was discovered [6–111].

Current Developments

For some time there has been general dissatisfaction with the current bulk sales law. The National Conference of Commissioners on Uniform State Laws has prepared a draft revision to UCC Article 6 (Bulk Sales) for consideration by the states; at the same time, the commissioners have voted to recommend to the states that they repeal Article 6 and do without a bulk sales law. Thus, the future for bulk sales laws is in doubt. At the time this book was published, 16 states had adopted the revised version.

1. Suppose you are the owner of a small jewelry store that sells new and antique jewelry. A customer leaves a family heirloom—an elaborate diamond ring—with you for cleaning and resetting. By mistake, a clerk in your store sells it to another customer. What would you do? If you were the buyer of the ring and had given it to your fiancé as a gift and then were informed of the circumstances, what would you do?

2. Under the pre-Code law, most issues relating to risks and insurable interests in goods were determined on the basis of who was technical title owner at the particular moment the problem of a right or liability arose. What policy considerations do you believe were involved in the decision by the drafters of the Code to provide for resolution of issues concerning risk of loss and insurable interest independent of who was the technical title owner?

3. In the *In Re Auclair* case, the owner that made the firearms available to the retailer for resale lost out to other creditors of the retailers when they filed for bankruptcy. Does this strike you as a reasonable result? What policy considerations underlie the Code provisions on which the court based its decision?

PROBLEMS AND PROBLEM CASES

1. Mr. and Mrs. Abelman engaged the Capitol Termite and Pest Control Company to treat their home for a termite infestation. The chemical used by Capitol was Gold Crest Termite manufactured by Velsicol Chemical Corporation. Velsicol sold the Gold Crest Termite to a distributor, which in turn sold it to Capitol in bulk—in 55-gallon drums. Capitol did not specifically buy materials for each termite job. One 55-gallon drum would service many homes. Employees of Capitol pumped the chemical from the 55-gallon drums into a 5-gallon pail at Capitol's premises. The solution was then poured from the 5-gallon pail into a 1-gallon pail, which they filled half full. Next, the half-gallon of Gold Crest Termite was poured into a fixed 50-gallon tank on the back of Capitol's trucks and then the tank was filled to capacity with water. This solution was then applied to the Abelman's residence by employees of Capitol. The Abelmans abandoned their home the day after Capitol completed treatment. Three years later they brought suit against Capitol and Velsicol contending that the termiticide had caused personal injuries and property damages. Among other things, they claimed there was a breach of express and implied warranties provided by the Uniform Commercial Code (discussed in Chapter 20). Velsicol and Capitol sought to dismiss these claims on the ground that there had not been a sale of goods and thus no warranties had arisen. Was the contract to obtain treatment for termites a sale of goods under the Uniform Commercial Code?

2. ▪ *Video Case.* See "Software Horror Story." Chuck Mason, a computer consultant, was hired to develop customized software for a client, Clark. Mason's plan was to purchase off-the-shelf software and to modify it to meet the customer's need. After identifying several software packages that might meet his need, he contacted a software retailer, Bits and Bytes, by phone and explained that he needed to be able to modify the package at the source code level and to have the source code. He then asked Bits and Bytes to recommend a package that would meet these criteria and be easy to modify. After receiving the recommended software (D-Base Hit) from Bits and Bytes, Chuck modified the software but was unable to get it to work as envisioned. Bits and Bytes refused to take it back because Chuck's modifications prevented it from being resold or returned to the software publisher. Chuck refused to pay Bits and Bytes for the package. Chuck then purchased a different software package (Customized Amazing Base) and customized it for his customer. However, the customized software never functioned satisfactorily for the client, and she refused to pay Chuck for it. Does the UCC apply to the sale of the software by the retailer? Does it apply to the sale of the customized software by Chuck to the customer?

3. Keith Russell, a boat dealer, contracted to sell a 19-foot Kinsvater boat to Robert Clouser for

$8,500. The agreement stipulated that Clouser was to make a down payment of $1,700, with the balance due when he took possession of the boat. According to the contract, Russell was to retain possession of the boat in order to install a new engine and drive train. While the boat was still in Russell's possession, it was completely destroyed when it struck a seawall. Transamerica, Russell's insurance company, refused to honor Russell's claim for the damages to the boat. The insurance policy between Transamerica and Russell covered only watercraft under 26 feet in length that were not owned by Russell. Transamerica argued that the boat was not covered by the policy since Russell still owned it at the time of the accident. Did Russell have title to the boat at the time of the accident?

4. Williams agreed to sell his car to an individual named Hodge and accepted a cashier's check from Hodge as payment. He signed the certificate of title as seller, although he did not indicate on the certificate that Hodge was the purchaser, and delivered the document and the car to Hodge. The next day, Hodge, representing himself to be Williams, offered to sell the car to Charles Evans BMW, Inc. When a price was agreed upon, Hodge presented to Evans BMW the certificate of title bearing Williams's signature as payee and Evans BMW gave Hodge a check that named Williams as payee. The check was cashed at a local bank when Hodge produced a Kentucky driver's license bearing the same number as had been issued to Williams. After the car had been purchased by Evans BMW from Hodge, Williams was notified that the cashier's check he had accepted from Hodge was a forgery. By the time Evans BMW was made aware of the fact it had not actually purchased the car from Williams, but rather from Hodge representing himself to be Williams, it had already resold the car. At the direction of the local police officials, the car and the certificate of title were returned to Evans BMW and the purchase price refunded. Evans BMW then initiated an action against Williams seeking to establish that it held good title to the car. Did Evans BMW obtain good title to the car when it purchased it from Hodge, a person who had obtained title through criminal fraud by giving the original owner a check that was subsequently dishonored?

5. ▣ *Video Case.* See "TV Repair." Arnold took his old TV to an appliance store for repair. The appliance store developed financial problems and was unable to pay its debts to its creditors as they became due. Facing bankruptcy, the appliance store held a going-out-of-business sale and sold everything in the store, including Arnold's TV, to individual customers who had no knowledge of anyone else's interest in the goods. Does Arnold have the legal right to recover the TV from the person who bought it at the going-out-of-business sale?

6. In June, Ramos entered into a contract to buy a motorcycle from Big Wheel Sports Center. He paid the purchase price of $893 and was given the papers necessary to register the cycle and get insurance on it. Ramos registered the cycle but had not attached the license plates to it. He left on vacation and told the salesperson for Big Wheel Sports Center that he would pick up the cycle on his return. While Ramos was on vacation, there was an electric power blackout in New York City and the cycle was stolen by looters. Ramos then sued Big Wheel Sports Center to get back his $893. Did Big Wheel Sports Center have the risk of loss of the motorcycle?

7. Legendary Homes, a home builder, purchased various appliances from Ron Mead T.V. & Appliance, a retail merchant selling home appliances. They were intended to be installed in one of Legendary Homes's houses and were to be delivered on February 1. At 5 o'clock on that day, the appliances had not been delivered. Legendary Homes's employees closed the home and left. Sometime between 5 and 6:30, Ron Mead delivered the appliances. No one was at the home so the deliveryman put the appliances in the garage. During the night, someone stole the appliances. Legendary Homes denied it was responsible for the loss and refused to pay Ron Mead for the appliances. Ron Mead then brought suit for the purchase price. Did Legendary Homes have the risk of loss of the appliances?

8. ▣ *Video Case.* See "Sour Grapes." Jelly Manufacturer, a food processor in Chicago, placed a phone order with Grape Grower, a grower in California, for a quantity of perishable produce. The shipping term was CIF with payment to be made on delivery (COD). Grower delivered the goods called for in the contract to a carrier and contracted for their shipment. However, it neglected to provide that the goods be shipped under refrigeration. The goods were loaded on a nonrefrigerated boxcar and as a result the produce was spoiled when it reached Chicago. Who had the risk of loss, Grape Grower or Jelly Manufacturer?

9. The Cedar Rapids YMCA bought a large number of cases of candy from Seaway Candy under an agreement by which any unused portion could be returned. The YMCA was to sell the candy to raise money to send boys to camp. The campaign was less than successful, and 688 cases remained unsold. They were returned to Seaway Candy by truck. When delivered to the common carrier, the candy was in good condition; when it arrived at Seaway four days later, it had melted and was completely worthless. Seaway then brought suit against the YMCA to recover the purchase price of the candy spoiled in transit. Between Seaway and the YMCA, which had the risk of loss?

10. W. N. Provenzano was a manufacturer and wholesaler of jewelry located in New York City. On November 3, 1980, Arthur Jervis, its representative, left two rings with Monahan & Co., a retail jewelry business. At that time, a memorandum agreement was signed by Jervis and an employee of Monahan. The agreement stated:

The goods described and valued as below are delivered to you for EXAMINATION AND INSPECTION ONLY and remain our property subject to our order and shall be returned to us on demand. Such merchandise, until returned to us and actually received, are at your risk from all hazards. NO RIGHT OR POWER IS GIVEN TO YOU TO SELL, PLEDGE, HYPOTHECATE OR OTHERWISE DISPOSE of this merchandise regardless of prior transactions. A sale of this merchandise can only be effected and title will pass only if, as and when we the said owner shall agree to such sale and a bill of sale rendered therefore.

The agreement also had the address of Provenzano printed on it. Filled in on the agreement was a description of the two rings in question. Jervis also wrote by hand on the agreement, "To work with Customer." In January and February 1981, Provenzano made several demands for the return of the two rings. The rings were not returned. On February 2, 1981, Monahan filed a voluntary Chapter 11 bankruptcy petition. Sometime thereafter, Monahan sold the two rings, one for $4,250 and the other to an unknown purchaser for an unknown amount. Provenzano brought suit, claiming that the goods were delivered to Monahan on a bailment and not for resale and that Monahan, as bailee, had therefore unlawfully converted the goods. Provenzano claimed that it was entitled to $15,000, the asserted fair market value of the rings. Did Provenzano have a better right to the rings, or their value, than the other creditors of Monahan?

Product Liability

S uppose that you are the president of a firm making products for sale to the public. One of your worries would be the company's exposure to civil liability for defects in those products. In particular, you might worry about changes in the law that make such liability more likely or more expensive. In other situations, however, the same changes might appeal to you. This is especially true if *you* are harmed by defective products you purchase as a consumer. You might also appreciate such changes if your firm wants to sue a supplier that has sold it defective products.

Each of these situations involves the law of *product liability*. Product liability law is the body of legal rules governing civil suits for losses resulting from defective goods.[1] After sketching product liability law's historical evolution, this chapter discusses the most important *theories of product liability recovery*. These theories are rules of law saying that, once plaintiffs prove certain facts, they recover for losses resulting from defective goods. The second part of the chapter considers certain legal problems that are common to all the theories of recovery but that may be resolved differently from theory to theory. ⌾

THE EVOLUTION OF PRODUCT LIABILITY LAW

The 19th Century

A century or so ago, the rules governing suits for defective goods were very much to sellers' and

---

[1]Chapter 47 discusses federal consumer protection and product safety regulation.

manufacturers' advantage. This was the era of *caveat emptor* (let the buyer beware). In contract suits involving defective goods, there usually was no liability unless the seller had made an express promise to the buyer and the goods did not conform to that promise. Some courts even required that the words *warrant* or *guarantee* accompany the promise before liability would exist. In negligence suits, the "no liability without fault" principle was widely accepted, and plaintiffs often had difficulty proving negligence because the necessary evidence was under the defendant's control. In both contract and negligence cases, finally, the doctrine of "no liability outside privity of contract"—that is, no liability without a direct contractual relationship between plaintiff and defendant—often prevented plaintiffs from recovering against parties with whom they had not directly dealt.

One reason for these prodefendant rules was the laissez-faire values that strongly influenced public policy and the law. One expression of those values was the belief that sellers and manufacturers should be contractually bound only when they deliberately assumed such liability by actually making a promise to someone with whom they dealt directly. Another factor limiting manufacturers' liability for defective products, some say, was the desire to promote industrialization by preventing potentially crippling damage recoveries against infant industries. Yet another explanation for this limited liability is that it might not have been too harmful to plaintiffs. Chains of distribution tended to be short, so the no-liability-outside-privity defense was not always available to sellers. Because goods tended to be simple, buyers sometimes could inspect them for defects. Before the emergence of large corporations late in the 19th century, sellers and buyers often were of relatively equal size, sophistication, and bargaining power. Thus, they could deal on a relatively equal footing.

The 20th Century

Today, laissez-faire values, while still influential, do not pack the weight they did a century ago. Instead, a more protective, interdependent climate has emerged. With the development of a viable industrial economy, there has been less perceived need to protect manufacturers from liability for defective goods. The emergence of long chains of distribution

has meant that consumers often do not deal directly with the parties responsible for defects in the products they buy. Because large corporations tend to dominate the economy, consumers are less able to bargain equally with such parties in any event. Finally, the growing complexity of goods has made buyer inspections more difficult.

In response to all these changes, product liability law has moved from its earlier *caveat emptor* emphasis to a stance of *caveat venditor* (let the seller beware). To protect consumers, modern courts and legislatures intervene in private contracts for the sale of goods and impose liability regardless of fault. As a result, sellers and manufacturers face greater liability and higher damage recoveries for defects in their products. Underlying the shift toward *caveat venditor* is the belief that sellers, manufacturers, and their insurers are best able to bear the economic costs associated with product defects, and that they usually can pass on these costs through higher prices. Thus, the economic risk associated with defective products has been effectively spread throughout society, or "socialized."

The Current "Crisis" in Product Liability Law

Modern product liability law and its socialization-of-risk strategy have come under increasing attack over the past 20-odd years. Such attacks often focus on the difficulty sellers and manufacturers encounter in obtaining product liability insurance and the increased costs of such insurance. Some observers blame the insurance industry for these developments, while others trace them to the increased liability and greater damage recoveries just discussed. Whatever their origin, these problems have put sellers and manufacturers in a bind. Businesses unwilling or unable to buy expensive product liability insurance run the risk of being crippled by large damage awards unless they self-insure, which can be an expensive option today. Firms that purchase insurance, on the other hand, often must pay higher prices for it. In either case, the resulting costs may be difficult to pass on to consumers. In addition, those costs may deter the development and marketing of innovative new products.

For these reasons and others, recent years have witnessed many efforts to scale back the proplaintiff thrust of modern product liability law. This is one aspect of the tort reform movement discussed in Chapter 7. However, despite the introduction of many federal reform bills, Congress has yet to make significant changes in product liability law. As we note later in this chapter, however, some tort reform efforts have occurred in the states.

THEORIES OF PRODUCT LIABILITY RECOVERY

Some theories of product liability recovery are contractual and some are tort-based. The contract theories involve a product **warranty**—a contractual promise about the nature of the product sold. In warranty cases, plaintiffs claim that the product failed to live up to the seller's promise. In tort cases, on the other hand, plaintiffs usually argue that the defendant was negligent or that strict liability should apply.[2]

Express Warranty

Creating an Express Warranty   UCC section 2–313(1) states that an **express warranty** is created in any of three ways.

1. Any *affirmation of fact or promise* regarding the goods creates an express warranty that the goods will conform to that affirmation. For instance, a computer manufacturer's statement that a computer has a certain amount of memory creates an express warranty to that effect.

2. Any *description* of the goods creates an express warranty that the goods will conform to the description. Descriptions include: (1) statements that goods are of a certain brand, type, or model (e.g., an IBM dot-matrix computer printer); (2) adjectives that characterize the product (e.g., shatterproof glass); and (3) drawings, blueprints, and technical specifications.

3. A *sample* or *model* of goods to be sold creates an express warranty that the rest of the goods will conform to the sample or model. A sample is an object drawn from an actual collection of goods to be sold, while a model is a replica offered for the buyer's inspection when the goods themselves are unavailable.

The first two kinds of express warranties probably overlap; also, each can be either written or oral. In addition, magic words like *warrant* or *guarantee* no longer are needed to create an express warranty.

Value, Opinion, and Sales Talk   Statements of *value* ("This chair would bring you $2,000 at an auction") or *opinion* ("I think that this chair is a genuine antique Louis XIV") do not create an express warranty. The same is true of statements that amount to *sales talk* or *puffery* ("This chair is a good buy"). No sharp line separates such statements from express warranties. In close cases, a statement is more likely to be an express warranty if it is specific rather than indefinite, if it is stated in the sales contract rather than elsewhere,[3] or if it is unequivocal rather than hedged or qualified. The relative knowledge possessed by the seller and the buyer also matters. For instance, a car salesperson's statement about a used car is more likely to be an express warranty where the buyer knows little about cars than where the buyer is another car dealer. The following *Hall Farms* case discusses some of the points made in this paragraph.

The Basis-of-the-Bargain Problem   Under pre-Code law, there was no recovery for breach of an express warranty unless the buyer significantly *relied* on that warranty in making the purchase. The UCC, however, ambiguously requires that the warranty be *part of the basis of the bargain.* Some courts read the Code's basis-of-the-bargain test as saying that significant reliance still is necessary. Others only require that the seller's warranty have been a *contributing factor* in the buyer's decision to purchase. Still others do not require any reliance on the buyer's part.

Advertisements   Statements made in advertisements, catalogs, or brochures may be express warranties. However, such sources often are filled with sales talk. Also, basis-of-the-bargain problems may arise if it is unclear whether or to what degree the statement really induced the buyer to make the purchase. For example, suppose that the buyer read an advertisement containing an express warranty one month before actually purchasing the product.

---

[2]Negligence and strict liability are discussed in Chapter 7.

[3]Parol evidence rule problems can arise in express warranty cases. For example, a seller who used a written sale contract may argue that the rule excludes an alleged oral warranty. On the parol evidence rule, see Chapter 16.

Multiple Express Warranties What happens when a seller gives two or more express warranties and those warranties arguably conflict? UCC section 2–317 says that such warranties should be read as consistent with each other and as cumulative if this is reasonable. If not, the parties' intention controls. In determining that intention: (1) exact or technical specifications defeat a sample, a model, or general descriptive language; and (2) a sample defeats general descriptive language.

MARTIN RISPENS & SON v. HALL FARMS, INC.   601 N.E.2d 429 (Ind. Ct. App. 1992)

Hall Farms, Inc. ordered 40 pounds of Prince Charles watermelon seed from Martin Rispens & Son, a seed dealer. Rispens had obtained the seed from Petoseed Company, Inc., a seed producer. The label on Petoseed's can stated that the seeds are "top quality seeds with high vitality, vigor and germination." Hall Farms germinated the seeds in a greenhouse, before transplanting the small watermelon plants to its fields. Although the plants had a few abnormalities, they grew rapidly. By mid-July, however, purple blotches had spread over most of the crop, and by the end of July the crop was ruined. It was later determined that the crop had been destroyed by "watermelon fruit blotch." Hall Farms' lost profits on the crop came to $180,000.

Hall Farms sued Petoseed for, among other things, breach of express warranty. Petoseed moved for summary judgment, but the trial court denied the motion. Petoseed appealed. ∞

Baker, Judge An express warranty is created by an affirmation of fact or promise made by the seller to the buyer which relates to the goods and becomes part of the basis of the bargain; it warrants that the goods shall conform to the affirmation or promise. It is not necessary that the seller use formal words such as "warrant" or "guarantee" or that he have a specific intention to make a warranty. On the other hand, an affirmation merely of the value of the goods or a statement purporting to be merely the seller's opinion or commendation of the goods does not create a warranty.

Whether a given representation is a warranty or merely an expression of the seller's opinion is determined in part by considering whether the seller asserts a fact of which the buyer is ignorant, or merely states an opinion or judgment on a matter of which the seller has no special knowledge and on which the buyer may be expected also to have an opinion and to exercise his judgment. Courts must also consider the degree of specificity expressed in the representation.

The label on Petoseed's can stated that the seeds are "top quality seeds with high vitality, vigor and germination." We consider the words "top quality seeds" as a classic example of puffery. The precise meaning of "top quality" is subject to considerably different interpretations.

Petoseed [also] claimed that its seeds possessed "high vitality, vigor and germination." Although reasonable people may differ as to the particular degree of vitality, vigor, and germination meant by the word "high," Petoseed did expressly warrant that its seeds would possess at least a modicum of vitality, vigor, and germination. If this affirmation became a basis of the bargain, an express warranty was created. We need not address this question, however, because even assuming Hall Farms relied on the affirmation, no breach occurred.

"Vitality" is the capacity to live, grow, or develop. "Vigor" is the capacity for natural growth and survival. "Germination" is the beginning of growth or sprouting. Here, there is no dispute that the watermelon seeds sprouted, grew, and developed a normal fruit set. Thus, the seeds conformed to the affirmation on Petoseed's labels; consequently, there was no breach. Partial summary judgment is appropriate when there is no conflict over facts dispositive of a portion of the litigation. Hall Farms may not recover from Petoseed based on an express warranty theory.

Trial court decision denying Petoseed's motion for summary judgment on Hall Farms' express warranty claim reversed.

Implied Warranty of Merchantability

An **implied warranty** is a warranty created by *operation of law* rather than the seller's express statements. UCC section 2–314(1) creates the Code's **implied warranty of merchantability** by stating that "a warranty that the goods shall be merchantable is implied in a contract for their sale if the seller is a merchant with respect to goods of that kind." This is a clear example of the 20th-century tendency for government to intervene in private contracts to protect consumers.

In an implied warranty of merchantability case, the plaintiff argues that the seller breached the warranty by selling nonmerchantable goods. Under section 2–314, such claims can succeed only where the seller is a *merchant with respect to goods of the kind sold.*[4] A housewife's sale of homemade preserves or a hardware store owner's sale of a used car, for example, do not trigger the implied warranty of merchantability.

UCC section 2–314(2) states that, to be merchantable, goods must at least: (1) pass without objection in the trade; (2) be fit for the ordinary purposes for which such goods are used; (3) be of even kind, quality, and quantity within each unit (case, package, or carton); (4) be adequately contained, packaged, and labeled; (5) conform to any promises or statements of fact made on the con-

tainer or label; and (6) in the case of fungible goods, be of fair average quality. The most important of these requirements is that the goods must be *fit for the ordinary purposes for which such goods are used.* The goods need not be perfect to be fit for their ordinary purposes. Rather, they need only meet the reasonable expectations of the average consumer.

This broad, flexible test of merchantability is almost inevitable given the wide range of products sold in the United States today and the varied defects they can present. Still, a few generalizations about merchantability determinations are possible. Goods that fail to function properly or that have harmful side effects normally are not merchantable. A computer that fails to work properly or that destroys the owner's programs, for example, is not fit for the ordinary purposes for which computers are used. In cases involving allergic reactions to drugs or other products, courts frequently find the defendant liable if it was reasonably foreseeable that an appreciable number of consumers would suffer the reaction. As the following *Marriott* case reveals, there is some disagreement about the standard for food products that are alleged to be nonmerchantable because they contain harmful objects or substances. Under the *foreign–natural* test, the defendant is liable if the object or substance is "foreign" to the product, but not liable if it is "natural" to that product. Increasingly, however, courts ask whether the food product met the consumer's *reasonable expectations.*

---

[4]The term *merchant* is defined in Chapter 9.

YONG CHA HONG v. MARRIOTT CORPORATION   3 UCC Rep. Serv. 2d 83 (D. Md. 1987)

Yong Cha Hong bought some take-out fried chicken from a Roy Rogers Family Restaurant owned by the Marriott Corporation. While eating a chicken wing from her order, she bit into an object that she perceived to be a worm. Claiming permanent injuries and great physical and emotional upset from this incident, Hong sued Marriott for $500,000 in federal district court under the implied warranty of merchantability. After introducing an expert's report alleging that the object in the chicken wing was not a worm, Marriott moved for summary judgment. It claimed that the case involved no disputed issues of material fact, and that there was no breach of the implied warranty of merchantability as a matter of law.

Smalkin, District Judge   It appears that the item encountered by plaintiff was probably not a worm or other parasite, although plaintiff, in her deposition, steadfastly maintains that it was a worm. If it

was not a worm (i.e., if the expert analysis is correct), it was either one of the chicken's major blood vessels (the aorta) or its trachea, both of which would appear worm-like (although not meaty like a worm, but hollow). For [present] purposes, the court will assume that the item was not a worm. Precisely how the aorta or trachea wound up in this hapless chicken's wing is a fascinating, but as yet unanswered (and presently immaterial), question.

Does Maryland law provide a breach of warranty remedy for personal injury flowing from an unexpected encounter with an inedible part of the chicken's anatomy in a piece of fast food fried chicken? Marriott contends that there can be no recovery unless the offending item was a foreign object, i.e., not part of the chicken itself.

In many cases that have denied [implied] warranty recovery as a matter of law, the injurious substance was, as in this case, a natural (though inedible) part of the edible item consumed. Thus, in *Shapiro v. Hotel Statler Corp.* (1955), recovery was denied for a fish bone in "Hot Barquette of Seafood Mornay." But in all these cases the natural item was reasonably to be expected in the dish by its very nature, under the prevailing expectation of any reasonable consumer. Indeed, precisely this "reasonable expectation" test has been adopted in a number of cases. The reasonable expectation test has largely displaced the foreign–natural test adverted to by Marriott. This court is confident that Maryland would apply the reasonable expectation rule.

The court cannot conclude that the presence of a trachea or an aorta in a fast food fried chicken wing is so reasonably to be expected as to render it merchantable, as a matter of law. This is not like the situation [in a previous case] involving a one centimeter bone in a piece of fried fish. Everyone but a fool knows that tiny bones may remain in even the best filets of fish. This case is more like [another decision], where the court held that the issue was for the trier of fact, on a claim arising from a cherry pit in cherry ice cream. Thus, a question is presented that precludes the grant of summary judgment. The jury must determine whether a piece of fast food fried chicken is merchantable if it contains an inedible item of the chicken's anatomy. Of course, the jury will be instructed that the consumer's reasonable expectations form a part of the merchantability concept.

Marriott's motion for summary judgment denied.

Implied Warranty of Fitness

UCC section 2–315's **implied warranty of fitness for a particular purpose** arises where: (1) the seller has reason to know a particular purpose for which the buyer requires the goods, (2) the seller has reason to know that the buyer is relying on the seller's skill or judgment to select suitable goods, and (3) the buyer actually relies on the seller's skill or judgment in purchasing the goods. If these tests are met, there is an implied warranty that the goods will be fit for the buyer's *particular* purpose.

In many fitness warranty cases, buyers effectively put themselves in the seller's hands by making their needs known and saying that they are relying on the seller to select goods that will satisfy those needs. This may happen, for example, where a seller sells a computer system specially manufactured or customized for a buyer's particular needs. But sellers also can be liable where the circumstances reasonably indicate that the buyer has a particular purpose and is relying on the seller to satisfy that purpose, even though the buyer fails to make either explicit. However, buyers may have trouble recovering where they are more expert than the seller, submit specifications for the goods they wish to buy, inspect the goods, actually select them, or insist on a particular brand.

As the following *Dempsey* case states, the implied warranty of fitness differs from the implied warranty of merchantability. The tests for the creation of each warranty plainly are different. Under section 2–315, moreover, sellers only warrant that the goods are fit for the buyer's *particular* purposes, not the *ordinary* purposes for which such goods are used. If a 400-pound man asks a department store for a hammock that will support his weight but is sold a hammock that only can support normally sized people, there is a breach of the implied warranty of fitness but no breach of the implied warranty of merchantability. If the hammock cannot support *anyone's* weight, however, both warranties are breached.

R uby Dempsey purchased a nine-week-old pedigreed male poodle from the American Kennels Pet Stores. She named the poodle Mr. Dunphy. Dempsey later testified that before making the purchase, she told the salesperson that she wanted a dog suitable for breeding purposes. Five days after the sale, she had Mr. Dunphy examined by a veterinarian, who discovered that the poodle had one undescended testicle. This condition did not seriously affect Mr. Dunphy's fertility, but it was a genetic defect that would probably be passed on to any offspring sired. Also, a dog with this condition could not be used as a show dog.

Dempsey demanded a refund from American Kennels, but her demand was denied. She then sued in small claims court, alleging that American Kennels had breached the implied warranty of fitness. ∞

Saxe, Judge UCC sections 2–314 and 2–315 make it clear that the warranty of fitness for a particular purpose is narrower, more specific, and more precise than the warranty of merchantability, which involves fitness for the *ordinary* purposes for which goods are used. The following are the conditions that are not required by the implied warranty of merchantability, but that must be present if a plaintiff is to recover on the basis of the implied warranty of fitness: (1) the seller must have reason to know the buyer's particular purpose, (2) the seller must have reason to know that the buyer is relying on the seller's skill or judgment to furnish appropriate goods, and (3) the buyer must, in fact, rely upon the seller's skill or judgment.

I find that the warranty of fitness for a particular purpose has been breached. Dempsey testified that

she specified to the salesperson that she wanted a dog that was suitable for breeding purposes. Although this is disputed by the defendant, the credible testimony supports Dempsey's version of the event. Further, it is reasonable for the seller of a pedigreed dog to assume that the buyer intends to breed it. But it is undisputed by the experts here (for both sides) that Mr. Dunphy was as capable of siring a litter as a male dog with two viable and descended testicles. This, the defendant contends, compels a finding in its favor. I disagree. While it is true that Mr. Dunphy's fertility level may be unaffected, his stud value, because of this hereditary condition (which is likely to be passed on to future generations), is severely diminished.

Judgment for Dempsey.

Negligence

Product liability suits based on the **negligence** theory discussed in Chapter 7 usually allege that the seller or manufacturer breached a duty to the plaintiff by failing to eliminate a reasonably foreseeable risk of harm associated with the product.[5] Such suits typically claim one or more of the following: (1) negligent *manufacture* of the goods (including improper materials and packaging), (2) negligent *inspection,* (3) a negligent failure to provide *adequate warnings* of hazards or defects, and (4) negligently defective *design.*

Negligent Manufacture   Negligence suits alleging the manufacturer's improper assembly, materials, or packaging often encounter problems because the evidence needed to prove a breach of duty is under the defendant's control. However, liberal modern discovery rules and the doctrine of *res ipsa loquitur* can help plaintiffs establish a breach in such situations.[6]

Improper Inspection   Manufacturers have a duty to inspect their products for defects that create a reasonably foreseeable risk of harm, if such an inspection would be practicable and effective. As before, *res ipsa loquitur* and modern discovery rules

---

[5]Occasionally, such suits may proceed under the theory of *negligence per se* discussed in Chapter 7—for example, where the product violates a consumer product safety regulation or pure food law.

[6]Chapter 2 discusses discovery, and Chapter 7 discusses *res ipsa loquitur.*

can help plaintiffs prove their case against the manufacturer.

Most courts have held that middlemen such as retailers and wholesalers have a duty to inspect the goods they sell only when they have actual knowledge or reason to know of a defect. In addition, such parties generally have no duty to inspect where this would be unduly difficult, burdensome, or time-consuming. Unless the product defect is obvious, for example, middlemen usually are not liable for failing to inspect goods sold in the manufacturer's original packages or containers.

On the other hand, sellers who prepare, install, or repair the goods they sell ordinarily have a duty to inspect those goods. Examples include restaurants, automobile dealers, and installers of household products. In general, the scope of the inspection need only be consistent with the preparation, installation, or repair work performed. Thus, it is unlikely that such sellers must unearth hidden or latent defects.

If there is a duty to inspect and the inspection reveals a defect, further duties can arise. For example, a seller or manufacturer may be required not to sell the product in its defective state, or at least to give a suitable warning.

Failure to Warn   Sellers and manufacturers have a duty to give an appropriate warning when their products pose a reasonably foreseeable risk of harm. But in determining whether there was a duty to warn and whether the defendant's warning was adequate, courts often consider other factors besides the reasonable foreseeability of the risk. These include the *magnitude or severity* of the likely harm, the *ease or difficulty of providing an appropriate warning,* and the likely *effectiveness of a warning.* As the following *Daniell* case makes clear, moreover, there is no duty to warn where the risk is *open and obvious.*

Design Defects   Manufacturers have a duty to design their products so as to avoid reasonably foreseeable risks of harm. Like failure-to-warn cases, however, design defect cases frequently involve other factors besides reasonable foreseeability. As before, one of these factors is the *magnitude or severity* of the foreseeable harm. Three others are *industry practices* at the time the product was manufactured, the *state of the art* (the state of existing scientific and technical knowledge) at that time, and the product's compliance or noncompliance with *government safety regulations.*[7]

Sometimes courts employ *risk–benefit analysis* when weighing these factors. In such analyses, three other factors—the design's *social utility,* the *effectiveness of alternative designs,* and the *cost of safer designs*—may figure in the weighing process. Even where the balancing process indicates that the design was not defective, courts still may require a suitable warning.

---

[7]Some states have statutes stating that a product's compliance with state or federal product safety regulations creates a rebuttable presumption that it was not defective. Also, a few states have a statutory state-of-the-art defense.

DANIELL v. FORD MOTOR COMPANY   581 F. Supp. 728 (D.N.M. 1984)

Connie Daniell attempted to commit suicide by locking herself inside the trunk of her 1973 Ford LTD. Daniell remained in the trunk for nine days, but survived after finally being rescued. Later, Daniell sued Ford in negligence to recover for her resulting physical and psychological injuries. She contended that the LTD was defectively designed because its trunk did not have an internal release or opening mechanism. She also argued that Ford was liable for negligently failing to warn her that the trunk could not be unlocked from within. Ford moved for summary judgment. ∞

Baldock, District Judge   As a general principle, a design defect is actionable only where the condition of the product is unreasonably dangerous to the user or consumer. Under negligence, a manufacturer has a duty to consider only those risks of injury which are foreseeable. A risk is not foreseeable where a product is used in a manner which could not reasonably be anticipated by the manufacturer and that use is the cause of the plaintiff's injury.

The purposes of an automobile trunk are to transport, stow, and secure the spare tire, luggage, and other goods and to protect those items from the weather. The design features of a trunk make it well near impossible that an adult intentionally would enter the trunk and close the lid. The dimensions of a trunk, the height of its sill and its load floor, and the efforts to first lower the lid and then to engage its latch, are among the design features which encourage closing and latching the trunk lid while standing outside the vehicle. The court holds that the plaintiff's use of the trunk compartment as a means to attempt suicide was an unforeseeable use as a matter of law. Therefore, the manufacturer had no duty to design an internal release or opening mechanism that might have prevented this occurrence.

Nor did the manufacturer have a duty to warn the plaintiff of the danger of her conduct, given the plaintiff's unforeseeable use of the product. Another reason why the manufacturer had no duty to warn the plaintiff of the risk inherent in crawling into an automobile trunk and closing the lid is [that] such a risk is obvious. There is no duty to warn of known dangers. Moreover, the potential efficacy of any warning, given the plaintiff's use of the trunk for a deliberate suicide attempt, is questionable.

Having held that the plaintiff's conception of the manufacturer's duty is in error, the court need not reach the issues of comparative negligence or other defenses such as assumption of risk.

Ford's motion for summary judgment granted; Daniell loses.

Strict Liability

Strict products liability is a relatively recent development. Only during the 1960s did courts begin to impose such liability in significant numbers. The movement toward strict liability received a big boost when the American Law Institute promulgated section 402A of the *Restatement (Second) of Torts* in 1965. By now, the vast majority of the states have adopted some form of strict products liability. The most important reason is the socialization-of-risk strategy discussed earlier. By not requiring plaintiffs to prove a breach of duty, strict liability makes it easier for them to recover; and sellers then are supposed to pass on the costs of this liability through higher prices. Another justification for strict products liability is that it stimulates manufacturers to design and build safer products.

Section 402A's Requirements   Because it is the most common version of strict products liability, we limit our discussion of the subject to section 402A. Section 402A provides that a "seller . . . engaged in the business of selling" a particular product is liable for physical harm or property damage suffered by the ultimate user or consumer of that product, if the product was "in a defective condition unreasonably dangerous to the user or consumer or to his property." This rule applies even though "the seller has exercised all possible care in the preparation and sale of his product." Thus, section 402A states a rule of strict liability that does not require plaintiffs to prove a breach of duty.

However, the liability imposed by section 402A is not absolute, for the section applies only if certain tests are met.

1. The seller must be *engaged in the business of selling the product that harmed the plaintiff.* Thus, section 402A only binds parties who resemble UCC merchants because they regularly sell the product at issue. For example, the section does not apply to a college professor's or a clothing store's sale of a used car.

2. The product must be in a *defective condition* when sold, and also must be *unreasonably dangerous* because of that condition. The usual test of a product's defective condition is whether the product meets the reasonable expectations of the average consumer. An unreasonably dangerous product is one that is dangerous to an extent beyond the reasonable contemplation of the average consumer. For example, good whiskey is not unreasonably dangerous even though it can cause harm, but whiskey contaminated with a poisonous substance qualifies. Some courts balance the product's social utility against its danger when determining whether it is unreasonably dangerous. As the following *Rauscher* case makes clear, defective condition and unreasonable danger determinations often are for the jury.

Due to section 402A's unreasonably dangerous requirement, it covers a smaller range of product defects than the implied warranty of merchantability. A power mower that simply fails to operate is not unreasonably dangerous, although it would not be merchantable. Some courts, however, blur the defective condition and unreasonably dangerous requirements, and a few have done away with the latter test.

3. Finally, defendants can avoid section 402A liability where the product was *substantially modified* by the plaintiff or another party after the sale, and the modification contributed to the plaintiff's injury or other loss.

Applications of Section 402A   Design defect and failure-to-warn suits can be brought under section 402A. Even though section 402A is a strict liability provision, the standards applied in such cases resemble the negligence standards discussed in the previous section.

Because it applies to sellers, section 402A covers retailers and other middlemen who market goods containing defects that they did not create and may not have been able to discover. Even though such parties often escape negligence liability, some courts have found them liable under section 402A's strict liability rule. However, other states have given middlemen some protection against 402A liability, and/or have required the manufacturer or other responsible party to indemnify them.

What about products, such as some drugs, that have great social utility, but that pose serious risks that cannot be eliminated? Imposing strict liability on such "unavoidably unsafe" products might deter manufacturers from developing and marketing them. Where products of this kind cause harm and a lawsuit follows, many courts follow comment k to section 402A. Comment k says that unavoidably unsafe products are neither defective nor unreasonably dangerous if they are properly prepared and accompanied by proper directions and a proper warning. For this rule to apply, the product must be genuinely incapable of being made safer.

RAUSCHER v. GENERAL MOTORS CORPORATION   905 S.W.2d 158 (Mo. Ct. App. 1995)

D*avid Rauscher bought a new Buick Century automobile in March 1981. In May of that year, with the car's odometer showing 2,476 miles, Rauscher took it to a local Buick dealer for service because the car's engine would sometimes hesitate and die. The dealer failed to fix the problem, which intermittently continued over the next five years despite at least five additional service trips by* Rauscher.

On June 5, 1986, Rauscher's daughter Madonna drove the Buick to school. When she pulled out from a stop sign to make a left turn on U.S. 40, the car stalled. It then was struck by another car proceeding along U.S. 40, causing personal injury to Madonna.

Madonna sued General Motors, among others, in a Missouri trial court. After the court directed a verdict for General Motors, she appealed.

Blackmar, Senior Judge   The case against General Motors is based on strict liability, as stated in section 402A, *Restatement (Second) of Torts* and adopted by the Supreme Court of Missouri. The essential elements of a strict product liability claim may be paraphrased as follows: (1) the defendant sold a product in the course of its business; (2) the product was then in a defective condition, unreasonably dangerous; (3) the product was used in a manner reasonably anticipated; and (4) the plaintiff was damaged as a direct result of such defective condition.

The plaintiff's evidence would permit a jury to find that each of these elements had been established. The jury has broad authority to determine whether a defective and unreasonably dangerous condition is present. A jury could surely find that an automobile subject to unpredictable stalls and stops, which might occur in traffic, was in a defective condition, and that the condition was unreasonably dangerous. Expert testimony would not be needed; jurors themselves could appreciate the danger by reason of their own experience. The danger is demonstrated by the [condition's] recurrence at unpredictable intervals, which might contribute to accidents such as the plaintiff sustained.

The jury could find that the condition was present at the time David purchased the car new. The problem first appeared within a few months, with less than 2,500 miles on the odometer. The same difficulty appeared, intermittently, up to the time of the accident. Prior to the first [service] trip the automobile was driven only on roads, and had no abnormal incidents. There was also evidence, in the form of General Motors service bulletins and the testimony of mechanics, that some 1981 Buick Centuries were prone to stall and die.

The jury, therefore, could have returned a verdict for the plaintiff. By no means was it compelled to do so. We reiterate the caution that trial judges should direct verdicts only in clear cases. It is better to take the jury's verdict and then take appropriate action on post-trial motions.

Directed verdict in favor of General Motors reversed; case returned to the trial court for retrial.

Other Theories of Recovery

Warranty of Title   Normally, a seller of goods impliedly warrants that: (1) the title he conveys is good and transfer of that title is rightful, and (2) the goods are free from any lien or security interest of which the buyer lacks knowledge. Thus, a buyer may recover damages against his seller where, for example, the seller has marketed stolen goods or goods that are subject to a third party's security interest. Also, a seller who is a merchant in goods of the kind sold normally warrants that the goods are free of any rightful patent or trademark infringement claim, or any similar claim, by a third party.

The Magnuson-Moss Act   The relevant civil-recovery provisions of the federal Magnuson-Moss Warranty Act apply to sales of *consumer products* costing more than *$10 per item*.[8] A consumer

---

[8]Other portions of the Magnuson-Moss Act are discussed later in this chapter and in Chapter 47.

C O N C E P T   R E V I E W

Comparing the Major Product Liability Theories—The Basics

THEORY	TORT OR CONTRACT	TYPE OF DEFENDANT	NATURE OF GOODS SOLD	REMARKS
Express Warranty	Contract	Seller of goods	Not as warranted by affirmation of fact or promise, description, sample, or model	Exemption for statements of value, opinion, or sales talk
Implied Warranty of Merchantability	Contract	Merchant for goods sold	Not merchantable; usually, not fit for ordinary purposes for which such goods used	Merchantability has other aspects
Implied Warranty of Fitness	Contract	Seller of goods	Not fit for buyer's particular purposes	Seller must have reason to know of buyer's needs and buyer's reliance, and buyer must actually rely.
Negligence	Tort	Manufacturer or seller of goods	"Defective" due to improper manufacture, inspection, design, or failure to give suitable warning	Limited inspection duty for middlemen
Section 402A	Tort	Seller engaged in business of selling product sold	Defective and unreasonably dangerous	Strict liability; design defect and failure-to-warn suits possible

product is tangible personal property normally used for personal, family, or household purposes. If a seller gives a *written warranty* for such a product to a *consumer,* the warranty must be designated full or limited. A seller who gives a full warranty promises to: (1) *remedy* any defects in the product and (2) *replace* the product or *refund* its purchase price if, after a reasonable number of attempts, it cannot be repaired.[9] A seller who gives a limited warranty is bound to whatever promises it actually makes. However, neither warranty applies if the seller simply declines to give a written warranty.

Misrepresentation   Section 402B of the *Restatement (Second) of Torts* lets *consumers* recover for *personal injury* resulting from certain *misrepresentations* about goods they have purchased. The misrepresentation must: (1) be made by a party engaged in the business of selling goods of the kind purchased; (2) be made to the public by advertising, labels, or similar means; (3) concern a fact *material* to the goods purchased; and (4) be *actually* and *justifiably* relied upon by the consumer. Suppose the manufacturer of a laxative states in its advertising that the laxative has no adverse side effects if used as directed. Smith, who has been influenced by the advertisements and has no reason to doubt their accuracy, buys a bottle of the laxative. If, after using it according to directions, Smith suffers injury to his digestive system, he can recover from the manufacturer for that injury.

INDUSTRYWIDE LIABILITY

The development we call industrywide liability is a way for plaintiffs to bypass problems of *causation* that exist where several firms within an industry have manufactured a harmful standardized product, and it is impossible for the plaintiff to prove which firm produced the product that injured her. The main reasons for these proof problems are the number of firms producing the product and the time lag between exposure to the product and the appearance of the injury. Many of the cases presenting such problems have involved DES (an antimiscarriage drug that has produced various ailments in daughters of the women to whom it was administered) or diseases resulting from long-term exposure to asbestos. In such cases, each manufacturer of the product can argue that the plaintiff should lose because she cannot show that its product harmed her.

How do the courts handle these cases? Some continue to deny recovery under traditional causation rules. However, using various theories whose many details are beyond the scope of this text, other courts have made it easier for plaintiffs to recover. Where recovery is allowed, some of these courts have *apportioned* damages among the firms that might have produced the harm-causing product. Typically, the apportionment is based on market share at some chosen time.

TIME LIMITATIONS

At this point, we begin to consider several problems that are common to each major theory of product liability recovery but that may be resolved differently from theory to theory.[10] One such problem is the time within which the plaintiff must sue or else lose the case. Traditionally, the main time limits on product liability suits have been the applicable contract and tort **statutes of limitations.** The usual UCC statute of limitations for express and implied warranty claims is four years after the seller offers the defective goods to the buyer (usually, four years after the sale).[11] In negligence and strict liability cases, the applicable tort statute of limitations generally is shorter, but it only begins to run when the defect was or should have been discovered—often, the time of the injury.

Due in part to tort reform, some states now impose various other limitations on the time within which product liability suits must be brought. Often, these limitations apply only to claims for death, personal injury, and property damage, but they override the states' other time limitations where they do apply. Among these additional time limitations are: (1) special statutes of limitations for product liability cases involving death, personal injury,

---

[9]Also, many states have enacted so-called lemon laws that may apply only to motor vehicles or to various other consumer products as well. The versions applying to motor vehicles generally require the manufacturer to replace the vehicle or refund its purchase price once certain conditions are met. These conditions may include the following: a serious defect covered by warranty, a certain number of unsuccessful attempts at repair or a certain amount of downtime due to attempted repairs, and the manufacturer's failure to show that the defect is curable.

[10]We do not consider how these problems are resolved under the warranty of title, the Magnuson-Moss Act, or section 402B.

[11]Also, in express and implied warranty cases, the buyer must notify the seller of the breach within a reasonable time after the buyer discovers or should have discovered it. There is no notice requirement for negligence and strict liability suits.

or property damage (e.g., from one to three years after the time the death or injury occurred or should have been discovered); (2) special time limits for "delayed manifestation" injuries such as those resulting from exposure to asbestos; (3) useful safe life defenses (which prevent plaintiffs from suing once the product's "useful safe life" has passed); and (4) statutes of repose (whose aim is similar). Statutes of repose usually run for a 10 to 12-year period that begins when the product is sold to the first buyer not purchasing for resale—usually an ordinary consumer. In a state with a 10-year statute of repose, for example, such parties cannot recover for injuries that occur more than 10 years after they purchased the product causing the injury. This is true even when the suit is begun quickly enough to satisfy the applicable statute of limitations.

DAMAGES IN PRODUCT LIABILITY SUITS

The damages obtainable under each theory of product liability recovery strongly influence a plaintiff's strategy. Here, we describe the major kinds of damages awarded in products liability cases, along with the theories under which each can be recovered. One lawsuit can involve claims for all these sorts of damages.

1. *Basis of the bargain damages.* Buyers of defective goods have not received full value for the goods' purchase price. The resulting loss, usually called basis-of-the-bargain damages or direct economic loss, is the value of the goods as promised under the contract, minus the value of the goods as received.

As the following *Peachtree* case suggests, basis-of-the-bargain damages usually are *not* awarded in *negligence* and *strict liability* cases. In *express* and *implied warranty* suits, however, basis-of-the-bargain damages are recoverable where there was *privity of contract* (a direct contractual relation) between the plaintiff and the defendant. As discussed in the next section, however, only occasionally will a warranty plaintiff who lacks privity with the defendant obtain basis-of-the-bargain damages. Such recoveries most often occur where an express warranty was made to a remote plaintiff through advertising, brochures, or labels.

2. *Consequential damages.* Consequential damages include: **personal injury, property damage** (dam-

age to the plaintiff's other property), and **indirect economic loss** (e.g., lost profits or lost business reputation) resulting from a product defect. Consequential damages also include **noneconomic loss**— for example, pain and suffering, physical impairment, mental distress, loss of enjoyment of life, loss of companionship or consortium, inconvenience, and disfigurement. Noneconomic loss usually is part of the plaintiff's personal injury claim. Recently, several states have limited noneconomic loss recoveries, typically by imposing a dollar cap on them.

Plaintiffs in *negligence* and *strict liability* cases normally can recover for personal injury and property damage. Recoveries for foreseeable indirect economic loss sometimes are allowed.

In *express* and *implied warranty* suits where *privity exists* between the plaintiff and the defendant, the plaintiff can recover for: (1) personal injury and property damage, if either proximately resulted from the breach of warranty; and (2) indirect economic loss, if the defendant had reason to know that this was likely. As discussed in the next section, a UCC plaintiff who *lacks privity* with the defendant has a fairly good chance of recovering for personal injury or property damage. But recovery for indirect economic loss is rare because remote sellers usually cannot foresee such losses.

3. *Punitive Damages.* Punitive damages are intended to punish defendants who have acted in an especially outrageous fashion, and to deter them and others from so acting in the future. Of the various standards for awarding punitive damages, perhaps the most common is the defendant's conscious or reckless disregard for the safety of those likely to be affected by the goods. Examples include concealment of known product hazards, knowing violation of government or industry product safety standards, failure to correct known dangerous defects, and grossly inadequate product testing or quality control procedures. Due to their perceived frequency, size, and effect on business and the economy, punitive damages have been subjected to state tort reform regulation throughout the 1980s and 1990s. The approaches taken by these statutes vary. Some set the standards for punitive damage recovery and the plaintiff's burden of proof; some articulate factors courts should consider when ruling on punitive damage awards; and some create special procedures for punitive damage determinations. Also, many states have limited the size of punitive damage recoveries, usually by restricting them to some

FIGURE I

When the Various Kinds of Damages Are Recoverable

Types of Damages	Express and Implied Warranty	Negligence and Section 402A
Basis of the Bargain	Within privity: Yes Outside privity: Occasionally	Rarely
Personal Injury and Property Damage	Within privity: If proximate result of breach Outside privity: Fairly good chance	Yes
Indirect Economic Loss	Within privity: If defendant has reason to know this likely Outside privity: Rarely	Sometimes
Punitive Damages	Rarely	Yes, in appropriate cases

multiple of the plaintiff's actual damages or by putting a flat dollar cap on them.

Assuming that the standards just described have been met, punitive damages are recoverable in *negligence* and *strict liability* cases. Due to the traditional rule that punitive damages are not avail-

able in contract cases, they usually are not awarded in *express* and *implied warranty* suits.

Figure 1 summarizes the plaintiff's chances of recovering the most important kinds of damages in contract and tort cases.

OCEANSIDE AT PINE POINT CONDOMINIUM OWNERS ASSOCIATION v. PEACHTREE DOORS, INC.
659 A.2d 267 (Me. Sup. Jud. Ct. 1995)

O*n June 25, 1986, a general contractor completed the Oceanside at Pine Point Condominium. In the construction, the contractor used windows manufactured by Peachtree Doors, Inc. Peachtree delivered the windows to the contractor in December 1985. After sale of the condominium units to the public, the condominium building suffered significant water damage around the windows. Pine Point's owners' association brought a class action product liability suit against Peachtree on December 31, 1991. The trial court entered summary judgment in Peachtree's favor on the association's warranty and tort claims. It held that the statute of limitations had run on the warranty claims and that the plaintiffs sought damages not recoverable under their tort claims. The plaintiffs appealed.* ∞

Clifford, Justice A lawsuit alleging damage or injury from a defective product may be based on a number of theories, including strict liability, negligence, and breach of warranty. Under tort theories, recovery is permitted for personal injuries and physical damage to property other than the defective product. Courts generally do not permit tort recovery for a defective product's damage to itself [basis-of-the-bargain damages]. Damage to a product itself means simply that the product has not met the customer's expectations, or that the customer has received insufficient product value. The maintenance of product value and quality is precisely the purpose of express and implied warranties. The failure of the product to function properly is distinguishable from those situations, traditionally within

the purview of tort, where the plaintiff has been exposed, through a hazardous product, to an unreasonable risk of injury to his person or property.

Whether a product has injured only itself may be a difficult question to answer. We follow the approach taken by courts when considering facts analogous to those before us, and look to the product purchased by the plaintiff, as opposed to the product sold by the defendant, to determine whether a product has injured only itself [citing cases]. The plaintiffs here purchased finished condominium units, not individual components of the units. Because the windows were integrated into the finished product, the damages caused by any defects in the windows constituted damage to the product itself, not damage to other property. Plaintiffs' claims for economic damages are properly addressable under a warranty theory. The plaintiffs may not recover for these damages in tort.

The statute of limitations applying to most breach of warranty claims is four years from the date of accrual, which occurs when tender of delivery is made. The cause of action accrued either when the windows were delivered [to the contrac-

tor] in December 1985, or when the project was completed in June 1986. Accordingly, the claim expired prior to the institution of this lawsuit in December 1991.

Trial court decision granting Peachtree summary judgment on the plaintiffs' warranty and tort claims affirmed.

THE NO-PRIVITY DEFENSE

Today, defective products often move through long chains of distribution before reaching the person they harm. This means that a product liability plaintiff often has not dealt directly with the party ultimately responsible for his losses. Figure 2 depicts a hypothetical chain of distribution in which goods defectively produced by a manufacturer of component parts move vertically through the manufacturer of a product in which those parts are used, a wholesaler, and a retailer, ultimately reaching the buyer. The defect's consequences may move horizontally as well, affecting members of the buyer's family, guests in his home, and even bystanders. If the buyer or one of these parties suffers loss due to the defect in the component parts, can he successfully sue the component parts manufacturer or any other party in the vertical chain of distribution with whom he did not directly deal?

Such suits were unlikely to succeed under 19th-century law. At that time, there was no recovery for defective goods without privity of contract between the plaintiff and the defendant. In the example above, the buyer would have been required to sue his dealer. If the buyer was successful, the retailer might have sued the wholesaler, and so on up the chain. For various reasons (including a middleman's limited negligence liability for failure to inspect), the party ultimately responsible for the defect often escaped liability.

Negligence and Strict Liability Cases

By now, the old no-liability-outside-privity rule has been severely eroded in tort suits. It has little, if any, effect in *strict liability* cases, where even bystanders can recover against remote manufacturers. In *negligence* cases, a plaintiff generally recovers against a

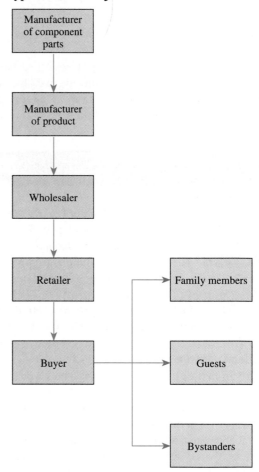

FIGURE **2**

A Hypothetical Chain of Distribution

remote defendant if the plaintiff's loss was a reasonably foreseeable consequence of the defect. Depending on the circumstances, therefore, bystanders and other distant parties might recover against a manufacturer in negligence as well.

Warranty Cases

The no-privity defense still retains some vitality in UCC cases. Unfortunately, the "law" on this subject is complex and confusing. Under the Code, the privity question is formally governed by section 2–318, which comes in three alternative versions. Section 2–318's language, however, is a questionable guide to the courts' actual behavior in UCC privity cases.

UCC Section 2–318   Alternative A to section 2–318 says that a seller's express or implied warranty runs to natural persons in the family or household of *his* (the seller's) buyer and to guests in his buyer's home, if they suffer personal injury and if it was reasonable to expect that they might use, consume, or be affected by the goods sold. On its face, Alternative A does little to undermine the traditional no-privity defense. In Figure 2, Alternative A would merely allow the buyer, his family, and guests in his home to sue the *retailer* for their personal injury.

Alternatives B and C go much further. Alternative B extends the seller's express or implied warranty to any natural person who has suffered personal injury, if it was reasonable to expect that this person would use, consume, or be affected by the goods. Alternative C is much the same, but it extends the warranty to any person (not just natural persons) and to those suffering injury in general (not just personal injury). If the reasonable-to-expect test is met, these two provisions should extend the warranty to many remote parties, including bystanders.

Departures from Section 2–318   For various reasons, section 2–318's literal language is of questionable relevance in UCC privity cases. Some states have adopted privity statutes that differ from any version of 2–318. Also, one of the comments to section 2–318 lets courts extend liability farther than the section expressly permits. Finally, versions B and C are fairly open ended as written. Thus, the plaintiff's ability to recover outside privity in warranty cases varies from state to state and situation to situation. The most important factors affecting resolution of this question are:

1. Whether it is *reasonably foreseeable* that a party like the plaintiff would be harmed by the product defect in question.
2. The *status of the plaintiff*. On average, consumers and other natural persons fare better outside privity than corporations and other business concerns.
3. The *type of damages* the plaintiff has suffered. In general, remote plaintiffs are: *(a)* most likely to recover for personal injury, *(b)* somewhat less likely to recover for property damage, *(c)* occasionally able to obtain basis of the bargain damages, and *(d)* rarely able to recover for indirect economic loss. Recall from the previous section that a remote plaintiff is most likely to receive basis of the bargain damages where an express warranty was made to him through advertising, brochures, or labels.

DISCLAIMERS AND REMEDY LIMITATIONS

A product liability **disclaimer** is a clause in the sales contract whereby the seller tries to eliminate its *liability* under one or more theories of recovery. A **remedy limitation** is a clause attempting to block recovery of certain *damages*. Disclaimers attack the plaintiff's theory of recovery; if a disclaimer is effective, no damages of any sort are recoverable under that theory. A successful remedy limitation prevents the plaintiff from recovering certain types of damages but does not attack the plaintiff's theory of recovery. Damages not excluded still may be recovered because the theory is left intact.

The main justification for enforcing disclaimers and remedy limitations is freedom of contract. But why would any rational contracting party freely accept a disclaimer or remedy limitation? Because sellers need not insure against lawsuits for defective goods accompanied by an effective disclaimer or remedy limitation, they should be able to sell those goods more cheaply. Thus, enforcing such clauses allows buyers to get a lower price by accepting the economic risk of a product defect. For purchases by ordinary consumers and other unsophisticated buyers, however, this argument often is illusory. Normally sellers present the disclaimer or remedy limitation in a standardized, take-it-or-leave-it fashion. More importantly, it is doubtful whether many consumers read disclaimers and remedy limitations at the time of purchase, or would comprehend them if they were read. As a result, there usually is little or no genuine bargaining over disclaimers or remedy limitations in consumer situations. Instead, they

FIGURE 3

The Enforceability of Implied Warranty Disclaimers

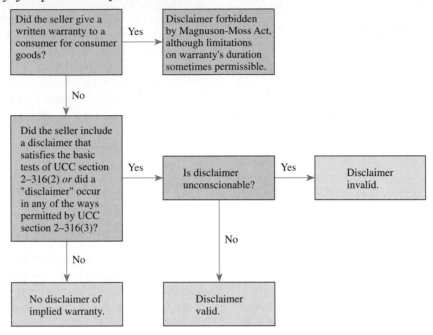

are effectively dictated by a seller with superior size and organization. These observations, however, are less valid where the buyer is a business entity with the capability to engage in genuine bargaining with sellers.

Because the realities surrounding the sale differ from situation to situation, and because some theories of recovery are more hospitable to contractual limitation than others, the law on product liability disclaimers and remedy limitations is complicated. We begin with a lengthy discussion of implied warranty disclaimers. Then we examine disclaimers of express warranty liability, negligence liability, and strict liability, before considering remedy limitations separately.

Implied Warranty Disclaimers

To determine the enforceability of implied warranty disclaimers, we must consider several sets of legal rules.[12] Figure 3 structures the steps in this analysis.

The Basic Tests of UCC Section 2–316(2)   UCC section 2–316(2) apparently makes it easy for sell-

ers to disclaim the implied warranties of merchantability and fitness for a particular purpose. The section states that to exclude or modify the implied warranty of *merchantability,* a seller must: (1) use the word *merchantability,* and (2) make the disclaimer conspicuous if it is written. To exclude or modify the implied warranty of *fitness,* a seller must: (1) use a writing, and (2) make the disclaimer conspicuous. A disclaimer is conspicuous if it is written so that a reasonable person ought to have noticed it. Capital letters, larger type, contrasting type, and contrasting colors usually suffice.

Unlike the fitness warranty disclaimer, a disclaimer of the implied warranty of merchantability can be oral. Also, while disclaimers of the latter warranty must use the word *merchantability,* no special language is needed to disclaim the implied warranty of fitness. For example, a conspicuous written statement that "THERE ARE NO WARRANTIES WHICH EXTEND BEYOND THE DESCRIPTION ON THE FACE HEREOF" disclaims the implied warranty of fitness but not the implied warranty of merchantability.

Other Ways to Disclaim Implied Warranties: Section 2–316(3)   According to UCC section 2–316(3)(a), sellers also can disclaim either implied

---

[12]The same rules probably apply where a seller tries to modify an implied warranty or to limit its duration.

warranty by using such terms as "with all faults," "as is," and "as they stand." Some courts have held that these terms must be conspicuous to be effective as disclaimers.

UCC section 2–316(3)(b) describes two situations where the buyer's *inspection* of the goods or her *refusal to inspect* can act as a disclaimer. If a buyer examines the goods before the sale and fails to discover a defect that should have been reasonably apparent to her, there can be no implied warranty suit based on that defect. Also, if a seller requests that the buyer examine the goods and the buyer refuses, the buyer cannot base an implied warranty suit on a defect that would have been reasonably apparent had she made the inspection. The definition of a reasonably apparent defect varies with the buyer's expertise. Unless the defect is blatant, ordinary consumers may have little to fear from section 2–316(3)(b).

Finally, UCC section 2–316(3)(c) says that an implied warranty can be excluded or modified by *course of dealing* (the parties' previous conduct), *course of performance* (the parties' previous conduct under the same contract), or *usage of trade* (any practice regularly observed in the trade). For example, if it is accepted in the local cattle trade that buyers who inspect the seller's cattle and reject certain animals must accept all defects in the cattle actually purchased, such buyers cannot mount an implied warranty suit for those defects.

Unconscionable Disclaimers   From the previous discussion, it seems that any seller who retains a competent attorney can escape implied warranty liability at will. In fact, however, a seller's ability to disclaim implied warranties sometimes is restricted by the doctrine of **unconscionability** established by UCC section 2–302 and discussed in Chapter 15. By now, almost all courts apply section 2–302's unconscionability standards to implied warranty disclaimers even though those disclaimers satisfy UCC section 2–316(2). Despite a growing willingness to protect smaller firms that deal with corporate giants, however, courts still tend to reject unconscionability claims where business parties have contracted in a commercial context. But implied warranty disclaimers often are declared unconscionable in personal injury suits by ordinary consumers.

The Impact of Magnuson-Moss   The Magnuson-Moss Act also limits a seller's ability to disclaim implied warranties. If a seller gives a consumer a full warranty on consumer goods whose price exceeds $10, the seller may not disclaim, modify, or limit the duration of any implied warranty. If a limited warranty is given, the seller may not disclaim or modify any implied warranty but may limit its duration to the duration of the limited warranty if this is done conspicuously and if the limitation is not unconscionable. These are significant limitations on a seller's power to disclaim implied warranties. Presumably, however, a seller still can disclaim by refusing to give a written warranty while placing the disclaimer on some other writing.

Express Warranty Disclaimers

UCC section 2–316(1) says that an express warranty and a disclaimer should be read consistently if possible, but that the disclaimer must yield if such a reading is unreasonable. Because it normally is unreasonable for a seller to exclude with one hand what he has freely and openly promised with the other, it is difficult to disclaim an express warranty.

Negligence and Strict Liability Disclaimers

Disclaimers of negligence liability and strict liability are usually ineffective in cases involving ordinary consumers. However, some courts enforce such disclaimers where both parties are business entities that: (1) dealt in a commercial setting, (2) had relatively equal bargaining power, (3) bargained the product's specifications, and (4) negotiated the risk of loss from product defects (e.g., the disclaimer itself).

Limitation of Remedies

Due to the expense they can create for sellers, consequential damages are the usual target of remedy limitations. Where a limitation of consequential damages succeeds, buyers of the product may suffer. For example, suppose that Dillman buys a computer system for $20,000 under a contract that excludes consequential damages and limits the buyer's remedies to the repair or replacement of defective parts. Suppose also that the system never works properly, causing Dillman to suffer $10,000 in lost profits. If the remedy limitation is enforceable, Dillman could only have the system replaced or repaired by the seller and could not recover his $10,000 in consequential damages.

In negligence and strict liability cases, the tests for the enforceability of remedy limitations resemble the previous tests for disclaimers. Under the UCC, however, the standards for remedy limitations differ from those for disclaimers. UCC section 2–719(3) allows the limitation of consequential damages in express and implied warranty cases but also states that such a limitation may be unconscionable. The section adds that a limitation of consequential damages is very likely to be unconscionable where the sale is for *consumer goods* and the plaintiff has suffered *personal injury.* Where the loss is "commercial," however, the limitation may or may not be unconscionable. The following case applies this provision, along with the Code's basic implied warranty disclaimer rules.

FARM FAMILY MUTUAL INSURANCE CO. v. MOORE BUSINESS FORMS, INC.
625 N.Y.S.2d 798 (N.Y. Sup. Ct.,Albany County 1995)

T *he Farm Family Mutual Insurance Company purchased various insurance forms, including New York cancellation notices, from Moore Business Forms, Inc. The cancellation notices turned out to be unsuited for their task due to a change in New York law. Consequently, Farm Family was compelled to make payments under policies it thought it had cancelled.*

Farm Family sued Moore for, among other things, breach of the UCC's implied warranties of merchantability and fitness. Moore argued that it had disclaimed these warranties and also had excluded the consequential damages Farm Family was seeking. Moore's standard form contract said that Moore did not warrant its forms' fitness for their intended use, and limited a buyer's remedies to the replacement or reworking of defective forms or the return of their purchase price. Then it stated: "THIS WARRANTY IS GIVEN IN LIEU OF ANY OTHER REPRESENTATION OR WARRANTY, EXPRESS OR IMPLIED, INCLUDING BUT NOT LIMITED TO THE IMPLIED WARRANTY OF MERCHANTABILITY OR FITNESS FOR A PARTICULAR PURPOSE." After this, the contract said that "except for personal injuries, in no event shall Moore be liable for incidental or consequential damages arising from any cause whatsoever." Both parties then moved for summary judgment. ∽

Harris, Justice   UCC section 2–719(3) states that "[c]onsequential damages may be limited or excluded unless the limitation or exclusion is unconscionable. Limitation of consequential damages for injury to the person in the case of consumer goods is prima facie unconscionable but limitation of damages where the loss is commercial is not." The limitation of consequential damages clause herein relates to commercial loss and not to personal injury. It therefore is not prima facie unconscionable.

Where, as here, businessmen contract in a commercial setting, a presumption of conscionability arises. As a general rule, unconscionability requires some showing of an absence of meaningful choice on the part of one of the parties together with contract terms which are unreasonably favorable to the other party. Prior to entering into a contractual relationship with Moore, Farm Family purchased its forms from another company. Therefore, Farm Family did not lack a meaningful choice. Accordingly, Moore effectively excluded consequential damages as a matter of law.

UCC section 2–316(2) states that "to exclude or modify the implied warranty of merchantability or any part of it the language must mention merchantability and in case of a writing must be conspicuous, and to exclude or modify any implied warranty of fitness the exclusion must be in writing and conspicuous." UCC section 1–210(10) states that " [a] term or clause is conspicuous when it is so written that a reasonable person against whom it is to operate might have noticed it. A printed heading in capitals (as: NON-NEGOTIABLE BILL OF LADING) is conspicuous. Language in the body of a form is 'conspicuous' if it is in larger or other contrasting type or color." Moore's disclaimers satisfy, as a matter of law, [these] conspicuousness requirements.

Moore's summary judgment motion on Farm Family's implied warranty claims granted; Farm Family's summary judgment motion denied.

DEFENSES

Many things—for example, the absence of privity or a valid disclaimer—can be considered defenses to a product liability suit. Here, however, our concern is with product liability defenses that involve the plaintiff's behavior.

The Traditional Defenses

Traditionally, the three main defenses in a product liability suit have been the overlapping trio of product misuse, assumption of risk, and contributory negligence.[13] **Product misuse** (or abnormal use) occurs when the plaintiff uses the product in some unusual, unforeseeable way, and this causes the loss for which she sues. Examples include ignoring the manufacturer's instructions, mishandling the product, and using the product for purposes for which it was not intended. But if the defendant had reason to foresee the misuse and failed to take reasonable precautions against it, there is no defense. Product misuse usually is a defense in warranty, negligence, and strict liability cases.

Assumption of risk is the plaintiff's voluntary consent to a known danger. It can occur any time the plaintiff willingly exposes herself to a known product hazard—for example, by consuming obviously adulterated food. Like product misuse, assumption of risk ordinarily is a defense in warranty, negligence, and strict liability cases.

Contributory negligence is the plaintiff's failure to act with reasonable, prudent self-protectiveness. In the product liability context, perhaps the most common example is the simple failure to notice a hazardous product defect. Contributory negligence clearly is a defense in a negligence suit,

but courts disagree about whether or when it should be a defense in warranty and strict liability cases.

Comparative Principles

Where they are allowed and proven, the three traditional product liability defenses completely absolve the defendant from liability. Dissatisfaction with this all-or-nothing situation has spurred the increasing use of *comparative* principles in product liability cases.[14] Rather than letting the traditional defenses completely absolve the defendant, courts and legislatures now apportion damages on the basis of relative fault. They do so by requiring that the factfinder establish the plaintiff's and the defendant's percentage shares of the total fault for the injury and then award the plaintiff his total provable damages times the defendant's percentage share of the fault.

Unsettled questions persist among the states that have adopted comparative principles. First, it is not always clear what kinds of fault will reduce the plaintiff's recovery. However, some state comparative negligence statutes have been read as embracing assumption of risk and product misuse, and state comparative fault statutes usually define fault broadly. Second, comparative principles may assume either the *pure* or the *mixed* forms described in Chapter 7. In "mixed" states, for example, the defendant has a complete defense where the plaintiff is more at fault than the defendant. Finally, there is some uncertainty about the theories of recovery and the types of damage claims to which comparative principles apply.

The following case involves a modern comparative fault statute that includes product misuse and several other kinds of fault.

---

[13]Chapter 7 discusses contributory negligence and assumption of risk.

[14]Comparative negligence and comparative fault are discussed in Chapter 7. Although courts and commentators often use the terms *comparative fault* and *comparative negligence* interchangeably, comparative fault usually includes forms of blameworthiness other than negligence.

JIMENEZ v. SEARS ROEBUCK & CO.   904 P.2d 861 (Ariz. Sup. Ct. 1995)

 ichard Jimenez was injured when a disc for the hand-held electric disc grinder he had purchased from Sears Roebuck shattered while he used the grinder to smooth down a steel weld. When Jimenez sued Sears in strict liability, Sears argued that he had misused the grinder. However, the trial court denied Sears's request for a comparative fault jury instruction. Instead, the court *instructed the jury that Sears should win if Jimenez's alleged misuse was the sole cause of his injury, but that Jimenez should recover full damages if that misuse was only a concurrent cause. After the jury awarded Jimenez $112,000, Sears appealed. The intermediate appellate court reversed, and Jimenez appealed to the Arizona Supreme Court.* ∽

Feldman, Chief Justice   In 1978, the legislature codified the common-law defense of misuse. In [a 1987 case], we held that [under this statute] misuse is a complete defense only if: (1) the plaintiff misused the product, and (2) misuse was the sole proximate cause of the injury. Under the comparative fault rules of the 1987 version of the Uniform Contribution Among Tortfeasors Act (UCATA), however, a jury can reduce a plaintiff's damages in an amount proportionate to the relative degree of the plaintiff's fault that proximately caused the injury. This of course [would] recognize the misuse defense in cases in which it is a contributing cause rather than the sole cause of injury. Thus, the jury would be instructed to determine whether the plaintiff's misuse contributed to the plaintiff's injuries, and, if so, to compare the plaintiff' share of misuse-causation with the causal contribution of the product's defect. The judge would then reduce the plaintiff's damage recovery by the percentage of cause the jury attributed to the plaintiff. We turn next to the question whether our comparative fault statutes encompass the defense of product misuse.

The 1987 UCATA amendments apparently broadened the scope of torts subject to comparative fault. Section 12–2506(F)(2) was added to define apportionable fault:

"Fault" means an actionable breach of legal duty, act or omission proximately contributing to injury or damages sustained by a person seeking recovery, including negligence in all of its degrees, contributory negligence, assumption of risk, strict liability, breach of express or implied warranty of a product, products liability, and misuse, modification, or abuse of a product.

We interpret [this provision] to encompass product misuse in the jury's allocation of comparative fault. In so concluding, we are supported by substantial authority. Our state is not alone in applying comparative fault principles to strict liability defenses. The drafters of the third revision of the *Restatement of Torts* recommend that defenses against product liability plaintiffs be subject to the apportionment rules in jurisdictions that have adopted the comparative responsibility rules.

On this record, therefore, the trial court erred in refusing to give the jury comparative fault instructions on the statutory defense of product misuse.

Case returned to the trial court for further action consistent with the Supreme Court's decision.

ETHICAL AND PUBLIC POLICY CONCERNS

1. As suggested earlier in the chapter, one explanation for the prodefendant thrust of 19th-century product liability law is the courts' desire to protect infant industries by preventing them from suffering potentially crippling damage awards. If this explanation is accurate, it means that those injured by defective products and the survivors of those killed by such products were denied compensation so that the country might be industrialized. Is this right? Should people's rights be sacrificed in this way? In answering this question, assume for the sake of argument that these denials of recovery actually were necessary for industrialization to proceed.

2. Courts are much more likely to find disclaimers and remedy limitations enforceable when the plaintiff is a business firm than when the plaintiff is an ordinary consumer. What is the justification for this difference in treatment?

One possible way to get around the arguments against enforcing disclaimers and remedy limitations in consumer cases is to enforce them when the seller has used various kinds of "superdisclosure" to make buyers aware of the disclaimer. Possibilities include: positioning the disclaimer or limitation outside the product package, using signs to alert buyers to it, explaining it to buyers, and requiring the buyer to sign separately near a conspicuous disclaimer or limitation. Try to think of some problems with superdisclosure itself and with allowing disclaimers and remedy limitations to be enforced on this basis.

3. Most likely, consumers would pay a somewhat lower price for the products they purchase if the implied warranty of merchantability did not exist. Why is this so? Assuming that it is so, why shouldn't consumers have the choice whether to buy products with the "insurance policy" the warranty provides or to get a lower price by forgoing this protection? Or would this choice be too difficult for individual sellers and manufacturers to provide? Nonetheless, shouldn't consumers at least know what deal sellers are offering so that they can pick the seller whose terms they prefer? In theory, how does current law make this possible? What probably would *really* be necessary for consumers to get the necessary information? *Hint:* Look at the second paragraph of the previous question.

PROBLEM CASES

1.  *Video Case.* See "TV Repair." Allen, a salesperson for an electronics store, is talking to Arnold, a customer, while Arnold picks up a portable TV and puts it on the counter preparatory to buying it. Allen tells Arnold that he "won't have any problems" with the set because he's "buying the best." He also tells Arnold that "I'm sure you'll enjoy your new set." After buying the set, taking it home, and plugging it in, Arnold finds that the set does not work. Assuming that Allen has the authority to bind the store, has the store breached an express warranty to Arnold? Assuming that the store is a merchant and has not disclaimed the implied warranty of merchantability, is it liable under that theory?

2. Ewers, who owns a saltwater aquarium with tropical fish, bought several seashells, a piece of coral, and a driftwood branch from the Verona Rock Shop. Just before the purchase, the salesclerk told Ewers that these items were "suitable for saltwater aquariums, if they [are] rinsed." After making the purchase, Ewers took the items home, rinsed them for 20 minutes in a saltwater solution, and put them in his aquarium. Within a week, 17 of his tropical fish died. The "rinsing" required to prevent their deaths is a week-long cleansing process that involves soaking the shells and the coral in boiling water. Suppose that you are Ewers's attorney in his express warranty suit against the shop. Make an argument that the clerk's statement is an express warranty. Make an argument that this warranty was breached. Assume that Ewers did not know the correct "rinsing" procedure.

3. Steven Taterka purchased a 1972 Ford Mustang from a Ford dealer in January 1972. In October 1974, after Taterka had put 75,000 miles on the car and Ford's express warranty had expired, he discovered that the taillight assembly gaskets on his Mustang had been installed in such a way that water was permitted to enter the taillight assembly, causing rust to form. Even though the rusting problem was a recurrent one of which Ford was aware, Ford did nothing for Taterka. Is Ford liable to Taterka under the implied warranty of merchantability?

4. Peter Vamos purchased a sealed bottle of Diet Coke at a grocery store. After Vamos drank from the bottle, he discovered that it contained two AA batteries. Vamos testified that he then became ill for several days. However, there apparently was no evidence that the liquid Vamos drank was poisonous or noxious. Can the Coca-Cola Bottling Company of New York, which bottled the liquid Vamos drank, be liable to him under the implied warranty of merchantability if the liquid in fact was harmless? If so, what result under the foreign–natural test? What result under the reasonable consumer expectations test?

5.  *Video Case.* See "Software Horror Story." Chuck contacts the Bits and Bites Computer Superstore to get a software package suitable for some customized computer program work he is performing for a client. He tells the store's salesperson that he needs a database management system that he can customize at the source code level. However, there is little discussion of his other needs, including the work Chuck is doing for the client. The salesperson recommends a system called "D-Base Hit" for $649, and Chuck relies on the salesperson's judgment in buying that package. As it turns out, D-Base Hit *can* be modified at the source code level, but it is otherwise unsuitable for the job Chuck is doing. Assuming that Article 2 of the UCC applies, has Bits and Bites breached the implied warranty of fitness for a particular purpose?

6. Kathryn Morris, a minor, was injured when a clothing display rack tipped over and fell on her at a Goodwill store. The store had bought the rack from Munsingwear, Inc. at a one-time liquidation sale.

Munsingwear claimed that it had not ever been engaged in the business of selling clothing racks, and, the liquidation sale aside, there was no evidence that it ever had been so engaged. Assuming that the rack was defective, is Munsingwear liable to Morris under either the implied warranty of merchantability or section 402A? Assume that the traditional privity defense would *not* block Morris's claim.

7. Billy Toney suffered severe injuries to his left leg when his Kawasaki 750 motorcycle was struck from the side by a truck while he was riding the cycle on a highway. The Kawasaki 750 lacked leg-protection devices. Does this lack make Kawasaki liable for defective design under section 402A?

8. Gari West used Ovulen-28, a birth control medication manufactured by Searle & Company. She claimed that the Ovulen-28 caused her to develop a hepatic adenoma (a benign liver tumor), which eventually ruptured, causing a life-threatening situation. Assuming that the Ovulen-28 actually caused West's problem, what argument can Searle make to avoid the imposition of strict liability under section 402A? *Hint*: Assume that the Ovulen-28 has considerable social utility and cannot feasibly be made safer than it now is.

9. Curtis Hagans lost the ring finger of his left hand while operating an industrial table saw manufactured by the Oliver Machinery Company. The saw originally was equipped with a detachable blade guard assembly that would have prevented Hagans's injury had it been attached to the saw while Hagans was working. This assembly was detachable rather than permanently affixed to the saw because many common woodworking functions could not be performed with the assembly in place. Also, the saw exceeded industry safety practices and national and associational safety standards in effect at the time of its manufacture. In addition, few competing manufacturers included blade guards as standard equipment, and none offered a table saw with a permanently affixed blade guard.

Hagans sued Oliver in negligence and under section 402A, alleging that the saw was defectively designed because it did not include a permanent blade guard assembly. Did Hagans win? You can assume that injuries of the kind Hagans suffered were foreseeable consequences of manufacturing the saw without a permanent guard, and that Hagans was not careless in his operation of the saw.

10. Arlyn and Rose Spindler were dairy farmers who leased a feed storage silo from Agristor Leasing. The silo was supposed to limit the oxygen reaching the feed and thus to hinder its spoilage. The Spindlers alleged that the silo was defective and that the dairy feed it contained was spoiled as a result. They further alleged that due to the spoilage of the feed, their dairy herd suffered medically and reproductively and their milk production dropped. The Spindlers sued Agristor in negligence and under section 402A for their resulting lost income. What *type* of damages are they claiming? Under the majority rule, can they recover for such damages in negligence or under section 402A? Would your answer be different if the Spindlers had sued for the damage to the *dairy feed* itself? Assume for purposes of argument that both section 402A and negligence suits are possible under this equipment lease.

11. 🎦 *Video Case.* See "Car Deals." Jake, a car salesman, is discussing a particular car with Jones, a customer at Jake's dealership. Jake tells Jones that "you won't find a car like this at any price. This car is a crown jewel." Later, Jake says that he bought the car at an auction in Kentucky. Influenced by these statements, Jones buys the car. The bill of sale conspicuously says that the car is being sold "AS IS," and that no warranties or representations concerning the car have been made or given, except as stated in the bill of sale. Later, Jones discovers that the car's brakes are so defective that the car is unsafe to drive.

Which, if any, of Jake's statements are express warranties? Which, if any, have been breached here? Does the language in the bill of sale disclaim any express warranties that might exist? Does that language disclaim the implied warranty of merchantability? If the implied warranty of merchantability has not been disclaimed, is it breached here?

12. Duane Martin, a small farmer, placed an order for cabbage seed with the Joseph Harris Company, a large national producer and distributor of seed. Harris's order form included the following language:

NOTICE TO BUYER: Joseph Harris Company, Inc. warrants that seeds and plants it sells conform to the label descriptions as required by Federal and State seed laws. IT MAKES NO OTHER WARRANTIES, EXPRESS OR IMPLIED, OF MERCHANTABILITY, FITNESS FOR PURPOSE, OR OTHERWISE, AND IN ANY EVENT ITS LIABILITY FOR BREACH OF ANY WARRANTY

OR CONTRACT WITH RESPECT TO SUCH SEEDS OR PLANTS IS LIMITED TO THE PURCHASE PRICE OF SUCH SEEDS OR PLANTS.

All of Harris's competitors used similar clauses in their contracts.

After Martin placed his order, and unknown to Martin, Harris stopped using a cabbage seed treatment that had been effective in preventing a certain cabbage fungus. Later, Martin planted the seed he had ordered from Harris, but a large portion of the resulting crop was destroyed by fungus because the seed did not contain the treatment Harris had previously used. Martin sued Harris for his losses under the implied warranty of merchantability.

Which portion of the notice quoted above is an attempted disclaimer of implied warranty liability, and which is an attempted limitation of remedies? Will the disclaimer language disclaim the implied warranty of merchantability under UCC section 2–316(2)? If Martin had sued under the implied warranty of fitness for a particular purpose, would the disclaimer language disclaim that implied warranty as well? Assuming that the disclaimer and the remedy limitation contained the correct legal boilerplate needed to make them effective, what argument could Martin still make to block their operation? What are his chances of success with this argument?

13. Moulton purchased a 1969 Ford LTD from Hull-Dobbs, a Ford dealer. His sales contracts with Ford and Hull-Dobbs contained valid disclaimers of the implied warranty of merchantability that satisfied UCC section 2–316(2). One year later, while Moulton was driving his car along an interstate highway, the Ford suddenly veered to the right, jumped the guardrail, and fell 26 feet to the street below. The accident was caused by a defect in the car's steering mechanism, and Moulton was seriously injured. Moulton sued Ford under the implied warranty of merchantability. Ford defended on the basis of its disclaimer. Moulton argued that the disclaimer was invalid in a personal injury case under UCC section 2–719(3), which makes the exclusion of consequential damages unconscionable in a case involving consumer goods and personal injury. Did Moulton's argument succeed?

14. Lloyd States was injured after falling from a step ladder at a construction site. He had placed the ladder's front feet (which are on the same side of the ladder as its steps) on a sidewalk, with its rear feet on the surface of an unfinished parking lot that was six to nine inches below the front feet. This was contrary to manufacturer's instructions for the use of the ladder, which were affixed to it. Then States climbed the ladder, turned on the steps so that his back was to them, and leaned over toward a building. He did so in order to attach a sign to the building with a power wrench while the sign was being held in place by an overhead crane. States pressed against the sign with one hand while using his other hand to apply pressure on the power wrench. As he did so, the ladder moved away from him and he fell.

States sued the manufacturer of the ladder under section 402A. Assuming that States had misused the ladder, what effect would a product misuse defense have in this case? Specifically, what effect would it have under the traditional rules discussed in the text? What effect would it have under a modern comparative fault statute like the statute in the *Jimenez* case? Assume for the sake of argument that the manufacturer would otherwise be liable under section 402A.

Performance of Sales Contracts

I n the two previous chapters, we discussed the formation and terms of sales contracts, including those terms concerning express and implied warranties. In this chapter, the focus is on the legal rules that govern the performance of contracts. Among the topics covered are the basic obligations of the buyer and seller with respect to delivery and payment, the rights of the parties when the goods delivered do not conform to the contract, and the circumstances that may excuse the performance of a party's contractual obligations. ∞

GENERAL RULES

The parties to a contract for the sale of goods are obligated to perform the contract according to its terms. The Uniform Commercial Code (UCC or Code) gives the parties great flexibility in deciding between themselves how they will perform a contract. The practices in the trade or business as well as any past dealings between the parties may supplement or explain the contract. The Code gives both the buyer and the seller certain rights, and it also sets out what is expected of them on points that they did not deal with in their contract. It should be kept in mind that the Code changes basic contract law in a number of respects.

Good Faith

The buyer and seller must act in **good faith** in the performance of a sales contract [1–203].[1] Good

---

[1]The numbers in brackets refer to sections of the Uniform Commercial Code.

faith is defined to mean "honesty in fact" in performing the duties assumed in the contract or in carrying out the transaction [1–201(19)]. Thus, if the contract requires the seller to select an assortment of goods for the buyer, the selection must be made in good faith; the seller should pick out a reasonable assortment [2–311]. It would not, for example, be good faith to include only unusual sizes or colors.

Course of Dealing

The terms in the contract between the parties are the primary means for determining the obligations of the buyer and seller. The meaning of those terms may be explained by looking at any performance that has already taken place. For example, a contract may call for periodic deliveries of goods. If the seller has made a number of deliveries without objection by the buyer, the way the deliveries were made shows how the parties intended them to be made. Similarly, if there were any past contracts between the parties, the way the parties interpreted those contracts is relevant to the interpretation of the present contract. If there is a conflict between the express terms of the contract and the past course of dealing between the parties, the express terms of the contract prevail [1–205(4)].

Usage of Trade

In many kinds of businesses, there are customs and practices of the trade that are known by people in the business and that are usually assumed by parties to a contract for goods of that type. Under the Code, the parties and courts may use these trade customs and practices—known as usage of trade—in interpreting a contract [2—202; 1–205]. If there is a conflict between the express terms of the contract and trade usage, the express terms prevail [1–205(4)]. The *Weisz Graphics v. Peck Industries* case illustrates how a court may consider the terms of a contract, the course of dealing between the parties, and trade usage in determining the interpretation of a contract between merchants.

WEISZ GRAPHICS v. PECK INDUSTRIES, INC. 403 S.E.2d 146 (S.C. Ct. App. 1991)

W*eisz Graphics is a custom manufacturer and seller of decals, markings, and other graphic materials and competes in a national market. Weisz manufactures its products to customer specifications based on blueprints, samples, art, or mechanical drawings. It manufactures only to order and does not maintain a general inventory. However, it regularly engages in what are known as "release programs" with its customer; such programs are common in the industry. Under a release program, Weisz manufactures a large quantity of goods to customer order, then warehouses the goods for the customer. As the customer needs the goods, Weisz releases them in specified lots and bills the buyer when it ships the goods. Release programs in the industry are generally limited to one year, due in part to the shelf life of the goods.*

Peck Industries, a manufacturer of commercial signs for national and Memphis, Tennessee, accounts, uses pressure sensitive vinyl letters, numbers, and other products. Beginning in 1985, Peck began purchasing some of its requirements from Weisz; some contracts were for immediate manufacture and delivery while others were for extended delivery under a release program. A November 1985 order (P.O. 4426) provided: "BREAK UP INTO MULTIPLE SHIPMENTS." Weisz's acknowledgment contained the following shipment term: "On Releases Bill & Ship on release for 12 months." In April 1986, Peck sent a purchase order (P.O. 5885) for a quantity of goods that provided "TO BE BILLED AND SHIPPED AS RELEASED." Weisz sent back its standard acknowledgment form on which a clerk had typed "On Releases over 12 months." Other orders (P.O. 4037 and P.O. 4426)) were placed by Peck that stated on their face: "ORDER AS NEEDED FOR A PERIOD OF 1 YEAR." In each case Weisz immediately manufactured the items ordered and over a period of a year released and billed shipments at Peck's request. At the end of the 12 months, Weisz refused to make further shipments until Peck paid in full the remaining balance on the shipment. Peck refused to pay, choosing instead to obtain its requirements from other manufacturers at higher prices. Weisz then brought suit for the balance due on the goods sold to Peck. ∽

396 Part 4 Sales

Bell, Judge   Section 1−205(3) states:

A course of dealing between parties and any usage of trade in the . . . trade in which they are engaged or should be aware [*sic*] give particular meaning to supplement or qualify terms of the agreement.

Similarly, section 2−208(1) provides that a course of performance between the parties which is accepted or acquiesced in without objection by a party with opportunity to object is relevant to determine the meaning of the agreement.

As to Purchase Order 4037, Peck itself specified that delivery was on release for one year. There is no evidence that Weisz's acknowledgment contained a similar notation. However, Weisz did not object and began delivering the goods on release.

Purchase Order 4426 specified multiple shipments, but no release period. Weisz's uncontradicted evidence showed that a time limitation is standard in the industry. It also showed that its prior course of dealing with Peck had been to ship on 12-month release. None of its release contracts with Peck exceeded 12 months. Moreover, Peck accepted performance of Order 4426 without objection. Therefore, under sections 1−205(3) and 2−208(1) the 12-month release period that supplemented the express provisions of the written form was part of the contract.

The same is true of Purchase Order 5885. Like Purchase Order 4426, it specified no release period. However, its express provisions were supplemented by trade usage and prior course of dealing which established the 12 month release period as a term of the contract.

In the alternative, the 12-month release period became a term of the contract under section 2−207(2). In response to Purchase Order 4426 and 5885, Weisz's acknowledgment forms added a 12-month release period. Neither of Peck's orders expressly limited Weisz's acceptance to the express terms of its standard form. Nor did Peck give Weisz a notification of objection to the acknowledgments. Instead, Peck began accepting performance of the contract without objection. Finally, the 12-month limit was not a material alteration of the contract. Because it conformed to existing trade usage and prior course of dealing between the parties, it did not result in unreasonable surprise or hardship. Accordingly, both contracts incorporated a term for delivery on 12-month release. Payment in full of the balance on the purchase price was due at the end of the 12th month.

Judgment for Weisz.

Modification

Under the Code, consideration is not required to support a modification or rescission of a contract for the sale of goods. However, the parties may specify in their agreement that modification or rescission must be in writing, in which case a signed writing is necessary for enforcement of any modification to the contract or its rescission [2−209].

Waiver

In a contract that entails a number of instances of partial performance (such as deliveries or payments) by one party, the other party must be careful to object to any late deliveries or payments. If the other party does not object, it may waive its rights to cancel the contract if other deliveries or payments are late [2−208(3), 2−209(4)]. For example, a contract calls for a fish market to deliver fish to a supermarket every Thursday and for the supermarket to pay on delivery. If the fish market regularly delivers the fish on Friday and the supermarket does not object, the supermarket will be unable to cancel the contract for that reason. Similarly, if the supermarket does not pay cash but sends a check the following week, then unless the fish market objects, it will not be able to assert the late payments as grounds for later canceling the contract. A party that has waived rights to a portion of the contract not yet performed may retract the waiver by giving reasonable notice to the other party that strict performance will be required. The retraction of the waiver is effective unless it would be unjust because of a material change of position by the other party in reliance on the waiver [2−209(5)].

Assignment

Under the Code, the buyer and/or the seller may delegate their duties to someone else. If there is a strong reason for having the original party perform the duties, perhaps because the quality of the performance might differ otherwise, the parties may not delegate their duties. Also, they may not delegate their duties if the parties agree in the contract that there is to be no assignment of duties. However, they may assign rights to receive performance—for example, the right to receive goods or payment [2–210].

DELIVERY

Basic Obligation

The basic duty of the seller is to deliver the goods called for by the contract. The basic duty of the buyer is to accept and pay for the goods if they conform to the contract [2–301]. The buyer and seller may agree that the goods are to be delivered in several lots or installments. If there is no such agreement, then a single delivery of all the goods must be made. Where delivery is to be made in lots, the seller may demand the price of each lot upon delivery unless there has been an agreement for the extension of credit [2–307].

Place of Delivery

The buyer and seller may agree on the place where the goods will be delivered. If no such agreement is made, then the goods are to be delivered at the seller's place of business. If the seller does not have a place of business, then delivery is to be made at his home. If the goods are located elsewhere than the seller's place of business or home, the place of delivery is the place where the goods are located [2–308].

Seller's Duty of Delivery

The seller's basic obligation is to tender delivery of goods that conform to the contract with the buyer. Tender of delivery means that the seller must make the goods available to the buyer. This must be done during reasonable hours and for a reasonable period of time, so that the buyer can take possession of the goods [2–503]. The contract of sale may require the seller merely to ship the goods to the buyer but not to deliver the goods to the buyer's place of business. If this is the case, the seller must put the goods into the possession of a carrier, such as a trucking

company or a railroad. The seller must also make a reasonable contract with the carrier to take the goods to the buyer. Then, the seller must notify the buyer that the goods have been shipped [2–504]. Shipment terms were discussed in Chapter 19, Formation and Terms of Sales Contracts.

If the seller does not make a reasonable contract for delivery or notify the buyer and a material delay or loss results, the buyer has the right to reject the shipment. Suppose the goods are perishable, such as fresh produce, and the seller does not ship them in a refrigerated truck or railroad car. If the produce deteriorates in transit, the buyer can reject the produce on the ground that the seller did not make a reasonable contract for shipping it.

In some situations, the goods sold may be in the possession of a bailee such as a warehouse. If the goods are covered by a negotiable warehouse receipt, the seller must indorse the receipt and give it to the buyer [2–503(4)(a)]. This enables the buyer to obtain the goods from the warehouse. Such a situation exists when grain being sold is stored at a grain elevator. The law of negotiable documents of title, including warehouse receipts, is discussed in Chapter 33, Checks and Documents of Title.

If the goods in the possession of a bailee are not covered by a negotiable warehouse receipt, then the seller must notify the bailee that it has sold the goods to the buyer and must obtain the bailee's consent to hold the goods for delivery to the buyer or release the goods to the buyer. The risk of loss as to the goods remains with the seller until the bailee agrees to hold them for the buyer [2–503(4)(b)].

INSPECTION AND PAYMENT

Buyer's Right of Inspection

Normally, the buyer has the right to inspect the goods before he accepts or pays for them. The buyer and seller may agree on the time, place, and manner in which the buyer will inspect the goods. If no agreement is made, then the buyer may inspect the goods at any reasonable time and place and in any reasonable manner [2–513(1)].

If the shipping terms are cash on delivery (COD), then the buyer must pay for the goods before inspecting them unless they are marked "Inspection Allowed." However, if it is obvious even without inspection that the goods do not conform to the contract, the buyer may reject them without paying for them first [2−512(1)(a)]. For example, if a farmer contracted to buy a bull and the seller delivered a cow, the farmer would not have to pay for it. The fact that a buyer may have to pay for goods before inspecting them does not deprive the buyer of remedies against the seller if the goods do not conform to the contract [2−512(2)].

If the goods conform to the contract, the buyer must pay the expenses of inspection. However, if the goods are nonconforming, he may recover his inspection expenses from the seller [2−513(2)].

Payment

The buyer and seller may agree in their contract that the price of the goods is to be paid in money or in other goods, services, or real property. If all or part of the price of goods is payable in real property, then only the transfer of goods is covered by the law of sales of goods. The transfer of the real property is covered by the law of real property [2−304].

The contract may provide that the goods are sold on credit to the buyer and that the buyer has a period of time to pay for them. If there is no agreement for extending credit to the buyer, the buyer must pay for them upon delivery. The buyer usually can inspect goods before payment except where the goods are shipped COD, in which case the buyer must pay for them before inspecting them.

Unless the seller demands cash, the buyer may pay for the goods by personal check or by any other method used in the ordinary course of business. If the seller demands cash, the seller must give the buyer a reasonable amount of time to obtain it. If payment is made by check, the payment is conditional on the check being honored by the bank when it is presented for payment [2−511(3)]. If the bank refuses to pay the check, the buyer has not satisfied the duty to pay for the goods. In that case, the buyer does not have the right to retain the goods and must give them back to the seller.

ACCEPTANCE, REVOCATION, AND REJECTION

Acceptance

Acceptance of goods occurs when a buyer, after having a reasonable opportunity to inspect them, either indicates that he will take them or fails to reject them. To **reject** goods, the buyer must notify the seller of the rejection and specify the defect or nonconformity. If a buyer treats the goods as if he owns them, the buyer is considered to have accepted them [2−606].

For example, Ace Appliance delivers a new color television set to Baldwin. Baldwin has accepted the set if, after trying it and finding it to be in working order, she says nothing to Ace or tells Ace that she will keep it. Even if the set is defective, Baldwin is considered to have accepted it if she does not give Ace timely notice that she does not want to keep it because it is not in working order. If she takes the set on a vacation trip even though she knows that it does not work properly, this is also an acceptance. In the latter case, her use of the television set would be inconsistent with its rejection and the return of ownership to the seller.

If a buyer accepts any part of a **commercial unit** of goods, he is considered to have accepted the whole unit [2−606(2)]. A commercial unit is any unit of goods that is treated by commercial usage as a single whole. It can be a single article (such as a machine), a set or quantity of articles (such as a dozen, bale, gross, or carload), or any other unit treated as a single whole [2−105(6)]. Thus, if a bushel of apples is a commercial unit, then a buyer purchasing 10 bushels of apples who accepts 8½ bushels is considered to have accepted 9 bushels.

In the case that follows, *Ford v. Star Fireworks, Inc.,* the buyer was considered to have accepted goods that it had handled inconsistently with a claim of rejection and return of ownership of the goods to the seller.

FORD v. STARR FIREWORKS, INC.   874 P.2d 230 (Wyo. Sup. Ct. 1994)

I *n the spring of 1991, Vince Ford, a retailer, contracted with a wholesaler, Starr Fireworks, for the purchase of various types of fireworks at an agreed price of $6,748.86. In May 1991, Starr delivered the 138 cases of fireworks in one lot to Ford's warehouse in Lusk, Wyoming. Ford did not immediately inspect the fireworks; instead, he distributed them to his retail outlets throughout Wyoming for resale to the public.*

Approximately 10 days after the fireworks were distributed to the retail outlets, Ford discovered that some fireworks were unsalable because of water damage and packaging problems. However, Ford did not inspect the remainder of the fireworks from the shipment. Ford telephoned Starr's representative to report the problems. Although Ford claimed that he instructed his employees not to sell any products received from Starr, a month later one of his stores sold several cases of the fireworks that had been purchased from Starr to another fireworks retailer. The buyer reported no problem with those fireworks, and they were subsequently resold to customers without reported problems.

After several unsuccessful efforts by Starr representatives to pick up the fireworks, they did pick up 10 cases of fireworks, worth $1,476.87, on August 3, 1991. At that time, Ford signed an acknowledgment that he still owed $5,251.99 to Starr. Ford claimed to have returned the remaining fireworks to Starr's Denver office on August 13, 1991. He said that no one was available in the office so he left the fireworks outside a side door; Starr never received those fireworks.

Starr brought suit to recover the balance due on the fireworks that Ford had acknowledged retaining. Ford claimed that he had rejected the entire shipment on the grounds they were unmerchantable and counterclaimed for damages he asserted he had sustained. Ford contended that his inspection of some of the fireworks disclosed packages with torn wrappings, mold, or mildew on some fireworks, and paper wrapping that fell apart, exposing the fireworks. Ford argued that from this sampling it was reasonable to assume all the goods delivered by Starr were unmerchantable. ∽

Taylor, Justice The Uniform Commercial Code, as enacted in Wyoming, permits a buyer to return nonconforming goods to a seller. If the goods or tender or delivery fail in any respect to conform to the contract, the buyer is permitted to reject the whole, accept the whole, or accept any commercial unit or units and reject the remainder. Section 2–601(a). The substance of this dispute involves which of the three alternatives Ford exercised in returning the fireworks. Ford broadly argues that he rejected the whole. The evidence, however, supports a conclusion that Ford effectively rejected some commercial units. Those units were returned to Starr and Ford's account was properly credited. Meanwhile, Ford's exercise of ownership over the other commercial units which he claimed to have rejected constituted an acceptance of those goods.

The evidence established that at least some of the fireworks Ford claimed were unmerchantable passed without objection in the trade. After Ford rejected the fireworks, Ford sold two to three cases of the bottle rockets received from Starr to another fireworks dealer. This resale implies the merchantability of at least some of the fireworks. If the fireworks were unmerchantable within trade standards, another retailer would not have purchased the bottle rockets. Also, no customer complaints were ever received about the merchantability of the fireworks sold by the second retailer from the lot delivered to Ford by Starr. Furthermore, Starr indicated that it received no complaints from any other purchaser of the remaining fireworks from the same

shipment Ford claimed was unmerchantable. Accordingly, we hold that the fireworks which Ford did not inspect or return to Starr were merchantable.

Next, Ford argues that the district court erred in concluding that Ford had wrongly exercised ownership of the rejected goods. While Ford admits he sold some of the rejected goods, he argues that the remainder was effectively rejected. Ford also contends that holding the goods at his retail outlets was not unreasonable.

A buyer who takes any action which is inconsistent with the claim that the goods have been rejected risks accepting the goods. A buyer's rejection can be converted into an acceptance by acts which are inconsistent with the seller's ownership rights.

Lorenzo Banfi di Banfi Renzo & Co. v. Davis Congress Shops, Inc. (N.D. Ill. 1983) illustrates the obligation of a buyer to avoid the exercise of ownership of goods which the buyer claims are unmerchantable. The buyer, a retailer of men's shoes, purchased over 500 pairs of shoes from the seller. After the buyer allegedly rejected the shipment, the buyer placed the shoes in inventory in his store, offered the shoes for sale, and sold a number of these shoes to customers. The buyer's actions in placing the shoes in inventory and offering the shoes for sale were an exercise of ownership by the buyer. Furthermore, the court found that offering allegedly defective goods for retail sale was not a reasonable use of the goods consistent with rejection. The court held the buyer's actions constituted an acceptance of the goods.

Similarly, Ford placed the rejected fireworks in inventory at his retail outlets. While he claimed to have withdrawn the goods from sale after the defects were discovered, Ford later sold several cases of the rejected bottle rockets to another retailer. Ford also held the rejected fireworks for at least two months after providing notice of rejection to Starr. As a result Starr's agents made two unsuccessful trips to Ford's warehouse to obtain the goods. In an industry with seasonal sales peaks, such a delay in making the rejected fireworks available to Starr was unreasonable. We hold Ford wrongfully exercised ownership of the rejected fireworks.

Although Ford did not have any duty to return the fireworks to Denver, section 2–602(b)(ii) requires a buyer to use reasonable care in holding the fireworks for the seller. A buyer who is also a merchant (section 2–104(a)) has a duty to follow any reasonable instructions received from the seller. Section 2–603(a). Once Ford gratuitously offered to return the fireworks to Starr's Denver location, Ford was under a duty to return the fireworks in a reasonable manner. Starr's sales representatives informed Ford that the fireworks were to be delivered to a responsible person at Starr. The evidence discloses that Ford left the fireworks unattended outside Starr's downtown Denver business location. We agree with the district court that leaving the fireworks unattended outside a business on a busy street is unreasonable. We hold that Ford failed to follow reasonable instructions in returning the fireworks to Starr.

Judgment for Starr affirmed.

Effect of Acceptance

Once a buyer has accepted goods, he cannot later reject them unless at the time they were accepted, the buyer had reason to believe that the nonconformity would be cured. By accepting goods, the buyer does not forfeit or waive remedies against the seller for any nonconformities in the goods. However, if the buyer wishes to hold the seller responsible, he must give the seller timely notice that the goods are nonconforming.

The buyer is obligated to pay for goods that are accepted. If the buyer accepts all of the goods sold, she is, of course, responsible for the full purchase price. If the buyer accepts only part of the goods, she must pay for that part at the contract rate [2–607(1)].

Revocation of Acceptance

Under certain circumstances, a buyer may **revoke** or undo the acceptance. A buyer may revoke acceptance of nonconforming goods where: (1) the nonconformity substantially impairs the value of the goods and (2) the buyer accepted them without knowledge of the nonconformity because of the difficulty of discovering the nonconformity, or the buyer accepted the goods because of the seller's assurances that it would cure the defect [2–608(1)].

The buyer must exercise her right to revoke acceptance within a reasonable time after the buyer discovers or should have discovered the nonconformity. Revocation is not effective until the buyer notifies the seller of the intention to revoke acceptance. After a buyer revokes acceptance, her rights are the same as they would have been if the goods had been rejected when delivery was offered [2–608].

The right to revoke acceptance could arise, for example, where Arnold buys a new car from Dealer. While driving the car home, Arnold discovers that it has a seriously defective transmission. When she returns the car to Dealer, Dealer promises to repair it, so Arnold decides to keep the car. If the dealer does not fix the transmission after repeated efforts to fix it, Arnold could revoke her acceptance on the grounds that the nonconformity substantially impairs the value of the car, that she took delivery of the car without knowledge of the nonconformity, and that her acceptance was based on Dealer's assurances that he would fix the car. Similarly, revocation of acceptance might be involved where a serious problem with the car not discoverable by inspection shows up in the first month's use.

Revocation must occur prior to any substantial change in the goods, however, such as serious damage in an accident or wear and tear from using them for a period of time. What constitutes a "substantial impairment in value" and when there has been a "substantial change in the goods" are questions that courts frequently have to decide when an attempted revocation of acceptance results in a lawsuit. The case below of *North River Homes, Inc. v. Bosarge* illustrates a number of the issues that arise in situations where a buyer is seeking to revoke her acceptance.

NORTH RIVER HOMES, INC. v. BOSARGE   17 UCC Rep.2d 121 (Miss. Sup. Ct. 1992)

O n August 20, 1983, Elmer and Martha Bosarge purchased from J & J Mobile Home Sales a furnished mobile home manufactured by North River Homes. The mobile home, described by a J & J salesperson as the "Cadillac" of mobile homes, cost $23,900. Upon moving into their new home, the Bosarges immediately discovered defect after defect. The defects included a bad water leak that caused water to run all over the trailer and into the insulation, which in turn caused the trailer's underside to balloon downward, loose moldings, a warped dishwasher door, a warped bathroom door, holes in the walls, a defective heating and cooling system, cabinets with chips and holes in them, furniture that fell apart, rooms that remained moldy and mildewed, a closet that leaked rainwater, and spaces between the doors and windows and their frames that allowed the elements to come in. The Bosarges had not been able to spot the defects before taking delivery because they viewed the mobile home at night on J & J's lot and there was no light on in the mobile home.

The Bosarges immediately and repeatedly notified North River Homes of the defects, but it failed to repair the home satisfactorily. In November 1983, the Bosarges informed North River of their decision to revoke their acceptance of the defective home. On some occasions, repairmen came but did not attempt to make repairs, saying they would come back. Other times, the repairs were inadequate. For example, while looking for the water leak, a repairman cut open the bottom of the mobile home and then taped it back together with masking tape that failed to hold and resulted in the floor bowing out. Another repairman inadvertently punctured a septic line and did not properly repair the puncture, resulting in a permanent stench. Other repairmen simply left things off at the home, such as a new dishwasher door and a countertop, saying they did not have time to make the repairs.

In June 1984, the Bosarges provided North River with an extensive list of problems that had not been corrected. When they did not receive a satisfactory response, they sent a letter on October 4, 1984, saying they would make no further payments. North River made no further efforts to correct the problems. In March 1986, the Bosarges's attorney wrote to North River formally revoking acceptance of the mobile home because of its substantially impaired value, tendering the mobile home back to it, and advising North River that it could pick the home up at its earliest convenience. They then brought a lawsuit requesting return of the purchase price and seeking damages for breach of various warranties. ∞

Prather, Justice   When a consumer has accepted goods and subsequently discovers defects or a breach of implied merchantability, the consumer may invoke statutory and case law which conditions revocation of acceptance on:

(1) a nonconformity [or defect] which substantially impairs the value of the "lot or commercial unit;"
(2) an acceptance
   (a) (with discovery of the defect) on the reasonable assumption that the nonconformity [or defect] would be cured or
   (b) (without discovery) reasonably induced by the difficulty of the discovery or by the seller's assurances;

(3) revocation within a reasonable time after the nonconformity [or defect] was discovered or should have been discovered; and
(4) revocation before a substantial change occurs in the condition of the goods not caused by their own defects.

Once the consumer has properly notified the seller of his or her intent to revoke acceptance, the seller has a right to attempt to cure the alleged defect. This right is not unlimited; that is, Mississippi law does not permit a seller to postpone revocation in perpetuity by fixing everything that goes wrong with the good. "There is a time when enough is enough"—when a consumer no longer must tolerate or endure a seller's repeated (though good faith) attempts to cure the defect. As aptly stated by a Florida Court of Appeals:

The buyer . . . is not bound to permit the seller to tinker with the article indefinitely in the hope it may ultimately be made to comply with the warranty. At some point in time, if major problems continue . . ., it must become obvious to all people that a particular [article] simply cannot be repaired or parts replaced so that the same is made free of defect.

When the "time has come," the consumer may revoke once and for all.

North River contends that the Bosarges' failure to move out of their mobile home after "rejecting it" constituted an exercise of ownership (or dominion) and waiver of their right to revoke acceptance. The Bosarges did not move out of their home in November 1983 and in October 1984—the dates when they notified North River of their intention to revoke acceptance—because they were repeatedly assured that the defects would be repaired. Their mistaken belief that North River would fulfill its assurances to repair the defects is but one reason why the Bosarges did not move out of their home. Another reason is simple and understandable:

When you tie up all your savings into purchasing a home, you cannot take it and park it somewhere. You have to live in it until you can get the people to clear your lot so you can put another one on it. Its just not like a car you can drive on the lot and hand them the keys and say, its yours. (Testimony of Martha Bosarge).

North River's contention that the Bosarges should have moved out reflects ignorance of case law which requires a consumer, who expresses an intention to revoke acceptance, to provide a seller with a reasonable attempt to cure the defect. The evidence unequivocally shows that the Bosarges complied with this law; indeed, one could arguably contend that they complied to an unnecessary extent. But the Bosarges' great patience is not surprising in view of their financial inability to move elsewhere.

Any excessive or unreasonable use of the home by the Bosarges may be remedied through quantum meruit recovery—*not* through ineffectuation of revocation.

North River also contends that the Bosarges "failed to prove that the mobile home in question was substantially impaired." The Bosarges counter "that the evidence showed that their North River trailer was literally falling apart." The Bosarges testimony revealed that each North River repairman who visited their home admitted to the Bosarges that their home was so defective that it "ought to be replaced." Notably, Ronnie Wilson, a HUD mobile home inspector provided testimony which is also supportive of the jury's finding; when asked if he would live in that kind of home (heating, cooling, leaking roof, mildew, ice), he answered "No, sir, my wife wouldn't let me, sir."

In sum the record is replete with evidence to support the jury's finding that the Bosarges' home was substantially impaired.

Judgment for Bosarges affirmed.

Buyer's Rights on Improper Delivery

If the goods delivered by the seller do not conform to the contract, the buyer has several options. The buyer can (1) reject all of the goods, (2) accept all of them, or (3) accept any commercial units and reject the rest [2–601]. The buyer, however, cannot accept only part of a commercial unit and reject the rest. The buyer must pay for the units accepted at the price per unit provided in the contract.

Where the contract calls for delivery of the goods in separate installments, the buyer's options are more limited. The buyer may reject an installment delivery only if the nonconformity *substantially affects the value* of that delivery and *cannot be corrected* by the seller in a timely fashion. If the nonconformity is relatively minor, the buyer must accept the installment. The seller may offer to replace the defective goods or give the buyer an allowance in the price to make up for the nonconformity [2–612].

Where the nonconformity or defect in one installment impairs the value of the whole contract, the buyer may treat it as a breach of the whole contract but must proceed carefully so as not to reinstate the remainder of the contract [2–612(3)].

Rejection

If a buyer has a basis for rejecting a delivery of goods, the buyer must act within a *reasonable time* after delivery. The buyer must also give the seller *notice* of the rejection, preferably in writing [2–602]. The buyer should be careful to state all of the defects on which he is basing the rejection, including all of the defects that a reasonable inspection would disclose. This is particularly important if these are defects that the seller might cure (remedy) and the time for delivery has not expired. In that case, the seller may notify the buyer that he intends to redeliver conforming goods.

If the buyer fails to state in connection with his rejection a particular defect that is ascertainable by reasonable inspection, he cannot use the defect to justify his rejection if the seller could have cured the defect had he been given reasonable notice of it. In a transaction taking place between merchants, the seller has, after rejection, a right to a written statement of all the defects in the goods on which the buyer bases his right to reject, and the buyer may not later assert defects not listed in justification of his rejection [2–605].

Right to Cure

If the seller has some reason to believe that the buyer would accept nonconforming goods, then the seller can take a reasonable time to reship conforming goods. The seller has this opportunity even if the original time for delivery has expired. For example, Ace Manufacturing contracts to sell 200 red baseball hats to Sam's Sporting Goods, with delivery to be made by April 1. On March 1, Sam's receives a package from Ace containing 200 blue baseball hats and refuses to accept them. Ace can notify Sam's that it intends to cure the improper delivery by supplying 200 red hats, and it has until April 1 to deliver the red hats to Sam's. If Ace thought that Sam's would accept the blue hats because on past shipments Sam's did not object to the substitution of blue hats for red, then Ace has a reasonable time even after April 1 to deliver the red hats [2–508]. The following case, *Central District Alarm, Inc., v. Hal-Tuc, Inc.,* illustrates a situation where the seller did not comply with the requirements for establishing a right to cure.

CONCEPT REVIEW

Acceptance, Revocation, and Rejection

Acceptance	1. Occurs when buyer, having had a reasonable opportunity to inspect goods, either (a) indicates he will take them or (b) fails to reject them.
	2. If buyer accepts any part of a commercial unit, he is considered to have accepted the whole unit.
	3. If buyer accepts goods, he cannot later reject them *unless* at the time they were accepted buyer had reason to believe that the nonconformity would be cured.
	4. Buyer is obligated to pay for goods that are accepted.
Revocation	1. Buyer may revoke acceptance of nonconforming goods where (a) the nonconformity *substantially impairs the value* of the goods and (b) buyer accepted the goods without knowledge of the nonconformity because of the difficulty of discovering the nonconformity *or* buyer accepted because of assurances by the seller.
	2. Right to revoke must be exercised within a *reasonable* time after buyer discovers *or* should have discovered the nonconformity.
	3. Revocation must be invoked before there is any *substantial* change in the goods.
	4. Revocation is not effective until buyer notifies seller of his intent to revoke acceptance.
Rejection	1. Where the goods delivered do not conform to the contract, buyer may (a) reject all of the goods, (b) accept all of the goods, or (c) accept any commercial unit and reject the rest. Buyer must pay for goods accepted.
	2. Where the goods are to be delivered in installments, an installment delivery may be rejected *only if* the nonconformity substantially affects the value of that delivery and cannot be corrected by the seller.
	3. Buyer must act within a reasonable time after delivery.

CENTRAL DISTRICT ALARM, INC. v. HAL-TUC, INC.   886 S.W.2d 210 (Mo. Ct. App. 1994)

Prior to January 1991, John Halton, president of Hal-Tuc, Inc., a company that operates retail lingerie and novelty stores, contacted Ron Weber, a security consultant for Central District Alarm (CDA), about purchasing a video surveillance system for one of its stores. Weber recommended a Javelin system and designed a system for Hal-Tuc.

On January 3, 1991, CDA and Hal-Tuc entered into a written sales agreement that provided that CDA would sell and install security equipment as described on an equipment list attached to the contract. This list included a Javelin VCR. The equipment was supposed to be new. The contract price was $7,692, of which $2,533 was paid when the contract was executed, with the balance to become due after CDA installed the equipment.

CDA ordered a new Javelin VCR but its supplier sent a new JVC VCR. CDA's supplier told CDA it would take another month to get a Javelin. When the system was installed on January 28, 1991, CDA installed a used JVC VCR instead of a new Javelin VCR. CDA did not install the new JVC VCR sent by its supplier because it would not be able to return the VCR after it had replaced it with the Javelin.

Halton called Weber the day after the installation and complained that the equipment was not Javelin and that the VCR was a used JVC VCR. Weber told Halton that the equipment was not used and that a JVC VCR was better than a Javelin. Halton telephoned other CDA personnel over a two-week period during which they denied that the equipment was used. After two weeks, when CDA's installation manager, Brian Modglin, went to the store to see the equipment, Modglin admitted for the first time that the VCR was used. No one from CDA advised Halton in advance that CDA was installing used equipment temporarily. After CDA admitted it had supplied a used JVC VCR, it offered to replace it with a new Javelin as soon as one arrived, which would take one or two months. Halton asked CDA to return Hal-Tuc's $2,533 deposit in exchange for CDA taking its equipment back. CDA refused to return the deposit. Hal-Tuc put all the equipment in boxes and stored it.

CDA brought suit against Hal-Tuc seeking damages for breach of contract. Hal-Tuc filed a counterclaim alleging fraud. The trail court found for Hal-Tuc, and CDA appealed. ∞

Crane, Judge   In this case there is no dispute that CDA supplied a VCR that did not conform. CDA argues that it has a right to cure under section 2–508(2) which provides:

(2) Where the buyer rejects a nonconforming tender which the seller had reasonable grounds to believe would be acceptable with or without money allowance the seller may if he seasonably notifies the buyer have a further reasonable time to substitute a conforming tender.

Under section 2–508(2) the seller must "seasonably" notify the buyer of the intention to cure. Seasonably means "within a reasonable time." Section 1–204(3). A "reasonable time" depends on the nature, purpose and circumstances of such action. Section 1–204(2). There was evidence from which the trial court could conclude that CDA did not seasonably notify Hal-Tuc of an intent to cure. CDA did not advise Hal-Tuc in advance that it did not have the new equipment knowingly and not by mistake. Hal-Tuc notified CDA after it discovered that CDA had installed the wrong equipment. Only after inspecting the equipment two weeks later did

CDA admit the equipment was used and offer to cure with new equipment. These circumstances support a finding that CDA did not seasonably notify Hal-Tuc of its intention to cure.

Further, in order to establish a right to cure under section 2–508(2), the seller must have had reasonable grounds to believe the nonconforming tender would be acceptable. Such reasonable grounds can lie in prior course of dealing, course of performance or usage of trade as well as in the particular circumstances surrounding the making of the contract. CDA did not show any prior course of dealing, course of performance or usage of trade by which used equipment could be substituted for new equipment. CDA argues that CDA had reasonable grounds to believe the used JVC would be acceptable until the new Javelin could be obtained because Hal-Tuc wanted the security system installed as soon as possible. Although there was evidence that Hal-Tuc wanted a security system installed as soon as possible, there was no evidence that Hal-Tuc told or otherwise indicated to CDA that time was more essential than new equipment.

Under these circumstances, CDA could not have had reasonable grounds to believe that a used VCR would be acceptable when a new one had been ordered. Further, CDA could not have had reasonable grounds to believe the tender of a used VCR would be acceptable until a new one could be supplied where that tender was not accompanied by a disclosure that a used VCR was only being supplied on a temporary basis. Without such a

communication, the tender was strictly a tender of a used VCR in lieu of a new VCR.

Because it did not establish seasonable notification and reasonable grounds, CDA did not establish a right to cure under section 2–508.

Judgment affirmed for Hal-Tuc on the breach of contract claim.

If the buyer wrongfully rejects goods, she is liable to the seller for breach of the sales contract [2–602(3)].

Buyer's Duties after Rejection

If the buyer is a merchant, then the buyer owes certain duties concerning the goods that he rejects. First, the buyer must follow any reasonable instructions that the seller gives concerning disposition of the goods. The seller, for example, might request that the rejected goods be shipped back to the seller. If the goods are perishable or may deteriorate rapidly, then the buyer must make a reasonable effort to sell the goods. The seller must reimburse the buyer for any expenses that the buyer incurs in carrying out the seller's instructions or in trying to resell perishable goods. In reselling goods, the buyer must act reasonably and in good faith [2–603(2) and (3)].

If the rejected goods are not perishable or if the seller does not give the buyer instructions, then the buyer has several options. First, the buyer can store the goods for the seller. Second, the buyer can reship them to the seller. Third, the buyer can resell them for the seller's benefit. If the buyer resells the goods, the buyer may keep his expenses and a reasonable commission on the sale. If the buyer stores the goods, the buyer should exercise care in handling them. The buyer also must give the seller a reasonable time to remove the goods [2–604]. The *Ford v. Starr Fireworks, Inc.* case, which appears earlier in this chapter at page 398, discusses the obligations of a buyer who receives nonconforming goods.

If the buyer is not a merchant, then her obligation after rejection is to hold the goods with reasonable care for a sufficient time to give the seller an opportunity to remove them. The buyer is not obligated to ship the goods back to the seller [2–602].

ASSURANCE, REPUDIATION, AND EXCUSE

Assurance

The buyer or seller may become concerned that the other party may not be able to perform his contract obligations. If there is a reasonable basis for that concern, the buyer or seller can demand **assurance** from the other party that the contract will be performed. If such assurances are not given within a reasonable time not exceeding 30 days, the party is considered to have repudiated the contract [2–609].

For example, a farmer contracts to sell 1,000 bushels of apples to a canner, with delivery to be made in September. In March, the canner learns that a severe frost has damaged many of the apple blossoms in the farmer's area and that 50 percent of the crop has been lost. The canner has the right to demand assurances in writing from the farmer that he will be able to fulfill his obligations in light of the frost. The farmer must provide those assurances within 30 days. Thus, he might advise the canner that his crop sustained only relatively light damage or that he had made commitments to sell only a small percentage of his total crop and expects to be able to fulfill his obligations. If the farmer does not provide such assurances in a timely manner, he is considered to have repudiated the contract. The canner then has certain remedies against the farmer for breach of contract. These remedies are discussed in the next chapter.

The *LNS Investment Company, Inc. v. Phillips 66 Company* case, which follows, illustrates a situation where a buyer became concerned about the seller's ability to perform and demanded assurances from the seller.

LNS INVESTMENT CO., INC. v. PHILLIPS 66 CO., 731 F. Supp. 1484 (D. Kansas 1990)

 NS Investment Company is the successor to the Compu-Blend Corporation (CBC) which blended, labeled, and packaged quart plastic bottles of motor oil for, among others, the Phillips 66 Company. On July 29, Peter Buhlinger, Phillip's manager of lubricants, wrote a letter to CBC that read as follows:

This will confirm our verbal agreement whereby Phillips will purchase additional quantities of plastic bottles from CBC during 1986.

CBC, in an effort to increase their packaging capacity, has committed to purchase several additional molds to blow the Phillips one-quart container. In order to amortize the cost of the additional equipment, Phillips has agreed to take delivery of a maximum of 4,000,000 bottles to be made available by December 31, 1986. This agreement includes the production available now and to be supplemented by the additional equipment. Should CBC be not able to produce the full 4,000,000 quarts by December 31, 1986, this agreement shall be considered satisfied.

Phillips' desire is to receive as many bottles packaged with Phillips motor oil in 1986 from CBC as possible. It is our intention to change to a different type of plastic one-quart container beginning in 1987 and therefore this agreement cannot extend past the December 31, 1986 deadline. All production would have to be of high resaleable [*sic*] plastic quarts filled with the appropriate Phillips products and labeled accordingly. The production would be required to be available on an even weekly basis in order to facilitate movement of the product to the warehouse and customers.

Although the agreement called for CBC to increase its production capacity, CBC experienced numerous problems in maintaining even its precontract capacity. Moreover, the quality of goods CBC was able to deliver was frequently unacceptable to Phillips. On September 18, a Phillips representative wrote to CBC complaining about the quality of goods Phillips was receiving, specifically mentioning neck finish and label application problems. The letter also noted that if Phillips had known how CBC would perform, it would not have committed to purchase CBC's hoped-for increase in production. CBC's chairman responded on September 29, acknowledging certain deficiencies, offering a number of reasons for the inability to perform, and stating that he was sure CBC would be showing "marked improvement in deliveries in the coming week and even more in another two or three weeks."

On October 15, the Phillips representative reiterated its continued dissatisfaction with CBC's products, indicating "we definitely do not want bottles on the shelf of the quality submitted." And, on December 16, he advised CBC that Phillips would not renew any commitments to purchase goods from CBC after March 31, 1987, because of CBC's poor performance under the July 29 agreement. In May 1987, CBC brought suit against Phillips, alleging that Phillips breached the July 29 agreement by failing to purchase CBC's full output of plastic bottles through December 31, 1986.

O'Connor, Chief Judge CBC's failure to provide either the quantity or quality of goods contemplated by the July 29 agreement entitled Phillips to suspend its performance. Section 2–609 of the Code states as follows:

Right to adequate assurance of performance.

(1) A contract for sale imposes an obligation on each party that the other's expectations will not be impaired. When reasonable grounds for insecurity arise with respect to the performance of either party, the other may in writing demand adequate assurance of due performance and until he receives such assurance may if commercially reasonable suspend any performance for which he has not already received the agreed return.

(2) Between merchants the reasonableness of grounds for insecurity and the adequacy of any assurance offered shall be determined according to commercial standards.

(3) Acceptance of any improper delivery or payment does not prejudice the aggrieved party's right to demand adequate assurance of future performance.

(4) After receipt of a justified demand failure to provide within a reasonable time not exceeding 30 days such assurance of due performance as is adequate under the circumstances of the particular case is a repudiation of the contract.

To suspend its performance pursuant to this section, Phillips must (1) have had reasonable grounds for insecurity regarding CBC's performance under the contract, (2) have demanded in writing adequate assurance of CBC's future performance and (3) have not received from CBC such assurances.

Phillips had reasonable grounds for insecurity regarding CBC's performance. The evidence conclusively demonstrated that CBC suffered numerous setbacks in its attempt to increase its capacity to produce plastic bottles for Phillips. Specifically, both the quantity and quality of the bottles were chronically poor. Indeed, Phillips was arguably entitled to cancel the contract soon after CBC's unacceptable performance began. Sec. 2–607(3)(a); 2–711(1). Although Phillips lost its right to cancel the contract by failing to elect that remedy within a reasonable time, the above circumstances were sufficient to establish Phillip's right to adequate assurance of CBC's future performance under Section 2–609.

Phillips demanded, in writing, assurance from CBC regarding CBC's future performance. Phillips

notified CBC of the inadequacies of CBC's goods and requested assurance that CBC would take steps to rectify the same. Thus it was incumbent on CBC to provide adequate assurance of its future performance to Phillips.

CBC failed to provide Phillips with adequate assurance of its future performance. CBC's continual excuses for failing to perform, unaccompanied by corresponding remedial action, cannot be deemed adequate assurance under the Code. Accordingly, Phillips was entitled to suspend its own performance of the contract by refusing to place orders with CBC and/or canceling orders already placed, 30 days after either or both the September 18, 1986, and October 15, 1986, letters. In view of this conclusion, Phillips did not breach the contract by suspending performance in December, 1986.

Judgment for Phillips.

Anticipatory Repudiation

Sometimes, one of the parties to a contract repudiates the contract by advising the other party that he does not intend to perform his obligations. When one party repudiates the contract, the other party may suspend his performance. In addition, he may either await performance for a reasonable time or use the remedies for breach of contract that are discussed in Chapter 22 [2–610].

Suppose the party who repudiated the contract changes his mind. Repudiation can be withdrawn by clearly indicating that the person intends to perform his obligations. The repudiating party must do this before the other party has canceled the contract or has materially changed position by, for example, buying the goods elsewhere [2–611].

Excuse

Unforeseen events may make it difficult or impossible for a person to perform his contractual obligations. The Code rules for determining when a person is excused from performing are similar to the general contract rules. General contract law uses the test of **impossibility.** In most situations, however, the Code uses the test of **commercial impracticability.**

The Code attempts to differentiate events that are unforeseeable or uncontrollable from events that were part of the risk borne by a party. If the goods required for the performance of a contract are destroyed without fault of either party prior to the time that the risk of loss passed to the buyer, the contract is voided [2–613]. Suppose Jones agrees to sell and deliver an antique table to Brown. The table is damaged when Jones's antiques store is struck by lightning and catches fire. The specific table covered by the contract was damaged without fault of either party prior to the time that the risk of loss was to pass to Brown. Under the Code, Brown has the option of either canceling the contract or accepting the table with an allowance in the purchase price to compensate for the damaged condition [2–613].

If unforeseen conditions cause a delay or the inability to make delivery of the goods and thus make performance impracticable, the seller is excused from making delivery. However, if a seller's capacity to deliver is only partially affected, the seller must allocate production in any fair and reasonable manner among his customers. The seller has the option of including any regular customer not then under contract in his allocation scheme. When the seller allocates production, he must notify the buyers [2–615]. When a buyer receives this notice, the buyer may either terminate the contract or agree to accept the allocation [2–616].

For example, United Nuclear contracts to sell certain quantities of fuel rods for nuclear power plants to a number of electric utilities. If the federal government limits the amount of uranium that United has access to, so that United is unable to fill all of its contracts, United is excused from full performance on the grounds of commercial impracticability. However, United may allocate its production of fuel rods among its customers by reducing each customer's share by a certain percentage and giving the customers notice of the allocation. Then, each utility can decide whether to cancel the contract or accept the partial allocation of fuel rods.

In the absence of compelling circumstances, courts do not readily excuse parties from their contractual obligations, particularly where it is clear that the parties anticipated a problem and sought to provide for it in the contract.

ETHICAL AND PUBLIC POLICY CONCERNS

1. Problem case 1 in this chapter illustrates a problem that can arise in situations where supplies of the goods that are the subject of a contract are either in significantly shorter or more plentiful supply than when the agreement was made and/or there has been a significant change in the market price. When, if ever, is a buyer or seller ethically justified in trying to find a way out of a contractual obligation because the supply or market price conditions have so changed that he can make a better deal elsewhere? Concomitantly, are there circumstances under which the other party, acting in an ethically responsible manner, should voluntarily release the disadvantaged party from her contractual commitment?

2. Suppose that you recently purchased a new automobile. The automobile has a number of problems that the dealer is unable to completely fix after you have left it with the dealer on two occasions. Although the dealer indicates a willingness to fix the remaining problems and confidence that they can be remedied quickly and completely, you have now concluded that you would prefer to have a car made by another manufacturer. Are there any ethical considerations involved in a decision on your part to attempt to revoke your acceptance of the automobile?

3. Where a contract calls for delivery in installments, the buyer can reject an installment delivery containing nonconforming goods only where the nonconformity substantially affects the value of the delivery and cannot be corrected; where the defects are relatively minor, the buyer has to keep the installment if the seller, for example, offers an allowance to make up for the nonconformity. Suppose you are a seller with some goods you know have minor defects that you would like to get rid of. Would it be ethical for you to send them to a customer with whom you have a contract for installment deliveries of the goods, knowing that they do not conform to the contract and that the customer will have to accept them as long as you give him a price allowance?

PROBLEMS AND PROBLEM CASES

1. Baker was a buyer and distributor of popcorn. Ratzlaff was a farmer who grew popcorn. Baker and Ratzlaff entered into a written contract pursuant to which Ratzlaff agreed that in the current year he would raise 380 acres of popcorn and sell the popcorn to Baker. Baker agreed to furnish the seed popcorn and to pay $4.75 per hundred pounds of popcorn. The popcorn was to be delivered to Baker as he ordered it, and Baker was to pay for the popcorn as it was delivered. At Baker's request, the first delivery was made on February 2 of the following year and the second on February 4. On neither occasion did Ratzlaff ask Baker to pay or Baker offer to pay. During that week, Ratzlaff and Baker had several phone conversations about further deliveries, but there was no discussion about payments. On February 11, Ratzlaff sent written notice to Baker that he was terminating the contract because Baker had not paid for the two loads of popcorn that had been delivered. In the meantime, Ratzlaff sold his remaining 1.6 million pounds of popcorn to another buyer at $8 per 100 pounds. Baker then sued Ratzlaff for breach of contract. Did Ratzlaff act in good faith in terminating the contract?

2. Harold Ledford agreed to purchase three used Mustang automobiles (a 1966 Mustang coupe, a 1965 fastback, and a 1966 convertible) from J. L. Cowan for $3,000. Ledford gave Cowan a cashier's check for $1,500 when he took possession of the coupe, with the understanding he would pay the remaining $1,500 on the delivery of the fastback and the convertible. Cowan arranged for Charles Canterberry to deliver the remaining vehicles to Ledford. Canterberry dropped the convertible off at a lot owned by Ledford and proceeded to Ledford's residence to deliver the fastback. He refused to unload it until Ledford paid him $1,500. Ledford refused to make the payment until he had an opportunity to inspect the convertible, which he suspected was not in the same condition that it had been in when he purchased it. Canterberry refused this request and returned both the fastback and the convertible to Cowan. Cowan then brought suit against Ledford to recover the balance of the purchase price. Was Ledford entitled to inspect the car before he paid the balance due on it?

3. Spada, an Oregon corporation, agreed to sell Belson, who operated a business in Chicago, two carloads of potatoes at "4.40 per sack, FOB Oregon shipping point." Spada had the potatoes put aboard railroad cars; however, it did not have floor racks placed under the potatoes, as was customary during the winter months. As a result, there was no warm air circulating and the potatoes were frozen while in transit. Spada claims that its obligations ended with the delivery to the carrier and that the risk of loss was on Belson. What argument would you make for Belson?

4. In April, Reginald Bell contracted to sell potatoes to Red Ball Potato Company for fall delivery. The contract specified that the potatoes were to be "85 percent U.S. 1's." In Red Ball's dealings with Bell and other farmers, potatoes were delivered and paid for in truckload quantities. In the fall, Bell delivered several truckloads of potatoes. Samples of each load were taken for testing, and most of the loads were determined to be below 85 percent U.S. No 1. What options are open to Red Ball?

5. James Shelton is an experienced musician who operates the University Music Center in Seattle, Washington. On Saturday, Barbara Farkas and her 22-year-old daughter, Penny, went to Shelton's store to look at violins. Penny had been studying violin in college for approximately nine months. Mrs. Farkas and Penny advised Shelton of the price range in which they were interested, and Penny told him she was relying on his expertise. He selected a violin for $368.90, including case and sales tax. Shelton claimed that the instrument was originally priced at $465 but that he discounted it because Mrs. Farkas was willing to take it on an "as is" basis. Mrs.

Farkas and Penny alleged that Shelton represented that the violin was "the best" and "a perfect violin for you" and that it was of high quality. Mrs. Farkas paid for it by check. On the following Monday, Penny took the violin to her college music teacher, who immediately told her that it had poor tone and a crack in the body and that it was not the right instrument for her. Mrs. Farkas telephoned Shelton and asked for a refund. He refused, saying that she had purchased and accepted the violin on an "as is" basis. Had Farkas "accepted" the violin so that it was too late for her to "reject" it?

6. On May 23, 1978, Deborah McCullough, a secretary, purchased a 1978 Chrysler LeBaron from Bill Swad Chrysler-Plymouth. The automobile was covered by both a limited warranty and a vehicle service contract (extended warranty). Following delivery, McCullough advised the salesperson that she had noted problems with the brakes, transmission, air conditioning, paint job, and seat panels, as well as the absence of rust proofing. The next day, the brakes failed and the car was returned to the dealer for the necessary repairs. When the car was returned, McCullough discovered that the brakes had not been properly repaired and that none of the cosmetic work had been done. The car was returned several times to the dealer to correct these problems and others that developed subsequently. On June 26, the car was again returned to the dealer, who kept it for three weeks. Many of the defects were not corrected, however, and new problems with the horn and brakes arose. While McCullough was on a shopping trip, the engine abruptly shut off and the car had to be towed to the dealer. Then, while she was on her honeymoon, the brakes again failed. The car was taken back to the dealer with a list of 32 defects that needed correction. After repeated efforts to repair the car were unsuccessful, McCullough sent a letter to the dealer calling for rescission of the purchase, requesting return of the purchase price, and offering to return the car on receipt of shipping instructions. She received no answer and continued to drive it. McCullough then filed suit. In May 1979, the dealer refused to do any further work on the car, claiming that it was in satisfactory condition. By the time of the trial, in June 1980, it had been driven 35,000 miles, approximately 23,000 of which had been logged after McCullough mailed her notice of revocation. By continuing to operate the vehicle after notifying the seller of her intent to rescind the sale, did McCullough waive her right to revoke her original acceptance?

7. Tai Wah Manufactory Ltd., a Hong Kong company, is a manufacturer of electronic goods. Ambassador Imports Ltd., a New York company, is an importer and wholesale distributor of various products, including electronic goods. The two companies had been doing business with each other for about five years when in February 1985, Ambassador placed an order with Tai Wah for 2,000 stereo cassette recorders, which were delivered to and accepted by Ambassador in Los Angeles on April 15. On April 4, Ambassador placed another order for cassette recorders with Tai Wah, this time for 2,040 units. Ambassador claimed that in May, it began to receive complaints from its customers about the recorders from the first shipment and several hundred units were returned to Ambassador before June 24. On May 31 and June 7, Ambassador sent telexes to Tai Wah advising it of problems with the quality of plastic in the dial and with breakage of the cassette door, and asking that the problem be corrected for all future orders. On June 1, Tai Wah indicated that it was trying to improve the quality of the plastic and that future orders would be corrected. It also advised Ambassador that the second shipment had been sent on May 24. Despite the complaints about the quality of the recorders, Ambassador picked up the second shipment of recorders in Los Angeles on June 24. It made no effort to inspect the goods. On June 29, it notified Tai Wah that it did not want the second shipment, that it had picked it up only to hold as collateral to assure that it would be compensated for its damages on the first shipment, and that it would return the second shipment when such compensation was arranged. Tai Wah then brought a lawsuit against Ambassador to recover the contract price of the second shipment of recorders. Did Ambassador make an effective rejection of the second shipment, thus relieving itself of the obligation to pay for it?

8. [▣] *Video Case.* See "Sour Grapes." Jelly Manufacturer, a food processor in Chicago, placed a phone order with Grape Grower, a grower in California, for a quantity of perishable produce. The shipping term was CIF with payment to be made on delivery (COD). Grower delivered the goods called for in the contract to a carrier and contracted for their shipment. However, it neglected to provide that the goods be shipped under refrigeration. The goods were loaded on a nonrefrigerated boxcar and as a result the produce was spoiled when it reached Chicago. Jelly Manufacturer, as required by the COD term, paid for the produce by check before discovering the spoilage. By paying for the produce, has Jelly Manufacturer accepted the goods so that it cannot subsequently reject them as nonconforming?

When Jelly Manufacturer called Grower to complain, Grower offered to rush a replacement shipment. Jelly Manufacturer declined the offer, stating that it would not arrive in time for the produce to be processed and delivered to Grocery Chain in time to meet Jelly Manufacturer's contract with Grocery Chain. Was Jelly Manufacturer required to accept Grower's promise to make a replacement shipment?

9. Walters, a grower of Christmas trees, contracted to supply Traynor with "top quality trees." When the shipment arrived and was inspected, Traynor discovered that some of the trees were not top quality. Within 24 hours, Traynor notified Walters that he was rejecting the trees that were not top quality. Walters did not have a place of business or an agent in the town where Traynor was. Christmas was only a short time away. The trees were perishable and would decline in value to zero by Christmas Eve. Walters did not give Traynor any instructions, so Traynor sold the trees for Walters's account. Traynor then tried to recover from Walters the expenses he incurred in caring for and selling the trees. Did Walters act properly in rejecting the trees and reselling them for the seller?

10. Haralambos Fekkos purchased from Lykins Sales & Service a Yammar Model 165D, 16-horsepower diesel tractor and various implements. On Saturday, April 27, Fekkos gave Lykins a check for the agreed-on purchase price, less trade-in, of $6,596, and the items were delivered to his residence. The next day, while attempting to use the tractor for the first time, Fekkos discovered it was defective. The defects included a dead battery requiring jump starts, overheating while pulling either the mower or tiller, missing safety shields over the muffler and the power takeoff, and a missing water pump. On Monday, Fekkos contacted Lykins's sales representative who believed his claims to be true and agreed to have the tractor picked up from Fekkos's residence; Fekkos also stopped payment on his check. Fekkos placed the tractor with the tiller attached in his front yard as near as possible to the front door without driving it onto the landscaped area closest to the house. Fekkos left the tractor on the lawn because his driveway was broken up for renovation and his garage was inaccessible, and because the tractor would have to be jump-started

by Lykins's employees when they picked it up. On Tuesday, Fekkos went back to Lykins's store to purchase an Allis-Chalmers tractor and reminded Lykins's employees that the Yammar tractor had not been picked up and remained on his lawn. On Wednesday, May 1, at 6:00 A.M., Fekkos discovered that the tractor was missing although the tiller had been unhitched and remained in the yard. Later that day, Lykins picked up the remaining implements. The theft was reported to the police. On several occasions, Fekkos was assured that Lykins's insurance would cover the stolen tractor, that it was Lykins's fault for not picking it up, and that Fekkos had nothing to worry about. However, Lykins subsequently brought suit against Fekkos to recover the purchase price of the Yammar tractor. Was Fekkos liable for the purchase price of the tractor that had been rejected and was stolen while awaiting pickup by the seller?

11. Whelan ordered fuel oil from Griffith to be delivered to his farm home, which was located on a country road. The oil was to be delivered on a COD basis. Griffith made two attempts to deliver the oil, but each time no one was found at home. The morning after a heavy snow, the heaviest in 20 years, Griffith equipped the truck with chains and made a third attempt to deliver the oil but found on arrival that the driveway to the house was impassable due to snowdrifts approximately 6 feet high. When the driver drove past the house and attempted to turn around, the truck became stuck in the snow and had to be towed back to the main highway. Whelan ran out of oil and, as a result of having no fuel, his heating plant froze, causing substantial damage to it. Whelan sued Griffith to recover for the damage to the heating plant, claiming the breach of the contract to deliver the oil was the cause of the damage. Should Griffith be held liable?

Remedies for Breach of Sales Contracts

U sually, both parties to a contract for the sale of goods perform the obligations that they assumed in the contract. Occasionally, however, one of the parties to a contract fails to perform his obligations. When this happens, the Uniform Commercial Code (UCC or Code) provides the injured party with a variety of remedies for breach of contract. This chapter will set forth and explain the remedies available to an injured party, as well as the Code's rules that govern buyer-seller agreements as to remedies and the Code's statute of limitations. The objective of the Code remedies is to put the injured person in the same position that he would have been in if the contract had been performed. Under the Code, an injured party may not recover consequential or punitive damages unless such damages are specifically provided for in the Code or in another statute [1–106].[1] ∞

AGREEMENTS AS TO REMEDIES

The buyer and seller may provide their own remedies in the contract, to be applied in the event that one of the parties fails to perform. They may also limit either the remedies that the law makes available or the damages that can be covered [2–719(1)]. If the parties agree on the amount of damages that will be paid to the injured party, this amount is known as **liquidated damages.** An agreement for liquidated damages is enforced if the amount is

---

[1]The numbers in brackets refer to sections of the Uniform Commercial Code.

reasonable and if actual damages would be difficult to prove in the event of a breach of the contract. The amount is considered reasonable if it is not so large as to be a penalty or so small as to be unconscionable [2–718(1)].

For example, Carl Carpenter contracts to build and sell a display booth for $5,000 to Hank Hawker for Hawker to use at the state fair. Delivery is to be made to Hawker by September 1. If the booth is not delivered on time, Hawker will not be able to sell his wares at the fair. Carpenter and Hawker might agree that if delivery is not made by September 1, Carpenter will pay Hawker $2,750 as liquidated damages. The actual sales that Hawker might lose without a booth would be very hard to prove, so Hawker and Carpenter can provide some certainty through the liquidated damages agreement. Carpen-

ter then knows what he will be liable for if he does not perform his obligation. Similarly, Hawker knows what he can recover if the booth is not delivered on time. The $2,750 amount is probably reasonable. If the amount were $500,000, it likely would be void as a penalty because it is way out of line with the damages that Hawker would reasonably be expected to sustain. And if the amount were too small, say $1, it might be considered unconscionable and therefore not enforceable.

If a liquidated damages clause is not enforceable because it is a penalty or unconscionable, the injured party can recover the actual damages that he suffered. The *Baker v. International Record Syndicate, Inc.* case, which follows, illustrates a situation where a court enforced a liquidated damages clause in a contract.

BAKER v. INTERNATIONAL RECORD SYNDICATE, INC. 812 S.W.2d 53 (Tex. Ct. App. 1991)

I nternational Record Syndicate (IRS) hired Jeff Baker to take photographs of the musical group Timbuk-3. Baker mailed 37 "chromes" (negatives) to IRS via the business agent of Timbuk-3. When the chromes were returned to Baker, holes had been punched in 34 of them. Baker brought an action for breach of contract to recover for the damage done to the chromes.

A provision printed on Baker's invoice to IRS stated: "[r]eimbursement for loss or damage shall be determined by a photograph's reasonable value which shall be no less than $1,500 per transparency."

Enoch, Chief Judge The Uniform Commercial Code provides:

Damages for breach by either party may be liquidated in the agreement but only at an amount which is reasonable in light of the anticipated harm caused by the breach, the difficulties of proof of loss, and the inconvenience or nonfeasibility of otherwise obtaining an adequate remedy. A term fixing unreasonably large liquidated damages is void as a penalty.

Under Texas law a liquidated damages provision will be enforced when the court finds (1) the harm caused by the breach is incapable of estimation, and (2) the amount of liquidated damages is a reasonable forecast of just compensation. This might be termed the "anticipated harm" test. The party asserting that a liquidated damages clause is, in fact, a penalty provision has the burden of proof. Evidence related to the difficulty of estimation and the reasonable forecast must be viewed as of the time the contract was executed.

Baker testified that he had been paid as much as $14,000 for a photo session, which resulted in 24

photographs and that several of these photographs had also been resold. Baker further testified that he had received as little as $125 for a single photograph. Baker also testified that he once sold a photograph for $500. Subsequently, he sold reproductions of the same photograph three additional times at various prices; the total income from this one photograph was $1,500. This particular photograph was taken in 1986 and was still producing income in 1990. Baker demonstrated, therefore, that an accurate demonstration of the damages from a single photograph is virtually impossible.

Timbuk-3's potential for fame was also an important factor in the valuation of the chromes. At the time of the photo session, Timbuk-3's potential was unknown. In view of the difficulty in determining the value of a piece of art, the broad range of values and long-term earning power of photographs, and the unknown potential for fame of the subject, $1,500 is not an unreasonable estimate of Baker's actual damages.

Additionally, liquidated damages must not be disproportionate to actual damages. If the liquidated damages are shown to be disproportionate to the actual damages, then the liquidated damages can be declared a penalty and recovery limited to actual damages proven. This might be called the "actual harm" test. The burden of proving this defense is upon the party seeking to invalidate the clause. The party asserting this defense is required to prove the amount of the other party's actual damages, if any, to show that the actual loss was not an approximation of the stipulated sum.

While evidence was presented that showed the value of several of Baker's other projects, this was not evidence of the photographs in question. The evidence clearly shows that photographs are unique items with many factors bearing on their actual value. Each of the 34 chromes may have had a different value. Proof of this loss is difficult; where damages are real but difficult to prove, injustice will be done the injured party if the court substitutes the requirements of judicial proof for the parties' own informed agreement as to what is a reasonable measure of damages. The evidence offered to prove Baker's actual damages lacks probative force. IRS failed to establish Baker's actual damages as to these particular photographs.

Judgment reversed in favor of Baker.

Liability for consequential damages resulting from a breach of contract (such as lost profits or damage to property) may also be limited or excluded by agreement. The limitation or exclusion is not enforced if it would be unconscionable. Any attempt to limit consequential damages for injury caused to a person by consumer goods is considered prima facie unconscionable [2–719(3)].

Suppose an automobile manufacturer makes a warranty as to the quality of an automobile that is purchased as a consumer good. It then tries to disclaim responsibility for any person injured if the car does not conform to the warranty and to limit its liability to replacing any defective parts. The disclaimer of consequential injuries in this case would be unconscionable and therefore would not be enforced. Exclusion of or limitation on consequential damages is permitted where the loss is commercial, as long as the exclusion or limitation is not unconscionable.

The *Hartzell v. Justus Co., Inc.* case, which follows, illustrates how the Code applies to a situation where circumstances cause a limited remedy agreed to by the parties to fail in its essential purpose. When this happens, the limited remedy is not enforced and the general Code remedies are available to the injured party.

HARTZELL v. JUSTUS CO., INC. 693 F.2d 770 (8th Cir. 1982)

*D*r. Allan Hartzell purchased a log home construction kit manufactured by Justus Homes. Hartzell purchased the package for $38,622 from Del Carter, who was Justus Homes's dealer for the Sioux Falls area. He also hired Carter's construction company to build the house, which eventually cost about $150,000. Hartzell was dissatisfied with the house in many respects. His chief complaints were that knotholes in the walls and ceilings leaked rain profusely and that the home was not weathertight because flashings were not included in the roofing materials and because the timbers were not kiln-dried and therefore shrank. He also complained that an undersized support beam, which eventually cracked, was included in the package. This defect resulted in floor cracks and in inside doors that would not close. Hartzell claimed that the structural defects were only partially remediable and that the fair market value of the house was reduced even after all practicable repairs had been made.

Hartzell brought suit against Justus Homes, alleging negligence and breach of implied and express warranties and seeking damages for loss in value and the cost of repairs. A jury awarded Hartzell a verdict of $34,794.67. Justus Homes appealed. ∽

Arnold, Circuit Judge Justus Homes contends the district court failed to adequately consider a limitation-of-remedies clause contained in its contract with Hartzell. Justus Homes relies on Clause 10c of the contract, which says that Justus will repair or replace defective materials, and Clause

10d, which states that this limited repair or replacement clause is the exclusive remedy available against Justus. These agreements, Justus asserts, are valid under the Uniform Commercial Code Section 2–719(1) states:

(1) Subject to the provisions of subsections (2) and (3) of this section and of section 2–718 on liquidation and limitation of damages,

(a) The agreement may provide for remedies in addition to or in substitution for those provided in this article and may limit or alter the measure of damages recoverable under this article, as by limiting the buyer's remedies to return of the goods and repayment of the price or to repair and replacement of nonconforming goods or parts; and

(b) Resort to a remedy as provided is optional unless the remedy is expressly agreed to be exclusive, in which case it is the sole remedy.

Subsection (1) of section 2–719 is qualified by subsection (2): "Where circumstances cause an exclusive or limited remedy to fail of its essential purpose, remedy may be had as provided in this title." The jury's verdict for Hartzell in an amount almost exactly equal to Hartzell's evidence of cost of repairs plus diminution in market value means it must have found that the structural defects were not entirely remediable. Such a finding necessarily means that the limited warranty failed of its essential purpose.

Two of our recent cases support this conclusion. In *Soo Line R.R. v. Fruehauf Corp.,* the defendant claimed, relying on a limitation-of-remedies clause similar to the one involved here, that the plaintiff's damages should be limited to the reasonable cost of repairing the railroad cars that plaintiff had bought from defendant. The jury verdict included, among other things, an award for the difference between the value of the cars as actually manufactured and what they would have been worth if they had measured up to the defendant's representations. This court affirmed the verdict for the larger amount. We held, construing the Minnesota UCC, which is identical to 2–719 as adopted in South Dakota, that the limitation-of-remedies clause was ineffective because the remedy as thus limited failed of its essential purpose. The defendant, though called upon to make the necessary repairs, had refused to do so, and the repairs as performed by the plaintiff itself "did not fully restore the cars to totally acceptable operating conditions."

Here, Justus Homes attempted to help with the necessary repairs, which is more than Fruehauf did in the *Soo Line* case, but after the repairs had been completed, the house was still, according to the jury verdict, not what Justus had promised it would be. The purpose of a remedy is to give to a buyer what the seller promised him—that is, a house that did not leak. If repairs alone do not achieve that end, then to limit the buyer's remedy to repair would cause that remedy to fail of its essential purpose.

An analogous case is *Select Port, Inc. v. Babcock Swine, Inc.,* applying 2–719 as adopted in Iowa. The defendant had promised to deliver to plaintiff certain extraordinary pigs known as Midwestern Gilts and Meatline Boars. Instead, only ordinary pigs were delivered. Plaintiff sued for breach of warranty, and defendant claimed that its damages, if any, should be limited to a return of the purchase price by an express clause to that effect in the contract. The district court held that the clause was unenforceable because it was unconscionable, see section 2–719(3), and because it failed of its essential purpose. We affirmed. "Having failed to deliver the highly-touted special pigs, defendants may not now assert a favorable clause to limit their liability."

So here, where the house sold was found by the jury to fall short of the seller's promises, and where repairs could not make it right, Justus Homes's liability cannot be limited to the cost of repairs. If the repairs had been adequate to restore the house to its promised condition, and if Dr. Hartzell had claimed additional consequential damages, for example, water damage to a rug from the leaky roof, the limitation-of-remedies clause would have been effective. But that is not this case.

The evidence in the record all demonstrates that the repair or replacement clause was a failure under the circumstances of this case. Some of the house's many problems simply could not be remedied by repair or replacement. The clause having failed of its essential purpose, that is, effective enjoyment of implied and express warranties, Dr. Hartzell was entitled, under UCC 2–719(2), to any of the buyer's remedies provided by the Code. Among these remedies are consequential damages as provided in 2–714 and 2–715(2).

Judgment for Hartzell affirmed.

Statute of Limitations

The Code provides that a lawsuit for breach of a sales contract must be filed within four years after the breach occurs. The parties to a contract may shorten this period to one year, but they may not extend it for longer than four years [2–725]. Normally, a breach of warranty is considered to have occurred when the goods are delivered to the buyer. However, if the warranty covers future performance of goods (for example, a warranty on a tire for four years or 40,000 miles), then the breach occurs at the time the buyer should have discovered the defect in the product. If, for example, the buyer of the tire discovers the defect after driving 25,000 miles on the tire over a three-year period, he would have four years from that time to bring any lawsuit to remedy the breach.

In the *Wilson v. Hammer Holdings, Inc.* case, which follows, the court rejected the argument that a warranty given in connection with the sale of a painting extended to the future performance of the painting.

WILSON v. HAMMER HOLDINGS, INC.   6 UCC Rep.2d 321 (1st Cir. 1988)

I n 1961, Dorothy and John Wilson purchased a painting entitled *Femme Debout* from the Hammer Galleries. They paid $11,000 for the work that was expressly guaranteed to be an original work of art by Edouard Vuillard. The purchase agreement stated that "the authenticity of this picture is guaranteed." In 1984, in preparation for selling it, the Wilsons had the picture examined by an expert. He determined that the painting was not done by the French artist Vuillard, and he refused to authenticate it.

The Wilsons returned the painting to the Hammer Galleries, and then brought a lawsuit seeking damages for breach of warranty. Hammer Galleries asserted that the claim was barred by the UCC's four-year statute of limitations. The district court held that the claim was barred by the statute of limitations, and the Wilsons appealed. ∞

Coffin, Circuit Judge The Massachusetts statute of limitations for breach of a sales contract is set out in section 2–725. That section provides that

(1) An action for breach of any contract for sale must be commenced within four years after the cause of action has accrued.

(2) A cause of action accrues when the breach occurs, regardless of the aggrieved party's lack of knowledge of the breach. A breach of warranty occurs when tender of delivery is made, except that where a warranty explicitly extends to future performance of the goods and discovery must await the time of such performance, the cause of action accrues when the breach is or should have been discovered.

There is no question that the Wilsons' action was untimely under this statute if it accrued at the time they purchased the painting and received the warranty because those events occurred 26 years before suit was filed. The Wilsons therefore contend that this case falls within the exception to section 2–725(2), and they argue that their cause of action accrued upon their discovery in 1985 that the painting was not authentic.

The district court found the exception in section 2–725(2) to be inapplicable because Hammer's warranty made no explicit reference to future performance as required by the statute. The Wilsons do not argue that the district court erred in reading the warranty to lack an explicit promise of future performance. Rather, they argue that a warranty of authenticity necessarily relates to the future condition of the artwork, despite the absence of explicit language to that effect, and for that reason, they claim that the exception in section 2–725(2) should apply to them. Section 2–725(2) refers to a warranty of "future performance," and so the Wilsons' theory depends first on extending the concept of a "performance" to a painting. They concede that paintings, unlike consumer goods like automobiles and washing machines, generally are not purchased based on how they "perform" or "function." They suggest, however, that a painting "performs" "by being what it is represented to be." In this case, they say, "Femme Debout" could "perform" only by being an authentic Vuillard.

Accepting at least for the sake of argument that a painting does "perform" by being genuine, the question then becomes whether Hammer's express warranty of authenticity not only guaranteed the present "being" of the painting as an authentic Vuillard but also extended, as required by section 2–725(2), to the future existence of a painting as a Vuillard. On this point, the Wilsons argue that because the authenticity of a painting does not change over time, Hammer's warranty necessarily guaranteed the present and future existence of the painting as an authentic Vuillard. Therefore, they contend, explicit words warranting future performance would be superfluous in this context.

One difficulty with this argument, however, is that it asks us to ignore the literal language of the statute requiring an explicit promise of future performance. The Wilsons argue essentially that because the statutory exception's requirement of an explicit prospective warranty does not make sense in the context of the sale of paintings, we should dispense with that requirement. We are reluctant, however, to waive the specific eligibility requirements established by the legislature for what, it must be remembered, is an exception to the general limitations rule.

Even if we were to accept the Wilsons' argument that Hammer's warranty necessarily extended to future performance of the painting, and thus met the prospective warranty requirement of section 2–725(2), we nevertheless would conclude that their action is time-barred. The statute also requires that discovery of the breach "must await" the time of such future performance. That is not the case here. Because of the static nature of authenticity, the Wilsons were no less capable of discovering that "Femme Debout" was a fake at the time of purchase than they were at a later time.

Our reluctance to enlarge the scope of the exception in section 2–725(2) is strengthened by the recognition that the statute of limitations for art buyers could run indefinitely. Indeed, in this case suit was filed 26 years after the purchase. Although Massachusetts legislators may choose to provide perpetual protection for consumers of artistic products, it would be presumptuous for us to assume they would. Moreover, we think it is more likely that, if Massachusetts chooses to extend protection to art buyers in the way the Wilsons suggest, the legislature would fix some endpoint to the seller's possible liability—perhaps similar to the 20-year limitations period for an action seeking the recovery of land.

Judgment in favor of Hammer Galleries affirmed.

SELLER'S REMEDIES

Remedies Available to an Injured Seller

A buyer may breach a contract in a number of ways. The most common are: (1) by wrongfully refusing to accept goods, (2) by wrongfully returning goods, (3) by failing to pay for goods when payment is due, and (4) by indicating an unwillingness to go ahead with the contract. When a buyer breaches a contract, the seller has a number of remedies under the Code, including the right to:

- Cancel the contract [2–703(f)].
- Withhold delivery of undelivered goods [2–703(a)].
- Resell the goods covered by the contract and recover damages from the buyer [2–706].
- Recover from the buyer the profit that the seller would have made on the sale or the damages that the seller sustained [2–708].
- Recover the purchase price of goods delivered to or accepted by the buyer [2–709].

In addition, a buyer may become insolvent and thus unable to pay the seller for goods already delivered or for goods that the seller is obligated to deliver. When a seller learns of a buyer's insolvency, the seller has a number of remedies, including the right to:

- Withhold delivery of undelivered goods [2–703(a)].
- Recover goods from a buyer upon the buyer's insolvency [2–702].
- Stop delivery of goods that are in the possession of a carrier or other bailee [2–705].

Cancellation and Withholding of Delivery

When a buyer breaches a contract, the seller has the right to cancel the contract and to hold up her own performance of the contract. The seller may then set aside any goods that were intended to fill her obligations under the contract [2–704].

If the seller is in the process of manufacturing the goods, she has two choices. She may complete manufacture of the goods, or she may stop manufacturing and sell the uncompleted goods for their scrap or salvage value. In choosing between these alternatives, the seller should select the alternative that will minimize the loss [2–704(2)]. Thus, a seller would be justified in completing the manufacture of goods that could be resold readily at the contract price. However, a seller would not be justified in completing specially manufactured goods that could not be sold to anyone other than the buyer who ordered them.

The purpose of this rule is to permit the seller to follow a reasonable course of action to mitigate (minimize) the damages. In *Madsen v. Murrey & Sons Co., Inc.,* which follows, the seller, who did not complete the manufacture of goods on the buyer's repudiation, but rather dismantled and largely scrapped the existing goods, was held not to have acted in a commercially reasonable manner.

MADSEN v. MURREY & SONS CO., INC.   743 P.2d 1212 (Utah Sup. Ct. 1987)

urrey & Sons Co., Inc. (Murrey), was engaged in the business of manufacturing and selling pool tables. Erik Madsen was working on an idea to develop a pool table that, through the use of electronic devices installed in the rails of the table, would produce lighting and sound effects in a fashion similar to a pinball machine. Murrey and Madsen entered into a written contract whereby Murrey agreed to manufacture 100 of its M1 4-foot by 8-foot six-pocket coin operated pool tables with customized rails capable of incorporating the electronic lighting and sound effects desired by Madsen. Under the agreement, Madsen would design the rails and provide the drawings to Murrey, who would manufacture them to Madsen's specifications. Madsen was to design, manufacture, and install the electronic components for the tables. Madsen agreed to pay $550 per table or a total of $55,000 for the 100 tables and made a $42,500 deposit on the contract.

Murrey began the manufacture of the tables while Madsen continued to work on the design of the rails and electronics. Madsen encountered significant difficulties and notified Murrey that he would be unable to take delivery of the 100 tables. Madsen then brought suit to recover the $42,500 he had paid Murrey.

Following Madsen's repudiation of the contract, Murrey dismantled the pool tables and used salvageable materials to manufacture other pool tables. A good portion of the material was simply used as firewood. Murrey made no attempt to market the 100 pool tables at a discount or at any other price in order to mitigate the damages. It claimed the salvage value of the materials it reused as $7,448. The trial court ordered Murrey to return $21,250 to Madsen and Murrey appealed. ∽

Howe, Justice Murrey contends that the trial court erred in concluding that it had failed to mitigate or minimize its damages in a commercially reasonable manner by not attempting to sell the 100 pool tables on the open market. It is a well-settled rule of the law of damages that "no party suffering a loss as the result of a breach of contract is entitled to any damages which could have been avoided if the aggrieved party had acted in a reasonably diligent manner in attempting to lessen his losses as a consequence of that breach." We have held:

Where a contractual agreement has been breached by a party thereto, the aggrieved party is entitled to those damages that will put him in as good a position as he would have been had the other party performed pursuant to the agreement. A corollary to this rule is that the aggrieved party may not, either by action or inaction, aggravate the injury occasioned by the breach, but has a duty actively to mitigate his damages.

Murrey asserts that it sufficiently mitigated its damages by dismantling the pool tables and salvaging various components that could be used to manufacture other pool tables. The salvage value to Murrey was claimed to be $7,448. Murrey presented testimony that selling the tables as "seconds" would damage its reputation for quality and that the various holes, notches and routings placed in the tables to accommodate the electrical components to be installed by buyer weakened the structure of the tables so as to submit seller to potential liability if they were sold on the market.

On the other hand, Ronald Baker, who had been involved with the manufacturing and marketing of pool tables for 25 years testified on behalf of the buyer that the notches, holes and routings made in the frame to accommodate electrical wiring would not adversely affect the quality or marketability of the 100 pool tables. According to Baker, the tables could have been sold at full value or at a discounted price. In addition to this testimony, the trial court had the opportunity to view the experimental table developed by Madsen and his associates and observe the holes, notches, and routings necessary for the electrical components.

The trial court found that Murrey's action in dismantling the tables and using the materials for salvage and firewood, rather than attempting to sell

or market the tables at full or discounted price, was not commercially reasonable. The court then concluded that seller had a duty to mitigate its damages and failed to do so. The finding is supported by competent evidence.

Applying the trial court's finding that the pool tables, if completed, could have been sold for at least $21,250, Murrey's damages are the difference between the market price ($21,250) and the contract price ($55,000) or $33,750. The trial court found that Murrey was not entitled to any incidental damages. Under section 2–718(2), (3), Madsen's right to restitution of advance payments on the contract ($42,500) is subject to offset to the extent that seller establishes damages ($33,750), for a total recovery of $8,750.

Judgment for Madsen affirmed, with the recovery set at $8,750.

Resale of Goods

If the seller sets aside goods intended for the contract or completes the manufacture of such goods, he is not obligated to try to resell the goods to someone else. However, he may resell them and recover damages. The seller must make any resale in good faith and in a commercially reasonable manner. If the seller does so, he is entitled to recover from the buyer as damages the difference between the resale price and the price the buyer agreed to pay in the contract [2–706].

If the seller resells, he may also recover incidental damages, but the seller must give the buyer credit for any expenses that the seller saved because of the buyer's breach of contract. Incidental damages include storage charges and sales commissions paid when the goods were resold [2–710]. Expenses saved might be the cost of packaging the goods and/or shipping them to the buyer.

If the buyer and seller have agreed as to the manner in which the resale is to be made, the courts will enforce the agreement unless it is found to be unconscionable [2–302]. If the parties have not entered into an agreement as to the resale of the goods, they may be resold at public or private sale, but in all events the resale must be made in good faith and in a commercially reasonable manner. The

seller should make it clear that the goods he is selling are those related to the broken contract.

If the goods are resold at private sale, the seller must give the buyer reasonable notification of his intention to resell [2–706(3)]. If the resale is a public sale, such as an auction, the seller must give the buyer notice of the time and place of the sale unless the goods are perishable or threaten to decline in value rapidly. The sale must be made at a usual place or market for public sales if one is reasonably available; and if the goods are not within the view of those attending the sale, the notification of the sale must state the place where the goods are located and provide for reasonable inspection by prospective bidders. The seller may bid at a public sale [2–706(4)].

The purchaser at a public sale who buys in good faith takes free from any rights of the original buyer even though the seller has failed to conduct the sale in compliance with the rules set out in the Code [2–706(5)]. The seller is not accountable to the buyer for any profit that the seller makes on a resale [2–706(6)].

Recovery of the Purchase Price

In the normal performance of a contract, the seller delivers conforming goods (goods that meet the contract specifications) to the buyer. The buyer accepts the goods and pays for them. The seller is entitled to the purchase price of all goods accepted by the buyer. She also is entitled to the purchase price of all goods that conformed to the contract and were lost or damaged after the buyer assumed the risk for their loss [2–709].

For example, a contract calls for Frank, a farmer, to ship 1,000 dozen eggs to Sutton, a grocer, with shipment "FOB Frank's Farm." If the eggs are lost or damaged while on their way to Sutton, she is responsible for paying Frank for them. Risk of loss is discussed in Chapter 19, Formation and Terms of Sales Contracts.

In one other situation, the seller may recover the purchase or contract price from the buyer. This is where the seller has made an honest effort to resell the goods and was unsuccessful or where it is apparent that any such effort to resell would be unsuccessful. This might happen where the seller manufactured goods especially for the buyer and the goods are not usable by anyone else. Assume that Sarton's Supermarket sponsors a bowling team. Sarton's orders six green-and-red bowling shirts to be embroidered with "Sarton's Supermarket" on the back and the names of the team members on the pocket. After the shirts are completed, Sarton's wrongfully refuses to accept them. The manufacturer will be able to recover the agreed purchase price if it cannot sell the shirts to someone else.

If the seller sues the buyer for the contract price of the goods, she must hold the goods for the buyer. Then, the seller must turn the goods over to the buyer if the buyer pays for them. However, if resale becomes possible before the buyer pays for the goods, the seller may resell them. Then, the seller must give the buyer credit for the proceeds of the resale [2–709(2)].

Damages for Rejection or Repudiation

When the buyer refuses to accept goods that conform to the contract or repudiates the contract, the seller does not have to resell the goods. The seller has two other ways of determining the damages that the buyer is liable for because of the breach of contract: (1) the difference between the contract price and the market price at which the goods are currently selling and (2) the "profit" that the seller lost when the buyer did not go through with the contract [2–708].

The seller may recover as damages the difference between the contract price and the market price at the time and place the goods were to be delivered to the buyer. The seller also may recover any incidental damages, but must give the buyer credit for any expenses that the seller has saved [2–708(1)]. This measure of damages most commonly is sought by a seller when the market price of the goods dropped substantially between the time the contract was made and the time the buyer repudiated the contract.

For example, on January 1, Toy Maker, Inc., contracts with the Red Balloon Toy Shop to sell the shop 100,000 trolls at $3.50 each, with delivery to be made in Boston on June 1. By June 1, the troll fad has passed and trolls are selling for $1 each in Boston. If Toy Shop repudiates the contract on June 1 and refuses to accept delivery of the 100,000 trolls, Toy Maker is entitled to the difference between the contract price of $350,000 and the June 1 market price in Boston of $100,000. Thus, Toy Maker could recover $250,000 in damages plus any incidental expenses, but less any expenses saved by it in not having to ship the trolls to Toy Shop (such as packaging and transportation costs).

If getting the difference between the contract price and the market price would not put the seller in as good a financial position as the seller would have been in if the contract had been performed, the seller may choose an alternative measure of damages based on the lost profit and overhead that the seller would have made if the sale had gone through. The seller can recover this lost profit and overhead plus any incidental expenses. However, the seller must give the buyer credit for any expenses saved as a result of the buyer's breach of contract [2–708(2)].

Using the troll example, assume that the direct labor and material cost to Toy Maker of making the trolls was 75 cents each. Toy Maker could recover as damages from Toy Shop the profit Toy Maker lost when Toy Shop defaulted on the contract. Toy Maker would be entitled to the difference between the contract price of $350,000 and its direct cost of $75,000. Thus, Toy Maker could recover $275,000 plus any incidental expenses and less any expenses saved.

Seller's Remedies Where Buyer Is Insolvent

If the seller has not agreed to extend credit to the buyer for the purchase price of goods, the buyer must make payment on delivery of the goods. If the seller tenders delivery of the goods, he may withhold delivery unless the agreed payment is made. Where the seller has agreed to extend credit to the buyer for the purchase price of the goods, but discovers before delivery that the buyer is insolvent, the seller may refuse delivery unless the buyer pays cash for the goods together with the unpaid balance for all goods previously delivered under the contract [2–702(1)].

At common law, a seller had the right to rescind a sales contract induced by fraud and to recover the goods unless they had been resold to a bona fide purchaser for value. Based on this general legal principle, the Code provides that where the seller discovers that the buyer has received goods while insolvent, the seller may reclaim the goods upon demand made within 10 days after their receipt. This right granted to the seller is based on constructive deceit on the part of the buyer. Receiving goods

while insolvent is equivalent to a false representation of solvency. To protect his rights, all the seller must do is to make a demand within the 10-day period; he need not actually repossess the goods.

If the buyer has misrepresented his solvency to this particular seller in writing within three months before the delivery of the goods, the 10-day limitation on the seller's right to reclaim the goods does not apply. However, the seller's right to reclaim the goods is subject to the prior rights of purchasers in the ordinary course of the buyer's business, good faith purchasers for value, creditors with a perfected lien on the buyer's inventory [2–702(2) and (3)], and a trustee in bankruptcy. The relative rights of creditors to their debtor's collateral are discussed in Chapter 28, Security Interests in Personal Property.

The case that follows, *Conoco, Inc. v. Braniff, Inc.,* illustrates some of issues that may arise when a creditor seeks to reclaim goods from an insolvent buyer.

CONOCO, INC. v. BRANIFF, INC.   11 UCC Rep.2d 519 (Bankr. M.D. Fla. 1990)

B*raniff, an airline, had an agreement with Conoco whereby Conoco supplied Braniff with its needs for Jet A aviation fuel. The fuel was sent through an interstate common carrier pipeline used by numerous suppliers, including Conoco. The pipeline contained breakout points where fuel was directed out of the pipeline and into tank farm storage facilities operated by Ogden Allied Aviation Services, Braniff's designated fueling agent, at the Dallas–Fort Worth and Kansas City airports.*

The agreement called for Braniff to make advance payments for its designated fuel needs for the following week, with settlement of overages or shortages on a monthly basis. Braniff made a payment of $320,000 on September 20, 1989, for its anticipated needs through September 27 and was scheduled to make a $420,000 payment on September 27, 1989. The payment was not made on September 27, and early the next morning Braniff filed a petition in bankruptcy under Chapter 11 of the Bankruptcy Code.

On September 29, 1989, Conoco sent Braniff a "Notice of Reclamation" seeking reclamation of unpaid fuel delivered into the tank farms at the Dallas–Fort Worth airports and Kansas City during the previous 10-day period. The reclamation notice identified the fuel it sought to reclaim by specifying 14 bills of lading representing unpaid shipments occurring from September 19 through September 27. ∞

Corcoran, Bankruptcy Judge   In order to establish entitlement to reclamation from a debtor under section 2–702 of the UCC and section 546 of the Bankruptcy Code, a reclaiming seller must satisfy the following four-part test:

1. The debtor was insolvent at the time the goods were delivered by the seller;

2. A written demand was made on the debtor within 10 days after the goods were delivered to the debtor;

3. The goods were identifiable at the time the demand was made; and

4. The goods were in the possession and control of the debtor at the time the demand was made.

Braniff contends that the fuel at issue here was neither identifiable nor in its possession and control at the time the reclamation demand was made because of the commingling that occurred in the common carrier pipelines and at the airport tank farms. Braniff points out that the fuel was pumped through a common carrier pipeline from Conoco's refineries with petroleum products belonging to numerous other suppliers. Once the fuel was received at the Ogden Allied tank farms, it was then commingled in large tanks with fuel supplied by other suppliers and allocated to and for the use of numerous users. At Dallas–Fort Worth, the commingled fuel allocated to Braniff had been supplied solely by Conoco. At Kansas City, the fuel allocated to Braniff had been supplied by four suppliers, including Conoco.

In the case of fungible, bulk petroleum products, such as jet fuel, the "identification" and "possession and control" requirements of the Code and the UCC mandate that the reclaiming party:

trace the [fuel] from its possession into an identifiable mass and to show that the mass contains only [fuel] of like kind and grade. If the mass of [fuel into which the fuel is traced] is subject to [the debtor's] control, then it is both "identifiable" and "in the possession of the debtor."

In this case the jet fuel type A was shipped from Conoco's refineries through a common carrier pipeline where it was commingled with other jet fuel type A refined by other suppliers and sold to other users. The commingling further occurred in the airport tank farms, from which many airlines withdrew the fuel that was ultimately pumped into airplanes. Plainly, on these facts, Conoco has traced its fuel into an identifiable mass containing only fuel of like grade and quality.

Likewise Conoco has shown that the mass of fuel in the airport tank farms was subject to Braniff's control. The tank farms were owned and operated by Braniff's fueling agent. The fueling agent would then draw down from the fuel in the storage tanks the amount needed to fuel Braniff aircraft. On this record, it is clear that the fueling agent abided by Braniff's instructions.

The fact that the tanks contained fuel allocated to other airlines, by itself, is irrelevant to the "identification" and "possession and control" issue. The inquiry here deals solely with the fuel in the tanks allocated to Braniff.

The fact that the fueling agent also served as fueling agent for other airlines and that other airlines controlled their allocable portion of the fuel in the tank farm storage tanks does not diminish the control Braniff exercised over its allocable portion. The point, of course, is that Braniff had the ability and authority to control the disposition of its fuel at the time the reclamation notice was received.

Conoco desires to reclaim 284,107 gallons for which it is unpaid from the ending pool of 397,735. In effect, Conoco wants the court to assume that Braniff used during the 10-day reclamation period the fuel that it had on hand before the period began, the fuel that Conoco supplied during the reclamation period for which payment was made, and the fuel provided by three other suppliers during the reclamation period. In other words, Conoco says only Conoco fuel for which payment had not been made was left in the tank at the end of the reclamation period and that Conoco can now claim this "identified" fuel.

Braniff, of course, contends just the opposite. Braniff would have the court assume that Braniff used during the 10-day reclamation period the Conoco fuel for which payment was not made so that the fuel remaining in the tank at the end of the period represents only fuel that was there before the reclamation period began, fuel supplied by Conoco for which payment was made during the reclamation period, and fuel supplied by other suppliers.

The court concludes that it is required to reject both approaches. Where, as here, there are several suppliers delivering fungible, bulk goods into a common tank, the supplier must do more than merely trace its fungible, bulk goods into the pool. The supplier must go further and show what quantity of goods was in the pool at the beginning of the relevant reclamation period. The supplier must also show when, and how much of the goods, each of the suppliers contributed to the pool during that period. Finally, the supplier must show how much of the total remained in the pool at the end of the relevant period. With that information the court can then determine the amount of each bulk shipment that was consumed by the debtor during the period. The court also can determine to which supplier the amount remaining in the tank at the end of the period should be attributed or the proportional way in which the amount remaining should be allocated among the suppliers. Implicit in the rule the court states here is a "first in, first out" theory of bulk fuel use to be used in cases such as this where fungible, bulk goods are pooled or commingled.

On the evidence presented, Conoco established its right to reclaim only the 100,002 gallons of fuel it delivered to Dallas–Fort Worth on September 26.

Judgment for Conoco.

CONCEPT REVIEW

Seller's Remedies (on breach by buyer)

PROBLEM	SELLER'S REMEDY
Buyer Refuses to Go Ahead with Contract and Seller Has Goods	1. Seller may cancel contract, suspend performance, and set aside goods intended to fill the contract. a. If seller is in the process of manufacturing, he may complete manufacture or stop and sell for scrap, picking alternative that in his judgment at the time will minimize the seller's loss. b. Seller can resell goods covered by contract and recover difference between contract price and proceeds of resale. c. Seller may recover purchase price where resale is not possible. d. Seller may recover damages for breach based on difference between contract price and market price, or in some cases based on lost profits.
Goods Are in Buyer's Possession	1. Seller may recover purchase price. 2. Seller may reclaim goods in possession of insolvent buyer by making a demand within 10 days after their receipt. If the buyer represented solvency to the seller in writing within three months before delivery, the 10-day limitation does not apply.
Goods Are in Transit	1. Seller may stop any size shipment if buyer is insolvent. 2. Seller may stop carload, truckload, planeload, or other large shipment for reasons other than buyer's insolvency.

Seller's Right to Stop Delivery

If the seller discovers that the buyer is insolvent, he has the right to stop the delivery of any goods that he has shipped to the buyer, regardless of the size of the shipment. If a buyer repudiates a sales contract or fails to make a payment due before delivery, the seller has the right to stop delivery of any large shipment of goods, such as a carload, a truckload, or a planeload [2–705].

To stop delivery, the seller must notify the carrier or other bailee in time for the bailee to prevent delivery of the goods. After receiving notice to stop delivery, the carrier or other bailee owes a duty to hold the goods and deliver them as directed by the seller. The seller is liable to the carrier or other bailee for expenses incurred or damages resulting from compliance with his order to stop delivery. If a nonnegotiable document of title has been issued for the goods, the carrier or other bailee does not have a duty to obey a stop-delivery order issued by any person other than the person who consigned the goods to him [2–705(3)].

Liquidated Damages

If the seller has justifiably withheld delivery of the goods because of the buyer's breach, the buyer may recover any money or goods he has delivered to the seller over and above the agreed amount of liquidated damages. If there is no such agreement, the seller may not retain an amount in excess of $500 or 20 percent of the value of the total performance for which the buyer is obligated under the contract, whichever is smaller. This right of restitution is subject to the seller's right to recover damages under other provisions of the Code and to recover the amount of value of benefits received by the buyer directly or indirectly by reason of the contract [2–718].

BUYER'S REMEDIES

Buyer's Remedies in General

A seller may breach a contract in a number of ways. The most common are: (1) failing to make an agreed delivery, (2) delivering goods that do not conform to the contract, and (3) indicating that he does not intend to fulfill the obligations under the contract.

A buyer whose seller breaks the contract is given a number of alternative remedies. These include:

- Buying other goods (covering) and recovering damages from the seller based on any additional expense that the buyer incurs in obtaining the goods [2–712].
- Recovering damages based on the difference between the contract price and the current market price of the goods [2–713].
- Recovering damages for any nonconforming goods accepted by the buyer based on the difference in value between what the buyer got and what he should have gotten [2–714].
- Obtaining specific performance of the contract where the goods are unique and cannot be obtained elsewhere [2–716].

In addition, the buyer can in some cases recover consequential damages (such as lost profits) and incidental damages (such as expenses incurred in buying substitute goods).

Buyer's Right to Cover

If the seller fails or refuses to deliver the goods called for in the contract, the buyer can purchase substitute goods; this is known as cover. If the buyer does purchase substitute goods, the buyer can recover as damages from the seller the difference between the contract price and the cost of the substitute goods [2–712]. For example, Frank Farmer agrees to sell Ann's Cider Mill 1,000 bushels of apples at $10 a bushel. Farmer then refuses to deliver the apples. Cider Mill can purchase 1,000 bushels of similar apples, and if it has to pay $11 a bushel, it can recover the difference ($1 a bushel) between what it paid ($11) and the contract price ($10). Thus, Cider Mill could recover $1,000 from Farmer.

The buyer can also recover any incidental damages sustained, but must give the seller credit for any expenses saved. In addition, he may be able to obtain consequential damages. The buyer is not required to cover, however. If he does not cover, the other remedies under the Code are still available [2–712].

The case that follows, *KGM Harvesting Co. v. Fresh Network*, illustrates a situation where the aggrieved buyer chose to seek damages based on its cost of cover from the defaulting seller.

KGM HARVESTING CO. v. FRESH NETWORK 26 UCC Rep.2d 1028 (Cal. App. 1995)

*K*GM Harvesting Company, a California lettuce grower and distributor, and Fresh Network, an Ohio lettuce broker, began dealing with each other in 1989, and over the years the terms of the agreement were modified. As of May 1991, their agreement called for KGM to deliver 14 "loads" of lettuce a week at a price of 9 cents a pound. A load of lettuce consists of 40 bins, each of which weighs 1,000 to 1,200 pounds. At an average bin weight of 1,100 pounds, one load would equal 44,000 pounds, and the 14 loads called for in the contract would weigh 616,000 pounds. At 9 cents per pound, the cost would be approximately $55,440 per week.

Fresh Network, in turn, resold all of the lettuce to another broker (Castellani Company) who sold it to Club Chef, a company that chopped and shredded it for the fast food industry (specifically, Burger King, Taco Bell, and Pizza Hut). The transactions between Fresh Network and Castellani, and in turn between Castellani and Club Chef, were on a cost-plus basis. This meant each paid its buyer its actual cost plus a small commission.

In May and June 1991, when the price of lettuce went up dramatically, KGM refused to supply Fresh Network with lettuce at the contract price of 9 cents per pound. Instead, it sold the lettuce to others at a profit between $800,000 and $1,100,000. Fresh Network then went out on the open market and purchased lettuce to satisfy its obligations to Castellani Company. Castellani covered all of Fresh Network's extra expense except for $70,000. Fresh Network then sought to recover from KGM as damages the difference between what it was forced to spend to buy replacement lettuce and the contract price of 9 cents a pound (approximately $700,000). KGM objected on the grounds that Fresh Network had been able to pass some of the increased cost along to Castellani.

Cottle, Presiding Judge   Section 2–711 of the California Uniform Commercial Code provides a buyer with several alternative remedies for a seller's breach of contract. The buyer can " 'cover' by making in good faith and without unreasonable delay any reasonable purchase of . . . goods in substitution for those due from the seller." (Sec. 2–712(1)). In that case, the buyer "may recover from the seller as damages the difference between the cost of cover and the contract price." (Sec. 2–712(2)). If the buyer is unable to cover or chooses not to cover, the measure of damages is the difference between the market price and the contract price. (Sec. 2–713).

In the instant case, buyer "covered" in order to fulfill its own contractual obligations to the Castellani Company. Accordingly, it was awarded the damages called for in cover cases—the difference between the contract price and the cover price.

In appeals from judgments rendered pursuant to section 2–712, the dispute typically centers on whether the buyer acted in "good faith," whether the "goods in substitution" differed substantially from the contracted for goods, whether the buyer unreasonably delayed in purchasing substitute goods in the mistaken belief the price would go down, or whether the buyer paid too much for the substitute goods.

In this case, however, none of these typical issues is in dispute. Seller does *not* contend that buyer paid too much for the substitute lettuce or that buyer was guilty of "unreasonable delay" or lack of "good faith" in its attempt to obtain substitute lettuce. Nor does seller contend that the lettuce purchased was of a higher quality or grade and therefore not a reasonable substitute.

Instead, seller takes issue with section 2–712 itself, contending that despite the unequivocal language of section 2–712, a buyer who covers should not *necessarily* recover the difference between the cover price and the contract price. Seller points out that because of buyer's "cost plus" contract with

Castellini Company, buyer was eventually able to pass on the extra expenses (except for $70,000) occasioned by seller's breach and buyer's consequent purchase of substitute lettuce on the open market. It urges this court under these circumstances not to allow buyer to obtain a "windfall."

The basic premise of contract law is to effectuate the expectations of the parties to the agreement, to give them the "benefit of the bargain" they struck when they entered into the agreement. In this case, the damage formula of section 2–712 put buyer in the identical position performance would have: it gave buyer the contracted for 14 loads of lettuce with which to carry on its business at the contracted for price of 9 cents per pound.

Despite the obvious applicability and appropriateness of section 2–712, seller argues in this appeal that the contract-cover differential of section 2–712 is inappropriate in cases, as here, where the aggrieved buyer is ultimately able to pass on its additional costs to other parties. Seller contends that section 1–106's remedial injunction to put the aggrieved party "in as good a position as if the other party had fully performed" demands that all subsequent events impacting on *buyer's* ultimate profit or loss be taken into consideration (specifically, that buyer passed on all but $70,000 of its loss to Castellini Company, which passed on all of its loss to Club Chef, which passed on most of its loss to its fast food customers).

No section 2–712 case has ever held that cover damages must be limited by section 1–106. The obvious reason is that the cover-contract differential puts a buyer who covers in the exact same position as performance would have done. This is precisely what is called for in section 1–106. In this respect, the cover/contract differential of section 2–712 is very different than the market/contract differential of section 2–713, which need bear no close relation to the buyer's actual loss.

Judgment affirmed for Fresh Network.

Incidental Damages

Incidental damages include expenses that the buyer incurs in receiving, inspecting, transporting, and storing goods shipped by the seller that do not conform to those called for in the contract. Incidental damages also include any reasonable expenses or charges that the buyer has to pay in obtaining substitute goods [2–715(1)].

Consequential Damages

In certain situations, an injured buyer is able to recover consequential damages, such as the buyer's lost profits caused by the seller's breach of contract. The buyer must be able to show that the seller knew or should have known at the time the contract was made that the buyer would suffer special damages if the seller did not perform his obligations. The buyer must also show that he could not have prevented the damage by obtaining substitute goods [2–715(2)].

Suppose Knitting Mill promises to deliver 15,000 yards of a special fabric to Dorsey by September 1. Knitting Mill knows that Dorsey wants to acquire the material to make garments suitable for the Christmas season. Knitting Mill also knows that in reliance on the contract with it, Dorsey will enter into contracts with department stores to deliver the finished garments by October 1. If Knitting Mill fails to deliver the fabric or delivers the fabric after September 1, it may be liable to Dorsey for any consequential damages that she sustains if she is unable to acquire the same material elsewhere in time to fulfill her October 1 contracts.

Consequential damages can also include an injury to a person or property caused by a breach of warranty. For example, an electric saw is defective. Hanson purchases the saw, and while he is using it, the blade comes off and severely cuts his arm. The injury to Hanson is consequential damage resulting from a nonconforming or defective product.

Damages for Nondelivery

If the seller fails or refuses to deliver the goods called for by the contract, the buyer has the option of recovering damages for the nondelivery. Thus, instead of covering, the buyer can get the difference between the contract price of the goods and their market price at the time he learns of the seller's breach. In addition, the buyer may recover any incidental damages and consequential damages, but must give the seller credit for any expenses saved [2–713].

Suppose Biddle agreed on June 1 to sell and deliver 1,500 bushels of wheat to a grain elevator on September 1 for $7 per bushel and then refused to deliver on September 1 because the market price was then $10 per bushel. The grain elevator could recover $4,500 damages from Biddle, plus incidental damages that could not have been prevented by cover.

The *Simeone v. First Bank National Association* case, which follows, illustrates the application of the measure of damages for nondelivery.

SIMEONE v. FIRST BANK NATIONAL ASS'N. 28 UCC Rep.2d 1062 (8th Cir. 1996)

Leland Gohlike defaulted on a loan obligation to First Bank National Association, and First Bank repossessed four 1920– to 1930-era vintage Mercedes-Benz automobiles and parts. The vehicles included a one-of-a-kind 1929 Mercedes-Benz SS Roadster, two 1930-era Mercedes-Benz Roadsters (of which a total of only 114 were ever manufactured), and a 1928 Mercedes-Benz SSK (1 of only 39 ever manufactured), which had been owned by the son of Sir Arthur Conan-Doyle, the creator of Sherlock Holmes. In addition, there were thousands of loose parts, including fenders, seat cushions, and wheels, which were no longer manufactured and which were themselves extraordinarily rare.

On October 26, 1985, after receiving inquiries from several potential purchasers, First Bank entered into an agreement to sell the repossessed automobiles and parts to Frederick Simeone, a collector of vintage automobiles, for $450,000. Simeone paid 10 percent of the contract price as a down payment.

On November 4, 1985, the date set for the conveyance of title to Simeone, Gohlike obtained a temporary restraining order (TRO) to prevent the sale of the collateral for his loan. Thereafter, First Bank refused Simeone's proffered tender of the balance of the purchase price. Prior to obtaining the TRO, Gohlike instituted a lawsuit against First Bank, claiming a violation of due process and seeking $13 million in damages.

First Bank entered into negotiations with Gohlike and James Torseth, his neighbor, to sell the automobiles and parts to Torseth in exchange for Gohlike's dismissal of his lawsuit and a purchase price slightly in excess of Simeone's. Believing that it no longer had an obligation to sell the property to Simeone because of a condition in the agreement, First Bank subsequently sold the cars and parts to SMB, Inc., a corporation created by Torseth for the purchase and resale of the automobiles and parts, and Gohlike dismissed his suit *against the bank. SMB, Inc., later sold all of the cars and parts for $1,114,960, including $470,000 that Simeone himself paid for the purchase of the 1929 Mercedes-Benz SS Roadster. Two experts at a later trial testified that by late 1987 or early 1988, the vehicles and parts were worth over $3 million.*

First Bank returned Simeone's down payment with interest, and Simeone filed suit alleging breach of contract and fraud. The district court granted summary judgment for First Bank, finding that a condition precedent was not satisfied and the bank was not obligated by the contract. The Eighth Circuit vacated the summary judgment, concluding that First Bank had breached the contract by failing to convey the property, and remanded the case for an assessment of damages. The jury awarded Simeone $2,405,000 for breach of contract, including $585,000 in compensatory damages, $225,000 in incidental damages, and $1,595,000 in consequential damages. First Bank appealed. ∞

Ross, Circuit Judge   In its challenge to the compensatory damages award, First Bank argues the district court erroneously allowed Simeone's experts to rely on the collector market as the relevant market in appraising the fair market value of the vehicles and parts at the time of the breach. Instead, First Bank contends the relevant market was the market of "repossessed goods in bank foreclosure sales."

Section 2–713(1) provides the proper measure of damages for a seller's breach of contract:

The difference between the market price at the time when the buyer learned of the breach and the contract price together with any incidental and consequential damages.

"Market price" is the price for goods of the same kind and in the same "branch of trade." Section 2–713, UCC Comment 2. According to First Bank, the "branch of trade" in this case was the resale market of repossessed goods, not a collector automobile market. The Uniform Commercial Code, as adopted in Minnesota, permits opinion evidence as to the value of the goods in question:

Where the unavailability of a market price is caused by a scarcity of goods of the type involved . . . such scarcity conditions . . . indicate that the price has risen and under the section providing for liberal administration of *remedies, opinion evidence as to the value of the goods would be admissible in the absence of a market price* and a liberal construction of allowable consequential damages should also result. Section 2–713, UCC Comment 3 (emphasis added).

At trial the evidence showed that the vehicles were rare, and in some cases unique, classic automobiles of historic significance. The disassembled parts, as well, were scarce commodities. At trial, an expert in vintage automobiles valued the cars and parts at $1,355,000 at the time of the breach. Based on the evidence presented at trial, the jury concluded the total market value of the property was $1,035,000. The difference between this fair market

value and the $450,000 contract price is $585,000, the amount of compensatory damages awarded. The evidence clearly supports the jury's determination and the award of compensatory damages is affirmed.

First Bank next raises several challenges to the consequential damages assessed against it. The jury awarded $1,595,000 in consequential damages, which was derived from expert testimony as to what the automobiles and parts were worth in late 1987, two years after the breach, minus the market price of the property at the time of the breach. First Bank now argues that evidence is insufficient to establish the foreseeability requirement to support the $1,595,000 consequential damages award.

Under Minnesota law, recoverable consequential damages include:

Any loss resulting from general or particular requirements and needs of which the seller at the time of contracting had reason to know and which could not reasonably be prevented by cover or otherwise. Section 2–715(2)(a).

Under this section, consequential damages are not available in every case, but instead are only proper if the seller had reason to foresee the particular requirements of the buyer, and even then only if such loss could not be prevented. The focus is on what the buyer had reason to know.

According to First Bank, Simeone repeatedly stated prior to contract formation that he was not in the business of selling automobiles and parts and therefore First Bank neither knew nor had reason to know that Simeone intended to trade or resell the automobiles and parts at any profit, let alone a profit of $1,595,000. First Bank contends the award of damages erroneously treats the agreement as one for the purchase of goods for resale when that was clearly not the case.

The question of whether the buyer's consequential damages were foreseeable by the seller is one of fact to be determined by the trier of fact. First Bank asks that this court conclude as a matter of law that the damages were not foreseeable. We decline to so hold. Mr. Garretson, commercial banking officer of First Bank and acting on behalf of the Bank during the relevant negotiations with Simeone, testified that he was aware that collectors may trade vehicles to enhance their collection. Further, Simeone testified he told First Bank's broker that he intended to use the cars and parts for trading or possible resale to obtain additional cars. Finally, Simeone contracted to purchase hundreds of automotive parts that the jury would reasonably presume would have to be either resold or assembled into something of increased value. The jury's determination that it was foreseeable that Simeone would seek to further his collection by engaging in sale or trade was not clearly erroneous.

First Bank next claims the evidence does not support the jury's award of incidental damages. Under Minnesota law, incidental damages resulting from a seller's breach are defined as:

Expenses reasonably incurred in inspection, receipt, transportation and care and custody of goods rightfully rejected, any commercially reasonable charges, expenses or commissions in connection with affecting cover and any other reasonable expense incident to the delay or other breach.

Here, the jury awarded Simeone $225,000 in incidental damages. Simeone speculates that this amount represents his cost of cover in purchasing the 1929 SS Roadster ($470,000 purchase price minus $250,000 contract price, plus $5,000 for dismissal of SMB, Inc., from a civil action). However, the difference between the cost of cover and the contract price is not properly characterized as incidental damages. Rather, incidental damages are, among other things, the "charges," "expenses" and "commissions" incurred in effecting cover. In contrast, the award of damages for the difference between Simeone's purchase price of the Roadster and the contract price falls under section 2–712 as "cover" damages. The jury's award of incidental damages in this case represents a double recovery to the extent that it compensates Simeone for the difference between the contract price and the price he actually paid for the Roadster. Simeone was compensated for the difference between the contract price and the purchase price through both the compensatory and consequential damages awards. Since there is no other evidence of incidental damages, the award of incidental damages must be reversed.

Judgment affirmed in part in favor of Simeone and reversed in part in favor of First Bank.

Damages for Defective Goods

If a buyer accepts defective goods and wants to hold the seller liable, the buyer must give the seller notice of the defect within a reasonable time after the buyer discovers the defect [2–607(3)]. Where goods are defective or not as warranted and the buyer gives the required notice, he can recover damages. The buyer is entitled to recover the difference between the value of the goods received and the value the goods would have had if they had been as warranted. He may also be entitled to incidental and consequential damages [2–714].

For example, Al's Auto Store sells Anders an automobile tire, warranting it to be four-ply construction. The tire goes flat when it is punctured by a nail, and Anders discovers that the tire is really only two-ply. If Anders gives the store prompt notice of the breach, she can keep the tire and recover from Al's the difference in value between a two-ply and a four-ply tire.

Buyer's Right to Specific Performance

Sometimes, the goods covered by a contract are unique and it is not possible for a buyer to obtain substitute goods. When this is the case, the buyer is entitled to specific performance of the contract.

Specific performance means that the buyer can require the seller to give the buyer the goods covered by the contract [2–716]. Thus, the buyer of an antique automobile such as a 1910 Ford might have a court order the seller to deliver the specified automobile to the buyer because it was one of a kind. On the other hand, the buyer of grain in a particular storage bin could not get specific performance if he could buy the same kind of grain elsewhere.

Buyer and Seller Agreements as to Remedies

As mentioned earlier in this chapter, the parties to a contract may provide remedies in addition to or as

Buyer's Remedies (on breach by seller)

PROBLEMS	BUYER'S REMEDY
Seller Fails to Deliver Goods or Delivers Nonconforming Goods that Buyer Rightfully Rejects or Justifiably Revokes Acceptance of	1. Buyer may cancel the contract and recover damages. 2. Buyer may "cover" by obtaining substitute goods and recover difference between contract price and cost of cover. 3. Buyer may recover damages for breach based on difference between contract price and market price.
Seller Delivers Nonconforming Goods That Are Accepted by Buyer	Buyer may recover damages based on difference between value of goods received and value of goods if they had been as warranted.
Seller Has the Goods but Refuses to Deliver Them and Buyer Wants Them	Buyer may seek specific performance if goods are unique and cannot be obtained elsewhere, or buyer may replevy (obtain from the seller) goods identified to contract if buyer cannot obtain cover.

substitution for those expressly provided in the Code [2–719]. For example, the buyer's remedies may be limited by the contract to the return of the goods and the repayment of the price or to the replacement of nonconforming goods or parts. However, a court looks to see whether such a limitation was freely agreed to or whether it is unconscionable. In the latter case, the court does not enforce the limitation and the buyer has all the rights given to an injured buyer by the Code.

ETHICAL AND PUBLIC POLICY CONCERNS

1. In the *Wilson v. Hammer Holdings, Inc.,* case, the court held that the statute of limitations barred a claim of breach of warranty. Even if the gallery is not legally obligated to make good on its "guarantee" of authenticity, does it have any ethical responsibility to the purchaser for selling a painting that was not painted by the artist to whom it was attributed at the time of the sale?

2. Problem case 7 involves the sale of a yacht as new that previously had sunk in salt water. How would you assess the ethicality of the representations made by the salesperson to the purchaser in response to his question? In a case like this, should it be incumbent on a purchaser to ask the "right" questions in order to protect himself, or should there be an ethical obligation on the seller to disclose voluntarily material facts that may be relevant to the purchaser making an informed decision?

3. Suppose you own an automobile dealership. The manufacturer whose cars you sell produces a limited edition of a particular model, sets a sticker price of $60,000 on it, and makes only two of the cars available to you. You agree to sell one of the cars to a customer for $60,000. Before you deliver the car, another customer, who collects rare and classic cars, offers you a $30,000 per car premium over the sticker price if you will sell both cars to him. Would you accept his offer? What ethical considerations are involved in making your decision?

PROBLEM CASES

1. Lobianco contracted with Property Protection, Inc., for the installation of a burglar alarm system. The contract provided in part:

Alarm system equipment installed by Property Protection, Inc., is guaranteed against improper function due to manufacturing defects of workmanship for a period of 12 months. The installation of the above equipment carries a 90-day warranty. The liability of Property Protection, Inc., is limited to repair or replacement of security alarm equipment and does not include loss or damage to possessions, persons, or property.

As installed, the alarm system included a standby battery source of power in the event that the regular source of power failed. During the 90-day warranty period, burglars broke into Lobianco's house and stole $35,815 worth of jewelry. First, they destroyed the electric meter so that there was no electric source to operate the system, and then they entered the house. The batteries in the standby system were dead, and thus the standby system failed to operate. Accordingly, no outside siren was activated and a telephone call that was supposed to be triggered was not made. Lobianco brought suit, claiming damage in the amount of her stolen jewelry because of the failure of the alarm system to work properly. Did the disclaimer effectively eliminate any liability on the alarm company's part for consequential damages?

2. Parzek purchased from New England Log Homes a log home kit consisting of hand-peeled logs, window frames, and door frames. The brochure that Parzek had seen before buying the log home kit contained a statement that the logs were treated with a preservative "to protect the treated wood against decay, stain, termites, and other insects." Other statements indicated the maintenance-free nature of the logs, and there was a guarantee against any materials and engineering defects. The logs were delivered in May 1974 to the construction site, where they were stored in stacks covered with heavy tarpaulins. By fall 1976, the walls were erected and the roof was on. In 1979, Parzek discovered 15 medium-sized blue metallic beetles on the interior walls of the home. He was assured by the dealer for New England Log Homes that the problem was not serious. The following April, however, Parzek observed several hundreds of beetles and discovered larvae and "excavation channels" in the logs. When he contacted New England Log Homes, he was told that it did not guarantee that its logs were insect free. Parzek had the home treated by an exterminator and then brought suit against New England Log Homes. Relying on Section 2–725 of the Code, New England Log Homes contended that the lawsuit was filed more than four years after the date of delivery. Was the lawsuit barred by the statute of limitations because it was filed more than four years after the date of delivery?

3. Kohn ordered a custom-made suit from Meledani Tailors. A few days later, before much work had been completed, Kohn told the tailors that he did not want the suit. They, therefore, stopped its manufacture and filed suit for the entire contract price. Is Kohn liable for the full purchase price?

4. Cohn advertised a 30-foot sailboat for sale in *The New York Times.* Fisher saw the ad, inspected the sailboat, and offered Cohn $4,650 for the boat. Cohn accepted the offer. Fisher gave Cohn a check for $2,535 as a deposit on the boat. He wrote on the check, "Deposit on aux sloop, D'arc Wind, full amount $4,650." Fisher later refused to go through

with the purchase and stopped payment on the deposit check. Cohn readvertised the boat and sold it for the highest offer he received, which was $3,000. Cohn then sued Fisher for breach of contract. He asked for damages of $1,679.50. This represented the $1,650 difference between the contract price and the sale price plus $29.50 in incidental expenses in reselling the boat. Is Cohn entitled to this measure of damages?

5. McCain Foods sold on credit and delivered a quantity of frozen french fries to Flagstaff Food Service Company. Several days later, when the potatoes had not yet been paid for, McCain discovered that Flagstaff was insolvent and had just filed a petition in bankruptcy. What would you advise McCain Foods to do?

6. Kneale bought two chairs from Modernage Furniture that were on sale for $97.50 apiece. The regular price of the chairs was $147.57 each, or $50.07 more than the sale price. Because the store had oversold that particular chair, it failed to deliver the items to Kneale, although she had paid the full purchase price in cash. She brought suit for breach of contract against Modernage Furniture. Modernage contended that its liability was limited to return of the purchase price. Was Modernage's liability for breach of contract limited to return of the purchase price?

7. Barr purchased from Crow's Nest Yacht Sales a 31-foot Tiara pleasure yacht manufactured by S-2 Yachts. He had gone to Crow's Nest knowing the style and type yacht he wanted. He was told that the retail price was $102,000 but that he could purchase the model they had for $80,000. When he asked about the reduction in price he was told that Crow's Nest had to move it because there was a change in the model and they had new ones coming in. He was assured that the yacht was new, that there was nothing wrong with it, and that it only had 20 hours on the engines. Barr installed a considerable amount of electronic equipment on the boat. When he began to use it, he experienced tremendous difficulties with equipment malfunctions. On examination by a marine expert it was determined that the yacht had earlier been sunk in salt water, resulting in significant rusting and deterioration in the engine, equipment, and fixtures. Other experts concluded that significant replacement and repair was required, that the engines would have only 25 percent of their normal expected life, and that following its sinking, the yacht would have only half of its original value. Barr then brought suit against Crow's Nest and S-2 Yachts for breach of warranty. To what measure of damages is Barr entitled to recover for breach of warranty?

8. Certina USA is a watch manufacturer that sells its watches through traveling salespeople paid by it. Migerobe, Inc., owns and operates jewelry counters in McRae's department stores, which are located throughout the Southeast. In the summer of 1987, Migerobe contacted Gerald Murff, a Certina salesperson from whom it had previously purchased watches. It notified him that Migerobe was interested in buying Certina watches if the company decided to sell a large portion of its inventory at reduced prices. Migerobe had some reason to believe that Certina had excess inventory, and Certina in fact decided to eliminate its inventory as a result of a corporate decision to withdraw its watches from the U.S. market. Migerobe was hoping to acquire the Certina watches so that they could be used as "doorbusters" for an after-Thanksgiving sale. Doorbusters or "loss leaders" are items offered at a low price, which are designed to increase the traffic flow through a store and, thereby, increase corollary sales (the sale of nonadvertised items). On October 29, the parties agreed on the sale of over 2,000 watches at a price of $45 per watch. On November 4, the national accounts manager for Certina called Migerobe to say that Certina would not ship the watches. Migerobe brought suit against Certina to recover damages for breach of contract, including consequential damages in the form of lost profits on corollary sales. Migerobe asserted that the Certina salesperson was aware of its plan to use the watches as a loss leader by featuring them in a doorbuster Thanksgiving advertisement at a 50 percent discount. It also had data that showed it previously had increased its corollary sales by 69 to 87 percent when it had used similar doorbuster promotions. Was Migerobe entitled to recover the lost profits on corollary sales as consequential damages caused by Certina's breach of contract?

9. De La Hoya bought a used handgun for $140 from Slim's Gun Shop, a licensed firearms dealer. At the time, neither De La Hoya nor Slim's knew that the gun had been stolen prior to the time Slim's bought it. While De La Hoya was using the gun for target shooting, he was questioned by a police officer. The officer traced the serial number of the gun, determined that it had been stolen, and arrested De La Hoya. De La Hoya had to hire an attorney to defend himself against the criminal charges. De La Hoya then brought a lawsuit against Slim's Gun Shop for breach of warranty of title. He sought to recover the purchase price of the gun plus $8,000, the amount of his attorney's fees, as "consequential damages." Can a buyer who does not get good title to the goods he purchased recover from the seller consequential damages caused by the breach of warranty of title?

10. In 1972, Schweber contracted to purchase a certain black 1973 Rolls-Royce Corniche automobile from Rallye Motors. He made a $3,500 deposit on the car. Rallye later returned his deposit to him and told him that the car was not available. However, Schweber learned that the automobile was available to the dealer and was being sold to another customer. The dealer then offered to sell Schweber a similar car, but with a different interior design. Schweber brought a lawsuit against the dealer to prevent it from selling the Rolls-Royce Corniche to anyone else and to require that it be sold to him. Rallye Motors claimed that he could get only damages and not specific performance. Approximately 100 Rolls-Royce Corniches were being sold each year in the United States, but none of the others would have the specific features and detail of this one. Is the remedy of specific performance available to Schweber?

11. [CD] *Video Case.* See "Sour Grapes." Jelly Manufacturer, a food processor in Chicago, placed a phone order with Grape Grower, a grower in California, for a quantity of perishable produce. The shipping term was CIF with payment to be made on delivery (COD). Grape Grower delivered the goods called for in the contract to a carrier and contracted for their shipment. However, it neglected to provide that the goods be shipped under refrigeration. The goods were loaded on a nonrefrigerated boxcar and as a result the produce was spoiled when it reached Chicago. Jelly Manufacturer, as required by the COD term, paid for the produce by check before discovering the spoilage. When Jelly Manufacturer called Grape Grower to complain, Grower offered to rush a replacement shipment. Jelly Manufacturer declined the offer, stating that it would not arrive in time for the produce to be processed and delivered to Grocery Chain in time to meet processor's contract with Grocery Chain. Jelly Manufacturer arranged for a rush replacement shipment from a nearby source, but had to pay 150 percent of the prevailing market price for the produce. Even so, Jelly Manufacturer was unable to deliver the finished products to Grocery Chain and was required to pay a penalty for late delivery as provided in its contract with Grocery Chain. Can Jelly Manufacturer recover damages from George Grower for breach of contract? If so, what elements can be recovered? Can Grocery Chain recover the penalty from Jelly Manufacturer?

Property

Personal Property and Bailments

The concept of property is crucial to the organization of society. The essential nature of a particular society is often reflected in the way it views property, including the degree to which property ownership is concentrated in the state, the extent to which it permits individual ownership of property, and the rules that govern such ownership. History is replete with wars and revolutions that arose out of conflicting claims to, or views concerning, property. Significant documents in our own Anglo-American legal tradition, such as the Magna Carta and the Constitution, deal explicitly with property rights. This chapter will discuss the nature and classification of property. It will also examine the various ways that interests in personal property can be obtained and transferred, such as by production, purchase, or gift. The last half of the chapter explores the law of bailments. A bailment is involved, for example, when you check your coat in a coatroom at a restaurant or when you park your car in a public parking garage and leave your keys with the attendant. ☜

NATURE OF PROPERTY

The word **property** is used to refer to something that is capable of being owned. It is also used to refer to a right or interest that allows a person to exercise dominion over a thing that may be owned or possessed.

When we talk about ownership of property, we are speaking of a bundle of rights that the law recognizes and enforces. For example, ownership of a building includes the exclusive right to use, enjoy, sell, mortgage, or rent the building. If someone else tries to use the property without the owner's consent, the owner may use the courts and legal procedures to eject that person. Ownership of a patent includes the rights to sell it, license others to use it, and to produce the patented article personally.

In the United States, private ownership of property is protected by the Constitution, which provides that the government shall deprive no person of "life, liberty or property without due process of law." We recognize and encourage the rights of individuals to acquire, enjoy, and use property. These rights, however, are not unlimited. For example, a person cannot use property in an unreasonable manner that injures others. Also, the state has **police power** through which it can impose reasonable regulations on the use of property, tax it, and take it for public use by paying the owner compensation for it.

Property can be divided into a number of categories based on its characteristics. The same piece of property may fall into more than one class. The following discussion explores the meaning of **personal property** and the numerous ways of classifying property.

CLASSIFICATIONS OF PROPERTY

Personal Property versus Real Property

Personal property is defined by process of exclusion. The term *personal property* is used in contrast to *real property*. Real property is the earth's crust and all things firmly attached to it.[1] For example, land, office buildings, and houses are all considered to be real property. All other objects and rights that can be owned are personal property. Clothing, books, and stock in a corporation are all examples of personal property.

Real property can be turned into personal property if it is detached from the earth. Personal property, if attached to the earth, becomes real property. For example, marble in the ground is real property. When the marble is quarried, it becomes personal property, but if it is used in constructing a building, it becomes real property again. Perennial vegetation that does not have to be seeded every year, such as trees, shrubs, and grass, is usually treated as part of the real property on which it is growing. When trees and shrubs are severed from the land, they become personal property. Crops that must be planted each year, such as corn, oats, and potatoes, are usually treated as personal property. However, if the real property on which they are growing is sold, the new owner of the real property also becomes the owner of the crops.

When personal property is attached to, or used in conjunction with, real property in such a way as to be treated as part of the real property, it is known as a **fixture.** The law concerning fixtures is discussed in the next chapter.

Tangible versus Intangible Personal Property

Personal property may be either tangible or intangible. Tangible property has a physical existence. Cars, animals, and computers are examples. Property that has no physical existence is called intangible property. For example, rights under a patent, copyright, or trademark would be intangible property.[2]

The distinction between tangible and intangible property is important primarily for tax and estate planning purposes. Generally, tangible property is subject to tax in the state in which it is located, whereas intangible property is usually taxable in the state where its owner lives.

Public and Private Property

Property is also classified as public or private based on the ownership of the property. If the property is owned by the government or a governmental unit, it is public property. If it is owned by an individual, a group of individuals, a corporation, or some other business organization, it is private property.

ACQUIRING OWNERSHIP OF PERSONAL PROPERTY

Production or Purchase

The most common ways of obtaining ownership of property are by producing it or purchasing it. A

---

[1]The law of real property is treated in Chapter 24.

[2]These important types of intangible property are discussed in Chapter 8.

person owns the property that she makes unless the person has agreed to do the work for another party. In that case, the other party is the owner of the product of the work. For example, a person who creates a painting, knits a sweater, or develops a computer program is the owner unless she has been retained by someone to create the painting, knit the sweater, or develop the program. Another major way of acquiring property is by purchase. The law regarding the purchase of tangible personal property (that is, sale of goods) is discussed in Chapter 19.

Possession of Unowned Property

In very early times, the most common way of obtaining ownership of personal property was simply by taking possession of unowned property. For example, the first person to take possession of a wild animal became its owner. Today, one may still acquire ownership of personal property by possessing it if the property is unowned. The two major examples of unowned property that may be acquired by possession are wild animals and abandoned property. Abandoned property will be discussed in the next section, which focuses on the rights of finders.

The first person to take possession of a wild animal normally becomes the owner.[3] To acquire ownership of a wild animal by taking possession, a person must obtain enough control over it to deprive it of its freedom. If a person fatally wounds a wild animal, the person becomes the owner. Wild animals caught in a trap or fish caught in a net are usually considered to be the property of the person who set the trap or net. If a captured wild animal escapes and is caught by another person, that person generally becomes the owner. However, if that person knows that the animal is an escaped animal and that the prior owner is chasing it to recapture it, then he does not become the owner.

Rights of Finders of Lost, Mislaid, and Abandoned Property

The old saying "finders keepers, losers weepers" is not a reliable way of predicting the legal rights of those who find personal property that originally belonged—or still belongs—to another. The rights of the finder will be determined according to whether the property he finds is classified as abandoned, lost, or mislaid.

1. *Abandoned property.* Property is considered to be abandoned if the owner intentionally placed the property out of his possession with the intent to relinquish ownership of it. For example, Norris takes his TV set to the city dump and leaves it there. The finder who takes possession of abandoned property with intent to claim ownership becomes the owner of the property. This means he acquires better rights to the property than anyone else in the world, including the original owner. For example, if Fox finds the TV set, puts it in his car, and takes it home, Fox becomes the owner of the TV set.

2. *Lost property.* Property is considered to be lost when the owner did not intend to part with possession of the property. For example, if Barber's camera fell out of her handbag while she was walking down the street, it would be considered lost property. The person who finds lost property does not acquire ownership of it, but he acquires better rights to the lost property than anyone other than the true owner. For example, suppose Lawrence finds Barber's camera in the grass where it fell. Jones then steals the camera from Lawrence's house. Under these facts, Barber is still the owner of the camera. She has the right to have it returned to her if she discovers where it is—or if Lawrence knows that it belongs to Barber. As the finder of lost property, however, Lawrence has a better right to the camera than anyone else except Barber. This means that Lawrence has the right to require Jones to return it to him if he finds out that Jones has it.

If the finder does not know who the true owner is or cannot easily find out, the finder must still return the property when the real owner shows up and asks for the property. If the finder of lost property knows who the owner is and refuses to return it, the finder is guilty of conversion and must pay the owner the fair value of the property.[4] A finder who sells the property that he has found can only pass to the purchaser those rights that he has; he cannot pass any better title to the property than he himself has. Thus, the true owner could recover the property from the purchaser.

---

[3]As wildlife is increasingly protected by law, however, some wild animals cannot be owned because it is illegal to capture them (e.g., endangered species).

---

[4]The tort of conversion is discussed in Chapter 6.

The *Powell* case, which follows shortly, provides further discussion of the rights of a finder of lost property.

3. *Mislaid property.* Property is considered to be mislaid if the owner intentionally placed the property somewhere and accidentally left it there, not intending to relinquish ownership of the property. For example, Fields places her backpack on a coatrack at Campus Bookstore while shopping for textbooks. Forgetting the backpack, Fields leaves the store and goes home. The backpack would be considered to be mislaid rather than lost because Fields intentionally and voluntarily placed it on the coatrack. The consequences of property being classified as mislaid are that the finder acquires no rights to the property. Rather, the person in possession of the real property on which the personal property was mislaid has the right to hold the property for the true owner and has better rights to the property than anyone other than the true owner. For example, if Stevens found Fields's backpack in

Campus Bookstore, Campus Bookstore would have the right to hold the mislaid property for Fields. Stevens would acquire neither possession nor ownership of the backpack.

The rationale for this rule is that it increases the chances that the property will be returned to its real owner. A person who knowingly placed the property somewhere but forgot to pick it up might well remember later where she left the property and return for it.

Some states have a statute that allows finders of property to clear their title to the property. The statutes generally provide that the person must give public notice of the fact that the property has been found, perhaps by putting an ad in a local newspaper. All states have statutes of limitations that require the true owner of property to claim it or bring a legal action to recover possession of it within a certain number of years. A person who keeps possession of lost or unclaimed property for longer than that period of time will become its owner.

POWELL v. FOUR THOUSAND SIX HUNDRED DOLLARS U.S. CURRENCY   904 P.2d 153 (Okl. Ct. App. 1995)

While driving home from a Valentine's Day party late in the evening of February 14, 1994, Martin and Robyn Hoel and their children came upon what they thought was money scattered along a road in Logan County, Oklahoma. They then decided to drive to the nearby home of some friends. While Mrs. Hoel contacted law enforcement officials, Mr. Hoel and the Hoels' son drove back to where they had seen the money. A Logan County deputy sheriff arrived at the scene, as did Mrs. Hoel. Mr. Hoel assisted the deputy in his search for the money. The search yielded $4,600 in hundred dollar bills. Before the deputy departed, Mr. and Mrs. Hoel told him that they wanted the money if the authorities could not locate its rightful owner.

An Oklahoma statute allows a county sheriff to seek court permission to deposit in a Sheriff's Training Fund money (including stolen, lost, and abandoned money) "which has come into [the sheriff's] possession," if the true owner is unknown and the sheriff has held the money for at least six months. The statutory procedure requires the sheriff to file an application requesting that the appropriate district court issue an order authorizing the deposit of the money. A hearing must be held on the application. According to the statute, if no one appears at the hearing and "prove[s] ownership," the court is to approve the deposit of the money in the training fund.

More than six months after the February 14, 1994, events described earlier, the Logan County sheriff, R. Douglas Powell, filed an application requesting the district court's permission to deposit the found money in his Sheriff's Training Fund. The Hoels appeared at the hearing and objected to the application. The district court ruled in favor of Sheriff Powell and issued an order approving the deposit of the money in the training fund. The Hoels, who were allowed to join the case as parties, appealed. ∞

Jones, Judge   Mr. Hoel testified [at the hearing on the sheriff's application] that he and his son returned to the place they had discovered the money in order "to secure the area," by which he meant

that he wanted to "[m]ake sure nobody else comes along and picks it up . . . [W]e wanted to make sure nobody touched it." Apparently Mrs. Hoel picked up one or two of the bills, which the deputy examined for signs of forgery. Deciding that the money was indeed genuine legal tender, the deputy then instructed the Hoels not to pick up any more money, because he wanted to check it for fingerprints and drug traces.

[The Hoels] rely on [statutory] and common law defining a finder's right to assert their claim to the money. By [Oklahoma] statute, if one chooses to take charge of lost goods he finds, he acquires both the rights and the obligations of a bailee for hire of the property owner. And, it is a basic maxim of the law that a finder of property acquires rights in found property which are superior to all claims except that of the rightful owner. [Sheriff Powell] contends this case should be governed by [the Oklahoma statute allowing the sheriff to] apply for court authority to deposit money "which has come into his possession" into the Sheriff's Training Fund. [The Hoels], by their own admission, assert no *prior* ownership of the money (i.e., prior to their discovery on the night of February 14, 1994). [Sheriff Powell therefore] argues that the "owner" of the money has not claimed it, and [that the Hoels] cannot "prove ownership," within the meaning of [the statute].

[The Hoels and the sheriff agree] that the money was truly "lost," i.e., that somehow the original owner(s) parted with the money involuntarily and unintentionally, and that he or she or they did not know that it lay scattered along the road where the Hoels discovered it. Two issues are presented here for us to resolve: first, whether the finder of lost property may qualify as an "owner" of the property, and so obtain sufficient legal rights in the property which would defeat a sheriff's application [under the statute]; and, second (assuming we give an affirmative answer to the first issue), whether the Hoels qualify as "finders" of the money.

The first issue has not been previously decided in this state. However, we conclude that [the Hoels], if

they qualified as finders of the money, acquired a sufficient ownership interest in the money to be "owners" of the money as that term is used in the unclaimed property statute. The Legislature did not intend to negate the common or statutory law granting legal rights to finders of lost property. By interpreting the unclaimed property statute in this manner, both legal principles at issue here can be harmonized without undue violence to either.

Having decided that a finder of lost property acquires rights which are superior to the sheriff's rights under the unclaimed property statute, we must next determine whether [the Hoels] qualify as "finders" under the circumstances presented in this case. It is stated by general authorities that the finder of lost property is one who first reduces it to possession, or at least such possession of the thing as its nature and circumstances will permit. [The Oklahoma statute dealing with finders of lost items] expresses a related notion in its opening clause; thus in order to obtain the rights of a finder under the statute, one must "take charge" of [the property].

[I]t is undisputed that Mr. Hoel and his eldest son returned to where the money had been discovered in order to prevent any third person from interfering with the recovery of the money. We should not penalize [the Hoels] for their legitimate concern that the money might have some evidentiary value. In fact, the deputy who subsequently appeared on the scene directed [the Hoels] *not* to pick up the money, precisely because of the possibility it might bear fingerprints or trace evidence. Under these rather unique circumstances, we hold that [the Hoels] "took charge" of the money before the deputy sheriff arrived, and so acquired the rights of a finder under our statutory and common law.

District court's judgment in favor of Sheriff Powell reversed and remanded.

Leasing

A lease of personal property is a transfer of the right to possess and use personal property belonging to another.[5] Although the rights of one who leases personal property (a lessee) do not constitute own-

ership of personal property, leasing is mentioned here because it is becoming an increasingly important way of acquiring the use of many kinds of personal property, from automobiles to farm equipment.

Article 2 and Article 9 of the UCC may sometimes be applied to personal property leases by analogy. However, rules contained in these articles are sometimes inadequate to resolve special prob-

---

[5]A lease of personal property is a form of bailment, a "bailment for hire." Bailments are discussed later in this chapter.

Rights of Finders of Personal Property

CHARACTER OF PROPERTY	DESCRIPTION	RIGHTS OF FINDER	RIGHTS OF ORIGINAL OWNER
Lost	Owner unintentionally parted with possession	Rights superior to everyone except the owner	Retains ownership; has the right to the return of the property
Mislaid	Owner intentionally put property in a place but unintentionally left it there	None; person in possession of real property on which mislaid property was found holds it for the owner, and has rights superior to everyone except owner	Retains ownership; has the right to the return of the property
Abandoned	Owner intentionally placed property out of his possession with intent to relinquish ownership of it	Finder who takes possession with intent to claim ownership acquires ownership of property	None

lems presented by leasing. For this reason, a new article of the UCC dealing exclusively with leases of goods, Article 2A, was written in 1987. Article 2A has been presented to state legislatures for possible adoption. Approximately 40 states have adopted Article 2A as of the time of this writing.

Gifts

Title to personal property may be obtained by **gift.** A gift is a voluntary transfer of property to the **donee** (the person who receives a gift), for which the **donor** (the person who gives the gift) gets no consideration in return. To have a valid gift, all three of the following elements are necessary:

1. The donor must *intend* to make a gift.
2. The donor must make *delivery* of the gift.
3. The donee must *accept* the gift.

The most critical requirement is delivery. The person who makes the gift must actually give up possession and control of the property either to the donee or to a third person who is to hold it for the donee. Delivery is important because it makes clear to the donor that he is voluntarily giving up ownership without getting something in exchange. A promise to make a gift is usually not enforceable;[6] the person must actually part with the property. In some cases, the delivery may be symbolic or con-

structive. For example, handing over the key to a strongbox can be symbolic delivery of the property in the strongbox. *King v. Trustees of Boston University,* which appears in this chapter's examination of bailments, discusses various issues concerning gifts and promises to make gifts for charitable purposes.

There are two kinds of gifts: gifts *inter vivos* and gifts *causa mortis.* A gift *inter vivos* is a gift between two living persons. For example, when Melissa's parents give her a car for her 21st birthday, that is a gift inter vivos. A gift *causa mortis* is a gift made in contemplation of death. For example, Uncle Earl, who is about to undergo a serious heart operation, gives his watch to his nephew, Bart, and says that he wants Bart to have it if he does not survive the operation.

A gift *causa mortis* is a conditional gift and is effective unless any of the following occurs:

1. The donor recovers from the peril or sickness under fear of which the gift was made, or
2. The donor revokes or withdraws the gift before he dies, or
3. The donee dies before the donor.

If one of these events takes place, ownership of the property goes back to the donor.

Conditional Gifts

Sometimes a gift is made on condition that the donee comply with certain restrictions or perform

---

[6]The idea is discussed in Chapter 12.

certain actions. A conditional gift is not a completed gift. It may be revoked by the donor before the donee complies with the conditions. Gifts in contemplation of marriage, such as engagement rings, are a primary example of a conditional gift. Such gifts are generally considered to have been made on an implied condition that marriage between the donor and donee will take place. If the donee breaks the engagement without legal justification or if the engagement is broken by mutual consent, the donor will be able to recover the ring or other engagement gift. However, if the engagement is unjustifiably broken by the donor, he or she is generally not entitled to recover gifts made in contemplation of marriage. As is detailed in *Fierro v. Hoel,* which follows, these rules are not uniformly applied in all states. Some states have enacted legislation prescribing the rules applicable to the return of engagement presents.

FIERRO v. HOEL   465 N.W.2d 669 (Ct. App. Iowa 1990)

John Fierro and Janan Hoel became engaged to be married shortly before Thanksgiving in 1987. At the time of the proposal, Fierro presented Hoel with a 1.37 carat diamond in a platinum setting. The ring was valued at approximately $9,000. The couple shared the news of their engagement with family and friends and began making wedding plans. After they located a condominium to purchase in New York City, Hoel refused to sign mortgage documents recognizing that Fierro's parents had loaned them money to make the purchase. Shortly thereafter, in March 1988, Fierro broke off the engagement. He asked Hoel to return the ring but she refused.

Fierro then filed a lawsuit seeking to establish ownership of the ring. He asserted that the ring was symbolic of the parties' intent to marry and inherently conditioned on their subsequent marriage. He contended that when a couple terminates an engagement, the ring must be returned to the donor. Hoel, on the other hand, took the position that Fierro had not expressly stated the condition when he gave the ring to her and that it should be viewed as a completed gift. The trial court entered judgment for Hoel and Fierro appealed.

Donielson, Judge The question before us is whether an engagement ring is a conditional gift or a completed gift upon delivery. The district court concluded that because John Fierro had placed no express conditions on the ring at the time possession was transferred to Janan Hoel, the engagement ring was a completed gift upon delivery. We hold an engagement ring is an inherently conditional gift and therefore reverse.

An engagement ring given in contemplation of marriage is an impliedly conditional gift. The jurisdictions which have considered cases dealing with the gift of an engagement ring uniformly hold that marriage is an implied condition of the transfer of title and that the gift does not become absolute until the marriage occurs. One court explained:

Where a gift of personal property is made with the intent to take place irrevocably, and is fully executed by unconditional delivery, it is a valid gift *inter vivos.* Such a gift is absolute and, once made, cannot be revoked. A gift, however, may be conditioned on the performance of some act by the donee, and if the condition is not fulfilled the donor may recover the gift. We find the conditional gift theory particularly appropriate when the contested property is an engagement ring. The inherent symbolism of this gift forecloses the need to establish an express condition that marriage will ensue. Rather the condition may be implied in fact or imposed by law in order to prevent unjust enrichment.

Once we recognize an engagement ring is a conditional gift, the question still remains: who gets the gift when the condition is not fulfilled. The obvious answer is the gift must be returned to the donor. However, an older majority line of cases follows the general principle that the donor of an engagement ring can recover the gift only if the engagement is dissolved by agreement or if the engagement is unjustifiably broken by the donee. The critical inquiry in cases following this principle is who was at "fault" for the termination of the relationship. The party to an engagement who was unjustifiably jilted became the owner of the ring—a type of "consolation prize."

What fact justifies the breaking of an engagement? The absence of a sense of humor? Differing musical tastes? Differing political views? The painfully learned fact is that marriages are made on earth, not in heaven. They must be approached with intelligent care and should not happen without a decent assurance of success. When either party lacks that assurance, for whatever reason, the engagement should be broken. No justification is needed. Either party may act. Fault, impossible to fix, does not count. This court believes fault, in an engagement setting, is irrelevant.

This court adopts the "no fault" approach followed in a minority of jurisdictions. Since the major purpose of the engagement period is to allow a couple time to test the permanency of their feelings, it would seem highly ironic to penalize the donor for taking steps to prevent a possibly unhappy marriage.

In summary, we hold an engagement ring given in contemplation of marriage is an impliedly conditional gift; it is a completed gift only upon marriage. If the wedding is called off, for whatever reason, the gift is not capable of becoming a completed gift and must be returned to the donor.

Reversed in favor of Fierro.

Hayden, Judge, dissenting The additional factual background in this case is John had given Janan a pin that belonged to his grandmother. He told Janan explicitly the pin was to be returned to him if they ever broke up. Later when John gave her the ring he placed no conditions on it when she received it. The trial court weighed and considered this evidence. The trial court ruled John had ended the engagement and had placed no conditions on the ring as he had done on the heirloom pin.

The question before us in this case is was the ring a gift conditioned on marriage or was the ring an unconditional gift. The Iowa Supreme Court has stated what the appropriate burden of proof should be when it is claimed there is a conditional gift: If an unqualified transfer to the donee is proved, one asserting the delivery was made on some condition or trust has the burden of establishing such condition or trust. Thus, if the gift elements are proven,

John has the burden of proof to show the gift was conditioned on marriage.

The three essential elements for an *inter vivos* gift are donative intent, delivery and acceptance. There is no question there has been a delivery and an acceptance. The remaining question is what was John's intent at the time he gave Janan the ring.

In this case the intention of John was evident from the testimony presented. Janan was responsible for the purchase and payment of the insurance on the ring. Also the ring was referred to by the parties at all times as "her ring." Finally, a demand for the ring was not made until nearly 30 days after John called off the engagement. Thus, it is evident the requirements for a gift were completed unless a condition was proved otherwise.

If John had imposed a condition of marriage on the gift of the ring, such a requirement must have been explicit and known. Thus, if John had wanted such a condition on the gift, he should have made this known and clearly understood at the time he gave possession of the ring to Janan.

There is evidence John was aware of the need to clearly express such a condition when giving this type of gift. John had made a condition of marriage a requirement for the previous gift of heirloom jewelry he had given to Janan. If the engagement was broken, the piece of heirloom jewelry would be returned. After the engagement was broken, the piece of heirloom jewelry was promptly returned. If John wanted the ring returned, he could have expressed such a condition as he did with the heirloom jewelry. Absent any such evidence of condition, I determine the giving of the ring is a valid completed gift.

I acknowledge parties are free to return engagement gifts. However, proper social etiquette does not demand their return, and neither should the courts as a matter of law.

Uniform Transfers to Minors Act

The Uniform Transfers to Minors Act, which has been adopted in one form or another in every state, provides a fairly simple and flexible method for making gifts and other transfers of property to minors.[7] As defined in this act, a minor is anyone

under the age of 21. Under the act, an adult may transfer money, securities, real property, insurance policies, and other property. The specific ways of doing this vary according to the type of property transferred. In general, however, the transferor (the person who gives or otherwise transfers the property) delivers, pays, or assigns the property to, or registers the property with, a custodian who acts for the benefit of the minor "under the Uniform Transfers to Minors Act." The custodian is given fairly

---

[7]This statute was formerly called, and is still called in some states, the Uniform Gift to Minors Act.

broad discretion to use the gift for the minor's benefit and may not use it for the custodian's personal benefit. The custodian may be the transferor himself, another adult, or a trust company, depending again on the type of property transferred. If the donor or other transferor fully complies with the Uniform Transfers to Minors Act, the transfer is considered to be irrevocable.

Will or Inheritance

Ownership of personal property may also be transferred upon the death of the former owner. The property may pass under the terms of a will if the will was validly executed. If there is no valid will, the property is transferred to the heirs of the owner according to state laws. Transfer of property at the death of the owner will be discussed in Chapter 26, Estates and Trusts.

Confusion

Title to personal property may be obtained by **confusion.** Confusion is the intermixing of different owners' goods in such a way that they cannot later be separated. For example, suppose wheat belonging to several different people is mixed in a grain elevator. If the mixing was by agreement or if it resulted from an accident without negligence on anyone's part, each person owns his proportionate share of the entire quantity of wheat. However, a different result would be reached if the wheat was wrongfully or negligently mixed. Suppose a thief steals a truckload of Grade #1 wheat worth $8.50 a bushel from a farmer. The thief dumps the wheat into his storage bin, which contains a lower-grade wheat worth $4.50 a bushel, with the result that the mixture is worth only $4.50 a bushel. The farmer has first claim against the entire mixture to recover the value of his wheat that was mixed with the lower-grade wheat. The thief, or any other person whose intentional or negligent act results in confusion of goods, must bear any loss caused by the confusion.

Accession

Ownership of personal property may also be acquired by **accession.** Accession means increasing the value of property by adding materials, labor, or both. As a general rule, the owner of the original property becomes the owner of the improvements. This is particularly likely to be true if the improvement was done with the permission of the owner. For example, Hudson takes his automobile to a shop that replaces the engine with a larger engine and puts in a new four-speed transmission. Hudson is still the owner of the automobile as well as the owner of the parts added by the auto shop.

Problems can arise if materials are added or work is performed on personal property without the consent of the owner. If property is stolen from one person and improved by the thief, the original owner can get it back and does not have to reimburse the thief for the work done or the materials used in improving it. For example, a thief steals Rourke's used car, puts a new engine in it, replaces the tires, and repairs the muffler. Rourke is entitled to get his car back from the thief and does not have to pay him for the engine, tires, and muffler.

The result is less easy to predict, however, if property is mistakenly improved in good faith by someone who believes that he is the owner of the property. In such a case, a court must weigh the respective interests of two innocent parties: the original owner and the improver.

For example, Johnson, a stonecarver, finds a block of limestone by the side of the road. Assuming that it has been abandoned, he takes it home and carves it into a sculpture. In fact, the block was owned by Hayes. Having fallen off a flatbed truck during transportation, the block is merely lost property, which Hayes ordinarily could recover from the finder. In a case such as this, a court could decide the case in either of two ways. The first alternative would be to give the original owner (Hayes) ownership of the improved property, but to allow the person who has improved the property in good faith (Johnson) to recover the cost of the improvements. The second alternative would be to hold that the improver, Johnson, has acquired ownership of the sculpture, but that he is required to pay the original owner the value of the property as of the time he obtained it. The greater the extent to which the improvements have increased the value of the property, the more likely it is that the court will choose the second alternative and permit the improver to acquire ownership of the improved property.

BAILMENTS

Nature of Bailments

A **bailment** is the delivery of personal property by its owner or one who has the right to possess it (the **bailor**) to another person (the **bailee**) who accepts it and is under an express or implied agreement to return it to the bailor or to someone designated by the bailor. Only personal property can be the subject of bailments.

Although the legal terminology used to describe bailments might be unfamiliar to most people, everyone is familiar with transactions that constitute bailments. For example, Lincoln takes his car to a parking garage where the attendant gives Lincoln a claim check and then drives the car down the ramp to park it. Charles borrows his neighbor's lawn mower to cut his grass. Tara, who lives next door to Kyle, agrees to take care of Kyle's cat while Kyle goes on a vacation. These are just a few of the everyday situations that involve bailments. The case of *York v. Jones,* which follows, involves a bailment that is much more unusual but possesses the essential characteristics.

YORK v. JONES   717 F. Supp. 421 (E.D. Va. 1989)

---

teven York and Risa Adler-York contacted the Jones Institute for Reproductive Medicine to determine whether they were viable candidates for in vitro fertilization (IVF). This process involves removing one or more oocytes or eggs from the woman's body, fertilizing those eggs in vitro (outside of the womb) with the husband's sperm, and then depositing the developing masses into the woman's uterus. The Yorks were accepted into the Jones Institute's IVF program.

In May 1987, the Yorks signed a Cryopreservation Agreement outlining the procedure for cryopreservation or freezing of pre-zygotes and detailing the Yorks' rights in the frozen pre-zygote. The agreement explained that the cryopreservation procedure is available if more than five pre-zygotes are retrieved during the IVF treatment, so that the possibility for multiple births could be reduced while maintaining optimal chances for pregnancy. The agreement also provided in part:

We may withdraw our consent and discontinue participation at any time . . . and we understand our pre-zygotes will be stored only as long as we are active IVF patients at . . . Jones Institute . . . We have the principal responsibility to decide the disposition of our pre-zygotes. Our frozen pre-zygotes will not be released from storage for the purpose of intrauterine transfer without the written consent of us both. In the event of divorce, we understand legal ownership of any stored pre-zygotes must be determined in a property settlement . . . Should we for any reason no longer wish to attempt to initiate a pregnancy, we understand we may choose one of three fates for our pre-zygotes that remain in frozen storage. Our pre-zygotes may be: 1) donated to another infertile couple . . . 2) donated for approved research investigation, and 3) thawed but not allowed to undergo further development.

The Yorks underwent IVF treatment on four occasions. Six eggs were removed from Mrs. York and fertilized with her husband's sperm, creating six embryos. Five of these embryos were transferred to Mrs. York's uterus. The remaining embryo was cryogenically preserved in accordance with the procedures outlined in the Cryopreservation Agreement. None of the in vitro fertilization attempts resulted in pregnancy.

During the course of treatment, the Yorks moved to California. They sought to have the remaining frozen pre-zygote transferred from the Jones Institute in Norfolk, Virginia, to the Institute for Reproductive Research in Los Angeles, where the Yorks planned to attempt in vitro fertilization again. The Yorks arranged for proper transportation and handling of the pre-zygote, but the Jones Institute refused to allow such a transfer.

The Yorks brought suit against the Jones Institute and its physicians, claiming that its continued dominion and control over the pre-zygote was contrary to law and the parties' agreement. The Jones Institute filed a motion to dismiss, alleging that the Yorks' complaint did not state a claim on which relief could be granted. This is the trial court's ruling on that motion. ∽

Clarke, Jr., District Judge   The Yorks' complaint in this case raises an issue of first impression in the rapidly developing field of human reproductive technology. The Jones Institute argues that the Yorks' proprietary rights in the pre-zygote are limited to the "three fates" enumerated in the [Cryopreservation Agreement] because there is no established protocol for the inter-institutional transfer of pre-zygotes.

The court begins its analysis by noting that the Cryopreservation Agreement created a bailor-bailee relationship between the Yorks and Jones Institute. While the parties in this case expressed no intent to create a bailment, under Virginia law, no formal contract or actual meeting of the minds is necessary. Rather, all that is needed is the element of lawful possession however created, and duty to account for the thing as the property of another that creates the bailment. The essential nature of a bailment relationship imposes on the bailee, when the purpose of the bailment has terminated, an absolute obligation to return the subject matter of the bailment to the bailor. The obligation to return the property is implied from the fact of lawful possession of the personal property of another.

In the instant case, the requisite elements of a bailment relationship are present. The Jones Institute consistently refers to the pre-zygote as the "property" of the Yorks. Although the Cryopreservation Agreement constitutes a bailment contract, the Agreement is nevertheless governed by the same principles as apply to other contracts.

The Cryopreservation Agreement should be more strictly construed against the Jones Institute, the parties who drafted the Agreement. The Jones Institute has defined the extent of its possession interest as bailee of the pre-zygote by the following provision of the Agreement: "We may withdraw our consent and discontinue participation at any time . . . and . . . our pre-zygote will be stored only as long as we are active IVF patients at the [Jones Institute.]" The Jones Institute has further defined the limits of its possessory interest by recognizing the Yorks' proprietary rights in the pre-zygote. The Agreement repeatedly refers to "our pre-zygote" and further provides that the Yorks have the "principal responsibility to decide the disposition" of the pre-zygote.

The Jones Institute takes the position that the plain language of the Cryopreservation Agreement limits the Yorks' proprietary right to the pre-zygote to the "three fates" listed in the Agreement. The Court finds, however, that the applicability of the three fates is limited by the following language, "Should we for any reason no longer wish to initiate a pregnancy, we understand we may choose one of three fates for our pre-zygotes . . ." The allegations of the Yorks' complaint and the entire thrust of this litigation suggest that the Yorks continue to desire to achieve pregnancy. The Agreement does not state that the attempt to initiate a pregnancy is restricted to procedures employed at the Jones Institute. The "three fates" are therefore inapplicable to the case at bar. For the reasons stated, the Court finds that the Yorks' complaint states a claim upon which relief can be granted.

Motion to dismiss denied in favor of the Yorks.

Elements of a Bailment

The essential elements of a bailment are:

1. The bailor must own or have the right to possess the property.
2. The bailor must deliver exclusive possession of and control over the property to the bailee.
3. The bailee must knowingly accept the property with the understanding that he owes a duty to return the property as directed by the bailor.

Creation of a Bailment

A bailment is created by an express or implied contract. Whether the elements of a bailment have been fulfilled is determined by examining all the facts and circumstances of the particular situation. For example, a patron goes into a restaurant and hangs his hat and coat on an unattended rack. It is unlikely that this created a bailment, because the restaurant owner never assumed exclusive control over the hat and coat. However, if there is a

FIGURE 1

Creation of a Bailment

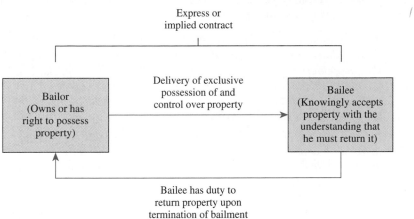

checkroom and the hat and coat are checked with the attendant, a bailment will arise.

If a customer parks her car in a parking lot, keeps the keys, and can drive the car out herself whenever she wishes, a bailment has not been created. The courts treat this situation as a lease of space. Suppose, however, that she takes her car to a parking garage where an attendant, after giving her a claim check, parks the car. There is a bailment of the car because the parking garage has accepted delivery and possession of the car. However, a distinction is made between the car and packages locked in the trunk. If the parking garage was not aware of the packages, it would probably not be a bailee of them as it did not knowingly accept possession of them. The creation of a bailment is illustrated in Figure 1. The conclusion that a bailment was created proved to be critical to the outcome in *King v. Trustees of Boston University*, which follows.

KING v. TRUSTEES OF BOSTON UNIVERSITY   647 N.E.2d 1196 (Mass. Sup. Jud. Ct. 1995)

pproximately four years prior to his death, Dr. Martin Luther King, Jr., provided Boston University with possession of some of his correspondence, manuscripts, and other papers. He did so pursuant to a letter, which read as follows:

On this 16th day of July, 1964, I name the Boston University Library the Repository of my correspondence, manuscripts, and other papers, along with a few of my awards and other materials which may come to be of interest in historical or other research.

In accordance with this action I have authorized the removal of most of the above-mentioned papers and other objects to Boston University, including most correspondence through 1961, at once. It is my intention that after the end of each calendar year, similar files of materials for an additional year should be sent to Boston University.

All papers and other objects which thus pass into the custody of Boston University remain my legal property until otherwise indicated, according to the statements below. However, if, despite scrupulous care, any such materials are damaged or lost while in custody of Boston University, I absolve Boston University of responsibility to me for such damage or loss.

I intend each year to indicate a portion of the materials deposited with Boston University to become the absolute property of Boston University as an outright gift from me, until all shall have been thus given to the

University. In the event of my death, all such materials deposited with the University shall become from that date the absolute property of Boston University.

Sincerely yours,

Martin Luther King, Jr.

Acting in her capacity as administrator of Dr. King's estate, his widow, Coretta Scott King, sued Boston University for conversion. (Conversion is discussed in Chapter 6.) The plaintiff alleged that the King estate, and not BU, held title to the papers that had been housed in the BU library's special collection since the 1964 delivery of them. BU contended that it owned the deposited papers because Dr. King had made an enforceable charitable pledge to give them to BU. The case was tried before a jury, which ruled in BU's favor. In response to questions posed by the trial judge on a special verdict form, the jury determined that in his July 16, 1964, letter, Dr. King had made a promise to give BU title to his papers and that this promise was an enforceable charitable pledge supported by consideration or reliance. (See Chapter 12 for a discussion of the concepts of consideration and reliance.) When the trial judge denied her motion for judgment notwithstanding the verdict or for a new trial, the plaintiff appealed. ∞

Abrams, Justice [T]he jury found that BU had acquired rightful ownership of the papers via a charitable pledge. [T]here is scant Massachusetts case law in the area of charitable pledges and subscriptions. A charitable subscription is an oral or written promise to do certain acts or to give real or personal property to a charity or for a charitable purpose. To enforce a charitable subscription in Massachusetts, a party must establish that there was a promise to give some property to a charitable institution and that the promise was supported by consideration or reliance.

The plaintiff argues that the terms of the letter promising "to indicate a portion of the material deposited with [BU] to become the absolute property of [BU] as an outright gift . . . until all shall have been thus given to [BU]," could not as a matter of basic contract law constitute a promise sufficient to establish an inter vivos charitable pledge because there is no indication of a bargained for exchange which would have bound Dr. King to his promise. The plaintiff asserts that the above-quoted excerpt (hereinafter "first statement") from the letter merely described an unenforceable unilateral and gratuitous mechanism by which he might make a gift of the papers in the future. In support of her position that Dr. King did not intend to bind himself to his statement of intent to make a gift of the papers he deposited with BU, the plaintiff points to the [letter's statement] that "[a]ll papers and other objects which thus pass into the custody of [BU] remain my legal property until otherwise indicated, according to the statements below." According to

the plaintiff, because of Dr. King's initial retention of legal ownership, BU could not reasonably rely on the letter's statements of intent to make a gift of the papers. We do not agree.

The letter contains two sentences which might reasonably be construed as a promise to give personal property to a charity or for a charitable purpose. The first statement, quoted above, is that Dr. King intended in subsequent installments to transfer title to portions of the papers in BU's custody until all the papers in its custody became its property. The second statement immediately follows the first, expressing an intent that "i]n the event of [Dr. King's] death, all . . . materials deposited with [BU] shall become from that date the absolute property of [BU]" (hereinafter "second statement"). BU claims that these two sentences should be read together as a promise to make a gift of all of the papers deposited with it at some point between the first day of deposit and at the very latest, . . . Dr. King's death.

A primary concern in enforcing charitable subscriptions, as with enforcement of other gratuitous transfers such as gifts and trusts, is ascertaining the intent of the donor. If donative intent is sufficiently clear, we shall give effect to that intent to the extent possible without abandoning basic contractual principles, such as specificity of the donor's promise, consideration, and reasonableness of the charity's reliance. In determining the intent of Dr. King as expressed in the letter and the understanding BU had of that letter, we look first to the language of the letter, in its entirety, but also consider the circumstances and relationship of the parties.

First Statement

The plaintiff contends that [the first statement] is not a promise but a mere statement of intent to do something in the future. We might agree that the first statement could induce nothing more than a hope or mere expectation on BU's part, if the statement were considered in a vacuum. However, our interpretation of that first statement is strongly influenced by the bailor-bailee relationship the letter unequivocally established between Dr. King and BU.

A bailment is established by "delivery of personalty for some particular purpose, or on mere deposit, upon a contract, express or implied, that after the purpose has been fulfilled, it shall be redelivered to the person who delivered it, or otherwise dealt with according to his directions, or kept until he reclaims it, as the case may be (quoting *Williston on Contracts* (3d ed. 1967)). The terms of the letter establish a bailment in which certain "correspondence, manuscripts and other papers, along with a few of [Dr. King's] awards" were placed in "the custody of [BU]." The bailed papers were to "remain [Dr. King's] property until otherwise indicated." By accepting delivery of the papers, BU assumed the duty of care as bailee set forth in the letter, that of "scrupulous care."

Generally there will be a case for the jury as to donative intent if property allegedly promised to a charity or other eleemosynary institution is placed by the donor in the custody of the donee. The bailor-bailee relationship established in the letter could be viewed by a rational factfinder as a security for the promise to give a gift in the future of the bailed property, and thus as evidence in addition to the [letter's] statement of an intent of the donor to be bound. Furthermore, while we have been unwilling to abandon fundamental principles of contract law in determining the enforceability of charitable subscriptions, we do recognize that the "meeting of minds" between a donor and a charitable institution differs from the understanding we require in the context of enforceable arm's-length commercial agreements. Charities depend on donations for their existence, whereas their donors may give personal property on conditions they choose, with or without . . . demanding consideration. In combination with the letter and in the context of a disputed pledge to a charity, the bailment of Dr. King's letters provided sufficient evidence of donative intent to submit to the jury the questions whether there was a promise to transfer ownership of the bailed property and whether there was consideration [for] or reliance on that promise.

Second Statement

The parties agree that a testamentary transfer of the papers by means of the July 16, 1964 letter would be invalid because the letter did not comply with the Statute of Wills ([which requires] testamentary dispositions to be subscribed by two or more competent witnesses). However, the Statute of Wills does not prevent an owner of property from stipulating by contract for the disposition of his property at the time of his death. The parties dispute whether the statement of intent to transfer title on Dr. King's death comports with the Statute of Frauds for contracts to make testamentary dispositions. Although the letter was a writing signed by Dr. King, the plaintiff asserts that [it] does not satisfy the Statute of Frauds because it did not contain all the terms of an enforceable agreement. We do not agree. The Statute of Frauds was not applicable because the letter was not a contract to make a will, but rather was a promise to give BU absolute title to all papers in its possession either at some future point in Dr. King's life or upon his death. [Even if the Statute of Frauds applied here], the first statement of intent to make gifts during his lifetime of the bailed papers could have been interpreted by the jury as a promise to give gifts on which BU reasonably relied or for which BU rendered consideration. The second statement that papers not yet transferred to BU but in its custody at the time of Dr. King's death could have been interpreted by the jury as a statement of the latest date on which Dr. King intended to make a gift to BU of the bailed property. Such an interpretation states all terms of an enforceable agreement. Thus, [even if] the Statute of Frauds governing contracts to make testamentary dispositions [applied here, it] would be satisfied.

Evidence of Consideration or Reliance

The judge did not err in submitting the second question on charitable pledge, regarding whether there was consideration for or reliance on the promise, to the jury. There was evidence that BU undertook indexing of the papers, made the papers available to researchers, and provided trained staff to care for the papers and assist researchers. BU held a convocation to commemorate receipt of the papers. Dr. King spoke at the convocation. In a speech at that time, he explained why he chose BU as the repository for his papers.

As we explained above, the letter established that so long as BU, as bailee, attended the papers with "scrupulous care," Dr. King, as bailor, would release them from liability for "any such materials . . . damaged or lost while in [its] custody." The jury could conclude that certain actions of BU, including indexing of the papers, went beyond the obligations BU assumed as a bailee to attend the papers with "scrupulous care" and constituted reliance [on] or consideration for the promises Dr. King included in the letter to transfer ownership of all bailed papers to BU at some future date or at his death. We conclude that the letter could have been read to contain a promise supported by consideration or reliance.

Judgment in favor of Boston University affirmed.

Types of Bailments

Bailments are commonly divided into three different categories:

1. Bailments for the sole benefit of the bailor.
2. Bailments for the sole benefit of the bailee.
3. Bailments for mutual benefit.

The type of bailment involved in a case can be important in determining the liability of the bailee for loss of or damage to the property. As will be discussed later, however, some courts no longer rely on these distinctions when they determine whether the bailee is liable.

Bailments for Benefit of Bailor A bailment for the sole benefit of the bailor is one in which the bailee renders some service but does not receive a benefit in return. For example, Brown allows his neighbor, Reston, to park her car in Brown's garage while she is on vacation. Brown does not ask for any compensation. Here, Reston, the bailor, has received a benefit from the bailee, Brown, but Brown has not received a benefit in return.

Bailments for Benefit of Bailee A bailment for the sole benefit of the bailee is one in which the owner of the goods allows someone else to use them free of charge. For example, Anderson lends a lawn mower to her neighbor, Moss, so he can cut his grass.

Bailments for Mutual Benefit If both the bailee and the bailor receive benefits from the bailment, it is a bailment for mutual benefit. For example, Sutton rents china for his daughter's wedding from E-Z Party Supplies for an agreed-on price. Sutton, the bailee, benefits by being able to use the china; E-Z benefits from his payment of the rental charge. On some occasions, the benefit to the bailee is less tangible. For example, a customer checks a coat at an attended coatroom at a restaurant. Even if no charge is made for the service, it is likely to be treated as a bailment for mutual benefit because the restaurant is benefiting from the customer's patronage.

Special Bailments

Certain professional bailees, such as innkeepers and common carriers, are treated somewhat differently by the law and are held to a higher level of responsibility than is the ordinary bailee. The rules applicable to common carriers and innkeepers are detailed later in this chapter.

Duties of the Bailee

The bailee has two basic duties:

1. To take care of the property that has been entrusted to her.
2. To return the property at the termination of the bailment.

The following discussion examines the scope of these duties.

Duty of Bailee to Take Care of Property

The bailee is responsible for taking steps to protect the property during the time she has possession of it. If the bailee does not exercise proper care and the property is lost or damaged, the bailee is liable for negligence. The bailee would then be required to reimburse the bailor for the amount of loss or damage. If the property is lost or damaged without the fault or negligence of the bailee, however, the bailee is not liable to the bailor. The degree of care required of the bailee traditionally has depended in large part on the type of bailment involved.

1. *Bailment for the benefit of the bailor.* If the bailment is solely for the benefit of the bailor, the bailee is expected to exercise only a minimal, or slight, degree of care for the protection of the bailed property. He would be liable, then, only if he were grossly negligent in his care of the bailed property. The rationale for this rule is that if the bailee is doing the bailor a favor, it is not reasonable to expect him to be as careful as when he is deriving some benefit from keeping the goods.

2. *Bailment for mutual benefit.* When the bailment is a bailment for mutual benefit, the bailee is expected to exercise ordinary or reasonable care. This degree of care requires the bailee to use the same care a reasonable person would use to protect his own property in the relevant situation. If the bailee is a professional that holds itself out as a professional bailee, such as a warehouse, it must use the degree of care that would be used by a person in the same profession. This is likely to be more care than the ordinary person would use. In addition, there is usually a duty on a professional bailee to explain any loss or damage to property—that is, to show it was not negligent. If it cannot do so, it will be liable to the bailor.

3. *Bailment for the benefit of the bailee.* If the bailment is solely for the benefit of the bailee, the bailee is expected to exercise a high degree of care. For instance a person who lends a sailboat to a neighbor would probably expect the neighbor to be even more careful with the sailboat than the owner might be. In such a case, the bailee would be liable for damage to the property if his action reflected a relatively small degree of negligence.

A number of courts today view the type of bailment involved in a case as just one factor to be considered in determining whether the bailee should be liable for loss of or damage to bailed goods. The modern trend appears to be moving in the direction of imposing a duty of reasonable care on bailees, regardless of the type of bailment. This flexible standard of care permits courts to take into account a variety of factors such as the nature and value of the property, the provisions of the parties' agreement, the payment of consideration for the bailment, and the experience of the bailee. In addition, the bailee is required to use the property only as was agreed between the parties. For example, Jones borrows Morrow's lawn mower to mow his lawn. If Jones uses the mower to cut the weeds on a trash-filled vacant lot and the mower is damaged, he would be liable because he was exceeding the agreed purpose of the bailment—to cut his lawn.

Bailee's Duty to Return the Property

One of the essential elements of a bailment is the duty of the bailee to return the property at the termination of the bailment. If the bailed property is taken from the bailee by legal process, the bailee should notify the bailor and must take whatever action is necessary to protect the bailor's interest. In most instances, the bailee must return the identical property that was bailed. A person who lends a 1996 Mercury Sable to a friend expects to have that particular car returned. In some cases, the bailor does not expect the return of the identical goods. For example, a farmer who stores 1,500 bushels of Grade #1 wheat at a local grain elevator expects to get back 1,500 bushels of Grade #1 wheat when the bailment is terminated, but not the identical wheat he deposited.

The bailee must return the goods in an undamaged condition to the bailor or to someone designated by the bailor. If the goods have been damaged, destroyed, or lost, there is a rebuttable presumption of negligence on the part of the bailee. To overcome the presumption, the bailee must come forward with evidence showing that he exercised the relevant level of care. The operation of the rebuttable presumption can be seen in the *Magee v. Walbro* case, which follows. If the property is lost or damaged without the fault or negligence of the bailee, however, the bailee is not liable to the bailor.

MAGEE v. WALBRO, INC., 525 N.E.2d 975 (Ill. Ct. App. 1988)

Walbro, Inc., doing business as Mysel Furs, was in the business of storing furs. It had arranged for United Parcel Service (UPS) to pick up furs from its customers and deliver them to Mysel's. In May 1982, Mysel's solicited Crella Magee's agreement that Mysel's could store her furs for the summer. Magee so agreed. Pursuant to an arrangement with Mysel's to pick up three furs from Magee, UPS delivered three empty boxes, which were labeled with unique call numbers, to Magee on May 25. Magee inserted a fur in each of the boxes. UPS then picked up the three boxes and gave Magee's husband three tickets bearing call numbers identical to those marked on the boxes. UPS delivered the boxes to Mysel's on May 26. A Mysel's employee signed for the boxes but did not check to be sure that each box had a fur in it. In July, Mysel's provided Magee with a storage receipt that showed only two furs. This storage receipt also contained a term that limited Mysel's liability for lost property to $100. Magee called Mysel's immediately and received assurances that the three furs were in storage.

When Magee went to pick up her three furs in October 1982, however, one of them—a blue fox jacket worth $3,400—was missing. Mysel's did not compensate Magee, arguing that its liability for lost articles was limited to $100. Magee then brought suit against Walbro, Mysel's, and UPS for breach of bailment and conversion. The trial court ruled for the defendants, and Magee appealed. (Magee voluntarily dismissed her case against UPS, so its liability was not involved in the appeal.) ∞

O'Connor, Justice Establishing a prima facie case of bailment raises a presumption of negligence by the defendant, which the defendant must rebut with evidence sufficient to support a finding of the nonexistence of the presumed fact. The trial court ruled that the evidence established a bailment between Magee and Walbro and Mysel's, thus raising the presumption of negligence. Walbro and Mysel produced no evidence, however, to rebut the presumption of negligence.

Based on the evidence presented, the trial court ruled that the lost jacket was delivered to Mysel Furs. Walbro and Mysel's argued that, assuming delivery of the jacket, any presumption of negligence was defeated by the procedures used in storing furs. The furs were placed in a locked, alarmed vault to which several, identifiable Mysel's employees had access. Mysel's then prepared and issued a storage receipt to the customer. Walbro presented no evidence to show that these procedures were followed for Magee's furs, and the storage receipt was not issued until six weeks after the jacket was delivered. It is reasonable to assume that the defendants' procedures and security precautions customarily resulted in the return of the customer's fur. Magee's fur was not returned; therefore, without showing more than the mere existence of safety and security measures, the defendants failed to rebut the presumption of negligence. Magee was therefore entitled to recover her damages.

Finally, the defendants asserted the defense of limitation of liability. Walbro and Mysel's argue that they effectively limited their liability to $100, citing *Schoen v. Wallace,* which upheld an agreement between a fur owner and fur storage company to limit the storage company's liability to $100. *Schoen* and [other cases] indicate, however, that the customer was aware of the limitation of liability before the furs were placed in storage. The *Schoen* decision was based in part on the fact that the plaintiff had dealt with the defendant before, knew of its insurance practices, [and] could have chosen another furrier had she found the limitation objectionable.

In the instant case, Magee testified that she was not told of the limitation until after the fur was lost. Defendants rely on the receipt of July 1982, which stated that liability was limited to $100. Magee should have known of the limitation after she received the receipt in July, but by that time her furs had been at Mysel's for six weeks.

The limitation does not apply in the instant case because Magee had no knowledge of the limitation before agreeing to store her furs. In *Schoen,* the court stated that it would be "unjust to permit the plaintiff to repudiate [the agreement to limit liability] because the coat was lost." In the instant case, it would be unjust to permit Mysel and Walbro to assert a limitation that was not made clear at the time that the bailment contract was made because the coat was lost. We therefore hold that the $100 limitation of liability is inapplicable in this case.

For the foregoing reasons, judgment in favor of the defendants is reversed, and this case is remanded to the trial court to enter judgment against Walbro and Mysel's and in favor of Magee in the amount of $3,400.

Reversed and remanded in favor of Magee.

Bailee's Liability for Misdelivery

The bailee is also liable to the bailor if he misdelivers the bailed property at the termination of the bailment. The property must be returned to the bailor or to someone specified by the bailor.

The bailee is in a dilemma if a third person, claiming to have rights that are superior to those of the bailor, demands possession of the bailed property. If the bailee refuses to deliver the bailed property to the third-party claimant and the claimant is entitled to its possession, the bailee is liable to the claimant. If the bailee delivers the bailed property to the third-party claimant and the claimant is not entitled to possession, the bailee is liable to the bailor. The circumstances may be such that the conflicting claims of the bailor and the third-party claimant can be determined only by judicial decision. In some cases, the bailee may protect himself by bringing the third-party claimant into a lawsuit along with the bailor so that all the competing claims can be adjudicated by the court before the bailee releases the property. This remedy is not always available, however.

Limits on Liability

Bailees may try to limit or relieve themselves of liability for the bailed property. Some examples include the storage receipt purporting to limit liability to $100 in the *Magee v. Walbro, Inc.* case, signs near checkrooms such as "Not responsible for loss of or damage to checked property," and disclaimers on claim checks such as "Goods left at owner's risk." The standards used to determine whether such limitations and disclaimers are enforceable are discussed in detail in Chapter 15.

Any attempt by the bailee to be relieved of liability for intentional wrongful acts is against public policy and will not be enforced. A bailee's ability to be relieved of liability for negligence is also limited. Courts look to see whether the dis-

claimer or limitation of liability was communicated to the bailor at the time of the bailment. Did the attendant point out the sign near the checkroom to the customer when her coat was checked? Did the parking lot attendant call the car owner's attention to the disclaimer on the back of the claim check?

If not, as in the *Magee* case, the court may hold that the disclaimer was not communicated to the bailor and did not become part of the bailment contract. Even if the bailor was aware of the disclaimer, it still may not be enforced on the ground that it is contrary to public policy.

If the disclaimer was offered on a take-it-or-leave-it basis and was not the subject of arm's-length bargaining, it is less likely to be enforced than if it has been negotiated and voluntarily agreed to by the parties. A bailee may be able to limit liability to a certain amount or to relieve himself of liability for certain perils. Ideally, the bailee will give the bailor a chance to declare a higher value and to pay an additional charge in order to be protected up to the declared value of the goods. Common carriers, such as railroads and trucking companies, often take this approach. Courts do not look with favor on efforts by a person to be relieved of liability for negligence. For this reason, terms limiting the liability of a bailee stand a better chance of being enforced than do terms completely relieving the bailee of liability.

An implied agreement as to the bailee's duties may arise from a prior course of dealing between the bailor and the bailee, or from the bailor's knowledge of the bailee's facilities or method of doing business. The bailee may, if he wishes, assume all the risks incident to the bailment and contract to return the bailed property undamaged or to pay for any damage to or loss of the property.

Right to Compensation

The express or implied contract creating the bailment controls whether the bailee has the right to receive compensation for keeping the property or must pay for having the right to use it. If the bailment is made as a favor, then the bailee is not entitled to compensation even though the bailment is for the sole benefit of the bailor. If the bailment is the rental of property, then the bailee must pay the agreed rental rate. If the bailment is for the storage or repair of property, then the bailee is entitled to the contract price for the storage or repair services. If no specific price was agreed on, but compensation was contemplated by the parties, the bailee is entitled to the reasonable value of the services provided.

In many instances, the bailee will have a lien (a charge against property to secure the payment of a debt) on the bailed property for the reasonable value of the services. For example, Silver takes a chair to Ace Upholstery to have it recovered. When the chair has been recovered, Ace has the right to keep it until the agreed price—or, if no price was set, the reasonable value of the work—is paid. This is an example of an **artisan's lien,** which is discussed in greater detail in Chapter 28.

Bailor's Liability for Defects in the Bailed Property

When personal property is rented or loaned, the bailor makes an implied warranty that the property has no hidden defects that make it unsafe for use. If the bailment is for the sole benefit of the bailee, the bailor is liable for injuries that result from defects in the bailed property only if the bailor knew about the defects and did not tell the bailee. For example, Price lends his car, which he knows has bad brakes, to Sloan. If Price does not tell Sloan about the bad brakes and Sloan is injured in an accident because the brakes fail, Price is liable for Sloan's injuries.

If the bailment is a bailment for mutual benefit, the bailor has a greater obligation. The bailor must use reasonable care in inspecting the property and seeing that it is safe for the purpose for which it is intended. The bailor is liable for injuries suffered by the bailee because of defects that the bailor either knew about or should have discovered through reasonable inspection. For example, Acme Rent-All, which rents trailers, does not inspect the trailers after they are returned. A wheel has come loose on a trailer that Acme rents to Hirsch. If the wheel comes off while Hirsch is using the trailer and the goods Hirsch is carrying in it are damaged, Acme is liable to Hirsch.

In addition, product liability doctrines that apply a higher standard of legal responsibility have been applied to bailors who are commercial lessors of personal property.[8] Express or implied warranties of quality under either Article 2 or Article 2A of the UCC may apply. Liability under these warranties does not depend on whether the bailor knew about or should have discovered the defect. The only question is whether the property's condition complied with the warranty. Some courts have also imposed strict liability on the commercial lessor-bailor of defective, unreasonably dangerous goods that cause personal injury or property damage to the lessee-bailee. This liability is imposed regardless of whether the lessor was negligent.

SPECIAL BAILMENTS

Common Carriers

Bailees that are common carriers are held to a higher level of responsibility than are bailees that are private carriers. Common carriers are licensed by governmental agencies to carry the property of anyone who requests the service. Airlines licensed by the Department of Transportation and trucks and buses licensed by the Interstate Commerce Commission are examples of common carriers. Private contract carriers carry goods only for persons selected by the carrier.

Both common carriers and private contract carriers are bailees. However, the law makes the common carrier a near-absolute insurer of the goods it carries. The common carrier is responsible for virtually any loss of or damage to goods entrusted to it. The common carrier can avoid responsibility only if it can show that the loss or damage was caused by one of the following:

1. An act of God.
2. An act of a public enemy.
3. An act or order of the government.
4. An act of the person who shipped the goods.
5. The nature of the goods themselves.

The common carrier is liable if goods entrusted to it are stolen by some unknown person, but not if the goods are destroyed when a tornado hits the warehouse. If goods are damaged because the shipper

---

[8]Product liability doctrines are discussed in Chapter 20.

Duties of Bailees and Bailors

TYPE OF BAILMENT	DUTIES OF BAILEE	DUTIES OF BAILOR
Sole Benefit of Bailee	1. Must use great care; liable for even slight negligence. 2. Must return goods to bailor or dispose of them at his direction. 3. May have duty to compensate bailor.	1. Must notify the bailee of any known defects.
Mutual Benefit	1. Must use reasonable care; liable for ordinary negligence. 2. Must return goods to bailor or dispose of them at his direction. 3. May have duty to compensate bailor.	1. Must notify bailee of all known defects and any defects that could be discovered on reasonable inspection. 2. Commercial lessors may be subject to warranties of quality and/or strict liability in tort. 3. May have duty to compensate bailee.
Sole Benefit of Bailor	1. Must use at least slight care; liable for gross negligence. 2. Must return goods to bailor or dispose of them at his direction.	1. Must notify bailee of all known defects and any hidden defects that are known or could be discovered on reasonable inspection. 2. May have duty to compensate bailee.

improperly packages or crates them, the carrier is not liable. Similarly, if perishable goods are not in suitable condition to be shipped and therefore deteriorate in the course of shipment, the carrier is not liable so long as it used reasonable care in handling them.

Common carriers are usually permitted to limit their liability to a stated value unless the bailor declares a higher value for the property and pays an additional fee.

Hotelkeepers

Hotelkeepers are engaged in the business of offering food and/or lodging to transient persons. They hold themselves out to serve the public and are obligated to do so. As is the common carrier, the hotelkeeper is held to a higher standard of care than that of the ordinary bailee. The hotelkeeper, however, is not a bailee in the strict sense of the word. The guest does not usually surrender the exclusive possession of his property to the hotelkeeper. Even so, the hotelkeeper is treated as the virtual insurer of the guest's property. The hotelkeeper is not liable for loss of or damage to property if she can show that it was caused by one of the following:

1. An act of God.
2. An act of a public enemy.

3. An act of a governmental authority.
4. The fault of a member of the guest's party.
5. The nature of the goods.

Most states have passed laws that limit the hotelkeeper's liability, however. Commonly, the law requires the hotel owner to post a notice advising guests that any valuables should be checked into the hotel vault. The hotelkeeper's liability is then limited, usually to a fixed amount, for valuables that are not so checked.

Safe-Deposit Boxes

If a person rents a safe-deposit box at a local bank and places some property in the box, the box and the property are in the physical possession of the bank. However, it takes both the renter's key and the key held by the bank to open the box. In most cases, the bank does not know the nature, amount, or value of the goods in the box. Although a few courts have held the rental of a safe-deposit box not to be a bailment, most courts have found that the renter of the box is a bailor and the bank is a bailee. As such, the bank is not an insurer of the contents of the box. It is obligated, however, to use due care and to come forward and explain loss of or damage to the property entrusted to it.

Involuntary Bailments

Suppose a person owns a cottage on a beach. After a violent storm, a sailboat washed up on his beach. As the finder of lost or misplaced property, he may be considered the **involuntary bailee** or **constructive bailee** of the sailboat. This relationship may arise when a person finds himself in possession of someone else's property without having agreed to accept possession.

The duties of the involuntary bailee are not well defined. The bailee does not have the right to destroy or use the property. If the true owner shows up, the property must be returned to him. Under some circumstances, the involuntary bailee may be under an obligation to assume control of the property or to take some minimal steps to ascertain the owner's identity, or both.

ETHICAL AND PUBLIC POLICY CONCERNS

1. Does a finder of lost or mislaid property have an ethical duty to look for the owner of the property? How effective are the legal principles that you learned in encouraging a finder to do so?

2. What part does ethical conduct play in determining whether a person acquires ownership of personal property by confusion? By accession?

3. You learned that in determining the degree of care a bailee must exercise over bailed property, courts traditionally have applied standards based on the amount of relative benefit the parties derive from the bailment. When both parties benefit, reasonable care is required; when the bailee alone benefits, great care is required; and when the bailor alone benefits, only slight care is required. Modern courts, however, seem to be moving in the direction of applying a standard of reasonable care to all bailments. Which approach is preferable, and why?

PROBLEMS AND PROBLEM CASES

1. In 1945, Lieber was serving in the U.S. Army. He was one of the first soldiers to occupy Munich, Germany. He and other soldiers entered Adolf Hitler's apartment and removed various items of Hitler's personal belongings. Lieber brought his share to his home in Louisiana. It included Hitler's uniform jacket and cap and some of his decorations and personal jewelry. Lieber's possession of these items was well known. There were several newspaper articles about them, and they were occasionally displayed to the public. Many years later, Lieber's chauffeur stole the collection and sold it to a dealer of historical material in New York. The dealer sold it to Mohawk Arms, which had no knowledge that it had been stolen. Lieber learned that Mohawk Arms had the collection and demanded that the company return it. Mohawk Arms claimed that it did not have to return the collection to Lieber because the collection properly belonged to the occupational military authority or to the Bavarian government and not to Lieber. Was Lieber entitled to the return of the collection that had been stolen from him?

2. First National Bank of Chicago (First Chicago) sold a number of used file cabinets on an "as is" basis to Zibton, an office supply and furniture dealer. Zibton later sold some of these cabinets to Strayve, who gave one of the cabinets—a locked one with no keys—to his friend, Richard Michael. Approximately six weeks later, Michael was moving the file cabinet in his garage. The cabinet fell over, and some of the locked drawers opened. Inside were more than 1,600 certificates of deposit (CDs), including seven recently matured CDs that had not been canceled or stamped paid. Those seven CDs were worth a total of more than $6 million. Six of them were payable to "Bearer." First Chicago had placed the CDs in the cabinet a few months earlier, when the responsibility for storing paid CDs was changed to a different unit of the bank. The CDs were moved from a vault to file cabinets at that time. Each drawer had been labeled with a card stating "Paid Negotiable CDs" and indicating the numbers of the CDs contained in the drawer. The new unit responsible for storing CDs had determined that it could not use the file cabinets, so the CDs were transferred to tote boxes. First Chicago employees randomly checked to determine whether the file cabinets were empty, and then transferred the cabinets to the warehouse for sale. After he discovered the CDs, Michael called the FBI, which took possession of them. Michael and his wife then filed a declaratory judgment action in an effort to have the court determine who owned the CDs. The Michaels contended that the CDs were abandoned property, and that they, as finders of the CDs, should therefore be considered the owners of the CDs. Were the Michaels correct in this contention?

3. Bernice Paset, a customer of the Old Orchard Bank, found $6,325 in currency on the seat of a chair in an examination booth in the bank's safety-deposit vault. The chair was partially under a table. Paset notified officers of the bank and turned the money over to them. She was told by bank officials that the bank would try to locate the owner and that she could have the money if the owner was not located within one year. The bank wrote to everyone who had been in the safety-deposit vault area either on the day of, or on the day preceding, the discovery. The bank's letter stated that some property had been found and invited the customers to describe any property they might have lost. No one reported the loss of any currency. The money remained unclaimed a year after it had been found. The bank refused to deliver the money to Paset, contending that it was mislaid, not lost, property and that it had a better right to it. Was the money mislaid property?

4. In October 1973, Richard Welton, a businessman in his late 60s, met Florence Gallagher, a widow in her late 40s. Welton subsequently underwent several operations for cancer. After he was released from the hospital, Gallagher devoted much time and attention to him. In 1975, she helped him operate an ice cream business he had purchased. Shortly thereafter, he moved into her house and spent considerable money fixing it up. Welton later moved out to live with Gallagher's niece, Sandra Kwock, a woman in her 20s. Kwock had agreed to take care of Welton for the rest of his life in return for his giving her $25,000 in bearer bonds. Kwock left town with the bonds, much to Welton's dismay. In April 1976, Welton moved back in with Gallagher, gave her $20,000 in bearer bonds, and told her to place them in her safe-deposit box. Gallagher said that he told her he wanted her to have them as a gift because she was much more deserving than her niece. Later in 1976, Welton and Gallagher ended their relationship. He moved out of her house and demanded that she return the bonds, but she refused. Had Welton made a completed *inter vivos* gift of the bonds to Gallagher?

5. Ochoa's Studebaker automobile was stolen. Eleven months later, the automobile somehow found its way into the hands of the U.S. government, which sold it to Rogers at a "junk" auction for $85. At the time it was purchased by Rogers, no part of the car was intact. It had no top except a part of the frame; it had no steering wheel, tires, rims, cushions, or battery; the motor, radiator, and gears were out of the car; one wheel was gone, as was one axle; the fenders were partly gone; and the frame was broken. It was no longer an automobile but a pile of broken and dismantled parts. Having purchased these parts, Rogers used them in the construction of a delivery truck at an expense of approximately $800. When the truck was completed, he put it to use in his furniture business. Several months later, Ochoa passed Rogers's place of business and recognized the vehicle from marks on the hood and the radiator. He discovered that the serial and engine numbers matched those of the car he had owned. Ochoa demanded the vehicle from Rogers, who refused to surrender it. Ochoa brought suit to recover possession of the property. In the alternative, he asked for the value of the vehicle at the time of the suit (allegedly $1,000) and for the value of the use of the car from the time Rogers purchased it from the government. Was Ochoa entitled to recover possession of his property, which Rogers had substantially improved?

6. Luis and Susan Bulas took their Mercedes-Benz to Bill Ussery Motors, Inc., for an oil change and routine maintenance. The technician who was servicing the car parked it in a lot across the street from Ussery's main facility. This lot, which was within view of the Coral Gables, Florida, police department, was used by Ussery for the servicing of vehicles and for employee parking. The technician was checking the Mercedes-Benz's transmission fluid when two women approached him. One woman was armed with a gun; the other carried a bottle of mace. They held the technician at gunpoint and stole the car. The Bulases filed a claim with their automobile insurer, State Farm Fire & Casualty Co., which paid the Bulases' claim. State Farm then sought to enforce its subrogation interest by suing Ussery on the theory that Ussery, as a bailee of the car, had been negligent and that this negligence led to the Bulases' loss. Should Ussery be held liable?

7. Georgie Simon entrusted 14 gold and silver coins to her ex-husband, Hardie Maloney, to take to a coin show in Atlanta, Georgia. He was to try to sell the coins, for which he would receive a 7 percent commission. Maloney traveled to the coin show along with his girlfriend, Ann Williams, and a male friend, Herbert Pellegrini, with whom he had previously traveled to 40 or 50 coin shows. Just before they got ready to leave the Waverly Hotel, where the show had been held, Maloney and Williams went up to Pellegrini's room. Pellegrini would not permit Williams to use the bathroom because he wanted to check out before the deadline and avoid being charged for another day. Williams and Maloney helped Pellegrini carry his three pieces of luggage to the lobby. While Pellegrini checked out, Williams went to the ladies' room in the lobby of the hotel. While Williams was in the bathroom, Maloney went to get his car, on the suggestion and insistence of Pellegrini. He initially resisted the suggestion because he was carrying a briefcase containing Georgie Simon's coins, as well as the coins he had brought to, and purchased at, the show. Maloney wanted to wait until they could all walk over to the car together for protection. However, after being assured by Pellegrini that he would watch the briefcase, Maloney went to get the car. Maloney set the briefcase down beside Pellegrini's three bags in front of the hotel. When Maloney returned with the car, Pellegrini walked up to the vehicle carrying all three pieces of his luggage. He left Maloney's briefcase in front of the hotel. When Maloney asked about the whereabouts of the briefcase, Pellegrini replied that he did not know where it was. It was never found. Georgie Simon brought suit against Maloney for $19,000, the value of the coins she had entrusted to him. Maloney, in turn, filed a claim against Pellegrini for the loss of those coins as well as for the $12,300 in coins that he had entrusted to Pellegrini. Was Pellegrini liable for the loss of the coins entrusted to him?

8. Pringle, the head of the drapery department at Wardrobe Cleaners, went to the Axelrods' home to inspect some dining room draperies for dry-cleaning purposes. He spent about 30 minutes looking at the drapes and inspecting both the drapes and the lining. He pointed out some roach spots on the lining that could not be removed by cleaning, but this was not of concern to the Axelrods. He did not indicate to them that the fabric had deteriorated from sunburn, age, dust, or air conditioning so as to make it unsuitable for dry cleaning. He took the drapes and had them dry cleaned. When the drapes were returned, they were unfit for use. The fabric had been a gold floral design on an eggshell-white background. When returned, it was a blotchy gold.

Wardrobe Cleaners stated that it was difficult to predict how imported fabrics would respond to the dry-cleaning process and that the company was not equipped to pretest the fabric to see whether it was colorfast. The Axelrods sued Wardrobe Cleaners for $1,000, the replacement value of the drapes. Was Wardrobe Cleaners liable for the damage caused to the drapes during the dry-cleaning process?

9. In April, Carter brought her fur coat to Reichlin Furriers for cleaning, glazing, and storage until the next winter season. She was given a printed form of receipt, upon the front of which an employee of Reichlin had written $100 as the value of the coat. There was no discussion of the value of the coat. Carter did not realize that such a value had been written on the receipt, which she did not read at the time. A space for the customer's signature on the front of the receipt was left blank. Below this space in prominent type appeared a notice to "see reverse side for terms and conditions." The other side of the receipt stated that it was a storage contract and that by its acceptance, the customer would be deemed to have agreed to its terms unless objections were given within 10 days. Fifteen conditions were listed. One of the conditions was as follows: "Storage charges are based upon valuation herein declared by the depositor, and amount recoverable for loss or damage to the article shall not exceed its actual value or the cost of repair or replacement with materials of like kind and quality or the depositor's valuation appearing in this receipt, whichever is less." In the fall of the year, after Carter had paid the bill for storage and other services on the coat, Reichlin informed her that the coat was lost. At that time, the fair market value of the coat was $450. Carter sued Reichlin for loss of the coat and sought $450 damages. Reichlin claimed that its liability was limited to $100. Is this correct?

10. Marvin Gooden checked into a Day's Inn in Atlanta, paying in advance for two days' lodging. The next day he temporarily left his room. He left behind, in the room, a paper bag filled with approximately $9,000. Shortly after Gooden left, housekeeper Mary Carter entered his room to clean it. Carter found the bag of money. Because she saw no other personal effects, Carter assumed that Gooden had checked out. She therefore turned the bag of money over to her supervisor, Vivian Clark. Clark gave the bag to Dempsey Wilson, who was responsible for general supervision and maintenance of the grounds. During the three years he had worked for Day's Inn, Wilson had occasionally been given items of value to turn in at the hotel's office. In the past, he had always turned in the items. This time, however, he absconded with the bag of money. There was a safe on the Day's Inn premises. Day's Inn had posted, on the door of Gooden's room, a notice concerning the safe's availability for use by guests who had valuables with them. Gooden, who had never sought the use of the safe, brought a tort action against Day's Inn, Clark, and Carter in an effort to collect $9,000 in damages. Day's Inn argued that it was protected against liability by the following Georgia statute: "The innkeeper may provide a safe or other place of deposit for valuable articles and, by posting a notice thereof, may require the guests of the innkeeper to place such valuable articles therein or the innkeeper shall be relieved from responsibility for such articles." Gooden contended, however, that the statute could not insulate an innkeeper from liability when the loss of a guest's valuables is occasioned by the negligent (or other tortious) conduct of the innkeeper's employees. Should Gooden prevail against Day's Inn, Clark, and Carter?

Real Property

L and's special importance in the law has long been recognized. In the agrarian society of previous eras, land served as the basic measure and source of wealth. In today's industrialized society, land functions not only as a source of food, clothing, and shelter but also as an instrument of commercial and industrial development. It is not surprising, then, that a complex body of law—the law of *real property*—exists regarding the ownership, acquisition, and use of land.

This chapter discusses the scope of real property and the various legal interests in it. In addition, the chapter examines the ways in which real property is transferred and the controls society places on an owner's use of real property. ∞

SCOPE OF REAL PROPERTY

Real property includes not only land but also things firmly attached to or embedded in land. Buildings and other permanent structures thus are considered real property. The owner of a tract of real property also owns the air above it, the minerals below its surface, and any trees or other vegetation growing on the property.[1]

Unlike readily movable personal property, real property is immovable or attached to something immovable. Distinguishing between real and per-

---

[1]Ownership of air above one's property is not an unlimited interest, however. Courts have held that the flight of aircraft above property does not violate the property owner's rights, so long as it does not unduly interfere with the owner's enjoyment of her land.

sonal property is important because rules of law governing real property transactions such as sale, taxation, and inheritance are frequently different from those applied to personal property transactions.

Fixtures

An item of personal property may, however, be attached to or used in conjunction with real property in such a way that it ceases being personal property and instead becomes part of the real property. This type of property is called a **fixture.**

Fixtures belong to the owner of the real property. One who provides or attaches fixtures to real property without a request to that effect from the owner of the real property is normally not entitled to compensation from the owner. A conveyance (transfer of ownership) of real property also conveys the fixtures associated with that property, even if the fixtures are not specifically mentioned.

People commonly install items of personal property on the real property they own or rent. Disputes may arise regarding rights to such property. Suppose that Jacobsen buys an elaborate ceiling fan and installs it in his home. When he sells the house to Orr, may Jacobsen remove the ceiling fan, or is it part of the home Orr has bought? Suppose that Luther, a commercial tenant, installs showcases and tracklights in the store she leases from Nelson. May Luther remove the showcases and the lights when her lease expires, or do the items now belong to Nelson? If the parties' contracts are silent on these matters, courts will resolve the cases by applying the law of fixtures. As later discussion will reveal, Jacobsen probably cannot remove the ceiling fan because it is likely to be considered part of the real property purchased by Orr. Luther, on the other hand, may be entitled to remove the showcases and the lights under the special rules governing trade fixtures.

Factors Indicating Whether an Item Is a Fixture
There is no mechanical formula for determining whether an item has become a fixture. Courts tend, however, to consider these factors:

1. *Attachment.* One factor helping to indicate whether an item is a fixture is the degree to which the item is **attached** or **annexed** to the real property. If firmly attached to the real property so that it cannot be removed without damaging the property, the item is likely to be considered a fixture. An item of personal property that may be removed with little or no injury to the property is less likely to be considered a fixture.

Actual physical attachment to real property is not necessary, however. A close physical connection between the item of personal property and the real property may enable a court to conclude that the item is **constructively annexed.** For example, heavy machinery or remote control devices for automatic garage doors may be considered fixtures even though they are not physically attached to real property.

2. *Adaptation.* Another factor to be considered is **adaptation**—the degree to which the item's use is necessary or beneficial to the use of the real property. Adaptation is a particularly relevant factor when the item is not physically attached to the real property or is only slightly attached. When an item would be of little value except for use with certain real property, the item is likely to be considered a fixture even if it is unattached or could easily be removed. For example, keys and custom-sized window screens and storm windows have been held to be fixtures.

3. *Intent.* The third factor to be considered is the **intent** of the person who installed the item. Intent is judged not by what that person subjectively intended, but by what the circumstances indicate he intended. To a great extent, intent is indicated by the annexation and adaptation factors. An owner of real property who improves it by attaching items of personal property presumably intended those items to become part of the real estate. If the owner does not want an attached item to be considered a fixture, he must specifically reserve the right to keep the item. For instance, if a seller of a house wants to keep an antique chandelier that has been installed in the house, she should either replace the chandelier before the house is shown to prospective purchasers or specify in the contract of sale that the chandelier will be excluded from the sale.

Ford v. Venard presents a typical judicial analysis of whether an item of personal property has become a fixture.

FORD v. VENARD   340 N.W.2d 270 (Iowa Sup. Ct. 1983)

I n 1973, Norman Van Sickle moved his double wide mobile home to a plot of land owned by Luelia Jedlicka. Van Sickle had the real estate landscaped, a foundation poured, concrete blocks set, and steel girders aligned on the blocks. After removing the hitches and wheels from the mobile home, he had the mobile home set on and hooked to the foundation. Thereafter, Van Sickle substantially modified his double-wide unit by welding it into a single unit, placing a roof over the entire building, and joining the exterior with siding. As a result, the structure could not be disassembled without tearing it apart and could not be moved as one unit except by a house mover.

Van Sickle had paid Jedlicka $500 as a down payment for the purchase of the land back in 1973, but had never made any further payments. He had never been asked to pay taxes and was told by Jedlicka that she paid them. Van Sickle had been told by the bank holding a security interest on the mobile home that the house would become part of Jedlicka's real estate after it was set on a foundation. Van Sickle did not consider himself the owner of the real estate; he believed the land belonged to Jedlicka.

In 1977, Henry Edsel Ford contracted with Jedlicka to buy the land. A clause in the Ford-Jedlicka contract specified that all "attached fixtures" were included as part of the real estate being sold. The question of ownership of the mobile home came to a head in 1982, when William Venard, a creditor of Van Sickle's, attempted to enforce a judgment against Van Sickle by attaching the mobile home and executing against it. Ford brought this action, claiming that he owned the mobile home and requesting an injunction to restrain Venard from executing against the mobile home. The trial court granted the injunction. Venard appealed. ∞

Harris, Justice   The question is whether the mobile home was a fixture included under the terms of the land contract between Jedlicka and Ford. We think it plainly was. Under our common law rule, personal property becomes a fixture when:

(1) it is actually annexed to the realty, or to something appurtenant thereto;

(2) it is put to the same use as the realty with which it is connected; and

(3) the party making the annexation intends to make a permanent accession to the freehold.

The intention of the party annexing the improvement is the "paramount factor" in determining whether the improvement is a fixture. Physical attachment of the structure to the soil or to an appurtenance thereto is not essential to make the structure a part of the realty. On the other hand, a building which cannot be removed without destruction of a substantial part of its value becomes almost unavoidably an integral part of the real estate.

Venard argues that Van Sickle's home was not physically annexed to the realty and that Van Sickle never intended for his home to be permanently attached to the freehold. Ford, on the other hand, relies on these facts: the home's tongues and wheels have been removed; the home was set on a foundation and girders; it has been extensively remodeled into a single unit; and its removal would be expensive and damaging. He points out that the home was used as a homestead, which is the use for which the realty had been appropriated. He points to the bank's advice to Van Sickle that his home would become the property of Jedlicka when set on her land.

We have found buildings to be fixtures in a number of cases. We are convinced the home became attached to the land. It could not be removed from its present location except in the sense that any permanent home could be. We hold that it has become an integral part of the real estate. The trial court was correct in ordering the issuance of the permanent injunction.

Affirmed in favor of Ford.

Express Agreement   If the parties to an express agreement have clearly stated their intent about whether a particular item is to be considered a fixture, a court will generally enforce that agreement. For example, the buyer and seller of a house might agree to permit the seller to remove a fence or shrubbery that would otherwise be considered a fixture.

Trade Fixtures   An exception to the usual fixture rules is recognized when a *tenant* attaches personal property to leased premises for the purpose of carrying on her trade or business. Such fixtures, called **trade fixtures,** remain the personal property of the tenant and may normally be removed at the termination of the lease. This trade fixtures exception encourages commerce and industry. It recognizes that the commercial tenant who affixed the item of personal property did not intend a permanent improvement of the leased premises.

The tenant's right to remove trade fixtures is subject to two limitations. First, the tenant cannot remove the fixtures if doing so would cause substantial damage to the landlord's realty. Second, the tenant must remove the fixtures by the end of the lease if the lease is for a definite period; if the lease is for an indefinite period, the tenant usually has a reasonable time after the expiration of the lease to remove the fixtures. Trade fixtures not removed within the appropriate time become the landlord's property.

Leases may contain terms expressly addressing the parties' rights in any fixtures. A lease might give the tenant the right to attach items or make other improvements, and to remove them later. The reverse may also be true. The lease could state that any improvements made or fixtures attached will become the landlord's property at the termination of the lease. Courts generally enforce parties' agreements on fixture ownership.

Security Interests in Fixtures   Special rules apply to personal property subject to a lien or security interest at the time it is attached to real property. Assume, for example, that a person buys a dishwasher on a time-payment plan from an appliance store and has it installed in his kitchen. To protect itself, the appliance store takes a security interest in the dishwasher and perfects that interest by filing a financing statement in the appropriate real estate records office within the period of time specified by the Uniform Commercial Code. The appliance store then is able to remove the dishwasher if the buyer defaults in his payments. The store could be liable, however, to third parties such as prior real estate mortgagees for any damage removal of the dishwasher caused to the real estate. The rules governing security interests in personal property that will become fixtures are explained more fully in Chapter 28.

CONCEPT REVIEW

Fixtures

Concept	A *fixture* is an item of personal property attached to or used in conjunction with real property in such a way that it is treated as being part of the real property.
Significance	A conveyance of the real property will also convey the fixtures on that property.
Factors Considered in Determining Whether Property Is a Fixture	1. Attachment: Is the item physically attached or closely connected to the real property? 2. Adaptation: How necessary or beneficial is the item to the use of the real property? 3. Intent: Did the person who installed the item manifest intent for the property to become part of the real property?
Express Agreement	Express agreements clearly stating intent about whether property is a fixture are generally enforceable.
Trade Fixtures (Tenants' Fixtures)	Definition of *trade fixture:* personal property attached to leased real property by a tenant for the purpose of carrying on his trade or business. Trade fixtures can be removed and retained by the tenant at the termination of the lease except when any of the following applies: 1. Removal would cause substantial damage to the landlord's real property. 2. Tenant fails to remove the fixtures by the end of the lease (or within a reasonable time, if the lease is for an indefinite period of time). 3. An express agreement between the landlord and tenant provides otherwise.

RIGHTS AND INTERESTS IN REAL PROPERTY

When we think of real property ownership, we normally envision one person owning all of the rights in a particular piece of land. Real property, however, involves a bundle of rights subject to ownership—sometimes by different people. This discussion examines the most common forms of present *possessory interests* (rights to exclusive possession of real property): **fee simple absolute** and **life estate.** It also explores the various ways in which two or more persons may share ownership of a possessory interest. Finally, it discusses the interests and rights one may have in another person's real property, such as the right to use the property or restrict the way the owner uses it.

Estates in Land

The term **estate** is used to describe the nature of a person's ownership interest in real property. Estates in land are classified as either **freehold estates** or **nonfreehold estates.** Nonfreehold (or leasehold) estates are those held by persons who lease real property. They will be discussed in the next chapter, which deals with landlord–tenant law. Freehold estates are ownership interests of uncertain duration. The most common types of freehold estates are fee simple absolute and life estates.

Fee Simple Absolute   The **fee simple absolute** is what we normally think of as "full ownership" of land. One who owns real property in fee simple absolute has the right to possess and use the property for an unlimited period of time, subject only to governmental regulations or private restrictions. She also has the unconditional power to dispose of the property during her lifetime or upon her death. A person who owns land in fee simple absolute may grant many rights to others without giving up fee simple ownership. For example, she may grant a mortgage on the property to a party who has loaned her money, lease the property to a tenant, or grant rights such as those to be discussed later in this section.

Life Estate   The property interest known as a **life estate** gives a person the right to possess and use property for a time measured by his or another person's lifetime. For example, if Haney has a life estate (measured by his life) in a tract of land known as Greenacre, he has the right to use Greenacre for the remainder of his life. At Haney's death, the property will revert to the person who conveyed the estate to him or will pass to some other designated person. Although a life tenant such as Haney has the right to use the property, he is obligated not to commit acts that would result in permanent injury to the property.

Co-Ownership of Real Property

Co-ownership of real property exists when two or more persons share the same ownership interest in the same property. The co-owners do not have separate rights to any portion of the real property; each has a share in the whole property. Seven types of co-ownership are recognized in the United States.

Tenancy in Common   Persons who own property under a **tenancy in common** have undivided interests in the property and equal rights to possess it. When property is transferred to two or more persons without specification of their co-ownership form, it is presumed that they acquire the property as tenants in common. The respective ownership interests of the tenants in common may be, but need not be, equal. One tenant, for example, could have a two-thirds ownership interest in the property, with the other tenant having a one-third interest.

Each tenant in common has the right to possess and use the property. Individual tenants, however, cannot exclude the other tenants in common from also possessing and using the property. If the property is rented or otherwise produces income, each tenant is entitled to share in the income in proportion to her ownership share. Similarly, each tenant must pay her proportionate share of property taxes and necessary repair costs. If a tenant in sole possession of the property receives no rents or profits from the property, she is not required to pay rent to her cotenant unless her possession is adverse to or inconsistent with her cotenant's property interests.

A tenant in common may dispose of his interest in the property during life and at death. Similarly, his interest is subject to his creditors' claims. When a tenant dies, his interest passes to his heirs or, if he has made a will, to the person or persons specified in the will. Suppose Peterson and Sievers own Blackacre as tenants in common. Sievers dies, having executed a valid will in which he leaves his

Blackacre interest to Johanns. In this situation, Peterson and Johanns become tenants in common.

Tenants in common may sever the cotenancy by agreeing to divide the property or, if they are unable to agree, by petitioning a court for *partition.* The court will physically divide the property if that is feasible, so that each tenant receives her proportionate share. If physical division is not feasible, the court will order that the property be sold and that the proceeds be appropriately divided.

Joint Tenancy   A **joint tenancy** is created when equal interests in real property are conveyed to two or more persons by means of a document specifying that they are to own the property as joint tenants. The rights of use, possession, contribution, and partition are the same for a joint tenancy as for a tenancy in common. The joint tenancy's distinguishing feature is that it gives the owners the **right of survivorship,** which means that upon the death of a joint tenant, the deceased tenant's interest automatically passes to the surviving joint tenant(s). The right of survivorship makes it easy for a person to transfer property at death without making a will. For example, Devaney and Osborne purchase Redacre and take title as joint tenants. At Devaney's death, his Redacre interest will pass to Osborne even if Devaney did not have a will setting forth such an intent. By the same token, even if Devaney had a will that purported to leave his Redacre interest to someone other than Osborne, the will's Redacre provision would be ineffective.

A joint tenant may mortgage, sell, or give away her interest in the property during her lifetime. Her interest in the property is subject to her creditors' claims. When a joint tenant transfers her interest, the joint tenancy is severed and a tenancy in common is created as to the share affected by the transaction. When a joint tenant sells her interest to a third person, the purchaser becomes a tenant in common with the remaining joint tenant(s).

Tenancy by the Entirety   Approximately half of the states permit married couples to own real property under a **tenancy by the entirety.** This tenancy is essentially a joint tenancy with the added requirement that the owners be married. As does the joint tenancy, the tenancy by the entirety features the right of survivorship. Neither spouse can transfer the property by will if the other is still living. Upon the death of the husband or wife, the property passes automatically to the surviving spouse.[2]

A tenancy by the entirety cannot be severed by the act of only one of the parties. Neither spouse can transfer the property unless the other one also signs the deed. Thus, a creditor of one tenant cannot claim an interest in that person's share of property held in tenancy by the entirety. Divorce, however, severs a tenancy by the entirety and transforms it into a tenancy in common. Figure 1 compares the features

---

[2]In states that do not recognize the tenancy by the entirety, married couples often own real property in joint tenancy, but they are not required to elect that co-ownership form.

FIGURE **I**

Tenancy in Common, Joint Tenancy, and Tenancy by the Entirety

	TENANCY IN COMMON	JOINT TENANCY	TENANCY BY THE ENTIRETY
Equal Possession and Use?	Yes	Yes	Yes
Share Income?	Yes	Yes	Presumably
Contribution Requirement?	Generally	Generally	Generally
Free Conveyance of Interest?	Yes; transferee becomes tenant in common	Yes, but joint tenancy is severed on conveyance and reverts to tenancy in common	Both must agree; divorce severs tenancy
Effect of Death?	Interest transferable at death by will or inheritance	Right of survivorship; surviving joint tenant takes decedent's share	Right of survivorship; surviving spouse takes decedent's share

of tenancy in common, joint tenancy, and tenancy by the entirety.

Community Property   A number of western and southern states recognize the **community property** system of co-ownership of property by married couples. This type of co-ownership assumes that marriage is a partnership in which each spouse contributes to the family's property base. Property acquired during the marriage through a spouse's industry or efforts is classified as *community* property. Each spouse has an equal interest in such property regardless of who produced or earned the property. Because each spouse has an equal share in community property, neither can convey community property without the other's joining in the transaction. Various community property states permit the parties to dispose of their interests in community property at death. The details of each state's community property system vary, depending on the specific provisions of that state's statutes.

Not all property owned by a married person is community property, however. Property a spouse owned before marriage or acquired during marriage by gift or inheritance is *separate* property. Neither spouse owns a legal interest in the other's separate property. Property exchanged for separate property also remains separately owned.

Tenancy in Partnership   When a partnership takes title to property in the partnership's name, the co-ownership form is called **tenancy in partnership.** This form of co-ownership is discussed in Chapter 36.

Condominium Ownership   Condominiums have become very common in the United States in recent years, even in locations outside urban and resort areas. Under condominium ownership, a purchaser takes title to her individual unit and becomes a tenant in common with other unit owners in shared facilities such as hallways, elevators, swimming pools, and parking areas. The condominium owner pays property taxes on her individual unit and makes a monthly payment for the maintenance of the common areas. She may generally mortgage or sell her unit without the other unit owners' approval. For federal income tax purposes, the condominium owner is treated as if she owned a single-family home, and is thus allowed to deduct her property taxes and mortgage interest expenses.

Cooperative Ownership   In a cooperative, a building is owned by a corporation or group of persons. One who wants to buy an apartment in the building purchases stock in the corporation and holds his apartment under a long-term, renewable lease called a *proprietary lease.* Frequently, the cooperative owner must obtain the other owners' approval to sell or sublease his unit.

INTERESTS IN REAL PROPERTY OWNED BY OTHERS

In various situations, a person may hold a legally protected interest in real property owned by someone else. Such interests, to be discussed below, are not possessory because they do not give their holder the right to complete dominion over the land. Rather, they give him the right to use another person's property or to limit the way in which the owner uses the property.

Easements

An **easement** is the right to make certain uses of another person's property (*affirmative easement*) or the right to prevent another person from making certain uses of his own property (*negative easement*). The right to run a sewer line across someone else's property would be an affirmative easement. Suppose an easement prevents Rogers from erecting, on his land, a structure that would block his neighbor McFeely's solar collector. Such an easement would be negative in nature.

If an easement qualifies as an **easement appurtenant,** it will pass with the land. This means that if the owner of the land benefited by an easement appurtenant sells or otherwise conveys the property, the new owner also acquires the right contemplated by the easement. An easement appurtenant is primarily designed to benefit a certain tract of land, rather than merely giving an individual a personal right. For example, Agnew and Nixon are next-door neighbors. They share a common driveway that runs along the borderline of their respective properties. Each has an easement in the portion of the driveway that lies on the other's property. If Agnew sells his property to Ford, Ford also obtains the easement in the driveway portion on Nixon's land. Nixon, of course, still has an easement in the driveway portion on Ford's land.

Creation of Easements

Easements may be acquired in any of the following ways:

1. *By grant.* When an owner of property expressly provides an easement in his property to another while retaining ownership of the property, he is said to **grant** an easement. For example, Monroe may sell or give Madison, who owns adjoining property, the right to go across Monroe's land to reach an alley behind that land.

2. *By reservation.* When one transfers ownership of her land but retains the right to use it for some specified purpose, she is said to **reserve** an easement in the land. For example, Smythe sells land to Jones but reserves the mineral rights to the property as well as an easement to enter the land to remove the minerals.

3. *By prescription.* An easement by **prescription** is created when one person uses another's land openly, continuously, and in a manner adverse to the owner's rights for a period of time specified by state statute (the necessary period of time varying state to state). In such a situation, the property owner presumably is on notice that someone else is acting as if she possesses rights to use the property. If the property owner does not take action during the statutory period to stop the other person from making use of his property, he may lose his right to stop that use. Suppose, for instance, that State X allows easements by prescription to be obtained through 15 years of prescriptive use. Tara, who lives in State X, uses the driveway of her next-door neighbor, Kyle. Tara does this openly, on a daily basis, and without Kyle's permission. If this use by Tara continues for the 15-year period established by statute and Kyle takes no action to stop Tara within that time span, Tara will obtain an easement by prescription. In that event, Tara will have the right to use the driveway not only while Kyle owns the property but also when Kyle sells the property to another party. Easements by prescription resemble *adverse possession,* a concept discussed later in this chapter.

4. *By implication.* Sometimes, easements are implied by the nature of the transaction rather than created by express agreement of the parties. Such easements, called **easements by implication,** take either of two forms: easements by prior use and easements by necessity.

An *easement by prior use* is created when land is subdivided and a path, road, or other apparent and beneficial use exists when part of the land is conveyed to another person. In this situation, the new owner of the conveyed portion of the land has an easement to continue using the path, road, or other prior use running across the nonconveyed portion of the land. Assume, for example, that a private road runs through Greenacre from north to south, linking the house located on Greenacre's northern portion to the public highway that lies south of Greenacre. Douglas, the owner of Greenacre, sells the northern portion to Kimball. On these facts, Kimball has an easement by implication to continue using the private road even where it runs across the portion of Greenacre retained by Douglas. To prevent such an easement from arising, Douglas and Kimball would need to have specified in their contract of sale that the easement would not exist.

An *easement by necessity* is created when real property once held in common ownership is subdivided in such a fashion that the only reasonable way a new owner can gain access to her land is through passage over another's land that was once part of the same tract. Such an easement is based on the necessity of obtaining access to property. Assume, for instance, that Tinker, the owner of Blackacre, sells Blackacre's northern 25 acres to Evers and its southern 25 acres to Chance. In order to have any reasonable access to her property, Chance must use a public road that runs alongside and just beyond the northern border of the land now owned by Evers; Chance must then go across Evers's property to reach hers. On these facts, Chance is entitled to an easement by necessity to cross Evers's land in order to go to and from her property.

Easements and the Statute of Frauds   As interests in land, easements are potentially within the coverage of the statute of frauds. To be enforceable, an express agreement granting or reserving an easement must be evidenced by a suitable writing signed by the party to be charged.[3] An express grant of an easement normally must be executed with the same formalities observed in executing the grant of a fee simple interest. However, easements not granted expressly (such as easements by prior use, necessity,

---

[3]Chapter 16 discusses the statute of frauds and compliance with the writing requirement it imposes when it is applicable.

or prescription) are enforceable despite the lack of a writing.

Profits

A **profit** is a right to enter another person's land and remove some product or part of the land. Timber, gravel, minerals, and oil are among the products and parts frequently made the subject of profits. Generally governed by the same rules applicable to easements, profits are sometimes called *easements with a profit*.

Licenses

A **license** is a temporary right to enter another's land for a specific purpose. Ordinarily, licenses are more informal than easements. Licenses may be created orally or in any other manner indicating the landowner's permission for the licensee to enter the property. Because licenses are considered to be personal rights, they are not true interests in land. The licensor may revoke a license at his will unless the license is coupled with an interest (such as the licensee's ownership of personal property located on the licensor's land) or the licensee has paid money or provided something else of value either for the license or in reliance on its existence. For example, Branch pays Leif $900 for certain trees on Leif's land. Branch is to dig up the trees and haul them to her own property for transplanting. Branch has an irrevocable license to enter Leif's land to dig up and haul away the trees.

Restrictive Covenants

Within certain limitations, real estate owners may create enforceable agreements that restrict the use of real property. These private agreements are called **restrictive covenants.** For example, Grant owns two adjacent lots. She sells one to Lee subject to the parties' agreement that Lee will not operate any liquor-selling business on the property. This use restriction appears in the deed Grant furnishes Lee. As another illustration, a subdivision developer sells lots in the subdivision and places a provision in each lot's deed regarding the minimum size of house to be built on the property.

The validity and enforceability of such private restrictions on the use of real property depend on the purpose, nature, and scope of the restrictions. A restraint that violates a statute or other expression of public policy will not be enforced. For example, the federal Fair Housing Act (discussed later in this chapter) would make unlawful an attempt by a seller or lessor of residential property to refuse to sell or rent to certain persons because of an existing restrictive covenant that purports to disqualify those prospective buyers or renters on the basis of their race, color, religion, sex, handicap, familial status, or national origin.

Public policy generally favors the unlimited use and transfer of land. A restrictive covenant therefore is unenforceable if it effectively prevents the sale or transfer of the property. Similarly, ambiguous language in a restrictive covenant is construed in favor of the less restrictive interpretation. A restraint is enforceable, however, if it is clearly expressed and neither unduly restrictive of the use and transfer of the property nor otherwise violative of public policy. Restrictions usually held enforceable include those relating to minimum lot size, building design and size, and maintenance of an area as a residential community.

An important and frequently arising question is whether subsequent owners of property are bound by a restrictive covenant even though they were not parties to the original agreement that established the covenant. Under certain circumstances, restrictive covenants are said to "run with the land" and thus bind subsequent owners of the restricted property. For a covenant to run with the land, it must have been *binding* on the original parties to it, and those parties must have *intended that the covenant bind their successors*. The covenant must also *"touch and concern"* the restricted land. This means that the covenant must involve the use, value, or character of the land, rather than being merely a personal obligation of one of the original parties. In addition, a covenant will not bind a subsequent purchaser unless she had notice of the covenant's existence when she took her interest. This notice would commonly be provided by the recording of the deed (a subject discussed later in this chapter) or other document containing the covenant.

Restrictive covenants may be enforced by the parties to them, by persons meant to benefit from them, and—if the covenants run with the land—by successors of the original parties to them. If restrictive covenants amounting to a general building scheme are contained in a subdivision plat (recorded description of a subdivision), property owners in the subdivision may be able to enforce them against noncomplying property owners.

Mains Farm Homeowners Association v. Worthington illustrates the difficult interpretation, enforceability, and public policy questions sometimes presented by litigation over restrictive covenants that run with the land.

MAINS FARM HOMEOWNERS ASSOCIATION v. WORTHINGTON   854 P.2d 1072 (Wash. Sup. Ct. 1993)

A *declaration of restrictive covenants for the platted Mains Farm subdivision was recorded in 1962. Worthington purchased a residential lot in Mains Farm in 1987. A house already existed on the property. Before purchasing, Worthington obtained and read a copy of the restrictive covenants, which stated, in pertinent part, that all lots in Mains Farm "shall be designated as 'Residence Lots' and shall be used for single family residential purposes only." Worthington later began occupying the residence along with four adults who paid her for 24-hour protective supervision and care. These four adults, who were not related to Worthington, were unable to do their own housekeeping, prepare their own meals, or attend to their personal hygiene. In providing this supervision and care on a for-profit basis, Worthington complied with the licensing and inspection requirements established by Washington law governing such enterprises.*

The Mains Farm Homeowners Association (Association), which consisted of owners of property in the subdivision, filed suit against Worthington and asked the court to enjoin her from using her property as an adult family home business. Association asserted that Worthington's use violated the restrictive covenants quoted above. The trial court granted Association's motion for summary judgment and issued the requested injunction against Worthington's use. The Washington Court of Appeals affirmed. Worthington appealed to the Washington Supreme Court. Various organizations representing the interests of disabled adults submitted amicus curiae (friend of the court) briefs urging reversal. ⌒

Brachtenbach, Justice *Before* defendant Worthington bought the premises, she *read* the restrictive covenants. Written opposition by other property owners was made known to her immediately after her purchase. Despite that knowledge, Worthington applied for a building permit to add a fifth bedroom to the house. She was advised by the county that her intended facility did not comply with applicable zoning. Worthington later obtained the permit by stating that only her family would be living with her. In her words: "I told them what they wanted to hear." These equitable considerations must be kept in mind when we interpret the restrictive covenants at issue here. Our analysis leads to the conclusion that Worthington's commercial use is prohibited.

To reach this conclusion, we consider the meaning of "single family." The cases interpreting "family" are legion. Any of the cases must be used with caution. Some involve a state statute which bears a different relationship to zoning powers than to vested property rights embodied in a restrictive covenant. No purpose will be served by examining and comparing in detail the numerous cases which define "family." Because of the widely differing documents being interpreted, the contexts in which the word is used, and the fact-specific circumstances, it is impossible to arrive at a single, all-purpose definition of "family." The possibilities range from the traditional notion of persons related by blood, marriage, or adoption to the broader concept of a group of people who live, sleep, cook, and eat upon the premises as a single housekeeping unit. Likewise, attempting to use one of the many dictionary classifications solves nothing. For similar reasons, the use of a phrase or two out of a dictionary to define "residential" for purposes of this covenant is not acceptable.

Some reflection leads us to attribute certain characteristics to a concept of "family," even in an extended sense. These include: (1) a sharing of responsibilities among the members and a mutual caring whether physical or emotional, (2) some commonality whether it be friendship, shared employment, mutual social or political interest, (3) some degree of existing or contemplated permanency to the relationship, and (4) a recognition of some common purpose—persons brought together by reasons other than a referral by a state agency.

Here, we have four persons, all strangers before arriving at this residence. By law, they cannot be related to Worthington by birth, adoption, or marriage. By law, they cannot be below the age of 18. By regulatory definition, they must require 24-hour protective supervision and care. Worthington could not form this "family" without a license from the State, which must approve the site and is free to inspect it. Worthington meets these qualifications and provides around-the-clock care as a means of making a living.

These are not the characteristics of a single family residence. Our primary goal is to ascertain the intent of the restrictive covenants and to accord the words their ordinary and common usage. The reasonable expectations of the other lot owners who bought their family houses in reliance on the long recorded covenants would not include a State-licensed, 24-hour operating business. In this case, Worthington's main use of her property is not to provide a single family residence, but to provide 24-hour protective care and supervision in exchange for money. It must therefore be concluded that the other lot owners are entitled in equity to the injunction granted by the trial court.

As an alternative ground for reversing the trial court, Worthington argues that the restrictive covenant violates a legislative declaration of public policy and is therefore void. The public policy question should not be resolved in this case, for various reasons. First, the record made in the trial court is not adequate to identify the facts and bases upon which such a significant public policy should be considered. It is true that the Legislature has found "that adult family homes are an important part of the state's long-term care system" [citation to statute omitted]. Unfortunately, this record shows little more. We know that the Legislature has not implemented this finding beyond declaring that such homes are considered residential for *zoning* purposes. We know nothing of the number of persons qualified for adult family homes or of whether that need is being met. We know nothing of the situation along those lines in the community or county in which the Mains Farm subdivision is located. We do not know whether there exists an adequate supply of adult family homes in areas not subject to restrictive covenants. We are unaware whether efforts by individual or governmental units have been successful in locating such homes either without neighborhood opposition or by successful negotiation with concerned owners. We have not been made aware of what coordinated efforts, if any, are being made by state or local agencies to establish adult family homes. All of these considerations would be relevant to any possible court finding that a significant public policy overrides the existing restrictive covenants at issue in this case.

In addition, the statute relied upon by Worthington as the source of a legislative declaration of public policy favoring adult family homes was not effective until after the written opinion of the trial court, and was not cited to the trial court. Moreover, the statute, in stating that an adult family home should be permitted in an area zoned for single-family dwellings, is by its very terms limited to *zoning*. When the Legislature intends to affect a *private land use restriction* (i.e., a covenant) as compared to *zoning,* it normally does so explicitly.

The cases from other jurisdictions cited by Worthington either do not reach the policy conflict presented here or are based upon entirely different statutory direction or even constitutional dictates. The various amici curiae raise a claimed violation of the federal Fair Housing Act. We do not consider issues raised first and only by amicus.

We hold that under the equities of these particular facts, the discretionary grant of an injunction was proper. We caution that the interpretation of a particular restrictive covenant is largely dependent upon the facts of the case at hand. Our holding should not be construed as an encompassing declaration concerning covenants and uses under other circumstances. Likewise, our rejection of the claimed public policy is limited to the facts herein, especially due to the record's lack of any comprehensive presentation of governmental goals, efforts, needs, and successes existing in fact.

Injunction in favor of Association and against Worthington's use of property affirmed.

Termination of Restrictive Covenants Restrictive covenants may be terminated in a variety of ways, including voluntary relinquishment or *waiver.* They may also be terminated *by their own terms* (such as when the covenant specifies that it is to exist for a certain length of time) or *by dramatically* *changed circumstances.* If Oldcodger's property is subject, for instance, to a restrictive covenant allowing only residential use, the fact that all of the surrounding property has come to be used for industrial purposes may operate to terminate the covenant. When a restrictive covenant has been terminated or held invalid, the deed containing the restriction remains a valid instrument of transfer but is treated as if the restriction had been removed from the document.

ACQUISITION OF REAL PROPERTY

Title to real property may be obtained in various ways, including purchase, gift, will or inheritance, tax sale, and adverse possession. Original title to land in the United States was acquired either from the federal government or from a country that held the land prior to its acquisition by the United States. The land in the 13 original colonies had been granted by the king of England either to the colonies or to certain individuals. The states ceded the land in the Northwest Territory to the federal government, which in turn issued grants or patents of land. Original ownership of much of the land in Florida and the southwest came by grants from Spain's rulers.

Acquisition by Purchase

Selling one's real property is a basic ownership right. Unreasonable restrictions on an owner's right to sell her property are considered unenforceable as against public policy. Most owners of real property acquired title by purchasing the property. Each state sets the requirements for proper conveyances of real property located in that state. The various elements of selling and buying real property are discussed later in this chapter.

Acquisition by Gift

Real property ownership may be acquired by gift. For a gift of real property to be valid, the donor must deliver a properly executed deed to the property to the donee or to some third person who is to hold it for the donee. Neither the donee nor the third person needs to take actual possession of the property. The gift's essential element is delivery of the deed. Suppose that Fields executes a deed to the family farm and leaves it in his safe-deposit box for delivery to his daughter (the intended donee) when he dies. The attempted gift will not be valid, because Fields did not deliver the gift during his lifetime.

Acquisition by Will or Inheritance

The owner of real property generally has the right to dispose of the property by will. The requirements for a valid will are discussed in Chapter 26. If the owner of real property dies without a valid will, the property passes to his heirs as determined under the laws of the state in which the property is located.

Acquisition by Tax Sale

If taxes assessed on real property are not paid when due, they become a *lien* on the property. This lien has priority over other claims to the land. If the taxes remain unpaid, the government may sell the land at a tax sale. Although the purchaser at the tax sale acquires title to the property, a number of states have statutes giving the original owner a limited time (such as a year) within which to buy the property from the tax sale purchaser for the price paid by the purchaser, plus interest.

Acquisition by Adverse Possession

Each state has a statute of limitations that gives an owner of land a specific number of years within which to bring suit to regain possession of her land from someone who is trespassing on it. This period varies from state to state, generally ranging from 5 to 20 years. If someone wrongfully possesses land and acts as if he were the owner, the actual owner must take steps to have the possessor ejected from the land. If the owner fails to do this within the statutory period, she loses her right to eject the possessor.

Assume, for example, that Titus owns a vacant lot next to Holdeman's house. Holdeman frequently uses the vacant lot for a variety of activities and appears to be the property's only user. In addition, Holdeman regularly mows and otherwise maintains the vacant lot. He has also placed a fence around it. By continuing such actions and thus staying in possession of Titus's property for the statutory period (and by meeting each other requirement about to be discussed), Holdeman may position himself to acquire title to the land by **adverse possession.**

To acquire title by adverse possession, one must possess land in a manner that puts the true owner on notice of the owner's cause of action against the possessor. The adverse possessor's acts of possession must be (1) *open,* (2) *actual,* (3) *continuous,* (4) *exclusive,* and (5) *hostile* (or adverse) *to the owner's rights.* The hostility element is not a matter of subjective intent. Rather, it means that the adverse possessor's acts of possession must be inconsistent with the owner's rights. If a person is in possession of another's property under a lease, as a cotenant, or with the permission of the owner, his possession is not hostile. In some states, the possessor of land must also pay the property taxes in order to gain title by adverse possession.

It is not necessary that the same person occupy the land for the statutory period. The periods of possession of several adverse possessors may be "tacked" together when calculating the period of possession if each possessor claimed rights from another possessor. The possession must, however, be continuous for the requisite time.

TRANSFER BY SALE

Steps in a Sale

The major steps normally involved in the sale of real property are:

1. Contracting with a real estate broker to locate a buyer.
2. Negotiating and signing a contract of sale.
3. Arranging for the financing of the purchase and satisfying other requirements, such as having a survey conducted or acquiring title insurance.
4. Closing the sale, which involves payment of the purchase price and transfer of the deed, as well as other matters.
5. Recording the deed.

Contracting with a Real Estate Broker

Although engaging a real estate broker is not a legal requirement for the sale of real property, it is common for one who wishes to sell his property to "list" the property with a broker. A listing contract empowers the broker to act as the seller's agent in procuring a ready, willing, and able buyer and in managing details of the property transfer. A number of states' statutes of frauds require listing contracts to be evidenced by a writing and signed by the party to be charged.

Real estate brokers are regulated by state and federal law. They owe *fiduciary duties* (duties of trust and confidence) to their clients. Chapter 34 contains additional information regarding the duties imposed on such agents.

Types of Listing Contracts Listing contracts specify such matters as the listing period's duration, the terms on which the seller will sell, and the amount and terms of the broker's commission. There are different types of listing contracts.

1. *Open listing.* Under an open listing contract, the broker receives a *nonexclusive* right to sell the property. This means that the seller and third parties (for example, other brokers) also are entitled to find a buyer for the property. The broker operating under an open listing is entitled to a commission only if he was the first to find a ready, willing, and able buyer.

2. *Exclusive agency listing.* Under an exclusive agency listing, the broker earns a commission if he *or any other agent* finds a ready, willing, and able buyer during the period of time specified in the contract. Thus, the broker operating under such a listing would have the right to a commission even if another broker actually procured the buyer. Under the exclusive agency listing, however, the seller has the right to sell the property himself without being obligated to pay the broker a commission.

3. *Exclusive right to sell.* An exclusive right to sell contract provides the broker the exclusive right to sell the property for a specified period of time and entitles her to a commission no matter who procured the buyer. Under this type of listing, a seller must pay the broker her commission even if it was the seller or some third party who found the buyer during the duration of the listing contract.

Contract of Sale

The contract formation, performance, assignment, and remedies principles about which you read in earlier chapters apply to real estate sales contracts. Such contracts identify the parties and subject property, and set forth the purchase price, the type of deed the purchaser will receive, the items of personal property (if any) included in the sale, and other important aspects of the parties' transaction. Real estate sales contracts often make the closing of the sale contingent on the buyer's obtaining financing at a specified rate of interest, on the seller's procurement of a survey and title insurance, and on the property's passing a termite inspection. Because they are within the statute of frauds, real estate sales contracts must be evidenced by a suitable writing signed by the party to be charged in order to be enforceable.

Fair Housing Act

The Fair Housing Act, enacted by Congress in 1968 and substantially revised in 1988, is designed to prevent discrimination in the housing market. Its provisions apply to real estate brokers, sellers (other than those selling their own single-family dwellings without the use of a broker), lenders, lessors, and appraisers. Originally, the act prohibited discrimination on the basis of race, color, religion, sex, and national origin. The 1988 amendments added handicap and "familial status" to this list. The familial status category was intended to prevent discrimination in the housing market against pregnant women and families with children.[4] "Adult" or "senior citizen" communities restricting residents' age do not violate the Fair Housing Act even though they exclude families with children, so long as the housing meets the requirements of the act's "housing for older persons" exemption.[5]

The act prohibits discrimination on the above-listed bases in a wide range of matters relating to the sale or rental of housing. These matters include refusals to sell or rent, representations that housing is not available for sale or rental when in fact it is, and discriminatory actions regarding terms, conditions, or privileges of sale or rental or regarding the provision of services and facilities involved in sale or rental.[6] The act also prohibits discrimination in connection with brokerage services, appraisals, and financing of dwellings.

Included within prohibited discrimination on the basis of handicap are refusals to permit a handicapped person to make (at his own expense) reasonable modifications to the property and refusals to make reasonable accommodations in property-related rules, policies, practices, or services when such modifications or accommodations are necessary to afford the handicapped person full enjoyment of the property. The act also outlaws the building of multifamily housing that is inaccessible to persons with handicaps.

A violation of the Fair Housing Act can result in a civil action brought by either the government or the aggrieved individual. If the aggrieved individual brings suit and prevails, the court may issue injunctions, award actual and punitive damages, assess attorney's fees and costs, and grant other appropriate relief. Finally, the Fair Housing Act invalidates any state or municipal law requiring or permitting an action that would be a discriminatory housing practice under federal law. *City of Edmonds v. Oxford House, Inc.,* which appears later in the chapter, illustrates the role of the Fair Housing Act when a city zoning ordinance allegedly has the effect of discriminating on the basis of handicap.

Financing the Purchase   The various arrangements for financing the purchase of real property—such as mortgages, land contracts, and deeds of trust—are discussed in Chapter 27.

Deeds

Each state's statutes set out the formalities necessary to accomplish a valid conveyance of land. As a general rule, a valid conveyance is brought about by the execution and delivery of a **deed,** a written instrument that transfers title from one person (the grantor) to another (the grantee). Three types of deeds are in general use in the United States: *quitclaim deeds, warranty deeds,* and *deeds of bargain and sale* (also called *grant deeds*). The precise rights contemplated by a deed depend on the type of deed the parties have used.

[4]"Familial status" is defined as an individual or individuals under the age of 18 who is/are domiciled with a parent, some other person who has custody over him/her/them, or the designee of the parent or custodial individual. The familial status classification also applies to one who is pregnant or in the process of attempting to secure custody of a child or children under the age of 18.

[5]The Fair Housing Act defines "housing for older persons" as housing provided under any state or federal program found by the Secretary of HUD to be specifically designed and operated to assist elderly persons, housing intended for and solely occupied by persons 62 years old or older, or housing that meets the requirements of federal regulations and is intended and operated for occupancy by at least one person 55 years old or older.

[6]Chapter 25 discusses the Fair Housing Act's application to rentals of residential property.

Quitclaim Deeds A **quitclaim deed** conveys whatever title the grantor has at the time he executes the deed. It does not, however, contain warranties of title. The grantor who executes a quitclaim deed does not claim to have good title—or any title, for that matter. The grantee has no action against the grantor under a quitclaim deed if the grantee does not acquire good title. Quitclaim deeds are frequently used to cure technical defects in the chain of title to property.

Warranty Deeds A **warranty deed,** unlike a quitclaim deed, contains covenants of warranty. Besides conveying title to the property, the grantor who executes a warranty deed guarantees the title she has conveyed. There are two types of warranty deeds.

1. *General warranty deed.* Under a general warranty deed, the grantor warrants against (and agrees to defend against) all title defects and encumbrances (such as liens and easements), including those that arose before the grantor received her title.

2. *Special warranty deed.* Under a special warranty deed, the grantor warrants against (and agrees to defend against) title defects and encumbrances that arose after she acquired the property. If the property conveyed is subject to an encumbrance such as a mortgage, a long-term lease, or an easement, the grantor frequently provides a special warranty deed that contains a provision excepting those specific encumbrances from the warranty.

Deed of Bargain and Sale In a **deed of bargain and sale** (also known as a **grant deed**), the grantor makes no covenants. The grantor uses language such as "I grant" or "I bargain and sell" or "I convey" property. Such a deed does contain, however, the grantor's implicit representation that he owns the land and has not previously encumbered it or conveyed it to another party.

Form and Execution of Deed

Some states' statutes suggest a form for deeds. Although the requirements for execution of deeds are not uniform, they do follow a similar pattern. As a general rule, a deed states the *name of the grantee,* contains a *recitation of consideration and a description of the property conveyed,* and is *signed by the grantor.* Most states require that the deed be notarized (acknowledged by the grantor before a notary

public or other authorized officer) in order to be eligible for recording in public records.

No technical words of conveyance are necessary for a valid deed. Any language is sufficient if it indicates with reasonable certainty the grantor's intent to transfer ownership of the property. The phrases "grant, bargain, and sell" and "convey and warrant" are commonly used. Deeds contain recitations of consideration primarily for historical reasons. The consideration recited is not necessarily the purchase price of the property. Deeds often state that the consideration for the conveyance is "one dollar and other valuable consideration."

The property conveyed must be described in such a manner that it can be identified. This usually means that the legal description of the property must be used. Several methods of legal description are used in the United States. In urban areas, descriptions are usually by lot, block, and plat. In rural areas where the land has been surveyed by the government, property is usually described by reference to the government survey. It may also be described by a metes and bounds description that specifies the boundaries of the tract of land.

Recording Deeds

Delivery of a valid deed conveys title from a grantor to a grantee. Even so, the grantee should promptly **record** the deed in order to prevent his interest from being defeated by third parties who may claim interests in the property. The grantee must pay a fee to have the deed recorded, a process that involves depositing and indexing the deed in the files of a government office designated by state law. A recorded deed operates to provide the public at large with notice of the grantee's property interest.

Recording Statutes Each state has a **recording statute** that establishes a system for the recording of all transactions affecting real property ownership. These statutes are not uniform in their provisions. In general, however, they provide for the recording of all deeds, mortgages, land contracts, and similar documents.

Types of Recording Statutes State recording statutes also provide for priority among competing claimants to rights in real property, in case conflicting rights or interests in property should be deeded to (or otherwise claimed by) more than one person.

(Obviously, a grantor has no right to issue two different grantees separate deeds to the same property, but if this should occur, recording statutes provide rules to decide which grantee has superior title.) These priority rules apply only to grantees who have given value for their deeds or other interest-creating documents (primarily purchasers and lenders), and not to donees. A given state's recording law will set up one of three basic types of priority systems: race statutes, notice statutes, and race-notice statutes. Figure 2 explains these priority systems. Although the examples used in Figure 2 deal with recorded and unrecorded deeds, recording statutes apply to other documents that create interests in real estate. Chapter 27 discusses the recording of mortgages, as well as the adverse security interest–related consequences a mortgagee may experience if its mortgage goes unrecorded.

Methods of Assuring Title

In purchasing real property, the buyer is really acquiring the seller's ownership interests. Because the buyer does not want to pay a large sum of money for something that proves to be of little or no value, it is important for her to obtain assurance that the seller has good title to the property. This is commonly done in one of three ways:

1. *Title opinion.* In some states, it is customary to have an attorney examine an **abstract of title.** An abstract of title is a history of what the public records show regarding the passage of title to, and other interests in, a parcel of real property. It is not a guarantee of good title. After examining the abstract, the attorney renders an opinion about whether the grantor has **marketable title** to the property. Marketable title is title free from defects or reasonable doubt about its validity. If the grantor's title is defective, the nature of the defects will be stated in the attorney's title opinion.

2. *Torrens system.* A method of title assurance available in a few states is the **Torrens system** of title registration. Under this system, one who owns land in fee simple obtains a certificate of title. When the property is sold, the grantor delivers a deed and a certificate of title to the grantee. All liens and encumbrances against the title are noted on the certificate, thus assuring the purchaser that the title is good except as to the liens and encumbrances noted on the certificate. However, some claims or encumbrances, such as those arising from adverse possession, do not appear on the records and must be discovered through an inspection of the property. In some Torrens states, encumbrances such as tax liens, short-term leases, and highway rights are valid against the purchaser even though they do not appear on the certificate.

FIGURE 2

Three Basic Types of Priority Systems for Recording Deeds

Race Statutes	Under a race statute—so named because the person who wins the race to the courthouse wins the property ownership "competition"—the first grantee who records a deed to a tract of land has superior title. For example, if Grantor deeds Blackacre to Kerr on March 1 and to Templin on April 1, Templin will have superior title to Blackacre if she records her deed before Kerr's is recorded. Race statutes are relatively uncommon today.
Notice Statutes	Under a notice system of priority, a later grantee of property has superior title if he acquired his interest without notice of an earlier grantee's claim to the property under an unrecorded deed. For example, Grantor deeds Greenacre to Jonson on June 1, but Jonson does not record his deed. On July 1, Marlowe purchases Greenacre without knowledge of Jonson's competing claim. Grantor executes and delivers a deed to Marlowe. In this situation, Marlowe would have superior rights to Greenacre even if Jonson ultimately records his deed before Marlowe's is recorded.
Race-Notice Statutes	The race-notice priority system combines elements of the systems just discussed. Under race-notice statutes, the grantee having priority is the one who *both takes his interest without notice* of any prior unrecorded claim and *records first.* For example, Grantor deeds Redacre to Frazier on September 1. On October 1 (at which time Frazier has not yet recorded his deed), Grantor deeds Redacre to Gill, who is then unaware of any claim by Frazier to Redacre. If Gill records his deed before Frazier's is recorded, Gill has superior rights to Redacre.

3. *Title insurance.* Purchasing a policy of **title insurance** provides the preferred and most common means of protecting title to real property. Title insurance obligates the insurer to reimburse the insured grantee for loss if the title proves to be defective. In addition, title insurance covers litigation costs if the insured grantee must go to court in a title dispute. Lenders commonly require that a separate policy of title insurance be obtained for the lender's protection. Title insurance may be obtained in combination with the other previously discussed methods of ensuring title.

SELLER'S RESPONSIBILITIES REGARDING THE QUALITY OF RESIDENTIAL PROPERTY

Buyers of real estate normally consider it important that any structures on the property be in good condition. This factor becomes especially significant if the buyer intends to use the property for residential purposes. The rule of *caveat emptor* (let the buyer beware) traditionally applied to the sale of real property unless the seller committed misrepresentation or fraud or made express warranties about the property's condition. In addition, sellers had no duty to disclose hidden defects in the property. In recent years, however, the legal environment for sellers—especially real estate professionals such as developers and builder-vendors of residential property—has changed substantially. This section examines two important sources of liability for sellers of real property.

Implied Warranty of Habitability

Historically, sellers of residential property were not regarded as making any **implied warranty** that the property was habitable or suitable for the buyer's use. The law's attitude toward the buyer–seller relationship in residential property sales began to shift, however, as product liability law underwent rapid change in the late 1960s. Courts began to see that the same policies favoring the creation of implied warranties in the sale of goods applied with equal force to the sale of residential real estate.[7] Both goods and housing are frequently mass-produced. The disparity of knowledge and bargain-

ing power often existing between a buyer of goods and a professional seller is also likely to exist between a buyer of a house and a builder-vendor (one who builds and sells houses). Moreover, many defects in houses are not readily discoverable during a buyer's inspection. This creates the possibility of serious loss, because the purchase of a home is often the largest single investment a person ever makes.

For these reasons, courts in most states now hold that builders, builder-vendors, and developers make an implied warranty of habitability when they build or sell real property for residential purposes. An ordinary owner who sells her house—in other words, a seller who was neither the builder nor the developer of the residential property—does not make an implied warranty of habitability.

The implied warranty of habitability amounts to a guarantee that the house is free of latent (hidden) defects that would render it unsafe or unsuitable for human habitation. A breach of this warranty subjects the defendant to liability for damages, measured by either the cost of repairs or the loss in value of the house.[8]

A related issue that has led to considerable litigation is whether the implied warranty of habitability extends to subsequent purchasers of the house. For example, PDQ Development Co. builds a house and sells it to Johnson. If Johnson later sells the house to McClure, may McClure successfully sue PDQ for breach of warranty if a serious defect renders the house uninhabitable? Although some courts have rejected implied warranty actions brought by subsequent purchasers, many courts today hold that an implied warranty made by a builder-vendor or developer would extend to a subsequent purchaser.

May the implied warranty of habitability be *disclaimed* or *limited* in the contract of sale? It appears at least possible to disclaim or limit the warranty by a contract provision, subject to limitations imposed by the unconscionability doctrine, public policy concerns, and contract interpretation principles.[9] Courts construe attempted disclaimers very strictly against the builder-vendor or developer, and often reject disclaimers that are not specific regarding rights supposedly waived by the purchaser.

---

[7]See Chapter 20 for a discussion of the development of similar doctrines in the law of product liability.

[8]Measures of damages are discussed in Chapter 18.

[9]The unconscionability doctrine and public policy concerns are discussed in Chapter 15. Chapter 16 addresses contract interpretation.

Duty to Disclose Hidden Defects

Traditional contract law provided that a seller had no duty to disclose to the buyer defects in the property being sold, even if the seller knew about the defects and the buyer could not reasonably find out about them on his own. The seller's failure to volunteer information, therefore, could not constitute misrepresentation or fraud. This traditional rule of nondisclosure was another expression of the prevailing *caveat emptor* notion. Although the non-disclosure rule was subject to certain exceptions,[10] the exceptions seldom applied. Thus, there was no duty to disclose in most sales of real property.

Today, courts in many jurisdictions have substantially eroded the traditional nondisclosure rule and have placed a duty on the seller to disclose any known defect that materially affects the property's value and is not reasonably observable by the buyer. The seller's failure to disclose such defects effectively amounts to an assertion that the defects do not exist—an assertion on which a judicial finding of misrepresentation or fraud may be based.[11] *Strawn v. Canuso* illustrates the trend toward expansion of the duty to disclose by holding that certain sellers of residential property may be obligated to reveal the existence of significant *off-site* physical conditions.

---

[10]These exceptions are discussed in Chapter 13.

[11]Misrepresentation and fraud are discussed in Chapter 13.

STRAWN v. CANUSO 657 A.2d 420 (N.J. Sup. Ct. 1995)

The Buzby Landfill was operated from 1966 to 1978. Although the landfill was not licensed to receive liquid industrial or chemical wastes, large amounts of hazardous materials and chemicals were dumped there. Toxic wastes began to escape from the landfill because it had no liner or cap. Tests performed by the New Jersey Department of Environmental Protection and Energy (DEPE) revealed ground water contamination due to hazardous waste seepage from the landfill.

High levels of methane gas also emanated from the dump site. Various contaminants were released because there were gas leaks in a venting system that had been installed at the site to vent excessive levels of methane gas. The federal Environmental Protection Agency (EPA) investigated the situation and recommended that the Buzby Landfill site be considered for cleanup under the federal Superfund law. The cleanup did not take place, however.

During the 1980s, Canetic Corp. and Canuso Management Corp. developed a housing subdivision near the closed Buzby Landfill. Some homes in the subdivision were within half a mile of the old landfill. Twenty-six families filed a class action lawsuit against Canetic and Canuso Management on behalf of all purchasers (approximately 150 families) who bought new homes in the subdivision between 1984 and 1987. Other defendants were John B. Canuso, Sr., and John B. Canuso, Jr., who were principals in the corporations mentioned above, and Fox & Lazo, Inc., a brokerage firm that acted as selling agent for the homes in the development. Alleging fraud, negligent misrepresentation, and a violation of the New Jersey Consumer Fraud Act, the plaintiffs contended that prior to selling the plaintiffs their homes, the defendants should have disclosed that the housing development was located near an abandoned hazardous waste dump. According to the plaintiffs, the defendants had received considerable information from the EPA and the DEPE concerning the dangers of placing a housing development in the vicinity of the closed landfill. Nevertheless, the defendants followed a policy of nondisclosure to prospective purchasers.

The trial court granted summary judgment to the defendants, holding that they did not owe prospective purchasers a duty to disclose the condition "of somebody else's property." The New Jersey Appellate Division reversed, holding that Canetic, Canuso Management, and Fox & Lazo had a duty to inform potential buyers of the existence of the nearby, closed landfill. The affected defendants appealed to the Supreme Court of New Jersey. ∞

O'Hern, Justice [T]he doctrine of *caveat emptor* survived [as part of real property law] into the first half of the twentieth century. *[C]aveat emptor* dic-tates that in the absence of express agreement, a seller is not liable to the buyer or others for the condition of the land existing at the time of transfer.

In *Michaels v. Brookchester, Inc.* (1958), this Court recognized that ... *caveat emptor* no longer applied to leasehold interests in property. We stated [that even though *caveat emptor* was] "suitable for the agrarian setting in which it was conceived, [it] lagged behind changes in dwelling habits and economic realities." Exceptions to the broad immunity of *caveat emptor* inevitably developed in the sale of land. In *Schipper v. Levitt & Sons, Inc.* (1965), the Court held that a builder-developer ... gave an implied warranty that the structure it built would be properly constructed—a warranty of its habitability. The Court said [that] "*[c]aveat emptor* developed when the buyer and seller were in an equal bargaining position ... Buyers of mass produced development homes are not on an equal footing with the builder vendors."

In *McDonald v. Mianecki* (1979), the Court extended the principles of *Schipper* to a small-scale builder of new homes. The Court [noted that applying] *caveat emptor* "to new houses [would be] an anachronism patently out of harmony with modern home buying practices." Finally, in *Weintraub v. Krobatsch* (1974), the Court ruled that a seller of real estate had an obligation to disclose the existence of roach infestation unknown to the buyers. The Court noted that in certain circumstances, "silence may be fraudulent."

Other jurisdictions have limited the doctrine of *caveat emptor.* In California, when the seller knows of facts materially affecting the value or desirability of property and the seller also knows that such facts are not known to, or within the reach of the diligent attention and observation of the buyer, the seller is subject to a duty to disclose those facts to the buyer. [A California court decision classifies] the real estate agent or broker representing the seller [as] a party to the business transaction [and, therefore, as a party with the same duty of disclosure as the seller]. Several jurisdictions have ... adopted mandatory disclosure laws [or] similar laws [that impose disclosure obligations on real property sellers and their brokers].

In the absence of such legislation or other regulatory requirements affecting real estate brokers, the question is whether our common-law precedent would require disclosure of off-site conditions that materially affect the value of property. By its favorable citation of California precedent, *Weintraub* establishes that a seller of real estate or a broker representing the seller would be liable for nondisclosure of on-site defective conditions if those conditions were known to them and unknown and not readily observable by the buyer. Such conditions, for example, would include radon contamination and a polluted water supply. California cases have extended this duty [of disclosure] to some off-site conditions. Whether and to what extent we should extend this duty to off-site conditions depends on an assessment of the various policies that have shaped the development of our law.

[T]he principal factors shaping the duty to disclose have been the difference in bargaining power between the professional seller of real estate and the purchaser of such housing, and the difference in access to information between the seller and the buyer. The first factor causes us to limit our holding to professional sellers of residential housing (persons engaged in the business of building or developing residential housing) and the brokers representing them. Neither the reseller of residential real estate nor the seller of commercial property has that same advantage in the bargaining process. Regarding the second factor, professional sellers of residential housing and their brokers enjoy markedly superior access to information. Hence, we believe that it is reasonable to extend to such professionals a similar duty to disclose off-site conditions that materially affect the value or desirability of the property.

[In this case, the] silence of the Fox & Lazo representative and the Canuso Management Corporation's principals and employees created a mistaken impression on the part of the purchaser. Defendants used sales-promotion brochures, newspaper advertisements, and a fact sheet to sell the homes in the development. That material portrayed the development as located in a peaceful, bucolic setting with an abundance of fresh air and clean lake waters. Although the literature mentioned how far the property was from malls, country clubs, and train stations, neither the brochures, the newspaper advertisements, nor any sales personnel mentioned that a landfill [was] located within half a mile of some of the homes.

Is the nearby presence of a toxic-waste dump a condition that materially affects the value of property? Surely, Lois Gibbs would have wanted to know that the home she was buying in Niagara Falls, New York, was within one-quarter mile of the abandoned Love Canal site. *See* Lois M. Gibbs, *Love Canal: My Story* (1982) (recounting residents' political struggle concerning a leaking toxic-chemical dump near their homes). In the case of on-site conditions, courts have imposed affirmative obligations on sellers to disclose information materially affecting the value of property. There is no logical reason why a certain class of sellers and brokers should not disclose off-site matters that materially affect the value of property.

We know that the physical effects of abandoned dump sites are not limited to the confines of the dump. [E]ven without physical intrusion, a landfill may cause diminution in the fair market value of real property located nearby. [O]ur precedent and policy offer reliable evidence that the value of property may be materially affected by adjacent or nearby landfills. Professional sellers in southern New Jersey could not help but have been aware of the potential effects of such conditions.

In December 1983, the Real Estate Commission wrote to the Camden County Board of Realtors, stating that "[b]ecause of the potential effects on health, and because of its impact on the value of property, location of property near a hazardous waste site is a bit of information that should be supplied to potential buyers." In addition, [a New Jersey statute] requires that a broker "make reasonable effort to ascertain all pertinent information concerning every property for which he accepts an agency" [and that the broker] "shall reveal all information material to any transaction to his client or principal and when appropriate to any other party." Although not dispositive of the issues in this case, those sources certainly suggest that profes-sionals should have been aware of some changing duty requiring them to be more forthcoming with respect to conditions affecting the value of property.

The duty that we recognize is not unlimited. We do not hold that sellers and brokers have a duty to investigate or disclose transient social conditions in the community that arguably affect the value of property. In the absence of a purchaser communicating specific needs, builders and brokers should not be held to decide whether the changing nature of a neighborhood, the presence of a group home, or the existence of a school in decline are facts material to the transaction. Rather, we root in the land the duty to disclose off-site conditions that are material to the transaction.

We hold that a builder-developer of residential real estate or a broker representing it is not only liable to a purchaser for affirmative and intentional misrepresentation, but is also liable for nondisclosure of off-site physical conditions known to it and unknown and not readily observable by the buyer, if the existence of those conditions is of sufficient materiality to affect the habitability, use, or enjoyment of the property and, therefore, render the property less desirable or valuable to the objectively reasonable buyer. Ultimately, a jury will decide whether the presence of a landfill is a factor that materially affects the value of property; whether the presence of a landfill was known by defendants and not known or readily observable by plaintiffs; and whether the presence of a landfill has indeed affected the value of plaintiffs' property.

Decision of Appellate Division affirmed.

OTHER PROPERTY CONDITION– RELATED OBLIGATIONS OF REAL PROPERTY OWNERS AND POSSESSORS

In recent years, the law has increasingly required real property owners and possessors to take steps to further the safety of persons on the property and to make the property more accessible to disabled individuals. This section discusses two legal developments along these lines: the trend toward expansion of *premises liability* and the inclusion of property-related provisions in the *Americans with Disabilities Act.*

Expansion of Premises Liability

Premises liability is the name sometimes used for negligence cases in which property owners or possessors (such as business operators leasing commercial real estate) are held liable to persons injured while on the property. As explained in Chapter 7, property owners and possessors face liability when their *failures to exercise reasonable care* to keep their property reasonably safe result in injuries to persons lawfully on the property.[12] The traditional premises liability case was one in which a property owner's or possessor's negligence led to the existence of a potentially hazardous condition on the property (e.g., a dangerously slick floor or similar physical condition at a business premises), and a person justifiably on the premises (e.g., a business customer) sustained personal injury upon encountering that unexpected condition (e.g., by slipping and falling).

Security Precautions against Foreseeable Criminal Acts Recent years have witnessed a judicial inclination to expand premises liability to cover other situations in addition to the traditional scenario. A key component of this expansion has been many courts' willingness to reconsider the once-customary holding that a property owner or possessor had no legal obligation to implement security measures to protect persons on the property from the wrongful acts of third parties lacking any connection with the owner or possessor. Today, courts frequently hold that a property owner's or possessor's duty to exercise reasonable care includes the obligation to take *reasonable security precautions* designed to protect persons lawfully on the premises from *foreseeable* wrongful (including criminal) acts by third parties.

This expansion has caused hotel, apartment building, and convenience store owners and operators to be among the defendants held liable—sometimes in very large damage amounts—to guests, tenants, and customers on whom violent third-party attackers inflicted severe physical injuries. In such cases, the property owners' or possessors' negligent failures to take security precautions restricting such wrongdoers' access to the premises served as at least a *substantial factor* leading to the plaintiffs' injuries.[13] The security lapses amounting to a lack of reasonable care in a particular case may

have been, for instance, failures to install deadbolt locks, provide adequate locking devices on sliding glass doors, maintain sufficient lighting, or employ security guards.

Determining Foreseeability The security precautions component of the reasonable care duty is triggered only when criminal activity on the premises is foreseeable. It therefore becomes important to determine whether the foreseeability standard has been met. In making this determination, courts look at such factors as whether previous crimes had occurred on or near the subject property (and if so, the nature and frequency of those crimes), whether the property owner or possessor knew or should have known of those prior occurrences, and whether the property was located in a high-crime area. The fact-specific nature of the foreseeability and reasonable care determinations makes the outcome of a given premises liability case difficult to predict in advance. Nevertheless, there is no doubt that the current premises liability climate gives property owners and possessors more reason than ever before to be concerned about security measures.

Americans with Disabilities Act

In 1990, Congress enacted the broad-ranging Americans with Disabilities Act (ADA). This statute was designed to eliminate longstanding patterns of discrimination against disabled persons in matters such as employment, access to public services, and access to business establishments and similar facilities open to the public. The ADA's Title III focuses on places of *public accommodation*.[14] It imposes on certain property owners and possessors the obligation to take reasonable steps to make their property accessible to disabled persons (individuals with a physical or mental impairment that substantially limits one or more major life activities).

Places of Public Accommodation Title III of the ADA classifies numerous businesses and nonbusiness enterprises as places of **public accommodation.** These include hotels, restaurants, bars, theaters, concert halls, auditoriums, stadiums, shopping centers, stores at which goods are sold or rented,

---

[12]Chapter 7 explains the law's traditional view that real property owners and possessors owe persons who come on the property certain duties that vary depending on those persons' invitee, licensee, or trespasser status. It also discusses courts' increasing tendency to merge the traditional invitee and licensee classifications and to hold that property owners and possessors owe invitees and licensees the duty to exercise reasonable care to keep the premises reasonably safe.

[13]See Chapter 7's discussion of the *causation* element of a negligence claim.

[14]42 U.S.C. §§ 12181-12189 (1990). These sections examine only Title III of the ADA. Chapter 50 discusses the employment-related provisions set forth elsewhere in the statute.

service-oriented businesses (running the gamut from gas stations to law firm offices), museums, parks, schools, social services establishments (day care centers, senior citizen centers, homeless shelters, and the like), places of recreation, and various other enterprises, facilities, and establishments. Private clubs and religious organizations, however, are not treated as places of public accommodation for purposes of the statute.

Modifications of Property   Under the ADA, the owner or operator of a place of public accommodation cannot exclude disabled persons from the premises or otherwise discriminate against them in terms of their ability to enjoy the public accommodation. Avoiding such exclusion or other discrimination may require alteration of the business or nonbusiness enterprise's practices, policies, and procedures. Moreover, using language contemplating the possible need for physical modifications of property serving as a place of public accommodation, the ADA includes within prohibited discrimination the property owner's or possessor's "failure to take such steps as may be necessary to ensure that no individual with a disability is excluded" or otherwise discriminated against in terms of access to what nondisabled persons are provided. The failure to take these steps does not violate the ADA, however, if the property owner or possessor demonstrates that implementing such steps would "fundamentally alter the nature" of the enterprise or would "result in an undue burden."

Prohibited discrimination may also include the "failure to remove architectural barriers and communication barriers that are structural in nature," if removal is "readily achievable." When the removal of such a barrier is not readily achievable, the property owner or possessor nonetheless engages in prohibited discrimination if he, she, or it does not adopt "alternative methods" to ensure access to the premises and what it has to offer (assuming that the alternative methods are themselves readily achievable). The ADA defines *readily achievable* as "easily accomplishable and able to be carried out without much difficulty or expense." The determination of whether an action is readily achievable involves consideration of factors such as the action's nature and cost, the nature of the enterprise conducted on the property, the financial resources of the affected property owner or possessor, and the effect the

action would have on expenses and resources of the property owner or possessor.

New Construction   Newly constructed buildings on property used as a place of public accommodation must contain physical features making the buildings *readily accessible* to disabled persons. The same is true of additions built on to previous structures. The ADA is supplemented by federal regulations setting forth property accessibility guidelines designed to lend substance and specificity to the broad legal standards stated in the statute. In addition, the federal government has issued technical assistance manuals and materials in an effort to educate public accommodation owners and operators regarding their obligations under the ADA.

Remedies   A person subjected to disability-based discrimination in any of the respects discussed above may bring a civil suit for injunctive relief. An injunction issued by a court must include "an order to alter facilities" to make the facilities "readily accessible to and usable by individuals with disabilities to the extent required" by the ADA. The court has discretion to award attorney's fees to the prevailing party. The U.S. Attorney General also has the legal authority to institute a civil action alleging a violation of Title III of the ADA. In such a case, the court may choose to grant injunctive and other appropriate equitable relief, award compensatory damages to aggrieved persons (when the Attorney General so requests), and assess civil penalties (up to $50,000 for a first violation and up to $100,000 for any subsequent violation) "to vindicate the public interest." When determining the amount of any such penalty, the court is to give consideration to any good faith effort by the property owner or possessor to comply with the law. The court must also consider whether the owner or possessor could reasonably have anticipated the need to accommodate disabled persons.

LAND USE CONTROL

Although a real property owner generally has the right to use his property as he desires, society has placed certain limitations on this right. This section examines the property use limitations imposed by nuisance law and by zoning and subdivision ordinances. It also discusses the ultimate land use restriction—the eminent domain power—which enables the government to deprive property owners of their land.

Nuisance Law

One's enjoyment of her own land depends to a great extent on the uses her neighbors make of their land. When the uses of neighboring landowners conflict, the aggrieved party frequently institutes litigation to resolve the conflict. A property use that unreasonably interferes with another person's ability to use or enjoy her own property may lead to an action for **nuisance** against the landowner or possessor engaging in the objectionable use.

The term *nuisance* has no set definition. It is often regarded, however, as encompassing any property-related use or activity that unreasonably interferes with the rights of others. Property uses potentially constituting nuisances include uses that are inappropriate to the neighborhood (such as using a vacant lot in a residential neighborhood as a garbage dump), bothersome to neighbors (such as keeping a pack of barking dogs in one's backyard), dangerous to others (such as storing large quantities of gasoline in 50-gallon drums in one's garage), or of questionable morality (such as operating a house of prostitution). To amount to a nuisance, a use need not be illegal. The fact that relevant zoning laws allow a given use does not mean that the use cannot be a nuisance. The use's having been in existence before complaining neighbors acquired their property does not mean that the use cannot be a nuisance, though it does lessen the likelihood that the use would be held a nuisance.

The test for determining the presence or absence of a nuisance is necessarily flexible and highly dependent on the individual case's facts. Courts balance a number of factors, such as the social importance of the parties' respective uses, the extent and duration of harm experienced by the aggrieved party, and the feasibility of abating (stopping) the nuisance.

Nuisances may be private or public. To bring a *private nuisance* action, the plaintiff must be a landowner or occupier whose enjoyment of her own land is substantially lessened by the alleged nuisance. The remedies for private nuisance include damages and injunctive relief designed to stop the offending use. A *public nuisance* occurs when a nuisance harms members of the public, who need not be injured in their use of property. For example, if a power plant creates noise and emissions posing a health hazard to pedestrians and workers in nearby buildings, a public nuisance may exist even though the nature of the harm has nothing to do with any loss of enjoyment of property. Public nuisances involve a broader class of affected parties than do private nuisances. The action to abate a public nuisance must usually be brought by the government. Remedies generally include injunctive relief and civil penalties that resemble fines. Private parties may sue for abatement of a public nuisance or for damages caused by one only when they suffered unique harm different from that experienced by the general public.

Wood v. Picillo illustrates the application of nuisance law to a property owner who maintained a hazardous waste dump.

WOOD v. PICILLO   443 A.2d 1244 (R.I. Sup. Ct. 1982)

The Picillos maintained a chemical dump site on a clearing on their land. The site was a huge trench about 200 feet long, 15- to 30-feet wide, and 15- to 20-feet deep. A thick layer of pungent, varicolored liquid covered the trench bottom. Along the periphery of the pit lay more than 100 55-gallon drums and 5-gallon pail containers. Some of these were upright and sealed, some were tipped, and some were partially buried. About 600 feet downhill from this site was a marshy wetland that drained into a river and several ponds. A witness testified that he saw the operator of a truck knock barrels marked "Combustible" off the truck's tailgate directly to the ground, where chemicals poured freely from the damaged barrels into the trench. Neighbors smelled "sickening," "heavy," and "terrible" odors that forced them to stay inside their homes. Several neighbors were made ill by the odors.

The attention of state officials was drawn to the site when an enormous explosion erupted into 50-foot flames in a trench on the Picillos' land, and the fire could not be extinguished. Investigators from the state environmental management department began an investigation of the site. The state fire marshal ordered the *dumping to cease, but dumping operations continued. Edward Wood and other plaintiffs brought a nuisance action against the Picillos. The trial court found that the dumping operation was a nuisance. It issued an injunction against further chemical disposal operations on the Picillo property and ordered the Picillos to finance the cleanup and removal of the toxic wastes. The Picillos appealed.* 🖉

Weisberger, Judge   The dump site proper might best be described in the succinct expression of the trial justice as "a chemical nightmare." At trial expert witnesses developed a scientific connection between the neighbors' experiences and the Picillos' operations. Laboratory analyses of samples taken from the trench, monitoring wells, and adjacent waters revealed the presence of five chemicals: toluene, xylene, chloroform, III trichloroethane, and trichloroethylene. According to the experts, the chemicals present on the Picillos' property and in the marsh, if left unchecked, would eventually threaten wildlife and humans well downstream from the dump site. Expert testimony further revealed that the chemicals had traveled and would continue to travel from the dump site into the marsh at the rate of about one foot per day. From the marsh, predicted the experts, the chemicals would flow into waters inhabited by fish and used by humans for recreational and agricultural purposes.

The Picillos contend that the evidence adduced at trial was insufficient to support a finding of public and private nuisance. We find this to be without merit. The essential element of an actionable nuisance is that persons have suffered harm or are threatened with injuries that they ought not to have to bear. Distinguished from negligence liability, liability in nuisance is predicated upon unreasonable injury rather than upon unreasonable conduct. Thus, plaintiffs may recover in nuisance despite the otherwise nontortious nature of the conduct which creates the injury.

The Picillos have accurately stated that the injury produced by an actionable nuisance "must be real and not fanciful or imaginary." The Picillos next suggest that the injuries in the case at bar are of the insubstantial, unactionable type. It is this statement, however, rather than the purported injuries, that is fanciful. The testimony to which reference is made in this opinion clearly establishes that the Picillos' dumping operations have already caused substantial injury to their neighbors and threaten to cause incalculable damage to the general public. The Picillos' neighbors have displayed physical symptoms of exposure to toxic chemicals and have been restricted in the reasonable use of their property. Moreover, expert testimony showed that the chemical presence on the Picillos' property threatens both aquatic wildlife and human beings with possible death, cancer, and liver disease. Thus, there was ample evidence at trial to support the finding of substantial injury.

For the reasons stated, the Picillos' appeal is dismissed.

Judgment for Wood affirmed.

Eminent Domain

The Fifth Amendment to the Constitution provides that private property shall not be taken for public use without "just compensation." Implicit in this provision is the principle that the government has the power to take property for public use if it pays "just compensation" to the owner of the property. This power, called the power of **eminent domain,** makes it possible for the government to acquire private property for highways, water control projects, municipal and civic centers, public housing, urban renewal, and other public uses. Governmental units can delegate their eminent domain power to private corporations such as railroads and utility companies.

Although the eminent domain power is a useful tool of efficient government, there are problems inherent in its use. Determining when the power can be properly exercised presents an initial problem. When the governmental unit itself uses the property taken, as would be the case with property acquired for construction of a municipal building or a public highway, the exercise of the power is proper. The use of eminent domain is not so clearly justified, however, when the government acquires the property and resells it to a private developer. Although such acquisitions may be more vulnerable to challenge, recent cases have applied a very lenient standard in determining what constitutes a public use.[15]

Determining *just compensation* in a given case poses a second and frequently encountered eminent domain problem. The property owner is entitled to receive the "fair market value" of his property. Critics assert, however, that this measure of compensation falls short of adequately compensating the owner for her loss, because *fair market value* does not cover such matters as the lost goodwill of a business or one's emotional attachment to his home.

A third problem sometimes encountered is determining when there has been a "taking" that triggers the government's just compensation obligation. The answer is easy when the government institutes a formal legal action to exercise the eminent domain power (often called an action to *condemn* property). In some instances, however, the government causes or permits a serious physical invasion of a landowner's property without having instituted formal condemnation proceedings. For example, the government's dam-building project results in persistent flooding of a private party's land. Courts have recognized the right of property owners in such cases to institute litigation seeking compensation from the governmental unit whose actions effectively amounted to a physical taking of their land. In these so-called **inverse condemnation** cases, the property owner sends the message that "you have taken my land; now pay for it."

Zoning and Subdivision Laws

State legislatures commonly delegate to cities and other political subdivisions the power to impose reasonable regulations designed to promote the public health, safety, and welfare (often called the *police power*). Zoning ordinances, which regulate real property use, stem from the exercise of the police power. Normally, zoning ordinances divide a city or town into various districts and specify or limit the uses to which property in those districts may be put. They also contain requirements and restrictions regarding improvements built on the land.

Zoning ordinances frequently contain direct restrictions on land use, such as by limiting property use in a given area to single-family or high-density residential uses, or to commercial, light industry, or heavy industry uses. Other sorts of use-related provisions commonly found in zoning ordinances include restrictions on building height, limitations on the portion of a lot that can be covered by a building, and specifications of the distance buildings must be from lot lines (usually called *setback* requirements). Zoning ordinances also commonly restrict property use by establishing population density limitations. Such restrictions specify the maximum number of persons who can be housed on property in a given area and dictate the amount of living space that must be provided for each person occupying residential property. In addition, zoning ordinances often establish restrictions designed to maintain or create a certain aesthetic character in the community. Examples of this type of restriction include specifications of buildings' architectural style, limitations on billboard and sign use, and designations of special zones for historic buildings.

Many local governments also have ordinances dealing with proposed subdivisions. These ordinances often require the subdivision developer to meet certain requirements regarding lot size, street and sidewalk layout, and sanitary facilities. They also require that the city or town approve the proposed development. Such ordinances are designed to further general community interests and to protect prospective buyers of property in the subdivision by ensuring that the developer meets minimum standards of suitability.

Nonconforming Uses A zoning ordinance has *prospective* effect. This means that the uses and buildings already existing when the ordinance is passed (**nonconforming uses**) are permitted to continue. The ordinance may provide, however, for the gradual phasing out of nonconforming uses and buildings that do not fit the general zoning plan.

Relief from Zoning Ordinances A property owner who wishes to use his property in a manner prohibited by a zoning ordinance has more than one potential avenue of relief from the ordinance. He may, for instance, seek to have the ordinance **amended**—in other words, attempt to get the law changed—on the ground that the proposed amendment is consistent with the essence of the overall zoning plan.

A different approach would be to seek permission from the city or political subdivision to deviate

---

[15]This issue is discussed further in Chapter 3, as are other issues relating to eminent domain.

from the zoning law. This permission is called a **variance.** A person seeking a variance usually claims that the ordinance works an undue hardship on her by denying her the opportunity to make reasonable use of her land. Examples of typical variance requests include a property owner's seeking permission to make a commercial use of her property even though it is located in an area zoned for residential purposes, or permission to deviate from normal setback or building size requirements.

Attempts to obtain variances and zoning ordinance amendments frequently clash with the interests of other owners of property in the same area—owners who have a vested interest in maintaining the status quo. As a result, variance and amendment requests often produce heated battles before local zoning authorities.

Challenges to the Validity of the Zoning Ordinance A disgruntled property owner might also attack the zoning ordinance's validity on constitutional grounds. Litigation challenging zoning ordinances has become frequent in recent years, as cities and towns have used their zoning power to achieve social control. For example, assume that a city creates special zoning requirements for adult bookstores or other uses considered moral threats to the community. Such uses of the zoning power have been challenged as unconstitutional restrictions on freedom of speech. In *City of Renton v. Playtime Theatres, Inc.,* however, the Supreme Court upheld a zoning ordinance that prohibited the operation of adult bookstores within 1,000 feet of specified uses such as residential areas and schools.[16] The Court established that the First Amendment rights of operators of adult businesses would not be violated by such an ordinance so long as the city provided them a "reasonable opportunity to open and operate" their businesses within the city. The reasonable opportunity test was satisfied in *City of Renton* even though the ordinance at issue effectively restricted

adult bookstores to a small area of the community in which no property was then available to buy or rent. As lower court cases reveal, however, the fact-specific nature of the inquiry contemplated by the reasonable opportunity test means that the government is not guaranteed of passing the test in every case.[17]

Other litigation has stemmed from ordinances by which municipalities have attempted to "zone out" residential facilities such as group homes for mentally retarded adults. In a leading case, the Supreme Court held that the Constitution's Equal Protection Clause was violated by a zoning ordinance that required a special use permit for a group home for the mentally retarded.[18] (For a case indicating that similar issues nonetheless may be treated differently in the *restrictive covenant*—as opposed to zoning—setting, see *Mains Farm Homeowners Association v. Worthington,* which appears earlier in this chapter.) The Fair Housing Act, which forbids discrimination on the basis of handicap and familial status, has also been used as a basis for challenging decisions that zone out group homes. Such a challenge has a chance of success when the plaintiff demonstrates that the zoning board's actions were a mere pretext for discrimination.[19] Certain applications of zoning ordinances that establish single-family residential areas may also raise Fair Housing Act–based claims of handicap discrimination. *City of Edmonds v. Oxford House, Inc.,* which follows shortly, is such a case.

Many cities and towns have attempted to restrict single-family residential zones to living units of traditional families related by blood or marriage. In enacting ordinances along those lines, municipalities have sought to prevent the presence of groups

---

[16]475 U.S. 41 (U.S. Sup. Ct. 1986). A later case, *FW/PBS, Inc. v. City of Dallas,* 493 U.S. 215 (U.S. Sup. Ct. 1990), presented a different sort of restriction on adult businesses and resulted in a different outcome. There, the Court held that a comprehensive ordinance requiring licensing of adult cabarets and other adult entertainment establishments violated the First Amendment because the ordinance did not have appropriate procedural safeguards against arbitrary denials of licenses. The ordinance's chief defect was its failure to establish a time limit within which city authorities were required to act on license applications.

[17]See, for example, *Topanga Press, Inc. v. City of Los Angeles,* 989 F.2d 1524 (9th Cir. 1993). In that case, the Ninth Circuit Court of Appeals upheld the trial court's issuance of a preliminary injunction against the city's *City of Renton*–like zoning ordinance regarding adult businesses. The reasonable opportunity test was not passed by the city, given that much of the real estate supposedly still "available" for relocation of the adult businesses was submerged beneath the Pacific Ocean or was used as a landfill, for petroleum storage, for airport runways, or for some other purpose inconsistent with the notion that the property could somehow become available for use by adult businesses.

[18]*City of Cleburne v. Cleburne Living Centers,* 473 U.S. 432 (U.S. Sup. Ct. 1985).

[19]See, for example, *Baxter v. City of Nashville,* 720 F. Supp. 720 (S.D. Ill. 1989), which involves a challenge by a hospice for AIDS patients to a city's denial of a special use permit.

of unrelated students, commune members, or religious cult adherents by specifically defining the term *family* in a way that excludes these groups. In *Belle Terre v. Boraas*,[20] the Supreme Court upheld such an ordinance as applied to a group of unrelated students. The Court later held, however, that an ordinance defining *family* so as to prohibit a grand-

mother from living with her grandsons was an unconstitutional intrusion on personal freedom regarding family life.[21] Restrictive definitions of *family* have been held unconstitutional under state constitutions in some cases but narrowly construed by courts in other cases.

---

[20]416 U.S. 1 (U.S. Sup. Ct. 1974).

[21]*Moore v. City of East Cleveland*, 431 U.S. 494 (U.S. Sup. Ct. 1977).

CITY OF EDMONDS v. OXFORD HOUSE, INC.   514 U.S. 725 (U.S. Sup. Ct. 1995)

*T*he zoning code of the City of Edmonds, Washington, allows only single-family dwelling units in certain designated areas of the city. One of this code's ordinances defines family as "an individual or two or more persons related by genetics, adoption, or marriage, or a group of five or fewer persons who are not related by genetics, adoption, or marriage." Oxford House, Inc., opened a group home on leased property in an area of Edmonds that was zoned for single-family residences. This group home was for 10 to 12 adults who were recovering from alcoholism and drug addiction. Upon learning that the group home was being operated, Edmonds issued criminal citations to the owner and a resident of the house. Because the Oxford House facility housed more than five unrelated persons in a single-family area, it did not conform to the Edmonds zoning code.

In an effort to keep the group home open, Oxford House relied on the federal Fair Housing Act (FHA), which bars discrimination in the sale or rental of real property on various bases, including the handicap of a buyer or renter. For purposes of the litigation described below, all parties stipulated that the residents of the Oxford House group home were recovering alcoholics or drug addicts and were therefore handicapped persons within the meaning of the FHA. Discrimination prohibited by the FHA includes the refusal to make "reasonable accommodations in rules, policies, practices, or services, when such accommodations may be necessary to afford [handicapped] persons equal opportunity to use and enjoy a dwelling." Oxford House asked Edmonds to make what Oxford House saw as a reasonable accommodation—allowing it to continue to operate the group home in the single-family residential dwelling it had leased. Edmonds denied this request.

Edmonds sued Oxford House in federal court, seeking a declaration that the FHA does not limit the operation of the city's zoning code rule defining family. The city based its case on an FHA provision that exempts from the FHA's antidiscrimination provisions "any reasonable local, State, or Federal restrictions regarding the maximum number of occupants permitted to occupy a dwelling" (FHA section 3607(b)(1)). Oxford House counterclaimed under the FHA, alleging that in refusing to permit maintenance of the group home in a single-family zone, Edmonds had failed to make a reasonable accommodation. Holding that the Edmonds zoning code's definition of family was a reasonable maximum occupancy restriction for purposes of the FHA exemption set out in section 3607(b)(1), the federal district granted summary judgment in favor of Edmonds. The Ninth Circuit Court of Appeals reversed. It held that section 3607(b)(1)'s exemption did not apply to the Edmonds ordinance. The U.S. Supreme Court granted the city's petition for certiorari. ∞

Ginsburg, Justice   The sole question before the Court is whether Edmonds' family composition rule qualifies as a "restrictio[n] regarding the maximum number of occupants permitted to occupy a dwelling" within the meaning of the FHA's absolute exemption [section 3607(b)(1)]. In answering this question, we are mindful of the Act's stated policy

"to provide . . . for fair housing throughout the United States." We also note precedent recognizing the FHA's "broad and inclusive" compass (quoting *Trafficante v. Metropolitan Life Insurance Co.* (1972). Accordingly, we regard this case as an instance in which an exception to "a general statement of policy" is sensibly read "narrowly in order to preserve the primary operation of the [policy]" (quoting *Commissioner v. Clark* (1989)).

Congress enacted section 3607(b)(1) against the backdrop of an evident distinction between municipal land use restrictions and maximum occupancy restrictions. Land use restrictions designate "districts in which only compatible uses are allowed and incompatible uses are excluded" (quoting D. Mandelker, *Land Use Law* (3d ed. 1993)). These restrictions typically categorize uses as single-family residential, multiple-family residential, commercial, or industrial. Land use restrictions aim to prevent problems caused by the "pig in the parlor instead of the barnyard" (quoting *Village of Euclid v. Ambler Realty Co.* (1926)). [R]eserving land for single-family residences preserves the character of neighborhoods. To limit land use to single-family residences, a municipality must define the term "family"; thus, family composition rules are an essential component of single-family residential uses.

Maximum occupancy restrictions, in contradistinction, cap the number of occupants per dwelling, typically in relation to available floor space or the number and types of rooms. These restrictions ordinarily apply uniformly to *all* residents of *all* dwelling units. Their purpose is to protect health and safety by preventing dwelling overcrowding.

Section 3607 (b)(1)'s language—"restrictions regarding the maximum number of occupants permitted to occupy a dwelling"—surely encompasses maximum occupancy restrictions. But the formulation does not fit family composition rules typically tied to land use restrictions. In sum, rules that cap the total number of occupants in order to prevent overcrowding of a dwelling [clearly] fall within section 3607(b)(1)'s absolute exemption from the FHA's governance; rules designed to preserve the family character of a neighborhood, fastening on the composition of households rather than on the total number of occupants living quarters can contain, do not.

Turning specifically to the City's [zoning code], we note that the provisions Edmonds invoked against Oxford House [the ordinance establishing single-family residential zoning for the area where the home was located and the ordinance defining *family*] are classic examples of a use restriction and complementing family composition rule. These provisions do not cap the number of people who may live in a dwelling. In plain terms, they direct that dwellings be used only to house families. A separate [Edmonds ordinance] caps the number of occupants a dwelling may house, based on the floor area. Th[e] space and occupancy standard [set forth in this separate ordinance] is a prototypical maximum occupancy restriction.

Edmonds nevertheless argues that its family composition rule falls within . . . the FHA exemption for maximum occupancy restrictions, because the rule caps at five the number of unrelated persons allowed to occupy a single-family dwelling. But Edmonds' family composition rule surely does not answer the question: "What is the maximum number of occupants permitted to occupy a house?" So long as they are related "by genetics, adoption, or marriage," any number of people can live in a house.

Family living, not living space per occupant, is what [the family composition ordinance] describes. Defining family primarily by biological and legal relationships, the provision also accommodates another group association: five or fewer unrelated people are allowed to live together as though they were family. This accommodation is the peg on which Edmonds rests its plea for section 3607(b)(1) exemption. It is curious reasoning indeed that converts a family values preserver into a maximum occupancy restriction once a town adds to a related persons prescription [a reference to a limited number of unrelated persons].

The parties have presented, and we have decided, only a threshold question: Edmonds' zoning code provision describing who may compose a "family" is not a maximum occupancy restriction exempt from the FHA under section 3607(b)(1). It remains for the lower courts to decide whether Edmonds' actions against Oxford House violate the FHA's prohibitions against discrimination.

Judgment of Ninth Circuit Court of Appeals affirmed.

Land Use Regulation and Taking

Another type of litigation seen with increasing frequency in recent years centers around zoning laws and other land use regulations that make the use of property less profitable for development.[22] Affected property owners have challenged the application of such regulations as unconstitutional takings of property without just compensation, even though these cases do not involve the actual physical invasions present in the inverse condemnation cases discussed earlier in this chapter.

States normally have broad discretion to use their police power for the public benefit, even when that means interfering to some extent with an owner's right to develop her property as she desires. Some regulations, however, may interfere with an owner's use of his property to such an extent that they constitute a taking.

For instance, in *Nollan v. California Coastal Commission,*[23] the owners of a beach-front lot (the Nollans) wished to tear down a small house on the lot and replace that structure with a larger house. The California Coastal Commission conditioned the grant of the necessary coastal development permit on the Nollans' agreeing to allow the public an easement across their property. This easement would have allowed the public to reach certain nearby public beaches more easily. The Nollans challenged the validity of the Coastal Commission's action.

Ultimately, the Supreme Court concluded that the Coastal Commission's placing the easement condition on the issuance of the permit amounted to an impermissible regulatory taking of the Nollans' property. In reaching this conclusion, the Court held that the state could not avoid paying compensation to the Nollans by choosing to do by way of the regulatory route what it would have had to pay for if it had followed the formal eminent domain route. In *Dolan v. City of Tigard,* which follows shortly, the Supreme Court further developed the analysis suggested in *Nollan.*

Regulations Denying Economically Beneficial Uses   What about a land use regulation that allows the property owner no *economically beneficial use*

of his property? *Lucas v. South Carolina Coastal Commission*[24] was brought by a property owner, Lucas, who had paid nearly $1 million for two residential beach-front lots before South Carolina enacted a coastal protection statute. This statute's effect was to bar Lucas from building any permanent habitable structures on the lots. The trial court held that the statute rendered Lucas's property "valueless" and that an unconstitutional taking had occurred, but the South Carolina Supreme Court reversed. The U.S. Supreme Court, however, held that when a land use regulation denies "all economically beneficial use" of property, there normally has been a taking for which just compensation must be paid. The exception to this rule, according to the Court, would be when the economically productive use being prohibited by the land use regulation was already disallowed by nuisance law or other comparable property law principles. The Court therefore reversed and remanded the case for determination of whether there had been a taking under the rule crafted by the Court, or instead an instance in which the "nuisance" exception applied. On remand, the South Carolina Supreme Court concluded that a taking calling for compensation had occurred (and, necessarily, that the nuisance exception did not apply to Lucas's intended residential use).[25]

The mere fact that a land use regulation deprives the owner of the *highest and most profitable use* of his property does not mean, however, that there has been a taking. If the regulation still allows a use that is economically beneficial in a meaningful sense— even though not the most profitable use—the *Lucas* analysis would seem to indicate that an unconstitutional taking probably did not occur. At the same time, *Lucas* offered hints that less-than-total takings (in terms of restrictions on economically beneficial uses) may sometimes trigger a right of compensation on the landowner's part. Thus, it appears that even as to land use regulations that restrict some but not all economically beneficial uses, property owners are likely to continue arguing (as they have in recent years) that the regulations go "too far" and amount to a taking.

There is no set formula for determining whether a regulation has gone too far. Courts look at the

---

[22]This issue is also discussed in Chapter 3.
[23]483 U.S. 825 (U.S. Sup. Ct. 1987).

[24]505 U.S. 1003 (U.S. Sup. Ct. 1992).
[25]424 S.E.2d 484 (S.C. Sup. Ct. 1992).

relevant facts and circumstances and weigh a variety of factors, such as the economic impact of the regulation, the degree to which the regulation interferes with the property owner's reasonable expectations, and the character of the government's invasion. The weighing of these factors occurs against the backdrop of a general presumption that state and local governments should have reasonably broad

discretion to develop land use restrictions pursuant to the police power. As a result, the outcome of a case in which *regulatory taking* allegations are made is less certain than when a *physical taking* (a physical invasion of the sort addressed in the earlier discussion of inverse condemnation cases) appears to have occurred.

DOLAN v. CITY OF TIGARD   512 U.S. 374 (U.S. Sup. Ct. 1994)

T*he City of Tigard, Oregon, developed a comprehensive land use plan and codified it in its Community Development Code (CDC). This plan identified congestion in the city's central business district as a problem whose severity could be lessened if pedestrian and bicycle pathways were developed. The CDC therefore required that appropriate land development projects facilitate the plan by dedicating land for pedestrian and bicycle pathways.*

Tigard's land use plan also noted that flooding had been a problem along Fanno Creek, and that the increase in impervious surfaces associated with continued urbanization would exacerbate the flooding problems. The CDC therefore required that the Fanno Creek Basin be improved through channel excavation and other modifications, that areas in and adjacent to the floodplain be maintained as greenways free of structures, and that the cost of the flood-control-related improvements be borne by owners of property located along the waterway.

Florence Dolan owned a plumbing and electric supply store that was located on a 1.67-acre parcel in Tigard's central business district. Fanno Creek flows through a corner of Dolan's property and along one of its boundaries. The creek's flow renders the area within its 100-year floodplain virtually unusable for commercial development.

Dolan wished to redevelop her property, so she sought a permit from the city for that purpose. Her plans called for nearly doubling her store's size and for paving a gravel parking lot. The City Planning Commission granted Dolan's permit application, subject to certain conditions. These conditions, which were based on CDC requirements, called for Dolan to dedicate (1) the portion of her property lying within the floodplain for improvement of a storm drainage system along Fanno Creek, and (2) a 15-foot strip of land adjacent to the floodplain for use as a "greenway" and as a public pedestrian/bicycle pathway.

Dolan requested that the City Planning Commission grant her a variance (i.e., an exemption from the CDC-based conditions). In denying this request, the Planning Commission made these findings: (1) it was reasonable to assume that the pedestrian/bicycle pathway could help alleviate traffic congestion in the central business district; and (2) the floodplain dedication was reasonably related to Dolan's proposed redevelopment because her project would be likely to increase storm water flow to an already strained drainage basin. The Tigard City Council approved the Planning Commission's action. So did the Land Use Board of Appeals, which rejected Dolan's argument that the conditions imposed by the city were a taking of her property. The Oregon Court of Appeals and the Supreme Court of Oregon each affirmed, concluding that the conditions were appropriately related to Dolan's proposed project. Dolan sought a writ of certiorari from the U.S. Supreme Court. ∞

Rehnquist, Chief Justice   We granted certiorari to resolve a question left open by our decision in *Nollan v. California Coastal Commission* (1987)[:] [W]hat is the required degree of connection between the exactions imposed by the city and the projected impacts of the proposed development[?]

The Takings Clause of the Fifth Amendment . . . provides: "[N]or shall private property be taken for public use, without just compensation." One of the principal purposes of the Takings Clause is "to bar Government from forcing some people alone to bear public burdens which, in all fairness and justice, should be borne by the public as a whole" (quoting *Armstrong v. United States* (1960)). Without question, had the city simply required [Dolan] to dedicate a strip of land along Fanno Creek for public use, rather than conditioning the grant of her permit to redevelop her property on such a dedication, a taking would have occurred.

On the other side of the ledger, the authority of state and local governments to engage in land use planning has been sustained against constitutional challenge as long ago as our decision in *Euclid v. Ambler Realty Co.* (1926). A land use regulation does not effect a taking if it "substantially advance[s] legitimate state interests" and does not "den[y] an owner economically viable use of his land" (quoting *Agins v. Tiburon* (1980)). The ... land use regulations discussed in the cases just cited, however, differ in two relevant particulars from the present case. First, they involved essentially legislative determinations classifying entire areas of the city, whereas here the city made an adjudicative decision to condition [Dolan's permit approval] on an individual parcel. Second, the conditions imposed were not simply a limitation on the use [Dolan] might make of her own parcel, but a requirement that she deed portions of the property to the city. In *Nollan,* we held that governmental authority to exact such a condition was circumscribed by the Fifth and Fourteenth Amendments.

[Dolan] contends that the city has forced her to choose between the building permit and her right ... to just compensation for the public easements. [She] does not quarrel with the city's authority to exact some forms of dedications as a condition for the grant of a building permit, but challenges the showing made by the city to justify these exactions. In evaluating [Dolan's] claim, we must first determine whether [an] "essential nexus" exists between the "legitimate state interest" and the permit condition exacted by the city (quoting *Nollan*). If we find that a nexus exists, we must then decide the required degree of connection between the exactions and the projected impact of the proposed development. We were not required to reach this question in *Nollan,* because we concluded that the [required nexus between the permit condition and the government interest was not present].

[In *Nollan,* the] absence of a nexus left [the government] in the position of simply trying to obtain an easement through gimmickry, which con-

verted a valid regulation of land use into [a taking]. No such gimmicks are associated with the permit conditions imposed by the city in this case. Undoubtedly, the prevention of flooding along Fanno Creek and the reduction of traffic in the Central Business District qualify as ... legitimate public purposes. It seems equally obvious that a nexus exists between preventing flooding along Fanno Creek and limiting development within the creek's 100-year floodplain. [Dolan] proposes to double the size of her retail store and to pave her now-gravel parking lot, thereby expanding the impervious surface on the property and increasing the amount of stormwater run-off into Fanno Creek.

The same may be said for the city's attempt to reduce traffic congestion by providing for alternative means of transportation. In theory, a pedestrian/bicycle pathway provides a useful alternative means of transportation for workers and shoppers.

The second part of our analysis requires us to determine whether the degree of the exactions demanded by the city's permit conditions bear the required relationship to the projected impact of [Dolan's] proposed development. The question for us is whether th[e] findings [of the City Planning Commission when it denied Dolan's request for a variance] are constitutionally sufficient to justify the conditions imposed by the city. We think a term such as "rough proportionality" best encapsulates what we hold to be the [test required under] the Fifth Amendment [for the appropriate degree of connection between the required land dedication and the projected impact of the proposed development]. No precise mathematical calculation is required, but the city must make some sort of individualized determination that the required dedication is related both in nature and extent to the impact of the proposed development. We turn now to analysis of whether the [city's] findings ... satisfied [the rough proportionality test].

It is axiomatic that increasing the amount of impervious surface will increase the quantity and rate of storm-water flow from [Dolan's] property. Therefore, keeping the floodplain open and free from development would likely confine the pressures on Fanno Creek created by [Dolan's] development. But the city demanded more—it not only wanted [Dolan] not to build in the floodplain, but it also wanted [her] property along Fanno Creek for its greenway system. The city has never said why a public greenway, as opposed to a private one, was required in the interest of flood control. The difference to [Dolan], of course, is the loss of her ability to exclude others. [T]his right to exclude others is "one of the most essential sticks in the bundle of rights that are commonly characterized as property" (quoting *Kaiser Aetna v. United States* (1979)). It is difficult to see why recreational visitors trampling along petitioner's floodplain easement are sufficiently related to the city's legitimate interest in reducing flooding problems along Fanno Creek. [T]he city has not attempted to make any individualized determination to support this part of its request.

[T]he city wants to impose a permanent recreational easement upon [Dolan's] property that borders Fanno Creek. [Dolan] would lose all rights to regulate the time in which the public entered onto the greenway, regardless of any interference it might pose with her retail store. Her right to exclude would not be regulated, it would be eviscerated. If [Dolan's] proposed development had somehow encroached on existing greenway space in the city, it would have been reasonable to require [her] to provide some alternative greenway space for the public either on her property or elsewhere. But that is not the case here. We conclude that the findings upon which the city relies do not show the required reasonable relationship between the floodplain easement and [Dolan's] proposed new building.

With respect to the pedestrian/bicycle pathway, we have no doubt that the city was correct in finding that the large retail sales facility proposed by [Dolan] will increase traffic on the streets of the Central Business District. The city estimates that the proposed development would generate roughly 435 additional trips per day. Dedications for streets, sidewalks, and other public ways are generally reasonable exactions to avoid excessive congestion from a proposed property use. But on the record before us, the city has not met its burden of demonstrating that the additional number of vehicle and bicycle trips generated by [Dolan's] development reasonably relate to the city's requirement for a dedication of the pedestrian/bicycle easement. As Justice Peterson of the Supreme Court of Oregon explained in his dissenting opinion, "[t]he findings of fact that the bicycle pathway system '*could* offset some of the traffic demand' is a far cry from a finding that the bicycle pathway system *will,* or is *likely to,* offset some of the traffic demand." [Emphasis in original.] No precise mathematical calculation is required, but the city must make some effort to quantify its findings in support of the dedication for the pedestrian/bicycle pathway beyond the conclusory statement that it could offset some of the traffic demand generated.

The city's goals of reducing flooding hazards and traffic congestion, and providing for public greenways, are laudable, but there are outer limits as to how this may be done. "A strong public desire to improve the public condition [will not] warrant achieving the desire by a shorter cut than the constitutional way of paying for the change" (quoting *Pennsylvania Coal Co. v. Mahon* (1922).

Decision of Supreme Court of Oregon reversed, and case remanded for further proceedings.

ETHICAL AND PUBLIC POLICY CONCERNS

1. You read that a person may acquire title to another person's real property by adversely possessing that property for a certain period of time. What are some justifications for this doctrine?

2. As you read, restrictive covenants and zoning ordinances are sometimes relied upon by opponents of plans to place group homes for the retarded or disabled in certain residential neighborhoods. What are the major ethical considerations suggested by such uses of restrictive covenants and zoning ordinances? What are the major ethical considerations suggested by attempts to place group homes in certain locations despite arguably contrary language in restrictive covenants and zoning ordinances?

3. In recent years, the law has placed increasing duties on sellers of real property regarding the quality of their property, such as the implied warranty of habitability and a seller's duty to disclose hidden defects in property. Do these developments constitute steps in the right direction? Should the law go farther and impose the implied warranty of habitability on all sellers, not just on builder-vendors and developers? Should it require disclosure of all defects, not just hidden ones?

1. In 1971, Swafford bought three metal buildings and installed them on his ranch. The buildings included (1) a horse barn with a dirt floor middle; (2) an office, a trophy room, and a tack room; and (3) an open-air hay shed with no siding. The buildings were prefabricated at a factory and were assembled at the ranch by Swafford's agent and bolted to concrete slabs. They were never moved after their assembly and installation. In 1973, Swafford mortgaged the property to Kerman. Swafford later defaulted on the debt, and Kerman instituted foreclosure proceedings. Kerman bought the ranch at the foreclosure sale. Swafford claims that the portable buildings belong to him and that he can remove them. Do they belong to Swafford?

2. In 1957 or 1958, the Hibbards cleared their land of overgrowth and set up a trailer park. There was no obvious boundary between their land and that of their neighbor to the east, so the Hibbards cleared the land up to a deep drainage ditch. They also built a road for use in entering and leaving the trailer park. In 1960, the Hibbards' neighbor, McMurray, discovered through a survey that the Hibbards had encroached on his land (the eastern parcel) by 20 feet. He so informed the Hibbards. The western parcel later changed hands several times until the Sanderses bought it in 1976. The use of the western parcel changed little over the years. The road remained in continuous use in connection with the trailer park. The area between the road and the drainage ditch was also used by trailer park residents for parking, storage, garbage removal, and picnicking. Trailer personnel and tenants mowed grass up to the drainage ditch and planted flowers. The Sanderses installed underground wiring and surface power poles in the area between the road and the drainage ditch. In 1978, the Chaplins bought the eastern parcel. Shortly thereafter, they had a survey conducted. This survey revealed the Sanderses' encroachments. The Chaplins then sued to quiet title to the road and its shoulder (Parcel A) and the area between the road and the drainage ditch (Parcel B). With 10 years being the relevant possession period under state law, the Sanderses asserted that they owned Parcels A and B by virtue of adverse possession. Were the Sanderses correct?

3. The Wakes owned a tract of land. They used one part of the tract as a farm and the other part as a cattle ranch. Each spring and fall, the Wakes drove cattle from the ranch over an access road on the farm to Butler Springs, which was also located on the farm. From Butler Springs, they ranged the cattle eastward to adjacent government land, where they held grazing rights. In December 1956, the Wakes sold the farm portion of the land on contract to the Hesses. The contract of sale expressly reserved an easement in the Wakes to use the Butler Springs water and the right-of-way from Butler Springs across the property to the federal land. The contract described the Butler Springs area but did not describe the access road leading to Butler Springs from the county road. In 1963, the Hesses sold the farm to the Johnsons. These parties' contract referred to the Wakes' easement. The Wakes continued to use the access road and Butler Springs until 1964, when they sold their ranch and granted the Butler Springs easement to the purchasers. The ranch later changed hands several times, but each owner continued to use the access road and Butler Springs. In 1978, shortly after the Nelsons bought the ranch, the Johnsons sent them a letter "revoking permission" to use the access road. The Johnsons later placed locks on the gates across the access road. The Nelsons alleged that they had easement rights in the Butler Springs area and the access road leading to it. Were they correct?

4. Major developed a subdivision in which he built a number of houses and offered them for sale. The Rozells bought one of the houses. Upon the first rain, water entered under the crawl space of the house. Water then accumulated to a depth of 17 inches in a room where the furnace and water heater were located. This frequently caused the water heater not to work. Major's attempts to keep the water out were unsuccessful. Water continued to accumulate in the room whenever there was a rainfall of any consequence. As a result, the house was damp and had a peculiar odor. Mildew also became a problem. Did the Rozells have a cause of action against Major? If so, what cause of action?

5. A restrictive covenant applicable to most lots in an industrial park was recorded in 1957. The restrictive covenant prohibited property improvements taller than 45 feet. It also forbade billboards and advertising signs except those identifying the name, business, and products of the person or firm occupying the property on which the billboards or signs appeared. In other words, billboards or signs promoting businesses located elsewhere (off-premises advertising) were prohibited. The City of Rolling Meadows acquired property in the industrial park in 1960. Shortly thereafter, approximately one-tenth of the park's 201 acres were condemned so that a new public highway, Route 53, could run through the park. National Advertising Company and Universal Outdoor, Inc., leased industrial park property during the 1980s and began constructing billboards on their leased property. They intended these billboards to be between 49 and 56 feet tall and available for advertising use by other businesses (i.e., for off-premises advertising). The City of Rolling Meadows learned of the restrictive covenant shortly after construction of the billboards began. The city then filed suit against National and Universal in an effort to enforce the restrictive covenant and halt the billboard construction. National and Universal argued, among other things, that the character of the industrial park area had changed substantially and that the restrictive covenant therefore should no longer be enforceable. As of the time of the litigation, Route 53 was a six-lane highway carrying approximately 100,000 to 150,000 cars per day through the industrial park. Was there a sufficient change in circumstances to justify a conclusion that the restrictive covenant was no longer enforceable?

6. The Parkers used part of their property for housing, breeding, raising, and selling German shepherd dogs. As many as 25 dogs were on the Parkers' property at one time. Many of the dogs were trained as guard, protection, or attack dogs. The dogs' barking and offensive odors annoyed adjacent property owners. The Parkers sometimes let some of the dogs wander around the neighborhood unsupervised. This caused neighbors to be concerned about the safety of their children. The Parkers' property was subject to a restriction prohibiting noxious or offensive activity and providing that no animal could be raised, bred, or kept for any purpose other than serving as household pets. Three owners of adjacent homes brought suit against the Parkers, seeking to have them enjoined from keeping a number of dogs. The Parkers argued that the subdivision restriction did not prohibit them from keeping the dogs. Were the neighbors entitled to obtain an injunction against the Parkers? If so, on what grounds?

7. Morton and Edna Davis entered into a contract to buy a house from Clarence and Dana Johnson for $310,000. The house was three years old. The contract required a $5,000 initial deposit payment and an additional $26,000 deposit payment within five days. After the Davises had paid the initial $5,000 deposit but before they had paid the $26,000 deposit, Mrs. Davis noticed some buckling and peeling plaster around the corner of a window frame, as well as stains on ceilings in several rooms. When Mrs. Davis inquired about this, Mr. Johnson told her that the window had had a minor problem which was corrected long ago and that the stains were wallpaper glue. The Davises then paid the remaining $26,000 deposit, and the Johnsons moved out of the house. Several days later, following a heavy rain, Mrs. Davis entered the house and discovered water gushing in from around the window frame, the ceiling of the family room, the light fixtures, the glass doors, and the stove in the kitchen. The Davises hired roofers, who reported that the roof was inherently defective and that any repairs would be temporary because the roof was "slipping." Only a new roof, at a cost of $15,000, could be watertight. The Davises then filed this action alleging, among other things, fraud on the part of the Johnsons. The Davises sought rescission of the contract and return of their deposit payments. Did the Johnsons commit fraud?

8. Elliot and Davis owned property in Athens, Georgia, where the University of Georgia is located. Their property was in an area whose residential-purpose zoning allowed an unlimited number of related persons to occupy the same residence but no more than four unrelated persons to occupy the same residence. Elliott and Davis sought to sell their property to The Potter's House, an entity that planned to operate an alcohol and drug rehabilitation center on the property. This center would house 12 rehabilitation program participants (all unrelated persons) plus an employee of The Potter's House. The rehabilitation center therefore would not have complied with applicable zoning. The sale from Elliott and Davis to The Potter's House was conditional on the ability to obtain zoning changes to accommodate the rehabilitation center. After the City of Athens refused requests that the area's zoning be altered to accommodate the rehabilitation center, Elliott, Davis, and The Potter's House sued the city on the theory that the city's refusal to make a zoning accommodation violated the federal Fair

Housing Act's provisions prohibiting discrimination on the basis of handicap. All parties to the case agreed that the rehabilitation center's inhabitants would be considered handicapped for purposes of the Fair Housing Act. The city argued, however, that it qualified for an exemption set forth in the Fair Housing Act for reasonable maximum occupancy restrictions imposed by local law. According to the city, its ordinance restricting the number of unrelated persons who could live together was designed to regulate the large university student population in Athens and to guard against extreme density-oriented problems in areas near the University of Georgia. Was the zoning ordinance a reasonable maximum occupancy restriction exempting the city from responsibility under the Fair Housing Act?

9. Mobile home owners commonly place their mobile homes on small plots of land (often called *pads*) they have leased in a mobile home park. In 1978, California enacted the Mobilehome Residency Law. This statute prohibited mobile home park owners from evicting mobile home owners from leased pads unless the mobile home owner defaulted on rental payments or violated park rules, or the park owner decided to change the property from a mobile home park to a different land use. The statute also prohibited the park owner from requiring that a mobile home be removed from a pad when the mobile home was sold to a responsible purchaser who wished to lease the same pad from the park owner. In the late 1980s, the City of Escondido enacted a mobile home rent control ordinance. This ordinance rolled back rents charged by park owners to their 1986 levels and required park owners to obtain City Council approval before raising rents. John and Irene Yee owned two mobile home parks in Escondido. They and other park owners (referred to here collectively as "the Yees") sued the city. The Yees alleged that Escondido's rent control ordinance, when viewed against the backdrop of California's Mobilehome Residency Law, amounted to a *physical taking* of their property without just compensation. Specifically, the Yees asserted that the rent control ordinance "had the effect of depriv-

ing the plaintiffs of all use and occupancy of [their] real property and granting to the tenants of mobile-homes . . . the right to physically permanently occupy and use the [plaintiffs'] real property." Were the Yees correct in arguing that the rent control ordinance's effect amounted to a *physical* taking?

10. Emma Yocum was married to James Yocum as of the time of her death in 1990. She and James had begun living together in March 1959. In July 1959, by way of a warranty deed that referred to them as "husband and wife," Emma and James took ownership of a home. She and James, however, were not yet married. Emma was still married to Joseph Perez, from whom she was divorced in April 1960. Emma and James were married in July 1960. When they acquired their home in 1959, James had provided the down payment. A mortgage executed by Emma and James at that time also referred to them as husband and wife even though they were not then married. After Emma's death in 1990, her children by her marriage to Joseph Perez filed suit in an effort to have the court determine present ownership of the home Emma and James had owned during her lifetime. Had Emma and James owned the home as *tenants in common* (meaning that Emma's interest in the property would pass to her estate, in which her children were entitled to share), or instead as either *tenants by the entirety* or *joint tenants* (meaning that James would then solely own the home by virtue of the right of survivorship)?

11. The Duchaines leased their property to Southern Massachusetts Broadcasters for a five-year period. While occupying the leased property, Southern installed a radio tower, which it used to transmit radio broadcasts. The tower was a 390-foot steel-frame structure that stood on three legs and was attached by iron bolts to 5-foot-square cement foundations. Although it was possible to remove the tower from the property, Southern neither attempted to remove it nor claimed the right to do so until two and one-quarter years after vacating the Duchaines' property. Southern then filed suit, claiming ownership of the tower. Was Southern entitled to prevail?

Landlord and Tenant

Landlord–tenant law has undergone dramatic change during the past three decades, due in large part to the changing nature of the relationship between landlords and tenants. In England and in early America, farms were the usual subjects of leases. The tenant's primary object was to lease land on which to grow crops or graze cattle. Accordingly, traditional landlord–tenant law viewed the lease as primarily a conveyance of land and paid relatively little attention to its contractual aspects.

In today's industrialized society, however, the landlord–tenant relationship is typified by the lease of property for residential or commercial purposes. The tenant occupies only a small portion of the total property. He bargains primarily for the use of structures on the land rather than for the land itself. He is likely to have signed a form lease provided by the landlord, the terms of which he may have had little opportunity to negotiate. In areas with a shortage of affordable housing, a residential tenant's ability to bargain for favorable lease provisions is further hampered. Because the typical landlord–tenant relationship can no longer fairly be characterized as one in which the parties have equal knowledge and bargaining power, it is not always realistic to presume that tenants are capable of negotiating to protect their own interests.

Although it was initially slow to recognize the changing nature of the landlord–tenant relationship, the law now tends to place greater emphasis than it once did on the contract components of the relationship. As a result, modern contract doctrines such as unconscionability, constructive conditions, the duty to mitigate damages, and implied warranties are applied to leases. Such doctrines may operate to compensate for tenants' lack of bargaining power. In addition, state legislatures and city councils have enacted statutes and ordinances that increasingly regulate leased property and the landlord–tenant relationship.

This chapter's discussion of landlord–tenant law will focus on the nature of leasehold interests, the traditional rights and duties of landlords and tenants, and recent statutory and judicial developments affecting those rights and duties. ∞

LEASES AND TENANCIES

Nature of Leases

A **lease** is a contract under which an owner of property, the **landlord** (also called the *lessor*), conveys to the **tenant** (also called the *lessee*) the exclusive right to possess property for a period of time. The property interest conveyed to the tenant is called a **leasehold estate.**

Types of Tenancies

The duration of the tenant's possessory right depends upon the type of **tenancy** established by or resulting from the lease. There are four main types of tenancies.

1. *Tenancy for a term.* In a **tenancy for a term** (also called a *tenancy for years*), the landlord and tenant have agreed on a specific duration of the lease and have fixed the date on which the tenancy will terminate. For example, if Dudley, a college student, leases an apartment for the academic year ending May 29, 1998, a tenancy for a term will have been created. The tenant's right to possess the property ends on the date agreed upon without any further notice, unless the lease contains a provision permitting extension.

2. *Periodic tenancy.* A **periodic tenancy** is created when the parties agree that rent will be paid in regular successive intervals until notice to terminate is given, but do not agree on a specific lease duration. If the tenant pays rent monthly, the tenancy is from month to month; if the tenant pays yearly, as is sometimes done under agricultural leases, the tenancy is from year to year. (Periodic tenancies therefore are sometimes called *tenancies from month to month* or *tenancies from year to year.*) To terminate a periodic tenancy, either party must give advance notice to the other. The precise amount of notice required is often defined by state statutes. For example, to terminate a tenancy from month to month, most states require that the notice be given at least one month in advance.

3. *Tenancy at will.* A **tenancy at will** occurs when property is leased for an indefinite period of time and either party may choose to conclude the tenancy at any time. Generally, tenancies at will involve situations in which the tenant either does not pay rent or does not pay it at regular intervals. For example, Landon allows her friend Trumbull to live in the apartment over her garage. Although this tenancy's name indicates that it is terminable "at [the] will" of either party, most states require that the landlord give reasonable advance notice to the tenant before exercising the right to terminate the tenancy.

4. *Tenancy at sufferance.* A **tenancy at sufferance** occurs when a tenant remains in possession of the property (holds over) after a lease has expired. In this situation, the landlord has two options: (1) treating the holdover tenant as a trespasser and bringing an action to eject him; and (2) continuing to treat him as a tenant and collecting rent from him. Until the landlord makes her election, the tenant is a tenant at sufferance. Suppose that Templeton has leased an apartment for one year from Larson. At the end of the year, Templeton holds over and does not move out. Templeton is a tenant at sufferance. Larson may have him ejected or may continue treating him as a tenant. If Larson elects the latter alternative, a new tenancy is created. The new tenancy will be either a tenancy for a term or a periodic tenancy, depending on the facts of the case and any presumptions established by state law. Thus, a tenant who holds over for even a few days runs the risk of creating a new tenancy he might not want.

Execution of a Lease

As transfers of interests in land, leases may be covered by the statute of frauds. In most states, a lease for a term of more than one year from the date it is made is unenforceable unless it is evidenced by a suitable writing signed by the party to be charged. A few states, however, require leases to be evidenced by a writing only when they are for a term of more than three years.

CONCEPT   REVIEW

Types of Tenancies

TYPE OF LEASE	CHARACTERISTICS	TERMINATION
Tenancy for a Term	Landlord and tenant agree on a specific duration of the lease and fix the date on which the tenancy will end	Ends automatically on the date agreed upon; no additional notice necessary
Periodic Tenancy	Landlord and tenant agree that tenant will pay rent at regular, successive intervals (e.g., month to month)	Either party may terminate by giving the amount of advance notice required by state law
Tenancy at Will	Landlord and tenant agree that tenant may possess property for an indefinite amount of time, with no agreement to pay rent at regular, successive intervals	May be terminated "at will" by either party, but state law requires advance notice
Tenancy at Sufferance	Tenant remains in possession after the termination of one of the leaseholds described above, until landlord brings ejectment action against tenant or collects rent from him	Landlord has choice of: 1. Treating tenant as a trespasser and bringing ejectment action against him, or 2. Accepting rent from tenant, thus creating a new leasehold

Good business practice demands that leases be carefully drafted to make clear the parties' respective rights and obligations. Care in drafting leases is especially important in cases of long-term and commercial leases. Lease provisions normally cover such essential matters as the term of the lease, the rent to be paid, the uses the tenant may make of the property, the circumstances under which the landlord may enter the property, the parties' respective obligations regarding the condition of the property, and the responsibility (as between landlord and tenant) for making repairs. In addition, leases often contain provisions allowing a possible extension of the term of the lease and purporting to limit the parties' rights to assign the lease or sublet the property. State or local law often regulates lease terms. For example, the Uniform Residential Landlord and Tenant Act (URLTA) has been enacted in a substantial minority of states. The URLTA prohibits the inclusion of certain lease provisions, such as a clause by which the tenant supposedly agrees to pay the landlord's attorney's fees in an action to enforce the lease. In states that have not enacted the URLTA, lease terms are likely to be regulated at least to a moderate degree by some combination of state statutes, common law principles, and local housing codes.

RIGHTS, DUTIES, AND LIABILITIES OF THE LANDLORD

Landlord's Rights

The landlord is entitled to receive the *agreed rent* for the term of the lease. Upon expiration of the lease, the landlord has the right to the *return of the property in as good a condition as it was when leased,* except for normal wear and tear and any destruction caused by an act of God.

Security Deposits   Landlords commonly require tenants to make security deposits or advance payments of rent. Such deposits operate to protect the landlord's right to receive rent as well as her right to reversion of the property in good condition. In recent years, many cities and states have enacted statutes or ordinances designed to prevent landlord abuse of security deposits. These laws typically limit the amount a landlord may demand and require that the security deposit be refundable, except for portions withheld by the landlord due to the tenant's nonpayment of rent or tenant-caused property damage beyond ordinary wear and tear. Some statutes or ordinances also require the landlord to place the funds in interest-bearing accounts when the lease is for more than a minimal period of time. As a general rule, these laws require landlords to provide tenants a written accounting regarding their security deposits and any portions being withheld. Such an accounting normally must be provided within a specified period of time (30 days, for example) after the termination of the lease. The landlord's failure to comply with statutes and ordinances regarding security deposits may cause the landlord to experience adverse consequences that vary state by state.

Landlord's Duties

Fair Housing Act As explained in Chapter 24, the Fair Housing Act prohibits housing discrimination on the basis of race, color, sex, religion, national origin, handicap, and familial status.[1] The Fair Housing Act prohibits discriminatory practices in various transactions affecting housing, including the rental of dwellings.[2] Included within the act's prohibited instances of discrimination against a protected person are refusals to rent property to such a person, discrimination against him or her in the terms, conditions, or privileges of rental, publication of any advertisement or statement indicating any preference, limitation, or discrimination operating to the disadvantage of a protected person, and repre-

sentations that a dwelling is not available for rental to such a person when, in fact, it is available.

The act also makes it a discriminatory practice for a landlord to refuse to permit a tenant with a handicap to make—at his own expense—reasonable modifications to leased property. The landlord may, however, condition this permission on the tenant's agreement to restore the property to its previous condition upon termination of the lease, reasonable wear and tear excepted. In addition, landlords are prohibited from refusing to make reasonable accommodations in rules, policies, practices, or services if such accommodations are necessary to afford a handicapped tenant equal opportunity to use and enjoy the leased premises. When constructing certain types of multifamily housing for first occupancy, property owners and developers risk violating the act if they fail to make the housing accessible to persons with handicaps.

Due to a perceived increase in the frequency with which landlords would refuse to rent to families with children, the act prohibits landlords from excluding families with children. If, however, the dwelling falls within the act's "housing for older persons" exception, this prohibition does not apply.[3]

In *Walker v. Crigler,* which follows, the court demonstrates the importance of the public policy notions underlying the Fair Housing Act by holding that a property owner may be held liable for his agent's discriminatory actions even if the property owner has instructed the agent to comply with applicable antidiscrimination laws.

---

[1]Familial status is defined in Chapter 24.

[2]The act provides an exemption for certain persons who own and rent single-family houses. To qualify for this exemption, owners must not use a real estate broker or an illegal advertisement and cannot own more than three such houses at one time. It also exempts owners who rent rooms or units in dwellings in which they themselves reside, if those dwellings house no more than four families.

---

[3]The "housing for older persons" exception is described in Chapter 24.

WALKER v. CRIGLER 976 F.2d 900 (4th Cir. 1992)

A lleging that the following facts amounted to discrimination on the basis of sex in the rental of housing and that the Fair Housing Act was therefore violated, Darlene Walker filed suit against property owner Frank Whitesell and his property manager, Constance Crigler. Walker, a single mother of one son, worked in Falls Church, Virginia, and wished to rent an apartment there for herself and her son. In July 1989, Walker sought the assistance of the Town and Country Properties (TCP) firm. TCP agents showed Walker the Multiple Listing Service (MLS) listings of available rental properties in Falls Church. After reviewing these listings, Walker became interested in an apartment located at 124 Falls Avenue. Whitesell owned this property. Crigler, a professional realtor, served as Whitesell's property manager for 124 Falls Avenue and other rental properties owned by Whitesell. Crigler's responsibilities included finding financially qualified tenants for Whitesell's properties.

The MLS listing for 124 Falls Avenue specified $600 per month as the rent and described the property as a two-bedroom apartment that was "ideal for two men." Walker decided that she wanted to rent the apartment because it was close to a school for her son and was accessible to public transportation facilities. A TCP agent testified at trial that when he told Crigler he intended to submit the rental application of a financially qualified single mother (Walker), Crigler stated that she would not rent to a female applicant under any circumstances. Another TCP agent contacted Crigler on Walker's behalf; Crigler reiterated her policy of not renting to women. Walker testified that when she personally telephoned Crigler regarding the apartment, Crigler stated essentially the same thing and added that in the past, boyfriends of single female tenants had caused problems. Roughly two months after these conversations took place, the 124 Falls Avenue apartment was rented to two men who paid a total monthly rent of $580—$20 per month less than what Walker had been willing to pay.

Crigler testified that she never told anyone she would not rent the apartment to a single woman. The evidence revealed that in January 1989 (approximately six months before Walker's unsuccessful attempt to rent the apartment), Whitesell's awareness of housing discrimination suits against landlords caused him to send Crigler a memorandum instructing her to comply with applicable antidiscrimination laws in screening possible tenants for his rental properties.

An instruction given by the trial judge to the jury stated that if the jury found Fair Housing Act violations on Crigler's part, Whitesell would also be liable if Crigler was Whitesell's agent and was acting within the scope of her employment at the time she engaged in discrimination. The jury returned a verdict in Walker's favor against Crigler for $5,000 in compensatory damages. The jury ruled in Whitesell's favor, however, on Walker's claim against him. The trial judge denied Walker's motions for judgment notwithstanding the verdict and for a new trial. Walker appealed. ⌒⌒

Murnaghan, Circuit Judge   The jury ruled in Whitesell's favor, holding, apparently, that Crigler [despite clearly being Whitesell's agent] was not acting in the scope of her employment when she denied Walker's attempts to rent the 124 Falls Avenue premises because Walker was a woman. The sole evidence to support the jury's conclusion that Whitesell was not liable for damages for the discrimination was the evidence indicating that Crigler was instructed not to refuse to rent on discriminatory grounds. In denying the motion for judgment notwithstanding the verdict, the trial judge concluded that the evidence of Whitesell's instruction was sufficient to support the jury's verdict. We find, however, that the court's conclusion is based on an erroneous theory of law. Since there is no unsettled question of fact to be submitted for decision by the jury, it is appropriate to reverse the judgment that Whitesell was not liable for compensatory damages and to direct entry of judgment against Whitesell in Walker's favor in the amount of $5,000.

The evidence is sufficient to support the conclusion that Whitesell specifically intended that Crigler not discriminate. In many cases involving issues other than housing discrimination, such a finding would refute the assertion that Crigler acted within the scope of employment and would concurrently shield Whitesell from any liability as principal.

However, the arguable conclusion that Crigler acted outside the scope of employment is irrelevant in the present case, for Whitesell could not insulate himself from liability for sex discrimination in regard to living premises owned by him and managed for his benefit merely by relinquishing the responsibility for preventing such discrimination to another party. We adopt the general rule applied by other federal courts that the duty of a property owner not to discriminate in the leasing or sale of that property is nondelegable.

We are not unmindful of the arguable incongruity of applying liability to Whitesell and . . . similarly situated [property owners] who are apparently non-culpable in a housing discrimination instance but must still bear the burden of liability. The central question to be decided in a case such as this, however, is which innocent party—the owner whose agent acted contrary to his instruction, or the potential renter who felt the direct harm of the agent's discriminatory failure to offer the residence for rental—will ultimately bear the burden of the harm caused. It is clear that the overriding societal priority of the provision of "fair housing throughout the United States" (clearly set out in the Fair Housing Act) indicates that the one innocent party with the power to control the acts of the agent—the owner of the property or other responsible superior—must act to compensate the injured party for the harm and to ensure that similar harm will not occur in the future.

It must not be overlooked that although the property owner's duty to prevent discrimination is nondelegable, the owner [usually] will not be subjected to liability for the full amount of all successful claims, [because] contribution from other liable parties may offset some or all of the payment for which the owner is responsible. [Although Crigler, in a separate legal proceeding, filed for bankruptcy and obtained a discharge of her judgment debt to Walker and any contribution-related obligation to Whitesell,] we may assume in the great majority of cases that real estate agents will not turn bankrupt or otherwise [become] judgment-proof. They will remain liable for damages flowing from flaunting a principal's intentions.

Just as we feel no qualms in holding a property owner responsible for paying property taxes, meet-

ing health code safety requirements, or ensuring that other responsibilities to protect the public are met—and we refuse to allow the owner to avoid these responsibilities with an assertion that he conferred the duty to another—we must hold those who benefit from the sale and rental of property to the public to the specific mandates of antidiscrimination law if the goal of equal housing opportunity is to be reached. Whitesell, despite forbidding discrimination on the part of Crigler, cannot, under the Fair Housing Act, dispose of his duty to prevent sexual discrimination in the rental of 124 Falls Avenue, a property which he owned and which was operated for his benefit.

Judgment in favor of Whitesell reversed; trial court ordered to enter judgment in favor of Walker and against Whitesell for $5,000 in compensatory damages.

Implied Warranty of Possession   Landlords have certain obligations that are imposed by law whenever property is leased. One of these obligations stems from the landlord's **implied warranty of possession.** This warranty guarantees the tenant's right to possess the property for the term of the lease. Suppose that Turner rents an apartment from Long for a term to begin on September 1, 1997, and to end on August 31, 1998. When Turner attempts to move in on September 1, 1997, she finds that Carlson, the previous tenant, is still in possession of the property. In this case, Long has breached the implied warranty of possession.

Implied Warranty of Quiet Enjoyment   By leasing property, the landlord also makes an **implied warranty of quiet enjoyment** (or *covenant of quiet enjoyment*). This covenant guarantees that the tenant's possession will not be interfered with as a result of the landlord's act or omission. In the absence of a contrary provision in the lease or an emergency that threatens the property, the landlord may not enter the leased property during the term of the lease. If he does, he will be liable for trespass. In some cases, courts have held that the covenant of quiet enjoyment was violated when the landlord failed to stop third parties, such as trespassers or other tenants who make excessive noise, from inter-

fering with the tenant's enjoyment of the leased premises.

Constructive Eviction   The doctrine of **constructive eviction** may aid a tenant when property becomes unsuitable for the purposes for which it was leased because of the landlord's act or omission, such as the breach of a duty to repair or the covenant of quiet enjoyment. Under this doctrine, which applies both to residential and commercial property, the tenant may terminate the lease because he has effectively been evicted as a result of the poor condition or the objectionable circumstances there. Constructive eviction gives a tenant the right to vacate the property without further rent obligation if he does so *promptly* after giving the landlord reasonable notice and an opportunity to correct the problem. Because constructive eviction requires the tenant to vacate the leased premises, it is an unattractive option, however, for tenants who cannot afford to move or do not have a suitable alternative place to live.

Landlord's Responsibility for Condition of Leased Property

The common law historically held that landlords made no implied warranties regarding the *condition* or *quality* of leased premises. As an adjunct to the landlord's right to receive the leased property in good condition at the termination of the lease, the common law imposed on the *tenant* the duty to make repairs. Even when the lease contained a landlord's express warranty or express promise to make repairs, a tenant was not entitled to withhold rent if the landlord failed to carry out his obligations. This was because a fundamental contract performance principle—that a party is not obligated to perform if the other party fails to perform—was considered inapplicable to leases. In recent years, however, changing views of the landlord-tenant relationship have resulted in dramatically increased legal responsibility on the part of landlords for the condition of leased residential property.

Implied Warranty of Habitability   The legal principle that landlords made no implied warranty regarding the condition of leased property arose during an era when tenants used land primarily for agricultural purposes. Buildings existing on the property were frequently of secondary importance. They also tended to be simple structures, lacking modern conveniences such as plumbing and wiring. These buildings were fairly easily inspected and repaired by the tenant, who was generally more self-sufficient than today's typical tenant. In view of the relative simplicity of the structures, landlord and tenant were considered to have equal knowledge of the property's condition upon commencement of the lease. Thus, a rule requiring the tenant to make repairs seemed reasonable.

The position of modern residential tenants differs greatly from that of an earlier era's agricultural tenants. The modern residential tenant bargains not for the use of the ground itself but for the use of a building (or portion thereof) as a dwelling. The structures on land today are complex, frequently involving systems (such as plumbing and electrical systems) to which the tenant does not have physical access. Besides decreasing the likelihood of perceiving defects during inspection, this complexity compounds the difficulty of making repairs—something at which today's tenant already tends to be less adept than his grandparents were. Moreover, placing a duty on tenants to negotiate for express warranties and duties to repair is no longer feasible. Residential leases are now routinely executed on standard forms provided by landlords.

For these reasons, statutes or judicial decisions in most states now impose an **implied warranty of habitability** on landlords leasing residential property. According to the vast majority of cases, this warranty is applicable only to *residential* property, and not to property leased for commercial uses. The implied warranty of habitability's content in lease settings is basically the same as in the sale of real estate—the property must be safe and suitable for human habitation. In lease settings, however, the landlord not only must deliver a habitable dwelling at the beginning of the lease but also must *maintain* the property in a habitable condition during the term of the lease. Various statutes and judicial decisions provide that the warranty includes an obligation that the leased property comply with any applicable housing codes. From a tenant's point of view, the implied warranty of habitability is superior to constructive eviction because a tenant does not have to vacate the leased premises in order to seek a remedy for breach of the warranty.

Remedies for Breach of Implied Warranty of Habitability   The particular remedies for breach of the implied warranty of habitability differ from state to state. Some of the remedies a tenant may pursue include:

1. *Action for damages.* The breach of the implied warranty of habitability violates the lease and renders the landlord liable for damages. The damages generally are measured by the diminished value of the leasehold. Nevertheless, damages for personal injury are sometimes available, as in *Johnson v. Scandia Associates, Inc.,* which follows shortly. The landlord's breach of the implied warranty of habitability may also be asserted by the tenant as a counterclaim and defense in the landlord's action for eviction and/or nonpayment of rent.

2. *Termination of lease.* In extreme cases, the landlord's breach of the implied warranty of habitability may justify the tenant's termination of the lease. For this remedy to be appropriate, the landlord's breach must have been substantial enough to constitute a material breach.

3. *Rent abatement.* Some states permit rent abatement, a remedy under which the tenant withholds part of the rent for the period during which the landlord was in breach of the implied warranty of habitability. Where authorized by law, this approach allows the tenant to pay a reduced rent that reflects the *actual* value of the leasehold in its defective condition. There are different ways of computing this value. State law determines the amount by which the rent will be reduced.

4. *Repair-and-deduct.* A growing number of states have statutes permitting the tenant to have defects repaired and to deduct the repair costs from her rent. The repairs authorized in these statutes are usually limited to essential services such as electricity and plumbing. They also require that the tenant give the landlord notice of the defect and an adequate opportunity to make the repairs himself.

Housing Codes   Many cities and states have enacted housing codes that impose duties on property owners with respect to the condition of leased property. Typical of these provisions is Section 2304 of the District of Columbia Housing Code, which provides: "No person shall rent or offer to rent any habitation or the furnishing thereof unless such habitation and its furnishings are in a clean, safe and sanitary condition, in repair and free from rodents or vermin." Such codes commonly call for the provision and maintenance of necessary services such as heat, water, and electricity, as well as suitable bathroom and kitchen facilities. Housing codes also usually require that specified minimum space-per-tenant standards be met, that windows, doors, floors, and screens be kept in repair, that the property be painted and free of lead paint, that keys and locks meet certain specifications, and that the landlord issue written receipts for rent payments. A landlord's failure to comply with an applicable housing code may result in a fine or in liability for injuries resulting from the property's disrepair. The noncompliance may also result in the landlord's losing part or all of his claim to the agreed-upon rent. Some housing codes establish that tenants have the right to withhold rent until necessary repairs have been made and the right to move out in cases of particularly egregious violations of housing code requirements.

JOHNSON v. SCANDIA ASSOCIATES, INC.   641 N.E.2d 51 (Ind. Ct. App. 1994)

Terri Johnson lived in an apartment building owned by Scandia Associates, Inc. She suffered electric shock–related personal injuries when she simultaneously touched the oven and the refrigerator in her apartment. Johnson sued Scandia on the theories of negligence and breach of the implied warranty of habitability. Because the trial court granted Scandia's motion to dismiss the breach of implied warranty of habitability claim, the case went to trial solely on the negligence claim. The jury concluded that Scandia was not negligent. Johnson appealed the dismissal of her breach of implied warranty of habitability claim. ⌒

Najam, Judge   Johnson raises only one issue for our review: whether the implied warranty of habitability in a residential lease agreement includes damages resulting from personal injury [such as the electric shock–related injury she suffered in her apartment]. Johnson acknowledges that our courts have not held that this warranty applies to claims for personal injuries. However, she contends that the implied warranty of habitability in residential leases should be extended to personal injury claims to carry out the reasonable expectations of the parties.

[W]e find guidance in our supreme court's decision [in *Barnes v. Mac Brown & Co.* (1976), in which the court held that a builder-vendor of a new home makes an implied warranty of habitability that may sometimes be invoked by a subsequent purchaser of a home]. [In *Barnes,*] the court observed: "The contention that a distinction should be drawn between mere 'economic loss' and personal injury is without merit. Why there should be a difference between an economic loss resulting from injury to property and an economic loss resulting from personal injury has not been revealed to us." We are likewise unconvinced that, upon a breach of the implied warranty of habitability in a residential lease, a distinction exists between recovery of damages for economic loss and recovery of damages for personal injury.

A landlord's warranty of habitability is an implied promise to "avoid hidden defects or concealed dangers" (quoting *Barnes*). Therefore, when a dangerous condition exists in the leased premises which is hidden or concealed from the tenant, damages for personal injury caused by the dangerous condition are within the contemplation of the parties as the probable result of the landlord's breach of the warranty. There is no rational reason to preclude recovery of damages for personal injury when such damages arise naturally from the condition of the premises.

Barnes demonstrate[s] that the implied warranty of habitability in a residential lease has its origins in the law of residential sales. Further, our supreme court has noted that with respect to the implied warranty of habitability, the sale of real estate should not be treated differently from the sale of personal property. Accordingly, we find guidance in the provisions of our commercial code governing recovery of damages for the sale of defective goods. [A] warranty of merchantability is implied in a contract for the sale of goods if the seller is a merchant with respect to goods of that kind. [R]ecovery of damages for personal injury [is allowed in a case of] breach of an implied warranty for the sale of goods.

In the landlord and tenant context, the analog to the merchant seller is the professional landlord that is in the business of renting dwellings to tenants. The analogy to damages for a merchant's breach of an implied warranty in the sale of goods was made complete by our decision in *Zimmerman v. Moore* (1982), where we held that the implied warranty of habitability does not extend to a non-merchant lessor. There, we noted the two principal philo-

sophical justifications supporting the implied warranty doctrine: (1) the requirement of a sale by a merchant . . . or person engaged in the business presupposes a superior expertise and knowledge not possessed by the consumer and (2) the merchant is in a better position to absorb the loss and spread it throughout the industry. We reasoned in *Zimmerman* that both philosophical underpinnings are absent when a non-merchant lessor casually rents a single-family dwelling. The requirement of a professional landlord, found lacking in *Zimmerman,* is [allegedly] present in this case. [C]onstrued most favorably to Johnson, the complaint demonstrates that Scandia is a professional landlord in the business of renting apartments and is in a better position to absorb and spread the costs of liability for personal injury claims.

Implied warranties are imposed by operation of law for the protection of the consumer, and they must be liberally construed in favor of the consumer. Therefore, we hold that the implied warranty of habitability in a residential lease extends to claims for personal injuries that result from a dangerous condition in the leased premises which is hidden or concealed. [T]he plaintiff's implied warranty claim for personal injuries is actionable only if (1) the landlord is a professional landlord in the business of renting dwellings on a regular basis and (2) the plaintiff is a tenant in privity of contract with the landlord.

Judgment for Scandia reversed and case remanded for further proceedings.

Americans with Disabilities Act   Landlords leasing property constituting a *place of public accommodation* (primarily commercial property as opposed to private residential property) must pay heed to Title III of the Americans with Disabilities Act. Under Title III, owners and possessors of real property that is a place of public accommodation may be expected to make reasonable accommodations, including physical modifications of the property, in order to allow disabled persons to have access to the property. Chapter 24 contains a detailed discussion of Title III's provisions.

Landlord's Tort Liability

Traditional No-Liability Rule   There were two major effects of the traditional rule that a landlord had no legal responsibility for the condition of the leased property. The first effect—that the uninhabitability of the premises traditionally did not give a tenant the right to withhold rent, assert a defense to nonpayment, or terminate a lease—has already been discussed. The second effect was that landlords normally could not be held liable in tort for injuries suffered by tenants on leased property. This state of affairs stemmed from the notion that the tenant had the ability and responsibility to inspect the property for defects before leasing it. By leasing the property, the tenant was presumed to take it as it was, with any existing defects. As to any defects that might arise during the term of the lease, the landlord's tort immunity was seen as justified by his lack of control over the leased property once he had surrendered it to the tenant.

Traditional Exceptions to No-Liability Rule
Even before the current era's protenant legal developments, however, courts created exceptions to the no-liability rule. In the following situations, landlords have traditionally owed the tenant (or an appropriate third party) a duty, the breach of which could constitute a tort:

1. *Duty to maintain common areas.* Landlords have a duty to use reasonable care to *maintain the common areas* (such as stairways, parking lots, and elevators) over which they retain control. If a tenant or a tenant's guest sustains injury as a result of the landlord's negligent maintenance of a common area, the landlord is liable.

2. *Duty to disclose hidden defects.* Landlords have the duty to disclose hidden defects about which they know, if the defects are not reasonably discoverable by the tenant. The landlord is liable if a tenant or appropriate third party suffers injury because of a hidden danger that was known to the landlord but undisclosed.

3. *Duty to use reasonable care in performing repairs.* If a landlord repairs leased property, he must *exercise reasonable care in making the repairs.* The landlord may be liable for the consequences stemming from negligently performed repairs, even if he was not obligated to perform them.

4. *Duty to maintain property leased for admission to the public.* The landlord has a duty to suitably maintain property that is leased for *admission to the public.* A theater would be an example.

5. *Duty to maintain furnished dwellings.* The landlord who rents a *fully furnished dwelling* for a short time impliedly warrants that the premises are safe and habitable.

Except for the above circumstances, the landlord traditionally was not liable for injuries suffered by the tenant on leased property. Note that none of these exceptions would apply to one of the most common injury scenarios—when the tenant was injured by a defect in her own apartment and the defect resulted from the landlord's failure to repair rather than from negligently performed repairs.

Current Trends in Landlord's Tort Liability
Today, there is a strong trend toward abolition of the traditional rule of landlord tort immunity. The proliferation of housing codes and the development of the implied warranty of habitability have persuaded a sizable number of courts to impose on landlords the duty to use *reasonable care* in their maintenance of the leased property. As discussed earlier, a landlord's duty to keep the property in repair may be based on an express clause in the lease, the implied warranty of habitability, or provisions of a housing code or statute. The landlord now may be liable if injury results from her negligent failure to carry out her duty to make repairs. As a general rule, a landlord will not be liable unless she had *notice* of the defect and a reasonable opportunity to make repairs.

The duty of care landlords owe tenants has been held to include the duty to take reasonable steps to protect tenants from substantial risks of harm created by other tenants. Courts have held landlords liable for tenants' injuries resulting from dangerous conditions (such as vicious animals) maintained by other tenants when the landlord knew or had reason to know of the danger.

It is not unusual for landlords to attempt to insulate themselves from negligence liability to tenants by including an *exculpatory clause* in the standard form leases they expect tenants to sign. An exculpatory clause purports to relieve the landlord from legal responsibility that the landlord could otherwise face (on negligence or other grounds) in certain instances of premises-related injuries suffered by tenants. In recent years, a number of state legislatures and courts have frowned upon exculpatory clauses when they are included in leases of residential property. *Crawford v. Buckner,* which follows, illustrates the increasing judicial tendency to limit the effect of exculpatory clauses or declare them unenforceable on public policy grounds when they are included in residential leases.

I n order to rent an apartment in a building owned by Tobe McKenzie and McKenzie Development Corporation (MDC), Linda Crawford was required to sign a standard form lease provided by McKenzie and MDC. This lease contained an exculpatory clause stating that McKenzie and MDC "shall not be liable" to Crawford "for any injury to [Crawford's] person or loss of or damage to property for any cause." Two months after Crawford rented the apartment (which was located on the building's second floor), a fire broke out in the first-floor apartment of Debra and Larry Buckner. The fire spread to Crawford's apartment and blocked Crawford from escaping through the front (and only) door of her apartment. To escape the fire, Crawford jumped from a second-story window. When she landed, she sustained numerous injuries, partly due to debris on the ground behind the apartment building.

Crawford filed a negligence suit against the Buckners, McKenzie, and MDC. She alleged that McKenzie and MDC were negligent in failing to maintain the building's fire alarm system, in failing to maintain the ground area behind the apartment building, and in continuing to allow the Buckners to reside in the apartment complex despite numerous complaints to McKenzie and MDC about the Buckners' behavior. McKenzie and MDC asserted that the exculpatory clause in their lease with Crawford barred her negligence claim against them. The trial court agreed and granted those defendants' motion for summary judgment. When Tennessee's intermediate court of appeals affirmed, Crawford appealed to the Tennessee Supreme Court. ᴄᴏ

Anderson, Justice   The determinative issue raised in this appeal is whether an exculpatory clause in a residential lease bars recovery against the landlord for negligence which caused the tenant injury. An exculpatory clause in the context of a landlord-tenant relationship refers to a clause which deprives the tenant of the right to recover damages . . . by releasing the landlord from liability for future acts of negligence. [T]he argument for enforceability of such clauses has often been based upon the doctrine of freedom of contract. Some cases, especially older ones, have reasoned that the relationship of landlord and tenant is in no event a matter of public interest, but is purely a private affair, so that such clauses cannot be held void on public policy grounds. However, because of the burden-shifting effect of such clauses, which [purport to] grant immunity from [liability], it is not surprising that their validity has been challenged and that courts have reached different conclusions as to their enforceability.

McKenzie and MDC contend that freedom to contract in the residential lease setting is the majority rule in the United States, and that holding exculpatory provisions in residential leases invalid on public policy grounds would require this court to adopt the minority rule. We find, as the Washington Supreme Court found in *McCutcheon v. United Homes Corp.* (1971), that there is no majority rule,

"only numerous conflicting decisions . . . and a disposition of the courts to emasculate such exculpatory clauses by means of strict construction."

Tennessee courts have long recognized that, subject to certain exceptions, parties may contract that one shall not be liable for his negligence to another. We held in *Olson v. Molzen* (1977), however, that if an exculpatory provision [adversely affects] the public interest, it is void as against public policy, despite the general rule that parties may contract that one shall not be liable for his negligence to another. In *Olson,* we said that a exculpatory clause signed by a patient as a condition of receiving medical treatment is invalid as contrary to public policy and may not be pleaded as a bar to the patient's suit for negligence.

Crawford contends in this case that the exculpatory provision in her lease falls squarely within criteria set forth in *Olson* [and that] the exculpatory provision [should therefore be held] void as against public policy. In order to determine whether an exculpatory provision [adversely] affects the public interest, we adopted the following criteria in *Olson:*

1. It concerns a business of a type generally thought suitable for public regulation.

2. The party seeking exculpation is engaged in performing a service of great importance to the public (often a matter of practical necessity for some members of the public).

3. The party [seeking exculpation] holds himself out as willing to perform this service for any member of the public who seeks it, or at least for any member coming within certain established standards.

4. As a result of the essential nature of the service, in the economic setting of the transaction, the party invoking exculpation possesses a decisive advantage of bargaining strength against any member of the public who seeks his services.

5. In exercising a superior bargaining power, that party confronts the public with a standardized adhesion contract of exculpation, and makes no provision whereby a purchaser [or lessee] may pay additional reasonable fees and obtain protection against negligence.

6. As a result of the transaction, the person or property of the purchaser [or lessee] is placed under the control of the seller [or lessor], subject to the risk of carelessness by the seller [or lessor] or his agents.

In adopting these factors, we stated that "it is not necessary that all be present . . . , but generally a transaction that has some of these characteristics would be offensive."

[W]e conclude that a residential lease concerns a business of a type generally thought suitable for public regulation. Our conclusion is bolstered by the fact that the legislature of this state has seen fit to regulate [some aspects of the residential landlord-tenant relationship]. [W]e no longer live in a society where land, not housing, was the important part of a rental agreement. Residential landlords offer shelter, a basic necessity of life, to more than a million inhabitants of this state. Accordingly, it is self-evident that a residential landlord is engaged in performing a service of great importance to the public [and that this service] is often a matter of practical necessity for some members of the public. In addition, a residential landlord holds itself out as willing to perform a service for any member of the public who seeks it.

As a result of the essential nature of the service and the economic setting of the transaction, a residential landlord has a decisive advantage in bargaining strength against any member of the public who seeks its services. A potential tenant is usually confronted with a "take it or leave it" form contract, which the tenant is powerless to alter. Moreover, due to its superior bargaining position, a residential landlord confronts the public with a standardized adhesion contract of exculpation, which contains no provision whereby a tenant can pay additional reasonable fees to obtain protection from the landlord's negligence. Finally, we conclude that by definition, a residential lease places the person and the property of the tenant under the control of the landlord, subject to the risk of carelessness by the landlord and his agents. The allegations of this case [provide] common examples of landlord negligence [allegedly] causing injury to either the person or property of the tenant.

Accordingly, we find that the residential landlord-tenant relationship here satisfies all six of the public interest criteria adopted in *Olson v. Molzen.* However, McKenzie and MDC insist that a residential lease between a landlord and a tenant is a purely private affair. We disagree. We find persuasive the reasoning of the Washington Supreme Court, which, in response to the very same argument, stated:

[W]e are not faced merely with the theoretical duty of construing a provision in an isolated contract specifically bargained for by *one landlord and one tenant* as a purely private affair. Considered realistically, we are asked to construe an exculpatory clause, the generalized use of which may have an impact upon thousands of potential tenants.

McCutcheon v. United Homes Corp. (1971) (emphasis in original).

Based on the foregoing, we conclude that the exculpatory clause in the residential lease in this case is contrary to public policy. In reaching this conclusion, we join a growing number of states, [which either by statute or judicial decision] have declared exculpatory clauses [in residential leases] void as against public policy.

Summary judgment for McKenzie and MDC reversed; case remanded to trial court for further proceedings.

Landlord's Liability for Injuries Resulting from Others' Criminal Conduct Another aspect of the trend toward increasing landlords' legal accountability is that many courts have imposed on landlords the duty to take reasonable steps to protect tenants and others on their property from foreseeable criminal conduct.[4] Although landlords are not insurers of the safety of persons on their property, an increasing number of courts have found them liable for injuries sustained by individuals who were criminally attacked on the landlord's property if the attack was facilitated by the landlord's failure to comply with housing codes or maintain reasonable security. This liability has been imposed on residential and commercial landlords (such as shopping mall owners). Some courts have held that the implied warranty of habitability includes the obligation to provide reasonable security. In most states that have imposed this type of liability, however, principles of negligence or negligence per se furnish the controlling rationale.[5] *Erichsen v. No-Frills Supermarkets of Omaha, Inc.,* which follows, applies negligence principles in this fashion.

---

[4]Chapter 24 contains a more extensive discussion of courts' recent inclination to impose this duty on owners and possessors of property.

[5]The law of negligence is covered in detail in Chapter 7.

ERICHSEN v. NO-FRILLS SUPERMARKETS OF OMAHA, INC.   518 N.W. 2d 116 (Neb. Sup. Ct. 1994)

No-Frills Supermarkets of Omaha, Inc., operated a supermarket at a shopping center location leased from the center's owner, Harold Cooperman. Janice Erichsen had been shopping at this supermarket and was returning to her car, which was parked in the store's parking lot. Before Erichsen reached her car, she was robbed and beaten by an assailant. In the course of the attack, Erichsen, who was outside the assailant's vehicle, became entangled in the vehicle's safety belt. She was then dragged on the pavement for 1.6 miles. She sustained serious injuries as a result.

Erichsen sued No-Frills and Cooperman, alleging that they had negligently failed to warn her or take other reasonable steps to protect her against allegedly foreseeable criminal activities. Erichsen alleged that on at least 10 occasions within a 16-month period prior to the attack on her, similar crimes, including theft, purse-snatching, and robbery, had been committed in the No-Frills parking lot or in immediately surrounding areas. Erichsen also contended that No-Frills and Cooperman had a duty to foresee the type of criminal activity to which she fell victim and to take appropriate steps to guard against such harm. The district court sustained the demurrer of No-Frills and Cooperman, holding that they did not owe Erichsen a duty of reasonable care. Erichsen appealed. ∞

Lanphier, Justice For actionable negligence to exist, there must be a legal duty on the part of the defendant to [use reasonable care to] protect the plaintiff from injury, a failure to discharge that duty, and damage proximately resulting from such undischarged duty. A duty . . . may be defined as an obligation, to which the law will give recognition and effect, to conform to a particular standard of conduct toward another. Foreseeability is a factor in establishing a defendant's duty.

We have . . . held that a landlord is under a duty to exercise reasonable care to protect his patrons. Such care may require giving a warning or providing greater protection where there is a *likelihood* that third persons will endanger the safety of the visitors. We have applied these principles in several cases. In *Harvey v. Van Aelstyn* (1982), we held that no liability attached to the owner of a bar where [the plaintiff], a patron, was assaulted by a third party while in the bar. The assailant had not been present in the bar, but . . . entered the bar suddenly, went straight for [the plaintiff], and struck him. The assailant had been violent in the establishment on *one* prior occasion a year or more prior to the incident at issue. We stated that the possessor of the premises was not bound to anticipate the unforeseeable independent acts of third persons, nor did she have a duty to take precautionary measures to protect against such acts, because those acts could not reasonably be anticipated.

[An earlier] case, *Hughes v. Coniglio* (1946), denied recovery against a restaurant owner where a patron suffered injuries from an assault by another patron. This court noted that there was no history of any fights in the establishment and that the assault occurred suddenly and unexpectedly where no precautionary measures would have prevented the assault. In *C.S. v. Sophir* (1985), the plaintiff, a tenant in the defendant landlord's apartment complex, was sexually assaulted. There had been one prior assault in the complex. We held that it would be unfair to impose liability upon a landlord based on a *single* prior assault at the complex.

The most recent case involving landlord liability for the acts of third persons is *K.S.R. v. Novak & Sons, Inc.* (1987). In *K.S.R.,* [the plaintiff] was sexually assaulted in the apartment complex owned by [the defendant]. The assailant had been seen by the building manager several times near the complex exhibiting inappropriate sexual behavior in public. In *K.S.R.,* we held that unlike *Sophir,* there was a history of criminal activity on the premises, and therefore the assault perpetrated against [the plaintiff] was foreseeable. [We concluded] that liability could be imposed against a landlord for reasonably foreseeable criminal acts of third parties.

This court has denied relief where the [plaintiff] based his or her allegations of negligence on a single act of violence. However, as *K.S.R.* demonstrates, a duty to undertake reasonable precautionary measures will be imposed on the landlord when there is a sufficient amount of criminal activity to make further criminal acts reasonably foreseeable. The trial court was in error in determining that the prior criminal activity must all involve the same suspect to make further criminal acts reasonably foreseeable. Under our standard of review, the allegation of many occasions of "similar" criminal activity in one fairly contiguous area in a limited timespan may make further such acts sufficiently foreseeable to create a duty to a business invitee.

[By referring in her petition to at least 10 instances of criminal activity at or near the No-Frills parking lot, Erichsen has alleged facts that] are legally sufficient to support [her] assertion that [No-Frills and Cooperman] owed her a duty of reasonable care which they breached. Although [Erichsen] concedes that not all of the criminal activities took place in the No-Frills parking lot, she did allege that at least some of the incidents of criminal activity, including a purse-snatching, actually took place on the area of the parking lot assigned to No-Frills. Criminal acts that occur near the premises in question give notice of the risk that crime may travel to the premises of the business owner. Accordingly, the district court erred in sustaining the demurrer.

District court decision reversed and case remanded for further proceedings.

RIGHTS, DUTIES, AND LIABILITIES OF THE TENANT

Rights of the Tenant

The tenant has the right to *exclusive possession* and *quiet enjoyment* of the property during the term of the lease. The landlord is not entitled to enter the leased property without the tenant's consent, unless an emergency threatens the property or the landlord is acting under an express lease provision giving her the right to enter. The tenant may use the leased premises for any lawful purpose that is reasonable and appropriate, unless the purpose for which it may be used is expressly limited in the lease. Furthermore, the tenant has both the right to receive leased residential property in a habitable condition at the beginning of the lease and the right to have the property maintained in a habitable condition for the duration of the lease.

Duty to Pay Rent

The tenant, of course, has the duty to pay rent in the agreed amount and at the agreed times. If two or more persons are cotenants, their liability under the lease is *joint and several.* This means that each cotenant has complete responsibility—not just partial responsibility—for performing the tenants' duties under the lease. For example, Alberts and Baker rent an apartment from Caldwell, with both Alberts and Baker signing a one-year lease. If Alberts moves out after three months, Caldwell may hold Baker responsible for the entire rent, not just half of it. (Naturally, Alberts remains liable on the lease—as well as to Baker under any rent-sharing agreement the two of them had—but Caldwell is free to proceed against Baker solely if Caldwell so chooses.)

Duty Not to Commit Waste

The tenant also has the duty not to commit **waste** on the property. This means that the tenant is responsible for the routine care and upkeep of the property and that he has the duty not to commit any act that would harm the property. In the past, fulfillment of this duty required that the tenant perform necessary repairs. Today, the duty to make repairs has generally been shifted to the landlord by court ruling, statute, or lease provision. The tenant now has no duty to make major repairs unless the relevant damage was caused by his own negligence. When damage exists through no fault of the tenant and the tenant therefore is not obligated to make the actual repairs, the tenant nonetheless has the duty to take reasonable interim steps to prevent further damage from the elements. This duty would include, but not necessarily be limited to, informing the landlord of the problem. The duty would be triggered, for instance, when a window breaks or the roof leaks.

Assignment and Subleasing

As with rights and duties under most other types of contracts, the rights and duties under a lease may generally be assigned and delegated to third parties. **Assignment** occurs when the landlord or the tenant transfers all of her remaining rights under the lease to another person. For example, a landlord may sell an apartment building and assign the relevant leases to the buyer, who will then become the new landlord. A tenant may assign the remainder of her lease to someone else, who then acquires whatever rights the original tenant had under the lease (including, of course, the right to exclusive possession of the leased premises).

Subleasing occurs when the tenant transfers to another person some, but not all, of his remaining right to possess the property. The relationship of

FIGURE 1
Comparison of Assignment and Sublease

	ASSIGNMENT	SUBLEASE
Does the tenant transfer to the third party *all* his remaining rights under the lease?	Yes	No
Does the tenant remain liable on the lease?	Yes	Yes
Does the third party (assignee or sublessee) acquire rights and duties under the tenant's lease with the landlord?	Yes	No

tenant to sublessee then becomes one of landlord and tenant. For example, Dorfman, a college student whose 18-month lease on an apartment is to terminate on December 31, 1998, sublets his apartment to Wembley for the summer months of 1998. This is a sublease rather than an assignment, because Dorfman has not transferred all of his remaining rights under the lease.

The significance of the assignment–sublease distinction is that an assignee acquires rights and duties under the lease between the landlord and the original tenant, but a sublessee does not. An assignee steps into the shoes of the original tenant and acquires any rights she had under the lease.[6] For example, if the lease contained an option to renew, the assignee would have the right to exercise this option if he desired to do so. The assignee, of course, becomes personally liable to the landlord for the payment of rent.

Under both an assignment and a sublease, the original tenant remains liable to the landlord for the commitments made in the lease. If the assignee or sublessee fails to pay rent, for example, the tenant has the legal obligation to pay it. Figure 1 compares the characteristics of assignments and subleases.

Lease Provisions Limiting Assignment Leases commonly contain limitations on assignment and subleasing. This is especially true of commercial leases. Such provisions typically require the landlord's

[6]Assignment is discussed in detail in Chapter 17.

consent to any assignment or sublease, or purport to prohibit such a transfer of the tenant's interests. Provisions requiring the landlord's consent are upheld by the courts, although some courts hold that the landlord cannot withhold consent unreasonably. Total prohibitions against assignment may be enforced as well, but they are disfavored in the law. Courts usually construe them narrowly, resolving ambiguities against the landlord.

Tenant's Liability for Injuries to Third Persons

The tenant is normally liable to persons who suffer harm while on the portion of the property over which the tenant has control, *if the injuries resulted from the tenant's negligence.*

TERMINATION OF THE LEASEHOLD

A leasehold typically terminates because the lease term has expired. Sometimes, however, the lease is terminated early because of a party's material breach of the lease or because of mutual agreement.

Eviction

If a tenant breaches the lease (most commonly, by nonpayment of rent), the landlord may take action to **evict** the tenant. State statutes usually establish a relatively speedy eviction procedure. The landlord who desires to evict a tenant must be careful to comply with any applicable state or city regulations governing evictions. These regulations usually forbid self-help measures on the landlord's part, such as forcible entry to change locks. At common law, a landlord had a lien on the tenant's personal property. The landlord therefore could remove and hold such property as security for the rent obligation. This lien has been abolished in many states. Where the lien still exists, it is subject to constitutional limitations requiring that the tenant be given notice of the lien, as well as an opportunity to defend and protect his belongings before they can be sold to satisfy the rent obligation.

Agreement to Surrender

A lease may terminate prematurely by mutual agreement between landlord and tenant to **surrender** the lease (i.e., return the property to the landlord prior to the end of the lease). A valid surrender discharges the tenant from further liability under the lease.

Abandonment

Abandonment occurs when the tenant unjustifiably and permanently vacates the leased premises before the end of the lease term, and defaults in the payment of rent. If a tenant abandons the leased property, he is making an offer to surrender the leasehold. As shown in Figure 2, the landlord must make a decision at this point. If the landlord's conduct shows acceptance of the tenant's offer of surrender, the tenant is relieved of the obligation to pay rent for the remaining period of the lease. If the landlord does not accept the surrender, she may sue the tenant for the rent due until such time as she rents the property to someone else, or, if she cannot find a new tenant, for the rent due for the remainder of the term.

At common law, the landlord had no obligation to mitigate (decrease) the damages caused by the abandonment by attempting to rent the leased property to a new tenant. In fact, taking possession of the property for the purpose of trying to rent it to someone else was a risky move for the landlord—her retaking of possession might be construed as acceptance of the surrender. Many states now place the duty on the landlord to attempt to mitigate damages by making a reasonable effort to rerent the property. These states also hold that the landlord's retaking of possession for the purpose of rerenting does not constitute a waiver of her right to pursue an action to collect unpaid rent.

ETHICAL AND PUBLIC POLICY CONCERNS

1. Suppose you own an older house and have rented it to a family with three young children. A state statute forbids painting new property with lead-based paint, but it does not forbid renting older property previously painted with lead-based paint. Should you disclose the lead-based paint to your tenants? Would current landlord–tenant law require you to do so?

2. As discussed earlier, the implied warranty of habitability guarantees that leased residential prop-

FIGURE 2

Termination of a Leasehold by Abandonment

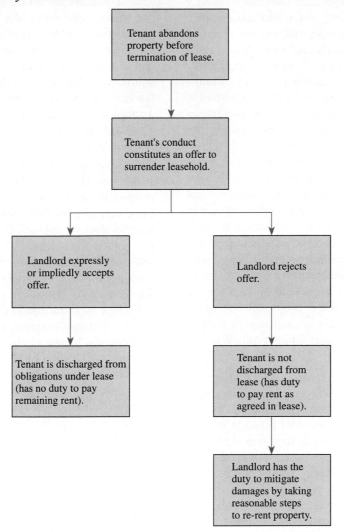

erty will be fit for human habitation and that the landlord will take the actions necessary to keep it in this condition during the term of the lease. Should this warranty be applied to landlords who are not in the business of leasing property but make occasional rentals? Should it apply to obviously rundown housing leased at very low rents?

3. When two or more persons lease property together, they are jointly and severally liable on the lease. This means that any one of them could be held liable to the landlord for 100 percent of the rent or damages. Is it ethical for one tenant to abandon leased property and leave his fellow cotenants with this liability?

PROBLEMS AND PROBLEM CASES

1. Dr. Kaminsky performed elective abortions in his medical practice. He leased office space from Fidelity in the Red Oak Atrium Building for a two-year term, beginning June 1983. The written lease included an express covenant of quiet enjoyment. In June 1984, antiabortion demonstrators began picketing at the building on Saturdays, when Dr. Kaminsky scheduled abortions. Singing and chanting demonstrators picketed in the building's parking lot, inner lobby, and atrium area. They approached patients to discourage them from entering the building, accused Dr. Kaminsky of killing babies, and distributed literature. The demonstrators frequently occupied the stairs leading to Dr. Kaminsky's office and prevented patients from entering the office by blocking the doorway. Occasionally, they gained access to the office waiting area. Dr. Kaminsky asked Fidelity for help in keeping the demonstrators away, but became frustrated by Fidelity's failures to respond. No security personnel were present on Saturdays, even though the lease obligated Fidelity to provide security service on Saturdays. Fidelity's attorneys prepared a notice to inform the demonstrators that they risked prosecution by not leaving when asked to do so, but Fidelity's agent did not distribute the notice. The Sheriff's office refused to ask the demonstrators to leave without a directive from Fidelity, whose only response was to state that it was aware of Dr. Kaminsky's problems. In early December 1984, Dr. Kaminsky abandoned the property and ceased paying rent. Fidelity sued for the balance due under the lease. Dr. Kaminsky argued that Fidelity constructively evicted him by breaching the covenant of quiet enjoyment. Was Dr. Kaminsky correct?

2. Dan Maltbie and John Burke, students at Indiana University, entered into a one-year written lease with Breezewood Management Company for the rental of an apartment in an older house in Bloomington, Indiana. The agreed rent was $235 per month. When Maltbie and Burke moved in, they discovered numerous defects: rotting porch floorboards, broken and loose windows, an inoperable front door lock, leaks in the plumbing, a back door that would not close, a missing bathroom door, inadequate water pressure, falling plaster, exposed wiring over the bathtub, and a malfunctioning toilet. Later, they discovered more leaks in the plumbing, a leaking roof, the absence of heat and hot water, cockroach infestation, and pigeons in the attic. The City of Bloomington had a housing code in effect at that time. Code enforcement officers inspected the apartment and found over 50 violations, 11 of which were "life-safety" violations (defined as conditions that might be severely "hazardous to health of the occupant"). These conditions remained largely uncorrected after notice by the code officers and further complaints by Maltbie and Burke. Maltbie vacated the apartment before the lease term expired, notified Breezewood, and refused to pay any further

rent. Breezewood agreed to let Burke remain and pay $112.50 per month. Breezewood then filed suit against Maltbie and Burke for $610.75, which was the balance due under the written rental contract plus certain charges. Maltbie and Burke filed counterclaims against Breezewood, claiming damages and abatement of the rent for breach of the implied warranty of habitability. Should Breezewood win the case, or should Maltbie and Burke?

3. Skiver rented an apartment from Brighton for a 12-month period beginning May 1, 1990. His monthly rent was $430.83. Skiver paid Brighton a $350 security deposit. Skiver moved elsewhere in June 1990. He paid $100 toward the June rent, and nothing thereafter. A substitute tenant was not located until March 1991. Brighton retained Skiver's security deposit and sued him in small claims court for unpaid rent. State law allowed landlords to retain security deposits to satisfy all or part of a rent arrearage and to compensate for "actual damages to the rental unit." However, a state statute also provided that "[i]n the case of damage to the rental unit or other obligation against the security deposit, the landlord shall mail to the tenant, within 45 days after the termination of occupancy, an itemized list of damages claimed for which the security deposit may be used." Another statute stated that if the landlord failed to provide such a list within the 45-day period, the landlord was obligated to refund the full security deposit and was disqualified from recovering damages from the tenant. Brighton provided no itemized list to Skiver. The small claims court concluded that Skiver owed Brighton eight months' rent plus the unpaid portion of the June 1990 rent. It granted Brighton a judgment of $2,650 (the court's $3,000 jurisdictional limit minus the retained security deposit). The court determined that Brighton did not need to provide an itemized list because Brighton did not claim that Skiver had caused any physical damage to the premises. Skiver appealed. Was Brighton entitled to retain the security deposit? Was Brighton entitled to judgment against Skiver for the rent arrearage exceeding the security deposit amount?

4. Kridel entered into a lease with Sommer, owner of the Pierre Apartments, to lease apartment 6-L for two years. Kridel, who was to be married in June, planned to move into the apartment in May. His parents and future parents-in-law had agreed to assume responsibility for the rent, because Kridel was a full-time student who had no funds of his own. Shortly before Kridel was to have moved in, his engagement was broken. He wrote Sommer a letter explaining his situation and stating that he could not take the apartment. Sommer did not answer the letter. When another party inquired about renting apartment 6-L, the person in charge told her that the apartment was already rented to Kridel. Sommer did not enter the apartment or show it to anyone until he rented apartment 6-L to someone else when there were approximately eight months left on Kridel's lease. He sued Kridel for the full rent for the period of approximately 16 months before the new tenant's lease took effect. Kridel argued that Sommer should not be able to collect rent for the first 16 months of the lease because he did not take reasonable steps to rerent the apartment. Was Sommer entitled to collect the rent he sought?

5. Brock, the administrator of Jackson's estate, sued Levie and Watts Realty in a wrongful death action. Prior to her death, Jackson lived in a Birmingham, Alabama, apartment building owned by Levie. Watts Realty had leased the apartment to Jackson. In her complaint, Brock alleged that Jackson had twice asked the defendants to repair the locks on the back door of Jackson's apartment, but that the defendants had failed to respond. After Jackson made these requests, she notified the police that a prowler was at the "back part" of the apartment. When the police came to the apartment to investigate, they discovered that Jackson had been fatally stabbed. Brock's complaint alleged that Jackson's murderer acquired access to the apartment because of the broken locks on the back door, and that Levie and Watts Realty should be held liable because they violated two Birmingham ordinances in failing to maintain the locks. These ordinances required locks on exterior doors and specified that the locks must be kept "in sound working condition and good repair." Apparently concluding as a matter of law that Levie and Watts Realty could not be held liable for Jackson's death at the hand of a murderer, the trial judge granted summary judgment in favor of Levie and Watts Realty. Was the trial judge correct in doing so?

6. Miguel Muniz, a nine-year-old boy, was permanently blinded when he was shot in the head while passing in front of a building owned by Lefran Realty. The bullet that struck Miguel was shot from inside Lefran Realty's building during a robbery of

the illegal "drug supermarket" operated by the tenant of a store located in the building. The illegal use of the store was well known to many people prior to the day when Miguel was shot. Although it had been raided by police on five occasions, the store reopened with the sale of drugs and narcotics soon after each raid. The building superintendent stated that patrons of the store went there to buy drugs rather than clothing and that he had reported the misuse of the store to the landlord several times before the shooting. The executive director of the neighborhood association had received many complaints about the store from persons in the neighborhood. Miguel and his mother brought a negligence suit against Lefran Realty. The trial court granted summary judgment in favor of Lefran Realty. Was the trial court correct in doing so?

7. From 1984 to 1986, Hardy occupied an apartment at 18 Arthur Street, which she leased from Griffin. Griffin had painted the apartment, but the previous coat of paint had not been scraped off. It was described as "thick, chipped, and peeling." Hardy saw her young son, Verron, eating paint chips in the apartment. This prompted her to have him tested for the presence of lead in his blood. She learned that Verron had abnormally high levels of lead in his blood and that this condition was due to his exposure to the lead-based paint present at 18 Arthur Street. Verron suffered severe brain damage as a result. Griffin admitted that in January 1987, he had received notice from the city about the presence of lead paint at 18 Arthur Street. On previous occasions, he had been put on notice that repairs to Hardy's unit were necessary. A state statute provided that "[t]he presence of paint which does not conform to federal standards as required in accordance with the Lead-Based Paint Poisoning Prevention Act . . . or of cracked, chipped, blistered, flaking, loose or peeling paint which constitutes a health hazard on accessible surfaces in any dwelling unit, tenement or any real property intended for human habitation shall be construed to render such dwelling unit . . . unfit for human habitation . . ." A city ordinance imposed a duty on landlords to "make all repairs and do whatever is necessary to put and keep the premises in a fit and habitable condition." Hardy brought suit against Griffin for Verron's injuries. Should Griffin be liable?

8. In October 1981, Cook entered into an oral lease to rent a residence to Melson. Melson agreed to pay

$400 per month, in advance, as rent. In November 1987, Cook sent Melson a letter advising that the rent would be increased to $525 per month, effective January 1, 1988, and asking whether Melson was going to pay. On December 10, 1987, Melson replied that he would not pay the increased rent. On January 2, 1988, Melson sent Cook a check for $400 as rent for January. Cook returned the check and stated that the rent was now $525. Melson did not vacate the premises until February 1, 1988. Cook brought a suit against Melson for $525, allegedly the unpaid rent for the month of January. Was Melson liable for the $525?

9. Sippin owned property on Main Street in Monroe, Connecticut. He rented this property to Longo and Ellam pursuant to a written lease, which stipulated that the premises was to be used exclusively for Longo's and Ellam's real estate business. Longo and Ellam did not know that the deed by which Sippin had acquired the property contained a restrictive covenant barring any commercial use of the property. After Longo and Ellam had been in possession of the property for a few months, the local zoning enforcement agency ordered them to remove a commercial real estate sign and to cease operating their business on the property because it was located in a residential zone. Although the residential zoning of the property was in effect at the time they entered into their lease with Sippin, Longo and Ellam had not previously known of this zoning designation. Further zoning enforcement action caused Longo and Ellam to wind up their real estate business and to vacate the property (without paying further rent) prior to the expiration of the term contemplated by their lease with Sippin. Sippin sued Longo and Ellam in an effort to recover the unpaid rent (as called for by the lease) for the remainder of the lease term, or, in the alternative, to recover the fair rental value of the premises pursuant to a line of Connecticut cases allowing landlords to collect the fair rental value of property from any tenant at sufferance. When the trial court ruled in favor of Long and Ellam, Sippin appealed. Was Sippin entitled to a judgment for the unpaid rent contemplated by the lease? Alternatively, did the line of cases dealing with tenants at sufferance entitle Sippin to a judgment for the fair rental value of the premises?

10. Norman owned a three-bedroom duplex in Dane County, Wisconsin. He adopted a policy of renting to married persons (and their families) or to a divorced, widowed, separated, or single person. Norman would not, however, rent to any *group of unrelated* individuals. A Dane County ordinance prohibited landlords from discriminating against potential tenants on the basis of "marital status." When Norman refused to rent his duplex to a group of three single women and to a later group consisting of two women plus a child of one of the women, Dane County instituted legal proceedings against Norman. The county alleged that he violated the ordinance referred to above. Did Norman violate the ordinance?

Estates and Trusts

One of the basic features of the ownership of property is the right to dispose of the property during life and at death. You have already learned about the ways in which property is transferred during the owner's life. The owner's death is another major event for the transfer of property. Most people want to be able to choose who will get their property when they die. There are a variety of ways in which a person may control the ultimate disposition of his property. He may take title to the property in a form of joint ownership that gives his co-owner a right of survivorship. He may create a trust and transfer property to it to be used for the benefit of a spouse, child, elderly parent, or other beneficiary. He may execute a will in which he directs that his real and personal property be distributed to persons named in the will. If, however, a person makes no provision for the disposition of his property at his death, his property will be distributed to his heirs as defined by state law. This chapter focuses on the transfer of property at death and on the use of trusts for the transfer and management of property, both during life and at death. ⌖

THE LAW OF ESTATES AND TRUSTS

Each state has its own statutes and common law regulating the distribution of property upon death. Legal requirements and procedures may vary from state to state, but many general principles can be stated. The **Uniform Probate Code (UPC)** is a comprehensive, uniform law that has been enacted in 18 states. It is intended to update and unify state law concerning the disposition and administration of property at death. Several relevant UPC provisions will be discussed in this chapter.

Estate Planning

A person's **estate** is all of the property owned by that person. **Estate planning** is the popular name for the complicated process of planning for the transfer of a person's estate in later life and at death. Estate planning also concerns planning for the possibility of prolonged illness or disability. An attorney who is creating an estate plan will take an inventory of the client's assets, learn the client's objectives, and draft the instruments necessary to carry out the plan. This plan is normally guided by the desire to reduce the amount of tax liability and to provide for the orderly disposition of the estate.

WILLS

Right of Disposition by Will

The right to control the disposition of property at death has not always existed. In the English feudal system, the king owned all land. The lords and knights had only the right to use land for their lifetime. A landholder's rights in land terminated upon his death, and no rights descended to his heirs. In 1215, the king granted the nobility the right to pass their interest in the land they held to their heirs. Later, that right was extended to all property owners. In the United States, each state has enacted statutes that establish the requirements for a valid will, including the formalities that must be met to pass property by will.

Nature of a Will

A **will** is a document executed with specific legal formalities by a **testator** (person making a will) that contains his instructions about the way his property will be disposed of at his death. A will can dispose only of property belonging to the testator at the time of his death. Furthermore, wills do not control property that goes to others through other planning devices (such as life insurance policies) or by operation of law (such as by right of survivorship). For example, property held in joint tenancy or tenancy by the entirety is not controlled by a will, because the property passes automatically to the surviving cotenant by right of survivorship. In addition, life insurance proceeds are controlled by the insured's designation of beneficiaries, not by any provision of a will. (Because joint tenancy and life insurance are ways of directing the disposition of property, they are sometimes referred to as "will substitutes.")

Common Will Terminology

Some legal terms commonly used in wills include the following:

1. *Bequest.* A **bequest** (also called **legacy**) is a gift of personal property or money. For example, a will might provide for a bequest of a family heirloom to the testator's daughter. Since a will can direct only property that is owned by the testator at the time of his death, a specific bequest of property that the testator has disposed of before his death is ineffective. This is called **ademption.** For example, Samuel's will states that Warren is to receive Samuel's collection of antique guns. If the guns are destroyed before Warren's death, however, the bequest is ineffective because of ademption.

2. *Devise.* A **devise** is a gift of real property. For example, the testator might devise his family farm to his grandson.

3. *Residuary.* The **residuary** is the balance of the estate that is left after specific devises and bequests are made by the will. After providing for the disposition of specific personal and real property, a testator might provide that the residuary of his estate is to go to his spouse or be divided among his descendants.

4. *Issue.* A person's **issue** are his lineal descendants (children, grandchildren, great-grandchildren, and so forth). This category of persons includes adopted children.

5. *Per capita.* This term and the next one, *per stirpes,* are used to describe the way in which a group of persons are to share a gift. **Per capita** means that each of that group of persons will share equally. For example, Grandfather dies, leaving a will that provides that the residuary of his estate is to go to his issue or descendants *per capita*. Grandfather had two children, Mary and Bill. Mary has two children, John and James. Bill has one child, Margaret. Mary and Bill die before Grandfather (in legal terms, *predecease* him), but all three of Grandfather's grandchildren are living at the time of his death. In this case, John, James, and Margaret would each take one-third of the residuary of Grandfather's estate.

6. *Per stirpes.* When a gift is given to the testator's issue or descendants **per stirpes** (also called **by right of representation**), each surviving descendant divides the share that his or her parent would have taken if the parent had survived. In the preceding example, if Grandfather's will had stated that the residuary of his estate was to go to his issue or descendants *per stirpes,* Margaret would take one-half and John and James would take one-quarter each (that is, they would divide the share that would have gone to their mother).

Testamentary Capacity

The capacity to make a valid will is called **testamentary capacity.** To have testamentary capacity, a person must be *of sound mind* and *of legal age,* which is 18 in most states. A person does not have to be in perfect mental health to have testamentary capacity. Because people often delay executing wills until they are weak and in ill health, the standard for mental capacity to make a will is fairly low. To be of "sound mind," a person need only be sufficiently rational to be capable of understanding the nature and character of his property, of realizing that he is making a will, and of knowing the persons who would normally be the beneficiaries of his affection. A person could move in and out of periods of lucidity and still have testamentary capacity if he executed his will during a lucid period.

Lack of testamentary capacity is a common ground upon which wills are challenged by persons who were excluded from a will. *Fraud* and *undue influence* are also common grounds for challenging the validity of a will.[1]

Execution of a Will

Unless a will is executed with the formalities required by state law, it is *void.* The courts are strict in interpreting statutes concerning the execution of wills. If a will is declared void, the property of the deceased person will be distributed according to the provisions of state laws that will be discussed later.

The formalities required for a valid will differ from state to state. For that reason, an individual should consult the laws of his state before making a

will. If he should move to another state after having executed a will, he should consult a lawyer in his new state to determine whether a new will needs to be executed. All states require that a will be *in writing.* State law also requires that a formal will be *witnessed,* generally by two or three *disinterested* witnesses (persons who do not stand to inherit any property under the will), and that it be *signed* by the testator or by someone else at the testator's direction. Most states also require that the testator *publish* the will—that is, declare or indicate at the time of signing that the instrument is his will. Another formality required by most states is that the testator sign the will in the presence and the sight of the witnesses and that the witnesses sign in the presence and the sight of each other. As a general rule, an **attestation clause,** which states the formalities that have been followed in the execution of the will, is written following the testator's signature. These detailed formalities are designed to prevent fraud. Section 2–502 of the UPC requires that a will must be in writing, signed by the testator (or in the testator's name by some other individual in the testator's conscious presence and by the testator's direction), and signed by at least two individuals, each of whom signed within a reasonable time after he witnessed either the signing of the will or the testator's acknowledgment of that signature or will. Also, under the UPC, any individual who is generally competent to be a witness may witness a will, and the fact that the witness is an interested party does not invalidate the will [2–505]. When a testator has made a technical error in executing a will, however, the UPC permits the document to be treated as if it had been executed properly if it can be proven by clear and convincing evidence that the testator intended the document to constitute his will [2–503].

In some situations, a lawyer might arrange to have the execution of a will *videotaped* to provide evidence relating to the testator's capacity and the use of proper formalities. (Note that the will is executed in the normal way; the videotape merely records the execution of the will.) Some state probate codes specifically provide that videotapes of the executions of wills are admissible into evidence.

Incorporation by Reference

In some situations, a testator might want his will to refer to and incorporate an existing writing. For

---

[1]Fraud and undue influence are discussed in detail in Chapter 13.

example, the testator may have created a list of specific gifts of personal property that he wants to incorporate in the will. A writing such as this is called an **extrinsic document**—that is, a writing apart from the will. In most states, the contents of extrinsic documents can be essentially incorporated into the will when the circumstances satisfy rules that have been designed to ensure that the document is genuine and that it was intended by the testator to be incorporated in the will. This is called **incorporation by reference.** For an extrinsic document to be incorporated by reference, it must have been *in existence at the time the will was executed.* In addition, the writing and the will must refer to each other so that the extrinsic document can be identified and so that it is clear that the testator intended the extrinsic document to be incorporated in the will. Under the UPC, incorporation by reference is allowed when the extrinsic document was in existence when the will was executed, the language of the will manifests the intent to incorporate the writing, and the will describes the writing sufficiently to identify it [2–510].

Informal Wills

Some states recognize certain types of wills that are not executed with these formalities. These are:

1. *Nuncupative wills.* A **nuncupative** will is an oral will. Such wills are recognized as valid in some states, but only under limited circumstances and to a limited extent. In a number of states, for example, nuncupative wills are valid only when made by soldiers in military service and sailors at sea, and even then they will be effective only to dispose of personal property that was in the actual possession of the person at the time the oral will was made. Other states place low dollar limits on the amount of property that can be passed by a nuncupative will.

2. *Holographic wills.* **Holographic wills** are wills that are written and signed in the testator's handwriting. You will see an example of a holographic will in *Foster v. Foster,* which appears later in this chapter. The fact that holographic wills are not properly witnessed makes them suspect. They are recognized in about half of the states and by section 2–502(b) of the UPC, even though they are not executed with the formalities usually required of valid wills. For a holographic will to be valid in the states that recognize them, it must evidence testa-

mentary intent and must actually be *handwritten* by the testator. A typed holographic will would be invalid. Some states require that the holographic will be *entirely* handwritten—although the UPC requires only that the signature and material portions of the will be handwritten by the testator [2–502(b)]—and some also require that the will be dated.

Joint and Mutual Wills

In some circumstances, two or more people—a married couple, for example—decide together on a plan for the disposition of their property at death. To carry out this plan, they may execute a **joint will** (a single instrument that constitutes the will of both or all of the testators and is executed by both or all) or they may execute **mutual wills** (joint or separate, individual wills that reflect the common plan of distribution).

Underlying a joint or mutual will is an agreement on a common plan. This common plan often includes an express or implied contract (a contract to make a will or not to revoke the will). One issue that sometimes arises is whether a testator who has made a joint or mutual will can later change his will. Whether joint and mutual wills are revocable depends on the language of the will, on state law, and on the timing of the revocation. For example, a testator who made a joint will with his spouse may be able to revoke his will during the life of his spouse, because the spouse still has a chance to change her own will, but he may be unable to revoke or change the will after the death of his spouse. The UPC provides that the mere fact that a joint or mutual will has been executed does *not* create the presumption of a contract not to revoke the will or wills [2–514].

Construction of Wills

Even in carefully drafted wills, questions sometimes arise as to the meaning or legal effect of a term or provision. Disputes about the meaning of the will are even more likely to occur in wills drafted by the testator himself, such as holographic wills. To interpret a will, a court will examine the entire instrument in an attempt to determine the testator's intent. The following case, *Foster v. Foster,* provides a good example of the methods and principles courts use to interpret wills.

FOSTER v. FOSTER   472 S.E.2d 678 (W. Va. Ct. App. 1996)

n March 23, 1994, Evelyn Foster died, leaving a house and nearly 400 acres of land in Mercer County along with personal property. She had executed a holographic will, which was offered for probate. The will states in part:

I—Evelyn Foster—being of sound Mind and Body—do hereby declare—In the event of my death—I herby [*sic*] will the farm—house + contents to go to Judy Foster Monk—any Monies shall be divided equally—after the funeral Expenses—between Greg Foster + Judy Foster Monk—also I do herby [*sic*] request that the Farm *not be sold!* Any personal items shall be equally divided—
Sincerely—
Evelyn Foster
If you have any doubt about this—Contact Charlie Smith.

Foster's son, Gregory, filed this action requesting the court to construe the meaning of the will. The trial court held that the will was ambiguous and therefore invalid. Foster's daughter, Judy, appealed.

Per Curiam   The sole issue on appeal is whether it is possible to put a meaning upon the language used in the will. In all other respects, the instrument meets the requirements necessary for a holographic will. Judy contends that her mother's holographic will is legible, coherent, and capable of interpretation. She asserts the real estate and house were clearly devised to her along with the contents of the house. Gregory argues that his mother only devised a "farm-house + contents" to his sister and the will leaves open the question of how the acreage surrounding the house should be distributed except for the provision that it should not be sold. He contends a differentiation should be made between the farmhouse and the farmland. He also asserts that should this Court hold that the will devised the farm and house to Judy, our decision would have the effect of nearly disinheriting him because the farm is the major asset of the estate.

In analyzing the parties' contentions, we must bear in mind two points of law. First, the law favors testacy over intestacy. Second, when at all possible, an attempt should be made to ascertain the meaning of a will so that it may be put into effect. The modern tendency is not to hold a will void for intestacy unless it is absolutely impossible to put a meaning upon it.

As a general rule, a devise of a farm includes the parcel of land used for farming purposes or incidental to the operation of a farm, along with any noncontiguous parcels owned by the testator that were used for farming. In this particular case, however, there is no dispute as to what constitutes the "farm." Gregory's contention that the will is ambiguous rests not on the language used in the will, but on the will's punctuation. He urges this Court to read the dash used between the words "farm" and "house" as a hyphen that links the two words into one. This construction would have the effect of conveying unto Judy only the "farmhouse" and leaves the question of who should receive the "farm" unanswered. Such interpretation violates the presumption against intestacy as to the whole or any part of the estate.

In ascertaining the testator's intentions, a court must consider the will as a whole and not focus upon isolated clauses or sentences. When we examine Ms. Foster's will, it is clear she substituted dashes in place of commas and addition signs in place of the word "and" throughout the instrument. A letter written by Ms. Foster that was admitted into evidence demonstrates it was her practice to use dashes in lieu of commas. For instance, a fair interpretation of the opening clause of the will, "I—Evelyn Foster—being of sound Mind + Body, do herby [*sic*] will the farm—house + contents to go to Judy Foster Monk," is "[in the event of my death, I hereby will the farm, house and contents to go to Judy Foster Monk."

Finally, Gregory's contention that the above conclusion renders him disinherited is unpersuasive. While he certainly receives a much smaller share of his mother's estate than he would have had she died intestate, he is specifically mentioned in the will. Under the terms of the will, he receives a portion of the estate and is not disinherited.

Based on the foregoing principles, we hold that the testamentary instrument in this case is a valid holographic will which evidences Ms. Foster's intentions to leave Judy the 400-acre farm, house, and contents of the house. The two children are to equally divide the personal property of their mother and the monetary assets of the estate remaining after payment of the funeral expenses.

Reversed and remanded in favor of Judy Foster Monk.

Limitations on Disposition by Will

A person who takes property by will takes it subject to all outstanding claims against the property. For example, if real property is subject to a mortgage or other lien, the beneficiary who takes the property gets it subject to the mortgage or lien. In addition, the rights of the testator's creditors are superior to the rights of beneficiaries under his will. Thus, if the testator was insolvent (his debts exceeded his assets), persons named as beneficiaries do not receive any property by virtue of the will.

Under the laws of most states, the surviving spouse of the testator has statutory rights in property owned solely by the testator that cannot be defeated by a contrary will provision. This means that a husband cannot effectively disinherit his wife, and vice versa. Even if the will provides for the surviving spouse, he or she can elect to take the share of the decedent's estate that would be provided by state law rather than the amount specified in the will. In some states, personal property, such as furniture, passes automatically to the surviving spouse.

At common law, a widow had the right to a life estate in one-third of the lands owned by her husband during their marriage. This was known as a widow's **dower right.** A similar right for a widower was known as **curtesy.** A number of states have changed the right by statute to give a surviving spouse a one-third interest in fee simple in the real and personal property owned by the deceased spouse at the time of his or her death. (Naturally, a testator can leave his spouse more than this if he desires.) Under UPC 2–201, the surviving spouse's elective share varies depending on the length of the surviving spouse's marriage to the testator—the elective share increases with the length of marriage.

As a general rule, a surviving spouse is given the right to use the family home for a stated period as well as a portion of the deceased spouse's estate. In community property states, each spouse has a one-half interest in community property that cannot be defeated by a contrary will provision. (Note that the surviving spouse will obtain *full* ownership of any property owned by the testator and the surviving spouse as joint tenants or tenants by the entirety.)

Children of the testator who were born or adopted after the will was executed are called **pretermitted** children. There is a presumption that the testator intended to provide for such a child, unless there is evidence to the contrary. State law gives pretermitted children the right to a share of the testator's estate. For example, under section 2–302 of the Uniform Probate Code, a pretermitted child has the right to receive the share he would have received under the state intestacy statute unless it appears that the omission of this child was intentional, the testator gave substantially all of his estate to the child's other parent, or the testator provided for the child outside of the will.

Revocation of Wills

One important feature of a will is that it is *revocable* until the moment of the testator's death. For this reason, a will confers *no present interest* in the testator's property. A person is free to revoke a prior will and, if she wishes, to make a new will. Wills can be revoked in a variety of ways. Physical destruction and mutilation done with intent to revoke a will constitute revocation, as do other acts such as crossing out the will or creating a writing that expressly cancels the will.

In addition, a will is revoked if the testator later executes a valid will that expressly revokes the earlier will. A later will that does not *expressly* revoke an earlier will operates to revoke only those portions of the earlier will that are inconsistent with the later will. Under the UPC, a later will that does not expressly revoke a prior will operates to revoke it by inconsistency if the testator intended the subsequent will to *replace* rather than *supplement* the prior will [2–507(b)]. Furthermore, the UPC presumes that the testator intended the subsequent will to replace rather than supplement the prior will if the subsequent one makes a complete disposition of her estate, but it presumes that the testator intended merely to supplement and not replace the prior will if the subsequent will disposes of only part of her estate [2–507(c), 2–507(d)]. In some states, a will is presumed to have been revoked if it cannot be located after the testator's death, although this presumption can be rebutted with contrary evidence.

Wills can also be revoked by operation of law without any act on the part of the testator signifying revocation. State statutes provide that certain changes in relationships operate as revocations of a will. In some states, marriage will operate to revoke a will that was made when the testator was single. Similarly, a divorce may revoke provisions in a will made during marriage that leave property to the divorced spouse. Under the laws of some states, the birth of a child after the execution of a will may operate as a partial revocation of the will.

Codicils

A **codicil** is an amendment of a will. If a person wants to change a provision of a will without making an entirely new will, she may amend the will by executing a codicil. One may *not* amend a will by merely striking out objectionable provisions and inserting new provisions. The same formalities are required for the creation of a valid codicil as for the creation of a valid will.

ADVANCE DIRECTIVES: PLANNING FOR DISABILITY

Advances in medical technology now permit a person to be kept alive by artificial means, even in many cases in which there is no hope of the person being able to function without life support. Many people are opposed to their lives being prolonged with no chance of recovery. In response to these concerns, almost all states have enacted statutes permitting individuals to state their choices about the medical procedures that should be administered or withheld if they should become incapacitated in the future and cannot recover. Collectively, these devices are called **advance directives.** An advance directive is a written document (such as a living will or durable power of attorney) that directs others how future health care decisions should be made in the event that the individual becomes incapacitated.

Living Wills

Living wills are documents in which a person states in advance his intention to forgo or obtain certain life-prolonging medical procedures. Almost all states have enacted statutes recognizing living wills. These statutes also establish the elements and formalities required to create a valid living will and describe the legal effect of living wills. Currently, the law concerning living wills is primarily a matter of state law and differs from state to state. Living wills are typically included with a patient's medical records. Many states require physicians and other health care providers to follow the provisions of a valid living will. Because living wills are created by statute, it is important that all terms and conditions of one's state statute be followed. Figure 1 shows an example of a living will form.

The importance of living wills and durable powers of attorney (which are discussed in the next section) was underscored in a 1990 U.S. Supreme Court case, *Cruzan v. Director, Missouri Department of Health. Cruzan,* which follows, held that it was constitutionally permissible for a state to refuse to permit the guardians of an incompetent person to terminate life support without clear and convincing evidence that the incompetent person would consent to such termination.

FIGURE   I

Living Will

LIVING WILL DECLARATION

Declaration made this _____ day of _____ , _____ . I, _____ , being at least eighteen (18) years of age and of sound mind, willfully and voluntarily make known my desires that my dying shall not be artificially prolonged under the circumstances set forth below, and I declare:

If at any time I have an incurable injury, disease, or illness certified in writing to be a terminal condition by my attending physician, and my attending physician has determined that my death will occur within a short time, and the use of life prolonging procedures would serve only to artificially prolong the dying process, I direct that such procedures be withheld or withdrawn and that I be permitted to die naturally with only the provision of appropriate nutrition and hydration and the administration of medication and the performance of any medical procedure necessary to provide me with comfort, care, or to alleviate pain.

In the absence of my ability to give directions regarding the use of life prolonging procedures, it is my intention that his declaration be honored by my family and physicians as the final expression of my legal right to refuse medical or surgical treatment and accept the consequences of the refusal.

I understand the full import of this declaration,

Signed: _____
City, County, and State of Residence

The declarant has been personally known to me, and I believe (him/her) to be of sound mind. I did not sign the declarant's signature above for or at the direction of the declarant. I am not a parent, spouse, or child of the declarant. I am not entitled to any part of the declarant's estate or directly financially responsible for the declarant's medical care. I am competent and at least eighteen (18) years of age.

Witness _____ Date _____
Witness _____ Date _____

CRUZAN v. DIRECTOR, MISSOURI DEPARTMENT OF HEALTH   110 S. Ct. 2841 (U.S. S. Ct. 1990)

On the night of January 11, 1983, 25-year-old Nancy Cruzan lost control of her car while driving down Elm Road in Jasper County, Missouri. The vehicle overturned and Cruzan was discovered lying face down in a ditch without detectable respiratory or cardiac function. Paramedics were able to restore her breathing and heartbeat at the accident site and she was transported to a hospital. There she was diagnosed as having sustained probable cerebral contusions compounded by significant anoxia (lack of oxygen). She remained in a coma for three weeks and then progressed to an unconscious state in which she was able to orally ingest some nutrition. To ease feeding and further her recovery, surgeons implanted a gastrostomy feeding and hydration tube. She then remained in a Missouri state hospital in what is commonly referred to as a persistent vegetative state.

After it became apparent that Cruzan had virtually no chance of regaining her mental faculties, her parents (also her legal guardians) asked hospital employees to terminate the artificial nutrition and hydration procedures, which would cause her death. The employees refused to do so without court approval. The parents then sought authorization from the state trial court for termination. Cruzan had not executed a living will, but a former roommate of Cruzan's testified that Cruzan had told her that if she were sick or injured she would not wish to continue her life unless she could live at least halfway normally. The trial court granted authorization to terminate nutrition and hydration, holding that a person in Cruzan's position had a fundamental constitutional right to refuse or direct the withdrawal of "death prolonging procedures." It also found that Cruzan's conversation with her roommate indicated that she would not want to continue with life support. The Supreme Court of Missouri reversed on the ground that no one can assume the choice regarding termination of medical treatment for an incompetent person in the absence of the formalities required under the Living Will

Statute or clear and convincing evidence, which evidence it found to be lacking in this case. The U.S. Supreme Court then granted certiorari to consider whether the U.S. Constitution would require the hospital to withdraw life-sustaining treatment from Cruzan under these circumstances. ∞

Rehnquist, Chief Justice Petitioners insist that the forced administration of life-sustaining medical treatment, and even of artificially-delivered food and water essential to life, would implicate a competent person's liberty interest. For purposes of this case, we assume that the United States Constitution would grant a competent person a constitutionally protected right to refuse lifesaving hydration and nutrition.

Petitioners go on to assert that an incompetent person should possess the same right in this respect as is possessed by a competent person. The difficulty with petitioner's claim is that an incompetent person is not able to make an informed and voluntary choice to exercise a hypothetical right to refuse treatment or any other right. Such a "right" must be exercised for her, if at all, by some sort of surrogate. Here, Missouri has in effect recognized that under certain circumstances a surrogate may act for the patient in electing to have hydration and nutrition withdrawn in such a way as to cause death, but it has established a procedural safeguard to assure that the action of the surrogate conforms as best it may to the wishes expressed by the patient while competent. Missouri requires that evidence of the incompetent's wishes as to the withdrawal of treatment be proved by clear and convincing evidence. The question, then, is whether the United States Constitution forbids the establishment of this procedural requirement by the State. We hold that it does not.

The choice between life and death is a deeply personal decision of obvious and overwhelming finality. We believe Missouri may legitimately seek to safeguard the personal element of this choice through the imposition of heightened evidentiary requirements. It cannot be disputed that the Due Process Clause protects an interest in life as well as an interest in refusing life-sustaining medical treatment. Not all incompetent patients will have loved ones available to serve as surrogate decisionmakers. And even where family members are present, there will, of course, be some unfortunate situations in which family members will not act to protect a patient. A State is entitled to guard against potential abuses in such situations. Similarly, a State is entitled to consider that a judicial proceeding to make a determination regarding an incompetent's wishes may very well not be an adversarial one, with the added guarantee of accurate factfinding that the adversary process brings with it. Finally, we think a State may properly decline to make judgments about the "quality" of life that a particular individual may enjoy, and simply assert an unqualified interest in the preservation of human life to be weighed against the constitutionally protected interests of the individual.

It is also worth noting that most, if not all, States simply forbid oral testimony entirely in determining the wishes of parties in transactions which, while important, simply do not have the consequences that a decision to terminate a person's life does. In most states, the parol evidence rule prevents the variations of the terms of a written contract by oral testimony. The statute of frauds makes unenforceable oral contracts to leave property by will, and statutes regulating the making of wills universally require that those instruments be in writing. There is no doubt that [these statutes] on occasion frustrate effectuation of the intent of a particular decedent just as Missouri's requirement of proof in this case may have frustrated the effectuation of the not-fully-expressed desires of Nancy Cruzan. But the Constitution does not require general rules to work faultlessly; no general rule can.

In sum, we conclude that a State may apply a clear and convincing evidence standard in proceedings where a guardian seeks to discontinue nutrition and hydration of a person diagnosed to be in a persistent vegetative state. The Supreme Court of Missouri held that the testimony adduced at trial did not amount to clear and convincing proof of the patient's desire to have hydration and nutrition withdrawn. We cannot say that the Supreme Court of Missouri committed constitutional error in reaching the conclusion that it did.

Judgment for the Missouri Department of Health affirmed.

Durable Power of Attorney

Another technique of planning for the eventuality that one may be unable to make decisions for oneself is to execute a document that gives another person the legal authority to act on one's behalf in the case of mental or physical incapacity. This document is called a **durable power of attorney.**

A *power of attorney* is an express statement in which one person (the **principal**) gives another person (the **attorney in fact**) the authority to do an act or series of acts on his behalf. For example, Andrews enters into a contract to sell his house to Willis, but he must be out of state on the date of the real estate closing. He gives Paulsen a power of attorney to attend the closing and execute the deed on his behalf. Ordinary powers of attorney terminate upon the principal's incapacity. By contrast, the *durable power of attorney* is not affected if the principal becomes incompetent.

A durable power of attorney permits a person to give someone else extremely broad powers to make decisions and enter transactions such as those involving real and personal property, bank accounts, and health care, and to specify that those powers will not terminate upon incapacity. The durable power of attorney is an extremely important planning device. For example, a durable power of attorney executed by an elderly parent to an adult child at a time in which the parent is competent would permit the child to take care of matters such as investments, property, bank accounts, and hospital admission. Without the durable power of attorney, the child would be forced to apply to a court for a guardianship, which is a more expensive and often less efficient manner in which to handle personal and business affairs.

Durable Power of Attorney for Health Care

The majority of states have enacted statutes specifically providing for **durable powers of attorney for health care** (sometimes called **health care representatives**). This is a type of durable power of attorney in which the principal specifically gives the attorney in fact the authority to make certain health care decisions for him if the principal should become incompetent. Depending on state law and the instructions given by the principal to the attorney in fact, this could include decisions such as consenting or withholding consent to surgery, admitting the

principal to a nursing home, and possibly withdrawing or prolonging life support. Note that the durable power of attorney becomes relevant only in the event that the principal becomes incompetent. So long as the principal is competent, he retains the ability to make his own health care decisions. This power of attorney is also revocable at the will of the principal. The precise requirements for creation of the durable power of attorney differ from state to state, but all states require a written and signed document executed with specified formalities, such as witnessing by disinterested witnesses.

Federal Law and Advance Directives

A federal statute, The Patient Self-Determination Act,[2] requires health care providers to take active steps to educate people about the opportunity to make advance decisions about medical care and the prolonging of life and to record the choices that they make. This statute, which became effective in 1992, requires health care providers such as hospitals, nursing homes, hospices, and home health agencies, to provide written information to adults receiving medical care about their rights concerning the ability to accept or refuse medical or surgical treatment, the health care provider's policies concerning those rights, and their right to formulate advance directives. The act also requires the provider to document in the patient's medical record whether the patient has executed an advance directive, and it forbids discrimination against the patient based on the individual's choice regarding an advance directive. In addition, the provider is required to ensure compliance with the requirements of state law concerning advance directives and to educate its staff and the community on issues concerning advance directives.

INTESTACY

If a person dies without making a will, or if he makes a will that is declared invalid, he is said to have died **intestate.** When that occurs, his property will be distributed to the persons designated as the intestate's heirs under the appropriate state's **intestacy** or **intestate succession** statute. The intestate's real property will be distributed according to the

---

[2]42 U.S.C. section 1395cc (1993).

intestacy statute of the state in which the property is located. His personal property will be distributed according to the intestacy statute of the state in which he was **domiciled** at the time of his death. A domicile is a person's permanent home. A person can have only one domicile at a time. Determinations of a person's domicile turn on facts that tend to show that person's intent to make a specific state his permanent home.

Characteristics of Intestacy Statutes

The provisions of intestacy statutes are not uniform. Their purpose, however, is to distribute property in a way that reflects the *presumed intent* of the deceased—that is, to distribute it to the persons most closely related to him. In general, such statutes first provide for the distribution of most or all of a person's estate to his surviving spouse, children, or grandchildren. If no such survivors exist, the statutes typically provide for the distribution of the estate to parents, siblings, or nieces and nephews. If no relatives at this level are living, the property may be distributed to surviving grandparents, uncles, aunts, or cousins. Generally, persons with the same degree of relationship to the deceased person take equal shares. If the deceased had no surviving relatives, the property **escheats** (goes) to the state.

Figure 2 shows an example of a distribution scheme under an intestacy statute.

Special Rules

Under intestacy statutes, a person must have a relationship to the deceased person through blood or marriage in order to inherit any part of his property. State law includes adopted children within the definition of "children," and treats adopted children in the same way as it treats biological children. (An adopted child would inherit from his adoptive parents, not from his biological parents.) Half brothers and half sisters are usually treated in the same way as brothers and sisters related by whole blood. An illegitimate child may inherit from his mother, but as a general rule, illegitimate children do not inherit from their fathers unless paternity has been either acknowledged or established in a legal proceeding.

A person must be alive at the time the decedent dies to claim a share of the decedent's estate. An exception may be made for pretermitted children or other descendants who are born *after* the decedent's death. If a person who is entitled to a share of the decedent's estate survives the decedent but dies before receiving his share, his share in the decedent's estate becomes part of his own estate.

Simultaneous Death

A statute known as the Uniform Simultaneous Death Act provides that where two persons who would inherit from each other (such as husband and

---

FIGURE 2

Example of a Distribution Scheme under an Intestacy Statute

PERSON DYING INTESTATE IS SURVIVED BY	RESULT
1. Spouse* and child or issue of a deceased child	Spouse ½, Child ½
2. Spouse and parent(s) but no issue	Spouse ¾, Parent ¼
3. Spouse but no parent or issue	All of the estate to spouse
4. Issue but no spouse	Estate is divided among issue
5. Parent(s), brothers, sisters, and/or issue of deceased brothers and sisters but no spouse or issue	Estate is divided among parent(s), brothers, sisters, and issue of deceased brothers and sisters
6. Issue of brothers and sisters but no spouse, issue, parents, brothers, and sisters	Estate is divided among issue of deceased brothers and sisters
7. Grandparents, but no spouse, issue, parents, brothers, sisters, or issue of deceased brothers and sisters	All of the estate goes to grandparents
8. None of the above	Estate goes to the state

*Note, however, second and subsequent spouses who had no children by the decedent may be assigned a smaller share.

wife) die under circumstances that make it difficult or impossible to determine who died first, each person's property is to be distributed as though he or she survived. This means, for example, that the husband's property will go to his relatives and the wife's property to her relatives.

ADMINISTRATION OF ESTATES

When a person dies, an orderly procedure is needed to collect his property, settle his debts, and distribute any remaining property to those who will inherit it under his will or by intestate succession. This process occurs under the supervision of a probate court and is known as the **administration process** or the **probate process.** Summary (simple) procedures are sometimes available when an estate is relatively small—for example, when it has assets of less than $7,500.

The Probate Estate

The probate process operates only on the decedent's property that is considered to be part of his **probate estate.** The probate estate is that property belonging to the decedent at the time of his death other than property held in joint ownership with right of survivorship, proceeds of insurance policies payable to a trust or a third party, property held in a revocable trust during the decedent's lifetime in which a third party is the beneficiary, or retirement benefits, such as pensions, payable to a third party. Assets that pass by operation of law and assets that are transferred by other devices such as trusts or life insurance policies do not pass through probate.

Note that the decedent's probate estate and his *taxable estate* for purposes of federal estate tax are two different concepts. The taxable estate includes all property owned or controlled by the decedent at the time of his death. For example, if a person purchased a $1 million life insurance policy made payable to his spouse or children, the policy would be included in his taxable estate, but not in his probate estate.

Determining the Existence of a Will

The first step in the probate process is to determine whether the deceased left a will. This may require a search of the deceased person's personal papers and safe-deposit box. If a will is found, it must be *proved* to be admitted to probate. This involves the testimony of the persons who witnessed the will, if they are still alive. If the witnesses are no longer alive, the signatures of the witnesses and the testator will have to be established in some other way. In many states and under UPC section 2–504, a will may be proved by an affidavit (declaration under oath) sworn to and signed by the testator and the witnesses at the time the will was executed. This is called a **self-proving affidavit.** If a will is located and proved, it will be admitted to probate and govern many of the decisions that must be made in the administration of the estate.

Selecting a Personal Representative

Another early step in the administration of an estate is the selection of a personal representative to administer the estate. If the deceased left a will, it is likely that he designated his personal representative in the will. The personal representative under a will is also known as the **executor.** Almost anyone could serve as an executor. The testator may have chosen, for example, his spouse, a grown child, a close friend, an attorney, or the trust department of a bank.

If the decedent died intestate, or if the personal representative named in a will is unable to serve, the probate court will name a personal representative to administer the estate. In the case of an intestate estate, the personal representative is called an **administrator.** A preference is usually accorded to a surviving spouse, child, or other close relative. If no relative is available and qualified to serve, a creditor, bank, or other person may be appointed by the court.

Most states require that the personal representative *post a bond* in an amount in excess of the estimated value of the estate to ensure that her duties will be properly and faithfully performed. A person making a will often directs that his executor may serve without posting a bond, and this exemption may be accepted by the court.

Responsibilities of the Personal Representative

The personal representative has a number of important tasks in the administration of the estate. She must see that an inventory is taken of the estate's assets and that the assets are appraised. Notice must then be given to creditors or potential claimants against the estate so that they can file and prove their claims within a specified time, normally five months. As a general rule, the surviving spouse of the deceased person is entitled to be paid an allowance during the time the estate is being settled. This allowance has priority over other debts of the estate. The personal representative must see that any properly payable funeral or burial expenses are paid and that the creditors' claims are satisfied.

Both federal and state governments impose estate or inheritance taxes on estates of a certain size. The personal representative is responsible for filing estate tax returns. The federal tax is a tax on the deceased's estate, with provisions for deducting items such as debts, expenses of administration, and charitable gifts. In addition, an amount equal to the amount left to the surviving spouse may be deducted from the gross estate before the tax is computed. State inheritance taxes are imposed on the person who receives a gift or statutory share from an estate. It is common, however, for wills to provide that the estate will pay all taxes, including inheritance taxes, so that the beneficiaries will not have to do so. The personal representative must also make provisions for filing an income tax return and for paying any income tax due for the partial year prior to the decedent's death.

When the debts, expenses, and taxes have been taken care of, the remaining assets of the estate are distributed to the decedent's heirs (if there was no will) or to the beneficiaries of the decedent's will. Special rules apply when the estate is too small to satisfy all of the bequests made in a will or when some or all of the designated beneficiaries are no longer living.

When the personal representative has completed all of these duties, the probate court will close the estate and discharge the personal representative.

TRUSTS

Nature of a Trust

A **trust** is a legal relationship in which a person who has legal title to property has the duty to hold it for the use or benefit of another person. The person benefited by a trust is considered to have **equitable title** to the property, because it is being maintained for his benefit. This means that he is the real owner even though the trustee has the legal title in his or her name. A trust can be created in a number of ways. An owner of property may *declare* that he is holding certain property in trust. For example, a mother might state that she is holding 100 shares of General Motors stock in trust for her daughter. A trust may also arise *by operation of law.* For example, when a lawyer representing a client injured in an automobile accident receives a settlement payment from an insurance company, the lawyer holds the settlement payment as trustee for the client. Most commonly, however, trusts are created through *express instruments* whereby an owner of property transfers title to the property to a trustee who is to hold, manage, and invest the property for the benefit of either the original owner or a third person. For example, Long transfers certain stock to First Trust Bank with instructions to pay the income to his daughter during her lifetime and to distribute the stock to her children after her death.

Trust Terminology

A person who creates a trust is known as a **settlor** or **trustor.** The person who holds the property for the benefit of another person is called the **trustee.** The person for whose benefit the property is held in trust is the **beneficiary.** Figure 3 illustrates the relationship between these parties. A single person may occupy more than one of these positions; however, if there is only one beneficiary, he cannot be the sole trustee. The property held in trust is called the **corpus** or **res.** A distinction is made between the property in trust, which is the principal, and the income that is produced by the principal.

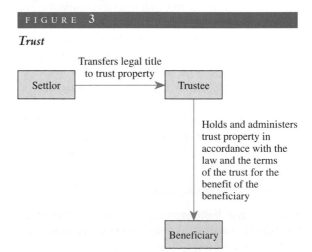

FIGURE 3

Trust

Transfers legal title to trust property

Settlor → Trustee

Holds and administers trust property in accordance with the law and the terms of the trust for the benefit of the beneficiary

Beneficiary

A trust that is established and effective during the settlor's lifetime is known as an **inter vivos trust.** A trust can also be established in a person's will. Such trusts take effect only at the death of the settlor. They are called **testamentary trusts.**

Why People Create Trusts

Bennett owns a portfolio of valuable stock. Her husband has predeceased her. She has two children and an elderly father for whom she would like to provide. Why might it be advantageous to Bennett to transfer the stock to a trust for the benefit of the members of her family?

First, there may be income tax or estate tax advantages in doing so, depending on the type of trust she establishes and the provisions of that trust. For example, she can establish an irrevocable trust for her children and remove the property transferred to her trust from her estate so that it is not taxable at her death. In addition, the trust property can be used for the benefit of others and may even pass to others after the settlor's death without the necessity of having a will. Many people prefer to pass their property by trust rather than by will because trusts afford more privacy: unlike a probated will, they do not become an item of public record. Trusts also afford greater opportunity for postgift management than do outright gifts and bequests. If Bennett wants her children to enjoy the income of the trust property during their young adulthood without distributing unfettered ownership of the property to them before she considers them able to manage it properly, she can accomplish this through a trust provision. A trust can prevent the property from being squandered or spent too quickly. Trusts can be set up so that a beneficiary's interest cannot be reached by his creditors in many situations. Such trusts, called **spendthrift trusts,** will be discussed later.

Placing property in trust can operate to increase the amount of property held for the beneficiaries if the trustee makes good investment decisions. Another important consideration is that a trust can be used to provide for the needs of disabled beneficiaries who are not capable of managing funds.

Creation of Express Trusts

There are five basic requirements for the creation of a valid express trust, although special and somewhat less restrictive rules govern the establishment of charitable trusts. The requirements for forming an express trust are:

1. *Capacity.* The settlor must have had the **legal capacity** to convey the property to the trust. This means that the settlor must have had the capacity needed to make a valid contract if the trust is an *inter vivos* trust or the capacity to make a will if the trust is a testamentary trust. For example, a trust would fail under this requirement if at the time the trust was created, the settlor had not attained the age required by state law for the creation of valid wills and contracts (age 18 in most states).

2. *Intent and formalities.* The settlor must *intend* to create a trust at the present time. To impose enforceable duties on the trustee, the settlor must meet certain formalities. Under the laws of most states, for example, the trustee must accept the trust by signing the trust instrument. In the case of a trust of land, the trust must be in writing so as to meet the statute of frauds. If the trust is a testamentary trust, it must satisfy the formal requirements for wills.

3. *Conveyance of specific property.* The settlor must convey *specific property* to the trust. The property conveyed must be property that the settlor has the *right to convey.*

4. *Proper purpose.* The trust must be created for a *proper purpose.* It cannot be created for a reason that is contrary to public policy, such as the commission of a crime.

5. *Identity of the beneficiaries.* The *beneficiaries* of the trust must be described clearly enough so that their identities can be ascertained. Sometimes, beneficiaries may be members of a specific class, such as "my children."

Charitable Trusts

A distinction is made between private trusts and trusts created for charitable purposes. In a private trust, property is devoted to the benefit of specific persons, whereas in a charitable trust, property is devoted to a charitable organization or to some other purposes beneficial to society. While some of the rules governing private and charitable trusts are the same, a number of these rules are different. For example, when a private trust is created, the beneficiary must be known at the time or ascertainable within a certain time (established by a legal rule known as the **rule against perpetuities**). However, a charitable trust is valid even though no definitely ascertainable beneficiary is named and even though it is to continue for an indefinite or unlimited period.

Doctrine of Cy Pres

A doctrine known as **cy pres** is applicable to charitable trusts when property is given in trust to be applied to a particular charitable purpose that becomes impossible, impracticable, or illegal to carry out. Under the doctrine of *cy pres,* the trust will not fail if the settlor indicated a general intention to devote the property to charitable purposes. If the settlor has not specifically provided for a substitute beneficiary, the court will direct the application of the property to some charitable purpose that falls within the settlor's general charitable intention.

Totten Trusts

A **Totten trust** is a deposit of money in a bank or other financial institution in the name of the depositor *as trustee* for a named beneficiary. For example, Bliss deposits money in First Bank in trust for his daughter, Bessie. The Totten trust creates a revocable living trust. At Bliss's death, if he has not revoked this trust, the money in the account will belong to Bessie.

Powers and Duties of the Trustee

In most express trusts, the settlor names a specific person to act as trustee. If the settlor does not name a trustee, the court will appoint one. Similarly, a court will replace a trustee who resigns, is incompetent, or refuses to act.

The trust codes of most states contain provisions giving trustees broad management powers over trust property. These provisions can be limited or expanded by express provisions in the trust instrument. The trustee must use a *reasonable degree of skill, judgment, and care* in the exercise of his duties unless he holds himself out as having a greater degree of skill, in which case he will be held to a higher standard. Section 7–302 of the UPC provides that the trustee is held to the standard of a prudent person dealing with the property of another, and if he has special skills or is named trustee based on a representation of special skills, he is required to

use those special skills. He *may not commingle* the property he holds in trust with his own property or with that of another trust.

A trustee owes a *duty of loyalty* (fiduciary duty) to the beneficiaries. This means that he must administer the trust for the benefit of the beneficiaries and avoid any conflict between his personal interests and the interest of the trust. For example, a trustee cannot do business with a trust that he administers without express permission in the trust agreement. He must not prefer one beneficiary's interest to another's, and he must account to the beneficiaries for all transactions. Unless the trust agreement provides otherwise, the trustee must make the trust productive. He may not delegate the performance of discretionary duties (such as the duty to select investments) to another, but he may delegate the performance of ministerial duties (such as the preparation of statements of account).

A trust may give the trustee discretion as to the amount of principal or income paid to a beneficiary. In such a case, the beneficiary cannot require the trustee to exercise his discretion in the manner desired by the beneficiary.

Allocating between Principal and Income   One of the duties of the trustee is to distribute the principal and income of the trust in accordance with the terms of the trust instrument. Suppose Wheeler's will created a testamentary trust providing that his wife was to receive the income from the trust for life, and at her death, the trust property was to be distributed to his children. During the duration of the trust, the trust earns profits, such as interest or rents, and has expenses, such as taxes or repairs. How should the trustee allocate these items as between Wheeler's surviving spouse, who is an **income beneficiary,** and his children, who are **remaindermen**?

The terms of the trust and state law bind the trustee in making this determination. As a general rule, ordinary profits received from the investment of trust property are allocated to income. For example, interest on trust property or rents earned from leasing real property held in trust would be allocated to income. Ordinary expenses such as insurance premiums, the cost of ordinary maintenance and repairs of trust property, and property taxes, would be chargeable to income. The principal of the trust includes the trust property itself and any extraordinary receipts, such as proceeds or gains derived from the sale of trust property. Extraordinary expenses—for example, the cost of long-term permanent improvements to real property or expenses relating to the sale of property—would ordinarily be charged against principal.

Liability of Trustee

A trustee who breaches any of the duties of a trustee or whose conduct falls below the standard of care applicable to trustees may incur personal liability. For example, if the trustee invests unwisely and imprudently, the trustee may be personally liable to reimburse the trust estate for the shortfall. The language of the trust affects the trustee's liability and the level of care owed by the trustee. A settlor might, for example, include language lowering the trustee's duty of care or relieving the trustee of some liability that he might otherwise incur. The following *Neuhaus v. Richards* case discusses both trustee liability and the extent to which a trust instrument can limit the trustee's liability.

The trustee can also have liability to third persons who are injured by the operation of the trust. Because a trust is not in itself a legal entity that can be sued, a third party who has a claim (such as a tort claim or a claim for breach of contract) must file his claim against the trustee of the trust. The trustee's actual personal liability to a third party depends on the language of the trust and of any contracts he might enter on behalf of the trust as well as the extent to which the injury complained of by the third party was a result of the personal fault or omission of the trustee.

NEUHAUS v. RICHARDS   846 S.W.2d 70 (Tex. Ct. App. 1992)

*I*n 1976, V. F. and Gertrude Neuhaus executed a Trust Indenture Creating the Neuhaus Family Trusts, which established a number of separate individual trusts for the benefit of their children and grandchildren, Vernon and Lacey Neuhaus. The trusts were both managed by the same cotrustees, Grace Neuhaus Richards and Robert Schwarz. The initial corpus of both trusts consisted of stock in McAllen State Bank. However, in 1982, First City Bancorporation of Texas acquired all the stock of McAllen State Bank, and First City substituted its own stock for the McAllen State Bank Stock in the trusts. From 1985 through 1987, the First City stock declined in value, but the trustees refused to sell until the stock in Lacey Neuhaus's trust became virtually worthless, and they delayed selling the stock in Vernon Neuhaus's trust until significant losses had been sustained. The Neuhauses sued both trustees alleging a breach of fiduciary duties, including a failure to exercise judgment and care, willful misconduct, and conscious disregard for the rights and welfare of the beneficiaries, among other claims. The trial court granted a summary judgment against the Neuhauses, and the Neuhauses appealed.* ∽

Hinojosa, Justice The fundamental duties of a trustee include the use of the skill and prudence that an ordinary, capable, and careful person would use in the conduct of his own affairs and loyalty to the beneficiaries of the trust. In particular, one of the basic duties of a trustee is to make the assets of the trust productive while at the same time preserving the assets. Under these principles, it would appear in the present case that the trustees could be held liable for failing to sell the First City stock if their decision not to sell was imprudent. However, the settlor may within the trust instrument relieve the trustee of certain duties, restrictions, responsibilities, and liabilities imposed by statute. However, exculpatory clauses are strictly construed, and the trustee is relieved of liability only to the extent that the trust instrument clearly provides that he shall be excused.

In the present case, the trustees point to two supposedly exculpatory provisions in the present trust indenture: section V(k) and section V(v). Section V(k) provides that:

All property transferred by gift to any trust and any property acquired by the Trustees . . . shall be deemed a proper investment, and the Trustees shall be under no obligation to dispose of or convert any such property.

The trustees suggest that section V(k) completely relieves them of any duty to sell the First City stock. However, we hold that this provision is ambiguous.

Section V(k) leaves uncertain whether the trustees are still under a duty to prudently manage and, if need be, sell an investment that is otherwise deemed proper, and whether the obligation to dispose of assets includes the generalized duty to manage the trust prudently or merely relieves the trustees of any specific obligation to sell a particular kind or class of investments. Even if we were to accept the trustees' interpretation that this section generally relieved them of a duty to sell or of liability for failing to sell the First City stock, nevertheless, it could not have validly relieved them of all liability for failing to sell the stock. Under Texas law, an exculpatory provision in the trust instrument is not effective to relieve the trustee of liability for action taken in bad faith or for acting intentionally adverse or with reckless indifference to the interests of the beneficiary. Courts have held that the trust instrument may relieve the trustee of the duty to act as a prudent man in determining to retain unproductive property, but not of the duty to do so honestly, in good faith, and without willful misconduct or reckless indifference to the interests of the beneficiaries. In other words, the trustee's determination to retain

unproductive investments is generally protected as long as that determination was not made dishonestly, in bad faith, recklessly, or with the intent to harm the trust.

Turning to the second exculpatory provision relied upon by the trustees, section V(v) provides that "no Trustee shall be liable for negligence or error of judgment but shall be liable only for his willful misconduct or personal dishonesty." Thus, under this general exculpatory provision, the trustees are not held to the prudent person standard but may be liable only for willful misconduct or personal dishonesty. As we stated earlier, the Neuhauses alleged that in failing to sell the First City stock the trustees not only failed to act prudently but also that they acted out of willful misconduct. Because the trustees made no attempt by summary judgment evidence to negate these allegations of willful misconduct, summary judgment should not have been granted in their favor on the basis of exculpatory provisions of the trust indenture.

Reversed in favor of the Neuhauses and remanded for trial.

Spendthrift Trusts

Generally, the beneficiary of a trust may voluntarily assign his rights to the principal or income of the trust to another person. In addition, any distributions to the beneficiary are subject to the claims of his creditors. Sometimes, however, trusts contain provisions known as **spendthrift clauses,** which restrict the voluntary or involuntary transfer of a beneficiary's interest. Such clauses are generally enforced, and they preclude assignees or creditors from compelling a trustee to recognize their claims to the trust. The enforceability of such clauses is subject to four exceptions, however:

1. A person cannot put his own property beyond the claims of his own creditors. Thus, a spendthrift clause is not effective in a trust when the settlor makes himself a beneficiary.
2. Divorced spouses and minor children of the beneficiary can compel payment for alimony and child support.
3. Creditors of the beneficiary who have furnished necessaries can compel payment.

4. Once the trustee distributes property to a beneficiary, it can be subject to valid claims of others.

Termination and Modification of a Trust

Normally, a settlor cannot revoke or modify a trust unless he reserves the power to do so at the time he establishes the trust. However, a trust may be modified or terminated with the consent of the settlor and all of the beneficiaries. When the settlor is dead or otherwise unable to consent, a trust can be modified or terminated by consent of all the persons with a beneficial interest, but only when this would not frustrate a material purpose of the trust. Because trusts are under the supervisory jurisdiction of a court, the court can permit a deviation from the terms of a trust when unanticipated changes in circumstances threaten accomplishment of the settlor's purpose.

Implied and Constructive Trusts

Under exceptional circumstances in which the creation of a trust is necessary to effectuate a settlor's intent or avoid unjust enrichment, the law *implies* or imposes a trust even though no express trust exists or an express trust exists but has failed. One trust of this type is a **resulting trust,** which arises when there has been an incomplete disposition of trust property. For example, if Hess transferred property to Wickes as trustee to provide for the needs of Hess's grandfather and the grandfather died before the trust funds were exhausted, Wickes will be deemed to hold the property in a resulting trust for Hess or Hess's heirs. Similarly, if Hess had transferred the property to Wickes as trustee and the trust had failed because Hess did not meet one of the requirements of a valid trust, Wickes would not be permitted to keep the trust property as his own. A resulting trust would be implied.

A **constructive trust** is a trust created by operation of law to avoid fraud, injustice, or unjust enrichment. This type of trust imposes on the constructive trustee a duty to convey property he holds to another person on the ground that the constructive trustee would be unjustly enriched if he were allowed to retain it. For example, when a person procures the transfer of property by means of fraud or duress, he becomes a constructive trustee and is under an obligation to return the property to its original owner.

ETHICAL AND PUBLIC POLICY CONCERNS

1. What are some of the ethical implications a state legislature should take into account before adopting a living will statute or a durable power of attorney for health care statute?

2. Why should the law require so much formality to create a valid will? Would it be preferable for the law to lift some of the formalities surrounding wills and allow people to make valid wills orally, by informal letters, or by videotapes or audio recordings?

3. What is the ethical basis of a constructive trust?

PROBLEMS AND PROBLEM CASES

1. Cunningham died in 1983, leaving a writing that purported to be his will. The writing was on a preprinted will form in which the first and last part of the will were printed and the rest of the will was handwritten by Cunningham. The first paragraph reads: "In the name of God, Amen. I," which is printed, followed by the handwriting: "Thomas John Cunningham—Social Security number 55–24–3083," which in turn is followed by printing: "being of sound mind, memory and understanding, do make and publish this my Last Will and Testament, in the manner following, that is to say: . . ." This is followed by the body of the will in Cunningham's handwriting, which gives instructions concerning the donation of bodily remains, specific bequests, and the distribution of the remainder of his estate. A printed clause appears after the body of the will, and immediately below this clause is a printed line upon which a testator normally signs his name, at the end of which is printed "Seal." Cunningham did not sign his name on this line; instead, the line contains the signature of a Notary Public of New Jersey, together with his notarial seal impressed over the printed word "Seal." Two people, a realtor (who was also the notary) and the realtor's secretary, witnessed the writing. Cunningham came to the realtor's office with the proposed will fully completed except for the witnesses' signatures. The writing was offered for probate as a will. Is the will valid?

2. Davidson died in a nursing home at the age of 90, leaving an estate in excess of $2 million. For a number of years before Davidson's death, Goodner had served as her lawyer. Goodner and his wife also ran personal errands for Davidson. In 1984, Goodner prepared a will for Davidson in which he was appointed her executor and was given, after other bequests, the residue and remainder of her property. Later, in 1985, Goodner prepared another will for Davidson in which he was named coexecutor and from which he was dropped as residual beneficiary in favor of Davidson's nephews, John and William Forrester. Over the next three years, Davidson gave Goodner and his wife gifts totaling $60,000. Following Davidson's death in 1989, her 1984 will was admitted to probate. William Forrester challenged the will on the ground of undue influence and Davidson's allegedly unsound mind. After the will contest was filed, Goodner found Davidson's 1985 will behind a dishwasher in her house. A petition to admit the 1985 will to probate was filed, and that will was contested by Forrester on the same grounds—undue influence and unsound mind. The probate court decided that the 1985 will revoked the

1984 will and it admitted the 1985 will to probate and appointed Goodner as executor. The court also found that Davidson was "in all respects competent, and was not acting under restraint or undue influence." Forrester appealed, seeking to invalidate both the 1984 and the 1985 wills on the ground of lack of testamentary capacity and to have the estate pass by intestacy. Will he prevail?

3. Roy and Icie Johnson established two revocable *inter vivos* trusts in 1966. The trusts provided that upon Roy and Icie's deaths, income from the trusts was to be paid in equal shares to their two sons, James and Robert, for life. Upon the death of the survivor of the sons, the trust was to be *divided equally between all of my grandchildren, per stirpes.* James had two daughters, Barbara and Elizabeth. Robert had four children, David, Rosalyn, Catherine, and Elizabeth. James and Robert disclaimed their interest in the trust in 1979, and a dispute arose about how the trust should be distributed to the grandchildren. The trustee filed an action seeking instructions on how the trusts should be distributed. What should the court hold?

4. Kenneth Haag owned Front Royal Supply Co. Smoot had worked for Haag as the manager of the Front Royal store for a number of years. Stickley was the manager of the company's Winchester store, but had not worked for Haag as long as Smoot had. Blye was assistant manager of the Winchester store, and had worked for the company for a lesser amount of time than had Stickley. Printz was also an employee of Haag's, but was fired in 1984–85. On January 20, 1983, Haag executed a holographic will. The will contained a specific bequest of stock to his employees who were still with Front Royal at the time of his death. Read the will as shown in Figure 4.

In October 1985, Haag executed a holographic codicil. This codicil provided that "In case Chs. Smoot is deceased or any other receipitent [*sic*] their stare [*sic*] will go back in the estate." Haag died in 1986. His will was admitted to probate, and his former wife, Helen, was named executor. At the time of Haag's death, he owned 689 shares of Front Royal stock, the value of which was at least $254,000. A dispute arose between Mrs. Haag, as executor, and Stickley and Blye about whether they were entitled to any shares. Mrs. Haag maintained that the will should be interpreted to give 500 shares of stock to Smoot, and none to Stickley and Blye, with the remaining 189 shares going into the residuary of the estate. Stickley and Blye filed this action asking the court to construe and interpret the will in order to determine their rights to the shares of stock. The court determined that Smoot should get the first 500 shares, and the remaining 189 shares should be divided equally between Stickley and Blye, with the odd share going to the person with longer service. Was this ruling correct?

Haag's Will

5. Crawshaw bequeathed the bulk of his estate to two residuary beneficiaries, the Salvation Army and Marymount College. Crawshaw's will provided for 15 percent of the residue to go to the Salvation Army outright and 85 percent to Marymount College in trust. The stated purpose of this trust was to provide loans to nursing and other students at Marymount. Marymount ceased operation on June 30, 1989. It sought to have the trust funds directed to Marymount Memorial Educational Trust Fund. The Salvation Army challenged this, arguing that Crawshaw did not intend to benefit students attending colleges other than Marymount. It asked that the court distribute the trust funds to the Salvation Army as the remaining beneficiary of Crawshaw's residuary estate. What should the court do?

6. Gaines, an elderly and infirm woman, maintained certain savings deposits and certificates in the Jefferson Federal Savings and Loan Association. During her lifetime, she had the name of her son, Billy Gaines, placed on the accounts along with her own. Her purpose in doing this was not to make a gift to Billy but rather to enable him to handle the funds for her support and benefit in the event she became incapacitated. Because of her deteriorating physical condition, she had to leave her residence and be cared for in Billy's home. She stayed there for about two years before being moved to a nursing home for about four months preceding her death. During the time Gaines was living with Billy, he took control of and disposed of all of the funds which were formerly on deposit at Jefferson Federal together with Gaines's Social Security checks. Billy invested some of the funds in his own personal newspaper business and used some of the funds for Gaines's support and maintenance. On Gaines's death, her estate claimed that a constructive trust arose between Billy and Gaines whereby he was obligated to reasonably use the funds for Gaines's benefit and to account for the balance. Is the estate correct?

7. Fickes, a resident of Washington, died in December 1943, leaving a will dated November 19, 1940. The will provided for the creation of a trust upon his death. The will also provided that upon the death of Fickes's last surviving child, one-half of the trust property was to be distributed to Rensselaer Polytechnic Institute and the other half of the trust property distributed "in equal portions" between Fickes's "grandchildren then living." At the time of death of Fickes's last surviving child, there were four biological grandchildren living. In addition, there were four adopted grandchildren living. Two of them, grandsons, had been adopted by Fickes's son while Fickes was still living. The other two, granddaughters, were adopted by Fickes's son in 1962 and 1965, long after Fickes's death. Were the granddaughters entitled to share in the trust distribution?

Credit

Introduction to Credit and Secured Transactions

In the United States, a substantial portion of business transactions involves the extension of credit. The term *credit* has many meanings. In this chapter, it will be used to mean transactions in which goods are sold, services are rendered, or money is loaned in exchange for a promise to pay for them at some future date.

In some of these transactions, a creditor is willing to rely on the debtor's promise to pay at a later time; in others, the creditor wants some further assurance or security that the debtor will make good on his promise to pay. This chapter will discuss the differences between secured and unsecured credit and will detail various mechanisms that are available to the creditor who wants to obtain security. These mechanisms include obtaining liens or security interests in personal or real property, sureties, and guarantors. Security interests in real property, sureties and guarantors, and common law liens on personal property will be covered in this chapter, and the Uniform Commercial Code (UCC or Code) rules concerning security interests in personal property will be covered in Chapter 28, Security Interests in Personal Property. The last chapter in this part deals with bankruptcy law, which may come into play when a debtor is unable to fulfill his obligation to pay his debts when they are due. ༠

CREDIT

Unsecured Credit

Many common transactions are based on unsecured credit. For example, a person may have a charge account at a department store or a MasterCard account. If the person buys a sweater and charges it to his charge account or MasterCard account, unsecured credit has been extended to him. He has received goods in return for his promise to pay for them later. Similarly, if a person goes to a dentist to have a tooth filled and the dentist sends her a bill payable by the end of the month, services have been rendered on the basis of unsecured credit. Consumers are not the only people who use unsecured credit. Many transactions between businesspeople utilize it. For example, a retailer buys merchandise or a manufacturer buys raw materials, promising to pay for the merchandise or materials within 30 days after receipt.

The unsecured credit transaction involves a maximum of risk to the creditor—the person who extends the credit. When goods are delivered, services are rendered, or money is loaned on unsecured credit, the creditor gives up all rights in the goods, services, or money. In return, the creditor gets a promise by the debtor to pay or to perform the promised act. If the debtor does not pay or keep the promise, the creditor's options are more limited than if he had obtained security to ensure the debtor's performance. One course of action is to bring a lawsuit against the debtor and obtain a judgment. The creditor might then have the sheriff execute the judgment on any property owned by the debtor that is subject to execution. The creditor might also try to **garnish** the wages or other moneys to which the debtor is entitled. However, the debtor might be **judgment-proof;** that is, the debtor may not have any property subject to execution or may not have a steady job. Under these circumstances, execution or garnishment would be of little aid to the creditor in collecting the judgment.

A businessperson may obtain credit insurance to stabilize the credit risk of doing business on an unsecured credit basis. However, he passes the costs of the insurance to the business, or of the unsecured credit losses that the business sustains, on to the consumer. The consumer pays a higher price for goods or services purchased, or a higher interest rate on any money borrowed, from a business that has high credit losses.

Secured Credit

To minimize his credit risk, a creditor may contract for security. The creditor may require the debtor to convey to the creditor a security interest or lien on the debtor's property. Suppose a person borrows $3,000 from a credit union. The credit union might require her to put up her car as security for the loan or might ask that some other person agree to be liable if she defaults. For example, if a student who does not have a regular job goes to a bank to borrow money, the bank might ask that the student's father or mother cosign the note for the loan.

When the creditor has security for the credit he extends and the debtor defaults, the creditor can go against the security to collect the obligation. Assume that a person borrows $18,000 from a bank to buy a new car and that the bank takes a security interest (lien) on the car. If the person fails to make his monthly payments, the bank has the right to repossess the car and have it sold so that it can recover its money. Similarly, if the borrower's father cosigned for the car loan and the borrower defaults, the bank can sue the father to collect the balance due on the loan.

Development of Security

Various types of security devices have been developed as social and economic need for them arose. The rights and liabilities of the parties to a secured transaction depend on the nature of the security— that is, on whether (1) the security pledged is the promise of another person to pay if the debtor does not, or (2) a security interest in goods, intangibles, or real estate is conveyed as security for the payment of a debt or obligation.

If personal credit is pledged, the other person may guarantee the payment of the debt—that is, become a guarantor—or the other person may join the debtor in the debtor's promise to pay, in which case the other person would become surety for the debt.

The oldest and simplest security device was the pledge. To have a pledge valid against third persons with an interest in the goods, such as subsequent purchasers or creditors, it was necessary that the property used as security be delivered to the pledgee or a pledge holder. Upon default by the pledger, the pledgee had the right to sell the property and apply the proceeds to the payment of the debt.

Situations arose in which it was desirable to leave the property used as security in the possession of the debtor. To accomplish this objective, the debtor would give the creditor a bill of sale to the property, thus passing title to the creditor. The bill of sale would provide that if the debtor performed his promise, the bill of sale would become null and void, thus revesting title to the property in the debtor. A secret lien on the goods was created by this device, and the early courts held that such a transaction was a fraud on third-party claimants and void as to them. An undisclosed or secret lien is unfair to creditors who might extend credit to the debtor on the strength of property that they see in the debtor's possession but that in fact is subject to the prior claim of another creditor. Statutes were enacted providing for the recording or filing of the bill of sale, which was later designated as a chattel mortgage. These statutes were not uniform in their provisions. Most of them set up formal requirements for the execution of the chattel mortgage and also stated the effect of recording or filing on the rights of third-party claimants.

To avoid the requirements for the execution and filing of the chattel mortgage, sellers of goods would sell the goods on a "conditional sales contract" under which the seller retained title to the goods until their purchase price had been paid in full. Upon default by the buyer, the seller could (a) repossess the goods or (b) pass title and recover a judgment for the unpaid balance of the purchase price. Abuses of this security device gave rise to some regulatory statutes. About one-half of the states enacted statutes providing that the conditional sales contract was void as to third parties unless it was filed or recorded.

No satisfactory device was developed whereby inventory could be used as security. The inherent difficulty is that inventory is intended to be sold and turned into cash and the creditor is interested in protecting his interest in the cash rather than in maintaining a lien on the sold goods. Field warehousing was used under the pledge, and an after-acquired property clause in a chattel mortgage on a stock of goods held for resale partially fulfilled this

need. One of the devices used was the trust receipt. This short-term marketing security arrangement had its origin in the export–import trade. It was later used extensively as a means of financing retailers of consumer goods having a high unit value.

Security Interests in Personal Property

Chapter 28, Security Interests in Personal Property, will discuss how a creditor can obtain a security interest in the personal property or fixtures of a debtor. It will also explain the rights to the debtor's property of the creditor, the debtor, and other creditors of the debtor. These security interests are covered by Article 9 of the Uniform Commercial Code, which sets out a comprehensive scheme for regulating security interests in personal property and fixtures. The Code abolishes the old formal distinctions between different types of security devices used to create security interests in personal property.

Security Interests in Real Property

Three types of contractual security devices have been developed by which real estate may be used as security: (1) the real estate mortgage, (2) the trust deed, and (3) the land contract. In addition to these contract security devices, all of the states have enacted statutes granting the right to mechanic's liens on real estate. Security interests in real property are covered later in this chapter.

SURETYSHIP AND GUARANTY

Sureties and Guarantors

As a condition of making a loan, granting credit, or employing someone (particularly as a fiduciary), a creditor may demand that the debtor, contractor, or employee provide as security for his performance the liability of a third person as surety or guarantor. The purpose of the contract of suretyship or guaranty is to provide the creditor with additional protection against loss in the event of default by the debtor, contractor, or employee.

A **surety** is a person who is *liable for the payment of another person's debt or for the performance of another person's duty*. The surety joins with the person primarily liable in promising to make the payment or to perform the duty. For example, Kathleen Kelly, who is 17 years old, buys a used car on credit from Harry's Used Cars. She signs a promissory note, agreeing to pay $75 a month on the note until the note is paid in full. Harry's has Kathleen's father cosign the note; thus, her father is a surety. Similarly, the city of Chicago hires the B&B Construction Company to build a new sewage treatment plant. The city will probably require B&B to have a surety agree to be liable for B&B's performance of its contract. There are insurance companies that, for a fee, will agree to be a surety on the contract of a company such as B&B.

If the person who is primarily liable (the principal) defaults, the surety is liable to pay or perform. Upon default, the creditor may ask the surety to pay even if he has not asked the principal debtor to pay. If the surety makes good on his contract of suretyship, he is entitled to be reimbursed by the principal. While a contract of surety does not have to be in writing to be enforceable, it normally is.

A guaranty contract is similar to a suretyship contract in that the promisor agrees to answer for the obligation of another. However, a guarantor does not join the principal in making a promise; rather, a guarantor makes a separate promise and agrees to be liable upon the happening of a certain event. For example, a father tells a merchant, "I will guarantee payment of my daughter Rachel's debt to you if she does not pay it," or "If Rachel becomes bankrupt, I will guarantee payment of her debt to you." While a surety is *primarily liable,* a guarantor is *secondarily* liable and can be held to his guarantee only after the principal defaults and cannot be held to his promise or payment. Generally, a guarantor's promise must be made in writing to be enforceable under the statute of frauds.

The rights and liabilities of the surety and the guarantor are substantially the same. No distinction will be made between them in this chapter except where the distinction is of basic importance. Moreover, most commercial contracts and promissory notes today that are to be signed by multiple parties provide for the parties to be "jointly and severally" liable, thus making the surety relationship the predominate one.

Creation of Principal and Surety Relation

The relationship of principal and surety, or that of principal and guarantor, is created by contract. The basic rules of contract law apply in determining the existence and nature of the relationship as well as the rights and duties of the parties.

Defenses of a Surety

Suppose Jeffrey's mother agrees to be a surety for Jeffrey on his purchase of a motorcycle. If the motorcycle was defectively made and Jeffrey refuses to make further payments on it, the dealer might try to collect the balance due from Jeffrey's mother. As a surety, Jeffrey's mother can use any defenses against the dealer that Jeffrey has if they go to the merits of the primary contract. Thus, if Jeffrey has a valid defense of breach of warranty against the dealer, his mother can use it as a basis for not paying the dealer.

Other defenses that go to the merits include (1) lack or failure of consideration, (2) inducement of the contract by fraud or duress, and (3) breach of contract by the other party. Certain defenses of the principal cannot be used by the surety. These defenses include lack of capacity, such as minority or insanity, and bankruptcy. Thus, if Jeffrey is only 17 years old, the fact that he is a minor cannot be used by Jeffrey's mother to defend against the dealer. This defense of Jeffrey's lack of capacity to contract does not go to the merits of the contract between Jeffrey and the dealer and cannot be used by Jeffrey's mother.

A surety contracts to be responsible for the performance of the principal's obligation. If the principal and the creditor change that obligation by agreement, the surety is relieved of responsibility unless the surety agrees to the change. This is because the surety's obligation cannot be changed without his consent.

For example, Fredericks cosigns a note for his friend Kato, which she has given to Credit Union to secure a loan. Suppose the note was originally for $2,500 and payable in 12 months with interest at 11 percent a year. Credit Union and Kato later agree that Kato will have 24 months to repay the note but that the interest will be 13 percent per year. Unless Fredericks consents to this change, he is discharged from his responsibility as surety. The obligation he agreed to assume was altered by the changes in the repayment period and the interest rate.

The most common kind of change affecting a surety is an extension of time to perform the contract. If the creditor merely allows the principal more time without the surety's consent, this does not relieve the surety of responsibility. The surety's consent is required only where there is an actual binding agreement between the creditor and the principal as to the extension of time.

In addition, the courts usually make a distinction between **accommodation sureties** and **compensated sureties.** An accommodation surety is a person who acts as a surety without compensation, such as a friend who cosigns a note as a favor. A compensated surety is a person, usually a professional such as a bonding company, who is paid for serving as a surety.

The courts are more protective of accommodation sureties than of compensated sureties. Accommodation sureties are relieved of liability unless they consent to an extension of time. Compensated sureties, on the other hand, must show that they will be harmed by an extension of time before they are relieved of responsibility because of a binding extension without their consent. A compensated surety must show that a change in the contract was both material and prejudicial to him if he is to be relieved of his obligation as surety.

Creditor's Duties to Surety

The creditor is required to disclose any material facts about the risk involved to the surety. If he does not do so, the surety is relieved of liability. For example, a bank (creditor) knows that an employee, Arthur, has been guilty of criminal conduct in the past. If the bank applies to a bonding company to obtain a bond on Arthur, the bank must disclose this information about Arthur. Similarly, suppose the bank has an employee, Alison, covered by a bond and discovers that Alison is embezzling money. If the bank agrees to give Alison another chance but does not report her actions to the bonding company, the bonding company is relieved of responsibility for further wrongful acts by Alison.

If the debtor posts security for the performance of an obligation, the creditor must not surrender the security without the consent of the surety. If the creditor does so, the surety is relieved of liability to the extent of the value surrendered.

The following *Camp* case illustrates the creditor's duty to the surety.

CAMP v. FIRST FINANCIAL FEDERAL SAVINGS AND LOAN ASSOCIATION 772 S.W.2d 602 (Sup. Ct. Ark. 1989)

R usty Jones, a used car dealer, applied to First Financial Federal Savings and Loan Association for a $50,000 line of credit to purchase an inventory of used cars. First Financial refused to make the loan to Jones alone but agreed to do so if Worth Camp, an attorney and friend of Jones, would cosign the note. Camp agreed to cosign as an accommodation maker or surety. The expectation of the parties was that the loans cosigned by Camp would be repaid from the proceeds of the car inventory.

The original note for $25,000 was signed on August 2, 1984, and renewals were executed on January 25, 1985, September 11, 1985, and March 15, 1986, and the amount was eventually increased to $50,000. In August 1985, as Camp was considering whether to sign the September renewal note, he was advised by First Financial's loan officer that the interest on the loan had been paid. In fact, interest payments were four months delinquent. In addition, unknown to Camp, as the $50,000 credit limit was approached, First Financial began making side, or personal, loans to Jones totaling around $25,000, which were also payable out of the proceeds of the used car inventory. Camp knew nothing of these loans and thought that Jones's used car business was making payments only on the loans he had cosigned.

Jones defaulted on the $50,000 note cosigned by Camp, and First Financial brought suit against Camp on his obligation as surety on the note. The trial court entered a judgment against Jones and Camp, jointly and severally, in the amount of $52,180 plus interest at the rate of 12 percent and attorneys' fees of $5,218. Camp appealed. ∞

Dudley, Justice   Under the facts of this case Camp is an accommodation party and a surety.

Sureties may have simple contract defenses. One of the defenses involves the creditor's failure to disclose facts which materially increase a surety's

risk. A number of courts have adopted Section 124(1) of the Restatement of Security (1940) to define the creditor's duty to disclose. We adopt the section which provides:

Section 124. Non-disclosure by Creditor.

(1) Where before the surety has undertaken his obligation the creditor knows facts unknown to the surety that materially increase the risk beyond that which the creditor has reason to believe the surety intends to assume, and the creditor also has reason to believe that these facts are unknown to the surety and has a reasonable opportunity to communicate them to the surety, failure of the creditor to notify the surety of such facts is a defense to the surety.

Comment (b) to that section states that:

Among facts that are material are the financial condition of the principal, secret agreements between the parties, or the relations of third parties to the principal. If the surety requests information, the creditor must disclose it. Where he realizes that the surety is acting or is about to act upon a mistaken belief about the principal in respect to a matter material to the surety's risk, he should afford the surety the benefit of his information if he has an opportunity to do so.

In this case the original note was executed on August 2, 1982, and the renewals were executed on January 25, 1985, September 11, 1985, and March 15, 1986. Camp testified that on August 15, 1985, just before the September 1985 renewal, the loan officer of First Financial "advised me that the loan was coming up for renewal and he advised me that the interest had been paid. First Federal offered no evidence to the contrary. In truth, interest payments were four (4) months delinquent. Camp testified that he would not have executed the September 11, 1985, renewal if he had known that interest was not current.

First Federal's conduct toward Camp was even more egregious in a different regard. All of the witnesses agreed that First Federal would not make the loan to Jones alone. First Federal's president testified that "the loan would not have been made without Mr. Camp as co-borrower." However, once Camp signed as a co-maker, and the loan limits were practically reached, first Federal began making side loans, or personal loans, to Jones. For example, when $24,861 or the guaranteed $25,000 line of credit had been reached, First Federal made a side loan to Jones of $3,250. When $48,019 of the $50,000 guaranteed line of credit had been reached, First Federal made side loans of almost $10,000. These side loans to Jones amounted to $25,038 and were repaid from cars which were mortgaged to First Federal. Yet, all parties understood that the loans which Camp co-signed were to be repaid by the sale of the car inventory. Camp knew nothing of the side loans and naturally thought that Jones' used car business was making payments only on the loans which he cosigned.

Both of these actions, the failure to disclose and the secret side loans, materially increased the surety's contemplated risk, and the creditor was aware of the surety's ignorance of the facts. Yet, the creditor, First Federal, chose to misrepresent the truth about the currency of the interest payments and to secret the side loans.

As a result of the actions, the surety assumed a risk well beyond that which he intended. First Federal was aware of the facts, and although given an opportunity, failed to communicate them to the surety. Such actions by a creditor discharge a surety. Accordingly, the judgment is reversed and the complaint is dismissed.

Judgment reversed in favor of Camp.

Subrogation, Reimbursement, and Contribution

If the surety has to perform or pay the principal's obligation, then the surety acquires all of the rights that the creditor had against the principal. This is known as the surety's **right of subrogation.** The rights acquired could include the right to any collateral in the possession of the creditor, any judgment right the creditor had against the principal on the obligation, and the rights of a creditor in bankruptcy proceedings.

If the surety performs or pays the principal's obligation, she is entitled to recover her costs from the principal; this is known as the surety's **right to reimbursement.** For example, Amado cosigns a promissory note for $250 at the credit union for her friend Anders. Anders defaults on the note, and the credit union collects $250 from Amado on her suretyship obligation. Amado then not only gets the credit union's rights against Anders under the right of subrogation, but also the right to collect $250 from Anders under the right of reimbursement.

Suppose several persons (Tom, Dick, and Harry) are cosureties of their friend Sam. When Sam defaults, Tom pays the whole obligation. Tom is entitled to collect one-third from both Dick and Harry since he paid more than his prorated share. This is known as the cosurety's **right to contribution.** The relative shares of cosureties, as well as any limitations on their liability, are normally set out in the contract of suretyship.

LIENS ON PERSONAL PROPERTY

Common Law Liens

Under the common—or judge-made—law, artisans, innkeepers, and common carriers (such as airlines and trucking companies) were entitled to liens to secure the reasonable value of the services they performed. An artisan such as a furniture upholsterer or an auto mechanic uses his labor or materials to improve personal property that belongs to someone else. The improvement becomes part of the property and belongs to the owner of the property. Therefore, the artisan who made the improvement is given a **lien** on the property until he is paid.

For example, the upholsterer who recovers a sofa for a customer is entitled to a lien on the sofa. The innkeeper and common carrier are in business to serve the public and are required by law to do so. Under the common law, the innkeeper, to secure payment for his reasonable charges for food and lodging, was allowed to claim a lien on the property that the guest brought to the hotel or inn. Similarly, the common carrier, such as a trucking company, was allowed to claim a lien on the goods carried for the reasonable charges for the service. The justification for such liens was that the innkeeper and common carrier were entitled to the protection of a lien because they were required by law to provide the service to anyone seeking it.

Statutory Liens

While common law liens are still generally recognized today, many states have incorporated this concept into statutes. Some of the state statutes have created additional liens, while others have modified the common law liens to some extent. The statutes commonly provide a procedure for foreclosing the lien. **Foreclosure** is the method by which the rights of the property owner are cut off so that the lienholder can realize her security interest. Typically, the statutes provide for a court to authorize the sale of the personal property subject to the lien so that the creditor can obtain the money to which she is entitled.

Carriers' liens and warehousemen's liens are provided for in Article 7, Documents of Title, of the Uniform Commercial Code. They are covered in Chapter 33, Checks and Documents of Title.

Characteristics of Liens

The common law lien and most of the statutory liens are known as **possessory liens.** They give the artisan or other lienholder the right to keep possession of the debtor's property until the reasonable charges for services have been paid. For the lien to come into play, possession of the goods must have been entrusted to the artisan. Suppose a person takes a chair to an upholsterer to have it repaired. The upholsterer can keep possession of the chair until the person pays the reasonable value of the repair work. However, if the upholsterer comes to the person's home to make the repair, the upholsterer would not have a lien on the chair as the person did not give up possession of it.

The two essential elements of the lien are: (1) possession by the improver or the provider of services and (2) a debt created by the improvement or the provision of services concerning the goods. If the artisan or other lienholder gives up the goods voluntarily, he loses the lien. For example, if a person has a new engine put in his car and the mechanic gives the car back to him before he pays for the engine, the mechanic loses the lien on the car to secure the person's payment for the work and materials. However, if the person uses a spare set of keys to regain possession, or does so by fraud or another illegal act, the lien is not lost. Once the debt has been paid, the lien is terminated and the artisan or other lienholder no longer has the right to retain the goods. If the artisan keeps the goods after the debt has been paid, or keeps the goods without the right to a lien, he is liable for conversion or unlawful detention of goods.

Another important aspect of common law liens is that the work or service must have been performed at the request of the owner of the property. If the work or service is performed without the consent of the owner, no lien is created. This is one of the issues raised in the *Navistar Financial Corporation v. Allen's Corner Garage and Towing Service, Inc.* case that follows.

Wieslaw Wik was the owner of a truck tractor on which Navistar Financial Corporation held a lien to secure a purchase loan agreement. On February 21, 1986, Wik was driving his truck tractor and pulling a trailer owned by the V. Seng Teaming Company. The tractor/trailer unit overturned in a ditch. Allen's Corner Garage and Towing Service was called by the Illinois State Police. Its crew removed the cargo from the trailer and hoisted the tractor and trailer out of the ditch and onto the highway. They then took the truck, trailer, and cargo to Allen's garage for storage. The uprighting and towing of semitrailer trucks is an intricate process and involves a good deal of specialized equipment. Allen's was licensed by the Interstate Commerce Commission and the Illinois Commerce Commission as a common carrier and owned over 50 specialized trucks and trailers for such operations.

Wik defaulted on his loan agreement with Navistar and the right to possession passed to Navistar. One of its employees contacted Allen's and offered to pay the towing plus storage charges on the truck in exchange for possession of it. Allen's refused, saying it would not release the truck unless the charges for the truck, trailer, and cargo were all paid. Navistar then brought suit against Allen's to recover possession of the truck. Subsequently, V. Seng Teaming Company paid $13,000 in towing and storage charges on the trailer and cargo and took possession of them. Navistar then reiterated its willingness to pay the towing charges but refused to pay any storage charges accruing after its initial offer.

The trial court held that Allen's had a common law artisan's lien against the tractor for towing charges but not for storage fees. It held that Navistar was entitled to possession of the tractor, subject to payment of $1,162 for towing. Allen's appealed and Navistar cross-appealed the portion of the order granting Allen's a common law lien for towing. ∞

Unverzagt, Judge   Illinois recognizes the common law possessory lien. Such liens are fundamentally consensual in nature and can be created only by agreement, by some fixed rule of law, or by usage of trade or commerce. The common law lien has no provision for forfeiture and sale, but is limited to the right to possession of the chattel until all charges are paid. The lien applies to categories of persons: (1) those who impart added value to the property and (2) common carriers who are bound by law to accept and carry the goods. In Illinois, a common carrier has a lien on goods delivered to it for carriage; the carrier is not bound to part with the goods until the charges are paid.

Allen's argues that its services fall within both categories of common law liens. It claims that its towing and cargo salvaging operations are so specialized as to qualify it as an artisan, or alternatively, that it is a common carrier. Navistar responds that Allen's is not an artisan, citing a number of cases from Illinois and from foreign jurisdictions for the principle that mere towing of a vehicle, no matter how difficult or specialized, does not give rise to a common law lien. Most of these cases are distinguishable as they involve towing of a vehicle without the owner's consent. Nonetheless, we agree

with Navistar that mere towing of a vehicle from one place to another does not add anything of value to the "intrinsic value" of the vehicle towed.

We agree with Allen's, however, that it is entitled to a lien as a common carrier. As a common carrier, it is entitled to a lien for carriage charges. Navistar does not directly challenge this conclusion, but argues that Allen's towed the tractor without its consent. As an agreement is a necessary element of a common law lien, Navistar's lack of consent would defeat Allen's lien. Although police have the power to remove disabled vehicles from highways, they may not create a lien upon a vehicle without the owner's consent. John Allen testified that a representative from Seng was at the scene when he arrived and that the entire unit was under Seng's control. Allen also testified that the driver came to Allen's place of business the following day. Testifying later, Allen stated unequivocally that Allen's Corner Garage was authorized to make the tow. The court could have concluded that the representative of Seng was authorized to and did give his consent to the towing, or that the driver subsequently ratified these actions.

Having decided that Allen's was entitled to a common law lien as a common carrier, we now turn to the question of whether it may also claim a lien for storage charges. The rule has been stated that when a common carrier hauls freight and then stores it at the destination until claimed by the receiver, the carrier becomes a warehouseman and obtains a lien for storage charges. [Citations omitted.] In those cases, the commodities involved, coal and grain, required special handling and storage. The carrier in each case sustained some inconvenience or expense by storing the property until the receiver was ready to remove it.

In the present case, Allen's did not keep the truck on the lot for the benefit of Navistar, but did so only to preserve its lien right. A garage owner is not entitled to a lien for storage in a garage. Since Allen's retained and stored the truck for no reason other than to be able to insist on its lien rights, the trial court was correct in denying it a lien for storage charges.

Judgment affirmed.

Foreclosure of Lien

The right of a lienholder to possess goods does not automatically give the lienholder the right to sell the goods or to claim ownership if his charges are not paid. Commonly, there is a procedure provided by statute for selling property once it has been held for a certain period of time. The lienholder is required to give notice to the debtor and to advertise the proposed sale by posting or publishing notices. If there is no statutory procedure, the lienholder must first bring a lawsuit against the debtor. After obtaining a judgment for his charges, the lienholder can have the sheriff seize the property and have it sold at a judicial sale.

SECURITY INTERESTS IN REAL PROPERTY

There are three basic contract devices for using real estate as security for an obligation: (1) the real estate mortgage, (2) the deed of trust, and (3) the land contract. In addition, the states have enacted statutes giving mechanics such as carpenters and plumbers, and materialmen such as lumberyards, a right to a lien on real property into which their labor or materials have been incorporated.

Historical Developments of Mortgages

A **mortgage** is a security interest in real property or a deed to real property that is given by the owner (the **mortgagor**) as security for a debt owed to the creditor (the **mortgagee**). The real estate mortgage was used as a form of security in England as early as the middle of the 12th century, but our present-day mortgage law developed from the common law mortgage of the 15th century. The common law mortgage was a deed that conveyed the land to the mortgagee, with the title to the land to return to the mortgagor upon payment of the debt secured by the mortgage. The mortgagee was given possession of the land during the term of the mortgage. If the mortgagor defaulted on the debt, the mortgagee's title to the land became absolute. The land was forfeited as a penalty, but the forfeiture did not discharge the debt. In addition to keeping the land, the mortgagee could sue on the debt, recover a judgment, and seek to collect the debt.

The early equity courts did not favor the imposition of penalties and would relieve mortgagors from such forfeitures, provided that the mortgagor's default was minor and was due to causes beyond his control. Gradually, the courts became more lenient in permitting redemptions and allowed the mortgagor to **redeem** (reclaim his property) if he tendered performance without unreasonable delay. Finally, the courts of equity recognized the mortgagor's right to redeem as an absolute right that would continue until the mortgagee asked the court of equity to decree that the mortgagor's right to redeem be foreclosed and cut off. Our present law regarding the foreclosure of mortgages developed from this practice.

Today, the mortgage is generally viewed as a lien on land rather than a conveyance of title to the land. There are still some states where the mortgagor goes through the process of giving the mortgagee some sort of legal title to the property. Even in these states, however, the mortgagee's title is minimal and the real ownership of the property remains in the mortgagor.

FIGURE   I

A Mortgage

MORTGAGE

THIS INDENTURE, made this 18th day of October, A.D. 1997, BETWEEN Raymond A. Dole and Deborah H. Dole, hereinafter called the Mortgagor, and First Federal Savings and Loan Association, hereinafter called the Mortgagee,

WITNESSETH, That the said Mortgagor, for and in consideration of the sum of One Dollar, to us in hand paid by the said Mortgagee, the receipt whereof is hereby acknowledged, have granted, bargained, and sold to the said Mortgagee, its heirs and assigns forever, the following described land situate, lying and being in the County of Genesee, State of Michigan, to wit:

All that certain plot, piece, or parcel of land located in the County of Genesee, State of Michigan and known and described as Lot number Thirty-nine (39) in William D. Green's subdivision of part of Lot numbered Twenty-two (22) in Square numbered Twelve Hundred Nineteen (1219), as per plot recorded in the Office of the Surveyor for the County of Genesee in Liber 30 at folio 32, together with the buildings and improvements thereon, and the said Mortgagor do hereby fully warrant the title to said land, and will defend the same against the lawful claims of all persons whomsoever.

PROVIDED ALWAYS, That if said Mortgagor, their heirs, legal representatives, or assigns shall pay unto the said Mortgagee, its legal representatives or assigns, a certain promissory note dated the 18th day of October, A.D. 1997, for the sum of Thirty-eight Thousand Dollars ($38,000.00), payable in monthly installments of Three Hundred Fifteen Dollars ($315.00) with interest at ten percent (10%) beginning on November 18, 1997, and signed by Raymond A. Dole and Deborah H. Dole and shall perform, comply with, and abide by this mortgage, and shall pay all taxes which may accrue on said land and all costs and expenses said Mortgagee may be put to in collecting said promissory note by foreclosure of this mortgage or otherwise, including a reasonable attorney's fee, then this mortgage and the estate hereby created shall cease and be null and void.

IN WITNESS WHEREOF, the said Mortgagor hereunto set their hands and seals the day and year first above written. Signed, sealed, and delivered in presence of us:

John R. Bacon)
James A. Brown)   *Raymond A. Dole*
)   *Deborah H. Dole*

ACKNOWLEDGMENT OF MORTGAGE
State of Michigan)
County of Genesee) ˢ ˢ

I, an officer authorized to take acknowledgments according to the laws of the State of Michigan, duly qualified and acting, HEREBY CERTIFY that Raymond A. Dole and Deborah H. Dole to me personally known, this day personally appeared and acknowledged before me that they executed the foregoing Mortgage, and I further certify that I know the said persons making said acknowledgment to be the individuals described in and who executed the said Mortgage.
Susan B. Clark
Notary Public

Susan B. Clark
Susan B. Clark
Notary Public

Form, Execution, and Recording

Because the real estate mortgage conveys an interest in real property, it must be executed with the same formality as a deed. Unless it is executed with the required formalities, it will not be eligible for recording in the local land records. Recordation of the mortgage does not affect its validity as between the mortgagor and the mortgagee. However, if it is not recorded, it will not be effective against subsequent purchasers of the property or creditors, including other mortgagees, who have no notice of the earlier mortgage. It is important to the mortgagee that the mortgage be recorded so that the world will be on notice of the mortgagee's interest in the property. See Figure 1 for an example of a mortgage.

Rights and Liabilities

The owner (mortgagor) of property subject to a mortgage can sell the interest in the property without the consent of the mortgagee. However, the sale does not affect the mortgagee's interest in the property or the mortgagee's claim against the mortgagor. In some cases, the mortgage may provide that if the property is sold, then any remaining balance becomes immediately due and payable. This is known as a "due on sale" clause.

Suppose Erica Smith owns a lot on a lake. She wants to build a cottage on the land, so she borrows $55,000 from First National Bank. She signs a note for $55,000 and gives the bank a $55,000 mortgage on the land and cottage as security for her repayment of the loan. Several years later, Smith sells her land and cottage to Melinda Mason. The mortgage she gave First National might make the unpaid balance due on the mortgage payable on sale. If it does not, Smith can sell the property with the mortgage on it. If Mason defaults on making the mortgage payments, the bank can foreclose on the mortgage. If at the foreclosure sale the property does not bring enough money to cover the costs, interest, and balance due on the mortgage, First National is entitled to a deficiency judgment against Smith. However, some courts are reluctant to give deficiency judgments where real property is used as security for a debt. If on foreclosure the property sells for more than the debt, Mason is entitled to the surplus.

A purchaser of mortgaged property may buy it **subject to** the mortgage or may **assume** the mortgage. If she buys subject to the mortgage and there is a default and foreclosure, the purchaser is not personally liable for any deficiency. The property is liable for the mortgage debt and can be sold to satisfy it in case of default; in addition, the original mortgagor remains liable for its payment. If the buyer assumes the mortgage, then she becomes personally liable for the debt and for any deficiency on default and foreclosure.

The creditor (mortgagee) may assign his interest in the mortgaged property. To do this, the mortgagee must assign the mortgage as well as the debt for which the mortgage is security. In most jurisdictions, the negotiation of the note carries with it the right to the security and the holder of the note is entitled to the benefits of the mortgage.

Foreclosure

Foreclosure is the process by which any rights of the mortgagor or the current property owner are cut off. Foreclosure proceedings are regulated by statute in the state in which the property is located. In many states, two or more alternative methods of foreclosure are available to the mortgagee or his assignee. The methods in common use today are (1) strict foreclosure, (2) action and sale, and (3) power of sale.

A small number of states permit what is called **strict foreclosure.** The creditor keeps the property in satisfaction of the debt, and the owner's rights are cut off. This means that the creditor has no right to a deficiency and the debtor has no right to any surplus. Strict foreclosure is normally limited to situations where the amount of the debt exceeds the value of the property.

Foreclosure by **action and sale** is permitted in all states, and it is the only method of foreclosure permitted in some states. Although the state statutes are not uniform, they are alike in their basic requirements. In a foreclosure by action and sale, suit is brought in a court having jurisdiction. Any party having a property interest that would be cut off by the foreclosure must be made a defendant, and if any such party has a defense, he must enter his appearance and set up his defense. After the case is tried, a judgment is entered and a sale of the property ordered. The proceeds of the sale are applied to the payment of the mortgage debt, and any surplus is paid over to the mortgagor. If there is a deficiency, a deficiency judgment is, as a general rule, entered against the mortgagor and such other persons as are liable on the debt. Deficiency judgments are generally not permitted where the property sold is the residence of the debtor.

The right to foreclose under a **power of sale** must be expressly conferred on the mortgagee by the terms of the mortgage. If the procedure for the exercise of the power is set out in the mortgage, that procedure must be followed. Several states have enacted statutes that set out the procedure to be followed in the exercise of a power of sale. No court action is required. As a general rule, notice of the default and sale must be given to the mortgagor. After the statutory period, the sale may be held. The sale must be advertised, and it must be at auction. The sale must be conducted fairly, and an effort must be made to sell the property at the highest price obtainable. The proceeds of the sale are applied to the payment of costs, interest, and the principal of the debt. Any surplus must be paid to the mortgagor. If there is a deficiency and the mortgagee wishes to recover a judgment for the deficiency, she must bring suit on the debt.

Right of Redemption

At common law and under existing statutes, the mortgagor or an assignee of the mortgagor has what is called an **equity of redemption** in the mortgaged real estate. This means that he has the absolute right to discharge the mortgage when due and to have title to the mortgaged property restored free and clear of the mortgage debt. Under the statutes of all states, the mortgagor or any party having an interest in the mortgaged property that will be cut off by the foreclosure may redeem the property after default and before the mortgagee forecloses the mortgage. In several states, the mortgagor or any other party in interest is given by statute what is known as a redemption period (usually six months or one year, beginning either after the foreclosure proceedings are started or after a foreclosure sale of the mortgaged property has been made) in which to pay the mortgaged debt, costs, and interest and to redeem the property.

As a general rule, if a party in interest wishes to redeem, he must, if the redemption period runs after the foreclosure sale, pay to the purchaser at the foreclosure sale the amount that the purchaser has paid plus interest up to the time of redemption. If the redemption period runs before the sale, the party in interest must pay the amount of the debt plus the costs and interest. The person who wishes to redeem from a mortgage foreclosure sale must redeem the entire mortgage interest; he cannot redeem a partial interest by paying a proportionate amount of the debt or by paying a proportionate amount of the price bid at the foreclosure sale.

Deed of Trust

States typically use either the mortgage or the **deed of trust** as the primary mechanism for holding a security interest in real property. There are three parties to a deed of trust: (1) the owner of the property who borrows the money (the debtor), (2) the trustee who holds legal title to the property put up as security, and (3) the lender who is the beneficiary of the trust. The trustee serves as a fiduciary for both the creditor and the debtor. The purpose of the deed of trust is to make it easy for the security to be liquidated. However, most states treat the deed of trust like a mortgage in giving the borrower a relatively long period of time to redeem the property, thereby defeating this rationale for the arrangement.

In a deed of trust transaction, the borrower deeds to the trustee the property that is to be put up as security. See Figure 2 for an example of a deed of trust. The trust agreement usually gives the trustee the right to foreclose or sell the property if the debtor fails to make a required payment on the debt. Normally, the trustee does not sell the property until the lender notifies him that the borrower is in default and demands that the property be sold. The trustee must notify the debtor that he is in default and that the land will be sold. The trustee advertises the property for sale. After the statutory period, the trustee will sell the property at a public or private sale. The proceeds are applied to the costs of the foreclosure, interest, and debt. If there is a surplus, it is paid to the borrower. If there is a deficiency, the lender has to sue the borrower on the debt and recover a judgment.

Land Contracts

The **land contract** is a device for securing the balance due the seller on the purchase price of real estate. Essentially, it is an installment contract for the purchase of land. The buyer agrees to pay the purchase price over a period of time. The seller agrees to convey title to the property to the buyer when the full price is paid. Usually, the buyer takes possession of the property, pays the taxes, insures the property, and assumes the other obligations of an owner. However, the seller keeps legal title and does not turn over the deed until the purchase price is paid.

If the buyer defaults, the seller usually has the right to declare a forfeiture and take over possession of the property. The buyer's rights to the property are cut off at that point. Most states give the buyer on a land contract a limited period of time to redeem

FIGURE 2

A Deed of Trust

DEED OF TRUST

THIS DEED made this 14th day of August, 1997, by and between Harold R. Holmes, grantor, party of the first part, and Frederick B. Cannon, trustee, party of the second part, and Sarah A Miles, party of the third part,

WITNESSETH:

The party of the first part does hereby grant unto the party of the second part, the following described property located in the District of Columbia and known as Lot number One Hundred Fourteen (114) in James B. Nicholson's subdivision in Square numbered Twelve Hundred Forty-seven (1247), formerly Square numbered Seventy-seven (77), "Georgetown," as per plat recorded in the Office of the Surveyor for the District of Columbia in Liber Georgetown 2 at folio 34, in trust, however, to secure the balance only of the purchase price of the above described premises, evidenced by the following described obligation:

Promissory note executed by the party of the first part, payable to the party of the third part and dated August 14, 1997, in the principal sum of Sixty-four Thousand Dollars ($64,000.00) bearing interest at the rate of ten percent (10%) per annum until paid. Said principal and interest are payable in monthly installments of Seven Hundred Thirty-five Dollars ($735.00) on the 14th day of each and every month beginning September 14, 1997, and continuing every month thereafter, with the unpaid balance of said principal and interest due and payable in full on August 14, 2007.

IN WITNESS WHEREOF, the party of the first part has set his hand and seal this the day and year first above written.

Harold R. Holmes

(SEAL)

Acknowledgment

This Deed of Trust accepted this 14th day of August, 1997.

Frederick B. Cannon

Trustee

his interest. Moreover, some states require the seller to go through a foreclosure proceeding. Generally, the procedure for declaring a forfeiture and recovering property sold on a land contract is simpler and less time-consuming than foreclosure of a mortgage. In most states, the procedure in case of default is set out by statute. If the buyer, after default, voluntarily surrenders possession to the seller, no court procedure is necessary; the seller's title will become absolute, and the buyer's equity will be cut off.

Purchases of farm property are commonly financed through the use of land contracts. See Figure 3 for an example of a land contract. As an interest in real estate, a land contract should be in writing and recorded in the local land records so as to protect the interests of both parties.

As can be seen in the following case, *Looney v. Farmers Home Administration,* some courts have invoked the equitable doctrine against forfeitures and have required that the seller on a land contract must foreclose on the property in order to avoid injustice to a defaulting buyer.

FIGURE 3

A Land Contract

LAND CONTRACT

THIS AGREEMENT, made this 15th day of September, A.D. 1997, between Sarah A. Collins, a single woman, hereinafter designated "Vendor," and Robert H. Bowen, a single man, hereinafter designated "Vendee," in the manner following: The Vendor hereby agrees to sell and the Vendee agrees to buy all that certain piece or parcel of land being in the Township of Fenton, County of Genesee and State of Michigan, and more particularly described as follows:

Part of the Northeast $\frac{1}{4}$ of the Northwest $\frac{1}{4}$ of Section 20, Township 5 North, Range 5 East, described as follows: Beginning at a point on the North line of said Section 20, which is West along said North line, 797.72 feet from the North $\frac{1}{4}$ corner of said Section 20; thence continuing West along said North line, 522.72 feet; thence South 0 degrees, 18 minutes, 12 seconds East along the West $\frac{1}{8}$ line of said Section, 1000.0 feet; thence East parallel to the North line of said Section, 522.72 feet; thence North 0 degrees, 18 minutes, 12 seconds West parallel to said West $\frac{1}{8}$ line 1000.0 feet to the point of beginning, containing 12.0 acres of land, more or less, and known as 1135 Long Lake Road.

Subject to all easements, laws, ordinances, reservations, applying to this property.

For the sum of Sixty-four Thousand Nine Hundred Dollars ($64,900.00), payable as follows: Ten Thousand Dollars ($10,000.00), cash in hand, receipt of which is hereby acknowledged before the signing of this contract and the balance payable as follows: Three Hundred Dollars ($300.00) or more payable on the 1st day of November, 1997, and a like amount on the 1st day of each and every month thereafter until the full sum of both interest and principal has been paid in full. Interest at the rate of ten percent (10%) per annum, starting October 1, 1997, shall be deducted from each and every monthly payment and the balance applied on the principal. The entire balance, both principal and interest, to be paid in full on or before 5 years from date of closing. It is understood and agreed that the above monthly payment includes taxes and insurance that may become due and payable subsequent to the date of this contract; said amounts to be paid by Vendor and added to the principal balance.

Vendee also agrees to pay all taxes and assessments extraordinary as well as ordinary that may be levied thereon, including taxes for the year 1997, and also deferred payments on special assessments that shall become due and payable after the date thereof to be prorated to date.

The Vendee agrees to keep the buildings upon or to be placed upon the premises insured against damage by fire and wind, in such company and amount as is approved by the Vendor, for the benefit of all parties in interest; such policies shall be delivered to and held by the Vendor.

And Vendee agrees to keep the buildings and other improvements on the premises in good repair. In case the Vendee shall fail to pay taxes, effect insurance, or make necessary repairs, the Vendor may do any or all of these things and the amount paid therefore by the Vendor shall be deemed a part of the principal sum under this contract and become payable immediately with interest at the rate of ten percent (10%) per annum until paid.

The Vendor on receiving payment in full of the principal and interest, and of all other sums chargeable under the contract, agrees, at his own proper cost and expense, to execute and deliver to the Vendee, or to his assigns, upon surrender of this contract, a good and sufficient conveyance in fee simple of the above described premises, free and clear of all liens and encumbrances, except such as may have accrued thereon subsequent to the date of this contract by or through the acts or negligences of others than the Vendor, and at the option of the Vendor furnish the Vendee an abstract of title or a policy of title insurance in an amount equal to the purchase price under this contract. The Vendor hereby reserves the right to mortgage said premises at any time in an amount not in excess of the amount then due on this contract, and the Vendee agrees that the said mortgage shall be a first lien on the premises.

It is mutually agreed that the Vendee shall have possession of said premises from and after October 1, 1997.

If the Vendee shall fail to comply with the terms of this contract, the Vendor may take possession of the property and all the improvements on it and treat the Vendee as a tenant holding over without permission and remove him therefrom and retain any money paid hereon as stipulated damages for nonperformance of this contract. It is hereby expressly understood and declared that time is and shall be taken as of the very essence of this contract. Notice of said forfeiture may be given by depositing the notice in post office, addressed to Vendee at his last known address.

It is agreed that the stipulations contained in this contract are to apply to and bind the heirs, executors, administrators, and assigns of the respective parties to this contract.

In witness whereof, the said parties have set their hands and seals the day and year first above written. Signed, sealed and delivered in presence of:

Harriet Greene)   *Sarah A. Collins*
                            Sarah A. Collins

Samuel A. Giggs)   *Robert H. Bowen*
                            Robert H. Bowen

LOONEY v. FARMERS HOME ADMINISTRATION 794 F.2d 310 (7th Cir. 1986)

On October 7, 1976, Lowry and Helen McCord entered into a land contract to purchase a 260-acre farm from John and Esther Looney for $250,000. The contract specified that this was to be amortized over a 20-year period at an annual interest rate of 7 percent. The McCords were to make annual payments of $23,280 on November 15 of each year until the purchase price and all accrued interest was paid. They also agreed to pay real estate taxes, insurance, and maintenance costs for the property.

Four years later, the McCords received an economic emergency loan of $183,000 from the Farmers Home Administration (FmHA). They signed a promissory note for the amount of the loan with interest at 11 percent and, as security, also granted the FmHA a second mortgage on the land subject to the land sales contract.

The McCords subsequently defaulted on their obligations to the Looneys. At the time of the default, the McCords had paid $123,280 to the Looneys but still owed $249,360.12 on the contract price. At the time, the property was worth $455,000. The Looneys brought suit against the McCords and the FmHA seeking to eject the McCords from the property and forfeiture of the contract. The FmHA objected to the proposed forfeiture and argued that the court should order foreclosure proceedings.

The district court denied the FmHA's motion for foreclosure. It held that the traditional presumption under Indiana law did not apply because the McCords had made only minimal payments on the contract and had not paid their fall taxes or insurance installments. Because $249,360.12 was still owed on an initial base price of $250,000, the court found the McCords's equity to be $639.88, only .26 percent of the principal. The court therefore found forfeiture appropriate, awarded the FmHA $639.88 and extinguished the FmHA's mortgage. The FmHA appealed. ∽

Cudahy, Circuit Judge Under Indiana law a conditional land sales contract is considered in the nature of a secured transaction, "the provisions of which are subject to all proper and just remedies at law and in equity." *Skendzel v. Marshall.* Recognizing the common law maxim that "equity abhors forfeitures," the *Skendzel* court concluded that "judicial foreclosure of a land sales contract is in consonance with the notions of equity developed in American jurisprudence." Foreclosure generally protects the rights of all parties to a contract. Upon judicial sale the proceeds are first applied to the balance of the contract principal and interest owed the seller. Then, any junior lienholders take their share. Any surplus goes to the buyer.

Skendzel recognized, however, two instances where forfeiture was the appropriate remedy:

In the case of an abandoning, absconding vendee, forfeiture is a logical and equitable remedy. Forfeiture would also be appropriate where the vendee has paid a minimal amount on the contract at the time of default and seeks to retain possession while the vendor is paying taxes, insurance, and other upkeep in order to preserve the premises.

The district court did not rely on the first *Skendzel* exception in finding forfeiture appropriate. No evidence in the record supports such a finding.

If forfeiture is justified, then, it is only because the second *Skendzel* exception is met. This requires that the vendee have paid only a minimum amount on the contract at the time of default. In this case, the district court concluded that "this is patently a situation contemplated by the court in *Skendzel* in which forfeiture is the logical and equitable remedy."

However, the buyers in *Skendzel* had in fact paid more than a minimum amount on the contract and the court cited no examples of what would "patently" constitute a "minimum amount." Rather, later Indiana cases have interpreted *Skendzel* as requiring a case by case analysis that examines the totality of circumstances surrounding the contract and its performance. Here, while $123,280 was paid to the Looneys, the court considered all but $639.88 to be interest rather than a part of the contract price. The court equated contract price with what was paid to reduce principal. But nothing in Indiana law compels the district court's construction of payments on the contract. On the contrary, several Indiana courts have considered and given weight to both payments to reduce principal and those to reduce interest in determining whether a buyer falls within the second *Skendzel* exception.

Even where no principal is paid, a buyer's stake in the property may be sufficient to justify foreclosure.

Here, two uncontested affidavits indicate the property to be worth over $200,000 more than the McCords owe the Looneys. With the evidence of appreciation, the court was incorrect to conclusively value the McCords' equity at only $639.88.

When the second *Skendzel* exception has been invoked it frequently has been because the vendee is contributing to a decline in the value of the security. There is no allegation or evidence of waste in this case. Even the Looneys admit that the buyers "had paid substantial monies pursuant to the terms of the contracts." The Looneys received $123,280 and the McCords paid the necessary real estate taxes, insurance premiums and upkeep expenses for over six years. The Looneys make no showing that foreclosure would not satisfy their interest and the court below made no such determination. While foreclosure would appear to satisfy all parties' needs, forfeiture leaves the FmHA with a $639.88 recovery on a $183,800 loan. In view of the "totality of circumstances" this result seems inequitable.

Judgment reversed in favor of Farmers Home Administration.

CONCEPT   REVIEW

Security Interests in Real Property

TYPE OF SECURITY INSTRUMENT	PARTIES	FEATURES
Mortgage	1. Mortgagor (property owner/debtor) 2. Mortgagee (creditor)	1. Mortgagee holds a security interest (and in some states, title) in real property as security for a debt. 2. If mortgagor defaults on her obligation, mortgagee must *foreclose* on property to realize on his security interest. 3. Mortgagor has a limited time after foreclosure to *redeem* her interest.
Deed of Trust	1. Owner/debtor 2. Lender/creditor 3. Trustee	1. Trustee holds legal title to the real property put up as security. 2. If debt is satisfied, the trustee conveys property back to owner/debtor. 3. If debt is not paid as agreed, creditor notifies trustee to sell the property. 4. While intended to make foreclosure easier, most states treat it like a mortgage for purposes of foreclosure.
Land Contract	1. Buyer 2. Seller	1. Seller agrees to convey title when full price is paid. 2. Buyer usually takes possession, pays property taxes and insurance, and maintains the property. 3. If buyer defaults, seller may declare a forfeiture and retake possession (most states) after buyer has limited time to redeem; some states require foreclosure.

MECHANIC'S AND MATERIALMAN'S LIENS

Each state has a statute that permits persons who contract to furnish labor or materials to improve real estate to claim a lien on the property until they are paid. There are many differences among states as to exactly who can claim such a lien and the requirements that must be met to do so.

Rights of Subcontractors and Materialmen

A general contractor is a person who has contracted with the owner to build, remodel, or improve real property. A subcontractor is a person who has contracted with the general contractor to perform a stipulated portion of the general contract. A materialman is a person who has contracted to furnish certain materials needed to perform a designated general contract.

Two distinct systems—the New York system and the Pennsylvania system—are followed by the states in allowing mechanic's liens on real estate to subcontractors and materialmen. The New York system is based on the theory of subrogation, and the subcontractors or materialmen cannot recover more than is owed to the contractor at the time they file a lien or give notice of a lien to the owner. Under the Pennsylvania system, the subcontractors or materialmen have direct liens and are entitled to liens for the value of labor and materials furnished, irrespective of the amount due from the owner to the contractor. Under the New York system, the general contractor's failure to perform his contract or his abandonment of the work has a direct effect on the lien rights of subcontractors and materialmen, whereas under the Pennsylvania system, such breach or abandonment by the general contractor does not directly affect the lien rights of subcontractors and materialmen.

Basis for Mechanic's or Materialman's Lien

Some state statutes provide that no lien shall be claimed unless the contract for the improvement is in writing and embodies a statement of the materials to be furnished and a description of the land on which the improvement is to take place and of the work to be done. Other states permit the contract to be oral, but in no state is a licensee or volunteer entitled to a lien. No lien can be claimed unless the work is done or the materials are furnished in the performance of a contract to improve specific real property. A sale of materials without reference to the improvement of specific real property does not entitle the person furnishing the materials to a lien on real property that is, in fact, improved by the use of the materials at some time after the sale.

Unless the state statute specifically includes sub-materialmen, they are not entitled to a lien. For example, if a lumber dealer contracts to furnish the lumber for the erection of a specific building and orders from a sawmill a carload of lumber that is needed to fulfill the contract, the sawmill will not be entitled to a lien on the building in which the lumber is used unless the state statute expressly provides that submaterialmen are entitled to a lien.

At times, the question has arisen as to whether materials have been furnished. Some courts have held that the materialman must prove that the material furnished was actually incorporated into the structure. Under this ruling, if material delivered on the job is diverted by the general contractor or others and not incorporated into the structure, the materialman will not be entitled to a lien. Other courts have held that the materialman is entitled to a lien if he can provide proof that the material was delivered on the job under a contract to furnish the material.

Requirements for Obtaining Lien

The requirements for obtaining a mechanic's or materialman's lien must be complied with strictly. Although there is no uniformity in the statutes as to the requirements for obtaining a lien, the statutes generally require the filing of a notice of lien with a county official such as the register of deeds or the county clerk, which notice sets forth the amount claimed, the name of the owner, the names of the contractor and the claimant, and a description of the property. Frequently, the notice of lien must be verified by an affidavit of the claimant. In some states, a copy of the notice must be served on the owner or be posted on the property.

The notice of lien must be filed within a stipulated time. The time varies from 30 to 90 days, but the favored time is 60 days after the last work performed or after the last materials furnished. Some statutes distinguish between labor claims, materialmen's claims, and claims of general contractors as to time of filing. The lien, when filed, must be foreclosed within a specified time, which generally varies from six months to two years.

Priorities and Foreclosure

The provisions for priorities vary widely, but most of the statutes provide that a mechanic's lien has priority over all liens attaching after the first work is performed or after the first materials are furnished. This statutory provision creates a hidden lien on the property, in that a mechanic's lien, filed within the allotted period of time after completion of the work, attaches as of the time the first work is done or the first material is furnished, but no notice of lien need be filed during this period. And if no notice of lien is filed during this period, third persons would have no means of knowing of the existence of a lien. There are no priorities among lien claimants under the majority of the statutes.

The following case, *In Re Skyline Properties*, illustrates a number of issues that can arise when a mechanic's claim that he has a lien on certain property because of work he did concerning it is challenged by another party claiming a competing interest in the property.

IN RE SKYLINE PROPERTIES, INC.
CENTURY NATIONAL BANK AND TRUST CO. v. SKYLINE PROPERTIES, INC.   134 B.R. 830 (Bankr. W.E.Pa. 1992)

I n 1987, Skyline Properties commenced development of an integrated, multifaceted resort encompassing approximately 1,000 acres to be known as Hunter's Station. David Mealy was engaged to perform excavating and grading work on the project and commenced visible work on April 20, 1987. Mealy's work included bulldozing new roads, constructing parking areas, digging footers and drainage ditches, grading a basement for a new building used as a tack shop, excavation of crawl spaces for new additions to an existing building subsequently used as a sales office, grading an area for a new horse barn, and the installation of drains and fencing on the property. The sales office was substantially complete and opened for business on June 4, 1987, while work continued on construction of the tack shop.

On June 5, 1987, Century National Bank extended $150,000 credit to Skyline, took as collateral a mortgage on several of the parcels in the development, and recorded the mortgage on June 5, 1987. Mealy completed his work on August 3, 1987, and filed a notice of a mechanics' lien claim on September 23, 1987. Pennsylvania law requires that claims for such liens be filed within four months after the completion of the work.

In October 1988, the bank filed a mortgage foreclosure action against Skyline's property that it held as security for the loan. In September 1989, Mealy obtained a judgment on his claim and scheduled a Sheriff's sale of the Skyline property. The sale was halted by the filing of a involuntary petition in bankruptcy. One of the issues in the bankruptcy proceeding was the relative priority of the claims of the bank and Mealy to the Skyline property. ☜

Bemtz, Bankruptcy Judge   A mechanics' lien for services which constitute alterations and repairs takes effect and has priority as of the date the mechanics' lien claim is filed. 49 Pa. Stat. Ann. Sec. 1508(b). In the case of services constituting erection and construction, the lien of a claim takes effect and has priority "as of the date of the visible commencement upon the ground of the work of erecting or constructing the improvement." 49 Pa.Stat. Ann. Sec. 1508(a).

This matter involves the following relevant dates:

Visible commencement of construction:	April 20, 1987
Bank's mortgage:	June 5, 1987
Mealy Claim filed:	September 23, 1987

Thus, if Mealy's work is erection and construction, Mealy's claim has priority over the Bank; if the work is alteration or repair, the Bank's mortgage takes priority.

Section 1201(10) of the Mechanics' Lien Law defines "erection and construction" as follows:

"Erection and construction" means the erection and construction of a new improvement or of a substantial addition to an existing improvement or any adaption of an existing improvement rendering the same fit for a new or distinct use and effecting a material change in the interior or exterior thereof.

The Bank asserts that no buildings were erected or constructed in conjunction with Mealy's work and Mealy's lien is for alterations and repairs. Thus the Bank asserts that Mealy's lien takes priority as of the date of filing of the Claim and not the date of visible commencement of the work.

The concern in determining whether the work is "erection and construction" or "alterations or repairs" is whether a substantial change to the existing structure has occurred such that any third party, such as the Bank, would be on notice that potential liens could exist. A change in the appearance or use of a building is sufficient to give such notice.

In the present case, the evidence reveals that a farmhouse on the property, formerly used as a residential dwelling, was converted into a sales office used to sell ownership interests in the development. Skyline converted an existing farmhouse into a sales office by essentially "gutting" the structure and constructing additions to the original dwelling. The appearance of the house was transformed into a commercial building and the use was altogether different. The addition to the building made it substantially larger than it had been as a private residence. The additions are substantial enough to be considered new construction. The work was substantially completed and the sales office open for business on June 4, 1987, one day *before* the Bank recorded its mortgage. Had the Bank, which was aware of the scope of the planned construction, viewed the property at the time it recorded its mortgage, it certainly would have known that potential liens could exist.

The tack shop was built on existing concrete blocks which had served as the foundation for a building that had previously fallen down or been removed. The tack shop has both a "new use" and a "new appearance" and constitutes erection and construction.

Grading and excavation is the type of work which is properly lienable as incident to the erection or construction of an improvement. Another way of

stating the test utilized by the Pennsylvania courts in determining whether a certain type of work is lienable is whether the work is incident to the construction of an improvement. Mealy graded the area for four structures—the sales office, the tack shop, the horse barn and arena, and the guardhouse. Mealy dug footers and drainage ditches for the sales office and the guardhouse and installed drains for the tack shop. The work Mealy performed was incident to the construction of these improvements and also designed to enhance their value by building a resort around them.

Mealy's lienable work, incident to the erection and construction of four structures, as opposed to merely alteration and repair, entitles Mealy to a claim which relates back in time to the date upon which work was commenced and therefore, is prior to the Bank's mortgage interest.

Order upholding Mealy's lien claim.

The procedure followed in the foreclosure of a mechanic's lien on real estate follows closely the procedure followed in a court foreclosure of a real estate mortgage. The rights acquired by the filing of a lien and the extent of the property covered by the lien are set out in some of the mechanic's lien statutes. In general, the lien attaches only to the interest that the person has in the property that has been improved at the time the notice is filed. Some statutes provide that the lien attaches to the building and to the city lot on which the building stands, or if the improvement is to farm property, the lien attaches to a specified amount of land.

Waiver of Lien

The question often arises as to the effect of an express provision in a contract for the improvement of real estate that no lien shall attach to the property for the cost of the improvement. In some states, there is a statute requiring the recording or filing of the contract and making such a provision ineffective if the statute is not complied with. In some states, courts have held that such a provision is effective against everyone; in other states, courts have held that the provision is ineffective against everyone except the contractor; and in still other states, courts

have held that such a provision is ineffective as to subcontractors, materialmen, and laborers. Whether the parties to the contract have notice of the waiver of lien provision plays an important part in several states in determining their right to a lien.

It is common practice that before a person who is having improvements made to his property makes final payment, he requires the contractor to sign an affidavit that all materialmen and subcontractors have been paid and to supply him with a release of lien signed by the subcontractors and materialmen.

ETHICAL AND PUBLIC POLICY CONCERNS

1. Suppose you operate an appliance store in an inner city neighborhood. Many of your potential customers do not have sufficient income to pay cash for goods such as television sets, VCRs, and stereo sets and they also have difficulty qualifying for credit cards or store charge accounts. You develop a "lease to buy" sales program whereby you offer those prospective customers the opportunity to lease a TV, VCR, or stereo on a weekly rental basis and after they have leased it for two years, they will be the owner of it. The total amount they would pay as rent for the item over the two years is about three times the retail cash price for the item. This element is not disclosed in your ads; rather, the focus is on the "opportunity to own" and the "low weekly payment." What ethical considerations are involved in your proposed sales program?

2. Suppose you own and operate a small loan business. A young man applies for a $1,000 loan. When you run a credit check on him, you find that he has had difficulty holding a job and has a terrible credit record. You conclude that he is a poor credit risk and inform him that you are willing to make the requested loan only if he can find someone who has a good credit rating to cosign a promissory note with him. The next day he comes by the office with a young woman who meets your criteria for a good credit rating and who indicates she is willing to cosign the note. Do you have any ethical obligation to share with the young woman the information you have about the young man's employment and credit history?

3. Suppose you have sold a farm to a young couple on a land contract that calls for them to pay off the purchase price over a 10-year period. After the couple has paid about a third of the purchase price, a serious drought damages their crop and they miss several payments, triggering your right to declare a default and reclaim possession of the property. Are there any ethical considerations involved in your taking such an action that you are otherwise legally entitled to take? If you proceed with a forfeiture action in court, what policy considerations should the court take into account in deciding whether to grant your request?

PROBLEM AND PROBLEM CASES

1. Mr. and Mrs. Marshall went to Beneficial Finance to borrow money but were deemed by Beneficial's office manager, Puckett, to be bad credit risks. The Marshalls stated that their friend Garren would be willing to cosign a note for them if necessary. Puckett advised Garren not to cosign because the Marshalls were bad credit risks. This did not dissuade Garren from cosigning a note for $480 but it prompted him to ask Beneficial to take a lien or security interest in Marshall's custom-built Harley-Davidson motorcycle, then worth over $1,000. Beneficial took and perfected a security

interest in the motorcycle. Marshall defaulted on the first payment. Beneficial gave notice of the default to Garren and advised him that it was looking to him for payment. Garren then discovered that Beneficial and Marshall had reached an agreement whereby Marshall would sell his motorcycle for $700; he was to receive $345 immediately, which was to be applied to the loan, and he promised to pay the balance of the loan from his pocket. Marshall paid Beneficial $89.50 and left town without giving the proceeds of the sale to Beneficial. Because Beneficial was unable to get the proceeds from Marshall, it brought suit against Garren on his obligation as surety. When Beneficial released the security for the loan (the motorcycle) without Garren's consent, was Garren relieved of his obligation as surety for repayment of the loan?

2. Bayer was the general contractor on a Massachusetts state highway contract. He hired Deschenes as a subcontractor to do certain excavation work. Deschenes was to start the job by November 24, 1988, and to complete it on or before March 1, 1989. Deschenes was required to furnish a bond of $91,000 to ensure his faithful performance of the subcontract, and he purchased such a bond from Aetna Insurance Company. Deschenes began the work on December 1, 1988, and quit on June 22, 1989, after completing only about half of the work. Bayer had made numerous efforts to get Deschenes to do the work and then completed the job himself when Deschenes walked off the job. Bayer then brought a lawsuit against Aetna on the bond, and Aetna claimed that it was discharged by the extension of the time given to Deschenes. Should Bayer recover on the bond?

3. International Automobiles, Ltd. was a company engaged in the sale and purchase of "collectors" cars. In 1975, International employed Eland Motor Car Company, a registered automotive repair shop, and its principal, Andrew Bach, to restore, repair, maintain, and store its collection of vehicles. Bach received a monthly fee of $4,000 for overseeing the collection as well as a 10 percent finder's fee for any cars he located for International and an additional 10 percent commission, both to be paid to Bach at the time of the sale of any such car. Over time, International ceased paying Eland and Bach for their services. In 1988, Eland asserted a garage owner's lien pursuant to New York Lien Law section 184 on the International vehicles still in its possession for the portion of the outstanding debt pertaining solely to the garage services. Section 184 of the Lien Law provides in pertinent part that a person keeping a registered motor vehicle repair shop or garage "and who in connection therewith tows, stores, maintains, keeps or repairs any motor vehicle . . . at the request or with the consent of the owner . . . has a lien upon such motor vehicle for the sum due for such [services] . . . and may detain such motor vehicle . . . at any time it may be lawfully in his possession until such sum is paid."

Eland arranged to conduct a garage keeper's lien sale in November 1988 to sell several of International's cars remaining in its possession to satisfy International's unpaid repair and storage bills. Eland duly served International with notices of the lien and sale. National Union Fire Insurance Company had become a money judgment creditor of International's for over $500,000. It brought a proceeding against Eland to compel it to turn over the cars in its possession that were owned by International. Pursuant to court order, Eland conducted a sale of the vehicles on June 9, 1990, and deposited the proceeds with the clerk of the court. Was Eland entitled to a priority garage keeper's lien on the vehicles in its possession because it had provided repair and storage services concerning those vehicles to International?

4. During May and June, John Shumate regularly parked his automobile on a vacant lot in downtown Philadelphia. At that time, no signs were posted prohibiting parking on the lot or indicating that vehicles parked there without authorization would be towed. On July 7, Shumate again left his car on the lot. When he returned two days later, the car was gone and the lot was posted with signs warning that parking was prohibited. Shumate learned that his car had been towed away by Ruffie's Towing Service and that the car was being held by Ruffie's at its place of business. Ruffie's refused to release the car until Shumate paid a towing fee of $44.50 plus storage charges of $4 per day. Shumate refused to pay the fee, and Ruffie's kept possession of the car. Did Ruffie's have a common law possessory lien on the car?

5. On July 18, Anna Parker conveyed certain land to Benjamin Coombs and took back a mortgage to secure the payment of $16,160, which was the balance due on the purchase price. The mortgage was recorded on November 11 of that year. Several days earlier, on October 30, Coombs executed a mortgage

to Mayham on that same property to secure the payment of $12,690. Mayham recorded his mortgage on October 30. Coombs defaulted on the Mayham mortgage and Mayham brought suit to foreclose it. Parker contended that her mortgage had priority over Mayham's because Mayham knew of it at the time he received his mortgage. The state law provides that mortgages "shall take effect from the time they are recorded." Which mortgage has priority?

6. Philip and Edith Beh purchased some property from Alfred M. Gromer and his wife. Sometime earlier, the Gromers had borrowed money from City Mortgage. They had signed a note and had given City Mortgage a second deed of trust on the property. There was also a first deed of trust on the property at the time the Behs purchased it. In the contract of sale between the Behs and the Gromers, the Behs promised to "assume" the second deed of trust of approximately $5,000 at 6 percent interest. The Behs later defaulted on the first deed of trust. Foreclosure was held on the first deed of trust, but the proceeds of the sale left nothing for City Mortgage on its second deed of trust. City Mortgage then brought a lawsuit against the Behs to collect the balance due on the second deed of trust. When the Behs "assumed" the second deed of trust, did they become personally liable for it?

7. Pope agreed to sell certain land to Pelz and retained a mortgage on the property to secure payment of the purchase price. The mortgage contained a clause providing that if Pelz defaulted, Pope had the "right to enter upon the above-described premises and sell the same at public sale" to pay the balance of the purchase price, accounting to Pelz for any surplus realized on the sale. What type of foreclosure does this provision contemplate: (1) strict foreclosure, (2) action and sale, or (3) private power of sale?

8. In October 1972, Verda Miller sold her 107-acre farm for $30,000 to Donald Kimball, who was acting on behalf of his own closely held corporation, American Wonderlands. Under the agreement, Miller retained title and Kimball was given possession pending full payment of all installments of the purchase price. The contract provided that Kimball was to pay all real estate taxes. If he did not pay them, Miller could discharge them and either add the amounts to the unpaid principal or demand immediate payment of the delinquencies plus interest. Miller also had the right to declare a forfeiture of the contract and regain possession if the terms of the agreement were not met. In 1975, Miller had to pay the real estate taxes on the property in the amount of $672.78. She demanded payment of this amount plus interest from Kimball. She also served a notice of forfeiture on him that he had 30 days to pay. Kimball paid the taxes but refused to pay interest of $10.48. Miller made continued demands on Kimball for two months, then filed notice of forfeiture with the county recorder in August 1975. She also advised Kimball of this. Was Miller justified in declaring a forfeiture and taking back possession of the land?

9. Edwin Bull was the owner of an 80-foot fishing trawler named the *Bull Head* that had been leased for use in dismantling a bridge over the Illinois River at Pekin, Illinois. At the termination of the lease, the *Bull Head* was towed upriver to Morris, Illinois, not operating on its own power. At Morris, a tugboat owned by Iowa Marine Repair Corporation was used to remove the *Bull Head* from the tow and to move it to the south bank of the river where it was tied up. Several months later, the *Bull Head* was moved across the river by Iowa Marine and moored at a place on the north bank where it maintained its fleeting operations. The *Bull Head* remained there for several years and greatly deteriorated. Iowa Marine sent Bull a bill for switching, fleeting, and other services. Bull refused to pay and brought suit against Iowa Marine to recover possession of the boat. In turn, Iowa Marine claimed that it

had a mechanic's lien on the *Bull Head* and that the boat should be sold to satisfy the lien. Illinois law provides that:

any architect, contractor, subcontractor, materialman, or other person furnishing services, labor, or material for the purpose of, or in constructing, building, altering, repairing or ornamenting a boat, barge, or watercraft shall have a lien on such boat for the value of such services, labor, or material in the same manner as in this act provided for the purpose of building, altering, repairing, or ornamenting a house or other building.

Does Iowa Marine have a valid mechanic's lien on the boat for its switching, fleeting, and storage services?

10. Bowen-Rodgers Hardware Company was engaged in the business of furnishing materials for the construction of buildings. It delivered a quantity of materials to property owned by Ronald and Carol Collins. The materials were for the use of a contractor who was building a home for the Collinses as well as several other houses in the area. The hardware company was not paid for the materials by the contractor, and it sought to obtain a mechanic's lien against the Collinses' property. The Collinses claimed that even though the materials were delivered to their home, they were actually used to build other houses in the area. Was the Collinses' property subject to a mechanic's lien because payment had not been made for materials delivered to it?

Security Interests in Personal Property

I n many credit transactions the creditor, in order to protect his investment, takes a security interest, or lien, in personal property belonging to the debtor. The law covering security interests in personal property is set forth in Article 9 of the Uniform Commercial Code. Article 9, entitled Secured Transactions, applies to situations that consumers and businesspeople commonly face; for example, the financing of an automobile, the purchase of a refrigerator on a time-payment plan, or the financing of business inventory. ∞

ARTICLE 9

If a creditor wants to obtain a security interest in the personal property of the debtor, he also wants to be sure that his interest is superior to the claims of other creditors. To do so, the creditor must carefully comply with Article 9. In Part IV, Sales, we pointed out that businesspersons sometimes leave out important terms in a contract or insert vague terms to be worked out later. Such looseness is a luxury that is not permitted in secured transactions. If a debtor gets into financial difficulties and cannot meet her obligations, even a minor noncompliance with Article 9 may cause the creditor to lose his preferred claim to the personal property of the debtor. A creditor who loses his secured interest is only a general creditor if the debtor is declared bankrupt. As a general creditor in bankruptcy proceedings, he may have little chance of recovering the money owed by the debtor because of the relatively low priority of such claims. Chapter 29, Bankruptcy, covers this in detail.

Article 9 has not been adopted in exactly the same form in every state. The law of each state must be examined carefully to determine the procedure for obtaining a secured interest and the rights of creditors and debtors in that state. The general concepts are the same in every state, however, and these concepts are the basis of our discussion in this chapter.

SECURITY INTERESTS UNDER THE CODE

Security Interests

Basic to a discussion of secured consumer and commercial transactions is the term **security interest.** A security interest is an interest in personal property or fixtures obtained by a creditor to secure payment or performance of an obligation [1-201(37)].[1] For example, when a person borrows money from a bank to buy a new car, the bank takes a security interest, or puts a lien, on the car until the loan is repaid. If the person defaults on the loan, the bank can repossess the car and have it sold to cover the unpaid balance. A security interest is a property interest in the collateral.

While one usually thinks of goods as being put up as collateral, the Code actually covers secured interests in a much broader grouping of personal property. The Code breaks down personal property into a number of different classifications that are important in determining how a creditor acquires an enforceable security interest in a particular collateral. The Code classifications are:

1. *Instruments.* This category includes checks, notes, drafts, stocks, bonds, and other investment securities [9–105(I)].

2. *Documents of title.* This category includes bills of lading, dock warrants, dock receipts, and warehouse receipts.

3. *Accounts.* This category includes rights to payment for goods sold or leased or for services rendered that are not evidenced by instruments or chattel paper but are carried on open account. The category includes such rights to payment whether or not they have been earned by performance [9–106].

4. *Chattel paper.* This category includes written documents that evidence both an obligation to pay money and a security interest in specific goods [9–105]. A typical example of chattel paper is what is commonly known as a conditional sales contract. This is the type of contract that a consumer might sign when she buys a large appliance such as a refrigerator on a time-payment plan.

5. *General intangibles.* Among the items in this catchall category are patents, copyrights, literary royalty rights, franchises, and money [9–106].

6. *Goods.* Goods are divided into several classes; the same item of collateral may fall into different classes at different times, depending on its use.

a. *Consumer goods.* These goods are used or bought for use primarily for personal, family, or household purposes. They include automobiles, furniture, and appliances.

b. *Equipment.* This includes goods used or bought for use primarily in business, including farming and professions.

c. *Farm products.* These are crops, livestock, or supplies used or produced in farming operations as long as they are still in the possession of a debtor engaged in farming.

d. *Inventory.* This includes goods held for sale or lease or for use under contracts of service as well as raw materials, work in process, and materials used or consumed in a business.

e. *Fixtures.* These are goods so affixed to real property as to be considered a part of it [9–109].

In different situations, an item such as a stove could be classified as inventory, equipment, or consumer goods. In the hands of the manufacturer or an appliance store, the stove is "inventory" goods. If it is used in a restaurant, it is "equipment." If it was purchased by a consumer for use in her home, it is "consumer goods."

Obtaining a Security Interest

The goal of a creditor is to obtain a security interest in certain personal property that will be good against: (1) the debtor, (2) other creditors of the debtor, and (3) a person who might purchase the property from the debtor. In case the debtor defaults on the debt, the creditor wants to have a better right to claim the property than anyone else. Obtaining an enforceable security interest is a two-step process—attachment and perfection.

---

[1]The numbers in brackets refer to sections of the Uniform Commercial Code.

ATTACHMENT OF THE SECURITY INTEREST

Attachment

A security interest is not legally enforceable against a debtor until it is attached to one or more particular items of the debtor's property. The **attachment** of the security interest takes place in a legal sense rather than in a physical sense. There are three basic requirements for a security interest to be attached to the goods of a debtor [9–203]. First is an *agreement* in which the debtor grants the creditor a security interest in particular property (collateral) in which the debtor has an interest. Second, the debtor must have *rights in the collateral*. Third, the creditor must give value to the debtor. The creditor must, for example, lend money or advance goods on credit to the debtor. Unless the debtor owes a debt to the creditor, there can be no security interest. The purpose of obtaining a security interest is to secure a debt.

The Security Agreement

The agreement in which a debtor grants a creditor a security interest in the debtor's property must generally be in writing and signed by the debtor. A written agreement is required in all cases except where the creditor has possession of the collateral [9–203]. Suppose Cole borrows $50 from Fox and gives Fox her wristwatch as a security for the loan. The agreement whereby Cole put up her watch as collateral does not have to be in writing to be enforceable. Because the creditor (Fox) is in possession of the collateral, an oral agreement is sufficient.

The security agreement must reasonably describe the collateral so that it can readily be identified. For example, it should list the year, make, and serial number of an automobile. The security agreement usually spells out the terms of the arrangement between the creditor and the debtor. Also, it normally contains a promise by the debtor to pay certain amounts of money in a certain way. The agreement specifies which events, such as nonpayment by the buyer, constitute a default. In addition, it may contain provisions that the creditor feels are necessary to protect his security interest. For example, the debtor may be required to keep the collateral insured, not to move it without the creditor's consent, or to periodically report sales of secured inventory goods. See Figure 1 for an example of a security agreement.

In the case that follows, *Sears, Roebuck & Co. v. Silch,* Sears was deemed to have obtained a valid security agreement from its debtor even though the document constituting it was missing certain critical terms.

SEARS, ROEBUCK & CO. v. SILCH   28 UCC Rep.2d 1995 (Mo. Ct. App. 1995)

 n May 19, 1990, Richard Silch purchased a camcorder at Sears Roebuck by charging it to his Sears charge account. Printed on the face of the sales ticket made at that time was the following:

This credit purchase is subject to the terms of my Sears Charge Agreement which is incorporated herein by reference and identified by the above account number. I grant Sears a security interest or lien in this merchandise, unless prohibited by law, until paid in full.

Silch's signature appeared immediately below that language on the sales ticket. The ticket also contained the brand name of the camcorder and a stock number.

Silch subsequently filed a Chapter 7 bankruptcy proceeding and was eventually discharged. Sears filed a petition to recover the camcorder from Silch, contending that it had a valid and enforceable security interest in the camcorder. The trial court ruled for Silch, holding that as a matter of law the sales ticket did not constitute a valid and enforceable security agreement. Sears appealed. ⌒

Garrison, Presiding Judge   The parties agree that the controlling issue here is whether the sales ticket constituted a valid security agreement which resulted in Sears having an enforceable security interest in the camcorder. Section 9–203 provides, in pertinent part:

(1) . . . a security interest is not enforceable against the debtor or third parties with respect to the collateral and does not attach unless

(a) . . . the debtor has signed a security agreement which contains a description of the collateral . . .

(b) value has been given; and

(c) the debtor has rights in the collateral.

FIGURE I

A Security Agreement

	Account No.
~~Mr. and Mrs.~~	
~~Mrs.~~	
BUYER Miss *Cheryl Cole*	
ADDRESS *542 Oakdale*	*C-1005*
CITY *Chicago, Il.* TEL. NO. *828-0290*	Date
DELIVER TO: *542 Oakdale*	

SECURITY AGREEMENT
ACE APPLIANCE

THIS AGREEMENT, executed between Ace Appliance, as Secured Party ("Seller"), and Buyer named above, as Debtor ("Buyer"): Seller agrees to sell and Buyer agrees to purchase, subject to the terms, conditions, and agreements stated in this agreement, the goods described below (the "Collateral"), Seller reserving and Buyer granting a purchase money security interest in the Collateral to secure the payment of the balance owed (Item 7) and all other present and future obligations of Buyer to Seller.

DESCRIPTION OF COLLATERAL				TERMS	
Quan.	Article	Unit Price	Total		
1	*Refrig*	*545* —	*545*	(1) Cash Price	*104 ⁰⁰*
1	*Stove*	*495* —	*495*	(2) Down Payment	*100 ⁰⁰*
				Trade-in	
				Unpaid Principal	
				(3) Balance Owed	*94 ⁰⁰*
				(4) Finance Charge	*100 ⁰⁰*
				Time Balance	
				(5) Owed	*1040 ⁰⁰*
				(6) Sales tax	*40 ⁰⁰*
				(7) Balance Owed	*1080 ⁰⁰*

Buyer agrees to pay Seller, without relief from valuation and appraisement laws, the balance owed (Item 7) of $ *1080 ⁰⁰*

in *11* successive ~~weekly~~ installments of $ *90 ⁰⁰* each and a final installment of $ *90 ⁰⁰* , commencing on   monthly

Jan. 1 , 19 *90* and continuing thereafter on the same day of each ~~week~~ until paid, together with all deliquent month charges, costs of repossession, collection, disposition, maintenance, and other like charges, allowed by law, and reasonable attorney's fees.

This sale is made subject to the terms, conditions, and agreements stated above on the reverse side. Buyer represents that the correct name and address of Buyer is as stated above, and that all statements made by buyer as to financial condition and credit information are true.

Buyer acknowledges delivery by Seller to Buyer of a copy of this agreement.

Buyer warrants and represents that the Collateral will be kept at Buyer's address unless otherwise specified as follows: _____

and will be used or is purchased for use primarily for: (check one) family or household purposes ☒; business use ☐; farming operations ☐. The Collateral will not be affixed to real estate unless checked here ☐. If the Collateral is to be affixed to real estate, a description of the real estate is as follows: _____

and the name of the record owner is _____

FIGURE I

(continued)

IN WITNESS WHEREOF, the parties have executed this agreement on this *1st* day of *Dec*, 19 *97*

BUYER'S SIGNATURE (Ace Appliance) Seller (as Secured party) *Cheryl Cole*   *Frank Singer*

By   (as debtor)

TERMS, CONDITIONS, AND AGREEMENTS

1. The security interest of Seller shall extend to all replacements, proceeds (including tort claims and insurance), and accessories, and shall continue until full performance by Buyer of all conditions and obligations under this agreement.

2. Buyer shall maintain the Collateral in good repair, pay all taxes and other charges levied upon the Collateral when due, and shall defend the Collateral against any claims. Buyer shall not permit the Collateral to be removed from the place where kept without the prior written consent of Seller. Buyer shall give prompt witten notice to Seller of any transfer, pledge, assignment, or any other process or action taken or pending, voluntary or involuntary, whereby a third party is to obtain or is attempting to obtain possession of or any interest in the Collateral. Seller shall have the right to inspect the Collateral at all reasonable times. At its option, but without obligation to Buyer and without relieving Buyer from any default, Seller may discharge any taxes, liens, or other encumbrances levied or placed upon the Collateral for which Buyer agrees to reimburse Seller upon demand.

3. If the Collateral is damaged or destroyed in any manner, the entire balance remaining unpaid under this agreement (the "Agreement Balance") shall immediately become due and payable and Buyer shall first apply any insurance or other receipts compensating for such loss to the Agreement Balance. Buyer shall fully insure the Collateral, for the benefit of both Seller and Buyer, against loss of fire, theft, and other casualties by comprehensive extended coverage insurance in an amount equal to the balance owed under this agreement.

4. Buyer shall pay all amounts payable when due at the store of Seller from which this sale is made or at Seller's principal office in *Gary*, Indiana, and upon default shall pay the maximum delinquent charges permitted by law. Upon prepayment of the Agreement Balance, Seller shall allow the minimum discount permitted by law.

5. Time is of the essence of this agreement. Buyer agrees that the following shall constitute an event of default under this Security Agreement: (*a*) the failure of Buyer to perform any condition or obligation contained in this agreement; (*b*) when any statement, representation, or warranty made by Buyer shall be found to have been untrue in any material respect when made; or (*c*) if Seller in good faith believes that the prospect of payment or performance is impaired. Upon a default, Seller, at its option and without notice or demand to Buyer, shall be entitled to declare the Agreement Balance immediately due and payable, take immediate possession of the Collateral and enter the premises at which the Collateral is located for such purpose or to render the Collateral unusable. Upon request, Buyer shall assemble and make the Collateral available to Seller at a place to be designated by Seller which is reasonably convenient to both parties. Upon repossession, Seller may retain or dispose of any or all of the collateral in the manner prescribed by the Indiana Uniform Commercial Code and the proceeds of any such disposition shall be first applied in the following order: (*a*) to the reasonable expenses of retaking, holding, preparing for sale, selling, and the like; (*b*) to the reasonable attorney's fees and legal expenses incurred by Seller; and (*c*) to the satisfaction of the indebtedness secured by this security interest. Buyer convenants to release and hold harmless Seller from any and all claims arising out of the repossession of the Collateral. No waiver of any default or any failure or delay to exercise any right or remedy by Seller shall operate as a waiver of any other default, or of the same default in the future or as a waiver of any right or remedy with respect to the same or any other occurrence.

6. All rights and remedies of seller specified in this agreement are cumulative and are in addition to, and shall not exclude, any rights and remedies Seller may have by law.

7. Seller shall not be liable for any damages, including special or consequential damages, for failure to deliver the Collateral or for any delay in delivery of the Collateral to Buyer.

8. Buyer agrees that Seller may carry this agreement, together with any other agreements and accounts, with Buyer in one account upon its records and unless otherwise instructed in writing by Buyer, any payment of less than all amounts then due on all agreements and accounts shall be applied to any accrued delinquent charges, costs of collection and maintenance, and to the balances owing under all agreements or accounts in such oder as Seller in its discretion shall determine.

9. Buyer authorizes Seller to execute and file financing statements signed only by Seller covering the Collateral described.

10. Any notice required by this agreement shall be deemed sufficient when mailed to Seller (state Seller's address), or to Buyer at the address at which the Collateral is kept.

11. Buyer shall have the benefit of manufacturers' warranties, if any; however, Seller makes no express warranties (except a warranty of title) and no implied warranties, including any warranty of MERCHANTABILITY or FITNESS. Buyer agrees that there are no promises or agreements between the parties not contained in this agreement. Any modification or rescission of this agreement shall be ineffective unless in writing and signed by both Seller and Buyer.

12. ANY HOLDER OF THIS CONSUMER CREDIT CONTRACT IS SUBJECT TO ALL CLAIMS AND DEFENSES WHICH THE DEBTOR COULD ASSERT AGAINST THE SELLER OF GOODS OR SERVICES OBTAINED WITH THE PROCEEDS HEREOF. RECOVERY HEREUNDER BY THE DEBTOR SHALL NOT EXCEED AMOUNTS PAID BY THE DEBTOR HEREUNDER.

(2) A security interest attaches when it becomes enforceable against the debtor with respect to the collateral. Attachment occurs as soon as all of the events specified in subsection (1) have taken place unless explicit agreement postpones the time of attaching.

In the instant case, there is no dispute that Sears delivered the camcorder to Silch who took possession of it as owner. There is no issue, therefore, with respect to the requirements of section 9–203 (1) (b) and (c). The issue is whether (a) was satisfied.

Section 9–105 defines a "security agreement" as "an agreement which provides for a security interest." In *Bradley v. K & E Investments, Inc.,* this court said that "although no precise words are required by the definition of *security agreement,* the definition indicates there must be some language in the agreement that actually conveys a security interest." In the instant case, the sales ticket signed by Silch stated that he granted "Sears a security interest or lien in this merchandise, unless prohibited by law, until paid in full."

Silch argues that the sales ticket does not set out the terms of the agreement, "parameter" or "consequences" of default, whether each item purchased stands only for its own debt or secures all debt to Sears, or the method of allocating payments on the account between different items purchased. He notes that whether the "SearsCharge Agreement" which was incorporated by reference in the sales ticket contained such information is unknown because it was not produced and there was no indication of its terms.

Silch cites no authority for the proposition that a valid security agreement under the UCC must contain all such information. *In re Hardage,* however, involved the validity of a similar sales ticket as a security agreement where the underlying Sears charge agreement was not produced. There, the debtor purchased personal property from Sears and signed a sales ticket which included the following; "I agree that Sears retains a security interest under the Uniform Commercial Code in the merchandise purchased until fully paid." The court, noting that no special words or form is required to show a possible security interest, held that the sales ticket was sufficient as a security agreement for the items purchased.

In the instant case, the sales ticket contained language expressly conveying a security interest. There being no issue about the signature of Silch on the sales ticket or the sufficiency of the description of the collateral, it complied with the requirements of a security agreement.

Judgment reversed in favor of Sears.

Future Advances

A security agreement may stipulate that it covers advances of credit to be made at some time in the future [9–204(3)]. Such later extensions of credit are known as **future advances.** Future advances would be involved where, for example, a bank grants a business a line of credit for $100,000 but initially advances only $20,000. When the business draws further against its line of credit, it has received a future advance and the bank is considered to have given additional "value" at that time. The security interest that the creditor obtained earlier also covers these later advances of money.

After-Acquired Property

A security agreement may be drafted to grant a creditor a security interest in the **after-acquired property** of the debtor. After-acquired property is property that the debtor does not currently own or have rights in but that he may acquire in the future. However, the security interest does not attach until the debtor actually obtains some rights to the new property [9–204].[2] For example, Dan's Diner borrows $25,000 from the bank and gives it a security interest in all of its present restaurant equipment as well as all of the restaurant equipment that it may "hereafter acquire." If Dan's owns only a stove at the time, then the bank has a security interest only in the stove. However, if a month later Dan's buys a refrigerator, the bank's security interest would

---

[2]The Code imposes an additional requirement as to security interests in after-acquired consumer goods. Security interests do not attach to consumer goods other than accessions unless the consumer acquires them within 10 days after the secured party gave value [9–204(2)].

"attach" to the refrigerator when Dan's acquires some rights to it.

A security interest in after-acquired property may not have priority over certain other creditors if the debtor acquires his new property subject to what is known as a **purchase money security interest.** When the seller of goods retains a security interest in goods until they are paid for, or when money is loaned for the purpose of acquiring certain goods and the lender takes a security interest in those goods, the security interest is a purchase money security interest. Later in this chapter, the section entitled Priority Rules discusses the rights of the holder of a purchase money security interest versus the rights of another creditor who filed earlier on after-acquired property of the debtor.

Proceeds

The creditor is commonly interested in having his security interest cover not only the collateral described in the agreement but also the **proceeds** on the disposal of the collateral by the debtor. For example, if a bank lends money to Dealer to enable Dealer to finance its inventory of new automobiles and the bank takes a security interest in the inventory, the bank wants its interest to continue in any cash proceeds obtained by Dealer when the automobiles are sold to customers. Under the 1972 amendments to Article 9, these proceeds are automatically covered unless the security agreement specifically excludes them [9–203(3)].

Assignment

In the past, installment sales contracts and security agreements commonly included a provision that the buyer would not assert against the assignee of a sales contract any claims or defenses that the buyer had against the seller. Such clauses made it easier for a retailer to assign its installment sales contracts, or security agreements, to a financial institution such as a bank. The bank knew that it could collect from the buyer without having to worry about any claims that the buyer had against the retailer, such as for breach of warranty. The waiver clauses were usually presented to the buyer on a take-it-or-leave-it basis.

Such clauses can operate to the disadvantage of the buyer. For example, Ellen Horn agrees to buy some storm windows from Ace Home Improvement Company. She signs an installment sales contract, or security agreement, promising to pay $50 a month for 24 months and giving the company a security interest in the windows. The contract contains a waiver of defenses clause. Ace assigns the contract to First Bank and goes out of business. If the storm windows were of a poorer quality than was called for by the contract, Horn would have a claim of breach of warranty against Ace. She would not have to pay Ace the full amount if it tried to collect from her. Under these circumstances, however, Horn has to pay the full amount to the bank; then she can try to collect from Ace for breach of warranty. Here, Horn might be out of luck.

Under the Uniform Commercial Code, an express or implied waiver of defenses is generally valid and enforceable by an assignee who takes his assignment for value, in good faith, and without notice of a claim or defense [9–206(1)]. The two exceptions to this rule are (1) the waiver is not effective as to any type of defense that could be asserted against a holder in due course of a negotiable instrument; (2) the waiver is not effective if a statute or court decision establishes a different rule for buyers of consumer goods [9–206(1)].

Some states have enacted comprehensive legislation to abolish waiver of defenses clauses in consumer contracts, and other states have limited their use. The Uniform Consumer Credit Code (UCCC), which has been adopted by a number of states, gives the adopting states two alternatives regarding waiver of defenses clauses: Alternative A provides that an assignee of a consumer sales contract takes subject to all of the defenses that the buyer has against the seller arising out of the sale, regardless of whether the contract contains a waiver of defenses clause. Alternative B permits the enforcement of such clauses only by an assignee who is not related to the seller and who acquires the assignment of the contract in good faith and for value, gives the buyer notice of the assignment, and is not advised by the buyer in writing within three months that the buyer has any claims or defenses against the seller.

In addition, the Federal Trade Commission has promulgated a regulation that applies to situations in which a buyer signs a waiver of defenses clause as part of an installment sales contract. For a detailed discussion of this regulation, see Chapter 31,

Negotiation and Holder in Due Course. The FTC regulation requires that a seller or financing agency insert in all consumer contracts and direct loan agreements a clause putting any holder of the contract on notice that the holder is subject to all of the claims and defenses that the buyer-debtor could assert against the seller of the goods or services covered by the contract.

PERFECTING THE SECURITY INTEREST

Perfection

While attachment of a security interest to collateral owned by the debtor gives the creditor rights vis-à-vis the debtor, a creditor is also concerned about making sure that she has a better right to the collateral than any other creditor if the debtor defaults. In addition, a creditor may be concerned about protecting her interest in the collateral if the debtor sells it to someone else. The creditor gets protection against other creditors or purchasers of the collateral by perfecting her security interest. Perfection is not effective without an attachment of the security interest [9–303].

Under the Code, there are three main ways of perfecting a security interest:

1. By filing a public notice of the security interest.
2. By the creditor taking possession of the collateral.
3. In certain transactions, by mere attachment of the security interest; this is known as automatic perfection.

Perfection by Public Filing

The most common way of perfecting a security interest is to file a **financing statement** in the appropriate public office. The financing statement serves as constructive notice to the world that the creditor claims an interest in collateral that belongs to a certain named debtor. The financing statement usually consists of a multicopy form that is available from the office of the secretary of state (see Figure 2). However, the security agreement can be filed as the financing statement if it contains the required information and has been signed by the debtor.

To be sufficient, the financing statement must (1) contain the names of the debtor and of the secured party, or creditor; (2) be signed by the debtor; (3) give an address of the secured party from which additional information about the security interest can be obtained; (4) give a mailing address for the debtor; and (5) contain a statement listing the collateral or a description of the collateral. If the financing statement covers goods that are to become fixtures, a description of the real estate must be included.

Each state specifies by statute where the financing statement has to be filed. In all states, a financing statement that covers fixtures must be filed in the office where a mortgage on real estate would be filed [9–401]. To obtain maximum security, the secured party acquiring a security interest in property that is a fixture or is to become a fixture should double file—that is, file the security interest as a fixture and as a nonfixture.

In regard to collateral other than fixtures, the state may require only central filing, usually in the office of the secretary of state. However, most states require the local filing of local transactions, such as transactions in which the collateral is equipment used in farming operations; farm products; accounts, contract rights, or general intangibles arising from or relating to the sale of farm products by a farmer; or consumer goods.

A financing statement is effective for a period of five years from the date of filing, and it lapses then unless a continuation statement has been filed before that time. An exception is made for real estate mortgages that are effective as fixture filings—they are effective until the mortgage is released or terminates [9–403].

A **continuation statement** may be filed within six months before the five-year expiration date. The continuation statement must be signed by the secured party, identify the original statement by file number, and state that the original statement is still effective. Successive continuation statements may be filed [9–403(3)].

When a consumer debtor completely fulfills all debts and obligations secured by a financing statement, she is entitled to a **termination statement** signed by the secured party or an assignee of record. Failure of the affected secured party to furnish a termination statement after proper demand subjects him to a fine of $100 plus damages for any loss caused to the debtor by such failure [9–404].

FIGURE 2

A Financing Statement

UNIFORM COMMERCIAL CODE	STATE OF INDIANA FINANCING STATEMENT	FORM UCC-1

INSTRUCTIONS

1. Please type this form. Fold only along perforation for mailing.
2. Remove Secured Party and Debtor copies and send other three copies with interleaved carbon paper to the filing officer. Enclose filing fee of $1.00. (plus $ .50 if collateral is or to become a fixture).
3. When filing is to be with more than one office, Form UCC-2 may be placed over this set to avoid double typing.
4. If the space provided for any item(s) is inadequate, the item(s) may be continued on additional sheets, preferably 5"x 8" or sizes convenient to secured party in case of long schedules, indentures, etc. Only one sheet is required. Extra names of debtors may be continued below box "1" in space for description of property.
5. If the collateral is crops or goods which are or are to become fixtures, describe the goods and also the real estate with the name of the record owner if he is other than the debtor.
6. Persons filing a security agreement (as distinguished from a financing statement) are urged to complete this form with or without signature and send with security agreement.
7. If collateral is goods which are or are to become fixtures, use Form UCC-1a over this Form to avoid double typing, and enclose regular fee plus $ .50
8. The filing officer will return the third page of this Form as an acknowledgment. Secured party at a later time may use third page as a Termination Statement by dating and signing the termination legend on that page.

This Financing Statement is presented to Filing Officer for filing pursuant to the UCC:		3. Maturity Date (if any):
1. Debtor(s) (Last Name First) and Address(es)	2. Secured Party(ies) and Address(es)	For Filing Officer (Date, Time, Number, and Filing Office)

4. This financing statement covers the following types (or items) of property (also describe realty where collateral is crops or fixtures):

Assignee of Secured Party

This statement is filed without the debtor's signature to perfect a security interest in collateral (check ☐ if so)

☐ under a security agreement signed by debtor authorizing secured party to file this statement, or
☐ already subject to a security interest in another jurisdiction when it was brought into this state, or
☐ which is proceeds of the following described original collateral which was perfected:

Check ☐ if covered: ☐ Proceeds of Collateral are also covered. ☐ Products of Collateral are also covered. No. of additional Sheets presented:

Filed with: ☐ Secretary of State ☐ Recorder of _____ County

By: _____
Signature(s) of Debtor(s)

By: _____
Signature(s) of Secured Party(ies)

(1) Filing Officer Copy—Alphabetical
FORM UCC-1—INDIANA UNIFORM COMMERCIAL CODE

Approved by: _____
Secretary of State

Possession by Secured Party as Public Notice

Public filing of a security interest is intended to put any interested members of the public on notice of the security interest. A potential creditor of the debtor, or a potential buyer of the collateral, can check the records to see whether anyone else claims an interest in the debtor's collateral. The same objective can be reached if the debtor gives up possession of the collateral to the creditor or to a third person who holds the collateral for the creditor. If a debtor does not have possession of collateral that he claims to own, then a potential creditor or debtor is on notice that someone else may claim an interest in it. Thus, a security interest is perfected by change of possession of collateral from the debtor to the creditor/secured party or his agent [9–302(1)(a)]. For example, Simpson borrows $50 from a pawnbroker and leaves his guitar as collateral for the loan. The pawnbroker's security interest in the guitar is perfected by virtue of her possession of the guitar.

Generally, possession by the secured party is the means for perfecting a security interest in instruments such as checks or notes and in money.[3]

---

[3]Sections 9–304(4) and (5) permit a 21-day temporary perfection.

Possession of the collateral by the secured party is an alternative means, and often the most satisfactory means, of perfecting a security interest in chattel paper and negotiable documents of title. Possession is also a possible means for perfecting a security interest in inventory. This is sometimes done through the **field warehousing** arrangement, whereby part of the debtor's inventory is fenced off and withdrawals from it are permitted only on the approval of the secured party or his on-the-scene representative.

Possession by the secured party is usually not a practical means for perfecting a security interest in equipment or consumer goods because the debtor normally wants to retain possession to make use of the equipment or goods. Of course, possession by the secured party is not possible at all with accounts or general intangibles. The person to whom the collateral is delivered holds it as bailee, and he owes the duties of a bailee to the parties in interest [9–207].

Perfection by Attachment

Perfection by mere attachment of the security interest, sometimes known as automatic perfection, is the only form of perfection that occurs without the giving of public notice. It occurs automatically when all the requirements of attachment are com- plete. This form of perfection is limited to certain classes of collateral; in addition, it may be only a temporary perfection in some situations.[4]

A creditor who sells goods to a consumer on credit, or who lends money to enable a consumer to buy goods, can obtain limited perfection of a secu- rity interest merely by attaching the security interest to the goods. A creditor under these circumstances has what is called a **purchase money security interest in consumer goods.** For example, an ap- pliance store sells a television set to Margaret Morse on a conditional sales contract, or time-payment plan. The store does not have to file its purchase money security interest in the set. The security interest is considered perfected just by virtue of its attachment to the set in the hands of the consumer.

In the case that follows, *In Re Phillips,* the court rejected a creditor's claims that its security interest was perfected by attachment, holding that the goods were equipment and not consumer goods.

---

[4]Temporary perfection without filing or possession is auto- matically obtained for 21 days after attachment of the security interest in instruments and negotiable documents [9–304]. To get protection beyond the 21-day period, the secured party must perfect by filing or possession. During the 21-day period of temporary perfection, however, any holder in due course of commercial paper or any bona fide purchaser of a security or a negotiated document will prevail over the secured party relying on temporary perfection [9–309].

IN RE PHILLIPS
CREDITWAY OF AMERICA v. PHILLIPS   42 UCC Rep. 679 (Bankr. W.D. Va. 1985)

J acob Phillips and his wife, Charlene, jointly owned the Village Variety 5&10 Store in Bluefield, Virginia. In addition, Mrs. Phillips was a computer science teacher at the Wytheville Community College. On December 1, 1984, Mrs. Phillips entered into a retail installment sales contract with Holdren's, Inc., for the purchase of a Leading Edge color computer and a Panasonic printer. The contract, which was also a security agreement, provided for a total payment of $3,175.68, with monthly payments of $132.32 to begin on March 5, 1985. On December 1, 1984, Holdren's assigned the contract to Creditway of America.

At the time of purchase, Mrs. Phillips advised Holdren's that she was purchasing the computer for professional use in her teaching assignments as well as for use in the variety store. One of the software programs purchased was a practical accounting program for business transactions. Mrs. Phillips also received a special discount price given by Holdren's to state instructors buying for their teaching use. She used the computer in the Village Variety 5&10 Store until it closed in April 1985. In June, the Phillips' filed a petition under Chapter 7 of the Bankruptcy Act. At the time, they owed $2,597.79 on the computer. No financing statement was ever filed.

Creditway filed a motion in the bankruptcy proceeding, claiming that it had a valid lien on the computer and seeking to be permitted to repossess it. ⌘

Pearson, Bankruptcy Judge The key factor in determining whether to grant Creditway's motion for relief is the classification of the collateral. Virginia Code Section 9–302(1)(d) provides that "a financing statement shall be filed to perfect all security interests except a purchase money security interest in consumer goods." If the computer goods are classified as consumer goods, then Creditway, as assignee of Holdren's, would not need to file a financing statement to have a perfected security interest in the collateral. However, if the computer items are classified as equipment, then, pursuant to Section 9–401(1)(c), it would be necessary for Creditway to have a dual filing to perfect its security interest.

Virginia Code Section 9–109 outlines the classification of collateral. In pertinent part it provides that

Goods are:
(1) "consumer goods" if they are used or bought for use primarily for personal, family, or household purposes;
(2) "equipment" if they are used or bought for use primarily in business (including farming or a profession).

The test for the classification of goods is the owner's use of the goods. The two classes of goods are mutually exclusive. The same property cannot be in two classes at the same time and as to the same person. Thus, an item cannot, for example, be classified as both consumer goods and equipment.

The evidence before this court indicates that the computer items were purchased for use primarily in business rather than for personal, family, or household purposes. Mrs. Phillips' uncontradicted testimony is that at the time of purchase she informed the salesperson at Holdren's that the computer would be used for her teaching assignments as well as in the variety store. She received a special discount as a state instructor for purchase of the items for use in teaching. Mrs. Phillips also indicated that she purchased this computer with its memory capability to handle business transactions, and that she purchased a software package on Practical Accounting for business billing. These facts and circumstances should have provided sufficient notice of the use of the items for classification purposes such that financing statements could have been filed properly to perfect the security interest.

Courts have held without exception that the Uniform Commercial Code filing requirements are mandatory and that the filing of a financing statement in an improper place or not in all the places required is ineffective to perfect a security interest. Although the application of rules in a given case may be harsh, any other result would invite inconsistency which the Uniform Commercial Code was enacted to avoid. On the evidence presented the collateral should be found to be classified as equipment and, having not filed in all places required, Creditway holds an unperfected security interest against the debtor.

Motion of Creditway to repossess the collateral denied.

Perfection by attachment is not effective if the consumer goods are motor vehicles for which the state issues certificates of title and has only limited effectiveness if the goods are fixtures [9–302]. A later section of this chapter discusses the special rules covering these kinds of collateral.

There are also major limitations to the perfection by attachment principle. As discussed in the Priority section of this chapter, relying on attachment for perfection does not, in some instances, provide as much protection to the creditor as does public filing.

One potential concern for a creditor is that the use of the collateral will change from that anticipated when the security interest was obtained. For example, in the *Phillips* case, assume that the computer was originally purchased to be used in the home and later converted to use in the business. It is important that the creditor properly perfect the security interest initially so that it will not be adversely affected by a subsequent change in use and will continue to have the benefit of its initial perfection.

Motor Vehicles

If state law requires a certificate of title for motor vehicles, then a creditor who takes a security interest in a motor vehicle (other than a creditor holding a security interest in inventory held for sale by a person in the business of selling goods of that kind) must have the security interest noted on the title [9–302]. Suppose a credit union lends Carlson money to buy a new car in a state that requires certificates of title for cars. The credit union cannot rely on filing or on attachment of its security interest in the car to perfect that interest; rather, it must have its security interest noted on the certificate of title.

This requirement protects the would-be buyer of the car or another creditor who might extend credit based on Carlson's ownership of the car. By checking the certificate of title to Carlson's car, a potential buyer or creditor would learn about the credit union's security interest in the car. If no security interest is noted on the certificate of title, the buyer can buy—or the creditor can extend credit—with confidence that there are no undisclosed security interests that would be effective against him.

Fixtures

The Code also provides special rules for perfecting security interests in consumer goods that become fixtures by virtue of their attachment to or use with real property. A creditor with a security interest in consumer goods (including consumer goods that will become fixtures) obtains perfection merely by attachment of her security interest to a consumer good. However, as discussed in the Priority section of this chapter, a creditor who relies on attachment for perfection will not, in some instances, prevail against other creditors who hold an interest in the real estate to which the consumer good is attached unless a financing statement is filed with the real estate records to perfect the security interest [9–401(1)(a)].

Removal of Collateral

Even where a creditor has a perfected security interest in the collateral of her debtor, she needs to be concerned about the possibility that the debtor can take the collateral from the state where the creditor has filed on it to another state where the creditor does not have her claim filed on the public record. Commonly, the security agreement between the creditor and the debtor provides where the collateral is to be kept and stipulates that it is not to be moved unless the debtor gives notice to and/or obtains the permission of the creditor. There is,

---

C O N C E P T   R E V I E W

Obtaining an Enforceable Security Interest

STEP	PURPOSE	NECESSARY ACTION
Attachment of Security Interest	To secure a debt. The debtor gives the creditor rights in the debtor's property to secure the debt owed by the creditor to the debtor.	1. Agreement by the debtor giving the creditor a security interest in specific property (collateral) in which the debtor has a legal interest. This can include after-acquired property and proceeds of the collateral. 2. The debtor must have a legal interest in the collateral. 3. The creditor must give value to the debtor (e.g., money or goods). Future advances are value when actually given to the debtor.
Perfection	To obtain protection against other creditors of the debtor and against purchasers of the collateral from the debtor.	1. *Public filing.* Filing a financing statement with the appropriate state or local office to put the world on notice that the creditor claims an interest in specific collateral belonging to the debtor; or in the case of a motor vehicle, noting the security interest on the certificate of title; or 2. *Possession by creditor.* The creditor may take possession of the collateral, thus putting other creditors and potential purchasers on notice that the creditor has an interest in the collateral (this is not practical for all kinds of collateral); or 3. *Perfection by attachment.* Limited perfection merely by attachment of the security interest is obtained where (a) a creditor sells consumer goods to a consumer on credit or (b) a creditor loans money to a consumer to enable him to buy consumer goods.

however, no absolute assurance that the debtor will be faithful to such an agreement.

Under the Code, a secured creditor who has perfected his security interest generally has four months after the collateral is brought into the new state to perfect his security interest in that state. If the creditor does not reperfect within the four months, his security interest becomes unperfected and he could lose the collateral to a person who purchases it, or takes an interest in it, after it has been removed [9–103(1)]. If the creditor has not perfected his security interest by the time the collateral is removed, or within the time period that the creditor has to perfect his security interest in the former location of the collateral, then his interest is unperfected and he does not obtain the advantage of the four-month grace period.

The Code rules that govern the removal of collateral covered by a state certificate of title—such as an automobile—are more complicated. If an automobile covered by a certificate of title on which a security interest is noted is moved to another state, the perfected security interest is perfected for four months in the new state, or until the automobile is registered in the new state. If the original state did not require that security interests be noted on the title, and if a new title is used in the second state without notation of the security interest, then under certain circumstances a buyer of the automobile can take free of the original security interest. To qualify, the buyer must not be in the business of buying and selling automobiles and must (1) give value, (2) take delivery after issuance of the new title, and (3) buy without notice of the security interest [9–103(2)].[5]

PRIORITY RULES

Importance of Determining Priority

Because several creditors may claim a security interest in the same collateral of a debtor, the Code establishes a set of rules for determining which of the conflicting security interests has priority. Determining which creditor has priority or the best claim takes on particular importance in bankruptcy situa-

tions, where, unless a creditor has a preferred secured interest in collateral that fully protects the obligation owed to him, the creditor may realize nothing or only a few cents on every dollar owed to him.

General Priority Rules

The basic rule established by the Code is that when more than one security interest in the same collateral has been filed or otherwise perfected, the first security interest to be filed or perfected has priority over any that are filed or perfected later. If only one security interest has been perfected, for example, by filing, then that security interest has priority. However, if none of the conflicting security interests has been perfected, then the first security interest to be attached to the collateral has priority [9–312(5)].

Thus, if Bank A filed a financing statement covering a retailer's inventory on February 1, 1997, and Bank B filed a financing statement covering that same inventory on March 1, 1997, Bank A would have priority over Bank B even though Bank B might have made its loan and attached its security interest to the inventory before Bank A did so. However, if Bank A neglected to perfect its security interest by filing and Bank B did perfect, then Bank B, as the holder of the only perfected security interest in the inventory, would prevail.

If both of the creditors neglected to perfect their security interest, then the first security interest that attached would have priority. For example, if Bank Y has a security agreement covering a dealer's equipment on June 1, 1997, and advances money to the dealer on that date, whereas Bank Z does not obtain a security agreement covering that equipment or advance money to the dealer until July 1, 1997, then Bank Y would have priority over Bank Z. In connection with the last situation, unperfected secured creditors do not enjoy a preferred position in bankruptcy proceedings, thus giving additional impetus to the desirability of filing or otherwise perfecting a security interest.

Purchase Money Security Interests in Inventory

There are several very important exceptions to the general priority rules: First, a *perfected purchase money security interest in inventory* has priority

---

[5] Other rules are set out in the Code for accounts, general intangibles, chattel paper, and mobile goods removed to other states [9–103(3) and (4)].

over a conflicting security interest in the same inventory *if the purchase money security interest is perfected at the time the debtor receives possession of the inventory* and if the purchase money secured party gives *notification in writing* to the prior secured creditor *before* the debtor receives the inventory [9–312(3)].

Assume that Bank A takes and perfects a security interest in all the present and after-acquired inventory of a debtor. Then, the debtor acquires some additional inventory from a wholesaler, who retains a security interest in the inventory until the debtor pays for it and perfects this security interest. The wholesaler has a purchase money security interest in inventory goods and has priority over the prior secured creditor (Bank A) if the wholesaler has

perfected the security interest by the time the collateral reaches the debtor and if the wholesaler sends notice of her purchase money security interest to Bank A before shipping the goods. Thus, to protect itself, the wholesaler must check the public records to see whether any of the debtor's creditors are claiming an interest in the debtor's inventory. When the wholesaler discovers that some are claiming an interest, it should file its own security interest and give notice to the existing creditors.

As the following *Borg-Warner Acceptance Corp.* case illustrates, the subsequent seller of inventory can obtain a priority position if it files a financing statement and notifies the prior secured party in a timely fashion.

BORG-WARNER ACCEPTANCE CORP. v. TASCOSA NATIONAL BANK   784 S.W.2d 129 (Tex. Ct. App. 1990)

 n March 1, 1982, the Tascosa National Bank of Amarillo (Bank) extended a loan to T & L Ventures, Inc., doing business as The Video Connection (T & L) in the amount of $30,006. A financing statement was obtained and filed with the secretary of state on March 4, 1982. The Bank's financing statement described the collateral as:

Video software and hardware, computer games hardware and software, all inventory, furniture, fixtures of above located at Amarillo, Potter County, Texas.

From time to time, the indebtedness was renewed and extended and additional funds were provided T & L, with the last note dated April 18, 1986, in the principal amount of $153,613.84. All indebtedness was evidenced by notes and secured by the same collateral.

On March 7, 1982, Borg-Warner Acceptance Corporation (Borg-Warner) entered into an Inventory Security Agreement pursuant to which T & L granted to Borg-Warner a security interest in its inventory purchased with the proceeds of loans made by Borg-Warner. Borg-Warner perfected its security interest as a purchase money security interest (PMSI) under section 9–312(3) by: (1) filing on March 11, 1982, a financing statement describing the collateral with the secretary of state's office; and (2) notifying the Bank of Borg-Warner's interest in T & L's inventory.

Following the perfection of Borg-Warner's PMSI, Borg-Warner commenced financing the acquisition of inventory by T & L and continued such financing through May 22, 1986. Pursuant to a "floor-planning arrangement," Borg-Warner purchased from vendors and paid directly to vendors the invoice purchase price of inventory acquired by T & L for resale. Indebtedness to Borg-Warner was not incurred for any purpose other than the purchase of inventory.

T & L defaulted on its indebtedness. On May 11, 1986, the Bank repossessed T & L's inventory, removed it from T & L's premises, and placed it in a warehouse. Borg-Warner demanded that the Bank deliver the inventory to it on the grounds it had a superior claim to it. The Bank refused and Borg-Warner brought suit against the Bank. The trial court granted summary judgment in favor of the Bank, and Borg-Warner appealed. ⌾

Dodson, Judge   The determinative issue on Borg-Warner's appeal is the priority of liens question. If Borg-Warner's security interest qualifies as a PMSI under section 9–312(3), Borg-Warner prevails.

However, if Borg-Warner's security interest does not so qualify, then the Bank prevails under the "first to file rule." Section 9–312(5)(1).

The Uniform Commercial Code defines two types of PMSI's, those claimed by sellers and those claimed by financing agencies:

A security interest is a "purchase money security interest" to the extent that it is

(1) taken or retained by the seller of the collateral to secure all or part of its price; or

(2) taken by a person who by making advances or incurring an obligation gives value to enable the debtor to acquire rights in or the use of collateral if such value is so used. Section 9–107.

We reiterate, the general rule of priority among conflicting security interests in the same collateral where both interests are perfected by filing, is that the secured party who first files a financing statement prevails. Section 9–312(5)(1). However, section 9–312(3) states a special rule for a PMSI in inventory. That subsection reads in full as follows:

(3) A perfected purchase money security interest in inventory has priority over a conflicting security interest in the same inventory and also has priority in identifiable cash proceeds received on or before the delivery of the inventory to a buyer if

(1) the purchase money security interest is perfected at the time the debtor receives possession of the inventory; and

(2) except where excused by section 9–319 (oil and gas production), the purchase money secured party gives notification in writing to the holder of the conflicting security interest if the holder had filed a financing statement covering the same types of inventory (i) before the date of the filing made by the purchase money secured party, or (ii) before the beginning of the 21-day period where the purchase money security interest is temporarily perfected without filing or possession (subsection (e) of Section 9–304); and

(3) the holder of the conflicting security interest receives any required notification within five years before the debtor receives possession of the inventory; and

(4) the notification states that the person giving the notice has or expects to acquire a purchase money security interest in inventory of the debtor, describing such inventory by item or type. Section 9–312(3).

Under the above provisions, Borg-Warner's security interest is a PMSI to the extent that it is taken by Borg-Warner who by incurring an obligation gave value to enable T & L to acquire rights in or the use of collateral if such value was in fact used.

In determining the priority between Borg-Warner and the Bank, we note that the legislature has provided that a PMSI in inventory such as Borg-Warner's has priority over a conflicting security interest in the same inventory if: (1) the PMSI was perfected at the time T & L received possession of the inventory; (2) Borg-Warner gave notice in writing to the Bank who had filed a financing statement covering the same type of inventory before the date of the filing by Borg-Warner; (3) the Bank received any required notification within five years before T & L received possession of the inventory; and (4) the notification stated that Borg-Warner expected to acquire a PMSI in the inventory of T & L, describing such inventory by item or type. Section 9–312(3).

Our earlier explication of the undisputed facts reveal that Borg-Warner complied with the statutory code requirements.

Judgment reversed in favor of Borg-Warner.

Purchase Money Security Interests in Noninventory Collateral

The second exception to the general priority rule is that a purchase money security interest in collateral other than inventory has priority over a conflicting security interest in the same collateral if the purchase money security interest is perfected at the time the debtor receives the collateral or within 10 days afterward [9–312(4)].

Assume that Bank B takes and perfects a security interest in all the present and after-acquired equipment belonging to a debtor. Then, a supplier sells some equipment to the debtor, reserving a security interest in the equipment until it is paid for. If the supplier perfects the purchase money security interest by filing at the time the debtor obtains the collateral or within 10 days thereafter, it has priority over Bank B. This is because its purchase money security interest in noninventory collateral prevails over a prior perfected security interest if the purchase money security interest is perfected at the time the debtor takes possession or within 10 days afterward.

Rationale for Protecting Purchase Money Security Interests

The preference given to purchase money security interests, provided that their holders comply with the statutory procedure in a timely manner, serves several ends. First, it prevents a single creditor from closing off all other sources of credit to a particular debtor and thus possibly preventing the debtor from obtaining additional inventory or equipment needed to maintain his business. Second, the preference makes it possible for a supplier to have first claim on inventory or equipment until it is paid for, at which time it may become subject to the after-acquired property clause of another creditor's security agreement. By requiring that the first perfected creditor be given notice of a purchase money security interest at the time the new inventory comes into the debtor's inventory, the Code serves to alert the first creditor to the fact that some of the inventory on which it may be relying for security is subject to a prior secured interest until it is paid for.

Buyers in the Ordinary Course of Business

A third exception to the general priority rule is that a **buyer in the ordinary course of business** (other than a person buying farm products from a person engaged in farming operations) takes free from a security interest created by his seller even though the security interest is perfected and even though the buyer knows of its existence [9–307(1)]. For example, a bank loans money to a dealership to finance that dealership's inventory of new automobiles and takes a security interest in the inventory, which it perfects by filing. Then, the dealership sells an automobile out of inventory to a customer. The customer takes the automobile free of the bank's security interest even though the dealership may be in default on its loan agreement and even if the customer knows about the bank's interest. As long as the customer is a buyer in the ordinary course of business, she is protected. The reasons for this rule are that a bank really expects to be paid from the proceeds of the dealership's automobile sales and that the rule is necessary to the smooth conduct of commerce. Customers would be very reluctant to buy goods if they could not be sure they were getting clear title to them from the merchants from whom they buy.

In the following case, *DBC Capital Fund, Inc. v. Snodgrass,* a buyer of an automobile from a dealer obtained title free of a security interest previously given by the dealer to his creditor.

DBC CAPITAL FUND, INC. v. SNODGRASS   551 N.E.2d 475 (Ind. Ct. App. 1990)

n February 19, 1988, DBC Capital Fund, Inc. (DBC), entered into an agreement with the owner of Devers Auto Sales whereby DBC obtained a security interest in the automobile inventory maintained by Devers. This security interest was perfected by filing with the secretary of state on February 25, 1988.

On March 24, 1989, Cheryl Snodgrass purchased a 1984 Oldsmobile from Devers for $5,000 in cash. This automobile was taken from the inventory covered by DBC's security interest, although Snodgrass was not made aware of the financing agreement between Devers and DBC. When Snodgrass took possession of the Oldsmobile, Devers told her that the automobile's certificate of title would be mailed to her. In the meantime, she was issued a temporary registration.

On April 28, 1989, Snodgrass was informed by letter that DBC had physical possession of the certificate of title for the Oldsmobile and that DBC considered itself to have a valid lien on the automobile. In a later telephone conversation, DBC's attorney informed Snodgrass that DBC would not release the certificate of title to the 1984 Oldsmobile until Snodgrass paid DBC $4,200.

On April 25, 1989, the temporary registration issued to Snodgrass by Devers expired. Because Snodgrass was not in possession of the certificate of title for the Oldsmobile, she was unable to obtain proper licensing for the vehicle and, therefore, could not use the automobile. In an effort to obtain the certificate of title, Snodgrass then filed suit against DBC. The trial court entered judgment in her favor on June 28, 1989, awarding her $1,920 in triple damages and $1,748.45 in attorney's fees. DBC appealed.

Ratliff, Judge DBC first contends that the trial court erred in determining that Snodgrass was a buyer in the ordinary course of business, and that, therefore, the trial court failed to recognize that, as a holder of a valid secured interest, DBC was entitled to possession of the certificate of title to the 1984 Oldsmobile. We disagree.

At the hearing the parties stipulated to the fact that DBC had a valid security interest in the 1984 Oldsmobile. The main issue litigated at trial was whether Snodgrass was in a legal position which would make her claim to the automobile superior to that of DBC. Under the relevant provision of the Uniform Commercial Code (UCC) the interest of a "buyer in the ordinary course of business" is superior to that of a holder of valid secured interest. Section 9–307(1).

DBC claims that Snodgrass cannot be considered a buyer in the ordinary course of business "because she failed to require delivery of the title at the time of purchase." According to DBC Snodgrass was charged with knowledge of Indiana Code sections 9-1-2-2(a) and 9-1-2-3(b) which made it unlawful for Devers to fail to deliver the certificate of title at the time of purchase. Because Devers failed to deliver the certificate of title at the time of sale, Snodgrass knew or should have known that the sale of the 1984 Oldsmobile was in violation of the ownership rights of a third party. DBC concludes that because Snodgrass was not a buyer in the ordinary course of business, Snodgrass cannot defeat DBC's valid security interest.

It is true that if there are grounds for suspecting that a security interest is being imperiled by a mode of dealing, a transaction cannot be considered in the ordinary course of business. However, we conclude that DBC has failed to prove that the mode of dealing in the present case was grounds for such a suspicion. DBC's analysis is flawed in that it rests on the supposition that sections 9-1-2-2(a) and 9-1-2-3(b) were enacted to protect the interests of secured creditors. Such simply is not the case. The plain purpose for enacting these statutes was to impede the trade in stolen vehicles. As stated by Judge Posner of the United States Court of Appeals, "as the statute is intended to protect purchasers . . . rather than lenders, there would be a considerable paradox in interpreting the statute to defeat the purchaser's interest." Therefore, we reject DBC's contention that these statutes create a duty on behalf of a purchaser to demand delivery of the certificate of title to an automobile at the time of sale.

Absent such a duty, nothing in the evidence suggests that Snodgrass' purchase of the 1984 Oldsmobile was outside the ordinary course of business. Therefore, under the provisions of section 9–307(1), as a buyer in the ordinary course of business, Snodgrass took free of the security interest held by DBC.

Judgment in favor of Snodgrass.

Artisan's and Mechanic's Liens

The Code also provides that certain liens arising by operation of law (such as an artisan's lien) have priority over a perfected security interest in the collateral [9–310]. For example, Marshall takes her automobile, on which a credit union has a perfected security interest, to Frank's Garage to have it repaired. Under common or statutory law, Frank's may have a lien on the car to secure payment for the repair work; such a lien permits Frank's to keep the car until it receives payment. If Marshall defaults on her loan to the credit union, refuses to pay Frank's for the repair work, and the car is sold to satisfy the liens, Frank's is entitled to its share of the proceeds before the credit union gets anything.

Liens on Consumer Goods Perfected by Attachment

A retailer of consumer goods who relies on attachment of a security interest to perfect it prevails over other creditors of the debtor-buyer. However, the retailer does not prevail over someone who buys the collateral from the debtor if the buyer (1) has no knowledge of the security interest; (2) gives value for the goods; and (3) buys the goods for his personal, family, or household use [9–307(2)]. The retailer does not have priority over such a **bona fide purchaser** unless it filed its security interest.

For example, an appliance store sells a television set to Arthur for $750 on a conditional sales contract, reserving a security interest in the set until

Arthur has paid for it. The store does not file a financing statement, but relies on attachment for perfection. Arthur later borrows money from a credit union and gives it a security interest in the television set. When Arthur defaults on his loans and the credit union tries to claim the set, the appliance store has a better claim to the set than does the credit union. The credit union then has the rights of an unsecured creditor against Arthur.

Now, suppose Arthur sells the television set for $500 to his neighbor Andrews. Andrews is not aware that Arthur still owes money on the set to the appliance store. Andrews buys it to use in her home. If Arthur defaults on his obligation to the store, it cannot recover the television set from Andrews. To be protected against such a purchaser from its debtor, the appliance store must file a financing statement rather than relying on attachment for perfection.

Fixtures

A separate set of problems arise when the collateral is goods that become fixtures by being so related to particular real estate that an interest in them arise under real estate law. Determining the priorities among a secured party with an interest in the fixtures, subsequent purchasers of the real estate, and those persons who have a secured interest—such as a mortgage—on the real property can involve both real estate law and the Code. However, the Code does set out rules for determining when the holder of a perfected security interest in fixtures has priority over an encumbrancer or owner of the real estate. Some of the Code priority rules are as follows:

First, the holder of the secured interest in a fixture has priority if: (1) her interest is a purchase money security interest obtained prior to the time the goods become fixtures; (2) the security interest is perfected by "fixture filing"; that is, by filing in the recording office where a mortgage on the real estate would be filed prior to, or within 10 days of, the time when the goods become fixtures; and (3) the debtor has a recorded interest in the real estate or is in possession of it [9–313(4)(a)].

For example, Restaurant Supply sells Arnold Schwab, the operator of Arnie's Diner, a new gas stove on a conditional sales contract, reserving a security interest until the purchase price of the stove is paid. The stove, a replacement for an existing stove, is to be installed in a building owned by

Arnold Schwab on which First National Bank holds a real estate mortgage. Restaurant Supply can ensure that its security interest in the stove has priority over any claims to it by First National Bank. To do this, Restaurant Supply must (1) enter into a security agreement with Schwab before the stove is delivered to him; and (2) perfect its security interest by fixture filing before the stove is hooked up by a plumber or within 10 days of that time.

Second, the secured party whose interest in fixtures is perfected has priority where: (1) the fixtures are removable factory or office machines or readily removable replacements of domestic appliances that are consumer goods; and (2) the security interest was perfected before the goods became fixtures [9–313(4)(c)]. For example, Harriet Hurd's dishwasher breaks down and she contracts with The Appliance Store to buy a new one on a time-payment plan. The mortgage on Hurd's house provides that it covers the real property along with all kitchen appliances, or their replacements. The Appliance Store's security interest in the dishwasher has priority over the interest of the holder of the mortgage if The Appliance Store perfects its security interest before the new dishwasher is installed in Hurd's home. Perfection in consumer goods can, of course, be obtained merely by attaching the security interest through the signing of a valid security agreement.

Note that a creditor holding a security interest in consumer goods that become fixtures who relies on attachment for perfection prevails over other creditors with an interest in the real property *only* where the consumer goods are "readily removable replacements for domestic appliances."

Suppose a hardware store takes a security interest in some storm windows. Because the storm windows are likely to become fixtures through their use with the homeowner's home, the hardware store cannot rely merely on attachment to protect its security interest. It should file a financing statement to protect that security interest against other creditors of the homeowner with an interest in his home. This rule helps protect a person interested in buying the real property or a person considering lending money based on the real property. By checking the real estate records, the potential buyer or creditor would learn of the hardware store's security interest in the storm windows.

Once a secured party has filed his security interest as a fixture filing, he has priority over purchasers or encumbrancers whose interests are filed after that of the secured party [9–313(4)(b) and (d)].

Where the secured party has priority over all owners and encumbrancers of the real estate, he generally has the right on default to remove the collateral from the real estate. However, he must make reimbursement for the cost of any physical injury caused to the property by the removal [9–313(8)].

CAPITAL FEDERAL SAVINGS & LOAN ASS'N v. HOGER   880 P.2d 281 (Kan. Ct. App. 1994)

apital Federal Savings and Loan Association held a real estate mortgage on the home of Paul and Margaret Hoger that was recorded in Johnson County on August 15, 1984. In 1990, the Hogers purchased a new furnace and air conditioner from The Kansas City Power and Light Company (now known as Western Resources, Inc.). On March 2, 1990, the Hogers and KPL entered into an installment contract and the Hogers executed a promissory note to finance the purchase of the furnace and air conditioner. They were installed on March 20, and on March 23, 1990, KPL filed financing statements covering the furnace and air conditioner in Johnson County on March 23, 1990.

The Hogers defaulted on both the Capital Federal and the KPL/Western Resources loans. Capital Federal filed a mortgage foreclosure action on December 28, 1992, and named both the Hogers and Western Resources as defendants. Western Resources answered and counterclaimed for the $2,887.50 amount the Hogers still owed on their installment contract, claiming a first and prior right to the real estate mortgage proceeds. Capital Federal contended that it had a priority in the real estate foreclosure sale proceeds over Western Resource's purchase money security interest. The trial court awarded Western Resources the first priority in the foreclosure proceeds and Capital Federal appealed. ∽

Briscoe, Chief Judge   The parties do not dispute that the furnace and air conditioner purchased by the Hogers have become fixtures and that Western Resources obtained a priority interest of some type in those fixtures.

The real question is whether the UCC permits Western Resources to proceed against the foreclosure sale proceeds. Western Resources' remedy, as provided by the UCC, is as follows:

When the secured party has priority over all owners and encumbrancers of the real estate, he may, on default, subject to the provisions of part 5, remove his collateral from the real estate but he must reimburse any encumbrancer or owner of the real estate who is not the debtor and who has not otherwise agreed for the cost of repair or physical injury, but not for any diminution in value of the real estate caused by the absence of the goods removed or by any necessity of replacing them. A person entitled to reimbursement may refuse permission to remove until the secured party gives adequate security for the performance of this obligation. Sec. 9–313(8).

Capital Federal argues repossession of the furnace and air conditioner or bringing its claim against the collateral to judgment under Sec. 9–501 were the only remedies available to Western Resources. Western Resources did not pursue an action pursuant to Sec. 9–501 and does not rely on Sec. 9–501 for its claim here. Instead, Western Resources relies upon Sec. 9–313(8) as the basis for its claim. Western Resources emphasizes that Sec. 9–313(8) states that a secured party "may" repossess the collateral and that use of this term implies that other remedies are available. Western Resources argues that once Capital Federal instituted the foreclosure proceedings, Western Resources was entitled to have its lien paid first from the proceeds of the sale.

Neither the language of Sec. 9–313(8) nor the comments answer the question with which we are presented. There are only a few authorities that address the issue, and there are no Kansas cases among those authorities.

A recent case, *Maplewood Bank v. Sears Roebuck,* contains facts similar to those here. Plaintiff bank held a first and prior mortgage and Sears later secured and held a priority interest in a number of kitchen fixtures. The fact that Sears was secured and held a priority interest in those fixtures was undisputed. When defendants defaulted on both obligations, the bank filed for foreclosure. Sears answered, seeking a declaration of priority and requesting that the court order the bank to pay Sears the amount due under its agreement. Sears' response was rejected and it eventually appealed, arguing it should be entitled to receive from the proceeds of a foreclosure sale the difference between the value of the realty with Sear's collateral and the value of the realty after that collateral had been removed. After reviewing the language of Sec. 9–313(8) as adopted in New Jersey, the court stated: "Sears has two options: removal of the fixtures or foregoing the removal of the fixtures." The court noted that the approach advocated by Sears had only been adopted in Louisiana, where the legislature had added the following language to Sec. 9–313(8): "A secured party may also demand separate appraisal of the fixtures to fix his interest in the receipts of the sale thereof in any proceedings in which the real estate is sold pursuant to execution upon it by a mortgagee or any other encumbrancer."

The *Maplewood* court concluded:

We decline to . . . legislat[e]. We prefer the approach followed in Louisiana where the legislature, upon its preference and initiative, provided the innovative remedy sought by Sears. To adopt Sears' argument in the absence of legislation would mean that a mortgagee's security interest could be impaired substantially without the Legislature pronouncing an intention to do so. Any modification of long established fundamental property rights of purchase money mortgagees, must be done in some straightforward manner and may not be implied from the existing statute. The fact that fixtures may be custom made does not require any different result.

After reviewing the authorities, we find *Maplewood* persuasive. Clearly, the UCC does not grant Western Resources an interest in real estate beyond its interest in the furnace and air conditioner as fixtures. To allow it to proceed against the real estate beyond its interest in the fixtures because on default the Hogers, Western Resources' possibility of recouping the amounts it claims would be tied not simply to the value of its collateral, but to the value of the real estate. As is the case here, Western Resources would be recovering the entire amount of its claim, despite the actual value of the fixtures. Even if the fixtures were approximately valued, the fixture creditor would benefit from the synergy of the fixture–real estate relationship. Although the law is such that a mortgagee may benefit by the addition of personal property to real estate (see Sec. 9–313 [7]), there is nothing in the UCC that indicates the interests of fixture creditors should be enhanced by the real estate to which personal property is affixed.

Judgment reversed in favor of Capital Resources.

DEFAULT AND FORECLOSURE

Default

Usually, the creditor and debtor state in their agreement which events constitute a default by the buyer. The Code does not define what constitutes default. Defining default is left to the parties' agreement, subject to the Code requirement that the parties act in good faith in doing so. If the debtor defaults, the secured creditor has several options:

1. Forget the collateral, and sue the debtor on his note or promise to pay.
2. Repossess the collateral, and use strict foreclosure—in some cases—to keep the collateral in satisfaction of the remaining debt.
3. Repossess and foreclose on the collateral, and then, depending on the circumstances, either sue for any deficiency or return the surplus to the debtor.

Right to Possession

The agreement between the creditor and the debtor may authorize the creditor to repossess the collateral in case of default. If the debtor does default, the creditor is entitled under the Code to possession of the collateral. If through self-help the creditor can obtain possession peaceably, he may do so. However, if the collateral is in the possession of the debtor and cannot be obtained without disturbing the peace, then the creditor must take court action to repossess the collateral [9–503]. See the *Ivy v. General Motors Acceptance Corp.* case, which follows shortly, for a discussion of what constitutes repossession without breach of the peace.

If the collateral is intangible, such as accounts, chattel paper, instruments, or documents, and performance has been rendered to the debtor, the secured party may give notice and have payments made or performance rendered to her [9–502].

CONCEPT   REVIEW

Priority Rules

PARTIES	RULE
Buyer of Collateral from Debtor versus Creditor with a Security Interest in the Collateral	1. A *buyer in ordinary course of business* (other than a person buying farm products from a person engaged in farming operations) takes *free* of a security interest created by his seller even though the security interest is *perfected* and even though the buyer knows of its existence. 2. A *bona fide purchaser* of collateral that is *consumer goods* from a debtor has priority over a creditor who holds a prior purchase money security interest in the collateral but did not file its security interest if the buyer (*a*) has no knowledge of the security interest, (*b*) gives value for the goods, and (*c*) buys them for her own personal, family, or household use. 3. Otherwise, buyers take subject to perfected or known security interests but free of unperfected and unknown security interests.

Secured Creditor versus Other Creditors	1. As to collateral *other than fixtures,* the general rule is that when more than one security interest in the same collateral has been filed (or otherwise perfected), the first security interest to be filed or perfected has priority over other security interests.
	2. Exceptions to this general rule are:
	  a. Inventory. A perfected purchase money security interest in inventory has priority over a conflicting security interest in the same inventory *if* the purchase money security interest is perfected at the time the debtor receives possession of the inventory *and* if the purchase money secured party gives notification in writing to the prior secured creditor *before* the debtor receives the inventory.
	  b. Noninventory. A purchase money security interest in noninventory collateral prevails over a prior perfected security interest *if* the purchase money security interest is perfected at the time the debtor takes possession or within 10 days afterward.
	  c. Liens by operation of law. Liens that arise by operation of law—such as artisan's liens—have priority over even perfected security interests in collateral.
	3. If none of the conflicting security interests has been perfected, then the *first* security interest to be *attached* to the collateral has priority.

Secured Creditor versus Other Persons with an Interest in Real Property on which Fixture Is Located	1. As to collateral that will become a *fixture:*
	  a. A creditor with a secured interest in a fixture has priority if (1) the interest is a purchase money security interest that was obtained prior to the time the goods became fixtures; (2) the security interest was perfected by fixture filing prior to, or within 10 days of, the time when the goods became fixtures; and (3) the debtor has a recorded interest in the real estate or is in possession of it.
	  b. A creditor with a perfected secured interest in fixtures will have priority where: (1) the fixtures are removable factory or office machines or readily removable replacements of domestic appliances that are consumer goods; and (2) the security interest is perfected *prior* to the time the goods become fixtures.

Sale of the Collateral

The secured party may dispose of the collateral by sale or lease or in any manner calculated to produce the greatest benefit to all parties concerned. However, the method of disposal must be commercially reasonable [9–504]. Notice of the time and place of a public sale must be given to the debtor, as must notice of a private sale. If the creditor decides to sell the collateral at a public sale such as an auction, then the creditor must give the debtor notice of the time and place of the public sale. Similarly, if the creditor proposes to make a private sale of the collateral, notice must be given to the debtor. This gives the debtor a chance to object to the proposed private sale if she considers it not to be commercially reasonable or to otherwise protect her interests [9–504].

Until the collateral is actually disposed of by the creditor, the buyer has the right to *redeem* it. This means that if the buyer tenders fulfillment of all obligations secured by the collateral as well as of the expenses incurred by the secured party in retaking, holding, and preparing the collateral for disposition, she can recover the collateral from the creditor [9–506].

Consumer Goods

If the creditor has a security interest in consumer goods and the debtor has paid 60 percent or more of the purchase price or debt (and has not agreed in writing to a strict foreclosure), the creditor must sell the repossessed collateral. If less than 60 percent of the purchase price or debt related to consumer goods has been paid, and as to any other security interest, the creditor may propose to the debtor that the seller keep the collateral in satisfaction of the debt. The consumer-debtor has 21 days to object in writing. If the consumer objects, the creditor must sell the collateral. Otherwise, the creditor may keep the collateral in satisfaction of the debt [9–505].

Distribution of Proceeds

The Code sets out the order in which any proceeds are to be distributed after the sale of collateral by the creditor. First, any expenses of repossessing, storing, and selling the collateral, including reasonable attorney's fees, are paid. Second, the proceeds are used to satisfy the debt. Third, any junior liens are paid. Finally, if any proceeds remain, the debtor is entitled to them. If the proceeds are not sufficient to satisfy the debt, then the creditor is usually entitled to a **deficiency judgment.** This means that the debtor remains personally liable for any debt remaining after the sale of the collateral [9–504].

For example, suppose a loan company lends Christy $5,000 to purchase a car and takes a security interest. After making several payments and reducing the debt to $4,800, Christy defaults. The loan company pays $50 to have the car repossessed and then has it sold at an auction, where it brings $4,500, thus incurring a sales commission of 10 percent ($450) and attorney's fees of $150. The repossession charges, sales commission, and attorney's fees, totaling $650, are paid first from the $4,500 proceeds. The remaining $3,850 is applied to the $4,800 debt, leaving a balance due of $950. Christy remains liable to the loan company for the $950.

Liability of Creditor

A creditor who holds a security interest in collateral must be careful to comply with the provisions of Article 9 of the Code. A creditor acting improperly in repossessing collateral or in its foreclosure and sale is liable to the parties injured. Thus, a creditor can be liable to a debtor if she acts improperly in repossessing or selling collateral [9–507]. This potential liability is illustrated in the case of *Ivy v. General Motors Acceptance Corp.,* which follows.

IVY v. GENERAL MOTORS ACCEPTANCE CORP.   612 So.2d 1108 (Miss. Sup. Ct. 1992)

 ester Ivy borrowed money from General Motors Acceptance Corp. (GMAC) to purchase a van, and GMAC acquired a security interest in the van. The security agreement contained a so-called insecurity clause that provided GMAC with the right to immediately repossess the van upon default; notice was not a prerequisite to repossession. Ivy defaulted on his obligation on the loan, and

GMAC hired American Lenders Service of Jackson to repossess Ivy's van. About 6:30 A.M., Dax Freeman and Jonathan Baker of American Lenders Service drove to Ivy's home. They drove on Ivy's gravel driveway, which is about a quarter-mile long, past a chicken house and the van parked near Ivy's mobile home. They quietly attempted to start the van, but their attempt failed. They then hitched the van to their tow truck and towed it away.

When Freeman and Baker reached the end of Ivy's driveway, Freeman stopped the tow truck and checked the van. At that point he saw someone running from the chicken house toward the mobile home. Ivy testified that prior to running toward the mobile home, he ran toward the tow truck "hollering and flagging for them to stop" but Freeman and Baker apparently did not see or hear Ivy at the time Freeman jumped back into the tow truck, drove off Ivy's property, and onto an adjacent road. Ivy decided to chase after Freeman and Baker because he thought they were stealing his van. He jumped into a pickup truck, passed Freeman and Baker, and—according to them—pulled in front of the tow truck, and slammed on his brakes. Freeman claimed he was forced to slam on his brakes but was unable to avoid a slight collision with the rear bumper of Ivy's truck. Ivy claimed that he stopped well ahead of the tow truck, affording Freeman plenty of time to stop, but that he revved the engine and "rammed him." Ivy claimed that his head hit the rear window of the truck as a result of the collision and that he sustained a "severe vertical sprain." However, Ivy's medical bill totaled only $20 and he did not miss any work.

When Ivy exited his truck, Freeman showed him some "official looking documents," advised him that he worked for American Lenders, and stated that they were repossessing his truck at GMAC's request. There was a dispute as to whether Ivy sought to have the sheriff called concerning the accident. Freeman allowed Ivy to retrieve some personal belongings from the van and gave Ivy a telephone number to call to get his van back; at that point, they all departed the scene.

Seven months later, on October 20, Ivy filed a complaint against GMAC and American Lenders contending that the repossession of his van was invalid because there was a breach of the peace and he had been caused "personal injuries." Ivy sought actual and punitive damages. At the conclusion of a jury trial, the jury awarded Ivy $5,000 in actual damages and $100,000 in punitive damages. The trial court judge set aside the punitive damage award and both parties appealed. ◠

Prather, Judge GMAC contends that its agents did not breach the peace and, therefore, it should not have been liable for actual damages. Ivy, of course, disagrees.

Mississippi law authorizes a creditor or secured party to repossess collateral without judicial process if he or she can do so without breaching the peace. Sec. 9–503. The legislature did not define "breach of peace," but this Court has provided some indication. For example, this court has held that entering a private driveway to repossess collateral without use of force does not constitute a breach of peace. This Court has also held that a creditor, who repossesses collateral despite the fact that the debtor has withheld his or her consent or has strongly objected, did not breach the peace. And, courts in other jurisdictions have generally held that the use of trickery or deceit to peaceably repossess collateral does not constitute a breach of peace.

On the other hand, a Florida Court of Appeal opined that a debtor's "physical objection"—"even from a public street"—bars repossession. A Georgia Court of Appeal found a breach of peace in a case in which: (1) the creditor repossessed the debtor's au-

tomobile by blocking it with another automobile; (2) the creditor informed the debtor that he could just "walk his a__ home"; and (3) the debtor "unequivocally protested" the manner of repossession. The Ohio Supreme Court opined that the use of intimidation or acts "fraught with the likelihood of violence" constitutes a breach of peace.

In sum, much of the litigation involving self-help repossession statutes involves the issue of whether a breach of peace has occurred. Disposition of this issue is not a simple task: Since physical violence will ordinarily result in a breach of peace, the secured party's right to repossession will end if repossession evokes physical violence, either on the part of the debtor or the secured party. At the other end from physical violence, a secured party may peaceably persuade the debtor to give up the collateral so that no breach of peace occurs. Between those two extreme situations—one in which violence occurs and the other in which the debtor peaceably gives up the collateral—lies the line which divides those cases in which the secured party may exercise self-help repossession and those in which he must resort to the courts. As with most dividing lines, the line between the two extremes is sometimes hard to locate, and even if it is located, it sometimes moves.

Application of the foregoing principles to the evidence viewed in the light most favorable to the verdict leads this Court to conclude that a breach of peace did occur. This Court, therefore, affirms on this issue.

Judgment affirmed awarding actual damages and denying punitive damages.

McRae, Justice, concurring in part and dissenting in part.   The majority complains that Mississippi case law provides little guidance on determining whether a creditor or agent's conduct is so malicious, oppressive or fraudulent that an award of punitive damages is warranted. While it is true that this Court has not often confronted this issue, the principle is well settled throughout the jurisdictions that punitive damages are proper where creditors seize property in a manner that reflects malice, fraud, oppression, gross negligence, or reckless disregard of the rights of the chattel holder.

In *Kirkwood v. Hickman,* perhaps the only Mississippi case to directly address this question, the Court found that when a creditor commits a trespass to retrieve secured property in an "intentional and highhanded manner," punitive damages are in order even if the trespass involved no violence. What could possibly be more "highhanded" than going onto a debtor's property without permission, hooking the debtor's van to a tow truck, and hauling it away in plain view of the debtor with no explanation whatsoever? In such circumstances the debtor would naturally think his property was being stolen and would set about to recapture the property. If the conduct of GMAC and American Lenders does not qualify as "reckless disregard for the rights of the chattel holder," then I am at a loss to imagine what might fit the description.

Clearly, given Ivy's version of the events the jury was justified in concluding that the conduct of GMAC and American Lenders was oppressive, highhanded and recklessly unmindful of Ivy's rights.

This entire misadventure might have been avoided if the creditor had simply followed the replevin procedures set out in the Mississippi Code. While Mississippi still permits creditors to employ the remedy of self-help when retrieving their property from chattel holders, creditors follow that path at their peril. GMAC and American Lenders in this case took the law into their own hand, and so could be held fully responsible for the consequences. I would reverse the judgment not withstanding the verdict and reinstate the jury's award of punitive damages.

Constitutional Requirements in Regard to Repossession

In 1972, in *Fuentes v. Shevin,*[6] the U.S. Supreme Court held that state repossession statutes that authorize summary seizure of goods and chattels by state agents such as a sheriff, on an application by some private person who claims he is lawfully entitled to the property and posts a bond, are unconstitutional. This is because these statutes deny the current possessor of the property an opportunity to be heard in court before the property is taken from him. The Court did not accept the argument that because the possessors of the property in question had signed conditional sales contracts authorizing the sellers to take back or repossess the property on default, they had waived their rights to a hearing. This decision raised some speculation that the pro- visions of the Code permitting secured parties to repossess collateral, in some cases without even judicial process, might be constitutionally defective.

Then, in 1974, in *Mitchell v. W. T. Grant,*[7] the Supreme Court limited the *Fuentes* holding to a requirement that where only property rights are involved, there must be some opportunity for a judicial hearing prior to any final determination of the rights of the parties claiming an interest in the property in question. This decision permits property to be seized by state officials, following the filing of an application and the posting of a bond, so long as the person from whom the property is seized has a later opportunity in court to assert his rights to the property.

The repossession provisions of the Code have been attacked in court as lacking in due process. However, the courts to date have upheld the Code repossession provisions as they relate to private

---

[6]407 U.S. 67 (1972).

[7]407 U.S. 600 (1974).

repossession without judicial process.[8] Where judicial process is used, the procedures must conform to the standards laid down in *Fuentes* and *Mitchell.*

1. In the *Ivy v. GMAC* case presented earlier in this chapter, a car was repossessed by towing it away from the debtor's residence early in the morning. In Problem case 10 of this chapter, the car was repossessed by driving it away from the owner's residence at 2:00 A.M. In another recent case, an automobile was repossessed by forcing it off the road and then forcing the driver to drive it to the dealer-creditor. Are the repossession techniques used in these cases ethical?

2. Should creditors be able to obtain deficiency judgments against consumers who default on their obligations in connection with the time-purchase of consumer goods and where the proceeds on resale are not sufficient to satisfy the balance due? Or should the creditor have to look solely to the collateral for his security?

3. Suppose that you own an appliance business in a working-class neighborhood that makes most of its sales on credit. What considerations would you take into account in determining whether and when to foreclose or repossess items on which customers have fallen behind in making their payments? Should you be swayed by the personal circumstances of your debtor or look only to protecting your financial interests? For example, would you consider the value of the item to the debtor—such as whether it is a necessity for her life, such as a refrigerator, or a luxury? Would you consider the reason the person had fallen behind—that is, whether she had been ill or had recently lost her job?

PROBLEMS AND PROBLEM CASES

1. Symons, a full-time insurance salesperson, bought a set of drums and cymbals from Grinnel Brothers. A security agreement was executed between them but was never filed. Symons purchased the drums to supplement his income by playing with a band. He had done this before, and his income from his two jobs was about equal. He also played several other instruments. Symons became bankrupt, and the trustee tried to acquire the drums and cymbals as part of his bankruptcy estate. Grinnel's claimed that the drums and cymbals were consumer goods and thus it had a perfected security interest merely by attachment of the security interest. Were the drums and cymbals consumer goods?

2. Robert and Billie Brown operated a paint and gift store. They borrowed $36,628.31 from the First National Bank of Dewey and gave the bank a security interest in "all goods, wares, merchandise, gifts, inventory, fixtures, and accounts receivable owned or thereafter acquired and used in the business." The security agreement also covered "all additions, accessions, and substitutions" to or for collateral and required the Browns to insure the collateral for the benefit of the bank. The bank perfected its security interest. The Browns obtained fire insurance but did not name the bank as a loss payee. The Browns's business was destroyed by fire, and the Browns received a $25,000 check from the insurance company for the loss of inventory. The bank then filed suit to obtain the check. Shortly thereafter, the Browns were adjudicated bankrupt. Does the bank have a perfected security interest in the insurance check?

3. Nicolosi bought a diamond ring on credit from Rike-Kumber as an engagement present for his fiancée. He signed a purchase money security agreement giving Rike-Kumber a security interest in the ring until it was paid for. Rike-Kumber did not file a financing statement covering its security interest. Nicolosi filed for bankruptcy. The bankruptcy trustee claimed that the diamond ring was part of the bankruptcy estate because Rike-Kumber did not perfect its security interest. Rike-Kumber claimed that it had a perfected security interest in the ring. Did Rike-Kumber have to file a financing statement to perfect its security interest in the diamond ring?

4. On October 28, 1983, Steve Gresham, doing business as Midway Cycle Sales, entered into a Wholesale Financing Agreement with ITT Commercial Finance Corporation. The agreement was to finance the purchase of new motorcycles from Suzuki Motor Corporation. ITT filed a financing statement with the Indiana secretary of state on December 16, 1983. The description of the collateral in which ITT asserted a security interest included "all

---

[8]See, for example, *Gibbs v. Titleman,* 502 F.2d 1107 (3rd Cir. 1974) and cases cited therein.

inventory . . . replacements and proceeds." On January 9, 1984, Union Bank filed a financing statement with the Indiana secretary of state claiming it was engaged in "floor planning of new motorcycles" for Midway Cycle Sales. In August 1984, ITT began paying Suzuki invoices for Gresham. In July 1985, ITT sent a letter to Union Bank notifying it that it expected to acquire purchase money security interests in the inventory of Stephan Gresham d/b/a Midway Cycle Sales. In early 1986, Union Bank began loaning money to Gresham under its floor planning agreement with him. Actually, Gresham was "double floor planning"—that is, he was taking invoices for motorcycles that had been paid for by ITT to the Union Bank and claiming that he had paid for the motorcycles but had decided to floor plan them. When Union Bank advanced money to him, he used the money to make payments on the loans to ITT. He made no payments to Union Bank and did not pay off all of his loan to ITT. Midway Cycle Sales went bankrupt when Union Bank repossessed 22 new Suzuki motorcycles. ITT brought suit against Union Bank, claiming it had paid for the motorcycles and had a perfected security interest in the motorcycles that had priority over Union Bank's security interest in them. Did ITT's security interest have priority over Union Bank's security interest?

5. On November 18, Firestone & Company made a loan to Edmund Carroll, doing business as Kozy Kitchen. To secure the loan, a security agreement was executed, which listed the items of property included, and concluded as follows: "together with all property and articles now, and which may hereafter be, used or mixed with, added or attached to, and/or substituted for any of the described property." A financing statement that included all the items listed in the security agreement was filed with the town clerk on November 18 and with the secretary of state on November 22. On November 25, National Cash Register Company delivered a cash register to Carroll on a conditional sales contract. National Cash Register filed a financing statement on the cash register with the town clerk on December 20 and with the secretary of state on December 21. Carroll defaulted in his payments to both Firestone and National Cash Register. Firestone repossessed all of Carroll's fixtures and equipment covered by its security agreement, including the cash register, and then sold the cash register. National Cash Register claimed that it was the title owner of the cash register and brought suit against

Firestone for conversion. Did Firestone or National Cash Register have the better right to the cash register?

6. Glatfelter purchased a stereo set under a purchase money security agreement from Mahaley's Store. This agreement was not perfected by filing. She sold the set to Colonial Trading Company, which in turn resold it. When Glatfelter did not meet her obligations, Mahaley's sued Colonial Trading for conversion of the stereo set in which it claimed a security interest. Is Colonial Trading liable for selling the stereo set in which Mahaley has a security interest?

7. Grimes purchased a new Dodge car from Hornish, a franchised Dodge dealer. The sale was made in the ordinary course of Hornish's business. Grimes paid Hornish the purchase price of the car at the time of the sale. Hornish had borrowed money from Sterling Acceptance and had given it a perfected security interest in its inventory, including the car Grimes bought. Hornish defaulted on its loan to Sterling and Sterling then tried to recover the Dodge from Grimes. Was the car Grimes bought from Hornish still subject to Sterling Acceptance's security interest?

8. On April 10, Benson purchased a new Ford Thunderbird automobile. She traded in her old automobile and financed the balance of $4,325 through the Magnavox Employees Credit Union, which took a security interest in the Thunderbird. In July, the Thunderbird sustained major damage in two accidents. It was taken to ACM Garage for repairs that took seven months to make and resulted in charges of $2,139.54. Benson was unable to pay the charges, and ACM claimed a garage man's lien. Does Magnavox Credit Union's lien or ACM's lien have priority?

9. Kahn applied for a home improvement loan to construct an in-ground swimming pool. Union National Bank approved the loan, and construction began on Kahn's land. State Bank held a valid mortgage on this land. After the pool was completed, Union National gave Kahn the money with which he paid the contractor. Union National then perfected its interest by filing. State Bank later attempted to foreclose on its mortgage. Union National claimed the value of the pool. Is Union National entitled to recover the value of the pool?

10. In August 1979, Norma Wade purchased a Ford Thunderbird automobile and gave Ford Motor Credit a security interest in it to secure her payment of the $7,000 balance of the purchase price. When Wade fell behind on her monthly payments, Ford engaged the Kansas Recovery Bureau to repossess the car. On February 10, 1980, an employee of the Recovery Bureau located the car in Wade's driveway, unlocked the door, got in, and started it. He then noticed a discrepancy between the serial number of the car and the number listed in his papers. He shut off the engine, got out, and locked the car. When Wade appeared at the door to her house, he advised her that he had been sent by Ford to repossess the car but would not do so until he had straightened out the serial number. She said that she had been making payments, that he was not going to take the car, and that she had a gun, which she would use. He suggested that Wade contact Ford to straighten out the problem. She called Ford and advised its representative that if she caught anybody on her property again trying to take her car, she would use her gun to "leave him laying right where I saw him." Wade made several more payments, but Ford again contracted to have the car repossessed. At 2:00 A.M. on March 5, 1980, the employee of the Kansas Recovery Bureau successfully took the car from Wade's driveway. She said that she heard a car burning rubber, looked out of her window, and saw that her car was missing. There was no confrontation between Wade and the employee since he had safely left the area before she discovered that the car had been taken. Wade then brought a lawsuit against Ford claiming that the car had been wrongfully repossessed. She sought actual and punitive damages, plus attorney's fees. Should Ford be held liable for wrongful repossession?

11. Gibson, a collector of rare old Indian jewelry, took two of his pieces to Hagberg, a pawnbroker. The two pieces, a silver belt and a silver necklace, were worth $500 each. Hagberg loaned only $45 on the belt and $50 on the necklace. Gibson defaulted on both loans, and immediately and without notice, the necklace was sold for $240. A short time later, the belt was sold for $80. At the time of their sale, Gibson owed interest on the loans of $22. Gibson sued Hagberg to recover damages for improperly disposing of the collateral. Is Gibson entitled to damages because of Hagberg's actions in disposing of the collateral?

12. 📼 *Video Case.* See "A Good Night's Sleep." Appliance Dealer needed additional working capital, so it obtained a loan from the bank, which took—and perfected by filing— a security interest

in all present and after-acquired inventory and equipment of the store. Subsequently, Appliance Dealer obtained inventory on credit from Wholesaler, who retained and perfected a security interest in the inventory until Appliance Dealer paid for it. Appliance Dealer also purchased from Computer Retailer a computer for use in the store; the Computer Retailer took and perfected a security interest in the computer before it was delivered. Can the bank obtain a security interest in the inventory and computer even though Appliance Dealer did not own them at the time it borrowed the money from the bank and gave it a security interest?

Cook, a customer, buys a microwave oven and built-in range/oven on credit from Appliance Dealer; both items were among the inventory that Appliance Dealer had purchased from Wholesaler but it has not yet paid Wholesaler for either item. Appliance Dealer retained a security interest in the items it sold to Cook but it did not file a financing statement. Cook sold the microwave to her neighbor for about 60 percent of the price she agreed to pay Appliance Dealer. If Cook subsequently defaulted on her obligation to Appliance Dealer, could it recover the stove from Cook? Would your answer be different if the oven had been installed in a building on which Mortgage Company held a mortgage? Who would have the better right to the oven, Appliance Dealer or Mortgage Company? Does Appliance Dealer have the right to recover the microwave from Cook's neighbor?

If Appliance Dealer subsequently defaulted on its obligations to Bank, to Wholesaler, and to Computer Retailer, who would have the priority security interest in the appliances that remain in the Appliance Dealer's inventory, Bank or Wholesaler? Would either have the legal right to recover the microwave or the stove that was sold to Cook? Who would have the priority security interest in the computer, Bank or Computer Retailer?

13. 📼 *Video Case.* See "TV Repair." Appliance Store acquired inventory on credit from TV Manufacturer, which retained and perfected a security interest in the TV sets until they were paid for. Appliance Store subsequently experienced financial difficulties and held a going-out-of-business sale. If TV Manufacturer had not been paid for the TV sets, would it have the legal right to recover them from individual customers who purchased them at the going-out-of-business sale?

Bankruptcy

When an individual, a partnership, or a corporation is unable to pay its debts to creditors, problems can arise. Some creditors may demand security for past debts or start court actions on their claims in an effort to protect themselves. Such actions may adversely affect other creditors by depriving them of their fair share of the debtor's assets. Also, quick depletion of the debtor's assets may effectively prevent the debtor who needs additional time to pay off his debts from having an opportunity to do so.

At the same time, creditors need to be protected against the actions a debtor in financial difficulty might be tempted to take to their detriment. For example, the debtor might run off with his remaining assets or might use them to pay certain favored creditors, leaving nothing for the other creditors. Finally, a means is needed by which a debtor can get a fresh start financially and not continue to be saddled with debts beyond his ability to pay. This chapter focuses on the body of law and procedure that has developed to deal with the competing interests when a debtor is unable to pay his debts in a timely manner. ∽

THE BANKRUPTCY ACT

The Bankruptcy Act is a federal law that provides an organized procedure under the supervision of a federal court for dealing with insolvent debtors. Debtors are considered insolvent if they are unable or fail to pay their debts as they become due. The power of Congress to enact bankruptcy legislation is provided in the Constitution. Through the years, there have been many amendments to the Bankruptcy Act. Congress completely revised the act in

1978 and then passed significant amendments to it in 1984, 1986, and 1994.

The Bankruptcy Act has several major purposes. One is to ensure that the debtor's property is fairly distributed to the creditors and that some creditors do not obtain unfair advantage over the others. At the same time, the act protects all of the creditors against actions by the debtor that would unreasonably diminish the debtor's assets to which they are entitled. The act also provides the honest debtor with a measure of protection against the demands for payment by his creditors. Under some circumstances, the debtor is given additional time to pay the creditors, freeing him of those pressures creditors might otherwise exert. If the debtor makes a full and honest accounting of his assets and liabilities and deals fairly with his creditors, the debtor may have most—if not all—of the debts discharged so as to have a fresh start.

At one time, **bankruptcy** carried a strong stigma for the debtors who became involved in it. Today, this is less true. It is still desirable that a person conduct her financial affairs in a responsible manner. However, there is a greater understanding that such events as accidents, natural disasters, illness, divorce, and severe economic dislocations are often beyond the ability of individuals to control and may lead to financial difficulty and bankruptcy.

Bankruptcy Proceedings

The Bankruptcy Act covers a number of bankruptcy proceedings. In this chapter, our focus will be on:

1. Straight bankruptcy (liquidations).
2. Reorganizations.
3. Family farms.
4. Consumer debt adjustments.

The Bankruptcy Act also contains provisions regarding municipal bankruptcies, which are not covered in this chapter.

Liquidations

A liquidation proceeding, traditionally called **straight bankruptcy,** is brought under Chapter 7 of the Bankruptcy Act. The debtor must disclose all of the property she owns and surrender this bankruptcy estate to the **bankruptcy trustee.** The trustee separates out certain property that the debtor is permitted to keep and then administers, liquidates, and distributes the remainder of the bankrupt debtor's estate. There is a mechanism for determining the relative rights of the creditors, for recovering any preferential payments made to creditors, and for disallowing any preferential liens obtained by creditors. If the bankrupt person has been honest in his business transactions and in the bankruptcy proceedings, she is usually given a **discharge** (relieved) of her debts.

Reorganizations

Chapter 11 of the Bankruptcy Act provides a proceeding whereby a debtor can work out a plan to solve its financial problems under the supervision of a federal court. A reorganization plan is essentially a contract between a debtor and its creditors. The proceeding is intended for debtors, particularly businesses, whose financial problems may be solvable if they are given some time and guidance and if they are relieved of some pressure from creditors.

Family Farms

Historically, farmers have been accorded special attention in the Bankruptcy Code. Chapter 12 of the Bankruptcy Act provides a special proceeding whereby a debtor involved in a family farming operation can develop a plan to work out his financial difficulties. Generally, the debtor remains in possession of the farm and continues to operate it while the plan is developed and implemented.

Consumer Debt Adjustments

Under Chapter 13 of the Bankruptcy Act, individuals with regular incomes who are in financial difficulty can develop plans under court supervision to satisfy their creditors. Chapter 13 permits compositions (reductions) of debts and/or extensions of time to pay debts out of the debtor's future earnings.

The Bankruptcy Courts

Bankruptcy cases and proceedings are filed in federal district courts. The district courts have the authority to refer the cases and proceedings to bankruptcy judges, who are considered to be units of the district court. If a dispute falls within what is known as a **core proceeding,** the bankruptcy judge can hear and determine the controversy. Core proceedings include a broad list of matters related to the administration of a bankruptcy estate. However, if a dispute is not a core proceeding but rather involves a state law claim, then the bankruptcy judge can only hear the case and prepare draft findings and conclusions for review by the district court judge.

Certain proceedings affecting interstate commerce have to be heard by the district court judge if any party requests that this be done. Moreover, even the district courts are precluded from deciding certain state law claims that could not normally be brought in federal court, even if those claims are related to the bankruptcy matter. Bankruptcy judges are appointed by the president for terms of 14 years.

CHAPTER 7: LIQUIDATION PROCEEDINGS

Petitions

All bankruptcy proceedings, including liquidation proceedings, are begun by the filing of a petition. The petition may be either a **voluntary petition** filed by the debtor or an **involuntary petition** filed by a creditor or creditors of the debtor. A voluntary petition in bankruptcy may be filed by an individual, a partnership, or a corporation. However, municipal, railroad, insurance, and banking corporations and savings or building and loan associations are not permitted to file for straight bankruptcy proceedings. A person filing a voluntary petition need not be insolvent—that is, her debts need not be greater than her assets. However, the person must be able to allege that she has debts. The primary purpose for filing a voluntary petition is to obtain a discharge from some or all of the debts.

Involuntary Petitions

An involuntary petition is a petition filed by creditors of a debtor. By filing it, they seek to have the debtor declared bankrupt and his assets distributed to the creditors. Involuntary petitions may be filed against many debtors. However, involuntary petitions in straight bankruptcy cannot be filed against (1) farmers; (2) ranchers; (3) nonprofit organizations; (4) municipal, railroad, insurance, and bank-

ing corporations; (5) credit unions; and (6) savings or building and loan associations.

If a debtor has 12 or more creditors, an involuntary petition to declare him bankrupt must be signed by at least 3 creditors. If there are fewer than 12 creditors, then an involuntary petition can be filed by a single creditor. The creditor or creditors must have valid claims against the debtor exceeding the value of any security they hold by $10,000 or more. To be forced into involuntary bankruptcy, the debtor must be generally not paying his debts as they become due—or have had a custodian for his property appointed within the previous 120 days.

If an involuntary petition is filed against a debtor engaged in business, the debtor may be permitted to continue to operate the business. However, the court may appoint an **interim trustee** if this is necessary to preserve the bankruptcy estate or to prevent loss of the estate. A creditor who suspects that a debtor may dismantle her business or dispose of its assets at less than fair value may apply to the court for protection.

Automatic Stay Provisions

The filing of a bankruptcy petition operates as an automatic stay, holding in abeyance various forms of creditor action against a debtor or her property. These actions include: (1) beginning or continuing judicial proceedings against the debtor; (2) actions to obtain possession of the debtor's property; (3) actions to create, perfect, or enforce a lien against the debtor's property; and (4) setoff of indebtedness owed to the debtor before commencement of the bankruptcy proceeding. A court may give a creditor relief from the stay if the creditor can show that the stay does not give her "adequate protection" and jeopardizes her interest in certain property. The relief to the creditor might take the form of periodic cash payments or the granting of a replacement lien or an additional lien on property.

The case that follows, *In Re Ionosphere Clubs, Inc.,* is an example of creditors trying to proceed independent of a bankruptcy court and having their efforts blocked.[1]

---

[1]While this case involved a petition for relief under Chapter 11 (Reorganization), the automatic stay provisions of the bankruptcy title of the U.S. Code are applicable to both Chapter 7 and Chapter 11 proceedings.

n March 4, 1989, the International Association of Machinists and Aerospace Workers, AFL-CIO (IAM), initiated a strike against Eastern Air Lines, Inc. Thereafter, both the Airline Pilots Association (ALPA) and the Transport Workers Union of America (TWU) initiated a sympathy strike. As a result, on March 9, 1989, Eastern and its affiliate, Ionosphere Clubs, Inc., each filed a voluntary petition for relief under Chapter 11. After the bankruptcy filing, Eastern and Ionosphere continued to operate their businesses as debtors in possession.

During the strike, Eastern hired new pilots as permanent replacements for the striking pilots. On November 22, 1989, the ALPA notified Eastern that the sympathy strike had been concluded and that the approximately 2,000 striking pilots were willing to return to work. Eastern was not willing to displace the replacement pilots to make room for the returning strikers.

In February 1990, Morteson Rolleston and 17 formerly striking pilots filed a class action lawsuit in federal district court in Atlanta, claiming, among other things, that Eastern had failed to fund its pilot pension plan and to pay interest on certain pension benefits that had already been paid. The lawsuit sought to freeze the assets of Eastern until amounts allegedly due to certain benefit plans were paid. Eastern sought an injunction from the bankruptcy court enjoining the Rolleston lawsuit as a violation of the automatic stay provisions of the Bankruptcy Act. ⌒

Lifland, Chief Judge Section 362(a)(3) of the Code provides in pertinent part as follows:

(a) . . . a petition filed under . . . this title . . . operates as a stay, applicable to all entities, of

(1) the commencement or continuation . . . of a judicial, administrative or other proceeding against the debtor that was or could have been commenced before the commencement of the case under this title, or to recover a claim against the debtor that arose before the commencement of the case under this title;

* * * * *

(3) an act to obtain possession of the property of the estate or of property from the estate or to exercise control over property of the estate;

* * * * *

(6) any act to collect, assess or recover a claim against the debtor that arose before the commencement of the case under this title.

It is beyond dispute that the Rolleston Plaintiffs seek to exercise control of at least $281 million of the cash assets of Eastern's estate by seeking to secure a court order "freezing" Eastern's assets and directing Eastern to pay this amount to the pilot pension plans. Additionally, the Rolleston Plaintiffs appear to request a temporary restraining order that would prohibit distributions under a reorganization plan, because "if the assets are distributed to creditors, it will be impossible for Plaintiffs to recover those assets." This direct attempt to secure preferred status for a discrete group of creditors runs directly counter to the distribution and oversight scheme established by the Code.

The Rolleston Plaintiffs also allege that the funds they seek to recover from Eastern on behalf of the pension plans "are not Eastern's assets but . . . are assets of the [Rolleston] Plaintiffs." It would appear that the Rolleston Plaintiffs are merely asserting unliquidated, contingent pre-petition claims against the Eastern estate and have no specific interest (other than the interest that all of Eastern's creditors have in property of the estate) in the property which they are attempting to gain control over.

Any attempt to "freeze" Eastern's assets and obtain an order requiring Eastern to transfer cash from its estate to the pilot pension plans is a direct and blatant attempt to assert control over the assets of the estate for the benefit of the Rolleston Plaintiffs. Such a distribution will reduce the amount to be paid to creditors and have an adverse effect on the feasibility of any plan of reorganization.

Additionally, the Rolleston lawsuit interferes with this court's jurisdiction over essential core matters in the Eastern case, including claims issues and confirmation of a plan of reorganization.

Judgment in favor of Eastern enjoining the Rolleston lawsuit.

Concerned that debtors were taking advantage of the automatic stay provisions to the substantial detriment of some creditors, such as creditors whose claims were secured by an interest in a single real estate asset, in 1994 Congress provided specific relief from the automatic stay for such creditors. Debtors must either file a plan of reorganization that has a reasonable chance of being confirmed within a reasonable time or must be making monthly payments to each such secured creditor that are in an amount equal to interest at a current fair market rate on the value of the creditor's interest in the real estate.

The 1994 amendments also specifically provide that the automatic stay provisions are not applicable to actions to establish paternity, to establish or modify orders for alimony, support, or maintenance, or for the collection of alimony, maintenance, or support from property that is not the property of the bankruptcy estate.

Order of Relief

Once a bankruptcy petition has been filed, the first step is a court determination that relief should be ordered. If a voluntary petition is filed by the debtor, or if the debtor does not contest an involuntary petition, this step is automatic. If the debtor contests an involuntary petition, then a trial is held on the question of whether the court should order relief. The court orders relief only (1) if the debtor is generally not paying his debts as they become due, or (2) if within 120 days of the filing of the petition a custodian was appointed or took possession of the debtor's property. The court also appoints an interim trustee pending election of a trustee by the creditors.

Meeting of Creditors and Election of Trustee

The bankrupt person is required to file a list of her assets, liabilities, and creditors and a statement of her financial affairs. Then a meeting of the creditors is called by the court. Prior to the conclusion of the meeting of creditors, the U.S. Trustee is required to examine the debtor to make sure he is aware of: (1) the potential consequences of seeking a discharge in bankruptcy, including the effects on credit history; (2) the debtor's ability to file a petition under other chapters (such as 11, 12, or 13) of the bankruptcy act; (3) the effect of receiving a discharge of debts; and (4) the effect of reaffirming a debt (discussed later in this chapter).

The creditors may elect a creditors' committee. The creditors also elect a **trustee** who, if approved by the judge, takes over administration of the bankrupt's estate. The trustee represents the creditors in handling the estate. At the meeting, the creditors have a chance to ask the debtor questions about her assets, liabilities, and financial difficulties. These questions commonly focus on whether the debtor has concealed or improperly disposed of assets. (See Figure 1.)

Duties of the Trustee

The trustee takes possession of the debtor's property and has it appraised. The debtor must also turn over her records to the trustee. For a time, the trustee may operate the debtor's business. The trustee sets aside the items of property that a debtor is permitted to keep under state exemption statutes or federal law.

The trustee examines the claims filed by various creditors and objects to those that are improper in any way. The trustee separates the unsecured property from the secured and otherwise exempt property. He also sells the bankrupt's nonexempt property as soon as possible, consistent with the best interest of the creditors.

The trustee is required to keep an accurate account of all the property and money he receives and to promptly deposit moneys into the estate's accounts. At the final meeting of the creditors, the trustee presents a detailed statement of the administration of the bankruptcy estate.

Exemptions

Even in a liquidation proceeding, the bankrupt is generally not required to give up all of his property; he is permitted to **exempt** certain items of property. Under the new Bankruptcy Act, the debtor may choose to keep certain items or property either exempted by state law, or exempt under federal law unless state law specifically forbids use of the federal exemptions. However, any such property concealed or fraudulently transferred by the debtor may not be retained.

FIGURE   I

Order and Notice of Chapter 7 Bankruptcy Filing

B16A United States Bankruptcy Court for the District of Maryland	ORDER AND NOTICE OF CHAPTER 7 BANKRUPTCY FILING, MEETING OF CREDITORS, AND FIXING OF DATES (Individual or Joint Debtor No Asset Case)

A. GENERAL INFORMATION

Name of Debtor
  John B. Jones
  D/B/A THE BATH SHOP
	Address of Debtor
	  195 MAIN STREET
	  ANNAPOLIS MD. 21401	

	Date Filed 01/24/97	Case Number 9060300-SD	Soc. Sec. Nos./Tax ID Nos. 050-30-4701

Addressee:
  WICKER PRODUCTS, INC.
  2000 SMITH PIKE
  ALMA, MI 48030
	Address of the Clerk of the Bankruptcy Court
	  United States Bankruptcy Court
	  101 W. Lombard Street
	  Baltimore, MD 21201

Name and Address of Attorney for Debtor
  MARC A. BURNS
  215 WATER STREET,
  BALTIMORE MD 21202
	Name and Address of Trustee
	  BRUCE A. SMITH
	  136 S. CHARLES STREET,
	  BALTIMORE MD 21201

B. DATE, TIME AND LOCATION OF MEETING OF CREDITORS
February 28, 1997, 09:15 A.M., U.S. Trustee, Fallon Federal Bldg., Rm. G-13, 31 Hopkins Plaza, Baltimore, MD 21201

C. DISCHARGE OF DEBTS
Deadline to File a Complaint Objecting to the Discharge of the Debtor or Dischargeability of a Debt: April 30, 1997

D. BANKRUPTCY INFORMATION

THERE APPEAR TO BE NO ASSETS AT THIS TIME FROM WHICH PAYMENT MAY BE MADE TO CREDITORS. DO NOT FILE A PROOF OF CLAIM UNTIL YOU RECEIVE NOTICE TO DO SO.

FILING OF A BANKRUPTCY CASE. A bankruptcy petition has been filed in this court for the person or persons named above as the debtor, and an order for relief has been entered. You will not receive notice of all documents filed in this case. All documents which are filed with the court, including lists of the debtor's property and debts, are available for inspection at the office of the clerk of the bankruptcy court.

CREDITORS MAY NOT TAKE CERTAIN ACTIONS. Anyone to whom the debtor owes money or property is a creditor. Under the bankruptcy law, the debtor is granted certain protection against creditors. Common examples of prohibited actions are contacting the debtor to demand repayment, taking action against the debtor to collect money owed to creditors or to take property of the debtor, except as specifically permitted by the bankruptcy law, and starting or continuing foreclosure actions, repossessions, or wage deductions. If unauthorized actions are taken by a creditor against a debtor, the court may punish that creditor. A creditor who is considering taking action against the debtor or the property of the debtor should review 11 U.S.C. § 362 and may wish to seek legal advice. The staff of the clerk's office is not permitted to give legal advice to anyone.

MEETING OF CREDITORS. The debtor (both husband and wife in a joint case) shall appear at the meeting of creditors at the date and place set forth above in box 'B' for the purpose of being examined under oath. ATTENDANCE BY CREDITORS AT THE MEETING IS WELCOMED, BUT NOT REQUIRED. At the meeting the creditors may elect a trustee as permitted by law, elect a committee of creditors, examine the debtor, and transact such other business as may properly come before the meeting. The meeting may be continued or adjourned from time to time without further written notice to the creditors.

LIQUIDATION OF THE DEBTOR'S PROPERTY. A trustee has been appointed in this case to collect the debtor's property, if any, and turn it into money. At this time, however, it appears from the schedules of the debtor that there are no assets from which any dividend can be paid to creditors. If at a later date it appears that there are assets from which a dividend may be paid, creditors will be notified and given an opportunity to file claims.

EXEMPT PROPERTY. Under state and federal law, the debtor is permitted to keep certain money or property as exempt. If a creditor believes that an exemption of money or property is not authorized by law, the creditor may file an objection. Any objection must be filed no later than 30 days after the conclusion of the meeting of creditors.

DISCHARGE OF DEBTS. The debtor is seeking a discharge of debts. A discharge means that certain debts are made unenforceable. Creditors whose claims against the debtor are discharged may never take action to collect the discharged debts. If a creditor believes the debtor should not receive a discharge under 11 U.S.C. § 727 or a specific debt should not be discharged under 11 U.S.C. § 523(c) for some valid reason specified in the bankruptcy law, the creditor must take action to challenge the discharge. The deadline for challenging a discharge is set forth above in box 'C.' Creditors considering taking such action may wish to seek legal advice.

DO NOT FILE A PROOF OF CLAIM UNLESS YOU RECEIVE A COURT NOTICE TO DO SO

For the Court:	
January 31, 1997	Michael Kostishak
Date	Clerk of the Bankruptcy Court

The debtor must elect to use *either* the set of exemptions provided by the state or the set provided by the federal bankruptcy law; she may not pick and choose between them. A husband and wife involved in bankruptcy proceedings must both elect either the federal or the state exemptions; where they cannot agree, the federal exemptions are deemed elected.

The **exemptions** permit the bankrupt person to retain a minimum amount of the assets considered necessary to life and to his ability to continue to earn a living. They are part of the fresh start philosophy that is one of the purposes of the Bankruptcy Act. The general effect of the federal exemptions is to make a minimum exemption available to debtors in all states. States that wish to be more generous to debtors can provide more liberal exemptions.

The specific items that are exempt under state statutes vary from state to state. Some states provide fairly liberal exemptions and are considered "debtors havens." For example, in Florida none of the equity in the debtor's homestead can be used to pay off unsecured creditors, thus allowing even relatively well-off individuals to shield significant assets from creditors. Items that are commonly made exempt from sale to pay debts owed creditors include the family Bible; tools or books of the trade; life insurance policies; health aids, such as wheelchairs and hearing aids; personal and household goods; and jewelry, furniture, and motor vehicles worth up to a certain amount.

The case that follows, *In re Griffin,* illustrates a claim by a debtor for an exemption under a state statute.

IN RE GRIFFIN   139 B.R. 415 (Bankr. W.D. Tex. 1992)

 roy Griffin was a debtor in a Chapter 7 bankruptcy proceeding. He claimed that his 1985 Hobie Magnum sailboat was exempt from his creditors under a Texas statute that provided an exemption for "athletic and sporting" equipment. A creditor objected to the claim of exemption. ∞

King, Bankruptcy Judge   The question in this case is whether a sailboat may be claimed as exempt under the "athletic and sporting equipment" category of section 42,002(a)(8) of the Texas Property Code. This Court holds that a sailboat is not included within the Texas exemption for athletic and sporting equipment, and, therefore, the objection to the claim of exemption is sustained and the exemption is denied.

The exemption statutes in Texas were amended in May, 1991. Prior to the amendments, certain items of personal property were not exempt unless the property was reasonably necessary for the family or single adult. After the amendments, however, athletic and sporting equipment were no longer required to be reasonably necessary for the family to qualify as exempt property.

The most extensive discussion of the athletic and sporting equipment exemption is found in an unreported opinion by Judge Clark, *In re Schwarzbach,* in which he determined that a 16-foot bass boat was not exempt as athletic or sporting equipment. *Schwarzbach* agreed with the analysis of an earlier

case that "athletic and sporting equipment" is limited to small items for personal use. *Schwarzbach* also compared the language of two different exemptions and concluded that the Legislature contemplated an exemption for a boat only if the boat is used in a trade or profession. At the time *Schwarzbach* was decided, section 42.002(3)(B) allowed an exemption for "tools, equipment, books, and apparatus, including a boat, used in a trade or profession." Today, that section includes "boats and motor vehicles." In contrast, the current 42.002(a)(8) exemption for athletic and sporting equipment expressly includes bicycles, but not boats.

The purpose of exemption laws is to work a balance between protecting the debtor from destitution and allowing creditors to obtain payment on legitimate debts from the debtor's assets. This court agrees with *Schwarzbach* in holding that "athletic and sporting equipment" under the Texas exemption statute should be limited to small items for individual use. Allowing exemption of a sailboat or ski boat as "athletic and sporting equipment" would permit debtors to take undue advantage of the exemption laws and shield assets which are not necessary to a fresh start from the just claims of creditors. As so aptly stated by *In re Henricksen,*

"Bankruptcy is intended to provide debtors with a fresh start, not with a fine finish."

Claim of exemption denied.

Eleven categories of property are exempt under the federal exemptions, which the debtor may elect in lieu of the state exemptions. The federal exemptions include:

1. The debtor's interest (not to exceed $15,000 in value) in real or personal property that the debtor or a dependent of the debtor uses as a residence.

2. The debtor's interest (not to exceed $2,400 in value) in one motor vehicle.

3. The debtor's interest (not to exceed $400 in value for any particular item) up to a total of $8,000 in household furnishings, household goods, wearing apparel, appliances, books, animals, crops, or musical instruments that are held primarily for the personal, family, or household use of the debtor or a dependent of the debtor.

4. The debtor's aggregate interest (not to exceed $1,000 in value) in jewelry held primarily for the personal, family, or household use of the debtor or a dependent of the debtor.

5. $800 in value of any other property of the debtor's choosing, plus up to $7,500 of any unused homestead exemption.

6. The debtor's aggregate interest (not to exceed $1,500 in value) in any implements, professional books, or tools of the trade.

7. Life insurance contracts.

8. Interest up to $8,000 in specified kinds of dividends or interest in certain kinds of life insurance policies.

9. Professionally prescribed health aids.

10. Social security, disability, alimony, and other benefits reasonably necessary for the support of the debtor or his dependents.

11. The debtor's right to receive certain insurance and liability payments.

The term **value** means "fair market value as of the date of the filing of the petition." In determining the debtor's interest in property, the amount of any liens against the property must be deducted.

Avoidance of Liens

The debtor is also permitted to **void** certain liens against exempt properties that impair her exemptions. Liens that can be voided on this basis are judicial liens or nonpossessionary, nonpurchase money security interests in: (1) household furnishings, household goods, wearing apparel, appliances, books, animals, crops, musical instruments, or jewelry that are held primarily for the personal, family, or household use of the debtor or a dependent of the debtor; (2) implements, professional books, or tools of the trade of the debtor or a dependent of the debtor; and (3) professionally prescribed health aids for the debtor or a dependent of the debtor. Debtors are also permitted to **redeem** exempt personal property from secured creditors by paying them the value of the collateral. Then, the creditor is an unsecured creditor as to any remaining debt owed by the debtor.

Preferential Payments

A major purpose of the Bankruptcy Act is to ensure equal treatment for the creditors of an insolvent debtor. The act also seeks to prevent an insolvent debtor from distributing her assets to a few favored creditors to the detriment of the other creditors. Thus, the trustee has the right to recover for the benefit of the bankruptcy estate all **preferential payments** in excess of $600 made by the bankrupt person.[2] A preferential payment is a payment made by an insolvent debtor within 90 days before the filing of the bankruptcy petition that enables a

---

[2]In the case of an individual debtor whose debts are primarily consumer debts, the trustee is not entitled to avoid preferences unless the aggregate value of the property is $600 or more.

creditor to obtain a greater percentage of a preexisting debt than other similar creditors of the debtor. It is irrelevant whether the creditor knew that the debtor was insolvent. A debtor is presumed to have been insolvent on and during the 90 days immediately preceding the filing of a petition.

For example, Fredericks has $1,000 in cash and no other assets. He owes $650 to his friend Roberts, $1,500 to a credit union, and $2,000 to a finance company. If Fredericks pays $650 to Roberts and then files for bankruptcy, he has made a preferential payment to Roberts. Roberts has had his debt paid in full, whereas only $350 is left to satisfy the $3,500 owed to the credit union and finance company. They stand to recover only 10 cents on each dollar that Fredericks owes them. The trustee has the right to get the $650 back from Roberts.

If the favored creditor is an insider—a relative of an individual debtor or an officer, director, or related party of a company—who had reasonable cause to believe the debtor was insolvent at the time the transfer was made, then a preferential payment made to that creditor up to one year prior to the filing of the petition can be recovered by the trustee.

The 1994 amendments to the Bankruptcy Act provided that the trustee may not recover as preferential payments any bona fide payments of debts to a spouse, former spouse, or child of the debtor for alimony, maintenance, or support pursuant to a separation agreement, divorce decree, or other court order.

Preferential Liens

Preferential liens are treated in a similar manner. A creditor might try to obtain an advantage over other creditors by obtaining a lien on the debtor's property to secure an existing debt. The creditor might seek to get the debtor's consent to a lien or to obtain a lien by legal process. Such liens are considered *preferential* and are invalid if they are obtained on property of an insolvent debtor within 90 days before the filing of a bankruptcy petition and if their purpose is to secure a preexisting debt. A preferential lien obtained by an insider (who had reasonable cause to believe the debtor was insolvent at the time the lien was obtained) up to one year prior to the filing of the bankruptcy petition can be avoided.

Transactions in the Ordinary Course of Business

The Bankruptcy Act provides several exceptions to the trustee's avoiding power that are designed to allow a debtor and his creditors to engage in ordinary business transactions. The exceptions include (1) transfers that are intended by the debtor and creditor to be a contemporaneous exchange for new value or (2) the creation of a security interest in new property where new value was given by the secured party to enable the debtor to obtain the property and where the new value was in fact used by the debtor to obtain the property.

For example, George Grocer is insolvent. He is permitted to purchase and pay cash for new inventory, such as produce or meat, without the payment being considered preferential. His assets have not been reduced. He has simply traded money for goods to be sold in his business. Similarly, he could buy a new display counter and give the seller a security interest in the counter until he has paid for it. This would not be considered a preferential lien. The seller of the counter has not gained an unfair advantage over other creditors, and Grocer's assets have not been reduced by the transaction. The unfair advantage comes where an existing creditor tries to take a lien or obtain a payment of more than his share of the debtor's assets. Then, the creditor has obtained a preference over other creditors, which is what the trustee is allowed to avoid.

The Bankruptcy Act also excepts transfers made in payment of a debt incurred in the ordinary course of the business or financial affairs of the debtor and the transferee made in the ordinary course of business or financial affairs of the debtor and the transferee and made according to ordinary business terms. The payment (transfer by the debtor) must be made not later than 45 days after the debt was incurred in the ordinary course of business. Thus, for example, a consumer could pay her monthly utility bills in a timely fashion without the creditor/utility being vulnerable to having the transfer of funds avoided by a trustee. The purpose of this exception is to leave undisturbed normal financial relations, and it is consistent with the general policy of the preference section of the Act to discourage *unusual action* by either a debtor or her creditors when the debtor is moving toward bankruptcy.

Exceptions to the trustee's avoidance power are also made for certain statutory liens, certain other perfected security interests, and cases filed by individual debtors whose debts are primarily consumer debts and the aggregate value of all property affected by the transfer is less than $600.

Fraudulent Transfers

If a debtor transfers property or incurs an obligation with *intent to hinder, delay, or defraud creditors,* the transfer is *voidable* by the trustee. Transfers of property for less than reasonable value are similarly voidable. Suppose Kasper is in financial difficulty. She "sells" her $15,000 car to her mother for $100 so that her creditors cannot claim it. Kasper did not receive fair consideration for this transfer. The transfer could be declared void by a trustee if it was made within a year before the filing of a bankruptcy petition against Kasper. The provisions of law concerning **fraudulent transfers** are designed to prevent a debtor from concealing or disposing of his property in fraud of creditors. Such transfers may also subject the debtor to criminal penalties and prevent discharge of the debtor's unpaid liabilities.[3]

Claims

If creditors wish to participate in the estate of a bankrupt debtor, they must file a **proof of claim** in the estate within a certain time, usually six months after the first meeting of creditors. Only unsecured creditors are required to file proofs of claims. However, a secured creditor whose secured claim exceeds the value of the collateral is an unsecured creditor to the extent of the deficiency. That creditor must file a proof of claim to support the recovery of the deficiency.

Allowable Claims

The fact that a proof of claim is filed does not ensure that a creditor can participate in the distribution of the assets of the bankruptcy estate. The claim

---

[3]Bulk sales of a debtor's materials, supplies, merchandise, or other inventory of the business in bulk and not in the ordinary course of business have the potential to defraud creditors. See Chapter 19, Formation and Terms of Sales Contracts, page 366 for a discussion of Article 6: Bulk Transfers, and the rights it provides to creditors.

must also be allowed. If the trustee has a valid defense to the claim, he can use the defense to disallow or reduce it. For example, if the claim is based on goods sold to the debtor and the seller breached a warranty, the trustee can assert the breach as a defense. All of the defenses available to the bankrupt person are available to the trustee.

Secured Claims

The trustee must also determine whether a creditor has a lien or secured interest to secure an allowable claim. If the debtor's property is subject to a secured claim of a creditor, that creditor has first claim to it. The property is available to satisfy claims of other creditors only to the extent that its value exceeds the amount of the debt secured.

Priority Claims

The Bankruptcy Act declares certain claims to have **priority** over other claims. The nine classes of priority claims are:

1. Expenses and fees incurred in administering the bankruptcy estate.
2. Unsecured claims in involuntary cases that arise in the ordinary course of the debtor's business after the filing of the petition but before the appointment of a trustee or the order of relief.
3. Unsecured claims of up to $4,000 per individual (including vacation, severance, and sick pay) for employees' wages earned within 90 days before the petition was filed.
4. Contributions to employee benefit plans up to $4,000 per person (moreover, the claim for wages plus pension contribution is limited to $4,000 per person).
5. Unsecured claims (*a*) for grain or the proceeds of grain against a debtor who owns or operates a grain storage facility or (*b*) up to $4,000 by a U.S. fisherman against a debtor who operates a fish produce storage or processing facility and who has acquired fish or fish produce from the fisherman.
6. Claims of up to $1,800 each by individuals for deposits made in connection with the purchase, lease, or rental of property or the purchase of

goods or services for personal use that were not delivered or provided.

7. Allowed for claims for debts to a spouse, former spouse, or child of the debtor for alimony to, maintenance for, or support of such spouse or child in connection with a separation agreement, divorce decree, or other court order (but not if assigned to someone else).

8. Certain taxes owed to governmental units.

9. Allowed unsecured claims based on a commitment by the debtor to a federal depositary institution regulatory agency (such as the FDIC).

Distribution of the Debtor's Estate

The priority claims are paid *after* secured creditors realize on their collateral but *before* other unsecured creditors are paid. Payments are made to the nine priority classes, in order, to the extent there are funds available. Each class must be paid in full before the next class is entitled to receive anything. To the extent there are insufficient funds to satisfy all the creditors within a class, each class member receives a pro rata share of his claim.

Unsecured creditors include: (1) those creditors who had not taken any collateral to secure the debt owed to them; (2) secured creditors to the extent their debt was not satisfied by the collateral they held; and (3) priority claimholders to the extent their claims exceed the limits set for priority claims.

Unsecured creditors, to the extent any funds are available for them, share in proportion to their claims. Unsecured creditors frequently receive little or nothing on their claims. Secured claims, trustee's fees, and other priority claims often consume a large part of the bankruptcy estate.

Special rules are set out in the Bankruptcy Act for distribution of the property of a bankrupt stockbroker or commodities broker.

DISCHARGE IN BANKRUPTCY

Discharge

A bankrupt person who has not been guilty of certain dishonest acts and has fulfilled his duties as a bankrupt is entitled to a **discharge in bankruptcy.**

A discharge relieves the bankrupt person of further responsibility for dischargeable debts and gives him a fresh start. A corporation or a partnership is not eligible for a discharge in bankruptcy. A bankrupt person may file a written waiver of his right to a discharge. An individual may not be granted a discharge if she obtained one within the previous six years.

Objections to Discharge

After the bankrupt has paid all of the required fees, the court gives creditors and others a chance to file objections to the discharge of the bankrupt. Objections may be filed by the trustee, a creditor, or the U.S. attorney. If objections are filed, the court holds a hearing to listen to them. At the hearing, the court must determine whether the bankrupt person has committed any act that is a bar to discharge. If the bankrupt has not committed such an act, the court grants the discharge. If the bankrupt has committed an act that is a bar to discharge, the discharge is denied. The discharge is also denied if the bankrupt fails to appear at the hearing on objections or if he refused earlier to submit to the questioning of the creditors.

Acts That Bar Discharge

Discharges in bankruptcy are intended for honest debtors. Therefore, the following acts bar a debtor from being discharged: (1) the unjustified falsifying, concealing, or destroying of records; (2) making false statements, presenting false claims, or withholding recorded information relating to the debtor's property or financial affairs; (3) transferring, removing, or concealing property in order to hinder, delay, or defraud creditors; (4) failing to account satisfactorily for any loss or deficiency of assets; and (5) failing to obey court orders or to answer questions approved by the court.

The *In Re Woodfield* case, which follows, illustrates the attempt of some debtors in anticipation of bankruptcy to put some of their assets beyond the reach of their creditors and the effort of a creditor to avoid the transfer as fraudulent and to prevent the debtors' discharge in bankruptcy.

Distribution of Debtor's Estate

Secured Creditors

Secured creditors proceed directly against the collateral. If debt is fully satisfied, they have no further interest; if debt is only partially satisfied, they are treated as general creditors for the balance.

Debtor's Estate Is Liquidated and Distributed

↓

Priority Creditors (9 classes)

*Distribution is made to 9 classes of priority claims in order.
*Each class must be fully paid before next class receives anything.
*If funds not sufficient to satisfy everyone in a class, then each member of the class receives same proportion of claim.

1. Costs and expenses of administration.

2. If involuntary proceeding, expenses incurred in the ordinary course of business after petition filed but before appointment of trustee.

3. Claims for wages, salaries, and commissions earned within 90 days of petition; limited to $4,000 per person.

4. Contributions to employee benefit plans arising out of services performed within 180 days of petition; limit of $4,000 (including claims for wages, salaries, and commissions) per person.

5. Unsecured claims *(a)* for grain or the proceeds of grain against a debtor who owns or operates a grain storage facility or *(b)* up to $4,000 by a U.S. fisherman against a debtor who operates a fish produce or processing facility and who has acquired fish or fish produce from the fisherman.

6. Claims of individuals, up to $1,800 per person, for deposits made on consumer goods or services that were not received.

7. Allowed-for claims for debts to a spouse, former spouse, or child of the debtor for alimony to, maintenance for, or support of such spouse or child in connection with a separation agreement, divorce decree, or other court order (if not assigned to someone else).

8. Government claims for certain taxes.

9. Allowed unsecured claims based on a commitment by the debtor to a federal depository institution regulatory agency.

↓

General Creditors

If funds are not sufficient to satisfy all general creditors, then they each receive the same proportion of their claims.

1. General unsecured creditors.
2. Secured creditors for the portion of their debt that was not satisfied by collateral.
3. Priority creditors for amounts beyond priority limits.

↓

Debtor

Debtor receives any remaining funds.

Blair and Marie Woodfield and Parley and Deanna Pearce, as partners, operated two "Wendy's Famous Hamburgers" restaurants in Walla Walla, Washington, and LaGrande, Oregon, pursuant to a franchise from Wendy's International, Inc. On March 10, 1989, the Woodfields and Pearces filed petitions for bankruptcy under Chapter 7. Within 10 days prior to the filing, the Woodfields and Pearces formed a new corporation, Quality Foods, Inc. (QFI), in which they each held a 50 percent interest. They then transferred to this corporation the franchise operating rights to the two Wendy's Restaurants; the equipment and fixtures used in the operation of those restaurants valued at $40,000; and inventory and restaurant supplies valued at $11,000. They gave their creditors a "Notice of Bulk Transfer" of these transactions. The Woodfields and Pearces received the stock of QFI in exchange for the assets. Apart from this exchange, Woodfield transferred $10,100 in cash and Pearce transferred $6,954 in cash to QFI. These transfers also occurred within 10 days before the bankruptcy filing.

At the creditors' meeting on April 25, the trustee in bankruptcy filed a "no assets report." Having received a forbearance agreement from Wendy's, the Woodfields and the Pearces continued to operate the two restaurants. On July 15 they agreed to dissolve QFI; the Woodfields acquired sole ownership of Wendy's in Walla Walla and the Pearces acquired sole ownership of Wendy's in LaGrande.

On June 26, 1989, an unsecured creditor, Emmett Valley Associates (EVA), objected to the proposed discharge of the Pearces and Woodfields, stating its belief that they had "fraudulently misrepresented the true value of their assets" and had transferred the operation of the two Wendy's to a new corporation in recognition of a value in the franchises in excess of what they had disclosed. EVA moved for a turnover of certain properties of the Woodfields and the Pearces and the voidance of the transfers to QFI.

In August 1989, the trustee formally moved to abandon the assets of the two Wendy's. The bankruptcy court approved the abandonment. In an opinion essentially prepared by the attorney for the debtors, it stated that the transfer of the $17,000 was "necessary to meet payroll due in the next few days and cover checks already written on the partnership debts relative to the restaurant operations." It also concluded that the debtors had no fraudulent intent in making the transfers and neglecting to list them on their state of affairs and that no one had been hindered or misled by them. The district court affirmed, and EVA appealed. ∞

Noonan, Circuit Judge   EVA argues that the Debtors intended to hinder or defraud their creditors in their transfer of cash to QFI. It urges the court to refuse to discharge the Debtors' obligations under 11 U.S.C. section 727(a)(2).

To deny a discharge under this section, the court must find that the Debtors harbored actual intent to hinder, delay or defraud a creditor or officer of the estate. We may infer this intent from the circumstances surrounding the transaction. Certain "badges of fraud" strongly suggest that a transaction's purpose is to defraud creditors unless some other convincing explanation appears. These factors, not all of which need be present, include: (1) a close relationship between the transferor and the transferee; (2) that the transfer was in anticipation of a pending suit; (3) that the transferor Debtor was insolvent or in poor financial condition at the time; (4) that all or substantially all of the Debtor's property was transferred; (5) that the transfer so com-

pletely depleted the Debtor's assets that the creditor has been hindered or delayed in recovering any part of the judgment; and (6) that the Debtor received inadequate compensation for the transfer.

The transaction here carried many of these badges of fraud. The relationship between the Debtors and the corporation could not have been closer; the Debtors created and operated the transferee corporation. The transfer was admittedly made in anticipation of the bankruptcy filing. The partnership was admittedly in poor financial condition at the time, having defaulted on several obligations. Substantially all of the partnership's property relating to the Wendy's franchises was transferred leaving nothing to satisfy and judgments; hence the trustee abandoned claims on the estate.

More than a dry checklist of badges of fraud demonstrates the Debtors' intent, however. The Debtors concededly were trying to delay or prevent seizure of the assets. They omitted the transfers from their statement of affairs in bankruptcy. They offer a justification for the transfer of cash that does not fit the facts, as explained below. They performed a second transfer, in which the QFI stock, which supposedly replaced the $17,000 in the estate, was rendered worthless. The net effect of the scheme was to remove $17,000 from the hands of the creditors and place it in the hands of the Debtors beyond the apparent reach of the creditors, who were thereby hindered and defrauded.

Woodfield and Pearce contend that the cash was transferred to pay wages that they owed; since they believed that the wage claimants would have had priority over general creditors, they argue, there was no intent to hinder or defraud. In fact, however, both Debtors admitted that the funds were used for many purposes other than paying wages. Woodfield admitted that after the transfer the account containing the $10,000 paid for advertising, a philanthropic donation, food, utilities, office supplies, and storage rental.

Pearce admitted that the $6,954 was what happened to be in the partnership account when the account was turned over to QFI. Several checks from that account also paid for non-payroll items. Postpetition restaurant revenues were commingled with the transferred monies.

All of this suggests that a random amount of cash, unconnected to the amount expected to be paid out in back wages, was put into a general-purpose account and used for general purposes, and no attempt was made to ensure that the cash was used only for wage claims. The bankruptcy court clearly erred in holding that the cash transfers were necessary to pay wages and clearly erred in holding that the Debtors' intent was not fraudulent. The Debtors intended to put the cash beyond the creditors' reach.

Judgment in favor of Debtors reversed.

Nondischargeable Debts

Certain debts are not affected by the discharge of a bankrupt debtor. The Bankruptcy Act provides that a discharge in bankruptcy releases a debtor from all provable debts except those that:

1. Are due as a tax or fine to the United States or any state or local unit of government.
2. Result from liabilities for obtaining money by false pretenses or false representations.
3. Are due for willful or malicious injury to a person or his property.
4. Are due for alimony or child support.
5. Were created by the debtor's larceny or embezzlement or by the debtor's fraud while acting in a fiduciary capacity.
6. Are certain kinds of educational loans that became due within five years prior to the filing of the petition.
7. Were not scheduled in time for proof and allowance because the creditor holding the debt did not have notification of the proceeding even though the debtor was aware that he owed money to that creditor.
8. Secured claims in exempt assets.

The 1984 amendments established several additional grounds for nondischargeability relating to debts incurred in contemplation of bankruptcy—and the 1994 amendments made changes to them. Congress was concerned about debtors who ran up large expenditures on credit cards shortly before filing for bankruptcy relief. Cash advances in excess of $1,500 obtained by use of a credit card and a revolving line of credit at a credit union obtained within 60 days of filing a bankruptcy petition are presumed to be nondischargeable. Similarly, a debtor's purchase of more than $1,500 in *luxury goods or services* on credit from a single creditor within 60 days of filing a petition is presumed to be nondischargeable.

There are also exceptions from dischargeability for debts: (1) reflected in a judgment arising out of a debtor's operation of a motor vehicle while legally intoxicated; (2) incurred to pay a tax to the United States that would be nondischargeable; and (3) incurred by a debtor in the course of a separation agreement or divorce decree *unless* the debtor does not have the ability to pay the debt from income or property not reasonably necessary for the support of the debtor or a dependant or discharging the debt would result in a benefit to the debtor that outweighs the detrimental consequences to a spouse, former spouse, or child of the debtor.

All of these nondischargeable debts are provable debts. The creditor who owns these claims can participate in the distribution of the bankrupt's estate. However, the creditor has an additional advantage: His right to recover the unpaid balance is not cut off by the bankrupt's discharge. All other provable debts are dischargeable; that is, the right to recover them is cut off by the bankrupt's discharge.

Reaffirmation Agreements

Sometimes, creditors put pressure on debtors to reaffirm, or to agree to pay, debts that have been discharged in bankruptcy. When the 1978 amendments to the Bankruptcy Act were under consideration, some individuals urged Congress to prohibit such agreements. They argued that reaffirmation agreements were inconsistent with the fresh start philosophy of the Bankruptcy Act. Congress did not agree to a total prohibition; instead, it set up a rather elaborate procedure for a creditor to go through to get a debt reaffirmed. Essentially, the agreement must be made *before* the discharge is granted and must contain a clear statement that advises the debtor (1) that the agreement may be rescinded at any time prior to discharge or within 60 days after filing with the court and (2) the agreement contains a clear and conspicuous statement advising the debtor that the reaffirmation is not required by the bankruptcy law and any other law or agreement. The agreement must be filed with the court accompanied by a statement from the debtor's attorney that (1) it represents a voluntary agreement by the debtor, (2) that it does not impose an undue hardship on the debtor, and (3) the attorney fully apprised the debtor of the legal affect and consequences of the agreement and of any default under such an agreement. Court approval is not required for the reaffirmation of loans secured by real property. Also, a debtor may voluntarily pay any dischargeable obligation without entering into a reaffirmation agreement.

Dismissal for Substantial Abuse

As it considered the 1984 amendments to the Bankruptcy Act, Congress was concerned that too many individuals with an ability to pay their debts over time pursuant to a Chapter 13 plan were filing petitions to obtain Chapter 7 discharges of liability. The consumer finance industry urged Congress to preclude Chapter 7 petitions where a debtor had the prospect of future disposable income to satisfy more than 50 percent of his prepetition unsecured debts. Although Congress rejected this approach, it did authorize Bankruptcy Courts to dismiss cases that they determined were a **substantial abuse** of the bankruptcy process. This provision appears to cover situations where a debtor has acted in bad faith or where she has the present or future ability to pay a significant portion of her current debts. The case that follows, *In re Huckfeldt,* illustrates a situation where the court concluded that a petition in bankruptcy had been filed in bad faith.

IN RE HUCKFELDT   39 F.3d 829 (8th Cir. 1994)

During their 12 years of marriage, Roger and Georgianne Huckfeldt accumulated over $250,000 in debts while Roger completed college, medical school, and six years of residency in surgery and while Georgianne completed college and law school. These debts included $166,000 in student loans to Huckfeldt and $47,000 jointly borrowed from Georgianne's parents. The Huckfeldts divorced on March 26, 1992. The divorce decree ordered Roger to pay his student loans, one-half of the debt to Georgianne's parents, and other enumerated debts totaling some $241,000. The decree also ordered Roger to hold Georgianne harmless for these debts but otherwise denied Georgianne's request for maintenance.

On June 4, 1992, six months before Roger would complete his residency in surgery, he filed a voluntary Chapter 7 petition, listing assets of $1,250 and liabilities of $546,857. After filing the petition, Roger accepted a fellowship at Oregon Health Sciences University, a one- or two-year position paying $45,000 per year, substantially less than the income he could likely earn during the pendency of his Chapter 7 proceeding. Following Roger's petition, creditors of the debts assigned to him in the divorce decree began pursuing Georgianne for repayment. She filed for bankruptcy protection in March 1993.

In September 1992, Georgianne and her parents filed a motion to dismiss Roger's Chapter 7 petition on the ground that it was filed in bad faith. They alleged that Roger had threatened to file for bankruptcy during the *divorce proceeding and had commenced the bankruptcy proceeding in defiance of the divorce decree for the purpose of shifting responsibility for assigned debts to Georgianne. They also alleged that Roger had deliberately taken steps to reduce his annual income to avoid payment of his debts through the Chapter 7 liquidation.*

After a hearing, the bankruptcy court granted the motion to dismiss the proceeding on the grounds it was filed in bad faith, finding, among other things, that Roger could be earning $110,000 to $120,000 after expenses. The district court affirmed the decision, and Roger appealed to the court of appeals. ∞

Loken, Circuit Judge After finding that Roger could be earning $110,000 to $120,000 per year, after all expenses except income tax, the bankruptcy court stated:

It is the purpose of the bankruptcy system to provide a fresh start for the honest but unfortunate debtor. It is not the purpose of the bankruptcy system to eliminate the obligations of a party who is capable of paying the same. The Court believes debtor filed this bankruptcy petition in bad faith and with the deliberate intention of unloading debt, particularly that to his spouse, which he could shortly begin to repay. Further this Court believes it was the intent of the debtor to leave his ex-spouse with all the debts and obligations incurred over the 12 years and force her into a bankruptcy situation also . . . Accordingly the court concludes that his case was filed in bad faith and concludes that good faith is a requirement for the filing of a bankruptcy petition no matter what the chapter.

Huckfeldt filed a Chapter 7 petition to frustrate the divorce court decree and to push his ex-wife into

bankruptcy. He then manipulated his immediate earnings to ensure the Chapter 7 proceeding would achieve these noneconomic motives. That conduct meets the standard for bad faith. Indeed, such conduct has long been considered unworthy of bankruptcy protection.

The petition in this case was not filed for the purpose of a just liquidation by composition with creditors but to defeat the wife from a right of possession in and to the real estate which was to be awarded to her under the divorce proceedings. This violates the purpose and intent of the statute and, as said by the Supreme Court of the United States, under that situation, the proceedings will be halted at the outset. Huckfeldt is not an "honest but unfortunate debtor" entitled to the equitable relief of a Chapter 7 liquidation.

Judgment against Roger Huckfeldt affirmed.

CHAPTER 11: REORGANIZATIONS

Reorganization Proceeding

Sometimes, creditors benefit more from the continuation of a bankrupt debtor's business than from the liquidation of the debtor's property. Chapter 11 of the Bankruptcy Act provides a proceeding whereby, under the supervision of the Bankruptcy Court, the debtor's financial affairs can be reorganized rather than liquidated. Chapter 11 proceedings are available to individuals and to virtually all business enterprises, including individual proprietorships, partnerships, and corporations (except banks, savings and loan associations, insurance companies, commodities brokers, and stockbrokers).

Petitions for reorganization proceedings can be filed voluntarily by the debtor or involuntarily by its creditors. Once a petition for a reorganization proceeding is filed and relief is ordered, the court usually appoints (1) a committee of creditors hold-

ing unsecured claims, (2) a committee of equity security holders (shareholders), and (3) a trustee. The trustee may be given the responsibility for running the debtor's business. He is also usually responsible for developing a plan for handling the various claims of creditors and the various interests of persons such as shareholders.

The reorganization plan is essentially a contract between a debtor and its creditors. This contract may involve recapitalizing a debtor corporation and/or giving creditors some equity, or shares, in the corporation in exchange for part or all of the debt owed to them. The plan must (1) divide the creditors into classes; (2) set forth how each creditor will be satisfied; (3) state which claims, or classes of claims, are impaired or adversely affected by the plan; and (4) provide the same treatment to each creditor in a particular class, unless the creditors in that class consent to different treatment.

The plan is then submitted to the creditors for approval. Approval generally requires that creditors holding two-thirds in amount and one-half in number of each class of claims impaired by the plan must accept it. Once approved, the plan goes before the court for confirmation. If the plan is confirmed, the debtor is responsible for carrying it out.

The case that follows, *Official Committee of Equity Security Holders v. Mabey,* shows that until a plan is confirmed, the bankruptcy court has no authority to distribute a portion of the bankruptcy assets to a portion of the unsecured creditors.

OFFICIAL COMMITTEE OF EQUALITY SECURITY HOLDERS v. MABEY   832 F.2d 299 (4th Cir. 1987)

*T**he A. H. Robins Company is a publicly held company that filed a voluntary petition for relief under Chapter 11 of the Bankruptcy Code. Robins sought refuge in Chapter 11 because of a multitude of civil actions filed against it by women who alleged they were injured by use of the Dalkon Shield intrauterine device that it manufactured and sold as a birth control device. Approximately 325,000 notices of claim against Robins were received by the Bankruptcy Court.*

In 1985, the court appointed the Official Committee of Equity Security Holders to represent the interest of Robins's public shareholders. In April 1987, Robins filed a proposed plan of reorganization but no action was taken on the proposed plan because of a merger proposal submitted by Rorer Group, Inc. Under this plan, Dalkon Shield claimants would be compensated out of a $1.75 billion fund, all other creditors would be paid in full, and Robins's stockholders would receive stock of the merged corporation. However, at the time of other critical activity in the bankruptcy proceeding, no revised plan incorporating the merger proposal had been filed or approved.

Earlier, in August 1986, the court had appointed Ralph Mabey as an examiner to evaluate and suggest proposed elements of a plan of reorganization. On Mabey's suggestion, a proposed order was put before the district court supervising the proceeding that would require Robins to establish a $15 million emergency treatment fund "for the purpose of assisting in providing tubal reconstructive surgery or in-vitro fertilization to eligible Dalkon Shield claimants." The purpose of the emergency fund was to assist those claimants who asserted that they had become infertile as a consequence of their use of the product. A program was proposed for administering the fund and for making the medical decisions required.

On May 21, 1987, the district court ordered that the emergency treatment fund be created, and the action was challenged by the committee representing the equity security holders. ∞

Chapman, Circuit Judge The May 21, 1987, order of the district court approving the Emergency Treatment Fund makes no mention of its authority to establish such a fund prior to the allowance of the claims of the women who would benefit from the fund, and prior to the confirmation of a plan of reorganization of Robins. In its order denying the Equity Committee's Motion for a Stay Pending Appeal of the May 21 order, the district court relied on the "expansive equity power" of the court to justify its action.

While one may understand and sympathize with the district court's concern for the Dalkon Shield claimants who may desire reconstructive surgery or in-vitro fertilization, the creation of the Emergency Treatment Fund at this stage of the Chapter 11 bankruptcy proceedings violates the clear language and intent of the Bankruptcy Code, and such action

may not be justified as an exercise of the court's equitable powers.

The Bankruptcy Code does not permit a distribution to unsecured creditors in a Chapter 11 proceeding except under and pursuant to a plan of reorganization that has been properly presented and approved. Sections 1122–1129 of the Bankruptcy Code set forth the required contents of the reorganization plan, the classification of claims, the requirements of disclosure of the contents of the plan, the method for accepting the plan, the hearing required on confirmation of the plan, and the requirements for confirmation. The clear language of these statutes does not authorize the payment in part or full, or the advance of monies to or for the benefit of unsecured claimants prior to the approval of the plan of reorganization. The creation of the Emergency Treatment Fund has no authority to support it in the Bankruptcy Code and violates the clear policy of Chapter 11 reorganizations by allowing piecemeal pre-confirmation payments to certain unsecured creditors. Such action also violates Bankruptcy Rule 3021 which allows distribution to creditors only after the allowance of claims and the confirmation of a plan.

Judgment reversed in favor of Official Committee of Equity Security Holders.

Use of Chapter 11

During the 1980s, attempts by a number of corporations to seek refuge in Chapter 11 as a means of escaping problems they were facing received considerable public attention. Some of the most visible cases involved efforts to obtain some protection against massive product liability claims and judgments for damages for breach of contract and to escape from collective bargaining agreements. Thus, for example, Johns-Manville Corporation filed under Chapter 11 because of the claims against it arising out of its production and sale of asbestos years earlier, while A. H. Robins Company, as illustrated in the preceding case, was concerned about a surfeit of claims arising out of its sale of the Dalkon Shield, an intrauterine birth control device. And, in 1987, Texaco, Inc., faced with a $10.3 billion judgment in favor of Pennzoil in a breach of contract action, filed a petition for reorganizational relief under Chapter 11. Companies such as LTV and Allegheny Industries sought changes in retirement and pension plans, and other companies such as Eastern Airlines sought refuge in Chapter 11 while embroiled in labor disputes.

As the 1990s began, a number of companies that were the subject of highly leveraged buyouts (LBOs) financed with so-called junk bonds, including a number of retailers, resorted to Chapter 11 to seek restructuring and relief from their creditors. Similarly, companies such as Pan Am and TWA that were hurt by economic slowdown and increase in fuel prices filed Chapter 11 petitions.

In recent years, Chapter 11 has been the subject of significant criticism and calls for its revision. Critics point out that many of the Chapter 11 cases are permitted to drag on for years, thus depleting the assets of the debtor through payments to trustees and lawyers involved in administration and diminishing the assets available to creditors.

Collective Bargaining Agreements

Collective bargaining contracts pose special problems. Prior to the 1984 amendments, there was concern that some companies would use Chapter 11 reorganizations as a vehicle to avoid executed collective bargaining agreements. The concern was heightened by the Supreme Court's 1984 decision in *NLRB v. Bildisco and Bildisco.* In that case, the Supreme Court held that a reorganizing debtor did not have to engage in collective bargaining before modifying or rejecting portions of a collective bargaining agreement and that such unilateral alterations by a debtor did not violate the National Labor Relations Act.

Congress then acted to try to prevent the misuse of bankruptcy proceedings for collective bargaining purposes. The act's 1984 amendments adopt a rigorous multistep process that must be compiled with in determining whether a labor contract can be rejected or modified as part of a reorganization. Among other things that must be done before a debtor or trustee can seek to avoid a collective bargaining agreement are the submission of a proposal to the employees' representative that details the "necessary" modifications to the collective bargaining agreement and ensures that "all creditors, the debtor and all affected parties are fairly treated." Then, before the bankruptcy court can authorize a rejection of the original collective bargaining agreement, it must review the proposal and find that (1) the employees' representative refused to accept it without good cause, and (2) the balance of equities clearly favors the rejection of the original collective bargaining agreement.

The following case, *In Re Maxwell Newspapers, Inc.,* shows the scrutiny that the court gives to the action of a debtor seeking to avoid a collective bargaining agreement.

IN RE MAXWELL NEWSPAPERS, INC.
NEW YORK TYPOGRAPHICAL UNION NO. 6 v. MAXWELL NEWSPAPERS, INC.
981 F.2d 85 (2nd Cir. 1992)

I *n July 1974, the New York Typographical Union No. 6 agreed in a collective bargaining agreement with the* Daily News, *a daily newspaper in New York City, to automation of the typesetting function in return for a guarantee of lifetime employment for its members then working at the newspaper. Between 1982 and 1992, the* Daily News *lost approximately $100 million and its owner, Maxwell Newspapers, Inc., had filed for relief under Chapter 11. Maxwell sought a buyer for the* Daily News *with sufficient resources to satisfy not only its creditors and employees but also to modernize its printing plant so that it could compete in the New York metropolitan market.*

In September 1992, Mortimer Zuckerman, through his affiliate New DN Company, entered negotiations with the Daily News *to buy its assets. These negotiations included a so-called stand-alone plan of reorganization that was conditioned on union support. One crucial component of the plan was concessions by Local No. 6 with respect to the July 1974 collective bargaining agreement that guaranteed the printers lifetime employment.*

On October 1, 1992, Maxwell, in tandem with Zuckerman, proposed to the union that the collective bargaining agreement be modified to eliminate: (1) any obligation of Maxwell to require the purchaser of the assets of the Daily News *to employ any member of the union, (2) any obligation of Maxwell to continue to employ any member of the union if Maxwell ceased publication or sold the* Daily News *pursuant to the bankruptcy proceeding, and (3) any obligation to arbitrate any controversy regarding these matters. Maxwell also provided documentation of the impact of the union's collective bargaining agreement on the financial stability of the* Daily News *and asserted that it had sought in vain prospective purchasers who would honor the labor agreement.*

The union made a counterproposal on October 14 in which it expressed a willingness to forgo the lifetime job guarantees. The union proposed a progressive reduction in the number of shifts worked conditioned on a cash buyout for each union member, three years' contribution to the pension and welfare funds, and an early retirement enhancement. Negotiations, including a series of counteroffers, continued until October 21, when Zuckerman, on the eve of a October 22 hearing in the bankruptcy case, made a final offer. He offered a reduced number of guaranteed shifts and jobs that fell to 15 jobs a year after a new printing plant was opened. The jobs would then be guaranteed for 13 years and he proposed to make a one-time contribution of $1 million to the pension and welfare funds.

The union rejected Zuckerman's final offer to modify the collective bargaining agreement, and negotiations broke down. Maxwell asked the bankruptcy court to reject the contract with Local No. 6 and to approve the proposed sale of the Daily News *to Zuckerman. The bankruptcy court granted the motions, and the union appealed. The district court reversed the bankruptcy court concerning the rejection of the collective bargaining agreement, holding that the union had "good cause" to reject Zuckerman's final offer.* ∞

Cardamone, Circuit Judge We first analyze whether the union in fact had "good cause" to refuse Zuckerman's final offer. Section 1113 of the Bankruptcy code controls the rejection of collective bargaining agreements in Chapter 11 proceedings. The statute puts in place "safeguards designed to insure that employers did not use Chapter 11 as medicine to rid themselves of corporate indigestion." Employers may only propose those "necessary modifications in the employees benefits and protections that are "necessary to permit" the effective reorganization of the debtor. A debtor may sell the assets of the business unencumbered by a collective bargaining agreement if that agreement has been rejected pursuant to section 1113. This statute requires unions to face those changed circumstances that occur when a company becomes insolvent, and it requires all affected parties to compromise in the face of financial hardship. At the same time, section 1113 also imposes requirements on the debtor to prevent it from using bankruptcy as a judicial hammer to break the union. Rejection of a collective bargaining agreement is permitted only if the debtor fulfills the requirements of section 1113(b)(1), the union fails to reject the debtor's proposal with good cause, and the balance of equities clearly favors rejection.

More importantly, the statute imposes the obligation on the parties to negotiate in good faith. This obligation is properly analyzed under section 1113(c)(2), which permits rejection of a labor agreement only when the union has rejected the debtor's proposal without good cause.

The district court reasoned that the statute covers not only the contents of an employer's proposed modification of a labor contract, but also how the offer is made. It ruled because the offer was made on October 21—on the eve of the bankruptcy hearing—and on a take-it-or-leave-it basis, the union had no meaningful opportunity to consider and make a counter-proposal.

What "good cause" means is difficult to answer in the abstract apart from the moorings of a given case. A more constructive and perhaps more answerable inquiry is why this term is in the statute. We think good cause serves as an incentive to the debtor trying to have its labor contract modified to propose in good faith only those changes necessary to its successful reorganization, while protecting it from the union's refusal to accept the changes without a good reason.

To that end, the entire thrust of section 1113 is to ensure that well-informed and good faith negotiations occur in the market place, not as part of the judicial process. Reorganization proceedings are designed to encourage such a negotiated voluntary modification. Knowing that it cannot turn down an employer's proposal without good cause gives the union an incentive to compromise on modifications of the collective bargaining agreement, so as to prevent its complete rejection. Because the employer has the burden of proving its proposals are necessary, the union is protected from an employer whose proposals may be offered in bad faith.

The bankruptcy court found that the debtor measures its workforce by calculating "full time equivalents" (FTEs) derived from dividing payroll expenses by five, which is the number of days in a week worked by a full-time employee. The bankruptcy judge further found that from September 1990 to August 1992, FTEs for debtor's employees declined as follows: for managers 58 percent, guild members 34 percent, drivers 46 percent, pressmen 47 percent, mailers 45 percent, paperhandlers 54 percent, machinists and electricians 21 percent, engravers and stereotypers 27 percent. In stark contrast, the Local 6 typographers workforce declined only 13 percent, and these employees are by far the highest hourly paid employees of the debtor. No other employees or unions suffered so small an FTE cut as Local No. 6.

Moreover, unsecured creditors, the court observed, are estimated to obtain only 13 to 18 cents on the dollar and the value of stockholders' equity is nearly worthless. Yet, the bankruptcy judge declared, the union did not offer an alternative that focused on the needs of its employer's organization, but instead adhered to its position that Local 6's excess employees had to be given an incentive to induce them to leave. Neither the debtor or purchaser could fund this demand.

We reverse the district court's ruling not only on the contents of the rejection order but also concerning the manner in which Zuckerman made his final offer to the union. First, Local No. 6 did not complain that it had too little time to respond to the employer's proposal on October 21. In addition, parties to collective bargaining agreements routinely negotiate for many hours under imperative deadlines. In that negotiating universe, 10 hours is ample time to consider and respond to a proposal. Consequently, the bankruptcy court correctly concluded that Local No. 6 rejected the employer's proposal without good cause.

Judgment reversed in favor of Maxwell Newspapers, Inc.

CHAPTER 12: FAMILY FARMS

Relief for Family Farmers

Historically, farmers have been accorded special treatment in the Bankruptcy Code. In the 1978 act, as in earlier versions, small farmers were exempted from involuntary proceedings. Thus, a small farmer who filed a voluntary Chapter 11 or 13 petition could not have the proceeding converted into a Chapter 7 liquidation over his objection so long as he complied with the act's requirements in a timely fashion. Additional protection was also accorded through the provision allowing states to opt out of the federal exemption scheme and to provide their own exemptions. A number of states used this flexibility to provide generous exemptions for farmers so they would be able to keep their tools and implements.

Despite these provisions, the serious stress on the agricultural sector in the mid-1980s led Congress in 1986 to further amend the Bankruptcy Act by adding a new Chapter 12 targeted to the financial problems of the family farm. During the 1970s and 1980s, farmland prices appreciated and many farmers borrowed heavily to expand their productive capacity, creating a large debt load in the agricultural sector. When land values subsequently dropped and excess production in the world kept farm product prices low, many farmers faced extreme financial difficulty.

Chapter 12 is modeled after Chapter 13, which is discussed next. It is available only for family farmers with regular income. To qualify, a farmer and spouse must have not less than 80 percent of their total noncontingent, liquidated debts arising out of their farming operations. The aggregate debt must be less than $1.5 million and at least 50 percent of an individual's or couple's income during the year preceding the filing of the petition must have come from the farming operation. A corporation or partnership can also qualify, provided that more than 50 percent of the stock or equity is held by one family or its relatives and they conduct the farming operation. Again, 80 percent of the debt must arise from the farming operation; the aggregate debt ceiling is $1.5 million.

The debtor is usually permitted to remain in possession to operate the farm. Although the debtor in possession has many of the rights of a Chapter 11 trustee, a trustee is appointed under Chapter 12 and the debtor is subject to his supervision. The trustee is permitted to sell unnecessary assets, including farmland and equipment, without the consent of secured creditors and before a plan is approved. However, the secured creditor's interest attaches to the proceeds of the sale.

The debtor is required to file a plan within 90 days of the filing of the Chapter 12 petition—although the bankruptcy court has the discretion to extend the time. A hearing is held on the proposed plan, and it can be confirmed over the objection of creditors. The debtor may release to any secured party the collateral that secures the claim to obtain confirmation without the acceptance by that creditor.

Unsecured creditors are required to receive at least liquidation value under the Chapter 12 plan. If an unsecured creditor or the trustee objects to the plan, the court may still confirm the plan despite the objection so long as it calls for full payment of the unsecured creditor's claim or it provides that the debtor's disposable income for the duration of the plan is applied to making payments on it. A debtor who fulfills his plan, or is excused from full performance because of subsequent hardship, is entitled to a discharge.

CHAPTER 13: CONSUMER DEBT ADJUSTMENTS

Relief for Individuals

Chapter 13 of the Bankruptcy Act, entitled Adjustments of Debts for Individuals, gives individuals who do not want to be declared bankrupt an opportunity to pay their debts in installments under the protection of a federal court. Under Chapter 13, the debtor has this opportunity free of such problems as garnishments and attachments of her property by creditors. Only individuals with regular incomes (including sole proprietors of businesses) who owe individually (or with their spouse) liquidated, unsecured debts of less than $250,000 and secured debts of less than $750,000 are eligible to file under Chapter 13. Under the pre-1978 Bankruptcy Act, Chapter 13 proceedings were known as "wage earner plans." The 1978 amendments expanded the coverage of these proceedings.

Procedure

Chapter 13 proceedings are initiated only by the voluntary petition of a debtor filed in the Bankruptcy Court. Creditors of the debtor may not file an involuntary petition for a Chapter 13 proceeding. The debtor in the petition states that he is insolvent or unable to pay his debts as they mature and that he desires to effect a composition or an extension, or both, out of future earnings or income. A **composition of debts** is an arrangement whereby the amount the person owes is reduced, whereas an **extension** provides the person a longer period of time in which to pay his debts. Commonly, the debtor files at the same time a list of his creditors as well as a list of his assets, liabilities, and executory contracts.

Following the filing of the petition, the court calls a meeting of creditors, at which time proofs of claims are received and allowed or disallowed. The debtor is examined, and she submits a plan of payment. The plan is submitted to the secured creditors for acceptance. If they accept the plan and if the court is satisfied that the plan is proposed in good faith, meets the legal requirements, and is in the interest of the creditors, the court approves the plan. The court then appoints a trustee to carry out the plan. The plan must provide for payments over three years or less, unless the court approves a longer period of up to five years.

No plan may be approved if the trustee or an unsecured creditor objects, unless the plan provides for the objecting creditor to be paid the present value of what he is owed or provides for the debtor to commit all of his projected disposable income for a three-year period to pay his creditors.

The case that follows, *In re Tucker,* deals with the issue of whether a proposed plan that provided for the commitment of all disposable income for a four-year period should be rejected because it unfairly discriminated against a class of unsecured creditors.

IN RE TUCKER 159 B.R. 325 (Bankr. D.Mont. 1993)

D aniel and Betty Tucker filed a voluntary Chapter 13 petition on March 10, 1993, listing personal property totaling $3,015. They claimed virtually all of their personal property as exempt, except for $180 worth of an automobile that exceeded the allowed exemption. Their real property was either encumbered or exempt, leaving little available for distribution to unsecured creditors in the event of liquidation under Chapter 7. They also listed unsecured claims in the amount of $14,208, of which $4,183 were claims for student loans. The remainder of claims were for services and purchases, all of which would be dischargeable.

In August 1993, the Tuckers filed a Chapter 13 plan that provided for monthly payments in the amount of $115, which corresponded to the difference between their current income and expenditures as shown on the schedules they filed with their petition. The plan provided for payment in full of the student loan debts over a 48-month period and 29 percent of the claims to the other unsecured creditors. The trustee, relying on objections from unsecured creditors, filed an objection to the plan on the grounds that it discriminated unfairly against a class of unsecured claims. ∞

Peterson, Bankruptcy Judge At issue is whether the Plan unfairly discriminates against the unsecured creditors in violation of Bankruptcy Code section 1322(b)(1) by paying nondischargeable student loan debts in full while only paying a 29 percent dividend on the other secured claims. The Tuckers argue that the discrimination in the Plan is fair because it allows them to pay the student loans in full, which fulfills the intent of Congress in making student loans nondischargeable; the Plan pays 29 percent to the unsecured creditors where they would receive virtually nothing if the case were in Chapter 7; and finally, it gives the Tuckers a "fresh start."

In determining whether a Plan discriminates unfairly against a class of unsecured claims, courts have developed a four-part test: (1) whether the discrimination has a reasonable basis; (2) whether the Debtor can carry out a Plan without discrimination; (3) whether the discrimination is proposed in good faith; and (4) whether the degree of discrimi-

nation is directly related to the basis or rationale for the discrimination.

The court in *In re Smallberger* (Bankr. D. Or. 1993) found discrimination in favor of student loans unfair and refused to allow separate classification simply on the basis that they were nondischargeable or in the interests of the debtor's "fresh start." The court in *In re Tucker* (Bankr. N.D. Ohio 1992) likewise found unfair discrimination in a plan which proposed paying 100 percent of student loans over 48 months while paying the unsecured claims 5 percent. The court deemed repayment of nondischargeable student loans to be the debtor's problem "which he cannot foist off on his other unsecured creditors."

Even the court in *Smallberger* notes that a "debtor might accomplish the result sought here by filing a Chapter 7 case and then a Chapter 13 case to deal with the nondischargeable obligations." This focuses the inquiry on whether the discrimination is indeed "unfair." Debtors in Chapter 13 have the unwaivable right to convert to Chapter 7 at any time. The parties agree that if the Debtors converted this case to Chapter 7, all of the unsecured claims would get virtually nothing after administrative expenses and their claims would be discharged with the exception of the student loan debts. The student loan debts, while not discharged, would be paid voluntarily by the Debtors from post-petition income in Chapter 7 as they would be under the proposed Chapter 13 Plan. By preventing the discrimination in favor of nondischargeable student loans, the courts in *Smallberger* and *Tucker* encourage debtors to utilize Chapter 7 instead of Chapter 13, despite Congressional intent favoring Chapter 13.

This court, looking at the facts on a case-by-case basis, deems a liquidation analysis highly significant. If this case is converted to a Chapter 7 case, the unsecured creditors will receive nothing and have their claims discharged. If the Plan is confirmed, they will receive 29 percent of their claims. The fairer treatment for the creditors is clearly the 29 percent dividend in Chapter 13 which Congress encourages Debtors to use in lieu of Chapter 7. The creditors who filed the rejections of the proposed Plan cannot hope to thereby force a larger dividend upon these Debtors (the Tuckers), who have nothing to lose by converting to Chapter 7, except all the unsecured claims which are not student loan debts.

Turning to the four-part test, I first find that the discrimination has a reasonable basis, i.e. that it provides for the payment in full of nondischargeable student loans. Second, I find that the Debtor cannot carry out a Plan without the discrimination. The Debtors already have extended the Plan period to four years, longer than the three year period of Bankruptcy Code section 1322(c). If the discrimination is not allowed the Plan payments would be completed without the student loans paid in full, thereby leaving the Debtors saddled with debt after four years under a Plan and defeating their "fresh start."

Third, I find that the discrimination is proposed in good faith. There is nothing to suggest that these Debtors proposed the discrimination in bad faith. Fourth, I find the degree of discrimination is directly related to the basis or rationale for the discrimination. They commit their disposable income for four years to the Plan, thereby providing a 29 percent dividend for creditors who would otherwise be left out in the cold in Chapter 7. The Plan pays in full a nondischargeable student loan and provides the Debtors with a "fresh start" at the end of 48 months free from all debts.

Objections to confirmation overruled.

Under the 1984 amendments, a Chapter 13 debtor must begin making the installment payments proposed in her plan within 30 days after the plan is filed. The interim payments must continue to be made until the plan is confirmed or denied. If the plan is denied, the money, less any administrative expenses, is returned to the debtor by the trustee. The interim payments give the trustee an opportunity to observe the debtor's performance and thus to be in a better position to make a recommendation about whether the plan should be approved.

Once approved, a plan may be subsequently modified on petition of a debtor or a creditor where there is a material change in the debtor's circumstances.

Suppose Curtis Brown has a monthly take-home pay of $1,000 and a few assets. He owes $1,500 to the credit union, borrowed for the purchase of furniture; he is supposed to repay the credit union $75 per month. He owes $1,800 to the finance company on the purchase of a used car; he is supposed to repay the company $90 a month. He has also run up charges of $1,200 on a MasterCard account, primarily for emergency repairs to his car; he must pay $60 per month to MasterCard. His rent is $350 per month, and food and other living expenses run him another $425 per month. Curtis was laid off from his job for a month and fell behind on his payments to his creditors. He then filed a Chapter 13 petition. In his plan, he might, for example, offer to repay the credit union $50 a month, the finance company $60 a month, and MasterCard $40 a month—with the payments spread over three years rather than the shorter time for which they are currently scheduled.

Comparison of Major Forms of Bankruptcy Proceedings

PURPOSE	CHAPTER 7 LIQUIDATION	CHAPTER 11 REORGANIZATION	CHAPTER 12 ADJUSTMENTS OF DEBTS	CHAPTER 13 ADJUSTMENTS OF DEBTS
Eligible Debtors	Individuals, partnerships, and corporations *except* municipal corporations, railroads, insurance companies, banks, and savings and loan associations. Farmers and ranchers are eligible only if they petition voluntarily.	Generally, same as Chapter 7 except a railroad may be a debtor, and a stockholder and commodity broker may not be a debtor under Chapter 11.	Family farmer with regular income, at least 50 percent of which comes from farming, and less than $1.5 million in debts, at least 80 percent of which is farm related.	Individual with regular income with liquidated unsecured debts less than $250,000 and secured debts of less than $750,000.
Initiation of Proceeding	Petition by debtor (voluntary). Petition by creditors (involuntary).	Petition by debtor (voluntary). Petition by creditors (involuntary).	Petition by debtor.	Petition by debtor.
Basic Procedure	1. Appointment of trustee. 2. Debtor retains exempt property. 3. Nonexempt property is sold and proceeds distributed based on priority of claims. 4. Dischargeable debts are terminated.	1. Appointment of trustee and committees of creditors and equity security holders. 2. Debtor submits reorganization plan. 3. If plan is approved and implemented, debts are discharged.	1. Trustee is appointed but debtor usually remains in possession of farm. 2. Debtor submits a plan in which unsecured creditors must receive at least liquidation value. 3. If plan is approved and fulfilled, debtor is entitled to a discharge.	1. Debtor indicates in petition that he is seeking a composition of debts or an extension. 2. If plan is approved after submitted to creditors, then trustee is appointed. 3. If plan is approved and fulfilled, debts covered by plan are discharged.
Advantages	After liquidation and distribution of assets, most or all of debts may be discharged and debtor gets a fresh start.	Debtor remains in business and debts are liquidated through implementation of approved reorganization plan.	Debtor generally remains in possession and has opportunity to work out of financial difficulty over period of time (usually three years) through implementation of approved plan.	Debtor has opportunity to work out of financial difficulty over period of time (usually three years) through implementation of approved plan.

Discharge

When the debtor has completed her performance of the plan, the court issues an order that discharges her from the debts covered by the plan. The debtor may also be discharged even though she did not complete her payments within the three years if the court is satisfied that the failure is due to circumstances for which the debtor cannot justly be held accountable. An active Chapter 13 proceeding stays, or holds in abeyance, any straight bankruptcy proceedings and any actions by creditors to collect consumer debts. However, if the Chapter 13 proceeding is dismissed (for example, because the debtor fails to file an acceptable plan or defaults on an accepted plan), straight bankruptcy proceedings may begin.

Advantages of Chapter 13

A debtor may choose to file under Chapter 13 to avoid the stigma of bankruptcy or to retain more of his property than is exempt from bankruptcy under state or federal law. Non-exempt property would have to be surrendered to the Trustee in a Chapter 7 liquidation proceeding. Chapter 13 can provide some financial discipline to a debtor as well as an opportunity to get his financial affairs back in good shape. It also gives him relief from the pressures of individual creditors so long as he makes the payments called for by the plan. The debtor's creditors may benefit by recovering a greater percentage of the debt owed to them than would be obtainable in straight bankruptcy.

ETHICAL AND PUBLIC POLICY CONCERNS

1. If a person receives a discharge of debts in bankruptcy, should the person feel an ethical obligation to reaffirm or to repay the debts that were discharged?

2. Is it ethical for a person facing the prospect of seeking relief under the bankruptcy laws to try to convert nonexempt property into exempt property on the eve of the filing of his petition? Does the relative economic condition of the debtor have any bearing on your response to this question?

3. As you have learned in this chapter, during the past decade corporations have filed petitions under Chapter 11 in order to deal with a variety of problems, including the threat of massive product liability claims and the desire of the company to get out of labor contracts. Is it ethical for a company to use Chapter 11 to try to get out of, or to modify, labor contracts or pension agreements that it now deems unfavorable to its interests? Is it ethical for a company to seek the shelter of Chapter 11 when faced with claims for product liability? Is the decision of the appeals court in *Official Committee of Equity Security Holders v. Mabey* to disallow the proposed emergency treatment fund good public policy?

4. As was discussed in this chapter, the federal bankruptcy law makes special provision for small farmers, and some states are particularly generous in the exemptions they make available to farmers. Is this special treatment of farmers justifiable as sound and fair public policy?

1. Gilbert and Kimberly Barnes filed a voluntary Chapter 7 petition in the U.S. Bankruptcy Court for the District of Maryland. Subsequently they moved to avoid a nonpurchase money lien held by ITT Financial Services on their exempt "household goods." Among the goods that the Barneses were claiming as "household goods" were a videocassette recorder (VCR), a 12-gauge pump shotgun, a 20-gauge shotgun, a 30-06 rifle, and a .22 pistol. ITT contended that the VCR and the firearms were not household goods that they could exempt. Under Maryland law, household goods are items of personal property reasonably necessary for the day-to-day existence of people in the context of their homes. Should the court consider the VCR and firearms to be "household goods"?

2. In September 1985, Richard and Nancy Beckman believed they collectively owned assets in excess of $3 million and had a joint net worth in excess of $1.5 million. However, after consulting an attorney and having their assets appraised, it became apparent during October 1985 that they had a negative net worth, that they were insolvent, and that bankruptcy was inevitable. In December, the Beckmans each signed applications to Bankers National Life Insurance Company to purchase $100,000 worth of additional life insurance. At the time, Richard Beckman already had $300,000 in term life insurance, $100,000 in accidental life insurance, $10,000 in whole life, and $14,000 in credit life insurance. On January 11, 1986, Richard Beckman delivered $15,000 in cash to Bankers Life as the initial premium on the two policies ($10,000 on his policy and $5,000 on her policy). The source of the funds was fees earned in his dentistry practice during the preceding October through December. The beneficiaries on all of the insurance policies (except the credit life policy) were either the Beckmans or their children. On January 9, 1986, the Beckmans signed a Chapter 7 bankruptcy petition, and it was filed on January 14, 1986. The trustee sought to avoid the purchase of insurance from Bankers Life as a fraud on creditors. Should the purchase of insurance be avoided?

3. William Kranich, Jr., was the sole shareholder in the DuVal Financial Corporation (DFC). On November 10, 1981, Kranich filed a voluntary petition for relief under Chapter 7; on January 6, 1982, DFC also filed a voluntary petition under Chapter 7. Prior to the commencement of the Chapter 7 proceedings, Kranich conveyed his personal residence in Clearwater, Florida, to DFC. The transfer was wholly without consideration. Shortly thereafter, DFC transferred the property to William Kranich III and June Elizabeth Kranich, Kranich's son and daughter, as tenants in common. This transfer was also without consideration. The bankruptcy trustee brought suit to recover the property from the son and daughter on the grounds that the transfer was fraudulent. Could the trustee recover the property on the grounds that its transfer, without consideration, was fraudulent?

4. David Hott was a college graduate with a degree in business administration who was employed as an insurance agent. He and his wife graduated from college in 1986. At the time he graduated, Hott had outstanding student loans of $14,500 for which he was given a grace period before he had to repay them. Hott became unemployed. Bills began to accumulate and a number of his outstanding bills were near the credit limits on his accounts. About that time, he received a promotional brochure by mail from Signal Consumer Discount Company, offering the opportunity to borrow several thousand dollars. The Hotts decided it appeared to be an attractive vehicle for them to use to consolidate their debts. Hott went to the Signal office and filled out a credit application. He did not list the student loan as a current debt. He later claimed that someone in the office told him he didn't have to list it if he owned an automobile but there was significant doubt about the credibility of this claim. Had he listed it, he would not have met the debt–income ratio required by Signal and it would not have made the loan. As it was, Signal agreed to make the loan on the condition Hott pay off a car debt in order to reduce his debt–income ratio and Hott agreed to do so. On March 30, 1987, Signal loaned the Hotts $3,458.01. On June 24, 1988, the Hotts filed for bankruptcy. Signal objected to discharge of the balance remaining on its loan on the ground it had been obtained through the use of a materially false financial statement. Was discharge of the debt barred on the ground it had been obtained through the use of a materially false financial statement?

5. While attending college, Barbara Barrington obtained a student loan from the New York State Higher Education Services Corporation. Barrington had depressive illnesses all her life, as had previous generations in her family. Her grandmother was institutionalized, and her mother had been on medication for a long time. Barrington was discharged by Eastman Kodak Company because she could not face the problems and stress of her job. Since that time, she had stayed at home, slept a lot, and played with her dog. She made little or no effort to find other employment because of her depressed condition. She also filed for bankruptcy. In the bankruptcy proceeding, one of the questions was whether payment of her student loan would impose an undue hardship on Barrington, and thus whether the loan was dischargeable. Should the student loan be discharged?

6. On December 19, 1986, Brian Scholz was involved in an automobile collision with a person insured by The Travelers Insurance Company. At the time, Scholz was cited for, and plead no contest to, a criminal charge of driving under the influence of alcohol arising out of the accident. The Travelers paid its insured $4,303.68 and was subrogated to the rights of its insured against Scholz. Subsequently, The Travelers filed a civil action against Scholz to recover the amount it had paid, and a default judgment was entered against Scholz. Eleven months later, Scholz sought relief from the bankruptcy court by filing a voluntary petition under Chapter 7. One of the questions in the bankruptcy proceeding was whether the debt owing to The Travelers was nondischargeable. Is the debt dischargeable?

7. Bryant filed a Chapter 7 petition on January 7, 1984. On March 8, she filed an application to reaffirm an indebtedness owed to General Motors Acceptance Corporation (GMAC) on her 1980 Cadillac automobile. Bryant was not married, and she supported two teenage daughters. She was not currently employed, and she collected $771 a month in unemployment benefits and $150 a month in rental income from her mother. Her monthly house payments were $259. The present value of the Cadillac was $9,175; she owed $7,956.37 on it, and her monthly payments were $345.93. Bryant indicated that she wanted to keep the vehicle because it was reliable. GMAC admitted that Bryant had been, and continued to be, current in her payments. GMAC said that the car was in no danger of being repossessed but that, absent reaffirmation, it might decide to repossess it. Should the court grant Bryant's application to reaffirm her indebtedness to GMAC?

8. Royal Composing Room, Inc., is an advertising typography company, and one of the last unionized shops in an industry that was subjected to considerable stress as computer technology replaced the Linotype machine. Royal was a party to a collective bargaining agreement with Typographical Union No. 6. Royal was a profitable company until 1982, when its gross revenues declined by $2 million; over the next four years, it sustained operating losses. Confronted with these difficulties, in 1983 Royal began to cut expenses by sharply cutting the compensation of its principal executives, freezing the salaries of salespeople and middle management foremen, eliminating company automobiles, and moving to a smaller location to save rent. At the start of 1986, Royal lost its largest customer, Doyle Dane Bernbach, Inc., and sought to convince the union, which theretofore had not made any sacrifices or concessions, to forgo a 3 percent wage increase agreed to earlier. When the union refused, Royal filed a petition for reorganization under Chapter 11 and sought to reject its collective bargaining agreement. Under section 1113(b) of the Bankruptcy Code, before it could reject the collective bargaining agreement, Royal was required to make a proposal to the union "which provides for those necessary modifications in the employees' benefits and protections that are necessary to permit the reorganization of the debtor and assures that all creditors, the debtor and all of the affected parties are treated fairly and equally." Royal held a meeting with officials of the union and offered a proposal that included a reduction of benefits, changes in work rules, the elimination of the scheduled wage increase, and the elimination of the union's right to arbitration as the way to change the contract. The union rejected the proposal and did not negotiate. Should the bankruptcy court approve the rejection of the collective bargaining agreement?

9. Winifred Doersam was the borrower on three student loans made to her by First Federal Savings and Loan and guaranteed by the state of Ohio Student Loan Commission (OSLC) totaling $10,000 to finance her graduate education at the University of Dayton. Doersam also signed as the cosigner for a $5,000 student loan for her daughter, also made by First Federal and guaranteed by OSLC. With the use of the loans, she was able to obtain a position as a systems analyst with NCR Corporation, which required her to obtain a master's degree in order to retain her position at an annual salary of $24,000. Approximately six weeks before her graduation, and before the first payment on her student loans was due, Doersam filed a petition and plan under Chapter 13. In her plan, she proposed to pay $375 a month to her unsecured creditors over a 36-month period. Doersam's total unsecured debt was $18,418, 81 percent of which was comprised of the outstanding student loans. Her schedules provided for payment of rent of $300 per month and food of $400 per month. Her listed dependents included her 23-year-old daughter and her 1-year-old granddaughter. At the time, her daughter was employed in the Ohio Work Program, a program designed to help welfare recipients, for which she was paid a small salary. The OLSC objected to the plan proposed by Doersam on the grounds that it was filed in bad faith. Should the bankruptcy court refuse to confirm the plan on the grounds it was not filed in good faith?

10. On July 13, 1980, Robert Leal purchased a new 1980 Ford Bronco for $12,000. The down payment consisted of $1,000 borrowed from Fidelity Financial Services and two cars that were traded in. The remainder of the purchase price was financed by Ford Motor Credit Company, which took a first lien on the vehicle. Leal gave Fidelity a security interest in certain household goods and a second lien on the Bronco. Leal never made a payment to Fidelity. On August 1, 1980, Leal executed a Chapter 13 plan that, among other things, proposed to treat Fidelity as an unsecured creditor, valued the collateral held by Ford—the Bronco—at $8,600, and offered $1 per claim to Fidelity and 10 other holders of unsecured claims whose debts were scheduled at $18,447. Leal offered to repay Ford the full amount owed to it. Fidelity objected to confirmation of the plan on the ground of lack of good faith. Should Fidelity's objection be sustained?

Commercial Paper

Negotiable Instruments

As commerce and trade developed, people moved beyond exclusive reliance on barter to the use of money and then to the use of substitutes for money. The term *commercial paper* encompasses substitutes in common usage today such as checks, promissory notes, and certificates of deposit.

History discloses that every civilization that engaged to an appreciable extent in commerce used some form of commercial paper. Probably the oldest commercial paper used in the carrying on of trade is the promissory note. Archaeologists found a promissory note made payable to bearer that dated from about 2100 B.C. The merchants of Europe used commercial paper—which, under the law merchant, was negotiable—in the 13th and 14th centuries. Commercial paper does not appear to have been used in England until about A.D. 1600.

This chapter and the three following chapters outline and discuss the body of law that governs commercial paper. Of particular interest are those kinds of commercial paper having the attribute of *negotiability*—that is, they can generally be transferred from party to party and accepted as a substitute for money. This chapter discusses the nature and benefits of negotiable instruments and then outlines the requirements an instrument must meet to qualify as a negotiable instrument. Subsequent chapters discuss transfer and negotiation of instruments, the rights and liabilities of parties to negotiable instruments, and the special rules applicable to checks. ∾

NATURE OF NEGOTIABLE INSTRUMENTS

When a person buys a television set and gives the merchant a check drawn on his checking account, that person uses a form of negotiable commercial paper. Similarly, a person who goes to a bank or a credit union to borrow money might sign a promissory note agreeing to pay the money back in 90 days. Again, the bank and borrower use a form of negotiable commercial paper.

Commercial paper is basically a *contract for the payment of money*. It may serve as a substitute for money payable immediately, such as a check. Or, it can be used as a means of extending credit. When a television set is bought by giving the merchant a check, the check is a substitute for money. If a credit union loans a borrower money now in exchange for the borrower's promise to repay it later, the promissory note signed by the borrower is a means of extending credit.

Uniform Commercial Code

The law of commercial paper is covered in Article 3 (Negotiable Instruments) and Article 4 (Bank Deposits and Collections) of the Uniform Commercial Code. Other negotiable documents, such as investment securities and documents of title, are treated in other articles of the Code. The original Code Articles 3 and 4, adopted initially in the 1960s, generally followed the basic, centuries-old rules governing the use of commercial paper; but at the same time they adopted modern terminology and coordinated, clarified, and simplified the law. However, business practices continued to evolve and new technological developments have changed the way that banks process checks. Accordingly, in 1990, a joint effort by the American Law Institute and the National Conference of Commissioners on Uniform State Laws produced a Revised Article 3 and related amendments to Articles 1 and 4. The purpose was to clarify Articles 3 and 4, to bring them into better harmony with current business practice, and to acknowledge recent technological developments.

Because a majority of the states have adopted the 1990 revision to Article 3 and the related amendments have now been adopted by a majority of the states, we use them as the basis for this edition of the textbook. The reader should ascertain whether the state in which she lives has adopted the revised article/amendments and also should keep in mind that instruments may be interpreted under the version of the Code that was in effect when the instruments were issued. Moreover, for the period between the first adoption of the revised article/amendments by a state (Arkansas) and the adoption by the last state or the District of Columbia, the "uniform law" concerning negotiable instruments will be anything but uniform.

For the student of negotiable instruments law, this is an interesting—but also a particularly difficult—time to study this area of the law. Revised Article 3 and the related amendments introduce new concepts, change definitions and the wording of key elements, and delete numerous provisions from the original version of Article 3. As a result, in drafting this chapter and the three chapters that follow, the authors have relied heavily on tracking the language of the revised article and on statements by the drafters as to their intent. Further complicating the picture is the fact that, in a number of respects, the revision is more complex than the original version. Moreover, while more than 30 years of case law had helped flesh out the meaning of the original Article 3, the revision has diminished much of the value of that case law. Virtually all of the cases to date arose under the original version of Article 3 and are of mixed—and sometimes very limited—value in trying to assess how courts will decide issues under the revision.

Just as these factors posed a challenge to the authors of this edition of the textbook, they will pose a challenge to you and your instructor as you work your way through the material on negotiable instruments. More questions are likely to be left up in the air than is true in other, more settled areas of the law. It will take a number of years, considerable experience, and new case law to clarify the updated law of negotiable instruments.

Negotiable Instruments

The two basic types of negotiable instruments are *promises to pay money* and *orders to pay money*. Promissory notes and certificates of deposit issued by banks are promises to pay someone money. Checks and drafts are orders to another person to pay money to a third person. A check, which is a type of draft, is an order directed to a certain kind of person, namely a bank, to pay money from a person's account to a third person.

Negotiability

Negotiable instruments are a special kind of commercial paper that can pass readily through our financial system and is accepted in place of money. This gives negotiable instruments many advantages.

For example, Searle, the owner of a clothing store in New York, contracts with Amado, a swimsuit manufacturer in Los Angeles, for $10,000 worth of swimsuits. If negotiable instruments did not exist, Searle would have to send or carry $10,000 across the country, which would be both inconvenient and risky. If someone stole the money along the way, Searle would lose the $10,000 unless he could locate the thief. By using a check in which Searle orders his bank to pay $10,000 from his account to Amado, or to someone designated by Amado, Searle makes the payment in a far more convenient manner. He sends only a single piece of paper to Amado. If the check is properly prepared and sent, sending the check is less risky than sending money. Even if someone steals the check along the way, Searle's bank may not pay it to anyone but Amado or someone authorized by Amado. And, because the check gives Amado the right either to collect the $10,000 or to transfer the right to collect it to someone else, the check is a practical substitute for cash to Amado as well as to Searle.

In this chapter and in the three following chapters, we discuss the requirements necessary for a contract for the payment of money to qualify as a negotiable instrument. We also explain the features that not only distinguish a negotiable instrument from a simple contract but also led to the widespread use of negotiable instruments as a substitute for money.

KINDS OF NEGOTIABLE INSTRUMENTS

Promissory Notes

The promissory note is the simplest form of commercial paper; it is simply a promise to pay money. A **promissory note** is a two-party instrument in which one person (known as the **maker**) makes an unconditional promise in writing to pay another person (the **payee**), a person specified by that person, or the bearer of the instrument, a fixed amount of money, with or without interest, either on demand or at a specified, future time [3–104].[1]

The promissory note, shown in Figures 1 and 2, is a credit instrument; it is used in a wide variety of transactions in which credit is extended. For example, if a person purchases an automobile using money borrowed from a bank, the bank has the person sign a promissory note for the unpaid balance of the purchase price. Similarly, if a person borrows money to purchase a house, the lender who makes the loan and takes a mortgage on the house has the person sign a promissory note for the amount due on the loan. The note probably states that it is secured by a mortgage. The terms of payment on the note should correspond with the terms of the sales contract for the purchase of the house.

---

[1]The numbers in brackets refer to the sections of the 1990 Revised Article 3 (and the conforming amendments to Articles 1 and 4) of the Uniform Commercial Code.

FIGURE I

Promissory Note

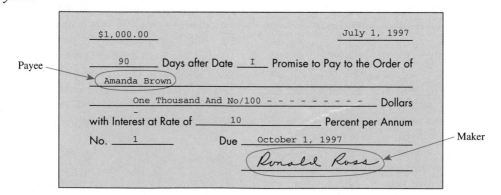

FIGURE 2

Promissory Note (Consumer Loan Note)

The National
**BANK OF
WASHINGTON**
CONSUMER LOAN NOTE
Date___November 21,___, 19_97_

The words I and me mean all borrowers who signed this note. The word bank means The National Bank of Washington.

Promise to Pay

___30___ months from today, I promise to pay to the order of The National Bank of Washington

Seventy-Eight Hundred Seventy Five and no/100 - - - - - - - - - - -dollars ($___7,875.00_).

Payee ⟶

Responsibility

Although this note may be signed below by more than one person, I understand that we are each as individuals responsible for paying back the full amount.

Breakdown of Loan

This is what I will pay:

Amount of loan	1.$	6,800.00
Credit Life Insurance (optional)	2.$	100.00
Other (describe)	3.$	-0-
Amount Financed (Add 1 and 2 and 3)	4.$	6,900
FINANCE CHARGE	5.$	975.00
Total of Payments (Add 4 and 5)	$	7,875.00
ANNUAL PERCENTAGE RATE		10.5%

Repayment

This is how I will repay:
I will repay the amount of this note in___30___equal uninterrupted monthly installments of $_262.50_ each on the __1st__ day of each month starting on the _1st_ day of _December_, 19_97_ and ending on ___May 1_, _____ _1999_

Prepayment

I have the right to prepay the whole outstanding amount of this note at any time. If I do, or if this loan is refinanced—that is, replaced by a new note—you will refund the unearned finance charge, figured by the rule of 78—a commonly used formula for figuring rebates on installment loans.

Late Charge

Any installment not paid within ten days of its due date shall be subject to a late charge of 5% of the payment, not to exceed $5.00 for any such late installment.

Security

To protect the National Bank of Washington, I give what is known as a security interest in my auto and/or other: (Describe) _Ford Thunderbird_____

_____# Serial #115117-12-_____

See the security agreement.

Credit Life Insurance

Credit life insurance is not required to obtain this loan. The bank need not provide it and I do not need to buy it unless I sign immediately below. The cost of credit life insurance is $___100.00___ for the term of the loan.

Signed: *A. J. Smith*_____

Date: ___November 21, 1997_____

Default

If for any reason I fail to make any payment on time, I shall be in default. The bank can then demand immediate payment of the entire remaining unpaid balance of this loan, without giving anyone further notice. If I have not paid the full amount of the loan when the final payment is due, the bank will charge me interest on the unpaid balance at six percent (6%) per year.

Right of Offset

If this loan becomes past due, the bank will have the right to pay this loan from any deposit or security I have at this bank without telling me ahead of time. Even if the bank gives me an extension of time to pay this loan, I still must repay the entire loan.

Collection Fees

If this note is placed with an attorney for collection, then I agree to pay an attorney's fee of fifteen percent (15%) of the unpaid balance. This fee will be added to the unpaid balance of the loan.

Co-borrowers

If I am signing this note as a co-borrower, I agree to be equally responsible with the borrower for this loan. The bank does not have to notify me that this note has not been paid. The bank can change the terms of payment and release any security without notifying or releasing me from responsibility for this loan.

Copy Received

I received a completely filled in copy of this note. If I have signed for Credit Life Insurance, I received a copy of the Credit Life Insurance certificate.

Borrower: *A. J. Smith* ⟵ **Maker**
A. J. Smith
3412 Brookdale, S. W. Washington D.C.
Address_____

Co-borrower: *Andrea H Smith* ⟵ **Co-maker**
Andrea H. Smith
3412 Brookdale, S. W. Washington D.C.
Address_____

Co-borrower:_____

Address_____

CONSUMER CREDIT HOTLINE: If you have any questions, please call us immediately at (202) 624-3450.
NBW 437 (Rev. 11-78)   1-Bank's copy   2-File copy   3-Customer's copy

Source: The National Bank of Washington.

Certificates of Deposit

The certificate of deposit given by a bank or a savings and loan association when a deposit of money is made is a type of note, namely a note of a bank. A **certificate of deposit** is an instrument containing (1) an acknowledgment by a bank that it has received a deposit of money and (2) a promise by the bank to repay the sum of money [3–104(j)]. Figure 3 is an example of a certificate of deposit.

FIGURE 3

Certificate of Deposit

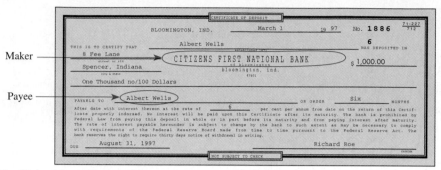

Source: Citizens First National Bank of Bloomington.

Many banks no longer issue certificates of deposit (CD) in paper form. Rather, the bank maintains an electronic deposit and provides the customer with a statement indicating the amount of principal held on a CD basis and the terms of the CD, such as the maturity and interest rate. In these instances, the certificate of deposit is not in negotiable instrument form.

Drafts

A **draft** is a form of commercial paper that involves an *order* to pay money rather than a promise to pay money [3–104(e)]. The most common example of a draft is a check. A draft has three parties to it: one person (known as the **drawer**) orders a second person (the **drawee**) to pay a certain sum of money to a third person (the **payee**), to a person specified by that person, or to bearer.

Drafts other than checks are used in a variety of commercial transactions. If Brown owes Ames money, Ames may draw a draft for the amount of the debt, naming Brown as drawee and herself or her bank as payee, and send the draft to Brown's bank for payment. Alternatively, Ames might send a draft providing for payment on a certain day in the future to Brown for "acceptance." Brown could "accept" the draft by signing his name to it, thereby obligating himself to pay the amount specified in the draft on that day in the future to Ames or to someone specified by Ames.

In freight shipments in which the terms are "cash on delivery," the seller commonly ships the goods to the buyer on an "order bill of lading" consigned to himself at the place of delivery. The seller then indorses the bill of lading and attaches a draft naming the buyer as drawee. He then sends the bill of lading and the draft through banking channels to the buyer's bank. A bank in the buyer's locale presents the draft to the buyer's bank for payment, and when the former bank receives payment, delivers the bill of lading to the buyer. Through this commercial transaction, the buyer gets the goods and the seller gets his money.

When credit is extended, the same procedure is followed, but the seller uses a time draft—a draft payable at some future time (see Figure 4). In such a transaction, the buyer "accepts" the draft (instead of paying it) and obligates herself to pay the amount of the draft when due. In these cases, the *drawee* (now called the **acceptor**) should date her signature so that the date at which payment is due is clear to all [3–409(c)].

Checks

A **check** is a *draft payable on demand* and drawn on a bank (i.e., a bank is the drawee or person to whom the order to pay is addressed). Checks are the most widely used form of commercial paper. The issuer of a check orders the bank at which she maintains an account to pay a specified person, or someone designated by that person, a fixed amount of money from the account. For example, Elizabeth Brown has a checking account at the National Bank of Washington. She goes to Sears Roebuck and agrees to buy a washing machine priced at $459.95. If she writes a check to pay for it, she is the drawer of the check, the National Bank of Washington is the drawee, and Sears is the payee. By writing the

FIGURE 4

Draft

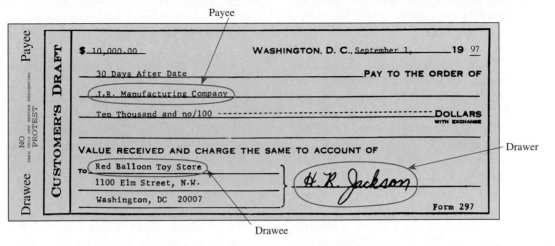

Payee

Drawer

Drawee

FIGURE 5

Check

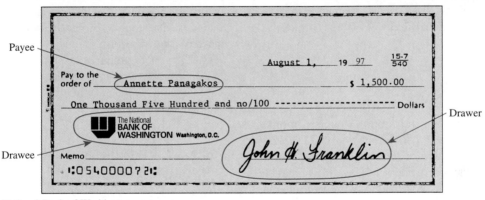

Payee

Drawer

Drawee

Source: The National Bank of Washington.

check, Elizabeth is ordering her bank to pay $459.95 from her account to Sears or to Sears's order—that is, to whomever Sears asks the bank to pay the money (see Figure 5).

An instrument may qualify as a "check" and be governed by Article 3 even though it is described on its face by another term, such as "money order." The Code definition of a "check" includes a "cashier's check" and a "teller's check." A **cashier's check** is a draft on which the drawer and drawee are the same bank (or branches of the same bank); a **teller's check** is a draft drawn by a bank (as drawer) on another bank or payable at or through a bank [3–104(g) and (h)]. For example, a check drawn by

a credit union on its account at a federally insured bank would be a teller's check.

BENEFITS OF NEGOTIABLE INSTRUMENTS

Rights of an Assignee of a Contract

As we noted in Chapter 17, Rights of Third Parties, the assignee of a contract can obtain no greater rights than the assignor had at the time of the assignment. For example, Frank Farmer and Neam's Market enter into a contract providing that Farmer will sell Neam's a dozen crates of fresh eggs a week for a year and that Neam's will pay Farmer $4,000 at the end of the year. If at the end of the year Farmer assigns to Bill Sanders his rights under the contract—including the right to collect the money from Neam's—then Sanders has whatever rights Farmer had at that time. If Farmer has delivered all the eggs to Neam's as he promised, then Farmer would be entitled to $4,000 and Sanders would obtain that right from him. However, if Farmer has not delivered all the eggs that he had promised to deliver, or if the eggs he delivered were not fresh, then Neam's might have a valid defense or reason to refuse to pay the full $4,000. In that case, Sanders would have only what rights Farmer had and also would be subject to the defense Neam's has against full payment.

Taking an assignment of a contract involves assuming certain risks. The assignee (Sanders) may not be aware of the nature and extent of any defenses that the party liable on the contract (Neam's) might have against the assignor (Farmer). An assignee who does not know what rights he is getting, or which risks he is assuming, may be reluctant to take an assignment of the contract.

Rights of a Holder of a Negotiable Instrument

The object of a negotiable instrument is to have it accepted readily as a substitute for money. In order to accept it readily, a person must be able to take it free of many of the risks assumed by the assignee of a regular contract. Under the law of negotiable instruments, this is possible if two conditions are met: (1) the contract for the payment of money must meet the formal requirements to qualify as a negotiable instrument; and (2) the person who acquires the instrument must qualify as a holder in due course. Basically, a *holder in due course* is a person who has good title to the instrument, paid value for it, acquired it in good faith, and had no notice of certain claims or defenses against payment. In addition, the instrument cannot bear facial irregularities (evidence of forgery or alteration or questions concerning its authenticity).

The next section of this chapter discusses the formal requirements for a negotiable instrument. Chapter 31, Negotiation and Holder in Due Course, outlines the requirements that a person must meet to qualify as a holder in due course.

A holder in due course of a negotiable instrument takes the instrument free of all defenses and claims to the instrument except those that concern its validity. For example, a holder in due course of a note given in payment for goods may enforce the obligation in spite of the buyer's claim that the seller breached a warranty. However, if the maker of a note wrote it under duress, such as a threat of force, or was a minor, then even a holder in due course is subject to the defenses of duress or infancy to the extent other law (1) would nullify the obligation for duress or (2) would permit infancy as a defense to a simple contract. The person who holds the note could not obtain the payment from the maker but would have to recover from the person from whom he got the note.

The Federal Trade Commission (FTC) has adopted a regulation that alters the rights of a holder in due course in consumer purchase transactions. This regulation allows a consumer who gives a negotiable instrument to use additional defenses (breach of warranty or fraudulent inducement) against payment of the instrument against even a holder in due course. Similarly, some states have enacted the Uniform Consumer Credit Code (UCCC), which produces a similar result. Chapter 31, Negotiation and Holder in Due Course, discusses the rights of a holder in due course, as well as the FTC rule.

FORMAL REQUIREMENTS FOR NEGOTIABILITY

Basic Requirements

An instrument such as a check or a note must meet certain formal requirements to be a negotiable instrument. If the instrument does not meet these requirements, it is non-negotiable; that is, it is treated as a simple contract and not as a negotiable instrument. A primary purpose for these formal requirements is to ensure the willingness of prospective purchasers of the instrument, particularly financial institutions such as banks, to accept it as a substitute for money.

For an instrument to be negotiable, it must:

1. Be in writing.
2. Be signed by the issuer (the *maker* in the case of a person undertaking to pay or the *drawer*

in the case of a person giving an order or instruction to pay).

3. Contain an unconditional promise or order to pay a fixed amount of money, with or without interest or other charges described in the promise or order.

4. Be payable to order or to bearer at the time it is issued or first comes into possession of a holder.

5. Be payable on demand or at a definite time.

6. Not state any other undertaking or instruction by the person promising or ordering to do any act in addition to the payment of money (but it may contain (*a*) an undertaking or promise relative to collateral to secure payment, (*b*) an authorization for confession of judgment, or (*c*) a waiver of benefit of any law intended for the advantage or protection of an obligor) [3–103; 3–104].

In addition, an instrument that otherwise qualifies as a check can be negotiable even if it is not explicitly payable to order or to bearer [3–104(c)]. As explained later, this means that a check that reads "pay John Doe" could be negotiable even though the normal form for a check is "pay to the order of _____ ."

A promise or order other than a check is not a negotiable instrument if at the time it is issued or first comes into the possession of a holder it contains a conspicuous statement that the promise or order is not negotiable or is not an instrument governed by Article 3 [3–104(d)]. For example, if a promissory note contained the legend "NON-NEGOTIABLE," it would not qualify as a negotiable instrument even if it otherwise met the formal requirements for one.

Importance of Form

Whether or not an instrument satisfies these formal requirements is important only for the purpose of determining whether an instrument is negotiable or non-negotiable. Negotiability should not be confused with validity or collectibility. If an instrument is negotiable, the law of negotiable instruments in the Code controls in determining the rights and liabilities of the parties to the instrument. If an instrument is non-negotiable, the general rules of contract law control. The purpose of determining negotiability is to ascertain whether a possessor of the instrument can become a holder in due course.

An instrument that meets all of the formal requirements is a negotiable instrument even though it is void, voidable, unenforceable, or uncollectible for other reasons. Negotiability is a matter of form and nothing else. Suppose a person gives an instrument in payment of a gambling debt in a state that has a statute declaring that any instrument or promise given in payment of a gambling debt is void. The instrument is a negotiable instrument if it is negotiable in form even though it is absolutely void. Also, an instrument that is negotiable in form is a negotiable instrument even though it is issued by a minor. The instrument is voidable at the option of the minor if state law makes infancy a defense to a simple contract, but it is negotiable.

IN WRITING

To be negotiable, an instrument must be in writing. An instrument that is handwritten, typed, or printed is considered to be in writing [1–201(46)]. The writing does not have to be on any particular material; all that is required is that the instrument be in writing. A person could create a negotiable instrument in pencil on a piece of wrapping paper. It would be poor business practice to do so, but the instrument would meet the statutory requirement that it be in writing.

SIGNED

To qualify as a negotiable instrument, an instrument in the form of a note must be signed by the person undertaking to pay (the maker) and an instrument in the form of a draft must be signed by the person giving the instruction to pay (the drawer) [3–103]. An instrument has been signed if the maker or drawer has put a name or other symbol on it with the intention of validating it [3–401(b)]. Normally, the maker or drawer signs an instrument by writing his name on it; however, this is not required. A person or company may authorize an agent to sign instruments for it. A typed or rubber-stamped signature is sufficient if it was put on the instrument to validate it. A person who cannot write her name might make an X and have it witnessed by someone else.

UNCONDITIONAL PROMISE OR ORDER

Requirement of a Promise or Order

If an instrument is promissory in nature, such as a note or a certificate of deposit, it must contain an unconditional promise to pay or it cannot be negotiable. Merely acknowledging a debt is not sufficient [3–103(9)]. For example, the statement "I owe you $100," does not constitute a promise to pay. An IOU in this form is not a negotiable instrument.

If an instrument is an order to pay, such as a check or a draft, it must contain an unconditional order. A simple request to pay as a favor is not sufficient; however, a politely phrased demand, such as "please pay," can meet the requirement. Checks commonly use the language "Pay to the order of." This satisfies the requirement that the check contain an order to pay. The order is the word "pay," not the word "order." The word "order" has another function—that of designating the instrument as payable "to order" or "to bearer" for purposes of negotiability.

FORD MOTOR CREDIT OC. v. ALL WAYS, INC. 546 N.W.2d 807 (Neb. Sup. Ct. 1996)

ll Ways, Inc., and its president, Gary L. Ross, signed two retail installment contracts for the purchase of a Lincoln passenger car and a Ford truck from Seward County Ford Lincoln Mercury, Inc. The two contracts were secured by liens on the vehicles. Seward Country Ford Lincoln Mercury assigned its interests in the contracts to Ford Motor Credit.

On October 27, 1993, All Ways and Ross tendered to Ford two "certified money orders" as payment in full for the two vehicles. The two documents were made out to Ford for $20,500 and $25,200. The documents stated that the sums were to be paid:

On Demand, Money of account of the United States, as required by law at Section 20 of Coinage Act of 1792 from the time of official determination of said money; OR, in UCC 1–201(24) Credit Money.

The documents stated they were:

REDEEMABLE AT FULL FACE VALUE WHEN PRESENTED[;] To: O.M.B. [;] W.D. McCALL[;] P.O. BOX 500-284[;] VICTORIA, TEXAS POSTAL ZONE 77901.

Upon receiving the documents, Ford applied the purported payments to the defendants' accounts and deposited the documents in a bank. The documents were returned by the bank as non-negotiable because there were no bank routing numbers on the documents, and no bank was identified through which to charge. Without routing numbers, a bank would have no obligation to accept or make payment on the documents.

Ford informed All Ways and Ross that the documents were not acceptable and that they would need to pay Ford in U.S. legal tender. However, no payments were forthcoming and the account was in default. Ford brought suit to compel All Ways and Ross to either return the vehicles to Ford or to pay $35,810. The trial court held that the documents tendered by All Ways and Ross did not order the payment of money and contained stipulations not contemplated by the Nebraska Uniform Commercial Code and awarded judgment to Ford. All Ways and Ross appealed. ∽

Per Curiam Whether the documents tendered by All Ways and Ross were negotiable instruments is governed by Nebraska's Uniform Commercial Code.

A negotiable instrument is an unconditional promise or order to pay a fixed amount of money. Revised section 3–104(a). The tendered documents are not within the definition of a negotiable instrument. The documents purport to provide the creditor an unspecified "Credit Money" when presented to a post office box. This cannot be construed as an unconditional promise or order to pay a fixed sum of money.

Judgment affirmed for Ford Motor Credit.

Promise or Order Must Be Unconditional

An instrument is not negotiable unless the promise or order is unconditional. For example, a note that provides, "I promise to pay to the order of Karl Adams $100 if he replaces the roof on my garage," is not negotiable because it is payable on a condition.

To be negotiable, an instrument must be written so that a person can tell from reading the instrument alone what the obligations of the parties are. If a note contains the statement, "Payment is subject to the terms of a mortgage dated November 20, 1995," it is not negotiable. To determine the rights of the parties on the note, one would have to examine another document—the mortgage.

However, a reference to another document for a statement of rights with respect to collateral, prepayment, or acceleration does not destroy the negotiability of a note [3–106(b)]. For example, a note could contain this statement: "This note is secured by a mortgage dated August 30, 1997" without affecting its negotiability. In this case, the mortgage does not affect rights and duties of the parties to the note. It would not be necessary to examine the mortgage document to determine the rights of the parties to the note; the parties only need examine the note.

The negotiability of an instrument is not affected by a statement of the consideration for which the instrument was given or by a statement of the transaction that gave rise to the instrument. For example, a negotiable instrument may state that it was given in payment of last month's rent or that it was given in payment of the purchase price of goods. The statement does not affect the negotiability of the instrument.

A check may reference the account to be debited without making the check non-negotiable. For example, a check could contain the notation, "payroll account" or "petty cash." Similarly, the account number that appears on personal checks does not make the instrument payable only out of a specific fund. Under original Article 3, a check (other than a governmental check) that stated that it was payable only out of a specific fund or account was treated as a conditional order and thus was not negotiable. Revised Article 3 changed this rule so that limiting payment to a particular fund or source does not make the promise or order conditional [3–106(b)].

Revised Article 3 also addresses the negotiability of traveler's checks that commonly require, as a condition to payment, a countersignature of a person whose specimen signature appears on the draft. Under the revision, the condition does not prevent the instrument from meeting the "unconditional promise or order" requirement [3–106(c)]. However, if the person whose specimen signature appears on the instrument fails to countersign it, the failure to sign becomes a defense to the obligation of the issuer to pay. This concept will be discussed in the following chapter.

A conditional *indorsement* does not destroy the negotiability of an otherwise negotiable instrument. The Code determines negotiability at *issuance,* so that indorsements do not affect the underlying negotiability of the instrument. We discuss conditional indorsements in Chapter 31, Negotiation and Holder in Due Course.

FIXED AMOUNT OF MONEY

Fixed Amount

The promise or order in an instrument must be to pay a fixed amount of money, with or without interest or other charges described in the promise or order. The requirement of a "fixed amount" applies only to principal; the amount of any interest payable is that described in the instrument. Interest may be stated in an instrument as a fixed or variable amount of money or it may be expressed as a fixed or variable rate or rates. If a variable rate of interest is prescribed, the amount of interest is calculated by reference to the formula or index referenced in the instrument. For example, a note might provide for interest at "three percent (3.00%) over Chase Manhattan Prime Rate to be adjusted monthly." If the description of interest in the instrument does not allow the amount of interest to be ascertained, then interest is payable at the judgment rate in effect at the place of payment at the time interest first accrues [3–112]. The judgment rate is the rate of interest courts impose on losing parties until they pay the winning parties.

Under the original version of Article 3, a promise or order had to be to pay a "sum certain." Generally, to meet this requirement, a person had to be able to compute from the information in the instrument the amount required to discharge—or pay off—the instrument at any given time. Among other things, this caused problems when applied to variable rate instruments that came into common commercial usage in the United States after the original Article 3 was drafted. Some state courts held that instruments providing for variable interest rates ascertainable through reference to indexes outside the instrument were not negotiable; other courts sought to interpret the Code to accommodate this new commercial practice. As noted above, the negotiability of instruments that provide for variable interest rates has now been resolved in Revised Article 3.

Payable in Money

The amount specified in the instrument must be payable in money, which is a medium of exchange authorized or adopted by a domestic or foreign government and includes a monetary unit of account established by an intergovernmental organization or by agreement between two or more nations [1–201(24)]. Unless the instrument otherwise provides, an instrument that states the amount payable in foreign money may be paid in the foreign money or in an equivalent dollar amount [3–107]. If the person obligated to pay off an instrument can do something other than pay money, the instrument is not negotiable. For example, if a note reads, "I promise to pay to the order of Sarah Smith, at my option, $40 or five bushels of apples, John Jones," the note is not negotiable.

PAYABLE ON DEMAND OR AT A DEFINITE TIME

To be negotiable, the promise or order must be payable either on demand or at a specified time in the future. This is so that the time when the instrument is payable can be determined with some certainty. An instrument that is payable on the happening of some uncertain event is not negotiable. Thus, a note payable "when my son graduates from college" is not negotiable, even though the son does graduate subsequently.

Payable on Demand

A promise or order is "payable on demand" if (1) it states that it is payable on "demand" or "sight" (or otherwise at the will of the holder of the instrument) or (2) does not state any time for payment [3–108(a)]. For example, if the maker forgets to state when a note is payable, it is payable immediately at the request of the holder of the note.

An instrument may be antedated or postdated, and normally an instrument payable on demand is not payable before the date of the instrument [3–113(a)]. Revised Article 3 makes an important exception for checks; a payor bank (a bank that is the drawee of a draft) may pay a postdated check before the stated date *unless* the drawer has notified the bank of postdating pursuant to a procedure set out in the Code [3–113(a); 4–401(c)].

Payable at a Definite Time

A promise or order is "payable at a definite time" if it is payable at a fixed date or dates or at a time or times readily ascertainable at the time the promise or order is issued [3–108(b)]. Thus, a note dated March 25, 1997, might be made payable at a fixed time after a stated date, such as "30 days after date."

Under the Code, an instrument that names a fixed date or time for payment—without losing its negotiable character—also may contain a clause permitting the time for payment to be accelerated at the option of the maker. Similarly, an instrument may allow an extension of time at the option of the holder or allow a maker or acceptor to extend payment to a further definite time. Or, the due date of a note might be triggered by the happening of an event, such as the filing of a petition in bankruptcy against the maker. The Code permits these clauses so long as one can determine the time for payment with certainty [3–108].

A promise or order also is "payable at a definite time" if it is payable on elapse of a definite period of time after "sight" or "acceptance." A draft payable at a specified time—such as "15 days after sight"—is, in effect, payable at a fixed time after the draft is presented to the drawee for acceptance.

If an instrument is undated, its "date" is the date it is issued by the maker or drawer [3–113(b)].

PAYABLE TO ORDER OR BEARER

Except for checks, to be negotiable an instrument must be "payable to order or to bearer." A note that provides, "I promise to pay to the order of Sarah Smith" or "I promise to pay to Sarah Smith or bearer" is negotiable. However, one that provides "I promise to pay to Sarah Smith" is not. The words "to the order of" or "to bearer" show that the drawer of a draft, or the maker of a note, intends to issue a negotiable instrument. The drawer or maker is not restricting payment of the instrument to just Sarah Smith but is willing to pay someone else designated by Sarah Smith. This is the essence of negotiability.

In the original version of Article 3, an order in the form of a check also had to be "payable to order or bearer" to qualify as a negotiable instrument. However, the drafters of Revised Article 3 created an exception for instruments that otherwise meet the requirements for a negotiable instrument as well as the definition of a check [3–104(c)]. Under the revised article, a check that reads "Pay John Doe" could qualify as a negotiable instrument. As a result, the Code treats checks, which are payment instruments, as negotiable instruments whether or not they contain the words "to the order of." The drafters explained that most checks are preprinted with these words but that occasionally the drawer may strike out the words before issuing the check and that a few check forms have been in use that do not contain these words. In these instances, the drafters preferred not to limit the rights of holders of

such checks who may pay money or give credit for a check without being aware that it is not in the conventional form for a negotiable instrument.

A promise or order is considered to be payable "to order" if it is payable (1) to the order of an identified person or (2) to an identified person or that person's order [3–109(b)]. Examples would include: "Pay to the order of Sandy Smith" and "Pay to Sandy Smith or order." The most common forms of a promise or order being payable to bearer use the words "payable to bearer," "payable to the order of bearer," "payable to cash," or "payable to the order of cash," [3–109(a)]. A check sent with the payee line blank is payable to bearer. However, it is also considered an incomplete instrument, the rules concerning which will be discussed in the following two chapters.

The case that follows, *Universal Premium Acceptance Corp. v. York Bank & Trust Co.*, illustrates an instrument that some of the parties treated as negotiable when, in fact, it did not meet the requirements for negotiability.

UNIVERSAL PREMIUM ACCEPTANCE CORP. v. YORK BANK & TRUST CO.   28 UCC REP.2d 1 (3RD CIR. 1995)

*U*niversal Premium Acceptance Corporation, with its principal office in St. Louis, Missouri, provides financing to policyholders to pay their insurance premiums. In the fall of 1991, Walter Talbot of the W. Talbot Insurance Agency in Lancaster, Pennsylvania, requested Universal to provide financing for his customers who needed funds to pay premiums on policies issued by the Great American Insurance Company.

Universal accepted Talbot's proposal and sent him the necessary documents, including blank drafts. The face of each instrument contained Universal's name and address in the top left-hand corner and a large UPAC logo in the top center. Below UPAC's address was printed "PAY AND DEPOSIT ONLY TO THE CREDIT OF: _____ INSURANCE CO." with a space for the amount. On the lower right side of the instrument were blanks for the policyholder's name, the insurance agency name, and a line for "SIGNATURE OF PRODUCER OF RECORD/BROKER/AGENT." In the lower right side beneath the signature line appeared the name and address of the Landmark Bank.

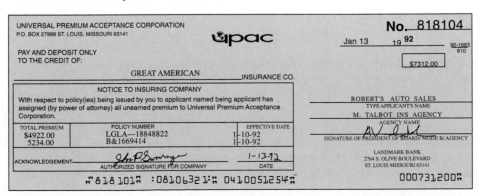

The back of each instrument contained preprinted language: "Acceptance of this draft acknowledges Universal Premium Acceptance Corporation's interest in the unearned or return premium(s) and that we have issued a policy(ies) to the named applicant (insured) in the amount of the premium indicated."

Between September 1991 and July 1992, Talbot signed drafts for more than $1 million in favor of Great American but did not deliver them to the insurance company. Instead, he arranged for his confederate to forge the indorsement of Great American and deposit the drafts in an account they opened at York Bank & Trust Co. under the name of "Small Businessman's Service Corporation." York transmitted the drafts to Landmark Bank, Universal's bank in St. Louis.

As part of the scheme, Talbot and his associates set up a dummy "Great American Insurance Company" in Lancaster and furnished its address and telephone number to Universal. To verify that Great American had issued a policy, Universal would contact that office. After assurance from Talbot's cohorts there that the transaction was in order, Universal would then authorize Landmark to pay the draft.

After the fraud was discovered, Talbot was convicted and imprisoned. Universal recovered part of its loss from Talbot and then filed suit against York Bank & Trust. The trial court ruled that, among other things, the drafts should be treated as if they were negotiable and applied the UCC. Universal appealed. ∞

Weis, Circuit Judge One of the requirements for negotiability under section 3–104(a)(3) is that an instrument must be "payable to order or to bearer." How the parties regard or characterize the instrument is immaterial. The drafts here did not meet the terms of section 3–104.

The language on the drafts, "PAY AND DEPOSIT ONLY TO THE CREDIT OF: Great American Insurance Company," does not meet the requirements for a negotiable instrument. Not only did these drafts lack "to the order of," they contained specific instructions—"deposit only to the credit of." Implicit in such language is a warning of non-negotiability.

The drafts demonstrate that they were not meant to be freely transferrable, but were to be "deposited" and "only" to the credit of the insurance company. "Deposited" implies that the instruments were to have a limited use and a short transactional life. "Only" can be understood to modify "deposited" or the payee, but, in either instance, the language is quite restrictive. The terms on the face were meant to preclude transfer.

Judgment in favor of York reversed on other grounds.

Note: Because the incidents in this case took place before July 9, 1993, the effective date of the revised edition of Articles 3 & 4 of the Uniform Commercial Code presently in effect in Pennsylvania, the older version, rather than the current one, was applied by the court. However, the same result would be expected under revised Articles 3 and 4.

The original payee of a draft or a note can transfer the right to receive payment to someone else. By making the instrument payable "to the order of " or "to bearer," the drawer or maker is giving the payee the chance to negotiate the instrument to another person and to cut off certain defenses that the drawer or maker may have against payment of the instrument.

An instrument that is payable to the order of a specific person is known as "order paper." Order paper can be negotiated or transferred only by indorsement. An instrument payable "to bearer" or "to cash" is known as "bearer paper"; it can be negotiated or transferred by delivery of possession without indorsement [3–201(b)]. The rules governing negotiation of instruments will be detailed in the next chapter.

An instrument can be made payable to two or more payees. For example, a check could be drawn payable "to the order of John Jones and Henry Smith." Then, both Jones and Smith have to be involved in negotiating it or enforcing its payment. An instrument also can be made payable to alternative persons— for example, "to the order of Susan Clark or Betsy Brown." In this case, either Clark or Brown could negotiate it or enforce its payment [3–110(d)].

A number of recent cases have addressed the use of the virgule (/) to separate the names of the payees. The following case, *Purina Mills, Inc. v. Security Bank & Trust,* illustrates how the courts typically have applied the UCC to such situations.

F*rom February 10, 1992, to June 17, 1992, K-R Summers & Sons Livestock drew 10 checks totaling over $21,000 on its account at Security Bank & Trust. The checks were made payable to International Livestock/Purina Mills." International Livestock indorsed the checks and presented them to Mid America Bank in Wisconsin. Mid America honored the checks and presented them to Security as the drawee bank, which also honored the checks without Purina's indorsement. Purina filed a lawsuit to recover the amount of the checks from Security. Security filed a motion for summary judgment, which the trial court granted. Purina appealed.* ⌒

Reilly, Judge   Whether the virgule separating the names of two or more payees on an instrument indicates that the instrument is payable to all parties listed, or to the parties in the alternative, is an issue of first impression in Michigan.

Courts in other jurisdictions that have decided this issue have concluded that its use indicates that the instrument is payable in the alternative.

We agree with these authorities that a check drawn to payees whose names are separated by a virgule allows payment to the payees alternatively. A virgule is defined as "an oblique stroke (/) used between two words to show that an appropriate one

may be chosen to complete the sense of the text." The Random House Dictionary, Revised Edition (1975). Thus the virgule is used to separate alternatives. According to UCC Section 3–110(d), "[i]f an instrument is payable to two or more persons alternatively, it is payable to any of them and may be negotiated, discharged, or enforced by any of them in possession of the instrument." The banks properly honored the checks that were presented with the indorsement of one of the payees.

Judgment affirmed for Security Bank & Trust.

SPECIAL TERMS

Additional Terms

Generally, if an instrument is to qualify as a negotiable instrument, the person promising or ordering payment may not state undertakings or instructions in addition to the payment of money [3–104(a)(3)]. However, the instrument may include clauses concerning (1) giving, maintaining, or protecting collateral to secure payment, (2) an authorization to confess judgment or to realize on or dispose of collateral, and (3) waiving the benefit of any law intended for the protection or benefit of any person obligated on the instrument.

Thus, a term authorizing the confession of judgment on an instrument when it is due does not affect the negotiability of the instrument. A confession of judgment clause authorizes the creditor to go into court if the debtor defaults and, with the debtor's acquiescence, to have a judgment entered against the debtor. However, some states prohibit confessions of judgment.

Banks and other businesses often use forms of commercial paper that meet their particular needs. These forms may include certain other terms that do

not affect the negotiability of an instrument. For example, a note may designate a place of payment without affecting the instrument's negotiability. Where the instrument does not specify a place of payment, the Code sets out rules for ascertaining where payment is to be made [3–111].

Ambiguous Terms

Occasionally, a person may write or receive a check on which the amount written in figures differs from the amount written in words. Or a note may have conflicting terms or an ambiguous term. Where a conflict or an ambiguous term exists, there are general rules of interpretation that are applied to resolve the conflict or ambiguity: Typewritten terms prevail over printed terms, handwritten terms prevail over printed and typewritten terms, and where words and numbers conflict, the words control the numbers [3–114].

The following *Galatia Community State Bank v. Kindy* case involves a check on which there was a difference between the numbers on the check placed there by a check-writing machine and those written by hand.

C O N C E P T   R E V I E W

Requirements for Negotiability

REQUIREMENT	BASIC RULES
Must Be in Writing	1. The instrument may be handwritten, typed, or printed.
Must Be Signed by the Maker or Drawer	1. Person issuing the instrument must sign with intent of validating his or her obligation. 2. Person issuing may affix the signature in a variety of ways—for example, by word, mark, or rubber stamp. 3. Agent or authorized representative may supply the "signature."
Must Contain a Promise or Order to Pay	1. Promise must be more than acknowledgment of a debt. 2. Order requirement is met if the drawer issues an instruction to "pay".
Promise or Order Must Be Unconditional	1. Entire obligation must be found in the instrument itself and not in another document or documents. 2. Payment cannot be conditioned on the occurrence of an event.
Must Call for Payment of a Fixed Amount of Money	1. Must be able to ascertain the principal from the face of the instrument. 2. May contain a clause providing for payment of interest or other charges such as collection or attorney's fees.
Must Be Payable in Money	1. Obligation must be payable in a medium of exchange authorized or adopted by a government or by an international organization or agreement between two or more nations. 2. Maker or drawer cannot have the option to pay in something other than money.
Must Be Payable on Demand or at a Definite Time	1. Requirement is met if instrument says it is payable on demand or, if no time for payment is stated, it is payable on demand. 2. Requirement is met if it is payable on a stated date, at a fixed time after a stated date, or a fixed time "after sight." 3. Instrument may contain an acceleration clause or a clause allowing maker or holder to extend the payment date.
Generally Must Be Payable to Bearer or to Order	1. Bearer requirement is met if instrument is payable "to bearer" or "to cash." 2. Order requirement is met if instrument is payable "to the order of" a specified person or persons. 3. Exception from requirement is made for instruments meeting both the definition of a check and all the other requirements for a negotiable instrument.
May Not State Any Other Undertaking or Instruction by the Person Promising or Ordering Payment to Do Any Act in Addition to the Payment of Money	1. However, it may contain (*a*) an undertaking or power to give, maintain, or protect collateral to secure payment, (*b*) an authorization or power to the holder to confess judgment or realize on or dispose of collateral, or (*c*) a waiver of the benefit of any law intended for the advantage or protection of an obligor on the instrument.

alatia Community State Bank honored a check it took for collection for $5,550, which was the amount imprinted by a check-writing machine in the center underlined section of the check commonly used for stating the amount in words. The imprint looked like this:

Registered
No. 497345 **5550 DOL'S 00 CTS

*The impression made by the check-writing machine could be felt on the front and back of the check, and "**5550 DOL'S 00 CTS" was imprinted in red ink. In the box on the right-hand side of the check commonly used for numbers, "6,550.00" appeared in handwriting. The check was in partial payment of the purchase price of two engines that Eugene Kindy was buying from the payee on the check, Tony Hicks. Kindy postdated the check by a month and deliberately placed two different amounts on the check because he thought the bank would check with him before paying it. Kindy wanted to be sure that the engines had been delivered to Canada before he paid the $6,550 balance of the purchase price.*

After the check was deposited in the Galatia Bank and Hicks was given $5,550, an employee of the bank altered the "6" by hand to read "5." Because Kindy had stopped payment on the check, the drawee bank refused to pay it to Galatia Bank. Galatia Bank then brought suit against Kindy as the drawer of the check. One of the issues in the lawsuit was how the check should be constructed. The trial court found that the rules on construction provided in the Code were not helpful because they were contradictory. The trial court held in favor of Kindy, and Galatia Bank appealed. ∽

Newbern, Justice   The trial court reviewed Code section 3–118(b) and (c) (1987) which has since been superseded by section 3–114 (1991) but which was in effect at the time in question in this case. The statute provided in relevant part:

3–118. Ambiguous terms and rules of construction.
The following rules apply to every instrument:

* * * * *

(b) Handwritten terms control typewritten and printed terms, and typewritten control printed.

(c) Words control figures except that if the words are ambiguous figures control.

The frustration expressed by the trial court with respect to section 3–118 which stated the applicable rules of construction for negotiable instruments is understandable.

The $5550.00 amount imprinted by the check writing machine upon the line customarily used for words is expressed in figures and not in words. One question is whether imprinted numbers located where words are customarily placed on a check control figures placed where figures are customarily placed. Another question is whether handwritten figures control printing.

We find both questions satisfactorily answered in *St. Paul Fire & Marine Ins. Co. v. Bank of Salem*. In that case, there was a conflict between an amount imprinted by a check imprinting machine and numbers expressed in typewritten figures. The court recognized the imprinted amount was not expressed in words but held "the purposes of the UCC are best served by considering an amount imprinted by a check writing machine as 'words' for the purpose of resolving an ambiguity between an amount and an amount entered upon the line usually used to express the amount in figures." The court quoted from a pre-UCC case, *United States Fidelity and Guar-*

anty Co. v. First National Bank of South Carolina (1964), as follows:

A prime purpose, as we see it, of making a sum payable when expressed in words controlling over the sum payable expressed in figures is the very fact that words are much more difficult to alter. The perforated imprinting by a check-writing machine, while fully expressing the sum payable in figures, is even more difficult to successfully alter than a sum payable in written words.

Because a check imprinting machine's purpose is to protect against alterations, the amount shown on the imprint should control whether the number is in words or figures.

Turning to the question of whether typewriting controls printing, the court in *United States Fidelity and Guaranty Co.* stated:

As the section makes clear, in the event of an ambiguity between printed terms and typewritten terms, the latter would control. We do not consider the impression made by the check imprinter to be 'printed terms' under this section.

A conflict between the two amounts on a check would be resolved by section 3–118 which states that words control figures. Arguably, the amount imprinted by the check writing machine upon the line customarily expressing the amount in words, is expressed in figures . . . We think, however, that the purposes of the UCC are best served by considering an amount imprinted by a check writing machine as 'words' for the purpose of resolving an ambiguity between that amount and an amount entered upon the line usually used to express the amount in figures.

Although the court did not say specifically that it regarded the portion written by the check writing machine was the equivalent of handwriting, that is the clear effect of the decision.

In *United States v. Hibernia National Bank,* a typed numerical amount was located in the place customarily used for words. The amount conflicted with the amount located in the place customarily used for figures. The court found the typed amount controlling despite the fact it was not expressed in words.

Judgment for Kindy reversed on other grounds.

Note: Although, as the court notes, this case was decided under the original version of Article 3, the dilemma posed, and the conclusion reached by the court on the construction of the check, would likely be the same under Revised Article 3.

ETHICAL AND PUBLIC POLICY CONCERNS

1. The Uniform Commercial Code currently provides that in the case of ambiguity or conflict between the words and numbers on a negotiable instrument, the words control the numbers. A group of banks argue that in an era of computers, they encode checks based on the amount stated in figures and that the Code should be changed to provide for the dominance of figures over words. What policy considerations are involved in deciding whether or not the bank's position should be adopted in the Code?

PROBLEMS AND PROBLEM CASES

1. Is the following instrument a note, a check, or a draft? Why? If it is not a check, how would you have to change it to make it a check?

To: Arthur Adams January 1, 1998
TEN DAYS AFTER DATE PAY TO THE ORDER OF:
Bernie Brown
THE SUM OF: Ten thousand and no/100 DOLLARS
SIGNED: Carl Clark

2. Wiley, Tate & Irby, buyers and sellers of used cars, sold several autos to Houston Auto Sales. Houston wrote out the order for payment on the outside of several envelopes. He signed them and they were drawn on his bank, Peoples Bank & Trust Co., to be paid on the demand of Wiley, Tate & Irby. Can the envelopes qualify as negotiable instruments?

3. Is the following a negotiable instrument?

IOU, A. Gay, the sum of seventeen and 5/100 dollars for value received.
John R. Rooke

4. Holly Hill Acres, Ltd., executed a promissory note and mortgage and delivered them to Rogers. The note contained the following stipulation:

This note with interest is secured by a mortgage on real estate of even date herewith, made by the maker hereof in favor of the said payee, and shall be construed and enforced according to the laws of the State of Florida. The terms of said mortgage are by this reference made a part hereof.

Is the note a negotiable instrument?

5. Strickland ordered a swimming pool from Kafko Manufacturing and gave it a check for the purchase price that included the following words in the space following the word memo: "for pool kit to be delivered." Is the check negotiable?

6. Olde Town Investment Corporation borrowed $18,000 from VMC Mortgage Company and signed a promissory note secured by a deed of trust on land it owned. The note provided for interest at "three percent (3.00%) over Chase Manhattan Prime to be adjusted monthly." Is a note providing for a variable amount of interest, not ascertainable from the face of the note, a negotiable instrument?

7. In 1964, S. Gentilotti wrote a check for $20,000 payable to the order of his son, Edward J. Gentilotti. He postdated the check November 4, 1984, which would be his son's 20th birthday. The father also wrote on the check that it should be paid from his estate if he died prior to November 4, 1984. The father then gave the check to Edward's mother for safekeeping. On May 31, 1972, the father died. The check was then presented for payment but the bank refused to pay it. The mother and the son then brought a lawsuit against the executor of the father's estate to require payment. The executor claimed that the check was not a valid negotiable instrument because it had been postdated. Can a check be a negotiable instrument if it is postdated 20 years?

8. Nation-Wide Check Corporation sold money orders to drugstores. The money orders contained the words, "Payable to," followed by a blank. Can the money order qualify as a negotiable instrument?

9. Holliday made out a promissory note to Anderson, leaving the date of payment of the note blank. Anderson filled in the words "on demand" in the blank without Holliday's knowledge. Does this alter the rights or obligations of the parties?

10. Louis Canino signed the following instrument:

No. *922B*. INSTALLMENT NOTE

$27,000.00   *March 11, 1980*

LOUIS G. CANINO for value received, does promise to pay to the order of *CARL MESS* the sum *Two Hundred Twenty-Five* ... Dollars at *Lakewood, Colorado,* said principal payable *on the first day of each and every month*

commencing April 1, 1980, with interest at the rate of 8 percent per annum.

/s/Louis G. Canino

When Mess sued Canino on the note, Canino argued that the words "Two Hundred Twenty-Five Dollars" should control the figures "$27,000" and that he was obligated to pay only $225. Is this a valid argument?

Negotiation and Holder in Due Course

The preceding chapter discussed the nature and benefits of negotiable instruments. It also outlined the requirements an instrument must meet to qualify as a negotiable instrument and thus possess the qualities that allow it to be accepted as a substitute for money.

This chapter focuses on negotiation—the process by which rights to a negotiable instrument pass from one person to another. Commonly, this involves an indorsement and transfer of the instrument. This chapter also develops the requirements that a transferee of a negotiable instrument must meet to qualify as a holder in due course and thus attain special rights under negotiable instruments law. These rights, which put a holder in due course in an enhanced position compared to an assignee of a contract, are discussed in some detail. ∞

NEGOTIATION

Nature of Negotiation

Under Revised Article 3, **negotiation** is the transfer of possession (whether voluntary or involuntary) of a negotiable instrument by a person (other than the issuer) to another person who becomes its *holder* [3–201]. A person is a **holder** if she is in possession of an instrument (1) that is payable to bearer or (2) made payable to an identified person and she is that identified person [1–201(20)].[1]

---

[1]The numbers in parentheses refer to sections of the Uniform Commercial Code (UCC), which is reproduced in the appendix.

For example, when an employer gives an employee, Susan Adams, a paycheck payable "to the order of Susan Adams," she is the holder of the check because she is in possession of an instrument payable to an identified person (Susan Adams) and she is that person. When she indorses (writes her name) on the back of the check and exchanges it for cash and merchandise at Ace Grocery, she has negotiated the check to the grocery store and the store is now the holder because it is in possession by transfer of a check and unless she specifies the grocery store by name, the check now is payable to bearer. Similarly, if Susan Adams indorsed the check "Pay to the Order of Ace Grocery, Susan Adams" and transferred it to the grocery store, it would be a holder through the negotiation of the order check to it. The grocery store would be in possession of an instrument payable to an identified person (Ace Grocery) and is the person identified in the check.

In certain circumstances, Revised Article 3 allows a person to become a holder by negotiation even though the transfer of possession is involuntary. For example, if a negotiable instrument is payable to bearer and is stolen by Tom Thief or found by Fred Finder, Thief or Finder becomes the holder when he obtains possession. The involuntary transfer of possession of a bearer instrument results in a negotiation to Thief or Finder.

Formal Requirements for Negotiation

The formal requirements for negotiation are very simple. If an instrument is payable to the order of a specific payee, it is called **order paper** and it can be negotiated by transfer of possession of the instrument after indorsement by the person specified [3–201(b)].

For example, if Rachel's father gives her a check payable "to the order of Rachel Stern," then Rachel can negotiate the check by indorsing her name on the back of the check and giving it to the person to whom she wants to transfer it. Note that the check is order paper, not because the word *order* appears on the check but rather because it named a specific payee, Rachel Stern.

If an instrument is payable "to bearer" or "to cash," it is called **bearer paper** and negotiating it is even simpler. An instrument payable to bearer may be negotiated by transfer of possession alone [3–201(b)]. Thus, if someone gives you a check that is made payable "to the order of cash," you can negotiate it simply by giving it to the person to whom you wish to transfer it. No indorsement is necessary to negotiate an instrument payable to bearer. However, the person who takes the instrument may ask for an indorsement for her protection. By indorsing the check, you agree to be liable for its payment to that person if it is not paid by the drawee bank when it is presented for payment. This liability will be discussed in Chapter 32, Liability of Parties.

Nature of Indorsement

An indorsement is made by adding the signature of the holder of the instrument to the instrument, usually on the back of it, either alone or with other words. **Indorsement** is defined to mean "a signature (other than that of a maker, drawer or acceptor) that alone or accompanied by other words, is made on an instrument for purpose of (i) negotiating the instrument, (ii) restricting payment of the instrument, or (iii) incurring indorser's liability on the instrument" [3–204(a)]. The negotiation and restriction of payment aspects of indorsements will be discussed below; indorser's liability will be covered in the next chapter.

The signature constituting an indorsement can be supplied or written either by the holder or by someone who is authorized to sign on behalf of the holder. For example, a check payable to "H&H Meat Market" might be indorsed "H&H Meat Market by Jane Frank, President," if Jane is authorized to do this on behalf of the market.

Wrong or Misspelled Name

When indorsing an instrument, the holder should spell his name in the same way as it appears on the instrument. If the holder's name is misspelled or wrong, then legally the indorsement can be made either in his name or in the name that is on the instrument. However, any person who pays the instrument or otherwise gives value for it may require the indorser to sign both names [3–204(d)].

Suppose Joan Ash is issued a check payable to the order of "Joanne Ashe." She may indorse the check as either "Joan Ash" or "Joanne Ashe ." However, if she takes the check to a bank to cash, the bank may require her to sign both "Joanne Ashe" and "Joan Ash."

Checks Deposited without Indorsement

Occasionally, when a customer deposits a check to her account with a bank, she may forget to indorse the check. It is common practice for depositary banks to receive unindorsed checks under what are known as "lock-box" arrangements with customers who receive a high volume of checks. Normally, a check payable to the order of an identified person would require the indorsement of that person in order for a negotiation to the depositary bank to take place and for it to become a holder. Under the original Article 3, the depositary bank, in most cases, had the right to supply the customer's indorsement. Instead of actually signing the customer's name to the check as the indorsement, the bank might just stamp on it that it was deposited by the customer or credited to her account. Banks did not have the right to put the customer's indorsement on a check that the customer has deposited if the check specifically required the payee's signature. Insurance and government checks commonly require the payee's signature.

The revision to Article 3 and the conforming amendments to Articles 1 and 4 address the situation where a check is deposited in a depositary bank without indorsement differently. The depositary bank becomes a holder of an item delivered to it for collection, whether or not it is indorsed by the customer, if the customer at the time of delivery qualified as a holder [4–205]. Concomitantly, the depositary bank warrants to other collecting banks, the payor bank (drawee), and the drawer that it paid the amount of the item to the customer or deposited the amount to the customer's account.

Transfer of Order Instrument

Except for the special provisions concerning depositary banks, if an order instrument is transferred without indorsement, the instrument has not been negotiated and the transferee cannot qualify as a holder. For example, Sue Brown gives a check payable "to the order of Susan Brown" to a drugstore in payment for some cosmetics. Until Sue indorses the check, she has not "negotiated" it and the druggist could not qualify as a "holder" of the check.

Transfer of an instrument, whether or not the transfer is a negotiation, vests in the transferee, such as the drug store, any right of Sue, the transferor, to enforce the instrument. However, the transferee cannot obtain the rights of a holder in due course (discussed later in this chapter) if he is engaged in any fraud or illegality affecting the instrument. Unless otherwise agreed, if an instrument is transferred for value but without a required indorsement, the transferee has the right to obtain the unqualified indorsement of the transferor; however, the "negotiation" only takes place when the transferor applies her indorsement [3–203(c)].

INDORSEMENTS

Effects of an Indorsement

There are three functions to an indorsement. First, an indorsement is necessary in order for the negotiation of an instrument that is payable to the order of a specified person. Thus, if a check is payable "to the order of James Lee, " James must indorse the check before it can be negotiated. Second, the form of the indorsement that the indorser uses also affects future attempts to negotiate the instrument. For example, if James indorses it "Pay to the order of Sarah Hill," Sarah must indorse it before it can be negotiated further.

Third, an indorsement generally makes a person liable on the instrument. By indorsing an instrument, a person incurs an obligation to pay the instrument if the person primarily liable on it (for example, the maker of a note) does not pay it. We discuss the contractual liability of indorsers in Chapter 32. In this chapter, we discuss the effect of an indorsement on further negotiation of an instrument.

Kinds of Indorsements

There are three basic kinds of indorsements: (1) special, (2) blank, and (3) restrictive. In addition, an indorsement may be "qualified."

Special Indorsement A **special indorsement** contains the signature of the indorser along with words indicating to whom, or to whose order, the instrument is payable. For example, if a check is drawn "Pay to the Order of Marcia Morse" and

Marcia indorses it "Pay to the Order of Sam Smith, Marcia Morse," or "Pay to Sam Smith, Marcia Morse," it has been indorsed with a special indorsement. An instrument that is indorsed with a special indorsement remains "order paper." It can be negotiated only with the indorsement of the person specified [3–205(a)]. In this example, Sam Smith must indorse the check before he can negotiate it to someone else.

Blank Indorsement   If an indorser merely signs his name and does not specify to whom the instrument is payable, he has indorsed the instrument **in blank.** For example, if a check drawn "Pay to the Order of Natalie Owens" is indorsed "Natalie Owens" by Natalie, Natalie has indorsed it in blank. An instrument indorsed in blank is payable to the bearer (person in possession of it) and from that act is "bearer paper." As such, the bearer negotiates it by transfer alone and no further indorsement is necessary for negotiation [3–205(b)].

If Natalie indorsed the check in blank and gave it to Kevin Foley, Kevin would have the right to convert the blank indorsement into a special indorsement [3–205(c)]. He could do this by writing the words "Pay to the Order of Kevin Foley" above Natalie's indorsement. Then Kevin would have to indorse the check before it could be further negotiated.

If Kevin took the check indorsed in blank to a bank and presented it for payment or for collection, the bank normally would ask him to indorse the check. It does this not because it needs his indorsement for the check to be negotiated to it; the check indorsed in blank can be negotiated merely by delivering it to the bank cashier. Rather, the bank asks for his indorsement because it wants to make him liable on the check if it is not paid when the bank sends it to the drawee bank for payment. Chapter 32, Liability of Parties, discusses the liability of indorsers.

Restrictive Indorsement   A **restrictive indorsement** is one that specifies the purpose of the indorsement or specifies the use to be made of the instrument. Among the more common restrictive indorsements are:

1. Indorsements for deposit. For example, "For Deposit Only" or "For Deposit to My Account at First National Bank."

2. Indorsements for collection, which are commonly put on by banks involved in the collection process. For example, "Pay any bank, banker, or trust company" or "For collection only."

3. Indorsements indicating that the indorsement is for the benefit of someone other than the person to whom it is payable. For example, "Pay to Arthur Attorney in Trust for Mark Minor."

Generally, the person who takes an instrument with a restrictive indorsement must pay or apply any money or other value he gives for the instrument consistently with the indorsement. In the case of a check indorsed "for deposit" or "for collection," any person other than a bank who purchases the check is considered to have **converted** the check unless (1) the indorser received the amount paid for it or (2) the bank applied the amount of the check consistently with the indorsement (e.g., deposited it to the indorser's account). Similarly, a depositary bank (a bank that takes an item for collection) or payor bank (the drawee bank) that takes an instrument for deposit or for immediate payment over the counter that has been indorsed "for deposit" or "for collection" will be liable for conversion unless the indorser received the amount paid for the instrument or the proceeds or the bank applied the amount consistently with the indorsement [3–206(c)].[2]

By way of illustration, assume that Robert Franks has indorsed his paycheck "For Deposit to My Account No. 4068933 at Bank One." While on his way to the bank he loses the check, and Fred Finder finds it. If Finder tries to cash the check at a check-cashing service, the service must ensure that any value it gives for the check either is deposited to Franks' account at Bank One or is received by Franks. If it gives the money to Finder, it will be liable to Franks for converting his check. This principle is illustrated in the following case, *Lehigh Presbytery v. Merchants Bancorp, Inc.,* which involves a bank that failed to apply value given for checks consistently with restrictive indorsements on the checks.

---

[2]Otherwise, a payor bank as well as an intermediary bank may disregard the indorsement and is not liable if the proceeds of the instrument are not received by the indorser or applied consistently with the indorsement [3–206(c)(4)].

Mary Ann Hunsberger was hired by the Lehigh Presbytery as a secretary/bookkeeper. In this capacity, she was responsible for opening the Presbytery's mail, affixing a rubber-stamp indorsement to checks received by the Presbytery, and depositing the checks into the Presbytery's account at Merchants Bancorp, Inc. Over a period of more than five years, Hunsberger deposited into her own account 153 of these checks. Each check was indorsed: "For Deposit Only To The Credit of Presbytery of Lehigh, Ernest Hutcheson, Treas." The bank credited the checks to Hunsberger's account, despite the rubber stamp restrictive indorsement, because it relied solely on the account number handwritten on the deposit slips submitted by Hunsberger with the checks at the time of deposit. Hunsberger obtained the deposit slips in the lobby of the bank, wrote the proper account title, "Lehigh Presbytery," but inserted her own account number rather than the account number of her employer.

When Lehigh Presbytery discovered the diversionary scheme, it sued the bank to recover the funds credited to Hunsberger's account. The primary issue in the case was whether the bank was bound to follow the restrictive indorsements on the 153 checks that it instead had deposited to the personal account of Hunsberger. The trial court ruled in favor of the bank and Lehigh Presbytery appealed. ∞

McEwen, Judge UCC Section 3–205 provides:

An indorsement is restrictive which either:

* * * * *

(3) includes the words "for collection," "for deposit," "pay any bank," or like terms signifying a purpose of deposit or collection; or

* * * * *

It is undisputed that the indorsement stamped on each check by Ms. Hunsberger is a restrictive indorsement within the meaning of section 3–205.

Section 3–206 of the UCC addresses the effect of such an indorsement and provides, in pertinent part:

(c) Conditional or specified purpose indorsement.— Except for an intermediary bank, any transferee under an indorsement which is conditional or includes the words "for collection," "for deposit," "Pay any bank," or like terms (section 3–205(1) and (3) (relating to restrictive indorsements) must pay or apply any value given by him for or on the security of the instrument consistently with the indorsement and to the extent he does he becomes a holder for value.

Thus, the UCC mandates application of the value of the checks consistently with the indorsement, i.e. for deposit to Lehigh Presbytery's account.

Courts considering the significance of a restrictive indorsement have consistently concluded that the UCC imposes an unwaivable obligation upon the bank to follow the indorsement. New York State's highest court has held that "[t]he presence of a restriction imposes upon the depositary bank an obligation not to accept that item other than in accord with the restriction. By disregarding the restriction, it not only subjects itself to liability for any losses resulting from its actions, but it also passes up what may be the best opportunity to prevent the fraud."

Judgment reversed in favor of Lehigh Presbytery.

Note: Although this case was decided under the original version of Article 3, the same result would be expected under Revised Article 3.

Some indorsements indicate payment to the indorsee as an agent, trustee, or fiduciary. A person who takes an instrument containing such an indorsement from the indorsee may pay the proceeds to the indorsee without regard to whether the indorsee violates a fiduciary duty to the indorser *unless* he is on *notice* of any breach of fiduciary duty that the indorser may be committing [3–206(d)]. A person would have such notice if he took the instrument in any transaction that benefited the indorsee personally [3–307]. Suppose a person takes a check indorsed to "Arthur Attorney in Trust for Mark Minor." The money given for the check should be put in Mark Minor's trust account. A person would not be justified in taking the check in exchange for a television set that he knew Attorney was acquiring for his own—rather than Minor's—use.

There are two other kinds of indorsements that the original Article 3 treated as restrictive indorsements but that the revised Article 3 no longer considers as restrictive indorsements. They are:

1. Indorsements purporting to prohibit further negotiation. For example, "Pay to Carl Clark Only."
2. Conditional indorsements, which indicate that they are effective only if the payee satisfies a certain condition. For example, "Pay to Bernard Builder Only if He Completes Construction on My House by November 1, 1995."

Under Revised Article 3, any indorsement that purports to limit payment to a particular person, or to prohibit further transfer or negotiation of the instrument, is not effective to prevent further transfer or negotiation [3–206(a)]. Thus, if a note is indorsed "Pay to Carl Clark Only" and given to Clark, he may negotiate the note to subsequent holders who may ignore the restriction on the indorsement.

Indorsements that state a condition to the right of the indorsee to receive payment do not affect the right of the indorsee to enforce the instrument. Any person who pays the instrument or takes it for value or for collection may disregard the condition. Moreover, the rights and liabilities of the person are not affected by whether the condition has been fulfilled [3–206(b)].

Qualified Indorsement   A **qualified indorsement** is one where the indorser disclaims her liability to make the instrument good if the maker or drawer defaults on it. Words such as "Without Recourse" are used to qualify an indorsement. They can be used with either a blank indorsement or a special indorsement and thus make it a qualified blank indorsement or a qualified special indorsement. The use of a qualified indorsement does not change the negotiable nature of the instrument. Its effect is to eliminate the contractual liability of the particular indorser. Chapter 32, Liability of Parties, will discuss this liability in detail.

C O N C E P T   R E V I E W

Indorsements
(Assume a check is payable "To The Order of Mark Smith.")

TYPE	EXAMPLE	CONSEQUENCES
Blank	Mark Smith	1. Satisfies the indorsement requirement for the negotiation of order paper. 2. The instrument becomes bearer paper and can be negotiated by delivery alone. 3. The indorser becomes obligated on the instrument. (See Chapter 32, Liability of Parties.)
Special	Pay to the Order of Joan Brown, Mark Smith	1. Satisfies the indorsement requirement for the negotiation of order paper. 2. The instrument remains order paper and Joan Brown's indorsement is required for further negotiation. 3. The indorser becomes obligated on the instrument. (See Chapter 32.)
Restrictive	For deposit only to my account in First American Bank Mark Smith	1. Satisfies the indorsement requirement for the negotiation of order paper. 2. The person who pays value for the instrument is obligated to pay it consistent with the indorsement (i.e., to pay it into Mark Smith's account at First American Bank). 3. The indorser becomes obligated on the instrument. (See Chapter 32.)
Qualified	Mark Smith (without recourse)	1. Satisfies the indorsement requirement for negotiation of order paper. 2. Eliminates the indorser's obligation. (See Chapter 32.)

Rescission of Indorsement

Negotiation is effective to transfer an instrument even if the negotiation is (1) made by a minor, a corporation exceeding its powers, or any other person without contractual capacity; (2) obtained by fraud, duress, or mistake of any kind; (3) made in breach of duty; or (4) part of an illegal transaction. A negotiation made under the preceding circumstances is subject to **rescission** before the instrument has been negotiated to a transferee who can qualify as a holder in due course or a person paying the instrument in good faith and without knowledge of the factual basis for rescission or other remedy [3–202]. The situation in such instances is analogous to a sale of goods where the sale has been induced by fraud or misrepresentation. In such a case, the seller may rescind the sale and recover the goods, provided that the seller acts before the goods are resold to a bona fide purchaser for value.

HOLDER IN DUE COURSE

A person who qualifies as a holder in due course of a negotiable instrument gets special rights. Normally, the transferee of an instrument—like the assignee of a contract—gets only those rights in the instrument that are held by the person from whom he got the instrument. But a holder in due course can get better rights. A holder in due course takes a negotiable instrument free of all **personal defenses, claims to the instrument,** and **claims in recoupment** either of the obligor or of a third party. A holder in due course does not take free of the **real defenses,** which go to the validity of the instrument or of claims that develop after he becomes a holder. We develop the differences between "personal" and "real defenses" in more detail later in this chapter and also explain claims to the instrument and claims in recoupment. The following example illustrates the advantage that a holder in due course of a negotiable instrument may have.

Assume that Carl Carpenter contracts with Helen Hawkins to build her a garage for $9,500, payable on October 1 when he expects to complete the garage. Assume further that Carpenter assigns his right to the $9,500 to First National Bank in order to obtain money for materials. If the bank tries to collect the money from Hawkins on October 1 but Carpenter has not finished building the garage, then Hawkins may assert the fact that the garage is not complete as a defense to paying the bank. As assignee of a simple contract, the bank has only those rights that its assignor, Carpenter, has and is subject to all claims and defenses that Hawkins has against Carpenter.

Now assume that instead of simply signing a contract with Hawkins, Carpenter had Homeowner give him a negotiable promissory note in the amount of $9,500 payable to the order of Carpenter on October 1 and that Carpenter then negotiated the note to the bank. If the bank is able to qualify as a holder in due course, it may collect the $9,500 from Hawkins on October 1 even though she might have a personal defense against payment of the note because Carpenter had not completed the work on the garage. Hawkins cannot assert that personal defense against a holder in due course. She would have to pay the note to the bank and then independently seek to recover from Carpenter for breach of their agreement. The bank's improved position is due to its status as a holder in due course of a negotiable instrument. If the instrument in question was not negotiable, or if the bank could not qualify as a holder in due course, then it would be in the same position as the assignee of a simple contract and would be subject to Homeowner's personal defense.

We turn now to a discussion of the requirements that must be met for the possessor of a negotiable instrument to qualify as a holder in due course.

General Requirements

In order to become a **holder in due course,** a person who takes a negotiable instrument must be a *holder,* and take the instrument for *value,* in *good faith, without notice* that it is *overdue* or has been *dishonored* or that there is any uncured default with respect to payment of another instrument issued as part of the same series, *without notice* that the instrument *contains an unauthorized signature or has been altered, without notice* of any *claim of a property or possessory interest in it,* and *without notice* that any party has any *defense against it* or *claim in recoupment to it* [3–302].

In addition, the revision to Article 3 requires "that the instrument when issued or negotiated to the holder does not bear such *apparent evidence of forgery or alteration* or is not otherwise so *irregular* or *incomplete* as to call into question its authenticity" [3–302(a)(1)].

If a person who takes a negotiable instrument does not meet these requirements, he is not a holder in due course. Then the person is in the same position as an assignee of a contract.

Holder

To be a **holder** of a negotiable instrument, a person must have possession of an instrument that is either payable to "bearer" or that is payable to him. For example, if Teresa Gonzales is given a check by her grandmother that is made payable "to the order of Teresa Gonzales," Teresa is a holder of the check because it is made out to her. If Teresa indorses the check "Pay to the order of Ames Grocery, Teresa Gonzales" and gives it to Ames Hardware in payment for some merchandise, then Ames Hardware is the holder of the check. Ames Hardware is a holder because it is in possession of a check that is indorsed to its order. If Ames Hardware indorses the check "Ames Hardware" and deposits it in its account at First National Bank, the bank becomes the holder. The bank is in possession of an instrument that is indorsed in blank and thus is payable to bearer.

It is important that all indorsements on the instrument at the time it is payable to the order of someone are *authorized indorsements*. With limited exceptions (discussed later), a forged indorsement is not an effective indorsement and prevents a person from becoming a holder.

To be a holder, a person must have a complete chain of authorized indorsements. Suppose the Internal Revenue Service mails to Robert Washington an income tax refund check payable to him. Tom Turner steals the check from Washington's mailbox, signs (indorses) "Robert Washington" on the back of the check, and cashes it at a shoe store. The shoe store is not a holder of the check because its transferor, Turner, was not a holder and because it needs Washington's signature to have a good chain of authorized indorsements. Robert Washington has to indorse the check in order for there to be a valid chain of indorsements. Turner's signature is not effective for this purpose because Washington did not authorize him to sign Washington's name to the check [1–201(20); 3–403(a); 3–416(a)(2)].

The case that follows, *La Junta State Bank v. Travis,* illustrates that a party in possession of a check indorsed in blank is a holder of the instrument.

LA JUNTA STATE BANK v. TRAVIS 727 P.2d 48 (Sup. CT. Colo. 1986)

O*n November 15, 1979, Katherine Warnock purchased a cashier's check in the amount of $53,541.93 payable to her order and drawn on the Pueblo Bank and Trust Company. At some time between November 15 and November 30, Warnock indorsed "Katherine Warnock" on the reverse side of the check, and Warnock's attorney, Jerry Quick, wrote the words "deposit only" under Warnock's indorsement. On November 30, Quick deposited the check into a trust account he maintained at the La Junta State Bank. Warnock did not maintain any type of account with La Junta State Bank. La Junta collected the amount of the check from Pueblo Bank.*

Warnock died on November 10, 1981. Robert Travis, Warnock's personal representative, was unable to find a receipt in her personal papers for the sum of $53,541.93. On June 24, Travis demanded that the La Junta Bank repay that sum to Warnock's estate. At the time, no funds remained in Quick's trust account at the bank. When the La Junta Bank refused the representative's demand, he brought suit against the bank claiming it had improperly paid the check by allowing it into any account other than one in Warnock's name. The trial court determined that Warnock had indorsed the check in blank and delivered it to Quick, that the check therefore became bearer paper upon Warnock's indorsement, and that the check was negotiable on delivery alone; it granted judgment to the bank. A divided court of appeals reversed in favor of the representative, holding that Quick's addition of the words "deposit only" below Warnock's signature created a restrictive indorsement and that because the bank failed to treat it as such, it was liable to the representative for the full amount of the check. The bank appealed. ∽

Kirshbaum, Justice It is undisputed that when Warnock indorsed the check in blank and delivered

it to Quick, it was converted from order paper to bearer paper, negotiable by delivery alone until specially indorsed [3–204(2)]. The trial court also concluded that Quick's addition of "deposit only" below Warnock's signature did not convert Warnock's blank indorsement into a special indorsement.

Implicit in the trial court's conclusions is the assumption that Quick added the words "deposit only" to the check some time after Warnock's indorsement thereof. This implicit finding is supported by the stipulation of facts and the evidence disclosed by the record. Therefore, we also conclude that when Warnock indorsed the check in blank and delivered it to Quick, Quick became a holder of the instrument in bearer form with the right to transfer or negotiate it by delivery alone.

Warnock's representative argues that, assuming Quick was initially a holder of a check in bearer form, his act of affixing the words "deposit only" to the check deprived him of that status, destroyed the negotiability of the check, and converted Warnock's blank indorsement into a restrictive indorsement. This argument is untenable.

Quick, as holder of an instrument, was not authorized by any Code provision to convert this transferor's blank indorsement into a restrictive one (see section 3–204(3): "The holder may convert a blank indorsement by writing over the signature of the indorser in blank any contract consistent with the character of the indorsement."). Furthermore, the representative incorrectly assumes that a blank indorsement and a restrictive indorsement create mutually exclusive methods for negotiation. As UCC section 3–206 official comment 5 (1978) indicates, "indorsements 'for collection' or 'for deposit' may be either special or blank." A single indorsement, therefore, may be both in blank and restrictive. The nonrestrictive character of Warnock's indorsement was determined when she affixed her signature to the check.

The fact that Quick was a holder of bearer paper does not end the inquiry into the propriety of the bank's conduct. Section 3–206(3) of the Code requires a depository bank, upon being presented with a negotiable instrument containing an indorsement which includes the words "for deposit" or like terms, to "pay or apply any value given by him for or on the security of the instrument consistently with the indorsement. . ." This obligation affords protection to payees or endorsers who indorse items "for deposit" in the belief that such indorsement will guard against further negotiation of the instrument to a holder in due course by a finder or a thief.

In this case the bank, as a depository bank, received a check containing what appeared to be a restrictive indorsement by Katherine Warnock. The record does not reveal who actually delivered the check and deposit slip to the bank. Thus, at the moment it received the restrictively indorsed check, the bank appeared to owe a duty to Warnock to either comply with the directions of the indorsement or to inquire further concerning the transaction because of the simultaneous receipt of a deposit slip into an account other than Warnock's. However, because the check was bearer paper when Quick received it, he was free to direct its deposit in any manner he elected. Any inquiry by the bank would have revealed that, although the language inscribed on the instrument appeared to constitute a restrictive indorsement by Katherine Warnock, the words "deposit only" had been added by Quick on his own behalf; and the bank owed a duty to Quick on November 30, 1979, to honor his restrictive indorsement. Under the circumstances of the case, the bank owed no duty to Warnock and Warnock's representative is entitled to no damages.

Judgment for La Junta State Bank.

Note: Although this case was decided under the original version of Article 3, the same result would be anticipated under Revised Article 3.

Value

To qualify as a holder in due course of a negotiable instrument, a person must give **value** for it. Value is not identical to simple consideration. Under the provisions of the Revised Article 3, a holder takes for value if: (1) the agreed-upon promise of performance has been performed—for example, if the instrument was given in exchange for a promise to deliver a refrigerator and the refrigerator has been delivered; (2) he acquires a security interest in, or a lien on, the instrument; (3) he takes the instrument in payment of, or as security for, an antecedent claim; (4) he gives a negotiable instrument for it; or (5) he makes an irrevocable commitment to a third person [3–303]. Thus, a person who gets a check as a gift or merely makes an executory promise in return for a check has not given value for it and cannot qualify as a holder in due course.

A bank or any person who discounts an instrument in the *regular course of trade* has given value for it. In this context the discount essentially is a means for increasing the return or the rate of interest on the instrument. Likewise, if a loan is made and an instrument is pledged as security for the repayment of the loan, the secured party has given value for the instrument to the amount of the loan. If Axe, who owes Bell a past-due debt, indorses and delivers to Bell, in payment of the debt or as security for its repayment, an instrument issued to Axe, Bell has given value for the instrument. If a bank allows a customer to draw against a check deposited for collection, it has given value to the extent of the credit drawn against.

If the promise of performance that is the consideration for an instrument has been partially performed, the holder may assert rights as a holder in due course of the instrument only to the fraction of the amount payable under the instrument equal to the partial performance divided by the value of the promised performance [3–302(d)]. For example, Arthur Wells agrees to purchase a note payable to the order of Helda Parks. The note is for the sum of

$5,000. Wells pays Parks $1,000 on the negotiation of the note to him and agrees to pay the balance of $4,000 in 10 days. Initially, Wells is a holder in due course for one-fifth of the amount of the note. If he later pays the $4,000 due he may become a holder in due course for the full amount.

Good Faith

To qualify as a holder in due course of a negotiable instrument, a person must take it in **good faith,** which means that the person obtained it honestly and in the observance of reasonable commercial standards of fair dealing [3–103(a)(4)]. If a person obtains a check by trickery or with knowledge that it has been stolen, the person has not obtained the check in good faith and cannot be a holder in due course. A person who pays too little for an instrument, perhaps because she suspects that something may be wrong with the way it was obtained, may have trouble meeting the good faith test. Suppose a finance company works closely with a door-to-door sales company that engages in shoddy practices. If the finance company buys the consumers' notes from the sales company, it will not be able to meet the good faith test and qualify as a holder in due course of the notes.

TRIFFIN v. DILLABOUGH   670 A.2d 684 (Penn. Super. Ct. 1996)

On December 11, 1990, two American Express money orders in the amounts of $550 and $650, respectively, which were payable to Stacey Anne Dillabough, were presented to Chuckie Enterprise, Inc. (Chuckie's), a check-cashing operation in Philadelphia. The money orders were duly indorsed, and photo identifications were provided by the payee; whereupon, Chuckie's paid the face amounts minus a 2 percent fee.

The two money orders had been stolen from the premises of an American Express agent. When stolen, the money orders were signed with the preprinted signature of the Chairman of American Express, but were blank as to payee, date, sender, and amount. When presented to Chuckie's, however, they had been completed by persons unknown.

The money orders were passed through the usual banking channels and were presented for payment at United Bank of Grand Junction, Colorado. American Express, having noted on its "fraud log" that the money orders were stolen, returned the money orders marked "Reported Lost or Stolen—Do Not Redeposit." American Express refused to pay the amounts of the money orders.

The back of the money orders contained the following legend:

IMPORTANT
DO NOT CASH FOR STRANGERS
This money order will not be paid if it has been altered or
stolen or if an indorsement is missing or forged. Be sure
you have effective recourse against your customer.

PAYEE'S INDORSEMENT

Triffin, a commercial discounter, purchased the dishonored money orders for cash from Chuckie's and took an assignment of all of Chuckie's rights, claims, and interests in the money orders. Triffin brought suit against Dillabough and American Express demanding payment of their stolen money orders. Judgment was entered against Dillabough by default, and the trial court entered a verdict in favor of American Express. Triffin appealed. ∞

Wieand, Judge The issue in this appeal is whether blank money orders, which were stolen prior to being sold and subsequently completed without authorization, are negotiable instruments, and, if so, whether a holder in due course has a right to payment on the instrument despite a lack of initial consideration and the absence of delivery.

Under section 3–407, a holder in due course may in all cases enforce the instrument according to its original tenor, and when an incomplete instrument has been completed, he may enforce it as completed. A holder in due course is a "holder who takes the instrument: (1) for value; (2) in good faith; and (3) without notice that it is overdue or has been dishonored or of any defense against or claim to it on the part of any person. Good faith is "honesty in fact in the conduct or transaction concerned."

It is not disputed that if Chuckie's, as Triffin's assignor, was a holder in due course, then Triffin also stands in the shoes of a holder in due course. The trial court made no specific determination that Chuckie's was a holder in due course, but, after hearing the evidence, the court did express its belief that Chuckie's had acted in good faith when it paid value for the money orders. American Express asserts that the legend printed on the reverse side of each instrument, together with the circumstances surrounding the transactions, created a heightened duty of inquiry upon Chuckie's for the purpose of establishing "good faith" and served as notice of voidability sufficient to present notice of a defense.

The evidence showed that Charles Giunta, president of Chuckie's enterprise, a check cashing business operated by Giunta since 1989, followed his customary procedures during the underlying transactions. He required and obtained photo identification from Dillabough. He recognized her as a previous customer. The instruments were complete and regular on their face when presented; and Chuckie's paid the face amount of the money orders, minus its regular fee. The surname of the sender on the Dillabough instruments was not decipherable. Giunta testified that he was familiar with money orders and that he had no reason to believe the money orders in question would not be paid

when presented. The evidence also shows that Giunta cashed the money orders presented by Dillabough within 30 days of the completed date on the money orders.

American Express disputes that Chuckie's attained holder in due course status because, under the circumstances, Chuckie's failed to ascertain information about the senders on the instruments and should have contacted American Express to determine if the money orders were properly payable before cashing them.

Contrary to American Express's position, we hold that the circumstances surrounding the subject transactions were not of a sufficiently suspicious nature as to require heightened inquiry by Chuckie's in order to establish the "good faith" element necessary for holder in due course status. Chuckie's required Dillabough to produce proper photo identification. Chuckie's also recognized the customer from prior transactions. The mere illegibility of the sender's surname did not suggest that lack of further inquiry arose from a suspicion that inquiry would disclose a vice or defect in the title.

American Express also argues that because the instruments state "[t]his money order will not be paid if it has been altered or stolen," Chuckie's should have inquired of American Express as to whether the money orders were properly payable. Given the general rule in Pennsylvania that there is no affirmative duty to inquire, we find no reason that the legend established such a duty, nor will we find that the mere presence of the legend would raise suspicion as to a vice or defect in the title. Therefore, we hold that Chuckie's was a holder in due course of the two American Express money orders which were stolen from American Express and completed without authorization by persons unknown. Triffin, by assignment, holds the same rights in the instruments as was previously held by Chuckie's.

Judgment in favor of American Express reversed.

Note: While Pennsylvania has adopted Revised Article 3, all of the transactions at issue in this case were completed prior to the effective date of the amendments and the court applied and cited the original version of Article 3. However, the same result would be expected if the court was applying Revised Article 3. The requirement under Revised Article 3 is that in order to be accorded the rights of a holder in due course, the person claiming that status must have taken the instrument in good faith. The expanded definition of good faith includes observance of reasonable commercial standards of fair dealing. See Revised Sections 3–302 and 3–103(a)(4).]

Overdue or Dishonored

In order to qualify as a holder in due course, a person must take a negotiable instrument before he has notice that it either is **overdue** or has been **dishonored.** The reason for this is that one should perform obligations when they are due. If a negotiable instrument is not paid when it is due, the Code considers the person taking it to be on notice that there may be defenses to the payment of it.

Overdue Instruments   If a negotiable instrument is payable on demand, it is overdue: (1) the day after demand for payment has been made in a proper manner and form; (2) 90 days after its date if it is a check; and (3) if it is an instrument other than a check, when it has been outstanding for an unreasonably long period of time in light of the nature of the instrument and trade practice [3–304(a)]. Thus, a check becomes stale after 90 days. For other kinds of instruments, one must consider trade practices and the facts of the particular case. In a farming community, the normal period for loans to farmers may be six months. A demand note might be outstanding for six or seven months before it is considered overdue. On the other hand, a demand note issued in an industrial city where the normal period of such loans is 30 to 60 days would be considered overdue in a much shorter period of time.

If a negotiable instrument due on a certain date is not paid by that date, normally then it will be overdue at the beginning of the next day after the due date. For example, if a promissory note dated January 1 is payable "30 days after date," it is due on January 31. If it is not paid by January 31, it is overdue beginning on February 1.

As to instruments payable at a definite time, Revised Article 3 sets out the following rules: (1) if the principal is not payable in installments and the due date has not been accelerated, the instrument is overdue on the day after the due date; (2) if the principal is due in installments and a due date has not been accelerated, the instrument is overdue upon default for nonpayment of an installment and remains overdue until the default is cured; (3) if a due date for the principal has been accelerated, the instrument is overdue on the day after the accelerated due date; and (4) unless the due date of the principal has been accelerated, an instrument does not become overdue if there is a default in payment of interest but no default in payment of principal [3–304(b)].

Dishonored Instruments   To be a holder in due course, a person not only must take a negotiable instrument before he has notice that it is overdue but also must take it before it has been dishonored. A negotiable instrument has been *dishonored* when the holder has *presented* it for payment (or acceptance) and payment (or acceptance) has been refused.

For example, Susan writes a check on her account at First National Bank that is payable "to the order of Sven Sorensen." Sven takes the check to First National Bank to cash it but the bank refuses to pay it because Susan has insufficient funds in her account to cover it. The check has been dishonored. If Sven then takes Susan's check to Harry's Hardware and uses it to pay for some paint, Harry's cannot be a holder in due course of the check if it is on notice that the check has been dishonored. Harry's would have such notice if First National had stamped the check "Payment Refused NSF" (not sufficient funds).

Similarly, suppose Carol Carson signs a 30-day note payable to Ace Appliance for $500 and gives it to Ace as payment for a stereo set. When Ace asks Carol for payment, she refuses to pay because the stereo does not work properly. If Ace negotiates the note to First National Bank, First National cannot be a holder in due course if it knows about Carol's refusal to pay.

Notice of Unauthorized Signature or Alteration

A holder who has notice that an instrument contains an unauthorized signature or has been altered cannot qualify as a holder in due course of the instrument.

For example, Frank makes out a check in the amount of $5 payable to George Grocer and gives it to his daughter, Jane, to take to the grocery store to purchase some groceries. The groceries Frank wants cost $20 and Jane changes the check to read $25, giving it to Grocer in exchange for the groceries and $5 in cash. Grocer cannot qualify as a holder in due course if he sees Jane make the alteration to the check or otherwise is on notice of it. [See 3–302(a)(1).]

Notice of Claims

If a person taking a negotiable instrument is *on notice of an adverse claim* to the instrument by someone else (for example, that she is the rightful owner of the instrument) or that someone is seeking to rescind a prior negotiation of the instrument, the current holder cannot qualify as a holder in due course. For example, a U.S. Treasury check is payable to Susan Samuels. Samuels loses the check and it is found by Robert Burns. Burns takes the check to a hardware store, signs "Susan Samuels" on the back of the check in the view of a clerk, and seeks to use it in payment of merchandise. The hardware store cannot be a holder in due course because it is on notice of a potential claim to the instrument by Susan Samuels.

Notice of Breach of Fiduciary Duty One situation in which the Code considers a person to be on notice of a claim is if she is taking a negotiable instrument from a fiduciary, such as a trustee. If a negotiable instrument is payable to a person as a trustee or an attorney for someone, then any attempt by that person to negotiate it for his own behalf or for his use (or benefit) or to deposit it in an account other than that of the fiduciary puts the person on notice that the beneficiary of the trust may have a claim [3–307].

For example, a check is drawn "Pay to the order of Arthur Adams, Trustee for Mary Minor." Adams takes the check to Credit Union, indorses his name to it, and uses it to pay off the balance on a loan Adams had from Credit Union. Credit Union cannot be a holder in due course because it should know that the negotiation of the check is in violation of the fiduciary duty Adams owes to Mary Minor. Ace should know this because Adams is negotiating the check for his own benefit, not Mary's.

Notice of Defenses and Claims in Recoupment

To qualify as a holder in due course, a person must also acquire a negotiable instrument without notice that any party to it has any **defenses** or **claims in recoupment.** Potential defenses include infancy, duress, fraud, and failure of consideration. Thus, if a person knows that a signature on the instrument was obtained by fraud, misrepresentation, or duress, the person cannot be a holder in due course.

A *claim in recoupment* is a claim of the obligor against the original payee of the instrument. The claim must arise from the transaction that gave rise to the instrument. An example of a claim in recoupment would be as follows: Buyer purchases a used automobile from Dealer for $8,000, giving the dealer a note for $8,000 payable in one year. Because the automobile is not as warranted, Buyer has a breach of warranty claim that could be asserted against Dealer as counterclaim or "claim in recoupment" to offset the amount owing on the note.

The following case, *Parkhill v. Nusor,* illustrates the factors a court may consider in determining whether a person should be on notice of possible defenses or adverse claims by a party to a negotiable instrument and thus not able to claim the status of a holder in due course.

IN RE NUSOR;
PARKHILL v. NUSOR   13 UCC Rep. 2d 773 (Bankr. App., 9th Cir. 1991)

I n the fall of 1987, Irene Nusor was behind in her mortgage payments. She received advertisements from Best Financial Consultants offering attractive refinancing opportunities. On October 14, 1987, she attended a meeting with Best representatives at a McDonald's restaurant who told her that Best would arrange for a complete refinancing of her home in the amount of $98,000, pay off the two existing lienholders, and provide Nusor with an additional $5,000 in spending money. In consideration for these services, Nusor was told that she would owe Best only $4,000.

Nusor agreed to the arrangement and proceeded to sign a fee agreement and a promissory note entitled "Installment Note" that was blank at the time and Best representatives later completed. As completed, it provided that Best would loan her a total sum of $14,986.61 payable in full in 60 days (on December 23, 1987) with an annual interest rate of 18 percent. Where the note provided for the name of the promisor to be filled in, the following words had been typed in: "I, the undersigned, Irene Vazquez Nusor, a married woman, as her sole and separate property." The note was payable to "Best Financial Consultants, a California Sole Proprietorship, or order." The note also contained the following statement: "This note is a junior [sic] to a first deed of trust of record." On November 13, 1987, Nusor went to a second meeting with Best representatives and signed a "short form deed of trust and assignment of rents." The deed indicated that it was secured by a promissory note in the amount of $14,986.61.

On December 2, 1987, Best assigned the note to Robin Parkhill for the discounted price of $13,812.19. Over the term of the note, Parkhill's total anticipated return was $1,624.02, representing the equivalent of an annual interest rate of over 203 percent. Parkhill, who responded to a newspaper ad placed by Best, bought the note without actual notice of the misrepresentations made to Nusor by Best. Nusor received only a single payment of $5,997.25 from Best to one of her lienholders; Best never refinanced Nusor's home or fulfilled its other promises. In June 1988, Nusor filed a Chapter 13 Bankruptcy Petition. One of the questions in the Bankruptcy Proceeding was the status of the promissory note that Parkhill claimed Nusor owed to her. A key issue was whether Parkhill was a holder in due course of a negotiable promissory note and thus not subject to the defenses of fraud in the inducement and failure of consideration that Nusor had against Best. The trial court held in favor of Nusor and Parkhill appealed. ∽

Volinn, Bankruptcy Judge   Whether Parkhill is a holder in due course turns on Parkhill satisfying the requirements of Code Section 3–302. Nusor argues that Parkhill fails to meet this standard because of the note's clumsy draftsmanship and its exceptional rate of return (i.e., the maturation of the discounted note 21 days from the date of the assignment) gave Parkhill at least constructive notice of Nusor's defenses. Nusor states that these "irregularities . . . would certainly cause a reasonably prudent person to question the note's validity and thereby be placed on notice." We agree and hold that Parkhill was not a holder in due course.

Code section 3–304(1) sets forth the conditions under which "irregularities" in the instrument puts the holder on notice:

(1) The purchaser has *notice of a claim or defense* if (a) the instrument is so incomplete, bears such visible evidence of forgery or alteration, or *is otherwise so irregular as to call into question its validity, terms or ownership* or to create an ambiguity as to the party to pay; *(Emphasis added.)*

The term "notice" is further defined in section 1–201(25)(c), which provides that one has notice of a fact when "[f]rom all the facts and circumstances known to him at the time in question he or she has *reason to know* that it exists." (Emphasis added.)

In this case, Parkhill did not seek interest income in the usual manner. She answered a newspaper advertisement. Presumably, after communicating with Best, she calculated the rate of return. The content of the Installment Note, particularly its extraordinarily favorable terms, clearly indicated that this was an unusual type of commercial transaction. For the discounted price of $13,812.19, Parkhill was assigned a note designed to provide her in 21 days (on December 23, 1987) the face value of the Installment Note ($14,986.61) plus 18% per annum interest that would accrue over the term of the note. Thus, Parkhill's total anticipated return was $1,624.02. This amount represents the equivalent of an annual rate of return of over 203%, a return far in excess of the reasonable expectations of any investor who in good faith seeks a favorable rate of return. In addition, we find it significant that Parkhill made no inquiry about the note's origins notwithstanding its manifestly unusual terms. See *Stewart v. Thornton* (holder in due course protection cannot be used to shield one who simply refuses to investigate when the facts known to him suggest an irregularity concerning the commercial paper he purchases).

The imprecise form of the Installment Note, combined with its exorbitant rate of return, were sufficient to divest Parkhill of holder in due course status and to subject her to Nusor's defenses against the note's enforceability. Accordingly, we hold that Parkhill is not a holder in due course and is therefore subject to Nusor's defenses of fraud in the inducement and failure of consideration.

Judgment in favor of Nusor affirmed.

Note: Although this case was decided under the original Article 3, the same result would be anticipated under Revised Article

3. And, as noted below, Revised Article 3 explicitly provides that a person cannot become a holder in due course of an instrument that is so irregular as to call into question its authenticity [3–302(a)(1)].

Irregular and Incomplete Instruments

A person cannot be a holder in due course of a negotiable instrument if, when she takes it, the instrument is irregular or some important or **material term** is blank. If the negotiable instrument contains a facial irregularity, such as an obvious alteration in the amount, then it is considered to be **irregular paper.** If you take an irregular instrument, you are considered to be on notice of any possible defenses to it. For example, Kevin writes a check for "one dollar" payable to Karen. Karen inserts the word "hundred" in the amount, changes the figure "$1" to "$100," and gives the check to a druggist in exchange for a purchase of goods. If the alterations in the amount should be obvious to the druggist, perhaps because there are erasures, different handwritings, or different inks, then the druggist cannot be a holder in due course. She would have taken irregular paper and would be on notice that there might be defenses to it. These defenses include Kevin's defense that he is liable for only $1 because that is the amount for which he made the check.

Similarly, if someone receives a check that has been signed but the space where the amount of the check is to be written is blank, then the person cannot be a holder in due course of that check. The fact that a material term is blank means that the instrument is **incomplete** and should put the person on notice that the drawer may have a defense to payment of it. To be material, the omitted term must be one that affects the legal obligation of the parties to the negotiable instrument. Material terms include the amount of the instrument and the name of the payee. If a negotiable instrument is unauthorizedly completed after the obligor signed it but before a person acquires it, the person can qualify as a holder in due course if she had no notice about the unauthorized completion. A person has notice if she knows or should know of the unauthorized completion.

Payee as Holder in Due Course

The original Article 3 provided explicitly that a *payee* could be a holder in due course if he com-plied with all the requirements for a holder in due course. Revised Article 3 drops the explicit statement; the drafters stated that they intended no change in the law but that they were concerned that the explicit provision suggested that use of holder-in-due-course status by payees was the normal situation. It is not the normal situation, because a payee usually will have notice or knowledge of any defenses to the instrument and will know whether it is overdue or has been dishonored; consequently, the payee is unlikely to qualify as a holder in due course. For example, Drew draws a check on First Bank as drawee, payable to the order of Parks, but leaves the amount blank. Drew delivers the check to Axe, his agent, and instructs Axe to fill in $300 as the amount. Axe, however, fills in $500 as the amount, and Parks gives Axe $500 for the check. Axe then gives Drew $300 and absconds with the extra $200. In such a case, Parks, as payee, is a holder in due course of the check because he has taken it for value, in good faith, and without notice of defenses.

Similarly, assume that Jarvis owes Fields $200. Jarvis agrees to sell Kirk a used television set for $200; Jarvis assures Kirk it is in working condition. In fact, the set is broken. Jarvis asks Kirk to make her check for $200 payable to Fields and then delivers the check to Fields in payment of the debt. Fields, as the payee, can be a holder in due course of the check if he is not aware of the misrepresentation that Jarvis made to Kirk in order to obtain the check.

Shelter Rule

The transferee of an instrument—whether or not the transfer is a negotiation—obtains those rights that the transferor had, including (1) the transferor's right to enforce the instrument and (2) any right as a holder in due course [3–203(b)]. This means that any person who can trace his title to an instrument back to a holder in due course receives rights similar of a holder in due course even if he cannot meet the requirements himself. This is known as the **shelter rule** in Article 3. For example, Archer

CONCEPT   REVIEW

Requirements for a Holder in Due Course

REQUIREMENT	RULE
1. Must be a *holder*	A holder is a person in possession of an instrument payable to bearer or payable to an identified person and he is that person.
2. Must take *for value*	A holder has given value: *a.* To the extent the agreed-on consideration has been paid or performed. *b.* To the extent a security interest or lien has been obtained in the negotiable instrument. *c.* By taking the negotiable instrument in payment of—or as security for—an antecedent claim. *d.* By giving a negotiable instrument for it. *e.* By making an irrevocable commitment to a third person.
3. Must take in *good faith*	Good faith means honesty in fact and the observance of reasonable commercial standards of fair dealing.
4. Must take *without notice* that the instrument is *overdue*	An instrument payable on demand is overdue the day after demand for payment has been duly made. A check is overdue 90 days after its date. If it is an instrument other than a check and payable on demand, when it has been outstanding for an unreasonably long period of time in light of nature of the instrument and trade practice. If it is an instrument due on a certain date, then it is overdue at the beginning of the next day after the due date.
5. Must take *without notice* that the instrument has been *dishonored*.	An instrument has been dishonored when the holder has presented it for payment (or acceptance) and payment (or acceptance) has been refused.
6. Must take *without notice* of any *uncured default* with respect to payment of another instrument issued as part of the same series.	If there is a series of notes, holder must take without notice that there is an uncured default as to any other notes in the series.
7. Must take *without notice* that the instrument contains an *unauthorized signature* or has been *altered*.	Notice of unauthorized signature or alteration—that is, a change in a material term—prevents holder from obtaining HDC status.
8. Must take *without notice* of any *claim of a property or possessory interest* in it.	Claims of property or possessory interest include: *a.* Claim by someone that she is the rightful owner of the instrument. *b.* Person seeking to rescind a prior negotiation of the instrument. *c.* Claim by a beneficiary that a fiduciary negotiated the instrument for his own benefit.
9. Must take *without notice* that any party has a *defense* against it.	Defenses include real defenses that go to the validity of the instrument and personal defenses that commonly are defenses to a simple contract.
10. Must take *without notice* of a *claim in recoupment* to it.	A claim in recoupment is a claim of the obligor on the instrument against the original payee that arises from the transaction that gave rise to the instrument.
11. The instrument must not bear *apparent evidence of forgery or alteration* or be *irregular* or *incomplete*.	The instrument must not contain obvious reasons to question its authenticity.

makes a note payable to Bryant. Bryant negotiates the note to Carlyle, who qualifies as a holder in due course. Carlyle then negotiates the note to Darby, who cannot qualify as a holder in due course because she knows the note is overdue. Because Darby can trace her title back to a holder in due course (Carlyle), Darby has rights like a holder in due course when she seeks payment of the note from Archer.

There is, however, a limitation on the shelter rule. A transferee who has himself been a party to any fraud or illegality affecting the instrument cannot improve his position by taking, directly or indirectly, from a later holder in due course [3–203(b)]. For example, Archer, through fraudulent representations, induced Bryant to execute a negotiable note payable to Archer and then negotiated the instrument to Carlyle, who took as a holder in due course. If Archer thereafter took the note for value from Carlyle, Archer could not acquire Carlyle's rights as a holder in due course. Archer was a party to the fraud that induced the note, and, accordingly, cannot improve his position by negotiating the instrument and then reacquiring it.

RIGHTS OF A HOLDER IN DUE COURSE

Claims and Defenses Generally

Revised Article 3 establishes four categories of claims and defenses. They are:

1. *Real defenses*—which go to the validity of the instrument.
2. *Personal defenses*—which generally arise out of the transaction that gave rise to the instrument.
3. *Claims to an instrument*—which generally concern property or possessory rights in an instrument or its proceeds.
4. *Claims in recoupment*—which also arise out of the transaction that gave rise to the instrument.

These defenses and claims are discussed in some detail below.

Importance of Being a Holder in Due Course

In the preceding chapter, we discussed that one advantage of negotiable instruments over other kinds of contracts is that they are accepted as substitutes for money. People are willing to accept them as substitutes for money because, generally, they can take them free of claims or defenses to payment between the original parties to the instrument. On the other hand, a person who takes an assignment of a simple contract gets only the same rights as the person had who assigned the contract.

There are two qualifications to the ability of a person who acquires a negotiable instrument to be free of claims or defenses between the original parties. First, the person in possession of a negotiable instrument must be a *person entitled to enforce the instrument* as well as a *holder in due course* (or must be a holder who has the rights of a holder in due course through the shelter rule). If the person is neither, then she is subject to all claims or defenses to payment that any party to it has. Second, the only claims or defenses that the holder in due course has to worry about are so-called real defenses—those that affect the validity of the instrument—or claims that arose after she became a holder. For example, if the maker or drawer did not have legal capacity because she was a minor, the maker or drawer has a real defense. The holder in due course does not have to worry about other defenses and claims that do not go to the validity of the instrument—the so-called personal defenses.

Real Defenses

There are some claims and defenses to payment of an instrument that go to the validity of the instrument. These claims and defenses are known as **real defenses.** They can be used as reasons against payment of a negotiable instrument to any holder, including a holder in due course (or a person who has the rights of a holder in due course). Real defenses include:

1. Minority or infancy that under state law makes the instrument void or voidable. For example, if Mark Miller, age 17, signs a promissory note as maker, he can use his lack of capacity to contract as a defense against paying it even to a holder in due course.

2. Incapacity that under state law makes the instrument void. For example, if a person has been declared mentally incompetent by a court, then the person has a real defense if state law declares all

contracts entered into by the person after the adjudication of incompetency to be void.

3. Duress that voids or nullifies the obligation of a party liable to pay the instrument. For example, if Harold points a gun at his grandmother and forces her to execute a promissory note, the grandmother can use duress as a defense against paying it even to a holder in due course.

4. Illegality that under state law renders the obligation void. For example, in some states, checks and notes given in payment of gambling debts are void.

5. Fraud in the essence (or fraud in the factum). This occurs where a person signs a negotiable instrument without knowing or having a reasonable opportunity to know that it is a negotiable instrument or of its essential terms. For example, Amy Jones is an illiterate person who lives alone. She signs a document that is actually a promissory note but she is told that it is a grant of permission for a television set to be left in her house on a trial basis. Amy has a real defense against payment of the note even to a holder in due course. Fraud in the essence

is distinguished from fraud in the inducement, discussed below, which is only a personal defense.

6. Discharge in bankruptcy. For example, if the maker of a promissory note has had the debt discharged in a bankruptcy proceeding, she no longer is liable on it and has a real defense against payment [3–305(a)(1)].

Real defenses can be asserted even against a holder in due course of a negotiable instrument because it is more desirable to protect people who have signed negotiable instruments in these situations than it is to protect persons who have taken negotiable instruments in the ordinary course of business.

The following case, *Kedzie & 103rd Currency Exchange, Inc. v. Hodge,* involves the question of whether a drawer who issued a check to an unlicensed plumber has a real defense of illegality that can be asserted against a holder in due course. It also highlights the difficult public policy issue inherent in section 3–305.

KEDZIE & 103RD CURRENCY EXCHANGE, INC. v. HODGE   21 UCC Rep. 2d 682 (Ill. Sup. Ct. 1993)

Pursuant to a written "work order," Fred Fentress agreed to install a "flood control system" at the home of Eric and Beulah Hodge of Chicago for $900. In partial payment for the work, Beulah Hodge drafted a personal check payable to "Fred Fentress—A-OK Plumbing" for $500 from the Hodges' joint account at Citicorp Savings.

The system's components were not delivered to the Hodges' home as scheduled. And, when Fentress failed to appear on the date set for installation, Eric Hodge telephoned Fentress to advise him the contract was "canceled." Hodge also told Fentress that he would order Citicorp Savings not to pay the check Fentress had been given. Later that day Citicorp received a stop-payment order from Hodge.

Fentress presented the check at the Kedzie & 103rd Street Currency Exchange, indorsing it as "sole owner" of A-OK Plumbing and obtained payment. However, when the Currency Exchange later presented the check for payment at Citicorp Savings, payment was refused in accordance with the stop-payment order.

The Currency Exchange, alleging that it was a holder in due course, then sued Beulah Hodge as the drawer of the check, and Fentress. Hodge moved to dismiss the action against her on the grounds that under section 3–305 she had a defense against payment that could be asserted against a holder in due course, namely that the transaction was illegal because Fentress was not a licensed plumber as required by Illinois law. The circuit court granted the motion and the appeals court affirmed. Currency Exchange then appealed to the Illinois Supreme Court. ∞

Freeman, Justice The Illinois Plumbing License Law requires that all plumbing, including "installation . . . or extension of" drains be performed by plumbers licensed under the Act. The affidavits establish that Fentress was not licensed either by the City of Chicago or the State of Illinois. That failure

is a violation of the Illinois Plumbing License Law and is punishable as a misdemeanor. No counter affidavit was supplied.

No material fact remains to be resolved. The question is simply whether Hodge is entitled, as a matter of law, to a judgment of dismissal in view of the defense asserted under section 3–305. Section 3–305 provides, in relevant part:

> [A] holder in due course . . . takes the instrument free from. . .
>> (2) all defenses of any party to the instrument with whom the holder has not dealt except. . .
>>> (b) . . . illegality of the transaction, as renders the obligation of the party a nullity.

The concern is whether noncompliance by Fentress with the Illinois Plumbing License Law gives rise to "illegality of the transaction" with respect to the contract for plumbing services as to bar the claim of the Currency Exchange, a holder in due course of the check initially given to Fentress.

The issue of "illegality" arises under a variety of statutes. In view of the diverse constructions to which statutory enactments are given, "illegality" is, accordingly, a matter "left to the local law." Even so, it is only when an obligation is made "entirely null and void" under "local law" that "illegality" exists as one of the "real defenses" under section 3–305 to defeat the claim of a holder in due course. In effect, the obligation must be no obligation at all. If it is "merely voidable" at the election of the obligor, the defense is unavailable.

Historically, this court has recognized "illegality" to arise only in view of legislative declaration affecting both the underlying contract or transaction and the instrument exchanged upon it. A contract or transaction which is void must certainly negate the obligation to pay arising from it as between the contracting parties. But, unless an instrument memorializing the obligation is also made void, an innocent third party who has no knowledge of the circumstances of the initial contract or transaction may yet claim payment of it against the drawer or maker.

Thus, "illegality" has been held to defeat the claims of holders in due course in cases involving contracts of a gaming nature or for retirement of gambling debts. Owing to a deep-seated hostility toward nongovernmental sanctioned gambling, our legislature has declared that any instrument associated with such activity is void, independent of the status of who may possess it. The absence of a similar legislative declaration as for an instrument given upon a usurious contract must account, in part, for a conclusion that usury has not been held to give rise to "illegality" as a defense against a holder in due course.

Several other jurisdictions also find reason to draw a distinction between the voidness of a negotiable instrument and the underlying contract or obligation upon which it is exchanged. A plaintiff is precluded from recovering on a suit involving an illegal contract because the plaintiff is a wrongdoer. But a holder in due course is an innocent third party.

In adopting the UCC and, in particular section 3–305, our legislature chose to confer on a holder in due course of a negotiable instrument considerable protection against claims by persons to it. Our legislature also continues to declare certain obligations void because of the circumstances of the agreements from which they arise and without regard to the status of who may claim ownership. The selective negation of obligations reflects a legislative aim to declare what will and will not give rise to "illegality" in cases now governed by the UCC. As legislative direction indicates which obligations are always void, legislative silence indicates when the protection afforded a holder in due course must be honored.

We therefore reaffirm today, the view this court has consistently recognized in cases predating the UCC. Unless the instrument arising from a contract or transaction is, itself, made void by statute, the "illegality" defense under section 3–305 is not available to bar the claim of a holder in due course.

Judgment for Hodge reversed.

Bilandic, Justice, dissenting   I would affirm the trial court's dismissal of the Currency Exchange's complaint. The majority here incorporates into section 3–305 of the UCC an additional requirement that must be met before the defense of illegality can be met to defeat the claim of an alleged holder in due course. That additional requirement is not found anywhere in the plain language of section 3–305, however.

With respect to the defenses of duress and illegality, the comments to section 3–305 state, in pertinent part, that "[t]hey are primarily a matter of local concern and local policy. All such matters are therefore left to the local law. If under that law the effect of the duress or the illegality is such to make the *obligation* entirely null and void, the defense may be asserted against a holder in due course.

The plain language of section 3–305 and the comments to the section make it clear that where the illegality of a transaction renders the *obligation* of the maker of an instrument a nullity, the illegal transaction can be raised as a defense by the maker of the instrument, even against a holder in due course. Section 3–305 does not state that illegality is a defense only where the *instrument* arising from a contract or transaction has been expressly declared void by the legislature due to the illegality of the transaction. Had the legislature intended for illegality to be a defense only where it had expressly declared an instrument void due to the illegality of the underlying transaction, it could easily have done so.

The only inquiry necessary to resolve the issue presented in this case then is whether the contract between Hodge and Fentress is void on the grounds of illegality. An examination of the statute providing for the licensing of plumbers, the public policy behind the statute, and the Illinois case law concerning contracts made in contravention of professional licensing laws establishes that the contract between Hodge and Fentress is illegal and void.

Courts in other states have ruled that the defense of illegality of the contract may be asserted against a holder in due course without requiring that a negotiable instrument in question be expressly declared void by statute. In *Wilson v. Steele* (Cal. 1989), the court held that a contract made by an unlicensed home contractor was void and illegal and that this defense could be asserted against a holder in due course. In *Columbus Check Cashiers, Inc. v. Stiles* (Ohio 1990), the court likewise held that a check given as consideration for a contract between a homeowner and an unlicensed home contractor is illegal and void and that the defense of illegality could be asserted against the holder in due course.

In *Columbus Check Cashiers* and *Wilson,* as in the instant case, the subject matter of the contract, performance by an unlicensed individual was prohibited by law. Accordingly, the courts held the contract was illegal and void and that this defense could be asserted against a holder in due course. More importantly, the courts in these two cases did not require that a statute expressly declare the note in question void in order for the defense of illegality

to be available. Such a requirement is likewise not a part of Illinois version of section 3–305. In contrast, under New Jersey law, which the majority here purports to follow, the comments to that state's version of section 3–305 expressly state that "[i]n New Jersey, a holder in due course takes free and clear of the defense of illegality, *unless the statute which declares the act illegal also indicates that payment thereunder is void." (Emphasis added.)*

The majority asserts that to bar recovery by Currency Exchange in this case would be unfair because the Currency Exchange is an innocent third party which had no knowledge of the circumstances of the contract between Hodge and Fentress. However, section 3–305 clearly provides that the general policy favoring free negotiability is not absolute. There is a competing policy disfavoring certain transactions, such as those involving infancy, duress, illegality or misrepresentation as to the true nature of an instrument (i.e. fraud in the factum). Pursuant to section 3–305, the Currency Exchange takes a check subject to these and certain other real defenses. The Illinois legislature has provided that, by definition, a holder in due course is one who does not have notice of *any* of the real defenses listed in section 3–305. By statute, the innocence of the holder in due course cannot defeat *any* of the real defenses listed in section 3–305, including illegality. Accordingly, the argument that the Currency Exchange could not have known that the underlying transaction was illegal is simply misplaced. Such reasoning would lead to the conclusion that all of the defenses listed in section 3–305 should be unavailable to defeat the claim of a holder in due course, a conclusion obviously contrary to the provisions of section 3–305.

For the above reasons, I dissent. I would affirm the judgment of the appellate court which affirmed the circuit court's dismissal of the Currency Exchange's action against Hodge.

Note: Although this case was decided under the original version of Article 3, the same result would be anticipated under Revised Article 3.

In addition to the real defenses discussed above, there are several other reasons why a person otherwise liable to pay an instrument would have a defense against payment that would be effective even against a holder in due course. They include:

1. Forgery. For example, if a maker's signature has been put on the instrument without his authorization and without his negligence, the maker has a defense against payment of the note.

2. Alteration of a completed instrument. This is a partial defense against a holder in due course (or a person having the rights of a holder in due course) and a complete defense against a nonholder in due course. A holder in due course can enforce an altered instrument against the maker or drawer according to its original tenor (terms).

3. Discharge. If a person takes an instrument with knowledge that the obligation of any party obligated on the instrument has been discharged, the person takes subject to the discharge even if the person is a holder in due course.

Personal Defenses

Personal defenses are legal reasons for avoiding or reducing liability of a person who is liable on a negotiable instrument. Generally, personal defenses arise out of the transaction in which the negotiable instrument was issued and are based on negotiable instruments law or contract law. A holder in due course of a negotiable instrument (or one who can claim the rights of one) is not subject to any personal defenses or claims that may exist between the original parties to the instrument. Personal defenses include:

1. Lack or failure of consideration. For example, a promissory note for $100 was given to someone without intent to make a gift and without receiving anything in return [3–303(b)].

2. Breach of contract, including breach of warranty. For example, a check was given in payment for repairs to an automobile but the repair work was defective.

3. Fraud in the inducement of any underlying contract. For example, an art dealer sells a lithograph to Cheryl, telling her that it is a Picasso, and takes Cheryl's check for $500 in payment. The art dealer knows that the lithograph is not a genuine Picasso but a forgery. Cheryl has been induced to make the purchase and to give her check by the art dealer's fraudulent representation. Because of this fraud, Cheryl has a personal defense against having to honor her check to the art dealer.

4. Incapacity to the extent that state law makes the obligation voidable, as opposed to void. For example, where state law makes the contract of a person of limited mental capacity but who has not been adjudicated incompetent voidable, the person has a personal defense to payment.

5. Illegality that makes a contract voidable, as opposed to void. For example, where the payee of a check given for certain professional services was required to have a license from the state but did not have one.

6. Duress, to the extent it is not so severe as to make the obligation void but rather only voidable. For example, if the instrument was signed under a threat to prosecute the maker's son if it was not signed, the maker might have a personal defense.

7. Unauthorized completion or alteration of the instrument. For example, the instrument was completed in an unauthorized manner, or was altered after it left the maker's or drawer's possession.

8. Nonissuance of the instrument, conditional issuance, and issuance for a special purpose. For example, the person in possession of the instrument obtained it by theft or by finding it, rather than through an intentional delivery of the instrument to him [3–105(b)].

9. Failure to countersign a traveler's check [3–106(c)].

10. Modification of the obligation by a separate agreement [3–117].

11. Payment that violates a restrictive indorsement [3–206(f)].

12. Breach of warranty when a draft is accepted (discussed in following chapter) [3–417(b)].

The following example illustrates the limited extent to which a maker or drawer can use personal defenses as a reason for not paying a negotiable instrument he signed. Suppose Trent Tucker bought a used truck from Honest Harry's and gave Harry a 60-day promissory note for $2,750 in payment for the truck. Honest Harry's "guaranteed" the truck to be in "good working condition," but in fact the truck had a cracked engine block. If Harry tries to collect the $2,750 from Trent, Trent could claim breach of warranty as a reason for not paying Harry the full $2,750 because Harry is not a holder in due course. However, if Harry negotiated the note to First National Bank and the bank was a holder in due course, the situation would be changed. If the bank tried to collect the $2,750 from Trent, Trent would have to pay the bank. Trent cannot use his defense or claim of breach of warranty as a reason for not paying the bank, which qualified as a holder in due course. It is a personal defense. Trent must pay the bank the $2,750 and then pursue his breach of warranty claim against Harry.

The rule that a holder in due course takes a negotiable instrument free of any personal defenses or claims to it has been modified to some extent, particularly in relation to instruments given by consumers. These modifications will be discussed in the next section of this chapter.

Claims to the Instrument

For purposes of Revised Article 3, the term *claims* to an instrument can include:

1. A claim to ownership of the instrument by one who asserts that he is the owner and was wrongfully deprived of possession.
2. A claim of a lien on the instrument.
3. A claim for rescission of an indorsement.

A holder in due course takes free of claims that arose before he became a holder but is subject to those arising when or after she becomes a holder in due course. For example, if a holder impairs the collateral given for an obligation, he may be creating a defense for an obligor.

Claims in Recoupment

A *claim in recoupment* is not actually a defense to an instrument but rather an *offset to liability*. For example, Ann Adams purchases a new automobile from Dealership, giving it a note for the balance of the purchase price beyond her down payment. After accepting delivery, she discovers a breach of warranty that the dealer fails to remedy. If Dealer has sold the note to a bank that subsequently seeks payment on the note from Adams, she has a claim in recoupment for breach of warranty. If the bank is a

---

Claims and Defenses against Payment of Negotiable Instruments

CLAIM OR DEFENSE	EXAMPLES
Real Defense Valid against all holders, including holders in due course and holders who have the rights of holders in due course.	1. Minority that under state law makes the contract void or voidable. 2. Other lack of capacity that makes the contract void. 3. Duress that makes the contract void. 4. Illegality that makes the contract void. 5. Fraud in the essence (fraud in the factum). 6. Discharge in bankruptcy.
Personal Defense Valid against plain holders of instruments—but not against holders in due course or holders who have the rights of in due course holders through the shelter rule.	1. Lack or failure of consideration. 2. Breach of contract (including breach of warranty). 3. Fraud in the inducement. 4. Lack of capacity that makes the contract voidable (except minority). 5. Illegality that makes the contract voidable. 6. Duress that makes the contract voidable. 7. Unauthorized completion of an incomplete instrument, or material alteration of the instrument. 8. Nonissuance of the instrument. 9. Failure to countersign a traveler's check. 10. Modification of the obligation by a separate agreement. 11. Payment that violates a restrictive indorsement. 12. Breach of warranty when a draft is accepted.
Claim to an Instrument	1. Claim of ownership by someone who claims to be the owner and that he was wrongfully deprived of possession. 2. Claim of a lien on the instrument. 3. Claim for rescission of an indorsement.
Claims in Recoupment	1. Breach of warranty in the sale of goods for which the instrument was issued.

holder in due course, the claim in recoupment cannot be asserted against it. However, if the bank is not a holder in due course, then Adams can assert the claim in recoupment to reduce the amount owing on the instrument at the time the action is brought against her on the note. Her claim could only serve to reduce the amount owing and not as a basis for a net recovery from the bank. However, if Dealer was the person bringing an action to collect the note, Adams could assert the breach of warranty claim as a counterclaim and potentially might recover from Dealer any difference between the claim and the damages due for breach of warranty.

The obligor may assert a claim up to the amount of the instrument if the holder is the original payee but cannot assert claims in recoupment against a holder in due course. In addition, the obligor may assert a claim against a transferee who does not qualify as a holder in due course, but only up to the amount owing on the instrument at the time it brought the claim in recoupment.

CHANGES IN THE HOLDER IN DUE COURSE RULE

Consumer Disadvantages

The rule that a holder in due course of a negotiable instrument is not subject to personal defenses between the original parties to it makes negotiable instruments a readily accepted substitute for money. This rule can also result in serious disadvantages to consumers. Consumers sometimes buy goods or services on credit and give the seller a negotiable instrument such as a promissory note. They often do this without knowing the consequences of their signing a negotiable instrument. If the goods or services are defective or not delivered, the consumer would like to withhold payment of the note until the seller corrects the problem or makes the delivery. Where the note is still held by the seller, the consumer can do this because any defenses of breach of warranty or nonperformance are good against the seller.

However, the seller may have negotiated the note at a discount to a third party such as a bank. If the bank qualifies as a holder in due course, the consumer must pay the note in full to the bank. The consumer's personal defenses are not valid against a holder in due course. The consumer must pay the holder in due course and then try to get her money back from the seller. This may be difficult if the seller cannot be found or will not accept responsibility. The consumer would be in a much stronger position if she could just withhold payment, even against the bank, until the goods or services are delivered or the performance is corrected.

State Consumer Protection Legislation

Some state legislatures and courts have limited the holder in due course rule, particularly as it affects consumers. State legislation limiting the doctrine typically amended state laws dealing with consumer credit transactions. For example, some state laws prohibit a seller from taking a negotiable instrument other than a check from a consumer in payment for consumer goods and services. Other states require promissory notes given by consumers in payment for goods and services to carry the words *consumer paper*. Holders of instruments with the legend "consumer paper" are not eligible to be holders in due course.[3] [3–106(d)]

Federal Trade Commission Regulation

The Federal Trade Commission (FTC) has promulgated a regulation designed to protect consumers against operation of the holder in due course rule. The FTC rule applies to persons who sell to consumers on credit and have the consumer sign a note or an installment sale contract or arrange third-party financing of the purchase. The seller must ensure that the note or the contract contains the following clause:

NOTICE: ANY HOLDER OF THIS CONSUMER CREDIT CONTRACT IS SUBJECT TO ALL CLAIMS AND DEFENSES WHICH THE DEBTOR COULD ASSERT AGAINST THE SELLER OF THE GOODS OR SERVICES OBTAINED PURSUANT HERETO OR WITH THE PROCEEDS HEREOF. RECOVERY HEREUNDER BY THE DEBTOR SHALL NOT EXCEED AMOUNTS PAID BY THE DEBTOR HEREUNDER.

---

[3]Revised Article 3 expressly deals with these state variations in section 3–106(d) and Official Comments 3 to 3–106 and Comments 3 to 3–305. Section 3–106(d) permits instruments containing legends or statements required by statutory or administrative law that preserve the obligor's right to assert claims or defenses against subsequent holders as within Article 3 except that no holder can be a holder in due course.

The effect of the notice is to make a potential holder of the note or contract subject to all claims and defenses of the consumer. This is illustrated in the *Ford Motor Credit Company v. Morgan* case, which follows. If the note or contract does not include the clause required by the FTC rule, the consumer does not gain any rights that he would not otherwise have under state law, and a subsequent holder may qualify as a holder in due course. However, the FTC does have the right to seek a fine of as much as $10,000 against the seller who failed to include the notice.

FORD MOTOR CREDIT COMPANY v. MORGAN   536 N.E.2d 587 (Sup. Jud. Ct. Mass. 1989)

R*ose and William Morgan purchased a new Mercury automobile from Neponset Lincoln Mercury, Inc. In order to finance their purchase through Ford Motor Credit Company, they signed a Note/Massachusetts Retail Installment Contract, a standard printed form contract prepared by Ford Credit. Printed in capital letters at the bottom of the first page of the form was the following statement:*

NOTICE: ANY HOLDER OF THIS CONSUMER CREDIT CONTRACT IS SUBJECT TO ALL CLAIMS AND DEFENSES WHICH THE DEBTOR COULD ASSERT AGAINST THE SELLER OF GOODS OR SERVICES OBTAINED PURSUANT HERETO OR WITH THE PROCEEDS HEREOF. RECOVERY HEREUNDER BY THE DEBTOR SHALL NOT EXCEED AMOUNTS PAID BY THE DEBTOR HEREUNDER.

Ford Credit financed the car for $3,833 with payment to be made in 36 consecutive monthly installments of $137.13. During the first 18 months they owned the car, the Morgans experienced problems with it. These included water leaking into the trunk, a faulty head gasket, rust, hood misalignment, lack of shine, and, when left unattended, the car would shift from "park" to "reverse" and would have to be shifted back to "park" before it could be started. After making 15 payments totaling $2,056.95, the Morgans defaulted on their remaining obligation to Ford Credit. Before the car could be resold by Ford Credit, it was extensively vandalized; the Morgans had not maintained insurance coverage on it and it was a total loss.

Ford Credit sued the Morgans on the note, seeking recovery of $2,628.87 plus attorney's fees. The Morgans counterclaimed, seeking recovery against Ford Credit of claims for fraud and deceit, unfair and deceptive practices, and breach of express and implied warranties. In a special verdict, a jury found that the dealer knowingly made false representations to the Morgans, on which the Morgans relied. In turn, the trial court judge determined that this gave the Morgans a valid defense that extinguished the claim of Ford Motor Credit for the balance due on the credit contract. He also denied the Morgan's claim for an affirmative recovery against Ford Motor Credit on their counterclaim. The Morgans appealed to the Appeals Court, which transferred the case to the Supreme Judicial Court. ∽

O'Connor, Justice   The Morgans' first contention is that the explicit language of the notice provision contained in the contract, which subjects holder to all "claims and defenses which the debtor could assert against the seller" permits them to recover from Ford Credit for the dealer's wrongdoing. As the Morgans acknowledge, that notice provision is mandated by a Federal Trade Commission (FTC) rule that provides that it is an unfair or deceptive act or practice to take or receive a consumer credit contract which fails to include that provision. Therefore, we look to the FTC's purpose in enacting the rule as a guide to our interpretation of the contract provision.

The rule was designed to preserve the consumer's claims and defenses by cutting off the creditor's rights as a holder in due course. Under the holder in due course principle, which would apply were it not for the contract provision mandated by the FTC rule, the creditor could "assert his right to be paid by the consumer" despite misrepresentation, breach of warranty or contract, or even fraud on the part of the seller, and despite the fact that the consumer's debt was generated by the sale. Thus, "being prevented from asserting the seller's breach of warranty or failure to perform against the assignee of the consumer's instrument, the consumer would be deprived of his most effective weapon—

nonpayment." Eliminating holder in due course status prevents the assignee from demanding further payment when there has been assignor wrongdoing, and rearms the consumer with the "weapon" of nonpayment.

The FTC anticipated that in addition to nonpayment, affirmative recovery, a judgment for damages against the assignee-creditor, would be available in limited circumstances. Thus, in its statement of policy and purpose, the FTC spelled out the avenues of relief under the rule as follows: "A consumer can (1) defend a creditor suit for payment of an obligation by raising a valid claim against a seller as a set-off, and (2) maintain an affirmative action against a creditor who has received for a return of moneys paid on account." However, the FTC made clear that "the latter alternative will only be available where a seller's breach is so substantial that a court is persuaded that rescission and restitution are justified. The most typical example of such a case would involve non-delivery, where delivery was scheduled after the date payments to a creditor commenced."

The FTC re-emphasized this point in stating, "consumers will not be in a position to obtain an affirmative recovery, unless they have actually commenced payments and received little or nothing of value from the seller. In the case of non-delivery, we believe the consumer is entitled to a refund of monies paid on account." Finally, the FTC anticipated that the rule would allow the courts to weigh the equities in the underlying sale, and "remain the final arbiters of equities between a seller and a consumer." Thus, the function of the rule is to allow consumers to stop payments, and, in limited circumstances not present here, where equity requires, to provide for a return of monies paid. The FTC did not intend that the rule would, as a matter of course, entitle a consumer to a full refund of monies paid on account. It follows, of course, that there is no merit to the Morgans' assertions that the contractual language allows them affirmative recovery even beyond the amount they paid in. To expose a creditor to further affirmative recovery would not only contravene the intention of the FTC, but "would place the creditor in the position of an absolute insurer or guarantor of the seller's performance." This we decline to do.

Judgment affirmed.

ETHICAL AND PUBLIC POLICY CONCERNS

1. If you are in the business of buying commercial paper—such as consumer notes—from businesses such as home improvement companies, how much of an ethical obligation, if any, do you have to look into the sales practices and performance records of the companies to whom the consumers have made the notes payable?

2. Suppose you have given a check in payment of a gambling debt in a state that makes such obligations void. Are there any ethical considerations involved as to whether you should assert the real defense of illegality against payment of the check to a holder in due course?

3. The *Kedzie & 103rd Currency Exchange, Inc. v. Hodge* case presents the public policy question of whether instruments issued in connection with transactions that are unenforceable between the original parties because of illegality can be enforced against holders in due course. If you were a legisla-tor in Illinois who was confronting this question following the decision in this case, what position would you take? Why?

PROBLEMS AND PROBLEM CASES

1. Stone & Webster drew three checks in the total amount of $64,755.44 payable to the order of Westinghouse Electric Corporation. An employee of Stone & Webster obtained possession of the checks, forged Westinghouse's indorsement to them, and cashed them at the First National Bank & Trust Company and put the proceeds to his own use. The first two checks were indorsed in typewriting, "For Deposit Only: Westinghouse Electric Corporation By: Mr. O. D. Costine, Treasury Representative," followed by the ink signature "O. D. Costine." The third check was indorsed in typewriting, "Westing-house Electric Corporation by: [Sgd.] O. D. Costine, Treasury Representative." Were the checks negotiated to the bank?

2. A bank cashed the checks of its customer, Dental Supply, Inc., presented to the bank by an employee of Dental Supply named Wilson. The checks were indorsed in blank with a rubber stamp of Dental Supply, Inc. Wilson had been stealing the checks by taking cash rather than depositing them to Dental Supply, Inc.'s account. What could Dental Supply have done to avoid this situation?

3. Raye Walker was a bookkeeper for O.K. Moving & Storage Company. She opened a checking account in her name at Elgin National Bank. She then took checks that were made payable to O.K. Moving & Storage, indorsed them "For Deposit Only, O.K. Moving & Storage Co., 80 Carson Drive, N.E., Fort Walton, Florida," and deposited them in her individual account at Elgin National Bank. In a period of one year, she deposited, and Elgin Bank accepted for deposit to her account, checks totaling $19,356.01. When O.K. Moving & Storage discovered this, it sued Elgin Bank for $19,356.01 for conversion of its checks. Should Elgin Bank have permitted the checks restrictively indorsed "For Deposit Only" to a corporation's account to be deposited to an individual account?

4. Reggie Bluiett worked at the Silver Slipper Gambling Hall and Saloon. She received her weekly paycheck made out to her from the Silver Slipper. She indorsed the check in blank and left it on her dresser at home. Fred Watkins broke into Bluiett's house and stole the check. Watkins took the check to the local auto store, where he bought two tires at a cost of $71.21. He obtained the balance of the check in cash. Could the auto store qualify as a holder in due course?

5. Horton wrote a check for $20,000 to Axe, who in turn indorsed it to Halbert. In return, Halbert advanced $8,000 in cash to Axe and promised to cancel a $12,000 debt owed him by Axe. The check, when presented by Halbert to the bank, was not paid due to insufficient funds. Halbert thus never regarded the debt as canceled. To what extent can Halbert be a holder in due course of the check?

6. Charles Alcombrack was appointed guardian for his son, Chad Alcombrack, who was seven years old and the beneficiary of his grandfather's life insurance policy. The insurance company issued a check for $30,588.39 made payable to "Charles Alcombrack, Guardian of the Estate of Chad Stephen Alcombrack, a Minor." The attorney for the son's estate directed the father to take the check, along with the letters of guardianship issued to the father, to the bank and open up a guardianship savings and checking account. Instead, the father took the check, without the letters of guardianship, to the Olympic Bank and opened a personal checking and a personal savings account. Despite the fact that the check was payable to the father in his guardianship capacity, the bank allowed the father to place the entire amount in his newly opened personal accounts. The father used all but $320.60 of the trust money for his personal benefit. A new guardian, J. David Smith, was appointed for Chad. Smith brought suit against the Olympic Bank, on Chad's behalf, to recover the amount of the check. Was the bank a holder in due course of the check?

7. Two smooth-talking salesmen for Rich Plan of New Orleans called on Leona and George Henne at their home. They sold the Hennes a home food plan. One of the salesmen suggested that the Hennes sign a blank promissory note. The Hennes refused. The salesman then wrote in ink "$100" as the amount and "4" as the number of installments in which the note was to be paid, and the Hennes signed the note. Several days later, the Hennes received a payment book from Nationwide Acceptance. The payment book showed that a total of $843.38 was due, payable in 36 monthly installments. Rich Plan had erased the "$100" and "4" on the note and typed in the figures "$843.38" and "36." The erasures were cleverly done but were visible to the naked eye. Rich Plan then negotiated the Hennes's note to Nationwide Acceptance. The Hennes refused to pay the note. Nationwide claimed that it was a holder in due course and was entitled to receive payment. Was Nationwide Acceptance a holder in due course?

8. A representative of Gracious Living, Inc., called on the Hutchinsons and identified himself as a "demonstrator" of water-softening equipment. After explaining the cost of the equipment, he told the Hutchinsons that Gracious Living would install it for a four-month trial. In return, the Hutchinsons were to give him a list of their friends and neighbors and permit a demonstration in their house. They were to receive a bonus if sales were made to any of their friends and neighbors. The Hutchinsons claimed that the man "asked them to sign a form that he could show to his boss to prove he had made the demonstration and also as a bond to cover the unit while it was on the Hutchinson's property." They signed the form. Later, the Hutchinsons received a payment book from the Reading Trust Company. They then realized that they had been tricked into signing a contract and a note. Hutchinson was a high school graduate, and his wife had completed her junior year in high school. Both could read and write the English language. Reading Trust had obtained the note from Gracious Living. It had no notice of Gracious Living's business practice and was a holder in due course. The Hutchinsons refused to pay the note, and Reading Trust sued them to collect on it. Did the Hutchinsons have a real defense that they could use against the Reading Trust Company even though it was a holder in due course?

9. Panlick, the owner of an apartment building, entered into a written contract with Bucci, a paving contractor whereby Bucci was to install asphalt paving on the parking lot of the building. When Bucci finished the job, Panlick gave Bucci a check for $6,500 and a promissory note for $7,593 with interest at 10 percent due six months from its date. When the note came due, Panlick refused to pay it. Bucci brought suit to collect the note, and Panlick claimed that there had been a failure of consideration because the asphalt was defectively installed. Can Panlick assert this defense against Bucci?

10. Ralph Herrmann wrote a check for $10,000 payable to Ormsby House, a hotel-casino in Carson City, Nevada, and exchanged it for three counter checks he had written earlier that evening to acquire gaming chips. Ormsby House was unable to collect the proceeds from the check because Herrmann had insufficient funds in his account. The debt evidenced by the check was assigned to Sea Air Support, Inc., d/b/a Automated Accounts Associates, for collection. Sea Air was also unsuccessful in its attempts to collect and filed a lawsuit against Herrmann to recover on the dishonored check. Nevada law then provided that all instruments drawn for the purpose of reimbursing or repaying any money knowingly lent or advanced for gaming are "utterly void, frustrate, and of none effect." Is Herrmann still liable to Sea Air?

11. **[CD]** *Video Case.* See "TV Repair." Arnold takes his old TV set to an appliance store for repair and purchases a new TV from the store. He signs a promissory note, which provides for installment payments, for the balance due on the new set. The note contains the notice that the FTC requires be included in consumer credit instruments. Arnold discovers that the TV is defective after making the first payment on the note to the appliance store. The appliance store assigns the promissory note to Acme Finance Company, which notifies Arnold of its interest in the note and that he should make his payments on the note to it. Arnold advises Acme Finance that he will not make any further payments on the promissory note until the TV is repaired. If Arnold has a valid claim for breach of warranty of merchantability of the TV set, can he assert this as a defense against paying the note to the appliance store and/or to Acme Finance?

Liability of Parties

T hus far in Part 7, Commercial Paper, the focus has been on the nature of, and requirements for, negotiable instruments as well as the rights that an owner of an instrument can obtain and how to obtain them. Another important aspect to negotiable instruments concerns how a person becomes liable on a negotiable instrument and the nature of the liability incurred.

When a person signs a promissory note, he expects to be liable for paying the note on the day it is due. Similarly, when a person signs a check and mails it off to pay a bill, she expects that the drawee bank will pay it from funds in her checking account and that if her account contains insufficient funds to cover it, she will have to make it good out of other funds she has. These liabilities concerning instruments are commonly understood.

However, there are a number of other ways in which a person can become liable on a negotiable instrument. For example, a person who indorses a paycheck assumes liability on it; and a bank that cashes a check with a forged indorsement on it is liable for conversion of the check. This chapter and the following chapter discuss the liabilities of the various parties to a negotiable instrument. These two chapters also explain what happens when an instrument is not paid when it is supposed to be paid. For example, a check should not be paid if the drawer's account contains insufficient funds or if the check has been forged. In addition, this chapter discusses the ways in which liability on an instrument can be discharged. ∞

LIABILITY IN GENERAL

Liability on negotiable instruments flows from signatures on the instruments as well as actions taken concerning them. It can arise from the fact that a person has signed a negotiable instrument or has authorized someone else to sign it. The liability depends on the capacity in which the person signs the instrument. Liability also arises from (1) transfer or presentment of an instrument, (2) negligence relating to the issuance, alteration, or indorsement of the instrument, (3) improper payment, or (4) conversion.

CONTRACTUAL LIABILITY

When a person signs a negotiable instrument, whether as maker, drawer, indorser, or in some other capacity, she generally becomes contractually liable on the instrument. As mentioned above, this contractual liability depends on the capacity in which the person signed the instrument. The terms of the contract of the parties to a negotiable instrument are not set out in the text of the instrument. Rather, Article 3 of the Uniform Commercial Code supplies the terms, which are as much a part of the instrument as if they were part of its text.

Primary and Secondary Liability

A party to a negotiable instrument may be either *primarily liable* or *secondarily liable* for payment of it. A person who is primarily liable has agreed to pay the negotiable instrument. For example, the maker of a promissory note is the person who is primarily liable on the note. A person who is secondarily liable is like a guarantor on a contract; Article 3 requires a secondary party to pay the negotiable instrument only if a person who is primarily liable defaults on that obligation. Chapter 27, Introduction to Credit and Secured Transactions, discusses guarantors.

Obligation of a Maker

The **maker** of a promissory note is primarily liable for payment of it. The maker makes an unconditional promise to pay a fixed amount of money and is responsible for making good on that promise. The obligation of the maker is to pay the negotiable instrument according to its terms at the time he issues it or, if it is not issued, then according to its terms at the time it first came into possession of a holder [3–412].[1] If the material terms of the note are not complete when the maker signs it, then the maker's obligation is to pay the note as it is completed, provided that the terms filled in are as authorized. If the instrument is incomplete when the maker signs it and it is completed in an unauthorized manner, then the maker's liability will depend on whether the person seeking to enforce the instrument can qualify as a holder in due course.

The obligation of the maker is owed to (1) a *person entitled to enforce the instrument* or (2) any indorser who paid the instrument pursuant to her indorser's liability (discussed below). A person entitled to enforce an instrument includes: (1) the holder of the instrument; (2) a nonholder in possession of the instrument who has the rights of a holder; and (3) a person not in possession of the instrument who has the right to enforce the instrument under section 3–309, which deals with lost, destroyed, or stolen instruments.

Revised Article 3 provides that the *drawer of a cashier's check* has the same obligation as the maker or issuer of a note. Thus, it treats a draft drawn on a bank drawer the same as a note for purposes of the issuer's liability rather than treating the issuer as a drawer of a draft [3–412].

Obligation of a Drawee or an Acceptor

The **acceptor** of a draft is obligated to pay the draft according to the terms at the time of its acceptance. As was discussed in Chapter 30, acceptance is the drawee's signed engagement to honor the draft as presented—and is commonly indicated by the signature of the acceptor on the instrument itself. The acceptor's obligation extends to (1) a person entitled to enforce the draft, (2) the drawer, and (3) an indorser who paid the instrument pursuant to her indorser's liability [3–413].

If the certification of a check or other acceptance of a draft states the amount certified or accepted, the obligation of the acceptor is that amount. If the certification or acceptance does not state an amount, or if the amount of the instrument is subsequently raised and then the instrument is negotiated to a holder in due course, the obligation of the acceptor

---

[1]The numbers in brackets refer to sections of the Uniform Commercial Code (UCC), which is reproduced in the appendix.

is the amount of the instrument at the time a holder in due course takes it [3–413(b)].

At the time a payee receives possession of a check or other draft, the payee gets the drawer's contract to pay the instrument if the drawee—bank or buyer of goods—does not pay. (This liability is discussed elsewhere in this chapter.) *Issuance* of the check or draft, however, does not obligate the *drawee* to pay it. Like other Article 3 contracts discussed in this chapter, the drawee does not have liability on the instrument until it *signs* the instrument.

The drawer or a holder of the check may ask the drawee bank to accept or certify the check. The drawee bank certifies the check by signing its name to the check and, with that act, accepts liability as acceptor. The drawee bank debits, or takes the money out of, the drawer's account and holds the money to pay the check. If the drawee bank certifies the check, it becomes primarily, or absolutely, liable for paying the check as it reads at the time of its acceptance [3–413], and its acceptance discharges the drawer and indorsers who indorsed before the acceptance. Similarly, when a trade draft is presented for acceptance or payment, and the named drawee accepts it, then the drawee accepts the obligation set forth in the instrument and the drawer and earlier indorsers are discharged.

A drawee has no liability on a check or other draft unless it certifies or accepts the check or draft—that is, agrees to be liable on it. However, a drawee bank that refuses to pay a check when it is presented for payment may be liable to the drawer for wrongfully refusing payment, assuming the drawer had sufficient funds in his checking account to cover it. The next chapter discusses this liability of a drawee bank.

Obligation of a Drawer

The **drawer**'s obligation is that if the drawee dishonors an unaccepted check (or draft), the drawer will pay the check (or draft) according to its terms at the time he issued it or, if it was not issued, according to its terms at the time it first came into possession of a holder. If the draft was not complete when issued but was completed as authorized, then the obligation is to pay it as completed. If any completion is not authorized, then the obligation will depend on whether the person seeking to enforce the instrument can qualify as a holder in due course. A person entitled to enforce the draft or an indorser who paid the draft pursuant to his indorser's liability may enforce the drawer's obligation [3–414(b)].

For example, Janis draws a check on her account at First National Bank payable to the order of Collbert. If First National does not pay the check when Collbert presents it for payment, then Janis is liable to Collbert on the basis of her drawer's obligation.

If a draft is accepted by a bank—for example, if the drawee bank certifies a check—the drawer is discharged of her drawer's obligation. If someone other than a bank accepts a draft, then the obligation of the drawer to pay the draft, if the draft is dishonored, is the same as an indorser (discussed next) [3–414(c) and (d)].

The case that follows, *First American Bank of Virginia v. Litchfield Company of South Carolina, Inc.*, illustrates circumstances under which a drawer might be liable on its drawer's contractual obligation.

FIRST AMERICAN BANK OF VIRGINIA v. LITCHFIELD COMPANY OF SOUTH CAROLINA, INC.
353 S.E.2D 143 (S.C. Ct. App. 1987)

On February 9, 1983, Litchfield Company drew a check payable to Jensen Farley Pictures, Inc., in the amount of $13,711.11, on its account with Bankers Trust of South Carolina. Litchfield sent the check to Jensen Farley, which negotiated the check on September 16 to First American Bank of Virginia with whom it had a checking account. First American gave Jensen Farley immediate credit on the check and forwarded it to Bankers Trust for payment. Unknown to First American, Litchfield had given Bankers Trust an oral stop-payment order on the check. On September 19, Jensen Farley withdrew most of the balance in its First American account; it subsequently filed for bankruptcy. On September 21, Bankers Trust returned the Litchfield check to First American marked "payment stopped."

First American then sued Litchfield, claiming that as drawer of the check, it was liable to First American, a holder in due course of the check. The trial court awarded First American Bank judgment for $9,369.37 (representing the amount it had been unable to recover from Jensen Farley), and Litchfield appealed.

Bell, Judge The drawer of a check engages that upon dishonor he will pay the amount of the draft to a holder in due course. Section 3–413(2). The drawer has the right to stop payment, but remains liable on the instrument to a holder in due course. Section 4–403 and comment 8; section 3–413(2). Since Litchfield has conceded First American was a holder in due course, Litchfield remains liable on the instrument unless it can establish a valid defense or set off.

Litchfield argues that its liability was discharged by First American's failure to give timely notice the check had been dishonored. This defense is unavailing for two reasons.

First, failure to give notice of dishonor discharges a drawer only to the extent he is deprived of funds maintained with the drawee bank to cover the check because the drawee bank became insolvent during the delay. Sections 3–501(2)(b) and 3–502(1)(b). A drawer is not otherwise discharged. In this case, Litchfield was not deprived of any funds in its account with Bankers Trust nor did Bankers Trust become insolvent during the delay.

Second, notice of dishonor is excused when the party to be charged has himself countermanded payment. Section 3–511(2)(b). Since Litchfield ordered payment stopped, it was not entitled to notice of dishonor.

Litchfield argues strenuously that it is unfair to apply section 3–511(2)(b) to the drawer of a check who has no means of knowing whether the check has been negotiated to a holder. This reasoning misses the mark. The maker of an outstanding negotiable instrument is presumed to know the instrument is subject to transfer to a holder in due course. The drawer is often without actual knowledge that his check has been negotiated, but that ignorance in no way diminishes the rights of a holder in due course. To hold otherwise would, as a practical matter, destroy the negotiability of a check.

Judgment for First American affirmed.

Note: Although this case was decided under the original Article 3 and Revised Article 3 restates the obligation of a drawer, the same result would be anticipated under Revised Article 3.

Obligation of an Indorser

A person who indorses a negotiable instrument usually is secondarily liable. Unless the indorser qualifies or otherwise disclaims liability, the **indorser**'s obligation on dishonor of the instrument is to pay the amount due on the instrument according to its terms at the time he indorsed it or if he indorsed it when incomplete, then according to its terms when completed, provided that it is completed as authorized. The indorser owes the obligation to a person entitled to enforce the instrument or to any subsequent indorser who had to pay it [3–415].

The indorser can avoid this liability only by qualifying his indorsement, such as "without recourse," on the instrument when he indorses it [3–415(b)].

Indorsers are liable to each other in the chronological order in which they indorse, from the last indorser back to the first. For example, Mark Maker gives a promissory note to Paul Payee. Payee indorses it and negotiates it to Fred First, who indorses it and negotiates it to Shirley Second. If Maker does not pay the note when Second takes it to him for payment, then Second can require First to pay it to her. First is secondarily liable on the basis of his indorsement. First, in turn, can require Payee to pay him because Payee also became secondarily liable when he indorsed it. Then, Payee is left to try to collect the note from Maker. Second also could have skipped over First and proceeded directly against Payee on his indorsement. First has no liability to Payee, however, because First indorsed after Payee indorsed the note.

If a bank accepted a draft (for example, by certifying a check) after an indorsement is made, the acceptance discharges the liability of the indorser [3–415(d)]. If notice of dishonor is required and proper notice is not given to the indorser, she is discharged of liability [3–415(c)]. And, where no one presents a check or gives it to a depositary bank for collection within 30 days after the date of an indorsement, the indorser's liability is discharged [3–415(e)].

Obligation of an Accommodation Party

An **accommodation party** is a person who signs a negotiable instrument for the purpose of lending her credit to another party to the instrument but is not a direct beneficiary of the value given for the instrument. For example, a bank might be reluctant to lend money to—and take a note from—Payee because of his shaky financial condition. However, the bank may be willing to lend money to Payee if he signs the note and has a relative or a friend also sign the note as an accommodation maker.

The obligation of an accommodation party depends on the capacity in which the party signs the instrument [3–419]. If Maker has his brother Sam sign a note as an accommodation maker, then Sam has the same contractual liability as a maker. Sam is primarily liable on the note. The bank may ask Sam to pay the note before asking Maker to pay. However, if Sam pays the note to the bank, he has the right to recover his payment from Maker, the person on whose behalf he signed.

Similarly, if a person signs a check as an accommodation indorser, his contractual liability is that of an indorser. If the accommodation indorser has to make good on that liability, he can collect in turn from the person on whose behalf he signed.

Signing an Instrument

No person is contractually liable on a negotiable instrument unless she or her authorized agent has signed it and the signature is binding on the represented person. A signature can be any name, word, or mark used in place of a written signature [3–401]. As discussed earlier, the capacity in which a person signs an instrument determines his liability on the instrument.

Signature by an Authorized Agent

An authorized agent can sign a negotiable instrument. If Sandra Smith authorized her attorney to sign checks as her agent, then she is liable on any checks properly signed by the attorney as her agent. All negotiable instruments signed by corporations have to be signed by an agent of the corporation who is authorized to sign negotiable instruments.

If a person purporting to act as a representative signs an instrument by signing either the name of the represented person or the name of the signer, that signature binds the represented person to the same extent she would be bound if the signature were on a simple contract. If the represented person has authorized the signature of the representative, it is the "authorized signature of the represented

person" and the represented person is liable on the instrument, whether or not identified in the instrument. This brings the Code in line with the general principle of agency law that binds an undisclosed principal on a simple contract. For example, if Principal authorizes Agent to borrow money on Principal's behalf and Agent signs her name to a note without disclosing that the signature was on behalf of Principal, Agent is liable on the note. In addition, if the person entitled to enforce the note can show that Principal authorized Agent to sign on his behalf, then Principal is liable on the note as well.

When a representative signs an authorized signature to an instrument, then the representative is not bound provided the signature shows "unambiguously" that the signature was made on behalf of the represented person who is named in the instrument [3–402(b)(1)]. For example, if a note is signed "XYZ, Inc. by Flanigan, Treasurer," Flanigan is not liable on the instrument in his own right but XYZ, Inc., is liable.

If an authorized representative signs his name as the representative of a drawer of a check without noting his representative status but the check is payable from an account of the represented person who is identified on the check, the signer is not liable on the check as long as his signature was authorized [3–402(c)]. The rationale for this provision is that because most checks today identify the person on whose account the check is drawn, no one is deceived into thinking that the person signing the check is meant to be liable.

Except for the check situation noted above, a representative is personally liable to a holder in due course that took the instrument without notice that the representative was not intended to be liable if (1) the form of the signature does not show unambiguously that the signature was made in a representative capacity or (2) the instrument does not identify the represented person. As to persons other than a holder in due course without notice of the representative nature of the signature, the representative is liable *unless* she can prove that the original parties did not intend her to be liable on the instrument [3–402(b)(2)].

Thus, if an agent or a representative signs a negotiable instrument on behalf of someone else, the agent should indicate clearly that he is signing as the representative of someone else. For example, Kim Darby, the president of Swimwear, Inc., is authorized to sign negotiable instruments for the company. If Swimwear borrows money from the bank and the bank asks her to sign a 90-day promissory note, Darby should sign it either "Swimwear, Inc., by Kim Darby, President" or "Kim Darby, President, for Swimwear, Inc." If Kim Darby signed the promissory note merely "Kim Darby," she could be personally liable on the note. Similarly, if Clara Carson authorizes Arthur Ander-

son, an attorney, to sign checks for her, Anderson should make sure either that the checks identify Clara Carson as the account involved or should sign them "Clara Carson by Arthur Anderson, Agent." Otherwise, he risks being personally liable on them.

The liability of an authorized representative is discussed in the case that follows, *Mestco Distributors, Inc., v. Stamps.*

MESTCO DISTRIBUTORS, INC. v. STAMPS   17 UCC Rep.2d 174 (Tex Ct. App. 1992)

 n seven separate occasions between May 1985 and December 1986, Mestco Distributors, Inc., loaned funds for business operations to Innovative Timber Specialties, Inc. (ITS), in which Mestco was a shareholder. The seven notes were signed as follows:

Promissory note 1—May 17, 1985, signed:
    I.T.S. Inc.
    by Ralph W. Stamps
    Secty. Treas

Promissory note 2—June 25, 1985, signed:
    Ralph W. Stamps

Promissory note 3—December 23, 1985, signed:
    Innovative Timber Specialties Inc.
    by Secty-Treas
    Ralph W. Stamps

Promissory note 4—July 16, 1985, signed:
    Ralph W. Stamps
    Secty-Treas. I.T.S. Inc.

Promissory note 5—December 9, 1985, signed:
    Ralph W. Stamps

Promissory note 6—August 6, 1986, signed:
    Innovative Timber Specialties Inc.
    by Ralph W. Stamps

Promissory note 7—December 31, 1986, signed:
    Ralph W. Stamps
    Innovative Timber Specialties Inc.
    by: Secretary

The notes were not paid and Mestco sued Stamps, seeking to hold him personally liable for paying the seven notes. The trial court held in favor of Stamps and Mestco appealed. ∞

Ellis, Judge   Mestco argues that none of the promissory notes meet the requirements of Section 3–403, and, therefore, Stamps was required to present evidence to overcome the presumption of individual liability as to all seven notes. We disagree.

Section 3–403(c) provides that a signature is established as being in a representative capacity *if it has the name of an organization preceded or fol-*

lowed by an authorized individual's name and office. Four of the promissory notes meet these requirements (May 17, 1985; December 23, 1885; July 16, 1986; December 31, 1986). Clearly, these notes listed the names of the organization followed or preceded by Ralph Stamps' name and his office, designated as Secretary or Secty-Treas. Accordingly, there was evidence to support the trial court's finding that these four notes were executed in a representative capacity.

Three of the promissory notes clearly did not meet the requirements of Section 3–403. Two notes were signed solely with Ralph Stamps' name and one note was signed "Innovative Timber Specialties, Inc. by Ralph W. Stamps." As Mestco correctly points out, if a signature is not shown to be in a representative capacity pursuant to Section 3–403(c), the signer/maker, in a dispute between the immediate parties, has the burden to offer proof that he signed only in a representative capacity.

Although there is no evidence in the present case that Stamps actually told Mestco that he was signing the notes in a representative capacity, there was evidence of prior dealings between the parties as well as circumstances that communicated to Mestco that Stamps was executing the notes in a representative capacity.

The evidence before the court was as follows. Henry Mest was president and owner of Mestco Distributors, Inc. He was in business for 30 years in La Marque, Texas. Stamps and Mest knew each other for more than 30 years. Stamps approached Mest regarding investing in ITS after its original formation in 1982. They each became shareholders in ITS, neither being majority shareholders. Both became officers and Mest became a director. The chief operating officer and president resigned in 1985 and Mest took over. In 1985 Mest went to ITS's job site once or twice a week and was fully aware of what was going on with the business.

Stamps managed ITS from 1985 to 1986 per an agreement with Mest. Stamps would also let Mestco know of ITS's financial need. Mestco and Stamps both from time to time loaned money to ITS as needed. In 1986, both Mestco and Stamps repaid in equal amounts a loan made to ITS in the amount of $150,000. Mestco received at least seven notes in addition to the notes the subject of this suit. These notes were later written off by Mestco as bad debts. The seven promissory notes involved in the present suit were prepared at Mest's direction. The payment of each of the notes was a promise of ITS's named in the subject notes and there was no understanding that the loans represented loans to Stamps individually. The funding of the notes was to ITS directly and the funds were often deposited to ITS's bank account by Mestco's accountant. Also the notes were carried on Mestco's books as notes receivable from ITS and not as notes receivable from Stamps. Further, the notes were charged-off by Mestco in 1986 and 1987.

Accordingly, there was sufficient evidence showing that Mestco knew the notes were executed in a representative capacity and not Stamps individually, and past dealings supported that Stamps executed in a representative capacity.

Judgment for Stamps affirmed.

Note: Although this case was decided under the original version of Article 3, the same result would likely be reached under Revised Article 3.

Unauthorized Signature

If someone signs a person's name to a negotiable instrument without that person's authorization or approval, the signature does not bind the person whose name appears. However, the signature is effective as the signature of the unauthorized signer in favor of any person who in good faith pays the instrument or takes it for value [3–403(a)]. For example, if Tom Thorne steals Ben Brown's checkbook and signs Brown's name to a check, Brown is not liable on the check because Brown had not authorized Thorne to sign Brown's name. Thorne can be liable on the check, however, because he did sign it, even though he did not sign it in his own name. Thorne's forgery of Brown's signature operates as Thorne's signature. Thus, if Thorne cashed the check at the bank, Thorne would be liable to it or if he negotiated it to a store for value, he would be liable to the store to make it good.

Even though a signature is not "authorized" when it is put on an instrument initially, it can be ratified later by the person represented [3–403(a)]. It also should be noted that if more than one person must sign to constitute the authorized signature of an organization, the signature of the organization is unauthorized if one of the required signatures is lacking [3–403(b)]. Corporate and other accounts sometimes require multiple signatures as a matter of maintaining sound financial control.

CONTRACTUAL LIABILITY IN OPERATION

To bring the contractual liability of the various parties to a negotiable instrument into play, it generally is necessary that the instrument be *presented for payment*. In addition, to hold the parties that are secondarily liable on the instrument to their contractual liability, it generally is necessary that the instrument be *presented for payment* and *dishonored*.

Presentment of a Note

The maker of a note is primarily liable to pay it when it is due. Normally, the holder takes the note to the maker at the time it is due and asks the maker to pay it. Sometimes, the note may provide for payment to be made at a bank or the maker sends the payment to the holder at the due date. The party to whom the holder presents the instrument, without dishonoring the instrument, may (1) require the exhibition of the instrument, (2) ask for reasonable identification of the person making presentment, (3) ask for evidence of his authority to make it if he is making it for another person, or (4) return the instrument for lack of any necessary indorsement, (5) ask that a receipt be signed for any payment made, and (6) surrender the instrument if full payment is made [3–501].

Dishonor of a note occurs if the maker does not pay the amount due when: (1) it is presented in the case of (*a*) a demand note or (*b*) a note payable at or through a bank on a definite date that is presented on or after that date, or (2) if it is not paid on the date payable in the case of a note payable on a definite date but not payable at or through a bank [3–502]. If the maker or payor dishonors the note, the holder can seek payment from any persons who indorsed the note before the holder took it. The basis for going after the indorsers are that they are secondarily liable. To hold the indorsers to their contractual obligation, the holder must give them notice of the dishonor. The notice can be either written or oral [3–503].

For example, Susan Strong borrows $1,000 from Jack Jones and gives him a promissory note for $1,000 at 9 percent annual interest payable in 90 days. Jones indorses the note "Pay to the order of Ralph Smith" and negotiates the note to Ralph Smith. At the end of the 90 days, Smith takes the note to Strong and presents it for payment. If Strong pays Smith the $1,000 and accrued interest, she can have Smith mark it "paid" and give it back to her. If Strong does not pay the note to Smith when he presents it for payment, then she has dishonored the note. Smith should give notice of the dishonor to Jones and advise him that he intends to hold Jones secondarily liable on his indorsement. Smith may collect payment of the note from Jones. Jones, after making the note good to Smith, can try to collect the note from Strong on the ground that she defaulted on the contract she made as maker of the note. Of course, Smith also could sue Strong on the basis of her maker's obligation.

Presentment of a Check or a Draft

The holder should present a check or draft to the drawee. The presentment can be either for payment or for acceptance (certification) of the check or draft. Under Revised Article 3, the presentment may be made by any commercially reasonable means, including a written, oral, or electronic communication [3–501]. The drawee is not obligated on a check or draft unless it accepts (certifies) it [3–408]. An acceptance of a draft is the drawee's signed commitment to honor the draft as presented. The acceptance must be written on the draft, and it may consist of the drawee's signature alone [3–409].

A drawer who writes a check issues an order to the drawee to pay a certain amount out of the drawer's account to the payee (or to someone authorized by the payee). This order is not an assignment of the funds in the drawer's account [3–408]. The drawee bank does not have an obligation to the payee to pay the check unless it certifies the check. However, the drawee bank usually does have a separate contractual obligation (apart from Article 3) to the drawer to pay any properly payable checks for which funds are available in the drawer's account.

For example, Janet Payne has $100 in a checking account at First National Bank and writes a check for $10 drawn on First National and payable to Ralph Smith. The writing of the check is the issuance of an order by Payne to First National to pay $10 from her account to Smith or to whomever Smith requests it to be paid. First National owes no obligation to Smith to pay the $10 unless it has certified the check. However, if Smith presents the check for payment and First National refuses to pay it even though there are sufficient funds in Payne's account, then First National is liable to Payne for breaching its contractual obligation to her to pay items properly payable from existing funds in her account. Chapter 33, Checks and Documents of Title, discusses the liability of a bank for wrongful dishonor of checks in more detail.

If the drawee bank does not pay or certify a check when it is properly presented for payment or acceptance (certification), the drawee bank has dishonored the check [3–502]. Similarly, if a draft is not paid on the date it is due (or accepted by the drawee on the due date for acceptance), it has been dishonored. The holder of the draft or check then can proceed against either the drawer or any indorsers on their liability. To do so, the holder must give them notice of the dishonor [3–503]. Notice of dishonor, like presentment, can be by any commercially reasonable means, including oral, written, or electronic communication. Under certain circumstances, set out in section 3–504, presentment or notice of dishonor may be excused.

Suppose Matthews draws a check for $100 on her account at a bank payable to the order of Williams. Williams indorses the check "Pay to the order of Clark, Williams" and negotiates it to Clark. When Clark takes the check to the bank, it refuses to pay the check because there are insufficient funds in Matthews's account to cover the check. The check has been presented and dishonored. Clark has two options: He can proceed against Williams on Williams's secondary liability as an indorser (because by putting an unqualified indorsement on the check, Williams is obligated to make the check good if it was not honored by the drawee). Or, he can proceed against Matthews on Matthews's obligation as drawer because in drawing the check, Matthews must pay any person entitled to enforce the check if it is dishonored and he is given notice. Because Clark dealt with Williams, Clark is probably more likely to return the check to Williams for payment. Williams then has to go against Matthews on Matthews's liability as drawer.

Time of Presentment

If an instrument is payable at a definite time, the holder should present it for payment on the due date. In the case of a demand instrument, the nature of the instrument, trade or bank usage, and the facts of the particular case determine a reasonable time for presentment for acceptance or payment. In a farming community, for example, a reasonable time to present a promissory note that is payable on demand may be six months or within a short time after the crops are ready for sale, because the holder commonly expects payment from the proceeds of the crops.

WARRANTY LIABILITY

Whether or not a person signs a negotiable instrument, a person who transfers such an instrument or presents it for payment or acceptance may incur liability on the basis of certain implied warranties. These warranties are (1) **transfer warranties,** which persons who transfer negotiable instruments make to their transferees; and (2) **presentment warranties,** which persons who present negotiable instruments for payment or acceptance (certification) make to those who pay or accept.

Transfer Warranties

A person who transfers a negotiable instrument to someone else and for consideration makes five warranties to his immediate transferee. If the transfer is by indorsement, the transferor makes these warranties to all subsequent transferees. The five **transfer warranties** are:

1. The warrantor is a person entitled to enforce the instrument. (In essence the transferor warrants that there are no unauthorized or missing indorsements that prevent the transferor from making the transferee a person entitled to enforce the instrument.)

2. All signatures on the instrument are authentic or authorized.

3. The instrument has not been altered.

4. The instrument is not subject to a defense or a claim in recoupment that any party can assert against the warrantor.

5. The warrantor has no knowledge of any insolvency proceedings commenced with respect to the maker or acceptor or, in the case of an unaccepted draft, the drawer [3–416(a)]. Note that this is not a warranty against difficulty in collection or insolvency—the warranty stops with the warrantor's knowledge.

Revised Article 3 provides that in the event of a breach of a transfer warranty, a beneficiary of the transfer warranties who took the instrument in good faith may recover from the warrantor an amount equal to the loss suffered as a result of the breach. However, the damages recoverable may not be more than the amount of the instrument plus expenses and loss of interest incurred as a result of the breach [3–416(b)].

Transferors of instruments other than checks may disclaim the transfer warranties. Unless the warrantor receives notice of a claim for breach of warranty within 30 days after the claimant has reason to know of the breach and the identity of the warrantor, the delay in giving notice of the claim may discharge the warrantor's liability to the extent of any loss the warrantor suffers from the delay, such as the opportunity to proceed against the transferor [3–416(c)].

Although contractual liability often furnishes a sufficient basis for suing a transferor when the party primarily obligated does not pay, warranties are still important. First, they apply even when the transferor did not indorse. Second, unlike contractual liability, they do not depend on presentment, dishonor, and notice, but may be utilized before presentment has been made or after the time for giving notice has expired. Third, a holder may find it easier to return the instrument to a transferor on the ground of breach of warranty than to prove her status as a holder in due course against a maker or drawer.

Presentment Warranties

Persons who present negotiable instruments for payment or drafts for acceptance also make warranties, but their warranties differ from those transferors make. If an unaccepted draft (such as a check) is presented to the drawee for payment or acceptance and the drawee pays or accepts the draft, then the person obtaining payment or acceptance warrants to the drawee making payment or accepting the draft in good faith that:

1. The warrantor is, or was, at the time the warrantor transferred the draft, a person entitled to enforce the draft or authorized to obtain payment or acceptance of the draft on behalf of a person entitled to enforce the draft.

2. The draft has not been altered.

3. The warrantor has no knowledge that the signature of the drawer of the draft has not been authorized [3–417(a)].

These warranties also are made by any prior transferor of the instrument at the time the person transfers the instrument; the warranties run to the drawee who makes payment or accepts the draft in good faith. Such a drawee would include a drawee bank paying a check presented to it for payment directly or through the bank collection process.

The effect of the third presentment warranty is to leave with the drawee the risk that the drawer's

---

CONCEPT REVIEW

Transfer Warranties

The five transfer warranties made by a person who transfers a negotiable instrument to someone else for consideration are:

1. The warrantor is entitled to enforce the instrument.
2. All signatures on the instrument are authentic or authorized.
3. The instrument has not been altered.
4. The instrument is not subject to a defense or a claim in recoupment that any party can assert against the warrantor.
5. The warrantor has no knowledge of any insolvency proceedings commenced with respect to the maker or acceptor or, in the case of an unaccepted draft, the drawer.

WHO	WHAT WARRANTIES	TO WHOM
Nonindorsing Transferor	Makes all five transfer warranties	To his immediate transferee only
Indorsing Transferor	Makes all five transfer warranties	To his immediate transferee and all subsequent transferees

signature is unauthorized, unless the person presenting the draft for payment, or a prior transferor, had knowledge of any lack of authorization.

A drawee who makes payment may recover as damages for any breach of a presentment warranty an amount equal to the amount paid by the drawee less the amount the drawee received or is entitled to receive from the drawer because of the payment. In addition, the drawee is entitled to compensation for expenses and loss of interest resulting from the breach [3–417(b)]. The drawee's right to recover damages for breach of warranty is not affected by any failure on the part of the drawee to exercise ordinary care in making payment.

If a drawee asserts a claim for breach of a presentment warranty based on an unauthorized indorsement of the draft or an alteration of the draft, the warrantor may defend by showing that the indorsement is effective under the *impostor* or *fictitious payee* rules (discussed later in this chapter) or that the drawer's negligence precludes him from asserting against the drawee the unauthorized indorsement or alteration (also discussed below) [3–417(c)].

If (1) a *dishonored draft* is presented for payment to the drawer or an indorser or (2) any other instrument (such as a note) is presented for payment to a party obligated to pay the instrument and the presenter receives payment, the presenter makes the following presentment warranty:

The person obtaining payment is a person entitled to enforce the instrument or authorized to obtain payment on behalf of a person entitled to enforce the instrument [3–417(d)].

On breach of this warranty, the person making the payment may recover from the warrantor an amount equal to the amount paid plus expenses and loss of interest resulting from the breach.

With respect to checks, the party presenting the check for payment cannot disclaim the presentment warranties [3–417(e)]. Unless the payor or drawee provides notice of a claim for breach of a present-ment warranty to the warrantor within 30 days after the claimant has reason to know of the breach and the identity of the warrantor, the warrantor is discharged to the extent of any loss caused by the delay in giving notice of the claim of breach.

Payment or Acceptance by Mistake

A longstanding general rule of negotiable instruments law is that payment or acceptance is final in favor of a holder in due course or payee who changes his position in reliance on the payment or acceptance. Revised Article 3 retains this concept by making payment final in favor of a person who took the instrument in good faith and for value. However, payment is not final—and may be recovered from—a person who does not meet these criteria where the drawee acted on the mistaken belief that (1) payment of a draft or check has not been stopped, and (2) the signature of the purported drawer of the draft was authorized [3–418(a)]. In some jurisdictions, the drawee's mistaken belief that the account held available funds also could serve as a basis for recovery of the payment [3–418(b)].

As a result, this means that if the drawee bank mistakenly paid a check over a stop-payment order, paid a check with a forged or unauthorized drawer's signature on it, or paid despite the lack of sufficient funds in the drawer's account to cover the check, the bank cannot recover if it paid the check to a presenter who had taken the instrument in good faith and for value. In that case, the drawee bank would have to pursue someone else, such as the forger or unauthorized signer, or seller whose goods proved to be defective. On the other hand, if the presenter had not taken in good faith or for value, the bank could, in these enumerated instances, recover from the presenter the payment it made by mistake.

The *Garnac Grain Co., Inc. v. Boatmen's Bank & Trust Co. of Kansas City* case, which follows, illustrates the operation of presentment and transfer warranties.

GARNAC GRAIN CO., INC. v. BOATMEN'S BANK & TRUST CO. OF KANSAS CITY 694 F. Supp. 1389 (W.D. Mo. 1988)

K atherine Millison was employed by the Garnac Grain Company as a bookkeeper. She developed a scheme to embezzle money from Garnac whereby she would take home fully executed and valid checks payable to freight vendors and type "or L. R. Millison" (her husband's name) under the named payee with her manual typewriter. She would then indorse the check "L. R. Millison" on the back and deposit the check in a joint account she and her husband maintained at the State Bank of Oskaloosa. The bank forwarded the altered checks through the Federal Reserve System (through First National Bank of Kansas City), which presented them for payment to the drawee bank, Boatmen's Bank & Trust Company of Kansas City. Boatmen's paid the checks. Millison then would intercept the monthly bank statements from Boatmen's Bank & Trust, remove the altered checks, and obliterate the "or L. R. Millison" on the face of the checks and the indorsement on the back.

The scheme was discovered and Millison was convicted of embezzlement. Garnac brought suit against Boatmen's Bank & Trust, alleging that it wrongfully paid the altered checks. It settled with Garnac and then sued the State Bank of Oskaloosa, contending that it breached the UCC transfer warranties when it forwarded the altered checks for payment. ∽

Hunter, Senior District Judge Boatmen's and First National contend that Oskaloosa is liable for the amount of their settlement with Garnac because it breached the UCC transfer warranties it made to them when it sent the checks altered by Millison to First National for payment by Boatmen's. Specifically it alleges that Oskaloosa breached the good title, material alterations, and genuine signature warranties.

Section 4–207 provides in pertinent part:

(1) Each customer or collecting bank who obtains payment or acceptance of an item and each prior customer and collecting bank warrants to the payor bank or other payor who in good faith pays or accepts the item that

(a) he has good title to the item or is authorized to obtain payment or acceptance on behalf of one who has a good title; and

(b) he has no knowledge that the signature of the maker or drawer is unauthorized . . . ; and

(c) the item has not been materially altered . . .

(2) Each customer and collecting bank who transfers an item and receives a settlement or other consideration for it warrants to his transferee and to any subsequent collecting bank who takes the item in good faith that

(a) he has a good title to the item or is authorized to obtain payment or acceptance on behalf of one who has a good title and the transfer is otherwise rightful; and

(b) all signatures are genuine and authorized; and

(c) the item has not been materially altered;

Under this system, a payor bank in possession of a check containing, for example, a material alteration has the choice of bringing a warranty claim against the bank that transferred the check to it, or any other intermediate collecting bank or the depository bank. If the payor bank brings the action against a bank other than the depository bank, that bank can bring a claim against its transferor bank or any other previous collecting bank. As between the banks involved in the collection process, the liability for a materially altered check falls on the depository bank. This is in accord with the loss allocation framework of Articles 3 and 4 of the UCC which generally places the loss of a forged or altered item on the person or bank who dealt with the wrongdoer if the wrongdoer cannot be found or is judgment proof. Since there is no knowledge or notice requirement with respect to the material alteration warranties, the question of whether or not a party breached these warranties is simply a question of whether or not the checks were materially altered.

There seems to be no serious dispute among the parties but that the alterations made by Millison were material. Each check was drawn on Garnac's account at Boatmen's, was properly made out to barge freight vendors, and was properly signed by authorized representatives of Garnac. Millison altered the checks by typing "or L. R. Millison" underneath the payee's name. The court finds that, as a matter of law, an alteration which adds an alternative payee is a material alteration as that term is used in the UCC. See section 3–407. Thus, both Oskaloosa and First National breached their 3–207 (1) warranties of no material alteration to Boatmen's;

Oskaloosa breached its 4−207 (2) warranty of no material alterations.

There is also no question that Oskaloosa breached its warranty of good title. Without the indorsement of the intended payees on the checks (i.e., the barge freight vendors) Oskaloosa could not obtain good title to the checks. The only indorsement on the back of the checks was "L. R. Millison." Neither Millison nor her husband was authorized to indorse the checks on behalf of the barge freight vendors shown as payees on the altered checks. Since Oskaloosa did not have good title when it transferred the checks to First National, it breached its section 4−207(1)(a) warranty to Boatmen's and its 4−207(2)(a) warranty to First National.

Summary judgment in favor of Boatmen's on its claims that the State Bank of Oskaloosa breached its warranties of good title and no material alterations.

Note: The court found that there were issues of material fact as to whether Garnac had exercised reasonable care and promptness in examining its bank statement to discover unauthorized signatures and alterations and whether Boatmen's had exercised ordinary care in paying the checks in question. This case was decided under the original version of Article 3 and 4. Revised Article 3 and the conforming amendments to Articles 1 and 4 changes the wording of the transfer and presentment warranties and the warranties appear under different section numbers. However, the result reached in this case would be the same under the revisions to the Code.

Operation of Warranties

Following are three scenarios that show how the transfer and presentment warranties shift the liability back to a wrongdoer or to the person who dealt immediately with a wrongdoer and thus was in the best position to avert the wrongdoing.

Scenario 1   Arthur makes a promissory note for $200 payable to the order of Betts. Carlson steals the note from Betts, indorses her name on the back, and gives it to Davidson in exchange for a television set. Davidson negotiates the note for value to Earle, who presents the note to Arthur for payment. Assume that Arthur refuses to pay the note because

Betts has advised him that it has been stolen and that he is the person entitled to enforce the instrument. Earle then can proceed to recover the face amount of the note from Davidson on the grounds that as a transferor Davidson has warranted that he is a person entitled to enforce the note and that all signatures were authentic. Davidson, in turn, can proceed against Carlson on the same basis—if he can find Carlson. If he cannot, then Davidson must bear the loss caused by Carlson's wrongdoing. Davidson was in the best position to ascertain whether Carlson was the owner of the note and whether the indorsement of Betts was genuine. Of course, even though Arthur does not have to pay the

C O N C E P T   R E V I E W

Presentment Warranties

If an unaccepted draft (such as a check) is presented for payment or acceptance and the drawee pays or accepts the draft, then the person and prior transferors obtaining payment or acceptance warrants to the drawee:

1. The warrantor is a person entitled to enforce payment or authorized to obtain payment or acceptance on behalf of a person entitled to enforce the draft.
2. The draft has not been altered.
3. The warrantor has no knowledge that the signature of the drawer of the draft has not been authorized.

If (*a*) a dishonored draft is presented for payment to the drawer or indorser or (*b*) any other instrument (such as a note) is presented for payment to a party obligated to pay the instrument and the presenter receives payment, the presenter (as well as a prior transferor of the instrument) makes the following warranty to the person making payment in good faith:

The person obtaining payment is a person entitled to enforce the instrument or authorized to obtain payment on behalf of a person entitled to enforce the instrument.

note to Earle, Arthur remains liable for his underlying obligation to Betts.

Scenario 2 Anderson draws a check for $10 on her checking account at First Bank payable to the order of Brown. Brown cleverly raises the check to $110, indorses it, and negotiates it to Carroll. Carroll then presents the check for payment to First Bank, which pays her $110 and charges Anderson's account for $110. Anderson then asks the bank to recredit her account for the altered check, and it does so. The bank can proceed against Carroll for breach of the presentment warranty that the instrument had not been altered, which she made to the bank when she presented the check for payment. Carroll in turn can proceed against Brown for breach of her transfer warranty that the check had not been altered—if she can find her. Unless she was negligent in drawing the check, Article 3 limits Anderson's liability to $10 because her obligation is to pay the amount in the instrument at the time she issued it.

Scenario 3 Bates steals Albers's checkbook and forges Albers's signature to a check for $100 payable to "cash," which he uses to buy $100 worth of groceries from a grocer. The grocer presents the check to Albers's bank. The bank pays the amount of the check to the grocer and charges Albers's account. Albers then demands that the bank recredit his account. The bank can recover against the grocer only if the grocer knew that Albers's signature had been forged. Otherwise, the bank must look for Bates. The bank had the responsibility to recognize the true signature of its drawer, Albers, and not to pay the check that contained an unauthorized signature. The bank may be able to resist recrediting Albers's account if it can show he was negligent. The next section of this chapter discusses negligence.

OTHER LIABILITY RULES

Normally, a bank may not charge against (debit from) the drawer's account a check that has a forged payee's indorsement. Similarly, a maker does not have to pay a note to the person who currently possesses the note if the payee's signature has been forged. If a check or note has been altered—for example, by raising the amount—the drawer or maker usually is liable only for the instrument in the amount for which he originally issued it. However, there are a number of exceptions to these usual rules. These exceptions, as well as liability based on conversion of an instrument, are discussed below.

Negligence

A person can be so negligent in writing or signing a negotiable instrument that he in effect invites an alteration or an unauthorized signature on it. If a person has been negligent, Article 3 precludes her from using the alteration or lack of authorization as a reason for not paying a person that in good faith pays the instrument or takes it for value [3–406]. For example, Mary Maker makes out a note for $10 in such a way that someone could alter it to read $10,000. Someone alters the note and negotiates it to Katherine Smith, who can qualify as a holder in due course. Smith can collect $10,000 from Maker. Maker's negligence precludes her from claiming alteration as a defense to paying it. Maker then has to find the person who "raised" her note and try to collect the $9,990 from him.

Where the person asserting the preclusion failed to exercise ordinary care in taking or paying the instrument and that failure substantially contributed to the loss, Article 3 allocates the loss between the two parties based on their comparative negligence [3–406(b)]. Thus, if a drawer was so negligent in drafting a check that he made it possible for the check to be altered and the bank that paid the check, in the exercise of ordinary care, should have noticed the alteration, then any loss occasioned by the fact that the person who made the alteration could not be found would be split by the drawer and the bank based on their comparative fault.

Impostor Rule

Article 3 establishes special rules for negotiable instruments made payable to impostors and fictitious persons. An impostor is a person who poses as someone else and convinces a drawer to make a check payable to the person being impersonated—or to an organization the person purports to be authorized to represent. When this happens, the Code makes any indorsement "substantially similar" to that of the named payee effective [3–404(a)]. Where the impostor has impersonated a person authorized to act for a payee, such as claiming to be Jack Jones, the president of Jones Enterprises, the impostor has the power to negotiate a check to Jones Enterprises.

An example of a situation involving the impostor rule would be the following: Arthur steals Paulsen's automobile and finds the certificate of title in the automobile. Then, representing himself as Paulsen, he sells the automobile to Berger Used Car Company. The car dealership draws its check payable to Paulsen for the agreed purchase price of the automobile and delivers the check to Arthur. Any person can negotiate the check by indorsing it in the name of Paulsen.

The rationale for the impostor rule is to put the responsibility for determining the true identity of the payee on the drawer or maker of a negotiable instrument. The drawer is in a better position to do this than some later holder of the check who may be entirely innocent. The impostor rule allows that later holder to have good title to the check by making the payee's signature valid although it is not the signature of the person with whom the drawer or maker thought he was dealing. It forces the drawer or maker to find the wrongdoer who tricked him into signing the negotiable instrument or to bear the loss himself.

Fictitious Payee Rule

A fictitious payee commonly arises in the following situation: A dishonest employee draws a check payable to someone who does not exist—or to a real person who does business with the employer but to whom the dishonest employee does not intend to send the check. If the employee has the authority to do so, he may sign the check himself. If he does not have such authority, he gives the check to his employer for signature and represents that the employer owes money to the person named as the payee of the check. The dishonest employee then takes the check, indorses it in the name of the payee, presents it for payment, and pockets the money. The employee may be in a position to cover up the wrongdoing by intercepting the canceled checks or juggling the company's books.

The Code allows any indorsement in the name of the fictitious payee to be effective as the payee's indorsement in favor of any person that pays the instrument in good faith or takes it for value or for collection [3–404(b) and (c)]. For example, Anderson, an accountant in charge of accounts payable at Moore Corporation, prepares a false invoice naming Parks, Inc., a supplier of Moore Corporation, as having supplied Moore Corporation with goods, and draws a check payable to Parks, Inc., for the amount of the invoice. Anderson then presents the check to Temple, Treasurer of Moore Corporation, together with other checks with invoices attached. Temple signs all of these checks and returns them to Anderson for mailing. Anderson then withdraws the check payable to Parks, Inc. Anyone, including Anderson, can negotiate the check by indorsing it in the name of Parks, Inc.

The rationale for the fictitious payee rule is similar to that for the impostor rule. If someone has a dishonest employee or agent who is responsible for the forgery of some checks, the employer of the wrongdoer should bear the immediate loss of those checks rather than some other innocent party. In turn, the employer must locate the unfaithful employee or agent and try to recover from him.

The *C & N Contractors, Inc. v. Community Bancshares, Inc.* case, which follows, illustrates the operation of the fictitious payee rule. As you read the case, determine how the contractor might have prevented the loss it suffered.

C & N CONTRACTORS v. COMMUNITY BANCSHARES, INC.   646 So.2d 1357 (Sup. Ct. Ala. 1994)

C *& N Contractors is a construction and general contracting company in Gardendale, Alabama, that performs work at job sites throughout the southeastern United States. Mary Bivens was employed by C & N and performed general administrative duties for it.*

Each Wednesday morning, the foreman at each job site telephoned Bivens and gave her the names of the employees working on the job site and the number of hours they had worked. Bivens then conveyed this information to Automatic Data Processing (ADP), whose offices are in Atlanta, Georgia. ADP prepared payroll checks based on the information given by Bivens and sent the checks to the offices of C & N in Gardendale for authorized signatures. Bivens was not an authorized signatory. After the checks were signed, Bivens sent the checks to the job site foreman for delivery to the employees.

In 1991, Bivens began conveying false information to ADP about employees and hours worked. On the basis of this false information, ADP prepared payroll checks payable to persons who were actual employees but had not worked the hours Bivens had indicated. After obtaining authorized signatures from C & N, Bivens intercepted the checks, forged the indorsement of the payees, and either cashed the checks at Community Bancshares or deposited them into her account at Community Bancshares, often presenting numerous checks at one time. Bivens continued this practice for almost a year, forging over 100 checks, until Jimmy Nation, vice president of C & N, discovered the embezzlement after noticing payroll checks payable to employees who had not recently performed services for the corporation. Bivens subsequently admitted forging the indorsements.

C & N brought suit against Community Bancshares for conversion when it cashed or accepted for deposit the numerous payroll checks containing forged payee indorsements. The trial court awarded summary judgment to Community Bancshares, and C & N Contractors appealed. ∽

Almon, Justice   With regard to the claim of conversion, the circuit court, in its summary judgment, held that under the "padded payroll" rule of section 3–405(1)(c) the forged indorsement of Bivens was effective and that, therefore, the loss caused by the forged indorsements fell on C & N. Section 3–405 provides in pertinent part:

(1) An indorsement by any person in the name of a named payee is effective if:
(c) An agent or employee of the maker or drawer has supplied him with the name of the payee intending the latter to have no interest in the instrument.

A forged indorsement is ordinarily ineffective to pass title to an instrument to a collecting bank or, generally, to authorize a drawee bank to pay the instrument. Section 3–405(1) creates a limited exception to these general rules.

Although section 3–405(1) does not explicitly impose liability on the drawer for the loss caused by the payment of a forged instrument, it has the general legal effect of shifting liability to the drawer from the party who took from the forger. By making effective an otherwise ineffective indorsement in the special circumstances provided in section 3–405 (1)(a), (b) and (c), section 3–405(1) generally precludes the liability of a drawee bank to a drawer under section 4–401 and the liability of a collecting bank to a drawee/payor bank under section 4–207.

Under section 4–207, each party who obtains payment from the drawee and each prior transferor warrants to the party who pays the check that he has good title to the instrument. This warranty is breached when the check has a forged or unauthorized signature. If in good faith and in accordance with commercially reasonable standards, a depositary or collecting bank accepts a check with a forged indorsement and then presents it for payment to the drawee/payor bank and if the drawee/payor bank pays the check, the drawee/payor bank is generally liable to the drawer under section 4–401 because it did not properly pay the check to the drawer's order.

After recrediting the drawer's account, the drawee/payor bank may seek indemnification against the collecting bank that made presentment under section 4–207, alleging breach of warranty of good title. Liability on the basis of breach of warranty travels backward through the chain of collection and is ultimately placed on the party who took the check from the forger. Thus, when a depositary bank accepts a forged instrument, it is generally liable for the amount of the check paid by the payor. The rationale for this system of allocating liability is that the party who took from the forger should be liable for the loss because that party is in the best position to prevent such fraud by checking the authenticity of indorsements.

Section 3–405(1) is a narrow exception to this general system of allocating loss. Because this section makes an indorsement on a forged signature effective, the drawee/payor bank is authorized to pay the instrument and is generally not liable, therefore, to the drawer under section 4–401. Further, because this section makes an indorsement on a forged signature effective, title to the instrument passes, as though there had been no forgery, and a collecting bank is entitled to payment from parties liable on the instrument. Thus, no conversion action by the drawer against either the drawee or the depositary bank will lie where section 3–405 controls. The official comment to section 3–405 states the rationale for allocating liability to the drawer in the circumstances covered by section 3–405(1):

The principle followed is that the loss should fall upon the employer as a risk of his business enterprise rather than upon the subsequent holder or drawee. The reasons are that the employer is normally in a better position to prevent such forgeries by reasonable care in the supervision of his employees, or, if he is not, is at least in a better position to cover the loss by fidelity insurance; and that the cost of such insurance is properly a cost of the business rather than of the holder or drawee.

The circuit court held, and Community Bancshares argues, that under section 3–405(1)(c) Community Bancshares is not liable in the circumstances of this case because Bivens, an employee of C & N, supplied her employer with the names of the payees of the payroll checks with the intent that the payees would take no interest in them. Community Banc-

shares argues that this is a "padded payroll" case and that by virtue of section 3–405(1)(c) the loss falls on the drawer of the checks, C & N.

We conclude that the circuit court correctly held an action for conversion will not be because there is no genuine issue of material fact regarding the application of section 3–405(1)(c) in the circumstances of this case.

Judgment affirmed for Community Bancshares.

Note: This case was decided under the original version of Article 3. Although Revised Article 3 changes the wording of the "fictitious payee rule" and sets it out in section 3–404 of Revised Article 3, the result would be the same under the revision.

Comparative Negligence Rule Concerning Impostors and Fictitious Payees

Revised Article 3 also establishes a comparative negligence rule if (1) the person, in a situation covered by the impostor or fictitious payee rule, pays the instrument or takes it for value or collection without exercising ordinary care in paying or taking the instrument, and (2) that failure substantially contributes to the loss resulting from payment of the instrument. In these instances, the person bearing the loss may recover an allocable share of the loss from the person who did not exercise ordinary care [3–404(d)].

Fraudulent Indorsements by Employees

Revised Article 3 specifically addresses employer responsibility for fraudulent indorsements by employees and adopts the principle that the risk of loss for such indorsements by employees who are entrusted with responsibilities for instruments (primarily checks) should fall on the employer rather than on the bank that takes the check or pays it [3–405]. As to any person who in good faith pays an instrument or takes it for value, a fraudulent indorsement by a responsible employee is effective as the indorsement of the payee if it is made in the name of the payee or in a substantially similar name [3–405(b)]. If the person taking or paying the instrument failed to exercise ordinary care and that failure substantially contributed to loss resulting

from the fraud, the comparative negligence doctrine guides the allocation of the loss.

A fraudulent indorsement includes a forged indorsement purporting to be that of the employer on an instrument payable to the employer; it also includes a forged indorsement purporting to be that of the payee of an instrument on which the employer is drawer or maker [3–405(a)(2)]. "Responsibility" with respect to instruments means the authority to (1) sign or indorse instruments on behalf of the employer, (2) process instruments received by the employer, (3) prepare or process instruments for issue in the name of the employer, (4) control the disposition of instruments to be issued in the name of the employer, or (5) otherwise act with respect to instruments in a responsible capacity. "Responsibility" does not cover those who simply have access to instruments as they are stored, transported, or that are in incoming or outgoing mail [3–405(a)(3)].

Conversion

Conversion of an instrument is an unauthorized assumption and exercise of ownership over it. A negotiable instrument can be converted in a number of ways. For example, it might be presented for payment or acceptance, and the person to whom it is presented might refuse to pay or accept and refuse to return it. An instrument also is converted if a person pays an instrument to a person not entitled to payment—for example, if it contains a forged indorsement.

Revised Article 3 modifies and then expands the previous treatment of conversion and provides that the law applicable to conversion of personal property applies to instruments. It also specifically provides that conversion occurs if (1) an instrument lacks an indorsement necessary for negotiation and (2) it is (*a*) purchased, (*b*) taken for collection, or (*c*) paid by a drawee to a person not entitled to payment. An action for conversion may not be brought by (1) the maker, drawer, or acceptor of the instrument or (2) a payee or an indorsee who did not receive delivery of the instrument either directly or through delivery to an agent or copayee [3–420].

Thus, if a bank pays a check that contains a forged indorsement, the bank has converted the check by wrongfully paying it. The bank then becomes liable for the face amount of the check to the person whose indorsement was forged [3–420]. For example, Arthur Able draws a check for $50 on his account at First Bank, payable to the order of Bernard Barker. Carol Collins steals the check, forges Barker's indorsement on it, and cashes it at First Bank. First Bank has converted Barker's property, because it had no right to pay the check without Barker's valid indorsement. First Bank must pay Barker $50, and then it can try to locate Collins to get the $50 back from her.

As is true under the original version of Article 3, if a check contains a restrictive indorsement (such as "for deposit" or "for collection") that shows a purpose of having the check collected for the benefit of a particular account, then any person who purchases the check or any depositary bank or payor bank that takes it for immediate payment converts the check unless the indorser receives the proceeds or the bank applies them consistent with the indorsement [3–206]. This principle is illustrated in the case that follows, *Kelly v. Central Bank & Trust Co. of Denver.*

KELLY v. CENTRAL BANK & TRUST CO. OF DENVER   794 P.2d 1037 (Colo. Ct. App. 1990)

number of investors, including Kelly, invested in a Cayman Islands entity, Tradecom, Ltd., a business involved in precious metals arbitrage. Their investments, in the form of cashier's checks, were payable to Tradecom and delivered to Arvey Down, Tradecom's agent. Down indorsed the checks and deposited them at the Central Bank & Trust Company of Denver into a checking account.

Most of the 934 checks, which were worth $11,227,473, were indorsed:

Tradecom Limited For deposit only 072 575

Other checks, totaling $576,850, were indorsed:

For deposit only 072 575

This included one check for $57,000, which apparently was deposited without indorsement and was indorsed by Central Bank's officer:

For deposit only 072 575 Tradecom
by Mark E. Thompson Commercial Loan officer

The referenced account, No. 072 575, was not that of Tradecom (which had no accounts at Central Bank) but rather was that of Equity Trading Corporation, a company owned and managed by Down, also purportedly an agent of Tradecom.

The investors subsequently lost most of their investments in Tradecom and they sued Central Bank for, among other things, conversion. They alleged that: (1) neither Down nor Equity Trading was an agent of Tradecom and that the check indorsements were unauthorized and ineffective; (2) over the course of 13 months, the bank negligently or recklessly permitted Down to divert the checks payable to Tradecom into Equity Trading's checking account; and (3) Central Bank did not follow reasonable commercial standards. Central Bank moved for summary judgment and in support of its motion submitted an executed power of attorney that indicated Down had the authority to indorse checks on behalf of Tradecom. The trial court awarded summary judgment to the Central Bank and the investors appealed. ∞*

Tursi, Judge   Because there was no triable issue of fact concerning Down's agency and authority to indorse and deposit the cashier's checks, and because proof of a forged or unauthorized indorsement is a necessary predicate to Central Bank's liability, the investors could not prevail as to the 11 million dollars of checks that contained an indorsement which included the "Tradecom Limited" name. Consequently, with respect to the checks indorsed with Tradecom's name, we conclude that the trial court properly granted summary judgment for Central Bank.

The trial court erred, however, in granting Central Bank summary judgment on the $57,000 check indorsed by Central Bank's commercial loan officer. In order for Central Bank to have become a holder under this indorsement, and thus have obtained title, Central Bank would have had to have been authorized to provide Tradecom's indorsement under section 4–205(1). This, however, was impossible since Tradecom was not Central Bank's "customer." Consequently, this indorsement is unauthorized as a matter of law, and summary judgment should not have been ordered for Central Bank on this check.

The investors also contend that the trial court erred in granting summary judgment for Central Bank on the remaining $519,850 of cashier's checks lacking any signature and merely indorsed "For deposit only 072 575." We agree.

Under section 3–419(1)(c), a check is converted when it is paid on a forged indorsement. In this context, a collecting or paying bank "pays" a check when it credits its customer's account with the proceeds of a check collected from the drawee bank. If such a payment occurs on a check with no indorsement or a missing indorsement, it is the legal equivalent of payment on a forged indorsement.

The term "indorsement" is generally understood to mean the indorser's writing of his or her signature on the instrument or the affixing of the indorser's name or some designation identifying the indorser on the instrument. A check simply inscribed "For deposit only" to an account other than payee's account and without the payee's signature is not an effective "indorsement." If the instrument is order paper and the depository bank does not, or cannot, supply the missing indorsement of its customer, the absence of the indorsement can be fatal to negotiation and transfer of title. One such situation is when the depository bank's customer and the payee are not the same person. In this case, the depository bank is unauthorized to, and cannot, supply the missing indorsement of the payee since the payee is not the bank's "customer" under section 4–205. In this situation, the depository bank does not become a holder of the checks and does not obtain good title to them. Payment of such proceeds to its depositor subjects the depository bank to liability for conversion.

In this case it was undisputed that Down, or someone in his employ, deposited $519,850 worth of cashier's checks at Central Bank bearing the simple inscription "For Deposit only 072 575." These checks, which bore no signature indorsement of the payee, Tradecom, or anyone else, were paid and credited to account 072 575. This was not an account of Tradecom, which was not a customer of Central Bank. Under these circumstances, Central Bank was not a holder of these checks by negotiation. It obtained no title to these checks. It is, consequently, subject to conversion liability under section 3–419(1)(c) for making payment on the equivalent of a forged indorsement.

Judgment for Central Bank reversed in part.

Note: Although this case was decided under original Article 3, the same result would be expected under Revised Article 3.

DISCHARGE OF NEGOTIABLE INSTRUMENTS

Discharge of Liability

The obligation of a party to pay an instrument is discharged (1) if he meets the requirements set out in Revised Article 3 or (2) by any act or agreement that would discharge an obligation to pay money on a simple contract. Discharge of an obligation is not effective against a person who has the rights of a holder in due course of the instrument and took the instrument without notice of the discharge [3–601].

The most common ways that an obligor is discharged from her liability are:

1. Payment of the instrument.
2. Cancellation of the instrument.
3. Alteration of the instrument.

4. Modification of the principal's obligation that causes loss to a surety or impairs the collateral.

5. Unexcused delay in presentment or notice of dishonor with respect to a check (discussed earlier in this chapter).

6. Acceptance of a draft [3-414(c) or (d); 3-415(d)]; as noted earlier in the chapter, a drawer is discharged of liability of a draft that is accepted by a bank (e.g., if a check is certified by a bank) because at that point the holder is looking to the bank to make the instrument good.

Discharge by Payment

Generally, payment in full discharges liability on an instrument to the extent payment is (1) by or on behalf of a party obligated to pay the instrument and (2) to a person entitled to enforce the instrument. For example, Arthur makes a note of $100 payable to the order of Bryan. Bryan indorses the note "Pay to the order of my account no. 16154 at First Bank, Bryan." Bryan then gives the note to his employee, Clark, to take to the bank. Clark takes the note to Arthur, who pays Clark the $100. Clark then runs off with the money. Arthur is not discharged of his primary liability on the note because he did not make his payment consistent with the restrictive indorsement. To be discharged, Arthur has to pay the $100 into Bryan's account at First Bank.

To the extent of payment, the obligation of a party to pay the instrument is discharged even though payment is made with knowledge of a claim to the instrument by some other person. However, the obligation is not discharged if: (1) there is a claim enforceable against the person making payment and payment is made with knowledge of the fact that payment is prohibited by an injunction or similar legal process, or (2) in the case of an instrument other than a cashier's, certified, or teller's check, the person making the payment had accepted from the person making the claim indemnity against loss for refusing to make payment to the person entitled to enforce payment. The obligation also is not discharged if he knows the instrument is a stolen instrument and pays someone he knows is in wrongful possession of the instrument [3-602].

Discharge by Cancellation

A person entitled to enforce a negotiable instrument may discharge the liability of the parties to the instrument by canceling or renouncing it. If the holder mutilates or destroys a negotiable instrument with the intent that it no longer evidences an obligation to pay money, the holder has canceled it [3-604]. For example, a grandfather lends $1,000 to his grandson for college expenses. The grandson gives his grandfather a promissory note for $1,000. If the grandfather later tears up the note with the intent that the grandson no longer owes him $1,000, the grandfather has canceled the note.

An accidental destruction or mutilation of a negotiable instrument is not a cancellation and does not discharge the parties to it. If an instrument is lost, mutilated accidentally, or destroyed, the person entitled to enforce it still can enforce the instrument. In such a case, the person must prove that the instrument existed and that she was its holder when it was lost, mutilated, or destroyed.

Altered Instruments; Discharge by Alteration

A person paying a fraudulently altered instrument, or taking it for value, in good faith and without notice of the alteration, may enforce the instrument (1) according to its original terms or (2) in the case of an incomplete instrument later completed in an unauthorized manner, according to its terms as completed [3-407(c)]. An alteration occurs if there is (1) an unauthorized change that modifies the obligation of a party to the instrument or (2) an unauthorized addition of words or numbers or other change to an incomplete instrument that changes the obligation of any party [3-407]. A change that does not affect the obligation of one of the parties, such as dotting an *i* or correcting the grammar, is not considered to be an alteration.

Two examples illustrate the situations in which Revised Article 3 allows fraudulently altered instruments to be enforced. First, assume the amount due on a note is fraudulently raised from $10 to $10,000. The contract of the maker has been changed: the maker promised to pay $10, but after the change has been made, he would be promising to pay much more. If the note is negotiated to or paid by a person who was without notice of the alteration, that person can enforce the note against the maker only according to its original terms. It would pursue the alterer or the person taking from the alterer for the balance on a presentment or transfer warranty. [3-417; 3-416]. If the maker's negligence substantially contributed to the alteration, then the maker would be responsible for as much as the entire $10,000 [3-407(c); 3-406].

Second, assume Swanson draws a check payable to Frank's Nursery, leaving the amount blank. He gives it to his gardener with instructions to purchase some fertilizer at Frank's and to fill in the purchase price of the fertilizer when it is known. The gardener fills in the check for $100 and gives it to Frank's in exchange for the fertilizer ($7.25) and the difference in cash ($92.75). The gardener then leaves town with the cash. If Frank's had no knowledge of the unauthorized completion, it could enforce the check for $100 against Swanson. A similar situation is illustrated in the case that follows, *American Federal Bank, FSB v. Parker.*

AMERICAN FEDERAL BANK, FSB v. PARKER   392 SE2d 798 (Ct. App. S.C. 1990)

homas Kirkman was involved in the horse business and was a friend of John Roundtree, a loan officer for American Federal Bank. Kirkman and Roundtree conceived a business arrangement in which Kirkman would locate buyers for horses and the buyers could seek financing from American Federal. Roundtree gave Kirkman blank promissory notes and security agreements from American Federal. Kirkman was to locate the potential purchaser, take care of the paperwork, and bring the documents to the bank for approval of the purchaser's loan.

Kirkman entered into a purchase agreement with Gene Parker, a horse dealer, to copurchase for $35,000 a horse named Wills Hightime that Kirkman represented he owned. Parker signed the American Federal promissory note in blank and also executed in blank a security agreement that authorized the bank to disburse the funds to the seller of the collateral. Kirkman told Parker he would cosign the note and fill in the details of the transaction with the bank. While Kirkman did not cosign the note, he did complete it for $85,000 as opposed to $35,000. Kirkman took the note with Parker's signature to Roundtree at American Federal and received two checks from the bank payable to him in the amounts of $35,000 and $50,000. Kirkman took the $35,000 and gave it to the real owner of the horse. Parker then received the horse.

Parker began making payments to the bank and called on Kirkman to assist in making the payments pursuant to their agreement. However, Kirkman skipped town, taking the additional $50,000 with him. Parker repaid the $35,000 but refused to pay any more. He argued that he only agreed to borrow $35,000 and the other $50,000 was unauthorized by him. American Federal Bank filed suit to recover the balance due on the note. The trial court held in favor of the bank and Parker appealed. ❧

Cureton, Judge   Parker executed a promissory note in blank. Under the Uniform Commercial Code, the maker of a note agrees to pay the instrument according to its tenor at the time of engagement "or as completed pursuant to Section 3–115 on incomplete instruments." Under Section 3–115(2) if the completion of an instrument is unauthorized the rules as to material alteration apply. Under Section 3–407(1)(b) the completion of an incomplete instrument otherwise than as authorized is considered an alteration. However, under Section 3–407(3) a subsequent holder in due course may enforce an incomplete instrument as completed. Official Comment 4 indicates that where blanks are filled or an incomplete instrument is otherwise completed, the loss is placed upon the party who left the instrument incomplete and the holder is permitted to enforce it according to its completed form.

We agree with the trial court that the bank was entitled to the directed verdicts. The responsibility for the situation rests with Parker. He and Kirkman negotiated their deal. Parker signed a blank promissory note. He relied upon Kirkman to cosign the note and fill it in for $35,000. Parker's negligence substantially contributed to the material alteration as a matter of law.

Parker argues that it was not reasonable commercial practice for American Federal to give Kirkman possession of blank promissory notes. After the fact, Parker argues the bank should have contacted him or checked to be sure everything was correct before disbursing the proceeds of the loan to Kirkman. There is no evidence in the record to establish the bank had any reason to inquire into the facial validity of the note. The note was complete when presented to the bank and there were no obvious alterations on it.

The record establishes American Federal took the note in good faith and without notice of any defense to it by Parker. American Federal gave value for the note when it disbursed the funds to Kirkman. As a holder in due course, American Federal may enforce the note against Parker as completed. Sections 3–302; 3–407(3).

Judgment for American Federal affirmed.

Note: Although this case was decided under the original version of Article 3, the same result would be reached under Revised Article 3 so long as the court found Kirkman's completion (alteration) to be fraudulent.

In any other case, a fraudulent alteration **discharges** any party whose obligation is affected by the alteration *unless* (1) the party assents or (2) is precluded from asserting the alteration (e.g. because of the party's negligence). Assume that Anderson signs a promissory note for $100 payable to Bond. Bond indorses the note "Pay to the order of Connolly, Bond" and negotiates it to Connolly. Connolly changes the $100 to read $100,000. Connolly's change is unauthorized and fraudulent. As a result, Anderson is discharged from her liability as maker of the note and Bond is discharged from her liability as indorser. Neither of them has to pay Connolly. The obligations of both Anderson and Bond were changed because the amount for which they are liable was altered.

No other alteration—that is, one that is not fraudulent—discharges any party and a holder may enforce the instrument according to its *original* terms. Thus, there would no discharge if a blank is filled in the honest belief that it is authorized or if a change is made, without any fraudulent intent, to give the maker on a note the benefit of a lower interest rate.

Discharge of Indorsers and Accommodation Parties

If a person entitled to enforce an instrument agrees, with or without consideration, to a material modification of the obligation of a party to the instrument, including an extension of the due date, then any accommodation party or indorser who has a right of recourse against the person whose obligation is modified is discharged *to the extent the modification causes a loss to the indorser or accommodation party*. Similarly, if collateral secures the obligation of a party to an instrument and a person entitled to enforce the instrument impairs the value of the collateral, the obligation of the indorser or accommodation party having the right of recourse against the obligor is discharged to the extent of the impairment. These discharges are not effective unless the

person agreeing to the modification or causing the impairment knows of the accommodation or has notice of it. Also, no discharge occurs if the obligor assented to the event or conduct, or if the obligor has waived the discharge [3–605].

For example, Frank goes to Credit Union to borrow $4,000 to purchase a used automobile. The credit union has Frank sign a promissory note and takes a security interest in the automobile (i.e., takes it as collateral for the loan). It also asks Frank's brother, Bob, to sign the note as an accommodation maker. Subsequently, Frank tells the credit union he wants to sell the automobile and it releases its security interest. Because release of the collateral adversely affects Bob's obligation as accommodation maker, he is discharged from his obligation as accommodation maker in the amount of the value of the automobile.

ETHICAL AND PUBLIC POLICY CONCERNS

1. Suppose you have taken a promissory note for $1,000 as payment for some carpentry work you did for a friend. You have some reason to believe that the maker is having some financial difficulty and may not be able to pay the note when it is due. You discuss the possible sale of the note to a local physician as an investment and she agrees to buy it. Would it be ethical for you to indorse the note with a qualified indorsement ("without recourse")?

2. In Problem case 11, a creditor made a mistake and returned a note marked "canceled" to the maker without collecting all of the interest due on it. Suppose instead that the maker/borrower realized that Crown Financial had made an error in not including in the subsequent note the interest due on the original note. Should the maker/borrower feel compelled by ethical considerations to pay the interest, even if not legally required to do so?

1. Terance Fitzgerald drew a check for $4,000 payable to New Look Auto Trim and Upholstery and delivered it to Yuvonne Goss and Benii Arrazza, the owners of New Look. Goss and Arrazza each indorsed the check in blank and deposited it in Goss's personal account at the Cincinnati Central Credit Union. When the Credit Union presented the check to Fitzgerald's bank, the check was dishonored for insufficient funds. The Credit Union then demanded that Goss and Arrazza honor the check. Are Goss and Arrazza obligated to make the check good to Credit Union?

2. Janota's signature appeared on a note under the name of a corporation acknowledging a $1,000 debt. No other wording appeared other than Janota's name and the corporate name. The holder of the note sues Janota on the note. What will Janota argue, and what will be the result?

3. J. M. Cook, then treasurer of Arizona Auto Auction, signed three corporate checks totaling $9,795 payable to Central Motors Company, which deposited them in its corporate account at Valley National Bank. The checks were boldly imprinted at the top "Arizona Auto Auction, Inc." "Arizona Auto Auction, Inc." was also imprinted above the signature line in the lower right-hand corner. Cook did not indicate on the check that she was signing as a representative of Arizona Auto Auction. When Valley National Bank sent the checks to the drawee bank, payment was refused because a stop-payment order had been put on them. Valley National Bank charged back the checks to the account of Central Motors, but it was unable to recover the money from Central Motors. Valley National Bank then brought suit against Arizona Auto Auction and J. M. Cook. Was Cook personally liable on the corporate checks she signed as corporate treasurer because she did not indicate she was signing in a representative capacity?

4. Clay Haynes was the bookkeeper for Johnstown Manufacturing, Inc. He had express check-signing authority, and his signature was on the signature card for the account that Johnstown maintained at BancOhio National Bank. Haynes was also the bookkeeper of another corporation, Lynn Polymers, Inc., which was operated by the same individuals that operated Johnstown. Over a period of a year,

Haynes engaged in a check-cashing scheme from which he pocketed approximately $70,000. Haynes wrote 35 corporate checks to the order of BancOhio National Bank, and the bank, in return, gave the cash to Haynes. Johnstown brought suit against BancOhio to recover $300 for the one check written on the Johnstown account that the bank paid to Haynes. Johnstown claimed that the check was written without the express authority of the corporation, and thus it contained an "unauthorized" signature. Was Haynes's signature on the check "unauthorized" as that term is used in the Uniform Commercial Code?

5. First National Bank certified Smith's check in the amount of $29. After certification, Smith altered the check so that it read $2,900. He presented the check to a merchant in payment for goods. The merchant then submitted the check to the bank for payment. The bank refused, saying it had only certified the instrument for $29. Can the merchant recover the $2,900 from the bank?

6. A check was drawn on First National Bank and made payable to Howard. It came into the possession of Carson, who forged Howard's indorsement and cashed it at Merchant's Bank. Merchant's Bank then indorsed it and collected payment from First National. Assuming that Carson is nowhere to be found, who bears the loss caused by Carson's forgery?

7. Mrs. Gordon Neely hired Louise Bradshaw as the bookkeeper for a Midas Muffler shop they owned and operated as a corporation, J. Gordon Neely Enterprises, Inc. (Neely). Bradshaw's duties included preparing company checks for Mrs. Neely's signature and reconciling the checking account when the company received bank statement and canceled checks each month. Bradshaw prepared several checks payable to herself and containing a large space to the left of the amount written on the designated line. When Mrs. Neely signed the checks, she was aware of the large gaps. Subsequently, Bradshaw altered the checks by adding a digit or two to the left of the original amount and then cashed them at American National Bank, the drawee bank. Several months later, the Neelys hired a new accountant, who discovered the altered checks. Neely brought suit against American National Bank to have its account recredited for the altered checks, claiming that American was liable for paying out on altered instruments. The bank contended that Neely's negligence substantially contributed to alterations of the instruments and thus Neely was precluded from asserting the alteration against the bank. Between Neely and American National Bank, who should bear the loss caused by Bradshaw's fraud?

8. Mrs. Johnson mailed a loan application to First National Bank in her husband's name and without his knowledge. Having dealt with her husband before, the bank approved the application and mailed a check in the amount requested to Mr. Johnson. Mrs. Johnson then indorsed the check in her husband's name and cashed it at Merchant's Bank. Merchant's Bank indorsed the check and presented it for payment. First National, having discovered the deception, refused to pay. Is First National liable on the check?

9. [▸] *Video case.* See "Cafeteria Conversion." Steve, an individual with a gambling and substance abuse problem, works in the accounts payable department of a company. He issues checks drawn on his employer's account that are made payable to suppliers who do business with his employer but who are not currently owed money. Then he forges the signature of the named payees, obtains payment of the checks from the drawee bank, and uses the funds to support his habits. Because Steve's responsibilities include reconciling the bank statements, his forgery scheme is not discovered for a considerable period of time. When it is discovered, is the drawee bank required to recredit the employer's account for the forged checks that were paid from it?

10. Stockton's housekeeper stole some of his checks, forged his name as drawer, and cashed them at Gristedes Supermarket where Stockton maintained check-cashing privileges. The checks were presented to Stockton's bank and honored by it. Over the course of 18 months, the scheme netted the housekeeper in excess of $147,000 on approximately 285 forged checks. Stockton brought suit against Gristedes Supermarket for conversion, seeking to recover the value of the checks it accepted and for which it obtained payment from the drawee bank. Was Gristedes Supermarket liable to Stockton for conversion for accepting and obtaining payment of the stolen and forged checks?

11. Charles Peterson, a farmer and rancher, was indebted to Crown Financial Corporation on a $4,450,000 promissory note that was due on December 29, 1992. Shortly before the note was due, Crown sent Peterson a statement of interest due on the note ($499,658.850). Petersen paid the interest and executed a new note in the amount of $4,450,000 that was to mature in December 1995. The old note was then marked "canceled" and returned to Peterson. In 1995, Crown billed Peterson for $363,800 in interest that had been due on the first note but apparently not included in the statement. Peterson claimed that the interest had been forgiven and that he was not obligated to pay it. Was Peterson still obligated to pay interest on the note that had been returned to him marked "canceled"?

Checks and Documents of Title

or most people, a checking account provides the majority of their contact with negotiable instruments. This chapter focuses on the relationship between the drawer with a checking account and the drawer's bank, known as the drawee bank. It addresses such common questions as: What happens when a bank refuses to pay a check even though the depositor has sufficient funds in her account? Does the bank have the right to create an overdraft in a depositor's account by paying an otherwise properly payable check? What are the depositor's rights and the bank's obligation when the depositor stops payment on a check? What is the difference between a certified check and a cashier's check? What are the depositor's responsibilities when she receives her monthly statement and canceled checks? The second half of the chapter discusses the Code rules that apply to negotiable documents of title such as warehouse receipts and bills of lading. ∞

THE DRAWER–DRAWEE RELATIONSHIP

There are two sources that govern the relationship between the depositor and the drawee bank: the deposit agreement and Articles 3 and 4 of the Code. Article 4, which governs Bank Deposits and Collections, allows the depositor and drawee bank (which Article 4 calls the "payor bank") to vary Article 4's provisions with a few important exceptions. The deposit agreement cannot disclaim the bank's responsibility for its own lack of good faith or failure to exercise ordinary care or limit the measure of damages for the lack or failure; however, the parties may determine by agreement the standards by which to measure the bank's responsibility so long as the standards are not manifestly unreasonable [4–103].

The deposit agreement establishes many important relationships between the depositor and drawee/payor bank. The first of these is their relationship as creditor and debtor, respectively, so that when a person deposits money in an account at the bank, the law no longer considers him the owner of the money. Instead, he is a creditor of the bank to the extent of his deposits and the bank becomes his debtor. Also, when the depositor deposits a check to a checking account, the bank also becomes his agent for collection of the check. The bank as the person's agent owes a duty to him to follow his reasonable instructions concerning payment of checks and other items from his account and a duty of ordinary care in collecting checks and other items deposited to the account.

Bank's Duty to Pay

When a bank receives a properly drawn and payable check on a person's account and there are sufficient funds to cover the check, the bank is under a duty to pay it. If the person has sufficient funds in the account and the bank refuses to pay, or dishonors, the check, the bank is liable for the actual damages proximately caused by its wrongful dishonor as well as consequential damages [4–402]. Actual damages may include charges imposed by retailers for returned checks as well as damages for arrest or prosecution of the customer. Consequential damages include injury to the depositor's credit rating that results from the dishonor.

For example, Donald Dodson writes a check for $1,500 to Ames Auto Sales in payment for a used car. At the time that Ames Auto presents the check for payment at Dodson's bank, First National Bank, Dodson has $1,800 in his account. However, a teller mistakenly refuses to pay the check and stamps it NSF (not sufficient funds). Ames Auto then goes to the local prosecutor and signs a complaint against Dodson for writing a bad check. As a result, Dodson is arrested. Dodson can recover from First National the damages that he sustained because the bank wrongfully dishonored his check, including the damages involved in his arrest, such as his attorney's fees.

In the case that follows, *Buckley v. Trenton Savings Fund Society,* the bank is potentially liable for consequential damages sustained by the drawer because it wrongfully dishonored a customer's checks. In reading the case, you should keep in mind that Revised Article 3 deletes any reference to "mistake" by the bank as contained in the original provision; thus, the proof and measure of damages no longer turns on whether the bank can establish that it dishonored a check by "mistake."

BUCKLEY v. TRENTON SAVINGS FUND SOCIETY 524 A.2d 886 (N.J. Super. Ct. 1987)

Buckley *maintained a checking account at the Trenton Savings Fund Society. In 1981, he separated from his wife, Linda, and entered into a consent agreement with her in which he agreed to pay her $150 per week for food and support for her and their children. On January 13, 1984, Buckley wrote a check for $150 and gave it to his wife. The next Saturday, she presented it for payment at one of Trenton Savings' branches but payment was refused even though Buckley had $900 in the account at the time. The following Monday, she took it to another branch where payment was refused again. The bank told Linda that it would not cash the check for her because Linda did not have an account at the bank. Subsequently, the bank agreed to cash checks for Linda, but on March 4, 1984, the bank again refused to pay one of Buckley's checks that she presented for payment. Linda was known to the bank because it held a mortgage on the home that she and Buckley jointly owned.*

Shortly after Trenton Bank's failure to cash the two checks, Buckley received an irate call from Linda. He also received calls from his parents, his sister, and his best friend inquiring as to why he was not making the support payments. In addition, his children inquired "why daddy wouldn't give them food money." Buckley incurred severe emotional distress over the matter. He brought suit against Trenton Savings for wrongful *dishonor and sought compensatory damages, as well as punitive damages, for the mental anguish he sustained. The trial court entered judgment for Buckley based on a jury verdict for $25,000 as compensatory damages, and the bank appealed.* ∽

Stern, Judge The bank contends that the jury should not have been permitted to award damages for emotional distress under the facts of this case. A bank's liability for wrongful dishonor of a customer's check is defined in section 4–402 of the Uniform Commercial Code:

A payor bank is liable to its customer for damages proximately caused by the wrongful dishonor of an item. When the dishonor occurs through mistake, liability is limited to actual damages proved. If so proximately caused and proved, damages may include damages for an arrest or prosecution of the customer or other consequential damages. Whether any consequential damages are proximately caused by the wrongful dishonor is a question of fact to be determined in each case.

The UCC does not indicate the theory or basis for a bank's liability for wrongful dishonor. As explained in the UCC official comment to section 4–402, "The liability of the drawee for dishonor has sometimes been stated as one for breach of contract, sometimes as for negligence or other breach of a tort duty, and sometimes as for defamation." The drafters of the UCC did not intend to exclude the possibility of mental distress damages upon a wrongful dishonor by a bank. Since section 4–402 is silent on any restriction of damages when the dishonor is grounded on an action other than mistake, it implies that these damages are not precluded by the Code. Thus, out-of-state courts interpreting section 4–402 have concluded that mental suffering is compensable under this section.

The Legislature adopted section 4–402 as promulgated in the Uniform Commercial Code without substantive change. The section expressly limits recovery for "actual damages" when the dishonor results from "mistake" but otherwise expressly permits recovery of "consequential damages" proximately caused. As White and Summers explains:

When wrongful dishonors occur not "through mistake" but willfully, the court may impose damages greater than "actual damages."

* * * * *

Might one argue that "actual damages" excludes recovery for mental distress? We think not. In the first place, the drafters went to great efforts to assure that customers can recover for arrest and prosecution. It is inconsistent to allow recovery for embarrassment and mental distress deriving from arrest and prosecution and to deny similar recovery in other cases. Moreover, cases under the predecessor to 4–402, the American Association Statute, held that "actual damages" includes damages for mental distress. Thus we believe . . . that the Code drafters intended to allow recovery for mental distress and other intangible injury.

In this case the judge's instructions failed to delineate the distinction between mistake and intentional mistake and an intentional breach or wilful, wanton or reckless conduct. As a result, the matter must be remanded for a new trial and for a determination of damages based on appropriate instructions.

We preclude an award of punitive damages. Punitive damages are not generally recoverable for breach of contract, at least when the breach of contract does not also constitute a tort for which punitive damages are recoverable.

Reversed and remanded for new trial

Note: This case was decided under the original version of Article 3, under which courts found that the Code appeared to allow a different measure of damages if the dishonor was other than by mistake. Revised Article 3 eliminates any distinction turning on mistake and provides that the depositor may recover actual damages, including consequential damages, proximately caused by a dishonor.

Bank's Right to Charge to Customer's Account

The drawee bank has the right to charge any properly payable check to the account of the customer or drawer. The bank has this right even though payment of the check creates an overdraft in the account [4–401]. If an account is overdrawn, the customer owes the bank the amount of the overdraft and the bank may take that amount out of the next deposit that the customer makes or from another account that the depositor maintains with the bank. Alternatively, the bank might seek to collect the amount directly from the customer. If there is more than one customer who can draw from an account, only that customer—or those customers—who sign the item or who benefit from the proceeds of an overdraft are liable for the overdraft.

Stale Checks The bank does not owe a duty to its customer to pay any checks out of the account that are more than six months old. Such checks are called stale checks. However, the bank acting in good faith may pay a check that is more than six months old and charge it to the drawer-depositor's account [4–404].

Altered and Incomplete Items If the bank in good faith pays a check drawn by the drawer-depositor but subsequently altered, it may charge the customer's account with the amount of the check as originally drawn. Also, if an incomplete check of a customer gets into circulation, is completed, and is presented to the drawee bank for payment, and the bank pays the check, the bank can charge the amount as completed to the customer's account even though it knows that the check has been completed, unless it has notice that the completion was improper [4–401(d)]. The respective rights, obligations, and liabilities of drawee banks and their drawer-customers concerning forged and altered checks are discussed in more detail later in this chapter.

Limitations on Bank's Right or Duty Article 4 recognizes that the bank's right or duty to pay a check or to charge the depositor's account for the check (including exercising its right to set off an amount due to it by the depositor) may be terminated, suspended, or modified by the depositor's order to stop payment (which is discussed in the next section of this chapter). In addition, it may be stopped by events external to the relationship between the depositor and the bank. These external events include the filing of a bankruptcy petition by the depositor or by the depositor's creditors, and the garnishment of the account by a creditor of the depositor. The bank must receive the stop-payment order from its depositor or the notice of the bankruptcy filing or garnishment before the bank has certified the check, paid it in cash, settled with another bank for the amount of the item without a

right to revoke the settlement, or otherwise become accountable for the amount of the check under Article 4, or the cut-off hour on the banking day after the check is received if the bank established a cut-off hour. [4–303]. These restrictions on the bank's right or duty to pay are discussed in later sections of this chapter.

Postdated Checks Under original Articles 3 and 4, a postdated check was not properly payable by the drawee bank until the date on the check. The recent amendments to Article 4 change this. Under the revision, an otherwise properly payable post-dated check that is presented for payment before the date on the check may be paid and charged to the customer's account *unless* the customer has given notice of it to the bank. The customer must give notice of the postdating in a way that describes the check with reasonable certainty. It is effective for the same time periods as Article 4 provides for stop-payment orders (discussed below). The customer must give notice to the bank at such time and in such a manner as to give the bank an opportunity to act on it before the bank takes any action with respect to paying the check. If the bank charges the customer's account for a postdated check before the date stated in the notice given to the bank, the bank is liable for damages for any loss that results. Such damages might include those associated with the dishonor of subsequent items [3–113(a); 4–401(c)].

There are a variety of reasons why a person might want to postdate a check. For example, a person might have a mortgage payment due on the first of the month at a bank located in another state. To make sure that the check arrives on time, the customer may send the payment by mail several days before the due date. However, if the person is depending on a deposit of her next monthly paycheck on the first of the month to cover the mortgage payment, she might postdate the check to the first of the following month. Under the original version of Articles 3 and 4, the bank could not properly pay the check until the first of the month. However, under the revisions it could be properly paid by the bank before that date if presented earlier. To avoid the risk that the bank would dishonor the check for insufficient funds if presented before the first, the customer should notify the drawee bank in a manner similar to that required for stop payment of checks.

Stop-Payment Order

A stop-payment order is a request made by a customer of a drawee bank instructing it not to pay or certify a specified check. As the drawer's agent in the payment of checks, the drawee bank must follow the reasonable orders of the drawer-customer about payments made on the drawer's behalf. Any person authorized to draw a check may stop payment of it. Thus, any person authorized to sign a check on the account may stop payment even if she did not sign the check in question [4–403(a)].

To be effective, a payor bank must receive the stop-payment order in time to give the bank a reasonable opportunity to act on the order. This means that the bank must receive the stop-payment order before it has paid or certified the check. In addition, the stop-payment order must come soon enough to give the bank time to instruct its tellers and other employees that they should not pay or certify the check [4–403(a)]. The stop-payment order also must describe the check with "reasonable certainty" so as to provide the bank's employees the ability to recognize it as the check corresponding to the stop-payment order.

The customer may give a stop-payment order orally to the bank, but it is valid for only 14 days unless the customer confirms it in writing during that time. A written stop-payment order is valid for six months and the customer can extend it for an additional six months by giving the bank instructions in writing to continue the order [4–403(b)]. (See Figure 1.)

Sometimes the information given the bank by the customer concerning the check on which payment is to be stopped is incorrect. For example, there may be an error in the payee's name, the amount of the check, or the number of the check. The question then arises whether the customer has accorded the bank a reasonable opportunity to act on his request. A common issue is whether the stop-payment order must have the dollar amount correct to the penny. Banks often take the position that the stop-payment order must be correct to the penny because they program and rely on computers to focus on the customer's account number and the amount of the check in question to avoid paying an item subject to a stop-payment order. The amendments to Article 4 do not resolve this question. In the Official Comments, the drafters indicate that "in describing an item, the customer, in the absence of a contrary agreement, must meet the standard of what information allows the bank under the technology then existing to identify the check with reasonable certainty." In the Stop Payment Request in Figure 1, the bank takes a more lenient approach than some: it asks for the range of number or low and high dollar of the check the customer does not want the bank to pay.

Stop-Payment Order

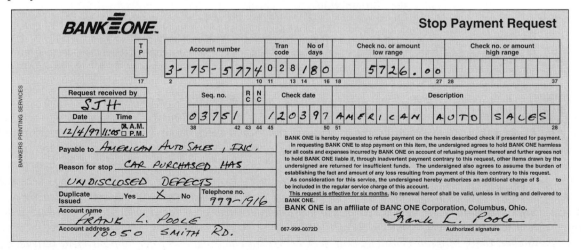

Source: Bank One

Bank's Liability for Payment after Stop-Payment Order

While a stop-payment order is in effect, the drawee bank is liable to the drawer of a check that it pays for any loss that the drawer suffers by reason of such payment. However, the drawer-customer has the burden of establishing the fact and amount of the loss. To show a loss, the drawer must establish that the drawee bank paid a person against whom the drawer had a valid defense to payment. To the extent that the drawer has such a defense, he has suffered a loss due to the drawee's failure to honor the stop-payment order.

For example, Brown buys what is represented to be a new car from Foster Ford and gives Foster Ford his check for $12,280 drawn on First Bank. Brown then discovers that the car is in fact a used demonstrator model and calls First Bank, ordering it to stop payment on the check. If Foster Ford presents the check for payment the following day and First Bank pays the check despite the stop-payment order, Brown can require the bank to recredit his account. (The depositor-drawer bases her claim to recredit on the fact that the bank did not follow her final instruction—the instruction not to pay the check.) Brown had a valid defense of misrepresentation that she could have asserted against Foster Ford if it had sued her on the check. Foster Ford would have been required to sue on the check or on Brown's contractual obligation to pay for the car.

Assume, instead, that Foster Ford negotiated the check to Smith and that Smith qualified as a holder in due course. Then, if the bank paid the check to Smith over the stop-payment order, Brown would not be able to have her account recredited, because Brown would not be able to show that she sustained any loss. If the bank had refused to pay the check, so that Smith came against Brown on her drawer's liability, Brown cannot use her personal defense of misrepresentation of the prior use of the car as a reason for not paying Smith. Brown's only recourse would be to pursue Foster Ford on her misrepresentation claim.

The bank may ask the customer to sign a form in which the bank tries to disclaim or limit its liability for the stop-payment order, or, as in Figure 1, for damages if it fails to obey the stop-payment order. As explained at the beginning of this chapter, the bank cannot disclaim its responsibility for its failure to act in good faith or to exercise ordinary care in paying a check over a stop-payment order [4–103].

If a bank pays a check after it has received a stop-payment order and has to reimburse its customer for the improperly paid check, it acquires all the rights of its customer against the person to whom it originally made payment, including rights arising from the transaction on which the check was based [4–407]. In the previous example involving Brown and Foster Ford, assume that Brown was able to have her account recredited because First Bank had paid the check to Foster Ford over her stop-payment order. Then, the bank would have any rights that Brown had against Foster Ford for the misrepresentation.

The following case, *Morgan Guaranty Trust Co. of New York v. Hauser,* illustrates a situation where a bank paid a check despite a stop-payment order and became subrogated to the rights of the payee of the check.

MORGAN QUARANTY TRUST CO. OF NEW YOUK v. HAUSER   28 UCC Rep.2d 851 (N.Y. Sup. Ct. 1994)

 ertrude Sackler and Enrique Hauser were married in 1985, but by October 1986 divorce proceedings were imminent. At that time, a series of incidents occurred that culminated in Morgan Guaranty Trust disregarding a stop-payment order on a check in the amount of $150,000 drawn on Sackler's account and payable to Hauser.

Sackler claimed that she discovered a "blank signed check (No. 122)" was missing from her safe in an office she shared with Hauser and immediately called Morgan Guaranty to ascertain whether the check had been cashed. On learning it had not been cashed, she orally requested a stop-payment order, which she was informed would be issued. At the request of Morgan Guaranty, she prepared a written stop-payment order which she submitted to the bank on October 20, 1986.

In November 1986, Morgan Guaranty sent Sackler written confirmation of her stop-payment instruction. The confirmation stated as follows:

The above check has not been paid since the opening of business 10/1/86. Paid checks and bank reports in your possession must be examined by you before issuing replacement checks. Please contact us within five business days after the date placed if the above details are incorrect. Failure to do so will constitute your authorization of the action taken above. The instruction to stop payment will remain in effect for 12 months unless you notify to cancel or renew before 10/20/87.

The stop payment was not honored by the bank and it allowed the check that Hauser had deposited into his own account with the bank to clear.

Hauser offered a different version of events. He maintained that Sackler and he were engaged in an art business in Europe with certain foreign investors. However, because the marriage was falling apart, the investors, who allegedly were friends of Hauser, decided to discontinue their investment in the business. Therefore, Hauser asserted, Sackler agreed to return the investors' money and did so by giving him the check for $150,000. Hauser stated that he deposited the check in his account and once it cleared, he transferred it to a third party, Brugal Investments. Hauser contended that after issuing the check, Sackler had changed her mind and attempted to stop payment on the check.

Morgan Guaranty never debited Sackler's account for the check. Instead, in January 1987, it brought suit against Hauser and later it added Sackler as a defendant. The bank advanced three claims against Sackler: (1) that it was entitled to charge her account because it had paid, pursuant to a check in the amount of $150,000 signed by her; (2) that she had improperly stopped payment after having given Hauser the check; and (3) that it had the right of subrogation pursuant to section 4–407. In May 1989, Hauser and Brugal provided Sackler with a general release of liability. ∞

Schlesinger, Judge   Stop payment orders are regulated by section 4–403. Subdivisions 1 & 2 of this section provide in relevant part:

1. A customer may by order to his bank stop payment of any item payable for his account but the order must be received at such time and in such manner as to afford the bank a reasonable opportunity to act on it prior to any action by the bank with respect to the item . . .
2. . . . An oral order is binding upon the bank only for 14 calendar days unless confirmed in writing within the period. A written order is effective for only six months unless renewed in writing.

Therefore, under this section Ms. Sackler had the absolute right to stop payment on the check. Morgan Guaranty was given a reasonable opportunity to act. It confirmed in writing that "the check has not been paid since the opening of business 10-1-86." The bank's date stamp on the back of the check indicates that the check was not cashed until November 3, 1986. Thus, the check was cashed within 14 business days of Ms. Sackler's stop payment order.

Morgan Guaranty questions whether Ms. Sackler ever submitted a written stop order. Even assuming that Ms. Sackler did not do so, the bank agreed, pursuant to its written confirmation that the stop payment would be effective for 12 months. Accordingly, the bank is deemed to have waived the requirements of section 4–403(2) by agreeing to be bound by Sackler's order for 12 months.

In view of the above, Ms. Sackler is entitled to summary judgment on Morgan Guaranty's first and second causes of action.

Morgan Guaranty's third cause of action alleges that it is entitled to $150,000 pursuant to section 4–407. The operation of section 4–407 is straightforward. In essence, it is a right of restitution. In order to prevent unjust enrichment, a bank is "subrogated to the rights of any holder in due course on the item against the drawer or maker either on the item or on the transaction out of which the item arose, and of the drawer or maker against any other holder of the item with respect to the transaction out of which the item arose."

Counsel for Ms. Sackler argues that the third cause of action must be dismissed as well. He asserts that since the alleged debt was owed to a third party, Brugal Investments N.V., Hauser does not have a claim against Sackler with respect to the check. Therefore, the bank does not have a subrogation claim against her either.

This argument is not persuasive. Even if Hauser was merely a conduit for the money transfer to Brugal Investments, section 4–407 permits the bank to raise the transaction and assert the rights of the payee or any holder against the drawer. Thus, to prevent unjust enrichment at the expense of the bank paying an alleged debt owed by Ms. Sackler, Morgan Guaranty is subrogated to the rights of either Hauser or Brugal and is permitted to recoup any loss that it has suffered.

Alternatively, Sackler contends that even if the bank has a valid subrogation claim, the claim is subject to the defense of release. Even assuming, arguendo, that Ms. Sackler had contemplated the claims involving the check at the time the releases were executed, it would be inequitable to permit this private agreement to defeat the bank's subrogation rights which were acquired prior to the execution of the releases.

The competing allegations made by Mr. Hauser and Ms. Sackler with respect to the circumstances surrounding the $150,000 check raise triable issues of fact.

Motions for summary judgment on count three denied.

If a person stops payment on a check and the bank honors the stop-payment order, the person may still be liable to the holder of the check. Suppose Peters writes a check for $450 to Ace Auto Repair in payment for repairs to her automobile. While driving the car home, she concludes that the car was not repaired properly. She calls her bank and stops payment on the check. Ace Auto negotiated the check to Sam's Auto Parts, which took the check as a holder in due course. When Sam's takes the check to Peters's bank, the bank refuses to pay because of the stop-payment order. Sam's then comes after Peters on her drawer's liability. All Peters has is a personal defense against payment, which is not good against a holder in due course. So, Peters must pay Sam's the $450 and pursue her claim separately against Ace. If Ace were still the holder of the check, however, the situation would be different. Peters could use her personal defense concerning the faulty work against Ace to reduce or possibly to cancel her obligation to pay the check.

Certified Check

Normally, a drawee bank is not obligated to certify a check. When a drawee bank does certify a check, it substitutes its undertaking (promise) to pay the check for the drawer's undertaking and becomes obligated to pay the check. At the time the bank certifies a check, the bank usually debits the customer's account for the amount of the certified check and shifts the money to a special account at the bank. It also adds its signature to the check to show that it has accepted primary liability for paying it. The bank's signature is an essential part of the certification: the bank's signature must appear on the check [3–409]. If the holder of a check chooses to have it certified, rather than seeking to have it paid at that time, the holder has made a conscious decision to look to the certifying bank for payment and no longer may rely on the drawer or the indorsers to pay it. See Figure 2 for an example of a certified check.

If the drawee bank certifies a check, then the drawer and any persons who previously indorsed the check are discharged of their liability on the check [3–414(c); 3–415(d)].

Cashier's Check

A cashier's check differs from a certified check. A check on which a bank is both the drawer and the drawee is a cashier's check. The bank is primarily liable on the cashier's check. See Figure 3 for an example of a cashier's check. A teller's check is similar to a cashier's check. It is a check on which one bank is the drawer and another bank is the drawee. An example of a teller's check is a check drawn by a credit union on its account at a bank.

Death or Incompetence of Customer

Under the general principles of agency law, the death or incompetence of the principal terminates the agent's authority to act for the principal. However, slightly different rules apply to the authority of a bank to pay checks out of the account of a deceased or incompetent person. The bank has the right to pay the checks of an incompetent person until it has notice that a court has determined that the person is incompetent. Once the bank learns of this fact, it loses its authority to pay that person's checks—because the depositor is not competent to issue instructions to pay.

FIGURE 2

Certified Check

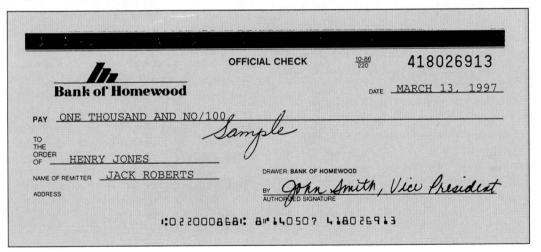

Source: Bank One

FIGURE 3

Cashier's Check

Source: Bank of Homewood

Similarly, a bank has the right to pay the checks of a deceased customer until it has notice of the customer's death. Even if a bank knows of a customer's death, for a period of 10 days after the customer's death, it can pay checks written by the customer prior to his death. However, the deceased person's heirs or other persons claiming an interest in the account can order the bank to stop payment [4–405].

FORGED AND ALTERED CHECKS

Bank's Right to Charge Account

A check that bears a forged signature of the drawer or payee is generally not properly payable from the customer's account because the bank is not following the instructions of the depositor precisely as he gave them. The bank is expected to be familiar with the authorized signature of its depositor. If it pays such a check, Article 4 will treat the transaction as one in which the bank paid out its own funds, rather than the depositor's funds.

Similarly, a check that was altered after the drawer made it out—for example, by increasing the amount of the check—is generally not properly payable from the customer's account. However, as noted earlier, if the drawer is negligent and contributes to the forgery or alteration, he may be barred from claiming it as the reason that a particular check should not be charged to his account.

For example, Barton makes a check for $1 in a way that makes it possible for someone to easily alter it to read $101, and it is so altered. If the drawee bank pays the check to a holder in good faith, it can charge the $101 to Barton's account if Barton's negligence contributed to the alteration. Similarly, if a company uses a mechanical check writer to write checks, it must use reasonable care to see that unauthorized persons do not have access to blank checks and to the check writer.

If the alteration is obvious, the bank should note that fact and refuse to pay the check when it is presented for payment. Occasionally, the alteration is so skillful that the bank cannot detect it. In that case, the bank is allowed to charge to the account the amount for which the check originally was written.

The bank has a duty to exercise "ordinary care" in the processing of negotiable instruments; it must observe the reasonable commercial standards prevailing among other banks in the area in which it does business. In the case of banks that take checks for collection or payment using automated means, it is important to note that reasonable commercial standards do not require the bank to examine every item *if* the failure to examine does not violate the bank's prescribed procedures and those procedures do not vary unreasonably from general banking practice or are not disapproved by the Code [3–107(a)(7); 4–103(c)]. For example, the bank's practice may be to examine those checks for more than $1,000 and a sample of smaller checks. Thus, if it did not examine a particular check in the amount of $250 for evidence of alteration or forgery, its action would be commercially reasonable so long as (1) it followed its own protocol, (2) that protocol was not a great variance from general banking

usage, and (3) the procedure followed was not specifically disallowed in the Code.

In a case where both a bank and its customer fail to use ordinary care, a comparative negligence standard is used [4–406(e)].

Customer's Duty to Report Forgeries and Alterations

A bank must send a monthly (or quarterly) statement listing the transactions in an account and commonly returns the canceled checks to the customer. Revised Article 3 recognizes the modern bank practice of truncating (or retaining) checks and permits the bank to supply only a statement showing the item number, amount, and date of payment [4–406(a)]. When the bank does not return the paid items to the customer, the bank must either retain the items or maintain the capacity to furnish legible copies of the items for seven years after their receipt. The customer may request an item and the bank has a reasonable time to provide either the item or a legible copy of it [4–406(b)].

If the bank sends or makes available a statement of account or items, the customer must exercise reasonable promptness to examine the statement or items to determine whether payment was not authorized because of an alteration of any item or because a signature of the customer was not authorized. If, based on the statement or items provided, the customer should discover the unauthorized payment, the customer must notify the bank of the relevant facts promptly [4–406(c)].

Multiple Forgeries or Alterations Revised Article 3 provides a special rule to govern the situation in which the same wrongdoer makes a series of unauthorized drawer's signatures or alterations. The customer generally cannot hold the bank responsible for paying, in good faith, any such checks after the statement of account or item that contained the first unauthorized customer's signature or an alteration was available to the customer for a reasonable period, not exceeding 30 calendar days. This rule holds (1) if the customer did not notify the bank of the unauthorized signature or alteration, and (2) the bank proves it suffered a loss because of the customer's failure to examine his statement and notify the bank [4–406(d)]. Unless the customer has notified the bank about the forgeries or alterations that he should have discovered by reviewing the statement or item, the customer generally bears responsibility for any subsequent forgeries or alterations by the same wrongdoer.

Suppose that Allen employs Farnum as an accountant and that over a period of three months, Farnum forges Allen's signature to 10 checks and cashes them. One of the forged checks is included in the checks returned to Allen at the end of the first month. Within 30 calendar days after the return of these checks, Farnum forges two more checks and cashes them. Allen does not examine the returned checks until three months after the checks that included the first forged check was returned to her. The bank would be responsible for the first forged

check and for the two checks forged and cashed within the 30-day period after it sent the first statement and the canceled checks (unless the bank proves that it suffered a loss because of the customer's failure to examine the checks and notify it more promptly). It would not be liable for the seven forged checks cashed after the expiration of the 30-day period.

The case that follows, *Rhode Island Hospital Trust National Bank v. Zapata,* illustrates how the UCC applies to a series of forgeries. It was decided under the original version of Article 3, which provided only a 14-day period for a customer to review a statement and notify the bank of any alterations or unauthorized signatures of the customer.

RHODE ISLAND HOSPITAL TRUST NATIONAL BANK v. ZAPATA CORP. 6 UCC Rep.2d 1 (1st Cir. 1988)

I n early 1985, an employee of the Zapata Corporation stole some blank checks from the company. She wrote a large number of forged checks, almost all in amounts of $150 to $800 each, on Zapata's account at Rhode Island Hospital Trust National Bank. The bank, from March through July 1985, received and paid them. Bank statements that the bank regularly sent Zapata first began to reflect the forged checks in early 1985. Zapata failed to examine its statements closely until July 1985, when it found the forgeries. It immediately notified the bank, which then stopped clearing the checks. The bank already had processed and paid checks containing forged drawer's signatures totaling $109,247.16. Zapata then brought suit against the bank to have its account recredited for the checks.

The district court held that the bank was liable to reimburse Zapata for the checks that it paid before April 25, 1985 (two weeks after Zapata received the first statement containing the forged checks), but held in favor of the bank as to the remaining checks. Zapata appealed. ⌇

Breyer, Circuit Judge The issue that this appeal presents is whether Zapata Corporation has shown that the system used by Rhode Island Hospital Trust National Bank for detecting forged checks—a system used by a majority of American banks—lacks the "ordinary care" that a bank must exercise under the Uniform Commercial Code section 4–406(3). The question arises out of the following district court determinations, all of which are adequately supported by the record and by Rhode Island law.

The Bank will (and legally must) reimburse Zapata in respect to all checks it cleared before April 25 (or for at least two weeks after Zapata received the statement that reflected the forgeries). See sections 3–401(1), 4–406(2). In respect to checks cleared on and after April 25, the Bank need not reimburse Zapata because Zapata failed to "ex-

ercise reasonable care and promptness to examine the [bank] statements." Section 4–406(1).

The question before us is whether this last-mentioned conclusion is correct or whether Zapata can recover for the post–April 24 checks on the theory that, even if it was negligent, so was the Bank.

To understand this question, one must examine UCC section 4–406. Ordinarily a bank must reimburse an innocent customer for forgeries that it honors, section 3–401(1), but section 4–406 makes an important exception to the liability rule. The exception operates in respect to a series of forged checks, and it applies once a customer has had a chance to catch the forgeries by examining his bank statements and notifying the bank but has failed to do so.

The statute, in relevant part, reads as follows:

(1) When a bank sends to its customer a statement of account accompanied by items paid in good faith in support of the debit entries or holds the statement and items pursuant to a request or instructions of its customer or otherwise in a reasonable manner makes the statement and items available to the customer, the customer must exercise reasonable care and promptness to examine the statement and items to discover his unauthorized signature or any alteration on an item and must notify the bank promptly after discovery thereof.

(2) If the bank establishes that the customer failed with respect to an item to comply with the duties imposed on the customer by subsection (1) the customer is precluded from asserting against the bank (a) His unauthorized signature or any alteration on the item if the bank also establishes that it suffered a loss by reason of such failure; and (b) An unauthorized signature or alteration by the same wrongdoer on any other item paid in good faith by the bank after the first item and statement was available to the customer for a reasonable period not exceeding fourteen (14) calendar days and before the bank receives notification from the customer of any such unauthorized signature or alteration. Section 4–406(1) and (2). (Emphasis added.)

The statute goes on to specify an important exception. It says:

(3) The preclusion under subsection (2) does not apply if the customer establishes lack of ordinary care on the part of the bank in paying the item(s). Section 4–406(3).

Zapata's specific claim on this appeal is that it falls within this "exception to the exception"—that the bank's treatment of the post-April 24 checks lacked "ordinary care." The statute places the burden of proof on Zapata. It says that strict bank liability terminates 14 days after the customer receives the bank's statement unless "the customer establishes lack of ordinary care." The record convinces us that Zapata failed to carry its burden of establishing "lack of ordinary care" on the part of the Bank.

First the Bank described its ordinary practices as follows: The Bank examines all signatures on checks for more than $1,000. It examines signatures on checks between $100 and $1,000 (those at issue here) if it has reason to suspect a problem, e.g., if a customer has warned it of a possible forgery or if the check was drawn on an account with insufficient funds. It examines the signatures of a randomly chosen 1 percent of all other checks between $100 and $1,000. But it does not examine the signatures on other checks between $100 and $1,000. Through expert testimony, the Bank also established that most other banks in the nation follow this practice and that banking industry experts recommend it. Indeed, the Bank's practices are conservative in this regard, as most banks set $2,500 or more, not $1,000, as the limit beneath which they will not examine each signature. This testimony made out a prima facie case of "ordinary care."

Second, both bank and industry experts pointed out that this industry practice, in general and in the particular case of the Bank, saved considerable expense, compared with the Bank's pre-1981 practice of examining each check by hand. To be specific, the change saved the Bank about $125,000 annually.

Third, both a Bank official and an industry expert testified that changing from an "individual signature examination" system to the new "bulk-filing" system led to no significant increase in the number of forgeries that were detected. Under the Bank's prior "individual signature examination" some forgeries still slipped through.

Fourth, even if one assumes, contrary to this uncontradicted evidence, that the new system meant some increase in the number of undetected forged checks, Zapata still could not prevail, for it presented no evidence tending to show any such increased loss unreasonable in light of the costs that the new practice would save.

Judgment for Rhode Island Hospital Trust National Bank affirmed.

Regardless of which party may have been negligent, a customer must discover and report to the bank any unauthorized customer's signature or any alteration within one year from the time after the statement or items are made available to him. If the customer does not do so, he cannot require the bank to recredit his account for such items. [4–406(f)].

CHECK COLLECTION AND FUNDS AVAILABILITY

Check Collection

As Chapter 30, Negotiable Instruments, describes, checks and other drafts collected through the banking system usually have at least three parties—the drawer, the drawee bank, and the payee. If the payee deposits the check at the same bank as the drawee bank, the latter will take a series of steps necessary to reflect the deposit as a credit to the payee's account and to decide whether to pay the check from the drawer's account. In connection with its handling of the deposit for the payee's benefit, it will make one ledger entry showing the deposit as a credit to the payee's account. In connection with its decision to pay, the bank's employees and computers will perform several steps commonly referred to as the process of posting. Original Article 4 contained special rules describing the process of posting and the legal effect. The amendments to Article 4 deleted these special rules because automated check processing limited the legal significance of particular acts in posting [4–109, 4–213(a), and 4–303(a)]. These steps need not be taken in any particular order, but they customarily include determining whether there are sufficient funds to pay, debiting the drawer's account for the amount of the check, and placing the check into a folder for later return to the drawer (to satisfy its obligations under the "bank statement" rule) [4–406]. Banks in those states that have not enacted the amendments to Article 4 will also compare the drawer's signature on the check with that on the deposit agreement as part of this process.

If the payee deposits the check at a bank other than the drawee bank, the depositary bank, acting as the agent of the payee, will make the ledger entry showing the deposit as a credit to the payee's account. The next step of the collection process depends on where the depositary bank is located. If the drawee and depositary banks are in the same town or county, the depositary bank will indorse the check and deliver (present)it to the drawee bank for payment. It may deliver it by courier or through a local association of banks known as a "clearing house" [4–104(1)(d)]. The drawee-payor bank must settle for the check before midnight of the banking day of its receipt of the check, which means that it must give the depositary bank funds or a credit

equal to the amount of the check. Once it settles for the check, the drawee-payor bank has until midnight of the banking day after the banking day of receipt to pay the check or to return the check or send notice of dishonor. This deadline for the drawee-payor bank's action on the check is known as the bank's "midnight deadline" [4–104(1)(h)]. The drawee-payor bank's failure to settle by midnight of the banking day of receipt, or its failure to pay or return the check, or send notice of dishonor, results in the drawee-payor bank becoming "accountable" for the amount of the check, which means it must pay the amount of the check [4–302(a)].

If the drawee and depositary banks are located in different counties, or in different states, the depositary bank will use an additional commercial bank, and one or more of the regional Federal Reserve Banks, in the collection of the check. In these cases, the depositary bank will send the check on to the drawee-payor bank through these "collecting banks." Each bank in the sequence must use ordinary care in presenting the check or sending it for presentment, and in sending notice of dishonor or returning the check after learning that the check has not been paid [4–202(a)]. The depositary and collecting banks have until their respective midnight deadlines—or, in some cases, a further reasonable time—to take the action required of them in the sequence of collection steps.

If the drawee-payor bank dishonors the check prior to its midnight deadline or shortly after the midnight deadline under circumstances specified in "Regulation CC" of the Federal Reserve Board (described in the next section of this chapter), it will send the check back to the depositary bank. Until September 1, 1988, the drawee-payor bank customarily sent the dishonored check back to the collecting bank from which it received the check, and the collecting bank sent it back to the bank from which it had received it, and through any other bank that handled the check in the "forward collection" process until the check again reached the depositary bank. The provisions of Article 4 still describe this sequence as the "return collection" process, although Regulation CC imposes new responsibilities on the payor bank and on any other "returning bank." Each bank in the return sequence adjusts its accounts to reflect the return and has until its midnight deadline to send the check back to the bank from which it originally had received the check. After September 1, 1988 (or in states that previously had adopted "direct return" [Original 4–212(b)], the drawee-payor bank may return the check directly to the depositary bank—skipping all of the collecting banks and the delay represented by the midnight deadlines that each bank otherwise would have had.

Direct return also increases the likelihood that the depositary bank will know whether the check has been dishonored by the day on which Regulation CC requires the depositary bank to allow the payee to write checks or otherwise make withdrawals against the deposit. The next section of this chapter discusses this aspect of Regulation CC in more detail.

On receipt of the dishonored check, the depositary bank will return the check or otherwise notify its depositor (the payee) of the dishonor and will debit or charge back her account for the check it did not collect. The depositary bank may charge back the deposit even if it previously had allowed the payee-depositor to withdraw against the credit given for the deposit.

When the depositor receives the notice of dishonor and returned check it will take one of several steps, depending on whether it received the check directly from the drawer or took it by indorsement from another person. If the depositor was not the original payee of the check, it usually will prefer to return the check—giving notice of dishonor unless already given by the drawee bank or another collecting bank—to the person who negotiated the check to her, the prior indorser. Recall that an indorser is obligated to pay the check following dishonor and notice of dishonor [3–415].

If the depositor received the check directly from the drawer, for example as payee, the depositor normally will demand payment from the drawer. Recall that the drawer is obligated to pay the check upon dishonor [3–414]; alternatively, the payee may seek to enforce the underlying obligation for which the drawer originally issued the check, such as the purchase of groceries or an automobile.

Funds Availability

When a bank takes a check for deposit to a customer's account, it typically places a hold on the funds represented by the deposited check because it runs a number of risks in allowing a customer to withdraw deposits that it has not collected from the drawee

bank. The risks that the check may be returned include: (1) there may be insufficient funds in the drawer's account or the account may have been closed; (2) the check may contain a forged drawer's or indorser's signature, or there may have been a material alteration of the check; (3) the possibility that the drawer is kiting checks or playing two accounts off against each other; or (4) a stop-payment order may have been placed against the check. These are real concerns to a depositary bank, and it has a significant interest in protecting itself against these possibilities.

Until recently, the risks run by a depositary bank were complicated by a very slow process used by drawee-payor banks in returning a dishonored check or notifying the bank of the dishonor. Moreover, depositary banks did not get direct notice from drawee-payor banks when they paid checks. Accordingly, banks often restricted the depositor's use of the deposit by placing relatively long holds on checks deposited with them for collection; these sometimes ran 15 to 20 days for items drawn on other than local banks.

The extensive use of holds, and a growing public sentiment that they were excessive and often unfair, led to the passage by Congress in 1987 of the Expedited Funds Availability Act. In the act, Congress set out mandatory schedules limiting check holds and specifying when funds are to be made available to customers by depositary institutions. The act also delegated to the Federal Reserve Board the authority to speed up the check-processing system. The regulations adopted by the Board to speed up check processing supersede the provisions of Article 4 of the UCC (Bank Deposits and Collections) in a number of respects but will not be covered in this text.

The key elements of the mandatory funds availability schedules, which are set out in Federal Reserve Board Regulation CC are:

1. Local checks (those drawn on banks in the same Federal Reserve check region as the depositary bank) must be made available for the depositor to draw against by the second business day following deposit.

2. Nonlocal checks (those drawn on banks located in the United States but outside the Federal Reserve check processing region in which the depositary bank is located) must be made available by the fifth business day following deposit.

3. Certain items must be made available by the next day after the day of deposit. These include:

  a. Cash deposits where the deposit is made in person to an employee of the depositary bank (i.e., not at an ATM).

  b. Electronic payments.

  c. Checks drawn on the U.S. Treasury.

  d. U.S. Postal Service money orders.

  e. Checks drawn on a Federal Reserve Bank or Federal Home Loan Bank.

  f. Checks drawn by a state or a unit of local government (under certain conditions).

  g. Cashier's, certified, or teller's checks.

  h. Checks drawn on the depositary bank.

  i. The lesser of $100 or the aggregate deposit on any one banking day.

4. If the next-day items are not deposited in person with an employee of the depositary institution but rather are deposited in an ATM machine or by mail, then the deposit does not have to be made available for withdrawal until the second business day after deposit.

5. Generally, the depositary bank must begin accruing interest to a depositor's interest-bearing account from the day it receives credit for cash and check deposits to an interest-bearing account.

There are six major exceptions to the mandatory availability schedules set out above that are designed to safeguard depositary banks against higher risk situations. The exceptions are:

1. *New account exception.* The depositary bank may suspend the availability rules for new accounts and can limit the next-day and second-day availability to the first $5,000 deposited.

2. *Large deposit exception.* The hold periods can be extended to the extent the aggregate deposit on any banking day exceeds $5,000.

3. *Redeposited check exception.* The hold period can be extended where a check has been returned one or more times.

4. *Repeated overdraft exception.* A longer hold period may be required for deposits to accounts that have been overdrawn repeatedly.

5. *Reasonable cause exception.* The scheduled availability may be extended where the bank has reasonable cause to believe the check is uncollectible.

6. *Emergency conditions exception.* The scheduled availability may be extended under certain emergency conditions such as a communications interruption or a computer failure.

Banks are required to disclose their funds availability policy to all of their customers; they may provide different policies to different classes or categories of customers.

ELECTRONIC BANKING

With the development of computer technology, many banks are encouraging their customers to transfer funds electronically by using computers rather than paper drafts and checks. A bank customer may use a specially coded card at terminals provided by the bank to make deposits to an account, to transfer money from one checking or savings account to another, to pay bills, or to withdraw cash from an account. These new forms of transferring money have raised questions about the legal rules that apply to them, and the questions are only beginning to be resolved.

Electronic Funds Transfer Act

The consumer who used electronic funds transfer systems (EFTs), the so-called cash machines or electronic tellers, in the early years often experienced problems in identifying and resolving mechanical errors resulting from malfunctioning EFTs. In response to these problems, Congress passed the Electronic Funds Transfer Act in 1978 to provide "a basic framework, establishing the rights, liabilities, and responsibilities of participants in electronic funds transfer systems" and especially to provide "individual consumer rights."

The four basic EFT systems are automated teller machines; point-of-sale terminals, which allow consumers to use their EFT cards like checks at retail establishments; preauthorized payments, such as automatic paycheck deposits or mortgage or utility payments; and telephone transfers between accounts or to pay specific bills by phone.

Similar to the Truth in Lending Act and the Fair Credit Billing Act (FCBA) discussed in Chapter 47, the EFT Act requires disclosure of the terms and conditions of electronic fund transfers at the time the consumer contracts for the EFT service. Among the nine disclosures required are the following: the consumer's liability for unauthorized electronic fund transfers (those resulting from loss or theft), the nature of the EFT services under the consumer's account, any pertinent dollar or frequency limitations, any charges for the right to make EFTs, the consumer's right to stop payment of a preauthorized transfer, the financial institution's liability to the consumer for failure to make or stop payments, and the consumer's right to receive documentation of transfers both at the point or time of transfer and periodically. The act also requires 21 days' notice prior to the effective date of any change in the terms or conditions of the consumer's account that pertains to the required disclosures.

The EFT Act does differ from the Fair Credit Billing Act in a number of important respects. For example, under the EFT Act, the operators of EFT systems have a maximum of 10 working days to investigate errors or provisionally recredit the consumer's account, whereas issuers of credit cards have a maximum of 60 days under the FCBA. The liability of the consumer also is different if an EFT card is lost or stolen than it is if a credit card is lost or stolen.

The case that follows, *Kruser v. Bank of America NT & SA,* illustrates the application of the EFT Act's provisions that require a customer to provide timely notification of any unauthorized use of his card in order to limit his liability for the unauthorized use of the card.

KRUSER v. BANK OF AMERICA NT & SA 281 Cal.Rptr. 463 (Cal. Ct. App. 1991)

Lawrence and Georgene Kruser maintained a joint checking account with the Bank of America. The bank issued each of them a "Versatel" card and separate personal identification numbers that would allow access to funds in their account from automatic teller machines. The Krusers also received with their cards a "Disclosure Booklet" that provided to the Krusers a summary of consumer liability, the bank's business hours, and the address and telephone number by which they could notify the bank in the event they believed an unauthorized transfer had been made.

The Krusers believed Mr. Kruser's card had been destroyed in September 1986. The December 1986 account statement mailed to the Krusers by the bank reflected a $20 unauthorized withdrawal of funds by someone using Mr. Kruser's card at an automatic teller machine. The Krusers reported this unauthorized transaction to the bank when they discovered it in August or September 1987.

Mrs. Kruser underwent surgery in late 1986 or early 1987 and remained hospitalized for 11 days. She then spent a period of six or seven months recuperating at home. During this time, she reviewed the statements the Krusers received from the bank.

In September 1987, the Krusers received bank statements for July and August 1987 that reflected 47 unauthorized withdrawals totaling $9,020 made from an automatic teller machine, again by someone using Mr. Kruser's card. They notified the bank of these withdrawals within a few days of receiving the statements. The bank refused to credit the Kruser's account with the amount of the unauthorized withdrawals. The Krusers sued the bank claiming damages for the unauthorized withdrawals from their account. The trial court ruled in favor of the bank on the grounds that the Krusers had failed to comply with the note and reporting requirements of the Electronic Funds Transfer Act (EFTA). The Krusers appealed.

Stone, Associate Justice The ultimate issue we address is whether, as a matter of law, the unauthorized $20 withdrawal which appeared on the December 1986 statement barred the Krusers from recovery for the losses incurred in July and August 1987. Resolution of the issue requires the interpretation of the EFTA and section 205.6 of Regulation E, one of the regulations prescribed by the Board of Governors of the Federal Reserve System in order to carry out the EFTA.

Section 205.6 of Regulation E mirrors [the EFTA] and in particular provides:

(b) Limitations on the amount of liability. The amount of a consumer's liability for an unauthorized electronic fund transfer or a series of related unauthorized transfers shall not exceed $50 or the amount of unauthorized transfers that occur before notice to the financial institution . . . whichever is less, unless one of the following exceptions apply:

* * * * *

(2) If the consumer fails to report within 60 days of transmittal of the periodic statement any unauthorized electronic fund transfer that appears on the statement, the consumer's liability shall not exceed the sum of (i) The lesser of $50 or the amount of unauthorized electronic fund transfers that appear on the periodic statement during the 60-day period and (ii) The amount of unauthorized electronic fund transfers that occur after the close of the 60 days and before notice to the financial institution and that the financial institution establishes would not have occurred but for the failure of the consumer to notify the financial institution within that time.

* * * * *

(4) If a delay in notifying the financial statements was due to extenuating circumstances, such as extended travel or hospitalization, the time periods specified above shall be extended to a reasonable time.

The trial court concluded the Bank was entitled to judgment as a matter of law because the unauthorized withdrawals of July and August 1987 occurred more than 60 days after the Krusers received a statement which reflected an unauthorized transfer in December 1986. The court relied upon section 205.6(b)(2) of Regulation E.

The Krusers contend the December withdrawal of $20 was so isolated in time and minimal in an amount that it cannot be considered in connection with the July and August withdrawals. They assert the court's interpretation of section 205.6(b)(2) of Regulation E would have absurd results which would be inconsistent with the primary objective of the EFTA—to protect the consumer. They argue that if a consumer receives a bank statement which reflects an unauthorized minimal electronic transfer and fails to report the transaction to the bank within 60 days of transmission of the bank statement, unauthorized transfers many years later, perhaps totaling thousands of dollars, would remain the responsibility of the consumer.

The result the Krusers fear is avoided by the requirement that the bank establish the subsequent unauthorized transfers could have been prevented had the consumer notified the bank of the first unauthorized transfer. Here, although the unauthorized transfer of $20 occurred approximately seven months before the unauthorized transfers totaling $9,020, it is undisputed that all transfers were made by using Mr. Kruser's card which the Krusers believed had been destroyed prior to December 1986. According to the declaration of Yvonne Maloon, the Bank's Versatel risk manager, the Bank could have and would have canceled Mr. Kruser's card had it been timely notified of the December unauthorized transfer. In that event Mr. Kruser's card could not have been used to accomplish the unauthorized transactions in July and August.

In the alternative, the Krusers contend the facts establish that Mrs. Kruser, who was solely responsible for reconciling the bank statements, was severely ill and was also caring for a terminally ill relative when the December withdrawal occurred. Therefore they claim they were entitled to an extension of time within which to notify the bank.

The evidence the Krusers rely upon indicates in late 1986 or early 1987 Mrs. Kruser underwent surgery and remained in the hospital for 11 days. She left her house infrequently during the first six or seven months of 1987 during which she was recuperating. Mrs. Kruser admits, however, she received and reviewed bank statements during her recuperation. Therefore, we need not consider whether Mrs. Kruser's illness created circumstances which might have excused her failure to notice the unauthorized withdrawal pursuant to the applicable sections. She in fact did review the statements in question.

Judgment for Bank of America affirmed.

DOCUMENTS OF TITLE

Introduction

Storing or shipping goods, giving a warehouse receipt or bill of lading representing the goods, and transferring such a receipt or bill of lading as representing the goods are practices of ancient origin. The warehouseman or the common carrier is a bailee of the goods who contracts to store or transport the goods and to deliver them to the owner or to act otherwise in accordance with the lawful directions of the owner. The warehouse receipt or the bill of lading may be either negotiable or non-negotiable. To be negotiable, a warehouse receipt, bill of lading, or other document of title must provide that the goods are to be delivered to the bearer or to the order of a named person [7–104(1)]. The primary differences between the law of negotiable instruments and the law of negotiable documents of title are based on the differences between the obligation to pay money and the obligation to deliver specific goods.

Warehouse Receipts

A warehouse receipt, to be valid, need not be in any particular form, but if it does not embody within its written or printed form each of the following, the warehouseman is liable for damages caused by the omission to a person injured as a result of it: (1) the location of the warehouse where the goods are stored; (2) the date of issue; (3) the consecutive number of the receipt; (4) whether the goods are to be delivered to the bearer or to the order of a named person; (5) the rate of storage and handling charges; (6) a description of the goods or of the packages containing them; (7) the signature of the warehouse-man or his agent; (8) whether the warehouseman is the owner of the goods, solely, jointly, or in common with others; and (9) a statement of the amount of the advances made and of the liabilities incurred for which the warehouseman claims a lien or security interest. Other terms may be inserted [7–202].

A warehouseman is liable to a purchaser for value in good faith of a warehouse receipt for nonreceipt or misdescription of goods. The receipt may conspicuously qualify the description by a statement such as "contents, condition, and quantity unknown" [7–203].

Because a warehouseman is a bailee of the goods, he owes to the holder of the warehouse receipt the duties of a mutual benefit bailee and must exercise reasonable care [7–204]. Chapter 23, Personal Property and Bailments, discusses the duties of a bailee in detail. The warehouseman may terminate the relation by notification where, for example, the goods are about to deteriorate or where they constitute a threat to other goods in the warehouse [7–206]. Unless the warehouse receipt provides otherwise, the warehouseman must keep separate the goods covered by each receipt; however, different lots of fungible goods such as grain may be mingled [7–207].

A warehouseman has a lien against the bailor on the goods covered by his receipt for his storage and other charges incurred in handling the goods [7–209]. The Code sets out a detailed procedure for enforcing this lien [7–210].

Bills of Lading

In many respects, the rights and liabilities of the parties to a negotiable bill of lading are the same as the rights and liabilities of the parties to a negotiable warehouse receipt. The contract of the issuer of a bill of lading is to transport goods, whereas the contract of the issuer of a warehouse receipt is to store goods. Like the issuer of a warehouse receipt, the issuer of a bill of lading is liable for nonreceipt or misdescription of the goods, but he may protect himself from liability where he does not know the contents of packages by marking the bill of lading "contents or condition of packages unknown" or similar language. Such terms are ineffective when the goods are loaded by an issuer who is a common carrier unless the goods are concealed by packages [7–301].

Duty of Care

A carrier who issues a bill of lading, or a warehouse operator who issues a warehouse receipt, must exercise the same degree of care in relation to the goods as a reasonably careful person would exercise under similar circumstances. Liability for damages not caused by the negligence of the carrier may be imposed on him by a special law or rule of law. Under tariff rules, a common carrier may limit her liability to a shipper's declaration of value, provided that the rates are dependent on value [7–309]. In the case that follows, *Calvin Klein Ltd. v. Trylon Trucking Corp.,* a court enforced a $50 per shipment limitation that had been part of a long series of shipping contracts where the customer had the opportunity to declare a higher value and failed to do so.

CALVIN KLEIN LTD. v. TRYLON TRUCKING CORP. 892 F.2d 191 (2d Cir. 1989)

 rylon Trucking Corporation is a New Jersey trucking firm that engaged in the business of transporting goods from New York City's airports for delivery to its customers' facilities. For three years prior to 1986, Calvin Klein, a New York clothing company, used the services of Trylon involving hundreds of shipments. Calvin Klein, through its customs broker, would contact Trylon to pick up the shipment from the airport for delivery to Calvin Klein's facility. After completing the delivery carriage, Trylon would forward to Calvin Klein an invoice, which contained a limitation of liability provision as follows:

> In consideration of the rate charged, the shipper agrees that the carrier shall not be liable for more than $50.00 on any shipment accepted for delivery to one consignee unless a greater value is declared, in writing, upon receipt at time of shipment and charge for such greater value paid, or agreed to be paid, by the shipper.

A shipment of 2,833 blouses from Hong Kong arrived at John F. Kennedy International Airport for Calvin Klein on March 27, 1986. Calvin Klein arranged for Trylon to pick up the shipment and deliver it to Calvin Klein's New Jersey warehouse. On April 2, Trylon dispatched its driver, J. Jefferson, to pick up this shipment. Jefferson signed a receipt for the shipment from Calvin Klein's broker. Later, on April 2, the parties discovered that Jefferson had stolen Trylon's truck and its shipment. The shipment was never recovered.

Calvin Klein sent a claim letter to Trylon for the full value of the lost blouses. When it did not receive a response from Trylon, Calvin Klein filed suit against Trylon, seeking to recover $150,000, the alleged value of the blouses. In the pleadings before the court, the parties agreed that Trylon was liable to Calvin Klein for the loss of the shipment and that it had been grossly negligent in the hiring and supervision of Jefferson. They also agreed that "the terms and conditions of Trylon's carriage were that liability for loss or damage to cargo is limited to $50 in accordance with the provision in Trylon's invoice forms." Calvin Klein conceded that it was aware of the limitation of liability and that it did not declare a value on the blouses at the time of shipment.

Trylon contended that its liability was limited to $50 in accordance with the provision in its invoice forms. Calvin Klein argued that the limitation clause was not enforceable for two reasons: (1) no agreement existed between it and Trylon as to the limitation of liability; and (2) even if an agreement existed, public policy would prevent its enforcement because of Trylon's gross negligence. The district court held that Calvin Klein had not assented to the limitation clause for this shipment and awarded damages to Calvin Klein of $101,542.62. Trylon appealed. ∞

Miner, Circuit Judge A common carrier is strictly liable for the loss of goods in its custody. Where the loss is not due to excepted causes [that is, act of God or public enemy, inherent nature of goods, or shipper's fault], it is immaterial whether the carrier was negligent or not. Even in the case of loss from theft by third parties, liability may be imposed upon a negligent common carrier. A shipper and a common carrier may contract to limit the carrier's liability in cases of loss to an amount agreed to by the parties, so long as the language of the limitation is clear, the shipper is aware of the terms of the limitation, and the shipper can change the terms by indicating the true value of the goods being shipped. Section 7–309(2). Such a limitation agreement is generally valid and enforceable despite carrier negligence. The limitation of liability provision involved here clearly provides that, at the time of delivery, the shipper may increase the limitation by written notice of the value of the goods to be delivered and by payment of a commensurately higher fee.

The parties stipulated to the fact that the $50 limitation of liability was a term and condition of carriage and that Calvin Klein was aware of that limitation. This stipulated fact removes the first

issue, namely whether an agreement existed as to a liability limitation between the parties. Calvin Klein's argument that it never previously acknowledged this limitation by accepting only $50 in settlement of a larger loss does not alter this explicit stipulation. The district court erred in not accepting the limitation of liability as stipulated.

The remaining issue concerns the enforceability of the limitation clause in the light of Trylon's conceded gross negligence.

Since carriers are strictly liable for loss of shipments in their custody and are insurers of those goods, the degree of carrier negligence is immaterial. The common carrier must exercise reasonable care in relation to the shipment in its custody. Section 7–309(2). Carriers can contract with their shipping customers on the amount of liability each party will bear for the loss of a shipment, regardless of the amount of carrier negligence. Unlike a merchant acquiring a burglar alarm, the shipper can calculate the specific amount of its potential damages in advance, declare the value of the shipment based on that calculation, can pay a commensurately higher rate to carry the goods, in effect buying additional insurance from the common carrier.

In this case Calvin Klein and Trylon were business entities with an ongoing commercial relationship involving numerous carriages of Calvin Klein goods by Trylon. Where such entities deal with each other in a commercial setting, and no special relationship exists between the parties, clear limitations between them will be enforced. Here, each carriage was under the same terms and conditions as the last, including a limitation of Trylon's liability. This is not a case in which the shipper was dealing with the common carrier for the first time or contracting under new or changed conditions. Calvin Klein was aware of the terms and was free to adjust the limitation upon a written declaration of the value of a given shipment, but failed to do so with the shipment at issue here. Since Calvin Klein failed to adjust the limitation, the limitation applies here, and no public policy that dictates otherwise can be identified.

Calvin Klein also argues that the limitation is so low as to be void. The amount is immaterial because Calvin Klein had the opportunity to negotiate the amount of coverage by declaring the value of the shipment. Commercial entities can easily negotiate the degree of risk each party will bear and which party will bear the cost of insurance. Calvin Klein had the opportunity to declare a higher value and we find all of its arguments relating to the unreasonableness of the limitation to be without merit.

District court judgment reversed with instructions to enter judgment for Calvin Klein for $50.

Negotiation of Document of Title

A negotiable document of title and a negotiable instrument are negotiated in substantially the same manner. If the document of title provides for the delivery of the goods to bearer, it may be negotiated by delivery. If it provides for delivery of the goods to the order of a named person, it must be indorsed by that person and delivered. If an order document of title is indorsed in blank, it may be negotiated by delivery unless it bears a special indorsement following the blank indorsement, in which event it must be indorsed by the special indorsee and delivered [7–501].

A person taking a negotiable document of title takes as a bona fide holder if she takes in good faith and in the regular course of business. The bona fide holder of a negotiable document of title has substantially the same advantages over a holder who is not a bona fide holder or over a holder of a non-negotiable document of title as does a holder in due course of a negotiable instrument over a holder who is not a holder in due course or over a holder of a non-negotiable instrument.

Rights Acquired by Negotiation

A person who acquires a negotiable document of title by due negotiation acquires (1) title to the document, (2) title to the goods, (3) the right to the goods delivered to the bailee after the issuance of the document, and (4) the direct obligation of the issuer to hold or deliver the goods according to the terms of the document [7–502(1)].

Under the broad general principle that a person cannot transfer title to goods he does not own, a thief—or the owner of goods subject to a perfected security interest—cannot, by warehousing or shipping the goods on a negotiable document of title and then negotiating the document of title, transfer to the purchaser of the document of title a better title than he has [7–503].

Warranties of Transferor of Document of Title

The transferor of a negotiable document of title warrants to his immediate transferee, in addition to any warranty of goods, only that the document is genuine, that he has no knowledge of any facts that would impair its validity or worth, and that his negotiation or transfer is rightful and fully effective with respect to the title to the document and the goods it represents [7–507].

ETHICAL AND PUBLIC POLICY CONCERNS

1. Suppose you take your car to a garage to have it repainted. When you go to pick it up, you are not happy with the quality of the work, but the garage owner refuses to release the car to you unless you pay him in full for the work. You give him a check in the amount requested, and on the way home stop at your bank and request that the bank stop payment on the check you have just written, an action you decided to take when you were writing out the check. Have you acted ethically?

2. Some banks take the position that because they process checks with the use of computers, a customer seeking to stop payment on a check must provide them with the amount of the check with every digit correct in order for the bank to be able to stop payment. What policy considerations are involved in deciding whether the bank's position should establish the minimum information required for a bank to have a "reasonable opportunity" to respond to the customer's request?

3. Suppose that you own and operate a warehouse. A local liquor store owner occasionally uses your facilities to store shipments of wine from France until he has room for the wine in his store. You are aware that from time to time your warehouse employees "borrow" a bottle from the crates of wine being stored in your warehouse. After a number of crates with a total of four bottles missing are delivered to the liquor store, the store owner queries you about the missing bottles and you tell him that they must have been broken in transit to your warehouse. Have you acted ethically?

PROBLEMS AND PROBLEM CASES

1. J. E. B. Stewart received a check in the amount of $185.48 in payment of a fee from a client. Stewart presented the check, properly indorsed, to the Citizen's & Southern Bank. The bank refused to cash the check even though there were sufficient funds in the drawer's account. Stewart then sued the bank for actual damages of $185.48 and for punitive damages of $50,000 for its failure to cash a valid check drawn against a solvent account in the bank. Should Stewart recover both the actual and punitive damages he seeks?

2. Louise Kalbe signed a check drawn on her account at the Pulaski State Bank; later, that check was lost or stolen. The check was drafted for $7,260 payable to cash. The bank paid the check, which created an overdraft of $6,542.12 in Kalbe's ac-

count. The bank brought a lawsuit against Kalbe to recover the overdraft. Kalbe asserted that the check was not properly payable from her account. Was the bank legally entitled to pay a check that exceeded the balance in her account and to recover the overdraft from her?

3. RPM Pizza, Inc., a Domino's Pizza franchisee, maintained a checking account at Bank One-Cambridge. On May 29, 1992, RPM erroneously issued a $96,000 check drawn on its account at the bank and payable to a computer broker, Systems Marketing. After mailing the check, RPM realized its error, and on June 2, 1992, RPM placed a stop-payment order on the check. As stated in its account agreement with Bank One (and in the UCC as adopted in Ohio), written stop-payment orders are effective for six months. The stop-payment order expired on December 6, 1992, and RPM failed to renew it. On December 22, 1992, Systems Marketing deposited the check in its account at the Bank of Tampa, Florida. When the Bank of Tampa received the check, it was more than six months old and was therefore "stale" according to standard banking procedures. The Bank of Tampa credited the check to Systems Marketing's account and sent it forward to Bank One-Cambridge, which charged it against RPM's checking account. RPM brought suit against Bank One, claiming that the bank had not exercised ordinary care or acted in good faith in paying the stale check. The bank established that it routinely paid stale checks and that its internal operating procedures simply required it to perform a signature authorization on checks of more than $50,000, which it did in this case. Did the bank violate the duty it owed to its customer, RPM, when it paid a check that was more than six months old?

4. Dr. Sherrill purchased a Buick Skylark from Frank Morris Buick. He gave the auto dealer a check for $4,960.61 drawn on his account at First Alabama Bank. The check was dated on "2/6/1996," was payable "to the order of Frank Morris Buick," and was not numbered. After buying the Skylark, Sherrill became concerned about whether he had received valid title to it. The day after he gave the dealer the check, he called in an oral stop-payment order on it. He later confirmed the stop-payment order in writing. In the stop-payment order, Sherrill stated that the check was not numbered, was payable to "Walter Morris Buick," was dated "6/3/96," and was in the amount of

$4,960.61. The bank paid the check when it was presented for payment. Sherrill then claimed that the bank should recredit his account for $4,960.61 because it paid the check over a valid stop-payment order. Did the stop-payment order describe the check accurately enough to constitute a valid stop payment order?

5.   **[icon]** *Video case.* See "Sour Grapes." Jelly Manufacturer orders some grapes by phone from Grape Grower in California on a COD basis. When the grapes arrive, Jelly Manufacturer pays for them by check before discovering that they had spoiled en route because they had been shipped in a nonrefrigerated truck. After calling Grape Grower to complain, Jelly Manufacturer calls its bank and places a stop-payment order on the check. The bank's computer fails to catch the check and the check is paid to Grape Grower. Does Jelly Manufacturer have any recourse against the bank for paying the check over the stop-payment order?

6.   In December, Whalley Company hired Nancy Cherauka as its bookkeeper. Her duties included preparing checks, taking deposits to the bank, and reconciling the monthly checking account statements. She was not authorized to sign or cash checks. Between the following January 24 and May 31, Cherauka forged 49 checks on the Whalley account at National City Bank. Each month, National City Bank sent Whalley a statement and the canceled checks (including the forgeries) it had paid the previous month. The president of Whalley looked at the statement to see the balance in the account but he did not look at the individual checks. Then he gave the statement and checks to the bookkeeper. The January 24 forged check was sent to Whalley on February 3. In June, Whalley discovered that Cherauka was forging checks and fired her. It then brought a lawsuit against National City Bank to force it to recredit Whalley's account with the total amount of the 49 checks. Whalley claimed that the checks were not properly payable from the account. Is National City required to recredit Whalley's account?

7.   In January 1980, Mrs. Baker began forging her husband's checks. In June 1981, Mr. Baker notified the bank that he had not been receiving his checking account statements. The missing statements were then personally delivered to Mr. Baker. Mr. Baker balanced his account statements in February 1983. In March 1983, he notified the bank that 25 of the

checks that they had cashed were forgeries. Does the bank or Mr. Baker bear the liability for the forgeries?

8.   On August 16, 1981, Frederick Ognibene went to the ATM area at a Citibank branch and activated one of the machines with his Citibank card, provided his personal identification code, and withdrew $20. When he approached the machine a person was using the customer service telephone located between two ATM machines and appeared to be telling customer service that one of the machines was malfunctioning. As Ognibene was making his withdrawal, the person said into the telephone, "I'll see if his card works in my machine." He then asked Ognibene if he could use his card to see if the other machine was working. Ognibene handed his card to him and saw him insert it into the adjoining machine at least two times while saying into the telephone, "Yes, it seems to be working." When Ognibene received his Citibank statement, it showed that two withdrawals of $200 each from his account were made at 5:42 P.M. and 5:43 P.M., respectively, on August 16. His own $20 withdrawal was made at 5:41 P.M. At the time, Ognibene was unaware that any withdrawals from his account were being made from the adjoining machine. Ognibene sought to have his account recredited for $400, claiming that the withdrawals had been unauthorized. Citibank had been aware for some time of a scam being perpetrated against its customers by persons who observed the customer inserting his personal identification number into an ATM and then obtaining access to the customer's ATM card in the same manner as Ognibene's card was obtained. After learning about the scam, Citibank posted signs in ATM areas containing a red circle approximately 2½ inches in diameter in which was written "Do Not Let Your Citicard Be Used For Any Transaction But Your Own." Was Citibank required under the Electronic Fund Transfer Act to recredit Ognibene's account on the grounds that the withdrawal of the $400 was unauthorized?

9.   Griswold and Bateman Warehouse Company stored 337 cases of Chivas Regal Scotch Whiskey for Joseph H. Reinfeld, Inc., in its bonded warehouse. The warehouse receipt issued to Reinfeld limited Griswold and Bateman's liability for negligence to 250 times the monthly storage rate, a total of $1,925. When Reinfeld sent its truck to pick up the whiskey, 40 cases were missing. Reinfeld then

brought suit seeking the wholesale market value of the whiskey, $6,417.60. Reinfeld presented evidence of the delivery of the whiskey, the demand for its return, and the failure of Griswold and Bateman to return it. Reinfeld claimed that the burden was on Griswold and Bateman to explain the disappearance of the whiskey. Griswold and Bateman admitted that it had been negligent, but sought to limit its liability to $1,925. Is Griswold and Bateman's liability limited to $1,925?

10. Everlens Mitchell entered into a written contract with All American Van & Storage to transport and store her household goods. She was to pay the storage charges on a monthly basis. As security, she granted All American a warehouseman's lien. All American had the right to sell the property if the charges remained unpaid for three months and if, in the opinion of the company, such action was necessary to protect the accrued charges. Mitchell fell eight months behind on her payments. On October 20, 1985, she received notice that if the unpaid charges, totaling $804.30, were not paid by October 31, her goods would be sold on November 7.

Mitchell advised All American that she had a claim pending with the Social Security Administration and would soon receive a large sum of money. This was confirmed to All American by several government officials. However, All American sold Mitchell's property on November 7 for $925.50. At the end of the month, Mitchell received a $5,500 disability payment. She sued All American for improperly selling her goods. The trial court awarded judgment to All American. Should the decision be reversed on appeal?

11. On October 15, Young delivered 207 bags of rice to Atteberry's warehouse and received a non-negotiable receipt. Young then transferred the receipt to Brock for a valuable consideration, and Brock notified Atteberry of the transfer on November 3. Prior to November 3, however, Young had procured a negotiable receipt for the rice along with some other rice he had deposited with Atteberry. Brock presented his non-negotiable receipt to Atteberry and demanded delivery of the rice. Atteberry contended that no rice was being held at the warehouse on Brock's account. Who is correct?

Agency Law

THIRTY-FOUR

The Agency Relationship

Often, businesses are legally bound by the actions of their employees or other representatives. For example, corporations frequently are liable on contracts their employees make or for torts their employees commit. We take such liability for granted, but why should we? A corporation is an artificial legal person distinct from the officers, employees, and other representatives who contract on its behalf and who may commit torts while on the job. Similarly, a sole proprietor is distinct from the people he may employ. How can these and other business actors be bound on contracts they did not make or for torts they did not commit? The reason is the law of **agency.**

Agency is a two-party relationship in which one party (the **agent**) is authorized to act on behalf of, and under the control of, the other party (the **principal**). Simple examples include hiring a salesperson to sell goods, retaining an attorney, and engaging a real estate broker to sell a house. Agency law's most important social function is to stimulate commercial activity. It does so by enabling businesses to increase the number of transactions they can complete within a given time. Without agency, for instance, a sole proprietor's ability to engage in trade would be limited by the need to make each of her purchase or sale contracts in person. As artificial persons, moreover, corporations can *only* act through their agents.

Agency law divides into two rough categories. The first involves legal relations *between the principal and the agent*. These include the rules governing formation of an agency, the duties the principal and the agent owe each other, and the ways an agency can be terminated. These topics are the main concern of this chapter. Chapter 35 discusses the principal's and the agent's relations with *third parties*. Here, our main concerns are the principal's and the agent's liability on contracts the agent makes and for torts the agent commits. ∽

CREATION OF AN AGENCY AND RELATED SUBJECTS

Formation

An agency is created by the manifested agreement of two parties that one party (the agent) will act for the benefit of the other (the principal) under the principal's direction.[1] As the term *manifested* suggests, the test for an agency's existence is *objective*. If the parties' behavior and the surrounding facts and circumstances indicate an agreement that one person is to act for the benefit and under the control of another, the relationship exists. If the facts establish an agency, neither party need know about the agency's existence or subjectively desire that it exist. In fact, an agency may be present even where the parties expressly say that they do not intend to create it, or intend to create some other legal relationship instead.

Often, parties create an agency by a written contract. But an agency contract may be oral unless state law provides otherwise.[2] Some states, for example, require written evidence of contracts to

pay an agent a commission for the sale of real estate. More importantly, the agency relation need not be contractual at all. Thus, consideration is not necessary to form an agency. As the following *Warren* case illustrates, courts sometimes imply an agency from the parties' behavior and the surrounding circumstances without discussing the need for a contract or for consideration.

Capacity

A principal or agent who lacks the necessary mental capacity when the agency is formed ordinarily can release himself from the agency at his option. Examples include those who are minors or are mentally incapacitated when the agency is created. Of course, incapacity may occur at other times as well; we discuss such situations later in this chapter and in Chapter 35.

As you have seen, corporations can and must appoint agents. In a partnership, each partner normally acts as the agent of the partnership in transacting partnership business,[3] and partnerships can appoint nonpartner agents as well. In addition, corporations, partnerships, and other business organizations themselves can act as agents.

Nondelegable Obligations

Certain duties or acts must be performed personally and cannot be delegated to an agent. Examples include making statements under oath, voting in public elections, and signing a will. The same is true for service contracts in which the principal's personal performance is crucial—for example, certain contracts by lawyers, doctors, artists, and entertainers.

---

[1]Sometimes it is said that an agency may also be created by *ratification, estoppel,* or *operation of law.* Usually, however, ratification and estoppel are regarded as ways of binding the principal to an agent's actions, not as ways of forming an agency in the first place. Ratification is discussed in Chapter 35, and estoppel resembles the concept of apparent authority discussed later in this chapter and in Chapter 35. It is unusual for an agency to be created by operation of law. An example might be a statute designating a state's secretary of state as an out-of-state motorist's "agent" for purposes of receiving a summons and a complaint in a lawsuit against the motorist.

[2]Usually, the state law in question is the statute of frauds, which is discussed in Chapter 16. Also, it sometimes is said that

if the contract the agent is to form must be in writing, the agency agreement likewise must be written. However, it is doubtful whether this "equal dignity rule" enjoys widespread acceptance.

[3]Chapter 37 discusses how agency law operates in the partnership context.

---

 or two years, Bobby and Modell Warren took their cotton crops to certain cotton gins that ginned and baled the cotton. After being so instructed by the Warrens, the gins obtained bids for the cotton from prospective buyers and the Warrens told the gins which bids to accept. Then the gins sold the cotton to the designated buyers, collecting the proceeds. At the Warrens' instruction, the gins *deferred payment of the proceeds to the Warrens until the year after the year in which each sale was made.*

The Warrens did not report the proceeds as taxable income for the year when the gins received the proceeds, instead including the proceeds in the return for the following year. After an IRS audit, the Warrens were compelled to treat the proceeds as taxable income for the year when the proceeds were received, and to pay accordingly. The Warrens eventually won a refund action in federal district court. The government appealed, arguing that the gins were agents of the Warrens. Because receipt of proceeds by an agent is receipt by the principal, this would mean that the proceeds were taxable income for the year when they were received by the gins. ∽

Johnson, Circuit Judge The relationship between the Warrens and the gins for the purpose of selling the cotton was indisputably that of principal and agent. The Warrens instructed the gins to solicit bids, the Warrens decided whether to accept the highest price offered, and the Warrens determined whether or not to instruct the gins to hold the proceeds from the sale until the following year. The gins' role in the sale of the cotton was to adhere to the Warrens' instructions. The Warrens were the owners of the cotton held for sale; the Warrens were in complete control of its disposition.

This case is distinguishable from those cases where it was recognized that proceeds from the sale of a crop by a farmer, pursuant to a bona fide arm's-length contract between the buyer and seller calling for payment in the taxable year following delivery, are includable in gross income for the taxable year in which payment is received. In the case at bar the bona fide arm's-length agreement was not between the buyer and seller but rather between the seller and his agent. The income was received by the Warrens' agents in the year of the sale. The fact that the Warrens restricted their access to the sales proceeds does not change the tax status of the money received.

Judgment reversed in favor of the government.

AGENCY CONCEPTS, DEFINITIONS, AND TYPES

Agency law includes various concepts, definitions, and distinctions. These matters often determine the rights, duties, and liabilities of the principal, the agent, and third parties. In addition, they sometimes are important outside agency law. Because these basic topics are so crucial in so many different situations, we outline them together here.

Authority

Although agency law lets people multiply their dealings by employing agents, a principal is not liable for any deal his agent concludes. Normally, an agent can bind his principal only when the agent has **authority** to do so. Authority is an agent's ability to affect his principal's legal relations. It comes in two main forms: **actual authority** and **apparent authority.** Each is based on the principal's manifested consent that the agent may act for and bind the principal. For actual authority this consent must be communicated to the *agent,* while for apparent authority it must be communicated to the *third party.*

Actual authority comes in two forms: **express authority** and **implied authority.** Express authority is created by the principal's *actual words* (whether written or oral). Thus, an agent has express authority to bind her principal in a certain fashion only when the principal has made a fairly precise statement to that effect. However, it is often impractical for a principal to specify the agent's authority fully and exactly. To avoid unnecessarily restricting an agent's ability to represent her principal, agency law also gives agents implied authority to bind their principals. An agent generally has implied authority to do whatever it is reasonable to assume that the principal wanted him to do, given the principal's express statements and the surrounding circumstances. Relevant factors include the principal's express statements, the nature of the agency, the acts reasonably necessary to carry on the agency business, and the acts customarily done when conducting that business.

Sometimes an agent who lacks actual authority may still *appear* to have such authority, and third parties may reasonably rely on this appearance of authority. To protect third parties in such situations, agency law lets agents bind the principal on the basis of their apparent authority. Apparent authority arises when the principal's behavior causes a third party to reasonably believe that the agent is authorized to act in a certain way. Apparent authority depends on what the principal communicates to the third party—either directly or through the agent. A principal might clothe an agent with apparent authority by making direct statements to the third party, telling an agent to do so, or allowing an agent to behave in a way that creates an appearance of authority. Communications to the agent are irrelevant unless they become known to the third party or affect the agent's behavior. Also, agents cannot give themselves apparent authority, and apparent authority does not exist where an agent creates an appearance of authority without the principal's consent. Finally, the third party must *reasonably* believe in the agent's authority. Trade customs and business practices can help courts determine whether such a belief was reasonable.

Authority is important in a number of agency contexts. Chapter 35 examines its most important agency application—determining a principal's liability on contracts made by his agent. As the following *Stieger* case illustrates, moreover, authority is used outside agency law as well.

STIEGER v. CHEVY CHASE SAVINGS BANK 666 A.2d 479 (D.C. Ct. App. 1995)

P aul Stieger gave his Chevy Chase Bank credit card to a Ms. Garrett during a business trip. He told her only to use the card for a car rental and for hotel lodging. After Stieger returned from the trip, he found that Garrett had made 15 unauthorized uses of his card. For 13 of these purchases, Garrett signed Stieger's name to the charge slip; for the other two, she signed her own name.

Stieger eventually obtained a $3,200 judgment against Garrett but was only able to collect $750 on that judgment. After Chevy Chase refused to cancel Garrett's unauthorized charges, Stieger sued for a declaration that he should not be liable for those charges. The trial court ruled in Chevy Chase's favor on all 15 charges, and an appellate court ruled in the bank's favor on the 13 charges Garrett signed in Stieger's name. Stieger appealed this ruling.

Pryor, Senior Judge The Truth-in-Lending Act was enacted to protect credit cardholders from unauthorized use by those able to obtain possession of a card from its original owner. The act limits liability for the cardholder to a maximum of $50 for charges made by third parties that are "unauthorized." However, the act does not limit liability for third-party charges that are made with "actual, implied or apparent authority." Since actual and implied authority are not alleged in this case, the issue is whether Garrett had apparent authority to use the card.

Apparent authority arises when a principal places an agent in a position which causes a third person to reasonably believe that the principal had consented to the exercise of authority the agent purports to hold. Where a credit cardholder voluntarily permits the use of his credit card by another person, the cardholder has authorized the use of that card and is thereby responsible for any charges as a result of that use, even if he requested that the other person not charge over a certain amount or make charges only for specified purposes. Nearly every jurisdiction that has addressed a factual situation where a cardholder voluntarily and knowingly allows another to use his card and that person subsequently misuses the card, has determined that the agent had apparent authority and therefore was not an unauthorized user.

Stieger argues that he had the right to expect Garrett to use the card only for the charges he authorized, and that he cannot be liable for [Garrett's] acting beyond the scope of her authority. Stieger also asserts that Garrett could not reasonably present herself as Paul Stieger, and that a merchant should be required to give greater scrutiny to the person using the card. [However,] Stieger placed Garrett, by voluntarily giving her the card, in such a position as to mislead third persons into believing that [she was] clothed with authority which in fact she [did] not possess. To a merchant, voluntary relinquishment combined with the matching of a signature is generally a reasonable indication of apparent authority to use the credit card. However, the same cannot be said of the two charges where Garrett signed her own name. It is an unreasonable extension of apparent authority for a merchant to accept charges, where the signatures do not match, without any additional factors to mislead the merchant into believing that the person presenting the card is the agent of the cardholder.

Lower court decision in Chevy Chase's favor on 13 of the 15 charges affirmed.

General and Special Agents

Although it may be falling out of favor with courts, the blurred distinction between general agents and special agents still has some importance. A **general agent** is continuously employed to conduct a series of transactions, while a **special agent** is employed to conduct a single transaction or a small, simple group of transactions. Thus, a continuously employed general manager, construction project supervisor, or purchasing agent normally is a general agent; and a person employed to buy or sell a few objects on a one-shot basis usually is a special agent. In addition to being employed on a continuous basis, general agents often serve for longer periods, perform more acts, and deal with more parties than do special agents.

Gratuitous Agents

An agent who receives no compensation for his services is called a **gratuitous agent.** Gratuitous agents have the same power to bind their principals as do paid agents with the same authority. However, the fact that an agent is gratuitous sometimes lowers the duties principal and agent owe each other and also may increase the parties' ability to terminate the agency without incurring liability.

Subagents

A **subagent** basically is an agent of an agent. More precisely, a subagent is a person appointed by an agent to perform tasks that the agent has undertaken to perform for his principal. For example, if you retain an accounting firm as your agent, the accountant actually handling your affairs is the firm's agent and your subagent. For a subagency to exist, an agent must have the authority to make the subagent *his agent* for conducting the principal's business. Sometimes, however, a party appointed by an agent is not a subagent because the appointing agent only had authority to appoint agents *for the principal*. For instance, sales agents appointed by a corpora-tion's sales manager probably are agents of the corporation, not agents of the sales manager.

When an agent appoints a true subagent, the agent becomes a principal with respect to the subagent, his agent. Thus, the legal relations between agent and subagent closely parallel the legal relations between principal and agent. But a subagent is also the *original principal's* agent. Here, though, the normal rules governing principals and agents do not always apply. We occasionally refer to such situations in the pages ahead.

Employees and Independent Contractors

Many legal questions depend on whether an agent or some other party who contracts with the principal is classed as an **employee** (or servant) or as an **independent contractor.**[4] No sharp line separates employees from independent contractors; the following *Circle C* case lists some factors considered in making such determinations. The most important of these factors is the principal's *right to control the physical details of the work.* Employees typically are subject to such control. Independent contractors, on the other hand, generally contract with the principal to produce some result, and determine for themselves how that result will be accomplished.

Although many employees perform physical labor or are paid on an hourly basis, corporate officers usually are employees as well. Professionals such as brokers, accountants, and attorneys often are independent contractors, although they sometimes are employees. Consider the difference between a cor-

---

[4]When are employees and independent contractors agents? Although there is little consensus on this question, this text follows the *Restatement (Second)* position. According to the *Restatement,* employees *always* are agents, while independent contractors *may or may not* be agents. An independent contractor is an agent when the tests for the existence of an agency—most importantly, sufficient control by the principal—are met. See *Restatement (Second) of Agency* §§; 2, 14N, 25, and the Introductory Note following § 218 (1959).

poration represented by an attorney engaged in her own practice and a corporation that maintains a staff of salaried in-house counsel. Finally, franchisees usually are independent contractors.

As Chapter 35 makes clear, the employee–independent contractor distinction often is crucial in determining the principal's liability for an agent's torts. The distinction also helps define the coverage of some employment laws discussed in Chapter 50. Unemployment compensation, the Fair Labor Standards Act (the subject of *Circle C*), and workers' compensation are clear examples.

REICH v. CIRCLE C INVESTMENTS, INC.   998 F.2d 324 (5th Cir. 1993)

ircle C Investments operated two nightclubs featuring topless dancers. The secretary of labor sued to compel Circle C to observe the minimum-wage, maximum-hours, and record-keeping provisions of the Fair Labor Standards Act (FLSA). Following a bench trial, the district court concluded that because the dancers were employees, the FLSA applied to Circle C's nightclubs. Thus, the court enjoined Circle C from further violating the FLSA, and also restrained it from withholding $539,630 in back wages. Circle C appealed. ∞

Reavley, Circuit Judge   To determine employee status under the FLSA, we focus on whether the alleged employee, as a matter of economic reality, is economically dependent upon the business to which she renders her services. Our focal inquiry is whether the individual is, as a matter of economic reality, in business for herself. We consider five factors: (1) the degree of control exercised by the alleged employer, (2) the relative investments of the worker and the alleged employer, (3) the degree to which the worker's opportunity for profit and loss is determined by the alleged employer, (4) the skill and initiative required in performing the job, and (5) the permanency of the relationship. These factors are merely aids in determining the underlying question of dependency, and no single factor is determinative.

Degree of Control

The dancers are required to comply with weekly work schedules. Circle C instructs the dancers to charge at least $10 for table dances and $20 for couch dances. The dancers supply their own costumes, but the costumes must meet standards set by Circle C. The dancers can express a preference for a certain type of music, but they do not have the final say. Dancers were expected to mingle with customers when not dancing. Circle C has promulgated many other rules. Circle C enforces [all] these rules by fining infringers. The record fully supports the district court's finding of significant control.

Relative Investment of Worker and Alleged Employer

A dancer's investment is limited to her costumes and a padlock. (One dancer testified that she spends $600 per month on costumes, while another testified that she spends approximately $40 per month.) [However,] a dancer's investment is relatively minor [compared] to the considerable investment Circle C has in operating a nightclub.

Degree to Which Employee's Profit and Loss Determined by Employer

A dancer's initiative, hustle, and costume significantly contribute to the amount of her tips. But Circle C has a significant role in drawing customers to its nightclubs. Circle C is responsible for advertising, location, business hours, maintenance, aesthetics, and beverages and food. Given its control over determinants of customer volume, Circle C exercises a high degree of control over a dancer's opportunity for "profit." The dancers are far more akin to wage earners toiling for a living, than to entrepreneurs seeking a return on their capital investments.

Skill and Initiative Required

The dancers do not need long training or highly developed skills to dance at a Circle C nightclub. The ability to develop and maintain rapport with customers is not the type of "initiative" [relevant here]. A dancer's initiative is essentially limited to decisions involving her costumes and dance routines. The dancers do not exhibit the skill or initiative indicative of persons in business for themselves.

Permanency of the Relationship

The parties agree, and the district court found, that most dancers have short-term relationships with Circle C.

On balance, the five factors favor employee status. A dancer has no specialized skills and her only real investment is in her costumes. Circle C exercises significant control over a dancer's behavior and opportunity for "profit." The transient nature of the work force is not enough to remove the dancers from the protections of the FLSA. Here, the economic reality is that the dancers are not in business for themselves but are dependent upon finding employment in the business of others.

District court decision on the FLSA's applicability affirmed; case vacated and remanded on other issues.

DUTIES OF AGENT TO PRINCIPAL

If an agency is created by contract, the agent must perform according to its terms. Regardless of whether the relationship is contractual, agency law also establishes certain *fiduciary duties* that the agent owes the principal.[5] These duties supplement the duties created by an agency contract. They exist because agency is a relationship of trust and confidence. (Often, however, the parties may eliminate or modify fiduciary duties by agreement.) The principal's many remedies for an agent's breach of her fiduciary duties are beyond the scope of this text.

Agent's Duty of Loyalty

Because agency is a relationship of trust and confidence, an agent has a **duty of loyalty** to his principal. Thus, an agent must subordinate his personal concerns by: (1) avoiding conflicts of interest with the principal, and (2) not disclosing confidential information received from the principal.

Conflicts of Interest   An agent whose interests conflict with the principal's interests may be unable to represent his principal effectively. When conducting the principal's business, therefore, an agent is forbidden to *deal with himself*. For example, an agent authorized to sell property cannot sell that property to himself. Many courts extend the rule to include transactions with the agent's relatives or business associates or with business organizations in which the agent has an interest. However, an agent may engage in self-dealing transactions if the principal consents. For this consent to be effective, the agent must disclose all relevant facts to the principal before dealing with the principal on his own behalf.

Unless the principal agrees otherwise, an agent also is forbidden to *compete with the principal* regarding the agency business so long as he remains an agent. Thus, an agent employed to purchase specific property may not buy it himself if the principal still desires it. As the following *Chernow* case states, moreover, an agent ordinarily may not solicit customers for a planned competing business while still employed by the principal.

Finally, an agent who is authorized to make a certain transaction cannot *act on behalf of the other party* to the transaction unless the principal knowingly consents. Thus, one ordinarily cannot act as agent for both parties to a transaction without first disclosing the double role to, and obtaining the consent of, both principals. Here, the agent must disclose to each principal all the factors reasonably affecting that principal's decision. Occasionally, though, an agent who acts as a middleman may serve both parties to a transaction without notifying either. For instance, an agent may simultaneously be employed as a "finder" by a firm seeking suitable businesses to acquire and a firm looking for prospective buyers, so long as neither principal expects the agent to advise it or negotiate for it.

---

[5]Despite certain exceptions noted later, a *gratuitous agent* usually has the same fiduciary duties as a paid agent. But this is true only so long as a gratuitous agent continues to act as an agent. In other words, a gratuitous agent need not perform as promised, he normally can terminate the agency without incurring liability, and his fiduciary duties cease once the agency ends. However, a gratuitous agent *is* liable for failing to perform as promised when his promise causes the principal to rely upon him to undertake certain acts, and the principal suffers losses because she refrained from performing those acts herself.

A *subagent* owes the agent (his principal) all the duties agents owe their principals. A subagent who knows of the original principal's existence also owes that principal all the duties agents owe their principals, except for duties arising solely from the original principal's contract with the agent. Finally, the agent who appointed the subagent generally is liable to the original principal when the principal is harmed by the subagent's conduct.

CHERNOW v. REYES   570 A.2d 1282 (N.J. Ct. App. 1990)

R onald Chernow is in the business of auditing telephone bills for customers. Typically, he determines whether the customers' phone equipment is in place, properly billed, and in working order; checks for overcharges; and receives half of any overcharge refund the customer receives from the telephone company. In October 1982, Chernow hired Angelo Reyes as an auditor. The employment lasted until July 1983, when Reyes either quit or was fired.

Prior to leaving Chernow's employ and without his knowledge, Reyes took various steps to form and operate a business that competed with Chernow's business. Most importantly, he obtained three auditing contracts and performed work under those contracts during that period. He also solicited a fourth account, but did no work for that firm until after ceasing to work for Chernow. None of these businesses was an existing customer of Chernow. In addition, Reyes's soliciting and auditing activities did not take place during his regular working hours, which he devoted to Chernow's business.

Chernow sued Reyes for breach of his agent's duty of loyalty. The trial court held for Reyes. Its main reason was that Reyes's customers were neither clients of Chernow nor within the pool of businesses Chernow was soliciting. Chernow appealed. ∞

Stein, Judge   An employee owes a duty of loyalty to the employer and must not, while employed, act contrary to the employer's interest. "Unless otherwise agreed, an agent is subject to a duty not to compete with the principal concerning the subject matter of his agency." *Restatement (Second) of Agency* section 393. Comment e to section 393 states:

. . . [B]efore the end of his employment, [the agent] can properly purchase a rival business and upon termination of employment immediately compete. *He is not, however, entitled to solicit customers for such rival business before the end of his employment nor can he properly do other similar acts in direct competition with the employer's business.* [Emphasis added.]

By engaging in a competitive enterprise, Reyes crossed the line between permissible preparation to change jobs and actionable conduct. Chernow was entitled to expect that a person on his payroll would not undertake to pursue competitive commercial opportunities. The protection accorded is not limited to the diversion of an employer's customers. It extends to pursuing and transacting business within the larger pool of potential customers who might have been solicited by the employer.

Judgment reversed in favor of Chernow.

Confidentiality   Unless otherwise agreed, an agent may not *use or disclose confidential information* acquired through the agency. Confidential information means facts that are valuable to the principal because they are not widely known or that would harm the principal's business if they became widely known. Examples include the principal's business plans, financial condition, contract bids, technological discoveries, manufacturing methods, customer files, and other trade secrets.[6] In the absence of an agreement to the contrary,[7] an agent may compete with her principal after termination of the agency. But as the following *ABKCO* case illustrates, the

duty not to use or disclose confidential information continues.[8] The former agent may, however, utilize general knowledge and skills acquired during the agency.

---

[6]Liability for misappropriation of trade secrets is discussed in Chapter 8.

[7]Agreements not to compete are discussed in Chapter 15.

[8]On the patent and trade secrets problems that arise when an employee or a former employee tries to utilize ideas, discoveries, or inventions found or created during the course of her employment, see Chapter 8.

I n 1963, a song called "He's So Fine" was a huge hit in the United States and Great Britain. In February 1971, Bright Tunes Music Corporation, the copyright holder of "He's So Fine," sued ex-Beatle George Harrison and Harrisongs, Music, Ltd. in federal district court. Bright Tunes claimed that the Harrison composition "My Sweet Lord" infringed its copyright to "He's So Fine." At this time, Harrison's business affairs were handled by ABKCO Music, Inc. and Allen B. Klein, its president. Shortly after the suit began, Klein unsuccessfully tried to settle it by having ABKCO purchase Bright Tunes.

Shortly thereafter, Bright Tunes went into receivership, and it did not resume the suit until 1973. At this time, coincidentally, ABKCO's management contract with Harrison expired. In late 1975 and early 1976, however, Klein continued his efforts to have ABKCO purchase Bright Tunes. As part of these efforts, he gave Bright Tunes three schedules summarizing Harrison's royalty income from "My Sweet Lord," information he possessed because of his previous service to Harrison. Throughout the 1973–76 period, Harrison's attorneys had been trying to settle the copyright infringement suit with Bright Tunes. Because Klein's activities not only gave Bright Tunes information about the economic potential of its suit but also gave it an economic alternative to settling with Harrison, Klein may have impeded Harrison's efforts to settle.

When the copyright infringement suit finally came to trial in 1976, the court found that Harrison had infringed Bright Tunes' copyright. The issue of damages was scheduled for trial at a later date and this trial was delayed for some time. In 1978, ABKCO purchased the "He's So Fine" copyright and all rights to the infringement suit from Bright Tunes. This made ABKCO the plaintiff in the 1979 trial for damages on the infringement suit. At trial, Harrison counterclaimed for damages resulting from Klein's and ABKCO's alleged breaches of the duty of loyalty. Finding a breach of duty, the district judge issued a complex order reducing ABKCO's recovery. ABKCO appealed. ∽

Pierce, Circuit Judge The relationship between Harrison and ABKCO prior to termination of the management agreement in 1973 was that of principal and agent. An agent has a duty not to use confidential knowledge acquired in his employment in competition with his principal. This duty exists as well after the employment as during its continuance. On the other hand, use of information based on general business knowledge is not covered by the rule, and the former agent is permitted to compete with his former principal in reliance on such publicly available information. The principal issue before us, then, is whether Klein (hence, ABKCO) improperly used confidential information, gained as Harrison's former agent, in negotiating for the purchase of Bright Tunes' stock in 1975–76.

One aspect of this inquiry concerns the nature of the schedules of "My Sweet Lord" earnings which Klein furnished to Bright Tunes in connection with the 1975–76 negotiations. It appears that at least some of [this] information was confidential. The evidence is not at all convincing that the information was publicly available.

Another aspect of the breach of duty issue concerns the timing and nature of Klein's entry into the negotiation picture and the manner in which he became a plaintiff in this action. We find this case analogous to those where an employee, with the use of information acquired through his former employment, completes for his own benefit a transaction originally undertaken on the former employer's behalf. Klein had commenced a purchase transaction with Bright Tunes in 1971 on behalf of Harrison, which he pursued on his own account after termination of his fiduciary relationship with Harrison. Klein pursued the later discussions armed with the intimate knowledge not only of Harrison's business affairs, but of the value of this lawsuit. Taking all of these circumstances together, we agree that Klein's conduct during the period 1975–78 did not meet the standard required of him as a former fiduciary.

District court decision in Harrison's favor on the breach of duty issue affirmed.

Agent's Duty to Obey Instructions

Because an agent acts under the principal's control and for the principal's benefit, she has a duty to *obey the principal's reasonable instructions* for carrying out the agency business. However, a gratuitous agent need not obey his principal's order to continue to act as an agent. Also, agents generally have no duty to obey orders to behave illegally or unethically. Thus, a sales agent need not follow directions to misrepresent the quality of the principal's goods, and professionals such as attorneys and accountants are not obligated to obey directions that conflict with the ethical rules of their professions.

Agent's Duty to Act with Care and Skill

A paid agent must *possess and exercise the degree of care and skill* that is standard in the locality for the kind of work the agent performs. A gratuitous agent need only exercise the care and skill required of nonagents who perform similar gratuitous undertakings. Paid agents who represent that they possess a higher than customary level of skill may be held to a correspondingly higher standard of performance.

Similarly, an agent's duty may change if the principal and the agent agree that the agent must possess and exercise greater or lesser than customary care and skill.

Agent's Duty to Notify the Principal

An agent must promptly communicate to the principal matters within the agent's knowledge that are reasonably relevant to the agency business and that he knows or should know are of concern to the principal. As the following *Levin* case suggests, this **duty to notify** sometimes is treated as one facet of the duty to act with care and skill. The basis for the duty to notify is the principal's interest in being informed of matters that are important to the agency business.

However, there is no duty to notify where the agent receives privileged or confidential information. For example, an attorney may acquire confidential information from a client and thus be obligated not to disclose it to a second client. If the attorney cannot properly represent the second client without revealing this information, he should refuse to represent that client.

LEVIN v. KASMIR WORLD TRAVEL   540 N.Y.S.2d 639 (N.Y. Civ. Ct. 1989)

I*n July 1987, Marsha Levin bought her daughter a round-trip plane ticket from New York City to Paris from Kasmir World Travel, Inc. Upon arriving in Paris, Mrs. Levin's daughter was denied entry and was placed on the next return flight to the United States because she did not have a visa. The apparent reason for the visa requirement was the French government's effort to deal with terrorist activities directed at Americans abroad. Neither Mrs. Levin nor her daughter was aware of the requirement; indeed, a few years earlier Mrs. Levin had traveled to France without being required to present a visa.*

Levin sued Kasmir for failing to notify her about the visa requirement. Kasmir moved to dismiss her complaint. ∞

Saxe, Judge   The duty of a travel agent includes such responsibilities as verifying or confirming reservations. Travel agents are required to have the degree of skill and knowledge requisite to the calling; to exercise good faith and reasonable skill, care, and diligence; and to possess reasonable knowledge of the types of carriers, lines, and accommodations that they select for their principals, and all significant attendant matters. Beyond the duty to confirm travel reservations, travel agents

should provide information which is necessary and of importance to the traveler.

Kasmir had a duty to notify the traveler about the need for a visa before entering France. This is in accord with the expanding role of the travel agent to provide all relevant and necessary information to the consumer who reasonably relies on the agent's expertise. Here, it was reasonable to expect Kasmir to alert its [principal] to important changes in the visa requirements of foreign nations. It was also reasonable for Mrs. Levin to rely on Kasmir to supply this information. The travel agency was clearly in a position to assemble and disseminate this basic and significant type of travel information.

I am aware of Kasmir's contention that its relationship to the claimant was merely that of a ticketing agent, and that consequently duties beyond the actual sale of the ticket could not implicate such an agent. [But] information concerning entry or visa requirements into foreign lands is so basic to the purchase or sale of the ticket that the seller must be obliged to furnish it to all affected consumers.

Kasmir's motion to dismiss denied.

Agent's Duties to Account

An agent's duties of loyalty and care require that she give the principal any money or property received in the course of the agency business. This includes profits resulting from the agent's breach of the duty of loyalty, or other duties. It also includes incidental benefits received through the agency business. Examples include bribes, kickbacks, and gifts from parties with whom the agent deals on the principal's behalf. However, the principal and the agent may agree that the agent can retain certain benefits received during the agency. Courts may imply such an agreement when it is customary for agents to retain tips or accept entertainment while doing the principal's business.

Another type of **duty to account** concerns agents whose business involves collections, receipts, or expenditures. Such agents must keep accurate records and accounts of all transactions and disclose these to the principal once the principal makes a reasonable demand for them. Also, an agent who obtains or holds property for the principal usually may not commingle that property with her own property. For example, an agent ordinarily cannot deposit the principal's funds in her own name or in her own bank account.

DUTIES OF PRINCIPAL TO AGENT

If an agency is formed by contract, the contract normally states the duties the principal owes the agent. In addition, the law implies certain duties from the existence of an agency relationship, however formed. The most important of these duties are the principal's obligations to **compensate** the agent, to **reimburse** the agent for money spent in the principal's service, and to **indemnify** the agent for losses suffered in conducting the principal's busi-

ness.[9] These duties generally can be eliminated or modified by agreement between the parties. The agent's various remedies for breach of these duties are beyond the scope of this text.

Duty to Compensate Agent

If the agency contract states the compensation the agent is to receive, it usually controls questions about the agent's pay. In other cases, the relationship of the parties and the surrounding circumstances determine whether and in what amount the agent is to be compensated. If there is no contract provision on compensation, for example, a principal generally is not required to pay for undertakings that she did not request, services to which she did not consent, and tasks that typically are undertaken without pay. Also, a principal usually need not compensate an agent who has materially breached the agency contract or has committed a serious breach of a fiduciary duty. Where compensation is due but its amount is not expressly stated, the amount is the market price or the customary price

---

[9]Although there is no duty to compensate a gratuitous agent, the principal still owes such an agent the other two duties in the absence of an agreement to the contrary. An agent's duties to a subagent are the same as a principal's duties to an agent. If there is no agreement to the contrary, however, the original principal has no contractual liability to a subagent. For example, such a principal normally is not obligated to compensate a subagent. But a principal must reimburse and indemnify subagents as he would agents.

A principal may also have other duties besides the three listed, including the duties to provide the agent with an opportunity for service, not interfere with the agent's work, keep accounts, act in a manner not harmful to the agent's reputation or self-esteem, and (in the case of employees) maintain a safe workplace. The last duty has been greatly affected, if not superseded, by workers' compensation systems and the Occupational Safety and Health Act, which are discussed in Chapter 50.

for the agent's services or, if neither is available, their reasonable value.

Sometimes an agent's compensation depends on the accomplishment of a specific result. For instance, a plaintiff's attorney may be retained on a contingent fee basis (being paid a certain percentage of the recovery if the suit succeeds or is settled), or a real estate broker may be entitled to a fee only if a suitable buyer is found. In such cases, the agent is not entitled to compensation unless he achieves the result within the time stated or, if no time is stated, within a reasonable time. This is true no matter how much effort or money the agent expends. However, the principal must cooperate with the agent in achieving the result and must not do anything to frustrate the agent's efforts. Otherwise, the agent is entitled to compensation despite the failure to perform as specified.

Duties of Reimbursement and Indemnity

If an agent makes expressly or impliedly authorized expenditures while acting on the principal's behalf, the agent normally is entitled to **reimbursement** for those expenditures. Unless otherwise agreed, for example, an agent requested to make overnight trips as part of his agency duties can recover reasonable transportation and hotel expenses.

A principal's duty of reimbursement overlaps with her duty of **indemnity.** Agency law implies a promise by the principal to indemnify an agent for losses that result from the agent's authorized activities. These include authorized payments made on the principal's behalf and payments on contracts on which the agent was authorized to become liable. A principal may also have to indemnify an agent if the agent's authorized acts constitute a breach of contract or a tort for which the agent is required to pay damages to a third party.

So long as the principal did not benefit from such behavior, however, he is *not* required to indemnify an agent for losses resulting: (1) from unauthorized acts, or (2) solely from the agent's negligence or other fault. Even where the principal directed the agent to commit a tortious act, moreover, there is no duty to indemnify if the agent knew the act was tortious. But the principal must indemnify the agent for tort damages resulting from authorized conduct that the agent did not believe was tortious. For

example, if a principal directs his agent to repossess goods located on another's property and the agent, believing her acts legal, becomes liable for conversion or trespass, the principal must indemnify the agent for the damages the agent pays.

TERMINATION OF AN AGENCY

An agency can terminate in many ways.[10] These fall under two general headings: (1) termination by act of the parties, and (2) termination by operation of law.

Termination by Act of the Parties

Termination by act of the parties occurs:

1. *At a time or upon the happening of an event stated in the agreement.* If no such time or event is stated, the agency terminates after a reasonable time.

2. *When a specified result has been accomplished, if the agency was created to accomplish a specified result.* For example, if an agency's only objective is to sell certain property, the agency terminates when the property is sold.

3. *By mutual agreement of the parties,* at any time.

4. *At the option of either party.* This is called **revocation** when done by the principal and **renunciation** when done by the agent. Revocation or renunciation occurs when either party manifests to the other that he does not wish the agency to continue. This includes conduct inconsistent with the agency's continuance. For example, an agent may learn that his principal has hired another agent to perform the same job.

A party can revoke or renounce even if this violates the agency agreement. However, although either party has the *power* to terminate in such cases, there is no *right* to do so. This means that where one party terminates in violation of the agreement, she need not perform any further, but she may be liable for damages to the other party.

---

[10]The rules stated below generally apply to the termination of a subagent's authority as well. In general, a subagency terminates when relations between either the principal and the agent or the agent and the subagent are terminated in any of the ways to be described.

However, a gratuitous agency normally is terminable by either party without liability. Also, the terminating party is not liable where the revocation or renunciation is justified by the other party's serious breach of a fiduciary duty.

Termination by Operation of Law

Termination by operation of law usually involves situations where it is reasonable to believe that the principal would not wish the agent to act further, or where accomplishment of the agency objectives has become impossible or illegal. Although courts may recognize exceptions in certain cases, an agency relationship usually is terminated by:

1. *The death of the principal.* This normally is true even where the agent has no notice of the principal's death.

2. *The death of the agent.*

3. *The principal's permanent loss of capacity.* This is a *permanent* loss of capacity occurring *after* creation of the agency—most often, due to the principal's insanity. The principal's permanent incapacity ends the agency even without notice to the agent. But a brief period of insanity may only temporarily suspend the agency for the time the principal is insane.

4. *The agent's loss of capacity to perform the agency business.* The scope of this basis for termination is unclear. As Chapter 35 states, an agent who becomes insane or otherwise incapacitated after the agency is formed still can bind his principal to contracts with third parties. Thus, it probably makes little sense to treat the agency as terminated in such cases. As a result, termination under this heading may be limited to such situations as the loss of a license needed to perform agency duties.

5. *Changes in the value of the agency property or subject matter* (e.g., a significant decline in the value of land to be sold by an agent).

6. *Changes in business conditions* (e.g., a much lower supply and a much increased price for goods to be purchased by an agent).

7. *The loss or destruction of the agency property or subject matter or the termination of the principal's interest therein* (e.g., where a house to be sold by a real estate broker burns down or is taken by a mortgage holder to satisfy a debt owed by the principal).

8. *Changes in the law that make the agency business illegal* (e.g., where drugs to be sold by an agent are banned by the government).

9. *The principal's bankruptcy*—as to transactions the agent should realize the principal no longer desires. For example, consider the likely effect of the principal's bankruptcy on an agency to purchase antiques for the principal's home versus its likely effect on an agency to purchase necessities of life for the principal.

10. *The agent's bankruptcy*—where the agent's financial condition affects his ability to serve the principal. This could occur where an agent is employed to purchase goods on his own credit for the principal.

11. *Impossibility of performance by the agent.* This covers various events, some of which fall within the categories just stated. The *Restatement*'s definition of impossibility, for example, includes: (*a*) destruction of the agency subject matter, (*b*) termination of the principal's interest in the agency subject matter (as, for example, by the principal's bankruptcy), and (*c*) changes in the law or in other circumstances that make it impossible for the agent to accomplish the agency's aims.

12. *A serious breach of the agent's duty of loyalty.*

13. *The outbreak of war*—where this leads the agent to the reasonable belief that his services are no longer desired. An example might be the outbreak of war between the principal's country and the agent's country.

Termination of Agency Powers Given as Security

An agency power given as security for a duty owed by the principal, sometimes called an *agency coupled with an interest,* is an exception to some of the termination rules just discussed. Here, the agent has an interest in the subject matter of the agency that is distinct from the principal's interest and that is not exercised for the principal's benefit. This interest exists to benefit the agent or a third person by securing performance of an obligation owed by the principal. A common example is a secured loan agreement authorizing a lender (the agent) to sell property used as security if the debtor (the principal) defaults. For instance, suppose that Allen lends Peters $100,000 and Peters gives Allen a lien or security interest on Peters's land to secure the loan. The agreement might authorize Allen to act as Peters's "agent" to sell the land if Peters fails to repay the loan.

Because the power given the "agent" in such cases is not for the principal's benefit, it sometimes is said that an agency coupled with an interest is not truly an agency. In any event, courts distinguish it from genuine agency relations in which the agent is compensated from the profits or proceeds of property held for the principal's benefit. For example, if an agent is promised a commission for selling the principal's property, the relationship is not an agency coupled with an interest. Here, the power exercised by the agent (selling the principal's property) benefits the principal. The following *Smith* case provides another example.

Why is the agency coupled with an interest important? The main reason is that it is *not terminated* by: (1) the principal's revocation, (2) the principal's or the agent's loss of capacity, (3) the agent's death, and (4) (usually) the principal's death. However, unless an agency coupled with an interest is held for the benefit of a third party, the agent can voluntarily surrender it. Of course, an agency coupled with an interest terminates when the principal performs her obligation.

Effect of Termination on Agent's Authority

Sometimes former agents continue to act on their ex-principals' behalf even though the agency has ended. Do such "agents" still have authority to bind their former principals? As Figure 1 states, once an agency terminates by any of the means just described, the agent's *express* and *implied* authority end as well.

Third parties who are unaware of the termination, however, may reasonably believe that an ex-agent still has authority. To protect third parties who rely on such a reasonable appearance of authority, an agent's *apparent authority* often persists after termination. Thus, a former agent may be able to bind the principal under his apparent authority even though the agency has ended. But as Figure 1 also states, apparent authority ends where the termination was caused by: (1) the principal's death, (2) the principal's loss of capacity, or (3) impossibility.[11] Note from the previous discussion that certain other bases for termination may also end the agent's apparent authority because they fit within the broad category of impossibility.

Notice to Third Parties   Apparent authority also ends when the third party receives appropriate *notice* of the termination. In general, any facts known to the third party that reasonably indicate the agency's termination constitute suitable notice. Some bases for termination by operation of law (e.g., changed business conditions) may provide such notice.

To protect themselves against unwanted liability, however, prudent principals may want to notify third parties themselves. The required type of notification varies with the third party in question.

1. *For third parties who have previously dealt with the agent or who have begun to deal with the agent,* **actual notification** *is necessary.* This can be accomplished by: (1) a direct personal statement to the third party; or (2) a writing delivered to the third party personally, to his place of business, or to some other place reasonably believed to be appropriate.

2. *For all other parties,* **constructive notification** *suffices.* Usually, these other parties are aware of the

---

[11]*Restatement (Second) of Agency* § 124A, comment a; and § 133 (1959).

FIGURE 1

Termination of an Agent's Authority after Termination of the Agency

TYPE OF TERMINATION	ACTUAL AUTHORITY	APPARENT AUTHORITY
By Acts of the Parties	Ceases	Persists unless appropriate notice or notification to third party
By Operation of Law	Ceases	Ceases if termination by principal's death or loss of capacity, or by impossibility; persists in other cases unless appropriate notice or notification to third party

agency but did no business with the agent. Constructive notification normally can be accomplished by advertising the agency's termination in a newspaper of general circulation in the place where the agency business regularly was carried on. If no suitable publication exists, notification by other means reasonably likely to inform third parties—for example, posting a notice in public places—may be enough.

SMITH v. CYNFAX CORPORATION   618 A.2d 937 (N.J. Super. Ct. 1992)

Brenda Smith was injured by a falling ceiling in a building owned by the Cynfax Corporation. She retained Floyd Goldsman as her attorney, and Goldsman sued Cynfax on her behalf. On February 4, 1992, Cynfax's insurer, the Cumberland Mutual Fire Insurance Company, made Smith a $7,000 settlement offer through Goldsman. Goldsman immediately tried to inform Smith of the offer but learned that she had died on February 2.

Goldsman later accepted Cumberland's offer to Smith. Still later, Cumberland refused to pay Smith's estate the $7,000. Smith's estate then moved to enforce the alleged settlement agreement. One issue before the court was whether Goldsman had authority to accept Cumberland's offer on Smith's behalf. ⌒

Yanoff, Judge   As Mrs. Smith's attorney, Goldsman was an agent of his client. For Goldsman to have accepted the settlement offer, his agency must have survived the death of his client. Goldsman's agency immediately ceased when his client died. It makes no difference that the settlement negotiations were undertaken in good faith and in ignorance of Smith's death. A general principle of agency is that the death of the principal terminates the authority of the agent. Knowledge of the principal's death only becomes an issue where the agency is derived from a written power of attorney [citing a New Jersey statute].

An agency coupled with an interest survives the principal, even after notice of his death. This requires that the agent have some interest, such as a security interest, in the subject-matter of the agency independent of the power conferred upon him by the principal. An interest merely in the proceeds which will arise from the exercise of the power of the agency is not sufficient for this purpose. Goldsman's agency was controlled by an agreement which provided that "the law firm will protect your legal rights and do all necessary legal work to represent you in this matter" in exchange for a percentage contingency fee. This created an interest in the proceeds of a successful exercise of the powers of the agency, not in its subject-matter. An attorney's contingent fee contract creates an agency which is not coupled with an interest and which terminates upon the death of the principal.

Motion of Smith's estate denied; Cumberland wins.

ETHICAL AND PUBLIC POLICY CONCERNS

1. Under one of the agent's duties to account, an agent might be required to return to the principal gifts from third parties with whom the agent deals on the principal's behalf. Where the gift is a genuine token of appreciation, the principal may be getting a windfall. What can justify this result?

2. A well-known ethical theory called utilitarianism generally asserts that the moral worth of actions should be judged by their tendency to promote net aggregate satisfaction. Some people regard the maximization of social wealth as a reasonable measuring rod for net aggregate satisfaction. Under a wealth-maximization criterion, does the rule forbidding ex-agents from using or disclosing confidential information make sense? How might the rule promote wealth-maximization? How might it hinder wealth-maximization? In attempting to answer this question, you might consult the introduction to the section on trade secrets in Chapter 8.

What other ethical considerations might justify the rule against the disclosure of confidential information by an ex-agent? Are they utilitarian in the sense defined above?

PROBLEM CASES

1. VIP Tours, Inc. arranged tours of central Florida's attractions. Cynthia Hoogland conducted 29 such tours for VIP between July 1980 and March 1981. Both Hoogland and VIP considered Hoogland an independent contractor. She worked for VIP only when it needed her services, and could reject particular assignments. She was also free to work for other tour services, and did so.

Once Hoogland accepted a job from VIP, she was told where to report and was given instructions about the job. She also had to use a VIP-furnished vehicle and wear a uniform with the VIP logo when conducting tours. Aside from ensuring that she departed on time, however, VIP did not tell her how long to stay or what kind of tour to conduct at each tourist attraction. Finally, Hoogland was paid on a per tour basis.

Hoogland later filed a claim for unemployment compensation benefits with the Florida Division of Labor and Employment Security. The Division concluded that she was entitled to these benefits because she was VIP Tours' employee. Was Hoogland an employee or an independent contractor?

2. Tadlock was a tenant on Lest's farm. Without any authorization from Lest, Tadlock ordered a new irrigation pump for the farm from Killinger. Tadlock told Killinger that he was Lest's tenant and that he had authority to purchase a new pump on Lest's behalf. Killinger then installed a new pump and billed Lest for $2,048. Lest denied liability on this bill, claiming that Tadlock's purchase was unauthorized. Tadlock did not have actual authority to purchase the pump, but was his statement to Killinger enough to give him *apparent* authority to make the purchase?

3. 📼 *Video Case.* Jack runs a video card shop. Linda, who knows little or nothing about baseball or baseball cards, agreed to run the shop for Jack while he went out for dinner. Jack told Linda that she could sell any card for the price marked on the card. Then, he pointed to a case containing the more expensive cards, and said that he might negotiate the price on those cards if customers would wait until he returned. Shortly after Jack left, Linda sold a small boy an Ernie Banks rookie card for $12. The card bore a price sticker which stated: "1200." The boy apparently was unaware of the card's true value

and did not try to negotiate its price. Did Linda have express, implied, or apparent authority to sell the card for $12? In any event, on what bases might Jack sue her for his losses?

4. 📼 *Video Case.* See "Martin Manufacturing." Martin, the president of Martin Manufacturing, fires a purchasing agent named Mitch because Mitch has been taking kickbacks from suppliers. Martin also withholds Mitch's last paycheck until Martin can determine how much Mitch's misbehavior has cost him.

Has Mitch breached any fiduciary duty or duties to Martin? If so, which ones? Will Mitch be required to give Martin the amount of any kickbacks he has received? Can Martin fire Mitch without incurring liability under these circumstances? Finally, is Martin justified in withholding Mitch's paycheck?

5. Productive Automated Systems Corporation (PASCO), which builds palletizers for use in industrial packaging systems, entered into a Sales Agency Agreement with CPI Systems, Inc. The agreement said that CPI would serve as PASCO's sales representative in Arkansas, Louisiana, Oklahoma, and Texas. Previously, CPI had bought products from PASCO for resale to others, and that relationship continued after completion of the Sales Agency Agreement. Later, CPI submitted a bid to BASF Corporation, a New Jersey firm, to supply a system for a BASF plant in Pennsylvania. After getting the bid, CPI ordered a PASCO palletizer to help complete the system. Later, though, CPI canceled both the order and the Sales Agency Agreement, and bought a palletizer from one of PASCO's competitors.

Did CPI breach its duty of loyalty to PASCO under the Sales Agency Agreement?

6. Ted and Sharon Markland arranged for a trip to the Virgin Islands with Travel Travel Southland, Inc. Travel Travel made the necessary arrangements with Eastern Airlines, which was having financial problems. The Marklands then paid Travel Travel $6,548 for the trip. There was conflicting testimony as to whether Travel Travel warned the Marklands about Eastern's difficulties, and for purposes of this question assume that it did not. It is also unclear how much the Marklands knew about Eastern's troubles, but assume that they had at least a general knowledge of them.

Ten days after the Marklands reached the Virgin Islands, their hotel informed them that their reservations no longer were valid because Eastern had not paid for them and (due to its declaring bankruptcy) most likely would not. The Marklands wound up having to pay the hotel an additional $4,900, and also had to expend another $1,756 for a return flight to the United States. Afterwards, they sued Travel Travel for failing to advise them about Eastern's precarious position. Did Travel Travel breach either its duty of care and skill or its duty to notify?

7. In February 1989, Thomas Fix arranged for a Florida vacation package for himself and his sister with Travel Help, a travel agency. The travel agent selected an Eastern Airlines package that included Eastern vouchers for a rental car, Howard Johnson's Fountain Park, and Sea World. Aware of the labor and other problems Eastern was experiencing at that time, Fix's sister contacted the agent several times requesting that all the arrangements be made with another airline. The agent assured her that the flights could be changed and that the vouchers would be honored. After Eastern went into bankruptcy on March 9, 1989, the agent arranged for Fix and his sister to be transported to Florida on a different airline. After they arrived, however, the providers of the voucher bookings refused to honor Eastern's vouchers. Did the agent breach a duty to Fix (and his sister)? If so, which one? You can assume that the travel agent was acting for both Fix and his sister, and that the communications to the agent by Fix's sister were communications to an agent by his principal.

8. Southeastern Agri-Systems, Inc. was an agent for Otto Niederer. James Stanford was Agri-Systems' president and sole employee. Niederer instructed Stanford to accept payment for the sale of some equipment owned by Niederer, to deduct his commission from the payment, and to wire the remainder to Niederer. Instead, Stanford diverted the funds to his own purposes and refused to pay Niederer the amount due. When sued individually for breach of the agent's duty to obey, Stanford argued that Niederer had employed Agri-Systems as its agent, that he was merely an employee of Agri-Systems, and that he thus owed no duty to Niederer. Is Stanford correct?

9. Wormhoudt Lumber Company employed Jon Cloyd to find construction jobs that would utilize Wormhoudt's materials. Cloyd would find property owners seeking to build, and link them up with construction contractors. Cloyd computed costs for materials and labor, including a profit for the contractor; if the contractor and the owner were satisfied with the terms, they would make a contract between themselves. If the contractor bought his materials from Wormhoudt and paid it within 30 days of the billing, it would get a 10 percent discount. Cloyd persuaded several contractors to split the 10 percent discount with him, in exchange for being recommended by him. Has Cloyd breached his duty to account?

10. Stanley Mazur owned an Oldsmobile Cutlass and a small Subaru pickup truck. He asked his insurance agent, Ken Curtis, to arrange "full coverage" on the truck similar to the coverage on his Cutlass. Although the policy on the Cutlass included personal injury protection, Curtis negligently failed to include such protection in the policy he obtained for the Subaru. Later, Mazur suffered personal injury from an accident in which he was involved while driving the Subaru. Because the policy did not cover such injury, he was unable to recover for it from the insurer, the Selected Risks Insurance Company.

Mazur recovered against Curtis for Curtis's failure to procure the requested coverage. Curtis then sued to have Selected indemnify him for this loss. Is Selected required to indemnify Curtis? Why or why not? Assume that Curtis was acting as an agent for Selected as well as for Mazur.

11. 🎞 *Video Case.* See "Martin Manufacturing." Immediately after being fired by Martin Manufacturing in Problem case 4 of this chapter, Mitch decides to squeeze one last bit of profit from his relationship with Martin. He calls a supplier with whom he has dealt on many occasions and orders several cases of fasteners on Martin's behalf. Later, he resells the fasteners himself, pocketing the price. Is Martin liable to the supplier for the fasteners? In any event, what should Martin do in order to protect itself in cases like this one?

Third-Party Relations of the Principal and the Agent

By letting principals contract through their agents and thereby multiply their dealings, agency law stimulates business activity. For this process to succeed, there must be rules for determining when the principal and the agent are liable on the agent's contracts. Principals need to predict and control their liability on agreements their agents make. Also, third parties need assurance that such agreements really bind the principal. Furthermore, both agents and third parties have an interest in knowing when an *agent* is bound on these contracts. The first half of this chapter discusses the principal's and the agent's contract liability.

While acting on the principal's behalf, agents sometimes harm third parties. Normally, this makes the agent liable to the injured party in tort. Sometimes, moreover, a *principal* is liable for his agent's torts. Because tort judgments can be expensive, the rules for determining the principal's and the agent's tort liability are of great concern to principals, their agents, and third parties. Thus, we examine these subjects in this chapter's second half. ∞

CONTRACT LIABILITY OF THE PRINCIPAL

A principal normally is liable on a contract made by his agent if the agent had **express, implied,** or **apparent authority** to make the contract. Occasionally, however, a principal's contract liability may be affected by other factors. Even where the agent lacked authority to contract, moreover, a principal may bind herself by later **ratifying** the agent's contract.

Express Authority

As discussed in Chapter 34, **express authority** is created by a principal's *words* to his agent, whether written or oral. Thus, an agent has express authority to bind her principal to a contract if the principal clearly told the agent that she could make that contract on the principal's behalf. For example, suppose that Payne instructs his agent Andrews to contract to sell a specific antique chair for $400 or more. If Andrews contracts to sell the chair to Tucker for $425, Payne is liable to Tucker on the basis of Andrews's express authority. However, Andrews would not have express authority to sell the chair for $375, or to sell a different chair.

Implied Authority

Often it is difficult for a principal to specify his agent's authority completely and precisely. Thus, agents can also bind their principals on the basis of the agent's **implied authority.** As Chapter 34 states, an agent generally has implied authority to do whatever it is reasonable to assume that his principal wanted him to do, in light of the principal's express statements and the surrounding circumstances. Relevant factors include the principal's express statements, the nature of the agency, the acts reasonably necessary to carry on the agency business, the acts customarily done when conducting that business, and the relations between principal and agent.

Implied authority usually derives from a grant of express authority by the principal. On occasion, however, implied authority may exist even though there is no relevant grant of express authority. Here, courts generally derive implied authority from the nature of the agency business, the relations between principal and agent, customs in the trade, and other facts and circumstances. For example, there may be implied authority to make a certain contract if the agent has made similar past contracts with the principal's knowledge and without his objection.

No matter what its source, an agent's implied authority cannot conflict with the principal's express statements. Thus, there is no implied authority to contract where a principal has limited her agent's authority by express statement or clear implication and the contract would conflict with that limitation. But as we will see, *apparent authority* may still exist in such cases.

Examples of Implied Authority   Courts have created general rules or presumptions for determining the implied authority of certain agents in certain situations. For example:

1. An agent hired to *manage a business* normally has implied authority to make contracts that are reasonably necessary for conducting the business or that are customary in the business. These include contracts for obtaining equipment and supplies, making repairs, employing employees, and selling goods or services. As the following *Hausam* case suggests, however, a manager ordinarily has no power to borrow money or issue negotiable instruments in the principal's name unless the principal is a banking or financial concern regularly performing such activities.

2. An agent given *full control over real property* has implied authority to contract for repairs and insurance and may rent the property if this is customary. But such an agent may not sell the property or allow any third-party liens or other interests to be taken on it.

3. Agents appointed to *sell the principal's goods* may have implied authority to make customary warranties on those goods. In states that still recognize the distinction, the general agent described in Chapter 34 is more likely to have such authority than a special agent.

Apparent Authority

As Chapter 34 stated, **apparent authority** arises when the *principal's behavior* causes a third party to form a *reasonable belief* that the agent is authorized to act in a certain way. In other words, apparent authority is based on: (1) communications by the principal to the third party, (2) that create a reasonable appearance of authority in the agent. Background factors such as trade customs and established business practices often determine whether it is reasonable for the third party to believe that the agent has authority.

Principals can give their agents apparent authority through the statements they make, or tell their agents to make, to third parties; and through the actions they knowingly allow their agents to take. Thus, a principal might create apparent authority by telling a third party that the agent has certain authority, or by directing the agent to do the same. A principal might also create apparent authority by appointing his agent to a position that customarily involves the authority to make certain contracts. For instance, if Peter makes Albert his sales manager, and if that position customarily involves the power to sell the firm's goods, Albert would have apparent authority to contract to sell those products. Here, Peter's behavior in appointing Albert to the position of sales manager, as reasonably interpreted in light of business customs, gives Albert apparent authority. However, because agents cannot give themselves apparent authority, there would be no such authority if, without Peter's knowledge or permission, Albert falsely told third parties that he had been promoted to sales manager.

Apparent authority protects third parties who reasonably rely on the principal's manifestations that the agent has authority. It assumes special importance in cases where the principal has told the agent not to make certain contracts that the agent ordinarily would have actual authority to make, but the third party knows nothing about this limitation and has no reason to know about it. For example, a sales agent often can bind his principal to warranties that the principal has forbidden the agent to make, if those warranties are customary in the trade. In states that still recognize the distinction, general agents are more likely to have this kind of apparent authority than are special agents. Suppose that Perry employs Arthur as general sales agent for his manufacturing business. Certain warranties customarily accompany the products Perry sells, and agents like Arthur ordinarily are empowered to give these warranties. But Perry tells Arthur not to make any such warranties to buyers, thus cutting off Arthur's express and implied authority. Despite Perry's orders, however, Arthur makes the usual warranties in a sale to Thomas, who is familiar with customs in the trade. If Thomas did not know about the limitation on Arthur's authority, Perry is bound by Arthur's warranties.

HAUSAM v. SCHNABL   887 P.2d 1076 (Idaho Ct. App. 1994)

John Schnabl ran RW Logging as a sole proprietorship. When John experienced health problems early in 1989, he placed his son Wade in charge of the business. John told Wade that he had authority to hire and fire employees, to seek logging contracts, to assign jobs, and to pay himself whatever he wanted. However, John did not explicitly give Wade the authority to borrow money on the business's behalf.

Nonetheless, Wade borrowed $20,000 for RW in January 1990. He signed a promissory note obligating the business to pay the lender, Neal Hausam, $28,000 on or before July 31, 1990. After Hausam forwarded the $28,000 to RW early in 1990, Wade stopped managing the business and it ceased operations early in 1991. Never having been repaid, Hausam sued John and Wade on the loan obligation. After Hausam obtained a default judgment against Wade, the court dismissed his claim against John. Among other things, the court held that Wade was not authorized to borrow money on RW's behalf. Hausam appealed.

Walters, Chief Judge   Both express and implied authority are forms of actual authority. Express authority refers to that authority which the principal has explicitly granted the agent. Implied authority is necessary, usual, and proper to accomplish or perform express authority. Apparent authority is created when the principal voluntarily places an agent in such a position that a person of ordinary prudence, conversant with the business usages and the nature of a particular business, is justified in believing that the agent is acting pursuant to existing authority.

In the instant case, there clearly was express authority for Wade to operate his father's business.

However, there was not express authority for Wade to borrow money. Therefore, Wade's authority to borrow money, if it existed, must have arisen from either implied or apparent authority.

Hausam asserts that included in the express authority to run a business is the implied authority to acquire the money necessary to operate that business. However, the trial court found that although John had placed Wade in charge of the day-to-day operations of the business, there was no evidence that the authority to borrow money was necessary to those functions. John's uncontradicted testimony was that the business did not need to borrow money at the time Wade obtained the loan from Hausam. John testified that even if the company had been in need of money, he would not have borrowed it from a "stranger." There was no implied authority for Wade to borrow money on behalf of the business.

The apparent authority of the agent is determined by the acts of the principal, not by the acts of the agent. The declarations of an agent, standing alone, are insufficient to prove the grant of power exercised by the agent and to bind the principal to third parties. To establish apparent authority, the principal must do something to lead the third party to believe that the agent has authority. In the instant case, John placed Wade in charge of the day-to-day operations of RW Logging. It cannot be said that such an action could lead Hausam to believe that Wade had authority to borrow money on behalf of RW. An agent with actual authority for one purpose does not thereby become an apparent agent for all other types of transactions.

Trial court judgment in John's favor affirmed on the question of John's contract liability on the loan. However, the court found John liable to Hausam in quasi-contract.

Other Factors Affecting a Principal's Contract Liability

Agent's Notification and Knowledge Sometimes the general agency rules regarding *notification* and *knowledge* affect a principal's contract liability. If a third party gives proper notification to an agent with actual or apparent authority to receive it, the principal is bound as if the notification had been given directly to him. For example, where a contract between Phillips and Thomas made by Phillips's agent Anderson contains a clause allowing Thomas to cancel if she notifies Phillips, she can cancel by notifying Anderson if Anderson has actual or apparent authority to receive the notification. Similarly, notification *to* a third party *by* an agent with the necessary authority is considered notification by the principal.

In certain circumstances, an agent's knowledge of facts is imputed to the principal. This means that the principal's rights and liabilities are what they would have been if the principal had known what the agent knew. Generally, an agent's knowledge is imputed to a principal when it is relevant to activities that the agent is authorized to undertake, or when the agent is under a duty to disclose the knowledge to the principal. Suppose that Ames contracts with Timmons on Pike's behalf, knowing that Timmons is completely mistaken about a matter material to the contract. Even though Pike knew nothing about Timmons's unilateral mistake, Timmons probably can avoid his contract with Pike.[1]

Incapacity of Principal or Agent As we saw in Chapter 34, a principal who lacks capacity at the time an agency is formed usually may avoid the agency, and a principal's permanent loss of capacity after the agency's formation terminates the agency. Where the agency continues to exist, is a principal of limited mental capacity such as a minor or an insane person bound on contracts made by an agent? Subject to the exceptions discussed in Chapter 14, such contracts are voidable at the principal's option. These contracts normally would be voidable if made by the principal himself, and it is difficult to see why acting through an agent should increase the principal's capacity.

Like the principal, an agent can avoid the agency agreement if she lacks capacity at the time it is formed. Where the agency survives, however, the agent's incapacity usually does *not* affect the contract liability of a principal who has capacity. Just as

---

[1]Unilateral mistake is discussed in Chapter 13.

an agent cannot increase the principal's capacity, neither can she diminish it. However, the principal may sometimes escape liability where an agent's incapacity is so extreme that the agent cannot receive or convey ideas, or cannot follow the principal's instructions.

Ratification

Ratification is a process whereby a principal binds himself to an unauthorized act done by an agent, or by a person purporting to act as an agent. Usually, the act in question is a contract. Ratification relates back to the time when the contract was made. It binds the principal as if the agent had possessed authority at that time.

Conduct Amounting to Ratification   Ratification can be express or implied. An *express ratification* occurs when the principal communicates an intent to ratify by words, whether written or oral. *Implied ratification* arises when the principal's behavior evidences an intent to ratify. Examples include the principal's part performance of a contract made by an agent, or the principal's acceptance of benefits under such a contract. Sometimes even a principal's silence, acquiescence, or failure to repudiate the transaction may constitute ratification. This can occur where the principal would be expected to object if he did not consent to the contract, the principal's silence leads the third party to believe that he does consent, and the principal is aware of all relevant facts.

Additional Requirements   Even if a principal's words or behavior indicate an intent to ratify, other requirements must be met before ratification occurs. These requirements have been variously stated; the following list is typical.

1.   The act ratified must be one that was *valid* at the time it was performed. For example, an agent's illegal contract cannot be made binding by the principal's subsequent ratification. However, a contract that was voidable when made due to the principal's incapacity may be ratified by a principal who has later attained or regained capacity.

2.   The principal must have been *in existence* at the time the agent acted. However, as discussed in Chapter 41, corporations may bind themselves to their promoters' preincorporation contracts by adopting such contracts.

3.   When the contract or other act occurred, the agent must have indicated to the third party that she was acting for a principal and not for herself. But the agent need not have disclosed the principal's identity.

4.   The principal must be *legally competent* at the time of ratification. For instance, an insane principal cannot ratify.

5.   As the following *Huppman* case makes clear, the principal must have *knowledge of all material facts* regarding the prior act or contract at the time it is ratified. Here, an agent's knowledge is not imputed to the principal.

6.   The principal must ratify the *entire* act or contract. He cannot ratify the beneficial parts of a contract and reject those that are detrimental.

7.   In ratifying, the principal must use the *same formalities* required to give the agent authority to execute the transaction. As Chapter 34 stated, few formalities normally are needed to give an agent authority. But where the original agency contract requires a writing, ratification likewise must be written.

Intervening Events   Certain events occurring after an agent's contract but before the principal's ratification may cut off the principal's power to ratify. These include: (1) the third party's *withdrawal* from the contract; (2) the third party's *death or loss of capacity;* (3) the principal's *failure to ratify within a reasonable time* (assuming that the principal's silence did not already work a ratification); and (4) *changed circumstances* (especially where the change places a greater burden on the third party than he assumed when the contract was made).

HUPPMAN v. TIGHE   642 A.2d 309 (Md. Ct. App. 1994)

I   *n April 1987, Harry Tighe opened an investment account with Legg Mason Wood Walker, Inc., a Baltimore investment firm. Tighe's authorization was required for all investments. When Tighe received his first monthly statement from Legg Mason in May 1987, however, he saw that his Legg Mason broker, L. Reed Huppman, had made an unauthorized $220,500 purchase constituting 8,820* *units of Mid-Atlantic Centers (MAC), a limited partnership that invested in shopping centers. Tighe immediately telephoned Huppman, profanely asking him what right he had to purchase the MAC units without Tighe's permission. Later, Huppman came to Tighe's home to explain the situation. According to Huppman's later testimony, he persuaded Tighe to hold the MAC investment to see how well it performed. According to Tighe, he held on to the MAC units only because Huppman convinced him that they were not readily marketable. In reality, however, the units probably were marketable.*

Despite this unauthorized purchase, Tighe did not close out his Legg Mason account or complain to Huppman's superiors, but instead continued to buy securities through Huppman for nearly two years. Over roughly that same period, he received over $52,000 in distributions from MAC, which were deposited in his Legg Mason account. In May 1989, Tighe finally complained to a Legg Mason compliance officer about the deal. Even then, however, he did not say that he wanted MAC removed from his account.

In 1990, Tighe sued Legg Mason and Huppman under various theories for damages resulting from Huppman's MAC purchase. After a jury trial, Tighe won a $234,426 judgment. After Legg Mason and Huppman unsuccessfully moved for judgment notwithstanding the verdict, they appealed that ruling. One of their arguments was that by his subsequent behavior, Tighe had ratified the unauthorized purchase of MAC units. ∽

Davis, Judge   If there exists any legally competent evidence, however slight, from which the jury could have found as it did, a judgment notwithstanding the verdict would be improper. A principal will be bound by the unauthorized acts of his agent if the transaction is ratified. A principal who, with knowledge of the material facts surrounding his agent's unauthorized act, receives and retains the benefits of the unauthorized act has ratified the act.

We affirm the trial court's ruling because the record provides sufficient evidence for a jury to have found that Tighe was not made aware of the material facts of the unauthorized transaction. Tighe's testimony reasonably infers that Huppman was intentionally misleading Tighe into believing that he could not get his money returned immedi-

ately because there was no market into which to sell the MAC investment. Thus, Tighe would have no choice but to hold on to the MAC investment until Legg Mason and Huppman could sell it. In contrast, Legg Mason's and Huppman's brief [admits at one point]: "The evidence . . . indicated that had Tighe unequivocally repudiated the transaction, Legg Mason would have been able to resell the units at full price and minimize its loss." If Huppman could have expeditiously sold the MAC investment, he kept this information from Tighe. Thus Tighe did not have all of the material facts undergirding the unauthorized transaction and thus could not have ratified the purchase.

Trial court judgment in Tighe's favor affirmed.

Contracts Made by Subagents

The rules governing a principal's liability for her agent's contracts generally apply to contracts made by her subagents. If an agent has authorized his subagent to make a certain contract and this authorization is within the authority granted the agent by his principal, the principal is bound to the subagent's contract.[2] Suppose that Peters employs the

Ajax Company to sell her personal property while she is out of the country, with the understanding that one of Ajax's agents will handle the sale from start to finish. If Ajax authorizes its agent Sampson (Peters's subagent) to contract to sell the property and Sampson does so, Peters is bound to the contract.

CONTRACT LIABILITY OF THE AGENT

When are *agents* liable on contracts they make on their principals' behalf? For the most part, this question depends on a different set of variables than

---

[2]Also, a subagent contracting within the authority conferred by her principal (the agent) bind the *agent* in an appropriate case. In addition, both the principal and the agent probably can ratify the contracts of subagents.

FIGURE I

Agent's Contractual Liability: The Basic Rules

TYPE OF PRINCIPAL	DOES THIRD PARTY KNOW OR HAVE REASON TO KNOW ABOUT P'S EXISTENCE?	DOES THIRD PARTY KNOW OR HAVE REASON TO KNOW P'S IDENTITY?	RESULT
Disclosed	Yes	Yes	A not liable unless A agrees to be liable or A lacks authority
Partially Disclosed	Yes	No	A liable
Undisclosed	No	No	A liable

the variables determining the principal's liability.[3] The most important of these variables is the *nature of the principal.* Thus, this section first examines the liability of agents who contract for several different kinds of principals. Then it discusses two ways that an agent can be bound after contracting for *any* type of principal.

The Nature of the Principal

Disclosed Principal   A principal is **disclosed** if a third party knows or has reason to know: (1) that the agent is acting for a principal, and (2) the principal's identity. Unless he agrees otherwise, an agent who represents a disclosed principal is *not liable* on authorized contracts made for such a principal. Suppose that Adkins, a sales agent for Parker, calls on Thompson and presents a business card clearly identifying her as Parker's agent. If Adkins contracts to sell Parker's goods to Thompson with authority to do so, Adkins is not bound because Parker is a disclosed principal. This rule usually is consistent with the third party's intentions; for example, Thompson probably intended to contract only with Parker.

Partially Disclosed Principal   A principal is **partially disclosed** if the third party: (1) knows or has reason to know that the agent is acting for *a* principal, but (2) lacks knowledge or reason to know the principal's *identity.* This can occur where an agent simply neglects to disclose his principal's identity. Also, a principal may tell her agent to keep

her identity secret to preserve her bargaining position.

Among the factors affecting anyone's decision to contract are the integrity, reliability, and creditworthiness of the other party to the contract. Where the principal is partially disclosed, the third party ordinarily cannot judge these matters. As a result, he usually depends on the agent's reliability to some degree. For this reason, and to give the third party additional protection, an agent is liable on contracts made for a partially disclosed principal unless the parties agree otherwise.

Undisclosed Principal   A principal is **undisclosed** where the third party lacks knowledge or reason to know *both* the principal's existence and the principal's identity. This can occur where a principal judges that he will get a better deal if his existence and identity remain secret, or where the agent neglects to make adequate disclosure.

A third party who deals with an agent for an undisclosed principal obviously cannot assess the principal's reliability, integrity, and creditworthiness. Indeed, here the third party reasonably believes that the *agent* is the other party to the contract. Thus, an agent is liable on contracts made for an undisclosed principal.

Two Other Kinds of Principals   Unless there is an agreement to the contrary, an agent who purports to act for a **legally nonexistent** principal such as an unincorporated association is personally liable. This is true even where the third party knows that the principal is nonexistent.

As you saw earlier, a principal who lacks contractual capacity due to insanity or infancy can avoid contracts made by his agent. In this case, the *agent* also escapes liability unless: (1) she misrepresents

---

[3]The rules stated here generally should govern the contract liability of subagents as well as agents. See *Restatement (Second) of Agency* § 361 (1959).

the capacity of her principal, or (2) she has reason to believe that the third party is unaware of the principal's incapacity and she fails to disclose this. Also, unless the parties agree otherwise, an agent is liable on contracts made for a *wholly incompetent* principal such as a person who has been adjudicated insane.

Not every court would decide the following case as it was decided here. Still, the decision contains an important message: If you want to escape contractual liability when you act as an agent, disclose your status as agent and fully disclose the name and business form of your principal.

AFRICAN BIO-BOTONICA, INC. v. LEINER 624 A.2d 1003 (N.J. Superior Ct. 1993)

Sally Leiner was the sole shareholder, director, and president of Ecco Bella, Inc., a New Jersey Corporation. On various occasions, African Bio-Botanica, Inc. sold Leiner and/or Ecco Bella merchandise. To all appearances, African gave little thought to the party with whom it was dealing. Initially, its records listed Sally Leiner as the customer; later, this was changed to Ecco Bella, but without any indication that Ecco Bella was a corporation. The checks with which Leiner paid for her orders and her firm's stationery bore the name Ecco Bella but likewise did not indicate that the firm was a corporation.

Eventually, Leiner did not pay for a shipment from African, and African sued her personally for damages in a New Jersey trial court. Leiner's defense was that only the corporation was liable. After the trial court awarded African $1,530 in damages, Leiner appealed. ∞

Brochin, Judge A corporation acts only through its agents. Unless the parties agree otherwise, an agent who enters into a contract for an undisclosed or a partially disclosed principal is personally liable on the contract; an agent who contracts on behalf of a disclosed principal is not personally liable on the contract. The court found as a fact, with adequate support in the record, that African was not informed and did not know that Ecco Bella was a corporation. The record gives no indication that African was informed of other facts from which it had reason to know that Ecco Bella was a corporation.

The agent who seeks protection from his status as agent has the means and the motive to communicate that status to the person with whom he is dealing. If the person with whom the agent is dealing does not know of the agency and has no reasonable way to know except by asking, the agent has the burden of disclosing his agency and the identity of his principal in order to avoid liability on contracts he makes. If an agent conducts business candidly as an agent for a disclosed principal, he should be readily able to prove that he disclosed his agency.

Leiner entered into an oral purchase contract. If Leiner was acting as an agent for her corporation, she was an agent for an undisclosed or partially disclosed principal and she was therefore personally liable on its purchase contracts.

Trial court judgment in African's favor affirmed.

Liability of Agent by Agreement

An agent may bind herself to contracts she makes for a principal by *expressly agreeing* to be liable. This is true regardless of the principal's nature. An agent may expressly bind herself by: (1) making the contract in her own name rather than in the principal's name, (2) joining the principal as an obligor on the contract, or (3) acting as surety or guarantor for the principal.

Problems of contract interpretation can arise when it is claimed that an agent has expressly promised to be bound. The two most important factors affecting the agent's liability are the wording of the contract and the way the agent has signed it. An agent who wishes to avoid liability should make no express promises in her own name and should try to ensure that the agreement only obligates the principal. In addition, the agent should use a signature form that clearly identifies the principal and indicates the agent's representative capacity—for example, "Parker, by Adkins," or "Adkins, for Parker." Simply adding the word "agent" when signing her name ("Adkins, Agent") or signing without any indication of her status ("Adkins") could subject the agent to liability. Sometimes, as in the following *Wired Music* case, the body of the agreement suggests one result and the signature form another. Here, and generally, oral evidence or other extrinsic evidence of the parties' understanding may help resolve the uncertainty.[4]

---

[4]However, the introduction of such evidence may be blocked by the parol evidence rule. See Chapter 16.

WIRED MUSIC, INC. v. GREAT RIVER STEAMBOAT CO.   554 S.W.2d 466 (Mo. Ct. App. 1977)

 sales representative of Wired Music, Inc. sold Frank Pierson, president of the Great River Steamboat Company, a five-year Muzak Program Service for a riverboat and restaurant owned by Great River. Pierson signed a form contract drafted by Wired Music in the following manner:

By /s/ Frank C. Pierson, Pres.
          Title

The Great River Steamboat Co.
~~Port of St. Louis Investments, Inc.~~
     For the Corporation

In signing, Pierson crossed out "Port of St. Louis Investments, Inc.," which had been incorrectly listed as the name of the corporation, and inserted the proper name. The contract included the following clause arguably making Pierson a surety or guarantor for Great River: "The individual signing this agreement for the subscriber guarantees that all of the above provisions shall be complied with."

Great River made approximately four payments under the contract and then ceased to pay. Wired Music brought an action for contract damages against Pierson personally. The trial court ruled in Pierson's favor, and Wired Music appealed. ∞

Gunn, Judge   The general rule regarding liability incurred by an individual who signs an instrument on behalf of another party is: where the principal is disclosed and the capacity in which the individual signs is evident, e.g., president, secretary, agent, the liability is the principal's and not that of the individual signing for the principal. Of course, where the circumstances surrounding the transaction disclose a mutual intention to impose personal responsibility on the individual executing the agreement, the individual may be personally liable even though the form of the signature is that of the agent.

The determinative issue here is whether, in view of the form of the signature to the agreement, the language of the so-called guaranty clause is sufficient to manifest a clear and explicit intent by Pierson to assume a personal guaranty contract. We hold that standing alone it does not. The contract language imposing a personal obligation is inconsistent with the form of execution, which positively limited Pierson's participation to his official corporate capacity and not as an individual. Such inconsistency creates at least a latent ambiguity which permits the admission of parol evidence to explain the true intent of the parties.

Pierson has stressed that he neglected to read the contract prior to its signing. One who signs a contract is presumed to have known its contents and accepted its terms. Thus, Pierson's failure to examine the terms of the instrument would afford no defense to the corporation regarding its obligations under the contract, as his signature was sufficient to bind the corporation. Such neglect *is* a relevant circumstance, however, in ascertaining Pierson's intent to assume personal liability, as his personal signature appeared nowhere on the instrument. Without knowledge of the guaranty clause he could not have possessed the requisite intent to assume obligations under it. The record is destitute of any indication that Pierson was ever made aware of potential personal liability under the guaranty clause, and he steadfastly denied any such knowledge. Wired Music drafted the contract, and its agents procured Pierson's corporate signature without explanation of or bargaining over its terms. Under these circumstances we find that there was an absence of the meeting of the minds as to the nature and the extent of the personal obligations imposed, essential to the formation of a binding guaranty.

Judgment for Pierson affirmed.

Agent's Liability on Unauthorized Contracts

An agent also may be liable to a third party if he contracts for the principal while *lacking authority* to do so. Here, the principal is not bound, and it is arguably unfair to leave the third party without any recovery. Thus, an agent normally is bound on the theory that he made an implied warranty of his authority to contract.[5] This liability exists regardless of whether the agent is otherwise bound to the third party.

To illustrate, suppose that Allen is a salesperson for Prine, a seller of furs. Allen has actual authority to receive offers for the sale of Prine's furs but not to make sale contracts, which must be approved by Prine himself. Prine has long followed this practice, and it is customary in the markets where his agents work. Representing himself as Prine's agent but saying nothing about his authority, Allen contracts to sell Prine's furs to Thatcher on Prine's behalf. Thatcher, who should have known better, honestly believes that Allen has authority to contract to sell Prine's furs. Prine is not liable on Allen's contract because Allen lacked actual or apparent authority to bind him. But Allen is liable to Thatcher for breaching his implied warranty of authority.

However, an agent is *not* liable for making an unauthorized contract if:

1. The third party *actually knows* that the agent lacks authority. However, note from the previous example that the agent still is liable where the third party had *reason to know* that authority was lacking.

2. The principal subsequently *ratifies* the contract. Here, the principal is bound, and there is arguably little reason to bind the agent.

3. The agent adequately *notifies* the third party that he does not warrant his authority to contract.

Contract Suits against Principal and Agent

Figure 2 sketches the most important situations in which the principal, the agent, or both are liable due to the agent's contracts. As it suggests, a third party usually has *someone* to sue if neither the principal nor the agent performs.

Without ratification, a principal is not liable on contracts made by an agent who lacks authority. Here, though, the agent usually is bound under an implied warranty of authority. In addition, the agent is bound on the contract where the principal was partially disclosed, undisclosed, or legally nonexist-

---

[5]An agent who intentionally misrepresents his authority may also be liable to the third party in tort. In addition, some states may allow tort liability for negligent misrepresentations. Where the third party has a tort suit, he may often elect to recover damages or to rescind the contract.

FIGURE **2**

Contract Liability of Principal and Agent: The Major Possibilities

	AGENT'S AUTHORITY		
PRINCIPAL	ACTUAL	APPARENT	NONE
Disclosed	P liable: A not liable unless agreement	P liable; A not liable unless agreement	P not liable; A usually liable
Partially Disclosed	P liable; A liable	P liable; A liable	P not liable; A liable
Undisclosed	P liable; A liable	Impossible	P not liable; A liable

ent.[6] Authorized contracts for a disclosed principal do not bind an agent unless he has agreed to be bound. But here the agent's actual or apparent authority binds the principal.

As Figure 2 further illustrates, in certain situations both principal and agent are liable on a contract made by the agent. This can occur where an agent with appropriate authority contracts on behalf of a partially disclosed or undisclosed principal. Also, an agent can bind himself by express agreement in situations where the principal also is bound. In such cases, which party ultimately is responsible to the third person? The complicated rules governing this question are beyond the scope of this text.

TORT LIABILITY OF THE PRINCIPAL

Besides contracting on the principal's behalf, an agent may also commit torts. A principal's liability for those torts involves four distinct subjects, which we consider in turn.[7]

Respondeat Superior Liability

Under the doctrine of **respondeat superior** (let the master answer), a principal who is an **employer** is liable for torts committed by agents: (1) who are **employees** and (2) who commit the tort while acting within the **scope of their employment**. *Respondeat superior* makes the principal liable both for an employee's negligence and for her intentional torts. Chapter 34 outlined the main factors courts consider when determining whether an agent is an employee. The most important of these factors is a principal's right to control the physical details of an agent's work.

Respondeat superior is a rule of *imputed* or *vicarious* liability because it bases an employer's liability on his relationship with the employee rather than his own fault. This imputation of liability reflects the following beliefs: (1) that the economic burdens of employee torts can best be borne by employers, (2) that employers often can protect themselves against such burdens by self-insuring or purchasing insurance, and (3) that the resulting costs frequently can be passed on to consumers, thus "socializing" the economic risk posed by employee torts. *Respondeat superior* also motivates employers to ensure that their employees avoid tortious behavior. Because they typically control the physical details of the work, employers are fairly well positioned to do so.

Scope of Employment *Respondeat superior*'s scope-of-employment requirement has been stated in many ways and is notoriously ambiguous. In the past, for example, some courts considering this question asked whether the employee was on a "frolic" of his own, or merely made a "detour" from his assigned activity. According to the *Restatement*,[8] an employee's conduct is within the scope of his employment if it meets *each* of the following four tests:

1. It was of the *kind* that the employee was employed to perform. To meet this test, an employee's conduct need only be of the same general nature as work expressly authorized or be incidental to its performance. The following *Haddon* case discusses this requirement at length.

2. It occurred substantially within the authorized *time* period. This is simply the employee's assigned time of work. Beyond this, there is an extra period of time during which the employment may continue. For instance, a security guard whose regular quitting time is 5:00 probably meets the time test if he unjustifiably injures an intruder at 5:15. Doing the same thing three hours later, however, would put the guard outside the scope of employment.

3. It occurred substantially within the *location* authorized by the *employer.* This includes locations not unreasonably distant from the authorized location. For example, a salesperson told to limit her activities to New York City probably would satisfy the location requirement while pursuing the employer's business in suburbs just outside the city limits but not while pursuing the same business in

---

[6]Note, however, that it is impossible for an agent for an undisclosed principal to have apparent authority. Apparent authority exists when the principal's communications to the third party cause that party to reasonably believe that the agent has authority to contract for another. This cannot occur when the principal is undisclosed.

[7]In addition to the various forms of tort liability discussed in this section, a principal can also *ratify* an agent's torts. Furthermore, the *Restatement* says that the rules governing a principal's liability for an agent's torts generally control a principal's liability for the torts of subagents. *Restatement (Second) of Agency* § 255 (1959).

---

[8]*Restatement (Second) of Agency* § 228(1) (1959). This section adds that if an employee intentionally uses force on another, this must have been "not unexpectable" by the employer to be within the scope of employment.

Philadelphia. Generally, the smaller the authorized area of activity, the smaller the departure from that area needed to put the employee outside the scope of employment. For example, consider the different physical distance limitations that should apply to a factory worker and a traveling salesperson.

4. It was motivated *at least in part* by the *purpose* of serving the employer. This test is met where the employee's conduct was motivated *to any appreciable extent* by the desire to serve the employer. Thus, an employee's tort may be within the scope of employment even if the motives for committing it were partly personal. For example, suppose that a delivery employee is behind schedule and for that reason has an accident while speeding to make a delivery in his employer's truck. The employee would be within the scope of employment even if another reason for his speeding was to impress a friend who was riding with him.

Strictly speaking, the following *Haddon* case does not involve *respondeat superior*. But *Haddon* does involve something similar—a federal law under which the U.S. government is made liable for certain torts committed by its employees within the scope of their employment. More importantly, the case says quite a bit about the first element of the *Restatement*'s scope-of-employment test.

HADDON v. UNITED STATES   68 F.3d 1420 (D.C. Cir. 1995)

J*effrey Freeburger, a White House electrician, allegedly told Sean Haddon, a White House assistant chef, that he would "beat the shit out of" Haddon unless Haddon withdrew an equal employment opportunity claim that he had filed against the White House's chief usher. Haddon's EEO claim did not involve Freeburger in any way.*

Haddon sued Freeburger for, among other things, assault and intentional infliction of emotional distress. As permitted by the Federal Employees Liability Reform and Tort Compensation Act of 1988 (the Westfall Act), Freeburger moved to substitute the federal government for himself as the sole defendant in the case. This required that Freeburger have been acting within the scope of his employment when he committed the alleged torts. The federal district court held that Freeburger indeed had been acting within the scope of his employment. Haddon's resulting suit against the federal government was governed by the Federal Tort Claims Act, which requires that the plaintiff exhaust his administrative remedies before suing. Because Haddon had not done so, the court dismissed his claim. Haddon appealed. His main argument was that because Freeburger did not *act within the scope of employment when he made the alleged threat, Freeburger should be reinstated as the sole defendant.* ∽

Tatel, Circuit Judge According to the *Restatement (Second) of Agency,* the conduct of an employee is within the scope of employment if, but only if: (1) it is of the kind he is employed to perform; (2) it occurs substantially within the authorized time and space limits; (3) it is actuated, at least in part, by a purpose to serve the employer; and (4) if force is intentionally used by the employee against another, the use of force is not unexpected by the employer. Because the complaint states that the threat occurred during the workday on White House premises and contains no allegation that Freeburger used any force, only the first and third criteria are at issue.

Finding that Freeburger's alleged threat was connected to a "job-related controversy,"—Haddon's EEO complaint—the district court concluded that Freeburger acted within the scope of his employment. Although the existence of a job-related controversy may support a determination that an employee was at least partially motivated to further the employer's interests (the third prong of the *Restatement* test), it cannot support a conclusion that the employee's conduct was of the kind he was employed to perform (the first prong). The plaintiff must satisfy both criteria to establish that an employee acted within the scope of employment.

To qualify as conduct of the kind he was employed to perform, Freeburger's actions must have either been of the same general nature as that authorized, or incidental to the conduct authorized. The White House employed Freeburger to work as an electrician, not to threaten kitchen staff. Freeburger's alleged conduct was thus not of the same general nature as the work he was hired to perform. Conduct is incidental to an employee's duties if it is a direct outgrowth of the employee's instructions or job assignment. It is not enough that an employee's job provides an opportunity to commit an intentional tort. In *Johnson v. Weinberg,* the D.C. Court of Appeals ruled that a laundromat could be liable for injuries inflicted when an employee responsible for removing clothes from washing machines shot a customer during a dispute over missing shirts. [On the other hand,] in *Boykin v. District of Columbia* the court held the District not liable to an elementary school student who alleged that the city's coordinator of programs for deaf and blind children sexually assaulted her in a school cafeteria. The coordinator's action was not a direct outgrowth of his authorized duties [because he] was not perform-

ing his [assigned] responsibilities during the encounter with the student.

Freeburger's alleged tort did not arise directly out of his instructions or job assignment as a White House electrician. Unlike the shooting in *Johnson,* his threat did not stem from a dispute over the performance of his work. He [also] was not performing his assigned duties at the time of the incident. His threat related to an EEO complaint not involving him in any way. This case is thus closer to the assault in *Boykin.* Freeburger's action was therefore not within the scope of his employment.

District court decision in Freeburger's and the government's favor reversed. Haddon's suit against Freeburger can proceed.

Direct Liability

As the following *Victory Tabernacle* case makes clear, a principal's **direct liability** for an agent's torts differs considerably from *respondeat superior* liability. Here, the principal *himself* is at fault, and there is no need to impute liability to him. Also, no scope-of-employment requirement exists in direct liability cases, and the agent need not be an employee. Of course, a principal might incur both direct liability and *respondeat superior* liability in cases where due to the principal's fault, an employee commits a tort within the scope of her employment.

A principal is directly liable for an agent's tortious conduct if the principal *directs* that conduct and *intends* that it occur. In such cases, the *agent's* behavior might be intentional, reckless, or negligent. For instance, if Petty tells his agent Able to

beat up Tabler and Able does so, Petty is directly liable to Tabler. Petty also would be liable for harm to third parties that results from his telling Able to do construction work in a negligent, substandard fashion.

The typical direct liability case, however, involves harm caused by the principal's *negligence* regarding the agent. Examples of direct liability for negligence include: (1) giving the agent improper or unclear instructions; (2) failing to make and enforce appropriate regulations to govern the agent's conduct; (3) hiring an unsuitable agent; (4) failing to discharge an unsuitable agent; (5) furnishing an agent with improper tools, instruments, or materials; and (6) carelessly supervising an agent. Today, suits for negligent hiring are common; the following case is an example.

J. v. VICTORY TABERNACLE BAPTIST CHURCH   372 S.E.2d 391 (Va. Sup. Ct. 1988)

A woman sued the Victory Tabernacle Baptist Church, alleging that due to its negligence her 10-year-old daughter had been repeatedly raped and sexually assaulted by a church employee. The plaintiff's complaint claimed that when the church hired the employee, it knew or should have known that he had recently been convicted of aggravated sexual assault on a young girl, that he was on probation for this offense, and that a condition of his probation was that he not be involved with children. Despite all this, the complaint continued, the employee's duties allowed him freely to come into contact with children, including the plaintiff's daughter, and he was given keys enabling him to lock and unlock all the church's doors.

The complaint alleged (among other things) negligent hiring on the church's part. The church filed a demurrer to the complaint, and the trial court sustained the demurrer. The plaintiff appealed this decision, and the case reached the Virginia Supreme Court. ☞

Thomas, Justice   We decide only whether the allegations of negligent hiring state a cause of action in Virginia. Victory Baptist argues that the trial court properly sustained the demurrer on [this] question because plaintiff failed to allege that the harm to the victim was caused by negligence on the part of the employee. According to this argument, the negligent hiring cause of action requires that the negligently hired individual negligently injured the plaintiff. We disagree. The very thing that allegedly should have been foreseen in this case is that the employee would commit a violent act upon a child. To say that a negligently hired employee who acts willfully or criminally thus relieves his employer of liability for negligent hiring when willful or criminal conduct is precisely what the employer should have foreseen would rob the tort of vitality.

Victory Baptist also argues that the [plaintiff's] allegations do not establish a sufficient nexus among the employer's breach of duty, the employee's conduct, and the employee's employment. In oral argument, counsel explained that there were no allegations that the employee was engaged in the church's business when the child was injured—no allegation, for example, that the employee was on duty for the church at the time the girl was raped. Counsel then made clear that what he was com-plaining about was that there were no allegations to bring the employee's conduct within the scope of his employment.

This argument demonstrates that Victory Baptist is confusing the doctrine of *respondeat superior* with the tort of negligent hiring. This distinction was succinctly stated in a recent law review article:

Under *respondeat superior,* an employer is vicariously liable for an employee's tortious acts committed within the scope of employment. In contrast, negligent hiring is a doctrine of primary liability; the employer is principally liable for negligently placing an unfit person in an employment situation involving an unreasonable risk of harm to others. Negligent hiring, therefore, enables plaintiffs to recover in situations where *respondeat superior*'s scope of employment limitation previously protected employers from liability.

Thus, Victory Baptist's contention is misplaced.

In our opinion, the [complaint] was fully sufficient to state a claim of negligent hiring, and thus it was error for the trial court to sustain the demurrer on that issue.

Judgment for the church on the negligent hiring claim reversed. Case remanded for trial consistent with the Supreme Court's opinion.

Liability for Torts of Independent Contractors

A principal ordinarily is *not* liable for torts committed by **independent contractors.** As compared with employees, independent contractors are more likely to have the size and resources to insure against tort liability and to pass on the resulting costs themselves. Sometimes, therefore, the risk still can be socialized if only the independent contractor is held responsible. Because the principal does not control the manner in which an independent contractor's work is performed, moreover, he has less ability to prevent a contractor's torts than an employer has to prevent an employee's torts. Thus, imposing liability on principals for the torts of independent contractors may do little to eliminate the contractor's torts.

However, the rule that principals are not liable for torts committed by independent contractors has exceptions. For example:

1. A principal can be *directly* liable for tortious behavior connected with the retention of an independent contractor. One example is the hiring of a dangerously incompetent independent contractor.

2. A principal is liable for harm resulting from the independent contractor's failure to perform a *nondelegable duty.* A nondelegable duty is a duty whose proper performance is so important that a principal cannot avoid liability by contracting it away. Examples include a carrier's duty to transport its passengers safely, a municipality's duty to keep its streets in repair, a railroad's duty to maintain safe crossings, and a landlord's duties to make repairs and to use care in doing so. Thus, a landlord who retains

FIGURE 3

The Principal's Tort Liability

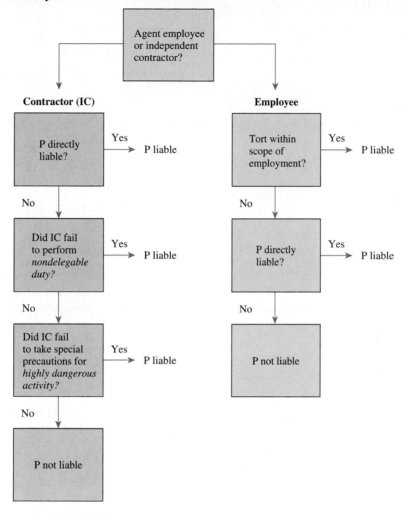

Note: The figure does not include liability for the agent's misrepresentations.

an independent contractor to repair the stairs in an apartment building is liable for injuries caused by the contractor's failure to repair the stairs properly.

3. A principal is liable for an independent contractor's negligent failure to take the special precautions needed to conduct certain *highly dangerous* or *inherently dangerous* activities.[9] Examples of such activities include excavations in publicly traveled areas, the clearing of land by fire, the construction of a dam, and the demolition of a building. For example, a contractor engaged in demolishing a building presumably has duties to warn pedestrians and to keep them at a safe distance. If injury results from the independent contractor's failure to meet these duties, the principal is liable. (See Figure 3.)

Liability for Agent's Misrepresentations

Special rules apply when a third party sues a principal for **misrepresentations** made by her agent.[10] In most cases where the principal is liable

---

[9]The range of activities considered "highly dangerous" or "inherently dangerous" is probably greater than the range of activities considered "ultrahazardous" or "abnormally dangerous" for strict liability purposes. On the latter activities, see Chapter 7.

[10]On fraud and misrepresentation in the tort and contract contexts, see Chapters 6 and 13.

An Outline of the Principal's Tort Liability

Respondeat Superior	1. Agent must be an employee, *and* 2. Employee must act within scope of employment while committing tort
Direct Liability	1. Principal intends and directs agent's intentional tort, recklessness, or negligence, *or* 2. Principal is negligent regarding agent
Torts of Independent Contractors	1. Principal generally is *not* liable 2. Exceptions for direct liability, highly dangerous activities, and nondelegable duties
Misrepresentation	1. Direct liability 2. Vicarious liability where agent had authority to make true statements on the subject of the misrepresentation 3. An exculpatory clause may eliminate the principal's tort liability, but the third party still can rescind
Torts of Subagents	The preceding rules govern the principal's liability, but their application varies

under these rules, the third party can elect to recover in tort, or to rescind the transaction.

A principal is *directly* liable for misrepresentations made by her agent during authorized transactions if she *intended* that the agent make the misrepresentations. In some states, a principal also may be directly liable if she *negligently* allows the agent to make misrepresentations. Even where a principal is not directly at fault, she may be liable for an agent's misrepresentations if the agent had *actual or apparent authority to make true statements on the subject.* Suppose that an agent authorized to sell farmland falsely states that a stream on the land has never flooded the property when in fact it does so almost every year, and that this statement induces a third party to buy the land. The principal is directly liable if she intended that the agent make this false statement. Even if the principal is personally blameless, she is liable if the agent had actual or apparent authority to make true statements about the spring.

After contemplating their potential liability under the rules just discussed, both honest and dishonest principals may try to escape liability for an agent's misrepresentations by including an *exculpatory clause* in contracts the agent makes with third parties. Such clauses typically state that the agent only has authority to make the representations contained in the contract and that only those representations bind the principal. Exculpatory clauses do not protect a principal who intends or expects that an agent will make false statements. Otherwise, though, they insulate the principal from *tort* liability

if the agent misrepresents. But the third party still may *rescind* the transaction, because it would be unjust to let the principal benefit from the transaction while disclaiming responsibility for it.

TORT LIABILITY OF THE AGENT

Agents are usually liable for their own torts.[11] Normally, they are not absolved from liability just because they acted at the principal's command. However, there are exceptions to this generalization.

1. An agent can escape liability if she is *exercising a privilege of the principal.* Suppose that Tingle grants Parkham a right-of-way to transport his farm products over a private road crossing Tingle's land. Parkham's agent Adams would not be liable in trespass for driving across Tingle's land to transport farm products if she did so at Parkham's command. However, an agent must not exceed the scope of the privilege and must act for the purpose for which the privilege was given. Thus, Adams would not be protected if she took her Jeep on a midnight joyride across Tingle's land. Also, the privilege given the agent must be delegable in the first place. If Tingle had given the easement to Parkham exclusively, Adams would not be privileged to drive across Tingle's land.

---

[11]The rules stated in the previous section generally govern an agent's liability for torts committed by his subagents. *Restatement (Second) of Agency* § 362 (1959).

2. A principal who is *privileged to take certain actions in defense of his person or property* may often authorize an agent to do the same. In such cases, the agent escapes liability if the principal could have done so. For example, a properly authorized agent may use force to protect the life or property of his principal if the principal could have done the same.

3. An agent who makes *misrepresentations* while conducting the principal's business is not liable in tort unless he either *knew or had reason to know* their falsity. Suppose Parker authorizes Arnold to sell his house, falsely telling Arnold that the house is fully insulated. Arnold does not know that the statement is false and could not discover its falsity through a reasonable inspection. If Arnold tells Thomas that the house is fully insulated and Thomas relies on this statement in purchasing the house, Parker is directly liable to Thomas, but Arnold is not liable.

4. An agent is not liable for injuries to third persons caused by *defective tools or instrumentalities* furnished by the principal unless the agent had actual knowledge or reason to know of the defect.

TORT SUITS AGAINST PRINCIPAL AND AGENT

Both principal and agent sometimes are liable for an agent's torts. Here, the parties are *jointly and severally* liable. This means that a third party may join the principal and the agent in one suit and get a judgment against each, or may sue either or both individually and get a judgment against either or both. However, once a third party actually collects in full from either the principal or the agent, no further recovery is possible.

In some cases, therefore, either the principal or the agent has to satisfy the judgment alone despite the other party's liability. Here, the other party sometimes is required to *indemnify* the party who has satisfied the judgment. As discussed in Chapter 34, for example, sometimes a principal is required to indemnify an agent for tort liability the agent incurs. On the other hand, some torts committed by agents may involve a breach of duty to their principal, and the principal may be able to recover from an agent on this basis.

ETHICAL AND PUBLIC POLICY CONCERNS

1. One of the justifications for *respondeat superior* is that employers are in a relatively good position to absorb the liability of employee torts, to insure against such liability, and to pass on the resulting costs. What are the advantages and disadvantages of applying this reasoning to make principals liable for all torts committed by *independent contractors* within the scope of their employment?

2. If the purposes underlying *respondeat superior* are sound ones, why limit the doctrine to employee torts committed within the scope of employment? In other words, why not make employers liable for *all* torts committed by their employees?

PROBLEM CASES

1. The Capital Dredge and Dock Corporation sued the city of Detroit for damages associated with certain construction work it had been performing for the city. One of the city's defenses was that Capital had released the city from liability on some of Capital's present claims during earlier, related litigation between Capital and the city. The releases were part of a settlement document signed by Capital Dredge's attorney, Alteri. Capital Dredge had held Alteri out as having authority to represent it in the relevant litigation, and this included authority to negotiate a settlement. However, unknown to the city, Capital Dredge also had specifically told Alteri not to compromise some of the claims he later settled. Under these circumstances, could Alteri have had implied authority to settle the claims in question? Could he have had apparent authority to do so?

2. Nick Bikos was an apartment manager for the Sagewood Apartments. Bikos had actual authority to collect the rent from tenants but did not have actual authority to write checks on the account in which the rents were deposited. After getting in financial trouble, Bikos devised a plan to sell the tenants short-term savings deposits in Sagewood's name. In addition to bearing Sagewood's name, the certificates showed Bikos's name as manager and a fictitious name signed by Bikos as treasurer. The certificates also purported to pay a rate exceeding that paid by any bank or savings association in the area. After Bikos's scheme fell apart and he was arrested for felony theft, the tenants sued Sagewood for the $20,200 they had paid Bikos for the worthless certificates. Did Bikos have implied or apparent authority to issue the savings certificates in Sagewood's name?

3. Rosia Adams, a warehouse employee at a school board warehouse, was injured when she slipped on a wet floor at the warehouse. The floor was wet because it had been mopped to clean up a spill from a defective Coca-Cola vending machine leased to the school district by a local Coca-Cola bottling company (Coke). The written lease for the machine required the school board to indemnify Coke for injuries like those suffered by Adams. The lease was signed by a warehouse inventory clerk. His job was simply to receive and inventory goods delivered to the school board's warehouse.

Adams sued Coke and got a judgment against it. Coke filed a third-party suit against the school board, arguing that the lease obligated the school board to compensate Coke for Adams's injuries. Based on the facts just presented, did the warehouse clerk have express, implied, or apparent authority to bind the school board to this particular term in the lease?

4. Roma Funk, who co-owned a piece of land along with her seven brothers and sisters, contracted to sell the land to her neighbors. It was unclear whether Funk had authority to sell the land on behalf of her siblings. For certain, there was no writing giving her such authority. Funk's siblings eventually backed out of the deal, and the buyers sued for specific performance. They argued that Funk's siblings had ratified her contract by failing to come forward and repudiate it. Can a contract ever be ratified in this way? Regardless of your answer to this question, there is a reason why Funk's siblings could not have ratified this particular contract. What is it? Assume that in this state an agent who executes an agreement conveying an interest in land on behalf of his principal must be authorized in writing.

5. Two attorneys ordered deposition transcripts from a court reporter. They did so as part of some litigation work they were performing for their clients. The attorneys did not tell the court reporter that they were acting on their clients' behalf in ordering the transcripts, nor did they specifically identify those clients' names to the court reporter.

However, the depositions contained captions identifying the clients and identifying the attorneys as their legal representatives. After the attorneys placed their order, their clients went bankrupt. Thus, the court reporter tried to recover against the attorneys for the cost of the transcripts. What *kind* of principal was each of the clients? What would this normally means for the attorneys' liability to the court reporter?

6. Seascape Restaurants, Inc. operated a restaurant called The Magic Moment. Jeff Rosenberg was one-third owner and president of Seascape. Van D. Costas, the president of Van D. Costas, Inc., contracted to construct a "magical entrance" to the Magic Moment. Jeff Rosenberg signed the contract on a line under which appeared the words "Jeff Rosenberg, the Magic Moment." The contract did not refer to Seascape, and Costas knew nothing of Seascape's existence. After a dispute over performance of the contract, Costas sued Rosenberg for breach of contract. Is Rosenberg personally liable to Costas?

7. Twelve people joined together to sponsor and promote a group of Little League baseball teams called the Golden Spike Little League. They arranged to purchase $3,900 in equipment for the league from a local sporting goods store. When the store sued the 12 individuals for refusing to pay the $3,900, they defended by arguing that they were agents for a disclosed principal, the league. Did this defense work?

8. Dale F. Everett did business as the Dale F. Everett Company, Inc. (the Company). He also formed a retail business known as The Clubhouse, which had no legal status aside from its registration as a trade name for the Company. Everett contracted with James Smith for $8,424 of advertising time. Everett signed his contract with Smith as follows: "THE CLUBHOUSE, Client, By Dale F. Everett." Smith later sent billing statements for the ads to "The Clubhouse, Inc." Everett never paid Smith the $8,424, and Smith sued Everett personally. Is Everett personally liable on the contract with Smith?

9. Redford had been a backhoe operator for five years. Although he had worked for other sign companies, he had spent 90 percent of his time during the past three years working for Tube Art Display, Inc. Redford generally dug holes exactly as directed by the sign company employing him. He did, however, pay his own business taxes, and he did not participate in any of the fringe benefits available to Tube Art employees.

Tube Art obtained a permit to install a sign in the parking lot of a combination commercial and apartment building. Telling Redford how to proceed, Tube Art's service manager laid out the exact location of a 4 × 4-foot square on the asphalt surface with yellow paint and directed that the hole be 6 feet deep. After Redford began the job, he struck a small natural gas pipeline with the backhoe. He examined the pipe, and, finding no indication of a leak or break, concluded that the line was not in use and left the worksite. Later, an explosion and fire occurred in the building serviced by the line. As a result, a business owned by Massey was destroyed. Massey sued Tube Art for Redford's negligence under the doctrine of *respondeat superior.* Will Massey recover? Assume that Redford was negligent.

10. John Hondzinski delivered newspapers in his own car for a newspaper called the *News Herald.* Under the contract between Hondzinski and the *News Herald,* Hondzinski was obligated to pick up and promptly deliver newspapers provided by the *News Herald,* but the means and the routes for doing so were within Hondzinski's control. While making deliveries for the *News Herald* one day, Hondzinski negligently allowed his car to collide with a car driven by Peter Janice. Janice sued the *News Herald* for Hondzinski's negligence. Can Janice recover against the *News Herald* under the doctrine of *respondeat superior?* Why or why not?

11. A. J. Gatzke, a district manager for the Walgreen Company, spent several weeks in Duluth, Minnesota, supervising the opening of a new Walgreen restaurant there. He remained at the restaurant approximately 17 hours a day, and he was on call 24 hours a day. While in Duluth, he lived at the Edgewater Motel at Walgreen's expense. After some heavy drinking late one night, Gatzke returned to his motel room and began filling out an expense account required by his employer. Shortly after Gatzke went to bed, a fire broke out in his motel room. Gatzke escaped, but fire damage to the motel totaled over $330,000. Assume that the fire was caused by Gatzke's dumping a burning cigarette or match in a wastebasket near the desk at which he worked.

Edgewater sued Walgreen for Gatzke's negligence. Under the *Restatement* test in the text, did Gatzke act within the scope of his employment when he negligently started the fire? Consider all four elements of the test.

12. Susie Mae Woodson's husband was killed due to a cave-in at a construction site where he was laying sewer pipe in a trench dug by an independent contractor of Davidson & Jones, Inc. (D&J). The trench in which Mr. Woodson was working had not been braced or shored to prevent a cave-in, which was a violation of federal occupational safety regulations. Mrs. Woodson sued D&J for the independent contractor's negligence. Will she recover? Assume that D&J was not in any way *directly* liable regarding the independent contractor.

13. Edward J. Opatz maintained an investment account with John G. Kinnard and Company. Byron Jensen, a Kinnard broker, handled Opatz's account. In January 1985, Jensen told Opatz that he would buy three-fourths of a $24,000 investment unit if Opatz would buy the remaining fourth. Relying on this statement and believing that the transaction was within Jensen's authority, Opatz gave Jensen a $6,000 check payable to Jensen. One week later, Jensen admitted to Opatz that he had never purchased the unit, and gave Opatz a personal check for $6,000. Still later, the check bounced and Jensen disappeared. Is Kinnard liable to Opatz for the $6,000? Assume that: (1) Jensen's statement that he would invest the $6,000 was actionable fraud, (2) Kinnard was not directly liable for Jensen's behavior, and (3) Kinnard did not expressly or impliedly authorize Jensen's statements to Opatz.

14. 📼 *Video Case.* See "Martin Manufacturing." Martin, the president of Martin Manufacturing, was talking with Arnold, a new traveling salesperson, about Arnold's first week on the road. Arnold told Martin that he had hit one of Martin's customers in the customer's store. The blow came after Arnold and the customer got into an argument, during which the customer ordered Arnold out of his store. In striking the customer, Arnold was motivated at least in part by a feeling that no Martin employee should have to endure such disrespect.

Then, Arnold also told Martin that he had gotten into an accident while driving a company van. The accident occurred after Arnold negligently ran a stop sign while thinking about the fight. The driver of the other car was seriously injured in the accident.

Assuming that Arnold is an employee, is Martin liable to the customer for any battery Arnold committed, and to the driver of the car for Arnold's negligence?

Partnerships

Introduction to Forms of Business and Formation of Partnerships

I n this chapter, you begin your study of business organizations. Early in this chapter, you will preview the basic characteristics of the most important forms of business and learn how to select an appropriate form for a business venture. Following that introduction, you will begin your in-depth study of partnerships, learning their characteristics and the formalities for their creation. ∞

CHOOSING A FORM OF BUSINESS

One of the most important decisions made by a person beginning a business is choosing a **form of business.** This decision is important because the business owner's liability and control of the business vary greatly among the many forms of business. In addition, some business forms offer significant tax advantages to their owners.

Although other forms of business exist, usually a person starting a business will wish to organize the business as a sole proprietorship, partnership, limited liability partnership, limited partnership, corporation, or limited liability company.

Sole Proprietorship

A **sole proprietorship** has only one owner. The sole proprietorship is merely an extension of its only owner, the **sole proprietor.**

As the only owner, the sole proprietor has the right to make all the management decisions of the business. In addition, all the profits of the business are his. A sole proprietor assumes great liability: He is personally liable for all the obligations of the business. All the debts of the business, including debts on contracts signed only in the name of the business, are his debts. If the assets of the business are insufficient to pay the claims of its creditors, the creditors may require the sole proprietor to pay the claims using his individual, nonbusiness assets such as money from his bank account and the proceeds from the sale of his house. A sole proprietor may lose everything if his business becomes insolvent. Hence, the sole proprietorship is a risky form of business for its owner.

Despite this risk, there are two reasons why a person may organize a business as a sole proprietorship. First, the sole proprietorship is formed very easily and inexpensively. No formalities are necessary. Second, few people consider the business form decision. They merely begin their businesses. Thus, by default, a person going into business by herself automatically creates a sole proprietorship when she fails to choose another business form. These two reasons explain why the sole proprietorship is the most common form of business in the United States.

Because the sole proprietorship is merely an extension of its owner, it has no life apart from its owner. Therefore, while the business of a sole proprietorship may be freely sold to someone else, legally the sole proprietorship as a form of business cannot be transferred to another person. The buyer of the business must create his own form of business to continue the business.

A sole proprietorship is not a legal entity. It cannot sue or be sued. Instead, creditors must sue the owner. The sole proprietor—in his own name—must sue those who harm the business.

A sole proprietor may hire employees for the business, but they are employees of the sole proprietor. Under the law of agency, the sole proprietor is responsible for her employees' authorized contracts and for the torts they commit in the course of their employment. Also, a sole proprietorship is not a tax-paying entity for federal income tax purposes. All of the income of a sole proprietorship is income to its owner and must be reported on the sole proprietor's individual federal income tax return. Likewise, any business losses are deductible without limit on the sole proprietor's individual tax return. This loss-deduction advantage explains why some wealthier taxpayers use the sole proprietorship for selected business investments—when losses are expected in the early years of the business, yet the risk of liability is low. Such an investor may form a sole proprietorship and hire a professional manager to operate the business.

Many sole proprietorships have trade names. For example, Caryl Stanley may operate her bagel shop under the name Caryl's Bagel Shop. Caryl would be required to file the trade name under a state statute requiring the registration of fictitious business names. If she were sued by a creditor, the creditor would address his complaint to "Caryl Stanley, doing business as Caryl's Bagel Shop."

Partnership

A **partnership** has two or more owners, called **partners.** The partners have the right to make all the management decisions for the business. In addition, all the profits of the business are shared by the partners.

The partners assume personal liability for all the obligations of the business. All the debts of the business are the debts of all the partners. Likewise, partners are liable for the torts committed in the course of business by their partners or by partnership employees. If the assets of the business are insufficient to pay the claims of its creditors, the creditors may require one or more of the partners to pay the claims using their individual, nonbusiness assets. Thus, a partner may have to pay more than his share of partnership liabilities.

Like the sole proprietorship, the partnership is not a tax-paying entity for federal income tax purposes. All of the income of the partnership is income to its partners and must be reported on the individual partner's federal income tax return. Likewise, any business losses are deductible without limit on the partner's individual tax return.

The partnership has no life apart from its owners. When a partner dies or otherwise leaves the business, the partnership is dissolved. A partner's ownership interest in a partnership is not freely transferable: A purchaser of the partner's interest is not a partner of the partnership, unless the other partners agree to admit the purchaser as a partner.

Why would persons organize a business as a partnership? Formation of a partnership requires no formalities and may be formed by default. A partnership is created automatically when two or more persons own a business together without selecting another form. Also, each partner's right to manage the business and the deductibility of partnership losses on individual tax returns are attractive features.

Limited Liability Partnership

Reacting to the large personal liability sometimes imposed on lawyers and accountants for the professional malpractice of their partners, Texas enacted in 1991 the first statute permitting the formation of **limited liability partnerships (LLP).** An LLP is similar to a partnership except that a partner's liability for his partners' professional malpractice is limited to the partnership's assets; a partner retains unlimited liability for his *own* malpractice and, in most states, for all *non*professional obligations of the partnership.

An LLP is managed by its partners, who have equal say in the business of the partnership, unless they agree otherwise. An LLP has no life apart from its partners, and a partner's ownership interest in an LLP is not freely transferable: The purchaser will not be a partner of the partnership, unless the other partners agree that the purchaser may join the LLP.

LLPs will be taxed like partnerships: The partnership pays no federal income tax; instead each partner reports his share of the LLP's profits and losses on his individual federal income tax return.

The formation of an LLP requires filing a form with the secretary of state; some states require LLPs to maintain adequate professional liability insurance or have a high net worth.

The LLP is an especially good form of business for professionals such as accountants, allowing them flexibility of management, while insulating them in part from personal liability. As more states adopt LLP statutes, the LLP will become the preferred form of business for professionals who do not incorporate. As of March 1997, 48 states and the District of Columbia had passed LLP statutes. Only Vermont and Wyoming do not have LLP statutes.

Limited Partnership

A **limited partnership** has one or more general partners and one or more limited partners. General partners have rights and liabilities similar to partners in a partnership. They manage the business of the limited partnership and have unlimited liability for the obligations of the limited partnership. Typically, however, the only general partner is a corporation, thereby protecting the human managers from unlimited liability.

The typical limited partnership is not a taxpaying entity for federal income tax purposes. General partners report their shares of the limited partnership's income and losses on their individual federal income tax returns. For general partners, losses of the business are deductible without limit.

Limited partners usually have no liability for the obligations of the limited partnership once they have paid their capital contributions to the limited partnership. Limited partners have no right to manage the business and may lose their limited liability for the business's obligations if they do manage the business.

A limited partner must pay federal income tax on his share of the profits of the business, but he may deduct his share of losses only to the extent of his investment in the business. As a passive investor, a limited partner may use the losses only to offset income from other passive investments.

A limited partnership may have a life apart from its owners. When a limited partner dies or otherwise leaves the business, the limited partnership is not dissolved. When a general partner dies or withdraws, however, the limited partnership is dissolved in the absence of a contrary agreement. A general or limited partner's rights may not be wholly transferred to another person unless the other partners agree to admit the new person as a partner.

Unlike a sole proprietorship or partnership, a limited partnership may be created only by complying with a state statute permitting limited partnerships. Thus, no limited partnership may be created by default.

There are three main reasons why persons organize a business as a limited partnership. First, by using a corporate general partner, no human will have unlimited liability for the debts of the business. Second, losses of the business are deductible on the owners' federal income tax returns. Third, investors may contribute capital to the business yet avoid unlimited liability and the obligation to manage the business. Thus, the limited partnership has the ability to attract large amounts of capital, much more than the sole proprietorship, which has only one owner, or the partnership, whose partners' fear of unlimited liability restricts the size of the business. Hence, for a business needing millions of dollars of capital and expecting to lose money in its early years, the limited partnership is a particularly good form of business.

Corporation

A **corporation** is owned by shareholders who elect a board of directors to manage the business. The board of directors often selects officers to run the day-to-day affairs of the business. Consequently, ownership and management of a corporation may be completely separate: No shareholder has the right to manage, and no officer or director needs to be a shareholder.

Shareholders have limited liability for the obligations of the corporation, even if a shareholder is elected as a director or selected as an officer. Directors and officers have no liability for the contracts they or the corporation's employees negotiate in the name of the corporation. While managers have liability for their own misconduct, they have no liability for corporate torts committed by other corporate managers or employees. Therefore, shareholders, officers, and directors have limited liability for the obligations of the business.

The usual corporation is a tax-paying entity for federal income tax purposes. The corporation pays taxes on its profits. Shareholders do not report their shares of corporation profits on their individual federal income tax returns. Instead, only when the corporation distributes its profits to the shareholders in the form of dividends or the shareholders sell their investments at a profit do the shareholders report income on their individual returns. This creates a double-tax possibility, as profits are taxed once at the corporation level and again at the shareholder level when dividends are paid.

Also, shareholders do not deduct corporate losses on their individual returns. They may, however, deduct their investment losses after they have sold their shares of the corporation.

There is one important exception to these corporate tax rules. The shareholders may elect to have the corporation and its shareholders taxed under Subchapter S of the Internal Revenue Code. By electing **S Corporation** status, the corporation and its shareholders are taxed nearly entirely like a partnership: Income and losses of the business are reported on the shareholders' individual federal income tax returns. A corporation electing S Corporation status may have no more than 75 shareholders, have only one class of shares, and be owned only by individuals and trusts.

A corporation has a life separate from its owners and its managers. When a shareholder or manager dies or otherwise leaves the business, the corporation is not dissolved. A shareholder may sell his shares of the corporation to other persons without limitation unless there is a contrary agreement. The purchaser becomes a shareholder with all the rights of the selling shareholder.

There are several reasons why persons organize a business as a corporation. First, no human has unlimited liability for the debts of the business. As a result, businesses in the riskiest industries—such as manufacturing—incorporate. Second, because investors may contribute capital to the business, avoid unlimited liability, escape the obligation to manage the business, and easily liquidate their investments by selling their shares, the corporation has the ability to attract large amounts of capital, even more than the limited partnership, whose partnership interests are not as freely transferable. Thus, the corporation has the capacity to raise the largest amount of capital.

The S Corporation has an additional advantage: Losses of the business are deductible on individual federal income tax returns. However, because the S Corporation is limited to 75 shareholders, its ability to raise capital is severely limited. Also, while legally permitted to sell their shares, S corporation shareholders may be unable to find investors willing to buy their shares or may be restricted from selling their shares pursuant to an agreement between the shareholders.

Limited Liability Company

A **limited liability company (LLC)** is a business form intended to combine the nontax advantages of corporations with the favorable tax treatment of partnerships. An LLC is owned by members, who may manage the LLC themselves or elect the manager or managers who will operate the business. Members have limited liability for the obligations of the LLC.

The LLC has the purported federal taxation advantage of the partnership—no federal income taxation at the firm level. Instead, LLC owners pay taxes on their shares of the firm's profits. However, there is a lack of free transferability of the members' ownership interests: Transfer of membership interests is prohibited without the consent of all the members or a provision in the LLC agreement permitting transfer. In addition, the death, retirement, or bankruptcy of any member dissolves and forces the liquidation of the LLC, unless all the remaining members vote to continue the business or the LLC agreement prevents dissolution.

What are the advantages of the LLC? The LLC has the limited liability advantage and the management advantage of the corporation. The LLC and its members receive the same federal tax treatment as the S Corporation and its shareholders, yet the LLC has no limit on the number or type of owners, as does an S Corporation.

See Figure 1 for a summary of the general characteristics of business forms.

Franchising

Franchising is an agreement by which a **franchisee** has the right to sell goods or services under a marketing plan prescribed in substantial part by a **franchisor.** Thus, when a franchisee purchases a franchise, the franchisee buys a *business opportunity,* which the franchisee may choose to operate as any form of business. For example, if you obtain a McDonald's restaurant franchise for the south side of Santa Fe, you will probably choose to operate the business as a corporation.

Franchising has advantages for both the franchisee and the franchisor. The franchisee receives the franchisor's assistance in setting up the business and training employees. In addition, the franchisee may benefit from the franchisor's national advertising and strong trademark and goodwill. For example, a McDonald's franchisee obtains instant visibility and credibility from displaying the McDonald's golden arches. In return for this assistance, the franchisee usually pays a substantial purchase price plus a fee based on income, sales, or the purchase price of specified supplies. For example, an ice-cream restaurant franchise may pay its franchisor 15 percent of the price it pays for its ice-cream mix. The fee is collected for the franchisor by an authorized supplier of the mix.

The franchisor also benefits. Instead of making a high investment in several business locations, the franchisor shifts most of the investment risk to the franchisees. Yet the franchisor receives income from the franchisees' operation of their businesses. And while the franchisor's profits are tied to the franchisees' success, the franchisees typically have a sizable investment in the franchises and have a strong incentive to succeed. Also, the franchisor can adopt standards to ensure it selects high-quality franchisees with superior financial strength. Using franchising allows a franchisor to exploit its trademark and goodwill yet also protect itself by requiring franchisees to adopt uniform image and marketing practices.

Nature of Franchisor/Franchisee Relationship Because a franchisor may exercise some control over parts of a franchisee's business, there is a risk that the franchisor may be liable for the torts and contracts of the franchisee. Most franchising agreements provide that the franchisee is not an agent or partner of the franchisor. Some courts refuse to accept this characterization of the relationship, especially when the degree and type of control by the franchisor suggest an agency relationship. For example, when a franchisor has the right to control a franchisee's prices, the franchisor may be responsible for any resulting antitrust violation resulting from the franchisee's pricing decisions.

Franchisee Protection   In response to abuses by franchisors, the courts, the Federal Trade Commission, and the state legislatures have created rules that protect franchisees. The typical franchising agreement gives a franchisor wide latitude to terminate a franchisee. Some courts have invalidated such termination power or required that terminations be made in good faith. The Federal Trade Commission has issued a franchise disclosure rule and guidelines requiring franchisors to disclose their financial fees and charges, the franchisees' obligations to purchase supplies, and territorial restrictions on the franchisees. In addition, most of the states require disclosure and termination protection for franchisees.

PARTNERSHIPS

The basic concept of partnership is as ancient as the history of collective human activity. Partnerships were known in ancient Babylonia, ancient Greece, and the Roman Empire. Hammurabi's Code of 2300 B.C. regulated partnerships. The definition of a partnership in the 6th-century Justinian Code of the Roman Empire does not differ materially from that in our laws today. The partnership was likewise

FIGURE I

General Characteristics of Forms of Business

	SOLE PROPRIETORSHIP	PARTNERSHIP	LIMITED LIABILITY PARTNERSHIP	LIMITED PARTNERSHIP	CORPORATION	S CORPORATION	LIMITED LIABILITY COMPANY
Formation	When one person owns a business without forming a corporation	By agreement of owners *or* by default when two or more owners conduct business together without forming a limited partnership or a corporation	By agreement of owners; must comply with limited liability partnership statute	By agreement of owners; must comply with limited partnership statute	By agreement of owners; must comply with corporation statute	By agreement of owners; must comply with corporation statute; must elect S Corporation status under Subchapter S of Internal Revenue Code	By agreement of owners; must comply with limited liability company statute
Duration	Terminates on death or withdrawal of sole proprietor	Dissolves on death or withdrawal of partner	Dissolves on death or withdrawal of partner	Dissolves on death or withdrawal of general partner	Unaffected by death or withdrawal of shareholder	Unaffected by death or withdrawal of shareholder	Dissolves on death or withdrawal of member
Management	By sole proprietor	By partners	By partners	By general partners	By board of directors	By board of directors	By managers or members
Owner Liability	Unlimited	Unlimited	Usually unlimited for general obligations of partnership; limited to capital contribution for professional malpractice of a fellow partner	Unlimited for general partners; limited to capital contribution for limited partners	Limited to capital contribution	Limited to capital contribution	Limited to capital contribution
Transferability of Owners' Interest	None	None	None	None, unless agreed otherwise	Freely transferable, although shareholders may agree otherwise	Freely transferable although shareholders usually agree otherwise	None
Federal Income Taxation	Only sole proprietor taxed	Only partners taxed	Only partners taxed	Usually only partners taxed; may elect to be taxed like a corporation	Corporation taxed; shareholders taxed on dividends (double tax)	Only shareholders taxed	Only members taxed

known in Asian countries, including China. During the Middle Ages, much trade between nations was carried on by partnerships.

By the close of the 17th century, the partnership was recognized in the English common law. When the United States became an independent nation and adopted the English common law in 1776, the English law of partnerships became a part of American law. In the early part of the 19th century, the partnership became the most important form of association in the United States.

Today, the American common law of partnership has been largely replaced by statutory law. Every state has a statute on partnership law. The Uniform Partnership Act (UPA) of 1914 is the law in about 40 states and the District of Columbia. The UPA is a model partnership statute that is the product of the National Conference of Commissioners on Uniform State Laws, a group of practicing lawyers, judges, and law professors. The aims of the UPA are to codify partnership law in one document, to make that law more nearly consistent with itself, and to attain uniformity throughout the country.

A Revised Uniform Partnership Act (RUPA) was proposed in 1992 and amended in 1994. As of March 1997, about 10 states had adopted the RUPA. The RUPA has been heavily criticized for changing partnership rules protecting creditors of partnerships. The UPA is the framework of your study of partnerships.

Entity and Aggregate Theories

Studying the list of partnership characteristics in Figure 2, you may perceive that in some respects the partnership is treated as an **entity**—that is, as a

---

FIGURE 2

Principal Characteristics of Partnerships under the UPA

1. A partnership may be created with no formalities. Two or more people merely need to agree to own and conduct a business together in order to create a partnership (aggregate theory).
2. Partners have unlimited liability for the obligations of the business (aggregate theory). However, a partner's personal creditors have first priority to that partner's assets, while partnership creditors have first priority to partnership assets (entity theory).
3. Each partner, merely by being an owner of the business, has a right to manage the business of the partnership (aggregate theory). He is an agent of the partnership and may make the partnership liable for contracts, torts, and crimes (entity theory). Because partners are liable for all obligations of the partnership, in effect each partner is an agent of the other partners. Each partner may hire agents, and every partner is liable for the agents' authorized contracts and for torts that the agents commit in the course of their employments (aggregate theory).
4. A partnership is not an employer of the partners, for most purposes. As a result, for example, a partner who leaves a partnership is not entitled to unemployment benefits (aggregate theory).
5. Partners are fiduciaries of the partnership. They must act in the best interests of the partnership, not in their individual best interests (entity theory).
6. The profits or losses of the business are shared by the partners, who report their shares of the profits or losses on their individual federal income tax returns, because the partnership does not pay federal income taxes (aggregate theory). Nonetheless, a partnership does keep its own financial records and must file an information return with the Internal Revenue Service (entity theory).*
7. A partnership may own property in its own name (entity theory).
8. A partnership may not sue or be sued in its own name. The partners must sue or be sued (aggregate theory).
9. A partner may not sue her partners. Her sole remedy is to seek an accounting between the partners (aggregate theory).
10. A partner's ownership interest in a partnership is not freely transferable. A purchaser of a partner's interest does not become a partner, but is entitled to receive only the partner's share of the partnership's profits (aggregate theory).
11. Generally, a partnership has no life apart from its owners. If a partner dies, the partnership dissolves and may be terminated (aggregate theory). Under certain circumstances, however, the partnership may continue after the death of a partner (entity theory).

*The federal income tax return filed by a partnership is merely an information return in which the partnership indicates its gross income and deductions and the names and addresses of its partners (IRC Sec. 6031). The information return allows the Internal Revenue Service to determine whether the partners accurately report partnership income on their individual returns.

person separate and distinct from its partners. In other respects, the partnership is viewed as an **aggregate** of the partners, with no life or powers apart from them. The UPA recognizes the partnership primarily as an aggregate of the partners. In a few situations, however, the UPA confers entity status on a partnership.

CREATION OF PARTNERSHIP

No formalities are necessary to create a partnership. Two or more persons may become partners in accordance with a written partnership contract (articles of partnership), they may agree orally to be partners, or they may become partners merely by arranging their affairs as if they were partners. If partners conduct business under a trade name, they must file the name with the secretary of state in compliance with state statutes requiring the registration of fictitious business names.

When people decide to become partners, they should employ a lawyer to prepare a written partnership agreement. Although such **articles of partnership** are not required to form a partnership, they are highly desirable for the same reasons that written contracts are generally preferred. In addition, the statute of frauds requires a writing for a partnership having a term exceeding one year.

When there is no written partnership agreement, a dispute may arise over whether persons who are associated in some enterprise are partners. For example, someone may assert that she is a partner and, therefore, claim a share of the value of a successful enterprise. More frequently, an unpaid creditor may seek to hold a person liable for a debt incurred by another person in the same enterprise. To determine whether there is a partnership in the absence of an express agreement, the courts use the definition of partnership in the UPA.

UPA Definition of Partnership

The UPA defines a partnership as an "association of two or more persons to carry on as co-owners a business for profit." If the definition is satisfied, then the courts will treat those involved as partners. A relationship may meet the UPA definition of partnership even when a person does not believe he is a partner, and occasionally, even if the parties agree that they are not partners.

Association of Two or More Persons   As an association, a partnership is a *voluntary and consensual relationship*. It cannot be imposed on a person; a person must agree expressly or impliedly to have a person associate with her. For example, a partner cannot force her partners to accept her daughter into the partnership.

No person can be a partner with herself—a partnership must have *at least two partners*. A person may be a partner with her spouse.

Nearly everyone or everything may be a partner. An individual, partnership, limited partnership, corporation, or other association may be a partner. Most states do not permit a trust to be a partner, but they allow the trustee of the trust to be a partner for the benefit of the trust.

Carrying On a Business   Any trade, occupation, or profession may qualify as a business. Carrying on a business usually requires a series of transactions conducted over a period of time. For example, a group of farmers that buys supplies in quantity to get lower prices is not carrying on a business but only part of one. If the group buys harvesting equipment with which it intends to harvest crops for others for a fee for many years, it is carrying on a business.

Co-Ownership   Partners must *co-own the business* in which they associate. There is no requirement that the capital contributions or the assets of the business be co-owned.

Also, by itself, co-ownership of assets does not establish a partnership. For example, two persons who own a building as joint tenants are not necessarily partners. To be partners, they must co-own a business.

The two most important factors in establishing co-ownership of the business are the sharing of profits and the sharing of management of the business. The UPA declares that a person's **sharing the profits** of a business is *prima facie* evidence that she is a partner in the business. This means that persons sharing profits are partners, unless other evidence exists to disprove they are partners. The rationale for this rule is that a person ordinarily would not be sharing the profits of a business unless she were a co-owner. This rule brings under partnership law many persons who fail to realize that they are partners. For example, two college students who purchase college basketball tickets, resell them, and split the profits are partners.

Sharing the gross revenues of a business does not create a presumption of partnership. The profits, not the gross receipts, must be shared. For example, a broker who receives a commission on a sale of land is not a partner of the seller of that land.

Although sharing profits usually is prima facie proof of partnership, the UPA provides that **no** presumption of partnership may be made when a share of profits is received:

1. By a creditor as payment on a debt.
2. By a creditor as interest on a loan.
3. By an employee as wages.
4. By a landlord as rent.
5. By a widow, widower, or representative of a deceased partner for the value of that partner's share of the partnership.
6. As consideration to the transferor of a business or other property for his sale of the goodwill of the business or other property.

These exceptions reflect the normal expectations of the parties that no partnership exists in such situations.

Sharing management of a business is additional evidence tending to prove the existence of a partnership. However, by itself, participation in management is not conclusive proof of the existence of a partnership. For example, a creditor may be granted considerable control in a business, such as a veto power over partnership decisions and the right of consultation, without becoming a partner. Also, a sole proprietor may hire someone to manage his business, yet the manager will not be a partner of the sole proprietor.

However, when the parties claim that they share profits for one of the six reasons above, the sharing of management may overcome the presumption that they are not partners. When the parties arrange their affairs in a manner that otherwise establishes an objective intent to create a partnership, the courts find that a partnership exists. For example, when a nonmanagerial employee initially shares profits as a form of employment compensation, the employee is not a partner of his employer. But when the employer and employee modify their relationship by having the employee exercise the managerial control of a partner and fail to reaffirm that the manager is merely an employee, a partnership may exist.

Creditors occupy a privileged position. Many cases have permitted creditors to share profits and to exercise considerable control over a business without becoming partners. Creditor control is often justified on the grounds that it is merely reasonable protection for the creditor's risk.

For Profit   The owners of an enterprise must *intend to make a profit* to create a partnership. If the enterprise suffers losses, yet the owners intend to make a profit, a partnership may result. When an endeavor is carried on by several people for charitable or other nonprofit objectives, it is not a partnership. For example, Alex and Geri operate a restaurant booth at a county fair each year to raise money for a Boy Scout troop. Their relationship is not a partnership but merely an association. (Nonetheless, like partners, they may be individually liable for the debts of the enterprise.)

Intent   Frequently, courts say that there must be intent to form a partnership. This rule is more correctly stated as follows: *The parties must intend to create a relationship that the law recognizes as a partnership.* A partnership may exist even if the parties entered it inadvertently, without considering whether they had created a partnership. A written agreement to the effect that the parties do not intend to form a partnership is not conclusive if their actions provide evidence of their intent to form a relationship that meets the UPA partnership test.

There are several important consequences of being a partner. See Figure 3 for a summary of the most important consequences.

Creation of Joint Ventures

Courts frequently distinguish **joint ventures** from partnerships. A joint venture may be found when a court is reluctant to call an arrangement a partnership because the purpose of the arrangement is not to establish an ongoing business involving many transactions; instead, it is limited to a single project. For example, an agreement to buy, develop, and resell for profit a particular piece of real estate is likely to be viewed as a joint venture rather than a partnership. In all other respects, joint ventures are created just as partnerships are created. The joint venturers may have a formal written agreement. In its absence, a court applies the UPA definition of partnership—modified so as not to require the car-

FIGURE 3

Important Consequences of Being a Partner

1. You share ownership of the business. For example, you want to bring an employee into your business, which is worth $250,000. If you and the employee conduct your affairs like partners, your employee will own half of your business.
2. You share the profits of the business.
3. You share management of the business. Your partner must be allowed to participate in management decisions.
4. Your partner is your agent. You are liable for your partner's torts and contracts made in the ordinary course of business.
5. You owe fiduciary duties to your partnership and your partner, such as the duties to devote full time to the business, not to compete with the business, not to self-deal, and not to disclose confidential matters.
6. You have unlimited personal liability for all the obligations of the partnership.

rying on of a business—to determine whether a joint venture has been created.

The legal implications of the distinction between a partnership and a joint venture are not entirely clear. Generally, partnership law applies to joint ventures. For example, all of the participants in a joint venture are personally liable for its debts, and joint venturers owe each other the fiduciary duties imposed on partners. Joint ventures are treated as partnerships for federal income tax purposes. The most significant difference between joint venturers and partners is that joint venturers are usually held to have *less implied and apparent authority* than partners, due to the limited scope of the enterprise.

The following case applies partnership law to the question of whether a joint venture has been created by players of the Illinois state lottery.

FITCHIE v. YURKO   570 N.E.2d 892 (Ill. App. Ct. 1991)

P*hyllis Huisel operated a coffee shop called the Hitching-A-Ride, from which she sold tickets for the Illinois state lottery. A regular customer, Rick Yurko, frequently purchased lottery tickets from Phyllis. In mid-February 1990, Yurko purchased $100 dollars worth of $1 Fortune Hunt lottery tickets. The lottery tickets were the scratch-off variety, which revealed instant winners when the* lottery player scratched off a film covering the tickets. Yurko asked Phyllis to help him scratch off the tickets, but she suggested that Judy Fitchie, one of her employees, should scratch off the tickets because Judy was luckier than Phyllis. Yurko placed several tickets in front of Judy and Frances Vincent, another customer at the coffee shop, and invited them to help him scratch them off. Yurko stated that if they would help him scratch off the lottery tickets, they would be his partners and would share in any winnings.

After playing for some time, Judy uncovered three television sets and announced that she had a winner. The ticket scratched by Judy gave the owner a chance to compete for a $100,000 prize. The owner of the ticket was required to complete the back of ticket, indicating the name, address, and phone number of the owner. Completed tickets were to be mailed to the Illinois Department of the Lottery; six tickets would be drawn and their owners would appear on the lottery television show.

Judy placed the ticket near Phyllis, and Yurko urged Phyllis to fill it out. Phyllis did not want to appear on television. Yurko indicated he would appear on television, and after discussion, Phyllis, Judy, Frances, and Yurko agreed that Yurko would be their representative and go on television. Yurko then printed on the back of the ticket "F.J.P. Rick Yurko." F.J.P. represented the first initials of Frances, Judy, and Phyllis. When Yurko started filling out the ticket, he told Phyllis that he was going to put all their initials and his name on the ticket and that they would be partners no matter what they might win.

The ticket was mailed to the Lottery and was one of six drawn for the lottery television show. Yurko appeared on the show and won the $100,000 prize. Thereafter, Yurko claimed all the $100,000 for himself. Phyllis, Judy, and Frances sued Yurko to recover shares of the winnings. The trial court held that they were partners or joint venturers entitled to an equal share of the winnings. Yurko appealed to the Appellate Court of Illinois. ∞

Bowman, Justice   The evidence indicates that the arrangement between Yurko, Phyllis, Judy, and Frances constituted a joint venture. A joint venture is essentially a partnership carried on for a single enterprise.

A joint venture is an association of two or more persons to carry out a single enterprise for profit. Whether a joint venture exists is a question of the intent of the parties. The elements to be considered in determining the parties' intent are: an agreement to carry on an enterprise; a demonstration of intent by the parties to be joint venturers; a joint interest, as reflected in the contribution of property, finances, effort, skill, or knowledge by each party; a measure of proprietorship or joint control over the enterprise; and a provision for sharing of profits and losses. A formal agreement is not essential to establish a joint venture. Rather, the existence of a joint venture may be inferred from facts and circumstances demonstrating that the parties, in fact, undertook a joint enterprise.

The parties entered into an agreement and showed their intent to be joint venturers when they started playing the lottery together. Yurko invited the women, both verbally and by placing tickets in front of them, to play the lottery with him. Yurko told them that if they would help him scratch tickets they would be his partners and would share in any prize winnings. They expressed agreement with Yurko's proposal when they began scratching off the tickets.

Both Judy and Frances uncovered tickets that were good for small cash prizes or more tickets. None of the players tried to claim any of those prizes as their own. Rather, the tickets were turned in for more tickets, and the players kept on scratching. After the winning ticket was revealed, there was discussion amongst all the parties as to who would appear on the television show. Together, not individually, they decided that Yurko would be the one to go. Yurko impliedly acknowledged a joint effort when he printed the women's initials right alongside his own name on the back of the winning ticket, again amidst talk that he and the women were partners.

A joint interest in the effort to win the lottery is also found in the evidence. It is undisputed that Yurko paid for the tickets. Frances and Judy expended their time and energy and put forth effort to scratch the tickets. While Phyllis's part in this is not altogether clear, Phyllis scratched off a couple of tickets, and it is evident the other parties considered her part of the enterprise.

Finally, with regard to provision for sharing of profits, Yurko told the women they would share in anything that was won if they helped scratch the tickets. Yurko also wrote the women's initials next to his own on the line provided on the lottery ticket for the ticket holder's name. This evidence proves that the joint venturers planned to share equally in any lottery prize ultimately won.

We acknowledge the informality of the arrangement between Yurko and the women. Nonetheless, the parties should be bound by the terms of their agreement to jointly carry out an enterprise for profit.

Judgment for Fitchie, Huisel, and Vincent affirmed.

Creation of Mining Partnerships

Although similar to an ordinary partnership or a joint venture, a mining partnership is recognized as a distinct relationship in a number of states. Persons who cooperate in the working of either a mine or an oil or gas well are treated as mining partners if there is (1) joint ownership of a mineral interest, (2) joint operation of the property, and (3) sharing of profits and losses. Joint operation requires more than merely financing the development of a mineral interest, but it does not require active physical participation in operations; it may be proved by furnishing labor, supplies, services, or advice. The delegation of sole operating responsibility to one of the participants does not bar treatment as a mining partnership.

Creation of Limited Liability Partnerships

Unlike an ordinary partnership, a limited liability partnership (LLP) may not be created merely by partners conducting a business together. The partners must expressly agree to create an LLP by complying with a limited liability partnership statute. The formation of an LLP requires filing a form with the secretary of state, paying an annual fee, and adding the words "Registered Limited Liability

Partnership" or the acronym "LLP" to the partnership's name. Some states, like California, also require an LLP to maintain at least $5,000,000 of professional liability insurance or have a net worth of $10,000,000 or more.

PARTNERSHIP BY ESTOPPEL

Two persons may not be partners, yet in the eyes of a third person they may **appear** to be partners. If the third person deals with one of the apparent partners, he may be harmed and seek to recover damages from both of the apparent partners. The question, then, is whether the third person may collect damages from both of the apparent partners.

For example, Thomas thinks that Wilson, a wealthy person, is a partner of Porter, a poor person. Thomas decides to do business with Porter on the grounds that if Porter does not perform as agreed, he can recover damages from Wilson. If Thomas is wrong and Wilson is not Porter's partner, Thomas ordinarily has no recourse against Wilson. UPA Section 7(1) states that "persons who are not partners as to each other are not partners as to third persons." However, if Thomas can prove that Wilson misled him to believe that Wilson and Porter were partners, he may sue Wilson for damages suffered when Porter failed to perform as agreed. This is an application of the doctrine of **partnership by estoppel.**

Partnership by estoppel is based on substantial, detrimental reliance on the appearance of partnership. Partnership by estoppel has three elements:

1. A person holds herself out or consents to being held out as a partner of another person.
2. A third party justifiably relies on the holding out.
3. The third person is injured as a result of the reliance.

The third party who is damaged may recover his loss from the person who held herself out or consented to being held out as the partner of the other person.

Holding Out

A person might hold himself out as a partner by referring to himself as another person's partner. Or he might appear frequently in the office of a purported partner and confer with him. Perhaps he and another person share office space, have one door to an office with both of their names on it, have one telephone number, and share a secretary who answers the phone giving the names of both persons.

More difficult is determining when a person *consents* to being held out as another's partner. Mere knowledge that one is being held out as a partner is not consent. But a person's silence in response to a statement that the person is another's partner is consent. For example, suppose Chavez tells Eaton that Gold is a partner in Birt's new retail shoe business. In fact, Gold is not Birt's partner. Later, Gold learns of the conversation between Chavez and Eaton. Gold does not have to seek out Chavez and Eaton to tell them that he is not Birt's partner in order to avoid being held liable as a partner for Birt's business debts. Had Chavez made the statement to Eaton in Gold's presence, however, Gold must deny the partnership relation or he will be held liable for Eaton's subsequent reliance on Gold's silence.

Reasonable Reliance and Injury

A partner by estoppel is liable only to those persons who reasonably rely on the holding out and suffer injury thereby. This means that partnership by estoppel is determined on a case-by-case basis.

A third person's reliance on the appearance of a partnership must be reasonable. When a person has information that would prevent a reasonable person from relying on the holding out, no partnership by estoppel may result. For example, Litz knows that Frank and Stump are employer and employee. Frank calls Stump "my partner" in the presence of Stump and Litz. Frank and Stump are not partners by estoppel. Because Litz knows that Frank and Stump are employer and employee, she may not reasonably rely on Frank's calling Stump "my partner."

The injury suffered by the third person must be the result of her reliance. If the third person would have done business with another person whether or not that person was a partner of someone held out as a partner, there is no injury as a result of reliance. Hence, there is no partnership by estoppel.

Effect of Partnership by Estoppel

Once partnership by estoppel has been proved, the person who held himself out or who consented to being held out is liable as though he were a partner. He is liable on contracts entered into by third persons on their belief that he was a partner. He is liable for torts committed during the course of relationships entered by third persons who believed he was a partner.

Although two parties are partners by estoppel to a person who knows of the holding out and who justifiably relies on it to his injury, the partners by estoppel are *not partners in fact* and do not share the profits, management, or value of the business of the purported partnership. Partnership by estoppel is merely a device to allow creditors to sue parties who mislead them into believing that a partnership exists.

In the following case, the court refused to find a partnership by estoppel because there was no reliance on the appearance of a partnership.

MILANO v. FREED 64 F.3d 91 (2d Cir. 1995)

Before Michael Milano was born, his mother met with Dr. Jay Freed, a pediatrician. Based on Dr. Freed's description of his pediatric practice, Michael's parents chose Dr. Freed's medical group as the pediatricians for Michael. The Freed Group included Drs. Jay Freed, Mitchell Kleinberg, and Stephanie Citerman. Two weeks after his birth, Michael was examined by Dr. Citerman. The visit was uneventful except for some minor concerns about jaundice.

When Michael was three weeks old, his parents noticed that he had abnormal stomach movements when he breathed, limited leg movement, a strange shaking of his legs when touched, frequent vomiting after feedings, a weak cry, a tendency to lean to the right, and a restricted ability to lift his head. Michael and his mother visited Dr. Kleinberg. After a quick exam, Dr. Kleinberg expressed no concern and suggested that Michael's mother was overfeeding Michael.

Over the next few weeks, Michael's symptoms worsened. Michael's mother immediately scheduled another visit with her pediatricians. After a five-minute examination, Dr. Freed explained that he attributed any problems with Michael's legs to an underdeveloped circulatory or nervous system, which he said was common in babies. He declared that Michael's other ailments were because he was a "slow starter" or "lazy." Dr. Freed told Michael's mother that she overfed Michael and "was just being a very nervous, first-time mother."

A month later, Michael's condition having worsened, he and his parents visited Dr. Kleinberg, who now suspected that Michael had craniosynostosis, a condition in which the bones in an infant's head grow together prematurely. Two weeks later, a CAT scan and a 3-D reconstruction of Michael's head revealed he did not suffer from craniosynostosis. The results of the test were given to Michael's mother 13 days later. Nonetheless, Michael's condition worsened, and his parents sought a second opinion from a pediatric neurosurgeon, who conjectured after reviewing Michael's medical history that his problems related to his brain, not his skull. Chest X rays revealed that 4½-month-old Michael Milano was suffering from a cancerous tumor on his spine. Although chemotherapy eradicated the tumor, Michael suffered permanent damage, including paralysis below his waist.

On behalf of Michael, his parent's sued the physicians in the Freed Group on the grounds that his injuries were aggravated by the failure to detect his tumor at an earlier date. First, the District Court found that there was no evidence that Dr. Citerman was a partner of the other physicians in the Freed Group. Next, the District Court found no evidence that Drs. Freed and Kleinberg had deviated from accepted medical practice. After the District Court refused to let the jury hear the case, the Milanos appealed to the court of appeals. The court of appeals found that there was sufficient evidence of malpractice by Drs. Freed and Kleinberg to allow a jury to hear the case. The court of appeals then considered whether Dr. Citerman could be vicariously liable for the malpractice of Drs. Freed and Kleinberg. ∞

Calabresi, Circuit Judge The Milanos's complaint named Dr. Citerman as a defendant, not because of any alleged malpractice on her part but as a vicariously liable partner in the Freed Group.

On appeal, the Milanos concede that Dr. Citerman was not an actual partner in the Freed Group; they seek instead to hold her liable under the New York doctrine of "partnership by estoppel." Section 27 of

New York's Partnership Law states that when "a person, by words spoken or written or by conduct, represents himself, or consents to another representing him to any one, as a partner in an existing partnership . . ., he is liable to any such person to whom such representation has been made, who has, on the faith of such representation, given credit to the actual or apparent partnership."

There is some evidence—most notably a bill for the Freed Group with Dr. Citerman's name prominently displayed—which might allow a jury to conclude that Dr. Citerman represented herself, or consented to another representing her, as a partner in the Freed Group. But we find nothing in the record to indicate that the Milanos, "on the faith of such representation, [gave] credit to the actual or apparent partnership." There is no evidence suggesting that the Milanos relied upon representations that Dr. Citerman was a partner in the Freed Group when they decided to use the partnership as Michael's pediatricians. Since such evidence is essential to establish liability through partnership by estoppel, the action against Dr. Citerman must be dismissed.

Judgment for Dr. Citerman affirmed.

PARTNERSHIP CAPITAL

When a partnership or limited liability partnership is formed, partners contribute cash or other property to the partnership. The partners' contribution is called **partnership capital.** To supplement beginning capital, other property may be contributed to the partnership as needed, such as by the partners permitting the partnership to retain some of its profits. Partnership capital is the equity of the business.

Loans made by partners to a partnership are not partnership capital but instead are liabilities of the business. Partners who make loans to a partnership are both owners and creditors.

PARTNERSHIP PROPERTY

A partnership or limited liability partnership may own all or only a part of the property it uses. For example, it may own the business and perhaps a small amount of working capital in the form of cash or a checking account, yet own no other assets. All other tangible and intangible property used by the partnership may be individually or jointly owned by one or more of the partners or rented by the partnership from third parties. A determination of what is partnership property becomes essential when the partnership is dissolved and the assets are being distributed and when creditors of either the partnership or one of the partners is seeking assets to satisfy a debt.

The UPA provides that (1) all property originally brought into the partnership or subsequently acquired by purchase or otherwise, on account of the partnership, is partnership property, and (2) unless the contrary intention appears, property acquired with partnership funds is partnership property.

The intent of the partners controls whether the partnership or an individual partner owns the property. It is best to have a written record of the partners' intent as to ownership of all property used by the partnership, such as in the articles of partnership. Other writings—such as accounting records—show the partnership assets; assets appearing in the partnership's books are presumed to belong to the partnership. Also, the partnership's paying rent on property provides strong evidence that the property belongs to the partner receiving the rent.

The presumption is very strong that property purchased with partnership funds and used in the partnership is partnership property. No such presumption is accorded to a partner who purchases property with her own funds and then allows the partnership to use the property; other factors besides the partner's funding the purchase determine who owns the property.

If title is taken in the partnership name, it is presumed that the property is partnership property. However, the presumption is not as strong that real property held in the name of a partner is individual property. Other indicia may prove that property held in a partner's name belongs to the partnership. For example, the partnership's payment of property taxes or insurance premiums, the maintainance, repair, and improvement of property by the partnership, and the deduction of these expenses on the partnership income tax return are indications of the intent of the partners that property belongs to the partnership, despite title being held in the name of a partner.

Examples

A tax accountant discovers that a partnership is using a building to which a partner, Jacob Smith, holds title. The partnership pays rent monthly to Smith, but the partnership pays for all maintenance and repairs on the building. The accountant wants to know whether the partnership or Smith should be paying real property taxes on the building. Smith is the owner and should be paying taxes on it because his partners' intent to allow Smith to retain ownership is evidenced by the partnership paying rent to Smith.

Changing the facts, suppose the partnership pays no rent to Smith, the partnership maintains and repairs the building, and the partnership pays real property taxes on the building, but the title is in Smith's name. Who owns the building? The property belongs to the partnership, because all the objective criteria of ownership point toward partnership ownership, especially the payment of taxes. Therefore, when the partnership is liquidated, the building will be sold along with other partnership assets, and the proceeds of its sale will be distributed to partnership creditors and to all of the partners.

In the following case, the court held that land held in a partner's name was partnership property.

HOLMES v. HOLMES 849 P.2d 1140 (Ore. Ct. App. 1993)

From 1957 to 1960, Steve Holmes and his father-in-law, Bill Foss, owned a construction business, Foss & Holmes Construction. Steve continued the business after Bill's death. In 1975, Steve's son Mike joined Foss & Holmes, which was operated as a partnership.

Steve also owned a ranch from which he generated hay sales of $30,000 to $50,000 per year. In 1984 and 1985, irrigation equipment was purchased for the ranch; for tax reasons, title to the irrigation equipment was placed in Mike's name. Beginning in 1984, Steve and Mike's joint books show that the funds of the ranch and Foss & Holmes were commingled. Money and assets were shifted from the two businesses' various bank accounts as necessary to achieve tax advantages and to protect property from Steve's creditors. Ranch activities and Foss & Holmes activities were reported to and considered together by Mike and Steve's accountant for tax purposes. Mike and Steve reported their income for tax purposes not necessarily to reflect their actual distribution of income between them but to minimize their overall tax liability.

In 1985, Mike signed loan agreements with the Bank of Eastern Oregon, the proceeds of which were used by Foss & Holmes and the ranch. In 1986, Steve obtained an FHA loan to pay off the loans by Bank of Eastern Oregon. In 1987, Steve learned of a special, low-interest FHA loan available for the purchase of property from a parent. Solely to obtain the benefits of the low-interest loan, Steve deeded the ranch to Mike. No money changed hands. Mike never paid Steve for the ranch. The transfer was not treated as a sale on Steve's and Mike's books. Mike did not claim ranch income as his own after the transfer. There were no changes in ranch operations. Steve continued to operate the ranch, and the money from hay sales was used to repay loans for both Foss & Holmes and the ranch.

Eventually, a dispute arose between Steve and Mike regarding Mike's compensation and liability arising out of ranch operations. To resolve the festering dispute, Steve brought a legal action against Mike to dissolve their partnership and distribute its assets. Steve argued that he and Mike were partners in the operation of not only Foss & Holmes but also the ranch. Steve testified that the ranch was a partnership asset that should be sold to pay claims against the partnership. Mike countered that he and Steve were not partners in the ranch; Mike testified that although they never intended to give title to the ranch to him, he nonetheless owned it as compensation for money owed him by Steve. The trial court held that the ranch was partnership property; Mike appealed. ∽

Rossman, Presiding Judge In view of the fact that the trial court has observed the witnesses' demeanor, its findings are entitled to substantial weight, particularly when the facts are in dispute and the credibility of the witnesses is an important factor. The trial court said that it was impressed by the testimony of Steve, who outlined the affairs of the parties without embellishment and with a genuine desire to get the matter concluded. The trial court was not impressed with Mike's testimony, and expressed its belief that Mike was so motivated by greed that his entire testimony was suspect.

We find that Steve and Mike were partners in the operation of the ranch, and that Steve contributed the ranch to the partnership. The fact that Steve later transferred the ranch to Mike did not end the partnership or remove the ranch as a partnership asset, if Steve and Mike intended that it would remain a partnership asset.

It is well established that title to the real property of a partnership may reside in one of the members rather than in the entity and that the locus of the title does not necessarily affect either the entity's rights in the property or the entity's existence. *Fenton v. State Ind. Acc. Com.* (1953).

We find that the purpose of the transfer of the ranch from Steve to Mike was to lessen the partnership's overall expenses, and that there never was an intention to remove it from the partnership. We agree with the trial court that the ranch continued to be a partnership asset.

Judgment for Steve Holmes affirmed.

PARTNERS' PROPERTY RIGHTS

In a partnership or limited liability partnership, a partner has three property rights:

1. Her rights in specific partnership property.
2. Her partnership interest.
3. Her right to participate in the management of the business.

The first two rights are discussed here. The management right is discussed in Chapter 37, Operation of Partnership and Related Forms.

Rights in Partnership Property

Partnership property is owned by partners as **tenants in partnership.** This means that the partners as a group own partnership property as a whole; the partners as individuals do not own proportionate interests in separate items of partnership property.

As a tenant in partnership, each partner has the right to possess partnership property for partnership purposes. A partner has no individual right to use or possess partnership property for her own purposes, such as paying a personal debt, unless she has the consent of the other partners. Likewise, a partner's personal creditor may not make a claim against partnership assets.

On the death or other withdrawal of a partner, his rights in partnership property pass to the surviving partners. This is called the **right of survivorship.**

Partnership Interest

As a co-owner of a partnership, a partner has an ownership interest in the partnership. A partner's ownership interest is called a **partnership interest** and is part of his personal property. Although a partner may not give his personal creditors any interest in separate items of partnership property, a partner may sell or **assign his partnership interest** to a creditor. And although a partner's personal creditor has no right to seize separate items of partnership property, a creditor may obtain rights in a partner's partnership interest by obtaining a **charging order** against that interest.

Assignment The sale or **assignment of a partnership interest** is a voluntary act of a partner. It entitles the buyer or assignee to receive the assigning partner's share of the partnership's profits. Although the assignee is the owner of the partnership interest, the assignee does not become a partner of the partnership: The assignee has no right to inspect the partnership's books and records or to manage the partnership. The assignee's only other right beyond receiving a share of the profits is to ask a court to dissolve the partnership, but only if the partnership is at will. (A partnership at will has no term and may rightfully be dissolved by a partner at any time.) An assignee who obtains a judicial dissolution may obtain liquidation of the partnership's assets and obtain payment from the proceeds of the sale of the partnership's assets.

By itself a partner's assignment of his partnership interest does not dissolve the partnership; the assigning partner remains a partner and can continue to manage the partnership.

The nonassigning partners may not exclude the assigning partner from the partnership. They may, however, rightfully dissolve the partnership by their unanimous agreement, even if the term or objective of the partnership has not been met.

The following case illustrates that an assignee of a partnership interest has the right to receive profits but has no liability to partnership creditors due to the assignment.

CONNORS v. MIDDLE FORK CORP. 790 F.Supp. 6 (D.D.C. 1992)

In 1983, Odell Rogers, John Lockhart, and Caleb Cooley formed MFC Partnership, a partnership formed under the laws of Kentucky. In 1984, Odell Rogers made a gift of his 41 percent interest in MFC to his three sons: 4-year-old Shannon Rogers, 19-year-old James Rogers, and 20-year-old Arthur Rogers. Odell made the gift for the purpose of providing income to his sons to pay their college expenses. The Rogers sons received income from MFC, which was reported on both the partnership's and the sons' individual federal income tax returns. The sons were identified as partners on MFC's unaudited balance sheet of December 31, 1985. In addition, MFC's 1986 income statement listed the sons as partners.

In 1987, MFC incurred liability to an employee pension fund under the federal Employee Retirement Income Security Act (ERISA). Joseph Connors, a trustee for the fund, contended that the Rogers sons were partners of MFC and therefore were personally liable to the fund on MFC's ERISA liability. The Rogers sons asked the trial court to grant a summary judgment for the sons on the grounds that they were merely assignees of their father's partnership interest and had no liability for MFC's obligations.

Revercomb, District Judge Under the Uniform Partnership Act, the receipt of profits from a business is *prima facie* evidence that one is a partner in the business. One may rebut this presumption by showing that one falls within a statutorily protected relationship. The Rogers sons argue that the 1984 transfer to them was no more than an assignment of Odell Rogers's partnership interest. An assignment of a partnership interest merely entitles the assignee to receive the assignor's profits from the firm but does not entitle the assignee to interfere otherwise in the management of the firm. Assignees are not partners and cannot be held personally liable for the firm's obligations.

Although the sharing of profits and losses is prima facie evidence of a partnership, the issue of control is the more important criterion in determining the existence of a partnership. Both Arthur and James Rogers did none of the acts which usually denote management or control of a partnership: request information about the firm's finances, attend its meetings or vote, attempt to withdraw its money, represent the firm to third parties, or even speak with the other partners about the firm. Neither James nor Arthur knew where the offices of MFC Partnership were located. Neither Arthur nor James was employed by MFC.

Connors notes that the Rogers sons on one occasion received "management fees" totalling $3,000, without any further showing of what these "fees" were paid for. The Court regards such evidence as no more than a mere scintilla upon which a jury could not reasonably find for Connors.

Thus, there can be *no* doubt that the transfer conveyed *less* than full partnership status. Connors has failed to carry his burden of proof of showing sufficient indicia of partnership. It follows that the Rogers sons are not jointly or severally liable to the pension fund as partners.

Motion for summary judgment granted in favor of the Rogers sons.

Charging Order A partner's personal creditor with a judgment against the partner may ask a court to issue a **charging order**—that is, an order charging the partner's partnership interest with payment of the unsatisfied amount of the judgment. Unlike assignment, a charging order is obtained without the partner's consent. As with assignment, however, the partner remains a partner and may manage the partnership, and the creditor is entitled to receive only the partner's share of the profits. If the profits are insufficient to pay the debt, the creditor may ask the court to order foreclosure and to sell the partner's interest to satisfy the charging order.

Neither the issuance of a charging order nor the purchase of a partnership interest at a foreclosure sale causes a dissolution. But the purchaser of a partnership interest at the foreclosure sale may ask a court to dissolve a partnership at will. The other partners may eliminate this potential threat to the continuation of the partnership by **redeeming the charging order.** To redeem a charging order, the other partners must pay the creditor the amount due on the judgment against the partner. If the other partners so choose, however, they may dissolve the partnership by their unanimous agreement, even if the term or objective of the partnership has not been met.

Joint Venturers and Mining Partners   Transfers of interests in joint ventures are treated in the same way as transfers of partnership interests. However, a mining partner's interest is *freely transferable*. The transferee becomes a partner with all the rights of ownership and management, and the transferor loses all of his partnership rights. The other mining partners cannot object to the transfer, and their consent to a transfer is not required.

ETHICAL AND PUBLIC POLICY CONCERNS

1. A person who carefully considers which business form to use for his one-person business can achieve nearly any combination of characteristics desirable to him. For example, by incorporating and electing S Corporation status, a person can limit his personal liability, deduct business losses on his individual federal income tax return, yet control the business by electing himself to the board of directors. Why should a careful planner obtain such advantages, while a person who merely begins his business without selecting a form has unlimited liability as a sole proprietor? Is the business of the careful planner more valuable to our society than the business of the person who does not choose a business form?

2. Why should all the partners in a partnership be individually liable for all the obligations of the partnership, while shareholders and managers of a corporation have no liability beyond their capital contributions? Is the corporate form of business or the business conducted by corporations more important to society than the partnership form or the business conducted by partnerships? Would benefits that businesses provide to society be reduced if limited liability were not extended to shareholders and managers of corporations?

3. What are the ethical underpinnings of partnership by estoppel? Why should a person be held liable for the business debts of another person when he does not benefit from the business? Could the person who relied on the appearance of partnership have protected himself by making inquiries? Should he be required to make such inquiries?

PROBLEMS AND PROBLEM CASES

1.  *Video Case.* See "The Reunion." When friends reunite at a wedding, they reveal their plans for future business ventures. Al and Amy, an unmarried couple, propose opening a Thai restaurant. Al is a dentist, and Amy is director of public relations for a publishing company. Amy will quit her job eventually to manage the restaurant. They will hire a chef whose restaurant is about to close.

Carl is a successful real estate agent who wants to open his own real estate firm.

Bob has tried several business ventures, but all have failed, including a venture to manufacture ski racks for motorcycles.

Dave and Donna, the newly married couple, plan to quit their jobs, move to Wyoming, and open a software development business. They want the business to have few investors. They have lined up potential clients who will finance their initial efforts in return for software customization.

What business forms should they use for their business ventures? What additional questions do you want to ask to help you determine the best business forms for their ventures?

2. Daon Corporation developed a housing subdivision, improving the building lots for resale. To promote the sales of lots, Daon created a marketing scheme, named Showcase of Homes, that involved area builders. The builders, including Raymond Driesel, purchased lots from Daon and built custom homes on the homesites. Daon advertised the Showcase of Homes, decorated and furnished model homes, and provided a landscaping plan to the builders. Both Driesel and Daon benefited from the Showcase program. Driesel benefited from Daon's advertising and the chance to show his home, leading to future home-building jobs. Daon benefited from having homes constructed in the subdivision, proving to prospective lot buyers the feasibility and desirability of buying a lot from Daon, leading to further lot sales. Theo Dority purchased the home built by Driesel. All negotiations and documents for the sale were between Dority and Driesel. The home was defective. Driesel promised to correct the defects, but he failed to do so. Dority corrected the defects at a cost of $20,000. Will Dority successfully sue Daon for $20,000 on the grounds that Daon and Driesel were partners?

3. OWLP, a Hawaii limited partnership, owned the Outrigger West Hotel. OWLP and Hawaii Hotels Operating Company (HHOC) agreed that OWLP and HHOC would jointly operate the hotel and share its revenues, allocating 73 percent to OWLP and 27 percent to HHOC. The agreement provided that revenues would be collected from the hotel and allocated daily according to the percentages above. However, the allocation percentages were changed six times during a four-year period to permit each party to recover out-of-pocket expenses and to provide a return of 98 percent of the net income to OWLP and of 2 percent of the net income to HHOC. Thus, any amount recovered by each party according to the predetermined percentage in excess of its expenses would be its profit. Losses were shared pro rata like the profits. Are OWLP and HHOC partners?

4. Alvin and Carol Volkman decided to build a house. They contacted David McNamee for construction advice. McNamee informed the Volkmans that he was doing business with Phillip Carroll. The Volkmans received a letter from McNamee on DP Associates stationery. They assumed that the DP was derived from the first names of McNamee and Carroll. At DP Associates' office before the contract was signed, McNamee introduced Alvin Volkman to Carroll, who said, "I hope we'll be working together." Carroll stated that McNamee would be the person at DP Associates primarily doing business with the Volkmans, but indicated that he also would be available for consultation. After the contract was signed, DP Associates failed to perform it. When the

Volkmans sued Carroll, the trial court concluded that Carroll was not a partner of McNamee and therefore was not liable to the Volkmans. Can the Volkman's prove that Carroll is liable to them as McNamee's partner by estoppel?

5. ▣ *Video Case.* See "The Partnership." Art, Ben, and Diedre are partners of Alphabet Builders, a partnership in the construction business. They meet at a restaurant with a prospective new partner, Don, who says he will decide whether to enter the partnership after discussing the matter with his wife. During the meeting, they are approached by John, with whom the partnership has been attempting to do business. Art introduces Don to John, stating, "We're celebrating Don's joining Alphabet Builders." Don and John shake hands, and John says, "Congratulations! Alphabet Builders has a very good reputation. In fact, I'm about to become one of your new clients. I signed the contract this morning." Don says nothing in response to John's statement. Subsequently, however, Don decides not to join Alphabet Builders. Nonetheless, when Alphabet Builders breaches its contract with John, John sues Don on the contract. Is Don liable to John?

6. Richard DeLong and Ken Birch formed a partnership to build houses. They agreed that all sales proceeds would be deposited in a partnership bank checking account and that both of them must sign all checks. For two years, Birch and DeLong signed all checks, but then DeLong agreed that Birch could sign partnership checks by himself. Six years later, DeLong discovered that Birch paid some of his personal expenses with partnership checks. DeLong reported his discovery to the Washington state prosecuting attorney, who prosecuted Birch for the crime of embezzlement. Embezzlement was defined in the Washington statute as exerting unauthorized control over the property of another. Has Birch committed embezzlement?

7. Padgett Carroll and Walter Fulton operated as a partnership a trucking business under the name of C & F Trucking. Carroll contributed a semi truck, which Fulton drove for the business. Carroll used $4,600 of his personal funds to purchase a used 42-foot trailer for C & F Trucking. The seller's invoice listed C & F Trucking as the purchaser of the trailer. The trailer's certificate of title listed C & F Trucking as the owner. Fulton's personal financial problems forced him to file for bankruptcy. May Fulton claim ownership of the trailer among his assets?

8. Claude Gauldin and Joe Corn formed a partnership to raise cattle and hogs on land owned by Corn. Partnership funds were used to build two buildings on the land for use by the partnership. Gauldin and Corn did not discuss who owned the buildings. Gauldin knew when the buildings were constructed that they would be permanent improvements to the land and would become part of it. The partnership paid no rent for the land, and there was no agreement to consider the use of the land as a contribution by Corn. The taxes on the land were paid by Corn, as was the cost of upkeep. When Corn left the partnership, Gauldin claimed that the buildings were partnership assets and that he was entitled to half of their fair market value. Was Gauldin correct?

Operation of Partnership and Related Forms

wo relationships are important during the operation of a partnership business: (1) the relation of the partners to each other and the partnership; and (2) the relation of the partners to third parties who are affected by the business of the partnership. ∞

DUTIES OF PARTNERS TO THE PARTNERSHIP AND EACH OTHER

The relation between partners and the partnership is a fiduciary relation of the highest order. It is one of mutual trust, confidence, and honesty. Therefore, partners owe to the partnership and each other the highest degree of *loyalty and good faith* in all partnership matters. The duties partners owe each other are the same in ordinary partnerships and in limited liability partnerships.

Profiting Secretly

Unless there is a contrary agreement, a partner's sole compensation from partnership affairs is a share of partnership profits. Therefore, a partner may not make a secret profit out of the transaction of partnership business. For example, a partner may not profit personally by receiving an undisclosed kickback from a partnership supplier. In addition, a partner may not profit secretly when she makes a contract with her partnership, such as selling a building she owns to her partnership without disclosing her ownership or her profit to her partners.

When a partner receives a secret profit, she has a conflict of interests, and there is a risk that she may prefer her own interests over those of the partnership. Therefore, the law permits a partner to profit personally from partnership transactions only if she deals in good faith, makes a full disclosure of all material facts affecting the transaction, and obtains approval from her partners. The remedy for a breach of this duty not to make a secret profit is a return of the profit that she made in the transaction with the partnership.

Competing against the Partnership

A partner may not compete against his partnership unless he obtains consent from the other partners. For example, a partner of a retail clothing store may not open a clothing store nearby. However, he may open a grocery store and not breach his fiduciary duty. The partnership has the remedy of recovering the profits of the partner's competing venture.

Duty to Serve

The duty to serve requires a partner to undertake his share of responsibility for running the day-to-day operations of the partnership business. The basis of this duty is the expectation that all partners will work. Sometimes, this duty is termed the duty to devote full time to the partnership.

Partners may agree to relieve a partner of the duty to serve. So-called *silent partners* merely contribute capital to the partnership. Silent partners do not have the duty to serve, but they have the same liability for partnership debts as any other partner.

The remedies for breach of the duty to serve include assessing the partner for the cost of hiring a person to do his work and paying the other partners additional compensation.

Duty of Care

In transacting partnership business, each partner owes a duty to use **reasonable skill and care.** A partner is not liable to her partnership for losses resulting from honest errors in judgment, but a partner is liable for losses resulting from her negli-

gence or lack of skill and care. She must make a **reasonable investigation** before making a decision so that she has an adequate basis for making the decision. The decision she makes must be that of an **ordinarily prudent business manager** in her position.

For example, a grocery store has stocked avocados for three years and has always sold them. If one of the partners buys the same amount of avocados as usual but they do not sell, the partner is not liable for the loss to the partnership. Her decision appears reasonable as of the time she made it. If prior to the time she made the decision, however, sales of avocados have fallen and trade magazines that she should have read published customer surveys showing lower expected sales of avocados, she would be liable.

Duty to Act within Actual Authority

A partner has the duty not to exceed the authority granted him by the partnership agreement or, if there is no agreement, the authority normally held by partners in his position. He is responsible to the partnership for losses resulting from unauthorized transactions negotiated in the name of the partnership. For example, suppose partners agree that no partner shall purchase supplies from Jasper Supply Company, which is unaware of the limitation on the partners' authority. When one partner purchases supplies from Jasper and the partnership suffers a loss because the supplies are of low quality, the wrongdoing partner must bear the loss due to her breach of the partnership agreement.

Duty to Account

Partners have a duty to account for their use or disposal of partnership funds and partnership property, as well as their receipt of any benefit or profit without the consent of the other partners. Partnership property should be used for partnership purposes, not for a partner's personal use.

For example, when a partner of a firm that leases residential property to college students allows his daughter to live in a partnership-owned apartment, the partner must collect rent for the partnership from his daughter or risk breaching the duty to account.

Each partner owes a duty to keep a reasonable record of all business transacted by him for the partnership and to make such records available to the person keeping the partnership books. The books must be kept at the partnership's principal place of business. Every partner must at all times have access to them and may inspect and copy them.

In addition to a right to inspect the books of the partnership, a partner has a right to a formal **accounting** of the partnership affairs. It is generally by an accounting that a partner can recover from his partners for their breaches of their fiduciary duties.

An accounting is not merely a presentation of financial statements. It is a judicial review of all partnership and partners' transactions to determine whether partners have properly used partnership assets and to award each partner his rightful share of partnership assets. The court takes into consideration breaches of fiduciary duties and adjusts appropriately the amounts payable to the partners.

An accounting is an extreme action and is ordinarily taken only after dissolution of a partnership. The Uniform Partnership Act (UPA), however, specifically permits an accounting prior to dissolution.

Closely related to the duty to account is the right of a partner to be **indemnified** for expenditures made from personal funds and for personal liabilities incurred during the ordinary conduct of the business. For example, a partner uses her own truck to pick up some partnership supplies, which she pays for with her personal check. The partner is entitled to be reimbursed for the cost of the supplies and for her cost of picking up the supplies, including fuel.

Other Duties

A partner must maintain the **confidentiality** of partnership information such as a trade secret or a customer list. This means a partner should not disclose to third parties confidential information of the partnership unless disclosure benefits the partnership.

On the other hand, each partner owes a duty to disclose to the other partners all information that is material to the partnership business. She also owes a duty to inform the partners of notices she has received that affect the rights of the partnership. For example, Gordon Gekko, a partner of a stock brokerage firm, learns that National Motors Corporation is projecting a loss for the current year. The projection reduces the value of National stock, which the firm has been recommending that its customers buy. Gekko has a duty to disclose the projection to his partners to allow them to advise customers of the brokerage.

In the following case, the court considered whether one partner breached the duty to disclose material information and whether the other partner breached the duty not to compete against the partnership.

LUND v. ALBRECHT   936 F.2d 459 (9th Cir. 1991)

In 1971, Bill Lund and Don Albrecht formed a partnership, Terramics Associates, that was involved in real estate acquisitions, development, and sales. Among the real estate properties was a 190-acre parcel known as Parcel D. In 1983, Lund and Albrecht agreed to terminate their partnership, with Albrecht purchasing Lund's interest in the partnership. On April 6, 1984, Albrecht sent a letter to Lund outlining the possible methods of terminating their relationship. Termination negotiations continued until June 4, 1984, when Lund and Albrecht signed a formal written agreement detailing all aspects of Albrecht's purchase of Lund's partnership interest.

Prior to signing the June 4 agreement, during May 1984, Albrecht received four offers for Parcel D ranging from $9.95 million to $12 million. These offers valued Parcel D at $2 to $4 million higher than the price placed on Parcel D during the negotiations leading to the June 4 agreement. Lund was not aware of these offers, and Albrecht did not inform Lund of the offers. In January 1985, Parcel D sold for $12.8 million.

After discovering Albrecht's failure to disclose the May 1984 offers, Lund sued Albrecht for breach of fiduciary duty. Albrecht filed a counterclaim against Lund, alleging Lund had failed to disclose that he had competed with the partnership by having a general partnership interest in Wilshire Redevelopment Company. The trial court held that Albrecht had breached his fiduciary duty to Lund; the court also found that Lund had disclosed his interest in the competing business to Albrecht. The trial court awarded Lund damages and interest of almost $2.2 million. Albrecht appealed.

Hug, Circuit Judge The district court concluded that Albrecht owed fiduciary obligations to Lund at least through June 4, 1984. The rule in California is that upon consummation of the sale of a partnership interest, the selling partner's interest and participation in the partnership are terminated. In California, consummation occurs, and a partner's fiduciary duty ends, when the parties have formed and signed a contract to purchase the partnership interest.

If the partnership existed until June 4, 1984, Albrecht's non-disclosure of the offers for Parcel D was a breach of fiduciary duty. However, if the partnership terminated on April 11, as Albrecht contends, then Albrecht's non-disclosure to Lund is not a breach of fiduciary duty.

After reviewing the April 6 letter, we agree that it does not constitute an agreement between Lund and Albrecht to terminate the partnership. The April 6 letter was merely an outline of what the parties had discussed. It was an agreement about the alternative methods of terminating their partnership.

The June 4 agreement was a complete, detailed, 10-page agreement prepared by the parties' attorneys dealing with the complexities of the multiple properties held by the partnership. It dealt with the entities to be transferred, the entities not affected, on-going indebtedness relating to the entities, assumption of liability, indemnification, representations, warranties, and a myriad of other important legal provisions governing the obligations of the parties. It was signed not only by Albrecht and Lund, but also by their spouses, a vital legal consideration in California, a community property state. The opening sentence of the agreement stated, "This Agreement is made and entered into as of this 4th day of June, 1984."

The district court correctly concluded that the June 4 agreement was the actual agreement for the sale and transfer of partnership assets. Albrecht breached his fiduciary duty, and the district court applied a constructive trust as an appropriate remedy for Lund, a victim of Albrecht's breach of fiduciary duty. The district court awarded Lund a 50% interest in Albrecht's excess profits from Parcel D. Such a measure of damages is justified because Lund is entitled to recover a money judgment for all losses occasioned by Albrecht's breach of fiduciary duty, regardless of whether such losses were anticipated. A breaching co-partner is required to account for all profits or benefits, even if the other co-partner has not suffered a loss.

In his counterclaim, Albrecht alleged that Lund had breached his fiduciary duties by failing to disclose his ownership as a general partner in the Wilshire properties, which were competing with the Albrecht/Lund partnership. The district court found that Albrecht was aware of Lund's involvement with Wilshire prior to signing the June 4 agreement. Further, the June 4 agreement specifically mentioned the Wilshire properties and provided that Albrecht waived and released any claim he might have had against Lund arising from Lund's participation in Wilshire.

Albrecht argues that he did not know that the June 4 agreement would serve as a release with regard to his counterclaim against Lund. Nonetheless, the express terms of the June 4 agreement acknowledged that Lund was an "owner of record" of Wilshire, that Albrecht "disclaims any interest" in Wilshire, that Wilshire belongs to Lund, and that Albrecht would make no claim against Lund with respect to Wilshire. The objective language of the June 4 agreement, not Albrecht's undisclosed subjective intention regarding the June 4 agreement, is what is legally binding upon the parties. Therefore, we hold that Albrecht had released all claims he had with regard to Wilshire in the June 4 agreement.

Judgment for Lund affirmed.

Joint Ventures and Mining Partnerships

The fiduciary duties of partners also exist in joint ventures and mining partnerships, although there are a few special rules regarding their enforcement. For example, a joint venturer may seek an accounting to settle claims between the joint venturers, or he may sue his joint venturers to recover joint property or to be indemnified for expenditures that he has made on behalf of the joint venture. A mining partner's remedy against his partners is an accounting; however, a mining partner has a lien against his partners' shares in the mining partnership for his expenditures on behalf of the mining partnership. The lien can be enforced against purchasers of his partners' shares.

Partner's Duties

1. Duty not to make a secret profit while transacting for the partnership.
2. Duty not to compete with the partnership.
3. Duty to serve the partnership.
4. Duty to exercise the skill and care of the ordinarily prudent business manager.
5. Duty to act within the actual authority possessed by the partner.
6. Duty to account for the use and disposal of partnership funds and property.
7. Duty to indemnify other partners for expenditures they made from their personal funds and for liabilities they incurred on behalf of the partnership.
8. Duty to maintain the confidentiality of partnership information.
9. Duty to disclose to the other partners information material to the partnership business.
10. Duty to inform partners of notices he has received.

COMPENSATION OF PARTNERS

A partner's compensation for working for a partnership or limited liability partnership is a share of the profits of the business. Ordinarily, a partner is not entitled to a salary or wages, even if he spends a disproportionate amount of time conducting the business of the partnership.

Profits and Losses

Unless there is an agreement to the contrary, partners share partnership profits equally, according to the number of partners, and not according to their capital contributions or the amount of time that each devotes to the partnership. For example, a partnership has two partners, Juarez, who contributes $85,000 of capital to the partnership and does 35 percent of the work, and Easton, who contributes $15,000 and does 65 percent of the work. If they have made no agreement how to share profits, when the partnership makes a $50,000 profit in the first year, each partner receives $25,000, half of the profits.

Losses   When the partnership agreement is silent on how to share losses, losses are shared in the same proportion that profits are shared. The basis of this rule is the presumption that partners want to share benefits and detriments in the same proportions.

Nonetheless, the presumption does not work in reverse. If a partnership agreement specifies how losses are shared but does not specify how profits are shared, profits are shared equally by the partners, not as losses are shared.

Examples   For example, when there is no agreement regarding how profits or losses are shared, profits are shared equally, and because losses are shared like profits, losses are shared equally as well. When two partners agree to share profits 70–30 and make no agreement on losses, both profits and losses are shared 70–30.

However, when two partners make no agreement how to share profits but agree to share losses 60–40, losses are shared in that proportion but profits are shared equally.

Partners may agree to split profits on one basis and losses on another basis for many reasons, including their making different capital and personal service contributions or a partner's having higher outside income than the other partners, which better enables him to use a partnership loss as a tax deduction.

Effect of Agreement on Creditors' Rights   Each partner has unlimited personal liability to partnership creditors. Loss-sharing agreements between partners do not bind partnership creditors unless the creditors agree to be bound. For example, two partners agree to share losses 60–40, the same proportion in which they contributed capital to the partnership. After the partnership assets have been distributed to the creditors, $50,000 is still owed to them. The creditors may collect the entire $50,000 from the partner who agreed to assume only 60

percent of the losses. That partner may, however, collect $20,000—40 percent of the amount—from the other partner.

In the following case, the court held that the partners' oral agreement regarding partners' compensation bound the partners.

WARREN v. WARREN   784 S.W.2d 247 (Mo. App. 1989)

I n 1969, brothers Harold and Ray Warren formed a partnership to operate a funeral home in Columbia, Missouri. In 1970, they created a second partnership, The Warren Yard and Tree Service. The brothers based their partnerships solely on oral agreements, never putting them in writing. They adopted a system under which each partner drew from the partnerships' funds a reasonable compensation for his actual services rendered to the two businesses.

After a few years, Harold—a licensed embalmer and funeral director—spent an increasing amount of his time in the funeral home, performing all the lab work and specialized mortuary services. By 1978, Harold spent nearly all his time at the funeral home. Ray—licensed only as a funeral director—devoted most of his time to the tree service partnership, spending only a few hours each week assisting with funerals. Consequently, during the term of their partnership, Harold drew large sums of compensation from the funeral home partnership and only about $400 from the tree service partnership. Ray drew his primary compensation from the tree service partnership and a smaller compensation from the funeral home partnership. Because the funeral home was the more profitable business, Harold's total compensation exceeded Ray's by a considerable amount.

In 1983, Ray sued Harold, claiming that he was entitled to receive compensation equal to Harold for the entire 14-year term of the funeral home partnership. Ray asked the trial court to order Harold to pay Ray an amount that would equalize their 14-year compensation. The trial court held that Ray was not entitled to additional compensation, and Ray appealed. ⌢

Nugent, Chief Judge   Ray Warren first asserts that the trial court erred in finding that an oral agreement bound each partner to draw compensation commensurate with his services. The Warren brothers adopted a compensation system abstruse as to a method of payment but clear as to intent and business customs. There was an agreement between Ray and Harold under which Ray would run the tree service, Harold the funeral home, and each would draw compensation commensurate with his input of services. For nearly 15 years, Ray knew of and did not protest the perquisites afforded his brother by the funeral home partnership, such as use of an apartment above the funeral home and of a car.

Section 18 of the Uniform Partnership Act enunciates the rules determining the rights and duties of a partner: "The rights and duties of the partners in relation to the partnership shall be determined, subject to any agreement between them, by the following rules: . . . (f) No partner is entitled to

remuneration for acting in the partnership business." The oral agreement between the brothers negates the statute's proscription of compensation to partners. Missouri law recognizes the validity of oral and implied agreements between partners. Indeed, for more than a century, Missouri has recognized that, in the presence of an agreement linking compensation to a partner's efforts, partners providing services vital to the enterprise, or those devoting much of their time to the partnership's commonweal, deserve compensation often far in excess of that owed partners providing less important services or those giving only a little time to the business.

Harold provided the expert services vital to the partnership. His skills in the mortuary business far exceeded Ray's. The brothers agreed that Harold would run the funeral home and Ray, the tree service. Thus, implicitly if not expressly, they acknowledged each other's expertise, and, accordingly, each concentrated his efforts in the area of his own ability.

Moreover, Ray derived substantial financial benefit from the funeral home, to which he contributed but minimal efforts. Concomitantly, Harold succeeded in continuing to operate the business despite the effective withdrawal of Ray. Thus, Harold became entitled to suitable compensation for his efforts.

Judgment for Harold Warren affirmed.

Partners' Share of Profits and Losses

Profits	Partners share profits equally, unless the partners agree otherwise.
Losses	Partners share losses in the same way they share profits, unless the partners agree to share losses in a different manner.
Tax Effect	A partner's share of partnership profits is income to the partner, on which the partner pays federal income tax. A partner's share of partnership losses may be deducted on the partner's individual federal income tax return.
Right of Contribution	A partner who pays more than his share of a partnership loss may collect the excess paid from those partners whose shares he paid.

MANAGEMENT POWERS OF PARTNERS

Individual Authority of Partners

In a partnership or limited liability partnership, every partner is a general manager of the business. This power is expressed in the UPA, which states that a partnership is bound by the act of every partner for apparently carrying on in the usual way the business of the partnership. Such authority is implied from the nature of the business. It permits a partner to bind the partnership and his partners for acts within the ordinary course of business. The scope of this **implied authority** is determined with reference to what is usual business for partnerships of the same general type in the locality.

Implied authority of a partner may not contradict a partner's **express authority,** which is created by agreement of the partners. An agreement among the partners can expand, restrict, or even completely eliminate the implied authority of a partner. For example, the partners in a newspaper publishing business may agree that one partner shall have the authority to purchase a magazine business for the partnership and that another partner shall not have the authority to sell advertising space in the newspaper. The partners may agree also that all partners must consent to borrow money for the partnership.

The partners' implied authority to be general managers is modified in accordance with these express agreements.

Express authority may be stated orally or in writing, or it may be obtained by acquiescence. Regardless of the method of agreement, all of the partners must agree to the modification of implied authority. Together, a partner's express and implied authority constitute her **actual authority.**

Apparent Authority   **Apparent authority** exists because it reasonably appears to a third party that a partner has authority to do an act. Often, the implied authority and apparent authority of a partner are coincident. However, when a partner's implied authority is restricted or eliminated, the partnership risks the possibility that **apparent authority** to do a denied act will remain. To prevent apparent authority from continuing when there is a limitation of a partner's actual authority, third persons with whom the partner deals must have knowledge of the limitation of his actual authority. Just as a principal must notify third persons of limitations of an agent's authority, so must a partnership notify its customers, suppliers, and others of express limitations of the actual authority of partners.

Suppose that Carroll, Melton, and Ramirez are partners and that they agree that Carroll will be the only purchasing agent for the partnership. This agreement must be communicated to third parties selling goods to the partnership, or Melton and Ramirez will have apparent authority to bind the partnership on purchase contracts. Melton and Ramirez do not have express authority to purchase goods, because they have agreed to such a restriction on their authority. They do not have implied authority to purchase, because implied authority may not contradict express authority.

Ratification   A partnership may ratify the unauthorized acts of partners. Essentially, **ratification** occurs when the partners accept an act of a partner who had no actual or apparent authority to do the act when it was done.

For example, suppose Cabrillo and Boeglin are partners in an accounting firm. They agree that only Cabrillo has authority to make contracts to perform audits of clients, an agreement known by Mantron Company. Nonetheless, Boeglin and Mantron contract for the partnership to audit Mantron's financial statements. At this point, the partnership is not liable on the contract, because Boeglin has no express, implied, or apparent authority to make the contract. But suppose Boeglin takes the contract to Cabrillo, who reads it and says, "OK, we'll do this audit." Cabrillo, as the partner with express authority to make audit contracts, has ratified the contract and thereby bound the partnership to the contract.

Special Transactions

The validity of some partner's actions is affected by special partnership rules that reflect a concern for protecting important property and the credit standing of partners. This concern is especially evident in the rules for conveying the partnership's real property and for borrowing money in the name of the partnership.

Power to Convey Partnership Real Property   To bind the partnership, an individual partner's conveyance of a partnership's real property must be expressly, impliedly, or apparently authorized or be ratified by the partnership. For example, the partners may expressly agree that a partner may sell the partnership's real property.

The more difficult determination is whether a partner has *implied* and *apparent* authority to convey real property. A partner has implied and apparent authority to sell real property if a partnership sells real property in the usual course of the partner-

ship business. Such would be the case with the partner of a real estate investment partnership that buys and sells land as its regular business. By contrast, a partner has no implied or apparent authority to sell the building in which the partnership's retail business is conducted. Here, unanimous agreement of the partners is required, since the sale of the building may affect the ability of the firm to continue. In addition, a partner has no implied or apparent authority to sell land held for investment not in the usual course of business. A sale of such land would be authorized only if the partners concurred.

When title to partnership real property is recorded in the name of the partners and not the partnership, those partners in whose name title is recorded have apparent authority to convey title to a bona fide purchaser unaware of the partnership's interest in the real property.

Borrowing Money   Partnership law restricts the ability of a partner to borrow money in the name of a partnership. Essentially, a partner must possess express, implied, or apparent authority to borrow. Express authority presents few problems. Finding implied and apparent authority to borrow is more difficult.

Although the UPA does not explicitly recognize the distinction, a number of courts have distinguished between trading and nontrading partnerships for purposes of determining whether a partner has implied or apparent authority to borrow money on behalf of the partnership. A **trading partnership** has an inventory; that is, its regular business is buying and selling merchandise, such as retailing, wholesaling, importing, or exporting. For example, a toy store and a clothing store are trading partnerships. Since there is a time lag between the date they pay for their inventory and the date they sell inventory to their customers, these firms ordinarily need to borrow to avoid cash flow problems. Therefore, a partner of a trading partnership has implied and apparent authority to borrow money for the partnership.

A **nontrading partnership** has no substantial inventory and is usually engaged in providing services—for example, accounting services or real estate brokerage. Such partnerships have no normal borrowing needs. Therefore, a partner of a nontrading partnership has no implied or apparent authority to borrow money for the partnership.

The distinction between trading and nontrading partnerships is not always clear. Businesses such as general contracting, manufacturing, and dairy farming, although not exclusively devoted to buying and selling inventory, have been held to be trading partnerships. The rationale for their inclusion in this category is that borrowing is necessary in the ordinary course of business to augment their working capital.

This suggests why the distinction between trading partnerships and nontrading partnerships is useless or misleading. There is no necessary connection between borrowing money and buying and selling. The more important inquiry should be whether a partner's borrowing is in the ordinary course of business. When borrowing is in the ordinary course of business, a partner has implied and apparent authority to borrow money. If borrowing is not in the ordinary course of business, then no individual partner has implied or apparent authority to borrow money.

If a court finds that a partner has authority to borrow money, the partnership is liable for his borrowings on behalf of the partnership. There is a limit, however, to a partner's capacity to borrow. A partner may have authority to borrow, yet borrow beyond the ordinary needs of the business. A partnership will not be liable for any loan whose amount exceeds the ordinary needs of the business, unless otherwise agreed by the partners.

The power to borrow money on the firm's credit will ordinarily carry with it the power to grant the lender a lien or security interest in firm assets to secure the repayment of the borrowed money. Security interests are a normal part of business loan transactions.

Issuing Negotiable Instruments   A partner who has the authority to borrow money also has authority to issue negotiable instruments such as promissory notes for that purpose. When a partnership has a checking account and a partner's name appears on the signature card filed with the bank, the partner has express authority to draw checks. A partner whose name is not on the signature card filed with the bank has apparent authority to issue checks, but only in respect to a third person who has no knowledge of the limitation on the partner's authority.

Negotiating Instruments   A partnership receives many negotiable instruments during the course of its business. For example, an accounting firm's clients often pay fees by check. Even though borrowing money and issuing negotiable instruments may be beyond a partner's implied and apparent authority, a partner usually has implied and apparent authority to transfer or negotiate instruments on behalf of the partnership.

For example, when a partnership has a bank account, a partner has implied and apparent authority to indorse and deposit in the account checks drawn payable to the partnership. As a general rule, a partner also has implied and apparent authority to indorse and cash checks drawn payable to the order of the partnership. Likewise, partners have implied authority to indorse drafts and notes payable to the order of the partnership and to sell them at a discount.

In the following case, a partner possessed authority to bind the partnership on a promissory note.

UNITED STATES LEATHER, INC. v. H & W PARTNERSHIP   60 F.3d 222 (5th Cir. 1995)

ean Wilkerson and Walter Helms formed DWA of Tennessee, Inc., a corporation operating a furniture manufacturing facility in Armory, Mississippi. Shortly thereafter, Wilkerson and Helms created H & W Partnership, a general partnership, for the purpose of purchasing DWA's furniture manufacturing facility and leasing it back to DWA. In 1990, DWA began purchasing leather from Lackawanna Leather Company, a division of United States Leather, Inc. By December 1990, DWA had purchased but not yet paid for $350,000 of leather. In May 1991, Lackawanna's chief financial officer visited the Armory plant to collect the debt. DWA promised to repay the debt, and in June 1991, Lackawanna delivered two additional shipments of leather on a COD basis. DWA's checks for those shipments bounced, and by the end of June DWA owed Lackawanna over $438,000.

In August 1991, Wilkerson met with Lackawanna officials and gave them a promissory note for the balance of the debt. Wilkerson signed the note on behalf of DWA. A few days before the first payment on the note was due, Wilkerson requested an extension of time. Lackawanna agreed on the inclusion of H & W as a maker of the note. The changes were made, and Wilkerson signed the note on behalf of DWA and H & W.

Payment was never made on the note. Because DWA was out of business, United States Leather sued Wilkerson, Helms, and H & W. The trial court found Wilkerson liable on the note. In addition, the trial court found Helms and H & W liable on the note on the grounds that Wilkerson's signing the note was within the scope of the partnership business because there was a direct relationship between DWA and H & W. Helms and H & W appealed. ∞

Wood, Circuit Judge   The controlling law is section 9 of the Uniform Partnership Act. That section of the UPA provides:

(1) Every partner is an agent of the partnership for the purpose of its business, and the act of every partner, including the execution in the partnership name of any instrument, for apparently carrying on in the usual way the business of the partnership of which the partner is a member binds the partnership, unless the partner so acting has in fact no authority to act for the partnership in the particular matter, and the person with whom the partner is dealing has knowledge of the fact that the partner has no such authority.

Under the statute, the determinative issue is whether Wilkerson acted within the scope of the partnership business.

The Wisconsin Supreme Court has set out the appropriate test for determining whether the partner's acts were within the scope of the partnership business: the acts of a partner will bind the partnership if they are done to further or benefit the partnership. It is not disputed that there is a direct relationship between DWA and H & W. H & W's own viability depended on the continuation of DWA because H & W relied on the rental income from DWA to pay its mortgagees. Therefore, in order to keep DWA in business, DWA needed raw materials, including leather from Lackawanna, and it was the business of the partnership to ensure DWA had access to financing so it could acquire these materials. The acts of Wilkerson in executing the promissory note in favor of Lackawanna indirectly, but with certainty, benefited the partnership.

Helms and H & W argue that the determinative factor is whether the partner's acts were consistent with the historic practices of the partnership. They contend that under this standard there was no evidence to suggest that either H & W was created for any other purpose than to own the property it rented to DWA, or that H & W's dealings with DWA were anything more than the receipt of a rent check each month. Helms and H & W contend the evidence clearly established that Lackawanna had never transacted with H & W before the August 8 promissory note.

We first note that the historical practices of the partnership are a factor to be considered in determining the scope of the partnership business or whether the partner had actual authority. Moreover, merely shifting the focus of the analysis to the historical practices of the partnership reveals other evidence that obtaining financing for DWA was an integral part of H & W's business. As mentioned previously, it is undisputed that H & W relied on DWA's rental income for its own viability, and therefore had an interest in keeping DWA in business. It has also been shown that Wilkerson executed a similar promissory note with Quaker Fabric Corporation and had even encouraged Lackawanna to inquire into that arrangement. In addition to the Quaker note, there were two other times H & W executed agreements in order to facilitate financing for DWA. On May 1, 1991, Wilkerson and Helms signed a Hypothecation Agreement in favor of Trustmark National Bank pledging H & W's assets so DWA could get additional money on a loan of credit. Also in August 1991, H & W executed a UCC Financing Statement in favor of Trustmark National Bank for the purpose of lending money to DWA. Helms argues that these incidents are "exceptions" to the way business was usually done because both partners signed the agreements. Both partners, however, signed the Lackawanna security agreement shortly after the August 8 promissory note was executed. What is reasonably apparent from these transactions is that H & W Partnership had a continued and necessary interest in obtaining financing for DWA that would subsequently benefit the partnership. The prior transactions further substantiate that this practice was an ordinary and consistent manner in which the partnership carried out its business. Wilkerson's actions were within the scope of the partnership business when he executed the note in favor of Lackawanna.

Judgment for United States Leather affirmed.

Admissions and Notice A partnership is bound by admissions or representations made by a partner concerning partnership affairs that are within her express, implied, or apparent authority. Likewise, notice to a partner is considered to be received by the partnership. Also, a partner's knowledge of material information relating to partnership affairs is **imputed** to the partnership. These rules reflect the reality that a partnership speaks, sees, and hears through its partners.

Disagreement among Partners

Usually, partners will discuss management decisions among themselves before taking action, even when doing so is not required by a partnership agreement and even when a partner has the implied authority to take the action by herself. When partners discuss a prospective action, they will usually vote on what action to take. Each partner has one vote, regardless of the relative sizes of their partnership interests or their shares of the profits. The vote of a majority of the partners controls ordinary business decisions and, thereby, limits the actual authority of the partners. Nonetheless, the apparent authority of the partners to bind the partnership on contracts in the ordinary course of business is unaffected by the majority vote of partners, unless the limitation on the partners' actual authority is communicated to third parties.

Effect of Partnership Agreement

The partners may modify the rules of management by their unanimous agreement. They may agree that a partner will relinquish his management right, thus removing the partner's express and implied authority to manage the partnership. They may grant sole authority to manage the business to one or more partners. Such removals or delegations of management powers will not, however, eliminate a partner's apparent authority to bind the partnership for his acts within the usual course of business.

A partnership agreement may create classes of partners, some of which will have the power to veto certain actions. Some classes of partners may be given greater voting rights. Unequal voting rights are often found in very large partnerships, such as an accounting firm with several hundred partners.

In the following case, a partnership agreement that was designed to prevent and resolve conflicts between the two partners eventually caused serious disagreements, illustrating the necessity for careful drafting of partnership agreements.

NBN BROADCASTING, INC. v. SHERIDAN BROADCASTING NETWORKS, INC. 105 F.3d 72 (2d Cir. 1997)

N BN Broadcasting, Inc., and Sheridan Broadcasting Networks, Inc., operated competing radio networks. In 1991, NBN and Sheridan agreed to form American Urban Radio Network (AURN), a Pennsylvania partnership that combined NBN's and Sheridan's networks into a single radio network. Sheridan owned 51% of the partnership; NBN owned 49%. They agreed to maintain NBN's offices in New York and Sheridan's offices in Pittsburgh to allow direct oversight and input by AURN's cochairmen and co-CEOs, Sydney Small (chairman of NBN) and Ronald R. Davenport (chairman of Sheridan). As the only partners, NBN and Sheridan wanted equal rights in management of the partnership. The partners' equal right to manage AURN was modified by the partnership agreement in sections 5.2 and 5.3. Section 5.2 created a five-member Management Committee comprising two members selected by NBN and two by Sheridan; a seat on the Management Committee was to be vacant and would be filled only when the Management Committee was deadlocked. Section 5.2 also provided:

> The Management Committee shall be responsible for the following functions of the partnership and contractual arrangements relating thereto:
> (i) Sales and marketing;
> (ii) Promotions and public relations;
> (iii) Affiliate relations and compensation;
> (iv) Network programming;
> (v) Personnel administration; and
> (vi) Budgeting, accounting, and finance.

Section 5.3 provides:

(a) In the event that three of the four members of the Management Committee are unable to reach agreement on any issue or issues relating to items (i) through (v) above and remain so unable for a period of thirty days, then Ronald R. Davenport, Chairman of Sheridan, shall have the right to fill the vacant seat on the Management Committee for the purpose of reaching an agreement, and only until an agreement is reached, on such issue or issues.

Section 5.3 did not authorize appointment of a fifth member of the Management Committee when there was a deadlock regarding budgeting, accounting, or finance or any matter other than those listed in Section 5.2(i) through (v). As to budgeting, accounting, and finance and matters not listed in Section 5.2(i) through (v), NBN and Sheridan were equal partners, and all decisions on such matters required their agreement.

At a Management Committee meeting on September 14, 1995, Davenport proposed that AURN open an expensive new office in Washington, D.C., hire Skip Finley as chief operating officer, and employ Richard Boland. When NBN's representatives opposed opening the new office and hiring Finley and Boland, Davenport scheduled a meeting solely to appoint a fifth member to break the deadlock. On September 15, NBN asked a Pennsylvania state trial court to grant a preliminary injunction and a permanent injunction against Sheridan's opening a new AURN office in Washington and hiring Finley and Boland, on the grounds that the proposals related to budgeting, accounting, and finance and were, therefore, not subject to the deadlock voting provision. On October 13, the state trial court denied NBN's motion for a preliminary injunction. The state trial court held that Sheridan had the right to invoke the deadlock provision to "make additions to personnel" by hiring Finley and Boland. The trial court did not rule on NBN's request for a permanent injunction.

At an October 16 Management Committee meeting, Davenport appointed a fifth member of the committee. By a 3–2 vote, the Management Committee voted to hire Finley and Boland, with NBN's representatives opposing. At that meeting, Davenport also proposed to relocate AURN's New York offices from NBN's office space in New York to other office space in the New York area; to transfer to Pittsburgh from New York AURN's traffic, billing, and collection functions; and to require Finley to make cuts in AURN's New York–based marketing and research personnel. NBN's representatives opposed the proposals, and Davenport scheduled a meeting on November 28 to break the deadlock.

Sensing that the Pennsylvania state trial court would dismiss its request for a permanent injunction and hoping to litigate the issues at a later time, NBN sought to withdraw its motion for a permanent injunction. On November 28, 1995, while the state trial court judge was considering NBN's request to withdraw its lawsuit, a meeting of AURN's Management Committee was held. Davenport again invoked the deadlock provision and appointed his son as fifth member of the Management Committee. By a 3–2 vote, the Management Committee agreed to relocate AURN's New York offices from NBN's office space, to transfer AURN functions to Pittsburgh from New York, and to authorize Finley to make cuts in AURN's New York–based marketing and research personnel. Davenport also proposed to promote Finley to chief executive officer and Boland to vice president of administration. NBN Chairman Small objected, and Davenport scheduled another meeting to break the deadlock.

On November 29 and 30, the state trial court, wanting to put "a final end to this unnecessary litigation," ordered the discontinuance of NBN's lawsuit with prejudice, meaning that NBN could appeal the ruling to an appellate court but would not be permitted to have another trial court litigate the same issues. NBN chose not to appeal the decision of the Pennsylvania state trial court.

After the November 28 meeting, Sheridan located new office space for AURN in New York and entered a new lease with a minimum annual liability of $900,000, yet Sheridan never revealed the location of the space to NBN or sought NBN approval of the relocation or new lease. On January 18, 1996, at the next Management Committee meeting, Davenport again appointed his son as the fifth member. By a 3–2 vote, with NBN's representatives opposing, the Management Committee appointed Finley as CEO and Boland as vice president of administration.

On January 31, 1996, NBN filed a federal lawsuit seeking an injunction against Sheridan's alleged violations of the equal management rights of the partners by hiring Finley and Boland, interfering with AURN's personnel and customer relations, and relocating AURN's New York offices. Sheridan asked the federal district court to dismiss the suit on the grounds of res judicata; *that is, Sheridan argued that NBN was raising legal issues that the Pennsylvania state trial court had already considered or that NBN should have brought to the Pennsylvania trial court. Thus, Sheridan argued, because the Pennsylvania trial court had already dismissed NBN's request for an injunction with prejudice, the federal district court should not reconsider these issues. The federal district court agreed with Sheridan and dismissed NBN's lawsuit. NBN appealed to the federal court of appeal.* ∞

Pollack, Judge A discontinuance with prejudice is deemed a final adjudication on the merits for res judicata purposes on the claims asserted or which could have been asserted in the suit. Any issue concerning the relocation of the New York Office could not have been raised in the State Court suit commenced on September 15, 1995, or until the voting deadlock thereon on November 28, 1995. The NBN claim on the relocation of the New York Office was a claim based on new conduct that could have only arisen long after the filing of NBN's State Court suit. Since a plaintiff has no obligation to expand its suit in order to add a claim that it could not have asserted at the time the suit was commenced, a later suit based on subsequent conduct is not barred by res judicata.

The res judicata effect is limited to those claims that had arisen at the time that NBN brought the State Court Action. They did not include the relocation of the New York office, which had not yet even been brought to an initial vote. There was no submission to the State Court of NBN's equal right to decide whether the New York Office should be moved from its existing location as part of NBN's premises.

The doctrine of res judicata embraces all claims of NBN, excluding those claims relating to the relocation of the New York Office, which were passed on by the Management Committee prior to the filing of NBN's State Court action; the claims asserted therein and the dismissal thereof on the grounds of res judicata is affirmed.

Judgment for Sheridan affirmed in part; judgment in part reversed in favor of NBN. Remanded to the district court.

Unanimous Partners' Agreement Required

Some partnership actions are so important that one partner should not be able to do them by himself. To make clear that no single partner has implied or apparent authority to do certain acts, in the absence of a contrary agreement, the UPA requires unanimity for several actions. These actions are:

1. Assignment of partnership property for the benefit of creditors.
2. Disposal of the goodwill of the business (such as selling the right to do business with a firm's customers to another business).
3. Action making it impossible to carry on the ordinary business of the partnership (such as the distress sale of the entire inventory of a retailing partnership).
4. Confession of judgment against the partnership.
5. Submission of a partnership claim or liability to arbitration.
6. An agreement for the partnership to pay or assume an individual debt of a partner.
7. An agreement for the partnership to serve as a surety or guarantor of the debt of another (unless the partnership's ordinary business is suretyship and guaranty).
8. Any act not apparently for the carrying on of business of the partnership in the usual way.

Essentially, this list contains acts that are not in the usual course of business of the partnership. Such actions must be approved by all partners, unless there is a contrary agreement. For example, a decision to merge one accounting partnership with another partnership must be approved by all partners. Similarly, the decision of a grocery store partnership to move the business to another city requires unanimous partner approval. To the contrary, in the *United States Leather* case presented earlier in this chapter, a partner bound the partnership as a surety because the partner served the interests of the partnership.

Joint Ventures and Mining Partnerships

Most of the authority rules of partnerships apply to joint ventures and mining partnerships. These business organizations are in essence partnerships with limited purposes. Therefore, their members have less implied and apparent authority than do partners. Joint venturers have considerable apparent authority if third persons are unaware of the limited scope of the joint venture. A mining partner has no implied authority to borrow money or issue negotiable instruments. As with partners, joint venturers and mining partners may by agreement expand or restrict each other's agency powers.

LIABILITY FOR TORTS AND CRIMES

Torts

The standards and principles of agency law's respondeat superior are applied in determining the liability of the partnership and of the other partners for the torts of a partner and other partnership employees. In addition, the partnership and the other partners are liable for the torts of a partner committed within the ordinary course of partnership business or within the ordinary authority of that partner. Finally, when a partner commits a breach of trust, the partnership and all of the partners are liable. For example, all of the partners in a stock brokerage firm are liable for a partner's embezzlement of a customer's securities and funds.

Intentional Torts   While the doctrine of respondeat superior usually imposes liability on a partnership and its partners for a partner's negligence, the doctrine does not usually impose liability for a partner's intentional torts. The reason for this rule is that intentional torts are not usually within the ordinary scope of business or within the ordinary authority of a partner.

A few intentional torts impose liability on a partnership and its partners. For example, a partner who repossesses consumer goods from debtors of the partnership may trespass on consumer property or batter a consumer. Such activities have been held to be in the ordinary course of business. Also, a partner who authorizes a partner to commit an intentional tort is liable for such torts.

In the following case, a partner was not held liable for the intentional tort of her partner.

VRABEL v. ACRI   103 N.E.2d 564 (Ohio Sup. Ct. 1952)

On February 17, 1947, Stephen Vrabel and a companion went into the Acri Cafe in Youngstown, Ohio, to drink a few beers. While Vrabel and his companion were sitting at the bar drinking, a partner of the bar, Michael Acri, without provocation drew a .38-caliber handgun, shot and killed Vrabel's companion, and shot and seriously injured Vrabel. Michael Acri was convicted of murder and sentenced to a life term in the state prison.

Since 1933, Florence and Michael Acri, as partners, had owned and operated the Acri Cafe. From the time of his marriage to Florence in 1931 until 1946, Michael had been in and out of hospitals, clinics, and sanitaria for the treatment of mental disorders and nervousness. Although Michael beat Florence when they had marital difficulties, he had not attacked, abused, or mistreated anyone else. Florence and Michael separated in September 1946, and Florence sued Michael for divorce soon afterward. Before their separation, Florence had operated and managed the cafe primarily only when Michael was ill. Following the marital separation and up until the time he shot Vrabel, Michael was in exclusive control of the management of the cafe.

Vrabel brought suit against Florence to recover damages for his injuries on the ground that, as Michael's partner, she was liable for Michael's tort of battery of Vrabel. The trial court ordered Florence to pay Vrabel damages of $7,500. Florence appealed. ∞

Zimmerman, Judge   When a partnership is shown to exist, each member of the partnership project acts both as principal and agent of the others as to those things done within the apparent scope of the business of the project and for its benefit.

However, it is equally true that where one member of a partnership commits a wrongful and malicious tort not within the actual or apparent scope of the agency or the common business of the particular venture, to which the other members have not assented and which has not been concurred in or ratified by them, they are not liable for the harm thereby caused.

Because at the time of Vrabel's injuries and for a long time prior thereto Florence had been excluded from the Acri Cafe and had no voice or control in its management, and because Florence did not know or have good reason to know that Michael was a dangerous individual prone to assault cafe patrons, the theory of negligence urged by Vrabel is hardly tenable. The willful and malicious attack by Michael Acri upon Vrabel in the Acri Cafe cannot reasonably be said to have come within the scope of the business of operating the cafe, so as to have rendered the absent Florence accountable.

Since the liability of a partner for the acts of his associates is founded upon the principles of agency, the statement is in point that an intentional and willful attack committed by an agent or employee, to vent his own spleen or malevolence against the injured person, is a clear departure from his employment, and his principal or employer is not responsible therefor.

Judgment reversed in favor of Florence Acri.

Partners' Remedies   When a partnership and the other partners are held liable for a partner's tort, they may, during an accounting, recover the amount of their vicarious liability from the wrongdoing partner. This rule places ultimate liability on the wrongdoing partner without affecting the ability of tort victims to obtain recovery from the partnership or the other partners.

Tort Liability and Limited Liability Partnerships

State legislatures created the limited liability partnership (LLP) as a means of reducing the personal liability of professional partners, such as accountants. Consequently, an innocent partner of an LLP has liability for the professional malpractice of his partners, but *limited to the assets of the partnership.* Arguably, LLP statutes grant partners broad protection, eliminating an innocent partner's liability for errors, omissions, negligence, incompetence, or malfeasance of his partners or employees.

That is the limit of protection, however. The LLP itself is liable for the tort of a wrongdoing partner or employee under the doctrine of respondeat superior. In addition, a wrongdoing partner is liable for his own malpractice or negligence. Also, the partner supervising the work of the wrongdoing partner has unlimited liability for the wrongdoing partner's tort. Thus, the LLP's assets, the wrongdoing partner's personal assets, and the supervising partners' personal assets are at risk. Finally, the LLP and, in most states, its partners have unlimited liability for other debts of the business, such as a supplier's bill, lease obligations, and bank loans.

Crimes

When a partner commits a crime in the course and scope of transacting partnership business, rarely are his partners criminally liable. But when the partners have participated in the criminal act or authorized its commission, they are liable. They may also be liable when they know of a partner's criminal tendencies yet place him in a position in which he may commit a crime.

Until recent times, a partnership could not be held liable for a crime in most states because it was not viewed as a legal entity. However, modern criminal codes usually define a partnership as a "person" that may commit a crime when a partner, acting within the scope of his authority, engages in a criminal act.

LAWSUITS BY AND AGAINST PARTNERSHIPS AND PARTNERS

Under the UPA, a partnership may not sue in its own name; instead, all of the partners must join in the suit. This means that if the partnership wants to sue someone for breaching a contract or defaming the partnership business, all of the partners must agree to bring the suit. Especially for large partnerships, this requirement is cumbersome. Today, many state statutes differ from the UPA by permitting a partnership to sue in its own name.

Because the UPA imposes on partners a different type of liability for torts than it does for contracts, different rules apply to tort actions than apply to contract actions against the partnership and its partners. Partners are **jointly and severally** liable for partnership **torts.** This means that a tort victim may sue all of the partners (jointly) or sue fewer than all of the partners (severally). If a tort victim sues all of the partners jointly, the judgment may be satisfied against assets of the partnership and assets of the individual partners. If fewer than all of the partners are sued severally, the judgment may generally be satisfied from only the individual assets of the partners sued.

If fewer than all of the partners are sued and made to pay the entire amount of the tort victim's damages, those partners may seek **indemnification** or **contribution** from the other partners for their shares of the liability.

Partners are **jointly liable** for **contractual** obligations of the partnership. This means that all of the partners must be sued if the partnership has breached a contract. Otherwise, no individual partner may be required to pay a judgment and the assets of the partnership cannot be used to satisfy the contract creditor's judgment.

Courts and legislatures have fashioned many modifications to this requirement of joining all the partners in contract actions. Some states make partners jointly and severally liable for contracts. Others have joint debtor statutes that permit creditors—both contract and tort claimants—to sue fewer than all of the partners and yet collect from partnership property. Some courts refuse to permit partners to be sued on contract actions until partnership assets have been exhausted.

The UPA does not permit a partnership to be sued in its own name. This prohibition is especially cumbersome for a party suing for breach of contract because the UPA imposes joint liability on partners for partnership contracts. Thus, it is necessary to sue each of the partners, which is especially difficult when the partners live in a number of states.

Many states have responded to this difficulty by enacting statutes that make all joint obligations joint and several. In addition, *common-name statutes* permit suits against the partnership even if fewer than all of the partners are notified of the suit. Pursuant to such statutes, a judgment against the partnership is enforceable against the assets of the partnership and against the individual assets of those partners who have been served with process.

ETHICAL AND PUBLIC POLICY CONCERNS

1. Should the law require partners to owe each other fiduciary duties? Does a partner's breach of his fiduciary duty harm only the partners, or is society at large also harmed? Should partners be allowed to agree that they do not owe fiduciary duties to each other?

2. Why should a partner have greater implied authority than an agent who is a general manager of another's business? Is there a greater risk that an agent will do something imprudent with a business that belongs entirely to someone else than that a partner will do something imprudent with a business that belongs in part to that partner?

3. Is it fair that a partner is liable for the contracts of his partners? Is it fair that a partner is liable for the torts of his partners? Should a partnership be entirely a beneficial relationship for the partners, by which the partners reap the benefits of their relationship with each other but suffer none of the detriments?

PROBLEMS AND PROBLEM CASES

1. Walter Levy and Henry Disharoon formed a partnership to purchase a jet airplane and to operate a charter airline business. Disharoon located a jet and informed Levy that the price was $963,000. After Levy approved the purchase, Disharoon contracted to buy the jet for $860,000. The partnership borrowed $975,000 to pay for the jet. Disharoon paid the seller $860,000 and deposited in Disharoon's personal bank account the $103,000 difference between the actual purchase price and the purchase price represented to Levy. Has Disharoon breached a fiduciary duty?

2. Larry Rose, Paul G. Veale, Sr., Paul G. Veale, Jr., Gary Gibson, and James Parker offered professional accounting services as partners under the firm name of Paul G. Veale and Co. Their written partnership agreement expressed the general duties of the partners, but it recognized that Veale, Sr., and

Rose had outside investments and a number of other business commitments. All of the partners were allowed to pursue other business activities so long as the activities did not conflict with the partnership practice of public accounting or materially interfere with the partners' duties to the partnership. While a partner, Larry Rose performed accounting services for Right Away Foods and Ed Payne. He was paid personally by those clients. Rose was an officer and shareholder of Right Away. In addition, Rose used the partnership's employees and computers to service those clients. Has Rose breached a fiduciary duty owed to his partners?

3. Holiday Inns, Inc., and L & M Enterprises, Inc. (L & M), were 50–50 partners of Marina Associates, a partnership formed to develop a gambling casino in Atlantic City. Holiday Inns conducted the day-to-day operation of Marina. The partnership was unprofitable during its early years, and rather than contribute more capital to the partnership, L & M agreed to sell most of its 50 percent interest to Holiday Inns. Subsequently, the casino became profitable, a fact that was a matter of public record. Also, L & M was aware that Marina had become highly profitable. Nonetheless, L & M sold its remaining 1 percent interest to Holiday Inns. After a newspaper article suggested that Holiday Inns had taken advantage of L & M, L & M sued Holiday Inns. L & M argued that Holiday Inns breached a fiduciary duty by failing to provide to L & M a 35-year financial forecast prepared by Holiday Inns, which projected large cash flows and high profits for the casino. Was Holiday Inns held liable to L & M?

4. Russel Daub, Daniel Smith, and Frederick Stehlik formed a partnership. No formal partnership agreement was executed. During 1980, profits were distributed monthly, with Daub receiving $3,000 per month, Smith $1,500, and Stehlik $1,500. In the latter months of 1980, Stehlik received $1,700 per month, but the 1980 partnership tax return indicated that profits were divided 50 percent to Daub and 25 percent each to Smith and Stehlik. During 1981, profits were distributed 50 percent to Daub and 25 percent each to Smith and Stehlik. The 1981 partnership tax return showed the 50–25–25 profit ratio at the beginning of the year, but it showed a year-end ratio of one-third to each partner. In 1982, profits were distributed 50–25–25. When the partnership was dissolved and liquidated, Smith and Stehlik argued that each was entitled to one-third of

the profits and one-third of the value of the partnership. Are they correct?

5. Two brothers, Sydney and Ashley Altman, operated several partnerships in Pennsylvania. They shared equally in the management of the partnerships. They agreed that each would receive identical salaries and that each was permitted to charge an equal amount of personal expenses to the partnerships. After Sydney moved to Florida, Sydney commuted to Pennsylvania every week to work for two to three days. After a year passed, Sydney told Ashley that he was considering retiring and remaining in Florida permanently. They tried to reach an agreement on Ashley's purchase of Sydney's partnership interests but were unable to do so. Ashley continued to manage the businesses by himself for nearly four years. During that time, Ashley paid himself salaries in excess of what the brothers had agreed. Has Ashley received excessive compensation as a partner?

6. Mervin Grosberg and Sheldon Goldman, as partners, constructed and operated the Chatham Fox Hills Shopping Center. Grosberg and Goldman had agreed that Goldman would receive rental checks from the shopping center's tenants and deposit them in an account in Grosberg's name at Manufacturers National Bank. Without Grosberg's knowledge or permission, Goldman opened an account in both their names at Michigan National Bank. Goldman deposited in that account checks relating to the partnership business that were payable to the partnership or its partners. Goldman indorsed each check by signing the name of the partnership or the partners. Later, Goldman embezzled $112,000 of the deposited funds. At no time was Michigan National Bank aware that Grosberg and Goldman were partners. Will Grosberg recover the $112,000 from Michigan National Bank on the grounds that Goldman had no authority to indorse and deposit partnership checks in the account in Michigan National Bank?

7. [CD] *Video Case.* See "The Partnership." Art is a partner of Alphabet Builders, a partnership in the construction business. The three partners of Alphabet Builders have agreed that the partnership may not borrow money unless all the partners approve the borrowing. In the name of the partnership but without the consent of his partners, Art borrows money from a bank. Art tells the bank that the partnership will use the money for general

purposes. Art indorses the loan check in the name of the partnership but deposits the money in his personal account. Art uses the money to purchase commodities futures. Art loses money on the futures and is unable to repay the loan. The bank sues Alphabet Builders and its partners. Are Alphabet Builders and its partners liable to the bank on the loan? Does Art have any liability to his partners?

8. L. G. Patel and S. L. Patel, husband and wife, owned the City Center Motel in Eureka, California. The Patels formed a partnership with their son, Raj, to own and operate the motel. The partnership agreement required Raj's approval of any sale of the motel building. Real estate records were not changed, however, and the motel building remained recorded only in the names of L. G. and S. L. Patel. L. G. and S. L. contracted to sell the motel building to P. V. and Kirit Patel, who were unaware of Raj's interest as a partner. When Raj was informed of the contract to sell the motel building, he refused to grant his approval. Is the contract enforceable against the partnership?

9. Alvin Meyer was a resident of 100 Central Park South, an apartment building in Manhattan, New York, owned by a partnership, Park South Associates. Meyer sued the partnership and one of its partners, Donald Trump, on three grounds: for violation of the lease between Meyer and the partnership, for breach of the warranty of habitability, and for the tort of intentional infliction of emotional distress due to the partnership's harassment of Meyer. Meyer did not allege in his complaint that Park South Associates was insolvent or otherwise unable to pay its obligations. Trump asked the trial court to dismiss the suit against him on the grounds that he personally could not be sued on partnership obligations unless it was insolvent or otherwise unable to pay its obligations. Did the court agree with Trump?

Dissolution, Winding Up, and Termination of Partnerships

This chapter is about the death of partnerships. Three terms are important in this connection: dissolution, winding up, and termination. Dissolution is a change in the relation of the partners, as when a partner dies. Winding up, which may follow dissolution, is the orderly liquidation of the partnership assets and the distribution of the proceeds to those having claims against the partnership. Termination, the end of the partnership's existence, automatically follows winding up. A limited liability partnership is dissolved, wound up, and terminated in the same manner as an ordinary partnership. ∞

DISSOLUTION

Dissolution is defined in the Uniform Partnership Act (UPA) as "the change in the relation of the partners caused by any partner ceasing to be associated in the carrying on as distinguished from the winding up of the business." A dissolution may be caused by a partner's retirement, death, or bankruptcy, among other things. Whatever the cause of dissolution, however, it is characterized by a partner's *ceasing to take part in the carrying on of the partnership's business.*

Dissolution is the starting place for the winding up (liquidation) and termination of a partnership. Although winding up does not always follow dissolution, it often does. Winding up usually has a severe effect on a business: It usually ends the business, because the assets of the business are sold and the proceeds of the sale are distributed to creditors and partners.

A partner has the *power* to dissolve the partnership *at any time,* such as by withdrawing from the partnership. A partner does not, however, always have the *right* to dissolve a partnership. A partner has the right to dissolve a partnership only when a dissolution does not violate the partnership agreement. For example, a partner has the power to withdraw from a partnership with a 20-year term before the term expires, but has no right to do so.

When a partner's dissolution does not violate the partnership agreement, the partner has the right to dissolve the partnership: Such a dissolution is **nonwrongful.** When a partner's dissolution violates the partnership agreement, the partner has the power—but not the right—to dissolve the partnership: Such a dissolution is **wrongful.** The consequences that follow a nonwrongful dissolution may differ from those that follow a wrongful dissolution.

Nonwrongful Dissolution

A dissolution is nonwrongful when the dissolution does not violate the partnership agreement. The following actions are nonwrongful dissolutions:

1. Automatic dissolution at the end of the term stated in the partnership agreement. For example, a partnership with a 20-year term is automatically dissolved at the expiration of that term.

2. Automatic dissolution on the partnership's accomplishment of its objective. For example, a partnership organized to build 15 condominiums dissolves when it completes their construction.

3. Withdrawal of a partner at any time from a partnership at will. A partnership at will is a partnership whose partnership agreement does not specify any specific term or objective.

4. Withdrawal of a partner in accordance with the partnership agreement. For example, a partnership agreement allows the partners to retire at age 55. A partner who retires at age 60 has dissolved the partnership nonwrongfully.

5. Expulsion of a partner in accordance with the partnership agreement. For example, the removal of a partner who has stolen partnership property dissolves the partnership if the partnership agreement allows removal on such grounds.

6. Unanimous agreement of the partners who have not assigned their partnership interests or suffered charging orders against their partnership interests.

7. The illegality of the partnership business.

8. The death of a partner.

9. The bankruptcy of a partner. The partner must be adjudicated a bankrupt. Mere insolvency does not effect a dissolution.

In addition, a partner or other may go to court to request that a judge order a judicial dissolution in several situations. The following grounds for **judicial dissolution** are nonwrongful:

10. The adjudicated insanity of a partner.

11. The inability of a partner to perform the partnership contract. For example, a two-person partnership that remodels kitchens may be dissolved by a court when one of the partners becomes paralyzed in an automobile accident.

12. The inability of the partnership to conduct business except at a loss. For example, a partnership may not make a profit because of irreconcilable differences among the partners that prevent the business from being conducted beneficially.

13. At the request of a purchaser of a partnership interest in a partnership at will. This allows the creditor to whom a partner has assigned his partnership interest to obtain a dissolution and then to seek a winding up. During winding up, the creditor is paid from the debtor/partner's share of the proceeds of the sale of partnership assets.

Consequences of Nonwrongful Dissolution   When a dissolution is nonwrongful, each partner, including the dissolving partner, may demand that the business of the partnership be wound up; also, each partner—unless deceased or bankrupt—may participate in the winding-up process. In addition, by their unanimous agreement, the partners—including the nonwrongfully dissolving partner—may decide to allow one or more of the partners to continue the business using the partnership's name. If unanimity to continue the business cannot be obtained, any partner may force the business to wind up.

Wrongful Dissolution

A partner wrongfully dissolves a partnership when she dissolves her partnership in violation of the partnership agreement. For example, a partner wrongfully dissolves a partnership by retiring before the partnership accomplishes its stated objective of building vacation homes in Aspen, Colorado.

In addition, some judicial dissolutions on the following grounds are wrongful dissolutions for the wrongdoing partner: (1) when a partner's conduct prejudicially affects the business, or (2) when a partner willfully and persistently breaches the partnership agreement or her fiduciary duties. For example, a partner may continually insult customers, causing a loss of business; or a partner may persistently and substantially use partnership property for his own benefit; or three partners may refuse to allow a fourth partner to manage the partnership's business. In all of these situations, the harmed partners may seek judicial dissolution. As to the harmed partners, the dissolution would be non-wrongful. As to the wrongdoing partners, the dissolution would be wrongful.

Consequences of Wrongful Dissolution   A partner who wrongfully dissolves a partnership (1) has no right to demand that the business be wound up; (2) has no right to participate in the winding up if the business is wound up; (3) has no right to have the goodwill of the business taken into account in valuing his partnership interest; (4) may not use the firm's name in connection with any business he conducts after dissolution; and (5) is liable for damages for breach of the partnership agreement, such as loss of profits. Nonetheless, a wrongfully dissolving partner is entitled to his share of the value of the partnership, minus his share of the partnership goodwill and the damages he caused the partnership.

Right to Continue   In the event of a wrongful dissolution, the innocent partners may continue the business themselves or with new partners. They may continue to use the partnership's name. This right to continue the business prevents a wrongfully dissolving partner from forcing a liquidation of the partnership. In addition, each of the innocent partners has all of the rights that are possessed by partners when there is a nonwrongful dissolution. This means that if there is a wrongful dissolution, any innocent partner may force a winding up.

Usually, innocent partners choose to continue the business.

Acts Not Causing Dissolution

A partner's assignment of his partnership interest does not dissolve a partnership, and neither does a creditor's obtaining a charging order. Also, the addition of a partner to a partnership does not dissolve the partnership, because no one disassociates from the partnership.

Mere disagreements, even irreconcilable differences, between the partners are expectable, but they are not grounds for dissolution. If the disagreements threaten partnership assets or profitability, then a court may order dissolution.

The partnership agreement may state that death or withdrawal shall not cause a dissolution. Although death or withdrawal clearly disassociates a partner from the carrying on of the business, several states permit the partners to vary the definition of dissolution by their agreement. Other states permit the partners to eliminate the right to demand a winding up after the death or withdrawal of a partner.

Joint Ventures and Mining Partnerships

Essentially, the partnership rules of dissolution apply to joint ventures. It is more likely in a joint venture than in a partnership that a member's death will not dissolve the joint venture or not permit a demand to wind up; courts often find that joint venturers made an implied agreement that the limited objective of the joint venture be completed, as in *Rhue v. Dawson,* which follows.

Mining partnerships are more difficult to dissolve than general partnerships due to the free transferability of mining partnership interests. The death or bankruptcy of a mining partner does not effect a dissolution. In addition, a mining partner may sell his interest to another person and disassociate himself from the carrying on of the mining partnership's business without causing a dissolution. The other rules of partnership dissolution apply to mining partnerships.

J ames Rhue and John Dawson formed a partnership or joint venture to acquire and develop a shopping center. They named the enterprise Shopping Center Enterprises of Arizona (SCEA). Rhue had shopping center expertise and handled day-to-day details. Dawson contributed most of the capital and promised to seek bank financing for the project. They agreed to share profits and equity equally. They did not immediately put their agreement in writing, although drafts of an agreement were circulated.

Rhue located two adjacent shopping centers that the partnership purchased for $7.2 million. The estimated cost of renovating the combined shopping centers was $4.6 million. To obtain bank financing of the purchase and development of the combined shopping centers, Dawson obtained an appraisal of the projected value of the combined shopping center assuming redevelopment according to the plans prepared by SCEA. The appraisal projected the value at $15.6 million, indicating a projected profit of $3.8 million for the venture. Rhue's one-half share of the projected profits would have been $1.9 million.

Seven days after receiving the appraisal, Dawson asked Rhue to sign a form entitled "Joint Venture Agreement." Dawson pressured Rhue to sign the agreement before Rhue could read it. Rhue specifically asked whether certain changes that they had discussed and agreed on were in the written agreement. Dawson replied that they were included; however, Dawson failed to tell Rhue that the agreement contained an "Option to Purchase" clause. Previous drafts lacked this clause. The clause allowed Dawson to buy Rhue's interest in the partnership merely by returning Rhue's capital contribution. Because Rhue contributed mostly expertise, not capital, this clause was highly favorable to Dawson. Rhue signed the agreement without reading it.

Two months later, Rhue learned about the "Option to Purchase" clause and indicated to Dawson that he did not intend to be bound by it. Dawson answered by notifying Rhue of his intent to exercise the buyout provision. Dawson then locked Rhue out of the partnership's offices. Rhue sued Dawson, claiming wrongful dissolution by Dawson and asking for lost profits. The trial judge held that Dawson had wrongfully dissolved the partnership and ordered Dawson to pay Rhue $8.4 million, which included Rhue's attorney's fees, punitive damages of $2 million, and the profits Rhue would have made on the venture, which were tripled under Arizona's racketeering statute. Dawson appealed. ∞

Lankford, Judge   Arizona law recognizes three types of partnerships differentiated by term: a partnership at will, a partnership for a particular undertaking, and a partnership for a definite term. A partnership for a definite term or for a particular undertaking may be dissolved without violating the partnership agreement only at the end of the term or on completion of the undertaking. Only a partnership having no specified definite term or particular undertaking is a partnership at will. Such a partnership is subject to dissolution by express will of a partner without violating the partnership agreement.

Evidence supports a finding of a partnership other than one at will. Rhue and Dawson contemplated purchase of a single shopping center. They anticipated no other undertakings. This suggests a partnership for a particular undertaking.

Dawson could dissolve the partnership only in accordance with the terms of the agreement. Dawson delivered a letter notifying Rhue of the buyout

and dissolving the partnership. Dawson locked Rhue out of the partnership offices. These actions effectively ousted Rhue as a partner. Dawson's conduct wrongfully dissolved the partnership in contravention of the parties' agreement.

A partner who has been wrongfully excluded from the partnership has the right, as against the partner who wrongfully excluded him, to damages for breach of the agreement, including loss of probable profits. To prove lost profits, Rhue must establish a reasonably certain factual basis for computation of lost profits. Dawson objects to the lost profits as too uncertain because SCEA was a new business.

While SCEA was a new business association, the two pieces of property held by SCEA had been operated in the commercial real estate market for many years. The appraiser estimated the value of the property based on the assumption that the property was to be developed in accordance with

SCEA's plans and specifications. Dawson himself had utilized the same appraisal after the dissolution in various financial statements to a lending institution. Valuation methods utilized by the appraiser included comparable sales, net income, discounted cash flows, and replacement costs. The evidence was sufficient to support an award of lost profits.

Dawson next argues that his conduct was not sufficiently outrageous to justify an award of punitive damages. Rhue's claim for punitive damages is proper. Both fraud and deliberate, overt, dishonest dealings will suffice to sustain punitive damages. Dawson deliberately misled Rhue and intended to injure Rhue. Moreover, the relationship between the parties affects whether punitive damages can be awarded. Rhue and Dawson were partners. Dawson failed to discharge his fiduciary duty and his duty to exercise the utmost good faith and to discharge the obligation of loyalty, fairness, and honesty in his dealings with Rhue.

Dawson acted with an evil mind. Dawson deliberately failed to disclose to Rhue that the agreement signed by the parties contained a buyout provision. Dawson locked Rhue out of the partnership offices. Dawson's actions were consciously malicious.

Dawson also questions whether punitive damages may be imposed in addition to civil racketeering treble damages. Appellate courts will not interfere with the trial court's verdict on damages unless the verdict is not supported by the evidence or unless it is so outrageously excessive as to suggest passion or prejudice. We remand for the trial court to review the amount of punitive damages in light of the trebled compensatory damages to ensure that the former are not excessive.

Judgment for Rhue affirmed; remanded to trial court for review of the punitive damage award.

CONCEPT REVIEW

Causes of Dissolution and Acts Not Causing Dissolution

Causes of Dissolution	**Wrongful Dissolutions**
	1. Any dissolution that violates the partnership agreement.
	2. Judicial dissolution due to a partner's conduct prejudicially affecting the business.
	3. Judicial dissolution due to a partner's willful and persistent breach of the partnership agreement or her fiduciary duties.
	Nonwrongful Dissolutions
	1. End of the term stated in the partnership agreement.
	2. The partnership's accomplishment of its objective.
	3. Withdrawal of a partner at any time from a partnership at will.
	4. Withdrawal of a partner in accordance with the partnership agreement.
	5. Expulsion of a partner in accordance with the partnership agreement.
	6. Unanimous agreement of the partners who have not assigned their partnership interests or suffered charging orders against their partnership interests.
	7. Illegality of the partnership business.
	8. Death of a partner.
	9. Bankruptcy of a partner.
	10. Judicial dissolution due to the adjudicated insanity of a partner.
	11. Judicial dissolution due to the inability of a partner to perform the partnership contract.
	12. Judicial dissolution due to the inability of the partnership to conduct business except at a loss.
	13. Judicial dissolution at the request of a purchaser of a partnership interest in a partnership at will.
Acts Not Causing Dissolution	1. A partner's assignment of a partnership interest.
	2. A creditor's obtaining a charging order against a partnership interest.
	3. Addition of a partner to a partnership.
	4. Disagreement among the partners that does not threaten partnership assets or profitability.
	5. Death or withdrawal of a partner, when the partnership agreement states that death or withdrawal shall not cause a dissolution.

WINDING UP THE PARTNERSHIP BUSINESS

When a partnership is to be terminated, the next step after dissolution is **winding up** the partnership's affairs. This involves the orderly liquidation—or sale—of the assets of the business. Liquidation may be accomplished asset by asset; that is, each asset may be sold separately. It may also be accomplished by a sale of the business as a whole. Or it may be accomplished by a means somewhere between these two extremes.

Winding up does not always require the sale of the assets or the business. When a partnership has valuable assets, the partners may wish to receive the assets rather than the proceeds from their sale. Such *distributions-in-kind* are rarely permitted. They are allowed when there are no creditors' claims against the partnership, the value of the assets can be ascertained, and the assets can be distributed in a manner that is fair to each partner.

During winding up, the partners continue as fiduciaries to each other, especially in negotiating sales or making distributions of partnership assets to members of the partnership. Nonetheless, there is a termination of the fiduciary duties unrelated to winding up. For example, a partner who is not winding up the business may compete with his partnership during winding up.

Demanding and Performing Winding Up

A partner who has not wrongfully dissolved the partnership may demand winding up. Thus, when a partnership has been dissolved nonwrongfully, any partner, even the dissolving partner, may demand winding up. If the partnership has been wrongfully dissolved, only the innocent partners may demand winding up.

Any surviving, nonbankrupt partner who has not wrongfully dissolved the partnership may perform the winding up. A partner who has wrongfully dissolved the partnership has no right to wind up the business. When a dissolution is caused by the death or bankruptcy of a partner, the surviving partners and the nonbankrupt partners have the right to wind up the business.

If the dissolution is by court decree, usually no partner winds up. Instead, a *receiver* is appointed by the court to wind up the business.

The compensation to a winding up partner is only his share of the profits, unless the partners agree to give special compensation to the winding up partner. In addition, when the winding up partner provides extraordinary services or is the sole surviving partner after dissolution by death, he is entitled to the reasonable value of his winding up services.

Partner's Authority during Winding Up

Express and Implied Authority   During winding up, a partner has the express authority to act as the partners have agreed. The implied authority of a winding up partner is the power to do those acts *reasonably necessary to the winding up* of the partnership affairs. That is, he has the power to bind the partnership in any transaction necessary to the liquidation of the assets. He may collect money due, sue to enforce partnership rights, prepare assets for sale, sell partnership assets, pay partnership creditors, and do whatever else is appropriate to wind up the business. He may maintain and preserve assets or enhance them for sale, for example, by painting a building or by paying a debt to prevent foreclosure on partnership land. A winding up partner may temporarily continue the business when the effect is to preserve the value of the partnership.

Performing Executory Contracts   The implied authority of a winding up partner includes the power to perform executory contracts (made before dissolution but not yet performed). A partner may not enter into *new* contracts unless the contracts aid the liquidation of the partnership's assets. For example, a partner may fulfill a contract to deliver coal if the contract was made before dissolution. She may not make a new contract to deliver coal unless doing so disposes of coal that the partnership owns or has contracted to purchase.

Borrowing Money   Usually, the implied authority of a winding up partner includes no power to borrow money in the name of the partnership. Nonetheless, when a partner can preserve the assets of the partnership or enhance them for sale by borrowing money, he has implied authority to engage in new borrowing. For example, a partnership may have a valuable machine repossessed and sold far below its value at a foreclosure sale unless it can refinance a loan. A partner may borrow the money needed to refinance the loan, thereby preserving the asset. A partner may also borrow money to perform executory contracts.

Apparent Authority Winding up partners have apparent authority to conduct business as they did before dissolution, when notice of dissolution is not given to those persons who knew of the partnership prior to its dissolution. For example, a construction partnership dissolves and begins winding up but does not notify anyone of its dissolution. After dissolution, a partner makes a contract with a customer to remodel the customer's building. The partner would have no implied authority to make the contract, because the contract is new business and does not help liquidate assets. Nonetheless, the contract may be within the partner's apparent authority, because to persons unaware of the dissolution, it appears that a partner may continue to make contracts that have been in the usual course of business.

To eliminate this apparent authority to conduct business in the normal way, the partnership must do both of the following:

1. Give **actual**—or personal—**notice** of the dissolution to persons who extended credit to the partnership prior to dissolution, and
2. Give either actual notice or **constructive notice** of the dissolution to persons who were not creditors but had merely done business with the partnership without extending credit or had

merely been aware of the existence of the partnership.

Actual notice may be given by telephone or by a letter mailed or faxed to the creditor's place of business. Creditors may also receive actual notice by hearing of the dissolution by word of mouth or reading of it in a newspaper.

Constructive notice is notice published in a newspaper of general circulation in the places where the partnership did business. Constructive notice eliminates apparent authority of the partners as to noncreditors even if the notice is not read by the noncreditors.

For persons who were previously unaware of the partnership's existence, no notice of any type need be given to eliminate apparent authority.

Disputes among Winding Up Partners When more than one partner has the right to wind up the partnership, the partners may disagree concerning which steps should be taken during winding up. For decisions in the ordinary course of winding up, the decision of a majority of the partners controls. When the decision is an extraordinary one, such as continuing the business for an extended period of time, unanimous partner approval is required.

In the following case, the court found that the business of the partnership to train and race a horse should continue during winding up.

PACIARONI v. CRANE   408 A.2d 946 (Del. Ct. Ch. 1979)

Black Ace, a harness racehorse of exceptional speed, was the fourth best pacer in the United States in 1979. He was owned by a partnership: Richard Paciaroni owned 50 percent; James Cassidy, 25 percent; and James Crane, 25 percent. Crane, a professional trainer, was in charge of the daily supervision of Black Ace, including training. It was understood that all of the partners would be consulted on the races in which Black Ace would be entered, the selection of drivers, and other major decisions; however, the recommendations of Crane were always followed by the other partners because of his superior knowledge of harness racing.

In 1979, Black Ace won $96,969 through mid-August. Seven other races remained in 1979, including the prestigious Little Brown Jug and the Messenger at Roosevelt Raceway. The purse for these races was $600,000.

A disagreement among the partners arose when Black Ace developed a ringbone condition and Crane followed the advice of a veterinarian not selected by Paciaroni and Cassidy. The ringbone condition disappeared, but later Black Ace became uncontrollable by his driver, and in a subsequent race he fell and failed to finish the race. Soon thereafter, Paciaroni and Cassidy sent a telegram to Crane rightfully dissolving *the partnership and directing him to deliver Black Ace to another trainer they had selected. Crane refused to relinquish control of Black Ace, so Paciaroni and Cassidy sued him in August 1979, asking the court to appoint a receiver who would race Black Ace in the remaining 1979 stakes races and then sell the horse. Crane objected to allowing anyone other than himself to enter the horse in races. Before the trial court issued the following decision, Black Ace had entered three additional races and won $40,000.*

Brown, Vice Chancellor   It is generally accepted that once dissolution occurs, the partnership continues only to the extent necessary to close out affairs and complete transactions begun but not then finished. It is not generally contemplated that new business will be generated or that new contractual commitments will be made. This, in principle, would work against permitting Black Ace to participate in the remaining few races for which he is eligible.

However, in Delaware, there have been exceptions to this. Where, because of the nature of the partnership business, a better price upon final liquidation is likely to be obtained by the temporary continuation of the business, it is permissible, during the winding up process, to have the business continue to the degree necessary to preserve or enhance its value upon liquidation, provided that such continuation is done in good faith with the intent to bring affairs to a conclusion as soon as reasonably possible. And one way to accomplish this is through an application to the Court for a winding up under UPA Section 37, which carries with it the power of the Court to appoint a receiver for that purpose.

The business purpose of the partnership was to own and race Black Ace for profit. The horse was bred to race. He has the ability to be competitive with the top pacers in the country. He is currently "racing fit" according to the evidence. He has at best only seven more races to go over a period of the next six weeks, after which time there are established horse sales at which he can be disposed of to the highest bidder. The purse for these remaining stake races is substantial. The fact that he could possibly sustain a disabling injury during this six-week period appears to be no greater than it was when the season commenced. Admittedly, an injury could occur at any time. But this is a fact of racing life which all owners and trainers are forced to accept. And the remaining stake races are races in which all three partners originally intended that he would compete, if able.

Under these circumstances, I conclude that the winding up of the partnership affairs should include the right to race Black Ace in some or all of the remaining 1979 stakes races for which he is now eligible. The final question, then, is who shall be in charge of racing him.

On this point, I rule in favor of Paciaroni and Cassidy. They may, on behalf of the partnership, continue to race the horse through their new trainer, subject, however, to the conditions hereafter set forth. Crane does have a monetary interest in the partnership assets that must be protected if Paciaroni and Cassidy are to be permitted to test the whims of providence in the name of the partnership during the next six weeks. Accordingly, I make the following ruling:

1. Paciaroni and Cassidy shall first post security in the sum of $100,000 so as to secure to Crane his share of the value of Black Ace.

2. If Paciaroni and Cassidy are unable or unwilling to meet this condition, then they shall forgo the right to act as liquidating partners. In that event, each party, within seven days, shall submit to the Court the names of two persons who they believe to be qualified, and who they know to be willing, to act as receiver for the winding up of partnership affairs.

3. In the event that no suitable person can be found to act as receiver, or in the event that the Court should deem it unwise to appoint any person from the names so submitted, then the Court reserves the power to terminate any further racing by Black Ace and to require that he simply be maintained and cared for until such time as he can be sold as a part of the final liquidation of the partnership.

Judgment for Paciaroni and Cassidy.

Partner's Authority during Winding Up

Express Authority	To do anything the partners agree a partner may perform.
Implied Authority	To do those acts reasonably necessary to winding up. • Preserve and enhance assets • Sell assets • Complete executory contracts
Apparent Authority	To conduct business in the usual way, unless proper notice of dissolution has been given. • Actual notice—must be given to prior creditors of the partnership. • Constructive notice (or actual notice)—must be given to noncreditors who conducted business with the partnership. • Constructive notice (or actual notice)—must be given to persons who did not conduct business with the partnership but knew of its existence. • No notice—to persons who previously were unaware of the partnership's existence.

WHEN THE BUSINESS IS CONTINUED

Cessation of business need not follow dissolution of a partnership. The remaining partners could purchase the business during winding up, someone else could purchase the business, or the partnership agreement could provide that there will be no winding up and that the business may be carried on by the remaining partners.

When there is no winding up and the business is continued, the claims of creditors against the partnership and the partners may be affected, because old partners are no longer with the business and new partners may enter the business.

Successor's Liability for Predecessor's Obligations

When the business of a partnership is continued after dissolution, creditors of the old partnership are creditors of the person or partnership continuing the business. In addition, the original partners remain liable for obligations incurred prior to dissolution unless there is agreement with the creditors to the contrary. Thus, partners may not usually escape liability by forming a new partnership or a corporation to carry on the old business of the partnership.

Outgoing Partner's Liability for Obligations Incurred While a Partner

Outgoing partners remain liable to partnership creditors for partnership liabilities incurred while they were partners; however, an outgoing partner's liability may be eliminated by the process of **novation.** Novation occurs when the following two conditions are met:

1. The continuing partners release an outgoing partner from liability on a partnership debt, and

2. A partnership creditor releases the outgoing partner from liability on the same obligation.

Partners usually expressly release an outgoing partner from liability, but the release may be implied as well. To complete the requirements for novation, an outgoing partner must also secure his release by the partnership's creditors. A creditor's agreement to release an outgoing partner from liability may be express, but usually it is implied. *Implied* novation may be proved by a creditor's knowledge of a partner's withdrawal and his continued extension of credit to the partnership. In addition, a *material modification* of an obligation operates as a novation for an outgoing partner, when the creditor has knowledge that the continuing partners have released the outgoing partner from liability.

When former partners release an outgoing partner from liability but creditors do not, there is not a novation. As a result, creditors may enforce a partnership liability against an outgoing partner. However, the outgoing partner may recover from his former partners who have agreed to release him from liability.

Nonetheless, an outgoing partner may not enforce a release-of-liability agreement when he obtains the release by failing to disclose material facts to the partners or creditors. For example, an outgoing partner who obtains release from the partners without disclosing that he has bound the partnership on a contract retains his liability to the other partners.

In the following case, an outgoing partner was not released from liability on a loan.

WEISS v. COMMISSIONER OF INTERNAL REVENUE   956 F.2d 242 (11th Cir. 1992)

Robert Weiss was the owner of Personal Management Services, Inc. (Weiss/PMS), a motel management business. In December 1978, Weiss formed a partnership with David Hillman, Martin Thaler, and Melvin Lenkin (the Hillman Group), for the purpose of purchasing and operating the Hawaiian Village Motel in Tampa, Florida. The partners had agreed that the Hillman Group would finance the purchase of the motel and provide working capital and that Weiss/PMS would manage the motel. They agreed that Weiss would receive 50 percent of the partnership's profits; the Hillman Group would receive the remaining 50 percent. The partnership entered a management contract with Weiss to manage the motel through Weiss/PMS. The management contract could be terminated at the option of the partnership if the motel's annual net cash flow fell below $250,000. The partnership agreement stated that Weiss forfeited his partnership interest if the management contract with Weiss/PMS were terminated or if Weiss failed to contribute capital to the partnership as requested by the partnership.

In February 1979, the partnership borrowed $300,000 from Flagship Bank of Tampa. Flagship required that Weiss and the other partners personally guarantee the loan. By late-summer 1979, the day-to-day operations of the motel were in disarray under Weiss's management. It was determined that an immediate capital infusion of $400,000 was necessary to cover the deficit between current assets and current liabilities. On October 4, Hillman terminated the management contract with Weiss/PMS. The next day, Hillman made a capital call to the partners for $400,000, of which Weiss's share was $200,000. The Hillman Group satisfied its capital call by obtaining an additional $200,000 loan from Flagship Bank, but Weiss did not. On November 19, Hillman notified Weiss that Weiss's partnership interest had been forfeited to the partnership as of November 15, 1979, due to Weiss's failure to meet the capital call.

After reviewing Weiss's 1979 federal income tax return, the Internal Revenue Service issued a notice of deficiency, stating that because Weiss's partnership interest was terminated and because he was relieved of partnership liabilities incurred before November 15, 1979, Weiss realized a short-term capital gain on his share of the partnership liabilities for which he was no longer responsible. Therefore, the IRS stated that Weiss had understated his 1979 income. Weiss asked the tax court to review the decision of the IRS. When the tax court agreed with the IRS, Weiss appealed to the court of appeals. ∽

Edmondson, Circuit Judge We conclude that Weiss was not relieved of partnership liability in 1979 and, therefore, that the Tax Court erred in determining Weiss's taxable gain in 1979. Weiss could only have realized a taxable gain if he was relieved of partnership liability. We have found nothing to indicate that Weiss was relieved of his personal guarantee on Flagship's $300,000 partnership loan.

In concluding that Weiss continued to be liable on his guarantee of the Flagship's loan, we reject the Tax Court's interpretation of Florida partnership law. The Tax Court relied on two Florida statutes to decide that Weiss had been relieved of partnership liability. The Tax Court looked at Fla. Stat. section 620.67(6), which states:

When a partner is expelled and the remaining partners continue the business, either alone or with others without liquidation of the partnership affairs, creditors of the dissolved partnership are also creditors of the person or partnership continuing the business.

While this statute protects partnership creditors, it does not divest them of their legal right to go after an ex-partner to whom they extended credit or an ex-partner who personally guaranteed a loan to the partnership. In fact, another Florida statute expressly states that "the dissolution of the partnership of itself does not discharge the existing liability of any partner." Fla. Stat. section 620.735(1).

The Tax Court, though, overlooked section 620.735(1) and went straight to Fla. Stat. section 620.735(2):

A partner is discharged from any existing liability upon dissolution of the partnership by an agreement to that effect between himself, the partnership creditor and the person or partnership continuing the business. The agreement may be inferred from the course of dealing between the creditor having knowledge of the dissolution and the person or partnership continuing the business.

No express or inferred agreement existed here. There was no express agreement between Weiss and the Hillman Group partners relieving Weiss of liability; Flagship did not expressly release Weiss from his personal guarantee, and nothing in the course of dealings between the Hillman Group and Flagship permits the inference that Flagship released Weiss from his personal guarantee.

Because the Tax Court did not indicate what course of dealings showed that Weiss was relieved of liability, we suppose that Flagship's extension of a $200,000 line of credit to the Hillman Group somehow influenced the Tax Court. But this credit extension is in no way inconsistent with the fact that Flagship still considered Weiss personally liable on his guarantee of the earlier loan. Without a clear inconsistency between the written guarantee and later conduct by Flagship, we see no reason to infer that Weiss had been discharged from his obligation pursuant to the guarantee. For example, we *might* decide that Weiss was relieved from liability by the course of dealings if, without expressly releasing Weiss, Flagship had substituted a new written guarantee from the Hillman Group or one of its members after Weiss's partnership interest was terminated. Or, for another example, we *might* also have decided that Weiss was released if, in the course of dealings, Flagship had been forced to recover on its loan participation and sought recovery only from the Hillman Group and not from Weiss. But here nothing in the record shows that Flagship had released Weiss from his personal guarantee. The Tax Court, therefore, erred in holding that Weiss was relieved of partnership liability.

Judgment reversed in favor of Weiss.

Outgoing Partner's Liability for Obligations Incurred after Leaving the Partnership

Ordinarily, an outgoing partner has no liability on partnership obligations incurred after he leaves the partnership because he no longer controls the partnership or shares as a co-owner in its profits. Nonetheless, outgoing partners may be liable for obligations incurred by a person or partnership continuing the business after their departure, under the theory of *partnership by estoppel*. There is no such liability to creditors who are aware of the change in partners. Also, the risk of estoppel liability can be eliminated by giving the appropriate notice that the partner has left the partnership.

Actual—or personal—notice must be given to those persons who extended credit to the partnership prior to dissolution. Such notice may be either oral or written and must be actually delivered or received. Constructive notice—notice published several times in a newspaper of general circulation—is sufficient for those who knew of the partnership but were not prior creditors. No notice need be given to persons who were not previously aware of the partnership's existence or who knew of the dissolution.

Liability of Incoming Partners

A person joining an existing partnership has unlimited liability for all partnership obligations incurred *after* she becomes a partner. For partnership obligations incurred *before* she became a partner, she is liable as if she had been a partner when the obligations were incurred; however, her liability is limited to the partnership's assets. Once partnership assets are exhausted, she has no further liability for partnership obligations that were incurred prior to her affiliation with the partnership. Nonetheless, if she has expressly or impliedly agreed to undertake unlimited liability for prior obligations, her liability will be unlimited. For example, she may agree with an outgoing partner to assume the outgoing partner's partnership obligations. The creditors may enforce the contract against the incoming partner under creditor beneficiary theory. Thus, the incoming partner is liable on obligations incurred by the partnership before she became a partner.

In the following case, an incoming partner was not liable for interest that accrued when she was a partner on a debt that was incurred when she was not a partner.

CONKLIN FARM v. LEIBOWITZ   658 A.2d 1257 (N.J. Sup. Ct. 1995)

*I*n December 1986, Paula Hertzberg, Elliot Leibowitz, and Joel Leibowitz formed a partnership, LongView Estates, for the purpose of acquiring 100 acres of land from Conklin Farm, where the partnership intended to build a condominium complex. Paula owned 40 percent of the partnership, Elliot 30 percent, and Joel 30 percent. The same day, LongView executed a promissory note promising to pay Conklin $9 million in exchange for the 100 acres of land. The note was signed by the partners on behalf of the partnership and individually as guarantors of the note. The note provided for monthly payments of interest only: 8¼ percent annual interest for the first year and 9 percent thereafter. The principal was due January 15, 1992.

On March 15, 1990, Joel's wife, Doris Leibowitz, joined the partnership. Seventeen months later, on August 30, 1991, Doris left the partnership. During those 17 months, interest of 9 percent per annum accrued on the $9 million note held by Conklin.

LongView's condominium project failed, and LongView defaulted to Conklin. Conklin seized the land to satisfy the principal obligation, but the partnership's assets were exhausted and the interest was not paid. Eventually, Paula Hertzberg, Elliot Leibowitz, and Joel Leibowitz filed for personal bankruptcy protection and were discharged from any personal liability on the note, including interest.

Conklin then sued Doris Leibowitz to collect the interest that accrued while she was a LongView partner. The trial court held that the interest was a debt that existed before Doris entered the partnership, not new debt incurred while she was a partner, and therefore, Doris was not personally liable for the interest. Conklin appealed to the appellate division, which reversed, holding Doris personally liable for the interest that accrued on the note while she was a partner of LongView. Doris appealed to the New Jersey Supreme Court. ∞

Garibaldi, Judge   N.J.S.A. 42:1-17 defines the liability of new partners entering an existing partnership:

A person admitted as a partner into an existing partnership is liable for all the obligations of the partnership arising before his admission as though he had been a partner when such obligations were incurred, except *that his liability shall be satisfied only out of partnership property.* (Emphasis added.)

Under this statute, although the original partners are personally liable for preexisting debt, the incoming partner's liability for preexisting debt is limited to partnership property. The source for that statute is section 17 of the Uniform Partnership Act.

In addition, section 41(1) of the Uniform Partnership Act, adopted by New Jersey, provides that when a new partner is admitted and the business continues, the creditors of the previous partnership are also creditors of the partnership continuing the

business. The result is that preexisting creditors are protected, but incoming partners are not exposed to personal liability to cover preexisting debts.

The Conklin note was executed by the partnership prior to Doris's having any interest in LongView. She did not sign or guarantee payment of that note. Thus, she is not personally liable for the debt. The parties agree that the principal of the note was preexisting debt. However, while Doris argues that the interest that accrued while she was a partner was part of that preexisting debt, Conklin argues that it was new debt that arose each month as it became due. Thus, according to Conklin, Doris is personally liable for the interest that accrued while she was a partner. We disagree.

That the interest is not an independent or new debt is reflected in the method Conklin used to calculate the claimed liability; Conklin referred to the promissory note executed prior to Doris's admission as a partner. Conklin referred to the preexisting note because no other source exists to define the interest obligation. Conklin's own claim demonstrates that interest is part of contractual debt, and that the obligation to pay interest *arises,* if at all, at the time that the parties execute the note or other debt instrument.

Conklin argues that just as a rent obligation arises for a current use of property, an interest obligation arises for current use of principal. Conklin relies primarily on *Ellingson v. Walsh, O'Connor & Barneson* (1940), in which the California Supreme Court held that an incoming partner was personally liable for rent due after his admission, even though he was not a partner when the partnership signed the lease. Significantly, the court did not hold that the incoming partner was personally liable for the preexisting lease obligation. Rather, the court held that section 17 of the Uniform Partnership Act did not shield the incoming partner from personal liability for the common-law obligation to pay rent based on current tenancy. That common-law obligation arises with each period of tenancy, and it arises even in the absence of a lease. Hence, the common-law obligation to pay rent—entirely independent of the contractual obligation under the lease—arose as a new debt each time the rent became due.

There is another crucial difference between rent and interest: Whereas all obligations and entitlements related to a loan are generally fixed at the time of executing the debt instrument, the same is not true of a lease. The obligation to pay rent under a lease is contingent on the landlord's fulfilling the *continuing* obligation to allow occupancy by the tenant. That characteristic of leases justifies the view that rent, even under a lease, may not arise as debt until its due date.

That characteristic also significantly differentiates a lease from a promissory note. The note from LongView in favor of Conklin provided for only one obligation on Conklin's part: the conveyance of the property in return for LongView's promise to pay $9 million plus interest. On execution of the deed to the land, Conklin had fulfilled its obligation. LongView's obligation to repay principal and to pay interest thus arose at the time that the note was executed. Unlike a tenant's obligation to pay rent, LongView's obligation to pay interest was not contingent on any further performance by Conklin.

Moreover, there is no prejudice to Conklin in the fact that it may look to only the original partners for payment of the preexisting debt and interest. In executing the note, Conklin considered the personal credit of only Paula Hertzberg, Elliot Leibowitz, and Joel Leibowitz, all of whom guaranteed the loan. Conklin did not rely on the personal credit of Doris. When lenders loan money, they rely on the financial statements of the general partners, and not of some future, unknown general partner. Furthermore, lenders can protect themselves by providing in the promissory note that if new partners enter the partnership, the partnership will terminate, and the note will be accelerated unless the new partner agrees to sign or guarantee the note.

We find that contractual interest is not new debt. It is not a separate and distinct obligation, but is an integral part of the debt itself. Accordingly, LongView's obligation to pay interest arose when it executed the Conklin note, before Doris Leibowitz became a partner. Hence, the interest on the note was preexisting debt and Doris Leibowitz is not personally liable for its payment.

Judgment reversed in favor of Doris Leibowitz.

Rights of Outgoing Partners

An outgoing partner is entitled to receive the value of his partnership interest. He becomes a creditor of the new partnership for the value of his partnership interest, but his claim is subordinate to the claims of other creditors of the partnership.

Valuation of the Outgoing Partner's Interest
The value of an outgoing partner's interest in the partnership is determined at the time of the dissolution. Often, the partnership agreement includes a method for calculating the value of a partnership interest.

The value of a partnership includes its goodwill. **Goodwill** is the well-founded expectation of continued public patronage of a business. It represents the difference between the going-concern value of a business and the liquidation value of its assets.

When a partnership business is continued after dissolution, it is frequently difficult to determine the value of the goodwill that is transferred to the continuing partners. In service partnerships, the goodwill may be so closely tied to the individual partners that no goodwill remains with the business when valuable partners withdraw from the partnership. These difficulties and uncertainties also make it advisable to have a partnership agreement on valuing the partnership, including the value of its goodwill.

Payment Options   In the absence of a contrary agreement, when dissolution results from death or retirement, the outgoing partner may choose one of the following payment options:

1. Taking the value of his partnership interest at the time of dissolution plus interest, or
2. Taking the value of his partnership interest at the time of dissolution plus a pro rata share of subsequent profits.

These options provide incentive for the continuing partners to settle promptly with an outgoing partner.

When there is no agreement and dissolution results from a cause other than death or retirement—as with dissolutions caused by bankruptcy or by willful, persistent breaches of the partnership agreement—the partner is entitled to receive the value of her interest at the time of dissolution. The outgoing partner may insist on immediate payment and receive interest for late payment.

Valuation of Interest of Wrongfully Dissolving Partner   A wrongfully dissolving partner must be paid the value of his partnership interest in cash by the continuing partners, or the partners must post a bond to have the privilege of continuing the business. In addition, they must agree to release him from all present and future partnership liabilities. However, goodwill is excluded from the valuation of the partnership interest of a partner who has wrongfully caused dissolution, and the valuation of that interest is further reduced by the damages that he has caused his partners due to his dissolution.

DISTRIBUTION OF ASSETS

After the partnership's assets have been sold during winding up, the proceeds are distributed to those persons who have claims against the partnership. Not only creditors but also partners have claims

against the proceeds. As you might expect, the claims of creditors must be satisfied before the claims of partners may be paid. The UPA states the order of distribution of the partnership assets:

1. Those owing to creditors other than partners.
2. Those owing to partners other than for capital and profits.
3. Those owing to partners in respect of capital.
4. Those owing to partners in respect of profits.

Note that item 2 places partners who are also creditors of the partnership subordinate to other creditors. This is done to prevent partners from underfunding a partnership to the detriment of creditors. The subordination of partner-creditors also emphasizes that the partners are liable for all the partnership's liabilities.

A partner who is also a creditor of the partnership, however, is paid his claim as a creditor before any partner receives any return of his capital contribution. Thus, for example, a partner's loan to the partnership is repaid before any partner has his capital returned.

If a partnership has not suffered losses that impair its capital, few problems are presented in the distribution of its assets. Everyone having an interest in the partnership is paid in full. If there is a disagreement about the amount due to a claimant, the dispute is usually resolved by an accounting ordered by the court.

Distribution of Assets of Insolvent Partnership

When a partnership has suffered losses, distribution of the assets may be troublesome. For example, partnership creditors may compete with the creditors of individual partners to obtain payment from partnership assets and the assets of individual partners. Also, the partnership losses must be allocated among partners. In adjusting the rights of partnership creditors and the creditors of individual partners, the rule is usually that partnership creditors have first claim on partnership assets and that individual creditors have first claim on individual assets. This is called **marshaling of assets.**

Example   The distribution of assets and allocation of losses of an insolvent partnership can best be explained with an example. Suppose that Alden,

Bass, and Casey form a partnership and that Alden contributes $25,000, Bass contributes $15,000, and Casey contributes $10,000. After operating for several years, the firm suffers losses and becomes insolvent. When the partnership is liquidated, its assets total $30,000 in cash. It owes $40,000 to partnership creditors. Therefore, the capital balance (net worth) of the partnership is a negative $10,000. This means that partnership losses totaled $60,000 ($50,000 of capital already contributed and lost plus the $10,000 negative net worth). The situation could be represented by the following equation:

Profit = Ending owner's capital − Beginning owner's capital

−$60,000 =   −$10,000   − $50,000

Because the profit is negative, this is a loss of $60,000.

In the absence of a provision in the partnership agreement concerning the partners' shares of profits and losses, they are shared equally. Therefore, each partner's **share of the loss** is one-third of the loss, $20,000. Their shares of the loss reduce the partners' capital claims against partnership assets, as shown in the following table.

	CAPITAL AT BEGINNING		SHARE OF LOSS		CAPITAL AT LIQUIDATION
Alden	$25,000	−	$20,000	=	$5,000
Bass	15,000	−	20,000	=	(5,000)
Casey	10,000	−	20,000	=	(10,000)
Totals	$50,000	−	$60,000	=	$(10,000)

The table shows that while each partner should have assumed $20,000 of the loss, Alden has taken $25,000 of the loss due to her $25,000 capital contribution. Therefore, unless she has $5,000 of her capital returned, she has assumed $5,000 of the loss she should not have assumed. Bass and Casey, on the other hand, have assumed too little of the loss, because their capital contributions were less

than $20,000. Bass should undertake $5,000 more of the loss, and Casey should assume $10,000 more, amounts reflected in the last column of the table.

Now we shall distribute partnership assets and pay the claims against the partnership. Following the order of distribution in the UPA, the $30,000 in cash from the liquidation is distributed pro rata to pay the nonpartner creditors of the partnership. Because the creditors are owed $40,000, the $30,000 payment leaves $10,000 of partnership debts to outsiders unpaid. The partners are liable for the remaining $10,000. Because the partnership assets are gone, the partners must pay the debt from their individual assets.

To undertake their **shares of the partnership liabilities,** Bass is legally liable to contribute $5,000 and Casey $10,000 to the partnership, the negative amounts in the Capital at Liquidation column in the table. This permits completion of the payment of the partnership creditors ($10,000) and the return of Alden's capital to the extent that it exceeded her share of the partnership loss—the $5,000 figure in the Capital at Liquidation column.

Unpaid partnership creditors have a right to collect from any solvent partner. Had they chosen to collect the entire amount from Alden, she would then have had to proceed against Bass and Casey for the amount she paid that Bass and Casey should have paid.

Termination

After the assets of a partnership have been distributed, **termination** of the partnership occurs automatically.

In the following case, not only was a partner denied a return of capital when the partnership's assets were insufficient to pay all the partnership's creditors, but also the partner was ordered to contribute additional funds to pay all claims of partnership creditors.

WESTON v. DONNELLY   927 F.2d 369 (8th Cir. 1991)

 ichard Donnelly and Robert Narmont each held a 50 percent interest in a partnership that owned a vacation home in Florida. In October 1983, William Weston agreed to purchase Narmont's interest in the house. Weston issued a check to Donnelly for $26,000, and Donnelly signed a promissory note promising to repay Weston the same amount, $26,000, on demand with no interest.

Donnelly then issued a check to Narmont for $26,000. Over the next 15 months, Weston stayed at the Florida home on at least eight separate occasions, using the home as a vacation retreat for his family and friends. Donnelly and Weston registered the name Cheshire Partnership under Missouri's fictitious-name statute, and held themselves out as partners of Cheshire. They borrowed $100,000 from a bank, signing the promissory note as partners of Cheshire Partnership. Weston also advanced $13,000 to the partnership to make improvements to the house.

In April 1985, Weston's business failed and he informed Donnelly he wanted all of his money back. Donnelly and Weston could not agree on the value of the partnership. For the next three years, Donnelly paid the interest on the partnership's debts and also paid for upkeep of the house. In March 1988, Donnelly sold the house for $110,000. Weston then sued to force Donnelly to repay the $26,000 promissory note. Donnelly answered that the note represented only Weston's capital contribution to the partnership. Donnelly asked the court for a partnership accounting. The trial court found that the promissory note represented not a loan by Weston but Weston's capital contribution to the partnership. The trial court also ordered Weston to undertake his share of the partnership's expenses and losses that Donnelly had incurred during the final years and the winding up of the partnership. The court ordered Weston to pay Donnelly $19,000. Weston appealed. ∞

Bright, Senior Circuit Judge Weston challenges the district court's finding that the promissory note executed by Donnelly did not represent a bona fide loan but rather an investment in the partnership. Weston has utterly failed to sustain his burden of establishing that this finding is clearly erroneous. On numerous occasions, Weston held himself out as a partner with Donnelly in Cheshire Partners. Both parties signed and filed a Registration of Fictitious Name with the State of Missouri, registering themselves as equal partners in the Cheshire Partnership. When Weston filed a personal financial condition form with the Mark Twain Parkway Bank in order to secure a note to cover the mortgage on the Florida home, Weston listed as personal assets a one-half interest in the Florida house. Notably, Weston did not list the promissory note as an asset. Weston and Donnelly, acting as partners of Cheshire Partnership, signed a note for $100,000 with the Mark Twain Parkway Bank. After reviewing the record, we are satisfied that the record abundantly supports the court's finding that the promissory note was an investment in the partnership.

Weston contends that the district court erred in calculating Donnelly's damage awards. According to Weston, the district court erred by failing to credit Weston with his initial cash contribution. We reject Weston's contention.

Partnership assets must be applied to satisfy outstanding debts in the following order:

(a) Those owing to creditors other than partners;
(b) Those owing to partners other than for capital and profits;
(c) Those owing to partners in respect of capital;
(d) Those owing to partners in respect of profits.

The outstanding partnership liabilities owed to Donnelly for expenses incurred on behalf of the partnership were for expenses other than capital and profits. Thus, those debts had to be completely satisfied before the partners could recoup their capital contributions.

In the present case, however, the partnership was operating at a loss and lacked sufficient assets to satisfy the debts which must be paid before the partners may seek a return of their capital contributions. Thus, there was no reason for the district court to consider Weston's capital contribution in its damage calculations. Put simply, both partners lost their capital contributions because the partnership's higher priority debts exceeded its assets.

Judgment for Donnelly affirmed.

1. Why should a partner have the power to dissolve a partnership at any time, while in general a shareholder of a corporation has no such power? Is it important to your answer that a partner has liability for his partners' contracts and torts, while a shareholder generally has no liability for the contracts or the torts of the corporation? Why should a partner not have the right to dissolve a partnership at any time? Who should determine when a partner has the right to dissolve a partnership? Should only the partners determine the scope of this right, or does society have the right to limit a partner's right to dissolve?

2. Why should a partnership give notice of the dissolution of a partnership? Why is the partnership liable to creditors who do not receive proper notice of the dissolution? Is fairness promoted by such a rule? Is economic efficiency promoted by such a rule?

3. Is it fair that a wrongfully dissolving partner is not entitled to receive a share of the value of the partnership's goodwill? What is goodwill? How much goodwill does the business lose when a dissolving partner leaves the partnership? Is more goodwill lost when a partner dissolves wrongfully than when he dissolves nonwrongfully? Do partners expect wrongful dissolutions? Do the expectations of the partners provide a rationale to deny goodwill to a wrongfully dissolving partner?

4. Do you think it is right that a partner who enters an existing partnership has liability limited to the partnership's assets? What argument can you make that the incoming partner should have unlimited liability? Are the partnership assets the sole extent of the benefit accruing to new partners? Shouldn't a new partner know the financial position of the partnership—including its liabilities—prior to entering the partnership? Why should preexisting creditors bear the risk rather than incoming partners? Are you convinced that the court in *Conklin Farm v. Leibowitz* made the correct decision that interest on a promissory note accrued when the note was made, not monthly as the interest is earned, and that therefore, the incoming partner was not liable on the interest due during her tenure as a partner? Are you convinced by the court's reasoning that interest is different from rent?

PROBLEMS AND PROBLEM CASES

1. Hilolani Acres Joint Venture was a partnership of 42 partners, including Benjamin Aiu. Four of the partners were designated managing partners. The partnership agreement stated that the purpose of the partnership was "dealing with" the Hilolani Acres, a housing development in Hawaii. The partnership agreement also provided for continuation of the business of the partnership in the event of a withdrawal of partners from the partnership. In 1971, three of the managing partners withdrew from the partnership; in addition, title to Hilolani Acres was transferred to Great Hawaiian Mortgage Corporation, which would manage the development of Hilolani Acres for the partnership; Great Hawaiian received 35 percent of the profits from Hilolani Acres, the remainder going to the partnership. The nonmanaging partners claimed that these acts dissolved the partnership, and they sought to wind it up. Were they right?

2. Robert Cowan was a partner in a six-person law firm. The partnership agreement provided that the firm would not dissolve upon the withdrawal of a partner. Cowan initially indicated that he would withdraw from the partnership but later changed his mind. By that time, however, the other partners had resolved to force Cowan from the partnership. The other partners transferred all partnership funds to accounts in their names only. However, a few days later, they set up an escrow account to protect the value of Cowan's partnership interest. Did the other partners' actions entitle Cowan to obtain a judicial dissolution of the partnership?

3. Kenneth Flynn and Rick Haddad were partners owning a beachfront lot with a small inn on it. Title to the lot was in both partners' names. Flynn gave Haddad a deed to Flynn's interest in the property, which was effective only upon Flynn's nonpayment of a loan. When the inn was destroyed by fire, the partners began construction of a new inn, but construction was stopped because it violated local zoning laws. The effect of halting construction was also to eliminate the market of potential buyers of the property. Haddad decided to sever his relationship with Flynn and, consequently, filed the deed to the property that had earlier been executed by Flynn, although Flynn had already repaid the loan.

Has the partnership been dissolved? Should the property be sold during winding up, or should Haddad receive title to it and be required to pay Flynn his share of the value of the property?

4. Brothers Eugene and Marlowe Mehl operated a family farm as a partnership. Each partner was active in the partnership until Marlowe suffered a stroke. Eleven years later, the partnership was dissolved, and Eugene by himself wound up the partnership's affairs. Was Eugene entitled to wages as compensation for winding up the partnership?

5. Ralph Neitzert and his brother were the only partners of Jolly Jug Liquors, a retail liquor store. The partners signed a contract to lease refrigeration equipment from Colo-Tex Leasing, Inc. A month later, Ralph sold his interest in the partnership to his sister. Ralph did not notify Colo-Tex that he sold his interest to his sister. A year later, when the partnership breached the lease, Colo-Tex sued Ralph, his brother, and his sister. Is Ralph liable to Colo-Tex?

6. Junior Nestle and Eric Ellis owned Red Rocks Meat and Deli, a partnership, which they operated in a building that they leased from Wester & Company. Nestle left the partnership, and Wester received notice that Nestle was no longer a partner. Wester did not object to the change in partners or request that Nestle remain liable. A year later, Wester and Ellis modified the lease to include adjacent space and to increase the rent. Four months later, Ellis failed to pay the rent; Wester sued Nestle. Was Nestle liable to Wester?

7. Weintraub, Gold & Alper, a law firm partnership, was dissolved. The firm's partners continued to occupy the same office space and to use the firm's name and letterhead as an aid in the partners' transition to individual law practices. Roger Allen sought a $60,000 loan from Royal Bank. Allen told Royal Bank that the $60,000 would be kept in an escrow account of his lawyers, the firm of Weintraub, Gold & Alper. Allen gave Royal Bank a letter on the law firm's stationery addressed to Allen and signed by Weintraub acknowledging that the money would be placed in a firm escrow account. Royal Bank discovered that Weintraub, Gold, and Alper were listed separately in a lawyer directory as practicing law at the address given on the firm stationery. Royal Bank also found the firm listing in the current New York phone book at the address and phone number on the letterhead. When Royal Bank dialed the number, the receptionist answered, "Weintraub, Gold and Alper." Royal Bank spoke with Weintraub, who confirmed the escrow arrangement. That same day, Royal Bank made the loan to Allen, giving him a check payable to the law firm. The check was deposited in the escrow account. When the loan was due, the escrowed check was not returned and the loan was not repaid. Royal Bank sued Gold and Alper to recover the $60,000. Were Gold and Alper liable to Royal Bank?

8. As partners, Joseph Kalichman and Joseph Klein owned and managed an apartment building in the Bronx. The partnership borrowed $189,000 from National Savings Bank of Albany. Joseph Klein died; his interest in the partnership passed to his sons, Jack and Frank, who received Joseph Klein's share of the partnership income. Jack and Frank did not, however, share in the management of the partnership business. The partnership defaulted on the loan from National Savings Bank, which sued Jack and Frank. Are Jack and Frank liable to National Savings Bank?

9. ☐☐☐ *Video Case.*   See "The Partnership." Art retires from Alphabet Builders, a partnership with Ben and Diedre. Zack agrees to replace Art in the partnership. Zack signs an agreement with Art assuming Art's liability for all partnership obligations. After Art leaves the partnership, Alphabet Builders falls behind in payments to its creditors, including the following:

a. The bank from which Art obtained a loan in the name of the partnership prior to his leaving the partnership. Art pocketed the bank loan and used it for his personal investment in commodities futures. Art did not disclose the loan to his partners or to Zack.

b. The creditor who leases office equipment to Alphabet Builders. The lease agreement predates the time Art left the partnership.

c. Subcontractors owed money on contracts entered into after Art left and Zack entered the partnership.

What is Art's liability on these obligations? What is Zack's liability on these obligations? What other facts do you need to help you answer these questions?

10. NFL Associates was a partnership of three partners: Herb Friedman, Strelsa Lee Langness, and the O Street Carpet Shop, Inc. When the partnership was created, O Street Carpet contributed a contract worth $9,000, Langness contributed $14,000 in cash, and Friedman contributed his legal services, which were not valued. The partners used part of Langness's contribution to make an $8,000 payment to O Street Carpet. They used the remaining $6,000 to purchase investment property and to provide working capital for the partnership. Later, O Street Carpet contributed an additional $4,005 in capital. The partners agreed that Friedman would receive 10 percent of the profits and that each of the other two partners would receive 45 percent of the profits.

They also agreed that Langness would receive payments of $116.66 each month. During the term of the partnership, Langness received monthly checks from the partnership totaling $6,300.30. Langness did not pay income tax on these monthly payments, and the partnership did not take expense deductions for the payments. When the partnership was dissolved and wound up, the partnership assets were sold for $52,001.20. Partnership creditors were owed $3,176.79. Who received what amounts from the proceeds of the sale of partnership assets?

Limited Partnerships and Limited Liability Companies

While the taxation advantages of the partnership form of business may attract investors to a partnership, the partners' unlimited liability for partnership debts scares away some investors. State legislatures and the Internal Revenue Service have cooperated to permit the creation of two business forms that offer taxation advantages similar to the partnership, yet extend limited liability to the owners of the business. These forms are the limited partnership and the limited liability company. ∞

LIMITED PARTNERSHIPS

The partnership form—with managerial control and unlimited liability for all partners—is not acceptable for all business arrangements. Often, business managers want an infusion of capital into a business yet are reluctant to surrender managerial control to those contributing capital. Investors wish to contribute capital to a business and share in its profits yet limit their liability to the amount of their investment and be relieved of the obligation to manage the business.

The **limited partnership** serves these needs. The limited partnership has two classes of owners: **general partners,** who contribute capital to the business, manage it, share in its profits, and possess unlimited liability for its obligations; and **limited partners,** who contribute capital and share profits,

FIGURE 1

Principal Characteristics of Limited Partnerships

1. A limited partnership may be *created only in accordance with a statute.*
2. A limited partnership has two types of partners: *general partners* and *limited partners.* It must have one or more of each type.
3. All partners, limited and general, *share the profits* of the business.
4. Each general partner has *unlimited liability* for the obligations of the business. Each limited partner has liability *limited to his capital contribution* to the business.
5. Each general partner has a *right to manage* the business, and she is an agent of the limited partnership. A limited partner has *no right to manage* the business or to act as its agent, but he does have the right to vote on fundamental matters. If a limited partner does manage the business, he may incur unlimited liability for partnership obligations.
6. General partners, as agents, are *fiduciaries* of the business. Limited partners are not fiduciaries.
7. A partner's interest in a limited partnership *is not freely transferable.* An assignee of a general or limited partnership interest is not a partner, but is entitled only to the assigning partner's share of capital and profits, absent a contrary agreement.
8. Withdrawal of a general partner *dissolves* a limited partnership absent a contrary agreement of the partners. The withdrawal of a limited partner does not automatically dissolve a limited partnership.
9. Usually, a limited partnership *pays no federal income taxes.* Its partners report their shares of the profits and losses on their individual federal income tax returns. A limited partnership files an *information return* with the Internal Revenue Service, notifying the IRS of each partner's share of the year's profit or loss.

but possess no management powers and have liability limited to their investments in the business.

In 1822, New York and Connecticut were the first states to recognize the limited partnership. Today, every state has a statute permitting the creation of limited partnerships, although Louisiana calls them partnerships *in commendam.*

The Uniform Limited Partnership Acts

The National Conference of Commissioners on Uniform State Laws—a body of lawyers, judges, and legal scholars—drafted the Uniform Limited Partnership Act (ULPA) in 1916. In 1976, the commissioners drafted the Revised Uniform Limited Partnership Act (RULPA), which more clearly and comprehensively states the law of limited partnership. The RULPA was amended in several significant ways in 1985. Forty-eight states have adopted the RULPA, Vermont follows the ULPA, and Louisiana follows neither. The RULPA as amended in 1985 forms the foundation of the discussion in this chapter. References are made to the Uniform Partnership Act (UPA), which applies to limited partnerships in the absence of an applicable provision in the RULPA. As shown in Figure 1, many characteristics of a limited partnership under the RULPA are similar to those of a partnership under the UPA.

Use of Limited Partnerships

The limited partnership form is used primarily in tax shelter ventures and activities such as real estate investment, oil and gas drilling, and professional sports. Usually, limited partnerships operate as tax shelters by allowing partners to reduce their personal federal income tax liability by deducting limited partnership losses on their individual income tax returns. General partners, however, receive a greater tax shelter advantage than do limited partners. Losses of the business allocated to a general partner offset his income from any other sources. Losses of the business allocated to limited partners may be used to offset only income from other *passive* investments and only to the extent limited partners are *at risk,* that is, to the extent of their capital contributions to the limited partnership. If a limited partner has sold her limited partnership interest or the limited partnership has terminated, her loss offsets any income.

CREATION OF LIMITED PARTNERSHIPS

A limited partnership may be created only by complying with the applicable state statute. Yet the statutory requirements of the RULPA are minimal. A **certificate of limited partnership** must be executed and filed with the secretary of state. The

FIGURE 2

Contents of Certificate of Limited Partnership

The following must be in the certificate:

1. The name of the limited partnership, which must contain the words *limited partnership*. The name may not include the surname of a limited partner, unless it is the same as the surname of a general partner or unless the business of the limited partnership has been carried on under that name prior to the admission of the limited partner.
2. The name and address of each general partner. Each general partner must sign the certificate.
3. The latest date the limited partnership will dissolve.
4. The name and address of an agent for service of process. Designating an agent for service of process in the certificate eases a creditor's obligation to notify a limited partnership that it is being sued by the creditor.

certificate must be signed by all general partners. A limited partnership begins its existence at the time the certificate is filed with the office of the secretary of state or at any later time specified in the certificate. Figure 2 lists the contents of the certificate of limited partnership.

The certificate is not required to state the names of the limited partners, the partners' capital contributions, the partners' shares of profits and other distributions, or the acts that cause a dissolution of the limited partnership. Nonetheless, the partners will usually include those and other matters in the certificate or in a separate **limited partnership agreement.**

Any *person* may be a general or limited partner. Persons include a natural person, partnership, limited partnership, trust, estate, association, or corporation. Hence, as commonly occurs, a corporation may be the sole general partner of a limited partnership.

The RULPA permits partners to make capital contributions of cash, property, services rendered, a promissory note, or a binding promise to contribute cash, property, or services.

Defective Compliance with Limited Partnership Statute

The RULPA requires at least *substantial compliance* with the previously listed requirements to create a limited partnership. If the persons attempting to create a limited partnership do not substantially comply with the RULPA, a limited partnership does not exist; therefore, a limited partner may lose her limited liability and become liable as a general partner. A lack of substantial compliance might result from failing to file a certificate of limited partnership or from filing a defective certificate. A defective certificate might, for example, misstate the name of the limited partnership.

Infrequently, a person will believe that she is a limited partner but discover later that she has been designated a general partner or that the general partners have not filed a certificate of limited partnership. In such circumstances and others, she may be liable as a general partner unless she in good faith believes she is a limited partner and upon discovering she is not a limited partner she either:

1. Causes a proper certificate of limited partnership (or an amendment thereto) to be filed with the secretary of state, or
2. Withdraws from future equity participation in the firm by filing a certificate declaring such withdrawal with the secretary of state.

However, such a person remains liable as a general partner to third parties who previously believed in good faith that the person was a general partner.

A limited partnership must keep its filed certificate current. Current filings allow creditors to discover current facts, not merely those facts that existed when the original certificate was filed. For example, a certificate amendment must be filed when a general partner is admitted or withdraws.

In the following case, the court considered the liability of new investors who believed they were limited partners although a limited partnership certificate had not been filed.

BRIARGATE CONDOMINIUM ASSOC. v. CARPENTER   976 F.2d 868 (4th Cir. 1992)

I n 1984, Judith Carpenter invested in Briargate Homes, a business that purchased several condominium units in the Briargate Condominium complex. Although Carpenter believed that Briargate was a limited partnership and that she was a limited partner, in fact Briargate Homes was a partnership and she was a general partner. No attempt had been made to achieve actual or substantial compliance with the North Carolina limited partnership statute.

Carpenter never signed the partnership agreement or saw copies of the partnership's K-1 tax returns, which clearly identified her as a general partner. However, deductions for partnership losses that Carpenter claimed on her individual income tax returns were allowable only if she was a general partner. In early 1987, Carpenter or her attorneys had possession of documents explicitly stating that Briargate Homes was a general partnership and that her interest was one of a general partner. In June and December 1987, Carpenter received additional documents identifying Briargate Homes as a general partnership. Carpenter was an experienced businesswoman, served on the board of directors of a bank, and had ready access to legal and other professional advice.

As an owner of condominiums, the partnership was liable to the Briargate Condominium Association for assessments for maintenance, repair, and replacement of common areas in the complex. In late 1987 and early 1988, the partnership failed to pay the Association assessed fees of $85,106. The Association sued the partnership and its partners.

On February 5, 1988, Carpenter notified the other partners and the Association that she was withdrawing from any equity participation and renouncing any interest in the profits of the partnership.

At the trial, Carpenter contended that because she believed she was a limited partner, she should not be liable to the Association for the fees. The district court found that because Carpenter had not promptly withdrawn from the partnership upon discovering she was a general partner, she was liable for the full amount of the debt. Carpenter appealed. ∞

Hamilton, Circuit Judge Carpenter's defense is grounded in the Revised Uniform Partnership Act sec. 304, which provides:

(a) Except as provided in subsection (b), a person who makes a contribution to a business enterprise and erroneously but in good faith believes that he has become a limited partner in the enterprise is not a general partner in the enterprise and is not bound by its obligations, . . . if, on ascertaining the mistake, he:
>   (1) Causes an appropriate certificate of limited partnership to be executed and filed; or
>   (2) Withdraws from future equity participation in the enterprise.

(b) A person who makes a contribution of the kind described in subsection (a) is liable as a general partner to any third party who transacts business with the enterprise (i) before the person withdraws from the enterprise, or (ii) before the person gives notice to the partnership of his withdrawal from future equity participation, but only if the third party actually believed in good faith that the person was a general partner at the time of the transaction.

First, the person must have a good faith belief that he has become a limited partner. Second, the person must on ascertaining the mistake take one of two courses of action. He may file an appropriate certificate of limited partnership. Under this option, the person may continue in the business with limited liability. In the alternative, the person may give notice and withdraw completely from future equity participation in the business. If the two elements are met, then the person is liable *only* as a limited

partner, effectively cutting off all personal liability of a general partner, unless subsection (b) applies.

Subsection (b) sets forth the *only* circumstances under which a person who meets the requirements of subsection (a) may incur liability like a general partner. Personal liability to third parties arises when the third party transacts business with the enterprise before the person files a proper certificate or withdraws. Imposition of liability is limited, however, by the requirement that at the time he transacts business, the third party actually believed in good faith that the person was a general partner at the time of the transaction. Reliance of the third party in the resources of the general partner is absolutely essential before liability may be imposed for transactions occurring before withdrawal.

Unlike its predecessor statute, RULPA sec. 304 does not specify how quickly a proper certificate or notice of withdrawal must be filed after a person ascertains he is not a limited partner. The current statute deletes the word "promptly" contained in the prior statute. The present statute also added the language in subsection (b) regarding reliance. This difference between the old and new statutes reflects a shift in emphasis away from the speed with which withdrawal is effected to an emphasis on protection of reliance by third parties. The key to liability is reliance by the third party on a person's apparent status as a general partner.

Given this interpretation of the statute, we believe the judgment of the district must be vacated, and the case remanded to the district court for additional findings. First, the district court must determine whether or not Carpenter held a good faith belief that she was a limited partner at the time she initially joined and contributed to the partnership. The district court did conclude that by at least mid-1987, Carpenter could not have held a good faith belief she was a limited partner, but the key date is the date of the contribution to the enterprise. Should the district court conclude that Carpenter did not have a good faith belief that she was a limited partner at the time of the initial contribution, then the statute affords her no relief.

Second, assuming Carpenter demonstrates a good faith belief at the time she invested, then her notice of withdrawal effectively cut off liability for any fees accrued after such notice. To hold Carpenter liable for fees accrued prior to the notice, the district court must determine if and when the Association actually believed in good faith that Carpen-

ter was a general partner. Carpenter may be held liable only for those assessments made in reliance on the belief that the Association could look to assets of Carpenter as a general partner to satisfy the debt.

Carpenter points to statements indicating that agents of the Association apparently believed they were dealing with a limited partnership and were totally unaware of Carpenter's interest in the partnership until the time of her notice withdrawing from any equity participation and renouncing any interest in the profits of the partnership. We decline, however, to rule on the issue. It does not appear that this issue received much attention at trial. The district court should, on remand, review the record and may take additional evidence if necessary to aid its fact-finding on this issue.

Judgment for the Association vacated; remanded to the district court.

Foreign Limited Partnerships

A limited partnership is **domestic** in the state in which it is organized; it is **foreign** in every other state. The RULPA makes it clear that the laws of the domestic state apply to the internal affairs of the limited partnership, allowing a limited partner protection regardless of where business is conducted.

Nonetheless, to be privileged to do business in a foreign state, a limited partnership must *register* to do business in that state. To register, a limited partnership must file an **application for registration** with the secretary of state of the foreign state. The application must include the name and address of the limited partnership, the names and addresses of the general partners, the name and address of an agent for service of process, and the address of the office where the names, addresses, and capital contributions of the limited partners are kept. The application must be accompanied by the payment of a fee. The secretary of state reviews the application and, if all requirements are met, issues a **certificate of registration.**

There are few penalties for failing to register as a foreign limited partnership. Although the RULPA does not impose fines for a failure to register, a few states have amended it to do so. In addition, an unregistered foreign limited partnership may not use

the foreign state's courts to sue to enforce any right or contract. Once it registers, a limited partnership may use the state's courts, even when it sues to enforce a contract that was made before it registered.

Failure to register does not invalidate any contracts made in the foreign state or prevent a limited partnership from defending itself in a suit brought in the state's courts. The failure to register, by itself, does not make a limited partner liable as a general partner.

RIGHTS AND LIABILITIES OF PARTNERS IN LIMITED PARTNERSHIPS

The partners of a limited partnership have many rights and liabilities. Some are identical to those of partners in an ordinary partnership, but others are special to limited partnerships. Some are common to both general and limited partners, while others are not shared.

Rights and Liabilities Shared by General and Limited Partners

Capital Contributions   A partner is obligated to contribute as capital the cash, property, or other services that he promised to contribute. This obligation may be enforced by the limited partnership or by any of its creditors, illustrated by the *Builders Steel* case, which follows this section.

Share of Profits and Losses Under the RULPA, profits and losses are shared on the basis of the value of each partner's capital contribution unless there is a written agreement to the contrary. For example, if 2 general partners contribute $1,000 each and 20 limited partners contribute $20,000 each, and the profit is $40,200, each general partner's share of the profits is $100 and each limited partner's share is $2,000.

Because most limited partnerships are tax shelters, partnership agreements often provide for limited partners to take all the losses of the business, up to the limit of their capital contributions.

Voting Rights The partnership agreement may require that certain transactions be approved by general partners, by limited partners, or by all the partners. The agreement may give each general partner more votes than it grants limited partners, or vice versa. The RULPA makes it clear that limited partners have no inherent right to vote on any matter as a class. They may receive such a right only by agreement of the partners.

Admission of New Partners No new partner may be admitted unless each partner has consented to the admission. New partners may be admitted by unanimous written consent of the partners or in accordance with the limited partnership agreement.

Partnership Interest Each partner in a limited partnership owns a partnership interest. It is his personal property. He may sell or assign it to others, such as his personal creditors. Or his personal creditor may obtain a charging order against it. Generally, a buyer or assignee—or a creditor with a charging order—is entitled to receive only the partner's share of distributions.

Nonetheless, when the limited partnership agreement so provides or all the partners consent, a buyer or assignee of a limited or a general partnership interest may become a limited partner. The new limited partner then assumes all the rights and liabilities of a limited partner, except for liabilities unknown to her at the time she became a partner.

A partner's assignment of his partnership interest terminates his status as a partner. The assignment does not, however, relieve him of liability for illegal distributions or for false filings with the secretary of state. When a court grants a charging order to a creditor, however, the partner remains a partner.

Right to Withdraw Partners in a limited partnership have the power to withdraw from the partnership and receive the fair value of their partnership interests. Fair value includes the going concern value of the partnership business—that is, its goodwill.

A general partner may withdraw from a limited partnership at any time; if a general partner's withdrawal breaches the limited partnership agreement, the value of her interest is reduced by the damages suffered by the limited partnership. A limited partner may withdraw after giving six months' prior notice to each general partner.

When a partner withdraws from a limited partnership, the partner may receive a return of his capital contribution. However, the return of capital may not impair the limited partnership's ability to pay its creditors. After the withdrawal of capital, the fair value of partnership assets must at least equal the limited partnership's liabilities to creditors.

BUILDERS STEEL CO. v. HYCORE, INC. 877 P.2d 1168 (Okla. Ct. App. 1994)

Max A. Heidenreich, as general partner, formed a limited partnership, Brookside Realty, Ltd. (BRL), for the purpose of purchasing and developing a commercial and retail center to be known as Brookside Center. BRL's limited partners included Gilbert Grubbs, Ray Phillips, Jack Herrold, Donald Herrold, and Ron Main. The limited partnership certificate stated the limited partners' contributions as follows: Grubbs agreed to contribute $20,000 cash, assume personal liability of $225,000, render no services, and be liable for a future assessment of $145,000; Phillips agreed to contribute $5,000 cash, assume personal liability of $127,500, render no services, and be liable for a future assessment of $72,500; the Herrolds and Main each agreed to contribute $5,000 cash, assume personal liability of $63,750, render no services, and be liable for a future assessment of $36,250.

Builders Steel was one of the suppliers that sold materials on credit to BRL for the construction of the Brookside Center. When Builders Steel was not paid in full, Heidenreich, as the general partner, sought to escape personal liability under the federal bankruptcy code, but was denied discharge on the grounds that he defrauded the creditors. Nonetheless, Builders Steel sued the limited partners of BRL. Because the limited partners had not paid all the assessments required by the limited partnership certificate, Builders Steel claimed that as a creditor of BRL, Builders Steel was entitled to require the payment of those assessments to the extent of BRL's indebtedness to Builders Steel. The trial court granted the limited partners' motion for summary judgment that they were not liable to Builders Steel. Builders Steel appealed. ∾

Brightmire, Judge   Builders Steel contends that it has a right under Oklahoma law, as a creditor of the partnership, to require payment of the assessments by the limited partners. They cite 54 O.S.1991 section 329(C):

Unless otherwise provided in the partnership agreement, the obligation of a partner to make a contribution or return money or other property paid or distributed in violation of this act may be compromised only by consent of all the partners. Notwithstanding the compromise, a creditor of a limited partnership who extends credit or otherwise acts in reliance on that obligation after the partner signs a writing which reflects this obligation and before the amendment or cancellation thereof to reflect the compromise, may enforce the original obligation.

In this regard, Builders Steel attached to its response a copy of the certificate of limited partnership filed with the Oklahoma Secretary of State which does in fact list specific future assessments owed by each of the limited partners, and copies of correspondence from Max Heidenreich to various limited partners discussing the assessments.

The limited partners, however, argue that paragraph 5 of the first amendment to the Certificate of Limited Partnership is a disclaimer and therefore eliminates any basis for Builders Steel's reliance on the limited partners' future liability to the partnership. Paragraph 5, as amended, provides:

Future assessments indicated above may be called only for limited purposes specifically authorized by the general partner and pursuant to the terms of the Partnership Agreement. No other creditor may rely on the above information as a representation of future assessments for the purpose of any claim.

The trouble is this argument overlooks the notice limitation of 54 O.S.1991 section 316:

The fact that a certificate of limited partnership is on file in the Office of the Secretary of State is notice that the partnership is a limited partnership and the persons designated therein as general partners are general partners, *but it is not notice of any other fact.*

We conclude, therefore, that the trial court was not justified in basing a summary judgment on a finding that no further obligations are due to the limited partnership from the limited partners.

Judgment reversed in favor of Builders Steel.

Other Rights of General Partners

A general partner has the same right to manage and the same agency powers as a partner in an ordinary partnership. He has the express authority to act as the partners have agreed he should and the implied authority to do what is in the usual course of business. In addition, he may have apparent authority to bind the partnership to contracts when his implied authority is limited yet no notice of the limitation has been given to third parties.

A general partner has no right to compensation beyond his share of the profits, absent an agreement to the contrary. Since most limited partnerships are tax shelters that are designed to lose money during their early years of operation, most limited partnership agreements provide for the payment of salaries to general partners.

Other Liabilities of General Partners

A general partner has unlimited liability to creditors of his limited partnership. In addition, a general partner is in a position of trust when he manages the business, and therefore owes fiduciary duties to the limited partnership and the limited partners (e.g., he may not profit secretly from limited partnership transactions or compete with the limited partnership). The following case imposed fiduciary liability on a general partner for misusing partnership property.

IN RE THE MONETARY GROUP 2 F.3d 1098 (11th Cir. 1993)

The Securities Group (TSG), The Monetary Group (TMG), and The Securities Group 1980 (TSG80) were New York limited partnerships. The Securities Groups (Groups) was a New York general partnership whose general partners included TSG, TMG, and TSG80. Charles Barnett and Randall Atkins were general partners of TSG; they were limited partners of TMG. Barnett was also a limited partner of TSG80.

In need of office space, TSG entered negotiations to purchase the Hotel Nassau and the adjacent Olivetti Building at 500 Park Avenue in New York City from Olivetti Properties. Eventually, it was decided that a Kentucky limited partnership—500 Park Avenue Associates (Associates)—would purchase the buildings for $22 million and lease three floors of the Olivetti Building to Groups. Atkins was a limited partner in Associates, which Atkins helped form for the express purpose of buying the buildings.

Under the lease agreement, Associates received a $1 million cash rent security deposit and a $4 million damage deposit from Groups. The $4 million damage deposit comprised marketable securities. Associates immediately gave the $1 million cash to Olivetti as a down payment on the buildings. Associates financed the remainder of the purchase price with a mortgage loan from Manufacturers Hanover Trust Company. Security for the loan was the buildings and the $4 million in marketable securities that Associates received from Groups. When Manufacturers Hanover required an additional $2.8 million collateral, Groups gave Associates another $2.8 million in marketable securities, which Associates transferred to Manufacturers Hanover.

Immediately after completing its purchase of the buildings, Associates placed the buildings on the market. A year and a half later, Associates sold the buildings to Equitable Life Assurance Company for $54.5 million plus a share of Equitable's future profits from developments on the Hotel Nassau site. As part of the sale, Associates assigned its lease with Groups to Equitable.

After six years, TMS, TMG, TMS80, and Groups sought Chapter 11 bankruptcy protection. The court-appointed administrator for the partnerships sued Barnett and Atkins on behalf of the partnerships, alleging that they had breached their fiduciary duty to the partnerships. The bankruptcy court found Barnett and Atkins liable for all gains received by them from the sale of the property, almost $32 million. Barnett and Atkins appealed to the district court, which affirmed the bankruptcy court's decision. Barnett and Atkins then appealed to the court of appeals. ∞

Per Curiam A general partner in a limited partnership stands in a fiduciary relationship with the limited partners of that limited partnership. Atkins was general partner of TSG. Thus, Atkins owed a fiduciary duty to TSG's limited partners. Additionally, TSG was a general partner of Groups. Therefore, Atkins' fiduciary duty extended to Groups.

A limited partner is liable to the other limited partners of a partnership where that limited partner acts in concert with a general partner of that partnership in derogation of that general partner's fiduciary duty. Atkins was a limited partner of TMG. TSG and TMG were partners operating as Groups. Thus, if Atkins violated his duty to TSG as general partner by participating in diverting partnership assets, then Atkins can be said to have joined in the wrong against TMG thereby necessitating the finding that Atkins is liable to the other limited partners of TMG.

A partner breaches his fiduciary where that partner diverts for non-partnership purposes monies belonging to the partnership. Partners are liable to each other for such wrongfully appropriated partnership property.

Funds and other assets of TSG, TMG, TSG80, and Groups were misused, thus enabling Associates to purchase the buildings. Negotiations were initiated on TSG's behalf. Even after Associates assumed the role of purchaser, the deal depended on the use of Groups' assets. The security deposits were obviously tailored to meet Associates' needs.

Atkins contends that such a transaction constitutes a valid lease agreement and should not be characterized as a misappropriation of partnership property. This court, however, need not determine whether the dubious lease agreement is an indirect misappropriation of partnership property, because there is ample evidence of a direct misappropriation of partnership property. When Associates' lender required an additional $2.8 million in security, the malefactors simply transferred an additional $2.8 million from Groups to Associates as an additional security. The additional $2.8 million was not transferred pursuant to an agreement. Groups was under no contractual obligation to pay Associates an additional security. The transfer of an extra $2.8 million represented nothing more than a naked misuse of the partnerships' property for Associates' benefit. Thus, Associates directly misappropriated at least $2.8 million worth of the partnerships' securities.

We must next consider whether Atkins was guilty of any wrongdoing. Atkins actively participated in the purchase of the property and facilitated the transfer of the security deposit from Groups to Associates. Moreover, Atkins enjoyed a personal windfall from the transactions through his limited partnership interest in Associates. Atkins' conduct directly violated his fiduciary duty as a partner of TSG and TMG to refrain from personally profiting from the misuse of partnership assets.

The bankruptcy court found that Barnett was liable by virtue of his position as a general partner of TSG. An innocent general partner may be held liable to third parties for the wrongful conduct of a fellow partner even though that partner had no knowledge of the offending partners' action. No cases have applied this principle of partnership liability in other than the third-party context. At least one state court has held that an innocent general partner does not bear agency liability to limited partners for another general partner's misuse of partnership funds. We decline to extend this principle of agency liability to the interpartnership suit context. Potentially, such an extension would make all innocent general partners in a partnership liable to each other for the secret misappropriation of partnership funds by one general partner. The bankruptcy court erred by imposing such liability on Barnett.

Judgment affirmed in favor of TMG against Atkins; judgment reversed in favor of Barnett.

Other Rights of Limited Partners

Limited partners have the right to be informed about partnership affairs. The RULPA obligates the general partners to provide financial information and tax returns to the limited partners on demand. In addition, a limited partner may inspect and copy a list of the partners, information concerning contributions by partners, the certificate of limited partnership, tax returns, and partnership agreements.

A limited partner may sue to enforce a limited partnership right of action against a person who has harmed the limited partnership. This right of action is called a **derivative suit** or a derivative action because it derives from the limited partnership. Any recovery obtained by the limited partner goes to the limited partnership, since it is the entity that was harmed. In addition, when a limited partnership is sued and the general partners fail to assert a defense, a limited partner may appear on behalf of the limited partnership and assert the defense.

Other Liabilities of Limited Partners

Once a limited partner has contributed all of his promised capital contribution, generally he has no further liability for partnership losses or obligations. In return for limited liability, however, a limited partner gives up the right to participate in the management of a limited partnership. When a limited partner engages in management activities, he may lose his limited liability.

Limited Partner Engaged in Management A limited partner who participates in the control of the business may be liable to creditors of the limited partnership. Under the RULPA, a limited partner who participates in control is liable only to those persons who transact with the limited partnership reasonably believing, based on the limited partner's conduct, that the limited partner is a general partner. Thus, three elements must be met in order for a limited partner to be liable as a general partner due to his participation in management:

1. The limited partner must participate in the control of the limited partnership.

2. That participation must lead a person to believe reasonably that the limited partner is a general partner.

3. That person must transact with the limited partnership while holding that belief.

For example, Larry Link is a limited partner whom the general partners have allowed to make management decisions. A creditor of the partnership observes Link's management of the partnership, with the result that the creditor extends $10,000 credit to the limited partnership believing that Link is a general partner. Link is liable on the $10,000 debt to the creditor.

It is sometimes difficult to determine whether a limited partner's acts amount to control of the limited partnership. Control is best defined as participation in the firm's day-to-day management decisions as contrasted with isolated involvement with major decisions. For example, a limited partner of a real estate investment partnership participates in control if she regularly decides which real estate the limited partnership should purchase. A limited partner who only once vetoed a loan agreement with a bank is not participating in control.

The RULPA lists the kinds of management activities that limited partners may perform without becoming personally liable for partnership debts. Therefore, a limited partner may perform these acts and still retain his limited liability. The list of such activities appears in Figure 3.

For most well-planned limited partnerships, the general partner is a corporation. Usually, the only shareholders, directors, and officers of the corporate general partner are the individuals who manage the limited partnership. Sometimes, these individuals are limited partners as well. These individuals will not have the liability of a general partner, because the RULPA permits limited partners to be officers,

---

FIGURE **3**

Activities Not Constituting Control by a Limited Partner

1. Being *an agent, an employee,* or *a contractor* for the limited partnership or a general partner; or being an officer, director, or shareholder of a general partner that is a corporation.
2. Being a *consultant* or *adviser* to a general partner.
3. Acting as a *surety* for the limited partnership or guaranteeing or assuming specific obligations of the limited partnership. However, a limited partner who specifically assumes liability on a partnership obligation is liable on that obligation.
4. Pursuing a derivative suit on behalf of the limited partnership.
5. Requesting or attending a meeting of partners.
6. Proposing or voting on such partnership matters as dissolution, sale of substantially all the assets, changes in the nature of the business, admissions and removals of general or limited partners, and amendments to the partnership agreement.
7. Winding up the limited partnership as permitted by the RULPA.

---

directors, or shareholders of a general partner (see item 1 of Figure 3).

In the following case, the court held that a limited partner had not exercised sufficient control over the limited partnership to render the limited partner liable as a general partner.

ALZADO v. BLINDER, ROBINSON & CO.   752 P.2d 544 (Colo. Sup. Ct. 1988)

I*n 1979, Blinder, Robinson & Co. as limited partner and Combat Promotions, Inc., as general partner created Combat Associates to promote an eight-round exhibition boxing match between Muhammad Ali and Lyle Alzado, the pro football player. Combat Promotions was owned entirely by Alzado, his accountant, and his professional agent. Alzado was also vice president of Combat Promotions. Combat Associates agreed to pay Alzado $100,000 for his participation in the match.*

Few tickets were sold, and the match proved to be a financial debacle. Alzado received no payments for participating in the boxing match. Alzado sued Blinder, Robinson, claiming that because of its conduct, Blinder, Robinson must be deemed a general partner of Combat Associates and, therefore, liable to Alzado under the agreement between Alzado and the limited partnership for Alzado's participation in the match. The trial court agreed with Alzado, but Blinder, Robinson appealed to the court of appeals, which held that Blinder, Robinson had no liability to Alzado. Alzado appealed to the Supreme Court of Colorado. ∽

Kirshbaum, Justice A limited partner may become liable to partnership creditors as a general partner if the limited partner assumes control of partnership business. RULPA Section 303 provides that a limited partner does not participate in the

control of partnership business solely by doing one or more of the following:

(a) Being a contractor for or an agent or employee of the limited partnership or of a general partner;

(b) Being an officer, director, or shareholder of a corporate general partner;

(c) Consulting with and advising a general partner with respect to the business of the limited partnership . . . .

Any determination of whether a limited partner's conduct amounts to control over the business affairs of the partnership must be determined by consideration of several factors, including the purpose of the partnership, the administrative activities undertaken, the manner in which the entity actually functioned, and the nature and frequency of the limited partner's purported activities.

The record here reflects that Blinder, Robinson used its Denver office as a ticket outlet, gave two parties to promote the exhibition match, and provided a meeting room for many of Combat Associates' meetings. Meyer Blinder, president of Blinder, Robinson, personally appeared on a television talk show and gave television interviews to promote the match. Blinder, Robinson made no investment, ac-counting or other financial decisions for the partnership; all such fiscal decisions were made by officers or employees of Combat Promotions, the general partner. The evidence established at most that Blinder, Robinson engaged in a few promotional activities. It does not establish that it took part in the management or control of the business affairs of the partnership.

Alzado finally asserts that Blinder, Robinson fostered the appearance of being in control of Combat Associates, that such actions rendered Blinder, Robinson liable as a general partner and that this conduct allowed third parties to believe that Blinder, Robinson was in fact a general partner. The evidence does not support this argument. Certainly, as Vice President of Combat Promotions, Alzado had no misconception concerning the function and role of Blinder, Robinson as a limited partner only.

Judgment for Blinder, Robinson affirmed.

Limited Partner's Name in Firm Name   Including a limited partner's *surname* in the name of a limited partnership may mislead a creditor to believe that a limited partner is a general partner. Under the RULPA, a limited partner who *knowingly* permits her name to be included in the firm name is liable to creditors who have *no actual knowledge* that she is a limited partner, unless a general partner has the same surname as that of the limited partner or the business of the limited partnership was conducted under that name prior to the limited partner's admission to the limited partnership.

DISSOLUTION AND WINDING UP OF A LIMITED PARTNERSHIP

Dissolution

A limited partnership may be dissolved and its affairs wound up. There are five causes of dissolution:

1. Expiration of the term specified in the certificate of limited partnership. For example, the certificate may provide that a limited partnership has a 20-year term.

2. Upon the happening of events specified in writing in the partnership agreement. For example, a written partnership agreement may provide for dissolution of a limited partnership after it has accomplished its objective of building a shopping mall.

3. By the written consent of all the partners.

4. Upon the withdrawal of a *general* partner, with few exceptions. Such a withdrawal includes retirement, death, bankruptcy, assignment of a general partnership interest, removal by the other partners, and adjudicated insanity. For a general partner that is not a natural person, such as a partnership or a corporation, its own dissolution is a withdrawal causing a dissolution of the limited partnership. The RULPA specifically permits a limited partnership to avoid dissolution after the withdrawal of a general partner if a written partnership agreement permits the business to be conducted by the remaining general partners or if all of the partners agree in writing to continue the business.

5. By court order, when it is *not reasonably practicable* to carry on the business in conformity with the limited partnership agreement. Judicial dissolution has frequently been granted when general partners continually violate their fiduciary duties, such as by secretly profiting from self-dealing with the limited partnership.

The RULPA requires a limited partnership to file a **certificate of cancellation** upon its dissolution and the commencement of winding up. The certificate of cancellation cancels the certificate of limited partnership. However, the failure to file a certificate of cancellation does not prevent a dissolution.

Winding Up

Winding up is the orderly liquidation of the limited partnership's assets and payment of the proceeds to creditors and other claimants. Dissolution requires the winding up of a limited partnership's affairs. The only way to prevent winding up is to prevent dissolution, such as by an agreement of the partners that an event shall not cause a dissolution.

General partners who have *not wrongfully dissolved* a limited partnership may perform the winding up. Wrongful dissolution includes a dissolution in violation of the limited partnership agreement or wrongful conduct that leads to a judicial dissolution, such as a general partner's breach of his fiduciary duties. Limited partners may wind up if there are no surviving general partners. In addition, any partner may *ask a court* to perform a winding up.

The winding up partner has express authority to act as the partners have agreed he should act. More importantly, he has the implied authority to do those acts that are reasonably necessary to liquidate the assets. He possesses the apparent authority to do all of the acts that he was able to do before dissolution, unless appropriate notice is given to persons who dealt with the partnership or knew of its existence.

Distribution of Assets   After the assets have been sold during winding up, the proceeds of the sale of assets are distributed to those persons having claims against the limited partnership. Figure 4 states the RULPA rule for distribution of limited partnership assets.

Continuation of the Business   Usually, the assets of a limited partnership are sold individually during winding up. However, all the assets of the business of the limited partnership could be sold to someone who desires to continue the business. For example, some of the partners may wish to continue the business despite dissolution. The continuing partners are required to pay the outgoing partners the fair value of their partnership interests, including goodwill.

Events Not Causing Dissolution   The death, bankruptcy, insanity, or withdrawal of a *limited*

FIGURE 4

Order of Distribution of Limited Partnership Assets during Winding Up

1. To firm *creditors,* including partners who are creditors, except for unpaid distributions to partners.
2. To partners for *unpaid distributions,* including the return of capital to previously withdrawn partners.
3. To partners to the extent of their *capital contributions.*
4. To partners in the proportion in which they share distributions. Hence, the partners share the proceeds that remain after all other claimants have been paid.

Between partners, the order of distribution may be changed by a partnership agreement. For example, a limited partnership agreement may combine priorities (2) and (3) to provide that unpaid distributions to partners shall be paid at the same time capital contributions are returned. However, the priority of creditors may not be harmed by a partner's agreement, such as an agreement to pay creditors *after* partners have received the return of their capital.

---

partner does not result in dissolution unless the certificate of limited partnership compels dissolution. Also, the *addition* of a partner—general or limited—does not cause a dissolution.

LIMITED LIABILITY COMPANIES

The limited liability company (LLC) is the product of attempts by state legislators to create a new business organization that combines the nontax advantages of the corporation and the favorable tax status of the partnership. Wyoming, in 1977, passed the first LLC statute. Florida followed in 1982. LLC members usually elect for the LLC to be recognized as a partnership for federal income tax purposes. As a result, the LLC pays no federal income tax. Instead, all income and losses of the LLC are reported by the LLC's owners on their individual income tax returns. Typically, the LLC is a tax shelter for wealthy investors, allowing such investors to reduce their taxable income by deducting LLC losses on their federal income tax returns to the extent they are *at risk,* that is, their capital contributions to the LLC. Moreover, passive investors in an LLC, like limited partners in a limited partnership, may use their shares of LLC losses to offset only income from other *passive* investments. Every state and the District of Columbia have enacted LLC statutes.

Formation of LLCs

To create an LLC, one or more persons must file **articles of organization** with the secretary of state. The articles must include the name of the LLC, its duration, and the name and address of its registered agent. The name of the LLC must include the words "limited liability company" or some other words indicating that the liability of its owners is limited.

Although not required, an LLC will typically have an **operating agreement,** which is an agreement of the owners as to how the LLC will be operated.

Many states also require an LLC to file an annual report with the secretary of state. The annual report may include financial information such as the capital accounts of the owners and the LLC's balance sheet.

Owners of LLCs

Owners of LLCs are called **members.** Some statutes require an LLC to have at least two members at all times, although there is no maximum limit on members. An individual, partnership, corporation, and even another LLC may be a member of an LLC.

A member has no personal liability for LLC obligations. A member must, however, make capital contributions to the LLC as she has agreed.

LLC statutes allow LLCs to restrict the members' ability to sell their interests in the LLC. An LLC interest is the personal property of the member and may be transferred as stated in the operating agreement; however, the transferee has no right to become a member or participate in management unless the other members consent to the transfer. The transferee who does not become a member is entitled only to the transferring member's share of profits. A member who sells his LCC interest has terminated his interest in the LLC.

A member is entitled to withdraw from the LLC and receive either the value of his interest or a return of his capital contribution. Such a distribution of assets to a member may be executed only if the LLC's assets exceed its liabilities after the distribution.

LLC as an Entity

The LLC is an entity separate from its owners. It may sue and be sued in its own name. It can buy, hold, and sell property. It can make contracts and incur liabilities.

Because the LLC is an entity liable for its own obligations, the members have no individual liability on LLC obligations. However, a court will pierce the veil between the LLC and its members and impose personal liability on the members when the LLC is used to defraud creditors. For example, suppose the members provide very little capital to an LLC that is engaging in a highly risky business. As a result, the business is unsuccessful and unable to pay its creditors. A court will likely require the members to pay the obligations of the business.

Management of LLCs

Members of an LLC share management power in proportion to their capital contributions to the LLC. If there is no member vote restricting the actual authority of a member, however, members have considerable implied and apparent authority to bind the LLC on transactions in the ordinary course of business.

The members may agree to entrust management to managers selected by the members. Managers of an LLC are comparable to directors of a corporation.

The members or managers who manage the LLC are fiduciaries of the LLC. They must manage the LLC in the best interest of the LLC and not prefer their individual interests over the interests of the LLC.

Dissolution of LLCs

Dissolution of an LLC is caused by the death, retirement, bankruptcy, or dissolution of any member. However, the remaining members may avoid liquidation by *unanimously* agreeing to continue the business. Under most statutes, an LLC's term cannot exceed 30 years.

In the following case, the court refused to allow corporate officers to use an LLC to evade a fiduciary duty that would have otherwise existed.

BARBIERI v. SWING-N-SLIDE CORP. 1997 Del. Ch. LEXIS 9 (Del. Ch. Ct. 1997)

R *ichard C. Mueller, president, chief executive officer, and a director of Swing-N-Slide Corp. (SNS), and several officers of SNS were the sole members of a limited liability company, Greengrass Management, LLC. Mueller and the officers formed Greengrass Management solely to act as one of two general partners of a partnership, Greengrass Holdings (Holdings). Holdings's only purpose was to make a public tender offer to purchase SNS's common shares from SNS shareholders. The terms of the tender offer were negotiated by and agreed to by SNS and Holdings: Holdings would pay $6.50 per share in cash for up to 60 percent of SNS's shares tendered by shareholders; Holdings also had the right to buy SNS shares from SNS at $4.80 per share if the management of SNS changed.*

Robert Barbieri, a shareholder of SNS, sued SNS, Mueller, the officers who were members of Greengrass Management, and Greengrass Management, LLC, on the grounds that the parties had breached a fiduciary duty to SNS's shareholders because the director and officers had a conflict of interest during the tender offer negotiations. Greengrass Management moved to dismiss the action on the grounds that it owed no fiduciary duty to SNS shareholders because it was not an officer, director, or majority shareholder of SNS. ∽

Steele, Vice Chancellor The underlying theory advanced in support of Barbieri's claim against Greengrass Management is succinctly stated as follows: Because defendant Mueller, a Swing-N-Slide director and president and chief executive officer, and other Swing-N-Slide officers are the owners of Greengrass Management, Greengrass Management owes fiduciary duties to the Swing-N-Slide shareholders. I address only the narrow issue whether Greengrass Management owes fiduciary obligations to SNS and its shareholders.

I start with the basic proposition that directors and officers of a corporation owe fiduciary duties to the corporation and its shareholders. In this instance, it is alleged that Mueller, a director and officer, and the senior management officers of SNS organized Greengrass Management. Those persons forming Greengrass Management therefore owed fiduciary duties to SNS. Unfortunately, none of the cases cited by either party answer the necessary question: Must their fiduciary obligations be imputed to the entity they formed? Surprisingly, I do not find any case within this jurisdiction addressing this issue.

I conclude, however, that the fiduciary duties of the SNS director and officers must be imputed to the limited liability company they formed. Accepting Barbieri's allegation as true, the complaints support the following: A single director and the management officers of SNS together formed a limited liability company. It is not suggested that there are other persons or entities involved in the LLC. Nor is it suggested that Greengrass Management was formed for or has carried out any other objective than one related to the SNS tender offer. I therefore fairly conclude that persons in positions owing fiduciary responsibility to SNS and its shareholders together formed a separate entity for purposes solely related to that company. Neither Mueller nor the others would escape their fiduciary obligations to SNS had they not formed Greengrass Management. To allow them to use this State's laws allowing the formation of the limited liability company as a vehicle to avoid those very duties would be unconscionable. Therefore, where, as here, the allegations of the complaint support the conclusion that an entity was formed and controlled by fiduciaries for purposes solely related to the entity to which those persons owed fiduciary duties, the entity may be considered to take on the same fiduciary obligations.

Judgment for Barbieri.

ETHICAL AND PUBLIC POLICY CONCERNS

1. Is it fair that a limited partner has limited liability for the obligations of a limited partnership?

Is it fair that a general partner has unlimited liability while a limited partner has limited liability?

2. Limited partners have a limited right to deduct limited partnership losses on their individual federal income tax returns, while general partners are not restricted. Is this fair? Are the general partners' investments or activities more socially desirable than the limited partners' investments or activities?

3. By having a corporation as the sole general partner of a limited partnership, no human will have unlimited liability for the obligations of the limited partnership. Is this fair? Does this produce a socially desirable result?

4. Why would anyone want to form a limited partnership when an LLC has the same tax benefits as the limited partnership and less liability for its members than the limited partnership, yet permits complete flexibility in determining who will manage the business? Have the states gone too far in serving the interests of businesses by allowing the creation of LLCs? Are businesses the only ones that benefit from the creation of LLCs?

PROBLEMS AND PROBLEM CASES

1. Brookwood Fund was a limited partnership formed to trade investment securities. The original certificate of limited partnership filed in April 1987 listed Kenneth Stein as the "General Partner" and Barbara Stein as the "Original Limited Partner." Between May and August 1987, additional limited partners were added to Brookwood. The new limited partners did not participate in the management of Brookwood. However, an amended certificate of limited partnership reflecting the new limited partners was not filed. What should the new limited partners do to protect themselves from having the liability of general partners?

2. Virginia Partners, Ltd., a limited partnership organized in Florida, was in the business of drilling oil wells. When Virginia Partners injected acid into an oil well in Kentucky, a bystander, Robert Day, was injured by acid that sprayed on him from a ruptured hose. Virginia Partners had failed to register as a foreign limited partnership in Kentucky. Are the limited partners of Virginia Partners liable to Day for his injuries?

3. Palmetto Federal Savings & Loan Association made real estate loans to Beacon Reef Limited Partnership. When Beacon Reef defaulted on the loans, Palmetto Federal sued Beacon Reef. Beacon Reef's general partners decided not to raise the defense that Palmetto Federal charged a usurious rate on the loan. May Howard Wulsin, the only limited partner, on behalf of Beacon Reef, assert the defense of usury against Palmetto Federal?

4. Dr. Medicherla Kumar, a medical doctor, was a limited partner of Metropolitan Hospital, L.P., a limited partnership, the owner of Metropolitan Hospital in Richmond, Virginia. While making rounds visiting patients at Metropolitan Hospital, Dr. Kumar slipped on some stairs, fell, and was injured. As a limited partner, may Dr. Kumar sue his limited partnership to recover damages for his injuries?

5. Cornel Peleo was a general partner of Livonia Associates, a limited partnership. On December 3, 1971, Peleo and his wife purchased land for $9,000. On April 15, 1972, they sold the land to Livonia Associates for $18,000. Peleo told one limited partner that he had an interest in the property, but he did not tell him the amount. Has Peleo breached a fiduciary duty?

6. Carol Humphreys was an employee at Medical Towers, Ltd. (MTL), a limited partnership. Diva Corporation was the sole general and managing partner of MTL. David Lawson was the president and sole shareholder of Diva Corporation. Effectively, Lawson was the general manager of MTL, controlling all aspects of the business; in addition, Lawson was a limited partner of MTL. Humphreys believed that Lawson was the general partner of MTL. Lawson never told her that he was not the general partner of MTL. Humphreys was initially employed as Lawson's assistant. After her promotion to business manager, Humphreys was continually sexually harassed by MTL employees Roger Bailey and Drew Crispin. Humphreys sued Lawson. Is Lawson liable for the sexual harassment of Bailey and Crispin?

7. The Securities Group 1980, a limited partnership, was created to provide tax deferral advantages for its limited partners. To offset a potential adverse tax consequence when the tax laws changed, the general partners arranged a sale of the limited partnership interests to a new partnership owned by the Securities Group's general partners. The limited partners received cash and promissory notes worth 105 percent of the net asset value of Securities Group. At that time, Securities Group was indebted to various creditors. The new partnership subsequently became insolvent, with the result that the Securities Group creditors were unpaid. Are the Securities Group creditors able to collect from the former limited partners of Securities Group?

8. OKC Corporation adopted a plan to become a limited partnership. Under the plan, the shareholders became limited partners in OKC Limited Partnership. They did not receive actual possession of their limited partnership interests. Instead, the limited partnership interests were deposited in MBank of Dallas, which then issued depositary receipts to the limited partners. The depositary receipts were traded on the Pacific Stock Exchange. Some of the limited partners sold their depositary receipts to other investors. In 1987, a committee of receipt holders attempted to replace the general partners, an action within the powers of the limited partners under the limited partnership agreement. The general partners opposed the action and claimed that only the original limited partners who were still receipt holders could vote to replace the general partners. Were the general partners correct?

9. Excel Associates was a New York limited partnership. Lipkin was Excel's only individual general partner. Tribute Music Inc. was the only other general partner. Chalpin, the only limited partner, was also the president and sole shareholder and director of Tribute Music. Chalpin hired Bernabe Gonzales to be the superintendent of Excel's apartment building in Long Beach, Long Island, New York. Later, Chalpin hired Gonzales to renovate the building. Chalpin signed all Excel's checks paying Gonzales. Chalpin did not name Tribute Music on the checks or indicate that he was signing in a representative capacity. Chalpin terminated Gonzales's employment with Excel. Gonzales sued Excel for breach of an employment contract. Gonzales also claimed that Chalpin was liable on the breached contract. On what grounds did Gonzales base his argument for Chalpin's liability?

10. Canal East Company was a limited partnership formed to operate a commercial real estate project known as Packett's Landing. John Flowers was the sole general partner. Scott Arrington, William May, and Robert Klimasewski were the only limited partners. Fishers Development Company was another partnership in which Arrington, May, and Klimasewski were the only limited partners. Fishers Development bought restaurant equipment and leased it to a restaurant-tenant at Packett's Landing. Flowers and Arrington were guarantors of the lease obligation to Fishers Development. When the restaurant-tenant became bankrupt, Flowers and Arrington obtained possession of the equipment pursuant to an assignment from the restaurant-tenant. They assigned the equipment lease to Canal East, which agreed to assume Flowers and Arrington's guaranty of the lease and to indemnify them from their liabilities under the lease or guaranty. Flowers and Arrington signed the agreement as assignors. In addition, Flowers signed the agreement as the general partner of Canal East, the assignee. May and Klimasewski sought judicial dissolution of the limited partnership, claiming that Flowers and Arrington breached fiduciary duties. Will the court order dissolution?

Corporations

History and Nature of Corporations

The modern corporation has facilitated the rapid economic development of the last 150 years by permitting businesses to attain economies of scale. Businesses organized as corporations can attain such economies because they have a greater capacity to raise capital than do other business forms. This capital-raising advantage is ensured by corporation law, which allows persons to invest their money in a corporation and become owners without imposing unlimited liability or management responsibilities on themselves. Many people are willing to invest their savings in a large, risky business if they have limited liability and no management responsibilities. Far fewer are willing to invest in a partnership or other business form in which owners have unlimited liability and management duties. ∞

HISTORY OF CORPORATIONS

Although modern corporation law emerged only in the last 150 years, ancestors of the modern corporation existed in the times of Hammurabi, ancient Greece, and the Roman Empire. As early as 1248 in France, privileges of incorporation were given to mercantile ventures to encourage investment for the benefit of society. In England, the corporate form was used extensively before the 16th century.

The famous British trading companies—such as the Massachusetts Bay Company—were the forerunners of the modern corporation. The British government gave these companies monopolies in trade and granted them powers to govern in the

FIGURE I

Principal Characteristics of Corporations

1. *Creation.* A corporation may be created only by *permission of a government.*
2. *Legal status.* A corporation is a legal person and a legal entity independent of its owners (*shareholders*) and its managers (officers and the *board of directors*). Its life is unaffected by the retirement or death of its shareholders, officers, and directors. A corporation is a person under the Constitution of the United States.
3. *Powers.* A corporation may *acquire, hold, and convey property* in its own name. A corporation may *sue and be sued* in its own name. Harm to a corporation is not harm to the shareholders; therefore, with few exceptions, a shareholder may not sue to enforce a claim of the corporation.
4. *Management.* Shareholders elect a board of directors, which manages the corporation. The board of directors may delegate management duties to officers. A shareholder has *no right or duty to manage* the business of a corporation, unless he is elected to the board of directors or is appointed an officer. The directors and officers need not be shareholders.
5. *Owners' liability.* The shareholders have *limited liability.* With few exceptions, they are not liable for the debts of a corporation after they have paid their promised capital contributions to the corporation.
6. *Transferability of owner's interest.* Generally, the ownership interest in a corporation is *freely transferable.* A shareholder may sell her shares to whomever she wants whenever she wants. The purchaser becomes a shareholder with the same rights that the seller had.
7. *Taxation.* A corporation pays *federal income taxes* on its income. Shareholders have personal income from the corporation only when the corporation makes a distribution of its income to them. For example, a shareholder would have personal income from the corporation when the corporation pays him a dividend. This creates a *double-taxation* possibility: The corporation pays income tax on its profits, and when the corporation distributes the after-tax profits as dividends, the shareholders pay tax on the dividends.

areas they colonized. They were permitted to operate as corporations due to the benefits they would confer on the British empire, such as the development of natural resources. Although these trading companies were among the few corporations of the time whose owners were granted limited liability, they sought corporate status primarily because the government granted them monopolies and governmental powers.

American Corporation Law

Beginning in 1776, corporation law in the United States evolved independently of English corporation law. Early American corporations received **special charters** from state legislatures. These charters were granted one at a time by special action of the legislatures; few special charters were granted.

In the late 18th century, general incorporation statutes emerged in the United States. Initially, these statutes permitted incorporation only for limited purposes beneficial to the public, such as operating toll bridges and water systems. Incorporation was still viewed as a privilege, and many restrictions were placed on corporations: incorporation was permitted for only short periods of time; maximum limits on capitalization were low; and ownership of real and personal property was often restricted.

During the last 150 years, such restrictive provisions have disappeared in most states. Today, modern incorporation statutes are mostly enabling, granting the persons who control a corporation great flexibility in establishing, financing, and operating it.

See Figure 1 for a statement of the characteristics of corporations.

CLASSIFICATIONS OF CORPORATIONS

Corporations may be divided into three classes: (1) corporations **for profit,** (2) corporations **not for profit,** and (3) **government-owned** corporations. State corporation statutes establish procedures for the incorporation of each of these classes and for their operation. In addition, a large body of common law applies to all corporations.

Most business corporations are **for-profit corporations.** For-profit corporations issue stock to their shareholders, who invest in the corporation with the expectation that they will earn a profit on their investment. That profit may take the form of dividends paid by the corporation or increased market value of their shares.

Nearly all for-profit corporations are incorporated under the **general incorporation law** of a state. All of the states require professionals who wish to incorporate, such as physicians, dentists, lawyers, and accountants, to incorporate under **professional corporation acts.** In addition, for-profit corporations that especially affect the public interest, such as banks, insurance companies, and savings and loan associations, are usually required to incorporate under special statutes.

For-profit corporations range from huge international organizations such as General Motors Corporation to small, one-owner businesses. GM is an example of a **publicly held corporation** because its shares are generally available to public investors. The publicly held corporation tends to be managed by professional managers who own small percentages of the corporation. Nearly all the shareholders of the typical publicly held corporation are merely investors who are not concerned in the management of the corporation.

Corporations with very few shareholders whose shares are not available to the general public are called **close corporations.** In the typical close corporation, the controlling shareholders are the only managers of the business.

Usually, close corporations and publicly held corporations are subject to the same rules under state corporation law. Many states, however, allow close corporations greater latitude in the operation of their internal affairs than is granted to public corporations. For example, the shareholders of a close corporation may be permitted to dispense with the board of directors and manage the close corporation as if it were a partnership.

A Subchapter S corporation, or **S Corporation,** is a special type of close corporation. It is treated nearly like a partnership for federal tax purposes. Its shareholders report the earnings or losses of the business on their individual federal income tax returns. This means that an S Corporation's profits are taxed only once—at the shareholder level, eliminating the double-taxation penalty of incorporation. All shareholders must consent to an S corporation election. The Internal Revenue Code requires an S corporation to have only one class of shares and 75 or fewer shareholders. Shareholders may be only individuals or trusts.

Not-for-profit corporations do not issue stock and do not expect to make a profit. Instead, they provide services to their members under a plan that eliminates any profit motive. These corporations have **members** rather than shareholders, and none of the surplus revenue from their operations may be distributed to their members. Since they generally pay no income tax, nonprofit corporations can reinvest a larger share of their incomes in the business than can for-profit corporations. Examples of nonprofit corporations are charities, churches, fraternal organizations, community arts councils, cooperative grocery stores, and cooperative farmers' feed and supplies stores.

Some corporations are owned by governments and perform governmental and business functions. A municipality (city) is one type of **government-owned corporation.** Other types are created to furnish more specific services—for example, school corporations and water companies. Others—such as the Tennessee Valley Authority and the Federal Deposit Insurance Corporation—operate much like for-profit corporations except that at least some of their directors are appointed by governmental officials, and some or all of their financing frequently comes from government. The TVA and the FDIC are chartered by Congress, but government-owned corporations may also be authorized by states. Government-operated businesses seek corporate status to free themselves from governmental operating procedures, which are more cumbersome than business operating procedures.

REGULATION OF FOR–PROFIT CORPORATIONS

To become a corporation, a business must **incorporate** by complying with an incorporation statute. Incorporation is a fairly simple process usually requiring little more than paying a fee and filing a document with a designated government official—usually the secretary of state of the state of incorporation. Incorporation of for-profit businesses has been entrusted primarily to the governments of the 50 states.

State Incorporation Statutes

State incorporation statutes set out the basic rules regarding the relationship between the corporation, its shareholders, and its managers. For example, an incorporation statute sets the requirements for a business to incorporate, the procedures for shareholders' election of directors, and the duties directors and officers owe to the corporation. Although a corporation may do business in several states, usually the relationship between the corporation, its shareholders, and its managers is regulated only by the state of incorporation.

The American Bar Association's Committee on Corporate Laws has prepared a *model* statute for adoption by state legislatures. The purpose of the model statute is to improve the rationality of corporation law. It is called the **Model Business Corporation Act (MBCA).** The MBCA has been amended many times, and it was completely revised in 1984.

The revised MBCA is the basis of corporation law in most states. Your study of statutory corporation law in this book concentrates on the revised MBCA. Delaware and several other major commercial and industrial states such as New York and California do not follow the MBCA. Therefore, selected provisions of the Delaware and other acts will be addressed.

Several states have special provisions or statutes that are applicable only to close corporations. The ABA's Committee on Corporate Laws has adopted the *Statutory Close Corporation Supplement to the Model Business Corporation Act.* The Supplement is designed to provide a rational, statutory solution to the special problems facing close corporations.

State Common Law of Corporations

Although nearly all of corporation law is statutory law, including the courts' interpretation of the statutes, there is a substantial body of common law of corporations (judge-made law). Most of this common law deals with creditor and shareholder rights. For example, the law of piercing the corporate veil, which you will study later in this chapter, is common law protecting creditors of corporations.

REGULATION OF NONPROFIT CORPORATIONS

Nonprofit corporations are regulated primarily by the states. Nonprofit corporations may be created only by complying with a nonprofit incorporation statute. Incorporation under state law requires delivering articles of incorporation to the secretary of state. The existence of a nonprofit corporation begins when the secretary of state files the articles.

Most states have statutes based on the revised **Model Nonprofit Corporation Act (MNCA).** Because of constitutional protection of freedom of religion, many states have special statutes regulating nonprofit religious organizations.

The law applied to nonprofit corporations is substantially similar to for-profit corporation law. At various points in the corporations chapters of this book, you will study the law of nonprofit corporations and examine how this form of business and its laws differ from the for-profit corporation and its laws. The Model Nonprofit Corporation Act will be the basis of your study of nonprofit corporation law.

REGULATION OF FOREIGN AND ALIEN CORPORATIONS

A corporation may be incorporated in one state yet do business in many other states in which it is not incorporated. The corporation's contacts with other persons in those states may permit the states to regulate the corporation's transactions with their citizens, to subject the corporation to suits in their courts, or to tax the corporation. The circumstances under which states may impose their laws on a business incorporated in another state is determined by the law of foreign corporations.

A corporation is a **domestic corporation** in the state that has granted its charter; it is a **foreign corporation** in all the other states in which it does business. For example, a corporation organized in Delaware and doing business in Florida is domestic in Delaware and foreign in Florida. Note that a corporation domiciled in one country is an **alien corporation** in other countries in which it does business. Many of the rules that apply to foreign corporations apply as well to alien corporations.

Generally, a state may impose its laws on a foreign corporation if such imposition does not violate the Constitution of the United States, notably the Due Process Clause of the Fourteenth Amendment and the Commerce Clause.

Due Process Clause

The Due Process Clause requires that a foreign corporation have sufficient contacts with a state before a state may exercise jurisdiction over the corporation. The leading case in this area is the

International Shoe case.[1] In that case, the Supreme Court ruled that a foreign corporation must have "certain minimum contacts" with the state such that asserting jurisdiction over the corporation does not offend "traditional notions of fair play and substantial justice." The Supreme Court justified its holding with a **benefit theory**: When a foreign corporation avails itself of the protection of a state's laws, it should suffer any reasonable burden that the state imposes as a consequence of such benefit. In other words, a foreign corporation should be required to pay for the benefits that it receives from the state.

Commerce Clause

Under the Commerce Clause, the power to regulate interstate commerce is given to the federal government. The states have no power to exclude or to discriminate against foreign corporations that are engaged solely in *interstate* commerce. Nevertheless, a state may require a foreign corporation doing interstate business in the state to comply with its laws if the application of these laws does not unduly burden interstate commerce. When a foreign corporation enters interstate commerce to do *intrastate* business in a state, the state may regulate the corporation's activities, provided again that the regulation does not unduly burden interstate commerce.

A state statute does not unduly burden interstate commerce if (1) the statute serves a legitimate state interest, (2) the state has chosen the least burdensome means of promoting that interest, and (3) that legitimate state interest outweighs the statute's burden on interstate commerce. Because conducting intrastate business increases a corporation's contact with a state, it is easier to prove that the state has a legitimate interest and that there is no undue burden on interstate commerce when the corporation is conducting intrastate business.

Doing Business To aid their determination of whether a state may constitutionally impose its laws on a foreign corporation, courts have traditionally used the concept of **doing business.** Courts have generally held that a foreign corporation is subject to the laws of a state when it is doing business in the state. The activities that constitute doing business differ, however, depending on the purpose of the determination. There are four such purposes: (1) to determine whether a corporation is subject to a lawsuit in a state's courts, (2) to determine whether the corporation's activities are subject to taxation, (3) to determine whether the corporation must qualify to carry on its activities in the state, and (4) to determine whether the state may regulate the internal affairs of the corporation.

Subjecting Foreign Corporations to Suit

The Supreme Court of the United States has held that a foreign corporation may be brought into a state's court in connection with its activities within the state, provided that the state does not violate the corporation's due process rights under the Fourteenth Amendment of the Constitution and its rights under the Commerce Clause.

The *International Shoe* minimum contacts test must be met. Subjecting the corporation to suit cannot offend "traditional notions of fair play and substantial justice." A court must weigh the corporation's contacts within the state against the inconvenience to the corporation of requiring it to defend a suit within the state. The burden on the corporation must be reasonable in relation to the benefit that it receives from conducting activities in the state.

Under the minimum contacts test, even an isolated event may be sufficient to confer jurisdiction on a state's courts. For example, driving a truck from Arizona through New Mexico toward a final destination in Florida provides sufficient contacts with New Mexico to permit a suit in New Mexico's courts against the foreign corporation for its driver's negligently causing an accident within New Mexico.

Most of the states have passed **long-arm statutes** to permit their courts to exercise jurisdiction under the decision of the *International Shoe* case. These statutes frequently specify several kinds of corporate activities that make foreign corporations subject to suit within the state, such as the commission of a tort, the making of a contract, or the ownership of property. Most of the long-arm statutes grant jurisdiction over causes of action growing out of any transaction within the state.

The following case applied the Florida long-arm statute to an alien corporation.

---

[1]*International Shoe Co. v. State of Washington,* 326 U.S. 310 (1945).

Sculptchair, Inc., a Florida corporation, owned a patent for a type of chair cover that it marketed under the Sculptchair trademark. In February 1991, Sculptchair signed a contract with Century Arts, Ltd., a Canadian corporation, granting to Century Arts an exclusive license to manufacture, use, sell, and lease the chair covers under the Sculptchair name in Canada. In return, Century Arts paid Sculptchair a monthly fee. Canadian residents Mary Bien and Phyllis Rich were the only officers, directors, and shareholders of Century Arts.

Almost immediately, Century Arts experienced financial difficulties and ceased making payments to Sculptchair in early 1992. In April 1992, Sculptchair terminated the contract with Century Arts; shortly thereafter, Century Arts was dissolved. Mary Bien and Phyllis Rich then formed a new corporation, Chair Decor, Inc., a Canadian corporation that also marketed chair covers. Mary Bien and Phyllis Rich were the only officers, directors, and shareholders of Chair Decor. In her spare time, Phyllis Rich's daughter, Deena Rich, who attended a Florida college, sold Chair Decor's products in Florida for a commission.

In May 1994, Sculptchair believed that Chair Decor was infringing Sculptchair's chair cover patent and trademark. Sculptchair sued Chair Decor in a trial court in Florida for patent and trademark infringement and breach of contract. Chair Decor asked the district court to dismiss the suit on the grounds that the court in Florida had no jurisdiction over Chair Decor, a Canadian corporation. The district court agreed with Chair Decor and dismissed the case. Sculptchair appealed. ∞

Gibson, Circuit Judge We must determine whether the Florida long-arm statute provides a basis for personal jurisdiction over Chair Decor. Florida's long-arm statute, Fla. Stat. ch. 48.193, provides in relevant part:

(1) Any person, whether or not a citizen or resident of this state, who personally or through an agent does any of the acts enumerated in this subsection thereby submits himself . . . to the jurisdiction of the courts of this state for any cause of action arising from the doing of any of the following acts:

(a) Operating, conducting, engaging in, or carrying on a business or business venture in this state or having an office or agency in this state.

(g) Breaching a contract in this state by failing to perform acts required by the contract to be performed in this state.

To establish that a defendant was carrying on a business or business venture in the state, either itself or through an agent, the activities of the defendant must be considered collectively and show a general course of business activity in the State for pecuniary benefit. Deena Rich admittedly operated as an independent contractor and sporadic sales representative for Chair Decor in her spare time while attending school in Florida. While most of her sales were based strictly on word of mouth, Deena Rich admitted that she had circulated a price list to 10 or so individuals describing Chair Decor's product line

and bearing the number of a local telephone answering machine. She also traveled to four or five Florida businesses and gave them product presentations. When a potential customer would leave a message, she would forward the order to Chair Decor in Canada where it would be filled. Deena Rich maintained no regular office, maintained no inventory, and received no regular salary, her salary consisting solely of commissions. Deena Rich's total sales efforts amounted to three to five transactions grossing an estimated $3,000. Although her sales efforts were sporadic at best and the revenue generated therefrom was relatively insignificant, we are left with the inescapable conclusion that her marketing efforts, viewed collectively, qualify as a general course of business activity in Florida for pecuniary benefit.

Because there is no evidence that Chair Decor ever directly manufactured, sold, leased, or solicited orders for chair covers or any other products in Florida, the question whether Chair Decor was ever carrying on a business or business activity in Florida necessarily hinges on whether Deena Rich's activities may be attributed to Chair Decor as its agent in Florida. The facts in this case indicate that Deena Rich was acting as an independent contractor as opposed to an agent. There is no evidence whatsoever that Chair Decor exercised any type of meaningful control over the means employed by Deena

Rich to market the product line. In fact, she set her own hours and chose her own marketing methods, relying principally on word of mouth. Deena Rich herself characterized her own position as that of an independent contractor, and we agree. As a result, we conclude that Chair Decor was not carrying on a business or business venture in Florida through the acts of Deena Rich.

Sculptchair next seeks to invoke section 48.193(1)(g), which provides for personal jurisdiction over persons breaching a contract within Florida by failing to perform acts required by the contract to be performed in Florida. Specifically, it claims that Chair Decor breached Paragraph Eleven of the exclusive licensing agreement by marketing similar chair covers.

This argument overlooks the salient fact that Chair Decor was not a party to that particular contract. As the very first clause of the agreement states, "THIS AGREEMENT is made between SCULPTCHAIR, INC. and CENTURY ARTS, LIMITED." Nonetheless, Sculptchair contends that Chair Decor should be bound by the terms of Century Arts' contract as its corporate successor in interest under Florida's "mere continuation of business doctrine." We agree. The concept of continua-

tion of business arises where the successor corporation is merely a continuation or reincarnation of the predecessor corporation under a different name. A "mere continuation of business" will be found where one corporation is absorbed by another, as evidenced by an identity of assets, location, management, personnel, and stockholders. There is an unmistakable identity of officers, directors, shareholders, and location in this particular case. Once Century Arts had been dissolved, its officers/directors/shareholders formed Chair Decor to market the same type of product out of the same address but without the contractual obligations of its predecessor corporation. Chair Decor assumed Century Arts' modus operandi and apparently remained in contact with its former clients. Because these facts indicate that Chair Decor is nothing more than Century Arts operating under a new name, we hold Chair Decor to the continuing contractual obligations undertaken by its corporate predecessor in interest. As such, we conclude that Sculptchair has met its burden of proving personal jurisdiction over Chair Decor.

Judgment reversed in favor of Sculptchair.

Taxation

A state may tax a foreign corporation if such taxation does not violate the Due Process Clause or the Commerce Clause. Generally, a state's imposition of a tax must serve a legitimate state interest and be reasonable in relation to a foreign corporation's contacts with the state. For example, a North Carolina corporation's property located in Pennsylvania is subject to property tax in Pennsylvania. The corporation enjoys Pennsylvania's protection of private property. It may be required to pay its share of the cost of such protection.

Greater contacts are needed to subject a corporation to state income and sales taxation in a state than are needed to subject it to property taxation. A state tax does not violate the Commerce Clause when the tax (1) is applied to an activity with a substantial connection with the taxing state, (2) is fairly apportioned, (3) does not discriminate against interstate commerce, and (4) is fairly related to the services provided by the state.

For example, New Jersey has been permitted to tax a portion of the entire net income of a corporation for the privilege of doing business, employing or owning capital or property, or maintaining an office in New Jersey when the portion of entire net income taxed is determined by an average of three ratios: in-state property to total property, in-state to total receipts, and in-state to total wages, salaries, and other employee compensation.[2] However, Pennsylvania could not assess a flat tax on the operation of all trucks on Pennsylvania highways. The flat tax imposed a disproportionate burden on interstate trucks as compared with intrastate trucks because interstate trucks traveled fewer miles per year on Pennsylvania highways.[3]

---

[2]*Amerada Hess Corp. v. Director of Taxation,* 490 U.S. 66 (1989).

[3]*American Trucking Assns., Inc. v. Scheiner,* 483 U.S. 266 (1987).

Qualifying to Do Business

A state may require that foreign corporations **qualify** to conduct **intrastate** business in the state. The level of doing business that constitutes intrastate business for qualification purposes has been difficult to define. To help clarify the confusion in this area, the MBCA lists several activities that do *not* require qualification. For example, soliciting— by mail or through employees—orders that require acceptance outside the state is not doing intrastate business requiring qualification. Selling through independent contractors or owning real or personal property does not require qualification.

Also classified as not doing business for qualification purposes is conducting an **isolated transaction** that is completed within 30 days and is not one in the course of repeated transactions of a like nature. This isolated transaction safe harbor allows a tree grower to bring Christmas trees into a state in order to sell them to one retailer. However, a Christmas tree retailer who comes into a state for 29 days before Christmas and sells to consumers from a street corner is required to qualify. Although both merchants have consummated their transactions within 30 days, the grower has engaged in only one transaction, but the retailer has engaged in a series of transactions.

Maintaining an office to conduct intrastate business, selling personal property not in interstate commerce, entering into contracts relating to local business or sales, or owning or using real estate for general corporate purposes does constitute doing intrastate business. Passive ownership of real estate for investment, however, is not doing intrastate business.

Maintaining a stock of goods within a state from which to fill orders, even if the orders are taken or accepted outside the state, is doing intrastate business requiring qualification. Performing service activities such as machinery repair and construction work may be doing intrastate business.

Qualification Requirements   To qualify to do intrastate business in a state, a foreign corporation must apply for a **certificate of authority** from the secretary of state, pay an application fee, maintain a registered office and a registered agent in the state, file an annual report with the secretary of state, and pay an annual fee.

Doing intrastate business without qualifying usually subjects a foreign corporation to a fine, in some states as much as $10,000. The MBCA disables the corporation to use the state's courts to bring a lawsuit until it obtains a certificate of authority. The corporation may defend itself in the state's courts, however, even if it has no certificate of authority.

In the following case, the Texas court of appeals allowed a Delaware corporation to sue in a Texas court even though the corporation had not obtained a certificate of authority.

GOSCH v. B & D SHRIMP, INC.   830 S.W.2d 652 (Tex. Ct. App. 1992)

B & D Shrimp, Inc., a Delaware corporation, entered a contract in Texas with Donald Gosch and Jesse Bach. The contract required Gosch and Bach to purchase a commercial shrimp boat from Shrimp, Inc. Gosch and Bach paid $5,000 down and received immediate possession of the boat; Gosch and Bach would get marketable title to the shrimp boat after transferring a cabin cruiser to Shrimp, Inc., and paying 15 percent of the cash proceeds generated from the shrimp boat's daily shrimp catches for the next calendar year. When Gosch and Bach defaulted on its obligation, Shrimp, Inc., sued Gosch. After the trial court found Gosch liable to Shrimp, Inc., Gosch asked the trial court to set aside its judgment on the grounds that Shrimp, Inc., had not obtained a certificate of authority to do business from the Texas secretary of state and, therefore, was not allowed to use Texas's courts to enforce the contract. The trial court denied Gosch's request, and Gosch appealed. ∽

O'Connor, Justice   The Texas Business Corporation Act prohibits a foreign corporation from maintaining any action in this State until it has obtained a certificate of authority to do business. Shrimp, Inc. argues that it was not necessary for it to obtain a certificate. A corporation is not considered to be transacting business in Texas if it conducts an isolated transaction that is completed within 30 days and the transaction is not in the course of a number of repeated transactions that are similar. Shrimp, Inc. contends that it fell within this exception to the statute requiring a certificate of authority. We disagree. Here, it is implicit in the agreement that the transaction could not be completed within 30 days. The transfer of title would not occur until, in addition to two other conditions, 15 percent of the cash proceeds generated from the daily shrimp catches for the *next calendar year* were paid.

Shrimp, Inc. also contends it was within the trial court's discretion to disregard Gosch's plea. We agree. Here, Gosch did not raise the issue of Shrimp, Inc.'s authority until 20 days after the judgment was signed, in a motion to set aside the judgment. By waiting until after the trial, Gosch waived the issue of Shrimp, Inc.'s capacity to prosecute the suit. Even if Gosch had not waived the issue, at the hearing on the motion to set aside the judgment, Shrimp, Inc. filed a certificate of authority. The trial court did not abuse its discretion in overruling the motion to set aside the judgment.

Judgment for B & D Shrimp, Inc. affirmed.

Regulation of a Corporation's Internal Affairs

Regulation of the internal affairs of a corporation—that is, the relation between the corporation and its directors, officers, and shareholders—is usually only exercised by the state of incorporation. Nonetheless, a foreign corporation may conduct most of its business in a state other than the one in which it is incorporated. Such a corporation is called a **pseudo-foreign corporation** in the state in which it conducts most of its business.

A few states subject pseudo-foreign corporations to extensive regulation of their internal affairs, regulation similar to that imposed on their domestic corporations. California's statute requires corporations that have more than 50 percent of their business and ownership in California to elect directors by cumulative voting, to hold annual directors' elections, and to comply with California's dividend payment restrictions. Foreign corporations raise many constitutional objections to the California statute, including violations of the Commerce Clause and the Due Process Clause.

REGULATION OF FOREIGN NONPROFIT CORPORATIONS

The Model Nonprofit Corporation Act and other laws impose the same requirements and penalties on nonprofit corporations as are imposed on for-profit corporations. For example, the MNCA requires a foreign nonprofit corporation to qualify to do intrastate business in a state. The failure to qualify prevents the foreign nonprofit corporation from using the state's courts to bring lawsuits and subjects it to fines for each day it transacts intrastate business without a certificate of authority.

PIERCING THE CORPORATE VEIL

A corporation is a legal entity separate from its shareholders. Corporation law erects an imaginary wall between a corporation and its shareholders that protects shareholders from liability for a corporation's actions. Once shareholders have made their promised capital contributions to the corporation, they have no further financial liability. This means that contracts of a corporation are not contracts of its shareholders, and debts of a corporation are not debts of its shareholders.

Nonetheless, in order *to promote justice and to prevent inequity,* courts will sometimes ignore the separateness of a corporation and its shareholders by **piercing the corporate veil.** The primary consequence of piercing the corporate veil is that a corporation's shareholders may lose their limited liability.

Two requirements must exist for a court to pierce the corporate veil: (1) **domination** of a corporation by its shareholders; and (2) use of that domination for an **improper purpose.**

As an entity separate from its shareholders, a corporation should act for itself, not for its shareholders. If the shareholders cause the corporation to act to its detriment and to the personal benefit of shareholders, *domination*—the first requirement for piercing the corporate veil—is proved. For example, shareholders' directing a corporation to pay a shareholder's personal expenses is domination. Domination is also proved if the shareholders cause the corporation to fail to observe corporate formalities (such as failing to hold shareholder and director meetings or to maintain separate accounting records). Some courts say that shareholder domination makes the corporation the *alter ego* (other self) of the shareholders. Other courts say that domination makes the corporation an *instrumentality* of the shareholders.

To prove domination, it is not sufficient, or even necessary, to show that there is only one shareholder. Many one-shareholder corporations will never have their veils pierced. However, nearly all corporations whose veils are pierced are close corporations, since domination is more easily accomplished in a close corporation than in a publicly held one.

In addition to domination, there must be an *improper use* of the corporation. The improper use may be any of three types: defrauding creditors, circumventing a statute, or evading an existing obligation.

Shareholders must organize a corporation with sufficient capital to meet the initial capital needs of the business. Inadequate capitalization, called **thin capitalization,** is proved when capitalization is very small in relation to the nature of the business of the corporation and the risks the business necessarily entails.

Thin capitalization defrauds creditors of a corporation. An example of thin capitalization is forming a business with a high debt-to-equity ratio, such as a $10-million-asset business with only $1,000 of equity capital, with the shareholders sometimes contributing the remainder of the needed capital as secured creditors. By doing so, the shareholders elevate a portion of their bankruptcy repayment priority to a level above that of general creditors, thereby reducing the shareholders' risk. The high debt-to-equity ratio harms nonshareholder-creditors by failing to provide an equity cushion sufficient to protect their claims. In such a situation, either the shareholders will be liable for the corporation's debts or the shareholders' loans to the corporation will be subordinated to the claims of other creditors. As a result, the nonshareholder-creditors are repaid all of their claims prior to the shareholder-creditors receiving payment from the corporation.

Transfers of corporate assets to shareholders for less than fair market value (called **looting**) also defraud creditors. For example, shareholder-managers loot a corporation by paying themselves excessively high salaries or by having the corporation pay their personal credit card bills. When such payments leave insufficient assets in the corporation to pay creditors' claims, a court will hold the shareholders liable to the creditors.

Frequently, the same shareholders may own two corporations that transact with each other. The shareholders may cause one corporation to loot the other. When such looting occurs between corporations of common ownership, courts pierce the veils of these corporations. This makes each corporation liable to the creditors of the other corporation. For example, a shareholder-manager operates two corporations from the same office. Corporation 1 transfers inventory to Corporation 2, but it receives less than fair market value for the inventory. Also, both corporations employ the same workers, but all of the wages are paid by Corporation 1. In such a situation, the veils of the corporations will be pierced, allowing the creditors of Corporation 1 to satisfy their claims against the assets of Corporation 2.

Looting may occur also when one corporation (called the **parent corporation**) owns at least a majority of the shares of another corporation (called the **subsidiary corporation**). Ordinarily, the parent is liable for its own obligations and the subsidiary is liable for its own obligations, but the parent is not liable for its subsidiary's debts and the subsidiary is not liable for the parent's debts. Nonetheless, because a parent corporation is able to elect the directors of its subsidiary and therefore can control the management of the subsidiary, the parent may cause its subsidiary to transact with the parent in a manner that benefits the parent but harms the subsidiary.

For example, a parent corporation may direct its subsidiary to sell its assets to the parent for less than fair market value. Because the subsidiary has given more assets to the parent than it has received from the parent, creditors of the subsidiary have been defrauded. Consequently, a court will pierce the veil between the parent and its subsidiary and hold the parent liable to the creditors of the subsidiary.

A corporation should not engage in a course of conduct that is prohibited by a statute. For example, a city ordinance prohibits retail businesses from being open on consecutive Sundays. To avoid the statute, a retail corporation forms a subsidiary owned entirely by the retail corporation; on alternate weeks, it leases its building and inventory to the subsidiary. A court will pierce the veil because

FIGURE 2

Examples of Piercing the Corporate Veil

Event	Proof of Domination	Proof of Improper Purpose	Result
Sole shareholder/ director causes corporation to pay shareholder's personal debt.	Sole shareholder/ director controls corporation's use of assets.	Creditors defrauded when corporate assets used to pay shareholder's debt, not corporation's debt.	Shareholder liable to creditors of corporation.
Shareholders/ directors fail to hold annual shareholders' and directors' meetings.	Shareholders and directors control corporation's decision to hold meetings.	Circumvention of incorporation statute requiring annual meetings.	Shareholders liable to creditors of corporation.
To avoid union contract, shareholders vote to transfer business of corporation to new corporation owned by the same shareholders.	Shareholders' vote controlled corporation's decision to transfer business to new corporation.	Obligation to employees evaded by the business.	New corporation liable to employees under union contract.
Parent of wholly owned subsidiary causes subsidiary to buy asset from parent at price higher than fair market value.	Parent owns 100% of subsidiary, elects its directors, and therby controls subsidiary.	Creditors of subsidiary defrauded when parent gives fewer assets to subsidiary than subsidiary gives to parent.	Parent liable to creditors of subsidiary.
Shareholders organize corporation by contributing $1,000 of capital and by loaning $99,000 to corporation. The loan is secured by all the corporation's assets.	Shareholders control organization of corporation.	Nonshareholder creditors defrauded by thin capitalization.	Part or all of loans treated as capital, thereby subordinating shareholder's loans to claims of nonshareholders.

the purpose of creating the subsidiary corporation is to circumvent the statutory prohibition. Consequently, both the parent and the subsidiary will be liable for violating the statute.

Sometimes, a corporation will attempt to escape liability on a contract by reincorporating or by forming a subsidiary corporation. The new corporation will claim that it is not bound by the contract, even though it is doing the same business as was done by the old corporation. In such a situation, courts pierce the corporate veil and hold the new corporation liable on the contract.

For example, to avoid an onerous labor union contract, a corporation creates a wholly owned subsidiary and sells its entire business to the subsidiary. The subsidiary will claim that it is not a party to the labor contract and may hire nonunion labor. A court will pierce the veil between the two corpora-tions because the subsidiary was created only to avoid the union contract.

Nonprofit Corporations

Like a for-profit corporation, a nonprofit corporation is an entity separate and distinct from its members. A member is not personally liable for a nonprofit corporation's acts or liabilities merely by being a member. However, a court may pierce the veil of a nonprofit corporation if it is used to defraud creditors, circumvent a statute, or evade an existing obligation, the same grounds on which a for-profit corporation's veil may be pierced.

For a summary of the law of piercing the corporate veil, see Figure 2.

In the following case, the court considered a full range of reasons to pierce a corporation's veil.

BINGHAM v. GOLDBERG, MARCHESANO, KOLMAN, INC.   637 A.2d 81 (D.C. App. 1994)

I n the summer 1983, Joan Bingham, Mortimer Zuckerman, and Anne Peretz formed a corporation, PFP, Inc., to explore the feasibility of publishing a weekly newspaper in Washington, D.C. The newspaper would be named The Washington Weekly. Initially, they contributed $50,000 to the corporation. At the organization meeting, Bingham, Zuckerman, and Peretz were named initial directors, Bingham was elected president, and James Glassman was appointed vice president, treasurer, secretary, and acting publisher. In December 1983, after it was determined that such a newspaper would be feasible, further contributions were made to the PFP. Bingham contributed $427,500, Anne Peretz invested $125,500, the Peretz Family Investments put in $100,000, Zuckerman contributed $100,000, and Martin Peretz added $7,000.

In late 1983, PFP hired Goldberg, Marchesano, Kohlman, Inc. (GMK) to assist with advertising and marketing The Washington Weekly. Glassman signed the contract for PFP. The contract provided for continuing the relationship on a month-to-month basis.

In April 1984, in order to raise additional capital for the newspaper, a limited partnership, Washington Weekly Limited (WWL), was formed. The sole general partner of WWL was PFP. Bingham signed the limited partnership agreement as president of the general partner, PFP. When WWL was formed, PFP contributed capital of $1,022,727 to the limited partnership, including all ownership of the newspaper The Washington Weekly. None of PFP's liabilities were transferred to WWL. PFP retained cash assets of $79,000. PFP also expected to receive management fees from WWL in exchange for its managing WWL as the general partner.

GMK provided advertising and marketing services to The Washington Weekly until September 1984. PFP made payments of more than $77,000 to GMK after the limited partnership was formed, but was delinquent in other payments to GMK. In late August, GMK contacted PFP about the late payments. In response, James Rice, The Washington Weekly's general manager, sent a letter to GMK terminating the monthly retainer agreement with GMK. The letter included Bingham's signature and listed her as publisher. In late September, Bingham wrote to Goldberg confirming the termination of the monthly retainer agreement and concluding, "We really appreciated all your good advice." Between February and September 1984, PFP paid GMK over $79,000, but still owed over $46,000.

Subsequently, The Washington Weekly *was unprofitable and the decision was made to cease its publication. The assets of PFP were insufficient to pay the remaining $46,000 debt owed to GMK. GMK then sued Bingham, claiming that she was personally liable to GMK. The trial court found Bingham liable to GMK, and Bingham appealed.* ∽

Wagner, Associate Judge   GMK contends that Bingham used the corporation as an alter-ego and so dominated its affairs that she should be subject to personal liability for the debt owed by PFP to GMK. The general rule has been that the corporate entity will be respected and that its obligations will not be imposed upon a particular individual unless a party seeking to disregard the corporate entity has proved that there is (1) unity of ownership and interest, and (2) use of the corporate form to perpetrate fraud or wrong. We have recognized a modification to this rule which rejects the requirement that fraud must be shown. Instead, considerations of justice and equity may justify piercing the corporate veil. Whether there is sufficient showing of a unity of ownership and interest will depend upon such factors as (1) whether corporate formalities have been disregarded, (2) whether corporate funds and assets have been extensively intermingled with personal assets, (3) inadequate initial capitalization, and (4) fraudulent use of the corporation to protect personal business from the claims of creditors.

When the evidence is viewed against these standards, there is no basis to conclude that there was a unity of ownership and interest. The record contains numerous documents evidencing the corporation's observance of corporate formalities. Among them are copies of the articles, the D.C. Certificate of Incorporation, the Resolution for Bank Accounts, minutes of meetings of the Board of Directors and of shareholders, consent to postponement of meet-

ing, corporate by-laws, and stock certificates. Final decision-making authority rested with the Board of Directors of the corporation, and it was the Board's decision to terminate publication of the paper.

There is also no evidence that Bingham's personal funds were commingled with the corporation's assets or that the corporation made a preferential payment to her. What the evidence shows is that, in addition to her capital contribution to the corporation, Bingham loaned the corporation $300,000 and that she later forgave the debt. Contrary to GMK's assertion, there is no evidence that Bingham actually seized the corporation's computer equipment, although there is evidence that she had a security interest in it. Thus, we do not agree with GMK that there was either a commingling of assets or a preferential payment.

Finally, there is no basis to conclude that the corporation was undercapitalized initially or that the transfer of assets to PFP was undertaken as a fraud on creditors. On the contrary, cash in excess of $1 million was invested into the corporation initially. We find no attempt to defraud creditors in the formation of WWL and PFP's purchase of a general partnership interest in the partnership. Thus, the basic elements for disregarding the corporate entity are absent here. The trial court's ruling imposing personal liability upon Bingham cannot be premised upon piercing the corporate veil.

Judgment reversed in favor of Bingham.

---

1. Do you think it is right that shareholders of corporations have no liability for the obligations of their corporation once they have paid their promised capital contribution? What benefits does society receive from extending such a privilege to shareholders? What detriments does society suffer?

2. Should businesses be permitted to incorporate in a state that has a business incorporation law that

extends the greatest freedom to managers of the business? Who benefits from businesses incorporating in such states? Who is harmed? Can the persons who are harmed protect themselves?

3. When a corporation engages in interstate business, should its managers attempt to reduce the risk that foreign states' courts will have jurisdiction over the corporation? Should the managers attempt to avoid taxation by foreign states? Should they try to avoid qualification requirements? Is it enough that the corporation complies exactly with the laws of the foreign states, or should the corporation attempt to return to the state—such as through taxes and qualification fees—an amount appropriate to the benefits it receives from customers in the foreign state? Is the corporation the only person benefiting from its doing business in a foreign state? What risk may arise if a state aggressively regulates foreign corporations?

4. Why should courts and corporation statutes require corporations to be adequately capitalized? Who is harmed by thin capitalization? Is it possible for creditors harmed by thin capitalization to protect themselves by examining the financial position of the corporation prior to extending credit to the corporation? Why should a court protect creditors who knowingly or carelessly extend credit to thinly capitalized corporations? Should a court treat a corporation's *contract* creditors differently from its *tort* creditors? Are a thinly capitalized corporation's *contract* creditors better able to protect themselves than are the corporation's *tort* victims?

PROBLEMS AND PROBLEM CASES

1. In September 1991, Jerry Tanner was working as a machinist on a construction project in Multnomah County, Oregon. Needing to repair broken equipment, he went to a local NAPA auto parts store and bought a product called Epoxy Mending Putty packaged under the Balkamp and NAPA labels. Following the directions on the epoxy's label, he rubbed the epoxy in his hands. The packaging did not warn about skin sensitivity, toxicity of epoxy resin, or the need to use gloves or a barrier cream when using the product. Tanner immediately reacted adversely to the epoxy. His condition spread to other parts of his body. As a result, he was disabled; he had trouble walking and performing other daily functions. Balkamp, Inc., supplied the epoxy to the NAPA store. Balkamp is affiliated with NAPA and sells only to NAPA stores. The epoxy was manufactured in 1984 by Hermetite UK. Hermetite was incorporated and had its operations in England. Hermetite UK sold some of this batch to Hermetite US, which marketed the epoxy in the United States. Balkamp bought the epoxy from Hermetite US. Tanner sued Balkamp in an Oregon trial court. Does the Oregon trial court have jurisdiction over Balkamp?

2. Debra Hervish, a resident of Florida, purchased 14 pieces of furniture from Growables, Inc., a furniture store incorporated and doing business in Florida. Planning to move to Louisiana, she asked Growables to ship the furniture to Louisiana. Growables hired Ryder Truck Lines to ship the furniture to Louisiana. When the furniture arrived in Louisiana, Hervish found that every piece was damaged. Hervish sued Growables in a Louisiana trial court. Does the Louisiana trial court have jurisdiction over Growables?

3. A Hawaiian statute imposed a 20 percent wholesale excise tax on liquor sold in Hawaii. To encourage the development of Hawaiian liquor, the statute exempted from taxation Okolehao, a brandy distilled from the root of the ti plant, a native Hawaiian shrub. Bacchus Imports, a liquor wholesaler, claimed that the excise tax violated the Commerce Clause. Was Bacchus correct?

4. Campaign Works, Ltd., a business incorporated in Florida, was a consultant to candidates for political office. Campaign Works had offices in Florida and Washington, D.C. It had no office and no employees in Missouri and had not qualified to do business in Missouri. Campaign Works contracted to provide political consulting services to Doug Hughes, a candidate to the U.S. Congress for Missouri. The contract was negotiated by telephone and concluded by mail between Campaign Works in Florida or Washington and Hughes in Missouri. The contract called for consultations with Hughes in Missouri and political research appropriate to his election campaign. Campaign Works actually performed election research for Hughes from its offices in Florida and Washington, and its president traveled to Missouri twice to consult with Hughes and his staff. The parties terminated the contract, with Hughes owing Campaign Works nearly $9,000. Hughes failed to pay this amount, and Campaign Works sued Hughes in a Missouri trial court. Does Campaign Works's failure to qualify to do business in Missouri prevent it from suing Hughes in a Missouri court?

5. The National Steeplechase and Hunt Association (NSHA) was a New York corporation that sanctioned, regulated, and supervised steeplechase races. NSHA sanctioned three steeplechase races in Kentucky. Each sanctioned event lasted no more than four days each year. NSHA promulgated steeplechase rules; approved the racecourses, race officials, and the financial responsibility of the sponsoring organization; received entries for each event by telephone or mail; assembled the information on the events; and prepared a booklet and identification badges for each meet. All these functions were performed in NSHA's New York office. The NSHA had no employees or offices in Kentucky. All communications were conducted by telephone or mail. NSHA leased fences and jumps to the sponsoring organization; the NSHA driver did not assist the local organization in setting up the equipment. Was NSHA required to qualify to do business in Kentucky.

6. Section 2115 of the California General Corporation Law requires that a foreign corporation doing a majority of its business in California (on the basis of its property, payroll, and sales) and having a majority of its outstanding voting securities owned by persons with addresses in California comply with certain internal governance provisions of the California corporation law, including section 708, which provides for the cumulative voting of shares for the election of directors. Louisiana-Pacific Resources, Inc., was a Utah corporation. The average of its property, payroll, and sales in California exceeded 50 percent, and more than 50 percent of its shareholders entitled to vote resided in California. Except for being domiciled in Utah and having a transfer agent there, Louisiana-Pacific had virtually no business connections with Utah. Its principal place of business was in California; its meetings of shareholders and directors were held in California; and all of its employees and bank accounts were in California. Louisiana-Pacific argued that application of section 2115 to Louisiana-Pacific violated the Constitution of the United States. Is it correct?

7. Pacific Development, Inc., was incorporated in the District of Columbia in 1968 to engage in the business of international brokerage and consulting. Tongsun Park was Pacific's founder, president, and sole shareholder. It was doubtful whether Pacific had a board of directors prior to December 1974. The directors met infrequently after 1974. When they did meet, they approved without discussion or question corporate decisions made by Park. Park wrote checks on Pacific's bank accounts to cover his unrelated personal and business expenses. Pacific employees served as Park's household servants. Park made loans with Pacific funds to politically influential people and then forgave the loans. Pacific

personnel provided administrative and managerial services for Park's other business ventures, and Pacific's profits were assigned to Park or to his other companies. In 1977, the Internal Revenue Service assessed $4.5 million in back income taxes against Park. To collect the taxes, the IRS seized some of Pacific's assets, claiming that the company was a mere alter ego of Park. Was the IRS correct?

8. Eric Dahlbeck incorporated Viking Construction, Inc., with an initial capital of $3,000. Dahlbeck also made a $7,000 loan to Viking. Viking had as assets 65 lots of land held for development, which lots cost $430,000. Viking became unable to pay its creditors, who sought to pierce the corporate veil and hold Dahlbeck liable. Were the creditors successful?

9. New York law required that every taxicab company carry $10,000 of accident liability insurance for each cab in its fleet. The purpose of the law was to ensure that passengers and pedestrians injured by cabs operated by these companies would be adequately compensated for their injuries. Carlton organized 10 corporations, each owning and operating two taxicabs in New York City. Each of these corporations carried $20,000 of liability insurance. Carlton was the principal shareholder of each corporation. The vehicles, the only freely transferable assets of these corporations, were collateral for claims of secured creditors. The 10 corporations were operated more or less as a unit with respect to supplies, repairs, and employees. Walkovszky was severely injured when he was run down by one of the taxicabs. He sued Carlton personally, alleging that the multiple corporate structure amounted to fraud upon those who might be injured by the taxicabs. Should the court pierce the corporate veil to reach Carlton individually?

10. Castleberry, Branscum, and Byboth each owned one-third of the shares of a furniture-moving business, Texan Transfer, Inc. Branscum formed Elite Moving Company, a business that competed with Texan Transfer. Castleberry objected and sued to claim part ownership of Elite Moving. Branscum threatened Castleberry that he would not receive any return on his investment in Texan Transfer unless he abandoned his claim of ownership of Elite Moving. Consequently, Castleberry sold his shares back to Texan Transfer for a $42,000 promissory note. Gradually, Elite Moving took over more and more of the business of Texan Transfer. Texan

Transfer allowed Elite Moving to use its employees and trucks. Elite Moving advertised for business, while Texan Transfer did not. Elite Moving prospered, while Texan Transfer's business declined. As a result, Castleberry was paid only $1,000 of the $42,000 promissory note. Did Castleberry have any grounds to hold Branscum liable for the unpaid portion of the note?

11. Maintenance Contractors, Inc., owed $13,600 to Westinghouse Electric Supply Co. Robert Pilkerton, the majority shareholder of Maintenance Contractors, caused Maintenance Contractors to cease operations. Twelve days later, Robert Pilkerton incorporated R.E. Pilkerton, Inc., which carried on the same business as Maintenance Contractors. Are Pilkerton and R.E. Pilkerton, Inc., liable to Westinghouse on the $13,600 debt?

Organization and Financial Structure of Corporations

A person desiring to incorporate a business must comply with the applicable corporation law. Failing to comply can create various problems. For example, a person may make a contract on behalf of the corporation before it is incorporated. Is the corporation liable on this contract? Is the person who made the contract on behalf of the prospective corporation liable on the contract? Do the people who thought that they were shareholders of a corporation have limited liability, or do they have unlimited liability as partners of a partnership? ∽

PROMOTERS AND PREINCORPORATION TRANSACTIONS

A **promoter** of a corporation incorporates a business, organizes its initial management, and raises its initial capital. Typically, a promoter discovers a business or an idea to be developed, finds people who are willing to invest in the business, negotiates the contracts necessary for the initial operation of the proposed venture, incorporates the business, and helps management start the operation of the business. Consequently, a promoter may engage in many acts prior to the incorporation of the business. As a result, the promoter may have liability on the contracts he negotiates on behalf of the prospective corporation. In addition, the corporation may *not* be liable on the contracts the promoter makes on its behalf.

Corporation's Liability on Preincorporation Contracts

A nonexistent corporation has no liability on contracts made by a promoter prior to its incorporation. This is because the corporation does not exist.

Even when the corporation comes into existence, it does not automatically become liable on a preincorporation contract made by a promoter on its behalf. It cannot be held liable as a principal whose agent made the contracts because the promoter was not its agent and the corporation was not in existence when the contracts were made.

The only way a corporation may become bound on a promoter's preincorporation contracts is by the corporation's **adoption** of the promoter's contracts. For a corporation to adopt a promoter's contract, the corporation must accept the contract with knowledge of all its material facts.

Acceptance may be express or implied. The corporation's knowing receipt of the benefits of the contract is sufficient for acceptance. For example, a promoter makes a preincorporation contract with a genetic engineer, requiring the engineer to work for a prospective corporation for 10 years. After incorporation, the promoter presents the contract to the board of directors. Although the board takes no formal action to accept the contract, the board allows the engineer to work for the corporation for one year as the contract provides and pays him the salary required by the contract. The board's actions constitute an acceptance of the contract, binding the corporation to the contract for its 10-year term.

Promoter's Liability on Preincorporation Contracts

A promoter and her copromoters are jointly and severally liable on preincorporation contracts the promoter negotiates in the name of the nonexistent corporation. This liability exists even when the promoters' names do not appear on the contract. Promoters are also jointly and severally liable for torts committed by their copromoters prior to incorporation.

A promoter retains liability on a preincorporation contract until **novation** occurs. For novation to occur, the corporation and the third party must agree to release the promoter from liability and to substitute the corporation for the promoter as the party liable on the contract. Usually, novation will occur by express or implied agreement of all the parties.

If the corporation is not formed, a promoter remains liable on a preincorporation contract unless the third party releases the promoter from liability. In addition, the mere formation of the corporation does not release a promoter from liability. A promoter remains liable on a preincorporation contract even after the corporation's adoption of the contract, since adoption does not automatically release the promoter. The corporation cannot by itself relieve the promoter of liability to the third party; the third party must also agree, expressly or impliedly, to release the promoter from liability.

A few courts have held that a promoter is not liable on preincorporation contracts if the third party *knew of the nonexistence* of the corporation yet insisted that the promoter sign the contract on behalf of the nonexistent corporation. Other courts have found that the promoter is not liable if the third party clearly stated that he would *look only to the prospective corporation* for performance.

Recently, courts have held that the Model Business Corporation Act (MBCA) permits a promoter to escape liability for preincorporation contracts when the promoter has made some effort to incorporate the business and believes the corporation is in existence. The MBCA rule is discussed below in the section titled, Defective Attempts to Incorporate. The *Sivers* case, which follows that section, is an example of the application of the MBCA promoter liability rule.

Obtaining a Binding Preincorporation Contract

While it may be desirable for the promoter to escape liability on a preincorporation contract, there is one disadvantage: Only when the promoter is liable on the preincorporation contract is the other party liable on the contract. This means that when the promoter is not liable on the contract, the other party to the contract may rescind the contract at any time prior to adoption by the corporation. Once the corporation has adopted the contract, the corporation and the third party are liable on it, and the contract cannot be rescinded without the consent of both parties.

To maintain the enforceability of a preincorporation contract prior to adoption, a promoter may want to be liable on a preincorporation contract at least until the corporation comes into existence and adopts the contract. To limit his liability, however, the promoter may wish to have his liability cease automatically upon adoption. The promoter should ensure that the contract has an **automatic novation clause.** For example, a preincorporation contract may read that "the promoter's liability on this contract shall terminate upon the corporation's adoption of this contract."

Instead of using automatic novation clauses, today most well-advised promoters incorporate the business prior to making any contracts for the corporation. By doing so, only the corporation and the third party—and not the promoter—have liability on the contract.

Preincorporation Share Subscriptions

Promoters sometimes use **preincorporation share subscriptions** to ensure that the corporation will have adequate capital when it begins its business. Under the terms of a share subscription, a prospective shareholder offers to buy a specific number of the corporation's shares at a stated price. Under the Model Business Corporation Act (MBCA), a prospective shareholder may not revoke a preincorporation subscription for a six-month period, in the absence of a contrary provision in the subscription. Generally, corporate acceptance of preincorporation subscriptions occurs by action of the board of directors after incorporation.

Promoters have no liability on preincorporation share subscriptions. They have a duty, however, to make a good faith effort to bring the corporation into existence. When a corporation fails to accept a preincorporation subscription or becomes insolvent, the promoter is not liable to the disappointed subscriber, in the absence of fraud or other wrongdoing by the promoter.

Today, most promoters incorporate the business and obtain promises to buy shares from prospective shareholders. These promises, which may take the

form of postincorporation subscriptions, are discussed later in this chapter.

Relation of Promoter and Prospective Corporation

A promoter of a nonexistent corporation is not an agent of the prospective corporation but nonetheless owes fiduciary duties to it. A promoter is not an agent of prospective investors in the business because they did not appoint him and they have no power to control him.

Although not an agent of the proposed corporation or its investors, a promoter owes a **fiduciary duty** to the corporation and to its prospective investors. A promoter owes such parties a duty of full disclosure and honesty. For example, a promoter breaches this duty when she diverts money received from prospective shareholders to pay her expenses, unless the shareholders agree to such payment. The fiduciary duty also prevents a promoter from diverting a business opportunity from the corporation and giving it to himself instead. In addition, the promoter may not purchase shares of the corporation at a price lower than that paid by the public shareholders.

A promoter may not profit personally by transacting secretly with the corporation in his personal capacity. The promoter's failure to disclose her interest in the transaction and the material facts permits the corporation to rescind the transaction or to recover the promoter's secret profit. On the other hand, the promoter's full disclosure of her interest and the material facts of the transaction to an independent board of directors that approves the transaction prevents the corporation from recovering the promoter's profit. Note, however, that when a promoter is a director, approval of the transaction by the board of directors is not sufficient; the transaction must be intrinsically fair to the corporation.

In the following case, the court held that promoters are fiduciaries of the corporation they organize.

SMITH v. BITTER 319 N.W.2d 196 (Iowa Sup. Ct. 1982)

J oseph J. Smith, Steve J. Smith, and Joseph Bitter planned to open a tavern in the college town of Dubuque, Iowa. In the name of Gomer's, Inc., a corporation not yet formed, all three signed an offer to purchase a building in which to operate the tavern. After Gomer's, Inc., had been incorporated, the Smiths as corporate officers signed a contract to purchase the building in the name of the corporation. Soon after business began, differences arose between the Smiths and Bitter. Despite

Bitter's protests, the Smiths assumed control of the corporation, including the building. Bitter sued the Smiths, asking the court to declare that Bitter and the Smiths as individuals owned the building and that Gomer's, Inc., had no interest in the building. The trial court held that Gomer's, Inc., owned the building. Bitter appealed to the Supreme Court of Iowa. ∞

LeGrand, Justice   This litigation culminates what started as a business venture among friends and terminated in acrimony and distrust.

In negotiating for the purchase of the real estate, Bitter and the Smiths were promoters acting for the corporation they were then in the process of organizing. A promoter stands in a fiduciary position toward both the corporation and its stockholders and is prohibited from acquiring a secret personal advantage from any action taken on behalf of the corporation.

The Smiths and Bitter owed a fiduciary duty to the corporation for which they were acting and to its shareholders. The fact that the promoters themselves were the stockholders does not alter that obligation. The record is clear that all negotiations for purchase of the real estate were made on behalf of Gomer's, Inc., which the Smiths and Bitter were then organizing. Bitter cannot profit personally from this transaction nor can he assert personal ownership of the real estate against those toward whom he was bound to exercise the utmost good faith.

Judgment for the Smiths affirmed.

Liability of Corporation to Promoter

Valuable as the services of a promoter may be to a prospective corporation and to society, a corporation is generally not required to compensate a promoter for her promotional services, or even her expenses, unless the corporation has agreed expressly to compensate the promoter. The justification for this rule is that the promoter is self-appointed and acts for a corporation that is not in existence.

Nonetheless, a corporation may choose to reimburse the promoter for her reasonable expenses and to pay her the value of her services to the corporation. Corporations often compensate their promoters with shares. The MBCA permits the issuance of shares for a promoter's preincorporation services.

To ensure that she is compensated for her services, a promoter may tie herself to a person or property that the corporation needs to succeed. For example, a promoter may purchase the invention that the corporation was formed to exploit. Another way to ensure compensation is by the promoter dominating the board of directors during the early months of its life. By doing so, the promoter may direct the corporation to compensate her.

CONCEPT   REVIEW

Preincorporation Contracts

Promoter Liability	A promoter is liable on a preincorporation contract unless either: 1. The third party knows of the nonexistence of the corporation and insists that the promoter sign in the name of the corporation, or 2. The third party knows of the nonexistence of corporation and agrees only to look to prospective corporation for performance, or 3. Novation occurs either: *a.* By agreement of the corporation and the third party, or *b.* By use of an automatic novation clause.
Corporation Liability	A corporation is *not* liable on a preincorporation contract until the board of directors adopts the contract.
Third-Party Liability	A third party is liable on a preincorporation contract if either the promoter or the corporation is liable on the contract.

INCORPORATION

Anyone seeking to incorporate a business must decide where to do so. If the business of a proposed corporation is to be primarily *intrastate,* it is usually cheaper to incorporate in the state where the corporation's business is to be conducted. For the business that is primarily *interstate,* however, the business may benefit by incorporating in a state different from the state in which it has its principal place of business.

Incorporation fees and taxes, annual fees, and other fees such as those on the transfer of shares or the dissolution of the corporation vary considerably from state to state. Delaware has been a popular state in which to incorporate because its fees tend to be low.

Promoters frequently choose to incorporate in a state whose corporation statute and court decisions grant managers broad management discretion. For example, it is easier to pay a large dividend and to effect a merger in Delaware than in many other states.

Steps in Incorporation

There are only a few requirements for incorporation. It is a fairly simple process and can be accomplished inexpensively in most cases. The steps prescribed by the incorporation statutes of the different states vary, but they generally include the following, which appear in the MBCA:

1. Preparation of articles of incorporation.
2. Signing and authenticating the articles by one or more incorporators.
3. Filing the articles with the secretary of state, accompanied by the payment of specified fees.
4. Receipt of a copy of the articles of incorporation stamped "Filed" by the secretary of state, accompanied by a fee receipt. (Some states retain the old MBCA rule requiring receipt of a certificate of incorporation issued by the secretary of state.)
5. Holding an organization meeting for the purpose of adopting bylaws, electing officers, and transacting other business.

Articles of Incorporation   The basic governing document of the corporation is the **articles of incorporation** (sometimes called the charter). The articles are similar to a constitution. They state many of the rights and responsibilities of the corporation, its management, and its shareholders. Figure 1 lists the contents of the articles.

The corporation must have a name that is distinguishable from the name of any other corporation incorporated or qualified to do business in the state. The name must include the word *corporation, incorporated, company,* or *limited,* or the abbreviation *corp., inc., co.,* or *ltd.*

The MBCA does not require the inclusion of a statement of purpose in the articles. When a purpose is stated, it is sufficient to state, alone or together with specific purposes, that the corporation may engage in "any lawful activity."

The MBCA permits a corporation to have perpetual existence. If desired, the articles of incorporation may provide for a shorter duration.

Most of the state corporation statutes require the articles to recite the initial capitalization of the business. Usually, the statutes require that there be a minimum amount of initial capital, such as $1,000. Since such a small amount of capital is rarely enough to protect creditors adequately, the MBCA dispenses with the need to recite a minimum amount of capital.

The articles may contain additional provisions not inconsistent with law for managing the corpora-

---

FIGURE   I

*Contents of Articles of Incorporation
(pursuant to MBCA)*

The following *must* be in the articles:

1. The name of the corporation.
2. The number of shares that the corporation has authority to issue.
3. The address of the initial registered office of the corporation and the name of its registered agent.
4. The name and address of each incorporator.

The following *may* be included in the articles:

1. The names and addresses of the individuals who are to serve as the initial directors.
2. The purpose of the corporation.
3. The duration of the corporation.
4. The par value of shares of the corporation.
5. Additional provisions not inconsistent with law for managing the corporation, regulating the internal affairs of the corporation, and establishing the powers of the corporation and its directors and shareholders.

tion, regulating the internal affairs of the corporation, and establishing the powers of the corporation and its directors and shareholders. For example, these additional provisions may contain the procedures for electing directors, the quorum requirements for shareholders' and directors' meetings, and the dividend rights of shareholders.

The MBCA specifies that one or more persons, including corporations, partnerships, and unincorporated associations, may serve as the **incorporators.** Incorporators have no function beyond lending their names and signatures to the process of bringing the corporation into existence. No special liability attaches to a person merely because she serves as an incorporator.

Filing Articles of Incorporation   The articles of incorporation must be delivered to the office of the secretary of state, and a filing fee must be paid. The office of the secretary of state reviews the articles of incorporation that are delivered to it. If the articles contain everything that is required, the secretary of state stamps the articles "Filed" and returns a copy of the stamped articles to the corporation along with a receipt for payment of incorporation fees. Some states require a duplicate filing of the articles with an office—usually the county recorder's office—in the county in which the corporation has its principal place of business.

The existence of the corporation begins when the articles are filed by the secretary of state. Filing of the articles is conclusive proof of the existence of the corporation.

Because the articles of incorporation embody the basic contract between a corporation and its shareholders, shareholders must approve most changes in the articles. For example, when the articles are amended to increase the number of authorized shares, shareholder approval is required.

The Organization Meeting   After the articles of incorporation have been filed by the secretary of state, an organization meeting is held. Usually, it is the first formal meeting of the directors. Frequently, only bylaws are adopted and officers elected. The function of the bylaws is to supplement the articles of incorporation by defining more precisely the powers, rights, and responsibilities of the corporation, its managers, and its shareholders and by stating other rules under which the corporation and its activities will be governed. Its common contents are listed in Figure 2.

FIGURE **2**

Contents of the Bylaws

1. The authority of the officers and the directors, specifying what they may or may not do.
2. The time and place at which the annual shareholders' meetings will be held.
3. The procedure for calling special meetings of shareholders.
4. The procedures for shareholders' and directors' meetings, including whether more than a majority is required for approval of specified actions.
5. Provisions for special committees of the board, defining their membership and the scope of their activities.
6. The procedures for the maintenance of share records.
7. The machinery for the transfer of shares.
8. The procedures and standards for the declaration and payment of dividends.

The MBCA gives the incorporators or the initial directors the power to adopt the initial bylaws. The board of directors holds the power to repeal and to amend the bylaws, unless the articles reserve this power to the shareholders. Under the MBCA, the shareholders, as the ultimate owners of the corporation, always retain the power to amend the bylaws, even if the directors also have such power. To be valid, bylaws must be consistent with the law and with the articles of incorporation.

If the organization meeting is the first meeting of the board of directors, the board may adopt a corporate seal for use on corporate documents, approve the form of share certificates, accept share subscriptions, authorize the issuance of shares, adopt preincorporation contracts, authorize reimbursement for promoters' expenses, and fix the salaries of officers.

Filing Annual Report   To retain its status as a corporation in good standing, a corporation must file an annual report with the secretary of state of the state of incorporation and pay an annual franchise fee or tax. The amount of annual franchise tax varies greatly from state to state. While the annual report includes very little information and repeats information already filed in the articles of incorporation, failure to file an annual report or pay the annual fee or tax may result in a dissolution of the corporation and an imposition of monetary penalties.

Close Corporation Elections

Close corporations face problems that normally do not affect publicly held corporations. In recognition of these problems, nearly half of the states have statutes that attend to the special needs of close corporations. For example, some corporation statutes allow a close corporation to be managed by its shareholders.

To take advantage of these close corporation statutes, most statutes require that a corporation make an *election* to be treated as a close corporation. The Statutory Close Corporation Supplement to the MBCA permits a corporation with *fewer than 50 shareholders* to elect to become a close corporation. The Close Corporation Supplement requires the articles of incorporation to state that the corporation is a statutory close corporation.

There is no penalty for a corporation's failure to make a close corporation election. The only consequence of a failure to meet the requirements is that the close corporation statutory provisions are inapplicable. Instead, statutory corporation law will treat the corporation as it treats any other general corporation.

Note, however, that even when a corporation fails to meet the statutory requirements for treatment as a close corporation, a court may decide to apply special *common law* rules applicable only to close corporations.

DEFECTIVE ATTEMPTS TO INCORPORATE

When business managers attempt to incorporate a business, sometimes they fail to comply with all the conditions for incorporation. For example, the incorporators may not have filed articles of incorporation or the directors may not have held an organization meeting. These are examples of **defective attempts to incorporate.**

One possible consequence of defective incorporation is to make the managers and the purported shareholders *personally liable* for the obligations of the defectively formed corporation. For example, an employee of an insolvent corporation drives the corporation's truck over a pedestrian. If the pedestrian proves that the corporation was defectively formed, he may be able to recover damages for his injuries from the managers and the shareholders.

A second possible consequence of defective incorporation is that a party to a contract involving the purported corporation may claim nonexistence of the corporation in order to avoid a contract made in the name of the corporation. For example, a person makes an ill-advised contract with a corporation. If the person proves that the corporation was defectively formed, he may escape liability on the contract because he made a contract with a nonexistent person, the defectively formed corporation. As an alternative, the defectively formed corporation may escape liability on the contract on the grounds that its nonexistence makes it impossible for it to have liability.

The courts have tried to determine when these two consequences should arise by making a distinction between de jure corporations, de facto corporations, corporations by estoppel, and corporations so defectively formed that they are treated as being nonexistent.

De Jure Corporation

A de jure corporation is formed when the promoters substantially comply with each of the **mandatory conditions precedent** to the incorporation of the business. Mandatory provisions are distinguished from directory provisions by statutory language and the purpose of the provision. Mandatory provisions are those that the corporation statute states "shall" or "must" be done or those that are necessary to protect the public interest. Directory provisions are those that "may" be done and that are unnecessary to protect the public interest.

For example, statutes provide that the incorporators shall file the articles of incorporation with the secretary of state. This is a mandatory provision, due not only to the use of the word *shall* but also to the importance of the filing in protecting the public interest. Other mandatory provisions include conducting an organization meeting. Directory provisions include minor matters such as the inclusion of the incorporators' addresses in the articles of incorporation.

If a corporation has complied with each mandatory provision, it is a de jure corporation and is treated as a corporation for all purposes. The validity of a de jure corporation cannot be attacked, except in a few states in which the state, in a *quo warranto* proceeding, may attack the corporation for noncompliance with a condition subsequent to incorporation, such as a failure to file an annual report with the secretary of state.

De Facto Corporation

A de facto corporation exists when the incorporators fail in some material respect to comply with all of the mandatory provisions of the incorporation statute yet comply with most mandatory provisions. There are three requirements for a de facto corporation:

1. There is a valid statute under which the corporation could be organized.
2. The promoters or managers make an honest attempt to organize under the statute. This requires substantial compliance with the mandatory provisions taken as a whole.
3. The promoters or managers exercise corporate powers. That is, they act as if they were acting for a corporation.

Generally, failing to file the articles of incorporation with the secretary of state will prevent the creation of a de facto corporation. However, a de facto corporation will exist despite the lack of an organization meeting or the failure to make a duplicate filing of the articles with a county recorder.

A de facto corporation is treated as a corporation against either an attack by a third party or an attempt of the business itself to deny that it is a corporation. The state, however, may attack the claimed corporate status of the business in a *quo warranto* action.

Corporation by Estoppel

When people hold themselves out as representing a corporation or believe themselves to be dealing with a corporation, a court will estop those people from denying the existence of a corporation. This is called **corporation by estoppel.** For example, a manager states that a business has been incorporated and induces a third person to contract with the purported corporation. The manager will not be permitted to use a failure to incorporate as a defense to the contract because he has misled others to believe reasonably that a corporation exists.

Under the doctrine of estoppel, each contract must be considered individually to determine whether either party to the contract is estopped from denying the corporation's existence.

Liability for Defective Incorporation

If people attempt to organize a corporation but their efforts are so defective that not even a corporation by estoppel is found to exist, the courts have generally held such persons to be partners with unlimited liability for the contracts and torts of the business. However, most courts impose the unlimited *contractual* liability of a partner only on those who are *actively engaged in the management* of the business or who are responsible for the defects in its organization. *Tort* liability, however, is generally imposed on everyone—the managers and the purported shareholders of the defectively formed corporation.

Modern Approaches to the Defective Incorporation Problem

As you can see, the law of defective incorporation is confusing. It becomes even more confusing when you consider that many of the defective incorporation cases look like promoter liability cases, and vice versa. A court may have difficulty deciding whether to apply the law of promoter liability or the law of defective incorporation to preincorporation contracts. It is not surprising, therefore, that modern corporation statutes have attempted to eliminate this confusion by adopting simple rules for determining the existence of a corporation and the liability of its promoters, managers, and shareholders.

The MBCA states that incorporation occurs when the articles are filed by the secretary of state. The **filing** of the articles is **conclusive proof** of the existence of the corporation, except in a proceeding brought by the state. Consequently, the incorporators may omit even a mandatory provision, yet create a corporation, provided that the secretary of state has filed the articles of incorporation. Conversely, courts have held that a failure to obtain a filing of the articles is conclusive proof of the nonexistence of the corporation, on the grounds that the MBCA eliminates the concepts of de facto corporation and corporation by estoppel.

Figure 3 summarizes the preceding discussion.

Liability for Defective Incorporation under the MBCA The MBCA imposes joint and several liability on those persons who purport to act on

FIGURE   3

Defective Attempts to Incorporate

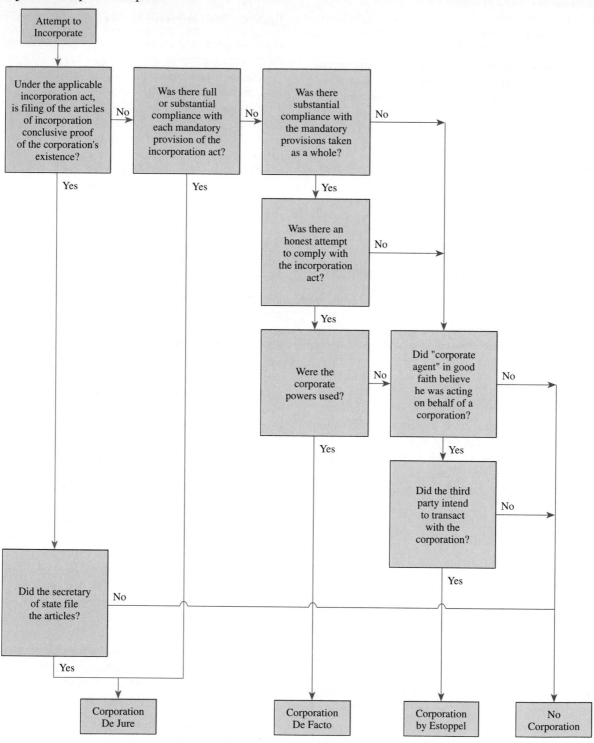

behalf of a corporation and know that there has been no incorporation. Thus, managers and shareholders who both (1) *participate* in the operational decisions of the business and (2) *know* that the corporation does not exist are liable for the purported corporation's contracts and torts.

The MBCA releases from liability shareholders and others who either (1) take no part in the management of the defectively formed corporation *or* (2) mistakenly believe that the corporation is in existence. Consequently, *passive* shareholders have no liability for the obligations of a defectively formed corporation even when they know that the corporation has not been formed. Likewise, managers of a defectively formed corporation have no liability when they believe that the corporation exists.

In the following case, a promoter who mistakenly thought the corporation was in existence was not liable on a preincorporation contract he made on behalf of the corporation.

SIVERS v. R & F CAPITOL CORP. 858 P.2d 895 (Ore. Ct. App. 1995)

Dennis Sivers owned a warehouse in Milwaukee, Oregon. On January 12, 1990, purporting to act on behalf of R & F Capital Corporation in the position of chairman, Roy Rose signed a contract to lease the warehouse from Sivers. R & F was not yet incorporated when Rose signed the lease on behalf of R & F; R & F did not come into existence until February 9, 1990. Later in 1990, R & F breached the lease, and Sivers sued Rose claiming that Rose was personally liable on the lease. Rose asked the trial court for a directed verdict, but the trial court denied Rose's motion. Rose appealed to the Oregon Court of Appeals. ∞

Warren, Judge   Ore. Rev. Stat. 60.054 provides:

All persons purporting to act as or on behalf of a corporation, knowing there was no corporation, are jointly and severally liable for liabilities created while so acting.

This provision was adopted in 1987 as part of SB 303 and is virtually identical to section 2.04 of the Revised Model Business Corporation Act (RMBCA). Section 2.04 is a codification of the judicial exceptions to the general rule that those who prematurely act as, or on behalf of, a corporation are personally liable on all transactions entered into or liabilities incurred before incorporation.

In proposing adoption of section 2.04 of the RMBCA in Oregon, the Task Force of the Oregon State Bar Business Law Section, which authored SB 303, wrote:

The Bill protects participants who act honestly but subject to the mistaken belief that the articles have been filed. This section is consistent with the Revised Uniform Limited Partnership Act, which provides that limited partners who contribute capital to a partnership with a mistaken belief that a limited partnership certificate has been filed are protected from liability.

The wording of Ore. Rev. Stat. 60.054 and the drafters' comments clearly indicate that the test for imposition of personal liability is one of actual knowledge.

Sivers argues that there are facts from which the jury could find that Rose knew that R & F was not incorporated when he signed the lease. We disagree.

Rose testified that he was a businessman who created financing packages to buy companies. His highest net worth at one point was $56 million. He had been involved in setting up many corporations. However, he had no specific experience with incorporating, because his attorneys handled those aspects of his business. For example, he did not know when a corporation formally began its existence, although he understood that documents need to be filed with the state and a copy would be returned upon incorporation.

With respect to R & F, Rose had no participation in its daily operation, other than attending board meetings and signing documents as "chairman." He entrusted Flaherty, a director of R & F, with those daily duties. Rose did not read the articles of incorporation of R & F until he was sued. He recalled that the document was given to him and he signed it in December, 1989.

Rose and another R & F director testified that Flaherty was entrusted to incorporate R & F in December of 1989, but failed to do that. They both believed that R & F was incorporated in December of 1989. Rose also testified that he started investing based on that belief, and that he would not have signed any document on behalf of a corporation if he had known that it was not incorporated.

Sivers does not argue that there is direct evidence that Rose knew that the corporation had not been formed when he signed the lease. To support his argument that there was circumstantial evidence, he points to Rose's vast experience as a businessman, his failure to read the articles of incorporation, and his complete lack of responsibility for filing necessary corporate documents with the Secretary of State. His reliance on those facts is misplaced. At most they show Rose should have inquired into R & F's status and should have known that the corporation was not formed. They do not rise to the level of knowledge required by Ore. Rev. Stat. 60.054. Sivers would have us require a test of constructive knowledge. However, had the legislature intended to adopt such a test, it would not have used the unmodified term "knowing."

A more fundamental argument Sivers raises is that, although Rose testified that he believed that R & F was incorporated at the time he signed the lease, the jury could disbelieve him and affirmatively find that he had the requisite actual knowledge. That argument goes too far. Although a jury may disbelieve a witness based on demeanor, bias, motives, interest, or inconsistent statements, there must be evidence, direct or circumstantial, from which the jury can *reasonably* find that a defendant possesses the requisite knowledge. In this case, Rose maintained throughout the trial that he honestly believed that R & F was incorporated when he signed the lease. Sivers produced nothing to contradict that. The trial court should have granted Rose's motion for a directed verdict.

Judgment reversed in favor of Rose.

INCORPORATION OF NONPROFIT CORPORATIONS

Nonprofit corporations are incorporated in substantially the same manner as for-profit corporations. One or more persons serve as incorporators and deliver articles of incorporation to the secretary of state for filing. A nonprofit corporation's articles must include the name and address of the corporation and state its registered agent. Unlike a for-profit corporation, a nonprofit corporation must state that it is either a public benefit corporation, a mutual benefit corporation, or a religious corporation. A public benefit corporation is incorporated primarily for the benefit of the public—for example, a community arts council that promotes the arts. A mutual benefit corporation is designed to benefit its members—for example, a golf country club. An example of a religious corporation is a church.

A nonprofit corporation's articles must also state whether it will have members. While it is typical for nonprofit corporations to have members, the Model Nonprofit Corporation Act (MNCA) does not require a nonprofit corporation to have members. An example of a nonprofit corporation having no members is a public benefit corporation established to promote business development in a city, whose directors are appointed by the city's mayor.

A nonprofit corporation's articles may include the purpose of the corporation, its initial directors, and any matter regarding the rights and duties of the corporation and its directors and members. Each incorporator and director named in the articles must sign the articles.

A nonprofit corporation's existence begins when the secretary of state files the articles. After incorporation, the initial directors or incorporators hold an organization meeting to adopt bylaws and conduct other business.

Liability for Preincorporation Transactions

Nonprofit corporation status normally protects the members and managers from personal liability. However, when a nonprofit corporation is not formed or is defectively formed, promoters and others who transact for the nonexistent nonprofit corporation have the same liability as promoters and others who transact for a nonexistent for-profit corporation. The MNCA states the same rule as the MBCA: Persons who act on behalf of a corporation knowing there is no corporation are jointly and severally liable for all liabilities created while so acting.

Similarly, promoters have no authority to make contracts for a nonexistent nonprofit corporation.

The corporation becomes liable on preincorporation contracts when its board of directors adopts the contracts.

FINANCING FOR–PROFIT CORPORATIONS

Any business needs money to operate and to grow. One advantage of incorporation is the large number of sources of funds that are available to businesses that incorporate. One such source is the sale of corporate **securities,** including shares, debentures, bonds, and long-term notes payable.

In addition to obtaining funds from the sale of securities, a corporation may be financed by other sources. A bank may lend money to the corporation in exchange for the corporation's short-term promissory notes, called commercial paper. Earnings provide a source of funds once the corporation is operating profitably. In addition, the corporation may use normal short-term financing, such as accounts receivable financing and inventory financing.

In this section, you will study only one source of corporate funds—a corporation's sale of securities. A corporate security may be either (1) a share in the corporation or (2) an obligation of the corporation. These two kinds of securities are called equity securities and debt securities.

Equity Securities

Every business corporation issues equity securities, which are commonly called stock or **shares.** The issuance of shares creates an ownership relationship: the holders of the shares—called stockholders or **shareholders**—are the owners of the corporation.

Modern statutes permit corporations to issue several classes of shares and to determine the rights of the various classes. Subject to minimum guarantees contained in the state business corporation law, the shareholders' rights are a matter of contract and appear in the articles of incorporation, in the bylaws, in a shareholder agreement, and on the share certificates.

Common Shares   Common shares (or common stock) are a type of equity security. Ordinarily, the owners of common shares—called **common shareholders**—have the exclusive right to elect the directors, who manage the corporation.

The common shareholders often occupy a position inferior to that of other investors, notably creditors and preferred shareholders. The claims of common shareholders are subordinate to the claims of creditors and other classes of shareholders when liabilities and dividends are paid and when assets are distributed upon liquidation.

In return for this subordination, however, the common shareholders have an exclusive claim to the corporate earnings and assets that exceed the claims of creditors and other shareholders. Therefore, the common shareholders bear the major risks of the corporate venture, yet stand to profit the most if it is successful.

Preferred Shares   Shares that have preferences with regard to assets or dividends over other classes of shares are called preferred shares (or preferred stock). **Preferred shareholders** are customarily given liquidation and dividend preferences over common shareholders. A corporation may have several classes of preferred shares. In such a situation, one class of preferred shares may be given preferences over another class of preferred shares. Under the MBCA, the preferences of preferred shareholders must be set out in the articles of incorporation.

The **liquidation preference** of preferred shares is usually a stated dollar amount. During a liquidation, this amount must be paid to each preferred shareholder before any common shareholder or other shareholder subordinated to the preferred class may receive his share of the corporation's assets.

Dividend preferences may vary greatly. For example, the dividends may be cumulative or noncumulative. Dividends on **cumulative** preferred shares, if not paid in any year, accumulate until paid. The entire accumulation must be paid before any dividends may be paid to common shareholders. Dividends on **noncumulative** preferred shares do not accumulate if unpaid. For such shares, only the current year's dividends must be paid to preferred shareholders prior to the payment of dividends to common shareholders.

Participating preferred shares have priority up to a stated amount or percentage of the dividends to be paid by the corporation. Then, the preferred shareholders participate with the common shareholders in additional dividends paid.

Some close corporations attempt to create preferred shares with a **mandatory dividend** right. These mandatory dividend provisions have generally been held illegal as unduly restricting the powers of the board of directors. Today, a few courts and some special close corporation statutes permit mandatory dividends.

A **redemption** provision in the articles allows a corporation at its option to repurchase preferred shareholders' shares at a price stated in the articles, despite the shareholders' unwillingness to sell. Some statutes permit the articles to give the shareholders the right to force the corporation to redeem preferred shares.

Preferred shares may be **convertible** into another class of shares, usually common shares. A **conversion** right allows a preferred shareholder to exchange her preferred shares for another class of shares, usually common shares. The conversion rate or price is stated in the articles.

Preferred shares have **voting rights** unless the articles provide otherwise. Usually, most voting rights are taken from preferred shares, except for important matters such as voting for a merger or a change in preferred shareholders' dividend rights. Rarely are preferred shareholders given the right to vote for directors, except in the event of a corporation's default in the payment of dividends.

Authorized, Issued, and Outstanding Shares

Authorized shares are shares that a corporation is permitted to issue by its articles of incorporation. A corporation may not issue more shares than are authorized. **Issued** shares are shares that have been sold to shareholders. **Outstanding** shares are shares that are currently held by shareholders. The distinctions between these terms are important. For example, a corporation pays cash, property, and share dividends only on outstanding shares. Only outstanding shares may be voted at a shareholders' meeting.

Canceled Shares Sometimes, a corporation will purchase its own shares. A corporation may cancel repurchased shares. Canceled shares do not exist: they are neither authorized, issued, nor outstanding. Since canceled shares do not exist, they cannot be reissued.

Shares Restored to Unissued Status Repurchased shares may be restored to unissued status instead of being canceled. If this is done, the shares are merely authorized and they may be reissued at a later time.

Treasury Shares If repurchased shares are neither canceled nor restored to unissued status, they are called **treasury shares.** Such shares are authorized and issued, but not outstanding. They may be sold by the corporation at a later time. The corporation may not vote them at shareholders' meetings, and it may not pay a cash or property dividend on them.

The MBCA abolishes the concept of treasury shares. It provides that repurchased shares are restored to unissued status and may be reissued, unless the articles of incorporation require cancellation.

Options, Warrants, and Rights

Equity securities include options to purchase common shares and preferred shares. The MBCA expressly permits the board of directors to issue **options** for the purchase of the corporation's shares. Share options are often issued to top-level managers as an incentive to increase the profitability of the corporation. An increase in profitability should increase the market value of the corporation's shares, resulting in increased compensation to the employees who own and exercise share options.

Warrants are options evidenced by certificates. They are sometimes part of a package of securities sold as a unit. For example, they may be sold along with notes, bonds, or even shares. Underwriters may receive warrants as part of their compensation for aiding a corporation in selling its shares to the public.

Rights are short-term certificated options that are usually transferable. Rights are used to give present security holders an option to subscribe to a proportional quantity of the same or a different security of the corporation. They are most often issued in connection with a **preemptive right** requirement, which obligates a corporation to offer each existing shareholder the opportunity to buy the corporation's newly issued shares in the same proportion as the shareholder's current ownership of the corporation's shares.

Debt Securities

Corporations have inherent power to borrow money necessary for their operations by issuing debt securities. Debt securities create a debtor-creditor relationship between the corporation and the security holder. With the typical debt security, the corporation is obligated to pay interest periodically and to pay the amount of the debt (the principal) on the maturity date. Debt securities include debentures, bonds, and notes payable.

Debentures are long-term, unsecured debt securities. Typically, a debenture has a term of 10 to 30 years. Debentures usually have indentures. An indenture is a contract that states the rights of the debenture holders. For example, an indenture defines what acts constitute default by the corporation and what rights the debenture holders have upon default. It may place restrictions on the corporation's right to issue other debt securities.

Bonds are long-term, secured debt securities that usually have indentures. They are identical to debentures except that bonds are secured by collateral. The collateral for bonds may be real property such as a building, or personal property such as a commercial airplane. If the debt is not paid, the bondholders may force the sale of the collateral and take the proceeds of the sale.

Generally, **notes** have a shorter duration than debentures or bonds. They seldom have terms exceeding five years. Notes may be secured or unsecured.

It is not uncommon for notes or debentures to be **convertible** into other securities, usually preferred or common shares. The right to convert belongs to the holder of the convertible note or debenture. This conversion right permits an investor to receive interest as a debt holder and, after conversion, to share in the increased value of the corporation as a shareholder.

CONSIDERATION FOR SHARES

The board of directors has the power to issue shares on behalf of the corporation. The board must decide at what *price* and for what *type of consideration* it will issue the shares. Corporation statutes restrict the discretion of the board in accepting specified kinds of consideration and in determining the value of the shares it issues.

Quality of Consideration for Shares

Not all kinds of consideration in contract law are acceptable as legal consideration for shares in corporation law. To protect creditors and other share-holders, the statutes require legal consideration to have *real value*. Modern statutes, however, place few limits on the type of consideration that may be received for shares. The MBCA permits shares to be issued in return for any tangible or intangible *property* or *benefit to the corporation,* including cash, promissory notes, services performed for the corporation, contracts for services *to be performed* for the corporation, and securities of the corporation or another corporation. The rationale for the MBCA rule is a recognition that future services and promises of future services have value that is as real as that of tangible property. Consequently, for example, a corporation may issue common shares to its president in exchange for the president's commitment to work for the corporation for three years or in exchange for bonds of the corporation or debentures issued by another corporation. In addition, the MBCA permits corporations to issue shares to their promoters in consideration for their promoters' pre-incorporation services. This rule acknowledges that a corporation benefits from a promoter's preincorporation services.

Several states' constitutions place stricter limits on permissible consideration for shares. They provide that shares may be issued only for money paid to the corporation, labor done for the corporation, or property actually received by the corporation. Such a rule prohibits a corporation from issuing its shares for a promise to pay money or a promise to provide services to the corporation in the future.

Quantity of Consideration for Shares

The board is required to issue shares for an adequate dollar amount of consideration. Whether shares have been issued for an adequate amount of consideration depends in part on the *par value* of the shares. The more important concern, however, is whether the shares have been issued for *fair value*.

Par Value   Par value is an arbitrary dollar amount that may be assigned to the shares by the articles of incorporation. Par value does not reflect the fair market value of the shares, but par value is the minimum amount of consideration for which the shares may be issued.

Shares issued for less than par value are called **discount shares.** The board of directors is liable to the corporation for issuing shares for less than par value. A shareholder who purchases shares from the corporation for less than par value is liable to the corporation for the difference between the par value and the amount she paid.

Fair Value   It is not always enough, however, for the board to issue shares for their par value. Many times, shares are worth more than their par value. In addition, many shares today do not have a par value. In fact, the MBCA purports to eliminate the concept of par value as it affects the issuance of shares. In all cases, the board must exercise care to ensure that the corporation receives the *fair value* of the shares it issues. If there are no par value problems, the board's judgment as to the amount of consideration that is received for the shares is *conclusive* when the board acts in good faith, exercises the care of ordinarily prudent directors, and acts in the best interests of the corporation.

Disputes may arise concerning the value of property that the corporation receives for its shares. The board's valuation of the consideration is conclusive if it acts in good faith with the care of prudent directors and in a manner it reasonably believes to be in the best interests of the corporation. When the board impermissibly overvalues the consideration for shares, the shareholder receives **watered shares.** Both the board and the shareholder are liable to the corporation when there is a watered shares problem.

When a shareholder pays less than the amount of consideration determined by the board of directors, the corporation or its creditors may sue the shareholder to recover the deficit. When a shareholder has paid the proper amount of consideration, the shares are said to be *fully paid and nonassessable.*

In the following case, the court held that shares were validly issued for services rendered to the corporation.

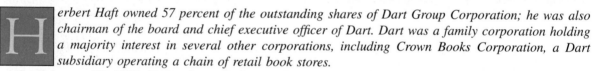

HAFT v. DART GROUP CORP.   841 F.Supp. 549 (D. Del. 1993)

Herbert Haft owned 57 percent of the outstanding shares of Dart Group Corporation; he was also chairman of the board and chief executive officer of Dart. Dart was a family corporation holding a majority interest in several other corporations, including Crown Books Corporation, a Dart subsidiary operating a chain of retail book stores.

On February 28, 1987, Herbert's son Robert Haft assumed the positions of president and chief executive officer of Crown. For the following two years, Robert Haft served as president and CEO. On June 7, 1989, Crown's board of directors authorized the issuance of 100,000 common shares to Robert Haft for a total price of $203,750. The terms of the issuance were contained in an incentive stock agreement, and the issuance was effected on August 30, 1989. The incentive stock agreement acknowledged payment by Robert Haft "in sum of $203,750, in the form of an unsecured, non-interest bearing promissory note due January 2, 2004, in full payment of the shares." Crown issued Stock Certificate No. 5464 to Robert Haft, representing 100,000 shares of Crown common stock.

In 1993, relations between Herbert and Robert Haft soured when a Wall Street Journal article, based on an interview with Robert Haft, referred to Robert Haft as "de facto chief executive" of Dart. Herbert resolved to oust Robert from his positions as president and CEO of Crown. On June 30, 1993, Robert Haft was removed as president and CEO of Crown; Herbert Haft was elected in his place. On August 4, Crown sought to cancel Robert Haft's purchase of the 100,000 common shares on the grounds that Robert Haft did not pay legal consideration for the shares. Robert Haft then sued Dart and Crown for breach of the incentive stock agreement. The trial court considered whether Robert Haft had paid legal consideration for the shares.

Schwartz, District Judge   Article IX of the Delaware Constitution requires certain types of consideration for stock: "No corporation shall issue stock, except for money paid, labor done or personal property, or real estate or leases thereof actually acquired by such corporation."

The Incentive Stock Agreement between Crown and Haft provides that "the Corporation hereby acknowledges payment by Haft of the sum of $203,750, in the form of a non-interest bearing promissory note due January 2, 2004 in full payment of the Shares." Crown notes that, in Delaware, "a promissory note, being a mere unsecured promise to pay, is not property actually acquired by the corporation" and thus not valid consideration. That Haft tendered such a note, however, does not end the inquiry. Haft alleges other, potentially valid forms of consideration which may be sufficient to support the stock issuance by themselves. The question becomes, then, whether Haft's past services can constitute valid consideration for the issuance of his shares under the agreement.

A corporation may compensate its officers and agents for services rendered. Such compensation may include stock option, stock incentive, and other compensation plans. In addition, the General Corporation Law confers broad discretion upon a corporation, through its directors, when it contracts to issue stock, stock options, and other rights in stock. Most significantly, in the absence of actual fraud in the transaction, the judgment of the directors as to the value of such consideration shall be conclusive.

The Incentive Stock Agreement provides for the issuance of shares "in recognition of Robert M. Haft's contribution to the Corporation," in other words, in recognition of his past services rendered.

Past services constitute valid consideration as "labor done." Haft had performed some services for Crown prior to the issuance of his shares. Because this consideration exists, the judgment of Crown's directors as to its value is conclusive in the absence of actual fraud. In order to establish actual fraud, however, Crown must make two showings: first, Crown must offer evidence of "gross overvaluation," which would establish constructive fraud; and second, Crown must allege other facts which, considered in connection with the "gross overvaluation," may be grounds for inferring actual fraud. A showing of no more than excessive valuation is insufficient to overcome the conclusiveness of the directors' judgment.

Crown, asserting the defense of lack of consideration, bears the burden of proving that defense. Crown has neither pleaded facts nor placed any evidence in the record which would suggest actual fraud in the formation of the Incentive Stock Agreement. Summary judgment on the applicability of this defense must therefore be granted Haft.

Motion for summary judgment granted to Haft.

Accounting for Consideration Received The consideration received by a corporation for its equity securities appears in the equity or capital accounts in the shareholders' equity section of the corporation's balance sheet. The **stated capital** account records the product of the number of shares outstanding multiplied by the par value of each share. When the shares are sold for more than par value, the excess or surplus consideration received by the corporation is **capital surplus.**

Under the MBCA, the terms *stated capital* and *capital surplus* have been eliminated. All consideration received for shares is lumped under one accounting entry for that class of shares, such as common equity.

Resales of Shares The par value of shares is important *only when the shares are issued* by the corporation. Since treasury shares are issued but not outstanding, the corporation does not issue treasury shares when it resells them. Therefore, the board may sell treasury shares for less than par, provided that it sells the shares for an amount equal to their fair value.

Because par value and fair value are designed to ensure only that the corporation receives adequate consideration for its shares, a shareholder may buy shares from another shareholder for less than par value or fair value and incur no liability. However, if the purchasing shareholder *knows* that the selling shareholder bought the shares from the corporation for less than par value, the purchasing shareholder is liable to the corporation for the difference between the par value and the amount paid by the selling shareholder.

SHARE SUBSCRIPTIONS

Under the terms of a **share subscription,** a prospective shareholder promises to buy a specific number of shares of a corporation at a stated price. If the subscription is accepted by the corporation and the subscriber has paid for the shares, the subscriber is a shareholder of the corporation, even if the shares have not been issued. Under the MBCA, subscriptions need not be in writing to be enforceable. Usually, however, subscriptions are written.

Promoters use written share subscriptions in the course of selling shares of a proposed corporation to ensure that equity capital will be provided once the corporation comes into existence. These are called **preincorporation subscriptions,** which were covered in this chapter's discussion of promoters. Preincorporation subscriptions are not contracts binding on the corporation and the shareholders until the corporation comes into existence and its board of directors accepts the share subscriptions.

Close corporations may use share subscriptions when they seek to sell additional shares after incorporation. These are examples of **postincorporation subscriptions,** subscription agreements made *after* incorporation. A postincorporation subscription is a contract between the corporation and the subscriber at the time the subscription agreement is made.

A subscription may provide for payment of the price of the shares on a specified day, in installments, or upon the demand of the board of directors. The board may not discriminate when it demands payment: It must demand payment from all the subscribers of a class of shares or from none of them.

A share certificate may not be issued to a share subscriber until the price of the shares has been fully paid. If the subscriber fails to pay as agreed, the corporation may sue the subscriber for the amount owed.

ISSUANCE OF SHARES

Uniform Commercial Code (UCC) Article 8 regulates the issuance of securities. Under Article 8, a corporation has a duty to issue only the number of shares authorized by its articles. Overissued shares are void.

When a person is entitled to overissued shares, the corporation may not issue the shares. However, the person has two remedies. The corporation must obtain identical shares and deliver them to the person entitled to issuance or the corporation must reimburse the person for the value paid for the shares plus interest.

The directors may incur liability, including criminal liability, for an overissuance of shares. To prevent overissuance through error in the issuance or transfer of their shares, corporations often employ a bank or a trust company as a registrar.

A share certificate is evidence that a person has been issued shares, owns the shares, and is a share-

holder. The certificate states the corporation's name, the shareholder's name, and the number and class of shares. A person can be a shareholder without receiving a share certificate, such as a holder of a share subscription. Under the MBCA, a corporation is not required to issue share certificates.

TRANSFER OF SHARES

Because share certificates are evidence of the ownership of shares, their transfer is evidence of the transfer of the ownership of shares. UCC Article 8 covers the registration and transfer of shares, as represented by certificates.

Share certificates are issued in *registered* form; that is, they are registered with the corporation in the name of a specific person. The indorsement of a share certificate on its back by its registered owner and the delivery of the certificate to another person transfers ownership of the shares to the other person. The transfer of a share certificate without naming a transferee creates a *street certificate.* The transfer of a street certificate may be made by delivery without indorsement. Any holder of a street certificate is presumed to be the owner of the shares it represents. Therefore, a transferee should ask the corporation to reregister the shares in his name.

Under the UCC, a corporation owes a duty to register the transfer of any registered shares presented to it for registration, provided that the shares have been properly indorsed. If the corporation refuses to make the transfer, it is liable to the transferee for either conversion or specific performance.

When an owner of shares claims that his certificate has been lost, destroyed, or stolen, the corporation must issue a new certificate to the owner if the corporation has not received notice that the shares have been acquired by a bona fide purchaser, the owner files with the corporation a sufficient indemnity bond, and the owner meets any other reasonable requirements of the corporation. A **bona fide purchaser** is a purchaser of the shares for value in good faith with no notice of any adverse claim against the shares.

If, after the issuance of the new certified shares, a bona fide purchaser of the original shares presents them for registration, the corporation must register the transfer, unless overissuance would result. In addition, the corporation may recover the new certified shares from the original owner.

Restrictions on Transferability of Shares

Historically, a shareholder has been free to sell her shares to whomever she wants whenever she wants. The courts have been reluctant to allow restrictions on the free transferability of shares, even if the shareholder agreed to a restriction on the transfer of her shares. Gradually, the courts and the legislatures have recognized that there are good reasons to permit the use of some restrictions on the transfer of shares. Today, modern corporation statutes allow most transfer restrictions, especially for close corporations.

Types of Restrictions on Transfer   There are four categories of transfer restrictions that may be used to accomplish the objectives addressed above: (1) rights of first refusal and option agreements, (2) buy-and-sell agreements, (3) consent restraints, and (4) provisions disqualifying purchasers.

A **right of first refusal** grants to the corporation or the other shareholders the right to match the offer that a selling shareholder receives for her shares. An **option agreement** grants the corporation or the other shareholders an option to buy the selling shareholder's shares at a price determined by the agreement. An option agreement will usually state a formula used to calculate the price of the shares.

A **buy-and-sell agreement** compels a shareholder to sell his shares to the corporation or to the other shareholders at the price stated in the agreement. It also obligates the corporation or the other shareholders to buy the selling shareholder's shares at that price. The price of the shares is usually determined by a stated formula.

A **consent restraint** requires a selling shareholder to obtain the consent of the corporation or the other shareholders before she may sell her shares. A **provision disqualifying purchasers** may be used in rare situations to exclude unwanted persons from the corporation. For example, a transfer restriction may prohibit the shareholders from selling to a competitor of the business.

Uses of Transfer Restrictions   A corporation and its shareholders may use transfer restrictions to maintain the balance of shareholder power in the corporation. For example, four persons may own 25 shares each in a corporation. No single person can control such a corporation. If one of the four can buy 26 additional shares from the other shareholders, he will acquire control. The shareholders may

therefore agree that each shareholder is entitled or required to buy an equal amount of any shares sold by any selling shareholder. The right of first refusal, option agreement, or buy-and-sell agreement may serve this purpose.

A buy-and-sell agreement may be used to guarantee a shareholder a market for his shares. For example, in a close corporation, there may be no ready market for the shares of the corporation. To ensure that a shareholder can obtain the value of her investment upon her retirement or death, the shareholders or the corporation may be required to buy a shareholder's shares upon the occurrence of a specific event such as death or retirement.

A buy-and-sell agreement may also be used to determine who should be required to sell and who should be required to buy shares when there is a severe disagreement between shareholders that threatens the profitability of the corporation.

In a close corporation, the shareholders may want only themselves or other approved persons as shareholders. A buy-and-sell agreement or right of first refusal may be used to prevent unwanted persons from becoming shareholders.

A provision disqualifying purchasers may be used in limited situations, such as when the purchaser is a competitor of the business or has a criminal background.

A consent restraint is used to preserve a close corporation or Subchapter S taxation election. Close corporation statutes and Subchapter S of the Internal Revenue Code limit the number of shareholders that a close corporation or S Corporation may have. A transfer restriction may prohibit the shareholders from selling shares if, as a result of the sale, there would be too many shareholders to preserve a close corporation or S Corporation election. A consent restraint is also used to preserve an exemption from registration of a securities offering. Under the Securities Act of 1933 and the state securities acts, an offering of securities is exempt from registration if the offering is to a limited number of investors, usually 35. A transfer restriction may require a selling shareholder to obtain permission from the corporation's legal counsel, which permission will be granted upon proof that the shareholder's sale of the shares does not cause the corporation to lose its registration exemption.

Legality of Transfer Restrictions   Corporation statutes permit the use of option agreements, rights of first refusal, and buy-and-sell agreements with virtually no restrictions. The MBCA authorizes transfer restrictions for any reasonable purpose. The reasonableness of a restraint is judged in light of the character and needs of the corporation.

Consent restraints and provisions disqualifying purchasers may be used if they are not *manifestly unreasonable*. The MBCA makes per se reasonable any consent restraint that maintains a corporation's status when that status is dependent on the number or identity of shareholders, as with close corporation or S Corporation status. The MBCA also makes per se reasonable any restriction that preserves registration exemptions under the Securities Act of 1933 and state securities laws.

Enforceability To be enforceable against a shareholder, a transfer restriction must be contained in the articles of incorporation, the bylaws, an agreement among the shareholders, or an agreement between the corporation and the shareholders. In addition, the shareholder must either agree to the restriction or purchase the shares with notice of the restriction. Under the MBCA, a purchaser of the shares has notice of a restriction if it is noted conspicuously on the face or the back of a share certificate or if it is a restriction of which he has knowledge.

In the following case, the court considered whether a right of first refusal was invoked by the corporation's decision to sell all its assets and to dissolve.

STUFFT v. STUFFT   916 P.2d 104 (Mont. Sup. Ct. 1996)

Stufft Farms, Inc., was a Montana corporation that owned and operated a family farm. Esther Stufft owned 17,077 shares of the corporation, Carmen Stufft 17,018 shares, Carol Stufft Larson 20 shares, Dorene Stufft Badgett 20 shares, and David Stufft 20 shares. To maintain control of the corporation in the hands of the Stufft family, the bylaws of the corporation included a right of first refusal share transfer restriction. Article XII, entitled Restrictions on Transfer of Shares, reads in relevant part:

No shareholder shall have the right or power to pledge, sell or otherwise dispose of, except by will, any share or shares of this company, without first offering the said share or shares for sale to the company and shareholders at the then book value.

On December 27, 1994, the board of directors of Stufft Farms adopted a resolution to dissolve and liquidate the corporation. Neil Johnson emerged as a possible purchaser of the corporation's assets, but tax considerations caused the shareholders to consider selling their shares instead of the corporation's assets. On February 24, 1995, Johnson offered to buy all of Stufft Farms's shares; the offer was contingent on all shareholders selling their shares to Johnson. All the shareholders, except David Stufft, agreed to accept Johnson's offer. On March 9, 1995, David Stufft attempted to invoke Article XII of the bylaws and to exercise his right of first refusal to buy the other shareholders' shares. David Stufft argued that the other shareholders' offer to sell their stock to Johnson triggered Article XII, giving him a right of first refusal to purchase their stock at book value. The other shareholders refused David Stufft's demand to sell to them at book value, and instead, they offered to sell their shares to David Stufft at the same price Johnson offered. David Stufft rejected their offer, and the other shareholders elected not to sell their shares to anyone. On March 27, 1995, the board of directors approved the sale of Stufft Farms's assets to Johnson. David Stufft sued the other shareholders and Stufft Farms to void the asset sale to Johnson on the grounds that his rights under Article XII made him the equitable owner of all the shares. He argued that only he should have been entitled to vote all the shares of stock and, therefore, the agreement to sell the corporation's assets to Johnson was void. The district court dismissed David Stufft's suit, and he appealed to the Supreme Court of Montana. ∞

Turnage, Chief Justice David Stufft argues that his right of first refusal was triggered by the other stockholders' acceptance of Johnson's February 24, 1995, offer to purchase all of the corporation's

outstanding stock, and again by the March 10, 1995 offer of the majority stockholders to sell their stock to him at the price at which the stock had been offered to Johnson, a price not shown or claimed to be book value. He maintains that the right of first refusal is triggered by a willingness, a desire, or an attempt by stockholders to dispose of their stock, citing *Weintz v. Bumgarner* (Mont. Sup. Ct. 1967).

A critical distinction between *Weintz* and the present case is that in *Weintz,* not only was there a willingness to sell on the part of the property owners, but actual agreements were reached to sell the various interests in the subject property. In the present case, no agreements were reached to sell the stock at issue.

Johnson's offer to purchase the stock in Stufft Farms, Inc., was an offer to purchase *all* of the stock in the corporation. Johnson's offer was not accepted by shareholder David Stufft. Because of the contingent nature of Johnson's offer, when Stufft elected not to sell, Johnson's offer to buy was withdrawn. Therefore, no agreement was reached. The corporation did not accept Johnson's offer.

Similarly, the other shareholders' March 10 offer to sell stock to David Stufft on the same terms as those offered by Johnson was counteroffer to David Stufft's March 9 offer to purchase the stock at book value. David Stufft's offer was not accepted. The counteroffer was not accepted.

Stufft's right of first refusal to purchase Stufft Farms, Inc., stock was not triggered, because the other shareholders did not "pledge, sell or otherwise dispose of" their shares of stock. The other stockholders still own their stock in the corporation.

Stufft also contends that the other shareholders and Johnson are attempting to circumvent his right of first refusal. The District Court noted:

The court is very aware of the purpose of corporate restrictive stock transfer bylaws and in particular those of a closely held family corporation. The purpose of such restrictions is to facilitate keeping the corporation closely held and to restrict the transfer of stock beyond family members. Such restrictive agreements and bylaws are specifically allowed under Montana law. However, neither the state statute nor restrictive agreements were intended to prohibit liquidation of a corporation and the sale of its assets.

We agree. The wording of Article XII does not suggest that it applies to an intended sale of the entire corporation or its assets. We conclude that David Stufft's right of first refusal was not violated.

Judgment for the other shareholders affirmed.

Statutory Solution to Close Corporation Share Transfer Problems   Although transfer restrictions are important to close corporations, many close corporation shareholders fail to address the share transferability problem. Therefore, a few states provide statutory resolution of the close corporation transferability problem. In these states, statutes offer solutions to the transferability problem that are similar to the solutions that the shareholders would have provided had they thought about the problem. Not all transferability problems are settled by the Close Corporation Supplement, however. For example, there is no statutory buy-and-sell provision.

FINANCING NONPROFIT CORPORATIONS

Nonprofit corporations are financed differently from for-profit corporations. This is especially true of a public benefit corporation such as a public television station, which obtains annual financing from government sources, private foundations, members, and public contributors. A religious corporation such as a church received weekly offerings from its congregation and may occasionally conduct capital drives to obtain additional funding from its members. A mutual benefit corporation, such as a fraternal or social organization like an Elks Club or golf country club, obtains initial funding from its original members to build facilities and assesses its members annually and monthly to pay operating expenses. In addition, nonprofit corporations have the power to obtain debt financing, such as borrowing from a bank or issuing notes and debentures.

A nonprofit corporation may admit members whether or not they pay consideration for their membership. There is no statutory limit on the number of members a nonprofit corporation may admit, although the articles may place a limit on the number of members. Social clubs typically limit the number of members. Members must be admitted in compliance with procedures stated in the articles or the bylaws.

Generally, memberships in a nonpublic corporation are not freely transferable. No member of a public benefit corporation or religious corporation may transfer her membership or any rights she possesses as a member. A member of a mutual benefit corporation may transfer her membership and rights only if the articles or bylaws permit. When transfer rights are permitted, restrictions on transfer are valid only if approved by the members, including the affected member.

ETHICAL AND PUBLIC POLICY CONCERNS

1. Suppose that a promoter of a prospective business, Promoter 1, chooses to incorporate the business prior to making any contracts for the prospective business. Because incorporation is a fairly simple process, Promoter 1 has done little more than Promoter 2, who makes preincorporation contracts. Yet Promoter 1 will not ordinarily have liability on contracts signed in the name of the corporation, while Promoter 2 will have liability. Does this distinction seem fair to both promoters? Is it fair to other parties to the contract? Would your answers change if Promoter 1 incorporated the business with the minimum amount of capital required by the incorporation statute and then negotiated contracts obligating the business in amounts exceeding $100,000?

2. Under the Model Business Corporation Act, investors who believe that they have contributed capital to a corporation have no personal liability for the debts of the corporation even if it has been defectively formed. Why should such investors not be held liable as partners? Is it fair that the defectively formed corporation's creditors cannot sue the investors? Should it matter whether the investors are involved in the operation of the defectively formed corporation? Should it matter whether the creditors believed there was no corporation and thought the investors were partners? Should it matter whether the creditors are contract creditors (who could have checked into the status of the corporation and its investors prior to contracting with the business) or tort creditors (who have little ability to investigate the corporation and its investors prior to being injured by the person acting on behalf of the defectively formed corporation)?

3. Why should the law impose limits on the use of share transfer restrictions? Who may be harmed if there are no legal limits? Is it possible for those who would be harmed to be protected in ways other than by limiting the use of share transfer restrictions?

PROBLEMS AND PROBLEM CASES

1. RKO-Stanley Warner Theatres, Inc., contracted to sell a theater to Jack Jenofsky and Ralph Graziano, who were in the process of forming a corporation to be known as Kent Enterprises, Inc. The contract included the following, added by Jenofsky and Graziano's lawyer:

It is understood by the parties hereto that it is the intention of the Purchaser to incorporate. Upon condition that such incorporation be completed by the closing date, all agreements contained herein shall be construed to have been made between Seller and the resultant corporation.

Subsequently, Kent Enterprises, Inc., was incorporated. A final closing date was set, but the sale was never completed. RKO sued Jenofsky and Graziano on the contract. Jenofsky claimed that the quoted provision in the contract released him from any personal liability. Was he correct?

2. Garry Fox met with Coopers & Lybrand to request a tax opinion and other accounting services. Fox told Coopers that he was acting on behalf of a corporation that he was in the process of forming, to be named G. Fox and Partners, Inc. Coopers knew that the corporation was not in existence. Fox and Coopers had no agreement regarding Fox's personal liability for payment of the fee for the services. G. Fox and Partners, Inc., was incorporated, and a few weeks later Coopers completed its work. The corporation did not pay for the work, so Coopers sued Fox. Is Fox liable to Coopers?

3. Stuart Lakes Club, Inc., a New York corporation, was a private game club owning 75 acres of land, two lakes, and a clubhouse. The board of directors adopted a bylaw provision that stated, "When any member ceases to be a member of the Club, either by death, resignation, or otherwise, his share shall be considered void and the certificate returned to the Treasurer for cancellation." The purpose of the bylaw provision was to make the last surviving member of the club its sole owner and therefore the beneficial owner of the club's valuable land and clubhouse. Has the board of directors adopted an enforceable bylaw?

4. Warthan and Knettel owned an insurance agency in St. Cloud, Minnesota. Koltes, McMahill, and Ketlin owned an insurance agency in Minnetonka, Minnesota. They agreed to transfer their businesses to a newly formed corporation, to be named Midwest Consolidated Insurance Agencies, Inc. (MCIA), equally owned by the St. Cloud and the Minnetonka groups. Articles of incorporation for MCIA were filed with the Minnesota secretary of state. The two groups had difficulties combining their operations. No shares of stock were issued, no formal shareholder or directors meetings were held. Although bylaws were drafted, they were never approved. Has MCIA's existence begun?

5. Eugene Levy agreed to buy a retail record business from Martin Robertson. Levy submitted for filing the articles of incorporation for Record Shack, Inc., but they were rejected by the secretary of state. Six days later, Robertson sold the assets of the business to the Record Shack and received a promissory note for the purchase price signed "Penn Ave. Record Shack, Inc., by Eugene M. Levy, President." Subsequently, Levy resubmitted the articles, and a certificate of incorporation of Penn Ave. Record Shack, Inc., was issued. Robertson accepted one payment on the promissory note from the corporation, but within six months, Record Shack ceased doing business; no assets remained. Robertson sued Levy for the balance of the promissory note. Was Levy liable on the promissory note?

6. Dale Frey intended to develop a 33-acre apartment complex, to be operated by Mt. Carmel Apartments, Inc., a corporation not yet formed. To promote and develop the complex, Frey contracted with Jess Burge. Their agreement provided that Burge would receive $70,000 payable in 12.5 percent of the shares of the corporation. Subsequently, Burge consulted with architects, calculated construction costs, executed a loan application, and consulted with prospective contractors on behalf of the complex. After incorporation of Mt. Carmel Apartments, Inc., the board of directors accepted the agreement between Frey and Burge, placed a $70,000 value on his services performed prior to incorporation, and issued 12.5 percent of the corporation's shares to Burge. After a dispute arose between Burge and the corporation, Frey claimed

that the corporation acted wrongly by issuing the shares to Burge. Was Frey correct?

7. Kirk's Auto Electric, Inc., issued 11 shares of common stock to Billy Bone, 10 shares to Andre Bone, and 5 shares to Joe Bone. In exchange, the Bones gave the corporation unsecured interest-bearing promissory notes payable on demand. No payments were ever made on the notes. Have the Bones paid proper consideration for the shares?

8. John Gazda, Anthony Kolinski, and John Giamartino formed a corporation to operate Big Boy restaurants, with each owning one-third of the shares. After a dispute resulted in the removal of Gazda as an officer, Kolinski and Giamartino as controlling directors voted to issue shares of the corporation for $100 per share. At the time, the book value of the corporation was $266 per share and the fair market value was between $497 and $572 per share. Gazda opposed the issuance of the shares. Was he successful with stopping the issuance?

9. [icon] *Video Case.* See "The Stock Option." An employee of FAMCO purchases common shares of FAMCO through its fringe benefit plan. Transfer of the shares purchased under the plan is restricted in two ways. First, when employment terminates for any reason, FAMCO has an option to purchase the shares at book value. Second, if an employee attempts to sell the shares while employed, FAMCO has a right of first refusal to purchase the shares at the sale price. FAMCO informs an employee that for the good of the company, she must sell her shares to FAMCO. She believes that she will be terminated unless she sells the shares to FAMCO, but nonetheless she sells the shares on the open market at a price much greater than book value. Can FAMCO invalidate the employee's sale of the shares?

10. Bruce Bowman received 1,500 shares of Ling and Company Class A common shares. The shares were the subject of an option agreement contained in the articles of incorporation requiring Bowman to offer the shares to the corporation before selling them to any other person. On the front of Bowman's share certificate, in small print, it was stated that transfer of the shares was subject to the provisions of the articles, that a copy of the articles could be obtained from Ling or from the secretary of state, and that the back of the share certificate stated which sections of the articles contained the content of the option agreement. On the back of the share certificate, in small print, the reference to the restriction was again made, and specific reference was given to Article 4 of the articles of incorporation, in which the restriction was contained. Bowman borrowed money from Trinity Savings and Loan. When Bowman defaulted on the loan, Trinity attempted to sell the shares, but Ling objected, invoking the option agreement. Is the option agreement enforceable against Trinity?

11. Alice Marr owned 800 of the 11,340 shares outstanding of Gloucester Ice & Storage Co., a closely held corporation with no ready market for its shares. When Marr died, Thomas Goode, the administrator of her will, demanded that Gloucester or its majority shareholder purchase Marr's shares. No provision restricting the transfer of shares or requiring the corporation or remaining shareholders to purchase shares on the death of a shareholder appeared in the corporation's articles of incorporation, bylaws, or agreement among shareholders. Is Gloucester or its majority shareholder required to purchase Marr's shares at fair market value?

Management of Corporations

lthough shareholders own a corporation, they traditionally have possessed no right to manage the business of the corporation. Instead, shareholders elect individuals to a *board of directors*, to which management is entrusted. Often, the board delegates much of its management responsibilities to *officers*.

This chapter explains the legal aspects of the board's and officers' management of the corporation. Their management of the corporation must be consistent with the objectives and powers of the corporation, and they owe duties to the corporation to manage it prudently and in the best interests of the corporation and the shareholders as a whole. ∞

CORPORATE OBJECTIVES

The traditional objective of the business corporation has been to *enhance corporate profits and shareholder gain.* According to this objective, the managers of a corporation must seek the accomplishment of the profit objective to the exclusion of all inconsistent goals. Interests other than profit maximization may be considered, provided that they do not hinder the ultimate profit objective.

Nonetheless, some courts have permitted corporations to take *socially responsible actions* that are *beyond the profit maximization requirement.* In addition, every state recognizes corporate powers that are not economically inspired. For example, corporations may make contributions to colleges, political campaigns, child abuse prevention centers, literary associations, and employee benefit plans, regardless of economic benefit to the corporations. Also, every state expressly recognizes the right of shareholders to choose freely the extent to which profit maximization captures all of their interests and all of their sense of responsibility.

In the following case, the court held that the board of directors acted improperly by failing to maximize shareholder profit.

REVLON, INC. v. MACANDREWS & FORBES HOLDINGS, INC. 506 A.2d 173 (Del. Sup. Ct. 1986)

I*n 1985, Pantry Pride, Inc., informed Revlon, Inc., of its intent to acquire Revlon. Pantry Pride planned to "bust up" Revlon after the acquisition by selling its various lines of businesses individually. Revlon's board of directors rejected Pantry Pride's plan. Nonetheless, Pantry Pride made a hostile takeover bid for Revlon's shares at $47.50 per share.*

In response to Pantry Pride's bid, Revlon's board sought to reduce the number of shares Pantry Pride could acquire by repurchasing some of its shares in exchange for new Senior Notes. The contract with the new Senior Noteholders protected the noteholders with covenants limiting Revlon's ability to incur more debt, sell assets, or pay dividends. The covenants, however, could be waived by the board's independent directors.

When this defense failed to deter Pantry Pride, the board recognized that a takeover was inevitable. Consequently, the board agreed to a friendly acquisition by Forstmann Little & Co. for $56 per share. Realizing the inevitability of a bust-up, Revlon's board agreed to break up its assets by selling its cosmetic division; Forstmann planned to sell two other divisions after the purchase.

In addition, Revlon's independent directors agreed to waive the Senior Note covenants. As a result, the value of the Senior Notes dropped 12 percent. Angry Senior Noteholders threatened to sue Revlon's directors. Concerned about their personal liability to the Senior Noteholders, the Revlon directors amended their agreement with Forstmann. Forstmann increased its offer to $57.25 per share and agreed to support the value of the Senior Notes. In return, Revlon gave Forstmann a lock-up option, promising to sell two valuable divisions to Forstmann at nearly $200 million below their market value if Pantry Pride was successful in taking over Revlon.

Pantry Pride sued Revlon to invalidate the lock-up option as beyond the objectives of the corporation. The trial court enjoined Revlon's directors from making concessions to Forstmann. Revlon appealed to the Supreme Court of Delaware. ↺

Moore, Justice The lock-up with Forstmann had as its emphasis shoring up the market value of the Senior Notes. The directors made support of the Senior Notes an integral part of the company's dealings with Forstmann, even though their primary responsibility at this stage was to the shareholders.

The original threat posed by Pantry Pride—the break-up of the company—had become a reality that even the directors embraced. Selective dealing to fend off a hostile bidder was no longer a proper objective. Instead, obtaining the highest price for the benefit of the shareholders should have been the central theme guiding director action.

The Revlon board argued that it acted in good faith in protecting the Senior Noteholders because Delaware law permits consideration of other corporate constituencies. Although such considerations may be permissible, there are fundamental limitations upon that prerogative. A board may have regard for various constituencies, provided there are rationally related benefits accruing to the shareholders. However, such concern for non-shareholder interests is inappropriate when an auction among active bidders is in progress, and the object no longer is to protect or maintain the corporate enterprise but to sell it to the highest bidder.

Revlon also contended that it had contractual obligations to the Senior Noteholders. However, any such duties are limited to the principle that one may not interfere with contractual relationships by improper actions. Here the rights of the Senior Noteholders were fixed by agreement, and there is nothing to suggest that any of those terms were violated. The Senior Notes covenants specifically contemplated a waiver.

In granting an asset option lock-up to Forstmann, the directors allowed considerations other than the maximization of shareholder profit to affect their judgment to the ultimate detriment of shareholders. No such defensive measure can be sustained.

Judgment for Pantry Pride affirmed.

The decision in *Revlon* prodded most of the states to enact **corporate constituency statutes,** which broaden the legal objectives of corporations. Such statutes permit or require directors to take into account the interests of constituencies other than shareholders. These statutes direct the board to act in the best interests of the corporation, not just the interests of the shareholders, and to maximize corporate profits *over the long term.* The new laws promote the view that a corporation is a collection of interests working together for the purpose of producing goods and services at a profit, and that the goal of corporate profit maximization over the long term is not necessarily the same as the goal of stock price maximization over the short term. For an example of the new statutes, see the excerpt from the Indiana statute in Figure 1.

CORPORATE POWERS

The actions of management are limited not only by the objectives of business corporations but also by the *powers* granted to business corporations. Such limitations may appear in the state statute, the articles of incorporation, and the bylaws.

The primary source of a corporation's powers is the corporation statute of the state in which it is incorporated. Some state corporation statutes expressly specify the powers of corporations. These powers include making gifts for charitable and educational purposes, lending money to corporate officers and directors, and purchasing and disposing of the corporation's shares. Other state corporation statutes limit the powers of corporations, such as prohibiting the acquisition of agricultural land by corporations.

Modern statutes attempt to authorize corporations to engage in any activity. The Model Business Corporation Act (MBCA) states that a corporation has the power to do *anything that an individual may do.*

Purpose Clauses in Articles of Incorporation

Most corporations state their purposes in the articles of incorporation. The purpose is usually phrased in broad terms, even if the corporation has been formed with only one type of business in mind. Most corporations have purpose clauses stating that they may engage in any lawful business.

Under the MBCA, the inclusion of a purpose clause in the articles is optional. Any corporation incorporated under the MBCA has the purpose of engaging in any lawful business, unless the articles state a narrower purpose.

The Ultra Vires Doctrine   Historically, an act of a corporation beyond its powers was a nullity, as it was *ultra vires,* which is Latin for "beyond the powers." Therefore, any act not permitted by the corporation statute or by the corporation's articles of incorporation was void due to lack of capacity.

This lack of capacity or power of the corporation was a defense to a contract assertable either by the corporation or by the other party that dealt with the corporation. Often, *ultra vires* was merely a convenient justification for reneging on an agreement that was no longer considered desirable. This misuse of the doctrine has led to its near abandonment.

Today, the *ultra vires* doctrine is of small importance for two reasons. First, nearly all corporations have broad purpose clauses, thereby preventing any *ultra vires* problem. Second, the MBCA and most other statutes do not permit a corporation or the other party to an agreement to avoid an obligation on the ground that the corporate action is *ultra vires.*

Under the MBCA, *ultra vires* may be asserted by only three types of persons: (1) by a shareholder seeking to enjoin a corporation from executing a proposed action that is *ultra vires,* (2) by the corporation suing its management for damages caused by exceeding the corporation's powers, and (3) by the state's attorney general, who may have the power to enjoin an *ultra vires* act or to dissolve a corporation that exceeds its powers.

POWERS OF NONPROFIT CORPORATIONS

Nonprofit corporations, like for-profit corporations, have the power to transact business granted by the incorporation statute, the articles, and the bylaws. The Model Nonprofit Corporation Act (MNCA), like the MBCA, grants nonprofit corporations the power to engage in any lawful activity and to do anything an individual may do. Thus, a nonprofit corporation may sue and be sued, purchase, hold, and sell real property, lend and borrow money, and make charitable and other donations, among its many powers.

Commonly, a nonprofit corporation's articles will limit its powers pursuant to a purpose clause. For example, a nonprofit corporation established to operate a junior baseball league may limit its powers to that business and matters reasonably connected to it. When a nonprofit corporation limits its powers, a risk arises that the corporation may commit an *ultra vires* act. The MNCA adopts the same rules for *ultra vires* contracts as does the MBCA: Generally, neither the corporation nor the other party may use *ultra vires* as a defense to a contract.

THE BOARD OF DIRECTORS

Traditionally, the **board of directors** has had the authority and the duty to manage the corporation. Yet in a large publicly held corporation, it is impossible for the board to manage the corporation on a day-to-day basis, because many of the directors are high-level executives in other corporations and devote most of their time to their other business interests. Therefore, the MBCA permits a corporation to be managed *under the direction of* the board of directors. Consequently, the board of directors delegates major responsibility for management to committees of the board such as an executive committee, to individual board members such as the chairman of the board, and to the officers of the corporation, especially the chief executive officer (CEO). In theory, the board supervises the actions of its committees, the chairman, and the officers to ensure that the board's policies are being carried out and that the delegatees are managing the corporation prudently. Figure 2 lists the results of a survey of directors concerning their primary responsibilities.

Board Authority under Corporation Statutes

A corporation's board of directors has the authority to do almost everything within the powers of the corporation. The board's authority includes not only the general power to manage or direct the corporation in the ordinary course of its business but also the power to issue shares of stock and to set the price of shares. Among its other powers, the board may repurchase shares, declare dividends, adopt and amend bylaws, elect and remove officers, and fill vacancies on the board.

Some corporate actions require *board initiative* and shareholder approval. That is, board approval is

---

FIGURE **2**

Primary Responsibilities of Directors

	PERCENT*
1. Ensure integrity of corporation's operations	60%
2. Counsel top management	58
3. Ensure strategic plan for the future	55
4. Monitor performance of the CEO	47
5. Ensure management succession	43
6. Serve the public interest	15
7. Monitor financial reporting	9

*Percent of directors surveyed citing each responsibility.
Source: Survey of directors, published by Arthur Young Executive Resource Consultants in *The New Director: Changing Views of the Board's Role* (1989).

necessary to *propose such actions to the shareholders,* who then must approve the action. Board initiative is required for important changes in the corporation, such as amendment of the articles of incorporation, merger of the corporation, the sale of all or substantially all of the corporation's assets, and voluntary dissolution.

Committees of the Board

Most publicly held corporations have committees of the board of directors. These committees, which have fewer members than the board has, can more efficiently handle management decisions and exercise board powers than can a large board. Only directors may serve on board committees.

Although many board powers may be delegated to committees of the board, some decisions are so important that corporation statutes require their *approval by the board as a whole.* Under the MBCA, the powers that may not be delegated concern important corporate actions such as declaring dividends, filling vacancies on the board or its committees, adopting and amending bylaws, approving issuances of shares, and approving repurchases of the corporation's shares.

The most common board committee is the **executive committee.** It is usually given authority to act for the board on most matters when the board is not in session. Generally, it consists of the inside directors and perhaps one or two outside directors who can attend a meeting on short notice. An inside director is an officer of the corporation who devotes substantially full time to the corporation. Outside directors have no such affiliation with the corporation.

Audit committees recommend independent public accountants and supervise the public accountants' audit of the corporate financial records. Nearly all publicly held firms have audit committees comprising independent directors.

Nominating committees choose management's slate of directors that is to be submitted to shareholders at the annual election of directors. Nominating committees also often plan generally for management succession. Nominating committees wholly or largely comprise outside directors.

Compensation committees review and approve the salaries, bonuses, stock options, and other benefits of high-level corporate executives. Although compensation committees usually comprise directors who have no affiliation with the executives or directors whose compensation is being approved, compensation committees may also set the compensation of their members. Directors of a typical corporation receive annual compensation between $30,000 to $60,000.

A **shareholder litigation committee** is given the task of determining whether a corporation should sue someone who has allegedly harmed the corporation. Usually, this committee of disinterested directors is formed when a shareholder asks the board of directors to cause the corporation to sue some or all of the directors for mismanaging the corporation.

Powers, Rights, and Liabilities of Directors as Individuals

A director is not an agent of the corporation *merely* by being a director. The directors may manage the corporation only when they act as a board, unless the board of directors grants agency powers to the directors individually.

A director has the *right to inspect* corporate books and records that contain corporate information essential to the director's performance of her duties. The director's right of inspection is denied when the director has an interest adverse to the corporation, as in the case of a director who plans to sell a corporation's trade secrets to a competitor.

Normally, a director does not have any personal liability for the contracts and torts of the corporation.

Election of Directors

Generally, any individual may serve as a director of a corporation. A director need not even be a shareholder. Nonetheless, a corporation is permitted to specify qualifications for directors in the articles of incorporation.

A corporation must have the number of directors required by the state corporation law. The MBCA and several state corporation statutes require a minimum of one director, recognizing that in close corporations with a single shareholder-manager, additional board members are superfluous. Several statutes, including the New York statute, require at least three directors, unless there are fewer than three shareholders, in which case the corporation may have no fewer directors than it has shareholders.

A corporation may have more than the minimum number of directors required by the corporation statute. The articles of incorporation or bylaws will state the number of directors of the corporation. Most large publicly held corporations have boards with more than 10 members.

Directors are elected by the shareholders at the annual shareholder meeting. Usually, each shareholder is permitted to vote for as many nominees as there are directors to be elected. The shareholder may cast as many votes for each nominee as he has shares. The top votegetters among the nominees are elected as directors. This voting process, called **straight voting,** permits a holder of more than 50 percent of the shares of a corporation to dominate the corporation by electing a board of directors that will manage the corporation as he wants it to be managed.

To avoid domination by a large shareholder, some corporations allow class voting or cumulative voting. **Class voting** may give certain classes of shareholders the right to elect a specified number of directors. **Cumulative voting** permits shareholders to multiply the number of their shares by the number of directors to be elected and to cast the resulting total of votes for one or more directors. As a result, cumulative voting may permit minority shareholders to obtain representation on the board of directors.

Directors usually hold office for only one year, but they may have longer terms. The MBCA permits *staggered terms* for directors. A corporation having a board of nine or more members may establish either two or three approximately equal classes of directors, with only one class of directors coming up for election at each annual shareholders' meeting. If there are two classes of directors, the directors serve two-year terms; if there are three classes, they serve three-year terms.

The original purpose of staggered terms was to permit continuity of management. Staggered terms also frustrate the ability of minority shareholders to use cumulative voting to elect their representatives to the board of directors.

The Proxy Solicitation Process   Most individual investors purchase corporate shares in the public market to increase their wealth, not to elect or to influence the directors of corporations. Nearly all institutional investors—such as pension funds, mutual funds, and bank trust departments—have the same profit motive. Generally, they are passive investors with little interest in exercising their

shareholder right to elect directors by attending shareholder meetings.

Once public ownership of the corporation's shares exceeds 50 percent, the corporation cannot conduct any business at its shareholder meetings unless some of the shares of these passive investors are voted. This is because the corporation will have a shareholder quorum requirement, which usually requires that 50 percent or more of the shares be voted for a shareholder vote to be valid. Since passive investors rarely attend shareholder meetings, the management of the corporation must solicit **proxies** if it wishes to have a valid shareholder vote. Shareholders who will not attend a shareholder meeting must be asked to appoint someone else to vote their shares for them. This is done by furnishing each such shareholder with a proxy form to sign. The proxy designates a person who may vote the shares for the shareholder.

Management Solicitation of Proxies   To ensure its perpetuation in office and the approval of other matters submitted for a shareholder vote, the corporation's management solicits proxies from shareholders for directors' elections and other important matters on which shareholders vote, such as mergers. The management designates an officer, a director, or some other person to vote the proxies received. The person who is designated to vote for the shareholder is also called a proxy. Typically, the chief executive officer (CEO) of the corporation, the president, or the chairman of the board of directors names the person who serves as the proxy.

Usually, the proxies are merely signed and returned by the public shareholders, including the institutional shareholders. Passive investors follow the **Wall Street rule:** Either support management or sell the shares. As a result, management almost always receives enough votes from its proxy solicitation to ensure the reelection of directors and the approval of other matters submitted to the shareholders, even when other parties solicit proxies in opposition to management.

Management's solicitation of proxies may produce a result quite different from the theory of corporate management that directors serve as representatives of the shareholders. The CEO usually nominates directors of his choice, and they are almost always elected. The directors appoint officers chosen by the CEO. The CEO's nominees for director are not unduly critical of his programs or of

FIGURE 3

Influence of Board on Key Management Decisions

	STRONG	MODERATE	NONE OR UNKNOWN
Compensation of top management	71%	27%	2%
Mergers and acquisitions	62	33	5
Capital expenditures	32	60	8
Selection of senior executives	22	64	14
Long-range planning	21	70	9

Note: Figures are percentages of directors surveyed citing the board's influence as strong, moderate, none, or unknown.
Source: Survey of directors, published by Arthur Young Executive Resource Consultants in *The New Director: Changing Views of the Board's Role* (1989).

his methods for carrying them out. This is particularly true if a large proportion of the directors are officers of the company and thus are more likely to be dominated by the CEO. In such situations, the board of directors may not function effectively as a representative of the shareholders in supervising and evaluating the CEO and the other officers of the corporation. The board members and the other officers are subordinates of the CEO, even though the CEO is not a major shareholder of the corporation.

Proposals for improving corporate governance in public-issue corporations seek to develop a board that is capable of functioning independently of the CEO by changing the composition or operation of the board of directors. Some corporate governance critics propose that a federal agency such as the Securities and Exchange Commission (SEC) appoint one or more directors to serve as watchdogs of the public interest. Other critics would require that shareholders elect at least a majority of directors without prior ties to the corporation, thus excluding shareholders, suppliers, and customers from the board. The New York Stock Exchange requires a minimum of two directors independent of management for its listed companies.

Other proposals recommend changing the method by which directors are nominated for election. One proposal would encourage shareholders to make nominations for directors. Supporters of this proposal argue that in addition to reducing the influence of the CEO, it would also broaden the range of backgrounds represented on the board. The SEC recommends that publicly held corporations establish a nominating committee composed of outside directors. Many publicly held corporations have nomination committees.

Mostly due to SEC and public pressures for changes in corporate governance, current boards of directors operate significantly differently from the boards of the 1960s and the early 1970s. Boards supervise officers more closely. More directors are outside rather than inside directors. Boards meet more frequently, and more important, they have working committees that assume specific responsibilities. In addition, today's directors *perceive* themselves as being more nearly independent of the CEO. As a consequence, they *are* more nearly independent of the CEO. See Figure 3.

In the following case, the court considered whether a board of directors abdicated its duty to direct the corporation by delegating unlimited power to the CEO.

GRIMES v. DONALD   673 A.2d 1207 (Del. Sup. Ct. 1996)

ames Donald was the chief executive officer of DSC Communications, a Delaware corporation headquartered in Plano, Texas. In 1990, DSC's board of directors entered an employment agreement with Donald that ran until his 75th birthday. The employment agreement provided that Donald "shall be responsible for the general management of the affairs of the company and report *to the Board." Donald's employment could be terminated by death, disability, for cause, and without cause. The agreement provided, however, that Donald could declare a "Constructive Termination Without Cause" by DSC, if there was "unreasonable interference, in the good faith judgment of Donald, by the Board or a substantial stockholder of DSC, in Donald's carrying out of his duties and responsibilities." When there was termination without cause, the employment agreement provided that Donald was entitled to payment of his annual base salary ($650,000) for the remainder of the contract, his annual incentive award ($300,000), and other benefits. The total amount of payments and benefits for the term of the contract was about $20,000,000.*

C. L. Grimes, a DSC shareholder, sued Donald on behalf of the corporation asking the court to invalidate the employment agreement between Donald and DSC on the grounds that the agreement illegally delegates the duties and responsibilities of DSC's board of directors to Donald. The Delaware Chancery Court dismissed the case, and Grimes appealed to the Supreme Court of Delaware. ⌒

Veasey, Chief Justice Grimes claims that the potentially severe financial penalties which DSC would incur in the event that the Board attempts to interfere in Donald's management will inhibit and deter the Board from exercising its duties. We disagree.

Grimes has pleaded, at most, that Donald would be entitled to $20 million in the event of a Constructive Termination. In light of the financial size of DSC, this amount would not constitute a *de facto* abdication.

Directors may not delegate duties which lie at the heart of the management of the corporation. A court cannot give legal sanction to agreements which have the effect of removing from directors in a very substantial way their duty to use their own best judgment on management matters. The Donald agreement does not formally preclude the DSC board from exercising its statutory powers and fulfilling its fiduciary duty.

With certain exceptions, an informed decision to delegate a task is as much an exercise of business judgment as any other. Likewise, business decisions are not an abdication of directorial authority merely because they limit a board's freedom of future action. A board which has decided to manufacture bricks has less freedom to decide to make bottles. In a world of scarcity, a decision to do one thing will commit a board to a certain course of action and make it costly and difficult to change course and do another. This is an inevitable fact of life and is not an abdication of directorial duty.

If the market for senior management, in the business judgment of the board, demands significant severance packages, boards will inevitably limit their future range of action by entering into employment agreements. Large severance payments will deter boards, to some extent, from dismissing senior officers. If an independent and informed board, acting in good faith, determines that the services of a particular individual warrant large amounts of money, whether in the form of current salary or severance provisions, the board has made a business judgment. That judgment normally will receive the protection of the business judgment rule unless the facts show that such amounts, compared with services to be received in exchange, constitute waste or could not otherwise be the product of a valid exercise of business judgment.

The Board of DSC retains the ultimate freedom to direct the strategy and affairs of DSC. If Donald disagrees with the Board, DSC may or may not be required to pay a substantial amount of money in order to pursue its chosen course of action. So far, we have only a rather unusual contract, but not a case of abdication.

Judgment for Donald affirmed.

Vacancies on the Board

The MBCA permits the directors to fill vacancies on the board. A majority vote of the remaining directors is sufficient to select persons to serve out unexpired terms, even though the remaining directors are less than a quorum.

Removal of Directors

Modern corporation statutes permit shareholders to remove directors *with or without cause*. The rationale for the modern rule is that the shareholders should have the power to judge the fitness of directors at any time.

However, most corporations have provisions in their articles authorizing the shareholders to remove directors *only for cause*. Cause for removal would include mismanagement or conflicts of interest. Before removal for cause, the director must be given notice and an opportunity for a hearing.

A director elected by a class of shareholders may be removed only by that class of shareholders, thereby protecting the voting rights of the class. A director elected by cumulative voting may not be removed if the votes cast against her removal would have been sufficient to elect her to the board, thereby protecting the voting rights of minority shareholders.

The court in the following case validated the shareholders' removal of a director at a meeting that was originally called as a board of directors meeting.

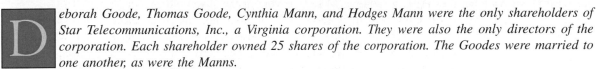

GOODE v. GOODE   29 Va. Cir. 409 (Va. Cir. Ct. 1992)

Deborah Goode, Thomas Goode, Cynthia Mann, and Hodges Mann were the only shareholders of Star Telecommunications, Inc., a Virginia corporation. They were also the only directors of the corporation. Each shareholder owned 25 shares of the corporation. The Goodes were married to one another, as were the Manns.

In the summer of 1991, the Goodes had marital difficulties that led to their separation. On October 3, 1991, Star Telecommunications' corporate counsel gave notice of a directors' meeting for October 11, 1991, the stated purpose of which was to remove Mrs. Goode from her position as director. The Manns and Goodes met at the office of the corporate counsel. The corporate attorney and Mrs. Goode's divorce attorney were also present. A vote was taken to remove Mrs. Goode as a director of the corporation. Mr. and Mrs. Mann voted in favor of the motion, Mrs. Goode voted against the motion, and Mr. Goode abstained. Mrs. Goode objected to her removal, and she sued to invalidate her removal on the grounds that before the meeting her husband and the Manns had conspired to divest her of involvement in the business affairs of the corporation, without cause. She also contends that her removal was not valid because of a lack of a majority vote. ∞

Ledbetter, Judge   The first step of an analysis of this dispute is to determine the nature of the October 11, 1991, meeting. The notice called for a meeting of the board of directors. Corporate counsel wrote a letter to Mrs. Goode's divorce attorney informing him of "a directors' meeting." The transcript of the meeting is entitled meeting of "stockholders and board of directors." At the beginning of the meeting, Mrs. Goode's divorce attorney asked what kind of meeting was being held. Mr. Goode said, "This is a stockholders' meeting." When Mrs. Goode's divorce attorney pointed out that the notice was for a directors' meeting, Mr. Mann interjected, "It's a directors' meeting." The point was never clarified.

The court is of the opinion that the meeting, in reality, was both a meeting of the shareholders and a meeting of the directors, jointly, for the special purpose stated in the notice. All shareholders and all directors (being the same people, of course) were present, all of them participated, all of them were aware of the purpose for which the meeting was called, all of them voted (except Mr. Goode, who abstained) on the action taken at the meeting. Mrs.

Goode's protest of the vote count—i.e., the result of the action taken—was not an objection to the meeting itself.

At common law, shareholders of a corporation could remove directors but only for cause. Under Virginia statute, the shareholders' right to remove directors has been expanded so that the right may be exercised with or without cause.

Directors of stock corporations have no authority to remove fellow directors. The bylaw of Star Telecommunications that allowed removal of a director for cause "by action of the board" is inconsistent with law, and, thus, a nullity.

As we have seen, the persons in attendance at the meeting owned all the outstanding stock of the corporation. They attended the meeting fully informed of its purpose, and they participated from beginning to end. Because the business being conducted required action of shareholders rather than directors, for the reasons explained above, their vote was a vote of shareholders.

To hold otherwise would elevate form over substance and would invite ridiculous results in closely-held corporations. Where a small group of people own all the stock and serve as officers and directors and attend a meeting fully informed of the agenda, it would be absurd to predicate the validity of their votes on whether the meeting was properly labelled and whether each vote was accurately identified as an action of the "shareholders," "directors," or whatever. So long as they are all the same people and were not surprised by the actions taken, what real difference does it make what they may have thought they were wearing at the time a vote was taken?

Therefore, the court holds that the action taken at the meeting on October 11, 1991, to remove Mrs. Goode from the board of directors was an action taken by shareholders, all of whom were present and participating with advance knowledge of the meeting's purpose. Because shareholders may remove directors at will pursuant to statute and the corporation bylaws, the action was appropriate without the need to show just cause.

Most of the parties' arguments about the vote tally (two in favor of removal, one opposed, one abstention) missed the point. Shareholders do not vote per capita. Each outstanding share is entitled to one vote on each matter voted on (with some exceptions not pertinent here). It follows that the actual vote count on the motion to remove Mrs. Goode was: 100 total shares outstanding, all represented at the meeting; 50 shares for the motion; 25 shares opposed to the motion; and 25 shares abstaining.

Fifty out of 100 shares is not a majority. However, only 75 shares were voted. If, as here, a quorum exists, an action is approved if the votes cast favoring the action exceed the votes cast opposing the action. In this case, the 50 shares voted in favor of removal clearly exceeded the 25 votes cast opposing the removal. Hence, the motion carried and the action was approved. Mrs. Goode was properly removed from the board of directors by a vote of the shareholders.

It does not matter that the other shareholders discussed and agreed beforehand that Mrs. Goode should be removed; no "deceptive voting practices" or fraud were involved as a matter of law; the shareholders did not breach a duty to Mrs. Goode in removing her as a director; and the possibility that a "less harmful course of action" may have been available is immaterial. Regardless of the truth of the allegations, no cause of action has been stated for which monetary damages may be recovered.

Judgment for Thomas Goode, Cynthia Mann, and Hodges Mann.

DIRECTORS' MEETINGS

Traditionally, directors could act only when they were properly convened as a board. They could not vote by proxy or informally, as by telephone. This rule was based on a belief in the value of consultation and collective judgment.

Today, the corporation laws of a majority of the states and the MBCA specifically permit action by the directors without a meeting if all of the directors consent in writing to the action taken. Such authorization is useful for dealing with routine matters or for formally approving an action based on an earlier policy decision made after full discussion.

The MBCA also permits a board to meet by telephone or television hookup. This section permits a meeting of directors who may otherwise be unable to convene. The only requirement is that the directors be able to hear one another simultaneously.

Directors are entitled to reasonable notice of all *special meetings,* but not of regularly scheduled meetings. The MBCA does not require the notice for a special meeting to state the purpose of the meeting. A director's attendance at a meeting waives any required notice, unless at the beginning of the meeting the director objects to the lack of notice.

For the directors to act, a *quorum* of the directors must be present. The quorum requirement ensures that the decision of the board will represent the views of a substantial portion of the directors. A quorum is usually a *majority* of the number of directors.

Each director has *one vote.* If a quorum is present, a vote of a majority of the directors present is an act of the board, unless the articles or the bylaws require the vote of a greater number of directors. Such *supermajority voting provisions* are common in close corporations but not in publicly held corporations. The use of supermajority voting provisions by close corporations is covered later in this chapter.

OFFICERS OF THE CORPORATION

The board of directors has the authority to appoint the officers of the corporation. Many corporation statutes provide that the officers of a corporation shall be the *president,* one or more *vice presidents,* a *secretary,* and a *treasurer.* Usually, any two or more offices may be held by the same person, except for the offices of president and secretary.

The MBCA requires only that there be an officer performing the duties normally granted to a corporate secretary. Under the MBCA, one person may hold several offices, including the offices of president and secretary.

The officers are agents of the corporation. As agents, officers have *express authority* conferred on them by the bylaws or the board of directors. In addition, officers have *implied authority* to do the things that are reasonably necessary to accomplish their express duties. Also, officers have *apparent authority* when the corporation leads third parties to believe reasonably that the officers have authority to act for the corporation. Like any principal, the corporation may *ratify* the unauthorized acts of its officers. This may be done expressly by a resolution of the board of directors or impliedly by the board's acceptance of the benefits of the officer's acts.

The most perplexing issue with regard to the authority of officers is whether an officer has *inherent authority* merely by virtue of the title of his office. Courts have held that certain official titles confer authority on officers, but such powers are much more restricted than you might expect.

Traditionally, a *president* possesses no power to bind the corporation by virtue of the office. Instead, she serves merely as the presiding officer at shareholder meetings and directors' meetings. A president with an additional title such as *general manager* or *chief executive officer* has broad implied authority to make contracts and to do other acts in the ordinary business of the corporation.

A *vice president* has no authority by virtue of that office. An executive who is vice president of a specified department, however, such as a vice president of marketing, will have the authority to transact the normal corporate business falling within the function of the department.

The *secretary* usually keeps the minutes of directors' and shareholder meetings, maintains other corporate records, retains custody of the corporate seal, and certifies corporate records as being authentic.

Although the secretary has no authority to make contracts for the corporation by virtue of that office, the corporation is bound by documents certified by the secretary.

The *treasurer* has custody of the corporation's funds. He is the proper officer to receive payments to the corporation and to disburse corporate funds for authorized purposes. The treasurer binds the corporation by his receipts, checks, and indorsements, but he does not by virtue of that office alone have authority to borrow money, to issue negotiable instruments, or to make other contracts on behalf of the corporation.

Like any agent, a corporate officer ordinarily has *no liability on contracts* that he makes on behalf of his principal, the corporation, if he signs for the corporation and not in his personal capacity.

Officers serve the corporation at the pleasure of the board of directors, which may remove an officer at any time with or without cause. An officer who has been removed without cause has no recourse against the corporation, unless the removal violates an employment contract between the officer and the corporation.

MANAGING CLOSE CORPORATIONS

Many of the management formalities that you have studied in this chapter are appropriate for publicly held corporations yet inappropriate for close corporations. Close corporations tend to be more loosely managed than public corporations. For example, they may have few board meetings. Each shareholder may want to be *involved in management* of the close corporation. If a shareholder is not involved in management, he may want to protect his interest by placing *restrictions on the managerial discretion* of those who do manage the corporation.

Modern close corporation statutes permit close corporations to dispense with most, if not all, management formalities. The Statutory Close Corporation Supplement to the MBCA permits a close corporation to *dispense with a board of directors* and to be *managed by the shareholders.* The California General Corporation Law permits the close corporation to be managed *as if it were a partnership.*

Because a minority shareholder of a close corporation may be dominated by the shareholders who control the board of directors, close corporation shareholders have resorted to two devices: **super-majority voting** requirements for board actions and **restrictions on the managerial discretion** of the board of directors.

Any corporation may require that board action be possible only with the approval of more than a majority of the directors, such as three-fourths or unanimous approval. A supermajority vote is often required to terminate the employment contract of an employee-shareholder, to reduce the level of dividends, and to change the corporation's line of business. Supermajority votes are rarely required for ordinary business matters, such as deciding with which suppliers the corporation should deal.

Traditionally, shareholders could not restrict the managerial discretion of directors. This rule recognized the traditional roles of the board as manager and of the shareholders as passive owners. Modern close corporation statutes permit shareholders to intrude into the sanctity of the boardroom. The Statutory Close Corporation Supplement grants the shareholders *unlimited* power to restrict the discretion of the board of directors. For example, the shareholders may agree that the directors may not terminate or reduce the salaries of employee-shareholders and may not lower or eliminate dividends. And, as was stated above, close corporation statutes even permit the shareholders to dispense with a board of directors altogether and to manage the close corporation as if it were a partnership.

MANAGING NONPROFIT CORPORATIONS

A nonprofit corporation is managed under the direction of a board of directors. The board of directors must have at least three directors. All corporate powers are exercised by or under the authority of the board of directors. Any person may serve as a director; however, the Model Nonprofit Corporation Act has an optional provision stating that no more than 49 percent of directors of a public service corporation may be financially interested in the business of the public service corporation. An interested person is, for example, the musical director of a city's symphony orchestra who receives a salary from the nonprofit corporation operating the orchestra.

If a nonprofit corporation has members, typically the members elect the directors. However, the ar-

ticles may provide for the directors to be appointed or elected by other persons. Directors serve for one year, unless the articles or bylaws provide otherwise. Directors who are elected may not serve terms longer than five years, but appointed directors may serve longer terms.

Directors may be elected by straight or cumulative voting and by class voting. Members may elect directors in person or by proxy. Directors may be removed at any time with or without cause by the members or other persons who elected or appointed the directors. When a director engages in fraudulent or dishonest conduct or breaches a fiduciary duty, members holding at least 10 percent of the voting power may petition a court to remove the wrongdoing director. Generally, a vacancy may be filled by the members or the board of directors; however, if a removed director was elected by a class of members or appointed by another person, only the class or person electing or appointing the director may fill the vacancy.

The board is permitted to set directors' compensation. Typically, directors of public benefit corporations and religious corporations are volunteers and receive no compensation.

Directors of a nonprofit corporation usually act at a meeting at which all directors may simultaneously hear each other, such as a meeting in person or by telephone conference call. The board may also act without a meeting if all directors consent in writing to the action. The board has the power to do most actions that are within the powers of the corporation, although some actions, such as mergers and amendments of the articles, require member action also. Ordinarily, an individual director has no authority to transact for a nonprofit corporation.

The board of directors of a nonprofit corporation may delegate some of its authority to committees of the board and to officers. A nonprofit corporation is not required to have officers, except for an officer performing the duties of corporate secretary. If a corporation chooses to have more officers, one person may hold more than one office. The board may remove an officer at any time with or without cause.

Officers have the authority granted them by the bylaws or by board resolution. However, a nonprofit corporation is bound by a contract signed by both the presiding officer of the board and the president, when the other party had no knowledge that the signing officers had no authority. The corporation is also bound to a contract signed by either the presiding officer or the president which is also signed by either a vice president, the secretary, the treasurer, or the executive director.

DIRECTORS' AND OFFICERS' DUTIES TO THE CORPORATION

Directors and officers are in positions of trust; they are entrusted with property belonging to the corporation and with power to act for the corporation. Therefore, directors and officers owe **fiduciary duties** to the corporation. They are the duties to act within the authority of the position and within the objectives and powers of the corporation, to act with due care in conducting the affairs of the corporation, and to act with loyalty to the corporation.

Acting within Authority

An officer or director has a duty to **act within the authority** conferred on her by the articles of incorporation, the bylaws, and the board of directors. The directors and officers must act within the scope of the powers of the corporation. An officer or a director may be liable to the corporation if it is damaged by an act exceeding that person's or the corporation's authority.

Duty of Care

Directors and officers are liable for losses to the corporation resulting from their lack of *care or diligence.* The MBCA expressly states the standard of care that must be exercised by directors and officers. MBCA Section 8.30 states:

(a) A director shall discharge his duties as a director, including his duties as a member of a committee:

    (1) in good faith;

    (2) with the care an ordinarily prudent person in a like position would exercise under similar circumstances; and

    (3) in a manner he reasonably believes to be in the best interests of the corporation.

Managers need merely meet the standard of the **ordinarily prudent person in the same circumstances,** a standard focusing on the basic manager attributes of common sense, practical wisdom, and informed judgment. The duty of care does not hold directors and officers to the standard of a prudent businessperson, a person of some undefined level of business skill. A director or officer's performance is evaluated at the time of the decision, thereby preventing the application of hindsight in judging her performance.

The MBCA duty of care test requires that a director or officer make a **reasonable investigation** and **honestly believe** that her decision is in the **best interests of the corporation.** For example, the board of directors decides to purchase an existing manufacturing business for $15 million without inquiring into the value of the business or examining its past financial performance. Although the directors may believe that they made a prudent decision, they have no reasonable basis for that belief. Therefore, if the plant is worth only $5 million, the directors will be liable to the corporation for its damages—$10 million—for breaching the duty of care.

The Business Judgment Rule The directors' and officers' duty of care is sometimes expressed as the **business judgment rule:** Absent bad faith, fraud, or breach of fiduciary duty, the judgment of the board of directors is conclusive. When directors and officers have complied with the business judgment rule, they are protected from liability to the corporation for their unwise decisions. The business judgment rule precludes the courts from substituting their business judgment for that of the corporation's managers. The business judgment rule recognizes that the directors and officers—not the shareholders and the courts—are best able to make business judgments and should not ordinarily be vulnerable to second-guessing. Shareholders and the courts are ill-equipped to make better business decisions than those made by the officers and directors of a corporation, who have more business experience and are more familiar with the needs, strengths, and limitations of the corporation.

Three requirements must be met for the business judgment rule to protect managers from liability:

1. The managers must make an **informed decision.** They must take the steps necessary to become informed about the relevant facts by making a **reasonable investigation** before making a decision. These steps may include merely listening to a proposal, reviewing written materials, or making inquiries. Managers

may rely on information collected and presented by other persons. In essence, the informed-decision component means that managers should do their homework if they want the protection of the business judgment rule.

2. The managers may have **no conflicts of interest.** The managers may not benefit personally—other than as shareholders—when they transact on behalf of the corporation.

3. The managers must have a **rational basis** for believing that the decision is in the best interests of the corporation. The rational basis element requires only that the managers' decision have a *logical connection to the facts* revealed by a reasonable investigation or that the decision *not be manifestly unreasonable.* Some courts have held that the managers' wrongdoing must amount to *gross negligence* for the directors to lose the protection of the business judgment rule.

If the business judgment rule does not apply because one or more of its elements are missing, a court may *substitute its judgment* for that of the managers.

Nonetheless, courts rarely refuse to apply the business judgment rule. As a result, the rule has been criticized frequently as providing too much protection for the managers of corporations. In one famous case, the court applied the business judgment rule to protect a 1965 decision made by the board of directors of the Chicago Cubs not to install lights and not to hold night baseball games at Wrigley Field.[1] Yet the business judgment rule is so flexible that it protected the decision of the Cubs' board of directors to install lights in 1988.

The *Trans Union* case[2] is one of the few cases that have held directors liable for failing to comply with the business judgment rule. The Supreme Court of Delaware found that the business judgment rule was not satisfied by the board's approval of an acquisition of the corporation for $55 per share. The board approved the acquisition after only two hours' consideration. The board received no documentation to support the adequacy of the $55 price. Instead, it relied entirely on a 20-minute *oral* report of the chairman of the board. No written summary of the acquisition was presented to the board. The directors failed to obtain an investment banker's report, prepared after careful consideration, that the acquisition price was fair.

In addition, the court held that the mere fact that the acquisition price exceeded the market price by $17 per share did not legitimize the board's decision. The board had frequently made statements prior to the acquisition that the market had undervalued the shares, yet the board took no steps to determine the intrinsic value of the shares. Consequently, the court found that at a minimum, the directors had been grossly negligent.

In the following case, the court considered whether a bank loan officer complied with the business judgment rule.

---

[1]*Shlensky v. Wrigley,* 237 N.E.2d 776 (Ill. Ct. App. 1968).
[2]*Smith v. Van Gorkom,* 488 A.2d 858 (Del. Sup. Ct. 1985).

OMNIBANK OF MANTEE v. UNITED SOUTHERN BANK 607 So.2d 76 (Miss. Sup. Ct. 1992)

J ames R. Gray was president and managing officer of the Peoples Bank and Trust Company in Olive Branch, Mississippi, a branch bank owned by United Southern Bank (USB). Gray had complete charge of the day-to-day banking business of Peoples Bank. He had discretionary loan authority, subject to USB's limits for all senior loan officers: $75,000 for unsecured loans and $150,000 for secured loans.

Frank Piecara was an established customer of Peoples Bank. Piecara was president of Mirage Construction, Inc., which was obligated on a subcontract to provide earthwork and roadwork for Rogers Construction Company at the Pacacho Pumping Plant in Arizona. Gray directed Peoples Bank to make loans in the amount of $536,000 to a trust managed by Piecara. The loan proceeds were used to provide working capital for Mirage. In addition, Gray directed Peoples Bank to issue a $300,000 irrevocable letter of credit to Rogers Construction for the purpose of securing Mirage's performance as Rogers's subcontractor. Gray called USB's senior vice president, Edward P. Peacock III, to request authorization of the letter of credit. Gray and

Peacock each had $150,000 authority to make secured loans, which they combined to issue the letter of credit. As security for the loans and letter of credit, Gray obtained a security interest in Mirage's accounts receivable and contract rights, in particular the payments Rogers might make to Mirage under the subcontract. Gray did not perfect the security interest in the subcontract. Gray did not notify Rogers or the owner of the Pacacho Pumping Plant of the security interest or require Rogers or the owner to remit subcontract payments directly to Peoples Bank.

Piecara and Mirage defaulted on the loans and letter of credit, with USB suffering a loss of almost $600,000. USB sued Gray alleging his breach of a fiduciary duty. The trial court found Gray liable to USB. Gray appealed to the Mississippi Supreme Court. ᢙ

Robertson, Justice The law devolves upon those in the upper echelons of a corporate entity certain duties owing to the entity, over and above those of an ordinary agent or employee. The question is whether Gray is one of those so burdened. We doubt a definitional line may be drawn with precision or permanence. For the moment, we are prepared to accept that

"Officer" means (a) the chief executive, operating, financial, legal and accounting officers of a corporation; (b) to the extent not encompassed by the foregoing, the chairman of the board of directors . . ., president, treasurer, and secretary, and a *vice-president or vice-chairman who is in charge of a principal business unit, division,* or function . . . and (c) any other individual designated by the corporation as an officer.
American Law Institute, *Principles of Corporate Governance: Analysis and Recommendations,* section 1.27.

His title aside, Gray served USB as the chief operating official at Peoples Bank where he had substantial discretionary authority. We think a banking office such as the Peoples Bank branch is one of USB's principal business units. Gray was the man in charge. He presided over a branch worth over twenty million dollars, had substantial loan authority, and had considerable autonomy in directing the day-to-day operations of the branch. The trial court was correct in treating Gray as an officer of USB.

By law, officer Gray owed USB two principal duties: a duty of care and a duty of loyalty and fair dealing. These duties differ in nature and content, though they doubtless intersect and overlap. There is a bit of lore born no doubt of thought of failed banks and helpless widows that we ought demand more of bank officers than one who runs a foundry or a pest control company.

We begin with the duty of care. A director or officer has a duty to the corporation to perform the director's or officer's functions in good faith, in a manner he or she reasonably believes to be in the best interests of the corporation, and with the care that an ordinarily prudent person would reasonably be expected to exercise in a like position and under similar circumstances. The duty includes the obligation to make, or cause to make, an inquiry when, but only when, the circumstances would alert a reasonable director or officer to the need therefor. The extent of such inquiry shall be such as the director or officer reasonably believes to be necessary.

We long ago recognized this duty in a banking setting and said an officer who "very negligently" makes unreasonably risky loans may on his borrowers' default be held personally to make good the bank's loss.

The duty of care is subject to a well-settled common law, known as the business judgment rule. That rule has recently been stated with care:

A director or officer who makes a business judgment in good faith fulfills the duty . . . [of care] if the director or officer:
(1) is not interested . . . in the subject of the business judgment;
(2) is informed with respect to the subject of the business judgment to the extent the director or officer reasonably believes to be appropriate under the circumstances; and
(3) rationally believes that the business judgment is in the best interests of the corporation.
Principles of Corporate Governance, section 4.01. *See* MBCA section 8.42.

Gray's defaults in the Piecara loans are apparent. To be sure, there is nothing improper about a banker securing a credit by taking a security interest in contract rights or assignment of accounts. On the other hand, there are risks associated with the receivables form of collateral not associated with more tangible security, and a prudent loan officer must reasonably assess and control these risks. These risks are exacerbated where, as here, the subcontract is to be performed some 1,500 miles away.

Gray made no inquiry of the financial responsibility of Rogers or the owner of the Picacho Pumping Plant. A prudent loan officer taking such collateral will give notice of his bank's interest to the prime contractor and the owner and demand that all payments due under the subcontract be routed through the bank. Gray did none of this, nor did he monitor performance of the subcontract and have Piecara remit as his company was paid. Gray failed to perfect the security interest. Moreover, it appears clear the value of the collateral was far below what prudently should have been required for credit of this size. We accept the trial court's holding that Gray breached his duty of care to USB in handling the Piecara loans.

Gray's argument in reply is laced with implied references to the business judgment rule. He insists he acted in subjective good faith at all times, and of this there is little doubt. The trial court found Gray had no "interest" in any of the credits at issue. Gray insists he reasonably believed the debtors would respond to their obligations in a reasonably timely fashion. Gray insists he thought the risks reasonable and, where unsecured, backed by adequate financial statements. Reports of these loans, their terms, and periodic status were routinely available to USB, which offered nothing but praise until a state bank examiner's probe in January, 1985.

These are not irrelevancies. They are evidence that Gray may have acted with reasonable business judgment. Most assuredly, the duty of care holds no truck with Monday morning quarterbacking, and the business judgment rule stands to prevent this. A loan officer is no guarantor of the success of each credit extension. The prudence of the practice is judged objectively in the circumstances then existing and reasonably knowable by the officer.

The defense ultimately founders. The trial court impliedly found unreasonable Gray's belief regarding the extent to which he should have informed himself at the time regarding these debtors. Further, the court impliedly found there was no rational basis for a belief that his handling of these matters was in USB's best interest.

Judgment for United Southern Bank affirmed.

Recent Changes in the Duty of Care

In response to the *Trans Union* case and insurance companies' increasing unwillingness to insure directors and officers for breaches of their duty of care (and the resulting exodus of outside directors from corporate boards of directors), many state legislatures changed the wording of the duty of care, typically imposing liability only for willful or wanton misconduct or for gross negligence.

For example, Ohio protects directors from monetary liability except when clear and convincing evidence demonstrates the directors' deliberate intent to injure the corporation or the directors' reckless disregard for its welfare. Delaware corporation law and the MBCA allow corporations to amend their articles to reduce or eliminate directors' liability for monetary damages for breaches of the duty of care. Figure 4 contains the MBCA provision.

Board Opposition to Acquisition of Control of a Corporation

In the last 30 years, many outsiders have attempted to acquire control of publicly held corporations.

FIGURE **4**

MBCA Section 2.02

(b) The articles of incorporation may set forth:

(4) a provision eliminating or limiting the liability of a director to the corporation or its shareholders for money damages for any action taken or any failure to take any action, as a director, except liability for

(A) the amount of financial benefit received by a director to which he is not entitled;

(B) an intentional infliction of harm on the corporation or the shareholders;

(C) a violation of Section 8.33 [illegal payment of dividends]; or

(D) an intentional violation of criminal law.

Typically, these outsiders (called **raiders**) will make a **tender offer** for the shares of a corporation (called the **target**). A tender offer is an offer to the shareholders to buy their shares at a price above the current market price. The raider hopes to acquire a

FIGURE   5

Tender Offer Defenses

Greenmail

The target's repurchase of its shares from the raider at a substantial profit to the raider, upon the condition that the raider sign a standstill agreement in which it promises not to buy additional shares of the target for a stated period of time.

White Knight

A friendly tender offeror whom management prefers over the original tender offeror — called a black knight. The white knight rescues the corporation from the black knight (the raider) by offering more money for the corporation's shares. In the *Revlon* case that appeared earlier in the chapter, Forstmann was a white knight for Revlon.

Pac-Man

The target corporation turns the tables on the tender offeror or raider (which is often another publicly held corporation) by making a tender offer for the raider's shares. As a result, two tender offerors are trying to buy each other's shares. This is similar to the Pac-Man video game, in which Pac-Man and his enemies chase each other.

Golden Parachutes

Justified as an incentive to attract high-quality business managers, a golden parachute requires a corporation to make a large severance payment to a top-level executive such as the CEO when there is a change in control of the corporation. Payments to an individual executive may approach $100 million. The golden parachute arguably is an effective tender offer defense because the severance payment increases the raider's acquisition cost, but in the face of billion dollar takeovers, it is doubtful that such payments are large enough to deter a raider. The severance agreement in *Grimes v. Donald* (which appears earlier in this chapter) requiring payment upon a change in control of the corporation was a golden parachute.

Lock-Up Option

Used in conjunction with a white knight to ensure the success of the white knight's bid. The target and the white knight agree that the white knight will buy a highly valuable asset of the target at a very attractive price for the white knight (usually a below-market price) if the raider succeeds in taking over the target. For example, in the *Revlon* case, Revlon gave a lock-up option to Forstmann to reduce the amount of profit that Pantry Pride would make had it completed its takeover of Revlon.

Friendly Shareholders

Establishing employee stock option plans (ESOPs), by which employees of the corporation purchase the corporation's shares, and selling the corporation shares to other shareholders likely to be loyal to management, such as employee pension funds and people in the community in which the corporation conducts its business, may create a significant percentage of friendly shareholders that are not likely to tender their shares to a raider who may be perceived as hostile to the continuation of the corporation's business in the local community. Thus, building and maintaining a base of friendly shareholders make it easier to defeat a raider.

Poison Pill

Also called a shareholders' rights plan. There are many types, but the typical poison pill involves the target's issuance of a new class of preferred shares to its common shareholders. The preferred shares have rights (share options) attached to them. These rights allow the target's shareholders to purchase shares of the raider or shares of the target at less than fair market value. The poison pill deters hostile takeover attempts by threatening the raider and its shareholders with severe dilutions in the value of the shares they hold.

---

majority of the shares, which will give it control of the target corporation.

Most tender offers are opposed by the target corporation's management. The defenses to tender offers are many and varied, and they carry interesting names, such as the Pac-Man defense, the white knight, greenmail, the poison pill, and the lock-up option. See Figure 5 for definitions of these defenses.

When takeover defenses are successful, shareholders of the target may lose the opportunity to sell their shares at a price up to twice the market price of the shares prior to the announcement of the hostile bid. Frequently, the loss of this opportunity upsets shareholders, who then decide to sue the directors who have opposed the tender offer. Shareholders contend that the directors have opposed the tender offer only to preserve their corporate jobs. Shareholders also argue that the target corporation's interests would have been better served if the tender offer had succeeded.

Generally, courts have refused to find directors liable for opposing a tender offer because the business judgment rule applies to a board's decision to oppose a tender offer.

Nonetheless, the business judgment rule will not apply when the directors make a decision to oppose the tender offer before they have carefully studied it. In addition, if the directors' actions indicate that they opposed the tender offer in order to preserve their jobs, they will be liable to the corporation.

Court decisions have seemingly modified the business judgment rule as it is applied in the tender offer context. For example, in *Unocal Corp. v. Mesa Petroleum Co.,*[3] the Supreme Court of Delaware upheld the application of the business judgment rule to a board's decision to block a hostile tender offer by making a tender offer for its own shares that excluded the raider.[4] But in so ruling, the court held that the board may use only those defense tactics that are *reasonable* compared to the takeover threat. The board may consider a variety of concerns, including the inadequacy of the price offered, nature and timing of the offer, questions of illegality, the impact on constituencies other than shareholders (i.e., creditors, customers, employees, and perhaps even the community generally), the risk of nonconsummation, and the quality of securities being offered in the exchange.

In *Unocal,* the threat was a two-tier, highly coercive tender offer. In the typical two-tier offer, the raider first offers cash for a majority of the shares. After acquiring a majority of the shares, the offeror initiates the second tier, in which the remaining shareholders are forced to sell their shares for a package of securities less attractive than the first tier. Because shareholders fear that they will be forced to take the less attractive second-tier securities if they fail to tender during the first tier, shareholders—including those who oppose the offer—are coerced into tendering during the first tier. *Unocal* and later cases specifically authorize the use of defenses to defeat a coercive two-tier tender offer.

Since its decision in *Unocal,* the Supreme Court of Delaware has applied this modified business judgment rule to validate a poison pill tender offer defense tactic in *Moran v. Household Int'l, Inc.*[5] and to invalidate a lock-up option tender offer defense in the *Revlon* case, which appears earlier in this chapter. These cases confirmed the *Unocal* holding that the board of directors must show that:

1. It had reasonable grounds to believe that a danger to corporate policy and effectiveness was posed by the takeover attempt.

2. It acted primarily to protect the corporation and its shareholders from that danger.

3. The defense tactic was reasonable in relation to the threat posed to the corporation.

Such a standard appeared to impose a higher standard on directors than the rational basis requirement of the business judgment rule, which historically has been interpreted to require only that a decision of a board not be manifestly unreasonable. In addition, the *Revlon* case required the board to establish an auction market for the company and to sell it to the highest bidder when the directors have abandoned the long-term business objectives of the company by embracing a bust-up of the company.

In the following case, the Supreme Court of Delaware expanded board discretion in fighting hostile takeovers, holding that a board may oppose a hostile takeover provided the board had a *preexisting, deliberately conceived corporate plan* justifying its opposition. The existence of such a plan enabled Time's board to meet the reasonable-tactic element of the *Unocal* test.

---

[3]493 A.2d 946 (Del. Sup. Ct. 1985).

[4]Discriminatory tender offers are now illegal pursuant to Securities Act Rule 13e-4.

---

[5]500 A.2d 346 (Del. Sup. Ct. 1985).

PARAMOUNT COMMUNICATIONS, INC. v. TIME, INC.   571 A.2d 1140 (Del. Sup. Ct. 1989)

 ince 1983, Time, Inc., had considered expanding its business beyond publishing magazines and books, owning Home Box Office and Cinemax, and operating television stations. In 1988, Time's board approved in principle a strategic plan for Time's acquisition of an entertainment company. The board gave management permission to negotiate a merger with Warner Communications, Inc.

The board's consensus was that a merger of Time and Warner was feasible, but only if Time controlled the resulting corporation, preserving the editorial integrity of Time's magazines. The board concluded that Warner was the superior candidate because Warner could make movies and TV shows for HBO, Warner had an international distribution system, Warner was a giant in the music business, Time and Warner would control half of New York City's cable TV system, and the Time network could promote Warner's movies.

Negotiations with Warner broke down when Warner refused to agree to Time dominating the combined companies. Time continued to seek expansion, but informal discussions with other companies terminated when it was suggested the other companies purchase Time or control the resulting board. In January 1989, Warner and Time resumed negotiations, and on March 4, 1989, they agreed to a combination by which Warner shareholders would own 62 percent of the resulting corporation, to be named Time-Warner. To retain the editorial integrity of Time, the merger agreement provided for a board committee dominated by Time representatives.

On June 7, 1989, Paramount Communications, Inc., announced a cash tender offer for all of Time's shares at $175 per share. (The day before, Time shares traded at $126 per share.) Time's financial advisers informed the outside directors that Time's auction value was materially higher than $175 per share. The board concluded that Paramount's $175 offer was inadequate. Also, the board viewed the Paramount offer as a threat to Time's control of its own destiny and retention of the Time editorial policy; the board found that a combination with Warner offered greater potential for Time.

In addition, concerned that shareholders would not comprehend the long-term benefits of the merger with Warner, on June 16, 1989, Time's board recast its acquisition with Warner into a two-tier acquisition, in which it would make a tender offer to buy 51 percent of Warner's shares for cash immediately and later buy the remaining 49 percent for cash and securities. The tender offer would eliminate the need for Time to obtain shareholder approval of the transaction.

On June 23, 1989, Paramount raised its offer to $200 per Time share. Three days later, Time's board rejected the offer as a threat to Time's survival and its editorial integrity; the board viewed the Warner acquisition as offering greater long-term value for the shareholders. Time shareholders and Paramount then sued Time and its board to enjoin Time's acquisition of Warner. The trial court held for Time. Paramount and Time shareholders appealed to the Supreme Court of Delaware.

Horsey, Justice Our decision does not require us to pass on the wisdom of the board's decision. That is not a court's task. Our task is simply to determine whether there is sufficient evidence to support the initial Time-Warner agreement as the product of a proper exercise of business judgment.

We have purposely detailed the evidence of the Time board's deliberative approach, beginning in 1983–84, to expand itself. Time's decision in 1988 to combine with Warner was made only after what could be fairly characterized as an exhaustive appraisal of Time's future as a corporation. Time's board was convinced that Warner would provide the best fit for Time to achieve its strategic objectives. The record attests to the zealousness of Time's executives, fully supported by their directors, in seeing to the preservation of Time's perceived editorial integrity in journalism. The Time board's decision to expand the business of the company through its March 4 merger with Warner was entitled to the protection of the business judgment rule.

The revised June 16 agreement was defense-motivated and designed to avoid the potentially disruptive effect that Paramount's offer would have had on consummation of the proposed merger were it put to a shareholder vote. Thus, we decline to apply the traditional business judgment rule to the revised transaction and instead analyze the Time board's June 16 decision under *Unocal.*

In *Unocal,* we held that before the business judgment rule is applied to a board's adoption of a defensive measure, the burden will lie with the board to prove (a) reasonable grounds for believing that a danger to corporate policy and effectiveness existed; and (b) that the defensive measure adopted was reasonable in relation to the threat posed.

Paramount argues a hostile tender offer can pose only two types of threats: the threat of coercion that results from a two-tier offer promising unequal treatment for nontendering shareholders; and the threat of inadequate value from an all-shares, all-cash offer at a price below what a target board in good faith deems to be the present value of its shares.

Paramount would have us hold that only if the value of Paramount's offer were determined to be clearly inferior to the value created by management's plan to merge with Warner could the offer be viewed—objectively—as a threat.

Paramount's position represents a fundamental misconception of our standard of review under *Unocal* principally because it would involve the court in substituting its judgment as to what is a "better" deal for that of a corporation's board of directors. The usefulness of *Unocal* as an analytical tool is precisely its flexibility in the face of a variety of fact scenarios. Thus, directors may consider, when evaluating the threat posed by a takeover bid, the inadequacy of the price offered, nature and timing of the offer, questions of illegality, the impact on constituencies other than shareholders, the risk of nonconsummation, and the quality of securities being offered in the exchange.

The Time board reasonably determined that inadequate value was not the only threat that Paramount's all-cash, all-shares offer could present. Time's board concluded that Paramount's offer posed other threats. One concern was that Time shareholders might elect to tender into Paramount's cash offer in ignorance or a mistaken belief of the strategic benefit which a business combination with Warner might produce.

Paramount also contends that Time's board had not duly investigated Paramount's offer. We find that Time explored the available entertainment companies, including Paramount, before determining that Warner provided the best strategic "fit." In addition, Time's board rejected Paramount's offer because Paramount did not serve Time's objectives or meet Time's needs. Time's board was adequately informed of the potential benefits of a transaction with Paramount. Time's failure to negotiate cannot be fairly found to have been uninformed. The evidence supporting this finding is materially enhanced by the fact that 12 of Time's 16 board members were outside independent directors.

We turn to the second part of the *Unocal* analysis. The obvious requisite to determining the reasonableness of a defensive action is a clear identification of the nature of the threat. This requires an evaluation of the importance of the corporate objective threatened; alternative methods of protecting that objective; impacts of the defensive action; and other relevant factors.

The fiduciary duty to manage a corporate enterprise includes the selection of a time frame for achievement of corporate goals. Directors are not obliged to abandon a deliberately conceived corporate plan for a short-term shareholder profit unless there is clearly no basis to sustain the corporate strategy. Time's responsive action to Paramount's tender offer was not aimed at "cramming down" on its shareholders a management-sponsored alternative, but rather had as its goal the carrying forward of a pre-existing transaction in an altered form. Thus, the response was reasonably related to the threat. The revised agreement did not preclude Paramount from making an offer for the combined Time-Warner company or from changing the conditions of its offer so as not to make the offer dependent upon the nullification of the Time-Warner agreement. Thus, the response was proportionate.

Judgment for Time affirmed.

The *QVC* Decision   In February 1994, the Delaware Supreme Court confirmed its holdings in *Unocal* and *Revlon*. In *Paramount Communications Inc. v. QVC Network Inc.,*[6] the Delaware Supreme Court enjoined defensive measures taken by Paramount's board of directors. The defensive tactics were designed to facilitate a friendly takeover of Paramount by Viacom Inc. (at $85 per share) and to thwart a more valuable unsolicited takeover bid by QVC (at $90 per share). The Paramount-Viacom agreement provided that Paramount's board would make Paramount's poison pill rights agreement inapplicable to Viacom's bid and grant Viacom a lock-up option to purchase almost 20 percent of Paramount's shares at a bargain price. In addition, Paramount promised to pay Viacom a termination fee of $100 million if Paramount's directors terminated the merger because of a competing transaction, if the directors recommended a competing merger, or if the shareholders failed to approve the merger. When Paramount's board rejected QVC's $90 offer, QVC sued

---

[6] 637 A.2d 34 (Del. Sup. Ct. 1994).

Paramount to enjoin enforcement of the defense tactics preferring Viacom.

The Delaware Supreme Court pointed out that the Paramount-Viacom merger would result in a transfer of control of Paramount from public shareholders to a single shareholder, with the public shareholders receiving a minority voting position in the surviving company. Once control shifted, the public shareholders would have no leverage to demand another premium for transferring control to the majority shareholder. As a result, the Delaware court held that the public shareholders of Paramount were entitled to receive "a control premium and/or protective devices of significant value." The court held that when a corporation undertakes a transaction that will cause a change in corporate control, the directors have an obligation "to seek the best value reasonably available to the shareholders." Having decided to sell control of Paramount, the directors were obligated "to evaluate critically whether or not all material aspects of the Paramount-Viacom merger (separately and in the aggregate) were reasonable and in the best interests of the public stockholders."

Applying the standard above, the Delaware Supreme Court found that the Paramount directors' process was not reasonable and the result achieved for the shareholders was not reasonable. The court ruled that the Paramount directors had the opportunity to improve the economic terms of the Paramount-Viacom transaction, but failed to do so, ultimately squandering their "final opportunity to negotiate on the stockholders' behalf and to fulfill their obligation to seek the best value reasonably available." Rather than taking advantage of the opportunity, the Paramount directors "chose to wall themselves off from material information that was reasonably available and to hide behind defensive measures as a rationalization for refusing to negotiate with QVC or seeking other alternatives." Consequently, the Delaware Supreme Court affirmed the lower court's grant of a preliminary injunction.

Duties of Loyalty

Directors and officers owe a duty of **utmost loyalty and fidelity** to the corporation. Judge Benjamin Cardozo stated this duty of trust. He declared that a director:

owes loyalty and allegiance to the corporation—a loyalty that is undivided and an allegiance that is influenced by no consideration other than the welfare of the corporation. Any adverse interest of a director will be subjected to a scrutiny rigid and uncompromising. He may not profit at the expense of his corporation and in conflict with its rights; he may not for personal gain divert unto himself the opportunities which in equity and fairness belong to his corporation.[7]

Directors and officers owe the corporation the same duties of loyalty that agents owe their principals, though many of these duties have special names in corporation law. The most important of these duties of loyalty are the duties not to *self-deal,* not to *usurp a corporate opportunity,* not to *oppress minority shareholders,* and not to *trade on inside information.*

Interested Person Transactions

A director or officer is an interested person when a director or officer deals with his corporation. The director or officer has a **conflict of interest** and may prefer his own interests over those of the corporation. The director's or officer's interest may be *direct,* such as his interest in selling his land to the corporation, or it may be *indirect,* such as his interest in having another business of which he is an owner, director, or officer supply goods to the corporation. When a director has a conflict of interest, the director's transaction with the corporation may be voided or rescinded.

Under the MBCA, an interested person transaction will not be voided merely on the grounds of a director's conflict of interest when *any one* of the following is true:

1. The transaction has been approved by a majority of informed, disinterested directors,
2. The transaction has been approved by a majority of the shares held by informed, disinterested shareholders, or
3. The transaction is fair to the corporation.

Nonetheless, even when disinterested directors' or shareholders' approval has been obtained, courts will void a conflict-of-interest transaction that is

---

[7]*Meinhard v. Salmon,* 164 N.E.2d 545, 546 (N.Y. Ct. App. 1928).

unfair to the corporation. Therefore, every corporate transaction in which a director has a conflict of interest must be fair to the corporation. If the transaction is fair, the interested director is excused from liability to the corporation. A transaction is fair if reasonable persons in an *arm's-length bargain* would have bound the corporation to it. This standard is often called the **intrinsic fairness standard.**

The function of disinterested director or disinterested shareholder approval of a conflict-of-interest transaction is merely to shift the burden of proving unfairness. Under the MBCA, the burden of proving fairness lies initially on the interested director. The burden of proof shifts to the corporation that is suing the interested officer or director if the transaction was approved by the board of directors or the shareholders. Nonetheless, when disinterested directors approve an interested person transaction, substantial deference is given to the decision in accordance with the business judgment rule, especially when the disinterested directors compose a majority of the board.

Generally, *unanimous* approval of an interested person transaction by informed shareholders *conclusively* releases an interested director or officer from liability even if the transaction is unfair to the corporation. The rationale for this rule is that fully informed shareholders should know what is best for themselves and their corporation.

Loans to Directors   Under early corporation law, *loans* by the corporation *to directors* or *officers* were illegal, on the grounds that such loans might result in the looting of corporate assets. The MBCA allows loans to directors only after certain procedures have been followed. Either the shareholders must approve the loan, or the directors, after finding that the loan benefits the corporation, must approve it.

Parent–Subsidiary Transactions   Self-dealing is a concern when a parent corporation *dominates* a subsidiary corporation. Often, the subsidiary's directors will be directors or officers of the parent also. When persons with dual directorships approve transactions between the parent and the subsidiary, the opportunity for *overreaching* arises. There may

be *no arm's-length bargaining* between the two corporations. Hence, such transactions must meet the *intrinsic fairness* test.

Usurpation of a Corporate Opportunity

Directors and officers may steal not only assets of their corporations (such as computer hardware and software) but also *opportunities* that their corporations could have exploited. Both types of theft are equally wrongful. As fiduciaries, directors and officers are liable to their corporation for **usurping corporate opportunities.**

The opportunity must come to the director or officer *in her corporate capacity*. Clearly, opportunities received at the corporate offices are received by the manager in her corporate capacity. In addition, courts hold that CEOs and other high-level officers are nearly always acting in their corporate capacities, even when they are away from their corporate offices.

The opportunity must have a *relation or connection* to an *existing or prospective* corporate activity. Some courts apply the *line of business test,* considering how closely related the opportunity is to the lines of business in which the corporation is engaged. Other courts use the *interest or expectancy test,* requiring the opportunity to relate to property in which the corporation has an existing interest or in which it has an expectancy growing out of an existing right.

The corporation must be *able financially* to take advantage of the opportunity. Managers are required to make a good faith effort to obtain external financing for the corporation, but they are not required to use their personal funds to enable the corporation to take advantage of the opportunity.

A director or officer is free to exploit an opportunity that has been rejected by the corporation.

In the following case, the court found that an opportunity to become the manufacturer of Pepsi-Cola syrup was usurped by the president of a corporation that manufactured beverage syrups and operated soda fountains.

L *oft, Inc., manufactured and sold candies, syrups, and beverages and operated 115 retail candy and soda fountain stores. Loft sold Coca-Cola at all of its stores, but it did not manufacture Coca-Cola syrup. Instead, it purchased its 30,000-gallon annual requirement of syrup and mixed it with carbonated water at its various soda fountains.*

In May 1931, Charles Guth, the president and general manager of Loft, became dissatisfied with the price of Coca-Cola syrup and suggested to Loft's vice president that Loft buy Pepsi-Cola syrup from National Pepsi-Cola Company, the owner of the secret formula and trademark for Pepsi-Cola. The vice president said he was investigating the purchase of Pepsi syrup.

Before being employed by Loft, Guth had been asked by the controlling shareholder of National Pepsi, Megargel, to acquire the assets of National Pepsi. Guth refused at that time. However, a few months after Guth had suggested that Loft purchase Pepsi syrup, Megargel again contacted Guth about buying National Pepsi's secret formula and trademark for only $10,000. This time, Guth agreed to the purchase, and Guth and Megargel organized a new corporation, Pepsi-Cola Company, to acquire the Pepsi-Cola secret formula and trademark from National Pepsi. Eventually, Guth and his family's corporation owned a majority of the shares of Pepsi-Cola Company.

Very little of Megargel's or Guth's funds were used to develop the business of Pepsi-Cola. Instead, without the knowledge or consent of Loft's board of directors, Guth used Loft's working capital, credit, plant and equipment, and executives and employees to produce Pepsi-Cola syrup. In addition, Guth's domination of Loft's board of directors ensured that Loft would become Pepsi-Cola's chief customer.

By 1935, the value of Pepsi-Cola's business was several million dollars. Loft sued Guth, asking the court to order Guth to transfer to Loft his shares of Pepsi-Cola Company and to pay Loft the dividends he had received from Pepsi-Cola Company. The trial court found that Guth had usurped a corporate opportunity and ordered Guth to transfer the shares and to pay Loft the dividends. Guth appealed. ∞

Layton, Chief Justice Public policy demands of a corporate officer or director the most scrupulous observance of his duty to refrain from doing anything that would deprive the corporation of profit or advantage. The rule that requires an undivided and unselfish loyalty to the corporation demands that there shall be no conflict between duty and self-interest.

The real issue is whether the opportunity to secure a very substantial stock interest in a corporation to be formed for the purpose of exploiting a cola beverage on a wholesale scale was so closely associated with the existing business activities of Loft, and so essential thereto, as to bring the transaction within that class of cases where the acquisition of the property would throw the corporate officer purchasing it into competition with his company.

Guth suggests a doubt whether Loft would have been able to finance the project. The answer to this suggestion is two-fold. Loft's net asset position was amply sufficient to finance the enterprise, and its plant, equipment, executives, personnel and facilities were adequate. The second answer is that Loft's resources were found to be sufficient, for Guth made use of no other resources to any important extent.

Guth asserts that Loft's primary business was the manufacturing and selling of candy in its own chain of retail stores, and that it never had the idea of turning a subsidiary product into a highly advertised, nation-wide specialty. It is contended that the Pepsi-Cola opportunity was not in the line of Loft's activities, which essentially were of a retail nature.

Loft, however, had many wholesale activities. Its wholesale business in 1931 amounted to over $800,000. It was a large company by any standard, with assets exceeding $9 million, excluding goodwill. It had an enormous plant. It paid enormous rentals. Guth, himself, said that Loft's success depended upon the fullest utilization of its large plant facilities. Moreover, it was a manufacturer of syrups and, with the exception of cola syrup, it supplied its own extensive needs. Guth, president of Loft, was an able and experienced man in that field. Loft, then, through its own personnel, possessed the technical knowledge, the practical business experience, and the resources necessary for the development of the Pepsi-Cola enterprise. Conceding that the essential of an opportunity is reasonably within the scope of a corporation's activities, latitude should be allowed for development and expansion. To deny this would be to deny the history of industrial development.

We cannot agree that Loft had no concern or expectancy in the opportunity. Loft had a practical and essential concern with respect to some cola syrup with an established formula and trademark. A cola beverage has come to be a business necessity for soft drink establishments; and it was essential to the success of Loft to serve at its soda fountains an acceptable five-cent cola drink in order to attract into its stores the great multitude of people who have formed the habit of drinking cola beverages.

When Guth determined to discontinue the sale of Coca-Cola in the Loft stores, it became, by his own act, a matter of urgent necessity for Loft to acquire a constant supply of some satisfactory cola syrup, secure against probable attack, as a replacement; and when the Pepsi-Cola opportunity presented itself, Guth having already considered the availability of the syrup, it became impressed with a Loft interest and expectancy arising out of the circumstances and the urgent and practical need created by him as the directing head of Loft.

The fiduciary relation demands something more than the morals of the marketplace. Guth did not offer the Pepsi-Cola opportunity to Loft, but captured it for himself. He invested little or no money of his own in the venture, but commandeered for his own benefit and advantage the money, resources, and facilities of his corporation and the services of his officials. He thrust upon Loft the hazard, while he reaped the benefit. In such a manner he acquired for himself 91 percent of the capital stock of Pepsi-Cola, now worth many millions. A genius in his line he may be, but the law makes no distinction between the wrongdoing genius and the one less endowed.

Judgment for Loft affirmed.

Oppression of Minority Shareholders

Directors and officers owe a duty to manage a corporation in the best interests of the corporation and the shareholders as a whole. When, however, a group of shareholders has been isolated for beneficial treatment to the detriment of another isolated group of shareholders, the disadvantaged group may complain of **oppression.**

For example, oppression may occur when directors of a close corporation who are also the majority shareholders pay themselves high salaries yet refuse to pay dividends or to hire minority shareholders as employees of the corporation. Since there is no market for the shares of a close corporation (apart from selling to the other shareholders), these oppressed minority shareholders have investments that provide them no return. They receive no dividends or salaries, and they can sell their shares only to the other shareholders, who are usually unwilling to pay the true value of the shares.

Generally, courts treat oppression of minority shareholders the same way courts treat director self-dealing: The transaction must be intrinsically fair to the corporation and the minority shareholders.

A special form of oppression is the **freeze-out.** A freeze-out is usually accomplished by merging a corporation with a newly formed corporation under terms by which the minority shareholders do not receive shares of the new corporation but instead receive only cash or other securities. The minority shareholders are thereby *frozen out as shareholders.*

Going private is a special term for a freeze-out of shareholders of *publicly owned corporations.* Some public corporations discover that the burdens of public ownership—such as the periodic disclosure requirements of the SEC—exceed the benefits of being public. Many of these publicly owned companies choose to freeze out their minority shareholders to avoid such burdens. Often, going private transactions appear abusive because the corporation goes public at a high price and goes private at a much lower price.

Some courts have adopted a fairness test and a business purpose test for freeze-outs. Most states apply the **total fairness test** to freeze-outs. In the freeze-out context, total fairness has two basic aspects: *fair dealing* and *fair price.* Fair dealing requires disclosing material information to directors and shareholders and providing an opportunity for negotiation. A determination of fair value requires the consideration of all the factors relevant to the value of the shares, except speculative projections.

Some states apply the **business purpose test** to freeze-outs. This test requires that the freeze-out accomplish some legitimate business purpose and not serve the special interests of the majority shareholders or the managers.

Other states place no restrictions on freeze-outs provided a shareholder has a **right of appraisal,** which permits a shareholder to require the corporation to purchase his shares at a fair price.

In addition, the SEC requires a *publicly held* company to make a statement on the fairness of its proposed going private transaction and to discuss in detail the material facts on which the statement is based.

In the next case, the court required that a freeze-out of minority shareholders of the New England Patriots football team meet both the business purpose and intrinsic fairness tests. The court held that freezing out the minority shareholders merely to allow the corporation to repay the majority shareholder's personal debts was not a proper business purpose.

COGGINS v. NEW ENGLAND PATRIOTS FOOTBALL CLUB, INC.   492 N.E.2d 1112 (Mass. Sup. Jud. Ct. 1986)

In 1959, the New England Patriots Football Club, Inc. (Old Patriots), was formed with one class of voting shares and one class of nonvoting shares. Each of the original 10 voting shareholders, including William H. Sullivan, purchased 10,000 voting shares for $2.50 per share. The 120,000 nonvoting shares were sold for $5 per share to the general public in order to generate loyalty to the Patriots football team. In 1974, Sullivan was ousted as president of Old Patriots. In November 1975, Sullivan succeeded in regaining control of Old Patriots by purchasing all 100,000 voting shares for $102 per share. He again became a director and president of Old Patriots.

To finance his purchase of the voting shares, Sullivan borrowed $5,350,000 from two banks. The banks insisted that Sullivan reorganize Old Patriots so that its income could be used to repay the loans made to Sullivan and its assets used to secure the loans. To make the use of Old Patriots' income and assets legal, it was necessary to freeze out the nonvoting shareholders. In November 1976, Sullivan organized a new corporation called the New Patriots Football Club, Inc. (New Patriots). Sullivan was the sole shareholder of New Patriots. In December 1976, the shareholders of Old Patriots approved a merger of Old Patriots and New Patriots. Under the terms of the merger, Old Patriots went out of business, New Patriots assumed the business of Old Patriots, Sullivan became the only owner of New Patriots, and the nonvoting shareholders of Old Patriots received $15 for each share they owned.

David A. Coggins, a Patriots fan from the time of its formation and owner of 10 Old Patriots nonvoting shares, objected to the merger and refused to accept the $15 per share payment for his shares. Coggins sued Sullivan and Old Patriots to obtain rescission of the merger. The trial judge found the merger to be illegal and ordered the payment of damages to Coggins and all other Old Patriots shareholders who voted against the merger and had not accepted the $15 per share merger payment. Sullivan and Old Patriots appealed to the Massachusetts Supreme Judicial Court.

Liacos, Justice When the director's duty of loyalty to the corporation is in conflict with his self-interest, the court will vigorously scrutinize the situation. The dangers of self-dealing and abuse of fiduciary duty are greatest in freeze-out situations like the Patriots merger, when a controlling shareholder and corporate director chooses to eliminate public ownership. Because the danger of abuse of fiduciary duty is especially great in a freeze-out merger, the court must be satisfied that the freeze-out was for the advancement of a legitimate corporate purpose. If satisfied that elimination of public ownership is in furtherance of a business purpose, the court should then proceed to determine if the transaction was fair by examining the totality of the circumstances. Consequently, Sullivan and Old Patriots bear the burden of proving, first, that the merger was for a legitimate business purpose, and second, that, considering the totality of circumstances, it was fair to the minority.

Sullivan and Old Patriots have failed to demonstrate that the merger served any valid corporate objective unrelated to the personal interests of Sullivan, the majority shareholder. The sole reason for the merger was to effectuate a restructuring of Old Patriots that would enable the repayment of the

personal indebtedness incurred by Sullivan. Under the approach we set forth above, there is no need to consider further the elements of fairness of a transaction that is not related to a valid corporate purpose.

Judgment for Coggins affirmed as modified.

Trading on Inside Information

Officers and directors have *confidential access* to nonpublic information about the corporation. Sometimes, directors and officers purchase their corporation's securities with knowledge of confidential information. Often, disclosure of previously nonpublic, **inside information** affects the value of the corporation's securities. Therefore, directors and officers may make a profit when the prices of the securities increase after the inside information has been disclosed publicly. Shareholders of the corporation claim that they have been harmed by such activity, either because the directors and officers misused confidential information that should have been used only for corporate purposes or because the directors and officers had an unfair informational advantage over the shareholders.

In this century, there has been a judicial trend toward finding a duty of directors and officers to disclose information that they have received confidentially from the corporation before they buy or sell the corporation's securities. As will be discussed fully in Chapter 37, Securities Regulation, the illegality of insider trading is already federal law under the Securities Exchange Act; however, it remains only a minority rule under state corporation law.

Director's Right to Dissent

A director who assents to an action of the board of directors may be held liable for the board's exceeding its authority or its failing to meet its duty of due care or loyalty. A director who attends a board meeting is deemed to have assented to any action taken at the meeting, unless he dissents.

Under the MBCA, to register his **dissent** to a board action, and thereby to protect himself from liability, the director must **not vote in favor** of the action and **must make his position clear** to the other board members. His position is made clear

either by requesting that his dissent appear in the minutes or by giving written notice of his dissent to the chairman of the board at the meeting or to the secretary immediately after the meeting. These procedures ensure that the dissenting director will attempt to dissuade the board from approving an imprudent action.

Generally, directors are not liable for failing to attend meetings. However, a director is liable for *continually failing* to attend meetings, with the result that the director is unable to prevent the board from harming the corporation by its self-dealing.

DUTIES OF DIRECTORS AND OFFICERS OF NONPROFIT CORPORATIONS

Directors and officers of nonprofit corporations owe fiduciary duties to their corporations that are similar to the duties owed by managers of for-profit corporations. Directors and officers owe a duty of care and duties of loyalty to the nonprofit corporation. They must act in good faith, with the care of an ordinarily prudent person, and with a reasonable belief that they are acting in the best interests of the corporation. In addition, a director should not have a conflict of interest in any transaction of the nonprofit corporation. As with for-profit corporations, conflict-of-interest transactions must meet the intrinsic fairness standard. Finally, a nonprofit corporation may not lend money to a director.

Liability concerns of directors of nonprofit corporations, especially public benefit corporations in which directors typically receive no compensation, have made it difficult for some nonprofit corporations to find and retain directors. Therefore, the Model Nonprofit Corporation Act permits nonprofit corporations to limit or eliminate the liability of directors for breach of the duty of care. The articles may not limit or eliminate a director's liability for failing to act in good faith, engaging in intentional misconduct, breaching the duty of loyalty, or having a conflict of interest.

CORPORATE AND MANAGEMENT LIABILITY FOR TORTS AND CRIMES

When directors, officers, and other employees of the corporation commit torts and crimes while conducting corporate affairs, the issue arises concerning who has liability. Should the individuals committing the torts and crimes be held liable, the corporation, or both?

Liability of the Corporation

For **torts,** the vicarious liability rule of *respondeat superior* applies to corporations. The only issue is whether an employee acted within the scope of her employment, which encompasses not only acts the employee is authorized to commit but may also include acts that the employee is expressly instructed to avoid. Generally, under the doctrine of *respondent superior,* a corporation is liable for an employee's tort that is reasonably connected to the authorized conduct of the employee.

The traditional view was that a corporation could not be guilty of a **crime** because criminal guilt required intent. A corporation, not having a mind, could form no intent. Other courts held that a corporation was not a person for purposes of criminal liability.

Today, few courts have difficulty holding corporations liable for crimes. Modern criminal statutes either expressly provide that corporations may commit crimes or define the term *person* to include corporations. In addition, some criminal statutes designed to protect the public welfare do not require intent as an element of some crimes, thereby removing the grounds used by early courts to justify relieving corporations of criminal liability.

Courts are especially likely to impose criminal liability on a corporation when the criminal act is requested, authorized, or performed by:

1. The board of directors,
2. An officer,
3. Another person having responsibility for formulating company policy, or
4. A high-level administrator having supervisory responsibility over the subject matter of the offense and acting within the scope of his employment.

In addition, courts hold a corporation liable for crimes of its agent or employee committed within the scope of his authority, even if a higher corporate official has no knowledge of the act and has not ratified it.

DIRECTORS' AND OFFICERS' LIABILITY FOR TORTS AND CRIMES

A person is always *liable for his own torts and crimes,* even when committed on behalf of his principal. Every person in our society is expected to exercise independent judgment and not merely to follow orders. Therefore, directors and officers are personally liable when they commit torts or crimes during the performance of their corporate duties.

A director or officer is usually not liable for the torts of employees of the corporation, since the corporation, not the director or the officer, is the principal. He will have **tort** liability, however, if he *authorizes* the tort or *participates* in its commission. A director or officer has **criminal** liability if she *requests, authorizes, conspires,* or *aids and abets* the commission of a crime by an employee.

In the next case, the court considered the liability of the sole officers and directors of a corporation that illegally dumped toxic waste.

 tlantic Disposal Service, Inc. (ADS), was in the business of hauling waste from commercial and industrial firms. Alvin White and Charles Carite were the sole shareholders, directors, and officers of ADS, each owning 50 percent of the shares. One of ADS's clients was a plant operated by USX Corporation in Camden, New Jersey. In 1976, the local county dump refused to accept ADS's truckload of 55-gallon drums of toxic liquid waste from USX; ADS then arranged to dispose of the drums on a one-acre wooded parcel in Tabernacle, New Jersey, owned by an ADS employee. In 1982, health department investigators discovered 193 barrels and containers at the Tabernacle site. Sampling by the Environmental Protection Agency revealed a release of hazardous substances to the soil and groundwater. After the EPA cleaned the site, it brought an action in a federal district court to recover the cost from ADS, White, and Carite under section 107(a)(4) of the Comprehensive Environmental Response, Compensation, and Liability Act (CERCLA). Section 107(a)(4) imposes liability on any person—commonly referred to as a "transporter"— who accepts hazardous substances for transport to a disposal facility selected by that person, from which there is a release of a hazardous substance. ADS was held liable as a transporter based on its employees' transportation of the drums of toxic waste to the Tabernacle site. White and Carite were held liable on the grounds they exercised control over ADS in 1976 when the drums were dumped at the Tabernacle site. ADS, White, and Carite appealed to the court of appeals. ∞

Vanaskie, Judge Congress enacted CERCLA to facilitate cleanup of potentially dangerous hazardous waste sites, with a view to the preservation of the environment and human health. *Tippins, Inc. v. USX* (1994). One of the principal purposes of CERCLA is to force polluters to pay for costs associated with remedying their pollution.

Liability of a "transporter" is established by showing that a person accepted hazardous substances for transport and either selected the disposal facility or had substantial input into deciding where the hazardous substance should be disposed. The United States presented the testimony of the ADS mechanic who leased the Tabernacle site and who had been paid by ADS to accept the drummed liquid waste for storage. The United States also presented the testimony of the ADS mechanic's former wife, who said that she witnessed the dumping of barrels from ADS trucks on the Tabernacle site. The ADS dispatcher at the time said that he had sent drummed liquid to the Tabernacle site. At least one of the drums found at the sight had attached to it USX shipping documents, and other drums bore the name USX. Accordingly, the judgment that ADS is liable for cleanup costs is affirmed.

The appeal from the judgment against White and Carite presents an issue of first impression in this Court: what standard of liability did Congress intend to establish under CERCLA for principal shareholders and officers of a closely-held corporation that transports hazardous substances?

In *Tippins,* we held that section 107(a)(4) imposed liability on a waste transportation corporation not only if it ultimately selects the disposal facility, but also when it actively participates in the disposal decision to the extent of having had substantial input into which facility was ultimately chosen. This

"active participation" standard advances the objectives of CERCLA by recognizing the reality that transporters often play an influential role in the decision to dispose of waste at a given facility.

The express terms of section 107(a)(4) limit liability to those persons who accept hazardous substances for transport and have a substantial input into the selection of the disposal facility. Thus, section 107(a)(4) plainly imposes liability on corporate officers and shareholders if they participate in the liability-creating conduct.

The United States contends that Congress also intended to impose liability on those who control the affairs of a responsible corporation, irrespective of whether those in control actually participate in the liability-creating conduct. According to the United States, the courts have generally construed CERCLA as permitting recovery from those corporate officers who participated in the management of or exercised control over a corporate entity. Extending liability to those controlling a corporation, according to the United States, is consistent with CERCLA's goal of placing the ultimate responsibility for cleanup on those responsible for problems caused by the disposal of chemical poisons.

CERCLA, of course, is to be construed liberally to effectuate its goals. Liberal construction, however, may not be employed as a means for filling in the blanks so as to discern a congressional intent to impose liability under nearly every conceivable scenario. In light of the established principle of limited liability that protects corporate officers or employees who do not actually participate in liability-creating conduct, there must be some basis in the statute itself, beyond its general purpose, to support the conclusion that Congress intended to impose liability on those who control the corporation's day-to-day activities.

Congress could have specified that majority shareholders or officers of corporations engaged in the waste hauling business are personally responsible for releases of hazardous substances from disposal facilities selected by their companies. On the contrary, the sparse legislative history indicates that Congress anticipated that issues of liability not resolved by CERCLA shall be governed by evolving principles of common law. Under these circumstances, it is appropriate to limit liability to those persons who are clearly made liable by the language Congress used—those who actively participate in the process of accepting hazardous substances for transport and have a substantial role in the selection of the disposal site.

Contrary to the assertion of White and Carite, however, liability under section 107(a)(4) is not limited to those who personally participated in the transportation of hazardous wastes. It is not necessary that the officer personally accept the waste for transport. Nor is it necessary that the officer participate in the selection of the disposal facility. Liability may be imposed where the officer is aware of the acceptance of materials for transport and of his company's substantial participation in the selection of the disposal facility. An officer who has authority to control disposal decisions should not escape liability when she has actual knowledge that a subordinate has selected a disposal site and, effectively, acquiesces in the subordinate's actions.

Although there was indeed substantial evidence that White and Carite were actively involved in the day-to-day affairs of ADS at the time of the disposal of waste drums at the Tabernacle site, there was also countervailing evidence that White and Carite were not "hands on" managers during the relevant time period. Moreover, White disavowed knowledge of disposal of drums at the Tabernacle site. Corroboration for White's assertion may be inferred from the fact that during the relevant time frame he supervised the sales and administrative staff and did not have active involvement in the operational aspects of the business.

Tony Carite, the younger brother of Charles Carite, testified that Charles Carite had few specific responsibilities in the day-to-day business. Tony Carite was the operations manager of ADS. The ADS dispatcher and truck drivers at the time of the dumping testified that they reported directly to Tony Carite and had little, if any, involvement with Charles Carite.

Under these circumstances, the United States was not entitled to summary judgment against White and Carite.

Judgment against ADS affirmed; judgment reversed in favor of White and Carite.

INSURANCE AND INDEMNIFICATION

The extensive potential liability of directors deters many persons from becoming directors. They fear that their liability for their actions as directors may far exceed their fees as directors. To encourage persons to become directors, corporations **indemnify** them for their outlays associated with defending lawsuits brought against them and paying judgments and settlement amounts. In addition, or as an alternative, corporations purchase **insurance** that will make such payments for the directors. Indemnification and insurance are provided for officers, also.

Mandatory Indemnification of Directors

Under the MBCA, a director is entitled to *mandatory indemnification* of her reasonable litigation expenses when she is sued and *wins completely* (is *wholly successful*). The greatest part of such expenses is attorney's fees. Because indemnification is mandatory in this context, when the corporation refuses to indemnify a director who has won completely, she may ask a court to order the corporation to indemnify her.

Permissible Indemnification of Directors

Under the MBCA, a director who loses a lawsuit *may* be indemnified by the corporation. This is called *permissible indemnification,* because the corporation is permitted to indemnify the director but is not required to do so.

The corporation must establish that the director acted in *good faith* and reasonably believed that she acted in the *best interests* of the corporation. When a director seeks indemnification for a *criminal* fine, the corporation must establish a third requirement—that the director had no reasonable cause to believe that her conduct was unlawful. Finally, any permissible indemnification must be approved by someone independent of the director receiving indemnification—a disinterested board of directors, disinterested shareholders, or independent legal counsel. Permissible indemnification may cover not only the director's reasonable expenses but also fines and damages that the director has been ordered to pay.

A corporation may not elect to indemnify a director who was found to have received a *financial benefit* to which he was not entitled. Such a rule tends to prevent indemnification of directors who acted from self-interest. If a director received no financial benefit but was held liable to his corporation or paid an amount to the corporation as part of a *settlement,* the director may be indemnified only for his reasonable expenses, not for the amount that he paid to the corporation. The purpose of these rules is to avoid the circularity of having the director pay damages to the corporation and then having the corporation indemnify the director for the same amount of money.

Advances   A director may not be able to afford to make payments to her lawyer prior to the end of a lawsuit. More important, a lawyer may refuse to defend a director who cannot pay legal fees. Therefore, the MBCA permits a corporation to make advances to a director to allow the director to afford a lawyer, if the director affirms that she meets the requirements for permissible indemnification and she promises to repay the advances if she is found not entitled to indemnification.

Court-Ordered Indemnification   A court may order a corporation to indemnify a director if it determines that the director meets the standard for *mandatory* indemnification or if the director is *fairly and reasonably* entitled to indemnification in view of all the relevant circumstances.

Indemnification of Nondirectors   Under the MBCA, officers and employees who are not directors are entitled to the same mandatory indemnification rights as directors.

Insurance

The MBCA does not limit the ability of a corporation to purchase insurance on behalf of its directors, officers, and employees. Insurance companies, however, are unwilling to insure all risks. In addition, some risks are *legally uninsurable as against public policy.* Therefore, liability for misconduct such as self-dealing, usurpation, and securities fraud is uninsurable.

Nonprofit Corporations

A nonprofit corporation may obtain insurance and indemnify its officers and directors for liabilities incurred in the course of their performance of their official duties. The MNCA requires indemnification when the director or officer wins the lawsuit completely. A corporation is permitted to indemnify an officer or director who is found liable if he acted in good faith and reasonably believed he acted in the best interests of the corporation.

ETHICAL AND PUBLIC POLICY CONCERNS

1. Do you agree that the primary objective of a corporation should be to maximize profits for its shareholders? What other objectives should a corporation have in addition to or instead of maximizing profits? Should the board of directors engage in an activity that maximizes profits but harms the community in which the corporation is located? Is it possible for a board to maximize profits and to be socially responsible to the community in which the corporation is located?

2. Should corporation law absolutely prevent CEO domination of a corporation or merely allow shareholders to restrict CEO power if shareholders choose? Why do shareholders invest in a corporation in which the CEO dominates the corporation? Why don't shareholders elect directors who control the CEO?

3. Should corporation law allow a board of directors great discretion in fighting hostile takeovers of a corporation? Is your answer affected by whether the raider is able to manage the corporation better than current management? Is your answer affected by whether the raider intends to move the operations of the target to another community? What other factors might affect your view of the law we have concerning takeover defenses? Suppose the raider plans to break up the corporation and to sell the divisible parts of the corporation's business to other corporations. Is board opposition to such a hostile bid more justifiable? Does society benefit from such a bust-up takeover?

1. Pilot House Motor Inns, Inc., issued demand promissory notes for $540,000 to Marvin Herkowitz. No meeting of the directors was held to approve the issuance of the notes, but minutes of a supposed meeting at which the corporation resolved to issue the notes was signed by all the directors. The minutes stated, "We, the undersigned directors, hereby ratify and confirm the actions reflected in the foregoing minutes." Has the board officially acted to authorize the issuance of the notes?

2. Jacob Lehman and Shlomo Piontkowski were surgeons who practiced together in a professional corporation. They were the only directors and only shareholders, Lehman owning six shares and Piontkowski owning four shares. Each was an employee of the corporation. Piontkowski's employment contract granted to the board of directors of the corporation the power to terminate his employment for "personal misconduct of such a material nature as to be professionally detrimental to the corporation." From 1977 to 1979, Lehman and Piontkowski disagreed on the distribution of the corporation's income. Dissatisfied with his share of the income, Piontkowski canceled surgery, informed his patients that he was on vacation, and planned to open his own office nearby. At a special shareholder meeting, Lehman proposed that Piontkowski be removed as a director and voted his six shares to oust Piontkowski. Piontkowski did not vote his four shares. Lehman then nominated himself as sole director, voted his shares to elect himself sole director, and adjourned the shareholder meeting. Lehman then called the special directors' meeting to order and, as the sole director, dismissed Piontkowski as an employee. Has Piontkowski been properly removed as a director and employee?

3. Lillian Pritchard was a director of Pritchard & Baird Corporation, a business founded by her husband. After the death of her husband, her sons took control of the corporation. For two years, they looted the assets of the corporation through theft and improper payments. The corporation's financial statements revealed the improper payments to the sons, but Mrs. Pritchard did not read the financial statements. She did not know what her sons were doing to the corporation or that what they were doing was unlawful. When Mrs. Pritchard was sued for failing to protect the assets of the corporation, she argued that she was a figurehead director, a simple housewife who served as a director as an accommodation to her husband and sons. Was Mrs. Pritchard held liable?

4. The Chicago National League Ball Club, Inc. (Chicago Cubs), operated Wrigley Field, the Cubs' home park. Through the 1965 baseball season, the Cubs were the only major league baseball team that played no home games at night because Wrigley Field had no lights for nighttime baseball. Philip K. Wrigley, director and president of the corporation, refused to install lights because of his personal opinion that baseball was a daytime sport and that installing lights and scheduling night baseball games would result in the deterioration of the surrounding neighborhood. The other directors assented to this policy. From 1961 to 1965, the Cubs suffered losses from their baseball operations. The Chicago White Sox, whose weekday games were generally played at night, drew many more fans than did the Cubs. A shareholder sued the board of directors to force them to install lights at Wrigley Field and to schedule night games. What did the court rule?

5. Paul Brane, Kenneth Richison, Ralph Dawes, and John Thompson were directors of LaFontaine Grain Co-op, a grain elevator cooperative. Co-op hired Eldon Richison as its manager with authority to buy and sell grain, which accounted for 90 percent of its business. After Co-op suffered a substantial loss in 1979, its independent accountant recommended to the directors that Co-op hedge its grain positions to protect itself from future losses. The directors authorized Eldon Richison to hedge for Co-op, but he was inexperienced in hedging. Moreover, the board failed to attain knowledge of the basic fundamentals of hedging to be able to direct hedging activities and supervise Eldon Richison. He hedged only $20,050 in 1980, whereas Co-op had $7,300,000 in grain sales. Co-op lost over $400,000 in 1980, due primarily to the failure to hedge. Did the directors have liability to Co-op?

6. The management of MacMillan Corporation recognized that it would not be able to prevent a takeover of the corporation. Therefore, management convinced the directors to authorize an auction of the company. Only two bidders emerged: Kohlberg Kravis Roberts & Co. (KKR) and Robert Maxwell. Management preferred KKR and took steps to ensure that KKR would win the auction. Only hours before the deadline for bids, MacMillan's chairman and CEO tipped KKR that Maxwell's bid was lower than KKR's. MacMillan's auctioneer understood that Maxwell would top any KKR bid yet allowed Maxwell to believe that he had made the higher bid. The board granted KKR a lock-up option of MacMillan's crown jewels—its most valuable assets. Has MacMillan's board acted properly?

7. CSX Corp. owned 100 percent of the stock of Chesapeake & Ohio Railway (C&O). C&O owned 98 percent of the stock of Baltimore & Ohio Railroad (B&O). B&O owed 66 percent of the stock of Western Maryland Railway Company; C&O owned 20 percent of Western Maryland. C&O also owned 100 percent of the stock of Peakbay Corporation. The directors of B&O were also the directors of C&O and Western Maryland. First Boston, an investment banking firm, prepared a study for CSX in which financial data for Western Maryland was compared with that of other railroad companies. Paul Goodwin, the senior vice president for finance for B&O and C&O, and his staff formulated a value of $55 per share for Western Maryland's stock. CSX proposed a merger of Western Maryland and Peakbay, by which each share of Western Maryland would be converted into the right to receive $55 cash or CSX common shares of equivalent value. The book value of Western Maryland shares was $63.43 per share; the market price of the shares, which were traded over-the-counter, was $31.50. The merger was approved by the appropriate boards of directors and shareholders. B&O elected to receive cash of $64 million for its Western Maryland shares. A minority B&O shareholder sued the B&O directors, alleging that the sale price was less than B&O would have received had it solicited bids from outside parties for the controlling interest in Western Maryland. What standard did the court apply in determining whether the B&O directors acted properly? Did the directors sell the shares for insufficient consideration?

8. Lindenhurst Drugs, Inc., was owned equally by Allen Becker, Burton Steinberg, and Marvin Steinberg. Each was also an officer and director. The corporation operated a drugstore in leased space in the Linden Plaza Shopping Center. Burton was the manager of the drugstore. In 1979, wanting more retail space to expand their product lines, Becker and the Steinbergs offered to purchase the Ben Franklin store franchise in the Linden Plaza Shopping Center. Their offer was rejected, but the corporation still had an interest in buying the Ben Franklin store. In 1981, the Linden Plaza Shopping Center notified the corporation that its lease would not be renewed at the end of the year. Becker did not immediately inform the Steinbergs of the termination notice. He did nothing to find a new space for the store. Instead, Becker purchased the Ben Franklin store in the name of his own corporation and leased space for the Ben Franklin store from Linden Plaza Shopping Center. Has Becker done anything wrong?

9. Brothers Theodore and Lawrence Lerner were the only shareholders of Lerner Corporation, a real estate development and management company in Washington, D.C. Theodore owned 70 shares and Lawrence 25 shares of the corporation. Each was an officer and director. In April 1983, Lawrence discovered that Theodore was excluding Lawrence from the benefit of investment opportunities that had been developed through Lawrence's efforts and the use of the corporation's resources. Lawrence sued for judicial dissolution of the corporation. The suit was publicized in a Washington newspaper. Theodore believed that Lawrence would challenge future salary decisions and otherwise engage in behavior that would adversely affect the morale and productivity of key employees. He also believed that word of mouth and the newspaper notoriety about dissension in the corporation would cause prospective customers to prefer other real estate management companies. Theodore removed Lawrence as an officer and director and removed him from the payroll. Theodore also proposed to amend the articles to effect a 1-for-35 reverse stock split, by which Theodore's 70 shares would become 2 shares and Lawrence's 25 shares would become a fractional share. Corporation law allowed the corporation to purchase Lawrence's fractional share, which would result in Lawrence being forced to sell his interest in the corporation for $241,000. The articles amendment was approved by a majority of the outstanding shares. Lawrence sued to enjoin the reverse stock split. Should he be successful?

10. Butch Stanko was an officer and shareholder of Cattle King Packing Company, Inc, which operated a meatpacking plant in Adams County, Colorado. Gary Waderich was a general sales manager primarily responsible for commercial sales of meat food products and for the daily operation of Cattle King. Stanko set company policies and practices to circumvent the Federal Meat Inspection Act (FMIA), which policies and practices he instructed Waderich and other employees to follow. When Stanko returned to his home in Scottsbluff, Nebraska, he monitored operations by phone and visits to the plant to make certain that the policies and practices that he had established were being followed. For example, spoiled meat rejected by a buyer and returned to Cattle King was in bags that were puffy with gas caused by the spoilage. On instructions by Waderich, an employee reworked the meat by poking the bags to release the gas, and the meat was reshipped to the same buyer. Were Waderich, Stanko, and Cattle King guilty of criminal violations of the FMIA?

11. Shareholders collectively owning 80 percent of the shares of the Bank of New Mexico Holding Company made a shareholder's buy-sell agreement. Those shareholders included directors of the corporation. One of the agreeing shareholders sued the other shareholders, including the directors, to obtain a determination of the price of the shares under the agreement. The corporation reimbursed the legal expenses of the directors who, as shareholders, were defendants in the litigation. Did the corporation act properly in indemnifying the directors?

Shareholders' Rights and Liabilities

T he *shareholders* are the ultimate owners of a corporation, but a shareholder has *no right to manage* the corporation. Instead, a corporation is managed by its board of directors and its officers for the benefit of its shareholders.

The shareholders' role in a corporation is limited to electing and removing directors, approving certain important matters, and ensuring that the actions of the corporation's managers are consistent with the applicable state corporation statute, the articles of incorporation, and the bylaws.

Shareholders also assume a few responsibilities. For example, all shareholders are required to pay the promised consideration for shares. Shareholders are liable for receiving dividends beyond the lawful amount. In addition, controlling shareholders may owe special duties to minority shareholders.

Close corporation shareholders enjoy rights and owe duties beyond the rights and duties of shareholders of publicly owned corporations. In addition, some courts have found close corporation shareholders to be fiduciaries of each other.

This chapter's study of the rights and responsibilities of shareholders begins with an examination of shareholders' meetings and voting rights. ∽

SHAREHOLDERS' MEETINGS

The general corporation statutes of most states and the Model Business Corporation Act (MBCA) provide that an **annual meeting of shareholders** shall be held. The purpose of an annual shareholders' meeting is to elect new directors and to conduct other necessary business. Often, the shareholders are asked to approve the corporation's independent auditors and to vote on shareholders' proposals.

Special meetings of shareholders may be held whenever a corporate matter arises that requires immediate shareholders' action, such as the approval of a merger that cannot wait until the next annual shareholders' meeting. Under the MBCA, a special shareholders' meeting may be called by the board of directors or by a person authorized to do so by the bylaws, usually the president or the chairman of the board. In addition, the holders of at least 10 percent of the shares entitled to vote at the meeting may call a special meeting.

Notice of Meetings

To permit shareholders to arrange their schedules for attendance at shareholders' meetings, the MBCA requires the corporation to give shareholders **notice** of annual and special meetings of shareholders. Notice of a *special meeting* must list the purpose of the meeting. Under the MBCA, notice of an *annual meeting* need not include the purpose of the meeting unless shareholders will be asked to approve extraordinary corporate changes—for example, amendments to the articles of incorporation and mergers.

Notice need be given only to shareholders entitled to vote who are **shareholders of record** on a date fixed by the board of directors. Shareholders of record are those whose names appear on the share-transfer book of the corporation. Usually, only shareholders of record are entitled to vote at shareholders' meetings.

Conduct of Meetings

To conduct business at a shareholders' meeting, a **quorum** of the outstanding shares must be represented at the meeting. If the approval of more than one class of shares is required, a quorum of each class of shares must be present. A quorum is a majority of shares outstanding, unless a greater percentage is established in the articles. The president or the chairman of the board usually presides at shareholders' meetings. Minutes of shareholders' meetings are usually kept by the secretary.

A majority of the votes cast at the shareholders' meeting will decide issues that are put to a vote. If the approval of more than one class of shares is required, a majority of the votes cast by each class must favor the issue. The articles may require a greater than majority vote. Ordinarily, a shareholder is entitled to cast as many votes as he has shares.

Shareholders have a right of *full participation* in shareholders' meetings. This includes the right to offer resolutions, to speak for and against proposed resolutions, and to ask questions of the officers of the corporation.

Typical shareholder resolutions are aimed at protecting or enhancing the interests of minority shareholders and promoting current social issues. Proposals have included limiting corporate charitable contributions, restricting the production of nuclear power, banning the manufacture of weapons, and requiring the protection of the environment.

Shareholder Action without a Meeting

Generally, shareholders can act only at a properly called meeting. However, the MBCA permits shareholders to act without a meeting if *all of the shareholders entitled to vote consent in writing* to the action.

SHAREHOLDERS' ELECTION OF DIRECTORS

The most important shareholder voting right exercised at a shareholder meeting is the right to elect the directors. Normally, directors are elected by a single class of shareholders in **straight voting,** in which each share has one vote for each new director to be elected. With straight voting, a shareholder may vote for as many nominees as there are directors to be elected; a shareholder may cast for each such nominee as many votes as she has shares. For example, in a director election in which 15 people have been nominated for 5 director positions, a shareholder with 100 shares can vote for up to 5 nominees and can cast up to 100 votes for each of those 5 nominees.

Under straight voting, the nominees with the most votes are elected. Consequently, straight voting allows a majority shareholder to elect the entire board of directors. Thus, minority shareholders are unable to elect any representatives to the board without the cooperation of the majority shareholder.

Straight voting is also a problem in close corporations in which a few shareholders own equal numbers of shares. In such corporations, no shareholder individually controls the corporation, yet if the holders of a majority of the shares act together, those holders will elect all of the directors and control the corporation. Such control may be exercised to the detriment of the other shareholders.

Two alternatives to straight voting aid minority shareholders' attempts to gain representation on the board and prevent harmful coalitions in close corporations: cumulative voting and class voting.

Cumulative Voting   With cumulative voting, a corporation allows a shareholder to cumulate her votes by multiplying the number of directors to be elected by the shareholder's number of shares. A shareholder may then allocate her votes among the nominees as she chooses. She may vote only for as many nominees as there are directors to be elected, but she may vote for fewer nominees. For example, she may choose to cast all of her votes for only one nominee.

See Figure 1 for a further explanation of the mechanics of cumulative voting.

Classes of Shares   A corporation may have several classes of shares. The two most common classes are *common shares* and *preferred shares,* but a corporation may have several classes of common shares and several classes of preferred shares. Many close corporations have two or more classes of common shares with different voting rights. Each class may be entitled to elect one or more directors, in order to balance power in a corporation.

For example, suppose a corporation has four directors and 100 shares held by four shareholders— each of whom owns 25 shares. With straight voting and no classes of shares, no shareholder owns enough shares to elect himself as a director, because 51 shares are necessary to elect a director. Suppose, however, that the corporation has four classes of shares, each with the right to elect one of the directors. Each class of shares is issued to only one shareholder. Now, as the sole owner of a class of shares entitling the class to elect one director, each shareholder can elect himself to the board.

Shareholder Control Devices

While cumulative voting and class voting are two useful methods by which shareholders can allocate

FIGURE   1

Cumulative Voting Formula

The formula for determining the minimum number of shares required to elect a desired number of directors under cumulative voting is:

$$X = \frac{S \times R}{D + 1} + 1$$

X = Number of shares needed to elect the desired number of directors

S = Total number of shares voting at the shareholders' meeting

R = Number of director representatives desired

D = Total number of directors to be elected at the meeting

Example: Sarah Smiles wants to elect two of the five directors of Oates Corporation. One thousand shares will be voted. In this case:

$S = 1,000$

$R = 2$

$D = 5$

Therefore:

$$X = 334.33$$

Fractions are ignored; thus, Sarah will need to hold at least 334 shares to be able to elect two directors.

or acquire voting control of a corporation, there are other devices that may also be used for these purposes: voting trusts; shareholder voting agreements; and proxies, especially irrevocable proxies.

Voting Trusts   With a **voting trust,** shareholders transfer their shares to one or more voting trustees and receive voting trust certificates in exchange. The shareholders retain many of their rights, including the right to receive dividends, but the voting trustees vote for directors and other matters submitted to shareholders.

The purpose of a voting trust is to control the corporation through the concentration of shareholder voting power in the voting trustees, who often are participating shareholders. If several minority shareholders collectively own a majority of the shares of a corporation, they may create a voting trust and thereby control the corporation. You may ask why shareholders need a voting trust when they are in apparent agreement on how to vote their shares. The reason is that they may have disputes in the future that could prevent the shareholders from agreeing on how to vote. The voting trust ensures that the shareholder group will control the corporation despite the emergence of differences.

The MBCA limits the duration of voting trusts to 10 years, though the participating shareholders may agree to extend the term for another 10 years. Also, a voting trust must be made public, with copies of the voting trust document available for inspection at the corporation's offices.

Shareholder Voting Agreements   As an alternative to a voting trust, shareholders may merely agree how they will vote their shares. For example, shareholders collectively owning a majority of the shares may agree to vote for each other as directors, resulting in each being elected to the board of directors.

A shareholder voting agreement must be written; only shareholders signing the agreement are bound by it. When a shareholder refuses to vote as agreed, courts specifically enforce the agreement.

Shareholder voting agreements have two advantages over voting trusts. First, their duration may be *perpetual*. Second, they may be kept secret from the other shareholders; they usually do not have to be filed in the corporation's offices.

Proxies   A shareholder may appoint a **proxy** to vote his shares. If several minority shareholders collectively own a majority of the shares of a corporation, they may appoint a proxy to vote their shares and thereby control the corporation. The ordinary proxy has only a limited duration—11 months under the MBCA—unless a longer term is specified. Also, the ordinary proxy is *revocable* at any time. As a result, there is no guarantee that control agreements accomplished through the use of revocable proxies will survive future shareholder disputes.

However, a proxy is *irrevocable* if it is coupled with an interest. A proxy is coupled with an interest when, among other things, the person holding the proxy is a party to a shareholder voting agreement or a buy-and-sell agreement. The principal use of irrevocable proxies is in conjunction with shareholder voting agreements.

In the next case, the court considered the legality of a shareholder voting agreement.

SCHREIBER v. CARNEY   447 A.2d 17 (Del. Ch. Ct. 1982)

*T*exas *International Airlines, Inc. (TIA), proposed a new corporate structure in order to strengthen its financial position. To effect the restructuring, TIA would merge with Texas Air Company. The merger required approval of each of the four classes of TIA shareholders. Jet Capital Corporation owned all of the shares of Class C stock. Although Jet Capital believed that the merger would benefit TIA and the other shareholders, Jet Capital would suffer adverse tax consequences if the merger was effected. Thus, Jet Capital decided to vote against the merger. Jet Capital's adverse tax burden was due to its ownership of warrants to purchase TIA shares. Jet Capital could eliminate the merger's adverse tax impact by exercising the warrants prior to the merger, an alternative that Jet Capital was unwilling to choose since it would require a cash payment of over $3 million. Beyond its shares of TIA, Jet Capital had assets of only $200,000. To borrow the $3 million at market interest rates was too expensive.*

Therefore, TIA and Jet Capital agreed that TIA would loan Jet Capital $3 million at a below-market interest rate. Since Jet Capital would give the cash from the loan immediately back to TIA when it exercised the warrants, the loan had virtually no impact on TIA's cash position. As a condition of the loan, Jet Capital agreed to vote in favor of the merger. The loan agreement was approved by a majority of the shares held by shareholders other than Jet Capital. Subsequently, the merger was approved by the TIA shareholders.

Leonard Schreiber, a TIA shareholder, brought a derivative suit on behalf of TIA against TIA's directors, including Robert Carney. Schreiber argued that the loan transaction constituted vote-buying and, therefore, was an illegal voting agreement. ☜

Hartnett, Vice Chancellor   There are essentially two principles regarding vote-buying that appear in the Delaware caselaw. The first is that vote-buying is illegal *per se* if its object or purpose is to defraud or disenfranchise the other shareholders.

The second principle is that vote-buying is illegal *per se* as a matter of public policy, the reason being that each shareholder should be entitled to rely upon the independent judgment of his fellow shareholders.

The agreement in question was entered into primarily to further the interests of TIA's other shareholders. Indeed, the shareholders voted overwhelmingly in favor of the loan agreement. Thus, the underlying rationale for the argument that vote-buying is illegal *per se,* as a matter of public policy, ceases to exist when measured against the undisputed reason for the transaction.

Moreover, the rationale that vote-buying is, as a matter of public policy, illegal *per se* is founded upon considerations of policy that are now outmoded as a necessary result of an evolving corporate environment. According to 5 Fletcher *Cyclopedia Corporation* (Perm.Ed.) section 2066:

The theory that each shareholder is entitled to the personal judgment of each other shareholder expressed in his vote, and that any agreement among shareholders frustrating it was invalid, is obsolete because it is both impracticable and impossible of application to modern corporations with many widely scattered shareholders.

In *Ringling Bros.-Barnum & Bailey Combined Shows v. Ringling* (1947), the Delaware Supreme Court adopted a liberal approach to voting agreements. The court stated:

Generally speaking, a shareholder may exercise wide liberality of judgment in the matter of voting, and it is not objectionable that his motives may be for personal profit, or determined by whims or caprice, so long as he violates no duty owed his fellow shareholders.

It is clear that Delaware has discarded the presumption against voting agreements. Thus, an agreement involving the transfer of share voting rights without the transfer of ownership is not necessarily illegal and each arrangement must be examined in light of its object or purpose. To hold otherwise would be to exalt form over substance. Voting agreements in whatever form, therefore, should not be considered to be illegal *per se* unless the object or purpose is to defraud or in some way disenfranchise the other shareholders. This is not to say, however, that vote-buying accomplished for some laudable purpose is automatically free from challenge. Because vote-buying is so easily susceptible of abuse, it must be viewed as a voidable transaction subject to a test for intrinsic fairness.

Schreiber's motion for summary judgment is denied.

FUNDAMENTAL CORPORATE CHANGES

Other matters besides the election of directors require shareholder action, some because they make fundamental changes in the structure or business of the corporation.

Because the articles of incorporation embody the basic contract between a corporation and its shareholders, shareholders must approve most **amendments of the articles of incorporation.** For example, when the articles are amended to increase the number of authorized shares or reduce the dividend rights of preferred shareholders, shareholder approval is needed.

A **merger** is a transaction in which one corporation merges into a second corporation. Usually, the first corporation dissolves; the second corporation takes all the business and assets of both corporations and becomes liable for the debts of both corporations. Usually, the shareholders of the dissolved corporation become shareholders of the surviving corporation. Ordinarily, both corporations' shareholders must approve a merger.

A **consolidation** is similar to a merger except that both old corporations go out of existence and a new corporation takes the business, assets, and liabilities of the old corporations. Both corporations' shareholders must approve the consolidation. Modern corporate practice makes consolidations obsolete, since it is usually desirable to have one of the old corporations survive. The MBCA does not recognize consolidations. However, the effect of a consolidation can be achieved by creating a new corporation and merging the two old corporations into it.

A **share exchange** is a transaction by which one corporation becomes the owner of all of the outstanding shares of a second corporation through a *compulsory* exchange of shares: The shareholders of the second corporation are compelled to exchange their shares for shares of the first corporation. The second corporation remains in existence and becomes a wholly owned subsidiary of the first corporation. Only the selling shareholders must approve the share exchange.

A **sale of all or substantially all of the assets** of the business other than in the regular course of business must be approved by the shareholders of the selling corporation, since it drastically changes the shareholders' investment. Thus, a corporation's sale of all its real property and equipment is a sale of substantially all its assets, even though the corporation continues its business by leasing the assets back from the purchaser. However, a corporation that sells its building, but retains its machinery with the intent of continuing operations at another location, has not sold all or substantially all of its assets.

A **dissolution** is the first step in the termination of the corporation's business. The typical dissolution requires shareholder approval. Dissolution of corporations is covered more fully at the end of this chapter.

The articles of incorporation and the bylaws may require or permit other matters to be submitted for shareholder approval. For example, loans to officers, self-dealing transactions, and indemnifications of managers for litigation expenses may be approved by shareholders. Also, many of the states require shareholder approval of share option plans for high-level executive officers, but the MBCA does not.

Procedures Required

Similar procedures must be met to effect each of the above fundamental changes. The procedures include approval of the board of directors, notice to all of the shareholders whether or not they are entitled to vote, and majority approval of the votes held by shareholders entitled to vote under the statute, articles, or bylaws. Majority approval will be insufficient if a corporation has a supermajority shareholder voting requirement, such as one requiring two-thirds approval.

If there are two or more classes of shares, the articles may provide that matters voted on by shareholders must be approved by each class substantially affected by the proposed transaction. For example, a merger may have to be approved by a majority of the preferred shareholders and a majority of the common shareholders. As an alternative, the articles may require only the approval of the shareholders as a whole.

Under the MBCA, voting by classes is required for mergers, share exchanges, and amendments of the articles if these would substantially affect the rights of the classes. For example, the approval of preferred shareholders is required if a merger would change the dividend rights of preferred shareholders.

In many states, no approval of shareholders of the *surviving corporation* is required for a merger *if* the merger does not fundamentally alter the character of the business or substantially reduce the shareholders' voting or dividend rights.

Also, many statutes, including the MBCA, permit a merger between a parent corporation and its subsidiary without the approval of the shareholders of either corporation. Instead, the board of directors of the parent approves the merger and sends a copy of the merger plan to the subsidiary's shareholders. This simplified merger is called a **short-form merger.** It is available only if the parent owns a high percentage of the subsidiary's shares—90 percent under the MBCA and the Delaware statute.

DISSENTERS' RIGHTS

Many times, shareholders approve a corporate action by less than a unanimous vote, indicating that some shareholders oppose the action. For the most part, the dissenting shareholders have little recourse. Their choice is to remain shareholders or to sell their shares. For close corporation shareholders, there is no choice—the dissenting close corporation shareholder has no ready market for her shares, so she will remain a shareholder.

Some corporate transactions, however, so materially change a shareholder's investment in the corporation or have such an adverse effect on the value of a shareholder's shares that it has been deemed unfair to require the dissenting shareholder either to remain a shareholder (because there is no fair market for the shares) or to suffer a loss in value when he sells his shares on a market that has been adversely affected by the news of the corporate action. Corporate law has therefore responded by creating **dissenters' rights** (a right of appraisal) for shareholders who disagree with specified fundamental corporate transactions. Dissenters' rights require the corporation to pay dissenting shareholders the *fair value* of their shares.

Under the MBCA, the dissenters' rights cover mergers, short-form mergers, share exchanges, significant amendments of the articles of incorporation, and sales of all or substantially all the assets other than in the ordinary course of business. Some statutes cover consolidations also.

A dissenting shareholder seeking payment of the fair value of his shares must have the *right to vote* on the action to which he objects; however, a shareholder of a subsidiary in a short-form merger has dissenters' rights despite his lack of voting power. In addition, the shareholder must *not vote in favor* of the transaction. The shareholder may either vote against the action or abstain from voting.

Many states' statutes exclude from dissenters' rights shares that are traded on a recognized securities exchange such as the New York Stock Exchange. Instead, these statutes expect a shareholder to sell his shares on the stock exchange if he dissents to the corporate action. The MBCA has no such exclusion, on the grounds that the market price may be adversely affected by the news of the proposed or consummated corporate action to which the shareholder objects.

Generally, a shareholder must notify the corporation of his intent to seek payment before the shareholders have voted on the action. Next, the corporation informs a dissenting shareholder how to demand payment. After the dissenting shareholder demands payment, the corporation and the shareholder negotiate a mutually acceptable price. If they cannot agree, a court will determine the fair value of the shares and order the corporation to pay that amount.

To determine fair value, most judges use the **Delaware Block Method,** a weighted average of several valuation techniques—such as market value, comparisons with other similar companies, capitalization of earnings, and book value. Ironically, the Supreme Court of Delaware has abandoned the Delaware Block Method, recognizing the need for courts to value shares by methods generally considered acceptable to the financial community. The following case further elaborates on the modern Delaware method of appraising shares.

CEDE & CO. v. CINERAMA, INC. 684 A.2d 289 (Del. Sup. Ct. 1996)

Technicolor, Inc., was a Delaware corporation engaged in a number of businesses, including videocassette duplicating (one of the largest facilities in the world), photographic film processing for professionals, and motion picture licensing. In May 1981, Technicolor's CEO and chairman, Morton Kamerman, proposed—and its board of directors approved—an ambitious venture to develop a nationwide network of one-hour consumer film processing stores. Unfortunately, execution of the venture fell behind schedule, and Technicolor suffered severe fiscal problems, reporting an 80 percent decline in net income.

In late summer 1982, Ronald Perelman, controlling shareholder of MacAndrews & Forbes Group, Inc. (MAF), identified Technicolor as an attractive takeover target. Negotiations between Perelman and Kamerman resulted in MAF and Technicolor's agreement to MAF's two-step acquisition of Technicolor. The first step was an all-cash tender offer of $23 per share for all of Technicolor's outstanding shares; if not all Technicolor shareholders tendered their shares to MAF, the second step was a merger of MAF and Technicolor, by which all remaining Technicolor shareholders would receive $23 per share and Technicolor would merge with MAF. By December 3, 1982, MAF had acquired 82 percent of Technicolor's shares under the first step of the acquisition. Immediately, as controlling shareholder, MAF began looking for buyers of Technicolor's less profitable divisions, including the one-hour consumer film processing business. On January 24, 1983, Technicolor's shareholders approved the second step.

Several Technicolor shareholders, including Cinerama, Inc., which owned 201,200 shares, dissented from the merger and sought to have the Delaware Court of Chancery appraise their shares under their statutory dissenters' rights. Cinerama argued that the chancery court should value Technicolor with regard to the strategies that had been conceived and implemented by MAF and Perelman as of the merger date (the Perelman Plan). Technicolor argued that the court of chancery should consider Technicolor without regard to the

Perelman Plan and only as Technicolor existed prior to October 29, 1982, with the strategies implemented by Kamerman (the Kamerman Plan). The dispute was whether the trial court should value Perelman's Technicolor—a company whose business plans and strategies focused on the processing and duplication of film and videotape and expected to generate $50 million in cash during 1983 from the sale of unwanted or unprofitable business; or Kamerman's Technicolor—a company that had diversified away from a concentration on film processing and videotape duplication for the professional market toward consumer-oriented businesses. The chancery court valued Technicolor as of October 29, 1982, holding that the value added by the Perelman Plan was excluded from the appraisal because it was value arising from the merger or its expectations. Cinerama appealed to the Delaware Supreme Court. ∞

Holland, Justice   The Delaware appraisal statute provides that the Court of Chancery:

shall appraise the shares, determining their fair value exclusive of any element of value arising from the accomplishment or expectation of the merger or consolidation. In determining such fair value, the Court shall take into account all relevant factors. Del. Code section 262(h).

In *Weinberger v. UOP* (1983), the Delaware Supreme Court reconciled the dual mandates of section 262(h), which direct the court to determine fair value based on all relevant factors, but to exclude any element of value arising from the accomplishment or expectation of the merger. In making that reconciliation, the *Weinberger* court said:

Only the speculative elements of value that may arise from the "accomplishment or expectation" of the merger are excluded. We take this to be a very narrow exception to the appraisal process, designed to eliminate use of pro forma data and projections of a speculative variety relating to the completion of a merger. But elements of future value, including the nature of the enterprise, which are known or susceptible of proof as of the date of the merger and not the product of speculation, may be considered. Fair value also includes any damages, resulting from the taking, which the stockholders sustain as a class. If that was not the case, then the obligation to consider "all relevant factors" in the valuation process would be eroded.

The underlying assumption in an appraisal valuation is that the dissenting shareholders would be willing to maintain their investment position had the merger not occurred. Accordingly, the Court of Chancery's task in an appraisal proceeding is to value what has been taken from the shareholder, i.e., the proportionate interest in the going concern. To that end, the corporation must be valued as an operating entity. We conclude that the Court of Chancery did not adhere to this principle.

The Court of Chancery determined that Perelman had a fixed view of how Technicolor's assets would

be sold before the merger and had begun to implement it prior to January 24, 1983. Consequently, the Court of Chancery found that the Perelman Plan for Technicolor was the operative reality on the date of the merger. Nevertheless, the Court of Chancery held that Cinerama was not entitled to an appraisal of Technicolor as it was actually functioning on the date of the merger pursuant to the Perelman Plan. The Court of Chancery reasoned that valuing Technicolor as a going concern, under the Perelman Plan, on the date of the merger, would be tantamount to awarding Cinerama a proportionate share of a control premium, which the Court of Chancery deemed economically undesirable. Thus, the Court of Chancery concluded that value added by a majority acquiror is not a part of the going concern in which a dissenting shareholder has a legal right to participate.

In a two-step merger, to the extent that value has been added following a change in majority control before cash-out, it is still value attributable to the going concern, i.e., the extant "nature of the enterprise," on the date of the merger. Consequently, value added to the going concern by the majority acquiror during the transient period of a two-step merger, accrues to the benefit of all shareholders and must be included in the appraisal process on the date of the merger.

By failing to accord Cinerama the full proportionate value of its shares in the going concern on the date of the merger, the Court of Chancery imposed a penalty upon Cinerama for lack of control. Consequently, the Court of Chancery permitted MAF to reap a windfall from the appraisal process by cashing out a dissenting shareholder for less than the fair value of its interest in Technicolor as a going concern on the date of the merger.

Technicolor must be viewed and valued as an on-going enterprise, and occupying a particular market position in the light of future prospects. All elements of future value, including the nature of the enterprise, which are known or susceptible of proof as of the date of the merger and not the product of speculation, may and should be considered.

This appraisal action will be remanded to the Court of Chancery for a recalculation of Technicolor's fair value on the date of the merger. It is within the Court of Chancery's discretion to select one of the parties' valuation models as its general frame-work, or fashion its own. Its choice of framework does not require it to adopt any one expert's model, methodology, or mathematical calculation in toto.

Judgment reversed in favor of Cinerama; remanded to the Court of Chancery for appraisal of the shares.

SHAREHOLDERS' INSPECTION AND INFORMATION RIGHTS

Inspecting a corporation's books and records is sometimes essential to the exercise of a shareholder's rights. For example, a shareholder may be able to decide how to vote in a director election only after examining corporate financial records that reveal whether the present directors are managing the corporation profitably. Also, a close corporation shareholder may need to look at the books to determine the value of his shares.

Many corporate managers are resistant to shareholders inspecting the corporation's books and records, charging that shareholders are nuisances or that shareholders often have improper purposes for making such an inspection. Sometimes, management objects solely on the ground that it desires secrecy.

Most of the state corporation statutes specifically grant shareholders inspection rights. The purpose of these statutes is to facilitate the shareholder's inspection of the books and records of corporations whose managements resist or delay proper requests by shareholders. A shareholder's lawyer or accountant may assist the shareholder's exercise of his inspection rights.

The MBCA grants shareholders an **absolute right of inspection** of an alphabetical listing of the shareholders entitled to notice of a meeting, including the number of shares owned. Access to a shareholder list allows a shareholder to contact other shareholders about important matters such as shareholder proposals.

The MBCA also grants an absolute right of inspection of, among other things, the articles, bylaws, and minutes of shareholder meetings within the past three years.

Shareholders have a **qualified right to inspect** other records, however. To inspect accounting records, board and committee minutes, and shareholder minutes more than three years old, a shareholder must make the demand in *good faith* and have a *proper purpose*. Proper purposes include inspecting the books of account to determine the value of shares or the propriety of dividends. On the other hand, learning business secrets and aiding a competitor are clearly improper purposes.

In the following case, the court held that only shareholders of record are entitled to enforce inspection rights in a stock corporation.

SHAW v. AGRI-MARK, INC.   663 A.2d 464 (Del. Sup. Ct. 1995)

A gri-Mark, Inc., is a cooperative stock corporation organized under the Delaware General Corporation Law. It was formed to process and market milk and other dairy products for its members, dairy farmers in New England and New York. Members agree to sell all their milk to Agri-Mark, which agrees to sell the milk to the public. Agri-Mark's equity consists of contributions from its members and retained earnings; the members are not, however, shareholders of the corporation. The only shareholders are the directors. Each director is issued one share for one dollar; when a director's term expires, he must resell the share to the corporation for one dollar. Only directors are permitted to vote at shareholder meetings. Agri-Mark is managed by the board of directors, who are elected by the regional delegates who represent a region of the area served by Agri-Mark. The delegates, in turn, are elected by members in that region.

Members Karen Shaw and Forrest Foster, dairy farmers in Vermont, brought an action to compel Agri-Mark to allow them to inspect Agri-Mark's members list and the compensation of Agri-Mark's five highest paid executives. The trial court found Shaw and Foster entitled to inspect the records even though they were not shareholders, on the grounds that they were equity owners and had averred a proper purpose to inspect the records. Agri-Mark appealed the decision. ∞

Walsh, Justice It is well established that, as a matter of common law, a stockholder of a Delaware corporation possessed a qualified right to inspect or examine the stock ledger, as well as the books and records of the corporation. The common law right of inspection was not absolute. In order to enforce inspection rights, the stockholder demanding inspection had to show that the inspection was for proper purposes. In addition to the common law right of inspection, the right has been codified in some form in Delaware since the turn of the century. The stockholder's right to inspect the stock ledger is currently codified at Del. Code section 220:

(a) As used in this section, "stockholder" means a stockholder of record.

(b) Any stockholder, in person or by attorney or other agent, shall have the right to inspect for any proper purpose the corporation's stock ledger, a list of its stockholders, and its other books and records. A proper purpose shall mean a purpose reasonably related to such person's interest as a stockholder.

Establishing oneself as a stockholder of record is a mandatory condition precedent to the right to make a demand for inspection. In this regard, the corporation may look to its stock ledger as the sole evidence in identifying those shareholders of record who are entitled to inspection. It is obvious that the only persons who are integrated with a corporation as stockholders are those persons who are stockholders of record on the stock books of the corporation. To hold otherwise would lead to corporate chaos.

This Court has yet to decide whether a member of a Delaware non-stock corporation has a right to inspection of the corporation's books and records. We need not reach the issue here because we decide only the case before us. Agri-Mark is a *stock* corporation, and the rights of its members must be evaluated from this perspective.

Both at common law and under the specific statutory provisions, the right of inspection is essentially a right of stockholders, being an incident of stock ownership. As such, the right of inspection of a *stock* corporation's books and records under Delaware common law is exclusively reserved to the stockholders of the corporation.

Shaw and Foster's argument that they should be recognized as stockholders of Agri-Mark since they are the real owners of the cooperative is unconvincing. While Shaw and Foster may assert certain rights arising out of the fiduciary relationship between themselves as equity owners and those who manage the affairs of the corporation, those rights do not extend to or include the attributes of record stockholders. Our corporate law has traditionally limited the right of stockholders to stockholders of record. We continue to recognize the long-established rule that a corporation may rely on its stock ledger in determining which stockholders are eligible to vote or exercise the important rights of a stockholder.

In this case, Shaw and Foster are not stockholders of Agri-Mark, let alone shareholders of record. Agri-Mark has issued one share of stock to each member of its board of directors. As the only stockholders of Agri-Mark, the directors exclusively enjoy the rights incident to their share ownership. In contrast, Shaw and Foster, as members of a stock corporation, do not enjoy any of the rights exclusively reserved for stockholders under either Delaware common law or the Delaware General Corporation Law. Just as a beneficial owner must recognize the risks inherent in choosing to register his or her shares in a "street name" and thereby cede the rights of share ownership to the record owner of stock, so too have Shaw and Foster ceded the rights of stock ownership to the actual stockholders of Agri-Mark. We hold, therefore, that a member of a Delaware *stock* corporation must be a stockholder of record to be entitled to inspect the books and records of the corporation under our common law.

Judgment reversed in favor of Agri-Mark.

Shareholders also have the right to receive from the corporation **information** that is important to their voting and investing decisions. The MBCA requires a corporation to furnish its shareholders *financial statements,* including a balance sheet, an income statement, and a statement of changes in shareholders' equity. The Securities Exchange Act of 1934 also requires publicly held companies to furnish such statements, as well as other information that is important to a shareholders' voting and investing decisions.

PREEMPTIVE RIGHT

The market price of a shareholder's shares will be reduced if a corporation issues additional shares at a price less than the market price. In addition, a shareholder's proportionate voting, dividend, and liquidation rights may be adversely affected by the issuance of additional shares. For example, if a corporation's only four shareholders each own 100 shares worth $10 per share, then each shareholder has shares worth $1,000, a 25 percent interest in any dividends declared, 25 percent of the voting power, and a claim against 25 percent of the corporation's assets after creditors' claims have been satisfied. If the corporation subsequently issues 100 shares to another person for only $5 per share, the value of each shareholder's shares falls to $900 and his dividend, voting, and liquidation rights are reduced to 20 percent. In a worse-scenario, the corporation issues 201 shares to one of the existing shareholders, giving that shareholder majority control of the corporation and reducing the other shareholders' interests to less than 17 percent each. As a result, the minority shareholders will be dominated by the majority shareholder and will receive a greatly reduced share of the corporation's dividends.

Such harmful effects of an issuance could have been prevented if the corporation had been required to offer each existing shareholder a percentage of the new shares equal to her current proportionate ownership. If, for example, in the situation described above, the corporation had offered 50 shares to each shareholder, each shareholder could have remained a 25 percent owner of the corporation; her interests in the corporation would not have been reduced, and her total wealth would not have been decreased.

Corporation law recognizes the importance of giving a shareholder the option of maintaining the value of his shares and retaining his proportionate interest in the corporation. This is the shareholder's **preemptive right,** an option to subscribe to a new issuance of shares in proportion to the shareholder's current interest in the corporation.

The MBCA adopts a comprehensive scheme for determining preemptive rights. It provides that the preemptive right does not exist except to the extent provided by the articles. The MBCA permits the corporation to state expressly when the preemptive right arises.

When the preemptive right exists, the corporation must notify a shareholder of her option to buy shares, the number of shares that she is entitled to buy, the price of the shares, and when the option must be exercised. Usually, the shareholder is issued a **right,** a written option that she may exercise herself or sell to a person who wishes to buy the shares.

DISTRIBUTIONS TO SHAREHOLDERS

During the life of a corporation, shareholders may receive distributions of the corporation's assets. Most people are familiar with one type of distribution—dividends—but there are other important types of distributions to shareholders, including payments to shareholders upon the corporation's repurchase of its shares.

There is one crucial similarity among all the types of distributions to shareholders: Corporate assets are transferred to shareholders. Consequently, an asset transfer to shareholders may harm the corporation's creditors and others with claims against the corporation's assets. For example, a distribution of assets may impair a corporation's ability to pay its creditors. In addition, a distribution to one class of shareholders may harm another class of shareholders that has a liquidation priority over the class of shareholders receiving the distribution. The existence of these potential harms compels corporation law to restrict the ability of corporations to make distributions to shareholders.

Dividends

One important objective of a business corporation is to make a profit. Shareholders invest in a corporation primarily to share in the expected profit either through appreciation of the value of their shares or through dividends. There are two types of dividends: *cash or property dividends* and *share dividends.* Only cash or property dividends are distributions of the corporation's assets. Share dividends are *not* distributions.

Cash or Property Dividends   Dividends are usually paid in cash. However, other assets of the corporation—such as airline discount coupons or shares of another corporation—may also be distributed as dividends. Cash or property dividends are declared by the board of directors and paid by the corporation on the date stated by the directors. Once declared, dividends are *debts* of the corporation and shareholders may sue to force payment of the dividends. The board's dividend declaration, including the amount of dividend and whether to declare a dividend, is protected by the business judgment rule.

Preferred shares nearly always have a set dividend rate stated in the articles of incorporation. Even so, unless the preferred dividend is mandatory, the board has discretion to determine whether to pay a preferred dividend and what amount to pay. Most preferred shares are *cumulative preferred shares,* on which unpaid dividends cumulate. The entire accumulation must be paid before common shareholders may receive any dividend. Even when preferred shares are noncumulative, the current dividend must be paid to preferred shareholders before any dividend may be paid to common shareholders.

The following is one of the few cases in which a court ordered the payment of a dividend to common shareholders. The court found that Henry Ford had the wrong motives for causing Ford Motor Company to refuse to pay a dividend.

DODGE v. FORD MOTOR CO.   170 N.W. 668 (Mich. Sup. Ct. 1919)

I n 1916, brothers John and Horace Dodge owned 10 percent of the common shares of the Ford Motor Company. Henry Ford owned 58 percent of the outstanding common shares and controlled the corporation and its board of directors. Starting in 1911, the corporation paid a regular annual dividend of $1.2 million, which was 60 percent of its capital stock of $2 million but only about 1 percent of its total equity of $114 million. In addition, from 1911 to 1915, the corporation paid special dividends totaling $41 million.

The policy of the corporation was to reduce the selling price of its cars each year. In June 1915, the board and officers agreed to increase production by constructing new plants for $10 million, acquiring land for $3 million, and erecting an $11 million smelter. To finance the planned expansion, the board decided not to reduce the selling price of cars beginning in August 1915 and to accumulate a large surplus.

A year later, the board reduced the selling price of cars by $80 per car. The corporation was able to produce 600,000 cars annually, all of which, and more, could have been sold for $440 instead of the new $360 price, a forgone revenue of $48 million. At the same time, the corporation announced a new dividend policy of paying no special dividend. Instead, it would reinvest all earnings except the regular dividend of $1.2 million.

Henry Ford announced his justification for the new dividend policy in a press release: "My ambition is to employ still more men, to spread the benefits of this industrial system to the greatest possible number, to help them build up their lives and their homes." The corporation had a $112 million surplus, expected profits of $60 million, total liabilities of $18 million, $52.5 million in cash on hand, and municipal bonds worth $1.3 million.

The Dodge brothers sued the corporation and the directors to force them to declare a special dividend. The trial court ordered the board to declare a dividend of $19.3 million. Ford Motor Company appealed. ∞

Ostrander, Chief Justice   It is a well-recognized principle of law that the directors of a corporation, and they alone, have the power to declare a dividend of the earnings of the corporation, and to determine its amount. Courts will not interfere in the management of the directors unless it is clearly made to appear that they are guilty of fraud or misappropriation of the corporate funds, or they refuse to declare

a dividend when the corporation has a surplus of net profits which it can, without detriment to the business, divide among its stockholders, and when a refusal to do so would amount to such an abuse of discretion as would constitute a fraud, or breach of that good faith that they are bound to exercise towards the shareholders.

The testimony of Mr. Ford convinces this court that he has to some extent the attitude towards shareholders of one who has dispensed and distributed to them large gains and that they should be content to take what he chooses to give. His testimony creates the impression that he thinks the Ford Motor Company has made too much money, has had too large profits, and that, although large profits might be still earned, a sharing of them with the public, by reducing the price of the output of the company, ought to be undertaken. We have no doubt that certain sentiments, philanthropic and altruistic, creditable to Mr. Ford, had large influence in determining the policy to be pursued by the Ford Motor Company.

There should be no confusion of the duties that Mr. Ford conceives that he and the shareholders owe to the general public and the duties that in law he and his co-directors owe to protesting, minority shareholders. A business corporation is organized and carried on primarily for the profit of the shareholders. The powers of the directors are to be employed for that end.

We are not, however, persuaded that we should interfere with the proposed expansion of the Ford Motor Company. In view of the fact that the selling price of products may be increased at any time, the ultimate results of the larger business cannot be certainly estimated. The judges are not business experts. It is recognized that plans must often be made for a long future, for expected competition, for a continuing as well as an immediately profitable venture. We are not satisfied that the alleged motives of the directors, in so far as they are reflected in the conduct of the business, menace the interests of shareholders.

Assuming the general plan and policy of expansion were for the best ultimate interest of the company and therefore of its shareholders, what does it amount to in justification of a refusal to declare and pay a special dividend? The Ford Motor Company was able to estimate with nicety its income and profit. It could sell more cars than it could make. The profit upon each car depended upon the selling price. That being fixed, the yearly income and profit was determinable, and, within slight variations, was certain.

There was appropriated for the smelter $11 million. Assuming that the plans required an expenditure sooner or later of $10 million for duplication of the plant, and for land $3 million, the total is $24 million. The company was a cash business. If the total cost of proposed expenditures had been withdrawn in cash from the cash surplus on hand August 1, 1916, there would have remained $30 million.

The directors of Ford Motor Company say, and it is true, that a considerable cash balance must be at all times carried by such a concern. But there was a large daily, weekly, monthly receipt of cash. The output was practically continuous and was continuously, and within a few days, turned into cash. Moreover, the contemplated expenditures were not to be immediately made. The large sum appropriated for the smelter plant was payable over a considerable period of time. So that, without going further, it would appear that, accepting and approving the plan of the directors, it was their duty to distribute on and near the 1st of August 1916, a very large sum of money to stockholders.

Judgment for the Dodge brothers affirmed.

To protect the claims of the corporation's creditors, all of the corporation statutes limit the extent to which dividends may be paid. The MBCA imposes two limits: (1) the *solvency test* and (2) the *balance sheet test.*

Solvency Test   A dividend may not make a corporation insolvent; that is, unable to pay its debts as they come due in the usual course of business. This means that a corporation may pay a dividend to the extent it has *excess solvency*—that is, liquidity that it does not need to pay its currently maturing obligations. This requirement protects creditors, who are concerned primarily with the corporation's ability to pay debts as they mature.

Balance Sheet Test   After the dividend has been paid, the corporation's assets must be sufficient to cover its liabilities and the liquidation preference of shareholders having a priority in liquidation over the shareholders receiving the dividend. This means that a corporation may pay a dividend to the extent it has *excess assets*—that is, assets it does not need to cover its liabilities and the liquidation preferences of shareholders having a priority in liquidation over the shareholders receiving the dividends. This requirement protects not only creditors but also preferred shareholders. It prevents a corporation from paying to common shareholders a dividend that will impair the liquidation rights of preferred shareholders.

Example   Batt Company has $27,000 in excess liquidity that it does not need to pay its currently maturing obligations. It has assets of $200,000 and liabilities of $160,000. It has one class of common shareholders. Its one class of preferred shareholders has a liquidation preference of $15,000. Examining these facts, we find that Batt's excess solvency is $27,000, but its excess assets are only $25,000 ($200,000 − 160,000 − 15,000). Therefore, Batt's shareholders may receive a maximum cash or property dividend of $25,000, which will eliminate all of Batt's excess assets and leave Batt with $2,000 of excess solvency.

Share Dividends and Share Splits   Corporations sometimes distribute additional shares of the corporation to their shareholders. Often, this is done in order to give shareholders something instead of a cash dividend so that the cash can be retained and reinvested in the business. Such an action may be called either a **share dividend** or a **share split.**

A **share dividend** of a *specified percentage of outstanding shares* is declared by the board of directors. For example, the board may declare a 10 percent share dividend. As a result, each shareholder will receive 10 percent more shares than she currently owns. A share dividend is paid on outstanding shares only. Unlike a cash or property dividend, a share dividend may be revoked by the board after it has been declared.

A **share split** results in shareholders receiving a specified number of shares in exchange for each share that they currently own. For example, shares may be split two for one. Each shareholder will now have two shares for each share that he previously owned. A holder of 50 shares will now have 100 shares instead of 50.

The MBCA recognizes that a share split or a share dividend in the same class of shares does not affect the value of the corporation or the shareholders' wealth, because no assets have been transferred from the corporation to the shareholders. The effect is like that produced by taking a pie with four pieces and dividing each piece in half. Each person may receive twice as many pieces of the pie, but each piece is worth only half as much. The total amount received by each person is unchanged.

Therefore, the MBCA permits share splits and share dividends of the same class of shares to be made merely by action of the directors. The directors merely have the corporation issue to the shareholders the number of shares needed to effect the share dividend or split. The corporation must have a sufficien number of authorized, unissued shares to effect the share split or dividend; when it does not, its articles must be amended to create the required number of additional authorized shares.

Reverse Share Split   A *reverse share split* is a decrease in the number of shares of a class such that, for example, two shares become one share. Most of the state corporation statutes require shareholder action to amend the articles to effect a reverse share split because the number of authorized shares is reduced. The purpose of a reverse share split is usually to increase the market price of the shares.

Share Repurchases

Declaring a cash or property dividend is only one of the ways in which a corporation may distribute its assets. A corporation may also distribute its assets by repurchasing its shares from its shareholders. Such a repurchase may be either a *redemption* or an *open-market repurchase.*

The right of **redemption** (or a call) is usually a right of the corporation to force an *involuntary* sale by a shareholder at a fixed price. The shareholder must sell the shares to the corporation at the corporation's request; in most states, the shareholder cannot force the corporation to redeem the shares.

Under the MBCA, the right of redemption must appear in the articles of incorporation. It is common for a corporation to issue preferred shares subject to redemption at the corporation's option. Usually, common shares are not redeemable.

In addition, a corporation may repurchase its shares **on the open market.** A corporation is empowered to purchase its shares from any shareholder who is willing to sell them. Such repurchases are *voluntary* on the shareholder's part, requiring the corporation to pay a current market price to entice the shareholder to sell.

A corporation's repurchase of its shares may harm creditors and other shareholders. The MBCA requires a corporation repurchasing shares to meet tests that are the same as its cash and property dividend rules, recognizing that financially, a repurchase of shares is no different from a dividend or any other distribution of assets to shareholders.

1. *Solvency Test:* The repurchase may not make the corporation insolvent, that is—unable to pay its debts as they come due in the usual course of business. This means that a corporation may repurchase shares to the extent it has *excess solvency.*

2. *Balance Sheet Test:* After the repurchase of shares, the corporation's assets must be sufficient to cover its liabilities and the liquidation preference of shareholders having a priority in liquidation over the shareholders whose shares were repurchased. This means that a corporation may repurchase shares to the extent that it has *excess assets.*

SHAREHOLDERS' LAWSUITS

Shareholders' Individual Lawsuits

A shareholder has the right to sue in his own name to prevent or redress a breach of the shareholder's contract. For example, a shareholder may sue to recover dividends declared but not paid or dividends that should have been declared, to enjoin the corporation from committing an *ultra vires* act, to enforce the shareholder's right of inspection, and to enforce preemptive rights.

Shareholder Class Action Suits

When several people have been injured similarly by the same persons in similar situations, one of the injured people may sue for the benefit of all the people injured. Likewise, if several shareholders have been similarly affected by a wrongful act of another, one of these shareholders may bring a **class action** on behalf of all the affected shareholders.

An appropriate class action under state corporation law would be an action seeking a dividend payment that has been brought by a preferred shareholder for all of the preferred shareholders.

Any recovery is prorated to all members of the class.

A shareholder who successfully brings a class action is entitled to be reimbursed from the award amount for his *reasonable expenses,* including attorney's fees. If the class action suit is unsuccessful and has no reasonable foundation, the court may order the suing shareholder to pay the defendants' reasonable litigation expenses, including attorney's fees.

Shareholders' Derivative Actions

When a corporation has been harmed by the actions of another person, the right to sue belongs to the corporation and any damages awarded by a court belong to the corporation. Hence, as a general rule, a shareholder has no right to sue in his own name when someone has harmed the corporation, and he may not recover for himself damages from that person. This is the rule even when the value of the shareholder's investment in the corporation has been impaired.

Nonetheless, one or more shareholders are permitted under certain circumstances to bring an action for the benefit of the corporation when the directors have failed to pursue a corporate cause of action. For example, if the corporation has a claim against its chief executive for wrongfully diverting corporate assets to her personal use, the corporation is unlikely to sue the chief executive because she controls the board of directors. Clearly, the CEO should not go unpunished. Consequently, corporation law authorizes a shareholder to bring a **derivative action** (or derivative suit) against the CEO on behalf of the corporation and for its benefit. Such a suit may also be used to bring a corporate claim against an outsider.

If the derivative action succeeds and damages are awarded, the damages ordinarily go to the corporate treasury for the benefit of the corporation. The suing shareholder is entitled only to reimbursement of his reasonable attorney's fees that he incurred in bringing the action.

Eligible Shareholders Although allowing shareholders to bring derivative suits creates a viable procedure for suing wrongdoing officers and directors, this procedure is also susceptible to abuse. **Strike suits** (lawsuits brought to gain out-of-court settlements for the complaining shareholders personally or to earn large attorney's fees, rather than to obtain a recovery for the corporation) have not been uncommon. To discourage strike suits, the person bringing the action must be a current shareholder who also held his shares at the time the alleged wrong occurred. In addition, the shareholder must fairly and adequately represent the interests of shareholders similarly situated in enforcing the right of the corporation.

One exception to these rules is the **double derivative suit,** a suit brought by a shareholder of a parent corporation on behalf of a subsidiary corporation owned by the parent. Courts regularly permit double derivative suits.

Demand on Directors Since a decision to sue someone is ordinarily made by corporate managers, a shareholder must first **demand** that the board of directors bring the suit. A demand informs the board that the corporation may have a right of action against a person that the board, in its business judgment, may decide to pursue. Therefore, if a demand is made and the board decides to bring the suit, the shareholder may not institute a derivative suit.

Ordinarily, a shareholder's failure to make a demand on the board prevents her from bringing a derivative suit. Nonetheless, the shareholder may initiate the suit if she proves that a demand on the board would have been useless or **futile.** Demand is futile, and therefore **excused,** if the board is unable to make a disinterested decision regarding whether to sue. Futility may be proved when all or a majority of the directors are interested in the challenged transaction, such as in a suit alleging that the directors issued shares to themselves at below-market prices.

If a shareholder makes a demand on the board and it **refuses** the shareholder's demand to bring a suit, ordinarily the shareholder is not permitted to continue the derivative action. The decision to bring a lawsuit is an ordinary business decision appropriate for a board of directors to make. The business judgment rule, therefore, is available to insulate from court review a board's decision not to bring a suit.

Of course, if a shareholder derivative suit accuses the board of harming the corporation, such as by misappropriating the corporation's assets, the board's refusal will not be protected by the business judgment rule because the board has a conflict of interest in its decision to sue. In such a situation, the shareholder may sue the directors despite the board's refusal.

Shareholder Litigation Committees In an attempt to ensure the application of the business judgment rule in demand refusal and demand futility situations, interested directors have tried to isolate themselves from the decision whether to sue by creating a special committee of the board, called a *shareholder litigation committee* (SLC) (or independent investigation committee) whose purpose is to decide whether to sue. The SLC should consist of directors who are not defendants in the derivative suit, who are not interested in the challenged action, are independent of the defendant directors, and if possible, were not directors at the time the wrong occurred. Usually, the SLC has independent legal counsel that assists its determination whether to sue. Because the SLC is a committee of the board, its decision may be protected by the business judgment rule. Therefore, an SLC's decision not to sue may prevent a shareholder from suing.

Shareholders have challenged the application of the business judgment rule to an SLC's decision to dismiss a shareholder derivative suit against some of the directors. The suing shareholders argue that it is improper for an SLC to dismiss a shareholder derivative suit because there is a *structural bias.* That is, the SLC members are motivated by a desire to avoid hurting their fellow directors and adversely affecting future working relationships within the board.

When demand is **not futile,** most of the courts that have been faced with this question have upheld the decisions of special litigation committees that comply with the business judgment rule. The courts require that the SLC members be *independent* of the defendant directors, be *disinterested* with regard to the subject matter of the suit, make a *reasonable investigation* into whether to dismiss the suit, and act in *good faith.*

When demand is **futile or excused,** most courts faced with the decision of an SLC have applied the rule of the *Zapata* case, which follows.

Z *apata Corporation had a share option plan that permitted its executives to purchase Zapata shares at a below-market price. Most of the directors participated in the share option plan. In 1974, the directors voted to advance the share option exercise date in order to reduce the federal income tax liability of the executives who exercised the share options, including the directors. An additional effect, however, was to increase the corporation's federal tax liability.*

William Maldonado, a Zapata shareholder, believed that the board action was a breach of a fiduciary duty and that it harmed the corporation. In 1975, he instituted a derivative suit in a Delaware court on behalf of Zapata against all of the directors. He failed to make a demand on the directors to sue themselves, alleging that this would be futile since they were all defendants.

The derivative suit was still pending in 1979, when four of the defendants were no longer directors. The remaining directors then appointed two new outside directors to the board and created an Independent Investigation Committee consisting solely of the two new directors. The board authorized the committee to make a final and binding decision regarding whether the derivative suit should be brought on behalf of the corporation. Following a three-month investigation, the committee concluded that Maldonado's derivative suit should be dismissed as against Zapata's best interests.

Zapata asked the Delaware court to dismiss the derivative suit. The court refused, holding that Maldonado possessed an individual right to maintain the derivative action and that the business judgment rule did not apply. Zapata appealed to the Supreme Court of Delaware. ∽

Quillen, Justice We find that the trial court's determination that a shareholder, once demand is made and refused, possesses an independent, individual right to continue a derivative suit for breaches of fiduciary duty over objection by the corporation, as an absolute rule, is erroneous.

Derivative suits enforce corporate rights, and any recovery obtained goes to the corporation. We see no inherent reason why a derivative suit should automatically place in the hands of the litigating shareholder sole control of the corporate right throughout the litigation. Such an inflexible rule would recognize the interest of one person or group to the exclusion of all others within the corporate entity.

When, if at all, should an authorized board committee be permitted to cause litigation, properly initiated by a derivative stockholder in his own right, to be dismissed? The problem is relatively simple. If, on the one hand, corporations can consistently wrest bona fide derivative actions away from well-meaning derivative plaintiffs through the use of the committee mechanism, the derivative suit will lose much, if not all, of its effectiveness as an intracorporate means of policing boards of directors. If, on the other hand, corporations are unable to rid themselves of meritless or harmful litigation and strike suits, the derivative action, created to benefit the corporation, will produce the opposite, unin-

tended result. It thus appears desirable to us to find a balancing point where bona fide shareholder power to bring corporate causes of action cannot be unfairly trampled on by the board of directors, but the corporation can rid itself of detrimental litigation.

We are not satisfied that acceptance of the business judgment rationale at this stage of derivative litigation is a proper balancing point. We must be mindful that directors are passing judgment on fellow directors in the same corporation and fellow directors, in this instance, who designated them to serve both as directors and committee members. The question naturally arises whether a "there but for the grace of God go I" empathy might not play a role. And the further question arises whether inquiry as to independence, good faith and reasonable investigation is sufficient safeguard against abuse, perhaps subconscious abuse.

We thus steer a middle course between those cases that yield to the independent business judgment of a board committee and this case as determined below, which would yield to unbridled shareholder control.

We recognize that the final substantive judgment whether a particular lawsuit should be maintained requires a balance of many factors—ethical, commercial, promotional, public relations, employee relations, fiscal, as well as legal. We recognize the danger of judicial overreaching but the alternatives seem to us to be outweighed by the fresh view of a judicial outsider.

After an objective and thorough investigation of a derivative suit, an independent committee may cause its corporation to file a motion to dismiss the derivative suit. The Court should apply a two-step test to the motion. First, the Court should inquire into the independence and good faith of the committee and the bases supporting its conclusions. The corporation should have the burden of proving independence, good faith, and reasonable investigation, rather than presuming independence, good faith, and reasonableness. If the Court determines either that the committee is not independent or has not shown reasonable bases for its conclusions, or if the Court is not satisfied for other reasons relating to the process, including but not limited to the good faith of the committee, the Court shall deny the corporation's motion to dismiss the derivative suit.

The second step provides the essential key in striking the balance between legitimate corporate claims as expressed in a derivative stockholder suit and a corporation's best interests as expressed by an independent investigating committee. The Court should determine, applying its own independent business judgment, whether the motion should be granted. The second step is intended to thwart instances where corporate actions meet the criteria of step one, but the result does not appear to satisfy its spirit, or where corporate actions would simply prematurely terminate a stockholder grievance deserving of further consideration in the corporation's interest. The Court of course must carefully consider and weigh how compelling the corporate interest in dismissal is when faced with a nonfrivolous lawsuit. The Court should, when appropriate, give special consideration to matters of law and public policy in addition to the corporation's best interests.

The second step shares some of the same spirit and philosophy of the statement of the trial court: "Under our system of law, courts and not litigants should decide the merits of litigation."

Judgment reversed in favor of Zapata. Case remanded to the trial court.

Litigation Expenses   If a shareholder is successful in a derivative suit, she is entitled to a reimbursement of her reasonable litigation expenses out of the corporation's damage award. On the other hand, if the suit is unsuccessful and has been brought without reasonable cause, the shareholder must pay the defendants' expenses, including attorney's fees. The purpose of this rule is to deter strike suits by punishing shareholders who litigate in bad faith.

Defense of Corporation by Shareholder

Occasionally, the officers or managers will refuse to defend a suit brought against a corporation. If a shareholder shows that the corporation has a valid defense to the suit and that the refusal or failure of the directors to defend is a breach of their fiduciary duty to the corporation, the courts will permit the shareholder to defend for the benefit of the corporation, its shareholders, and its creditors.

SHAREHOLDER LIABILITY

Shareholders have many responsibilities and liabilities in addition to their many rights. You have already studied shareholder liability when a shareholder pays too little consideration for shares, when a corporation is defectively formed, and when a corporation's veil is pierced. In this section, four other grounds for shareholder liability are discussed.

Shareholder Liability for Illegal Distributions

Dividends and other distributions of a corporation's assets received by a shareholder with *knowledge of their illegality* may be recovered on behalf of the corporation. Under the MBCA, primary liability is placed on the directors who, failing to comply with the business judgment rule, authorized the unlawful distribution. However, the directors are entitled to contribution from shareholders who received an asset distribution knowing that it was illegally made. These liability rules enforce the limits on asset distributions that were discussed earlier in this chapter.

Shareholder Liability for Corporate Debts

One of the chief attributes of a shareholder is his *limited liability*: Ordinarily, he has no liability for corporate obligations beyond his capital contribution. Defective attempts to incorporate and piercing the corporate veil are grounds on which a shareholder may be held liable for corporate debts beyond his capital contribution. In addition, a few states impose personal liability on shareholders for *wages owed to corporate employees,* even if the shareholders have fully paid for their shares.

Sale of a Control Block of Shares

The per share value of the shares of a majority shareholder of a corporation is greater than the per share value of the shares of a minority shareholder. This difference in value is due to the majority shareholder's ability to control the corporation and to cause it to hire her as an employee at a high salary. Therefore, a majority shareholder can sell her shares for a *premium* over the fair market value of minority shares.

Majority ownership is not always required for control of a corporation. In a close corporation it is required, but in a publicly held corporation with a widely dispersed, hard-to-mobilize shareholder group, minority ownership of from 5 to 30 percent may be enough to obtain control. Therefore, a holder of minority control in such a corporation will also be able to receive a premium.

Current corporation law imposes no liability on any shareholder, whether or not the shareholder is a controlling shareholder, *merely* because she is able to sell her shares for a premium. Nonetheless, if the premium is accompanied by wrongdoing, controlling shareholders have been held liable either for the amount of the premium or for the damages suffered by the corporation.

For example, a seller of control shares is liable for selling to a purchaser who harms the corporation if the seller had or should have had a *reasonable suspicion* that the purchaser would mismanage or loot the corporation. A seller may be placed on notice of a purchaser's bad motives by facts indicating the purchasers' history of *mismanagement and personal use of corporate assets,* by the purchaser's *lack of interest in the physical facilities* of the corporation, or the purchaser's great *interest in the liquid assets* of the corporation. These factors tend to indicate that the purchaser has a short-term interest in the corporation.

The mere payment of a premium is not enough to put the seller on notice. If the *premium is unduly*

high, however, such as a $50 offer for shares traded for $10, a seller must doubt whether the purchaser will be able to recoup his investment without looting the corporation.

When a seller has, or should have, a reasonable suspicion that a purchaser will mismanage or loot the corporation, he must not sell to the purchaser unless a *reasonable investigation* shows there is no reasonable risk of wrongdoing.

A few courts find liability when a selling shareholder takes or sells a *corporate asset.* For example, if a purchaser wants to buy the corporation's assets and the controlling shareholder proposes that the purchaser buy her shares instead, the controlling shareholder is liable for usurping a corporate opportunity.

A more unusual situation existed in *Perlman v. Feldman.*[1] In that case, Newport Steel Corporation had excess demand for its steel production, due to the Korean War. Another corporation, in order to guarantee a steady supply of steel, bought at a premium a minority yet controlling block of shares of Newport from Feldman, its chairman and president. The court ruled that Feldman was required to share the premium with the other shareholders because he had sold a corporate asset—the ability to exploit an excess demand for steel. The court reasoned that Newport could have exploited that asset to its advantage.

Shareholders as Fiduciaries

A few courts have recognized a fiduciary duty of controlling shareholders to use their ability to control the corporation in a fair, just, and equitable manner that benefits all of the shareholders proportionately. This is a duty to be **impartial**—that is, not to prefer themselves over the minority shareholders. For example, controlling shareholders have a fiduciary duty not to cause the corporation to repurchase their own shares or to pay themselves a dividend unless the same offer is made to the minority shareholder.

One of the most common examples of impartiality is the **freeze-out** of minority shareholders, which is wrongful because of its **oppression** of minority shareholders. It occurs in close corporations when controlling shareholders pay themselves high sala-

---

[1] 219 F.2d 173 (2d Cir. 1955).

ries while not employing or paying dividends to noncontrolling shareholders. Since there is usually no liquid market for the shares of the noncontrolling shareholders, they have an investment that provides them no return, while the controlling shareholders reap large gains. Such actions by the majority are especially wrongful when the controlling shareholders follow with an offer to buy the minority's shares at an unreasonably low price.

Some courts have held that all close corporation shareholders—whether majority or minority owners—are fiduciaries of each other and the corporation, on the grounds that the close corporation is an incorporated partnership. Thus, like partners, the shareholders owe fiduciary duties to act in the best interests of the corporation and the shareholders as a whole.

Some statutes, such as the Statutory Close Corporation Supplement to the MBCA, permit close corporation shareholders to dispense with a board of directors or to arrange corporate affairs as if the corporation were a partnership. The effect of these statutes is to impose management responsibilities, including the fiduciary duties of directors, on the shareholders. In essence, the shareholders are partners and owe each other fiduciary duties similar to those owed between partners of a partnership.

In the following case, the court found that a minority shareholder of a close corporation breached his fiduciary duty to the corporation by taking the name of the corporation, even though he did so in retaliation for his being frozen out of the corporation by the controlling shareholders.

REXFORD RAND CORP. v. ANCEL   58 F.3d 1215 (7th Cir. 1995)

Rexford Rand Corporation was a chemical manufacturing firm incorporated in Illinois. A close corporation, its only shareholders were Selwyn Ancel, owner of 50 percent of the company, and his two sons, Gregory and Albert, each an owner of 25 percent of the company. Rexford Rand sold over 200 products to 5,800 customers in many states, generating annual sales of $1.75 million. The name "Rexford Rand" appeared on the corporation's business cards, product literature, labels, containers, packaging, invoices, stationery, advertising, and buildings. Rexford Rand sold primarily to repeat customers.

Albert was the president and CEO, Selwyn was chairman of the board, and Gregory the vice president and treasurer. Gregory's salary from the corporation was his sole source of income. In December 1991, Gregory was fired from his positions as vice president, treasurer, and employee of Rexford Rand. Gregory contended that he was frozen out by Albert and Selwyn. After his firing, he received neither salary nor other benefits from Rexford Rand. Rexford Rand had never paid dividends to its shareholders.

In 1993, Rexford Rand failed to file its annual report with the state of Illinois, and as a result, the corporation was administratively dissolved. The dissolution caused the name "Rexford Rand" to become available. Gregory discovered that the corporation had been dissolved but did not inform Albert or Selwyn. Instead, Gregory reserved the name Rexford Rand Corporation and filed articles of incorporation in the name of Rexford Rand Corporation. This action prevented Rexford Rand from reincorporating under its original name.

Rexford Rand sued Gregory on the grounds he breached his fiduciary duty as a minority shareholder in a close corporation. The trial court ordered the return of the original name to Rexford Rand and permanently enjoined Gregory from conducting business under the name Rexford Rand. Gregory appealed.

Flaum, Judge Generally, imposing a fiduciary duty on shareholders in a close corporation shields minority shareholders from oppressive conduct by the majority. Shareholders in close corporations have often invested a substantial percentage of their assets in the corporation, and their position in the corporation may provide them with their only source of income. Minority shareholders are vulner-

able to freeze-outs or squeeze-outs, where the majority, for personal rather than legitimate business reasons, deprives the minority shareholder of his office, employment, and salary. Moreover, because no active market exists for the corporation's stock (and prospective purchasers may be wary of buying into a small enterprise where dissension has already occurred), the minority stockholder most likely will not be able to sell his shares for any sum approaching their fair value. Consequently, an oppressed shareholder in a close corporation may seek a judicial remedy.

In addition, minority shareholders owe a duty of loyalty to a close corporation in certain circumstances. Minority shareholders have an obligation as de facto partners in the joint venture not to do damage to the corporate interests. Gregory acknowledges that, under normal circumstances, he would have owed a duty of loyalty to Rexford Rand. He argues, however, that his duty terminated after the alleged freeze-out, which deprived him of his position in the corporation as well as the benefits of his stock ownership.

The Illinois courts have never decided whether a freeze-out terminates a minority shareholder's duty of loyalty to a close corporation. Generally, a shareholder's fiduciary duty continues after he resigns as an officer, director, or employee of a close corporation. Only one court has addressed the question whether a freeze-out terminates a shareholder's fiduciary duty to a close corporation. In *J Bar H, Inc. v. Johnson* (1991), the Supreme Court of Wyoming stated that:

> where a shareholder/director/employee of a close corporation has been wrongfully terminated from employment with the corporation and has been unjustly prevented from fulfilling her function as a director or officer, she can no longer be considered to act in a fiduciary capacity for the corporation.

The court reasoned that the fiduciary duty not to compete depends on the ability to exercise the status which creates it. A minority shareholder who has been frozen out no longer exercises the influence over corporate affairs that gives rise to fiduciary duty. Consequently, no fiduciary duty should remain after a freeze-out.

While we understand the reluctance of the *J Bar H* court to place a fiduciary duty on a shareholder who has been frozen out, we do not believe that *J Bar H* achieves the optimal result. Gregory may have been the victim of oppressive activity, and he may have believed that reserving the Rexford Rand name for his own use would induce Albert and Selwyn to buy out his stock at a fair price. Gregory's desire to obtain a fair buyout is not itself objectionable; in fact, courts will occasionally order forced buyouts as a remedy for oppression. The method by which he sought to induce a settlement, however, is troubling. By appropriating the corporate name, Gregory threatened to cause serious damage to the well-being of the corporation, and to imperil Selwyn and Albert's investment as well as his own. The freeze-out did not deprive Gregory of his status as a shareholder, and as a shareholder in a close corporation, Gregory should have placed the interests of the corporation above his personal interests.

Illinois allows oppressed shareholders to seek a judicial remedy, and Gregory should have relied on his suit against Albert and Selwyn seeking damages. If shareholders take it upon themselves to retaliate any time they believe they have been frozen out, disputes in close corporations will only increase. Rather, if unable to resolve matters amicably, aggrieved parties should take their claims to court and seek judicial resolution.

Judgment for Rexford Rand affirmed.

MEMBERS' RIGHTS AND DUTIES IN NONPROFIT CORPORATIONS

In a for-profit corporation, the shareholders' rights to elect directors and to receive dividends are their most important rights. The shareholders' duty to contribute capital as promised is the most important responsibility. By contrast, in a nonprofit corporation, the members' rights and duties—especially in a mutual benefit corporation—are defined by the ability of the members to use the facilities of the corporation (as in a social club) or to consume its output (as in a cooperative grocery store) and by their obligations to support the enterprise periodically with their money (such as dues paid to a social club) or with their labor (such as the duty to work a specified number of hours in a cooperative grocery store).

Nonprofit corporation law grants a corporation and its members considerable flexibility in determining the rights and liabilities of its members. The Model Nonprofit Corporation Act (MNCA) provides that all members of a nonprofit corporation have equal rights and obligations with respect to voting, dissolution, redemption of membership, and transfer of membership, unless the articles or bylaws establish classes of membership with different rights and obligations. For other rights and obligations, the MNCA provides that all members have the same rights and obligations, unless the articles or bylaws provide otherwise.

For example, a mutual benefit corporation that operates a golf country club may have two classes of membership. A full membership may entitle a full member to use all the club's facilities (including the swimming pool and tennis courts), grant the full member two votes on all matters submitted to members, and require the full member to pay monthly dues of $500. A limited membership may give a limited member the right to play the golf course only, grant the limited member one vote on all matters submitted to members, and require the limited members to pay monthly dues of $300 per month.

While members are primarily concerned about their consumption rights and financial obligations—such as those addressed above—that are embodied in the articles and the bylaws, they have other rights and obligations as well, including voting, inspection, and information rights similar to those held by shareholders of for-profit corporations.

Members' Meeting and Voting Rights

A nonprofit corporation must hold an annual meeting of its members and may hold meetings at other times as well. Members holding at least 5 percent of the voting power may call for a special meeting of members at any time.

All members of record have one vote on all matters submitted to members, unless the articles or bylaws grant lesser or greater voting power. The articles or bylaws may provide for different classes of members. Members of one class may be given greater voting rights than the members of another class. The articles or bylaws may provide that a class has no voting power.

Members may not act at a meeting unless a quorum is present. Under the MNCA, a quorum is 10 percent of the votes entitled to be cast on a matter. However, unless at least one third of the voting power is present at the meeting, the only matters that may be voted on are matters listed in the meeting notice sent to members. The articles or bylaws may require higher percentages.

Members may elect directors by straight or cumulative voting and by class voting. The articles or bylaws may also permit members to elect directors on the basis of chapter or other organizational unit, by region or other geographical unit, or by any other reasonable method. For example, a national humanitarian fraternity such as Lions Club may divide the United States into seven regions whose members are entitled to elect one director. Members also have the right to remove directors they have elected with or without cause.

In addition to the rights to elect and to remove directors, members have the right to vote on most amendments of the articles and bylaws, merger of the corporation with another corporation, sale of substantially all the corporation's assets, and dissolution of the corporation. Ordinarily, members must approve such matters by two thirds of the votes cast or a majority of the voting power, whichever is less. This requirement is more lenient than the rule applied to for-profit corporations. Combined with the 10 percent quorum requirement, members with less than 7 percent of the voting power may approve matters submitted to members.

However, the unfairness of such voting rules is offset by the MNCA's notice requirement. A members' meeting may not consider important matters such as mergers and articles amendments unless the corporation gave members fair and reasonable notice that such matters were to be submitted to the members for a vote.

In addition, the MNCA requires approval of each class of members whose rights are substantially affected by the matter. This requirement may increase the difficulty of obtaining member approval. For example, full members of a golf country club may not change the rights of limited members without the approval of the limited members. In addition, the articles or bylaws may require third person approval as well. For example, a city industrial development board may not be permitted to amend its articles without the consent of the mayor.

Members may vote in person or by proxy. They may also have written voting agreements. However, member voting agreements may not have a term exceeding 10 years. Members may act without a meeting if the action is approved in writing by at least 80 percent of the voting power.

Member Inspection and Information Rights

A member may not be able to exercise his voting and other rights unless he is informed. Moreover, a member must be able to communicate with other members to be able to influence the way they vote on matters submitted to members. Consequently, the MNCA grants members inspection and information rights.

Members have an absolute right to inspect and copy the articles, bylaws, board resolutions, and minutes of members' meetings. Members have a qualified right to inspect and copy a list of the members. The members' demand to inspect the members' list must be in good faith and for a proper purpose—that is, a purpose related to the member's interest as a member. Improper purposes include selling the list or using the list to solicit money. Members also have a qualified right to inspect minutes of board meetings and records of actions taken by committees of the board.

A nonprofit corporation is required to maintain appropriate accounting records, and members have a qualified right to inspect them. Upon demand, the corporation must provide to a member its latest annual financial statements, including a balance sheet and statement of operations. However, the MNCA permits a religious corporation to abolish or limit the right of a member to inspect any corporate record.

Distributions of Assets

Because it is not intended to make a profit, a nonprofit corporation does not pay dividends to its members. In fact, a nonprofit corporation is generally prohibited from making any distribution of its assets to its members.

Nonetheless, a mutual benefit corporation may purchase a membership and thereby distribute its assets to the selling member, but only if the corporation is able to pay its currently maturing obligations and has assets at least equal to its liabilities. For example, when a farmer joins a farmers' purchasing cooperative, he purchases a membership interest having economic value—it entitles him to purchase supplies from the cooperative at a bargain price. The mutual benefit corporation may repurchase the farmer's membership when he retires from farming. Religious and public benefit corporations may not repurchase their memberships.

Resignation and Expulsion of Members

A member may resign at any time from a nonprofit corporation. When a member resigns, generally a member may not sell or transfer her membership to any other person. A member of a mutual benefit corporation may transfer her interest to a buyer if the articles or bylaws permit.

It is fairly easy for a nonprofit corporation to expel a member or terminate her membership. The corporation must follow procedures that are fair and reasonable and carried out in good faith. The MNCA does not require the corporation to have a proper purpose to expel or terminate a member but only to follow proper procedures. The MNCA places no limits on a religious corporation's expulsion of its members.

The MNCA does not require a nonprofit corporation to purchase the membership of an expelled member, and—as explained above—permits only a mutual benefit corporation to purchase a membership. Members of mutual benefit corporations who fear expulsion should provide for repurchase rights in the articles or bylaws.

Derivative Suits

Members of a nonprofit corporation have a limited right to bring derivative actions on behalf of the corporation. A derivative action may be brought by members having at least 5 percent of the voting power or by 50 members, whichever is less. Members must first demand that the directors bring the suit or establish that demand is futile. If the action is successful, a court may require the corporation to pay the suing members' reasonable expenses. When the action is unsuccessful and has been commenced frivolously or in bad faith, a court may require the suing members to pay the other party's expenses.

DISSOLUTION AND TERMINATION OF CORPORATIONS

The MBCA provides that a corporation doing business may be dissolved by action of its directors and shareholders. The directors must adopt a dissolution resolution, and a majority of the shares outstanding must be cast in favor of dissolution at a shareholders' meeting. For a **voluntary dissolution** to be effective, the corporation must file articles of dissolution with the secretary of state. The dissolution is effective when the articles are filed.

A corporation may be also dissolved **without its consent** by administrative action of the secretary of state or by judicial action of a court. The secretary of state may commence an administrative proceeding to dissolve a corporation that has not filed its annual report, paid its annual franchise tax, appointed or maintained a registered office or agent in the state, or whose period of duration has expired. **Administrative dissolution** requires that the secretary of state give written notice to the corporation of the grounds for dissolution. If, within 60 days, the corporation has not corrected the default or demonstrated that the default does not exist, the secretary dissolves the corporation by signing a certificate of dissolution.

The shareholders, secretary of state, or the creditors of a corporation may ask a court to order the involuntary dissolution of a corporation. Any **shareholder** may obtain judicial dissolution when there is a deadlock of the directors that is harmful to the corporation, when the shareholders are deadlocked and cannot elect directors for two years, or when the directors are acting contrary to the best interests of the corporation. The **secretary of state** may obtain judicial dissolution if it is proved that a corporation obtained its articles of incorporation by fraud or exceeded or abused its legal authority. **Creditors** may request dissolution if the corporation is insolvent.

Under the MBCA, a corporation that has not issued shares or commenced business may be dissolved by the vote of a majority of its incorporators or initial directors.

Many close corporations are nothing more than incorporated partnerships, in which all the shareholders are managers and friends or relatives. Recently, corporation law has reflected the special needs of those shareholders of close corporations who want to arrange their affairs to make the close corporation more like a partnership. The Close Corporation Supplement to the MBCA recognizes that a **close corporation shareholder** should have the same dissolution power as a partner. This section, like similar provisions in many states, permits the articles of incorporation to empower any shareholder to dissolve the corporation at will or upon the occurrence of a specified event such as the death of a shareholder.

Winding Up and Termination

A dissolved corporation continues its corporate existence but may not carry on any business except that appropriate to winding up its affairs. Therefore, winding up (liquidation) must follow dissolution. Winding up is the orderly collection and disposal of the corporation's assets and the distribution of the proceeds of the sale of assets. From these proceeds, the claims of creditors will be paid first. Next, the liquidation preferences of preferred shareholders will be paid. Then, common shareholders receive any proceeds that remain.

After winding up has been completed, the corporation's existence terminates. A person who purports to act on behalf of a terminated corporation has the liability of a person acting for a corporation prior to its incorporation. Some courts, like the court in the next case, impose similar liability on a person acting on behalf of a dissolved corporation, especially when dissolution is obtained by the secretary of state such as for the failure to file an annual report or to pay franchise taxes.

BODINE ALUMINUM CO., INC. v. MITAUER   776 S.W.2d 485 (Mo. Ct. App. 1989)

E ast Side Metals, Inc., a Missouri corporation, failed to file an annual registration statement required by the Missouri corporation statute. Consequently, in November 1984, its corporate charter was forfeited. On East Side's last annual registration statement, Harlin, Louis, and Bernice Mitauer were listed as its officers and directors. Although East Side's charter was forfeited, the Mitauers continued to operate the business. In 1985, the business purchased scrap aluminum from Bodine Aluminum Co., Inc. When the business failed to pay $17,064 of the purchase price, Bodine sued the Mitauers to recover the remainder. The trial court held that the Mitauers individually owed Bodine $17,064. The Mitauers appealed to the Missouri Court of Appeals. ∞

Grimm, Judge The Missouri corporation statute provides:

If any corporation: (1) Fails to comply with the provisions of this chapter with respect to its annual registration the corporate rights and privileges of the corporation shall be forfeited, and the secretary of state shall notify the corporation that its corporate existence and rights in this state have been forfeited and canceled, and the corporation dissolved; and the directors and officers in office when the forfeiture occurs shall be the trustees of the corporation, who shall have full authority to wind up its business and affairs; and the trustees shall be jointly and severally responsible to the creditors and shareholders of the corporation to the extent of its property and effects that shall have come into their hands.

This statute places a limit on the liability of officers and directors as they wind up the affairs of a corporation after its corporate rights and privileges have been forfeited. When, however, the officers and directors continue to operate the business after forfeiture, individual liability may be imposed on them.

East Side's charter was forfeited on November 1, 1984. The Mitauers then became statutory trustees for the purpose of winding up the affairs of the corporation. When no effort was made to wind up, all post-forfeiture debts became the personal liability of the Mitauers.

Judgment affirmed for Bodine.

CONCEPT REVIEW

Roles of Shareholders and the Board of Directors

CORPORATE ACTION	BOARD'S ROLE	SHAREHOLDERS' ROLE
Day-to-Day Management	Selects officers; supervises management	Elect and remove directors
Issuance of Shares	Issues shares	Protected by preemptive right
Merger and Share Exchange	Adopts articles of merger or share exchange	Vote to approve merger or share exchange; protected by dissenters' rights
Amendment of Articles of Incorporation	Proposes amendment	Vote to approve amendment
Dissolution	Proposes dissolution	Vote to approve dissolution
Dividends	Declares dividends	Receive dividends
Board of Directors Harms Individual Shareholder Rights	Has harmed shareholders	Bring individual or class action against directors or the corporation
Directors Harm Corporation	Sues wrongdoing directors	Bring derivative action against wrongdoing directors

---

Dissolution of Nonprofit Corporations

A nonprofit corporation may be dissolved voluntarily, administratively, or judicially. Voluntary dissolution will usually require approval of both the directors and the members. However, a nonprofit corporation may include a provision in its articles requiring the approval of a third person also. For example, such a third person might be a state governor who appointed some of the directors to the board of a nonprofit corporation organized to encourage industrial development in the state. The dissolution is effective when the corporation delivers articles of dissolution to the secretary of state and the secretary of state files them. The dissolved corporation continues its existence, but only for the purpose of liquidating its assets and winding up its affairs.

The secretary of state may administratively dissolve a nonprofit corporation that fails to pay incorporation taxes or to deliver its annual report to the secretary of state, among other things. Minority members or directors may obtain judicial dissolution by a court if the directors are deadlocked, the directors in control are acting illegally or fraudulently, or the members are deadlocked and cannot elect directors for two successive elections, among other reasons.

1. Why should shareholders in a close corporation be permitted to make a long-term voting agreement that permits them to control the corporation? Who benefits from shareholder voting agreements? Does the corporation benefit from such an agreement? Who is harmed by such an agreement? May such an agreement harm shareholders who are parties to the agreement? Is it possible for persons harmed by such agreements to protect themselves? Should there be a maximum legal time period for such agreements?

2. Are dissenters' rights to seek appraisal of their shares the only protection a shareholder needs when the corporation's board of directors proposes a merger harmful to the corporation? Should the shareholder be content with the fair value of his shares although he would rather stop the merger? How can shareholders use their dissenters' rights to deter the board of directors from effecting a merger harmful to the corporation?

3. Should a corporation be permitted to use a shareholder litigation committee (SLC) to decide the future of a shareholder derivative suit? Should the business judgment rule apply to the decision of a SLC, or should the *Zapata* two-step test apply? Do your answers depend on whether the shareholders are suing the directors or someone outside the corporation? How could it ever be in the best interests of a corporation not to sue directors who have personally profited by mismanaging the corporation?

4. Do you agree with the decision in the *Perlman v. Feldman* case, which is discussed on page 908? Do you agree that Newport Steel lost its ability to exploit excess demand for steel merely by being acquired by another corporation? After the acquisition, Newport became a subsidiary of the acquiring corporation. Thinking back to the discussion of piercing the corporate veil (Chapter 40, History and Nature of Corporations) and the discussion of conflicts of interests (Chapter 42, Management of Corporations), what price must the parent corporation pay when it buys steel from Newport?

PROBLEMS AND PROBLEM CASES

1. Facing billions of dollars of creditors' claims, Manville Corporation sought a bankruptcy reorganization. In 1985, Manville's management and its creditors agreed to a reorganization plan, but a group of Manville shareholders objected to the plan's intent to eliminate 90 percent of the shareholders' equity in Manville. The shareholders sued to force Manville to have a shareholders' meeting at which shareholders would remove the current directors and replace them with directors who would negotiate a reorganization plan that would better preserve the shareholders' equity. Manville had not held a shareholders' meeting since 1982. Manville claimed that holding a shareholders' meeting would obstruct its reorganization. Should the court grant the shareholders' request for a meeting?

2. Edward Carey owned 109,000 of the 2,700,341 outstanding shares of Pennsylvania Enterprises, Inc. (PEI). Concerned that Carey would attempt to take over PEI, its board of directors announced a proposal to widen the distribution of PEI shares. The proposal required shareholder approval. PEI announced that a special meeting of shareholders would be held on October 12, and its board of directors set the record date as September 2, 1988. Needing 1,350,171 votes to pass, the proposal received 1,373,968 votes in favor, passing with a margin of almost 24,000 votes. However, 79,118 of the shares voted in favor of the proposal were recorded in the names of Loriot & Co. and Cede & Co. but voted by other persons. Loriot and Cede were nominees for Manufacturer's Hanover Trust, which administered PEI's Dividend Reinvestment Plan (DRIP). Under the DRIP, PEI shareholders could opt to reinvest their cash dividends with PEI, which would issue new shares to the shareholders. Instead of registering the new shares in the names of the individual shareholders, however, PEI registered new shares to Loriot or Cede. A provision of the DRIP provided that the individual shareholders (beneficial shareholders), not Loriot and Cede, were able to vote the shares. At the special shareholders' meeting, the election judges permitted the DRIP beneficial shareholders to vote the DRIP shares in favor of the proposal. Did the election judges act properly?

3. Don Sanders owned 2 percent of the shares of Houston Sports Association (HSA). A group of minority shareholders, including Sanders, tried to enter a voting agreement with 51 percent of HSA shares. The purpose of the agreement was to oust from management John McMullen, the largest shareholder (34 percent) of HSA. However, McMullen promised Sanders that McMullen would vote his shares annually to elect Sanders to the HSA board of directors if Sanders agreed to withdraw his support from the minority shareholder group and to vote his shares to retain McMullen in management. Sanders agreed. Their agreement was only oral. Subsequently, McMullen was able to acquire 63 percent ownership of HSA, and Sanders—at McMullen's request—increased his holdings to 13 percent. Two years later, Sanders was not reelected to the board despite McMullen's majority ownership of shares. Sanders sued McMullen for violating their voting agreement. Was McMullen held liable?

4. Dale Waters was minority shareholder of Double L, Inc., a business engaged in manufacturing agricultural machinery and related products. When Double L became financially distressed, the directors agreed to sell to Pioneer Astro all of Double L's real property and equipment and to issue sufficient shares to make Pioneer Astro an 80 percent shareholder of Double L. To improve Double L's financial position, Pioneer Astro agreed to pay cash for the assets and shares and to loan money to Double L. To allow Double L to continue its business, Pioneer Astro agreed to lease the purchased assets back to Double L. At a shareholder meeting, shareholders approved the transaction with Pioneer Astro. Waters, however, abstained from voting and demanded that Double L pay him the fair value of his shares pursuant to dissenters' rights under Idaho law. Are dissenter's rights available in this context?

5. William Carter owned 317 shares of Wilson Construction Company. He also owned 20 percent of the shares of Wilson Equipment Leasing, Inc., a company that leased equipment to and engaged in other transactions with Wilson Construction. Carter worked for Wilson Construction until he resigned his position in November 1983. Immediately, he organized and became a part owner and employee of C & L Contracting, Inc., a competitor of Wilson Construction. Carter offered to sell his shares to Wilson Construction, but his offer was rejected. In 1984, Carter demanded that Wilson Construction make available to him its books, records of account, minutes, and record of shareholders, on the grounds that he had been told and believed that the financial condition of Wilson Construction had deteriorated due to improper management. In addition, he requested the information to determine the value of his shares, the financial condition of the corporation, and whether it was efficiently managed in the best interests of the corporation. Must Wilson Construction comply with Carter's request?

6. Historically, Liggett Group, Inc., had paid quarterly dividends to its shareholders in March, June, September, and December of each year. On May 14, 1980, the Liggett board of directors recommended that shareholders accept a tender offer by GM Sub Corporation at $69 per share. The tender offer provided that if GM Sub acquired more than 50 percent of the Liggett shares, GM Sub and Liggett would merge; the Liggett shareholders who did not tender during the tender offer would receive $69 per share under the merger. Subsequently, 87.4 percent of Liggett shareholders tendered their shares. The cash-out merger was effected on August 7. Because the Liggett board believed that it would have been unfair to the shareholders who accepted the tender offer, the board skipped the June 1980 dividend. The board believed that the shareholders who did not tender should not be rewarded for refusing to tender their shares to GM Sub knowing that they would receive the same price per share in the merger. Also, the board believed that $69 was a fair price for the shares. Gabelli & Co. surrendered its Liggett shares pursuant to the merger agreement but then sued Liggett to force payment of the June 1980 dividend. Did Gabelli succeed?

7. Fred and Maxine Brandon and their four children owned all the shares of Brandon Construction Co., a family corporation. Fred and Maxine owned a majority of the shares. In 1987, the shareholders agreed that Fred and Maxine each would receive a monthly salary of $12,500. Two months later, daughter Betty Brandon alleged that the salaries were excessive, and that Fred and Maxine were dismantling the corporation and distributing its assets to themselves, without regard for the children's rights as minority shareholders. She initiated a derivative action against her parents, but her siblings responded that Betty did not represent their interests as minority shareholders and that they were content with the salaries paid to their parents. Is Betty a proper person to bring a derivative suit?

8. Three brothers—Joseph, Myer, and Samuel Sugarman—owned equal amounts of the shares of Statler Tissue Corporation. Over time, Myer's son Leonard became the majority shareholder of the corporation: Samuel gave some of his shares to his son Hyman and to Hyman's children, James, Marjorie, and Jon Sugarman; Hyman sold his shares to Leonard; Joseph Sugarman's shares were repurchased by the corporation. By 1974, Leonard owned 61 percent of the shares and was president and chairman of the board. James, Marjorie, and Jon Sugarman owned 22 percent of the shares. Marjorie had sought employment with the corporation but was not hired. Jon was employed from 1974 until his discharge in 1978. James never sought employment with the company. After 1975, Myer's value to the corporation was nearly zero because he had Alzheimer's disease; nonetheless, Myer was employed by the corporation and received a salary equal to Hyman's salary. In 1980, Leonard caused the company to double Myer's salary to $85,000 for 1980 and 1981, when Myer was 87 and 88 years of age. Hyman received no such increase. When Myer retired in 1982, Leonard caused the corporation to pay Myer a yearly pension of $75,000. When Hyman retired in 1980, he received no pension. The corporation paid no dividends. In 1980, Leonard offered to buy Jon's and Marjorie's shares for $3.33 per share. At that time, Price Waterhouse had ad-

vised Leonard that the book value of the corporation's shares was $16.30 per share. Does Leonard have liability to Jon and Marjorie?

9. H. F. Ahmanson & Co. was the controlling shareholder of United Savings and Loan Association. There was very little trading in the Association's shares, however. To create a public market for their shares, Ahmanson and a few other shareholders of the Association incorporated United Financial Corporation and exchanged each of their Association shares for United shares. United then owned more than 85 percent of the shares of the Association. The minority shareholders of the Association were not given an opportunity to exchange their shares. United made two public offerings of its shares. As a result, trading in United shares was very active, while sales of Association shares decreased to half of the formerly low level, with United as virtually the only purchaser. United offered to purchase Association shares from the minority shareholders for $1,100 per share. Some of the minority shareholders accepted this offer. At that time, the shares held by the majority shareholders were worth $3,700. United also caused the Association to decrease its dividend payments. Has Ahmanson done anything wrong?

10. Albert Martin and Raymond Martin were brothers, each owning 50 percent of Martin's News Service, Inc., a retail store selling newspapers, lottery tickets, and cigarettes. Beginning in 1973, they had difficulty working together, eventually communicating only through their accountant. Directors' and shareholders' meetings ceased. In 1983, Albert fell ill and was unable to work in the store. In December 1983, Albert sued for a judicial dissolution of the corporation. Will the court order dissolution?

FORTY-FOUR

Securities Regulation

odern securities regulation arose from the rubble of the great stock market crash of October 1929. After the crash, Congress studied its causes and discovered several common problems in securities transactions, the most important ones being:

1. *Investors lacked the necessary information to make intelligent decisions whether to buy, sell, or hold securities.*

2. *Disreputable sellers of securities made outlandish claims about the expected performance of securities and sold securities in nonexistent companies.*

Faced with these perceived problems, Congress chose to require securities sellers to disclose the information that investors need to make intelligent investment decisions. Congress found that investors are able to make intelligent investment decisions if they are given sufficient information about the company whose securities they are to buy. This *disclosure scheme* assumes that investors need assistance from government in acquiring information but that they need no help in evaluating information. ∞

PURPOSES OF SECURITIES REGULATION

To implement its disclosure scheme, in the early 1930s Congress passed two major statutes, which are the hub of federal securities regulation in the United States today. These two statutes, the **Securities Act of 1933** and the **Securities Exchange Act of 1934,** have three basic purposes:

1. To require the disclosure of meaningful information about a security and its issuer to allow investors to make intelligent investment decisions.

2. To impose liability on those persons who make inadequate and erroneous disclosures of information.

3. To regulate insiders, professional sellers of securities, securities exchanges, and other self-regulatory securities organizations.

The crux of the securities acts is to impose on issuers of securities, other sellers of securities, and selected buyers of securities the affirmative duty to disclose important information, even if they are not asked by investors to make the disclosures. By requiring disclosure, Congress hoped to restore investor confidence in the securities markets. Congress wanted to bolster investor confidence in the honesty of the stock market and thus encourage more investors to invest in securities. Building investor confidence would increase capital formation and, it was hoped, help the American economy emerge from the Great Depression of the 1930s.

SECURITIES AND EXCHANGE COMMISSION

The Securities and Exchange Commission (SEC) was created by the 1934 Act. Its responsibility is to administer the 1933 Act, 1934 Act, and other securities statutes. Like other federal administrative agencies, the SEC has legislative, executive, and judicial functions. Its legislative branch promulgates rules and regulations; its executive branch brings enforcement actions against alleged violators of the securities statutes and their rules and regulations; its judicial branch decides whether a person has violated the securities laws.

SEC Actions

The SEC is empowered to investigate violations of the 1933 Act and 1934 Act and to hold hearings to determine whether the acts have been violated. Such hearings are held before an administrative law judge (ALJ), who is an employee of the SEC. The administrative law judge is a finder of both fact and law. Decisions of the ALJ are reviewed by the commis-

sioners of the SEC. Decisions of the commissioners are appealed to the U.S. courts of appeals. Most SEC actions are not litigated. Instead, the SEC issues consent orders, by which the defendant promises not to violate the securities laws in the future but does not admit to having violated them in the past.

The SEC has the power to impose civil penalties (fines) up to $500,000 and to issue **cease and desist orders.** A cease and desist order directs a defendant to stop violating the securities laws and to desist from future violations. Nonetheless, the SEC does not have the power to issue injunctions; only courts may issue injunctions. The 1933 Act and the 1934 Act empower the SEC only to ask federal district courts for injunctions against persons who have violated or are about to violate either act. The SEC may also ask the courts to grant ancillary relief, a remedy in addition to an injunction. Ancillary relief may include, for example, the disgorgement of profits that a defendant has made in a fraudulent sale or in an illegal insider trading transaction.

WHAT IS A SECURITY?

The first issue in securities regulation is the definition of a security. If a transaction involves no security, then the law of securities regulation does not apply. The 1933 Act defines the term **security** broadly:

Unless the context otherwise requires the term "security" means any note, stock, bond, debenture, evidence of indebtedness, certificate of interest of participation in any profit-sharing agreement, . . . preorganization certificate or subscription, . . . investment contract, voting trust certificate, . . . fractional undivided interest in oil, gas, or mineral rights, . . . or, in general, any interest or instrument commonly known as a "security."

The 1934 Act definition of security is similar, but excludes notes and drafts that mature not more than nine months from the date of issuance.

While typical securities like common shares, preferred shares, bonds, and debentures are defined as securities, the definition of a security also includes many contracts that the general public may believe are not securities. This is because the term **investment contract** is broadly defined by the courts. The Supreme Court's three-part test for an investment contract, called the *Howey* test, has been the guiding beacon in the area for the past 45 years.[1] The *Howey* test states that an investment contract is an investment of money in a common enterprise with an expectation of profits solely from the efforts of others.

In the *Howey* case, the sales of plots in an orange grove along with a management contract were held to be sales of securities. The purchasers had investment motives (they intended to make a profit from, not to consume the oranges produced by the trees).

---

[1]*SEC v. W. J. Howey Co.,* 328 U.S. 293 (U.S. Sup. Ct. 1946).

There was a common enterprise, because the investors were similarly affected by the efforts of the sellers who grew and sold the oranges for all investors. The sellers, not the buyers, did all of the work needed to make the plots profitable.

In other cases, sales of limited partnership interests, Scotch whisky receipts, and restaurant franchises have been held to constitute investment contracts and, therefore, securities.

In the following case, the court considered whether viatical agreements—which provide funding for AIDS victims—are securities.

SECURITIES AND EXCHANGE COMMISSION v. LIFE PARTNERS, INC.   87 F.3d 536 (D.C. Cir. 1996)

A *viatical settlement is a contract by which an investor purchases the life insurance policy of a terminally ill person—typically an AIDS victim—who is in need of immediate cash to pay mounting medical expenses. Depending on the insured's life expectancy, the buyer pays 60 to 80 percent of the death benefit. When the insured dies, the investor receives the death benefit. The investor's profit is the difference between the death benefit collected from the insurer and the discounted purchase price paid to the insured, less transaction costs, premiums paid, and other administrative expenses.*

Life Partners, Inc. (LPI), acts as a middleman between the insured and the investors. LPI performs several functions prior to the investors' purchases of an insurance policy: LPI evaluates the insured's medical condition, reviews his insurance policy, negotiates the purchase price, and prepares legal documents. LPI assembles the purchasers of each insurance policy, selling fractional interests for as little as $650 and 3 percent of the death benefits of the policy. The investors become the owners of the insurance policy purchased from the insured.

After the purchase, investors are given an option to use the service of Sterling Trust Company, an independent escrow agent. Acting for LPI, Sterling performs the following postpurchase services: monitoring the insured's health, ensuring that the policy does not lapse, and arranging for resale of the investor's interest when requested. Alternatively, an investor may choose to perform those services himself. When the purchase of an insurance policy is closed and an investor seeks the services of Sterling, Sterling collects a fee, escrows funds for expected premium payments, and delivers the balance to the insured. Sterling holds the policy, holds and disburses all funds, ensures that all paperwork is in order, and files the death claim when the insured dies.

The SEC contends that the viatical settlements marketed by LPI are securities and that LPI has violated the Securities Act of 1933 by selling them without first complying with the registration requirements of the Act. The district court agreed and preliminarily enjoined LPI from making further sales. LPI appealed the decision to the court of appeals. ∽

Ginsburg, Circuit Judge The district court acknowledged that LPI provides "valuable funds to AIDS patients in their final illness" and that after "an apparently exhaustive two-year investigation" the SEC could produce no evidence or even allegations "that any investor, terminally ill patient, or insurance company has been defrauded, misled, or is in any way dissatisfied with an LPI viatical settlement." The Commission, however, points out that the securities laws, and in particular the disclo-

sure requirements of the 1933 and 1934 Acts, are intended to prevent abuses before they arise.

Still, that neither policyholders nor investors have complained of any abuse may help to explain why the viatical settlements industry is not more regulated. A number of states have enacted laws protecting the insureds, but according to the SEC, no state has undertaken specifically to protect investors in viatical settlements. (In all states investors are still protected by the common law of fraud, of course.)

Although some promoters of viatical settlements do register them as securities under the federal securities laws, LPI observes that registration means higher costs for investors and correspondingly lower prices for terminally ill policyholders, and objects that any significant administrative delay might be fatal in this time-sensitive context. The Commission concedes that some policy-by-policy disclosure of risk factors would be required but ventures that the burden would not be prohibitive. The Commission also notes that some firms have sought and obtained an exemption from the federal securities laws for their viatical contracts; presumably a firm might also buy insurance policies for its own account or act as an agent, matching a single investor with a terminally ill insured, without running afoul of the securities laws.

We turn to the question whether the LPI contracts are properly characterized as securities within the terms of the 1933 Act. That determination is controlled by the Supreme Court's decision in *SEC v. Howey* (1946), which holds that an investment contract is a security subject to the Act if investors purchase with (1) an expectation of profits arising from (2) a common enterprise that (3) depends upon the efforts of others.

The SEC argues that the profits test requires only that the "investor could lose his investment, or that the value of his return could fluctuate," and that, although the death benefit that an investor gets from a viatical settlement is in a fixed dollar amount, the profitability of the investment can vary because of the uncertain interval of time between the date of investment and the date of the insured's death.

LPI maintains that profits must be derived from "either capital appreciation resulting from the development of the initial investment or a participation in earnings resulting from the use of the investors' funds," neither of which obtains with respect to viatical contracts.

We think that the expected profits must, in conformity with ordinary usage, be in the form of a financial return on the investment, not in the form of consumption. The asset acquired by an LPI investor is a claim on future death benefits. The buyer is obviously purchasing not for consumption—unmatured claims cannot be currently consumed—but rather for the prospect of a return on his investment. That is enough to satisfy the requirement that the investment be made in the expectation of profits.

The second element of the *Howey* test for a security is that there be a "common enterprise." So-called horizontal commonality—defined by the pooling of investment funds, shared profits, and shared losses—is ordinarily sufficient to satisfy the common enterprise requirement.

Here, LPI brings together multiple investors and aggregates their funds to purchase the death benefits of an insurance policy. If the insured dies in a relatively short time, then the investors realize profits; if the insured lives a relatively long time, then the investors may lose money or at best fail to realize the return they had envisioned; *i.e.,* they experience a loss of the return they could otherwise have realized in some alternative investment of equivalent risk. Any profits or losses from an LPI contract accrue to all of the investors in that contract; *i.e.,* it is not possible for one investor to realize a gain or loss without each other investor gaining or losing proportionately, based upon the amount that he invested. In that sense, the outcomes are shared among the investors; the sum that each receives is a predetermined portion of the aggregate death benefit.

We think that pooling is in practice an essential ingredient of the LPI program; that is, any individual investor would find that the profitability if not the completion of his or her purchase depends upon the completion of the larger deal. Because LPI's viatical settlements entail this implicit form of pooling, and because any profits or losses accrue to all investors (in proportion to the amount invested), we conclude that all three elements of horizontal commonality—pooling, profit sharing, and loss sharing—attend the purchase of a fractional interest through LPI.

The final requirement of the *Howey* test for an investment to be deemed a security is that the profits expected by the investor be derived from the efforts of others. In this connection, the SEC suggests that investors in LPI's viatical settlements are essentially passive; their profits, the Commission argues, depend predominantly upon the efforts of LPI, which provides pre-purchase expertise in identifying existing policyholders and, together with Sterling, provides post-purchase management of the investment.

Meanwhile, LPI argues that its pre-purchase functions are wholly irrelevant and that the post-purchase functions, by whomever performed, should not count because they are only ministerial. On this view, once the transaction closes, the investors do not look to the efforts of others for their profits because the only variable affecting profits is the timing of the insured's death, which is outside of LPI's and Sterling's control.

By its terms *Howey* requires that profits be generated "solely" from the efforts of others. Although the lower courts have given the Supreme Court's definition of a security broader sweep by requiring that profits be generated only "predominantly" from the efforts of others, they have never suggested that purely ministerial or clerical functions are by themselves sufficient; indeed, quite the opposite is true. Because post-purchase entrepreneurial activities are the "efforts of others" most obviously relevant to the question whether a promoter is selling a "security," we turn first to the distinction between those post-purchase functions that are entrepreneurial and those that are ministerial; thereafter, we consider the relevance of pre-purchase entrepreneurial services.

Ministerial Versus Entrepreneurial Functions, Post-Purchase

Sterling offered the following post-purchase services: holding the policy, monitoring the insured's health, paying premiums, converting a group policy into an individual policy where required, filing the death claim, collecting and distributing the death benefit (if requested), and assisting an investor who might wish to resell his interest. LPI characterizes these functions as clerical and routine, not managerial or entrepreneurial, and therefore unimportant to the source of investor expectations; in sum, anyone including the investor himself could supply these services. The district court agreed with LPI for it described them as "often ministerial in nature."

The Commission disputes the district court's characterization of post-purchase services as ministerial, but attempts to portray only one service in particular as entrepreneurial: the secondary market that LPI purportedly makes. By establishing a resale market, according to the SEC, LPI links the profitability of the investments it sells to the success of its own efforts. We find this argument unconvincing for several reasons. First, there is no evidence that investors actually seek to liquidate their investments prior to the receipt of death benefits. Second, there is no evidence that LPI's potential assistance adds value to the investment contract; an investor could get the same help with resale through any one of the many firms that sell viatical settlements. Third, LPI

is quite specific in warning its clients that viatical transactions are not liquid assets, and that LPI's practice is to assist in the resale of policies purchased by it, but there is no guarantee that any policy can be resold, or that resale will be at any given price. LPI's promise of help in arranging for the resale of a policy is not an adequate basis upon which to conclude that the fortunes of the investors are tied to the efforts of LPI, must less that their profits derive predominantly from those efforts.

Entrepreneurial Functions, Pre-Purchase

LPI asserts that its pre-purchase efforts are irrelevant. LPI performed highly specialized functions in identifying and evaluating individual policies suitable for purchase by investors. Still, the district court declared that pre-purchase activities cannot alone support a finding that investors' profits derive from the efforts of LPI. Instead, the court relied upon the pre-closing activities in addition to the post-closing activities that LPI continues to perform.

The Commission reminds us that the Supreme Court did not draw a bright line distinction in *Howey* between pre- and post-purchase efforts. Therefore, it would be hypertechnical, according to the Commission, to discount the importance of LPI's pre-purchase entrepreneurial functions simply because they occur before the moment of closing.

We cannot agree that the time of sale is an artificial dividing line. It is a legal construct but a significant one. If the investor's profits after the purchase depend predominantly upon the promoter's efforts, then the investor may benefit from the disclosure and other requirements of the federal securities law. But if the value of the promoter's efforts has already been impounded into the promoter's fees or into the purchase price of the investment, and if neither the promoter nor anyone else is expected to make further efforts that will affect the outcome of the investment, then the need for federal securities regulation is greatly diminished. While coverage under the 1933 Act might increase the quantity (and perhaps the quality) of information available to the investor prior to closing, the securities laws are not a broad federal remedy for all fraud. They are concerned only with securities fraud.

We see here no venture associated with the ownership of an insurance contract from which one's profit depends entirely upon the mortality of the insured. Nor is the combination of LPI's pre-purchase services as a finder-promoter and its largely ministerial post-purchase services enough to establish that the investors' profits flow predominantly from the efforts of others. Pre-purchase services cannot by themselves suffice to make the profits of an investment arise predominantly from the efforts of others. Ministerial functions should receive a good deal less weight than entrepreneurial activities.

In this case it is the length of the insured's life that is of overwhelming importance to the value of the viatical settlements marketed by LPI. As a result, the SEC is unable to show that the promoter's efforts have a predominant influence upon investors' profits; and because all three elements of the *Howey* test must be satisfied before an investment is characterized as a security risk, we must conclude that the viatical settlements marketed by LPI are not securities.

Judgment reversed in favor of LPI.

Courts have used the *Howey* test to hold that some contracts with typical security names are not securities. The courts point out that some of these contracts possess few of the typical characteristics of a security. For example, in *United Housing Foundation, Inc. v. Forman,*[2] the Supreme Court held that although tenants in a cooperative apartment building purchased contracts labeled as stock, the contracts were not securities. The "stock" possessed few of the typical characteristics of stock and the economic realities of the transaction bore few similarities to those of the typical stock sale: The stock gave tenants no dividend rights or voting rights in proportion to the number of shares owned, it was not negotiable, and it could not appreciate in value. More important, tenants bought the stock not for the purpose of investment but to acquire suitable living space.

However, when investors are misled to believe that the securities laws apply because a seller sold a contract bearing both the name of a typical security and significant characteristics of that security, the securities laws do apply to the sale of the security. The application of this doctrine led to the Supreme Court's rejection of the sale-of-business doctrine, which had held that the sale of 100 percent of the shares of a corporation to a single purchaser who would manage the corporation was not a security. The rationale for the sale-of-business doctrine was that the purchaser failed to meet element 3 of the *Howey* test because he expected to make a profit from his own efforts in managing the business. Today, when a business sale is effected by the sale of stock, the transaction is covered by the securities acts if the stock possesses the characteristics of stock.

In 1990, the Supreme Court further extended this rationale in *Reves v. Ernst & Young,*[3] adopting the **family resemblance test** to determine whether promissory notes were securities. The Supreme Court held that it is inappropriate to apply the *Howey* test to notes. Instead, applying the family resemblance test, the Court held that notes are presumed to be securities unless they bear a "strong family resemblance" to a type of note that is not a security. Types of notes that are not securities include consumer notes, mortgage notes, short-term notes secured by a lien on a small business, short-term notes secured by accounts receivable, and notes evidencing loans by commercial banks for current operations.

SECURITIES ACT OF 1933

The Securities Act of 1933 (1933 Act) is concerned primarily with public distributions of securities. That is, the 1933 Act regulates the sale of securities while they are passing from the hands of the issuer into the hands of public investors. An issuer selling securities publicly must make necessary disclosures at the time the issuer sells the securities to the public.

The 1933 Act has two principal regulatory components: (1) registration provisions and (2) liability provisions. The registration requirements of the 1933 Act are designed to give investors the information they need to make intelligent decisions whether to purchase securities when an issuer sells

---

[2]*United Housing Foundation, Inc. v. Forman,* 421 U.S. 837 (U.S. Sup. Ct. 1975).

[3]494 U.S. 56 (U.S. Sup. Ct. 1990).

its securities to the public. The various liability provisions in the 1933 Act impose liability on sellers of securities for misstating or omitting facts of material significance to investors.

REGISTRATION OF SECURITIES UNDER THE 1933 ACT

The 1933 Act requires that *every* offering of securities be registered with the SEC prior to any offer or sale of the securities, unless the offering or the securities are exempt from registration. That is, an issuer and its underwriters may not offer or sell securities unless the securities are registered with the SEC or exempt from registration. Over the next few pages, we will cover the registration process. Then the exemptions from registration will be addressed.

Mechanics of a Registered Offering

When an issuer makes a decision to raise money by a public offering of securities, the issuer needs to obtain the assistance of securities market professionals. The issuer will contact a managing underwriter, the primary person assisting the issuer in selling the securities. The managing underwriter will review the issuer's operations and financial statements and reach an agreement with the issuer regarding the type of securities to sell, the offering price, and the compensation to be paid to the underwriters. The issuer and the managing underwriter will determine what type of underwriting to use.

In a **stand-by underwriting,** the underwriters obtain subscriptions from prospective investors, but the issuer sells the securities only if there is sufficient investor interest in the securities. The underwriters receive warrants—options to purchase the issuer's securities at a bargain price—as compensation for their efforts. The stand-by underwriting is typically used only to sell common shares to existing shareholders pursuant to a preemptive rights offering.

With a **best efforts underwriting,** the underwriters are merely agents making their best efforts to sell the issuer's securities. The underwriters receive a commission for their selling efforts. The best efforts underwriting is used when an issuer is not well established and the underwriter is unwilling to risk being unable to sell the securities.

The classic underwriting arrangement is a **firm commitment underwriting.** Here the managing underwriter forms an underwriting group and a selling group. The underwriting group agrees to purchase the securities from the issuer at a discount from the public offering price—for example, 25 cents per share below the offering price. The selling group agrees to buy the securities from the underwriters also at a discount—for example, 12½ cents per share below the offering price. Consequently, the underwriters and selling group bear much of the risk with a firm commitment underwriting, but they also stand to make the most profit under such an arrangement.

Registration Statement and Prospectus

The 1933 Act requires the issuer of securities to register the securities with the SEC before the issuer or underwriters may offer or sell the securities. Registration requires filing a **registration statement** with the SEC. Historical and current data about the issuer and its business, full details about the securities to be offered, and the use of the proceeds of the issuance, among other information, must be included in the registration statement prepared by the issuer of the securities with the assistance of the managing underwriter, securities lawyers, and independent accountants. Generally, the registration statement must include audited balance sheets as of the end of each of the two most recent fiscal years, in addition to audited income statements and audited statements of changes in financial position for each of the last three fiscal years.

The registration statement becomes effective after it has been reviewed by the SEC. The 1933 Act provides that the registration statement becomes effective automatically on the 20th day after its filing, unless the SEC delays or advances the effective date.

The **prospectus** is the basic selling document of an offering registered under the 1933 Act. Most of the information in the registration statement must be included in the prospectus. It must be furnished to every purchaser of the registered security prior to or concurrently with the sale of the security to the purchaser. The prospectus enables an investor to base his investment decision on all of the relevant data concerning the issuer, not merely on the favorable information that the issuer may be inclined to disclose voluntarily.

CONCEPT   REVIEW

Communications with Investors by or on Behalf of Issuer Permitted by Section 5 during a 1933 Act Registration

	FILING DATE OF REGISTRATION STATEMENT		EFFECTIVE DATE OF REGISTRATION STATEMENT
TYPE OF COMMUNICATION	**PRE-FILING PERIOD**	**WAITING PERIOD**	**POST-EFFECTIVE PERIOD**
Annual Reports, Press Releases, and Quarterly Reports	Permitted, unless designed to assist the placement of securities or arouse interest in a prospective sale of securities	Permitted, unless designed to assist the placement of securities or arouse interest in a prospective sale of securities	Permitted, without restriction, if used contemporaneously with or after delivery of final prospectus
Notice of Proposed Offering (Rule 135)	Permitted	Permitted	Permitted
Tombstone Ad (Rule 134)	Not permitted	Permitted	Permitted
Offer by Preliminary Prospectus	Not permitted	Permitted	Not permitted
Offer by Final Prospectus	Not permitted	Not permitted	Permitted
Oral One-on-One Offers (including telephone calls)	Not permitted	Permitted	Permitted
Oral Offers at Sales Meeting	Not permitted	Permitted, if each investor has an opportunity to ask unlimited questions	Permitted, if each investor has an opportunity to ask unlimited questions, or if each investor has received a final prospectus
Written Offers Other than a Prospectus (so-called free writing)	Not permitted	Not permitted	Permitted, contemporaneously with or after delivery of final prospectus
Sales	Not permitted	Not permitted	Permitted, contemporaneously with or after delivery of final prospectus

Although most prospectuses are delivered in person or by mail, the growth of the Internet as a communication tool has resulted in many issuers transmitting their prospectuses in their Web pages.

Section 5: Timing, Manner, and Content of Offers and Sales

The 1933 Act restricts the issuer's and underwriter's ability to communicate with prospective purchasers of the securities. Section 5 of the 1933 Act states the basic rules regarding the timing, manner, and content of offers and sales. It creates three important periods of time in the life of a securities offering: (1) the pre-filing period, (2) the waiting period, and (3) the post-effective period.

The Pre-Filing Period   Prior to the filing of the registration statement (the pre-filing period), the issuer and any other person may **not offer or sell**

the securities to be registered. A prospective issuer, its directors and officers, and its underwriters must avoid publicity about the issuer and the prospective issuance of securities during the prefiling period. Press releases, advertisements, speeches, and press conferences may be deemed offers if their intent or effect is to condition the market to receive the securities.

SEC Rule 135 permits the issuer to publish a notice about a prospective offering during the prefiling period. The notice may contain only the name of the issuer and a basic description of the securities and the offering. It may not name the underwriters or state the price at which the securities will be offered.

The Waiting Period The waiting period is the time between the filing date and the effective date of the registration statement, when the issuer is waiting for the SEC to declare the registration statement effective. During the waiting period, Section 5 permits the securities to be **offered but not sold.** However, not all kinds of offers are permitted. Face-to-face oral offers (including personal phone calls) are allowed during the waiting period. However, written offers may be made only by a statutory prospectus, usually a **preliminary prospectus** that often omits the price of the securities. (A final prospectus will be available after the registration statement becomes effective. It will contain the price of the securities.)

General publicity during the waiting period may be construed as an illegal offer because it conditions the market to receive the securities. One type of general advertisement, called the **tombstone ad,** is permitted during the waiting period and thereafter. The tombstone ad, which appears in financial publications, is permitted by SEC Rule 134, which allows disclosure of the same information as is allowed by Rule 135 plus the general business of the issuer, the price of the securities, and the names of the underwriters who are helping the issuer to sell the securities. In addition, Rule 134 requires the tombstone ad to state that it is not an offer.

The waiting period is an important part of the regulatory scheme of the 1933 Act. It provides an investor with adequate time (at least 20 days) to judge the wisdom of buying the security during a period when he cannot be pressured to buy it. Not even a contract to buy the security may be made during the waiting period.

The Post-Effective Period After the effective date (the date on which the SEC declares the registration effective), Section 5 permits the security to be **offered and also to be sold,** provided that the buyer has received a **final prospectus** (a preliminary prospectus is not acceptable for this purpose). Written offers not previously allowed are permitted during the post-effective period, but only if the offeree has received a final prospectus.

Liability for Violating Section 5 Section 12(a)(1) of the 1933 Act imposes liability on any person who violates the provisions of Section 5. Liability extends to any *purchaser* to whom an illegal offer or sale was made. The purchaser's remedy is *rescission* or damages.

EXEMPTIONS FROM THE REGISTRATION REQUIREMENTS OF THE 1993 ACT

Complying with the registration requirements of the 1933 Act, including the restrictions of Section 5, is a burdensome, time-consuming, and expensive process. Planning and executing an issuer's first public offering may consume six months and cost in excess of $1 million. Consequently, some issuers prefer to avoid registration when they sell securities. There are two types of exemptions from the registration requirements of the 1933 Act: securities exemptions and transaction exemptions.

Securities Exemptions

Exempt securities never need to be registered, regardless who sells the securities, how they are sold, or to whom they are sold. The following are the most important securities exemptions.[4]

1. Securities issued or guaranteed by any government in the United States and its territories.

---

[4]Excluded from the list of securities exemptions are the intrastate offering and small offering exemptions. Although the 1933 Act denotes them (except for the section 4(6) exemption) as securities exemptions, they are in practice transaction exemptions. An exempt security is exempt from registration forever. But when securities originally sold pursuant to an intrastate or small offering exemption are resold at a later date, the subsequent sales may have to be registered. The exemption of the earlier offering does not exempt a future offering. The SEC treats these two exemptions as transaction exemptions. Consequently, this chapter also treats them as transaction exemptions.

2. A note or draft that has a maturity date not more than nine months after its date of issuance.

3. A security issued by a nonprofit religious, charitable, educational, benevolent, or fraternal organization.

4. Securities issued by banks and by savings and loan associations.

5. Securities issued by railroads and trucking companies regulated by the Interstate Commerce Commission.

6. An insurance policy or an annuity contract.

Although the types of securities listed above are exempt from the registration provisions of the 1933 Act, they are not exempt from the general antifraud provisions of the securities acts. For example, any fraud committed in the course of selling such securities can be attacked by the SEC and by the persons who were defrauded under Section 17(a) of the 1933 Act and Section 10(b) of the 1934 Act.

Transaction Exemptions

The most important 1933 Act registration exemptions are the transaction exemptions. If a security is sold pursuant to a transaction exemption, that sale is exempt from registration. Subsequent sales, however, are not automatically exempt. Future sales must be made pursuant to a registration or another exemption.

The transaction exemptions are exemptions from the registration provisions. The general antifraud provisions of the 1933 Act and the 1934 Act apply to exempted and nonexempted transactions.

The most important transaction exemptions are those available to issuers of securities. These exemptions are the intrastate offering exemption, the private offering exemption, and the small offering exemptions.

Intrastate Offering Exemption

Under section 3(a)(11), an offering of securities solely to investors in one state by an issuer resident and doing business in that state is exempt from the 1933 Act's registration requirements. The reason for the exemption is that there is little federal government interest in an offering that occurs in only one state. Although the offering may be exempt from SEC regulation, state securities law may require a registration. The expectation is that state securities regulation will adequately protect investors.

The SEC has defined the intrastate offering exemption more precisely in Rule 147. An issuer must have at least 80 percent of its gross revenues and 80 percent of its assets in the state and use at least 80 percent of the proceeds of the offering in the state. Resale of the securities is limited to persons within the state for nine months.

Rule 147, however, is not an exclusive rule. In the following case, the court applied only the statutory standard of section 3(a)(11).

BUSCH v. CARPENTER   827 F.2d 653 (10th Cir. 1987)

onic Petroleum, Inc., was incorporated in Utah for the purpose of acquiring, extracting, and marketing natural resources such as oil, gas, and coal. Its corporate office, books, and records were in Utah. During October and November 1980, Sonic publicly offered and sold 25 million shares entirely to residents of Utah. The proceeds were $500,000. Sonic did not file a Securities Act registration statement with the SEC, instead relying on the exemption from registration for intrastate offerings. At the time of the offering, Sonic had not undertaken any business activities in Utah or anywhere else.

Craig Carpenter, Sonic's president, negotiated Sonic's acquisition of an Illinois drilling corporation owned by William Mason. On May 25, 1981, Sonic issued a controlling block of its shares to Mason in exchange for Mason's corporation. Shortly thereafter, Sonic deposited in Illinois $350,000 of the proceeds from the sale of shares to Utah residents. At about the same time, Mason and Carpenter helped create a public market for Sonic shares. As a result, Paul and Linda Busch, who were California residents, purchased Sonic shares from Utah residents who had purchased shares in October and November 1980. When the shares' value dropped, the Busches sued Carpenter for selling unregistered securities. The trial court held that Sonic sold the shares pursuant to the intrastate offering exemption and, therefore, did not need to register the shares. The Busches appealed. ☞

Seymour, Circuit Judge Section 5 of the Securities Act of 1933 prohibits the offer or sale of any security unless a proper registration statement has first been filed with the SEC. However, Congress also recognized that the protections of the 1933 Act were not essential for those securities that could be supervised effectively by the states. Section 3(a)(11) therefore exempts from the Act's registration requirements

Any security which is part of an issue offered and sold only to persons resident within a single State or Territory, where the issuer of such security is a person resident and doing business within or, if a corporation, incorporated by and doing business within, such State or Territory.

In order to fall within the intrastate exemption, initial sales to state residents must be bona fide. The intrastate exemption becomes unavailable whenever sales or purchases by a subsequent purchaser circumvent the federal securities laws. The SEC has consistently maintained that a distribution of securities must have actually come to rest in the hands of the resident investors—persons purchasing for investment intent and not for purpose of resale.

The Busches contend that Sonic had the burden to prove that the original buyers bought with investment intent. We reject this argument. The intrastate offering exemption requires that the issue be "offered and sold only to persons resident within a single state." In face of Sonic's undisputed showing that all of the original buyers were Utah residents, the Busches were therefore required to produce evidence that the stock had not come to rest but had been sold to people who intended to resell it out of state. The interstate purchases of freely trading shares several months after the completion of the intrastate offering do not, without more, impugn the investment intent of the original buyers.

The Busches alternatively contend that Sonic was not entitled to the intrastate exemption because the corporate issuer was not doing business in Utah as required by section 3(a)(11). An issuer cannot claim the exemption simply by opening an office in a particular state. Conducting substantially all income-producing operations elsewhere defeats the exemption, as do the plans of recently organized companies to invest the net proceeds of initial public offerings only in other states.

Here Sonic never did more than maintain its office, books, and records in Utah. Sonic transferred essentially all of its assets to Illinois and made no prior efforts whatever at locating investment opportunities within Utah. Sonic may have been intending all along to invest its assets outside the state. A newly formed company may not claim the exemption while planning covertly to invest the proceeds of a local offering in other states.

Judgment reversed in favor of the Busches; remanded for trial.

Private Offering Exemption

Section 4(2) of the 1933 Act provides that the registration requirements of the 1933 Act "shall not apply to transactions by an issuer not involving any public offering." A private offering is an offering to a small number of purchasers who can protect themselves because they are wealthy or because they are sophisticated in investment matters and have access to the information that they need to make intelligent investment decisions.

To create greater certainty about what a private offering is, the SEC adopted Rule 506. Although an issuer may exempt a private offering under either the courts' interpretation of section 4(2) or Rule 506, the SEC tends to treat Rule 506 as the exclusive way to obtain the exemption.

Rule 506 Under Rule 506, which is part of Securities Act Regulation D, the issuer must reasonably believe that each purchaser is either (a) an accredited investor or (b) an unaccredited investor who "has such knowledge and experience in financial and business matters that he is capable of evaluating the merits and risks of the prospective investment." Accredited investors include institutional investors (such as banks and mutual funds), wealthy investors, and high-level insiders of the issuer (such as executive officers, directors, and partners).

An issuer may sell to no more than 35 unaccredited purchasers who have sufficient investment knowledge and experience; it may sell to an unlimited number of accredited purchasers, regardless of their investment sophistication.

Each purchaser must be given or have access to the information she needs to make an informed investment decision. For a public company making a nonpublic offering under Rule 506, purchasers must receive information in a form required by the 1934 Act, such as a 10-K or annual report. The issuer must provide the following audited financial statements: two years' balance sheets, three years' income statements, and three years' statements of changes in financial position.

For a nonpublic company making a nonpublic offering under Rule 506, the issuer must provide much of the same nonfinancial information required in a registered offering. A nonpublic company may, however, obtain some relief from the burden of providing audited financial statements to investors. When the amount of the issuance is $2 million or less, only one year's balance sheet need be audited. If the amount issued exceeds $2 million but not $7.5 million, only one year's balance sheet, one year's income statement, and one year's statement of changes in financial position need be audited. When the amount issued exceeds $7.5 million, the issuer must provide two years' balance sheets, three years'

income statements, and three years' statements of changes in financial position. In any offering of any amount by a nonpublic issuer, when auditing would involve unreasonable effort or expense, only an audited balance sheet is needed. When a limited partnership issuer finds that auditing involves unreasonable effort or expense, the limited partnership may use financial statements prepared by an independent accountant in conformance with the requirements of federal tax law.

Rule 506 prohibits the issuer from making any general public selling effort. This prevents the issuer from using the radio, newspapers, and television. However, offers to an individual one-on-one are permitted.

In addition, the issuer must take reasonable steps to ensure that the purchasers do not resell the securities in a manner that makes the issuance a public distribution rather than a private one. Usually, the investor must hold the security for a minimum of two years.

In the following case, the issuer failed to prove it was entitled to a private offering exemption under Rule 506.

MARK v. FSC SECURITIES CORP. 870 F.2d 331 (6th Cir. 1989)

F
SC Securities Corp., a securities brokerage, sold limited partnership interests in Malaga Arabian Limited Partnership to Mr. and Mrs. Mark. A total of 28 investors purchased limited partnership interests in Malaga. All investors were asked to execute subscription documents, including a suitability letter in which the purchaser stated his income level, that he had an opportunity to obtain relevant information, and that he had sufficient knowledge and experience in business affairs to evaluate the risks of the investment.

When the value of the limited partnership interests fell, the Marks sued FSC to rescind their purchase on the grounds that FSC sold unregistered securities in violation of the Securities Act of 1933. The jury held that the offering was exempt as an offering not involving a public offering. The Marks appealed. ∽

Simpson, Judge Section 4(2) of the Securities Act exempts from registration with the SEC "transactions by an issuer not involving any public offering." There are no hard and fast rules for determining whether a securities offering is exempt from registration under the general language of section 4(2).

However, the "safe harbor" provision of Regulation D, Rule 506, deems certain transactions to be not involving any public offering within the meaning of section 4(2). FSC had to prove that certain

objective tests were met. These conditions include the general conditions not in dispute here, and the following specific conditions:

(i) Limitation on number of purchasers. The issuer shall reasonably believe that there are no more than thirty-five purchasers of securities in any offering under this Section.

(ii) Nature of purchasers. The issuer shall reasonably believe immediately prior to making any sale that each purchaser who is not an accredited investor either alone or with his purchaser representative(s) has such knowledge and experience in financial and business matters that he is capable of evaluating the merits and risks of the prospective investment.

In this case, we take the issuer to be the general partners of Malaga. FSC is required to offer evidence of the issuer's reasonable belief as to the nature of each purchaser. The only testimony at trial competent to establish the issuer's belief as to the nature of the purchasers was that of Laurence Leafer, a general partner in Malaga. By his own admission, he had no knowledge about any purchaser, much less any belief, reasonable or not, as to the purchasers' knowledge and experience in financial and business matters.

Q: What was done to determine if investors were, in fact, reasonably sophisticated?

A: Well, there were two things. Number one, we had investor suitability standards that had to be met. You had to have a certain income, be in a certain tax bracket, this kind of thing. Then in the subscription documents themselves, they, when they sign it, supposedly represented that they had received information necessary to make an informed investment decision, and that they were sophisticated. And if they were not, they relied on an offering representative who was.

Q: Did you review the subscription documents that came in for the Malaga offering?

A: No.

Q: So do you know whether all of the investors in the Malaga offering met the suitability and sophistication requirements?

A: I don't.

FSC also offered as evidence the Marks' executed subscription documents, as well as a set of documents in blank, to establish the procedure it followed in the Malaga sales offering. Although the Marks' executed documents may have been sufficient to establish the reasonableness of any belief the issuer may have had as to the Marks' particular qualifications, that does not satisfy Rule 506. The documents offered no evidence from which a jury could conclude the issuer reasonably believed each purchaser was suitable. Instead, all that was proved was the sale of 28 limited partnership interests, and the circumstances under which those sales were intended to have been made. The blank subscriptions documents simply do not amount to probative evidence, when it is the answers and information received from purchasers that determine whether the conditions of Rule 506 have been met.

Having concluded that the Malaga limited-partnership offering did not meet the registration exemption requirement of Rule 506 of Regulation D, we conclude that the Marks are entitled to the remedy of rescission.

Judgment reversed in favor of the Marks; remanded to the trial court.

Small Offering Exemptions

Sections 3(b) and 4(6) of the 1933 Act permit the SEC to exempt from registration any offering by an issuer not exceeding $5 million. Several SEC rules and regulations permit an issuer to sell small amounts of securities and avoid registration. The rationale for these exemptions is that the dollar amount of the securities offered or the number of purchasers is too small for the federal government to be concerned with registration. State securities law may require registration, however.

Rule 504 SEC Rule 504 of Regulation D allows a nonpublic issuer to sell up to $1 million of securities in a 12-month period and avoid registration. Rule 504 sets no limits on the number of offerees or purchasers. The purchasers need not be sophisticated in investment matters, and the issuer need

disclose information only as required by state securities law. Rule 504 permits general selling efforts, and purchasers are free to resell the securities at any time.

Rule 505 Rule 505 of Regulation D allows any issuer to sell up to $5 million of securities in a 12-month period and avoid registration. No general selling efforts are allowed, and purchasers may not resell the securities for at least two years. The issuer may sell to no more than 35 unaccredited purchasers, but there is no limit on the number of accredited purchasers. The purchasers need not be sophisticated in investment matters. Rule 505 has the same disclosure requirements as Rule 506.

Regulation A Regulation A permits a nonpublic issuer to sell up to $5 million of securities in a one-year period. There is no limit on the number of purchasers, no purchaser sophistication requirement, and no purchaser resale restriction.

The Regulation A disclosure document is the offering circular, which must be filed with the SEC. The offering circular is required to contain a balance sheet dated within 90 days before the filing date of the offering circular. It must also contain two years' income statements, cash flow statements, and statements of shareholder equity. Ordinarily, the financial statements need not be audited unless the issuer is otherwise required to have audited financial statements.

There is a 20-day waiting period after the filing of the offering circular, during which offers may be made. Oral offers are permitted, as are brief advertisements and written offers by an offering circular. Sales are permitted after the waiting period.

Regulation A also permits issuers to determine investors' interest in a planned offering prior to undertaking the expense of preparing an offering circular.

Securities Offerings on the Internet

With the emergence of the Internet as a significant communication tool, small issuers have sought to make offerings to investors over the Internet. Such offerings can easily run afoul of Rules 505 and 506 of Regulation D, which prohibit public solicitations of investors. Spring Street Brewing Company, the first issuer to offer securities via the Web in 1995, avoided registration by using the Regulation A exemption. It is expected that the SEC will, in the next few years, create exemptions specifically for Internet offerings of securities. For example, the SEC might permit a nonpublic issuer to sell up to $5 million of securities to accredited or otherwise qualified purchasers.

Transaction Exemptions for Nonissuers

Although it is true that the registration provisions apply primarily to issuers and those who help issuers sell their securities publicly, the 1933 Act states that every person who sells a security is potentially subject to Section 5's restrictions on the timing of offers and sales. You must learn the most important rule of the 1933 Act: **Every transaction in securities must be registered with the SEC or be exempt from registration.**

This rule applies to every person, including the small investor who, through the New York Stock Exchange, sells securities that may have been registered by the issuer 15 years earlier. The small investor must either have the issuer register her sale of securities or find an exemption from registration that applies to the situation. Fortunately, most small investors who resell securities will have an exemption from the registration requirements of the 1933 Act. The transaction ordinarily used by these resellers is Section 4(1) of the 1933 Act. It provides an exemption for "transactions by an person other than an issuer, underwriter, or dealer."

For example, if you buy GM common shares on the New York Stock Exchange, you may freely resell them without a registration. You are not an issuer (GM is). You are not a dealer (because you are not in the business of selling securities). And you are not an underwriter (because you are not helping GM distribute the shares to the public).

Application of this exemption when an investor sells shares that are already publicly traded is easy; however, it is more difficult to determine whether an investor can use this exemption when the investor sells **restricted securities.**

Sale of Restricted Securities

Restricted securities are securities issued pursuant to Rules 505 and 506. Restricted securities are supposed to be held by the purchaser for at least two years. If they are sold earlier, the investor may be deemed an underwriter who has assisted the issuer in selling the securities to the general public. Consequently, both the issuer and the investor may have violated Section 5 of the 1933 Act by selling nonexempted securities prior to a registration of the securities with the SEC. As a result, all investors who purchased securities from the issuer in the Rule 506 offering may have the remedy of rescission under Section 12(a)(1), resulting in the issuer being required to return to investors all the proceeds of the issuance.

For example, an investor buys 10,000 common shares issued by Arcom Corporation pursuant to a Rule 506 private offering exemption. One month later, the investor sells the securities to 40 other investors. The original investor has acted as an underwriter because he has helped Arcom distribute the shares to the public. The original investor may

Comparison of 1933 Act Registration Exemptions

	TYPE OF ISSUER THAT MAY USE THE RULE	LIMIT OF AMOUNT SOLD	LIMIT OF NUMBER OF PURCHASERS
Rule 504	Only an issuer that is not a public issuer	$1 million	No limit
Rule 505	All issuers	$5 million	35 unaccredited purchasers; unlimited number of accredited purchasers
Rule 506	All issuers	No limit	35 unaccredited purchasers; unlimited number of accredited purchasers
Regulation A	Only an issuer that is not a public issuer	$5 million	No limit
Rule 147	Only an issuer organized and doing business in the same state as the offerees and purchasers (80% of assets, 80% of sales, 80% of proceeds used in that state)	No limit	No limit

not use the issuer's private offering exemption because it exempted only the issuer's sale to him. As a result, both the original investor and Arcom have violated Section 5. The 40 investors who purchased the securities from the original investor—and all other investors who purchased common shares from the issuer in the Rule 506 offering—may rescind their purchases under Section 12(a)(1) of the 1933 Act, receiving from their seller the return of their investment.

SEC Rule 144 allows purchasers of restricted securities to resell the securities and not be deemed underwriters. The resellers must hold the securities for at least two years. Investment information concerning the issuer of the securities must be publicly available. In any three-month period, the reseller may sell only a limited amount of securities—the greater of 1 percent of the outstanding securities or the average weekly volume of trading. The reseller must file a notice (Form 144) with the SEC.

If a purchaser who is not an insider of the issuer has held the restricted securities for at least three years, Rule 144 permits her to sell unlimited amounts of the securities. In addition, investment information concerning the issuer need not be publicly available.

Consequence of Obtaining a Securities or Transaction Exemption

When an issuer has obtained an exemption from the registration provisions of the 1933 Act, the Section 5 limits on when and how offers and sales may be made do not apply. Consequently, Section 12(a)(1)'s

MUST PURCHASERS MEET ANY REQUIREMENTS?	IS DISCLOSURE REQUIRED?	ARE GENERAL SOLICITATIONS PERMITTED?	IS RESALE RESTRICTED?	IS A FILING WITH THE SEC REQUIRED?
No	No	Yes	No	Yes; Form D must be filed not later than 15 days after the first sale.
No	Yes, unless selling to accredited purchasers only	No	Yes; for at least 2 years	Yes; Form D must be filed not later than 15 days after the first sale.
Yes; each purchaser must either be accredited or have such knowledge and experience in business and financial matters to be capable of evaluating the merits and risks of the investment.	Yes; unless selling to accredited purchasers only	No	Yes; for at least 2 years	Yes, Form D must be filed not later than 15 days after the first sale.
No	Yes; an offering circular must be given to investors	Yes	No	The offering circular and other offering material must be filed.
Yes; all offerees and purchasers must reside in the issuer's state.	No	Yes	Yes; for 9 months sales may not be made to persons resident outside the state of the issuance.	No

remedy of rescission is unavailable to an investor who has purchased securities in an exempt offering.

When an issuer has attempted to comply with a registration exemption and has failed to do so, any offer or sale of securities by the issuer may violate Section 5. Because the issuer has offered or sold nonexempted securities prior to filing a registration statement with the SEC, any purchaser may sue the issuer under Section 12(a)(1) of the 1933 Act.

Although the registration provisions of the 1933 Act do not apply to an exempt offering, the antifraud provisions of the 1933 Act and 1934 Act, which are discussed later, are applicable. For example, when an issuer gives false information to a purchaser in a Rule 504 offering, the issuer may have violated the antifraud provisions of the two acts. The purchaser may obtain damages from the

issuer under the antifraud rules even though the transaction is exempt from registration.

LIABILITY PROVISIONS OF THE 1933 ACT

To deter fraud, deception, and manipulation and to provide remedies to the victims of such practices, Congress included a number of liability provisions in the Securities Act of 1933.

Liability for Defective Registration Statements

Section 11 of the 1933 Act provides civil liabilities for damages when a 1933 Act registration statement on its effective date misstates or omits a material fact. A purchaser of securities issued pursuant to the defective registration statement may sue certain classes of persons that are listed in Section 11—the issuer, its chief executive officer, its chief accounting officer, its chief financial officer, the directors, other signers of the registration statement, the underwriter, and experts who contributed to the registration statement (such as auditors who issued opinions regarding the financial statements or lawyers who issued an opinion concerning the tax aspects of a limited partnership). The purchaser's remedy under Section 11 is for damages caused by the misstatement or omission. Damages are presumed to be equal to the difference between the purchase price of the securities less the price of the securities at the time of the lawsuit.

Section 11 is a radical liability section for three reasons. First, reliance is usually not required; that is, the purchaser need not show that she relied on the misstatement or omission in the registration statement. In fact, the purchaser need not have read the registration statement or have seen it. Second, privity is not required; that is, the purchaser need not prove that she purchased the securities from the defendant. All she has to prove is that the defendant is in one of the classes of persons liable under Section 11. Third, the purchaser need not prove that the defendant negligently or intentionally misstated or omitted a material fact. Instead, a defendant who otherwise would be liable under Section 11 may escape liability by proving that he exercised due diligence.

Section 11 Defenses A defendant can escape liability under Section 11 by proving that the purchaser knew of the misstatement or omission when she purchased the security. In addition, a defendant may raise the **due diligence defense.** It is the more important of the two defenses.

Any defendant except the issuer may escape liability under Section 11 by proving that he acted with due diligence in determining the accuracy of the registration statement. The due diligence defense basically requires the defendant to prove that he was not negligent. The exact defense varies, however, according to the class of defendant and the portion of the registration statement that is defective. Most defendants must prove that after a **reasonable investigation** they had **reasonable grounds to believe** and **did believe** that the registration statement was true and contained no omission of material fact.

Experts need to prove due diligence only in respect to the parts that they have contributed. For example, independent auditors must prove due diligence in ascertaining the accuracy of financial statements for which they issue opinions. Due diligence requires that an auditor at least comply with generally accepted auditing standards (GAAS).

Nonexperts meet their due diligence defense for parts contributed by experts if they had no reason to believe and did not believe that the expertised parts misstated or omitted any material fact. This defense does not require the nonexpert to investigate the accuracy of expertised portions, unless something alerted the nonexpert to problems with the expertised portions.

The following is the most famous case construing the due diligence defense of Section 11.

ESCOTT v. BARCHRIS CONSTRUCTION CORP. 283 F.Supp. 643 (S.D.N.Y. 1968)

BarChris Construction Corporation was in the business of constructing bowling centers. With the introduction of automatic pinsetters in 1952, there was a rapid growth in the popularity of bowling, and BarChris's sales increased from $800,000 in 1956 to over $9 million in 1960. By 1960, it was building about 3 percent of the lanes constructed, while Brunswick Corporation and AMF were building 97 percent. BarChris contracted with its customers to construct and equip bowling alleys for them. Under the contracts, a customer was required to make a small down payment in cash. After the alleys were constructed, customers gave BarChris promissory notes for the balance of the purchase price. BarChris discounted the notes with a factor. The factor kept part of the face value of the notes as a reserve until the customer paid the notes. BarChris was obligated to repurchase the notes if the customer defaulted.

In 1960, BarChris offered its customers an alternative financing method in which BarChris sold the interior of a bowling alley to a factor, James Talcott, Inc. Talcott then leased the alley either to a BarChris customer (Type A financing) or to a BarChris subsidiary that then subleased to the customer (Type B financing). Under

Type A financing, BarChris guaranteed 25 percent of the customer's obligation under the lease. With Type B financing, BarChris was liable for 100 percent of its subsidiaries' lease obligations. Under either financing method, BarChris made substantial expenditures before receiving payment from customers and, therefore, experienced a constant need of cash.

In early 1961, BarChris decided to issue debentures and to use part of the proceeds to help its cash position. In March 1961, BarChris filed with the SEC a registration statement covering the debentures. The statement became effective on May 16. The proceeds of the offering were received by BarChris on May 24, 1961. By that time, BarChris had difficulty collecting from some of its customers, and other customers were in arrears on their payments to the factors of the discounted notes. Due to overexpansion in the bowling alley industry, many BarChris customers failed. On October 29, 1962, BarChris filed a petition for bankruptcy. On November 1, it defaulted on the payment of interest on the debentures.

Escott and other purchasers of the debentures sued BarChris and its officers, directors, and auditors, among others, under Section 11 of the Securities Act of 1933. BarChris's registration statement contained material misstatements and omitted material facts. It overstated current assets by $609,689 (15.6 percent), sales by $653,900 (7.7 percent), and earnings per share by 10 cents (15.4 percent) in the 1960 balance sheet and income statement audited by Peat, Marwick, Mitchell & Co. The registration statement also understated BarChris's contingent liabilities by $618,853 (42.8 percent) as of April 30, 1961. It overstated gross profit for the first quarter of 1961 by $230,755 (92 percent) and sales for the first quarter of 1961 by $519,810 (32.1 percent). The March 31, 1961, backlog was overstated by $4,490,000 (186 percent). The 1961 figures were not audited by Peat, Marwick.

In addition, the registration statement reported that prior loans from officers had been repaid, but failed to disclose that officers had made new loans to BarChris totaling $386,615. BarChris had used $1,160,000 of the proceeds of the debentures to pay old debts, a use not disclosed in the registration statement. BarChris's potential liability of $1,350,000 to factors due to customer delinquencies on factored notes was not disclosed. The registration statement represented BarChris's contingent liability on Type B financings as 25 percent instead of 100 percent. It misrepresented the nature of BarChris's business by failing to disclose that BarChris was already engaged and was about to become more heavily engaged in the operation of bowling alleys, including one called Capitol Lanes, as a way of minimizing its losses from customer defaults.

Trilling, BarChris's comptroller, signed the registration statement. Auslander, a director, signed the registration statement. Peat, Marwick consented to being named as an expert in the registration statement. All three would be liable to Escott unless they could meet the due diligence defense of Section 11. ∽

McLean, District Judge   The question is whether Trilling, Auslander, and Peat, Marwick have proved their due diligence defenses. The position of each defendant will be separately considered.

Trilling

Trilling was BarChris's controller. He signed the registration statement in that capacity. Trilling entered BarChris's employ in October 1960. He was Kircher's [BarChris's treasurer] subordinate. When Kircher asked him for information, he furnished it.

Trilling was not a member of the executive committee. He was a comparatively minor figure in BarChris. The description of BarChris's management in the prospectus does not mention him. He was not considered to be an executive officer.

Trilling may well have been unaware of several of the inaccuracies in the prospectus. But he must have known of some of them. As a financial officer,

he was familiar with BarChris's finances and with its books of account. He knew that part of the cash on deposit on December 31, 1960, had been procured temporarily by Russo [BarChris's executive vice president] for window-dressing purposes. He knew that BarChris was operating Capitol Lanes in 1960. He should have known, although perhaps through carelessness he did not know at the time, that BarChris's contingent liability on Type B lease transactions was greater than the prospectus stated. In the light of these facts, I cannot find that Trilling believed the entire prospectus to be true.

But even if he did, he still did not establish his due diligence defenses. He did not prove that as to the parts of the prospectus expertised by Peat, Marwick he had no reasonable ground to believe that it was untrue. He also failed to prove, as to the parts of the prospectus not expertised by Peat, Marwick, that he made a reasonable investigation which afforded him a reasonable ground to believe that it was true. As far as appears, he made no investigation. He did what was asked of him and assumed that others would properly take care of supplying accurate data as to the other aspects of the company's business. This would have been well enough but for the fact that he signed the registration statement. As a signer, he could not avoid responsibility by leaving it up to others to make it accurate. Trilling did not sustain the burden of proving his due diligence defenses.

Auslander

Auslander was an outside director, i.e., one who was not an officer of BarChris. He was chairman of the board of Valley Stream National Bank in Valley Stream, Long Island. In February 1961, Vitolo [BarChris's president] asked him to become a director of BarChris. In February and early March 1961, before accepting Vitolo's invitation, Auslander made some investigation of BarChris. He obtained Dun & Bradstreet reports that contained sales and earnings figures for periods earlier than December 31, 1960. He caused inquiry to be made of certain of BarChris's banks and was advised that they regarded BarChris favorably. He was informed that inquiry of Talcott had also produced a favorable response.

On March 3, 1961, Auslander indicated his willingness to accept a place on the board. Shortly thereafter, on March 14, Kircher sent him a copy of BarChris's annual report for 1960. Auslander observed that BarChris's auditors were Peat, Marwick. They were also the auditors for the Valley Stream National Bank. He thought well of them.

Auslander was elected a director on April 17, 1961. The registration statement in its original form had already been filed, of course without his signature. On May 10, 1961, he signed a signature page for the first amendment to the registration statement which was filed on May 11, 1961. This was a separate sheet without any document attached. Auslander did not know that it was a signature page for a registration statement. He vaguely understood that it was something "for the SEC."

At the May 15 directors' meeting, however, Auslander did realize that what he was signing was a signature sheet to a registration statement. This was the first time that he had appreciated the fact. A copy of the registration statement in its earlier form as amended on May 11, 1961, was passed around at the meeting. Auslander glanced at it briefly. He did not read it thoroughly. At the May 15 meeting, Russo and Vitolo stated that everything was in order and that the prospectus was correct. Auslander believed this statement.

In considering Auslander's due diligence defenses, a distinction must be drawn between the expertised and nonexpertised portions of the prospectus. As to the former, Auslander knew that Peat, Marwick had audited the 1960 figures. He believed them to be correct because he had confidence in Peat, Marwick. He had no reasonable ground to believe otherwise.

As to the nonexpertised portions, however, Auslander is in a different position. He seems to have been under the impression that Peat, Marwick was responsible for all the figures. This impression was not correct, as he would have realized if he had read the prospectus carefully. Auslander made no investigation of the accuracy of the prospectus. He relied on the assurance of Vitolo and Russo, and upon the information he had received in answer to his inquiries back in February and early March. These inquiries were general ones, in the nature of a credit check. The information which he received in answer to them was also general, without specific reference to the statements in the prospectus, which was not prepared until some time thereafter.

It is true that Auslander became a director on the eve of the financing. He had little opportunity to familiarize himself with the company's affairs. The question is whether, under such circumstances, Auslander did enough to establish his due diligence.

Section 11 imposes liability upon a director, no matter how new he is. He is presumed to know his responsibility when he becomes a director. He can escape liability only by using that reasonable care to investigate the facts that a prudent man would employ in the management of his own property. In my opinion, a prudent man would not act in an important matter without any knowledge of the relevant facts, in sole reliance upon general information which does not purport to cover the particular case. To say that such minimal conduct measures up to the statutory standard would, to all intents and purposes, absolve new directors from responsibility merely because they are new. This is not a sensible construction of Section 11, when one bears in mind its fundamental purpose of requiring full and truthful disclosure for the protection of investors.

Auslander has not established his due diligence defense with respect to the misstatements and omissions in those portions of the prospectus other than the audited 1960 figures.

Peat, Marwick

The part of the registration statement purporting to be made upon the authority of Peat, Marwick as an expert was the 1960 figures. But because the statute requires the court to determine Peat, Marwick's belief, and the grounds thereof, "at the time such part of the registration statement became effective," for the purposes of this affirmative defense, the matter must be viewed as of May 16, 1961, and the question is whether at that time Peat, Marwick, after reasonable investigation, had reasonable ground to believe and did believe that the 1960 figures were true and that no material fact had been omitted from the registration statement which should have been included in order to make the 1960 figures not misleading. In deciding this issue, the court must consider not only what Peat, Marwick did in its 1960 audit, but also what it did in its subsequent S–1 review. The proper scope of that review must also be determined.

The 1960 Audit

Peat, Marwick's work was in general charge of a member of the firm, Cummings, and more immediately in charge of Peat, Marwick's manager, Logan. Most of the actual work was performed by a senior accountant, Berardi, who had junior assistants, one of whom was Kennedy.

Berardi was then about 30 years old. He was not yet a CPA. He had had no previous experience with the bowling industry. This was his first job as a senior accountant. He could hardly have been given a more difficult assignment.

It is unnecessary to recount everything that Berardi did in the course of the audit. We are concerned only with the evidence relating to what Berardi did or did not do with respect to those items which I have found to have been incorrectly reported in the 1960 figures in the prospectus. More narrowly, we are directly concerned only with such of those items as I have found to be material.

First and foremost is Berardi's failure to discover that Capitol Lanes had not been sold. This error affected both the sales figure and the liability side of the balance sheet. Fundamentally, the error stemmed

from the fact that Berardi never realized that Heavenly Lanes and Capitol were two different names for the same alley. Berardi assumed that Heavenly was to be treated like any other completed job.

Berardi read the minutes of the board of directors meeting of November 22, 1960, which recited that "the Chairman recommended that the Corporation operate Capitol Lanes." Berardi knew from various BarChris records that Capitol Lanes, Inc., was paying rentals to Talcott. Also, a Peat, Marwick work paper bearing Kennedy's initials recorded that Capitol Lanes, Inc., held certain insurance policies.

Berardi testified that he inquired of Russo about Capitol Lanes and that Russo told him that Capitol Lanes, Inc., was going to operate an alley someday but as yet it had no alley. Berardi testified that he understood that the alley had not been built and that he believed that the rental payments were on vacant land.

I am not satisfied with this testimony. If Berardi did hold this belief, he should not have held it. The entries as to insurance and as to "operation of alley" should have alerted him to the fact that an alley existed. He should have made further inquiry on the subject. It is apparent that Berardi did not understand this transaction.

He never identified this mysterious Capitol with the Heavenly Lanes which he had included in his sales and profit figures. The vital question is whether he failed to make a reasonable investigation which, if he had made it, would have revealed the truth.

Certain accounting records of BarChris, which Berardi testified he did not see, would have put him on inquiry. One was a job cost ledger card for job no. 6036, the job number which Berardi put on his own sheet for Heavenly Lanes. This card read "Capitol Theatre (Heavenly)." In addition, two accounts receivable cards each showed both names on the same card, Capitol and Heavenly. Berardi testified that he looked at the accounts receivable records but that he did not see these particular cards. He testified that he did not look on the job cost ledger cards because he took the costs from another record, the costs register.

The burden of proof on this issue is on Peat, Marwick. Although the question is a rather close one, I find that Peat, Marwick has not sustained that burden. Peat, Marwick has not proved that Berardi made a reasonable investigation as far as Capitol

Lanes was concerned and that his ignorance of the true facts was justified.

I turn now to the errors in the current assets. As to cash, Berardi properly obtained a confirmation from the bank as to BarChris's cash balance on December 31, 1960. He did not know that part of this balance had been temporarily increased by the deposit of reserves returned by Talcott to BarChris conditionally for a limited time. I do not believe that Berardi reasonably should have known this. It would not be reasonable to require Berardi to examine all of BarChris's correspondence files [which contained correspondence indicating that BarChris was to return the cash to Talcott] when he had no reason to suspect any irregularity.

The S–1 Review

The purpose of reviewing events subsequent to the date of a certified balance sheet (referred to as an S–1 review when made with reference to a registration statement) is to ascertain whether any material change has occurred in the company's financial position which should be disclosed in order to prevent the balance sheet figures from being misleading. The scope of such a review, under generally accepted auditing standards, is limited. It does not amount to a complete audit.

Berardi made the S–1 review in May 1961. He devoted a little over two days to it, a total of 20½ hours. He did not discover any of the errors or omissions pertaining to the state of affairs in 1961, all of which were material. The question is whether, despite his failure to find out anything, his investigation was reasonable within the meaning of the statute.

What Berardi did was to look at a consolidating trial balance as of March 31, 1961, which had been prepared by BarChris, compare it with the audited December 31, 1960 figures, discuss with Trilling certain unfavorable developments which the comparison disclosed, and read certain minutes. He did not examine any important financial records other than the trial balance.

In substance, Berardi asked questions, he got answers which he considered satisfactory, and he did nothing to verify them. Since he never read the prospectus, he was not even aware that there had ever been any problem about loans from officers. He made no inquiry of factors about delinquent notes in his S–1 review. Since he knew nothing about Kircher's notes of the executive committee meetings, he did not learn that the delinquency situation had grown worse. He was content with Trilling's assurance that no liability theretofore contingent had become direct. Apparently the only BarChris officer with whom Berardi communicated was Trilling. He could not recall making any inquiries of Russo, Vitolo, or Pugliese [a BarChris vice-president].

There had been a material change for the worse in BarChris's financial position. That change was sufficiently serious so that the failure to disclose it made the 1960 figures misleading. Berardi did not discover it. As far as results were concerned, his S–1 review was useless.

Accountants should not be held to a standard higher than that recognized in their profession. I do not do so here. Berardi's review did not come up to that standard. He did not take some of the steps which Peat, Marwick's written program prescribed. He did not spend an adequate amount of time on a task of this magnitude. Most important of all, he was too easily satisfied with glib answers to his inquiries.

This is not to say that he should have made a complete audit. But there were enough danger signals in the materials which he did examine to require some further investigation on his part. Generally accepted auditing standards require such further investigation under these circumstances. It is not always sufficient merely to ask questions.

Here again, the burden of proof is on Peat, Marwick. I find that burden has not been satisfied. I conclude that Peat, Marwick has not established its due diligence defense.

Judgment for Escott and the other purchasers.

Due Diligence Meeting Officers, directors, underwriters, accountants, and other experts attempt to reduce their Section 11 liability by holding a due diligence meeting just prior to the effective date of a registration statement. At the due diligence meeting, the participants obtain assurances and demand proof from each other that the registration statement contains no misstatements or omissions of material fact. If it appears from the meeting that there are inadequacies in the investigation of the information in the registration statement, the issuer will delay the effective date until an appropriate investigation is undertaken.

Statute of Limitations   Under section 11, a defendant has liability for only a limited period of time, pursuant to a statute of limitations. A purchaser must sue the defendant within one year after the misstatement or omission was or should have been discovered by the purchaser. In addition, the purchaser may sue the defendant not more than three years after the securities were offered to the public. Although the word "offered" is used in the statute, the three-year period does not usually begin until after the registered securities are first delivered to a purchaser.

Other Liability Provisions

Section 12(a)(2) of the 1933 Act prohibits misstatements or omissions of material fact in any written or oral communication in connection with the public offering of any security by an issuer (except government-issued or government-guaranteed securities). Section 17(a) prohibits the use of any device or artifice to defraud, or the use of any untrue or misleading statement, in connection with the offer or sale of any security. Two of the subsections of Section 17(a) require that the defendant merely act negligently, while the third subsection requires proof of scienter. Scienter is the intent to deceive, manipulate, or defraud the purchaser. Some courts have held that scienter also includes recklessness.

Since these liability sections are part of federal law, there must be some connection between the illegal activity and interstate commerce for liability to exist. Section 11 merely requires the filing of a registration statement with the SEC. Sections 12(a)(1), 12(a)(2), and 17(a) require the use of the mails or other instrumentality or means of interstate communication or transportation.

Criminal Liability

Section 24 of the 1933 Act provides for criminal liability for any person who willfully violates the Act or its rules and regulations. The maximum penalty is a $10,000 fine and five years' imprisonment. Criminal actions under the 1933 Act are brought by the attorney general of the United States, not by the SEC.

SECURITIES EXCHANGE ACT OF 1934

The Securities Exchange Act of 1934 is chiefly concerned with requiring the disclosure of material information to investors. Unlike the 1933 Act, which is primarily a one-time disclosure statute, the 1934 Act requires **periodic disclosure** by issuers with publicly held equity securities. An issuer with publicly traded equity securities must report annually to its shareholders and submit annual and quarterly reports to the SEC. Also, any material information about the issuer must be disclosed as the issuer obtains it, unless the issuer has a valid business purpose for withholding disclosure.

In addition, the 1934 Act regulates insiders' transactions in securities, proxy solicitations, tender offers, brokers and dealers, and securities exchanges. The 1934 Act also has several sections prohibiting fraud and manipulation in securities transactions. The ultimate purpose of the 1934 Act is to keep investors fully informed to allow them to make intelligent investment decisions at any time.

Registration of Securities under the 1934 Act

Under the 1934 Act, issuers must **register classes of securities.** This is different from the 1933 Act, which requires issuers to register issuances of securities. Under the 1933 Act, securities are registered only for the term of an issuance. Under the 1934 Act, registered classes of securities remain registered until the issuer takes steps to deregister the securities. The chief consequence of having securities registered under the 1934 Act is that the issuer is required to disclose information about itself to its owners and the SEC.

Registration Requirement   Two types of issuers must register securities with the SEC under the 1934 Act.

1. An issuer whose total assets exceed $10 million must register a class of equity securities held by at least 500 holders if the securities are traded in interstate commerce.

2. An issuer must register any security traded on a national security exchange, such as common shares traded on the American Stock Exchange.

To register the securities, the issuer must file a 1934 Act **registration statement** with the SEC. The information required in the 1934 Act registration statement is similar to that required in the 1933 Act registration statement, except that offering information is omitted.

Termination of Registration An issuer may avoid the expense and burden of complying with the periodic disclosure and other requirements of the 1934 Act if the issuer terminates its registration. A 1934 Act registration of a class of securities may be terminated if the issuer has fewer than 300 shareholders of that class. In addition, a registration may be terminated if the issuer has fewer than 500 shareholders of the registered class of equity securities and assets of no more than $10 million for each of the last three years. However, an issuer with securities listed on a national securities exchange would not be able to terminate a registration of the listed securities.

Periodic Reporting Requirement To maintain a steady flow of material information to investors, the 1934 Act requires public issuers to file periodic reports with the SEC. Three types of issuers must file such reports:

1. An issuer whose total assets exceed $10 million and who has a class of equity securities held by at least 500 holders, if the securities are traded in interstate commerce.

2. An issuer whose securities are traded on a national securities exchange.

3. An issuer who has made a registered offering of securities under the 1933 Act.

The first two types of issuers—which are issuers that must also register securities under the 1934 Act—must file several periodic reports, including an annual report (Form 10-K) and a quarterly report (Form 10-Q). They must file a monthly report (Form 8-K) when material events occur. Comparable reports must also be sent to their shareholders. The third type of issuer—an issuer who must dis-

close under the 1934 Act only because it has made a registered offering under the 1933 Act—must file the same reports as the other issuers, except that it need not provide an annual report to its shareholders. 1934 Act disclosure required of the third type of issuer is in addition to the disclosure required by the 1933 Act.

The 10-K annual report must include audited financial statements plus current information about the conduct of the business, its management, and the status of its securities. It includes management's description and analysis of the issuer's financial condition (the so-called MDA section) and the names of directors and executive officers, including their compensation (such as salary and stock options). The 10-K auditing requirements are the same as for a 1933 Act registration statement—two years' audited balance sheets, three years' audited income statements, and three years' audited statements of changes in financial position.

The quarterly report, the 10-Q, requires only a summarized, unaudited operating statement and unaudited figures on capitalization and shareholders' equity. The 8-K monthly report must be filed within 15 calendar days of the occurrence of the event, such as a change in the amount of securities, an acquisition or disposition of assets, a change in control of the company, a revaluation of assets, or "any materially important event."

The SEC permits issuers to file reports electronically, transmitting them by telephone or by sending computer tapes or disks to the SEC. These electronic filings are made with the SEC's Electronic Data Gathering, Analysis, and Retrieval system (EDGAR).

Suspension of Duty to File Reports An issuer's duty to file periodic reports with regard to a class of securities is suspended if the issuer has fewer than 300 holders of that class. In addition, a suspension occurs if the issuer has fewer than 500 holders of that class of securities and assets of no more than $10 million. However, an issuer with securities traded on a national securities exchange would remain obligated to file periodic reports with respect to those securities.

Holdings and Trading by Insiders

Section 16 of the 1934 Act is designed to promote investor confidence in the integrity of the securities markets by limiting the ability of insiders to profit from trading in the shares of their issuers. Section 16(a) requires statutory insiders to disclose their ownership of their company's securities within 10 days of becoming owners. In addition, statutory insiders must report any subsequent transaction in such securities within 10 days.

A statutory insider is a person who falls into any of the following categories:

1. An officer of a corporation having equity securities registered under the 1934 Act.
2. A director of such a corporation.
3. An owner of more than 10 percent of a class of equity securities registered under the 1934 Act.

Section 16(b) prevents an insider from profiting from short-swing trading in his company's shares. Any profit made by a statutory insider is recoverable by the issuer if the profit resulted from the purchase and sale (or the sale and purchase) of any class of the issuer's equity securities within less than a six-month period. This provision was designed to stop speculative insider trading on the basis of information that "may have been obtained by such owner, director, or officer by reason of his relationship to the issuer." The application of the provision is without regard to intent to use or actual use of inside information. However, a few cases have held that sales made by a statutory insider without actual access to inside information do not violate Section 16(b).

Proxy Solicitation Regulation

In a public corporation, shareholders rarely attend and vote at shareholder meetings. Many shareholders are able to vote at shareholder meetings only by **proxy,** a document by which shareholders direct other persons to vote their shares. Just as investors need information to be able to make intelligent investment decisions, shareholders need information to make intelligent voting and proxy decisions.

The 1934 Act regulates the solicitation of proxies. Regulation 14A requires any person soliciting proxies from holders of securities registered under the 1934 Act to furnish each holder with a **proxy statement** containing voting information. Usually, the only party soliciting proxies is the corporation's management, which is seeking proxies from common shareholders to enable it to reelect itself to the board of directors.

If the management of the corporation does not solicit proxies, it must nevertheless inform the shareholders of material information affecting matters that are to be put to a vote of the shareholders. This **information statement,** which contains about the same information as a proxy statement, must be sent to all shareholders that are entitled to vote at the meeting.

The primary purpose of the SEC rules concerning information that must be included in the proxy or information statement is to permit shareholders to make informed decisions while voting for directors and considering any resolutions proposed by the management or shareholders. Information on each director nominee must include the candidate's principal occupation, his shareholdings in the corporation, his previous service as a director of the corporation, his material transactions with the corporation (such as goods or services provided), and his directorships in other corporations. The total remuneration of the five directors or officers who are highest paid, including bonuses, grants under stock option plans, fringe benefits, and other perquisites, must also be included in the proxy statement.

SEC rules regarding the content of proxies ensure that the shareholder understands how his proxy will be voted. The proxy form must indicate in boldface type on whose behalf it is being solicited— for example, the corporation's management. Generally, the proxy must permit the shareholder to vote for or against the proposal or to abstain from voting on any resolutions on the meeting's agenda. The proxy form may ask for discretionary voting authority if the proxy indicates in bold print how the shares will be voted. For directors' elections, the shareholders must be provided with a means for withholding approval for each nominee.

SEC Rule 14a-9 prohibits misstatements or omissions of material fact in the course of a proxy solicitation. If a violation is proved, a court may enjoin the holding of the shareholders' meeting, void the proxies that were illegally obtained, or rescind the action taken at the shareholders' meeting.

Proxy Contests A shareholder may decide to solicit proxies in competition with management. Such a competition is called a proxy contest, and a solicitation of this kind is also subject to SEC rules. To facilitate proxy contests, the SEC requires the corporation either to furnish a shareholder list to shareholders who desire to wage a proxy contest or to mail the competing proxy material for them.

Shareholder Proposals In a large public corporation, it is very expensive for a shareholder to solicit proxies in support of a proposal for corporate action that she will offer at a shareholders' meeting. Therefore, she usually asks the management to include her proposal in its proxy statement. SEC Rule 14a-8 covers proposals by shareholders.

Under SEC Rule 14a-8, the corporation must include a shareholder's proposal in its proxy statement if, among other things, the shareholder owns at least 1 percent or $1,000 of the securities to be voted at the shareholders' meeting. A shareholder may submit only one proposal per meeting. The proposal and its supporting statement may not exceed 500 words.

Under Rule 14a-8, a corporation's management may exclude many types of shareholder proposals from its proxy statement. For example, a proposal is excludable if:

1. The proposal deals with the ordinary business operations of the corporation. For example, Pacific Telesis Group was permitted on this ground to omit a proposal that the board consider adding an environmentalist director and designate a vice president for environmental matters for each subsidiary. However, TRW, Inc., was required to include in its proxy statement a proposal that it establish a shareholder advisory committee that would advise the board of directors on the interests of shareholders.

2. The proposal relates to operations that account for less than 5 percent of a corporation's total assets and is not otherwise significantly related to the company's business. For example, Harsco Corp. could not omit a proposal that it sell its 50 percent interest in a South African firm even though the investment was arguably economically insignificant—only 4.5 percent of net earnings—because the issues raised by the proposal were significantly related to Harsco's business.

3. The proposal requires the issuer to violate a state or federal law. For example, one shareholder asked North American Bank to put a lesbian on the board of directors. The proposal was excludable because it may have required the bank to violate antidiscrimination laws.

4. The proposal relates to a personal claim or grievance. A proposal that the corporation pay the shareholder $1 million for damages that she suf-

fered from using one of the corporation's products would be excludable.

In addition, Rule 14a-8 prevents a shareholder from submitting a proposal similar to recent proposals that have been overwhelmingly rejected by shareholders in recent years.

LIABILITY PROVISIONS OF THE 1934 ACT

To prevent fraud, deception, or manipulation and to provide remedies to the victims of such practices, Congress included provisions in the 1934 Act that impose liability on persons who engage in wrongful conduct.

Liability for False Statements in Filed Documents

Section 18 is the 1934 Act counterpart to Section 11 of the 1933 Act. Section 18 imposes liability on any person responsible for a false or misleading statement of material fact in any document filed with the SEC under the 1934 Act. (Filed documents include the 10-K report, 8-K report, and proxy statements, but not the 10-Q report.) Any person who relies on a false or misleading statement in such a filed document may sue for damages. The purchaser need not prove that the defendant was at fault. Instead, the defendant has a defense that he acted in good faith and had no knowledge that the statement was false or misleading. This defense requires only that the defendant prove that he did not act with scienter.

Section 10(b) and Rule 10b-5

The most important liability section in the 1934 Act is Section 10(b), an extremely broad provision prohibiting the use of any manipulative or deceptive device in contravention of any rules that the SEC prescribes as "necessary or appropriate in the public interest or for the protection of investors." Rule 10b-5 was adopted by the SEC under Section 10(b). The rule states:

It shall be unlawful for any person, directly or indirectly, by use of any means or instrumentality of interstate commerce or of the mails, or of any facility of any national securities exchange,

(a) to employ any device, scheme, or artifice to defraud,

(b) to make any untrue statement of a material fact or to omit to state a material fact necessary in order to make the statements made, in the light of the circumstances under which they were made, not misleading, or

(c) to engage in any act, practice, or course of business which operates or would operate as a fraud or deceit upon any person, in connection with the purchase or sale of any security.

Rule 10b-5 applies to all transactions in all securities, whether or not registered under the 1933 Act or the 1934 Act.

Elements of a Rule 10b-5 Violation

The most important elements of a Rule 10b-5 violation are a misstatement or omission of material fact and scienter. In addition, private persons suing under the rule must be purchasers or sellers of securities who relied on the misstatement or omission.

Misstatement or Omission of Material Fact
Rule 10b-5 prohibits only *misstatements or omissions of material fact.* A person **misstates** material facts, for example, when a manager of an unprofitable business induces shareholders to sell their stock to him by stating that the business will fail, although he knows that the business has become potentially profitable.

Liability for an **omission of a material fact** arises when a person fails to disclose material facts when he has a duty to disclose. For example, a securities broker is liable to his customer for not disclosing that he owns the shares that he recommends to the customer. As an agent of the customer, he owes a fiduciary duty to his customer to disclose his conflict of interest. In addition, a person is liable for omitting to tell all of the material facts after he has chosen to disclose some of them. His incomplete disclosure creates the duty to disclose all of the material facts.

Materiality Under Rule 10b-5, the misstated or omitted fact must be **material.** In essence, material information is any information that is likely to have an impact on the price of a security in the market. A fact is material if there is a substantial likelihood that a reasonable investor would consider it important to his decision, that the fact would have assumed actual significance in the deliberations of the reasonable investor, and that the disclosure of the fact would have been viewed by the reasonable investor as having significantly altered the total mix of information made available.

When there is doubt whether an important event will occur, the *Texas Gulf Sulphur* case holds that materiality of the doubtful event can be determined by "a balancing of both the indicated probability that the event will occur and the anticipated magnitude of the event in light of the totality of the company activity."

Scienter Under Rule 10b-5, the defendant is not liable unless he acted with **scienter.** Scienter is an intent to deceive, manipulate, or defraud. Scienter probably includes gross recklessness of the defendant in ascertaining the truth of his statements. Mere negligence is not scienter.

Other Elements Rule 10b-5 requires that private plaintiffs seeking damages be **actual purchasers or sellers** of securities. Persons who were deterred from purchasing securities by fraudulent statements may not recover lost profits under Rule 10b-5.

Under Rule 10b-5, private plaintiffs alleging damages due to misstatements by the defendant must prove that they **relied** on the misstatement of material fact. The SEC as plaintiff need not prove reliance. For private plaintiffs, reliance is not usually required in omission cases; the investor need merely prove that the omitted fact was material. In addition, the misstatement or omission must **cause the investor's loss**.

The following case considers whether an investor was entitled to rely on the misstatements of a securities salesman that contradicted a writing disclosing the risks of an investment.

CARR v. CIGNA SECURITIES, INC. 95 F.3d 544 (7th Cir. 1996)

enny Carr was a professional basketball player in the National Basketball Association (NBA) when in 1984 he paid CIGNA Securities, Inc., $450,000 for limited-partner interests in two commercial real estate limited partnerships that CIGNA had created. Carr said that the CIGNA salesman told him the limited partnerships were safe, conservative investments. The CIGNA salesman gave Carr *documents that disclosed the riskiness of the investment, but Carr did not read or understand them. Carr also said that the salesman "knew that I didn't understand them. He said they were boilerplate kind of stuff, and breezed through them. He just explained them in his own words. He didn't say they were contrary to what he had told me. What I understood was what he told me."*

When the commercial real estate market collapsed in the late 1980s, Carr lost his entire investment. Carr sued CIGNA for fraudulently selling securities in violation of Securities Exchange Act Rule 10b-5. The district court dismissed the action, and Carr appealed. ☞

Posner, Chief Judge We are going to come directly to the merits of the fraud claim. Carr's claim is barred by a very simple, very basic, very sensible principle of the law of fraud. If a literate, competent adult is given a document that in readable and comprehensive prose says X (X might be, "this is a risky investment"), and the person who hands it to him tells him orally, not-X ("this is a safe investment"), our literate, competent adult cannot maintain an action for fraud against the issuer of the document. This principle is necessary to provide sellers of goods and services, including investments, with a safe harbor against groundless, or at least indeterminate, claims of fraud by their customers. Without such a principle, sellers would have no protection against plausible liars and gullible jurors. The sale of risky investments would be itself a very risky enterprise. Risky investments by definition often fizzle. If the documents an investor was given, warning him in capitals and bold face that it was a **RISKY** investment, do not preclude a suit, it will simply be his word against the seller's concerning the content of an unrecorded conversation.

Carr was a fully literate, fully competent adult investing $450,000, which even to an NBA player is not such chicken feed that a busy person could not realistically be expected to take the time to read a lot of fine-print legal mumbo-jumbo. Carr points out that he was not in 1984 a sophisticated investor, knowledgeable about limited partnerships or commercial real estate. He argues that CIGNA's salesman invited him to repose trust in the salesman's advice and by doing so created a fiduciary relationship. The general rule, however, is that a broker is not the fiduciary of his customer unless the customer entrusts him with discretion to select the customer's investments, which Carr did not do. But it hardly matters. A fiduciary relationship places on the fiduciary a duty of candor, and concomitantly

excuses the principal from having to take the same degree of care that is expected of a participant in an arm's length contractual relationship. But the fiduciary relationship does not excuse the principal from taking the most elementary precautions against a salesman's pitch, such as the precaution of reading a short and plain statement of what one is buying for one's $450,000.

We do not say that a written disclaimer provides a safe harbor in every fiduciary case. Not all principals of fiduciaries are competent adults; not all disclaimers are clear; and the relationship may involve such a degree of trust as to dispel any duty of self-protection by the principal. But we are dealing here with a case in which, if there is a fiduciary duty—and probably there is not—it lies at the outer limits of the fiduciary principle. In so attenuated a fiduciary relation, and with so much money at stake, the principal has a duty to read.

Carr points out that CIGNA handed him 427 pages of documents when he bought the shares of the limited partnerships. We agree that it would be unreasonable to expect Carr to pore through 427 pages of legal and accounting mumbo-jumbo looking for nuggets of intelligible warnings. But the subscription agreements for each of the limited partnership were only eight pages long and rich in lucid warnings, such as: "the Units are speculative investments which involve a high degree of risk of loss by the undersigned of his entire investment in the Partnership."

Professional athletes may be a common prey of financial predators. But their vulnerability does not justify a rule that would have the effect of making financial advisors the guarantors of risky investments.

Judgment for CIGNA affirmed.

Several courts have held that an investor's reliance on the availability of the securities on the market satisfies the reliance requirement of Rule 10b-5 because the securities market is defrauded as to the value of the securities. This **fraud-on-the-market theory** is based on the hypothesis that, in an open and developed securities market, the price of a company's stock is determined by the available material information regarding the company and its business. With the presence of a market, the market is interposed between seller and buyer and, ideally, transmits information to the investor in the processed form of a market price. Thus, the market is performing a substantial part of the valuation process performed by the investor in a face-to-face transaction. The market is acting as the unpaid agent of the investor, informing him that given all the information available to it, the value of the stock is the same as the market price. Misleading statements will therefore defraud purchasers of stock even if the purchasers do not directly rely on the misstatements and even if the defendants never communicated with the plaintiffs.

In *Basic, Inc. v. Levinson,* which follows this section, the Supreme Court held that the fraud-on-the-market theory permits a court to presume an investor's reliance merely from the public availability of material misrepresentations. That presumption, however, is rebuttable, such as by evidence that an investor knew the market price was incorrect.

For Rule 10b-5 to apply, the wrongful action must be accomplished *by the mails, with any means or instrumentality of interstate commerce,* or *on a national securities exchange.* This element satisfies the federal jurisdiction requirement. Use of the mails or a telephone within one state has been held to meet this element.

The scope of activities proscribed by Rule 10b-5 is not immediately obvious. While it is easy to understand that actual fraud and price manipulation are covered by the rule, two other areas are less easily mastered—the corporation's continuous disclosure obligation and insider trading.

Continuous Disclosure Obligation   The purpose of the 1934 Act is to ensure that investors have the information they need in order to make intelligent investment decisions at all times. The periodic reporting requirements of the 1934 Act are especially designed to accomplish this result. If important developments arise between the disclosure dates of reports, however, investors will not have all of the information they need to make intelligent decisions unless the corporation discloses the material information immediately. Rule 10b-5 requires a corporation to disclose material information immediately, unless the corporation has a valid business purpose for withholding disclosure. When a corporation chooses to disclose information or to comment on information that it has no duty to disclose, it must do so accurately.

Until 1988, courts had disagreed on whether Rule 10b-5 requires disclosure of merger and other acquisition negotiations prior to an agreement in principle. In the following case, the Supreme Court of the United States held that materiality of merger negotiations is to be determined on a case-by-case basis. The Court held that materiality depends on the probability that the transaction will be consummated and its significance to the issuer of the securities. In addition, the Court stated that a corporation that chooses to comment on acquisition negotiations must do so truthfully.

BASIC INC. v. LEVINSON   485 U.S. 224 (U.S. Sup. Ct. 1988)

F*or over a decade, Combustion Engineering, Inc. (CEI), had been interested in acquiring Basic, Inc. When antitrust barriers to such an acquisition were eliminated in 1976, CEI's secret strategic plan listed the acquisition of Basic as an objective. Between September 1976 and October 1977, the managements of Basic and CEI privately discussed several times a possible acquisition of Basic by CEI. Throughout 1977 and 1978, despite the secrecy of merger negotiations, there were repeated instances of abnormal trading in Basic's shares on the New York Stock Exchange. On October 19 and 20, 1977, the trading volume in Basic's shares rose from an average of 7,000 shares per day to 29,000 shares. On October 21, 1977, Max Muller, the president of Basic, made a public announcement, reported in a major newspaper, that "the company knew no reason for the stock's activity and that no negotiations were under way with any company for a merger."*

Secret contacts between Basic and CEI continued, however. On June 7, 1978, CEI offered $28 per share for Basic, which Basic rejected as too low. CEI stated it would make a better offer, but Muller told CEI to "hold off until we tell you," because Muller wanted to see an investment banker's valuation of Basic before evaluating any CEI offer. Muller and other Basic officials decided to ask CEI for its best offer. On July 10, 1978, Muller and CEI agreed that CEI would make an informal offer to Basic. CEI advised Muller to make no public disclosures about the negotiations.

On July 14, 1978, the price of Basic shares rose more than 12 percent to $27 per share on trading of 18,200 shares. The New York Stock Exchange called Basic and asked it to explain the trading in its shares. Basic denied that any undisclosed merger or acquisition plans or any other significant corporate development existed. On September 24, 1978, the price of Basic shares rose more than 2 points to $30 per share on volume of 31,900 shares. The next day, the price rose almost 3 points to $33 per share on volume of 28,500 shares, even though the Dow Jones Industrial Average fell more than 3 points. Again the Exchange asked Basic whether there were any undisclosed acquisition plans or any other significant corporate developments. Basic flatly denied that there were any corporate developments and issued a press release that stated:

> management is unaware of any present or pending corporate development that would result in the abnormally heavy trading activity and price fluctuation in company shares that have been experienced in the past few days.

Secret contacts between Basic and CEI continued. In early November, Basic sent a quarterly report to its shareholders in which it stated:

> With regard to the stock market activity in the Company's shares we remain unaware of any present or pending developments that would account for the high volume of trading and price fluctuations in recent months.

On November 27, 1978, CEI secretly offered to buy Basic's outstanding shares for $35 per share. Basic rejected the offer. On December 14, 1978, CEI offered $46 per share. The next day, Friday, December 15, the price of Basic's shares soared. Again Basic answered the Exchange's inquiry with a denial of corporate developments. On Monday, December 18, 1978, Basic asked the Exchange to suspend trading in Basic shares, because it had been "approached" concerning a possible merger. The next day, Basic accepted CEI's offer. On the following day, December 19, Basic announced its acceptance of CEI's offer to buy Basic's outstanding shares for $46 per share.

Max Levinson and several other Basic shareholders sold their Basic shares between October 21, 1977, and December 15, 1978, at a price lower than CEI's offer. They claimed that Basic's statements denying that any merger discussions were occurring violated Section 10(b) and Rule 10b-5 of the Securities Exchange Act of 1934. The district court held that the merger negotiations were not material. Levinson appealed to the Sixth Circuit Court of Appeals, which held that Basic possessed no general duty to disclose the merger negotiations. However, the court found that Basic released statements that were so incomplete as to be misleading. Basic appealed to the Supreme Court. ◌

Blackmun, Justice Underlying the adoption of extensive disclosure requirements of the 1934 Act was a legislative philosophy: There cannot be honest markets without honest publicity. Manipulation and dishonest practices of the market place thrive upon mystery and secrecy.

The Court previously has explicitly defined a standard of materiality under the securities laws, concluding in the proxy-solicitation context that "[a]n omitted fact is material if there is a substantial likelihood that a reasonable shareholder would consider it important in deciding how to vote." *TSC*

Industries, Inc. v. Northway, Inc. (1976). The Court was careful not to set too low a standard of materiality; it was concerned that a minimal standard might bring an overabundance of information within its reach, and lead management "simply to bury the shareholders in an avalanche of trivial information—a result that is hardly conducive to informed decisionmaking." To fulfill the materiality requirement "there must be a substantial likelihood that the disclosure of the omitted fact would have been viewed by the reasonable investor as having significantly altered the "total mix" of information made available." We now expressly adopt the *TSC Industries* standard of materiality for the Section 10(b) and Rule 10b-5 context.

The application of this materiality standard to preliminary merger discussions is not self-evident. Where the event is contingent or speculative in nature, it is difficult to ascertain whether the "reasonable investor" would have considered the omitted information significant at the time. Merger negotiations, because of the ever-present possibility that the contemplated transaction will not be effectuated, fall into this category.

Basic urges upon us the Third Circuit test for resolving this difficulty. Under this approach, preliminary merger discussions do not become material until "agreement-in-principle" as to the price and structure of the transaction has been reached between the would-be merger partners. See *Greenfield v. Heublein, Inc.* (3d Cir. 1984). By definition, then, information concerning any negotiations not yet at the agreement-in-principle stage could be withheld or even misrepresented without a violation of Rule 10b-5.

Three rationales have been offered in support of the "agreement-in-principle" test. The first derives from the concern that an investor not be overwhelmed by excessively detailed and trivial information and focuses on the substantial risk that preliminary merger discussions may collapse: because such discussions are inherently tentative, disclosure of their existence itself could mislead investors and foster false optimism. The other two justifications for the agreement-in-principle standard are based on management concerns: because the requirement of "agreement-in-principle" limits the scope of disclosure obligations, it helps preserve the confidentiality of merger discussions where earlier disclosure might prejudice the negotiations; and the test also provides a usable, bright-line rule for determining when disclosure must be made.

None of these policy-based rationales, however, purports to explain why drawing the line at agreement-in-principle reflects the significance of the information upon the investor's decision. The first rationale "assumes that investors are nitwits, unable to appreciate—even when told—that mergers are risky propositions up until the closing." *Flamm v. Eberstadt* (7th Cir. 1987).

The second rationale, the importance of secrecy during the early stages of merger discussions, also seems irrelevant to an assessment whether their existence is significant to the trading decision of a reasonable investor. To avoid a "bidding war" over its target, an acquiring firm often will insist that negotiations remain confidential and at least one Court of Appeals has stated that "silence pending settlement of the price and structure of a deal is beneficial to most investors, most of the time." *Flamm v. Eberstadt.*

We need not ascertain, however, whether secrecy necessarily maximizes shareholder wealth—although we note that the proposition is at least disputed as a matter of theory and empirical research—for this case does not concern the timing of a disclosure; it concerns only its accuracy and completeness. We face here the narrow question whether information concerning the existence and status of preliminary merger discussions is significant to the reasonable investor's trading decision. Arguments based on the premise that some disclosure would be "premature" in a sense are more properly considered under the rubric of an issuer's duty to disclose. The "secrecy" rationale is simply inapposite to the definition of materiality.

The final justification offered in support of the agreement-in-principle test seems to be directed solely at the comfort of corporate managers. A bright-line rule indeed is easier to follow than a standard that requires the exercise of judgment in light of all the circumstances. But ease of application alone is not an excuse for ignoring the purposes of the securities acts and Congress' policy decisions.

We therefore find no valid justification for artificially excluding from the definition of materiality information concerning merger discussions, which would otherwise be considered significant to the trading decision of a reasonable investor, merely because agreement-in-principle as to price and structure has not yet been reached by the parties or their representatives.

Even before this Court's decision in *TSC Industries,* the Second Circuit had explained the role of the materiality requirement of Rule 10b-5, with respect to contingent or speculative information or events. Under such circumstances, materiality "will depend at any given time upon a balancing of both the indicated probability that the event will occur and the anticipated magnitude of the event in light of the totality of the company activity." *SEC v. Texas Gulf Sulphur Co.* (2d Cir. 1968).

The late Judge Friendly applied the Texas Gulf Sulphur probability/magnitude approach in the specific context of preliminary merger negotiations. He stated:

Since a merger in which it is bought out is the most important event that can occur in a small corporation's life, to wit, its death, we think that inside information, as regards a merger of this sort, can become material at an earlier stage than would be the case as regards lesser transactions—and this even though the mortality rate of mergers in such formative stages is doubtless high. *SEC v. Geon Industries, Inc.* (2d Cir. 1976).

We agree with that analysis.

Whether merger discussions in any particular case are material therefore depends on the facts. Generally, in order to assess the probability that the event will occur, a factfinder will need to look to indicia of interest in the transaction at the highest corporate levels. Board resolutions, instructions to investment bankers, and actual negotiations between principals or their intermediaries may serve as indicia of interest. To assess the magnitude of the transaction to the issuer of the securities allegedly manipulated, a factfinder will need to consider such facts as the size of the two corporate entities and of the potential premiums over market value. No particular event or factor short of closing the transaction need be either necessary or sufficient by itself to render merger discussions material.

As we clarify today, materiality depends on the significance the reasonable investor would place on the withheld or misrepresented information. Because the standard of materiality we have adopted differs from that used by both courts below, we remand the case for reconsideration.

Judgment vacated and remanded to the Court of Appeals.

In response to the *Basic* decision, in 1989 the SEC released guidelines to help public companies decide whether they must disclose merger negotiations. A company is not required to disclose merger negotiations if all three of the following requirements are met:

1. The company did not make any prior disclosures about the merger negotiations,
2. Disclosure is not compelled by other SEC rules.
3. Management determines that disclosure would jeopardize completion of the merger transaction.

Trading on Inside Information   One of the greatest destroyers of public confidence in the integrity of the securities market is the belief that insiders can trade securities while possessing corporate information that is not available to the general public.

Rule 10b-5 prohibits **insider trading** on nonpublic corporate information. A person with nonpublic, confidential, inside information may not use that information when trading with a person who does not possess that information. He must either disclose the information before trading or refrain from trading. The difficult task in the insider trading area is determining when a person is subject to this **disclose-or-refrain** rule.

In *United States v. Chiarella*,[5] the Supreme Court laid down the test for determining an insider's liability for trading on nonpublic, corporate information:

The duty to disclose arises when one party has information that the other party is entitled to know because of a fiduciary or similar relation of trust and confidence between them. A relationship of trust and confidence exists between the shareholders of a corporation and those insiders who have obtained confidential information by reason of their position with that corporation. This relationship gives rise to a duty to disclose because of the necessity of preventing a corporate insider from taking unfair advantage of the uninformed stockholders.

Under this test, **insiders** include not only officers and directors of the corporation, but also anyone who is *entrusted with corporate information for a corporate purpose*. Insiders include outside consultants, lawyers, independent auditors, engineers, investment bankers, public relations advisers, news reporters, and personnel of government agencies who are given confidential corporate information for a corporate purpose.

Tippees are recipients of inside information (tips) from insiders. Tippees of insiders—such as

---

[5]445 U.S. 222 (U.S. Sup. Ct. 1980).

relatives and friends of insiders, stockbrokers, and security analysts—are forbidden to trade on inside information and are subject to recovery of their profits if they do.

In the following case, the Supreme Court stated the applicability of Rule 10b-5 to tippees. The Court held that a tippee has liability if (1) an insider has breached a fiduciary duty of trust and confidence to the shareholders by disclosing to the tippee and (2) the tippee knows or should know of the insider's breach. In addition, the court held that an insider has not breached her fiduciary duty to the shareholders unless she has received a personal benefit by disclosing to the tippee.

SEC v. DIRKS   463 U.S. 646 (U.S. Sup. Ct. 1983)

O*n March 6, 1973, Raymond Dirks, a security analyst in a New York brokerage firm, received nonpublic information from Ronald Secrist, a former officer of Equity Funding of America, a seller of life insurance and mutual funds. Secrist alleged that the assets of Equity Funding were vastly overstated as the result of fraudulent corporate practices. He also stated that the SEC and state insurance departments had failed to act on similar charges of fraud made by Equity Funding employees. Secrist urged Dirks to verify the fraud and to disclose it publicly.*

Dirks visited Equity Funding's headquarters in Los Angeles and interviewed several officers and employees of the corporation. The senior management denied any wrongdoing, but certain employees corroborated the charges of fraud. Dirks openly discussed the information he had obtained with a number of his clients and investors. Some of these persons sold their holdings of Equity Funding securities.

Dirks urged a Wall Street Journal *reporter to write a story on the fraud allegations. The reporter, fearing libel, declined to write the story.*

During the two-week period in which Dirks investigated the fraud and spread the word of Secrist's charges, the price of Equity Funding stock fell from $26 per share to less than $15 per share. The New York Stock Exchange halted trading in Equity Funding stock on March 27. On that date, Dirks voluntarily presented his information on the fraud to the SEC. Only then did the SEC bring an action for fraud against Equity Funding. Shortly thereafter, California insurance authorities impounded Equity Funding's records and uncovered evidence of the fraud. On April 2, The Wall Street Journal *published a front-page story based largely on information assembled by Dirks. Equity Funding immediately went into receivership.*

The SEC brought an administrative proceeding against Dirks for violating Rule 10b-5 by passing along confidential inside information to his clients. The SEC found that he had violated Rule 10b-5, but it merely censured him, since he had played an important role in bringing the fraud to light. Dirks appealed to the Court of Appeals, which affirmed the judgment. Dirks then appealed to the Supreme Court. ⌒

Powell, Justice   In *U.S. v. Chiarella* (1980), we accepted the two elements set out in *In re Cady, Roberts* (1961) for establishing a Rule 10b-5 violation: (i) the existence of a relationship affording access to inside information intended to be available only for a corporate purpose, and (ii) the unfairness of allowing a corporate insider to take advantage of that information by trading without disclosure. The Court found that a duty to disclose under Section 10(b) does not arise from the mere possession of nonpublic market information. Such a duty arises from the existence of a fiduciary relationship.

There can be no duty to disclose when the person who has traded on inside information was not the corporation's agent, was not a fiduciary, or was not a person in whom the sellers of the securities had placed their trust and confidence.

This requirement of a specific relationship between the shareholders and the individual trading on inside information has created analytical difficulties for the SEC and courts in policing tippees who trade on inside information. Unlike insiders who have independent fiduciary duties to both the corporation and its shareholders, the typical tippee has no such relationship. In view of this absence, it has been unclear how a tippee acquires the duty to refrain from trading on inside information.

Not only are insiders forbidden by their fiduciary relationship from personally using undisclosed corporate information to their advantage, but also they may not give such information to an outsider for the same improper purpose of exploiting the information for their personal gain. The transactions of those who knowingly participate with the fiduciary in such a breach are as forbidden as transactions on behalf on the trustee himself. Thus, the tippee's duty to disclose or abstain is derivative from that of the insider's duty. The tippee's obligation has been viewed as arising from his role as a participant after the fact in the insider's breach of a fiduciary duty.

A tippee assumes a fiduciary duty to the shareholders of a corporation not to trade on material nonpublic information only when the insider has breached his fiduciary duty to the shareholders by disclosing the information to the tippee and the tippee knows or should know that there has been a breach.

In determining whether a tippee is under an obligation to disclose or abstain, it thus is necessary to determine whether the insider's tip constituted a breach of the insider's fiduciary duty. Whether disclosure is a breach of duty therefore depends in large part on the purpose of the disclosure. Thus, the test is whether the insider personally will benefit, directly or indirectly, from his disclosure. Absent some personal gain, there has been no breach of duty to stockholders. And absent a breach by the insider, there is no derivative breach.

This requires courts to focus on objective criteria, *i.e.,* whether the insider receives a direct or indirect personal benefit from the disclosure, such as a pecuniary gain or a reputational benefit that will translate into future earnings. For example, there may be a relationship between the insider and the recipient that suggests a *quid pro quo* from the latter, or an intention to benefit the particular recipient. The elements of fiduciary duty and exploitation of nonpublic information also exist when an insider makes a gift of confidential information to a relative or friend who trades. The tip and trade resemble trading by the insider himself followed by a gift of the profits to the recipient.

Under the inside-trading and tipping rules set forth above, we find that there was no violation by Dirks. Dirks was a stranger to Equity Funding, with no pre-existing fiduciary duty to its shareholders. He took no action, directly or indirectly, that induced the shareholders or officers of Equity Funding to repose trust or confidence in him. There was no expectation by Dirks' sources that he would keep their information in confidence. Nor did Dirks misappropriate or illegally obtain the information about Equity Funding. Unless the insiders breached their *Cady, Roberts* duty to shareholders in disclosing the nonpublic information to Dirks, he breached no duty when he passed it on to investors as well as to *The Wall Street Journal.*

It is clear that neither Secrist nor the other Equity Funding employees violated their *Cady, Roberts* duty to the corporation's shareholders by providing information to Dirks. Secrist intended to convey relevant information that management was unlawfully concealing, and he believed that persuading Dirks to investigate was the best way to disclose the fraud. The tippers received no monetary or personal benefit for revealing Equity Funding's secrets, nor was their purpose to make a gift of valuable information to Dirks. The tippers were motivated by a desire to expose the fraud. In the absence of a breach of duty to shareholders by the insiders, there was no derivative breach by Dirks. Dirks therefore could not have been a participant after the fact in an insider's breach of a fiduciary duty.

Judgment reversed in favor of Dirks.

In June 1997, the Supreme Court held that Rule 10b-5 liability attaches to anyone who trades in securities for personal profit using confidential information misappropriated in a breach of fiduciary duty owed to the *source of the information.* Under the **misappropriation theory**, a person violates Rule 10b-5 not only when he steals confidential information from his company and trades in its shares, but also for example, if he steals confidential information about his firm's intent to make a tender offer for another firm and buys securities of the second firm.

Extent of Liability for Insider Trading Section 20A of the 1934 Act allows persons who traded in the securities at about the same time as the insider or tippee to recover damages from the insider or tippee. Although there may be several persons trading at about the same time, the insider or tippee's total liability cannot exceed the profit she has made or the loss she has avoided by trading on inside information.

This limitation, which merely requires disgorgement of profits, has been assailed as not adequately deterring insider trading, because the defendant may realize an enormous profit if her trading is not discovered, but lose nothing beyond her profits if it is. In response to this issue of liability, Congress passed an amendment to the 1934 Act permitting the SEC to seek a civil penalty of three times the profit gained or the loss avoided by trading on inside information. This treble penalty is paid to the Treasury of the United States. The penalty applies only to SEC actions; it does not affect the amount of damages that may be recovered by private plaintiffs. The 1934 Act also grants the SEC power to award up to 10 percent of any triple-damage penalty as a bounty to informants who helped the SEC uncover insider trading.

Liability for Aiding and Abetting   Persons who are not the primary actors that violate Rule 10b-5 but merely aid and abet another's violation of the rule nonetheless may be prosecuted by the SEC. To have aiding and abetting liability, there must be (1) a primary violation by another person, (2) the aider and abettor's knowledge of that violation, and (3) substantial assistance by the aider and abettor in the achievement of the primary violation. Although the SEC may prosecute aiders and abettors, investors harmed by a primary violation may recover their damages only from primary violators, not from aiders and abettors.

Statute of Limitations   A purchaser or seller bringing an action under Rule 10b-5 must file his suit in a timely fashion or else be precluded from litigating the issue. An action under Rule 10b-5 must be commenced within one year after discovery of the facts constituting a violation of Rule 10b-5 and within three years of the violation. In the following case, the court examined when investors should have discovered the violation.

LASALLE v. MEDCO RESEARCH, INC.   54 F.3d 443 (7th Cir. 1995)

edco Research, Inc., is a pharmaceutical company that develops drugs for the diagnosis and treatment of heart disease. In 1988, it had licensed Fujisawa-USA to manufacture Medco's first product, "Adenocard." The following year the Food and Drug Administration (FDA) approved Adenocard for sale in the United States. Sales grew rapidly, but Medco was anxious because all its revenues came from the sale of this one product and the product was beginning to face competition. Medco needed to develop another successful product and do it fast. Subsequently, Medco developed a related product, "Adenoscan," designed to simulate the physiological effects of a treadmill stress test for cardiac patients who are unable to take the test or to perform adequately on it. Again Medco licensed Fujisawa-USA to do the actual manufacturing. Before Adenoscan could be sold in the United States, it had to receive approval from the FDA.

Unfortunately, because of problems with safety and quality control at Fujisawa's plant, the application for FDA approval was in serious trouble, and it appeared that the approval would be substantially delayed. On April 7, 1992, about a week after Medco had temporarily withdrawn its application for approval of the sale of Adenoscan, Medco told its shareholders that its application was on track and that Adenoscan could be expected to be approved by the end of the year. In April 1993, a year later, with Adenoscan still not approved (it was not approved until December 14, 1993), Medco announced that it was going to sue Fujisawa. The suit was filed the following month. The announcement of the impending suit was publicized in the business press, revealing to investors the problems at Fujisawa's plant that had been responsible for Medco's inability to obtain timely approval of Adenoscan from the FDA, contradicting Medco's earlier representations that FDA approval was imminent.

Anthony LaSalle and other investors purchased Medco common shares between April 7, 1992, and April 1993. On September 1, 1993, LaSalle sued Medco, alleging a fraudulent nondisclosure of material facts in violation of Rule 10b-5. Medco defended on the grounds that LaSalle failed to comply with the statute of limitations, alleging that it had been more than a year since facts were available indicating the fraud. The trial court agreed with Medco, and LaSalle appealed. ∽

Posner, Chief Judge The one-year statute of limitations applicable to fraud suits brought under the SEC's Rule 10b-5 begins to run when the plaintiff first learned of facts that would have caused a reasonable person to suspect the possibility of a misrepresentation or misleading omission.

The question whether the suit is untimely depends therefore on whether LaSalle should have suspected before September 1, 1992, that Medco was engaged in fraud. In arguing that LaSalle should have suspected, Medco relies on two "critical" facts, in its words. The first is a precipitate decline in the price of Medco's stock. That price had peaked at $31.75 per share on January 24, 1992. By April 24, 1992, it had plunged to $15.25, a decline of slightly more than 50 percent, and while it rose a bit afterward it was still only $15.50 at the end of August of that year. The second allegedly critical fact is that on June 9 the FDA recalled several batches of Adenocard because of "short filling": presumably as a consequence of a manufacturing problem at Fujisawa's plant, some vials did not contain as much of the drug as they were supposed to.

We have great difficulty in seeing how these two facts, even in conjunction, would cause a reasonable investor to suspect fraud. Everyone knows that the process of obtaining the FDA's approval for a new drug is fraught with uncertainty; and when a drug company's entire earnings are from one declining product and it is counting on a new product for its financial salvation, unexpected delays in obtaining an approval without which the product cannot be sold are likely to have a devastating impact on the company's stock price. Stated differently but equivalently, much of the price of Medco stock during the relevant period must have represented simply a capitalization of the expected earnings from the sale of Adenoscan, and those earnings in turn depended critically on the timing of the FDA's approval. If that approval was long delayed, then as had happened with Adenocard, the earnings from the new drug would be eroded by competition in the market for new drugs, which is dynamic. It is misleading to point to the January 24, 1992, peak of $31.75. There can be no inference that it represented a stable value of Medco's shares. Three weeks before, the price had been only $25. Two and a half months before that it had been only $16.75. And in January of 1991, only a year before it reached its peak of $31.75, it had been only $6.75. What goes up fast sometimes comes down fast—without fraud.

As for the recall of Adenocard, product recalls have become a familiar feature of the American economy. How common they are in the drug industry we do not know. There is no evidence on the question, although the well-publicized recalls of pacemakers and other medical appliances and drugs are a matter of common knowledge and lead us to suspect that recalls in the industry are not all that uncommon. No doubt the recall of Adenocard was an indication that the Fujisawa plant had problems, problems that might lap over to Adenoscan, which was being manufactured at the same plant. It was an indication, in other words, of looming difficulties with the approval of Adenoscan. It does not follow that it was an indication of fraud.

Judgment reversed in favor of LaSalle; remanded to the district court.

Criminal Liability

Like the 1933 Act, the 1934 Act provides for liability for criminal violations of the Act. Section 32 provides that individuals may be fined up to $1 million and imprisoned up to 10 years for willful violations of the 1934 Act or the related SEC rules. Businesses may be fined up to $2.5 million.

TENDER OFFER REGULATION

Historically, the predominant procedure by which one corporation acquired another was the merger, a transaction requiring the cooperation of the acquired corporation's management. Since the early 1970s, the **tender offer** has become an often used acquisition device. A tender offer is a public offer by a **bidder** to purchase a **subject company's** equity securities directly from its shareholders at a specified price for a fixed period of time. The offering price is usually well above the market price of the shares. Such offers are often made even though there is opposition from the subject company's management. Opposed offers are called hostile tender offers. The legality of efforts opposing a tender offer is covered in Chapter 35.

The Williams Act amendments to the 1934 Act require bidders and subject companies to provide a shareholder with information on which to base his decision whether to sell his shares to a bidder. The aim of the Williams Act is to protect investors and to give the bidder and the subject company equal opportunities to present their cases to the shareholder. The intent is to encourage an auction of the shares with the highest bidder purchasing the shares. The Williams Act applies only when the subject company's equity securities are registered under the 1934 Act.

The Williams Act does not define a tender offer, but the courts have compiled a list of factors to determine whether a person has made a tender offer. The greater the number of people solicited and the lower their investment sophistication, the more likely it is that the bidder will be held to have made a tender offer. Also, the shorter the offering period, the more rigid the price, and the greater the publicity concerning the offer, the more likely it is that the purchase efforts of the bidder will be treated as a tender offer. Given these factors, a person who offers to purchase shares directly from several shareholders at a set price for only a few days risks having a court treat the offer like a tender offer. The Williams Act does not regulate a tender offer unless the bidder intends to become a holder of at least 5 percent of the subject company's shares.

A bidder making a tender offer must file a tender offer statement (Schedule 14D-1) with the SEC when the offer commences. The information in this schedule includes the terms of the offer (for example, the price), the background of the bidder, and the purpose of the tender offer (including whether the bidder intends to control the subject company).

The SEC requires the bidder to keep the tender offer open for at least 20 business days and prohibits any purchase of shares during that time. This rule is to give shareholders adequate time to make informed decisions regarding whether to tender their shares. Tendering shareholders may withdraw their tendered shares during the entire term of the offer. This rule allows the highest bidder to buy the shares, as in an auction.

All tender offers, whether made by the issuer or by a third-party bidder, must be made to all holders of the targeted class of shares. When a bidder increases the offering price during the term of the tender offer, all of the shareholders must be paid the higher price even if they tendered their shares at a lower price. If more shares are tendered than the bidder offered to buy, the bidder must prorate its purchases among all of the shares tendered. This proration rule is designed to foster careful shareholder decisions about whether to sell shares. Shareholders might rush to tender their shares if the bidder could accept shares on a first-come, first-served basis.

The management of the subject company is required to inform the shareholders of its position on the tender offer, with its reasons, within 10 days after the offer has been made. It must also provide the bidder with a list of the holders of the equity securities that the bidder seeks to acquire or mail the materials for the bidder.

SEC Rule 14e-3 prohibits persons who have knowledge of an impending tender offer from using such information prior to its public disclosure. The rule limits insider trading in the tender offer context.

Private Acquisitions of Shares

The Williams Act regulates private acquisitions of shares differently from tender offers. When the bidder privately seeks a controlling block of the subject company's shares on a stock exchange or in face-to-face negotiations with only a few shareholders, no advance notice to the SEC or disclosure to shareholders is required. However, a person making a private acquisition is required to file a Schedule 13D with the SEC and to send a copy to the subject company within 10 days after he becomes a holder of 5 percent of its shares. A Schedule 13G (which requires less disclosure than a 13D) must be filed when a 5 percent holder has purchased no more than 2 percent of the shares within the past 12 months.

The next case considers whether a bidder violated the "best price" rule by entering into an agreement with the controlling shareholder prior to the commencement of the tender offer.

LERRO v. QUAKER OATS CO. 84 F.3d 239 (7th Cir. 1996)

O n November 1, 1994, Quaker Oats Company and Snapple Beverage Corporation signed a Merger Agreement by which Quaker Oats would acquire Snapple in a two-step transaction: a tender offer for $14 per share followed by a merger in which shareholders that had not tendered their shares would receive $14 per share; shareholders who thought the merger price was too low could demand appraisal of their shares under Delaware corporation law. However, the success of the acquisition was assured because Snapple's controlling shareholder, Thomas Lee, supported the acquisition. Lee promised to tender his shares to Quaker Oats during the tender offer and to sell this shares to Quaker Oats if the tender offer were unsuccessful.

At the same time, Quaker Oats and Snapple also entered a new Distributor Agreement granting Select Beverages, Inc., the exclusive right to distribute Snapple and Gatorade in Indiana, Illinois, and Wisconsin. Thomas Lee controlled a majority of the stock of Select.

Subsequently, Quaker Oats acquired 96.5 percent of Snapple's shares pursuant to the tender offer, and immediately effected a short-form merger under Delaware law. Snapple shareholder Joseph Lerro sued Quaker Oats and Thomas Lee for allegedly violating the Williams Act and the regulations thereunder, on the grounds that the Distributor Agreement provided Lee with extra compensation for his shares. Lerro argued that the extra compensation violated Securities Exchange Act Rule 14d-10(a)(2), which requires that all holders who tender shares during a tender offer receive the same consideration. The district court dismissed the case on the grounds that the agreement had been signed before the tender offer began and, therefore, was not consideration paid during the tender offer. Lerro appealed. ∞

Easterbrook, Circuit Judge Rule 14d-10(a)(2) gives every investor whose shares are acquired as part of the offer "the highest consideration paid to any other security holder during such tender offer." Everyone who tenders receives the highest price paid "during the tender offer"—not the price paid at some other time. Before the offer is not "during" the offer. The difference between "during" and "before" (or "after") is not just linguistic. It is essential to permit everyone to participate in the markets near the time of a tender offer. Bidders are forbidden to buy or sell on the open market or via negotiated transactions during an offer, but they are free to transact until an offer begins, or immediately after it ends.

Purchases near in time to a tender offer, but outside it, may be essential to transactions that all investors find beneficial. Controlling shareholders often receive indirect or non-monetary benefits and are unwilling to part with their stock (and hence with control) for a price that outside investors find attractive. At the same time, potential bidders may be unable to profit by paying everyone the price essential to separate the insiders from their shares. Suppose a firm's stock is trading for $20, insiders who hold 30 percent of the firm would not sell for less than $30, and a potential bidder values the entire firm at $25 per share. An offer of $25 for all stock would not attract the insiders' shares; and as a practical matter, failure to attract the control bloc would doom the offer. The transaction would be feasible, however, if the acquiror could pay $30 to the control group before the bid commences and acquire the rest of the stock at $22 per share, for an average price of $24.40. Everyone is better off: the public investors prefer $22 to $20; the control group is happy; the bidder anticipates a profit of 60 cents per share. Treating the Williams Act as a mandate for an identical price across the board—as opposed to an identical price for all shares acquired in the offer—would make all investors worse off.

Just as those who sell for $15 today cannot complain if their trading partner pays $20 to someone else tomorrow, those who sell in the market a day before the offer starts are not entitled to the higher price paid to those who wait. The point of Rule 14d-10 is to demark clearly the periods during which the special Williams Act rules apply. Once the offer begins, professional investors and amateurs receive the same price. Persons who make tender offers do not lose their ability to participate as investors for undefined periods "near" the time of the offer. With millions or even billions of dollars at stake, precise definition of the blackout period is essential. The line is arbitrary, to be sure; but some line is essential, and it had best be a bright one.

Lerro alleges that the Distributor Agreement was integral to the transaction, in the sense that Quaker

Oats would not have launched the bid unless it knew that Lee was satisfied with the terms. The Distributor Agreement was signed on November 1, but its effect depended on the merger and obviously was bound up with the tender offer too. Nonetheless, this does not establish that Quaker Oats paid Lee more than $14 per share "during" the tender offer. The agreements were signed before the offer began, and were effective with a merger that occurred later. We reject any argument that a follow-up merger should be integrated with a tender offer. They are different transactions, under different bodies of law (federal law regulates the tender offer and state law the merger). Accepting Lerro's request to treat the tender offer and the merger as a single step would imperil countless ordinary transactions— from two-tier tender offer and merger sequences (with different prices, or different forms of securities, offered in the two tiers) to simple employment agreements under which the surviving entity promises to employ managers for stated terms or give severance pay. Yet none of the regulations implementing the Williams Act requires managerial salary, or Golden Parachute payments, to be imputed to stock and offered to non-management as well.

Because transactions before or after a tender offer are outside the scope of Rule 14d-10, we must decide whether the transactions at issue preceded the tender offer. Rule 14d-2(a) addresses this directly:

A tender offer shall commence at 12:01 A.M. on the date when the first of the following events occur:

(1) The long form publication of the tender offer is first published by the bidder;
(2) The summary advertisement of the tender offer is first published by the bidder;
(4) Definitive copies of a tender offer are first published or sent or given by the bidder to the security holders;
(5) The tender offer is first published or sent or given to security holder by the bidder by any means not otherwise referred to in paragraphs (a)(1) through (a)(4).

The Merger Agreement and Distributor Agreement were signed on November 1, 1994. News of the impending bid first reached the public, via the *Dow Jones News Wire,* on November 2, and the tender offer was formally announced on November 4, commencing it on that date.

Not so, Lerro insists. He believes that the offer commenced even before November 1 because it was given to Lee and other Snapple insiders before then. Lerro reads "security holders" in Rule 14d-2(a)(5) to mean *any* security holders, rather than investors in general; on Lerro's understanding, a tender offer "commences" as soon as a potential bidder opens negotiations with a potential target's management. Yet no case or administrative interpretation supports that understanding. Rule 14d-2 contemplates general publication or notice. "Tender offer" means the definitive announcement, not negotiations looking toward an offer.

Treating private acquisitions as the "commencement" of a tender offer would have effects far beyond requiring Quaker Oats to pay a little more than $14 per share to Snapple's public investors. For starters, it would forbid outright the kind of bargain that Quaker and Snapple's managers reached. Under Rule 10b-13(a), once a tender offer begins, the bidder cannot acquire shares in negotiated transactions. Inability to reach a modus vivendi would make bids less attractive, reduce the prices bidders are willing to pay, or both—to the detriment of the investors Congress set out to protect. If the offer commences when negotiations open, then potential bidders must get out of the public markets too. And that is not all. The Williams Act and the accompanying regulations are crammed with timetables measured from the commencement of the bid. The times for withdrawal, proration rights, and so on run from the time of commencement of the offer and would be disrupted if not nullified by a conclusion that a private negotiation marks the commencement. It would defeat the purposes of the Williams Act and the SEC's regulations to close the proration pool before the public learns of the offer. Everything depends on making the times start from a *public* announcement—and on making that time as clear as humanly possible.

Lerro reminds us that neither the Williams Act nor the SEC's regulations define "tender offer." That term has been frustratingly difficult to encapsulate. True enough, but our case is about "when" rather than "what." Quaker Oats made a traditional tender offer. The commencement date for such an offer is rigorously defined. This offer commenced at 12:01 A.M. on November 4, 1994. From this conclusion everything else follows.

Judgment for Quaker Oats affirmed.

State Regulation of Tender Offers

Statutes that apply to tender offers have been enacted by about two-thirds of the states. State statutes have become highly protective of subject companies. For example, the Indiana statute gives shareholders other than the bidder the right to determine whether the shares acquired by the bidder may be voted in directors' elections and other matters. The statute, which essentially gives a subject company the power to require shareholder approval of a hostile tender offer, has been copied by several states.

Other states, such as Delaware, have adopted business combination moratorium statutes. These statutes delay the effectuation of a merger of the corporation with a shareholder owning a large percentage of shares (such as 15 percent) unless the board of director's approval is obtained. Because the typical large shareholder in a public company is a bidder who has made a tender offer, these state statutes primarily affect the ability of a bidder to effectuate a merger after a tender offer and, therefore, may have the effect of deterring hostile acquisitions.

THE FOREIGN CORRUPT PRACTICES ACT

The Foreign Corrupt Practices Act (FCPA) was passed by Congress in 1977 as an amendment to the Securities Exchange Act of 1934. Its passage followed discoveries that more than 400 American corporations had given bribes or made other improper or questionable payments in connection with business abroad and within the United States. Many of these payments were bribes to high-level officials of foreign governments for the purpose of obtaining contracts for the sale of goods or services. Officers of the companies that had made the payments argued that such payments were customary and necessary in business transactions in many countries. This argument was pressed forcefully with regard to facilitating payments. Such payments were said to be essential to get lower-level government officials in a number of countries to perform their nondiscretionary or ministerial tasks, such as preparing or approving necessary import or export documents.

In a significant number of cases, bribes had been accounted for as commission payments, as normal transactions with foreign subsidiaries, or as payments for services rendered by professionals or other firms, or had in other ways been made to appear as normal business expenses. These bribes were then illegally deducted as normal business expenses in income tax returns filed with the Internal Revenue Service.

The Payments Prohibition

The FCPA makes it a crime for any American firm—whether or not it has securities registered under the 1934 Act—to offer, promise, or make payments or gifts of anything of value to foreign officials and certain others. Payments are prohibited if the person making the payment knows or should know that some or all of it will be used for the purpose of influencing a governmental decision, even if the offer is not accepted or the promise is not carried out. The FCPA prohibits offers or payments to foreign political parties and candidates for office as well as offers and payments to government officials. Payments of kickbacks to foreign businesses and their officers are not prohibited unless it is known or should be known that these payments will be passed on to government officials or other illegal recipients.

Facilitating or grease payments are not prohibited by the FCPA. For example, suppose a corporation applies for a radio license in Italy and makes a payment to the government official who issues the licenses. If the official grants licenses to every applicant and the payment merely speeds up the processing of the application, the FCPA is not violated.

Substantial penalties for violations may be imposed. A company may be fined up to $2 million. Directors, officers, employees, or agents participating in violations are liable for fines of up to $100,000 and prison terms of up to five years.

Record-Keeping and Internal Controls Requirements

The FCPA also establishes record-keeping and internal control requirements for firms subject to the periodic disclosure provisions of the Securities Exchange Act of 1934. The purpose of such controls is to prevent unauthorized payments and transactions and unauthorized access to company assets that may result in illegal payments.

The FCPA requires the making and keeping of records and accounts "which, in reasonable detail, accurately, and fairly reflect the transactions and dispositions of the assets of the issuer" of securities. It also requires the establishment and maintenance of a system of internal accounting controls that provides "reasonable assurances" that the firm's transactions are executed in accordance with management's authorization and that the firm's assets are used or disposed of only as authorized by management.

STATE SECURITIES LAW

State securities laws are frequently referred to as blue-sky laws, since the early state securities statutes were designed to protect investors from promoters and security salespersons who would "sell building lots in the blue sky." The first state to enact a securities law was Kansas, in 1911. All of the states now have such legislation.

The National Conference of Commissioners on Uniform State Laws has adopted the Uniform Securities Act of 1956. The act contains antifraud provisions, requires the registration of securities, and demands broker-dealer registration. About two-thirds of the states have adopted the act, but many states have made significant changes in it.

All of the state securities statutes provide penalties for fraudulent sales and permit the issuance of injunctions to protect investors from additional or anticipated fraudulent acts. Most of the statutes grant broad power to investigate fraud to some state official—usually the attorney general or his appointee as securities administrator. All of the statutes provide criminal penalties for selling fraudulent securities and conducting fraudulent transactions.

Registration of Securities

Most of the state securities statutes adopt the philosophy of the 1933 Act that informed investors can make intelligent investment decisions. The states with such statutes have a registration scheme much like the 1933 Act, with required disclosures for public offerings and exemptions from registration for small and private offerings. Other states reject the contention that investors with full information can make intelligent investment decisions. The securities statutes in these states have a **merit registration** requirement, giving a securities administrator power to deny registration on the merits of the security and its issuer. Only securities that are not unduly risky and promise an adequate return to investors may receive administrator approval.

All state statutes have a limited number of exemptions from registration. Most statutes have private offering exemptions that are similar to Securities Act Rule 506 of Regulation D. In addition, a person may avoid the registration requirements of state securities laws by not offering or selling securities.

Registration by Coordination   The Uniform Securities Act permits an issuer to register its securities by coordination. Instead of filing a registration statement under the Securities Act of 1933 and a different one as required by state law, registration by coordination allows an issuer to file the 1933 Act registration statement with the state securities administrator. Registration by coordination decreases an issuer's expense of complying with state law when making an interstate offering of its securities.

Capital Markets Efficiency Act of 1976   Congress passed the Capital Markets Efficient Act (CMEA) to facilitate offerings of securities by small investors. The CMEA preempts state registration of offers and sales of securities to "qualified purchasers," as defined by the SEC. The SEC has taken no steps to define "qualified purchasers," but it is expected that the SEC will use its authority to enable small issuers to make securities offerings on the Internet without having to comply with the registration provisions of the state securities statutes.

In the following case, the court considered whether a seller of securities violated the fraud and registration provisions of the Idaho Securities Act.

IDAHO v. SHAMA RESOURCES LIMITED PARTNERSHIP   899 P.2d 977 (Idaho Sup. Ct. 1995)

 hama Resources Limited Partnership was a limited partnership organized in Idaho. Lawrence McGary and Maranatha Corporation were Shama's general partners. On behalf of Shama, McGary offered and sold limited partnership interests in Shama to investors. The limited partnership interests were not registered with the Idaho Department of Finance; in addition, McGary and

Shama were not registered as brokers-dealers with the Department of Finance. McGary did not inform purchasers of the limited partnership interests that the securities, McGary, and Shama were not registered with the Department of Finance.

The Department of Finance filed an action against McGary, Maranatha, and Shama seeking to enjoin them from violating the Idaho Securities Act by selling unregistered securities by an unregistered broker and defrauding investors in connection with the sale of securities. A default judgment was entered against Shama and Maranatha. McGary defended the action on the grounds that the securities were exempt from registration under the nonpublic offer and limited offer exemptions of the Idaho Securities Act. He also argued that he had not committed fraud because he did not act with scienter. The trial found that the securities were required to be registered and that fraud had been committed and, therefore, enjoined McGary from selling the limited partnership interests. McGary appealed to the Idaho Supreme Court. ∽

McDevitt, Chief Justice   The Department alleged that McGary committed securities fraud under I.C. §§ 30-1403(2) and 1403(3). To establish fraud under I.C. § 30-1403(2), the Department must show that McGary made untrue statements of material fact or omitted any material facts in connection with the sale, offer, or purchase of any security. I.C. § 30-1403(2). To establish fraud under I.C. § 30-1403(3), the Department must show that McGary engaged in an act, practice, or course of business, which operated or would operate as a fraud or deceit upon any person. I.C. § 30-1403(3).

McGary argued that the Department was also required to show intent to establish fraud under the Securities Act. This Court has not previously determined whether the intent to defraud or deceive, scienter, is a required element to establish fraud under the Idaho Securities Act. Examining the literal words of the statute and giving the statutory language its plain and literal meaning, we conclude that intent is not an element of securities fraud under I.C. § 30-1403(2) or (3).

The relevant portions of the Idaho Securities Act make it unlawful for any person "to make any untrue statement of a material fact," "To omit to state a material fact," or "to engage in any act, . . . which operates . . . as a fraud or deceit upon any person." I.C. §§ 30-1403(2) and (3). There is nothing in the language of these provisions that indicates scienter is required to establish fraud. I.C. § 30-1403(2) prohibits the acts of omitting statements and making untrue statements of material fact and is not dependent upon the intent of the person committing those acts. I.C. § 30-1403(3), which prohibits any act that operates as to defraud, focuses on the effect of the act and not the intent of the actor. Under I.C. §§ 30-1403(2) and (3), it is sufficient that the person engage in those enumerated activities, in connection with the offer, sale or purchase of a security, to commit securities fraud under the relevant portions of the Idaho Securities Act. We conclude that the Department was not required to make a showing of scienter under I.C. §§ 30-1403(2) and (3).

The Department met its burden of establishing that McGary committed securities fraud under I.C. §§ 30-1403(2) and (3) through the affidavits of investors and offerees who stated that McGary omitted material facts to them about McGary not being a registered broker-dealer and about the Shama securities being unregistered.

McGary asserted the affirmative defenses of exemption from registration under the Idaho Securities Act pursuant to the nonpublic and limited offering exemptions, I.C. § 30-1435(1) and (8). The burden of proving an exemption rests upon McGary, the person claiming the exemption. The nonpublic offering exemption applies to securities that are offered or sold in an isolated transaction or pursuant to a private, nonpublic offering. I.C. § 30-1435(1). McGary's claim for exemption from registration under I.C. § 30-1435(1) is based on the offering being private in nature, and not based on an isolated transaction. Case law has established that a nonpublic offer exists where securities are offered only to those who "possess enough intelligence, information and expertise to make a sound business judgment" or those who have access to the type of information that would be contained in a registration statement.

The purpose of securities registration is to protect investors by promoting full disclosure of information, necessary to make informed investment decisions. Thus, an offering made to persons who are in need of protections of a registration statement and who are not able to fend for themselves, is not a nonpublic offering. To establish a nonpublic offer under I.C. § 30-1435(1), McGary must make a showing that each of the offerees had access to the type of information available in a registration statement such that they did not require the protections of a registration statement.

The second exemption sought by McGary applies to limited offers where the seller reasonably believes that all buyers are purchasing for investment purposes, and that no commission or other remuneration was paid or given directly or indirectly for soliciting any prospective buyer. I.C. § 30-1435(8). A limited offer is one where the offerings are made to not more than 10 persons within 12 consecutive months. To establish that the limited offering exemption applies, McGary must make a showing that the offer was limited in nature, that McGary reasonably believed that each of the offer-

ees and purchasers intended their purchase of Shama securities to be for investment purposes, and that McGary received no commission or remuneration for soliciting a prospective buyer.

The Department met its burden of showing that no genuine issue existed as to McGary's violation of the Idaho Securities Act when McGary offered and sold unregistered securities through an unregistered broker-dealer. The burden of establishing an exemption under the Idaho Securities Act rests with McGary. McGary did not present any evidence to the trial court in support of his claims. McGary failed to carry his burden under the nonpublic offer and limited offering exemptions.

Judgment for the Department of Finance affirmed.

ETHICAL AND PUBLIC POLICY CONCERNS

1. Should the federal and state governments require disclosure by issuers of securities? Are investors able to protect themselves by insisting that issuers provide relevant information prior to the investors' purchasing securities from issuers? How can current securities owners ensure that they will continue to receive relevant investment information? Could investors have contracted at the time of purchase to receive information as needed in the future? Do public companies othewise have economic incentives to publish relevant information about themselves?

2. Who are the primary beneficiaries of the securities laws; that is, who primarily buys and sells securities? Nearly all securities are owned by persons whose wealth places them in the top 10 percent of the population. Is securities regulation merely welfare for the wealthy? Does anyone else benefit from securities regulation? Does the benefit to those persons justify the costs of securities regulation?

3. Should insider trading be illegal? Is insider trading unfair? To whom is it unfair? What are the social and economic costs of insider trading? What are the social and economic benefits of insider trading? Does insider trading improve the efficiency of the securities markets? Should shareholders be

given the power to authorize insiders to trade on inside information? Why might shareholders want insiders to trade on inside information?

4. Should tender offers be regulated by the SEC? Why should all shareholders be entitled to tender their shares to the bidder? Why should a bidder be required to prorate its purchases of tendered shares rather than buy the shares of the first to tender? Why shouldn't shareholders that tender first—who are willing to take more risk—be allowed to benefit more than shareholders who wait to tender? Is it relevant to your analysis that after a successful tender offer, a public company that previously was not dominated by any one shareholder is now dominated by a single shareholder? Is this a normal risk of being a minority shareholder? Does a minority shareholder need the protection of securities law to protect her from this risk?

5. Should the payments prohibition part of the Foreign Corrupt Practices Act be repealed? What is unethical about an American corporation making bribes to foreign government officials and political parties? What benefits does the United States receive from the making of such payments? What detriments does the United States suffer from the making of such payments? Does the analysis change if bribery is a standard way of business life in a foreign country?

1. Beverly Chew and other promoters created 35 general partnerships, each of which purchased 80 acres of land for the purpose of farming jojoba, "the super bean of the future." Each general partner had one operating general partner and several other general partners. The general partners had full and exclusive control of the business of each partnership; however, none of the general partners had any experience in jojoba farming. Most were doctors, dentists, and their relatives. Even the operating general partners made decisions as directed by the promoters. Actual farming was under the control of the promoters. One person farmed all the acreage, because it was not feasible to farm jojoba in 80-acre parcels. The same business plan was followed for all the general partnerships. All the partnerships shared the same field office. When the general partnerships failed, the investors sued the promoters for selling unregistered securities. Were the general partnership interests securities?

2. Jim Long, Jerome Atchley, and Jon and Linda Coleman invested in a cattle-feeding program offered by Shultz Cattle Company, Inc. (SCCI). They participated in SCCI's individual feeding program, under which investors would purchase and raise their own cattle. Each investor was required to sign a consulting agreement by which SCCI agreed to provide advice regarding the purchase, feeding, and sale of the investor's cattle. SCCI received only a flat-rate consulting fee of $20 per head of cattle for these services and received no share of the investors' profits. To receive tax benefits from the investment, the tax laws required investors to participate actively in farming. Therefore, SCCI required each investor to represent that "He will exert substantial and significant control over, and will, exercising independent judgment, make all principal and significant management decisions concerning his cattle feeding operations." However, investors relied solely on the advice of SCCI: they followed SCCI's recommendations regarding the purchase of cattle, the choice of feedyard, the decision when to sell, and the decision to whom to sell. Long's, Atchley's, and the Colemans' cattle were fed, along with those of many other SCCI clients, in a feedyard in which the cattle were commingled. The cattle were tagged by pen number and not by individual investor. Each

investor therefore owned a percentage of the total pounds of cattle in the pen. If any cattle died, the loss was not attributed to a single investor but was distributed pro rata among the investors. Have Long, Atchley, and the Colemans purchased securities?

3. Attempting to reach as wide an audience as possible, a mutual fund company inserts prospectuses for the issuance of its shares in local newspapers and magazines. In subsequent editions of the newspapers and issues of the magazines, the company distributes additional sales materials. Has the company violated Section 5 of the Securities Act of 1933?

4. Western-Realco Limited Partnership sold $800,000 of its limited partnership interests through the services of securities brokers. Western-Realco did not supervise the brokers and was unaware of whether the brokers solicited their clients in a newsletter or to the public in general. Will Western-Realco be able to use the private offering exemption or Rule 504 to avoid a 1933 Act registration?

5. Capital Sunbelt Securities, Inc. (Sunbelt), and Phoenix Financial Corp. were two brokerages that sold limited partnership interests in Capital: Maple Leaf Estates, Ltd. (Capital) and Maple Leaf Estates, Ltd. (Maple Leaf). Capital was to purchase a mobile home park that would be operated by Maple Leaf. Sunbelt and Phoenix kept logs reflecting the persons to whom they distributed copies of the limited offering circulars for Capital and Maple Leaf. Ninety-six persons received copies of the Capital offering circular and 34 received the Maple Leaf circular. The circulars contained the same information as a 1933 Act registration statement. In addition, Capital and Maple Leaf promised to make available any additional information requested by investors. All offerees had a prior relationship with Phoenix or Sunbelt, and there were no seminars or meetings attended by the general public. There was no advertising, and each offering circular was addressed to a specific person. All investors were required to state that they were acquiring the limited partnership interests for investment. Proceeds of the offerings were $2,677,000 for Capital and $950,000 for Maple Leaf. Phoenix offered to sell Capital limited partnership interests to 228 persons and sold to 33 investors, 16 of which had a net worth in excess of $1 million. There were 187 offerees of the Maple Leaf limited partnership interests and 13 purchasers, 9 of whom had a net worth over $1 million. At the conclusion of the offerings, no Form D was filed with the SEC. Were the offerings exempt from registration under Section 4(2) or Rule 506 of the Securities Act?

6. Commonwealth Edison Co. registered 3 million common shares with the SEC and sold the shares for about $28 per share. The price of the purchasers' stock dropped to $21 when the Atomic Safety and Licensing Board denied ComEd's application to license one of its reactors. It was the first and only time the Board had denied a license application. ComEd assumed that the license would be granted; therefore, its registration statement failed to disclose the pendency of the license application. Did ComEd violate Section 11 of the Securities Act?

7. Joseph Crotty was a vice president of United Artists Communications, Inc. (UA), a corporation with equity securities registered under the Securities Exchange Act of 1934. Crotty was the head film buyer of UA's western division. He had virtually complete and autonomous control of film buying for the 351 UA theaters in the western United States, including negotiating and signing movie acquisition agreements, supervising movie distribution, and settling contracts after the movies had been shown. Crotty knew how many contracts were being negotiated at any one time and the price UA was paying for the rental of each movie. Crotty was required to consult with higher officers only if he wanted to exceed a certain limit on the amount of the cash advance paid to a distributor for a movie. This occurred no more than two or three times a year. The gross revenue from Crotty's division was about 35 percent of UA's gross revenue from movie exhibitions and around 17 percent of its total gross revenue. During a six-month period, Crotty purchased 7,500 shares of UA and sold 3,500 shares, realizing a large profit. Has Crotty violated Section 16(b) of the 1934 Act?

8. Potlatch Corporation was in the forests products industry, an industry that had experienced a wave of takeovers. The Potlatch board of directors approved a voting rights amendment to the articles of incorporation that granted four votes per share to current shareholders and other specified shareholders. New shareholders would have only one vote per share until they held the shares for four years. The effect of the amendment would be to deter and frustrate a hostile takeover of Potlatch. The board issued a proxy statement in connection with its solicitation

of proxies from the shareholders. A letter issued with the proxy statement stated that the intent of the voting rights amendment was to give long-term shareholders a greater voice in the affairs of Potlatch. The voting rights amendment was approved by shareholders. Potlatch shareholders sued the company under Section 14(a) of the 1934 Act, seeking to void the shareholders' approval of the voting rights amendment. They alleged that the shareholders' votes were procured by fraud because the board failed to disclose the real purpose of the voting rights amendment—entrenchment of current management. Should the shareholders succeed?

9. J. C. Harrelson, the president and chief shareholder of Alabama Supply and Equipment Company (ASECo), and Clarence Hamilton conspired to defraud investors. They induced Frisco City, Alabama, to create the Industrial Development Board of Frisco City to issue tax-exempt bonds to investors. The Board offered and sold bonds pursuant to an offering circular, which misstated or omitted several material facts, due to misrepresentations made by Harrelson and Hamilton. The Board used the proceeds of the bond issuance to build a manufacturing plant for ASECo. After the ASECo plant was constructed, ASECo ceased all operations and defaulted on its rental payments to the Board, causing the value of the bonds to drop precipitously. The bondholders received only $373.33 for each $1,000 bond. Clarence Bishop had purchased four of the bonds for $4,096. He never saw the offering circular or knew that one existed. He bought the bonds solely on his broker's oral representations that they were a good investment and that others in the community had purchased them. Can Bishop sue Harrelson and Hamilton under Rule 10b-5 even though he failed to read or even to seek to read the offering circular?

10. In May 1983, Phil Gutter read a report in *The Wall Street Journal* that listed certain corporate bonds as trading with interest. Relying on the report, Gutter purchased $36,000 of the bonds. In reality, the bonds were trading without interest. When *The Wall Street Journal* corrected its error, the price of the bonds fell, resulting in Gutter suffering a loss of $1,692. Is *The Wall Street Journal* liable to Gutter for his loss under Rule 10b-5?

11. When he was the Oklahoma Sooner football coach, Barry Switzer attended a track meet, where he spoke with friends and acquaintances, including

G. Platt, a director of Phoenix Corporation and chief executive officer of Texas International Company (TIC), a business that sponsored Switzer's coach's television show. TIC owned more than 50 percent of Phoenix's shares. Switzer moved around the bleachers at the track meet in order to talk to various people. After speaking with Platt and his wife Linda for the last of five times, Switzer lay down to sunbathe on a row of bleachers behind the Platts. G. Platt, unaware that Switzer was behind him, carelessly spoke too loud while talking with his wife about his desire to sell or liquidate Phoenix. He also talked about several companies making bids to buy Phoenix. Switzer also overheard that an announcement of a possible liquidation of Phoenix might be made within a week. Switzer used the information he obtained in deciding to purchase Phoenix shares. Did Switzer trade illegally on inside information?

12. Edper, Inc., identified Brascan, Inc., as a potential takeover target. On behalf of Edper, a securities broker contacted 40 institutional investors and 12 substantial individual holders of Brascan shares who were his clients. The broker told the investors that Edper was interested in buying 3 to 4 million shares. Eventually, Edper bought 6.3 million shares—nearly 25 percent of Brascan's outstanding shares—from these investors at a price that the broker and each individual investor agreed on. Did Edper make a tender offer for Brascan's shares that required it to file a Schedule 14D-1 prior to the making the offers to the investors?

13. First City Financial Corp., a Canadian company controlled by the Belzberg family, was engaged in the business of investing in publicly held American corporations. Marc Belzberg identified Ashland Oil Company as a potential target, and on February 11, 1986, he secretly purchased 61,000 shares of Ashland stock for First City. By February 26, additional secret purchases of Ashland shares pushed First City's holdings to just over 4.9 percent of Ashland's stock. These last two purchases were effected for First City by Alan "Ace" Greenberg, the chief executive officer of Bear Stearns, a large Wall Street brokerage. On March 4, Belzberg called Greenberg and told him, "It wouldn't be a bad idea if you bought Ashland Oil here." Immediately after the phone call, Greenberg purchased 20,500 Ashland shares for about $44 per share. If purchased for

First City, those shares would have increased First City's Ashland holdings above 5 percent. Greenberg believed he was buying the shares for First City under a put and call agreement, under which First City had the right to buy the shares from Bear Stearns and Bear Stearns had the right to require First City to buy the shares from it. Between March 4 and 14, Greenberg purchased an additional 330,700 shares. On March 17, First City and Bear Stearns signed a formal put and call agreement covering all the shares Greenberg purchased. On March 25, First City announced publicly for the first time that it intended to make a tender offer for all of Ashland's shares. First City filed a Schedule 13D on March 26. Has First City violated the Williams Act?

14. ▣ *Video Case.* See "Cafeteria Conversation." Steve has authority to write checks on the account of his employer, a public company under the Securities Exchange Act of 1934. Because Steve is a compulsive gambler and substance abuser, he needs a constant supply of cash to finance his habits. Steve regularly issues checks payable to actual suppliers not currently owed money, steals the checks, signs the names of the payees, and cashes the checks. Because Steve is also in charge of reconciling his employer's bank statements, his embezzlement scheme is not discovered by the employer's independent auditor during a routine audit. Is the independent auditor liable to its client for its losses resulting from Steve's embezzlement?

15. Amenity, Inc., was incorporated with 1 million authorized shares, which were issued to Capital General Corporation (CGC) for $2,000. CGC distributed 90,000 of those shares to about 900 of its clients, business associates, and other contacts to create and maintain goodwill among its clients and contacts. CGC did not receive any monetary or other direct financial consideration from those receiving the stock. Amenity had no actual business function at this time, and its sole asset was the $2,000 CGC had paid for the 1 million shares. Through CGC's efforts, Amenity was acquired by another company, which paid CGC $25,000 for its efforts. The Utah Securities Division sought to suspend the public trading of Amenity stock on the grounds that when CGC distributed the shares it had sold them in violation of the Utah Securities Act. Was CGC's distribution a sale of securities?

Legal and Professional Responsibilities of Accountants

This chapter covers the legal responsibilities of accountants. It considers the professional relationships of accountants with their clients and others who rely on their work. This chapter also covers the criminal and administrative sanctions for wrongful professional conduct by accountants. ∞

GENERAL STANDARD OF PERFORMANCE

The general duty that accountants owe to their clients and to other persons who are affected by their actions is to exercise the skill and care of the ordinarily prudent accountant in the same circumstances. Hence, accountants must act carefully and diligently; they are *not* guarantors of the accuracy of their work. The accountant's duty to exercise reasonable care is a subset of the negligence standard of tort law. Two elements compose the general duty of performance: skill and care.

An accountant must have the **skill of the ordinarily prudent accountant.** This element focuses on the education or knowledge of the accountant, whether acquired formally at school or by self-instruction. For example, to prepare tax returns, an accountant must know the tax laws as well as the ordinarily prudent accountant does. To audit financial records, an accountant must know generally accepted auditing standards (GAAS) and generally accepted accounting principles (GAAP). GAAS and GAAP are standards and principles embodied in the rules, releases, and pronouncements of the Securities and Exchange Commission, the American Institute of Certified Public Accountants (AICPA), and the Financial Accounting Standards Board (FASB).

The care element requires an accountant to act **as carefully as the ordinarily prudent accountant.** For example, in preparing a tax return, he must discover the income exclusions, the deductions, and the tax credits that the reasonably careful accountant would find are available to the client. When auditing financial statements, he must follow the rules of GAAS and GAAP.

Courts and legislatures usually defer to the members of the accounting profession in determining what the ordinarily prudent accountant would do. Such deference recognizes the lawmakers' lack of understanding of the nuances of accounting practice. However, the accounting profession will not be permitted to establish a standard of conduct that is harmful to the interests of clients or other members of society.

Originally, accountants were held to the standard of the ordinarily prudent accountant in his locality. This local standard has given way to a national standard in recent years. Due to improved means of communication in the modern world and the widespread availability of continuing accounting education courses, few accountants today can argue that they are unaware of modern accounting techniques.

ACCOUNTANTS' LIABILITY TO CLIENTS

Acountants are frequently sued by their clients. For example, an accountant may wrongfully claim deductions on a client's tax return. When the IRS discovers the wrongful deduction, the individual will have to pay the extra tax, interest, and perhaps a penalty. The individual may sue his accountant to recover the amount of the penalty. For another example, consider an accountant who prepares an income statement that understates a client's income. The client uses the income statement to apply for a loan, but is denied the loan because her stated net income is inadequate. The client may sue her accountant for damages caused by the erroneous income statement.

There are three principal bases of liability of an accountant to his client: contract, tort, and trust.

Contractual Liability

As a party to a contract with her client, an accountant owes a duty to the client to perform as she has agreed to perform. This includes an implied duty to perform the contract as the ordinarily prudent accountant would perform it. If the accountant fails to perform as agreed, ordinarily an accountant is liable only for those damages that are contemplated by the client and the accountant at the time the contract was made, such as the client's cost of hiring another accountant to complete the work. For example, an auditor agrees to provide audited financial statements for inclusion in a client's bank loan application. The loan will be used to expand the client's business. When the auditor fails to complete the audit on time, the auditor will not ordinarily be liable for the client's lost profits from the unexecuted expansion, unless the auditor had agreed to be liable for such lost profits.

An accountant is not liable for breach of contract if the client obstructs the accountant's performance of the contract. For example, an accounting firm is not liable for failing to complete an audit on time when the client refuses to give the firm access to needed records and property.

An accountant may not delegate his duty to perform a contract without the consent of the client. Delegation is not permitted because the performance of a contract for accounting services depends on the skill, training, and character of the accountant. As a result, for example, Price Waterhouse & Co., a public accounting firm, may not delegate to Ernst & Young, another public accounting firm, the contractual duty to audit the financial statements of GM, even though both firms are nearly equally skillful and careful.

Tort Liability

Accountants' tort liability to their clients may be based on the common law concepts of negligence and fraud or on the violation of a statute, principally the federal and state securities laws.

Negligence The essence of negligence is the failure of an accountant to exercise the skill and care of the ordinarily prudent accountant. An accountant is negligent when the accountant breaches the duty to act skillfully and carefully and proximately causes damages to the client. For example, a client may recover the interest on excess taxes that he paid as a result of his accountant's lack of due care in claiming allowable deductions on a tax return.

Sometimes, an accountant will audit a company, yet fail to uncover fraud, embezzlement, or other intentional wrongdoing by an employee of the company. Ordinarily, an accountant has no specific duty to uncover employee fraud or embezzlement. Nonetheless, an accountant must uncover employee fraud or embezzlement if an ordinarily prudent accountant would have discovered it. The accountant who fails to uncover such fraud or embezzlement is negligent and liable to his client. In addition, an accountant owes a duty to investigate suspicious circumstances that tend to indicate fraud, regardless of how he became aware of those circumstances. Also, an accountant has a duty to inform a proper party of his suspicions. It is not enough to inform or confront the person suspected of fraud.

When an accountant is hired to perform a fraud audit to investigate suspected fraud or embezzlement, she has a greater duty to investigate. She must be as skillful and careful as the ordinarily prudent auditor performing a fraud audit.

When an accountant negligently fails to discover embezzlement, generally he is liable to his client only for an amount equal to the embezzlement that occurred after he should have discovered the embezzlement. The accountant is usually not liable for any part of the embezzlement that occurred prior to the time he should have uncovered the embezzlement unless his tardy discovery prevented the client from recovering embezzled funds.

In the following case, an accounting firm was held liable to its client for failing to meet the standard of the profession.

DIVERSIFIED GRAPHICS LTD. v. GROVES   868 F.2d 293 (8th Cir. 1989)

*D*iversified Graphics, Ltd. (D.G.), hired Ernst & Whinney (E & W) to assist it in obtaining a computer system to fit its data processing needs. D.G. had a longstanding relationship with E & W during which D.G. developed great trust and reliance on E & W's services. Because D.G. lacked computer expertise, it decided to entrust E & W with the selection and implementation of an in-house computer data processing system. E & W had promised to locate a "turnkey" system, which would be fully operational without the need for extensive employee training. D.G. instead received a system that was difficult to operate and failed to meet its needs. D.G. sued E & W and its partners, including Ray Groves, for negligence. The jury found in favor of D.G.; E & W and its partners appealed. ☞

Lay, Chief Judge   D.G.'s theory for recovery based on negligence encompasses the notion of a consultant-client relationship and therefore the existence of a professional standard of care.

The degree of skill and care that may be required of a professional is a question of fact for the jury. We find that there was substantial evidence regarding the applicable standard of a professional consultant.

E & W's Guidelines to Practice incorporates the Management Advisory Services Practice Standards which were adopted by the American Institute of Certified Public Accountants, Inc. (AICPA Standards). The AICPA Standards require that "due professional care" is to be exercised in providing management advisory services. These standards in part generally provide:

In performing management advisory services, a practitioner must act with integrity and objectivity and be independent in mental attitude.

Engagements are to be performed by practitioners having competence in the analytical approach and process, and in the technical subject matter under consideration.

Due professional care is to be exercised in the performance of a management advisory services engagement.

Before accepting an engagement, a practitioner is to notify the client of any reservations he has regarding anticipated benefits.

Before undertaking an engagement, a practitioner is to inform his client of all significant matters related to the engagement.

Engagements are to be adequately planned, supervised, and controlled.

Sufficient relevant data is to be obtained, documented, and evaluated in developing conclusions and recommendations.

All significant matters relating to the results of the engagement are to be communicated to the client.

AICPA Standards Nos. 1–8.

D.G. had determined that it required a "turnkey" computer system that would fully perform all of its data processing in-house. The term "turnkey" is intended to describe a self-sufficient system which the purchaser need only "turn the key" to commence operation. The purchaser should not have to hire programmers, and current employees should not have to undergo extensive training to be able to operate the system. To procure this type of customized and fully operational system, great care must be taken to carefully detail a business's needs and to properly develop specifications for the computer system. Potential vendors must be carefully scrutinized to discover all of the inadequacies of their data processing systems. Once a vendor is chosen, proper implementation is imperative to ensure that the purchaser truly need only "turn the key" to commence full operation of the system. A fundamental part of implementation involves testing the system through parallel data processing operation. Finally, the existence of adequate documentation regarding the operation of the system is crucial once the system is up and running. As previously stated, employees will have had only minimal training and will depend heavily on the instructions for operation. Moreover, documentation is particularly important because this type of system is highly customized and standard instruction sources will have only limited value.

Thus, the jury could conclude that E & W's conduct fell short of adhering to the applicable professional standard of care.

Judgment for Diversified Graphics affirmed.

Contributory and Comparative Negligence of Client Courts are reluctant to permit an accountant to escape liability to a client merely because the client was **contributorily negligent.** Since the accountant has skills superior to those of the client, courts generally allow clients to rely on the accountant's duty to discover employee fraud, available tax deductions, and other matters for which the accountant is hired. The client is not required to exercise reasonable care to discover these things itself.

Nonetheless, some courts allow the defense of contributory negligence or the defense of **comparative negligence,** such as when clients negligently fail to follow an accountant's advice or when clients possess information that makes their reliance on the accountant unwarranted. The next case considers the limits of the comparative negligence defense.

SCIOTO MEMORIAL HOSPITAL ASS'N., INC. v. PRICE WATERHOUSE 659 N.E.2d 1268 (Ohio Sup. Ct. 1996)

*S*cioto Memorial Hospital Association, Inc., planned the construction of Richmond Place, a 170-unit residential retirement center in Lexington, Kentucky. Scioto hired Price Waterhouse (PW) to review the work of the architect, the financial underwriter, and the marketing consultant and to recommend whether Scioto should proceed with the Richmond Place investment. PW's engagement letter represented that PW would issue a preliminary feasibility study and review a detailed financial forecast of the project. Financial forecasts represent management's judgment of the most likely set of conditions and management's most likely course of action. Instead of reviewing a financial forecast for Richmond Place, PW reviewed only a financial projection compiled by the underwriter. As PW explained in its letter to Scioto, a projection "represents management's estimate of its possible, but not necessarily most probable, future course of action." PW's final report issued to Scioto assumed an occupancy rate of 98 percent.

During construction, presales were lagging, but PW assured Scioto's president that Richmond Place was a good project. When construction was 70 percent complete, fire destroyed most of the retirement center. Scioto used the insurance proceeds to rebuild, yet a year later, only 15 residents occupied Richmond Place.

Scioto sued PW alleging negligence and breach of contract on the grounds that PW failed adequately to assess and disclose to Scioto the risks associated with the project. Scioto claimed it would not have undertaken the project if PW's report had accurately reflected the financial forecast. PW defended on the grounds that Scioto's comparative negligence caused Scioto's damages: PW pointed to delays in construction after the fire and Scioto's lack of business-interruption insurance covering the six-month delay in construction due to the fire. The trial court held that PW could not raise the defense of Scioto's comparative negligence, and the jury found PW liable. PW appealed to an Ohio appeals court, which affirmed, but reduced PW's liability to $8,771,000. PW appealed to the Supreme Court of Ohio. ∞

Sweeney, Justice   The main issue before this court is whether the comparative negligence is applicable to a professional negligence claim of a client against its accountant. We find that the comparative negligence defense is applicable in accounting negligence cases.

The audit interference rule was set forth in *National Surety Corp. v. Lybrand* (1939). At that time, New York recognized contributory negligence as a complete bar to recovery. In *National Surety,* the New York Supreme Court, Appellate Division, held that contributory negligence constituted a defense for accountants only if the client's negligence contributed to the accountant's failure to perform his contract and to report the truth. While this rule was adopted by a number of jurisdictions, a review of these cases shows that none discusses its application in a state recognizing comparative negligence, with the exception of *Fullmer v. Wohlfeiler & Beck* (1990). The audit interference rule was made to soften what was then the harsh rule of negligence law which barred recovery of damages if there was any contributory negligence on the part of the plaintiff.

However, in light of Ohio's comparative negligence statute enacted in 1980, there is no need for a special rule and, thus, we reject the application of the audit interference rule in Ohio. Hence, any negligence by a client, whether or not it directly interferes with the accountant's performance of its duties, can reduce the client's recovery. In so holding, we note that virtually all courts that have expressly considered the applicability of the audit interference rule to their comparative negligence states have agreed and rejected the rule.

As to the application of the comparative negligence defense in the present case, we note that while accountants should exercise ordinary care in conducting their accounting activities, the persons who hire accountants, usually businesspersons, should also be required to conduct their business

activities in a reasonable and prudent manner. Accordingly, the trial court erred in granting the motion as to PW's comparative negligence defense and failing to give an instruction on comparative negligence to the jury.

However, despite the trial court's ruling, the record demonstrates that PW was not precluded from presenting extensive evidence tending to show that Scioto's own conduct was a cause of its losses, in addition to the negligence of PW. PW primarily argues about the trial court's exclusion of evidence regarding Scioto's business-interruption insurance. However, the $4,000,000 hole in Scioto's protective coverage was clearly and repeatedly presented to the jury. Moreover, failure to obtain such insurance constitutes comparative negligence only with regard to the damages attributable to the delays caused by the fire and not the other damages which the jury found Scioto to have sustained as a result of PW's negligence and breach of contract. The court of appeals recognized that the jury award improperly included damages that resulted from the fire and cured the error. Accordingly, we find that while the trial court should have allowed the comparative negligence defense, in this case the error was cured by the court of appeals and, therefore, did not constitute prejudicial error.

Likewise, the trial court's failure to give an instruction to the jury on comparative negligence was not prejudicial error in this case. Evidence pertaining to the negligent acts of Scioto was presented to the jury during the trial. The jury was instructed that if Scioto failed to act reasonably to avoid or reduce its losses, it could not recover any such damages. Despite these instructions, the jury still awarded Scioto all of its damages, indicating that the jury found PW the sole cause of the failure of Richmond Place. Thus, we find that even if the jury had been required to apportion the fault between the parties in this case, the outcome would have been the same. The jury found that PW was solely liable for Scioto's loss. Accordingly, since there was no prejudicial error, a new trial is not warranted.

Judgment for Scioto Memorial Hospital affirmed in part and reversed in part in favor of Price Waterhouse.

Fraud An accountant is liable to his client for fraud when he misstates or omits facts in communications with his client and acts with **scienter.** An accountant acts with scienter when he knows of the falsity of a statement or he recklessly disregards the truth. Thus, accountants are liable in fraud for their intentional or reckless disregard for accuracy in their work.

For example, an accountant chooses not to examine the current figures in a client's books of account, but relies on last year's figures because he is behind in his work for other clients. As a result, the accountant understates the client's income on an income statement that the client uses to apply for a loan. The client obtains a loan, but he has to pay a higher interest rate because his low stated income makes the loan a higher risk for the bank. Such misconduct by the accountant proves scienter and, therefore, amounts to fraud.

Scienter also includes recklessly ignoring facts, such as an auditor's finding obvious evidence of embezzlement yet failing to notify a client of the embezzlement.

The chief advantage of establishing fraud is that the client may get a higher damage award than when the accountant is merely negligent. Usually, a client may receive only compensatory damages for a breach of contract or negligence. By proving fraud, a client may be awarded punitive damages as well.

Breach of Trust

An accountant owes a duty of trust to his client. Information and assets that are entrusted to an accountant may be used only to benefit the client. The duty of trust requires the accountant to maintain the confidentiality of the client's information entrusted to the accounting firm. Therefore, an accountant may not disclose sensitive matters such as a client's income and wealth. In addition, an accountant may not use the assets of his client for his own benefit.

Securities Law

Federal and state securities law creates several rights of action for persons harmed in connection with the purchase or sale of securities. These rights of action are based in tort. Although available to clients of an accountant, they are rarely used for that purpose. Usually, only third parties (nonclients) sue under the securities law. The securities law sections that apply to accountants are discussed later in this chapter.

ACCOUNTANTS' LIABILITY TO THIRD PERSONS: COMMON LAW

Other persons besides an accountant's clients may use her work product. Banks may use financial statements prepared by a loan applicant's accountant in deciding whether to make a loan to the applicant. Investors may use financial statements certified by a company's auditors in deciding whether to buy or sell the company's securities. These documents prepared by an accountant may prove incorrect, resulting in damages to the nonclients who relied on them. For example, banks may lend money to a corporation only because an income statement prepared by an accountant overstated the corporation's income. When the corporation fails to repay the loan, the bank may sue the accountant to recover the damages it suffered.

Nonclients may sue accountants for common law negligence, common law fraud, and violations of the securities laws. In this section, common law negligence and fraud are discussed.

Negligence and Negligent Misrepresentation

When an accountant fails to perform as the ordinarily prudent accountant would perform, she risks having liability for negligence. Many courts have restricted the ability of nonclients to sue an accountant for damages proximately caused by the accountant's negligent conduct. These courts limit nonclient suits on the grounds that nonclient users of an accountant's work product have not contracted with the accountant and, therefore, are not in **privity of contract** with the accountant. Essentially, these courts hold that an accountant owes no duty to nonclients to exercise ordinary skill and care.

This judicial stance conflicts with the usual principles of negligence law under which a negligent person is liable to all persons who are reasonably foreseeably damaged by his negligence. The rationale for the restrictive judicial stance was expressed in the *Ultramares* case,[1] a decision of the highest court in New York. In that case, Judge Benjamin Cardozo refused to hold an auditor liable to third parties for mere negligence. His rationale was stated as follows:

If liability for negligence exists, a thoughtless slip or blunder, the failure to detect a theft or forgery beneath the cover of deceptive entries, may expose accountants to a liability in an indeterminate amount for an indeterminate time to an indeterminate class.

Ultramares dominated the thinking of judges for many years, and its impact is still felt today. However, many courts understand that many nonclients use and reasonably rely on the work product of accountants. To varying degrees, these courts have relaxed the privity requirement and expanded the class of persons who may sue an accountant for negligence conduct. Today, most courts adopt one of the following three tests to determine whether a nonclient may sue an accountant for negligence.

Primary Benefit Test The *Ultramares* court adopted a primary benefit test for imposing liability for negligence. Under this test, an accountant's duty of care extends only to those persons for whose primary benefit the accountant prepares financial reports and other documents. The accountant must actually foresee the nonclient's use and prepare the document primarily for use by a specified nonclient. That is, the nonclient must be a **foreseen user** of the

accountant's work product. The accountant must know two things: (1) the name of the person who will use the accountant's work product and (2) the particular purpose for which that person will use the work product.

Foreseen Users and Foreseen Class of Users Test By 1965, a draft of the *Restatement (Second) of Torts* proposed that the law of professional negligence expand the class of protected persons to **foreseen users** and **users within a foreseen class of users** of reports. Under this test, the accountant must know either the user of the work product or the use to be made of the work product. The protected persons are (1) those persons who an accountant knows will use the accountant's work product and (2) those persons who use an accountant's work product in a way the accountant knew the work product would be used.

For example, an accountant prepares an income statement that he knows his client will use to obtain a loan at Bank X. Any bank to which the client supplies the statement to obtain a loan, including Bank Y, may sue the accountant for damages caused by a negligently prepared income statement. Bank X is a foreseen user, and Bank Y is in a foreseen class of users. On the other hand, if an accountant prepares an income statement for a tax return and the client, without the accountant's knowledge, uses the income statement to apply for a loan from a bank, the bank is not among the protected class of persons—the accountant did not know that the tax return would be used for that purpose.

Foreseeable Users Test A few courts have applied traditional negligence causation principles to accountants' negligence. They have extended liability to **foreseeable users** of an accountant's reports who suffered damages that were proximately caused by the accountant's negligence. To be liable to a nonclient under this test, an accountant need merely be able to expect or foresee the nonclient's use of the accountant's work product. It is not necessary for the nonclient to prove that the accountant actually expected or foresaw the nonclient's use.

In the following case, the court rejected the foreseeable users test as too broad and instead adopted the *Restatement's* foreseen class of users test in the negligent misrepresentation context.

---

[1] *Ultramares Corp. v. Touche,* 174 N.E. 441 (N.Y. Ct. App. 1931).

BILY v. ARTHUR YOUNG & CO. 834 P.2d 745 (Cal. Sup. Ct. 1992)

Founded in 1980 by enterpreneur Adam Osborne, Osborne Computer Company manufactured the first personal computer for the mass market. By fall 1982, sales of the Osborne I computer reached $10 million per month, making Osborne Computer one of the fastest growing businesses in American history.

The company proposed an early 1983 public offering of its common shares. To obtain temporary financing until the company went public, Osborne Computer issued warrants to investors in exchange for the investors making or securing loans to Osborne Computer. The warrants entitled the investors to purchase Osborne Computer shares at a favorable price. It was expected that once the public offering was made, the investors holding warrants would make a substantial profit. The investors were individuals, pension funds, and capital investment firms. Other investors purchased common shares of Osborne Computer. Robert Bily, a director of the company, was one of the investors; he purchased 37,500 shares for $1.5 million from Adam Osborne.

The investors were given and relied on an unqualified audit opinion of Osborne Computer's 1982 financial statements. The audit opinion, issued by Arthur Young & Co., stated that Arthur Young had examined the financial statements in compliance with GAAS, that the statements had been prepared in compliance with GAAP, and that the statements presented fairly Osborne Computer's financial position. The 1982 financial statements revealed that Osborne Computer had a net operating profit of $69,000 on sales of $68 million. Arthur Young delivered 100 sets of the opinion to Osborne Computer.

In the first half of 1983, Osborne Computer's sales declined sharply because of manufacturing problems with its new Executive model computer. In June 1983, the IBM personal computer became a major factor in the small-computer market. Osborne never made a public offering of its shares, and on September 13, 1983, filed for bankruptcy. The investors lost their investments.

The investors sued Arthur Young, alleging professional negligence and negligent misrepresentation. At trial, evidence showed that Arthur Young did not comply with GAAS, resulting in its failure to find that Osborne Computer's liabilities were understated by $3 million. As a result, the supposed operating profit of $69,000 was actually a loss of $3 million. Also, Arthur Young had failed to detect weaknesses in Osborne Computer's accounting procedures and systems. The jury was instructed that liability for professional negligence extended to those third parties who reasonably and foreseeably relied on the audited financial statements. The court also instructed the jury that for Arthur Young to have liability for negligent misrepresentation, Arthur Young must have intended to induce the plaintiff or a particular class of persons to which the plaintiff belongs to rely on the audit opinion. The jury found Arthur Young liable for professional negligence but not negligent misrepresentation, and it awarded the investors damages of $4.3 million. The California Court of Appeals affirmed, and Arthur Young appealed to the Supreme Court of California. ∞

Lucas, Chief Justice We decline to permit all merely foreseeable third party users of audit reports to sue the auditor on a theory of professional negligence.

An auditor is a watchdog, not a bloodhound. Audits are performed in a client-controlled environment. The client typically prepares its own financial statements. Because the auditor cannot in the time available become an expert in the client's business and record-keeping systems, the client necessarily furnishes the information base for the audit. Moreover, an audit report is not a simple statement of verifiable fact that, like the weight of a load of beans, can be easily checked against uniform standards of indisputable accuracy. Rather, an audit report is a professional opinion based on numerous and complex factors, involving discretion and judgment on the part of the auditor at every stage.

Although the auditor's role in the financial reporting process is secondary, the liability it faces is primary and personal and can be massive. The client, its promoters, and its managers have generally left the scene, headed in most cases for bankruptcy. The auditor has now assumed center stage as the remaining solvent defendant and is faced with a claim for all sums of money ever loaned to or invested in the client. Such disproportionate liability cannot fairly be justified on moral, ethical, or economic grounds.

Investors, creditors, and others who read and rely on audit reports and financial statements possess considerable sophistication in analyzing financial information and are aware from training and experience of the limits of an audit report. The third party in an audit negligence case can "privately order" the risk of inaccurate financial reporting by contractual arrangements with the client. For example, a third party might expend its own resources to verify the client's financial statements. It might commission its own audit or investigation, thus establishing privity between itself and an auditor. In addition, it might bargain with the client for special security or improved terms in a credit or investment transaction. Finally, the third party could insist that an audit be conducted on its behalf or establish direct communications with the auditor.

As a matter of economic and social policy, third parties should be encouraged to rely on their own prudence, diligence, and contracting power. This kind of self-reliance promotes sound investment and credit practices and discourages the careless use of monetary resources. If, instead, third parties are simply permitted to recover from the auditor for mistakes in the client's financial statements, the auditor becomes an insurer of not only the financial statements, but also of bad loans and investments in general.

We doubt that a significant and desirable improvement in audit care would result from an expanded rule of liability. In view of the inherent dependence of the auditor on the client and the labor-intensive nature of auditing, we doubt whether audits can be done in ways that would yield significantly greater accuracy without disadvantages. Auditors may rationally respond to increased liability by simply reducing audit services in fledgling industries where the business failure rate is high, reasoning that they will inevitably be singled out and sued when their client goes into bankruptcy regardless of the care or detail of their audits. It might also be doubted whether auditors are the most efficient absorbers of the losses from inaccuracies in financial information. Investors and creditors can limit the impact of losses by diversifying investments and loan portfolios.

A foreseeability rule applied in this context inevitably produces large numbers of expensive and complex lawsuits of questionable merit as scores of investors and lenders seek to recoup business losses.

We hold that an auditor's liability for general negligence in the conduct of an audit of its client's financial statements is confined to the client, i.e., the person who contracts for or engages the audit services.

There is, however, a further narrow class of persons who, although not clients, may reasonably come to receive and rely on an audit report and whose existence constitutes a risk of auditing reporting that may fairly be imposed on the auditor. Such persons are specifically intended beneficiaries of the audited report who are known to the auditor and for whose benefit it renders the report. While such persons may not recover on a general negligence theory, we hold they may recover on a theory of negligent misrepresentation. Negligent misrepresentation is a separate and distinct tort. Where the defendant makes false statements, honestly believing that they are true, but without reasonable ground for such belief, he may be liable for negligent misrepresentation, a form of deceit.

Under certain circumstances, expressions of professional opinion are treated as representations of fact. When a party possesses superior knowledge or expertise regarding the subject matter and a plaintiff is so situated that it may reasonably rely on such supposed knowledge or expertise, the defendant's representation may be treated as one of material fact. There is no dispute that Arthur Young's statements in audit opinions fall within these principles.

But the person or class of persons entitled to rely upon the representations is restricted to those to whom or for whom the misrepresentations were made. Restatement Second of Tort section 552 is most consistent with the elements and policy foundations of the tort of negligent misrepresentation. By confining liability to those persons whom the engagement is designed to benefit, the Restatement rule requires that the supplier of information receive notice of potential third party claims, thereby allowing it to ascertain the potential scope of its liability and make rational decisions regarding the undertaking. Liability should be confined to cases in which the supplier *manifests* an intent to supply the information for the *sort of use* in which the plaintiff's loss occurs.

Having determined that intended beneficiaries of an audit report are entitled to recovery on a theory of negligent misrepresentation, we must consider whether they may also recover on a general negligence theory. We conclude they may not. Because the audit report, not the audit itself, is the foundation of the third person's claim, negligent misrepresentation more precisely captures the gravamen of the cause of action and more clearly conveys the elements essential to a recovery.

Based on our decision, the California standard jury instructions concerning negligent misrepresentation should be amended in future auditor liability cases to permit the jury to determine whether plaintiff belongs to the class of persons to whom or for whom the representations in the audit report were made. The representation must have been made with the intent to induce plaintiff, or a particular class of persons to which plaintiff belongs, to act in reliance upon the representation in a specific transaction, or a specific type of transaction, that defendant intended to influence. Defendant is deemed to have intended to influence its client's transaction with plaintiff whenever defendant knows with substantial certainty that plaintiff, or the particular class of persons to which plaintiff belongs, will rely on the representation in the course of the transaction. If others become aware of the representation and act upon it, there is no liability even though defendant should reasonably have foreseen such a possibility.

Judgment reversed in favor of Arthur Young.

CONCEPT   REVIEW

Common Law Bases of Liability of Accountant to Nonclients

PRIVITY TEST ADOPTED BY STATE	BASIS OF LIABILITY	
	NEGLIGENCE	FRAUD
Primary Benefit Test (*Ultramares*)	Accountant liable only to foreseen users (accountant knew name of user and purpose of the user's use)	
Restatement (Second) of Torts Test	Accountant liable to foreseen users and users in a foreseen class of users (accountant knew at least the purpose of the user's use)	Regardless of test adopted, accountant liable to all persons whose damages were caused by their reliance on accountant's fraud
Foreseeable Users Test	Accountant liable to all foreseeable users (accountant can expect or foresee the purpose of the user's use)	

Fraud

Fraud is such reprehensible conduct that all courts have extended an accountant's liability for fraud to all foreseeable users of his work product who suffered damages that were proximately caused by the accountant's fraud. Privity of contract, therefore, is not required when a person sues an accountant for fraud, even in a state that has adopted the *Ultramares* test for negligence actions. To prove fraud, a nonclient must establish that an accountant acted with scienter.

Some courts recognize a tort called constructive fraud that applies when an accountant misstates a material fact. For a misstatement to amount to constructive fraud, the accountant must have reck-lessly or grossly negligently failed to ascertain the truth of the statement. As with actual fraud, an accountant's liability for constructive fraud extends to all persons who justifiably rely on the misstatement.

ACCOUNTANT'S LIABILITY TO THIRD PARTIES: SECURITIES LAW

The slow reaction of the common law in creating a negligence remedy for third parties has led to an increased use of securities law by nonclients—that is, persons not in privity with an accountant. Many liability sections in these statutes either eliminate the privity requirement or expansively define privity.

Securities Act of 1933

There are several liability sections under the Securities Act of 1933 (1933 Act). The most important liability section of the Securities Act of 1933 is Section 11, but Sections 12(a)(2) and 17(a) are also important.

Section 11 Liability Section 11 imposes on auditors liability for misstatements or omissions of material fact in opinions regarding financial statements that they audit for Securities Act registration statements. The 1933 Act registration statement must be filed with the Securities and Exchange Commission by an issuer making a public distribution of securities. An auditor is liable to any purchaser of securities issued pursuant to a defective registration statement. The purchaser need not establish privity of contract with the auditor; he need merely prove that the auditor is a person who furnished an opinion regarding financial statements for inclusion in the registration statement. Usually, the purchaser need not prove he relied on the misstated or omitted material fact; he need not even have read or seen the defective financial statement.

For example, an auditor issues an unqualified opinion regarding a client's income statement that overstates net income by 85 percent. The defective income statement is included in the client's registration statement pursuant to which the client sells its preferred shares. Without reading the registration statement or the income statement, a person buys from the client 100 preferred shares for $105 per share. After the correct income figure is released, the price of the shares drops to $25 per share. The auditor will most likely be liable to the purchaser for $8,000.

Under Section 11, auditors may escape liability by proving that they exercised due diligence. This **due diligence defense** requires that an auditor issuing an opinion regarding financial statements prove that she made a reasonable investigation and that she reasonably believed that there were no misstatements or omissions of material fact in the financial statements at time the registration statement became effective. Because the effective date is often several months after an audit has been completed, an auditor must perform an additional review of the audited statements to ensure that the statements are accurate as of the effective date. In essence, due diligence means that an auditor was not negligent, which is usually proved by showing that she complied with GAAS and GAAP. The due diligence defense is explained more fully in *Escott v. BarChris Construction Corp.,* which appears in Chapter 44, Securities Regulation at page 934.

Under Section 11, an auditor has liability for only a limited period of time, pursuant to a **statute of limitations.** A purchaser must sue the auditor within one year after the misstatement or omission was or should have been discovered by the purchaser. In addition, a purchaser may sue the auditor no more than three years after the securities were offered to the public. Although the word "offered" is used in the statute, the three-year period does not usually begin until after the registered securities are first delivered to a purchaser.

Section 12(a)(2) Section 12(a)(2) imposes liability on any person who misstates or omits a material fact in connection with an offer or sale of a security that is part of a public offering of securities by an issuer. Privity of contract between the plaintiff and the defendant apparently is required, because Section 12(a)(2) states that the defendant is liable to the person *purchasing* the security *from him.*

Until recently, Section 12(a)(2) had been interpreted broadly to impose liability on auditors of financial statements that misstate or omit material facts. Recent decisions of the Supreme Court, including the *Central Bank* case that is mentioned in the next case, suggest that auditors are unlikely to be held liable under Section 12(a)(2) in the future. An accountant must have direct contact with a buyer of a security to be liable. Merely performing professional services, such as drafting or certifying financial statements, is not enough for Section 12(a)(2) liability. The accountant must actively solicit the sale, motivated at least by a desire to serve his own financial interest. Such a financial interest is unlikely to be met by an accountant whose compensation is a fee unconnected to the proceeds of the securities sale. In addition, the *Central Bank* case makes it fairly clear that auditors who merely *aid and abet* a client's Section 12(a)(2) violation will not have liability under Section 12(a)(2).

In the event that an accountant has sufficient contact with a purchaser to incur Section 12(a)(2) liability, the accountant may escape liability by proving that she did not know and could not reasonably have known of the untruth or omission; that is, she must prove that she was not negligent.

CONCEPT REVIEW

Liability Sections of the 1933 Act and 1934 Act

	WRONGFUL CONDUCT	COVERED COMMUNICATIONS	WHO MAY SUE?	MUST THE PLAINTIFF PROVE RELIANCE ON THE WRONGFUL CONDUCT?
Securities Act of 1933 Section 11	Misstatement or omission of material fact	1933 Act registration statement only	Any purchaser of securities issued pursuant to the registration statement	No
Securities Act of 1933 Section 12(a)(2)	Misstatement or omission of material fact	Any communication in connection with a public offering of securities by an issuer (except government issued or guaranteed securities)	Any purchaser of the securities offered or sold	No
Securities Act of 1933 Section 17(a)	Misstatement or omission of material fact	Any communication in connection with any offer to sell or sale of any security	Any purchaser of the securities offered or sold	Yes
Securities Exchange Act of 1934 Section 10(b) and Rule 10b-5	Misstatement or omission of material fact	Any communication in connection with a purchase or sale of any security	Any purchaser or seller of the securities	Yes
Securities Exchange Act of 1934 Section 18	False or misleading statement of material fact	Any document filed with the SEC under the 1934 Act (includes the 1934 Act registration statement, 10-K, 8-K, and proxy statements)	Any purchaser or seller of a security whose price was affected by the statement	Yes

WHO MAY BE SUED?	MUST THE PLAINTIFF AND DEFENDANT BE IN PRIVITY OF CONTRACT?	DEFENDANT'S LEVEL OF FAULT	WHO HAS THE BURDEN OF PROVING OR DISPROVING DEFENDANT'S LEVEL OF FAULT?	AMOUNT OF DEFENDANT'S LIABILITY TO PLAINTIFF
Issuer, underwriters, directors, selected officers, and experts who contribute to the registration statement (such as auditors of financial statements)	No	Negligence, except for the issuer. Issuer is liable without regard to fault.	Defendant, except issuer, may escape liability by proving he made a reasonable investigation and had reason to believe and did believe there were no misstatements or omissions of material fact	The price the purchaser paid for the securities less the market price of the securities at the time of the suit; may be reduced by defendant's proof that the loss was caused by factors other than the misstatement or omission
Any person who sells a security or actively solicits a sale of a security	Yes (although met by a defendant who has a financial interest in a sale of securities)	Negligence	Defendant may escape liability by proving he did not know and could not reasonably have known of the misstatement or omission of material fact	The price the purchaser paid for the securities (upon the purchaser's return of the securities)
Any person responsible for the misstatement or omission	No	Negligence for some parts of Section 17(a); scienter for one part	Plaintiff must prove the defendant acted negligently or with scienter	Plaintiff's damages caused by his reliance on the misstatement or omission
Any person primarily responsible for the misstatement or omission	No	Scienter	Plaintiff must prove the defendant acted with scienter	Plaintiff's damages caused by his reliance on the misstatement or omission
Any person who made or caused the statement to be made	No	Scienter	Defendant may escape liability by proving he acted in good faith with no knowledge that the statement was false or misleading	Plaintiff's damages caused by his reliance on the false or misleading statement

Section 17(a) Under Section 17(a), a purchaser of a security must prove his reliance on a misstatement or omission of material fact for which an accountant is responsible. Under two of the subsections of Section 17(a), the investor need prove only negligence by the accountant. Under the third, the investor must prove the accountant acted with scienter. Whether there is a private right of action for damages under Section 17(a) is unclear. The courts of appeals are in disagreement, and the Supreme Court has not ruled on the issue.

Securities Exchange Act of 1934

Two sections of the 1934 Act—Section 18 and Section 10(b)—especially affect the liability of accountants to nonclients.

Section 18 Section 18 of the 1934 Act imposes liability on accountants who furnish misleading and false statements of material fact in any report or document filed with the Securities and Exchange Commission under the 1934 Act. Such reports or documents include the annual 10-K report—which includes auditors' opinions regarding financial statements—the monthly 8-K report, and proxy statements.

Under Section 18, a purchaser or seller of a security may sue the accountant if he relied on the defective statement in the filed document and it caused his damages. Usually, this means that a plaintiff must have *read and relied* on the defective statement in the filed document. The purchaser or seller may sue the accountant even if they are not in privity of contract.

An accountant may escape Section 18 liability by proving that she acted in *good faith* and had *no knowledge* that the information was misleading. That is, she must show that she acted *without scienter.*

Section 10(b) and Rule 10b-5 Securities Exchange Act Rule 10b-5, pursuant to Section 10(b), has been the basis for most of the recent suits investors have brought against accountants. Rule 10b-5 prohibits any person from making a misstatement or omission of material fact in connection with the purchase or sale of any security. Rule 10b-5 applies to misstatements or omissions in any communications with investors, covering any use of audited financial statements resulting in a purchase

or sale of a security. The wrongful act must have a connection with interstate commerce, the mails, or a national securities exchange.

A purchaser or seller of a security may sue an accountant who has misstated or omitted a material fact. Privity is not required. The purchaser or seller must rely on the misstatement or omission. In omission cases, reliance may be inferred from materiality.

In addition, the accountant must act with scienter. In this context, scienter is an intent to deceive, manipulate, or defraud. Negligence is not enough.

Aiding and Abetting Until recently, a common way investors held an accountant liable under Rule 10b-5 was to prove that the accountant aided and abetted a client's fraud. Most courts had recognized accountants' aiding and abetting liability under Rule 10b-5 by requiring (1) a primary violation by another person (such as a client fraudulently overstating its earnings), (2) the accountant's knowledge of the primary violation, and (3) the accountant's substantial assistance in the achievement of the primary violation (such as an accountant's failure to disclose a client's fraud known to the accountant).

In 1994 in the *Central Bank* case that is mentioned in the next case, the Supreme Court of the United States held that those who merely aid and abet Rule 10b-5 violations have no liability to those injured by the fraud. The court drew a distinction between those **primarily** responsible for the fraud—who retain Rule 10b-5 liability—and those **secondarily** responsible—who no longer have liability under Rule 10b-5. The distinction between primary and secondary responsibility is unclear. Issuing unqualified opinions regarding false financial statements is primary fault and would impose Rule 10b-5 liability on the auditor. However, an independent accountant's work in connection with false unaudited statements or other financial information released by a client may be only secondary and may not impose Rule 10b-5 liability on the accountant.

Although auditors are not liable to private litigants for merely secondary activities, Congress has made it clear that the SEC may prosecute accountants for aiding and abetting a client's violation of Rule 10b-5. Even so, the risk of liability is slight, because Rule 10b-5 liability is imposed only on those who act with scienter.

Extent of Liability.   The Private Securities Litigation Reform Act of 1995 limits the liability of most auditors to the amount of an investor's loss for which the auditor is responsible. This means that an auditor has *proportionate liability* and need no longer fear being liable for investors' entire losses when a fraudulent client is unable to pay its share of the damages. The determination of the percentage of the loss for which an auditor is responsible is a question for the jury. Note, however, the Reform Act provides that when an auditor knowingly commits a violation of the securities laws, the auditor may be required to pay an investor's entire loss.

The following case explores the distinction between an auditor's primary violation of Section 10(b) and an auditor's merely aiding and abetting a client's violation of Section 10(b).

ANIXTER v. HOME-STAKE PRODUCTION CO.   77 F.3d 1215 (10th Cir. 1996)

More than 30 years ago, Home-Stake Production Company began offering securities registered with the Securities and Exchange Commission in the form of interests in oil and gas drilling programs. The securities represented units of participation in annual oil production subsidiaries Home-Stake established each year between 1964 and 1972, referred to as Program Operating Corporations (Programs). These offerings purported to present investors both the promise of return on investment and attractive tax deductions of intangible drilling costs. In fact, the Home-Stake venture resembled a classic Ponzi swindle. Instead of going to oil development, investments made in later-year Programs were paid to earlier-year investors as "income" from oil production. The scheme collapsed after investors had lost tens of millions of dollars.

From 1968 to 1971, Home-Stake's independent auditor was Norman Cross. Cross prepared documents used by Home-Stake, consented to have his name appear in registration statements filed with the SEC, and issued unqualified opinions regarding Home-Stake's financial statements. Cross prepared Home-Stake's consolidated financial statements for 1968 and 1969. He also prepared the start-up balance sheets for the 1969 and 1970 Programs, which were included in the 1969 and 1970 Program registration statements and prospectuses. The registration statements and attached prospectuses were filed with the SEC. Cross consented to the use of his reports on the 1969 and 1970 Program balance sheets in the SEC filings.

Cross also provided Home-Stake with opinions on the 1969 and 1970 Programs' beginning balance sheet he prepared. These opinions were also contained in the registration statements and prospectuses filed with the SEC. Cross also provided opinion letters for Home-Stake's consolidated financial statements for 1968–70. The opinion letters for Home-Stake's financial statements, addressed to the Home-Stake board of directors, were included in Home-Stake's 1969 and 1970 annual reports but were not included in the Program prospectuses or registration statements.

In 1969 and 1970, Home-Stake also published and mailed to Program participants documents known as "Program Books" or "Black Books." These documents, which included descriptions of specific oil recovery programs and estimates of anticipated returns, were not filed with the SEC and contained information inconsistent with or contradicting the prospectuses. Home-Stake's financial statements, audited by Cross, also were included either with the Program Books or as part of Home-Stake's sales kit. The Program Books and sales kits were the primary methods of marketing Program units; the SEC-filed prospectuses were made available to investors only upon request.

Finally, Cross was also involved in the prospectus for a rescission offer made to investors in the 1970 program. In 1971, the SEC filed a complaint against Home-Stake in federal district court, alleging that its officers and directors failed to meet information requirements to investors and misstated the use of investments in the 1970 Program. As part of a consent decree entered into with the SEC, Home-Stake made a rescission offer to its 1970 Program investors. The offer documents included a Rescission Offer Prospectus. The Rescission Offer Prospectus itself failed to disclose material facts. Cross prepared an opinion on Home-Stake's 1970 consolidated financial statement and an opinion on the beginning balance sheet of the 1970 Program, included as part of the 1970 Rescission Offer Registration Statement.

In March 1973, purchasers of interests in the programs, including Ivan Anixter, filed lawsuits against Home-Stake, its officers, its outside lawyers, Cross, and brokers who sold the interests, alleging violations of Section 10(b) and Rule 10b-5 of the Securities Exchange Act of 1934. The case went to trial in 1988, and Anixter and the other investors won jury verdicts totaling over $40 million. Cross appealed on the grounds that the court improperly instructed the jury that it could find him liable under Rule 10b-5 as an aider and abettor; he also claimed that he had not acted with scienter.

Lucero, Circuit Judge This securities fraud case, first filed in 1973, already has been the subject of four published opinions by this court. Over the past four years it has been ordered dismissed, reinstated, remanded, and now, appealed once more.

We must resolve whether again to dismiss or remand judgments against Home-Stake's outside auditor for violating § 10(b) of the Securities Exchange Act of 1934. The question dominating our review is whether we can let stand a general jury verdict returned on a securities fraud claim that included an instruction on aiding and abetting liability, an implied cause of action that has since been found invalid by the Supreme Court in *Central Bank of Denver* (1994). In the balance is a choice between a jury award plaintiffs won on claims filed more than 22 years ago, and maintaining judgments now totalling more than $40 million when the jury may have found liability on an invalid legal theory. We conclude the aiding and abetting instruction hopelessly taints the general verdict and that remand for a new trial is necessary.

We must first consider what acts make up a "primary" violation of § 10(b), and how they differ from those that could be characterized only as "aiding and abetting." Unfortunately, deciding when conduct constituting aiding and abetting rises to the level of prohibited primary conduct is not well settled.

Cross argues that none of his acts constituted fraudulent misrepresentations or omissions relied on by investing plaintiffs; at most the acts only aided Home-Stake in committing the alleged fraud. Anixter points to Cross's opinion letters as evidence that Cross himself made misrepresentations or omissions sufficient to subject him to primary liability.

To establish a primary liability claim under § 10(b), a plaintiff must prove the following facts: (1) that the defendant made an untrue statement of material fact, or failed to state a material fact; (2) that the conduct occurred in connection with the purchase or sale of a security; (3) that the defendant made the statement or omission with scienter; and (4) that plaintiff relied on the misrepresentation, and sustained damages as a proximate result of the misrepresentation. This contrasts with aider and abettor liability, which required plaintiff to prove (1) the existence of a primary violation of the securities laws by another; (2) knowledge of the primary violation by the alleged aider and abettor; and (3) substantial assistance by the alleged aider and abettor in achieving the primary violation. The critical element separating primary from aiding and abetting violations is the existence of a representation, either by statement or omission, made by the defendant, that is relied upon by the plaintiff. Reliance only on representations made by others cannot itself form the basis of liability.

Clearly, accountants may make representations in their role as auditor to a firm selling securities. Typical representations include issuing unqualified opinions regarding financial statements and other opinion letters. An accountant's false and misleading representations in connection with the purchase or sale of any security, if made with the proper state of mind and if relied upon by those purchasing or selling a security, can constitute a primary violation. There is no requirement that the alleged violator directly communicated misrepresentations to plaintiffs for primary liability to attach. Nevertheless, for an accountant's misrepresentation to be actionable as a primary violation, there must be a showing that he knew or should have known that his representation would be communicated to investors because § 10(b) and Rule 10b-5 focus on fraud made "in connection with the sale or purchase" of a security.

Reading the language of § 10(b) and 10b-5 through the lens of *Central Bank of Denver*, we conclude that in order for accountants to "use or employ" a "deception" actionable under the antifraud law, they must themselves make a false or misleading statement (or omission) that they know or should know will reach potential investors. In addition to being consistent with the language of the statute, this rule, though far from a bright line, provides more guidance to litigants than a rule allowing liability to attach to an accountant or other outside professional who provided "significant" or "substantial" assistance to the representations of others.

The record in this case contains much evidence that could sustain a finding of primary liability. Most of Anixter's arguments went to representations Cross made as Home-Stake's auditor. He issued opinions on the 1969 and 1970 Program's start up balance sheets. He issued unqualified opinions regarding Home-Stake's Consolidated financial statements for those years. Cross's opinions letters were reproduced in prospectuses, annual reports, registration statements, and other Home-Stake promotional material. The jury could have concluded that any or all of these representations were false and misleading, that Cross was reckless in making the representations, and that Cross knew or should have known that his representations would reach potential investors and that they would reasonably rely on them.

Although the record supports finding Cross liable for a primary violation of § 10(b), we still must determine whether the jury *did* find him liable as a primary violator. Cross urges us to remand for a new trial on the theory that it is not clear from the jury verdict whether his liability under Rule 10b-5 rested on finding a primary or aiding and abetting violation.

It is obvious from our discussion analyzing accountant behavior under § 10(b) that distinctions in conduct between primary and secondary liability are elusive. The verdicts shed no light on whether the jury found Cross liable of his substantial assistance to Home-Stake's independent fraudulent acts, or whether his liability rests on actual representations

he made that reached investors. The chances that the jury was confused by the aiding and abetting instructions cannot be dismissed as remote—and require us to remand.

Cross argues that remand is unnecessary, and that we should reverse the judgment because he only acted recklessly with respect to the Home-Stake fraud, and recklessness does not satisfy the scienter requirement for liability in a civil action under § 10(b). The district court correctly rejected this argument.

In *Ernst & Ernst v. Hochfelder* (1976), the Supreme Court expressly declined to address "the question whether, in some circumstances, reckless behavior is sufficient for civil liability under § 10(b) and Rule 10b-5." The Supreme Court has still not spoken on this question. In *Hackbart v. Holmes* (1982) this court held that "recklessness" satisfies the scienter requirement for a primary violation of § 10(b). We defined "recklessness" as "conduct that is an extreme departure from the standards of ordinary care, and which presents a danger of misleading buyers or sellers that is either known to the defendant or is so obvious that the actor must have been aware of it."

This circuit still maintains that recklessness as defined in *Hackbart* is sufficient scienter for finding civil § 10(b) primary violations.

This is a very old case, and it is with a heavy heart that we act to prolong it. Our decision, however, is mandated by a supervening change in the law of securities fraud.

Judgment reversed in favor of Cross; remanded to the trial court.

State Securities Law

All states have securities statutes with liability sections. Most of the states have a liability section similar to Section 12(2) of the Securities Act.

LIMITING ACCOUNTANTS' LIABILITY: PROFESSIONAL CORPORATIONS AND LIMITED LIABILITY PARTNERSHIPS

Every state permits professionals to incorporate their business under a professional incorporation

statute. Most statutes permit a professional accounting corporation to be owned only by accountants.

While there are significant taxation advantages to incorporation, the principal advantage of incorporation—*limited liability of the shareholders*—does not isolate accountants from liability for professional misconduct. For example, an accountant who injures his client by failing to act as the ordinarily prudent accountant would act has liability to his client, despite the incorporation of the accountant's business.

When two or more accountants conduct an accounting business as co-owners, incorporation may offer them limited liability. While partners in a partnership are jointly and severally liable for each other's negligence, some states permit incorporated accountants to escape liability for their associate's torts, unless the accountant actually supervised the wrongdoing associate or participated in the tort. Other states do not allow incorporated accountants to limit their liability for their associates' torts, making all the shareholder/accountants jointly and severally liable for the professional misconduct of any of its accountants.

Reacting to the large personal liability sometimes imposed on lawyers and accountants for the professional malpractice of their partners, Texas enacted in 1991 the first statute permitting the formation of limited liability partnerships (LLP). An LLP is similar to a partnership, except that a partner's liability for his partners' professional malpractice is limited to the partnership's assets, unless the partner supervised the work of the wrongdoing partner. A partner retains unlimited liability for his *own* malpractice and, in most states, for all *non*professional obligations of the partnership.

Nearly every state and the District of Columbia have passed LLP statutes. The LLP has become the preferred form of business for accountants who do not incorporate.

For more information on the limited liability partnership, see Chapter 36.

QUALIFIED OPINIONS, DISCLAIMERS OF OPINION, ADVERSE OPINIONS, AND UNAUDITED STATEMENTS

After performing an audit of financial statements, an independent auditor issues an opinion letter regarding the financial statements. The **opinion letter** expresses whether the audit has been performed in compliance with GAAS and whether, in the auditor's opinion, the financial statements fairly present the client's financial position and results of operations in conformity with GAAP. Usually, an auditor issues an **unqualified opinion**—that is, an opinion that there has been compliance with GAAS and GAAP. Sometimes, an auditor issues a qualified opinion, a disclaimer of opinion, or an adverse opinion. Up to this point, you have studied the liability of an auditor who has issued unqualified opinions yet has not complied with GAAS and GAAP.

What liability should be imposed on an auditor who discloses that he has not complied with GAAS and GAAP? An auditor is relieved of responsibility only to the extent that a qualification or disclaimer is specifically expressed in the opinion letter. Therefore, letters that purport to totally disclaim liability for false and misleading financial statements are too general to excuse an accountant from exercising ordinary skill and care.

For example, an auditor qualifies his opinion of the ability of financial statements to present the financial position of a company by indicating that there is uncertainty about how an antitrust suit against the company may be decided. He would not be held liable for damages resulting from an unfavorable verdict in the antitrust suit. He would remain liable, however, for failing to make an examination in compliance with GAAS that would have revealed other serious problems.

For another example, consider an auditor who, due to the limited scope of the audit, disclaims any opinion on the ability of the financial statements to present the financial position of the company. She would nonetheless be liable for the nondiscovery of problems that the limited audit should have revealed.

Likewise, an accountant who issued an adverse opinion that depreciation had not been calculated according to GAAP would not be liable for damages resulting from the wrongful accounting treatment of depreciation, but he would be liable for damages resulting from the wrongful treatment of receivables.

Merely preparing unaudited statements does not create a disclaimer as to their accuracy. The mere fact that the statements are unaudited only permits an accountant to exercise a lower level of inquiry. Even so, an accountant must act as the ordinarily prudent accountant would act under the same circumstances in preparing unaudited financial statements.

CRIMINAL, INJUNCTIVE, AND ADMINISTRATIVE PROCEEDINGS

In addition to being held liable for damages to clients and third parties, an accountant may be found criminally liable for his violations of securities, tax, and other laws. For criminal violations, he may be fined and imprisoned. His wrongful conduct may also result in the issuance of an injunction, which bars him from doing the same acts in the future. In addition, his wrongful conduct may be the subject of administrative proceedings by the Securities and Exchange Commission and state licensing boards. An administrative proceeding may result in the revocation of an accountant's license to practice or the suspension from practice. Finally, disciplinary proceedings may be brought against an accountant by professional societies such as the AICPA.

CRIMINAL LIABILITY UNDER THE SECURITIES LAWS

Both the Securities Act of 1933 and the Securities Exchange Act of 1934 have criminal provisions that can be applied to accountants. The 1933 Act imposes criminal liability for willful violations of any section of the 1933 Act, including Sections 11, 12(a)(2), and 17(a), or any 1933 Act rule or regulation. For example, willfully making an untrue statement or omitting any material fact in a 1933 Act registration statement imposes criminal liability on an accountant. The maximum penalty for a criminal violation of the 1933 Act is a $10,000 fine and five years' imprisonment.

The 1934 Act imposes criminal penalties for willful violations of any section of the 1934 Act, such as Sections 10(b) and 18, and any 1934 Act rule or regulation, such as Rule 10b-5. For example, willfully making false or misleading statements in reports that are required to be filed under the 1934 Act incurs criminal liability. Such filings include 10-Ks, 8-Ks, and proxy statements. An individual accountant may be fined up to $1 million and imprisoned for up to 10 years for a criminal violation of the 1934 Act; however, an individual accountant who proves that he had no knowledge of an SEC rule or regulation may not be imprisoned for violating that rule or regulation. An accounting firm may be fined up to $2.5 million.

Most of the states have statutes imposing criminal penalties on accountants who willfully falsify financial statements or other reports in filings under the state securities laws and who willfully violate the state securities laws or aid and abet criminal violations of these laws by others.

In the following case, accountants permitting a client to book unbilled sales after the close of the fiscal period subjected the accountants to the criminal penalties of the 1934 Act.

UNITED STATES v. NATELLI   527 F.2d 311 (2d Cir. 1975)

nthony Natelli was the partner in charge of the Washington, D.C., office of Peat, Marwick, Mitchell & Co., a large CPA firm. In August 1968, Peat, Marwick became the independent public auditor of National Student Marketing Corporation. Natelli was the engagement partner for the audit of Student Marketing. Joseph Scansaroli was Peat, Marwick's audit supervisor on that engagement.

Student Marketing provided its corporate clients with a wide range of marketing services to help them reach the lucrative youth market. In its financial statements for the nine months ended May 31, 1968, Student Marketing had counted as income the entire amount of oral customer commitments to pay fees in Student Marketing's "fixed-fee marketing programs," even though those fees had not yet been paid. They were to be paid for services that Student Marketing would provide over a period of several years. Standard accounting practice required that part of the unpaid fees be considered income in the present year but that part be deferred as income until the years when Student Marketing actually performed the services for which the fees were paid. Therefore, in making the year-end audit, Natelli concluded that he would use a percentage-of-completion approach on these commitments, taking as income in the present year only those fees that were to be paid for services in that year.

The customer fee commitments were oral only, making it difficult to verify whether they really existed. Natelli directed Scansaroli to try to verify the fee commitments by telephoning the customers but not by seeking written verification. However, Scansaroli never called Student Marketing's clients. Instead, Scansaroli accepted a schedule prepared by Student Marketing showing estimates of the percentage of completion of services for each corporate client and the amount of the fee commitment from each client. This resulted in an adjustment of $1.7 million for "unbilled accounts receivable." The adjustment turned a loss for the year into a profit twice that of the year before.

By May 1969, a total of $1 million of the customer fee commitments had been written off as uncollectible. The effect of the write-off was to reduce 1968 income by $209,750. However, Scansaroli, with Natelli's approval, offset this by reversing a deferred tax item of approximately the same amount.

Student Marketing issued a proxy statement in September 1969 in connection with a shareholders' meeting to consider merging six companies into Student Marketing. The proxy statement was filed with the Securities and Exchange Commission. It contained several financial statements, some of which had been audited by Peat, Marwick. Others had not been audited, but Peat, Marwick had aided in their preparation. In the proxy statement, a footnote to the financial statements failed to show that the write-off of customer fee commitments had affected Student Marketing's fiscal 1968 income.

The proxy statement required an unaudited statement of nine months' earnings through May 31, 1969. This statement was prepared by Student Marketing with Peat, Marwick's assistance. Student Marketing produced a $1.2 million commitment from the Pontiac Division of General Motors Corporation two months after the end of May, but it was dated April 28, 1969. At 3 A.M. on the day the proxy statement was to be printed, Natelli informed Randall, the chief executive officer and founder of Student Marketing, that this commitment could not be included because it was not a legally binding contract. Randall responded at once that he had "a commitment from Eastern Airlines" for a somewhat comparable amount attributable to the same period. Such a letter was produced at the printing plant a few hours later, and the Eastern commitment was substituted for the Pontiac sale in the proxy. Shortly thereafter, another Peat, Marwick accountant, Oberlander, discovered $177,547 in "bad" commitments from 1968. These were known to Scansaroli in May 1969 as being doubtful, but they had not been written off. Oberlander suggested to the company that these commitments plus others, for a total of $320,000, be written off, but Scansaroli, after consulting with Natelli, decided against the suggested write-off.

There was no disclosure in the proxy statement that Student Marketing had written off $1 million (20 percent) of its 1968 sales and over $2 million of the $3.3 million of unbilled sales booked in 1968 and 1969. A true disclosure would have shown that Student Marketing had made no profit for the first nine months of 1969.

Subsequently, it was revealed that many of Student Marketing's fee commitments were fictitious. The attorney general of the United States brought a criminal action against Natelli and Scansaroli for violating the Securities Exchange Act of 1934 by willfully and knowingly making false and misleading statements in a proxy statement. The district court jury convicted both Natelli and Scansaroli, and they appealed. ⌾

Gurfein, Circuit Judge The original action of Natelli in permitting the booking of unbilled sales after the close of the fiscal period in an amount sufficient to convert a loss into a profit was contrary to sound accounting practice. When the uncollectibility, and indeed, the nonexistence of these large receivables was established in 1969, the revelation stood to cause Natelli severe criticism and possible liability. He had a motive, therefore, intentionally to conceal the write-offs that had to be made.

Honesty should have impelled Natelli and Scansaroli to disclose in the footnote that annotated their own audited statement for fiscal 1968 that substantial write-offs had been taken, after year-end, to reflect a loss for the year. A simple desire to right the wrong that had been perpetrated on the stockholders and others by the false audited financial statement should have dictated that course.

The accountant owes a duty to the public not to assert a privilege of silence until the next audited annual statement comes around in due time. Since companies were being acquired by Student Marketing for its shares in this period, Natelli had to know that the 1968 audited statement was being used continuously.

Natelli contends that he had no duty to verify the Eastern commitment because the earnings statement within which it was included was unaudited. This raises the issue of the duty of the CPA in relation to an unaudited financial statement contained within a proxy statement where the figures are reviewed and to some extent supplied by the auditors. The auditors were associated with the statement and were required to object to anything they actually knew to be materially false. In the ordinary case involving an unaudited statement, the auditor would not be chargeable simply because he failed to discover the invalidity of booked accounts receivable, inasmuch as he had not undertaken an audit with verification. In this case, however, Natelli knew the history of post-period bookings and the dismal consequences later discovered.

In terms of professional standards, the accountant may not shut his eyes in reckless disregard of his knowledge that highly suspicious figures, known to him to be suspicious, were being included in the unaudited earnings figures in the proxy statement with which he was associated.

There is some merit to Scansaroli's point that he was simply carrying out the judgments of his superior, Natelli. The defense of obedience to higher authority has always been troublesome. There is no sure yardstick to measure criminal responsibility except by measurement of the degree of awareness on the part of a defendant that he is participating in a criminal act, in the absence of physical coercion such as a soldier might face. Here the motivation to conceal undermines Scansaroli's argument that he was merely implementing Natelli's instructions, at least with respect to concealment of matters that were within his own ken. The jury could properly have found him guilty on the specification relating to the footnote.

With respect to the Eastern commitment, Scansaroli stands in a position different from that of Natelli. Natelli was his superior. He was the man to make the judgment whether or not to object to the last-minute inclusion of a new commitment in the nine-months statement. There is insufficient evidence that Scansaroli engaged in any conversations about the Eastern commitment or that he was a participant with Natelli in any check on its authenticity. Since in the hierarchy of the accounting firm it was not his responsibility to decide whether to book the Eastern contract, his mere adjustment of the figures to reflect it under orders was not a matter for his discretion.

Conviction of Natelli affirmed. Conviction of Scansaroli affirmed in part and reversed in part.

Other Criminal Law Violations

Federal tax law imposes on accountants a wide range of penalties for a wide variety of wrongful conduct. At one end of the penalty spectrum is a $25 fine for failing to furnish a client with a copy of his income tax return or failing to sign a client's return. At the other end is a fine of $100,000 and imprisonment of three years for tax fraud. In between is the penalty for promoting abusive tax shelters. The fine is $1,000, or 20 percent of the accountant's income from her participation in the tax shelter, whichever is greater. In addition, all of the states impose criminal penalties for specified violations of their tax laws.

Several other federal statutes also impose criminal liability on accountants. The most notable of these statutes is the general mail fraud statute, which prohibits the use of the mails to commit fraud. To be held liable, an accountant must know or foresee that the mails will be used to transmit materials containing fraudulent statements provided by her.

In addition, the general false-statement-to-government-personnel statute prohibits fraudulent statements to government personnel. The false-statement-to-bank statute proscribes fraudulent statements on a loan application to a bank or other financial institution.

RICO The Racketeer Influenced and Corrupt Organizations Act (RICO) makes it a federal crime to engage in a pattern of racketeering activity. Although RICO was designed to attack the activities of organized crime enterprises, it applies to accountants who conduct or participate in the affairs of an enterprise in almost any pattern of business fraud. A pattern of fraud is proved by the commission of two predicate offenses within a 10-year period. Predicate offenses include securities law violations, mail fraud, and bribery. Individuals convicted of a RICO violation may be fined up to $25,000 and imprisoned up to 20 years.

A person who is injured in his business or property by reason of an accountant's conduct or participation, directly or indirectly, in an enterprise's affairs through a pattern of racketeering activity may recover treble damages (three times his actual damages) from the accountant. In *Reves v. Ernst & Young,*[2] the Supreme Court held that merely by auditing financial statements that substantially

---

[2] 113 S. Ct. 1163 (1993).

overvalued a client's assets, an accounting firm was not conducting or participating in the affairs of the client's business. The Court held that the accounting firm must participate in the "operation or management" of the enterprise itself to be liable under RICO.

Injunctions

Adminstrative agencies such as the SEC and the Internal Revenue Service may bring injunctive actions against an accountant in a federal district court. The purpose of such an injunction is to prevent an accountant from committing a future violation of the securities or tax laws.

After an injunction has been issued by a court, violating the injunction may result in serious sanctions. Not only may penalties be imposed for contempt, but a criminal violation may also be more easily proven.

Administrative Proceedings

The SEC has the authority to bring administrative proceedings against persons who violate the provisions of the federal securities acts. In recent years, the SEC has stepped up enforcement of SEC Rule of Practice 2(e). Rule 2(e) permits the SEC to bar temporarily or permanently from practicing before the SEC an accountant who has demonstrated a lack of the qualifications required to practice before it, such as an accountant who has prepared financial statements not complying with GAAP. Rule 2(e) also permits the SEC to take action against an accountant who has willfully violated or aided and abetted another's violation of the securities acts. An SEC administrative law judge hears the case and makes an initial determination. The SEC commissioners then issue a final order, which may be appealed to a federal court of appeals.

Rule 2(e) administrative proceedings can impose severe penalties on an accountant. By suspending an accountant from practicing before it, the SEC may take away a substantial part of an accountant's practice. Also, the SEC may impose civil penalties up to $500,000.

In addition, state licensing boards may suspend or revoke an accountant's license to practice if she engages in illegal or unethical conduct. If such action is taken, an accountant may lose her entire ability to practice accounting.

Securities Exchange Act Audit Requirements

The Private Securities Litigation Reform Act of 1995 imposes significant public duties on independent auditors that audit the financial statements of public companies. In part added to the Securities Exchange Act as Section 10A, the Reform Act requires auditors to take specific steps if they learn during the course of an audit that a client may have committed an illegal act (that is, a violation of any law, rule, or regulation). First, the auditor is required to determine whether an illegal act has in fact occurred. If the auditor determines that the client has committed an illegal act, the auditor must calculate the prospective impact on the client's financial statements, including fines, penalties, and liability costs such as damage awards to persons harmed by the client. As soon as practical, the auditor must inform the client's management and audit committee of the auditor's determination, unless the illegal act is clearly inconsequential.

If the client's management does not take appropriate remedial action with respect to an illegal act that has a material effect on the financial statements of the client—and if the failure to take remedial action is reasonably expected to result in the auditor's issuance of a nonstandard report or resignation from the audit engagement—the auditor must make a report to the client's board of directors. The board of directors has one business day to inform the SEC of the auditor's report; if the board does not submit a report to the SEC, the auditor has one additional business day to furnish a copy of its report to the SEC, whether or not the auditor also resigns from the audit engagement.

Section 10A imposes a significant whistleblowing duty on independent auditors, consistent with the watchdog function that Congress and the courts have continually assigned to auditors. To encourage auditors to make such reports, Section 10A also provides that an auditor will have no liability to a private litigant for any statement in the auditor's reports given to management, the board of directors, or the SEC.

OWNERSHIP OF WORKING PAPERS

The personal records that a client entrusts to an accountant remain the property of the client. An accountant must return these records to his client. Nonetheless, the working papers produced by independent auditors belong to the accountant, not the client.

Working papers are the records made during an audit. They include such items as work programs or plans for the audit, evidence of the testing of accounts, explanations of the handling of unusual matters, data reconciling the accountant's report with the client's records, and comments about the client's internal controls. The client has a right of access to the working papers. The accountant must obtain the client's permission before the working papers can be transferred to another accountant.

ACCOUNTANT–CLIENT PRIVILEGE

An accountant–client privilege of confidentiality protects many of the communications between accountants and their clients from the prying eyes of courts and other government agencies. In addition, it protects an accountant's working papers from the discovery procedures available in a lawsuit.

Although the common law does not recognize an accountant–client privilege, a large number of states have granted such a privilege by statute. The provisions of the statutes vary, but usually the privilege belongs to the client, and an accountant may not refuse to disclose the privileged material in a courtroom if the client consents to its disclosure.

Generally, the state-granted privileges are recognized in both state and federal courts deciding questions of state law. Nonetheless, federal courts do not recognize the privilege in matters involving federal questions, including antitrust and criminal matters.

In federal tax matters, for example, no privilege of confidentiality is recognized on the grounds that an accountant has a duty as a public watchdog to ensure that his client correctly reports his income tax liability. Consequently, an accountant can be required to bring his working papers into court and to testify as to matters involving the client's tax records and discussions with the client regarding tax matters. In addition, an accountant may be required by subpoena to make available his working papers involving a client who is being investigated by the IRS or who has been charged with tax irregularities. The same holds true for SEC investigations.

Although no accountant–client privilege exists in federal tax matters, an attorney–client privilege does exist. Moreover, the attorney–client privilege will protect communications between a client and its accountant when the accountant is assisting an attorney in rendering advice to the client. The next case discusses the limits of this use of the attorney–client privilege.

UNITED STATES v. ADLMAN   68 F.3d 1495 (2d Cir. 1995)

I n the spring of 1989, the management of Sequa Corporation considered combining two of its subsidiary corporations, Atlantic Research Corp. (ARC) and Chromalloy Gas Turbine Corp. To assess the likely tax consequences of the proposed combination, Sequa's vice president of taxes, Monroe Adlman, consulted with Paul Sheahen, an accountant and partner at Arthur Andersen & Co. (Andersen). Andersen had served as Sequa's accountant and auditor, and Sheahen specialized in evaluating the tax implications of corporate reorganizations.

After numerous discussions, Adlman, who was an attorney, directed Sheahen to prepare a draft memorandum discussing the probable tax consequences of the proposed restructuring. Sheahen presented the draft memo to Adlman in August 1989. After making several changes to address questions raised by Adlman, Sheahen sent Adlman the memorandum in final form on September 5, 1989. The final draft is 58 pages long and contains a detailed technical analysis of the tax implications of the proposed reorganization.

Two days after submitting the final memo to Adlman, Sheahen wrote to Gerald Gutterman, Sequa's executive vice president in charge of finance and administration, summarizing "our recommendations and conclusions." The letter also contained Andersen's recommendation as to the form the transaction should take—urging Sequa to sell a substantial majority interest in ARC to Chromalloy, recapitalize the remaining shares as preferred stock, and then sell the newly preferred stock to a third party. The transaction occurred in essentially the manner recommended by Andersen and was consummated by the end of 1989.

Andersen formalized its analysis of the transaction in two opinion letters dated April 20, 1990, and addressed to Adlman. In these letters, Andersen evaluated the reorganization in light of the federal tax code and concluded that the reorganization should result in a substantial capital loss for Sequa. On its 1989 tax return, Sequa claimed a tax loss of approximately $290 million from the transaction. Part of that loss was carried back to offset millions of dollars of Sequa's capital gains from 1986, thereby generating a large tax refund.

The Internal Revenue Service undertook an audit of Sequa's tax returns from 1986 to 1989. The IRS sent numerous informal information document requests for materials related to the restructuring. Sequa acknowledged the existence of the draft and final versions of the Andersen memo but claimed that they were protected from disclosure by the attorney–client privilege and the work-product doctrine. On September 23, 1993, the IRS served a summons on Adlman to compel disclosure of the Andersen memos. Adlman again refused to provide them on grounds of privilege and work product. Sequa contended that the memoranda were prepared in anticipation of litigation with the IRS over a $290 million loss claimed by Sequa in its 1989 tax return, resulting from a corporate reorganization.

The United States sued to force disclosure of the Andersen memos. The district court ruled that the memoranda were not protected by either the attorney–client privilege or the work-product rule. Sequa appealed. ✑

Leval, Circuit Judge The attorney–client privilege forbids an attorney from disclosing confidential communications obtained from the client during the course of professional consultations. The privilege is intended to encourage clients to be forthcoming and candid with their attorneys so that the attorney is sufficiently well-informed to provide sound legal advice. The privilege applies only to communications between lawyer and client; in general, communications between accountants and their clients enjoy no privilege.

Under certain circumstances, however, the privilege for communication with attorneys can extend to shield communications to others when the purpose of the communication is to assist the attorney in rendering advice to the client. Thus in *United States v. Kovel* (1961), we recognized that the privilege would extend to communications by an attorney's client to an accountant hired by the attorney to assist the attorney in understanding the client's financial information. Recognizing that the privilege would surely apply where a client who spoke only a foreign language furnished his confidential information to an interpreter employed by the attorney to translate for the attorney's benefit, Judge Friendly observed that accounting concepts can be as incomprehensible as a foreign language to attorneys. "Hence the presence of an accountant while the client is relating a complicated tax story to the lawyer, ought not destroy the privilege. What is vital to the privilege is that the communication be made *in confidence* for the purpose of obtaining *legal* advice *from the lawyer*. If what is sought is not

legal advice but only accounting service or if the advice sought is the accountant's rather than the lawyer's, no privilege exists."

The party claiming the benefit of the attorney-client privilege has the burden of establishing all the essential elements. The problem with Adlman's argument is that the facts are subject to competing interpretations. In many respects, the evidence supports the conclusion that Sequa consulted an accounting firm for tax advice, rather than that Adlman, as Sequa's counsel, consulted Andersen to help him reach the understanding he needed to furnish legal advice. Adlman himself serves not only as counsel to Sequa but also as one of its officers. Andersen, furthermore, is regularly employed by Sequa to furnish auditing, accounting, and advisory services. Andersen furnished extensive advisory services to Sequa in connection with the merger, including tax advice. If the facts were that Sequa furnished information to Andersen to seek Andersen's expert advice on the tax implications of the proposed transaction, no privilege would apply.

There is virtually no contemporaneous documentation supporting the view that Andersen, in this task alone, was working under a different arrangement from that which governed the rest of its work for Sequa. Andersen's billing statements lump the work done in this consultation together with its other accounting and advisory services to Sequa. By his own admission, Adlman lacked the expertise necessary to assess the tax implications of corporate reorganizations. It was Andersen, not Adlman, that prepared all the written analyses of the tax consequences of the transaction. These included not only the memos in question, but also two formal opinion letters dated April 20, 1990. Furthermore, by its letter dated September 7, 1989, Andersen sent a summary of its recommendations and conclusions directly to Sequa's management, offering "to discuss all related matters with a view toward prompt successful implementation [of the restructuring plan]." All of these factors favored the IRS contentions as to the proper understanding of the transaction. Sequa's interpretation was suggested primarily by litigation affidavits prepared by interested persons four years after the fact and lacking any support in contemporaneous documentation. The district court did not abuse its discretion or make clearly erroneous findings.

Sequa contends the Andersen memoranda are shielded from discovery by the "work product" rule. The work-product rule shields from disclosure materials prepared "in anticipation of litigation" by a party, or the party's representative, absent a showing of substantial need. The purpose of the doctrine is to establish a zone of privacy for strategic litigation planning and to prevent one party from piggybacking on the adversary's preparation.

Sequa contends it caused the memoranda to be written "in anticipation of litigation" with the IRS over Sequa's claimed tax loss. The district judge rejected Sequa's claim of entitlement to work-product protection for the sole reason that at the time of Andersen's creation of the memoranda, neither the litigation nor the events giving rise to it (the proposed merger) had yet occurred.

Although the non-occurrence of the events giving rise to the anticipated litigation is a factor that can argue against application of the work-product doctrine, especially when the expected litigation is merely a vague abstract possibility without precise form, there is no rule that bars application of work-product protection to documents created prior to the event giving rise to litigation. Nor do we see any reason for such a limitation. In many instances, the expected litigation is quite concrete, notwithstanding that the events giving rise to it have not yet occurred. We see no reason why work-product protection should not apply to preparatory litigation studies undertaken by a party.

We conclude that the district court barred work-product protection on the basis of an incorrect standard. We must therefore remand for a determination whether the work-product protection should apply. Our vacating the district court's ruling should not be understood to imply that work-product protection is applicable—only that the particular reason for denying it was invalid. The district court will need to consider whether, within the meaning of the rule, the Andersen memoranda were "prepared in anticipation of litigation," and if so, whether the government has shown "substantial need of the materials."

Judgment affirmed in part and reversed in part; remanded to the trial court.

ETHICAL AND PUBLIC POLICY CONCERNS

1. Is it enough that an accountant acts in accordance with the standards of the accounting profession? What risk arises if society entrusts the accounting profession with regulating itself? How great is the risk? Can clients collectively or individually reduce this risk? Is it fair that some clients cannot protect themselves from this risk and yet may have no legal recourse?

2. Should accountants have liability for negligence to persons who are not their clients? What are the social and economic costs of making accountants liable to all users of their work product? What are the social and economic costs of relieving accountants from liability to persons who are not their clients? Is it fair to allow an accountant to be negligent and not have liability to those who relied on the accountant's work product?

3. Should an accountant–client privilege exist? What are the social benefits and costs? In the tax context, why should an accountant be burdened with the public watchdog function when lawyers are not; that is, why must accountants ensure that their clients comply with the tax laws, when a lawyer is permitted to serve the best interests of his client? When a tax accountant is working for a client who also has a lawyer, how can the accountant's work product become privileged? Does the answer to that question suggest a logical or ethical inconsistency in the law?

PROBLEMS AND PROBLEM CASES

1. The 1136 Tenants' Corporation, a cooperative apartment house, hired Max Rothenberg & Co., a firm of certified public accountants, to perform accounting services for it. Rothenberg discovered that several invoices were missing from the financial records of the apartment house. These invoices were needed to prove that payments of $44,000 had been made to creditors of the apartment house and were not embezzled by someone with authority to make payments for the apartment house. Rothenberg noted the missing invoices on his worksheet but failed to notify the apartment house that there were missing invoices. In fact, there were no invoices. Jerome Riker, the apartment house manager, had embezzled the $44,000 from the apartment house by ordering it to make unauthorized payments to him. Riker embezzled more money after the audit was completed. Is Rothenberg liable to its client for failing to inform it of Riker's embezzlement?

2. Robert Burns hired Sheila Camenisch to prepare a life insurance trust for his daughters. Burns told Camenisch that he wanted to ensure financial security for himself and his wife, and that he did not want the proceeds of the life insurance policy to be taxable. Camenisch created the trust, telling Burns that the proceeds of the life insurance policy would not be taxed. Unfortunately, the trust did not accomplish its objective, with the result that the life insurance proceeds would be subject to a gift and estate tax of at least $25,000 and as much as $525,000 if Burns died within three years. Burns sued Camenisch for negligence. It addition to damages for payment of taxes, Burns sought damages of $1 million due to his suffering severe emotional distress. Burns claimed that the news that he would have to pay $525,000 in taxes if he died within three years caused him to suffer severe alarm, anxiety, shock, loss of sleep, and other stress. Did the court award Burns damages for emotional distress?

3. From 1983 to 1985, Baumann-Furrie & Co. provided accounting services to Halla Nursery, Inc. During this time, Halla's bookkeeper embezzled $135,000. In 1986, Halla sued Baumann-Furrie alleging it negligently failed to detect the embezzlement. Baumann-Furrie claimed that Halla negligently failed to put in place internal financial controls to protect the company from embezzlement. The jury found Halla 80 percent at fault and Baumann-Furrie 20 percent at fault. Is Baumann-Furrie nonetheless liable to Halla?

4. ▣ *Video Case.* See "Cafeteria Conversation." Steve has authority to write checks on the account of his employer, a public company under the Securities Exchange Act of 1934. Because Steve is a compulsive gambler and substance abuser, he needs a constant supply of cash to finance his habits. Steve regularly issues checks payable to actual suppliers not currently owed money, steals the checks, signs the names of the payees, and cashes the checks. Because Steve is also in charge of reconciling his employer's bank statements, his embezzlement scheme is not discovered by the employer's independent auditor during a routine audit. Is the independent auditor liable to its client for damages resulting from Steve's embezzlement?

5. When Robert Hicks offered to sell his shares in Intermountain Merchandising, Inc. (IMI), to Montana Merchandising (MM), IMI hired Alan Bloomgren, a CPA, to audit IMI. Based on Bloomgren's clean opinion on IMI's balance sheet, MM purchased Hicks's shares, advanced funds to IMI, and signed financial guaranties for IMI. Bloomgren knew that MM would rely on the audit and that the audit would be used to aid MM in buying out IMI, including making loans and guaranties. Bloomgren's audit was materially defective, failing to represent that IMI had a negative net worth. MM sued Bloomgren for negligence. Is Bloomgren liable to MM?

6. Max Mitchell & Co., a public accounting firm, performed an audit of the financial statements of C.M. Systems, Inc. At the time Mitchell performed the audit, it was not known that the audited financial statements would be used to obtain a loan from First Florida Bank. However, subsequent to preparing the audited financial statements, Mitchell negotiated a loan with First Florida Bank on behalf of C.M. and personally delivered the financial statements to the bank. Relying on the financial statements, First Florida loaned $500,000 to C.M. After C.M. defaulted on the loan, First Florida discovered that the financial statements materially understated C.M.'s liabilities and materially overstated its assets and net income. Is Mitchell liable to First Florida under the theory of negligence?

7. For the years 1973 to 1976, Timm, Schmidt & Co., an accounting firm, prepared financial statements for Clintonville Fire Apparatus, Inc. (CFA). For every year except 1973, Timm sent an opinion letter to CFA stating that the financial statements fairly presented the financial condition of CFA and that the statements were prepared in accordance with generally accepted accounting principles. In November 1975, CFA obtained a $300,000 loan from Citizens State Bank. Citizens made the loan to CFA after reviewing the financial statements that Timm had prepared. Citizens made additional loans to CFA in 1976. By the end of 1976, CFA owed Citizens $380,000. In early 1977, Timm employees discovered that the 1974 and 1975 financial statements contained a number of material errors totaling over $400,000. When Timm informed Citizens of the errors, Citizens called all of CFA's loans due. As a result, CFA was liquidated. CFA's assets were insufficient to pay the loans from Citizens. Citizens sued Timm, seeking to recover $152,000, the amount due on its loans to CFA. If Timm failed to comply with generally accepted auditing standards (GAAS) when it first audited the 1974 and 1975 financial statements, is Timm liable to Citizens for negligence?

8. To aid its decision whether to purchase all the shares of Gillespie Furniture Company, DMI Furniture, Inc., hired Arthur Young & Co. to review an audit of Gillespie's financial statements that had been performed by Brown, Kraft & Company. Arthur Young wrote a letter stating that Brown, Kraft had "performed a quality audit." Based on this letter, DMI decided to buy all of Gillespie's shares. When Gillespie became less profitable than DMI expected, DMI sued Arthur Young under Securities Exchange Act Rule 10b-5. DMI alleged that Arthur Young acted recklessly in failing to detect and to disclose that Brown, Kraft's audit report was inaccurate and misleading because it grossly overstated inventory and showed a profit when there was a loss. Do DMI's allegations establish that Arthur Young has violated Rule 10b-5?

9. In 1986 and 1988, the Colorado Springs–Stetson Hills Public Building Authority (Authority) issued $26 million in bonds to finance public improvements at Stetson Hills, a residential and commercial development in Colorado Springs. Central Bank served as the trustee for the bondholders, undertaking a fiduciary duty to the bondholders to ensure that the Authority complied with indenture provisions protecting bondholders. The bonds were secured by liens against 522 acres of land, and the indenture required that the land be worth at least 160 percent of the bonds' outstanding principal and interest. In January 1988, AmWest Development—the developer of Stetson Hills—gave Central Bank an appraisal of the land. The appraisal showed land values almost unchanged from a 1986 appraisal, even though property values were declining in Colorado Springs. Central Bank's in-house appraiser reviewed the 1988 appraisal and decided that it was optimistic. He suggested that Central Bank use an independent outside appraiser to review the 1988 appraisal. After an exchange of letters between Central Bank and AmWest in early 1988, Central Bank agreed to delay independent review of the appraisal until the end of 1988, six months after the 1988 bonds had been issued to investors. Before the independent review was complete, the Authority defaulted on the 1988 bonds. Is Central Bank liable to the bondholders under Section 10(b) of the Securities Exchange Act of 1934?

10. Bill Thomas, a CPA, was a member of Lawhon, Thomas, Holmes & Co. (LTH), a public accounting firm. When LTH performed accounting services for Xenerex Corp., LTH received 144,000 Xenerex shares instead of cash. LTH continued to hold the Xenerex shares when the three LTH members joined the accounting firm of Oppenheim, Appel, Dixon & Co. (OAD). LTH ceased operations and sold all its assets except the Xenerex shares to OAD. The three former LTH members, including Thomas, retained ownership of LTH. After he joined OAD, Thomas immediately solicited Xenerex as a client for OAD. Thomas, on behalf of OAD, signed a new client acceptance form for Xenerex, giving a negative response to the question, "Are there any known independence problems?" Thomas prepared and signed OAD's report on Xenerex's financial statements and annual report filed on Form 10-K with the SEC. Has Thomas violated SEC Rule of Practice 2(e)?

11. Robert Gatewood and two other limited partners entered a limited partnership agreement with United States Cellular Corporation (USCC), the sole general partner. The agreement provided that in the event the partners were unable to agree on the value of a cellular phone system in which they had an interest, each would select an appraiser, and the two appraisers would select a third. An impasse arose concerning the selection of this third appraiser, and a federal district court was asked to resolve the dispute. During litigation, USCC took the deposition of Terry Korn, a Pennsylvania certified public accountant and appraiser selected by the limited partners. USCC sought to inquire about the conduct and results of Korn's appraisal as well as any communications between Korn and the limited partners. The limited partners directed Korn not to respond to any of these questions, asserting that the communications were covered by Pennsylvania statutory accountant–client privilege. Are the limited partners correct?

12. While performing a routine audit of the tax returns of Amerada Hess Corporation, the Internal Revenue Service discovered questionable payments of $7,830. The IRS issued a summons to Arthur Young & Co., the accounting firm that had prepared the tax accrual working papers that might reveal the nature of the payments. The working papers had been prepared in the process of Arthur Young's review of Amerada Hess's financial statements, as required by federal securities law. In the summons, the IRS ordered Arthur Young to make available to the IRS all of its Amerada Hess files, including its tax accrual working papers. Amerada Hess directed Arthur Young not to comply with the summons on the grounds that they were protected by an accountant–client privilege. Is Amerada Hess correct?

Regulation of Business

FORTY-SIX

Administrative Agencies

Today's businesses operate in a highly regulated environment. The *administrative agency* serves as the fundamental vehicle for the creation and enforcement of modern regulation. As governmental bodies that are neither courts nor legislatures, administrative agencies have the legal power to take actions affecting the rights of private individuals and organizations. Supreme Court Justice Robert H. Jackson characterized the sweeping influence of administrative agencies this way:

The rise of administrative bodies probably has been the most significant legal trend of the last century and perhaps more values today are affected by their decisions than by those of all of the courts, review of administrative decisions apart. They also have begun to have important consequences on personal rights. . . . They have become a veritable fourth branch of the Government, which has deranged our three-branch legal theories as much as the concept of a fourth dimension unsettles our three-dimensional thinking.[1]

This chapter focuses on federal administrative agencies. It is important to remember, however, that the great growth in *federal* regulation during this century has been accompanied by a comparable growth in *state* and *local* regulation by agencies at those levels of government.

It is difficult to think of an area of modern individual life that is not somehow touched by the actions of administrative agencies. The energy that heats and lights your home and workplace, the clothes you wear, the food you eat, the medicines you take, the design of the car you drive, the programs you watch on television, and the contents of (and label on) the pillow on which you lay your

---

[1] *FTC v. Ruberoid Co.*, 343 U.S. 470 (U.S. Sup. Ct. 1952).

head at night are all shaped in some way by regulation. If anything, this observation is even more appropriate to corporations than to individuals. Virtually every significant aspect of contemporary corporate operations is regulated to the point that the *legal* consequences of a corporation's actions are nearly as important to its future success as the *business* consequences of its decisions.

Because administrative agencies have enormous power and some novel characteristics, they have always been objects of controversy. Are they protectors of the public or impediments to business efficiency? Are they guardians of competitive market structures or a shield behind which noncompetitive firms have sought refuge from more vigorous competitors? Have they been impartial, efficient agents of the public interest or are they more often overzealous, or inept, or "captives" of the industries they supposedly regulate? At various times, and where various agencies are concerned, each of the above allegations has probably been true. Why, then, did we resort to such controversial entities to perform the regulatory function? ∞

ORIGINS OF ADMINISTRATIVE AGENCIES

In the latter decades of the 19th century, the United States was in the midst of a dramatic transformation from an agrarian nation to a major industrial power. Improved means of transportation and communication facilitated a dramatic market expansion. Large business organizations acquired unheard of economic power, and new technologies promised additional social transformations.

The tremendous growth that resulted from these developments, however, was not attained without some cost. Large organizations sometimes abused their power at the expense of their customers, distributors, and competitors. New technologies often posed risks of harm to large numbers of citizens. Yet traditional institutions of legal control, such as courts and legislatures, were not particularly well suited to the regulatory needs of an increasingly complex, interdependent society in the throes of rapid change.

Courts, after all, are passive institutions that must await a genuine case or controversy before they can act. Courts may also lack the technical expertise necessary to address many regulatory issues intelligently. In addition, they are constrained by the formalistic rules of procedure and evidence that make litigation a time-consuming and expensive process.

Legislatures, on the other hand, are theoretically able to anticipate social problems and to act in a comprehensive fashion to minimize or avoid social harm. In reality, however, legislatures rarely act until a problem has become severe enough to generate strong political support for a regulatory solution. Legislatures may also lack (as do courts) the expertise necessary to make rational policy regarding highly technical activities.

What was needed, therefore, was a new type of governmental entity: one that would be exclusively devoted to monitoring a particular area of activity; one that could, by its exclusive focus and specialized hiring practices, develop a reservoir of expertise about the object of its efforts; and one that could provide the continuous attention and constant policy development demanded by a rapidly changing environment. Such new entities, it was thought, could best perform their regulatory tasks if they were given considerable latitude in the procedures they followed and the approaches they took to achieve regulatory goals.

In 1887, the modern regulatory era was born when Congress, in response to complaints about discriminatory ratemaking practices by railroads, passed the Interstate Commerce Act. This statute created the Interstate Commerce Commission and gave it the power to regulate transportation industry ratemaking practices. Thereafter, new administrative agencies have been added whenever *pressing social problems* (e.g., the threat to competition that led to the creation of the Federal Trade Commission) or *new technologies,* such as aviation (Federal Aviation Administration), communications (Federal Communications Commission), and nuclear power (Nuclear Regulatory Commission), have generated a political consensus in favor of regulation. More recently, developing scientific knowledge about the *dangers that modern technologies and industrial processes pose* to the environment and to industrial workers has led to the creation of new federal agencies empowered to regulate environmental pollution (Environmental Protection Agency) and promote workplace safety (Occupational Safety and

Health Administration). The following sections of this chapter examine the legal dimensions of the process by which such administrative agencies are created.

AGENCY CREATION

Enabling Legislation

Administrative agencies are created when Congress passes **enabling legislation** specifying the name, composition, and powers of the agency. For example, consider the following language from Section 1 of the Federal Trade Commission Act:

A commission is created and established, to be known as the Federal Trade Commission, which shall be composed of five commissioners, who shall be appointed by the President, by and with the advice and consent of the Senate.

This section creates the Federal Trade Commission (FTC). Section 5 of the FTC Act prohibits "unfair methods of competition" and "unfair or deceptive acts or practices in commerce" and empowers the FTC to prevent such practices.[2] Section 5 also describes the procedures the Commission must follow to charge persons or organizations with violations of the act, and provides for judicial review of agency orders. Subsequent portions of the statute give the FTC the power "to make rules and regulations for the purpose of carrying out the provisions of the Act," to conduct investigations of business practices, to require reports from interstate corporations concerning their practices and operations, to investigate possible violations of the antitrust laws,[3] to publish reports concerning its findings and activities, and to recommend new legislation to Congress.

Thus, Congress has given the FTC powers typically associated with the three traditional branches of government. The FTC may, for instance, act in a legislative fashion by *promulgating rules* that have binding legal effect on future behavior. It may also take the executive branch–like actions of *investigating* and *prosecuting* alleged violations. Finally, the FTC may act much as courts do and *adjudicate* disputes concerning alleged violations of the law.

Most other federal administrative agencies have a similarly broad mix of governmental powers, making these agencies potentially powerful agents of social control.

But great power to do good may also be great power to do evil. Regulatory bias, zeal, insensitivity, or corruption, if left unchecked, may infringe on the basic freedoms that are the essence of our system of government. Accordingly, the fundamental problem in administrative law—a problem that will surface repeatedly throughout this chapter—is how to design a system of control over agency action that minimizes the potential for arbitrariness and harm yet preserves the power and flexibility that make administrative agencies uniquely valuable instruments of public policy.

Administrative Agencies and the Constitution

Because administrative agencies are governmental bodies, administrative action is *governmental action* that is subject to the basic constitutional checks discussed in Chapter 3. As the *Mallen* case, which follows shortly, demonstrates, this "fourth branch of government" is bound by basic constitutional guaranties such as *due process, equal protection,* and *freedom of speech,* just as the three traditional branches are. The tobacco advertising regulations promulgated in 1996 by the Food & Drug Administration serve as a recent example of agency action that regulated parties perceive as a potential encroachment on constitutionally protected freedoms. Various tobacco companies and other affected parties instituted litigation in which they alleged that the tobacco advertising regulations violated the First Amendment guarantee of freedom of speech. As of early 1997, when this book went to press, the case remained pending.

One basic constitutional principle is uniquely important when the creation of administrative agencies is at issue—the principle of **separation of powers.** A fundamental attribute of our Constitution is its allocation of governmental power among the three branches of government. Lawmaking power is given to the legislative branch, law enforcing power to the executive branch, and law interpreting power to the judicial branch. By limiting the powers of each branch, and by giving each branch some checks on the exercise of power by the other branches, the Constitution seeks to ensure that

---

[2]Section 5 of the FTC Act is discussed in detail in Chapter 47.

[3]The antitrust laws are discussed in detail in Chapters 48 and 49.

governmental power remains accountable to the public will. (In reality, of course, this separation is never perfectly complete. As you learned in Chapter 1, for instance, courts often "make" law when developing common law doctrines or interpreting broadly worded statutes.)

Administrative agencies, which exercise powers resembling those of each of the three branches of government, create obvious concerns about separation of powers. In particular, the congressional delegation of legislative power to an agency in its enabling legislation may be challenged as violating the separation of powers principle if the legislation is so broadly worded as to indicate that Congress has abdicated its lawmaking responsibilities. Early judicial decisions exploring the manner in which Congress could delegate its power tended to require

enabling legislation to contain fairly specific guidelines and standards limiting the exercise of agency discretion.

More recently, courts have tended to sustain quite broad delegations of power to administrative agencies. For example, Section 5 of the FTC Act is such a delegation of power. A great range of unspecified behavior falls within the statute's prohibition of "unfair methods of competition" and "unfair or deceptive acts or practices." Courts tend to approve broad delegations of power when Congress has expressed an "intelligible principle" to guide the agency's actions.[4]

---

[4]*J. W. Hampton, Jr. & Co. v. United States,* 276 U.S. 394 (U.S. Sup. Ct. 1928).

FEDERAL DEPOSIT INSURANCE CORP. v. MALLEN 486 U.S. 230 (U.S. Sup. Ct. 1988)

*O*n December 10, 1986, James Mallen was indicted by a federal grand jury in Iowa for making false statements to the Federal Deposit Insurance Corporation (FDIC) and for making false statements to Farmers State Bank for the purpose of influencing the actions of the FDIC. At the time of the indictment, Mallen was the president and a director of a federally insured bank. On January 20, 1987, the FDIC issued an ex parte order finding that Mallen's continued service might "pose a threat to the interests of the bank's depositors or threaten to impair public confidence in the bank," suspending him as president and as a director of the bank and prohibiting him "from further participation in any manner in the conduct of the affairs of the Bank, or any other bank insured by the FDIC."

In issuing the suspension order without first holding a hearing on the matter, the FDIC was acting pursuant to a section of the Financial Institutions Supervisory Act of 1966 [12 U.S.C. section 1818(g)]. A copy of the order was served on Mallen on January 26, 1987, and four days later Mallen's attorney filed a written request for an "immediate administrative hearing" to commence no later than February 9, 1987. The FDIC set a hearing date for February 18, 1987, but on February 6, 1987, Mallen filed suit against the FDIC in the Federal District Court for the Northern District of Iowa. When the District Court ruled in Mallen's favor, entering a preliminary injunction against the suspension order, the FDIC appealed. ∞

Stevens, Justice The District Court expressed no opinion on the merits of the suspension; its decision rested entirely on the perceived procedural shortcomings in the post-suspension process. It is undisputed that Mallen's interest in the right to continue to serve as president of the bank and to participate in the conduct of its affairs is a property right protected by the Fifth Amendment Due Process Clause. The FDIC cannot arbitrarily interfere with Mallen's employment relationship with the bank, nor with his interest as a substantial stockholder in the bank's holding company. It is also undisputed that the FDIC's order effected a deprivation of this property interest.

Once it is determined that due process applies, the question remains what process is due. Mallen does not contend that he was entitled to an opportunity to be heard prior to the order of suspension. An important governmental interest, accompanied by a substantial assurance that the deprivation is not baseless or unwarranted, may in limited cases demanding prompt action justify postponing the opportunity to be heard until after the initial deprivation. In this case, the postponement of the hearing is supported by such an interest. The legislation under scrutiny is premised on the congressional finding that prompt suspension of indicted bank officers may be necessary to protect the interests of depositors and to maintain public confidence in our banking institutions.

Moreover, Mallen's suspension was supported by findings that assure that the suspension was not baseless. A grand jury had determined that there was probable cause to believe that he had committed a felony. Such an *ex parte* finding of probable cause provides sufficient basis for an arrest, which of course constitutes a temporary deprivation of liberty. It should certainly be sufficient to support the order entered in this case even though the FDIC did not provide Mallen with a separate pre-suspension hearing.

We cannot agree with the District Court that Mallen was denied a sufficiently prompt post-deprivation hearing. The District Court was properly concerned about the importance of providing prompt post-deprivation procedures in situations in which an agency's discretionary impairment of an individual's property is not preceded by an opportunity for a pre-deprivation hearing. However, the District Court seems to have been improperly concerned with the danger of an interminable delay by the agency, rather than by what would have happened in this case if the proceedings had not been interrupted, or indeed, if the FDIC had been as dilatory as the statute permits. For even though there is a point at which an unjustified delay in completing a post-deprivation proceeding would become a constitutional violation, the significance of such a delay cannot be evaluated in a vacuum.

Section 1818(g)(3) requires the FDIC to hold a hearing within 30 days of a written request for an opportunity to appear before the agency to contest a suspension and requires that it notify the suspended officer of its decision within 60 days of the hearing. Thus, at a maximum, the suspended officer receives a decision within 90 days of his or her request for a hearing. In this case, the agency reported that it would have been able to issue a written decision within 30 days after the hearing. In addition, the initial hearing was scheduled to take place 19 days after it was formally requested.

Mallen's interest in continued employment is without doubt an important interest that ought not be interrupted without substantial justification. Yet, even assuming that the FDIC required the complete 90 days to hear the case and reach its decision, we are not persuaded that this exceeds permissible limits. In fact, a suspended bank officer has an interest in seeing that a decision concerning his or her continued suspension is not made with excessive haste. The statute imposes a permissive standard for continuing a suspension, and presumably, when in doubt, the agency may give greater weight to the public interest and leave the suspension in place, particularly when the suspension does not impose the additional harm of a significant, incremental injury to reputation. Through the return of an indictment, the Government has already accused Mallen of serious wrongdoing. The incidental suspension is not likely to augment this injury to his reputation. We thus conclude that the 90 day period is not so long that it will always violate due process.

In many cases, perhaps most, it will be justified by an important government interest coupled with factors minimizing the risk of an erroneous deprivation. The magnitude of the public interest in a correct decision counsels strongly against any constitutional imperative that might require overly hasty decision making. Congress has determined that the integrity of the banking industry requires that indicted bank officers be suspended until it is determined that they do not pose a threat to the interests of the bank's depositors or threaten to undermine public confidence in the bank. To return these officers to a position of influence in the conduct of the bank's affairs prior to an opportunity to weigh the evidence carefully would threaten these interests in the same way as allowing them to remain in office from the start.

Moreover, there is little likelihood that the deprivation is without basis. The returning of the indictment establishes that an independent body has determined that there is probable cause to believe that the officer has committed a crime. This finding is relevant in at least two important ways. First, the finding of probable cause by an independent body demonstrates that the suspension is not arbitrary. Second, the indictment itself is an objective fact that will in most cases raise serious public concern that the bank is not being managed in a responsible manner.

The post-suspension procedure authorized by section 1818(g)(3) is not unconstitutional on its face; nor do we find any unfairness in the FDIC's use of that procedure in this case.

District Court preliminary injunction reversed.

AGENCY TYPES AND ORGANIZATION

Agency Types

Administrative agencies may be found under a variety of labels. They may be called "administration," "agency," "authority," "board," "bureau," "commission," "department," "division," or "service." They sometimes have a governing body, which may be appointed or elected. They almost invariably have an administrative head (variously called "Chairman," "Commissioner," "Director," etc.), and a staff. Because our focus is on federal administrative agencies, it is important for us to distinguish between the two basic types of federal administrative agencies: executive agencies and independent agencies.

Executive Agencies   Administrative agencies that reside within the Executive Office of the President or within the executive departments of the president's cabinet are called **executive agencies.** Examples of such executive agencies and their cabinet homes are: the Food and Drug Administration (Department of Health and Human Services); the Nuclear Regulatory Agency and the Federal Energy Regulatory Agency (Department of Energy); the Occupational Safety and Health Administration (Department of Labor); and the Internal Revenue Service (Treasury Department). In addition to their executive home, such agencies share one other important attribute. Their administrative heads serve "at the pleasure of the President"—they are appointed and removable at his will.

Independent Agencies   The Interstate Commerce Commission was the first independent administrative agency created by Congress. Much of the most significant regulation businesses face emanates from independent agencies such as the FTC, the National Labor Relations Board, the Consumer Product Safety Commission, the Equal Employment Opportunity Commission, the Environmental Protection Agency, and the Securities and Exchange Commission. Independent agencies are usually headed by a board or a commission (e.g., the FTC has five commissioners) whose members are appointed by the president "with the advice and consent of the Senate." Commissioners or board members are usually appointed for fixed terms (e.g., FTC commissioners serve seven-year, staggered terms) and are removable only for cause (e.g., FTC commissioners

may be removed only for "inefficiency, neglect of duty, or malfeasance in office"). Finally, it is quite common for enabling legislation to require political balance in agency appointments (e.g., the FTC Act provides that "[n]ot more than three of the commissioners shall be members of the same political party").

Agency Organization

As the organizational chart of the FTC reproduced in Figure 1 indicates, an agency's organizational structure is largely a function of its regulatory mission. Thus, the operational side of the FTC is divided into three bureaus: the Bureau of Competition, which enforces the antitrust laws and unfair competitive practices; the Bureau of Consumer Protection, which focuses on unfair or deceptive trade practices; and the Bureau of Economics, which gathers data, compiles statistics, and furnishes technical assistance to the other bureaus. The Commission is headquartered in Washington, D.C., but it also maintains regional offices in Atlanta, Boston, Chicago, Cleveland, Dallas, Denver, Los Angeles, New York, San Francisco, and Seattle. This regional office system enhances the Commission's enforcement, investigative, and educational missions by locating Commission staff closer to the public it serves.

AGENCY POWERS AND PROCEDURES

Nature, Types, and Source of Powers

The powers administrative agencies possess may be classified in a variety of ways. Some agencies' powers are largely *ministerial*—concerned primarily with the routine performance of duties imposed by law. The most important administrative agencies, however, have broad *discretionary* powers that necessitate the exercise of significant discretion and judgment when they are employed. The most important formal discretionary powers agencies can posess are **investigative power, rulemaking power,** and **adjudicatory power.**

The formal powers an agency possesses are those granted by its enabling legislation. Important federal agencies such as the FTC normally enjoy significant levels of each of the formal discretionary powers. As the following sections illustrate, however, even such powerful agencies face significant limitations on the exercise of their powers. In addition to

FIGURE I

Federal Trade Commission

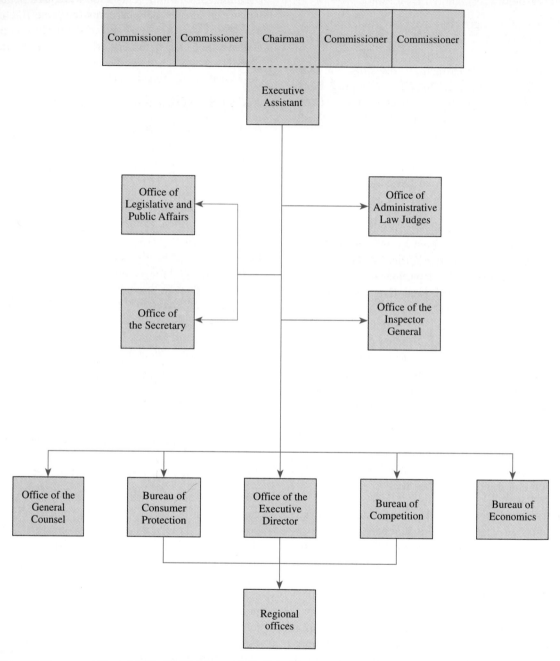

Source: *U.S. Government Manual 1995–96* (Washington, D.C.: U.S. Government Printing Office, 1995), p. 575.

explicit limits on agency proceedings contained in enabling legislation, basic constitutional provisions restrict agency action.

A federal agency's exercise of its rulemaking and adjudicatory powers is also constrained by the *Ad-* *ministrative Procedure Act (APA).* The APA was enacted by Congress in 1946 in an attempt to standardize federal agency procedures and to respond to critics who said that administrative power was out of control. The APA applies to all federal agencies, although it will not displace stricter procedural requirements contained in a particular agency's enabling legislation. In addition to specifying agency procedures, the APA plays a major role in shaping the conditions under which courts will review agency actions and the standards courts will use when conducting such a review. Most states have adopted "baby APAs" to govern the activities of state administrative agencies.

Finally, as later parts of this chapter will confirm, each of the three traditional branches of government possesses substantial powers to mold and constrain the powers of the "fourth branch." That being said, one final point needs to be made before we turn to a detailed examination of formal agency powers and procedures. An agency's formal powers also confer on it significant *informal* power. Agency "advice," "suggestions," or "guidelines," which technically lack the legal force of formal agency regulations or rulings, may nonetheless play a major role in shaping the behavior of regulated industries because they carry with them the implicit or explicit threat of formal agency action in the event that they are ignored. Such gentle persuasion can be a highly effective regulatory tool, and one that is subject to far fewer constraints than formal agency action.

Investigative Power

Effective regulation is impossible without accurate information. Administrative agencies need information about business practices and activities not only so that they can detect and prosecute regulatory violations, but also to enable them to identify areas in which new rules are needed or existing rules require modification. Much of the information agencies require to do their jobs is readily available. "Public interest" groups, complaints from customers or competitors, and other regulatory agencies are all important sources of information.

However, much of the information necessary to effective agency enforcement can come only from sources that may be strongly disinclined to provide it—the individuals and business organizations who are subject to regulation. This reluctance may be due to the desire to avoid or delay the regulation or regulatory action that disclosure would generate. It might also be the product, however, of more legitimate concerns, such as a desire to protect personal privacy, a desire to prevent competitors from acquiring trade secrets and other sensitive information

from agency files, or a reluctance to incur the costs that may accompany compliance with substantial information demands. Agencies, therefore, need the means to compel unwilling possessors of information to comply with legitimate demands for information. The two most important (and most intrusive) investigative tools employed by administrative agencies are *subpoenas* and *searches and seizures.*

Subpoenas   There are two basic types of subpoena: the subpoena *ad testificandum* and the subpoena *duces tecum.* Subpoenas *ad testificandum* may be used by an agency to compel unwilling witnesses to appear and testify at agency hearings. Subpoenas *duces tecum* may be used by an agency to compel the production of most types of documentary evidence, such as accounting records and office memoranda.

It should be obvious that unlimited agency subpoena power would sacrifice individual liberty and privacy in the name of regulatory efficiency. Accordingly, the courts have formulated a number of limitations that seek to balance an agency's legitimate need to know against an investigatory target's legitimate privacy interests.

Agency investigations must be *authorized by law* and *conducted for a legitimate purpose.* The former requirement means that the agency's enabling legislation must have granted the agency the investigatory power it is seeking to assert. The latter requirement prohibits bad faith investigations pursued for improper motives (e.g., Internal Revenue Service investigations undertaken solely to harass political opponents of an incumbent administration).

Even when the investigation is legally authorized and is undertaken for a legitimate purpose, the information sought must be *relevant to that lawful purpose.* The Fourth Amendment to the Constitution is the source of this limitation on agency powers. However, an agency issuing an administrative subpoena need not possess the "probable cause" that the Fourth Amendment requires in support of regular search warrants.[5] In the words of the Supreme Court, an agency "can investigate merely on the suspicion that the law is being violated, or even just because it wants assurance that it is not."[6] This

---

[5]The Fourth Amendment's Warrant Clause is discussed in Chapter 5.

[6]*United States v. Morton Salt,* 338 U.S. 632 (U.S. Sup. Ct. 1950).

lesser standard makes sense in the agency context, since the only evidence of many regulatory violations is documentary and "probable cause" might be demonstrable only after inspection of the target's records. In such cases, a probable cause requirement would effectively negate agency enforcement power.

Similarly, agency information demands must be *sufficiently specific* and *not unreasonably burdensome*. This requirement also derives from the Fourth Amendment's prohibition against "unreasonable searches and seizures."[7] It means that agency subpoenas must describe adequately the information the agency seeks. It also means that the cost to the target of complying with the agency's demand (e.g., the cost of assembling and reproducing the data, the disruption of business operations, or the risk that proprietary information will be indirectly disclosed to competitors) must not be unreasonably disproportionate to the agency's interest in obtaining the information.

Finally, the information sought *must not be privileged*. Various statutory and common law privileges

_____

[7]The Fourth Amendment's guarantee against unreasonable searches and seizures is discussed in Chapter 5.

can, at times, limit an agency's power to compel the production of information. By far the most important privilege in this respect is the Fifth Amendment *privilege against compelled testimonial self-incrimination,* or "the right to silence." As you learned in Chapter 5, however, this privilege is subject to serious limitations in the business context. The right to silence in the administrative context is further limited by the fact that it is only available in *criminal* proceedings. In some regulatory contexts, the potential sanctions for violation may be labeled "civil penalties" or "forfeitures." Only when such sanctions are essentially punitive in their intent or effect will they be considered "criminal" for the purpose of allowing the invocation of the privilege.

Public policy concerns provide another subpoena power limitation that may apply even if neither the Fifth Amendment nor another privilege bars production of the documents sought by an agency. As indicated in the *Collins* case, which follows, courts may conclude that an agency subpoena should not be enforced if its enforcement would tend to compromise important operations being conducted by another agency or arm of the government.

COMMODITY FUTURES TRADING COMMISSION v. COLLINS   997 F.2d 1230 (7th Cir. 1993)

*T*he Commodity Futures Trading Commission (CFTC) was investigating Thomas Collins for possible civil violations of the Commodity Exchange Act. Among the violations of which Collins was suspected was the trading of commodities futures contracts other than on a commodities exchange. The CFTC's staff suspected that these trades were spurious trades, which (the staff theorized) were intended to enable Collins to reallocate losses to persons who would reap the maximum tax benefits from the losses. As part of this investigation, the CFTC issued a subpoena directing Collins to produce copies of his federal income tax returns for examination by the CFTC's staff. The staff's reasoning was that the presence of tax motives would be evidence of a likely violation of rules enforced by the CFTC.

Collins resisted the subpoena on the ground that it would force him to incriminate himself. Collins argued that the tax returns contained information that could be evidence—or could lead to evidence—of felony violations of federal law. The CFTC argued that the tax returns were required records and that compelling their disclosure therefore would not violate the Fifth Amendment. [See Chapter 5's discussion of the required-records doctrine, which operates to eliminate Fifth Amendment privilege claims regarding the contents of such records.] The district court agreed with the CFTC and entered an enforcement order requiring Collins to obey the subpoena. Collins appealed.

In a portion of its opinion not set forth here, the Seventh Circuit Court of Appeals concluded that the required-records doctrine was inapplicable because the subpoena sought a taxpayer's copies of his tax returns—copies that the taxpayer was not required by law to make—rather than the actual tax returns whose preparation and filing with the Internal Revenue Service were required by law. The Seventh Circuit then (as set forth below) continued its analysis of Collins's Fifth Amendment argument and addressed other policy concerns triggered by the CFTC's subpoena. ∽

Posner, Judge [The inapplicability of the required-records doctrine] does not end our inquiry. The [required-records] doctrine only comes into play if, were it not for the doctrine, the government would be forcing a person to incriminate himself. *Garner v. United States* (1976) holds that the tax-payer who includes incriminating information on his return is like the witness who blurts out incriminating testimony rather than invoking the Fifth Amendment and keeping mum: he has not been compelled to testify against himself, so he has no Fifth Amendment claim. *Garner* . . . is consistent with the cases which hold that there is no Fifth Amendment privilege in already created documents, because the disclosures in them were not compelled. *Garner* and [the cases dealing with already created documents] make the required-records exception to the Fifth Amendment privilege largely, perhaps entirely, superfluous, because records that are not required are by the same token not privileged. And those decisions suggest another reason for doubting that Collins has any Fifth Amendment claim: Collins created copies of his tax returns voluntarily, so any information in the copies, however incriminating, was not compelled by the government.

In light of all this it is doubtful that Collins has any constitutional leg to stand on. No matter. All constitutional concerns to one side, we think it was an abuse of discretion for the district judge to enforce this subpoena. Income tax returns are highly sensitive documents; that is why [federal law provides that agencies such as the CFTC] cannot get Collins's tax returns directly from the Internal Revenue Service. The self-reporting, self-assessing character of the income tax system would be compromised were they promiscuously disclosed to agencies enforcing regulatory programs unrelated to tax collection itself. The CFTC made no showing that it needed Collins's tax returns. All it legitimately wants to know is whether Collins traded off the exchange and if so, why. It can ask him. If it doubts his answer, it can ask for substantiation. If he refuses to furnish it on the ground that it would compel him to incriminate himself, the CFTC can draw the appropriate inference—for example, that he was trading off the exchange in order to reap tax benefits. No law forbids a regulatory agency to draw the logical inference from a regulated entity's refusing on Fifth Amendment grounds to play ball with the agency. Should the government want to prosecute Collins criminally the Fifth Amendment would be a potential bar—but a very feeble one, in light of our previous discussion.

We are not experts in the investigation of violations of the commodity laws, so we may have overlooked reasons why, despite appearances, the effectiveness of the CFTC's investigation of Collins depends on its having access to his tax returns. The CFTC has not advanced any such reasons. It asked for and obtained the enforcement of the subpoena as a matter of rote, upon its bare representation that the tax returns might contain information germane to the investigation. That is not enough, if an appropriate balance is to be struck between the privacy of income tax returns and the needs of law enforcement. [L]arger interests are at stake than those of the immediate parties—namely the interest, unrepresented by . . . the parties to this case (for the CFTC is not represented by the Department of Justice, which might be assumed to be speaking for the Internal Revenue Service as well), in the effective administration of the federal tax laws.

District court order enforcing subpoena reversed in favor of Collins.

Searches and Seizures Sometimes the evidence necessary to prove a regulatory violation can be obtained only by entering private property such as a home, an office, or a factory. When administrative agencies seek to gather information by such an entry, the Fourth Amendment's prohibition against unreasonable searches and seizures and its warrant requirement come into play. Owners of commercial property, although afforded less Fourth Amendment protection than the owners of private dwellings, do have some legitimate expectations of privacy in their business premises.

Not all agency information-gathering efforts, however, will be considered so intrusive as to amount to a prohibited search and seizure. In *Dow Chemical Co. v. United States,*[8] for instance, the Environmental Protection Agency's warrantless

---

[8]476 U.S. 227 (U.S. Sup. Ct. 1986).

aerial photography of one of Dow's plants was upheld. Furthermore, in *State of New York v. Burger,*[9] the Supreme Court upheld the constitutionality of warrantless administrative inspections of the premises of "closely regulated" businesses so long as three criteria are satisfied: (1) there must be a substantial government interest in the regulatory scheme in question, (2) the warrantless inspections must be necessary to further the scheme, and (3) the inspection program must provide a constitutionally adequate substitute for a warrant by giving owners of commercial property adequate notice that their property is subject to inspection and by limiting the discretion of inspecting officers.

Rulemaking Power

An agency's rulemaking power derives from its enabling legislation. For example, the FTC Act gives the FTC the power "to make rules and regulations for the purpose of carrying out the provisions of this Act." The Administrative Procedure Act (APA) defines a rule as "an agency statement of general or particular applicability and future effect designed to complement, interpret or prescribe law or policy." All agency rules are compiled and published in the *Code of Federal Regulations.*

Types of Rules Administrative agencies create three types of rules: procedural rules, interpretive rules, and legislative rules.

Procedural rules specify how the agency will conduct itself. For instance, agencies typically have procedural rules dealing with such matters as the manner in which advance notice of agency rulemaking proceedings will be disseminated.

Interpretive rules are designed to advise regulated individuals and entities of the manner in which an agency interprets the statutes it enforces. For example, the FTC has promulgated a rule interpreting the term *consumer product,* as used in the Magnuson-Moss Warranty Act (a statute the FTC has the legal responsibility to enforce).[10] Interpretive rules technically do not have the force of law. Therefore, they are not binding on businesses and

the courts. Courts interpreting regulatory statutes often give agency interpretations substantial weight, however, in deference to the agency's familiarity with the statutes it administers and its presumed expertise in the general area being regulated. Business is also likely to pay attention to agency interpretive rules because such rules indicate the circumstances in which an agency is likely to take formal enforcement action.

If consistent with an agency's enabling legislation and the Constitution, and if created in accordance with the procedures dictated by the APA, *legislative rules* have the full force and effect of law. Legislative rules thus are binding on the courts, the public, and the agency. Federal agencies have promulgated very large numbers of legislative rules, many of which address highly specific matters. For example, an FTC legislative rule states that if a party sells a quick-freeze aerosol spray product designed for the frosting of beverage glasses and the product contains an ingredient known as Fluorocarbon 12, the seller must issue a warning (on the product label) that the product should not be inhaled in concentrated form, due to the risk that such behavior may lead to severe harm or death.[11]

Given the greater relative importance of legislative rules, you should not be surprised to learn that the process by which they are promulgated—unlike the process by which procedural and interpretive rules are created—is highly regulated by the APA and closely scrutinized by the courts. At present, there are three basic types of agency rulemaking: informal rulemaking, formal rulemaking, and hybrid rulemaking.

Informal Rulemaking *Informal rulemaking* (or "notice and comment" rulemaking) is the method most commonly employed by administrative agencies that are not forced by their enabling legislation to follow the more stringent procedures of formal rulemaking. The informal rulemaking process commences with the publication of a *"Notice of Proposed Rulemaking"* in the *Federal Register.* The APA requires that such notices contain: a statement of the time and place at which the proceedings will be held; a statement of the nature of the proceedings; a statement of the legal authority for the proceedings (usually the agency's enabling legisla-

---

[9]482 U.S. 691 (U.S. Sup. Ct. 1987).

[10]16 *Code of Federal Regulations* § 700.1. The Magnuson-Moss Warranty Act and FTC regulations related to it are discussed in Chapters 20 and 47.

[11]16 *Code of Federal Regulations* § 417.6.

tion); and either a statement of the terms of the proposed rule or a description of the subjects or issues to be addressed by the rule.

Publication of notice must then be followed by a *comment period* during which interested parties may submit to the agency written comments detailing their views about the proposed rule. After comments have been received and considered, the agency must publish the regulation in its final form in the *Federal Register.* As a general rule, the rule cannot become effective until at least 30 days after this final publication. The APA, however, recognizes a "good cause" exception to the 30-day waiting period requirement, and to the notice of rulemaking requirement as well, when notice would be impractical, unnecessary, or contrary to the public interest.

Agencies tend to favor the informal rulemaking process because it allows quick and efficient regulatory action. Such quickness and efficiency, however, are purchased at a significant cost—a relatively minimal opportunity for interested parties to participate in the rule-formation process. Giving interested parties the opportunity to be heard may, in some cases, ultimately further regulatory goals. For example, the vigorous debate about a proposed rule that a public hearing can provide may contribute to the creation of more effective rules. Also, providing interested parties with what they perceive to be an adequate opportunity to participate in the rulemaking process lends credibility to that process and the rules it produces, thereby enhancing the chances of voluntary compliance by the regulated industry.

Formal Rulemaking   *Formal rulemaking* (or "on the record" rulemaking) is designed to give interested parties a far greater opportunity to make their views heard than that afforded by informal rulemaking. As does informal rulemaking, formal rulemaking begins with publication of a *"Notice of Proposed Rulemaking"* in the *Federal Register.* Unlike the notice employed to announce informal rulemaking procedures, however, this notice must include notice of a time and place at which a public hearing concerning the proposed rule will be held. Such hearings resemble trials in that the agency must produce evidence justifying the proposed regulation, and interested parties are likewise allowed to present evidence in opposition to it. Both sides are entitled to examine each other's exhibits and to cross-examine each other's witnesses. At the con-

clusion of the proceedings, the agency must prepare a formal, written document detailing its findings based on the evidence presented in the hearing.

Although the formal rulemaking process affords interested parties greatly enhanced opportunities to be heard, this greater access is purchased at significant expense and at the risk that some parties will abuse their access rights to impede the regulatory process. By tireless cross-examination of government witnesses and lengthy presentations of their own, opponents seeking to derail or delay regulation may consume months, or even years, of agency time. The classic example of such behavior would be the Food and Drug Administration's hearings on a proposed rule requiring that the minimum peanut content of peanut butter be set at 90 percent. Industry forces favored an 87 percent minimum and were able to delay regulation for almost 10 years.

Hybrid Rulemaking   Frustration over the lack of access afforded by informal rulemaking and the potential for paralyzing the regulatory process that is inherent in formal rulemaking have led some courts and legislators to attempt the creation of a rulemaking process embodying some of the elements of informal and formal procedures. Although hybrid rulemaking procedures are insufficiently established and standardized at this point to permit a detailed discussion of them, some general tendencies are evident. Hybrid procedures bear some resemblance to those of formal rulemaking in that both involve some sort of hearing. Unlike formal rulemaking procedures, however, hybrid procedures tend to limit the right of interested parties to cross-examine agency witnesses.

Adjudicatory Power

Most major federal agencies possess substantial adjudicatory powers. Besides having the authority to investigate alleged behaviors and to produce regulations that have legal effect, they have the power to instigate and conduct proceedings to determine whether regulatory or statutory violations have occurred. The administrative adjudication process is at once similar to, but substantially different from, the judicial process you studied in Chapter 2.

The administrative adjudication process normally begins with a complaint filed by the agency. The party charged in the complaint (called the *respondent*) files an answer. Respondents are normally

FIGURE 2

Administrative Agencies and Separation of Powers

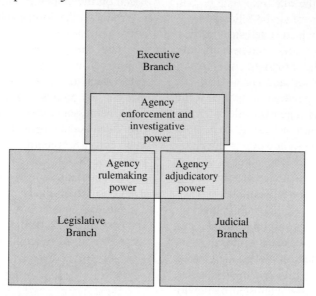

entitled to a hearing before the agency. At this hearing, they may confront and cross-examine agency witnesses and present evidence of their own. Respondents may be represented by legal counsel. No juries are present in administrative adjudications, however. The cases are heard by an agency employee usually called an **administrative law judge (ALJ).** Also, unlike criminal prosecutions, the burden of proof in administrative proceedings is normally the civil *preponderance of the evidence* standard. Constitutional procedural safeguards such as the exclusionary rule do not protect the respondent.[12]

The agency, in effect, functions as police officer, prosecutor, judge, and jury. The APA attempts to deal with the obvious potential for abuse inherent in this combination in a number of ways. First, the APA attempts to ensure that ALJs are as independent as possible by requiring internal separation between an agency's judges and its investigative and prosecutorial functions. (Note, for example, the organizational separation of the FTC's Office of Administrative Law Judges, as depicted in Figure 1.)

The APA also prohibits ALJs from having private consultations with anyone who is a party to an agency proceeding and shields them from agency disciplinary action other than for "good cause." Finally, insufficient separation between an agency's adjudication function and its other functions can be contrary to basic due process requirements.

After each party to the proceeding has been heard, the ALJ renders a decision stating her findings of fact and conclusions of law, and imposing whatever penalty she deems appropriate within the parameters established by the agency's enabling legislation (e.g., a fine or a cease and desist order). If neither party challenges the ALJ's decision, it becomes final. The losing party, however, may appeal an ALJ's decision, in which case it will be subjected to a **de novo review** by the governing body of the agency (e.g., appeals from FTC ALJ decisions are heard by the five FTC commissioners). *De novo review* means that the agency's governing body may treat the proceedings as if they were occurring for the first time and may totally ignore the ALJ's findings. Often, however, the agency's governing body will adopt the ALJ's findings. In any event, those findings will be part of the record if a disappointed respondent seeks judicial review of an agency's decision.

Finally, when considering agency adjudicatory powers it is important to note that many agency

---

[12]*INS v. Lopez-Mendoza,* 468 U.S. 1032 (U.S. Sup. Ct. 1984). The exclusionary rule and the beyond a reasonable doubt standard employed in criminal cases are discussed in Chapter 5. The preponderance of the evidence standard is discussed in Chapter 6.

proceedings are settled by a **consent order** before completion of the adjudication process. Consent orders are similar to the nolo contendere pleas discussed in Chapter 5. Respondents who sign consent orders do not admit wrongdoing, but they waive all rights to judicial review, agree to accept a specific sanction imposed by the agency, and commonly agree to discontinue the business practice that triggered the agency action.

Figure 2 depicts the major powers of this "fourth branch" of the government.

CONTROLLING ADMINISTRATIVE AGENCIES

By this point in our discussion of administrative agencies, we have already encountered several legal controls on agency action, such as the terms of an agency's enabling legislation, the procedural requirements imposed by the APA, and the basic constraints that the Constitution places on all governmental action. The following sections continue to focus on the important theme of agency control by examining the various devices, both formal and informal, through which the three traditional branches of government influence and control the actions of administrative agencies.

Presidential Controls

The executive branch has at its disposal a number of tools that can be employed to shape agency action. The most obvious among them is the president's power to appoint and remove agency administrators. For example, in Chapters 48 and 49, you will learn that President Reagan's appointees to the Department of Justice and the FTC made major changes in governmental antitrust enforcement policies because of their commitment to "Chicago School" antitrust ideas. This presidential power is obviously more limited in the case of independent agencies than it is where executive agencies are concerned, but the president generally has the power to appoint the heads of independent agencies and demote the prior chairpersons without cause. Skillful use of the new chair's managerial powers, probably the most important of which is the power to influence agency hiring policies, can eventually effect substantial changes in agency policy. Also, significant and sustained policy differences between an independent agency and the executive branch often eventually trigger resignations by agency commissioners, thus providing the president with the opportunity to appoint new members whose philosophies are more congruent with his own.

The executive branch also exercises significant control over agency action through the Office of Management and Budget (OMB). The OMB plays a major role in the creation of the annual executive budget the president presents to Congress. In the process, the OMB reviews, and sometimes modifies, the budgetary requests of executive agencies. In addition, an executive order requires executive agencies to prepare cost-benefit and least-cost analyses for all major proposed rules and to submit this information to the OMB for review prior to seeking public comments. This and a subsequent executive order requiring agencies to give the OMB early warning of possible rule changes have made the OMB a powerful player in the rulemaking process.

Finally, the president's power to *veto* legislation concerning administrative agencies represents another point of executive influence over agency operations.

Congressional Controls

The legislative branch possesses a number of devices, both formal and informal, by which it may influence agency action. Obvious avenues of congressional control include the Senate's "advice and consent" role in agency appointments, the power to amend an agency's enabling legislation (what Congress has given, Congress can take away), and the power to pass legislation that mandates changes in agency practices or procedures. Examples of the latter include the National Environmental Policy Act (NEPA), which dictated that administrative agencies file *environmental impact statements* for every agency action that might significantly affect the quality of the environment, and the Regulatory Flexibility Act, which ordered changes in agency rulemaking procedures designed to give small businesses improved notice of agency rulemaking activities that may have a substantial impact on them. Congress can also pass *sunset legislation* providing for the automatic expiration of an agency's authority unless Congress expressly extends it by a specified date. Such legislation ensures periodic congressional review of the initial decision to delegate legislative authority to an administrative agency.

Congress also enjoys several other less obvious, but no less important, points of influence over agency action. For example, Congress must authorize agency budgetary appropriations. Thus, Congress may limit or deny funding for agency programs with which it disagrees. Also, the Governmental Operations Committees of both houses of Congress exercise significant oversight over agency activities. These committees review agency programs and conduct hearings concerning proposed agency appointments and appropriations. Finally, individual members of Congress may seek to influence agency action through "casework"—informal contacts with an agency on behalf of constituents who are involved with the agency.

Judicial Review

As important as the roles of the executive and legislative branches are in controlling agency action, the courts exercise the greatest amount of control over agency behavior. This may be due, in part, to the fact that they are the branch of government most accessible to members of the public aggrieved by agency action. The APA provides for judicial review of most agency action, which takes place either in one of the U.S. courts of appeals or a U.S. district court, depending on the nature of the agency action at issue. The Supreme Court, if it chooses to grant certiorari, is the court of last resort for review of agency action.

Not all agency actions are subject to judicial review. Moreover, only certain parties may challenge those that are reviewable. An individual or organization seeking judicial review must demonstrate that the agency action being challenged is *reviewable,* that the challenging party has *standing to sue,* that *necessary administrative remedies have been exhausted,* and that the dispute is *ripe for judicial review.* These requirements are discussed below.

Reviewability Only reviewable agency actions may be challenged by dissatisfied individuals and organizations. Normally, it is not difficult for aggrieved parties to show that the agency action is reviewable because the APA creates a strong presumption in favor of reviewability. This presumption may be overcome only by a showing that "statutes preclude review" or that the decision in question is "committed to agency discretion by law." These limitations on reviewability come from Congress's power to dictate the jurisdiction of the federal courts and from judicial deference to the proper functions of the other branches of government (e.g., a decision relating to matters of foreign policy is likely to be seen as outside the proper province of the judiciary).

Standing to Sue Once reviewability of an agency action has been established, the challenging party must demonstrate that he, she, or it has standing to sue. This means that the individual or organization seeking judicial review is "an aggrieved party" whose interests have been substantially affected by the agency action. Initially, courts took a relatively restrictive view of this basic requirement, requiring plaintiffs to show harm to a legally protected interest. More recently, however, courts have liberalized the standing requirement somewhat, requiring plaintiffs to demonstrate that they have suffered an "injury" to an interest that lies within the "zone of interests" protected by the statute or constitutional provision that serves as the basis of their challenge. Demonstrating an economic loss remains the surest way to satisfy the "injury" requirement, but emotional, aesthetic, and environmental injuries have been found sufficient on occasion.

Lujan v. Defenders of Wildlife, which follows, demonstrates that even though the standing requirement has been liberalized over the years, an asserted injury that is overly abstract, speculative, or tenuous in nature will be insufficient to confer standing on the plaintiff.

LUJAN v. DEFENDERS OF WILDLIFE 504 U.S. 555 (U.S. Sup. Ct. 1992)

S *ection 7(a)(2) of the Endangered Species Act of 1973 divides responsibilities as to protection of endangered species between the Secretary of the Interior and the Secretary of Commerce. The statute also requires each federal agency to consult with the relevant secretary in order to ensure that any action funded by the agency would be unlikely to jeopardize the existence or habitat of an endangered or threatened species. In 1978, the secretaries referred to above promulgated a joint regulation stating that the obligations imposed by Section 7(a)(2) extend not only to actions taken in the United States but also to actions taken in foreign nations. A revised joint regulation, reinterpreting Section 7(a)(2) to require consultation only for actions taken in the United States or on the high seas, was promulgated in 1986. Defenders of Wildlife (DOW), an organization dedicated to wildlife conservation and other environmental causes, sued the Secretary of the Interior, seeking a declaratory judgment that the 1986 regulation erroneously interpreted the geographic scope of Section 7(a)(2). DOW also sought an injunction requiring the secretary to develop a new regulation restoring the interpretation set forth in the 1978 regulation. The district court denied the secretary's motion for summary judgment on the issue of whether DOW had standing to sue, granted DOW's motion for summary judgment on all issues, and ordered the secretary to develop a revised regulation. After the Eighth Circuit Court of Appeals affirmed, the Supreme Court granted certiorari.* ∽

Scalia, Justice   The preliminary issue, and the only one we reach, is whether DOW has standing to seek judicial review [of the 1986 regulation]. [Article III of the U.S. Constitution] limits the jurisdiction of federal courts to "Cases" and "Controversies." Though some of its elements express merely prudential considerations that are part of judicial self-government, the core component of standing is an essential and unchanging part of the case-or-controversy requirement of Article III.

Over the years, our cases have established that the irreducible constitutional minimum of standing contains three elements: First, the plaintiff must have suffered an injury in fact—an invasion of a legally-protected interest which is (a) concrete and particularized, and (b) actual or imminent, not conjectural or hypothetical. Second, there must be a causal connection between the injury and the conduct complained of. Third, it must be likely, as opposed to merely speculative, that the injury will be redressed by a favorable decision.

The party invoking federal jurisdiction bears the burden of establishing these elements. When the suit is one challenging the legality of government action or inaction, the nature and extent of facts [necessary] to establish standing depends considerably upon whether the plaintiff is himself an object of the action (or foregone action) at issue. If he is, there is ordinarily little question that the action or inaction has caused him injury, and that a judgment preventing or requiring the action will redress it. When, however, as in this case, a plaintiff's asserted injury arises from the government's allegedly unlawful regulation (or lack of regulation) of **someone else,** . . . standing is not precluded, but it is ordinarily substantially more difficult to establish [the necessary elements outlined above].

DOW's claim to injury is that the lack of consultation with respect to certain funded activities abroad "increases the rate of extinction of endangered and threatened species." Of course, the desire to use or observe an animal species, even for purely aesthetic purposes, is undeniably a cognizable interest for purpose of standing. "But the 'injury in fact' test requires more than an injury to a cognizable interest. It requires that the party seeking review be himself among the injured." *Sierra Club v. Morton* (1972). We shall assume for the sake of argument that [the affidavits of two DOW members, offered by DOW in opposition of the secretary's motion for summary judgment on the standing issue,] contain facts showing that certain agency-funded projects threaten listed species [a variety of crocodile in Egypt and the Asian elephant and the leopard in Sri Lanka]. [The affidavits] plainly contain no facts, however, showing how damage to the species will produce "imminent" injury to [the affiants]. That the affiants "had visited" the areas of the projects before the projects commenced proves nothing. And the affiants' profession of an "intent" to return to the places they had visited before—where they will presumably, this time, be deprived of the opportunity to observe animals of the endangered species—is simply not enough. Such "some day" intentions—without any description of concrete plans, or indeed any specification of *when* the some day will be—do not support a finding of the "actual or imminent" injury that our cases require.

[DOW also asserts theories] called, alas, the "animal nexus" approach, whereby anyone who has an interest in studying or seeing the endangered animals anywhere on the globe has standing; and the "vocational nexus" approach, under which anyone with a professional interest in such animals can sue. Under these theories, anyone who goes to see elephants in the Bronx Zoo, and anyone who is a keeper of Asian elephants in the Bronx Zoo, has standing to sue because the Director of AID did not consult with the Secretary regarding the AID-funded project in Sri Lanka. This is beyond all reason. Standing is not "an ingenious academic exercise in the conceivable." *U.S. v. Students Challenging Regulatory Agency Procedures* (1973). [Instead, standing requires] a factual showing of perceptible harm. It is clear that the person who observes or works with a particular animal threatened by a federal decision is facing perceptible harm, since the very subject of his interest will no longer exist. It is even plausible—though it goes to the outermost limit of plausibility—to think that a person who observes or works with animals of a particular species in the very area of the world where that species is threatened by a federal decision is facing such harm, since some animal that might have been the subject of his interest will no longer exist. It goes beyond the limit, however, and into pure speculation and fantasy, to say that anyone who observes or works with an endangered species, anywhere in the world, is appreciably harmed by a single project affecting some portion of that species with which he has no more specific connection.

The Court of Appeals found that DOW had standing for an additional reason: because it had suffered a "procedural injury" [by virtue of the Endangered Species Act's so-called "citizen-suit" provision stating that "any person" may bring suit to enjoin a violation of the statute]. The court held that . . . the citizen-suit provision [allows] *anyone* [to] file suit in federal court to challenge the Secretary's (or presumably any other official's) failure to follow the assertedly correct consultative procedure, notwithstanding their inability to allege any discrete injury flowing from that failure. The court held that the injury-in-fact requirement [for standing purposes] had been satisfied by congressional conferral upon *all* persons of an abstract, self-contained, noninstrumental "right" to have the Executive [branch] observe the procedures required by law. We reject this view. We have consistently held that a plaintiff raising only a generally available grievance about government—claiming only harm to his and every citizen's interest in proper application of the Constitution and laws, and seeking relief that no more directly and tangibly benefits him than it does the public at large—does not state an Article III case or controversy.

[I]t is clear that in suits against the government, at least, the concrete injury requirement must remain. We hold that DOW lacks standing to bring this action.

Decision of Eighth Circuit Court of Appeals reversed in favor of Secretary of Interior.

Exhaustion and Ripeness Once standing has been established, two further obstacles—exhaustion and ripeness—confront the party challenging an agency action. Courts do not want to allow regulated parties to short-circuit the regulatory process. They also want to give agencies the chance to correct their own mistakes and to develop fully their positions in disputed matters. Accordingly, they normally insist that aggrieved parties *exhaust necessary administrative remedies* before they will grant judicial review.[13] The requirement that a dispute be *ripe* for judicial review is a general requirement emanating from the Constitution's insistence that only "cases or controversies" are judicially resolvable. In determining ripeness, the courts weigh the hardship to the parties of withholding judicial review against the degree of refinement of the issues still possible (e.g., might further administrative action alter the nature of the issues or eliminate the need for judicial review?).

Legal Bases for Challenging Agency Actions Assuming that the above prerequisites to judicial review are met, there are several legal theories on which agency action may be attacked. It may be alleged that the agency's action was *ultra vires* (exceeded its authority as granted by its enabling legislation) or that the agency *substantially deviated from procedural requirements* contained in the APA or in the agency's enabling legislation. Agency action may also be challenged as *unconstitutional* or

---

[13]Necessary administrative remedies are those a statute or regulation establishes as mandatory steps to be completed before judicial review can be sought. In *Darby v. Cisneros*, 509 U.S. 137 (U.S. Sup. Ct. 1993), the Supreme Court held that federal courts do not have the authority to require plaintiffs to exhaust available administrative remedies before seeking judicial review unless the relevant statutes or agency rules specifically mandate exhaustion as a prerequisite to judicial review.

as the product of an *erroneous interpretation of statutes*. (The *Sweet Home* case, which follows shortly, illustrates the latter line of attack.) Finally, agency action may be overturned if it is *unsubstantiated by the facts* before the agency when it acted.

Standards of Review The degree of scrutiny that courts will apply to agency action depends on the nature of issues under dispute and the type of agency proceedings that produced the challenged action. Courts are least likely to defer to agency action when *questions of law* are at issue. Although courts afford substantial consideration to an agency's interpretations of the statutes it enforces, the courts are still the ultimate arbiters of the meaning of statutes and constitutional provisions.

When *questions of fact* or *policy* are at issue, however, courts are more likely to defer to the agency because it presumably has superior expertise and because the agency fact finders who heard and viewed the evidence were better situated to judge its merit. When agency factual judgments are at stake, the APA provides for three standards of review, the most rigorous of which is *de novo* review.

When conducting a *de novo* review, courts make an independent finding of the facts after conducting a new hearing. Efficiency considerations plainly favor limited judicial review of the facts. Accordingly, *de novo* review is employed only when required by statute, when inadequate fact-finding proceedings were used in an agency adjudicatory proceeding, or when new factual issues that were not before the agency are raised in a proceeding to enforce a nonadjudicatory agency action.

When courts review formal agency adjudications or formal rulemaking, the APA calls for the application of a **substantial evidence** test. Only agency findings that are "unsupported by substantial evidence" will be overturned. In conducting substantial evidence reviews, courts look at the reasonableness of an agency's actions in relation to the facts before it rather than conducting an independent fact-finding hearing (such as that done in *de novo* reviews). The substantial evidence test also tends to be employed in hybrid rulemaking cases.

The judicial standard of review used in cases involving informal agency adjudications or rulemaking is the **arbitrary and capricious** test. This is the least rigorous standard of judicial review, due to the great degree of deference it accords agency decisions. In deciding whether an agency's action was arbitrary and capricious, a reviewing court theoretically should not substitute its judgment for that of the agency. Instead, it should ask whether there was an adequate factual basis for the agency's action, and should sustain actions that do not amount to a "clear error of judgment." Although the substantial evidence and arbitrary and capricious tests are separate and distinct in theory, the distinctions often tend to blur in actual practice.

BABBITT v. SWEET HOME CHAPTER OF COMMUNITIES FOR A GREAT OREGON
115 S. Ct. 2407 (U.S. Sup. Ct. 1995)

Section 9 of the Endangered Species Act (ESA) makes it unlawful for any person to "take" an endangered or threatened species of fish or wildlife. A definition section in the ESA states that take means "to harass, harm, pursue, hunt, shoot, wound, kill, trap, capture, or collect, or to attempt to engage in any such conduct." The Secretary of the Department of the Interior (the Secretary) promulgated a regulation that defines the term harm for purposes of the statutory language just quoted. This regulation states that harm "means an act which actually kills or injures wildlife" and that "[s]uch act may include significant habitat modification or degradation where it actually kills or injures wildlife by significantly impairing essential behavioral patterns, including breeding, feeding or sheltering."

A declaratory judgment action attacking the validity of this regulation was brought against the Secretary by a group of landowners, logging companies, and families dependent on the forest products industries, and by organizations representing those parties' interests. The plaintiffs sought a judicial ruling that the regulation defining harm as including habitat modification or degradation was an unreasonable and erroneous interpretation of the ESA. The plaintiffs (referred to here collectively as "Sweet Home") alleged that they had been injured economically by the government's application of the harm regulation to the red-cockaded woodpecker, an endangered species, and the northern spotted owl, a threatened species. The federal district court upheld the regulation and granted summary judgment in favor of the Secretary. The U.S. Court of

Appeals for the District of Columbia Circuit reversed, however. The U.S. Supreme Court granted the Secretary's petition for a writ of certiorari. ∞

Stevens, Justice The text of the [ESA] provides three reasons for concluding that the Secretary's interpretation is reasonable. First, an ordinary understanding of the word "harm" supports it. The dictionary definition of the verb form of "harm" is "to cause hurt or damage; to injure" [quoting *Webster's Third New International Dictionary*]. In the context of the ESA, that definition naturally encompasses habitat modification that results in actual injury or death to members of an endangered or threatened species.

[Sweet Home argues] that the Secretary should have limited the purview of "harm" to direct applications of force against protected species, but the dictionary definition does not include the word "directly" or suggest in any way that only direct or willful action that leads to injury constitutes "harm." Moreover, unless the statutory term "harm" encompasses indirect as well as direct injuries, the word has no meaning that does not duplicate the meaning of other words that [the statutory definition section] uses to define "take." A reluctance to treat statutory terms as surplusage supports the reasonableness of the Secretary's interpretation.

Second, the broad purpose of the ESA supports the Secretary's decision to extend protection against activities that cause the precise harms Congress enacted the statute to avoid. As stated in section 2 of the [ESA], among its central purposes is "to provide a means whereby the ecosystems upon which endangered species and threatened species depend may be conserved." Given Congress' clear expression of the ESA's broad purpose to protect endangered and threatened wildlife, the Secretary's definition of "harm" is reasonable.

Third, . . . Congress in 1982 authorized the Secretary to issue permits for takings that [section 9] would otherwise prohibit, "if such taking is incidental to, and not the purpose of, the carrying out of an otherwise lawful activity," [quoting section 10 of the ESA]. [This authorization] strongly suggests that Congress understood [section 9] to prohibit indirect as well as deliberate takings. The permit process requires the applicant to prepare a "conservation plan" that specifies how he intends to "minimize and mitigate" the "impact" of the activity on endangered and threatened species, making clear

that Congress had in mind foreseeable rather than merely accidental effects on listed species. No one could seriously request an "incidental" take permit to avert section 9 lability for direct, deliberate action against a member of an endangered or threatened species, but [Sweet Home] would read "harm" so narrowly that the permit procedure would have little more than that absurd purpose. Congress' addition of the section 10 permit provision supports the Secretary's conclusion that activities not intended to harm an endangered species, such as habitat modification, may constitute unlawful takings under the ESA unless the Secretary permits them.

The Court of Appeals [erred] in asserting that "harm" must refer to a direct application of force because the words around it do. [T]he court's premise was flawed. Several of the words that accompany "harm" in the [statutory] definition of "take," especially "harass," "pursue," "wound," and "kill," refer to actions or effects that do not require direct applications of force. [The Court of Appeals gave] "harm" essentially the same function as other words in the definition, thereby denying it independent meaning. The statutory context of "harm" suggests that Congress meant that term to serve a particular function in the ESA, consistent with but distinct from the functions of the other verbs used to define "take." The Secretary's interpretation of "harm" to include indirectly injuring endangered animals through habitat modification permissibly interprets "harm" to have a character of its own.

We need not decide whether the statutory definition of "take" compels the Secretary's interpretation of "harm," because our conclusions that Congress did not unambiguously manifest its intent to adopt [Sweet Home's] view and that the Secretary's interpretation is reasonable suffice to decide this case. The latitude the ESA gives the Secretary in enforcing the statute, together with the degree of regulatory expertise necessary to its enforcement, establishes that we owe some degree of deference to the Secretary's reasonable interpretation.

When it enacted the ESA, Congress delegated broad administrative and interpretive power to the Secretary. The task of defining and listing endangered and threatened species requires an expertise and attention to detail that exceeds the normal province of Congress. Fashioning appropriate standards for issuing permits under section 10 for takings that would otherwise violate section 9 necessarily requires the exercise of broad discretion. The proper interpretation of a term such as "harm" involves a complex policy choice. When Congress has entrusted the Secretary with broad discretion, we are especially reluctant to substitute our views of wise policy for his. In this case, that reluctance accords with our conclusion . . . that the Secretary reasonably construed the intent of Congress when he defined "harm" to include "significant habitat modification or degradation that actually kills or injures wildlife."

Judgment of Court of Appeals reversed.

INFORMATION CONTROLS

Over the last three decades, Congress has enacted three major statutes aimed at controlling administrative agencies through the regulation of information. Each of these statutes represents a compromise between competing social interests of significant importance. On one hand, we have a strong democratic preference for public disclosure of governmental operations, believing that "government in the dark" is less likely to be consistent with the public interest than is "government in the sunshine." On the other hand, we recognize that some sensitive governmental activities must be shielded from the scrutiny of unfriendly parties, and that disclosure of some information may unjustifiably invade personal privacy, hinder government law enforcement efforts, or provide the competitors of a company about which information is being disclosed with proprietary information that could be used unfairly to the competitors' advantage.

Freedom of Information Act

Congress passed the *Freedom of Information Act* (FOIA) in 1966 and amended it in 1974. The FOIA was designed to enable private citizens to have access to documents in the government's possession. Agencies must normally respond to public requests for documents within 10 days after such a request has been received. An agency bears the burden of justifying any denial of any FOIA request. Denials are appealable to an appropriate federal district court. Successful plaintiffs may recover their costs and attorney's fees.

Not all government-held documents are obtainable under the FOIA, however. The FOIA exempts from disclosure documents that:

1. Must be kept secret in the interest of national security.

2. Concern an agency's internal personnel practices.

3. Are specifically exempted from disclosure by statute.

4. Contain trade secrets or other confidential or privileged commercial or financial information.

5. Reflect internal agency deliberations on matters of policy or proceedings.

6. Appear in individual personnel or medical files, or in similar files if disclosure would constitute a clearly unwarranted invasion of personal privacy.

7. Would threaten the integrity of a law enforcement agency's investigations or jeopardize an individual's right to a fair trial.

8. Relate to the supervision or regulation of financial institutions.

9. Contain geological or geophysical data.

Frequent users of the FOIA include the media, industry trade associations, public interest groups, and companies seeking to obtain useful information about their competitors. *Oregon Natural Desert Association v. Bibles,* which follows shortly, illustrates an unsuccessful attempt by a government agency to invoke the privacy exemption as a justification for not releasing information requested by a public interest group. It is important to note that although the FOIA allows agencies to refuse to disclose exempted documents, it does not impose on them the affirmative duty to do so. The Supreme Court has held that individuals cannot compel an agency to deny an FOIA request for allegedly exempt documents that contain sensitive information about them.[14]

The FOIA has recently been the focus of considerable controversy on two points. First, budgetary

---

[14]*Chrysler Corp. v. Brown,* 441 U.S. 281 (U.S. Sup. Ct. 1980).

cutbacks have combined with growing numbers of requests for information to produce agency delays as long as two years in responding to information requests. Courts tend to tolerate agency delays if the agency can show that it is making a "due diligence" effort to respond. Second, the dramatic increase in computerized information storage that has occurred since the passage of the FOIA has created problems not specifically contemplated by the statute, which focuses on information stored in documentary form. Do interested parties have the same rights of access to data stored in agency computers that they have to government documents? May the government destroy electronic mail messages, or must it save them? Future legislative or judicial action will be necessary to resolve such questions.

OREGON NATURAL DESERT ASSOCIATION v. BIBLES 83 F.3d 1168 (9th Cir. 1996)

The Oregon Natural Desert Association (ONDA), a nonprofit organization interested in desert preservation, made a Freedom of Information Act (FOIA) request for the list of names and addresses of persons who receive a newsletter published by the Bureau of Land Management (BLM). The newsletter provides information about the BLM's activities and plans affecting the Oregon desert. [R]efusing to release the list, the BLM invoked an FOIA exemption that protects files whose disclosure would constitute "a clearly unwarranted invasion of personal privacy." ONDA appealed to the Department of the Interior, which concluded that the names and addresses of organizations should be released but that the names and addresses of private individuals were protected by the privacy exemption.

ONDA then filed an FOIA suit against the BLM and its Oregon director, D. Dean Bibles, in an effort to obtain the complete list. According to its complaint, ONDA sought the list in order to identify the parties to whom the government was directing "selected" information about the high desert. ONDA planned to provide those recipients with more complete information. The federal district court ruled in favor of ONDA and ordered that the complete list be released. The BLM appealed. ∽

Schroeder, Circuit Judge The FOIA mandates broad disclosure of government documents [by providing that] "each agency, upon a request for records which (A) reasonably describes such record and (B) is made in accordance with published rules stating the time, place, fees (if any), and procedures to be followed, shall make the records promptly available to any person." The FOIA request must be granted unless the information requested falls within one of the nine statutory exemptions. The government has the burden of establishing that an exemption applies, and exemptions are construed narrowly.

The FOIA's privacy exemption 6 applies to "personnel and medical files and similar files the disclosure of which would constitute a clearly unwarranted invasion of personal privacy." Although a list of names and addresses . . . is clearly not a "medical" or "personnel" file, the provision for "similar" files is broad enough to encompass government records containing information about particular individuals. We have recognized that a government list of names and addresses meets the threshold requirements of exemption 6.

The relevant question is thus whether the disclosure of [the BLM] mailing list would constitute a "clearly unwarranted invasion of personal privacy." We know from an early Supreme Court decision that resolving this question involves balancing the individual's right of privacy against the goal of FOIA to "open agency action to the light of public scrutiny" (quoting *Department of the Air Force v. Rose* (1976)). The parties do not dispute that outside of ONDA's FOIA request, there are no alternative means to obtain the requested information. Additionally, the parties agree that [we are] to consider . . . the public's interest in disclosure and the degree of invasion of personal privacy.

ONDA argues persuasively . . . that in addition to the overarching [FOIA] presumption favoring disclosure, . . . there is also a substantial public interest in knowing to whom the government is directing information, or as ONDA characterizes it, "propaganda," so that those persons may receive information from other sources that do not share the BLM's self-interest in presenting government activities in the most favorable light. We agree and therefore conclude that there is more than a minimal public interest served by disclosure in this case.

We next must consider whether this public interest in disclosure is outweighed by the invasion of privacy that would result from disclosure of the list. The BLM has argued that dissemination of its mailing list would cause the persons listed to be flooded with unsolicited mail. Yet the district court aptly observed that these individuals are already on a mailing list, on which the majority of the individuals asked to be placed, in order to receive mailings about BLM activities. [T]he privacy interests implicated in th[is] case are minimal in light of the mailings already received by the individuals and the similar subject matter of the mailings likely to be received as a result of the disclosure.

The Supreme Court's decision in *United States Department of Defense v. F.L.R.A.* (1994) [referred to here as "*DOD*"], fully supports the district court's analysis, which measures the privacy interest at stake in terms of the nature and likelihood of probable contacts stemming from the particular disclosure. *DOD* further supports the district court's conclusion that in this case the invasion of privacy would be minimal. In *DOD,* the Court denied a union's FOIA request for a list of government employees in the union's own bargaining unit, even though the union requested the list to further federal labor policies as embodied in the federal labor statutes. The Court said that the *DOD* employees had a "nontrivial privacy interest in nondisclosure, and in avoiding the influx of union-related mail, and perhaps union-related telephone calls or visits that would follow from disclosure." The employees [in *DOD*] had chosen not to provide the union with their addresses. In this case, the persons on the BLM's mailing list have, for the most part, affirmatively indicated their interest in receiving mailings on subjects related to ONDA's interest. Furthermore, recipients of the BLM news are unlikely to be targeted for the same type of aggressive, high stakes personal contact that the Court was wary of in *DOD*. In short, the effect of disclosure is much smaller than in *DOD*.

Because the privacy interests at stake are minimal, and because there is a significant public interest in knowing with whom the government has chosen to communicate and in providing those persons with additional information, we conclude that disclosure of the mailing list would not result in a clearly unwarranted invasion of privacy.

District court decision in favor of ONDA affirmed.

Privacy Act of 1974

The **Privacy Act of 1974** allows individuals to inspect files that agencies maintain on them and to request that erroneous or incomplete records be corrected. It also attempts to prevent agencies from gathering unnecessary information about individuals, and forbids the disclosure of an individual's records without his written permission, except in certain specifically exempted circumstances. For example, records may be disclosed to employees of the agency that collected the information if those employees need the records to perform their duties (the "need to know" exception), to law enforcement agencies, to other agencies' personnel for "routine use" (uses for purposes compatible with the purpose for which the record was collected), and to persons filing legitimate FOIA requests. In addition, records may be disclosed if a court order requires disclosure.

Government in the Sunshine Act

The *Government in the Sunshine Act* of 1976 was designed to ensure that "[e]very portion of every meeting of an agency shall be open to public observation." However, complete public access to all agency meetings could have the same negative consequences that unrestrained public access to agency records can sometimes produce. Accordingly, the Sunshine Act exempts certain agency meetings from public scrutiny under circumstances similar to those under which documents are exempt from disclosure under the FOIA.

ISSUES IN REGULATION

"Old" Regulation versus "New" Regulation

Some interested observers of regulatory developments over roughly the past 40 years have noted significant differences between the regulations that originated during the Progressive (1902 to 1914) and New Deal (1933 to 1938) eras and many regulations promulgated more recently.[15] They argue not only that the number and scope of regulatory controls have increased substantially in recent years, but also that the focus and the impact of regulation have changed significantly.

Whereas earlier regulation often focused on business practices that harmed the economic interests of specific segments of society (e.g., workers, small-business owners, investors), many modern regulations focus on the health and safety of all citizens. Furthermore, whereas earlier regulations often focused on a particular industry or group of industries (e.g., the railroads or the securities industry), many modern regulations affect large segments of industry (e.g., Title VII of the Civil Rights Act of 1964 and regulations governing environmental pollution and workplace safety). Finally, whereas earlier congressional delegations of regulatory power tended to be quite broad (e.g., the FTC Act's prohibition of "unfair methods of competition" and "unfair or deceptive acts or practices"), many more recent regulatory statutes (e.g., the Clean Air Acts) have been extremely detailed.

What are the consequences of these changes in the nature of regulation? Far more businesses than ever before feel the impact of federal regulation, and far more areas of internal corporate decision-making are affected by regulation. These changes tend to erode the historic distinction between "regulated" and other industries, and to heighten the importance of business–government relations. Detailed regulatory statutes also increase Congress's role in shaping regulatory policy at the expense of administrative discretion, making regulatory policy arguably more vulnerable to legislative lobbying efforts.

"Captive" Agencies and Agencies' "Shadows"

Proponents of regulation have traditionally feared that regulatory agencies would become "captives" of the industries they were charged with regulating. Through "revolving door" appointments by which key figures move back and forth between government and the private sector, and through excessive reliance on "experts" beholden to industry, the independence of administrative agencies may be compromised and their effectiveness as regulators destroyed.

More recently, commentators sympathetic to business have argued that similar dangers to agency independence exist in the form of the nonindustry "shadow" groups that public interest organizations maintain to monitor agency actions (e.g., the Center for Auto Safety, which monitors the work of the Highway Transportation Safety Administration). Agencies may develop dependency relationships with their shadows or at least make decisions based in part on their shadows' anticipated reactions. Such informal means of shaping regulatory policy, when combined with the ability to challenge agency actions in court due to somewhat liberalized standing rules, have made public interest organizations important players in the contemporary regulatory process.

Deregulation versus Reregulation

A useful axiom for understanding the process of social and legal evolution is that *the cost of the status quo is easier to perceive than the cost of change.* Few things are more illustrative of the operation of this axiom than the history of regulation in the United States.

In the latter years of the 19th century, the social costs of living in an unregulated environment were readily apparent. Large business organizations often abused their power at the expense of their customers, suppliers, employees, and distributors, and sought to increase their power by acquiring their competitors or driving them out of business. Market forces, standing alone, were apparently unable to protect the public from defective, and in some cases dangerous, products. As a result of these and numerous other social and historical factors, this century has witnessed a tremendous growth in government and in government regulation of business.

Regulation, too, has its costs. Regulatory bureaucracies generate their own internal momentum and have their own interests to protect. They may become insensitive to the legitimate concerns of the industries they regulate and the public they supposedly serve. They may continue to seek higher and higher levels of safety, heedless of the fact that life necessarily involves some elements of risk and that

---

[15]See, for example, David Vogel, "The 'New' Social Regulation in Historical and Comparative Perspective," in *Regulation in Perspective,* ed. T. McGraw (Cambridge, MA: Harvard University Press, 1981), p. 155.

the total elimination of risk in a modern technological society may be impossible—or if possible, obtainable at a cost that we cannot afford to pay. At a time when many Americans are legitimately concerned about economic efficiency, as well as the ability of U.S. companies to compete effectively in world markets against competitors who operate in less regulated environments, these and other costs of regulation are also readily apparent.

As a result, in the last 15 to 20 years, we have witnessed substantial deregulation in a number of industries such as the airline, banking, railroad, and trucking industries. The results of these efforts are, at best, mixed. The case of airline regulation should suffice to make the point. Proponents of deregulation cite the generally lower fares that deregulation has produced. Opponents tend to point to increased airline overbooking practices, reduced or eliminated services to smaller communities, and increased safety problems, all of which, they argue, are products of deregulation. The costs of deregulation have generated predictable calls for reregulating the airline industry. The ultimate outcome of the deregulation versus reregulation debate will depend on which costs we as a society decide we would prefer to pay.

ETHICAL AND PUBLIC POLICY CONCERNS

1. Earlier in this chapter, you learned that agency formal rulemaking procedures are vulnerable to industry tactics aimed at delaying regulation (e.g., the example concerning the minimum peanut content of peanut butter). Are such industry tactics ethically justifiable?

2. In our discussion of the Freedom of Information Act, you learned that companies seeking to obtain useful information about their competitors frequently seek access to documents covered by the act. Is this an ethical way to gain access to information?

3. Although question 1 in this section focuses on delaying tactics practiced by industry, it is important to note that agencies have also been known to engage in delay and other tactics designed to frustrate citizens and organizations with whom they interact. For example, an agency may delay its response to an FOIA request, untruthfully arguing that staff shortages prevent a timely response, or it may refuse to turn over documents that it knows are

not exempt from disclosure, forcing those seeking disclosure to engage in expensive and time-consuming litigation to attain their ends. Are such agency tactics ethically justifiable?

PROBLEMS AND PROBLEM CASES

1. Title X of the Public Health Service Act provides federal funding for family-planning services. Section 1008 of the statute specifies that none of the federal funds provided under Title X are to be "used in programs where abortion is a method of family planning." In 1988, the Secretary of Health and Human Services issued new regulations that, among other things, prohibited family-planning services that receive Title X funds from engaging in counseling concerning the use of abortion as a method of family planning, referrals for abortion as a method of family planning, and activities amounting to encouragement or advocacy of abortion as a method of family planning. Various Title X grantees and physicians supervising Title X funds challenged the validity of the regulations and sought an injunction against their implementation. Were the regulations a permissible interpretation of Section 1008? Did the regulations violate constitutional guarantees?

2. In November 1984, the Federal Election Commission (FEC) began an investigation of the activities of the Lyndon Larouche Campaign for the Democratic Party's presidential nomination. The investigation centered on allegations that the campaign had falsified its records and obtained federal election matching funds by claiming that donations via credit cards had been made by individuals who denied making the donations. In December 1984, the FEC issued a subpoena requiring the campaign to produce records regarding the solicitation of contributions (including the names of solicitors and those solicited), contributions actually received, and all telephone records regarding the solicitation of funds. When the Larouche campaign failed to comply with the subpoena, the FEC brought an action in a federal district court to obtain enforcement. The district court ordered the campaign to comply with the subpoena. The Larouche campaign appealed on First Amendment grounds. Was the district court's compliance order proper?

3. In April 1982, the parents of an infant with Down's syndrome and other handicaps refused consent to surgery to remove an obstruction in the infant's esophagus that prevented oral feeding. In May 1982, after the child's death, the Secretary of Health and Human Services (HHS) promulgated regulations that, among other things, required hospitals and other health care providers to post notices that health care should not be withheld from infants on the basis of mental or physical handicap. The regulations were adopted pursuant to section 504 of the Rehabilitation Act of 1973, which permits the head of any executive branch agency to promulgate rules prohibiting discrimination against an "otherwise qualified handicapped individual . . . solely by reason of his handicap." The American Hospital Association (AHA) challenged the validity of the regulations. Did the Secretary of HHS possess an adequate rationale and supporting basis for the regulations?

4. Fenster, president and part owner of Utica Packing Company, was convicted of bribing a federal meat inspector, an employee of the United States Department of Agriculture (USDA). In a hearing before an administrative law judge (ALJ), the USDA sought a withdrawal of meat inspection services from Utica unless Fenster sold his ownership of Utica and withdrew from its management. The ALJ ruled in the USDA's favor, effectively eliminating Utica's ability to conduct its business. Utica appealed the decision to the USDA Judicial Officer, Donald Campbell, who had the power to make final adjudicative orders for the USDA. Campbell affirmed the ALJ's decision, and so did a federal District Court. The Sixth Circuit Court of Appeals, however, held that Campbell erred by not considering mitigating circumstances in the case. Upon reconsideration, Campbell reluctantly held that the mitigating circumstances prevented him from finding that Utica was unfit to receive inspection services. USDA executive officials strongly disagreed with Campbell's decision. They convinced the Secretary of Agriculture to replace Campbell with Deputy Assistant Secretary John Franke, who was not a lawyer and had no adjudicatory experience. Franke then reconsidered Campbell's decision at the USDA's request, finding that the mitigating circumstances were insufficient to justify Fenster's bribing the meat inspector. Utica appealed, arguing that its due process rights had been violated. Is Utica correct?

5. John Doe began work at the Central Intelligence Agency (CIA) in 1973 as a clerk-typist. Periodic

fitness reports consistently rated him as an excellent or outstanding employee. By 1977, he had been promoted to covert electronics technician. In January 1982, Doe voluntarily told a CIA security officer that he was a homosexual. Almost immediately, the CIA placed Doe on paid administrative leave and began an investigation of his sexual orientation and conduct. Doe submitted to an extensive polygraph examination during which he denied having sexual relations with foreign nationals and maintained that he had not disclosed classified information to any of his sexual partners. The polygraph officer told Doe that the test results indicated that his responses had been truthful. Nonetheless, a month later Doe was told that the CIA's Office of Security had determined that his homosexuality posed a threat to security. CIA officials declined, however, to explain the nature of the danger. Doe was asked to resign. When he refused to do so he was dismissed by CIA Director William Webster, who "deemed it necessary and advisable in the interests of the United States to terminate [Doe's] employment with this Agency pursuant to section 102(c) of the National Security Act." The statutory section cited by the director allows termination of a CIA employee whenever the director "shall deem such termination necessary or advisable in the interests of the United States." Doe filed suit against the CIA, arguing that his termination was unlawful under section 102(c) and various constitutional guarantees. The CIA moved to dismiss Doe's complaint, arguing that the director's decision was a decision committed to agency discretion by law and thus was not subject to judicial review. Was the CIA's argument correct?

6. Scott Armstrong submitted a Freedom of Information Act (FOIA) request that, among other things, called for the federal government to reveal a list of names of lower-level FBI agents who attended certain meetings at the White House during the mid-1980s. When the government refused to reveal the agents' names, Armstrong filed suit under the FOIA. Upholding this refusal, the district court agreed with the government's contention that the names of FBI agents should always be exempt from disclosure under the FOIA exemption for "personnel and medical files and similar files the disclosure of which would constitute a clearly unwarranted invasion of personal privacy." On appeal, Armstrong argued that the district court erred in concluding that the FOIA's privacy exemption justifies a categorical rule that FBI agents' names are exempt from disclosure. Was Armstrong correct?

7. On August 1, 1982, Larry Morrison, a pilot for Northwest Airlines, piloted a passenger airliner while he was intoxicated. Four days later, Northwest Airlines discharged him as an employee. The next day, Morrison began four weeks of voluntary alcoholism treatment. He attended weekly counseling sessions thereafter. On January 20, 1983, the Federal Aviation Administration (FAA) temporarily suspended his pilot certificate. Without a pilot certificate, Morrison could not pilot airplanes within the United States. On September 2, 1983, Morrison requested recertification, which the FAA granted subject to a few restrictions. Northwest Airlines sought judicial review of the FAA's recertification on the grounds that (1) recertifying Morrison would make the skies unsafe for Northwest airplanes, its crews, and its passengers and (2) the FAA's lenient recertification policy would make it more difficult for Northwest to deter drinking among its pilots and other employees. Were these injuries sufficient to give Northwest standing to seek judicial review of the FAA's decision to recertify Morrison?

8. The federal Clean Water Act provides for two sets of water quality measures: effluent limitations, which are promulgated by the Environmental Protection Agency (EPA), and water quality standards, which are promulgated by the states. The Clean Water Act generally prohibits the discharge of effluent into a navigable body of water unless the party making such a discharge obtains a permit to do so from a state with an EPA-approved permit program or from the EPA itself. The EPA issued a Fayetteville, Arkansas, sewage treatment plant a permit to discharge effluent into an Arkansas stream that ultimately reaches the Illinois River upstream from the Oklahoma border. The permit included conditions designed to make the Fayetteville discharge comply with Oklahoma's water quality standards. Oklahoma challenged the permit's issuance and terms. Following a hearing, an EPA administrative law judge affirmed the issuance of the permit. After the EPA's chief judicial officer did the same, Oklahoma sought judicial review in federal court. What standard of review should the court follow?

9. An agent of the Pennsylvania Department of Environmental Resources saw Disposal Service's loaded trash truck backing into a building that was used to compact waste to be loaded onto tractor-trailers for transportation and final disposal. Know-

ing the building's purpose and that Disposal Service did not have a permit to operate it as a transfer station, as required by the state Solid Waste Management Act (SWMA), the agent entered the property, went into the building, and observed the operation. Disposal Service was later prosecuted for operating a transfer station without a permit. Disposal Service moved to suppress the agent's evidence, arguing that his warrantless entry onto the property violated the Fourth Amendment. The state argued that the SWMA's provisions allowing such warrantless inspections were constitutional. Should the evidence be suppressed?

10. The *New York Times* (the *Times*) filed a Freedom of Information Act (FOIA) request with the National Aeronautics and Space Administration (NASA) for "transcripts of all voice and data communications recorded aboard the space shuttle *Challenger*" on the day when the shuttle self-destructed, killing all seven astronauts on board. The *Times* also requested copies of voice communication tapes. NASA provided a written transcript of the only voice recording made, but refused to turn over a copy of the tape itself, arguing that to do so would violate the privacy of the astronauts' families by exposing them to replays of their loved ones' voices. NASA argued that the tape was exempt from disclosure under Exemption 6 to the FOIA because the human voice, being unique to each individual, "clearly is information about the individual and identifiable as such." Should NASA turn over the tape?

11. Section 203(a) of the federal Communications Act required communications common carriers to file tariffs with the Federal Communications Commission (FCC). Section 203(b) of the same statute authorized the FCC to "modify any requirement made by or under" section 203. Relying on its modification authority under section 203(b), the FCC issued a series of orders during the 1980s and early 1990s. These orders made tariff filing optional for all nondominant long-distance carriers. American Telephone and Telegraph Co. (AT&T), the only long-distance carrier classified as dominant, asked the U.S. Court of Appeals for the District of Columbia Circuit to reverse these FCC orders. AT&T contended that making tariff filing optional for nondominant long-distance carriers was not a valid exercise of the FCC's modification authority under section 203(b). Was AT&T correct in this contention?

The Federal Trade Commission Act and Consumer Protection Laws

As Chapter 20 demonstrates, consumers' ability to recover damages for defective products increased dramatically during the 1960s and 1970s. *Direct government regulation* of consumer matters also grew tremendously during those decades. This chapter addresses federal consumer protection regulation. It begins with a general discussion of America's main consumer watchdog: the Federal Trade Commission (FTC). After describing how the FTC operates, the chapter examines its regulation of anticompetitive, deceptive, and unfair business practices. Then we discuss various other federal laws that regulate consumer matters, many of which involve consumer credit. ∞

THE FEDERAL TRADE COMMISSION

The Federal Trade Commission was formed shortly after the 1914 enactment of the Federal Trade Commission Act (FTC Act).[1] The FTC is an independent federal agency, which means that it is outside the executive branch of the federal government and is less subject to political control than

---

[1]See Chapter 46 for further discussion of the FTC's creation, organization, powers, and status as an independent agency.

agencies that are executive departments. The FTC is headed by five commissioners appointed by the president and confirmed by the Senate for staggered seven-year terms. The president designates one of the commissioners as chairman of the FTC. The FTC has a Washington headquarters and several regional offices located throughout the United States. Figure 1 in Chapter 46 sets out the Commission's internal organization.

The FTC's Powers

The FTC's principal missions are to keep the U.S. economy both *free* and *fair.* As Figure 1 suggests, Congress has given the Commission many tools for accomplishing these missions. By far the most important is section 5 of the FTC Act, which empowers the Commission to prevent: (1) unfair methods of competition, and (2) unfair or deceptive acts or practices. We examine these bases of FTC authority later in this chapter. The Commission also enforces the consumer protection and consumer credit measures discussed in the last half of the chapter. Finally, the FTC enforces various other federal acts, some of which are listed in Figure 1.

FTC Enforcement Procedures

The FTC has many legal tools for ensuring compliance with the statutes it administers. The three most important FTC enforcement devices are its procedures for facilitating voluntary compliance, its issuance of trade regulation rules, and its adjudicative proceedings.

FIGURE   **1**

Some of the Major Acts Enforced by the FTC

Regulation of Economic Competition
FTC Act Section 5 (including Sherman Act standards)—discussed in this chapter and in Chapter 48
Clayton Act—discussed in Chapter 49
Robinson-Patman Act—also discussed in Chapter 49
Hart-Scott-Rodino Antitrust Improvements Act of 1976—requires that certain companies planning mergers notify and provide information to FTC and Justice Department
Consumer Protection Measures Discussed in This Chapter
FTC Act Section 5
Telemarketing and Consumer Fraud and Abuse Prevention Act
Magnuson-Moss Warranty Act
Truth in Lending Act (including 1988 Fair Credit and Charge Card Disclosure Act and Home Equity Loan Consumer Protection Act)
Consumer Leasing Act
Fair Credit Reporting Act
Equal Credit Opportunity Act
Fair Credit Billing Act
Fair Debt Collection Practices Act
Other Measures
Export Trade Act—empowers FTC to supervise registration and operation of associations of American exporters engaged in export trade
Fair Packaging and Labeling Act—regulates packaging and labeling of consumer products to ensure accurate quality and value comparisons
Flammable Fabrics Act—regulates manufacture, sale, and importation of flammable fabrics, with FTC having some enforcement powers
Fur Products Labeling Act—regulates labeling, other identification, and advertising of fur products
Hobby Protection Act—regulates certain imitations of political campaign materials and certain imitation coins and paper money
Lanham Act—empowers FTC to petition for the cancellation of certain trademarks
Smokeless Tobacco Act—empowers FTC to approve manufacturers' plans for rotation and display of statements on smokeless tobacco packages and ads
Textile Fiber Products Identification Act—regulates labeling and other identification of textile fiber products
Wool Products Labeling Act—regulates labeling and other identification of wool products

Sources: *1995–96 United States Government Manual* and various statutes.

Voluntary Compliance   The FTC promotes voluntary, cooperative business behavior by issuing advisory opinions and industry guides. An **advisory opinion** is the Commission's response to a private party's query about the legality of proposed business conduct. The FTC is not obligated to furnish advisory opinions. The Commission may rescind a previously issued opinion when the public interest requires. When the FTC does so, however, it cannot proceed against the opinion's recipient for actions taken in good faith reliance on the opinion without giving the recipient notice of the rescission and an opportunity to discontinue those actions.

Industry guides are FTC interpretations of the laws it administers. Their purpose is to encourage businesses to abandon certain unlawful practices. To further this end, industry guides are written in lay language. Industry guides lack the force of law. Often, however, behavior that violates an industry guide also violates one of the statutes or other rules the Commission enforces.

Trade Regulation Rules   Unlike industry guides, FTC **trade regulation rules** are written in legalistic language and have the force of law. Thus, the FTC can proceed directly against those who engage in practices forbidden by a trade regulation rule. This may occur through the *adjudicative proceedings* discussed immediately below. The Commission may also obtain a federal district court *civil penalty* of up to $10,000 for each knowing violation of a rule. Furthermore, it may institute court proceedings to obtain various forms of *consumer redress,* including the payment of damages, the refund of money, the return of property, and the reformation or rescission of contracts.

FTC Adjudicative Proceedings   Often, the FTC proceeds against violators of statutes or trade regulation rules by administrative action within the Commission itself. The FTC obtains evidence of possible violations from private parties, government bodies, and its own investigations. If, after further investigation and discussion, it decides to proceed against the alleged offender (the *respondent*), it enters a formal complaint. The case is heard in a public administrative hearing called an *adjudicative proceeding*. An FTC administrative law judge presides over this proceeding.[2] The judge's decision can be appealed to the FTC's five commissioners and then to the federal courts of appeals and the U.S. Supreme Court.

The usual penalty resulting from a final decision against the respondent is an FTC **cease-and-desist order.** This is a command ordering the respondent to stop its illegal behavior. As you will see later in the chapter, however, courts have upheld FTC orders going beyond the command to cease and desist. The civil penalty for noncompliance with a cease-and-desist order is up to $10,000 per violation. Where there is a continuing failure to obey a final order, each day that the violation continues is considered a separate violation.

Many alleged violations are never adjudicated by the FTC. Instead, they are settled through a **consent order.** This is an order approving a negotiated agreement in which the respondent promises to cease certain activities. Consent orders normally provide that the respondent does not admit any violation of the law. The failure to observe a consent order is punishable by civil penalties.

ANTICOMPETITIVE BEHAVIOR

Section 5 of the FTC Act empowers the Commission to prevent "unfair methods of competition." This language allows the FTC to regulate anticompetitive practices made unlawful by the Sherman Act.[3] The Commission also has statutory authority to enforce the Clayton and Robinson-Patman Acts.[4]

For the most part, section 5's application to anticompetitive behavior involves the orthodox antitrust violations discussed in the following two chapters. Section 5, however, also reaches anticompetitive behavior *not covered by other antitrust statutes*. In addition, section 5 enables the FTC to proceed against *potential* or *incipient* antitrust violations.

DECEPTION AND UNFAIRNESS

Section 5 of the FTC Act also prohibits "unfair or deceptive acts or practices" in commercial settings. This language enables the FTC to regulate a wide range of activities that disadvantage consumers. In

---

[2]Chapter 46 describes federal administrative proceedings.

[3]Chapter 48 discusses the Sherman Act.

[4]Chapter 49 discusses the Clayton and Robinson-Patman Acts.

doing so, the Commission may seek to prove that the activity is *deceptive,* or that it is *unfair.* Here, we set out the general standards that the FTC uses to define each of these section 5 violations. Much of this discussion involves FTC regulation of advertising, but the standards we outline apply to many other misrepresentations, omissions, and practices. Although their details are beyond the scope of this text, the Commission also has enacted numerous trade regulation rules defining specific deceptive and unfair practices.

Deception

The FTC determines the deceptiveness of advertising and other business practices on a case-by-case basis. Courts often defer to the Commission's determinations. To be considered deceptive under the FTC's 1983 Policy Statement on Deception, an activity must: (1) involve a *material* misrepresentation, omission, or practice; (2) that is *likely to mislead* a consumer; (3) who acts *reasonably* under the circumstances.

Representation, Omission, or Practice Likely to Mislead   Sometimes, sellers *expressly* make false or misleading claims in their advertisements or other representations. As revealed in the *Kraft* case, which follows shortly, an advertiser's false or misleading claims of an *implied* nature may also be challenged by the FTC. The same is true of a seller's deceptive *omissions.* Finally, certain deceptive *marketing practices* may violate section 5. In one such case, encyclopedia salespeople gained entry to the homes of potential customers by posing as surveyors engaged in advertising research.

In all of these situations, the statement, omission, or practice must be *likely to mislead* a consumer. Actual deception is not required. Determining whether an ad or practice is likely to mislead requires that the FTC evaluate the accuracy of the seller's claims. In some cases, moreover, the Commission requires that sellers *substantiate* objective claims about their products by showing that they have a reasonable basis for making such claims.

The "Reasonable Consumer" Test   To be deceptive, the representation, omission, or practice must also be likely to mislead *reasonable consumers under the circumstances.* This requirement aims to protect sellers from liability for every foolish, ignorant, or outlandish misconception that some consumer might entertain. As the Commission noted some years ago, advertising an American-made pastry as "Danish Pastry" does not violate section 5 just because "a few misguided souls believe . . . that all Danish Pastry is made in Denmark."[5] Also, section 5 normally is not violated by statements of opinion, sales talk, or "puffing," statements about matters that consumers can easily evaluate for themselves, and statements regarding subjective matters such as taste or smell. Such statements are unlikely to deceive reasonable consumers.

Materiality   Finally, the representation, omission, or practice must be *material.* Material information is important to reasonable consumers and is likely to affect their choice of a product or service. Examples include statements or omissions regarding a product's cost, safety, effectiveness, performance, durability, quality, or warranty protection. In addition, the Commission presumes that express statements are material.

The *Kraft* case, which follows, illustrates the application of the FTC's deception test to an advertising claim of an implied nature. *Kraft* also reveals the Commission's broad discretion in fashioning appropriate orders once deceptive advertising has been proven.

---

[5]*Heinz v. W. Kirchner,* 63 F.T.C. 1282, 1290 (1963).

KRAFT, INC. v. FEDERAL TRADE COMMISSION   970 F.2d 311 (7th Cir. 1992)

I ndividually wrapped slices of cheese and cheeselike products come in two major types: process cheese food slices, *which must contain at least 51 percent natural cheese according to a federal regulation; and* imitation slices, *which contain little or no natural cheese. Kraft, Inc.'s "Kraft Singles" are process cheese food slices. In the early 1980s, Kraft began losing market share to other firms' less expensive imitation slices. Kraft responded with its "Skimp" and "Class Picture" advertisements, which were designed to inform consumers that Kraft Singles cost more because each slice is made from 5 ounces of milk. These advertisements, which ran nationally in print and broadcast media between 1985 and 1987, also stressed the calcium content of Kraft Singles.*

In the broadcast version of the Skimp advertisements, a woman stated that she bought Kraft Singles for her daughter rather than "skimping" by purchasing imitation slices. She noted that "[i]mitation slices use hardly any milk. But Kraft has 5 ounces per slice. Five ounces. So her little bones get calcium they need to grow." The commercial also showed milk being poured into a glass that bore the label "5 oz. milk slice." The glass was then transformed into part of the label on a package of Singles. In March 1987, Kraft added, as a subscript in the television commercial and as a footnote in the print media version, the disclosure that "one 3/4 ounce slice has 70% of the calcium of five ounces of milk."

The televised version of the Class Picture advertisements cited a government study indicating that "half the school kids in America don't get all the calcium recommended for growing kids." According to the commercial, "[t]hat's why Kraft Singles are important. Kraft is made from five ounces of milk per slice. So they're concentrated with calcium. Calcium the government recommends for strong bones and healthy teeth." The commercial also included the subscript disclaimer mentioned above.

The Federal Trade Commission instituted a deceptive advertising proceeding against Kraft under section 5 of the FTC Act. According to the FTC's complaint, the Skimp and Class Picture advertisements made the false implied *claim that a Singles slice contains the same amount of calcium as 5 ounces of milk (the* milk equivalency *claim). The FTC regarded the milk equivalency claim as false even though Kraft actually uses 5 ounces of milk in making each Singles slice because roughly 30 percent of the calcium contained in the milk is lost during processing.*

The administrative law judge (ALJ) concluded that the Skimp and Class Picture advertisements made the milk equivalency claim, which was false and material. He concluded that Kraft's subscript and footnote disclosures of the calcium loss were inconspicuous and confusing and therefore insufficient to dispel the misleading impression created by the advertisements. The ALJ ordered Kraft to cease and desist making the milk equivalency claim regarding any of its individually wrapped process cheese food slices or imitation slices. In addition, the ALJ ordered Kraft not to make other calcium or nutritional claims concerning its individually wrapped slices unless Kraft had reliable scientific evidence to support the claims.

Kraft appealed to the FTC commissioners (referred to here as "the Commission"). The Commission affirmed the ALJ's decision but modified it. According to the Commission, the Skimp and Class Picture advertisements made the false and material milk equivalency claim. The Commission modified the ALJ's orders by extending their coverage from Kraft's individually wrapped slices to "any product that is a cheese, related cheese product, imitation cheese, or substitute cheese." Kraft appealed to the U.S. Court of Appeals for the Seventh Circuit. (In a portion of the opinion not set forth here, the Seventh Circuit concluded, as had the ALJ and the Commission, that some of the Kraft advertisements made a further false claim of an implied nature: that Kraft Singles slices contain more calcium than imitation slices. The following portion of the Seventh Circuit's opinion addresses the milk equivalency claim.) ∞

Flaum, Circuit Judge [A]n advertisement is deceptive under [section 5 of the FTC Act] if it is likely to mislead consumers, acting reasonably under the circumstances, in a material respect. Our standard for reviewing FTC findings has been traditionally limited to the highly deferential, substantial evidence test.

In determining what claims are conveyed by a challenged advertisement, the Commission relies on two sources of information: its own viewing of the ad and extrinsic evidence. Its practice is to view the ad first and, if it is unable on its own to determine with confidence what claims are conveyed . . . , to turn to extrinsic evidence. The most convincing extrinsic evidence is a [consumer] survey . . . , but the Commission also relies on other forms of extrinsic evidence including consumer testimony, expert opinion, and copy tests of ads.

Kraft has no quarrel with this approach when it comes to determining whether an ad conveys *express* claims, but contends that the FTC should be required . . . to rely on extrinsic evidence rather than its own subjective analysis in all cases involving allegedly *implied* claims. The Commissioners, Kraft argues, are simply incapable of determining what implicit messages consumers are likely to perceive in an ad. Making matters worse, Kraft asserts that the Commissioners are predisposed to find implied claims because the claims have [already] been identified in the complaint.

Here, the Commission found implied claims based solely on its own intuitive reading of the ads (although it did reinforce that conclusion by examining the proffered extrinsic evidence). Had the Commission fully and properly relied on available extrinsic evidence, Kraft argues it would have conclusively found that consumers do not perceive the milk equivalency . . . claim in the ads. While Kraft's arguments may have some force as a matter of policy, they are unavailing as a matter of law. Courts, including the Supreme Court, have uniformly rejected imposing such a requirement on the FTC, and we decline to do so as well. We hold that the Commission may rely on its own reasoned analysis to determine what claims, including implied ones, are conveyed in a challenged advertisement, so long as those claims are reasonably clear from the face of the advertisement.

[Kraft relies on] the faulty premise that implied claims are inescapably subjective and unpredictable. In fact, implied claims fall on a continuum, ranging from the obvious to the barely discernible. The Commission does not have license to go on a fishing expedition to pin liability on advertisers for barely imaginable claims. However, when [implied] claims [are] conspicuous, extrinsic evidence is unnecessary because common sense and administrative experience provide the Commission with adequate tools to make its findings. The implied claims Kraft made are reasonably clear from the face of the advertisements, and hence the Commission was not required to utilize consumer surveys in reaching its decision.

Alternatively, Kraft argues that substantial evidence does not support the FTC's finding that the Class Picture ads convey a milk equivalency claim. We find substantial [supporting] evidence in the record. Although Kraft downplays the nexus in the ads between milk and calcium, the ads emphasize visually and verbally that five ounces of milk go into a slice of Kraft Singles; this image is linked to calcium content, strongly implying that the consumer gets the calcium found in five ounces of milk. Furthermore, the Class Picture ads contained one other element reinforcing the milk equivalency claim, the phrase "5 oz. milk slice" inside the image of a glass superimposed on the Singles package.

Kraft asserts that the literal truth of the . . . ads—[Kraft Singles] *are* made from five ounces of milk and they *do* have a high concentration of calcium—makes it illogical to render a finding of consumer deception. The difficulty with this argument is that even literally true statements can have misleading implications. Here, the average consumer is not likely to know that much of the calcium in five ounces of milk (30%) is lost in processing, which leaves consumers with a misleading impression about calcium content.

Kraft next asserts that the milk equivalency . . . claim, even if made, [is] not material to consumers. A claim is considered material if it involves information that is important to consumers and, hence, likely to affect their choice of, or conduct regarding, a product. In determining that the milk equivalency claim was material to consumers, the FTC cited Kraft surveys showing that 71% of respondents rated calcium content an extremely or very important factor in their decision to buy Kraft Singles, [and that a substantial percentage of respondents] reported significant personal concerns about adequate calcium consumption. [The Commission] rationally concluded that a 30% exaggeration of calcium content was a nutritionally significant claim that would affect consumer purchasing decisions. This finding was supported by expert witnesses who agreed that consumers would prefer a slice of cheese with 100% of the calcium in five ounces of milk over one with only 70%. [T]he FTC [also] found evidence in the record that Kraft designed the ads with the intent to capitalize on consumer calcium deficiency concerns.

Significantly, the FTC found further evidence of materiality in Kraft's conduct. Before the ads even ran, ABC television raised a red flag when it asked Kraft to substantiate the milk and calcium claims in the ads. Kraft's ad agency also warned Kraft in a legal memorandum to substantiate the claims before running the ads. Moreover, in October 1985, a consumer group warned Kraft that it believed the Skimp ads were potentially deceptive. Nonetheless, a high-level Kraft executive recommended that the ad copy remain unaltered because the "Singles business is growing for the first time in four years due in large part to the copy." Finally, the FTC and the California Attorney General's Office independently notified the company in early 1986 that investigations had been initiated to determine whether the ads conveyed the milk equivalency claims. Notwithstanding these warnings, Kraft continued to run the ads and even rejected proposed alternatives that would have allayed concerns over their deceptive nature. From this, the FTC inferred—we believe, reasonably—that Kraft thought the challenged milk equivalency claim induced consumers to purchase Singles and hence that the claim was material to consumers.

The Commission's cease and desist order prohibits Kraft from running the Skimp and Class Picture ads, as well as from advertising any calcium or nutritional claims not supported by reliable scientific evidence. This order extends not only to the product contained in the deceptive advertisements (Kraft Singles), but to all Kraft cheeses and cheese-related products.

First Amendment infirmities arise, according to Kraft, from the sweep of the order: by banning commercial speech that is only *potentially* misleading, the order chills some non-deceptive advertising deserving of constitutional protection. Kraft acknowledges that sweeping bans of this variety comport with traditional FTC practice, and have been repeatedly upheld against First Amendment challenges in the past. [Kraft nevertheless argues that a First Amendment problem exists because] the order is broader than reasonably necessary to prevent deception.

We reject Kraft's argument. To begin with, the Commission determined that the ads were *actually* misleading, not *potentially* misleading, thus justifying a total ban on the ads. Moreover, even if we were to assume the order bans some potentially misleading speech, it is only constitutionally defective if it is broader than reasonably necessary to prevent the deception. Kraft mischaracterized the [Commission's order] as a categorical ban on commercial speech when in fact it identifies with particularity two nutrient claims that the Commission found actually misleading and prohibits only those claims. It further places on Kraft the minor burden of supporting future nutrient claims with reliable data. This leaves Kraft free to use any advertisement it chooses, including the Skimp and Class Picture ads, so long as it either eliminates the elements specifically identified by the FTC as contributing to consumer deception or corrects this inaccurate impression by adding prominent, unambiguous disclosures. [T]he specific prohibitions imposed on Kraft in the FTC's cease and desist order are not broader than reasonably necessary to prevent deception and hence not violative of the First Amendment.

Alternatively, Kraft argues that the scope of the order is not reasonably related to Kraft's violation of the [FTC] Act because it extends to products that were not the subject of the challenged advertisements. The FTC has discretion to issue multi-product orders, so-called "fencing-in" orders, that extend beyond violations of the Act to prevent violators from engaging in similar deceptive practices in the future.

[The Commission] concluded that Kraft's violations were serious, deliberate, and easily transferable to other Kraft products, thus warranting a broad fencing-in order. We find substantial evidence to support the scope of the order. The Commission based its finding of seriousness on the size ($15 million annually) and duration (two and one-half years) of the ad campaign and on the difficulty most consumers would face in judging the truth or falsity of the calcium claims. [T]he FTC properly found that it is unreasonable to expect most consumers to perform the calculations necessary to compare the calcium content of Kraft Singles with five ounces of milk given the fact that the nutrient information given on milk cartons is not based on a five ounce serving.

As noted previously, the Commission [reasonably] found that Kraft's conduct was deliberate because it persisted in running the challenged ad copy despite repeated warnings from outside sources that the copy might be implicitly misleading. Kraft made three modifications to the ads, but two of them were implemented at the very end of the campaign, more than two years after it had begun. This dilatory response provided a sufficient basis for the Commission's conclusion. The Commission further [made the reasonable finding] that the violations were readily transferable to other Kraft cheese products given the general similarity between Singles and other Kraft cheeses.

Commission's order upheld and enforced.

Unfairness

Section 5's prohibition of *unfair* acts or practices enables the FTC to attack behavior that, while not necessarily deceptive, is objectionable for other reasons. As *International Harvester* demonstrates, the FTC focuses on *consumer injury* when it attacks unfair acts or practices. To violate section 5, this injury:

1. *Must be substantial.* Monetary loss and unwarranted health and safety risks usually constitute substantial harm, but emotional distress or the perceived offensiveness of certain advertisements generally do not.

2. *Must not be outweighed by any offsetting consumer or competitive benefits produced by the challenged practice.* This element requires the Commission to balance the harm caused by the act or practice against its benefits to consumers and to competition generally. A seller's failure to give a consumer complex technical data about a product, for example, may disadvantage the consumer, but it may also reduce the product's price. Only when an act or practice is injurious in its *net effects* can it be unfair under section 5.

3. *Must be one that consumers could not reasonably have avoided.* An injury is considered reasonably unavoidable when a seller's actions significantly interfered with a consumer's ability to make informed decisions that would have prevented the injury. For example, a seller may have withheld otherwise unavailable information about important product features, or used high-pressure sales tactics on vulnerable consumers.

Remedies

Several types of orders can result from a successful FTC adjudicative proceeding attacking deceptive or unfair behavior.[6] One possibility is an order telling the respondent to *cease* engaging in the deceptive or unfair conduct. Another is the *affirmative disclosure* of information whose absence made the advertisement deceptive or unfair. Yet another is *corrective advertising.* This requires the seller's future advertisements to correct false impressions created by its past advertisements. In certain cases, moreover, the FTC may issue an *all-products order* extending beyond the product or service whose advertisements violated section 5, and including future advertisements for other products or services marketed by the seller. The *Kraft* case, which appeared earlier in the chapter, illustrates such an order. Finally, the FTC may sometimes go to court to seek the civil penalties or consumer redress noted earlier or to seek injunctive relief.

---

[6]Such orders, and FTC regulation of deceptive and unfair advertising generally, may collide with the First Amendment protection of commercial speech discussed in Chapter 3. For the most part, however, the First Amendment has not been a major obstacle to the Commission. One reason is that the constitutional protection given commercial speech does not extend to false or misleading statements and thus does not protect deceptive advertising.

IN THE MATTER OF INTERNATIONAL HARVESTER COMPANY   104 F.T.C. 949 (1984)

Since at least the early 1950s, the International Harvester Company's gasoline-powered tractors had been subject to "fuel geysering." This was a phenomenon in which hot liquid gasoline would shoot from the tractor's gas tank when the filler cap was opened. The hot gasoline could cause severe burns and could ignite and cause a fire. Over the years, at least 90 fuel geysering incidents involving International Harvester tractors occurred. At least 12 of these involved significant burn injuries, and at least one caused a death.

International Harvester first discovered the full dimensions of the fuel geysering problem in 1963. In that year, it revised its owner's manuals to warn buyers of new gas-powered tractors not to remove the gas cap from a hot or running tractor. In 1976, it produced a new fuel tank decal with a similar warning. Due to an industrywide shift to diesel-powered tractors, however, this warning had a very limited distribution to buyers of new tractors, and it rarely reached former buyers. International Harvester never specifically warned either new or old buyers about the geysering problem until 1980, when it voluntarily made a mass mailing to 630,000 customers.

In 1980, the FTC issued a complaint against International Harvester, alleging that its failure to warn buyers of the fuel geysering problem for 17 years was both deceptive and unfair under FTC Act section 5. The administrative law judge agreed with the Commission on each charge. Due to International Harvester's notification program, however, he concluded that a cease-and-desist order was unnecessary. Both International Harvester and the FTC's complaint counsel appealed to the full Commission. The Commission concluded that International Harvester's failure to disclose the fuel geysering problem was not deceptive, primarily because only 12 of the approximately 1.3 million tractors sold by International Harvester during the relevant time period had been involved in geysering incidents that resulted in injury. In the following portion of its opinion, the Commission addressed the unfairness *claim.* ⌣

Douglas, Commissioner   Unfairness analysis focuses on three criteria: (1) whether the practice creates a serious consumer injury; (2) whether this injury exceeds any offsetting consumer benefits; and (3) whether the injury was one that consumers could not reasonably have avoided. We find that all three criteria are satisfied in the present case.

There clearly has been serious consumer injury. At least one person has been killed and eleven others burned. Many of the burn injuries have been major ones. It is true that [these injuries] involve only limited numbers of people, but conduct causing a very severe harm to a small number will be covered.

The second criterion states that the consumer injury must not be outweighed by any countervailing benefits to consumers or to competition that the practice also brings about. The principal trade-off to be considered in this analysis is that involving compliance costs. More information may be helpful to consumers, but such information can be produced only by incurring costs that are ultimately borne as higher prices by those same consumers. Harvester's program which finally led to an effective warning cost the company approximately $2.8 million. Here, however, Harvester's expenses were not large in relation to the injuries that could have been avoided. We therefore conclude that the costs and benefits in this case satisfy the second unfairness criterion.

Finally, the injury must be one that consumers could not reasonably have avoided. Here, tractor operators could have avoided their injuries if they had refrained from removing the cap from a hot or running tractor—something that both the owner's manuals and common knowledge suggested was a dangerous practice. However, whether some consequence is reasonably avoidable depends, not just on whether people know the steps to take to prevent it, but also on whether they understand the necessity of taking those steps. Farmers may have known that loosening the fuel cap was generally a poor practice, but they did not know the full consequences that might follow. Since fuel geysering was a risk that they were not aware of, they could not reasonably have avoided it. This is so even though they had been informed of measures to prevent it. Such information was not the same thing as an effective warning.

Having found that Harvester was engaged in unfair practices, we must now determine what corrective measures the public interest will require. Under the particular circumstances of this case, we will issue no order at all. First, Harvester's voluntary notification program has already provided all the relief that could be expected from a Commission order. Second, Harvester has not made a gasoline tractor since 1978 and does not appear likely to do so again in the future.

Decision of administrative law judge affirmed in part and reversed in part.

CONSUMER PROTECTION LAWS

The term *consumer protection* includes everything from Chapter 20's product liability law to the packaging and labeling regulations listed earlier in Figure 1. Here, we examine federal regulation of telemarketing practices, product warranties, consumer credit, and product safety.

Telemarketing and Consumer Fraud and Abuse Prevention Act

In the Telemarketing and Consumer Fraud and Abuse Prevention Act (Telemarketing Act), which was enacted in 1994, Congress required the FTC to promulgate regulations defining and prohibiting *deceptive* and *abusive* telemarketing acts or practices.

The FTC responded to this directive with the Telemarketing Sales Rule (TSR), which was promulgated in 1995.

For purposes of the TSR and the discussion in the following paragraphs, a *seller* is a party who (or which), in connection with a telemarketing transaction, offers or arranges to provide customers with goods or services in exchange for consideration. The TSR defines *telemarketer* as "any person who, in connection with telemarketing, initiates or receives telephone calls to or from a customer." It defines *telemarketing* as "a plan, program, or campaign which is conducted to induce the purchase of goods or services by use of one or more telephones and which involves more than one interstate telephone call." Exemptions from the telemarketing definition are provided for sellers that solicit sales through the mailing of a catalog and then receive customers' orders by telephone, and for sellers that make telephone calls of solicitation to a consumer but complete the transaction in a face-to-face meeting with the consumer.

A major feature of the TSR makes it a deceptive practice for telemarketers and sellers to fail to disclose certain information to a customer before she pays for the goods or services being telemarketed. The customer is regarded as having paid for goods or services once she provides information that may be used for billing purposes. The mandatory disclosures specified in the TSR include the total cost of the goods or services, any material restrictions or conditions on the purchase or use of the goods or services, and the terms of any refund or exchange policy mentioned in the solicitation (or, if the seller has a policy of not allowing refunds or exchanges, a disclosure of that policy). Various other mandatory disclosures are necessary if the telemarketing solicitation pertains to a prize promotion. The TSR also makes it a deceptive practice for a telemarketer or seller to misrepresent information required to be disclosed in the mandatory disclosures, or to misrepresent any other information concerning the performance, nature, or characteristics of the goods or services being offered for sale.

According to the TSR, a telemarketer or seller engages in an abusive practice if he: directs threats, intimidation, or profane or obscene language toward a customer; causes the telephone to ring, or engages a person in a telephone conversation, repeatedly and with the intent to harass, abuse, or annoy a person at the called number; or initiates a call to a person who

has previously stated that she does not wish to receive a call made by or on behalf of the seller whose goods or services are being offered. What would otherwise appear to transgress the last prohibition will not be considered a violation of the TSR, however, if the seller or telemarketer has adopted and implemented procedures designed to prevent further calls to a list of persons who have said they do not want to receive calls, and the making of a further call to a listed person was merely an error.

The TSR also makes it an abusive practice for a telemarketer to call a person's residence at any time other than between 8:00 A.M. and 9:00 P.M. local time at the called person's location. In addition, the telemarketer engages in an abusive practice if, in a telephone call he initiated, he does not promptly and clearly disclose the identity of the seller, the sales purpose of the call, the nature of the goods or services, and the fact that no purchase or payment is necessary in order to win a prize or participate in a prize promotion (if a prize or prize promotion is being offered). Still other abusive practices are enumerated in the TSR.

The FTC and state attorneys general may bring enforcement proceedings against violators of the Telemarketing Act and the TSR. Civil penalties of up to $10,000 per violation are among the available remedies in government-initiated proceedings. Under some circumstances, private citizens may sue violators for damages and injunctive relief.

The Magnuson-Moss Warranty Act

The Magnuson-Moss Warranty Act of 1975 mainly applies to *written warranties* for *consumer products*. Nothing in the act requires sellers to give a written warranty. Sellers who decline to provide such a warranty generally escape coverage. A consumer product is personal property that is ordinarily used for personal, family, or household purposes. In addition, many Magnuson-Moss provisions apply only when a written warranty is given in connection with the sale of a consumer product to a *consumer.* A consumer is a buyer or transferee of a consumer (one who does not use the product for resale or in his own business).

Chapter 20 discusses Magnuson-Moss's provisions giving consumers minimum warranty protection. Here, we examine its rules requiring that consumer warranties contain certain information and that this information be made available to buyers before the sale. Any failure to comply with these rules violates section 5 of the FTC Act and may trigger Commission action. Also, either the FTC or the attorney general may sue to obtain injunctive relief against such violations.

Required Warranty Information   The Magnuson-Moss Act and its regulations require the simple, clear, and conspicuous presentation of certain information in written warranties to consumers for consumer products costing more than $15.[7] That information includes: (1) the persons protected by the warranty when coverage is limited to the original purchaser or is otherwise limited; (2) the products, parts, characteristics, components, or properties covered by the warranty; (3) what the warrantor will do in case of a product defect or other failure to conform to the warranty; (4) the time the warranty begins (if different from the purchase date) and its duration; and (5) the procedure the consumer should follow to obtain the performance of warranty obligations. The act also requires that a warrantor disclose: (1) any limitations on the duration of implied warranties and (2) any attempt to limit consequential damages or other consumer remedies.[8]

Presale Availability of Warranty Information   The regulations accompanying Magnuson-Moss also contain detailed rules requiring that warranty terms be made available to a buyer before the sale. These rules generally govern sales to consumers of consumer products costing more than $15. They set out certain duties that must be met by sellers (usually retailers) and warrantors (usually manufacturers) of such products. For example:

1. *Sellers* must make the text of the warranty available for the prospective buyer's review before the sale, either by displaying the warranty in close proximity to the product or by furnishing the warranty upon request after posting signs informing buyers of its availability.

2. *Catalog or mail-order sellers* must clearly and conspicuously disclose in their catalog or solicitation either the full text of the warranty or the address from which a free copy can be obtained.

3. *Door-to-door sales.* To provide a concrete illustration of an FTC trade regulation rule, we include the full text of its door-to-door sales rule in Figure 2. As FTC rules go, this one is fairly short and straightforward.

4. *Warrantors* must give sellers the warranty materials necessary for them to comply with the duties stated in paragraph 1. Warrantors must also give catalog, mail-order, and door-to-door sellers copies of the warranties they need to meet their duties.

Truth in Lending Act

When Congress passed the Truth in Lending Act (TILA) in 1968, its main aims were to increase consumer knowledge and understanding of credit terms by compelling their *disclosure,* and to help consumers better shop for credit by commanding *uniform* disclosures. Now, however, the act protects consumers in other ways as well.

Coverage   The TILA generally applies to creditors who extend consumer credit to a debtor in an amount not exceeding $25,000.[9] A *creditor* is a party who regularly extends consumer credit. Examples include banks, credit card issuers, and savings and loan associations. Extending credit need not be a creditor's primary business. For instance, auto dealers and retail stores are creditors if they regularly extend credit. To qualify as a creditor, the party in question must also either impose a finance charge or by agreement require payment in more than four installments. *Consumer credit* is credit enabling the purchase of goods, services, or real estate used primarily for personal, family, or household purposes—not business or agricultural purposes. The TILA *debtor* must be a natural person; the act does not protect business organizations.

Disclosure Provisions   The TILA's detailed disclosure provisions break down into three categories.

1. *Open-end credit.* The TILA defines an open-end credit plan as one that contemplates repeated transactions and involves a finance charge that may be

---

[7]Actually, the act states a $5 figure, whereas the regulations accompanying it state a $15 figure.

[8]Chapter 20 discusses limitations on an implied warranty's duration and on a consumer's remedies.

[9]The $25,000 maximum does not apply where a creditor takes a security interest in a debtor's real property or in personal property, such as a mobile home, used as the debtor's principal dwelling. Here, the disclosure rules differ slightly from the rules for closed-end credit discussed shortly. In certain transactions of this kind, moreover, the debtor has a three-day rescission right whose details are beyond the scope of this text.

FIGURE **2**

The FTC's Door-to-Door Sales Rule: 16 C.F.R. Section 702.3(d)

(d) *Door-to-door sales.*

(1) For purposes of this paragraph:

(i) "Door-to-Door sale" means a sale of consumer products in which the seller or his representative personally solicits the sale, including those in response to or following an invitation by a buyer, and the buyer's agreement to offer to purchase is made at a place other than the place of business of the seller.

(ii) "Prospective buyer" means an individual solicited by a door-to-door seller to buy a consumer product who indicates sufficient interest in that consumer product or maintains sufficient contact with the seller for the seller reasonably to conclude that the person solicited is considering purchasing the product.

(2) Any seller who offers for sale to consumers consumer products with written warranties by means of door-to-door sales shall, prior to the consummation of the sale, disclose the fact that the sales representative has copies of the warranties for the warranted products being offered for sale, which may be inspected by the prospective buyer at any time during the sales presentation. Such disclosure shall be made orally and shall be included in any written materials shown to prospective buyers.

computed from time to time on the unpaid balance. Examples include credit card plans and revolving charge accounts offered by retail stores. Open-end credit plans require two forms of disclosure: (1) an *initial statement* made before the first transaction under the plan, and (2) a series of *periodic statements* (usually, one for each billing cycle). In each case, the required disclosures must be made clearly, conspicuously, and in meaningful sequence.

Among the disclosures required in the initial statement are: (1) when a finance charge is imposed and how it is determined, (2) the amount of any additional charges and the method for computing them, (3) the fact that the creditor has taken or will acquire a security interest in the debtor's property, and (4) the debtor's billing rights. Periodic statements require an even lengthier set of disclosures. Much of the information contained in a monthly credit card statement, for example, is compelled by the TILA.

2. *Closed-end credit.* The TILA requires a different set of disclosures for other credit plans, which generally involve closed-end credit. Closed-end credit such as a car loan or a consumer loan from a finance company is extended for a specific time period; the total amount financed, number of payments, and due dates are all agreed on at the time of the transaction. Examples of the disclosures necessary before the completion of a closed-end credit transaction include: (1) the total finance charge; (2) the annual percentage rate (APR); (3) the amount financed; (4) the total number of payments, their due dates, and the amount of each payment;

(5) the total dollar value of all payments; (6) any late charges imposed for past-due payments; and (7) any security interest taken by the creditor and the property that the security interest covers.

3. *Credit card applications and solicitations.* In 1988, Congress amended the TILA to impose disclosure requirements on credit card applications and solicitations. These elaborate requirements differ depending on whether the application or solicitation is made by direct mail, telephone, or other means such as catalogs and magazines. To take just one example, direct mail applications and solicitations must include information about matters such as the APR, annual fees, the grace period for paying without incurring a finance charge, and the method for computing the balance on which the finance charge is based.

Other TILA Provisions   The TILA has provisions dealing with *consumer credit advertising.* For example, the act prevents a creditor from "baiting" customers by advertising loan or down payment amounts that it does not usually make available. To help consumers put advertised terms in perspective, if ads for open-end consumer credit plans state any of the plan's specific terms, they must state various other terms as well. For instance, an advertisement using such terms as "$100 down payment," "8 percent interest," or "$99 per month" must also state other relevant terms such as the APR.

Due to a 1988 amendment, the TILA now regulates *open-end consumer credit plans involving an extension of credit secured by a consumer's principal dwelling*—basically, the popular home equity loans. The act controls *advertisements* for such plans, requiring certain information such as the APR if the ad states any specific terms and forbidding misleading terms such as "free money." It also imposes elaborate disclosure requirements on *applications* for such plans. These include matters such as interest rates, fees, repayment options, minimum payments, and repayment periods. Finally, the act also controls the *terms* of such a plan and the *actions* a creditor may take under it. For example: (1) if the plan involves a variable interest rate, the "index rate" to which changes in the APR are pegged must be based on some publicly available rate and must not be under the creditor's control; (2) a creditor cannot unilaterally terminate the plan and require immediate repayment of the outstanding balance unless a consumer has made material misrepresentations, has failed to repay the balance, or has adversely affected the creditor's security; and (3) the plan cannot allow a creditor to unilaterally alter its important terms.

Finally, the TILA includes rules concerning *credit cards.* The most important such rule limits a cardholder's liability for unauthorized use of the card to a maximum of $50. Unauthorized use is use by a person other than the cardholder, if this person lacks express, implied, or apparent authority for such use.[10]

Enforcement   Various federal agencies enforce the TILA. Except in areas committed to a particular agency, overall enforcement authority rests in the FTC. In addition, those who willfully and knowingly violate the act may face criminal prosecution. Civil actions by private parties, including class actions, are also possible.

Consumer Leasing Act

The Consumer Leasing Act, which was enacted in 1976, covers leases of personal property: (1) to natural persons (not organizations), (2) for consumer purposes, (3) for an amount not exceeding $25,000, and (4) for a period exceeding four months.

The act requires that a lessor make numerous written *disclosures* to a lessee before the consum-

mation of the lease transaction. Examples include: a description or identification of the leased property; the number, amount, and due dates of the lease payments; their total amount; any express warranties made by the lessor; and any security interest taken by the lessor. The act also requires that lease *advertisements* include certain additional information if they already state the amount of any payment, the number of required payments, the amount of the down payment, or that no down payment is required.

The Consumer Leasing Act subjects creditors that violate its disclosure requirements to the same civil suits permitted under the TILA. The FTC also enforces the act.

Fair Credit Reporting Act

The reports credit bureaus provide to various users may significantly affect one's ability to obtain credit, insurance, employment, and many of life's other goods. Often, affected individuals are unaware of the influence that credit reports had on such decisions. The Fair Credit Reporting Act (FCRA) was enacted in 1970 to give people some protection against abuses in the process of disseminating information about their creditworthiness.

Duties of Consumer Reporting Agencies   The FCRA imposes certain duties on consumer reporting agencies—agencies that regularly compile credit-related information on individuals for the purpose of furnishing consumer credit reports to users. A consumer reporting agency must adopt *reasonable procedures* to:

1. Ensure that *users employ* the information only for the following purposes: consumer credit sales, employment evaluations, the underwriting of insurance, the granting of a government license or other benefit, or any other business transaction where the user has a legitimate business need for the information.

2. Avoid including in a report *obsolete information* predating the report by more than a stated period. This period usually is 7 years; for a prior bankruptcy, it is 10 years. This duty does not apply to credit reports used in connection with certain life insurance policies, large credit transactions, and applications for employment.

---

[10]Express, implied, and apparent authority are discussed in Chapter 34.

3. Ensure *maximum possible accuracy* regarding the personal information in credit reports. The *Grant* case, which follows shortly, discusses this duty. However, the act does little to limit the *types* of data included in credit reports. In fact, all kinds of information about a person's character, reputation, personal traits, and mode of life seemingly are permitted.

Disclosure Duties on Users   The FCRA also imposes disclosure duties on *users* of credit reports—mainly credit sellers, lenders, employers, and insurers.[11] One of these duties applies to users who order an *investigative consumer report.* This is a credit report that includes information on a person's character, reputation, personal traits, or mode of living and is based on interviews with neighbors, friends, associates, and the like. If a user procures such a report on a person, it must inform him that the report has been requested, that the report may contain sensitive information, and that he has a right to obtain further disclosures about the user's investigation. If the person requests such disclosures within a reasonable time, the user must reveal the nature and scope of the investigation.

Another disclosure duty arises when, because of information contained in any credit report, a user: (1) rejects an applicant for consumer credit, insurance, or employment; or (2) charges a higher rate for credit or insurance. Here, the user must maintain *reasonable procedures* for advising the affected individual that it relied on the credit report in making its decision, and for stating the name and address of the consumer reporting agency that supplied the report.

---

[11]In addition to the duties stated here, the FCRA imposes disclosure duties on users who deny consumer credit, or increase the charge for such credit, because of information obtained from *someone other than a consumer reporting agency.*

Disclosure and Correction of Credit Report Information   After a request from a properly identified individual, a *consumer reporting agency* must normally disclose to that individual: (1) the nature and substance of all its information about the individual; (2) the sources of this information; and (3) the recipients of any credit reports that it has furnished within certain time periods. Then, a person disputing the completeness or accuracy of the agency's information can compel it to reinvestigate. As *Grant* makes clear, the credit bureau must delete the information from the person's file if it finds the information to be inaccurate or unverifiable. An individual who is not satisfied with the agency's investigation may file a brief statement setting forth the nature of her dispute with the agency. If so, any subsequent credit report containing the disputed information must note that it is disputed and must provide either the individual's statement or a clear and accurate summary of it. Also, an agency may be required to notify certain prior recipients of deleted, unverifiable, or disputed information if the individual requests this. However, there is no duty to investigate or to include the consumer's version of the facts if the credit bureau has reason to believe that the individual's request is frivolous or irrelevant.

Enforcement   Violations of the FCRA are violations of FTC Act section 5; the Commission may use its normal enforcement procedures in such cases. Other federal agencies may also enforce the FCRA in certain situations. The FCRA establishes criminal penalties for persons who knowingly and willfully obtain consumer information from a credit bureau under false pretenses, and for credit bureau officers or employees who knowingly or willfully provide information to unauthorized persons. Violations of the FCRA may also trigger private civil suits against consumer reporting agencies and users.

GRANT v. TRW, INC.   789 F. Supp. 690 (D. Md. 1992)

In 1989, Samuel Grant sued his landlord in a Maryland trial court. The landlord filed a counterclaim. Grant recovered $608 against the landlord, who recovered $476.10 against Grant. This left Grant with a net recovery of $131.90. In 1990, Texaco denied Grant's application for a credit card because a TRW, Inc., credit report obtained by Texaco stated that a judgment of $400 had been entered against Grant. After obtaining a credit report from TRW, Grant informed the credit bureau that the litigation involving his landlord had resulted in a net judgment in his (Grant's) favor. Eventually, TRW *sent Grant an "Updated Credit Profile" showing that the $400 judgment had been deleted from Grant's file.*

In May 1991, Grant again applied for a Texaco credit card. His application again was denied because the $400 debt appeared on his credit report. Grant then sued TRW under the FCRA in a Maryland trial court. After the case was removed to federal district court, TRW moved to dismiss Grant's claim. ⚭

Motz, District Judge   Grant first alleges that TRW violated the FCRA by failing to follow reasonable procedures assuring "maximum possible accuracy of the information concerning the individual about whom the report relates." In order to make out a prima facie violation of [this provision], a consumer must present evidence that a credit reporting agency prepared a report containing inaccurate information. Here, plaintiff concedes that the notation in the credit report that a judgment had been entered against him was accurate insofar as it went. There may be extreme instances in which a technically accurate statement is so inherently misleading that it would run afoul of the "maximum possible accuracy" requirement. For example, if a consumer were a victim of a credit card scam, it would hardly seem accurate for a consumer reporting agency to report that the person was "involved" in the scam. However, the possibility that such extreme cases might be presented does not justify rewriting the FCRA to render actionable the initial reporting of information which, although accurate, is deemed to be misleading because it is incomplete. "Accuracy" can be tested by verification, whereas a determination of "completeness" requires the exercise of judgment on potentially difficult questions concerning the meaning and effect of contextual information. Adding a "completeness" element substantially expands the duties imposed upon consumer reporting agencies and exposes them to dramatically increased litigation.

That is not the end of the matter, however. [The FCRA also] provides: "If the completeness or accuracy of any item of information contained in his file is disputed by a consumer, . . . the consumer reporting agency shall within a reasonable period of time reinvestigate and record the current status of that information unless it has reasonable grounds to believe that the dispute by the consumer is frivolous or irrelevant." This provision . . . places the burden upon the consumer to challenge incomplete information, but, once the challenge is made, it requires reinvestigation and recording of the information provided by the consumer. Here, Grant did notify TRW of the full circumstances surrounding the Maryland trial court judgment, but, inexplicably, after advising Grant that it would delete the challenged notation from his report, TRW neither effected the deletion nor recorded the information which Grant had provided. This dereliction is actionable under [the FCRA].

TRW's motion to dismiss denied.

Equal Credit Opportunity Act

The Equal Credit Opportunity Act (ECOA), originally passed in 1974, prohibits credit discrimination on the bases of sex, marital status, age, race, color, national origin, religion, and the obtaining of income from public assistance. The ECOA covers all entities that regularly arrange, extend, renew, or continue credit. Examples include banks, savings and loan associations, credit card issuers, and many retailers, auto dealers, and realtors. The act is not limited to consumer credit; it also covers business and commercial loans.

The ECOA governs all phases of a credit transaction. As authorized by the act, the Federal Reserve Board has promulgated regulations detailing permissible and impermissible creditor behavior at each stage. Even where the regulations do not specifically prohibit certain creditor behavior, that behavior may still violate the act itself. Moreover, a credit practice that is neutral on its face may result in an ECOA violation if the practice has an adverse statistical impact on one of the ECOA's protected classes.[12]

The ECOA also requires that creditors notify applicants of the action taken on a credit application within 30 days of its receipt or any longer reasonable time stated in the regulations. If the action is

---

[12]This resembles the adverse impact or disparate impact method of proof used in employment discrimination cases under Title VII of the 1964 Civil Rights Act. See Chapter 50.

unfavorable, an applicant is entitled to a statement of reasons from the creditor.

The ECOA is enforced by several federal agencies, with overall enforcement resting in the hands of the FTC. Which agency enforces the act depends on the type of creditor or credit involved. Civil actions by aggrieved private parties, including class actions, also are possible.

Fair Credit Billing Act

The Fair Credit Billing Act, which took effect in 1975, is mainly aimed at credit card issuers. Although the act regulates the credit card business in other ways, its most important provisions involve billing disputes.[13] To trigger these provisions, a cardholder must give the issuer written notice of an alleged error in a billing statement within 60 days of the time that the statement is sent to the cardholder. Then, within two complete billing cycles or 90 days (whichever is less), the issuer must either: (1) correct the cardholder's account; or (2) send the cardholder a written statement justifying the statement's accuracy. Until the issuer takes one of these steps, it may not: (1) restrict or close the cardholder's account because of her failure to pay the disputed amount; (2) try to collect the disputed amount; or (3) report or threaten to report the cardholder's failure to pay the disputed amount to a third party such as a consumer reporting agency.

Once an issuer has met the act's requirements, it must also give a cardholder at least 10 days to pay the disputed amount before making an unfavorable report to a third party. If the cardholder disputes the issuer's justification within the 10-day period allowed for payment, the issuer can make such a report only if it also tells the third party that the debt is disputed and gives the cardholder the third party's name and address. In addition, the issuer must report the final resolution of the dispute to the third party.

An issuer that fails to comply with any of these rules forfeits its right to collect $50 of the disputed amount from the cardholder. Because the issuer may still be able to collect the balance on large disputed debts, it is doubtful whether this provision does much to deter violations of the act.

---

[13]The Federal Reserve Board has promulgated regulations regarding the resolution of billing errors. The FTC has some enforcement authority under the act as well.

Fair Debt Collection Practices Act

Concern over abusive, deceptive, and unfair practices by debt collectors led Congress to pass the Fair Debt Collection Practices Act (FDCPA) in 1977. The act applies to debts that involve money, property, insurance, or services obtained by a *consumer* for *consumer purposes.* Normally, the act only covers those who are in the business of collecting debts owed to *others*. However, creditors who collect their own debts are covered when, by using a name other than their own name, they indicate that a third party is collecting the debt. The *Heintz* case, which follows shortly, focuses on whether attorneys involved in litigation over a consumer debt are subject to the FDCPA.

Communication Rules   Except when necessary to locate a debtor, the FDCPA generally prevents debt collectors from contacting third parties such as the debtor's employer, relatives, or friends. The act also limits a collector's contacts with the debtor himself. Unless the debtor consents, for instance, a collector cannot contact him at unusual or inconvenient times or places, or at his place of employment if the employer forbids such contacts. Also, a collector cannot contact a debtor if it knows that the debtor is represented by an attorney, unless the attorney consents to such contact or fails to respond to the collector's communications. In addition, a collector must cease most communications with a debtor if the debtor gives the creditor written notification that he refuses to pay the debt or that he does not desire further communications from the collector.

The FDCPA also requires a collector to give a debtor certain information about the debt within five days of the collector's first communication with the debtor. If the debtor disputes the debt in writing within 30 days after receiving this information, the collector must cease its collection efforts until it sends verification of the debt to the debtor.

Specific Forbidden Practices   The FDCPA sets out categories of forbidden collector practices and lists specific examples of each category. The listed examples, however, do not exhaust the ways that debt collectors can violate the act. The categories are:

1. *Harassment, oppression, or abuse.* Examples include threats of violence, obscene or abusive language, and repeated phone calls.

2. *False or misleading misrepresentations.* Among the FDCPA's listed examples are statements that a debtor will be imprisoned for failure to pay, that a collector will take an action it is not legally entitled to take, or does not intend to take, that a collector is affiliated with the government, and that misstate the amount of the debt.

3. *Unfair practices.* These include collecting from a debtor an amount not authorized by the agreement creating the debt, inducing a debtor to accept a collect call before revealing the call's true purpose, and falsely or unjustifiably threatening to take a debtor's property.

Enforcement The FTC is the main enforcement agency for the FDCPA, although other agencies enforce it in certain cases. The FDCPA also permits individual civil actions and class actions by the affected debtor or debtors.[14]

---

[14]Some debt collection practices might lead to tort liability for invasion of privacy or intentional infliction of emotional distress. Chapter 6 discusses these torts.

HEINTZ v. JENKINS   514 U.S. 291 (U.S. Sup. Ct. 1995)

Darlene Jenkins obtained a car loan from a bank. When she defaulted on the loan, the bank sued her to recover the balance due. The bank's attorney, George Heintz, wrote Jenkins a letter in an effort to settle the case. In the portion of the letter in which he stated the amount Jenkins allegedly owed, Heintz included $4,173 owed for insurance that the bank had purchased because Jenkins had not kept the car insured.

Jenkins sued Heintz under the Fair Debt Collection Practices Act (referred to below as "the Act"). She contended that Heintz's letter violated the Act's prohibition against attempting to collect an amount not "authorized by the agreement creating the debt," as well as its prohibition against making a "false representation of . . . the . . . amount . . . of any debt." Jenkins conceded that the loan agreement required her to keep the car insured "against loss or damage" and permitted the bank to buy such insurance to protect the car if she failed to do so. She asserted, however, that the $4,173 policy purchased by the bank was not the kind of policy the loan agreement contemplated, because it insured the bank not only against "loss or damage" but also against her failure to repay the loan. According to Jenkins, Heintz's representation about the amount of her "debt" violated the Act because the representation was false and part of an attempt to collect an amount not authorized by the loan agreement.

Reasoning that the Act does not apply to attorneys engaged in litigation, the federal district court dismissed Jenkins's lawsuit for failure to state a claim. The U.S. Court of Appeals for the Seventh Circuit reversed, holding that the Act applies to attorneys involved in litigation. This holding conflicted with the position the Court of Appeals for the Sixth Circuit had taken in a similar case. In order to resolve the conflict between circuits, the U.S. Supreme Court granted Heintz's petition for certiorari. ∞

Breyer, Justice The issue before us is whether the term "debt collector" in the Fair Debt Collection Practices Act applies to a lawyer who "regularly," *through litigation,* tries to collect consumer debts. The Act prohibits "debt collector[s]" from making false or misleading representations and from engaging in various abusive and unfair practices. The Act's definition of the term "debt collector" includes a person "who regularly collects or attempts to collect, directly or indirectly, [consumer] debts owed [to] another."

There are two rather strong reasons for believing that the Act applies to the litigating activities of lawyers. *First,* . . . [i]n ordinary English, a lawyer who regularly tries to obtain payment of consumer debts through legal proceedings is a lawyer who regularly "attempts" to "collect" those consumer debts. Second, in 1977, Congress enacted an earlier version of this statute, which contained an express exemption for lawyers. That exemption said that the term "debt collector" did not include "any attorney-at-law collecting a debt as an attorney on behalf of and in the name of a client." In 1986, however, Congress repealed this exemption in its entirety, without creating a narrower, litigation-related, exemption, to fill the void. Without more, then, one would think that Congress intended that lawyers be subject to the Act whenever they meet the general "debt collector" definition.

Heintz [asserts] that we should nonetheless read the statute as containing an implied exemption for those debt-collecting activities of lawyers that consist of litigating (including, he assumes, settlement efforts). He relies primarily on three arguments. *First,* Heintz argues that many of the Act's requirements, if applied directly to litigating activities, will create harmfully anomalous results that Congress simply could not have intended. Many of Heintz's "anomalies" are not particularly anomalous. For example, [Heintz notes a section of the Act that] forbids a "debt collector" to make any "threat to take an action that cannot legally be taken." [He argues] that, were the Act to apply to litigating activities, this provision automatically would make liable any litigating lawyer who brought, and then lost, a claim against a debtor. [W]e do not see how the fact that a lawsuit turns out ultimately to be unsuccessful could, by itself, make the bringing of it an "action that cannot legally be taken."

The remaining significant "anomalies" similarly depend for their persuasive force upon readings that courts seem unlikely to endorse. For example, Heintz's strongest "anomaly" argument focuses upon the Act's [provision that] requires a "debt collector" not to "communicate further" with a consumer who "notifies" the "debt collector" that he or she "refuses to pay" or wishes the debt collector to "cease further communication." In light of this provision, asks Heintz, how can an attorney file a lawsuit against (and thereby communicate with) a nonconsenting consumer or file a motion for summary judgment against that consumer?

We agree with Heintz that it would be odd if the Act empowered a debt-owing consumer to stop the "communications" inherent in [litigation] and thereby cause an ordinary debt-collecting lawsuit to grind to a halt. But, it is not necessary to read [the communications section of the statute] in that way. [The communications section contains] exceptions that permit communications "to notify the consumer that the debt collector or creditor may invoke" or "intends to invoke" a "specified remedy."

Courts can read these exceptions, plausibly, to imply that they authorize the actual invocation of the remedy that the collector "intends to invoke." The language permits such a reading, for an ordinary court-related document does, in fact, "notify" its recipient that the creditor may "invoke" a judicial remedy. Moreover, the interpretation is consistent with the statute's apparent objective of preserving creditors' judicial remedies. [I]t is easier to read [the communications provision of the statute] as containing some such additional, implicit, exception than to believe that Congress intended, silently and implicitly, to create a far broader exception, for all litigating attorneys, from the Act itself.

Second, Heintz points to a statement of Congressman Frank Annunzio, one of the sponsors of the 1986 amendment that removed from the Act the language creating a blanket exemption for lawyers. Representative Annunzio stated that, despite the exemption's removal, the Act still would not apply to lawyers' litigating activities. [He] said that the Act "regulates debt collection, not the practice of law. Congress repealed the attorney exemption to the Act, not because of attorneys' conduct in the courtroom, but because of their conduct in the backroom. Only collection activities, not legal activities, are covered by the Act." This statement, however, does not persuade us.

For one thing, the plain language of the Act itself says nothing about retaining the exemption in respect to litigation. The line the statement seeks to draw between "legal" activities and "debt collection activities" was not necessarily apparent to those who debated the legislation, for litigating, at first blush, seems simply one way of collecting a debt. For another thing, when Congress considered the Act, other Congressmen expressed fear that repeal would limit lawyers' ability to contact third parties in order to facilitate settlements and could very easily interfere with a client's right to pursue judicial remedies. They proposed alternative language designed to keep litigation activities outside the Act's scope, but that language was not enacted. Further, Congressman Annunzio made his statement not during the legislative process, but *after* the statute became law. It therefore is not a statement upon which other legislators might have relied in voting for or against the Act [;] it simply represents the views of one informed person on an issue about which others may (or may not) have thought differently.

Finally, Heintz points to a "Commentary" on the Act by the Federal Trade Commission's staff. It says that "[a]ttorneys or law firms that engage in traditional debt collecting activities (sending dunning letters, making collection calls to consumers) are covered by the [Act], but those whose practice is limited to legal activities are not covered." We cannot give conclusive weight to this statement. The Commentary of which this statement is a part says that it "is not binding on the Commission or the public." More importantly, we find nothing either in the Act or elsewhere indicating that Congress intended to authorize the FTC to create this exception from the Act's coverage—an exception that . . . falls outside the range of reasonable interpretations of the Act's express language.

For these reasons, we agree with the Seventh Circuit that the Act applies to attorneys who "regularly" engage in consumer debt-collection activity, even when that activity consists of litigation.

Decision of Seventh Circuit Court of Appeals affirmed.

Product Safety Regulation

Yet another facet of consumer protection law is federal regulation of product safety. As discussed in Chapter 20, sellers and manufacturers of dangerously defective products may be held civilly liable to those injured by such products. Damage recoveries, however, are at best an after-the-fact remedy for injuries caused by such products. Thus, federal law also seeks to promote product safety by *direct regulation* of consumer products.

The Consumer Product Safety Act The most important federal product safety measure is the Consumer Product Safety Act (CPSA). The CPSA established the Consumer Product Safety Commission (CPSC), an independent regulatory agency that is the main federal body concerned with the safety of consumer products. Among the CPSC's activities are the following: (1) issuing *consumer product safety standards* (which normally pertain to the performance of consumer products or require product warnings or instructions); (2) issuing rules *banning* certain *hazardous products*; (3) bringing suit in federal district court to eliminate the dangers presented by *imminently hazardous* consumer products (products that pose an immediate and unreasonable risk of death, serious illness, or severe personal injury); and (4) *ordering private parties to address "substantial product hazards"* after receiving notice of such hazards. The CPSA's remedies and enforcement devices include injunctions, the seizure of products, civil penalties, criminal penalties, and private damage suits.

Other Federal Product Safety Regulation Other federal statutes besides the CPSA regulate various specific consumer products. Among the subjects so regulated are toys, cigarette labeling and advertising, eggs, meat, poultry, smokeless tobacco, flammable fabrics, drugs, cosmetics, pesticides, and motor vehicles. Some of these laws are enforced by the CPSC and some by other bodies.

ETHICAL AND PUBLIC POLICY CONCERNS

1. In the *International Harvester* case earlier in this chapter, the FTC weighed the consumer injury caused by fuel geysering against the costs of providing effective warnings about it. In this case, 12 people had been seriously burned by fuel geysering over a period of about 40 years, and one person had been killed. The Commission concluded that the injuries that could have been avoided by a warning outweighed the $2.8 million apparently required for an effective warning. However, its method clearly left open the possibility that in some cases a practice's benefits to consumers or to competition might outweigh the harm it causes.

Is it morally right to balance personal injury and human life against economic gain? Doesn't this amount to putting a dollar value on human life? Isn't each human life infinitely precious? How can decisionmaking processes such as the FTC's ever be justified?

On the other hand, if you think that the Commission's balancing exercise *is* justifiable, how is one to strike the balance? How would you have decided the *International Harvester* case?

2. Over the years, some have argued that modern mass advertising for consumer products and services is much more *manipulative* than *informative.* The idea is that by playing on unconscious or semiconscious consumer impulses of all kinds, such advertising motivates consumers to buy products for reasons other than those products' innate attributes. Generally speaking, do you think that this charge is accurate or inaccurate? In answering, consider: (1) whether advertisers often try such ploys; and (2) whether they generally are effective when tried. Assuming for the sake of argument that the charge is generally accurate, does FTC Act section 5's ban on *deceptive* advertising do much to address the problem? What body of law discussed in this chapter might conceivably do so?

Again assuming that the charge is accurate, consider two other questions. First, how would manipulative advertising fare under the *utilitarian* ethical criteria discussed in Chapter 4? *Hint:* If advertising manipulates consumers, what happens to the idea that free competition maximizes consumer welfare by rewarding those who sell superior products and services and weeding out their inferior competitors? Second, how would manipulative advertising fare under the two versions of Kant's *categorical imperative* discussed in Chapter 4?

PROBLEMS AND PROBLEM CASES

1. For many years, advertisements for Listerine Antiseptic Mouthwash had impliedly claimed that Listerine was beneficial in the treatment of colds, cold symptoms, and sore throats. An FTC adjudicative proceeding concluded that these claims were false. Thus, the Commission ordered Warner-Lambert Company, the manufacturer of Listerine, to include the following statement in future Listerine advertisements: "Contrary to prior advertising, Listerine will not help prevent colds or sore throats or lessen their severity." Warner-Lambert argued that this order was invalid because it went beyond a command to simply cease and desist from illegal behavior. Is Warner-Lambert correct?

2. Pantron I Corp. sold a shampoo and conditioner known as the Helsinki Formula. Pantron promoted the Helsinki Formula as an aid in fighting male pattern baldness. According to Pantron, polysorbate was the main ingredient that made the Helsinki Formula effective in arresting hair loss and stimu-

lating hair growth. The Federal Trade Commission filed suit against Pantron on the theory that Pantron's advertisements made deceptive representations about the effectiveness of the Helsinki Formula, as well as deceptive representations that scientific evidence supported the effectiveness claims. The FTC sought injunctive and monetary relief. The evidence showed that the Helsinki Formula was effective for some users with male pattern baldness but that this effectiveness was probably due to the "placebo effect" (i.e., the effectiveness for some users stemmed from psychological reasons rather than from the inherent merit of the product). Because there was no scientifically valid evidence indicating that polysorbate is effective in treating hair loss or in inducing hair growth, the district court concluded that Pantron's advertisements were deceptive in representing that *scientific evidence* supported a conclusion that the Helsinki Formula was effective. The district court therefore issued an injunction that barred Pantron from representing, in its advertisements, that scientific evidence supports the alleged effectiveness of the Helsinki Formula in treating baldness or hair loss. However, because the Helsinki Formula did work for some users some of the time (whatever the reason), the district court concluded that the FTC had failed to carry its burden of proving that Pantron engaged in deceptive advertising when it represented that the Helsinki Formula was effective for persons with male pattern baldness. The court therefore refused to enjoin Pantron from making such a representation of effectiveness (i.e., a representation of effectiveness that did not go on to make the false claim of supporting scientific evidence). The court also refused to order monetary relief. In its appeal to the U.S. Court of Appeals for the Ninth Circuit, the FTC argued that when a product's effectiveness is due only to the placebo effect, an advertising claim of effectiveness is false and deceptive for purposes of the FTC Act. Was this FTC argument legally correct? Which party—the FTC or Pantron—was entitled to win the appeal?

3. World Travel Vacation Brokers, Inc., advertised Hawaii vacations by offering $29 certificates that could be redeemed for roundtrip airfare to Hawaii. To get these certificates, consumers had to book hotel reservations through World Travel for a minimum of eight days and seven nights at World Travel's "hotel cost." The ads stated that World

Travel could offer this $29 price because it had purchased excess frequent flyer coupons, its huge purchasing volume had enabled it to obtain big discounts from airlines, and the package was part of a promotional "deregulation special" offered by the airlines.

World Travel sold between 600,000 and 700,000 of the $29 Hawaii vacation certificates. Unfortunately for their purchasers, World Travel had effectively charged them full airfare by jacking up the "hotel cost." Language on the certificates, however, stated that "prices do not reflect actual hotel rates." Under the FTC's section 5 policy statement on deceptive advertising, did the consumers who purchased the certificates act reasonably under the circumstances?

4. Between 1966 and 1975, the Orkin Exterminating Company, the world's largest termite and pest control firm, offered its customers a "lifetime" guarantee that could be renewed each year by paying a definite amount specified in its contracts with the customers. The contracts gave no indication that the fees could be raised for any reasons other than certain narrowly specified ones. Beginning in 1980, Orkin unilaterally breached these contracts by imposing higher-than-agreed-upon annual renewal fees. Roughly 200,000 contracts were breached in this way. Orkin realized $7 million in additional revenues from customers who renewed at the higher fees. The additional fees did not purchase a higher level of service than that originally provided for in the contracts. Although some of Orkin's competitors may have been willing to assume Orkin's pre-1975 contracts at the fees stated therein, they would not have offered a fixed, locked-in "lifetime" renewal fee such as the one Orkin originally provided. Under the three-part test stated in the text, did Orkin's behavior violate FTC Act section 5's prohibition against *unfair* acts or practices?

5. Patron Aviation, Inc., an aviation company, bought an airplane engine from L&M Aircraft. The engine was assembled and shipped to L&M by Teledyne Industries, Inc. L&M installed the engine in one of Patron's airplanes. The engine turned out to be defective, so Patron sued L&M and Teledyne. One of the issues presented by the case was whether the Magnuson-Moss Act was applicable. Does the Magnuson-Moss Act apply to this transaction?

6. National Financial Services, Inc., a debt collection agency that serves magazine subscriptions clearinghouses, handled roughly 2.2 million accounts during 1986 and 1987. It sent letters to debtors whose accounts were delinquent. The average unpaid balance owed on these accounts was approximately $20. One letter sent by National Financial to a large number of debtors stated that their account "Will Be Transferred To An Attorney If It Is Unpaid After The Deadline Date!!!" Debtors who did not pay after receiving this letter received one or more letters that bore the letterhead of "N. Frank Lanocha, Attorney at Law." Lanocha prepared the text of these form letters and gave copies to National Financial's president, Smith. Smith then arranged for the letters to be prepared and mailed out. One of these letters contained the following statements: "Please Note I Am The Collection Attorney Who Represents American Family Publishers. I Have The Authority To See That Suit Is Filed Against You In This Matter." The letter also stated: "Unless This Payment Is Received In This Office Within Five Days Of The Date Of This Notice, I Will Be Compelled To Consider The Use Of The Legal Remedies That May Be Available To Effect Collection." The Federal Trade Commission sued National Financial, Smith, and Lanocha, alleging violations of the Fair Debt Collection Practices Act. How should the court rule?

7. Smith rented a television set from ABC Rental Systems. The rental agreement stated that the lease was a week-to-week arrangement and that it was terminable by either party at any time. The agreement stated the figures "$16.00/55.00" in a space provided for the rental rate. The $16 figure was the weekly rate; the $55 figure was a reduced monthly rate available to a consumer who wished to pay monthly. Smith was never provided with any of the disclosures required by the Consumer Leasing Act. Does the Consumer Leasing Act apply to this transaction?

8. In 1988, Vincent Mone quit his job at Sawyer of Napa, Inc., a California corporation whose president and CEO was Milton Dranow. When Mone established a competing firm, Dranow sued him for $5 million, alleging unfair competition. Three days before filing suit, Dranow had obtained a credit report on Mone from TRW, Inc., a credit reporting agency. Under the Fair Credit Reporting Act, did

TRW act properly in giving Dranow the credit report on Mone?

9. The Credit Bureau, Inc. (CBI), maintained credit records on consumers, among them a Mr. and Mrs. Rush. When the Rushes obtained a CBI report on themselves, they found an "R-9" credit rating (the lowest possible) next to the entry for their Macy's account. This poor credit rating caused the Rushes to be denied credit on several occasions. The Rushes sued Macy's under the Fair Credit Reporting Act. Will the Rushes win under the FCRA? Assume for purposes of argument that the entry was erroneous and was the fault of Macy's.

10. Sylvia Miller, a married woman, wanted to buy a pair of loveseats from a retail furniture store. The store offered to arrange financing for her through the Public Industrial Loan Company. Public later refused to extend credit to Miller unless her husband cosigned the debt obligation. The reason was a consumer reporting agency's unfavorable credit report on Miller. Was Public's action forbidden sex discrimination under the Equal Credit Opportunity Act? In any event, what other legal remedy might Miller have?

11. John E. Koerner & Co., Inc. applied for a credit card account with the American Express Company. The application was for a company account designed for business customers. Koerner asked American Express to issue cards bearing the company's name to Louis Koerner and four other officers of the corporation. Koerner was required to sign a company account form, under which he agreed that he would be jointly and severally liable with the company for all charges incurred through use of the company card. American Express issued the cards requested by the company. Thereafter, the cards were used almost totally for business purposes, although Koerner occasionally used his card for personal expenses. Later, a dispute regarding charges appearing on the company account arose. Does the Fair Credit Billing Act apply to this dispute?

12. Lenvil Miller owed $2,501.61 to a bank, which referred the collection of the debt to a collection agency, Payco-General American Credits, Inc. Payco sent Miller a one-page collection form whose front side listed Payco's address and provided infor-

mation about the creditor and the amount of the debt. In the middle of the page, in large, red, boldface type, was this statement: THIS IS A DEMAND FOR IMMEDIATE FULL PAYMENT OF YOUR DEBT. After that came these sentences: YOUR SERIOUSLY PAST DUE ACCOUNT HAS BEEN GIVEN TO US FOR IMMEDIATE ACTION. YOU HAVE HAD AMPLE TIME TO PAY YOUR DEBT, BUT YOU HAVE NOT. IF THERE IS A VALID REASON, PHONE US AT [telephone number] TODAY. IF NOT, PAY US—NOW. The bottom third of the form was almost completely filled by the word NOW, which appeared in white letters nearly two inches tall against a red background. At the bottom of the page in the smallest type appearing on the form was this statement: NOTICE: SEE REVERSE SIDE FOR IMPORTANT INFORMATION. The reverse side of the form contained the "validation notice" required by the Fair Debt Collection Practices Act (i.e., statements informing a consumer about how to obtain verification of the debt). Miller sued Payco, alleging that the form did not comply with the FDCPA. The federal district court granted summary judgment in favor of Payco. Was the district court correct in doing so?

13. 📼 *Video Case.* See "Henry and Wanda." Henry and Wanda, a married couple, had a joint charge account. Henry left Wanda following an argument over money. He then made many purchases on the account, eventually overdrawing it. As a result, Wanda received numerous phone calls at all hours of the day and night. In one of these calls, the caller referred to Wanda as a "deadbeat" because she would not pay her husband's debts. In another, the caller threatened to contact Wanda's employer. Eventually, one of the callers located Henry by contacting his mother. The caller told her that Henry's father had been involved in a serious accident, and that it was necessary to contact Henry so that he could donate blood to his father. Assuming that all these actions were taken by a covered debt collector and that Henry and Wanda are protected debtors, explain how these various practices *may* have violated the Fair Debt Collection Practices Act.

Antitrust: The Sherman Act

T he post–Civil War emergence and growth of large industrial combines and trusts significantly altered the business environment of earlier years. A major feature of this economic phenomenon was the tendency of various large business entities to acquire dominant positions in their industries by buying up smaller competitors or engaging in practices aimed at driving smaller competitors out of business. This behavior led to public demands for legislation to preserve competitive market structures and prevent the accumulation of great economic power in the hands of a few firms.

Although the common law had long held that contracts unreasonably restraining trade violated public policy, courts could implement this rule only by refusing to enforce such a contract if one of the parties objected to it. Legislation was therefore necessary to give the courts greater power to deal with the problem of anticompetitive practices. Congress responded in 1890 with the Sherman Act. It supplemented this response by enacting the Clayton Act in 1914 and the Robinson-Patman Act in 1936. ∞

PRESERVATION OF COMPETITION

In enacting the antitrust statutes, Congress adopted a public policy in favor of preserving and promoting free competition as the most efficient means of allocating social resources. The Supreme Court summarized the rationale for this faith in competition's positive effects when it said:

Basic to faith that a free economy best promotes the public weal is that goods must stand the cold test of competition;

that the public, acting through the market's impersonal judgment, shall allocate the nation's resources and thus direct the course its economic development will take.[1]

Congress thus presumed, in enacting the antitrust statutes, that competition was more likely to exist in an industrial structure characterized by a large number of competing firms than in concentrated industries dominated by a few large competitors. As Judge Learned Hand observed:

Many people believe that possession of an unchallenged economic power deadens initiative, discourages thrift, and depresses energy; that immunity from competition is a narcotic, and rivalry is a stimulant, to industrial progress; that the spur of constant stress is necessary to counteract an inevitable disposition to let well enough alone.[2]

Despite this longstanding policy in favor of competitive market structures, the antitrust laws have not been very successful in halting the trend toward concentration in American industry. The market structure in many important industries today is highly *oligopolistic,* with the bulk of production accounted for by a few dominant firms. Traditional antitrust concepts are often difficult to apply to the behavior of firms in these highly concentrated markets. Recent years have witnessed the emergence of new ideas that challenge various longstanding antitrust policy assumptions.

THE ANTITRUST POLICY DEBATE

Antitrust enforcement necessarily reflects fundamental public policy judgments about the economic activities to be allowed and the industrial structure best suited to foster desirable economic activity. Given the importance of such judgments to the future of the American economy, it is not surprising that antitrust policy spurs vigorous public debate.

Chicago School Theories

In recent years, traditional antitrust assumptions have faced a highly effective challenge from commentators and courts advocating the application of microeconomic theory to antitrust enforcement. These methods of antitrust analysis are commonly

called **Chicago School theories** because many of their major premises were advanced by scholars associated with the University of Chicago.

Chicago School advocates tend to view *economic efficiency* as the primary, if not the sole, goal of antitrust enforcement. They are far less concerned with the supposed effects of industrial concentration than are traditional antitrust thinkers. Even highly concentrated industries, they argue, may engage in significant forms of nonprice competition, such as competition in advertising, styling, and warranties. They also point out that concentration in a particular industry does not necessarily preclude *interindustry competition* among related industries. For example, a highly concentrated glass container industry may still face significant competition from the makers of metal, plastic, and fiberboard containers. Chicago School advocates are also quick to point out that many markets today are international in scope, so that highly concentrated domestic industries such as automobiles, steel, and electronics may nonetheless face effective foreign competition. In fact, they argue that the technological developments necessary for American industry to compete more effectively in international markets may require the great capital resources that result from concentration in domestic industry.

According to the Chicago School viewpoint, the traditional antitrust focus on the structure of industry has improperly emphasized protecting *competitors* rather than protecting *competition.* Chicago School theorists argue that the primary thrust of antitrust policy should involve *anticonspiracy* efforts rather than *anticoncentration* efforts. In addition, most of these theorists take a rather lenient view toward various vertically imposed restrictions on price and distribution that have been traditionally seen as undesirable because they believe that such restrictions can promote efficiencies in distribution. Thus, they tend to be more tolerant of attempts by manufacturers to control resale prices and establish exclusive distribution systems for their products.

Traditional Antitrust Theories

Traditional antitrust thinkers, however, contend that although economic efficiency is *an* important goal of antitrust enforcement, antitrust policy has historically embraced *political* as well as economic values. Concentrated economic power, they argue, is undesirable for a variety of noneconomic reasons. It may

---

[1]*Times-Picayune Co. v. United States,* 345 U.S. 594 (U.S. Sup. Ct. 1953).

[2]*United States v. Aluminum Co. of America, Inc.,* 148 F.2d 416 (2d Cir. 1945).

lead to antidemocratic concentrations of political power. Moreover, it may stimulate greater governmental intrusions into the economy in the same way that the post–Civil War activities of the trusts led to the passage of the antitrust laws. According to the traditional view, lessening concentration enhances individual freedom by reducing the barriers to entry that confront would-be competitors and by ensuring broader input into economic decisions having important social consequences. Judge Learned Hand summed up this perspective on antitrust policy:

> Great industrial consolidations are inherently undesirable, regardless of their economic results. Throughout the history of [sections 1 and 2 of the Sherman Act] it has been constantly assumed that one of their purposes was to perpetuate and preserve, for its own sake and in spite of possible cost, an organization of industry in small units which can effectively compete with each other.[3]

Effect of Chicago School Notions

Chicago School notions, however, have had a significant impact on the course of antitrust enforcement in recent years. The Supreme Court and many of President Reagan's appointees to the lower federal courts have given credence to Chicago School economic arguments in many cases. Some of President Reagan's appointees to the Department of Justice and the Federal Trade Commission were sympathetic to Chicago School policy views. Appointees during the Bush and Clinton administrations have been somewhat more inclined toward government enforcement of the antitrust laws than their Reagan administration predecessors were. Nevertheless, the presence on the federal bench of so many judges embracing Chicago School ideas means that those views are likely to continue to have an impact on the shape of antitrust law for the foreseeable future.

JURISDICTION, TYPES OF ANTITRUST CASES, AND STANDING

Jurisdiction

The Sherman Act outlaws monopolization and agreements in restraint of trade. Because the federal government's power to regulate business originates in the Commerce Clause of the U.S. Constitution, the federal antitrust laws apply only to behavior having some significant impact on *interstate* or *foreign* commerce.[4] Given the interdependent nature of our national economy, it is normally fairly easy to demonstrate that a challenged activity either involves interstate commerce (the "in commerce" jurisdiction test) or has a substantial effect on interstate commerce (the "effect on commerce" jurisdiction test). Various cases indicate that a business activity may have a substantial effect on interstate commerce even though the activity occurs solely within the borders of one state. Activities that are purely *intrastate* in their effects, however, are outside the scope of federal antitrust jurisdiction and must be challenged under state law.

The federal antitrust statutes have been extensively applied to activities affecting the international commerce of the United States. The activities of American firms operating outside U.S. borders may be attacked under our antitrust laws if those activities have an intended effect on our foreign commerce. Likewise, foreign firms "continuously engaged" in our domestic commerce are subject to federal antitrust jurisdiction. Determining the full extent of the extraterritorial reach of our antitrust laws often involves courts in difficult questions of antitrust exemptions and immunities (to be discussed in Chapter 49). The extraterritorial reach issue also suggests a troubling political prospect: Aggressive expansion of antitrust law's applicability may create tension between our antitrust policy and our foreign policy in general.

Types of Cases and the Role of Pretrial Settlements

Sherman Act violations may give rise to criminal prosecutions and civil litigation instituted by the federal government (through the Department of Justice), as well as to civil suits filed by private parties. A significant percentage of the antitrust cases brought by the Department of Justice are settled without trial through the use of *nolo contendere* pleas in criminal cases and *consent decrees* in civil cases. A defendant who pleads nolo contendere

---

[3]*United States v. Aluminum Co. of America, Inc.,* 148 F.2d 416 (2d Cir. 1945).

[4]Chapter 3 discusses the Commerce Clause in detail.

technically has not admitted guilt. The sentencing court, however, is free to impose the same penalty that would be appropriate in the case of a guilty plea or a conviction at trial. Consent decrees involve a defendant's consent to remedial measures aimed at remedying the competitive harm resulting from his actions. Because neither a nolo plea nor a consent decree is admissible as proof of a violation of the Sherman Act in a later civil suit filed by a private plaintiff, these devices are often attractive to antitrust defendants.

Criminal Prosecutions

Individuals criminally convicted of Sherman Act violations may receive a fine of up to $350,000 per violation and/or a term of imprisonment of up to three years. Corporations convicted of violating the Sherman Act may be fined up to $10 million per violation. Before an individual may be found criminally responsible under the Sherman Act, however, the government must prove an *anticompetitive effect* flowing from the challenged activity, as well as *criminal intent* on the defendant's part. The level of criminal intent required for a violation is a "knowledge of [the challenged activity's] probable consequences" rather than a specific intent to violate the antitrust laws.[5] Civil violations of the antitrust laws may be proved, however, by evidence of either an unlawful purpose or an anticompetitive effect.

Civil Litigation

The federal courts have broad injunctive powers to remedy civil antitrust violations. Courts may order convicted defendants to *divest* themselves of the stock or assets of acquired companies, to *divorce* themselves from a functional level of their operations (e.g., ordering a manufacturer to sell its captive retail outlets), to refrain from particular conduct in the future, and to cancel existing contracts. In extreme cases, courts may also enter a *dissolution decree* ordering a defendant to liquidate its assets and cease business operations. Private individuals and the federal Department of Justice may seek such injunctive relief regarding antitrust violations.

Treble Damages for Private Plaintiffs   Section 4 of the Clayton Act gives private parties a significant incentive to enforce the antitrust laws by providing that private plaintiffs injured by Sherman Act or Clayton Act violations are entitled to recover *treble damages* plus court costs and attorney's fees from the defendant. This means that once antitrust plaintiffs have demonstrated the amount of their actual losses (such as lost profits or increased costs) resulting from the challenged violation, this amount is tripled. The potential for treble damage liability plainly presents a significant deterrent threat to potential antitrust violators. For example, a famous antitrust case against General Electric Company and several other electrical equipment manufacturers resulted in treble damage awards in excess of $200 million. Some Chicago School critics have argued unsuccessfully that treble damages should be allowed only for *per se* antitrust violations, with plaintiffs who prove *"rule of reason"* violations being limited to recovering actual damages. (Per se and rule of reason violations are discussed later in this chapter.)

Standing

Private plaintiffs seeking to enforce the antitrust laws must first demonstrate that they have **standing** to sue. This means that they must show a *direct antitrust injury* as a result of the challenged behavior. An antitrust injury results from the unlawful aspects of the challenged behavior and is of the sort Congress sought to prevent by enacting the antitrust laws. For example, in *Brunswick Corp. v. Pueblo Bowl-o-Mat, Inc.,*[6] the operator of a chain of bowling centers (Pueblo) challenged a bowling equipment manufacturer's (Brunswick's) acquisition of various competing bowling centers that had defaulted on payments owed to Brunswick for equipment purchases. In essence, Pueblo asserted that if Brunswick had not acquired them, the failing bowling centers would have gone out of business—in which event Pueblo's profits presumably would have increased. The Supreme Court rejected Pueblo's claim because Pueblo's supposed losses flowed from Brunswick's having *preserved* competition by acquiring the failing centers. Allowing recovery for

---

[5]*United States v. U.S. Gypsum Co.,* 438 U.S. 422 (U.S. Sup. Ct. 1978).

[6]429 U.S. 477 (U.S. Sup. Ct. 1977).

such losses would be contrary to the antitrust purpose of *promoting* competition. The antitrust injury requirement is discussed further in the *Khan* case, which appears later in the chapter.

Importance of Direct Injury Proof that an antitrust injury is *direct* is critical because the Supreme Court has held that *indirect purchasers* lack standing to sue for antitrust violations. In *Illinois Brick Co. v. State of Illinois,*[7] the state of Illinois and several other governmental entities sought treble damages from concrete block suppliers who, they alleged, were guilty of illegally fixing the price of the block used in the construction of public buildings. The plaintiffs acknowledged that the builders hired to construct the buildings in question had actually paid the inflated prices for the blocks, but argued that these illegal costs probably had been passed on to them in the form of higher prices for building construction. The Supreme Court refused to allow recovery, however, holding that granting standing to indirect purchasers would create a risk of "duplicative recoveries" by purchasers at various levels in a product's chain of distribution. The Court also observed that affording standing to indirect purchasers would lead to difficult problems of tracing competitive injuries through several levels of distribution and assessing the extent of an indirect purchaser's actual losses.

A number of state legislatures responded to *Illinois Brick* by enacting statutes allowing indirect purchasers to sue under *state* antitrust statutes. The Supreme Court has held that the *Illinois Brick* holding does not preempt such statutes.[8]

SECTION I—RESTRAINTS OF TRADE

Concerted Action

Section 1 of the Sherman Act states that "[e]very contract, combination in the form of trust or otherwise, or conspiracy, in restraint of trade or commerce among the several states, or with foreign nations is declared to be illegal." A **contract** is any agreement, express or implied, between *two or more* persons or business entities to restrain competition; a **combination** is a continuing *partnership* in restraint of trade; a **conspiracy** occurs when *two or more* persons or business entities join for the purpose of restraining trade.

The above statutory language makes obvious the conclusion that section 1 of the Sherman Act is aimed at **concerted action** (i.e., *joint action*) in restraint of trade. *Purely unilateral action* by a competitor, on the other hand, cannot violate section 1. This statutory section reflects a basic public policy that businesspersons should make important competitive decisions on their own, rather than in conjunction with competitors. In his famous book *The Wealth of Nations* (1776), Adam Smith acknowledged both the danger to competition posed by concerted action and the tendencies of competitors to engage in such action. Smith observed that "[p]eople of the same trade seldom meet together, even for merriment and diversion, [without] the conversation end[ing] in a conspiracy against the public, or in some contrivance to raise prices."

Problems Posed by Concerted Action Requirement

Section 1's concerted action requirement poses two major problems. First, how separate must two business entities be before their joint activities are subject to the act's prohibitions? For example, it has long been held that a corporation cannot conspire with itself or its employees and that a corporation's employees cannot be guilty of a conspiracy in the absence of some independent party. What about conspiracies, however, among related corporate entities? In decisions more than 40 years ago, the Supreme Court appeared to hold that a corporation could violate the Sherman Act by conspiring with a wholly owned subsidiary. More recently, however, in *Copperweld Corp. v. Independence Tube Corp.,*[9] the Court repudiated the "intra-enterprise conspiracy doctrine." The Court held that a parent company is legally incapable of conspiring with a wholly owned subsidiary for Sherman Act purposes, because an agreement between parent and subsidiary does not create the risk to competition that results when two independent entities act in concert. It remains to be seen whether this approach extends to corporate subsidiaries and affiliates that are not wholly owned. *Copperweld's* logic would appear,

---

[7]431 U.S. 720 (U.S. Sup. Ct. 1977).

[8]*California v. ARC America Corp.,* 490 U.S. 93 (U.S. Sup. Ct. 1989).

---

[9]467 U.S. 752 (U.S. Sup. Ct. 1984).

however, to cover any subsidiary in which the parent firm has a controlling interest.

A second—and more difficult—problem frequently accompanies attempts to enforce section 1. This problem arises when courts are asked to *infer* (from the relevant circumstances) the existence of an agreement or conspiracy to restrain trade despite the lack of any *overt* agreement by the parties. Should parallel pricing behavior by several firms be enough, for instance, to justify the inference that a price-fixing conspiracy exists? Courts have consistently held that proof of pure *"conscious parallelism,"* standing alone, is **not** enough to establish a section 1 violation. Other evidence must be presented to show that the defendants' actions stemmed from an **agreement,** *express or implied,* rather than from independent business decisions. It therefore becomes quite difficult to attack *oligopolies* (a few large firms sharing one market) under section 1, because such firms may independently elect to follow the pricing policies of the industry "price leader" rather than risk their large market shares by engaging in vigorous price competition.

Per Se Analysis

Although section 1's language condemns "every" contract, combination, and conspiracy in restraint of trade, the Supreme Court has long held that the Sherman Act applies only to behavior that *unreasonably* restrains competition. In addition, the Court has developed two fundamentally different approaches to analyzing behavior challenged under section 1. According to the Court, some actions always have a negative effect on competition— an effect that cannot be excused or justified. Such actions are classified as **per se** unlawful. If a particular behavior falls under the per se heading, it is conclusively presumed to violate section 1. Per se rules are thought to provide reliable guidance to business. They also simplify otherwise lengthy antitrust litigation, because if per se unlawful behavior is proven, the defendant cannot assert any supposed justifications in an attempt to avoid liability.

Per se rules, however, are frequently criticized on the ground that they tend to oversimplify complex economic realities. Recent decisions indicate that for *some* economic activities, the Supreme Court is moving away from per se rules and instead adopting "rule of reason" analysis. This trend is consistent with the Court's increased inclination to consider new economic theories that seek to justify behavior previously held to be per se unlawful.

"Rule of Reason" Analysis

Behavior not classified as per se unlawful is judged under the **"rule of reason."** This approach requires a detailed inquiry into the actual competitive effects of the defendant's actions and includes consideration of any justifications that the defendant may advance. If the court concludes that the challenged activity had a significant anticompetitive effect that was not offset by any positive effect on competition or other social benefit such as enhanced economic efficiency, the activity will be held to violate section 1. On the other hand, if the court concludes that the justifications advanced by the defendant outweigh the harm to competition resulting from the defendant's activity, there is no section 1 violation.

The following subsections of the chapter examine some of the behaviors held to violate section 1 of the Sherman Act. The legal treatment (per se or rule of reason) given to the respective behaviors is also considered.

Horizontal Price-Fixing

An essential attribute of a free market is that the price of goods and services is determined by the free play of the impersonal forces of the marketplace. Attempts by competitors to interfere with market forces and control prices—called **horizontal price-fixing**—have long been held per se unlawful under section 1. Price-fixing may take the form of direct agreements among competitors about the price at which they sell or buy a particular product or service. It may also be accomplished by agreements on the quantity of goods to be produced, offered for sale, or bought. In one famous case, an agreement by major oil refiners to purchase and store the excess production of small independent refiners was held to amount to price-fixing because the purpose of the agreement was to affect the market price for gasoline by artificially limiting the available supply.[10]

Some commentators have suggested that agreements among competitors to fix *maximum* prices should be treated under a rule of reason approach

---

[10]*United States v. Socony-Vacuum Oil Co.,* 310 U.S. 150 (U.S. Sup. Ct. 1940).

rather than the harsher per se standard because, in some instances, such agreements may result in savings to consumers. In addition, lower courts have occasionally sought to craft exceptions to the rule that horizontal price-fixing triggers per se treatment. It is important to note, however, that the Supreme Court continues to adhere to the longstanding rule of per se illegality for any form of horizontal price-fixing. In the *Denny's Marina* case, which follows, a federal court of appeals overturned a district court's attempt to limit the applicability of the per se rule in the horizontal price-fixing context.

DENNY'S MARINA, INC. v. RENFRO PRODUCTIONS, INC. 8 F.3d 1217 (7th Cir. 1993)

enny's Marina, Inc. filed an antitrust action, described more fully below, against various defendants: the "Renfro Defendants" (Renfro Productions, Inc., Indianapolis Boat, Sport, and Travel Show, Inc., and individuals connected with those firms); "CIMDA" (the Central Indiana Marine Dealers Association); and the "Dealer Defendants" (various boat dealers who competed with Denny's in the sale of fishing boats, motors, trailers, and marine accessories in the central Indiana market). The Renfro Defendants operate two boat shows each year, one in the spring and one in the fall, at the Indiana State Fairgrounds. The spring show has occurred annually for more than 30 years and is one of the top three boat shows in the United States. It attracts between 160,000 and 191,000 consumers each year. The fall show is a smaller operation that has occurred each year since 1987. Numerous boat dealers participate in the two shows.

Denny's participated in the fall show in 1988, 1989, and 1990. It participated in the spring show in 1989 and 1990. According to allegations made by Denny's in its antitrust complaint, Denny's was quite successful at each of these shows, apparently because it urged customers to shop the other dealers and then return to Denny's for a lower price. After the 1989 spring show, some of the Dealer Defendants began to complain (according to Denny's) to the Renfro Defendants about the sales methods used by Denny's. In addition, Denny's alleged, the Dealer Defendants spent a significant part of a CIMDA meeting venting frustration about similar sales tactics used by Denny's at the 1990 spring show. Denny's also asserted that the Dealer Defendants' complaints to the Renfro Defendants escalated, and that as a result, the Renfro Defendants informed Denny's after the 1990 fall show that Denny's could no longer participate in the boat shows.

Denny's claimed that the above-described conduct of the defendants amounted to a conspiracy, prohibited by Sherman Act section 1, to exclude Denny's from participating in the boat shows because its policy was to "meet or beat" its competitors' prices at the shows. When the district court granted the defendants' motions for summary judgment, Denny's appealed to the Seventh Circuit Court of Appeals.

Cummings, Circuit Judge Because summary judgment was granted to the defendants, the facts alleged by Denny's and any inferences therefrom must be construed in its favor. Summary judgment will be denied if a reasonable jury could return a verdict for the plaintiff.

A successful claim under Section 1 of the Sherman Act requires proof of three elements: (1) a contract, combination, or conspiracy; (2) a resultant unreasonable restraint of trade in the relevant market; and (3) an accompanying injury. The district court noted that [for purposes of a ruling on their summary judgment motions] defendants do not dispute the first and third elements of proof. Hence the parties' only argument is whether Denny's has made a sufficient showing of the second element, unreasonable restraint of trade, to withstand defendants' motions for summary judgment.

There are two standards for evaluating whether an alleged restraint of trade is unreasonable: the rule of reason and the per se rule. The nature of the restraint determines which rule will be applied. Because the restraint alleged by Denny's constitutes a horizontal price-fixing conspiracy, it is per se an unreasonable restraint of trade [under a long line of Supreme Court decisions]. The conspiracy in this case was horizontal because it . . . consisted of Denny's competitors and their association. That the conspiracy was joined by the operators of the . . . boat shows does not transform it into a vertical agreement.

Likewise, the conspiracy was to fix prices. Price-fixing agreements need not include "explicit agreement on prices to be charged or that one party have the right to be consulted about the other's prices." *Palmer v. BRG of Georgia, Inc.* (1990). "Under the Sherman Act a combination formed for the purpose and with the effect of raising, depressing, fixing, pegging, or stabilizing the price of a commodity in interstate or foreign commerce is illegal per se." *United States v. Socony Vacuum-Oil Co.* (1940). Concerted action by dealers to protect themselves from price competition by discounters constitutes horizontal price-fixing. Hence the actions of the Dealer Defendants and CIMDA, joined by the Renfro Defendants, to prevent Denny's from participating in the boat shows constitutes a horizontal price-fixing conspiracy notwithstanding the apparent lack of an explicit agreement to set prices.

So far, the position of this court is similar to that of the court below. Nevertheless, having essentially found that Denny's had adduced sufficient evidence of a horizontal price-fixing conspiracy to withstand a motion for summary judgment, the court below refused to apply the per se rule that would allow it to conclude that there had been an unreasonable restraint of trade in the relevant market. Instead, before it would apply the per se rule the court required Denny's to demonstrate a substantial potential for impact on competition in the central Indiana market as a whole. Such an exception to the per se rule against price-fixing is unwarranted by cited precedent . . . [and] would effectively require plaintiffs to make a rule of reason demonstration in order to invoke the per se rule! [In cases governed by the rule of reason], both parties are likely to present extensive economic analysis of the relevant market. It is in part to avoid such excessive costs of litigation that the per se rule is applied in cases where the anti-competitive effect of certain practices may be presumed.

As far back as 1940, it has been clear that horizontal price-fixing is illegal per se without requiring a showing of actual or likely impact on a market. *See Socony-Vacuum Oil.* This is because joint action by competitors to suppress price-cutting has the requisite "substantial potential for impact on competition" to warrant per se treatment. *Federal Trade Commission v. Superior Court Trial Lawyers Association* (1990). The district court would require Denny's to demonstrate a particular potential for impact on the market, when one of the purposes of the per se rule is that in cases like this such a potential is so well-established as not to require individualized showings. The pernicious effects are conclusively presumed.

Since Denny's presented enough evidence for a court and jury to conclude that the defendants engaged in [per se behavior consisting of] a horizontal conspiracy to suppress price competition at boat shows, . . . the district court's grant of summary judgment to the defendants [was erroneous].

Summary judgment for defendants reversed in favor of Denny's; case remanded for trial.

Vertical Price-Fixing

Attempts by manufacturers to control the resale price of their products may also fall within the scope of section 1. This behavior, called **vertical price-fixing** or *resale price maintenance,* has long been held to be per se illegal. Manufacturers may lawfully state a suggested retail price for their products, because such an action is purely unilateral in nature and does not involve the concerted action necessary for a violation of section 1. Per se illegality is present, however, whenever there is a manufacturer-dealer *agreement* (express or implied) obligating the dealer to resell at a price dictated by the manufacturer. The latter scenario involves prohibited *concerted action.*

Consignment Sales   The section 1 emphasis on concerted action provides the basis for two indirect methods that some manufacturers may lawfully be able to use to control resale prices: *consignment sales* and *unilateral refusals to deal.* Consignments are agreements in which an owner of goods (the consignor) delivers them to another who is to act as the owner's agent in selling them (the consignee). Because the consignee is effectively the consignor's agent in selling the goods, and because the owners of goods generally have the right to determine the price at which their goods are sold, an early Supreme Court decision established that consignment sales were not covered by Section 1.[11]

More recent cases, however, have cast some doubt on the legality of resale price maintenance achieved by consignment dealing.[12] Consignment selling systems whose primary purpose is resale price maintenance may be held unlawful if they

---

[11] *United States v. General Electric Co.,* 272 U.S. 476 (U.S. Sup. Ct. 1926).

[12] See, for instance, *Simpson v. Union Oil Co. of California,* 377 U.S. 13 (U.S. Sup. Ct. 1964).

result in restraining price competition among a large number of consignees who would otherwise be in competition with one another. This is especially likely to be true in cases where the consignor has sufficient economic power over his consignees to permit him to refuse to deal with them on any basis other than a consignment. Finally, to have any hope of avoiding liability, the arrangement in question must be a true consignment. The consignor must retain title to the goods and bear the risk of loss of the goods while they are in the consignee's hands. In addition, the consignee must have the right to return unsold goods.

Unilateral Refusals to Deal   In *United States v. Colgate & Co.,*[13] the Supreme Court held that a manufacturer could *unilaterally refuse to deal* with dealers who failed to follow its suggested resale prices. The rationale underlying this holding was that a single firm may deal or not deal with whomever it chooses without violating section 1, because unilateral action is not the concerted action prohibited by the statute. Subsequent cases, however, have narrowly construed the "*Colgate* doctrine." Manufacturers probably will be held to have violated section 1 if they enlist the aid of dealers who are not price-cutting to help enforce their (the manufacturers') pricing policies, or if they engage in other joint action to further those policies.

---

[13]250 U.S. 300 (U.S. Sup. Ct. 1919).

Future of Per Se Illegality   Recent events have cast doubt on the long-term future of the rule of per se illegality for all resale price maintenance agreements. Chicago School theorists argue that many of the same reasons that have been held to justify rule of reason analysis of vertically imposed *nonprice* restraints on distribution (discussed later in this chapter) are equally applicable to vertical price-fixing agreements. In particular, these critics argue that vertical restrictions limiting the maximum price at which a dealer can resell may prevent dealers with dominant market positions from exploiting consumers through price-gouging. Although the Supreme Court had hinted in previous cases that it might be inclined to repudiate its longstanding rule that vertically imposed maximum price restraints trigger per se treatment, it had not formally done so as of early 1997, when this book went to press. In the *Khan* case, which follows, the Seventh Circuit Court of Appeals criticizes the application of per se treatment to vertical fixing of maximum prices but ultimately concludes that if rule of reason analysis is to be applied in such cases, the Supreme Court must first issue a clear holding along those lines. As this book went to press, the Supreme Court agreed to hear an appeal of the Seventh Circuit's decision in *Khan*. In agreeing to decide the case, the Court set the stage for what could be a definitive ruling on the appropriate treatment—per se or rule of reason—to be extended to vertical fixing of maximum prices.

KHAN v. STATE OIL CO.   93 F.3d 1358 (7th Cir. 1996)

B arkat Khan operated a service station in Illinois under a contract with State Oil Co. State Oil leased the station premises to Khan under a contract that also called for State Oil to supply him with gasoline and related products for resale purposes. When Khan failed to pay the agreed-upon rent, State Oil terminated the contract. Khan then sued State Oil, alleging that it had engaged in price-fixing in violation of section 1 of the Sherman Act. The district court held that the alleged price-fixing should be evaluated under the rule of reason approach rather than under the per se rule. The court also concluded that Khan had presented no evidence on essential elements of a rule of a reason case (such as market power), that the study conducted by Khan's economic expert was inadmissible, and that without the study he could not prove injury. The court therefore granted summary judgment in favor of State Oil. Khan appealed to the U.S. Court of Appeals for the Seventh Circuit. ∞

Posner, Chief Judge   The contract between State Oil and Khan provided that State Oil would establish a suggested retail price for the gasoline [it supplied to Khan for resale under the "Union 76"

brand name] and would sell the gasoline to Khan for 3.25 cents less than that price. If Khan believed the suggested retail price was too low he could ask State Oil to raise it, thus preserving his margin; but if State Oil refused and Khan went ahead and raised his price anyway, the contract required Khan to rebate the difference between his new price and the suggested price times the number of gallons sold at the new price. The contract thus required Khan to rebate the entire profit from raising his price without his supplier's permission above the retail price suggested by the supplier.

State Oil . . . denies that the provision in the contract pertaining to Khan's charging a price above the suggested retail price is a form of price fixing. It points out that Khan was free to charge as high a price as he wishes. This is true in the sense that it would not have been a breach of contract for Khan to raise his price. But the contract made it worthless for him to do so. [I]magine that the contract had forbidden Khan to exceed the suggested retail price and had provided that if he violated the prohibition the sanction would be for him to remit any resulting profit to State Oil. There is no practical difference between that form of words and permitting Khan to sell at a higher price but providing that if he does so the profit belongs to State Oil.

So State Oil engaged in maximum price fixing; the next question is whether this practice is illegal per se, meaning that all the plaintiff need prove to prevail is that the defendant engaged in the practice; investigations of its actual economic effects is pretermitted. Challenged practices that do not fall within any of the per se categories are subject to the broader-ranging inquiry into effect and motives that goes by the name of the ''rule of reason'' and that requires the plaintiff to prove that the defendant's conduct actually (or with a high likelihood) reduced competition. Price fixing has long been illegal per se. In its usual and most pernicious form, [price fixing involves] an agreement or conspiracy between competing forms to fix a minimum price for their product. By a modest extension it refers also to an agreement between competitors to fix either a minimum or a maximum price for the resale of their products by their dealers.

The questionable next step in the evolution of antitrust law was to affix the per se label to contracts in which a single supplier, not acting in concert with any of its competitors, fixed its dealers' retail prices. Here the economic difference between fixing a minimum resale price and fixing a maximum resale price becomes more pronounced, although most economists believe that neither form of price fixing is pernicious when the supplier is neither the cat's

paw of colluding distributors nor acting in concert with his competitors. A supplier acting unilaterally might fix a minimum resale price in order to induce his dealers to furnish valuable point-of-sale services (trained salesmen, clean restrooms—whatever) to customers, which they could not afford to do without a guaranteed margin to cover the costs of the services.

As for maximum resale price fixing, . . . the supplier [usually] cannot squeeze his dealers' margins below a competitive level; the attempt to do so would just drive the dealers into the arms of a competing supplier. A supplier might, however, fix a maximum resale price in order to prevent his dealers from exploiting a monopoly position. We do not know anything about the competitive environment in which Khan and State Oil operate—which is why the district judge was right to conclude that if the rule of reason is applicable, Khan loses. But suppose that State Oil, perhaps to encourage the dealer services that we mentioned, has spaced its dealers sufficiently far apart to limit competition among them (or even given each of them an exclusive territory); and suppose further that Union 76 is a sufficiently distinctive and popular brand to give the dealers in it a modicum of monopoly power. Then State Oil might want to place a ceiling on the dealers' resale prices in order to prevent them from exploiting that monopoly power fully. It would do this not out of disinterested malice, but in its commercial self-interest. The higher the price at which gasoline is resold, the smaller the volume sold, and so the lower the profit to the supplier if the higher profit per gallon at the higher price is being snared by the dealer.

Despite these points, the Supreme Court thus far has refused to reexamine the cases in which it has held that resale price fixing is illegal per se regardless of the competitive position of the price fixer or whether the price is a floor or a ceiling. The key precedent so far as the present case is concerned is *Albrecht v. Herald Co.* (U.S. Sup. Ct. 1968), where the Court held over a vigorous dissent that the action of a newspaper publisher in fixing a ceiling at which its distributors could resell the newspaper to the public was illegal per se. State Oil seeks to distinguish *Albrecht* by pointing out that the initiative for the newspaper to take action against the plaintiff distributor had come from another distributor, giving the scheme a ''horizontal'' flavor. True, but this was not a factor on which the Court relied.

It stated its holding broadly: maximum price fixing is illegal per se even if entirely "vertical," that is, even if the only parties in the picture are a single supplier and a single dealer, as in this case. The only use the Court made of the involvement of the other distributor was to show that it was not a case in which the supplier, as permitted by the *Colgate* doctrine (see below), had merely cut off a dealer for failing to adhere to a suggested price. It is not cricket to distinguish a precedent by pointing to a fact mentioned by the court in the previous opinion but clearly given no weight by it. Otherwise no precedent would have any force, for no two cases are exactly alike.

State Oil points out that a supplier has the right to suggest a retail price and terminate a dealer who does not adhere to it. True, [under] *United States v. Colgate & Co.* (U.S.Sup. Ct. 1919), but irrelevant. In such a case there is no agreement between the parties and so no basis for invoking section 1 of the Sherman Act, which is limited to contracts, combinations, and conspiracies, all of which involve an element of agreement. There was an explicit agreement that Khan could not make money if he sold above the suggested retail price. Had he raised the price above that level, State Oil would have had a contractual right to a rebate.

State Oil's main argument is that *Albrecht* is no longer the view of the Supreme Court. State Oil relied on a line of cases decided after *Albrecht* in which the Court established the concept of "antitrust injury." There is no right to maintain a suit under the antitrust laws unless the defendant's conduct has impaired the kind of interest that the antitrust laws were intended to protect. And there is no such interest in the maintenance of a monopoly price. If typically and here a resale price ceiling imposed by a seller merely prevents his dealers from reaping monopoly profits, the injury to the dealers from the ceiling—the loss, that is, of monopoly profits—will not support an antitrust suit. The requirement of proving antitrust injury is not waived in per se cases. In *Atlantic Richfield Co. v. USA Petroleum Co.* (1990), the Supreme Court held that a competitor of dealers prevented by their suppliers from raising their prices could not complain that the restriction was preventing him from raising his own prices.

We have considerable sympathy with the argument that *Albrecht* is inconsistent with the cases that establish the requirement of proving antitrust injury. In fact, we think the argument is right and that it may well portend the doom of *Albrecht*. In [an earlier case], we said we regarded the continued validity of *Albrecht* as an open question, albeit for a different reason: that after *Albrecht* the Supreme Court had (reversing its previous position) recognized that exclusive dealer territories may be procompetitive. [A] price ceiling is a natural and procompetitive incident to a scheme of territorial exclusivity. The majority opinion in *Albrecht* had rejected this argument on the ground that price fixing cannot be "justified because it blunts the pernicious consequences of another distribution practice," namely exclusive territories. We now know that the consequences of that other practice are not (not generally, at any rate) pernicious. So another prop beneath *Albrecht* has been knocked away.

Yet despite all its infirmities, its increasingly wobbly, moth-eaten foundations, *Albrecht* has not been *expressly* overruled. And the Supreme Court has told the lower federal courts, in increasingly emphatic, even strident, terms, not to anticipate an overruling of a decision by the Court; we are to leave the overruling to the Court itself. *Albrecht* was unsound when decided, and is inconsistent with later decisions by the Supreme Court. It should be overruled. Someday, we expect, it will be. The Supreme Court in the *Atlantic Richfield* case was willing to assume only *"arguendo"* that *Albrecht* had been correctly decided, and it cited at length the critical academic commentary on the case. But all this is an aside. We have been told by our judicial superiors not to read the sibylline leaves of the *U.S. Reports* for prophetic clues to overruling. It is not our place to overrule *Albrecht*; and *Albrecht* cannot fairly be distinguished from this case.

[The Seventh Circuit went on to conclude that the district court had erred in ruling that the study conducted by Khan's economic expert was inadmissible evidence of possible antitrust injury.]

District court's grant of summary judgment for State Oil reversed; case remanded for further proceedings.

Horizontal Divisions of Markets

It has traditionally been said that **horizontal division of markets** agreements—those agreements among competing firms to divide up the available market by assigning one another certain exclusive territories or certain customers—are illegal per se. Such agreements plainly represent agreements not to compete. They result in each firm being isolated from competition in the affected market.

More than 20 years ago, in *United States v. Topco Associates, Inc.*,[14] the Supreme Court reaffirmed this longstanding principle by striking down a horizontal division of markets agreement among members of a cooperative association of local and regional supermarket chains. The *Topco* decision was widely criticized, however, on the ground that its per se approach ignored an arguably important point—that the defendants' joint activities in promoting Topco brand products were aimed at enabling them to compete more effectively with national supermarket chains. Critics argued that when such horizontal restraints were ancillary to *procompetitive* behavior, they should be judged under the rule of reason.

Naked Restraints and Ancillary Restraints
Such criticism evidently has had an impact. Several decisions by lower federal courts have distinguished between "naked" horizontal restraints (those having no other purpose or effect except restraining competition) and "ancillary" horizontal restraints (those constituting a necessary part of a larger joint undertaking serving procompetitive ends).[15] Although these courts continue to apply the per se rule to naked horizontal restraints, they give rule of reason treatment to ancillary restraints. In determining whether ancillary restraints are lawful under the rule of reason, courts weigh the harm to competition resulting from such restraints against the alleged offsetting benefits to competition. One factor likely to be of substantial importance in this weighing process is the market strength of the defendants.

The idea here is that if an agreement restrains competition among firms lacking market power because they face strong competition from other firms not subject to the agreement, consumers are unlikely to be harmed. This is because the existence of competition limits the ability of the agreeing firms to exploit their agreement by raising prices.

Whether the Supreme Court ultimately will endorse such departures from *Topco* remains to be seen. However, the Court's post-*Topco* tendency to discard per se rules in favor of a rule of reason approach in other areas suggests that *Topco*'s critics may ultimately prevail with their arguments.

Vertical Restraints on Distribution

Vertical restraints on distribution (or *vertical nonprice restraints*) also fall within the scope of the Sherman Act. A manufacturer has always had the power to *unilaterally* assign exclusive territories to its dealers or to limit the dealerships it grants in a particular geographic area. However, manufacturers may run afoul of section 1 by causing dealers to *agree* not to sell outside their dealership territories or by placing other restrictions on their dealers' right to resell their products.

The Supreme Court once held that vertical restraints on distribution were per se illegal when applied to goods that the manufacturer had sold to its dealers (consignment sales being treated under the rule of reason). The Court changed course, however, in *Continental T.V., Inc. v. GTE Sylvania, Inc.*[16] In *Sylvania,* the Court abandoned the per se rule in favor of a rule of reason approach to most vertical restraints on distribution. The Court accepted many Chicago School arguments concerning the potential *economic efficiencies* that could result from vertical restraints on distribution. Most notably, such restraints were alleged to offer a chance for increased *interbrand* competition among the product lines of competing manufacturers at the admitted cost of restraining *intrabrand* competition among dealers in a particular manufacturer's product. The *Orson* case, which follows, illustrates this point.

Subsequent decisions on the legality of vertical restraints on distribution have emphasized the

---

[14]405 U.S. 596 (U.S. Sup. Ct. 1972).

[15]See, for example, *Polk Bros. v. Forest City Enterprises,* 776 F.2d 185 (7th Cir. 1985). In this case, two retailers were constructing a new building that they were to share. An agreement by the retailers not to compete in the sale of certain product lines was upheld as ancillary to their agreement to develop the joint facility.

[16]433 U.S. 36 (U.S. Sup. Ct. 1977).

importance of the market share of the manufacturer imposing the restraints. Restraints imposed by manufacturers with large market shares are more likely to be found unlawful under the rule of reason because the resultant harm to intrabrand competition is unlikely to be offset by significant positive effects on interbrand competition.

ORSON, INC. v. MIRAMAX FILM CORP. 79 F.3d 1358 (3D Cir. 1996)

O *rson, Inc., owned and operated the Roxy, a movie theater located in downtown Center City, Philadelphia, from January 1992 until the permanent closing of the theater in October 1994. The Roxy exhibited art films—as opposed to movies that may be characterized as mainstream—on two screens. The total seating capacity at the Roxy was 260. The Ritz theaters, which competed with the Roxy in the showing of art films in the Center City area, consisted of two five-screen facilities with a total seating capacity of approximately 1,800. The ticket prices at the Roxy and at the Ritz theaters (referred to collectively as "the Ritz") were essentially the same. In addition to the Roxy and the Ritz, there were six other Center City area theaters that showed art films at least part of the time.*

Miramax Film Corp., a nationwide distributor of feature-length motion pictures (including art films), distributed movies to all of the theaters in Center City and elsewhere in the greater metropolitan Philadelphia area. Miramax licensed films for exhibition for a limited period of time. Consistent with the usual practice in the motion picture industry, these licenses normally were exclusive—meaning that during the time period established in the license, the film would not be licensed to other theaters located in a specified area. Such licenses, called clearances, *contained compensation terms entitling Miramax to a portion of the exhibiting theater's box office gross.*

In the motion picture industry, a first run *is the initial exhibition of a film in a given geographic area. A* subsequent run *is an exhibition of that film in the same geographic area after the first run has expired. Between January 1992 and February 1994 (when discovery ended in the lawsuit described below), Miramax licensed 28 films on a first-run basis, as well as one on a subsequent-run basis, to the Ritz. During the same time period, Miramax granted the Roxy one first-run license and 14 subsequent-run licenses, and issued various first-run licenses to Center City area theaters other than the Roxy and the Ritz. In addition, during the same time period, 59 distributors other than Miramax granted a total of 73 first-run licenses to the Roxy.*

All of the first-run licenses Miramax granted to the Ritz were exclusive in nature. On occasion, Orson sought a first-run, nonexclusive license on a Miramax film and indicated that Orson would offer Miramax a higher percentage of the Roxy's box office receipts than the percentage the Ritz would pay. Nevertheless, Miramax did not grant Orson the licenses it had requested for the Roxy.

Orson sued Miramax in August 1993, alleging that it had violated section 1 of the Sherman Act by conspiring with the Ritz to exclude the Roxy from the art film market. According to Orson's complaint, this conspiracy involved an agreement to (1) make the Ritz Miramax's exclusive Philadelphia exhibitor for first-run art film features, and (2) grant the Ritz exclusive first-run rights to any Miramax film the Ritz wished to exhibit. The district court concluded that rule of reason analysis was appropriate because the supposed agreement between Miramax and the Ritz was "clearly a vertical agreement" between a distributor and an exhibitor. After undertaking such an analysis, the district court granted summary judgment in favor of Miramax. Orson appealed to the U.S. Court of Appeals for the Third Circuit. ∞

Mansmann, Circuit Judge In rule of reason cases, the plaintiff bears the intial burden of showing that the alleged combination or agreement produced adverse, anticompetitive effects within the relevant product and geographic markets. The plaintiff may satisfy this burden by proving the existence of actual anticompetitive effects, such as reduction of output, increase in price, or deterioration in quality of goods and services. Due to the difficulty of isolating the market effects of the challenged conduct, however, such proof is often impossible to make. Accordingly, the courts allow proof of the defendant's "market power" instead. Market power [is] the ability to raise prices above those that would prevail in a competitive market. If a plaintiff meets his initial burden of adducing adequate evidence of market power or actual anticompetitive effects, the burden shifts to the defendant to show that the challenged conduct promotes a sufficiently pro-competitive objective.

Agreements between entities at different market levels are termed "vertical restraints." The Supreme Court has instructed that vertical restraints of trade, which do not present an express or implied agreement to set resale prices, are evaluated under the rule of reason. The Supreme Court has also repeatedly confirmed in vertical restraint cases that inter-brand competition, as opposed to intrabrand competition, is the primary goal of the antitrust laws.

Miramax conceded for purposes of summary judgment that the relevant product market was art films and that the relevant geographic market was Center City, Philadelphia. The first issue we consider is the precise nature of the agreement between Miramax and the Ritz. Orson alleges that Miramax committed to make the Ritz its exclusive Philadelphia exhibitor for first-run art film features. [W]e disagree. The record is devoid of any proof of a promise [by Miramax] to grant first-run licenses . . . in Center City to the Ritz only. Moreover, the evidence is to the contrary; the Roxy received a first-run license from Miramax, as did [other Center City area theaters]. The record shows, instead, a series of clearances granted by Miramax to the Ritz, based on an understanding between the parties' respective principals that any time the Ritz was showing a first-run Miramax film, its license would be exclusive.

Before we consider the antitrust significance of the clearances, however, we will address the alleged conspiracy that we believe lies at the heart of Orson's . . . complaint. As we understand it, Orson's antitrust theory does not primarily challenge the clearances themselves; [instead, Orson] claims that the clearances were mere vehicles that Miramax and the Ritz used to further a secret conspiracy to drive the Roxy out of business by denying that theater first-run Miramax films.

[In a previous case in which a theater owner alleged the existence of a similar conspiracy between another theater owner and a motion picture distributor, the Third Circuit required the plaintiff to prove the defendants' conscious commitment to a scheme to achieve an unlawful objective. According to the Third Circuit's decision in that precedent case, such proof must include a showing that the defendants (1) acted in a manner contrary to their economic interests, and (2) had a motive to enter into the allegedly unlawful scheme.] Orson . . . contends that given its willingness to pay a higher percentage of the Roxy's gross for first-run Miramax films than paid by the Ritz, Miramax acted contrary to its economic well-being by choosing to grant clearances to the Ritz; [Orson] further maintains that Miramax was coerced into favoring the Ritz because the Ritz had made it clear that unless it was granted an exclusive arrangement it would use its clout and refuse to play Miramax films.

We do not find sufficient evidence in the record for either assertion. To the contrary, the evidence established that the clearances were consistent with Miramax's business interests, granted by the distributor to, as between the Roxy and the Ritz, the theater it reasonably predicted would generate greater income. The record demonstrated that the Ritz had [five times as many screens as the Roxy and nearly nine times the seating capacity of the Roxy, as well as] a solid history of box office receipts; by comparison, the Roxy was not nearly as profitable. The theaters which comprised the Ritz had been in continuous operation since their inception; the Roxy, on the other hand, had ceased operation from time to time over the years. Simply put, . . . Orson's position, premised solely on the financial terms of its offer, is insufficient to call into question the wisdom of Miramax's decision. [T]he evidence in the record is insufficient to permit the factfinder to conclude that Miramax acted contrary to its self-interest by choosing to license exclusively to the Ritz rather than the Roxy. Moreover, the deposition testimony that Orson offered to support its assertion that the Ritz had unduly pressured Miramax in its licensing decisions, even when viewed in Orson's favor, shows nothing of the kind. Orson failed to show that Miramax had a motive to conspire with the Ritz to drive the Roxy out of business. Therefore, we conclude that Orson failed to sustain its burden on summary judgment regarding the essential elements of its antitrust conspiracy claim.

Our inquiry does not end here. The fact remains that clearances existed between Miramax and the

Ritz, and that Orson contends that [the clearances themselves] violated section 1 of the Sherman Act. [C]learances, which involve entities at different levels of the film distribution industry, are vertical nonprice restraints of trade. As such, they are subject under section 1 to a rule of reason analysis.

Guided by applicable rules of federal antitrust law and [previous cases in which courts have considered the potential antitrust implications of clearances], we conclude that the reasonableness of a clearance under section 1 of the Sherman Act depends on the competitive stance of the theaters involved and the clearance's effect on competition. [Special attention must be paid to the effect on] interbrand competition, which, as the Supreme Court has instructed, is our primary concern in an antitrust action.

[W]e begin with the fact that the parties agreed that the Roxy and the Ritz were in competition. Thus, the clearances served their accepted purpose of assuring both Miramax and the Ritz that the return from one run of a particular Miramax film would not be diminished. Turning to the touchstone of the rule of reason, the clearances' competitive effects, the uncontroverted facts . . . reveal a market in which competition thrived at both the distributor

and exhibitor levels. In Center City, the Roxy, the Ritz, and [various other theaters] vied for the films of at least 59 distributors. Indeed, it is the indisputable existence of alternative sources of supply for the Roxy which negates the existence of anticompetitive effects in this case. Although the Miramax-Ritz clearances most certainly reduced intrabrand competition to some degree by disallowing the Roxy from showing on a first-run basis any Miramax film that the Ritz had selected, they undeniably promoted interbrand competition by requiring the Roxy to seek out and exhibit the films of other distributors, which it consistently accomplished. [T]he record conclusively establishes that the clearances did not produce the anticompetitive effects the Sherman Act was designed to prevent. On the contrary, competition in the relevant market was enhanced; art film consumers in Center City had more movies from which to choose. We thus conclude that Orson failed to present sufficient evidence to support its claim that the Miramax-Ritz clearances were unreasonable restraints of trade.

District court's grant of summary judgment for Miramax affirmed.

Group Boycotts and Concerted Refusals to Deal

Under the *Colgate* doctrine, a single firm may lawfully refuse to deal with certain firms. The same is not true, however, of *agreements* by two or more business entities to refuse to deal with others, to deal with others only on certain terms and conditions, or to coerce suppliers or customers not to deal with one of their competitors. Such agreements are *joint* restraints on trade. Historically, they have been per se unlawful under section 1. For example, when a trade association of garment manufacturers agreed not to sell to retailers that sold clothing or fabrics with designs pirated from legitimate manufacturers, the agreement was held to be a per se violation of the Sherman Act.[17]

Vertical Boycotts Recent antitrust developments, however, indicate that not all concerted refusals to

deal will receive per se analysis. If a manufacturer terminated a distributor in response to complaints from other distributors that the terminated distributor was selling to customers outside its prescribed sales territory, the manufacturer will be held to have violated section 1 only if the termination resulted in a significant harm to competition. This result follows logically from the *Sylvania* decision. If vertical restraints on distribution are judged under the rule of reason, the same standard should apply to a vertical boycott designed to enforce such restraints.

Even distributors claiming to have been terminated as part of a per se illegal vertical price-fixing scheme have found recovery increasingly difficult to obtain in recent years. In *Monsanto v. Spray-Rite Service Corp.,*[18] a manufacturer had terminated a discounting distributor after receiving complaints from its other distributors. The Supreme Court held that these facts would not trigger per se liability for vertical price-fixing in the absence of additional

[17]*Fashion Originators' Guild v. FTC,* 312 U.S. 457 (U.S. Sup. Ct. 1941).

[18]465 U.S. 752 (U.S. Sup. Ct. 1984).

evidence tending to exclude the possibility that the manufacturer and the nonterminated distributors acted independently. More recently, in *Business Electronics Corp. v. Sharp Electronics Corp.,*[19] the Court held that even proof of a conspiracy between a manufacturer and nonterminated distributors to terminate a price-cutter would not trigger per se liability unless it was accompanied by proof that the manufacturer and nonterminated dealers were also engaged in a vertical price-fixing conspiracy. *Monsanto* and *Sharp* have generated a substantial controversy, as well as proposals for legislation overruling them and codifying the per se rule for vertical price-fixing. As of the time this book went to press, no such legislation had been enacted.

Horizontal Boycotts   It also appears that the Supreme Court is willing to relax the per se rule for some *horizontal* boycotts. For instance, in *Northwest Wholesale Stationers, Inc. v. Pacific Stationery & Printing Co.,* members of an office supply retailers' purchasing cooperative had expelled a member retailer that engaged in some wholesale operations in addition to retail activities. The Court held that rule of reason treatment should be extended to the alleged boycott at issue, but declined to eliminate the per se rule for all horizontal boycotts. The Court has offered only general guidance for determining which horizontal boycotts trigger rule of reason analysis and which ones amount to per se violations. The appropriate legal treatment in a given case is therefore difficult to predict. Future decisions may resolve the uncertainty.

Tying Agreements

Tying agreements occur when a seller refuses to sell a buyer a certain product (the *tying product*) unless the buyer also agrees to purchase a different product (the *tied product*) from the seller. For example, a fertilizer manufacturer refuses to sell its dealers fertilizer (the tying product) unless they also agree to buy its line of pesticides (the tied product). The potential anticompetitive effect of a tying agreement is that the seller's competitors in the sale of the tied product may be foreclosed from competing with the seller for sales to customers that have entered into tying agreements with the seller. To the extent that tying agreements are coercively imposed, they also deprive buyers of the freedom to make independent decisions concerning their purchases of the tied product. Tying agreements may be challenged under both section 1 of the Sherman Act and section 3 of the Clayton Act.[20]

Elements of Prohibited Tying Agreements   Tying agreements are often said to be per se illegal under section 1. However, because a tying agreement must meet certain criteria before it is subjected to per se analysis, and because evidence of certain justifications is sometimes considered in tying cases, the rule against tying agreements is at best a "soft" per se rule. Before a challenged tying agreement is held to violate section 1, these must be demonstrated: (1) the agreement involves *two* separate and distinct items rather than integrated components of a larger product, service, or system of doing business; (2) the tying product cannot be purchased unless the tied product is also purchased; (3) the seller has sufficient economic power in the market for the tying product (such as a patent or a large market share) to appreciably restrain competition in the tied product market; and (4) a "not insubstantial" amount of commerce in the tied product is affected by the seller's tying agreements.[21] The following *Eastman Kodak* case contains a discussion of the elements of prohibited tying arrangements, with a focus on the third element: *market power as to the tying product.*

[19]485 U.S. 108 (U.S. Sup. Ct. 1988).

[20]Section 3 of the Clayton Act applies, however, only when both the tying and the tied products are commodities. Chapter 49 discusses Clayton Act standards for tying agreement legality.

[21]*U.S. Steel Corp. v. Fortner Enterprises, Inc.,* 429 U.S. 610 (U.S. Sup. Ct. 1977).

EASTMAN KODAK CO. v. IMAGE TECHNICAL SERVICES, INC.   504 U.S. 451 (U.S. Sup. Ct. 1992)

astman Kodak Co. (Kodak) manufactures and sells photocopiers and micrographic equipment. In addition, Kodak provides customers with service and replacement parts for its equipment. Kodak produces some of the parts itself. The other parts are made to order for Kodak by independent original equipment manufacturers (OEMs). Rather than selling a complete system of original equipment, lifetime parts, and lifetime service for a single price, Kodak furnishes service after an initial warranty period either through annual service contracts or on a per-call basis. Kodak provides between 80 and 95 percent of the service for Kodak machines.

In the early 1980s, independent service organizations (ISOs) began repairing and servicing Kodak equipment, as well as selling parts for it. ISOs kept an inventory of parts, purchased either from Kodak or from other sources (primarily OEMs). In 1985, Kodak adopted policies designed to limit ISOs' access to parts and to make it more difficult for ISOs to compete with Kodak in servicing Kodak equipment. Kodak began selling replacement parts only to Kodak equipment buyers who used Kodak service or repaired their own machines (i.e., buyers who did not use ISOs for service). In addition, Kodak sought to limit ISO access to other sources of Kodak parts by working out agreements with OEMs that they would sell parts for Kodak equipment to no one other than Kodak, and by pressuring Kodak equipment owners and independent parts distributors not to sell Kodak parts to ISOs.

Eighteen ISOs sued Kodak, claiming that these policies amounted to (1) unlawful tying of the sale of service for Kodak machines to the sale of parts (in violation of Sherman Act Section 1), and (2) monopolization or attempted monopolization of the sale of service for Kodak machines (in violation of Sherman Act Section 2). The U.S. District Court granted summary judgment in favor of Kodak on each of these claims. The Ninth Circuit Court of Appeals reversed, holding that summary judgment was inappropriate because there were genuine issues of material fact regarding the ISOs' claims. The Supreme Court granted Kodak's petition for a writ of certiorari. ∞

Blackmun, Justice Because this case comes to us on Kodak's motion for summary judgment, the evidence of the ISOs is to be believed, and all justifiable inferences are to be drawn in the ISOs' favor [for purposes of determining whether Kodak is entitled to summary judgment or whether a trial is instead necessary].

A tying arrangement is "an agreement by a party to sell one product but only on the condition that the buyer also purchases a different (or tied) product, or at least agrees that he will not purchase that product from any other supplier." *Northern Pacific Railway Co. v. United States* (1958). Such an arrangement violates Section 1 of the Sherman Act if the seller has "appreciable economic power" in the tying product market and if the arrangement affects a substantial volume of commerce in the tied market. *Fortner Enterprises, Inc. v. U.S. Steel Corp.* (1969). Kodak did not dispute that its arrangement affects a substantial volume of interstate commerce. It, however, did challenge whether its activities constituted a "tying arrangement" and whether Kodak exercised "appreciable economic power" in the tying market.

For the ISOs to defeat [Kodak's] motion for summary judgment, . . . a reasonable trier of fact must be able to find, first, that service and parts are two distinct products, and second, that Kodak has tied the sale of the two products. For service and parts to be considered two distinct products, there

must be sufficient consumer demand so that it is efficient for a firm to provide service separately from parts. Evidence in the record indicates that service and parts have been sold separately in the past and still are sold separately to self-service equipment owners. Kodak insists that because there is no demand for parts separate from service, there cannot be separate markets for service and parts. By that logic, we would be forced to conclude that there can never be separate markets, for example, for cameras and film, computers and software, or automobiles and tires. That is an assumption we are unwilling to make.

Kodak's assertion also appears to be incorrect as a factual matter. At least some consumers would purchase service without parts, because some service does not require parts, and some consumers, those who self-service for example, would purchase parts without service. Enough doubt is cast on Kodak's claim of a unified market that it should be resolved by the trier of fact. [T]he ISOs have [also] presented sufficient evidence of a tie between service and parts. The record indicates that Kodak would sell parts to third parties only if they agreed not to buy service from ISOs.

[We now] consider the other necessary feature of an illegal tying arrangement: appreciable economic power in the tying market. Market power is the power "to force a purchaser to do something that he would not do in a competitive market." *Jefferson*

Parish Hospital Dist. No. 2 v. Hyde (1984). The existence of such power ordinarily is inferred from the seller's possession of a predominant share of the market.

The ISOs contend that Kodak has more than sufficient power in the parts market to force unwanted purchases of the tied market, service. The ISOs [assert or] provide evidence that certain parts are available exclusively through Kodak, . . . that Kodak has control over the availability of parts it does not manufacture, [and that Kodak has both] prohibited independent manufacturers from selling Kodak parts to ISOs [and] pressured Kodak equipment owners and independent parts distributors to deny ISOs the purchase of Kodak parts. The ISOs also allege that Kodak's control over the parts market has excluded service competition, boosted service prices, and forced unwilling consumption of Kodak service. [They] offer evidence that consumers have switched to Kodak service even though they preferred ISO service, that Kodak service was of higher price and lower quality than the preferred ISO service, and that ISOs were driven out of business by Kodak's policies. Under our prior precedents, this evidence would be sufficient to entitle the ISOs to a trial on their claim of market power.

Kodak counters that even if it concedes monopoly *share* of the relevant parts market, it cannot actually exercise the necessary market *power* for a Sherman Act violation. This is so, according to Kodak, because competition exists in the equipment market. Kodak argues that it could not have the ability to raise prices of service and parts above the level that would be charged in a competitive market because any increase in profits from a higher price in the aftermarkets at least would be offset by a corresponding loss in profits from lower equipment sales as consumers began purchasing equipment with more attractive service costs. Kodak does not present any actual data on the equipment, service, or parts markets. Instead, it urges the adoption of a substantive legal rule that equipment competition precludes any finding of monopoly power in derivative aftermarkets. Legal presumptions that rest on formalistic distinctions rather than actual market realities are generally disfavored in antitrust law. This Court has preferred to resolve antitrust claims on a case-by-case basis, focusing on the particular facts disclosed by the record . . . and the economic reality of the market at issue.

Even if Kodak could not raise the price of service and parts one cent without losing equipment sales, that fact would not disprove market power in the aftermarkets. Kodak's [theory] is based on the false dichotomy that there are only two prices that can be charged [for parts and service]—a competitive price or a ruinous one. But there could easily be a middle, optimum price at which the increased revenues from the higher-priced sales of service and parts would more than compensate for the lower revenues from lost equipment sales. [Contrary to the assertion in Kodak's brief], there is no immutable physical law—no "basic economic reality"—insisting that competition in the equipment market cannot coexist with market power in the aftermarkets.

[Kodak also overlooks] the existence of significant information and switching costs. These costs could create a less responsive connection between service and parts prices and equipment sales. For the service-market price to affect equipment demand, consumers must inform themselves of the total cost of the "package"—equipment, service, and parts—at the time of purchase; that is, consumers must engage in accurate lifecycle pricing. The necessary information would include data on price, quality, and availability of parts needed to operate, upgrade, or enhance the initial equipment, as well as service and repair costs, including estimates of breakdown frequency, nature of repairs, price of service and parts, length of "down-time," and losses incurred from down-time. Much of this information is difficult—some of it impossible—to acquire at the time of purchase.

Moreover, even if consumers were capable of acquiring and processing the complex body of information, they may choose not to do so. Acquiring the information is expensive. [Consumers] may not find it cost-efficient to compile the information. [It therefore] makes little sense to assume, in the absence of any evidentiary support, that equipment-purchasing decisions are based on an accurate assessment of the total cost of equipment, service, and parts over the lifetime of the machine.

A second factor undermining Kodak's claim that supracompetitive prices in the service market lead to ruinous losses in equipment sales is the cost to current owners of switching to a different product. If the cost of switching is high, consumers who already have purchased the equipment, and are thus "locked-in," will tolerate some level of service-price increases before changing equipment brands. Under this scenario, a seller profitably could maintain supracompetitive prices in the aftermarket if the switching costs were high relative to the increase in service prices, and the number of locked-in customers were high relative to the number of new purchasers. Respondents have offered evidence that the heavy initial outlay for Kodak equipment, combined with the required support material that works only with Kodak equipment, makes switching costs very high for existing Kodak customers.

We conclude, then, that Kodak has failed to demonstrate that the ISOs' inference of market power in the service and parts markets is unreasonable. It is clearly reasonable to infer that Kodak has market power to raise prices and drive out competition in the aftermarkets, since the ISOs offer direct evidence that Kodak did so. It is also plausible . . . to infer that Kodak chose to gain immediate profits by exerting that market power where locked-in customers [and] high information costs . . . limited and perhaps eliminated any long-term loss.

In this case, . . . the balance tips against [granting Kodak's request for] summary judgment.

Denial of Kodak's motion for summary judgment affirmed in favor of the ISOs; case remanded for further proceedings.

Note: In another portion of the opinion not set forth here, the Court held that Kodak was not entitled to summary judgment on the ISOs' Sherman Act section 2 claim.

Possible Justifications for Tying Agreements
The first two of the above elements have been particularly significant in cases involving alleged tying agreements among franchisors and their franchised dealers. For example, a suit by a McDonald's franchisee alleged that McDonald's violated section 1 by requiring franchisees to lease their stores from McDonald's as a condition of acquiring a McDonald's franchise. The Eighth Circuit Court of Appeals rejected the franchisee's claim, however, holding that no tying agreement was involved. Instead, the franchise and the lease were integral components of a well-thought-out system of doing business.[22]

The lower federal courts have recognized two other possible justifications for tying agreements. First, tying arrangements that are instrumental in launching a new competitor with an otherwise uncertain future may be lawful until the new business has established itself in the marketplace. The logic of this "new business" exception is obvious: If a tying agreement enables a fledgling firm to become a viable competitor, the agreement's net effect on competition is positive. Second, some courts have recognized that tying agreements sometimes may be necessary to protect the reputation of the seller's product line. For example, one of the seller's products functions properly only if used in conjunction with another of its products. To qualify for this exception, however, the seller must convince the court that a tying arrangement is the only viable means to protect its goodwill.

Chicago School Views on Tying Agreements
Chicago School thinkers have long criticized the traditional judicial approach to tying agreements because they do not believe that most tie-ins result in any significant economic harm. They argue that sellers who try to impose a tie-in in competitive markets gain no increased profits as a result. This is so because instead of participating in a tying agreement, buyers may turn to substitutes for the tying product or may purchase the tying product from competing sellers. The net effect of a tie-in may therefore be that any increase in the seller's sales in the tied product is offset by a loss in sales of the tying product. Only when the seller has substantial power in the tying product market is there potential that a tie-in may be used to increase the seller's power in the tied product market. However, even when the seller has such market power in the tying product, Chicago School thinkers argue that no harm to competition is likely to result if the seller faces strong competition in the tied product market. For these and other reasons, Chicago School thinkers favor a rule of reason approach to all tying agreements. A majority of the Supreme Court has yet to accept these arguments. Some justices, however, appear willing to do so. If other members of the Court are similarly persuaded in the future, a substantial change in the legal criteria applied to tying agreements will be the likely result.

---

[22]*Principe v. McDonald's Corp.*, 631 F.2d 303 (4th Cir. 1980).

Reciprocal Dealing Agreements

Under a **reciprocal dealing agreement,** a buyer attempts to exploit its purchasing power by conditioning its purchases from suppliers on reciprocal purchases of some product or service offered for sale by the buyer. For example, an oil company with a chain of wholly owned gas stations refuses to purchase the tires it sells in those stations unless the tire manufacturer (the would-be supplier of the tires) agrees to purchase, from the oil company, the petrochemicals used in the tire manufacturing process. Reciprocal dealing agreements are quite similar in motivation and effect to tying agreements. Courts therefore tend to treat them in a similar fashion. In seeking to impose the reciprocal dealing agreement on the tire manufacturer, the oil company is attempting to gain a competitive advantage over its competitors in the petrochemical market. A court judging the legality of such an agreement would examine the oil company's economic power as a purchaser of tires and the dollar amount of petrochemical sales involved.

Exclusive Dealing Agreements

Exclusive dealing agreements require buyers of a particular product or service to purchase that product or service exclusively from a particular seller. For example, Standard Lawnmower Corporation requires its retail dealers to sell only Standard brand mowers. A common variation of an exclusive dealing agreement is the *requirements contract,* under which the buyer of a particular product agrees to purchase all of its requirements for that product from a particular supplier. For example, a candy manufacturer agrees to buy all of its sugar requirements from one sugar refiner. Exclusive dealing contracts present a threat to competition similar to that involved in tying contracts—they may reduce interbrand competition by foreclosing a seller's competitors from the opportunity to compete for sales to its customers. Unlike tying contracts, however, exclusive dealing agreements may sometimes enhance efficiencies in distribution and stimulate interbrand competition. Exclusive dealing agreements reduce a manufacturer's sales costs and provide dealers with a secure source of supply. They may also encourage dealer efforts to market the manufacturer's products more effectively, because a dealer selling only one product line has a greater stake in the success of that line than does a dealer who sells the products of several competing manufacturers.

Because many exclusive dealing agreements involve commodities, they may also be challenged under section 3 of the Clayton Act. The legal tests applicable to exclusive dealing agreements under both acts are identical. Therefore, we defer discussing those tests until the next chapter.

Joint Ventures by Competitors

A **joint venture** is a combined effort by two or more business entities for a limited purpose such as research. Because joint ventures may yield enhanced efficiencies by integrating the resources of more than one firm, they are commonly judged under the rule of reason. Under this approach, courts tend to ask whether any competitive restraints that are incidental to the venture are necessary to accomplish its lawful objectives and, if so, whether those restraints are offset by the venture's positive effects. Joint ventures whose primary purpose is illegal per se, however, have often been given per se treatment. An example of such a case would be two competing firms that form a joint sales agency and authorize it to fix the price of their products.

National Cooperative Research and Production Act   Antitrust critics have long argued that the threat of antitrust prosecution seriously inhibits the formation of joint research and development ventures, and that American firms are placed at a competitive disadvantage in world markets as a result. Such arguments have enjoyed more acceptance during roughly the past decade, given concerns about the American economy's performance. In 1984, Congress passed the National Cooperative Research Act (NCRA). This act applies to *"joint research and development ventures"* (JRDVs), which are broadly defined to include basic and applied research and joint activities in the licensing of technologies developed by such research. The NCRA requires the application of a reasonableness standard, rather than a per se rule, when a JRDV's legality is determined. It also requires firms contemplating a JRDV to provide the Department of Justice and the Federal Trade Commission with advance notice of their intent to do so. The NCRA provides that only actual (not treble) damages may be recovered for losses flowing from a JRDV ultimately found to be in violation of section 1. In addition, the NCRA contains a provision allowing the parties to a challenged JRDV to recover attorney's fees from an

Potentially Illegal Practices and Their Treatment under Sherman Act Section 1

POTENTIALLY ILLEGAL PRACTICE	JUDICIAL TREATMENT	
	PER SE	RULE OF REASON
Horizontal price-fixing	*	
Vertical price-fixing	*?	
Horizontal division of markets	*?	*?
Vertical division of markets		*
Horizontal boycotts	*	*
Vertical boycotts	*	*
Tying agreements	*?	*
Reciprocal dealing agreements	*?	*
Exclusive dealing agreements		*
Joint ventures	*	*

Note: an entry with an asterisk in both columns means the facts of the individual case determine the treatment. A question mark indicates that future treatment is in question.

unsuccessful challenger if the suit is shown to be "frivolous, unreasonable, without foundation, or in bad faith." Congress amended the statute in 1993 to extend its application to joint *production* ventures. In doing so, Congress renamed the statute the National Cooperative Research and Production Act.

Figure 1 summarizes the judicial treatment of potentially illegal practices under section 1 of the Sherman Act (as of early 1997, when this book went to press).

SECTION 2—MONOPOLIZATION

Introduction

Firms that acquire **monopoly power** in a given market have defeated the antitrust laws' objective of promoting competitive market structures. Monopolists, by definition, have the power to fix prices unilaterally because they have no effective competition. Section 2 of the Sherman Act was designed to

prevent the formation of monopoly power. It provides: "Every person who shall monopolize, or attempt to monopolize, or combine or conspire with any other person to monopolize any part of trade or commerce among the several states, or with foreign nations shall be deemed guilty of a felony." Section 2 does not, however, outlaw monopolies. Instead, it outlaws the act of *"monopolizing."* Under section 2, a *single firm* can be guilty of "monopolizing" or "attempting to monopolize" a part of trade or commerce. The proof of joint action required for violations of section 1 is required only when two or more firms are charged with a conspiracy to monopolize under section 2.

Monopolization

Monopolization is "the willful acquisition or maintenance of monopoly power in a relevant market as opposed to growth as a consequence of superior product, business acumen, or historical accident."[23] This means that to be guilty of monopolization, a defendant must have possessed not only monopoly power but also an **intent to monopolize.**

Monopoly Power *Monopoly power* is usually defined for antitrust purposes as the power to *fix prices* or *exclude competitors* in a given market. Such power is generally inferred from the fact that a firm has captured a predominant share of the relevant market. Although the exact percentage share necessary to support an inference of monopoly power remains unclear and courts often look at other economic factors (such as the existence in the industry of barriers to the entry of new competitors), market shares in excess of 70 percent have historically justified an inference of monopoly power.

Before a court can determine a defendant's market share, it must first define the **relevant market.** This is a crucial issue in section 2 cases because a broad definition of the relevant market normally results in a smaller market share for the defendant and a resulting reduction in the likelihood that the defendant will be found to possess monopoly power. The two components of a relevant market determination are the relevant **geographic market** and the relevant **product market.**

---

[23]*United States v. Grinnell Corp.,* 384 U.S. 563 (U.S. Sup. Ct. 1966).

Economic realities prevailing in the industry determine the relevant geographic market. In which parts of the country can the defendant effectively compete with other firms in the sale of the product in question? To whom may buyers turn for alternative sources of supply? Factors such as transportation costs may also play a critical role in relevant market determinations. Thus, the relevant market for coal may be regional in nature, but the relevant market for transistors may be national in scope.

The relevant product market is composed of those products meeting the *functional interchangeability* test, which identifies the products "reasonably interchangeable by consumers for the same purposes." This test recognizes that a firm's ability to fix the price for its products is limited by the availability of competing products that buyers view as acceptable substitutes. In a famous antitrust case, for example, Du Pont was charged with monopolizing the national market for cellophane because it had a 75 percent share. The Supreme Court concluded, however, that the relevant market was all "flexible wrapping materials," including aluminum foil, waxed paper, and polyethylene. Du Pont's 20 percent share of that product market was far too small to amount to monopoly power.[24]

May a *single brand* of a product or service ever be a relevant market for section 2 purposes? Although most section 2 cases would logically be expected to involve product markets consisting of more than one brand of a given type of product (and perhaps other products that are reasonably interchangeable for the same purposes), the Supreme Court refused to rule, in the *Eastman Kodak* case, that a single brand cannot be a relevant market. (*Eastman Kodak* involved claims under sections 1 and 2 of the Sherman Act. The case's major facts and the section 1 aspect of the Court's opinion were set forth in this chapter's discussion of tying arrangements.) Because *Eastman Kodak* dealt with allegedly anticompetitive practices regarding parts and service for Kodak equipment, the Court observed that "[t]he relevant market for antitrust purposes is determined by the choices available to Kodak equipment owners." The Court concluded that "[b]ecause service and parts for Kodak equip-

ment are not interchangeable with other manufacturers' service and parts, the relevant market from the Kodak-equipment owner's perspective is composed of only those companies that service Kodak machines." According to the Court, "prior cases support the proposition that in some instances one brand of a product can constitute a separate market." Evidence that Kodak controlled nearly 100 percent of the parts market and 80 to 95 percent of the service market for Kodak brand equipment was held to be sufficient evidence of monopoly power for purposes of the Court's ruling that Kodak was not entitled to summary judgment on the plaintiffs' section 2 claim against it.

Intent to Monopolize   Proof of monopoly power standing alone, however, is never sufficient to prove a violation of section 2. The defendant's **intent to monopolize** must also be shown. Early cases under section 2 required evidence that the defendant either acquired monopoly power by predatory or coercive means that violated antitrust rules (e.g., price-fixing or discriminatory pricing) or abused monopoly power in some way after acquiring it (such as by engaging in price-gouging). Contemporary courts focus on how the defendant acquired monopoly power. If the defendant *intentionally acquired it* or *attempted to maintain it* after acquiring it, the defendant possessed an intent to monopolize. Defendants are not in violation of section 2, however, if their monopoly power resulted from the superiority of their products or business decisions, or from historical accident (e.g., the owner of a professional sports franchise in an area too small to support a competing franchise).

Purposeful acquisition or maintenance of monopoly power may be demonstrated in various ways. A famous monopolization case involved Alcoa, which had a 90 percent market share of the American market for virgin aluminum ingot. Alcoa was found guilty of purposefully maintaining its monopoly power by acquiring every new opportunity relating to the production or marketing of aluminum, thereby excluding potential competitors.[25] As the *Grinnell* case indicates, firms that develop monopoly power by acquiring ownership or control of their competitors are very likely to be held to have demonstrated an intent to monopolize.

---

[24]*United States v. E. I. du Pont de Nemours & Co.*, 351 U.S. 377 (U.S. Sup. Ct. 1956).

[25]*United States v. Aluminum Co. of America, Inc.*, 148 F.2d 416 (2d Cir. 1945).

G rinnell manufactured plumbing supplies and fire sprinkler systems. It also owned 76 percent of the stock of ADT, 89 percent of the stock of AFA, and 100 percent of the stock of Holmes. ADT provided both burglary and fire protection services; Holmes provided burglary services alone; AFA supplied only fire protection service. Each offered a central station service under which hazard-detecting devices installed on the protected premises automatically transmitted an electrical signal to a central station. There were other forms of protective services. The record indicated, however, that subscribers to an accredited central station service (i.e., one approved by the insurance underwriters) received reductions in their insurance premiums substantially greater than the reductions received by the users of other protection services. In 1961, ADT, Holmes, and AFA were the three largest central station service companies in terms of revenue, with about 87 percent of the business.

In 1907, Grinnell and the other defendants entered into a series of agreements that allocated the major cities and markets for central station alarm services in the United States. Each defendant agreed not to compete outside the market areas allocated. Over the years, the defendants bought 30 other companies providing burglar or fire alarm services. After Grinnell acquired control of the other defendants, the latter continued in their attempts to acquire central station companies. Offers were made to at least eight companies between 1955 and 1961, including four of the five largest remaining companies in the business. When the present suit was filed, each of those defendants had outstanding an offer to purchase one of the four largest nondefendant companies.

Over the years, ADT reduced its minimum basic rates to meet competition and renewed contracts at substantially increased rates in cities where it had a monopoly of accredited central station service. ADT threatened retaliation against firms that contemplated inaugurating central station service.

The government filed suit against Grinnell under section 2 of the Sherman Act, asking that Grinnell be forced to divest itself of ADT, Holmes, and AFA and that other injunctive relief be granted. The district court ruled in favor of the government. Grinnell appealed. ∽

Douglas, Justice   The offense of monopolization under section 2 of the Sherman Act has two elements: (1) the possession of monopoly power in the relevant market and (2) the willful acquisition or maintenance of that power as distinguished from growth or development as a consequence of a superior product, business acumen, or historic accident. This second ingredient presents no major problem here, as what was done in building the empire was done plainly and explicitly for a single purpose. In *United States v. E. I. du Pont de Nemours & Co.,* we defined monopoly power as "the power to control prices or exclude competition." The existence of such power ordinarily may be inferred from the predominant share of the market. In *American Tobacco Co. v. United States,* we said that "over two thirds of the entire domestic field of cigarettes, and over 80 percent of the field of comparable cigarettes" constituted "a substantial monopoly." In *United States v. Aluminum Co. of America,* 90 percent of the market constituted monopoly power. In the present case, 87 percent of the accredited central station service business leaves no

doubt that these defendants have monopoly power—power which they did not hesitate to wield—if that business is the relevant market. The only remaining question therefore is, what is the relevant market?

A product may be of such a character that substitute products must also be considered, as customers may turn to them if there is a slight increase in the price of the main product. That is the teaching of the *Du Pont* case, that commodities reasonably interchangeable make up that "part" of trade or commerce which section 2 protects against monopoly power. The District Court treated the entire accredited central station service business as a single market and it was justified in so doing. Grinnell argues that the different central station services offered are so diverse that they cannot under *Du Pont* be lumped together to make up the relevant market. For example, burglar alarm services are not interchangeable with fire alarm services. It further urges that *Du Pont* requires that protective services other than those of the central station variety be included in the market definition.

We see no barrier to combining in a single market a number of different products or services where that combination reflects commercial realities. There is here a single basic service—the protection of property through use of a central service station—that must be compared with all other forms of property protection. There are, to be sure, substitutes for the accredited central station service. But none of them appears to operate on the same level as the central station service so as to meet the interchangeability test. What Grinnell overlooks is that the high degree of differentiation between central station protection and the other forms means that for many customers, only central station protection will do.

As the District Court found, the relevant market for determining whether the defendants have monopoly power is not the several local areas which the individual stations serve, but the broader national market that reflects the reality of the way in which they built and conduct their business. We have said enough about the great hold that the defendants have on this market. The percentage is so high as to justify the finding of monopoly. And this monopoly was achieved in large part by unlawful and exclusionary practices. The agreements that pre-empted for each company a segment of the market where it was free of competition of the others were one device. Pricing practices that contained competitors were another. The acquisitions by Grinnell of ADT, AFA, and Holmes were still another. Its control of the three other defendants eliminated any possibility of an outbreak of competition that might have occurred when the 1907 agreements terminated. By those acquisitions it perfected the monopoly power to exclude competitors and fix prices.

Judgment for the government affirmed.

Attempted Monopolization

Firms that have not yet attained monopoly power may nonetheless be liable for an **attempt to monopolize** in violation of section 2 if they are dangerously close to acquiring monopoly power and are employing methods likely to result in monopoly power if left unchecked. The *Spectrum Sports* case (which follows shortly) reveals that as part of the required proof of a dangerous probability that monopoly power will be acquired, plaintiffs in attempted monopolization cases must furnish proof of the relevant market—as in monopolization cases. Unlike monopolization cases, however, attempt cases also require proof that the defendant possessed a specific intent to acquire monopoly power through anticompetitive means.

A controversial issue that surfaces in many attempted monopolization cases concerns the role that *predatory pricing* may play in proving an intent to monopolize. The Supreme Court has defined predatory pricing as "pricing below an appropriate measure of cost for the purpose of eliminating competitors in the short run and reducing competition in the long run."[26] What constitutes "an appropriate measure of cost" in predatory pricing cases has long been a subject of debate among antitrust scholars. The Supreme Court has declined to resolve this debate definitively. What the Court's recent opinions do tell us is that the Court is likely to take a skeptical view of predatory pricing claims in the future. The Court has described predatory pricing schemes as "rarely tried, and even more rarely successful."[27] As part of this characterization of predatory pricing schemes, the Court indicated that it agrees with those economists who have argued that predatory pricing is often economically irrational because, to be successful, the predator must maintain monopoly power long enough after it has driven its competitors out of business to recoup the profits it lost through predatory pricing. The predator would be able to sustain monopoly power only if high barriers to entry prevented new competitors from being drawn into the market by the supracompetitive prices the predator would have to charge in order to recoup its losses.

Conspiracy to Monopolize

When two or more business entities **conspire to monopolize** a relevant market, section 2 may be

---

[26]*Cargill, Inc. & Excel Corp. v. Monfort of Colorado, Inc.,* 479 U.S. 484 (U.S. Sup. Ct. 1986).

[27]*Matsushita Electric Industrial Co., Ltd. v. Zenith Radio Corp.,* 475 U.S. 574 (U.S. Sup. Ct. 1986).

FIGURE 2

Elements of Section 2 Offenses

OFFENSE	MONOPOLY POWER	INTENT TO MONOPOLIZE	CONCERTED ACTION
Monopolization	Required	Required	Not required
Attempted monopolization	"Dangerously close"	Specific intent required	Not required
Conspiracy to monopolize	Not required	Specific intent required	Required

violated. This portion of section 2, however, largely overlaps section 1, because it is difficult to conceive of a conspiracy to monopolize that would not also amount to a conspiracy in restraint of trade. The lower federal courts have differed on the elements necessary to prove a conspiracy to monopolize. In addition to requiring proof of the existence of a conspiracy, some courts insist on proof of the relevant market, a specific intent to acquire monopoly power, and overt action in furtherance of the conspiracy. Other courts do not require extensive

proof of the relevant market. According to these courts, a violation is established through proof that the defendants conspired to exclude competitors from, or acquire control over prices in, some significant area of commerce. The Supreme Court's *Spectrum Sports* decision, however, would seem to cast doubt on the validity of an approach that deemphasizes the requirement of proof of the relevant market.

Figure 2 summarizes the elements of section 2 offenses.

SPECTRUM SPORTS, INC. v. McQUILLAN 506 U.S. 447 (U.S. Sup. Ct. 1993)

Sorbothane is a patented elastic polymer whose shock-absorbing characteristics make it useful in a variety of medical, athletic, and equestrian products. BTR, Inc., owns the patent rights to sorbothane. Prior to 1982, a BTR subsidiary, Hamilton-Kent Manufacturing Co. (H-K) produced and distributed sorbothane for BTR. Another BTR subsidiary, Sorbothane, Inc. (SI), was formed in 1982 to replace H-K as the manufacturer of sorbothane and holder of distribution rights regarding it.

H-K and Shirley and Larry McQuillan signed a letter of intent in 1980. This letter of intent granted the McQuillans, who were designing a horseshoe pad that used sorbothane, exclusive rights to purchase sorbothane for use in equestrian products. In 1981, H-K established five regional distributorships for sorbothane. The McQuillans were chosen as distributors of all sorbothane products, including medical products and shoe inserts, for the Southwest. Spectrum Sports, Inc., was selected as distributor for another region of the country. Spectrum's co-owner, Kenneth Leighton, Jr., was the son of Kenneth Leighton, Sr., the president of H-K and later the president of SI.

In January 1982, H-K shifted responsibility for selling medical products from five regional distributors to a single national distributor. Three months later, H-K told the McQuillans that it wanted them to relinquish their athletic shoe distributorship as a condition of being able to retain the right to develop and distribute equestrian products. In May 1982, SI (having succeeded H-K in handling the sorbothane business for BTR) made the same demand to the McQuillans. At a meeting scheduled to discuss a possible sale of the McQuillans' athletic shoe distributorship to Spectrum, Shirley McQuillan was told by Leighton, Jr., that if the McQuillans did not come to agreement with Spectrum, they would be "looking for work." The McQuillans refused to sell and continued to distribute athletic shoe inserts.

Leighton, Sr., informed the McQuillans during the fall of 1982 that another firm had been appointed as the national equestrian distributor, and that the McQuillans were "no longer involved in equestrian products." In January 1983, SI began marketing, through a national distributor, a sorbothane horseshoe pad that, according to the McQuillans, was indistinguishable from the one they had designed. SI named Spectrum as the national distributor of sorbothane athletic shoe inserts in August 1983. At roughly the same time, SI informed the

McQuillans that it would no longer accept their sorbothane orders. With the McQuillans thus being unable to obtain sorbothane, their business failed.

The McQuillans sued the other parties referred to above on various legal theories, including a claim of attempted monopolization in violation of section 2 of the Sherman Act. The jury returned a $1,743,000 verdict in favor of the McQuillans on the section 2 count. The district court trebled the jury's compensatory damages award. After the Ninth Circuit Court of Appeals affirmed, the Supreme Court granted the petition for a writ of certiorari filed by Spectrum and Leighton, Jr. ∞

White, Justice   On the section 2 issue . . . present here, the Court of Appeals . . . rejected [the] argument that attempted monopolization had not been established because the McQuillans had failed to prove that [the defendants] had a specific intent to monopolize a relevant market. The court also held that in order to show that [an] attempt to monopolize was likely to succeed, it was not necessary to present evidence of the relevant market or of the defendants' market power. In so doing, the Ninth Circuit relied on *Lessig v. Tidewater Oil Co.* (1964) [a Ninth Circuit decision] and its progeny. The Court of Appeals noted that these cases, in dealing with attempt to monopolize claims, had ruled that if evidence of unfair or predatory conduct is presented, [such evidence will also] satisfy both the specific intent and dangerous probability elements of the offense, without any proof of relevant market or the defendant's market power. The court went on to find [that the defendants] engaged in unfair or predatory conduct, [that the jury could therefore infer that the defendants] had the specific intent and the dangerous probability of success, [and that the McQuillans] did not have to prove [the] relevant market or the defendants' market power.

The decision below, and the *Lessig* line of decisions on which it relies, conflicts with holdings of courts in other circuits that proving an attempt to monopolize requires proof of a dangerous probability of monopolization of a relevant market. We granted certiorari to resolve this conflict.

Section 2 does not define the elements of the offense of attempted monopolization. Nor is there much guidance to be had in the scant legislative history of that provision. The legislative history does indicate that much of the interpretation of the necessarily broad principles of the Act was to be left for the courts in particular cases.

This Court first addressed the meaning of attempt to monopolize under section 2 in *Swift & Co. v. United States* (1905). The Court's opinion [set forth the elements of intent to bring about a monopoly and a dangerous probability that a monopoly would

occur]. The Court went on to explain, however, that not every act done with intent to produce an unlawful result constitutes an attempt: "It is a question of proximity and degree." *Swift* thus indicated that intent is necessary, but alone is not sufficient, to establish the dangerous probability of success that is the object of section 2's prohibition of attempts.

The Court's decisions since *Swift* have reflected the view that the plaintiff charging attempted monopolization must prove a dangerous probability of actual monopolization, which has generally required a definition of the relevant market and examination of market power. In *Walker Process Equipment, Inc. v. Food Machinery & Chemical Corp.* (1965), we found that enforcement of a fraudulently obtained patent claim could violate the Sherman Act. We stated that, to establish monopolization or attempt to monopolize under section 2 . . ., it would be necessary to appraise the exclusionary power of the illegal patent claim in terms of the relevant market for the product involved. The reason was that "without a definition of that market there is no way to measure ability to lessen or destroy competition." Similarly, this Court reaffirmed in *Copperweld Corp. v. Independence Tube Corp.* (1984) that . . . the conduct of a single firm [violates section 2] "only when it threatens actual monopolization."

The Courts of Appeals other than the Ninth Circuit have followed this approach. Consistent with our cases, it is generally required that to demonstrate attempted monopolization a plaintiff must prove (1) that the defendant has engaged in predatory or anticompetitive conduct with (2) a specific intent to monopolize and (3) a dangerous probability of achieving monopoly power. In order to determine whether there is a dangerous probability of monopolization, courts have found it necessary to consider the relevant market and the defendant's ability to lessen or destroy competition in that market.

Notwithstanding the array of authority contrary to *Lessig*, the Court of Appeals in this case reaffirmed its prior holdings. We are not at all inclined to embrace *Lessig*'s interpretation of section 2, for there is little if any support for it in the statute or the case law, and the notion that proof of unfair or predatory conduct alone is sufficient to make out the offense of attempted monopolization is contrary to the purpose and policy of the Sherman Act. The purpose of the Act is not to protect business from the working of the market; it is to protect the public from the failure of the market. The law directs itself not against conduct which is competitive, even severely so, but against conduct which unfairly tends to destroy competition itself. It does so not out of solicitude for private concerns but out of concern for the public interest.

Thus, this Court and other courts have been careful to avoid constructions of section 2 which might chill competition, rather than foster it. It is sometimes difficult to distinguish robust competition from conduct with long-term anticompetitive effects; moreover, single-firm activity is unlike concerted activity covered by Section 1, which inher-

ently is fraught with anticompetitive risk. For these reasons, section 2 makes the conduct of a single firm unlawful only when it actually monopolizes or dangerously threatens to do so.

The concern that section 2 might be applied so as to further anticompetitive ends is plainly not met by inquiring only whether the defendant had engaged in "unfair" or "predatory" tactics. Such conduct may be sufficient to prove the necessary intent to monopolize, which is something more than an intent to compete vigorously, but demonstrating the dangerous probability of monopolization in an attempt case also requires inquiry into the relevant product and geographic market and the defendant's economic power in that market.

Judgment reversed in favor of Spectrum and Leighton; case remanded for further proceedings consistent with Supreme Court's opinion.

ETHICAL AND PUBLIC POLICY CONCERNS

1. Early in this chapter, you read Judge Learned Hand's statement that "[g]reat industrial consolidations are inherently undesirable, regardless of their economic results." Yet you also learned that Chicago School antitrust thinkers, who have very different notions about the effects of industrial concentration, have had an important influence on antitrust policy in recent years. Identify two aspects of the current global business environment that might make today's American policymakers less willing than Judge Hand to "perpetuate and preserve, for its own sake and in spite of possible cost, an organization of industry in small units which can effectively compete with each other."

2. Some of the cases in this chapter recite the statement that antitrust was designed to protect competition, not competitors. How is this statement consistent with the ethical justification of markets as the most efficient form of economic organization? Consider the case of a competitor who is driven out of business by another competitor's ultimately unsuccessful predatory pricing efforts (unsuccessful because the predator could not maintain monopoly power long enough to recoup the profits lost through

predatory pricing). Although competition may not suffer in such a case, does such a competitor have any *ethical* claim to compensation? What public policy argument could be made in favor of compensation?

3. Tying arrangements that do not satisfy the criteria for per se illegality explained earlier in this chapter are judged under the rule of reason. This means that they will be judged lawful unless evidence demonstrates that they unreasonably restrain competition. Is there an *ethical* basis for arguing a seller's imposition of a tie-in is wrong, regardless of its effect on competition?

PROBLEMS AND PROBLEM CASES

1. Atlantic Richfield (ARCO) is an integrated oil company that sells gasoline to consumers both directly through its own stations and indirectly through ARCO-brand dealers. USA is an independent retail marketer of gasoline that buys gasoline from major petroleum companies for resale under its own brand name. USA competes directly with ARCO dealers at the retail level. Its outlets typically are low-overhead, high-volume "discount" stations that charge less than stations selling equivalent quality gasoline under major brand names. ARCO adopted a new marketing strategy in order to compete more effectively with independents such as USA. ARCO encouraged its dealers to match the retail gasoline prices offered by independents in various ways. These included making available to its dealers and distributors short-term discounts and reducing its dealers' costs by, for example, eliminating credit card sales. ARCO's strategy increased its sales and market share. When USA's sales dropped, it sued ARCO, charging that ARCO and its dealers were engaged in a per se illegal vertical price-fixing scheme. On these facts, could USA show an *antitrust injury* resulting from ARCO's actions (i.e., injury that flows from the unlawful aspects of the challenged behavior and is of a type that the antitrust laws were designed to prevent)? Does per se treatment apply to vertical price-fixing when the allegedly fixed price is of a *maximum* nature?

2. Co-Operative Theatres (Co-op), a Cleveland area movie theater booking agent, began seeking customers in southern Ohio. Shortly thereafter, Tri-State Theatre Services (Tri-State), a Cincinnati booking agent, began to solicit business in the Cleveland area. Later, however, Co-op and Tri-State allegedly entered into an agreement not to solicit each other's customers. The Justice Department prosecuted them for agreeing to restrain trade in violation of section 1 of the Sherman Act. Under a government grant of immunity, Tri-State's vice president testified that Co-op's vice president had approached him at a trade convention and threatened to start taking Tri-State's accounts if Tri-State did not stop calling on Co-op's accounts. He also testified that at a luncheon meeting he attended with officials from both firms, the presidents of both firms said that it would be in the interests of both firms to stop calling on each other's accounts. Several Co-op customers testified that Tri-State had refused to accept their business because of the agreement with Co-op. The trial court found both firms guilty of a per se violation of the Sherman Act, rejecting their argument that the rule of reason should have been applied and refusing to allow them to introduce evidence that the agreement did not have a significant anticompetitive effect. Should the rule of reason have been applied?

3. Advanced Health-Care Services (ACHS), a supplier of durable medical equipment (DME) such as wheelchairs, hospital beds, walkers, crutches, and other equipment used by persons convalescing at home after hospitalization, filed a Sherman Act suit against Radford Community Hospital and Radford's holding company owner, Southwest Virginia Health Services Corporation (Southwest). ACHS's complaint alleged, among other things, that Radford, which provided acute health care services to approximately 75 percent of the residents of the greater Radford, Virginia, region, had conspired with another wholly owned subsidiary of Southwest's to prevent Radford patients from dealing with ACHS and to induce them to purchase DME from the Southwest subsidiary instead. ACHS argued that Radford and Southwest were guilty of conspiring to restrain trade in violation of Sherman Act section 1, and of monopolization and conspiracy to monopolize in violation of Sherman Act section 2. Was the district court's summary dismissal of all of ACHS's claims proper?

4. The Maricopa Foundation for Medical Care was a nonprofit organization established by the Maricopa County Medical Society to promote fee-for-service medicine. Roughly 70 percent of the physicians in Maricopa County belonged to the foundation. The foundation's trustees set maximum fees that members could charge for medical services provided to policyholders of approved medical insurance plans. To obtain the foundation's approval, insurers had to agree to pay the fees of member physicians up to the prescribed maximum. Member physicians were free to charge less than the prescribed maximum, but had to agree not to seek additional payments in excess of the maximum from insured patients. The Arizona attorney general filed suit for injunctive relief against the Maricopa County Medical Society and the foundation, arguing that the fee agreement constituted per se illegal horizontal price-fixing. The district court denied the state's motion for a partial summary judgment. The Ninth Circuit Court of Appeals affirmed on the ground that the per se rule was not applicable to the case. Was the Ninth Circuit correct?

5. In 1986, Market Force, Inc. (MFI), began operating in the Milwaukee real estate market as a buyer's broker. MFI and prospective home buyers entered into exclusive contracts providing that MFI would receive a fee equal to 40 percent of the sales commission if it located a house that the buyer ultimately purchased. This 40 percent commission was the same commission selling brokers (those who ultimately produced a buyer, but whose duty of loyalty was to the seller) earned when they sold property placed on the local multiple listing service (MLS) by other brokers. MFI's contracts anticipated that the buyer would ask the listing broker (the one who had listed the property for sale on behalf of its owners and who received 60 percent of the commission when the property was sold) to pay MFI the commission at the time of the sale. If the listing broker agreed to do so, the buyer had no further obligation to MFI. For some time after MFI began operations, other real estate firms treated it inconsistently; some paid the full 40 percent commission but others paid nothing. In the fall of 1987, Wauwatosa Realty Co. and Coldwell Banker, the top two firms listing high-quality homes in Milwaukee, issued formal policies on splitting commissions with buyer's brokers. Wauwatosa said it would pay 20 percent of the selling agent's 40 percent commission. Coldwell Banker said it would pay 20 percent of the total sales commission. Several other real estate firms followed suit, setting their rates at 10 or 20 percent of the total sales commission, with the result that firms accounting for 31 percent of the annual listings of the MLS adopted policies and disseminated them to other MLS members. MFI filed suit against the brokers who had announced policies, arguing that they had conspired to restrain trade in violation of section 1 of the Sherman Act. At trial, the defendants introduced evidence of numerous business justifications for their policies and argued that their knowingly having adopted similar policies was not enough, standing alone, to justify a conclusion that the Sherman Act was violated. Was this argument correct?

6. When Triple-A Baseball Club Associates was in the process of building the Old Orchard Beach Ballpark, both Gemini Concerts, Inc., and Don Law Co., Inc., expressed interest in promoting concerts at the ballpark. Triple-A, however, had neither the time nor money to make the facility suitable for concerts. Gemini eventually ceased its efforts to use the facility. Law, however, persisted. After several years of discussions, Law and Triple-A signed an agreement giving Law the exclusive right to promote concerts at the ballpark for two years, with an option to renew for another five years. In return, Law paid for many of the capital improvements necessary to equip the ballpark for concerts and shared with Triple-A the cost of others. Gemini filed suit against Triple-A and Law, arguing that their exclusive dealing contract violated section 1 of the

Sherman Act. Should the trial court grant the restraining order requested by Gemini?

7. Concerned that its dealers might not have sufficient spare parts to make repairs on recently purchased Subaru cars, Subaru of America (SOA) decided in 1973 to require its dealers to keep certain spare parts kits on hand. Grappone, Inc., a New Hampshire Subaru dealer, also had AMC, Pontiac, Jeep, Toyota, and Peugot franchises. Grappone acquired its cars from Subaru of New England, Inc. (SNE), a regional Subaru distributor. Grappone objected when told by SNE that it needed to purchase two "dealer's kits" containing 88 parts for 1974 cars and two "supplemental kits" containing 44 parts each (the total number of different Subaru parts being somewhere between 4,000 and 5,000). SNE refused to give Grappone its 1974 car allotment until Grappone bought the kits. Grappone went 10 months without cars; it then agreed to take the kits. Grappone later sued SNE, arguing that SNE violated section 1 of the Sherman Act by tying the sale of the parts kits to the sale of cars. The evidence introduced at trial indicated that Subaru's national market share was under 1 percent and that its share of the New Hampshire market was 3.4 percent. Was the trial court correct in granting judgment in favor of Grappone?

8. McClain and others brought a private antitrust action under the Sherman Act against the Real Estate Board of New Orleans. They alleged price-fixing by means of fixed commission rates, fee splitting, and suppression of market information useful to buyers. The trial court granted the board's motion for dismissal on the ground that real estate brokerage activities were wholly local in nature and therefore lacked the effect on interstate commerce necessary to invoke the Sherman Act. Was the trial court correct?

9. In mid-1982, Indiana Grocery (Indiana) owned 28 supermarkets in the Indianapolis area and sold about 13 percent of the area's groceries. Indiana bought Preston-Safeway in 1985. After 1986, all of Indiana's Indianapolis stores operated under the Preston-Safeway name. The Kroger Company (Kroger) operates over 1,400 supermarkets throughout the United States. In 1983, Kroger operated 32 stores in the Indianapolis area and sold about 28 percent of the area's groceries. Super Valu Stores, Inc., is primarily a grocery wholesaler. Since 1980, however, it has owned and franchised Cub retail food stores in various states. Cub stores, which are substantially larger than conventional supermarkets, offer a low level of services to customers in exchange for prices that normally are 6 to 10 percent lower than those of conventional stores. Between 1983 and 1986, four Cub stores were opened in the Indianapolis area. This ushered in a period of intense price competition as Kroger and others, realizing that gains by Cub would come at their expense, sought to compete. Cub had captured a 15 percent share of Indianapolis retail grocery sales by early 1985. Nevertheless, as of 1987, Kroger (with 33 stores), Marsh (with 30), Indiana (with 24), O'Malia (with 9), Mr.D's (with 5), Aldi (with 5), and 7-Eleven (with 4), all remained in the Indianapolis market, as did other firms operating approximately 38 more supermarkets. Indiana filed suit in 1985 against Kroger. Indiana asserted, among other things, that Kroger used predatory pricing as a means of attempting to monopolize the Indianapolis retail grocery market. The district court granted summary judgment in Kroger's favor. Was the district court correct in doing so?

10. In July 1977, anesthesiologist Edwin G. Hyde applied for admission to the medical staff of East Jefferson Hospital in New Orleans. The credentials committee and the medical staff executive committee recommended approval, but the hospital board denied the application because the hospital was a party to a contract providing that all anesthesiological services required by the hospital's patients would be performed by Roux & Associates, a professional medical corporation. Hyde filed suit against the board, arguing that the contract violated section 1 of the Sherman Act. The district court ruled in favor of the board, finding that the anticompetitive effects of the contract were minimal and outweighed by the benefits of improved patient care. It noted that there were at least 20 hospitals in the New Orleans metropolitan area and that about 70 percent of the patients residing in Jefferson Parish went to hospitals other than East Jefferson. It therefore concluded that East Jefferson lacked any significant market power and could not use the contract for anticompetitive ends. The Fifth Circuit Court of Appeals reversed, holding that the relevant market was the East Bank Jefferson Parish rather than the New Orleans metropolitan area. The court therefore concluded that because 30 percent of the parish residents used East Jefferson and "patients tend to choose hospitals by location rather than price or quality," East Jefferson possessed sufficient market power to make the contract a per se illegal tying contract. Was the Fifth Circuit correct?

11. Häagen-Dazs was the first "super premium" ice cream manufacturer to achieve national distribution. Häagen-Dazs refused to sell its products to any distributor who also sold a comparable, competing ice cream brand. Two Count had been a Häagen-Dazs distributor in the San Francisco area since 1976. In 1985, Two Count agreed to become a distributor (in addition to being a Häagen-Dazs distributor) for Double Rainbow, another "super premium" ice cream manufacturer. When informed of this agreement, Häagen-Dazs terminated Two Count's distributorship. Two Count and Double Rainbow subsequently sued Häagen-Dazs, arguing, among other things, that Häagen-Dazs was guilty of monopolizing, or attempting to monopolize, the "super premium" ice cream market. At trial, Häagen-Dazs introduced uncontroverted evidence indicating that all grades of ice cream compete with one another for customer preference and space in retailers' freezers. Häagen-Dazs's share of the San Francisco ice cream market was 4 to 5 percent. Its national market share was in the same range. Should the trial court have granted Häagen-Dazs's motion for summary judgment on the section 2 claims?

The Clayton Act, The Robinson-Patman Act, and Antitrust Exemptions and Immunities

oncentration in the American economy continued despite the 1890 enactment of the Sherman Act. Early restrictive judicial interpretations of section 2 of the Sherman Act limited its effectiveness against many monopolists. Critics therefore sought legislation to thwart would-be monopolists before they achieved full-blown restraint of trade or monopoly power. In 1914, Congress responded by passing the Clayton Act.

Congress envisioned the Clayton Act as a vehicle for attacking some of the specific practices that monopolists had historically employed to acquire monopoly power. These practices included tying and exclusive dealing arrangements designed to squeeze competitors out of the market, mergers and acquisitions aimed at reducing competition through the elimination of competitors, interlocking corporate directorates designed to reduce competition by placing competitors under common leadership, and predatory or discriminatory pricing designed to force competitors out of business. Each of these practices will be discussed in the following pages.

In view of the congressional intent that the Clayton Act serve as a preventive measure, only a *probability* of a significant anticompetitive effect must be shown for most Clayton Act violations.

Because the Clayton Act focuses on probable harms to competition, there are no criminal penalties for violating its provisions. Private plaintiffs, however, may sue for treble damages or injunctive relief if they are injured, or threatened with injury, by another party's violation of the statute. The Justice Department and the Federal Trade Commission (FTC) share responsibility for enforcing the Clayton Act. Each has the authority to seek injunctive relief to prevent or remedy violations of the statute. In addition, the FTC has the power to enforce the Clayton Act through the use of cease and desist orders, which were discussed in Chapter 47. ∞

CLAYTON ACT SECTION 3

Section 3 of the Clayton Act makes it unlawful for any person engaged in interstate commerce to *lease or sell commodities,* or to *fix a price for commodities,* on the *condition, agreement, or understanding* that the lessee or buyer of the commodities will not use or deal in the commodities of the lessor's or seller's competitors, if the effect of doing so *may be* to *substantially lessen competition* or *tend to create a monopoly* in any line of commerce. Section 3 primarily targets two potentially anticompetitive behaviors: **tying agreements** and **exclusive dealing agreements.** As you learned in the preceding chapter, both of these types of contracts may amount to restraints of trade in violation of Sherman Act section 1. The language of section 3, however, contains limitations on the Clayton Act's application to such agreements.

A major limitation is that section 3 applies only to those tying agreements and exclusive dealing contracts involving *commodities.* Any such agreements involving services, real estate, or intangibles must therefore be attacked under the Sherman Act. In addition, section 3 applies only when there has been a *lease or sale* of commodities. It thus does not apply to true consignment agreements, because no sale or lease occurs in a consignment. Although section 3 speaks of sales and leases on the "condition, agreement, or understanding" that the buyer or lessee not deal in the commodities of the seller's or lessor's competitors, no formal agreement is required. Whenever a seller or lessor uses its economic power to prevent its customers from dealing with its competitors, potential Clayton Act concerns are triggered.

Tying Agreements

Many *tying agreements* plainly fall within at least the first portion of the relevant section 3 language. Any agreement that requires a buyer to purchase one product (the *tied product*) from a seller as a condition of purchasing another product (the *tying product*) from the same seller necessarily prevents the buyer from purchasing the tied product from the seller's competitors.

Only tying agreements that may *"substantially lessen competition or tend to create a monopoly,"* however, violate section 3. The lower federal courts are not in complete agreement on the nature of the proof necessary to demonstrate such a probable anticompetitive effect. More than 40 years ago, the Supreme Court appeared to indicate that a tying agreement would violate the Clayton Act if the seller either had monopoly power over the tying product or restrained a substantial volume of commerce in the tied product.[1]

Most lower federal courts today, however, require essentially the same elements of proof for a Clayton Act violation that they require for a violation of the Sherman Act: the challenged agreement must involve *two separate products, sale of the tying product must be conditioned* on an accompanying sale of the tied product, the seller must have *sufficient economic power in the market for the tying product* to appreciably restrain competition in the tied product market, and the seller's tying arrangements must restrain a *"not insubstantial"* amount of commerce in the tied product market. A few courts continue to apply a less demanding standard for Clayton Act tying liability by dispensing with proof of the seller's economic power in the market for the tying product as long as the seller's tying arrangements involve a "not insubstantial" amount of commerce in the tied product. The defenses to tying liability under the Sherman Act (discussed in the preceding chapter) are also applicable to tying claims brought under the Clayton Act.

Exclusive Dealing Agreements

In the preceding chapter, we discussed the nature of *exclusive dealing agreements.* Such contracts clearly fall under the initial portion of the relevant

---

[1]*Times-Picayune Publ. Co. v. United States,* 345 U.S. 594 (U.S. Sup. Ct. 1953).

section 3 language because buyers who agree to handle one seller's product exclusively, or to purchase all of their requirements for a particular commodity from one seller, are by definition agreeing not to purchase similar items from the seller's competitors. As with tying agreements, however, not all exclusive dealing agreements are unlawful. Section 3 outlaws only those agreements that may "substantially lessen competition or tend to create a monopoly."

Exclusive dealing agreements initially were treated in much the same way as tying agreements. Courts looked at the dollar amount of commerce involved and declared illegal those agreements involving a "not insubstantial" amount of commerce. This *quantitative substantiality* test was employed, for example, by the Supreme Court in *Standard Oil Co. v. United States.*[2] Standard Oil was the largest refiner and supplier of gasoline in several western states, holding approximately 14 percent of the retail market. Roughly half of these sales were made by retail outlets owned by Standard. The other half were made by independent dealers who had entered into exclusive dealing contracts with Standard. Standard's six major competitors had entered into similar contracts with their own independent dealers. The Court recognized that exclusive dealing contracts, unlike tying agreements, could benefit both buyers and sellers, but declared Standard's contracts illegal on the ground that nearly $58 million in commerce was involved.

The Court's decision in the *Standard Oil* case provoked considerable criticism. In *Tampa Electric Co. v. Nashville Coal Co.,* however, the Court applied a broader *qualitative substantiality* test to gauge the legality of a long-term requirements contract for the sale of coal to an electric utility.[3] In *Tampa Electric,* the Court looked at the "area of effective competition," which was the total market for coal in the geographic region from which the utility could reasonably purchase its coal needs. The Court then examined the percentage of this region's total coal sales accounted for by the challenged contract. Because that percentage share was less than 1 percent of the region's total coal sales, the Court upheld the agreement even though it represented more than $100 million in coal sales.

Tampa Electric, however, is distinguishable from *Standard Oil,* which, in any event, the Court has not overruled. Unlike *Standard Oil, Tampa Electric* involved parties with relatively equal bargaining power and an individual agreement, rather than an industrywide practice. In addition, there were obvious reasons why an electric utility such as Tampa Electric might want to lock in its coal costs by using a long-term requirements contract. Although lower court opinions employing each test may be found, the *qualitative* approach employed in *Tampa Electric* is the one more likely to be employed by the current Court.

CLAYTON ACT SECTION 7

Introduction

Section 7 of the Clayton Act was designed to attack **mergers**—a term used broadly in this chapter to refer to the acquisition of one company by another. Our historical experience indicates that one way in which monopolists acquired monopoly power was by acquiring control of their competitors. Section 7 prohibits any party engaged in commerce or in any activity affecting commerce from *acquiring the stock or assets* of another such party if the effect, in *any line of commerce* or *any activity affecting commerce* in any section of the country, *may be to substantially lessen competition* or *tend to create a monopoly.* Rather than adopting the Sherman Act section 2 approach of waiting until a would-be monopolist has acquired monopoly power or is dangerously close to doing so, section 7 attempts to "nip monopolies in the bud" by barring mergers that *may* have an anticompetitive effect.

Although section 7 is plainly an anticoncentration device, it has also been used (as the following text indicates) to attack mergers that have had no direct effect on concentration in a particular industry. As such, its future evolution is in doubt, given the influence of Chicago School economic theories on contemporary antitrust law and the more tolerant stance those theories take toward mergers. During the 1980s, the Justice Department signaled a more permissive approach to merger activity than the government had previously adopted. During the first term of the Clinton presidency, Justice Department and FTC officials undertook greater scrutiny of mergers in some industries, though not necessarily on an across-the-board basis. In fiscal 1995, the

---

[2]337 U.S. 293 (U.S. Sup. Ct. 1949).
[3]365 U.S. 320 (1961).

FTC took formal legal action concerning 35 mergers. This meant that the FTC challenged more mergers than it had in any fiscal year since 1980. The Justice Department challenged 16 mergers in fiscal 1995. This was the Department's second-highest total of merger challenges since 1990. As of the time this book went to press, it remained to be seen whether the Clinton administration would continue to pursue a stepped-up enforcement policy regarding mergers. Regardless of the enforcement approach chosen by the federal government, it should be remembered that private enforcement of section 7 is also possible.

Predictions regarding section 7's ultimate judicial treatment are complicated considerably by the fact that many of the important merger cases in recent years have been settled out of court. This leaves interested observers of antitrust policy with few definitive expressions of the Supreme Court's current thinking on many merger issues.

Relevant Market Determination

Regardless of the treatment section 7 ultimately receives in the courts, determining the **relevant market** affected by a merger is likely to remain a crucial component of any section 7 case. Before a court can determine whether a particular merger will have the *probable* anticompetitive effect required by the Clayton Act, it must first determine the *line of commerce* (or *relevant product market*) and the *section of the country* (or *relevant geographic market*) that are likely to be affected by the merger. If the court adopts a broad relevant market definition, this will usually enhance the government's or private plaintiff's difficulty in demonstrating a probable anticompetitive effect flowing from a challenged merger.

Relevant Product Market "Line of commerce" determinations under the Clayton Act have traditionally employed *functional interchangeability* tests similar to those employed in relevant product market determinations under section 2 of the Sherman Act. Which products do the acquired and acquiring firms manufacture (assuming a merger between competitors), and which products are reasonably interchangeable by consumers to serve the same purposes? The federal government's merger guidelines indicate that the relevant market includes those products that consumers view as good substitutes at prevailing prices. The guidelines also state that the relevant market includes any products that a significant percentage of current customers would shift to in the event of a "small, but significant and non-transitory increase" in price of the products of the merged firms. The *Olin* case, which follows, discusses the making of a relevant product market determination.

OLIN CORPORATION v. FEDERAL TRADE COMMISSION   986 F.2d 1295 (9th Cir. 1993)

anitizing agents are used to kill algae and bacteria in swimming pools. Pool owners may use any of three sanitizing agents. One of these is liquid pool bleach; the other two are chemicals sold in dry form. These dry sanitizers are isocyanurates (ISOS) and calcium hypochlorite (CAL/HYPO). The chemical cyanuric acid (CA) is a precursor in the manufacturing process of ISOS. When CAL/HYPO is used as a sanitizer, CA is used along with it as a stabilizer.

Olin Corporation was the market leader in CAL/HYPO production in the United States from 1980 through 1984, with a market share of 79 to 89 percent. Olin sought to increase its ability to produce and market ISOS. After technical problems doomed Olin's attempts to produce CA and ISOS during the late 1970s and early 1980s, Olin entered into a 1984 agreement with Monsanto Co. Under this agreement, Olin provided certain ISOS precursors to Monsanto, which then produced ISOS and provided them to Olin. Olin thus became a "repackager" of ISOS.

In 1985, Olin and FMC Corporation entered into an agreement under which Olin was to purchase FMC's swimming pool chemical business. The assets of that business included FMC's sanitizers manufacturing plant at South Charleston, West Virginia. The South Charleston plant produced both CA and ISOS. The Federal Trade Commission challenged the proposed acquisition on the theory that it would likely result in a substantial lessening of competition in the relevant markets, in violation of section 7 of the Clayton Act and section 5 of the FTC Act. To avoid a possible order that would have prohibited the acquisition, Olin agreed to maintain the acquired assets in such a way that divestiture would be possible if the FTC issued a final decision holding that the acquisition violated antitrust laws. In addition, Olin agreed to a graduated withdrawal from its agreement with Monsanto. Olin and FMC were therefore allowed to consummate their transaction, pending final review by the FTC.

After a hearing, the FTC administrative law judge (ALJ) concluded that the acquisition violated the Clayton and FTC Acts because it would likely result in a substantial lessening of competition in the relevant markets. The FTC commissioners (referred to below as "the Commission") upheld the ALJ's decision as well as the ALJ's proposed remedy of divestiture. The Commission therefore ordered Olin to divest itself of the South Charleston plant it had acquired from FMC. Olin petitioned the Ninth Circuit Court of Appeals for review of the Commission's decision and order. ⌒

Tang, Circuit Judge Normally, "a delineation of proper geographic and product markets is a necessary precondition to assessment of the probabilities of a substantial effect on competition within them." *United States v. General Dynamics Corp.* (U.S. Sup. Ct. 1974). There is no dispute in this case that the geographic market relevant to this case is the entire United States. The parties have further stipulated that one relevant United States product market consists solely of ISOS (the "ISOS-only" market). The Commission also identified over Olin's objection a second relevant United States product market, one comprised of both ISOS and CAL/HYPO (the "dry sanitizers" market). Olin contends that the finding of likely anticompetitive effect is erroneous because it is premised on . . . a relevant dry sanitizers market [whose] existence is not supported by substantial evidence. In analyzing the post-acquisition dry sanitizers market [the existence of which Olin does not concede], the Commission concluded that Olin's production capacity would be 57% of a market in which the four-firm concentration ratio was 95%.

[In *California v. American Stores Co.* (9th Cir. 1989), we] described the process of product market definition as follows:

"The outer boundaries of a product market are determined by the reasonable interchangeability of use or the cross-elasticity of demand between the product itself and substitutes for it" (quoting *Brown Shoe Co. v. United States* (U.S. Sup. Ct. 1962)). Where an increase in the price of one product leads to an increase in demand for another, both products should be included in the relevant product market.

In conducting its product market analysis for swimming pool sanitizers, the Commission discussed physical composition, usage, and technical characteristics of dry sanitizers. [T]he Commission observed that similarities in these categories "predominate over the minor [physical] differences between ISOS and CAL/HYPO. The following facts are particularly important: (1) both products are used to deliver chlorine to swimming pools; (2) each product is able to deliver chlorine with about the same efficiency—although a pool chlorinated with ISOS will remain chlorinated longer; (3) by virtue of both products' stability and other characteristics, "a pool owner can purchase a year's supply of either [product] in a single trip to the store"; and (4) both products are available to consumers in the same forms. In discussing these characteristics, the Commission apparently assumed that the relevant market is defined in terms of consumers who maintain their own pools. Although Olin challenged this assumption, we conclude there is substantial evidence in support of dealing with residential consumers as a distinct market.

Despite [the above] similarities, however, ISOS are perceived as more convenient than CAL/HYPO because, once applied, ISOS last longer than CAL/HYPO, and because CAL/HYPO requires use of a separate stabilizer (i.e., CA). Recognizing that the "convenience of [ISOS] is reflected in a price premium that [ISOS] maintain over [CAL/HYPO]," the Commission then analyzed whether this premium is sufficient to prevent inclusion of ISOS and CAL/HYPO in the same market. Ultimately, the Commission [applied a test set forth in the merger guidelines subscribed to by the Department of Justice and the FTC, and concluded that] "Olin could not profitably impose a small but significant and nontransitory increase in the price of [CAL/HYPO] because of the danger that consumers would then switch to [ISOS]." Given this indication of cross-elasticity of demand, the Commission concluded that ISOS and CAL/HYPO together compose a relevant product market (i.e., the dry sanitizers market).

Olin argues that it is inconsistent to recognize a larger, dry sanitizers market once a relevant ISOS-only market has been identified. However, relevant submarkets are common in merger analysis. Recognizing ISOS as a submarket of the dry sanitizers market is not inherently contradictory with recognizing a dry sanitizers market.

Olin charges that the Commission had no basis on which to conclude that any significant degree of elasticity existed between ISOS and CAL/HYPO. It is evident from its opinion that the Commission relied on a narrowing of the price gap between the two products in determining cross-elasticity. The opinion [stated that] "from 1977 to 1983, . . . the price of [CAL/HYPO] increased at a faster rate than that of [ISOS]." According to the opinion, this increase in the price of CAL/HYPO came about despite direct competition from Japanese CAL/HYPO, which was later the subject of an "antidumping" order. Olin argues that the narrowing of the price gap between CAL/HYPO and ISOS was artificial—and should not be used in determining cross-elasticity—because the Japanese were "dumping" ISOS on the American market. The Commission responds convincingly that, because CAL/HYPO was subject to the same pressures as the result of Japanese CAL/HYPO dumping, the narrowing in price was not artificial. Olin ignores this explanation and shifts its focus to the Commission concession that CAL/HYPO consumers would not switch to ISOS until the price of CAL/HYPO had risen at least 10%.

Olin . . . attempt[s] to emphasize the 5% factor normally used [by the Department of Justice and the FTC when they apply the merger guidelines' test that asks whether a "small but significant and nontransitory price increase" would cause consumers to switch to another product]. [However,] research has not disclosed a case that mandates [use of the 5% figure in] determining relevant product markets. Indeed, [the government's merger guidelines themselves acknowledge] that a higher percent increase in price is appropriate in determining the relevant product market in certain cases. Thus, a finding of cross-elasticity between ISOS and CAL/HYPO is not precluded by the fact that a higher price increase is necessary to induce a switch; a higher increase indicates only that the relationship between the two products is somewhat inelastic—but not necessarily so inelastic as to exclude the products from the same market, particularly under the substantial evidence standard of review.

[In making its cross-elasticity finding, the Commission also reasonably relied on] a statement Olin made to the International Trade Commission [in which Olin complained about Japanese "dumping" but appeared to acknowledge that CAL/HYPO faces competition from ISOS] and a statement made by an Olin competitor indicating a competitive relationship between CAL/HYPO and ISOS. [W]e find adequate support for the Commission's finding of cross-elasticity between ISOS and CAL/HYPO.

Finally, Olin attacks the exclusion of liquid pool bleach from a market composed of ISOS and CAL/HYPO. Olin essentially argues that the only rational basis for including CAL/HYPO and ISOS in the same market is that both products are used to sanitize swimming pools. If this is the determinative criterion, Olin continues, then liquid pool bleach must also be included in the relevant market. Olin's efforts to include liquid pool bleach in the relevant product market are intended to undermine the Commission's reliance on a dry sanitizers market in ordering divestiture [of the South Charleston plant].

The Commission cites several plausible reasons to separate liquid pool bleach from the dry sanitizers in defining a relevant market: Most pool bleach is consumed in discrete geographic regions; liquid pool bleach is inconvenient because a season's worth cannot be bought in one trip to the store, and because bleach spills can damage clothing and car interiors; liquid bleach is less expensive than dry sanitizers; and liquid pool bleach is sold [mainly] to pool service companies rather than to those who maintain their pools themselves. The Commission also discussed cross-elasticity of demand between dry sanitizers and liquid pool bleach, concluding that "circumstantial evidence indicates a low degree of substitution between dry and liquid sanitizers." Based on the foregoing, the Commission was justified in identifying a relevant dry sanitizers market that excluded liquid pool bleach.

[The Ninth Circuit went on to hold that the divestiture remedy ordered by the Commission was an appropriate exercise of the Commission's discretion.]

Olin's petition for review denied; decision and order of Commission upheld.

Relevant Geographic Market To determine a particular merger's probable anticompetitive effect on a section of the country, courts have traditionally asked where the effects of the merger will be "direct and immediate."[4] This means that the relevant geographic market may not be as broad as the markets in which the acquiring and acquired firms actually operate or, in the case of a merger between competitors, the markets in which they actually compete. The focus of the relevant market inquiry is on those sections of the country in which competition is most likely to be injured by the merger. As a result, the relevant geographic market in a given case could be drawn as narrowly as one metropolitan area or as broadly as the entire nation. All that is necessary to satisfy this aspect of section 7 is proof that the challenged merger might have a significant negative effect on competition in any economically significant geographic market.

The federal government's merger guidelines adopt a somewhat different approach to determining the relevant geographic market. They define the relevant geographic market as the geographic area in which a sole supplier of the product in question could profitably raise its price without causing outside suppliers to begin selling in the area. The guidelines contemplate beginning with the existing markets in which the parties to a merger compete, and then adding the markets of those suppliers that would enter the market in response to a "small, but significant and non-transitory increase" in price.

Horizontal Mergers

The analytical approach employed to gauge a merger's probable effect on competition varies according to the nature of the merger in question. **Horizontal mergers**—mergers among firms competing in the same product and geographic markets—have traditionally been subjected to the most rigorous scrutiny because they clearly lead to increased concentration in the relevant market.

Market Share of Resulting Firm To determine the legality of such a merger, courts look at the *market share of the resulting firm*. In *United States v. Philadelphia National Bank,* the Supreme Court indicated that a horizontal merger producing a firm

with an "undue percentage share" of the relevant market (33 percent in that case) and resulting in a "significant increase in concentration" of the firms in that market would be presumed illegal, absent convincing evidence that the merger would not have an anticompetitive effect.[5]

In the past, mergers involving firms with smaller market shares than those involved in *Philadelphia National Bank* were also enjoined if other economic or historical factors pointed toward a probable anticompetitive effect. Some of the factors that courts have traditionally considered relevant include:

1. *A trend toward concentration in the relevant market*: Has the number of competing firms decreased over time?

2. *The competitive position of the merging firms*: Are the defendants dominant firms despite their relatively small market shares?

3. *A past history of acquisitions by the acquiring firm*: Are we dealing with a would-be empire builder?

4. *The nature of the acquired firm*: Is it an aggressive, innovative competitor despite its small market share?

Recent Assessments of Merger Effects Recent developments, however, indicate that the courts and federal antitrust enforcement agencies have become increasingly less willing to presume that anticompetitive effects will necessarily result from a merger that produces a firm with a relatively large market share. Instead, a more detailed inquiry is made into the nature of the relevant market and of the merging firms in order to ascertain the likelihood of a probable harm to competition as a result of a challenged merger. The federal government's horizontal merger guidelines indicate that when regulators assess a merger's probable effect, the focus is on the existing concentration in the relevant market, the increase in concentration as a result of the proposed merger, and other nonmarket share factors. The more concentrated the existing market and the greater the increase in concentration that would result from the proposed merger, the more likely the merger is to be challenged by the government.

The nonmarket share factors considered by federal regulators are more traditional. They include: the existence (or absence) of barriers to the entry of

---

[4]See, for instance, *United States v. Phillipsburg National Bank,* 399 U.S. 350 (U.S. Sup. Ct. 1970).

[5]374 U.S. 321 (1963).

new competitors into the relevant market, the prior conduct of the merging firms, and the probable future competitive strength of the acquired firm. The last factor is particularly important because courts have acknowledged that a firm's current market share may not reflect its ability to compete in the future. For example, courts have long recognized a "failing company" justification for some mergers. If the acquired firm is a failing company and no other purchasers are interested in acquiring it, its acquisition by a competitor may be lawful under section 7. Similarly, if an acquired firm has financial problems that reflect some underlying structural weakness, or if it lacks new technologies that are necessary to compete effectively in the future, its current market share may overstate its future competitive importance.

Finally, given the increased weight being assigned to economic arguments in antitrust cases, two other merger justifications may be granted greater credence in the future. Some lower federal courts have recognized the notion that a merger between two small companies may be justifiable, despite the resulting statistical increase in concentration, if the merger enables them to compete more effectively with larger competitors. In a somewhat similar vein, some commentators have argued that mergers resulting in cost savings or other enhanced economic efficiencies should sometimes be allowed even though they may have some anticompetitive impact. Though Courts have not been very receptive to efficiency arguments in the past, the government's horizontal merger guidelines are flexible enough to allow the Justice Department and FTC to consider efficiency claims in deciding whether to challenge a merger.

UNITED STATES v. WASTE MANAGEMENT, INC.   743 F.2d 976 (2d Cir. 1984)

Waste Management, Inc. (WMI), a company in the solid waste disposal business, acquired the stock of EMW Ventures, Inc. EMW was a diversified holding company, one of whose subsidiaries was Waste Resources. WMI and Waste Resources each had subsidiaries operating in or near Dallas, Texas. The government challenged the merger, arguing that it violated section 7 of the Clayton Act. The trial court (Judge Griesa) agreed, defining the relevant market as including all forms of trash collection (except at single-family or multiple-family residences or small apartment complexes) in Dallas County plus a small fringe area. The combined WMI and Waste Resources subsidiaries had 48.8 percent of the market so defined. The trial court found this market share presumptively illegal. WMI appealed. ☜

Winter, Circuit Judge   A post-merger market share of 48.8% is sufficient to establish prima facie illegality under *United States v. Philadelphia National Bank.* That decision held that large market shares are a convenient proxy for appraising the danger of monopoly power resulting from a horizontal merger. Under its rationale, a merger resulting in a large market share is presumptively illegal, rebuttable only by a demonstration that the merger will not have anticompetitive effects. Thus, in *United States v. General Dynamics Corp.* (1974), the Court upheld a merger of two leading coal producers because substantially all of the production of one firm was tied up in long-term contracts and its reserves were insubstantial. Since that firm's future ability to compete was negligible, the Court reasoned that its disappearance as an independent competitor could not affect the market.

WMI does not claim that 48.8% is too small a share to trigger the *Philadelphia National Bank* presumption. Rather, it argues that the presumption is rebutted by the fact that competitors can enter the Dallas waste hauling market with such ease that the finding of a 48.8% market share does not accurately reflect market power. WMI argues that it is unable to raise prices over the competitive level because new firms would quickly enter the market and undercut them.

The Supreme Court has never directly held that ease of entry may rebut a showing of *prima facie* illegality under *Philadelphia National Bank.* However, on several occasions it has held that appraisal of the impact of a proposed merger upon competition must take into account potential competition from firms not presently active in the relevant product and geographic markets. Moreover, under *General Dynamics,* a substantial existing market share is insufficient to void a merger where that share is misleading as to actual future competitive effect. In that case, long-term contracts and declining reserves negated the inference of market power drawn from the existing market share. In the present case, a market definition artificially restricted to existing firms competing at one moment may yield market share statistics that are not an accurate proxy for market power when substantial potential competition able to respond quickly to price increases exists.

Finally, the *Merger Guidelines* issued by the government itself not only recognize the economic principle that ease of entry is relevant to appraising the impact upon competition of a merger but also state that it may override all other factors. Where entry is "so easy that existing competitors could not succeed in raising prices for any significant period of time," the government has announced that it will usually not challenge a merger.

Turning to the evidence in this case, we believe that entry into the relevant product and geographic market by new firms or by existing firms in the Fort Worth area is so easy that any anticompetitive impact of the merger before us would be eliminated more quickly by such competition than by litigation.

Judge Griesa specifically found that individuals operating out of their homes can acquire trucks and some containers and compete successfully "with any other company." His conclusion that "there is no showing of any circumstances, related to ease of entry or the trend of the business, which promises in and of itself to materially erode the [defendants'] competitive strength" is consistent with our decision. They may well retain their present market share. However, in view of the findings as to ease of entry, that share can be retained only by competitive pricing. Ease of entry constrains not only WMI, but every firm in the market. Should WMI attempt to exercise market power by raising prices, none of its small competitors would be able to follow the price increases because of the ease with which new competitors would appear. WMI would then face lower prices charged by all existing competitors as well as entry by new ones, a condition fatal to its economic prospects if not rectified.

Judgment reversed in favor of Waste Management, Inc.

Vertical Mergers

A **vertical merger** is a merger between firms that previously had, or could have had, a supplier–customer relationship. For example, a manufacturer may seek to vertically integrate its operations by acquiring a company that controls retail outlets at which the manufacturer's products could be sold. Alternatively, the manufacturer could vertically merge by acquiring a company that makes a product the manufacturer regularly uses in its production processes. Vertical mergers, unlike horizontal mergers, do not directly result in an increase in concentration. Nonetheless, they traditionally have been thought to threaten competition in various ways.

Foreclosing Competitors in Relevant Market First, vertical mergers may *foreclose competitors* from a share of the relevant market. For example, if a major customer for a particular product acquires a captive supplier of that product, the competitors of the acquired firm are thereafter foreclosed from competing with it for sales to the acquiring firm. Similarly, if a manufacturer acquires a captive retail outlet for its products, the manufacturer's competitors are foreclosed from competing for sales to that retail outlet. A vertical merger in the latter case may also result in reduced competition at the retail level. For instance, a shoe manufacturer acquires a retail shoe store chain that carries the brands of several competing manufacturers and has a dominant share of the retail market in certain geographic areas. If the retail chain carries only the acquiring manufacturer's brands after the merger occurs, competition among the acquiring manufacturer and its competitors is reduced in the retail market for shoes.

Creation of Increased Market Entry Barriers A second way in which vertical mergers threaten competition is that they may lead to *increased barriers to market entry* for new competitors. For example, if a major purchaser of a product acquires a captive supplier of that product, potential producers of the product may be discouraged from commencing production due to the merger-related contraction of the market for the product.

Elimination of Potential Competition in Acquired Firm's Market In addition, some vertical mergers threaten competition by *eliminating potential competition* in one of two ways. First, an acquiring firm may be perceived by existing competitors in the acquired firm's market as a likely potential entrant into that market. The threat of such a potential entrant "waiting in the wings" may moderate the behavior of existing competitors because they fear that pursuing pricing policies that exploit their current market position might cause the potential entrant to react by entering the market. The acquiring firm's entry into the market by the acquisition of an existing competitor means the end of its moderating influence as a potential entrant. Second, a vertical merger may deprive the market of the potential benefits that would have resulted if the acquiring firm had entered the market in a more competitive manner, such as by creating its own entrant into the market through internal expansion or by making a toehold acquisition of a small existing competitor and subsequently building it into a more significant competitor.

Historically, courts seeking to determine the legality of vertical mergers have tended to look at the *share of the relevant market foreclosed to competition.* If a more than insignificant market share is foreclosed to competition, courts consider other economic and historical factors. Factors viewed as aggravating the anticompetitive potential of a vertical merger include: a trend toward concentration or vertical integration in the industry, a past history of vertical integration in the industry, a past history of vertical acquisitions by the acquiring company, and significant barriers to entry resulting from the merger. This approach to determining the legality of vertical mergers has been criticized by some commentators. These critics argue that vertical integration may yield certain efficiencies of distribution and that vertical integration by merger may be more economically efficient than vertical integration by internal expansion. The Justice Department generally affords greater weight to efficiency arguments in cases involving vertical mergers than in cases involving horizontal mergers. The department generally applies the same criteria to all nonhorizontal mergers. We discuss these criteria in the following section.

Conglomerate Mergers

A **conglomerate merger** is a merger between two firms that neither compete with each other (because they do business in different product or geographic markets) nor have a supplier–customer relationship with each other. Conglomerate mergers may be either *market extension* mergers or *product extension* mergers. In a market extension merger, the acquiring firm expands into a new geographic market by purchasing a firm already doing business in that market. For example, a conglomerate that owns an east coast grocery chain buys a west coast grocery chain. In a product extension merger, the acquiring firm diversifies its operations by purchasing a company in a new product market. For example, a conglomerate with interests in the aerospace and electronics industries purchases a department store chain.

There is considerable disagreement over the economic effects of conglomerate acquisitions. As later discussion will reveal, conglomerate mergers have been attacked with some degree of success under section 7 if they involve **potential reciprocity,** serve to **eliminate potential competition,** or give an acquired firm an **unfair advantage** over its competitors. Nevertheless, there is significant sentiment that the Clayton Act is not well suited to dealing with conglomerate mergers. This realization has produced calls for specific legislation on the subject. Such legislation is probably desirable if we ultimately conclude that conglomerate merger activity is a proper subject for regulation.

Potential Reciprocity   Conglomerate mergers that involve *potential reciprocity* are among those sometimes held to be prohibited by section 7. A conglomerate merger may create a risk of potential reciprocity if the acquired firm produces a product regularly purchased by the acquiring firm's suppliers. Such suppliers, eager to continue their relationship with the acquiring firm, may thereafter purchase the acquired firm's products rather than those of its competitors.

Elimination of Potential Competition   Some conglomerate mergers may result in *elimination of potential competition* in ways similar to vertical mergers, and thus may be vulnerable to attack under section 7. If existing competitors perceive the acquiring company as a potential entrant in the acquired company's market, the acquiring company's entry by means of a conglomerate acquisition may result in the loss of the moderating influence that it had while waiting in the wings. In addition, when the acquiring company actually enters the new market by acquiring a well-established competitor rather than by starting a new competitor through internal expansion (a *de novo* entry) or by making a toehold acquisition, the market is deprived of the

Types of Mergers Covered by Section 7

CATEGORY	DESCRIPTION	EXAMPLE
Horizontal	Between competitors	One automobile manufacturer merges with another automobile manufacturer
Vertical	Between a supplier and its customer	An oil producer merges with an oil refiner
Conglomerate	Between two largely unrelated businesses	A candy company merges with a greeting card company

potential for increased competition flowing from the reduction in concentration that would have accompanied either of the latter strategies.

Relevant Supreme Court decisions suggest, however, that a high degree of proof is required before either of these potential competition arguments will be accepted. Arguments that a conglomerate merger eliminated a *perceived potential entrant* must be accompanied by proof that existing competitors actually perceived the acquiring firm as a potential entrant.[6] Arguments that a conglomerate acquisition eliminated an *actual* potential entrant (and thereby deprived the market of the benefits of reduced concentration) must be accompanied by evidence that the acquiring firm had the ability to enter the market by internal expansion or a toehold acquisition and that doing so would have ultimately yielded a substantial reduction in concentration.[7]

Unfair Advantage to Acquired Firm   Finally, conglomerate mergers may violate section 7 in certain instances when the acquired firm obtains an *unfair advantage* over its competitors. When a large firm acquires a firm that already enjoys a significant position in its market, the acquired firm may gain an unfair advantage over its competitors through its ability to draw on the greater resources and expertise of its new owner. This advantage may entrench the acquired firm in its market by deterring existing competitors from actively competing with it for market share and by causing other potential competitors to be reluctant to enter the market after the acquisition.

Virtually all of the important recent conglomerate merger cases have been settled out of court. As a result, we do not have a clear indication of the Supreme Court's current thinking on conglomerate merger issues. In recent years, the Justice Department has taken the position that the primary theories to be used by the department in attacking all *nonhorizontal* mergers are the *elimination of perceived and actual potential competition* theories. In employing these analytical tools, the department also considers other economic factors. These include: (1) the degree of concentration in the acquired firm's market; (2) the existence of barriers to entry into the market and the presence or absence of other firms with a comparable ability to enter; and (3) the market share of the acquired firm (with challenges being unlikely if this is 5 percent or less and likely if it is 20 percent or more). It remains to be seen whether the Supreme Court will accept this more restrictive view of the scope of section 7.

Figure 1 summarizes the types of mergers covered by section 7.

---

[6]*United States v. Falstaff Brewing Corp.*, 410 U.S. 526 (U.S. Sup. Ct. 1973).

[7]*United States v. Marine Bancorporation, Inc.*, 418 U.S. 602 (U.S. Sup. Ct. 1974).

TENNECO INC. v. FTC   689 F.2d 346 (2d Cir. 1982)

I n 1975, Tenneco, Inc., was the 15th largest industrial corporation in America. Tenneco's Walker Manufacturing Division produced and distributed a wide variety of automotive parts, the most important of which were exhaust system parts. Walker was the nation's leading seller of exhaust system parts in 1975 and 1976. Tenneco acquired control of Monroe Auto Equipment Company, a *leading manufacturer of automotive shock absorbers. Monroe was the number two firm in the national market for replacement shock absorbers. Monroe and Gabriel, the industry leader, accounted for over 77 percent of replacement shock absorber sales in 1976. General Motors and Questor Corporation, the third and fourth largest firms, controlled another 15 percent of the market.*

The replacement shock absorber market exhibited significant barriers to the entry of new competitors. Economies of scale in the industry dictated manufacturing plants of substantial size. Furthermore, the nature of the industry required would-be entrants to acquire significant new technologies and marketing skills unique to the industry. The Federal Trade Commission (Commission) concluded that Tenneco's acquisition of Monroe violated section 7 of the Clayton Act by eliminating both perceived and actual potential competition in the replacement shock absorber market. The Commission therefore ordered Tenneco to divest itself of Monroe. Tenneco appealed. ⌒

Meskill, Circuit Judge The Supreme Court has described the theory of perceived potential competition, which it has approved for application to cases brought under section 7 of the Clayton Act, as the principal focus of the potential competition doctrine. The Court has recognized that:

A market extension merger may be unlawful if the target market is substantially concentrated, if the acquiring firm has the characteristics, capabilities, and economic incentive to render it a perceived potential *de novo* entrant, and if the acquiring firm's presence on the fringe of the target market in fact tempered oligopolistic behavior on the part of existing participants in that market. *United States v. Marine Bancorporation, Inc.* (1974).

The actual potential competition theory, which has yet to receive sanction from the Supreme Court, would

proscribe a market extension merger solely on the ground that such a merger eliminates the prospect for long-term deconcentration of an oligopolistic market that in theory might result if the acquiring firm were forbidden to enter except through a *de novo* undertaking or through the acquisition of a small existing entrant.

We reject the Commission's finding that Tenneco was an actual potential entrant likely to increase competition in the market for replacement shock absorbers. Tenneco was actively considering entry into the market and was pursuing all leads to that end at least since the late 1960s or early 1970s. Moreover, Tenneco clearly possessed adequate financial resources to make the large initial investment needed to attempt to penetrate the market. The record, however, is deficient in evidence that there were viable toehold options available to Tenneco or that Tenneco would have entered the market *de novo*.

The Commission conceded that Tenneco never expressed any interest in entering the market for replacement shock absorbers "on a completely *de*

novo basis." However, the Commission found that Tenneco had expressed interest in entering the market essentially *de novo,* building the required production facilities from scratch and acquiring the necessary technology via a license from an established foreign shock absorber producer. The Commission concluded that Tenneco would likely have done so absent its acquisition of Monroe.

The Commission's reasoning is flawed. It ignores Tenneco's decision not to enter the market during the 1960s and early 1970s, a period of high profitability for shock absorber manufacturers, because of anticipated inadequate earnings during early years. The record is devoid of evidentiary support for the Commission's assertion that in the period relevant to this case, when industry earnings were in decline, Tenneco would have been willing to suffer the "cost disadvantage" inherent in the building of an efficient scale plant that would remain underutilized "for a number of years."

The Commission's conclusion that Tenneco would likely have entered the replacement shock absorber market through toehold acquisition is similarly flawed. The Commission identified Armstrong Patents, Ltd. ("Armstrong"), a British shock absorber manufacturer, DeCarbon Shock Absorber Co. ("DeCarbon"), a French company, and Blackstone Manufacturing Corp. ("Blackstone"), a small United States producer of shock absorbers, as potential toeholds. However, Tenneco in fact negotiated unsuccessfully with Armstrong and DeCarbon. Armstrong management indicated that Tenneco would have to offer a 100 percent premium over the market price of its stock to generate its interest. Tenneco's negotiations with DeCarbon, which were conducted through an independent broker, were equally fruitless. DeCarbon had asked a selling price of 100 times its earnings.

As for Blackstone, the Commission itself described that company as "a small, struggling domestic firm burdened with aged equipment, a less than complete product line, declining market share and a mediocre reputation." Since 1974 Blackstone had unsuccessfully sought a buyer for its business, soliciting, among others, Midas International Corp., which operates a chain of muffler installation shops, and Questor. Nevertheless, the Commission remarkably concluded that Blackstone "would have served as a viable method of toehold entry."

We also conclude that the record contains inadequate evidence to support the Commission's conclusion that Tenneco's acquisition of Monroe violated section 7 by eliminating Tenneco as a perceived potential competitor in the market for replacement shock absorbers. There is abundant evidence that the oligopolists in the market for replacement shock absorbers perceived Tenneco as a potential entrant. Industry executives testified that they considered Tenneco one of very few manufacturers with both the incentive and the capability to enter the market. This perception was based on Tenneco's financial strength and on the compatibility of shock absorbers with exhaust system parts produced by Tenneco's Walker Division.

However, the Commission's conclusion that the perception of Tenneco as a potential entrant actually tempered the conduct of oligopolists in the market must also be supported by substantial evidence. It is not. Tenneco argued that in the years immediately preceding its acquisition of Monroe the market for replacement shock absorbers had become highly competitive. The Commission apparently agrees with this assessment. The rate of increase in advertised retail prices for shock absorbers fell significantly behind inflation, and mass merchandisers such as Sears, Roebuck replaced traditional wholesale distributors as the leading purchasers of replacement shock absorbers from manufacturers. Sears's retail prices for shock absorbers were frequently below the prices that manufacturers charged wholesale distributors, who were several levels above the retail customer in the traditional chain of distribution.

The advent of increased sales by mass merchandisers coincided with aggressive competition among shock absorber manufacturers. Manufacturers offered substantial discounts off their circulated price sheets to traditional wholesalers and implemented "stocklifting," a practice in which a manufacturer buys a wholesaler's inventory of a competing manufacturer's product and replaces it with his own product.

While agreeing that competitive activity increased dramatically in the mid-1970s, the Commission stated:

> We disagree with [Tenneco] over the cause of that new competitive vigor. In brief, we find that the source of the improved economic performance lay in industry fears that Tenneco was likely to attempt entry—an actual "edge effect"—rather than in the buyer power supposedly asserted by mass merchants against their suppliers.

The Commission's hypothesis depends almost entirely on inferences drawn from the activity of Maremont [Gabriel's owner]. We have no doubt that direct evidence of an "edge effect" is not required to support a Commission finding of a Section 7 violation. In this case, however, direct evidence concerning Tenneco's "edge effect" on Maremont was elicited by the Commission, though it does not support the Commission's conclusion. During the testimony of Byron Pond, Senior Vice-President and Director of Maremont, the following colloquy occurred:

> *Q*: [by Commission Counsel]: Did the presence of Walker, IPC or Midas and/or TRW as likely potential entrants into the shock absorber market, have any effect on Maremont's decisions, business decisions?
> *A*: [by Mr. Pond]: I don't think that we looked specifically at competitors on a periodic basis or potential competitors in developing our strategy. I think we developed our strategy and approach to the business based on how we perceive it and how we perceived the opportunities.

Mr. Pond's testimony constitutes direct evidence that Tenneco had no direct effect on Maremont's business decisions or competitive activity. In the face of this contrary and unchallenged direct evidence, the substantiality of circumstantial evidence arguably suggesting an "edge effect" vanishes. Accordingly, we hold that the Commission's finding that Maremont's actions were probably taken in response to its desire to dissuade Tenneco from entering the market is unsupported by substantial evidence in the record.

Commission order set aside in favor of Tenneco.

CLAYTON ACT SECTION 8

If the same individuals control theoretically competing corporations, an obvious potential exists for collusive anticompetitive conduct such as price-fixing or division of markets. Section 8 of the Clayton Act was designed to minimize the risks posed by such interlocks. Initially, section 8 prohibited any person from serving as a *director* of two or more corporations (other than banks or common carriers) if either had "capital, surplus, and undivided profits aggregating more than $1,000,000" and the corporations were, or had been, competitors, "so that elimination of competition by agreement between them" would violate any of the antitrust laws. The Antitrust Amendments Act of 1990 amended section 8's original language to increase the amount required to trigger the statute from $1 million to $10 million (a figure to be adjusted annually by an amount equal to the percentage increase or decrease in the gross national product).

Section 8 establishes a per se standard of liability in the sense that a violation of the statute may be demonstrated without proof that the interlock harmed competition. Until recently, however, the statute's prohibition against interlocks was quite limited in scope because it barred only interlocking *directorates*. Nothing in the original language of section 8 prohibited a person from serving as an *officer* of two competing corporations, or as an officer of one firm and a director of its competitor. The Antitrust Amendments Act of 1990, however, expanded the scope of the statute by including senior *"officers"* (defined as officers elected or chosen by the board of directors) within its reach.

Although government enforcement of section 8 was historically lax, recent years have witnessed some signs of growing government interest in the statute. The Supreme Court, however, has indicated that section 8 should not be interpreted in an expansive fashion that strains the statutory language. *BankAmerica Corp. v. United States*[8] stemmed from a Justice Department attempt to police interlocking directorates between banks and insurance companies. Never before had an interlock involving a bank been challenged under section 8 because of the specific statutory language prohibit-

ing interlocks between corporations "other than banks." Concerned about the increasing areas in which banks and a variety of other businesses were competing in rapidly changing financial markets, the Justice Department argued that the statutory exception should apply only when both of the companies at issue were banks. Had the department been successful, the consequences for the banking industry could have been significant, given the long history of interlocking directorates between banks and other business corporations. The Supreme Court, however, rejected the government's broad reading of the statute, holding that the "most natural reading" of the statute was that the interlocking corporations must all be corporations "other than banks." The Antitrust Amendments Act of 1990 retained the statutory language exempting banks.

Signs of renewed government interest in section 8 produced significant concern in an era of conglomerate merger activity. Given the wide diversification that characterizes many large corporations, it would be increasingly easy to demonstrate some degree of competitive overlap among a substantial number of large, diversified corporations. Critics alleged that section 8 has operated to discourage qualified persons from serving as directors when no potential for actual competitive harm exists. In response to such criticism, the Antitrust Amendments Act of 1990 specified that individuals may serve as officers or directors of competing corporations when the "competitive overlap" between them is an insignificant part of either company's total sales.

THE ROBINSON-PATMAN ACT

Background

Section 2 of the Clayton Act originally prohibited *local and territorial price discrimination* by sellers, a practice monopolists frequently used to destroy smaller competitors. A large company operating in a number of geographic markets would sell at or below cost in markets where it faced local competitors, and would then make up its losses by selling at higher prices in areas where it faced no competition. Faced with such tactics, the smaller local competitors might eventually be driven out of business. Section 2 was aimed at such **primary level** (or *first line*) price discrimination.

---

[8]462 U.S. 122 (U.S. Sup. Ct. 1983).

FIGURE **2**

Levels of Price Discrimination

TYPE OF DISCRIMINATION	TYPE OF HARM	EXAMPLE
First Line	Injury to the seller's competitors	A seller subsidizes its low prices in an area of high competition by raising its prices in areas where it has little competition.
Second Line	Injury to the competitors of the favored buyer	A high-volume chain store induces its suppliers to give it discriminatorily low prices, enabling it to undersell its competitors.
Third Line	Injury to the competitors of the favored buyer's buyers	A wholesaler receiving discriminatorily low prices from its manufacturer passes the savings on to its retailers, enabling them to undersell their competitors.

During the 1930s, Congress was confronted with complaints that large chain stores were using their buying power to induce manufacturers to sell to them at prices lower than those offered to their smaller, independent competitors. Chain stores were also inclined to seek and obtain other payments and services their smaller competitors did not receive. Being able to purchase at lower prices and to obtain discriminatory payments and services arguably gave large firms a competitive advantage over their smaller competitors. Such price discrimination in sales to the competing customers of a particular seller is known as **secondary level** (or *second line*) price discrimination.

In addition, the customers of a manufacturer's favored customer (such as a wholesaler receiving a functional discount) may gain a competitive advantage over *their* competitors (for example, other retailers purchasing directly from the manufacturer at a higher price) if the favored customer passes on all or a portion of its discount to its customers. This form of price discrimination is known as **tertiary level** (or *third line*) price discrimination.

Congress responded to these problems by passing the Robinson-Patman Act in 1936. The Robinson-Patman Act preserved Clayton Act section 2's ban on primary level price discrimination. It also amended section 2 to outlaw secondary and tertiary level direct price discrimination, as well as indirect price discrimination in the form of discriminatory payments and services to a seller's customers. Since its enactment, the Robinson-Patman Act has been the subject of widespread dissatisfaction and criticism. Critics have long charged that the act often protects competitors at the expense of promot-

ing competition. Government enforcement of the act has been haphazard over the years, with prominent officials in the Justice Department and the Federal Trade Commission sometimes voicing disagreement with the act's underlying policies and assumptions. This government stance, when combined with Supreme Court decisions making private enforcement of the act difficult, raises questions about the act's future usefulness as a component of our antitrust laws.

Figure 2 summarizes the levels of price discrimination addressed by the Robinson-Patman Act.

Jurisdiction

The Robinson-Patman Act applies only to discriminatory acts that occur "in commerce." This test is narrower than the "affecting commerce" test employed under the Sherman Act. At least one of the discriminatory acts complained of must take place in interstate commerce. Thus, the act probably would not apply if a Texas manufacturer discriminated in price in sales to two Texas customers. Some lower federal courts have indicated, however, that even wholly intrastate sales may be deemed sufficiently "in commerce" if the nonfavored buyer bought the goods for resale to out-of-state customers.

Section 2(a)

Section 2(a) of the Robinson-Patman Act prohibits sellers, in certain instances, from *discriminating in price* "between different purchasers of commodities of like grade or quality." Such discrimination is prohibited when its effect may be to (1) "substantially ... lessen competition or tend to create a monopoly in any line of commerce," or (2) "injure, destroy, or prevent competition with any person who either grants [*primary level*] or knowingly receives [*secondary level*] the benefit of such discrimination, or with the customers of either of them [*tertiary level*]."

Price Discrimination   To violate section 2(a), a seller must have made two or more sales to different purchasers at different prices. Merely quoting a discriminatory price or refusing to sell except at a discriminatory price is not a violation of the statute, because no actual purchase is involved. For the same reason, price discrimination in lease or consignment transactions is not covered by section 2(a). Actual sales at different prices to different purchasers will not be treated as discriminatory unless the sales were fairly close in time.

For purposes of deciding whether discriminatory prices have been charged to two or more purchasers, the degree of control a parent corporation exercises over its subsidiaries sometimes assumes major im-portance. For example, a parent that sells a product directly to one customer at a low price may be found to have engaged in price discrimination if a wholesaler actively controlled by the parent contemporaneously sells the same product at a higher price to a competitor of the parent's customer. On the other hand, contemporaneous sales by a parent to a wholly owned subsidiary and to an independent competitor at different prices are not treated as price discrimination, because no true sale has been made to the subsidiary.

Finally, section 2(a) does not directly address the legality of *functional discounts*. Such discounts are sometimes granted to buyers at various levels in a product's chain of distribution because of differences in the functions those buyers perform in the distribution system. As indicated in the *Texaco* case, which follows shortly, the legality of such discounts depends on their competitive effect. If a seller charges wholesale customers lower prices than it charges retail customers, the Robinson-Patman Act is not violated unless the lower wholesale prices are somehow passed on to retailers in competition with the seller's retail customers.

TEXACO INC. v. HASBROUCK   496 U.S. 543 (U.S. Sup. Ct. 1990)

Ricky Hasbrouck and 11 other plaintiffs were Texaco retail service station dealers in the Spokane area. They purchased gasoline directly from Texaco and resold it at retail under the Texaco trademark. Throughout the relevant time period (1972–81), Texaco also supplied gasoline to two gasoline distributors, Dompier Oil Company and Gull Oil Company, at a price that was at various times between 2.5 cents and 5.75 cents per gallon lower than the price Hasbrouck paid.

Dompier and Gull sold the gasoline they purchased from Texaco to independent retail service stations. Dompier sold the gasoline to retailers under the Texaco trademark; Gull marketed it under private brand names. Gull's customers either sold their gasoline on consignment (in which case they set their own prices) or on commission (in which case Gull set their resale prices). Gull retained title until the gas was sold to a retail customer in either case. Some of the retail stations supplied by Dompier were owned and operated by Dompier's salaried employees. Both Dompier and Gull picked up gas at the Texaco bulk plant and delivered it to their retail customers, a service for which Dompier was compensated by Texaco at the common carrier rate.

Hasbrouck and the other dealers filed a price discrimination suit against Texaco under section 2(a) of the Robinson-Patman Act. At trial, Texaco argued that its lower prices to Gull and Dompier were lawful "functional discounts." The jury awarded the plaintiffs $1,349,700 in treble damages. When the Ninth Circuit Court of Appeals affirmed the jury award, Texaco appealed. ∞

Stevens, Justice   Section 2(a) contains no express reference to functional discounts. It does contain two affirmative defenses that provide protection for two categories of discounts—those that are justified by savings in the seller's cost of manufacture, delivery, or sale, and those that represent a good faith response to the equally low prices of a competitor. In order to establish a violation of the Act, plaintiffs had the burden of proving four facts: (1) that Texaco's sales to Gull and Dompier were made in interstate commerce; (2) that the gasoline sold to them was of the same grade and quality as that sold to plaintiffs; (3) that Texaco discriminated in price as between Gull and Dompier on the one hand and plaintiffs on the other; and (4) that the discrimination had a prohibited effect on competition.

The first two elements of plaintiffs' case are not disputed in this Court. Texaco does argue, however, that although it charged different prices, it did not "discriminate in price" within the meaning of the Act, and that, at least to the extent that Gull and Dompier acted as wholesalers, the price differentials did not injure competition. Texaco's first argument would create a blanket exception for all functional discounts. Indeed, carried to its logical conclusion, it would exempt all price differentials except those given to competing purchasers. The primary basis for Texaco's argument is the following comment by Congressman Utterback, an active sponsor of the Act:

In its meaning as simple English, a discrimination is more than a mere difference. Underlying the meaning of the word is the idea that some relationship exists between the parties to the discrimination which entitles them to equal treatment, whereby the difference granted to one casts some burden or disadvantage upon the other. . . . [W]here no such relationship exists, where the goods are sold in different markets and the conditions affecting those markets set different price levels for them, the sale to different customers at . . . different prices would not constitute discrimination within the meaning of this bill.

We have previously considered this excerpt from the legislative history, and have refused to draw from it the conclusion Texaco proposes. Although the excerpt does support Texaco's argument, we remain persuaded that the argument is foreclosed by the text of the Act itself. In a statute that plainly reveals a concern with competitive consequences at different levels of distribution, and carefully defines specific affirmative defenses, it would be anomalous to assume that Congress intended the term "discriminate" to have such a limited meaning. Since we have already decided that a price discrimination within the meaning of section 2(a) "is merely a price difference," we must reject Texaco's first argument.

In *FTC v. Morton Salt Co.* (1948), we held that an injury to competition may be inferred from evidence that some purchasers had to pay their supplier "substantially more for their goods than their competitors had to pay." Texaco, supported by the United States and the Federal Trade Commission as *amici curiae,* argues that this presumption should not apply to differences between prices charged to wholesalers and those charged to retailers. Moreover, they argue that it would be inconsistent with fundamental antitrust policies to construe the Act as requiring a seller to control his customers' resale prices. The seller should not be held liable for the independent pricing decisions of his customers. As the Government correctly notes, this argument endorses the position advocated 35 years ago in the Report of the Attorney General's Nation Committee to Study the Antitrust Laws (1955).

After observing that suppliers ought not to be held liable for the independent pricing decisions of their buyers, and that without functional discounts distributors might go uncompensated for the services they performed, the Committee wrote:

On the other hand, the law should tolerate no subterfuge. For instance, where a wholesaler-retailer *buys* only part of his goods as a wholesaler, he must not claim a functional discount on all. Only to the extent that a buyer *actually* performs certain functions, assuming all the risk, investment, and costs involved, should he legally qualify for a functional discount.

We generally agree with this description of the legal status of functional discounts. A supplier need not satisfy the rigorous requirements of the cost justification defense in order to prove that a particular functional discount is reasonable and accordingly did not cause any substantial lessening of competition between a wholesaler's customers and the supplier's direct customers. The record in this case, however, adequately supports the finding that Texaco violated the Act.

The hypothetical predicate for the Committee's entire discussion of functional discounts is a price differential "that merely accords due recognition and reimbursement for actual marketing functions." Such a discount is not illegal. In this case, however, both the District Court and the Court of Appeals concluded that there was no substantial evidence indicating that the discounts to Gull and Dompier constituted a reasonable reimbursement for the value to Texaco of their actual marketing functions. Indeed, Dompier was separately compensated for its hauling function, and neither Gull nor Dompier maintained any significant storage facilities.

Both Gull and Dompier received the full discount on all their purchases even though most of their volume was resold directly to consumers. The extra margin on those sales obviously enabled them to price aggressively in both their retail and their wholesale marketing. To the extent that Dompier and Gull competed with plaintiffs in the retail market, the presumption of adverse effect on competition recognized in the *Morton Salt* case becomes all the more appropriate. The evidence indicates, moreover, that Texaco affirmatively encouraged Dompier to expand its retail business and was fully informed about the persistent and marketwide consequences of its own pricing policies. Indeed, its own executives recognized that the dramatic impact on the market was almost entirely attributable to the magnitude of the distributor discount and the hauling allowance. The special facts of this case thus make it peculiarly difficult for Texaco to claim that it is being held liable for the independent pricing decisions of Gull or Dompier.

The competitive injury component of a Robinson-Patman Act violation is not limited to the injury to competition between the favored and disfavored purchaser; it also encompasses the injury to competition between their customers. This conclusion is compelled by the statutory language, which specifically encompasses not only the adverse effect of price discrimination on persons who either grant or knowingly receive the benefit of such discrimination, but also to the "customers of either of them." Such indirect competitive effects surely may not be presumed automatically in every functional discount setting, and, indeed, one would expect that most functional discounts will be legitimate discounts that do not harm competition. At the least, a functional discount that constitutes a reasonable reimbursement for the purchasers' actual marketing functions will not violate the Act. Yet it is also true that not every functional discount is entitled to a judgment of legitimacy, and that it will sometimes be possible to produce evidence showing that a particular discount caused a price discrimination of the sort that the Act prohibits. When such anticompetitive effects are proved—as we believe they were in this case—they are covered by the Act.

Judgment for Hasbrouck affirmed.

Commodities of Like Grade and Quality   Section 2(a) applies only to price discrimination in the sale of *commodities*. Price discrimination involving intangibles, real estate, or services must be challenged under the Sherman Act (as a restraint of trade or an attempt to monopolize) or under the FTC Act (as an unfair method of competition).[9] The essence of price discrimination is that two or more buyers are charged differing prices for the *same* commodity. Sales of commodities of varying grades or quality at varying prices, therefore, do not violate section 2(a) so long as uniform prices are charged for commodities of equal quality. Some *physical difference* in the grade or quality of two products must be shown to justify a price differential between them. Differences solely in the brand name or label under which a product is sold—such as the seller's standard brand and a "house" brand sold to a large customer for resale under the customer's label—do not justify discriminatory pricing.

Anticompetitive Effect   Only price discrimination having a *probable* anticompetitive effect is prohibited by section 2(a). Traditionally, courts have required a higher degree of proof of likely competitive injury in cases involving primary level price discrimination (which may damage the seller's competitors) than in cases involving secondary or tertiary level discrimination (which threatens competition among the seller's customers or its customers' customers). To prove a primary level violation, a market analysis must show that competitive harm has occurred as a result of the seller's engaging in significant and sustained price discrimination with the intent of punishing or disciplining a competitor. Proof of predatory pricing is often offered as evidence of a seller's anticompetitive

---

[9]The FTC Act was discussed in Chapter 47.

intent. The *Brown & Williamson case,* which follows shortly, addresses predatory pricing claims under the Robinson-Patman Act and emphasizes that likely harm to competition—not merely to a competitor—remains the critical focus.

In secondary or tertiary level cases, courts tend to infer the existence of competitive injury from evidence of substantial price discrimination between competing purchasers over time. Some qualifications on this point are in order, however. Price discrimination for a short period of time ordinarily does not support an inference of competitive injury. Likewise, if the evidence indicates that nonfavored buyers could have purchased the same goods from other sellers at prices identical to those the defendant seller charged its favored customers, no competitive injury is inferred. Finally, buyers seeking treble damages for secondary or tertiary level harm must still prove that they suffered actual damages as a result of a violation of the act.

BROOKE GROUP LTD. v. BROWN & WILLIAMSON TOBACCO CORP.   509 U.S. 209 (U.S. Sup. Ct. 1993)

Brown & Williamson Tobacco Corp. (BW) and Brooke Group Ltd. (referred to here by its former corporate name, Liggett Corp.) are two of only six firms of significant consequence in the oligopolistic cigarette manufacturing industry. In 1980, BW's share of the national cigarette market was roughly 12 percent. This share placed BW a distant third behind market leaders Philip Morris and R.J. Reynolds. Liggett's share was less than half of BW's. Liggett pioneered the development of the economy segment of the national cigarette market in 1980 by introducing a popular line of "black and white" generic cigarettes (low-priced cigarettes sold in plain white packages with simple black lettering). As Liggett's sales of generic cigarettes became substantial, other cigarette manufacturers started introducing economy-priced cigarettes. In 1984, BW introduced a black and white cigarette whose net price was lower than Liggett's. BW achieved this lower price by offering volume rebates to wholesalers.

Liggett sued BW, claiming that BW's volume rebates amounted to price discrimination having a reasonable probability of injuring competition, in violation of section 2(a) of the Robinson-Patman Act. Specifically, Liggett alleged that BW's rebates were integral to a scheme of predatory pricing, under which BW reduced its net prices for generic cigarettes below average variable costs. Liggett further alleged that this pricing by BW was designed to pressure Liggett to raise its list prices on generic cigarettes, so that the percentage price difference between generic and branded cigarettes would narrow. As a result, according to Liggett, the growth of the economy segment would be restrained and BW would thereby be able to preserve its supracompetitive profits on branded cigarettes. Liggett further asserted that it could not afford to reduce its wholesale rebates without losing market share to BW. Therefore, Liggett claimed that its only choice, if it wished to avoid prolonged losses on the generic line that had become its principal product, was to raise retail prices.

After a 115-day trial, the jury returned a verdict in Liggett's favor for $49.6 million in damages. The district court trebled this amount. After reviewing the trial record, however, the district court concluded that BW was entitled to prevail as a matter of law. The court therefore set aside the jury's verdict and entered judgment in BW's favor. Liggett appealed. The Fourth Circuit Court of Appeals affirmed, holding (apparently) that there cannot be liability for predatory price discrimination that allegedly takes place in the context of an oligopoly such as the cigarette industry. The Supreme Court granted Liggett's petition for a writ of certiorari. ∞

Kennedy, Justice   Liggett contends that BW's discriminatory volume rebates to wholesalers threatened substantial competitive injury by furthering a predatory pricing scheme designed to purge competition from the economy segment of the cigarette market. This type of injury, which harms direct competitors of the discriminating seller, is known as primary-line injury. [P]rimary-line competitive injury under the Robinson-Patman Act is of the same general character as the injury inflicted by predatory pricing schemes actionable under section 2 of the Sherman Act. [T]he essence of the claim under either statute is the same.

Accordingly, whether the claim alleges predatory pricing under section 2 of the Sherman Act or primary-line price discrimination under the Robinson-Patman Act, two prerequisites to recovery [exist]. First, a plaintiff seeking to establish competitive injury resulting from a rival's low prices must prove that the prices complained of are below an appropriate measure of its rival's costs. [Second, the plaintiff must demonstrate] that the competitor had a reasonable prospect [if the claim is brought under the Robinson-Patman Act], or . . . a dangerous probability [if the claim is brought under section 2 of the Sherman Act], of recouping its investment in below-cost prices. Recoupment is the ultimate object of an unlawful predatory-pricing scheme; it is the means by which a predator profits from predation. Without it, predatory pricing produces lower aggregate prices in the market, and consumer welfare is enhanced. That below-cost pricing may impose painful losses on its target is of no moment to the antitrust laws if competition is not injured.

For recoupment to occur, below-cost pricing must be capable . . . of producing the intended effects on the firm's rivals, whether driving them from the market, or, as was alleged to be the goal here, causing them to raise their prices to supracompetitive levels within a disciplined oligopoly. If circumstances indicate that below-cost pricing could likely produce its intended effect on the target, there is still the further question whether it would be likely to injure competition in the relevant market. The plaintiff must demonstrate that there is a likelihood that the predatory scheme alleged would cause a rise in prices above a competitive level that would be sufficient to compensate for the amounts expended on the predation. These prerequisites to recovery are not easy to establish, but . . . they are essential components of real market injury.

Liggett . . . allege[s] . . . that BW sought to preserve supracompetitive profits on branded cigarettes by pressuring Liggett to raise its generic cigarette prices through a process of tacit collusion with the other cigarette companies. Tacit collusion, sometimes called oligopolistic price coordination or conscious parallelism, describes the process, not in itself unlawful, by which firms in a concentrated market might in effect share monopoly power, setting their prices at a profit-maximizing, supracompetitive level by recognizing their shared economic interests and their interdependence with respect to price and output decisions.

In *Matsushita Electric Industrial Co. v. Zenith Radio Corp.* (1986), we remarked upon the general implausibility of predatory pricing. *Matsushita* observed that such schemes are even more improbable when they require coordinated action among several firms. However unlikely predatory pricing by multiple firms may be when they conspire, it is even less likely when, as here, there is no express coordination. Firms that seek to recoup predatory losses through the conscious parallelism of oligopoly must rely on uncertain and ambiguous signals to achieve concerted action. The signals are subject to misinterpretation and are a blunt and imprecise means of ensuring smooth cooperation, especially in the context of changing or unprecedented market circumstances. This anticompetitive minuet is most difficult to compose and to perform, even for a disciplined oligopoly.

[O]n the whole, tacit cooperation among oligopolists must be considered the least likely means of recouping predatory losses. In addition to the difficulty of achieving effective tacit coordination and the high likelihood that any attempt to discipline will produce an outbreak of competition, the predator's present losses in a case like this fall on it alone, while the later supracompetitive profits must be shared with every other oligopolist in proportion to its market share, including the intended victim. In this case, for example, BW, with its 11–12% share of the cigarette market, would have had to generate around $9 in supracompetitive profits for each $1 invested in predation; the remaining $8 would belong to its competitors, who had taken no risk.

[However,] [t]o the extent that the Court of Appeals may have held that the interdependent pricing of an oligopoly may never provide a means for achieving recoupment and so may not form the basis of a primary-line injury claim, we disagree. A predatory pricing scheme designed to preserve or create a stable oligopoly, if successful, can injure consumers in the same way, and to the same extent, as one designed to bring about a monopoly. However unlikely that possibility may be as a general matter, when the realities of the market and the record facts indicate that it has occurred and was likely to have succeeded, theory will not stand in the way of liability. The Robinson-Patman Act . . . suggests no exclusion from coverage when primary-line injury occurs in an oligopoly setting. We decline to create a per se rule of nonliability [under the Robinson-Patman Act] for predatory price discrimination when recoupment is alleged to take place through supracompetitive oligopoly pricing.

Although Liggett's theory of liability, as an abstract matter, is within the reach of the statute, we agree with the [lower courts] that Liggett was not entitled to submit its case to the jury. Liggett . . . failed to demonstrate competitive injury as a matter of law. The evidence is inadequate to show that in pursuing [an alleged below-cost pricing] scheme, BW had a reasonable prospect of recovering its losses from below-cost pricing through slowing the growth of generics.

The only means by which BW is alleged to have established oligopoly pricing . . . is through tacit price coordination with the other cigarette firms. Yet the situation facing the cigarette companies in the 1980s would have made such tacit coordination unmanageable. Tacit coordination is facilitated by a stable market environment, fungible products, and a small number of variables upon which the firms seeking to coordinate their pricing may focus. By 1984, however, the cigarette market was in an obvious state of flux. The introduction of generic cigarettes in 1980 represented the first serious price competition in the cigarette market since the 1930s. This development was bound to unsettle previous expectations and patterns of market conduct and to reduce the cigarette firms' ability to predict each other's behavior. The larger number of product types and pricing variables also decreased the probability of effective parallel pricing.

Even if all the cigarette companies were willing to participate in a scheme to restrain the growth of the generic segment, they would not have been able to coordinate their actions and raise prices above a competitive level unless they understood that BW's entry into the [economy] segment was not a genuine effort to compete with Liggett. If even one other firm misinterpreted BW's entry as an effort to expand share, a chain reaction of competitive responses would almost certainly have resulted, and oligopoly discipline would have broken down, perhaps irretrievably. Liggett argues that [BW's] maintaining existing list prices while offering substantial rebates to wholesalers was a signal to the other cigarette firms that BW did not intend to attract additional smokers to the generic segment by its entry. But a reasonable jury could not conclude that this pricing structure eliminated or rendered insignificant the risk that the other firms might misunderstand BW's entry as a competitive move.

We hold that the evidence cannot support a finding that BW's alleged scheme was likely to result in oligopolistic price coordination and sustained supracompetitive pricing in the generic segment of the national cigarette market. Without this, BW had no reasonable prospect of recouping its predatory losses and could not inflict the injury to competition the antitrust laws prohibit.

Judgment for BW affirmed.

Defenses to Section 2(a) Liability

There are three major statutory defenses to liability under section 2(a): *cost justification, changing conditions,* and *meeting competition in good faith.*

Cost Justification Section 2(a) specifically legalizes price differentials that do no more than make an appropriate allowance for differences in the "cost of manufacture, sale, or delivery resulting from the differing methods or quantities" in which goods are sold or delivered to buyers. This defense recognizes the reality that it may be less costly for a seller to service some buyers than others. Sales to buyers purchasing large quantities may in some cases be more cost-effective than small-quantity sales to their competitors. Sellers are allowed to pass on such cost savings to their customers.

Utilizing this *cost justification* defense is quite difficult and expensive for sellers, however, because quantity discounts must be supported by *actual evidence of cost savings.* Sellers are allowed to average their costs and classify their customers into categories based on their average sales costs. The customers included in any particular classification, however, must be sufficiently similar to justify similar treatment.

Changing Conditions Section 2(a) specifically exempts price discriminations that reflect "changing conditions in the market for or the marketability of the goods." The *changing conditions* defense has been narrowly confined to temporary situations caused by the physical nature of the goods. Examples include the deterioration of perishable goods and a declining market for seasonal goods. This defense also applies to forced judicial sales of the goods (such as during bankruptcy proceedings involving the seller) and to good faith sales by sellers that have decided to cease selling the goods in question.

Meeting Competition Section 2(b) of the Robinson-Patman Act states that price discrimination may be lawful if the discriminatory lower price was charged "in good faith to meet an equally low price of a competitor." This *meeting competition* defense is necessary to prevent the act from stifling the very competition it was designed to preserve. For example, suppose Sony Corporation has been selling a particular model of video recorder to its customers for $350 per unit. Sony then learns that Sharp Electronics is offering a comparable recorder to Acme Appliance Stores for $300 per unit. Acme, however, competes with Best Buy Video Stores, a Sony customer that has recently been charged the $350 price. Should Sony be forced to refrain from offering the lower competitive price to Acme for fear that Best Buy will charge Sony with price discrimination if it does so? If Sony cannot offer the lower competitive price to Acme, competition between Sony and Sharp will plainly suffer.

Section 2(b) avoids this undesirable result by allowing a seller to charge a lower price to certain customers if the seller has reasonable grounds for believing that the lower price is necessary to meet an equally low price offered by a competitor. Sellers may meet competition *offensively* (to gain a new customer) or *defensively* (to keep an existing customer). The meeting competition defense is subject to significant qualifications, however. First, the lower price must be necessary to meet a lower price charged by a competitor of the *seller,* not to enable a customer of the seller to compete more effectively with that customer's competitors. Second, the seller may lawfully seek only to *meet,* not *beat,* its competitor's price. A seller cannot, however, be held in violation of the act for beating a competitor's price if it did so unknowingly in a good faith attempt to meet competition. Third, the seller may

reduce its price only to meet competitors' prices for products of *similar quality.*

Courts also have held that the discriminatory price must be a response to an individual competitive situation rather than the product of a seller's wholesale adoption of a competitor's discriminatory pricing system. However, a seller's competitive response need not be on a customer-by-customer basis, so long as the lower price is offered only to those customers that the seller reasonably believes are being offered a lower price by the seller's competitors.

Indirect Price Discrimination

When Congress passed the Robinson-Patman Act, it also addressed **indirect price discrimination,** which takes the form of a seller's discriminating among competing buyers by making discriminatory payments to selected buyers or by furnishing certain buyers with services not made available to their competitors. Three sections of the act are designed to prevent such practices.

False Brokerage Section 2(c) prohibits sellers from granting, and buyers from receiving, any "commission, brokerage, or other compensation, or any allowance or discount in lieu thereof, except for services rendered in connection with the sale or purchase of goods." This provision prevents large buyers, either directly or through subsidiary brokerage agents, from receiving phony commissions or brokerage payments from their suppliers. The courts and the FTC originally interpreted section 2(c) as prohibiting any brokerage payments to a buyer or its agent, regardless of whether the buyer or agent had in fact provided sale-related services that would otherwise have been performed by the seller or an independent broker. This narrow interpretation drew heavy criticism, however, because it operated to create a closed shop for independent brokers by denying large buyers any incentive to create their own brokerage services. This interpretation also made it difficult for small, independent retailers to create cooperative buying organizations and thereby match more closely the buying power of their large competitors. More recent decisions have responded to these criticisms by allowing payments that are for services actually performed by buyers and represent actual cost savings to sellers.

Section 2(c), unlike section 2(a), establishes a per se standard of liability. No demonstration of probable anticompetitive effect is required for a violation. Neither the cost justification nor meeting competition defense is available in 2(c) cases. Individual plaintiffs still must prove that they have suffered some injury as a result of a 2(c) violation, however, before they are entitled to recover damages.

Discriminatory Payments and Services Sellers and their customers benefit from merchandising activities that customers employ to promote the sellers' products. Section 2(d) prohibits sellers from making *discriminatory payments* to competing customers for such customer-performed services as advertising and promotional activities or such customer-provided facilities as shelf space. Section 2(e) prohibits sellers from discriminating in the *services* they provide to competing customers, such as by providing favored customers with a display case or a demonstration kit.

A seller may lawfully make payments or provide services to customers only if the payments or services are made available to all competing customers on *proportionately equal terms.* This means that the seller must inform all customers of the availability of the payments or services and must distribute them on some rational basis, such as the quantity of goods bought by the customer. The seller must also devise a flexible plan that enables its various classes of customers to participate in the payment or services program in an appropriate way.

As does section 2(c), sections 2(d) and 2(e) create a per se liability standard. No proof of probable harm to competition is required for a violation; no cost justification defense is available. The meeting competition defense provided by section 2(b) is applicable, however, to actions under sections 2(d) and 2(e).

Buyer Inducement of Discrimination

Section 2(f) of the Robinson-Patman Act makes it illegal for a buyer *knowingly to induce or receive* a discriminatory price in violation of section 2(a). The logic of the section is that buyers who are successful in demanding discriminatory prices should face liability along with the sellers charging discriminatory prices. To violate section 2(f), the buyer must know that the price the buyer received was unjustifiably

discriminatory. This means that the price probably was neither cost-justified nor made in response to changing conditions. Section 2(f) does not apply to buyer inducements of discriminatory payments or services prohibited by sections 2(d) and 2(e). Such buyer actions may, however, be attacked as unfair methods of competition under section 5 of the FTC Act.

In *Great Atlantic and Pacific Tea Co. v. FTC,*[10] the Supreme Court further narrowed the effective reach of section 2(f) by holding that buyers who knowingly received a discriminatory price do not violate the act if their seller has a valid defense to the charge of violating section 2(a). The seller in *Great Atlantic* had a "meeting competition in good faith" defense under section 2(b). This fact was held to insulate the buyer from liability even though the buyer knew that the seller had beaten, rather than merely met, its competitor's price.

ANTITRUST EXCEPTIONS AND EXEMPTIONS

Introduction

A wide variety of economic activities occur outside the reach of the antitrust laws. This is so either because these activities have been specifically exempted by statute or because courts have carved out nonstatutory exceptions designed to balance our antitrust policy in favor of competition against other social policies. With critics charging that a number of existing exemptions are no longer justifiable, recent years have witnessed a judicial tendency to narrow the scope of many exemptions.

Statutory Exemptions

Labor Unions and Certain Union Activities Sections 6 and 20 of the Clayton Act and the Norris-LaGuardia Act of 1932 provide that *labor unions* are not combinations or conspiracies in restraint of trade and exempt certain union activities, including boycotts and secondary picketing, from antitrust scrutiny. This statutory exemption does not, however, exempt union combinations with nonlabor groups aimed at restraining trade or creating a monopoly. An example of such nonexempted

---

[10]440 U.S. 69 (U.S. Sup. Ct. 1979).

activity would be a labor union's agreement with Employer A to call a strike at Employer B's plants. In an attempt to accommodate the strong public policy in favor of collective bargaining, courts have also created a limited nonstatutory exemption for legitimate union-employer agreements arising from the collective bargaining context.

Agricultural Cooperatives and Certain Cooperative Actions Section 6 of the Clayton Act and the Capper-Volstead Act exempt the formation and collective marketing activities of *agricultural cooperatives* from antitrust liability. Courts have narrowly construed this exemption, however. Cooperatives including members not engaged in the production of agricultural commodities have been denied exempt status. One such example would be a cooperative including retailers or wholesalers who do not also produce the commodity in question. The agricultural cooperatives exemption extends only to legitimate collective marketing activities. It does not legitimize coercive or predatory practices that are unnecessary to accomplish lawful cooperative goals. For example, this exemption would not prevent the antitrust laws from being applied to a boycott designed to force nonmembers of the cooperative to adopt a pricing policy established by the cooperative.

Joint Export Activities The Webb-Pomerene Act exempts the *joint export activities* of American companies, so long as those activities do not "artificially or intentionally enhance or depress prices within the United States." The purpose of the act is to encourage export activity by allowing the formation of combinations to enable domestic firms to compete more effectively with foreign cartels. Some critics assert that this exemption is no longer needed because there are fewer foreign cartels today and American firms often play a dominant role in foreign trade. Others question whether any group of American firms enjoying significant domestic market shares in the sale of a particular product could agree on an international marketing strategy, such as the amounts that they will export, without indirectly affecting domestic supplies and prices.

Business of Insurance The McCarran-Ferguson Act exempts from federal antitrust scrutiny those aspects of the *business of insurance* that are subject to state regulation. The act provides, however, that state law cannot legitimize any agreement to boycott, coerce, or intimidate others. Because the insurance industry is extensively regulated by the states, many practices in the industry are outside the reach of the federal antitrust laws.

In recent years, however, courts have tended to decrease the scope of this exemption by narrowly construing the meaning of "business of insurance." For example, in *Union Labor Life Insurance Co. v. Pireno*,[11] the Supreme Court held that the exemption did not insulate from antitrust scrutiny a peer review system in which an insurance company used a committee established by a state chiropractic association to review the reasonableness of particular chiropractors' charges. The Court stated that to qualify for the business of insurance exemption, a challenged practice must have the effect of transferring or spreading policyholders' risk and must be an integral part of the policy relationship between the insured and the insurer. Therefore, only practices related to traditional functions of the insurance business, such as underwriting and risk-spreading, are likely to be exempt.

Calls from some quarters for repeal of the McCarran-Ferguson Act have led to the introduction of bills in Congress to that effect in recent years. These proposals for legislation typically contemplate, however, that insurers could continue to participate in certain joint activities, such as collecting and exchanging information on fraudulent claims, pooling historical loss data, and developing standardized policy forms. As of the time this book went to press, no such bill had been passed.

Other Regulated Industries Many other *regulated industries* enjoy various degrees of antitrust immunity. The airline, banking, utility, railroad, shipping, and securities industries traditionally have been regulated in the public interest. The regulatory agencies supervising such industries have frequently been given the power to approve industry practices such as rate-setting and mergers that would otherwise violate antitrust laws. In recent years, there has been a distinct tendency to deregulate many regulated industries. If this trend continues, a greater portion of the economic activity in these industries could be subjected to antitrust scrutiny.

---

[11]458 U.S. 119 (U.S. Sup. Ct. 1982).

State Action Exemption

In *Parker v. Brown*,[12] the Supreme Court held that a California state agency's regulation of the production and price of raisins was a state action exempt from the federal antitrust laws. The **state action exemption** developed in *Parker v. Brown* recognizes states' rights to regulate economic activity in the interest of their citizens. It also, however, may tempt business entities to seek "friendly" state regulation as a way of shielding anticompetitive activity from antitrust supervision. Recognizing this possibility, courts have placed important limitations on the scope of the state action exemption.

First, the exemption extends only to governmental actions by a state or to actions compelled by a state acting in its sovereign capacity. Second, as indicated in the *Ticor Title Insurance* case (which follows shortly), challenged activity cannot qualify for immunity under this exemption unless the activity is "clearly articulated and affirmatively expressed as state policy" and "actively supervised" by the state. In other words, the price of antitrust immunity is real regulation by the state. The Supreme Court placed a further limitation on the state action exemption by holding that it does not automatically confer immunity on the actions of municipalities.[13] Municipal conduct is immune only if it was authorized by the state legislature and its anticompetitive effects were a foreseeable result of the authorization. The Court's decision caused concern that the threat of treble damage liability might inhibit legitimate regulatory action by municipal authorities. As a result, Congress passed the Local Government Antitrust Act of 1984. This statute eliminates damage actions against municipalities and their officers, agents, and employees for antitrust violations and makes injunctive relief the sole remedy in such cases.

---

[12]317 U.S. 341 (U.S. Sup. Ct. 1943).

[13]*Community Communications Co. v. City of Boulder,* 455 U.S. 40 (U.S. Sup. Ct. 1982).

FEDERAL TRADE COMMISSION v. TICOR TITLE INSURANCE CO.   504 U.S. 621 (U.S. Sup. Ct. 1992)

The Federal Trade Commission filed an administrative complaint against six of the nation's title insurance companies, including Ticor Title Insurance Co. The complaint alleged that the title insurers engaged in horizontal price-fixing in their setting of uniform rates for title searches and title examinations. (According to the FTC, these uniform rates pertained to aspects of the business that did not involve insurance, as opposed to the setting of uniform rates for insurance against risk of loss from defective titles. The latter type of ratesetting, which was not challenged by the FTC in this case, would directly involve insurance and would likely be shielded from antitrust scrutiny by the McCarran-Ferguson Act.)

The challenged uniform ratesetting for title searches and title examinations occurred in various states through rating bureaus organized by the title insurers. These rating bureaus allegedly would set standard rates for search and examination services notwithstanding possible differences in efficiencies and costs as between individual title insurance companies. Though privately organized, these rating bureaus and the rates they set were potentially subject to oversight by the various states in which they operated.

Price-fixing by the title insurers was alleged, in the FTC complaint, to have occurred in four states: Connecticut, Wisconsin, Arizona, and Montana. The administrative law judge (ALJ) held that price-fixing had occurred in each of those four states, but that the requirements of the state action exemption from liability applied to the title insurer's actions in Arizona and Montana. As for the title insurers' actions in Connecticut and Wisconsin, the ALJ concluded that the requirements of the state action exemption were not met and that the title insurers therefore should face legal responsibility for their antitrust violations. The FTC commissioners, reviewing the ALJ's decision, concluded that the state action exemption did not apply to the title insurers' actions in any of the four states. On appeal, the Third Circuit Court of Appeals held that the state action exemption shielded the title insurers' actions in all four of the states.

The Supreme Court granted certiorari. (On the question whether the Third Circuit correctly stated and applied the law regarding the state action exemption, the FTC and the title insurers (referred to below simply *as "Ticor") confined their briefing—and the Supreme Court largely confined its discussion—to the regulatory regimes existing under Wisconsin and Montana law.)* ◌◌

Kennedy, Justice   [I]n *Parker v. Brown* (1943), we upheld a state-supervised market sharing scheme against a Sherman Act challenge. We announced the doctrine that federal antitrust laws are subject to supersession by state regulatory programs. Our decision was grounded in principles of federalism.

In *California Retail Liquor Dealers Association v. Midcal Aluminum, Inc.* (1980), we announced a two-part [state action immunity test] applicable to instances where private parties participate [with the state in allegedly anticompetitive conduct]: "First, the challenged restraint must be one clearly articulated and affirmatively expressed as state policy; second, the policy must be actively supervised by the State itself." *Midcal* confirms that while a State may not confer antitrust immunity on private parties by fiat, it may displace competition with active state supervision if the displacement is both intended by the State and implemented in its specific details. Actual state involvement, not deference to private price fixing arrangements under the general auspices of state law, is the precondition of immunity from federal law. Immunity is conferred out of respect for ongoing regulation by the State, not out of respect for the economics of price restraint.

The rationale was further elaborated in *Patrick v. Burget.* [In that case, it was noted that the *active supervision* element of the test set forth in *Midcal*] "mandates that the State exercise ultimate control over the challenged anticompetitive conduct" [and establishes that] "mere presence of some state involvement or monitoring does not suffice." [*Patrick* also contained the observation that the] "active supervision prong of the *Midcal* test requires that state officials have and exercise power to review particular anticompetitive acts of private parties and disapprove those that fail to accord with state policy."

Our decisions emphasize that the purpose of the active supervision inquiry . . . is to determine whether the State has exercised sufficient independent judgment and control so that the details of the rates or prices have been established as a product of deliberate state intervention, not simply by agreement among private parties. [T]he analysis asks whether the State has played a substantial role in determining the specifics of the economic policy.

The question is not how well the state regulation works but whether the anticompetitive scheme is the State's own.

In the case before us, the Court of Appeals relied upon [an erroneous] formulation of the active supervision requirement [in] rul[ing] that the active supervision requirement was met and in [holding] that the [title insurers'] conduct was entitled to state-action immunity from antitrust liability. Where prices or rates are set as an initial matter by private parties, subject only to a veto if the State chooses to exercise it, the party claiming immunity must show that state officials have undertaken the necessary steps to determine the specifics of the price-fixing or ratesetting scheme. The mere potential for state supervision is not an adequate substitute for a decision by the State. Under these standards, we must conclude that there was no active supervision in either Wisconsin or Montana.

[I]n Wisconsin and Montana, the rating bureaus filed rates with state agencies and . . . the so-called negative option rule prevailed. The rates became effective unless they were rejected within a set time. It is [asserted by Ticor] that as a matter of law in those States inaction signified substantive approval. This proposition cannot be reconciled, however, with the detailed findings, entered by the ALJ and adopted by the Commission[ers], which demonstrate that the potential for state supervision was not realized in fact. The ALJ found, and the Commission[ers] agreed, that at most the rate filings were checked for mathematical accuracy. Some were unchecked altogether. In Montana, a rate filing became effective despite the failure of the rating bureau to provide additional requested information. [There was a similar occurrence in Wisconsin.] These findings are fatal to Ticor's attempts to portray the state regulatory regimes as providing the necessary component of active supervision. The findings demonstrate that whatever the potential for state regulatory review in Wisconsin and Montana, active state supervision did not occur. In the absence of active supervision in fact, there can be no state-action immunity for what were otherwise private price fixing agreements.

This case involves horizontal price fixing under a vague imprimatur in form and agency inaction in fact. No antitrust offense is more pernicious than price fixing. In this context, we decline to formulate a rule that would lead to a finding of active state supervision when in fact there was none.

Judgment of court of appeals reversed in favor of Federal Trade Commission; case remanded for further proceedings and consideration of other issues.

The Noerr–Pennington Doctrine

In the *Noerr* and *Pennington* cases, the Supreme Court held that "the Sherman Act does not prohibit two or more persons from associating together in an attempt to persuade the legislature or the executive to take particular action with respect to a law that would produce a restraint or a monopoly."[14] This exemption recognizes that the right to petition government provided by the Bill of Rights takes prece-

dence over the antitrust policy favoring competition. In a later case, the Court extended the *Noerr–Pennington* exemption from liability by making it applicable to a party's filing of a lawsuit. The exemption does not, however, extend to sham activities that are attempts to interfere with the business activities of competitors rather than legitimate attempts to influence governmental action.[15] The *Professional Real Estate Investors* case, which follows, discusses the *Noerr–Pennington* doctrine and the sham exception to its application.

[14]*Eastern R.R. President's Conference v. Noerr Motor Freight, Inc.*, 365 U.S. 127 (U.S. Sup. Ct. 1961); *United Mine Workers v. Pennington*, 381 U.S. 657 (U.S. Sup. Ct. 1965).

[15]*California Motor Transport v. Trucking Unlimited*, 404 U.S. 508 (U.S. Sup. Ct. 1982).

PROFESSIONAL REAL ESTATE INVESTORS, INC. v. COLUMBIA PICTURES INDUSTRIES, INC.
508 U.S. 49 (U.S. Sup. Ct. 1993)

Professional Real Estate Investors, Inc. (PRE), operated a resort hotel in Palm Springs, California. PRE installed videodisc players in the hotel's rooms. It assembled a library of more than 200 motion picture titles and rented these videodiscs to guests for in-room viewing. PRE also sought to develop a market for the sale of videodisc players to other hotels that wished to offer in-room viewing of prerecorded material. Columbia Pictures Industries, Inc., and seven other major motion picture studios (referred to collectively as "Columbia") owned the copyrights on the motion pictures that appeared on the videodiscs PRE had purchased. Columbia also licensed the transmission of copyrighted motion pictures to hotel rooms through a wired cable system called Spectradyne. PRE therefore competed with Columbia not only for the viewing market at PRE's hotel but also for the broader market for in-room entertainment services in hotels.

Columbia sued PRE for copyright infringement on the basis of PRE's rental of videodiscs for viewing in hotel rooms. PRE counterclaimed, charging Columbia with violations of sections 1 and 2 of the Sherman Act. In particular, PRE alleged that Columbia's copyright action was a mere sham that cloaked underlying acts of monopolization and conspiracy to restrain trade. Each party sought summary judgment on Columbia's copyright infringement claim. Columbia conceded that the Copyright Act's "first sale" doctrine would allow PRE to sell or lease lawfully purchased videodiscs. PRE conceded that the playing of videodiscs constituted "performance" of motion pictures. As a result, summary judgement depended solely on whether rental of videodiscs for in-room viewing infringed Columbia's exclusive right, under the Copyright Act, to "perform the copyrighted work[s] publicly." (Emphasis added.) Ruling that such rental did not constitute public performance, the district court granted summary judgment in favor of PRE. The Ninth Circuit Court of Appeals affirmed, concluding that a hotel room was not a public place.

Columbia sought summary judgment on PRE's antitrust counterclaims. Columbia asserted—and the district court and the Ninth Circuit agreed—that its copyright infringement claim had not been a sham and that the Noerr-Pennington *doctrine therefore protected Columbia against antitrust attack. PRE opposed Columbia's motion for summary judgment on PRE's antitrust counterclaims by arguing that Columbia's copyright infringement claim was a sham because Columbia did not honestly believe that the claim was meritorious. The Ninth Circuit rejected PRE's contention that Columbia's subjective intent in bringing the lawsuit was a question of fact that precluded summary judgment. Instead, the court reasoned that the existence of probable cause for Columbia to bring the infringement claim "preclude[d] the application of the sham exception as a matter of law" because "a suit brought with probable cause does not fall within the sham exception to the* Noerr-Pennington *doctrine." Finally, the court observed that PRE's failure to show that "the copyright infringement action was baseless" rendered irrelevant any "evidence of [Columbia's] subjective intent." The U.S. Supreme Court granted PRE's petition for certiorari.* ∽

Thomas, Justice Those who petition government for redress are generally immune from antitrust liability. We first recognized in *Eastern R.R. Presidents Conference v. Noerr Motor Freight, Inc.* (1961) that "the Sherman Act does not prohibit . . . persons from associating together in an attempt to persuade the legislature or the executive to take particular action with respect to a law that would produce a restraint or a monopoly." Accord, *Mine Workers v. Pennington* (1965). In light of the government's "power to act in [its] representative capacity" and "to take actions . . . that operate to restrain trade," we reasoned [in *Noerr*] that the Sherman Act does not punish "political activity" through which "the people . . . freely inform the government of their wishes." Nor did we "impute to Congress an intent to invade" the First Amendment right to petition.

Noerr, however, withheld immunity from "sham" activities because "applications of the Sherman Act would be justified" when petitioning activity, "ostensibly directed toward influencing governmental action, is a mere sham to cover . . . an attempt to interfere directly with the business relationships of a competitor." In *Noerr* itself, we found that a publicity campaign by railroads seeking legislation harmful to truckers was no sham in that the "effort to influence legislation" was "not only genuine but also highly successful."

In *California Motor Transport Co. v. Trucking Unlimited* (1972), we . . . extended *Noerr* to "the approach of citizens . . . to administrative agencies . . . and to courts." We left unresolved the question presented by this case—whether litigation may be sham [and hence unprotected by the *Noerr-Pennington* doctrine] merely because a subjective expectation of success does not motivate the litigant. We now answer this question in the negative and hold that an objectively reasonable effort to litigate cannot be sham regardless of subjective intent.

Our original formulation of antitrust petitioning immunity required that unprotected activity lack objective reasonableness. *Noerr* rejected the contention that an attempt "to influence the passage and enforcement of laws" might lose immunity merely because the lobbyists' "sole purpose . . . was to destroy [their] competitors." We reasoned that "[t]he right of the people to inform their representatives in government of their desires with respect to the passage or enforcement of laws cannot properly be made to depend upon their intent in doing so. In short, [as the *Pennington* decision states,] 'Noerr shields from the Sherman Act a concerted effort to influence public officials regardless of intent or purpose.'

Nothing in *California Motor Transport* retreated from these principles. Indeed, we recognized that recourse to agencies and courts should not be condemned as sham until a reviewing court has "discern[ed] and draw[n]" the "difficult line" separating objectively reasonable claims from "a pattern of baseless, repetitive claims . . . which leads the factfinder to conclude that the administrative and judicial processes have been abused." [*California Motor Transport* establishes] that the institution of legal proceedings "without probable cause" will give rise to a sham if such activity effectively "bar[s] . . . competitors from meaningful access to adjudicatory tribunals and so . . . usurp[s] th[e] decisionmaking process."

Since *California Motor Transport,* we have consistently assumed that the sham exception contains an indispensable objective component. [W]e have repeatedly reaffirmed that evidence of anticompetitive intent or purpose alone cannot transform otherwise legitimate activity into a sham. Our . . . applications of *Noerr* immunity . . . demonstrate that neither *Noerr* immunity nor its sham exception turns on subjective intent alone. [F]idelity to precedent compels us to reject a purely subjective definition of "sham." The sham exception so construed would undermine, if not vitiate, *Noerr.*

We now outline a two-part definition of "sham" litigation. First, the lawsuit must be objectively baseless in the sense that no reasonable litigant could realistically expect success on the merits. If an objective litigant could conclude that the suit is reasonably calculated to elicit a favorable outcome, the suit is immunized under *Noerr,* and an antitrust claim premised on the sham exception must fail. A winning lawsuit is by definition a reasonable effort at petitioning for redress and therefore not a sham. On the other hand, when the antitrust defendant has lost the underlying litigation, a court must "resist the understandable temptation to engage in *post hoc* reasoning by concluding" that an ultimately unsuccessful "action must have been unreasonable or without foundation" (quoting *Christiansburg Garment Co. v. EEOC* (1978)).

Only if challenged litigation is objectively meritless may a court examine the litigant's subjective motivation. Under this second part of our definition of sham, the court should focus on whether the baseless lawsuit conceals "an attempt to interfere directly with the business relationships of a competitor" (quoting *Noerr*) through the "use [of] the governmental *process*—as opposed to the *outcome* of that process—as an anticompetitive weapon" (quoting *Columbia v. Omni Outdoor Advertising, Inc.* (1991)). This two-tiered process requires the plaintiff to disprove the challenged lawsuit's *legal* viability before the court will entertain evidence of the suit's *economic* viability. Of course, even a plaintiff who defeats the defendant's claim to *Noerr* immunity by demonstrating both the objective and the subjective components of a sham must still prove a substantive antitrust violation.

We conclude that the Court of Appeals properly affirmed summary judgment for Columbia on PRE's

antitrust counterclaim. The existence of probable cause to institute legal proceedings precludes a finding that an antitrust defendant has engaged in sham litigation. When the District Court entered summary judgment for PRE on Columbia's copyright claim in 1986, it was by no means clear whether PRE's videodisc rental activities intruded on Columbia's copyrights. At that time, the Third Circuit and a District Court within the Third Circuit had held that the rental of video cassettes for viewing in on-site, private screening rooms infringed on the copyright owner's right of public performance. Although the District Court and the Ninth Circuit distinguished these decisions by reasoning that hotel rooms offered a degree of privacy more akin to the home than to a video rental store, copyright scholars criticized both the reasoning and the outcome of the Ninth Circuit's decision. The Seventh Circuit expressly [rejected the Ninth Circuit's approach] and adopted instead the Third Circuit's definition of [what constitutes a public place]. In light of the unsettled condition of the law, Columbia plainly had probable cause to sue.

Any reasonable copyright owner in Columbia's position could have believed that it had some chance of winning an infringement suit against PRE. Even though it did not survive PRE's motion for summary judgment, Columbia's copyright action was arguably warranted by existing law. A court could reasonably conclude that Columbia's infringement action was an objectively plausible effort to enforce rights. Accordingly, we conclude that PRE failed to establish the objective prong of *Noerr's* sham exception.

Ninth Circuit's decision affirmed; grant of summary judgment in favor of Columbia on PRE's antitrust claims upheld.

Patent Licensing

There is a basic tension between the antitrust objective of promoting competition and the purpose of the patent law, which seeks to promote innovation by granting a limited monopoly to those who develop new products or processes.[16] In the early case

of *United States v. General Electric Company,*[17] the Supreme Court allowed General Electric to control the price at which other manufacturers sold light bulbs they had manufactured under patent licensing agreements with General Electric. The Court recognized that an important part of holding a patent was

---

[16]Chapter 8 discusses patent law in detail.

[17]272 U.S. 476 (U.S. Sup. Ct. 1926).

the right to license others to manufacture the patented item. This right effectively would be negated if licensees were allowed to undercut the prices that patent holders charged for their own sales of patented products.

Patent holders cannot, however, lawfully control the price at which patented items are resold by distributors purchasing them from the patent holder. Nor can patent holders use their patents to impose tying agreements on their customers by conditioning the sale of patented items on the purchase of nonpatented items, unless such agreements are otherwise lawful under the Sherman and Clayton Acts. Finally, firms that seek to monopolize an area by acquiring most or all of the patents related to that area of commerce may face liability for violating Sherman Act section 2 or Clayton Act section 7, because a patent has been held to be an asset within the meaning of section 7.

Foreign Commerce

When foreign governments are involved in commercial activities affecting the domestic or international commerce of the United States, our antitrust policy may be at odds with our foreign policy. Congress and the courts have created a variety of antitrust exemptions aimed at reconciling this potential conflict. The Foreign Sovereign Immunities Act of 1976 (FSIA) provides that the governmental actions of foreign sovereigns and their agents are exempt from antitrust liability. The commercial activities of foreign sovereigns, however, are not included within this **sovereign immunity** exemption. Significant international controversy exists concerning the proper criteria for determining whether a particular governmental act is commercial in nature. Under the FSIA, the courts employ a *nature of the act* test, holding that a commercial activity is one that an individual might customarily carry on for a profit.

The **act of state doctrine** provides that an American court cannot adjudicate a politically sensitive dispute whose resolution would require the court to judge the legality of a foreign government's sovereign act. This doctrine reflects judicial deference to the primary role of the executive and legislative branches in the adoption and execution of our foreign policy. The act of state doctrine recognizes (as does the doctrine of sovereign immunity) the importance of respecting the sovereignty of other nations. Unlike the doctrine of sovereign

immunity, however, the act of state doctrine also reflects a fundamental attribute of our system of government—the principle of separation of powers.

Finally, the **sovereign compulsion doctrine** provides private parties a defense if they have been compelled by a foreign sovereign to commit, within that sovereign's territory, acts that would otherwise violate the antitrust laws due to their negative impact on our international commerce. To employ this defense successfully, a defendant must show that the challenged actions were the product of actual compulsion—as opposed to mere encouragement or approval—by a foreign sovereign.

Figure 3 summarizes the various antitrust exceptions and exemptions.

ETHICAL AND PUBLIC POLICY CONCERNS

1. In the *Professional Real Estate Investors* (PRE) case, which appeared earlier in the chapter, the Supreme Court concluded that even if Columbia subjectively believed that it would not win its copyright infringement claim, any such subjective belief was not legally significant so long as Columbia had probable cause to bring the claim. Suppose that Columbia actually (i.e., subjectively) believed it would lose its copyright infringement claim. If so, did Columbia act *ethically* in filing the case? Explain your reasoning.

2. Refer to the facts of problem case 9 at the end of this chapter. Is paying a disguised bribe to win a contract ethically justifiable under such circumstances? Would your answer change if such bribes were a customary means of doing business in Nigeria rather than a violation of Nigerian law?

PROBLEMS AND PROBLEM CASES

1. Mercedes-Benz of North America (MBNA), the exclusive U.S. distributor of Mercedes-Benz (Mercedes) automobiles, was a wholly owned subsidiary of Daimler-Benz Aktiengesellschaft (DBAG), the manufacturer of Mercedes automobiles. MBNA required its approximately 400 franchised Mercedes dealers to agree not to sell or use (in the repair or servicing of Mercedes automobiles) any parts other than genuine Mercedes parts. Mozart, a wholesale automotive parts distributor, filed an antitrust suit

FIGURE   3

Antitrust Exceptions and Exemptions

EXCEPTION/EXEMPTION	ACTIVITIES COVERED	SOURCE
Statutory Labor	Legitimate union activities	Clayton Act, Norris-LaGuardia Act
Nonstatutory Labor	Collective bargaining agreements	Judicial decision (policy favoring collective bargaining)
Agricultural Cooperatives	Legitimate cooperative activities	Clayton Act, Capper-Volstead Act
Export Trade Associations	Joint export activities	Webb-Pomerene Act
Insurance	Business of insurance	McCarran-Ferguson Act
Regulated Industries	Anticompetitive activities shielded by federal regulation	Regulatory statutes
State Action	State authorized and supervised anticompetitive activities	Judicial decision (federalism)
***Noerr-Pennington* Doctrine**	Attempts to induce anticompetitive governmental action	Judicial decision (First Amendment)
Patent Licensing	Legitimate activities of patent holders	Judicial decision (patent laws)
Sovereign Immunity	Governmental acts of foreign sovereigns	Foreign Sovereign Immunities Act
Act of State Doctrine	Sovereign acts of foreign sovereigns	Judicial decision (separation of powers)
Sovereign Compulsion Doctrine	Private acts compelled by foreign sovereigns	Judicial decision

against MBNA. Mozart alleged, among other things, that MBNA had violated both section 1 of the Sherman Act and Section 3 of the Clayton Act by tying the sale of Mercedes parts to the sale of Mercedes automobiles. The trial court ruled in favor of MBNA. Was the trial court's ruling correct?

2. Sterling Electric manufactured electric motors and replacement parts for them. No one else made parts compatible with Sterling motors. After being acquired by A. O. Smith Corporation, Sterling instituted new distribution programs. Its new agreement with distributors who stocked its parts required that these "stocking" distributors buy and aggressively promote minimum quantities of Sterling motors, in return for their being able to buy parts for less than the prices Sterling charged "referral" distributors who merely passed on orders for Sterling parts. On October 1, 1982, Sterling terminated Parts and Electric Motors, Inc. (P&E), a stocking distributor, for insufficient motor purchases. P&E then filed suit against Sterling, arguing that the motor purchase requirement was a tying arrangement prohibited by

the Sherman and Clayton Acts. At trial, P&E introduced evidence that the purchase requirement forced dealers to increase their motor purchases by more than $250,000. Was the jury verdict in P&E's favor proper?

3. In 1961, Ford Motor Company acquired Autolite, a manufacturer of spark plugs, in order to enter the profitable aftermarket for spark plugs sold as replacement parts. Ford and the other major automobile manufacturers had previously purchased original equipment spark plugs (those installed in new cars when they leave the factory) from independent producers such as Autolite and Champion, either at or below the producer's cost. The independents were willing to sell original equipment plugs so cheaply because aftermarket mechanics often replace original equipment plugs with the same brand of spark plug. GM had already moved into the spark plug market by developing its own division. Ford decided to do so by means of a vertical merger under which it acquired Autolite. Prior to the Autolite acquisition, Ford bought 10 percent of the total

spark plug output. The merger left Champion as the only major independent spark plug producer. Champion's market share thereafter declined because Chrysler was the only major original equipment spark plug purchaser remaining in the market. The government filed a divestiture suit against Ford, arguing that Ford's acquisition of Autolite violated section 7 of the Clayton Act. Should Ford have been ordered to divest itself of Autolite?

4. Siemens, a diversified firm with interests in the medical equipment field, notified the Justice Department in 1979 that it intended to acquire control of Searle Diagnostics (SD), a manufacturer of nuclear medical equipment. Ten years earlier, Siemens had failed in an attempt to start its own nuclear medical equipment division. In 1972, it had considered trying to reenter the field but concluded that it would not be able to recoup the investment reentry required. The top four firms in the nuclear medical equipment market accounted for 77 percent of total sales in 1979. This figure, however, was down from 1975, when they accounted for 92 percent of total sales. Although SD was still first in 1979, it had seen its market share fall from 50 percent to 22 percent during the same five-year period. These facts, together with the fact that SD had lost money in 1978 and 1979, led SD's parent firm to agree to the sale to Siemens. The Justice Department sought a preliminary injunction against the merger, arguing that it would violate section 7 by eliminating both perceived and actual potential competition. The department, however, presented no evidence that any attractive toehold purchase was available to Siemens or that Siemens, as an acknowledged likely entrant, had had any actual impact on the conduct of existing firms in the market. Was a preliminary injunction appropriate?

5. In 1983, Warner Communications, Inc., the second-largest distributor of prerecorded music (18.9 percent market share) in the United States, agreed to merge part of its record operations and form a joint venture company with Polygram Records, Inc., the sixth largest (7.1 percent market share) distributor. The Federal Trade Commission applied for a preliminary injunction to block the joint venture. The FTC presented evidence that the top four distributors collectively commanded 67 percent of the domestic market and that if the joint venture were completed, their collective market share would increase to 75 percent. In addition, the

FTC presented evidence showing a trend toward concentration in the industry and the existence of high barriers to entry by new competitors. The trial court ruled that the FTC had failed to demonstrate the likelihood of ultimate success necessary to justify a preliminary injunction. Was that ruling correct?

6. First Comics, Inc., wanted to enter the comic book publishing business. First hired World Color Press to print its comics because World had a less expensive method of printing than other comic book printers did. World allegedly promised to charge First the same price it charged its larger customers such as Marvel Comics Group and DC Comics. When First discovered it was being charged 4.3 cents per copy more than Marvel, First demanded reimbursement or a future credit. When World refused, First filed a price discrimination suit against World under the Robinson-Patman Act. Does the Robinson-Patman Act apply to this case?

7. Indian Coffee Company, a coffee roaster in Pittsburgh, Pennsylvania, sold its Breakfast Cheer coffee in the Pittsburgh area, where it had an 18 percent market share, and in Cleveland, Ohio, where it had a significant, but smaller, market share. Late in 1971, Folger Coffee Company, then the leading seller of branded coffee west of the Mississippi, entered the Pittsburgh market for the first time. In its effort to gain market share in Pittsburgh, Folger granted retailers high promotional allowances in the form of coupons. Retail customers could use these coupons to obtain price cuts. Redeeming retailers could use the coupons as credits against invoices from Folger. For a time, Indian tried to retain its market share by matching Folger's price concessions, but because Indian only operated in two areas, it could not subsidize such sales with profits from other areas. Indian, which finally was forced out of business in 1974, later filed a Robinson-Patman suit against Folger. At trial, Indian introduced evidence that Folger's Pittsburgh promotional allowances were far higher than its allowances in other geographic areas, and that Folger's Pittsburgh prices were below green (unroasted) coffee cost, below material and manufacturing costs, below total cost, and below marginal cost or average variable cost. Was the trial court's directed verdict in favor of Folger proper?

8. Peugeot Motors of America, Inc. (PMA), the exclusive domestic importer of Peugeot products, controlled all U.S. Peugeot distributors except EAD, the exclusive distributor for Peugeot cars in the southeastern United States. EAD filed suit against PMA, arguing that PMA had violated sections 2(d) and 2(e) of the Robinson-Patman Act by providing cash incentives, training facilities, and parts repurchase programs (allowing dealers to return for credit a part of their obsolete parts inventory) to PMA's dealers without making such incentives, facilities, and programs available to EAD's dealers. The evidence at trial indicated that Memphis, Tennessee, was the only place in the United States where an EAD dealer was within 50 miles of a PMA dealer, and that less than 1 percent of national Peugeot sales were cross-border sales between PMA and EAD territories. EAD's president testified that he did not know the reason for any of the cross-border sales. He also admitted that some such sales occurred for reasons other than competition between the two sets of dealers. The trial court directed a verdict in favor of PMA. Was the trial court correct in doing so?

9. In 1982, a subsidiary of W. S. Kirkpatrick & Co. won a Nigerian Defense Ministry contract for the construction and equipment of an aeromedical center at a Nigerian Air Force base. Environmental Tectonics Corporation (Environmental), an unsuccessful bidder for the same contract, filed RICO and Robinson-Patman Act claims against Kirkpatrick. Environmental alleged that Kirkpatrick had won the contract by paying a 20 percent "commission" to bribe certain Nigerian officials. The parties agreed that the bribes, if paid, would violate Nigerian law. Was the trial court correct in holding that the act of state doctrine barred Environmental's claim?

10. Pocahontas Coal Company filed suit against a number of other companies engaged in the mining and production of coal in West Virginia. Pocahontas alleged that the defendants were involved in a conspiracy to control the production and pricing of coal. One of Pocahontas's specific claims was that the defendants had violated section 8 of the Clayton Act by "deputizing" various persons to sit on the boards of competing subsidiaries. The defendants moved for summary judgment on the section 8 claim, noting that Pocahontas's complaint contained no factual allegations that any of the defendants were competitors, failed to name any of the alleged "deputies," and was ambiguous because it alleged that certain persons were "officers and/or directors" of competing companies. The trial court offered Pocahontas the opportunity to clarify the complaint by bringing forth additional information on these points. Did the court properly grant the defendants summary judgment when Pocahontas declined to do so?

Employment Law

Years ago, it was unusual to see a separate employment law chapter in a business law text. At that time, the rights, duties, and liabilities accompanying employment usually were determined by basic legal institutions such as contract, tort, and agency. Today, these common law principles still control employer–employee relations unless displaced by government regulations or by new judge-made rules applying specifically to employment. By now, however, such rules and regulations are so numerous that they touch almost every facet of employment. This chapter discusses the most important of these modern legal controls on the employer–employee relation. ∞

SOME BASIC EMPLOYMENT STATUTES

Modern American employment law is so vast and complex a subject that texts designed for lawyers seldom address it in its entirety. Indeed, specialized subjects like labor law and employment discrimination often get book-length treatment in their own right. This chapter's overview of employment law emphasizes three topics that have attracted much recent attention—employment discrimination, employee privacy, and common law claims for wrongful discharge. But no discussion of employment law is complete without outlining certain basic regulations that significantly affect the conditions of employment for most Americans. Figure 1 notes these regulations and briefly states the functions they perform.

Workers' Compensation

Nineteenth-century law made it difficult for employees to recover when they sued their employer in

FIGURE I

The Ends and Means of Modern Employment Law

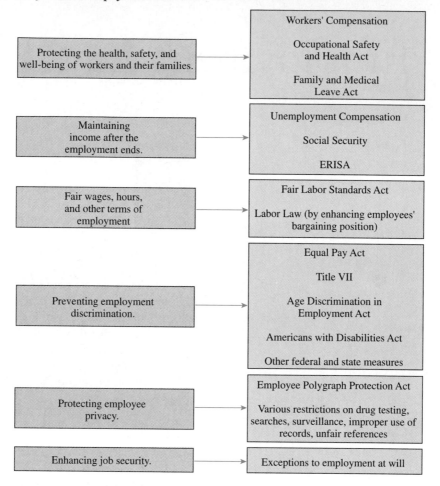

---

negligence for on-the-job injuries.[1] At that time, employers had an implied assumption of risk defense under which an employee assumed all the normal and customary risks of his employment simply by taking the job. If an employee's own carelessness played some role in his injury, employers often could avoid negligence liability under the traditional rule that even a slight degree of contributory negligence is a complete defense. Another employer defense, the fellow-servant rule, said that where an employee's injury resulted from the negligence of a coemployee (or fellow servant), the

employer was not liable. Finally, employees sometimes had problems proving the employer's negligence. State workers' compensation statutes, which first appeared early in the 20th century, were a response to all these problems. Today all 50 states have such systems.[2]

Basic Features Workers' compensation only protects employees, and not independent contractors.[3] However, many states exempt casual, agricultural,

---

[1]Chapter 7 discusses negligence law and most of the negligence defenses noted below.

[2]In addition, various federal statutes regulate on-the-job injuries suffered by employees of the federal government and other employees such as railroad workers, seamen, longshoremen, and harbor workers.

[3]Chapter 34 defines the terms *employee* and *independent contractor.*

and domestic employees, among others. State and local government employees may be covered by workers' compensation or by some alternative state system. Also, states usually exempt certain employers—for example, firms employing fewer than a stated number of employees (often three).

Where they apply, however, all workers' compensation systems share certain basic features. They allow injured employees to recover under *strict liability,* thus removing any need to prove employer negligence. They also eliminate the employer's three traditional defenses: contributory negligence, assumption of risk, and the fellow-servant rule. In addition, they make workers' compensation an employee's *exclusive remedy* against her employer for covered injuries. Usually, however, employees injured by their employer's intentional torts sue the employer outside workers' compensation.

Workers' compensation basically is a social compromise. Because it involves strict liability and eliminates the three traditional employer defenses, workers' compensation greatly increases the probability that an injured employee will recover. Such recoveries usually include: (1) hospital and medical expenses (including vocational rehabilitation), (2) disability benefits, (3) specified recoveries for the loss of certain body parts, and (4) death benefits to survivors and/or dependents. But the amount recoverable under each category of damages frequently is less than would be obtained in a negligence suit. Thus, as the following *Tolbert* case illustrates, injured employees sometimes deny that they are covered by workers' compensation so that they can pursue a tort suit against their employer instead.

Although workers' compensation is an injured employee's sole remedy against her employer, she may be able to sue other parties whose behavior helped cause her injury. One example is a product liability suit against a manufacturer who supplies an employer with defective machinery or raw materials that cause an on-the-job injury. However, many states immunize co-employees from ordinary tort liability for injuries they inflict on other employees. Complicated questions of contribution, indemnity, and subrogation can arise where an injured employee is able to recover against both an employer and a third party.

The Work-Related Injury Requirement Another basic feature of workers' compensation is that employees recover only for *work-related* injuries.

To be work-related, the injury must: (1) arise out of the employment, and (2) happen in the course of the employment. These tests have been variously interpreted.

The arising-out-of-the-employment test usually requires a sufficiently close relationship between the injury and the *nature* of the employment. As *Tolbert* illustrates, courts use different standards to define this requirement. A factory worker assaulted by a trespasser, for example, probably would be denied workers' compensation recovery under the "increased risk" test discussed in *Tolbert,* but probably would recover under the "positional risk" test described there. If the same trespasser assaulted an on-duty security guard, however, the guard should recover under either test.

The in-the-course-of-the-employment requirement inquires whether the injury occurred within the *time, place,* and *circumstances* of the employment. Employees injured off the employer's premises generally are outside the course of the employment. For example, injuries suffered while traveling to or from work usually are not compensable. But an employee may be covered where the off-the-premises injury occurred while she was performing employment-related duties such as going on a business trip or running an employment-related errand.

Other work-related injury problems on which courts have disagreed include mental injuries allegedly arising from the employment and injuries resulting from employee horseplay. Virtually all states, however, regard intentionally self-inflicted injuries as outside workers' compensation. Recovery for occupational diseases, on the other hand, usually is allowed today. An employee whose preexisting diseased condition is aggravated by her employment sometimes recovers as well.

Administration and Funding Workers' compensation systems usually are administered by a state agency that adjudicates workers' claims and administers the system. Its decisions on such claims normally are appealable to the state courts. The states fund workers' compensation by compelling covered employers to: (1) purchase private insurance, (2) self-insure (e.g., by maintaining a contingency fund), or (3) make payments into a state insurance fund. Because employers generally pass on the costs of insurance to their customers, workers' compensation tends to spread the economic risk of workplace injuries throughout society.

D*eborah Tolbert, a secretary employed by the Martin Marietta Corporation, was raped by a Martin Marietta janitor while on her way to lunch within the secured defense facility where she worked. She sued Martin Marietta, alleging that it had negligently hired the janitor and had negligently failed to make its premises safe for employees. Martin Marietta moved for summary judgment, claiming that Tolbert could not sue in negligence because workers' compensation was her sole remedy.* ∽

Carrigan, District Judge The sole issue is whether the Colorado Workmen's Compensation Act covers Tolbert's injury. If it does, workers' compensation is her exclusive remedy and this tort action is barred. Tolbert asserts that her injury is not covered by workers' compensation, presumably because she expects that a tort action would yield a larger recovery. Martin Marietta, on the other hand, apparently is willing to pay the workers' compensation award to avoid risking a large tort verdict.

Workers' compensation applies where the injury or death is proximately caused by an injury or occupational disease arising out of and in the course of the employee's employment and is not intentionally self-inflicted. Although her injury did arise in the course of her employment, Tolbert contends that it did not "arise out of" the employment. The "arising out of" condition [requires] that there be some causal relationship between the employment and the injury. Courts have interpreted the "arising out of" language in different ways. Unfortunately, Colorado courts have not consistently applied any single test. Martin Marietta argues that positional-risk analysis applies to categorize the case as one [making workers' compensation applicable]. The positional-risk doctrine has been defined thus:

An injury arises out of the employment if it would not have occurred but for the fact that the conditions and obligations of the employment placed claimant in the position where he was injured . . . This theory supports compensation in cases of stray bullets, roving lunatics and other situations in which the only connection of the employment with the injury is that its obligations placed the employee in the particular place at the particular time when he was injured by some neutral force, meaning by "neutral" neither personal to the claimant nor distinctly associated with the employment.

Invoking this rule, Martin Marietta asserts that Tolbert's injury is covered by workers' compensation because: (1) her employment placed her within the building where she was injured, and (2) the assault was a neutral force.

[However, a 1923 Colorado case] . . . applied the "increased-risk" test of causality. Under the increased-risk test, compensation is awarded only if the employment increases the worker's risk of injury above that to which the general public is exposed. If Colorado presently applies the increased-risk analysis, Tolbert would not be covered by workers' compensation. Certainly her employment as a secretary within a secured defense facility would not be expected to increase her risk of sexual assault above that to which women in the general public are exposed.

Colorado first applied positional risk analysis four years after [the 1923 case] was decided. [In this later positional-risk case,] the court upheld an award to a farmhand who was struck by lightning. It can readily be seen that the positional-risk test provides substantially broader coverage than does the increased-risk test. Unfortunately, the Colorado courts on several more recent occasions have departed from the positional-risk test to impose a higher standard of causal relationship to the employment.

The rape was a nonemployment-motivated act directed at the plaintiff because she was a woman. There is nothing to indicate that any other woman—whether or not a Martin employee—who happened to be in the same area at the time of the attack would not have become the victim. Tolbert was not raped because of the nature of her duties or the nature of her workplace environment, or because of any incident or quarrel growing out of the work.

Both applicable Colorado precedent and sound rationale support holding that the workers' compensation statute has not abolished Tolbert's tort claim. Adopting this position has the additional advantage of providing employers an incentive to make reasonable efforts to screen prospective employees so as to avoid hiring rapists or those having the identifiable characteristics of potential rapists. Tort law does not impose strict liability; Tolbert still has the burden of showing negligence, causation, and damages.

Martin Marietta's motion for summary judgment denied; case proceeds to trial on Tolbert's negligence theories.

The Occupational Safety and Health Act

Although it may stimulate employers to remedy hazardous working conditions, workers' compensation does not directly forbid such conditions. The most important measure directly regulating workplace safety is the federal Occupational Safety and Health Act of 1970. The Occupational Safety and Health Act applies to all employers engaged in a business affecting interstate commerce. Exempted, however, are the U.S. government, the states and their political subdivisions, and certain industries regulated by other federal safety legislation. The Occupational Safety and Health Act mainly is administered by the Occupational Safety and Health Administration (OSHA) of the Labor Department. It does not preempt state workplace safety regulation, but OSHA must approve any state regulatory plan.

The Occupational Safety and Health Act requires employers to provide their employees with employment and a place of employment free from recognized hazards that are likely to cause death or serious physical harm. It also requires employers to comply with the many detailed regulations promulgated by OSHA. OSHA can inspect places of employment for violations of the act and its regulations. If an employer is found to violate the act's general duty provision or any specific standard, OSHA issues a written citation. It must do so with reasonable promptness, and in no event more than six months after the violation. The citation becomes final after 15 workdays following its service on the employer, unless it is contested. Contested citations are reviewed by the Occupational Safety and Health Review Commission, a three-member body composed of presidential appointees. Further review by the federal courts of appeals is possible.

The main sanctions for violations of the act and the regulations are the various civil penalties imposed by OSHA. In addition, any employer who commits a willful violation resulting in death to an employee may suffer a fine, imprisonment, or both. Also, the secretary of labor may seek injunctive relief when an employment hazard presents an imminent danger of death or physical harm that cannot be promptly eliminated by normal citation procedures. Finally, the act imposes various record-keeping and reporting requirements on employers.

Social Security

Today, the law requires that employers help ensure their employees' financial security after the employment ends. One example is the federal social security system. Social security mainly is financed by the Federal Insurance Contributions Act (FICA). FICA imposes a flat percentage tax on all employee income below a certain base figure and requires employers to pay a matching amount. Self-employed people pay a different rate on a different wage base. FICA revenues finance various forms of financial assistance besides the old-age benefits that people usually call social security. These include survivors' benefits to family members of deceased workers, disability benefits, and medical and hospitalization benefits for the elderly (the medicare system).

Unemployment Compensation

Another way that the law protects employees after their employment ends is by providing unemployment compensation for discharged workers. Since 1935, federal law has authorized joint federal–state efforts in this area. Today, each state administers its own unemployment compensation system under federal guidelines. The system's costs are met by subjecting employers to federal and state unemployment compensation taxes.

Unemployment insurance plans vary from state to state but usually share certain features. States often condition the receipt of benefits on the recipient's having worked for a covered employer for a specified time period, and/or having earned a certain minimum income over such a period. Generally, those who voluntarily quit work without good cause, are fired for bad conduct, fail to actively seek suitable new work, or refuse such work are ineligible for benefits. Benefit levels vary from state to state, as do the time periods during which benefits can be received.

ERISA

Many employers voluntarily contribute to their employees' postemployment income by maintaining pension plans. For years, pension plan abuses such as arbitrary termination of participation in the plan, arbitrary benefit reduction, and mismanagement of fund assets were not uncommon. The Employee Retirement Income Security Act of 1974 (ERISA) was a response to these problems. ERISA does not require employers to establish or fund pension plans and does not set benefit levels. Instead, it tries to check abuses and to protect employees' expectations that promised pension benefits will be paid.

ERISA imposes *fiduciary duties* on pension fund managers. For example, it requires that managers diversify the plan's investments to minimize the risk of large losses, unless this is clearly imprudent. ERISA also imposes *record-keeping, reporting,* and *disclosure* requirements. For instance, it requires that covered plans provide annual reports to their participants and specifies the contents of those reports. In addition, the act has a provision *guaranteeing employee participation* in the plan. For example, certain employees who complete one year of service with an employer cannot be denied plan participation. Furthermore, ERISA contains *funding* requirements for protecting plan participants against loss of pension income. Finally, ERISA contains complex *vesting* requirements that determine when an employee's right to receive pension benefits becomes nonforfeitable. These requirements help prevent employers from using a late vesting date to avoid pension obligations to employees who change jobs or are fired before that date. ERISA's remedies include civil suits by plan participants and beneficiaries, equitable relief, and criminal penalties.

Labor Law

Entire legal treatises are devoted to labor law, and the subject can occupy a chapter in a business law text. What follows is only a brief historical outline of the subject. Early in the 19th century, some courts treated labor unions as illegal criminal conspiracies. After this restriction disappeared around mid-century, organized labor began its lengthy—and sometimes violent—rise to power. During the late 19th and early 20th centuries, unions' growing influence and wage earners' increasing presence in the electorate spurred the passage of many laws benefiting labor. These included statutes outlawing "yellow dog" contracts (under which employees agreed not to join or remain a union member), minimum wage and maximum hours legislation, laws regulating the employment of women and children, factory safety measures, and workers' compensation. But during this period, some say, the courts tended to represent business interests. Perhaps for this reason, some prolabor measures were struck down on constitutional grounds. Also, some courts were quick to issue temporary and permanent injunctions to restrain union picketing and boycotts and help quell strikes.

Organized labor's political power continued to grow during the first part of the 20th century. In 1926, Congress passed the Railway Labor Act, which regulates labor relations in the railroad industry, and which later included airlines. This was followed by the Norris-LaGuardia Act of 1932, which limited the circumstances in which federal courts could enjoin strikes and picketing in labor disputes, and also prohibited federal court enforcement of yellow-dog contracts.

The most important 20th-century American labor statute, however, was the National Labor Relations Act of 1935 (the NLRA or Wagner Act). The NLRA gave employees the *right to organize* by enabling them to form, join, and assist labor organizations. It also allowed them to *bargain collectively* through their own representatives. In addition, the Wagner Act prohibited certain *unfair labor practices* that were believed to discourage collective bargaining. These practices include: (1) interfering with employees' rights to form, join, and assist labor unions; (2) dominating or interfering with the formation or administration of a labor union, or giving a union financial or other support; (3) discriminating against employees in hiring, tenure, or any term of employment due to their union membership; (4) discriminating against employees because they have filed charges or given testimony under the NLRA; and (5) refusing to bargain collectively with any duly designated employee representative. The NLRA also established the National Labor Relations Board (NLRB). The NLRB's main functions are: (1) handling representation cases (which involve the process by which a union becomes the certified employee representative within a bargaining unit), and (2) deciding whether challenged employer or union activity is an unfair labor practice.

In 1947, Congress amended the NLRA by passing the Labor Management Relations Act (LMRA or Taft-Hartley Act). The act declared that certain acts by *unions* are unfair labor practices. These include: (1) restraining or coercing employees in the exercise of their guaranteed bargaining rights (e.g., their right to refrain from joining a union); (2) causing an employer to discriminate against an employee who is not a union member; (3) refusing to bargain collectively with an employer; (4) conducting a secondary strike or a secondary boycott for a specified illegal purpose;[4] (5) requiring employees covered by union-shop contracts to pay excessive or discriminatory initiation fees or dues; and (6) featherbedding (forcing an employer to pay for work not actually performed). The LMRA also established an 80-day cooling-off period for strikes that the president finds likely to endanger national safety or health. In addition, it created a Federal Mediation and Conciliation Service to assist employers and unions in settling labor disputes.

Congressional investigations during the 1950s uncovered corruption in internal union affairs and also revealed that the internal procedures of many unions were undemocratic. In response, Congress enacted the Labor Management Reporting and Disclosure Act (or Landrum-Griffin Act) in 1959. The act established a "bill of rights" for union members and attempted to make internal union affairs more democratic. It also amended the NLRA by adding to the LMRA's list of unfair union labor practices.

The Fair Labor Standards Act

Although federal labor law regulates several aspects of labor–management relations, it still permits many terms of employment to be determined by private bargaining. Nonetheless, sometimes the law directly

---

[4]These are strikes or boycotts aimed at a third party with which the union has no real dispute. Their purpose is to coerce that party not to deal with an employer with which the union *does* have a dispute, and thus to gain some leverage over the employer.

regulates such key terms of employment as wages and hours worked. The most important example is the Fair Labor Standards Act (FLSA) of 1938.

The FLSA regulates *wages and hours* by entitling covered employees to: (1) a specified minimum wage whose amount changes over time, and (2) a time-and-a-half rate for work exceeding 40 hours per week. The FLSA's complicated coverage provisions basically enable its wages-and-hours standards to reach most significantly sized businesses that are engaged in interstate commerce or produce goods for such commerce. Also covered are state and local employees. The many exemptions from the FLSA's wages-and-hours provisions include executive, administrative, and professional personnel.

The FLSA also forbids oppressive *child labor* by any employer engaged in interstate commerce or in the production of goods for such commerce, and also forbids the interstate shipment of goods produced in an establishment where oppressive child labor occurs. Oppressive child labor includes: (1) most employment of children below the age of 14; (2) employment of children aged 14–15, unless they work in an occupation specifically approved by the Department of Labor; and (3) employment of children aged 16–17 who work in occupations declared particularly hazardous by the Labor Department. These provisions do not apply to most agricultural employment.

Both affected employees and the Labor Department can recover any unpaid minimum wages or overtime, plus an additional equal amount as liquidated damages, from an employer that has violated the FLSA's wages-and-hours provisions. A suit by the Labor Department terminates an employee's right to sue, but the department pays the amounts it recovers to the employee. Violations of the act's child labor provisions may result in civil penalties. Other FLSA remedies include injunctive relief and criminal liability for willful violations.

The Family and Medical Leave Act

After concluding that proper child-raising, family stability, and job security require that employees get reasonable work leave for family and medical reasons, Congress passed the Family and Medical Leave Act (FMLA) in 1993. In general, the act covers those employed for at least 12 months, and for 1,250 hours during those 12 months, by an employer employing 50 or more employees. Covered employers include federal, state, and local government agencies.

Under the FMLA, covered employees are entitled to a total of 12 workweeks of leave during any 12-month period for one or more of the following reasons: (1) the birth of a child and the need to care for that child; (2) the adoption of a child; (3) the need to care for a spouse, child, or parent with a serious health condition; and (4) the employee's own serious health condition. Usually, the leave may be without pay. Upon the employee's return from leave, the employer ordinarily must restore her to the position she held when the leave began, or to an equivalent position, and not deny her any benefits accrued before the leave began.

Employers who deny any of an employee's FMLA rights are civilly liable to the affected employee for resulting lost wages or, if no wages were lost, for any other resulting monetary losses not exceeding 12 weeks' wages. Employees may also recover an additional equal amount as liquidated damages, unless the employer acted in good faith and had reasonable grounds for believing that it was not violating the act. Like the FLSA, the FMLA permits civil actions by the secretary of labor, with any sums recovered distributed to affected employees. Employees may also obtain equitable relief, including reinstatement and promotion.

The Equal Pay Act

The Equal Pay Act (EPA), which forbids *sex* discrimination regarding *pay,* was a 1963 amendment to the FLSA. Its coverage resembles the coverage of the FLSA's minimum wage provisions. Unlike the FLSA, however, the EPA covers executive, administrative, and professional employees.

The Equal Pay Act forbids gender-based pay discrimination against men. But the typical EPA case involves a woman who claims that she has received lower pay than a male employee performing substantially equal work for the same employer. The substantially-equal-work requirement is met if the plaintiff's job and the higher-paid male employee's job involve *each* of the following: (1) equal effort, (2) equal skill, (3) equal responsibility, and (4) similar working conditions.

Effort basically means physical or mental exertion. *Skill* refers to the experience, training, education, and ability required for the positions being compared. Here, the question is not whether the employees being compared have equal skills but whether *their jobs require or utilize* substantially the same skills. *Responsibility* (or accountability) involves such factors as the degree of supervision each job requires and the importance of each job to the employer. For instance, a retail sales position in which an employee may not approve customer checks probably is not equal to a sales position in which an employee has this authority. *Working conditions* refers to such factors as temperature, weather, fumes, ventilation, toxic conditions, and risk of injury. These need only be *similar,* not equal.

If the two jobs are substantially equal and they are paid unequally, an employer must prove one of the EPA's four defenses or it will lose the case. The employer has a defense if it shows that the pay disparity is based on: (1) seniority, (2) merit, (3) quality or quantity of production (e.g., a piecework system), or (4) any factor other than sex. The first three defenses require an employer to show some organized, systematic, structured, and communicated rating system with predetermined criteria that apply equally to employees of each sex. The any-factor-other-than-sex defense is a catchall category that includes shift differentials, bonuses paid because the job is part of a training program, and differences in the profitability of the products or services on which employees work. The following *Dey* case reads this defense broadly.

The EPA's remedial scheme resembles the FLSA's scheme. Under the EPA, however, employee suits are for the amount of *back pay* lost because of an employer's discrimination, not for unpaid minimum wages or overtime. An employee may also recover an equal sum as liquidated damages. The EPA is enforced by the Equal Employment Opportunity Commission (EEOC) rather than the Labor Department.[5] Unlike some of the employment discrimination statutes described later, however, the EPA does not require that private plaintiffs submit their complaints to the EEOC or a state agency before mounting suit.

---

[5]The EEOC is an independent federal agency with a sizable staff and many regional offices. Its functions include: (1) enforcing most of the employment discrimination laws discussed in this chapter through lawsuits that it initiates or in which it intervenes, (2) conciliating employment discrimination charges (e.g., by encouraging their negotiated settlement), (3) investigating discrimination-related matters, and (4) interpreting the statutes it enforces through regulations and guidelines.

A nne Dey worked as a controller for the Colt Construction and Development Corporation. Her duties included: maintaining Colt's payroll, payables, and receivables; making disbursements to various parties; paying office expenses; documenting project costs; and preparing various forms and reports. However, while Dey provided the data for Colt's income tax returns and its year-end financial statements, each was prepared by an outside accountant. Dey was fired from her job for reasons that are not completely clear. At that time, she was making $27,820 a year.

Unlike Dey, her successor with Colt, Larry Gagnon, was a CPA with an MBA degree. Gagnon's duties included the tasks performed by Dey, plus preparation of Colt's tax returns, computerization of its financial records, and analysis of real estate investments. Gagnon was hired at a salary of $50,000.

After Gagnon left Colt's employ, he was replaced by Steven Maloney. Maloney had an MBA but had failed to pass the CPA exam. Also, he was about to be laid off by his employer. Maloney had responsibilities similar to Dey's responsibilities. Unlike Dey, however, he could execute certain documents without getting a company officer to sign them, and he supposedly continued the computerization of Colt's financial records. Colt originally offered Maloney $30,000, but upped that figure to $32,400, the amount Maloney had been making with his then-employer.

Dey sued Colt, alleging that these pay disparities violated the Equal Pay Act. After Colt successfully moved for summary judgment on this claim, Dey appealed. ∽

Rovner, Circuit Judge   To establish a prima facie case under [the Equal Pay Act], Dey must show: (1) that different wages are paid to employees of the opposite sex; (2) that the employees do equal work which requires equal skill, effort, and responsibility; and (3) that the employees have similar working conditions. In assessing whether two jobs require equal skill, effort, and responsibility, we look to the duties actually performed by each employee, and not to his or her job description or title. If two employees have a common core of tasks, the second element of the test is satisfied unless the employer can show that the higher-paid employee was assigned additional tasks that made his job substantially different.

[The] difference between Dey's salary and that of her successors is sufficient to support an action under the EPA. Dey has conceded, however, that Gagnon's responsibilities were substantially different from her own, so that his higher salary was justified. She focuses only on Maloney, and we agree with the district court that there are factual questions whether the responsibilities of Maloney and Dey were substantially different. We therefore assume that Dey could establish a prima facie case and proceed to Colt's defenses.

Once the plaintiff makes out a prima facie case, the defendant bears the burden of showing that the pay disparity is due to: (1) a seniority system; (2) a merit system; (3) a system which measures earnings by quality or quantity or production; or (4) a differential based on any factor other than sex. The district court concluded that Colt had satisfied its burden by showing that Maloney had more advanced business degrees, and that Maloney had negotiated a salary comparable to what he had earned at [his previous employer]. The court found that both were based on factors other than sex.

The EPA's fourth affirmative defenses is a broad catch-all exception that embraces an almost limitless number of factors, so long as they do not involve sex. The factor need not be related to the requirements of the particular position in question, nor must it even be business-related. We ask only whether the factor is bona fide, whether it has been discriminatorily applied, and in some circumstances whether it may have a discriminatory effect.

Dey has been unable to dispute Colt's assertion that the pay disparity was based on a factor other than sex. Although Maloney was not a CPA, he did have [an MBA], which would justify Colt's paying him a higher salary to perform a controller's duties. Although Dey had no doubt garnered invaluable experience during her tenure with Colt, we may not second-guess the company's decision to pay more for an advanced business degree where there is no evidence that it paid women with similar degrees a lesser amount or that Maloney's degree was unrelated to the tasks assigned him.

It is not surprising that Maloney would be unwilling to become Colt's controller unless he was compensated at or near his previous rate. When we consider [this] in conjunction with Maloney's superior educational background and the fact that Colt hired Maloney almost a full year after Dey's last

pay raise, we are convinced that Maloney's higher salary is unrelated to his sex.

District court summary judgment in Colt's favor affirmed on Dey's Equal Pay Act claim.

TITLE VII

Unlike the other laws discussed in the previous section, the Equal Pay Act is an *employment discrimination* provision. Employment discrimination might be defined as employer behavior that penalizes certain individuals because of personal traits that they cannot control and that bear no relation to effective job performance. Such discrimination was common before the law began to attack it during the 1960s and 1970s. Today, however, employers confront a maze of legal rules forbidding various kinds of employment discrimination.

Of the many employment discrimination laws in force today, the most important is Title VII of the 1964 Civil Rights Act. Unlike the Equal Pay Act, which merely forbids sex discrimination regarding pay, Title VII is a wide-ranging employment discrimination provision. It prohibits discrimination based on *race, color, religion, sex,* and *national origin* in hiring, firing, job assignments, pay, access to training and apprenticeship programs, and most other employment decisions.

Basic Features of Title VII

In discussing Title VII, we first examine some general rules that govern all the kinds of discrimination it forbids. Then we examine each forbidden basis of discrimination in detail.

Covered Entities   Title VII covers all employers employing 15 or more employees and engaging in an industry affecting interstate commerce. Employers include individuals, partnerships, corporations, colleges and universities, labor unions and employment agencies (with respect to their own employees), and state and local governments.[6] Also, *referrals* by employment agencies are covered no matter

what the size of the agency, if an employer serviced by the agency has 15 or more employees. In addition, Title VII covers certain unions—mainly those with 15 or more members—in their capacity as *employee representative.*

Procedures   Although the EEOC sometimes sues to enforce Title VII, the usual Title VII suit is a private claim. The complicated procedures governing private Title VII suits are beyond the scope of this text, but a few points should be kept in mind. Private parties with a Title VII claim have no automatic right to sue. Instead, they first must file a *charge* with the EEOC, or with a state agency in states having suitable fair employment laws and enforcement schemes. This allows the EEOC or the state agency to investigate the claim, attempt conciliation if the claim has substance, or sue the employer itself. If a plaintiff files with a state agency and the state fails to act, the plaintiff still can file a charge with the EEOC. Even if the EEOC fails to act on the claim, a plaintiff still may mount her own suit. Here, the EEOC issues a "right-to-sue letter" enabling the plaintiff to sue.

Proving Discrimination   The permissible methods for *proving* a Title VII violation are critical to its effectiveness against employment discrimination. Proof of discrimination is easy in cases, such as the *Johnson Controls* decision later in the chapter, where the employer had an **express policy** disfavoring one of Title VII's protected classes. **Direct evidence** of a discriminatory motive such as testimony or written evidence obviously is useful to plaintiffs as well. However, because employers can discriminate without leaving such obvious tracks, the courts have devised other methods of proving a Title VII violation. As of late 1996, two such methods predominated. Because each method's many details are beyond the scope of this text, and because each may have changed by the time you read this section, we merely outline them here.

---

[6]Employment discrimination within the federal government is beyond the scope of this text.

Title VII **disparate treatment** suits usually involve an individual plaintiff who alleges some specific instance or instances of discrimination. In such suits, the plaintiff first must show a *prima facie case:* a case strong enough to create a presumption of discrimination and to require a counterargument from the defendant. The proof needed for a prima facie case varies with the nature of the challenged employment decision (e.g., hiring or promotion), but ordinarily it gives plaintiffs few difficulties. Once the plaintiff establishes a prima facie case, the employer must produce evidence that the challenged employment decision was taken for *legitimate, nondiscriminatory reasons* or it will lose the lawsuit. In a hiring case, for example, an employer might produce evidence that it rejected the plaintiff because she did not meet its criteria for the position in question. If the employer produces satisfactory reasons, the plaintiff then must *show that discrimination actually occurred.* She might do so by showing that the employer's alleged nondiscriminatory reasons were a *pretext* for a decision that really involved discrimination. For example, she might show that the employer's alleged hiring criteria were not applied to similarly situated male job applicants.

Title VII's **disparate impact** (or adverse impact) method is most often used when the alleged discrimination affects many employees. Here, the plaintiffs ordinarily maintain that the employer uses a *particular employment practice* that causes a *disparate impact* on the basis of race, color, religion, sex, or national origin. Often, the practice is an employer rule that is neutral on its face but has a disproportionate adverse effect on one of Title VII's protected groups—for example, a height, weight, or high school diploma requirement for hiring, or a written test for hiring or promotion. If the plaintiffs show a disparate impact, the employer loses unless it demonstrates that the challenged practice is *job-related for the position in question and consistent with business necessity.* For example, the employer might show that its promotion test really predicts effective job performance, and that effective performance in the relevant job is necessary for its operations. Even if the employer makes this demonstration, the plaintiffs have another option: to show that the employer's legitimate business needs can be advanced by an *alternative employment practice* that is *less discriminatory than the challenged practice.* For example, the plaintiffs might show that the

employer's legitimate needs can be met by a different promotion test that has less adverse impact on the protected group. If the employer refuses to adopt this practice, the plaintiffs win.

Defenses   Even if a plaintiff proves a Title VII violation, the employer still prevails if it can establish one of Title VII's defenses. The most important such defenses are:

1. *Seniority.* Title VII is not violated if the employer treats employees differently pursuant to a *bona fide seniority system.* To be bona fide, such a system at least must treat all employees equally on its face, not have been created for discriminatory reasons, and not operate in a discriminatory fashion.

2. *The various "merit" defenses.* An employer also escapes Title VII liability if it acts pursuant to: a *bona fide merit system,* a system basing earnings on *quantity or quality of production,* or the results of a *professionally developed ability test.* Presumably, such systems and tests at least must meet the general standards for seniority systems stated above. Also, the EEOC has promulgated lengthy *Uniform Guidelines on Employee Selection Procedures* that speak to these and other matters.

3. *The BFOQ Defense.* Finally, Title VII allows employers to discriminate on the bases of sex, religion, or national origin where one of those traits is a *bona fide occupational qualification (BFOQ) that is reasonably necessary to the business in question.* This BFOQ defense does not protect race or color discrimination. As the following *Johnson Controls* case makes clear, moreover, the defense is a narrow one even where it applies. Generally, it is available only where a certain gender, religion, or national origin is necessary for effective job performance. For example, a BFOQ probably would exist where a female is employed to model women's clothing or to fit women's undergarments, or a French restaurant hires a French chef. But the BFOQ defense usually is unavailable where the discrimination is based on stereotypes (e.g., that women are less aggressive than men) or on the preferences of co-workers or customers (e.g., the preference of airline travelers for female rather than male flight attendants). As *Johnson Controls* suggests, the defense also is unavailable where the employer's discriminatory practice promotes goals, such as fetal protection, that do not concern effective job performance.

J ohnson Controls, Inc., manufactures batteries. Lead is a primary ingredient in that manufacturing process. A female employee's occupational exposure to lead involves a risk of harm to any fetus she carries. For this reason, Johnson Controls excluded women who are pregnant or who are capable of bearing children from jobs that involve exposure to lead. Numerous plaintiffs, including a woman who had chosen to be sterilized to avoid losing her job, entered a federal district court class action alleging that Johnson Controls' policy constituted illegal sex discrimination under Title VII. The district court entered a summary judgment for Johnson Controls and the court of appeals affirmed. The plaintiffs appealed to the U.S. Supreme Court. ∞

Blackmun, Justice Johnson Controls' fetal-protection policy explicitly discriminates against women on the basis of their sex. The policy excludes women with childbearing capacity from lead-exposed jobs and so creates a facial classification based on gender. [But] an employer may discriminate on the basis of "religion, sex, or national origin in those certain instances where religion, sex, or national origin is a bona fide occupational qualification reasonably necessary to the normal operation of that particular business or enterprise." The BFOQ defense is written narrowly, and this Court has read it narrowly.

Johnson Controls argues that its fetal-protection policy falls within the so-called safety exception [of] the BFOQ. Discrimination on the basis of sex because of safety concerns is allowed only in narrow circumstances. In *Dothard v. Rawlinson* (1977), we allowed the employer to hire only male guards in contact areas of maximum-security male penitentiaries only because more was at stake than the individual woman's decision to weigh and accept the risks of employment. We found sex to be a BFOQ inasmuch as the employment of a female guard would create real risks of safety to others if [rape-related] violence broke out because the guard was a woman. Sex discrimination was tolerated because sex was related to the guard's ability to do the job—maintaining prison security. Similarly, some courts have approved airlines' layoffs of pregnant flight attendants on the ground that the employer's policy was necessary to ensure the safety of passengers. In two of these cases, the courts pointedly indicated that fetal, as opposed to passenger, safety was best left to the mother.

Therefore, the safety exception is limited to instances in which sex or pregnancy actually interferes with the employee's ability to perform the job . . . [Thus,] Johnson Controls cannot establish a BFOQ. Fertile women, as far as appears in the record, manufacture batteries as efficiently as anyone else. Johnson Controls' professed moral and ethical concerns about the next generation do not suffice to establish a BFOQ of female sterility. Decisions about the welfare of future children must be left to the parents who conceive, bear, support, and raise them rather than to the employers who hire those parents.

Judgment in favor of Johnson Controls reversed; case returned to the lower courts for further proceedings consistent with the Supreme Court's opinion.

Remedies Various remedies are possible once private plaintiffs or the EEOC win a Title VII suit. If intentional discrimination has caused lost wages, employees can obtain **back pay** accruing from a date two years before the filing of the charge. At the court's discretion, successful private plaintiffs also may recover reasonable **attorney's fees.** In addition, victims of intentional discrimination can recover **compensatory damages** for harms such as emotional distress, sickness, loss of reputation, or denial of credit. Victims of intentional discrimination also can recover **punitive damages** where the defendant discriminated with malice or with reckless indifference to the plaintiff's rights. However, the sum of the plaintiff's compensatory and punitive damages cannot exceed certain amounts that vary with the size of the employer. For example, they cannot total more than $300,000 for an employer with more than 500 employees.

Intentional discrimination may also entitle successful plaintiffs to **equitable relief.** Examples include orders compelling hiring, reinstatement, or retroactive seniority. On occasion, moreover, the courts have ordered quotalike preferences in Title VII cases involving race and (occasionally) gender discrimination. For example, a court might order that whites and minorities be hired on a 50–50 basis until minority representation in the employer's work force reaches some specified percentage. Generally speaking, such orders are permissible if: (1) an employer has engaged in severe, widespread, or longstanding discrimination; (2) the order does not unduly restrict the employment interests of white people; and (3) it does not force an employer to hire unqualified workers. Minority preferences also may appear in the **consent decrees** courts issue when approving the terms on which the parties have settled a Title VII case.[7]

Race or Color Discrimination

At this point, we consider each of Title VII's prohibited bases of discrimination in more detail. *Race or color* discrimination includes discrimination against blacks, other racial minorities, Eskimos, and American Indians, among others. Title VII also prohibits racial discrimination against whites. Nonetheless, voluntary racial preferences that favor minorities survive a Title VII attack if they: (1) are intended to correct a racial imbalance involving underrepresentation of minorities in traditionally segregated job categories, (2) do not "unnecessarily trammel" the rights of white employees or create an absolute bar to their advancement, and (3) are only temporary.[8] Note that here our concern is not the use of minority preferences as a *remedy* for a Title VII violation, but whether such preferences *themselves* violate Title VII when voluntarily established by an employer.

National Origin Discrimination

National origin discrimination includes discrimination based on: (1) the country of one's or one's ancestors' origin; or (2) one's possession of physical, cultural, or linguistic characteristics identified with people of a particular nation. Thus, plaintiffs in national origin discrimination cases need not have been born in the country at issue. In fact, if the discrimination is based on physical, cultural, or linguistic traits identified with a particular nation, even the plaintiff's ancestors need not have been born there. Thus, a person of pure French ancestry may have a Title VII case if she suffers discrimination because she looks like, acts like, or talks like a German.

Certain formally neutral employment practices can also constitute national origin discrimination. Employers who hire only U.S. citizens may violate Title VII if their policy has the purpose or effect of discriminating against one or more national origin groups. This could happen where the employer is located in an area where aliens of a particular nationality are heavily concentrated. Also, employment criteria such as height, weight, and fluency in English may violate Title VII if they have a disparate impact on a national origin group and are not job-related.

Religious Discrimination

For Title VII purposes, the term *religion* is broadly defined. Although all courts may not agree, the EEOC says that it includes any set of moral beliefs that are sincerely held with the same strength as traditional religious views. In fact, Title VII forbids religious discrimination against atheists. It also forbids discrimination based on religious *observances or practices*—for example, grooming, clothing, or the refusal to work on the Sabbath. But such discrimination is permissible if an employer cannot reasonably accommodate the religious practice without suffering undue hardship. Undue hardship exists when the accommodation imposes more than a minimal cost on an employer.

---

[7]As discussed in Chapter 3, recently the Supreme Court has held that federal government racial discrimination against whites gets the same full strict scrutiny as racial discrimination against blacks and other racial minorities. It remains to be seen whether this change will affect the courts' ability to order remedial minority preferences or to approve such preferences when they appear in consent decrees.

[8]*United Steelworkers v. Weber,* 443 U.S. 193 (1979), a portion of which is excerpted in Chapter 1. As of late 1996, it appeared that this test would block employers from pursuing racial diversity or racial balance for its own sake, if this requires discrimination against white people.

Sex Discrimination

Title VII's ban on sex discrimination aims at *gender-based* discrimination and does not forbid discrimination on the basis of homosexuality or transsexuality. Just as clearly, it applies to gender discrimination against *both men and women.* Still, voluntary employer programs favoring women in hiring or promotion survive a Title VII attack if they meet the previous tests for voluntary racial preferences (reformulated in terms of gender). Title VII also forbids discrimination on the bases of *pregnancy and childbirth,* and requires employers to treat these conditions like any other condition similarly affecting working ability in their sick leave programs, medical benefit and disability plans, and so forth. Finally, *sexual stereotyping* violates Title VII. This is employer behavior that either: (1) denies a woman employment opportunities by assuming that she must have traditionally "female" traits (e.g., unaggressiveness), or (2) penalizes her for lacking such traits (e.g., for acting aggressively).

Sexual Harassment Unwelcome sexual advances, requests for sexual favors, and other verbal or physical conduct of a sexual nature can violate Title VII under two different theories. The first, called *quid pro quo* sexual harassment, involves some express or implied linkage between an employee's submission to sexually oriented behavior and tangible job consequences. Quid pro quo cases usually arise when, due to an employee's refusal to submit, she suffers a *tangible job detriment* of an economic nature; indeed, courts usually require such a detriment for recovery. For example, suppose that a supervisor fires a secretary because she refuses to have sexual relations with him or refuses to submit to other sex-related behavior. Such conduct would violate Title VII whether or not the supervisor expressly told the secretary that she would be fired for refusing to submit. Title VII is also violated if a supervisor denies a subordinate a deserved promotion or other job benefit for refusing to submit.

However, no quid pro quo and no tangible job detriment are required when an employee is subjected to *work environment* sexual harassment. As the following *Harris* case states, this is unwelcome sex-related behavior that is sufficiently severe or pervasive to change the conditions of the victim's employment and create an abusive working environment. Work environment sexual harassment can be inflicted by both supervisors and co-workers. Because such behavior must be *unwelcome,* however, an employee may have trouble recovering if she instigated or contributed to the sex-related behavior. Also, the offending behavior must be sufficiently *severe or pervasive* to create an environment that a *reasonable person* would find hostile or abusive.

When is an *employer* liable for sexual harassment committed by its employees? Courts usually hold that: (1) employers are strictly liable for quid pro quo harassment, and (2) employers are liable for work environment harassment if they knew or should have known of the harassment and failed to take appropriate corrective action.

The reach of Title VII sexual harassment law continues to expand. Courts have long held that men can sue for sexual harassment by women. In addition, some courts have held that Title VII allows sexual harassment recovery when both the harasser(s) and the harassee are of the same gender—so-called same-sex sexual harassment. Finally, a few courts have granted Title VII recoveries for "sexual favoritism"—discrimination in favor of employees who submit to sexual harassment, benefit from a sexual relationship with a superior, or trade sex for personal advancement. However, other courts do not allow recovery for same-sex harassment and sexual favoritism.

HARRIS v. FORKLIFT SYSTEMS, INC. 510 U.S. 17 (U.S. Sup. Ct. 1993)

I n April 1985, Theresa Harris started work as a manager for Forklift Systems, Inc. (Forklift). During Harris's two and one-half years with Forklift, she was subjected to gender-based insults and unwanted sexual innuendos from Charles Hardy, the firm's president. Several times, for example, Hardy told Harris: "You're a woman, what do you know?" and "We need a man as the rental manager." Once, he suggested that he and Harris negotiate her raise at the Holiday Inn. Hardy also would ask Harris and other female employees to get coins from his front pants pocket, and to pick up objects that he threw on the ground. Most of these incidents occurred with other employees present.

After Harris complained to Hardy in August of 1987, he apologized and promised to stop his offensive behavior. In early September, however, he inquired whether Harris had promised sex to a customer with whom she had concluded a deal on Forklift's behalf. On October 1, Harris quit. She then sued Forklift for work environment sexual harassment in federal district court. Although it considered Harris's claim "a close case," the court found for Forklift. It did so in part because it concluded that Hardy's actions were not sufficiently severe to seriously affect Harris's psychological well-being. After the court of appeals affirmed, Harris appealed to the U.S. Supreme Court. ∞

O'Connor, Justice   Title VII makes it "an unlawful employment practice for an employer to discriminate against any individual with respect to his compensation, terms, conditions, or privileges of employment, because of such individual's race, color, religion, sex, or national origin." The phrase "terms, conditions, or privileges of employment" evinces a Congressional intent to strike at the entire spectrum of disparate treatment of men and women in employment, which includes requiring people to work in a discriminatorily hostile or abusive environment. When the workplace is permeated with discriminatory intimidation, ridicule, and insult that is sufficiently severe or pervasive to alter the conditions of the victim's employment and create an abusive working environment, Title VII is violated.

This standard takes a middle path between making actionable any conduct that is merely offensive and requiring the conduct to cause a tangible psychological injury. Conduct that is not severe or pervasive enough to create an environment that a reasonable person would find hostile or abusive is beyond Title VII's purview. Likewise, if the victim does not subjectively perceive the environment to be abusive, there is no Title VII violation.

But Title VII comes into play before the harassing conduct leads to a nervous breakdown. A discriminatorily abusive work environment, even one that does not seriously affect employees' psychological well-being, can and often will detract from

employees' job performance, discourage employees from remaining on the job, or keep them from advancing in their careers. We therefore believe the district court erred in relying on whether the conduct seriously affected plaintiff's psychological well-being or led her to suffer injury. Such an inquiry may needlessly focus the fact-finder's attention on concrete psychological harm, an element Title VII does not require. Certainly Title VII bars conduct that would seriously affect a reasonable person's psychological well-being, but the statute is not limited to such conduct. So long as the environment would reasonably be perceived, and is perceived, as hostile or abusive, there is no need for it also to be psychologically injurious.

This is not, and by its nature cannot be, a mathematically precise test. Whether an environment is "hostile" or "abusive" can be determined only by looking at all the circumstances. These may include the frequency of the discriminatory conduct; its severity; whether it is physically threatening or humiliating, or a mere offensive utterance; and whether it unreasonably interferes with an employee's work performance.

Court of appeals decision in Forklift's favor reversed. Case returned to the district court for proceedings consistent with the Supreme Court's opinion.

OTHER IMPORTANT EMPLOYMENT DISCRIMINATION PROVISIONS

Section 1981

Where it applies, a post-Civil War civil rights statute called section 1981 sets employment discrimination standards resembling those of Title VII. Section 1981 forbids public and private employment discrimination against blacks, people of certain racially characterized national origins such as Mexicans,

and ethnic groups such as gypsies and Jews. Included within such discrimination are most of the ways that an employer might disadvantage an employee.

Section 1981 is important because it gives covered plaintiffs certain advantages that Title VII does not provide. Although courts often use Title VII's methods of proof in section 1981 cases, Title VII's limitations on covered employers and its complex procedural requirements do not apply. Also, damages are apt to be greater under section 1981; in particular, Title VII's limits on compensatory and punitive damages are inapplicable. For these reasons, covered plaintiffs often include a section 1981 claim along with a Title VII claim in their complaint.

The Age Discrimination in Employment Act

The 1967 Age Discrimination in Employment Act (ADEA) prohibits age-based employment discrimination against employees who are *at least 40 years of age.* The favored employee may be either inside or outside the protected age group. In addition, the ADEA probably forbids age discrimination in favor of both younger and older employees.

Coverage The ADEA covers individuals, partnerships, labor organizations and employment agencies (as to their employees), and corporations that: (1) engage in an industry affecting interstate commerce, and (2) employ at least 20 persons. The act also regulates state and local governments.[9] *Referrals* by an employment agency to a covered employer are within the ADEA's scope regardless of the agency's size. In addition, the ADEA reaches labor union practices affecting *union members*; usually, unions with 25 or more members are covered. The ADEA protects against age discrimination in many employment contexts, including hiring, firing, pay, job assignment, and fringe benefits.

Procedural Requirements The complex procedural requirements for an ADEA suit are beyond the scope of this text. Before she can sue in her own right, a private plaintiff must file a charge with the EEOC or with an appropriate state agency. The EEOC also may sue to enforce the ADEA; such a suit precludes private suits arising from the same alleged violation. For both government and private suits, the statute of limitations is three years from the date of an alleged *willful* violation and two years from the date of an alleged *nonwillful* violation.

Proof Proving age discrimination is no problem where an employer uses an express age criterion, and may be easy where there is direct evidence of discrimination such as testimony or incriminating documents. However, many ADEA cases, like the following *Biggins* decision, are brought under the Title VII disparate treatment theory discussed earlier. A few courts have used Title VII's disparate impact theory in ADEA cases.

Defenses The ADEA allows employers to discharge or otherwise discipline an employee for *good cause,* and to use *reasonable factors other than age* in their employment decisions. It also allows employers to observe the terms of a *bona fide seniority system.* In addition, the ADEA has a *bona fide occupational qualification* (BFOQ) defense. Speaking very generally, an employer seeking to use this defense must show that its age classification is reasonably necessary to the proper performance—usually the safe performance—of the job in question. For example, an employer that refuses to hire anyone over 60 as a helicopter pilot should have a BFOQ defense if it has a reasonable basis for concluding that 60-and-over helicopter pilots pose significant safety risks, or that it is not feasible to test older pilots individually.

Remedies Remedies available after a successful ADEA suit include unpaid back wages and overtime pay resulting from the discrimination; an additional equal award of liquidated damages where the employer acted willfully; attorney's fees; and equitable relief, including hiring, reinstatement, and promotion. Most courts do not allow punitive damages and recoveries for pain, suffering, mental distress, and so forth.

---

[9]Age discrimination in the federal government is beyond the scope of this text.

HAZEN PAPER CO. v. BIGGINS   507 U.S. 604 (U.S. Sup. Ct. 1993)

Walter F. Biggins worked as a technical director for the Hazen Paper Company. In 1986, when Biggins was 62, Hazen fired him. Its justification was that Biggins had been doing business with Hazen's competitors. At the time of the firing, Biggins was within a few weeks of completing the 10-year vesting period for his employer-provided pension. There was also evidence that Hazen offered to retain Biggins as a consultant to the company, in which case he would not have been entitled to pension benefits.

After Biggins sued Hazen under the ADEA, a federal district court jury found in his favor. The court of appeals affirmed, and Hazen appealed to the U.S. Supreme Court. ∽

O'Connor, Justice The courts of appeals repeatedly have faced the question whether an employer violates the ADEA by acting on the basis of a factor, such as an employee's pension status or seniority, that is empirically correlated with age. We now clarify that there is no disparate treatment under the ADEA when the factor motivating the employer is some feature other than the employee's age.

We have long distinguished between disparate treatment and disparate impact theories of employment discrimination. The disparate treatment theory is available under the ADEA. By contrast, we have never decided whether a disparate impact theory of liability is available under the ADEA, and we need not do so here. Biggins claims only that he received disparate treatment.

In a disparate treatment case, liability depends on whether the protected trait (under the ADEA, age) actually motivated the employer's decision. It is the very essence of age discrimination for an older employee to be fired because the employer believes that productivity and competence decline with old age. The employer cannot rely on age as a proxy for an employee's remaining characteristics, such as productivity, but must instead focus on those factors directly.

When the employer's decision *is* wholly motivated by factors other than age, the problem of inaccurate and stigmatizing stereotypes disappears. This is true even if the motivating factor is correlated with age, as pension status typically is. Pension plans typically provide that an employee's accrued benefits will become nonforfeitable, or "vested," once the employee completes a certain number of years of service with the employer. On average, an older employee has had more years in the work force than a younger employee, and thus may well have accumulated more years of service with a particular employer. Yet an employee's age is analytically distinct from his years of service. An employee who is younger than 40, and therefore outside the class of older workers as defined by the ADEA, may have worked for a particular employer his entire career, while an older worker may have been newly hired. Because age and years of service are analytically distinct, an employer can take account of one while ignoring the other, and thus it is incorrect to say that a decision based on years of service is necessarily age-based.

We do not mean to suggest that an employer *lawfully* could fire an employee in order to prevent his pension benefits from vesting. Such conduct is actionable under [ERISA]. But it would not, without more, violate the ADEA.

Besides the evidence of pension interference, the court of appeals cited some additional evidentiary support for ADEA liability. Biggins was asked to sign a confidentiality agreement, even though no other employee had been required to do so, and his replacement was a younger man who was given a less onerous agreement. In the ordinary ADEA case, indirect evidence of this kind may well suffice to support liability if the plaintiff also shows that the employer's explanation for its decision—here, that Biggins had been disloyal to Hazen by doing business with its competitors—is unworthy of credence. But inferring age-motivation from the implausibility of the employer's explanation may be problematic in cases where other unsavory motives, such as pension interference, were present. We therefore remand the case for the court of appeals to reconsider whether the jury had sufficient evidence to find an ADEA violation.

Judgment reversed. Case returned to the court of appeals to consider whether, under the standards outlined in its opinion, there was sufficient evidence to find Hazen liable for age discrimination.

The Americans with Disabilities Act

Before the 1990s, federal regulation of employment discrimination against handicapped people mainly was limited to certain federal contractors and recipients of federal financial assistance. By passing Title I of the Americans with Disabilities Act of 1990 (ADA), however, Congress addressed this problem comprehensively. This portion of the ADA is primarily enforced by the EEOC, and its procedures and remedies are the same as for Title VII.

FIGURE 2

A Map through the ADA

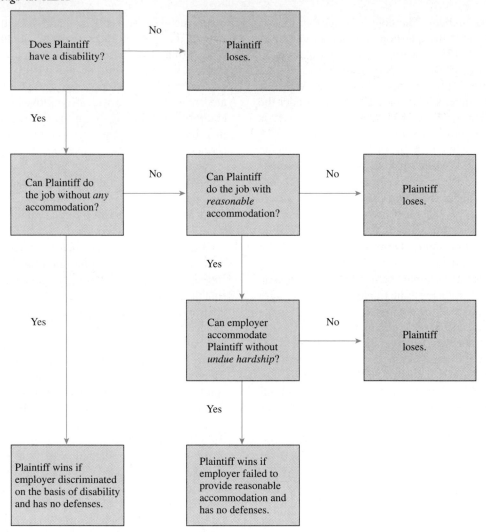

Covered Entities Title I covers employers who have 15 or more employees and who are engaged in an industry affecting interstate commerce. Employers include individuals, partnerships, corporations, colleges and universities, labor unions and employment agencies (regarding their own employees), and state and local governments. The act also covers certain labor unions in their capacity as employee representative, as well as employment agencies' discrimination against their clients.

Substantive Protections The ADA forbids covered entities from discriminating against *qualified* *individuals with a disability* because of that disability. It covers disability-related discrimination regarding hiring, firing, promotion, pay, and innumerable other employment decisions. The act defines a *disability* as: (1) a physical or mental impairment that substantially limits one or more of an individual's major life activities, (2) a record of such an impairment, or (3) one's being regarded as having such an impairment. (The last two categories protect those who have previously been misdiagnosed or who have recovered from earlier impairments.) Not protected, however, are those who suffer discrimination for currently engaging in the illegal use of drugs. Furthermore, homosexuality, bisexuality, transvestism, transsexualism, and various other sex-related traits or conditions are not considered disabilities.

A *qualified individual with a disability* is a person who can perform the essential functions of the relevant job either: (1) without reasonable accommodation, or (2) with such accommodation. Thus, the ADA protects both individuals who can perform their job despite their handicap, and individuals who could perform their job if reasonable accommodation is provided. In the latter case, employers illegally discriminate if they do not provide such accommodation. *Reasonable accommodation* includes: making existing facilities readily accessible and usable, acquiring new equipment, restruc-

turing jobs, modifying work schedules, and reassigning workers to vacant positions, among other options. The following *Johnston* case discusses these various requirements.

However, employers need not make reasonable accommodation where such accommodation would cause them to suffer *undue hardship*. Undue hardship is an act requiring significant difficulty or expense. Among the factors used to determine its existence are the cost of the accommodation, the covered entity's overall financial resources, and the accommodation's effect on the covered entity's activities. The ADA also protects employers whose allegedly discriminatory decisions are based on *job-related criteria and business necessity,* so long as proper job performance cannot be accomplished by reasonable accommodation.

JOHNSTON v. MORRISON, INC.   849 F. Supp. 777 (N.D. Ala. 1994)

G *eneva Johnston worked as a food server at a Morrison's L&N Seafood Restaurant. She claimed to suffer from a number of ailments, among them "panic attack disorder." These ailments affected her ability to perform her food server duties. For example, she had considerable difficulty handling changes in the restaurant's menu. After learning of Johnston's condition, the restaurant assigned her to its least busy workstation. This tactic met with some success until the night of December 31, 1992, when Johnston suffered what she described as a "meltdown" during an especially busy period for the restaurant. Apparently Johnston's inability to perform her duties on that night led to her being fired.*

Johnston sued Morrison under the ADA. Morrison then moved for summary judgment. ∞

Nelson, District Judge   Under the ADA, "[n]o covered entity shall discriminate against a qualified individual with a disability." A qualified individual with a disability is one "who, with or without reasonable accommodation, can perform the essential functions of the employment position that such individual holds or desires." Since the plaintiff's disability plainly prevented her from performing the essential functions required of a food server at the restaurant, with or without reasonable accommodation, the plaintiff is not a qualified individual and cannot prevail on her ADA claim.

The term *essential functions* means the fundamental job duties of the employment position. Morrison has the right to determine that an essential function of being a food server includes knowing and being able to communicate the ingredients, portion sizes, and prices of items on the menu. Johnston testified that Morrison constantly made

changes in what she was required to know and communicate to the customers. However, because of her disability, she could not handle such changes. She testified that changes of the kind described caused "a panic attack all the time," and [that] these attacks resulted in "constant headache, constant fear," and "confusion inside."

Johnston also testified that her disability prevented her from performing her duties when the restaurant became crowded. In order to accommodate her disability, Morrison assigned her to the restaurant's least busy area. Under the ADA, a reasonable accommodation may include "job restructuring [and] part-time or modified work schedules." However, "[a]n employer or other covered entity is not required to reallocate essential functions." Morrison was not required to provide another employee to handle Johnston's food server duties. Morrison also was not required to remove

Johnston from her work station when her work station became crowded. Johnston's position required her to perform her duties during all times she was at her work station, whether the situation presented slow or busy periods.

Morrison's motion for summary judgment on Johnston's ADA claim granted.

Executive Order 11246

Executive Order 11246, issued in 1965 and later amended, forbids race, color, national origin, religion, and sex discrimination by certain federal contractors. The order is enforced by the Labor Department's Office of Federal Contract Compliance Programs (OFCCP). In the past, OFCCP enforcement has included affirmative action requirements and occasionally quotalike preferences benefiting racial minorities.

State Antidiscrimination Laws

Most states have statutes that parallel Title VII, the EPA, the ADEA, and the ADA. These statutes sometimes provide more extensive protection than their federal counterparts. In addition, some states prohibit forms of discrimination not barred by federal law. Examples include discrimination on the bases of one's marital status, physical appearance, sexual orientation, political affiliation, AIDS infection, and off-the-job smoking.

Finally, some states and localities have adopted laws that adopt the employment discrimination theory called **comparable worth.** These laws, which typically apply only to public employees, often say that state governments should not discriminate in pay between female-dominated jobs and male-dominated jobs of comparable overall worth to the employer. The worth of different jobs may be determined by giving each job a point rating under factors such as skill, responsibility, effort, and working conditions; adding the ratings; and comparing the totals. It was once believed that comparable worth claims might find favor under Title VII, but that possibility has receded over the years.

CONCEPT   REVIEW

The Employment Discrimination Laws Compared

	PROTECTED TRAITS	COVERED EMPLOYER DECISIONS	NEED TO FILE CHARGE IN PRIVATE SUIT?
Equal Pay Act	Sex only	Pay only	No
Title VII	Race, color, national origin, religion, sex	Wide range	Yes
Section 1981	Race, racially characterized national origin, perhaps alienage	Wide range	No
Age Discrimination in Employment Act	Age, if victim 40 or over	Wide range	Yes
Americans with Disabilities Act	Existence of disability, if person qualified to perform job with or without reasonable accommodation	Wide range	Yes
Executive Order 11246	Race, color, religion, national origin, sex	Wide range	Not applicable; enforced by OFCCP

EMPLOYEE PRIVACY

The term *employee privacy* describes several employment issues that have assumed increasing importance recently. Uniting these issues is a concern with protecting employees' personal dignity and increasing their freedom from intrusions, surveillance, and the revelation of personal matters.

Polygraph Testing

Over the years, employers have made increasing use of polygraph and other lie detector tests—most often, to screen job applicants and to investigate employee thefts. This has led to concerns about the accuracy of such tests; the personal questions examiners sometimes ask; and the tests' impact on workers' job prospects, job security, and personal privacy. Besides provoking state restrictions on polygraph testing, such worries led Congress to pass the Employee Polygraph Protection Act in 1988.

The Employee Polygraph Protection Act mainly regulates lie detector tests, which include polygraph tests and certain other devices for assessing a person's honesty. Under the act, employers may not: (1) require, suggest, request, or cause employees or prospective employees to take any lie detector test; (2) use, accept, refer to, or inquire about the results of any lie detector test administered to employees or prospective employees; and (3) discriminate or threaten to discriminate against employees or prospective employees because of the results of any lie detector test, or because such parties failed or refused to take such a test. The act also has an antiretaliation provision.

However, certain employers and tests are exempt from these provisions. They include: (1) federal, state, and local government employers; (2) certain national defense and security-related tests by the federal government; (3) certain tests by security service firms; and (4) certain tests by firms manufacturing and distributing controlled substances. The act also contains a limited exemption for private employers that use polygraph tests when investigating economic losses caused by theft, embezzlement, industrial espionage, and so forth. Finally, the act restricts the disclosure of test results by examiners and by most employers.

The Polygraph Protection Act is enforced by the Labor Department, which has issued regulations in furtherance of that mission. It does not preempt state laws that prohibit lie detector tests or that set standards stricter than those imposed by federal law. Violations of the act or its regulations can result in civil penalties, suits for equitable relief by the Labor Department, and private suits for damages and equitable relief. Workers and job applicants who succeed in a private suit can obtain employment, reinstatement, promotion, and payment of lost wages and benefits.

Drug and Alcohol Testing

Due to their impact on employees' safe and effective job performance, employers have become increasingly concerned about both on-the-job and off-the-job drug and alcohol use. Thus, employers increasingly require employees and job applicants to undergo urine tests for drugs and/or alcohol. Because those who test positive may be either disciplined or induced to undergo treatment, and because the tests themselves can raise privacy concerns, some legal checks on their use have emerged.

Drug and alcohol testing by *public* employers can be attacked under the Fourth Amendment's search-and-seizure provisions. However, such tests generally are constitutional where there is a reasonable basis for suspecting that an employee is using drugs or alcohol, or drug use in a particular job could threaten the public interest or public safety. Due to the government action requirement discussed in Chapter 3, *private-sector* employees generally have no federal constitutional protection against drug and alcohol testing. Some state constitutions, however, lack a government action requirement. In addition, several states now regulate private drug and/or alcohol testing by statute. Tort suits for invasion of privacy or infliction of emotional distress may also be possible in some cases.[10]

Despite these protections, however, federal law *requires* private-sector drug testing in certain situations. Under a Defense Department rule, for example, employers who contract with the department must agree to establish a drug-testing program requiring, for instance, that employees who work in sensitive positions sometimes be tested. Also,

---

[10]Invasion of privacy and intentional infliction of emotional distress are discussed in Chapter 6, and negligent infliction of emotional distress is discussed in Chapter 7.

Transportation Department regulations require random testing of public and private employees occupying safety-sensitive or security-related positions in industries such as aviation, trucking, railroads, mass transit, and others.

Employer Searches

Employers concerned about theft, drug use, and other misbehavior by their employees sometimes conduct searches of those employees' offices, desks, lockers, files, briefcases, packages, vehicles, and even bodies to confirm their suspicions. The Supreme Court has held that public employees sometimes have a reasonable expectation of privacy in areas such as their offices, desks, or files. But it also held that searches of those areas are constitutional under the Fourth Amendment when they are reasonable under the circumstances. Determining reasonableness generally means balancing the employee's legitimate privacy expectations against the government's need for supervision and control of the workplace, with more intrusive searches demanding a higher degree of justification. Finally, the Court also said that neither probable cause nor a warrant is necessary for such searches to proceed.

As noted above, the U.S. Constitution ordinarily does not apply to private employment. Nonetheless, both private and public employees can mount common law invasion of privacy suits against employers who conduct searches. In such cases, courts usually try to weigh the intrusiveness of the search against the purposes justifying it and consider the availability of less intrusive alternatives that still would satisfy the employer's legitimate needs.

Employer Monitoring

Although employers have always monitored their employees' work, recent technological advances enable such monitoring to occur without those employees' knowledge. Examples include closed-circuit television, video monitoring, telephone monitoring, the monitoring of computer workstations (e.g., by counting keystrokes), and metal detectors at plant entrances. Such monitoring has encountered objections because employees often are unaware that it exists or may suffer stress when they do know or suspect its existence. Employers counter these objections by stressing that monitoring is highly useful in evaluating employee performance, improving efficiency, and reducing theft.

Telephone monitoring occasionally has been found illegal under federal wiretapping law. Although such claims have been uncommon, invasion of privacy suits may succeed in situations where an employer's need for surveillance is slight and it is conducted in areas, such as restrooms and lounges, in which employees have a reasonable expectation of privacy. Despite several state and federal bills proposing statutes regulating various forms of monitoring, little such legislation had passed as of late 1996.

Records and References

Many states allow both public and private employees at least some access to personnel files maintained by their employers. Also, some states limit third-party access to such records. In addition, employers who transmit such data to third parties—for example, in letters of reference—may be civilly liable for defamation or invasion of privacy.[11] However, truth is a defense in defamation cases. In both defamation and invasion of privacy suits, moreover, the employer's actions may be conditionally privileged. This defense and these privileges can protect employers who are sued for truthful, accurate, relevant, good faith statements made in references concerning former employees. Finally, a few states have allowed defamation suits for so-called compelled self-disclosure by job-seeking discharged employees who have been required to tell potential employers their former employer's alleged reasons for firing them.

WRONGFUL DISCHARGE

The Doctrine of Employment at Will

The traditional employment-at-will rule first appeared around 1870, and by the early 20th century most state courts had adopted it. The rule says that *either party can terminate an employment contract of indefinite duration.* Indefinite-duration contracts do not state a definite time period for the employ-

---

[11]Defamation and invasion of privacy are discussed in Chapter 6.

ment; included among such contracts are those for "steady," "regular," or "permanent" employment. The termination can occur at any time; and can be for good cause, bad cause, or no cause. However, employees may recover for work actually done.

The Common Law Exceptions

Because it allows employers to discharge indefinite-term employees with virtual impunity, employment at will has long been regarded as a force for economic efficiency but also as a threat to workers' job security. Although the doctrine remains important today, it has been eroded by many of the developments described in this chapter. For example, the NLRA forbids dismissal for union affiliation, and labor contracts frequently bar termination without just cause. Also, Title VII prohibits firings based on certain personal traits, the ADEA blocks discharges on the basis of age, and the ADA forbids terminations for covered personal disabilities.

Over the past 20 to 25 years, courts have been carving out further exceptions to employment at will. Here we discuss the three most important such exceptions. Although a few states do not recognize any of these exceptions, most states have adopted one or more of them. In such states, a terminated employee sometimes can recover against her employer for **wrongful discharge** or **unjust dismissal.** The remedies in successful wrongful discharge suits depend heavily on whether the plaintiff's claim sounds in contract or in tort, with tort remedies being more advantageous for plaintiffs.

The Public Policy Exception The public policy exception to employment at will, which has been recognized by over three-fourths of the states, is the most common basis for a wrongful discharge suit. It usually is a tort claim. In public policy cases, the terminated employee argues that his discharge was unlawful because it violated the state's public policy. How do courts determine the content of this public policy? Although there is some disagreement on the subject, most courts limit "public policy" to the policies furthered by existing laws such as constitutional provisions, statutes, and perhaps administrative regulations and common law rules. For this reason, employees often fail to recover where they are fired for ethical objections to job assignments or employer practices.

Successful suits under the public policy exception usually involve firings caused by an employee's: (1) refusal to commit an unlawful act (e.g., committing perjury or violating the antitrust laws), (2) performance of an important public obligation (e.g., jury duty or whistle-blowing),[12] or (3) exercise of a legal right or privilege (e.g., making a workers' compensation claim or refusing to take an illegal polygraph test). In each case, the act (or refusal to act) that caused the firing is consistent with some public policy; for this reason, the firing frustrates the policy. For example, firing an employee for filing a workers' compensation claim undermines the public policies underlying state workers' compensation statutes.

The Implied Covenant of Good Faith and Fair Dealing A wrongful discharge suit based on the implied covenant of good faith and fair dealing usually is a contract claim. Here, the employee argues that her discharge was unlawful because it was not made in good faith or did not amount to fair dealing, thus breaching the implied contract term. Only about 25 percent of the states have recognized this exception to employment at will, and most of these give it a narrow scope.

Promises by Employers Using various legal theories, courts have increasingly made employers liable for breaking promises to their employees regarding termination policy. Such promises typically are express statements made by employers during hiring or employee orientation, or in their employee manuals, handbooks, personnel policies, and benefit plans. Occasionally such promises are implied from business custom and usage as well. Here, our concern is with express or implied employer promises involving matters such as discharge policies and discharge procedures. If the employer fails to follow those promises when it fires an employee, it is liable for breach of contract. At least two-thirds of the states recognize this exception to employment at will. As the following *Progress Printing* case suggests, however, employers often succeed in disclaiming liability for their own promises.

---

[12]Whistle-blowers are employees who publicly disclose dangerous, illegal, or improper employer behavior. A few states have passed statutes protecting the employment rights of certain whistle-blowers.

On January 20, 1987, William H. Nichols began work as a pressman for the Progress Printing Company. At that time, Nichols was provided with a copy of the company's Employees' Handbook. The handbook stated that Progress would not discharge or suspend an employee "without just cause" and that the company "shall give at least one warning notice in writing" before termination, except under certain circumstances not relevant here.

On February 2, 1987, however, the firm's personnel director gave Nichols a form which stated in part:

I have received a copy of the Progress Printing Employee Handbook. I recognize that an understanding of this information is important to a successful relationship between Progress Printing and myself. I agree to follow the procedures and guidelines it contains. Any questions concerning Progress Printing's polices will be directed to the Personnel Director.

The employment relationship between Progress Printing and the employee is *at will and may be terminated by either party at any time*. [Emphasis in original.]

Nichols and the personnel director both signed the form.

On March 8, 1989, Nichols became upset over Progress's failure to correct a recurring defect in a print job, and he refused to complete that job assignment as a result. Nichols was fired on the following day, without the prior written notice promised by the Employee Handbook.

Nichols then sued for wrongful discharge in a Virginia trial court. After that court ruled in his favor and awarded him $9,000 in damages, Progress appealed. ∾

Lacy, Justice In Virginia, as in a majority of jurisdictions, the employment relationship is presumed to be "at will," which means that the employment term extends for an indefinite period and may be terminated for any reason. This presumption may be rebutted if sufficient evidence is produced to show that the employment is for a definite, rather than an indefinite, term. Progress argues that Nichols failed to rebut the presumption because the handbook did not constitute an enforceable employment contract and, even if it did, the subsequent execution of the acknowledgment form created an at-will employment relationship.

A number of jurisdictions have held that the employer can be bound by termination-for-cause provisions contained in employee handbooks where those provisions are communicated to the employee in a sufficiently specific manner. We have held that an employment condition which allows termination only for cause sets a definite term for the duration of the employment. We nevertheless agree with Progress that the acknowledgment form specifically superseded and replaced that [just cause] provision with the agreement that the employment relationship was at will. We base this holding on a number of grounds.

The termination-for-cause language of the handbook and the employment-at-will relationship agreed to in the subsequent acknowledgment form are in direct conflict and cannot be reconciled in any reasonable way. If the documents are considered a single contract, this conflict fails to provide sufficient evidence to rebut the presumption of employment at will.

[In any event,] the acknowledgment form was not a part of the handbook and was executed 13 days after Nichols began work. Under these circumstances, the form reflects an understanding between the parties separate from that contained in the handbook. Execution of the form memorialized reciprocal commitments that satisfy the requisites of a contract—there was an offer of employment at will; the employee continued service, which constituted the consideration; and the employee accepted by performance.

We conclude that the employment relationship between Nichols and Progress was at-will employment which either party could terminate at any time. Therefore, Progress did not breach the employment contract when it terminated Nichols.

Trial court decision on Nichols's employment-at-will claim reversed in favor of Progress.

1. Do you think that the employer in the immediately preceding *Progress Printing* case behaved ethically? Why or why not?

2. Over the past 150 years, a moral theory known as *utilitarianism* has been very influential. Utilitarianism basically asserts that the test for determining the rightness or wrongness of actions (including laws) is their ability to produce the greatest net balance of satisfactions over dissatisfactions throughout society as a whole. Give a utilitarian justification for the traditional employment-at-will rule. You can assume that economic well-being counts as a "satisfaction" for utilitarian purposes. You also can assume that the people fired under the traditional employment-at-will rule suffer from their firing.

PROBLEM CASES

1. Sheila Grove sued the Frostburg National Bank under the Equal Pay Act. She claimed that she was paid less than another employee named David Klink, who performed the same work she did. The bank claimed that it had a merit defense because Klink was a better worker than Grove. This determination was made by the bank's vice president, who based his judgments primarily on his own observations of employees and his "gut feeling" about them. Did the bank have a merit defense here?

2. Dianne Rawlinson, a female applicant who was rejected for employment as a prison guard in the Alabama prison system, challenged certain state rules restricting her employment prospects under Title VII. They were: (1) requirements that all prison employees be at least 5 feet 2 inches tall and weigh at least 120 pounds, and (2) a rule expressly prohibiting women from assuming close-contact prison guard positions in maximum-security prisons (most of which were all-male). What method of proving a Title VII case should Rawlinson use in attacking the height and weight requirements? Does she need to use one of these methods to attack the second rule? What argument should the state use if Rawlinson establishes that the height and weight requirements have an adverse impact? What Title

VII defense might the state have for the second rule? With regard to the second rule, assume that at this time Alabama's maximum security prisons housed their male prisoners barracks-style rather than putting them in cells, and that they did not separate sex offenders from other prisoners.

3. Jesse Cook, a Seventh Day Adventist, worked at a Chrysler Corporation plant. Because he lacked sufficient seniority in his job, Cook was assigned to the evening shift, which required him to work on Friday nights. Cook's religion prohibited him from working from sundown Friday until sundown Saturday. Cook was informed that under the relevant collective bargaining agreement, his shift could not be changed. Eventually, Cook was fired for his continuing Friday night absences from work. Accommodating Cook probably would have required Chrysler to make Cook a part-time employee while paying him full-time benefits. Also, it probably would have required Chrysler to use a temporary part-time employee (or floater) to replace Cook every Friday night. This would have meant that Chrysler either had to forgo using a floater elsewhere or hire another floater. Also, more repairs and lower efficiency are likely when a floater is used on the line.

Cook sued Chrysler and the union for religious discrimination under Title VII. Will the defendants succeed if they argue that they were not discriminating against Cook's *religion* as such but rather against his refusal to work on Friday nights? In any event, what other argument might they use? Will it work here?

4. Ann Hopkins, a senior manager at the accounting firm of Price Waterhouse, was denied partnership in the firm. A persistent theme in existing partners' written comments on Hopkins's candidacy was the belief that Hopkins acted in ways inappropriate for a woman to act. Thus, one partner described her as "macho," another wrote that she "overcompensated for being a woman," yet another advised that she take "a course at charm school," and still others objected to her use of profanity. Also, a partner who tried to help Hopkins through the process told her that to improve her chances, she should walk more femininely, dress more femininely, wear makeup, have her hair styled, and wear jewelry. Assuming that these opinions were the only reason for Hopkins's failure to make partner, was that denial illegal sex discrimination under Title VII?

5. Mechelle Vinson alleged that during her four years with the Meritor Savings Bank, her supervisor, Sidney Taylor, repeatedly demanded sexual favors from her and that she had sexual intercourse with him on 40 to 50 separate occasions. She also contended that Taylor fondled her in front of other employees, followed her into the women's restroom, exposed himself to her, and forcibly raped her on several occasions. Despite these allegations, however, Vinson apparently was well treated by her employer in other respects. She received three promotions during her time with the bank, and it was undisputed that her advancement was based solely on merit. Assuming that Vinson's allegations are true and that Taylor's behavior was unwelcome to her, can she recover against the bank for quid pro quo sexual harassment? Can she recover for work environment sexual harassment? Assume that the bank would be liable for Taylor's behavior.

6. At the age of 56, James O'Connor was fired by his employer. O'Connor's replacement was 40 years old. Was the replacement within the ADEA's protected age group? If so, does this prevent O'Connor from successfully suing for age discrimination under the ADEA?

7. William Guthrie managed a JC Penney Company store in Meridian, Mississippi. JC Penney originally had a policy requiring all store managers to retire at age 60, but this policy was changed after passage of the ADEA. In 1979, just before Guthrie's 60th birthday, various Penney employees made "friendly" inquiries about his retirement plans. Guthrie, however, continued to manage the Meridian store, receiving satisfactory performance ratings and making decent profits for JC Penney. In 1982, however, Guthrie's new Penney supervisor reprimanded Guthrie before other store employees, overrode several decisions ordinarily made by Guthrie, lowered Guthrie's performance ratings, and gave him some difficult new performance objectives. Feeling that his discharge was inevitable, Guthrie resigned. Under the younger store manager who succeeded him, the Meridian store did less well in sales and profits, but the new manager received satisfactory performance ratings and was allowed to run the store without interference.

Guthrie sued Penney for constructive discharge under the ADEA. What method of proof would his suit involve? Can that method be used under the ADEA?

9. Vern Peterson, a customs officer with a Utah corporation, was fired for refusing to falsify tax and customs documents in violation of federal and state law. What theory of wrongful discharge offers Peterson his best bet for recovery and why?

10. **[▶]** **Video Case.** See "How Safe Is Too Safe?" Mike, a factory worker at XYZ Manufacturing, suffers injury to his fingers while working for XYZ. The injury occurs while Mike is operating a table saw built by ABCO Assembly. The saw was designed with a detachable blade guard assembly. The blade guard assembly would have prevented Mike's injury had it been in place while he was using the saw, but it was detached at that time. Assuming for the sake of argument that Mike was contributorily negligent or that he assumed the risk of the injury he suffered, can XYZ use either of these defenses to prevent Mike from recovering under workers' compensation for his injuries? Suppose that Mike wants to mount a product liability suit against ABCO. Would workers' compensation block such a suit?

11. Robert Harmer worked in the headquarters of the Virginia Electric and Power Company. He worked in an unenclosed cubicle that exposed him to tobacco smoke from nearby workers. Harmer had severe bronchial asthma and the smoke aggravated it. Despite this problem, Harmer consistently received satisfactory job performance appraisals from Virginia Electric. Virginia Electric eventually took some steps to alleviate the smoke in Harmer's area. Apparently finding these steps insufficient, however, Harmer sued his employer under the Americans with Disabilities Act. Harmer argued that he was entitled to a complete smoking ban as a reasonable accommodation for his disability. Will Harmer win?

Environmental Regulation

Today's businessperson must be concerned with not only competing effectively against competitors but also complying with a myriad of regulatory requirements. For many businesses, particularly those that manufacture goods or that generate wastes, the environmental laws and regulations loom large in terms of the requirements and costs they impose. They can have a significant effect on the way businesses have to be conducted as well as on their profitability. This area of the law has expanded dramatically over the last two decades, and environmental issues are a major concern of people and governments around the world. This chapter will briefly discuss the development of environmental law and will outline the major federal statutes that have been enacted to control pollution of air, water, and land. ∞

Historical Perspective

Historically, people assumed that the air, water, and land around them would absorb their waste products. In recent times, however, it has become clear that nature's capacity to assimilate people's wastes is not infinite. Burgeoning population, economic growth, and the products of our industrial society can pose risks to human health and the environment. The societal challenge is to accommodate economic activity and growth and at the same time provide reasonable protection of human health and the environment.

Concern about the environment is not a recent phenomenon. In medieval England, Parliament passed smoke control acts making it illegal to burn soft coal at certain times of the year. Where the owner or operator of a piece of property is using it in such a manner as to unreasonably interfere with another owner's (or the public's) health or enjoyment of his property, the courts have long entertained suits to abate the nuisance. Nuisance actions, which are discussed in Chapter 24, Real Property, are frequently not ideal vehicles for dealing with widespread pollution problems. Rather than a hit-or-miss approach, a comprehensive across-the-board approach may be required.

Realizing this, the federal government, as well as many state and local governments, had passed laws to abate air and water pollution by the late 1950s and 1960s. As the 1970s began, concern over the quality and future of the environment produced new laws and fresh public demands for action. During the 1980s, these laws were refined and, in some cases, their coverage was extended. Environmental concerns continue to be prominent around the globe and many countries, both individually and collectively, have programs in place to address them. Accordingly, it is increasingly important that the businessperson be cognizant of the legal requirements and the public's environmental concerns in operating a business. These requirements and concerns not only may pose challenges to businesses but can provide opportunities for them as well.

The Environmental Protection Agency

In 1970, the Environmental Protection Agency was created to consolidate the federal government's environmental responsibilities. This was an explicit recognition that the problems of air and water pollution, solid waste disposal, water supply, and pesticide and radiation control were interrelated and required a consolidated approach. Congress subsequently passed comprehensive new legislation covering, among other things, air and water pollution, pesticides, ocean dumping, and waste disposal. Among the factors prompting these laws were protection of human health, aesthetics, economic costs of continued pollution, and protection of natural systems.

The initial efforts were aimed at problems that could largely be seen, smelled, or tasted. As control requirements have been put in place, implemented by industry and government, and significant

progress has been noted in the form of cleaner air and water, attention has focused increasingly on problems that are somewhat less visible but potentially more threatening—the problems posed by toxic substances. These problems have come into more prominence as scientific research indicates the risks posed by some substances, as new detection technology has enabled the detection of suspect substances in ever more minute quantities in the world around us, and as increased monitoring and testing is conducted. Determination of the degree of risk posed by any particular substance or proposed action—and deciding the most appropriate control strategy—frequently triggers strong disagreements within the society because of what is at stake in terms of economic costs and protection of health or the environment.

The National Environmental Policy Act

The National Environmental Policy Act (NEPA) was signed into law on January 1, 1970. The act required that an environmental impact statement be prepared for every recommendation or report on legislation and for every major federal action significantly affecting the quality of the environment. The environmental impact statement must: (1) describe the environmental impact of the proposed action, (2) discuss impacts that cannot be avoided, (3) discuss the alternatives to the proposed action, (4) indicate differences between short- and long-term impacts, and (5) detail any irreversible commitments of resources.

NEPA requires a federal agency to consider the environmental impact of a project before the project is undertaken. Other federal, state, and local agencies, as well as interested citizens, have an opportunity to comment on the environmental impact of a project before the agency can proceed. Where the process is not followed, citizens can and have gone to court to force compliance with NEPA. A number of states and local governments have passed their own environmental impact laws requiring NEPA-type statements for major public and private developments.

While the federal and state laws requiring the preparation of environmental impact statements appear directed at government actions, it is important to note that the government actions covered often include the granting of permits to private parties.

Thus, businesspeople may readily find themselves involved in the preparation of an environmental impact statement—for example, in connection with a marina to be built in a navigable waterway or a resort development that will impact wetlands, both of which require permits from the U.S. Army Corps of Engineers. Similarly, a developer seeking a local zoning change so she can build a major commercial or residential development may find that she is asked to finance a study of the potential environmental impact of her proposed project.

AIR POLLUTION

Background

Fuel combustion, industrial processes, and solid waste disposal are the major contributors to air pollution. People's initial concern with air pollution related to what they could see—visible or smoke pollution. For instance, in the 1880s, Chicago and Cincinnati enacted smoke control ordinances. As the technology became available to deal with smoke and particulate emissions, attention focused on other, less visible gases that could adversely affect human health and vegetation or that could increase the acidity of lakes, thus making them unsuitable for fish.

Clean Air Act

The comprehensive legislation enacted in 1970 and known as the **Clean Air Act** provides the basis for the present approach to air pollution control. In 1977, Congress modified the 1970 act and enacted provisions designed to prevent deterioration of the air in areas where its quality currently exceeds that required by federal law. Thirteen years then passed before Congress, in 1990, enacted a major revision to the act to deal with acid rain, toxic air pollutants, and urban smog problems that were not satisfactorily dealt with under the existing legislation.

Ambient Air Control Standards

The Clean Air Act established a comprehensive approach for dealing with air pollution. EPA is required to set **national ambient air quality standards** for the major pollutants that have an adverse impact on human health—that is, to regulate the

amount of a given pollutant that may be present in the air around us. The ambient air quality standards are set at two levels: (1) **primary standards** are designed to protect the public's health from harm; and (2) **secondary standards** are designed to protect vegetation, materials, climate, visibility, and economic values. Pursuant to this statutory mandate, EPA has set national ambient air quality standards for carbon monoxide, nitrogen oxide, sulfur oxide, ozone, lead, and particulate matter.

Each state is required to develop a **state implementation plan** for meeting national ambient air quality standards. This necessitates an inventory of the various sources of air pollution and their contribution to the total air pollution in the air quality region. The major emitters of pollutants are then required to reduce their emissions to a level that ensures that overall air quality meets the national standards. For example, a factory may be required to limit its emissions of volatile organic compounds (a contributor to ozone or smog) to a certain amount per unit of production or hour of operation; similarly, a power plant might have its emissions of sulfur oxides and nitrogen oxides limited to so many pounds per Btu of energy produced. The states have the responsibility for selecting which activities must be regulated or curtailed so that overall emissions at any point in the state or area do not exceed the national standards.

Because by the late 1980s many of the nation's major urban areas were still not in compliance with the health-based standards for ozone and carbon monoxide, Congress, in its 1990 amendments, imposed an additional set of requirements on the areas that were not in compliance. Thus, citizens living in the areas and existing businesses, as well as prospective businesses seeking to locate in the designated areas, face increasingly stringent control measures designed to bring the areas into attainment with the national standards. These new requirements will mean that businesses such as bakeries that are generally not thought of as major polluters of the air will have to further control their emissions, and that paints and other products that contain solvents may have to be reformulated.

Acid Rain Controls

Responding to the 1970 Clean Air Act, which sought to protect the air in the area near sources of air pollution, many electric generating facilities built tall smokestacks so that the emissions were dispersed over a broader area. Unwittingly, this contributed to long-range transport of some of the pollutants, which changed chemically enroute and fell to earth many miles away in the form of acid rain, snow, fog, or dry deposition. For a number of years, a considerable debate ensued over acid rain, in particular as to whether it was a problem, what kind of damage it caused, whether anything should be done about it, and who should pay for the cost of limiting it. The 1990 amendments address acid deposition by among other things placing a cap on the overall emissions of the contributors to it (the oxides of sulfur and nitrogen) and requiring electric utilities to reduce their emissions to specified levels in two steps over the next decade. This will require most electric generating facilities in the country to install large control devices known as scrubbers, to switch to lower sulfur coal, or to install so-called clean coal technologies. The 1990 amendments also provide an innovative system whereby companies whose emissions are cleaner than required by law can sell their rights to emit more sulfur oxide—known as *allowances*—to other companies that may be finding it more difficult to meet the standards.

Control of Toxic Air Pollutants

The 1970 Clean Air Act also required EPA to regulate the emission of toxic air pollutants. Under this authority, EPA only set standards for asbestos, beryllium, mercury, vinyl chloride, benzene, and radio nuclides. Unhappy with the slow pace of regulation of toxic air pollutants, Congress in 1990 specified a list of 189 chemicals for which EPA is required to issue regulations requiring the installation of the maximum available control technology. The regulations are to be developed and the control technology installed by industry in phases over the next decade. Thus, while many toxic emissions have largely gone unregulated, that situation will change in the next few years. In addition, a number of chemical companies have announced they are voluntarily reducing their emissions of toxic chemicals to levels below those they are required to meet by law.

The case that follows, *United States v. Midwest Suspension and Brake,* involves the enforcement of an EPA regulation that controls the management and disposal of asbestos and asbestos-containing materials.

UNITED STATES v. MIDWEST SUSPENSION AND BRAKE   49 F.3d 1197 (6th Cir. 1995)

M idwest Suspension and Brake is in the business of supplying parts for heavy-duty truck suspensions, steering systems, and brakes. One of the operations it performs concerning brake systems involves the collection and rehabilitation of used brake shoes for resale. During the rehabilitation process, brake shoes are disassembled and parts that may contain asbestos are discarded. Some brake shoes are delined, a procedure performed by removing rivets that hold the brake lining to the brake table and then cleaning, sandblasting, painting, and relining the table with a new brake block. Old brake blocks and brake linings, which contain asbestos, are discarded.

During an EPA inspection of the Midwest facility, numerous emissions of asbestos were documented and the shop floor yielded detectable amounts of asbestos. As a result, EPA issued a "finding of violation" of the "no visible emission" requirement of the National Emission Standard for Hazardous Air Pollutants (NESHAP) for asbestos. To resolve the matter, Midwest agreed to the issuance of an Administrative Order (AO) that required that Midwest comply with the Clean Air Act and the asbestos NESHAP, including the no visible emission requirement.

As a preventative measure, the AO specified waste management requirements for Midwest operations including the following: (1) that delining wastes fall into a sturdy cardboard box, instead of falling to the ground; (2) that the box be securely closed and wrapped so that it would not leak when discarded; and (3) that the box bear a warning label. The AO also required that the floor of the delining area be vacuumed, not swept, and that the vacuum residue be tightly sealed before disposal. Finally, the AO required that asbestos waste be segregated and separately disposed of, without compacting, at a landfill.

Subsequent EPA inspections of the Midwest facility found numerous violations of the AO—as did inspections by the Wayne County (Michigan) Health Department. Asbestos wastes were being compacted, resulting in visible emissions. Vacuum residue was not tightly sealed, and boxes of delining wastes were improperly taped, resulting in visible emissions during landfill disposal. Asbestos-containing materials were being dropped on the shop floor, and the floor was being broom cleaned rather than vacuumed.

When efforts to have Midwest comply with the AO were unsuccessful, EPA filed suit against it in federal court. EPA sought injunctive relief as well as civil penalties of up to $25,000 per day for each violation. The federal district court found that Midwest had violated the Clean Air Act and ordered it to pay a $50,000 civil penalty. Midwest appealed, contending, among other things, that it did not fall under the Clean Air Act or the asbestos NESHAP because it did not fabricate friction products containing asbestos within the meaning of the Act. ∞

Contie, Circuit Judge   According to the NESHAP definition of "fabrication," it includes *any* processing of a manufactured product. A plain reading of this definition is that "fabricating" is not limited to specific types of processes, such as preparing chemical substances, but entails *any* processing of a manufactured product containing asbestos. Moreover, the EPA has explained that the definition of "processing" includes operations which "cut, shape, assemble, mix, or otherwise alter" a manufactured product that contains commercial asbestos.

The district court found that Midwest's brake refurbishing operation clearly falls within this definition of processing, and therefore Midwest is considered a business that "fabricates" friction products containing commercial asbestos within the meaning of the Act. The court found that Midwest's business involves among other things, the production and sale of rebuilt brake shoes for medium and heavy duty trucks. As described by Robert Cuipak, Midwest's general manager, Midwest's process of making rebuilt brake shoes includes the following:

We take used brake shoes, deline them, inspect them to make sure that they are still to the manufacturer's specifications, clean them, paint them and then reline them with brake lining. And those are made available as second hand shoes.

The district court found that Midwest "fabricated" brake shoes by "cutting" and "altering" used brake shoes by removing their linings, which contain asbestos, and by assembling refurbished brake cores with new linings, which may contain asbestos, for sale as rebuilt shoes. The court found that the entire rebuilding operation is a "process," and that Midwest's production of rebuilt brake shoes which includes a delining process, a sandblasting process, an assembly of the cores and

linings, and, in some cases, the cutting, grinding, and drilling of strip stock, constitutes "fabrication" within the meaning of the Act.

We agree with the district court that these operations come within the definition of "fabrication"— the processing of friction materials containing asbestos—as contemplated by the Act. Substantial evidence in the record indicates that during Midwest's operations, particularly during the delining phase where the plow on the machines breaks and shatters the used brake linings containing asbestos, and during sandblasting, where asbestos fibers encapsulated in rust on the brake cores are pulverized into trillions of fibers, asbestos-containing material is plainly being "cut" and "otherwise altered."

Furthermore, there is evidence in the record to support the government's contention that the Asbestos NESHAP was amended specifically so that the regulations would apply to brake relining operations, such as Midwest's operation. In 1973, the EPA conducted an extensive investigation of fabricating facilities and concluded that facilities that process brake shoe linings generated significant amounts of asbestos dust. For that reason, in 1975, the EPA amended the Asbestos NESHAP to include the fabricating standard, which regulates facilities that "fabricate" friction products.

The friction product fabricating standards were promulgated in 1975 and published to provide a full opportunity for notice and comment by the public. Therefore, Midwest's allegation that the terms of the regulation were too broad to give it notice that its operations would be covered has no merit. Midwest, as a business dealing with asbestos, was under a duty to be aware of the published regulations and their interpretation.

Judgment against Midwest affirmed.

New Source Controls

The Clean Air Act requires that new stationary sources such as factories and power plants install the best available technology for reducing air pollution. EPA is required to establish the standards to be met by new stationary sources and has done so for the major stationary sources of air pollution. This means that a new facility covered by the regulations must install state of the art control technology, even if it is locating in an area where the air quality is much better than that required by law. Two major policy objectives underlie this requirement: (1) to provide a level playing field for new industry irrespective of where it locates and (2) to gradually improve air quality by requiring state of the art controls whenever a new facility is built.

Enforcement

The primary responsibility for enforcing air quality standards lies with the states, but the federal government has the right to enforce the standards where the states fail to do so. The Clean Air Act also provides for suits by citizens to force industry or the government to fully comply with the act's provisions.

Automobile Pollution

The Clean Air Act provides specifically for air pollution controls on transportation sources such as automobiles. The major pollutants from automobiles are carbon monoxide, hydrocarbons, and nitrogen oxides. Carbon monoxide is a colorless, odorless gas that can dull mental performance and even cause death when inhaled in large quantities. Hydrocarbons, in the form of unburned fuel, are part of a category of air pollutants known as volatile organic compounds (VOCs). VOCs combine with nitrogen oxides under the influence of sunlight to become ozone—we know it as smog.

The 1970 Clean Air Act required a reduction of 90 percent of the carbon monoxide and hydrocarbons emitted by automobiles by 1975 and a 90 percent reduction in the nitrogen oxides emitted by 1976. At the time, these requirements were "technology forcing"; that is, the manufacturers could not rely on already existing technology to meet the standards but rather had to develop new technology. Ultimately, most manufacturers had to go beyond simply making changes in engine design and utilize pollution control devices known as catalytic converters.

Subsequently, Congress addressed the question of setting even more stringent limits on automobile emissions while at the same time requiring that the new automobiles get better gas mileage. The 1990 amendments require further limitations on emissions from tailpipes, the development of so-called clean-fueled vehicles (such as electric and natural gas fueled vehicles) for use in cities with dirty air, and the availability of oxygenated fuels (which are cleaner burning) in specified areas of the country that are having difficulty meeting the air quality limits at least part of the year. These new requirements have significant ramifications for the oil and automobile industries.

Under the Clean Air Act, no manufacturer may sell vehicles subject to emission standards without prior certification from EPA that the vehicles meet the required standards. The tests are performed on prototype vehicles and if they pass, a certificate of conformity covering that type of engine and vehicle is issued. EPA subsequently can test vehicles on the assembly line to make sure that the production vehicles covered by the certificate are meeting the standards. The manufacturers are required to warrant that the vehicle, if properly maintained, will comply with the emission standards for its useful life. If EPA discovers that vehicles in actual use exceed the emission standards, it may order the manufacturer to recall and repair the defective models; this is a power that EPA has exercised on a number of occasions.

The act also provides for the regulation and registration of fuel additives such as lead. In the 1980s, lead was largely phased out of use as an octane enhancer in gasoline. As indicated previously, the 1990 amendments provide for the availability of alternative fuels based on ethanol and methanol.

International Air Problems

During the late 1970s and 1980s, concern developed that the release of chlorine-containing substances such as chlorofluorocarbons (CFCs) used in air conditioning, refrigeration, and certain foam products was depleting the stratospheric ozone layer. This could lead to more ultraviolet radiation reaching the earth and, in turn, more skin cancer. Subsequently, a number of nations, acting under the aegis of the United Nations, signed a treaty agreeing first to limit any increases in production of chlorine-containing substances and ultimately to significantly phase out their use. The 1990 amendments to the Clean Air Act implement the obligations of the United States under the treaty and provide for the phasedown and phaseout of a number of chlorofluorocarbons; accordingly, many businesses are trying to develop or to locate substitutes for those chemicals that will be available only in reduced quantities, if at all.

Other air pollution issues with international dimensions that may result in multinational control efforts are acid rain and global warming/climate change resulting, in part, from increased emissions of carbon dioxide to the atmosphere.

Indoor Air Pollution

As we increased the insulation and made our buildings airtight to conserve energy, we generally reduced the air exchange and increased the concentrations of pollutants in our homes and workplaces. In recent years, attention has focused on a range of indoor air problems, sometimes known under the term *sick building syndrome,* including radon gas, asbestos, the products of combustion from fireplaces and stoves, molds and pollens, formaldehyde, cigarette smoke, pesticides, and cleaning products. Some of these problems are being dealt with on a problem-by-problem, or product-by-product, basis under various laws. Others are being addressed by providing information to consumers so that they can take appropriate actions to protect themselves. In some cases, Congress and other legislative bodies have required that steps be taken to minimize the risks, such as the federal requirement for schools to inspect for asbestos and to remove it where certain conditions are found.

Radiation Control

In recent years, people have been concerned about radioactivity, particularly radioactivity from nuclear-fueled power plants. Some of these concerns were accentuated by the accident at Chernobyl in the former USSR and the one at Three Mile Island in the United States. Citizens are specifically concerned about the release of radioactivity into the environment during normal operation of the nuclear reactors, accidents through human error or mechanical failure, and disposal of the radioactive wastes generated by the reactors. They are also concerned that the discharge of heated water used to cool the reactor—thermal pollution—may cause damage to the environment. These issues are of particular concern to businesses such as utilities that operate nuclear-powered generating facilities and also to segments of the health industry—such as hospitals and other medical facilities—that may utilize low-level radioactive materials in their diagnostic and treatment activities.

Currently, the problems of reactor safety are under the jurisdiction of the Nuclear Regulatory Commission, which exercises licensing authority over nuclear power plants. EPA is responsible for setting standards for radioactivity in the overall environment and for dealing with the problem of disposal of some radioactive waste. EPA also handles the thermal pollution problem pursuant to its water pollution control authority. In addition, EPA is responsible for regulating emissions from a variety of other sources, such as uranium mill tailing piles and uranium mines.

WATER POLLUTION

Background

History is replete with plagues and epidemics brought on by poor sanitation and polluted water. Indeed, preventing waterborne disease has always been the major reason for combating water pollution. In the early 1970s, fishing and swimming were prohibited in many bodies of water, and game fish could no longer survive in some waters where they had formerly thrived. Lake Erie was becoming choked with algae and considered to be dying. The nation recognized that water pollution could affect public health, recreation, commercial fishing, agriculture, water supplies, and aesthetics. During the 1970s, Congress enacted three major statutes to protect our water resources: the Clean Water Act; the Marine Protection, Research, and Sanctuaries Act; and the Safe Drinking Water Act.

Early Federal Legislation

Federal water pollution legislation dates back to the 19th century when Congress enacted the River and Harbor Act of 1886. In fact, this statute, recodified

1136 Part 11 Regulation of Business

in the River and Harbor Act of 1899, furnished the legal basis for EPA's initial enforcement actions against polluters. The act provided that people had to obtain a discharge permit from the Army Corps of Engineers to deposit or discharge refuse into a navigable waterway. Under some contemporary court decisions, even hot water discharged from nuclear power plants was considered refuse. The permit system established pursuant to the "Refuse Act" was replaced in 1972 by a more comprehensive permit system now administered by EPA.

Congress passed the initial Federal Water Pollution Control Act (FWPCA) in 1948. Amendments to the FWPCA in 1956, 1965, 1966, and 1970 increased the federal government's role in water pollution abatement and strengthened its enforcement powers.

Clean Water Act

The 1972 amendments to the FWPCA—known as the Clean Water Act—were as comprehensive in the water pollution field as the 1970 Clean Air Act was in the air pollution field. They proclaimed two general goals for this country: (1) to achieve wherever possible by July 1, 1983, water clean enough for swimming and other recreational uses and clean enough for the protection and propagation of fish, shellfish, and wildlife; and (2) to have no discharges of pollutants into the nation's waters by 1985. These goals reflected a national frustration with the lack of progress in dealing with water pollution and a commitment to end such pollution. The new law set out a series of specific actions that federal, state, and local governments and industry were to take by certain dates and also provided strong enforcement provisions to back up the deadlines. In 1977 and again in 1987, Congress modified the 1972 act by adjusting some of the deadlines and otherwise fine-tuning the act.

State Role

Under the Clean Water Act, the states have the primary responsibility for preventing, reducing, and eliminating water pollution. The states have to do this within a national framework, and EPA is empowered to move in if the states do not fulfill their responsibilities.

Controls on Industrial Wastes

The act set a number of deadlines to control water pollution from industrial sources. It required industries discharging wastes into the nation's waterways to install the *best available water pollution control technology;* new sources of industrial pollution must use the best available demonstrated control technology. In each instance, EPA is responsible for issuing guidelines as to the best available technologies. Industries that discharge their wastes into municipal wastewater treatment systems are required to *pretreat* the wastes so that they do not interfere with the biological operation of the plant or pass through the plant without treatment.

Water Quality Standards

The act continued and expanded the previously established system of setting *water quality standards* by designating the uses of specific bodies of water for recreation, public water supply, propagation of fish and wildlife, and agricultural and industrial water supply. Then, the maximum daily loads of various pollutants are set so that the water is suitable for the designated use.

Discharge Permits

The act requires all municipal and industrial discharges to obtain permits—known as an *NPDES permit* or National Pollution Discharge Elimination System permit—that spell out the amounts and specific pollutants that permit holders are allowed to discharge and any steps that they must take to reduce their present or anticipated discharge. These permits are the vehicles for applying and enforcing the technology-based standards and the water quality–based limitations discussed above. Dischargers are also required to keep records, install and maintain monitoring equipment, and sample their discharges.

Enforcement

Both civil and criminal sanctions are included in the act. Criminal penalties for violating the law range from a minimum of $2,500 for a first offense up to $50,000 per day and two years in prison for subsequent violations. The act is enforced by federal and state governments. In addition, any citizen or group of citizens whose interests are adversely affected has the right to bring a court action against anyone violating an effluent standard, limitation, or order issued by EPA or a state. A significant number of cases have been brought by citizen-action groups against firms whose wastewater discharges exceeded the limits of their discharge permits. Citizens also have the right to take court action against EPA if it fails to carry out mandatory provisions of the law.

Wetlands

Another aspect of the Clean Water Act having the potential to affect businesses as well as individual property owners is the wetlands provision. Commonly, wetlands are transition zones between land and open water. Under Section 404 of the act, any *dredging or filling* activity in a wetland that is connected to the waters of the United States—as well as in any water of the United States—requires a permit before any activity begins. The permit program is administered by the Army Corps of Engineers, with the involvement of the Environmental Protection Agency.

As can be seen in the *Bersani v. U.S. Environmental Protection Agency* case, which follows, the permit requirement can significantly limit a landowner's use of his property where the fill activity is viewed as injurious to the values protected by the act.

BERSANI v. U.S. ENVIRONMENTAL PROTECTION AGENCY   674 F. Supp. 405 (N.D.N.Y. 1987)
aff'd 395 F.2d 36 (2d Cir. 1988)

*P*yramid Companies was an association of partnerships that was in the business of developing, constructing, and operating shopping centers; John Bersani was a principal in one of the partnerships. In 1983, Pyramid became interested in developing a shopping mall in the Attleboro, Massachusetts, area and focused its attention on an 82-acre site known as Sweden's Swamp along an interstate highway in South Attleboro. The project contemplated altering or filling some 32 acres of the 49.6 acres of wetlands on the property. At the same time, Pyramid planned to excavate 9 acres of uplands (nonwetlands) to create new wetlands and to alter some 13 acres of existing wetlands to enhance their value for fish and wildlife.

In 1984, Pyramid applied to the U.S. Army Corps of Engineers for a permit under Section 404 of the Clean Water Act to do the dredge and fill work in the wetlands. As part of its application, it was required to submit information on practicable alternative sites for its shopping mall. One site subsequently focused on by the Corps and the Environmental Protection Agency was about three miles north in North Attleboro. Pyramid relied on several factors in claiming that the site was not a practicable alternative to its proposed site: namely, the site lacked sufficient traffic volume and access from local roads, potential department store tenants had expressed doubts about the feasibility of the site, and previous attempts to develop the site had met with strong resistance from the surrounding community. However, after Pyramid examined the site, another major developer of shopping centers had taken an option to acquire the property.

The New England Division Engineer of the Corps recommended that the permit be denied because a practicable alternative with a less adverse effect on the environment existed. The Chief of Engineers directed that the permit be issued, noting that the alternative site was not available to Pyramid because it was owned by a competitor. He also believed that even if it was considered available, Pyramid had made a convincing case that the site would not fulfill its objectives for a successful project. EPA then exercised its prerogative under the Clean Water Act to veto the permit on the grounds that filling Sweden's Swamp to build the shopping mall would have an unacceptable adverse effect on the environment. In its view, another less environmentally damaging site had been available to Pyramid at the time it made its site selection; thus, any adverse effects on Sweden's Swamp were avoidable. Bersani and Pyramid then brought suit challenging the denial of its permit application. ⌒

McAvo, Judge   Section 404(a) authorizes the Secretary of the Army, acting through the Corps, to issue permits for the discharge of dredged or fill material at specified disposal sites. Criteria developed by the EPA in conjunction with the Corps govern these permitting decisions. Generally, the

Corps must employ a "practicable alternative" analysis in determining whether to allow a proposed discharge. Section 230.10 of the regulations provides:

(a) . . . no discharge of dredged or fill material shall be permitted if there is a practicable alternative to the proposed discharge which would have less adverse impact on the aquatic ecosystem, so long as the alternative does not have other significant adverse environmental consequences. (2) An alternative is practicable if it is available and capable of being done, after taking into account cost, existing technology, and logistics in light of overall project purposes. If it is otherwise a practicable alternative, an area not presently owned by the applicant which could reasonably be obtained, utilized, expanded or managed in order to fulfill the basic purpose of the proposed activity may be considered. (3) Where the activity associated with a discharge which is proposed for a special aquatic site (including a wetland) does not require access or proximity to or siting within the special aquatic site in question to fulfill its basic purpose (i.e., is not "water dependent"), practicable alternatives that do not involve special aquatic sites are presumed to be available unless clearly demonstrated otherwise. In addition, where a discharge is proposed for a special aquatic site, all practicable alternatives to the proposed discharge which do not involve a discharge into a special aquatic site are presumed to have less adverse impact on the aquatic ecosystem, unless clearly demonstrated otherwise.

Where the proposed discharge involves a special aquatic site such as wetlands, a more stringent standard is imposed. Indeed Section 230.10(a)(3) creates a presumption that a practicable alternative exists when the discharge involves wetlands and the activity, here a shopping mall, is not "water dependent." Then the applicant must "clearly demonstrate" that no such alternative does in fact exist.

Pyramid argues that EPA's determination of feasibility was based on its erroneous conclusion that the marketplace considered the North Attleboro site suitable for a virtually identical regional shopping mall. Pyramid notes that six other shopping center developers over the past 15 years have tried and failed to develop the North Attleboro site as a shopping center. It contends that EPA has substituted its own judgment for that of the marketplace in an area in which it cannot claim expertise. The EPA, however, contends that it did not simply substitute its judgment for that of the developer. Instead, the EPA argues that the evidence on the record demonstrates that the North Attleboro site is suitable in fact for a regional shopping center mall virtually identical to that proposed by Pyramid. In this respect, the fact that a competing developer, the New England Development Company, had found the site suitable for a similar shopping mall, and its own marketing analysis weighed in reaching this decision. The EPA also engaged in a review of the specific features that Pyramid found objectionable; namely, the distance from the primary trade area, lack of visibility from nearby highways, zoning, past failures of prior attempts to develop a shopping mall at the site, and various considerations. Consequently, the court finds that EPA's feasibility determination was not arbitrary.

Summary judgment granted for EPA.

Ocean Dumping

The Marine Protection, Research, and Sanctuaries Act of 1972 set up a permit system regulating the dumping of all types of materials into ocean waters. EPA has the responsibility for designating disposal sites and for establishing the rules governing ocean disposal. The Ocean Dumping Ban Act of 1987 required that all ocean dumping of municipal sewage sludge and industrial wastes be terminated by December 31, 1991. Thus, the major remaining questions of ocean dumping concern the disposal of dredge spoils from dredging to keep harbors open.

Drinking Water

In 1974, Congress passed, and in 1986 and in 1996 amended, the Safe Drinking Water Act that is designed to protect and enhance the quality of our drinking water. Under the act, EPA sets *primary drinking water standards,* minimum levels of quality for water consumed by humans. The act also establishes a program governing the injection of wastes into wells. The primary responsibility for complying with the federally established standards lies with the states. Where the states fail to enforce the drinking water standards, the federal government has the right to enforce them.

A significant number of suppliers of drinking water are privately owned—and they, as well as the publicly owned systems, have to be concerned with meeting the federal standards. In addition, factories, trailer parks, schools, and other entities that draw drinking water from wells and provide it within their facility can find that they are also subject to the drinking water regulations.

WASTE DISPOSAL

Background

Historically, concern about the environment focused on decreasing air and water pollution as well as protecting natural resources and wildlife. People paid relatively little attention to the disposal of wastes on land. Until the early 1970s, much of the solid and hazardous waste generated was disposed of in open dumps and landfills. Although some of the waste we produce can be disposed of without presenting significant health or environmental problems, some industrial, agricultural, and mining wastes—and even some household wastes—are hazardous and can present serious problems. Unless wastes are properly disposed of, they can cause air, water, and land pollution as well as contamination of the underground aquifers from which much of our drinking water is drawn. Once aquifers have been contaminated, they can take a very long time to cleanse themselves of pollutants.

In the 1970s, the discovery of abandoned dump sites such as Love Canal in New York and the Valley of the Drums in Kentucky heightened public concern about the disposal of toxic and hazardous wastes. Congress has enacted several laws regulating the generation and disposal of hazardous waste: the Resource Conservation and Recovery Act mandates proper management and disposal of wastes currently generated; and the Comprehensive Environmental Response, Compensation, and Liability Act focuses on cleaning up past disposal sites threatening public health and the environment.

The Resource Conservation and Recovery Act

Congress originally enacted the Resource Conservation and Recovery Act (RCRA) in 1976 and significantly amended it in 1984. RCRA provides the federal government and the states with the authority to regulate facilities that generate, treat, store, and dispose of hazardous waste. Most of the wastes defined as hazardous are subject to a cradle-to-the-grave tracking system and must be handled and disposed of in defined ways. RCRA requires persons who generate, treat, store, or transport specified quantities of hazardous waste to obtain permits, to meet certain standards and follow specified procedures in the handling of the wastes, and to keep records. Figure 1 illustrates the form that must accompany all shipments of hazardous waste from the point of generation until its final treatment or disposal.

In addition, operators of land waste disposal facilities must meet financial responsibility requirements and monitor groundwater quality. EPA determines whether certain wastes should be banned entirely from land disposal; a significant number of wastes must be treated before they can be disposed of in land disposal units.

Underground Storage Tanks

In 1984, Congress directed that EPA also regulate underground product storage tanks such as gasoline tanks to prevent and respond to leaks that might contaminate underground water. The regulations that EPA issued to implement these requirements impose significant costs on many businesses such as gasoline stations that utilize such storage tanks.

State Responsibilities

EPA sets minimum requirements for state RCRA programs and then delegates the responsibility for conducting programs to the states when they have the legal ability and interest to administer them. Until a state assumes partial or complete responsibility for a RCRA program, the federal government administers the program.

Enforcement

Failure to comply with the hazardous waste regulations promulgated under RCRA can subject violators to civil and criminal penalties. In the *United States v. Dean* case, which follows, an employee of a company that disposed of hazardous waste without a RCRA permit was held criminally liable. .

FIGURE I

Sample "Uniform Hazardous Waste Manifest" Form*

SAMPLE "UNIFORM HAZARDOUS WASTE MANIFEST" FORM

Please Print or type   (Form designed for use on elite (12-pitch) typewriter)   Form Approved OMB 2000-0404 Expires 7-31-99

UNIFORM HAZARDOUS WASTE MANIFEST	1. Generator's US EPA ID No. V A D 0 0 1 2 3 4 5 6 7 0 0 0 0 7	2. Page 1 of	Information in the shaded areas is not required by federal law

3. Generator's Name and Mailing Address
GENERAL METAL PROCESSING CO.
501 MAIN ST.
SMALLTOWN, VA 23000

A. State Manifest Document Number

4. Generator's Phone No. (804) 555-0509

B. State Generator's ID

5. Transporter 1 Company Name
SAFETY HAULER

6. US EPA ID Number V A D 0 0 8 9 1 2 3 4 5

C. State Transporter's ID

D. Transporter's Phone

7. Transporter 2 Company Name

8. US EPA ID Number

E. State Transporter's ID

F. Transporter's Phone

9. Designated Facility Name and Site Address
DISPOS-ALL, INC.
1800 NORTH AVE.
FRIENDLY TOWN, VA 2300

10. US EPA ID Number V A D 0 0 6 7 8 9 1 2 3

G. State Facility's ID

H. Facility's Phone

11. US DOT Description *(Including Proper Shipping Name, Hazard Class, and ID Number)*	12. Containers		13. Total Quantity	13. Unit Wt/Vol	I. Waste No.
	No.	Type			
a. HAZARDOUS WASTE, LIQUID OR SOLID, NOS ORM-E NA9189	0 0 2	D M	0 0 1 1 0	GAL	
b. WASTE CYANIDE SOLUTION, NOS UN1935	0 0 1	D M	0 0 0 5 5	GAL	
c. WASTE FLAMMABLE SOLUTION, NOS UN1993	0 0 1	D M	0 0 0 5 5	GAL	
d.					

J. Additional Descriptions for Materials Listed Above

K. Handling Codes for Wastes Listed Above

15. Special Handling Instructions and Additional Information

16. Generator's Certification: I hereby declare that the contents of this consignment are fully and accurately described above by proper shipping name and classified, packed, marked, labeled, and are in all respects in proper condition for transport by highway according to applicable international and national regulations.

Unless I am a small quantity generator who has been exempted by statute or regulation from the duty to make a waste minimization certification under Section 3002(b) of RCRA. I also certify that I have a program in place to reduce the volume and toxicity of waste generated to the degree I have determined to be economically practicable and I have selected the method of treatment, storage, or disposal currently available to me which minimizes the present and future threat to human health and the environment.

Printed/ Typed Name JOSEPHINE K. DOE	Signature *Josephine K. Doe*	Month Day Year 0 8 3 0 9 7

17. Transporter 1 Acknowledgement of Receipt of Materials

Printed/Typed Name	Signature	

18. Transporter 2 Acknowledgement of Receipt of Materials

Printed/Typed Name	Signature	Month Day Year

19. Discrepancy Indication Space

20. Facility Owner or Operator: Certification of receipt of hazardous materials covered by this manifest except as noted in Item 19.

Printed/Typed Name	Signature	Month Day Year

EPA Form 8700-22 (Rev. 4-85) Previous Edition is obsolete.

*Information in the shaded areas is not required by federal law, but this or other additional information may be required by your state.

eneral Metal Fabricators, Inc. (GMF), owned and operated a facility in Erwin, Tennessee, which was engaged in metal stamping, plating, and painting. The facility utilized hazardous chemicals and generated hazardous waste but did not have a RCRA permit nor did it maintain the required records of the treatment, storage, and disposal of hazardous substances. The hazardous waste disposal practices at GMF were discovered by chance by state waste-management authorities whose attention was caught, while driving to an appointment at another facility, by two 55-gallon drums abandoned among weeds on GMF's property.

The owners of GMF, Joseph and Jean Sanchez, as well as Clyde Griffith, the plant manager, and Gale Dean, the production manager, were indicted for conspiracy to violate RCRA, and, individually, for violations of various sections of RCRA. At his request, Dean's trial was severed from that of the other defendants.

As production manager, Dean had day-to-day supervision of GMF's production process and employees. Among his duties was the instruction of employees on hazardous waste handling and disposal. Numerous practices at GMF violated RCRA. GMF's plating operations utilized rinse baths, contaminated with hazardous chemicals, which were drained through a pipe into an earthen lagoon outside the facility. In addition, Dean instructed employees to shovel various kinds of solid wastes from the tanks into 55-gallon drums. Dean ordered the construction of a pit, concealed behind the facility, into which 38 drums of such hazardous waste were tossed. The contents spilled onto the soil from open or corroded drums. Chemical analyses of soil and solid wastes revealed that the pit and the lagoon were contaminated with chromium. In addition, the pit was contaminated with toluene and xylene solvents. All of these substances are considered hazardous under RCRA. Drums of spent chromic acid solution were also illegally stored on the premises.

Dean was familiar with the chemicals used in each of the tanks on the production line and with the manner in which the contents of the rinse tanks were deposited in the lagoon. Material Safety Data Sheets (MSDS) provided to GMF by the chemical manufacturer clearly stated that the various chemicals in use at GMF were hazardous and were subject to federal pollution control laws. Dean was familiar with the MSDS and knowledgeable about their contents. The MSDS delivered with the chromic acid made specific reference to RCRA and to related EPA regulations. Dean told investigators that he "had read this RCRA waste code but thought it was a bunch of bullshit."

Dean was convicted of conspiracy to violate RCRA as well as of (1) failure to file documentation of hazardous waste generation, storage, and disposal, (2) storage of spent chromic acid without a permit, (3) disposal of chromic acid rinse water and sludges in a lagoon without a permit, and (4) disposal of paint sludge and solvent wastes in a pit without a permit, all in violation of RCRA. Dean appealed his conviction. ∞

Joiner, Senior District Judge   The first of the issues raised by Dean is that the trial court erred in denying his motion for acquittal on the permit-related counts because there was no evidence that Dean knew of RCRA's permit requirement. Dean's characterization of the evidence is inaccurate, but moreover, we see no basis on the face of the statute for concluding that knowledge of the permit requirement is an element of the crime. The statute penalizes:

Any person who— ... (2) knowingly treats, stores or disposes of any hazardous waste identified or listed under this subchapter—(A) without a permit under this subchapter ... ; or (B) in knowing violation of any material condition or requirement of such permit; or (C) in know-

ing violation of any applicable interim status or regulations. 42 U.S.C. section 6928(d)(2).

Dean was convicted of violating subsection 6928(d)(2)(A).

The question of interpretation presented by this provision is the familiar one of how far the initial "knowingly" travels. Other courts of appeals have divided on this question. We agree with the reasoning of the Court of Appeals for the Ninth Circuit in *United States v. Hoflin.* The "knowingly" which begins section 6928(d)(2) cannot be read as extending to the subsections without rendering nugatory the word "knowing" contained in subsections 6928(d)(2)(B) and (C). Subsection 6928(d)(2)(A) requires knowing treatment (or knowing storage, or knowing disposal) of hazardous waste. It also requires proof that the treatment, storage or disposal was done without a permit. It does not require that the person charged must have known that a permit was required, and that knowledge is not relevant.

Dean also contends that the district court should have granted his motion for acquittal because subsection 6928(d)(2)(A) was not intended to reach employees who are not "owners" or "operators" of facilities. By its terms, the provision applies to "any person." "Person" is a defined term meaning "an individual ... " Dean would be hard pressed to convince the court that he is not an "individual." He argues, however, that because only owners and operators of facilities are required to obtain permits, the penalty imposed for hazardous waste handling without a permit must apply only to owners and operators.

This contention is unpersuasive for numerous reasons. Of primary importance is the fact that it is contrary to the unambiguous language of the statute.

Affirmed.

Solid Waste

Mining, commercial, and household activities generate a large volume of waste material that can present problems if not properly disposed. As population density has increased, causing a corresponding increase in the total volume of waste, it has become more difficult to find land or incinerators where the waste material can be disposed of properly. RCRA authorizes EPA to set minimum standards for such disposal, but states and local governments bear the primary responsibility for the siting and regulation of such activity.

As the cost and difficulty of disposing of waste increases, public attention focuses on reducing the waste to be disposed, on looking for opportunities to recycle some of the waste material, and on changing the characteristics of the material that must ultimately be disposed of so that it poses fewer environmental problems. One of the significant challenges faced by tomorrow's businessperson will be in designing products, packaging, and production processes so as to minimize the waste products that result. A significant problem for both government and industry is the difficulty in trying to site new waste facilities. The NIMBY, or not-in-my-backyard syndrome, is pervasive as people almost universally desire to have the wastes from their everyday lives and from the economic activity in their community disposed of in someone else's neighborhood—any place but their own. As governments try to cope with the reality of finding places to dispose of wastes in an environmentally safe manner and at the same time cope with public opposition to siting new facilities, the temptation is strong to try to bar wastes from other areas from being disposed of in local facilities.

In the landmark case, *City of Philadelphia v. New Jersey,* the U.S. Supreme Court struck down an attempt by the state of New Jersey to prohibit the importation of most solid waste originating outside the state. An ironic twist is that several decades later, we find a number of other eastern and midwestern states trying to find ways to block the importation of wastes from New Jersey into their states. In recent years, the Supreme Court has had occasion to reiterate its holding in *City of Philadelphia v. New Jersey* in a series of new cases involving efforts by states to block or limit the flow of solid and hazardous waste from outside their state to disposal sites within the state. One of the most recent cases in this series of cases, *Fort Gratiot Sanitary Landfill, Inc. v. Michigan Department of Natural Resources,* follows.

FORT GRATIOT SANITARY LANDFILL, INC. v. MICHIGAN DEPARTMENT OF NATURAL RESOURCES
112 S.Ct. 2019 (1992)

I n 1978, Michigan enacted its Solid Waste Management Act (SWMA), which required every Michigan county to estimate the amount of solid waste that would be generated in the county in the next 20 years and to adopt a plan providing for its disposal at facilities that comply with state health standards. After holding public hearings, the St. Clair County Board of Commissioners *adopted a solid waste plan for the St. Clair County. In 1987, the Michigan Department of Natural Resources issued a permit to Fort Gratiot Sanitary Landfill, Inc., to operate a sanitary landfill as a solid waste disposal area in the county. In December 1988, the Michigan Legislature amended the SWMA by adopting two provisions concerning the "acceptance of waste or ash generated outside the county of disposal area." The new provisions, which were effective immediately, prohibited the acceptance of out of county wastes unless the acceptance of such waste was explicitly authorized in the approved county solid waste management plan.*

In February 1989, Fort Gratiot submitted an application to the St. Clair County Solid Waste Planning Committee for authority to accept up to 1,750 tons per day of out-of-state waste at its landfill. In the application Fort Gratiot promised to reserve sufficient capacity to dispose of all solid waste generated in the county in the next 20 years. The planning committee denied the application. Because the county's management plan did not authorize the acceptance of any out-of-county waste, Fort Gratiot was effectively prevented from receiving any solid waste that did not originate in St. Clair County.

Fort Gratiot then brought a lawsuit seeking a judgment declaring that the waste import restrictions violated the Commerce Clause of the U.S. Constitution and thus were unconstitutional and enjoining their enforcement. Fort Gratiot contended that requiring a private landfill operator to limit its business to the acceptance of local waste constituted impermissible discrimination against interstate commerce. The District Court dismissed the lawsuit. It concluded, first, that the statute did not discriminate against interstate commerce because the limitation applied equally to Michigan counties outside the county as well as to out-of-state waste. It also noted that each county had discretion to accept out-of-state waste and that any incidental burden on interstate commerce was not excessive in relation to the public health and environmental benefits derived by Michigan from the statute. The Court of Appeals affirmed the ruling, and Fort Gratiot appealed to the U.S. Supreme Court. ❧

Stevens, Justice   In *Philadelphia v. New Jersey* (1978) we held that a New Jersey law prohibiting the importation of most "solid or liquid waste which originated or was collected outside the territorial limits of the State" violated the Commerce Clause of the United States Constitution. In this case petitioner challenges a Michigan law that prohibits private landfill operators from accepting solid waste that originates outside the county in which their facilities are located. Adhering to our holding in the *New Jersey* case we conclude that this Michigan statute is also unconstitutional.

Philadelphia v. New Jersey provides the framework for our analysis of this case. Solid waste, even if it has no value, is an article of commerce. Whether the business arrangements between out-of-state generators of waste and the Michigan operator of a waste disposal site are viewed as "sales" of garbage or "purchases" of transportation and disposal services, the commercial transactions unquestionably have an interstate character. The Commerce Clause thus imposes some constraints on Michigan's ability to regulate these transactions.

As we have long recognized, the "negative" or "dormant" aspect of the Commerce Clause prohibits States from advancing their own commercial interests by curtailing the movement of articles or commerce, either into or out of the state. A state

statute that clearly discriminates against interstate commerce is therefore unconstitutional unless the discrimination is demonstrably justified by a valid factor unrelated to economic protectionism.

The Waste Import Restrictions enacted by Michigan authorize each of its 83 counties to isolate itself from the national economy. Indeed, unless a county acts affirmatively to permit other waste to enter its jurisdiction, the statute affords local waste producers complete protection from competition from out-of-state waste producers who seek to use local waste disposal areas. In view of the fact that Michigan has not identified any reason, apart from its origin, why solid waste coming from outside the county should be treated differently from solid waste within the county, the foregoing reasoning would appear to control the disposition of this case.

Michigan and St. Clair County assert that the Waste Import Restrictions are necessary because they enable individual counties to make adequate plans for the safe disposal of future waste. Although accurate forecasts about the volume and composition of future waste flows may be an indispensable part of a comprehensive waste disposal plan, Michigan could attain that objective without discriminating between in- and out-of-state waste. Michigan could, for example, limit the amount of waste that landfill operators may accept each year. There is, however, no valid health and safety reason for limiting the amount of waste that a landfill operator may accept from outside the State, but not the amount that the operator may accept from inside the State. Of course our conclusion would be different if the imported waste raised health or other concerns not presented by Michigan waste.

For the foregoing reasons, the Waste Import Restrictions unambiguously discriminate against interstate commerce and are appropriately characterized as protectionist measures that cannot withstand scrutiny under the Commerce Clause.

Judgment of the Court of Appeals is reversed.

Rehnquist, Chief Justice, dissenting When confronted with a dormant Commerce Clause challenge, "the crucial inquiry must be directed to determining whether the challenged statute is basically a protectionist measure, or whether it can fairly be viewed as a law directed to legitimate local concerns with effects on interstate commerce that are only incidental. Because I think the Michigan statute is at least arguably directed to legitimate local concerns, rather than improper economic protectionism, I would remand this case for further proceedings.

The substantial environmental, aesthetic, health, and safety problems flowing from this country's waste piles were already apparent at the time we decided *Philadelphia.* Those problems have only risen in the intervening years. In part, this is due to increased waste volumes, volumes that are expected to continue to rise in the foreseeable future. It is no secret why capacity is not expanding sufficiently to meet the demand—the substantial risks attendant to waste sites make them extraordinarily unattractive neighbors. The result, of course, is that while many are willing to generate waste—indeed it is a practical impossibility to solve the waste problem by banning waste production—few are willing to help dispose of it. Those locales that do provide disposal capacity to serve foreign waste effectively are affording reduced environmental and safety risks to the States that will not take charge of their own waste.

The State of Michigan has stepped into this quagmire in order to address waste problems generated by its own populace. It has done so by adopting a comprehensive approach to the disposal of solid wastes generated within its borders. The legislation challenged today is simply one part of a broad package that includes a number of features: a state-mandated state-wide effort to control and plan for waste disposal; requirements that local units of government participate in the planning process; restrictions to assure safe transport; a ban on the operation of a waste disposal facility unless various design and technical requirements are satisfied and appropriate permits obtained; and commitments to promote source separation, composting, and recycling. The Michigan legislation is thus quite unlike the simple outright ban that we confronted in *Philadelphia.*

In adopting this legislation, the Michigan Legislature also appears to have concluded that, like the State, counties should reap as they have sown—hardly a novel proposition. It has accomplished this by prohibiting waste facilities from accepting waste generated from outside the county, unless special permits are obtained. In the process, of course, this facially neutral restriction (i.e. it applies equally to interstate and intrastate waste) also works to ban disposal from out-of-state sources unless appropriate permits are procured. But I cannot agree that such a requirement, when imposed as one part of a comprehensive approach to regulating in this difficult field is the stuff of which economic protectionism is made.

Michigan has limited the ability of its own population to despoil the environment and to create health and safety risks by excessive and uncontrolled waste disposal. It does not thereby violate the Commerce Clause when it seeks to prevent this resource from being exported—the result if Michigan is forced to accept foreign waste in its disposal facilities.

The Court today penalizes the State of Michigan for what to all appearances are its good-faith effort, in turn encouraging each State to ignore the waste problem in the hope that another will pick up the slack. The Court's approach fails to recognize that the latter option is quite real and quite attractive for many States—and becomes even more so when the intermediate option of solving its own problems, but only its own problems, is eliminated.

Superfund

In 1980, Congress passed the Comprehensive Environmental Response, Compensation, and Liability Act (CERCLA), commonly known as Superfund, to deal with the problem of uncontrolled or abandoned hazardous waste sites. In 1986, it strengthened and expanded the law. Under the Superfund law, EPA identified and assessed the sites in the United States where hazardous wastes had been spilled, stored, or abandoned.

Eventually, EPA expects to identify 30,000 such sites. The sites are ranked on the basis of the type, quantity, and toxicity of the wastes; the number of people potentially exposed to the wastes; the different ways (e.g., in the air or drinking water) in which they might be exposed; the risks to contamination of aquifers; and other factors. The sites with the highest ranking are put on the National Priority List to receive priority federal and/or state attention for cleanup. At these sites, EPA makes careful scientific and engineering studies to determine the most appropriate cleanup plans. Once a site has been cleaned up, the state is responsible for managing it to prevent future environmental problems. EPA also has the authority to quickly initiate actions at hazardous waste sites—whether or not the site is on the priority list—to address imminent hazards such as the risk of fire, explosion, or contamination of drinking water.

The cleanup activity is financed by a tax on chemicals and feedstocks. However, EPA is authorized to require that a site be cleaned up by those persons responsible for contaminating it, either as the owner or operator of the site, a transporter of wastes to the site, or the owner of wastes deposited at the site. Where EPA expends money to clean up a site, it has the legal authority to recover its costs from those who were responsible for the problem. The courts have held that such persons are "jointly and severally responsible for the cost of cleanup." Chapter 7, Negligence and Strict Liability, discusses the concept of joint liability.

The *Chem-Dyne* case, which follows, involves a challenge to the concept of joint and several liability by the contributors to a major hazardous waste site. Of concern to many businesspeople is the fact that this stringent and potentially very expensive liability can in some instances be imposed on a current owner of a site who had nothing to do with the contamination, such as a subsequent purchaser of the land or even a bank that financed the purchase of the property and subsequently took it over when the purchaser defaulted on its obligation to the bank.

UNITED STATES v. CHEM-DYNE CORP.   572 F. Supp. 802 (S.D. Ohio 1983)

*T*he United States brought a lawsuit under the Comprehensive Environmental Response, Compensation, and Liability Act (CERCLA) against 24 defendants who had allegedly generated or transported some of the hazardous substances located at the Chem-Dyne treatment facility in Ohio. The government sought to be reimbursed for money that it had spent in cleaning up hazardous wastes at the facility and asserted that each defendant was jointly and severally liable for the entire cost of the cleanup. The defendants contested the claim that they were jointly and severally liable and moved for summary judgment in their favor on this issue. ⌒

Rubin, Chief Judge   CERCLA was enacted both to provide rapid responses to the nationwide threats posed by the 30,000–50,000 improperly managed hazardous waste sites in this country as well as to induce voluntary responses to those sites. The legislation established a $1.6 billion trust fund ("Superfund"), drawn from industry and federal appropriations, to finance the clean-up and containment efforts. The state or federal government may then pursue rapid recovery of the costs incurred from persons liable to reimburse the Superfund money expended. This recovery task may prove difficult when several companies used a site, when dumped chemicals react with others to form new or more toxic substances, or when records are unavailable. Nevertheless, those responsible for the problems caused by the hazardous wastes were intended to bear the costs and responsibilities for remedying the condition. The House sponsor, Representative Florio, commented at length:

The liability provisions of this bill do not refer to the terms strict, joint and several liability, terms which were contained in the version of H.R. 7020 passed earlier by this body. The standard of liability in these amendments is intended to be strict liability ... I have concluded that despite the absence of these specific terms, the strict liability standard already approved by this body is preserved. Issues of joint and several liability not resolved by this bill shall be governed by traditional and evolving principles of common law. The terms "joint and several" have been deleted with the intent that the liability of joint tortfeasors be determined under common or previous statutory law.

Typically, as in this case, there will be numerous hazardous substance generators or transporters who have disposed of wastes at a particular site. The term joint and several liability was deleted from the express language of the statute in order to avoid its universal application to inappropriate circumstances. An examination of the common law reveals that when two or more persons acting independently cause a distinct or single harm for which there is a reasonable basis for division according to the contribution of each, each is subject to liability only for the portion of the total harm that he has himself caused. But where two or more persons cause a single and indivisible harm, each is subject to liability for the entire harm. Furthermore, where the conduct of two or more persons liable under CERCLA has combined to violate the statute, and one or more of the defendants seek to limit their liability on the ground that the entire harm is capable of apportionment, the burden of proof as to apportionment is upon each defendant.

The question of whether the defendants are jointly or severally liable for the clean-up costs turns on a fairly complex factual determination.

Read in the light most favorable to the United States, the following facts illustrate the nature of the problem. The Chem-Dyne facility contains a variety of hazardous waste from 289 generators or transporters, consisting of about 608,000 pounds of material. Some of the wastes have been commingled, but the identities of the sources of these wastes remain unascertained. The fact of the mixing of the wastes raises an issue as to the divisibility of the harm. Further, a dispute exists over which of the wastes have contaminated the groundwater, the degree of their migration, and the concomitant health hazard. Finally, the volume of waste of a particular generator is not an accurate predictor of the risk associated with the waste because the toxicity or migratory potential of a particular hazardous substance generally varies independently with the volume of the waste.

This case, as do most pollution cases, turns on the issue of whether the harm caused at Chem-Dyne is "divisible" or "indivisible." If the harm is divisible and if there is a reasonable basis for apportionment of damages, each defendant is liable only for the portion of harm he himself caused. In this situation, the burden of proof as to apportionment is upon each defendant. On the other hand, if the defendants caused an indivisible harm, each is subject to liability for the entire harm. The defendants have not carried their burden of demonstrating the divisibility of the harm and the degrees to which each defendant is responsible.

Defendants' motion for summary judgment is denied.

Community Right to Know and Emergency Cleanup

As part of its 1986 amendments to Superfund, Congress enacted a series of requirements for emergency planning, notification of spills and accidents involving hazardous materials, disclosure by industry to the community of the presence of certain listed chemicals, and notification of the amounts of various chemicals being routinely released into the environment in the area of a facility. This legislation was in response to the industrial accident at Bhopal, India, in 1984 and to several similar incidents in the United States. Firms subject to the requirements have to carefully plan how they will communicate with the surrounding community what chemicals are being regularly released and what precautions the facility has taken to protect the community from regular or accidental releases. Mindful of the difficulty of explaining to a community why large emissions of hazardous substances are taking place, a significant number of companies have undertaken to reduce those emissions below levels they are currently required to meet by law.

REGULATION OF CHEMICALS

Background

More than 60,000 chemical substances are manufactured in the United States and used in a variety of products. Although these chemicals contribute much to the standard of living we enjoy, some of them are toxic or have the potential to cause cancer, birth defects, reproductive failures, and other health-related problems. These risks may be posed in the manufacturing process, during the use of a product, or as a result of the manner of disposal of the chemical or product. EPA has two statutory authorities that give it the ability to prevent or restrict the manufacture and use of new and existing chemicals to remove unreasonable risks to human health or the environment. These authorities are the Federal Insecticide, Fungicide, and Rodenticide Act and the Toxic Substances Control Act.

Regulation of Agricultural Chemicals

The vast increase in the American farmer's productivity over the past few decades has been in large measure attributable to the farmer's use of chemicals to kill the insects, pests, and weeds that have historically competed with the farmer for crops. Some of these chemicals, such as pesticides and herbicides, were a mixed blessing. They enabled people to dramatically increase productivity and to conquer disease. On the other hand, dead fish and birds provided evidence that chemicals were not only building up in the food chain but also proving fatal to some species. Unless such chemicals are carefully used and disposed of, they can present a danger to the applier and to the consumer of food and water. Gradually, people realized the need to focus on the effects of using such chemicals.

EPA enforces the Federal Insecticide, Fungicide, and Rodenticide Act (FIFRA). This act gives EPA the authority to register pesticides before they can be sold, to provide for the certification of appliers of pesticides designated for restrictive use, to set limits on the pesticide residue permitted on crops that provide food for people or animals, and to register and inspect pesticide manufacturing establishments. As noted in *King v. E. I. DuPont De Nemours & Co.,* which follows, the FIFRA provides for a relatively small state role in the regulation of pesticides.

Ernest *King and Edward Higgins were employed by the Maine Department of Transportation (MDOT). As part of their employment duties, King and Higgins seasonally sprayed one or more herbicides manufactured by E. I. du Pont de Nemours and Company (Du Pont), the Dow Chemical Company (Dow), Velsicol Chemical Company (Velsicol), and Sandoz Corporation (Sandoz). As a result of their exposure to the herbicides they claimed to have experienced nausea, headaches, loss of appetite, irritability, loss of concentration, muscle pains, joint pain, memory loss, and continued deterioration of vision; in addition, Higgins claimed to suffer from numbness in his extremities.*

King and Higgins brought suit against Du Pont, Dow, Velsicol, and Sandoz seeking to impose liability for damages under state tort law theories of negligence and strict liability. They claimed that the chemical companies had failed to warn them about the safe and proper use of the herbicides as well as about the harm and danger of exposure to these products. The chemical companies moved for summary judgment in their favor. One of the key questions was whether the Federal Insecticide, Fungicide, and Rodenticide Act (FIFRA) preempted state tort claims based on failure to warn or inadequate warnings relating to products subject to the Act's labeling requirements. The parties stipulated that all of the product labels in question were submitted to and approved by the EPA in accordance with FIFRA.

Brody, District Judge Under FIFRA, the EPA cannot approve an herbicide unless it complies with the requirements established in FIFRA, and the EPA labeling regulations promulgated to implement the Act. The EPA regulations detail how warning labels are to be presented and provide specific requirements for the content, placement, type, size and promotion of the warnings. "Label" is defined under FIFRA to include "the written, printed or graphic matter on, or attached to the pesticide or device or any of its containers or wrappers. Required warnings are specified according to the degree to which ingestion or contact with an herbicide is toxic, and these warnings must include precautionary statements about risks posed to humans. The regulations also specify necessary directions on how to use each chemical.

The procedure for registration under FIFRA requires that each applicant file a statement with the Administrator of the EPA which includes the name of the chemical, a statement of all claims to be made for the product, any directions for the product's use and a full description of the tests made and the results thereof upon which the claims are based.

The data required to be submitted to EPA varies with the nature of the chemical and its intended use. On the basis of the information provided by the registrant, the EPA must register the product if it determines that:

(A) Its composition is such as to warrant the proposed claims for it;

(B) Its labeling and other material required to be submitted comply with the requirements of the [Act];

(C) It will perform its intended function without unreasonable adverse effects on the environment; and

(D) When used in accordance with widespread and commonly recognized practice it will not generally cause unreasonable adverse affects on the environment.

An unreasonable adverse effect on the environment is defined under the Act as "any unreasonable risk to man or the environment, taking into account the economic, social, and environmental costs and benefits of the use of any pesticide."

The 1972 Amendments to FIFRA added a section expressly setting forth the states' authority to regulate pesticides. This section states in relevant part:

(a) In general. A state may regulate the sale or use of any federally registered pesticide or device in the State, but only if and to the extent the regulation does not permit any sale or use prohibited by this [Act].

(b) Uniformity. Such State shall not impose or continue in effect any requirements for labeling or packaging different from those required under this [Act].

The statute's language, by itself, is a powerful limit on state power over labeling. A report accompanying the bill, as originally reported out of the House Committee, also indicates the limits on state power due to the division of authority between the federal and state governments: "In dividing the responsibility between the States and the Federal Government for the management of an effective pesticide program, the Committee had adopted language which is intended to completely preempt State authority in regard to packaging and labeling." Congress recognized that while the intent of the provision was to leave to the states the authority to impose stricter regulation on pesticide use than that required under the Act, subsection (b) preempted any State labeling or packaging requirements differing from such requirements under the Act.

Although King and Higgins have stipulated that all of the product labels underlying this controversy were submitted to and approved by EPA under FIFRA, they contend that the defendant chemical companies failed to adequately warn them of the dangers inherent in their products. The chemical companies argue that these claims are expressly preempted under subsection (b) because, if successful, such claims would constitute state-imposed "requirements for labeling or packaging in addition to or different from those required [under FIFRA]." Alternatively, they claim that FIFRA immediately preempts such claims.

There is a split among the circuit and district courts on the issue of whether FIFRA preempts state failure to warn claims. Prior to the Supreme Court's ruling in *Cippolone v. Liggett Group, Inc.,* courts examining the preemptive scope of FIFRA failed to apply express preemption analysis exclusively. Because *Cippolone* rested on express preemption under a statute containing language almost identical to the relevant statutory language in FIFRA, we are satisfied that under *Cippolone's* standards, the language of FIFRA presents a case of express preemption.

Chemical companies' motion for summary judgment in their favor was granted.

When the EPA administrator has reason to believe that continued use of a particular pesticide poses an "imminent hazard," he may suspend its registration and remove the product from the market. When the administrator believes that there is a less than imminent hazard but that the environmental risks of continuing to use a pesticide outweigh its benefits, the administrator may initiate a cancellation of registration proceeding. This proceeding affords all interested persons—manufacturers, distributors, users, environmentalists, and scientists—an opportunity to present evidence on the proposed cancellation. Cancellation of the registration occurs when the administrator finds that the product causes unreasonable adverse effects on the environment.

Companion regulations promulgated by EPA and enforced by the Food and Drug Administration control the amount of pesticide residue that can remain on raw and processed food intended for human or animal consumption. These regulations establish what are known as "tolerances."

Those involved in the food production and distribution process must keep a close watch on regulatory developments at EPA concerning the registration, cancellation, and suspension of products as well as actions it takes concerning permissible residues of pesticides on food products. During the 1980s, the agency took highly publicized actions concerning the use of ethylene dibromide (EDB), a fumigant, on citrus and grain products, sulfites on table grapes, alar on apples, and chlordane as a treatment against termite infestation. In each instance, the economic well-being of many businesses was at risk if they did not adequately anticipate and/or deal with the EPA's actions and the publicity that resulted from these actions.

Toxic Substances Control Act

The other major statute regulating chemical use focuses on toxic substances—such as asbestos and PCBs—and on the new chemical compounds that are developed each year. The Toxic Substances Control Act, enacted in 1976, requires that chemicals be tested by manufacturers or processors to determine their effect on human health or the environment before the chemicals are introduced into commerce. The act also gives EPA the authority to regulate chemical substances or mixtures that present an unreasonable risk of injury to health or the environment and to take action against any such substances or mixtures that pose an imminent hazard.

This legislation was enacted in response to the concern that thousands of new substances were being released into the environment each year, sometimes without adequate consideration of their

CONCEPT REVIEW

Major Environmental Laws

ACT	FOCUS
Clean Air Act	Protects quality of ambient (outdoor) air through national ambient air quality standards, state implementation plans, control of toxic air pollutants, new source performance standards, and controls on automobiles and fuels
Clean Water Act	Protects and enhances quality of surface waters by setting water quality standards and limiting discharges by industry and municipalities to those waters through permit system; also regulates dredging and filling of wetlands.
Marine Protection, Research, and Sanctuaries Act	Regulates dumping of all types of material into ocean waters
Safe Drinking Water Act	Protects and enhances quality of our drinking water. Also regulates disposal of wastes in wells
Resource Conservation and Recovery Act (RCRA)	Establishes a cradle-to-the-grave regulatory system for handling and disposal of hazardous wastes; also deals with solid waste
Comprehensive Environmental Response Compensation and Liability Act (Superfund)	Provides a program to deal with hazardous waste that was inadequately disposed of in the past; financed in part by tax on chemicals and feedstocks
Federal Insecticide, Fungicide, and Rodenticide Act (FIFRA)	Regulates the sale and use of chemicals to be used as pesticides and herbicides; companion legislation regulates residues permitted on crops intended for use as food
Toxic Substances Control Act (TSCA)	Requires preclearance of new chemicals and provides for regulation of existing chemicals that pose an unreasonable risk to health or the environment

potential for harm, and that it was not until damage from a substance occurs that its manufacture or use was properly regulated. At the same time, a goal of the act is not to unduly impede, or create unnecessary economic barriers to, technological innovation.

Biotechnology

The development of techniques to genetically manipulate organisms—often referred to generally as biotechnology—offers considerable promise to aid our ability to provide food and health care and to generate a range of new products and production processes. At the same time, they raise concerns about their potential to adversely affect human health or the environment. Responsibility for regulating research and use of biotechnology is shared in the federal government between the Food and Drug Administration, the Department of Agriculture, the Environmental Protection Agency, and the National Institutes of Health. Generally, a review is required of such activity before it takes place. This process is of considerable import to companies that are developing genetically engineered organisms for commercial purposes; it can affect both the speed at which they are able to get the products to market and the public's confidence that release of the organisms does not pose an unreasonable risk.

ETHICAL AND PUBLIC POLICY CONCERNS

1. Suppose that a multinational chemical company with its primary manufacturing facilities in the United States plans to build a manufacturing facility in a developing country where there are few, if any, real state-imposed environmental regulations. Is it sufficient for the company to simply meet the environmental requirements of the host country? Is there any ethical obligation to do more—for example, to build the facility to meet the requirements it would have to meet in this country?

2. Suppose a manufacturing facility emits a chemical into the air that it has reason to believe is inadequately regulated by EPA and that poses a significant threat to nearby residents even at levels lower than permitted by EPA. As manager of the facility, would you be satisfied to meet the EPA required level or would you install the additional controls you believe necessary to achieve a reasonably safe level?

3. Suppose that you own some valuable seashore property that contains some marshland and wetlands that are critical to the local ecology. In evaluating whether or not to develop your property, what weight would you give to the value that the marshland and wetlands have as a part of the local ecological system?

PROBLEM CASES

1. The Interstate Commerce Commission (ICC) has the power to approve or set the tariff rates that railroads charge shippers. As a result of past ICC approvals, the railroad tariffs call for higher shipping charges to carry scrap metals and paper than to carry virgin materials. This disparity operates as an economic discrimination against recycled goods. A group of law students has formed an organization known as SCRAP (Students Challenging Regulatory Agency Procedures). SCRAP is concerned that the ICC-approved rate structure discourages the environmentally desirable use of recycled goods. The ICC approved a 2.5 percent across-the-board surcharge in railroad shipping rates and indicated that no environmental impact statement was necessary because there was no environmental impact. SCRAP is concerned that the increase will further the discrimination against used materials and filed suit against the ICC to require that an environmental impact statement be prepared. Should the court decide that an environmental impact statement is required?

2. In July 1984, Vanguard Corporation began operating a metal furniture manufacturing plant in Brooklyn, New York. The plant is located in an area that has not attained the national ambient air quality standards for ozone. The plant is a major stationary source (i.e., has the potential to emit more than 100 tons a year) of volatile organic compounds that contribute to the production of ozone in the atmosphere. The New York state implementation plan (SIP) requires that metal-coating facilities use paint that contains less than three pounds of organic solvent (minus water) per gallon at the time of coating. On August 24, 1984, EPA notified Vanguard that it was not in compliance with the SIP provision concerning coatings and issued it a notice of violation. Vanguard sought to defend against the notice of violation on the grounds that it had used its best faith efforts to comply but that full compliance was technologically and economically infeasible. It indicated that it wanted 18 more months to come into compliance. Should Vanguard be held to be in violation of the Clean Air Act?

3. In August 1986, Tzavah Urban Renewal Corporation purchased from the city of Newark a building formerly known as the Old Military Park Hotel. While the buyer was given an opportunity to inspect the building, it was not informed by the city that the building was permeated with asbestos-containing material. At the time of the purchase, the building was in great disrepair and had been uninhabited for many years. Its proposed renovation was to be a major urban renewal project. In June 1987, Tzavah contracted with Greer Industrial Corporation to "gut" the building. While the work was going on, an EPA inspector visited the site and concluded that the hotel was contaminated with asbestos. He observed Greer employees throwing asbestos-laced objects out of the windows of the building and noted an uncovered refuse pile next to the hotel that contained asbestos. The workers were not wetting the debris before heaving it out the windows and the refuse pile was also dry. As a result, asbestos dust was being released into the air. Although the hotel was located in a commercial district, there were private homes nearby. Renovation of buildings contaminated with asbestos is regulated under the Clean Air Act. The EPA regulations require building owners or operators to notify EPA before commencing renovation or demolition and prescribe various procedures for storage and removal of the asbestos. Tzavah failed to provide the required notice or to comply with procedures required. After being notified by EPA of the violation of the law, Tzavah stopped the demolition work, left the building unsecured, and left the waste piles dry and uncovered. EPA tried informally to get Tzavah to complete the work in accordance with the asbestos regulations; when Tzavah did not take action, EPA brought a lawsuit against Tzavah to do so. Should the court issue an injunction requiring Tzavah to abate the hazard posed by the dry asbestos remaining in the hotel?

4. Mall Properties, Inc., was an organization that for many years sought to develop a shopping mall in the Town of North Haven, Connecticut, a suburb of New Haven. Because the proposed development would require the filling of some wetlands, Mall Properties was required to obtain a permit from the Corps of Engineers pursuant to section 404 of the

Clean Water Act. The City of New Haven opposed development of the mall—and the granting of the permit—on the grounds it would jeopardize the fragile economy of New Haven. The Corps of Engineers found the net loss of wetlands would be substantially compensated for by a proposed on-site wetland creation. Relying primarily on the socioeconomic concerns of the City of New Haven, the District Engineer rejected the proposed permit. Mall Properties then brought suit against the Corps of Engineers, claiming that the decision was arbitrary and capricious. Should the District Engineer have relied on socioeconomic factors unrelated to the project's environmental impacts in making a decision on the permit?

5. Charles Hanson owned land abutting Keith Lake, a freshwater lake that was subject to some tidal flooding as a result of its connection with tidal waters. In order to minimize the detrimental effects from the tidal activities and consequent flooding, Hanson deposited a large quantity of dirt, rock, bricks, sheet metal, and other debris along the shoreline of his property. He did so without obtaining a permit from the U.S. Army Corps of Engineers under section 404 of the Clean Water Act, which controls dumping and filling activities in navigable waters of the United States. Under the law, discharges of pollutants into navigable waters without a permit are forbidden. The term *pollutant* is defined to include "dredged spoil, solid waste, incinerator residue, sewage, garbage, sewage sludge, munitions, chemical wastes, biological materials, radioactive materials, heat, wrecked or discarded equipment, rock, sand, cellar dirt, and industrial, municipal and agricultural waste discharged into water." EPA brought an enforcement action against Hanson claiming he had violated the Clean Water Act. Should the court find that Hanson violated the act?

6. Johnson & Towers, Inc., is in the business of overhauling large motor vehicles. It uses degreasers and other industrial chemicals that contain chemicals classified as "hazardous wastes" under the Resource Conservation and Recovery Act (RCRA)—for example, methylene chloride and trichloroethylene. For some period of time, waste chemicals from cleaning operations were drained into a holding tank and, when the tank was full, pumped into a trench. The trench flowed from the plant property into Parker's Creek, a tributary of the Delaware River. Under RCRA, generators of such wastes must obtain a permit for disposal from the Environmental Protection Agency (EPA). EPA had neither issued, nor received an application for, a permit for the Johnson & Towers operations. Over a three-day period, federal agents saw workers pump waste from the tank into the trench, and on the third day toxic chemicals flowed into the creek. The company and two of its employees, Jack Hopkins, a foreman, and Peter Angel, the service manager, were indicted for unlawfully disposing of hazardous wastes. The company pled guilty. The federal district court dismissed the criminal charges against the two individuals, holding that RCRA's criminal penalty provisions imposing fines and imprisonment did not apply to employees. The government appealed. Can employees of a corporation be held criminally liable if their actions on behalf of the corporation violate the federal hazardous waste law?

7. In 1979, Anne Arundel County, Maryland, enacted two related ordinances. One absolutely prohibited the disposal in and the transportation through Anne Arundel County of various hazardous wastes not originating in that county. Another ordinance required a license to dispose of hazardous waste in Anne Arundel County; it also requires a license to transport hazardous wastes through the county. Browning-Ferris, Inc. (BFI), is the owner and operator of a landfill located in Anne Arundel County that is licensed by the state of Maryland to receive hazardous wastes. BFI is also a hauler of hazardous wastes within the county. The county notified BFI that it expected BFI to comply with the new regulations, and BFI filed a lawsuit challenging the ordinances and seeking to have them enjoined. How should the court rule?

8. The Royal McBee Corporation manufactured typewriters at a factory in Springfield, Missouri. As a part of the manufacturing process, Royal McBee generated cyanide-based electroplating wastes, sludge from the bottom of electroplating tanks, and spent plating bath solution. As part of their duties, Royal McBee employees dumped the wastes onto the surface of the soil on a vacant lot adjoining the factory. This took place between 1959 and 1962. Over time, the waste materials migrated outward and downward from the original dumping site, contaminating a large area. In 1970, the manufacturing facility and lot were sold to General Electric, which operated the plant but did not engage in the dumping of wastes on the vacant lot. In the mid-1980s, General Electric was required by EPA and the state of Missouri, under the authority of the federal Superfund law, to clean up the contamination at the site. General Electric then brought a lawsuit against the successor corporation of Royal McBee's typewriter business, Litton Business Systems, to recover for the costs incurred in cleaning up the site. Under the Superfund law, "any person who at the time of disposal of any hazardous substance owned or operated any facilities at which such hazardous substances were disposed of, shall be liable for any other necessary costs of response incurred by any other person" consistent with the Superfund law and regulations. Is General Electric entitled to recover its cleanup costs from Litton?

9. Chemlawn sells pesticide products for use on residential lawns. The active ingredients in Chemlawn's products are registered with the Environmental Protection Agency pursuant to the Federal Insecticide, Fungicide, and Rodenticide Act (FIFRA). Deborah Ryan brought a lawsuit against Chemlawn seeking damages in tort for injuries she claimed that she and her son Kevin sustained from the use of Chemlawn products. Ryan claims that the products are unsafe for commercial use and that they have been inadequately tested by the EPA. Chemlawn contends that Ryan should take her complaints to EPA, which has the responsibility for determining whether the products are safe to be sold. How should the court decide?

Special Topics

The Legal Environment for International Business

Since 1945, American businesses have steadily increased the number and size of transactions with people in foreign markets. American businesses export their goods to other countries, import foreign goods into the United States, establish manufacturing, drilling, and other operations on foreign soil, and license their patents and other technology to foreign businesses. With the economic changes that have swept eastern Europe after the December 1989 revolutions, foreign trade by American firms in the 1990s has accelerated. ∞

THE CHALLENGE OF INTERNATIONAL BUSINESS

Each international business transaction faces dozens of legal and practical problems. The answers to the legal problems come from a mix of the laws of our own country, those of the other country or countries involved, and doctrines of international law. For example, American exporters must comply with American laws concerning the export of goods and foreign laws that restrict the importation of goods. While many nations have signed agreements designed to remove importation restrictions, such international law is not binding on a signatory nation unless its legislature has passed a statute to implement the agreement.

When an American business enters a contract to sell goods to a foreign buyer, the buyer and seller may choose to follow American contract law or foreign contract law. They may use international law embodied in the United Nations Convention on Contracts for the International Sale of Goods (CISG). Usually, the CISG will not apply unless the seller's or buyer's nation has adopted the CISG.

When an American firm makes a direct foreign investment by establishing a manufacturing plant abroad, the firm must comply with all of the foreign nation's laws applicable to its operations, such as employee safety and dismissal laws, antitrust laws, and toxic waste disposal regulations. In addition, American firms doing business abroad must comply with other domestic laws of the host country. For example, many Arabic countries prohibit alcohol consumption and forbid women to operate motor vehicles. Many foreign nations require that any firm doing business within their boundaries be owned by their government or by their citizens. In addition, the foreign nation's laws may restrict the American firm's ability to take its profits back to the United States—reinvestment of profits in the foreign nation may be required. Also, several socialist countries have confiscated or expropriated the business assets of U.S. firms doing business in those countries.

Practical problems abound as well. There are language and cultural differences. Contract negotiations may be either more or less formal than in America. In addition, the parties to international transactions are much less likely to know each other well because they are separated by great distances, thereby increasing a seller's risk of nonpayment by the buyer and a buyer's risk of nondelivery by the seller. There are different currencies, some of which—like the Russian ruble—may be nearly worthless on the world market. Other currencies' values may quickly depreciate, increasing the risk that a buyer of goods will underpay for goods, unless the parties designate a stable currency in their sales contract.

The resolution of disputes is troublesome, as each party may seek to have a dispute resolved in his home court, applying law favorable to his side. Disputes between an American seller and a foreign buyer may be resolved in the courts of either nation or in an international arbitration tribunal. The court or tribunal may apply American law, foreign law, or international law.

Only some of the complexities of the law of international business transactions can be explored within the limited scope of this chapter. The intent of this chapter, therefore, is to give you a sense of the legal environment of international business by examining the most important legal questions that arise in connection with international sales, licensing, and investment. Because most international business transactions entered into by an American business must comply with trade restrictions imposed by the United States and other governments, this chapter begins with a consideration of trade limitations.

LIMITATIONS ON TRADE

Many governmentally imposed barriers to trade affect international business transactions. The most important are export and import controls, including tariffs.

Export Controls

For political or economic purposes, most nations place export controls on certain goods and technology leaving their countries. For example, in 1990, most nations placed an embargo on exports to Iraq in response to Iraq's invasion of Kuwait. Another example is the restriction on the sale of militarily sensitive technology by Western nations so that it is not obtained by countries whose governments are considered unfriendly. The restrictions are agreed on unanimously by Western countries who are members of the Paris-based Coordinating Committee for Multilateral Export Controls (COCOM). The restrictions are then enforced through laws passed in each country. Failure to abide by the restrictions can lead to imprisonment of the sellers of the restricted goods.

The Export Administration Act of 1985 The Export Administration Act of 1985 is the main law controlling **exports** from the United States. The act is enforced by the Office of Export Administration (OEA) of the Department of Commerce. The act is designed to accomplish three purposes:

1. To enhance national security.
2. To aid in the accomplishment of the objectives of American foreign policy.
3. To preserve commodities and technology essential to the protection of the American economy.

The OEA implements the act by administering a licensing procedure and maintaining a **commodity control list** of goods and technical data subject to the act. The OEA generally requires an exporter to obtain a **license** prior to exportation of the good or technology.

Before applying for a license, an exporter must consult the commodity control list to determine whether exports to the country of destination are restricted. For example, exports to Cuba, Cambodia, and North Korea are almost totally prohibited. Libya's role in international terrorism has resulted in heavy restrictions on exports to Libya. Exports to communist countries are restricted as well. Only recently have exports to Vietnam been permitted. Exports to most western hemisphere nations are not restricted.

When the commodity control list indicates that exportation of the good or technology to the destination country is prohibited, the exporter must abandon its attempt to export. When the exportation is legal, the exporter must consult the commodity control list to determine whether it needs a general or a validated license issued by the OEA.

A **general license** is a blanket authorization to export the covered goods or technology without obtaining permission for a specific export. A general license appears in the form of an administrative regulation and authorizes every exporter to export the covered goods or technology. Thus, for example, an exporter need not obtain specific OEA approval when the OEA has issued a general license to export beer to Canada.

A **validated license** authorizes a specific exporter to export a specific good or technology to a specific country. A validated license may validate one export or a series of exports. The OEA's refusal to grant a validated license may be appealed to the assistant secretary of commerce for trade administration. However, his decision is final; there is no judicial review of his administrative decision.

The commodity control list applies not merely to the exportation by an American firm to a foreign country. It also controls the **reexportation** of American goods and technology by the foreign buyer to a second foreign nation. As a result, when American goods are exported to Germany and reexported to Iraq, the OEA would regulate both the America-to-Germany and Germany-to-Iraq transactions.

The OEA does not have authority to issue licenses for all goods and technology. For example, weapons export is usually controlled by the State Department; the export of nuclear materials is licensed by the Nuclear Regulatory Commission.

Import Controls

Countries control the importation of goods and technology primarily to protect domestic industry. These restrictions commonly take the form of quotas, licensing requirements, import restrictions, or tariffs.

Quotas A quota is a limit on the number or poundage of an item that may be imported into a country. By setting a quota on the importation of Japanese automobiles, the United States has forced Japan to limit the number of automobiles it sells in the United States as a way of opening up the American market for American-made automobiles.

Licensing A license is a government-granted privilege to conduct a specific business. By requiring the licensing of foreign technology, Japan has improved the ability of its manufacturers to obtain more favorable bargaining terms. Instead of having different Japanese manufacturers compete with one another to get a desirable piece of technology from an American licensor, the Japanese licensing agency in effect tells the licensor that it will be excluded from the Japanese market unless it agrees to accept considerably less favorable terms than would have resulted without the regulation. In developing nations, licensing regulations may ensure that a country's scarce resources are not being used unless the imported technology fits into the country's basic development plans. To protect domestic employees, some nations require technical training of local personnel in return for license approval.

Prohibited Imports Most countries also maintain a list of prohibited imports. There are a large number of goods that may not be imported into the United States. For example, the American fur industry is protected by a prohibition on the import of furs from Russia. Public morals are protected by the exclusion of obscene materials and lottery tickets. The domestic fishing industry is served by prohibiting the importation of fish from nations that seize American fishing boats. In the following case, the court considered the president's prohibition of the importation into the United States of weapons from China, a response to China's domestic human rights violations.

B-*West Imports, Inc., was involved in the business of importing weapons manufactured in the Peoples Republic of China. On May 26, 1994, President Bill Clinton announced the renewal of most favored nation trading status for the People's Republic of China. At the same time, however, in light of "continuing human rights abuses" in China, he announced certain trading sanctions against that country. One of the sanctions was a ban on the importation of weapons from China. China is one of the countries on the State Department's "proscribed list," a list of countries as to which it is "the policy of the United States to deny licenses and other approvals" for the importation of munitions. Arms may not be imported from any country on the proscribed list without a special exception or suspension of the regulation by the Office of Defense Trade Controls in the Department of State.*

Prior to 1994, China was exempted from the effects of its inclusion on the proscribed list, meaning that arms could be imported from China by licensed importers who obtained import permits. On May 28, 1994, however, two days after the president announced the arms embargo against China, the Secretary of State advised the Secretary of the Treasury that China's exemption from the proscribed list was terminated "effective immediately on the basis of U.S. foreign policy." In light of the decision to revoke China's exemption from the proscribed list, the Secretary of State requested the Secretary of the Treasury to "take all necessary steps to prohibit the import of all defense articles enumerated in the U.S. Munitions List."

The two Treasury Department agencies responsible for enforcing arms import limits are the Bureau of Alcohol, Tobacco, and Firearms (ATF) and the Customs Service. On June 27, 1994, the ATF advised companies holding permits to import munitions from China—including B-West Imports—that their permits were revoked as of May 28. On August 5, 1994, the Customs Service directed that all shipments of weapons from China that entered the United States on or after May 28 be detained.

B-West Imports challenged the government's actions in the Court of International Trade. It argued three points: that the Arms Export Control Act (AECA) does not authorize the president or his delegates to impose an arms embargo; that the Customs Service exceeded its authority in detaining goods for which B-West held validly issued import permits and in declaring the permits null and void; and that the ATF exceeded its authority when it purported to revoke B-West's permit. The court rejected B-West's arguments, upholding the authority of the president, the ATF, and the Custom's Service. B-West appealed to the court of appeals. ∞

Bryson, Circuit Judge B-West argues that the AECA does not authorize an arms embargo. Although section 38 of the Act grants to the President the authority to "control" arms imports, B-West argues that the term "control" limits the President to creating and operating a licensing system for arms importation, and does not allow the President to ban the importation of arms for which import permits have been granted. B-West's argument is unconvincing. B-West concedes that the term "control" is broad enough to allow the President to ban imports by denying licenses or permits for future imports. Their contention is thus limited to the assertion that "control" does not include the right to revoke licenses and permits after they are granted. But if the term "control" includes the power to prohibit, we are unable to discern any basis of construing the statute to convey the power to deny permits and licenses in advance, but to withhold the power to revoke them once they have been issued.

Presidents acting under broad statutory grants of authority have imposed and lifted embargoes, prohibited and allowed exports, suspended and resumed commercial intercourse with foreign countries. Thus, the broad statutory delegation in the AECA incorporates the historical authority of the President in the fields of foreign commerce and importation into the country." We therefore agree with the Court of International Trade that the AECA authorizes the President not only to regulate arms importation through a licensing system, but also to prohibit particular importations altogether when the circumstances warrant.

B-West contends that the Customs Service and the ATF did not act lawfully in this case. Once again, we agree with the Court of International Trade, which held that the agencies did not exceed their lawful authority in putting the embargo into effect. The actions taken by the Secretary of State and the Secretary of the Treasury under the AECA were authorized by Executive Order 11958, which delegates the President's "control" authority under the AECA to the Secretary of the Treasury, guided by the views of the Secretary of State on matters affecting the foreign policy of the United States. State Department regulations further provide that "any license or other approval or exemption granted [for arms transaction invoking countries on the proscribed list] may be revoked, suspended, or amended without notice whenever the Department of State deems such action to be in furtherance of the foreign policy of the United States, or is otherwise advisable."

B-West is therefore incorrect in contending that they were entitled to continue importing munitions from China, pursuant to its previously issued permits, after the embargo became effective. The revocation of its permits was authorized not only by the broad authority granted under the AECA and delegated to the Treasury Department, but also by the regulation that specifically authorizes the revocation, without notice, of permits for importing goods from "proscribed list" countries.

B-West contends that the Customs Service had no lawful right to detain arms shipments from China that were supported by import permits, even after the declaration of the import ban. But a Treasury Department regulation notes that it is "the policy of the United States to deny licenses and other approvals" to import munitions from countries on the proscribed list, including countries "with respect to which the United States maintains an arms embargo." Following the declaration of the Chinese arms embargo and the cancellation of China's exemption from the proscribed list, Customs was therefore authorized to take steps to ensure that goods falling within the scope of the embargo were not admitted into the United States, regardless of whether the goods were supported by an import permit.

B-West next challenges the ATF's June 27 announcement revoking the importers' outstanding permits for importing arms from China. B-West contends that the ATF's own regulations prohibited it from revoking the importers' permits once they were granted. The ATF regulation that applies generally to permits to import munitions provides that import permits may be revoked without notice at any time. While the particular kinds of munitions that B-West was seeking to import are governed by a separate regulation, the regulation does not state or imply that the authorization, once granted, becomes irrevocable. Nor is there any reason to believe that the drafters of the ATF regulations intended to create irrevocable permits for the particular class of munitions B-West seeks to import, while providing that permits for the general class of munitions could be freely revoked at any time. Moreover, denying the ATF the right to revoke permits after their issuance would be perverse, as it would be contrary to other regulations governing arms imports, which make clear that munitions may be excluded whenever a ban on arms imports is declared for foreign policy reasons, even after the importer has obtained a permit. We therefore conclude that after China's exemption from the proscribed list was canceled, the ATF was authorized to withdraw its prior approval for the importation of arms from China and to announce to the importers that their permits had been revoked.

Judgment for United States affirmed.

Tariffs A tariff is a tax or duty assessed on goods, generally when they are imported into a country. The duty is **ad valorem**—that is, a percentage of the value of the goods, such as 10 percent. Through the use of tariffs, governments can discourage imports and protect domestic industry from foreign competition. A sufficiently high ad valorem duty makes the product so expensive that most consumers will refuse to buy it; consequently, consumers do without the good or buy a domestically produced equivalent.

In the United States, import duties are assessed and collected by the U.S. Customs Service. Imported goods are unloaded under the supervision of the Customs Service and taken to a warehouse, where they are kept until a formal entry into the United States is made. **Entry** is the presentation of documentation necessary to classify the goods and assess the duty. After a bond is posted to ensure payment of the duty, the goods are examined. If importation of the goods is prohibited or the goods are not listed on the invoices, the goods may be seized and criminal charges brought against the importer. If the goods pass examination, a tentative duty is assessed and the goods are released to the importer. The Customs Service has the right to charge an additional duty at a later time. The importer may protest or ask for review of the duty before an appraisal specialist at the Customs headquarters. Further reviews are heard by the Court of International Trade and the Court of Appeals for the Federal Circuit in Washington, D.C.

In the next case, the court was faced with the question whether the Nissan Pathfinder sport-utility vehicle should be categorized as a passenger vehicle dutiable at 2.5 percent or as a truck dutiable at 25 percent.

MARUBENI AMERICAN CORP. v. UNITED STATES   35 F.3d 530 (Fed. Cir. 1994)

Marubeni American Corp. and Nissan Motor Corporation USA import into the United States motor vehicles manufactured in Japan by Nissan. Vehicles imported included the 1989 and 1990 Nissan Pathfinder. The Pathfinder was a two door, two-wheel- or four-wheel-drive, dual-purpose or multipurpose passenger vehicle, generally referred to as a compact sport-utility vehicle. The Pathfinder does not have a cargo box or bed like a truck. Instead, its body is one unit that is configured much like an ordinary station wagon in that it has rear seats that fold forward, but not flat, for extra cargo space. These seats, however, are not removable. The spare tire is housed within the cargo space or alternatively, it may be attached outside the vehicle on the rear hatch. The rear hatch operates like those on a station wagon; it has a window that may be opened to place small packages in the cargo area without opening the tailgate. The Pathfinder is mechanically designed for both on- and off-road use.

The Pathfinder was classified by the U.S. Customs Service under 8704.30.00 of the Harmonized Tariff Schedule of the United States (HTSUS) as a "motor vehicle for the transport of goods," and a 25 percent ad valorem duty was assessed to Nissan. Nissan administratively protested the decision, claiming that the Pathfinder should be classified under 8703.23.00 of the HTSUS as a motor vehicle principally designed for the transport of persons, and thus should be assessed a duty of only 2.5 percent. This protest was denied, and Nissan then brought an action in the Court of International Trade (CIT). The CIT conducted a three-week trial that included test-driving the Pathfinder and comparison vehicles and videotape viewing. The CIT concluded that Customs' classification of the Pathfinder under 8704 HTSUS, "motor vehicle for the transport of goods," was incorrect, and that the correct classification was under 8703 HTSUS, "motor vehicle principally designed for the transport of persons." The United States appealed to the court of appeals. ∞

Rich, Circuit Judge   The two competing provisions of the HTSUS are set forth below.

8703   Motor cars and other motor vehicles principally designed for the transport of persons (other than those of heading 8702), including station wagons and racing cars.

8704   Motor vehicles for the transport of goods.

There are no legally binding notes to these headings that are relevant to the classification of dual-purpose vehicles such as the Pathfinder; therefore, we need only look to the common meaning of the terms as they appear above.

By the express language of 8703, "motor vehicle principally designed for the transport of persons," it is clear that the vehicle must be designed "more" for the transport of persons than goods. *Webster's*

Third New International Dictionary of the English Language, Unabridged (1986) defines "principally" as "in the chief place, chiefly;" and defines "designed" as "done by design or purposefully opposed to accidental or inadvertent; intended, planned." Thus, if the vehicle is equally designed for the transport of goods and persons, it would not be properly classified under 8703 HTSUS. There is nothing in the legislative history that indicates a different meaning.

The government argues that "the correct standard to be utilized in determining the principal design of any vehicle must be its construction—its basic structure, body, components, and vehicle layout—and the proper question to be asked is whether that construction is uniquely for passenger transportation." This standard is clearly at odds with Customs' interpretation in its March 1, 1989, memorandum providing guidance in applying these headings to sports utility vehicles. Customs stated:

Design features, whether they accommodate passenger transport or cargo transport, or both, *are of two types both of which are relevant in determining the proper classification of a sports-utility vehicle.* First are what may be regarded as *structures,* or *integral design features* such as basic body, chassis, and suspension design, . . . style and structure of the body [control access to rear]. The second type of design features, *auxiliary design features* which are relevant when determining whether, on the whole, the transport of persons was the principal design consideration. *Neither type by itself can be considered determinative on the issue of the purpose for which the vehicle was principally designed.* [Emphasis added.]

Thus, requiring that the resulting product be uniquely constructed for the purpose of transporting persons, to the exclusion of any other use, is a constrictive interpretation of the terms with which we cannot agree.

To answer the question whether a vehicle is principally designed for a particular purpose, not uniquely designed for the particular purpose, one must look at both the structural and auxiliary design features, as neither by itself is determinative.

Heading 8703 HTSUS specifically includes "station wagons," which are not uniquely designed for transport of persons, rather, they are designed as dual-purpose vehicles for the transport of goods and persons. The Pathfinder, like the station wagon, is a vehicle designed with a dual-purpose—to transport goods and persons.

The specific mention of "including station wagons" in 8703 can affect proper classification when dual-purpose vehicles are at issue. The Explanatory Notes define "station wagon" as "vehicles with a maximum seating capacity of nine persons (including the driver), the interior of which may be used, without structural alteration, for the transport of both persons and goods."

Notwithstanding the fact that a vehicle may fit the definition of a station wagon and that the term is expressly included in 8703 HTSUS, that vehicle is not automatically included in or excluded from 8703 HTSUS classification. It necessarily follows that correct interpretation of 8703 HTSUS requires a determination of whether or not the vehicle was "principally designed for the transport of persons," and not merely a finding that it is within the

definition of a "station wagon," unless of course it is unquestionably a station wagon. The Pathfinder is not the latter.

It is evident that the CIT carefully applied the proper standards in making its decision. In reaching its conclusion, the CIT evaluated the marketing and engineering design goals (consumer demands, off the line parts availability), the structural design necessary to meet both cargo and passenger carrying requirements for both on- and off-road use, as well as interior passenger amenities.

The CIT also recognized that the Pathfinder was basically derived from Nissan's Hardbody truck line, yet the Pathfinder was based on totally different design concepts than a truck. Specifically, the designers decided to adopt the Hardbody's frame side rails and the cab portion from the front bumper to the frame just behind the driver's seats so that they could quickly and economically reach the market. The front suspension system was also adopted from Nissan's truck line but the rear suspension was not. The fact that a vehicle is derived in-part from a truck or from a sedan is not, without more, determinative of its intended principal design objectives which were passenger transport and off-road capability.

Substantial structural changes were necessary to meet the design criterion of transporting passengers. The addition of the rear passenger seat required that the gas tank be moved to the rear and the spare tire relocated. This effectively reduces the cargo carrying capacity. Of particular importance was the design of a new rear suspension that was developed specifically to provide a smooth ride for passengers. New and different cross beams, not present on the Hardbody frame, were added to the Pathfinder's frame to accommodate the above changes.

Other design aspects that point to a principal design for passengers include: the spare tire and the rear seat when folded down intrude upon the cargo space; the cargo area is carpeted; a separate window opening in the pop-up tailgate accommodates passengers loading and unloading small packages without having to lower the tailgate. The CIT also found that the cargo volume is greatly reduced when the rear seat is up to accommodate passengers. Moreover, the axle and wheel differences are minor and consistent with the Pathfinder's off-road mission, particularly in the loaded condition. The Pathfinder has the same engine size as the Maxima passenger car.

Auxiliary design aspects, in addition to those merely relating to the structural derivation of the Pathfinder, that indicates passenger use over cargo use include: vehicle height was lowered 50 millimeters; the seat sides were improved yet similar to those on two door passenger sedans. Other auxiliary design features that point to transport of passengers include: rear seats that recline, are comfortable, and fold to make a fairly flat cargo bed but are not removable; rear seat stereo outlets, ashtrays, cubbyholes, arm rests, handholds, footwells, seat belts, child seat tie down hooks, and operable windows. The CIT noted that there is not much more that can be done to accommodate passengers in the rear seat. Moreover, the testimony of the three primary design engineers as well as the contemporaneous design development documents support the finding that the Pathfinder was principally designed for the transport of persons.

In its March 1, 1989, memorandum referred to above, Customs has drawn what appears to be a line between two door and four door versions of sports utility vehicles. Customs' conclusion, however, that vehicles that lack rear side passenger access doors are to be classified under 8704, is *de facto* affording determinative weight to this feature. This line, clas-

sifying two door dual-purpose vehicles for the transport of goods while classifying the four door version as principally designed for transport of persons, appears to be arbitrary.

Passenger cars with two doors also have restricted entry into the rear seat but this fact does not take these vehicles out of 8703 classification. Two-door passenger cars are equipped with a seat slide mechanism that effectively slides the front seat forward to provide easier access to the rear seat. The doors of two-door passenger cars are generally wider as well. The CIT found that the Pathfinder has both of these features so that passengers can be easily accommodated. Therefore, the two door Pathfinder accommodates passengers in the rear seat as well as two door passenger cars, if not as easily as four door sports utility vehicles. Consequently, the number of doors on a vehicle should not be determinative.

We hold that the court applied the correct legal standards, and that the evidence of record supports the CIT's decision that the Pathfinder is principally designed for the transport of persons.

Judgment for Nissan affirmed.

GATT   Tariffs have been the most common barrier to free trade, and as a result, many governments are cooperating to control or eliminate tariffs. One of the most comprehensive efforts at cooperation has been the rounds of negotiations under the **General Agreement on Tariffs and Trade (GATT),** a treaty subscribed to by more than 80 nations.

Negotiations under GATT have resulted in significant tariff reductions. The focus of GATT is much broader than tariff reduction, however; its purpose is to reduce all trade barriers and promote a stable world trade environment. Among other ways, it attempts to do this through a **most favored nation** clause, which requires a signatory nation (such as the United States) to offer all other signatory nations treatment as favorable as that granted to any other country. Thus, with some exceptions, this eliminates discrimination among countries on the basis of tariffs and duties.

GATS   The General Agreement on Trade in Services (GATS), like GATT, requires its member

nations to extend most favored nation treatment to services and service suppliers of other member nations—such as banking, accounting, and consulting firms. In addition, GATS requires its member nations to accord services and service suppliers of other member nations treatment no less favorable than it grants its own services and service suppliers. First effective in 1995, GATS attempts to strike down the same barriers to the international provision of services that are stricken by GATT in the goods sector.

Regional Trade Associations   Another way that tariffs and trade barriers have been reduced is through the formation of regional associations. Regional trade associations are formed in compliance with treaties signed by participating countries to foster free trade within the association. The **North American Free Trade Agreement (NAFTA)** is a regional trade association of the United States, Canada, and Mexico. The United States approved NAFTA in 1993. The purpose of NAFTA is to eliminate most trade barriers between the United States, Canada, and Mexico.

One of the best known economic unions is the **European Union (EU),** also known as the European Community (EC). Formed in 1957, the EU comprises most of the western European countries. The purpose of the EU is to establish an economic community by promoting free trade within its boundaries. It does this by eliminating tariffs among its members and establishing common tariffs for outside countries, promoting the free movement of workers, goods, and capital among its members, establishing a common monetary policy with the eventual goal of establishing a single monetary unit, and generally promoting the welfare of individuals within the union through economic development. Through this union, the member countries have created an economic force that is far greater than any individual member could have generated on its own.

The EU has supranational powers, requiring its member nations to bring their internal laws in compliance with EU law. This has caused squabbling between EU members concerning national interests, such as France's interest in protecting its farmers, threatening the achievement of the EU's goal to remove trade barriers between EU countries.

Dumping and Subsidized Goods One of the most common reasons the United States and other countries impose tariffs today is to counteract dumping and subsidizing goods. **Dumping** is the selling of goods at unfairly low prices. The selling of imported goods at these low prices means that domestic manufacturers cannot effectively compete with them. Thus, duties are imposed on the goods to offset the difference between the import price and the fair price as determined by the nation of import. In the United States, dumping is regulated by an **antidumping** law, the Trade Agreement Act of 1979. When dumping is alleged, the allegation is investigated by the International Trade Administration (ITA) of the Department of Commerce to determine if the goods are being sold at less than fair value. If such a violation is proved, the International Trade Commission (ITC) determines whether the dumping has injured a domestic industry. If both a violation and injury are proved, an antidumping duty can be assessed by the ITA.

Subsidized goods are goods that in some way have been economically supported by the govern-ment of their country of origin. For example, Spain has subsidized goods by rebating domestic taxes to its manufacturers. Because of this support, subsidized goods can then be sold for less than goods not receiving subsidies. Governments impose **countervailing duties** against subsidized imported goods to protect competing domestic goods. Both the United States and the EU have imposed duties against Japanese goods because of government subsidies. The Trade Agreement Act of 1979 applies to subsidized goods imported into the United States.

Counterfeit and Gray Market Goods Piracy and other unauthorized uses of American goods or technology protected by U.S. patent, copyright, and trademark law have become a major problem of American businesses. For example, foreign jeans manufacturers may without authorization place the Levi's label on their jeans, thereby damaging the business of Levi Strauss & Co. by depriving it of some of the jeans' market and damaging the value of the Levi trademark, especially if the imported jeans are of inferior quality. This is an example of **counterfeit goods,** goods unlawfully bearing a trademark. Counterfeit goods may also unlawfully appropriate patented technology or copyrighted material. For example, a foreign musical recording company may pirate the latest Madonna album and import thousands of copies of it into the United States without copyright permission.

American firms harmed by the importation of counterfeit goods may obtain injunctions and damages under the Tariff Act of 1930, the Lanham Trademark Act of 1946, the Copyright Act, and federal patent law. In addition, the Trademark Counterfeiting Act of 1984 establishes criminal penalties for counterfeiting goods. It also allows an American firm to recover from a counterfeiter three times its damages or three times the counterfeiter's profits (whichever is greater).

Patent, copyright, and trademark piracy is increasing in many parts of the world, especially in developing nations. Some developing nations believe that technology should be transferred freely to foster their economic growth. Consequently, they either encourage piracy or choose not to oppose it. This trend could be reversed if the proposed GATT Code on Discouraging Trade in Counterfeit Goods becomes international law.

Gray market goods are goods lawfully bearing trademarks or using patents and copyrighted material but entering the American market without authorization. For example, Parker Pen Co. may authorize a Japanese manufacturer to make and sell Parker pens only in Japan. When an American firm imports the Japanese-made Parker pens into the United States, the goods become gray market goods.

While importing gray market goods may violate the contract between the American firm and its foreign licensee, it is not clear in what contexts it violates U.S. importation, trademark, patent, or copyright law. Some courts find a Lanham Act or Tariff Act violation, but other courts do not. The Trademark Counterfeiting Act of 1984 specifically excludes gray market goods from its coverage.The Copyright Act covers gray market goods. As the following case illustrates, the Copyright Act prohibits importation only when it is not authorized by the copyright owner.

DISENOS ARTISTICOS E INDUSTRIALES, S.A. v. COSTCO WHOLESALE CORP.   97 F.3d 377 (9th Cir. 1996)

ladro figurines are decorative figurines designed for collection and display. They are copyrighted by Disenos Artisticos E Industriales, S.A. (DAISA), a Spanish Corporation. DAISA is part of a group of related corporations. Lladro Comercial, S.A., is the parent corporation, and through intermediaries, wholly owns DAISA.

DAISA, the copyright owner, does not manufacture the figurines itself, and the parent corporation, Lladro Comercial does not. Instead, DAISA licenses the copyright to four Spanish corporations, all affiliated with the Lladro group, and contracts with them to manufacture the figurines. The manufacturers are licensed not only to produce but also to sell the figurines "to all countries of the world, without the existence of any limitations or exclusions of territory." DAISA does not restrict its licensees at all with respect to distribution.

The licensed manufacturers do not, however, take advantage of their license from DAISA to sell to all countries of the world. Instead, each has a contract with the parent corporation, Lladro Comercial, to sell the entire output of the figurines to the parent corporation. The parent corporation then distributes the figures throughout the world. The manufacturers' contracts with the parent corporation provide that the parent corporation controls the means of sale, "selecting the appropriate category of the places to sell as well as the distributors and representatives."

The parent corporation then sells the figurines directly to retailers in some countries and to distributors in others. Lladro Comercial has granted Lladro USA, Inc., the exclusive right to sell Lladro figurines in the United States. Lladro USA's business strategy in the United States is to market the figurines only to select up-scale retailers. It spends considerable money on marketing to promote the reputation of the brand as high-quality collectors' items and supports auctions establishing a secondary market for the figurines. In its contract with Lladro USA, Inc., the parent corporation, Lladro Comercial, promises not to export the figurines to anyone but Lladro USA within the 50 states of the United States. The parent corporation further covenants that it "shall not knowingly cause any third party to sell the Product in the Territory, nor shall authorize any other party to distribute the Product within the Territory."

Lladro Comercial has at least three arrangements regarding reexport of Lladro figures. It has contracts with some distributors prohibiting commercial reexport and even sales of large quantities to other retailers who might themselves export. Other distributors are prohibited only from "carrying out an active marketing policy of the product outside the territory." In a third agreement, Lladro Comercial directly or through distributors sells to retailers without any contractual restrictions at all.

Costco Wholesale Corporation operates a chain of retail stores throughout the United States. From 1990 through 1994, Costco sold Lladro figurines in its stores. None of the figurines were pirated copies or fakes. All were genuine and were manufactured pursuant to the manufacturing license granted by DAISA. Lladro USA, however, has not sold figurines to Costco, or authorized Costco to sell them. Costco did not import any of the figurines. Some came from countries where they were sold directly to retailers without contractual restrictions. For example, some were imported by an American company from a store in Mexico that went out of business. The Mexican store had no contractual agreement with any Lladro affiliate restricting its right to market inventory in the United States or anywhere else.

DAISA and Lladro USA sued Costco in federal district court alleging that Costco's sale of Lladro figurines was unauthorized and in violation of section 602(a) of the Copyright Act of the United States. The district court granted summary judgment in favor of Lladro USA and DAISA, on the theory that the sale to Costco were not authorized; Costco appealed. ∞

Kleinfeld, Circuit Judge We begin with the statute upon which DAISA and Lladro rely, which prohibits importation of copyrighted goods into the United States "without the authority of the owner of copyright:"

Importation into the United States, without the authority of the owner of the copyright under this title, of copies or phonorecords of a work that has been acquired outside the United States is an infringement of the exclusive right to distribute copies. 17 U.S.C. § 602(a).

This statute is part of the legislative scheme for dealing with pirated and "gray market" goods. In the trademark context, "a gray market good is a foreign-manufactured good, bearing a valid United States trademark, that is imported without the consent of the United States trademark holder." Copyright and trademark owners fought a lengthy and intense legislative battle over the degree to which they would be able to use the customs service and federal law to control the flow of gray market goods. Copyright and trademark law are not the only means of protecting the integrity of a distributorship network, of course. To the extent that the copyright owner has enough market power to obtain and enforce them, it can use contractual restrictions on resale. It can also buy back unsold inventory, as chewing gum and magazine distributors typically do. Wholesalers and retailers may bargain for the right to sell back unsold inventory, or the freedom to liquidate it however they can. We should not put our thumb on the legislative scale. A court construing a statute should avoid adding to or detracting from the benefits Congress accorded to any of the competing interests.

Under section 602(a), the only authorization that counts is authorization by "the owner of the copyright." DAISA owns the copyright, not Lladro Comercial or Lladro USA. It is true that DAISA is a subsidiary of Lladro Comercial, but that does not mean that the parent owns the copyright. Lladro Comercial would have us pierce its own corporate veil. But a corporation is not entitled to establish and use its affiliates' separate legal existence for some purposes, yet have their own separate corporate existence disregarded for its own benefit against third parties.

Because DAISA owned the copyright, we determine whether importation was "without the authority of the owner" by examining the conduct of DAISA. DAISA's arrangements were with its licensees only. DAISA authorized its licensee manufacturers to sell the figurines to "all countries of the world." It did not require its licensees to restrict the sales in any way. So far as DAISA's contracts provided, any of the manufacturers could distribute any of the figurines directly or indirectly into the United States.

The authority to export to the United States must necessarily imply the authority to import into the United States, commercially as well as logically. Lladro USA's evidence shows how a secondary market supports a higher price.

Lladro USA manages the Lladro Collectors Society and publishes Expressions Magazine, both of which are dedicated to serving the needs of collectors of Lladro figurines. Lladro USA has also published two high quality "art" books devoted to the study of Lladro figurines.

Lladro USA promotes two annual auctions in the United States at which investors in Lladro figurines may buy and sell their figurines. Because of Lladro's high quality, high prestige reputation, many people are able to realize a return several times their investment at these auctions.

Likewise, the existence of a liquidation market could be expected to support a higher wholesale price. When a purchaser of Lladro figurines from Lladro Comercial bargains for the right to export them outside its territory, it can afford to pay more for them, because of the larger market for liquidation of excess inventory. Some of the Costco figurines were derived from a Mexican store which had closed. That store had purchased its figurines with no restriction upon its right to resell them. Had Lladro Comercial bargained with that store owner for a prohibition upon his right to sell them into the United States, then the store owner would have had to consider the smaller market available for liquidation when she considered how much money she could afford to commit to Lladro inventory. The right to export would be valueless if it did not imply a right to import.

Authorization by a copyright owner to export goods to anywhere in the world necessarily implies authority to import the goods into the United States. So do sales without restriction on export into the United States. Accordingly, in this case, the copy-right owner, DAISA, and Lladro USA failed to establish that the importation into the United States was "without the authority of the owner of the copyright."

Judgment reversed in favor of Costco.

FOREIGN SALES OF DOMESTICALLY MANUFACTURED PRODUCTS

Once an American exporter has determined that the sale of its product to a buyer in a foreign nation is permitted by American export law and the foreign nation's import law, the exporter may enter a contract with the foreign buyer. In addition to the logistical problems of negotiation at long distance perhaps in two languages, the primary legal questions are what contract law applies to the transaction and what terms the contract should include.

Regulation of International Sales Contracts

Countries have attempted to address some of the problems raised by international transactions through their agreement to codes that apply across national boundaries. Typically, countries agree to be bound by international codes, then adjust their internal laws in compliance with the laws laid out in the code.

An example of such an agreement is the United Nations Convention on Contracts for the International Sale of Goods (CISG), which has been adopted by many nations, including the United States and Canada. The CISG is designed to provide a uniform code for international contracts much the same way that the Uniform Commercial Code (UCC) provides uniformity and certainty for transactions among contracting parties from different states in the United States. The Convention provides rules governing the formation of international contracts and regulates the transfer of goods under those contracts.

There are substantial differences between the CISG and the UCC. The CISG does not require any sales contract to be written. Offers easily become irrevocable—the offeree need only reasonably believe that it is irrevocable. An attempted acceptance that changes the terms of the offer is not an acceptance. Acceptance is effective upon receipt, not dispatch. An offeree who accepts by performance is not required to notify the offeror. A contract must include not only the quantity of the goods sold but also the price. In the next case, the court applied the CISG to determine whether the seller delivered nonconforming goods and breached the contract and what damages the seller owed the buyer.

DELCHI CARRIER SPA v. ROTOREX CORP.   71 F.3d 1024 (2d Cir. 1995)

I n January 1988, Rotorex Corporation, a New York corporation, agreed to sell 10,800 compressors to Delchi Carrier SpA, an Italian manufacturer, for use in Delchi's "Ariele" line of portable room air conditioners. The air conditioners were scheduled to go on sale in the spring and summer of 1988. Prior to executing the contract, Rotorex sent Delchi a sample compressor and accompanying written performance specifications.

Rotorex sent the first shipment by sea on March 26. The shipment arrived at Delchi's Italian factory on April 20. Rotorex sent a second shipment of compressors on or about May 9. While the second shipment was en route, Delchi discovered that the first lot of compressors did not conform to the sample model and accompanying specifications: 93 percent of the compressors were rejected in quality control checks because they had lower cooling capacity and consumed more power than the sample model and specifications. After *several unsuccessful attempts to cure the defects in the compressors, Delchi asked Rotorex to supply new compressors conforming to the original sample and specifications. Rotorex refused, claiming that the performance specifications were not part of the contract because they were inadvertently communicated to Delchi.*

Delchi was unable to obtain in a timely fashion substitute compressors from other sources and thus suffered a loss in its sales volume of Ariele air conditioners during the 1988 selling season. Delchi sued Rotorex for breach of contract and failure to deliver conforming goods under the United Nations Convention on Contracts for the International Sale of Goods (CISG). The district court judge issued a summary judgment holding Rotorex liable to Delchi for $1,248,331.87. This amount included consequential damages for lost profits resulting from a diminished sales level of Ariele air conditioners. Rotorex appealed to the court of appeals, arguing that it did not breach the agreement, that Delchi is not entitled to lost profits because it maintained inventory levels in excess of the maximum number of possible lost sales, that the calculation of the number of lost sales was improper, and that the district court improperly excluded fixed costs and depreciation from the manufacturing cost in calculating lost profits.

Winter, Circuit Judge The instant matter is governed by the CISG, a self-executing agreement between the United States and other signatories, including Italy. Because there is virtually no case law under the CISG, we look to its language and to the general principles upon which it is based. The CISG directs that its interpretation be informed by its "international character and the need to promote uniformity in its application and the observance of good faith in international trade." Case law interpreting analogous provisions of Article 2 of the Uniform Commercial Code (UCC) may also inform a court where the language of the relevant CISG provisions tracks that of the UCC.

We first address the liability issue. Under the CISG, "the seller must deliver goods which are of the quantity, quality and description required by the contract," and "the goods do not conform with the contract unless they possess the qualities of goods which the seller has held out to the buyer as a sample or model." CISG art. 35. The CISG further states that "the seller is liable in accordance with the contract and this Convention for any lack of conformity." CISG art. 36.

The district court judge held that "there is no question that Rotorex's compressors did not conform to the terms of the contract between the parties" and noted that "there are ample admissions by Rotorex to that effect." We agree. The agreement between Delchi and Rotorex was based upon a sample compressor supplied by Rotorex and upon written specifications regarding cooling capacity and power consumption. Rotorex's engineering representative, Ernest Gamache, admitted in a May 13, 1988 letter to Delchi that the compressors would actually generate less cooling power and consume more energy than the specifications indicated. The president of Rotorex, John McFee, conceded in a May 17, 1988 letter to Delchi that the compressors supplied were less efficient than the sample and did not meet the specifications provided by Rotorex. Finally, in its answer to Delchi's complaint, Rotorex admitted "that some of the compressors did not conform to the nominal performance information." There was thus no genuine issue of material fact regarding liability, and summary judgment was proper.

Under the CISG, if the breach is "fundamental" the buyer may either require delivery of substitute goods (CISG art. 46) or seek damages. With regard to what kind of breach is fundamental, Article 25 provides:

> A breach of contract committed by one of the parties is fundamental if it results in such detriment to the other party as substantially to deprive him of what he is entitled to expect under the contract, unless the party in breach did not foresee and a reasonable person of the same kind in the same circumstances would not have foreseen such a result.

Because the cooling power and energy consumption of an air conditioner compressor are important determinants of the product's value, the district court's conclusion that Rotorex was liable for a fundamental breach of contract under the CISG was proper.

We turn now to the district court's award of damages. The CISG provides:

> Damages for breach of contract by one party consist of a sum equal to the loss, including loss of profit, suffered by the other party as a consequence of the breach. Such damages may not exceed the loss which the party in

breach foresaw or ought to have foreseen at the time of the conclusion of the contract, in the light of the facts and matters of which he then knew or ought to have known, as a possible consequence of the breach of contract. CISG art. 74.

This provision is "designed to place the aggrieved party in as good a position as if the other party had properly performed by contract."

Rotorex argues that Delchi is not entitled to lost profits because it was able to maintain inventory levels of Ariele air conditioning units in excess of the maximum number of possible lost sales. In Rotorex's view, therefore, there was no actual short-fall of Ariele units available for sale because of Rotorex's delivery of nonconforming compressors. Rotorex's argument goes as follows. The end of the air conditioner selling season is August 1. If one totals the number of units available to Delchi from March to August 1, the sum is enough to fill all sales. We may assume that the evidence in the record supports the factual premise. Nevertheless, the argument is fallacious. Because of Rotorex's breach, Delchi had to shut down its manufacturing operation for a few days in May, and the date on which particular units were available for sale was substantially delayed. For example, units available in late July could not be used to meet orders in the spring. As a result, Delchi lost sales in the spring and early summer. We therefore conclude that the district court's findings regarding lost sales are not clearly erroneous.

Rotorex contends, in the alternative, that the district court improperly awarded lost profits for unfilled orders from Delchi affiliates in Europe and from sales agents within Italy. We disagree. The CISG requires that damages be limited by the familiar principle of foreseeability. However, it was objectively foreseeable that Delchi would take orders for Ariele sales based on the number of compressors it had ordered and expected to have ready for the season. The district court was entitled to rely upon the documents and testimony regarding these lost sales and was well within its authority in deciding which orders were proven with sufficient certainty.

Rotorex also challenges the district court's exclusion of fixed costs and depreciation from the manufacturing cost used to calculate lost profits. The trial judge calculated lost profits by subtracting the 478,783 lire "manufacturing cost"—the total variable cost—of an Ariele unit from the 654,644 lire average sale price. The CISG does not explicitly state whether only variable expenses, or both fixed and variable expenses, should be subtracted from sales revenue in calculating lost profits. However, courts generally do not include fixed costs in the calculation of lost profits. This is, of course, because the fixed costs would have been encountered whether or not the breach occurred. In the absence of a specific provision in the CISG for calculating lost profits, the district court was correct to use the standard formula employed by most America courts and to deduct only variable costs from sales revenue to arrive at a figure for lost profits.

Judgment for Delchi affirmed.

Need for Written Sales Contracts   Even when the CISG applies to an international sales contract, the parties should not rely exclusively on its protections. Instead, they should draft a comprehensive contract that carefully addresses the major legal and practical problems that may arise in the performance of the contract. The content of the contract varies according to the manner of relationship between the buyer and the seller: (1) A firm may make direct sales to customers abroad, or (2) it may appoint one or more distributors for a particular country or region, which distributors purchase the product from the American firm and resell it to customers in their territories. These two methods of exploiting the world market can involve different

legal problems. The following discussion is based on the typical way these transactions are structured to deal with the international climate.

Direct Sale to a Foreign Buyer

When an American firm contracts to sell its goods to a foreign buyer, the buyer and the seller should execute a written contract to ensure their complete understanding of the basic terms and conditions of the contract. The interpretation and enforcement of most of these terms and conditions—such as price, method of payment, currency of payment, and product warranties—primarily involve contract law. To the extent that the CISG does not apply and there is a difference between the contract law of the seller's jurisdiction and that of the buyer, courts typically respect the choice of the parties as to which law applies if the parties, as is usual, have included a **choice of law clause** in the agreement.

In addition, international sales contracts should include a *force majeure* **clause,** which excuses performance due to conditions beyond the parties' control. For example, a *force majeure* clause may excuse a seller of oil from performing when the outbreak of war threatens shipping lanes in the Persian Gulf. *Force majeure* clauses reflect the risks known to have occurred in the past.

As an alternative or in addition to a *force majeure* clause, the CISG has a frustration defense that is similar to the commercial impracticability defense of the UCC. The CISG excuses nonperformance due to an impediment beyond a party's control that the party could not reasonably have been expected to take into account at the time the contract was made or to avoid or overcome at the time of performance.

An international sales contract should also specify the **currency** in which payment is to be made. American dollars are usually selected because their value is relatively stable, while the currencies of some nations—for example, Brazil—continually fall in value due to high inflation. To illustrate, suppose an American firm contracts to sell five trucks worth $100,000 to a Brazilian firm for 150,000 cruzados. If payment is delayed for three months, Brazilian inflation may cause the 150,000 cruzado payment to be worth only $90,000.

Assurance of Payment   Perhaps the most important provisions in the international sales contract cover the manner by which the buyer pays the seller. Frequently, a foreign buyer's contractual promise to pay when the goods arrive does not provide the seller with sufficient assurance of payment. The seller may not know the overseas buyer well enough to determine the buyer's financial condition or inclination to refuse payment if the buyer no longer wants the goods when they arrive. When the buyer fails to make payment, the seller will find it difficult and expensive to pursue its legal rights under the contract. Even if the seller is assured that the buyer will pay for the goods on arrival, the time required for shipping the goods often means that payment is not received until months after shipment.

To solve these problems, the seller often insists on receiving an **irrevocable letter of credit.** The buyer obtains a letter of credit from a bank in the buyer's country. The letter of credit obligates the buyer's bank to pay the amount of the sales contract to the seller. To obtain payment, the seller must produce a **negotiable bill of lading** and other documents proving that it shipped the goods required by the sales contract in conformity with the terms of the letter of credit.[1] A letter of credit is irrevocable when the buyer's bank cannot withdraw its obligation to pay without the consent of the seller and the buyer.

Letters of credit may be confirmed or advised. Under a **confirmed** letter of credit, the seller's bank agrees to assume liability on the letter of credit. Typically, under a confirmed letter of credit, the buyer's bank issues a letter of credit to the seller; the seller's bank confirms the letter of credit; the seller delivers the goods to a carrier; the carrier issues a negotiable bill of lading to the seller; the seller delivers the bill of lading to the seller's bank and presents a draft[2] drawn on the buyer demanding payment for the goods; the seller's bank pays the seller for the goods; the buyer's bank reimburses the seller's bank; and the buyer reimburses its bank. Figure 1 summarizes the confirmed letter of credit transaction.

With an **advised** letter of credit, the seller's bank merely acts as an agent for collection of the amount owed to the seller. The seller's bank acts as agent for the seller by collecting from the buyer's bank and giving the payment to the seller. The buyer's bank is reimbursed by the buyer.

The confirmed letter of credit is the least risky payment method for sellers. The confirmation is needed because the seller, unlike the confirming bank, may not know any more about the financial integrity of the issuing bank than it knows about that of the buyer. The seller has a promise of immediate payment from an entity it knows to be financially solvent—the confirming bank. If the draft drawn pursuant to the letter of credit is not paid, the seller may sue the confirming bank, which is a bank in his home country.

---

[1]A bill of lading is a document issued by a carrier acknowledging that the seller has delivered particular goods to it and entitling the holder of the bill of lading to receive these goods at the place of destination. Bills of lading are discussed in Chapter 33.

[2]A draft is a negotiable instrument by which the drawer (in this case, the seller) orders the drawee (the buyer) to pay the payee (the seller). Drafts are discussed in Chapter 30.

FIGURE I

Confirmed Letter of Credit Transaction

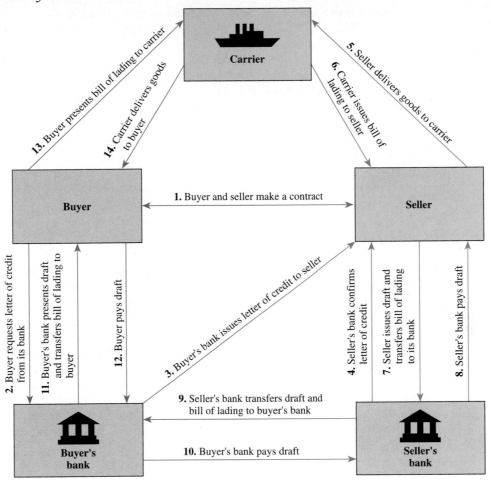

Under the confirmed letter of credit, payment is made to the seller well before the goods arrive. Thus, the buyer cannot claim that the goods are defective and refuse to pay for them. When the goods are truly defective on arrival, however, the customer can commence an action for damages against the seller based on their original sales contract.

Conforming and Nonconforming Documents   In a letter of credit transaction, the promises made by the buyer's and seller's banks are independent of the underlying sales contract between the seller and the buyer. Therefore, when the seller presents a bill of lading and other documents that *conform* to the terms of the letter of credit, the issuing bank and the confirming bank are required to pay, even if the buyer refuses to pay its bank or even, generally, if the buyer claims to know that the goods are defective. However, if the bill of lading or other required documents do not conform to the terms of the letter of credit, a bank may properly refuse to pay. A bill of lading is *nonconforming* when, for example, it indicates the wrong goods were shipped, states the wrong person to receive the goods, or states a buyer's address differently than the letter of credit.

In the following case, even though the seller shipped nonconforming goods to the buyer, the buyer's bank that issued the irrevocable letter of credit was required to pay when the seller presented a bill of lading and other documents that conformed to the letter of credit.

B enetton Services Corporation was an Italian clothing manufacturer. Benedot, Inc., was formed for the purpose of selling Benetton clothing at retail outlets in Dothan and Auburn, Alabama. Benedot placed several orders with Benetton over a period of approximately 36 months. All of the orders were delivered late, and all contained some nonconforming merchandise. Benetton told Benedot that Benetton had made changes in personnel, and that future orders would be conforming and would be delivered on time. Relying on this representation, Benedot placed an order with Benetton for spring and summer 1988 clothing.

As a condition to shipping Benedot's order, Benetton required Benedot to pay $20,000, and to have issued to Benetton an irrevocable letter of credit in the amount of $61,000. On behalf of Benedot, Southland Bank of Dothan issued an irrevocable letter of credit for $61,000 to Benetton.

The spring/summer 1988 order was delivered late and it contained nonconforming goods. Benedot accepted the shipment, because it was very difficult and expensive to return the goods to Italy. Nonetheless, to prevent Benetton from collecting for the goods, Benedot obtained a temporary restraining order directing Southland Bank not to pay Benetton. At a hearing, the trial court issued a preliminary injunction enjoining Southland Bank from paying Benetton. Benetton appealed to the Supreme Court of Alabama. ∞

Shores, Justice   Payment under an irrevocable letter of credit, upon compliance with its terms, is independent of the underlying contract. The issuer of a letter of credit must honor a draft drawn thereunder that complies with the terms of the letter of credit, regardless of whether the goods conform to the underlying contract.

Because the letter of credit represents an independent obligation of the issuer to the beneficiary, payment under an irrevocable letter of credit may not be enjoined absent evidence of forgery or fraud in the issuance of the letter or fraud in the underlying transaction for which the letter of credit was issued.

Benedot has failed to prove fraud. Benetton promised that, upon receipt of the $20,000 and a letter of credit, it would ship conforming goods and that delivery would be timely. This is clearly a promise to do an act in the future; to base a fraud claim on that promise, Benedot had to prove that Benetton, when it made the agreement, did not intend to comply with its terms. Also, Benedot had to prove that, at the time that promise was made, Benetton had an intent to deceive. The record is devoid of any such evidence. The evidence would support, at most, a finding that the promise was recklessly made. A reckless misrepresentation cannot support a fraud action where that misrepresentation relates to a future act. Furthermore, the failure to perform a promised act is not in itself evidence that the defendant, at the time the promise was made, intended to deceive.

The trial court's order granting the preliminary injunction is reversed and the case is remanded with instructions to release the funds due and owing to Benetton pursuant to the letter of credit issued by Southland.

Judgment reversed in favor of Benetton; remanded to the trial court.

Standby Letters of Credit   Although an ordinary letter of credit protects the seller, it leaves a buyer at risk if the seller ships defective goods. Therefore, the buyer may insist that the seller obtain a letter of credit from the seller's bank under which the seller's bank promises to pay the buyer if the seller defaults on the sales contract. Such a **standby letter of credit** operates as a guaranty or insurance for the buyer. The buyer pays the seller, expecting the seller to perform; if the seller defaults on the contract, such as by shipping defective goods, the buyer exercises its rights under the standby letter of credit and obtains payment from the seller's bank. (If the standby letter of credit is confirmed, the buyer would collect from the buyer's confirming bank, which would then collect from the seller's bank.) The seller's bank collects the amount of the payment from the seller, if it has not done so already.

Because the seller's bank is in the same city as the seller, it can more easily than the buyer obtain collection from the seller.

Dispute Resolution   Disputes between an American seller and a foreign buyer may be resolved in the courts of either nation or in an international arbitration tribunal. The court or tribunal may apply American law, foreign law, or international law.

The international sales contract should include a **choice of forum clause,** which designates which court or arbitration tribunal will resolve disputes between the parties. Of course, each party wants to have the dispute resolved in its national courts applying national or local law. As a compromise, an arbitration panel is often the forum of choice.

Arbitration, the settlement of disputes by a nonjudicial third party, may be cheaper, quicker, and more private than resolving disputes through litigation. Equally important, it can take place in a neutral location. The growing attractiveness of arbitration has resulted in the establishment of arbitration centers in London, Paris, Cairo, Hong Kong, Geneva, and New York.

After an American firm successfully litigates or obtains arbitration against a foreign firm, another problem may arise: enforcement of the judgment or decision. For example, an American firm may obtain a judgment in a U.S. court awarding it $50,000 against an Iranian firm. However, the firm may not have any assets in the United States. Moreover, when the American firm seeks enforcement of the judgment in Iran, an Iranian court may refuse to recognize the judgment or to enforce it. Thus, the firm may find it necessary to relitigate in Iran the issues decided by the American court.

Sales to Nonmarket Economies   The international sales transaction is complicated when an American buyer sells to a buyer in a nation that has a **nonmarket economy (NME).** NMEs exist in socialist nations, in which a central government owns and controls all significant means of production. This means that a sale by an American seller to an NME will usually be to a buyer that is authorized by its government to enter international sales contracts. Cuba is among the nations having NMEs.

The typical NME buyer is a **foreign trade corporation.** A socialist economy usually has several foreign trade corporations, each empowered to conduct the whole business of exporting or importing a particular good. Contract negotiations with a foreign trade corporation may be slow and costly, due to the unusually high but necessary precision with which the contract is written. Once agreement has been reached, however, foreign trade corporations have an excellent performance record.

Most foreign trade corporations insist that all disputes be resolved by arbitration in their country. This is normally not a great risk for an American seller because most socialist arbitration tribunals have a good record for efficiency and impartiality. When a foreign trade corporation is sued in a court outside its boundaries, it may raise the **doctrine of sovereign immunity.** The doctrine of sovereign immunity is international law; it holds that a nation may not be sued for causing harm. It is founded in the ancient principle that "The King Can Do No Wrong" and, therefore, a king could not be sued by his subjects. Nonetheless, the United States has rejected the doctrine of sovereign immunity in limited circumstances, by allowing actions against foreign governments under the Foreign Sovereign Immunity Act. The United States and other nations deny immunity to the commercial activities of governments, including the international business transactions of foreign trade corporations.

Countertrade   Often, a socialist nation will condition its agreement to buy goods from an American seller on the seller's agreement to purchase NME goods. This is known as a countertrade, of which two kinds are most common: the counterpurchase and the compensation transaction. In a **counterpurchase,** an American firm sells its goods to an NME nation and purchases from the NME nation goods unrelated to the goods it sells. For example, in a counterpurchase agreement with the former Soviet Union, PepsiCo sold bottling rights to Pepsi-Cola and purchased Stolychnaya vodka produced by the former Soviet Union.

In a **compensation or buy-back transaction,** an American firm sells equipment or technology to the NME nation and agrees to purchase some of the goods produced with the equipment or technology. For example, Occidental Petroleum sold to the former Soviet Union technology for the construction and operation of ammonia plants and purchased ammonia produced by the plants.

Countertrade is not to be confused with a **barter** transaction, which is a nonmoney transaction in which goods are exchanged. Countertrade involves two reciprocal sales in which each party is paid in money, usually the currency of the NME.

Accepting countertrade may benefit an American seller. It may be the only way an American firm can obtain access to an NME, and it does provide a greater assurance of payment. However, payment is in the NME currency, which either cannot be taken out of the NME nation or has little value on world monetary markets. Also, the goods obtained from the NME nation may not fit into an American firm's normal distribution network and may be of inferior quality. Therefore, an American firm may have difficulty disposing of countertraded goods.

Sales Abroad through a Distributor

If a U.S. firm believes that there is a substantial market for its product in some area abroad, it may find that appointing a distributor located in that area is a more effective and efficient way to exploit the market than selling directly to buyers. If so, it signs a distribution agreement, a contract between the seller and the distributor that sets forth a wide range of terms and conditions of the distributorship. This contract should be written and should contain provisions similar to those in a direct sales contract. However, a distributorship agreement may have additional provisions that cause violations of American and foreign antitrust laws.

Two possible provisions in an international distribution agreement can raise antitrust problems. The first is an exclusive dealing or requirements contract provision whereby the distributor promises not to distribute competing products of any other manufacturer. A seller often wants such a provision because it encourages the distributor to devote its full efforts to sales of the seller's product and not to sales of a competing product. Such an agreement may be illegal under American antitrust laws because it limits the ability of competing firms to export into that territory. The second provision, an exclusive distributorship whereby the seller promises that it will not appoint another distributor in the same territory, is more likely to be challenged under foreign antitrust laws. Distributors frequently want such a provision in order to protect their efforts to build up a base of customers.

The EU's antitrust laws apply to American firms operating in western Europe. Article 85 of the Treaty of Rome states: "all agreements which . . . may affect trade between member states and which have as their object or effect the prevention, restric-

tion or distortion of competition within the common market" are void, and fines may be imposed on parties entering into such agreements. Article 86 prohibits entities with a dominant market position in a substantial portion of the EU from taking improper advantage of that position. Exclusive distributorship agreements have been especially susceptible to challenge under Article 85.

Liability of Carriers of Goods

When an American firm ships goods to a foreign buyer, the goods may be shipped by ground, air, or water carrier. The duties and extent of liability of these various carriers is largely determined by domestic statutes and international law.

Ground Carriers   American trucking and railroad companies are regulated by the Interstate Commerce Commission pursuant to the Interstate Commerce Act. American carriers are liable for any loss or damage to the goods with few exceptions—for example, damage caused by acts of God and acts of the shipper (usually the seller of the goods), such as poorly packaging the goods. An American carrier may limit its liability by contract, provided it allows the shipper to obtain full liability by paying a higher shipping charge.

Most European trucking companies are covered by the Convention on the Contract for International Carriage of Goods by Road (CMR); most European railroads are governed by the International Convention Concerning Carriage of Goods by Rail (CIM). These international agreements place liability on carriers for damages to goods they carry with few exceptions—for example, defective packaging by the shipper and circumstances beyond the carrier's control. Each also limits a carrier's liability to an amount stated in the CMR or CIM, unless the shipper agrees to pay for greater liability.

Air Carriers   The Warsaw Convention governs the liability of international air carriers. Most nations have ratified the Warsaw Convention in its original or amended form. Under the Convention, an air carrier is liable to the shipper for damages to goods with few exceptions, including that it was impossible for the carrier to prevent the loss or that the damage was caused by the negligence of the shipper. The Warsaw Convention limits a carrier's liability to a stated amount per pound, unless the shipper pays for greater liability.

Water Carriers   The Hague Rules govern the liability of international water carriers. The Hague Rules were amended in Visby, Sweden, in 1968. The United States codified the Hague Rules in the Carriage of Goods by Sea Act (COGSA), but has not ratified the Visby amendments, which do not substantially change the liability of international water carriers.

The Hague–Visby Rules and the COGSA impose on international water carriers the duties to (1) furnish a seaworthy ship and (2) stow the cargo carefully to prevent it from breaking loose during storms at sea. When these duties are met, a water carrier will not usually be liable for damages to cargo. Water carriers have no liability for damages due to circumstances beyond their control—such as poor packaging, piracy, or acts of war. Under COGSA, liability is limited to $500 per package, unless the shipper agrees to pay a higher shipping fee. Under the Hague–Visby Rules, liability will be the value of the goods declared by the shipper.

Under COGSA or the Hague–Visby Rules, the owner of cargo will be liable for damage his cargo does to other cargo. Also, under the ancient maritime **doctrine of general average,** when a carrier sacrifices an owner's cargo, such as throwing it overboard in order to save the ship and the other cargo, the other owners have liability to the owner whose cargo was sacrificed; liability is pro rated to each owner according to the value of each owner's goods in relation to the value of the voyage (the value of the ship plus the value of the other owners' goods plus the carrier's total shipping fees).

The doctrine of general average is commonly expanded by the contract between the carrier and cargo owners in **New Jason clauses.**[3] Typically, a New Jason clause provides that in *all* cases when goods are damaged and the carrier is not liable under COGSA, the goods owner is entitled to general average contributions from all other cargo owners. The doctrine of general average, bolstered by a New Jason clause, also requires cargo owners to pay for damages to the ship when not the result of the carrier's fault.

[3]*The Jason,* 225 U.S. 32 (U.S. Sup. Ct. 1912) (upheld the validity of general average clauses in bills of lading).

LICENSING FOREIGN MANUFACTURERS

An American firm can also enter the world market by licensing its product or service to a foreign manufacturer. In exchange for granting a license to the foreign licensee, the American licensor will receive royalties from the sale of the licensed product or service. Usually, the licensed product or service or the name under which it is sold will be protected by American intellectual property law, such as patent, trade secret, copyright, or trademark law. Because American intellectual property law does not protect the property outside the boundaries of the United States, a licensor needs to take steps to ensure that its intellectual property will acquire protection in the foreign nation. Otherwise, the licensor risks that a competitor may appropriate the intellectual property without penalty.

Patents and Trade Secrets

A patent filing must be made in each nation in which protection is desired. It is not difficult for a firm to acquire parallel patents in each of the major countries maintaining a patent system, because many countries are parties to the Paris Convention for the Protection of Industrial Property. This convention recognizes the date of the first filing in any nation as the filing date for all, but only if subsequent filings are in fact made within a year of the first filing.

When technology is not patented, either because it is not patentable or because a firm makes a business decision not to patent it, a licensor may control its use abroad under **trade secret** law. For example, an American firm can license its manufacturing know-how to a foreign manufacturer for use in a defined territory in return for promises to pay royalties and to keep the trade secret confidential.

Copyright

An American firm may license a foreign manufacturer to produce literary, artistic, or musical materials for which the firm holds an American copyright. For example, a computer software development firm may grant a license to a foreign manufacturer of software. Also, the American owner of copyrights protecting the Beavis and Butt-head cartoon characters may license a Chinese firm to manufacture Beavis and Butt-head dolls.

International copyright protection is governed by the Berne Convention, which states that a copyright registration in one signatory nation grants the copyright owner rights in all signatory nations. The United States is a signatory of the Berne Convention.

The following case, involving the Beatles film *Yellow Submarine,* illustrates the importance of obtaining the protection of foreign intellectual property law, holding that American copyright law does not apply to an act of infringement that occurs exclusively outside the United States. The court left open the issue whether foreign copyright laws may have been violated.

SUBAFILMS, LTD. v. MGM-PATHE COMMUNICATIONS CO. 24 F.3d 1088 (9th Cir. 1994)

I n 1966, the musical group The Beatles, through Subafilms, Ltd., entered into a joint venture with the Hearst Corporation to produce the animated motion picture Yellow Submarine. In 1967, Hearst negotiated agreements with United Artists Corporation (UA) to distribute and finance the film. Pursuant to these agreements, UA distributed Yellow Submarine in theaters beginning in 1968 and later on television.

In the early 1980s, with the advent of the home video market, UA entered into several licensing agreements to distribute a number of its films on videocassette. Although one company expressed interest in Yellow Submarine, UA refused to license Yellow Submarine because of uncertainty over whether home video rights had been granted by the 1967 agreements. Nonetheless, in 1987, UA's successor company, MGM/UA Communications Co., authorized its subsidiary, MGM/UA Home Video, Inc., to distribute Yellow Submarine for the domestic home video market and notified Warner Bros., Inc., that Yellow Submarine had been cleared for international videocassette distribution. Warner, through its wholly owned subsidiary, Warner Home Video, Inc., in turn entered into agreements with third parties for distribution of Yellow Submarine on videocassette around the world.

In 1988, Subafilms and Hearst brought suit against MGM/UA, Warner, and their subsidiaries (collectively the Distributors), contending that the videocassette distribution of Yellow Submarine, both foreign and domestic, constituted copyright infringement under the U.S. Copyright Act and a breach of the 1967 agreements. The district court found the Distributors liable and awarded $2,228,000 in compensatory damages to Subafilms and Hearst, evenly split between foreign and domestic distribution. On appeal, a panel of the court of appeals affirmed that both the domestic and foreign distribution of Yellow Submarine constituted infringement under the Copyright Act. With respect to the foreign distribution of Yellow Submarine, the court of appeals concluded that although infringing actions that take place entirely outside the United States are not violations of the Copyright Act, infringement within the United States occurs—and is a violation of the Copyright Act—when the illegal authorization of international infringement takes place in the United States. The Distributors asked the court of appeals for an en banc rehearing on the grounds that the copyright law had been misapplied. ∞

Nelson, Circuit Judge Accepting that wholly extraterritorial acts of infringement cannot support a claim under the Copyright Act, we believe that the panel in this case erred in concluding that the mere authorization of such acts supports a claim for infringement under the Act.

The "undisputed axiom" that the United States' copyright laws have no application to extraterritorial infringement predates the 1909 Act. There is no clear expression of congressional intent in either the 1976 Act or other relevant enactments to alter the preexisting extraterritoriality doctrine. Furthermore, we note that Congress chose in 1976 to expand one specific "extraterritorial" application of the Act by declaring that the authorized importation of copyrighted works constitutes infringement even when the copies lawfully were made abroad. Had Congress been inclined to overturn the preexisting doctrine that infringing acts that take place wholly outside the United States are not actionable under the Copyright Act, it knew how to do so.

Subafilms and Hearst, however, propose that the presumption against extraterritorial application of U.S. laws may be "overcome" when denying such application would "result in adverse effects within the United States." More importantly, application of the presumption is particularly appropriate when "it serves to protect against unintended clashes between our laws and those of other nations which could result in international discord." Subafilms and Hearst contend that, if liability for "authorizing" acts of infringement depends on finding that the authorized acts themselves are cognizable under the Copyright Act, this court should find that the United States copyright laws *do extend* to extraterritorial acts of infringement when such acts "result in adverse effects within the United States." They buttress this argument with the contention that failure to apply the copyright laws extraterritorially in this case will have a disastrous effect on the American film industry, and that other remedies, such as suits in foreign jurisdictions or the application of foreign copyright laws by American courts, are not realistic alternatives.

We are not persuaded by Subafilms and Hearst's parade of horribles. The Supreme Court recently reminded us that "it is a long-standing principle of American law that legislation of Congress, unless a contrary intent appears, is meant to apply only within the territorial jurisdiction of the United States."

At the time that the international distribution of the videocassettes in this case took place, the United States was a member of the Universal Copyright Convention ("UCC"), and, in 1988, the United States acceded to the Berne Convention for the Protection of Literary and Artistic Works. The central thrust of these multilateral treaties is the principle of "national treatment." A work of an American national first generated in America will receive the same protection in a foreign nation as that country accords to the works of its own nationals.

It is commonly acknowledged that the national treatment principle implicates a rule of territoriality. Indeed, a recognition of this principle appears implicit in Congress's statements in acceding to the Berne Convention that "the primary mechanism for discouraging discriminatory treatment of foreign copyright claimants is the principle of national treatment," and that adherence to the Berne Convention will require "careful due regard for the values" of other nations.

In light of the concern with preventing international discord, we think it inappropriate for the courts to act in a manner that might disrupt Congress's efforts to secure a more stable international intellectual property regime unless Congress otherwise clearly has expressed its intent. The application of American copyright law to acts of infringement that occur entirely overseas clearly could have this effect. Extraterritorial application of American law would be contrary to the spirit of the Berne Convention, and might offend other member nations by effectively displacing their law in circumstances in which previously it was assumed to govern. Consequently, an extension of extraterritoriality might undermine Congress's objective of achieving "effective and harmonious copyright laws among all nations." Indeed, it might well send the signal that the United States does not believe that the protection accorded by the laws of other member nations is adequate, which would undermine two other objectives of Congress in joining the convention: "strengthening the credibility of the U.S. position in trade negotiations with countries where piracy is not uncommon" and "raising the likelihood that other nations will enter the Convention."

Accordingly, because an extension of the extraterritorial reach of the Copyright Act by the courts would in all likelihood disrupt the international regime for protecting intellectual property that Congress so recently described as essential to furthering the goal of protecting the works of American authors abroad, we reaffirm that the United States copyright laws do not reach acts of infringement that take place entirely abroad. It is for Congress, and not the courts, to take the initiative in this field.

Subafilms and Hearst raise a number of additional arguments. They maintain that they may recover damages for international distribution of "Yellow Submarine" based on the theory of direct infringement—reproduction of the negatives for "Yellow Submarine"—took place in the United States. In addition, they maintain that the Distributors are liable for the international distribution under foreign copyright law.

We resolve none of these questions, but leave them for the panel, in its best judgment to consider.

Judgment reversed in favor of the Distributors; remanded to the panel of the court of appeals.

Trademarks

The holder of an American trademark may license the use of its trademark in a foreign nation. For example, McDonald's may license a French firm to use the McDonald's name and golden arches at a restaurant on the Champs-Elysees. Or the holder of the Calvin Klein trademark may license a South Korean firm to manufacture Calvin Klein jeans. In addition to the gray market goods problem discussed earlier in this chapter, the holder of an American trademark that licenses its product or services abroad runs the risk of losing trademark protection in the foreign market.

Trademark registrations must be made in each nation in which protection is desired. Parallel trademark registrations may be made in compliance with the Paris Convention for the Protection of Industrial Property. Under the Paris Convention, the date of the first filing in any nation is the filing date for all nations, if the subsequent filings are made within six months of the first filing.

The EU allows a single filing to be effective in all EU nations. The Madrid Agreement also permits a firm to register a trademark in all its signatory nations simultaneously by filing an application for registration with the World Intellectual Property Organization in Geneva. The United States is not a signatory of the Madrid Agreement; therefore, an American trademark holder must register its trademark in a signatory nation to take advantage of the Madrid Agreement.

Antitrust Problems

International licensing of intellectual property, if done on an exclusive basis, can give rise to the same kinds of antitrust questions as do exclusive distributorships. An exclusive license of a product innovation means that no one other than the licensee, not even the licensor, can manufacture or sell the product or service in the designated territory. Competition among products using the same technology is limited and, therefore, may be illegal.

DIRECT FOREIGN INVESTMENT

An American firm may directly invest in a foreign economy, such as building a manufacturing plant and making its goods near foreign customers. For-eign production may give access to lower-priced labor and raw materials as well as avoid the tariff and other trade barriers erected by foreign nations.

Before an American firm decides to establish a manufacturing operation abroad, its officers must examine a wide variety of legal issues. Some of the issues are ones we have already discussed, such as protection of patents and trademarks. Foreign labor laws may be very different from American law and may impose long-term obligations on the employer. For example, Japanese custom is to hire an employee for life, and in the Netherlands, an employer must obtain governmental approval to dismiss an employee.

Import license requirements and high tariffs may force the firm to use local sources of supplies and raw materials and to manufacture locally a certain percentage of the parts used in assembling the final product. Some countries—for example, India—prohibit foreigners from having a majority equity interest in any operation within their borders. In socialist nations, direct foreign investment is usually prohibited, although some NME nations—for example, China—allow an American firm to co-own a business with a government-owned entity.

When these legal problems are surmounted and the American firm establishes a successful operation in a foreign nation, two additional problems may arise: (1) restrictions on investment repatriation and (2) expropriation.

Repatriation of Earnings and Investment

Repatriation is bringing back to the United States earnings from a direct foreign investment. Many countries, particularly those in the developing world, have regulations concerning the conversion of their currency into a foreign currency such as dollars, and the removal of the converted currency to another country such as the United States. When an American firm wishes to repatriate some of the earnings from an operation in a country with such regulations, it must obtain permission from the host nation's currency exchange authorities. These authorities operate under rules intended to encourage foreign firms to reinvest their earnings in the country rather than send them home. Some countries place an absolute limit, stated in terms of a set percentage of the amount that a firm has invested, on the amount of earnings that may be repatriated each year. Other countries place a substantial income withholding tax on repatriated earnings, which increases in percentage with the amount repatriated.

When an American firm wants to sell or liquidate its operations, all proceeds in excess of the original investment are usually considered dividends, and their repatriation may be either prohibited or taxed at a very high rate. The existence of such regulations in a country means that an American firm should normally not consider a major investment in that country unless it is prepared to make a long-term commitment.

Expropriation

One of the biggest fears of an American firm investing in a politically unstable country is expropriation, the taking of its facilities by the host government without adequate compensation. Since 1945, expropriations have been common, including the expropriation of hotels and banks in Cuba and oil fields and refineries in Iran, Saudi Arabia, and Libya.

American political leaders take the position that international law requires adequate, effective, and prompt compensation whenever a foreign government takes property belonging to someone who is not a citizen of that country. Although this position, which is consistent with our Constitution, is shared by most western nations, it is rejected by many developing countries and communist countries.

Some of these countries contend that international law requires only nondiscriminatory treatment of their citizens and noncitizens. Others recognize the principle that compensation is required, but assert that it may be delayed if immediate payment would frustrate what they view as vital state programs, as would almost always be the case where there is a social revolution that includes a program of massive expropriation of private property.

Regardless, there is difficulty persuading a court to take and listen to such a compensation case. American courts will usually not interfere on the grounds that a foreign government's expropriation action is entitled to deference as an act of state. The **act of state doctrine,** while not international law, is a matter of comity or courtesy between nations. It holds that a nation is not permitted to question the act of another nation committed within its own boundaries. In addition, a court may refuse to allow a foreign government to be sued by an American firm under the doctrine of sovereign immunity. A neutral foreign court is an even less likely forum because it is not anxious to put itself in the middle of a dispute between a citizen of one foreign country and the government of another.

As the following case shows, however, some courts are willing to find a duty to compensate fairly an American firm for the expropriation of its property when a treaty between the United States and the expropriating nation provides for such a remedy. Note, also, that the American court had jurisdiction over funds of the expropriating nation.

KALAMAZOO SPICE EXTRACTION CO. v. PROVISIONAL MILITARY GOVERNMENT OF SOCIALIST ETHIOPIA
729 F.2d 422 (6th Cir. 1984)

In 1966, Kalamazoo Spice Extraction Co. (Kal-Spice), an American corporation, entered a joint venture with Ethiopian citizens. They created the Ethiopian Spice Extraction Co. (ESESCO), an Ethiopian-based corporation that was to engage in the production of spices. Kal-Spice owned approximately 80 percent of the shares of ESESCO, contributed capital, built a production facility, and trained ESESCO's staff, which consisted of Ethiopian citizens. After four years of preparation, construction, and training, production began in 1970.

In 1974, the Provisional Military Government of Socialist Ethiopia (PMGSE) came to power. In February 1975, as part of its program to ensure that Ethiopian industries would "be operated according to the philosophy of Ethiopian socialism," the PMGSE announced the seizure of several businesses, including ESESCO. As a result of the expropriation, Kal-Spice's ownership interest in ESESCO was reduced to 39 percent. In December 1975, the PMGSE established a Compensation Commission, which in October 1981 offered Kal-Spice the equivalent of $450,000 in Ethiopian currency. Believing it was entitled to compensation of $11 million, Kal-Spice rejected the offer and, in retaliation, refused to pay for $1.9 million of spices that

ESESCO had shipped to Kal-Spice in Michigan. When ESESCO (controlled by the PMGSE) sued Kal-Spice for payment, Kal-Spice counterclaimed against the PMGSE for damages for expropriating part of its interest in ESESCO. The trial court decided that the act of state doctrine precluded adjudication of the claims against the PMGSE. Kal-Spice appealed. ∽

Keith, Judge The Act of State doctrine is an exception to the general rule that a court of the United States will decide cases by choosing the rules from among various sources of law, including international law. The roots of the doctrine can be traced to *Underhill v. Hernandez* (1897), where the Supreme Court held:

Every sovereign state is bound to respect the independence of every other sovereign state, and the courts of one country will not sit in judgment on the acts of the government of another done within its own territory.

Kal-Spice requests that this Court recognize a "treaty exception" to the Act of State doctrine. *Banco Nacional de Cuba v. Sabbatino* (1964) provides the basis for a treaty exception:

[T]he Judicial Branch will not examine the validity of a taking of property within its own territory by a foreign sovereign government, extant and recognized by this country at the time of suit, *in the absence of a treaty or other unambiguous agreement regarding controlling legal principles,* even if the complaint alleges that the taking violates customary international law. [Emphasis added.]

This language and the existence of a treaty between the United States and Ethiopia, asserts Kal-Spice, requires a "treaty" exception to the rule that a United States court will not exercise jurisdiction over a foreign sovereign for an act done by that sovereign within its borders. The treaty in existence between the United States and Ethiopia is the 1953 Treaty of Amity and Economic Relations. That treaty provides:

Property of nationals and companies of either High Contracting Party, including interests in property, shall receive the most constant protection and security within the territories of the other High Contracting Party. *Such property shall not be taken except for a public purpose, nor shall it be taken without prompt payment of just and effective compensation.* [Emphasis added.]

The standard of compensation provided for in the Treaty of Amity between Ethiopia and the United States can provide a basis for determining the extent of compensation to which Kal-Spice may be entitled. Numerous treaties employ the standard of compensation used in the 1953 Treaty of Amity between Ethiopia and the United States. Undoubtedly, the widespread use of this compensation standard is evidence that it is an agreed upon principle in international law.

There is a great national interest to be served in this case, i.e., the recognition and execution of treaties that we enter into with foreign nations. The failure of this court to recognize a properly executed treaty would indeed be an egregious error because of the position that treaties occupy in our body of law.

Judgment reversed in favor of Kal-Spice; remanded to the trial court.

The best protection against the risk of expropriation is insurance. To encourage American investment in developing countries, the U.S. government established the Overseas Private Investment Corporation (OPIC). OPIC offers low-cost expropriation insurance for certain investment projects in designated countries.

OFF–SHORE BANKING AND OTHER USES OF TAX HAVENS

Because differences in the business taxation rates of developed nations are minimal, tax shopping among developed nations provides little benefit to an international business. However, small countries in North America and Europe provide significant tax advantages to American firms. These **tax havens,** including the Bahamas, the Cayman Islands, and Bermuda, have no income tax. In addition, some tax havens, such as Switzerland, the Bahamas, and the Cayman Islands, not only have low or no income taxes but also protect the secrecy of banking accounts. Consequently, many American firms have established insurance, banking, and investment company subsidiaries in these tax havens.

Not surprisingly, many persons use tax havens to mask illegal activities, especially drug dealing. During the 1980s, the U.S. government pressured the

Swiss government to remove its bank secrecy protections to help the United States prosecute drug dealers and tax defrauders. The United States has not, however, exerted similar pressure against other tax havens that have strong bank secrecy laws.

The following case demonstrated how an offshore tax haven is used to launder money from illegal activities—and how the American government apprehends criminals who launder money using tax havens.

UNITED STATES v. GOULDING   26 F.3d 656 (7th Cir. 1994)

R*andall Goulding and Michael Ushijima were Illinois lawyers. In late 1984 or early 1985, Goulding told government informant James Evegelatos that he knew how to move money around the world to hide it from the government in order to avoid paying taxes. Goulding claimed to have bankers in Hong Kong, Switzerland, and the Cayman Islands, all of whom were acquainted with his system.*

From December 1986 until August 1987, International Revenue Service Special Agent Gregory Myre, using the name T. J. Ryder, posed as a businessman who during the past four years had acquired $400,000 in illegal income from bookmaking in Florida. Ryder was introduced to Goulding by Evegelatos in December 1986. Ryder informed Goulding that he wished to have use of his income without reporting it to the Internal Revenue Service. Goulding told Ryder that if Ryder declared his unreported income, the taxes, penalties, and interest might eat up the entire unreported amount. Goulding explained, however, that for $10,000 he could arrange for Ryder's money to be moved through a corporate account in the Cayman Islands and brought back to the United States as a non-taxable corporate loan. Goulding drew a flowchart to depict the system. He acknowledged that Ryder would be in a lot of trouble if anyone found out about the system but reassured Ryder that the system could be set up so that the Internal Revenue Service would not detect it. Goulding claimed his system "cleaned the money."

Later in February 1987, Ryder met with Goulding at the O'Hare Hilton Hotel in Chicago and was introduced to Ushijima. Ryder told Ushijima that he had cash income that had not been reported on his tax returns. Ushijima described his system of trusts and corporations to be set up in the United States and Cayman Islands to move the money. He said that a management company in the Caymans would provide an existing, dormant "shell" company. The company would be owned by a trust administered by a bank, which would take instructions from Ryder through "wish letters." He added that a domestic corporation would be set up in Minnesota to receive funds from the Cayman corporation and convey Ryder's money back to him as a "loan."

Ushijima indicated that his fee would be $5,000 and that the best way to send the money to the Caymans was in cash by courier rather than international wire transfers or mails. Ushijima warned Ryder that the courier would not declare the cash taken to the Caymans even though it was illegal to take more than $10,000 out of the United States without declaring it. Ushijima also warned Ryder that the cash could be seized if the courier were caught.

At this same meeting, Ushijima said that the fee for Goulding, himself and courier would be $15,000. Thereupon Ryder gave Goulding a $5,000 cashier's check in part payment and made arrangements to deliver $30,000 to Goulding and Ushijima to be sent through the Caymans, with $7,000 additional cash to go to Goulding and Ushijima as their fee and for expenses.

In March 1987, Ryder again met with Goulding at the O'Hare Hilton and gave Goulding $37,000 in $100 bills. Goulding recommended that Ryder report the income but added that the taxes, interest, and penalties would total close to 100 percent of Ryder's money. Ryder's $30,000 was transported by courier to the Caymans about March 7, 1987. No Customs Service report was filed. Ushijima also traveled to the Caymans on March 7 and Goulding followed on March 9. The two arranged there for the formation of a trust, a corporation known as Tarbet Investments, Ltd. C.I., and a corporate bank account in Tarbet's name. Ownership of Tarbet was put in the name of local Cayman nominees. Goulding later formed a domestic corporation (Tarbet Investments, Ltd. U.S.) in Minnesota and opened a corporate bank account there for that corporation.

On May 13, 1987, Trevor Lloyd, a Cayman resident acting on instructions of Ushijima, caused $28,000 of Ryder's money to be wire-transferred from the corporate account of Tarbet C.I. in the Caymans to the Minnesota bank account of Tarbet U.S. Goulding provided Ryder with fictitious documents showing a $15,000 *loan from Tarbet U.S. Goulding also provided Ryder with a bank promissory note to be used to create fictitious loan documents for subsequent money transfers pursuant to the scheme.*

On May 18, 1987, Ryder met with Ushijima in his law office in Des Plaines, Illinois, to arrange for the transfer of an additional $120,000 to the Caymans. Ushijima said he would deposit the money into his corporate escrow account in Chicago and convert $100,000 of the $120,000 into bearer bonds through his Chicago broker. He told Ryder that the bonds would be taken to the Caymans by the same courier who had transported the initial $30,000 and that once the bonds were in the Caymans, he would open an account in the name of Tarbet C.I. to sell the securities. The balance of Ryder's $120,000 was wire-transferred to Ushijima's corporate escrow account in the Caymans. When Ryder expressed concern about possible questioning of Ushijima about where the money came from, Ushijima replied that he would say it came from clients but would not identify them under the attorney–client privilege. Ryder and Ushijima made arrangements for the two of them and Goulding to meet the next day for Ryder to deliver the additional $120,000.

The next day Ryder met with Goulding at an Elk Grove, Illinois, motor lodge. Ryder thereupon gave Goulding $120,000 in cash. Goulding counted the cash and then left to meet Ushijima at his law office. $100,000 in bearer bonds were purchased as Ushijima had described and were transported by courier to the Caymans on June 6, 1987, and sold. Although required, no Customs report was filed when the bearer bonds were transported out of the United States. The additional $20,000 was wire-transferred to the Caymans and deposited, along with the proceeds of the sale of the bearer bonds, into the Tarbet C.I. bank account in the Caymans. On June 29, $118,000 was wire-transferred by Trevor Lloyd from the Tarbet C.I. account in the Caymans to the Tarbet U.S. Minnesota account.

Based on information provided by Ryder, the United States prosecuted Goulding and Ushijima for conspiracy to defraud the United States and illegal transportation of currency and monetary instruments. The jury found them guilty, and they were sentenced to six months in prison and five years' probation and ordered to perform 500 hours of community service. Goulding and Ushijima appealed their convictions to the court of appeals. ⌒

Cummings, Circuit Judge There was overwhelming evidence that from December 1986 until August 1987 defendants engaged in a conspiracy to defraud the federal government of taxes by laundering money from the United States through the Cayman Islands. They aided Ryder in his efforts to evade the payment of income taxes on $400,000, money they knew was from illegal bookmaking activity. They arranged for the formation of fictitious corporations and for corporate bank accounts here and in the Cayman Islands to launder money and to show that actual taxable income was only nontaxable corporate loans. The defendants warned Ryder to avoid using the international mails and telephones as to the Caymans while suggesting to him how to make the newly formed corporations appear legitimate, although they had no purpose except to "clean" Ryder's money. They violated currency laws about transportation of cash and monetary instruments out of the country; they admitted they were "cleaning" and "laundering" Ryder's illegal unreported income and that the attorney-client privilege was inapplicable to their conduct but nevertheless would be used by them to avoid investigation. Taken together, this evidence is clearly sufficient to establish that the defendants conspired to defraud the government.

The evidence also showed that defendants believed that Ryder owed taxes and that they conspired to deprive the government of information needed to collect the taxes and to deprive the government of those taxes. Goulding recognized that taxes, penalties and interest due on Ryder's $400,000 might total $400,000 and stated that his fee for laundering the money was cheaper than paying Ryder's taxes, penalties and interest. The defendants did not report the monetary transfer out of the United States and concealed the ownership of Ryder's money by creating bank accounts, corporations, nominee stockholders and false loan documents. They also coached Ryder to prevent the government from learning of his untaxed hoard of illegally obtained money. This was all done to keep the government from assessing and collecting taxes on Ryder's $400,000 of illegal income. There was clearly adequate evidence to support defendants' convictions under the conspiracy to defraud clause.

Defendants submit that their convictions for illegally transporting currency and monetary instruments out of the United States were unwarranted.

Despite the defendants' arguments to the contrary, there was sufficient evidence to convict. The evidence shows that they caused $30,000 in cash and $100,000 in bearer bonds to be transported from the United States to the Cayman Islands in March and June 1987. The evidence established that they knew that in such instances reports of the transportation had to be made to the government. Moreover, they made clear in advance that they were not planning to comply with the reporting requirement. Their convictions were therefore justified.

Goulding states that there was no evidence he had knowledge of the general reporting requirement, but this is untrue. The evidence showed that Goulding knew it was illegal to transport more than $100,000 out of the country without reporting it to the government. Ushijima told Ryder that in Goul-

ding's presence on February 24, 1987. Goulding also knew that bearer bonds were negotiable instruments and had to be reported because on February 24 he and Ushijima discussed that very subject. Goulding's knowledge also was shown by his refusal to take the bearer bonds to the Caymans on behalf of Ryder, saying that an attorney should know it was illegal to do so.

Moreover, when one defendant is a member of the conspiracy and his co-defendant commits an offense in furtherance or as a consequence of the conspiracy, the defendant can be found guilty of the offense. Consequently, Ushijima's knowledge of the reporting requirement and his culpability were attributable to Goulding and vice versa.

Conviction of Goulding and Ushijima affirmed.

THE FOREIGN CORRUPT PRACTICES ACT

In 1977, the Congress of the United States passed the Foreign Corrupt Practices Act (FCPA) in response to discoveries that over 400 American firms had made bribes to foreign businesses and government officials in connection with international business transactions. The FCPA makes it a crime for any American firm to offer, promise, or make payments or gifts of anything of value to a foreign official or any other person if the firm knows or should know that it will be used to influence a discretionary governmental decision. An American firm may be fined up to $2 million. Any officer or director who violates the payments prohibition may be fined up to $100,000 and imprisoned up to five years.

ETHICAL AND PUBLIC POLICY CONCERNS

1. Do you think it is right for nations to use export controls for political ends? Consider the 1990 and 1991 world embargo of Iraqi exports in response to its invasion of Kuwait. Did the benefits of such an embargo outweigh its costs? Does it matter that Iraqi citizens were harmed by an embargo that was aimed at Iraq's political leaders?

2. Do you think that foreign governments should restrict the repatriation of earnings and investment?

Why do foreign governments restrict repatriation? What are the long-term costs and benefits of restricting repatriation? Would you make a direct foreign investment in a country that has a history of expropriating American investments without adequate compensation? Do you think American firms have given as much to the economies of developing nations as they have taken out of the economies?

3. Do you think it is right for an American firm to establish a banking or other subsidiary in the Cayman Islands? Who benefits from such a decision? Who suffers by such a decision? Would you invest in an American firm that has a banking subsidiary in a tax haven?

PROBLEMS AND PROBLEM CASES

1. Roger Geissler was an exporter of military arms and parts. He exported tires for F-14 fighter jets to Iran for use by the Iranian Air Force. Geissler did not obtain a validated license to export the F-14 tires, even though the Commodity Control List required a validated license for the export of "Other aircraft parts and components, n.e.s. [not elsewhere specified]." The only other federal agency that could regulate the export of F-14 tires—the State Department—explicitly excluded F-14 aircraft tires from its jurisdiction. Has Geissler violated the Export Administration Act?

2. Edward Elkins, an American businessman, was approached about selling Lockheed aircraft to a buyer in Libya. The aircraft had potential military uses. The U.S. Department of State told Elkins the sale would not be approved because of a presidential order prohibiting trade to Libya. Elkins conceived of a plan to obtain validated licenses to sell the aircraft to a German company owned and operated by Libyans and to route the aircraft through Bordeaux, France, to Benin (a small African country), and then to Libya. Is the export of the aircraft in this manner a violation of the Export Administration Act?

3. Hasbro Industries, Inc., imported G.I. Joe Action Figures from Hong Kong. G.I. Joe figures are plastic, 3½ inches tall, and appear like humans dressed and equipped for war. They are lifelike; the head turns, and the arms are jointed at the shoulder and elbow. They can turn and bend at the waist. The legs have a wide range of movement. Each figure is packaged singly in a large plastic blister mounted on a large card that contains specific biographical information for each figure. For example, First Sergeant, Code Name: Duke, has the following personnel card:

File Name: Hauser, Conrad S.
Primary Military Specialty: Airborne Infantryman
Birthplace: St. Louis, MO Grade: E-8 (Master Sergeant)

Duke was fluent in French, German, and English when he enlisted in 1967. Graduated top of his class at airborne school, Fort Benning. Went Special Forces in 1979. Ran four different Special Forces schools. Turned down a commission in 1971. Statement after declining commission: "They tell me that an officer's job is to impel others to take the risks—so that the officer survives to take the blame in the event of total catastrophe. With all due respect, sir, if that's what an officer does, I don't want any part of it."

In addition, each figure comes with its own specialized accessories. For example, First Sergeant comes with plastic pieces representing binoculars, a helmet, an assault pack, and an M-32 submarine gun. In 1982 and 1983, the U.S. Customs Service classified G.I. Joe figures as "other dolls" under the Tariff Schedule of the United States and assessed a duty on the figures. Hasbro claimed that G.I. Joe was not a doll and should be importable free of duty. Is G.I. Joe a doll?

4. To encourage investment and development, the governments of Canada, Alberta, Ontario, and Saskatchewan gave investment tax credits and monetary grants to Canadian producers of tubular steel, including Ipsco Steel, Inc. Ipsco exported tubular steel to the United States. American producers claimed to be harmed by Ipsco's exports. What remedy is available to the American producers?

5. Manufacture des Montres Rolex S.A. Bienne (Bienne), a Swiss company, is the manufacturer of Rolex watches. Bienne is the owner of the ROLEX trademark in Switzerland. Bienne sold the American rights to the ROLEX trademark to Rolex Watch USA Inc., a New York corporation. The importation of Rolex watches into the United States was forbidden unless imported for the account of Rolex USA. The distributor of Rolex watches is Montres Rolex S.A. (Rolex Geneva), located in Geneva, Switzerland. Bienne manufactures the watch movements and sells them to Rolex Geneva, which places them in casings and then distributes the watches worldwide. Rolex USA is wholly owned by the Wilsdorf Foundation, which also owns 86 percent of Rolex Geneva. Wilsdorf owns no shares of Bienne. Bienne has a five-member board of directors and seven officers, none of whom are officers or directors of Rolex Geneva, Rolex USA, or Wilsdorf.

Sam's Wholesale Club had 83 Rolex watches in its inventory. The watches, bearing the ROLEX trademark, were imported by Rolex Geneva and sold to Sam's without Rolex USA's permission. The Customs Service attempted to seize the 83 Rolex watches, but Sam's argued that the watches were not gray market goods illegally imported into the United States because Rolex USA is under common ownership of control of a foreign company owning the trademark abroad, an exception to trademark infringement. May the Customs Service seize the 83 Rolex watches?

6. Asturquimica, S.A., a Spanish company, exported potassium permanganate to the United States in 1985 and 1986. During 1986, the value of the Spanish peso appreciated 13 percent in relation to the American dollar. Asturquimica increased its export price by 6 percent, except to American buyers to whom it was contractually committed to sell at the 1985 price. The result was that Asturquimica sold potassium permanganate in the United States at prices from 7 to 13 percent below the price in Spain. Carus, an American competitor of Asturquimica, asked the International Trade Administration to impose a countervailing duty against Asturquimica. Did the ITA assess the duty?

7. In 1980, National Oil Corporation (NOC), a company owned by the Libyan government, and Libyan Sun Oil Co., a Delaware corporation, agreed to drill for oil in Libya. Their contract contained a *force majeure* clause and provided for arbitration of any dispute by the International Chamber of Commerce (ICC) in Paris. When the United States banned the importation into the United States of Libyan oil, Sun Oil notified NOC that the *force majeure* clause excused its future performance. NOC requested and obtained arbitration before the ICC, which held that the *force majeure* clause did not excuse Sun Oil and found Sun Oil liable to NOC for $20 million. NOC sought to enforce the award of the ICC in a U.S. federal district court. Did the American court enforce the ICC award?

8. Dessaleng Beyene, an American resident, agreed to sell two prefabricated houses to Mohammed Sofan, a resident of Yemen. Sofan obtained a letter of credit from a Yemen bank. The letter of credit was confirmed by Irving Trust Company in New York. Beyene shipped the houses to Sofan and received a bill of lading addressed to "Mohammed So*ran*." When Beyene presented the bill of lading to Irving Trust, it refused to pay Beyene's draft drawn against the letter of credit. Has Irving Trust acted properly?

9. Deutsche Shell contracted to deliver crude oil to Placid Refining Co's. refinery in Port Allen, Louisiana. The oil tanker left Scotland, crossing the Atlantic with no difficulty. On reaching the Mississippi River, a compulsory river pilot guided the tanker upstream. On June 5, the ship passed through shallow water and experienced a vibration, after which its 10-cm radar failed. The captain requested service for the 10-cm radar and also the 3-cm radar, which had a weak picture. Further upstream, the tanker encountered a storm and the 3-cm radar failed, leaving the tanker without any operational radar. The captain was able to make the 3-cm radar operate intermittently, but the pilot, fearing that the 3-cm radar might fail completely, leaving the tanker in shipping lanes without radar, refused to proceed and directed the ship to anchor. Because the Mississippi was at flood stage, before the anchors could hold, the current swept the ship downstream, where it went aground. After a week of salvage efforts, the tanker was refloated and delivered the oil to Placid's refinery. Deutsche Shell sued Placid under the doctrine of general average and a New Jason clause in the shipping contract. Placid defended on grounds that Deutsche Shell negligently maintained the 3-cm radar, resulting in its failure: for example, a service report three years before the accident indicated that the upper antenna's array ball bearing needed to be replaced, yet there was no evidence that the recommendation was followed; also, the radar manufacturer's instructions advised that the antenna array should be overhauled every second year, yet there was no evidence that this was done during the 10 years after the 3-cm radar was installed. The 3-cm radar failed because of water intrusion into its antenna/wavelength components. Did the court find Placid liable to Deutsche Shell?

10. Soon after the Fidel Castro regime came to power in Cuba, the Cuban socialist government expropriated four Cuban branches of the Chase Manhattan Bank. The value of the branches was $6.9 million. The Cuban government made no payment to Chase. At the same time, Chase sold for $17 million collateral it held securing $10 million of loans Chase made to two government-owned Cuban banks. Chase kept the $7 million excess proceeds. In addition, Chase refused to repay $2.5 million that the government-owned Cuban Banks had on deposit at Chase. Banco Nacional de Cuba, a government-owned Cuban bank and the successor of the two government-owned Cuban banks, sued Chase in a U.S. court to recover the $9.5 million. Will the recovery of Banco Nacional be reduced by the value of the Chase bank branches expropriated by the government?

FIFTY-THREE

Insurance

Insurance serves as a frequent topic of discussion in various contexts in today's society. Advertisements for companies offering life, automobile, and property insurance appear daily on television and in the print media. Journalists report on issues of health insurance coverage and movements for reform. Persons engaged in business publicly and privately lament the excessive (from their perspective) costs of obtaining liability insurance. Insurance companies and insurance industry critics offer differing explanations for why those costs have reached their present levels.

Despite the frequency with which insurance matters receive public discussion and the perceived importance of insurance coverage, major legal aspects of insurance relationships remain largely unfamiliar to many persons. This chapter, therefore, examines important components of insurance law. We begin by discussing the nature of insurance relationships and exploring contract law's application to insurance policies in general. We then discuss other legal concepts and issues associated with specific types of insurance, most notably property insurance, liability insurance, and life insurance.[1] The chapter concludes with an examination of an important judicial trend—allowing insurers to be held liable for compensatory and punitive damages if they refuse in bad faith to perform their policy obligations. ∽

---

[1]The chapter also contains a brief discussion of health insurance. Another frequently encountered type of insurance, title insurance, was discussed in Chapter 24.

NATURE AND BENEFITS OF INSURANCE RELATIONSHIPS

Insurance relationships arise from an agreement under which a risk of loss that one party (normally the **insured**) otherwise would have to bear is shifted to another party (the **insurer**). The ability to obtain insurance enables the insured to lessen or avoid the adverse financial effects that would be likely if certain happenings were to take place. In return for the insured's payment of necessary consideration (the **premium**), the insurer agrees to shoulder the financial consequences stemming from particular risks if those risks should materialize in the form of actual events.

Each party presumably benefits from the insurance relationship. The insured obtains a promise of coverage for losses that, if they materialize, could easily exceed the amounts of the premiums paid. Along with this promise, the insured acquires the supposed "peace of mind" that insurance companies and agents like to emphasize. By collecting premiums from many insureds over a substantial period of time, the insurer stands to profit despite its obligation to make payments covering financial losses that stem from insured-against risks. The insured-against risks, after all, are just that: risks. In some instances, events triggering the insurer's payment obligation to a particular insured may never occur (e.g., the insured's property never sustains damage from a cause contemplated by the property insurance policy). The insurer nonetheless remains entitled to the premiums collected during the policy period. Other times, events that call the insurer's payment obligation into play in a given situation may occur infrequently (e.g., a particular insured under an automobile insurance policy has an accident only every few years) or only after many years of premium collection (e.g., an insured paid premiums on his life insurance policy for 35 years prior to his death).

INSURANCE POLICIES AS CONTRACTS

Interested Parties

Regardless of the type of insurance involved, the insurance relationship is fundamentally contractual. This relationship involves at least two—and frequently more than two—interested parties. As noted earlier, the insurer (usually a corporation), in exchange for the payment of consideration (the premium), agrees to pay for losses caused by specific events (sometimes called *perils*). The insured is the person who acquires insurance on real or personal property or insurance against liability, or, in the case of life or health insurance, the person whose life or health is the focus of the policy. The person to whom the insurance proceeds are payable is the **beneficiary.** Except in the case of life insurance, the insured and the beneficiary will often be the same person. In most but not all instances, the insured will also be the **owner** of the policy (the person entitled to exercise the contract rights set out in the insurance policy and in applicable law). In view of the contractual nature of the insurance relationship, insurance policies must satisfy all of the elements required for a binding contract.

Offer, Acceptance, and Consideration

The insurance industry's standard practice is to have the potential insured make an offer for an insurance contract by completing and submitting an application (provided by the insurer's agent), along with the appropriate premium, to the insurer. The insurer may then either accept or reject this offer. If the insurer accepts, the parties have an insurance contract under which the insured's initial premium payment and future premium payments furnish consideration for the insurer's promises of coverage for designated risks, and vice versa.

What constitutes acceptance of the offer set forth in the application may vary somewhat, depending on the type of insurance requested and the language of the application. As a general rule, however, acceptance occurs when the insurer (or agent, if authorized to do so) indicates to the insured an intent to accept the application. It is important to know the precise time when an acceptance occurs, because the insurer's contractual obligations to the insured do not commence until acceptance has taken place. If the insured sustains losses after the submission of the application (the making of the offer) but prior to an acceptance by the insurer, those losses normally must be borne by the insured rather than the insurer.

With property insurance and sometimes other types of insurance, the application may be worded

FIGURE   I

Creation of an Insurance Contract

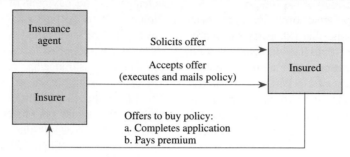

so that insurance coverage begins when the insured signs the application. This arrangement provides temporary coverage until the insurer either accepts or rejects the offer contained in the application. The same result may also be achieved by the use of a *binder,* an agreement for temporary insurance pending the insurer's decision to accept or reject the risk.

Figure 1 depicts the formation of an insurance contract.

Insurer's Delay in Acting on Application   A common insurance law problem is the effect of the insurer's delay in acting on the application. If the applicant suffers a loss after applying but before a delaying insurer formally accepts, who must bear the loss? As a general rule, the insurer's delay does not constitute acceptance. Some states, however, have held that an insurer's retention of the premium for an unreasonable time constitutes acceptance and hence obligates the insurer to cover the insured's loss.

Other states have allowed negligence suits against insurers for delaying unreasonably in acting on an application. The theory of these cases is that insurance companies have a public duty to insure qualified applicants and that an unreasonable delay prevents applicants from obtaining insurance protection from another source. A few states have enacted statutes establishing that insurers are bound to the insurance contract unless they reject the prospective insured's application within a specified period of time.

Effect of Insured's Misrepresentation

Applicants for insurance have a duty to reveal to insurers all the material (significant) facts about the nature of the risk so that the insurer may make an intelligent decision about whether to accept the risk.

When an insurance application includes a false statement by the insured regarding a material matter, the insured's misrepresentation, if relied on by the insurer, has the same effect produced by misrepresentation in connection with other contracts—the contract becomes voidable at the election of the insurer. This means that the insurer may avoid its obligations under the policy. The same result is possible if the insured failed, in the application, to disclose known material facts to the insurer, which issued a policy it would not have issued if the disclosures had been made. (As will be seen later in the chapter, however, certain clauses frequently appearing in life insurance policies may limit the ability of issuers of such policies to use the insured's misrepresentation as a way of avoiding all obligations under the policy.)

Warranty/Representation Distinction   It sometimes becomes important to distinguish between **warranties** and representations that the insured makes (usually in the application) to induce the insurer to issue an insurance policy. Warranties are *express terms in the insurance policy.* They are intended to operate as conditions on which the insurer's liability is based. The insured's breach of warranty terminates the insurer's duty to perform under the policy. For example, a property insurance policy on a commercial office building specifies that the insured must install and maintain a working sprinkler system in the building, but the insured never installs the sprinkler system. The sprinkler system requirement is a warranty, which the insured breached by failing to install the system. This means that the insurer may not be obligated to perform its obligations under the policy.

Traditionally, an insured's breach of warranty has been seen as terminating the insurer's duty to perform *regardless of whether the condition set forth in the breached warranty was actually material to the insurer's risk* (unlike the treatment given to the insured's misrepresentations, which do not make the insurance policy voidable unless they pertained to a material matter). In view of the potential harshness of the traditional rule concerning the effect of a breach of warranty, some states have refused to allow insurers to escape liability on breach of warranty grounds unless the condition contemplated by the breached warranty was indeed material.

Capacity of Parties

Generally speaking, a contract is not enforceable unless both parties to it had the legal capacity to bind themselves to an agreement. This is seldom a problem in the insurance context, whose typical contracting parties—a corporation and an adult—clearly would have capacity in nearly all instances. An insurance policy taken out by a minor may sometimes be treated differently, due to the usual rule that a minor's lack of capacity makes the minor's contract voidable at the election of the minor.[2] For purposes of the insurance setting, however, many states have departed from the usual rule by enacting statutes that make the insurance contracts of minors enforceable against them.

Legality

The law distinguishes between unlawful wagering contracts and valid insurance contracts. A wagering contract creates a new risk that did not previously exist. Such a contract is contrary to public policy and therefore illegal. An insurance contract, however, *transfers existing risks*—a permissible, even desirable, economic activity. A major means by which insurance law separates insurance contracts from wagering contracts is the typical requirement that the party who purchases a policy of property or life insurance must possess an **insurable interest** in the property or life being insured. Specific discussion of the insurable interest requirement appears in this chapter's later sections on property and life insurance.

Form and Content of Insurance Contracts

Writing   State law governs whether insurance contracts are within the statute of frauds and must be evidenced by a writing. Some states require specific types of insurance contracts to be in writing. Contracts for property insurance are not usually within the statute of frauds, meaning that they may be either written or oral unless they come within some general provision of the statute of frauds—for example, the "one-year" provision.[3] Even when a writing is not legally required, however, wisdom dictates that the parties reduce their agreement to written form whenever possible.

Reformation of Written Policy   As one would expect, insurance companies' customary practice is to issue written policies of insurance regardless of whether the applicable statute of frauds requires a writing. An argument sometimes raised by insureds is that the written policy issued by the insurer did not accurately reflect the content of the parties' actual agreement. For instance, after the occurrence of a loss for which the insured thought there was coverage under the insurance contract, the insured learns that the loss-causing event was excluded from coverage by the terms expressly stated in the written policy. In such a situation, the insured may be inclined to argue that the written policy should be judicially **reformed,** so as to make it conform to the parties' supposed actual agreement.

Although reformation is available in appropriate cases, courts normally presume that the written policy of insurance should be treated as the embodiment of the parties' actual agreement. Courts consider reformation an extreme remedy. Hence, they usually refuse to grant reformation unless either of two circumstances is present. The first reformation-triggering circumstance exists when the insured and the insurer, through its agent or agents, were *mutually mistaken* about a supposedly covered event or other supposed contract term (i.e., both parties believed an event was covered by, or some other term was part of, the parties' insurance agreement but the written policy indicated otherwise). The alternative route to reformation calls for proof that the insurer committed fraud as to the terms contained in the policy or otherwise engaged in inequitable

---

[2]An insurance contract taken out on the life of a minor (the insured) *by an adult* (the owner) is not voidable, however. Only when the minor is the owner of the policy does the usual concern over the minor's lack of capacity come into play.

[3]The usual provisions of the statute of frauds are discussed in detail in Chapter 16.

conduct. *Ridenour v. Farm Bureau Insurance Co.*, which follows, illustrates the judicial presumption that the written policy sets forth the parties' true agreement. The case also confirms that the insured's unilateral mistake—as opposed to the parties' mutual mistake—about policy terms will not warrant reformation.

RIDENOUR v. FARM BUREAU INSURANCE COMPANY   377 N.W.2d 101 (Neb. Sup. Ct. 1985)

I n August 1982, a hog confinement building owned by Charles Ridenour collapsed and was rendered a total loss. Some of Ridenour's hogs were killed as a further result of the collapse. Ridenour made a claim for these losses with his property insurer, Farm Bureau Insurance Company, whose Country Squire policy had been issued on Ridenour's property in July 1977 and had been renewed on a yearly basis after that. Farm Bureau denied the claim because the policy did not provide coverage for the collapse of farm buildings such as the hog confinement structure. Moreover, though the policy provided coverage for hog deaths resulting from certain designated causes, collapse of a building was not among the causes listed. Asserting that the parties' insurance contract was to have covered the peril of building collapse notwithstanding the terms of the written policy, Ridenour sued Farm Bureau. He asked the court to order reformation of the written policy so that it would conform to the parties' supposed agreement regarding coverage.

At trial, Ridenour testified about a February 1982 meeting in which he, his wife, and their son discussed insurance coverage with Farm Bureau agent Tim Moomey. Ridenour testified that he wanted to be certain there was insurance coverage if the hog confinement building collapsed because he had heard about the collapse of a similar structure owned by someone else. Therefore, he asked Moomey whether the Country Squire policy then in force provided such coverage. According to Ridenour, Moomey said that it did. Ridenour's wife, Thelma, testified that she asked Moomey (during the same meeting) whether there would be coverage if the floor slats of the hog confinement building collapsed and caused hogs to fall into the pit below the building. According to her testimony, Moomey responded affirmatively. The Ridenours' son, Tom, testified to the same effect. Mr. and Mrs. Ridenour both testified that they had not completely read the Country Squire policy and that because they did not understand the wording, they relied on Moomey to interpret the policy for them.

Moomey, who had ended his relationship with Farm Bureau by the time the case came to trial, testified that at no time did the Ridenours request that the hogs and the confinement building be insured so as to provide coverage for losses resulting from collapse of the building. Moomey knew that collapse coverage was not available from Farm Bureau for hog confinement buildings. In addition, Moomey testified that he met with Ridenour in April 1982 and conducted a "farm review" in which he discussed a coverage checklist and the Country Squire policy's declarations pages (which set forth the policy limits). This checklist, which Ridenour signed after Moomey reviewed it with him, made no reference to coverage for collapse losses. (Ridenour admitted in his testimony that he had signed the checklist after Moomey read off the listed items to him.) When Moomey was contacted by the Ridenours on the day the building collapsed, he had his secretary prepare a notice of loss report for submission to Farm Bureau. He also assigned an adjuster to inspect the property. Moomey and the adjuster discussed the fact that the Country Squire policy did not provide coverage for Ridenour's losses. Ridenour further testified that the day after the collapse occurred, Moomey told him he was sorry but that Farm Bureau's home office had said there was no coverage.

The trial court granted reformation, as Ridenour had requested. Farm Bureau appealed. ∽

Caporale, Judge   The principle upon which Ridenour relies is that reformation is decreed in order to effectuate the real agreement of the parties when a written instrument does not represent their true intent. In this jurisdiction reformation may be decreed where there has been a mutual mistake or where there has been a unilateral mistake caused by the fraud or in-equitable conduct of the other party. To obtain reformation the evidence must be clear, convincing, and satisfactory. Such evidence is present when there has been produced in the trier of fact a firm belief or conviction that a fact to be proved exists. Moreover, there is a strong presumption that a written instrument correctly expresses the intention of the parties to it.

The record does not produce in us a firm belief or conviction that there was a mutual mistake of fact. Moomey was a trained and experienced insurance agent who, after he had no relationship with Farm Bureau, testified he knew the coverage claimed by Ridenour was not available from Farm Bureau and who denied representing that such coverage existed under the policy. Ridenour argues that Moomey's expression of sorrow over the fact that Farm Bureau's home office said there was no coverage, coupled with the facts that he caused a notice of loss report to be prepared and arranged for an adjuster to inspect the property, establishes that Moomey did think collapse coverage for the hog building existed. We conclude otherwise. Prudence dictated that Ridenour's claim be noted and investigated. Investigation of this claim to determine the facts does not imply a thought that coverage exists. Neither does an expression of regret that the home office said coverage does not exist necessarily imply an earlier belief by Moomey that there was coverage. It may as easily imply regret at the confirmation of what Moomey already knew.

Any mistake which may have existed was therefore one made only by Ridenour. Under such a circumstance he must, in order to recover, clearly, convincingly, and satisfactorily establish that the mistake was either the result of fraud on the part of Farm Bureau or due to Farm Bureau's inequitable conduct. Ridenour concedes in his brief that there was no fraud, but argues that Farm Bureau engaged in inequitable conduct by not delivering the declarations pages until after the loss. The late delivery of the declarations pages is more than adequately explained, however, by the fact that Ridenour was tardy in paying his premium. Moreover, since Ridenour admits that he did not read the policy, he cannot be heard to complain that not having the declarations pages deprived him of an opportunity to discover that he had no collapse coverage on his hog confinement building.

The nature of the conflict in the evidence in this case is not unlike that present in . . . earlier cases which resulted in a denial of reformation. [In addition,] the principal cases relied upon by Ridenour in which reformation was decreed are distinguishable from the case presently before us [because in each of the cases cited by Ridenour, the insured and the insurer's agent both testified that the agent made coverage assumptions and representations that were inconsistent with the terms of the written policy]. Indeed, in [those cases] there was no evidentiary conflict as to what the agent represented; consequently, the only conclusion which could have been reached was that there had been a mutual mistake. In the case before us, however, the evidence falls short of overcoming the presumption that the policy as written correctly expresses the intention of the parties at the time it was renewed.

Judgment and decree of reformation reversed in favor of Farm Bureau.

Interpretation of Insurance Contracts   Modern courts realize that many persons who buy insurance do not have the training or background to fully understand the technical language often contained in insurance policies. As a result, courts tend to interpret insurance policy provisions as they would be understood by an average person. In addition, courts construe ambiguities in an insurance contract against the insurer, the drafter of the contract (and hence the user of the ambiguous language). This rule of construction means that if a word or phrase used in an insurance policy is equally subject to two possible interpretations, one of which favors the insurer and the other of which favors the insured, the court will adopt the interpretation that favors the insured. The *Cope* case, which follows shortly, illustrates the application of this rule of construction to an ambiguous provision in a liability insurance policy.

A number of states purport to follow the *reasonable expectations of the insured* approach to interpretation of insurance policies. Analysis of judicial decisions reveals, however, that this approach's content and effect vary among the states ostensibly subscribing to it. Some states do little more than attach the reasonable expectations label to the familiar principles of interpretation set forth in the preceding paragraph. A few states give the reasonable expectations approach a much more significant effect by allowing courts to effectively read clauses into or out of an insurance policy, depending on whether reasonable persons in the position of the insured would have expected such clauses to be in a policy of the sort at issue. When applied in the latter manner, the reasonable expectations approach tends to resemble reformation in its effect.

P roperty Owners Insurance Co. (POI) was the insurer and Thomas Cope was the insured under a liability policy that excluded coverage except in instances of liability "with respect to the conduct of a business" owned by Cope. Cope owned a roofing business. While the policy was in force, Cope traveled to Montana with Edward Urbanski, a person with whom Cope did significant business. While on this trip, Cope snowmobiled with a group of persons that included Gregory Johnson, who died in a snowmobiling accident. Johnson's estate brought a wrongful death suit against Cope in a Montana court. POI then filed a declaratory judgment action against Cope and Johnson's estate in the U.S. District Court for the Northern District of Indiana. In this suit, POI sought a judicial determination that it had no obligations to Cope and Johnson's estate under the liability insurance policy. The parties agreed that Indiana law would control the case, which came before the court on POI's motion for summary judgment. ∽

Moody, District Judge POI maintains that the Montana snowmobiling trip was a recreational event rather than "the conduct of a business" owned by Cope. Thus, argues POI, the Montana trip was not covered by the insurance contract. Cope, however, maintains that he intended the Montana trip to advance both business and pleasure, thus bringing it under the policy.

The parties have not briefed, nor has the court found, any Indiana law interpreting the words "conduct of a business" in the context of an exclusion in a contract to provide liability insurance to a business owner. The closest reported case is apparently *Unigard Mutual Insurance Co. v. Martin* (1982), [an Arizona Court of Appeals case] cited by POI. The evidence before the *Martin* court showed that the object of a large annual fishing trip was both recreation and the advancement of business. The *Martin* court . . . focused on the express terms of the [liability] insurance contract. [Noting that the fishing trip was heavily recreational but only incidentally business-connected, and stressing the policy's exclusion for "personal" activities that were not in "direct conduct of a business," the *Martin* court held that the policy at issue did not afford coverage.]

Applying *Martin* to this case, the court readily distinguishes the Arizona precedent on its facts. The *Martin* court relied heavily on [the] particular wording [of the policy involved there] in making its most important analytical point—namely, that the insurance contract was not ambiguous, but plainly excluded the fishing trip by its express terms. The *Martin* court focused especially on the words "direct conduct" in the exclusion before it, defining each word at length, and with particular emphasis on the word "direct." In the case at bar, the contract

language is different, the limitation on coverage arising by negative implication from the words "only with respect to the conduct of a business." The word "direct" does not modify "conduct" in this case, nor does the contract expressly contrast personal and business activities. Accordingly, the *Martin* case does not present a perfect template for dealing with this action.

Whether or not the *Martin* court properly read the contract before it as unambiguous, the policy issue before this court is not resolved by the familiar Indiana rule that where an insurance contract is clear and unambiguous, the language therein must be given its plain meaning. [T]his court holds that the words "with respect to the conduct of a business" are, in this context, not sufficiently self-defining in their plain meaning. Rather, those words are ambiguous and require construction because reasonable persons might well differ on the question of whether they exclude coverage for activities furthering dual purposes of recreation and profit.

[U]nder settled principles for the interpretation of ambiguous insurance contracts . . . , this court construes the policy in favor of the insured. Thus, the court holds that the language of the contract before it does not exclude, as a matter of law, coverage for activities that serve dual purposes of recreation and profit. If insurance companies operating in Indiana desire the benefit of such an exclusion, it is a simple enough matter for them to draft their policies to unambiguously exclude coverage for recreational activities furthering business objectives.

In this case, the record on summary judgment reveals a genuine dispute over the factual nature of the Montana snowmobiling trip. This dispute is certainly material, for the factual nature of the trip will, under the express terms of the contract at issue, determine the applicability of the policy's limit on liability. It remains, however, for the court to further explore the materiality of that dispute by detailing the applicable legal standard for assessing the facts. The *Martin* court, in this regard, paints an alarming picture of insurer liability leaping up in extreme situations, perhaps even with chance meetings at Little League games. On the other hand, if hypotheticals are brought to bear, this court can readily imagine a far different situation at the other extreme, one in which a business executive who enjoys his solitude, loathes the boors to whom he must sell his product, and hopes to retire at the earliest possible moment, must nevertheless occasionally invite customers to cocktails or sporting events for the purely fictional purpose of having fun. The *Martin* court, apparently concerned with the dubious horrors of the slippery slope, seems inclined to create a bright line rule denying coverage in both situations. Given the ambiguity in the contract at issue here, however, this court is prepared to seek out a test in the law capable of discriminating among situations of mixed profit and recreation motives.

Cope advances the workmen's compensation test applied in Indiana law for many years: [whether] the activity at issue was "required by or incidental to" the insured's business. The *Martin* court rejected this type of test because the liberal coverage policy motivating workmen's compensation statutes is not at play in a private insurance contract. In this case, however, the contract is ambiguous, which brings to bear Indiana's policy of construing insurance exclusions against insurers. Thus, a significant policy of Indiana insurance law—already employed in construing the contract to cover mixed motive activities—parallels the expansive coverage policy motivating workmen's compensation, and justifies application of the same test. Accordingly, this court holds that the test for coverage under the "conduct of a business" policy at issue is whether Cope's Montana snowmobiling trip was necessary or incidental to the pursuit of profit through his business.

Of course, nothing in this opinion should be read as establishing that the Montana snowmobiling trip was sufficiently related to the insured's business to support a jury verdict of liability under the policy. Rather, this opinion merely establishes Cope's right to present evidence against exclusion at trial.

POI's motion for summary judgment denied.

Clauses Required by Law The insurance business is highly regulated by the states, which recognize the importance of the interests protected by insurance and the difference in bargaining power that often exists between insurers and their insureds. In an attempt to remedy this imbalance, many states' statutes and insurance regulations require the inclusion of certain standard clauses in insurance policies. Many states also regulate such matters as the size and style of the print used in insurance policies. Laws in a growing number of states encourage or require the use of plain, straightforward language (rather than insurance jargon and legal terms of art) in policies whenever such language is possible to use.

Notice and Proof of Loss-Causing Event The insured (or, in the case of life insurance, the beneficiary) who seeks to obtain the benefits or protection provided by an insurance policy must notify the insurer that an event covered by the policy has occurred. In addition, the insured (or the benefi-

ciary) must furnish reasonable proof of the loss-causing event. Property insurance policies, for instance, ordinarily require the insured to furnish a sworn statement (called a *proof of loss*) in which the covered event and the resulting damage to the insured's property are described. Under life insurance policies, the beneficiary is usually expected to provide suitable documentation of the fact that the insured person has died. Liability insurance policies call for the insured to give the insurer copies of liability claims made against the insured.

Time Limits Insurance policies commonly specify that notice and proof of loss must be given within a specified time. Policies sometimes state that compliance with these requirements is a condition of the insured's recovery and that failure to comply terminates the insurer's obligation. Other times, policies merely provide that failure to comply suspends the insurer's duty to pay until proper compliance occurs. Some courts require the insurer to prove it was harmed by the insured's failure to give notice before allowing the insurer to avoid liability on the ground of tardy notice.

Cancellation and Lapse   When a party with the power to terminate an insurance policy (extinguish all rights under the policy) exercises that power, **cancellation** has occurred. **Lapse** occurs at the end of the term specified in a policy written for a stated duration, unless the parties take action to renew the policy for an additional period of time. Alternatively, lapse may occur as a result of the insured's failure to pay premiums or some other significant default on the part of the insured. Special issues regarding cancellation and lapse of property and life insurance will be discussed later in the chapter.

Third Parties and Insurance Contracts   As a general rule, contracts are assignable only when the assignment will not materially alter the promisor's burden of performance. The insured's identity, character, and traits are important elements of the risk in property, life, health, and liability insurance policies. Therefore, such policies are generally nonassignable. It is also common for insurance policies to contain express restrictions on assignability. After a loss covered by an insurance policy has occurred, however, the insured may normally assign to another party the right to receive benefits under the policy. Such an assignment is permissible because it involves no change in the insurer's risk.

Performance and Breach by Insurer

The insurer performs its obligations by paying out the sums (and taking other related actions) contemplated by the policy's terms within a reasonable time after the occurrence of an event that calls the duty to perform into play. If the insurer fails or refuses to pay despite the occurrence of a payment-triggering event, the insured of course may sue the insurer for breach of contract. By proving that the insurer's denial of the insured's claim for payment constituted a breach, the insured becomes entitled to recover compensatory damages in at least the amount that the insurer would have had to pay under the policy if the insurer had not breached.

What if the insurer's breach caused the insured to incur consequential damages that, when added to the amount due under the policy, would lead to a damages claim exceeding the dollar limits set forth in the policy? Assume that XYZ Computer Sales,

Inc.'s store building is covered by a property insurance policy with Secure Insurance Co., that the building is destroyed by an accidental fire (a covered peril), and that the extent of the destruction makes the full $300,000 policy limit owing from Secure to XYZ. Secure, however, denies payment because it believes—erroneously—that XYZ officials committed arson (a cause, if it had been the actual one, that would have relieved Secure from any duty to pay). Because it needs to rebuild and take other related steps to stay in business but is short on available funds due to Secure's denial of its claim, XYZ borrows the necessary funds from a bank. XYZ thereby incurs substantial interest costs, which are consequential damages XYZ would not have occurred if Secure had performed its obligation under the policy. Assuming that XYZ's consequential damages would have been foreseeable to Secure, most states would allow XYZ to recover the consequential damages in addition to the amount due from Secure under the policy.[4] This is so even though the addition of the consequential damages would cause XYZ's damages recovery to exceed the dollar limit set forth in the parties' insurance policy. The breaching insurer's liability may exceed the policy limits despite the insurer's good faith (though incorrect) basis for denying the claim, because a good faith but erroneous refusal to pay is nonetheless a breach of contract. If the insurer could point to the policy limits as a maximum recovery in this type of situation, it would have an all-too-convenient means of avoiding responsibility for harms that logically flowed from its breach of contract.

Due to similar reasoning, many states' laws provide that if an insured successfully sues her insurer for amounts due under the policy, the insured may recover interest on those amounts (amounts that, after all, should have been paid by

---

[4]Even though the terms of the insurance policy almost certainly would state that Secure's payment obligation is limited to costs of repair or replacement or to the property's actual cash value—that is, without any coverage for consequential harms experienced by the insured—Secure cannot invoke this policy language as a defense. If Secure had performed its contract obligation, its payment obligation would have been restricted to what the policy provided in that regard. Having breached the insurance contract, however, Secure stands potentially liable for consequential damages to the full extent provided for by general contract law. For additional discussion of damages for breach of contract, see Chapter 18.

the insurer much sooner and without litigation). Some states also have statutes providing that insureds who successfully sue insurers are entitled to awards of attorney's fees. Punitive damages are *not* allowed, however, when the insurer's breach of contract consisted of a *good faith (though erroneous) denial* of the insured's claim. Later in this chapter, we will explore the recent judicial trend toward allowing punitive damages when the insurer's breach was in *bad faith* and thus amounted to the tort of bad faith breach of contract.

PROPERTY INSURANCE

Owners of residential and commercial property always face the possibility that their property might be damaged or destroyed by any number of causes beyond their control. These causes include, to name a few notable ones, fire, lightning, hail, and wind. Although property owners may not be able to prevent harm to their property, they can secure some protection against resulting financial loss by contracting for property insurance and thereby transferring certain risks of loss to the insurer. Certain persons holding property interests that fall short of ownership may likewise seek to benefit, as will be seen, from the risk-shifting feature of property insurance.

The Insurable Interest Requirement

As noted earlier in this chapter, in order for a property insurance contract not to be considered an illegal wagering contract, the person who purchases the policy (the policy owner) must have an **insurable interest** in the property being insured. One has an insurable interest if he, she, or it possesses a legal or equitable interest in the property and that interest translates into an economic stake in the continued existence of the property and the preservation of its condition. In other words, a person has an insurable interest if he would suffer a financial loss in the event of harm to the subject property. If no insurable interest is present, the policy is void.

Examples of Insurable Interest   The legal owner of the insured property would obviously have an insurable interest. So might other parties whose legal or equitable interests in the property do not rise to the level of an ownership interest. For example, mortgagees and other lienholders would have insurable interests in the property on which they hold liens.[5] A nonexhaustive list of other examples would also include holders of life estates in real property, buyers under as-yet unperformed contracts for the sale of real property, and lessees of real estate.[6] In the types of situations just noted, the interested party stands to lose financially if the property is damaged or destroyed. *Crowell v. Delafield Farmers Mutual Fire Insurance Company,* which follows shortly, provides a further example of a property interest substantial enough to amount to an insurable interest.

Timing and Extent of Insurable Interest   A sensible and important corollary of the insurable interest principle is that the requisite insurable interest must exist *at the time of the loss* (i.e., at the time the subject property was damaged). If an insurable interest existed when the holder thereof purchased the property insurance but the interest was no longer present when the loss occurred, the policy owner is not entitled to payment for the loss. This would mean, for example, that a property owner who purchased property insurance would not be entitled to collect from the insurer for property damage that occurred after she had transferred ownership to someone else. Similarly, a lienholder who purchased property insurance could not collect under the policy if the loss took place after his lien had been extinguished by payment of the underlying debt or by another means.

The extent of a person's insurable interest in property is limited to the value of that interest. For example, Fidelity Savings & Loan extends Williams a $95,000 loan to purchase a home and takes a mortgage on the home as security. In order to protect this investment, Fidelity obtains a $95,000 insurance policy on the property. Several years later, the house is destroyed by fire, a cause triggering the insurer's payment obligation. At the time of the fire, the balance due on the loan is $84,000. Fidelity's recovery under the insurance policy is limited to $84,000, because that amount is the full extent of its

---

[5]Chapter 27 contains a detailed discussion of security interests in real property. Chapter 28 addresses security interests in personal property.

[6]Chapter 24 contains a discussion of life estates and an examination of contracts for the sale of real property. Leases of real estate are explored in Chapter 25.

insurable interest. (An alternative way by which mortgagees protect their interest is to insist that the property owner list the mortgagee as the *loss payee* under the property owner's policy. This means that if the property is destroyed, the insurer will pay the policy proceeds to the mortgagee. Once again, however, the mortgagee's entitlement to payment under this approach would be limited to the dollar value of its insurable interest, with surplus proceeds going to the insured property owner.)

CROWELL v. DELAFIELD FARMERS MUTUAL FIRE INSURANCE COMPANY   453 N.W.2d 724 (Minn. Ct. App. 1990)

Earl and Vonette Crowell owned and operated a farm in Cottonwood County, Minnesota. In 1980, the Crowells took out a mortgage on the property with Farm Credit Services. They also took out a fire insurance policy with Delafield Farmers Mutual Insurance Company. This policy ran from October 1985 until October 1988. The Crowells failed to make their mortgage payments and Farm Credit began foreclosure proceedings. Upon foreclosure, mortgagors such as the Crowells have a right of redemption for a specified time, during which they have the right to buy back their property after it has been sold to another. In November 1987, the Crowells' right of redemption ended. Under Minnesota law, however, farmers who lose their farms to corporate lenders are given an additional opportunity to repurchase their farms under a "right of first refusal." This right meant that Farm Credit was forbidden to sell the farm to anyone else before offering it to the Crowells at a price no higher than the highest price offered by a third party. Farm Credit allowed the Crowells to remain on the farm while they tried to secure financing to buy the property under their right of first refusal.

On November 27, 1987, the farmhouse was substantially destroyed by fire. The Crowells filed a claim for the loss with Delafield. Delafield paid the claim on the Crowells' personal effects inside the house, but denied the claim on the structure itself. It claimed that since the Crowells' period of redemption had expired, they no longer had an insurable interest in the farmhouse. The Crowells brought suit. When the trial court granted summary judgment for the Crowells, Delafield appealed. ∞

Kalitowski, Judge   To be entitled to recovery for a loss, an insured must have an insurable interest in the property covered by the policy. To have an insurable interest, the party must suffer a loss of property interest that is substantial and real. A person has an insurable interest in property when the relationship between him and the property is such that he has a reasonable expectation, based upon a real or legal right, of benefit to be derived from the continued existence of the property and of loss or liability from its destruction. The Minnesota Supreme Court has stated that it is not necessary that the insured should have an absolute right of property, and that he has an insurable interest if, by the destruction of the property, he will suffer a loss, whether he has or has not any title to, lien upon, or possession of the property itself.

Farm Credit foreclosed on the Crowells' farm mortgage. The Crowells remained on and continued to operate the farm. After the redemption period, Farm Credit became the absolute owner of the property. The record indicates Farm Credit allowed the Crowells to remain on the farm after the re-

demption period expired because it was involved in the Crowells' effort to secure financing to enable them to exercise their statutory right of first refusal. In addition, Farm Credit did not purchase and the Crowells did not cancel fire insurance on the property.

By creating a right of first refusal, the legislature gave financially distressed farmers who had lost their farms to corporate lenders an opportunity to repurchase the farms. The legislative purpose of this right of first refusal is to encourage and protect the family farm as a basic economic unit, to insure it as the most socially desirable mode of agricultural production, and to enhance and promote the stability and well-being of rural society in Minnesota and the nuclear family.

This right of first refusal gives family farmers some additional right or interest in the property they lost to corporate lenders. Based on this legal right in the property, the Crowells had a reasonable expectation to derive a benefit from the continued existence of the farmhouse. Although the Crowells no longer had title to the farm, they were allowed to remain on the land with all parties' knowledge and intention that they would exercise their right of first refusal and regain the farm. Therefore, they expected the benefit of living in the farmhouse until they exercised that right.

It is clear the Crowells suffered a loss from the destruction of the farmhouse. Since the fire the Crowells have been unable to live in the farmhouse. This situation forces the Crowells to live several miles from their farm and commute between their home and the farm, causing additional expenses and inconvenience. The advantage of living on the farm is clearly lost.

Under the facts of this case we hold the trial court was correct in holding this right gave the Crowells an insurable interest in the farm and its structures.

Judgment for the Crowells affirmed.

Covered and Excluded Perils

Property insurers usually do not undertake to provide coverage for losses stemming from any and all causes of harm to property. Instead, property insurers tend to either specify certain causes (**covered perils**) as to which the insured *will* receive payment for resulting losses—meaning that there is no coverage regarding a peril not specified—or set forth a seemingly broad statement of coverage but then specify certain perils concerning which there will be *no* payment for losses (**excluded perils**). (Sometimes, property insurers employ a combination of these two approaches by specifying certain covered perils and certain excluded perils.)

Typical Covered Perils   The effects of these approaches are essentially the same, as most property insurers tend to provide coverage for the same sorts of causes of harm to property. The perils concerning which property insurance policies typically provide benefits include fire, lightning, hail, and wind. In addition, property insurance policies often cover harms to property resulting from causes such as the impact of an automobile or aircraft (e.g., an automobile or aircraft crashes into an insured building), vandalism, certain collapses of buildings, and certain accidental discharges or overflows from pipes or heating and air-conditioning systems.

Fire as a Covered Peril   Historically, the importance of coverage against the peril of fire made *fire insurance* a commonly used term. Various insurance companies incorporated the term into their official firm name; the policies these companies issued came to be called *fire insurance policies* even when they covered perils in addition to fire (as policies increasingly have done in this century). As a result, judges, commentators, and persons affiliated with the insurance industry will sometimes refer to today's policies as fire insurance policies despite the usual property insurer's tendency to cover not only fire but also some combination of the other perils mentioned in the preceding paragraph. Whether the term used is *property insurance* (generally employed in this chapter) or *fire insurance,* reference is being made to the same type of policy.

Fire-related losses covered by property insurance policies are those resulting from accidental fires. An accidental fire is one other than a fire deliberately set by, or at the direction of, the insured for the purpose of damaging the property. In other words, the insured obtains no coverage for losses stemming from the insured's act of arson. This commonsense restriction on an insurer's duty to pay for losses also applies to other harms the insured deliberately caused to his property.

For purposes of fire coverage, insurance contracts often distinguish between *friendly fires,* which are those contained in a place intended for a fire (such as fires in a woodstove or fireplace), and *hostile fires,* which burn where no fire is intended to be (such as fires caused by lightning, outside sources, electrical shorts, or those that began as friendly fires but escaped their boundaries). Losses caused by hostile fires are covered; those stemming from friendly fires tend not to be. As a general rule, covered fire losses may extend beyond direct damage caused by the fire. Indirect damage caused by smoke and heat is usually covered, as is damage caused by firefighters in their attempts to put out the fire.

Typical Excluded Perils   Although flood-related harm to property may seem similar to harm stemming from some of the weather-related causes listed earlier among the typical covered perils, it does not usually receive the same treatment. Property insurance policies frequently exclude coverage for flood damage. On this point, however, as with other questions regarding perils covered or excluded, the actual language of the policy at issue must always be consulted before a coverage issue is resolved in any given case.[7] Other typical exclusions include earthquake damage and harm to property stemming from war or nuclear reaction, radiation, or contamination. As previously indicated, property insurance policies exclude coverage for losses caused by the insured's deliberate actions that were intended to cause harm to the property.

Additional Coverages   Even as to perils for which there may not be coverage in the typical property insurance policy, the property owner may sometimes be able to purchase a specialized policy (e.g., a flood insurance policy) that does afford coverage for such perils. Other times, even if coverage for a given peril is not provided by the terms of most standard property insurance policies, it may nonetheless be possible for the property owner to have coverage for that peril added to the policy by paying an additional premium. This is sometimes done, for example, by policy owners who desire earthquake coverage.

Personal Property Insurance   Although the broad term *property insurance* is what has been employed, the discussion so far in this section has centered around policies providing coverage for harm to *real* property. Items of *personal* property are, of course, insurable as well. Property insurance policies commonly known as homeowners' policies—because the real property serving as the policy's primary subject is the insured's dwelling—cover not only harm to the dwelling but also to personal property located inside the dwelling or otherwise on the subject real property. (Sometimes, depending on the policy language, there may be coverage even when the item of personal property was not located at the designated real property when the item was damaged.) Property insurance policies

covering office buildings and other commercial real estate often provide some level of personal property coverage as well. When personal property coverage is included in a policy primarily concerned with real property coverage, the perils insured against in the personal property coverage tend to be largely the same as, though not necessarily identical to, those applicable to the real property coverage.

Lessees of residential or commercial real estate may obtain insurance policies to cover their items of personal property that are on the leased premises. Such policies are highly advisable, because the apartment or office building owner's insurance policy on the real property is likely to furnish little or no coverage for the tenant's personal property.

Automobile insurance policies are in part personal property insurance policies because they provide coverage (under what are usually called the *comprehensive* and *collision* sections) for car damage resulting from such causes as fire, wind, hail, vandalism, or collision with an animal or tree. (As will be seen, automobile insurance policies also contain significant features of another major type of insurance policy to be discussed later—liability insurance.) Other specialized types of personal property insurance are also available. For example, some farmers purchase crop insurance in order to guard against the adverse financial effects that would result if a hailstorm or other covered peril severely damaged a season's crop.

Nature and Extent of Insurer's Payment Obligation

Property insurance policies are **indemnity** contracts. This means that the insurer is obligated to reimburse the insured for his actual losses associated with a covered harm to the insured property. The insured's recovery under the policy thus cannot exceed the extent of the loss sustained. Neither may it exceed the extent of the insured's insurable interest (as discussed earlier in this chapter) or the amount of coverage that the insured purchased (the **policy limits**).[8]

---

[7]It may be that a type of peril frequently excluded in property insurance policies is in fact a covered peril under the language of the policy at issue. Alternatively, losses that at first glance appear to have resulted from an excluded peril may sometimes be characterized as having resulted, at least in part, from a covered peril. In the latter event, there may be some coverage for the losses.

[8]Some insurers, however, provide (in exchange for a more substantial premium than would be charged for a policy without this feature) a homeowner's policy under which the insurer could become obligated to pay *more* than the policy limits if the insured's home was destroyed and the cost to replace it would actually exceed the policy limits.

Policy provisions other than the policy limits also help define the extent of the insurer's obligation to pay. When covered real property is damaged but not destroyed, the **cost of repair** is normally the relevant measure. Many policies provide that when covered real property is destroyed, the insurer must pay the **actual cash value** (or *fair market value*) of the property. Some policies, however, establish **cost of replacement** as the payment obligation in this situation. The policies that call for payment of the actual cash value frequently give the insurer the option to pay the cost of replacement, however, if that amount would be less than the actual cash value. As to covered personal property, the controlling standard is typically the least of the following: cost of repair, cost of replacement, or actual cash value.[9]

Many property insurance policies supplement the above provisions by obligating the insurer to pay the insured's reasonable costs of temporarily living elsewhere if the insured property was her residence and the damage to the residence made it uninhabitable pending completion of repairs or replacement. Comparable benefits may sometimes be provided in policies covering business property. Lost profits and similar consequential losses resulting from harm to or destruction of one's insured property, however, do not normally fall within the insurer's payment obligation unless a specific provision obligates the insurer along those lines.[10] Regardless of whether the damaged or destroyed property is real or personal in nature, the particular language of the policy at issue must always be consulted before a definite determination can be made concerning what is and is not within the insurer's duty to pay.

Valued and Open Policies   When insured real property is destroyed as a result of fire or another covered peril, the amount to be paid by the insurer

may be further influenced by the type of policy involved. Some property insurance contracts are **valued policies.** If real property insured under a valued policy is destroyed, the insured is entitled to recover the face amount of the policy regardless of the property's fair market value. For example, in 1985, Douglas purchased a home with a fair market value of $90,000. Douglas also purchased a valued policy with a face amount of $90,000 to insure the house against various risks, including fire. The home's fair market value decreased over the next several years because of deterioration in the surrounding neighborhood. In 1997, when the home had a fair market value of only $75,000, it was destroyed by fire. Douglas is entitled to $90,000 (the face amount of the valued policy) despite the reduction in the home's fair market value.

Most property insurance policies, however, are open policies. Open policies allow the insured to recover the fair market value (actual cash value) of the property at the time it was destroyed, up to the limits stated in the policy. Thus, if Douglas had had an open policy in the example presented in the previous paragraph, he would have been entitled to only $75,000 when the home was destroyed by fire. Suppose instead that Douglas's home had increased in value, so that at the time of the fire its fair market value was $105,000. In that event, it would not matter what type of policy (valued or open) Douglas had. Under either type of policy, his recovery would be limited to the $90,000 face amount of the policy.

Coinsurance Clause   Some property insurance policies contain a **coinsurance clause,** which may operate as a further limit on the insurer's payment obligation and the insured's right to recovery. A coinsurance clause provides that in order for the insured to be able to recover the full cost of partial losses, the insured must obtain insurance on the property in an amount equal to a specified percentage (often 80 percent) of the property's fair market value.

For example, PDQ Corporation has a fire insurance policy on its warehouse with Cooperative Mutual Insurance Group. The policy has an 80 percent coinsurance clause. The warehouse had a fair market value of $100,000, meaning that PDQ was required to carry at least $80,000 of insurance on the building. PDQ, however, purchased a policy with a face amount of only $60,000. A fire partially destroyed the warehouse, causing $40,000 worth of damage to the structure. Because of the coinsurance

---

[9]Concerning certain designated items of personal property such as furs or jewelry, policies often set forth a maximum insurer payout (such as $1,000) that is less than the general policy limits applicable to personal property. Such a payout limitation would operate as a further restriction on the extent of the insurer's obligation.

[10]Recall, however, that if the insurer violates its payment obligation by wrongfully failing or refusing to pay what the policy contemplates, the insurer has committed a breach of contract. As noted in this chapter's earlier discussion of insurance policies as contracts, fundamental breach of contract principles dictate that the breaching insurer is potentially liable for consequential damages.

FIGURE 2

Operation of Coinsurance Clause

FAIR MARKET VALUE AT TIME OF LOSS	FACE VALUE OF POLICY	AMOUNT OF INSURANCE REQUIRED	ACTUAL LOSS	RECOVERY
$100,000	$60,000	$80,000	$ 40,000	$30,000
100,000	60,000	80,000	100,000	60,000

clause, PDQ will recover only $30,000 from Cooperative. This figure was arrived at by taking the amount of insurance carried ($60,000) divided by the amount of insurance required ($80,000) times the loss ($40,000).

The coinsurance formula for recovery for partial losses is stated as follows:

$$\frac{\text{Amount of insurance carried}}{\text{Coinsurance percent} \times \text{Fair market value}} \times \text{Loss} = \text{Recovery}$$

Remember that the coinsurance formula applies only to *partial* losses (i.e., damage to, but not complete destruction of, property). If PDQ's warehouse had been totally destroyed by the fire, the formula would not have been used. PDQ would have recovered $60,000—the face amount of the policy—for the total loss. If the formula had been used, it would have indicated that Cooperative owed PDQ $75,000—more than the face amount of the policy. This result would be neither logical nor in keeping with the parties' insurance contract. Whether the loss is total or partial, the insured is not entitled to recover more than the face amount of the policy. The examples just discussed are depicted in Figure 2.

Pro Rata Clause With the limited exception of the valued policy (discussed above), the insured cannot recover more than the amount of the actual loss. A rule allowing the insured to recover more than the actual loss could encourage unscrupulous persons to purchase policies from more than one insurer on the same property (thus substantially overinsuring it) and then intentionally destroy the property in a way that appears to be a covered peril (e.g., committing arson but making the fire look accidental). In order to make certain that the insured does not obtain a recovery that exceeds the actual loss, property insurance policies commonly contain a *pro rata clause,* which applies when the insured has purchased insurance policies from more than one insurer. The effect of the pro rata clause is to apportion the loss among the insurance companies.

(Applicable state law sometimes contains a rule having this same effect.)

Under the pro rata clause, the amount any particular insurer must pay the insured depends on the percentage of total insurance coverage represented by that insurer's policy. For example, Mumford purchases two insurance policies to cover his home against fire and other risks. His policy from Security Mutual Insurance Corp. has a face amount of $50,000; his policy from Reliable Insurance Co. is for $100,000. Mumford's home is partially destroyed by an accidental fire, with a resulting loss of $30,000. As illustrated in Figure 3, Security Mutual must pay Mumford $10,000, with Reliable having to pay the remaining $20,000 of the loss.

The formula for determining each insurer's liability under a pro rata clause is stated as follows:

$$\frac{\text{Amount of insurer's policy}}{\text{Total coverage by all insurers}} \times \text{Loss} = \text{Liability of insurer}$$

Thus, Security Mutual's payment amount was calculated as follows:

$$\frac{\$50,000 \text{ (Security Mutual's policy)}}{\$150,000 \text{ (Total of both policies)}} \times \$30,000 \text{ (Loss)} = \$10,000$$

Reliable's payment amount could be similarly calculated by substituting $100,000 (Reliable's policy amount) for the $50,000 (Security Mutual's policy amount) in the numerator of the equation. This formula may be used for both partial and total losses. However, each company's payment obligation is limited by the face amount of its policy. Thus, Security Mutual could never be liable for more than $50,000. Similarly, Reliable's liability is limited to a maximum of $100,000.

Right of Subrogation

The insurer may be able in some instances to exercise a **right of subrogation** if it is required to

Operation of Pro Rata Clause

POLICY A	POLICY B	TOTAL INSURANCE (POLICY A PLUS POLICY B)	ACTUAL LOSS	LIABILITY OF INSURER A	LIABILITY OF INSURER B
$50,000	$100,000	$150,000	$30,000	$10,000	$20,000

pay for a loss under a property insurance contract. Under the right of subrogation, the insurer obtains all of the insured's rights to pursue legal remedies against anyone who negligently or intentionally caused the harm to the property. For example, Arnett purchased a property insurance policy on her home from Benevolent Insurance Company. Arnett's home was completely destroyed by a fire that spread to her property when her neighbor, Clifton, was burning leaves and negligently failed to control the fire. After Benevolent pays Arnett for her loss, Benevolent's right of subrogation entitles it to sue Clifton to recover the amount Benevolent paid Arnett. Arnett will be obligated to cooperate with Benevolent and furnish assistance to it in connection with the subrogation claim.

If the insured provides the liable third party a general release from liability, the insurer will be released from his payment obligation to the insured. Suppose that in the above scenario, Clifton persuaded Arnett to sign an agreement releasing him from liability for the fire. Because this action by Arnett would interfere with Benevolent's right of subrogation, Benevolent would not have to pay Arnett for the loss. A partial release of Clifton by Arnett would relieve Benevolent of responsibility to Arnett to the extent of her release.

Duration and Cancellation of Policy

Property insurance policies are usually effective for a designated period such as six months or a year. They are then extended for consecutive periods of like duration if the insured continues to pay the necessary premium and neither the insured nor the insurer elects to cancel the policy. The insured is normally entitled to cancel the policy at any time by providing the insurer written notice to that effect or by surrendering the policy to the insurer. Although property insurers usually have some right to cancel policies, terms of the policies themselves and/or governing law typically limit the grounds on which property insurers may do so. Permitted grounds for cancellation include the insured's nonpayment of the premium and, as a general rule, the insured's misrepresentation or fraud (see this chapter's discussion of contract law's applicability to insurance policies). Policy provisions and/or applicable law typically provide that if the property insurer intends to cancel the policy, the insured must be given meaningful advance written notice (often 30 days) of this intent before cancellation takes effect.

Another cancellation basis exists by virtue of the **increase of hazard** clauses that appear in many property insurance policies. An increase of hazard clause provides that the insurer's liability will be terminated if the insured takes any action materially increasing the insurer's risk. Some increase of hazard provisions also specify certain types of behavior that will cause termination. Common examples of such behavior include keeping highly explosive material on the property and allowing the premises to remain vacant for a lengthy period of time. *Good v. Continental Insurance Company,* which follows, illustrates the operation of an increase of hazard clause.

GOOD v. CONTINENTAL INSURANCE COMPANY   291 S.E.2d 198 (S.C. Sup. Ct. 1982)

Sims and Dorothy Good purchased a standard fire insurance policy on their home from Continental Insurance Company. The policy contained an "increase of hazard" clause stating that the insurer would not be liable if the risk of fire was increased "by any means within the control or knowledge of the insured." A November 1977 fire almost completely destroyed the house. While putting out the fire, firefighters discovered an illegal liquor still concealed in a false closet under the eaves of the roof. The still, encased by bricks and mortar, consisted of a 90-gallon copper vat over an 8- to 10-inch butane gas *burner. Firefighters also discovered 22 half-gallons of "moonshine" and many 55-gallon drums full or partially full of mash. A police department detective who dismantled and examined the still's burner after the fire offered the opinion that the still was in operation when the fire occurred. Good denied this, though he admitted installing the still two years earlier—after his insurance policy became effective. Continental refused to pay for the destruction on the ground that the still was an increased hazard.*

The Goods sued Continental to recover proceeds under the policy. When the trial court awarded damages to the Goods, Continental appealed. ∽

Harwell, Justice   In [previous cases], this court held that coverage under an insurance policy was suspended if the increased risk was permanent and continuous even though it did not produce the loss. However, if the increased risk caused the loss, an occasional, temporary increase of risk was sufficient to void a policy.

In addition to these guidelines, to void the policy the increase of hazard must be material and substantial such that the insurer could not reasonably be presumed to have contracted to assume it. Also, according to the policy, increased hazard must be accomplished by means solely within the control and knowledge of Good after the insurance contract was effected.

The evidence leads unmistakably to the following: the distillery was permanently installed; it was regularly used at least during the holiday season; Good installed the still after the insurance policy became effective; and only he operated the still. We conclude that the only reasonable inference from the evidence is that there had been an increase of hazard, thereby voiding the policy.

The use to which the Goods put their dwelling was so foreign to the normal uses of a dwelling as to become beyond the contemplation of the insurer. Surely the insurer did not contemplate providing insurance coverage on a residence which concealed an illegal still and the fruits of its operation.

Judgment reversed in favor of Continental.

LIABILITY INSURANCE

As its name suggests, liability insurance provides the insured the ability to transfer liability risks to the insurer. Under policies of liability insurance, the insurer agrees, among other things, to pay sums the insured becomes legally obligated to pay to another party. This enables the insured to minimize the troublesome or even devastating financial effects that he could experience in the event of his liability to someone else.

Types of Liability Insurance Policies

Liability insurance policies come in various types. These include, but are not limited to: **personal liability policies** designed to cover a range of liabilities an individual person could face; **business liability policies** (sometimes called *comprehensive general liability policies*) meant to apply to various liabilities that sole proprietors, partnerships, and corporations might encounter in their business operations; **professional liability policies** (sometimes called *malpractice insurance policies*) that cover physicians, attorneys, accountants, and members of other professions against liabilities to clients and sometimes other persons; and **workers' compensation policies** under which insurers agree to cover employers' statutorily required obligation to pay benefits to injured workers.

Some policies combine property insurance features with liability insurance components. Automobile insurance policies, for instance, afford property insurance when they cover designated automobiles owned by the insured against perils such as vandalism, hail, and collisions with animals, telephone poles, and the like. Other sections of automobile insurance policies provide liability insurance to the insured (the policy owner), members of her household, and sometimes other authorized drivers when their use of a covered automobile leads to an accident in which they face liability to another party. Typical homeowners' policies also combine property and liability insurance features. Besides covering the insured's home and contents against perils of the types discussed earlier in this chapter, these policies normally provide the insured coverage for a range of liabilities he may face as an individual.

Liabilities Insured Against

Although the different types of liability insurance policies discussed above contain different terms setting forth the liabilities covered and not covered, liability policies commonly afford coverage against the insured's liability for negligence but not against the insured's liability stemming from deliberate wrongful acts (most intentional torts and most behavior constituting a crime).[11] Liability policies tend to reach this common ground in the same sorts of ways property insurance policies define the scope of coverage—by listing particular liabilities that are covered and stating that an unlisted liability is not covered, by setting forth a seemingly broad statement of coverage and then specifying exclusions from coverage, or by employing a combination of the previous approaches (e.g., specifying certain covered liabilities and certain excluded liabilities).

Personal Liability and Homeowners' Policies Personal liability policies and the liability sections of homeowners' policies often state that coverage is restricted to instances of "bodily injury" and "property damage" experienced by a third party as a result of an "occurrence" for which the insured faces liability. These sorts of policies normally define *occurrence* as an "accident" resulting in bodily injury or property damage. The provisions just noted lead to the conclusion that intentional torts and most criminal behavior, if committed or engaged in by the insured, would fall outside the coverage of the policy at issue because they are not accidents (whereas instances of the insured's negligence would be). This conclusion is underscored by typical clauses purporting to exclude coverage for bodily injury or property damage the insured intended to cause. The occurrence, bodily injury, and property damage references in these policies also indicate that liabilities stemming from, for example, breach of contract would not be covered either (no accident, no bodily injury, no property damage). In addition, personal liability policies and liability sections of homeowners' policies also tend to

specify that if bodily injury or property damage results from the insured's business or professional pursuits, it is not covered.

Business Liability Policies Business liability policies also feature coverage for bodily injury and property damage stemming from the insured's actions. The relevant range of actions, of course, is broadened to include the insured's business pursuits or "conduct of business." A major focus remains on unintentional wrongful conduct (usually negligence) of the insured, with the insured's deliberate wrongful acts normally being specifically excluded from coverage. Another typical exclusion is the pollution exclusion, which deprives the insured of coverage for actions that lead to pollution of other parties' property, unless the pollution occurs suddenly and accidentally.

Business liability policies also tend to provide the insured coverage in instances where the insured would be liable for certain torts of his employees (normally under the *respondeat superior* doctrine).[12] In addition, business liability policies sometimes afford coverage broader than instances of tortious conduct producing physical injury or property damage. Some policies, for instance, contain a clause that contemplates coverage for the insured's defamation of another person or invasion of that person's privacy (though other policies specifically exclude coverage for those same torts). Furthermore, the broad "conduct of business" language in certain policies, as well as specialized clauses (in some policies) referring to liability stemming from advertising or unfair competition, may contemplate coverage for the insured's legal wrongs that cause others to experience economic harm. In the end, the particular liabilities covered by a business liability policy cannot be determined without a close examination of the provisions in the policy at issue. It may become necessary for a court to interpret a policy provision whose meaning is unclear or scope is uncertain. In the *Granite State Insurance* case, which follows, the court addressed the scope of an advertising injury clause that afforded coverage for acts of unfair competition.

---

[11]Workers' compensation liability policies are somewhat different, as later discussion in this chapter will reveal.

[12]The *respondeat superior* doctrine is discussed in Chapter 35. Although the insured's own intentional torts would not normally be covered, business liability policies sometimes provide that if the insured is liable on *respondeat superior* grounds for an employee's intentional tort such as battery, the insured will be covered unless the insured directed the employee to commit the intentional tort.

I n a class-action suit against Aamco Transmissions, Inc., consumers Joseph R. Tracy and Joseph P. Tracy claimed that Aamco and its network of franchisees used deceptive advertising that inaccurately described Aamco's services and lured many consumer purchasers of transmission services into paying excessively and for unnecessary repairs. The Tracys asserted that Aamco was liable under the Pennsylvania Unfair Trade Practices and Consumer Protection Law. Aamco was the insured under a comprehensive general liability insurance policy issued by Granite State Insurance Co. This policy provided liability coverage to Aamco "for personal injury or advertising injury . . . arising out of the conduct of" Aamco's business. The policy defined "advertising injury" as "injury arising . . . in the course of [Aamco's] advertising activities, if such injury arises out of libel, slander, defamation, violation of right of privacy, piracy, unfair competition, or infringement of copyright, title or slogan."

Contending that it had coverage under the "unfair competition" category of the advertising injury coverage, Aamco demanded that Granite defend and indemnify it in connection with the consumer class action case described above. When Granite declined to do so, Aamco settled the case on its own. Granite then brought a declaratory judgment action against Aamco in federal district court. Granite sought a ruling that it was not obligated to provide coverage for Aamco in the class action case brought by the Tracys. The district court concluded that the unfair competition term in the policy contemplated coverage only for common law–based claims against Aamco, not for any claims based on a state or federal statute. Because the Tracys' class action case was based on a supposed violation of a Pennsylvania statute, the district court held that Granite's policy did not furnish coverage to Aamco. In addition, the court held that the term unfair competition was not ambiguous and that Aamco could not have had a reasonable expectation that consumers' claims against it would be covered. Aamco appealed to the Third Circuit Court of Appeals. ∽

Greenberg, Circuit Judge   We will affirm, though we do not ground our result on the district court's reasoning as we do not agree with its conclusion that the phrase "unfair competition" unambiguously refers only to the traditional common law tort of that name. For one thing, the courts are not uniform in describing the tort of unfair competition. [Because *unfair competition* is a term used by courts to refer to various types of conduct,] it is not so easy to conclude that there is one narrow and clear category of the common law tort.

Furthermore, regardless of the scope of the common law tort of unfair competition, a person reading the term "unfair competition" as a category of "advertising injury" within an insurance policy would not necessarily understand the term to be limited to a common law definition. A broader interpretation of the term . . . would be particularly reasonable in Pennsylvania as that state's legislature has defined "[u]nfair methods of competition" to include a host of [different] activities. In short, we see no valid reason to exclude conduct described in the statute simply because it might not be regarded as unfair competition in a common law sense.

Yet even if the term "unfair competition" within an insurance policy is construed broadly with re-

spect to the character of an insured's conduct, that construction does not determine the class of persons who can present claims against the insured which will be regarded as being claims for unfair competition within the policy. Thus, in order for Aamco to succeed, it must show that claims by its customers injured by its own practices reasonably can be described as unfair competition claims within the context of the insurance coverage. In this endeavor it fails for, regardless of the nature of the insured's conduct, a claim by a consumer of its products or services arising from that conduct hardly can be characterized as a claim for unfair competition. After all, "competition" connotes an insured's relationship with other persons or entities supplying similar goods or services.

In fact, the Pennsylvania legislature itself recognized this point. The statute involved in the [consumer class-action case against Aamco] is not called the "Pennsylvania Unfair Competition Statute." Rather, it is the "Pennsylvania Unfair Trade Practices *and Consumer Protection Law*." It is a broad business fraud statute that by its very title demonstrates that it encompasses more than acts of unfair competition. The fact that the legislature deemed it expedient to combine the remedies for unfair competition and consumer fraud in one statute does not magically transform acts of "consumer fraud" into acts of "unfair competition." Accordingly, we think that the Supreme Court of Pennsylvania would hold that a competitor of the insured, but not its customer, can assert a claim which may be covered under the "unfair competition" category of the "advertising injury" coverage. While we acknowledge, as did the district court, that ambiguities in insurance policies should be resolved in an insured's favor, the Granite policy is not ambiguous with respect to the relationship required between a plaintiff in an underlying action and an insured for that plaintiff's claim to be considered unfair competition within the Granite policy.

We have not overlooked Aamco's argument that the proper focus regarding issues of coverage under insurance contracts is the reasonable expectation of the insured. Rather, we conclude that Aamco could not have expected to have insurance coverage for the Tracys' claims under the portion of a policy protecting it against claims of "unfair competition." [I]t would be expected that a claim arising from "competition" would be forwarded by a competitor of an insured. The Tracys and the class they represented were not competitors of Aamco.

District court's decision denying coverage to Aamco affirmed.

Other Liability Policies Professional liability policies also afford coverage for the insured's tortious conduct, this time in the practice of his or her profession. Negligent professional conduct producing harm to a third party (normally bodily injury in the medical malpractice setting but usually economic harm in the legal or other professional malpractice context) would be a covered liability. Wrongful professional conduct of an intentional nature typically would not be covered.

Automobile liability policies cover liability for physical injury and property damage stemming from the insured's (and certain other drivers') negligent driving. Once again, however, there is no coverage for liability arising from the insured's (or another driver's) deliberate vehicle operation acts of a wrongful nature.

Workers' compensation policies tend to approach coverage questions somewhat differently, primarily because injured employees need not prove negligence on the part of their employer in order to be entitled to benefits. Therefore, the insurer's obligation under a workers' compensation policy is phrased in terms of the liability the insured employer would face under state law.

Insurer's Obligations

Duty to Defend When another party makes a legal claim against the insured and the nature and allegations of the claim are such that the insurer would be obligated to cover the insured's liability if the claim were proven, the insurer has a **duty to**

defend the insured. A commonsense precondition of this duty's being triggered is that the insured must notify the insurer that the claim has been made against her. The duty to defend means that the insurer must furnish, at its expense, an attorney to represent the insured in litigation resulting from the claim against her. If the insurer fails to perform its duty to defend in an instance where the duty arose, the insurer has breached the insurance contract. Depending on the facts, the breaching insurer would at least be liable for compensatory damages (as indicated in this chapter's earlier discussion of insurance policies as contracts)[13] and potentially for punitive damages as well under the *bad faith* doctrine examined later in this chapter.

Sometimes it is quite clear that the insurer's duty to defend applies or does not apply, given the nature of the claim made against the insured. Other times, however, there may be uncertainty as to whether the claim alleged against the insured would fall within the scope of the liability insurance policy. Such uncertainty, of course, means that it is not clear whether the insurer has a duty to defend. Insurers tend to take one of two approaches in an effort to resolve this uncertainty. Under the first approach,

---

[13]The compensatory damages in such an instance would normally be the reasonable costs incurred by the insured in retaining an attorney and paying him to represent her. Of course, if the insured ended up being held liable in the third party's suit and the insurer wrongfully refused to pay the damages assessed against the insured in that case, the insured's compensatory damages claim against the breaching insurer would be increased substantially.

the insurer files a declaratory judgment suit against the insured. In this suit, the insurer asks the court to determine whether the insurer owes obligations to the insured under the policy (including the duty to defend as well as the payment obligation to be discussed shortly) in connection with the particular liability claim made against the insured by the injured third party. The other option insurers often pursue when it is unclear whether the liability policy applies is to retain an attorney to represent the insured in the litigation filed by the third party—thus fulfilling any duty to defend that may be owed—but to do so under a *reservation of rights* notice. By providing the reservation of rights notice to the insured, the insurer indicates that it reserves the right, upon acquisition of additional information, to conclude (or seek a later judicial determination) that it does not have the obligation to pay any damages that may be assessed against the insured as a result of the third party's claim. The insurer's reservation of rights also serves to eliminate an argument that by proceeding to defend the insured, the insurer waived the ability to argue that any actual liability would not be covered.

Duty to Pay Sums Owed by Insured If a third party's claim against the insured falls within the liabilities covered by the policy, the insurer is obligated to pay the compensatory damages held by a judge or jury to be due and owing from the insured to the third party. In addition, the insured's obligation to pay such expenses as court costs would also be covered. These payment obligations are subject, of course, to the policy limits of the insurance contract involved. For example, if the insured is held liable for compensatory damages and court costs totaling $150,000 but the policy limits of the relevant liability policy are $100,000, the insurer's contractual obligation to pay sums owed by the insured is restricted to $100,000.

Is the insurer also obligated to pay any *punitive damages* assessed against the insured as a result of a covered claim? As a general rule, the insurer will have no such obligation, either because of an insurance contract provision to that effect or because of judicial decisions holding that notions of public policy forbid arrangements by which one could transfer his punitive damages liability to an insurer. Not all courts facing this issue have so held, however, meaning that in occasional instances the insured's punitive damages liability may also be cov-

ered if the insurance policy's terms specifically contemplate such a result.

The liability insurer need not wait until litigation has been concluded (and damages are awarded or not awarded) to attempt to dispose of a liability claim made against the insured. Insurance policy provisions, consistent with our legal system's tendency to encourage voluntary settlements of claims, allow insurers to negotiate settlements with third parties who have made liability claims against the insured. These settlements involve payment of an agreed sum of money to the third party, in exchange for the third party's giving up her legal right to proceed with litigation against the insured. Settlements may occur regardless of whether litigation has been formally instituted by the third party or whether the claim against the insured consists of the third party's prelitigation demand for payment by the insured. If settlements are reached—and they are reached much more often than not—the substantial costs involved in taking a case all the way to trial may be avoided. The same is also true, from the insurer's perspective, of the damages that might have been assessed against the insured if the case had been tried. Note, however, that even if the defendant (the insured) wins a suit that does proceed to trial, the costs to the insurer are still substantial even though there is no award of damages to pay. Those costs include a considerable amount for attorney's fees for the insured (the insurer's obligation regardless of the outcome of the case) as well as other substantial expenses associated with protracted litigation. Accordingly, even when the insurer thinks that the insured probably would prevail if the case went to trial, the insurer may be interested in pursuing a settlement with the third party claimant if a reasonable amount (an amount less than what it would cost the insurer to defend the case) can be agreed upon.

Is There a Liability Insurance Crisis?

During roughly the past decade, the necessary premiums for liability insurance policies of various types (particularly business and professional liability policies) have risen considerably. Sometimes, the premiums charged by liability insurers have become so substantial that would-be insureds have concluded that they cannot afford liability insurance and therefore must go without it despite its importance. In addition, some insurers have ceased offering certain types of liability policies and/or have become much more restrictive in their decisions about which persons or firms to insure.

Insurance companies tend to blame the above state of affairs on what they see as a tort law regime under which plaintiffs win lawsuits too frequently and recover very large damage awards too often. As a result, insurers have been among the most outspoken parties calling for tort reform, a subject discussed in earlier chapters in this book. Plaintiffs' attorneys and critics of the insurance industry blame rising liability insurance premiums on, primarily, another alleged cause: questionable investment practices and other unsound business practices supposedly engaged in by insurance companies. The parties making these assertions thus oppose tort reform efforts as being unnecessary and unwise.

Liability insurance premiums in general may not be increasing as rapidly today as they did a few years ago, but they remain substantial in amount. So long as liability insurance remains unaffordable or otherwise difficult to obtain, there is a "crisis," given the adverse financial consequences that could beset an uninsured person. This is so regardless of which of the competing explanations set forth above bears greater legitimacy.

LIFE INSURANCE

Life insurance provides a means of lessening the financial hardships that result from the death of a given person. A few basic life insurance concepts were alluded to in this chapter's section on insurance policies as contracts. This section builds on the earlier discussion by examining specialized legal topics and issues that arise in connection with life insurance.

Parties Other than Insurer

Earlier in the chapter, we noted that in the property and liability insurance contexts, the same person will often be the insured (the purchaser of the insurance), the policy owner (the party entitled to enforce the contract rights set forth in the policy), and the beneficiary (the party entitled to payment under the policy). Life insurance, however, departs from this typical property and liability insurance model. In the life insurance setting, the insured is *the person whose life is insured* under the policy. That person may or may not have been the purchaser of the policy. Although the insured may also be the party entitled to enforce the policy's contract rights (the policy owner), it is not unusual for the policy owner to be someone other than the insured. The policy owner is typically the party who purchased the policy, but this is not always true.

Life insurance also departs from the property and liability model with regard to the identity of the beneficiary (the person entitled to payment when the insured dies). The beneficiary, who is designated by the policy owner, will often be one or more family members or friends of the insured, or sometimes business partners of the insured. Of course, the policy owner may double as the designated beneficiary. It is also possible that the insured's estate could be specified as the beneficiary instead of a particular individual (or individuals) being so designated. Life insurance policies often allow the policy owner to change the designated beneficiary prior to the insured's death. Some policies, however, contain terms under which the designation of a beneficiary is irrevocable, meaning that a different beneficiary cannot be substituted for the one already specified.

Insurable Interest

As discussed earlier in this chapter, an insurable interest is required in order to keep an insurance contract from being an illegal wagering contract. In the life insurance context, the requisite insurable interest *must exist at the time the policy was issued* but need not exist at the time of the insured's death. Persons who stand to suffer a financial loss in the event of the insured's death have the insurable interest necessary to support the purchase of a life insurance policy on the insured. The insured and his or her spouse, parents, children, and other dependents thus possess an insurable interest in the insured's life.

In addition, the business associates of the insured may also have an insurable interest in his or her life. Such persons would include the insured's employer, business partners, or shareholders in a closely held corporation with which the insured is connected. Creditors of the insured also have an insurable interest, but only to the extent of the debt owed by the insured.

Types of Life Insurance Policies

A life insurance contract is a valued policy because, upon the insured's death, the insurer must pay the beneficiary a set amount that equals the **face value** of the policy (the amount of insurance coverage purchased). The policy's face value helps determine the amount of the premiums that must be paid to keep the policy in force. A policy with a large face value will, of course, cost the purchaser of the policy more in premiums than will a policy with a smaller face value.

Two basic types of life insurance, **whole life policies** and **term policies,** merit discussion. Although both types are valued policies, they differ in important respects.

Whole Life Policies   *Whole life policies*—sometimes called *ordinary life* or *straight life* policies—contemplate that the insured (or the owner, if a person other than the insured) will pay a set premium for the remainder of his life or until a specified time when the obligation to pay further premiums will cease. The whole life policy does more than impose on the insurer the obligation to pay the policy's face value upon the insured's death. Such a policy possesses a savings feature, in that it develops a **cash surrender value** as premiums are paid. The insured policy owner may recover this value if the policy is terminated. In addition, whole life policies develop a loan value as premiums are paid. This sometimes enables the policy owner to borrow money from the insurer at favorable interest rates. Because of the investment feature and the potential for borrowing present in whole life policies, premiums that the policy owner must pay for such policies usually tend to be higher than the premiums required for term insurance—at least when the insured is in his 30s and perhaps his 40s.

Term Policies   *Term policies* are so named because they are designed to be in effect for a designated term or duration, such as one year. These policies provide insurance coverage only, without the cash surrender value and loan value features present in whole life insurance. In return for the payment of premiums during the term of the policy, the insurer agrees to pay the face amount of the policy if the insured dies during the term.

For many persons, having a suitable amount of insurance coverage in the event of the insured's death may be much more important than an added investment feature or the prospect of borrowing funds in the future. Term policies may be an economical way of obtaining coverage, because premiums for a term policy of a given face value often start lower than for a whole life policy of the same face value. This tends to be true if the term policy is purchased while the insured is in her 30s or early 40s. Although term policies are typically written for a one-year period, they frequently have a *guaranteed renewability* provision. This provision enables the insured (or the owner, if insured and owner are not one and the same) to renew the policy for successive additional terms up to a specified age, without having to undergo medical examinations designed to show that the insured is still in good health. Those desiring insurance coverage may thus keep the term policy in force.

In keeping a term policy in force year after year, however, they face the downside of term policies—annual premium increases. As the insured gets another year older, the premium necessary to keep the term policy in force rises. Although term insurance premiums typically begin lower than whole life premiums, term insurance premiums eventually will equal or exceed those for a whole life policy of the same face value. Therefore, owners of term policies may eventually face the need to decide whether to convert their term policies to whole life policies and thereby avoid the ever-increasing term premiums (plus acquire the added benefits of whole life policies). Term policies often contain a *guaranteed conversion option,* under which the insured may choose to convert the term policy to a whole life policy.

Other Special Issues and Policy Provisions

Misrepresentation Issues   As explained earlier in this chapter, an insurance applicant's misrepresentations concerning material matters may cause a resulting insurance contract to become voidable at the option of the insurer. In the life insurance setting, misrepresentations regarding the proposed insured's health condition become the focus of considerable attention. Whether the insurer is able to avoid its policy obligations on the basis of the insurance applicant's health-related misstatements or failures to disclose will depend on the seriousness of the matter misstated or not disclosed by the applicant, and on the degree to which knowledge of the truth would have influenced the insurer's decision on whether to issue a policy. If the insurer would not have issued the policy had it known the truth, the insurer is likely to be allowed to avoid its policy obligation.

Misstatement of Age Clauses   Two common provisions in life insurance policies help to offset the potentially harsh effect that might otherwise result from certain false representations by the insurance applicant. These provisions are *misstatement of age clauses* and *incontestability clauses.* Under a misstatement of age clause, the insurer is allowed to reduce the amount it must pay upon the insured's death if the insured's age listed in the application for insurance was lower than the insured's actual age at that time. The amount of the insurer's payment obligation will be lowered to reflect the amount of coverage that the premiums paid would have bought at the correct age's premium rates.

For example, having stated his age as 39, Wingfield purchases a $100,000 face-value policy on himself from Invincible Insurance Co. When Wingfield dies, Invincible learns he was actually 43 when he took out the policy. Because the premium rate for a 43-year-old would have been higher, the total amount of premiums actually paid by Wingfield would have purchased only $85,000 in coverage at the correct premium rate. Therefore, under the misstatement of age clause, Invincible would be obligated to pay Wingfield's beneficiary $85,000 rather than $100,000.

Incontestability Clauses   Under the incontestability clauses commonly seen in life insurance policies, insurers are barred from contesting their liability under the policy on the basis of certain misrepresentations by the insured if the policy has been in force for a specified period of time (frequently, two years). Incontestability clauses do not, however, prevent the insurer from contesting liability on the grounds that the requisite insurable interest was lacking, that an impostor filled in for the insured at the required medical exam, or that the policy purchaser took out the policy with the intent to kill the insured and collect the policy proceeds.

Special Cancellation and Lapse Issues   Insurers generally cannot cancel life insurance contracts as long as the necessary premiums are being paid. A contrary rule could tempt insurers to terminate policies covering seriously ill insureds and would thus poorly serve insureds, policy owners, and beneficiaries.

The policy owner may cancel a life insurance policy by surrendering it to the insurer. If the policy is a whole life policy, the owner is usually allowed under the policy provisions to recover the accumulated cash surrender value or to purchase a paid-up or extended policy. Under a paid-up policy, the owner acquires a fully paid-for policy on the insured. The policy's face value is the amount of coverage that the cash surrender value would purchase, in light of the insured's age. An extended policy is a term policy having the same face value as the original policy that was surrendered.

Lapse of a term insurance policy occurs upon the expiration of the stated duration, unless the policy is renewed. Any life insurance policy, whether term or whole life, lapses if the necessary premiums are not paid. When a whole life policy lapses due to nonpayment of premiums, the owner normally has the same rights to cash surrender value and a paid-up or extended policy as are made available to the owner who surrenders a whole life policy. The owner whose term insurance lapses because of nonpayment of premiums, however, has no such remedies.

In order to guard against the potentially harsh consequences stemming from lapsed life insurance policies (particularly lapsed term policies), many states have enacted statutes allowing policy owners a grace period within which they may pay past-due premiums and thereby avoid policy lapse or cancellation. A typical statutory grace period is 30 days. Life insurance policies themselves sometimes contain similarly motivated provisions, under which the owner whose life insurance policy has lapsed is given a limited time within which to pay past-due premiums and furnish proof of insurability (the insured's good health). By doing these things within the specified time, the owner obtains reinstatement of the policy.

HEALTH INSURANCE

With the costs of medical treatment, hospitalization, and medications having increased dramatically in recent years, health insurance has become a critical means by which insureds minimize the adverse financial consequences associated with illness and injury. The costs of serious illness or injury may be financially crippling unless insurance coverage exists.[14] Health insurance has thus become a virtual necessity in today's society, as demonstrated by the fact that a very large percentage of the U.S. population does have some form of health coverage.

Nature of Coverage

Health insurance policies typically provide coverage for medical expenses resulting from a broad range of illnesses and injuries experienced by the insured (or by the insured's family member, if family coverage was procured by the insured). In setting forth the illnesses or injuries covered under the policy, health insurers take approaches similar to the previously discussed methods used by property insurers when they stake out the scope of those policies' coverage. This means that health insurance policies tend to specify an exclusive list of covered illnesses and injuries, set forth a broad general statement of coverage but then specify certain excluded causes, or combine the two approaches by specifying certain covered illnesses and injuries and designating other causes as excluded.

Whichever approach is used, most illnesses and injuries tend to be covered in some fashion. The resulting expenses that stem from medically necessary treatment then become subject to the terms of the insurer's payment obligation, as discussed below. Excluded causes often include preexisting health conditions—the insured's (or family member's) illnesses or injuries that befell the insured (or family member) before the effective date of the policy.

Insurer's Payment Obligation

As a general rule, health insurance policies require the insured to pay up to a certain amount in medical expenses per year before the insurer's payment obligation is triggered. This amount is known as the **deductible.** The specific amount varies from policy to policy. Once the insured has met his or her deductible, the insurer becomes obligated to pay all or part of the insured's medically necessary expenses that result from a covered illness or injury. If the policy establishes a payment obligation that is a percentage of the medical expenses, 80 percent is fairly typical, though once again this differs from policy to policy. When the health insurer makes payment, it may either pay the insured if the insured has already paid the medical bill or pay the health care provider directly if the insured has not yet paid the bill.

Increasingly, policies tie the insurer's payment obligation to what the insurer establishes as the usual and customary cost of a particular medical procedure or treatment. If the health care provider's charge for a particular procedure or treatment exceeds this usual and customary cost, the excess is not covered. The insurer's payment obligation is then to pay all or the specified percentage (depending on the policy's provisions) of the usual and customary cost.

Health policies tend to make special provisions for covered conditions requiring long-term medical care or hospitalization. These special provisions establish somewhat different payment obligations for the insurer. Often, these provisions specify that the insurer will pay a designated percentage of hospital expenses up to a certain amount, and then all of the hospital expenses once that amount has been reached. The exact percentages and amounts in a given situation are determined by checking the terms of the particular policy at issue.

Special provisions defining the extent of the insurer's obligation to pay for prescription medication costs are not uncommon. In addition, health policies sometimes contain specifications of maximum dollar amounts that the insurer will pay for certain surgical procedures or other medical treatments. Often, policy provisions state that there is no payment obligation regarding experimental medical treatments (treatments that are not yet classifiable as generally accepted medical treatments).

Group Policies

Most persons' health insurance coverage comes through group policies, under which an employer or an organization contracts with a health insurer for

---

[14]Disability insurance, under which insureds obtain coverage against loss of income resulting from long-term disabilities that interfere with one's ability to perform one's job, addresses the same sorts of financial concerns. Disability insurance will not be discussed further in this chapter.

coverage to be made available to employees of that employer or members of that organization. From the perspective of insured employees or insured members of organizations, the chief advantage of group policies is that the necessary premiums are significantly lower than the premiums one would have to pay in order to obtain a nongroup policy. The cessation of one's employee or group membership status may lead to a loss of her group insurance benefits and therefore significantly higher costs to her if she is forced to seek nongroup coverage. Sometimes these added costs will simply be prohibitively high. Other times, the typical policy exclusion for preexisting conditions will prove to be a problem when the insured must seek new health insurance coverage because she has lost her group insurance. Congress has attempted to deal with these sorts of problems by establishing limited rights to continued coverage in certain instances where the insured's employee status or organization membership has ended. Nevertheless, the problems persist.

The Health Insurance Debate

Although most U.S. residents have health insurance coverage of some sort, millions do not. Access to affordable coverage has become a major concern in today's society. There has been ongoing debate in the federal and state political arenas concerning how to control spiraling health care costs and increase access to affordable health insurance. In recent years, differing proposals for potentially sweeping federal legislation governing health insurance availability and coverage were proposed and considered in Congress. These competing proposals advocated different approaches on such issues as whether there should be "universal" coverage (for all U.S. residents), whether employers should be required to make health insurance available to their employees, and whether large health insurance purchasing cooperatives should be instituted as a means of attempting to reduce premium costs. Another area of disagreement was the extent to which membership in health maintenance organizations (HMOs) should be encouraged by any federal legislation concerning the health insurance business. HMOs offer insurance plans under which member patients are treated by HMO-affiliated physicians under arrangements designed to control medical costs and presumably

lessen the premiums or fees that HMO members must pay for health care coverage.

Congress ultimately decided, during the mid-1990s, not to enact legislation that would make sweeping changes in the health insurance status quo. Instead, Congress enacted reforms of a more limited, incremental nature, such as the Health Insurance Portability and Accountability Act of 1996. This statute includes provisions designed to allow most employees who had health insurance coverage in connection with their employment to change jobs without fear of losing health insurance coverage. Regardless of whether Congress continues the present course of modest tinkering or changes direction and enacts more extensive reforms in the health insurance realm, difficult public policy questions will complicate the process.

BAD FAITH BREACH OF INSURANCE CONTRACT

Earlier in this chapter, we discussed the liability that an insurer will face if it breaches its policy obligations by means of a good faith but erroneous denial of coverage. That liability is for compensatory damages—damages designed to compensate the insured for the losses stemming from the insurer's breach—just as in breach of contract cases outside the insurance setting. Punitive damages are not available, however, when the insurer's wrongful failure or refusal to perform stemmed from a good faith (though erroneous) coverage denial. What if the insurer's failure or refusal to perform exhibited a lack of good faith? In this section, we examine the recent judicial tendency to go beyond the conventional remedy of compensatory damages and to assess punitive damages against the insurer when the insurer's refusal to perform its policy obligations amounted to the tort of **bad faith breach of contract.**

The special nature of the insurer–insured relationship tends to involve a "we'll take care of you" message that insurers communicate to insureds—at least at the outset of the relationship. Recognizing this, courts have displayed little tolerance in recent years for insurers' unjustifiable refusals to take care of insureds when taking care of them is clearly called for by the relevant policy's terms. When an insurer refuses to perform obvious policy obligations without a plausible, legitimate explanation for the refusal, the insurer risks more than being held liable for compensatory damages. If the facts and circumstances indicate that the insurer's refusal to perform stemmed not from a reasonable argument over coverage but from an intent to "stonewall," deny, or unreasonably delay paying a meritorious claim, or otherwise create hardship for the insured, the insurer's breach may be of the bad faith variety. Because bad faith breach is considered an independent tort of a flagrantly wrongful nature, punitive damages—in addition to compensatory damages—have been held to be appropriate. The purposes of punitive damages in this context are the same as in other types of cases that call for punitive damages: to punish the flagrant wrongdoer and to deter the wrongdoer (as well as other potential wrongdoers) from repeating such an action.

The past decade has witnessed bad faith cases in which many millions of dollars in punitive damages have been assessed against insurers. The types of situations in which bad faith liability has been found have included a liability insurer's unjustifiable refusal to defend its insured and/or pay damages awarded against the insured in litigation that clearly triggered the policy obligations. Various cases of very large punitive damages assessments for bad faith liability have stemmed from property insurers' refusals to pay for the insured's destroyed property when the cause was clearly a covered peril and the insurer had no plausible rationale for denying coverage. Still other bad faith cases in which liability was held to exist have included malpractice or other liability insurers' refusals to settle certain probably meritorious claims against the insured within the policy limits. Bad faith liability in these cases tends to involve a situation in which the insured is held legally liable to a plaintiff for an amount well in excess of the dollar limits of the liability policy (meaning that the insured would be personally responsible for the amount of the judgment in excess of the policy limits), after the liability insurer, without reasonable justification, refused the plaintiff's offer to settle the case for an amount less than or equal to the policy limits.

Whether bad faith liability exists in a given case depends, of course, on all of the relevant facts and circumstances. Although bad faith liability is not established in every case in which insureds allege it, cases raising a bad faith claim are of particular concern to insurers.

ETHICAL AND PUBLIC POLICY CONCERNS

1. The law requires that the purchaser of property insurance must have an insurable interest in the property being insured. Why? Does this requirement encourage ethical conduct?

2. Provisions in liability insurance policies often state that the insurer will have no obligation to pay any *punitive* damages assessed against the insured. In addition, controlling legal rules sometimes provide that any agreement to provide insurance coverage for punitive damages liability is unenforceable. Should one be able to insure himself or herself against punitive damages liability? Why or why not?

3. A young parent of two children contacts an insurance agent and indicates that she wishes to purchase a life insurance policy. This parent has a modest income. Her main concern, as stated to the agent, is that her children will be provided for financially if she should die before they reach adulthood. The agent knows that he will make more money if he sells her a *whole life* policy than if he sells her a *term* policy, because his commission is a percentage of the premium (which will be higher with a whole life policy than with a term policy). What ethical issues does the agent face under these circumstances?

PROBLEMS AND PROBLEM CASES

1. Eighteen-year-old Arthur Smith became intoxicated at a New Year's Eve party. At 11:00 P.M., Smith left the party and began walking home. Police officer Don Czopek saw Smith walking down the center of a road and weaving from side to side. Because Smith was interfering with traffic and placing himself at risk of physical harm, Czopek pulled his patrol car alongside Smith and attempted to talk him into getting off the road. Smith refused, became argumentative, and started shouting. Czopek parked his patrol car, got out, and approached Smith in an effort to calm him down. Smith became increasingly hostile and grabbed Czopek by the lapels of his coat. Officer Herdis Petty then arrived on the scene to assist Czopek. A struggle occurred as the two officers attempted to handcuff Smith and put him into a patrol car. Smith kicked, hit, and bit the officers during this struggle, which continued for a substantial length of time. Czopek suffered frostbite on one of his hands. Petty sustained broken ribs as a result of being kicked by Smith (plus other less serious injuries). Smith was later convicted of assault and battery. He admitted that he intentionally resisted arrest but said that he did not recall hitting or kicking anyone. Officers Czopek and Petty filed a civil suit against Smith's parents, whose homeowners' policy with Group Insurance Company of Michigan (GICOM) provided liability coverage to the insureds—a status that, under the policy's terms, included Arthur Smith—for third parties' personal injury claims resulting from an "occurrence." The policy defined "occurrence" as "an accident, including injurious exposure to conditions, which results . . . in bodily injury or property damage." The policy contained an exclusion from coverage for "bodily injury or property damage which is either expected or intended from the standpoint of the insured." GICOM filed a declaratory judgment suit in which it asked the court to declare that it had no duty to defend or indemnify Arthur Smith and his parents in connection with the litigation brought by Czopek and Petty. Was GICOM entitled to such a ruling by the court?

2. Herbert Prashker was a partner in a law firm. Pursuant to their partnership agreement, the firm's partners purchased two life insurance policies on Prashker's life. The partners were named as beneficiaries. These policies, whose face amounts totaled $1,350,000, were obtained because Prashker was the most significant partner in terms of business generation and size of capital account. Prashker later fell ill with cancer and could no longer practice law. The partners agreed to terminate the partnership business. Five months after the partnership ceased doing business, Prashker died. Prashker's former partners sought to recover the life insurance proceeds. So did Prashker's daughter. She argued that the former partners were not entitled to the insurance proceeds because their insurable interest ended when the partnership was terminated. Were Prashker's former partners entitled to the life insurance proceeds?

3. In a class action suit, the plaintiffs alleged that an automobile loan program instituted by Bank of the West (BOW) violated California's Unfair Business Practices Act. No common law unfair competition claim was made in the suit. The Unfair Business Practices Act did not allow courts to award

compensatory or punitive damages, but did authorize courts to order "the disgorgement of money" wrongfully obtained. BOW settled the class action suit by paying $500,000 and agreeing to make changes in the operation of the loan program. BOW contended that the $500,000 payment was covered by the terms of a liability policy issued to BOW by Industrial Indemnity Co. The policy provided coverage for "all sums which the insured shall become legally obligated to pay as damages because of advertising injury to which this insurance applies." The policy went on to define "advertising injury" as "injury arising out of . . . libel, slander, defamation, violation of right of privacy, unfair competition, or infringement of copyright, title or slogan." Industrial filed a declaratory judgment action in which it asked the court to determine that the policy did not cover the $500,000 payment made by BOW to settle the class action suit. The trial court ruled in Industrial's favor, but the intermediate appellate court reversed. It concluded that the policy afforded coverage because the term "unfair competition" was ambiguous and thus could refer to either the common law of unfair competition or statutory claims such as those under the Unfair Business Practices Act. Was the intermediate appellate court correct?

4. Benjamin Born applied for a life insurance policy from Medico Life Insurance Company. The application form called for a health history, which Born provided. In addition, the application form asked specific questions about preexisting medical conditions. Born's wife, Adeline, answered these questions by stating that Born had no preexisting medical problems and was in good health. After issuing the policy, Medico discovered that Born had a history of heart disease, degenerative arthritis, and urinary system disorders. Medico then rescinded the policy and provided Born a check representing a refund of the premiums he had paid. Taking the position that he was still insured, Born refused the refund check. On these facts, was Medico entitled to rescind the policy?

5. The Pecks owned a lawn and garden supply store. Standard Marine was the insurer of the store and its contents. The Pecks placed a fireworks display in the store, where it was subsequently set off by a young boy. A resulting fire damaged or destroyed much of the Pecks' merchandise. Standard Marine refused to reimburse the Pecks for their loss, citing this clause in the policy: "The Company shall not be liable for loss occurring while the hazard is increased by any means within the control or knowledge of the insured." Was Standard Marine obligated to pay the Pecks for their loss?

6. The Plummers owned a commercial building in which they operated two businesses. The building and its contents were insured by Indiana Insurance Company (IIC). After an explosion and fire destroyed the building, the Plummers filed a claim and proof of loss with IIC. After an investigation, IIC denied the claim due to its conclusion that the Plummers had intentionally set the fire. IIC then filed a declaratory judgment action in which it asked for a determination that it had no obligation to cover losses stemming from the fire. The Plummers counterclaimed, seeking damages for breach of contract as well as punitive damages. The jury returned a verdict in favor of the Plummers on all issues. The jury awarded the Plummers approximately $700,000 in compensatory damages (an amount that exceeded the policy limits set forth in the insurance policy at issue), plus $3.5 million in punitive damages. The $700,000 compensatory damages award included not only the value of the destroyed building and its contents (what would have been due under the policy) but also $200,000 in consequential damages allegedly incurred by the Plummers as a result of IIC's lengthy investigation of the fire and ultimate denial of the Plummers' claim. For the most part, the consequential damages represented interest costs and similar expenses incurred by the Plummers—costs and expenses they would not have incurred if IIC had paid their claim. Although the evidence IIC adduced at trial included experts' testimony that the fire had been intentionally set, the jury rejected that testimony and accepted the Plummers' contrary evidence. IIC appealed, arguing that its denial of the Plummers' claim was in good faith, that it therefore should have no liability for consequential damages and punitive damages, and that the damages awarded for breach of an insurance contract cannot exceed the policy limits set forth in the contract. Was IIC correct in these arguments?

7. In 1972, Betty DeWitt and her husband, Joseph, purchased a house. Title was taken in Betty's name. Seven years later, the DeWitts were divorced. Under the 1979 divorce decree, Joseph was given possession of the house and Betty was ordered to sign the deed over to him. Joseph died in January 1980. Soon thereafter, Betty moved into the house and purchased a fire insurance policy from American Family Mutual Insurance Company. The policy had a face value of $38,500. In August 1980, the house was completely destroyed by fire. At that time, American Family learned of her divorce and the decree ordering her to convey title to Joseph. American Family refused to pay on the policy, arguing that Betty did not have an insurable interest. Was American Family correct?

8. Robert Baer and Dareen Dahlstrom had been close friends for more than 20 years. Dahlstrom, who was in the process of separating from her husband, went to visit Baer in July 1988. On various occasions, Baer had used a recreational drug known as Ecstasy. For several years after its discovery, Ecstasy was not an illegal drug. It was, however, designated by federal law as a prohibited controlled substance beginning in March 1988. Baer believed that the use of Ecstasy had certain psychological and emotional benefits, and that using it might help Dahlstrom cope with the personal problems she was experiencing at the time of her July 1988 visit. After she and Baer discussed his beliefs regarding Ecstasy, Dahlstrom told him that she wanted to use the drug. Baer and Dahlstrom went through various rituals in preparation for use of the drug and recited a prayer that "this [may] bring harm to no one and blessing to all." Baer then removed some Ecstasy from his personal supply, which he had purchased prior to March 1988. Baer dissolved approximately one-half of his usual dose in a glass of water and gave it to Dahlstrom. She drank the mixture. Within approximately 30 minutes, she was dead. Dahlstrom's survivors filed a wrongful death suit against Baer, who asserted that the claim fell within the liability coverage provided to him by State Farm Insurance Company as part of his homeowner's policy. The policy afforded coverage for third parties' claims for physical injury resulting from an "occurrence," which was defined in terms of an "accident" that caused injury. The policy also contained an exclusion from coverage for injury that was either intended or expected by the insured. State Farm filed a declaratory judgment action in which it asked for a judicial determination that in light of the above provisions in the parties' insurance contract as well as public policy considerations, it owed Baer no coverage duties regarding the suit that stemmed from Dahlstrom's death. Was State Farm entitled to the relief it sought?

9. Jeffrey Lane was employed by Memtek, Inc., at its Arby's Restaurant. He was being trained as a cook. After 11:00 one evening, Lane finished work and clocked out. He remained in the restaurant's lobby, however, because he was waiting for the manager to complete her duties. As Lane waited, friends of other restaurant employees came to a door of the restaurant. Lane and the other employees became involved in a conversation with these persons, who included John Taylor. Lane told Taylor that he could not enter the restaurant because it was closed. Taylor did not attempt to force his way into the restaurant. Instead, he "dared" Lane to come outside. Lane left the restaurant "of [his] own will" (according to Lane's deposition) for what he assumed would be a fight with Taylor. In the fight that transpired, Lane broke Taylor's nose and knocked out three of his teeth. Lane later pleaded guilty to a criminal battery charge. Taylor filed a civil suit against Lane and Memtek in an effort to collect damages stemming from the altercation with Lane. American Family Mutual Insurance Company provided liability insurance for Memtek in connection with its restaurant. The policy stated that for purposes of American Family's duties to defend and indemnify, "the insured" included not only Memtek but also Memtek's "employees, . . . but only for acts within the scope of their employment." American Family filed a declaratory judgment action in which it asked the court to determine that it owed Lane neither a duty to defend nor a duty to indemnify in connection with the incident giving rise to Taylor's lawsuit. American Family's theory was that for purposes of that incident, Lane was not an insured within the above-quoted policy provision. Was American Family correct?

10. In December 1988, Counihan purchased a property insurance policy under which Allstate Insurance Co. insured her house against all risks of loss. In February 1989, the U.S. government seized the house and sought its forfeiture under federal law due to its connection with illegal drug activity that occurred in July 1988. After two trials and an appeal, the Second Circuit Court of Appeals affirmed the forfeiture of the property in 1993. A fire had destroyed the house in 1990, while Counihan's policy with Allstate allegedly was in force. Counihan filed a claim with Allstate to recover the value of the destroyed house. The forfeiture statute under which the government had sought forfeiture of Counihan's property stated that "[a]ll right, title, and interest in property [to which the government has been held entitled to forfeiture due to the property's connection with illegal drug activity] shall vest in the United States upon commission of the act giving rise to forfeiture under this section." Arguing that this statute's retroactive effect would mean that Counihan did not possess an insurable interest when she purchased the policy and when the fire destroyed the house, Allstate asserted that its insurance contract with Counihan was void and unenforceable. Did Counihan have the necessary insurable interest at the times in question?

Appendixes

The Constitution of the United States of America

PREAMBLE

We the People of the United States, in Order to form a more perfect Union, establish Justice, insure domestic Tranquility, provide for the common defense, promote the general Welfare, and secure the Blessings of Liberty to ourselves and our Posterity, do ordain and establish this Constitution for the United States of America.

ARTICLE I

Section 1   All legislative Powers herein granted shall be vested in a Congress of the United States, which shall consist of a Senate and House of Representatives.

Section 2   The House of Representatives shall be composed of Members chosen every second Year by the People of the several States, and the Electors in each State shall have the Qualifications requisite for Electors of the most numerous Branch of the State Legislature.

No Person shall be a Representative who shall not have attained to the age of twenty five Years, and been seven Years a Citizen of the United States, and who shall not, when elected, be an Inhabitant of that State in which he shall be chosen.

Representatives and direct Taxes shall be apportioned among the several States which may be included within this Union, according to their respective Numbers, which shall be determined by adding to the whole Number of free Persons, including those bound to Service for a Term of Years, and excluding Indians not taxed, three fifths of all other Persons.[1] The actual Enumeration shall be made within three Years after the first Meeting of the Congress of the United States, and within every subsequent Term of ten Years, in such Manner as they shall by Law direct. The Number of Representatives shall not exceed one for every thirty Thousand, but each State shall have at Least one Representative, and until such enumeration shall be made, the State of New Hampshire shall be entitled to choose three, Massachusetts eight, Rhode-Island and

Providence Plantations one, Connecticut five, New York six, New Jersey four, Pennsylvania eight, Delaware one, Maryland six, Virginia ten, North Carolina five, South Carolina five, and Georgia three.

When vacancies happen in the Representation from any State, the Executive Authority thereof shall issue Writs of Election to fill such Vacancies.

The House of Representatives shall chuse their Speaker and other Officers; and shall have the sole Power of Impeachment.

Section 3   The Senate of the United States shall be composed of two Senators from each State, chosen by the Legislature thereof,[2] for six Years; and each Senator shall have one Vote.

Immediately after they shall be assembled in Consequence of the first Election, they shall be divided as equally as may be into three Classes. The Seats of the Senators of the first Class shall be vacated at the Expiration of the second Year, of the second Class at the Expiration of the fourth Year, and of the third Class at the Expiration of the sixth Year, so that one third may be chosen every second Year; and if Vacancies happen by Resignation, or otherwise, during the Recess of the Legislature of any State, the Executive thereof may make temporary Appointments until the next Meeting of the Legislature, which shall then fill such Vacancies.[3]

No Person shall be a Senator who shall not have attained to the Age of thirty Years, and been nine Years a Citizen of the United States, and who shall not, when elected, be an Inhabitant of that State for which he shall be chosen.

The Vice President of the United States shall be President of the Senate, but shall have no Vote, unless they be equally divided.

The Senate shall chuse their other Officers, and also a President pro tempore, in the Absence of the Vice President, or when he shall exercise the Office of President of the United States.

---

[1]Changed by the Fourteenth Amendment.

[2]Changed by the Seventeenth Amendment.
[3]Changed by the Seventeenth Amendment.

The Senate shall have the sole Power to try all Impeachments. When sitting for that Purpose, they shall be on Oath or Affirmation. When the President of the United States is tried, the Chief Justice shall preside: And no Person shall be convicted without the Concurrence of two thirds of the Members present.

Judgment in Cases of Impeachment shall not extend further than to removal from Office, and disqualification to hold and enjoy any Office of honor, Trust or Profit under the United States: but the Party convicted shall nevertheless be liable and subject to Indictment, Trial, Judgment and Punishment, according to Law.

Section 4   The Times, Places and Manner of holding Elections for Senators and Representatives, shall be prescribed in each State by the Legislature thereof; but the Congress may at any time by Law make or alter such Regulations, except as to the Places of chusing Senators.

The Congress shall assemble at least once in every Year, and such Meeting shall be on the first Monday in December, unless they shall by Law appoint a different Day.[4]

Section 5   Each House shall be the Judge of the Elections, Returns and Qualifications of its own Members, and a Majority of each shall constitute a Quorum to do Business; but a smaller Number may adjourn from day to day, and may be authorized to compel the Attendance of absent Members, in such Manner, and under such Penalties as each House may provide.

Each House may determine the Rules of its Proceedings, punish its Members for disorderly Behaviour, and with the Concurrence of two thirds, expel a Member.

Each House shall keep a Journal of its Proceedings, and from time to time publish the same, excepting such Parts as may in their Judgment require Secrecy; and the Yeas and Nays of the Members of either House on any question shall, at the Desire of one fifth of those Present, be entered on the Journal.

Neither House, during the Session of Congress, shall, without the Consent of the other, adjourn for more than three days, nor to any other Place than that in which the two Houses shall be sitting.

Section 6   The Senators and Representatives shall receive a Compensation for their Services, to be ascertained by Law, and paid out of the Treasury of the United States. They shall in all Cases, except Treason, Felony and Breach of the Peace, be privileged from Arrest during their Attendance at the Session of their respective Houses, and in going to and returning from the same; and for any Speech or Debate in either House, they shall not be questioned in any other Place.

No Senator or Representative shall, during the Time for which he was elected, be appointed to any civil Office under the Authority of the United States, which shall have been created, or the Emoluments whereof shall have been encreased during such time; and no Person holding any Office under the United States, shall be a Member of either House during his Continuance in Office.

Section 7   All Bills for raising Revenue shall originate in the House of Representatives; but the Senate may propose or concur with Amendments as on other Bills.

Every Bill which shall have passed the House of Representatives and the Senate, shall, before it becomes a Law, be presented to the President of the United States; If he approves he shall sign it, but if not he shall return it, with his Objections to that House in which it shall have originated, who shall enter the Objections at large on their Journal, and proceed to reconsider it. If after such Reconsideration two thirds of that House shall agree to pass the Bill, it shall be sent, together with the Objections, to the other House, by which it shall likewise be reconsidered, and if approved by two thirds of that House, it shall become a Law. But in all such Cases the Votes of both Houses shall be determined by Yeas and Nays, and the Names of the Persons voting for and against the Bill shall be entered on the Journal of each House respectively. If any Bill shall not be returned by the President within ten Days (Sundays excepted) after it shall have been presented to him, the Same shall be a Law, in like Manner as if he had signed it, unless the Congress by their Adjournment prevent its Return, in which Case it shall not be a Law.

Every Order, Resolution, or Vote to which the Concurrence of the Senate and House of Representatives may be necessary (except on a question of Adjournment) shall be presented to the President of the United States; and before the Same shall take Effect, shall be approved by him, or being disapproved by him, shall be repassed by two thirds of the Senate and House of Representatives, according to the Rules and Limitations prescribed in the Case of a Bill.

Section 8   The Congress shall have Power To lay and collect Taxes, Duties, Imposts and Excises, to pay the Debts and provide for the common Defence and general Welfare of the United States; but all Duties, Imposts and Excises shall be uniform throughout the United States.

To borrow Money on the credit of the United States;

To regulate Commerce with foreign Nations, and among the several States, and with the Indian Tribes;

To establish an uniform Rule of Naturalization, and uniform Laws on the subject of Bankruptcies throughout the United States;

To coin Money, regulate the Value thereof, and of foreign Coin, and fix the Standard of Weights and Measures;

To provide for the Punishment of counterfeiting the Securities and current Coin of the United States;

---

[4]Changed by the Twentieth Amendment.

To establish Post Offices and post Roads;

To promote the Progress of Science and useful Arts, by securing for limited Times to Authors and Inventors the exclusive Right to their respective Writings and Discoveries;

To constitute Tribunals inferior to the supreme Court;

To define and punish Piracies and Felonies committed on the high Seas, and Offences against the Law of Nations;

To declare War, grant Letters of Marque and Reprisal, and make Rules concerning Captures on Land and Water;

To raise and support Armies, but no Appropriation of Money to that Use shall be for a longer Term than two Years;

To provide and maintain a Navy;

To make Rules for the Government and Regulation of the land and naval Forces;

To provide for calling forth the Militia to execute the Laws of the Union, suppress Insurrections and repel Invasions;

To provide for organizing, arming, and disciplining, the Militia, and for governing such Part of them as may be employed in the Service of the United States, reserving to the States respectively, the Appointment of the Officers, and the Authority of training the Militia according to the discipline prescribed by Congress;

To exercise exclusive Legislation in all Cases whatsoever, over such District (not exceeding ten Miles square) as may, by Cession of particular States, and the Acceptance of Congress, become the Seat of the Government of the United States, and to exercise like Authority over all Places purchased by the Consent of the Legislature of the State in which the Same shall be, for the Erection of Forts, Magazines, Arsenals, dock-Yards, and other needful Buildings;—And

To make all Laws which shall be necessary and proper for carrying into Execution the foregoing Powers, and all other Powers vested by this Constitution in the Government of the United States, or in any Department or Officer thereof.

Section 9   The Migration or Importation of such Persons as any of the States now existing shall think proper to admit, shall not be prohibited by the Congress prior to the Year one thousand eight hundred and eight, but a Tax or duty may be imposed on such Importation, not exceeding ten dollars for each Person.

The Privilege of the Writ of Habeas Corpus shall not be suspended, unless when in Cases of Rebellion or Invasion the public Safety may require it.

No Bill of Attainder or ex post facto Law shall be passed.

No Capitation, or other direct, Tax shall be laid, unless in Proportion to the Census of Enumeration herein before directed to be taken.[5]

_____
[5]Changed by the Sixteenth Amendment.

No Tax or Duty shall be laid on Articles exported from any State.

No Preference shall be given by any Regulation of Commerce or Revenue to the Ports of one State over those of another: nor shall Vessels bound to, or from, one State, be obliged to enter, clear, or pay Duties in another.

No Money shall be drawn from the Treasury, but in Consequence of Appropriations made by Law; and a regular Statement and Account of the Receipts and Expenditures of all public Money shall be published from time to time.

No Title of Nobility shall be granted by the United States: And no Person holding any Office of Profit or Trust under them, shall, without the Consent of the Congress, accept of any present, Emolument, Office, or Title, of any kind whatever, from any King, Prince, or foreign State.

Section 10   No State shall enter into any Treaty, Alliance, or Confederation; grant Letters of Marque and Reprisal; coin Money; emit Bills of Credit; make any Thing but gold and silver coin a Tender in Payment of Debts; pass any Bill of Attainder, ex post facto Law, or Law impairing the Obligation of Contracts, or grant any Title of Nobility.

No State shall, without the Consent of the Congress, lay any Imposts or Duties on Imports or Exports, except what may be absolutely necessary for executing its inspection Laws: and the net Produce of all Duties and Imposts, laid by any State on Imports or Exports, shall be for the Use of the Treasury of the United States; and all such Laws shall be subject to the Revision and Controul of the Congress.

No State shall, without the consent of Congress, lay any Duty of Tonnage, keep Troops, or Ships of War in time of Peace, enter into any Agreement or Compact with another State, or with a foreign Power, or engage in War, unless actually invaded, or in such imminent Danger as will not admit of delay.

ARTICLE II

Section 1   The executive Power shall be vested in a President of the United States of America. He shall hold his Office during the Term of four Years, and, together with the Vice President, chosen for the same Term, be elected, as follows

Each state shall appoint, in such Manner as the Legislature thereof may direct, a Number of Electors, equal to the whole Number of Senators and Representatives to which the State may be entitled in Congress: but no Senator or Representative, or Person holding an Office of Trust or Profit under the United States, shall be appointed an Elector.

The Electors shall meet in their respective States, and vote by Ballot for two Persons, of whom one at least shall not be an inhabitant of the same State with themselves. And they shall make a List of all the Persons voted for, and of the Number of Votes for each; which List they shall sign and certify, and transmit sealed to the Seat of the Government of the United States, directed to the President of the Senate. The President of the Senate shall, in the Presence of the Senate and House of Representatives, open all the Certificates, and the Votes shall then be counted. The Person having the greatest Number of Votes shall be the President, if such Number be a Majority of the whole Number of Electors appointed; and if there be more than one who have such Majority, and have an equal Number of Votes, then the House of Representatives shall immediately chuse by Ballot one of them for President; and if no Person have a Majority, then from the five highest on the List the said House shall in like Manner chuse the President. But in chusing the President, the Votes shall be taken by States, the Representation from each State having one Vote; A quorum for this purpose shall consist of a Member or Members from two thirds of the States, and a Majority of all the States shall be necessary to a Choice. In every Case, after the Choice of the President, the Person having the greatest Number of Votes of the Electors shall be the Vice President. But if there should remain two or more who have equal Votes, the Senate shall chuse from them by Ballot the Vice President.[6]

The Congress may determine the Time of chusing the Electors, and the Day on which they shall give their Votes; which Day shall be the same throughout the United States.

No Person except a natural born Citizen, or a Citizen of the United States, at the time of the Adoption of this Constitution, shall be eligible to the Office of President; neither shall any Person be eligible to that Office who shall not have attained to the Age of thirty five Years, and been fourteen Years a Resident within the United States.

In Case of the Removal of the President from Office, or of his Death, Resignation, or Inability to discharge the Powers and Duties of the said Office, the Same shall devolve on the Vice President, and the Congress may by Law provide for the Case of Removal, Death, Resignation or Inability, both of the President and Vice President, declaring what Officer shall then act as President, and such Officer shall act accordingly, until the Disability be removed, or a President shall be elected.[7]

The President shall, at stated Times, receive for his Services, a Compensation, which shall neither be increased nor diminished during the Period for which he shall have been elected, and he shall not receive within that Period any other Emolument from the United States, or any of them.

Before he enter on the Execution of his Office, he shall take the following Oath or Affirmation:—"I do solemnly swear (or affirm) that I will faithfully execute the Office of President of the United States, and will to the best of my Ability, preserve, protect, and defend the Constitution of the United States."

Section 2 The President shall be Commander in Chief of the Army and Navy of the United States, and of the Militia of the several States, when called into the actual Service of the United States; he may require the Opinion, in writing, of the principal Officer in each of the executive Departments, upon any Subject relating to the Duties of their respective Offices, and he shall have Power to grant Reprieves and Pardons for Offences against the United States, except in Cases of Impeachment.

He shall have Power, by and with the Advice and Consent of the Senate, to make Treaties, provided two thirds of the Senators present concur; and he shall nominate, and by and with the Advice and Consent of the Senate, shall appoint Ambassadors, other public Ministers and Consuls, Judges of the supreme Court, and all other Officers of the United States, whose Appointments are not herein otherwise provided for, and which shall be established by Law; but the Congress may by Law vest the Appointment of such inferior Officers, as they think proper, in the President alone, in the Courts of Law, or in the Heads of Departments.

The President shall have Power to fill up all Vacancies that may happen during the Recess of the Senate, by granting Commissions which shall expire at the End of their next Session.

Section 3 He shall from time to time give to the Congress Information of the State of the Union, and recommend to their Consideration such Measures as he shall judge necessary and expedient; he may, on extraordinary Occasions, convene both Houses, or either of them, and in Case of Disagreement between them, with Respect to the Time of Adjournment, he may adjourn them to such Time as he shall think proper; he shall receive Ambassadors and other public Ministers; he shall take Care that the Laws be faithfully executed, and shall Commission all the Officers of the United States.

Section 4 The President, Vice President and all civil Officers of the United States, shall be removed from Office on Impeachment for, and Conviction of, Treason, Bribery, or other high Crimes and Misdemeanors.

ARTICLE III

Section 1 The judicial Power of the United States, shall be vested in one supreme Court, and in such inferior Courts as the Congress may from time to time ordain and establish. The Judges, both of the supreme and inferior Courts, shall hold their Offices during good Behaviour, and shall, at stated Times, receive for their Services, a Compensation, which shall not be diminished during their Continuance in Office.

---

[6]Changed by the Twelfth Amendment.

[7]Changed by the Twenty-fifth Amendment.

Section 2   The judicial Power shall extend to all Cases, in Law and Equity, arising under this Constitution, the Laws of the United States, and Treaties made, or which shall be made, under their Authority;—to all Cases affecting Ambassadors, other public Ministers and Consuls;—to all Cases of admiralty and maritime Jurisdiction;—to Controversies to which the United States shall be a party;—to Controversies between two or more States;—between a State and Citizens of another State;[8]—between Citizens of different States;—between Citizens of the same State claiming Lands under Grants of different States, and between a State, or the Citizens thereof, and foreign States, Citizens or Subjects.

In all Cases affecting Ambassadors, other public Ministers and Consuls, and those in which a State shall be Party, the supreme Court shall have original Jurisdiction. In all the other Cases before mentioned, the supreme Court shall have appellate Jurisdiction, both as to Law and Fact, with such Exceptions, and under such Regulations as the Congress shall make.

The Trial of all Crimes, except in Cases of Impeachment, shall be by Jury: and such Trial shall be held in the State where the said Crimes shall have been committed; but when not committed within any State, the Trial shall be at such Place or Places as the Congress may by Law have directed.

Section 3   Treason against the United States, shall consist only in levying War against them, or in adhering to their Enemies, giving them Aid and Comfort. No Person shall be convicted of Treason unless on the Testimony of two Witnesses to the same overt Act, or on Confession in open Court.

The Congress shall have Power to declare the Punishment of Treason, but no Attainder of Treason shall work Corruption of Blood, or Forfeiture except during the Life of the Person attainted.

ARTICLE IV

Section 1   Full Faith and Credit shall be given in each State to the public Acts, Records, and judicial Proceedings of every other State. And the Congress may by general Laws prescribe the Manner in which such Acts, Records and Proceedings shall be proved, and the Effect thereof.

Section 2   The Citizens of each State shall be entitled to all Privileges and Immunities of Citizens in the several States.

A Person charged in any State with Treason, Felony, or other Crime, who shall flee from Justice, and be found in another State, shall on Demand of the executive Authority of the State from which he fled, be delivered up, to be removed to the State having Jurisdiction of the Crime.

No Person held to Service or Labour in one State, under the Laws thereof, escaping into another, shall, in Consequence of any Law or Regulation therein, be discharged from such Service or Labour, but shall be delivered up on Claim of the Party to whom such Service or Labour may be due.[9]

Section 3   New States may be admitted by the Congress into this Union; but no new State shall be formed or erected within the Jurisdiction of any other State; nor any State be formed by the Junction of two or more States, or Parts of States, without the Consent of the Legislatures of the States concerned as well as of the Congress.

The Congress shall have Power to dispose of and make all needful Rules and Regulations respecting the Territory or other Property belonging to the United States; and nothing in this Constitution shall be so construed as to Prejudice any Claims of the United States, or of any particular State.

Section 4   The United States shall guarantee to every State in this Union a Republican Form of Government, and shall protect each of them against Invasion; and on Application of the Legislature, or of the Executive (when the Legislature cannot be convened) against domestic Violence.

ARTICLE V

The Congress, whenever two thirds of both Houses shall deem it necessary, shall propose Amendments to this Constitution, or, on the Application of the Legislatures of two thirds of the several States, shall call a Convention for proposing Amendments, which, in either Case, shall be valid to all Intents and Purposes, as Part of this Constitution, when ratified by the legislatures of three fourths of the several States, or by Conventions in three fourths thereof, as the one or the other Mode of Ratification may be proposed by the Congress; Provided that no Amendment which may be made prior to the Year One thousand eight hundred and eight shall in any Manner affect the first and fourth Clauses in the Ninth Section of the first Article; and that no State, without its Consent, shall be deprived of its equal Suffrage in the Senate.

ARTICLE VI

All Debts contracted and Engagements entered into, before the Adoption of this Constitution, shall be as valid against the United States under this Constitution, as under the Confederation.

The Constitution, and the Laws of the United States which shall be made in Pursuance thereof; and all Treaties made, or which shall be made, under the Authority of the United States, shall be the supreme Law of the Land; and the Judges in every State shall be bound thereby, any Thing in the Constitution or Laws of any State to the Contrary notwithstanding.

---

[8]Changed by the Eleventh Amendment.

[9]Changed by the Thirteenth Amendment.

The Senators and Representatives before mentioned, and the Members of the several State Legislatures, and all executive and judicial Officers, both of the United States and of the several States, shall be bound by Oath or Affirmation, to support this Constitution; but no religious Test shall ever be required as a Qualification to any Office or public Trust under the United States.

ARTICLE VII

The Ratification of the Conventions of nine States, shall be sufficient for the Establishment of this Constitution between the States so ratifying the Same.

Done in Convention by the Unanimous Consent of the States present the Seventeenth Day of September in the Year of our Lord one thousand seven hundred and eighty seven and of the Independance of the United States of America the Twelfth. In witness whereof We have hereunto subscribed our Names.

AMENDMENTS

[The first 10 amendments are known as the "Bill of Rights."]

Amendment I (Ratified 1791)

Congress shall make no law respecting an establishment of religion, or prohibiting the free exercise thereof; or abridging the freedom of speech, or of the press; or the right of the people peaceably to assemble, and to petition the Government for a redress of grievances.

Amendment 2 (Ratified 1791)

A well regulated Militia, being necessary to the security of a free State, the right of the people to keep and bear Arms, shall not be infringed.

Amendment 3 (Ratified 1791)

No Soldier shall, in time of peace be quartered in any house, without the consent of the Owner, nor in time of war, but in a manner to be prescribed by law.

Amendment 4 (Ratified 1791)

The right of the people to be secure in their persons, houses, papers, and effects, against unreasonable searches and seizures, shall not be violated, and no Warrants shall issue, but upon probable cause, supported by Oath or affirmation, and particularly describing the place to be searched, and the persons or things to be seized.

Amendment 5 (Ratified 1791)

No person shall be held to answer for a capital, or otherwise infamous crime, unless on a presentment or indictment of a Grand Jury, except in cases arising in the land or naval forces, or in the Militia, when in actual service in time of War or public danger; nor shall any person be subject for the same offence to be twice put in jeopardy of life or limb; nor shall be compelled in any criminal case to be a witness against himself, nor be deprived of life, liberty, or property, without due process of law; nor shall private property be taken for public use, without just compensation.

Amendment 6 (Ratified 1791)

In all criminal prosecutions, the accused shall enjoy the right to a speedy and public trial, by an impartial jury of the State and district wherein the crime shall have been committed, which district shall have been previously ascertained by law, and to be informed of the nature and cause of the accusation; to be confronted with the witnesses against him; to have compulsory process for obtaining Witnesses in his favor, and to have assistance of counsel for his defence.

Amendment 7 (Ratified 1791)

In Suits at common law, where the value in controversy shall exceed twenty dollars, the right of trial by jury shall be preserved, and no fact tried by a jury, shall be otherwise re-examined in any Court of the United States, than according to the rules of the common law.

Amendment 8 (Ratified 1791)

Excessive bail shall not be required, nor excessive fines imposed, nor cruel and unusual punishments inflicted.

Amendment 9 (Ratified 1791)

The enumeration in the Constitution, of certain rights, shall not be construed to deny or disparage others retained by the people.

Amendment 10 (Ratified 1791)

The powers not delegated to the United States by the Constitution, nor prohibited by it to the States, are reserved to the States respectively, or to the people.

Amendment 11 (Ratified 1795)

The Judicial power of the United States shall not be construed to extend to any suit in law or equity, commenced or prosecuted against one of the United States by Citizens of another State, or by Citizens or Subjects of any Foreign State.

Amendment 12 (Ratified 1804)

The Electors shall meet in their respective states, and vote by ballot for President and Vice-President, one of whom, at least, shall not be an inhabitant of the same state with themselves; they shall name in their ballots the person voted for as President, and in distinct ballots the person voted for as Vice-President, and they shall make distinct lists of all persons voted for as President, and of all persons voted for as Vice-President, and of the number of votes for each, which lists they shall sign and certify, and transmit sealed to the seat of the government of the United States, directed to the President of the Senate;— The President of the Senate shall, in the presence of the Senate and House of Representatives, open all the certificates and the votes shall then be counted;—The person having the greatest number of votes for President, shall be the President, if such number be a majority of the whole number of Electors appointed; and if no person have such majority, then from the persons having the highest numbers not exceeding three on the list of those voted for as President, the House of Representatives shall choose immediately, by ballot, the President. But in choosing the President, the votes shall be taken by states, the representation from each state having one vote; a quorum for this purpose shall consist of a member or members from two-thirds of the states, and a majority of all the states shall be necessary to a choice. And if the House of Representatives shall not choose a President whenever the right of choice shall devolve upon them, before the fourth day of March next following, then the Vice-President shall act as president, as in the case of the death or other constitutional disability of the President.[10]—The person having the greatest number of votes as Vice-President, shall be the Vice-President, if such number be a majority of the whole number of Electors appointed, and if no person have a majority, then from the two highest numbers on the list, the Senate shall choose the Vice-President; a quorum for the purpose shall consist of two-thirds of the whole number of Senators, and a majority of the whole number shall be necessary to a choice. But no person constitutionally ineligible to the office of President shall be eligible to that of Vice-President of the United States.

Amendment 13 (Ratified 1865)

Section 1   Neither slavery nor involuntary servitude, except as a punishment for crime whereof the party shall have been duly convicted, shall exist within the United States, or any place subject to their jurisdiction.

Section 2   Congress shall have power to enforce this article by appropriate legislation.

Amendment 14 (Ratified 1868)

Section 1   All persons born or naturalized in the United States, and subject to the jurisdiction thereof, are citizens of the United States and of the State wherein they reside. No State shall make or enforce any law which shall abridge the privileges or immunities of citizens of the United States; nor shall any State deprive any person of life, liberty, or property, without due process of law; nor deny to any person within its jurisdiction the equal protection of the laws.

Section 2   Representatives shall be apportioned among the several States according to their respective numbers, counting the whole number of persons in each State, excluding Indians not taxed. But when the right to vote at any election for the choice of electors for President and Vice President of the United States, Representatives in Congress, the Executive and Judicial officers of a State, or the members of the Legislature thereof, is denied to any of the male inhabitants of such State, being twenty-one[11] years of age, and citizens of the United States, or in any way abridged except for participation in rebellion, or other crime, the basis of representation therein shall be reduced in the proportion which the number of such male citizens shall bear to the whole number of male citizens twenty-one years of age in such State.

Section 3   No person shall be a Senator or Representative in Congress, or elector of President and Vice President, or hold any office, civil or military, under the United States, or under any State, who, having previously taken an oath, as a member of Congress, or as an officer of the United States, or as a member of any State legislature, or as an executive or judicial officer of any State, to support the Constitution of the United States, shall have engaged in insurrection or rebellion against the same, or given aid or comfort to the enemies thereof. But Congress may by a vote of two-thirds of each House, remove such disability.

Section 4   The validity of the public debt of the United States, authorized by law, including debts incurred for payment of pensions and bounties for services in suppressing insurrection or rebellion, shall not be questioned. But neither the United States nor any State shall assume or pay any debt or obligation incurred in aid of insurrection or rebellion against the United States, or any claim for the loss or emancipation of any slave; but all such debts, obligations and claims shall be held illegal and void.

Section 5   The Congress shall have power to enforce, by appropriate legislation, the provisions of this article.

Amendment 15 (Ratified 1870)

Section 1   The right of citizens of the United States to vote shall not be denied or abridged by the United States

---

[10]Changed by the Twentieth Amendment.

[11]Changed by the Twenty-sixth Amendment.

or by any State on account of race, color, or previous condition of servitude.

Section 2   The Congress shall have power to enforce this article by appropriate legislation.

Amendment 16 (Ratified 1913)

The Congress shall have power to lay and collect taxes on incomes, from whatever source derived, without apportionment among the several States, and without regard to any census or enumeration.

Amendment 17 (Ratified 1913)

The Senate of the United States shall be composed of two Senators from each State, elected by the people thereof, for six years; and each Senator shall have one vote. The electors in each State shall have the qualifications requisite for electors of the most numerous branch of the State legislatures.

When vacancies happen in the representation of any State in the Senate, the executive authority of such State shall issue writs of election to fill such vacancies: *Provided,* That the legislature of any State may empower the executive thereof to make temporary appointments until the people fill the vacancies by election as the legislature may direct.

This amendment shall not be so construed as to affect the election or term of any Senator chosen before it becomes valid as part of the Constitution.

Amendment 18 (Ratified 1919; Repealed 1933)

Section 1   After one year from the ratification of this article the manufacture, sale, or transportation of intoxicating liquors within, the importation thereof into, or the exportation thereof from the United States and all territory subject to the jurisdiction thereof for beverage purposes is hereby prohibited.

Section 2   The Congress and the several States shall have concurrent power to enforce this article by appropriate legislation.

Section 3   This article shall be inoperative unless it shall have been ratified as an amendment to the Constitution by the legislatures of the several States, as provided in the Constitution, within seven years from the date of the submission hereof to the States by the Congress.[12]

Amendment 19 (Ratified 1920)

The right of citizens of the United States to vote shall not be denied or abridged by the United States or by any State on account of sex.

---

[12]Repealed by the Twenty-first Amendment.

Congress shall have power to enforce this article by appropriate legislation.

Amendment 20 (Ratified 1933)

Section 1   The terms of the President and Vice President shall end at noon on the 20th day of January, and the terms of Senators and Representatives at noon on the 3d day of January, of the years in which such terms would have ended if this article had not been ratified; and the terms of their successors shall then begin.

Section 2   The Congress shall assemble at least once in every year, and such meeting shall begin at noon on the 3d day of January, unless they shall by law appoint a different day.

Section 3   If, at the time fixed for the beginning of the term of the President, the President elect shall have died, the Vice President elect shall become President. If a President shall not have been chosen before the time fixed for the beginning of his term, or if the President elect shall have failed to qualify, then the Vice President elect shall act as President until a President shall have qualified; and the Congress may by law provide for the case wherein neither a President elect nor a Vice President elect shall have qualified, declaring who shall then act as President, or the manner in which one who is to act shall be selected, and such person shall act accordingly until a President or Vice President shall have qualified.

Section 4   The Congress may by law provide for the case of the death of any of the persons from whom the House of Representatives may choose a President whenever the right of choice shall have devolved upon them, and for the case of the death of any of the persons from whom the Senate may choose a Vice President whenever the right of choice shall have devolved upon them.

Section 5   Sections 1 and 2 shall take effect on the 15th day of October following the ratification of this article.

Section 6   This article shall be inoperative unless it shall have been ratified as an amendment to the Constitution by the legislatures of three-fourths of the several States within seven years from the date of its submission.

Amendment 21 (Ratified 1933)

Section 1   The eighteenth article of amendment to the Constitution of the United States is hereby repealed.

Section 2   The transportation or importation into any State, Territory, or possession of the United States for delivery or use therein of intoxicating liquors, in violation of the laws thereof, is hereby prohibited.

Section 3   This article shall be inoperative unless it shall have been ratified as an amendment to the Constitution by conventions in the several States, as provided in the Constitution, within seven years from the date of the submission hereof to the States by the Congress.

Amendment 22 (Ratified 1951)

Section 1   No person shall be elected to the office of the President more than twice, and no person who has held the office of President, or acted as President, for more than two years of a term to which some other person was elected President shall be elected to the office of the President more than once. But this Article shall not apply to any person holding the office of President when this Article was proposed by the Congress, and shall not prevent any person who may be holding the office of President, or acting as President, during the term within which this Article becomes operative from holding the office of President or acting as President during the remainder of such term.

Section 2   This Article shall be inoperative unless it shall have been ratified as an amendment to the Constitution by the legislatures of three-fourths of the several States within seven years from the date of its submission to the States by the Congress.

Amendment 23 (Ratified 1961)

Section 1   The District constituting the seat of Government of the United States shall appoint in such manner as the Congress may direct:

A number of electors of President and Vice President equal to the whole number of Senators and Representatives in Congress to which the District would be entitled if it were a State, but in no event more than the least populous State; they shall be in addition to those appointed by the States, but they shall be considered, for the purposes of the election of President and Vice President, to be electors appointed by a State; and they shall meet in the District and perform such duties as provided by the twelfth article of amendment.

Section 2   The Congress shall have power to enforce this article by appropriate legislation.

Amendment 24 (Ratified 1964)

Section 1   The right of citizens of the United States to vote in any primary or other election for President or Vice President, for electors for President or Vice President, or for Senator or Representative in Congress, shall not be denied or abridged by the United States or any State by reason of failure to pay any poll tax or other tax.

Section 2   The Congress shall have power to enforce this article by appropriate legislation.

Amendment 25 (Ratified 1967)

Section 1   In case of the removal of the President from office or of his death or resignation, the Vice President shall become President.

Section 2   Whenever there is a vacancy in the office of the Vice President, the President shall nominate a Vice President who shall take office upon confirmation by a majority vote of both Houses of Congress.

Section 3   Whenever the President transmits to the President pro tempore of the Senate and the Speaker of the House of Representatives his written declaration that he is unable to discharge the powers and duties of his office, and until he transmits to them a written declaration to the contrary, such powers and duties shall be discharged by the Vice President as Acting President.

Section 4   Whenever the Vice President and a majority of either the principal officers of the executive departments or of such other body as Congress may by law provide, transmit to the President pro tempore of the Senate and the Speaker of the House of Representatives their written declaration that the President is unable to discharge the powers and duties of his office, the Vice President shall immediately assume the powers and duties of the office as Acting President.

Thereafter, when the President transmits to the President pro tempore of the Senate and the Speaker of the House of Representatives his written declaration that no inability exists, he shall resume the powers and duties of his office unless the Vice President and a majority of either the principal officers of the executive department or of such other body as Congress may by law provide, transmit within four days to the President pro tempore of the Senate and the Speaker of the House of Representatives their written declaration that the President is unable to discharge the powers and duties of his office. Thereupon Congress shall decide the issue, assembling within forty-eight hours for that purpose if not in session. If the Congress, within twenty-one days after receipt of the latter written declaration, or, if Congress is not in session, within twenty-one days after Congress is required to assemble, determines by two-thirds vote of both Houses that the President is unable to discharge the powers and duties of his office, the Vice President shall continue to discharge the same as Acting President; otherwise, the President shall resume the powers and duties of his office.

Amendment 26 (Ratified 1971)

Section 1   The right of citizens of the United States, who are eighteen years of age or older, to vote shall not be denied or abridged by the United States or by any State on account of age.

Section 2   The Congress shall have power to enforce this article by appropriate legislation.

Amendment 27 (Ratified 1992)

No law, varying the compensation for the services of the Senators and Representatives, shall take effect, until an election of Representatives shall have intervened.

Uniform Commercial Code*

Title

An Act
To be known as the Uniform Commercial Code, Relating to Certain Commercial Transactions in or regarding Personal Property and Contracts and other Documents concerning them, including Sales, Commercial Paper, Bank Deposits and Collections, Letters of Credit, Bulk Transfers, Warehouse Receipts, Bills of Lading, other Documents of Title, Investment Securities, and Secured Transactions, including certain Sales of Accounts, Chattel Paper, and Contract Rights; Providing for Public Notice to Third Parties in Certain Circumstances; Regulating Procedure, Evidence and Damages in Certain Court Actions Involving such Transactions, Contracts or Documents; to Make Uniform the Law with Respect Thereto; and Repealing Inconsistent Legislation.

ARTICLE I GENERAL PROVISIONS

Part I Short Title, Construction, Application and Subject Matter of the Act

§ 1–101. Short Title
This Act shall be known and may be cited as Uniform Commercial Code.

§ 1–102. Purposes; Rules of Construction; Variation by Agreement
(1) This Act shall be liberally construed and applied to promote its underlying purposes and policies.
(2) Underlying purposes and policies of this Act are
    (a) to simplify, clarify and modernize the law governing commercial transactions;
    (b) to permit the continued expansion of commercial practices through custom, usage and agreement of the parties;
    (c) to make uniform the law among the various jurisdictions.
(3) The effect of provisions of this Act may be varied by agreement, except as otherwise provided in this Act and except that the obligations of good faith, diligence, reasonableness and care prescribed by this Act may not be disclaimed by agreement but the parties may by agreement determine the standards by which the performance of such obligations is to be measured if such standards are not manifestly unreasonable.
(4) The presence in certain provisions of this Act of the words "unless otherwise agreed" or words of similar import does not imply that the effect of other provisions may not be varied by agreement under subsection (3).
(5) In this Act unless the context otherwise requires
    (a) words in the singular number include the plural, and in the plural include the singular;
    (b) words of the masculine gender include the feminine and the neuter, and when the sense so indicates words of the neuter gender may refer to any gender.

§ 1–103. Supplementary General Principles of Law Applicable
Unless displaced by the particular provisions of this Act, the principles of law and equity, including the law merchant and the law relative to capacity to contract, principal and agent, estoppel, fraud, misrepresentation, duress, coercion, mistake, bankruptcy, or other validating or invalidating cause shall supplement its provisions.

§ 1–104. Construction Against Implicit Repeal
This Act being a general act intended as a unified coverage of its subject matter, no part of it shall be deemed to be impliedly repealed by subsequent legislation if such construction can reasonably be avoided.

§ 1–105. Territorial Application of the Act; Parties' Power to Choose Applicable Law
(1) Except as provided hereafter in this section, when a transaction bears a reasonable relation to this state and also to another state or nation the parties may agree that the law either of this state or of such other state or nation shall govern their rights and duties. Failing such agreement this Act applies to transactions bearing an appropriate relation to this state.
(2) Where one of the following provisions of this Act specifies the applicable law, that provision governs and a contrary agreement is effective only to the extent permitted by law (including the conflict of laws rules) so specified:
Rights of creditors against sold goods. Section 2–402.

*Excerpts from the Official Text—1990. Copyright © 1991 by The American Law Institute and the National Conference of Commissioners on Uniform State Laws. Reprinted with the permission of the Permanent Editorial Board for the Uniform Commercial Code.

Applicability of the Article on Leases. Sections 2A–105 and 2A–106.

Applicability of the Article on Bank Deposits and Collections. Section 4–102.

Governing Law in the Article on Funds Transfers. Section 4A–507.

Bulk transfers subject to the Article on Bulk Transfers. Section 6–103.

Applicability of the Article on Investment Securities. Section 8–106.

Perfection provisions of the Article on Secured Transactions. Section 9–103.

§ 1–106. Remedies to Be Liberally Administered

(1) The remedies provided by this Act shall be liberally administered to the end that the aggrieved party may be put in as good a position as if the other party had fully performed but neither consequential or special nor penal damages may be had except as specifically provided in this Act or by other rule of law.

(2) Any right or obligation declared by this Act is enforceable by action unless the provision declaring it specifies a different and limited effect.

§ 1–107. Waiver or Renunciation of Claim or Right After Breach

Any claim or right arising out of an alleged breach can be discharged in whole or in part without consideration by a written waiver or renunciation signed and delivered by the aggrieved party.

§ 1–108. Severability

If any provision or clause of this Act or application thereof to any person or circumstances is held invalid, such invalidity shall not affect other provisions or applications of the Act which can be given effect without the invalid provision or application, and to this end the provisions of this Act are declared to be severable.

§ 1–109. Section Captions

Section captions are parts of this Act.

Part 2 General Definitions and Principles of Interpretation

§ 1–201. General Definitions

Subject to additional definitions contained in the subsequent Articles of this Act which are applicable to specific Articles or Parts thereof, and unless the context otherwise requires, in this Act:

(1) "Action" in the sense of a judicial proceeding includes recoupment, counterclaim, set-off, suit in equity and any other proceedings in which rights are determined.

(2) "Aggrieved party" means a party entitled to resort to a remedy.

(3) "Agreement" means the bargain of the parties in fact as found in their language or by implication from other circumstances including course of dealing or usage of trade or course of performance as provided in this Act (Sections 1–205 and 2–208). Whether an agreement has legal consequences is determined by the provisions of this Act, if applicable; otherwise by the law of contracts (Section 1–103). (Compare "Contract.")

(4) "Bank" means any person engaged in the business of banking.

(5) "Bearer" means the person in possession of an instrument, document of title, or certificated security payable to bearer or indorsed in blank.

(6) "Bill of lading" means a document evidencing the receipt of goods for shipment issued by a person engaged in the business of transporting or forwarding goods, and includes an airbill. "Airbill" means a document serving for air transportation as a bill of lading does for marine or rail transportation, and includes an air consignment note or air waybill.

(7) "Branch" includes a separately incorporated foreign branch of a bank.

(8) "Burden of establishing" a fact means the burden of persuading the triers of fact that the existence of the fact is more probable than its nonexistence.

(9) "Buyer in ordinary course of business" means a person who in good faith and without knowledge that the sale to him is in violation of the ownership rights or security interest of a third party in the goods buys in ordinary course from a person in the business of selling goods of that kind but does not include a pawnbroker. All persons who sell minerals or the like (including oil and gas) at wellhead or minehead shall be deemed to be persons in the business of selling goods of that kind. "Buying" may be for cash or by exchange of other property or on secured or unsecured credit and includes receiving goods or documents of title under a pre-existing contract for sale but does not include a transfer in bulk or as security for or in total or partial satisfaction of a money debt.

(10) "Conspicuous": A term or clause is conspicuous when it is so written that a reasonable person against whom it is to operate ought to have noticed it. A printed heading in capitals (as: Non–Negotiable Bill of Lading) is conspicuous. Language in the body of a form is "conspicuous" if it is in larger or other contrasting type or color. But in a telegram any stated term is "conspicuous." Whether a term or clause is "conspicuous" or not is for decision by the court.

(11) "Contract" means the total legal obligation which results from the parties' agreement as affected by this Act and any other applicable rules of law. (Compare "Agreement.")

(12) "Creditor" includes a general creditor, a secured creditor, a lien creditor and any representative of creditors,

including an assignee for the benefit of creditors, a trustee in bankruptcy, a receiver in equity and an executor or administrator of an insolvent debtor's or assignor's estate.

(13) "Defendant" includes a person in the position of defendant in a cross-action or counterclaim.

(14) "Delivery" with respect to instruments, documents of title, chattel paper, or certificated securities means voluntary transfer of possession.

(15) "Document of title" includes bill of lading, dock warrant, dock receipt, warehouse receipt or order for the delivery of goods, and also any other document which in the regular course of business or financing is treated as adequately evidencing that the person in possession of it is entitled to receive, hold and dispose of the document and the goods it covers. To be a document of title a document must purport to be issued by or addressed to a bailee and purport to cover goods in the bailee's possession which are either identified or are fungible portions of an identified mass.

(16) "Fault" means wrongful act, omission or breach.

(17) "Fungible" with respect to goods or securities means goods or securities of which any unit is, by nature or usage of trade, the equivalent of any other like unit. Goods which are not fungible shall be deemed fungible for the purposes of this Act to the extent that under a particular agreement or document unlike units are treated as equivalents.

(18) "Genuine" means free of forgery or counterfeiting.

(19) "Good faith" means honesty in fact in the conduct or transaction concerned.

(20) "Holder," with respect to a negotiable instrument, means the person in possession if the instrument is payable to bearer, or in the case of an instrument payable to an identified person, if the identified person is in possession. "Holder" with respect to a document of title means the person in possession of the goods are deliverable to bearer or to the order of the person in possession.

(21) To "honor" is to pay or to accept and pay, or where a credit so engages to purchase or discount a draft complying with the terms of credit.

(22) "Insolvency proceedings" includes any assignment for the benefit of creditors or other proceedings intended to liquidate or rehabilitate the estate of the person involved.

(23) A person is "insolvent" who either has ceased to pay his debts in the ordinary course of business or cannot pay his debts as they become due or is insolvent within the meaning of the federal bankruptcy law.

(24) "Money" means a medium of exchange authorized or adopted by a domestic or foreign government as a part of its currency.

(25) A person has "notice" of a fact when

(a) he has actual knowledge of it; or

(b) he has received a notice or notification of it; or

(c) from all the facts and circumstances known to him at the time in question he has reason to know that it exists.

A person "knows" or has "knowledge" of a fact when he has actual knowledge of it. "Discover" or "learn" or a word or phrase of similar import refers to knowledge rather than to reason to know. The time and circumstances under which a notice or notification may cease to be effective are not determined by this Act.

(26) A person "notifies" or "gives" a notice or notification to another by taking such steps as may be reasonably required to inform the other in ordinary course whether or not such other actually comes to know of it. A person "receives" a notice or notification when

(a) it comes to his attention; or

(b) it is duly delivered at the place of business through which the contract was made or at any other place held out by him as the place for receipt of such communications.

(27) Notice, knowledge or a notice or notification received by an organization is effective for a particular transaction from the time when it is brought to the attention of the individual conducting that transaction, and in any event from the time when it would have been brought to his attention if the organization had exercised due diligence. An organization exercises due diligence if it maintains reasonable routines for communicating significant information to the person conducting the transaction and there is reasonable compliance with the routines. Due diligence does not require an individual acting for the organization to communicate information unless such communication is part of his regular duties or unless he has reason to know of the transaction and that the transaction would be materially affected by the information.

(28) "Organization" includes a corporation, government or governmental subdivision or agency, business trust, estate, trust, partnership or association, two or more persons having a joint or common interest, or any other legal or commercial entity.

(29) "Party," as distinct from "third party," means a person who has engaged in a transaction or made an agreement within this Act.

(30) "Person" includes an individual or an organization (See Section 1–102).

(31) "Presumption" or "presumed" means that the trier of fact must find the existence of the fact presumed unless and until evidence is introduced which would support a finding of its nonexistence.

(32) "Purchase" includes taking by sale, discount, negotiation, mortgage, pledge, lien, issue or reissue, gift or any other voluntary transaction creating an interest in property.

(33) "Purchaser" means a person who takes by purchase.

(34) "Remedy" means any remedial right to which an aggrieved party is entitled with or without resort to a tribunal.

(35) "Representative" includes an agent, an officer of a corporation or association, and a trustee, executor or

administrator of an estate, or any other person empowered to act for another.

(36) "Rights" includes remedies.

(37) "Security interest" means an interest in personal property or fixtures which secures payment or performance of an obligation. The retention or reservation of title by a seller of goods notwithstanding shipment or delivery to the buyer (Section 2–401) is limited in effect to a reservation of a "security interest." The term also includes any interest of a buyer of accounts or chattel paper which is subject to Article 9. The special property interest of a buyer of goods on identification of those goods to a contract for sale under Section 2–401 is not a "security interest," but a buyer may also acquire a "security interest" by complying with Article 9. Unless a consignment is intended as security, reservation of title thereunder is not a "security interest," but a consignment in any event is subject to the provisions on consignment sales (Section 2–326).

Whether a transaction creates a lease or security interest is determined by the facts of each case; however, a transaction creates a security interest if the consideration the lessee is to pay the lessor for the right to possession and use of the goods is an obligation for the term of the lease not subject to termination by the lessee, and

(a) the original term of the lease is equal to or greater than the remaining economic life of the goods,

(b) the lessee is bound to renew the lease for the remaining economic life of the goods or is bound to become the owner of the goods,

(c) the lessee has an option to renew the lease for the remaining economic life of the goods for no additional consideration or nominal additional consideration upon compliance with the lease agreement, or

(d) the lessee has an option to become the owner of the goods for no additional consideration or nominal additional consideration upon compliance with the lease agreement.

A transaction does not create a security interest merely because it provides that

(a) the present value of the consideration the lessee is obligated to pay the lessor for the right to possession and use of the goods is substantially equal to or is greater than the fair market value of the goods at the time the lease is entered into,

(b) the lessee assumes risk of loss of the goods, or agrees to pay taxes, insurance, filing, recording, or registration fees, or service or maintenance costs with respect to the goods,

(c) the lessee has an option to renew the lease or to become the owner of the goods.

(d) the lessee has an option to renew the lease for a fixed rent that is equal to or greater than the reasonably predictable fair market rent for the use of the goods for the term of the renewal at the time the option is to be performed, or

(e) the lessee has an option to become the owner of the goods for a fixed price that is equal to or greater than the reasonably predictable fair market value of the goods at the time the option is to be performed.

For purposes of this subsection (37):

(x) Additional consideration is not nominal if (i) when the option to renew the lease is granted to the lessee the rent is stated to be the fair market rent for the use of the goods for the term of the renewal determined at the time the option is to be performed, or (ii) when the option to become the owner of the goods is granted to the lessee the price is stated to be the fair market value of the goods determined at the time the option is to be performed. Additional consideration is nominal if it is less than the lessee's reasonably predictable cost of performing under the lease agreement if the option is not exercised;

(y) "Reasonably predictable" and "remaining economic life of the goods" are to be determined with reference to the facts and circumstances at the time the transaction is entered into; and

(z) "Present value" means the amount as of a date certain of one or more sums payable in the future, discounted to the date certain. The discount is determined by the interest rate specified by the parties if the rate is not manifestly unreasonable at the time the transaction is entered into; otherwise, the discount is determined by a commercially reasonable rate that takes into account the facts and circumstances of each case at the time the transaction was entered into.

(38) "Send" in connection with any writing or notice means to deposit in the mail or deliver for transmission by any other usual means of communication with postage or cost of transmission provided for and properly addressed and in the case of an instrument to an address specified thereon or otherwise agreed, or if there be none to any address reasonable under the circumstances. The receipt of any writing or notice within the time at which it would have arrived if properly sent has the effect of a proper sending.

(39) "Signed" includes any symbol executed or adopted by a party with present intention to authenticate a writing.

(40) "Surety" includes guarantor.

(41) "Telegram" includes a message transmitted by radio, teletype, cable, any mechanical method of transmission, or the like.

(42) "Term" means that portion of an agreement which relates to a particular matter.

(43) "Unauthorized" signature or indorsement means one made without actual, implied or apparent authority and includes a forgery.

(44) "Value." Except as otherwise provided with respect to negotiable instruments and bank collections (Sections 3–303, 4–208 and 4–209) a person gives "value" for rights if he acquires them

(a) in return for a binding commitment to extend credit or for the extension of immediately available credit whether or not drawn upon and whether or not a charge-back is provided for in the event of difficulties in collection; or

(b) as security for or in total or partial satisfaction of a preexisting claim; or

(c) by accepting delivery pursuant to a preexisting contract for purchase; or

(d) generally, in return for any consideration sufficient to support a simple contract.

(45) "Warehouse receipt" means a receipt issued by a person engaged in the business of storing goods for hire.

(46) "Written" or "writing" includes printing, typewriting or any other intentional reduction to tangible form.

§ 1–202. Prima Facie Evidence by Third Party Documents

A document in due form purporting to be a bill of lading, policy or certificate of insurance, official weigher's or inspector's certificate, consular invoice, or any other document authorized or required by the contract to be issued by a third party shall be prima facie evidence of its own authenticity and genuineness and of the facts stated in the document by the third party.

§ 1–203. Obligation of Good Faith

Every contract or duty within this Act imposes an obligation of good faith in its performance or enforcement.

§ 1–204. Time; Reasonable Time; "Seasonably"

(1) Whenever this Act requires any action to be taken within a reasonable time, any time which is not manifestly unreasonable may be fixed by agreement.

(2) What is a reasonable time for taking any action depends on the nature, purpose and circumstances of such action.

(3) An action is taken "seasonably" when it is taken at or within the time agreed or if no time is agreed at or within a reasonable time.

§ 1–205. Course of Dealing and Usage of Trade

(1) A course of dealing is a sequence of previous conduct between the parties to a particular transaction which is fairly to be regarded as establishing a common basis of understanding for interpreting their expressions and other conduct.

(2) A usage of trade is any practice or method of dealing having such regularity of observance in a place, vocation or trade as to justify an expectation that it will be observed with respect to the transaction in question. The existence and scope of such a usage are to be proved as facts. If it is established that such a usage is embodied in a written trade code or similar writing the interpretation of the writing is for the court.

(3) A course of dealing between parties and any usage of trade in the vocation or trade in which they are engaged or of which they are or should be aware give particular meaning to and supplement or qualify terms of an agreement.

(4) The express terms of an agreement and an applicable course of dealing or usage of trade shall be construed wherever reasonable as consistent with each other; but when such construction is unreasonable express terms control both course of dealing and usage of trade and course of dealing controls usage of trade.

(5) An applicable usage of trade in the place where any part of performance is to occur shall be used in interpreting the agreement as to that part of the performance.

(6) Evidence of a relevant usage of trade offered by one party is not admissible unless and until he has given the other party such notice as the court finds sufficient to prevent unfair surprise to the latter.

§ 1–206. Statute of Frauds for Kinds of Personal Property Not Otherwise Covered

(1) Except in the cases described in subsection (2) of this section a contract for the sale of personal property is not enforceable by way of action or defense beyond five thousand dollars in amount or value of remedy unless there is some writing which indicates that a contract for sale has been made between the parties at a defined or stated price, reasonably identifies the subject matter, and is signed by the party against whom enforcement is sought or by his authorized agent.

(2) Subsection (1) of this section does not apply to contracts for the sale of goods (Section 2–201) nor of securities (Section 8–319) nor to security agreements (Section 9–203).

§ 1–207. Performance or Acceptance Under Reservation of Rights

(1) A party who with explicit reservation of rights performs or promises performance or assents to performance in a manner demanded or offered by the other party does not thereby prejudice the rights reserved. Such words as "without prejudice," "under protest" or the like are sufficient.

(2) Subsection (1) does not apply to an accord and satisfaction.

§ 1–208. Option to Accelerate at Will

A term providing that one party or his successor in interest may accelerate payment or performance or require collateral or additional collateral "at will" or "when he deems himself insecure" or in words of similar import shall be construed to mean that he shall have power to do so only if he in good faith believes that the prospect of payment or performance is impaired. The burden of establishing lack of good faith is on the party against whom the power has been exercised.

§ 1–209. Subordinated Obligations

An obligation may be issued as subordinated to payment of another obligation of the person obligated, or a creditor may subordinate his right to payment of an obligation by agreement with either the person obligated or another creditor of the person obligated. Such a subordination does not create a security interest as against either the common debtor or a subordinated creditor. This section shall be construed as declaring the law as it existed prior to the enactment of this section and not as modifying it.

Note: This new section is proposed as an optional provision to make it clear that a subordination agreement does not create a security interest unless so intended.

ARTICLE 2 SALES

Part I Short Title, General Construction and Subject Matter

§ 2–101. Short Title

This Article shall be known and may be cited as Uniform Commercial Code—Sales.

§ 2–102. Scope; Certain Security and Other Transactions Excluded From This Article

Unless the context otherwise requires, this Article applies to transactions in goods; it does not apply to any transaction which although in the form of an unconditional contract to sell or present sale is intended to operate only as a security transaction nor does this Article impair or repeal any statute regulating sales to consumers, farmers or other specified classes of buyers.

§ 2–103. Definitions and Index of Definitions

(1) In this Article unless the context otherwise requires

    (a) "Buyer" means a person who buys or contracts to buy goods.

    (b) "Good faith" in the case of a merchant means honesty in fact and the observance of reasonable commercial standards of fair dealing in the trade.

    (c) "Receipt" of goods means taking physical possession of them.

    (d) "Seller" means a person who sells or contracts to sell goods.

(2) Other definitions applying to this Article or to specified Parts thereof, and the sections in which they appear are:

    "Acceptance." Section 2–606.
    "Banker's credit." Section 2–325.
    "Between merchants." Section 2–104.
    "Cancellation." Section 2–106(4).
    "Commercial unit." Section 2–105.
    "Confirmed credit." Section 2–325.
    "Conforming to contract." Section 2–106.
    "Contract for sale." Section 2–106.
    "Cover." Section 2–712.
    "Entrusting." Section 2–403.
    "Financing agency." Section 2–104.
    "Future goods." Section 2–105.
    "Goods." Section 2–105.
    "Identification." Section 2–501.
    "Installment contract." Section 2–612.
    "Letter of Credit." Section 2–325.
    "Lot." Section 2–105.
    "Merchant." Section 2–104.
    "Overseas." Section 2–323.
    "Person in position of seller." Section 2–707.
    "Present sale." Section 2–106.
    "Sale." Section 2–106.
    "Sale on approval." Section 2–326.
    "Sale or return." Section 2–326.
    "Termination." Section 2–106.

(3) The following definitions in other Articles apply to this Article:

    "Check." Section 3–104.
    "Consignee." Section 7–102.
    "Consignor." Section 7–102.
    "Consumer goods." Section 9–109.
    "Dishonor." Section 3–507.
    "Draft." Section 3–104.

(4) In addition Article 1 contains general definitions and principles of construction and interpretation applicable throughout this Article.

§ 2–104. Definitions: "Merchant"; "Between Merchants"; "Financing Agency"

(1) "Merchant" means a person who deals in goods of the kind or otherwise by his occupation holds himself out as having knowledge or skill peculiar to the practices or goods involved in the transaction or to whom such knowledge or skill may be attributed by his employment of an agent or broker or other intermediary who by his occupation holds himself out as having such knowledge or skill.

(2) "Financing agency" means a bank, finance company or other person who in the ordinary course of business makes advances against goods or documents of title or who by arrangement with either the seller or the buyer intervenes in ordinary course to make or collect payment due or claimed under the contract for sale, as by purchasing or paying the seller's draft or making advances against it or by merely taking it for collection whether or not documents of title accompany the draft. "Financing agency" includes also a bank or other person who similarly intervenes between persons who are in the position of seller and buyer in respect to the goods (Section 2–707).

(3) "Between merchants" means in any transaction with respect to which both parties are chargeable with the knowledge or skill of merchants.

§ 2-105. Definitions: Transferability; "Goods"; "Future Goods"; "Lot"; "Commercial Unit"

(1) "Goods" means all things (including specially manufactured goods) which are moveable at the time of identification to the contract for sale other than the money in which the price is to be paid, investment securities (Article 8) and things in action. "Goods" also includes the unborn young of animals and growing crops and other identified things attached to realty as described in the section on goods to be severed from realty (Section 2-107).

(2) Goods must be both existing and identified before any interest in them can pass. Goods which are not both existing and identified are "future" goods. A purported present sale of future goods or of any interest therein operates as a contract to sell.

(3) There may be a sale of a part interest in existing identified goods.

(4) An undivided share in an identified bulk of fungible goods is sufficiently identified to be sold although the quantity of the bulk is not determined. Any agreed proportion of such a bulk or any quantity thereof agreed upon by number, weight or other measure may to the extent of the seller's interest in the bulk be sold to the buyer who then becomes an owner in common.

(5) "Lot" means a parcel or a single article which is the subject matter of a separate sale or delivery, whether or not it is sufficient to perform the contract.

(6) "Commercial unit" means such a unit of goods as by commercial usage is a single whole for purposes of sale and division of which materially impairs its character or value on the market or in use. A commercial unit may be a single article (as a machine) or a set of articles (as a suite of furniture or an assortment of sizes) or a quantity (as a bale, gross, or carload) or any other unit treated in use or in the relevant market as a single whole.

§ 2-106. Definitions: "Contract"; "Agreement"; "Contract for Sale"; "Sale"; "Present Sale"; "Conforming to Contract"; "Termination"; "Cancellation"

(1) In this Article unless the context otherwise requires "contract" and "agreement" are limited to those relating to the present or future sale of goods. "Contract for sale" includes both a present sale of goods and a contract to sell goods at a future time. A "sale" consists in the passing of title from the seller to the buyer for a price (Section 2-401). A "present sale" means a sale which is accomplished by the making of the contract.

(2) Goods or conduct including any part of a performance are "conforming" or conform to the contract when they

are in accordance with the obligations under the contract.

(3) "Termination" occurs when either party pursuant to a power created by agreement or law puts an end to the contract otherwise than for its breach. On "termination" all obligations which are still executory on both sides are discharged but any right based on prior breach or performance survives.

(4) "Cancellation" occurs when either party puts an end to the contract for breach by the other and its effect is the same as that of "termination" except that the cancelling party also retains any remedy for breach of the whole contract or any unperformed balance.

§ 2-107. Goods to Be Severed From Realty: Recording

(1) A contract for the sale of minerals or the like (including oil and gas) or a structure or its materials to be removed from realty is a contract for the sale of goods within this Article if they are to be severed by the seller but until severance a purported present sale thereof which is not effective as a transfer of an interest in land is effective only as a contract to sell.

(2) A contract for the sale apart from the land of growing crops or other things attached to realty and capable of severance without material harm thereto but not described in subsection (1) or of timber to be cut is a contract for the sale of goods within this Article whether the subject matter is to be severed by the buyer or by the seller even though it forms part of the realty at the time of contracting, and the parties can by identification effect a present sale before severance.

(3) The provisions of this section are subject to any third party rights provided by the law relating to realty records, and the contract for sale may be executed and recorded as a document transferring an interest in land and shall then constitute notice to third parties of the buyer's rights under the contract for sale.

Part 2 Form, Formation and Readjustment of Contract

§ 2-201. Formal Requirements; Statute of Frauds

(1) Except as otherwise provided in this section a contract for the sale of goods for the price of $500 or more is not enforceable by way of action or defense unless there is some writing sufficient to indicate that a contract for sale has been made between the parties and signed by the party against whom enforcement is sought or by his authorized agent or broker. A writing is not insufficient because it omits or incorrectly states a term agreed upon but the contract is not enforceable under this paragraph beyond the quantity of goods shown in such writing.

(2) Between merchants if within a reasonable time a writing in confirmation of the contract and sufficient

against the sender is received and the party receiving it has reason to know its contents, it satisfies the requirements of subsection (1) against such party unless written notice of objection to its contents is given within 10 days after it is received.

(3) A contract which does not satisfy the requirements of subsection (1) but which is valid in other respects is enforceable

(a) if the goods are to be specially manufactured for the buyer and are not suitable for sale to others in the ordinary course of the seller's business and the seller, before notice of repudiation is received and under circumstances which reasonably indicate that the goods are for the buyer, has made either a substantial beginning of their manufacture or commitments for their procurement; or

(b) if the party against whom enforcement is sought admits in his pleading, testimony or otherwise in court that a contract for sale was made, but the contract is not enforceable under this provision beyond the quantity of goods admitted; or

(c) with respect to goods for which payment has been made and accepted or which have been received and accepted (Section 2–606).

§ 2–202. Final Written Expression: Parol or Extrinsic Evidence

Terms with respect to which the confirmatory memoranda of the parties agree or which are otherwise set forth in a writing intended by the parties as a final expression of their agreement with respect to such terms as are included therein may not be contradicted by evidence of any prior agreement or of a contemporaneous oral agreement but may be explained or supplemented

(a) by course of dealing or usage of trade (Section 1–205) or by course of performance (Section 2–208); and

(b) by evidence of consistent additional terms unless the court finds the writing to have been intended also as a complete and exclusive statement of the terms of the agreement.

§ 2–203. Seals Inoperative

The affixing of a seal to a writing evidencing a contract for sale or an offer to buy or sell goods does not constitute the writing of a sealed instrument and the law with respect to sealed instruments does not apply to such a contract or offer.

§ 2–204. Formation in General

(1) A contract for sale of goods may be made in any manner sufficient to show agreement, including conduct by both parties which recognizes the existence of such a contract.

(2) An agreement sufficient to constitute a contract for sale may be found even though the moment of its making is undetermined.

(3) Even though one or more terms are left open a contract for sale does not fail for indefiniteness if the parties have intended to make a contract and there is a reasonably certain basis for giving an appropriate remedy.

§ 2–205. Firm Offers

An offer by a merchant to buy or sell goods in a signed writing which by its terms gives assurance that it will be held open is not revocable, for lack of consideration, during the time stated or if no time is stated for a reasonable time, but in no event may such period of irrevocability exceed three months; but any such term of assurance on a form supplied by the offeree must be separately signed by the offeror.

§ 2–206. Offer and Acceptance in Formation of Contract

(1) Unless otherwise unambiguously indicated by the language or circumstances

(a) an offer to make a contract shall be construed as inviting acceptance in any manner and by any medium reasonable in the circumstances;

(b) an order or other offer to buy goods for prompt or current shipment shall be construed as inviting acceptance either by a prompt promise to ship or by the prompt or current shipment of conforming or nonconforming goods, but such a shipment of nonconforming goods does not constitute an acceptance if the seller seasonably notifies the buyer that the shipment is offered only as an accommodation to the buyer.

(2) Where the beginning of a requested performance is a reasonable mode of acceptance an offeror who is not notified of acceptance within a reasonable time may treat the offer as having lapsed before acceptance.

§ 2–207. Additional Terms in Acceptance or Confirmation

(1) A definite and seasonable expression of acceptance or a written confirmation which is sent within a reasonable time operates as an acceptance even though it states terms additional to or different from those offered or agreed upon, unless acceptance is expressly made conditional on assent to the additional or different terms.

(2) The additional terms are to be construed as proposals for addition to the contract. Between merchants such terms become part of the contract unless:

(a) the offer expressly limits acceptance to the terms of the offer;

(b) they materially alter it; or

(c) notification of objection to them has already been given or is given within a reasonable time after notice of them is received.

(3) Conduct by both parties which recognizes the existence of a contract is sufficient to establish a contract for sale although the writings of the parties do not otherwise establish a contract. In such case the terms of the particu-

lar contract consist of those terms on which the writings of the parties agree, together with any supplementary terms incorporated under any other provisions of this Act.

§ 2–208. Course of Performance or Practical Construction

(1) Where the contract for sale involves repeated occasions for performance by either party with knowledge of the nature of the performance and opportunity for objection to it by the other, any course of performance accepted or acquiesced in without objection shall be relevant to determine the meaning of the agreement.

(2) The express terms of the agreement and any such course of performance, as well as any course of dealing and usage of trade, shall be construed whenever reasonable as consistent with each other; but when such construction is unreasonable, express terms shall control course of performance and course of performance shall control both course of dealing and usage of trade (Section 1–205).

(3) Subject to the provisions of the next section on modification and waiver, such course of performance shall be relevant to show a waiver or modification of any term inconsistent with such course of performance.

§ 2–209. Modification, Rescission and Waiver

(1) An agreement modifying a contract within this Article needs no consideration to be binding.

(2) A signed agreement which excludes modification or rescission except by a signed writing cannot be otherwise modified or rescinded, but except as between merchants such a requirement on a form supplied by the merchant must be separately signed by the other party.

(3) The requirements of the statute of frauds section of this Article (Section 2–201) must be satisfied if the contract as modified is within its provisions.

(4) Although an attempt at modification or rescission does not satisfy the requirements of subsection (2) or (3) it can operate as a waiver.

(5) A party who has made a waiver affecting an executory portion of the contract may retract the waiver by reasonable notification received by the other party that strict performance will be required of any term waived, unless the retraction would be unjust in view of a material change of position in reliance on the waiver.

§ 2–210. Delegation of Performance; Assignment of Rights

(1) A party may perform his duty through a delegate unless otherwise agreed or unless the other party has a substantial interest in having his original promisor perform or control the acts required by the contract. No delegation of performance relieves the party delegating of any duty to perform or any liability for breach.

(2) Unless otherwise agreed all rights of either seller or buyer can be assigned except where the assignment would materially change the duty of the other party, or increase materially the burden or risk imposed on him by his contract, or impair materially his chance of obtaining return performance. A right to damages for breach of the whole contract or a right arising out of the assignor's due performance of his entire obligation can be assigned despite agreement otherwise.

(3) Unless the circumstances indicate the contrary a prohibition of assignment of "the contract" is to be construed as barring only the delegation to the assignee of the assignor's performance.

(4) An assignment of "the contract" or of "all my rights under the contract" or an assignment in similar general terms is an assignment of rights and unless the language or the circumstances (as in an assignment for security) indicate the contrary, it is a delegation of performance of the duties of the assignor and its acceptance by the assignee constitutes a promise by him to perform those duties. This promise is enforceable by either the assignor or the other party to the original contract.

(5) The other party may treat any assignment which delegates performance as creating reasonable grounds for insecurity and may without prejudice to his rights against the assignor demand assurance from the assignee (Section 2–609).

Part 3 General Obligation and Construction of Contract

§ 2–301. General Obligations of Parties

The obligation of the seller is to transfer and deliver and that of the buyer is to accept and pay in accordance with the contract.

§ 2–302. Unconscionable Contract or Clause

(1) If the court as a matter of law finds the contract or any clause of the contract to have been unconscionable at the time it was made the court may refuse to enforce the contract, or it may enforce the remainder of the contract without the unconscionable clause, or it may so limit the application of any unconscionable clause as to avoid any unconscionable result.

(2) When it is claimed or appears to the court that the contract or any clause thereof may be unconscionable the parties shall be afforded a reasonable opportunity to present evidence as to its commercial setting, purpose and effect to aid the court in making the determination.

§ 2–303. Allocation or Division of Risks

Where this Article allocates a risk or a burden as between the parties "unless otherwise agreed," the agreement may not only shift the allocation but may also divide the risk or burden.

§ 2–304. Price Payable in Money, Goods, Realty, or Otherwise

(1) The price can be made payable in money or otherwise. If it is payable in whole or in part in goods each party is a seller of the goods which he is to transfer.

(2) Even though all or part of the price is payable in an interest in realty the transfer of the goods and the seller's obligations with reference to them are subject to this Article, but not the transfer of the interest in realty or the transferor's obligations in connection therewith.

§ 2–305. Open Price Term

(1) The parties if they so intend can conclude a contract for sale even though the price is not settled. In such case the price is a reasonable price at the time for delivery if

(a) nothing is said as to price; or

(b) the price is left to be agreed by the parties and they fail to agree; or

(c) the price is to be fixed in terms of some agreed market or other standard as set or recorded by a third person or agency and it is not so set or recorded.

(2) A price to be fixed by the seller or by the buyer means a price for him to fix in good faith.

(3) When a price left to be fixed otherwise than by agreement of the parties fails to be fixed through fault of one party the other may at his option treat the contract as cancelled or himself fix a reasonable price.

(4) Where, however, the parties intend not to be bound unless the price be fixed or agreed and it is not fixed or agreed there is no contract. In such a case the buyer must return any goods already received or if unable so to do must pay their reasonable value at the time of delivery and the seller must return any portion of the price paid on account.

§ 2–306. Output, Requirements and Exclusive Dealings

(1) A term which measures the quantity by the output of the seller or the requirements of the buyer means such actual output or requirements as may occur in good faith, except that no quantity unreasonably disproportionate to any stated estimate or in the absence of a stated estimate to any normal or otherwise comparable prior output or requirements may be tendered or demanded.

(2) A lawful agreement by either the seller or the buyer for exclusive dealing in the kind of goods concerned imposes unless otherwise agreed an obligation by the seller to use best efforts to supply the goods and by the buyer to use best efforts to promote their sale.

§ 2–307. Delivery in Single Lot or Several Lots

Unless otherwise agreed all goods called for by a contract for sale must be tendered in a single delivery and payment is due only on such tender but where the circumstances give either party the right to make or demand delivery in lots the price if it can be apportioned may be demanded for each lot.

§ 2–308. Absence of Specified Place for Delivery

Unless otherwise agreed

(a) the place for delivery of goods is the seller's place of business or if he has none his residence; but

(b) in a contract for sale of identified goods which to the knowledge of the parties at the time of contracting are in some other place, that place is the place for their delivery; and

(c) documents of title may be delivered through customary banking channels.

§ 2–309. Absence of Specific Time Provisions; Notice of Termination

(1) The time for shipment or delivery or any other action under a contract if not provided in this Article or agreed upon shall be a reasonable time.

(2) Where the contract provides for successive performances but is indefinite in duration it is valid for a reasonable time but unless otherwise agreed may be terminated at any time by either party.

(3) Termination of a contract by one party except on the happening of an agreed event requires that reasonable notification be received by the other party and an agreement dispensing with notification is invalid if its operation would be unconscionable.

§ 2–310. Open Time for Payment or Running of Credit: Authority to Ship Under Reservation

Unless otherwise agreed

(a) payment is due at the time and place at which the buyer is to receive the goods even though the place of shipment is the place of delivery; and

(b) if the seller is authorized to send the goods he may ship them under reservation, and may tender the documents of title, but the buyer may inspect the goods after their arrival before payment is due unless such inspection is inconsistent with the terms of the contract (Section 2–513); and

(c) if delivery is authorized and made by way of documents of title otherwise than by subsection (b) then payment is due at the time and place at which the buyer is to receive the documents regardless of where the goods are to be received; and

(d) where the seller is required or authorized to ship the goods on credit the credit period runs from the time of shipment but post-dating the invoice or delaying its dispatch will correspondingly delay the starting of the credit period.

§ 2–311. Options and Cooperation Respecting Performance

(1) An agreement for sale which is otherwise sufficiently definite (subsection (3) of Section 2–204) to be a contract

is not made invalid by the fact that it leaves particulars of performance to be specified by one of the parties. Any such specification must be made in good faith and within limits set by commercial reasonableness.

(2) Unless otherwise agreed specifications relating to assortment of the goods are at the buyer's option and except as otherwise provided in subsection (1)(c) and (3) of Section 2–319 specifications or arrangements relating to shipment are at the seller's option.

(3) Where such specification would materially affect the other party's performance but is not seasonably made or where one party's cooperation is necessary to the agreed performance of the other but is not seasonably forthcoming, the other party in addition to all other remedies

(a) is excused for any resulting delay in his own performance; and

(b) may also either proceed to perform in any reasonable manner or after the time for a material part of his own performance treat the failure to specify or to cooperate as a breach by failure to deliver or accept the goods.

§ 2–312. Warranty of Title and Against Infringement; Buyer's Obligation Against Infringement

(1) Subject to subsection (2) there is in a contract for sale a warranty by the seller that

(a) the title conveyed shall be good, and its transfer rightful; and

(b) the goods shall be delivered free from any security interest or other lien or encumbrance of which the buyer at the time of contracting has no knowledge.

(2) A warranty under subsection (1) will be excluded or modified only by specific language or by circumstances which give the buyer reason to know that the person selling does not claim title in himself or that he is purporting to sell only such right or title as he or a third person may have.

(3) Unless otherwise agreed a seller who is a merchant regularly dealing in goods of the kind warrants that the goods shall be delivered free of the rightful claim of any third person by way of infringement or the like but a buyer who furnishes specifications to the seller must hold the seller harmless against any such claim which arises out of compliance with the specifications.

§ 2–313. Express Warranties by Affirmation, Promise, Description, Sample

(1) Express warranties by the seller are created as follows:

(a) Any affirmation of fact or promise made by the seller to the buyer which relates to the goods and becomes part of the basis of the bargain creates an express warranty that the goods shall conform to the affirmation or promise.

(b) Any description of the goods which is made part of the basis of the bargain creates an express warranty that the goods shall conform to the description.

(c) Any sample or model which is made part of the basis of the bargain creates an express warranty that the whole of the goods shall conform to the sample or model.

(2) It is not necessary to the creation of an express warranty that the seller use formal words such as "warrant" or "guarantee" or that he have a specific intention to make a warranty, but an affirmation merely of the value of the goods or a statement purporting to be merely the seller's opinion or commendation of the goods does not create a warranty.

§ 2–314. Implied Warranty: Merchantability; Usage of Trade

(1) Unless excluded or modified (Section 2–316), a warranty that the goods shall be merchantable is implied in a contract for their sale if the seller is a merchant with respect to goods of that kind. Under this section the serving for value of food or drink to be consumed either on the premises or elsewhere is a sale.

(2) Goods to be merchantable must be at least such as

(a) pass without objection in the trade under the contract description; and

(b) in the case of fungible goods, are of fair average quality within the description; and

(c) are fit for the ordinary purposes for which such goods are used; and

(d) run, within the variations permitted by the agreement, of even kind, quality and quantity within each unit and among all units involved; and

(e) are adequately contained, packaged, and labeled as the agreement may require; and

(f) conform to the promises or affirmations of fact made on the container or label if any.

(3) Unless excluded or modified (Section 2–316) other implied warranties may arise from course of dealing or usage of trade.

§ 2–315. Implied Warranty: Fitness for Particular Purpose

Where the seller at the time of contracting has reason to know any particular purpose for which the goods are required and that the buyer is relying on the seller's skill or judgment to select or furnish suitable goods, there is unless excluded or modified under the next section an implied warranty that the goods shall be fit for such purpose.

§ 2–316. Exclusion or Modification of Warranties

(1) Words or conduct relevant to the creation of an express warranty and words or conduct tending to negate or limit warranty shall be construed wherever reasonable as consistent with each other; but subject to the provisions of this Article on parol or extrinsic evidence (Section 2–202) negation or limitation is inoperative to the extent that such construction is unreasonable.

(2) Subject to subsection (3), to exclude or modify the implied warranty of merchantability or any part of it the language must mention merchantability and in case of a writing must be conspicuous, and to exclude or modify any implied warranty of fitness the exclusion must be by a writing and conspicuous. Language to exclude all implied warranties of fitness is sufficient if it states, for example, that "There are no warranties which extend beyond the description on the face hereof."

(3) Notwithstanding subsection (2)

(a) unless the circumstances indicate otherwise, all implied warranties are excluded by expressions like "as is," "with all faults" or other languages which in common understanding calls the buyer's attention to the exclusion of warranties and makes plain that there is no implied warranty; and

(b) when the buyer before entering into the contract has examined the goods or the sample or model as fully as he desired or has refused to examine the goods there is no implied warranty with regard to defects which an examination ought in the circumstances to have revealed to him; and

(c) an implied warranty can also be excluded or modified by course of dealing or course of performance or usage of trade.

(4) Remedies for breach of warranty can be limited in accordance with the provisions of this Article on liquidation or limitation of damages and on contractual modification of remedy (Section 2–718 and 2–719).

§ 2–317. Cumulation and Conflict of Warranties Express or Implied

Warranties whether express or implied shall be construed as consistent with each other and as cumulative, but if such construction is unreasonable the intention of the parties shall determine which warranty is dominant. In ascertaining that intention the following rules apply:

(a) Exact or technical specifications displace an inconsistent sample or model or general language of description.

(b) A sample from an existing bulk displaces inconsistent general language of description.

(c) Express warranties displace inconsistent implied warranties other than an implied warranty of fitness for a particular purpose.

§ 2–318. Third Party Beneficiaries of Warranties Express or Implied

Note: If this Act is introduced in the Congress of the United States this Section should be omitted. (States to select one alternative.)

Alternative A
A seller's warranty whether express or implied extends to any natural person who is in the family or household of his buyer or who is a guest in his home if it is reasonable to expect that such person may use, consume or be affected by the goods and who is injured in person by breach of the warranty. A seller may not exclude or limit the operation of this section.

Alternative B
A seller's warranty whether express or implied extends to any natural person who may reasonably be expected to use, consume or be affected by the goods and who is injured in person by breach of the warranty. A seller may not exclude or limit the operation of this section.

Alternative C
A seller's warranty whether express or implied extends to any person who may reasonably be expected to use, consume or be affected by the goods and who is injured by breach of the warranty. A seller may not exclude or limit the operation of this section with respect to injury to the person of an individual to whom the warranty extends.

§ 2–319. F.O.B. and F.A.S. Terms

(1) Unless otherwise agreed the term F.O.B. (which means "free on board") at a named place, even though used only in connection with the stated price, is a delivery term under which

(a) when the term is F.O.B. the place of shipment, the seller must at that place ship the goods in the manner provided in this Article (Section 2–504) and bear the expense and risk of putting them into the possession of the carrier; or

(b) when the term is F.O.B. the place of destination, the seller must at his own expense and risk transport the goods to that place and there tender delivery of them in the manner provided in this Article (Section 2–503);

(c) when under either (a) or (b) the term is also F.O.B. vessel, car or other vehicle, the seller must in addition at his own expense and risk load the goods on board. If the term is F.O.B. vessel the buyer must name the vessel and in an appropriate case the seller must comply with the provisions of this Article on the form of bill of lading (Section 2–323).

(2) Unless otherwise agreed the term F.A.S. vessel (which means "free alongside") at a named port, even though used only in connection with the stated price, is a delivery term under which the seller must

(a) at his own expense and risk deliver the goods alongside the vessel in the manner usual in that port or on a dock designated and provided by the buyer; and

(b) obtain and tender a receipt for the goods in exchange for which the carrier is under a duty to issue a bill of lading.

(3) Unless otherwise agreed in any case falling within subsection (1)(a) or (c) or subsection (2) the buyer must seasonably give any needed instructions for making de-

livery, including when the term is F.A.S. or F.O.B. the loading berth of the vessel and in an appropriate case its name and sailing date. The seller may treat the failure of needed instructions as a failure of cooperation under this Article (Section 2–311). He may also at his option move the goods in any reasonable manner preparatory to delivery or shipment.

(4) Under the term F.O.B. vessel or F.A.S. unless otherwise agreed the buyer must make payment against tender of the required documents and the seller may not tender nor the buyer demand delivery of the goods in substitution for the documents.

§ 2–320. C.I.F. and C. & F. Terms

(1) The term C.I.F. means that the price includes in a lump sum the cost of the goods and the insurance and freight to the named destination. The term C. & F. or C.F. means that the price so includes cost and freight to the named destination.

(2) Unless otherwise agreed and even though used only in connection with the stated price and destination, the term C.I.F. destination or its equivalent requires the seller at his own expense and risk to

(a) put the goods into the possession of a carrier at the port for shipment and obtain a negotiable bill or bills of lading covering the entire transportation to the named destination; and

(b) load the goods and obtain a receipt from the carrier (which may be contained in the bill of lading) showing that the freight has been paid or provided for; and

(c) obtain a policy or certificate of insurance, including any war risk insurance, of a kind and on terms then current at the port of shipment in the usual amount, in the currency of the contract, shown to cover the same goods covered by the bill of lading and providing for payment of loss to the order of the buyer or for the account of whom it may concern; but the seller may add to the price the amount of the premium for any such war risk insurance; and

(d) prepare an invoice of the goods and procure any other documents required to effect shipment or to comply with the contract; and

(e) forward and tender with commercial promptness all the documents in due form and with any indorsement necessary to perfect the buyer's rights.

(3) Unless otherwise agreed the term C. & F. or its equivalent has the same effect and imposes upon the seller the same obligations and risks as a C.I.F. term except the obligation as to insurance.

(4) Under the term C.I.F. & C. & F. unless otherwise agreed the buyer must make payment against tender of the required documents and the seller may not tender nor the buyer demand delivery of the goods in substitution for the documents.

§ 2–321. C.I.F. or C. & F.: "Net Landed Weights"; "Payment on Arrival"; Warranty of Condition on Arrival

Under a contract containing a term C.I.F. or C. & F.

(1) Where the price is based on or is to be adjusted according to "net landed weights," "delivered weights," "out turn" quantity or quality or the like, unless otherwise agreed the seller must reasonably estimate the price. The payment due on tender of the documents called for by the contract is the amount so estimated, but after final adjustment of the price a settlement must be made with commercial promptness.

(2) An agreement described in subsection (1) or any warranty of quality or condition of the goods on arrival places upon the seller the risk of ordinary deterioration, shrinkage and the like in transportation but has no effect on the place or time of identification to the contract for sale or delivery or on the passing of the risk of loss.

(3) Unless otherwise agreed where the contract provides for payment on or after arrival of the goods the seller must before payment allow such preliminary inspection as is feasible; but if the goods are lost delivery of the documents and payment are due when the goods should have arrived.

§ 2–322. Delivery "Ex-Ship"

(1) Unless otherwise agreed a term for delivery of goods "ex-ship" (which means from the carrying vessel) or in equivalent language is not restricted to a particular ship and requires delivery from a ship which has reached a place at the named port of destination where goods of the kind are usually discharged.

(2) Under such a term unless otherwise agreed

(a) the seller must discharge all liens arising out of the carriage and furnish the buyer with a direction which puts the carrier under a duty to deliver the goods; and

(b) the risk of loss does not pass to the buyer until the goods leave the ship's tackle or are otherwise properly unloaded.

§ 2–323. Form of Bill of Lading Required in Overseas Shipment: "Overseas"

(1) Where the contract contemplates overseas shipment and contains a term C.I.F. or C. & F. or F.O.B. vessel, the seller unless otherwise agreed must obtain a negotiable bill of lading stating that the goods have been loaded on board or, in the case of a term C.I.F. or C. & F., received for shipment.

(2) Where in a case within subsection (1) a bill of lading has been issued in a set of parts, unless otherwise agreed if the documents are not to be sent from abroad the buyer may demand tender of the full set; otherwise only one part of the bill of lading need be tendered. Even if the agreement expressly requires a full set

(a) due tender of a single part is acceptable within the provisions of this Article on cure of improper delivery (subsection (1) of Section 2–508); and

(b) even though the full set is demanded, if the documents are sent from abroad the person tendering an incomplete set may nevertheless require payment upon furnishing an indemnity which the buyer in good faith deems adequate.

(3) A shipment by water or by air or a contract contemplating such shipment is "overseas" insofar as by usage of trade or agreement it is subject to the commercial, financing or shipping practices characteristic of international deep water commerce.

§ 2–324. "No Arrival, No Sale" Term

Under a term "no arrival, no sale" or terms of like meaning, unless otherwise agreed,

(a) the seller must properly ship conforming goods and if they arrive by any means he must tender them on arrival but he assumes no obligation that the goods will arrive unless he has caused the nonarrival; and

(b) where without fault of the seller the goods are in part lost or have so deteriorated as no longer to conform to the contract or arrive after the contract time, the buyer may proceed as if there had been casualty to identified goods (Section 2–613).

§ 2–325. "Letter of Credit" Term; "Confirmed Credit"

(1) Failure of the buyer seasonably to furnish an agreed letter of credit is a breach of the contract for sale.

(2) The delivery to seller of a proper letter of credit suspends the buyer's obligation to pay. If the letter of credit is dishonored, the seller may on seasonable notification to the buyer require payment directly from him.

(3) Unless otherwise agreed the term "letter of credit" or "banker's credit" in a contract for sale means an irrevocable credit issued by a financing agency of good repute and, where the shipment is overseas, of good international repute. The term "confirmed credit" means that the credit must also carry the direct obligation of such an agency which does business in the seller's financial market.

§ 2–326. Sale on Approval and Sale or Return; Consignment Sales and Rights of Creditors

(1) Unless otherwise agreed, if delivered goods may be returned by the buyer even though they conform to the contract, the transaction is

(a) a "sale on approval" if the goods are delivered primarily for use, and

(b) a "sale or return" if the goods are delivered primarily for resale.

(2) Except as provided in subsection (3), goods held on approval are not subject to the claims of the buyer's creditors until acceptance; goods held on sale or return are subject to such claims while in the buyer's possession.

(3) Where goods are delivered to a person for sale and such person maintains a place of business at which he deals in goods of the kind involved, under a name other than the name of the person making delivery, then with respect to claims of creditors of the person conducting the business the goods are deemed to be on sale or return. The provisions of this subsection are applicable even though an agreement purports to reserve title to the person making delivery until payment or resale or uses such words as "on consignment" or "on memorandum." However, this subsection is not applicable if the person making delivery

(a) complies with an applicable law providing for a consignor's interest or the like to be evidenced by a sign, or

(b) establishes that the person conducting the business is generally known by his creditors to be substantially engaged in selling the goods of others, or

(c) complies with the filing provisions of the Article on Secured Transactions (Article 9).

(4) Any "or return" term of a contract for sale is to be treated as a separate contract for sale within the statute of frauds section of this Article (Section 2–201) and as contradicting the sale aspect of the contract within the provisions of this Article on parol or extrinsic evidence (Section 2–202).

§ 2–327. Special Incidents of Sale on Approval and Sale or Return

(1) Under a sale on approval unless otherwise agreed

(a) although the goods are identified to the contract the risk of loss and the title do not pass to the buyer until acceptance; and

(b) use of the goods consistent with the purpose of trial is not acceptance but failure seasonably to notify the seller of election to return the goods is acceptance, and if the goods conform to the contract acceptance of any part is acceptance of the whole; and

(c) after due notification of election to return, the return is at the seller's risk and expense but a merchant buyer must follow any reasonable instructions.

(2) Under a sale or return unless otherwise agreed

(a) the option to return extends to the whole or any commercial unit of the goods while in substantially their original condition, but must be exercised seasonably; and

(b) the return is at the buyer's risk and expense.

§ 2–328. Sale by Auction

(1) In a sale by auction if goods are put up in lots each lot is the subject of a separate sale.

(2) A sale by auction is complete when the auctioneer so announces by the fall of the hammer or in other customary manner. Where a bid is made while the hammer is falling in acceptance of a prior bid the auctioneer may in

his discretion reopen the bidding or declare the goods sold under the bid on which the hammer was falling.

(3) Such a sale is with reserve unless the goods are in explicit terms put up without reserve. In an auction with reserve the auctioneer may withdraw the goods at any time until he announces completion of the sale. In an auction without reserve, after the auctioneer calls for bids on an article or lot, that article or lot cannot be withdrawn unless no bid is made within a reasonable time. In either case a bidder may retract his bid until the auctioneer's announcement of completion of sale, but a bidder's retraction does not revive any previous bid.

(4) If the auctioneer knowingly receives a bid on the seller's behalf or the seller makes or procures such a bid, and notice has not been given that liberty for such bidding is reserved, the buyer may at his option avoid the sale or take the goods at the price of the last good faith bid prior to the completion of the sale. This subsection shall not apply to any bid at a forced sale.

Part 4 Title, Creditors and Good Faith Purchasers

§ 2–401. Passing of Title; Reservation for Security; Limited Application of This Section

Each provision of this Article with regard to the rights, obligations and remedies of the seller, the buyer, purchasers or other third parties applies irrespective of title to the goods except where the provision refers to such title. Insofar as situations are not covered by the other provisions of this Article and matters concerning title become material the following rules apply:

(1) Title to goods cannot pass under a contract for sale prior to their identification to the contract (Section 2–501), and unless otherwise explicitly agreed the buyer acquires by their identification a special property as limited by this Act. Any retention or reservation by the seller of the title (property) in goods shipped or delivered to the buyer is limited in effect to a reservation of a security interest. Subject to these provisions and to the provisions of the Article on Secured Transactions (Article 9), title to goods passes from the seller to the buyer in any manner and on any conditions explicitly agreed on by the parties.

(2) Unless otherwise explicitly agreed title passes to the buyer at the time and place at which the seller completes his performance with reference to the physical delivery of the goods, despite any reservation of a security interest and even though a document of title is to be delivered at a different time or place; and in particular and despite any reservation of a security interest by the bill of lading

(a) if the contract requires or authorizes the seller to send the goods to the buyer but does not require him to deliver them at destination, title passes to the buyer at the time and place of shipment; but

(b) if the contract requires delivery at destination, title passes on tender there.

(3) Unless otherwise explicitly agreed where delivery is to be made without moving the goods,

(a) if the seller is to deliver a document of title, title passes at the time when and the place where he delivers such documents; or

(b) if the goods are at the time of contracting already identified and no documents are to be delivered, title passes at the time and place of contracting.

(4) A rejection or other refusal by the buyer to receive or retain the goods, whether or not justified, or a justified revocation of acceptance revests title to the goods in the seller. Such revesting occurs by operation of law and is not a "sale."

§ 2–402. Rights of Seller's Creditors Against Sold Goods

(1) Except as provided in subsections (2) and (3), rights of unsecured creditors of the seller with respect to goods which have been identified to a contract for sale are subject to the buyer's rights to recover the goods under this Article (Section 2–502 and 2–716).

(2) A creditor of the seller may treat a sale or an identification of goods to a contract for sale as void if as against him a retention of possession by the seller is fraudulent under any rule of law of the state where the goods are situated, except that retention of possession in good faith and current course of trade by a merchant-seller for a commercially reasonable time after a sale or identification is not fraudulent.

(3) Nothing in this Article shall be deemed to impair the rights of creditors of the seller

(a) under the provisions of the Article on Secured Transactions (Article 9); or

(b) where identification to the contract or delivery is made not in current course of trade but in satisfaction of or as security for a pre-existing claim for money, security or the like and is made under circumstances which under any rule of law of the state where the goods are situated would apart from this Article constitute the transaction a fraudulent transfer or voidable preference.

§ 2–403. Power to Transfer; Good Faith Purchase of Goods; "Entrusting"

(1) A purchaser of goods acquires all title which his transferor had or had power to transfer except that a purchaser of a limited interest acquires rights only to the extent of the interest purchased. A person with voidable title has power to transfer a good title to a good faith purchaser for value. When goods have been delivered under a transaction of purchase the purchaser has such power even though

(a) the transferor was deceived as to the identity of the purchaser, or

(b) the delivery was in exchange for a check which is later dishonored, or

(c) it was agreed that the transaction was to be a "cash sale," or

(d) the delivery was procured through fraud punishable as larcenous under the criminal law.

(2) Any entrusting of possession of goods to a merchant who deals in goods of that kind gives him power to transfer all rights of the entruster to a buyer in ordinary course of business.

(3) "Entrusting" includes any delivery and any acquiescence in retention of possession regardless of any condition expressed between the parties to the delivery or acquiescence and regardless of whether the procurement of the entrusting or the possessor's disposition of the goods have been such as to be larcenous under the criminal law.

(4) The rights of other purchasers of goods and of lien creditors are governed by the Articles on Secured Transactions (Article 9), Bulk Transfers (Article 6) and Documents of Title (Article 7).

Part 5 Performance

§ 2–501. Insurable Interest in Goods; Manner of Identification of Goods

(1) The buyer obtains a special property and an insurable interest in goods by identification of existing goods as goods to which the contract refers even though the goods so identified are nonconforming and he has an option to return or reject them. Such identification can be made at any time and in any manner explicitly agreed to by the parties. In the absence of explicit agreement identification occurs

(a) when the contract is made if it is for the sale of goods already existing and identified;

(b) if the contract is for the sale of future goods other than those described in paragraph (c), when goods are shipped, marked or otherwise designated by the seller as goods to which the contract refers;

(c) when the crops are planted or otherwise become growing crops or the young are conceived if the contract is for the sale of unborn young to be born within twelve months after contracting or for the sale of crops to be harvested within twelve months or the next normal harvest season after contracting whichever is longer.

(2) The seller retains an insurable interest in goods so long as title to or any security interest in the goods remains in him and where the identification is by the seller alone he may until default or insolvency or notification to the buyer that the identification is final substitute other goods for those identified.

(3) Nothing in this section impairs any insurable interest recognized under any other statute or rule or law.

§ 2–502. Buyer's Right to Goods on Seller's Insolvency

(1) Subject to subsection (2) and even though the goods have not been shipped a buyer who has paid a part or all of the price of goods in which he has a special property under the provisions of the immediately preceding section may on making and keeping good a tender of any unpaid portion of their price recover them from the seller if the seller becomes insolvent within ten days after receipt of the first installment on their price.

(2) If the identification creating his special property has been made by the buyer he acquires the right to recover the goods only if they conform to the contract for sale.

§ 2–503. Manner of Seller's Tender of Delivery

(1) Tender of delivery requires that the seller put and hold conforming goods at the buyer's disposition and give the buyer any notification reasonably necessary to enable him to take delivery. The manner, time and place for tender are determined by the agreement and this Article, and in particular

(a) tender must be at a reasonable hour, and if it is of goods they must be kept available for the period reasonably necessary to enable the buyer to take possession; but

(b) unless otherwise agreed the buyer must furnish facilities reasonably suited to the receipt of the goods.

(2) Where the case is within the next section respecting shipment tender requires that the seller comply with its provisions.

(3) Where the seller is required to deliver at a particular destination tender requires that he comply with subsection (1) and also in any appropriate case tender documents as described in subsections (4) and (5) of this section.

(4) Where goods are in the possession of a bailee and are to be delivered without being moved

(a) tender requires that the seller either tender a negotiable document of title covering such goods or procure acknowledgment by the bailee of the buyer's right to possession of the goods; but

(b) tender to the buyer of a non-negotiable document of title or of a written direction to the bailee to deliver is sufficient tender unless the buyer seasonably objects, and receipt by the bailee of notification of the buyer's rights fixes those rights as against the bailee and all third persons; but risk of loss of the goods and of any failure by the bailee to honor the non-negotiable document of title or to obey the direction remains on the seller until the buyer has had a reasonable time to present the document or direction, and a refusal by the bailee to honor the document or to obey the direction defeats the tender.

(5) Where the contract requires the seller to deliver documents

(a) he must tender all such documents in correct form, except as provided in this Article with respect to bills of lading in a set (subsection (2) of Section 2–323); and

(b) tender through customary banking channels is sufficient and dishonor of a draft accompanying the documents constitutes non-acceptance or rejection.

§ 2–504. Shipment by Seller

Where the seller is required or authorized to send the goods to the buyer and the contract does not require him to deliver them at a particular destination, then unless otherwise agreed he must

(a) put the goods in the possession of such a carrier and make such a contract for their transportation as may be reasonable having regard to the nature of the goods and other circumstances of the case; and

(b) obtain and promptly deliver or tender in due form any document necessary to enable the buyer to obtain possession of the goods or otherwise required by the agreement or by usage of trade; and

(c) promptly notify the buyer of the shipment. Failure to notify the buyer under paragraph (c) or to make a proper contract under paragraph (a) is a ground for rejection only if material delay or loss ensues.

§ 2–505. Seller's Shipment Under Reservation

(1) Where the seller has identified goods to the contract by or before shipment:

(a) his procurement of a negotiable bill of lading to his own order or otherwise reserves in him a security interest in the goods. His procurement of the bill to the order of a financing agency or of the buyer indicates in addition only the seller's expectation of transferring that interest to the person named.

(b) a non-negotiable bill of lading to himself or his nominee reserves possession of the goods as security but except in a case of conditional delivery (subsection (2) of Section 2–507) a non-negotiable bill of lading naming the buyer as consignee reserves no security interest even though the seller retains possession of the bill of lading.

(2) When shipment by the seller with reservation of a security interest is in violation of the contract for sale it constitutes an improper contract for transportation within the preceding section but impairs neither the rights given to the buyer by shipment and identification of the goods to the contract nor the seller's powers as a holder of a negotiable document.

§ 2–506. Rights of Financing Agency

(1) A financing agency by paying or purchasing for value a draft which relates to a shipment of goods acquires to the extent of the payment or purchase and in addition to its own rights under the draft and any document of title securing it any rights of the shipper in the goods including the right to stop delivery and the shipper's right to have the draft honored by the buyer.

(2) The right to reimbursement of a financing agency which has in good faith honored or purchased the draft under commitment to or authority from the buyer is not impaired by subsequent discovery of defects with reference to any relevant document which was apparently regular on its face.

§ 2–507. Effect of Seller's Tender; Delivery on Condition

(1) Tender of delivery is a condition to the buyer's duty to accept the goods and, unless otherwise agreed, to his duty to pay for them. Tender entitles the seller to acceptance of the goods and to payment according to the contract.

(2) Where payment is due and demanded on the delivery to the buyer of goods or documents of title, his right as against the seller to retain or dispose of them is conditional upon his making the payment due.

§ 2–508. Cure by Seller of Improper Tender or Delivery; Replacement

(1) Where any tender or delivery by the seller is rejected because non-conforming and the time for performance has not yet expired, the seller may seasonably notify the buyer of his intention to cure and may then within the contract time make a conforming delivery.

(2) Where the buyer rejects a non-conforming tender which the seller had reasonable grounds to believe would be acceptable with or without money allowance the seller may if he seasonably notifies the buyer have a further reasonable time to substitute a conforming tender.

§ 2–509. Risk of Loss in the Absence of Breach

(1) Where the contract requires or authorizes the seller to ship the good by carrier

(a) if it does not require him to deliver them at a particular destination, the risk of loss passes to the buyer when the goods are duly delivered to the carrier even though the shipment is under reservation (Section 2–505); but

(b) if it does require him to deliver them at a particular destination and the goods are there duly tendered while in the possession of the carrier, the risk of loss passes to the buyer when the goods are there duly so tendered as to enable the buyer to take delivery.

(2) Where the goods are held by a bailee to be delivered without being moved, the risk of loss passes to the buyer.

(a) on his receipt of a negotiable document of title covering the goods; or

(b) on acknowledgment by the bailee of the buyer's right to possession of the goods; or

(c) after his receipt of a non-negotiable document of title or other written direction to deliver, as provided in subsection (4)(b) of Section 2–503.

(3) In any case not within subsection (1) or (2), the risk of loss passes to the buyer on his receipt of the goods if the seller is a merchant; otherwise the risk passes to the buyer on tender of delivery.

(4) The provisions of this section are subject to contrary agreement of the parties and to the provisions of this Article on sale on approval (Section 2–327) and on effect of breach on risk of loss (Section 2–510).

§ 2–510. Effect of Breach on Risk of Loss

(1) Where a tender or delivery of goods so fails to conform to the contract as to give a right of rejection the risk of their loss remains on the seller until cure or acceptance.

(2) Where the buyer rightfully revokes acceptance he may to the extent of any deficiency in his effective insurance coverage treat the risk of loss as having rested on the seller from the beginning.

(3) Where the buyer as to conforming goods already identified to the contract for sale repudiates or is otherwise in breach before risk of their loss has passed to him, the seller may to the extent of any deficiency in his effective insurance coverage treat the risk of loss as resting on the buyer for a commercially reasonable time.

§ 2–511. Tender of Payment by Buyer; Payment by Check

(1) Unless otherwise agreed tender of payment is a condition to the seller's duty to tender and complete any delivery.

(2) Tender of payment is sufficient when made by any means or in any manner current in the ordinary course of business unless the seller demands payment in legal tender and gives any extension of time reasonably necessary to procure it.

(3) Subject to the provisions of this Act on the effect of an instrument on an obligation (Section 3–802), payment by check is conditional and is defeated as between the parties by dishonor of the check on due presentment.

§ 2–512. Payment by Buyer Before Inspection

(1) Where the contract requires payment before inspection non-conformity of the goods does not excuse the buyer from so making payment unless

(a) the non-conformity appears without inspection; or

(b) despite tender of the required documents the circumstances would justify injunction against honor under the provisions of this Act (Section 5–114).

(2) Payment pursuant to subsection (1) does not constitute an acceptance of goods or impair the buyer's right to inspect or any of his remedies.

§ 2–513. Buyer's Right to Inspection of Goods

(1) Unless otherwise agreed and subject to subsection (3), where goods are tendered or delivered or identified to the contract for sale, the buyer has a right before payment or acceptance to inspect them at any reasonable place and time and in any reasonable manner. When the seller is required and authorized to send the goods to the buyer, the inspection may be after their arrival.

(2) Expenses of inspection must be borne by the buyer but may be recovered from the seller if the goods do not conform and are rejected.

(3) Unless otherwise agreed and subject to the provisions of this Article on C.I.F. contracts (subsection (3) of Section 2–321), the buyer is not entitled to inspect the goods before payment of the price when the contract provides

(a) for delivery "C.O.D." or on other like terms; or

(b) for payment against documents of title, except where such payment is due only after the goods are to become available for inspection.

(4) A place or method of inspection fixed by the parties is presumed to be exclusive but unless otherwise expressly agreed it does not postpone identification or shift the place for delivery or for passing the risk of loss. If compliance becomes impossible, inspection shall be as provided in this section unless the place or method fixed was clearly intended as an indispensable condition failure of which avoids the contract.

§ 2–514. When Documents Deliverable on Acceptance; When on Payment

Unless otherwise agreed documents against which a draft is drawn are to be delivered to the drawee on acceptance of the draft if it is payable more than three days after presentment; otherwise, only on payment.

§ 2–515. Preserving Evidence of Goods in Dispute

In furtherance of the adjustment of any claim or dispute

(a) either party on reasonable notification to the other and for the purpose of ascertaining the facts and preserving evidence has the right to inspect, test and sample the goods including such of them as may be in the possession or control of the other; and

(b) the parties may agree to a third party inspection or survey to determine the conformity or condition of the goods and may agree that the findings shall be binding upon them in any subsequent litigation or adjustment.

Part 6 Breach, Repudiation and Excuse

§ 2–601. Buyer's Rights on Improper Delivery

Subject to the provisions of this Article on breach in installment contracts (Section 2–612) and unless otherwise agreed under the sections on contractual limitations of remedy (Sections 2–718 and 2–719), if the goods or the tender of delivery fail in any respect to conform to the contract, the buyer may

(a) reject the whole; or

(b) accept the whole; or

(c) accept any commercial unit or units and reject the rest.

§ 2–602. Manner and Effect of Rightful Rejection

(1) Rejection of goods must be within a reasonable time after their delivery or tender. It is ineffective unless the buyer seasonably notifies the seller.

(2) Subject to the provisions of the two following sections on rejected goods (Sections 2–603 and 2–604),

(a) after rejection any exercise of ownership by the buyer with respect to any commercial unit is wrongful as against the seller; and

(b) if the buyer has before rejection taken physical possession of goods in which he does not have a security interest under the provisions of this Article (subsection (3) of Section 2–711), he is under a duty after rejection to hold them with reasonable care at the seller's disposition for a time sufficient to permit the seller to remove them; but

(c) the buyer has no further obligations with regard to goods rightfully rejected.

(3) The seller's rights with respect to goods wrongfully rejected are governed by the provisions of this Article on Seller's remedies in general (Section 2–703).

§ 2–603. Merchant Buyer's Duties as to Rightfully Rejected Goods

(1) Subject to any security interest in the buyer (subsection (3) of Section 2–711), when the seller has no agent or place of business at the market of rejection a merchant buyer is under a duty after rejection of goods in his possession or control to follow any reasonable instructions received from the seller with respect to the goods and in the absence of such instructions to make reasonable efforts to sell them for the seller's account if they are perishable or threaten to decline in value speedily. Instructions are not reasonable if on demand indemnity for expense is not forthcoming.

(2) When the buyer sells goods under subsection (1), he is entitled to reimbursement from the seller or out of the proceeds for reasonable expenses of caring for and selling them, and if the expenses include no selling commission then to such commission as is usual in the trade or if there is none to a reasonable sum not exceeding ten per cent on the gross proceeds.

(3) In complying with this section the buyer is held only to good faith and good faith conduct hereunder is neither acceptance nor conversion nor the basis of an action for damages.

§ 2–604. Buyer's Options as to Salvage of Rightfully Rejected Goods

Subject to the provisions of the immediately preceding section on perishables if the seller gives no instructions within a reasonable time after notification of rejection the buyer may store the rejected goods for the seller's account or reship them to him or resell them for the seller's account with reimbursement as provided in the preceding section. Such action is not acceptance or conversion.

§ 2–605. Waiver of Buyer's Objections by Failure to Particularize

(1) The buyer's failure to state in connection with rejection a particular defect which is ascertainable by reasonable inspection precludes him from relying on the unstated defect to justify rejection or to establish breach

(a) where the seller could have cured it if stated seasonably; or

(b) between merchants when the seller has after rejection made a request in writing for a full and final written statement of all defects on which the buyer proposes to rely.

(2) Payment against documents made without reservation of rights precludes recovery of the payment for defects apparent on the face of the documents.

§ 2–606. What Constitutes Acceptance of Goods

(1) Acceptance of goods occurs when the buyer

(a) after a reasonable opportunity to inspect the goods signifies to the seller that the goods are conforming or that he will take or retain them in spite of their nonconformity; or

(b) fails to make an effective rejection (subsection (1) of Section 2–602), but such acceptance does not occur until the buyer has had a reasonable opportunity to inspect them; or

(c) does any act inconsistent with the seller's ownership; but if such act is wrongful as against the seller it is an acceptance only if ratified by him.

(2) Acceptance of a part of any commercial unit is acceptance of that entire unit.

§ 2–607. Effect of Acceptance; Notice of Breach; Burden of Establishing Breach After Acceptance; Notice of Claim or Litigation to Person Answerable Over

(1) The buyer must pay at the contract rate for any goods accepted.

(2) Acceptance of goods by the buyer precludes rejection of the goods accepted and if made with knowledge of a nonconformity cannot be revoked because of it unless the acceptance was on the reasonable assumption that the non-conformity would be seasonably cured but acceptance does not of itself impair any other remedy provided by this Article for non-conformity.

(3) Where a tender has been accepted

(a) the buyer must within a reasonable time after he discovers or should have discovered any breach notify the seller of breach or be barred from any remedy; and

(b) if the claim is one for infringement or the like (subsection (3) of Section 2–312) and the buyer is sued as a result of such a breach he must so notify the seller within a reasonable time after he receives notice of the litigation or be barred from any remedy over for liability established by the litigation.

(4) The burden is on the buyer to establish any breach with respect to the goods accepted.

(5) Where the buyer is sued for breach of a warranty or other obligation for which his seller is answerable over

(a) he may give his seller written notice of the litigation. If the notice states that the seller may come in and defend and that if the seller does not do so he will be bound in any action against him by his buyer by any determination of fact common to the two litigations, then unless the seller after seasonable receipt of the notice does come in and defend he is so bound.

(b) if the claim is one for infringement or the like (subsection (3) of Section 2–312) the original seller may demand in writing that his buyer turn over to him control of the litigation including settlement or else be barred from any remedy over and if he also agrees to bear all expense and to satisfy any adverse judgment, then unless the buyer after seasonable receipt of the demand does turn over control the buyer is so barred.

(6) The provisions of subsections (3), (4) and (5) apply to any obligation of a buyer to hold the seller harmless against infringement or the like (subsection (3) of Section 2–312).

§ 2–608. Revocation of Acceptance in Whole or in Part

(1) The buyer may revoke his acceptance of a lot or commercial unit whose non-conformity substantially impairs its value to him if he has accepted it

(a) on the reasonable assumption that its non-conformity would be cured and it has not been seasonably cured; or

(b) without discovery of such non-conformity if his acceptance was reasonably induced either by the difficulty of discovery before acceptance or by the seller's assurances.

(2) Revocation of acceptance must occur within a reasonable time after the buyer discovers or should have discovered the ground for it and before any substantial change in condition of the goods which is not caused by their own defects. It is not effective until the buyer notifies the seller of it.

(3) A buyer who so revokes has the same rights and duties with regard to the goods involved as if he had rejected them.

§ 2–609. Right to Adequate Assurance of Performance

(1) A contract for sale imposes an obligation on each party that the other's expectation of receiving due performance will not be impaired. When reasonable grounds for inse-

curity arise with respect to the performance of either party the other may in writing demand adequate assurance of due performance and until he receives such assurance may if commercially reasonable suspend any performance for which he has not already received the agreed return.

(2) Between merchants the reasonableness of grounds for insecurity and the adequacy of any assurance offered shall be determined according to commercial standards.

(3) Acceptance of any improper delivery or payment does not prejudice the aggrieved party's right to demand adequate assurance of future performance.

(4) After receipt of a justified demand failure to provide within a reasonable time not exceeding thirty days such assurance of due performance as is adequate under the circumstances of the particular case is a repudiation of the contract.

§ 2–610. Anticipatory Repudiation

When either party repudiates the contract with respect to a performance not yet due the loss of which will substantially impair the value of the contract to the other, the aggrieved party may

(a) for a commercially reasonable time await performance by the repudiating party; or

(b) resort to any remedy for breach (Section 2–703 or Section 2–711), even though he has notified the repudiating party that he would await the latter's performance and has urged retraction; and

(c) in either case suspend his own performance or proceed in accordance with the provisions of this Article on the seller's right to identify goods to the contract notwithstanding breach or to salvage unfinished goods (Section 2–704).

§ 2–611. Retraction of Anticipatory Repudiation

(1) Until the repudiating party's next performance is due he can retract his repudiation unless the aggrieved party has since the repudiation cancelled or materially changed his position or otherwise indicated that he considers the repudiation final.

(2) Retraction may be by any method which clearly indicates to the aggrieved party that the repudiating party intends to perform, but must include any assurance justifiably demanded under the provisions of this Article (Section 2–609).

(3) Retraction reinstates the repudiating party's right under the contract with due excuse and allowance to the aggrieved party for any delay occasioned by the repudiation.

§ 2–612. "Installment Contract"; Breach

(1) An "installment contract" is one which requires or authorizes the delivery of goods in separate lots to be separately accepted, even though the contract contains a

clause "each delivery is a separate contract" or its equivalent.

(2) The buyer may reject any installment which is non-conforming if the non-conformity substantially impairs the value of that installment and cannot be cured or if the non-conformity is a defect in the required documents; but if the non-conformity does not fall within subsection (3) and the seller gives adequate assurance of its cure the buyer must accept that installment.

(3) Whenever non-conformity or default with respect to one or more installments substantially impairs the value of the whole contract there is a breach of the whole. But the aggrieved party reinstates the contract if he accepts a non-conforming installment without seasonably notifying of cancellation or if he brings an action with respect only to past installments or demands performance as to future installments.

§ 2–613. Casualty to Identified Goods

Where the contract requires for its performance goods identified when the contract is made, and the goods suffer casualty without fault of either party before the risk of loss passes to the buyer, or in a proper case under a "no arrival, no sale" term (Section 2–324) then

(a) if the loss is total the contract is avoided; and

(b) if the loss is partial or the goods have so deteriorated as no longer to conform to the contract the buyer may nevertheless demand inspection and at his option either treat the contract as avoided or accept the goods with due allowance from the contract price for the deterioration or the deficiency in quantity but without further right against the seller.

§ 2–614. Substituted Performance

(1) Where without fault of either party the agreed berthing, loading, or unloading facilities fail or an agreed type of carrier becomes unavailable or the agreed manner of delivery otherwise becomes commercially impracticable but a commercially reasonable substitute is available, such substitute performance must be tendered and accepted.

(2) If the agreed means or manner of payment fails because of domestic or foreign governmental regulation, the seller may withhold or stop delivery unless the buyer provides a means or manner of payment which is commercially a substantial equivalent. If delivery has already been taken, payment by the means or in the manner provided by the regulation discharges the buyer's obligation unless the regulation is discriminatory, oppressive or predatory.

§ 2–615. Excuse by Failure of Presupposed Conditions

Except so far as a seller may have assumed a greater obligation and subject to the preceding section on substituted performance:

(a) Delay in delivery or non-delivery in whole or in part by a seller who complies with paragraphs (b) and (c) is not a breach of his duty under a contract for sale if performance as agreed has been made impracticable by the occurrence of a contingency the nonoccurrence of which was a basic assumption on which the contract was made or by compliance in good faith with any applicable foreign or domestic governmental regulation or order whether or not it later proves to be invalid.

(b) Where the causes mentioned in paragraph (a) affect only a part of the seller's capacity to perform, he must allocate production and deliveries among his customers but may at his option include regular customers not then under contract as well as his own requirements for further manufacture. He may so allocate in any manner which is fair and reasonable.

(c) The seller must notify the buyer seasonably that there will be delay or non-delivery and, when allocation is required under paragraph (b), of the estimated quota thus made available for the buyer.

§ 2–616. Procedure on Notice Claiming Excuse

(1) Where the buyer receives notification of a material or indefinite delay or an allocation justified under the preceding section he may by written notification to the seller as to any delivery concerned, and where the prospective deficiency substantially impairs the value of the whole contract under the provisions of this Article relating to breach of installment contracts (Section 2–612), then also as to the whole,

(a) terminate and thereby discharge any unexecuted portion of the contract; or

(b) modify the contract by agreeing to take his available quota in substitution.

(2) If after receipt of such notification from the seller the buyer fails so to modify the contract within a reasonable time not exceeding thirty days the contract lapses with respect to any deliveries affected.

(3) The provisions of this section may not be negated by agreement except in so far as the seller has assumed a greater obligation under the preceding section.

Part 7 Remedies

§ 2–701. Remedies for Breach of Collateral Contracts Not Impaired

Remedies for breach of any obligation or promise collateral or ancillary to a contract for sale are not impaired by the provisions of this Article.

§ 2–702. Seller's Remedies on Discovery of Buyer's Insolvency

(1) Where the seller discovers the buyer to be insolvent he may refuse delivery except for cash including payment for

all goods theretofore delivered under the contract, and stop delivery under this Article (Section 2–705).

(2) Where the seller discovers that the buyer has received goods on credit while insolvent he may reclaim the goods upon demand made within ten days after the receipt, but if misrepresentation of solvency has been made to the particular seller in writing within three months before delivery the ten day limitation does not apply. Except as provided in this subsection the seller may not base a right to reclaim goods on the buyer's fraudulent or innocent misrepresentation of solvency or of intent to pay.

(3) The seller's right to reclaim under subsection (2) is subject to the rights of a buyer in ordinary course or other good faith purchaser under this Article (Section 2–403). Successful reclamation of goods excludes all other remedies with respect to them.

§ 2–703. Seller's Remedies in General

Where the buyer wrongfully rejects or revokes acceptance of goods or fails to make a payment due on or before delivery or repudiates with respect to a part or the whole, then with respect to any goods directly affected and, if the breach is of the whole contract (Section 2–612), then also with respect to the whole undelivered balance, the aggrieved seller may

(a) withhold delivery of such goods;

(b) stop delivery by any bailee as hereafter provided (Section 2–705);

(c) proceed under the next section respecting goods still unidentified to the contract;

(d) resell and recover damages as hereafter provided (Section 2–706);

(e) recover damages for non-acceptance (Section 2–708) or in a proper case the price (Section 2–709);

(f) cancel.

§ 2–704. Seller's Right to Identify Goods to the Contract Notwithstanding Breach or to Salvage Unfinished Goods

(1) An aggrieved seller under the preceding section may

(a) identify to the contract conforming goods not already identified if at the time he learned of the breach they are in his possession or control;

(b) treat as the subject of resale goods which have demonstrably been intended for the particular contract even though those goods are unfinished.

(2) Where the goods are unfinished an aggrieved seller may in the exercise of reasonable commercial judgment for the purposes of avoiding loss and of effective realization either complete the manufacture and wholly identify the goods to the contract or cease manufacture and resell for scrap or salvage value or proceed in any other reasonable manner.

§ 2–705. Seller's Stoppage of Delivery in Transit or Otherwise

(1) The seller may stop delivery of goods in the possession of a carrier or other bailee when he discovers the buyer to be insolvent (Section 2–702) and may stop delivery of carload, truckload, planeload or larger shipments of express or freight when the buyer repudiates or fails to make a payment due before delivery or if for any other reason the seller has a right to withhold or reclaim the goods.

(2) As against such buyer the seller may stop delivery until

(a) receipt of the goods by the buyer; or

(b) acknowledgment to the buyer by any bailee of the goods except a carrier that the bailee holds the goods for the buyer; or

(c) such acknowledgment to the buyer by a carrier by reshipment or as warehouseman; or

(d) negotiation to the buyer of any negotiable document of title covering the goods.

(3)(a) To stop delivery the seller must so notify as to enable the bailee by reasonable diligence to prevent delivery of the goods.

(b) After such notification the bailee must hold and deliver the goods according to the directions of the seller but the seller is liable to the bailee for any ensuing charges or damages.

(c) If a negotiable document of title has been issued for goods the bailee is not obliged to obey a notification to stop until surrender of the document.

(d) A carrier who has issued a non-negotiable bill of lading is not obliged to obey a notification to stop received from a person other than the consignor.

§ 2–706. Seller's Resale Including Contract for Resale

(1) Under the conditions stated in Section 2–703 on seller's remedies, the seller may resell the goods concerned or the undelivered balance thereof. Where the resale is made in good faith and in a commercially reasonable manner the seller may recover the difference between the resale price and the contract price together with any incidental damages allowed under the provisions of this Article (Section 2–710), but less expenses saved in consequence of the buyer's breach.

(2) Except as otherwise provided in subsection (3) or unless otherwise agreed resale may be at public or private sale including sale by way of one or more contracts to sell or of identification to an existing contract of the seller. Sale may be as a unit or in parcels and at any time and place and on any terms but every aspect of the sale including the method, manner, time, place and terms must be commercially reasonable. The resale must be reasonably identified as referring to the broken contract, but it is

not necessary that the goods be in existence or that any or all of them have been identified to the contract before the breach.

(3) Where the resale is at private sale the seller must give the buyer reasonable notification of his intention to resell.

(4) Where the resale is at public sale

(a) only identified goods can be sold except where there is a recognized market for a public sale of futures in goods of the kind; and

(b) it must be made at a usual place or market for public sale if one is reasonably available and except in the case of goods which are perishable or threaten to decline in value speedily the seller must give the buyer reasonable notice of the time and place of the resale; and

(c) if the goods are not to be within the view of those attending the sale the notification of sale must state the place where the goods are located and provide for their reasonable inspection by prospective bidders; and

(d) the seller may buy.

(5) A purchaser who buys in good faith at a resale takes the goods free of any rights of the original buyer even though the seller fails to comply with one or more of the requirements of this section.

(6) The seller is not accountable to the buyer for any profit made on any resale. A person in the position of a seller (Section 2–707) or a buyer who has rightfully rejected or justifiably revoked acceptance must account for any excess over the amount of his security interest, as hereinafter defined (subsection (3) of Section 2–711).

§ 2–707. "Person in the Position of a Seller"

(1) A "person in the position of a seller" includes as against a principal an agent who has paid or become responsible for the price of goods on behalf of his principal or anyone who otherwise holds a security interest or other right in goods similar to that of a seller.

(2) A person in the position of a seller may as provided in this Article withhold or stop delivery (Section 2–706) and recover incidental damages (Section 2–710).

§ 2–708. Seller's Damages for Non-Acceptance or Repudiation

(1) Subject to subsection (2) and to the provisions of this Article with respect to proof of market price (Section 2–723), the measure of damages for non-acceptance or repudiation by the buyer is the difference between the market price at the time and place for tender and the unpaid contract price together with any incidental damages provided in this Article (Section 2–710), but less expenses saved in consequence of the buyer's breach.

(2) If the measure of damages provided in subsection (1) is inadequate to put the seller in as good a position as

performance would have done then the measure of damages is the profit (including reasonable overhead) which the seller would have made from full performance by the buyer, together with any incidental damages provided in this Article (Section 2–710), due allowance for costs reasonably incurred and due credit for payments or proceeds of resale.

§ 2–709. Action for the Price

(1) When the buyer fails to pay the price as it becomes due the seller may recover, together with any incidental damages under the next section, the price

(a) of goods accepted or of conforming goods lost or damaged within a commercially reasonable time after risk of their loss has passed to the buyer; and

(b) of goods identified to the contract if the seller is unable after reasonable effort to resell them at a reasonable price or the circumstances reasonably indicate that such effort will be unavailing.

(2) Where the seller sues for the price he must hold for the buyer any goods which have been identified to the contract and are still in his control except that if resale becomes possible he may resell them at any time prior to the collection of the judgment. The net proceeds of any such resale must be credited to the buyer and payment of the judgment entitles him to any goods not resold.

(3) After the buyer has wrongfully rejected or revoked acceptance of the goods or has failed to make a payment due or has repudiated (Section 2–610), a seller who is held not entitled to the price under this section shall nevertheless be awarded damages for non-acceptance under the preceding section.

§ 2–710. Seller's Incidental Damages

Incidental damages to an aggrieved seller include any commercially reasonable charges, expenses or commissions incurred in stopping delivery, in the transportation, care and custody of goods after the buyer's breach, in connection with return or resale of the goods or otherwise resulting from the breach.

§ 2–711. Buyer's Remedies in General; Buyer's Security Interest in Rejected Goods

(1) Where the seller fails to make delivery or repudiates or the buyer rightfully rejects or justifiably revokes acceptance then with respect to any goods involved, and with respect to the whole if the breach goes to the whole contract (Section 2–612), the buyer may cancel and whether or not he has done so may in addition to recovering so much of the price as has been paid

(a) "cover" and have damages under the next section as to all the goods affected whether or not they have been identified to the contract; or

(b) recover damages for non-delivery as provided in this Article (Section 2–713).

(2) Where the seller fails to deliver or repudiates the buyer may also

(a) if the goods have been identified recover them as provided in this Article (Section 2–502); or

(b) in a proper case obtain specific performance or replevy the goods as provided in this Article (Section 2–716).

(3) On rightful rejection or justifiable revocation of acceptance a buyer has a security interest in goods in his possession or control for any payments made on their price and any expenses reasonably incurred in their inspection, receipt, transportation, care and custody and may hold such goods and resell them in like manner as an aggrieved seller (Section 2–706).

§ 2–712. "Cover"; Buyer's Procurement of Substitute Goods

(1) After a breach within the preceding section the buyer may "cover" by making in good faith and without unreasonable delay any reasonable purchase of or contract to purchase goods in substitution for those due from the seller.

(2) The buyer may recover from the seller as damages the difference between the cost of cover and the contract price together with any incidental or consequential damages as hereinafter defined (Section 2–715), but less expenses saved in consequence of the seller's breach.

(3) Failure of the buyer to effect cover within this section does not bar him from any other remedy.

§ 2–713. Buyer's Damages for Non-Delivery or Repudiation

(1) Subject to the provisions of this Article with respect to proof of market price (Section 2–723), the measure of damages for non-delivery or repudiation by the seller is the difference between the market price at the time when the buyer learned of the breach and the contract price together with any incidental and consequential damages provided in this Article (Section 2–715), but less expenses saved in consequence of the seller's breach.

(2) Market price is to be determined as of the place for tender or, in cases of rejection after arrival or revocation of acceptance, as of the place of arrival.

§ 2–714. Buyer's Damages for Breach in Regard to Accepted Goods

(1) Where the buyer has accepted goods and given notification (subsection (3) of Section 2–607) he may recover as damages for any non-conformity of tender the loss resulting in the ordinary course of events from the seller's breach as determined in any manner which is reasonable.

(2) The measure of damages for breach of warranty is the difference at the time and place of acceptance between the value of the goods accepted and the value they would have had if they had been as warranted, unless special circumstances show proximate damages of a different amount.

(3) In a proper case any incidental and consequential damages under the next section may also be recovered.

§ 2–715. Buyer's Incidental and Consequential Damages

(1) Incidental damages resulting from the seller's breach include expenses reasonably incurred in inspection, receipt, transportation and care and custody of goods rightfully rejected, any commercially reasonable charges, expenses or commissions in connection with effecting cover and any other reasonable expense incident to the delay or other breach.

(2) Consequential damages resulting from the seller's breach include

(a) any loss resulting from general or particular requirements and needs of which the seller at the time of contracting had reason to know and which could not reasonably be prevented by cover or otherwise; and

(b) injury to person or property proximately resulting from any breach of warranty.

§ 2–716. Buyer's Right to Specific Performance or Replevin

(1) Specific performance may be decreed where the goods are unique or in other proper circumstances.

(2) The decree for specific performance may include such terms and conditions as to payment of the price, damages, or other relief as the court may deem just.

(3) The buyer has a right of replevin for goods identified to the contract if after reasonable effort he is unable to effect cover for such goods or the circumstances reasonably indicate that such effort will be unavailing or if the goods have been shipped under reservation and satisfaction of the security interest in them has been made or tendered.

§ 2–717. Deduction of Damages From the Price

The buyer on notifying the seller of his intention to do so may deduct all or any part of the damages resulting from any breach of the contract from any part of the price still due under the same contract.

§ 2–718. Liquidation or Limitation of Damages; Deposits

(1) Damages for breach by either party may be liquidated in the agreement but only at an amount which is reasonable in the light of the anticipated or actual harm caused by the breach, the difficulties of proof of loss, and the inconvenience or nonfeasibility of otherwise obtaining an

adequate remedy. A term fixing unreasonably large liquidated damages is void as a penalty.

(2) Where the seller justifiably withholds delivery of goods because of the buyer's breach, the buyer is entitled to restitution of any amount by which the sum of his payments exceeds

(a) the amount to which the seller is entitled by virtue of terms liquidating the seller's damages in accordance with subsection (1), or

(b) in the absence of such terms, twenty percent of the value of the total performance for which the buyer is obligated under the contract or $500, whichever is smaller.

(3) The buyer's right to restitution under subsection (2) is subject to offset to the extent that the seller establishes

(a) a right to recover damages under the provisions of this Article other than subsection (1), and

(b) the amount or value of any benefits received by the buyer directly or indirectly by reason of the contract.

(4) Where a seller has received payment in goods their reasonable value or the proceeds of their resale shall be treated as payments for the purposes of subsection (2); but if the seller has notice of the buyer's breach before reselling goods received in part performance, his resale is subject to the conditions laid down in this Article on resale by an aggrieved seller (Section 2–706).

§ 2–719. Contractual Modification or Limitation of Remedy

(1) Subject to the provisions of subsections (2) and (3) of this section and of the preceding section on liquidation and limitation of damages,

(a) the agreement may provide for remedies in addition to or in substitution for those provided in this Article and may limit or alter the measure of damages recoverable under this Article, as by limiting the buyer's remedies to return of the goods and repayment of the price or to repair and replacement of non-conforming goods or parts; and

(b) resort to a remedy as provided is optional unless the remedy is expressly agreed to be exclusive, in which case it is the sole remedy.

(2) Where circumstances cause an exclusive or limited remedy to fail of its essential purpose, remedy may be had as provided in this Act.

(3) Consequential damages may be limited or excluded unless the limitation or exclusion is unconscionable. Limitation of consequential damages for injury to the person in the case of consumer goods is prima facie unconscionable but limitation of damages where the loss is commercial is not.

§ 2–720. Effect of "Cancellation" or "Rescission" on Claims for Antecedent Breach

Unless the contrary intention clearly appears, expressions of "cancellation" or "rescission" of the contract or the like shall not be construed as a renunciation or discharge of any claim in damages for an antecedent breach.

§ 2–721. Remedies for Fraud

Remedies for material misrepresentation or fraud include all remedies available under this Article for nonfraudulent breach. Neither rescission or a claim for rescission of the contract for sale nor rejection or return of the goods shall bar or be deemed inconsistent with a claim for damages or other remedy.

§ 2–722. Who Can Sue Third Parties for Injury to Goods

Where a third party so deals with goods which have been identified to a contract for sale as to cause actionable injury to a party to that contract

(a) a right of action against the third party is in either party to the contract for sale who has title to or a security interest or a special property or an insurable interest in the goods; and if the goods have been destroyed or converted a right of action is also in the party who either bore the risk of loss under the contract for sale or has since the injury assumed that risk as against the other;

(b) if at the time of the injury the party plaintiff did not bear the risk of loss as against the other party to the contract for sale and there is no arrangement between them for disposition of the recovery, his suit or settlement is, subject to his own interest, as a fiduciary for the other party to the contract;

(c) either party may with the consent of the other sue for the benefit of whom it may concern.

§ 2–723. Proof of Market Price: Time and Place

(1) If an action based on anticipatory repudiation comes to trial before the time for performance with respect to some or all of the goods, any damages based on market price (Section 2–708 or Section 2–713) shall be determined according to the price of such goods prevailing at the time when the aggrieved party learned of the repudiation.

(2) If evidence of a price prevailing at the times or places described in this Article is not readily available the price prevailing within any reasonable time before or after the time described or at any other place which in commercial judgment or under usage of trade would serve as a reasonable substitute for the one described may be used, making any proper allowance for the cost of transporting the goods to or from such other place.

(3) Evidence of a relevant price prevailing at a time or place other than the one described in this Article offered by one party is not admissible unless and until he has given the other party such notice as the court finds sufficient to prevent unfair surprise.

§ 2–724. Admissibility of Market Quotations

Whenever the prevailing price or value of any goods regularly bought and sold in any established commodity market is in issue, reports in official publications or trade journals or in newspapers or periodicals of general circulation published as the reports of such market shall be admissible in evidence. The circumstances of the preparation of such a report may be shown to affect its weight but not its admissibility.

§ 2–725. Statute of Limitations in Contracts for Sale

(1) An action for breach of any contract for sale must be commenced within four years after the cause of action has accrued. By the original agreement the parties may reduce the period of limitation to not less than one year but may not extend it.

(2) A cause of action accrues when the breach occurs, regardless of the aggrieved party's lack of knowledge of the breach. A breach of warranty occurs when tender of delivery is made, except that where a warranty explicitly extends to future performance of the goods and discovery of the breach must await the time of such performance the cause of action accrues when the breach is or should have been discovered.

(3) Where an action commenced within the time limited by subsection (1) is so terminated as to leave available a remedy by another action for the same breach such other action may be commenced after the expiration of the time limited and within six months after the termination of the first action unless the termination resulted from voluntary discontinuance or from dismissal for failure or neglect to prosecute.

(4) This section does not alter the law on tolling of the statute of limitations nor does it apply to causes of action which have accrued before this Act becomes effective.

ARTICLE 2A LEASES

Part I General Provisions

§ 2A–101. Short Title

This Article shall be known and may be cited as the Uniform Commercial Code—Leases.

§ 2A–102. Scope

This Article applies to any transaction, regardless of form, that creates a lease.

§ 2A–103. Definitions and Index of Definitions

(1) In this Article unless the context otherwise requires:

(a) "Buyer in ordinary course of business" means a person who in good faith and without knowledge that the sale to him [or her] is in violation of the ownership rights or security interest or leasehold interest of a third party in the goods buys in ordinary course from a person in the business of selling goods of that kind but does not include a pawnbroker. "Buying" may be for cash or by exchange of other property or on secured or unsecured credit and includes receiving goods or documents of title under a pre-existing contract for sale but does not include a transfer in bulk or as security for or in total or partial satisfaction of a money debt.

(b) "Cancellation" occurs when either party puts an end to the lease contract for default by the other party.

(c) "Commercial unit" means such a unit of goods as by commercial usage is a single whole for purposes of lease and division of which materially impairs its character or value on the market or in use. A commercial unit may be a single article, as a machine, or a set of articles, as a suite of furniture or a line of machinery, or a quantity, as a gross or carload, or any other unit treated in use or in the relevant market as a single whole.

(d) "Conforming" goods or performance under a lease contract means goods or performance that are in accordance with the obligations under the lease contract.

(e) "Consumer lease" means a lease that a lessor regularly engaged in the business of leasing or selling makes to a lessee who is an individual and who takes under the lease primarily for a personal, family, or household purpose [, if the total payments to be made under the lease contract, excluding payments for options to renew or buy, do not exceed $_____].

(f) "Fault" means wrongful act, omission, breach, or default.

(g) "Finance lease" means a lease with respect to which:

(i) the lessor does not select, manufacture, or supply the goods;

(ii) the lessor acquires the goods or the right to possession and use of the goods in connection with the lease; and

(iii) one of the following occurs:

(A) the lessee receives a copy of the contract by which the lessor acquired the goods or the right to possession and use of the goods before signing the lease contract;

(B) the lessee's approval of the contract by which the lessor acquired the goods or the right to possession and use of the goods is a condition to effectiveness of the lease contract;

(C) the lessee, before signing the lease contract, receives an accurate and complete statement designating the promises and warranties, and any disclaimers of warranties, limitations or modifications of remedies, or liquidated damages, including those of a third party, such as the manufacturer of the goods, provided to the lessor by the person supplying the goods in connection with or as part of the contract by which the lessor acquired the goods or the right to possession and use of the goods; or

(D) if the lease is not a consumer lease, the lessor, before the lessee signs the lease contract, informs the lessee in writing (a) of the identity of the person supplying the goods to the lessor, unless the lessee has selected that person and directed the lessor to acquire the goods or the right to possession and use of the goods from that person, (b) that the lessee is entitled under this Article to the promises and warranties, including those of any third party, provided to the lessor by the person supplying the goods in connection with or as part of the contract by which the lessor acquired the goods or the right to possession and use of the goods, and (c) that the lessee may communicate with the person supplying the goods to the lessor and receive an accurate and complete statement of those promises and warranties, including any disclaimers and limitations of them or of remedies.

(h) "Goods" means all things that are movable at the time of identification to the lease contract, or are fixtures (Section 2A–309), but the term does not include money, documents, instruments, accounts, chattel paper, general intangibles, or minerals or the like, including oil and gas, before extraction. The term also includes the unborn young of animals.

(i) "Installment lease contract" means a lease contract that authorizes or requires the delivery of goods in separate lots to be separately accepted, even though the lease contract contains a clause "each delivery is a separate lease" or its equivalent.

(j) "Lease" means a transfer of the right to possession and use of goods for a term in return for consideration, but a sale, including a sale on approval or a sale or return, or retention or creation of a security interest is not a lease. Unless the context clearly indicates otherwise, the term includes a sublease.

(k) "Lease agreement" means the bargain, with respect to the lease, of the lessor and the lessee in fact as found in their language or by implication from other circumstances including course of dealing or usage of trade or course of performance as provided in this Article. Unless the context clearly indicates otherwise, the term includes a sublease agreement.

(l) "Lease contract" means the total legal obligation that results from the lease agreement as affected by this Article and any other applicable rules of law. Unless the context clearly indicates otherwise, the term includes a sublease contract.

(m) "Leasehold interest" means the interest of the lessor or the lessee under a lease contract.

(n) "Lessee" means a person who acquires the right to possession and use of goods under a lease. Unless the context clearly indicates otherwise, the term includes a sublessee.

(o) "Lessee in ordinary course of business" means a person who in good faith and without knowledge that the lease to him [or her] is in violation of the ownership rights or security interest or leasehold interest of a third party in the goods, leases in ordinary course from a person in the business of selling or leasing goods of that kind but does not include a pawnbroker. "Leasing" may be for cash or by exchange of other property or on secured or unsecured credit and includes receiving goods or documents of title under a pre-existing lease contract but does not include a transfer in bulk or as security for or in total or partial satisfaction of a money debt.

(p) "Lessor" means a person who transfers the right to possession and use of goods under a lease. Unless the context clearly indicates otherwise, the term includes a sublessor.

(q) "Lessor's residual interest" means the lessor's interest in the goods after expiration, termination, or cancellation of the lease contract.

(r) "Lien" means a charge against or interest in goods to secure payment of a debt or performance of an obligation, but the term does not include a security interest.

(s) "Lot" means a parcel or a single article that is the subject matter of a separate lease or delivery, whether or not it is sufficient to perform the lease contract.

(t) "Merchant lessee" means a lessee that is a merchant with respect to goods of the kind subject to the lease.

(u) "Present value" means the amount as of a date certain of one or more sums payable in the future, discounted to the date certain. The discount is determined by the interest rate specified by the parties if the rate was not manifestly unreasonable at the time the transaction was entered into; otherwise, the discount is determined by a commercially reasonable rate that takes into account the facts and circumstances of each case at the time the transaction was entered into.

(v) "Purchase" includes taking by sale, lease, mortgage, security interest, pledge, gift, or any other voluntary transaction creating an interest in goods.

(w) "Sublease" means a lease of goods the right to possession and use of which was acquired by the lessor as a lessee under an existing lease.

(x) "Supplier" means a person from whom a lessor buys or leases goods to be leased under a finance lease.

(y) "Supply contract" means a contract under which a lessor buys or leases goods to be leased.

(z) "Termination" occurs when either party pursuant to a power created by agreement or law puts an end to the lease contract otherwise than for default.

(2) Other definitions applying to this Article and the sections in which they appear are:

"Accessions." Section 2A–310(1).

"Construction mortgage." Section 2A–309(1)(d).

"Encumbrance." Section 2A–309(1)(e).

"Fixtures." Section 2A–309(1)(a).

"Fixture filing." Section 2A–309(1)(b).

"Purchase money lease." Section 2A–309(1)(c).

(3) The following definitions in other Articles apply to this Article:

"Account." Section 9–106.

"Between merchants." Section 2–104(3).

"Buyer." Section 2–103(1)(a).

"Chattel paper." Section 9–105(1)(b).

"Consumer goods." Section 9–109(1).

"Document." Section 9–105(1)(f).

"Entrusting." Section 2–403(3).

"General intangibles." Section 9–106.

"Good faith." Section 2–103(1)(b).

"Instrument." Section 9–105(1)(i).

"Merchant." Section 2–104(1).

"Mortgage." Section 9–105(1)(j).

"Pursuant to commitment." Section 9–105(1)(k).

"Receipt." Section 2–103(1)(c).

"Sale." Section 2–106(1).

"Sale on approval." Section 2–326.

"Sale or return." Section 2–326.

"Seller." Section 2–103(1)(d).

(4) In addition Article 1 contains general definitions and principles of construction and interpretation applicable throughout this Article.

As amended in 1990.

§ 2A–104. Leases Subject to Other Law

(1) A lease, although subject to this Article, is also subject to any applicable:

(a) certificate of title statute of this State: (list any certificate of title statutes covering automobiles, trailers, mobile homes, boats, farm tractors, and the like);

(b) certificate of title statute of another jurisdiction (Section 2A–105); or

(c) consumer protection statute of this State, or final consumer protection decision of a court of this State existing on the effective date of this Article.

(2) In case of conflict between this Article, other than Sections 2A–105, 2A–304(3), and 2A–305(3), and a statute or decision referred to in subsection (1), the statute or decision controls.

(3) Failure to comply with an applicable law has only the effect specified therein.

As amended in 1990.

§ 2A–105. Territorial Application of Article to Goods Covered by Certificate of Title

Subject to the provisions of Sections 2A–304(3) and 2A–305(3), with respect to goods covered by a certificate of title issued under a statute of this State or of another jurisdiction, compliance and the effect of compliance or noncompliance with a certificate of title statute are governed by the law (including the conflict of laws rules) of the jurisdiction issuing the certificate until the earlier of (a) surrender of the certificate, or (b) four months after the goods are removed from that jurisdiction and thereafter until a new certificate of title is issued by another jurisdiction.

§ 2A–106. Limitation on Power of Parties to Consumer Lease to Choose Applicable Law and Judicial Forum

(1) If the law chosen by the parties to a consumer lease is that of a jurisdiction other than a jurisdiction in which the lessee resides at the time the lease agreement becomes enforceable or within 30 days thereafter or in which the goods are to be used, the choice is not enforceable.

(2) If the judicial forum chosen by the parties to a consumer lease is a forum that would not otherwise have jurisdiction over the lessee, the choice is not enforceable.

§ 2A–107. Waiver or Renunciation of Claim or Right After Default

Any claim or right arising out of an alleged default or breach of warranty may be discharged in whole or in part without consideration by a written waiver or renunciation signed and delivered by the aggrieved party.

§ 2A–108. Unconscionability

(1) If the court as a matter of law finds a lease contract or any clause of a lease contract to have been unconscionable at the time it was made the court may refuse to enforce the lease contract, or it may enforce the remainder of the lease contract without the unconscionable clause, or it may so limit the application of any unconscionable clause as to avoid any unconscionable result.

(2) With respect to a consumer lease, if the court as a matter of law finds that a lease contract or any clause of a lease contract has been induced by unconscionable conduct or that unconscionable conduct has occurred in the collection of a claim arising from a lease contract, the court may grant appropriate relief.

(3) Before making a finding of unconscionability under subsection (1) or (2), the court, on its own motion or that of a party, shall afford the parties a reasonable opportunity to present evidence as to the setting, purpose, and effect of the lease contract or clause thereof, or of the conduct.

(4) In an action in which the lessee claims unconscionability with respect to a consumer lease:

(a) If the court finds unconscionability under subsection (1) or (2), the court shall award reasonable attorney's fees to the lessee.

(b) If the court does not find unconscionability and the lessee claiming unconscionability has brought or maintained an action he [or she] knew to be groundless, the court shall award reasonable attorney's fees to the party against whom the claim is made.

(c) In determining attorney's fees, the amount of the recovery on behalf of the claimant under subsections (1) and (2) is not controlling.

§ 2A–109. Option to Accelerate at Will

(1) A term providing that one party or his [or her] successor in interest may accelerate payment or performance or require collateral or additional collateral "at will" or "when he [or she] deems himself [or herself] insecure" or in words of similar import must be construed to mean that he [or she] has power to do so only if he [or she] in good faith believes that the prospect of payment or performance is impaired.

(2) With respect to a consumer lease, the burden of establishing good faith under subsection (1) is on the party who exercised the power; otherwise the burden of establishing lack of good faith is on the party against whom the power has been exercised.

Part 2 Formation and Construction of Lease Contract

§ 2A–201. Statute of Frauds

(1) A lease contract is not enforceable by way of action or defense unless:

(a) the total payments to be made under the lease contract, excluding payments for options to renew or buy, are less than $1,000; or

(b) there is a writing, signed by the party against whom enforcement is sought or by that party's authorized agent, sufficient to indicate that a lease contract has been made between the parties and to describe the goods leased and the lease term.

(2) Any description of leased goods or of the lease term is sufficient and satisfies subsection (1)(b), whether or not it is specific, if it reasonably identifies what is described.

(3) A writing is not insufficient because it omits or incorrectly states a term agreed upon, but the lease contract is not enforceable under subsection (1)(b) beyond the lease term and the quantity of goods shown in the writing.

(4) A lease contract that does not satisfy the requirements of subsection (1), but which is valid in other respects, is enforceable:

(a) if the goods are to be specially manufactured or obtained for the lessee and are not suitable for lease or sale to others in the ordinary course of the lessor's business, and the lessor, before notice of repudiation is received and under circumstances that reasonably indicate that the goods are for the lessee, has made either a substantial beginning of their manufacture or commitments for their procurement;

(b) if the party against whom enforcement is sought admits in that party's pleading, testimony or otherwise in

court that a lease contract was made, but the lease contract is not enforceable under this provision beyond the quantity of goods admitted; or

(c) with respect to goods that have been received and accepted by the lessee.

(5) The lease term under a lease contract referred to in subsection (4) is:

(a) if there is a writing signed by the party against whom enforcement is sought or by that party's authorized agent specifying the lease term, the term so specified;

(b) if the party against whom enforcement is sought admits in that party's pleading, testimony, or otherwise in court a lease term, the term so admitted; or

(c) a reasonable lease term.

§ 2A–202. Final Written Expression: Parol or Extrinsic Evidence

Terms with respect to which the confirmatory memoranda of the parties agree or which are otherwise set forth in a writing intended by the parties as a final expression of their agreement with respect to such terms as are included therein may not be contradicted by evidence of any prior agreement or of a contemporaneous oral agreement but may be explained or supplemented:

(a) by course of dealing or usage of trade or by course of performance; and

(b) by evidence of consistent additional terms unless the court finds the writing to have been intended also as a complete and exclusive statement of the terms of the agreement.

§ 2A–203. Seals Inoperative

The affixing of a seal to a writing evidencing a lease contract or an offer to enter into a lease contract does not render the writing a sealed instrument and the law with respect to sealed instruments does not apply to the lease contract or offer.

§ 2A–204. Formation in General

(1) A lease contract may be made in any manner sufficient to show agreement, including conduct by both parties which recognizes the existence of a lease contract.

(2) An agreement sufficient to constitute a lease contract may be found although the moment of its making is undetermined.

(3) Although one or more terms are left open, a lease contract does not fail for indefiniteness if the parties have intended to make a lease contract and there is a reasonably certain basis for giving an appropriate remedy.

§ 2A–205. Firm Offers

An offer by a merchant to lease goods to or from another person in a signed writing that by its terms gives assurance it will be held open is not revocable, for lack of consideration, during the time stated or, if no time is stated, for a reasonable time, but in no event may the period of irrevocability exceed 3 months. Any such term of assurance on a form supplied by the offeree must be separately signed by the offeror.

§ 2A–206. Offer and Acceptance in Formation of Lease Contract

(1) Unless otherwise unambiguously indicated by the language or circumstances, an offer to make a lease contract must be construed as inviting acceptance in any manner and by any medium reasonable in the circumstances.

(2) If the beginning of a requested performance is a reasonable mode of acceptance, an offeror who is not notified of acceptance within a reasonable time may treat the offer as having lapsed before acceptance.

§ 2A–207. Course of Performance or Practical Construction

(1) If a lease contract involves repeated occasions for performance by either party with knowledge of the nature of the performance and opportunity for objection to it by the other, any course of performance accepted or acquiesced in without objection is relevant to determine the meaning of the lease agreement.

(2) The express terms of a lease agreement and any course of performance, as well as any course of dealing and usage of trade, must be construed whenever reasonable as consistent with each other; but if that construction is unreasonable, express terms control course of performance, course of performance controls both course of dealing and usage of trade, and course of dealing controls usage of trade.

(3) Subject to the provisions of Section 2A–208 on modification and waiver, course of performance is relevant to show a waiver or modification of any term inconsistent with the course of performance.

§ 2A–208. Modification, Rescission and Waiver

(1) An agreement modifying a lease contract needs no consideration to be binding.

(2) A signed lease agreement that excludes modification or rescission except by a signed writing may not be otherwise modified or rescinded, but, except as between merchants, such a requirement on a form supplied by a merchant must be separately signed by the other party.

(3) Although an attempt at modification or rescission does not satisfy the requirements of subsection (2), it may operate as a waiver.

(4) A party who has made a waiver affecting an executory portion of a lease contract may retract the waiver by reasonable notification received by the other party that strict performance will be required of any term waived, unless the retraction would be unjust in view of a material change of position in reliance on the waiver.

§ 2A–209. Lessee Under Finance Lease as Beneficiary of Supply Contract

(1) The benefit of a supplier's promises to the lessor under the supply contract and of all warranties, whether express or implied, including those of any third party provided in connection with or as part of the supply contract, extends to the lessee to the extent of the lessee's leasehold interest under a finance lease related to the supply contract, but is subject to the terms of the warranty and of the supply contract and all defenses or claims arising therefrom.

(2) The extension of the benefit of a supplier's promises and of warranties to the lessee (Section 2A–209(1)) does not: (i) modify the rights and obligations of the parties to the supply contract, whether arising therefrom or otherwise, or (ii) impose any duty or liability under the supply contract on the lessee.

(3) Any modification or rescission of the supply contract by the supplier and the lessor is effective between the supplier and the lessee unless, before the modification or rescission, the supplier has received notice that the lessee has entered into a finance lease related to the supply contract. If the modification or rescission is effective between the supplier and the lessee, the lessor is deemed to have assumed, in addition to the obligations of the lessor to the lessee under the lease contract, promises of the supplier to the lessor and warranties that were so modified or rescinded as they existed and were available to the lessee before modification or rescission.

(4) In addition to the extension of the benefit of the supplier's promises and of warranties to the lessee under subsection (1), the lessee retains all rights that the lessee may have against the supplier which arise from an agreement between the lessee and the supplier or under other law.

As amended in 1990.

§ 2A–210. Express Warranties

(1) Express warranties by the lessor are created as follows:

(a) Any affirmation of fact or promise made by the lessor to the lessee which relates to the goods and becomes part of the basis of the bargain creates an express warranty that the goods will conform to the affirmation or promise.

(b) Any description of the goods which is made part of the basis of the bargain creates an express warranty that the goods will conform to the description.

(c) Any sample or model that is made part of the basis of the bargain creates an express warranty that the whole of the goods will conform to the sample or model.

(2) It is not necessary to the creation of an express warranty that the lessor use formal words, such as "warrant" or "guarantee," or that the lessor have a specific intention to make a warranty, but an affirmation merely of

the value of the goods or a statement purporting to be merely the lessor's opinion or commendation of the goods does not create a warranty.

§ 2A–211. Warranties Against Interference and Against Infringement; Lessee's Obligation Against Infringement

(1) There is in a lease contract a warranty that for the lease term no person holds a claim to or interest in the goods that arose from an act or omission of the lessor, other than a claim by way of infringement or the like, which will interfere with the lessee's enjoyment of its leasehold interest.

(2) Except in a finance lease there is in a lease contract by a lessor who is a merchant regularly dealing in goods of the kind a warranty that the goods are delivered free of the rightful claim of any person by way of infringement or the like.

(3) A lessee who furnishes specifications to a lessor or a supplier shall hold the lessor and the supplier harmless against any claim by way of infringement or the like that arises out of compliance with the specifications.

§ 2A–212. Implied Warranty of Merchantability

(1) Except in a finance lease, a warranty that the goods will be merchantable is implied in a lease contract if the lessor is a merchant with respect to goods of that kind.

(2) Goods to be merchantable must be at least such as

(a) pass without objection in the trade under the description in the lease agreement;

(b) in the case of fungible goods, are of fair average quality within the description;

(c) are fit for the ordinary purposes for which goods of that type are used;

(d) run, within the variation permitted by the lease agreement, of even kind, quality, and quantity within each unit and among all units involved;

(e) are adequately contained, packaged, and labeled as the lease agreement may require; and

(f) conform to any promises or affirmations of fact made on the container or label.

(3) Other implied warranties may arise from course of dealing or usage of trade.

§ 2A–213. Implied Warranty of Fitness for Particular Purpose

Except in a finance lease, if the lessor at the time the lease contract is made has reason to know of any particular purpose for which the goods are required and that the lessee is relying on the lessor's skill or judgment to select or furnish suitable goods, there is in the lease contract an implied warranty that the goods will be fit for that purpose.

§ 2A–214. Exclusion or Modification of Warranties

(1) Words or conduct relevant to the creation of an express warranty and words or conduct tending to negate or limit a warranty must be construed wherever reasonable as consistent with each other; but, subject to the provisions of Section 2A–202 on parol or extrinsic evidence, negation or limitation is inoperative to the extent that the construction is unreasonable.

(2) Subject to subsection (3), to exclude or modify the implied warranty of merchantability or any part of it the language must mention "merchantability," be by a writing, and be conspicuous. Subject to subsection (3), to exclude or modify any implied warranty of fitness the exclusion must be by a 'writing and be conspicuous. Language to exclude all implied warranties of fitness is sufficient if it is in writing, is conspicuous and states, for example, "There is no warranty that the goods will be fit for a particular purpose".

(3) Notwithstanding subsection (2), but subject to subsection (4),

(a) unless the circumstances indicate otherwise, all implied warranties are excluded by expressions like "as is," or "with all faults," or by other language that in common understanding calls the lessee's attention to the exclusion of warranties and makes plain that there is no implied warranty, if in writing and conspicuous;

(b) if the lessee before entering into the lease contract has examined the goods or the sample or model as fully as desired or has refused to examine the goods, there is no implied warranty with regard to defects that an examination ought in the circumstances to have revealed; and

(c) an implied warranty may also be excluded or modified by course of dealing, course of performance, or usage of trade.

(4) To exclude or modify a warranty against interference or against infringement (Section 2A–211) or any part of it, the language must be specific, be by a writing, and be conspicuous, unless the circumstances, including course of performance, course of dealing, or usage of trade, give the lessee reason to know that the goods are being leased subject to a claim or interest of any person.

§ 2A–215. Cumulation and Conflict of Warranties Express or Implied

Warranties, whether express or implied, must be construed as consistent with each other and as cumulative, but if that construction is unreasonable, the intention of the parties determines which warranty is dominant. In ascertaining that intention the following rules apply:

(a) Exact or technical specifications displace an inconsistent sample or model or general language of description.

(b) A sample from an existing bulk displaces inconsistent general language of description.

(c) Express warranties displace inconsistent implied warranties other than an implied warranty of fitness for a particular purpose.

§ 2A–216. Third-Party Beneficiaries of Express and Implied Warranties

Alternative A

A warranty to or for the benefit of a lessee under this Article, whether express or implied, extends to any natural person who is in the family or household of the lessee or who is a guest in the lessee's home if it is reasonable to expect that such person may use, consume, or be affected by the goods and who is injured in person by breach of the warranty. This section does not displace principles of law and equity that extend a warranty to or for the benefit of a lessee to other persons. The operation of this section may not be excluded, modified, or limited, but an exclusion, modification, or limitation of the warranty, including any with respect to rights and remedies, effective against the lessee is also effective against any beneficiary designated under this section.

Alternative B

A warranty to or for the benefit of a lessee under this Article, whether express or implied, extends to any natural person who may reasonably be expected to use, consume, or be affected by the goods and who is injured in person by breach of the warranty. This section does not displace principles of law and equity that extend a warranty to or for the benefit of a lessee to other persons. The operation of this section may not be excluded, modified, or limited, but an exclusion, modification, or limitation of the warranty, including any with respect to rights and remedies, effective against the lessee is also effective against the beneficiary designated under this section.

Alternative C

A warranty to or for the benefit of a lessee under this Article, whether express or implied, extends to any person who may reasonably be expected to use, consume, or be affected by the goods and who is injured by breach of the warranty. The operation of this section may not be excluded, modified, or limited with respect to injury to the person of an individual to whom the warranty extends, but an exclusion, modification, or limitation of the warranty, including any with respect to rights and remedies, effective against the lessee is also effective against the beneficiary designated under this section.

§ 2A–217. Identification

Identification of goods as goods to which a lease contract refers may be made at any time and in any manner explicitly agreed to by the parties. In the absence of explicit agreement, identification occurs:

(a) when the lease contract is made if the lease contract is for a lease of goods that are existing and identified;

(b) when the goods are shipped, marked, or otherwise designated by the lessor as goods to which the lease contract refers, if the lease contract is for a lease of goods that are not existing and identified; or

(c) when the young are conceived, if the lease contract is for a lease of unborn young of animals.

§ 2A–218. Insurance and Proceeds

(1) A lessee obtains an insurable interest when existing goods are identified to the lease contract even though the goods identified are nonconforming and the lessee has an option to reject them.

(2) If a lessee has an insurable interest only by reason of the lessor's identification of the goods, the lessor, until default or insolvency or notification to the lessee that identification is final, may substitute other goods for those identified.

(3) Notwithstanding a lessee's insurable interest under subsections (1) and (2), the lessor retains an insurable interest until an option to buy has been exercised by the lessee and risk of loss has passed to the lessee.

(4) Nothing in this section impairs any insurable interest recognized under any other statute or rule of law.

(5) The parties by agreement may determine that one or more parties have an obligation to obtain and pay for insurance covering the goods and by agreement may determine the beneficiary of the proceeds of the insurance.

§ 2A–219. Risk of Loss

(1) Except in the case of a finance lease, risk of loss is retained by the lessor and does not pass to the lessee. In the case of a finance lease, risk of loss passes to the lessee.

(2) Subject to the provisions of this Article on the effect of default on risk of loss (Section 2A–220), if risk of loss is to pass to the lessee and the time of passage is not stated, the following rules apply:

(a) If the lease contract requires or authorizes the goods to be shipped by carrier

(i) and it does not require delivery at a particular destination, the risk of loss passes to the lessee when the goods are duly delivered to the carrier; but

(ii) if it does require delivery at a particular destination and the goods are there duly tendered while in the possession of the carrier, the risk of loss passes to the lessee when the goods are there duly so tendered as to enable the lessee to take delivery.

(b) If the goods are held by a bailee to be delivered without being moved, the risk of loss passes to the lessee on acknowledgment by the bailee of the lessee's right to possession of the goods.

(c) In any case not within subsection (a) or (b), the risk of loss passes to the lessee on the lessee's receipt of the goods if the lessor, or, in the case of a finance lease, the supplier, is a merchant; otherwise the risk passes to the lessee on tender of delivery.

§ 2A–220. Effect of Default on Risk of Loss

(1) Where risk of loss is to pass to the lessee and the time of passage is not stated:

(a) If a tender or delivery of goods so fails to conform to the lease contract as to give a right of rejection, the risk of their loss remains with the lessor, or, in the case of a finance lease, the supplier, until cure or acceptance.

(b) If the lessee rightfully revokes acceptance, he [or she], to the extent of any deficiency in his [or her] effective insurance coverage, may treat the risk of loss as having remained with the lessor from the beginning.

(2) Whether or not risk of loss is to pass to the lessee, if the lessee as to conforming goods already identified to a lease contract repudiates or is otherwise in default under the lease contract, the lessor, or, in the case of a finance lease, the supplier, to the extent of any deficiency in his [or her] effective insurance coverage may treat the risk of loss as resting on the lessee for a commercially reasonable time.

§ 2A–221. Casualty to Identified Goods

If a lease contract requires goods identified when the lease contract is made, and the goods suffer casualty without fault of the lessee, the lessor or the supplier before delivery, or the goods suffer casualty before risk of loss passes to the lessee pursuant to the lease agreement or Section 2A–219, then:

(a) if the loss is total, the lease contract is avoided; and

(b) if the loss is partial or the goods have so deteriorated as to no longer conform to the lease contract, the lessee may nevertheless demand inspection and at his [or her] option either treat the lease contract as avoided or, except in a finance lease that is not a consumer lease, accept the goods with due allowance from the rent payable for the balance of the lease term for the deterioration or the deficiency in quantity but without further right against the lessor.

Part 3 Effect of Lease Contract

§ 2A–301. Enforceability of Lease Contract

Except as otherwise provided in this Article, a lease contract is effective and enforceable according to its terms between the parties, against purchasers of the goods and against creditors of the parties.

§ 2A–302. Title to and Possession of Goods

Except as otherwise provided in this Article, each provision of this Article applies whether the lessor or a third party has title to the goods, and whether the lessor, the

lessee, or a third party has possession of the goods, notwithstanding any statute or rule of law that possession or the absence of possession is fraudulent.

§ 2A–303. Alienability of Party's Interest Under Lease Contract or of Lessor's Residual Interest in Goods; Delegation of Performance; Transfer of Rights

(1) As used in this section, "creation of a security interest" includes the sale of a lease contract that is subject to Article 9, Secured Transactions, by reason of Section 9–102(1)(b).

(2) Except as provided in subsections (3) and (4), a provision in a lease agreement which (i) prohibits the voluntary or involuntary transfer, including a transfer by sale, sublease, creation or enforcement of a security interest, or attachment, levy, or other judicial process, of an interest of a party under the lease contract or of the lessor's residual interest in the goods, or (ii) makes such a transfer an event of default, gives rise to the rights and remedies provided in subsection (5), but a transfer that is prohibited or is an event of default under the lease agreement is otherwise effective.

(3) A provision in a lease agreement which (i) prohibits the creation or enforcement of a security interest in an interest of a party under the lease contract or in the lessor's residual interest in the goods, or (ii) makes such a transfer an event of default, is not enforceable unless, and then only to the extent that, there is an actual transfer by the lessee of the lessee's right of possession or use of the goods in violation of the provision or an actual delegation of a material performance of either party to the lease contract in violation of the provision. Neither the granting nor the enforcement of a security interest in (i) the lessor's interest under the lease contract or (ii) the lessor's residual interest in the goods is a transfer that materially impairs the prospect of obtaining return performance by, materially changes the duty of, or materially increases the burden or risk imposed on, the lessee within the purview of subsection (5) unless, and then only to the extent that, there is an actual delegation of a material performance of the lessor.

(4) A provision in a lease agreement which (i) prohibits a transfer of a right to damages for default with respect to the whole lease contract or of a right to payment arising out of the transferor's due performance of the transferor's entire obligation, or (ii) makes such a transfer an event of default, is not enforceable, and such a transfer is not a transfer that materially impairs the prospect of obtaining return performance by, materially changes the duty of, or materially increases the burden or risk imposed on, the other party to the lease contract within the purview of subsection (5).

(5) Subject to subsections (3) and (4):

(a) if a transfer is made which is made an event of default under a lease agreement, the party to the lease contract not making the transfer, unless that party waives the default or otherwise agrees, has the rights and remedies described in Section 2A–501(2);

(b) if paragraph (a) is not applicable and if a transfer is made that (i) is prohibited under a lease agreement or (ii) materially impairs the prospect of obtaining return performance by, materially changes the duty of, or materially increases the burden or risk imposed on, the other party to the lease contract, unless the party not making the transfer agrees at any time to the transfer in the lease contract or otherwise, then, except as limited by contract, (i) the transferor is liable to the party not making the transfer for damages caused by the transfer to the extent that the damages could not reasonably be prevented by the party not making the transfer and (ii) a court having jurisdiction may grant other appropriate relief, including cancellation of the lease contract or an injunction against the transfer.

(6) A transfer of "the lease" or of "all my rights under the lease," or a transfer in similar general terms, is a transfer of rights and, unless the language or the circumstances, as in a transfer for security, indicate the contrary, the transfer is a delegation of duties by the transferor to the transferee. Acceptance by the transferee constitutes a promise by the transferee to perform those duties. The promise is enforceable by either the transferor or the other party to the lease contract.

(7) Unless otherwise agreed by the lessor and the lessee, a delegation of performance does not relieve the transferor as against the other party of any duty to perform or of any liability for default.

(8) In a consumer lease, to prohibit the transfer of an interest of a party under the lease contract or to make a transfer an event of default, the language must be specific, by a writing, and conspicuous.
As amended in 1990.

§ 2A–304. Subsequent Lease of Goods by Lessor

(1) Subject to Section 2A–303, a subsequent lessee from a lessor of goods under an existing lease contract obtains, to the extent of the leasehold interest transferred, the leasehold interest in the goods that the lessor had or had power to transfer, and except as provided in subsection (2) and Section 2A–527(4), takes subject to the existing lease contract. A lessor with voidable title has power to transfer a good leasehold interest to a good faith subsequent lessee for value, but only to the extent set forth in the preceding sentence. If goods have been delivered under a transaction of purchase, the lessor has that power even though:

(a) the lessor's transferor was deceived as to the identity of the lessor;

(b) the delivery was in exchange for a check which is later dishonored;

(c) it was agreed that the transaction was to be a "cash sale"; or

(d) the delivery was procured through fraud punishable as larcenous under the criminal law.

(2) A subsequent lessee in the ordinary course of business from a lessor who is a merchant dealing in goods of that kind to whom the goods were entrusted by the existing lessee of that lessor before the interest of the subsequent lessee became enforceable against that lessor obtains, to the extent of the leasehold interest transferred, all of that lessor's and the existing lessee's rights to the goods, and takes free of the existing lease contract.

(3) A subsequent lessee from the lessor of goods that are subject to an existing lease contract and are covered by a certificate of title issued under a statute of this State or of another jurisdiction takes no greater rights than those provided both by this section and by the certificate of title statute.
As amended in 1990.

§ 2A–305. Sale or Sublease of Goods by Lessee

(1) Subject to the provisions of Section 2A–303, a buyer or sublessee from the lessee of goods under an existing lease contract obtains, to the extent of the interest transferred, the leasehold interest in the goods that the lessee had or had power to transfer, and except as provided in subsection (2) and Section 2A–511(4), takes subject to the existing lease contract. A lessee with a voidable leasehold interest has power to transfer a good leasehold interest to a good faith buyer for value or a good faith sublessee for value, but only to the extent set forth in the preceding sentence. When goods have been delivered under a transaction of lease the lessee has that power even though:

(a) the lessor was deceived as to the identity of the lessee;

(b) the delivery was in exchange for a check which is later dishonored; or

(c) the delivery was procured through fraud punishable as larcenous under the criminal law.

(2) A buyer in the ordinary course of business or a sublessee in the ordinary course of business from a lessee who is a merchant dealing in goods of that kind to whom the goods were entrusted by the lessor obtains, to the extent of the interest transferred, all of the lessor's and lessee's rights to the goods, and takes free of the existing lease contract.

(3) A buyer or sublessee from the lessee of goods that are subject to an existing lease contract and are covered by a certificate of title issued under a statute of this State or of another jurisdiction takes no greater rights than those provided both by this section and by the certificate of title statute.

§ 2A–306. Priority of Certain Liens Arising by Operation of Law

If a person in the ordinary course of his [or her] business furnishes services or materials with respect to goods subject to a lease contract, a lien upon those goods in the possession of that person given by statute or rule of law for those materials or services takes priority over any interest of the lessor or lessee under the lease contract or this Article unless the lien is created by statute and the statute provides otherwise or unless the lien is created by rule of law and the rule of law provides otherwise.

§ 2A–307. Priority of Liens Arising by Attachment or Levy on, Security Interests in, and Other Claims to Goods

(1) Except as otherwise provided in Section 2A–306, a creditor of a lessee takes subject to the lease contract.

(2) Except as otherwise provided in subsections (3) and (4) and in Sections 2A–306 and 2A–308, a creditor of a lessor takes subject to the lease contract unless:

(a) the creditor holds a lien that attached to the goods before the lease contract became enforceable,

(b) the creditor holds a security interest in the goods and the lessee did not give value and receive delivery of the goods without knowledge of the security interest; or

(c) the creditor holds a security interest in the goods which was perfected (Section 9–303) before the lease contract became enforceable.

(3) A lessee in the ordinary course of business takes the leasehold interest free of a security interest in the goods created by the lessor even though the security interest is perfected (Section 9–303) and the lessee knows of its existence.

(4) A lessee other than a lessee in the ordinary course of business takes the leasehold interest free of a security interest to the extent that it secures future advances made after the secured party acquires knowledge of the lease or more than 45 days after the lease contract becomes enforceable, whichever first occurs, unless the future advances are made pursuant to a commitment entered into without knowledge of the lease and before the expiration of the 45-day period.

As amended in 1990.

§ 2A–308. Special Rights of Creditors

(1) A creditor of a lessor in possession of goods subject to a lease contract may treat the lease contract as void if as against the creditor retention of possession by the lessor is fraudulent under any statute or rule of law, but retention of possession in good faith and current course of trade by the lessor for a commercially reasonable time after the lease contract becomes enforceable is not fraudulent.

(2) Nothing in this Article impairs the rights of creditors of a lessor if the lease contract (a) becomes enforceable, not in current course of trade but in satisfaction of or as security for a pre-existing claim for money, security, or the like, and (b) is made under circumstances which under any statute or rule of law apart from this Article would constitute the transaction a fraudulent transfer or voidable preference.

(3) A creditor of a seller may treat a sale or an identification of goods to a contract for sale as void if as against the creditor retention of possession by the seller is fraudulent under any statute or rule of law, but retention of possession of the goods pursuant to a lease contract entered into by the seller as lessee and the buyer as lessor in connection with the sale or identification of the goods is not fraudulent if the buyer bought for value and in good faith.

§ 2A–309. Lessor's and Lessee's Rights When Goods Become Fixtures

(1) In this section:

(a) goods are "fixtures" when they become so related to particular real estate that an interest in them arises under real estate law;

(b) a "fixture filing" is the filing, in the office where a mortgage on the real estate would be filed or recorded, of a financing statement covering goods that are or are to become fixtures and conforming to the requirements of Section 9–402(5);

(c) a lease is a "purchase money lease" unless the lessee has possession or use of the goods or the right to possession or use of the goods before the lease agreement is enforceable;

(d) a mortgage is a "construction mortgage" to the extent it secures an obligation incurred for the construction of an improvement on land including the acquisition cost of the land, if the recorded writing so indicates; and

(e) "encumbrance" includes real estate mortgages and other liens on real estate and all other rights in real estate that are not ownership interests.

(2) Under this Article a lease may be of goods that are fixtures or may continue in goods that become fixtures, but no lease exists under this Article of ordinary building materials incorporated into an improvement on land.

(3) This Article does not prevent creation of a lease of fixtures pursuant to real estate law.

(4) The perfected interest of a lessor of fixtures has priority over a conflicting interest of an encumbrancer or owner of the real estate if:

(a) the lease is a purchase money lease, the conflicting interest of the encumbrancer or owner arises before the goods become fixtures, the interest of the lessor is perfected by a fixture filing before the goods become fixtures or within ten days thereafter, and the lessee has an interest of record in the real estate or is in possession of the real estate; or

(b) the interest of the lessor is perfected by a fixture filing before the interest of the encumbrancer or owner is of record, the lessor's interest has priority over any conflicting interest of a predecessor in title of the encumbrancer or owner, and the lessee has an interest of record in the real estate or is in possession of the real estate.

(5) The interest of a lessor of fixtures, whether or not perfected, has priority over the conflicting interest of an encumbrancer or owner of the real estate if:

(a) the fixtures are readily removable factory or office machines, readily removable equipment that is not primarily used or leased for use in the operation of the real estate, or readily removable replacements of domestic appliances that are goods subject to a consumer lease, and before the goods become fixtures the lease contract is enforceable; or

(b) the conflicting interest is a lien on the real estate obtained by legal or equitable proceedings after the lease contract is enforceable; or

(c) the encumbrancer or owner has consented in writing to the lease or has disclaimed an interest in the goods as fixtures; or

(d) the lessee has a right to remove the goods as against the encumbrancer or owner. If the lessee's right to remove terminates, the priority of the interest of the lessor continues for a reasonable time.

(6) Notwithstanding subsection (4)(a) but otherwise subject to subsections (4) and (5), the interest of a lessor of fixtures, including the lessor's residual interest, is subordinate to the conflicting interest of an encumbrancer of the real estate under a construction mortgage recorded before the goods become fixtures if the goods become fixtures before the completion of the construction. To the extent given to refinance a construction mortgage, the conflicting interest of an encumbrancer of the real estate under a mortgage has this priority to the same extent as the encumbrancer of the real estate under the construction mortgage.

(7) In cases not within the preceding subsections, priority between the interest of a lessor of fixtures, including the lessor's residual interest, and the conflicting interest of an encumbrancer or owner of the real estate who is not the lessee is determined by the priority rules governing conflicting interests in real estate.

(8) If the interest of a lessor of fixtures, including the lessor's residual interest, has priority over all conflicting interests of all owners and encumbrancers of the real estate, the lessor or the lessee may (i) on default, expiration, termination, or cancellation of the lease agreement but subject to the agreement and this Article, or (ii) if necessary to enforce other rights and remedies of the lessor or lessee under this Article, remove the goods from the real estate, free and clear of all conflicting interests of all owners and encumbrancers of the real estate, but the lessor or lessee must reimburse any encumbrancer or owner of the real estate who is not the lessee and who has not otherwise agreed for the cost of repair of any physical injury, but not for any diminution in value of the real estate caused by the absence of the goods removed or by any necessity of replacing them. A person entitled to reimbursement may refuse permission to remove until the party seeking removal gives adequate security for the performance of this obligation.

(9) Even though the lease agreement does not create a security interest, the interest of a lessor of fixtures, including the lessor's residual interest, is perfected by filing a financing statement as a fixture filing for leased goods that are or are to become fixtures in accordance with the relevant provisions of the Article on Secured Transactions (Article 9).
As amended in 1990.

§ 2A–310. Lessor's and Lessee's Rights When Goods Become Accessions

(1) Goods are "accessions" when they are installed in or affixed to other goods.

(2) The interest of a lessor or a lessee under a lease contract entered into before the goods became accessions is superior to all interests in the whole except as stated in subsection (4).

(3) The interest of a lessor or a lessee under a lease contract entered into at the time or after the goods became accessions is superior to all subsequently acquired interests in the whole except as stated in subsection (4) but is subordinate to interests in the whole existing at the time the lease contract was made unless the holders of such interests in the whole have in writing consented to the lease or disclaimed an interest in the goods as part of the whole.

(4) The interest of a lessor or a lessee under a lease contract described in subsection (2) or (3) is subordinate to the interest of

(a) a buyer in the ordinary course of business or a lessee in the ordinary course of business of any interest in the whole acquired after the goods became accessions; or

(b) a creditor with a security interest in the whole perfected before the lease contract was made to the extent that the creditor makes subsequent advances without knowledge of the lease contract.

(5) When under subsections (2) or (3) and (4) a lessor or a lessee of accessions holds an interest that is superior to all interests in the whole, the lessor or the lessee may (a) on default, expiration, termination, or cancellation of the lease contract by the other party but subject to the provisions of the lease contract and this Article, or (b) if necessary to enforce his [or her] other rights and remedies under this Article, remove the goods from the whole, free and clear of all interests in the whole, but he [or she] must reimburse any holder of an interest in the whole who is not the lessee and who has not otherwise agreed for the cost of repair of any physical injury but not for any diminution in value of the whole caused by the absence of the goods removed or by any necessity for replacing them. A person entitled to reimbursement may refuse permission to remove until the party seeking removal gives adequate security for the performance of this obligation.

§ 2A–311. Priority Subject to Subordination

Nothing in this Article prevents subordination by agreement by any person entitled to priority.
As added in 1990.

Part 4 Performance of Lease Contract: Repudiated, Substituted and Excused

§ 2A–401. Insecurity: Adequate Assurance of Performance

(1) A lease contract imposes an obligation on each party that the other's expectation of receiving due performance will not be impaired.

(2) If reasonable grounds for insecurity arise with respect to the performance of either party, the insecure party may demand in writing adequate assurance of due performance. Until the insecure party receives that assurance, if commercially reasonable the insecure party may suspend any performance for which he [or she] has not already received the agreed return.

(3) A repudiation of the lease contract occurs if assurance of due performance adequate under the circumstances of the particular case is not provided to the insecure party within a reasonable time, not to exceed 30 days after receipt of a demand by the other party.

(4) Between merchants, the reasonableness of grounds for insecurity and the adequacy of any assurance offered must be determined according to commercial standards.

(5) Acceptance of any nonconforming delivery or payment does not prejudice the aggrieved party's right to demand adequate assurance of future performance.

§ 2A–402. Anticipatory Repudiation

If either party repudiates a lease contract with respect to a performance not yet due under the lease contract, the loss of which performance will substantially impair the value of the lease contract to the other, the aggrieved party may:

(a) for a commercially reasonable time, await retraction of repudiation and performance by the repudiating party;

(b) make demand pursuant to Section 2A–401 and await assurance of future performance adequate under the circumstances of the particular case; or

(c) resort to any right or remedy upon default under the lease contract or this Article, even though the aggrieved party has notified the repudiating party that the aggrieved party would await the repudiating party's performance and assurance and has urged retraction. In addition, whether or not the aggrieved party is pursuing one of the foregoing remedies, the aggrieved party may suspend performance or, if the aggrieved party is the lessor, proceed in accordance with the provisions of this Article on the lessor's right to identify goods to the lease contract notwithstanding default or to salvage unfinished goods (Section 2A–524).

§ 2A–403. Retraction of Anticipatory Repudiation

(1) Until the repudiating party's next performance is due, the repudiating party can retract the repudiation unless, since the repudiation, the aggrieved party has canceled the lease contract or materially changed the aggrieved party's position or otherwise indicated that the aggrieved party considers the repudiation final.

(2) Retraction may be by any method that clearly indicates to the aggrieved party that the repudiating party intends to perform under the lease contract and includes any assurance demanded under Section 2A–401.

(3) Retraction reinstates a repudiating party's rights under a lease contract with due excuse and allowance to the aggrieved party for any delay occasioned by the repudiation.

§ 2A–404. Substituted Performance

(1) If without fault of the lessee, the lessor and the supplier, the agreed berthing, loading, or unloading facilities fail or the agreed type of carrier becomes unavailable or the agreed manner of delivery otherwise becomes commercially impracticable, but a commercially reasonable substitute is available, the substitute performance must be tendered and accepted.

(2) If the agreed means or manner of payment fails because of domestic or foreign governmental regulation:

(a) the lessor may withhold or stop delivery or cause the supplier to withhold or stop delivery unless the lessee provides a means or manner of payment that is commercially a substantial equivalent; and

(b) if delivery has already been taken, payment by the means or in the manner provided by the regulation discharges the lessee's obligation unless the regulation is discriminatory, oppressive, or predatory.

§ 2A–405. Excused Performance

Subject to Section 2A–404 on substituted performance, the following rules apply:

(a) Delay in delivery or nondelivery in whole or in part by a lessor or a supplier who complies with paragraphs (b) and (c) is not a default under the lease contract if performance as agreed has been made impracticable by the occurrence of a contingency the nonoccurrence of which was a basic assumption on which the lease contract was made or by compliance in good faith with any applicable foreign or domestic governmental regulation or order, whether or not the regulation or order later proves to be invalid.

(b) If the causes mentioned in paragraph (a) affect only part of the lessor's or the supplier's capacity to perform, he [or she] shall allocate production and deliveries among his [or her] customers but at his [or her] option may include regular customers not then under contract for sale or lease as well as his [or her] own requirements for further manufacture. He [or she] may so allocate in any manner that is fair and reasonable.

(c) The lessor seasonably shall notify the lessee and in the case of a finance lease the supplier seasonably shall notify the lessor and the lessee, if known, that there will be delay or nondelivery and, if allocation is required under paragraph (b), of the estimated quota thus made available for the lessee.

§ 2A–406. Procedure on Excused Performance

(1) If the lessee receives notification of a material or indefinite delay or an allocation justified under Section 2A–405, the lessee may by written notification to the lessor as to any goods involved, and with respect to all of the goods if under an installment lease contract the value of the whole lease contract is substantially impaired (Section 2A–510):

(a) terminate the lease contract (Section 2A–505(2)); or

(b) except in a finance lease that is not a consumer lease, modify the lease contract by accepting the available quota in substitution, with due allowance from the rent payable for the balance of the lease term for the deficiency but without further right against the lessor.

(2) If, after receipt of a notification from the lessor under Section 2A–405, the lessee fails so to modify the lease agreement within a reasonable time not exceeding 30 days, the lease contract lapses with respect to any deliveries affected.

§ 2A–407. Irrevocable Promises: Finance Leases

(1) In the case of a finance lease that is not a consumer lease the lessee's promises under the lease contract become irrevocable and independent upon the lessee's acceptance of the goods.

(2) A promise that has become irrevocable and independent under subsection (1):

(a) is effective and enforceable between the parties, and by or against third parties including assignees of the parties; and

(b) is not subject to cancellation, termination, modification, repudiation, excuse, or substitution without the consent of the party to whom the promise runs.

(3) This section does not affect the validity under any other law of a covenant in any lease contract making the lessee's promises irrevocable and independent upon the lessee's acceptance of the goods.

As amended in 1990.

Part 5 Default
A. In General

§ 2A–501. Default: Procedure

(1) Whether the lessor or the lessee is in default under a lease contract is determined by the lease agreement and this Article.

(2) If the lessor or the lessee is in default under the lease contract, the party seeking enforcement has rights and remedies as provided in this Article and, except as limited by this Article, as provided in the lease agreement.

(3) If the lessor or the lessee is in default under the lease contract, the party seeking enforcement may reduce the party's claim to judgment, or otherwise enforce the lease contract by self-help or any available judicial procedure or nonjudicial procedure, including administrative proceeding, arbitration, or the like, in accordance with this Article.

(4) Except as otherwise provided in Section 1–106(1) or this Article or the lease agreement, the rights and remedies referred to in subsections (2) and (3) are cumulative.

(5) If the lease agreement covers both real property and goods, the party seeking enforcement may proceed under this Part as to the goods, or under other applicable law as to both the real property and the goods in accordance with that party's rights and remedies in respect of the real property, in which case this Part does not apply.

As amended in 1990.

§ 2A–502. Notice After Default

Except as otherwise provided in this Article or the lease agreement, the lessor or lessee in default under the lease contract is not entitled to notice of default or notice of enforcement from the other party to the lease agreement.

§ 2A–503. Modification or Impairment of Rights and Remedies

(1) Except as otherwise provided in this Article, the lease agreement may include rights and remedies for default in addition to or in substitution for those provided in this Article and may limit or alter the measure of damages recoverable under this Article.

(2) Resort to a remedy provided under this Article or in the lease agreement is optional unless the remedy is expressly agreed to be exclusive. If circumstances cause an exclusive or limited remedy to fail of its essential purpose, or provision for an exclusive remedy is unconscionable, remedy may be had as provided in this Article.

(3) Consequential damages may be liquidated under Section 2A–504, or may otherwise be limited, altered, or excluded unless the limitation, alteration, or exclusion is unconscionable. Limitation, alteration, or exclusion of consequential damages for injury to the person in the case of consumer goods is prima facie unconscionable but limitation, alteration, or exclusion of damages where the loss is commercial is not prima facie unconscionable.

(4) Rights and remedies on default by the lessor or the lessee with respect to any obligation or promise collateral or ancillary to the lease contract are not impaired by this Article.

As amended in 1990.

§ 2A–504. Liquidation of Damages

(1) Damages payable by either party for default, or any other act or omission, including indemnity for loss or diminution of anticipated tax benefits or loss or damage to lessor's residual interest, may be liquidated in the lease agreement but only at an amount or by a formula that is reasonable in light of the then anticipated harm caused by the default or other act or omission.

(2) If the lease agreement provides for liquidation of damages, and such provision does not comply with subsection (1), or such provision is an exclusive or limited remedy that circumstances cause to fail of its essential purpose, remedy may be had as provided in this Article.

(3) If the lessor justifiably withholds or stops delivery of goods because of the lessee's default or insolvency (Section 2A–525 or 2A–526), the lessee is entitled to restitution of any amount by which the sum of his [or her] payments exceeds:

    (a) the amount to which the lessor is entitled by virtue of terms liquidating the lessor's damages in accordance with subsection (1); or

    (b) in the absence of those terms, 20 percent of the then present value of the total rent the lessee was obligated to pay for the balance of the lease term, or, in the case of a consumer lease, the lesser of such amount or $500.

(4) A lessee's right to restitution under subsection (3) is subject to offset to the extent the lessor establishes:

    (a) a right to recover damages under the provisions of this Article other than subsection (1); and

    (b) the amount or value of any benefits received by the lessee directly or indirectly by reason of the lease contract.

§ 2A–505. Cancellation and Termination and Effect of Cancellation, Termination, Rescission, or Fraud on Rights and Remedies

(1) On cancellation of the lease contract, all obligations that are still executory on both sides are discharged, but any right based on prior default or performance survives, and the cancelling party also retains any remedy for default of the whole lease contract or any unperformed balance.

(2) On termination of the lease contract, all obligations that are still executory on both sides are discharged but any right based on prior default or performance survives.

(3) Unless the contrary intention clearly appears, expressions of "cancellation," "rescission," or the like of the lease contract may not be construed as a renunciation or discharge of any claim in damages for an antecedent default.

(4) Rights and remedies for material misrepresentation or fraud include all rights and remedies available under this Article for default.

(5) Neither rescission nor a claim for rescission of the lease contract nor rejection or return of the goods may bar or be deemed inconsistent with a claim for damages or other right or remedy.

§ 2A–506. Statute of Limitations

(1) An action for default under a lease contract, including breach of warranty or indemnity, must be commenced within 4 years after the cause of action accrued. By the original lease contract the parties may reduce the period of limitation to not less than one year.

(2) A cause of action for default accrues when the act or omission on which the default or breach of warranty is based is or should have been discovered by the aggrieved party, or when the default occurs, whichever is later. A cause of action for indemnity accrues when the act or omission on which the claim for indemnity is based is or should have been discovered by the indemnified party, whichever is later.

(3) If an action commenced within the time limited by subsection (1) is so terminated as to leave available a remedy by another action for the same default or breach of warranty or indemnity, the other action may be commenced after the expiration of the time limited and within 6 months after the termination of the first action unless the termination resulted from voluntary discontinuance or from dismissal for failure or neglect to prosecute.

(4) This section does not alter the law on tolling of the statute of limitations nor does it apply to causes of action that have accrued before this Article becomes effective.

§ 2A–507. Proof of Market Rent: Time and Place

(1) Damages based on market rent (Section 2A–519 or 2A–528) are determined according to the rent for the use of the goods concerned for a lease term identical to the remaining lease term of the original lease agreement and prevailing at the times specified in Sections 2A–519 and 2A–528.

(2) If evidence of rent for the use of the goods concerned for a lease term identical to the remaining lease term of the original lease agreement and prevailing at the times or places described in this Article is not readily available, the rent prevailing within any reasonable time before or after the time described or at any other place or for a different lease term which in commercial judgment or under usage of trade would serve as a reasonable substitute for the one described may be used, making any proper allowance for the difference, including the cost of transporting the goods to or from the other place.

(3) Evidence of a relevant rent prevailing at a time or place or for a lease term other than the one described in this Article offered by one party is not admissible unless and until he [or she] has given the other party notice the court finds sufficient to prevent unfair surprise.

(4) If the prevailing rent or value of any goods regularly leased in any established market is in issue, reports in official publications or trade journals or in newspapers or periodicals of general circulation published as the reports of that market are admissible in evidence. The circumstances of the preparation of the report may be shown to affect its weight but not its admissibility.

As amended in 1990.

B. Default by Lessor

§ 2A–508. Lessee's Remedies

(1) If a lessor fails to deliver the goods in conformity to the lease contract (Section 2A–509) or repudiates the lease contract (Section 2A–402), or a lessee rightfully rejects the goods (Section 2A–509) or justifiably revokes acceptance of the goods (Section 2A–517), then with respect to any goods involved, and with respect to all of the goods if under an installment lease contract the value of the whole lease contract is substantially impaired (Section 2A–510), the lessor is in default under the lease contract and the lessee may:

    (a) cancel the lease contract (Section 2A–505(1));

    (b) recover so much of the rent and security as has been paid and is just under the circumstances;

    (c) cover and recover damages as to all goods affected whether or not they have been identified to the lease contract (Sections 2A–518 and 2A–520), or recover damages for nondelivery (Sections 2A–519 and 2A–520);

    (d) exercise any other rights or pursue any other remedies provided in the lease contract.

(2) If a lessor fails to deliver the goods in conformity to the lease contract or repudiates the lease contract, the lessee may also:

    (a) if the goods have been identified, recover them (Section 2A–522); or

    (b) in a proper case, obtain specific performance or replevy the goods (Section 2A–521).

(3) If a lessor is otherwise in default under a lease contract, the lessee may exercise the rights and pursue the remedies provided in the lease contract, which may include a right to cancel the lease, and in Section 2A–519(3).

(4) If a lessor has breached a warranty, whether express or implied, the lessee may recover damages (Section 2A–519(4)).

(5) On rightful rejection or justifiable revocation of acceptance, a lessee has a security interest in goods in the lessee's possession or control for any rent and security that has been paid and any expenses reasonably incurred in their inspection, receipt, transportation, and care and custody and may hold those goods and dispose of them in good faith and in a commercially reasonable manner, subject to Section 2A–527(5).

(6) Subject to the provisions of Section 2A–407, a lessee, on notifying the lessor of the lessee's intention to do so, may deduct all or any part of the damages resulting from any default under the lease contract from any part of the rent still due under the same lease contract.

As amended in 1990.

§ 2A–509. Lessee's Rights on Improper Delivery; Rightful Rejection

(1) Subject to the provisions of Section 2A–510 on default in installment lease contracts, if the goods or the tender or delivery fail in any respect to conform to the lease contract, the lessee may reject or accept the goods or accept any commercial unit or units and reject the rest of the goods.

(2) Rejection of goods is ineffective unless it is within a reasonable time after tender or delivery of the goods and the lessee seasonably notifies the lessor.

§ 2A–510. Installment Lease Contracts: Rejection and Default

(1) Under an installment lease contract a lessee may reject any delivery that is nonconforming if the nonconformity substantially impairs the value of that delivery and cannot be cured or the nonconformity is a defect in the required documents; but if the nonconformity does not fall within subsection (2) and the lessor or the supplier gives adequate assurance of its cure, the lessee must accept that delivery.

(2) Whenever nonconformity or default with respect to one or more deliveries substantially impairs the value of the installment lease contract as a whole there is a default with respect to the whole. But, the aggrieved party reinstates the installment lease contract as a whole if the aggrieved party accepts a nonconforming delivery without seasonably notifying of cancellation or brings an action with respect only to past deliveries or demands performance as to future deliveries.

§ 2A–511. Merchant Lessee's Duties as to Rightfully Rejected Goods

(1) Subject to any security interest of a lessee (Section 2A–508(5)), if a lessor or a supplier has no agent or place of business at the market of rejection, a merchant lessee, after rejection of goods in his [or her] possession or control, shall follow any reasonable instructions received from the lessor or the supplier with respect to the goods. In the absence of those instructions, a merchant lessee shall make reasonable efforts to sell, lease, or otherwise dispose of the goods for the lessor's account if they threaten to decline in value speedily. Instructions are not reasonable if on demand indemnity for expenses is not forthcoming.

(2) If a merchant lessee (subsection (1)) or any other lessee (Section 2A–512) disposes of goods, he [or she] is entitled to reimbursement either from the lessor or the supplier or out of the proceeds for reasonable expenses of caring for and disposing of the goods and, if the expenses include no disposition commission, to such commission as is usual in the trade, or if there is none, to a reasonable sum not exceeding 10 percent of the gross proceeds.

(3) In complying with this section or Section 2A–512, the lessee is held only to good faith. Good faith conduct hereunder is neither acceptance or conversion nor the basis of an action for damages.

(4) A purchaser who purchases in good faith from a lessee pursuant to this section or Section 2A–512 takes the goods free of any rights of the lessor and the supplier even though the lessee fails to comply with one or more of the requirements of this Article.

§ 2A–512. Lessee's Duties as to Rightfully Rejected Goods

(1) Except as otherwise provided with respect to goods that threaten to decline in value speedily (Section 2A–511) and subject to any security interest of a lessee (Section 2A–508(5)):

(a) the lessee, after rejection of goods in the lessee's possession, shall hold them with reasonable care at the lessor's or the supplier's disposition for a reasonable time after the lessee's seasonable notification of rejection;

(b) if the lessor or the supplier gives no instructions within a reasonable time after notification of rejection, the lessee may store the rejected goods for the lessor's or the supplier's account or ship them to the lessor or the supplier or dispose of them for the lessor's or the supplier's account with reimbursement in the manner provided in Section 2A–511; but

(c) the lessee has no further obligations with regard to goods rightfully rejected.

(2) Action by the lessee pursuant to subsection (1) is not acceptance or conversion.

§ 2A–513. Cure by Lessor of Improper Tender or Delivery; Replacement

(1) If any tender or delivery by the lessor or the supplier is rejected because nonconforming and the time for performance has not yet expired, the lessor or the supplier may seasonably notify the lessee of the lessor's or the supplier's intention to cure and may then make a conforming delivery within the time provided in the lease contract.

(2) If the lessee rejects a nonconforming tender that the lessor or the supplier had reasonable grounds to believe would be acceptable with or without money allowance, the lessor or the supplier may have a further reasonable time to substitute a conforming tender if he [or she] seasonably notifies the lessee.

§ 2A–514. Waiver of Lessee's Objections

(1) In rejecting goods, a lessee's failure to state a particular defect that is ascertainable by reasonable inspection precludes the lessee from relying on the defect to justify rejection or to establish default:

(a) if, stated seasonably, the lessor or the supplier could have cured it (Section 2A–513); or

(b) between merchants if the lessor or the supplier after rejection has made a request in writing for a full and final written statement of all defects on which the lessee proposes to rely.

(2) A lessee's failure to reserve rights when paying rent or other consideration against documents precludes recovery of the payment for defects apparent on the face of the documents.

§ 2A–515. Acceptance of Goods

(1) Acceptance of goods occurs after the lessee has had a reasonable opportunity to inspect the goods and

(a) the lessee signifies or acts with respect to the goods in a manner that signifies to the lessor or the supplier that the goods are conforming or that the lessee will take or retain them in spite of their nonconformity; or

(b) the lessee fails to make an effective rejection of the goods (Section 2A–509(2)).

(2) Acceptance of a part of any commercial unit is acceptance of that entire unit.

§ 2A–516. Effect of Acceptance of Goods; Notice of Default; Burden of Establishing Default After Acceptance; Notice of Claim or Litigation to Person Answerable Over

(1) A lessee must pay rent for any goods accepted in accordance with the lease contract, with due allowance for goods rightfully rejected or not delivered.

(2) A lessee's acceptance of goods precludes rejection of the goods accepted. In the case of a finance lease, if made with knowledge of a nonconformity, acceptance cannot be revoked because of it. In any other case, if made with knowledge of a nonconformity, acceptance cannot be revoked because of it unless the acceptance was on the reasonable assumption that the nonconformity would be seasonably cured. Acceptance does not of itself impair any other remedy provided by this Article or the lease agreement for nonconformity.

(3) If a tender has been accepted:

(a) within a reasonable time after the lessee discovers or should have discovered any default, the lessee shall notify the lessor and the supplier, if any, or be barred from any remedy against the party not notified;

(b) except in the case of a consumer lease, within a reasonable time after the lessee receives notice of litigation for infringement or the like (Section 2A–211) the lessee shall notify the lessor or be barred from any remedy over for liability established by the litigation; and

(c) the burden is on the lessee to establish any default.

(4) If a lessee is sued for breach of a warranty or other obligation for which a lessor or a supplier is answerable over the following apply:

(a) The lessee may give the lessor or the supplier, or both, written notice of the litigation. If the notice states that the person notified may come in and defend and that if the person notified does not do so that person will be bound in any action against that person by the lessee by any determination of fact common to the two litigations, then unless the person notified after seasonable receipt of the notice does come in and defend that person is so bound.

(b) The lessor or the supplier may demand in writing that the lessee turn over control of the litigation including settlement if the claim is one for infringement or the like (Section 2A–211) or else be barred from any remedy over. If the demand states that the lessor or the supplier agrees to bear all expense and to satisfy any adverse judgment, then unless the lessee after seasonable receipt of the demand does turn over control the lessee is so barred.

(5) Subsections (3) and (4) apply to any obligation of a lessee to hold the lessor or the supplier harmless against infringement or the like (Section 2A–211).

As amended in 1990.

§ 2A–517. Revocation of Acceptance of Goods

(1) A lessee may revoke acceptance of a lot or commercial unit whose nonconformity substantially impairs its value to the lessee if the lessee has accepted it:

(a) except in the case of a finance lease, on the reasonable assumption that its nonconformity would be cured and it has not been seasonably cured; or

(b) without discovery of the nonconformity if the lessee's acceptance was reasonably induced either by the lessor's assurances or, except in the case of a finance lease, by the difficulty of discovery before acceptance.

(2) Except in the case of a finance lease that is not a consumer lease, a lessee may revoke acceptance of a lot or commercial unit if the lessor defaults under the lease contract and the default substantially impairs the value of that lot or commercial unit to the lessee.

(3) If the lease agreement so provides, the lessee may revoke acceptance of a lot or commercial unit because of other defaults by the lessor.

(4) Revocation of acceptance must occur within a reasonable time after the lessee discovers or should have discovered the ground for it and before any substantial change in condition of the goods which is not caused by the nonconformity. Revocation is not effective until the lessee notifies the lessor.

(5) A lessee who so revokes has the same rights and duties with regard to the goods involved as if the lessee had rejected them.

As amended in 1990.

§ 2A–518. Cover; Substitute Goods

(1) After a default by a lessor under the lease contract of the type described in Section 2A–508(1), or, if agreed, after other default by the lessor, the lessee may cover by making any purchase or lease of or contract to purchase or lease goods in substitution for those due from the lessor.

(2) Except as otherwise provided with respect to damages liquidated in the lease agreement (Section 2A–504) or otherwise determined pursuant to agreement of the parties (Sections 1–102(3) and 2A–503), if a lessee's cover is by a lease agreement substantially similar to the original

lease agreement and the new lease agreement is made in good faith and in a commercially reasonable manner, the lessee may recover from the lessor as damages (i) the present value, as of the date of the commencement of the term of the new lease agreement, of the rent under the new lease agreement applicable to that period of the new lease term which is comparable to the then remaining term of the original lease agreement minus the present value as of the same date of the total rent for the then remaining lease term of the original lease agreement, and (ii) any incidental or consequential damages, less expenses saved in consequence of the lessor's default.

(3) If a lessee's cover is by lease agreement that for any reason does not qualify for treatment under subsection (2), or is by purchase or otherwise, the lessee may recover from the lessor as if the lessee had elected not to cover and Section 2A–519 governs.

As amended in 1990.

§ 2A–519. Lessee's Damages for Non-delivery, Repudiation, Default, and Breach of Warranty in Regard to Accepted Goods

(1) Except as otherwise provided with respect to damages liquidated in the lease agreement (Section 2A–504) or otherwise determined pursuant to agreement of the parties (Sections 1–102(3) and 2A–503), if a lessee elects not to cover or a lessee elects to cover and the cover is by lease agreement that for any reason does not qualify for treatment under Section 2A–518(2), or is by purchase or otherwise, the measure of damages for non-delivery or repudiation by the lessor or for rejection or revocation of acceptance by the lessee is the present value, as of the date of the default, of the then market rent minus the present value as of the same date of the original rent, computed for the remaining lease term of the original lease agreement, together with incidental and consequential damages, less expenses saved in consequence of the lessor's default.

(2) Market rent is to be determined as of the place for tender or, in cases of rejection after arrival or revocation of acceptance, as of the place of arrival.

(3) Except as otherwise agreed, if the lessee has accepted goods and given notification (Section 2A–516(3)), the measure of damages for nonconforming tender or delivery or other default by a lessor is the loss resulting in the ordinary course of events from the lessor's default as determined in any manner that is reasonable together with incidental and consequential damages, less expenses saved in consequence of the lessor's default.

(4) Except as otherwise agreed, the measure of damages for breach of warranty is the present value at the time and place of acceptance of the difference between the value of the use of the goods accepted and the value if they had been as warranted for the lease term, unless special circumstances show proximate damages of a different amount, together with incidental and consequential dam-

ages, less expenses saved in consequence of the lessor's default or breach of warranty.
As amended in 1990.

§ 2A–520. Lessee's Incidental and Consequential Damages

(1) Incidental damages resulting from a lessor's default include expenses reasonably incurred in inspection, receipt, transportation, and care and custody of goods rightfully rejected or goods the acceptance of which is justifiably revoked, any commercially reasonable charges, expenses or commissions in connection with effecting cover, and any other reasonable expense incident to the default.

(2) Consequential damages resulting from a lessor's default include:

(a) any loss resulting from general or particular requirements and needs of which the lessor at the time of contracting had reason to know and which could not reasonably be prevented by cover or otherwise; and

(b) injury to person or property proximately resulting from any breach of warranty.

§ 2A–521. Lessee's Right to Specific Performance or Replevin

(1) Specific performance may be decreed if the goods are unique or in other proper circumstances.

(2) A decree for specific performance may include any terms and conditions as to payment of the rent, damages, or other relief that the court deems just.

(3) A lessee has a right of replevin, detinue, sequestration, claim and delivery, or the like for goods identified to the lease contract if after reasonable effort the lessee is unable to effect cover for those goods or the circumstances reasonably indicate that the effort will be unavailing.

§ 2A–522. Lessee's Right to Goods on Lessor's Insolvency

(1) Subject to subsection (2) and even though the goods have not been shipped, a lessee who has paid a part or all of the rent and security for goods identified to a lease contract (Section 2A–217) on making and keeping good a tender of any unpaid portion of the rent and security due under the lease contract may recover the goods identified from the lessor if the lessor becomes insolvent within 10 days after receipt of the first installment of rent and security.

(2) A lessee acquires the right to recover goods identified to a lease contract only if they conform to the lease contract.

C. Default by Lessee

§ 2A–523. Lessor's Remedies

(1) If a lessee wrongfully rejects or revokes acceptance of goods or fails to make a payment when due or repudiates with respect to a part or the whole, then, with respect to

any goods involved, and with respect to all of the goods if under an installment lease contract the value of the whole lease contract is substantially impaired (Section 2A–510), the lessee is in default under the lease contract and the lessor may:

(a) cancel the lease contract (Section 2A–505(1));

(b) proceed respecting goods not identified to the lease contract (Section 2A–524);

(c) withhold delivery of the goods and take possession of goods previously delivered (Section 2A–525);

(d) stop delivery of the goods by any bailee (Section 2A–526);

(e) dispose of the goods and recover damages (Section 2A–527), or retain the goods and recover damages (Section 2A–528), or in a proper case recover rent (Section 2A–529).

(f) exercise any other rights or pursue any other remedies provided in the lease contract.

(2) If a lessor does not fully exercise a right or obtain a remedy to which the lessor is entitled under subsection (1), the lessor may recover the loss resulting in the ordinary course of events from the lessee's default as determined in any reasonable manner, together with incidental damages, less expenses saved in consequence of the lessee's default.

(3) If a lessee is otherwise in default under a lease contract, the lessor may exercise the rights and pursue the remedies provided in the lease contract, which may include a right to cancel the lease. In addition, unless otherwise provided in the lease contract:

(a) if the default substantially impairs the value of the lease contract to the lessor, the lessor may exercise the rights and pursue the remedies provided in subsections (1) or (2); or

(b) if the default does not substantially impair the value of the lease contract to the lessor, the lessor may recover as provided in subsection (2).
As amended in 1990.

§ 2A–524. Lessor's Right to Identify Goods to Lease Contract

(1) After default by the lessee under the lease contract of the type described in Section 2A–523(1) or 2A–523(3)(a) or, if agreed, after other default by the lessee, the lessor may:

(a) identify to the lease contract conforming goods not already identified if at the time the lessor learned of the default they were in the lessor's or the supplier's possession or control; and

(b) dispose of goods (Section 2A–527(1)) that demonstrably have been intended for the particular lease contract even though those goods are unfinished.

(2) If the goods are unfinished, in the exercise of reasonable commercial judgment for the purposes of avoiding loss and of effective realization, an aggrieved lessor or the supplier may either complete manufacture and wholly

identify the goods to the lease contract or cease manufacture and lease, sell, or otherwise dispose of the goods for scrap or salvage value or proceed in any other reasonable manner.

As amended in 1990.

§ 2A–525. Lessor's Right to Possession of Goods

(1) If a lessor discovers the lessee to be insolvent, the lessor may refuse to deliver the goods.

(2) After a default by the lessee under the lease contract of the type described in Section 2A–523(1) or 2A–523(3)(a) or, if agreed, after other default by the lessee, the lessor has the right to take possession of the goods. If the lease contract so provides, the lessor may require the lessee to assemble the goods and make them available to the lessor at a place to be designated by the lessor which is reasonably convenient to both parties. Without removal, the lessor may render unusable any goods employed in trade or business, and may dispose of goods on the lessee's premises (Section 2A–527).

(3) The lessor may proceed under subsection (2) without judicial process if it can be done without breach of the peace or the lessor may proceed by action.

As amended in 1990.

§ 2A–526. Lessor's Stoppage of Delivery in Transit or Otherwise

(1) A lessor may stop delivery of goods in the possession of a carrier or other bailee if the lessor discovers the lessee to be insolvent and may stop delivery of carload, truckload, planeload, or larger shipments of express or freight if the lessee repudiates or fails to make a payment due before delivery, whether for rent, security or otherwise under the lease contract, or for any other reason the lessor has a right to withhold or take possession of the goods.

(2) In pursuing its remedies under subsection (1), the lessor may stop delivery until

(a) receipt of the goods by the lessee;

(b) acknowledgment to the lessee by any bailee of the goods, except a carrier, that the bailee holds the goods for the lessee; or

(c) such an acknowledgement to the lessee by a carrier via reshipment or as warehouseman.

(3)(a) To stop delivery, a lessor shall so notify as to enable the bailee by reasonable diligence to prevent delivery of the goods.

(b) After notification, the bailee shall hold and deliver the goods according to the directions of the lessor, but the lessor is liable to the bailee for any ensuing charges or damages.

(c) A carrier who has issued a nonnegotiable bill of lading is not obliged to obey a notification to stop received from a person other than the consignor.

§ 2A–527. Lessor's Rights to Dispose of Goods

(1) After a default by a lessee under the lease contract of the type described in Section 2A–523(1) or 2A–523(3)(a) or after the lessor refuses to deliver or takes possession of goods (Section 2A–525 or 2A–526), or, if agreed, after other default by a lessee, the lessor may dispose of the goods concerned or the undelivered balance thereof by lease, sale, or otherwise.

(2) Except as otherwise provided with respect to damages liquidated in the lease agreement (Section 2A–504) or otherwise determined pursuant to agreement of the parties (Sections 1–102(3) and 2A–503), if the disposition is by lease agreement substantially similar to the original lease agreement and the new lease agreement is made in good faith and in a commercially reasonable manner, the lessor may recover from the lessee as damages (i) accrued and unpaid rent as of the date of the commencement of the term of the new lease agreement, (ii) the present value, as of the same date, of the total rent for the then remaining lease term of the original lease agreement minus the present value, as of the same date, of the rent under the new lease agreement applicable to that period of the new lease term which is comparable to the then remaining term of the original lease agreement, and (iii) any incidental damages allowed under Section 2A–530, less expenses saved in consequence of the lessee's default.

(3) If the lessor's disposition is by lease agreement that for any reason does not qualify for treatment under subsection (2), or is by sale or otherwise, the lessor may recover from the lessee as if the lessor had elected not to dispose of the goods and Section 2A–528 governs.

(4) A subsequent buyer or lessee who buys or leases from the lessor in good faith for value as a result of a disposition under this section takes the goods free of the original lease contract and any rights of the original lessee even though the lessor fails to comply with one or more of the requirements of this Article.

(5) The lessor is not accountable to the lessee for any profit made on any disposition. A lessee who has rightfully rejected or justifiably revoked acceptance shall account to the lessor for any excess over the amount of the lessee's security interest (Section 2A–508(5)).

As amended in 1990.

§ 2A–528. Lessor's Damages for Non-acceptance, Failure to Pay, Repudiation, or Other Default

(1) Except as otherwise provided with respect to damages liquidated in the lease agreement (Section 2A–504) or otherwise determined pursuant to agreement of the parties (Sections 1–102(3) and 2A–503), if a lessor elects to retain the goods or a lessor elects to dispose of the goods and the disposition is by lease agreement that for any reason does not qualify for treatment under Section 2A–527(2), or is by sale or otherwise, the lessor may

recover from the lessee as damages for a default of the type described in Section 2A–523(1) or 2A–523(3)(a), or, if agreed, for other default of the lessee, (i) accrued and unpaid rent as of the date of default if the lessee has never taken possession of the goods, or, if the lessee has taken possession of the goods, as of the date the lessor repossesses the goods or an earlier date on which the lessee makes a tender of the goods to the lessor, (ii) the present value as of the date determined under clause (i) of the total rent for the then remaining lease term of the original lease agreement minus the present value as of the same date of the market rent at the place where the goods are located computed for the same lease term, and (iii) any incidental damages allowed under Section 2A–530, less expenses saved in consequence of the lessee's default.

(2) If the measure of damages provided in subsection (1) is inadequate to put a lessor in as good a position as performance would have, the measure of damages is the present value of the profit, including reasonable overhead, the lessor would have made from full performance by the lessee, together with any incidental damages allowed under Section 2A–530, due allowance for costs reasonably incurred and due credit for payments or proceeds of disposition.

As amended in 1990.

§ 2A–529. Lessor's Action for the Rent

(1) After default by the lessee under the lease contract of the type described in Section 2A–523(1) or 2A–523(3)(a) or, if agreed, after other default by the lessee, if the lessor complies with subsection (2), the lessor may recover from the lessee as damages:

(a) for goods accepted by the lessee and not repossessed by or tendered to the lessor, and for conforming goods lost or damaged within a commercially reasonable time after risk of loss passes to the lessee (Section 2A–219), (i) accrued and unpaid rent as of the date of entry of judgment in favor of the lessor, (ii) the present value as of the same date of the rent for the then remaining lease term of the lease agreement, and (iii) any incidental damages allowed under Section 2A–530, less expenses saved in consequence of the lessee's default; and

(b) for goods identified to the lease contract if the lessor is unable after reasonable effort to dispose of them at a reasonable price or the circumstances reasonably indicate that effort will be unavailing, (i) accrued and unpaid rent as of the date of entry of judgment in favor of the lessor, (ii) the present value as of the same date of the rent for the then remaining lease term of the lease agreement, and (iii) any incidental damages allowed under Section 2A–530, less expenses saved in consequence of the lessee's default.

(2) Except as provided in subsection (3), the lessor shall hold for the lessee for the remaining lease term of the lease agreement any goods that have been identified to the lease contract and are in the lessor's control.

(3) The lessor may dispose of the goods at any time before collection of the judgment for damages obtained pursuant to subsection (1). If the disposition is before the end of the remaining lease term of the lease agreement, the lessor's recovery against the lessee for damages is governed by Section 2A–527 or Section 2A–528, and the lessor will cause an appropriate credit to be provided against a judgment for damages to the extent that the amount of the judgment exceeds the recovery available pursuant to Section 2A–527 or 2A–528.

(4) Payment of the judgment for damages obtained pursuant to subsection (1) entitles the lessee to the use and possession of the goods not then disposed of for the remaining lease term of and in accordance with the lease agreement.

(5) After default by the lessee under the lease contract of the type described in Section 2A–523(1) or Section 2A–523(3)(a) or, if agreed, after other default by the lessee, a lessor who is held not entitled to rent under this section must nevertheless be awarded damages for non-acceptance under Section 2A–527 or Section 2A–528.

As amended in 1990.

§ 2A–530. Lessor's Incidental Damages

Incidental damages to an aggrieved lessor include any commercially reasonable charges, expenses, or commissions incurred in stopping delivery, in the transportation, care and custody of goods after the lessee's default, in connection with return or disposition of the goods, or otherwise resulting from the default.

§ 2A–531. Standing to Sue Third Parties for Injury to Goods

(1) If a third party so deals with goods that have been identified to a lease contract as to cause actionable injury to a party to the lease contract (a) the lessor has a right of action against the third party, and (b) the lessee also has a right of action against the third party if the lessee:

(i) has a security interest in the goods;
(ii) has an insurable interest in the goods; or
(iii) bears the risk of loss under the lease contract or has since the injury assumed that risk as against the lessor and the goods have been converted or destroyed.

(2) If at the time of the injury the party plaintiff did not bear the risk of loss as against the other party to the lease contract and there is no arrangement between them for disposition of the recovery, his [or her] suit or settlement, subject to his [or her] own interest, is as a fiduciary for the other party to the lease contract.

(3) Either party with the consent of the other may sue for the benefit of whom it may concern.

§ 2A–532. Lessor's Rights to Residual Interest

In addition to any other recovery permitted by this Article or other law, the lessor may recover from the lessee an amount that will fully compensate the lessor for any loss of or damage to the lessor's residual interest in the goods caused by the default of the lessee.

As added in 1990.

[REVISED] ARTICLE 3
NEGOTIABLE INSTRUMENTS

Part I General Provisions and Definitions

§ 3–101. Short Title

This Article may be cited as Uniform Commercial Code—Negotiable Instruments.

§ 3–102. Subject Matter

(a) This Article applies to negotiable instruments. It does not apply to money, to payment orders governed by Article 4A, or to securities governed by Article 8.

(b) If there is conflict between this Article and Article 4 or 9, Articles 4 and 9 govern.

(c) Regulations of the Board of Governors of the Federal Reserve System and operating circulars of the Federal Reserve Banks supersede any inconsistent provision of this Article to the extent of the inconsistency.

§ 3–103. Definitions

(a) In this Article:

(1) "Acceptor" means a drawee who has accepted a draft.

(2) "Drawee" means a person ordered in a draft to make payment.

(3) "Drawer" means a person who signs or is identified in a draft as a person ordering payment.

(4) "Good faith" means honesty in fact and the observance of reasonable commercial standards of fair dealing.

(5) "Maker" means a person who signs or is identified in a note as a person undertaking to pay.

(6) "Order" means a written instruction to pay money signed by the person giving the instruction. The instruction may be addressed to any person, including the person giving the instruction, or to one or more persons jointly or in the alternative but not in succession. An authorization to pay is not an order unless the person authorized to pay is also instructed to pay.

(7) "Ordinary care" in the case of a person engaged in business means observance of reasonable commercial standards, prevailing in the area in which the person is located, with respect to the business in which the person is engaged. In the case of a bank that takes an instrument for processing for collection or payment by automated means, reasonable commercial standards do not require the bank to examine the instrument if the failure to examine does not violate the bank's prescribed procedures and the bank's procedures do not vary unreasonably from general banking usage not disapproved by this Article or Article 4.

(8) "Party" means a party to an instrument.

(9) "Promise" means a written undertaking to pay money signed by the person undertaking to pay. An acknowledgement of an obligation by the obligor is not a promise unless the obligor also undertakes to pay the obligation.

(10) "Prove" with respect to a fact means to meet the burden of establishing the fact (Section 1–201(8)).

(11) "Remitter" means a person who purchases an instrument from its issuer if the instrument is payable to an identified person other than the purchaser.

(b) Other definitions applying to this Article and the sections in which they appear are:

"Acceptance"	Section 3–409
"Accommodated party"	Section 3–419
"Accommodation party"	Section 3–419
"Alteration"	Section 3–407
"Anomalous indorsement"	Section 3–205
"Blank indorsement"	Section 3–205
"Cashier's check"	Section 3–104
"Certificate of Deposit"	Section 3–104
"Certified check"	Section 3–409
"Check"	Section 3–104
"Consideration"	Section 3–303
"Draft"	Section 3–104
"Holder in due course"	Section 3–302
"Incomplete instrument"	Section 3–115
"Indorsement"	Section 3–204
"Indorser"	Section 3–204
"Instrument"	Section 3–104
"Issue"	Section 3–105
"Issuer"	Section 3–105
"Negotiable instrument"	Section 3–104
"Negotiation"	Section 3–201
"Note"	Section 3–104
"Payable at a definite time"	Section 3–108
"Payable on demand"	Section 3–108
"Payable to bearer"	Section 3–109
"Payable to order"	Section 3–109
"Payment"	Section 3–602
"Person entitled to enforce"	Section 3–301
"Presentment"	Section 3–501

(c) The following definitions in other Articles apply to this Article:

(d) In addition, Article 1 contains general definitions and principles of construction and interpretation applicable throughout this Article.

§ 3-104. Negotiable Instrument

(a) Except as provided in subsections (c) and (d), "negotiable instrument" means an unconditional promise or order to pay a fixed amount of money, with or without interest or other charges described in the promise or order, if it:

(1) is payable to bearer or to order at the time it is issued or first comes into possession of a holder;

(2) is payable on demand or at a definite time; and

(3) does not state any other undertaking or instruction by the person promising or ordering payment to do any act in addition to the payment of money, but the promise or order may contain (i) an undertaking or power to give, maintain, or protect collateral to secure payment, (ii) an authorization or power to the holder to confess judgment or realize on or dispose of collateral, or (iii) a waiver of the benefit of any law intended for the advantage or protection of an obligor.

(b) "Instrument" means a negotiable instrument.

(c) An order that meets all of the requirements of subsection (a), except paragraph (1), and otherwise falls within the definition of "check" in subsection (f) is a negotiable instrument and a check.

(d) A promise or order other than a check is not an instrument if, at the time it is issued or first comes into possession of a holder, it contains a conspicuous statement, however expressed, to the effect that the promise or order is not negotiable or is not an instrument governed by this Article.

(e) An instrument is a "note" if it is a promise and is a "draft" if it is an order. If an instrument falls within the definition of both "note" and "draft," a person entitled to enforce the instrument may treat it as either.

(f) "Check" means (i) a draft, other than a documentary draft, payable on demand and drawn on a bank or (ii) a cashier's check or teller's check. An instrument may be a check even though it is described on its face by another term, such as "money order."

(g) "Cashier's check" means a draft with respect to which the drawer and drawee are the same bank or branches of the same bank.

(h) "Teller's check" means a draft drawn by a bank (i) on another bank, or (ii) payable at or through a bank.

(i) "Traveler's check" means an instrument that (i) is payable on demand, (ii) is drawn on or payable at or through a bank, (iii) is designated by the term "traveler's check" or by a substantially similar term, and (iv) requires, as a condition to payment, a countersignature by a person whose specimen signature appears on the instrument.

(j) "Certificate of deposit" means an instrument containing an acknowledgment by a bank that a sum of money has been received by the bank and a promise by the bank to repay the sum of money. A certificate of deposit is a note of the bank.

§ 3-105. Issue of Instrument

(a) "Issue" means the first delivery of an instrument by the maker or drawer, whether to a holder or nonholder, for the purpose of giving rights on the instrument to any person.

(b) An unissued instrument, or an unissued incomplete instrument that is completed, is binding on the maker or drawer, but nonissuance is a defense. An instrument that is conditionally issued or is issued for a special purpose is binding on the maker or drawer, but failure of the condition or special purpose to be fulfilled is a defense.

(c) "Issuer" applies to issued and unissued instruments and means a maker or drawer of an instrument.

§ 3-106. Unconditional Promise or Order

(a) Except as provided in this section, for the purposes of Section 3-104(a), a promise or order is unconditional unless it states (i) an express condition to payment, (ii) that the promise or order is subject to or governed by another writing, or (iii) that rights or obligations with respect to the promise or order are stated in another writing. A reference to another writing does not of itself make the promise or order conditional.

(b) A promise or order is not made conditional (i) by a reference to another writing for a statement of rights with respect to collateral, prepayment, or acceleration, or (ii) because payment is limited to resort to a particular fund or source.

(c) If a promise or order requires, as a condition to payment, a countersignature by a person whose specimen signature appears on the promise or order, the condition does not make the promise or order conditional for the purposes of Section 3–104(a). If the person whose specimen signature appears on an instrument fails to countersign the instrument, the failure to countersign is a defense to the obligation of the issuer, but the failure does not prevent a transferee of the instrument from becoming a holder of the instrument.

(d) If a promise or order at the time it is issued or first comes into possession of a holder contains a statement, required by applicable statutory or administrative law, to the effect that the rights of a holder or transferee are subject to claims or defenses that the issuer could assert against the original payee, the promise or order is not thereby made conditional for the purposes of Section 3–104(a); but if the promise or order is an instrument, there cannot be a holder in due course of the instrument.

§ 3–107. Instrument Payable in Foreign Money

Unless the instrument otherwise provides, an instrument that states the amount payable in foreign money may be paid in the foreign money or in an equivalent amount in dollars calculated by using the current bank-offered spot rate at the place of payment for the purchase of dollars on the day on which the instrument is paid.

§ 3–108. Payable on Demand or at Definite Time

(a) A promise or order is "payable on demand" if it (i) states that it is payable on demand or at sight, or otherwise indicates that it is payable at the will of the holder, or (ii) does not state any time of payment.

(b) A promise or order is "payable at a definite time" if it is payable on elapse of a definite period of time after sight or acceptance or at a fixed date or dates or at a time or times readily ascertainable at the time the promise or order is issued, subject to rights of (i) prepayment, (ii) acceleration, (iii) extension at the option of the holder, or (iv) extension to a further definite time at the option of the maker or acceptor or automatically upon or after a specified act or event.

(c) If an instrument, payable at a fixed date, is also payable upon demand made before the fixed date, the instrument is payable on demand until the fixed date and, if demand for payment is not made before that date, becomes payable at a definite time on the fixed date.

§ 3–109. Payable to Bearer or to Order

(a) A promise or order is payable to bearer if it:

(1) states that it is payable to bearer or to the order of bearer or otherwise indicates that the person in possession of the promise or order is entitled to payment:

(2) does not state a payee; or

(3) states that it is payable to or to the order of cash or otherwise indicates that it is not payable to an identified person.

(b) A promise or order that is not payable to bearer is payable to order if it is payable (i) to the order of an identified person or (ii) to an identified person or order. A promise or order that is payable to order is payable to the identified person.

(c) An instrument payable to bearer may become payable to an identified person if it is specially indorsed pursuant to Section 3–205(a). An instrument payable to an identified person may become payable to bearer if it is indorsed in blank pursuant to Section 3–205(b).

§ 3–110. Identification of Person to Whom Instrument Is Payable

(a) The person to whom an instrument is initially payable is determined by the intent of the person, whether or not authorized, signing as, or in the name or behalf of, the issuer of the instrument. The instrument is payable to the person intended by the signer even if that person is identified in the instrument by a name or other identification that is not that of the intended person. If more than one person signs in the name or behalf of the issuer of an instrument and all the signers do not intend the same person as payee, the instrument is payable to any person intended by one or more of the signers.

(b) If the signature of the issuer of an instrument is made by automated means, such as a check-writing machine, the payee of the instrument is determined by the intent of the person who supplied the name or identification of the payee, whether or not authorized to do so.

(c) A person to whom an instrument is payable may be identified in any way, including by name, identifying number, office, or account number. For the purpose of determining the holder of an instrument, the following rules apply:

(1) If an instrument is payable to an account and the account is identified only by number, the instrument is payable to the person to whom the account is payable. If an instrument is payable to an account identified by number and by the name of a person, the instrument is payable to the named person, whether or not that person is the owner of the account identified by number.

(2) If an instrument is payable to:

(i) a trust, an estate, or a person described as trustee or representative of a trust or estate, the instrument is payable to the trustee, the representative, or a successor of either, whether or not the beneficiary or estate is also named;

(ii) a person described as agent or similar representative of a named or identified person, the instrument is payable to the represented person, the representative, or a successor of the representative;

(iii) a fund or organization that is not a legal entity, the instrument is payable to a representative of the members of the fund or organization; or

(iv) an office or to a person described as holding an office, the instrument is payable to the named person, the incumbent of the office, or a successor to the incumbent.

(d) If an instrument is payable to two or more persons alternatively, it is payable to any of them and may be negotiated, discharged, or enforced by any or all of them in possession of the instrument. If an instrument is payable to two or more persons not alternatively, it is payable to all of them and may be negotiated, discharged, or enforced only by all of them. If an instrument payable to two or more persons is ambiguous as to whether it is payable to the persons alternatively, the instrument is payable to the persons alternatively.

§ 3–111. Place of Payment

Except as otherwise provided for items in Article 4, an instrument is payable at the place of payment stated in the instrument. If no place of payment is stated, an instrument is payable at the address of the drawee or maker stated in the instrument. If no address is stated, the place of payment is the place of business of the drawee or maker. If a drawee or maker has more than one place of business, the place of payment is any place of business of the drawee or maker chosen by the person entitled to enforce the instrument. If the drawee or maker has no place of business, the place of payment is the residence of the drawee or maker.

§ 3–112. Interest

(a) Unless otherwise provided in the instrument, (i) an instrument is not payable with interest, and (ii) interest on an interest-bearing instrument is payable from the date of the instrument.

(b) Interest may be stated in an instrument as a fixed or variable amount of money or it may be expressed as a fixed or variable rate or rates. The amount or rate of interest may be stated or described in the instrument in any manner and may require reference to information not contained in the instrument. If an instrument provides for interest, but the amount of interest payable cannot be ascertained from the description, interest is payable at the judgment rate in effect at the place of payment of the instrument and at the time interest first accrues.

§ 3–113. Date of Instrument

(a) An instrument may be antedated or postdated. The date stated determines the time of payment if the instrument is payable at a fixed period after date. Except as provided in Section 4–401(c), an instrument payable on demand is not payable before the date of the instrument.

(b) If an instrument is undated, its date is the date of its issue or, in the case of an unissued instrument, the date it first comes into possession of a holder.

§ 3–114. Contradictory Terms of Instrument

If an instrument contains contradictory terms, typewritten terms prevail over printed terms, handwritten terms prevail over both, and words prevail over numbers.

§ 3–115. Incomplete Instrument

(a) "Incomplete instrument" means a signed writing, whether or not issued by the signer, the contents of which show at the time of signing that it is incomplete but that the signer intended it to be completed by the addition of words or numbers.

(b) Subject to subsection (c), if an incomplete instrument is an instrument under Section 3–104, it may be enforced according to its terms if it is not completed, or according to its terms as augmented by completion. If an incomplete instrument is not an instrument under Section 3–104, but, after completion, the requirements of Section 3–104 are met, the instrument may be enforced according to its terms as augmented by completion.

(c) If words or numbers are added to an incomplete instrument without authority of the signer, there is an alteration of the incomplete instrument under Section 3–407.

(d) The burden of establishing that words or numbers were added to an incomplete instrument without authority of the signer is on the person asserting the lack of authority.

§ 3–116. Joint and Several Liability; Contribution

(a) Except as otherwise provided in the instrument, two or more persons who have the same liability on an instrument as makers, drawers, acceptors, indorsers who indorse as joint payees, or anomalous indorsers are jointly and severally liable in the capacity in which they sign.

(b) Except as provided in Section 3–419(e) or by agreement of the affected parties, a party having joint and several liability who pays the instrument is entitled to receive from any party having the same joint and several liability contribution in accordance with applicable law.

(c) Discharge of one party having joint and several liability by a person entitled to enforce the instrument does not affect the right under subsection (b) of a party having the same joint and several liability to receive contribution from the party discharged.

§ 3–117. Other Agreements Affecting Instrument

Subject to applicable law regarding exclusion of proof of contemporaneous or previous agreements, the obligation of a party to an instrument to pay the instrument may be modified, supplemented, or nullified by a separate agreement of the obligor and a person entitled to enforce the instrument, if the instrument is issued or the obligation is incurred in reliance on the agreement or as part of the same transaction giving rise to the agreement. To the extent an obligation is modified, supplemented, or nullified by an agreement under this section, the agreement is a defense to the obligation.

§ 3–118. Statute of Limitations

(a) Except as provided in subsection (e), an action to enforce the obligation of a party to pay a note payable at a definite time must be commenced within six years after the due date or dates stated in the note or, if a due date is accelerated, within six years after the accelerated due date.

(b) Except as provided in subsection (d) or (e), if demand for payment is made to the maker of a note payable on demand, an action to enforce the obligation of a party to pay the note must be commenced within six years after the demand. If no demand for payment is made to the maker, an action to enforce the note is barred if neither principal nor interest on the note has been paid for a continuous period of 10 years.

(c) Except as provided in subsection (d), an action to enforce the obligation of a party to an unaccepted draft to pay the draft must be commenced within three years after dishonor of the draft or 10 years after the date of the draft, whichever period expires first.

(d) An action to enforce the obligation of the acceptor of a certified check or the issuer of a teller's check, cashier's check, or traveler's check must be commenced within three years after demand for payment is made to the acceptor or issuer, as the case may be.

(e) An action to enforce the obligation of a party to a certificate of deposit to pay the instrument must be commenced within six years after demand for payment is made to the maker, but if the instrument states a due date and the maker is not required to pay before that date, the six-year period begins when a demand for payment is in effect and the due date has passed.

(f) An action to enforce the obligation of a party to pay an accepted draft, other than a certified check, must be commenced (i) within six years after the due date or dates stated in the draft or acceptance if the obligation of the acceptor is payable at a definite time, or (ii) within six years after the date of the acceptance if the obligation of the acceptor is payable on demand.

(g) Unless governed by other law regarding claims for indemnity or contribution, an action (i) for conversion of an instrument, for money had and received, or like action based on conversion, (ii) for breach of warranty, or (iii) to enforce an obligation, duty, or right arising under this Article and not governed by this section must be commenced within three years after the [cause of action] accrues.

§ 3–119. Notice of Right to Defend Action

In an action for breach of an obligation for which a third person is answerable over pursuant to this Article or Article 4, the defendant may give the third person written notice of the litigation, and the person notified may then give similar notice to any other person who is answerable over. If the notice states (i) that the person notified may come in and defend and (ii) that failure to do so will bind the person notified in an action later brought by the person giving the notice as to any determination of fact common to the two litigations, the person notified is so bound unless after seasonable receipt of the notice the person notified does come in and defend.

Part 2 Negotiation, Transfer, and Indorsement

§ 3–201. Negotiation

(a) "Negotiation" means a transfer of possession, whether voluntary or involuntary, of an instrument by a person other than the issuer to a person who thereby becomes its holder.

(b) Except for negotiation by a remitter, if an instrument is payable to an identified person, negotiation requires transfer of possession of the instrument and its indorsement by the holder. If an instrument is payable to bearer, it may be negotiated by transfer of possession alone.

§ 3–202. Negotiation Subject to Rescission

(a) Negotiation is effective even if obtained (i) from an infant, a corporation exceeding its powers, or a person without capacity, (ii) by fraud, duress, or mistake, or (iii) in breach of duty or as part of an illegal transaction.

(b) To the extent permitted by other law, negotiation may be rescinded or may be subject to other remedies, but those remedies may not be asserted against a subsequent holder in due course or a person paying the instrument in good faith and without knowledge of facts that are a basis for rescission or other remedy.

§ 3–203. Transfer of Instrument; Rights Acquired by Transfer

(a) An instrument is transferred when it is delivered by a person other than its issuer for the purpose of giving to the person receiving delivery the right to enforce the instrument.

(b) Transfer of an instrument, whether or not the transfer is a negotiation, vests in the transferee any right of the transferor to enforce the instrument, including any right as a holder in due course, but the transferee cannot acquire rights of a holder in due course by a transfer, directly or indirectly, from a holder in due course if the transferee engaged in fraud or illegality affecting the instrument.

(c) Unless otherwise agreed, if an instrument is transferred for value and the transferee does not become a holder because of lack of indorsement by the transferor, the transferee has a specifically enforceable right to the unqualified indorsement of the transferor, but negotiation of the instrument does not occur until the indorsement is made.

(d) If a transfer purports to transfer less than the entire instrument, negotiation of the instrument does not occur. The transferee obtains no rights under this Article and has only the rights of a partial assignee.

§ 3–204. Indorsement

(a) "Indorsement" means a signature, other than that of a signer as maker, drawer, or acceptor, that alone or accompanied by other words is made on an instrument for the purpose of (i) negotiating the instrument, (ii) restricting payment of the instrument, or (iii) incurring indorser's liability on the instrument, but regardless of the intent of the signer, a signature and its accompanying words is an indorsement unless the accompanying words, terms of the instrument, place of the signature, or other circumstances unambiguously indicate that the signature was made for a purpose other than indorsement. For the purpose of determining whether a signature is made on an instrument, a paper affixed to the instrument is a part of the instrument.

(b) "Indorser" means a person who makes an indorsement.

(c) For the purpose of determining whether the transferee of an instrument is a holder, an indorsement that transfers a security interest in the instrument is effective as an unqualified indorsement of the instrument.

(d) If an instrument is payable to a holder under a name that is not the name of the holder, indorsement may be made by the holder in the name stated in the instrument or in the holder's name or both, but signature in both names may be required by a person paying or taking the instrument for value or collection.

§ 3–205. Special Indorsement; Blank Indorsement; Anomalous Indorsement

(a) If an indorsement is made by the holder of an instrument, whether payable to an identified person or payable to bearer, and the indorsement identifies a person to whom it makes the instrument payable, it is a "special indorsement." When specially indorsed, an instrument becomes payable to the identified person and may be negotiated only by the indorsement of that person. The

principles stated in Section 3–110 apply to special indorsements.

(b) If an indorsement is made by the holder of an instrument and it is not a special indorsement, it is a "blank indorsement." When indorsed in blank, an instrument becomes payable to bearer and may be negotiated by transfer of possession alone until specially indorsed.

(c) The holder may convert a blank indorsement that consists only of a signature into a special indorsement by writing, above the signature of the indorser, words identifying the person to whom the instrument is made payable.

(d) "Anomalous indorsement" means an indorsement made by a person who is not the holder of the instrument. An anomalous indorsement does not affect the manner in which the instrument may be negotiated.

§ 3–206. Restrictive Indorsement

(a) An indorsement limiting payment to a particular person or otherwise prohibiting further transfer or negotiation of the instrument is not effective to prevent further transfer or negotiation of the instrument.

(b) An indorsement stating a condition to the right of the indorsee to receive payment does not affect the right of the indorsee to enforce the instrument. A person paying the instrument or taking it for value or collection may disregard the condition, and the rights and liabilities of that person are not affected by whether the condition has been fulfilled.

(c) If an instrument bears an indorsement (i) described in Section 4–201(b), or (ii) in blank or to a particular bank using the words "for deposit," "for collection," or other words indicating a purpose of having the instrument collected by a bank for the indorser or for a particular account, the following rules apply:

(1) A person, other than a bank, who purchases the instrument when so indorsed converts the instrument unless the amount paid for the instrument is received by the indorser or applied consistently with the indorsement.

(2) A depositary bank that purchases the instrument or takes it for collection when so indorsed converts the instrument unless the amount paid by the bank with respect to the instrument is received by the indorser or applied consistently with the indorsement.

(3) A payor bank that is also the depositary bank or that takes the instrument for immediate payment over the counter from a person other than a collecting bank converts the instrument unless the proceeds of the instrument are received by the indorser or applied consistently with the indorsement.

(4) Except as otherwise provided in paragraph (3), a payor bank or intermediary bank may disregard the

indorsement and is not liable if the proceeds of the instrument are not received by the indorser or applied consistently with the indorsement.

(d) Except for an indorsement covered by subsection (c), if an instrument bears an indorsement using words to the effect that payment is to be made to the indorsee as agent, trustee, or other fiduciary for the benefit of the indorser or another person, the following rules apply:

(1) Unless there is notice of breach of fiduciary duty as provided in Section 3–307, a person who purchases the instrument from the indorsee or takes the instrument from the indorsee for collection or payment may pay the proceeds of payment or the value given for the instrument to the indorsee without regard to whether the indorsee violates a fiduciary duty to the indorser.

(2) A subsequent transferee of the instrument or person who pays the instrument is neither given notice nor otherwise affected by the restriction in the indorsement unless the transferee or payor knows that the fiduciary dealt with the instrument or its proceeds in breach of fiduciary duty.

(e) The presence on an instrument of an indorsement to which this section applies does not prevent a purchaser of the instrument from becoming a holder in due course of the instrument unless the purchaser is a converter under subsection (c) or has notice or knowledge of breach of fiduciary duty as stated in subsection (d).

(f) In an action to enforce the obligation of a party to pay the instrument, the obligor has a defense if payment would violate an indorsement to which this section applies and the payment is not permitted by this section.

§ 3–207. Reacquisition

Reacquisition of an instrument occurs if it is transferred to a former holder, by negotiation or otherwise. A former holder who reacquires the instrument may cancel indorsements made after the reacquirer first became a holder of the instrument. If the cancellation causes the instrument to be payable to the reacquirer or to bearer, the reacquirer may negotiate the instrument. An indorser whose indorsement is canceled is discharged, and the discharge is effective against any subsequent holder.

Part 3 Enforcement of Instruments

§ 3–301. Person Entitled to Enforce Instrument

"Person entitled to enforce" an instrument means (i) the holder of the instrument, (ii) a nonholder in possession of the instrument who has the rights of a holder, or (iii) a person not in possession of the instrument who is entitled to enforce the instrument pursuant to Section 3–309 or 3–418(d). A person may be a person entitled to enforce the instrument even though the person is not the owner of the instrument or is in wrongful possession of the instrument.

§ 3–302. Holder in Due Course

(a) Subject to subsection (c) and Section 3–106(d), "holder in due course" means the holder of an instrument if:

(1) the instrument when issued or negotiated to the holder does not bear such apparent evidence of forgery or alteration or is not otherwise so irregular or incomplete as to call into question its authenticity; and

(2) the holder took the instrument (i) for value, (ii) in good faith, (iii) without notice that the instrument is overdue or has been dishonored or that there is an uncured default with respect to payment of another instrument issued as part of the same series, (iv) without notice that the instrument contains an unauthorized signature or has been altered, (v) without notice of any claim to the instrument described in Section 3–306, and (vi) without notice that any party has a defense or claim in recoupment described in Section 3–305(a).

(b) Notice of discharge of a party, other than discharge in an insolvency proceeding, is not notice of a defense under subsection (a), but discharge is effective against a person who became a holder in due course with notice of the discharge. Public filing or recording of a document does not of itself constitute notice of a defense, claim in recoupment, or claim to the instrument.

(c) Except to the extent a transferor or predecessor in interest has rights as a holder in due course, a person does not acquire rights of a holder in due course of an instrument taken (i) by legal process or by purchase in an execution, bankruptcy, or creditor's sale or similar proceeding, (ii) by purchase as part of a bulk transaction not in ordinary course of business of the transferor, or (iii) as the successor in interest to an estate or other organization.

(d) If, under Section 3–303(a)(1), the promise of performance that is the consideration for an instrument has been partially performed, the holder may assert rights as a holder in due course of the instrument only to the fraction of the amount payable under the instrument equal to the value of the partial performance divided by the value of the promised performance.

(e) If (i) the person entitled to enforce an instrument has only a security interest in the instrument and (ii) the person obliged to pay the instrument has a defense, claim in recoupment, or claim to the instrument that may be asserted against the person who granted the security interest, the person entitled to enforce the instrument may assert rights as a holder in due course only to an amount payable under the instrument which, at the time of enforcement of the instrument, does not exceed the amount of the unpaid obligation secured.

(f) To be effective, notice must be received at a time and in a manner that gives a reasonable opportunity to act on it.

(g) This section is subject to any law limiting status as a holder in due course in particular classes of transactions.

§ 3–303. Value and Consideration

(a) An instrument is issued or transferred for value if:

(1) the instrument is issued or transferred for a promise of performance, to the extent the promise has been performed;

(2) the transferee acquires a security interest or other lien in the instrument other than a lien obtained by judicial proceeding;

(3) the instrument is issued or transferred as payment of, or as security for, an antecedent claim against any person, whether or not the claim is due;

(4) the instrument is issued or transferred in exchange for a negotiable instrument; or

(5) the instrument is issued or transferred in exchange for the incurring of an irrevocable obligation to a third party by the person taking the instrument.

(b) "Consideration" means any consideration sufficient to support a simple contract. The drawer or maker of an instrument has a defense if the instrument is issued without consideration. If an instrument is issued for a promise of performance, the issuer has a defense to the extent performance of the promise is due and the promise has not been performed. If an instrument is issued for value as stated in subsection (a), the instrument is also issued for consideration.

§ 3–304. Overdue Instrument

(a) An instrument payable on demand becomes overdue at the earliest of the following times:

(1) on the day after the day demand for payment is duly made;

(2) if the instrument is a check, 90 days after its date; or

(3) if the instrument is not a check, when the instrument has been outstanding for a period of time after its date which is unreasonably long under the circumstances of the particular case in light of the nature of the instrument and usage of the trade.

(b) With respect to an instrument payable at a definite time the following rules apply:

(1) If the principal is payable in installments and a due date has not been accelerated, the instrument becomes overdue upon default under the instrument for nonpayment of an installment, and the instrument remains overdue until the default is cured.

(2) If the principal is not payable in installments and the due date has not been accelerated, the instrument becomes overdue on the day after the due date.

(3) If a due date with respect to principal has been accelerated, the instrument becomes overdue on the day after the accelerated due date.

(c) Unless the due date of principal has been accelerated, an instrument does not become overdue if there is default in payment of interest but no default in payment of principal.

§ 3–305. Defenses and Claims in Recoupment

(a) Except as stated in subsection (b), the right to enforce the obligation of a party to pay an instrument is subject to the following:

(1) a defense of the obligor based on (i) infancy of the obligor to the extent it is a defense to a simple contract, (ii) duress, lack of legal capacity, or illegality of the transaction which, under other law, nullifies the obligation of the obligor, (iii) fraud that induced the obligor to sign the instrument with neither knowledge nor reasonable opportunity to learn of its character or its essential terms, or (iv) discharge of the obligor in insolvency proceedings;

(2) a defense of the obligor stated in another section of this Article or a defense of the obligor that would be available if the person entitled to enforce the instrument were enforcing a right to payment under a simple contract; and

(3) a claim in recoupment of the obligor against the original payee of the instrument if the claim arose from the transaction that gave rise to the instrument; but the claim of the obligor may be asserted against a transferee of the instrument only to reduce the amount owing on the instrument at the time the action is brought.

(b) The right of a holder in due course to enforce the obligation of a party to pay the instrument is subject to defenses of the obligor stated in subsection (a)(1), but is not subject to defenses of the obligor stated in subsection (a)(2) or claims in recoupment stated in subsection (a)(3) against a person other than the holder.

(c) Except as stated in subsection (d), in an action to enforce the obligation of a party to pay the instrument, the obligor may not assert against the person entitled to enforce the instrument a defense, claim in recoupment, or claim to the instrument (Section 3–306) of another person, but the other person's claim to the instrument may be asserted by the obligor if the other person is joined in the action and personally asserts the claim against the person entitled to enforce the instrument. An obligor is not obliged to pay the instrument if the person seeking enforcement of the instrument does not have rights of a holder in due course and the obligor proves that the instrument is a lost or stolen instrument.

(d) In an action to enforce the obligation of an accommodation party to pay an instrument, the accommodation party may assert against the person entitled to enforce the instrument any defense or claim in recoupment under subsection (a) that the accommodated party could assert against the person entitled to enforce the instrument, except the defenses of discharge in insolvency proceedings, infancy, and lack of legal capacity.

§ 3–306. Claims to an Instrument

A person taking an instrument, other than a person having rights of a holder in due course, is subject to a claim of a property or possessory right in the instrument or its proceeds, including a claim to rescind a negotiation and to recover the instrument or its proceeds. A person having rights of a holder in due course takes free of the claim to the instrument.

§ 3–307. Notice of Breach of Fiduciary Duty

(a) In this section:

(1) "Fiduciary" means an agent, trustee, partner, corporate officer or director, or other representative owing a fiduciary duty with respect to an instrument.

(2) "Represented person" means the principal, beneficiary, partnership, corporation, or other person to whom the duty stated in paragraph (1) is owed.

(b) If (i) an instrument is taken from a fiduciary for payment or collection or for value, (ii) the taker has knowledge of the fiduciary status of the fiduciary, and (iii) the represented person makes a claim to the instrument or its proceeds on the basis that the transaction of the fiduciary is a breach of fiduciary duty, the following rules apply:

(1) Notice of breach of fiduciary duty by the fiduciary is notice of the claim of the represented person.

(2) In the case of an instrument payable to the represented person or the fiduciary as such, the taker has notice of the breach of fiduciary duty if the instrument is (i) taken in payment of or as security for a debt known by the taker to be the personal debt of the fiduciary, (ii) taken in a transaction known by the taker to be for the personal benefit of the fiduciary, or (iii) deposited to an account other than an account of the fiduciary, as such, or an account of the represented person.

(3) If an instrument is issued by the represented person or the fiduciary as such, and made payable to the fiduciary personally, the taker does not have notice of the breach of fiduciary duty unless the taker knows of the breach of fiduciary duty.

(4) If an instrument is issued by the represented person or the fiduciary as such, to the taker as payee, the taker has notice of the breach of fiduciary duty if the instrument is (i) taken in payment of or as security for a debt known by the taker to be the

personal debt of the fiduciary, (ii) taken in a transaction known by the taker to be for the personal benefit of the fiduciary, or (iii) deposited to an account other than an account of the fiduciary, as such, or an account of the represented person.

§ 3–308. Proof of Signatures and Status as Holder in Due Course

(a) In an action with respect to an instrument, the authenticity of, and authority to make, each signature on the instrument is admitted unless specifically denied in the pleadings. If the validity of a signature is denied in the pleadings, the burden of establishing validity is on the person claiming validity, but the signature is presumed to be authentic and authorized unless the action is to enforce the liability of the purported signer and the signer is dead or incompetent at the time of trial of the issue of validity of the signature. If an action to enforce the instrument is brought against a person as the undisclosed principal of a person who signed the instrument as a party to the instrument, the plaintiff has the burden of establishing that the defendant is liable on the instrument as a represented person under Section 3–402(a).

(b) If the validity of signatures is admitted or proved and there is compliance with subsection (a), a plaintiff producing the instrument is entitled to payment if the plaintiff proves entitlement to enforce the instrument under Section 3–301, unless the defendant proves a defense or claim in recoupment. If a defense or claim in recoupment is proved, the right to payment of the plaintiff is subject to the defense or claim, except to the extent the plaintiff proves that the plaintiff has rights of a holder in due course which are not subject to the defense or claim.

§ 3–309. Enforcement of Lost, Destroyed, or Stolen Instrument

(a) A person not in possession of an instrument is entitled to enforce the instrument if (i) the person was in possession of the instrument and entitled to enforce it when loss of possession occurred, (ii) the loss of possession was not the result of a transfer by the person or a lawful seizure, and (iii) the person cannot reasonably obtain possession of the instrument because the instrument was destroyed, its whereabouts cannot be determined, or it is in the wrongful possession of an unknown person or a person that cannot be found or is not amenable to service of process.

(b) A person seeking enforcement of an instrument under subsection (a) must prove the terms of the instrument and the person's right to enforce the instrument. If that proof is made, Section 3–308 applies to the case as if the person seeking enforcement had produced the instrument. The court may not enter judgment in favor of the person seeking enforcement unless it finds that the person required to pay the instrument is adequately protected against loss that might occur by reason of a claim by another person to enforce the instrument. Adequate protection may be provided by any reasonable means.

§ 3–310. Effect of Instrument on Obligation for Which Taken

(a) Unless otherwise agreed, if a certified check, cashier's check, or teller's check is taken for an obligation, the obligation is discharged to the same extent discharge would result if an amount of money equal to the amount of the instrument were taken in payment of the obligation. Discharge of the obligation does not affect any liability that the obligor may have as an indorser of the instrument.

(b) Unless otherwise agreed and except as provided in subsection (a), if a note or an uncertified check is taken for an obligation, the obligation is suspended to the same extent the obligation would be discharged if an amount of money equal to the amount of the instrument were taken, and the following rules apply:

(1) In the case of an uncertified check, suspension of the obligation continues until dishonor of the check or until it is paid or certified. Payment or certification of the check results in discharge of the obligation to the extent of the amount of the check.

(2) In the case of a note, suspension of the obligation continues until dishonor of the note or until it is paid. Payment of the note results in discharge of the obligation to the extent of the payment.

(3) Except as provided in paragraph (4), if the check or note is dishonored and the obligee of the obligation for which the instrument was taken is the person entitled to enforce the instrument, the obligee may enforce either the instrument or the obligation. In the case of an instrument of a third person which is negotiated to the obligee by the obligor, discharge of the obligor on the instrument also discharges the obligation.

(4) If the person entitled to enforce the instrument taken for an obligation is a person other than the obligee, the obligee may not enforce the obligation to the extent the obligation is suspended. If the obligee is the person entitled to enforce the instrument but no longer has possession of it because it was lost, stolen, or destroyed, the obligation may not be enforced to the extent of the amount payable on the instrument, and to that extent the obligee's rights against the obligor are limited to enforcement of the instrument.

(c) If an instrument other than one described in subsection (a) or (b) is taken for an obligation, the effect is (i) that stated in subsection (a) if the instrument is one on which a bank is liable as maker or acceptor, or (ii) that stated in subsection (b) in any other case.

§ 3–311. Accord and Satisfaction by Use of Instrument

(a) If a person against whom a claim is asserted proves that (i) that person in good faith tendered an instrument to the claimant as full satisfaction of the claim, (ii) the amount of the claim was unliquidated or subject to a bona fide dispute, and (iii) the claimant obtained payment of the instrument, the following subsections apply.

(b) Unless subsection (c) applies, the claim is discharged if the person against whom the claim is asserted proves that the instrument or an accompanying written communication contained a conspicuous statement to the effect that the instrument was tendered as full satisfaction of the claim.

(c) Subject to subsection (d), a claim is not discharged under subsection (b) if either of the following applies:

(1) The claimant, if an organization, proves that (i) within a reasonable time before the tender, the claimant sent a conspicuous statement to the person against whom the claim is asserted that communications concerning disputed debts, including an instrument tendered as full satisfaction of a debt, are to be sent to a designated person, office, or place, and (ii) the instrument or accompanying communication was not received by that designated person, office, or place.

(2) The claimant, whether or not an organization, proves that within 90 days after payment of the instrument, the claimant tendered repayment of the amount of the instrument to the person against whom the claim is asserted. This paragraph does not apply if the claimant is an organization that sent a statement complying with paragraph (1)(i).

(d) A claim is discharged if the person against whom the claim is asserted proves that within a reasonable time before collection of the instrument was initiated, the claimant, or an agent of the claimant having direct responsibility with respect to the disputed obligation, knew that the instrument was tendered in full satisfaction of the claim.

§ 3–312. Lost, Destroyed, or Stolen Cashier's Check, Teller's Check, or Certified Check

(a) In this section:

(1) "Check" means a cashier's check, teller's check, or certified check.

(2) "Claimant" means a person who claims the right to receive the amount of a cashier's check, teller's check, or certified check that was lost, destroyed, or stolen.

(3) "Declaration of loss" means a written statement, made under penalty of perjury, to the effect that (i) the declarer lost possession of a check, (ii) the declarer is the drawer or payee of the check, in the

case of a certified check, or the remitter or payee of the check, in the case of a cashier's check or teller's check, (iii) the loss of possession was not the result of a transfer by the declarer or a lawful seizure, and (iv) the declarer cannot reasonably obtain possession of the check because the check was destroyed, its whereabouts cannot be determined, or it is in the wrongful possession of an unknown person or a person that cannot be found or is not amenable to service of process.

(4) "Obligated bank" means the issuer of a cashier's check or teller's check or the acceptor of a certified check.

(b) A claimant may assert a claim to the amount of a check by a communication to the obligated bank describing the check with reasonable certainty and requesting payment of the amount of the check, if (i) the claimant is the drawer or payee of a certified check or the remitter or payee of a cashier's check or teller's check, (ii) the communication contains or is accompanied by a declaration of loss of the claimant with respect to the check, (iii) the communication is received at a time and in a manner affording the bank a reasonable time to act on it before the check is paid, and (iv) the claimant provides reasonable identification if requested by the obligated bank. Delivery of a declaration of loss is a warranty of the truth of the statements made in the declaration. The warranty is made to the obligated bank and any person entitled to enforce the check. If a claim is asserted in compliance with this subsection, the following rules apply:

(1) The claim becomes enforceable at the later of (i) the time the claim is asserted, or (ii) the 90th day following the date of the check, in the case of a cashier's check or teller's check, or the 90th day following the date of the acceptance, in the case of a certified check.

(2) Until the claim becomes enforceable, it has no legal effect and the obligated bank may pay the check or, in the case of a teller's check, may permit the drawee to pay the check. Payment to a person entitled to enforce the check discharges all liability of the obligated bank with respect to the check.

(3) If the claim becomes enforceable before the check is presented for payment, the obligated bank is not obligated to pay the check.

(4) When the claim becomes enforceable, the obligated bank becomes obliged to pay the amount of the check to the claimant if payment of the check has not been made to a person entitled to enforce the check. Subject to Section 4–302(a)(1), payment to the claimant discharges all liability of the obligated bank with respect to the check.

(c) If the obligated bank pays the amount of a check to a claimant under subsection (b)(4) and, after the claim became enforceable, the check is presented for payment by a person having rights of a holder in due course, the claimant is obliged to (i) refund the payment to the obligated bank if the check is paid, or (ii) pay the amount of the check to the person having rights of a holder in due course if the check is dishonored.

(d) If a claimant has the right to assert a claim under subsection (b) and is also a person entitled to enforce a cashier's check, teller's check, or certified check which is lost, destroyed, or stolen, the claimant may assert rights with respect to the check either under this section or Section 3–309.

Part 4 Liability of Parties

§ 3–401. Signature

(a) A person is not liable on an instrument unless (i) the person signed the instrument, or (ii) the person is represented by an agent or representative who signed the instrument and the signature is binding on the represented person under Section 3–402.

(b) A signature may be made (i) manually or by means of a device or machine, and (ii) by the use of any name, including a trade or assumed name, or by a word, mark, or symbol executed or adopted by a person with present intention to authenticate a writing.

§ 3–402. Signature by Representative

(a) If a person acting, or purporting to act, as a representative signs an instrument by signing either the name of the represented person or the name of the signer, the represented person is bound by the signature to the same extent the represented person would be bound if the signature were on a simple contract. If the represented person is bound, the signature of the representative is the "authorized signature of the represented person" and the represented person is liable on the instrument, whether or not identified in the instrument.

(b) If a representative signs the name of the representative to an instrument and the signature is an authorized signature of the represented person, the following rules apply:

(1) If the form of the signature shows unambiguously that the signature is made on behalf of the represented person who is identified in the instrument, the representative is not liable on the instrument.

(2) Subject to subsection (c), if (i) the form of the signature does not show unambiguously that the signature is made in a representative capacity or (ii) the represented person is not identified in the instrument, the representative is liable on the instrument to a holder in due course that took the instrument without notice that the representative was not intended to be liable on the instrument.

With respect to any other person, the representative is liable on the instrument unless the representative proves that the original parties did not intend the representative to be liable on the instrument.

(c) If a representative signs the name of the representative as drawer of a check without indication of the representative status and the check is payable from an account of the represented person who is identified on the check, the signer is not liable on the check if the signature is an authorized signature of the represented person.

§ 3–403. Unauthorized Signature

(a) Unless otherwise provided in this Article or Article 4, an unauthorized signature is ineffective except as the signature of the unauthorized signer in favor of a person who in good faith pays the instrument or takes it for value. An unauthorized signature may be ratified for all purposes of this Article.

(b) If the signature of more than one person is required to constitute the authorized signature of an organization, the signature of the organization is unauthorized if one of the required signatures is lacking.

(c) The civil or criminal liability of a person who makes an unauthorized signature is not affected by any provision of this Article which makes the unauthorized signature effective for the purposes of this Article.

§ 3–404. Impostors; Fictitious Payees

(a) If an imposter, by use of the mails or otherwise, induces the issuer of an instrument to issue the instrument to the imposter, or to a person acting in concert with the imposter, by impersonating the payee of the instrument or a person authorized to act for the payee, an indorsement of the instrument by any person in the name of the payee is effective as the indorsement of the payee in favor of a person who, in good faith, pays the instrument or takes it for value or for collection.

(b) If (i) a person whose intent determines to whom an instrument is payable (Section 3–110(a) or (b)) does not intend the person identified as payee to have any interest in the instrument, or (ii) the person identified as payee of an instrument is a fictitious person, the following rules apply until the instrument is negotiated by special indorsement:

(1) Any person in possession of the instrument is its holder.

(2) An indorsement by any person in the name of the payee stated in the instrument is effective as the indorsement of the payee in favor of a person who, in good faith, pays the instrument or takes it for value or for collection.

(c) Under subsection (a) or (b), an indorsement is made in the name of a payee if (i) it is made in a name substantially similar to that of the payee or (ii) the instrument, whether or not indorsed, is deposited in a depositary bank to an account in a name substantially similar to that of the payee.

(d) With respect to an instrument to which subsection (a) or (b) applies, if a person paying the instrument or taking it for value or for collection fails to exercise ordinary care in paying or taking the instrument and that failure substantially contributes to loss resulting from payment of the instrument, the person bearing the loss may recover from the person failing to exercise ordinary care to the extent the failure to exercise ordinary care contributed to the loss.

§ 3–405. Employer's Responsibility for Fraudulent Indorsement by Employee

(a) In this section:

(1) "Employee" includes an independent contractor and employee of an independent contractor retained by the employer.

(2) "Fraudulent indorsement" means (i) in the case of an instrument payable to the employer, a forged indorsement purporting to be that of the employer, or (ii) in the case of an instrument with respect to which the employer is the issuer, a forged indorsement purporting to be that of the person identified as payee.

(3) "Responsibility" with respect to instruments means authority (i) to sign or indorse instruments on behalf of the employer, (ii) to process instruments received by the employer for bookkeeping purposes, for deposit to an account, or for other disposition, (iii) to prepare or process instruments for issue in the name of the employer, (iv) to supply information determining the names or addresses of payees of instruments to be issued in the name of the employer, (v) to control the disposition of instruments to be issued in the name of the employer, or (vi) to act otherwise with respect to instruments in a responsible capacity. "Responsibility" does not include authority that merely allows an employee to have access to instruments or blank or incomplete instrument forms that are being stored or transported or are part of incoming or outgoing mail, or similar access.

(b) For the purpose of determining the rights and liabilities of a person who, in good faith, pays an instrument or takes it for value or for collection, if an employer entrusted an employee with responsibility with respect to the instrument and the employee or a person acting in concert with the employee makes a fraudulent indorsement of the instrument, the indorsement is effective as the indorsement of the person to whom the instrument is payable if it is made in the name of that person. If the person paying the instrument or taking it for value or for collection fails to exercise ordinary care in paying or taking the instrument and that failure substantially contributes to loss resulting from the fraud, the person bearing the loss may recover from the person failing to exercise ordinary care to the extent the failure to exercise ordinary care contributed to the loss.

(c) Under subsection (b), an indorsement is made in the name of the person to whom an instrument is payable if (i) it is made in a name substantially similar to the name of that person or (ii) the instrument, whether or not indorsed, is deposited in a depositary bank to an account in a name substantially similar to the name of that person.

§ 3–406. Negligence Contributing to Forged Signature or Alteration of Instrument

(a) A person whose failure to exercise ordinary care substantially contributes to an alteration of an instrument or to the making of a forged signature on an instrument is precluded from asserting the alteration or the forgery against a person who, in good faith, pays the instrument or takes it for value or for collection.

(b) Under subsection (a), if the person asserting the preclusion fails to exercise ordinary care in paying or taking the instrument and that failure substantially contributes to loss, the loss is allocated between the person precluded and the person asserting the preclusion according to the extent to which the failure of each to exercise ordinary care contributed to the loss.

(c) Under subsection (a), the burden of proving failure to exercise ordinary care is on the person asserting the preclusion. Under subsection (b), the burden of proving failure to exercise ordinary care is on the person precluded.

§ 3–407. Alteration

(a) "Alteration" means (i) an unauthorized change in an instrument that purports to modify in any respect the obligation of a party, or (ii) an unauthorized addition of words or numbers or other change to an incomplete instrument relating to the obligation of a party.

(b) Except as provided in subsection (c), an alteration fraudulently made discharges a party whose obligation is affected by the alteration unless that party assents or is precluded from asserting the alteration. No other alteration discharges a party, and the instrument may be enforced according to its original terms.

(c) A payor bank or drawee paying a fraudulently altered instrument or a person taking it for value, in good faith and without notice of the alteration, may enforce rights with respect to the instrument (i) according to its original terms, or (ii) in the case of an incomplete instrument altered by unauthorized completion, according to its terms as completed.

§ 3–408. Drawee Not Liable on Unaccepted Draft

A check or other draft does not of itself operate as an assignment of funds in the hands of the drawee available for its payment, and the drawee is not liable on the instrument until the drawee accepts it.

§ 3–409. Acceptance of Draft; Certified Check

(a) "Acceptance" means the drawee's signed agreement to pay a draft as presented. It must be written on the draft and may consist of the drawee's signature alone. Acceptance may be made at any time and becomes effective when notification pursuant to instructions is given or the accepted draft is delivered for the purpose of giving rights on the acceptance to any person.

(b) A draft may be accepted although it has not been signed by the drawer, is otherwise incomplete, is overdue, or has been dishonored.

(c) If a draft is payable at a fixed period after sight and the acceptor fails to date the acceptance, the holder may complete the acceptance by supplying a date in good faith.

(d) "Certified check" means a check accepted by the bank on which it is drawn. Acceptance may be made as stated in subsection (a) or by a writing on the check which indicates that the check is certified. The drawee of a check has no obligation to certify the check, and refusal to certify is not dishonor of the check.

§ 3–410. Acceptance Varying Draft

(a) If the terms of a drawee's acceptance vary from the terms of the draft as presented, the holder may refuse the acceptance and treat the draft as dishonored. In that case, the drawee may cancel the acceptance.

(b) The terms of a draft are not varied by an acceptance to pay at a particular bank or place in the United States, unless the acceptance states that the draft is to be paid only at that bank or place.

(c) If the holder assents to an acceptance varying the terms of a draft, the obligation of each drawer and indorser that does not expressly assent to the acceptance is discharged.

§ 3–411. Refusal to Pay Cashier's Checks, Teller's Checks, and Certified Checks

(a) In this section, "obligated bank" means the acceptor of a certified check or the issuer of a cashier's check or teller's check bought from the issuer.

(b) If the obligated bank wrongfully (i) refuses to pay a cashier's check or certified check, (ii) stops payment of a teller's check, or (iii) refuses to pay a dishonored teller's check, the person asserting the right to enforce the check is entitled to compensation for expenses and loss of interest resulting from the nonpayment and may recover consequential damages if the obligated bank refuses to pay after receiving notice of particular circumstances giving rise to the damages.

(c) Expenses or consequential damages under subsection (b) are not recoverable if the refusal of the obligated bank to pay occurs because (i) the bank suspends payments, (ii) the obligated bank asserts a claim or defense of the bank that it has reasonable grounds to believe is available against the person entitled to enforce the instrument, (iii) the obligated bank has a reasonable doubt whether the person demanding payment is the person entitled to enforce the instrument, or (iv) payment is prohibited by law.

§ 3–412. Obligation of Issuer of Note or Cashier's Check

The issuer of a note or cashier's check or other draft drawn on the drawer is obliged to pay the instrument (i) according to its terms at the time it was issued or, if not issued, at the time it first came into possession of a holder, or (ii) if the issuer signed an incomplete instrument according to its terms when completed, to the extent stated in Sections 3–115 and 3–407. The obligation is owed to a person entitled to enforce the instrument or to an indorser who paid the instrument under Section 3–415.

§ 3–413. Obligation of Acceptor

(a) The acceptor of a draft is obliged to pay the draft (i) according to its terms at the time it was accepted, even though the acceptance states that the draft is payable "as originally drawn" or equivalent terms, (ii) if the acceptance varies the terms of the draft, according to the terms of the draft as varied, or (iii) if the acceptance is of a draft that is an incomplete instrument, according to its terms when completed, to the extent stated in Sections 3–115 and 3–407. The obligation is owed to a person entitled to enforce the draft or to the drawer or an indorser who paid the draft under Section 3–414 or 3–415.

(b) If the certification of a check or other acceptance of a draft states the amount certified or accepted, the obligation of the acceptor is that amount. If (i) the certification or acceptance does not state an amount, (ii) the amount of the instrument is subsequently raised, and (iii) the instrument is then negotiated to a holder in due course, the obligation of the acceptor is the amount of the instrument at the time it was taken by the holder in due course.

§ 3–414. Obligation of Drawer

(a) This section does not apply to cashier's checks or other drafts drawn on the drawer.

(b) If an unaccepted draft is dishonored, the drawer is obliged to pay the draft (i) according to its terms at the time it was issued or, if not issued, at the time it first came into possession of a holder, or (ii) if the drawer signed an incomplete instrument, according to its terms when completed, to the extent stated in Sections 3–115 and 3–407. The obligation is owed to a person entitled to enforce the draft or to an indorser who paid the draft under Section 3–415.

(c) If a draft is accepted by a bank, the drawer is discharged, regardless of when or by whom acceptance was obtained.

(d) If a draft is accepted and the acceptor is not a bank, the obligation of the drawer to pay the draft if the draft is dishonored by the acceptor is the same as the obligation of an indorser under Section 3–415(a) and (c).

(e) If a draft states that it is drawn "without recourse" or otherwise disclaims liability of the drawer to pay the draft, the drawer is not liable under subsection (b) to pay the draft if the draft is not a check. A disclaimer of the liability stated in subsection (b) is not effective if the draft is a check.

(f) If (i) a check is not presented for payment or given to a depositary bank for collection within 30 days after its date, (ii) the drawee suspends payments after expiration of the 30-day period without paying the check, and (iii) because of the suspension of payments, the drawer is deprived of funds maintained with the drawee to cover payment of the check, the drawer to the extent deprived of funds may discharge its obligation to pay the check by assigning to the person entitled to enforce the check the rights of the drawer against the drawee with respect to the funds.

§ 3–415. Obligation of Indorser

(a) Subject to subsections (b), (c), and (d) and to Section 3–419(d), if an instrument is dishonored, an indorser is obliged to pay the amount due on the instrument (i) according to the terms of the instrument at the time it was indorsed, or (ii) if the indorser indorsed an incomplete instrument, according to its terms when completed, to the extent stated in Section 3–115 and 3–407. The obligation of the indorser is owed to a person entitled to enforce the instrument or to a subsequent indorser who paid the instrument under this section.

(b) If an indorsement states that it is made "without recourse" or otherwise disclaims liability of the indorser, the indorser is not liable under subsection (a) to pay the instrument.

(c) If notice of dishonor of an instrument is required by Section 3–503 and notice of dishonor complying with that section is not given to an indorser, the liability of the indorser under subsection (a) is discharged.

(d) If a draft is accepted by a bank after an indorsement is made, the liability of the indorser under subsection (a) is discharged.

(e) If an indorser of a check is liable under subsection (a) and the check is not presented for payment, or given to a depositary bank for collection, within 30 days after the day the indorsement was made, the liability of the indorser under subsection (a) is discharged.

§ 3–416. Transfer Warranties

(a) A person who transfers an instrument for consideration warrants to the transferee and, if the transfer is by indorsement, to any subsequent transferee that:

(1) the warrantor is a person entitled to enforce the instrument;

(2) all signatures on the instrument are authentic and authorized;

(3) the instrument has not been altered;

(4) the instrument is not subject to a defense or claim in recoupment of any party which can be asserted against the warrantor; and

(5) the warrantor has no knowledge of any insolvency proceeding commenced with respect to the maker or acceptor or, in the case of an unaccepted draft, the drawer.

(b) A person to whom the warranties under subsection (a) are made and who took the instrument in good faith may recover from the warrantor as damages for breach of warranty an amount equal to the loss suffered as a result of the breach, but not more than the amount of the instrument plus expenses and loss of interest incurred as a result of the breach.

(c) The warranties stated in subsection (a) cannot be disclaimed with respect to checks. Unless notice of a claim for breach of warranty is given to the warrantor within 30 days after the claimant has reason to know of the breach and the identity of the warrantor, the liability of the warrantor under subsection (b) is discharged to the extent of any loss caused by the delay in giving notice of the claim.

(d) A [cause of action] for breach of warranty under this section accrues when the claimant has reason to know of the breach.

§ 3–417. Presentment Warranties

(a) If an unaccepted draft is presented to the drawee for payment or acceptance and the drawee pays or accepts the draft, (i) the person obtaining payment or acceptance at the time of presentment, and (ii) a previous transferor of the draft, at the time of transfer, warrant to the drawee making payment or accepting the draft in good faith that:

(1) the warrantor is, or was, at the time the warrantor transferred the draft, a person entitled to enforce the draft or authorized to obtain payment or acceptance of the draft on behalf of a person entitled to enforce the draft;

(2) the draft has not been altered; and

(3) the warrantor has no knowledge that the signature of the drawer of the draft is unauthorized.

(b) A drawee making payment may recover from any warrantor damages for breach of warranty equal to the amount paid by the drawee less the amount the drawee received or is entitled to receive from the drawer because of the payment. In addition, the drawee is entitled to compensation for expenses and loss of interest resulting from the breach. The right of the drawee to recover damages under this subsection is not affected by any failure of the drawee to exercise ordinary care in making payment. If the drawee accepts the draft, breach of warranty is a defense to the obligation of the acceptor. If the acceptor makes payment with respect to the draft, the acceptor is entitled to recover from any warrantor for breach of warranty the amounts stated in this subsection.

(c) If a drawee asserts a claim for breach of warranty under subsection (a) based on an unauthorized indorsement of the draft or an alteration of the draft, the warrantor may defend by proving that the indorsement is effective under Section 3–404 or 3–405 or the drawer is precluded under Section 3–406 or 4–406 from asserting against the drawee the unauthorized indorsement or alteration.

(d) If (i) a dishonored draft is presented for payment to the drawer or an indorser or (ii) any other instrument is presented for payment to a party obliged to pay the instrument, and (iii) payment is received, the following rules apply:

(1) The person obtaining payment and a prior transferor of the instrument warrant to the person making payment in good faith that the warrantor is, or was, at the time the warrantor transferred the instrument, a person entitled to enforce the instrument or authorized to obtain payment on behalf of a person entitled to enforce the instrument.

(2) The person making payment may recover from any warrantor for breach of warranty an amount equal to the amount paid plus expenses and loss of interest resulting from the breach.

(e) The warranties stated in subsections (a) and (d) cannot be disclaimed with respect to checks. Unless notice of a claim for breach of warranty is given to the warrantor within 30 days after the claimant has reason to know of the breach and the identity of the warrantor, the liability of the warrantor under subsection (b) or (d) is discharged to the extent of any loss caused by the delay in giving notice of the claim.

(f) A [cause of action] for breach of warranty under this section accrues when the claimant has reason to know of the breach.

§ 3–418. Payment or Acceptance by Mistake

(a) Except as provided in subsection (c), if the drawee of a draft pays or accepts the draft and the drawee acted on the mistaken belief that (i) payment of the draft had not been stopped pursuant to Section 4–403 or (ii) the signature of the drawer of the draft was authorized, the drawee may recover the amount of the draft from the person to whom or for whose benefit payment was made or, in the case of acceptance, may revoke the acceptance. Rights of the drawee under this subsection are not affected by failure of the drawee to exercise ordinary care in paying or accepting the draft.

(b) Except as provided in subsection (c), if an instrument has been paid or accepted by mistake and the case is not covered by subsection (a), the person paying or accepting may, to the extent permitted by the law governing mistake and restitution, (i) recover the payment from the person to whom or for whose benefit payment was made or (ii) in the case of acceptance, may revoke the acceptance.

(c) The remedies provided by subsection (a) or (b) may not be asserted against a person who took the instrument in good faith and for value or who in good faith changed position in reliance on the payment or acceptance. This subsection does not limit remedies provided by Section 3–417 and 4–407.

(d) Notwithstanding Section 4–215, if an instrument is paid or accepted by mistake and the payor or acceptor recovers payment or revokes acceptance under subsection (a) or (b), the instrument is deemed not to have been paid or accepted and is treated as dishonored, and the person from whom payment is recovered has rights as a person entitled to enforce the dishonored instrument.

§ 3–419. Instruments Signed for Accommodation

(a) If an instrument is issued for value given for the benefit of a party to the instrument ("accommodated party") and another party to the instrument ("accommodation party") signs the instrument for the purpose of incurring liability on the instrument without being a direct beneficiary of the value given for the instrument, the instrument is signed by the accommodation party "for accommodation."

(b) An accommodation party may sign the instrument as maker, drawer, acceptor, or indorser and, subject to subsection (d), is obliged to pay the instrument in the capacity in which the accommodation party signs. The obligation of an accommodation party may be enforced notwithstanding any statute of frauds and whether or not the accommodation party receives consideration for the accommodation.

(c) A person signing an instrument is presumed to be an accommodation party and there is notice that the instrument is signed for accommodation if the signature is an anomalous indorsement or is accompanied by words indicating that the signer is acting as surety or guarantor with respect to the obligation of another party to the instrument. Except as provided in Section 3–605, the obligation of an accommodation party to pay the instrument is not affected by the fact that the person enforcing the obligation had notice when the instrument was taken by that person that the accommodation party signed the instrument for accommodation.

(d) If the signature of a party to an instrument is accompanied by words indicating unambiguously that the party is guaranteeing collection rather than payment of the obligation of another party to the instrument, the signer is obliged to pay the amount due on the instrument to a person entitled to enforce the instrument only if (i) execution of judgment against the other party has been returned unsatisfied, (ii) the other party is insolvent or in an insolvency proceeding, (iii) the other party cannot be served with process, or (iv) it is otherwise apparent that payment cannot be obtained from the other party.

(e) An accommodation party who pays the instrument is entitled to reimbursement from the accommodated party and is entitled to enforce the instrument against the accommodated party. An accommodated party who pays the instrument has no right of recourse against, and is not entitled to contribution from, an accommodation party.

§ 3–420. Conversion of Instrument

(a) The law applicable to conversion of personal property applies to instruments. An instrument is also converted if it is taken by transfer, other than a negotiation, from a person not entitled to enforce the instrument or a bank makes or obtains payment with respect to the instrument for a person not entitled to enforce the instrument or receive payment. An action for conversion of an instrument may not be brought by (i) the issuer or acceptor of the instrument or (ii) a payee or indorsee who did not receive delivery of the instrument either directly or through delivery to an agent or a co-payee.

(b) In an action under subsection (a), the measure of liability is presumed to be the amount payable on the instrument, but recovery may not exceed the amount of the plaintiff's interest in the instrument.

(c) A representative, other than a depositary bank, who has in good faith dealt with an instrument or its proceeds on behalf of one who was not the person entitled to enforce the instrument is not liable in conversion to that person beyond the amount of any proceeds that it has not paid out.

Part 5 Dishonor

§ 3–501. Presentment

(a) "Presentment" means a demand made by or on behalf of a person entitled to enforce an instrument (i) to pay the instrument made to the drawee or a party obliged to pay the instrument or, in the case of a note or accepted draft payable at a bank, to the bank, or (ii) to accept a draft made to the drawee.

(b) The following rules are subject to Article 4, agreement of the parties, and clearing-house rules and the like:

(1) Presentment may be made at the place of payment of the instrument and must be made at the place of payment if the instrument is payable at a bank in the United States; may be made by any commercially reasonable means, including an oral, written, or electronic communication; is effective when the demand for payment or acceptance is received by

the person to whom presentment is made; and is effective if made to any one of two or more makers, acceptors, drawees, or other payors.

(2) Upon demand of the person to whom presentment is made, the person making presentment must (i) exhibit the instrument, (ii) give reasonable identification and, if presentment is made on behalf of another person, reasonable evidence of authority to do so, and (. . .) sign a receipt on the instrument for any payment made or surrender the instrument if full payment is made.

(3) Without dishonoring the instrument, the party to whom presentment is made may (i) return the instrument for lack of a necessary indorsement, or (ii) refuse payment or acceptance for failure of the presentment to comply with the terms of the instrument, an agreement of the parties, or other applicable law or rule.

(4) The party to whom presentment is made may treat presentment as occurring on the next business day after the day of presentment if the party to whom presentment is made has established a cut-off hour not earlier than 2 P.M. for the receipt and processing of instruments presented for payment or acceptance and presentment is made after the cut-off hour.

§ 3–502. Dishonor

(a) Dishonor of a note is governed by the following rules:

(1) If the note is payable on demand, the note is dishonored if presentment is duly made to the maker and the note is not paid on the day of presentment.

(2) If the note is not payable on demand and is payable at or through a bank or the terms of the note require presentment, the note is dishonored if presentment is duly made and the note is not paid on the day it becomes payable or the day of presentment, whichever is later.

(3) If the note is not payable on demand and paragraph (2) does not apply, the note is dishonored if it is not paid on the day it becomes payable.

(b) Dishonor of an unaccepted draft other than a documentary draft is governed by the following rules:

(1) If a check is duly presented for payment to the payor bank otherwise than for immediate payment over the counter, the check is dishonored if the payor bank makes timely return of the check or sends timely notice of dishonor or nonpayment under Section 4–301 or 4–302, or becomes accountable for the amount of the check under Section 4–302.

(2) If a draft is payable on demand and paragraph (1) does not apply, the draft is dishonored if present-

ment for payment is duly made to the drawee and the draft is not paid on the day of presentment.

(3) If a draft is payable on a date stated in the draft, the draft is dishonored if (i) presentment for payment is duly made to the drawee and payment is not made on the day the draft becomes payable or the day of presentment, whichever is later, or (ii) presentment for acceptance is duly made before the day the draft becomes payable and the draft is not accepted on the day of presentment.

(4) If a draft is payable on elapse of a period of time after sight or acceptance, the draft is dishonored if presentment for acceptance is duly made and the draft is not accepted on the day of presentment.

(c) Dishonor of an unaccepted documentary draft occurs according to the rules stated in subsection (b)(2), (3), and (4), except that payment or acceptance may be delayed without dishonor until no later than the close of the third business day of the drawee following the day on which payment or acceptance is required by those paragraphs.

(d) Dishonor of an accepted draft is governed by the following rules:

(1) If the draft is payable on demand, the draft is dishonored if presentment for payment is duly made to the acceptor and the draft is not paid on the day of presentment.

(2) If the draft is not payable on demand, the draft is dishonored if presentment for payment is duly made to the acceptor and payment is not made on the day it becomes payable or the day of presentment, whichever is later.

(e) In any case in which presentment is otherwise required for dishonor under this section and presentment is excused under Section 3–504, dishonor occurs without presentment if the instrument is not duly accepted or paid.

(f) If a draft is dishonored because timely acceptance of the draft was not made and the person entitled to demand acceptance consents to a late acceptance, from the time of acceptance the draft is treated as never having been dishonored.

§ 3–503. Notice of Dishonor

(a) The obligation of an indorser stated in Section 3–415(a) and the obligation of a drawer stated in Section 3–414(d) may not be enforced unless (i) the indorser or drawer is given notice of dishonor of the instrument complying with this section or (ii) notice of dishonor is excused under Section 3–504(b).

(b) Notice of dishonor may be given by any person; may be given by any commercially reasonable means, including an oral, written, or electronic communication; and is sufficient if it reasonably identifies the instrument and indicates that the instrument has been dishonored or has not been paid or accepted. Return of an instrument given to a bank for collection is sufficient notice of dishonor.

(c) Subject to Section 3–504(c), with respect to an instrument taken for collection by a collecting bank, notice of dishonor must be given (i) by the bank before midnight of the next banking day following the banking day on which the bank receives notice of dishonor of the instrument, or (ii) by any other person within 30 days following the day on which the person receives notice of dishonor. With respect to any other instrument, notice of dishonor must be given within 30 days following the day on which dishonor occurs.

§ 3–504. Excused Presentment and Notice of Dishonor

(a) Presentment for payment or acceptance of an instrument is excused if (i) the person entitled to present the instrument cannot with reasonable diligence make presentment, (ii) the maker or acceptor has repudiated an obligation to pay the instrument or is dead or in insolvency proceedings, (iii) by the terms of the instrument presentment is not necessary to enforce the obligation of indorsers or the drawer, (iv) the drawer or indorser whose obligation is being enforced has waived presentment or otherwise has no reason to expect or right to require that the instrument be paid or accepted, or (v) the drawer instructed the drawee not to pay or accept the draft or the drawee was not obligated to the drawer to pay the draft.

(b) Notice of dishonor is excused if (i) by the terms of the instrument notice of dishonor is not necessary to enforce the obligation of a party to pay the instrument, or (ii) the party whose obligation is being enforced waived notice of dishonor. A waiver of presentment is also a waiver of notice of dishonor.

(c) Delay in giving notice of dishonor is excused if the delay was caused by circumstances beyond the control of the person giving the notice and the person giving the notice exercised reasonable diligence after the cause of the delay ceased to operate.

§ 3–505. Evidence of Dishonor

(a) The following are admissible as evidence and create a presumption of dishonor and of any notice of dishonor stated:

(1) a document regular in form as provided in subsection (b) which purports to be a protest;

(2) a purported stamp or writing of the drawee, payor bank, or presenting bank on or accompanying the instrument stating that acceptance or payment has been refused unless reasons for the refusal are stated and the reasons are not consistent with dishonor;

(3) a book or record of the drawee, payor bank, or collecting bank, kept in the usual course of business which shows dishonor, even if there is no evidence of who made the entry.

(b) A protest is a certificate of dishonor made by a United States consul or vice consul, or a notary public or other person authorized to administer oaths by the law of the place where dishonor occurs. It may be made upon information satisfactory to that person. The protest must identify the instrument and certify either that presentment has been made or, if not made, the reason why it was not made, and that the instrument has been dishonored by nonacceptance or nonpayment. The protest may also certify that notice of dishonor has been given to some or all parties.

Part 6 Discharge and Payment

§ 3–601. Discharge and Effect of Discharge

(a) The obligation of a party to pay the instrument is discharged as stated in this Article or by an act or agreement with the party which would discharge an obligation to pay money under a simple contract.

(b) Discharge of the obligation of a party is not effective against a person acquiring rights of a holder in due course of the instrument without notice of the discharge.

§ 3–602. Payment

(a) Subject to subsection (b), an instrument is paid to the extent payment is made (i) by or on behalf of a party obliged to pay the instrument, and (ii) to a person entitled to enforce the instrument. To the extent of the payment, the obligation of the party obliged to pay the instrument is discharged even though payment is made with knowledge of a claim to the instrument under Section 3–306 by another person.

(b) The obligation of a party to pay the instrument is not discharged under subsection (a) if:

(1) a claim to the instrument under Section 3–306 is enforceable against the party receiving payment and (i) payment is made with knowledge by the payor that payment is prohibited by injunction or similar process of a court of competent jurisdiction, or (ii) in the case of an instrument other than a cashier's check, teller's check, or certified check, the party making payment accepted, from the person having a claim to the instrument, indemnity against loss resulting from refusal to pay the person entitled to enforce the instrument; or

(2) the person making payment knows that the instrument is a stolen instrument and pays a person it knows is in wrongful possession of the instrument.

§ 3–603. Tender of Payment

(a) If tender of payment of an obligation to pay an instrument is made to a person entitled to enforce the instrument, the effect of tender is governed by principles of law applicable to tender of payment under a simple contract.

(b) If tender of payment of an obligation to pay an instrument is made to a person entitled to enforce the instrument and the tender is refused, there is discharge, to the extent of the amount of the tender, of the obligation of an indorser or accommodation party having a right of recourse with respect to the obligation to which the tender relates.

(c) If tender of payment of an amount due on an instrument is made to a person entitled to enforce the instrument, the obligation of the obligor to pay interest after the due date on the amount tendered is discharged. If presentment is required with respect to an instrument and the obligor is able and ready to pay on the due date at every place of payment stated in the instrument, the obligor is deemed to have made tender of payment on the due date to the person entitled to enforce the instrument.

§ 3–604. Discharge by Cancellation or Renunciation

(a) A person entitled to enforce an instrument, with or without consideration, may discharge the obligation of a party to pay the instrument (i) by an intentional voluntary act, such as surrender of the instrument to the party, destruction, mutilation, or cancellation of the instrument, cancellation or striking out of the party's signature, or the addition of words to the instrument indicating discharge, or (ii) by agreeing not to sue or otherwise renouncing rights against the party by a signed writing.

(b) Cancellation or striking out of an indorsement pursuant to subsection (a) does not affect the status and rights of a party derived from the indorsement.

§ 3–605. Discharge of Indorsers and Accommodation Parties

(a) In this section, the term "indorser" includes a drawer having the obligation described in Section 3–414(d).

(b) Discharge, under Section 3–604, of the obligation of a party to pay an instrument does not discharge the obligation of an indorser or accommodation party having a right of recourse against the discharged party.

(c) If a person entitled to enforce an instrument agrees, with or without consideration, to an extension of the due date of the obligation of a party to pay the instrument, the extension discharges an indorser or accommodation party having a right of recourse against the party whose obligation is extended to the extent the indorser or accommodation party proves that the extension caused loss to the indorser or accommodation party with respect to the right of recourse.

(d) If a person entitled to enforce an instrument agrees, with or without consideration, to a material modification of the obligation of a party other than an extension of the due date, the modification discharges the obligation of an indorser or accommodation party having a right of recourse against the person whose obligation is modified to the extent the modification causes loss to the indorser or accommodation party with respect to the right of recourse. The loss suffered by the indorser or accommodation party as a result of the modification is equal to the amount of the right of recourse unless the person enforcing the instrument proves that no loss was caused by the modification or that the loss caused by the modification was an amount less than the amount of the right of recourse.

(e) If the obligation of a party to pay an instrument is secured by an interest in collateral and a person entitled to enforce the instrument impairs the value of the interest in collateral, the obligation of an indorser or accommodation party having a right of recourse against the obligor is discharged to the extent of the impairment. The value of an interest in collateral is impaired to the extent (i) the value of the interest is reduced to an amount less than the amount of the right of recourse of the party asserting discharge, or (ii) the reduction in value of the interest causes an increase in the amount by which the amount of the right of recourse exceeds the value of the interest. The burden of proving impairment is on the party asserting discharge.

(f) If the obligation of a party is secured by an interest in collateral not provided by an accommodation party and a person entitled to enforce the instrument impairs the value of the interest in collateral, the obligation of any party who is jointly and severally liable with respect to the secured obligation is discharged to the extent the impairment causes the party asserting discharge to pay more than that party would have been obliged to pay, taking into account rights of contribution, if impairment had not occurred. If the party asserting discharge is an accommodation party not entitled to discharge under subsection (e), the party is deemed to have a right to contribution based on joint and several liability rather than a right to reimbursement. The burden of proving impairment is on the party asserting discharge.

(g) Under subsection (e) or (f), impairing value of an interest in collateral includes (i) failure to obtain or maintain perfection or recordation of the interest in collateral, (ii) release of collateral without substitution of collateral of equal value, (iii) failure to perform a duty to preserve the value of collateral owed, under Article 9 or other law, to a debtor or surety or other person secondarily liable, or (iv) failure to comply with applicable law in disposing of collateral.

(h) An accommodation party is not discharged under subsection (c), (d), or (e) unless the person entitled to enforce the instrument knows of the accommodation or has notice under Section 3–419(c) that the instrument was signed for accommodation.

(i) A party is not discharged under this section if (i) the party asserting discharge consents to the event or conduct that is the basis of the discharge, or (ii) the instrument or a separate agreement of the party provides for waiver of discharge under this section either specifically or by general language indicating that parties waive defenses based on suretyship or impairment of collateral.

ARTICLE 4 BANK DEPOSITS AND COLLECTIONS

Part I General Provisions and Definitions

§ 4–101. Short Title

This Article may be cited as Uniform Commercial Code—Bank Deposits and Collections.
As amended in 1990.

§ 4–102. Applicability

(a) To the extent that items within this Article are also within Articles 3 and 8, they are subject to those Articles. If there is conflict, this Article governs Article 3, but Article 8 governs this Article.

(b) The liability of a bank for action or non-action with respect to an item handled by it for purposes of present-ment, payment, or collection is governed by the law of the place where the bank is located. In the case of action or non-action by or at a branch or separate office of a bank, its liability is governed by the law of the place where the branch or separate office is located.
As amended in 1990.

§ 4–103. Variation by Agreement; Measure of Damages; Action Constituting Ordinary Care

(a) The effect of the provisions of this Article may be varied by agreement, but the parties to the agreement cannot disclaim a bank's responsibility for its lack of good faith or failure to exercise ordinary care or limit the measure of damages for the lack or failure. However, the parties may determine by agreement the standards by which the bank's responsibility is to be measured if those standards are not manifestly unreasonable.

(b) Federal Reserve regulations and operating circu-lars, clearing-house rules, and the like have the effect of agreements under subsection (a), whether or not specifi-cally assented to by all parties interested in items handled.

(c) Action or non-action approved by this Article or pursuant to Federal Reserve regulations or operating circulars is the exercise of ordinary care and, in the absence of special instructions, action or non-action con-sistent with clearing-house rules and the like or with a general banking usage not disapproved by this Article, is prima facie the exercise of ordinary care.

(d) The specification or approval of certain procedures by this Article is not disapproval of other procedures that may be reasonable under the circumstances.

(e) The measure of damages for failure to exercise ordinary care in handling an item is the amount of the item reduced by an amount that could not have been realized by the exercise of ordinary care. If there is also bad faith it includes any other damages the party suffered as a proximate consequence.
As amended in 1990.

§ 4–104. Definitions and Index of Definitions

(a) In this Article, unless the context otherwise re-quires:

(1) "Account" means any deposit or credit account with a bank, including a demand, time, savings, passbook, share draft, or like account, other than an account evidenced by a certificate of deposit;

(2) "Afternoon" means the period of day between noon and midnight;

(3) "Banking day" means the part of a day on which a bank is open to the public for carrying on substantially all of its banking functions;

(4) "Clearing house" means an association of banks or other payors regularly clearing items;

(5) "Customer" means a person having an account with a bank or for whom a bank has agreed to collect items, including a bank that maintains an account at another bank;

(6) "Documentary draft" means a draft to be pre-sented for acceptance or payment if specified documents, certificated securities (Section 8–102) or instructions for uncertificated securi-ties (Section 8–308), or other certificates, state-ments, or the like are to be received by the drawee or other payor before acceptance or pay-ment of the draft;

(7) "Draft" means a draft as defined in Section 3–104 or an item, other than an instrument, that is an order;

(8) "Drawee" means a person ordered in a draft to make payment;

(9) "Item" means an instrument or a promise or order to pay money handled by a bank for collection or payment. The term does not include a payment order governed by Article 4A or a credit or debit card slip;

(10) "Midnight deadline" with respect to a bank is midnight on its next banking day following the banking day on which it receives the relevant item or notice or from which the time for taking action commences to run, whichever is later;

(11) "Settle" means to pay in cash, by clearing-house settlement, in a charge or credit or by remittance, or otherwise as agreed. A settlement may be either provisional or final;

(12) "Suspends payments" with respect to a bank means that it has been closed by order of the supervisory authorities, that a public officer has been appointed to take it over, or that it ceases or

refuses to make payments in the ordinary course of business.

(b) Other definitions applying to this Article and the sections in which they appear are:

"Agreement for electronic presentment" Section 4–110.

"Bank"	Section 4–105.
"Collecting bank"	Section 4–105.
"Depositary bank"	Section 4–105.
"Intermediary bank"	Section 4–105.
"Payor bank"	Section 4–105.
"Presenting bank"	Section 4–105.
"Presentment notice"	Section 4–110.

§ 4–105. "Bank"; "Depositary Bank"; "Payor Bank"; "Intermediary Bank"; "Collecting Bank"; "Presenting Bank"

In this Article:

(1) "Bank" means a person engaged in the business of banking, including a savings bank, savings and loan association, credit union, or trust company;

(2) "Depositary bank" means the first bank to take an item even though it is also the payor bank, unless the item is presented for immediate payment over the counter;

(3) "Payor bank" means a bank that is the drawee of a draft;

(4) "Intermediary bank" means a bank to which an item is transferred in course of collection except the depositary or payor bank;

(5) "Collecting bank" means a bank handling an item for collection except the payor bank;

(6) "Presenting bank" means a bank presenting an item except a payor bank.

As amended in 1990.

§ 4–106. Payable Through or Payable at Bank: Collecting Bank

(a) If an item states that it is "payable through" a bank identified in the item, (i) the item designates the bank as a collecting bank and does not by itself authorize the bank to pay the item, and (ii) the item may be presented for payment only by or through the bank.

Alternative A

(b) If an item states that it is "payable at" a bank identified in the item, the item is equivalent to a draft drawn on the bank.

Alternative B

(b) If an item states that it is "payable at" a bank identified in the item, (i) the item designates the bank as a collecting bank and does not by itself authorize the bank to pay the item, and (ii) the item may be presented for payment only by or through the bank.

(c) If a draft means a nonbank drawee and it is unclear whether a bank named in the draft is a co-drawee or a collecting bank, the bank is a collecting bank.

As added in 1990.

§ 4–107. Separate Office of Bank

A branch or separate office of a bank is a separate bank for the purpose of computing the time within which and determining the place at or to which action may be taken or notices or orders shall be given under this Article and under Article 3.

As amended in 1962 and 1990.

§ 4–108. Time of Receipt of Items

(a) For the purpose of allowing time to process items, prove balances, and make the necessary entries on its books to determine its position for the day, a bank may fix an afternoon hour of 2 P.M. or later as a cutoff hour for the handling of money and items and the making of entries on its books.

(b) An item or deposit of money received on any day after a cutoff hour so fixed or after the close of the banking day may be treated as being received at the opening of the next banking day.

As amended in 1990.

§ 4–109. Delays

(a) Unless otherwise instructed, a collecting bank in a good faith effort to secure payment of a specific item drawn on a payor other than a bank, and with or without the approval of any person involved, may waive, modify, or extend time limits imposed or permitted by this [Act] for a period not exceeding two additional banking days without discharge of drawers or indorsers or liability to its transferor or a prior party.

(b) Delay by a collecting bank or payor bank beyond time limits prescribed or permitted by this [Act] or by instructions is excused if (i) the delay is caused by interruption of communication or computer facilities, suspension of payments by another bank, war, emergency conditions, failure of equipment, or other circumstances beyond the control of the bank, and (ii) the bank exercises such diligence as the circumstances require.

As amended in 1990.

§ 4–110. Electronic Presentment

(a) "Agreement for electronic presentment" means an agreement, clearing-house rule, or Federal Reserve regulation or operating circular, providing that presentment of an item may be made by transmission of an image of an item or information describing the item ("presentment notice") rather than delivery of the item itself. The agreement may provide for procedures governing retention, presentment, payment, dishonor, and other matters concerning items subject to the agreement.

(b) Presentment of an item pursuant to an agreement for presentment is made when the presentment notice is received.

(c) If presentment is made by presentment notice, a reference to "item" or "check" in this Article means the presentment notice unless the context otherwise indicates.

As added in 1990.

§ 4–111. Statute of Limitations

An action to enforce an obligation, duty, or right arising under this Article must be commenced within three years after the [cause of action] accrues.

As added in 1990.

Part 2 Collection of Items: Depositary and Collecting Banks

§ 4–201. Status of Collecting Bank as Agent and Provisional Status of Credits; Applicability of Article; Item Indorsed "Pay Any Bank"

(a) Unless a contrary intent clearly appears and before the time that a settlement given by a collecting bank for an item is or becomes final, the bank, with respect to an item, is an agent or sub-agent of the owner of the item and any settlement given for the item is provisional. This provision applies regardless of the form of indorsement or lack of indorsement and even though credit given for the item is subject to immediate withdrawal as of right or is in fact withdrawn; but the continuance of ownership of an item by its owner and any rights of the owner to proceeds of the item are subject to rights of a collecting bank, such as those resulting from outstanding advances on the item and rights of recoupment or setoff. If an item is handled by banks for purposes of presentment, payment, collection, or return, the relevant provisions of this Article apply even though action of the parties clearly establishes that a particular bank has purchased the item and is the owner of it.

(b) After an item has been indorsed with the words "pay any bank" or the like, only a bank may acquire the rights of a holder until the item has been:

(1) returned to the customer initiating collection; or

(2) specially indorsed by a bank to a person who is not a bank.

As amended in 1990.

§ 4–202. Responsibility for Collection or Return; When Action Timely

(a) A collecting bank must exercise ordinary care in:

(1) presenting an item or sending it for presentment;

(2) sending notice of dishonor or nonpayment or returning an item other than a documentary draft to the bank's transferor after learning that the item has not been paid or accepted, as the case may be;

(3) settling for an item when the bank receives final settlement; and

(4) notifying its transferor of any loss or delay in transit within a reasonable time after discovery thereof.

(b) A collecting bank exercises ordinary care under subsection (a) by taking proper action before its midnight deadline following receipt of an item, notice, or settlement. Taking proper action within a reasonably longer time may constitute the exercise of ordinary care, but the bank has the burden of establishing timeliness.

(c) Subject to subsection (a)(1), a bank is not liable for the insolvency, neglect, misconduct, mistake, or default of another bank or person or for loss or destruction of an item in the possession of others or in transit.

As amended in 1990.

§ 4–203. Effect of Instructions

Subject to Article 3 concerning conversion of instruments (Section 3–420) and restrictive indorsements (Section 3–206), only a collecting bank's transferor can give instructions that affect the bank or constitute notice to it, and a collecting bank is not liable to prior parties for any action taken pursuant to the instructions or in accordance with any agreement with its transferor.

As amended in 1990.

§ 4–204. Methods of Sending and Presenting; Sending Directly to Payor Bank

(a) A collecting bank shall send items by a reasonably prompt method, taking into consideration relevant instructions, the nature of the item, the number of those items on hand, the cost of collection involved, and the method generally used by it or others to present those items.

(b) A collecting bank may send:

(1) an item directly to the payor bank;

(2) an item to a nonbank payor if authorized by its transferor; and

(3) an item other than documentary drafts to a non-bank payor, if authorized by Federal Reserve regulation or operating circular, clearing-house rule, or the like.

(c) Presentment may be made by a presenting bank at a place where the payor bank or other payor has requested that presentment be made.

As amended in 1962 and 1990.

§ 4–205. Depositary Bank Holder of Unindorsed Item

If a customer delivers an item to a depositary bank for collection:

(1) the depositary bank becomes a holder of the item at the time it receives the item for collection if the customer at the time of delivery was a holder of the item, whether or not the customer indorses the item, and, if the bank satisfies the other requirements of Section 3–302, it is a holder in due course; and

(2) the depositary bank warrants to collecting banks, the payor bank or other payor, and the drawer that the amount of the item was paid to the customer or deposited to the customer's account.

As amended in 1990.

§ 4–206. Transfer Between Banks

Any agreed method that identifies the transferor bank is sufficient for the item's further transfer to another bank.

As amended in 1990.

§ 4–207. Transfer Warranties

(a) A customer or collecting bank that transfers an item and receives a settlement or other consideration warrants to the transferee and to any subsequent collecting bank that:

(1) the warrantor is a person entitled to enforce the item;

(2) all signatures on the item are authentic and authorized;

(3) the item has not been altered;

(4) the item is not subject to a defense or claim in recoupment (Section 3–305(a)) of any party that can be asserted against the warrantor; and

(5) the warrantor has no knowledge of any insolvency proceeding commenced with respect to the maker or acceptor or, in the case of an unaccepted draft, the drawer.

(b) If an item is dishonored, a customer or collecting bank transferring the item and receiving settlement or other consideration is obliged to pay the amount due on the item (i) according to the terms of the item at the time it was transferred, or (ii) if the transfer was of an incomplete item, according to its terms when completed as stated in Sections 3–115 and 3–407. The obligation of a transferor is owed to the transferee and to any subsequent collecting bank that takes the item in good faith. A transferor cannot disclaim its obligation under this subsection by an indorsement stating that it is made "without recourse" or otherwise disclaiming liability.

(c) A person to whom the warranties under subsection (a) are made and who took the item in good faith may recover from the warrantor as damages for breach of warranty an amount equal to the loss suffered as a result of the breach, but not more than the amount of the item plus expenses and loss of interest incurred as a result of the breach.

(d) The warranties stated in subsection (a) cannot be disclaimed with respect to checks. Unless notice of a claim for breach of warranty is given to the warrantor within 30 days after the claimant has reason to know of the breach and the identity of the warrantor, the warrantor is discharged to the extent of any loss caused by the delay in giving notice of the claim.

(e) A cause of action for breach of warranty under this section accrues when the claimant has reason to know of the breach.
As added in 1990.

§ 4–208. Presentment Warranties

(a) If an unaccepted draft is presented to the drawee for payment or acceptance and the drawee pays or accepts the draft, (i) the person obtaining payment or acceptance, at the time of presentment, and (ii) a previous transferor of the draft, at the time of transfer, warrant to the drawee that pays or accepts the draft in good faith that:

(1) the warrantor is, or was, at the time the warrantor transferred the draft, a person entitled to enforce the draft or authorized to obtain payment or acceptance of the draft on behalf of a person entitled to enforce the draft;

(2) the draft has not been altered; and

(3) the warrantor has no knowledge that the signature of the purported drawer of the draft is unauthorized.

(b) A drawee making payment may recover from a warrantor damages for breach of warranty equal to the amount paid by the drawee less the amount the drawee received or is entitled to receive from the drawer because of the payment. In addition, the drawee is entitled to compensation for expenses and loss of interest resulting from the breach. The right of the drawee to recover damages under this subsection is not affected by any failure of the drawee to exercise ordinary care in making payment. If the drawee accepts the draft (i) breach of warranty is a defense to the obligation of the acceptor, and (ii) if the acceptor makes payment with respect to the draft, the acceptor is entitled to recover from a warrantor for breach of warranty the amounts stated in this subsection.

(c) If a drawee asserts a claim for breach of warranty under subsection (a) based on an unauthorized indorsement of the draft or an alteration of the draft, the warrantor may defend by proving that the indorsement is effective under Section 3–404 or 3–405 or the drawer is precluded under Section 3–406 or 4–406 from asserting against the drawee the unauthorized indorsement or alteration.

(d) If (i) a dishonored draft is presented for payment to the drawer or an indorser or (ii) any other item is presented for payment to a party obliged to pay the item, and the item is paid, the person obtaining payment and a prior transferor of the item warrant to the person making payment in good faith that the warrantor is, or was, at the time the warrantor transferred the item, a person entitled to enforce the item or authorized to obtain payment on behalf of a person entitled to enforce the item. The person making payment may recover from any warrantor for breach of warranty an amount equal to the amount paid plus expenses and loss of interest resulting from the breach.

(e) The warranties stated in subsections (a) and (d) cannot be disclaimed with respect to checks. Unless notice of a claim for breach of warranty is given to the warrantor within 30 days after the claimant has reason to know of the breach and the identity of the warrantor, the warrantor is discharged to the extent of any loss caused by the delay in giving notice of the claim.

(f) A cause of action for breach of warranty under this section accrues when the claimant has reason to know of the breach.
As added in 1990.

§ 4–209. Encoding and Retention Warranties

(a) A person who encodes information on or with respect to an item after issue warrants to any subsequent collecting bank and to the payor bank or other payor that the information is correctly encoded. If the customer of a depositary bank encodes, that bank also makes the warranty.

(b) A person who undertakes to retain an item pursuant to an agreement for electronic presentment warrants to any subsequent collecting bank and to the payor bank or other payor that retention and presentment of the item comply with the agreement. If a customer of a depositary bank undertakes to retain an item, that bank also makes this warranty.

(c) A person to whom warranties are made under this section and who took the item in good faith may recover from the warrantor as damages for breach of warranty an amount equal to the loss suffered as a result of the breach, plus expenses and loss of interest incurred as a result of the breach.

As added in 1990.

§ 4–210. Security Interest of Collecting Bank in Items, Accompanying Documents and Proceeds

(a) A collecting bank has a security interest in an item and any accompanying documents or the proceeds of either:

(1) in case of an item deposited in an account, to the extent to which credit given for the item has been withdrawn or applied;

(2) in case of an item for which it has given credit available for withdrawal as of right, to the extent of the credit given, whether or not the credit is drawn upon or there is a right of charge-back; or

(3) if it makes an advance on or against the item.

(b) If credit given for several items received at one time or pursuant to a single agreement is withdrawn or applied in part, the security interest remains upon all the items, any accompanying documents or the proceeds of either. For the purpose of this section, credits first given are first withdrawn.

(c) Receipt by a collecting bank of a final settlement for an item is a realization on its security interest in the item, accompanying documents, and proceeds. So long as the bank does not receive final settlement for the item or give up possession of the item or accompanying documents for purposes other than collection, the security interest continues to that extent and is subject to Article 9, but:

(1) no security agreement is necessary to make the security interest enforceable (Section 9–203(1)(a));

(2) no filing is required to perfect the security interest; and

(3) the security interest has priority over conflicting perfected security interests in the item, accompanying documents, or proceeds.

As amended in 1990.

§ 4–211. When Bank Gives Value for Purposes of Holder in Due Course

For purposes of determining its status as a holder in due course, a bank has given value to the extent it has a security interest in an item, if the bank otherwise complies with the requirements of Section 3–302 on what constitutes a holder in due course.

As amended in 1990.

§ 4–212. Presentment by Notice of Item Not Payable by, Through, or at Bank; Liability of Drawer or Indorser

(a) Unless otherwise instructed, a collecting bank may present an item not payable by, through, or at a bank by sending to the party to accept or pay a written notice that the bank holds the item for acceptance or payment. The notice must be sent in time to be received on or before the day when presentment is due and the bank must meet any requirement of the party to accept or pay under Section 3–501 by the close of the bank's next banking day after it knows of the requirement.

(b) If presentment is made by notice and payment, acceptance, or request for compliance with a requirement under Section 3–501 is not received by the close of business on the day after maturity or, in the case of demand items, by the close of business on the third banking day after notice was sent, the presenting bank may treat the item as dishonored and charge any drawer or indorser by sending it notice of the facts.

As amended in 1990.

§ 4–213. Medium and Time of Settlement by Bank

(a) With respect to settlement by a bank, the medium and time of settlement may be prescribed by Federal Reserve regulations or circulars, clearing-house rules, and the like, or agreement. In the absence of such prescription:

(1) the medium or settlement is cash or credit to an account in a Federal Reserve bank of or specified by the person to receive settlement; and

(2) the time of settlement is:

(i) with respect to tender of settlement by cash, a cashier's check, or teller's check, when the cash or check is sent or delivered;

(ii) with respect to tender of settlement by credit in an account in a Federal Reserve Bank, when the credit is made;

(iii) with respect to tender of settlement by a credit or debit to an account in a bank, when the credit or debit is made or, in the case of tender of settlement by authority to charge an account, when the authority is sent or delivered; or

(iv) with respect to tender of settlement by a funds transfer, when payment is made pursuant to Section 4–406(a) to the person receiving settlement.

(b) If the tender of settlement is not by a medium authorized by subsection (a) or the time of settlement is not fixed by subsection (a), no settlement occurs until the tender of settlement is accepted by the person receiving settlement.

(c) If settlement for an item is made by cashier's check or teller's check and the person receiving settlement, before its midnight deadline:

(1) presents or forwards the check for collection, settlement is final when the check is finally paid; or

(2) fails to present or forward the check for collection, settlement is final at the midnight deadline of the person receiving settlement.

(d) If settlement for an item is made by giving authority to charge the account of the bank giving settlement in the bank receiving settlement, settlement is final when the charge is made by the bank receiving settlement if there are funds available in the account for the amount of the item.

As amended in 1990.

§ 4–214. Right of Charge-Back or Refund; Liability of Collecting Bank: Return of Item

(a) If a collecting bank has made provisional settlement with its customer for an item and fails by reason of dishonor, suspension of payments by a bank, or otherwise to receive settlement for the item which is or becomes final, the bank may revoke the settlement given by it, charge back the amount of any credit given for the item to its customer's account, or obtain refund from its customer, whether or not it is able to return the item, if by its midnight deadline or within a longer reasonable time after it learns the facts it returns the item or sends notification of the facts. If the return or notice is delayed beyond the bank's midnight deadline or a longer reasonable time after it learns the facts, the bank may revoke the settlement, charge back the credit, or obtain refund from its customer, but it is liable for any loss resulting from the delay. These rights to revoke, charge back, and obtain refund terminate if and when a settlement for the item received by the bank is or becomes final.

(b) A collecting bank returns an item when it is sent or delivered to the bank's customer or transferor or pursuant to its instructions.

(c) A depositary bank that is also the payor may charge back the amount of an item to its customer's account or obtain refund in accordance with the section governing return of an item received by a payor bank for credit on its books (Section 4–301).

(d) The right to charge back is not affected by:

(1) previous use of a credit given for the item; or

(2) failure by any bank to exercise ordinary care with respect to the item, but a bank so failing remains liable.

(e) A failure to charge back or claim refund does not affect other rights of the bank against the customer or any other party.

(f) If credit is given in dollars as the equivalent of the value of an item payable in foreign money, the dollar amount of any charge-back or refund must be calculated on the basis of the bank-offered spot rate for the foreign money prevailing on the day when the person entitled to the charge-back or refund learns that it will not receive payment in ordinary course.

As amended in 1990.

§ 4–215. Final Payment of Item by Payor Bank; When Provisional Debits and Credits Become Final; When Certain Credits Become Available for Withdrawal

(a) An item is finally paid by a payor bank when the bank has first done any of the following:

(1) paid the item in cash;

(2) settled for the item without having a right to revoke the settlement under statute, clearing-house rule, or agreement; or

(3) made a provisional settlement for the item and failed to revoke the settlement in the time and manner permitted by statute, clearing-house rule, or agreement.

(b) If provisional settlement for an item does not become final, the item is not finally paid.

(c) If provisional settlement for an item between the presenting and payor banks is made through a clearing house or by debits or credits in an account between them, then to the extent that provisional debits or credits for the item are entered in accounts between the presenting and payor banks or between the presenting and successive prior collecting banks seriatim, they become final upon final payment of the item by the payor bank.

(d) If a collecting bank receives a settlement for an item which is or becomes final, the bank is accountable to its customer for the amount of the item and any provisional credit given for the item in an account with its customer becomes final.

(e) Subject to (i) applicable law stating a time for availability of funds and (ii) any right of the bank to apply the credit to an obligation of the customer, credit given by a bank for an item in a customer's account becomes available for withdrawal as of right:

(1) if the bank has received a provisional settlement for the item, when the settlement becomes final and the bank has had a reasonable time to receive return of the item and the item has not been received within that time;

(2) if the bank is both the depositary bank and the payor bank, and the item is finally paid, at the

opening of the bank's second banking day following receipt of the item.

(f) Subject to applicable law stating a time for availability of funds and any right of a bank to apply a deposit to an obligation of the depositor, a deposit of money becomes available for withdrawal as of right at the opening of the bank's next banking day after receipt of the deposit. As amended in 1990.

§ 4–216. Insolvency and Preferences

(a) If an item is in or comes into the possession of a payor or collecting bank that suspends payment and the item has not been finally paid, the item must be returned by the receiver, trustee, or agent in charge of the closed bank to the presenting bank or the closed bank's customer.

(b) If a payor bank finally pays an item and suspends payments without making a settlement for the item with its customer or the presenting bank which settlement is or becomes final, the owner of the item has a preferred claim against the payor bank.

(c) If a payor bank gives or a collecting bank gives or receives a provisional settlement for an item and thereafter suspends payments, the suspension does not prevent or interfere with the settlement's becoming final if the finality occurs automatically upon the lapse of certain time or the happening of certain events.

(d) If a collecting bank receives from subsequent parties settlement for an item, which settlement is or becomes final and the bank suspends payments without making a settlement for the item with its customer which settlement is or becomes final, the owner of the item has a preferred claim against the collecting bank.
As amended in 1990.

Part 3 Collection of Items: Payor Banks

§ 4–301. Deferred Posting; Recovery of Payment by Return of Items; Time of Dishonor; Return of Items by Payor Bank

(a) If a payor bank settles for a demand item other than a documentary draft presented otherwise than for immediate payment over the counter before midnight of the banking day of receipt, the payor bank may revoke the settlement and recover the settlement if, before it has made final payment and before its midnight deadline, it

(1) returns the item; or
(2) sends written notice of dishonor or nonpayment if the item is unavailable for return.

(b) If a demand item is received by a payor bank for credit on its books, it may return the item or send notice of dishonor and may revoke any credit given or recover the amount thereof withdrawn by its customer, if it acts within the time limit and in the manner specified in subsection (a).

(c) Unless previous notice of dishonor has been sent, an item is dishonored at the time when for purposes of dishonor it is returned or notice sent in accordance with this section.

(d) An item is returned:
(1) as to an item presented through a clearing house, when it is delivered to the presenting or last collecting bank or to the clearing house or is sent or delivered in accordance with clearing-house rules; or
(2) in all other cases, when it is sent or delivered to the bank's customer or transferor or pursuant to instructions.
As amended in 1990.

§ 4–302. Payor Bank's Responsibility for Late Return of Item

(a) If an item is presented to and received by a payor bank, the bank is accountable for the amount of:
(1) a demand item, other than a documentary draft, whether properly payable or not, if the bank, in any case in which it is not also the depositary bank, retains the item beyond midnight of the banking day of receipt without settling for it or, whether or not it is also the depositary bank, does not pay or return the item or send notice of dishonor until after its midnight deadline; or
(2) any other properly payable item unless, within the time allowed for acceptance or payment of that item, the bank either accepts or pays the item or returns it and accompanying documents.

(b) The liability of a payor bank to pay an item pursuant to subsection (a) is subject to defenses based on breach of a presentment warranty (Section 4–208) or proof that the person seeking enforcement of the liability presented or transferred the item for the purpose of defrauding the payor bank.
As amended in 1990.

§ 4–303. When Items Subject to Notice, Stop-Payment Order, Legal Process, or Setoff; Order in Which Items May be Charged or Certified

(a) Any knowledge, notice, or stop-payment order received by, legal process served upon, or setoff exercised by a payor bank comes too late to terminate, suspend, or modify the bank's right or duty to pay an item or to charge its customer's account for the item if the knowledge, notice, stop-payment order, or legal process is received or served and a reasonable time for the bank to act thereon expires or the setoff is exercised after the earliest of the following:
(1) the bank accepts or certifies the item;
(2) the bank pays the item in cash;
(3) the bank settles for the item without having a right to revoke the settlement under statute, clearing-house rule, or agreement;

(4) the bank becomes accountable for the amount of the item under Section 4–302 dealing with the payor bank's responsibility for late return of items; or

(5) with respect to checks, a cutoff hour no earlier than one hour after the opening of the next banking day after the banking day on which the bank received the check and no later than the close of that next banking day or, if no cutoff hour is fixed, the close of the next banking day after the banking day on which the bank received the check.

(b) Subject to subsection (a), items may be accepted, paid, certified, or charged to the indicated account of its customer in any order.

As amended in 1990.

Part 4 Relationship Between Payor Bank and Its Customer

§ 4–401. When Bank May Charge Customer's Account

(a) A bank may charge against the account of a customer an item that is properly payable from the account even though the charge creates an overdraft. An item is properly payable if it is authorized by the customer and is in accordance with any agreement between the customer and bank.

(b) A customer is not liable for the amount of an overdraft if the customer neither signed the item nor benefited from the proceeds of the item.

(c) A bank may charge against the account of a customer a check that is otherwise properly payable from the account, even though payment was made before the date of the check, unless the customer has given notice to the bank of the postdating describing the check with reasonable certainty. The notice is effective for the period stated in Section 4–403(b) for stop-payment orders, and must be received at such time and in such manner as to afford the bank a reasonable opportunity to act on it before the bank takes any action with respect to the check described in Section 4–303. If a bank charges against the account of a customer a check before the date stated in the notice of postdating, the bank is liable for damages for the loss resulting from its act. The loss may include damages for dishonor of subsequent items under Section 4–402.

(d) A bank that in good faith makes payment to a holder may charge the indicated account of its customer according to:

(1) the original terms of the altered item; or

(2) the terms of the completed item, even though the bank knows the item has been completed unless the bank has notice that the completion was improper.

As amended in 1990.

§ 4–402. Bank's Liability to Customer for Wrongful Dishonor; Time of Determining Insufficiency of Account

(a) Except as otherwise provided in this Article, a payor bank wrongfully dishonors an item if it dishonors an item that is properly payable, but a bank may dishonor an item that would create an overdraft unless it has agreed to pay the overdraft.

(b) A payor bank is liable to its customer for damages proximately caused by the wrongful dishonor of an item. Liability is limited to actual damages proved and may include damages for an arrest or prosecution of the customer or other consequential damages. Whether any consequential damages are proximately caused by the wrongful dishonor is a question of fact to be determined in each case.

(c) A payor bank's determination of the customer's account balance on which a decision to dishonor for insufficiency of available funds is based may be made at any time between the time the item is received by the payor bank and the time that the payor bank returns the item or gives notice in lieu of return, and no more than one determination need be made. If, at the election of the payor bank, a subsequent balance determination is made for the purpose of reevaluating the bank's decision to dishonor the item, the account balance at that time is determinative of whether a dishonor for insufficiency of available funds is wrongful.

As amended in 1990.

§ 4–403. Customer's Right to Stop Payment; Burden of Proof of Loss

(a) A customer or any person authorized to draw on the account if there is more than one person may stop payment of any item drawn on the customer's account or close the account by an order to the bank describing the item or account with reasonable certainty received at a time and in a manner that affords the bank a reasonable opportunity to act on it before any action by the bank with respect to the item described in Section 4–303. If the signature of more than one person is required to draw on an account, any of these persons may stop payment or close the account.

(b) A stop-payment order is effective for six months, but it lapses after 14 calendar days if the original order was oral and was not confirmed in writing within that period. A stop-payment order may be renewed for additional six-month periods by a writing given to the bank within a period during which the stop-payment order is effective.

(c) The burden of establishing the fact and amount of loss resulting from the payment of an item contrary to a stop-payment order or order to close an account is on the customer. The loss from payment of an item contrary to a

stop-payment order may include damages for dishonor of subsequent items under Section 4–402.
As amended in 1990.

§ 4–404. Bank Not Obliged to Pay Check More Than Six Months Old

A bank is under no obligation to a customer having a checking account to pay a check, other than a certified check, which is presented more than six months after its date, but it may charge its customer's account for a payment made thereafter in good faith.

§ 4–405. Death or Incompetence of Customer

(a) A payor or collecting bank's authority to accept, pay, or collect an item or to account for proceeds of its collection, if otherwise effective, is not rendered ineffective by incompetence of a customer of either bank existing at the time the item is issued or its collection is undertaken if the bank does not know of an adjudication of incompetence. Neither death nor incompetence of a customer revokes the authority to accept, pay, collect, or account until the bank knows of the fact of death or of an adjudication of incompetence and has reasonable opportunity to act on it.

(b) Even with knowledge, a bank may for 10 days after the date of death pay or certify checks drawn on or before that date unless ordered to stop payment by a person claiming an interest in the account.
As amended in 1990.

§ 4–406. Customer's Duty to Discover and Report Unauthorized Signature or Alteration

(a) A bank that sends or makes available to a customer a statement of account showing payment of items for the account shall either return or make available to the customer the items paid or provide information in the statement of account sufficient to allow the customer reasonably to identify the items paid. The statement of account provides sufficient information if the item is described by item number, amount, and date of payment.

(b) If the items are not returned to the customer, the person retaining the items shall either retain the items or, if the items are destroyed, maintain the capacity to furnish legible copies of the items until the expiration of seven years after receipt of the items. A customer may request an item from the bank that paid the item, and that bank must provide in a reasonable time either the item or, if the item has been destroyed or is not otherwise obtainable, a legible copy of the item.

(c) If a bank sends or makes available a statement of account or items pursuant to subsection (a), the customer must exercise reasonable promptness in examining the statement or the items to determine whether any payment was not authorized because of an alteration of an item or because a purported signature by or on behalf of the customer was not authorized. If, based on the statement or items provided, the customer should reasonably have discovered the unauthorized payment, the customer must promptly notify the bank of the relevant facts.

(d) If the bank proves that the customer failed, with respect to an item, to comply with the duties imposed on the customer by subsection (c), the customer is precluded from asserting against the bank:

(1) the customer's unauthorized signature or any alteration on the item, if the bank also proves that it suffered a loss by reason of the failure; and

(2) the customer's unauthorized signature or alteration by the same wrongdoer on any other item paid in good faith by the bank if the payment was made before the bank received notice from the customer of the unauthorized signature or alteration and after the customer had been afforded a reasonable period of time, not exceeding 30 days, in which to examine the item or statement of account and notify the bank.

(e) If subsection (d) applies and the customer proves that the bank failed to exercise ordinary care in paying the item and that the failure substantially contributed to loss, the loss is allocated between the customer precluded and the bank asserting the preclusion according to the extent to which the failure of the customer to comply with subsection (c) and the failure of the bank to exercise ordinary care contributed to the loss. If the customer proves that the bank did not pay the item in good faith, the preclusion under subsection (d) does not apply.

(f) Without regard to care or lack of care of either the customer or the bank, a customer who does not within one year after the statement or items are made available to the customer (subsection (a)) discover and report the customer's unauthorized signature on or any alteration on the item is precluded from asserting against the bank the unauthorized signature or alteration. If there is a preclusion under this subsection, the payor bank may not recover for breach or warranty under Section 4–208 with respect to the unauthorized signature or alteration to which the preclusion applies.
As amended in 1990.

§ 4–407. Payor Bank's Right to Subrogation on Improper Payment

If a payor bank has paid an item over the order of the drawer or maker to stop payment, or after an account has been closed, or otherwise under circumstances giving a basis for objection by the drawer or maker, to prevent unjust enrichment and only to the extent necessary to prevent loss to the bank by reason of its payment of the item, the payor bank is subrogated to the rights

(1) of any holder in due course on the item against the drawer or maker;

(2) of the payee or any other holder of the item against the drawer or maker either on the item or under the transaction out of which the item arose; and

(3) of the drawer or maker against the payee or any other holder of the item with respect to the transaction out of which the item arose.

As amended in 1990.

Part 5 Collection of Documentary Drafts

§ 4–501. Handling of Documentary Drafts; Duty to Send for Presentment and to Notify Customer of Dishonor

A bank that takes a documentary draft for collection shall present or send the draft and accompanying documents for presentment and, upon learning that the draft has not been paid or accepted in due course, shall seasonably notify its customer of the fact even though it may have discounted or bought the draft or extended credit available for withdrawal as of right.

As amended in 1990.

§ 4–502. Presentment of "On Arrival" Drafts

If a draft or the relevant instructions require presentment "on arrival," "when goods arrive" or the like, the collecting bank need not present until in its judgment a reasonable time for arrival of the goods has expired. Refusal to pay or accept because the goods have not arrived is not dishonor; the bank must notify its transferor of the refusal but need not present the draft again until it is instructed to do so or learns of the arrival of the goods.

As amended in 1990.

§ 4–503. Responsibility of Presenting Bank for Documents and Goods; Report of Reasons for Dishonor; Referee in Case of Need

Unless otherwise instructed and except as provided in Article 5, a bank presenting a documentary draft:

(1) must deliver the documents to the drawee on acceptance of the draft if it is payable more than three days after presentment; otherwise, only on payment; and

(2) upon dishonor, either in the case of presentment for acceptance or presentment for payment, may seek and follow instructions from any referee in case of need designated in the draft or, if the presenting bank does not choose to utilize the referee's services, it must use diligence and good faith to ascertain the reason for dishonor, must notify its transferor of the dishonor and of the results of its effort to ascertain the reasons therefor, and must request instructions.

However the presenting bank is under no obligation with respect to goods represented by the documents except to follow any reasonable instructions seasonably received; it has a right to reimbursement for any expense incurred in following instructions and to prepayment of or indemnity for those expenses.

As amended in 1990.

§ 4–504. Privilege of Presenting Bank to Deal With Goods; Security Interest for Expenses

(a) A presenting bank that, following the dishonor of a documentary draft, has seasonably requested instructions but does not receive them within a reasonable time may store, sell, or otherwise deal with the goods in any reasonable manner.

(b) For its reasonable expenses incurred by action under subsection (a) the presenting bank has a lien upon the goods or their proceeds, which may be foreclosed in the same manner as an unpaid seller's lien. As amended in 1990.

ARTICLE 4A FUNDS TRANSFERS

Part 1 Subject Matter and Definitions

§ 4A–101. Short Title

This Article may be cited as Uniform Commercial Code—Funds Transfers.

§ 4A–102. Subject Matter

Except as otherwise provided in Section 4A–108, this Article applies to funds transfers defined in Section 4A–104.

§ 4A–103. Payment Order—Definitions

(a) In this Article:

(1) "Payment order" means an instruction of a sender to a receiving bank, transmitted orally, electronically, or in writing, to pay, or to cause another bank to pay, a fixed or determinable amount of money to a beneficiary if:

  (i) the instruction does not state a condition to payment to the beneficiary other than time of payment,

  (ii) the receiving bank is to be reimbursed by debiting an account of, or otherwise receiving payment from, the sender, and

  (iii) the instruction is transmitted by the sender directly to the receiving bank or to an agent, funds-transfer system, or communication system for transmittal to the receiving bank.

(2) "Beneficiary" means the person to be paid by the beneficiary's bank.

(3) "Beneficiary's bank" means the bank identified in a payment order in which an account of the beneficiary is to be credited pursuant to the order or which otherwise is to make payment to the beneficiary if the order does not provide for payment to an account.

(4) "Receiving bank" means the bank to which the sender's instruction is addressed.

(5) "Sender" means the person giving the instruction to the receiving bank.

(b) If an instruction complying with subsection (a)(1) is to make more than one payment to a beneficiary, the instruction is a separate payment order with respect to each payment.

(c) A payment order is issued when it is sent to the receiving bank.

§ 4A–104. Funds Transfer—Definitions

In this Article:

(a) "Funds transfer" means the series of transactions, beginning with the originator's payment order, made for the purpose of making payment to the beneficiary of the order. The term includes any payment order issued by the originator's bank or an intermediary bank intended to carry out the originator's payment order. A funds transfer is completed by acceptance by the beneficiary's bank of a payment order for the benefit of the beneficiary of the originator's payment order.

(b) "Intermediary bank" means a receiving bank other than the originator's bank or the beneficiary's bank.

(c) "Originator" means the sender of the first payment order in a funds transfer.

(d) "Originator's bank" means (i) the receiving bank to which the payment order of the originator is issued if the originator is not a bank, or (ii) the originator if the originator is a bank.

§ 4A–105. Other Definitions

(a) In this Article:

(1) "Authorized account" means a deposit account of a customer in a bank designated by the customer as a source of payment of payment orders issued by the customer to the bank. If a customer does not so designate an account, any account of the customer is an authorized account if payment of a payment order from that account is not inconsistent with a restriction on the use of that account.

(2) "Bank" means a person engaged in the business of banking and includes a savings bank, savings and loan association, credit union, and trust company. A branch or separate office of a bank is a separate bank for purposes of this Article.

(3) "Customer" means a person, including a bank, having an account with a bank or from whom a bank has agreed to receive payment orders.

(4) "Funds-transfer business day" of a receiving bank means the part of a day during which the receiving bank is open for the receipt, processing, and transmittal of payment orders and cancellations and amendments of payment orders.

(5) "Funds-transfer system" means a wire transfer network, automated clearing house, or other communication system of a clearing house or other association of banks through which a payment order by a bank may be transmitted to the bank to which the order is addressed.

(6) "Good faith" means honesty in fact and the observance of reasonable commercial standards of fair dealing.

(7) "Prove" with respect to a fact means to meet the burden of establishing the fact (Section 1–201(8)).

(b) Other definitions applying to this Article and the sections in which they appear are:

"Acceptance"	Section 4A–209
"Beneficiary"	Section 4A–103
"Beneficiary's bank"	Section 4A–103
"Executed"	Section 4A–301
"Execution date"	Section 4A–301
"Funds transfer"	Section 4A–104
"Funds-transfer system rule"	Section 4A–501
"Intermediary bank"	Section 4A–104
"Originator"	Section 4A–104
"Originator's bank"	Section 4A–104
"Payment by beneficiary's bank to beneficiary"	Section 4A–405
"Payment by originator to beneficiary"	Section 4A–406
"Payment by sender to receiving bank"	Section 4A–403
"Payment date"	Section 4A–401
"Payment order"	Section 4A–103
"Receiving bank"	Section 4A–103
"Security procedure"	Section 4A–201
"Sender"	Section 4A–103

(c) The following definitions in Article 4 apply to this Article:

"Clearing house"	Section 4–104
"Item"	Section 4–104
"Suspends payments"	Section 4–104

(d) In addition Article 1 contains general definitions and principles of construction and interpretation applicable throughout this Article.

§ 4A–106. Time Payment Order Is Received

(a) The time of receipt of a payment order or communication cancelling or amending a payment order is determined by the rules applicable to receipt of a notice stated in Section 1–201(27). A receiving bank may fix a cut-off time or times on a funds-transfer business day for the receipt and processing of payment orders and communications cancelling or amending payment orders. Different cut-off times may apply to payment orders, cancellations, or amendments, or to different categories of payment orders, cancellations, or amendments. A cut-off time may apply to senders generally or different cut-off times may apply to different senders or categories of payment orders. If a payment order or communication cancelling or amending a payment order is received after the close of a funds-transfer business day or after the appropriate cut-off time on a funds-transfer business day, the receiving bank may treat the payment order or communication as received at the opening of the next funds-transfer business day.

(b) If this Article refers to an execution date or payment date or states a day on which a receiving bank is required to take action, and the date or day does not fall on a funds-transfer business day, the next day that is a funds-transfer business day is treated as the date or day stated, unless the contrary is stated in this Article.

§ 4A–107. Federal Reserve Regulations and Operating Circulars

Regulations of the Board of Governors of the Federal Reserve System and operating circulars of the Federal Reserve Banks supersede any inconsistent provision of this Article to the extent of the inconsistency.

§ 4A–108. Exclusion of Consumer Transactions Governed by Federal Law

This Article does not apply to a funds transfer any part of which is governed by the Electronic Fund Transfer Act of 1978 (Title XX, Public Law 95-630, 92 Stat. 3728, 15 U.S.C. § 1693 et seq.) as amended from time to time.

Part 2 Issue and Acceptance of Payment Order

§ 4A–201. Security Procedure

"Security procedure" means a procedure established by agreement of a customer and a receiving bank for the purpose of (i) verifying that a payment order or communication amending or cancelling a payment order is that of the customer, or (ii) detecting error in the transmission or the content of the payment order or communication. A security procedure may require the use of algorithms or other codes, identifying words or numbers, encryption, callback procedures, or similar security devices. Comparison of a signature on a payment order or communication with an authorized specimen signature of the customer is not by itself a security procedure.

§ 4A–202. Authorized and Verified Payment Orders

(a) A payment order received by the receiving bank is the authorized order of the person identified as sender if that person authorized the order or is otherwise bound by it under the law of agency.

(b) If a bank and its customer have agreed that the authenticity of payment orders issued to the bank in the name of the customer as sender will be verified pursuant to a security procedure, a payment order received by the receiving bank is effective as the order of the customer, whether or not authorized, if (i) the security procedure is a commercially reasonable method of providing security against unauthorized payment orders, and (ii) the bank proves that it accepted the payment order in good faith and in compliance with the security procedure and any written agreement or instruction of the customer restrict-

ing acceptance of payment orders issued in the name of the customer. The bank is not required to follow an instruction that violates a written agreement with the customer or notice of which is not received at a time and in a manner affording the bank a reasonable opportunity to act on it before the payment order is accepted.

(c) Commercial reasonableness of a security procedure is a question of law to be determined by considering the wishes of the customer expressed to the bank, the circumstances of the customer known to the bank, including the size, type, and frequency of payment orders normally issued by the customer to the bank, alternative security procedures offered to the customer, and security procedures in general use by customers and receiving banks similarly situated. A security procedure is deemed to be commercially reasonable if (i) the security procedure was chosen by the customer after the bank offered, and the customer refused, a security procedure that was commercially reasonable for that customer, and (ii) the customer expressly agreed in writing to be bound by any payment order, whether or not authorized, issued in its name and accepted by the bank in compliance with the security procedure chosen by the customer.

(d) The term "sender" in this Article includes the customer in whose name a payment order is issued if the order is the authorized order of the customer under subsection (a), or it is effective as the order of the customer under subsection (b).

(e) This section applies to amendments and cancellations of payment orders to the same extent it applies to payment orders.

(f) Except as provided in this section and in Section 4A–203(a)(1), rights and obligations arising under this section or Section 4A–203 may not be varied by agreement.

§ 4A–203. Unenforceability of Certain Verified Payment Orders

(a) If an accepted payment order is not, under Section 4A–202(a), an authorized order of a customer identified as sender, but is effective as an order of the customer pursuant to Section 4A–202(b), the following rules apply:

(1) By express written agreement, the receiving bank may limit the extent to which it is entitled to enforce or retain payment of the payment order.

(2) The receiving bank is not entitled to enforce or retain payment of the payment order if the customer proves that the order was not caused, directly or indirectly, by a person (i) entrusted at any time with duties to act for the customer with respect to payment orders or the security procedure, or (ii) who obtained access to transmitting facilities of the customer or who obtained, from a source controlled by the customer and without authority of the receiving bank, information facilitating breach of the security procedure, regardless

of how the information was obtained or whether the customer was at fault. Information includes any access device, computer software, or the like.

(b) This section applies to amendments of payment orders to the same extent it applies to payment orders.

§ 4A–204. Refund of Payment and Duty of Customer to Report With Respect to Unauthorized Payment Order

(a) If a receiving bank accepts a payment order issued in the name of its customer as sender which is (i) not authorized and not effective as the order of the customer under Section 4A–202, or (ii) not enforceable, in whole or in part, against the customer under Section 4A–203, the bank shall refund any payment of the payment order received from the customer to the extent the bank is not entitled to enforce payment and shall pay interest on the refundable amount calculated from the date the bank received payment to the date of the refund. However, the customer is not entitled to interest from the bank on the amount to be refunded if the customer fails to exercise ordinary care to determine that the order was not authorized by the customer and to notify the bank of the relevant facts within a reasonable time not exceeding 90 days after the date the customer received notification from the bank that the order was accepted or that the customer's account was debited with respect to the order. The bank is not entitled to any recovery from the customer on account of a failure by the customer to give notification as stated in this section.

(b) Reasonable time under subsection (a) may be fixed by agreement as stated in Section 1–204(1), but the obligation of a receiving bank to refund payment as stated in subsection (a) may not otherwise be varied by agreement.

§ 4A–205. Erroneous Payment Orders

(a) If an accepted payment order was transmitted pursuant to a security procedure for the detection of error and the payment order (i) erroneously instructed payment to a beneficiary not intended by the sender, (ii) erroneously instructed payment in an amount greater than the amount intended by the sender, or (iii) was an erroneously transmitted duplicate of a payment order previously sent by the sender, the following rules apply:

(1) If the sender proves that the sender or a person acting on behalf of the sender pursuant to Section 4A–206 complied with the security procedure and that the error would have been detected if the receiving bank had also complied, the sender is not obliged to pay the order to the extent stated in paragraphs (2) and (3).

(2) If the funds transfer is completed on the basis of an erroneous payment order described in clause (i) or (iii) of subsection (a), the sender is not obliged to pay the order and the receiving bank is entitled to recover from the beneficiary any amount paid to the beneficiary to the extent allowed by the law governing mistake and restitution.

(3) If the funds transfer is completed on the basis of a payment order described in clause (ii) of subsection (a), the sender is not obliged to pay the order to the extent the amount received by the beneficiary is greater than the amount intended by the sender. In that case, the receiving bank is entitled to recover from the beneficiary the excess amount received to the extent allowed by the law governing mistake and restitution.

(b) If (i) the sender of an erroneous payment order described in subsection (a) is not obliged to pay all or part of the order, and (ii) the sender receives notification from the receiving bank that the order was accepted by the bank or that the sender's account was debited with respect to the order, the sender has a duty to exercise ordinary care, on the basis of information available to the sender, to discover the error with respect to the order and to advise the bank of the relevant facts within a reasonable time, not exceeding 90 days, after the bank's notification was received by the sender. If the bank proves that the sender failed to perform that duty, the sender is liable to the bank for the loss the bank proves it incurred as a result of the failure, but the liability of the sender may not exceed the amount of the sender's order.

(c) This section applies to amendments to payment orders to the same extent it applies to payment orders.

§ 4A–206. Transmission of Payment Order Through Funds-Transfer or Other Communication System

(a) If a payment order addressed to a receiving bank is transmitted to a funds-transfer system or other third-party communication system for transmittal to the bank, the system is deemed to be an agent of the sender for the purpose of transmitting the payment order to the bank. If there is a discrepancy between the terms of the payment order transmitted to the system and the terms of the payment order transmitted by the system to the bank, the terms of the payment order of the sender are those transmitted by the system. This section does not apply to a funds-transfer system of the Federal Reserve Banks.

(b) This section applies to cancellations and amendments of payment orders to the same extent it applies to payment orders.

§ 4A–207. Misdescription of Beneficiary

(a) Subject to subsection (b), if, in a payment order received by the beneficiary's bank, the name, bank account number, or other identification of the beneficiary refers to a nonexistent or unidentifiable person or account, no person has rights as a beneficiary of the order and acceptance of the order cannot occur.

(b) If a payment order received by the beneficiary's bank identifies the beneficiary both by name and by an identifying or bank account number and the name and number identify different persons, the following rules apply:

(1) Except as otherwise provided in subsection (c), if the beneficiary's bank does not know that the name and number refer to different persons, it may rely on the number as the proper identification of the beneficiary of the order. The beneficiary's bank need not determine whether the name and number refer to the same person.

(2) If the beneficiary's bank pays the person identified by name or knows that the name and number identify different persons, no person has rights as beneficiary except the person paid by the beneficiary's bank if that person was entitled to receive payment from the originator of the funds transfer. If no person has rights as beneficiary, acceptance of the order cannot occur.

(c) If (i) a payment order described in subsection (b) is accepted, (ii) the originator's payment order described the beneficiary inconsistently by name and number, and (iii) the beneficiary's bank pays the person identified by number as permitted by subsection (b)(1), the following rules apply:

(1) If the originator is a bank, the originator is obliged to pay its order.

(2) If the originator is not a bank and proves that the person identified by number was not entitled to receive payment from the originator, the originator is not obliged to pay its order unless the originator's bank proves that the originator, before acceptance of the originator's order, had notice that payment of a payment order issued by the originator might be made by the beneficiary's bank on the basis of an identifying or bank account number even if it identifies a person different from the named beneficiary. Proof of notice may be made by any admissible evidence. The originator's bank satisfies the burden of proof if it proves that the originator, before the payment order was accepted, signed a writing stating the information to which the notice relates.

(d) In a case governed by subsection (b)(1), if the beneficiary's bank rightfully pays the person identified by number and that person was not entitled to receive payment from the originator, the amount paid may be recovered from that person to the extent allowed by the law governing mistake and restitution as follows:

(1) If the originator is obliged to pay its payment order as stated in subsection (c), the originator has the right to recover.

(2) If the originator is not a bank and is not obliged to pay its payment order, the originator's bank has the right to recover.

§ 4A–208. Misdescription of Intermediary Bank or Beneficiary's Bank

(a) This subsection applies to a payment order identifying an intermediary bank or the beneficiary's bank only by an identifying number.

(1) The receiving bank may rely on the number as the proper identification of the intermediary or beneficiary's bank and need not determine whether the number identifies a bank.

(2) The sender is obliged to compensate the receiving bank for any loss and expenses incurred by the receiving bank as a result of its reliance on the number in executing or attempting to execute the order.

(b) This subsection applies to a payment order identifying an intermediary bank or the beneficiary's bank both by name and an identifying number if the name and number identify different persons.

(1) If the sender is a bank, the receiving bank may rely on the number as the proper identification of the intermediary or beneficiary's bank if the receiving bank, when it executes the sender's order, does not know that the name and number identify different persons. The receiving bank need not determine whether the name and number refer to the same person or whether the number refers to a bank. The sender is obliged to compensate the receiving bank for any loss and expenses incurred by the receiving bank as a result of its reliance on the number in executing or attempting to execute the order.

(2) If the sender is not a bank and the receiving bank proves that the sender, before the payment order was accepted, had notice that the receiving bank might rely on the number as the proper identification of the intermediary or beneficiary's bank even if it identifies a person different from the bank identified by name, the rights and obligations of the sender and the receiving bank are governed by subsection (b)(1), as though the sender were a bank. Proof of notice may be made by any admissible evidence. The receiving bank satisfies the burden of proof if it proves that the sender, before the payment order was accepted, signed a writing stating the information to which the notice relates.

(3) Regardless of whether the sender is a bank, the receiving bank may rely on the name as the proper identification of the intermediary or beneficiary's bank if the receiving bank, at the time it executes the sender's order, does not know that the name and number identify different persons. The receiving bank need not determine whether the name and number refer to the same person.

(4) If the receiving bank knows that the name and number identify different persons, reliance on either the name or the number in executing the sender's payment order is a breach of the obligation stated in Section 4A–302(a)(1).

§ 4A–209. Acceptance of Payment Order

(a) Subject to subsection (d), a receiving bank other than the beneficiary's bank accepts a payment order when it executes the order.

(b) Subject to subsections (c) and (d), a beneficiary's bank accepts a payment order at the earliest of the following times:

(1) when the bank (i) pays the beneficiary as stated in Section 4A–405(a) or 4A–405(b), or (ii) notifies the beneficiary of receipt of the order or that the account of the beneficiary has been credited with respect to the order unless the notice indicates that the bank is rejecting the order or that funds with respect to the order may not be withdrawn or used until receipt of payment from the sender of the order;

(2) when the bank receives payment of the entire amount of the sender's order pursuant to Section 4A–403(a)(1) or 4A–403(a)(2); or

(3) the opening of the next funds-transfer business day of the bank following the payment date of the order if, at that time, the amount of the sender's order is fully covered by a withdrawable credit balance in an authorized account of the sender or the bank has otherwise received full payment from the sender, unless the order was rejected before that time or is rejected within (i) one hour after that time, or (ii) one hour after the opening of the next business day of the sender following the payment date if that time is later. If notice of rejection is received by the sender after the payment date and the authorized account of the sender does not bear interest, the bank is obliged to pay interest to the sender on the amount of the order for the number of days elapsing after the payment date to the day the sender receives notice or learns that the order was not accepted, counting that day as an elapsed day. If the withdrawable credit balance during that period falls below the amount of the order, the amount of interest payable is reduced accordingly.

(c) Acceptance of a payment order cannot occur before the order is received by the receiving bank. Acceptance does not occur under subsection (b)(2) or (b)(3) if the beneficiary of the payment order does not have an account with the receiving bank, the account has been closed, or the receiving bank is not permitted by law to receive credits for the beneficiary's account.

(d) A payment order issued to the originator's bank cannot be accepted until the payment date if the bank is the beneficiary's bank, or the execution date if the bank is not the beneficiary's bank. If the originator's bank executes the originator's payment order before the execution date or pays the beneficiary of the originator's payment order before the payment date and the payment order is subsequently canceled pursuant to Section 4A–211(b),

the bank may recover from the beneficiary any payment received to the extent allowed by the law governing mistake and restitution.

§ 4A–210. Rejection of Payment Order

(a) A payment order is rejected by the receiving bank by a notice of rejection transmitted to the sender orally, electronically, or in writing. A notice of rejection need not use any particular words and is sufficient if it indicates that the receiving bank is rejecting the order or will not execute or pay the order. Rejection is effective when the notice is given if transmission is by a means that is reasonable in the circumstances. If notice of rejection is given by a means that is not reasonable, rejection is effective when the notice is received. If an agreement of the sender and receiving bank establishes the means to be used to reject a payment order, (i) any means complying with the agreement is reasonable and (ii) any means not complying is not reasonable unless no significant delay in receipt of the notice resulted from the use of the noncomplying means.

(b) This subsection applies if a receiving bank other than the beneficiary's bank fails to execute a payment order despite the existence on the execution date of a withdrawable credit balance in an authorized account of the sender sufficient to cover the order. If the sender does not receive notice of rejection of the order on the execution date and the authorized account of the sender does not bear interest, the bank is obliged to pay interest to the sender on the amount of the order for the number of days elapsing after the execution date to the earlier of the day the order is canceled pursuant to Section 4A–211(d) or the day the sender receives notice or learns that the order was not executed, counting the final day of the period as an elapsed day. If the withdrawable credit balance during that period falls below the amount of the order, the amount of interest is reduced accordingly.

(c) If a receiving bank suspends payments, all unaccepted payment orders issued to it are deemed rejected at the time the bank suspends payments.

(d) Acceptance of a payment order precludes a later rejection of the order. Rejection of a payment order precludes a later acceptance of the order.

§ 4A–211. Cancellation and Amendment of Payment Order

(a) A communication of the sender of a payment order cancelling or amending the order may be transmitted to the receiving bank orally, electronically, or in writing. If a security procedure is in effect between the sender and the receiving bank, the communication is not effective to cancel or amend the order unless the communication is verified pursuant to the security procedure or the bank agrees to the cancellation or amendment.

(b) Subject to subsection (a), a communication by the sender cancelling or amending a payment order is effective to cancel or amend the order if notice of the communication is received at a time and in a manner affording the receiving bank a reasonable opportunity to act on the communication before the bank accepts the payment order.

(c) After a payment order has been accepted, cancellation or amendment of the order is not effective unless the receiving bank agrees or a funds-transfer system rule allows cancellation or amendment without agreement of the bank.

(1) With respect to a payment order accepted by a receiving bank other than the beneficiary's bank, cancellation or amendment is not effective unless a conforming cancellation or amendment of the payment order issued by the receiving bank is also made.

(2) With respect to a payment order accepted by the beneficiary's bank, cancellation or amendment is not effective unless the order was issued in execution of an unauthorized payment order, or because of a mistake by a sender in the funds transfer which resulted in the issuance of a payment order (i) that is a duplicate of a payment order previously issued by the sender, (ii) that orders payment to a beneficiary not entitled to receive payment from the originator, or (iii) that orders payment in an amount greater than the amount the beneficiary was entitled to receive from the originator. If the payment order is canceled or amended, the beneficiary's bank is entitled to recover from the beneficiary any amount paid to the beneficiary to the extent allowed by the law governing mistake and restitution.

(d) An unaccepted payment order is canceled by operation of law at the close of the fifth funds-transfer business day of the receiving bank after the execution date or payment date of the order.

(e) A canceled payment order cannot be accepted. If an accepted payment order is canceled, the acceptance is nullified and no person has any right or obligation based on the acceptance. Amendment of a payment order is deemed to be cancellation of the original order at the time of amendment and issue of a new payment order in the amended form at the same time.

(f) Unless otherwise provided in an agreement of the parties or in a funds-transfer system rule, if the receiving bank, after accepting a payment order, agrees to cancellation or amendment of the order by the sender or is bound by a funds-transfer system rule allowing cancellation or amendment without the bank's agreement, the sender, whether or not cancellation or amendment is effective, is liable to the bank for any loss and expenses, including reasonable attorney's fees, incurred by the bank as a result of the cancellation or amendment or attempted cancellation or amendment.

(g) A payment order is not revoked by the death or legal incapacity of the sender unless the receiving bank knows of the death or of an adjudication of incapacity by a court of competent jurisdiction and has reasonable opportunity to act before acceptance of the order.

(h) A funds-transfer system rule is not effective to the extent it conflicts with subsection (c)(2).

§ 4A–212. Liability and Duty of Receiving Bank Regarding Unaccepted Payment Order

If a receiving bank fails to accept a payment order that it is obliged by express agreement to accept, the bank is liable for breach of the agreement to the extent provided in the agreement or in this Article, but does not otherwise have any duty to accept a payment order or, before acceptance, to take any action, or refrain from taking action, with respect to the order except as provided in this Article or by express agreement. Liability based on acceptance arises only when acceptance occurs as stated in Section 4A–209, and liability is limited to that provided in this Article. A receiving bank is not the agent of the sender or beneficiary of the payment order it accepts, or of any other party to the funds transfer, and the bank owes no duty to any party to the funds transfer except as provided in this Article or by express agreement.

Part 3 Execution of Sender's Payment Order by Receiving Bank

§ 4A–301. Execution and Execution Date

(a) A payment order is "executed" by the receiving bank when it issues a payment order intended to carry out the payment order received by the bank. A payment order received by the beneficiary's bank can be accepted but cannot be executed.

(b) "Execution date" of a payment order means the day on which the receiving bank may properly issue a payment order in execution of the sender's order. The execution date may be determined by instruction of the sender but cannot be earlier than the day the order is received and, unless otherwise determined, is the day the order is received. If the sender's instruction states a payment date, the execution date is the payment date or an earlier date on which execution is reasonably necessary to allow payment to the beneficiary on the payment date.

§ 4A–302. Obligations of Receiving Bank in Execution of Payment Order

(a) Except as provided in subsections (b) through (d), if the receiving bank accepts a payment order pursuant to Section 4A–209(a), the bank has the following obligations in executing the order:

(1) The receiving bank is obliged to issue, on the execution date, a payment order complying with the sender's order and to follow the sender's instructions concerning (i) any intermediary bank or funds-transfer system to be used in carrying out the funds transfer, or (ii) the means by which

payment orders are to be transmitted in the funds transfer. If the originator's bank issues a payment order to an intermediary bank, the originator's bank is obliged to instruct the intermediary bank according to the instruction of the originator. An intermediary bank in the funds transfer is similarly bound by an instruction given to it by the sender of the payment order it accepts.

(2) If the sender's instruction states that the funds transfer is to be carried out telephonically or by wire transfer or otherwise indicates that the funds transfer is to be carried out by the most expeditious means, the receiving bank is obliged to transmit its payment order by the most expeditious available means, and to instruct any intermediary bank accordingly. If a sender's instruction states a payment date, the receiving bank is obliged to transmit its payment order at a time and by means reasonably necessary to allow payment to the beneficiary on the payment date or as soon thereafter as is feasible.

(b) Unless otherwise instructed, a receiving bank executing a payment order may (i) use any funds-transfer system if use of that system is reasonable in the circumstances, and (ii) issue a payment order to the beneficiary's bank or to an intermediary bank through which a payment order conforming to the sender's order can expeditiously be issued to the beneficiary's bank if the receiving bank exercises ordinary care in the selection of the intermediary bank. A receiving bank is not required to follow an instruction of the sender designating a funds-transfer system to be used in carrying out the funds transfer if the receiving bank, in good faith, determines that it is not feasible to follow the instruction or that following the instruction would unduly delay completion of the funds transfer.

(c) Unless subsection (a)(2) applies or the receiving bank is otherwise instructed, the bank may execute a payment order by transmitting its payment order by first class mail or by any means reasonable in the circumstances. If the receiving bank is instructed to execute the sender's order by transmitting its payment order by a particular means, the receiving bank may issue its payment order by the means stated or by any means as expeditious as the means stated.

(d) Unless instructed by the sender, (i) the receiving bank may not obtain payment of its charges for services and expenses in connection with the execution of the sender's order by issuing a payment order in an amount equal to the amount of the sender's order less the amount of the charges, and (ii) may not instruct a subsequent receiving bank to obtain payment of its charges in the same manner.

§ 4A–303. Erroneous Execution of Payment Order

(a) A receiving bank that (i) executes the payment order of the sender by issuing a payment order in an

amount greater than the amount of the sender's order, or (ii) issues a payment order in execution of the sender's order and then issues a duplicate order, is entitled to payment of the amount of the sender's order under Section 4A–402(c) if that subsection is otherwise satisfied. The bank is entitled to recover from the beneficiary of the erroneous order the excess payment received to the extent allowed by the law governing mistake and restitution.

(b) A receiving bank that executes the payment order of the sender by issuing a payment order in an amount less than the amount of the sender's order is entitled to payment of the amount of the sender's order under Section 4A–402(c) if (i) that subsection is otherwise satisfied and (ii) the bank corrects its mistake by issuing an additional payment order for the benefit of the beneficiary of the sender's order. If the error is not corrected, the issuer of the erroneous order is entitled to receive or retain payment from the sender of the order it accepted only to the extent of the amount of the erroneous order. This subsection does not apply if the receiving bank executes the sender's payment order by issuing a payment order in an amount less than the amount of the sender's order for the purpose of obtaining payment of its charges for services and expenses pursuant to instruction of the sender.

(c) If a receiving bank executes the payment order of the sender by issuing a payment order to a beneficiary different from the beneficiary of the sender's order and the funds transfer is completed on the basis of that error, the sender of the payment order that was erroneously executed and all previous senders in the funds transfer are not obliged to pay the payment orders they issued. The issuer of the erroneous order is entitled to recover from the beneficiary of the order the payment received to the extent allowed by the law governing mistake and restitution.

§ 4A–304. Duty of Sender to Report Erroneously Executed Payment Order

If the sender of a payment order that is erroneously executed as stated in Section 4A–303 receives notification from the receiving bank that the order was executed or that the sender's account was debited with respect to the order, the sender has a duty to exercise ordinary care to determine, on the basis of information available to the sender, that the order was erroneously executed and to notify the bank of the relevant facts within a reasonable time not exceeding 90 days after the notification from the bank was received by the sender. If the sender fails to perform that duty, the bank is not obliged to pay interest on any amount refundable to the sender under Section 4A–402(d) for the period before the bank learns of the execution error. The bank is not entitled to any recovery from the sender on account of a failure by the sender to perform the duty stated in this section.

§ 4A–305. Liability for Late or Improper Execution or Failure to Execute Payment Order

(a) If a funds transfer is completed but execution of a payment order by the receiving bank in breach of Section 4A–302 results in delay in payment to the beneficiary, the bank is obliged to pay interest to either the originator or the beneficiary of the funds transfer for the period of delay caused by the improper execution. Except as provided in subsection (c), additional damages are not recoverable.

(b) If execution of a payment order by a receiving bank in breach of Section 4A–302 results in (i) noncompletion of the funds transfer, (ii) failure to use an intermediary bank designated by the originator, or (iii) issuance of a payment order that does not comply with the terms of the payment order of the originator, the bank is liable to the originator for its expenses in the funds transfer and for incidental expenses and interest losses, to the extent not covered by subsection (a), resulting from the improper execution. Except as provided in subsection (c), additional damages are not recoverable.

(c) In addition to the amounts payable under subsections (a) and (b), damages, including consequential damages, are recoverable to the extent provided in an express written agreement of the receiving bank.

(d) If a receiving bank fails to execute a payment order it was obliged by express agreement to execute, the receiving bank is liable to the sender for its expenses in the transaction and for incidental expenses and interest losses resulting from the failure to execute. Additional damages, including consequential damages, are recoverable to the extent provided in an express written agreement of the receiving bank, but are not otherwise recoverable.

(e) Reasonable attorney's fees are recoverable if demand for compensation under subsection (a) or (b) is made and refused before an action is brought on the claim. If a claim is made for breach of an agreement under subsection (d) and the agreement does not provide for damages, reasonable attorney's fees are recoverable if demand for compensation under subsection (d) is made and refused before an action is brought on the claim.

(f) Except as stated in this section, the liability of a receiving bank under subsections (a) and (b) may not be varied by agreement.

Part 4 Payment

§ 4A–401. Payment Date

"Payment date" of a payment order means the day on which the amount of the order is payable to the beneficiary by the beneficiary's bank. The payment date may be determined by instruction of the sender but cannot be earlier than the day the order is received by the beneficiary's bank and, unless otherwise determined, is the day the order is received by the beneficiary's bank.

§ 4A–402. Obligation of Sender to Pay Receiving Bank

(a) This section is subject to Sections 4A–205 and 4A–207.

(b) With respect to a payment order issued to the beneficiary's bank, acceptance of the order by the bank obliges the sender to pay the bank the amount of the order, but payment is not due until the payment date of the order.

(c) This subsection is subject to subsection (e) and to Section 4A–303. With respect to a payment order issued to a receiving bank other than the beneficiary's bank, acceptance of the order by the receiving bank obliges the sender to pay the bank the amount of the sender's order. Payment by the sender is not due until the execution date of the sender's order. The obligation of that sender to pay its payment order is excused if the funds transfer is not completed by acceptance by the beneficiary's bank of a payment order instructing payment to the beneficiary of that sender's payment order.

(d) If the sender of a payment order pays the order and was not obliged to pay all or part of the amount paid, the bank receiving payment is obliged to refund payment to the extent the sender was not obliged to pay. Except as provided in Sections 4A–204 and 4A–304, interest is payable on the refundable amount from the date of payment.

(e) If a funds transfer is not completed as stated in subsection (c) and an intermediary bank is obliged to refund payment as stated in subsection (d) but is unable to do so because not permitted by applicable law or because the bank suspends payments, a sender in the funds transfer that executed a payment order in compliance with an instruction, as stated in Section 4A–302(a)(1), to route the funds transfer through that intermediary bank is entitled to receive or retain payment from the sender of the payment order that is accepted. The first sender in the funds transfer that issued an instruction requiring routing through that intermediary bank is subrogated to the right of the bank that paid the intermediary bank to refund as stated in subsection (d).

(f) The right of the sender of a payment order to be excused from the obligation to pay the order as stated in subsection (c) or to receive refund under subsection (d) may not be varied by agreement.

§ 4A–403. Payment by Sender to Receiving Bank

(a) Payment of the sender's obligation under Section 4A–402 to pay the receiving bank occurs as follows:

(1) If the sender is a bank, payment occurs when the receiving bank receives final settlement of the obligation through a Federal Reserve Bank or through a funds-transfer system.

(2) If the sender is a bank and the sender (i) credited an account of the receiving bank with the sender, or (ii) caused an account of the receiving bank in another bank to be credited, payment occurs when the credit is withdrawn or, if not withdrawn, at midnight of the day on which the credit is withdrawable and the receiving bank learns of that fact.

(3) If the receiving bank debits an account of the sender with the receiving bank, payment occurs when the debit is made to the extent the debit is covered by a withdrawable credit balance in the account.

(b) If the sender and receiving bank are members of a funds-transfer system that nets obligations multilaterally among participants, the receiving bank receives final settlement when settlement is complete in accordance with the rules of the system. The obligation of the sender to pay the amount of a payment order transmitted through the funds-transfer system may be satisfied, to the extent permitted by the rules of the system, by setting off and applying against the sender's obligation the right of the sender to receive payment from the receiving bank of the amount of any other payment order transmitted to the sender by the receiving bank through the funds-transfer system. The aggregate balance of obligations owed by each sender to each receiving bank in the funds-transfer system may be satisfied, to the extent permitted by the rules of the system, by setting off and applying against that balance the aggregate balance of obligations owed to the sender by other members of the system. The aggregate balance is determined after the right of setoff stated in the second sentence of this subsection has been exercised.

(c) If two banks transmit payment orders to each other under an agreement that settlement of the obligations of each bank to the other under Section 4A–402 will be made at the end of the day or other period, the total amount owed with respect to all orders transmitted by one bank shall be set off against the total amount owed with respect to all orders transmitted by the other bank. To the extent of the setoff, each bank has made payment to the other.

(d) In a case not covered by subsection (a), the time when payment of the sender's obligation under Section 4A–402(b) or 4A–402(c) occurs is governed by applicable principles of law that determine when an obligation is satisfied.

§ 4A–404. Obligation of Beneficiary's Bank to Pay and Give Notice to Beneficiary

(a) Subject to Sections 4A–211(e), 4A–405(d), and 4A–405(e), if a beneficiary's bank accepts a payment order, the bank is obliged to pay the amount of the order to the beneficiary of the order. Payment is due on the payment date of the order, but if acceptance occurs on the payment date after the close of the funds-transfer business day of the bank, payment is due on the next funds-transfer

business day. If the bank refuses to pay after demand by the beneficiary and receipt of notice of particular circumstances that will give rise to consequential damages as a result of nonpayment, the beneficiary may recover damages resulting from the refusal to pay to the extent the bank had notice of the damages, unless the bank proves that it did not pay because of a reasonable doubt concerning the right of the beneficiary to payment.

(b) If a payment order accepted by the beneficiary's bank instructs payment to an account of the beneficiary, the bank is obliged to notify the beneficiary of receipt of the order before midnight of the next funds-transfer business day following the payment date. If the payment order does not instruct payment to an account of the beneficiary, the bank is required to notify the beneficiary only if notice is required by the order. Notice may be given by first class mail or any other means reasonable in the circumstances. If the bank fails to give the required notice, the bank is obliged to pay interest to the beneficiary on the amount of the payment order from the day notice should have been given until the day the beneficiary learned of receipt of the payment order by the bank. No other damages are recoverable. Reasonable attorney's fees are also recoverable if demand for interest is made and refused before an action is brought on the claim.

(c) The right of a beneficiary to receive payment and damages as stated in subsection (a) may not be varied by agreement or a funds-transfer system rule. The right of a beneficiary to be notified as stated in subsection (b) may be varied by agreement of the beneficiary or by a funds-transfer system rule if the beneficiary is notified of the rule before initiation of the funds transfer.

§ 4A–405. Payment by Beneficiary's Bank to Beneficiary

(a) If the beneficiary's bank credits an account of the beneficiary of a payment order, payment of the bank's obligation under Section 4A–404(a) occurs when and to the extent (i) the beneficiary is notified of the right to withdraw the credit, (ii) the bank lawfully applies the credit to a debt of the beneficiary, or (iii) funds with respect to the order are otherwise made available to the beneficiary by the bank.

(b) If the beneficiary's bank does not credit an account of the beneficiary of a payment order, the time when payment of the bank's obligation under Section 4A–404(a) occurs is governed by principles of law that determine when an obligation is satisfied.

(c) Except as stated in subsection (d) and (e), if the beneficiary's bank pays the beneficiary of a payment order under a condition to payment or agreement of the beneficiary giving the bank the right to recover payment from the beneficiary if the bank does not receive payment of the order, the condition to payment or agreement is not enforceable.

(d) A funds-transfer system rule may provide that payments made to beneficiaries of funds transfers made through the system are provisional until receipt of payment by the beneficiary's bank of the payment order it accepted. A beneficiary's bank that makes a payment that is provisional under the rule is entitled to refund from the beneficiary if (i) the rule requires that both the beneficiary and the originator be given notice of the provisional nature of the payment before the funds transfer is initiated, (ii) the beneficiary, the beneficiary's bank and the originator's bank agreed to be bound by the rule, and (iii) the beneficiary's bank did not receive payment of the payment order that it accepted. If the beneficiary is obliged to refund payment to the beneficiary's bank, acceptance of the payment order by the beneficiary's bank is nullified and no payment by the originator of the funds transfer to the beneficiary occurs under Section 4A–406.

(e) This subsection applies to a funds transfer that includes a payment order transmitted over a funds-transfer system that (i) nets obligations multilaterally among participants, and (ii) has in effect a loss-sharing agreement among participants for the purpose of providing funds necessary to complete settlement of the obligations of one or more participants that do not meet their settlement obligations. If the beneficiary's bank in the funds transfer accepts a payment order and the system fails to complete settlement pursuant to its rules with respect to any payment order in the funds transfer, (i) the acceptance by the beneficiary's bank is nullified and no person has any right or obligation based on the acceptance, (ii) the beneficiary's bank is entitled to recover payment from the beneficiary, (iii) no payment by the originator to the beneficiary occurs under Section 4A–406, and (iv) subject to Section 4A–402(e), each sender in the funds transfer is excused from its obligation to pay its payment order under Section 4A–402(c) because the funds transfer has not been completed.

§ 4A–406. Payment by Originator to Beneficiary; Discharge of Underlying Obligation

(a) Subject to Sections 4A–211(e), 4A–405(d), and 4A–405(e), the originator of a funds transfer pays the beneficiary of the originator's payment order (i) at the time a payment order for the benefit of the beneficiary is accepted by the beneficiary's bank in the funds transfer and (ii) in an amount equal to the amount of the order accepted by the beneficiary's bank, but not more than the amount of the originator's order.

(b) If payment under subsection (a) is made to satisfy an obligation, the obligation is discharged to the same extent discharge would result from payment to the beneficiary of the same amount in money, unless (i) the payment under subsection (a) was made by a means prohibited by the contract of the beneficiary with respect to the obligation, (ii) the beneficiary, within a reasonable time after

receiving notice of receipt of the order by the beneficiary's bank, notified the originator of the beneficiary's refusal of the payment, (iii) funds with respect to the order were not withdrawn by the beneficiary or applied to a debt of the beneficiary, and (iv) the beneficiary would suffer a loss that could reasonably have been avoided if payment had been made by a means complying with the contract. If payment by the originator does not result in discharge under this section, the originator is subrogated to the rights of the beneficiary to receive payment from the beneficiary's bank under Section 4A–404(a).

(c) For the purpose of determining whether discharge of an obligation occurs under subsection (b), if the beneficiary's bank accepts a payment order in an amount equal to the amount of the originator's payment order less charges of one or more receiving banks in the funds transfer, payment to the beneficiary is deemed to be in the amount of the originator's order unless upon demand by the beneficiary the originator does not pay the beneficiary the amount of the deducted charges.

(d) Rights of the originator or of the beneficiary of a funds transfer under this section may be varied only by agreement of the originator and the beneficiary.

Part 5 Miscellaneous Provisions

§ 4A–501. Variation by Agreement and Effect of Funds-Transfer System Rule

(a) Except as otherwise provided in this Article, the rights and obligations of a party to a funds transfer may be varied by agreement of the affected party.

(b) "Funds-transfer system rule" means a rule of an association of banks (i) governing transmission of payment orders by means of a funds-transfer system of the association or rights and obligations with respect to those orders, or (ii) to the extent the rule governs rights and obligations between banks that are parties to a funds transfer in which a Federal Reserve Bank, acting as an intermediary bank, sends a payment order to the beneficiary's bank. Except as otherwise provided in this Article, a funds-transfer system rule governing rights and obligations between participating banks using the system may be effective even if the rule conflicts with this Article and indirectly affects another party to the funds transfer who does not consent to the rule. A funds-transfer system rule may also govern rights and obligations of parties other than participating banks using the system to the extent stated in Sections 4A–404(c), 4A–405(d), and 4A–507(c).

§ 4A–502. Creditor Process Served on Receiving Bank; Setoff by Beneficiary's Bank

(a) As used in this section, "creditor process" means levy, attachment, garnishment, notice of lien, sequestration, or similar process issued by or on behalf of a creditor or other claimant with respect to an account.

(b) This subsection applies to creditor process with respect to an authorized account of the sender of a payment order if the creditor process is served on the receiving bank. For the purpose of determining rights with respect to the creditor process, if the receiving bank accepts the payment order the balance in the authorized account is deemed to be reduced by the amount of the payment order to the extent the bank did not otherwise receive payment of the order, unless the creditor process is served at a time and in a manner affording the bank a reasonable opportunity to act on it before the bank accepts the payment order.

(c) If a beneficiary's bank has received a payment order for payment to the beneficiary's account in the bank, the following rules apply:

(1) The bank may credit the beneficiary's account. The amount credited may be set off against an obligation owed by the beneficiary to the bank or may be applied to satisfy creditor process served on the bank with respect to the account.

(2) The bank may credit the beneficiary's account and allow withdrawal of the amount credited unless creditor process with respect to the account is served at a time and in a manner affording the bank a reasonable opportunity to act to prevent withdrawal.

(3) If creditor process with respect to the beneficiary's account has been served and the bank has had a reasonable opportunity to act on it, the bank may not reject the payment order except for a reason unrelated to the service of process.

(d) Creditor process with respect to a payment by the originator to the beneficiary pursuant to a funds transfer may be served only on the beneficiary's bank with respect to the debt owed by that bank to the beneficiary. Any other bank served with the creditor process is not obliged to act with respect to the process.

§ 4A–503. Injunction or Restraining Order With Respect to Funds Transfer

For proper cause and in compliance with applicable law, a court may restrain (i) a person from issuing a payment order to initiate a funds transfer, (ii) an originator's bank from executing the payment order of the originator, or (iii) the beneficiary's bank from releasing funds to the beneficiary or the beneficiary from withdrawing the funds. A court may not otherwise restrain a person from issuing a payment order, paying or receiving payment of a payment order, or otherwise acting with respect to a funds transfer.

§ 4A–504. Order in Which Items and Payment Orders May Be Charged to Account; Order of Withdrawals From Account

(a) If a receiving bank has received more than one payment order of the sender or one or more payment orders and other items that are payable from the sender's account, the bank may charge the sender's account with respect to the various orders and items in any sequence.

(b) In determining whether a credit to an account has been withdrawn by the holder of the account or applied to a debt of the holder of the account, credits first made to the account are first withdrawn or applied.

§ 4A–505. Preclusion of Objection to Debit of Customer's Account

If a receiving bank has received payment from its customer with respect to a payment order issued in the name of the customer as sender and accepted by the bank, and the customer received notification reasonably identifying the order, the customer is precluded from asserting that the bank is not entitled to retain the payment unless the customer notifies the bank of the customer's objection to the payment within one year after the notification was received by the customer.

§ 4A–506. Rate of Interest

(a) If, under this Article, a receiving bank is obliged to pay interest with respect to a payment order issued to the bank, the amount payable may be determined (i) by agreement of the sender and receiving bank, or (ii) by a funds-transfer system rule if the payment order is transmitted through a funds-transfer system.

(b) If the amount of interest is not determined by an agreement or rule as stated in subsection (a), the amount is calculated by multiplying the applicable Federal Funds rate by the amount on which interest is payable, and then multiplying the product by the number of days for which interest is payable. The applicable Federal Funds rate is the average of the Federal Funds rates published by the Federal Reserve Bank of New York for each of the days for which interest is payable divided by 360. The Federal Funds rate for any day on which a published rate is not available is the same as the published rate for the next preceding day for which there is a published rate. If a receiving bank that accepted a payment order is required to refund payment to the sender of the order because the funds transfer was not completed, but the failure to complete was not due to any fault by the bank, the interest payable is reduced by a percentage equal to the reserve requirement on deposits of the receiving bank.

§ 4A–507. Choice of Law

(a) The following rules apply unless the affected parties otherwise agree or subsection (c) applies:

(1) The rights and obligations between the sender of a payment order and the receiving bank are governed by the law of the jurisdiction in which the receiving bank is located.

(2) The rights and obligations between the beneficiary's bank and the beneficiary are governed by the

law of the jurisdiction in which the beneficiary's bank is located.

(3) The issue of when payment is made pursuant to a funds transfer by the originator to the beneficiary is governed by the law of the jurisdiction in which the beneficiary's bank is located.

(b) If the parties described in each paragraph of subsection (a) have made an agreement selecting the law of a particular jurisdiction to govern rights and obligations between each other, the law of that jurisdiction governs those rights and obligations, whether or not the payment order or the funds transfer bears a reasonable relation to that jurisdiction.

(c) A funds-transfer system rule may select the law of a particular jurisdiction to govern (i) rights and obligations between participating banks with respect to payment orders transmitted or processed through the system, or (ii) the rights and obligations of some or all parties to a funds transfer any part of which is carried out by means of the system. A choice of law made pursuant to clause (i) is binding on participating banks. A choice of law made pursuant to clause (ii) is binding on the originator, other sender, or a receiving bank having notice that the funds-transfer system might be used in the funds transfer and of the choice of law by the system when the originator, other sender, or receiving bank issued or accepted a payment order. The beneficiary of a funds transfer is bound by the choice of law if, when the funds transfer is initiated, the beneficiary has notice that the funds-transfer system might be used in the funds transfer and of the choice of law by the system. The law of a jurisdiction selected pursuant to this subsection may govern, whether or not that law bears a reasonable relation to the matter in issue.

(d) In the event of inconsistency between an agreement under subsection (b) and a choice-of-law rule under subsection (c), the agreement under subsection (b) prevails.

(e) If a funds transfer is made by use of more than one funds-transfer system and there is inconsistency between choice-of-law rules of the systems, the matter in issue is governed by the law of the selected jurisdiction that has the most significant relationship to the matter in issue.

ARTICLE 7 WAREHOUSE RECEIPTS, BILLS OF LANDING AND OTHER DOCUMENTS OF TITLE

Part I General

§ 7–101. Short Title
This article shall be known and may be cited as Uniform Commercial Code—Documents of Title.

§ 7–102. Definitions and Index of Definitions
(1) In this Article, unless the context otherwise requires:

(a) "Bailee" means the person who by a warehouse receipt, bill of lading or other document of title acknowledges possession of goods and contracts to deliver them.

(b) "Consignee" means the person named in a bill to whom or to whose order the bill promises delivery.

(c) "Consignor" means the person named in a bill as the person from whom the goods have been received for shipment.

(d) "Delivery order" means a written order to deliver goods directed to a warehouseman, carrier or other person who in the ordinary course of business issues warehouse receipts or bills of lading.

(e) "Document" means document of title as defined in the general definitions in Article 1 (Section 1–201).

(f) "Goods" means all things which are treated as movable for the purposes of a contract of storage or transportation.

(g) "Issuer" means a bailee who issues a document except that in relation to an unaccepted delivery order it means the person who orders the possessor of goods to deliver. Issuer includes any person for whom an agent or employee purports to act in issuing a document if the agent or employee has real or apparent authority to issue documents, notwithstanding that the issuer received no goods or that the goods were misdescribed or that in any other respect the agent or employee violated his instructions.

(h) "Warehouseman" is a person engaged in the business of storing goods for hire.

(2) Other definitions applying to this Article or to specified Parts thereof, and the sections in which they appear are:

"Duly negotiate." Section 7–501.

"Person entitled under the document." Section 7–403(4).

(3) Definitions in other Articles applying to this Article and the sections in which they appear are:

"Contract for sale." Section 2–106.

"Overseas." Section 2–323.

"Receipt" of goods. Section 2–103.

(4) In addition Article 1 contains general definitions and principles of construction and interpretation applicable throughout this Article.

§ 7–103. Relation of Article to Treaty, Statute, Tariff, Classification or Regulation
To the extent that any treaty or statute of the United States, regulatory statute of this State or tariff, classification or regulation filed or issued pursuant thereto is applicable, the provisions of this Article are subject thereto.

§ 7–104. Negotiable and Non-Negotiable Warehouse Receipt, Bill of Lading or Other Document of Title
(1) A warehouse receipt, bill of lading or other document of title is negotiable

(a) if by its terms the goods are to be delivered to bearer or to the order of a named person; or

(b) where recognized in overseas trade, if it runs to a named person or assigns.

(2) Any other documents are non-negotiable. A bill of lading in which it is stated that the goods are consigned to a named person is not made negotiable by a provision that the goods are to be delivered only against a written order signed by the same or another named person.

§ 7–105. Construction Against Negative Implication

The omission from either Part 2 or Part 3 of this Article of a provision corresponding to a provision made in the other Part does not imply that a corresponding rule of law is not applicable.

Part 2 Warehouse Receipts: Special Provisions

§ 7–201. Who May Issue a Warehouse Receipt; Storage Under Government Bond

(1) A warehouse receipt may be issued by any warehouseman.

(2) Where goods including distilled spirits and agricultural commodities are stored under a statute requiring a bond against withdrawal or a license for the issuance of receipts in the nature of warehouse receipts, a receipt issued for the goods has like effect as a warehouse receipt even though issued by a person who is the owner of the goods and is not a warehouseman.

§ 7–202. Forms of Warehouse Receipt; Essential Terms; Optional Terms

(1) A warehouse receipt need not be in any particular form.

(2) Unless a warehouse receipt embodies within its written or printed terms each of the following, the warehouseman is liable for damages caused by the omission to a person injured thereby:

(a) the location of the warehouse where the goods are stored;

(b) the date of issue of the receipt;

(c) the consecutive number of the receipt;

(d) a statement whether the goods received will be delivered to the bearer, to a specified person, or to a specified person or his order;

(e) the rate of storage and handling charges, except that where goods are stored under a field warehousing arrangement a statement of that fact is sufficient on a non-negotiable receipt;

(f) a description of the goods or of the packages containing them;

(g) the signature of the warehouseman which may be made by his authorized agent;

(h) if the receipt is issued for goods of which the warehouseman is owner, either solely or jointly or in common with others, the fact of such ownership; and

(i) a statement of the amount of advances made and of liabilities incurred for which the warehouseman claims a lien or security interest (Section 7–209). If the precise amount of such advances made or of such liabilities incurred is, at the time of the issue of the receipt, unknown to the warehouseman or to his agent who issues it, a statement of the fact that advances have been made or liabilities incurred and the purpose thereof is sufficient.

(3) A warehouseman may insert in his receipt any other terms which are not contrary to the provisions of this Act and do not impair his obligation of delivery (Section 7–403) or his duty of care (Section 7–204). Any contrary provisions shall be ineffective.

§ 7–203. Liability for Non-Receipt or Misdescription

A party to or purchaser for value in good faith of a document of title other than a bill of lading relying in either case upon the description therein of the goods may recover from the issuer damages caused by the non-receipt or misdescription of the goods, except to the extent that the document conspicuously indicates that the issuer does not know whether any part or all of the goods in fact were received or conform to the description, as where the description is in terms of marks or labels or kind, quantity or condition, or the receipt or description is qualified by "contents, condition and quality unknown," "said to contain" or the like, if such indication be true, or the party or purchaser otherwise has notice.

§ 7–204. Duty of Care; Contractual Limitation of Warehouseman's Liability

(1) A warehouseman is liable for damages for loss of or injury to the goods caused by his failure to exercise such care in regard to them as a reasonably careful man would exercise under like circumstances but unless otherwise agreed he is not liable for damages which could not have been avoided by the exercise of such care.

(2) Damages may be limited by a term in the warehouse receipt or storage agreement limiting the amount of liability in case of loss or damage, and setting forth a specific liability per article or item, or value per unit of weight, beyond which the warehouseman shall not be liable; provided, however, that such liability may on written request of the bailor at the time of signing such storage agreement or within a reasonable time after receipt of the warehouse receipt be increased on part or all of the goods thereunder, in which event increased rates may be charged based on such increased valuation, but that no such increase shall be permitted contrary to a lawful limitation of liability contained in the warehouseman's tariff, if any. No such limitation is effective with respect to the warehouseman's liability for conversion to his own use.

(3) Reasonable provisions as to the time and manner of presenting claims and instituting actions based on the

bailment may be included in the warehouse receipt or tariff.

(4) This section does not impair or repeal . . .

Note: Insert in subsection (4) a reference to any statute which imposes a higher responsibility upon the warehouseman or invalidates contractual limitations which would be permissible under this Article.

§ 7–205. Title under Warehouse Receipt Defeated in Certain Cases

A buyer in the ordinary course of business of fungible goods sold and delivered by a warehouseman who is also in the business of buying and selling such goods takes free of any claim under a warehouse receipt even though it has been duly negotiated.

§ 7–206. Termination of Storage at Warehouseman's Option

(1) A warehouseman may on notifying the person on whose account the goods are held and any other person known to claim an interest in the goods require payment of any charges and removal of the goods from the warehouse at the termination of the period of storage fixed by the document, or, if no period is fixed, within a stated period not less than thirty days after the notification. If the goods are not removed before the date specified in the notification, the warehouseman may sell them in accordance with the provisions of the section on enforcement of a warehouseman's lien (Section 7–210).

(2) If a warehouseman in good faith believes that the goods are about to deteriorate or decline in value to less than the amount of his lien within the time prescribed in subsection (1) for notification, advertisement and sale, the warehouseman may specify in the notification any reasonable shorter time for removal of the goods and in case the goods are not removed, may sell them at public sale held not less than one week after a single advertisement or posting.

(3) If as a result of a quality or condition of the goods of which the warehouseman had no notice at the time of deposit the goods are a hazard to other property or to the warehouse or to persons, the warehouseman may sell the goods at public or private sale without advertisement on reasonable notification to all persons known to claim an interest in the goods. If the warehouseman after a reasonable effort is unable to sell the goods he may dispose of them in any lawful manner and shall incur no liability by reason of such disposition.

(4) The warehouseman must deliver the goods to any person entitled to them under this Article upon due demand made at any time prior to sale or other disposition under this section.

(5) The warehouseman may satisfy his lien from the proceeds of any sale or disposition under this section but must hold the balance for delivery on the demand of any person to whom he would have been bound to deliver the goods.

§ 7–207. Goods Must Be Kept Separate; Fungible Goods

(1) Unless the warehouse receipt otherwise provides, a warehouseman must keep separate the goods covered by each receipt so as to permit at all times identification and delivery of those goods except that different lots of fungible goods may be commingled.

(2) Fungible goods so commingled are owned in common by the persons entitled thereto and the warehouseman is severally liable to each owner for that owner's share. Where because of overissue a mass of fungible goods is insufficient to meet all the receipts which the warehouseman has issued against it, the persons entitled include all holders to whom overissued receipts have been duly negotiated.

§ 7–208. Altered Warehouse Receipts

Where a blank in a negotiable warehouse receipt has been filled in without authority, a purchaser for value and without notice of the want of authority may treat the insertion as authorized. Any other unauthorized alteration leaves any receipt enforceable against the issuer according to its original tenor.

§ 7–209. Lien of Warehouseman

(1) A warehouseman has a lien against the bailor on the goods covered by a warehouse receipt or on the proceeds thereof in his possession for charges for storage or transportation (including demurrage and terminal charges), insurance, labor, or charges present or future in relation to the goods, and for expenses necessary for preservation of the goods or reasonably incurred in their sale pursuant to law. If the person on whose account the goods are held is liable for like charges or expenses in relation to other goods whenever deposited and it is stated in the receipt that a lien is claimed for charges and expenses in relation to other goods, the warehouseman also has a lien against him for such charges and expenses whether or not the other goods have been delivered by the warehouseman. But against a person to whom a negotiable warehouse receipt is duly negotiated a warehouseman's lien is limited to charges in an amount or at a rate specified on the receipt or if no charges are so specified then to a reasonable charge for storage of the goods covered by the receipt subsequent to the date of receipt.

(2) The warehouseman may also reserve a security interest against the bailor for a maximum amount specified on the receipt for charges other than those specified in subsection (1), such as for money advanced and interest. Such a security interest is governed by the Article on Secured Transactions (Article 9).

(3)(a) A warehouseman's lien for charges and expenses under subsection (1) or a security interest under subsection (2) is also effective against any person who so entrusted the bailor with possession of the goods that a pledge of them by him to a good faith purchaser for value would have been valid but is not effective against a person as to whom the document confers no right in the goods covered by it under Section 7–503.

(b) A warehouseman's lien on household goods for charges and expenses in relation to the goods under subsection (1) is also effective against all persons if the depositor was the legal possessor of the goods at the time of deposit. "Household goods" means furniture, furnishings, and personal effects used by the depositor in a dwelling.

(4) A warehouseman loses his lien on any goods which he voluntarily delivers or which he unjustifiably refuses to deliver.

§ 7–210. Enforcement of Warehouseman's Lien

(1) Except as provided in subsection (2), a warehouseman's lien may be enforced by public or private sale of the goods in block or in parcels, at any time or place and on any terms which are commercially reasonable, after notifying all persons known to claim an interest in the goods. Such notification must include a statement of the amount due, the nature of the proposed sale and the time and place of any public sale. The fact that a better price could have been obtained by a sale at a different time or in a different method from that selected by the warehouseman is not of itself sufficient to establish that the sale was not made in a commercially reasonable manner. If the warehouseman either sells the goods in the usual manner in any recognized market therefor, or if he sells at the price current in such market at the time of his sale, or if he has otherwise sold in conformity with commercially reasonable practices among dealers in the type of goods sold, he has sold in a commercially reasonable manner. A sale of more goods than apparently necessary to be offered to insure satisfaction of the obligation is not commercially reasonable except in cases covered by the preceding sentence.

(2) A warehouseman's lien on goods other than goods stored by a merchant in the course of his business may be enforced only as follows:

(a) All persons known to claim an interest in the goods must be notified.

(b) The notification must be delivered in person or sent by registered or certified letter to the last known address of any person to be notified.

(c) The notification must include an itemized statement of the claim, a description of the goods subject to the lien, a demand for payment within a specified time not less than ten days after receipt of the notification, and a conspicuous statement that unless the claim is paid within that time the goods will be advertised for sale and sold by auction at a specified time and place.

(d) The sale must conform to the terms of the notification.

(e) The sale must be held at the nearest suitable place to that where the goods are held or stored.

(f) After the expiration of the time given in the notification, an advertisement of the sale must be published once a week for two weeks consecutively in a newspaper of general circulation where the sale is to be held. The advertisement must include a description of the goods, the name of the person on whose account they are being held, and the time and place of the sale. The sale must take place at least fifteen days after the first publication. If there is no newspaper of general circulation where the sale is to be held, the advertisement must be posted at least ten days before the sale in not less than six conspicuous places in the neighborhood of the proposed sale.

(3) Before any sale pursuant to this section any person claiming a right in the goods may pay the amount necessary to satisfy the lien and the reasonable expenses incurred under this section. In that event the goods must not be sold, but must be retained by the warehouseman subject to the terms of the receipt and this Article.

(4) The warehouseman may buy at any public sale pursuant to this section.

(5) A purchaser in good faith of goods sold to enforce a warehouseman's lien takes the goods free of any rights of persons against whom the lien was valid, despite noncompliance by the warehouseman with the requirements of this section.

(6) The warehouseman may satisfy his lien from the proceeds of any sale pursuant to this section but must hold the balance, if any, for delivery on demand to any person to whom he would have been bound to deliver the goods.

(7) The rights provided by this section shall be in addition to all other rights allowed by law to a creditor against his debtor.

(8) Where a lien is on goods stored by a merchant in the course of his business the lien may be enforced in accordance with either subsection (1) or (2).

(9) The warehouseman is liable for damages caused by failure to comply with the requirements for sale under this section and in case of willful violation is liable for conversion.

◆

Part 3 Bills of Lading: Special Provisions

§ 7–301. Liability for Non-Receipt or Misdescription; "Said to Contain"; "Shipper's Load and Count"; Improper Handling

(1) A consignee of a non-negotiable bill who has given value in good faith or a holder to whom a negotiable bill has been duly negotiated relying in either case upon the description therein of the goods; or upon the date therein

shown; may recover from the issuer damages caused by the misdating of the bill or the non-receipt or misdescription of the goods, except to the extent that the document indicates that the issuer does not know whether any part or all of the goods in fact were received or conform to the description, as where the description is in terms of marks or labels or kind, quantity, or condition or the receipt or description is qualified by "contents or condition of contents of packages unknown," "said to contain," "shipper's weight, load and count" or the like, if such indication be true.

(2) When goods are loaded by an issuer who is a common carrier, the issuer must count the packages of goods if package freight and ascertain the kind and quantity if bulk freight. In such cases "shipper's weight, load and count" or other words indicating that the description was made by the shipper are ineffective except as to freight concealed by packages.

(3) When bulk freight is loaded by a shipper who makes available to the issuer adequate facilities for weighing such freight, an issuer who is a common carrier must ascertain the kind and quantity within a reasonable time after receiving the written request of the shipper to do so. In such cases "shipper's weight" or other words of like purport are ineffective.

(4) The issuer may by inserting in the bill the words "shipper's weight, load and count" or other words of like purport indicate that the goods were loaded by the shipper; and if such statement be true the issuer shall not be liable for damages caused by the improper loading. But their omission does not imply liability for such damages.

(5) The shipper shall be deemed to have guaranteed to the issuer the accuracy at the time of shipment of the description, marks, labels, number, kind, quantity, condition and weight, as furnished by him; and the shipper shall indemnify the issuer against damage caused by inaccuracies in such particulars. The right of the issuer to such indemnity shall in no way limit his responsibility and liability under the contract of carriage to any person other than the shipper.

§ 7–302. Through Bills of Lading and Similar Documents

(1) The issuer of a through bill of lading or other document embodying an undertaking to be performed in part by persons acting as its agents or by connecting carriers is liable to anyone entitled to recover on the document for any breach by such other persons or by a connecting carrier of its obligation under the document but to the extent that the bill covers an undertaking to be performed overseas or in territory not contiguous to the continental United States or an undertaking including matters other than transportation this liability may be varied by agreement of the parties.

(2) Where goods covered by a through bill of lading or other document embodying an undertaking to be performed in part by persons other than the issuer are received by any such person, he is subject with respect to his own performance while the goods are in his possession to the obligation of the issuer. His obligation is discharged by delivery of the goods to another such person pursuant to the document, and does not include liability for breach by any other such persons or by the issuer.

(3) The issuer of such through bill of lading or other document shall be entitled to recover from the connecting carrier or such other person in possession of the goods when the breach of the obligation under the document occurred, the amount it may be required to pay to anyone entitled to recover on the document therefor, as may be evidenced by any receipt. judgment, or transcript thereof, and the amount of any expense reasonably incurred by it in defending any action brought by anyone entitled to recover on the document therefor.

§ 7–303. Diversion; Reconsignment; Change of Instructions

(1) Unless the bill of lading otherwise provides, the carrier may deliver the goods to a person or destination other than that stated in the bill or may otherwise dispose of the goods on instructions from

(a) the holder of a negotiable bill; or

(b) the consignor on a non-negotiable bill notwithstanding contrary instructions from the consignee; or

(c) the consignee on a non-negotiable bill in the absence of contrary instructions from the consignor, if the goods have arrived at the billed destination or if the consignee is in possession of the bill; or

(d) the consignee on a non-negotiable bill if he is entitled as against the consignor to dispose of them.

(2) Unless such instructions are noted on a negotiable bill of lading, a person to whom the bill is duly negotiated can hold the bailee according to the original terms.

§ 7–304. Bills of Lading in a Set

(1) Except where customary in overseas transportation, a bill of lading must not be issued in a set of parts. The issuer is liable for damages caused by violation of this subsection.

(2) Where a bill of lading is lawfully drawn in a set of parts, each of which is numbered and expressed to be valid only if the goods have not been delivered against any other part, the whole of the parts constitute one bill.

(3) Where a bill of lading is lawfully issued in a set of parts and different parts are negotiated to different persons, the title of the holder to whom the first due negotiation is made prevails as to both the document and the goods even though any later holder may have received the goods from the carrier in good faith and discharged the carrier's obligation by surrender of his part.

(4) Any person who negotiates or transfers a single part of a bill of lading drawn in a set is liable to holders of that part as if it were the whole set.

(5) The bailee is obliged to deliver in accordance with Part 4 of this Article against the first presented part of a bill of lading lawfully drawn in a set. Such delivery discharges the bailee's obligation on the whole bill.

§ 7–305. Destination Bills

(1) Instead of issuing a bill of lading to the consignor at the place of shipment a carrier may at the request of the consignor procure the bill to be issued at destination or at any other place designated in the request.

(2) Upon request of anyone entitled as against the carrier to control the goods while in transit and on surrender of any outstanding bill of lading or other receipt covering such goods, the issuer may procure a substitute bill to be issued at any place designated in the request.

§ 7–306. Altered Bills of Lading

An unauthorized alteration or filling in of a blank in a bill of lading leaves the bill enforceable according to its original tenor.

§ 7–307. Lien of Carrier

(1) A carrier has a lien on the goods covered by a bill of lading for charges subsequent to the date of its receipt of the goods for storage or transportation (including demurrage and terminal charges) and for expenses necessary for preservation of the goods incident to their transportation or reasonably incurred in their sale pursuant to law. But against a purchaser for value of a negotiable bill of lading a carrier's lien is limited to charges stated in the bill or the applicable tariffs, or if no charges are stated then to a reasonable charge.

(2) A lien for charges and expenses under subsection (1) on goods which the carrier was required by law to receive for transportation is effective against the consignor or any person entitled to the goods unless the carrier had notice that the consignor lacked authority to subject the goods to such charges and expenses. Any other lien under subsection (1) is effective against the consignor and any person who permitted the bailor to have control or possession of the goods unless the carrier had notice that the bailor lacked such authority.

(3) A carrier loses his lien on any goods which he voluntarily delivers or which he unjustifiably refuses to deliver.

§ 7–308. Enforcement of Carrier's Lien

(1) A carrier's lien may be enforced by public or private sale of the goods, in block or in parcels, at any time or place and on any terms which are commercially reasonable, after notifying all persons known to claim an interest in the goods. Such notification must include a statement of the amount due, the nature of the proposed sale and the time and place of any public sale. The fact that a better price could have been obtained by a sale at a different time or in a different method from that selected by the carrier is not of itself sufficient to establish that the sale was not made in a commercially reasonable manner. If the carrier either sells the goods in the usual manner in any recognized market therefor or if he sells at the price current in such market at the time of his sale or if he has otherwise sold in conformity with commercially reasonable practices among dealers in the type of goods sold he has sold in a commercially reasonable manner. A sale of more goods than apparently necessary to be offered to ensure satisfaction of the obligation is not commercially reasonable except in cases covered by the preceding sentence.

(2) Before any sale pursuant to this section any person claiming a right in the goods may pay the amount necessary to satisfy the lien and the reasonable expenses incurred under this section. In that event the goods must not be sold, but must be retained by the carrier subject to the terms of the bill and this Article.

(3) The carrier may buy at any public sale pursuant to this section.

(4) A purchaser in good faith of goods sold to enforce a carrier's lien takes the goods free of any rights of persons against whom the lien was valid, despite noncompliance by the carrier with the requirements of this section.

(5) The carrier may satisfy his lien from the proceeds of any sale pursuant to this section but must hold the balance, if any, for delivery on demand to any person to whom he would have been bound to deliver the goods.

(6) The rights provided by this section shall be in addition to all other rights allowed by law to a creditor against his debtor.

(7) A carrier's lien may be enforced in accordance with either subsection (1) or the procedure set forth in subsection (2) of Section 7–210.

(8) The carrier is liable for damages caused by failure to comply with the requirements for sale under this section and in case of willful violation is liable for conversion.

§ 7–309. Duty of Care; Contractual Limitation of Carrier's Liability

(1) A carrier who issues a bill of lading whether negotiable or non-negotiable must exercise the degree of care in relation to the goods which a reasonably careful man would exercise under like circumstances. This subsection does not repeal or change any law or rule of law which imposes liability upon a common carrier for damages not caused by its negligence.

(2) Damages may be limited by a provision that the carrier's liability shall not exceed a value stated in the

document if the carrier's rates are dependent upon value and the consignor by the carrier's tariff is afforded an opportunity to declare a higher value or a value as lawfully provided in the tariff, or where no tariff is filed he is otherwise advised of such opportunity; but no such limitation is effective with respect to the carrier's liability for conversion to its own use.

(3) Reasonable provisions as to the time and manner of presenting claims and instituting actions based on the shipment may be included in a bill of lading or tariff.

Part 4 Warehouse Receipts and Bills of Lading: General Obligations

§ 7–401. Irregularities in Issue of Receipt or Bill or Conduct of Issuer

The obligations imposed by this Article on an issuer apply to a document of title regardless of the fact that

(a) the document may not comply with the requirements of this Article or of any other law or regulation regarding its issue, form or content; or

(b) the issuer may have violated laws regulating the conduct of his business; or

(c) the goods covered by the document were owned by the bailee at the time the document was issued; or

(d) the person issuing the document does not come within the definition of warehouseman if it purports to be a warehouse receipt.

§ 7–402. Duplicate Receipt or Bill; Overissue

Neither a duplicate nor any other document of title purporting to cover goods already represented by an outstanding document of the same issuer confers any right in the goods, except as provided in the case of bills in a set, overissue of documents for fungible goods and substitutes for lost, stolen or destroyed documents. But the issuer is liable for damages caused by his overissue or failure to identify a duplicate document as such by conspicuous notation on its face.

§ 7–403. Obligation of Warehouseman or Carrier to Deliver; Excuse

(1) The bailee must deliver the goods to a person entitled under the document who complies with subsections (2) and (3), unless and to the extent that the bailee establishes any of the following:

(a) delivery of the goods to a person whose receipt was rightful as against the claimant;

(b) damage to or delay, loss or destruction of the goods for which the bailee is not liable[, but the burden of establishing negligence in such cases is on the person entitled under the document];

Note: The brackets in (1)(b) indicate that State enactments may differ on this point without serious damage to the principle of uniformity.

(c) previous sale or other disposition of the goods in lawful enforcement of a lien or on warehouseman's lawful termination of storage;

(d) the exercise by a seller of his right to stop delivery pursuant to the provisions of the Article on Sales (Section 2–705);

(e) a diversion, reconsignment or other disposition pursuant to the provisions of this Article (Section 7–303) or tariff regulating such right;

(f) release, satisfaction or any other fact affording a personal defense against the claimant;

(g) any other lawful excuse

(2) A person claiming goods covered by a document of title must satisfy the bailee's lien where the bailee so requests or where the bailee is prohibited by law from delivering the goods until the charges are paid.

(3) Unless the person claiming is one against whom the document confers no right under Sec. 7–503(1), he must surrender for cancellation or notation of partial deliveries any outstanding negotiable document covering the goods, and the bailee must cancel the document or conspicuously note the partial delivery thereon or be liable to any person to whom the document is duly negotiated.

(4) "Person entitled under the document" means holder in the case of a negotiable document, or the person to whom delivery is to be made by the terms of or pursuant to written instructions under a non-negotiable document.

§ 7–404. No Liability for Good Faith Delivery Pursuant to Receipt or Bill

A bailee who in good faith including observance of reasonable commercial standards has received goods and delivered or otherwise disposed of them according to the terms of the document of title or pursuant to this Article is not liable therefor. This rule applies even though the person from whom he received the goods has no authority to procure the document or to dispose of the goods and even though the person to whom he delivered the goods had no authority to receive them.

Part 5 Warehouse Receipts and Bills of Lading: Negotiation and Transfer

§ 7–501. Form of Negotiation and Requirements of "Due Negotiation"

(1) A negotiable document of title running to the order of a named person is negotiated by his indorsement and delivery. After his indorsement in blank or to bearer any person can negotiate it by delivery alone.

(2)(a) A negotiable document of title is also negotiated by delivery alone when by its original terms it runs to bearer.

(b) When a document running to the order of a named person is delivered to him the effect is the same as if the document had been negotiated.

(3) Negotiation of a negotiable document of title after it has been indorsed to a specified person requires indorsement by the special indorsee as well as delivery.

(4) A negotiable document of title is "duly negotiated" when it is negotiated in the manner stated in this section to a holder who purchases it in good faith without notice of any defense against or claim to it on the part of any person and for value, unless it is established that the negotiation is not in the regular course of business or financing or involves receiving the document in settlement or payment of a money obligation.

(5) Indorsement of a non-negotiable document neither makes it negotiable nor adds to the transferee's rights.

(6) The naming in a negotiable bill of a person to be notified of the arrival of the goods does not limit the negotiability of the bill nor constitute notice to a purchaser thereof of any interest of such person in the goods.

§ 7–502. Rights Acquired by Due Negotiation

(1) Subject to the following section and to the provisions of Section 7–205 on fungible goods, a holder to whom a negotiable document of title has been duly negotiated acquires thereby:

   (a) title to the document;

   (b) title to the goods;

   (c) all rights accruing under the law of agency or estoppel, including rights to goods delivered to the bailee after the document was issued; and

   (d) the direct obligation of the issuer to hold or deliver the goods according to the terms of the document free of any defense or claim by him except those arising under the terms of the document or under this Article. In the case of a delivery order the bailee's obligation accrues only upon acceptance and the obligation acquired by the holder is that the issuer and any indorser will procure the acceptance of the bailee.

(2) Subject to the following section, title and rights so acquired are not defeated by any stoppage of the goods represented by the document or by surrender of such goods by the bailee, and are not impaired even though the negotiation or any prior negotiation constituted a breach of duty or even though any person has been deprived of possession of the document by misrepresentation, fraud, accident, mistake, duress, loss, theft or conversion, or even though a previous sale or other transfer of the goods or document has been made to a third person.

§ 7–503. Document of Title to Goods Defeated in Certain Cases

(1) A document of title confers no right in goods against a person who before issuance of the document had a legal interest or a perfected security interest in them and who neither

   (a) delivered or entrusted them or any document of title covering them to the bailor or his nominee with actual or apparent authority to ship, store or sell or with power to obtain delivery under this Article (Section 7–403) or with power of disposition under this Act (Section 2–403 and 9–307) or other statute or rule of law; nor

   (b) acquiesced in the procurement by the bailor or his nominee of any document of title.

(2) Title to goods based upon an unaccepted delivery order is subject to the rights of anyone to whom a negotiable warehouse receipt or bill of lading covering the goods has been duly negotiated. Such a title may be defeated under the next section to the same extent as the rights of the issuer or a transferee from the issuer.

(3) Title to goods based upon a bill of lading issued to a freight forwarder is subject to the rights of anyone to whom a bill issued by the freight forwarder is duly negotiated; but delivery by the carrier in accordance with Part 4 of this Article pursuant to its own bill of lading discharges the carrier's obligation to deliver.

§ 7–504. Rights Acquired in the Absence of Due Negotiation; Effect of Diversion; Seller's Stoppage of Delivery

(1) A transferee of a document, whether negotiable or non-negotiable, to whom the document has been delivered but not duly negotiated, acquires the title and rights which his transferor had or had actual authority to convey.

(2) In the case of a non-negotiable document, until but not after the bailee receives notification of the transfer, the rights of the transferee may be defeated

   (a) by those creditors of the transferor who could treat the sale as void under Section 2–402; or

   (b) by a buyer from the transferor in ordinary course of business if the bailee has delivered the goods to the buyer or received notification of his rights; or

   (c) as against the bailee by good faith dealings of the bailee with the transferor.

(3) A diversion or other change of shipping instructions by the consignor in a non-negotiable bill of lading which causes the bailee not to deliver to the consignee defeats the consignee's title to the goods if they have been delivered to a buyer in ordinary course of business and in any event defeats the consignee's rights against the bailee.

(4) Delivery pursuant to a non-negotiable document may be stopped by a seller under Section 2–705, and subject to the requirement of due notification there provided. A bailee honoring the seller's instructions is entitled to be indemnified by the seller against any resulting loss or expense.

§ 7–505. Indorser Not a Guarantor for Other Parties

The indorsement of a document of title issued by a bailee does not make the indorser liable for any default by the bailee or by previous indorsers.

§ 7–506. Delivery Without Indorsement: Right to Compel Indorsement

The transferee of a negotiable document of title has a specifically enforceable right to have his transferor supply any necessary indorsement but the transfer becomes a negotiation only as of the time the indorsement is supplied.

§ 7–507. Warranties on Negotiation or Transfer of Receipt or Bill

Where a person negotiates or transfers a document of title for value otherwise than as a mere intermediary under the next following section, then unless otherwise agreed he warrants to his immediate purchaser only in addition to any warranty made in selling the goods

(a) that the document is genuine; and

(b) that he has no knowledge of any fact which would impair its validity or worth; and

(c) that his negotiation or transfer is rightful and fully effective with respect to the title to the document and the goods it represents.

§ 7–508. Warranties of Collecting Bank as to Documents

A collecting bank or other intermediary known to be entrusted with documents on behalf of another or with collection of a draft or other claim against delivery of documents warrants by such delivery of the documents only its own good faith and authority. This rule applies even though the intermediary has purchased or made advances against the claim or draft to be collected.

§ 7–509. Receipt or Bill: When Adequate Compliance With Commercial Contract

The question whether a document is adequate to fulfill the obligations of a contract for sale or the conditions of a credit is governed by the Articles on Sales (Article 2) and on Letters of Credit (Article 5).

Part 6 Warehouse Receipts and Bills of Lading: Miscellaneous Provisions

§ 7–601. Lost and Missing Documents

(1) If a document has been lost, stolen or destroyed, a court may order delivery of the goods or issuance of a substitute document and the bailee may without liability to any person comply with such order. If the document was negotiable the claimant must post security approved by the court to indemnify any person who may suffer loss as a result of non-surrender of the document. If the document was not negotiable, such security may be required at the discretion of the court. The court may also in its discretion order payment of the bailee's reasonable costs and counsel fees.

(2) A bailee who without court order delivers goods to a person claiming under a missing negotiable document is liable to any person injured thereby, and if the delivery is not in good faith becomes liable for conversion. Delivery in good faith is not conversion if made in accordance with a filed classification or tariff or, where no classification or

tariff is filed, if the claimant posts security with the bailee if an amount at least double the value of the goods at the time of posting to indemnify any person injured by the delivery who files a notice of claim within one year after the delivery.

§ 7–602. Attachment of Goods Covered by a Negotiable Document

Except where the document was originally issued upon delivery of the goods by a person who had no power to dispose of them, no lien attaches by virtue of any judicial process to goods in the possession of a bailee for which a negotiable document of title is outstanding unless the document be first surrendered to the bailee or its negotiation enjoined, and the bailee shall not be compelled to deliver the goods pursuant to process until the document is surrendered to him or impounded by the court. One who purchases the document for value without notice of the process or injunction takes free of the lien imposed by judicial process.

§ 7–603. Conflicting Claims; Interpleader

If more than one person claims title or possession of the goods, the bailee is excused from delivery until he has had a reasonable time to ascertain the validity of the adverse claims or to bring an action to compel all claimants to interplead and may compel such interpleader, either in defending an action for non-delivery of the goods, or by original action, whichever is appropriate.

ARTICLE 9 SECURED TRANSACTIONS; SALES OF ACCOUNTS AND CHATTEL PAPER and Chattel Paper

Part 1 Short Title, Applicability and Definitions

§ 9–101. Short Title

This Article shall be known and may be cited as Uniform Commercial Code—Secured Transactions.

§ 9–102. Policy and Subject Matter of Article

(1) Except as otherwise provided in Section 9–104 on excluded transactions, this Article applies

(a) to any transaction (regardless of its form) which is intended to create a security interest in personal property or fixtures including goods, documents, instruments, general intangibles, chattel paper or accounts; and also

(b) to any sale of accounts or chattel paper.

(2) This Article applies to security interests created by contract including pledge, assignment, chattel mortgage, chattel trust, trust deed, factor's lien, equipment trust, conditional sale, trust receipt, other lien or title retention contract and lease or consignment intended as security. This Article does not apply to statutory liens except as provided in Section 9–310.

(3) The application of this Article to a security interest in a secured obligation is not affected by the fact that the obligation is itself secured by a transaction or interest to which this Article does not apply.

§ 9–103. Perfection of Security Interest in Multiple State Transactions

(1) Documents, instruments and ordinary goods.

(a) This subsection applies to documents and instruments and to goods other than those covered by a certificate of title described in subsection (2), mobile goods described in subsection (3), and minerals described in subsection (5).

(b) Except as otherwise provided in this subsection, perfection and the effect of perfection or non-perfection of a security interest in collateral are governed by the law of the jurisdiction where the collateral is when the last event occurs on which is based the assertion that the security interest is perfected or unperfected.

(c) If the parties to a transaction creating a purchase money security interest in goods in one jurisdiction understand at the time that the security interest attaches that the goods will be kept in another jurisdiction, then the law of the other jurisdiction governs the perfection and the effect of perfection or nonperfection of the security interest from the time it attaches until thirty days after the debtor receives possession of the goods and thereafter if the goods are taken to the other jurisdiction before the end of the thirty-day period.

(d) When collateral is brought into and kept in this state while subject to a security interest perfected under the law of the jurisdiction from which the collateral was removed, the security interest remains perfected, but if action is required by Part 3 of this Article to perfect the security interest.

(i) if the action is not taken before the expiration of the period of perfection in the other jurisdiction or the end of four months after the collateral is brought into this state, whichever period first expires, the security interest becomes unperfected at the end of that period and is thereafter deemed to have been unperfected as against a person who became a purchaser after removal;

(ii) if the action is taken before the expiration of the period specified in subparagraph (i), the security interest continues perfected thereafter;

(iii) for the purpose of priority over a buyer of consumer goods (subsection (2) of Section 9–307), the period of effectiveness of a filing in the jurisdiction from which the collateral is removed is governed by the rules with respect to perfection in subparagraphs (i) and (ii).

(2) Certificate of title.

(a) This subsection applies to goods covered by a certificate of title issued under a statute of this state or of another jurisdiction under the law of which indication of a security interest on the certificate is required as a condition of perfection.

(b) Except as otherwise provided in this subsection, perfection and the effect of perfection or non-perfection of the security interest are governed by the law (including the conflict of law rules) of the jurisdiction issuing the certificate until four months after the goods are removed from that jurisdiction and thereafter until the goods are registered in another jurisdiction, but in any event not beyond surrender of the certificate. After the expiration of that period, the goods are not covered by the certificate of title within the meaning of this section.

(c) Except with respect to the rights of a buyer described in the next paragraph, a security interest, perfected in another jurisdiction otherwise than by notation on a certificate of title, in goods brought into this state and thereafter covered by a certificate of title issued by this state is subject to the rules stated in paragraph (d) of subsection (1).

(d) If goods are brought into this state while a security interest therein is perfected in any manner under the law of the jurisdiction from which the goods are removed and a certificate of title is issued by this state and the certificate does not show that the goods are subject to the security interest or that they may be subject to security interests not shown on the certificate, the security interest is subordinate to the rights of a buyer of the goods who is not in the business of selling goods of that kind to the extent that he gives value and receives delivery of the goods after issuance of the certificate and without knowledge of the security interest.

(3) Accounts, general intangibles and mobile goods.

(a) This subsection applies to accounts (other than an account described in subsection (5) on minerals) and general intangibles (other than uncertificated securities) and to goods which are mobile and which are of a type normally used in more than one jurisdiction, such as motor vehicles, trailers, rolling stock, airplanes, shipping containers, road building and construction machinery and commercial harvesting machinery and the like, if the goods are equipment or are inventory leased or held for lease by the debtor to others, and are not covered by a certificate of title described in subsection (2).

(b) The law (including the conflict of laws rules) of the jurisdiction in which the debtor is located governs the perfection and the effect of perfection or non-perfection of the security interest.

(c) If, however, the debtor is located in a jurisdiction which is not part of the United States, and which does not provide for perfection of the security interest by filing or recording in that jurisdiction, the law of the jurisdiction in the United States in which the debtor has its major executive office governs the perfection and the effect of perfection or non-perfection of the security interest through filing. In the alternative, if the debtor is located in a jurisdiction which is not a part of the United States or Canada and the collateral is accounts or general intangibles for money due or to become due, the security interest may be perfected by notification to the account debtor. As used in this paragraph, "United States" includes its territories and possessions and the Commonwealth of Puerto Rico.

(d) A debtor shall be deemed located at his place of business if he has one, at his chief executive office if he has more than one place of business, otherwise at his residence. If, however, the debtor is a foreign air carrier under the Federal Aviation Act of 1958, as amended, it shall be deemed located at the designated office of the agent upon whom service of process may be made on behalf of the foreign air carrier.

(e) A security interest perfected under the law of the jurisdiction of the location of the debtor is perfected until the expiration of four months after a change of the debtor's location to another jurisdiction, or until perfection would have ceased by the law of the first jurisdiction, whichever period first expires. Unless perfected in the new jurisdiction before the end of that period, it becomes unperfected thereafter and is deemed to have been unperfected as against a person who became a purchaser after the change.

(4) Chattel paper. The rules stated for goods in subsection (1) apply to a possessory security interest in chattel paper. The rules stated for accounts in subsection (3) apply to a non-possessory security interest in chattel paper, but the security interest may not be perfected by notification to the account debtor.

(5) Minerals. Perfection and the effect of perfection or nonperfection of a security interest which is created by a debtor who has an interest in minerals or the like (including oil and gas) before extraction and which attaches thereto as extracted, or which attaches to an account resulting from the sale thereof at the wellhead or minehead are governed by the law (including the conflict of laws rules) of the jurisdiction wherein the wellhead or minehead is located.

(6) Uncertificated securities. The law (including the conflict of laws rules) of the jurisdiction or organization of the issuer governs the perfection and the effect of perfection or nonperfection of a security interest in uncertificated securities.

§ 9–104. Transactions Excluded From Article

This Article does not apply

(a) to a security interest subject to any statute of the United States, to the extent that such statute governs the rights of parties to and third parties affected by transactions in particular types of property; or

(b) to a landlord's lien; or

(c) to a lien given by statute or other rule of law for services or materials except as provided in Section 9–310 on priority of such liens; or

(d) to a transfer of a claim for wages, salary or other compensation of an employee; or

(e) to a transfer by a government or governmental subdivision or agency; or

(f) to a sale of accounts or chattel paper as part of a sale of the business out of which they arose, or an assignment of accounts or chattel paper which is for the purpose of collection only, or a transfer of a right to payment under a contract to an assignee who is also to do the performance under the contract or a transfer of a single account to an assignee in whole or partial satisfaction of a preexisting indebtedness; or

(g) to a transfer of an interest in or claim in or under any policy of insurance, except as provided with respect to proceeds (Section 9–306) and priorities in proceeds (Section 9–312); or

(h) to a right represented by a judgment (other than a judgment taken on a right to payment which was collateral); or

(i) to any right of set-off; or

(j) except to the extent that provision is made for fixtures to Section 9–313, to the creation or transfer of an interest in or lien on real estate, including a lease or rents thereunder; or

(k) to a transfer in whole or in part of any claim arising out of tort; or

(l) to a transfer of an interest in any deposit account (subsection (1) of Section 9–105), except as provided with respect to proceeds (Section 9–306) and priorities in proceeds (Section 9–312).

§ 9–105. Definitions and Index of Definitions

(1) In this Article unless the context otherwise requires:

(a) "Account debtor" means the person who is obligated on an account, chattel paper or general intangible;

(b) "Chattel paper" means a writing or writings which evidence both a monetary obligation and a security interest in or a lease of specific goods, but a charter or other contract involving the use or hire of a vessel is not chattel paper. When a transaction is evidenced both by such a security agreement or a lease and by an instrument or a series of instruments, the group of writings taken together constitutes chattel paper;

(c) "Collateral" means the property subject to a security interest, and includes accounts and chattel paper which have been sold;

(d) "Debtor" means the person who owes payment or other performance of the obligation secured, whether or not he owns or has rights in the collateral, and includes the seller of accounts or chattel paper. Where the debtor and the owner of the collateral are not the same person, the term "debtor" means the owner of the collateral in any provision of the Article dealing with the collateral, the obligor in any provision dealing with the obligation, and may include both where the context so requires;

(e) "Deposit account" means a demand, time, savings, passbook or like account maintained with a bank, savings and loan association, credit union or like organization, other than an account evidenced by a certificate of deposit;

(f) "Document" means document of title as defined in the general definitions of Article 1 (Section 1–201), and a receipt of the kind described in subsection (2) of Section 7–201;

(g) "Encumbrance" includes real estate mortgages and other liens on real estate and all other rights in real estate that are not ownership interests;

(h) "Goods" includes all things which are movable at the time the security interest attaches or which are fixtures (Section 9–313), but does not include money, documents, instruments, accounts, chattel paper, general intangibles, or minerals or the like (including oil and gas) before extraction. "Goods" also includes standing timber which is to be cut and removed under a conveyance or contract for sale, the unborn young of animals, and growing crops;

(i) "Instrument" means a negotiable instrument (defined in Section 3–104), or a certificated security (defined in Section 8–102) or any other writing which evidences a right to the payment of money and is not itself a security agreement or lease and is of a type which is in ordinary course of business transferred by delivery with any necessary indorsement or assignment;

(j) "Mortgage" means a consensual interest created by a real estate mortgage, a trust deed on real estate, or the like;

(k) An advance is made "pursuant to commitment" if the secured party has bound himself to make it, whether or not a subsequent event of default or other event not within his control has relieved or may relieve him from his obligation;

(l) "Security agreement" means an agreement which creates or provides for a security interest;

(m) "Secured party" means a lender, seller or other person in whose favor there is a security interest, including a person to whom accounts or chattel paper have been sold. When the holders of obligations issued under an indenture of trust, equipment trust agreement or the like are represented by a trustee or other person, the representative is the secured party;

(n) "Transmitting utility" means any person primarily engaged in the railroad, street railway or trolley bus business, the electric or electronics communications transmission business, the transmission of goods or pipeline, or the transmission or the production and transmission of electricity, steam, gas or water, or the provision of sewer service.

(2) Other definitions applying to this Article and the sections in which they appear are:

"Account."	Section 9–106.
"Attach."	Section 9–203.
"Construction mortgage."	Section 9–313(1).
"Consumer goods."	Section 9–109(1).
"Equipment."	Section 9–109(2).
"Farm products."	Section 9–109(3).
"Fixture."	Section 9–313(1).
"Fixture filing."	Section 9–313(1).
"General intangibles."	Section 9–106.
"Inventory."	Section 9–109(4).
"Lien creditor."	Section 9–301(3).
"Proceeds."	Section 9–306(1).
"Purchase money security interest."	Section 9–107.
"United States."	Section 9–103.

(3) The following definitions in other Articles apply to this Article:

"Check."	Section 3–104.
"Contract for sale."	Section 2–106.
"Holder in due course."	Section 3–302.
"Note."	Section 3–104.
"Sale."	Section 2–106.

(4) In addition Article 1 contains general definitions and principles of construction and interpretation applicable throughout this Article.

§ 9–106. Definitions: "Account"; "General Intangibles"

"Account" means any right to payment for goods sold or leased or for services rendered which is not evidenced by an instrument or chattel paper, whether or not it has been earned by performance. "General tangibles" means any personal property (including things in action) other than goods, accounts, chattel paper, documents, instruments, and money. All rights to payment earned or unearned under a charter or other contract involving the use or hire of a vessel and all rights incident to the charter or contract are accounts.

§ 9–107. Definitions: "Purchase Money Security Interest"

A security interest is a "purchase money security interest" to the extent that it is

(a) taken or retained by the seller of the collateral to secure all or part of its price; or

(b) taken by a person who by making advances or incurring an obligation gives value to enable the debtor to acquire rights in or the use of collateral if such value is in fact so used.

§ 9–108. When After-Acquired Collateral Not Security for Antecedent Debt

Where a secured party makes an advance, incurs an obligation, releases a perfected security interest, or otherwise gives new value which is to be secured in whole or in part by after-acquired property his security interest in the after-acquired collateral shall be deemed to be taken for new value and not as security for an antecedent debt if the debtor acquires his rights in such collateral either in the ordinary course of his business or under a contract of purchase made pursuant to the security agreement within a reasonable time after new value is given.

§ 9–109. Classification of Goods; "Consumer Goods"; "Equipment"; "Farm Products"; "Inventory"

Goods are

(1) "consumer goods" if they are used or bought for use primarily for personal, family or household purposes;

(2) "equipment" if they are used or bought for use primarily in business (including farming or a profession) or by a debtor who is a non-profit organization or a governmental subdivision or agency or if the goods are not included in the definitions of inventory, farm products or consumer goods;

(3) "farm products" if they are crops or livestock or supplies used or produced in farming operations or if they are products of crops or livestock in their unmanufactured states (such as ginned cotton, wool-clip, maple syrup, milk and eggs), and if they are in the possession of a debtor engaged in raising, fattening, grazing or other farming operations. If goods are farm products they are neither equipment nor inventory;

(4) "inventory" if they are held by a person who holds them for sale or lease or to be furnished under contracts of service or if he has so furnished them, or if they are raw materials, work in process or materials used or consumed in a business. Inventory of a person is not be classified as his equipment.

§ 9–110. Sufficiency of Description

For the purposes of this Article any description of personal property or real estate is sufficient whether or not it is specific if it reasonably identifies what is described.

§ 9–111. Applicability of Bulk Transfer Laws

The creation of a security interest is not a bulk transfer under Article 6 (see Section 6–103).

§ 9–112. Where Collateral Is Not Owned by Debtor

Unless otherwise agreed, when a secured party knows that collateral is owned by a person who is not the debtor, the owner of the collateral is entitled to receive from the secured party any surplus under Section 9–502(2) or under Section 9–504(1), and is not liable for the debt or for any deficiency after resale, and he has the same right as the debtor

(a) to receive statements under Section 9–208;

(b) to receive notice of and to object to a secured party's proposal to retain the collateral in satisfaction of the indebtedness under Section 9–505;

(c) to redeem the collateral under Section 9–506;

(d) to obtain injunctive or other relief under Section 9–507(1); and

(e) to recover losses caused to him under Section 9–208(2).

§ 9–113. Security Interests Arising under Article on Sales

A security interest arising solely under the Article on Sales (Article 2) or the Article on Leases (Article 2A) is subject to the provisions of this Article except that to the extent that and so long as the debtor does not have or does not lawfully obtain possession of the goods

(a) no security agreement is necessary to make the security interest enforceable; and

(b) no filing is required to perfect the security interest; and

(c) the rights of the secured party on default by the debtor are governed (i) by the Article on Sales (Article 2) in the case of a security interest arising solely under such Article or (ii) by the Article on Leases (Article 2A) in the case of a security interest arising solely under such Article.

§ 9–114. Consignment

(1) A person who delivers goods under a consignment which is not a security interest and who would be required to file under this Article by paragraph (3)(c) of Section 2–326 has priority over a secured party who is or becomes a creditor of the consignee and who would have a perfected security interest in the goods if they were the property of the consignee, and also has priority with respect to identifiable cash proceeds received on or before delivery of the goods to a buyer, if

(a) the consignor complies with the filing provision of the Article on Sales with respect to consignments (paragraph (3)(c) of Section 2–326) before the consignee receives possession of the goods; and

(b) the consignor gives notification in writing to the holder of the security interest if the holder has filed a financing statement covering the same types of goods before the date of the filing made by the consignor; and

(c) the holder of the security interest receives the notification within five years before the consignee receives possession of the goods; and

(d) the notification states that the consignor expects to deliver goods on consignment to the consignee, describing the goods by item or type.

(2) In the case of a consignment which is not a security interest and in which the requirements of the preceding

subsection have not been met, a person who delivers goods to another is subordinate to a person who would have a perfected security interest in the goods if they were the property of the debtor.

Part 2 Validity of Security Agreement and Rights of Parties Thereto

§ 9–201. General Validity of Security Agreement
Except as otherwise provided by this Act a security agreement is effective according to its terms between the parties, against purchasers of the collateral and against creditors. Nothing in this Article validates any charge or practice illegal under any statute or regulation thereunder governing usury, small loans, retail installment sales, or the like, or extends the application of any such statute or regulation to any transaction not otherwise subject thereto.

§ 9–202. Title to Collateral Immaterial
Each provision of this Article with regard to rights, obligations and remedies applies whether title to collateral is in the secured party or in the debtor.

§ 9–203. Attachment and Enforceability of Security Interest; Proceeds; Formal Requisites
(1) Subject to the provisions of Section 4–208 on the security interest of a collecting bank, Section 8–321 on security interests in securities and Section 9–113 on a security interest arising under the Article on Sales, a security interest is not enforceable against the debtor or third parties with respect to the collateral and does not attach unless:

(a) the collateral is in the possession of the secured party pursuant to agreement, or the debtor has signed a security agreement which contains a description of the collateral and in addition, when the security interest covers crops growing or to be grown or timber to be cut, a description of the land concerned;

(b) value has been given; and

(c) the debtor has rights in the collateral.

(2) A security interest attaches when it becomes enforceable against the debtor with respect to the collateral. Attachment occurs as soon as all of the events specified in subsection (1) have taken place unless explicit agreement postpones the time of attaching.

(3) Unless otherwise agreed a security agreement gives the secured party the rights to proceeds provided by Section 9–306.

(4) A transaction, although subject to this Article, is also subject to . . . .*, and in the case of conflict between the provisions of this Article and any such statute, the provisions of such statute control. Failure to comply with any applicable statute has only the effect which is specified therein.

*Note: At * in subsection (4) insert reference to any local statute regulating small loans, retail installment sales and the like.*

The foregoing subsection (4) is designed to make it clear that certain transactions, although subject to this Article, must also comply with other applicable legislation.

This Article is designed to regulate all the "security" aspects of transactions within its scope. There is, however, much regulatory legislation, particularly in the consumer field, which supplements this Article and should not be repealed by its enactment. Examples are small loan acts, retail installment selling acts and the like. Such acts may provide for licensing and rate regulation and may prescribe particular forms of contract. Such provisions should remain in force despite the enactment of this Article. On the other hand if a retail installment selling act contains provisions on filing, rights on default, etc., such provisions should be repealed as inconsistent with this Article except that inconsistent provisions as to deficiencies, penalties, etc., in the Uniform Consumer Credit Code and other recent related legislation should remain because those statutes were drafted after the substantial enactment of the Article and with the intention of modifying certain provisions of this Article as to consumer credit.

§ 9–204. After-Acquired Property; Future Advances
(1) Except as provided in subsection (2), a security agreement may provide that any or all obligations covered by the security agreement are to be secured by after-acquired collateral.

(2) No security interest attaches under an after-acquired property clause to consumer goods other than accessions (Section 9–314) when given as additional security unless the debtor acquires rights in them within ten days after the secured party gives value.

(3) Obligations covered by a security agreement may include future advances or other value whether or not the advances or value are given pursuant to commitment (subsection (1) of Section 9–105).

§ 9–205. Use or Disposition of Collateral Without Accounting Permissible
A security interest is not invalid or fraudulent against creditors by reason of liberty in the debtor to use, commingle or dispose of all or part of the collateral (including returned or repossessed goods) or to collect or compromise accounts or chattel paper, or to accept the return of goods or make repossessions, or to use, commingle or dispose of proceeds, or by reason of the failure of the secured party to require the debtor to account for proceeds or replace collateral. This section does not relax the requirements of possession where perfection of a

security interest depends upon possession of the collateral by the secured party or by a bailee.

§ 9–206. Agreement Not to Assert Defenses Against Assignee; Modification of Sales Warranties Where Security Agreement Exists

(1) Subject to any statute or decision which establishes a different rule for buyers or lessees of consumer goods, an agreement by a buyer or lessee that he will not assert against an assignee any claim or defense which he may have against the seller or lessor is enforceable by an assignee who takes his assignment for value, in good faith and without notice of a claim or defense, except as to defenses of a type which may be asserted against a holder in due course of a negotiable instrument under the Article on Commercial Paper (Article 3). A buyer who as part of one transaction signs both a negotiable instrument and a security agreement makes such an agreement.

(2) When a seller retains a purchase money security interest in goods the Article on Sales (Article 2) governs the sale and any disclaimer, limitation or modification of the seller's warranties.

§ 9–207. Rights and Duties When Collateral Is in Secured Party's Possession

(1) A secured party must use reasonable care in the custody and preservation of collateral in his possession. In the case of an instrument or chattel paper reasonable care includes taking necessary steps to preserve rights against prior parties unless otherwise agreed.

(2) Unless otherwise agreed, when collateral is in the secured party's possession

   (a) reasonable expenses (including the cost of any insurance and payment of taxes or other charges) incurred in the custody, preservation, use or operation of the collateral are chargeable to the debtor and are secured by the collateral;

   (b) the risk of accidental loss or damage is on the debtor to the extent of any deficiency in any effective insurance coverage;

   (c) the secured party may hold as additional security any increase or profits (except money) received from the collateral, but money so received, unless remitted to the debtor, shall be applied in reduction of the secured obligation;

   (d) the secured party must keep the collateral identifiable but fungible collateral may be commingled;

   (e) the secured party may repledge the collateral upon terms which do not impair the debtor's right to redeem it.

(3) A secured party is liable for any loss caused by his failure to meet any obligation imposed by the preceding subsections but does not lose his security interest.

(4) A secured party may use or operate the collateral for the purpose of preserving the collateral or its value or pursuant to the order of a court of appropriate jurisdiction or, except in the case of consumer goods, in the manner and to the extent provided in the security agreement.

§ 9–208. Request for Statement of Account or List of Collateral

(1) A debtor may sign a statement indicating what he believes to be the aggregate amount of unpaid indebtedness as of a specified date and may send it to the secured party with a request that the statement be approved or corrected and returned to the debtor. When the security agreement or any other record kept by the secured party identifies the collateral a debtor may similarly request the secured party to approve or correct a list of the collateral.

(2) The secured party must comply with such a request within two weeks after receipt by sending a written correction or approval. If the secured party claims a security interest in all of a particular type of collateral owned by the debtor he may indicate that fact in his reply and need not approve or correct an itemized list of such collateral. If the secured party without reasonable excuse fails to comply he is liable for any loss caused to the debtor thereby; and if the debtor has properly included in his request a good faith statement of the obligation or a list of the collateral or both the secured party may claim a security interest only as shown in the statement against persons misled by his failure to comply. If he no longer has an interest in the obligation or collateral at the time the request is received he must disclose the name and address of any successor in interest known to him and he is liable for any loss caused to the debtor as a result of failure to disclose. A successor in interest is not subject to this section until a request is received by him.

(3) A debtor is entitled to such a statement once every six months without charge. The secured party may require payment of a charge not exceeding $10 for each additional statement furnished.

Part 3 Rights of Third Parties; Perfected and Unperfected Security Interests; Rules of Priority

§ 9–301. Persons Who Take Priority over Unperfected Security Interests; Rights of "Lien Creditor"

(1) Except as otherwise provided in subsection (2), an unperfected security interest is subordinate to the rights of

   (a) persons entitled to priority under Section 9–312;

   (b) a person who becomes a lien creditor before the security interest is perfected;

   (c) in the case of goods, instruments, documents, and chattel paper, a person who is not a secured party and who is a transferee in bulk or other buyer not in ordinary course of business or is a buyer of farm products in ordinary course of business, to the extent that he gives value and receives delivery of the collateral without knowledge of the security interest and before it is perfected;

(d) in the case of accounts and general intangibles, a person who is not a secured party and who is a transferee to the extent that he gives value without knowledge of the security interest and before it is perfected.

(2) If the secured party files with respect to a purchase money security interest before or within ten days after the debtor receives possession of the collateral, he takes priority over the rights of a transferee in bulk or of a lien creditor which arise between the time the security interest attaches and the time of filing.

(3) A "lien creditor" means a creditor who has acquired a lien on the property involved by attachment, levy or the like and includes an assignee for benefit of creditors from the time of assignment, and a trustee in bankruptcy from the date of the filing of the petition or a receiver in equity from the time of appointment.

(4) A person who becomes a lien creditor while a security interest is perfected takes subject to the security interest only to the extent that it secures advances made before he becomes a lien creditor or within 45 days thereafter or made without knowledge of the lien or pursuant to a commitment entered into without knowledge of the lien.

§ 9–302. When Filing Is Required to Perfect Security Interest; Security Interests to Which Filing Provisions of This Article Do Not Apply

(1) A financing statement must be filed to perfect all security interests except the following:

(a) a security interest in collateral in possession of the secured party under Section 9–305;

(b) a security interest temporarily perfected in instruments or documents without delivery under Section 9–304 or in proceeds for a 10 day period under Section 9–306;

(c) a security interest created by an assignment of a beneficial interest in a trust or a decedent's estate;

(d) a purchase money security interest in consumer goods; but filing is required for a motor vehicle required to be registered; and fixture filing is required for priority over conflicting interests in fixtures to the extent provided in Section 9–313;

(e) an assignment of accounts which does not alone or in conjunction with other assignments to the same assignee transfer a significant part of the outstanding accounts of the assignor;

(f) a security interest of a collecting bank (Section 4–208) or in securities (Section 8–321) or arising under the Article on Sales (see Section 9–113) or covered in subsection (3) of this section;

(g) an assignment for the benefit of all the creditors of the transferor, and subsequent transfers by the assignee thereunder.

(2) If a secured party assigns a perfected security interest, no filing under this Article is required in order to continue the perfected status of the security interest against creditors of the transferees from the original debtor.

(3) The filing of a financing statement otherwise required by this Article is not necessary or effective to perfect a security interest in property subject to

(a) a statute or treaty of the United States which provides for a national or international registration or a national or international certificate of title or which specifies a place of filing different from that specified in this Article for filing of the security interest; or

(b) the following statutes of this state; [list any certificate of title statute covering automobiles, trailers, mobile homes, boats, farm tractors, or the like, and any central filing statute*]; but during any period in which collateral is inventory held for sale by a person who is in the business of selling goods of that kind, the filing provisions of this Article (Part 4) apply to a security interest in that collateral created by him as debtor; or

(c) a certificate of title statute of another jurisdiction under the law of which indication of a security interest on the certificate is required as a condition of perfection (subsection (2) of Section 9–103).

(4) Compliance with a statute or treaty described in subsection (3) is equivalent to the filing of a financing statement under this Article, and a security interest in property subject to the statute or treaty can be perfected only by compliance therewith except as provided in Section 9–103 on multiple state transactions. Duration and renewal of perfection of a security interest perfected by compliance with the statute or treaty are governed by the provisions of the statute or treaty; in other respects the security interest is subject to this Article.

*Note: *It is recommended that the provisions of certificate of title acts for perfection of security interests by notation on the certificates should be amended to exclude coverage of inventory held for sale.*

§ 9–303. When Security Interest Is Perfected; Continuity of Perfection

(1) A security interest is perfected when it has attached and when all of the applicable steps required for perfection have been taken. Such steps are specified in Section 9–302, 9–304, 9–305 and 9–306. If such steps are taken before the security interest attaches, it is perfected at the time when it attaches.

(2) If a security interest is originally perfected in any way permitted under this Article and is subsequently perfected in some other way under this Article, without an intermediate period when it was unperfected, the security interest shall be deemed to be perfected continuously for the purposes of this Article.

§ 9–304. Perfection of Security Interest in Instruments, Documents, and Goods Covered by Documents; Perfection by Permissive Filing; Temporary Perfection Without Filing or Transfer of Possession

(1) A security interest in chattel paper or negotiable documents may be perfected by filing. A security interest in money or instruments (other than certificated securities or instruments which constitute part of chattel paper) can be perfected only by the secured party's taking possession, except as provided in subsections (4) and (5) of this section and subsections (2) and (3) of Section 9–306 on proceeds.

(2) During the period that goods are in the possession of the issuer of a negotiable document therefor, a security interest in the goods is perfected by perfecting a security interest in the document, and any security interest in the goods otherwise perfected during such period is subject thereto.

(3) A security interest in goods in the possession of a bailee other than one who has issued a negotiable document therefor is perfected by issuance of a document in the name of the secured party or by the bailee's receipt of notification of the secured party's interest or by filing as to the goods.

(4) A security interest in instruments (other than certificated securities) or negotiable documents is perfected without filing or the taking of possession for a period of 21 days from the time it attaches to the extent that it arises from new value given under a written security agreement.

(5) A security interest remains perfected for a period of 21 days without filing where a secured party having a perfected security interest in an instrument (other than a certificated security), a negotiable document or goods in possession of a bailee other than one who has issued a negotiable document therefor

(a) makes available to the debtor the goods or documents representing the goods for the purpose of ultimate sale or exchange or for the purpose of loading, unloading, storing, shipping, transshipping, manufacturing, processing or otherwise dealing with them in a manner preliminary to their sale or exchange, but priority between conflicting security interests in the goods is subject to subsection (3) of Section 9–312; or

(b) delivers the instrument to the debtor for the purpose of ultimate sale or exchange or of presentation, collection, renewal or registration of transfer.

(6) After the 21 day period in subsections (4) and (5) perfection depends upon compliance with applicable provisions of this Article.

§ 9–305. When Possession by Secured Party Perfects Security Interest Without Filing

A security interest in letters of credit and advices of credit (subsection (2)(a) of Section 5–116), goods, instruments (other than certificated securities), money, negotiable documents, or chattel paper may be perfected by the secured party's taking possession of the collateral. If such collateral other than goods covered by a negotiable document is held by a bailee, the secured party is deemed to have possession from the time possession is taken without a relation back and continues only so long as possession is retained, unless otherwise specified in this Article. The security interest may be otherwise perfected as provided in this Article before or after the period of possession by the secured party.

§ 9–306. "Proceeds"; Secured Party's Rights on Disposition of Collateral

(1) "Proceeds" includes whatever is received upon the sale, exchange, collection or other disposition of collateral or proceeds. Insurance payable by reason of loss or damage to the collateral is proceeds, except to the extent that it is payable to a person other than a party to the security agreement. Money, checks, deposit accounts, and the like are "cash proceeds." All other proceeds are "non-cash proceeds."

(2) Except where this Article otherwise provides, a security interest continues in collateral notwithstanding sale, exchange or other disposition thereof unless the disposition was authorized by the secured party in the security agreement or otherwise, and also continues in any identifiable proceeds including collections received by the debtor.

(3) The security interest in proceeds is a continuously perfected security interest if the interest in the original collateral was perfected but it ceases to be a perfected security interest and becomes unperfected ten days after receipt of the proceeds by the debtor unless

(a) a filed financing statement covers the original collateral and the proceeds are collateral in which a security interest may be perfected by filing in the office or offices where the financing statement has been filed and, if the proceeds are acquired with cash proceeds, the description of collateral in the financing statement indicates the types of property constituting the proceeds; or

(b) a filed financing statement covers the original collateral and the proceeds are identifiable cash proceeds; or

(c) the security interest in the proceeds is perfected before the expiration of the ten day period. Except as provided in this section, a security interest in proceeds can be perfected only by the methods or under the circumstances permitted in this Article for original collateral of the same type.

(4) In the event of insolvency proceedings instituted by or against a debtor, a secured party with a perfected security interest in proceeds has a perfected security interest only in the following proceeds:

(a) in identifiable non-cash proceeds and in separate deposit accounts containing only proceeds;

(b) in identifiable proceeds in the form of money which is neither commingled with other money nor deposited in a deposit account prior to the insolvency proceedings;

(c) in identifiable cash proceeds in the form of checks and the like which are not deposited in a deposit account prior to the insolvency proceedings; and

(d) in all cash and deposit accounts of the debtor in which proceeds have been commingled with other funds, but the perfected security interest under this paragraph (d) is

(i) subject to any right to setoff; and

(ii) limited to an amount not greater than the amount of any cash proceeds received by the debtor within ten days before the institution of the insolvency proceedings less the sum of (I) the payments to the secured party on account of cash proceeds received by the debtor during such period and (II) the cash proceeds received by the debtor during such period to which the secured party is entitled under paragraph (a) through (c) of this subsection (4).

(5) If a sale of goods results in an account or chattel paper which is transferred by the seller to a secured party, and if the goods are returned to or are repossessed by the seller or the secured party, the following rules determine priorities:

(a) If the goods are collateral at the time of sale, for an indebtedness of the seller which is still unpaid, the original security interest attaches again to the goods and continues as a perfected security interest if it was perfected at the time when the goods were sold. If the security interest was originally perfected by a filing which is still effective, nothing further is required to continue the perfected status; in any other case, the secured party must take possession of the returned or repossessed goods or must file.

(b) An unpaid transferee of the chattel paper has a security interest in the goods against the transferor. Such security interest is prior to a security interest asserted under paragraph (a) to the extent that the transferee of the chattel paper was entitled to priority under Section 9–308.

(c) An unpaid transferee of the account has a security interest in the goods against the transferor. Such security interest is subordinate to a security interest asserted under paragraph (a).

(d) A security interest of an unpaid transferee asserted under paragraph (b) or (c) must be perfected for protection against creditors of the transferor and purchasers of the returned or repossessed goods.

§ 9–307. Protection of Buyers of Goods

(1) A buyer in ordinary course of business (subsection (9) of Section 1–201) other than a person buying farm products from a person engaged in farming operations takes free of a security interest created by his seller even though the security interest is perfected and even though the buyer knows of its existence.

(2) In a case of consumer goods, a buyer takes free of a security interest even though perfected if he buys without knowledge of the security interest, for value and for his own personal, family or household purposes unless prior to the purchase the secured party has filed a financing statement covering such goods.

(3) A buyer other than a buyer in ordinary course of business (subsection (1) of this section) takes free of a security interest to the extent that it secures future advances made after the secured party acquires knowledge of the purchase, or more than 45 days after the purchase, whichever first occurs, unless made pursuant to a commitment entered into without knowledge of the purchase and before the expiration of the 45 day period.

§ 9–308. Purchase of Chattel Paper and Instruments

A purchaser of chattel paper or an instrument who gives new value and takes possession of it in the ordinary course of his business has priority over a security interest in the chattel paper or instrument

(a) which is perfected under Section 9–304 (permissive filing and temporary perfection) or under Section 9–306 (perfection as to proceeds) if he acts without knowledge that the specific paper or instrument is subject to a security interest; or

(b) which is claimed merely as proceeds of inventory subject to a security interest (Section 9–306) even though he knows that the specific paper or instrument is subject to the security interest.

§ 9–309. Protection of Purchasers of Instruments, Documents and Securities

Nothing in this Article limits the rights of a holder in due course of a negotiable instrument (Section 3–302) or a holder to whom a negotiable document of title has been duly negotiated (Section 7–501) or a bona fide purchaser of a security (Section 8–302) and the holders or purchasers take priority over an earlier security interest even though perfected. Filing under this Article does not constitute notice of the security interest to such holders or purchasers.

§ 9–310. Priority of Certain Liens Arising by Operation of Law

When a person in the ordinary course of his business furnishes services or materials with respect to goods subject to a security interest, a lien upon goods in the possession of such person given by statute or rule of law for such materials or services takes priority over a perfected security interest unless the lien is statutory and the statute expressly provides otherwise.

§ 9–311. Alienability of Debtor's Rights: Judicial Process

The debtor's rights in collateral may be voluntarily or involuntarily transferred (by way of sale, creation of a security interest, attachment, levy, garnishment or other judicial process) notwithstanding a provision in the security agreement prohibiting any transfer or making the transfer constitute a default.

§ 9–312. Priorities among Conflicting Security Interests in the Same Collateral

(1) The rules of priority stated in other sections of this Part and in the following sections shall govern when applicable; Section 4–208 with respect to the security interests of collecting banks in items being collected, accompanying documents and proceeds; Section 9–103 on security interests related to other jurisdictions; Section 9–114 on consignments.

(2) A perfected security interest in crops for new value given to enable the debtor to produce the crops during the production season and given not more than three months before the crops become growing crops by planting or otherwise takes priority over an earlier perfected security interest to the extent that such earlier interest secures obligations due more than six months before the crops become growing crops by planting or otherwise, even though the person giving new value had knowledge of the earlier security interest.

(3) A perfected purchase money security interest in inventory has priority over a conflicting security interest in the same inventory and also has priority in identifiable cash proceeds received on or before the delivery of the inventory to a buyer if

(a) the purchase money security interest is perfected at the time the debtor receives possession of the inventory; and

(b) the purchase money secured party gives notification in writing to the holder of the conflicting security interest if the holder had filed a financing statement covering the same types of inventory (i) before the date of filing made by the purchase money secured party, or (ii) before the beginning of the 21 day period where the purchase money security interest is temporarily perfected without filing or possession (subsection (5) of Section 9–304); and

(c) the holder of the conflicting security interest receives the notification within five years before the debtor receives possession of the inventory; and

(d) the notification states that the person giving the notice has or expects to acquire a purchase money security interest in inventory of the debtor, describing such inventory by item or type.

(4) A purchase money security interest in collateral other than inventory has priority over a conflicting security interest in the same collateral or its proceeds if the purchase money security interest is perfected at the time the debtor receives possession of the collateral or within ten days thereafter.

(5) In all cases not governed by other rules stated in this section (including cases of purchase money security interests which do not qualify for the special priorities set forth in subsections (3) and (4) of this section), priority be-

tween conflicting security interests in the same collateral shall be determined according to the following rules:

(a) Conflicting security interests rank according to priority in time of filing or perfection. Priority dates from the time a filing is first made covering the collateral or the time the security interest is first perfected, whichever is earlier, provided that there is no period thereafter when there is neither filing nor perfection.

(b) So long as conflicting security interests are unperfected, the first to attach has priority.

(6) For the purposes of subsection (5) a date of filing or perfection as to collateral is also a date of filing or perfection as to proceeds.

(7) If future advances are made while a security interest is perfected by filing, the taking of possession, or under Section 8–321 on securities, the security interest has the same priority for the purposes of subsection (5) with respect to the future advances as it does with respect to first advance. If a commitment is made before or while the security interest is so perfected, the security interest has the same priority with respect to advances made pursuant thereto. In other cases a perfected security interest has priority from the date the advance is made.

§ 9–313. Priority of Security Interests in Fixtures

(1) In this section and in the provisions of Part 4 of this Article referring to fixture filing, unless the context otherwise requires

(a) goods are "fixtures" when they become so related to particular real estate that an interest in them arises under real estate law

(b) a "fixture filing" is the filing in the office where a mortgage on the real estate would be filed or recorded of a financing statement covering goods which are or are to become fixtures and conforming to the requirements of subsection (5) of Section 9–402

(c) a mortgage is a "construction mortgage" to the extent that it secures an obligation incurred for the construction of an improvement on land including the acquisition cost of the land, if the recorded writing so indicates.

(2) A security interest under this Article may be created in goods which are fixtures or may continue in goods which become fixtures, but no security interest exists under this Article in ordinary building materials incorporated into an improvement on land.

(3) This Article does not prevent creation of an encumbrance upon fixtures pursuant to real estate law.

(4) A perfected security interest in fixtures has priority over the conflicting interest of an encumbrancer or owner of the real estate where

(a) the security interest is a purchase money security interest, the interest of the encumbrancer or owner arises before the goods become fixtures, the security interest is perfected by a fixture filing before the goods become fixtures or within ten days thereafter, and the debtor has an interest of record in the real estate or is in possession of the real estate; or

(b) the security interest is perfected by a fixture filing before the interest of the encumbrancer or owner is of record, the security interest has priority over any conflicting interest of a predecessor in title of the encumbrancer or owner, and the debtor has an interest of record in the real estate or is in possession of the real estate; or

(c) the fixtures are readily removable factory or office machines or readily removable replacements of domestic appliances which are consumer goods, and before the goods become fixtures the security interest is perfected by any method permitted by this Article; or

(d) the conflicting interest is a lien on the real estate obtained by legal or equitable proceedings after the security interest was perfected by any method permitted by this Article.

(5) A security interest in fixtures, whether or not perfected, has priority over the conflicting interest of an encumbrancer or owner of the real estate where

(a) the encumbrancer or owner has consented in writing to the security interest or has disclaimed an interest in the goods as fixtures; or

(b) the debtor has a right to remove the goods as against the encumbrancer or owner. If the debtor's right terminates, the priority of the security interest continues for a reasonable time.

(6) Notwithstanding paragraph (a) of subsection (4) but otherwise subject to subsections (4) and (5), a security interest in fixtures is subordinate to a construction mortgage recorded before the goods become fixtures if the goods become fixtures before the completion of the construction. To the extent that it is given to refinance a construction mortgage, a mortgage has this priority to the same extent as the construction mortgage.

(7) In cases not within the preceding subsections, a security interest in fixtures is subordinate to the conflicting interest of an encumbrancer or owner of the related real estate who is not the debtor.

(8) When the secured party has priority over all owners and encumbrancers of the real estate, he may, on default, subject to the provisions of Part 5, remove his collateral from the real estate but he must reimburse any encumbrancer or owner of the real estate who is not the debtor and who has not otherwise agreed for the cost of repair of any physical injury, but not for any diminution in value of the real estate caused by the absence of the goods removed or by any necessity of replacing them. A person entitled to reimbursement may refuse permission to remove until the secured party gives adequate security for the performance of this obligation.

§ 9–314. Accessions

(1) A security interest in goods which attaches before they are installed in or affixed to other goods takes priority as to the goods installed or affixed (called in this section "accessions") over the claims of all persons to the whole except as stated in subsection (3) and subject to Section 9–315(1).

(2) A security interest which attaches to goods after they become part of a whole is valid against all persons subsequently acquiring interests in the whole except as stated in subsection (3) but is invalid against any person with an interest in the whole at the time the security interest attaches to the goods who has not in writing consented to the security interest or disclaimed an interest in the goods as part of the whole.

(3) The security interest described in subsections (1) and (2) do not take priority over

(a) a subsequent purchaser for value of any interest in the whole; or

(b) a creditor with a lien on the whole subsequently obtained by judicial proceedings; or

(c) a creditor with a prior perfected security interest in the whole to the extent that he makes subsequent advances if the subsequent purchase is made, the lien by judicial proceedings obtained or the subsequent advance under the prior perfected security interest is made or contracted for without knowledge of the security interest and before it is perfected. A purchaser of the whole at a foreclosure sale other than the holder of a perfected security interest purchasing at his own foreclosure sale is a subsequent purchaser within this section.

(4) When under subsections (1) and (2) and (3) a secured party has an interest in accessions which has priority over the claims of all persons who have interests in the whole, he may on default subject to the provisions of Part 5 remove his collateral from the whole but he must reimburse any encumbrancer or owner of the whole who is not the debtor and who has not otherwise agreed for the cost of repair of any physical injury but not for any diminution in value of the whole caused by the absence of the goods removed or by any necessity for replacing them. A person entitled to reimbursement may refuse permission to remove until the secured party gives adequate security for the performance of this obligation.

§ 9–315. Priority When Goods Are Commingled or Processed

(1) If a security interest in goods was perfected and subsequently the goods or a part thereof have become part of a product or mass, the security interest continues in the product or mass if

(a) the goods are so manufactured, processed, assembled or commingled that their identity is lost in the product or mass; or

(b) a financing statement covering the original goods also covers the product into which the goods have been manufactured, processed or assembled. In a case to which paragraph (b) applies, no separate security interest in that part of the original goods which have been manufactured, processed or assembled into the product may be claimed under Section 9-314.

(2) When under subsection (1) more than one security interest attaches to the product or mass, they rank equally according to the ratio that the cost of the goods to which each interest originally attached bears to the cost of the total product or mass.

§ 9-316. Priority Subject to Subordination

Nothing in this Article prevents subordination by agreement by any person entitled to priority.

§ 9-317. Secured Party Not Obligated on Contract of Debtor

The mere existence of a security interest or authority given to the debtor to dispose of or use collateral does not impose contract or tort liability upon the secured party for the debtor's acts or omissions.

§ 9-318. Defenses Against Assignee; Modification of Contract After Notification of Assignment; Term Prohibiting Assignment Ineffective; Identification and Proof of Assignment

(1) Unless an account debtor has made an enforceable agreement not to assert defenses or claims arising out of a sale as provided in Section 9-206 the rights of an assignee are subject to

(a) all the terms of the contract between the account debtor and assignor and any defense or claim arising therefrom; and

(b) any other defense or claim of the account debtor against the assignor which accrues before the account debtor receives notification of the assignment.

(2) So far as the right to payment or a part thereof under an assigned contract has not been fully earned by performance, and notwithstanding notification of the assignment, any modification of or substitution for the contract made in good faith and in accordance with reasonable commercial standards is effective against an assignee unless the account debtor has otherwise agreed but the assignee acquires corresponding rights under the modified or substituted contract. The assignment may provide that such modification or substitution is a breach by the assignor.

(3) The account debtor is authorized to pay the assignor until the account debtor receives notification that the amount due or to become due has been assigned and that payment is to be made to the assignee. A notification which does not reasonably identify the rights assigned is ineffective. If requested by the account debtor, the assignee must seasonably furnish reasonable proof that the assignment has been made and unless he does so the account debtor may pay the assignor.

(4) A term in any contract between an account debtor and an assignor is ineffective if it prohibits assignment of an account or prohibits creation of a security interest in a general intangible for money due or to become due or requires the account debtor's consent to such assignment or security interest.

Part 4 Filing

§ 9-401. Place of Filing; Erroneous Filing; Removal of Collateral

First Alternative Subsection (1)

(1) The proper place to file in order to perfect a security interest is as follows:

(a) when the collateral is timber to be cut or is minerals or the like (including oil and gas) or accounts subject to subsection (5) of Section 9-103, or when the financing statement is filed as a fixture filing (Section 9-313) and the collateral is goods which are or are to become fixtures, then in the office where a mortgage on the real estate would be filed or recorded;

(b) in all other cases, in the office of the [Secretary of State].

Second Alternative Subsection (1)

(1) The proper place to file in order to perfect a security interest is as follows:

(a) when the collateral is equipment used in farming operations, or farm products, or accounts or general intangibles arising from or relating to the sale of farm products by a farmer, or consumer goods, then in the office of the . . . . in the county of the debtor's residence or if the debtor is not a resident of this state then in the office of the . . . . in the county where the goods are kept, and in addition when the collateral is crops growing or to be grown in the office of the . . . . in the county where the land is located;

(b) when the collateral is timber to be cut or is minerals or the like (including oil and gas) or accounts subject to subsection (5) of Section 9-103, or when the financing statement is filed as a fixture filing (Section 9-313) and the collateral is goods which are or are to become fixtures, then in the office where a mortgage on the real estate would be filed or recorded;

(c) in all other cases, in the office of the [Secretary of State].

Third Alternative Subsection (1)

(1) The proper place to file in order to perfect a security interest is as follows:

(a) when the collateral is equipment used in farming operations, or farm products, or accounts or general intangibles arising from or relating to the sale of farm products by a farmer, or consumer goods, then in the office of the . . . . in the county of the debtor's residence or if the debtor is not a resident of this state then in office of the . . . . in the county where the goods are kept, and in addition when the collateral is crops growing or to be grown in the office of the . . . . in the county where the land is located;

(b) when the collateral is timber to be cut or is minerals or the like (including oil and gas) or accounts subject to subsection (5) of Section 9–103, or when the financing statement is filed as a fixture filing (Section 9–313) and the collateral is goods which are or are to become fixtures, then in the office where a mortgage on the real estate would be filed or recorded;

(c) in all other cases, in the office of the [Secretary of State] and in addition, if the debtor has a place of business in only one county of this state, also in the office of . . . . of such county, or, if the debtor has no place of business in this state, but resides in this state, also in the office of . . . . of the county in which he resides.

Note: One of the three alternatives should be selected as subsection (1).

(2) A filing which is made in good faith in an improper place or not in all of the places required by this section is nevertheless effective with regard to any collateral as to which the filing complied with the requirements of this Article and is also effective with regard to collateral covered by the financing statement against any person who has knowledge of the contents of such financing statement.

(3) A filing which is made in the proper place in this state continues effective even though the debtor's residence or place of business or the location of the collateral or its use, whichever controlled the original filing, is thereafter changed.

Alternative to Subsection (3)

[(3) A filing which is made in the proper county continues effective for four months after a change to another county of the debtor's residence or place of business or the location of the collateral, whichever controlled the original filing. It becomes ineffective thereafter unless a copy of the financing statement signed by the secured party is filed in the new county within said period. The security interest may also be perfected in the new county after the expiration of the four-month period; in such case perfection dates from the time of perfection in the new county. A change in the use of the collateral does not impair the effectiveness of the original filing.]

(4) The rules stated in Section 9–103 determines whether filing is necessary in this state.

(5) Notwithstanding the preceding subsections, and subject to subsection (3) of Section 9–302, the proper place to file in order to perfect a security interest in collateral, including fixtures, of a transmitting utility is the office of the [Secretary of State]. This filing constitutes a fixture filing (Section 9–313) as to the collateral described therein which is or is to become fixtures.

(6) For the purposes of this section, the residence of an organization is its place of business if it has one or its chief executive office if it has more than one place of business.

Note: Subsection (6) should be used if the state chooses the Second or Third Alternative Subsection (1).

§ 9–402. Formal Requisites of Financing Statement; Amendments; Mortgage as Financing Statement

(1) A financing statement is sufficient if it gives the names of the debtor and the secured party, is signed by the debtor, gives an address of the secured party from which information concerning the security interest may be obtained, gives a mailing address of the debtor and contains a statement indicating the types, or describing the items, of collateral. A financing statement may be filed before a security agreement is made or a security interest otherwise attaches. When the financing statement covers crops growing or to be grown, the statement must also contain a description of the real estate concerned. When the financing statement covers timber to be cut or covers minerals or the like (including oil and gas) or accounts subject to subsection (5) of Section 9–103, or when the financing statement is filed as a fixture filing (Section 9–313) and the collateral is goods which are or are to become fixtures, the statement must also comply with subsection (5). A copy of the security agreement is sufficient as a financing statement if it contains the above information and is signed by the debtor. A carbon, photographic or other reproduction of a security agreement or a financing statement is sufficient as a financing statement if the security agreement so provides or if the original has been filed in this state.

(2) A financing statement which otherwise complies with subsection (1) is sufficient when it is signed by the secured party instead of the debtor if it is filed to perfect a security interest in

(a) collateral already subject to a security interest in another jurisdiction when it is brought into this state, or when the debtor's location is changed to this state. Such a financing statement must state that the collateral was brought into this state or that the debtor's location was changed to this state under such circumstances; or

(b) proceeds under Section 9–306 if the security interest in the original collateral was perfected. Such a financing statement must describe the original collateral; or

(c) collateral as to which the filing has lapsed; or

(d) collateral acquired after a change of name, identity or corporate structure of the debtor (subsection (7)).

(3) A form substantially as follows is sufficient to comply with subsection (1):

Name of debtor (or assignor) . . . .

Address . . . .

Name of secured party (or assignee)..................

Address ....

1. This financing statement covers the following types (or items) of property:.........................
(Describe): ....
2. (If collateral is crops) The above described crops are growing or are to be grown on:..............
(Describe Real Estate) ....
3. (If applicable) The above goods are to become fixtures on:* ....
(Describe Real Estate) ....
and this financing statement is to be filed [for record] in the real estate records. (If the debtor does not have an interest of record) The name of a record owner is ....
4. (If products of collateral are claimed) Products of the collateral are also covered.
(Use whichever is applicable) ....
Signature of Debtor (or Assignor) ....
Signature of Secured Party (or Assignee) ....

*Note: *Where appropriate substitute either "The above timber is standing on . . ." or "The above minerals or the like (including oil and gas) or accounts will be financed at the wellhead or minehead of the well or mine located on . . ." Language in brackets is optional.*

(4) A financing statement may be amended by filing a writing signed by both the debtor and the secured party. An amendment does not extend the period of effectiveness of a financing statement. If any amendment adds collateral, it is effective as to the added collateral only from the filing date of the amendment. In this Article, unless the context otherwise requires, the term "financing statement" means the original financing statement and any amendments.

(5) A financing statement covering timber to be cut or covering minerals or the like (including oil and gas) or accounts subject to subsection (5) of Section 9–103, or a financing statement filed as a fixture filing (Section 9–313) where the debtor is not a transmitting utility, must show that it covers this type of collateral, must recite that it is to be filed [for record] in the real estate records, and the financing statement must contain a description of the real estate [sufficient if it were contained in a mortgage of the real estate to give constructive notice of the mortgage under the law of this state]. If the debtor does not have an interest of record in the real estate, the financing statement must show the name of a record owner.

(6) A mortgage is effective as a financing statement filed as a fixture filing from the date of its recording if

(a) the goods are described in the mortgage by item or type; and

(b) the goods are or are to become fixtures related to the real estate described in the mortgage; and

(c) the mortgage complies with the requirements for a financing statement in this section other than a recital that it is to be filed in the real estate records; and

(d) the mortgage is duly recorded.

No fee with reference to the financing statement is required other than the regular recording and satisfaction fees with respect to the mortgage.

(7) A financing statement sufficiently shows the name of the debtor if it gives the individual, partnership or corporate name of the debtor, whether or not it adds other trade names or names of partners. Where the debtor so changes his name or in the case of an organization its name, identity or corporate structure that a filed financing statement becomes seriously misleading, the filing is not effective to perfect a security interest in collateral acquired by the debtor more than four months after the change, unless a new appropriate financing statement is filed before the expiration of that time. A filed financing statement remains effective with respect to collateral transferred by the debtor even though the secured party knows of or consents to the transfer.

(8) A financing statement substantially complying with the requirements of this section is effective even though it contains minor errors which are not seriously misleading.

*Note: *Where the state has any special recording system for real estate other than the usual grantor-grantee index (as, for instance, a tract system or a title registration or Torrens system) local adaptations of subsection (5) and Section 9–403(7) may be necessary. See Mass. Gen. Laws Chapter 106, Section 9–409.*

§ 9–403. What Constitutes Filing; Duration of Filing; Effect of Lapsed Filing; Duties of Filing Officer

(1) Presentation for filing of a financing statement and tender of the filing fee or acceptance of the statement by the filing officer constitutes filing under this Article.

(2) Except as provided in subsection (6) a filed financing statement is effective for a period of five years from the date of filing. The effectiveness of a filed financing statement lapses on the expiration of the five year period unless a continuation statement is filed prior to the lapse. If a security interest perfected by filing exists at the time insolvency proceedings are commenced by or against the debtor, the security interest remains perfected until termination of the insolvency proceedings and thereafter for a period of sixty days or until expiration of the five year period, whichever occurs later. Upon lapse the security interest becomes unperfected, unless it is perfected without filing. If the security interest becomes unperfected upon lapse, it is deemed to have been unperfected as against a person who became a purchaser or lien creditor before lapse.

(3) A continuation statement may be filed by the secured party within six months prior to the expiration of the five

year period specified in subsection (2). Any such continuation statement must be signed by the secured party, identify the original statement by file number and state that the original statement is still effective. A continuation statement signed by a person other than the secured party of record must be accompanied by a separate written statement of assignment signed by the secured party of record and complying with subsection (2) of Section 9–405, including payment of the required fee. Upon timely filing of the continuation statement, the effectiveness of the original statement is continued for five years after the last date to which the filing was effective whereupon it lapses in the same manner as provided in subsection (2) unless another continuation statement is filed prior to such lapse. Succeeding continuation statements may be filed in the same manner to continue the effectiveness of the original statement. Unless a statute on disposition of public records provides otherwise, the filing officer may remove a lapsed statement from the files and destroy it immediately if he has retained a microfilm or other photographic record, or in other cases after one year after the lapse. The filing officer shall so arrange matters by physical annexation of financing statements to continuation statements or other related filings, or by other means, that if he physically destroys the financing statements of a period more than five years past, those which have been continued by a continuation statement or which are still effective under subsection (6) shall be retained.

(4) Except as provided in subsection (7) a filing officer shall mark each statement with a file number and with the date and hour of filing and shall hold the statement or a microfilm or other photographic copy thereof for public inspection. In addition the filing officer shall index the statement according to the name of the debtor and shall note in the index the file number and the address of the debtor given in the statement.

(5) The uniform fee for filing and indexing and for stamping a copy furnished by the secured party to show the date and place of filing for an original financing statement or for a continuation statement shall be $. . . . . . if the statement is in the standard form prescribed by the [Secretary of State] and otherwise shall be $. . . . . ., plus in each case, if the financing statement is subject to subsection (5) of Section 9–402, $. . . . . . The uniform fee for each name more than one required to be indexed shall be $. . . . . . The secured party may at his option show a trade name for any person and an extra uniform indexing fee of $. . . . . . shall be paid with respect thereto.

(6) If the debtor is a transmitting utility (subsection (5) of Section 9–401) and a filed financing statement so states, it is effective until a termination statement is filed. A real estate mortgage which is effective as a fixture filing under subsection (6) of Section 9–402 remains effective as a fixture filing until the mortgage is released or satisfied of

record or its effectiveness otherwise terminates as to the real estate.

(7) When a financing statement covers timber to be cut or covers minerals or the like (including oil and gas) or accounts subject to subsection (5) of Section 9–103, or is filed as a fixture filing, [it shall be filed for record and] the filing officer shall index it under the names of the debtor and any owner of record shown on the financing statement in the same fashion as if they were the mortgagors in a mortgage of the real estate described, and, to the extent that the law of this state provides for the indexing of mortgages under the name of the mortgagee, under the name of the secured party as if he were the mortgagee thereunder, or where indexing is by description in the same fashion as if the financing statement were a mortgage of the real estate described.

Note: In states in which writings will not appear in the real estate records and indices unless actually recorded the bracketed language in subsection (7) should be used.

§ 9–404. Termination Statement

(1) If a financing statement covering consumer goods is filed on or after . . . . . ., then within one month or within ten days following written demand by the debtor after there is no outstanding secured obligation and no commitment to make advances, incur obligations or otherwise give value, the secured party must file with each filing officer with whom the financing statement was filed, a termination statement to the effect that he no longer claims a security interest under the financing statement, which shall be identified by file number. In other cases whenever there is no outstanding secured obligation and no commitment to make advances, incur obligations or otherwise give value, the secured party must on written demand by the debtor send the debtor, for each filing officer with whom the financing statement was filed, a termination statement to the effect that he no longer claims a security interest under the financing statement, which shall be identified by file number. A termination statement signed by a person other than the secured party of record must be accompanied by a separate written statement of assignment signed by the secured party of record complying with subsection (2) of Section 9–405, including payment of the required fee. If the affected secured party fails to file such a termination statement as required by this subsection, or to send such a termination statement within ten days after proper demand therefor, he shall be liable to the debtor for one hundred dollars, and in addition for any loss caused to the debtor by such failure.

(2) On presentation to the filing officer of such a termination statement he must note it in the index. If he has received the termination statement in duplicate, he shall return one copy of the termination statement to the

secured party stamped to show the time of receipt thereof. If the filing officer has a microfilm or other photographic record of the financing statement, and of any related continuation statement, statement of assignment and statement of release, he may remove the originals from the files at any time after receipt of the termination statement, or if he has no such record, he may remove them from the files at any time after one year after receipt of the termination statement.

(3) If the termination statement is in the standard form prescribed by the [Secretary of State], the uniform fee for filing and indexing the termination statement shall be $. . . . ., and otherwise shall be $. . . . ., plus in each case an additional fee of $. . . . . for each name more than one against which the termination statement is required to be indexed.

Note: The date to be inserted should be the effective date of the revised Article 9.

§ 9–405. Assignment of Security Interest; Duties of Filing Officer; Fees

(1) A financing statement may disclose an assignment of a security interest in the collateral described in the financing statement by indication in the financing statement of the name and address of the assignee or by an assignment itself or a copy thereof on the face or back of the statement. On presentation to the filing officer of such a financing statement the filing officer shall mark the same as provided in Section 9–403(4). The uniform fee for filing, indexing and furnishing filing data for a financing statement so indicating an assignment shall be $. . . . . . if the statement is in the standard form prescribed by the [Secretary of State] and otherwise shall be $. . . . ., plus in each case an additional fee of $. . . . . for each name more than one against which the financing statement is required to be indexed.

(2) A secured party may assign of record all or part of his rights under a financing statement by the filing in the place where the original financing statement was filed of a separate written statement of assignment signed by the secured party of record and setting forth the name of the secured party of record and the debtor, the file number and the date of filing of the financing statement and the name and address of the assignee and containing a description of the collateral assigned. A copy of the assignment is sufficient as a separate statement if it complies with the preceding sentence. On presentation to the filing officer of such a separate statement, the filing officer shall mark such separate statement with the date and hour of the filing. He shall note the assignment on the index of the financing statement, or in the case of a fixture filing, or a filing covering timber to be cut, or covering minerals or the like (including oil and gas) or accounts subject to subsection (5) of Section 9–103, he shall index

the assignment under the name of the assignor as grantor and, to the extent that the law of this state provides for indexing the assignment of a mortgage under the name of the assignee, he shall index the assignment of the financing statement under the name of the assignee. The uniform fee for filing, indexing and furnishing filing data about such a separate statement of assignment shall be $. . . . . if the statement is in the standard form prescribed by the [Secretary of State] and otherwise shall be $. . . . ., plus in each case an additional fee of $. . . . . for each name more than one against which the statement of assignment is required to be indexed. Notwithstanding the provisions of this subsection, an assignment of record of a security interest in a fixture contained in a mortgage effective as a fixture filing (subsection (6) of Section 9–402) may be made only by an assignment of the mortgage in the manner provided by the law of this state other than this Act.

(3) After the disclosure or filing of an assignment under this section, the assignee is the secured party of record.

§ 9–406. Release of Collateral; Duties of Filing Officer; Fees

A secured party of record may by his signed statement release all or a part of any collateral described in a filed financing statement. The statement of release is sufficient if it contains a description of the collateral being released, the name and address of the debtor, the name and address of the secured party, and the file number of the financing statement. A statement of release signed by a person other than the secured party of record must be accompanied by a separate written statement of assignment signed by the secured party of record and complying with subsection (2) of Section 9–405, including payment of the required fee. Upon presentation of such a statement of release to the filing officer he shall mark the statement with the hour and date of filing and shall note the same upon the margin of the index of the filing of the financing statement. The uniform fee for filing and noting such a statement of release shall be $. . . . . if the statement is in the standard form prescribed by the [Secretary of State] and otherwise shall be $. . . . ., plus in each case an additional fee of $. . . . . for each name more than one against which the statement of release is required to be indexed.

[§ 9–407. Information from Filing Officer]

[(1) If the person filing any financing statement, termination statement, statement of assignment, or statement of release, furnishes the filing officer a copy thereof, the filing officer shall upon request note upon the copy the file number and date and hour of the filing of the original and deliver or send the copy to such person.]

[(2) Upon request of any person, the filing officer shall issue his certificate showing whether there is on file on the date and hour stated therein, any presently effective financing statement naming a particular debtor and any statement of assignment thereof and if there is, giving the date and hour of filing of each such statement and the names and addresses of each secured party therein. The uniform fee for such a certificate shall be $. . . . . . if the request for the certificate is in the standard form prescribed by the [Secretary of State] and otherwise shall be $. . . . . Upon request the filing officer shall furnish a copy of any filed financing statement or statement of assignment for a uniform fee of $. . . . . per page.]

Note: This section is proposed as an optional provision to require filing officers to furnish certificates. Local law and practices should be consulted with regard to the advisability of adoption.

§ 9–408. Financing Statements Covering Consigned or Leased Goods

A consignor or lessor of goods may file a financing statement using the terms "consignor," "consignee," "lessor," "lessee" or the like instead of the terms specified in Section 9–402. The provisions of this Part shall apply as appropriate to such a financing statement but its filing shall not of itself be a factor in determining whether or not the consignment or lease is intended as security (Section 1–201(37)). However, if it is determined for other reasons that the consignment or lease is so intended, a security interest of the consignor or lessor which attaches to the consigned or leased goods is perfected by such filing.

Part 5 Default

§ 9–501. Default; Procedure When Security Agreement Covers Both Real and Personal Property

(1) When a debtor is in default under a security agreement, a secured party has the rights and remedies provided in this Part and except as limited by subsection (3) those provided in the security agreement. He may reduce his claim to judgment, foreclose or otherwise enforce the security interest by an available judicial procedure. If the collateral is documents the secured party may proceed either as to the documents or as to the goods covered thereby. A secured party in possession has the rights, remedies and duties provided in Section 9–207. The rights and remedies referred to in this subsection are cumulative.

(2) After default, the debtor has the rights and remedies provided in this Part, those provided in the security agreement and those provided in Section 9–207.

(3) To the extent that they give rights to the debtor and impose duties on the secured party, the rules stated in the subsections referred to below may not be waived or varied except as provided with respect to compulsory disposition of collateral (subsection (3) of Section 9–504

and Section 9–505) and with respect to redemption of collateral (Section 9–506) but the parties may by agreement determine the standard by which the fulfillment of these rights and duties is to be measured if such standards are not manifestly unreasonable:

(a) subsection (2) of Section 9–502 and subsection (2) of Section 9–504 insofar as they require accounting for surplus proceeds of collateral;

(b) subsection (3) of Section 9–504 and subsection (1) of Section 9–505 which deal with disposition of collateral;

(c) subsection (2) of Section 9–505 which deals with acceptance of collateral as discharge of obligation;

(d) Section 9–506 which deals with redemption of collateral; and

(e) subsection (1) of Section 9–507 which deals with the secured party's liability for failure to comply with this Part.

(4) If the security agreement covers both real and personal property, the secured party may proceed under this Part as to the personal property or he may proceed as to both the real and the personal property in accordance with his rights and remedies in respect of the real property in which case the provisions of this Part do not apply.

(5) When a secured party has reduced his claim to judgment the lien of any levy which may be made upon his collateral by virtue of any execution based upon the judgment shall relate back to the date of the perfection of the security interest in such collateral. A judicial sale, pursuant to such execution, is a foreclosure of the security interest by judicial procedure within the meaning of this section, and the secured party may purchase at the sale and thereafter hold the collateral free of any other requirements of this Article.

§ 9–502. Collection Rights of Secured Party

(1) When so agreed and in any event on default the secured party is entitled to notify an account debtor or the obligor on an instrument to make payment to him whether or not the assignor was theretofore making collections on the collateral, and also to take control of any proceeds to which he is entitled under Section 9–306.

(2) A secured party who by agreement is entitled to charge back uncollected collateral or otherwise to full or limited recourse against the debtor and who undertakes to collect from the account debtors or obligors must proceed in a commercially reasonable manner and may deduct his reasonable expenses of realization from the collections. If the security agreement secures an indebtedness, the secured party must account to the debtor for any surplus, and unless otherwise agreed, the debtor is liable for any deficiency. But, if the underlying transaction was a sale of accounts or chattel paper, the debtor is entitled to any surplus or is liable for any deficiency only if the security agreement so provides.

§ 9–503. Secured Party's Rights to Take Possession After Default

Unless otherwise agreed a secured party has on default the right to take possession of the collateral. In taking possession a secured party may proceed without judicial process if this can be done without breach of the peace or may proceed by action. If the security agreement so provides the secured party may require the debtor to assemble the collateral and make it available to the secured party at a place to be designated by the secured party which is reasonably convenient to both parties. Without removal a secured party may render equipment unusable, and may dispose of collateral on the debtor's premises under Section 9–504.

§ 9–504. Secured Party's Right to Dispose of Collateral After Default; Effect of Disposition

(1) A secured party after default may sell, lease or otherwise dispose of any or all of the collateral in its then condition or following any commercially reasonable preparation or processing. Any sale of goods is subject to the Article on Sales (Article 2). The proceeds of disposition shall be applied in the order following to

(a) the reasonable expenses of retaking, holding, preparing for sale or lease, selling, leasing and the like and, to the extent provided for in the agreement and not prohibited by law, the reasonable attorney's fees and legal expenses incurred by the secured party;

(b) the satisfaction of indebtedness secured by the security interest under which the disposition is made;

(c) the satisfaction of indebtedness secured by any subordinate security interest in the collateral if written notification of demand therefor is received before distribution of the proceeds is completed. If requested by the secured party, the holder of a subordinate security interest must reasonably furnish reasonable proof of his interest, and unless he does so, the secured party need not comply with his demand.

(2) If the security interest secures an indebtedness, the secured party must account to the debtor for any surplus, and, unless otherwise agreed, the debtor is liable for any deficiency. But if the underlying transaction was a sale of accounts or chattel paper, the debtor is entitled to any surplus or is liable for any deficiency only if the security agreement so provides.

(3) Disposition of the collateral may be public or private proceedings and may be made by way of one or more contracts. Sale or other disposition may be as a unit or in parcels and at any time and place and on any terms but every aspect of the disposition including the method, manner, time, place and terms must be commercially reasonable. Unless collateral is perishable or threatens to decline speedily in value or is of a type customarily sold on a recognized market, reasonable notification of the time and place of any public sale or reasonable notifica-

tion of the time after which any private sale or other intended disposition is to be made shall be sent by the secured party to the debtor, if he has not signed after default a statement renouncing or modifying his right to notification of sale. In the case of consumer goods no other notification need be sent. In other cases notification shall be sent to any other secured party from whom the secured party has received (before sending his notification to the debtor or before the debtor's renunciation of his rights) written notice of a claim of an interest in the collateral. The secured party may buy at any public sale and if the collateral is of a type customarily sold in a recognized market or is of a type which is the subject of widely distributed standard price quotations he may buy at private sale.

(4) When collateral is disposed of by a secured party after default, the disposition transfers to a purchaser for value all of the debtor's rights therein, discharges the security interest under which it is made and any security interest or lien subordinate thereto. The purchaser takes free of all such rights and interests even though the secured party fails to comply with the requirements of this Part or of any judicial proceedings

(a) in the case of a public sale, if the purchaser has no knowledge of any defects in the sale and if he does not buy in collusion with the secured party, other bidders or the person conducting the sale; or

(b) in any other case, if the purchaser acts in good faith.

(5) A person who is liable to a secured party under a guaranty, indorsement, repurchase agreement or the like and who receives a transfer of collateral from the secured party or is subrogated to his rights has thereafter the rights and duties of the secured party. Such a transfer of collateral is not a sale or disposition of the collateral under this Article.

§ 9–505. Compulsory Disposition of Collateral; Acceptance of the Collateral as Discharge of Obligation

(1) If the debtor has paid sixty per cent of the case price in the case of a purchase money security interest in consumer goods or sixty per cent of the loan in the case of another security interest in consumer goods, and has not signed after default a statement renouncing or modifying his rights under this Part a secured party who has taken possession of collateral must dispose of it under Section 9–504 and if he fails to do so within ninety days after he takes possession the debtor at his option may recover in conversion or under Section 9–507(1) on secured party's liability.

(2) In any other case involving consumer goods or any other collateral a secured party in possession may, after default, propose to retain the collateral in satisfaction of the obligation. Written notice of such proposal shall be

sent to the debtor if he has not signed after default a statement renouncing or modifying his rights under this subsection. In the case of consumer goods no other notice need be given. In other cases notice shall be sent to any other secured party from whom the secured party has received (before sending his notice to the debtor or before the debtor's renunciation of his rights) written notice of a claim of an interest in the collateral. If the secured party receives objection in writing from a person entitled to receive notification within twenty-one days after the notice was sent, the secured party must dispose of the collateral under Section 9–504. In the absence of such written objection the secured party may retain the collateral in satisfaction of the debtor's obligation.

§ 9–506. Debtor's Right to Redeem Collateral

At any time before the secured party has disposed of collateral or entered into a contract for its disposition under Section 9–504 or before the obligation has been discharged under Section 9–505(2) the debtor or any other secured party may unless otherwise agreed in writing after default redeem the collateral by tendering fulfillment of all obligations secured by the collateral as well as the expenses reasonably incurred by the secured party in retaking, holding and preparing the collateral for disposition, in arranging for the sale, and to the extent provided in the agreement and not prohibited by law, his reasonable attorney's fees and legal expenses.

§ 9–507. Secured Party's Liability for Failure to Comply With This Part

(1) If it is established that the secured party is not proceeding in accordance with the provisions of this Part disposition may be ordered or restrained on appropriate terms and conditions. If the disposition has occurred the debtor or any person entitled to notification or whose security interest has been made known to the secured party prior to the disposition has a right to recover from the secured party any loss caused by a failure to comply with the provisions of this Part. If the collateral is consumer goods, the debtor has a right to recover in any event an amount not less than the credit service charge plus ten per cent of the principal amount of the debt or the time price differential plus 10 per cent of the cash price. (2) The fact that a better price could have been obtained by a sale at a different time or in a different method from that selected by the secured party is not of itself sufficient to establish that the sale was not made in a commercially reasonable manner. If the secured party either sells the collateral in the usual manner in any recognized market therefor or if he sells at the price current in such market at the time of his sale or if he has otherwise sold in conformity with reasonable commercial practices among dealers in the type of property sold he has sold in a commercially reasonable manner. The principles stated in the two preceding sentences with respect to sales also apply as may be appropriate to other types of disposition. A disposition which has been approved in any judicial proceeding or by any bona fide creditors' committee or representative of creditors shall conclusively be deemed to be commercially reasonable, but this sentence does not indicate that any such approval must be obtained in any case nor does it indicate that any disposition not so approved is not commercially reasonable.

Note: Articles 10 and 11 have been omitted as unnecessary for the purposes of this text.

abandonment To intentionally give up possession or claim to property with the intent of relinquishment of any ownership or claim.

abatement An action of stopping or removing.

ab initio From the beginning.

abstract of title A summary of the conveyances, transfers, and other facts relied on as evidence of title, together with all such facts appearing of record that may impair its validity.

abuse of process An intentional tort designed to protect against the initiation of legal proceedings for a primary purpose other than the one for which such proceedings were designed.

acceleration The shortening of the time for the performance of a contract or the payment of a note by the operation of some provision in the contract or note itself.

acceptance The actual or implied receipt and retention of that which is tendered or offered.

accession The acquisition of property by its incorporation or union with other property.

accommodation paper A negotiable instrument signed without consideration by a party as acceptor, drawer, or indorser for the purpose of enabling the payee to obtain credit.

accommodation party A person who signs a negotiable instrument for the purpose of adding his name and liability to another party to the instrument.

accord and satisfaction A legally binding agreement to settle a disputed claim for a definite amount.

account stated An account that has been rendered by one to another and which purports to state the true balance due and that balance is either expressly or impliedly admitted to be due by the debtor.

acquit To set free or judicially to discharge from an accusation; to release from a debt, duty, obligation, charge, or suspicion of guilt.

actionable Capable of being remedied by a legal action or claim.

act of God An occurrence resulting exclusively from natural forces that could not have been prevented or whose effect could not have been avoided by care or foresight.

act of state doctrine A doctrine of international law that no nation is permitted to judge the act of another nation committed within its own boundaries.

adjudge To give judgment; to decide.

adjudicate To adjudge; to settle by judicial decree.

ad litem During the pendency of the action or proceeding.

administrator The personal representative appointed by a probate court to settle the estate of a deceased person who died intestate (without leaving a valid will).

adoption In corporation law, a corporation's acceptance of a preincorporation contract by action of its board of directors, by which the corporation becomes liable on the contract.

advance directive A written document such as a living will or durable power of attorney that directs others how future health care decisions should be made in the event that the individual becomes incapacitated.

adverse possession Open and notorious possession of real property over a given length of time that denies ownership in any other claimant.

advised letter of credit See *letter of credit, advised.*

affidavit A signed writing containing statements of fact to whose accuracy the signing party has sworn. Used in a variety of judicial proceedings, including the motion for summary judgment.

affirm To confirm or uphold a former judgment or order of a court. Appellate courts, for instance, may affirm the decisions of lower courts.

after-acquired property Property of the debtor that is obtained after a security interest in the debtor's property has been created.

agency A legal relationship in which an agent acts under the direction of a principal for the principal's benefit. Also used to refer to government regulatory bodies of all kinds.

agent One who acts under the direction of a principal for the principal's benefit in a legal relationship known as agency. See *principal.*

aggregate theory In partnership law, the view that there is no distinction between a partnership and the partners who own it. See *entity theory.*

aggrieved One whose legal rights have been invaded by the act of another. Also, one whose pecuniary interest is directly affected by a judgment, or whose right of property may be divested by an action.

alienation The voluntary act or acts by which one person transfers his or her own property to another.

alien corporation   A corporation incorporated in one country that is doing business in another country. See *foreign corporation.*

allegation   A statement of a party to an action in a declaration or pleading of what the party intends to prove.

allege   To assert a statement of fact.

alteration   An addition or change in a document.

alter ego   Other self. In corporation law, a doctrine that permits a court to pierce a corporation's veil and to hold a shareholder liable for the actions of a corporation dominated by the shareholder.

alternative dispute resolution (ADR)   A general name applied to the many nonjudicial means of settling private disputes.

amortize   To provide for the payment of a debt by creating a sinking fund or paying in installments.

ancillary   Auxiliary to. An ancillary receiver is a receiver who has been appointed in aid of, and in subordination to, the primary receiver.

ancillary covenant not to compete   A promise that is ancillary to (part of) a valid contract whereby one party to a contract agrees not to compete with the other party for a specified time and within a specified location. Also called *non-competition clause.*

answer   The pleading of a defendant in which he or she may deny any or all the facts set out in the plaintiff's declaration or complaint.

anticipatory breach   A contracting party's indication before the time for performance that he cannot or will not perform the contract.

appearance   The first act of the defendant in court.

appellant   The party making an appeal.

appellate jurisdiction   Jurisdiction to revise or correct the work of a subordinate court.

appellee   A party against whom a favorable court decision is appealed. May be called the *respondent* in some jurisdictions.

applicant   A petitioner; one who files a petition or application.

appraisal, right of   A shareholder's right to receive the fair value of her shares from her corporation when she objects to a corporate transaction that significantly alters her rights in the corporation.

appurtenance   An accessory; something that belongs to another thing.

arbitrate   To submit some disputed matter to selected persons and to accept their decision or award as a substitute for the decision of a judicial tribunal.

argument   The discussion by counsel for the respective parties of their contentions on the law and the facts of the case being tried in order to aid the jury in arriving at a correct and just conclusion.

articles of incorporation   A document that must be filed with a secretary of state to create a corporation. Usually, it includes the basic rights and responsibilities of the corporation and the shareholders.

articles of partnership   A formal written contract between the partners of a partnership that states the rights and the responsibilities of the partners.

artisan's lien   A common law possessory security interest arising out of the improvement of property by one skilled in some mechanical art or craft; the lien entitles the improver of the property to retain possession in order to secure the agreed-on price or the value of the work performed.

assault   An intentional tort that prohibits any attempt or offer to cause harmful or offensive contact with another if it results in a well-grounded apprehension of imminent battery in the mind of the threatened person.

assent   To give or express one's concurrence or approval of something done.

assignable   Capable of being lawfully assigned or transferred; transferable; negotiable. Also, capable of being specified or pointed out as an assignable error.

assignee   A person to whom an assignment is made.

assignment   A transfer of property or some right or interest.

assignment of partnership interest   A partner's voluntary transfer of her partnership interest to the partner's personal creditor, giving the creditor the right to receive the partner's share of partnership profits.

assignor   The maker of an assignment.

assumption of risk   A traditional defense to negligence liability based on the argument that the plaintiff voluntarily exposed himself to a known danger created by the defendant's negligence.

assurance   To provide confidence or to inform positively.

attachment   In general, the process of taking a person's property under an appropriate judicial order by an appropriate officer of the court. Used for a variety of purposes, including the acquisition of jurisdiction over the property seized and the securing of property that may be used to satisfy a debt.

attest   To bear witness to; to affirm; to be true or genuine.

attorney-in-fact   An agent who is given express, written authorization by his principal to do a particular act or series of acts on behalf of the principal.

at will   See *employment at will.*

audit committee   In corporation law, a committee of the board that recommends and supervises the public accountant who audits the corporation's financial records.

authentication   Such official attestation of a written instrument as will render it legally admissible in evidence.

authority   In agency law, an agent's ability to affect his principal's legal relations with third parties. Also used to refer to an actor's legal power or ability to do something. In addition, sometimes used to refer to a statute, case, or other legal source that justifies a particular result.

authorized shares   Shares that a corporation is empowered to issue by its articles of incorporation.

automatic stay   Under the Bankruptcy Act, the suspension of all litigation against the debtor and his property, which is triggered by the filing of a bankruptcy petition.

averment   A statement of fact made in a pleading.

avoid   To nullify a contractual obligation.

bad faith   A person's actual intent to mislead or deceive another; an intent to take an unfair and unethical advantage of another.

bailee   The person to whom a bailment is made.

bailment   The transfer of personal property by its owner to another person with the understanding that the property will be returned to the owner in the future.

bailor   The owner of bailed property; the one who delivers personal property to another to be held in bailment.

bankruptcy   The state of a person who is unable to pay his or her debts without respect to time; one whose liabilities exceed his or her assets.

bar   As a collective noun, those persons who are admitted to practice law, members of the bar. The court itself. A plea or defense asserted by a defendant that is sufficient to destroy a plaintiff's action.

battery   An intentional tort that prohibits the harmful or offensive touching of another without his consent.

bearer   A person in possession of a negotiable instrument that is payable to him, his order, or to whoever is in possession of the instrument.

bench   Generally used as a synonym for the term *court* or the judges of a court.

beneficiary   The person for whose benefit an insurance policy, trust, will, or contract is established. In the case of a contract, the beneficiary is called a *third-party beneficiary*.

bequest   In a will, a gift of personal property or money. Also called a *legacy*.

bid   To make an offer at an auction or at a judicial sale. As a noun, an offer.

bilateral contract   A contract in which the promise of one of the parties forms the consideration for the promise of the other.

bill of exchange   An unconditional order in writing by one person to another, signed by the person giving it, requiring the person to whom it is addressed to pay on demand or at a fixed or determinable future time a sum certain in money to order or to bearer.

bill of lading   A written acknowledgment of the receipt of goods to be transported to a designated place and delivery to a named person or to his or her order.

bill of sale   A written agreement by which one person assigns or transfers interests or rights in personal property to another.

binder   Also called a *binding slip*. A brief memorandum or agreement issued by an insurer as a temporary policy for the convenience of all the parties, constituting a present insurance in the amount specified, to continue in force until the execution of a formal policy.

blue sky laws   The popular name for state statutes that regulate securities transactions.

bona fide   Made honestly and in good faith; genuine.

bona fide purchaser   An innocent buyer for valuable consideration who purchases goods without notice of any defects in the title of the goods acquired.

bond   A long-term debt security that is secured by collateral.

bonus shares   Also called *bonus stock*. Shares issued for no lawful consideration. See *discount shares* and *watered shares*.

breaking bulk   The division or separation of the contents of a package or container.

brief   A statement of a party's case or legal arguments, usually prepared by an attorney. Often used to support some of the motions described in Chapter 2, and also used to make legal arguments before appellate courts. Also, an abridgement of a reported case.

broker   An agent who bargains or carries on negotiations in behalf of the principal as an intermediary between the latter and third persons in transacting business relative to the acquisition of contractual rights, or to the sale or purchase of property the custody of which is not intrusted to him or her for the purpose of discharging the agency.

bulk transfer   The sale or transfer of a major part of the stock of goods of a merchant at one time and not in the ordinary course of business.

burden of proof   Used to refer both to the necessity or obligation of proving the facts needed to support a party's claim, and the persuasiveness of the evidence used to do so. Regarding the second sense of the term, the usual burden of proof in a civil case is a preponderance of the evidence; in a criminal case, it is proof beyond a reasonable doubt.

business judgment rule   A rule protecting business managers from liability for making bad decisions when they have acted prudently and in good faith.

buy-and-sell agreement   A share transfer restriction compelling a shareholder to sell his shares to the other shareholders or the corporation and obligating the other shareholders or the corporation to buy the shareholder's shares.

buyer in ordinary course of business A person who, in good faith and without knowledge that the sale to him is in violation of a third party's ownership rights or security interest in the goods, buys in ordinary course from a person who is in the business of selling goods of that kind.

bylaws In corporation law, a document that supplements the articles of incorporation and contains less important rights, powers, and responsibilities of a corporation and its shareholders, officers, and directors.

C&F The price of the goods includes the cost of the goods plus the freight to the named destination.

call See *redemption*. Also, a type of option permitting a person to buy a fixed number of securities at a fixed price at a specified time. See *put*.

canceled shares Previously outstanding shares repurchased by a corporation and canceled by it; such shares no longer exist.

cancellation The act of crossing out a writing. The operation of destroying a written instrument.

capacity The ability to incur legal obligations and acquire legal rights.

capital Contributions of money and other property to a business made by the owners of the business.

capital stock See *stated capital*.

capital surplus Also called *additional paid capital*. A balance sheet account; the portion of shareholders' contributions exceeding the par or stated value of shares.

case law The law extracted from decided cases.

cashier's check A draft (including a check) drawn by a bank on itself and accepted by the act of issuance.

causa mortis In contemplation of approaching death.

cause of action A legal rule giving the plaintiff the right to obtain some legal relief once certain factual elements are proven. Often used synonymously with the terms *claim* or *theory of recovery*.

caveat emptor Let the buyer beware.

caveat venditor Let the seller beware.

certificate of deposit An acknowledgment by a bank of the receipt of money with an engagement to pay it back.

certificate of limited partnership A document that must be filed with a secretary of state to create a limited partnership.

certification The return of a writ; a formal attestation of a matter of fact; the appropriate marking of a certified check.

certified check A check that has been accepted by the drawee bank and has been so marked or certified that it indicates such acceptance.

chancellor A judge of a court of chancery.

chancery Equity or a court of equity.

charge The legal instructions that a judge gives a jury before the jury begins its deliberations. In the prosecution of a crime, to formally accuse the offender or charge him with the crime.

charging order A court's order granting rights in a partner's partnership interest to a personal creditor of the partner; a creditor with a charging order is entitled to the partner's share of partnership profits.

charter An instrument or authority from the sovereign power bestowing the right or power to do business under the corporate form of organization. Also, the organic law of a city or town, and representing a portion of the statute law of the state.

chattel An article of tangible property other than land.

chattel mortgage An instrument whereby the owner of chattels transfers the title to such property to another as security for the performance of an obligation subject to be defeated on the performance of the obligation. Under the UCC, called merely a *security interest*.

chattel paper Written documents that evidence both an obligation to pay money and a security interest in particular goods.

check A written order on a bank or banker payable on demand to the person named or his order or bearer and drawn by virtue of credits due the drawer from the bank created by money deposited with the bank.

chose in action A personal right not reduced to possession but recoverable by a suit at law.

CIF An abbreviation for cost, freight, and insurance, used in mercantile transactions, especially in import transactions.

citation of authorities The reference to legal authorities such as reported cases or treatises to support propositions advanced.

civil action An action brought to enforce a civil right; in contrast to a criminal action.

civil law The body of law applicable to lawsuits involving two private parties.

class action An action brought on behalf of the plaintiff and others similarly situated.

close corporation A corporation with few shareholders generally having a close personal relationship to each other and participating in the management of the business.

COD Cash on delivery. When goods are delivered to a carrier for a cash on delivery shipment, the carrier must not deliver without receiving payment of the amount due.

code A system of law; a systematic and complete body of law.

codicil Some addition to or qualification of one's last will and testament.

collateral Property put up to secure the performance of a promise, so that if the promisor fails to perform as promised, the creditor may look to the property to make him whole.

collateral attack   An attempt to impeach a decree, a judgment, or other official act in a proceeding that has not been instituted for the express purpose of correcting or annulling or modifying the decree, judgment, or official act.

collateral contract   A contract in which one person agrees to pay the debt of another if the principal debtor fails to pay. See *guaranty.*

comaker   A person who with another or others signs a negotiable instrument on its face and thereby becomes primarily liable for its payment.

commercial impracticability   The standards used by the UCC, replacing the common law doctrine of impossibility, to define when a party is relieved of his or her contract obligations because of the occurrence of unforeseeable, external events beyond his or her control.

commercial law   The law that relates to the rights of property and persons engaged in trade or commerce.

commercial paper   Negotiable paper such as promissory notes, drafts, and checks that provides for the payment of money and can readily be transferred to other parties.

commercial unit   Under the UCC, any unit of goods that is treated by commercial usage as a single whole. It may, for example, be a single article or a set of articles such as a dozen, bale, gross, or carload.

common area   In landlord–tenant law, an area over which the landlord retains control but which is often used by or for the benefit of tenants. For example, hallways in an apartment building.

common carrier   One who undertakes, for hire or reward, to transport the goods of such of the public as choose to employ him.

common law   The law that is made and applied by judges.

common shareholders   Shareholders who claim the residual profits and assets of a corporation, and usually have the exclusive power and right to elect the directors of the corporation.

comparative fault   Often used synonymously with *comparative negligence.* But also sometimes used to refer to a defense that operates like comparative negligence but considers the plaintiff's and the defendant's overall fault rather than either's negligence alone.

comparative negligence   The contemporary replacement for the traditional doctrine of contributory negligence. The basic idea is that damages are apportioned between the parties to a negligence action in proportion to their relative fault. The details vary from state to state.

compensatory damages   See *damages, compensatory.*

complaint   The pleading in a civil case in which the plaintiff states his claim and requests relief.

composition with creditors   An agreement between creditors and their common debtor and between themselves whereby the creditors agree to accept the sum or security stipulated in full payment of their claims.

concealment   In contract law, taking active steps to prevent another from learning the truth.

concurrent   Running with; simultaneously with.

condemn   To appropriate land for public use. To adjudge a person guilty; to pass sentence on a person convicted of a crime.

condition   In contract law, a future, uncertain event that creates or extinguishes a duty of performance; a provision or clause in a contract that operates to suspend or rescind a party's duty to perform.

conditional acceptance   An acceptance of a bill of exchange containing some qualification limiting or altering the acceptor's liability on the bill.

conditional gift   A gift that does not become absolute or complete until the occurrence of some express or implied condition.

conditional sale   The term is most frequently applied to a sale in which the seller reserves the title to the goods, although the possession is delivered to the buyer, until the purchase price is paid in full.

condition precedent   A condition that operates to give rise to a contracting party's duty to perform.

condition subsequent   A condition that operates to relieve or discharge one from his obligation under a contract.

confession of judgment   An entry of judgment on the admission or confession of the debtor without the formality, time, or expense involved in an ordinary proceeding.

confirmed letter of credit   See *letter of credit, confirmed.*

confusion   The inseparable intermixture of property belonging to different owners.

consent decree or **consent order**   Used to refer to the order courts or administrative agencies issue when approving the settlement of a lawsuit or administrative action against some party.

consent restraint   A security transfer restriction requiring a shareholder to obtain the consent of the corporation or its shareholders prior to the shareholder's sale of her shares.

consequential damages   See *damages, consequential.*

conservator (of an incompetent person)   A person appointed by a court to take care of and oversee the person and estate of an incompetent person.

consideration   In contract law, a basic requirement for an enforceable agreement under traditional contract principles, defined in this text as legal value, bargained for and given in exchange for an act or promise. In corporation law, cash or property contributed to a corporation in exchange for shares, or a promise to contribute such cash or property.

consignee A person to whom goods are consigned, shipped, or otherwise transmitted, either for sale or for safekeeping.

consignment A bailment for sale. The consignee does not undertake the absolute obligation to sell or pay for the goods.

consignor One who sends goods to another on consignment. A shipper or transmitter of goods.

conspicuous Noticeable by a reasonable person, such as a term or clause in a contract that is in bold print, in capitals, or a contrasting color or type style.

constructive eviction In landlord–tenant law, a breach of duty by the landlord that makes the premises uninhabitable or otherwise deprives the tenant of the benefit of the lease and gives rise to the tenant's right to vacate the property and terminate the lease.

construe To read a statute or document for the purpose of ascertaining its meaning and effect, but in doing so the law must be regarded.

contempt Conduct in the presence of a legislative or judicial body tending to disturb its proceedings or impair the respect due to its authority, or a disobedience to the rules or orders of such a body, which interferes with the due administration of law.

continuation statement A document, usually a multi-copy form, filed in a public office to indicate the continuing viability of a financing statement. See *financing statement.*

contra Otherwise; disagreeing with; contrary to.

contract A legally enforceable promise or set of promises.

contract of adhesion A contract in which a stronger party is able to dictate terms to a weaker party, leaving the weaker party no practical choice but to adhere to the terms. If the stronger party has exploited its bargaining power to achieve unfair terms, the contract is against public policy.

contribution In business organization law, the cash or property contributed to a business by its owners.

contributory negligence A traditional defense to negligence liability based on the plaintiff's failure to exercise reasonable care for his own safety.

conversion Any distinct act of dominion wrongfully exerted over another's personal property in denial of or inconsistent with his rights therein. That tort committed by a person who deals with chattels not belonging to him in a manner that is inconsistent with the ownership of the lawful owner.

convertible securities Securities giving their holders the power to exchange those securities for other securities without paying any additional consideration.

conveyance A written instrument transferring the title to land or some interest therein from one person to another.

copartnership A partnership.

copyright A set of exclusive rights, protected by federal law, pertaining to certain creative works such as books, musical compositions, computer programs, works of art, and so forth. The rights are: (1) to reproduce the work in question, (2) to prepare derivative works based on it, (3) to sell or otherwise distribute it, and (4) to perform or display it publicly.

corporation A form of business organization that is owned by owners, called shareholders, who have no inherent right to manage the business, and is managed by a board of directors that is elected by the shareholders.

corporation by estoppel A doctrine that prevents persons from denying that a corporation exists when the persons hold themselves out as representing a corporation or believe themselves to be dealing with a corporation.

corporeal Possessing physical substance; tangible; perceptible to the senses.

counterclaim A legal claim made in response to the plaintiff's initial claim in a civil suit. Unlike a defense, the counterclaim is the defendant's affirmative attempt to obtain legal relief; in effect, it states a cause of action entitling the defendant to such relief. Often, the counterclaim must arise out of the occurrence that forms the basis for the plaintiff's claim.

counteroffer A cross-offer made by the offeree to the offeror.

countertrade A buyer's purchase of the seller's goods in exchange for the seller's agreement to purchase goods of the buyer or other person; usually required as a condition to selling goods to a foreign trade corporation.

course of dealing A sequence of previous conduct between the parties to a transaction that is fairly to be regarded as establishing a common basis for interpreting their contract.

covenant A contract; a promise.

cover To obtain substitute or equivalent goods.

credible As applied to a witness, competent.

creditor A person to whom a debt or legal obligation is owed, and who has the right to enforce payment of that debt or obligation.

crime An act prohibited by the state; a public wrong.

criminal law The body of law setting out public wrongs that the government attempts to correct by prosecuting wrongdoers.

culpable Blameworthy; denotes breach of legal duty but not necessarily criminal conduct.

cumulative voting A procedure for voting for directors that permits a shareholder to multiply the number of shares he owns by the number of directors to be elected and to cast the resulting total of votes for one or more directors. See *straight voting.*

curtesy At common law, a husband's right in property owned by his wife during her life.

custody The bare control or care of a thing as distinguished from the possession of it.

cy pres As near as possible. In the law of trusts, a doctrine applied to prevent a charitable trust from failing when the application of trust property to the charitable beneficiary designated by the settlor becomes illegal or impossible to carry out; in such a case, cy pres allows the court to redirect the distribution of trust property for some purpose that is as near as possible to the settlor's general charitable intent.

damages The sum of money recoverable by a plaintiff who has received a judgment in a civil case.

    compensatory Damages that will compensate a party for direct losses due to an injury suffered.

    consequential Damages that do not flow directly and immediately from an act but rather flow from the results of the act; damages that are indirect consequences of a breach of contract or certain other legal wrongs. Examples include personal injury, damage to property, and lost profits.

    incidental Collateral damages that result from a breach of contract, including all reasonable expenses that are incurred because of the breach; damages that compensate a person injured by a breach of contract for reasonable costs he incurs in an attempt to avoid further loss.

    liquidated Damages made certain by the prior agreement of the parties.

    nominal Damages that are recoverable when a legal right is to be vindicated against an invasion that has produced no actual present loss.

    punitive Damages designed to punish flagrant wrongdoers and to deter them and others from engaging in similar conduct in the future.

    special Actual damages that would not necessarily but because of special circumstances do in fact flow from an injury.

    treble Three times provable damages, as may be granted to private parties bringing an action under the antitrust laws.

date of issue As applied to notes, bonds, and so on of a series, the arbitrary date fixed as the beginning of the term for which they run, without reference to the precise time when convenience or the state of the market may permit their sale or delivery.

D/B/A Doing business as; indicates the use of a trade name.

deal To engage in transactions of any kind, to do business with.

debenture A long-term, unsecured debt security.

debtor A person who is under a legal obligation to pay a sum of money to another (the creditor).

decedent A person who has died.

deceit A tort involving intentional misrepresentation or cheating by means of some device.

decision The judgment of a court; the opinion merely represents the reasons for that judgment.

declaratory judgment One that expresses the opinion of a court on a question of law without ordering anything to be done.

decree An order or sentence of a court of equity determining some right or adjudicating some matter affecting the merits of the cause.

deed A writing, sealed and delivered by the parties; an instrument conveying real property.

deed of trust A three-party instrument used to create a security interest in real property in which the legal title to the real property is placed in one or more trustees to secure the repayment of a sum of money or the performance of other conditions.

de facto In fact, actual. Often used in contrast to *de jure* to refer to a real state of affairs.

de facto corporation A corporation that has complied substantially with the mandatory conditions precedent to incorporation, taken as a whole.

defalcation The word includes both embezzlement and misappropriation and is a broader term than either.

defamation An intentional tort that prohibits the publication of false and defamatory statements concerning another.

default Fault; neglect; omission; the failure of a party to an action to appear when properly served with process; the failure to perform a duty or obligation; the failure of a person to pay money when due or when lawfully demanded.

defeasible Regarding title to property, capable of being defeated. A title to property that is open to attack or that may be defeated by the performance of some act.

defend To oppose a claim or action; to plead in defense of an action; to contest an action suit or proceeding.

defendant The party who is sued in a civil case, or the party who is prosecuted in a criminal case.

defendant in error Any of the parties in whose favor a judgment was rendered that the losing party seeks to have reversed or modified by writ of error and whom he names as adverse parties.

defense A rule of law entitling the defendant to a judgment in his favor even if the plaintiff proves all elements of his claim or cause of action.

deficiency   That part of a debt that a mortgage was made to secure, not realized by the liquidation of the mortgaged property. Something that is lacking.

defraud   To deprive another of a right by deception or artifice.

de jure   According to the law; legitimate; by legal right.

de jure corporation   A corporation that has complied substantially with each of the mandatory conditions precedent to incorporation.

delegation   In constitutional law and administrative law, a process whereby a legislature effectively hands over some of its legislative power to an administrative agency that it has created, thus giving the agency power to make law within the limits set by the legislature. In contract law, a transaction whereby a person who owes a legal duty to perform under a contract appoints someone else to carry out his performance.

deliver   To surrender property to another person.

demand   A claim; a legal obligation; a request to perform an alleged obligation; a written statement of a claim. In corporation law, a request that the board of directors sue a person who has harmed the corporation; a prerequisite to a shareholder derivative suit.

demurrer   A civil motion that attacks the plaintiff's complaint by assuming the truth of the facts stated in the complaint for purposes of the motion, and by arguing that even if these facts are true, there is no rule of law entitling the plaintiff to recovery. Roughly similar to the motion to dismiss for failure to state a claim on which relief can be granted.

de novo   Anew; over again; a second time. A trial de novo, for example, is a new trial in which the entire case is retried.

deposition   A form of discovery consisting of the oral examination of a party or a party's witness by the other party's attorney.

deputy   A person subordinate to a public officer whose business and object is to perform the duties of the principal.

derivative suit   Also called *derivative action.* A suit to enforce a corporate right of action brought on behalf of a corporation by one or more of its shareholders.

descent   Hereditary succession. It is the title whereby, upon the death of an ancestor, the heir acquires the ancestor's estate under state law.

detriment   Any act or forbearance by a promisee. A loss or harm suffered in person or property.

devise   In a will, a gift of real property.

dictum   Language in a judicial opinion that is not necessary for the decision of the case and that, while perhaps persuasive, does not bind subsequent courts. Distinguished from *holding.*

directed verdict   A verdict issued by a judge who has, in effect, taken the case away from the jury by directing a verdict for one party. Usually, the motion for a directed verdict is made at trial by one party after the other party has finished presenting his evidence.

disaffirm   In contract law, a party's exercise of his power to avoid a contract entered before the party reached the age of majority; a minor's cancellation of his contract.

discharge   Release from liability.

discharge in bankruptcy   An order or decree rendered by a court in bankruptcy proceedings, the effect of which is to satisfy all debts provable against the estate of the bankrupt as of the time when the bankruptcy proceedings were initiated.

disclaimer   A term in a contract whereby a party attempts to relieve itself of some potential liability associated with the contract. The most common example is the seller's attempt to disclaim liability for defects in goods that it sells.

discount   A loan on an evidence of debt, where the compensation for the use of the money until the maturity of the debt is deducted from the principal and retained by the lender at the time of making the loan.

discount shares   Also called *discount stock.* Shares issued for less than their par value or stated value. See *bonus shares* and *watered shares.*

discovery   A process of information gathering that takes place before a civil trial. See *deposition* and *interrogatory.*

dishonor   The failure to pay or accept a negotiable instrument that has been properly presented.

dismiss   To order a cause, motion, or prosecution to be discontinued or quashed.

dissolution   In partnership law, the change in the relation of the partners caused by any partner ceasing to be associated with the carrying on of the business.

distribution   In business organization law, a business's gratuitous transfer of its assets to the owners of the business. Includes cash and property dividends and redemptions.

divided court   A court is so described when there has been a division of opinion between its members on a matter that has been submitted to it for decision.

dividends, cash or property   A corporation's distribution of a portion of its assets to its shareholders, usually corresponding to current or historical corporate profits; unlike a redemption, it is not accompanied by a repurchase of shares.

dividends, share   Also called *stock dividends.* A corporation's pro rata issuance of shares to existing shareholders for no consideration.

documents of title   A classification of personal property that includes bills of lading, warehouse receipts, dock warrants, and dock receipts.

domain   The ownership of land; immediate or absolute ownership. The public lands of a state are frequently termed the *public domain.*

domicile   A place where a person lives or has his home; in a strict legal sense, the place where he has his true, fixed, permanent home and principal establishment, and to which place he has, whenever he is absent, the intention of returning.

donee   A person to whom a gift is made.

donor   A person who makes a gift.

double jeopardy clause   A constitutional provision designed to protect criminal defendants from multiple prosecutions for the same offense.

dower   The legal right or interest that a wife has in her husband's real estate by virtue of their marriage.

draft   A written order drawn on one person by another, requesting him to pay money to a designated third person.

drawee   A person on whom a draft is drawn by the drawer.

drawer   The maker of a draft.

due bill   An acknowledgment of a debt in writing, not made payable to order.

dummy   One posing or represented as acting for himself, but in reality acting for another. A tool or "straw man" for the real parties in interest.

dumping   The selling of goods by a seller in a foreign nation at unfairly low prices.

durable power of attorney   A power of attorney that is not affected by the principal's incapacity. See *power of attorney* and *attorney-in-fact.*

durable power of attorney for health care   A durable power of attorney in which the principal specifically gives the attorney-in-fact the authority to make health care decisions for her in the event that the principal should become incompetent. Also called *health care representative.*

duress   Overpowering of the will of a person by force or fear.

earned surplus   Also called *retained earnings.* A balance sheet account; a corporation's profits that have not been distributed to shareholders.

earnest money   Something given as part of the purchase price to bind the bargain.

easement   The right to make certain uses of another person's property or to prevent another person from making certain uses of his own property.

edict   A command or prohibition promulgated by a sovereign and having the effect of law.

e.g.   For example.

ejectment   By statute in some states, an action to recover the immediate possession of real property.

eleemosynary corporation   A corporation created for a charitable purpose or for charitable purposes.

emancipate   To release; to set free. In contract law, a parent's waiver of his rights to control and receive the services of his minor child.

embezzlement   A statutory offense consisting of the fraudulent conversion of another's personal property by one to whom it has been intrusted, with the intention of depriving the owner thereof, the gist of the offense being usually the violation of relations of a fiduciary character.

eminent domain   A governmental power whereby the government can take or condemn private property for a public purpose on the payment of just compensation.

employment at will   A rule stating that if an employment is not for a definite time period, either party may terminate the employment without liability at any time and for any reason.

enabling legislation   The statute by which a legislative body creates an administrative agency.

en banc (in banc)   By all the judges of a court, with all the judges of a court sitting.

encumbrance   A right in a third person that diminishes the value of the land but is consistent with the passing of ownership of the land by deed.

endorsement   See *indorsement.*

entity theory   In partnership law, the view that a partnership is a legal entity distinct from the partners who own it. See *aggregate theory.*

entry   Recordation; noting in a record; going on land; taking actual possession of land.

environmental impact statement   A document that the National Environmental Policy Act requires federal agencies to prepare in connection with any legislative proposals or proposed actions that will significantly affect the environment.

equity   A system of justice that developed in England separate from the common law courts. Few states in the United States still maintain separate equity courts, though most apply equity principles and procedures when remedies derived from the equity courts are sought. A broader meaning denotes fairness and justice. In business organization law, the capital contributions of owners plus profits that have not been distributed to the owners; stated capital plus capital surplus plus earned surplus.

equity of redemption   The right of a mortgagee to discharge the mortgage when due and to have title to the mortgaged property free and clear of the mortgage debt.

error   A mistake of law or fact; a mistake of the court in the trial of an action.

escheat The reversion of land to the state in the event that a decedent dies leaving no heirs.

estate An interest in land. Property owned by a decedent at the time of his death.

estop To bar or stop.

estoppel That state of affairs that arises when one is forbidden by law from alleging or denying a fact because of his previous action or inaction.

et al. And another or and others. An abbreviation for the Latin *et alius,* meaning and another; also of *et alii,* meaning and others.

eviction Depriving the tenant of the possession of leased premises.

evidence That which makes clear or ascertains the truth of the fact or point in issue either on the one side or the other; those rules of law whereby we determine what testimony is to be admitted and what rejected in each case and what is the weight to be given to the testimony admitted.

exception An objection; a reservation; a contradiction.

exclusionary rule The rule that bars the admissibility in criminal proceedings of evidence seized in violation of the Fourth Amendment's prohibition against unreasonable searches and seizures.

exculpatory clause A clause in a contract or trust instrument that excuses a party from some duty.

executed When applied to written instruments, synonymous with the word *signed*; more frequently, it means everything has been done to complete the transaction; that is, the instrument has been signed, sealed, and delivered. An executed contract is one in which the object of the contract is performed.

execution A process of enforcing a judgment, usually by having an appropriate officer seize property of the defendant and sell it at a judicial sale. The final consummation of a contract or other instrument, including completion of all the formalities needed to make it binding.

executive order A legal rule issued by a chief executive (e.g., the president or a state governor), usually pursuant to a delegation of power from the legislature.

executor The personal representative appointed to administer the estate of a person who died leaving a valid will.

executory Not yet executed; not yet fully performed, completed, fulfilled, or carried out; to be performed wholly or in part.

exemption A release from some burden, duty, or obligation; a grace; a favor; an immunity; taken out from under the general rule, not to be like others who are not exempt.

exhibit A copy of a written instrument on which a pleading is founded, annexed to the pleading and by reference made a part of it. Any paper or thing offered in evidence and marked for identification.

ex post facto After the fact. The U.S. Constitution prohibits ex post facto criminal laws, meaning those that criminalize behavior that was legal when committed.

express warranty A warranty made in words, either oral or written.

expropriation A government's taking of a business's assets, such as a manufacturing facility, usually without just compensation.

ex ship A shipping term that does not specify a particular ship for transportation of goods but does not place the expense and risk of transportation on the seller until the goods are unloaded from whatever ship is used.

face value The nominal or par value of an instrument as expressed on its face; in the case of a bond, this is the amount really due, including interest.

factor An agent who is employed to sell goods for a principal, usually in his own name, and who is given possession of the goods.

false imprisonment An intentional tort that prohibits the unlawful confinement of another for an appreciable time without his consent.

FAS An abbreviation for the expression free alongside ship.

federal supremacy The ability of federal laws to defeat inconsistent state laws in case they conflict.

fee simple absolute The highest form of land ownership, which gives the owner the right to possess and use the land for an unlimited period of time, subject only to governmental or private restrictions, and unconditional power to dispose of the property during his lifetime or upon his death.

felony As a general rule, all crimes punishable by death or by imprisonment in a state prison.

fiction An assumption made by the law that something is true that is or may be false.

fiduciary One who holds goods in trust for another or one who holds a position of trust and confidence.

field warehousing A method of protecting a security interest in the inventory of a debtor whereby the creditor or his agent retains the physical custody of the debtor's inventory, which is released to the debtor as he complies with the underlying security agreement.

financing statement A document, usually a multicopy form, filed in a public office serving as constructive notice to the world that a creditor claims a security interest in collateral that belongs to a certain named debtor.

firm offer Under the Uniform Commercial Code, a signed, written offer by a merchant containing assurances that it will be held open, and which is not revocable for the time stated in the offer, or for a reasonable time if no such time is stated.

fixture A thing that was originally personal property and that has been actually or constructively affixed to the soil itself or to some structure legally a part of the land.

FOB An abbreviation of free on board.

force majeure clause A contract provision, commonly encountered in international agreements for the sale of goods, that excuses nonperformance that results from conditions beyond the parties' control.

foreclosure To terminate the rights of the mortgagor/owner of property.

foreign corporation A corporation incorporated in one state doing business in another state. See *alien corporation.*

foreign trade corporation A corporation in a NME nation that is empowered by the government to conduct the whole business of exporting or importing a particular product.

forwarder A person who, having no interest in goods and no ownership or interest in the means of their carriage, undertakes, for hire, to forward them by a safe carrier to their destination.

franchise A special privilege conferred by government on individuals, and which does not belong to the citizens of a country generally, of common right. Also a contractual relationship establishing a means of marketing goods or services giving certain elements of control to the supplier (franchisor) in return for the right of the franchisee to use the supplier's tradename or trademark, usually in a specific marketing area.

fraud Misrepresentation made with knowledge of its falsity and intent to deceive. See *misrepresentation.*

freeze-out In corporation law, a type of oppression by which only minority shareholders are forced to sell their shares.

fungible goods Goods any unit of which is from its nature or by mercantile custom treated as the equivalent of any other unit.

future advances Money or other value provided to a debtor by a creditor subsequent to the time a security interest in the debtor's collateral is taken by that creditor.

futures Contracts for the sale and future delivery of stocks or commodities, wherein either party may waive delivery, and receive or pay, as the case may be, the difference in market price at the time set for delivery.

garnishee Used as a noun, the third party who is subjected to the process of garnishment. Used as a verb, to institute garnishment proceedings; to cause a garnishment to be levied on the garnishee.

garnishment A statutory proceeding whereby money, property, wages, or credits of the defendant that are in the hands of a third party are seized to satisfy a judgment or legally valid claim that the plaintiff has against the defendant.

general partnership See *partnership.*

gift A voluntary transfer of property for which the donor receives no consideration in return.

good faith Honesty in fact; an honest intention to abstain from taking an unfair advantage of another.

goodwill The value of a business due to expected continued public patronage of the business.

grantee A person to whom a grant is made.

grantor A person who makes a grant.

gravamen The gist, essence, or central point of a legal claim or argument.

grey market goods Goods lawfully bearing trademarks or using patented or copyrighted material, but imported into a foreign market without the authorization of the owner of the trademark, patent, or copyright.

guarantor A person who promises to perform the same obligation as another person (called the *principal*), upon the principal's default.

guaranty An undertaking by one person to be answerable for the payment of some debt, or the due performance of some contract or duty by another person, who remains liable to pay or perform the same.

guardian A person (in some rare cases, a corporation) to whom the law has entrusted the custody and control of the person, or estate, or both, of an incompetent person.

habeas corpus Any of several common law writs having as their object to bring a party before the court or judge. The only issue it presents is whether the prisoner is restrained of his liberty by due process.

hearing The supporting of one's contentions by argument and, if need be, by proof.

hedging A market transaction in which a party buys a certain quantity of a given commodity at the price current on the date of the purchase and sells an equal quantity of the same commodity for future delivery for the purpose of getting protection against loss due to fluctuation in the market.

heirs Those persons appointed by law to succeed to the estate of a decedent who has died without leaving a valid will.

holder A person in possession of a document of title or an instrument payable or indorsed to him, his order, or to bearer.

holder in due course A person who is a holder of a negotiable instrument who took the instrument for value, in good faith, without notice that it is overdue or has been dishonored or that there is any uncured default with respect to payment of another instrument issued as part of the same series, without notice that the instrument contains an unauthorized signature or has been altered, without notice of any claim of a property or possessory interest in it, and without notice that any party has any defense against it or claim in recoupment to it.

holding Language in a judicial opinion that is necessary for the decision the court reached and that is said to be binding on subsequent courts. Distinguished from *dictum.*

holding company A corporation whose purpose or function is to own or otherwise hold the shares of other corporations either for investment or control.

holographic will A will written in the handwriting of the testator.

homestead In a legal sense, the real estate occupied as a home and also the right to have it exempt from levy and forced sale. It is the land, not exceeding a prescribed amount, upon which the owner and his family reside, including the house in which they reside as an indispensable part.

i.e. That is.

illusory Deceiving or intending to deceive, as by false appearances; fallacious. An illusory promise is a promise that appears to be binding but that in fact does not bind the promisor.

immunity A personal favor granted by law, contrary to the general rule.

impanel To place the names of the jurors on a panel; to make a list of the names of those persons who have been selected for jury duty; to go through the process of selecting a jury that is to try a cause.

implied warranty A warranty created by operation of law.

implied warranty of habitability Implied warranty arising in lease or sale of residential real estate that the property will be fit for human habitation.

impossibility A doctrine under which a party to a contract is relieved of his or her duty to perform when that performance has become impossible because of the occurrence of an event unforeseen at the time of contracting.

inalienable Incapable of being alienated, transferred, or conveyed; nontransferable.

in camera In the judge's chambers; in private.

incapacity A legal disability, such as infancy or want of authority.

inception Initial stage. The word does not refer to a state of actual existence but to a condition of things or circumstances from which the thing may develop.

inchoate Imperfect; incipient; not completely formed.

incidental damages See *damages, incidental.*

independent contractor A person who contracts with a principal to perform some task according to his own methods, and who is not under the principal's control regarding the physical details of the work. Under the *Restatement (Second) of Agency,* an independent contractor may or may not be an agent.

indictment A finding by a grand jury that there is probable cause to believe an accused committed a crime.

indorsement Writing on the back of an instrument; the contract whereby the holder of an instrument (such as a draft, check, or note) or a document (such as a warehouse receipt or bill of lading) transfers to another person his right to such instrument and incurs the liabilities incident to the transfer.

infant See *minor.*

information A written accusation of crime brought by a public prosecuting officer to a court without the intervention of a grand jury.

injunction An equitable remedy whereby the defendant is ordered to perform certain acts or to desist from certain acts.

in pari delicto Equally at fault in tort or crime; in equal fault or guilt.

in personam Against a person. For example, in personam jurisdiction.

in re In the matter of.

in rem Against a thing and not against a person; concerning the condition or status of a thing; for example, in rem jurisdiction.

inside information Confidential information possessed by a person due to his relationship with a business.

insolvency In corporation law, the inability of a business to pay its currently maturing obligations.

instrument Formal or legal documents in writing, such as contracts, deeds, wills, bonds, leases, and mortgages.

insurable interest Any interest in property such that the owner would experience a benefit from the continued existence of the property or a loss from its destruction.

inter alia Among other things.

interlocutory Something not final but deciding only some subsidiary matter raised while a lawsuit is pending.

interpleader An equitable remedy applicable where one fears injury from conflicting claims. Where a person does not know which of two or more persons claiming certain property held by him has a right to it, filing a bill of interpleader forces the claimants to litigate the title between themselves.

interrogatory Written questions directed to a party, answered in writing, and signed under oath.

inter se Between or among themselves.

interstate Between or among two or more states.

intervening cause An intervening force that plays so substantial a role in causing a particular plaintiff's injury that it relieves a negligent defendant of any responsibility for that injury. Also called *superseding cause*.

intervention A proceeding by which one not originally made a party to an action or suit is permitted, on his own application, to appear therein and join one of the original parties in maintaining his cause of action or defense, or to assert some cause of action against some or all of the parties to the proceeding as originally instituted.

inter vivos A transaction between living persons.

intestate Having died without leaving a valid will.

in toto Wholly, completely.

intrastate Within a particular state.

investment contract In securities law, a type of security encompassing any contract by which an investor invests in a common enterprise with an expectation of profits solely from the efforts of persons other than the investor.

invitee A person who is on private premises for a purpose connected with the business interests of the possessor of those premises, or a member of the public who is lawfully on land open to the public.

ipso facto By the fact itself; by the very fact.

irrevocable letter of credit See *letter of credit, irrevocable*.

issue Lineal descendants such as children and grandchildren. This category of persons includes adopted children.

issued shares A corporation's shares that a corporation has sold to its shareholders. Includes shares repurchased by the corporation and retained as treasury shares, but not shares canceled or returned to unissued status.

issuer In securities law, a person who issues or proposes to issue a security; the person whose obligation is represented by a security.

joint and several liability Liability of a group of persons in which the plaintiff may sue any member of the group individually and get a judgment against that person, or may sue all members of the group collectively.

joint bank account A bank account of two persons so fixed that they shall be joint owners thereof during their mutual lives, and the survivor shall take the whole on the death of other.

joint liability Liability of a group of persons in which, if one of these persons is sued, he can insist that the other liable parties be joined to the suit as codefendants, so that all must be sued collectively.

jointly Acting together or in concert or cooperating; holding in common or interdependently, not separately. Persons are jointly bound in a bond or note when both or all must be sued in one action for its enforcement, not either one at the election of the creditor.

joint tenancy An estate held by two or more jointly, with an equal right in all to share in the enjoyments of the land during their lives. An incident of joint tenancy is the right of survivorship.

joint venture A form of business organization identical to a partnership, except that it is engaged in a single project, not carrying on a business.

judgment A court's final resolution of a lawsuit or other proceeding submitted to it for decision.

judgment lien The statutory lien on the real property of a judgment debtor that is created by the judgment itself. At common law, a judgment imposes no lien on the real property of the judgment debtor, and to subject the property of the debtor to the judgment, it was necessary to take out a writ called an *elegit*.

judgment notwithstanding the verdict A judgment made by a judge contrary to a prior jury verdict whereby the judge effectively overrules the jury's verdict. Also called the *j.n.o.v.* or the *judgment non obstante veredicto*. Similar to the directed verdict, except that it occurs after the jury has issued its verdict.

judicial review The courts' power to declare the actions of the other branches of government unconstitutional.

jurisdiction The power of a court to hear and decide a case.

jurisprudence The philosophy of law. Also sometimes used to refer to the collected positive law of some jurisdiction.

jury A body of lay persons, selected by lot, or by some other fair and impartial means, to ascertain, under the guidance of the judge, the truth in questions of fact arising either in civil litigation or a criminal process.

kite To secure the temporary use of money by issuing or negotiating worthless paper and then redeeming such paper with the proceeds of similar paper. The word is also used as a noun, meaning the worthless paper thus employed.

laches The established doctrine of equity that, apart from any question of statutory limitation, its courts will discourage delay and sloth in the enforcement of rights. Equity demands conscience, good faith, and reasonable diligence.

land contract A conditional agreement for the sale and purchase of real estate in which the legal title to the property is retained by the seller until the purchaser has fulfilled the agreement, usually by completing the payment of the agreed-on purchase price.

larceny The unlawful taking and carrying away of personal property with the intent to deprive the owner of his property permanently.

last clear chance   Under traditional tort principles, a doctrine that allowed a contributorily negligent plaintiff to recover despite his failure to exercise reasonable care for his own safety by arguing that the defendant had the superior opportunity (last clear chance) to avoid the harm.

law merchant   The custom of merchants, or lex mercatorio, that grew out of the necessity and convenience of business, and that, although different from the general rules of the common law, was engrafted into it and became a part of it. It was founded on the custom and usage of merchants.

leading case   The most significant and authoritative case regarded as having settled and determined a point of law. Often, the first case to have done so in a definitive and complete fashion.

leading questions   Questions that suggest to the witness the answer desired or those that assume a fact to be proved that is not proved, or that, embodying a material fact, allow the witness to answer by a simple negative or affirmative.

lease   A contract for the possession and use of land or other property, including goods, on one side, and a recompense of rent or other income on the other; a conveyance to a person for life, or years, or at will in consideration of a return of rent or other recompense.

legacy   A bequest; a testamentary gift of personal property. Sometimes incorrectly applied to a testamentary gift of real property.

legal   According to the principles of law; according to the method required by statute; by means of judicial proceedings; not equitable.

letter of credit   An instrument containing a request (general or special) to pay to the bearer or person named money, or sell him or her some commodity on credit or give something of value and look to the drawer of the letter for recompense.

   advised   The seller's bank acts as the seller's agent to collect against the letter of credit issued by the buyer's bank.

   confirmed   The seller's bank agrees to assume liability on the letter of credit issued by the buyer's bank.

   irrevocable   The issuing bank may not revoke the letter of credit issued by the buyer's bank.

   standby   The seller's bank promises to pay the buyer if the seller defaults on his contract to deliver conforming goods.

levy   At common law, a levy on goods consisted of an officer's entering the premises where they were and either leaving an assistant in charge of them or removing them after taking an inventory. Today, courts differ as to what is a valid levy, but by the weight of authority there must be an actual or constructive seizure of the goods. In most states, a levy on land must be made by some unequivocal act of the officer indicating the intention of singling out certain real estate for the satisfaction of the debt.

libel   The defamation action appropriate to printed or written defamations, or to those that have a physical form.

license   A personal privilege to do some act or series of acts on the land of another, without possessing any ownership interest in the land. A permit or authorization to do something that, without a license, would be unlawful.

licensee   A person lawfully on land in possession of another for purposes unconnected with the business interests of the possessor.

lien   In its most extensive meaning, it is a charge on property for the payment or discharge of a debt or duty; a qualified right; a proprietary interest that, in a given case, may be exercised over the property of another.

life estate   A property interest that gives a person the right to possess and use property for a time that is measured by his lifetime or that of another person.

limited partner   An owner of a limited partnership who has no right to manage the business but who possesses liability limited to his capital contribution to the business.

limited partnership   A form of business organization that has one or more general partners who manage the business and have unlimited liability for the obligations of the business and one or more limited partners who do not manage and have limited liability.

liquidated damages   The stipulation by the parties to a contract of the sum of money to be recovered by the aggrieved party in the event of a breach of the contract by the other party.

liquidated debt   A debt that is due and certain. That is, one that is not the subject of a bona fide dispute either as to its existence or the amount that is owed.

lis pendens   A pending suit. As applied to the doctrine of lis pendens, it is the jurisdiction, power, or control that courts acquire over property involved in a suit, pending the continuance of the action, and until its final judgment.

listing contract   A so-called contract whereby an owner of real property employs a broker to procure a purchaser without giving the broker an exclusive right to sell. Under such an agreement, it is generally held that the employment may be terminated by the owner at will, and that a sale of the property by the owner terminates the employment.

litigant   A party to a lawsuit.

living will   A document executed with specific legal formalities stating a person's preference that heroic life support measures should not be used if there is no hope of the person's recovery.

long-arm statute   A state statute that grants to a state's courts broad authority to exercise jurisdiction over out-of-state persons who have contacts with the state.

looting   In corporation law, the transfer of a corporation's assets to its managers or controlling shareholders at less than fair value.

magistrate   A word commonly applied to the lower judicial officers such as justices of the peace, police judges, town recorders, and other local judicial functionaries. In a broader sense, a magistrate is a public civil officer invested with some part of the legislative, executive, or judicial power given by the Constitution. The president of the United States is the chief magistrate of the nation.

maker   A person who makes or executes an instrument. The signer of an instrument.

malfeasance   The doing of an act that a person ought not to do at all. It is to be distinguished from misfeasance—the improper doing of an act that a person might lawfully do.

malicious prosecution   An intentional tort designed to protect against the wrongful initiation of criminal proceedings.

mandamus   We command. It is a command issuing from a competent jurisdiction, in the name of the state or sovereign, directed to some inferior court, officer, corporation, or person, requiring the performance of a particular duty therein specified, which duty results from the official station of the party to whom it is directed, or from operation of law.

margin   A deposit by a buyer in stocks with a seller or a stockbroker, as security to cover fluctuations in the market in reference to stocks that the buyer has purchased but for which he has not paid. Commodities are also traded on margin.

marshals   Ministerial officers belonging to the executive department of the federal government, who with their deputies have the same powers of executing the laws of the United States in each state as the sheriffs and their deputies in such state may have in executing the laws of that state.

material   Important. In securities law, a fact is material if a reasonable person would consider it important in his decision to purchase shares or to vote shares.

materialman's lien   A claim created by law for the purpose of securing a priority of payment of the price or value of materials furnished in erecting or repairing a building or other structure.

mechanic's lien   A claim created by law for the purpose of securing a priority of payment of the price or value of work performed and materials furnished in erecting or repairing a building or other structure; as such, it attaches to the land as well as to the buildings erected therein.

memorandum   A writing.

mens rea   A guilty mind; criminal intent.

merchant   Under the Uniform Commercial Code, one who regularly deals in goods of the kind sold in the contract at issue, or holds himself out as having special knowledge or skill relevant to such goods, or who makes the sale through an agent who regularly deals in such goods or claims such knowledge or skill.

merchantable   Of good quality and salable, but not necessarily the best. As applied to articles sold, the word requires that the article shall be such as is usually sold in the market, of medium quality, and bringing the average price.

merger   In corporation law, traditionally, a transaction by which one corporation acquires another corporation, with the acquiring corporation being owned by the shareholders of both corporations and the acquired corporation going out of existence. Today, loosely applied to any negotiated acquisition of one corporation by another.

merger clause   A contract clause providing that the written contract is the complete expression of the parties' agreement. Also called *integration clause.*

mining partnership   A form of business organization used for mining and drilling mineral resources that is identical to a partnership, except that mining partnership interests are freely transferable and the death or bankruptcy of a mining partner does not cause a dissolution.

minor   A person who has not reached the age at which the law recognizes a general contractual capacity (called *majority*), which is 18 in most states.

misdemeanor   Any crime that is punishable neither by death nor by imprisonment in a state prison.

misrepresentation   The assertion of a fact that is not in accord with the truth. A contract can be rescinded on the ground of misrepresentation when the assertion relates to a material fact or is made fraudulently and the other party actually and justifiably relies on the assertion.

mistrial   An invalid trial due to lack of jurisdiction, error in selection of jurors, or some other fundamental requirement.

mitigation of damages   A reduction in the amount of damages due to extenuating circumstances.

mortgage   A conveyance of property to secure the performance of some obligation, the conveyance to be void on the due performance thereof.

mortgagee   The creditor to whom property has been mortgaged to secure the performance of an obligation.

mortgagor   The owner of the property that has been mortgaged or pledged as security for a debt.

motion to dismiss   A motion made by the defendant in a civil case to defeat the plaintiff's case, usually after the complaint or all the pleadings have been completed. The most common form of motion to dismiss is the motion to dismiss for failure to state a claim on which relief can be granted, which attacks the legal sufficiency of the plaintiff's complaint. See *demurrer.*

motive The cause or reason that induced a person to commit a crime.

mutuality Reciprocal obligations of the parties required to make a contract binding on either party.

national ambient air quality standards Federally established air pollution standards designed to protect the public health and welfare.

natural law A body of allegedly existing ethical rules or principles that is morally superior to positive law and that prevails over positive law in case of a clash between it and the natural law. See *positive law.*

necessaries That which is reasonably necessary for a minor's proper and suitable maintenance, in view of the income level and social position of the minor's family.

negligence The omission to do something that a reasonable person, guided by those considerations that ordinarily regulate human affairs, would do, or doing something that a prudent and reasonable person would not do.

negligence per se The doctrine that provides that a conclusive presumption of breach of duty arises when a defendant has violated a statute and thereby caused a harm the statute was designed to prevent to a person the statute was designed to protect.

negotiable Capable of being transferred by indorsement or delivery so as to give the holder a right to sue in his or her own name and to avoid certain defenses against the payee.

negotiable instrument An instrument that may be transferred or negotiated, so that the holder may maintain an action thereon in his own name.

negotiation The transfer of an instrument in such form that the transferee becomes a holder.

NME A nonmarket economy; a socialist economy in which a central government owns and controls all significant means of production, thereby setting prices and the levels of production.

nolo contendere A no contest plea by the defendant in a criminal case that has much the same effect as a guilty plea but that cannot be used as an admission of guilt in other legal proceedings.

nominal damages See *damages, nominal.*

non compos mentis Mentally incompetent.

nonfeasance In the law of agency, the total omission or failure of an agent to enter on the performance of some distinct duty or undertaking that he or she has agreed with the principal to do.

non obstante veredicto Notwithstanding the verdict. J.n.o.v. See *judgment notwithstanding the verdict.*

no-par value stock Stock of a corporation having no face or par value.

novation A mutual agreement, between all parties concerned, for the discharge of a valid existing obligation by the substitution of a new valid obligation on the part of the debtor or another, or a like agreement for the discharge of a debtor to his creditor by the substitution of a new creditor.

nudum pactum A naked promise, a promise for which there is no consideration.

nuisance That which endangers life or health, gives offense to the senses, violates the laws of decency, or obstructs the reasonable and comfortable use of property.

nuncupative will An oral will. Such wills are valid in some states, but only under limited circumstances and to a limited extent.

oath Any form of attestation by which a person signifies that he is bound in conscience to perform an act faithfully and truthfully.

obiter dictum That which is said in passing; a rule of law set forth in a court's opinion but not necessary to decide the case. See *dictum.*

objection In the trial of a case the formal remonstrance made by counsel to something that has been said or done, in order to obtain the court's ruling thereon.

obligee A person to whom another is bound by a promise or other obligation; a promisee.

obligor A person who is bound by a promise or other obligation; a promisor.

offer A proposal by one person to another that is intended to create legal relations on acceptance by the person to whom it is made.

offeree A person to whom an offer is made.

offeror A person who makes an offer.

opinion The opinion of the court represents merely the reasons for its judgment, while the decision of the court is the judgment itself.

oppression The officers, directors, or controlling shareholder's isolation of one group of shareholders for disadvantageous treatment to the benefit of another group of shareholders.

option A separate contract in which an offeror agrees not to revoke her offer for a stated period of time in exchange for some valuable consideration.

option agreement A share transfer restriction granting a corporation or its shareholders an option to buy a selling shareholder's shares at a price determined by the agreement.

ordinance A legislative enactment of a county or an incorporated city or town.

original jurisdiction The power to decide a case as a trial court.

outstanding shares A corporation's shares currently held by shareholders.

overdraft The withdrawal from a bank by a depositor of money in excess of the amount of money he or she has on deposit there.

overdue When an instrument is not paid when due or at maturity.

overplus That which remains; a balance left over.

owner's risk A term employed by common carriers in bills of lading and shipping receipts to signify that the carrier does not assume responsibility for the safety of the goods.

par Par means equal, and par value means a value equal to the face of a bond or a stock certificate.

parent corporation A corporation that owns a controlling interest of another corporation, called a *subsidiary corporation.*

parol Oral; verbal; by word of mouth.

parol evidence Where a written contract exists, evidence about promises or statements made prior to or during the execution of the writing that are not contained in the written contract.

parties All persons who are interested in the subject matter of an action and who have a right to make defense, control the proceedings, examine and cross-examine witnesses, and appeal from the judgment.

partition A proceeding the object of which is to enable those who own property as joint tenants or tenants in common to put an end to the tenancy so as to vest in each a sole estate in specific property or an allotment of the lands and tenements. If a division of the estate is impracticable, the estate ought to be sold and the proceeds divided.

partners The owners of a partnership.

partnership A form of business organization; specifically, an association of two or more persons to carry on as co-owners of a business for profit.

partnership by estoppel The appearance of partnership when there is no partnership; it arises when a person misleads a second person into believing that the first person is a partner of a third person; a theory that allows the second person to recover from the first person all reasonable damages the second person has suffered due to his reliance on the appearance of partnership.

partnership interest A partner's ownership interest in a partnership.

party to be charged The person against whom enforcement of a contract is sought; the person who is asserting the statute of frauds as a defense.

par value An arbitrary dollar amount assigned to shares by the articles of incorporation, representing the minimum amount of consideration for which the corporation may issue the shares and the portion of consideration that must be allocated to the stated capital amount.

patent A patent for land is a conveyance of title to government lands by the government; a patent of an invention is the right of monopoly secured by statute to those who invent or discover new and useful devices and processes.

patentee The holder of a patent.

pawn A pledge; a bailment of personal property as security for some debt or engagement, redeemable on certain terms, and with an implied power of sale on default.

payee A person to whom a payment is made or is made payable.

pecuniary Financial; pertaining or relating to money.

pendente lite During the litigation.

per capita A distribution of property in which each member of a group shares equally.

per curiam By the court as a whole, without an opinion signed by a particular judge.

peremptory challenge A challenge to a proposed juror that a defendant may make as an absolute right, and that cannot be questioned by either opposing counsel or the court.

perfection The process or method by which a secured party obtains a priority in certain collateral belonging to a debtor against creditors or claimants of a debtor; it usually entails giving notice of the security interest, such as by taking possession or filing a financial statement.

performance The fulfillment of a contractual duty.

periodic tenancy The tenancy that exists when the landlord and tenant agree that rent will be paid in regular successive intervals until notice to terminate is given but do not agree on a specific duration of the lease. A typical periodic tenancy is a tenancy from month to month.

perjury The willful and corrupt false swearing or affirming, after an oath lawfully administered, in the course of a judicial or quasi-judicial proceeding, as to some matter material to the issue or point in question.

per se In itself or as such.

personal property All objects and rights, other than real property, that can be owned. See *real property.*

per stirpes A distribution in which each surviving descendant divides the share that his or her parent would have taken if the parent had survived. Also called *by right of representation.*

petition In equity pleading, a petition is in the nature of a pleading (at least when filed by a stranger to the suit) and forms a basis for independent action.

petition (bankruptcy) The document filed with the appropriate federal court that initiates a bankruptcy proceeding. It may be either a voluntary petition (i.e., filed by the debtor) or an involuntary petition (i.e., filed by creditors).

piercing the corporate veil Holding a shareholder responsible for acts of a corporation due to a shareholder's domination and improper use of the corporation.

plaintiff The party who sues in a civil case.

plaintiff in error The unsuccessful party to the action who prosecutes a writ of error in a higher court.

plea A plea is an answer to a declaration or complaint or any material allegation of fact therein that, if untrue, would defeat the action. In criminal procedure, a plea is the matter that the accused, on his arraignment, alleges in answer to the charge against him.

pleadings The documents the parties file with the court when they state their claims and counterarguments early in a civil case. Examples include the complaint and the answer.

pledge A pawn; a bailment of personal property as security for some debt or engagement, redeemable on certain terms, and with an implied power of sale on default.

pledgee A person to whom personal property is pledged by a pledgor.

pledgor A person who makes a pledge of personal property to a pledgee.

police power The states' power to regulate to promote the public health, safety, morals, and welfare.

positive law Laws actually and specifically enacted or adopted by proper authority for the government of a jural society as distinguished from principles of morality or laws of honor.

possession Respecting real property, exclusive dominion and control such as owners of like property usually exercise over it. Manual control of personal property either as owner or as one having a qualified right in it.

postdated check A check dated with a date later than its date of issue.

power of attorney A written authorization by a principal to an agent to perform specified acts on behalf of the principal. See *attorney-in-fact.*

precedent A past judicial decision relied on as authority in a present case.

preemptive right A shareholder's option to purchase new issuances of shares in proportion to the shareholder's current ownership of the corporation.

preference The act of a debtor in paying or securing one or more of his creditors in a manner more favorable to them than to other creditors or to the exclusion of such other creditors. In the absence of statute, a preference is perfectly good, but to be legal it must be bona fide, and not a mere subterfuge of the debtor to secure a future benefit to himself or to prevent the application of his property to his debts.

preferential Having priority.

preferred shareholders Shareholders who have dividend and liquidation preferences over other classes of shareholders, usually common shareholders.

prenuptial contract A contract between prospective marriage partners respecting matters such as property ownership and division.

preponderance Most; majority; more probable than not.

prerogative A special power, privilege, or immunity, usually used in reference to an official or his office.

presentment A demand for acceptance or payment of a negotiable instrument made on the maker, acceptor, drawee, or other payor by or on behalf of the holder.

presumption A term used to signify that which may be assumed without proof, or taken for granted. It is asserted as a self-evident result of human reason and experience.

pretermitted In the law of wills, an heir born after the execution of the testator's will.

prima facie At first sight; a fact that is presumed to be true unless disproved by contrary evidence.

prima facie case A case sufficiently strong that, unless rebutted by the defendant in some fashion, it entitles the plaintiff to recover against the defendant.

principal In agency law, one under whose direction an agent acts and for whose benefit that agent acts.

priority Having precedence or the better right.

privilege Generally, a legal right to engage in conduct that would otherwise result in legal liability. Privileges are commonly classified as absolute (unqualified) or conditional (qualified). Occasionally, privilege is also used to denote a legal right to refrain from particular behavior (e.g., the constitutional privilege against self-incrimination).

privity of contract The existence of a direct contractual relation between two parties.

probate A term used to include all matters of which probate courts have jurisdiction, which in many states are the estates of deceased persons and of persons under guardianship.

procedural law The body of law controlling public bodies such as courts, as they create and enforce rules of substantive law. See *substantive law.*

proceeds Whatever is received on the sale, exchange, collection, or other disposition of collateral.

process Generally, the summons or notice of beginning of suit.

proffer To offer for acceptance or to make a tender of.

profit An interest in land giving a person the right to enter land owned by another and remove natural resources (e.g., timber) from the land. Also called *profit à prendre.*

promisee The person to whom a promise is made.

promisor A person who makes a promise to another; a person who promises.

promissory estoppel An equitable doctrine that protects those who foreseeably and reasonably rely on the promises of others by enforcing such promises when enforcement is necessary to avoid injustice, even though one or more of the elements normally required for an enforceable agreement is absent.

promissory note Commercial paper or instrument in which the maker promises to pay a specific sum of money to another person, to his order, or to bearer.

promoter A person who incorporates a business, organizes its initial management, and raises its initial capital.

property Something that is capable of being owned. A right or interest associated with something that gives the owner the ability to exercise dominion over it.

pro rata Proportionate; in proportion.

prospectus In securities law, a document given to prospective purchasers of a security that contains information about an issuer of securities and the securities being issued.

pro tanto For so much; to such an extent.

proximate cause A legal limitation on a negligent wrongdoer's liability for the actual consequences of his actions. Such wrongdoers are said to be relieved of responsibility for consequences that are too remote or not the proximate result of their actions. Various tests for proximate cause are employed by the courts.

proxy A person who is authorized to vote the shares of another person. Also, the written authorization empowering a person to vote the shares of another person.

pseudoforeign corporation A corporation incorporated under the laws of a state but doing most of its business in one other state.

publicly held corporation A corporation owned by a large number of widely dispersed shareholders.

punitive damages See *damages, punitive.*

purchase money security interest A security interest that is (1) taken or retained by the seller of collateral to secure all or part of its purchase price or (2) taken by a debtor to acquire rights in or the use of the collateral if the value is so used.

put A type of option permitting a person to sell a fixed number of securities at a fixed price at a specified time. See *call.*

qualified acceptance A conditional or modified acceptance. In order to create a contract, an acceptance must accept the offer substantially as made; hence, a qualified acceptance is no acceptance at all, is treated by the courts as a rejection of the offer made, and is in effect an offer by the offeree, which the offeror may, if he chooses, accept and thus create a contract.

quantum meruit As much as is deserved. A part of a common law action in assumpsit for the value of services rendered.

quash To vacate or make void.

quasi-contract The doctrine by which courts imply, as a matter of law, a promise to pay the reasonable value of goods or services when the party receiving such goods or services has knowingly done so under circumstances that make it unfair to retain them without paying for them.

quasi-judicial Acts of public officers involving investigation of facts and drawing conclusions from them as a basis of official action.

quiet title, action to An action to establish a claimant's title in land by requiring adverse claimants to come into court to prove their claim or to be barred from asserting it later.

quitclaim deed A deed conveying only the right, title, and interest of the grantor in the property described, as distinguished from a deed conveying the property itself.

quorum That number of persons, shares represented, or officers who may lawfully transact the business of a meeting called for that purpose.

quo warranto By what authority. The name of a writ (and also of the whole pleading) by which the government commences an action to recover an office or franchise from the person or corporation in possession of it.

ratification The adoption or affirmance by a person of a prior act that did not bind him.

real property The earth's crust and all things firmly attached to it.

rebuttal Testimony addressed to evidence produced by the opposite party; rebutting evidence.

receiver One appointed by a court to take charge of a business or the property of another during litigation to preserve it and/or to dispose of it as directed by the court.

recklessness Behavior that indicates a conscious disregard for a known high risk of probable harm to others.

recognizance At common law, an obligation entered into before some court of record or magistrate duly authorized, with a condition to do some particular act, usually to appear and answer to a criminal accusation. Being taken in open court and entered on the order book, it was valid without the signature or seal of any of the obligors.

recorder A public officer of a town or county charged with the duty of keeping the record books required by law to be kept in his or her office and of receiving and causing to be copied in such books such instruments as by law are entitled to be recorded.

redemption The buying back of one's property after it has been sold. The right to redeem property sold under an order or decree of court is purely a privilege conferred by, and does not exist independently of, statute.

redemption right Also called a call. In corporation law, the right of a corporation to repurchase shares held by existing shareholders.

redress Remedy; indemnity; reparation.

reformation An equitable remedy in which a court effectively rewrites the terms of a contract.

rejection In contract law, an express or implied manifestation of an offeree's unwillingness to contract on the terms of an offer. In sales law, a buyer's refusal to accept goods because they are defective or nonconforming.

release The giving up or abandoning of a claim or right to a person against whom the claim exists or the right is to be enforced or exercised. It is the discharge of a debt by the act of the party, in distinction from an extinguishment that is a discharge by operation of law.

remainderman One who is entitled to the remainder of the estate after a particular estate carved out of it has expired.

remand A process whereby an appellate court returns the case to a lower court (usually a trial court) for proceedings not inconsistent with the appellate court's decision.

remedy The appropriate legal form of relief by which a remediable right may be enforced.

remittitur The certificate of reversal issued by an appellate court upon reversing the order or judgment appealed from.

repatriation An investor's removal to the investor's nation of profits from his investment in a foreign nation.

replevin A common law action by which the owner recovers possession of his own goods.

repudiation Indicating to another party to a contract that the party does not intend to perform his obligations.

res The thing; the subject matter of a suit; the property involved in the litigation; a matter; property; the business; the affair; the transaction.

rescind As the word is applied to contracts, to terminate the contract as to future transactions or to annul the contract from the beginning.

rescission The rescinding or cancellation of a contract or transaction. In general, its effect is to restore the parties to their original precontractual position.

residue Residuary; all that portion of the estate of a testator of which no effectual disposition has been made by his will otherwise than in the residuary clause.

res ipsa loquitur Literally, the thing speaks for itself. A doctrine that, in some circumstances, gives rise to an inference that a defendant was negligent and that his negligence was the cause of the plaintiff's injury.

res judicata A matter that has been adjudicated; that which is definitely settled by a judicial decision.

respondeat superior A legal doctrine making an employer (or master) liable for the torts of an employee (servant) that are committed within the scope of the employee's employment.

respondent A term often used to describe the party charged in an administrative proceeding. The party adverse to the appellant in a case appealed to a higher court. In this sense, often synonymous with *appellee*.

Restatement(s) Collections of legal rules produced by the American Law Institute, covering certain subject matter areas. Although *Restatements* are often persuasive to courts, they are not legally binding unless adopted by the highest court of a particular state.

restitution A remedy whereby one is able to obtain the return of that which he has given the other party, or an amount of money equivalent to that which he has given the other party.

restrictive covenant An agreement restricting the use of real property.

reverse To reject or overturn a judgment or order of a court. An appellate court, for example, may reverse the decision of a trial court. See *affirm*.

revocation In general, the recalling or voiding of a prior action. In contract law, the withdrawal of an offer by the offeror prior to effective acceptance by the offeree.

right An interest given and protected by law. In corporation law, an option to purchase shares given to existing shareholders, permitting them to buy quantities of newly issued securities in proportion to their current ownership.

right of appraisal See *appraisal, right of.*

right of first refusal In corporation law, a share transfer restriction granting a corporation or its shareholders an option to match the offer that a selling shareholder receives for her shares. See also *option agreement.*

right of survivorship A feature of some types of co-ownership of property causing a co-owner's interest in property to be transferred on his death immediately and by operation of law to his surviving co-owner(s). See *tenancy by the entirety, tenant in partnership,* and *joint tenancy.*

riparian Pertaining to or situated on the bank of a river.

sale of goods The transfer of ownership to tangible personal property in exchange for money, other goods, or the performance of service.

sale on approval A conditional sale that is to become final only in case the buyer, after a trial, approves or is satisfied with the article sold.

sale or return A contract in which the seller delivers a quantity of goods to the buyer on the understanding that if the buyer desires to retain, use, or sell any portion of the goods, he will consider such part as having been sold to him, and that he will return the balance or hold it as bailee for the seller.

sanction The penalty that will be incurred by a wrongdoer for the violation of a law.

satisfaction A performance of the terms of an accord. If such terms require a payment of a sum of money, then satisfaction means that such payment has been made.

scienter In cases of fraud and deceit, the word means knowledge on the part of the person making the representations, at the time when they are made, that they are false. In an action for deceit, scienter must be proved.

S corporation   Also called *subchapter S corporation*. A close corporation whose shareholders have elected to be taxed essentially like partners are taxed under federal income tax law.

seal   At common law, a seal is an impression on wax or some other tenacious material, but in modern practice the letters *l.s.* (locus sigilli) or the word *seal* enclosed in a scroll, either written, or printed, and acknowledged in the body of the instrument to be a seal, are often used as substitutes.

security   An instrument commonly dealt with in the securities markets or commonly recognized as a medium of investment and evidencing an obligation of an issuer or a share, participation, or other interest in an enterprise.

security agreement   An agreement that creates or provides a security interest or lien on personal property. A term used in the UCC including a wide range of transactions in the nature of chattel mortgages, conditional sales, and so on.

security interest   A lien given by a debtor to his creditor to secure payment or performance of a debt or obligation.

service   As applied to a process of courts, the word ordinarily implies something in the nature of an act or proceeding adverse to the party served, or of a notice to him.

set off   That right that exists between two parties, each of whom, under an independent contract, owes an ascertained amount to the other, to calculate their respective debts by way of mutual deduction, so that, in any action brought for the larger debt, the residue only, after such deduction, shall be recovered.

settlor   A person who creates a trust. Also called *trustor.*

severable contract   A contract that is not entire or indivisible. If the consideration is single, the contract is entire; but if it is expressly or by necessary implication apportioned, the contract is severable. The question is ordinarily determined by inquiring whether the contract embraces one or more subject matters, whether the obligation is due at the same time to the same person, and whether the consideration is entire or apportioned.

share   An equity security, representing a shareholder's ownership of a corporation.

share dividend   See *dividends, share.*

shareholder   Also called *stockholder.* An owner of a corporation, who has no inherent right to manage the corporation but has liability limited to his capital contribution.

share split   Also called *stock split.* Traditionally, a corporation's dividing existing shares into two or more shares, thereby increasing the number of authorized, issued, and outstanding shares and reducing their par value. In modern corporation law, treated like a share dividend.

sight   A term signifying the date of the acceptance or that of protest for the nonacceptance of a bill of exchange; for example, 10 days after sight.

sinking fund   A fund established by an issuer of securities to accumulate funds to repurchase the issuer's securities.

situs   Location; local position; the place where a person or thing is, is his situs. Intangible property has no actual situs, but it may have a legal situs, and for the purpose of taxation, its legal situs is at the place where it is owned and not at the place where it is owed.

slander   The defamation action appropriate to oral defamation.

sole proprietor   The owner of a sole proprietorship.

sole proprietorship   A form of business under which one person owns and controls the business.

sovereign immunity   Generally, the idea that the sovereign (or state) may not be sued unless it consents to be sued. In antitrust law, the statutory immunity from antitrust liability for governmental actions that foreign governments enjoy under the Foreign Sovereign Immunities Act of 1976.

special damages   See *damages, special.*

specific performance   A contract remedy whereby the defendant is ordered to perform according to the terms of his contract.

stale check   A check more than six months past its date of issue.

standby letter of credit   See *letter of credit, standby.*

standing   The legal requirement that anyone seeking to challenge a particular action in court must demonstrate that such action substantially affects his legitimate interests before he will be entitled to bring suit.

stare decisis   A doctrine whereby a court is said to be bound to follow past cases that are like the present case on the facts and on the legal issues it presents, and that are issued by an authoritative court.

stated capital   Also called *capital stock.* A balance sheet account; shareholders' capital contributions representing the par value of par shares or stated value of no-par shares.

stated value   An arbitrary dollar amount assigned to shares by the board of directors, representing the minimum amount of consideration for which the corporation may issue the shares and the portion of consideration that must be allocated to the stated capital account.

state implementation plan   A document prepared by states in which the emissions to the air from individual sources are limited legally so that the area will meet the national ambient air quality standards.

status quo   The existing state of things. In contract law, returning a party to status quo or status quo ante means putting him in the position he was in before entering the contract.

statute of frauds   A statute that provides that no lawsuit may be brought to enforce certain classes of contracts unless there is a written note or memorandum signed by the party against whom enforcement is sought or by his agent.

statute of limitations   A statute that requires that certain classes of lawsuits must be brought within defined limits of time after the right to begin them accrued or the right to bring the lawsuit is lost.

stipulation   An agreement between opposing counsel in a pending action, usually required to be made in open court and entered on the minutes of the court, or else to be in writing and filed in the action, ordinarily entered into for the purpose of avoiding delay, trouble, or expense in the conduct of the action.

stock   A business's inventory. Also, as used in corporation and securities law, see *share.*

stock dividend   See *dividends, share.*

stockholder   See *shareholder.*

stock split   See *share split.*

stoppage in transitu   A right that the vendor of goods on credit has to recall them, or retake them, on the discovery of the insolvency of the vendee. It continues so long as the carrier remains in the possession and control of the goods or until there has been an actual or constructive delivery to the vendee, or some third person has acquired a bona fide right in them.

stop-payment order   A request made by the drawer of a check to the drawee asking that the order to pay not be followed.

straight voting   A form of voting for directors that ordinarily permits a shareholder to cast a number of votes equal to the number of shares he owns for as many nominees as there are directors to be elected. See *cumulative voting.*

strict liability   Legal responsibility placed on an individual for the results of his actions irrespective of whether he was culpable or at fault.

strike suit   In corporation law, a derivative suit motivated primarily by an intent to gain an out-of-court settlement for the suing shareholder personally or to earn large attorney's fees for lawyers, rather than to obtain a recovery for the corporation.

subchapter S corporation   See *S corporation.*

sub judice   Before a court.

sublease   A transfer of some but not all of a tenant's remaining right to possess property under a lease.

sub nom   Under the name of.

subpoena   A process for compelling a witness to appear before a court and give testimony.

subrogation   The substitution of one person in the place of another with reference to a lawful claim or right, frequently referred to as the doctrine of substitution. It is a device adopted or invented by equity to compel the ultimate discharge of a debt or obligation by the person who in good conscience ought to pay it.

subscription   In corporation law, a promise by a person to purchase from a corporation a specified number of shares at a specified price.

subsidiary corporation   A corporation owned and controlled by another corporation, called a *parent corporation.*

substantive law   The body of law setting out rights and duties that affect how people behave in organized social life. See *procedural law.*

sui generis   Of its own kind, unique, peculiar to itself.

summary judgment   A method of reaching a judgment in a civil case before trial. The standard for granting a motion for summary judgment is that there be no significant issue of material fact and that the moving party be entitled to judgment as a matter of law.

summary proceedings   Proceedings, usually statutory, in the course of which many formalities are dispensed with. But such proceedings are not concluded without proper investigation of the facts, or without notice, or an opportunity to be heard by the person alleged to have committed the act, or whose property is sought to be affected.

summons   A writ or process issued and served on a defendant in a civil action for the purpose of securing his appearance in the action.

superseding cause   See *intervening cause.*

supra   Above; above mentioned; in addition to.

surety   A person who promises to perform the same obligation as another person (the principal) and who is jointly liable along with the principal for that obligation's performance. See *guarantor.*

T/A   Trading as, indicating the use of a trade name.

tacking   The adding together of successive periods of adverse possession of persons in privity with each other, in order to constitute one continuous adverse possession for the time required by the statute, to establish title.

takeover   A tender offer; also applied generally to any acquisition of one business by another business.

tangible   Having a physical existence; real; substantial; evident.

tariff   A tax or duty imposed on goods by a nation when the goods are imported into that nation.

tax haven   A nation that has no or minimal taxation of personal, business, and investment income.

tenancy   General term indicating a possessory interest in property. In landlord–tenant law, a property owner's conveyance to another person of the right to possess the property exclusively for a period of time.

tenancy at sufferance   The leasehold interest that occurs when a tenant remains in possession of property after the expiration of a lease.

tenancy at will A leasehold interest that occurs when property is leased for an indefinite period of time and is terminable at the will of either landlord or tenant.

tenancy by the entirety A form of co-ownership of property by a married couple that gives the owners a right of survivorship and cannot be severed during life by the act of only one of the parties.

tenancy for a term A leasehold interest that results when the landlord and tenant agree on a specific duration for a lease and fix the date on which the tenancy will terminate.

tenancy in common A form of co-ownership of property that is freely disposable both during life and at death, and in which the co-owners have undivided interests in the property and equal rights to possess the property.

tenancy in partnership The manner in which partners co-own partnership property, much like a tenancy in common, except that partners have a right of survivorship.

tender An unconditional offer of payment, consisting in the actual production in money or legal tender of a sum not less than the amount due.

tender offer A public offer by a bidder to purchase a subject company's shares directly from its shareholders at a specified price for a fixed period of time.

testament A will; the disposition of one's property to take effect after death.

testator A deceased person who died leaving a will.

testimony In some contexts, the word bears the same import as the word *evidence,* but in most connections it has a much narrower meaning. Testimony is the words heard from the witness in court, and evidence is what the jury considers it worth.

thin capitalization In corporation law, a ground for piercing the corporate veil due to the shareholders' contributing too little capital to the corporation in relation to its needs.

third-party beneficiary A person who is not a party to a contract but who has the right to enforce it because the parties to the contract made the contract with the intent to benefit him.

title Legal ownership; also, a document evidencing legal rights to real or personal property.

tombstone advertisement A brief newspaper advertisement alerting prospective shareholders that an issuer is offering to sell the securities described in the advertisement.

tort A private (civil) wrong against a person or his property.

tortfeasor A person who commits a tort; a wrongdoer.

tortious Partaking of the nature of a tort; wrongful; injurious.

trade fixtures Articles of personal property that have been annexed to real property leased by a tenant during the term of the lease and that are necessary to the carrying on of a trade.

trademark A distinctive word, name, symbol, device, or combination thereof, which enables consumers to identify favored products or services and which may find protection under state or federal law.

trade secret A secret formula, pattern, process, program, device, method, technique, or compilation of information that is used in its owner's business and affords that owner a competitive advantage. Trade secrets are protected by state law.

transcript A copy of a writing.

transferee A person to whom a transfer is made.

transferor A person who makes a transfer.

treasury shares Previously outstanding shares repurchased by a corporation that are not canceled or restored to unissued status.

treble damages See *damages, treble.*

trespass An unauthorized entry on another's property.

trial An examination before a competent tribunal, according to the law of the land, of the facts or law put in issue in a cause, for the purpose of determining such issue. When the court hears and determines any issue of fact or law for the purpose of determining the rights of the parties, it may be considered a trial.

trust A legal relationship in which a person who has legal title to property has the duty to hold it for the use or benefit of another person. The term is also used in a general sense to mean confidence reposed in one person by another.

trustee A person in whom property is vested in trust for another.

trustee in bankruptcy The federal bankruptcy act defines the term as an officer, and he is an officer of the courts in a certain restricted sense, but not in any such sense as a receiver. He takes the legal title to the property of the bankrupt and in respect to suits stands in the same general position as a trustee of an express trust or an executor. His duties are fixed by statute. He is to collect and reduce to money the property of the estate of the bankrupt.

ultra vires Beyond the powers. In administrative law, it describes an act that is beyond the authority granted to an administrative agency by its enabling legislation. In corporation law, it describes a corporation's performing an act beyond the limits of its purposes as stated in its articles of incorporation.

unconscionable In contract law, a contract that is grossly unfair or one-sided; one that "shocks the conscience of the court."

unilateral contract A contract formed by an offer or a promise on one side for an act to be done on the other, and a doing of the act by the other by way of acceptance of the offer or promise; that is, a contract wherein the only acceptance of the offer that is necessary is the performance of the act.

unliquidated   Undetermined in amount.

usage of trade   Customs and practices generally known by people in the business and usually assumed by parties to a contract for goods of that type.

usurpation   In corporation law, an officer, director, or shareholder's taking to himself a business opportunity that belongs to his corporation.

usury   The taking of more than the law allows on a loan or for forbearance of a debt. Illegal interest; interest in excess of the rate allowed by law.

valid   Effective; operative; not void; subsisting; sufficient in law.

value   Under the Code (except for negotiable instruments and bank collections), generally any consideration sufficient to support a simple contract.

vendee   A purchaser of property. The word is more commonly applied to a purchaser of real property, the word *buyer* being more commonly applied to the purchaser of personal property.

vendor   A person who sells property to a vendee. The words *vendor* and *vendee* are more commonly applied to the seller and purchaser of real estate, and the words *seller* and *buyer* are more commonly applied to the seller and purchaser of personal property.

venire   The name of a writ by which a jury is summoned.

venue   A requirement distinct from jurisdiction that the court be geographically situated so that it is the most appropriate and convenient court to try the case.

verdict   Usually, the decision made by a jury and reported to the judge on the matters or questions submitted to it at trial. In some situations, however, the judge may be the party issuing a verdict, as, for example, in the motion for a directed verdict. See *directed verdict.*

versus   Against.

vest   To give an immediate fixed right of present or future enjoyment.

vicarious liability   The imposition of liability on one party for the wrongs of another. Also called *imputed liability.* For example, the civil liability of a principal for the wrongs his agent commits when acting within the scope of his employment. See *respondeat superior.* Such liability is also occasionally encountered in the criminal context (e.g., the criminal liability that some regulatory statutes impose on managers for the actions of employees under their supervision).

void   That which is entirely null. A void act is one that is not binding on either party and that is not susceptible of ratification.

voidable   Capable of being made void; not utterly null, but annullable, and hence that may be either voided or confirmed. See *avoid.*

voidable title   A title that is capable of, or subject to, being judged invalid or void.

voting trust   A type of shareholder voting arrangement by which shareholders transfer their voting rights to a voting trustee.

waive   To throw away; to relinquish voluntarily, as a right that one may enforce, if he chooses.

waiver   The intentional relinquishment of a known right. It is a voluntary act and implies an election by the party to dispense with something of value, or to forgo some advantage that he or she might have demanded and insisted on.

warehouse receipt   A receipt issued by a person engaged in the business of storing goods for hire.

warrant   An order authorizing a payment of money by another person to a third person. Also, an option to purchase a security. As a verb, the word means to defend; to guarantee; to enter into an obligation of warranty.

warrant of arrest   A legal process issued by competent authority, usually directed to regular officers of the law, but occasionally issued to private persons named in it, directing the arrest of a person or persons on grounds stated therein.

warranty   An undertaking relating to characteristics of a thing being sold; a guaranty.

waste   The material alteration, abuse, or destructive use of property by one in rightful possession of it that results in injury to one having an underlying interest in it.

watered shares   Also called *watered stock.* Shares issued in exchange for property that has been overvalued. See *bonus shares* and *discount shares.*

will   A document executed with specific legal formalities that contains a person's instructions about the disposition of his property at his death.

winding up   In partnership and corporation law, the orderly liquidation of the business's assets.

writ   A commandment of a court given for the purpose of compelling certain action from the defendant, and usually executed by a sheriff or other judicial officer.

writ of certiorari   An order of a court to an inferior court to forward the record of a case for reexamination by the superior court.

wrongful use of civil proceedings   An intentional tort designed to protect against the wrongful initiation of civil proceedings.

Spanish-English Equivalents for Important Legal Terms

abatement of nuisance   eliminación de un estorbo

abstract of title   resumen de título

acceptance   aceptación

accession   accesión

accommodation paper   documento de favor

accord and satisfaction   acuerdo y satisfacción

act of state   Acto de Gobierno

adjudicate   juzgar, adjudicar

administrator   administrador

adverse possession   posesión adversa

affirm   afirmar

affirmative action   acción afimativo

agent   agente

allegation   alegato

allege   alegar

answer   contestación

anticipatory breach   infracción anticipador

appelle   apelado

arbitrate   arbitrar

assignee   cesionario

assignment   cesión

assignor   cedente

bailee   depositario

bailment   depósito, entrega

bailor   depositante

bankruptcy   bancarrota

bearer   portador

beneficiary   beneficiario

bid   oferta

bill of lading   conocimiento de embarque

Prepared by Roberto Cisneros, Jr., Chaviano & Associates, Ltd., Chicago, Illinois.

G-24

blue sky laws   el nombre popular de leyes estatales hechas a proteger a inversionistas en la venta de valores

brief   breve, escrito

bulk transfer   transferencia a granel

burden of proof   carga de la prueba

case law   ley de causas, precedentes

cashier's check   cheque de caja, cheque bancario

cause of action   derecho de acción

caveat emptor   tenga cuidado el comprador

caveat venditor   tenga cuidado el vendedor

certification   certificación

certified check   cheque certificado

check   cheque

CIF   costo, seguro y flete

civil action   acción civil

class action   litigio entablado en representación de un grupo

COD "Cash on Delivery"   entrega contra pago

code   código

codicil   codicilo, cambio a un testamento

common carrier   transportador público

compensatory   (See *damages*) compensatario

complaint   queja, demanda

composition with creditors   concordato con acreedores

condition   condición

condition precedent   condición precedente

condition subsequent   condición subsiguiente

conditional gift   regalo condicional

consignee   consignatario

consignment   consignación

consignor   consignador

contract   contracto

conversion   conversión

corporation   corporación, sociedad autónoma
counterclaim   contrademanda
counteroffer   contraoferta
custody   custodia

damages   daños y perjucios
D/B/A   haciendo negocio como
debtor   deudor
deceit   engaño
decision   decisión
deed   escritura, título
defendant   accusado, demandado
defraud   estafar
deliver   entregar
de novo, trial   juicio de nuevo
deposition   deposición
derivative action   acción derivado de un accionista a beneficio de la corporación
dictum   opinión expresado por un tribunal
directed verdict   veredicto dirigido por el juez
discharge in bankruptcy   extinción de una obligación en bancarrota
dismiss   despedir, rechazar
donee   donatario
donor   donante
dower   los bienes del esposo fallecido que le corresponden a la viuda
draft   letra de cambio
drawee   girado
duress   por compulsión

easement   servidumbre
en banc   en el tribunal
equity   equidad, valor liquido
equity of redemption   derecho de rescate de una propiedad hipotecada
estoppel   impedimento por actas propias
ex ship   enviar al gasto y riesgo del vendedor
exculpatory clause   clausula exculpatoria
executor   albacea
executory   por cumplirse
executrix   albacea

FAS   franco muelle
felony   felonia, crimen
fiduciary   fiduciario
financing statement   declaración de seguridad
fixture   instalación fijo

FOB   libre a bordo
fungible goods   bienes fungibles

garnishment   embargo
gift   un regalo
good faith   buena fe
guarantor   garante
guaranty   garantía

heirs   herederos
holder in due course   tenedor de buena fe

illusory   illusorio
implied warranty   garantía implicita
incapacity   incapacidad
independent contractor   contratista independiente
indorsement   endorso
injunction   interdicto judicial
inpersonam   contra la persona
insolvency   insolvencia
in status quo   en stata quo
instrument   instrumento

jointly   conjuntamente
jointly and severally   conjuntamente y independiente-mente, solidariamente
joint tenancy   tenencia conjunta
judgment   juicio
judgment n.o.v.   sentencia contraria al veredicto
jurisdiction   jurisdicción

law merchant   derecho comercial
lease   contrato de arrendamiento
legal   legal
lien   gravamen, carga
litigant   litigante

magistrate   juez, magistrado
mechanic's lien   gravamen de constructor
mens rea   intención criminal
minitrial   mini juicio
minor   menor
misdemeanor   delito, ofensa menor
mistrial   juicio nulo
mitigation of damages   mitigación de daños
mortgage   hipoteca

necessaries   necesarios
negligence   negligencia

negotiable   negociable

negotiable instrument   instrumento negociable

negotiation   negociación

no arrival, no sale   si no llegan los bienes, no hay pago por ellos

nolo contendere   no contestare

non compos mentis   incapacitado mentalmente

novation   novación

oath   juramento

obligee   obligante

obligor   obligado

objection   objeción

offer   oferta

offeree   quien recibe una oferta

offeror   oferente

opinion   opinión

option   opción

ordinance   ordenanza

parol evidence   prueba extrínseca

partners   socios

payee   tenedor, beneficiaro de pago

per curiam   por el tribunal

perjury   perjurio

petition (bankruptcy)   petición de bancarrota

plaintiff   demandante

plea   alegato

polygraph   aparato para detectar mentiras

positive law   ley positiva

postdated check   cheque posfechado

power of attorney   poder actual

precedent   precedente

privity   relación juridica o contractual

probate   validación de testamento

promisee   a quien se promete

promisor   prometedor

promissory estoppel   impedimento promisorio

promoters   promotores

prospectus   prospecto

proximate cause   causa inmediata

quasi-contract   cuasicontracto

ratification   ratificación

rebuttal   refutación

recorder   registrador, grabador

redemption   redención

remand   devolver

remedy   remedio

res   asunto

respondent   respondiente

satisfaction   satisfacción

scienter   a sabiendas

security agreement   acuerdo de seguridad

shareholder   accionista

sovereign immunity   inmunidad soberana

specific performance   ejecución de lo estipulado en un contrato

stated capital   dicha capital

stare decisis   acaturse a los precedentas judiciales

status quo   el estado de las cosas en un momento dado

stockholder   accionista

subpoena   citación

summary judgment   sentencia sumaria

summons   emplazamiento

testimony   testimonio

tort   daño legal

tortious   dañoso

trial   juicio

transcript   transcripción

treble damages   daños triplcados

trustee in bankruptcy   síndico concursal

unliquidated debt   deuda no liquidada

ultra vires act   acta fuera de la facultad de una corporación

usury   usura

venue   lugar de jurisdicción

verdict   veredicto

versus   contra

void   nulo

voidable   anulable

waive   renunciar

waiver   renuncia

warranty   garantía

whistleblowing   un empleado que informa sobre actividades ilicitas en su empresa

writ   orden judicial

writ of certiorari   auto de avocación

writ of execution (or garnishment)   ejecutoria, mandamiento de ejecución